Gateway to the West

GATEWAY
to the
W·E·S·T

Volume 2

Compiled by

Ruth Bowers and Anita Short

Genealogical Publishing Co., Inc.

Gateway to the West was published quarterly between 1967 and 1978
as follows:
September 1967: Vol. 1, No. 1-A (trial issue)
1968-1977: Vol. 1, No. 1-Vol. 10, No. 4 (40 issues total)
1978: Vol. 11 (single, large issue)

This edition of *Gateway to the West* has been excerpted from the ori-
ginal numbers, consolidated, and reprinted in two volumes, with added
Publisher's Note, Tables of Contents, and Indexes, by Genealogical
Publishing Co., Inc. Baltimore, 1989.
Library of Congress Catalogue Card Number 88-82636
International Standard Book Number, Volume 2: 0-8063-1238-6
Set Number: 0-8063-1236-X
Made in the United States of America

Contents

Logan County

Common Pleas Court Records
1849-1850 (Vol. 6, No. 1) 1
1850-1851 (Vol. 8, No. 2) 7
Marriages, 1818-1825 (Vol. 2, No. 1) 11
Index to Estates, 1818-1831 (Vol. 1, No. 1) 16
Death Records, 1867-1870 (Vol. 3, No. 2) 20
Will Abstracts, 1818-1831 (Vol. 1, No. 1) 24

Lorain County

Marriages, 1822-1830 (Vol. 6, No. 1) 28
Death Records, 1867-1868 (Vol. 8, No. 4) 33
Greenwood Cemetery, Wellington (Vol. 7, No. 2) 37

Lucas County

Index to Guardianships, 1835-1850 (Vol. 5, No. 3) 38
Index to Wills and Estates, 1835-1850 (Vol. 5, No. 3) 40

Madison County

Deaths
1867-1870 (Vol. 1, No. 3) 43
1871-1875 (Vol. 4, No. 1) 46
Will Abstracts
1810-1825 (Vol. 1, No. 3) 50
1826-1835 (Vol. 2, No. 3) 54
1836-1848 (Vol. 7, No. 1) 57

Marion County

Deed Records
1824-1829 (Vol. 6, No. 4) 65

1830-1838 (Vol. 8, No. 3) 66

Medina County
Common Pleas Court Records, 1843-1844 (Vol. 7, No. 2) . . . 69
Death Records, 1867-1870 (Vol. 10, No. 3) 74

Meigs County
Marriages
1819-1825 (Vol. 4, No. 1) 76
1826-1828 (Vol. 9, No. 3) 82
Index to Wills, 1822-1844 (Vol. 5, No. 2) 86
Death Records, 1867-1872 (Vol. 8, No. 1) 87

Mercer County
Cemetery Records
Burntwoos Cemetery (Vol. 1, No. 3) 94
Zimmerman Cemetery and Coats-Gray Cemetery,
Black Creek Twp. (Vol. 7, No. 1) 95
Roebuck Cemetery (Vol. 5, No. 4) 96
Anderson Cemetery (Vol. 3, No. 1) 97
Pioneer Cemetery (Vol. 2, No. 3) 98
Will Abstracts
1823-1838 (Vol. 1, No. 1-A) 100
1838-1849 (Vol. 6, No. 3) 103
Death Records, 1867-1870 (Vol. 9, No. 1) 111
Index to Guardianships, 1837-1850 (Vol. 9, No. 2) 114

Miami County
Marriages
1807-1812 (Vol. 1, No. 1) 116
1813-1816 (Vol. 1, No. 4; Vol. 2, No. 1) 119
1817-1820 (Vol. 5, No. 3) 123
Divorces, 1818-1831 (Vol. 9, No. 3) 128
Will Abstracts, 1807-1826 (Vol. 10, No. 3) 130
Index to Guardianships
1807-1840 (Vol. 7, No. 3) 137
1841-1850 (Vol. 8, No. 4) 143
Indenture and Apprentice Records, 1828-1833
(Vol. 6, No. 1) 147

Cemetery Records
    Old Leatherwood Cemetery (Vol. 3, No. 4) 149
    Whitmer-Witmer Cemetery, Newberry Twp.
    (Vol. 5, No. 3) 151

Monroe County
    Deeds, 1814-1839 (Vol. 5, No. 4; Vol. 6, Nos. 1, 2, 3 & 4) . . 152

Montgomery County
Guardianships
    1803-1812 (Vol. 1, No. 4) 182
    1812-1820 (Vol. 7, No. 2) 184
    1821-1825 (Vol. 7, No. 4) 191
    1826-1829 (Vol. 8, No. 1) 198
    1830-1833 (Vol. 8, No. 2) 205
    1834-1837 (Vol. 8, No. 3) 211
Early Death Records (Vol. 1, No. 2) 219
Death Notices, Miamisburg, 1872-1873 (Vol. 2, No. 3) 222
Estates, 1803-1812 (Vol. 1, No. 4) 223
Naturalizations, 1818-1833 (Vol. 10, No. 2) 225
Deed Abstracts (Vol. 2, Nos. 2, 3 & 4; Vol. 3, No. 1;
Vol. 1, No. 4) 229
Baptisms, Stillwater Lutheran Church, 1834-1849
(Vol. 6, No. 1) 234
Cemetery Records
    Stillwater Lutheran Church Cemetery (Vol. 6, No. 1) 237
    Pontilus Cemetery, German Twp.; Hook Cemetery,
    Perry Twp.; Swank Cemetery, Perry Twp. (Vol. 5, No. 1) . . 240
    Mullendore Cemetery, Jackson Twp. (Vol. 5, No. 3) 241
    Munger-Butt Cemetery, Miami Twp. (Vol. 8, No. 2) 241
    Stetler Church Cemetery, Miami Twp. (Vol. 5, No. 1) 242
    Welbaum Cemetery, Perry Twp. (Vol. 5, No. 1) 244
    Bachman Cemetery, Clay Twp.; Marshall Cemetery,
    Clay Twp. (Vol. 5, No. 1) 245
    Swank Cemetery, Clay Twp. (Vol. 11) 246
Revolutionary Solider's Grave Marked (newspaper story)
(Vol. 8, No. 3) 246

Morgan County

Guardianships

1836-1843 (Vol. 4, No. 3) 247

1843-1847 (Vol. 5, No. 4) 253

Common Pleas Minute Book A (Vol. 11) 258

Morrow County

Baptismal Records, Peace Universal Church of Christ

(Vol. 10, No. 2) 276

Death Records, 1867-1870 (Vol. 4, No. 4) 278

Muskingum County

Land Grants (Vol. 1, No. 4; Vol. 4, No. 3) 282

Will Abstracts, 1832-1833 (Vol. 7, No. 3) 290

Will, Estate, and Guardianship Records, 1804-1814

(Vol. 3, No. 3) 294

Noble County

Death Records, 1867-1869 (Vol. 4, No. 4) 301

Index to Wills, 1852-1861 (Vol. 4, No. 4) 303

Common Pleas Court Records

1854-1859 (Vol. 7, No. 3) 305

1859-1864 (Vol. 8, No. 3) 310

Paulding County

Common Pleas Court Records (Vol. 9, No. 4)

Journal 1, 2, 3 - 1842-1855 316

Court Record A & C, 1840-1853 323

Cemetery Records

Ankney Cemetery (Vol. 7, No. 1) 326

Ankney Farm Cemetery (Vol. 7, No. 1) 327

Gordon Cemetery (Vol. 7, No. 1) 327

Hash Cemetery (Vol. 7, No. 1) 328

Clark Cemetery (Vol. 5, No. 2) 330

Death Records, 1867-1872 (Vol. 11) 333

Marriages (Vol. 10, No. 4)

1839-1845 335

1852-1853 336

Perry County

U.S. Land Grants (Vol. 2, No. 3) 338
Cemetery Records (Vol. 8, No. 2)
    Hopewell Baptist Cemetery 342
    Catholic Cemetery, Somerset 343
Partition Records, 1821-1830 (Vol. 3, No. 3) 347
Will Abstracts, 1818-1851 (Vol. 4, Nos. 1, 2, 3 & 4;
Vol. 5, No. 1) 353

Pickaway County

Marriages, 1810-1814 (Vol. 3, No. 2) 382
Declaration of Intention for Naturalization (Vol. 6, No. 3) . . .388
Will Abstracts, 1810-1820 (Vol. 2, No. 2) 390
Partition Records, 1836-1840 (Vol. 7, No. 3) 394
Death Records, 1856-1857 (Vol. 4, No. 3) 403

Pike County

Funeral Records, 1913-1917 (Vol. 3, No. 3) 408

Preble County

Mortality Schedule, 1860 (Vol. 3, No. 2) 413
Common Pleas Court Records (Vol. 1, No. 3) 415
Indenture and Apprentice Records, 1825-1831
(Vol. 2, No. 3) 416
Marriage Consents, 1846-1863 (Vol. 4, No. 4) 419
Newspaper Obituaries and Death Notices, 1850-1856
(Vol. 4, No. 2) 421
U.S. Land Patents Granted in Monroe Township
(Vol. 1, No. 1-A) 427
Index to Guardianships
    1815-1832 (Vol. 6, No. 1) 429
    1833-1850 (Vol. 9, No. 3) 432

Richland County

Common Pleas Court Records
    1822-1825 (Vol. 6, No. 3) 438
    1823-1833 (Vol. 4, No. 4) 445

Ross County
Marriages
  1798-1804 (Vol. 1, No. 3) 451
  1803-1807 (Vol. 3, No. 4) 454
  1806-1809 (Vol. 6, No. 2) 461
Territorial Court Order Book
  1798-1799 (Vol. 5, No. 2) 469
  1799-1800 (Vol. 8, No. 3) 476
Index to Estates and Guardianships
  1797-1814 (Vol. 1, No. 2) 487
  1815-1820 (Vol. 1, No. 4) 492

Sandusky County
Marriages, 1820-1832 (Vol. 6, No. 3) 495

Scioto County
Will Abstracts
  1809-1836 (Vol. 5, No. 3) 500
  1837-1840 (Vol. 7, No. 4) 508
Marriages, 1804-1815 (Vol. 9, No. 4) 511

Seneca County
Marriages, 1841-1842 (Vol. 5, No. 2) 518
Will Abstracts, 1830-1842 (Vol. 2, No. 4) 524
Ministers' Licenses (Vol. 4, No. 1) 531

Shelby County
Cemetery Records
  Lennox Cemetery, Franklin Twp. (Vol. 1, No. 1) 532
  Long Cemetery, Dinsmore Twp. (Vol. 1, No. 1) 533
  Old Ioramie Cemetery, Dinsmore Twp. (Vol. 1, No. 1) . . . 534
  Mills Cemetery (Vol. 3, No. 3) 537
  Montra Methodist Cemetery (Vol. 4, No. 1) 538
  Medaris Cemetery, Perry Twp. (Vol. 5, No. 3) 539
  Small Cemetery, Perry Twp. (Vol. 5, No. 3) 539
  Thompson Cemetery (Vol. 3, No. 4) 540
  Old Dunkard Cemetery, Perry Twp. (Vol. 5, No. 4) 540
  Elliott Cemetery (Vol. 4, No. 1) 541
  Galley Cemetery, Cynthian Twp. (Vol. 7, No. 2) 541

Index to Estates and Guardianships, 1819-1850
(Vol. 3, No. 1) 542
Marriages, 1830-1833 (Vol. 7, No. 1) 548
Wills and Estates in Deed Book A (Vol. 8, No. 3) 552

Stark County
Will Abstracts, 1811-1822 (Vol. 3, No. 3) 553

Tuscarawas County
Will Abstracts, 1809-1824 (Vol. 9, No. 4) 560
Marriages
    1808-1817 (Vol. 4, No. 2) 565
    1818-1823 (Vol. 8, No. 4) 570
Cemetery Records (includes Holmes County)
(Vol. 1, No. 1) 578

Union County
Death Records, 1867-1871 (Vol. 10, No. 1) 580
Marriages
    1820-1825 (Vol. 5, No. 1) 585
    1826-1836 (Vol. 8, No. 4) 588
Ministers' Licenses, 1826-1836 (Vol. 8, No. 4) 594
Wills, Estates, and Guardianships, 1821-1828
(Vol. 5, No. 1) 595

Van Wert County
Common Pleas Court Records, 1837-1847
(Vol. 10, No. 1) 599
Ministers' Licenses (Vol. 2, No. 2) 605
Marriages, 1840-1849 (Vol. 7, No. 3) 606
Willshire Cemetery (Vol. 10, No. 3) 611
U.S. Land Patents (Vol. 1, No. 2) 620
Will Abstracts, 1840-1850 (Vol. 4, No. 1) 625

Vinton County
Common Pleas Court Records, 1850-1854
(Vol. 5, No. 3) 628
Will Abstracts, 1853-1857 (Vol. 9, No. 1) 633

Warren County

Guardianships

1804-1817 (Vol. 10, No. 2) 638

1818-1826 (Vol. 11) 646

Marriages

1803-1810 (Vol. 1, No. 1-A) 657

1810-1812 (Vol. 4, No. 1) 664

Will Abstracts

1806-1815 (Vol. 3, No. 1) 668

Miscellaneous (Vol. 1, No. 1-A) 671

Common Pleas Court Records

1817-1818 (Vol. 5, No. 2) 672

1831-1832 (Vol. 8, No. 1) 676

1841-1843 (Vol. 9, No. 3) 681

Cemetery Records

Olive Branch Cemetery (Vol. 1, No. 3) 692

Old Franklin Cemetery (Vol. 11) 694

Caesars Creek (Friends) Cemetery (Vol. 4, No. 4) 697

Rosebud Acres Cemetery, Wagoner Estate Cemetery,

Hamilton Twp. (Vol. 6, No. 4) 702

Washington County

Declarations for Naturalization, 1826-1833 (Vol. 8, No. 2) . . .704

Death Records, 1867-1869 (Vol. 5, No. 3) 708

Marriages

1789-1798 (Vol. 2, No. 1) 713

1799-1802 (Vol. 2, No. 2) 716

Wills and Estates

1789-1799 (Vol. 7, No. 1) 720

1800-1805 (Vol. 10, No. 1) 727

Index to Land Entries (Vol. 10, No. 2) 731

Wayne County

Cemetery Records: Jefferson Cemetery (Vol. 1, No. 4) 734

Will Abstracts, 1840-1843 (Vol. 6, No. 2) 736

Williams County

Marriages, 1824-1837 (Vol. 7, No. 3) 744

xii

Death Records, 1867-1871 (Vol. 10, No. 3) 748
Will Abstracts, 1827-1850 (Vol. 6, No. 4) 750

Wood County
Chancery Records, 1839-1850 (Vol. 7, No. 4) 755
Will Abstracts, 1820-1850 (Vol. 6, No. 1) 760

Index 767

LOGAN COUNTY, OHIO - COMMON PLEAS COURT RECORDS 1849-1850

The following records were taken from "Chancery Record L" located in the Common Pleas, Clerk of Courts Office at Bellefontaine, Logan County court house. Pages on which the record may be found in the original are given in parenthesis.

5-15-1849 - Benjamin PLUMMER vs. Dorcas PLUMMER. Petition for Divorce. Filed 2-6-1849. Benjamin married Dorcas Plummer late Dorcas Kellison on 11-18-1842 in Logon Co., Ohio. Dorcus eloped in June or July 1848 with John W. Johnson and has gone to parts unknown. (1)

5-15-1849 - Jno. A. and Daniel L. LOUDER adms. of Anthony LOUDER, dec'd vs. Heirs of dec'd. Petition to complete real contract. Filed 3-31-1849. Anthony Louder in his lifetime contracted to sell 11 acres NW¼ Section 35, Township 3, Range 3 to Jacob Hover of Logan Co. Anthony Louder, dec'd, died in 1847. Heirs: Jno. A. Louder: Daniel L. Louder both of Logan Co.; Susan R. formerly Louder wife of John W. Tabler of Shelby Co., Ohio; Mortimer H. Louder of Logan Co.; Emeline (or Emily) A. Louder; George W. P. Louder; Jacob M. Louder; Henry I. Louder; and Samuel S. Louder; the last five named being minors and all of Shelby Co., Ohio. (3 & 24)

5-15-1849 - Wm. C. CHANEY vs. Widow and Heirs of John CHANEY, dec'd. Petition for Partition. Filed 8-11-1848. Land, 80 acres E½ NW¼ Section 11, Township 3, Range 13, patented to John Chaney. John Chaney, dec'd, died 2-29-1836 Logan Co., having formerly resided in Clark Co. Widow, Hannah Chaney of Logan Co., entitled to dower, Heirs 1/11th part, William C. Chaney formerly of Logan Co., now of Rock Island Co., Ill.; 1/11th part, Marquis L. Chaney; 1/11th part Joanna Chaney; 1/11th part, Perry M. Chaney; 1/11th part, Francis W. Chaney, a minor; 1/11th part, Jane Chaney; 1/11th part, Sarah Ann Chaney, a minor; 1/11th part, John McLease Chaney, a minor; the foregoing all of Logan Co., Ohio; 1/11th part, Nelson W. Chaney of Rock Island Co., Ill.; 1/11th part; Edward J. Chaney of Van Buren Co., Iowa; 1/11th part, Mary Ann late Chaney, dec'd, late wife of Abraham G. Craig, Mary Ann died 3-17-1847 leaving children--Emily Craig of Champaign Co., Ohio, William H. Craig and Perry W. Craig, all having minors with the last two named being of Logan Co., Ohio. (18)

7-31-1849 - John MARQUIS adms. of James MARQUIS, dec'd vs. Widow and Heirs. Petition to sell land. Filed 4-19-1848. Land, part Survey #3442 and also N½ in-lot 160 Bellefontaine. Widow, Mary Marquis. Heirs: Addison, Larissa, Ellhusa and Amanda Marquis. (32)

7-31-1849 - Orsamus SCOTT guardian of Mary PURCELL vs. Mary PURCELL and others. Petition to sell land. Filed 8-22-1848. George Purcell, dec'd, died nine years ago. Widow, Rhoda, now wife of Orsamus Scott of Logan Co., Ohio. Daughter, Mary Purcell. That George Purcell in his lifetime contracted with his father, Thomas Purcell to purchase a tract of land from him as recorded in Title Bond dated 2-28-1838 recorded in Book K, page 349 (Land Records) being part Section 30, Township 6, Range 8; but that Thomas never made deed. (37)

7-31-1849 - David STAUFFER vs. Widow and Heirs of David STAUFFER, dec'd. Petition for Partition and Dower. Filed 2-8-1849. Land, NW¼ Section 1, Township 2, Range 14, Pleasant twp. David Stauffer, dec'd, died intestate with Benjamin F. Phinegar as his adms. Widow, Elizabeth Stauffer. Children: 1/9th part, David Stauffer of Champaign Co., Ohio; 1/9th part, Elizabeth late Stauffer wife of Abraham Garber of Logan Co.; 1/9th part, Sarah late Stauffer wife of Samuel Garber of Logan Co.;

1

STAUFFER vs. STAUFFER - cont.
1/9th part, Susannah late Stauffer wife of Benjamin F. Phinegar of Logan Co.; 1/9th
part, Nancy late Stauffer wife of Solomon Garber of Tennessee; 1/9th part, Catharine
late Stauffer wife of John Clinger of Kosciusko Co., Indiana; 1/9th part, Joseph
Stauffer of Kosciusko Co., Indiana; 1/9th part, Abraham Stauffer of Vermillion Co.,
Indiana; 1/9th part, Mary late Stauffer, now dec'd bying before her father, late wife
of Christopher Grove of Hocking Co., Ohio, her children--Susannah, David, Catharine,
Martin, Samuel, Elizabeth and Mary Grove, all being minors of Hocking Co., Ohio. (42)

7-31-1849 - Sarah LAYPORT guardian of Heirs of her dec'd husband vs. Minor Heirs.
Petition to sell land and for Dower. Filed 5-10-1848. Land, part of Military Surveys
#4948, #9423 and #9876 in Virginia Military District. Charles D. Layport, dec'd.
Widow, Sarah Layport, appointed guardian of children at April Term 1847 Court.
Children: Catherine, Margaret, Robinson, James C. and Charles A.W. Layport, all
minors. (48)

7-31-1849 - Thos. F. McADEN adms. of Levi GARWOOD, dec'd vs. Sarah GARWOOD, widow
and others. Petition to sell land. Filed 8-28-1848. Land, 89 acres part of
Military Survey #4689, lines--Sandusky Road, 100 acre tract sold to John Garwood.
Levi Garwood, dec'd. Widow Sarah Garwood, entitled to dower. Heirs: Job Garwood;
Esther formerly Garwood wife of Samuel Hatcher; James Garwood; Synthia formerly
Garwood wife of Benj. Smith; William Garwood; Susan late Garwood wife of David P.
Lane; Aaron Garwood, dec'd, his children--Silas Garwood aged about 18 yrs., Clirinda
Garwood aged about 16 yrs., Sarah Jane Garwood aged about 14 yrs. and Carlisle H.
Garwood aged about 12 yrs.; John Garwood; Charles Garwood; (note: not clear as to
whether John and Charles are children of Aaron Garwood, dec'd or Levi Garwood, dec'd
--most likely the latter); Hope Reynolds, late Garwood, dec'd, her daughter--Serepta
Reynolds aged 14 yrs.; Rachel Dodson, late Garwood, dec'd, her son--John Dodson
aged 11 yrs.; Levi Garwood, dec'd his children--Alexander, Elizabeth and Nathaniel
Garwood, all minors and all last three named of Michigan. (54)

7-31-1849 - Walter SLICER vs. Isaac PICKERING. Petition for Partition. Filed
5-16-1849. Land, E' SW¼ Section 21, Township 3, Range 14. Daniel Pickering, dec'd.
Widow, Susan, now wife of George Kart, entitled to dower. 6/7th part, Walter Slicer
of Logan Co., by purchase from heirs of Daniel Pickering, dec'd; 1/7th part, Isaac
Pickering of Logan Co., a minor, son of Daniel Pickering, dec'd. (60)

7-31-1849 - Isaac MINSHALL guardian of William WILSON vs. William WILSON, minor.
Petition to sell land and for Dower. Filed 8-26-1848. William Wilson, dec'd.
Widow, Jane late Wilson, now wife of Isaac Minshall. Son, William Wilson, a minor.
Land, 40 acres NE¼ SE¼ Section 34, Township 3, Range 11, being land patented to
Cephas Dills and by him sold to Hugh Wilson who by deed dated 2-2-1840, then being
of Hardin Co., Ohio conveyed to William Wilson, also of Hardin Co., Ohio at that
time. (65)

7-31-1849 - John and Daniel W. FILMER vs. Elizabeth HUMPHRIES, et al. Partition.
Filed 3-6-1849; 60½ acres and 2 poles being part of Robert Powers Survey #3680 and
Duncan McArthur Survey #4953. Partition: 1/3rd part, widow Elizabeth Humphries
(late Elizabeth Sharp). 1/3rd part jointly John and Daniel W. Filmer by their next
friend Robert Filmer. 1/3rd part jointly, Eliza A., Lucilda, Andrew J. and Augustus
W. Humphries, all minors. (70)

7-31-1849 - John FARIS and Joseph STEVENSON, executors vs. Devisees of James KERR. Bill of Interpleader. Filed 5-14-1849. James Kerr, dec'd, executed will on 12-1-1841, executed codicil on 10-29-1844, departed this life 9-1-1846 and will proved and admitted to record on 9-9-1846. Widow, Mary Kerr, still in full life. Heirs; James Kerr of Muskingum Co., Ohio; George Kerr of Ohio Co., Virginia; Joseph Kerr of Logan Co.; Thomas L. Kerr of Logan Co.; David Kerr of Belmont Co., Ohio; Katherine Kerr of Logan Co.; John Kerr of Belmont Co., Ohio; William Kerr of Belmont Co., Ohio; Martha Kerr of Logan Co.; Morrison Kerr; Patterson Kerr; Robert S. Kerr; and Eliza Jane Kerr; the last four named being minors and all of Logan Co., Ohio. Will of James Kerr dated 12-1-1841 names wife, Martha to have all personal property for support of minor children and 150 acrs where testator lives during her natural life. Names sons, James Kerr, William Kerr, George Kerr, Joseph Kerr, Thomas L. Kerr, David Kerr, Morrison Kerr, Samuel Kerr, Patterson Kerr, Robert S. Kerr and Wily M. Kerr. Names daughters, Margaret Ann Stephenson and Katherine Kerr. Executors: Robert Patterson and brother, Wm. Kerr. Signed: James Kerr. Wit: Benjamin Staunton Jr. and John F. Davis. Codicil dated 10-29-1844 states that sons, Samuel Kerr and Wily M. Kerr have since departed this life and that daughter, Eliza Jane Kerr has been born. In lieu of executors appointed in will, now appoints John Faris and Joseph Stephenson Jr. as Executors. Signed: James Kerr. Wit: B. Staunton and Rodalphus Pettit. (77)

7-31-1849 - Mary PARKER vs. John PARKER. Petition for Divorce. Filed 4-25-1849. Married 3-4-1841 Logan Co., Ohio. John Parker now of parts unknown. (88)

5-15-1849 - Noah DEVALT adms. of Thomas PENDERGRASS vs. Widow and Heirs. Petition to sell land. Filed 4-28-1847. Land, Part of Thomas Pearsons Survey #9906. Thomas Pendergrass, dec'd. Widow, Mary formerly Pendergrass now wife of Morgan Tolen (Toland). Heirs: Mary A., Pattrick, Sophronia, John W. and Thomas Pendergrass. (103)

11-6-1849 - Nesbit JANUARY vs. Mary WILKINS, etal. Petition for Partition. Filed 4-7-1849. Land in Union Co. and Logan Co.; part Survey #3155; part George McCready's survey #3155 and part Survey #3351; also out-lot #3 adjoining town of Marysville. James January, dec'd, late of Logan Co. Widow, Catharine January of Logan Co. Heirs: 1/5 part, Nesbit January; 1/5th part, Mary wife of David Wilkins; 1/5th part, Martha January; 1/5th part, Elizabeth January; 1/5th part, Houston January. (124)

11-6-1849 - Alexander WEST adms. of William FINTON vs. Mary E. FINTON, widow and others. Petition to sell land. Filed 11-6-1847. Land, 80 acres E½ SE¼ and 20 acres S½ SE¼ NE¼ Section 15, Township 6, Range 8. William FINTON, dec'd, late of Logan Co., died intestate in April 1847. Widow, Mary E. Finton of Logan Co. Only child, Sarah Elizabeth Finton of Logan Co. (133)

5-13-1850 - Andrew WALKER guardian of James WILSON vs. James WILSON and James M. WILSON. In Chancery. Filed 7-9-1849. John Wilson, dec'd, died in Logan Co., Ohio leaving his only son, James Wilson, a minor with Andrew Walker of Muskingum Co., Ohio as his guardian. Land, 50 acres part Military Survey #3220 which was conveyed to John Wilson on 3-15-1841 by Joseph Marquis and wife as recorded in Deed Book L, pages 511 & 512. That on 5-21-1845 William Findlay who was then guardian of James Wilson filed his petition on Logan Co. Common Pleas Court to sell said land. That James M. Wilson then of Trumbull Co., Ohio purchased land. (139)

5-13-1850 - Samuel LEAS vs. Daniel G. LEAS, etal. In Chauncery. Filed 4-6-1849.
Samuel Leas of Muskingum Co., Ohio formerly of Logan Co. represents that on or
about 1-16-1846 and prior to that time Stephen Leas, father of said Samuel, was owner
of part of Military Survey #3439 on waters of Mad River being 38.16 acres being same
land conveyed from Stephen Leas to Daniel G. Leas and included in mortgage from
Daniel G. Leas to Stephen Leas. That Rebecca Jane Leas who was wife of Daniel G.
Leas in Nov. 1846 Term Court divorced said Daniel G. Leas.   (163)

5-13-1850 - David WALLACE adms. of Estate of Joseph WALLACE, dec'd vs. John P.
WALLACE and others, heirs of Joseph Wallace. In Chancery. Filed 1-31-1850.
Petition to Complete Contract. Land, part Military Survey #9903 which Joseph
Wallace on 10-26-1837 agreed to sell to Linus Cutting. Heirs: John P. Wallace
married Emeline Hover; Mary A. Wallace wife of Abraham Elder; James Wallace and
Alexander G. Wallace, both minors by Rev. James Wallace their guardian; Margaret
Wallace, a minor by Mary Wallace her guardian; Joseph Wallace by Eliza Walker his
guardian, he also a minor. (180 & 213)

5-13-1850 - Thomas BERRY and wife vs. John ROBERTS, et al. Partition. Filed
3-5-1850. Land, part Survey #9968 conveyed to John Moyer by James Taylor and wife.
John MOYER, dec'd. Widow, Dina Moyer of Logan Co., entitled to dower. Heirs:
1/8th part, Dina late Moyer wife of Thomas Berry of Logan Co.; 1/8th part, Catherine
late Moyer wife of John Roberts; 1/8th part, Leah late Moyer wife of Hampson Burner;
1/8th part, Sarah Johnson late Moyer; 1/8th part, Lydia Moyer, a minor of Logan Co.;
1/8th part, Elizabeth Moyer, a minor of Logan Co.; 1/8th part, Margaret Moyer, a
minor of Logan Co.; 1/8th part, George W. Moyer, a minor of Logan Co. (184)

5-13-1850 - Elon O. HAMMOND guardian of Heirs of D. W. HARRINGTON vs. The Heirs.
Petition to sell land. File 3-3-1848. David W. Harrington, dec'd, late of Logan
Co. Widow, Parmelia K. late Harrington, now wife of Elon O. Hammond. Children:
Mary Sophia and George S. Harrington, minors by Elon O. Hammond of Montpelier,
Washington Co., Vermont, their guardian. (190)

5-13-1850 - Anson R. THRALL adms. of Robert A. McCLURE, dec'd vs. John TAYLOR and
Widow and Heirs. Filed 3-13-1847. Robert McClure, dec'd, died intestate, late of
Logan Co. That Robert McClure died seized of undivided half of lot 208 Bellefontaine
with John Taylor owning the other undivided half. Widow, Martha McClure. Heirs:
Harriet, Ann, William Scott and Eliza McClure, all minors. (200)

5-13-1850 - Thomas MOORE adms. of Judith (Judah) CHAMBERLAIN vs. Calvin CHAMBERLAIN,
et al. Petition to sell land. Filed 6-25-1849. Land. 126 acres part S½ Section 13,
Township 3, Range 14. Widow, Phebe Chamberlain, entitled to dower. Heirs with next
estate of inheritance: Calvin Chamberlain of New York; Harriet late Chamberlain,
wife of Henry Hanford of Logan Co.; Lansing Chamberlain of Wyandot Co., Ohio; Vincent
Chamberlain of Madison Co., Ohio; and Warren Chamberlain of Logan Co. (205)

5-13-1850 - Oden HAYES adms. of James CRAIG, dec'd vs. Widow and Heirs. Petition to
sell land. Filed 6-26-1849. Land, S pt. E½ SE¼ Section 1, Township 7, Range 8, 52
acres, Washington twp. Widow, Delilah Craig. Heirs: Eliza Jane Craig, Elizabeth
Craig, Eliza Jane Preston and Rachel Ann formerly Craig wife of Joseph Hudwell.
(216)

4

5-13-1850 - Benjamin S. BROWN adms. of George SHAFFER, dec'd vs. Widow and Heirs.
Petition to sell land. Filed 10-4-1849. Land, lot 85 in Bellefontaine. Widow,
Hannah Shaffer. Heirs: William H., Samuel and Francis M. Shaffer. (220)

5-13-1850 - Zilpha Kellison vs. Eli Kellison. Divorce. File 1-31-1850. Married
1-1-1838 in Licking Co., Ohio. Eli Kellison eloped with one Mary Johnson in 1848
and is believed to be in Indiana. (223)

5-13-1850 - Andrew BASSART vs. Joseph PETTY, et al. In Partition. Filed 9-18-1849.
Land, 35 acres N end E½ SW¼ Section 16, Township 3, Range 14 being tract conveyed by
Jonathan Norton to James Prosser late of Allen Co., Ohio and of which James died
seized. James PROSSER, dec'd. Widow, Margaret late Prosser, now wife of Simeon
Bently of Allen Co., Ohio. Partition: 3/6ths part, Andrew Bassart (possibly by
purchase); 1/6th part, Nancy wife of Joseph Petty of Illinois; 1/6th part, Rebecca
wife of Anthony Hall, residence unknown; 1/6th part, Thomas Prosser, a minor of Allen
Co., Ohio by William Hubbard his guardian; the last three named being Heirs of James
Prosser, dec'd. (225)

5-13-1850 - Almon HOPKINS adms. of Dan HOPKINS, dec'd vs. Widow and Heirs. Petition
to sell land. Filed 6-28-1849. Land, lot 116 in Bellefontaine. Widow, Sarah Hopkins of Logan Co. entitled to dower. Heirs: Almon Hopkins; Jemima late Hopkins wife
of John Wilcox of Putnam Co., Ohio; Martha Ann late Hopkins wife of John Knox of
Wapello Co., Iowa; Hester Jane Hopkins; Elizabeth Hopkins, William Hopkins; Eliza
Hopkins; Owen Johnston Hopkins; Herty Hopkins and Frank Hopkins; the last seven
named all being minors and all of Logan Co. (229)

5-13-1850 - Alexander HENRY and Harriet Elizabeth HENRY by Wm. McCOLLOCH guardian
vs. Heirs and Devisees. Petition for Pa tition. Filed 6-1-1849. Land, two tracts
being 52 acres one tract and 10 acres other tract part of Alexander Dandridge's
Survey #3220 and patented to Thomas Worthington. James HENRY, dec'd, died in 1840
with will recorded in Probate Record C, pages 158-159. Widow, Priscilla Henry, to
have real estate during her life, then to go to children, Priscilla departed life
in March or April 1849. Children: 1/8th part, Sanford Henry of Logan Co.; 1/8th part,
Nancy McFaden, dec'd, late wife of Thomas McFadden who is still living, her children
--Thomas Vance and Sarah Elizabeth McFadden, both minors of Logan Co.; 1/8th part,
Mary Ann wife of John Reeder of Logan Co.; 1/8th part, Sarah wife of Newton Garwood
of Logan Co.; 1/8th part, Joel Henry of Indiana; 1/8th part, George Henry; 1/8th part,
Alexander Henry; 1/8th part, Harriet Elizabeth Henry; the last three named being
minors and all of Logan Co. (244)

7-27-1850 - Israel COPE, et al. vs. George FOLSOM, et al. In Chancery. Filed
8-13-1849 - Simeon HADLEY, dec'd, formerly of Pickaway Co., Ohio, died in 1818
leaving will proven in Probate Court of New Castle Co., Delaware with John Dixon of
Delaware amd Stephen Short of Pickaway Co., Ohio as executors and with will also
being entered and recorded in Pickaway Co., Ohio Probate Court. Heirs: Sister,
Elizabeth Dixon, dec'd, entitled to 1/5th part of all estate, her children--Rebecca
Woods, dec'd (died after Elizabeth Dixon), her children--Elizabeth Adamson, Samuel
Woods and Lydia Woods, all of Columbiana Co., Ohio; Ruth Cope, dec'd (died after
Elizabeth Dixon), her children--Simeon Cope of Columbiana Co., Ohio, Caleb Cope of
Wabash Co., Indiana, Edith wife of Ephraim Stratton of Wayne Co., Indiana and Mary
Paxon, dec'd (who died after Ruth Cope), her children--Ruth Ann formerly Paxon wife

COPE vs. FOLSOM - cont.
of John Pickerell, Eli Paxon, Nelson Paxon, Samuel Paxon, and Charles Paxon all of
Elkhart Co., Indiana; SIMON DIXON, dec"d (died after Elizabeth Dixon), his children--
Ruth formerly Dixon wife of John Elliott of Logan Co., Sarah Agee (or Agie) a widow
of Stark Co., Ohio, Cyrus Dixon of Columbiana Co., Ohio, John Dixon, Matilda formerly
Dixon wife of James Elliott of Logan Co., Mary wife of Benjamin Harrison; HENRY DIXON,
dec'd, who in his lifetime deeded his interest in his mother, Elizabeth Dixon's
estate to Israel Cope and William Harrison; MARGARET COPE, a widow, of Columbiana Co.,
Ohio; ELIZABETH wife of ISRAEL COPE of Columbiana Co., Ohio; MARY wife of WILLIAM
HARRISON of Columbiana Co., Ohio; EMMY COPE, dec'd (died after Elizabeth Dixon), her
children--Henry Cope of Columbiana Co., Ohio, Samuel Cope of Columbiana Co., Ohio,
Caleb Cope of Columbiana Co., Ohio, Eli Cope of Columbiana Co., Ohio, John Cope of
Wood Co., Ohio, Mary wife of John Boyce of Columbiana Co., Ohio. Other Heirs under
will of Simeon Hadley (note: no relationships given): Moses Pennock of Chester Co.,
Pa.; Mary Dixon of Wilmington, Delaware; David Willson of New Castle Co., Delaware;
Spencer Chandler and Eliza wife; Stephen Willson; Phebe Willson; Lydia Willson; the
last three named all of New Castle Co., Delaware; John Hadley and Ann wife of Chester
Co., Pa.; Simon Pennock and Sarah wife of Lancaster Co., Pa.; Elizabeth Pennock; Ann
Pennock; Phoebe Pennock; the last three named all of Chester Co., Pa.; Jacob Taylor
and Mary wife; Thomas Martin; Samuel Hadley and Phebe wife; Joshua Thompson and Phebe
wife; Joel Hoopes and Rebecca wife; Samuel Ma.tin and Rachael wife; George Martin and
Ann E. wife; Thomas Martin Jr. and Hannah wife; Simon Martin and Deborah wife; all of
Chester Co., Pa. Simeon Hadley entered the whole of Military Entry and Survey #3139
in the Virginia Military District, of this land, he sold a part being 1500 acres on
7-17-1815 to Joseph Garwood, then of Crawford Co., Pa. for the sum of $45,860.00.
Of the remaining land, part was apparently deeded to William Miller, still living, of
Pickaway Co., Ohio and also to Joshua Folsom and William Renick, both now deceased.
This last mentioned land appears to have been the subject of much litigation with
part being in the Pickaway Co. Common Pleas Court. WILLIAM RENICK, long since dec'd.
Heirs: Seymore G. Renick; Joseph O. B. Renick; Felix W. Renick; Eliza formerly Renick
wife of Samuel Adams; Ellen Renick of Pickaway Co., Ohio; Hiram Renick of Missouri;
James Whitcomb of Indiana; Martha Ann Whitcomb, a minor of Indiana, but now in Ross
Co., Ohio. JOSHUA FOLSOM, took possession of land by deed (apparently after litigation against Hadley in Pickaway Co., Ohio Common Pleas Court) in 1831 or 1832 and
continued to occupy same until his death on 12-23-1840, but that on 12-1-1840 Joshua
deeded for natural love and affection to son George Folsom 500 acres being part of
tract, Heirs of Joshua Folsom under his will: widow, Catharine Folsom of Pickaway Co.,
Ohio; son, George Folsom of Logan Co., Ohio; son, Charles Folsom (he received 600
acres of tract under will) of Logan Co., Ohio; son, Henry Folsom, now known by name of
Henry Folsom Paige, of Pickaway Co., Ohio; and daughter, Mary Folsom of Pickaway Co.,
Ohio. (254 & 279)

7-29-1850 - Joseph LAWRENCE adms. of James King MOORE, dec'd vs. Widow and Heirs.
Petition to sell land. Filed 4-11-1850. James King Moore died seized of one undivid-
ed sixth part of 96 Military Survey $5499 and 10 acres part Military survey
#3183 being premises which William Moore died seized. James King MOORE, dec'd.
Widow, Harriet E. Moore of Licking Co., Ohio, entitled to dower. Only child, Hannah
Elizabeth Moore, a minor of Licking Co., Ohio. William MOORE, dec'd, died several
years since leaving widow, Elizabeth Moore of Logan Co., and six children of whom
James King Moore was one and by which James King Moore inherited his 1/6th interest.
(316)

6

The following records were taken from "Chancery Record L" located in the Common Pleas, Clerk of Courts Office at the court house in Bellefontaine. Pages on which record may be found in the original are given in parenthesis.

7-29-1850 - Jonathan PLUM and Isaac PLUM vs Michael TROUT, Hannah KERNS, Abraham KERNS, et al. Petition for Partition. Filed 11-12-1849. Land, 340 acres fractional Section 25, Township 7, Range 8; NW fractional quarter Section 30, Township 6, Range 9, 72 acres; 37.66 acres SE fractional quarter and 46.40 acres NE fractional quarter Section 30, Township 7, Range 9. Michael Kerns, dec'd. Widow, Elizabeth Kerns. Partition 3/12ths part, Jonathan Plum of Logan Co.; 2/12ths part, Isaac Plum of Logan Co.; 3/12ths part, Michael Trout of Logan Co., by purchse and right of his wife Mary Trout a daughter of Michael Kerns, dec'd; 1/12th part, Hannah Kerns; 1/12th part, Abraham Kerns; 1/12th part, Lucinda Kerns; 1/12th part, George A. Kerns; all of Logan Co. and all minors, children of Michael Kerns, dec'd by William H. McKinnon and Gabriel H. Barnes their guardians. (322)

7-29-1850 - Oden HAYS adms. of Samuel McBETH, dec'd vs. Demarris McBETH, et al. Petition to sell land. Filed 10-4-1849. Land, 43 acres W pt. E½ SW¼ Section 35, Township 5, Range 13, E.G.M.R. Samuel McBeth, dec'd, late of Logan Co., died intestate. Widow, Demarris McBeth. Heirs: Letitia Ann, Margaret Francis, Catharine Sophia, James Henry, Martha Jane and Edward R. McBeth. (330)

7-29-1850 - William HENRY guardian of Isabella WILKINSON vs. Isabella WILKINSON. Petition to sell land. Filed 3-11-1850. Isabella Wilkinson an insane woman of Logan Co. is seized of part of Hezekiah Norton Survey #4498 being Lot 2 in division of Estate of Thomas Wilkinson and descending to Isabella from her father, said Thomas Wilkinson. (335)

7-29-1850 - Benjamin F. ROBB vs. Hannah ROBB, et al. Petition for Partition. Filed 10-11-1850. Land, 57.95 acres part Military Survey #9931. John Robb, dec'd, died 9-1-1848. Brothers and Sisters: 1/10th part, Benjamin F. Robb of Logan Co.; 1/10th part, Hannah Robb of Logan Co.; 1/10th part, Barbara Robb of Logan Co.; 1/10th part, Dorcus Robb of Logan Co.; 1/10th part, Samuel Robb of Muskingum Co., Ohio; 1/10th part, James Robb of Muskingum Co., Ohio; 1/10th part, Mary formerly Robb wife of Joseph Little of Beaver Co., Penna.; 1/10th part, Andrew Robb of Allegheny Co., Penna., but not heard from in 10 years; 1/10th part, David Robb of Hardin Co., Ohio; 1/10th part jointly or 1/20th part each, William Robb, dec'd, his children--Samuel and Dorcus Jane Robb, both minors of Logan Co. (338)

7-29-1850 - James W. HAMILTON vs. Clarinda GARWOOD, et al. Petition to sell land. Filed 10-4-1849. Land, 100 acres being E½ of a 200 acre lot on waters of Mill Creek part Survey #13315 which was conveyed to Levi Garwood by Duncan McArthur on 6-8-1836. Aaron Garwood, dec'd, late of Logan Co. Children: Clarinda, Jane, Silas and Carlisle H. Garwood, Minors by James W. Hamilton their guardian. (345)

7-29-1850 - Howell G. SMITH vs. Peter SMITH and others, Heirs and Devisees of Robert SMITH. Petition for Partition. Filed 7-6-1849. Land, 40 acres E pt. SW¼ Section 11, Township 4, Range 13. Widow, mentioned but not named. Children: 1/9th part, William Smith of Perry Co., Ohio; 1/9th part, Jane formerly Smith wife of Henry Hicks of Warren Co., New Jersey; 1/9th part, Howell G. Smith; 1/9th part, Peter Smith; 1/9th part, David Smith; 1/9th part, Sarah Elizabeth Smith; 1/9th part, Joseph Smith; 1/9th part, Irena Smith; 1/9th part, Alfred G. Smith; the last three named being minors. (348)

7-29-1850 - William JOSEPH adms. of Daniel JOSEPH vs. Annis JOSEPH, et al. Petition to sell land. Filed 4-24-1850. Land, pt. E½ SW¼ and S part W½ SE¼ Section 10, Township 4, Range 3. Widow, Annis Joseph. Heirs: John Joseph, William Joseph, David Joseph, Harvey Joseph, Eva Jane wife of Manlove Holmes, Daniel Joseph, Julianna Joseph, Mary Eleanor Joseph, Thomas Joseph, Isabella Joseph, Priscilla Joseph and Annis Joseph, the last six named being minors. (356)

7-29-1) - Philander BALDWIN vs. Widow and heirs of Abraham BRONSON. Petition for Partition. Filed 5-30-1850. Land, 100½ acres on waters of Mill Creek, Military Survey 4210. Abraham Bronson, dec;d, late of Logan Co. died about August 1842. Widow, Mary Bronson of Logan Co. Heirs: William Bronson of Allen Co., Indiana; John E. Bronson of Noble Co., Indiana; Sarah late Bronson wife of David Jones of Logan Co.; Robert Bronson; George W. Bronson; James H. Bronson; Rebecca B. Bronson; and Philana Ann Bronson; the last five named being minors and all of Logan Co. Each entitled to 1/8th part with Sarah and David Jones having sold their interest to Philander Baldwin. (359)

11-4-1850 - George IRWIN adms. of William JONSON, dec'd vs. Widow and Heirs. PETITION to sell land. Filed 11-7-1849. Land, 64 acres on waters of Big Miami being part of Survey 9975. Widow, Eleanor Johnston. Heirs: Elizabeth Johnson; Mary Johnson; Eleanor late Johnson, dec'd wife of George Irwin, her children-- Mary Ellen and William Irwin; Isaac Johnson; Adison Johnson; Hetty Ann Johnson; John W. Johnson; and Robert Johnson; the last six named being minors. (419)

11-4-1850 - Robert H. CANBY adms. of Joseph CANBY, dec'd vs. widow and Heirs. Petition to sell land. Filed 9-9-1847. Land, part fractional Section 24, Township 3, Range 13 on which there is a grist mill, said land conveyed to Joseph Canby by James R. Baldwin and wife as recorded in Book G, page 197; also 156 acres MW¼ Section 6, Township 3, Range 13 as recorded in Book C, page 463; also 147.37 acres W part fractional Section 23, Township 1, Range 8 and lots 9 & 19 in Canby's addition to Quincy; (note: also a number of other land descriptions). Widow, Margaret H. Canby. Children: Ann late Canby wife of Edward Kitchen of Miami Co., Ohio; Hannah late Canby wife of John Evans of Indiana; Robert H. Canby; Richard S. Canby; John Canby; Israel Canby; Noah H. Canby; Mary Canby; Sarah B. Canby and Lydia Canby; all of Logan Co. with Israel, Noah H. and Lydia being minors. (426)

11-4-1850 - William LEASE adms. of Silas C. DUFF, dec'd vs. Widow and Heirs. Petition to sell land. Filed 6-21-1850. Land, Lots 11 & 12 in town of Richland. Widow, Harriet Duff. Child, Julia Ann Duff, a minor. (474)

11-4-1850 - William PARKER, guardian vs. Calvin STRATTON. Petition to sell land. Filed 5-16-1830. Land, Land warrant #24511 for 160 acres issued by War Dept. on 8-26-1848. Joel STRATTON, dec'd, late Pvt. in Capt. Kings Co., 15th Regt., U.S. Inf. Child, Calvin Stratton, a minor of Logan Co. (478)

11-4-1850 - Geo. W. WILLIAMS adms. of Zimri BRATTAIN vs. Mary Ann BRATTAIN.
Petition to sell land. Filed 7-18-1849. Land, part Survey 3221 adj. Pickrelltown.
Widow, Mary Ann now wife of Thomas Allmon of Morrow Co., Ohio. No children. (482)

11-4-1850 - John HILLINGS vs. Margaret READ, et al. Petition to complete contract.
Filed 8-3-1850. That Obediah Read on 11-13-1841 contracted to sell Hillings
24 1/3 acres where Read then resided, which was conveyed to said Obediah Read
by Joseph Reed being part of Kinous(?) Survey. Obediah Read, dec'd. Widow,
Margaret Read. Four minor children: Edward, Rachel, Sarah and Mary Read, all
of Logan Co. (486)

11-4-1850 - Melissa C. REED vs. Orrin REED. Petition for Divorce. Filed 9-20-1850.
Married Oct. 1847. (499)

11-4-1850 - Joseph LONGFELLOW and wife vs. Heirs of Layton POLLOCK, dec'd. Petition
for Partition. Filed 5-20-1850. Land, 152 acres SW¼ Section 24, Township 4, Range
13. Partition: 1/8th part jointly, Sarah formerly Pollock, dec'd wife of Adam
Neher, her children--George and Rachel Ann Neher, minors with their father, Adam
Neher as guardian, all of Logan Co.; 1/8th part jointly, William Pollock, dec'd,
his children--Layton, Thomas, George Retty, Mary and William Pollock, all minors
and all of Iowa; 1/8th part jointly, Layton Pollock and Joseph Pollock; 1/8th part,
Robert Pollock of Logan Co.; 1/8th part, James Pollock of Illinois; 3/8ths part,
Mary formerly Pollock wife of Joseph Longfellow of Logan Co. with 1/8th part in
Mary's own right and the other 2/8ths part by purchase from Layton Pollock and
Joseph Pollock. (501 & 505)

11-4-1850 - Walter PAINTER vs. Isaac PAINTER, guardian. Petition for Partition.
Filed 9-9-1850. Land. 50 acres on waters of Mill Creek being pt. Survey #4210.
Alfred Painter, dec'd. Widow, Matilda Vanvoorhis, right to dower. Partition:
1/4th part, Walter Painter; 1/4th part, William R. Painter; 1/4th part, Robert
Painter; 1/4th part, Sophia Painter; the last three named being minors by Isaac
Painter their guardian; all of Logan Co.

11-4-1850 - James PARK vs. John WILKINSON, et al. Bill in Chancery. Filed
6-12-1850. That prior to the year 1815, Thomas Wilkinson was owner of part of
Hezekiah Morton Military Survey #4498 on waters of the Big Miami. Thomas Wilkinson,
dec'd died about year 1813 (note: in another portion of record it states he died in
1826). Widow, Catharine Wilkinson now Rifer, she having married Christopher Rifer
who died prior to about 1833 with said Catharine selling her interest to Moses
Marquis of Montgomery Co., Ohio and Joseph Marquis of Logan Co., Ohio, both of whom
later sold to Park. Four children: John Wilkinson and his wife Deborah now of
Michigan, conveyed their interest to the Marquis' in 1835; George Wilkinson; Nancy
wife of George Kellerman, conveyed her interest to Marquis' in 1835; Isabella
Wilkinson, her interest conveyed by court. (520)

11-4-1850 - Mary COOPER widow of Isaac COOPER, dec'd vs. Heirs. Petition for Dower.
Filed 5-20-1850. Land, 80 acres W½ SW½ and 80 acres E½ SW½ Section 13 and 40 acres
NE¼ NW¼ Section 24, Township 7, Range 8 (note: also a number of other land descrip-
tions). Isaac Cooper, dec'd, died in late part 1848 or early part 1849. Widow,
Mary Cooper. Heirs: Thomas B. Cooper; Nancy Ann formerly Cooper wife of Kemp G.
Carter; Abigail J. formerly Cooper widow of Andrew I. Cherry, he now being dec'd;

9

Mary J. formerly Cooper wife of Thomas Niven; Joseph L. Cooper; Alfred F. Cooper; and Isaac A. Cooper; all of Logan Co. with Mary Niven and last three named being minors. (526)

11-4-1850 - Henry Cowgill of Champaign Co., Ohio adms. of Estate of James W. MARMON, dec'd vs. Heirs. Petition to sell land. Filed 4-17-1850. Land, 3 4/5 acres Zanesfield part Survey #3137, Lots 43 & 46 Crawfordsville; also real estate in Wyandot Co., Ohio. James W. Marmon, dec'd, late of Wayne Co., Indiana. Left no widow. Children: Martin Marmon of Champaign Co., Ohio; Ann Marmon of Wayne Co., Ohio; Mary Marmon; Charles M. Marmon; and Daniel W. Marmon; the last three named being minors and all of Wayne Co., Indiana. (531)

5-5-1851 - James LEISTER and Margaret MARQUIS adms. of John MARQUIS, dec'd vs. Wm V. MARQUIS, et al. Petition to sell land. Filed 10-15-1850. Land, lot 99 and south side lot 106 Bellefontaine. Widow, Margaret Marquis. Children: Lucinda wife of James Leister, William Vance Marquis and Calvin Marquis. (557)

5-5-1851 - Alexander BLACK, adms. vs. Robert McILVAIN's Heirs. Petition to sell land. Filed 4-16-1850. Land, 160 acres SE¼ Section 12, Township 4, Range 13. Heirs: Moses McIlvain; Florence McIlvain; Robert McIlvain, a minor; all of Logan Co.; Rebecca McIlvain of Champaign Co., Ohio; Jane late McIlvain wife of William Smith; Elizabeth McIlvain; Mary Ellen McIlvain, a minor; all of Putnam Co., Ohio. (562)

5-5-1851 - Joseph WILLIAMSON vs. Wm. G. WILLIAMSON. Petition for Partition. Filed 2-25-1850. Land, 78½ acres W½ SW¼ and 75½ acres S½ NW¼ Section 12, Township 4, Range 13. William Williamson, dec'd, died in 1833 leaving will recorded in Book B. Widow, Isabella Williamson, to have use of estate during her life, then to descend to her children, she died in March 1848. Children: 1/7th part, Joseph Williamson of Logan Co.; 1/7th part, Hugh Williamson, sold his interest to Margaret Andrews; 1/7th part, Jane Morris, dec'd, late wife of Joseph Morris, her children--James and John Morris, both minors with Benjamin Morris of Clark Co. their guardian; 1/7th part, Anne Morris, dec'd, late wife of Benjamin Morris, her child--Thadeus Morris, a minor with Benjamin Morris his guardian; 1/7th part, Elizabeth Drummond, dec'd, late wife of John Drummond, her child--William Drummond, a minor; 1/7th part, Catharine wife of Nathan H. Mathews; 1/7th part, Wm. G. Williamson, a minor. (573)

5-5-1851 - John MADDINGTON vs Widow and Heirs of Jacob SESLER, dec'd. Petition for Partition. Filed 6-1-1849. Land, 100 acres part Virginia Military Survey 9972 on Big Miami. Sidow, Damarius Sesler. Children: 1/6th part, Harriet wife of John Madigan formerly of Logan Co. but now of Clark Co.; 1/6th part, sophronia Ann Sesler; 1/6th part, Elizabeth Groves Sesler; 1/6th part, William Hamilton Sesler; 1/6th part, Thomas Jefferson Sesler; 1/6th part, Mary Sesler. (581)

5-5-1851 - Martha A. READ vs. Nathaniel C. READ. Petition for Divorce. Filed 1-20-1851. Married in July 1831. Nathaniel living in Cincinnati in 1849. (602)

ALEXANDER, Joseph to Martha ALEXANDER		9-1-1822
ARSKIN, John to Polly McILVAIN		2-4-1819
AUSTIN, Carlisle H. to Rebecca REA		6-24-1824
BAILESS, Josiah to Hannah CURL		10-12-1820
BAILOR, Frederick to Elizabeth CRAIG		3-29-1821
BALDWIN, Jesse to Jane MARMON		12-22-1825
BALLENGER, John to Mary INSKIP		7-25-1820
BENNETT, Henry H. to Polly HERROD	Iss.	6-4-1825
BEST, Thomas to Margaret OHAVER		9-6-1822
BISHOP, James to Eliza INSKIP		12-5-1822
BISHOP, John to Sally GARWOOD		12-20-1819
BISHOP, William to Rachel BRANSEN		5-8-1823
BLACK, Joseph to Mercey KNOUSKOP		10-2-1825
BLAGG, Samuel to Catharine KELLEY		11-23-1820
BLAIR, Brice to Mary JOHNSON		9-29-1825
BLAYLOCK, Vachel to Anne COVINGTON		12-19-1824
BLUE, John to Mary HOBOUCH		12-23-1819
BLUE, William to Elizabeth IDLE		11-30-1824
BOTKIN, John to Elizabeth LOCKARD		5-5-1825
BRADEN, Robert to Lucinda McNAY		2-12-1822
BRANSEN, Abram to Mary MATHEWS		8-12-1821
BRATTIN, Stephen to Elizabeth LOWE		9-21-1819
BULLER, James to Obedience PATTERSON		3-9-1820
BURNSIDES, John to Nancy JONES		2-17-1825
CAIN, Henry to Rachel MENDENHALL		5-17-1821
CALHOUN, Abner to Mary HOIT		4-17-1823
CAMPBELL, George to Sally SKINNER		1-14-1819
CAMPBELL, James to Betsey MOON		12-14-182
CAMPBELL, William to Anne MOORE		2-13-1821
CARNER, Michael to Redy HEATH		4-11-1824
CARROL, William to Naome SCOTT		10-25-1821
CARTER, Jonathan to Nancy McARTHUR		6-10-1824
CASEBOLL, Robert to Hannah DAVIS		3-11-1819
CAUSHEN, William to Nancy HELTEN		6-5-1822
William of Highland County		
CHAPPELL, Joshua to Anne DUNN		1-10-1819
CLINE, Peter to Margaret SCOTT		9-22-1825
COE, William to Winney BAILY	Iss.	6-5-1822
COLVIN, Daniel to Nancy HILE		6-6-1820
CONNEL, James to Sally FIELDER		3-18-1824
CONNER, James to Mayet (Myet?) LEE		3-11-1825
CRAY, Mathias to Sally CARPENTER		1-2-1819
CREVISTON, Jacob to Martha POPE		5-9-1824
CROCKET, Payten to Matilda NEWELL		2-18-1823
CROSS, Solomon to Betsey SAWYER		4-28-1819
CRUCHER, Nathan to Sarah POLLOCK		10-28-1819
CURL, James R. to Louisa Ann BAILESS		5-10-1825
CURL, Joseph S. to Zillah GREGG		9-22-1825
CURL, Samuel to Catharine SMITH		6-17-1819
DANIEL, Samuel M. to Elenor CARRAGO	Iss.	5-28-1822
	Ret.	8-10-1822
DAULPH, Benjamin to Sarah WOOD		4-6-1824
DAVIDSON, William to Polly BEARD		5-23-1821

```
DAVIS, John to Matilda WOOD                            2-7-1822
DAVIS, William A. to Frances TELLIS      Iss.    7-20-1822
DAVIS, William H. to Mary JOHNSTON                1-28-1819
DEARDUFF, Daniel to Polly SURTS                   4-15-1824
DICKINSON, Richard to Peggy HENRY                10-29-1818
DICKSON, Thompson to Cynthia TURNER              12-2-1824
DILLIN, Frederick to Catharine PRICKET           8-11-1824
DILLIN, Isaac B. to Pamila SMITH                 8-11-1824
DODGE, Nathaniel to Betsey WORKMAN               3-13-1820
DUNLAP, Joseph to Nancy WHEELER                 10-17-1825
DUNN, George F. to Isabella McILVAIN            11-17-1818
DUNSTON, Thomas to Bulah PATRICK                 9-22-1825
EATON, William to Sally ELLENDER                 9-30-1819
EDWARDS, Justice to Margaret SMITH       Iss.   10-23-1821
ELLIS, John to Elizabeth CONNER                  2-27-1823
ENOCH, John to Betsey KELLY                      7-25-1822
EWINS, Joseph to Phebe HANES                    11-7-1823
FLOWERS, Adam to Betsey ARCHER                  11-10-1825
FORSYTHE, Robert A. to Almira HULL               1-17-1819
FRANKLIN, Henry to Elizabeth ARCHER              6-22-1822
FRANTZ, Abraham to Catharine HOUTZ               1-11-1824
GALLENTINE, John to Deborah COX                  1-9-1823
GARWOOD, Daniel to Elizabeth HUMPHREYS          11-28-1823
GARWOOD, James to Jane SMITH                     2-15-1824
GARWOOD, Jehu G. to Rachel HAIRCHUR              8-30-1821
GARWOOD, Job to Lydia GREGG                      2-3-1820
GARWOOD, William to Betsey BROWN                12-22-1824
GRAYUS, Doctor to Matilda ZANE           Iss.    7-14-1824
GREEN, George to Ruth WILLIAMS                   5-22-1823
GREEN, Nehmiah to Julia FRIER                   11-6-1825
GREEN, William to Hester LEIPER                 11-28-1826
GRETCHELL, David to Eliza LANE                   5-27-182?
GRUBS, Daniel to Sally CAIN                      6-24-1819
HAINES, Jesse to Delilah BAILESS                 9-22-1823
HAINES, Jesse to Rebecca COWGILL                 6-17-1824
HAINES, William H. to Atlanlick GRUBS            5-24-1825
HALL, John to Pamelia LEE                        3-22-1821
HALL, John to Susannah MORAHUSE          Iss.    8-17-1822
HARMAN, Thomas to Peggy TRUIT                   10-29-1818
HARPER, John to Rebecca WOOD                     8-8-1822
HASKINS, Collister to Fanny GUNN                 6-16-1818
HATCHER, Joshua to Ruth THOMAS                   8-15-1825
HENRY, George to Nancy THARP                    11-12-1823
HILL, James to Mary RICHEY                       5-18-1819
HOBOUCH, Solomon to Leah CARLILE                 3-5-1820
HOOVER, Sam'l to Sally HULL              Iss.   12-27-1821
HOPKINS, John H. to Isabel TAYLER                3-24-1825
HOUTZ, Henry to Betsey FRANTZ                    4-13-1819
HOWARD, Peter to Sarah MATTEN                   10-14-1824
HUBBARD, Owen to Margaret CRAIG                  8-1-1820
HUMPHREYS, Jacob to Margaret GREEN              11-10-1825
```

```
HUNT, Reuben to Margaret WILLIAMS          Iss.    7-27-1822
HUNTER, John to Ascy LEWALLEN                       5-13-1824
HUNTER, William to Rebecca LEWALLEN                 1-16-1823
INSKIP, Job to Sally SHARP                          11-2-1820
IRWIN, Thomas to Mary STANTER                       4-13-1819
JACOBS, John to Elizabeth EDGERTON                  12-21-1825
JAMES, Isaac to Hannah JONES                        1-29-1824
JAMES, Thomas to Mary SMITH                         10-14-1825
JOHNSON, David to Jane GILLILAND                    12-23-1825
JOHNSON, John to Margaret REED                      8-26-1824
JOHNSTON, Griffeth to Ruth PATTEN                   9-24-1818
JONES, Joseph to Sarah WOOLY                        11-28-1822
KELLY, James to Ann B. FYFFE               Iss.    12-6-1821
KELLY, Peter to Sally SMITH                Iss.    6-5-1822
KELSEY, Abner to Nancy PURDY               Iss.    3-12-1822
KENTON, Simeon to Sally DOWDEN                      12-1-1818
LADD, Jeremiah to Mary Ann Rebecca MARMON           8-16-1821
LANE, David Pitman to Susannah GARWOOD              9-14-1825
LAY, Lorenzo D. to Sarah HILL                       7-25-1825
LEEPER, George to Jane McNAY                        6-23-1825
LEVILL, Ezekiel to Rachel HOKECH           Iss.    9-7-1820
LEWIS, Silas to Lydia CHILSAN                       4-12-1819
LINGERAL, Jeremiah to Nelly ROGAN                   1-8-1824
LINKSWILER, George to Peggy HILL                    6-14-1820
LONG, Benjamin to Mary RANDALL             Iss.    ----1821
LONG, James to Martha TURNER                        11-8-1821
LORD, Abiel H. to Letitia McCLOUD                   5-27-1824
McARTHUR, Peter to Mina GRIFFIN                     7-8-1824
McFALL, John B. to Rachel PENNER           Iss.    12-2-1823
McILVAIN, James to Polly ARSKIN                     2-11-1819
McILVAIN, John I. to Betsey LEEPER                  2-4-1821
McILVAIN, Robert to Nancy WRAY                      3-25-1819
McKENNEN, Uriah to Nancy Star INSKIP                6-3-1821
        Uriah of Clark County
McMILLEN, Robert S. to Jane ELLIS                   8-13-1818
McNAY, John to Rachel ALEXANDER                     9-29-1825
McNEEL, John to Elenor I. HERRING                   10-26-1820
McPHARRIN, Silas to Polly RHODES                    6-9-1822
McPHERSON, Henry H. to Anne SMITH                   3-13-1820
McTEHU(?), John to Elizabeth STEWARD                8-24-1820
MARMAN, Stephen to Mary REED                        11-8-1818
MARMEN, Martin to Margaret RAY                      6-28-1821
MARMON, Peter to Maream COLYER                      3-24-1825
MARMON, Richard to Pricilla MARMON                  3-26-1818
MARSH, George to Julia VARNEY                       5-20-1819
MARSHALL, Walter to Matilda INSKIP                  11-22-1824
MARTIN, Archibald to Jane LEWALLEN                  2-13-1823
MARTIN, Daniel (or David) V. to Elenor WALL         12-5-1822
MILLER, Isaac to Elizabeth McCLOUD                  2-2-1819
MILLER, James to Jane HERROD                        11-29-1821
MONROE, Simeon to Polly HALE                        2-11-1820
MOORE (MOON?), Robert to Margaret MAKINSON          1-13-1825
MOORE, Thomas to Rebecca McCLEMSON                  3-8-1821
MOORE, William to Anne ARSKINS                      8-27-1818
```

13

```
MOORE, William to Mary MOORE                        11-4-1819
MOORE, Wm. G. to Elizabeth DAVIS          Iss.      12-15-1821
MOOTS, John to Elizabeth RANDALL                    1-8-1822
MORTS, George Jr. to Margaret HALL                  1-7-1819
MURPHY, David to Elizabeth CARPENTER                2-2-1819
MURRAY, Daniel to Abigail WARD                      3-13-1819
MURRY, Daniel to Polly KENTON                       2-20-1825
NEGLEY, John to Sarah E. PEACH                      1-16-1822
NICHELSON, David I. to Ruth BROWN                   12-8-1825
NORTON, David to Eliza DUNSTON                      2-1-1819
OHAVER, Asahel to Martha REAMS                      9-12-1821
OVERTON, Oliver to Mary JONES                       12-19-1823
PARKER, Thomas to Margaret STEPHENSON               8-17-1823
           Thomas of Champaign Co.
PATTEN, Shepherd to Margaret ALEXANDER              1-31-1822
PATTERSON, John to Patty SCOTT            Iss.      9-17-1825
PEACH, Richard I. (or J.) to Nancy WOOD             3-24-1825
PEARSON, Jonathan to Mary SNUFFIN                   8-18-1821
PHILIPS, James to Hannah BOGER                      12-22-1826
PICKERELL, John to Temperance DUNSTON               12-25-1825
POLLOCH, Geba to Margaret POLLUCH         Iss.      8-28-1821
                                          Ret.      10-27-1821
POLLOCK, Joseph to Martha CONNEL                    2-29-1820
POPE, Emsley to Susanna LUNDY                       10-28-1829
POWELL, Jacob F. to Sally McCLOUD                   7-15-1820
POWELL, William to Elizabeth COHEN        Iss.      1-14-1822
PRATER, John to Mary POPE                           1-20-1825
PRICE, William to Sarah FIRESTONE                   9-9-1819
PUGH, Thos. to Sally LAME                 Iss.      1-25-1822
PURDY, Francis to Margaret EASTEN                   2-24-1825
QUEEN(?), Michael to Polly MOORE                    4-25-1818
REA, Allen to Minah BISHOP                          1-25-1821
REA, David to Shady SKIDMORE                        12-20-1820
REA, David to Ruth SKIDMORE                         2-20-1823
REA, Robert to Mary GRUBS                           10-14-1819
REAMS, Aron to Lena JAMES                           2-1-1819
REAMS, Caleb to Elizabeth MARMIN                    3-11-1819
REAMS, Joel to Lettice MARMON                       12-20-1821
REAMS, Moses to Mahley NORTON                       5-23-1819
REAMS, Talner to Jane STEEL                         9-13-1821
REED, John to Jane S. Palmer                        5-19-1825
REED, Nathan to Peggy TINNIS                        4-17-1823
RICHEY, William to Elizabeth TICE                   7-28-1825
ROBENSON, James to Polly BEEKHAM                    11-15-1825
ROBERTSON, Joshua to Rachel WILLETS                 3-23-1821
ROBERTSON, Samuel to Polly McNEEL                   9-28-1820
RULE, Lawrence to Ellen ARINS                       1-29-1824
RUTLEDGE, Benjamin to Sarah GREY                    3-11-1825
RUTLEDGE, Samuel to Susannah HILL                   12-1-1825
SCHOOLER, William to Sarah DOUGLASS                 4-14-1825
SCOTT, John T. to Lucy HENRY                        1-15-1824
SCOTT, William to Jane LIPPENCOTT                   8-29-1821
```

```
SEELEY, James to Betsey BURGESS              Iss.    12-8-1821
SERGENT, John to Sally McCOY                 Iss.    12-7-1822
SHACKLEY, Richard to Susannah PAXTON                 4-30-1818
SHARP, Jesse to Rebecca HAINES                       11-4-1819
SHARP, Job to Sarah Ann HAINS                        12-2-1824
SHAW, George to Elizabeth WOODS                      5-2-1825
SHAW, Robert to Patsey CARTER                        3-8-1821
SKIDMORE, Joseph to Rebecca GARWOOD                  10-17-1822
SMITH, Benjamin to Cynthanetta GARWOOD               11-27-1822
SMITH, Enoch to Sophia DOWDEN                        11-7-1822
SMITH, James to Mary Ann TAYLER                      7-4-1822
SMITH, Spencer to Susan CARPENTER                    10-5-1825
SNODDY, Abner to Hannah KINDRICK                     12-18-1823
SPAIN, Thomas to Sarah WILLIAMS                      7-9-1818
SPARKS, Isaac to Martha BALLENGER                    10-12-1820
STANFIELD, Eli to Nicy Dunnis NEW            Iss.    3-30-1824
STANBERRY, Jeremiah to Nancy SERGENT         Iss.    1-22-1825
STANBURY, Daniel to Mary ALLEN               Iss.    10-13-1824
STARBUCK, Samuel to Rebecca DICKINSON        Iss.    2-16-1822
STARRAGE, Thomas to Rosanna RICE  Iss. 8-29-1821 Ret.10-27-1821
STARRAGE, William to Nancy FETCH             Iss.    2-23-1824
STEPHENSON, James to Unity NEWS                      1-23-1823
STEPHENSON, Jas. to Nancy REED               Iss.    1-25-1822
STERLING, Adam to Sarah RAGIN                        4-21-1825
TAYLOR, John to Margaret McILVAIN                    10-27-1821
TENNERY, Joseph L. to Zellah McCOLLOCH               6-11-1820
THARP, D. to Nancy D. DENSON                         7-9-1821
THARP, Henry D. to Susannah MOOTS                    12-11-1825
THOMAS, Abel to Rebecca HATCHER                      5-5-1825
TINNUS, David to Mary COLYER                         1-1-1824
TRUIT, William to Sally OWEN                         4-21-1819
TURNER, Thomas to Jane DIXON                         10-21-1824
UNDERWOOD, William to Nancy HILL                     4-12-1821
VANCE, Samuel to Catharine AMEL                      2-3-1819
VERTNER, John to Ellen JOHNSTON                      11-19-1823
WAGGONER, Peter to Syloy HOIT                        5-20-1824
WALL, Benjamin to Pruella KING                       2-17-1825
WATSON, Patrick to Lethe DOWDEN                      10-28-1823
WATSON, William to Sarah SHAW                        6-13-1824
WHITE, Joshua to Rachail WILLIAMS            Iss.    11-27-1821
WILKASEN, William to Jane STARAGE                    4-2-1821
WILKINSON, James to Nancy SKINNER                    12-14-1818
WILLETS, Rachel to Joshua ROBERTSON                  3-23-1821
WILLIAMS, Jesse to Hannah SOUTHERLAND                2-3-1825
WILLIAMS, Jonathan to Elizabeth ROBERTSON            4-26-1825
WILLIAMS, Nicholas to Faney STEWART                  8-10-1822
WILSEN, James L. to Mary STARAGE             Iss.    8-6-1821
                                             Ret.    10-27-1821
WILSON, William to Julia HAUBY                       12-24-1818
WOOD, Joseph to Patsey DAVIS                         3-22-1824
WOODFIELD, John to Mahala LEWIS                      6-17-1821
WRIGHT, James to Frances GARRAGO                     2-6-1823
```

15

Estate of JOHN ANDREWS, deceased - Adms. Docket A, page 476 - 4-8-1830
Eleazer Hunt, adms.

Estate of DAVID ARCHER, deceased - Adms. Docket A, page 71 - 10-6-1821
Elizabeth Archer, widow relinquishes right to administer estate -
David Scott, adms.

Estate of WILLIAM AUSTEN, deceased - Adms. Docket A, page 130
10-13-1823 - Mary Austen and William Sharp, adms.

Estate of JONATHAN BEAL, deceased - Adms. Docket A, page 297
8-6-1825 - Raphael Moore, adms.

Estate of WILLIAM BLAIR, deceased - Adms. Docket A, page 195
11-22-1824 - Brice Blair, adms.

Estate of JOHN BRIES, deceased - Adms. Docket A, page 95 - 12-22-1822
bond of $250. by Robert Briese and George McCulloch, adns.

Estate of WILLIAM BROWN, deceased - Adms. Docket A, page 55,8-28-1821
widow (not named) relinquishes right to administer estate. Bond of
$600 by John Turner, adms. with John Leach and Janes Moore as securities

Estate of REUBEN BUNDY, deceased - Adms. Docket A, page 315 10-5-1825
Sally Bundy, widow, relinquishes right to administer estate - William
McBeth, adms.

Estate of JOSHUA CAIN, deceased - Adms. Docket A, page 481 7-29-1830
Henry Cain, adms.

Estate of WILLIAM CARTER, deceased - Adms. Docket A, page 1. Letters
of administration granted to relict, Polly Carter and Janes LEEPER -
Bond dated 5-16-1818 of $1,00 by Polly Carter and James Leeper with
John WORKMAN, Thomas THOMPSON and Samuel Carter as secureties.

Estate of JAMES COWEN, deceased - Adms. Docket A, page 372 - 4-2-1827
Elizabeth Cowan and William Woods, adm

Estate of ROBERT CROCKET, deceased - Adms. Docket A, page 141
4-30-1823 - Patsy Crocket and John Newell, adms.

Estate of SAMUEL CURL, deceased - Adms. Docket A, page 112 - 10-25-1823
Mary Curl and John Garwood, adms.

Estate of THOMAS DAVIS, deceased - Adms. Docket A, page 87 10-24-1822
Bond of $1,200. by John Davis and Janes Davis, sons and heirs of
Thomas Davis, deceased - Letters of administration granted to John
Davis and Janes Davis

Estate of JOHN DAVIS, deceased - Adms. Docket A, page 105
10-13-1823 - William Davis, adms.

Estate of WILLIAM DAVIS, deceased - Adms. Docket A, page 172
9-8-1823 - Polly Davis and William C. Wood, adms.

16

Estate of DANIEL GARWOOD, deceased - Adms. Docket A, page 31 9-26-1820
Hepsabeth Garwood relinquishes right to administer estate of her deceased husband. Jesse H. Garwood and John Garwood, adms. with Levi Garwood and John Inskip as securities.

Estate of JOHN GARWOOD, Sr. deceased - Adms. Docket A, page 4   Samuel Ballenger and John Inskip adms., bond dated 7-1-1819 of $2,000 with Joseph Stokes and Daniel Garwood as securities.

Estate of NATHAN GILLIAN(D), deceased - Adms. Docket A, page 116
11-11-1823 - James Gillian and Nicholas Pickeral, adms.

Estate of NATHAN GUTHEY, deceased - Adms. Docket A, page 53
12-5-1821 Reubin Hale, adms.

Estate of CARLISLE HANES, deceased - Adms. Docket A, page 21
2-15-1820 Darcus Hanes, widow and Daniel Garwood, adms.; bond of $600.
with Levi Garwood and Jesse Sharp as securities.

Estate of WILLIAM E. HANKINS, deceased - Adms. Docket A, page 44.
Bond dated 4-18-1821 of $300 by John Cowgel, adms. with John Warner and James Stokes as securities.

Estate of WILLIA. B. HERRIN, deceased - Adms. Docket A, page 18
2-15-1820 Ellin J. Herrin, widow, adms. with James Wall, Sr. as security.

Estate of HENRY HOUTZ, deceased - Adms. Docket A, page 126 1-10-1824
Leonard Houtz and Abran Frantz, adms.

Estate of LEVI INSKIP, deceased - Adms. Docket A, page 375
10-31-1826 - Lot Inskip, adms.

Estate of MICHAEL KEITH, deceased - Adms. Docket A, page 193   10-16-1824
bond of $200 by Levi Keith, adms. with William Ellis and Robert F. Wilson as securities.

Estate of DAVID KING, deceased - Adms. Docket A, page 136
4-30-1823 - Priscilla King, adms.

Estate of GEORGE LINKSWILER, deceased - Adms. Docket A, page 393
11-27-1828 - John Shelby, adms.

Estate of DANIEL McCOY, deceased - Adms. Docket A, page 342
1-20-1827 - James McCoy, adms.

Estate of ROBERT McMILLEN, deceased - Adms. Docket A, page 78 12-29-1821
Bond of $200 by Jane S. McMillen, widow and William S. Douglass, adms.
with Robert Ellis and William Ellis as securities.

Estate of DAVID McNAY, deceased - Adms. Docket A, page 496
4-26-1831 - Rhoda McNay and James Steel, adms.

Estate of PHILIP MATHEWS, deceased - Adms. Docket A, page 198
3-22-1825 - Philip Mathews, adms.

Estate of PHILISH MATHEWS, deceased - Adms. Docket A, page 42
12-28-1822 Rachel Mathews, widow of deceased, and Philish Mathews,
son of deceased, granted letters of administration.

Estate of THOMAS NEWELL, deceased - Adms. Docket A, page 352
4-5-1824 Rosannah Newell, widow, relinquishes right to administer
estate - Nicholas Picheral and Samuel Newell, adms.

Estate of GEORGE T. PALMER, deceased - Adms. Docket A, page 83
8 -28-1821 Bond of $1,000 by Jane Palmer, adms. with James Brown and
Samuel Newell as securities.

Estate of NICHOLS PICHREL, deceased - Adms. Docket A, page 268
5-25-1825 - Henry Pichrel and Martin Marmon; adms.

Estate of JOSEPH POLOCK, deceased - Adms. Docket A, page 122
2-7-1824 - George Leonard and Jabez Crutcher (Crucher), adms.

Estate of BENJAMIN REA, deceased - Adms. Docket A, page 46   6-17-1822
Pricilla (mark) Rea relinquishes right to administer estate in favor of
Raphael Moore - 6-24-1822 Raphael Moore granted letters of administration

Estate of JOHN RHODES, deceased - Adms. Docket A, page 275
9-8-1824 - Mary Rhodes, Bennet Taber and Noah Z. McColloch, adms.

Estate of THOMAS RICHARDSON, deceased - Adms. Docket A, page 286
8-30-1828 - David Norton and Lydia Richardson, adms.

Estate of WILLIAM ROBERTS, deceased - Adms. Docket A, page 506
4-25-1831 Widow (not named) relinquishes right to administer estate -
Richard E. Roberts, adms.

Estate of HENRY ROBERTSON, deceased - Adms. Docket A, page 367
11-20-1827 Sally Robertson, widow, relinquishes her right to administer
estate - John Robertson, son of the deceased and Jonathan Williams, adms.

Estate of HELKIAH ROSEBROOK, deceased - Adms. Docket A, page 403
6-20-1829 - Susannah Rosebrook, widow and Henry Rosebrook, adms.

Estate of JOHN SHEPHERD, deceased - Adms. Docket A, page 491
10-22-1830 Anna Shepherd, widow, relinquishes right to administer
estate - Lanson Curtis, adms.

Estate of DAVID SHIELDS, deceased - Adms. Docket A, page 343   7-3-1827
Catharine Shields relinquishes her right to administer estate of her
late husband - Martin Shields and William McBeth, adms.

Estate of SAMUEL SHIELDS, Jr., deceased - Adms. Docket A, page 108
10-13-1823 - Joseph McBeth and John Dunn, adms.

Estate of JACOB SIDES, deceased - Adms. Docket A, page 464
8-14-1830 Widow (not named) relinquishes right to administer estate -
Isaac S. Gardner and Henry H. McPherson, adms.

Estate of RUTH SMITH, deceased - Adns. Docket A, page 381
10-2-1927 - Nathan Sprague, adns.

Estate of JAMES STEWART, deceased - Adn. Docket A, page 461   5-8-1830
Widow (not named) relinquishes right to administer estate - Joseph M.
Stewart, adns.

Estate of THOMAS STEWART, deceased - Adns. Docket A, page 499   6-6-1831
Susan Stewart, widow, relinquishes right to administer estate -
Samuel Scott, adns.

Estate of NICHOLAS STILWELL, Sr. - Adns. Docket A, page 498
7-9-1830 - Elizabeth Stilwell, widow, adns.

Estate of MATHEW TERREL, deceased - Adns. Docket A, page 120
11-14-1823 - William Terrel, adns.

Estate of JOHN WALL, deceased - Adns. Docket A, page 144
2-25-1823 - Polly Wall. Samuel Newell and Benjamin Wall, adns.

Estate of JOSEPH WILKINS, deceased - Adns. Docket A, page 475
4-3-1830 - Huldah Wilkins, widow, adns.

Estate of HEZEKIAH WILLCOX, deceased - Adns. Docket A, page 155
6-9-1823 - David McNay and Samuel Newell, adns.

Estate of JOHN WILLSON, deceased - Adns. Docket A, page 191
10-16-1824 - John Means, adns.

Estate of WILLIAM WOOD, deceased - Adns. Docket A, page 12
9-16-1819 Sarah Wood widow relinquishes right to administer estate.
Adns. Christopher Wood and William Wood with William Davis and John
Workman as securities on bond of $500.

Estate of WILLIAM ZANE, deceased - Adns. Docket A, page 378
4-3-1827 - Martin Marnan and James Crew, adns.

LOGAN COUNTY, OHIO - DEATH RECORDS 1867-1870

Persons 50 years of age or over.

Name	Date of) Death 1867	Age Years Mo.Da.	Place of Death or Residence	Marital Status	Place of Birth
COLTER, Philip	7-25	52 yrs.	Bellefontaine	mar.	Ireland
DETRICK, Peter	7-24	69-9-15	Union Twp.	mar.	Virginia
EMERY, Eliza	9-21	50 yrs.	Harrison Twp.	mar.	Penna.
HAMMER, Hulda	8-3	66y 6m	Quincy	wid.	Logan Co.
HULL, William	9-13	50 yrs.	Logan Co.	mar.	- - - - - -
McCOLLOCH, Samuel	9-12	54 yrs.	Rush Creek Twp.	mar.	Jefferson Twp.
NEER, Adam	9-22	52 yrs.	Logan Co.	mar.	- - - - - -
NEER, Martin	7-6	64y 3m	Quincy	mar.	- - - - - -
PRATT, John	8-3	84-3-12	Rush Creek Twp.	mar.	- - - - - -
ROSS, Almina	8-14	51-1-11	Liberty Twp.	single	Fayette Co. Pa.
ROBUCK, Naomi	9-25	75 yrs.	Richland Twp.	mar.	Kentucky
WAIT, Almida	8-16	52m 5m	Bellefontaine	mar.	New York
WILLIAMS, N.	9-27	74-6-10	Monroe Twp.	mar.	Virginia
HAINES, Auston	11-18	59y 3m	Perry Twp.	mar.	New Jersey
CORNELIUS, Benjamin	12-31	73-3-2	West Liberty	mar.	New Jersey
CARLISLE, Archibald	11-25	60 yrs.	Stokes Twp.	mar.	Stokes Twp.
HOUBERT, Margaret	12-24	69 yrs.	Bellefontaine	wid.	Penna.
HAINES, Samuel	10-28	87 yrs.	Jefferson Twp.	mar.	Virginia
HOOVER, John	10-21	60 yrs.	Stokes Twp.	mar.	Ohio
KNOWLES, Levi	12-27	58-8-17	Rush Creek Twp.	mar.	New Jersey
LEASE, Stephen	11-16	88 yrs.	Jefferson Twp.	mar.	Penna.
McDANIEL, William	10-26	89 yrs.	Monroe Twp.	wid.	Kentucky
SCOTT, Ann	10-4	55 yrs	McArthur Twp.	wid.	Maryland
SMITH, William	12-30	77-9-14	Monroe Twp.	mar.	Baltimore
	1868				
GRAY, Mrs.	2-29	65 yrs.	Richland Twp.	mar.	Ireland
GOOD, Jacob	3-24	74 yrs.	Harrison Twp.	wid.	Virginia
JOHNSTON, Stanton	2-26	56 yrs.	Richland Twp.	mar.	Ohio
MONROE, John	2-7	78 yrs.	Bellefontaine	mar.	Virginia
MOHR, Frederick	3-5	77 yrs.	Union Twp.	mar.	Germany
PETTY, Elam	3-4	58 yrs.	Pleasant Twp.	mar.	Virginia
ROBERTS, Thomas	2-21	78 yrs.	Bokes Creek Twp.	mar.	Penna.
REED, Allen	2-4	69 yrs.	Logan Co.	mar.	Logan Co.
STILES, E. D.	3-28	60 yrs.	Pleasant Twp.	mar.	Logan Co.
SECRIST, Henry	1-20	85 yrs.	Union Twp.	wid.	Virginia
BROWN, Isabell	4-8	60 yrs.	Liberty Twp.	single	Ireland
BLAIR, James	6-15	70 yrs.	Richland Twp.	mar.	Penna.
DAVIS, Elizabeth C.	5-7	61y 6m	Logan Co.	wid.	Ohio
HALL, Benjamin F.	4-12	72 yrs.	Bellefontaine	wid.	Cincinnati
KIRKWOOD, Nancy	5-9	74-2-10	Liberty Twp.	mar.	- - - - - -
REYMER, Rachel	6-20	70 yrs.	Perry Twp.	wid.	New Jersey

Name	Date of) Death 1868	Age Years Mo.Da.	Place of Death or Residence	Marital Status	Place of Birth
SMITH, Isaac	6-4	50 yrs.	Degraff	mar.	Virginia
ZEIGLER, Jacob	4-29	65 yrs.	West Liberty	mar.	Logan Co.
ASHBAUGH, Andrew	7-6	63 yrs.	Richland Twp.	mar.	- - - - -
AUSTON, Rebecca	9-28	64 yrs.	Perry Twp.	mar.	Virginia
BROWN, Elizabeth	9-19	69-11-8	West Liberty	mar.	Virginia
BALLINGER, John	8-14	72 yrs.	Logan Co	mar.	New Jersey
CHAMBERS, Absalom	9-21	75 yrs.	Quincy	mar.	Virginia
COCHRAN, Phebe	9-22	86 yrs.	W. Middleburg	wid.	Long Island
HILDEBRAND, Emely	8-27	85 yrs.	West Liberty	wid.	- - - - -
HILLENGS, Margaret	9-23	88 yrs.	W. Middlebury	wid.	Penna.
MURDOCK, Fanny	9-23	78 yrs.	Bokes Creek Twp.	wid.	Virginia
McLAUGHLEN, Robert J.	8-10	80 yrs.	Bellefontaine	mar.	Ireland
NEWELL, Joseph	9-12	61 yrs.	Bellefontaine	mar.	Logan Co.
PENNOCK, Thomas	8-17	68 yrs.	Zanesfield	mar.	Penna.
POLLOCH, John	8-7	58 yrs.	Logan Co.	mar.	Penna.
REA, David	9-10	76 yrs.	Perry Twp.	mar.	Ohio
DONNELS, Susan	12-13	81 yrs.	Monroe Twp.	single	- - - - -
DAVIS, Elizabeth	11-7	54-3-10	Logan Co.	wid.	Logan Co.
FRY, Mary	10-21	75 yrs.	Jefferson Twp.	mar.	- - - - -
HAYS, Alfred	11-15	62-7-3	Bellefontaine	wid.	Clark Co. Ohio
HAYS, Jemima	11-22	72y 3d	Bellefontaine	wid.	Morgan Co. Va.
KITCHEN, Ann	12-10	58-1-22	Logan Co.	mar.	Lebanon, Ohio
MARMON, Zylpha	12-17	70 yrs.	Logan Co.	mar.	N. Carolina
McMICHAEL, Eliza	10-24	57 yrs.	Logan Co.	mar.	Logan Co.
RICHARDS, John N.	10-25	72 yrs.	Logan Co.	mar.	Logan Co.
THOMPSON, James	10-3	73 yrs.	Logan Co.	mar.	Logan Co.
TAYLOR, Mahlon K.	10-10	60 yrs.	Lake Twp.	mar.	Virginia
	1869				
BOYD, Robert	2-5	76 yrs.	Richland Twp.	mar.	Ireland
BLACK, Jane	3-5	68 yrs.	McArthur Twp.	wid.	Penna.
BLAIR, Mary E.	3-28	67 yrs.	Richland Twp.	wid.	Penna.
FANCHER, Jane	2-25	65 yrs.	Liberty Twp.	wid.	Penna.
HARMON, Mary	1-18	65 yrs.	Rush Creek Twp.	wid.	Greene Co. Ohio
NICHOLS, Solomon C.	3-16	54 yrs.	Pleasant Twp.	mar.	Champaign Co. O.
POOL, Thomas A.	- -	51-2-24	Miami Twp.	mar.	Champaign Co. O.
STRAYER, Daniel	3-27	84 yrs.	Miami Twp.	wid.	Miami (?)
GROVER, Jonathan	5-26	65 yrs.	Perry Twp.	mar.	Virginia
MORRISON, Wm. V.	4-15	65 yrs.	Lake Twp.	mar.	Penna.
ARTIS, Jane	12-5	63-10-22	Monroe Twp.	mar.	N. Carolina
BARKMAN, Elizabeth	10-12	63y 20d	Stokes Twp.	mar.	- - - - -
BUSHONG, Nancy L.	11-21	75-11-23	Bokes Creek Twp.	wid.	So. Carolina
BUCKWATER, Henry	8-25	67y 7d	Harrison Twp.	mar.	Lancaster Co. Pa.
BUCKWATER, Susannah	10-24	61y 3d	Harrison Twp.	wid.	Lancaster Co. Pa.
COWGILL, Mary	4-20	93y 1m	Zane Twp.	wid.	New Jersey

21

Name	Date of) Death 1869	Age Years Mo.Da.	Place of Death or Residence	Marital Status	Place of Birth
DOW, Ann	1-4	65 yrs.	Harrison Twp.	mar.	Greene Co. Ohio
ELLIOTT, Martha	11-7	73-3-27	Perry Twp.	wid.	Penna.
GURNER, Martha	7-28	76 yrs.	Degraff	wid.	Kentucky
GABBY, Robert	11-26	73y 6m	Richland Twp.	- -	Logan Co. (?)
GROVER, Jonathan	5-22	68 yrs.	Perry Twp.	mar.	Virginia
HANKS, Rachel	12-5	69-9-13	Pleasant Twp.	mar.	Logan Co.
HARRIMAN, David	7-11	62-1-21	Perry Twp.	mar.	Washington Co. Pa.
HEATH, Hannah	9-19	79y 3m	Perry Twp.	mar.	- - - - -
HEATH, John	9-21	86y 8m	Perry Twp.	mar.	- - - - -
HENRY, Nancy	4-5	73-10-15	Monroe Twp.	mar.	Kentucky
HARPLE, Conrod	7-27	72-6-10	Jefferson Twp.	mar.	Penna
IRWIN, Nathaniel	6-10	90y 10m	Harrison Twp.	mar.	Ireland
KNOX, John	11-26	82 yrs.	Bellefontaine	mar.	Scotland
KNIGHT, John	9-11	78y 2m	Zanesfield	mar.	Virginia
LEMON, John A.	4-6	58-8-11	Union Twp.	mar.	Champaign Co. O.
MARTIN, Catharine	June	62 yrs.	Harrison Twp.	wid.	- - - - -
MILROY, Catharine	11-14	53y 10m	McArthur Twp.	wid.	Ireland
MOORE, Sarah	10-24	85-7-13	Zane Twp.	wid.	New Jersey
NEWSOM, Benjamin	9-2	89 yrs.	Pickrelltown	wid.	N. Carolina
NORTON, Jonathan	10-1	78-5-17	Union Twp.	mar.	New York
PICKRELL, Temperance	9-5	63-2-28	Monroe Twp.	wid.	Virginia
RHODES, William	9-13	79y 3d	Harrison Twp.	mar.	England
SIDESINGER, Leonard	12-22	82-6-6	Monroe Twp.	wid.	Penna.
SHARP, Isaac	9-23	70y 13d	Zane Twp.	mar.	Virginia
TALLMAN, Woodmince	9-7	80-1-17	Zane Twp.	mar.	New Jersey
WHITEHILL, John	10-20	56-8-20	Jefferson Twp.	mar.	Pennsylvania
WALL, Susan	12-7	64y 4m	Harrison Twp.	mar.	Virginia
WARREN, Joshua	2-5	51-7-10	Stokes Twp.	mar.	New York
WRIGHT, James	9-29	76 yrs.	Richland Twp.	mar.	Penna.
	1870				
BURILL, Lavina	3-10	71y 2m	Miami Twp.	wid.	Penna.
BALLINGER, Margaret	3-30	59-10-1	Perry Twp.	wid.	Clark Co. Ohio
DOAN, Lyman	2-18	69-7-4	Miami Twp.	mar.	Connecticut
ELLIS, John F.	1-27	70-3-12	Pleasant Twp.	mar.	Kentucky
ELLIS, Joannah	3-30	50-6-10	Degraff	mar.	- - - - -
GABBY, Sarah Ann	2-13	72 yrs.	Richland Twp.	mar.	Logan Co. (?)
HILL, Elizabeth	2-26	98y 10d	Bokes Creek Twp.	wid.	Virginia
JEFFERS, Barbara	3-15	74 yrs.	McArthur Twp.	wid.	Logan Co. (?)
KERN, Margaret	3-14	79 yrs.	Rush Creek Twp.	wid.	Logan Co. (?)
KING, Jacob	3-3	75y 2m	Rush Creek Twp.	mar.	Kentucky
KERSHAW, Jane	2-1	65-10-11	Bellefontaine	wid.	England
LAMONT, Mary	3-14	73-10-11	Rush Creek Twp.	mar.	Ireland
PLANK, John	3-8	68y 5m	Liberty Twp.	mar.	Penna
REAMS, Vincent	1-11	64-7-25	Bokes Creek Twp.	mar.	N. Carolina

Name	Date of) Death 1870	Age Years Mo.Da.	Place of Death or Residence	Marital Status	Place of Birth
SMITH, Margaret	1-11	61y 15d	Harrison Twp.	mar.	Logan Co.
STEEN, James	3-2	78y 5m	Lake Twp.	wid.	Virginia
WILSON, John	3-20	61-5-7	Bellefontaine	mar.	Penna.
BROWN, Joseph	12-19	67-2-19	McArthur Twp.	mar.	Virginia
CLARK, Anna	Oct.	79 yrs.	Lake Twp.	wid.	Penna.
Parents of Anna Clark = Rev. Thomas Marquis and Sarah Park					
DORWIN, Philo	10-6	75y 3m	Bellefontaine	mar.	Vermont
Parents of Philo Dorwin = Philo Dorwin and Mary Hichley					
EASTON, Charlotte	Aug.	66y 6m	Jefferson Twp.	mar.	Logan Co.
FAWCETT, Jesse	7-1	77-3-13	Rush Creek Twp.	mar.	Virginia
FURGESON, William	3-8	71-4-20	McArthur Twp.	single	Ireland
FIELDER, Matilda	10-23	64y 8m	Miami Twp.	mar.	Logan Co.
FULMER, Mary	11-15	63 yrs.	Bellefontaine	mar.	Penna.
Father of Mary Fulmer = A. Zimmerman					
GAFFIELD, Mary	11-3	97y 15d	Rush Creek Twp.	wid.	Vermont
GRAY, James	8-16	79 yrs.	Richland Twp.	wid.	Ireland
HEWS, Hiram	6-1	56-8-25	Rush Creek Twp.	mar.	Fairfield Co. O.
HOY, Matilda	11-24	66-4-10	Bloomfield	wid.	New York
HENPHILL, John	12-26	74-2-16	Bellefontaine	mar.	Kentucky
HANDRAHAM, Joshua	12-25	80 yrs.	Harrison Twp.	wid.	Ireland
HOVER, Susanah	10-17-	78 yrs.	Stokes Twp.	wid.	New Jersey
JEWELL, Walter	5-31	75 yrs.	Liberty Twp.	single	Connecticut
JACOBS, Elizabeth	12-20	100 yrs.	Harrison Twp.	wid.	Virginia
JOURDON, Catharine	6-10	74 yrs.	Liberty Twp.	mar.	Ireland
LONGBRAKE, Caroline	8-1	61 yrs.	Washington Twp.	mar.	Maryland
MYERS, Magdeline	10-28	65 yrs.	Harrison Twp.	wid.	Penna.
McKUNE, Squiss C.	9-20	79-10-20	Rush Creek Twp.	wid.	Scotland
PARKER, Joseph H.	3-28	51-2-14	Degraff	mar.	New Jersey
PUSEY, Mary	12-3	85y 6m	Bellefontaine	wid.	Penna.
PATTERSON, Joseph	8-20	60-8-14	Bellefontaine	mar.	Ireland
RAY, Mary	12-2	70-8-4	Liberty Twp.	single	Virginia
SHANTZ, Magdalina	9-25	83 yrs.	Union Twp.	wid.	France
WORRELL, Samuel	12-20	57-10-9	Zane Twp.	mar.	New Jersey
Father of Samuel Worrell = William Worrel					
WENNER, John	4-26	80-2-9	Perry Twp.	mar.	New Jersey
YODER, Magdalena	6-30	67-5-15	Liberty Twp.	wid.	Penna.

23

BEDILLAN (B. DILLANE), Isaac - Zane Twp. - Adms. Docket A page 323
Dated 3-23-1824 - Recorded 4-3-1827; Wife - Osilla Bedillan
Sons - Abraham Bedillin and Frederick Bedillin.
Grandsons - David Row Bedillin, not of age; Isaac and Benjamin
Bedillin. Mentions money in lands of Isaac Collins, Jr. in
Gloucester County, New Jersey. Executors - John Garwood and
son, Abraham Bedillin. Signed - Isaac B. Dillane
Witnesses - Joseph Curl, Henry Seaman and John Garwood
Note: Name is given as Bedillan/Bedillin throughout the will,
however signature is Isaac B. Dillane

BOUSMAN, John - Lake Twp. - Adms. Docket A, page 177
Dated 7-11-1822 - Recorded 11-22-1822; Wife - mentioned but not
named. Eight children - William, John, Eleanor, Nichodemus,
Sarah, Maximilla, Maria and Barbara. Mentions land in
Champaign County, Ohio. Executor - son, William Bousman
Signed - John (mark) Bousman
Witnesses - George Krouskap, Jr. and Andrew Grubb

BUSHENG, James - Adms. Docket A, page 159 Dated 1-1-1824
Recorded 4-6-1824 Wife - Nancy Busheng   Son - Jacob Busheng
Daughters - Delilee and Gemima Busheng Executor Alexander
McCLREG Signed - James Busheng
Witnesses - John Garwood, Thomas James and John Busheng

EVANS, Moses - Adms. Docket A page 350 Dated 12-25-1827
Recorded 1-5-1828 Wife - Rebecca   Son - William Daughter -
Thebe Stokes Grandsons - Joseph Evans, not of age, to have lot
in Urbana; Silas Evans. Mentions Polly Cowgele, but does not
give relationship; she is to have the new family Bible
Executors - John Inskip and son, William Evans
Signed - Moses (mark) Evans
Witnesses - Joseph Stokes and Elisha Cowgel

FIRESTONE, Daniel - Adms. Docket A, page 99 Dated 12-30-1822
Recorded 3-24-1823 Wife - Nancy Firestone Sons - Samuel and
George Daughters - Rebekah and Sally. Mentions Lot LOGAN of
Hawkin Co. (no state given). Executors - sons, Samuel and
George Firestone. Signed - Daniel Firestone.
Witnesses - Patrick McFALL and Leonard HOUTZ

HAINES, Philip - Verbal Will - Adms. Docket A, page 385
Will given 9-24-1828 - Philip Haines died 9-25-1828
Deposition given 9-27-1828 - Recorded 10-11-1828
Wife - mentioned but not named. Sons - Philip Haines and
Jonathan Haines. Daughters - mentioned but not named.
Executors - Peter KELLY and son, Philip Haines
Witnesses and deposition given and signed by - John Kelly
and Peter Kelly

INSKIP, Lot - Adrs. Docket A, page 419   Dated 11-5-1829;Recorded
2-19-1830   Wife - Annamaria Inskip   Daughter - Margaretann
Inskip   Executors - wife, Annamaria Inskip and John Garwood
Signed - Lot Inskip   Witnesses - John Garwood, John G.
Hewlings and Job Inskip

JENNINGS, Isaac - Adms. Docket A, page 423   Dated 2-27-1830
Dated 2-27-1830 - Recorded April 1830   Wife - Joana Jennings
Son - Cornelius Jennings   Son-in-law - John Andrews
Mentions Nathaniel BERT, relationship, if any, not given
Executors - wife, Joana Jennings and Eleazer Hunt
Signed - Isaac (mark) Jennings
Witnesses - George RODECHER and James ANDREWS

KELLY, Peter, Sr. - Adms. Docket A, page 305   Dated 11-27-1822
Recorded 3-27-1826   Wife - Mary Kelly   Sons - Nathaniel Kelly,
deceased, mentions three children but does not name; John Kelly
and Peter Kelly.   Daughters - Sally Hanver and her husband
Samuel Hanver; Patty Knox; Caty Blog; Betsy Enoch.   Mentions
Madison and David Walts (not of age), children of daughter Sally
by her first husband.   Mentions money in Virginia.
Executors - Robert SMITH and John SHELBY   Signed: Peter Kelly
Witnesses - James Smith and John Shelby

MARMIN, David - Champaign Co., Ohio - Adms. Docket A, page 15
Dated 8th day, 1st month, 1814 - Recorded (not given)
Wife - mentioned, but not named.   Sons - Peter, Edmond and David.
Executors - sons, Peter and Edmond. Signed - David Marmun
Witnesses - Daniel BULLER and Joseph CUTLAND

MARMIN, Peter - Adms. Docket A, page 27.   Dated 4th month, 5th day, 1820
Recorded 9-2-1820.   Wife - Dorothy Marmin   Mentions 3 children,
but does not name.   Executors - Martin Marmin and Aaron FROWN
Signed - Peter Marmin.   Witnesses - Robert (mark) Marmin, Peter
Marmin and Mary (mark) Marmin

MARMON, Robert - Adms. Docket A, page 516   Dated 2nd month, 4th day,
1826 - Recorded 11-3-1831.   Sons - Richmond, Joshua, Peter and
Stephen.   Daughters - Dorothy Marmon, Hannah Dougherty and
Obedience Watkins.   Executors - Martin Marmon and Joshua Marmon
Signed - Robert (mark) Marmon.   Witnesses: Daniel Buller,
Robert M. Marmon and James WATKINS

MARQUIS, Rev. Thomas - (formerly) Washington Co., Pennsylvania
Adms. Docket A, page 364   Dated 9-25-1827 - Recorded 10-2-1827
Wife - Jean (given as "Jane" in one place). Sons - William and
James.   Daughters - Sarah Stevenson, Susannah Marquis, Mary
Newell, Jane Coldwell, and Ann Marquis.
Executors - William RAY, Joseph STENESON and Samuel CALDWELL
Signed - Thomas (mark) Marquis
Witnesses - Joshua ROBB, James P. McCOY and A. H. LORD

MASSIE,Henry - Jefferson Co., Kentucky - Adns. Docket A, page 426
    Dated 2-6-1830 - Copy of will recorded 7-30-1830
    Wife - Helen Massie, also to serve as Executrix
    Brothers - Nathaniel, deceased; Thonas. Nieces - Constance
    Massie, Elizabeth Thonpson and Sally Hawes. Pephews -
    Nathaniel Massie of Ohio, son of deceased brother Nathaniel
    Massie; Heath Jones Miller of Louisville. Mentions - Henry
    Bullett son of Cuthbert Bullitt and Alexander Scott Bullitt
    son of William C. Bullitt (relationship not clearly stated,
    possibly nephews???). Mentions Courtland Massie - relationship
    not stated. Signed - H. Massie
    Witnesses - W. C. Galt, N. Bullitt and Edw'd Johnson

PATRICK, Samuel - Adns. Docket A, page 513 Dated (not given)
    Recorded 11-4-1831 Wife - nentioned but not naned
    Son -"Samuel Patrick Daughter - Phebe, her son, Hiram
    Other children not of age, nentioned but not naned
    Signed - Samuel Patrick
    Witnesses - Thonas (nark) PENDERGRASS and Joseph (nark) HALL

PAXTON, John, Sr. - Lake Twp. - Adns. Docket A, page 81
    Dated 18th day, 7th nonth, 1820 - Recorded 12-4-1820
    Wife - Mary Paxton Sons - John, Willian, Ruben and Jacob
    Daughters - Achsha PICHERAL, Abiel GARRETSON, Nancy PICHERAL,
    Nancy WILLIAMS and Susanna Paxton
    Executors - Sons, Reubin Paxton and John Paxton
    Signed - John Paxton
    Witnesses - Obadiah Willians and Henry Picheral

PENNER, John - Miani Twp. - Adns. Docket A, page 170
    Dated 7-20-1824 Recorded 9-9-1824 Wife - Rachel Penner
    Sons - John, oldest son, and Janes. Daughters - Sally Rector,
    Catharire Ellis, Nelly Penner, Rachel Penner and Rheda Penner
    Executor - John Turner. Signed - John Penner
    Witnesses - Christian SMITH, Janes STEWARD, Samuel FIRESTONE

PICHERAL, John - Monroe Twp. - Adns. Docket A, page 422
    Dated 2nd day, 8th nonth, 1828 - Recorded April 1830
    Wife - Catherine Son - John Executor - David NORTON
    Signed - John (nark) Picherall
    Witnesses - Obadiah WILLIAMS and Henry WILLIAMS

SHARP, Job - Zane Twp. - Adns. Docket A, page 66
    Dated 26th day, 7 nonth, 1821 - Recorded 1-26-1822
    Wife - Phebe Sharp Son - Joshua Sharp, also to serve executor
    Daughters - Achshah McWaid wife of Arthur McWADE, Esther Antrin
    wife of Thonas ANTRIM, Sarah wife of Sineon SMITH
    Grandson - Job H. Sharp. Mentions land in Chanpaing Co., Ohio.
    Signed - Job Sharp
    Witnesses - Abijah WARNER, Isaac WARNER and John E. FOSETH

SHARP, Samuel - Adns. Docket A, page 400 Dated 12-23-1828
    Recorded 1-3-1829 Wife - Mary, also to serve as guardian of
    children. Four children - Nancy, Elizabeth, Rachel and Maria
    Sharp. Executors - Job Sharp and John Sharp
    Signed - Samuel (mark) Sharp
    Witnesses - John D. ELBERT, Sr. and John CANTRIL

SHIELDS, Samuel - Adns. Docket A, page 39 Dated 7-31-1820
    Sons - John Shields, deceased; David Shields; Samuel Shields
    and Martin Shields. Daughters - Peggy McBeth wife of William
    McBETH and Polly Kirkwood wife of Joseph KIRKWOOD
    Daughter-in-law - formerly Rhoda Shields now Rhoda KIRKWOOD
    Grandchildren - Samuel and Betsy Shields, children of John
    Shields, deceased; Matilda NEWELL
    Executors - Samuel Newell and son, Samuel Shields
    Signed - Samuel (mark) Shields
    Witnesses - Thomas NEWELL and John MOORE
    Codicil dated 8-8-1822 - no additional information.

STANFIELD, Thomas, Sr. - Jefferson Twp. - Adns. Docket A, page 133
    Dated 7th day, 5th month, 1823 - Recorded (not given)
    Wife - Hannah Stanfield   Son - Thomas Stanfield
    Daughters - Lydia, deceased, wife of Edward WEST; Mary Stanfield;
    Nancy, wife of Jesse JOHNSTON; Hannah Stout, wife of Philip
    STOUT; Sarah, wife of Samuel LITTLER; Elizabeth wife of John
    LITTLER; Rebekah, widow of John TODHUNTER, deceased; Rachel,
    wife of Cephas FISHER; Phebe, wife of Thomas SOUTHERLAND.
    Grandson - Thomas West, son of daughter Lydia, deceased, and
    Edward West. Executors - wife, Hannah and son Thomas, Jr.
    Signed - Thomas Stanfield. Witnesses - Isaac MYERS, Hequis
    PARKER and Richard BALDWIN

STRATTON, Joseph - Adns. Docket A, page 92. Dated 24th day, 7th month,
    1820 - Recorded March 1823. Wife - Naomi Stratton
    Sons - Joel, Joseph, Benjamin and Jacob. Daughters - Hannah
    Stratton; Mary THOMAS, land where David THOMAS now lives.
    Grandson - Joseph Stratton, not of age, son of Joel
    Executors - Thomas JAMES, John GARWOOD and son, Jacob Stratton
    Signed - Joseph Stratton
    Witnesses - Moris (mark) EWERS, Levi ANTRIM and Samuel CURL

TELLUS (TILLUS, TULLES), John - Adns. Docket A, page 201. Dated (not
    given) - Recorded 8-6-1825 Wife - Frances Tellus
    Son - John Tellus. Granddaughter - Frances DAVIS formerly
    Frances Tellus and her husband William Davis
    Grandsons - James and Lewis Tellus. Grandchildren - Griffeth,
    John, Nancy, Rebecca, Bitsy, Dorothy, India and Lydia Tellus
    Executors - Friends, Robert SMITH and Samuel NEWELL

WILLIAMS, John - Lake Twp. - Adns. Docket A, page 8 Dated 7-7-1818
    Recorded 4-13-1819. Wife - Rebekah Williams; to serve Executrix.
    Children - Edwen, Sarah, Isaac, George and Lukena Williams
    William Williams to serve as guardian of children.
    Signed - John (mark) Williams
    Witnesses - Mary (mark) RAYNOLDS and Joseph WHITE

ABBOTT, Justin to Sally Powers	11-11-1826
ADAMS, Calvin to Eunice Smith	10-7-1828
ADAMS, Isaac N. to Marilla Emmons	12-2-1828
ADAMS, Milton M. to Eunice Emmons	1-18-1826
ANDREWS, Rodney to Amelia Peck (no day given)	June 1825
ANDREWS, Samuel to Elizabeth Wait	3-16-1829
AUSTIN, Henry to Jane Root	4-12-1827
BABCOCK, Abraham F. to Rosana Kimball both of Brownhelm	9-1-1828
BACON, Benjamin to Anna W. Graham	8-25-1828
BALEY (BAILEY), Charles to Marinda Newton	7-4-1827
BARNEY, Royal Jr. to Sarah Brooks	11-4-1829
BARNS, Sardis G. to Minerva Gillet.	8-7-1828
BARNUM, John to Eunice Bronson	11-23-1828
BARNUM, Leman to Pamela Barnum	1-25-1826
BARNUM, Sylvester to Mahitabel Keeler	5-9-1826
BEDORTHA, Theodore to Chloe McNeil	8-9-1826
BEEBE, Laurel to Lucinda Terrel	9-12-1828
BEEBE, Willis to Sally M. Brunson	3-18-1827
BEEMUS, Jonas to Matilda Disbrow	7-5-1826
BENNETT, David Jr. to Jane Galpin	2-7-1830
BLAKESLEE, James S. to Fanny S. Lilly	12-26-1829
BRADLEY, Jason to Hannah Moe	6-5-1825
BRANDENBURY, Aaron to Mary Clefford	11-10-1830
BRIGGS, Otis to Ressa Terrell	1-6-1825
BRONSON, Albert to Rheuby Adams	4-9-1827
BRONSON, Rev. C. P. to Nancy Sibley	10-4-1826
BROOKS, Calvin W. to Amanda M. Webster	11-13-1828
BROWN, Agusta to Maria Emmons	3-18-1830
BROWN, Thomas to Ann Smith	8-5-1830
BURGE, Adams to Marinda Close	12-10-1829
BURRELL, Isaac to Flava Adams	9-27-1825
BUTLER, Justus to Anna Clark	11-23-1829
BUTTOLPH, George to Dorothy Clark	12-31-1829
CAHOON, Jesse S. to Macena Moore	11-3-1830
CAHOON, Wilber Jr. to Thirza Moor both of Avon	4-6-1826
CARTER, William to Anna Van Alsdall (Vannasdoll)	1-24-1828
CASH, Israel to Ruth More	10-6-1824
CHAPMAN, Milton to Pamela Barnum	11-4-1829
CLARK, James to Charlotte Sergeant	9-18-1830
CLARK, John B. to Lucy Ferris	8-2-1829
CLARK, William of Brunswick. Medina Co., Ohio to Mary Murray of Ridgeville, Lorain Co.	12-19-1824
CLARKE, Oren to Clarissa Rathborn	5-24-1830
CLAY, John T. to Betsey Shupe	6-27-1830
CLEFFORD, Luther L. to Martha Chanter	7-1-1828
COLT, Richard E. to Chloe Jackson	10-28-1830
COMMONS, Lester to Mary P. Eldred	12-30-1828
COOLEY, Moses B. to Jane M. Peck	5-21-1829
COOLEY, Rensellear to Julia H. Wells	6-2-1825
COOLEY, Roger to Irene Allen both of Elyria	9-9-1824
COOPER, Reuben to Hannah Daily	11-18-1824

```
COSSETT, John to Elizabeth Curtis                                          4-24-1830
CUTLER, Jesse to Temperance Crawford                                      11-22-1827
CURTIS, Harvey A. to Ruth B. Harris                                        1-18-1830
CURTIS, Jared R. to Lydia C. Potter                                       10-28-1828
CURTIS, Lewis to Mary Goodwin                                             12-23-1830
CURTIS, Samuel J. of Grafton to Esther Prouty of Elyria                    1-1-1829
DAILEY, Andrew R. to Mariah Carpenter                                      4-9-1829
DAILY, Roswell to Lucy M. Greene                                          11-25-1830
DIMICK, Augustus R. to Alsina Crowel                                       7-2-1829
DISBROW, Jonathan to Delilah Wellman                                       3-4-1826
ELDRED, Aaron to Loisa Emmons                                             2-15-1827
ELDRED, Noah to Betsey Murray                                             12-6-1826
EMMONS, Ichabod to Dorcas Fuller                                          2-23-1830
EWING(S), James to Loami Davis                                            10-29-1828
EWINGS, James to Elizabeth Cooley                                          5-3-1825
FALCONER, Samuel to Margaret Bisset                                        1-5-1828
FARR, Philemon to Susan Greenslit                                         11-2-1828
FERRIS, Forest of Black River tp. to Mary Ann Wellman, Russia tp.1-1-1828
FLEM(N)ING, Abraham to Adaline Case                                        4-1-1829
FLORA, John to Alvira Mellen                                              6-23-1830
FORD, Albert to Rebecka Disbrow                                           7-12-1829
FOSTER, Archibald to Eliza Ann Mann                                        1-1-1828
FOUT, Ransom to Martha Smith                                              3-19-1828
FOX, Elijah of Wellington to Ellen S. Whitlock of Brighton               4-25-1825
FOX, Levi F. to Elizabeth Millard                                        5-13-1825
GARDNER, Archibald to Rhoda Thompson                                     8-15-1830
GATES, Lemuel B. to Jane Ann Holcomb                                     5-29-1825
GILLET, Gersham to Betsey Moe                                            3-16-1825
GODARD, Anson A. to Marietta Osborn                                       5-3-1829
GOTT, David Jr. to Emeline Rockwood                                      7-17-1828
GOULD, Enos to Philena Rice                                              9-10-1828
GOULD, Joseph to Mary Drake                                              3-18-1830
GREENSLIT, Moses to Lovicea McNeil                                      12-11-1828
HALL, Selden to Emily Smith                                              4-23-1828
HARDEN, Thomas to Sylvena Jain Edmonds                                   4-26-1825
HARPER, James to Hannah Blakesly                                          3-2-1828
HARPSTER, Daniel of Wayne Co. to Elizabeth Space                        11-23-1830
HART, Judah B. to Sarah Jones                                            5-3-1825
HEACOCK, Davis to Huldah Myers                                          12-22-1830
HEACOCK, Erastus to Eunice Burrell both of Sheffield                    12-6-1827
HERRINGTON, Benjamin to Phebe Atwell both of Avon twp.                  8-31-1826
HICKCOX, Harvey to Almancy Hoadley                                      7-18-1830
HIGBY, John to Amanda Culver                                            7-26-1824
HOADLEY, Calvin R. to Lucy E. Osborn                                     1-1-1827
HOADLEY, Nelson to Marietta Phelps                                      12-29-1828
HOLCOMB, Loami to Mrs. Patience Tiff                                     4-24-1827
HOWK, Alanson to Theadocia Clefford                                     10-1-1828
HUBBARD, Eber'n to Honor M. Kingsbury                                    1-2-1827
HUBBELL, Samuel to Sally M. Mann                                         3-2-1828
HURD, Horace to Sophronia Crandel(1)                                    11-13-1828
INGERSOLL, James to Mary Simmons                                        5-16-1827
```

```
JACKSON, Truman to Harriet Bacon                                          10-7-1830
JOHNSON, James to Mary Atkinson                                         12-31-1829
JOHNSON, Leonard to Chloe Cutler                                         2-3-1825
JOHNSON, Phinehas M. of Elyria to Orra Ann Collins of Black River 9-9-(1829)
JOHNSON, Samuel to Suzan Cousins                                         7-5-1826
JONES, Ebenezer to Sophia Ann Perry                                     6-27-1827
KEELER, George to Errilla Kellog                                   lic. 11-17-1827
KNAPP, Alfred to Semanthe Mead both of Wellington                       7-2-1828
KYES, Samuel to Mercy Daily                                            10-2-1830
LAYLIN, Charles of Norwalk to Julia Abbot of Black River               4-6-1825
LENDER, Charles F. (James F. on lic.) to
            Sophia Burk both of Columbia twp.                          11-30-1828
LENT, Nun M. to Orra Case                                             11-28-1826
LEWIS, Oliver H. to Almena Beebe                                      12-12-1830
LONG, Adam to Mary Chanter                                            12-23-1830
LOVELAND, Abner Jr. to Pamela D. Wolf                                  3-29-1826
MARSH, Clement to Hannah Gould                                          6-3-1830
MERRILL, Moses to Eliza Wilcox                                          6-1-1830
MILES, Thompson to Mary Eddy Green both of Elyria                       2-7-1830
MILLER, Adam to Agnesd Denison                                        11-11-1830
MILLER, Peter to Ruth Houseworth                                        1-3-1828
MINOTT, Henry C. to Emeline F. Hubbard                                  7-8-1829
MITCHELL, Sidney to Teresa Dismal                                      4-25-1830
MOE, Edwin to Mahitable Alcott                                        11-28-1826
MOON, Abraham A. to Polly Moe                                           7-8-1829
MOON, Heman to Sarah Ann Adams                                        11-22-1826
MOORE, Ransom to Elsa Austin                                          11-27-1826
MOORE, Shadrach N. to Philena Barney                                  11-27-1825
MORGAN, E. Wm to Lucy W. Stow                                          6-30-1830
MURRAY, Abner to Diadama Webb                                          1-27-1830
MYERS, John to Mrs. Persis Whelsley                                    9-10-1830
NILES, Jonathan to Esther Hart                                         6-7-1827
NORTH, Zelotus to Chloe Rice                                           1-1-1828
OSGOOD, Rowland to Maria Buck                                          8-1-1830
PALMER, Dennis to Olive I. Terrill                                     4-8-1826
PARKHURST, Edward to Cordelia James                                  11-29-1827
PATCH, John Patterson to Margaret Cummins                             7-14-1825
PEARSONS, Thorrel to Mary Page                                       11-24-1829
PECK, Elisha to Phedima Baldwin                                        1-26-1829
PELTON, Josiah S. to Sophia Leonard                                    5-22-1825
PERRY, Ebenezer to Julia Ann Fairman                                   2-1-1826
PORTER, James to Cynthia Buckland                                      5-21-1828
RATHBONE, George to Sally Ann Wait                                     4-21-1825
READER, John to Laura Curtis                                           6-22-1829
REDINGTON, Ransom to Pamela Manter                                   11-28-1826
RICHMOND, Freeman to Eunice Gillet                                    10-5-1824
ROBINSON, Joseph to Mercy Vannetten                                  12-9-1827
ROBBINS, Orin to Silence Braman                                      10-13-1830
ROCKWOOD, David to Mary Graves                                         6-26-1828
SACKETT, Noahdiah to Hannah Chapman                                   4-18-1830
SANDERS, Horace to Miranda Clark of Lagrange                         10-23-1828
```

SHERMAN, Justin to Wakeman, Huron Co., Ohio to
    Betsey Reading of Ridgeville, Lorain Co.   9-4-1825
SHOEMAKER, Christian to Harriet Barnum   11-18-1830
SHOLES, Stanton to Lucy Halsey   2-16-1829
SLOCUM, Elias of Richland Co. to Mary Banning of Lorain Co. 12-11-1829
SMITH, Azeriah to Ruth Tillotson   5-30-1830
SMITH, Bennet(t) to Caroline Beebe   12-25-1828
SMITH, Daniel to Maria Humphrey   6-18-1828
SMITH, David to Fanny Barns   10-10-1824
SMITH, Douglas to Sally Burrell   6-2-1824
SMITH, Isaac to Ludy Crosier   9-3-1826
SMITH, Joel to Nancy Beam   5-20-1827
SMITH, Roswell to Jane Whitlock both of Wellington   11-7-1827
SMITH, Warren to Amanda Barns   7-9-1826
SQUIER, Daniel to Polly Lent   lic. 10-18-1827
SQUIERS, Ezra to Emily Hurd   12-11-1826
SQUIRES, Amasa to Jerusha Carter   9-8-1830
STEDMAN, Almerin to Weltha Abbott   2-14-1828
STODDARD, Loammi to Hannah Bruce   2-8-1829
STOW, Norris O. to Julia West   2-13-1828
STRICKLAND, Peter to Jane Ray   10-25-1828
STRONG, Emory of Strongsville, Cuyahoga Co. to
    Irene Johnson of Carlisle   7-19-1830
STRONG, Samuel to Caroline A. Merwin   11-19-1829
STRONG, Warren of Strongsville, Cuyahoga Co. to
    Saloma Burrell of Sheffield, Lorain Co.   1-1-1829
TAYLOR, Franklin to Anne Mennell   11-8-1827
TAYLOR, George to Amanda Terrill   10-7-1827
TAYLOR, Paul to Harriet Terril   9-8-1828
TERREL, Randal to Sally Cole   11-23-1828
TERRELL, Randel to Elizabeth M. Terrell (License destroyed)lic. 9-21-1827
TERRIL, Albert G. to Sally Hoadley   6-22-1828
THURSTON, Henry to Abby Abbot   12-22-1826
TRYON, Truman to Marietta Squiers   12-24-1830
TURNER, John of Dover, Cuyahoga Co., Ohio to
    Lydia Murray of Ridgeville, Lorain Co.   5-20-1826
USHER, Elias P. to Margaret Keeler   5-30-1827
VAN DRESER, Eleazer to Polly Shupe   7-10-1824
WAINRIGHT, William to Martha Goodell   1-6-1830
WAIT, Thomas to Marietta Wait   1-6-1830
WAKELY, Lyman to Rachel Butolph   11-20-1825
WALKER, William to Polly Disbrow   8-4-1825
WARDEN, John to Mary Townsend   6-22-1830
WEBSTER, Milton B. to Sally Cash both of Black River twp. 10-26-1828
WEEDEN, Charles W. to Marenday Goodwin both of Columbia 4-8-1830
WELLES, Woolsey to Mary W. Brown   1-1-1828
WELLMAN, Isaac to Cynthia Ann Thomas   6-29-1826
WELLMAN, Joseph to Abigail Hosford   3-4-1829
WEST, Edmund to Julia Johnson   6-19-1822
WESTERN, Warren to Almira Hancock   9-27-1826
WHITING, Nathan to Marinda Corban   4-10-1828

WHITTLESEY, Frederick Esq. to Eliza Burrell   9-9-1830
WICK, Solomon to Emily Gillet   4-29-1827
WILCOX, Calvin to Harriet B. Hubbard   3-8-1827
WILLIAMS, George O. to Dorcas Young   11-9-1829
WILLIAMS, John to Lorain Root   11-25-1827
WILLIAMS, Justin to Renew Austin   4-11-1827
YOUNG, William to Elizabeth Osburn   11-10-1830

The following records were taken from Death Record Book 1-2. Page on which the
original record may be found is given in parenthesis. This list includes only
those 40 years of age and over. Place of residence is same as place of death
unless otherwise stated. Abbreviations used: d-died; a-age; m-married; w-widow
or widower; s-single; pd-place of death; pb-place of birth; res-residence. Although
there is a place for names of parents, this was rarily filled in unless the
deceased was a child.

DENT, Samuel - d 5-10-1867; a 63y; m; pd LaGrange twp.; pb Yorkshire, England.(2)
MOON, Oliver - d 4-2-1867; a 80y 7m 16d; m; pd Shefield twp.; pb Berkshire,
    Mass. (2)
ROWEL, Jerusha - d 6-11-1867; a 86y 1m 12d; w; pd Sheffeld twp; pb Conn. (2)
IRISH, Nathan - d 4-13-1867; a 64y 3m 15d; m; pd Sheffeld twp.; pb N. Y. (2)
RANNEY, Susan - d 4-20-1867; a 72y; m; pd Rockport, O.; pb Mass. (2)
JAMESON, Joseph B. - d 6-8-1867; a 79y 6m 8d; m; pd Avon; pb N.H. (2)
PORTER, Ebenezer - d 7-5-1867; a 90y 8m 27d; w; pc Ridgeville; pb Lee, Mass. (2)
JONES, Chloe - d 7-29-1867; a 72y; w; pd Sheffield; pb Conn. (2)
SIMPSON, Ann Eliza - d 8-22-1867; a 54y 7m 4d; m; pd Oberlin; pb N. Carolina. (2)
WALTERS, Old Man - d 9-10-1857; a 67y; pd Spencer; pb ------. (2)
FREEMAN, Anna - d 713-1867; a 72y 6m 2d; w; pd Amherst; pb Vermont. (2)
CALVIN, James - d 9-1-1867; a 45y 8m 9d; pd Oberlin; pb N.C. (2)
MADDOCK, Mary - d 7-17-1867; a 68y; m; pd Avon; pb England. (2)
CARPENTER, Lusenia - d-30-1867; a 76y 4m; w; pd Olmsted; pb Dover, Vt. (2)
JOHNSON, Anna - d 9-28-1867; a 73y; m; pd Oberlin; pb Vt. (2)
BROWN, Stephen - d 8-25-1867; a 68y; m; pd Brownhelm; pb N. Y.
GERHART, John - d 8-17-1867 a 59y; m; pd LaGrange; pb------(4)
FOOTE, Anna - d 4-19-1867; a 68y; m; pd Wellington; pb N.Y. (4)
BATTLE. Ithiel - d 5-3-1867; 77y 2m 27d; m; pd Wellington, pb Mass. (4)
BRIGGS, Charles - 5-5-1867; a 46y; m; pd Wellington; pb N.Y. (4)
STEWART, Elizabeth - d 10-14-1867; a 50y 10m; 10m; m;; pd Wellington; pb Mass.(4)
WEBSTER, David - d 10-14-1867; age 95y 11m; m; pd Wellington; pb Conn. (4)
RUGG, David - 9-28-1867; a 73y; m; pd Huntington; pb-------(4)
STOUDER, Peter - d 1-28-1867; a 62y; m; pd Avon; pb Germany. (4)
PETERS, Statira - d 11-15-1867; a 48y; m; pd Penfield; pb Penfield. (4)
HUMPHREY, Orson J. - d 12-3-1867; a 71y; m; pd Eaton; pb Conn. (4)
WEBSTER, Hannah - d 10-8-1867; a 68y 3m 22d; w; pd Sandusky City; pb N.Y.:
    res. Oberlin. (4)
MANNING, William - d 12-19-1867; a 77y; m; pd Wellington; pb---------. (4)
GATES, Mrs. Sarah T. - d 12-9-1867; a 47y; m; pd Russia; pb--------; res.
    Clarksfield, O. (4)
HOSKINS, Mary - d 12-16-1867; a 103y 6m 1d per Register of family or 108y 6m
    1d her report; w; pd Camden; pb Mass. (6)
BATTLE, Sarah - d 10-7-1867; a 75y 6m; w; pd Wellington; pd Mass. (6)
GRIEM, Cattiarina E.R.C.-d 1-1-1868; a 45y 3m 26d m; pd Amherst; pb Germany.(6)
ROBINSON, Joseph - d 12-15-1867; a 69y; m; pd Ridgeville; pb England. (6)
ALLIS, Polly A. - d 12-24-1867; a 58y 3m 24d; w; pd LaPorte; pb Conn. (6)
MARSH, Henry d 10-28-1867; a 77y 8d; m; pd Olmsted; pb England. (6)
VAUGHN, Samuel - d 11-25-1867; a 54y; m; pd N. Ridgeville; pb England. (6)
WING, Polly - d 12-11-1867; a 50y 6m 37d; w; pd Amherst; pb N.Y. (6)

RUST, Elijah - d 8-26-1868; a 74y; w; pd Oberlin; pb Mass. (16)
MORISON, Charlotte C. - d 10-6-1868; a 59y 2m 22d; w; pd Oberlin; pb N.Y. (16)
HOWEY, Aaron - d 8-16-1868; a 69y; m; pd Olmsted; pb N.Y. (16)
CHURCHWARD, Mary - d 10-12-1868; a 49y;m; pd Cuyahoga Co. O.; pb Conn.; res.
    Berea, Cuyahoga Co., O. (16)
KELLEY, Margaret - d 6-1-1868; a 43y 2m 14d; pd Carlisle; pb Canada. (16)
WILKINSON, Richard - d 5-3-1868; a 40y; m; pd Ridgeville; pb England. (16)
POWERS(?), Anna - d 8-24-1868; a 75y 7m; w; pd Carlisle; pb_____. (16)
HOPKINS, Arnal - d 9-21-1868; a 75y 23d; m; pd Eaton; pb R. Island. (16)
HART, Emma L. - d 8-1-1868; a 59y 9m 20d; m; pd Penfield; pb Ct. (16)
PERKINS, Darius M. - d 7-23-1868; a 59y 3m 23d; m; pd Wellington; pb Mass. (16)
SHEMKLIN, _____(blank) - d 8-11-1868; a 68y; m; pd Oberlin; pb_____; res. N.Y.(16)
BURRELL, Daniel H. - d 9-23-1868; a 80y 1m 20d; w; pd Ridgeville; pb Mass. (16)
CORBIN, Roxa - d 8-28-1868; a 82y; m; pd Carlisle; pb Mass. (16)
PRIOR, George - d 9-13-1868; a65y; m; pd Elyria; pb_____. (18)
WEBSTER, Catharine - d 9-23-1868; a 55y; m; pd Carlisle; pb_____. (18)
POWER, Anna - d 8-24-1868; a 75y 7m; pd Carlisle; pb_____. (18)
HEALY, Benjamin - d 10-11-1868; a 45y 9m 7d; m; pd Eaton; pb N.Y.. (18)
COLEMAN, Achsah S. - d 12-8-1868; a 94y 10m 11d; w; pd Oberlin; pb Mass. (18)
BAKER, George - d 10-15-1868; a 43y 5m 23d; m; pd Amherst; pb Germany. (18)
GLEASON, Alfred - d 10-31-1868; a 61y 4m 24d; s; pd Amherst; pb N. Y. (18)
BECKER, George - d 10-15-1868; a 43y 6m 21d; m; pd Amherst; pb Prussia. (18)
HAGEMAN, Anna Martha - d 10-21-1868; a 71y 3m 23d; m; pd Amherst; pb Prussia.(18)
JENS, Katharine M. - d 10-23-1868; a 65y 2m 8d; m; pd Russia; pb Germany. (18)
PENFIELD, Maria - d 10-10-1868; a 73y; pd Penfield; pb_____. (18)
BARRETT, Mrs. - d 11-2-1868; a 50y; w; pd Oberlin; pb unknown. (18)
PAYNE, Sally A. - d 11-8-1868; a 64y; w; pd Avon; pb Mass. (18)
BURRELL, Abraham - d 11-23-1868: a 69y 6m 23d; w; pd Elyria; pb N.Y. (18)
LANE, Luther - d 11-23-1868; z 85y 2m; w; pd Elyria; pb Mass. (18)
BRADFORD, Lucy - d 12-6-1868; a 67y 3m 16d; m; pd Elyria; pb Conn. (18)
CARPENTER, Barlow G. - d 11-8-1868; a 52y 3m 11d; m; pd Wellington; pb Vt. (18)
HOPPELBERGER, Elizabeth - d 11-15-1868; z 48y 5m 1d; pd Elyria; pb Ham. Co. (18)
HYDE, William - d 12-1-1868; a 706; m; pd Elyria; pb Ebtland. (18)
RUTCIL, John N. - d 12-30-1868; a 40y; m; pd Elyria; pb Germany. (18)
ARNOLD, Mary - d 1022-1868; a 62y; m; pd Columbia; pb England. (18)
GLEASON, Alford - d 10-30-1868; a 61y 4m 24d; s; pd Amherst; pb N.Y. (18)
(Note: Some deaths were reportee twice; they have been included twice if the
information given was different from first report.)

GREENWOOD CEMETERY - WELLINGTON - LORAIN COUNTY, OHIO

Contributed by: Lucy Bloomquist, 1156 Briarcliff Dr., Rantoul, Ill. 61866
Cemetery copied in part, not all inscriptions taken.

DICKSON..... Mary L. Manley wife of J. H. b May 12, 1832 d Apr 9, 1881
        Joseph H.   1825-1895
        Mary A. Laudon w/o J. H. 1841-1895

CRANDALL.... Sarah C. w/o Pardon b in Bradford, N.H. Oct. 11, 1811 d at Youngstown,
           Ohio Apr. 27, 1879
        Pardon s/o N. & S. S. b in Derby, Ct.(Vt.?) June 28, 1807, removed to
           Ohio in 1834, d. in Pittsfield, Ohio Oct. 4, 1868
        Joshua s/o P. & S. M. b Dec. 14, 1844, a Member of Co. C, 86th Regt.
           O.V., d at Cumberland Gap Oct. 30, 1863
        Daughters of P. & S. M.
        Aseneth D. b. Apr. 15, 1839 d July 23, 1840
        Mary L. b Nov. 3, 1855 d Mar. 4, 1862
        Maria H, b Sep. 24, 1848 d Feb. 27, 1868

AMES........ Orpheus Nelson b in Becket, Mass. Apr. 6, 1832 d at Sioux Rapids,
           Iowa Mar. 3, 1889
        Nellie Gordon wife of Nelson O. b Sept. 7, 1832 d Jan. 1, 1872

PHELPS...... Charles b in Otis, Mass. 1823 d at Wellington, Ohio 1904 m Ann
        Ames w/o Charles b in Becket, Mass. 1828 d at Wellington, O. 1910.

LONG........ Adam b May 31, 1806 d June 5, 1886
        Mary w/o Adam b Apr. 10, 1812 d May 18, 1880
        Celestia w/o Noah d June 23, 1874
        Tracey aged 6 months (no date)

THOMAS..... Almena B. w/o G. M. b Apr. 13, 1809 d Mar. 13, 1876

DAVIS...... Belle M. d Apr. 31, 1872 ae 18y 6m 16d
        Allie F. d at Richardson Neb. Nov. 3, 1858 ae 2y 6d
        Daughters of J. T. & M.
        John T. d June 17, 1870 ae 41y 6m 5d
        Mary Eglin w/o John T. d Jan. 12, 1921 ae 91y

CARPENTER... B. G. b in Dover, Vt., d Wellington, Ohio Nov. 8, 1868 ae 52y
        Lucinda w/o B. G. b in Waitsfield, Vt., d June 11, 1895 ae 71y

37

The following was taken from Adms. Docket 1. Case numbers used in this docket may
not be the same as packet case numbers.

Name	Date	Case #	Name	Date	Case #
BALDWIN, Cornell R.	1848	260	GNAGGY, Francis	1843	132
Urinia			Anna		
Eliza T.			GREEN, Olive S.	1842	118
BARCLANE, Sally	1845	182	Harriet T.		
BARNES, Christian	1846	186	Francis M.		
BARRETT, Louiza	1848	266	Milton A.		
Wesley			Simeon F.		
Harrison			HANCOCK, David	1848	249
Beanzer			Mary J.		
BERDAN, Peter Frederick	1842	112	HARE, Eliza	1843	129
John			Cha les		
Mary Margaret			HARRIS, George	1850.	343
George			aged 14y on 9 Apr. 1850		
BERKHOLDER, Moses - 7 yrs.	1844	154	HARROWN, Sarah Jane	1848	283
Salome - 5 yrs.			HEFFELBOWER, Sarah	1847	244
Jacob - 3 yrs.			Barbara		
BERRY, Isaac S.	1848	284	David		
Mary S.			HIBBARD, Oscar J.	1843-4?	226½
BRINER, Catharine	1849	311	James R.		
BRINER, John Gotleit	1849	312	HOLLOWAY, Mary Jane	1848	273
BROWN, Emma J.	1849	300	George		
CAVINAC, Wm.	1849	316	Herbert		
Mary Ellen			HOUSE, James	1849	307
ch. of Morgan Cavinac			Harriet		
DAGGETT, Henry Smith	1847	231	HOWDEN, Emely	1849	287
William F.			Thomas		
Sarah			Martha		
Caroline E.			Matilda		
DAGGET T, ' William Fred.	1849	290	minor ch. of John & Jane Howden		
Henry E.			HUBBELL, Calvin	1848	208
DANIELS, Mary C.	1850	329	HUBBELL, Thomas	1846	209
Lucy			Christiana		
Kate			Mary Ann		
Ellah			HUBBELL, Hannah	1847	226
Willard W.			HUBBELL, Thomas	1849	322
DARK, William H.	1847	218	HULINGS, Mary	1838	13,62
DEAPER, Susan	1833	139	JOHNSON, Guy	1846	196
DICKINSON, Barney R.	1840	69	Joel M.		
Ellen I.			Abner		
Augustus M.			JUSTICE, Ava	1849	315, 346
FLETCHER, Hannah	1848	272	Thos. Jefferson		
FROBES, Augustus Ernst	1849	328	Hannah Rosetta		
William Ernst			Westly		
Henry Ernst			Nancy		
ch. of Henry Ernst Frobes			ch. of John Justice		
GALE, James	1844	156	KEELER, Catharine	1846	199
GEAPAM, Margaret	1848	254	ch. of Coleman J. Keeler Jr.		

Name	Date	Case #	Name	Date	Case #
KELLER, Hezekiah	1844	150	NORTH, John	1848	251
KING, William George	1849	289	Alida		
KOOS, Margaret	1847	238	Harriet		
George			Geo.		
Christian			James		
KRONTZ, Jacob	1848	274	PEACOCK, Abigal	1840	72
Lucinda			PEACOCK, Peter	1840	71
Manuel			PHILLIPS, Celestia	1839	65
Simon			PRAY, Ambrose Rice	1843	133
Caroline			RICHIOIN (RICHISON), Henry	1843	138
LYUR, Samuel E.	1842	122	SHAFFER, John	1844	157
McCONKEY, William	1839	66	STAIR, John	1848	256
MACOON, Isaac	1846	205	STEELE, Barbary J.	1848	270
MANER, Julia Jane	1850	344	WALKER, Francis E.	1850	339
Lewis W.			WATKINS, Christopher	1847	234
exander P.			Alfred		
Mary Clarisa			Catharine A.		
MERCERAN, Ellen Ann	1850	340	Way, Andrew I. H.	1838	17
aged 16y on 12 Mar. 1850			WHEELER, Betsey A.	1837	60
MERCERAN, Sarah E.	1850	341	WHITE, Francis Ann	1849	319
aged 9y on 25 July 1849			WIGGINS, Richard	1846	134
			WILKISON, James H.	1850	337
			WILSON, William et al.	1839	50
			YOUNG, Sarah	1850	347
			Wm.		

39

Information given below was taken from Adms. Docket 1. Case numbers used in this docket may not be the same as packet case numbers. Wills are filed in packets in the same manner as intestate estates. The term "estate" seems to have been used rather loosely in this docket, thus, it is possible that some references listed as estates could also contain wills. The county seat of Lucas County is Toledo, with the county being formed in 1835 from Wood County. E-Estate; W-Will.

Name	Type	Date	Case #	Name	Type	Date	Case #
ADAMS, Isaac N.	E	1850	352	CASE, Albert	E	1850	357
ALLWOOD, William	E	1849	324	CAVINAC, Morgan	E	1849	318
AXTELL, Harriet	E	1849?	323	CHAMBERLAIN, Moses	E	1839	64
BAKER, Josiah	E	1838	11,33	CHAMBERS, Joseph	E	1842	100
BALDWIN, John N.	E.	1838	16	CHAMBERS, Robert	E	1845	161
BALDWIN, John T.	W	1839	52	CHAMPION, Orlando	E	1850	356
BARKHEIMER, Isaac	W	1843	135	CHARTER, Dennis	W	1843	196
BARKHEIMER, Jacob	E	1842	110	CHATFIELD, Albert A.	E	1842	96,136
BARRON (BARROW),				CHENEY. Roswell	W	1846	179,183
Lamard W.	W	1850	349	CLEMENS, Chesterfield W.	E	1842	113
BARTLEY, Simeon	E	1846	187	COFFIN, Benj. D.	E	1849	320
BATEMAN, Asahel	E	1844	153	CONNER, Boyne	E	1849	321
BATLEIS, Nathaniel	E	1844	143	COOKE, Charles	W	1850	342
BEAL, William	E	1843	166	COOKE, Richard	E	1840	73
BEBEE, Levi	E	1838	37,119	CORNWELL, Sylvester	E	1847	237
BEEKMAN, John C.	E	1842	90	CORY, John B.	E	1849	325
BEHRINES, John B.	E	1848	267	COWRSER, Edward	W	1842	124
BENNETT, Philo	E	1838	18	COY, Cyrus	E	1845	162
BERDAN, John	E	1841	85	COZEN, Horatio G.	E	1848	281
BERRY, Daniel	E	1844	155	CRAFT, Thomas	E	1838	22
BEST, Jacob	E	1849	293	CUNAGER, Joseph	E	1839	58
BEVIRES(?), George	E	1839	47	CUPLIVER, Philip	E	1850	330
BINDER, Jacob	W	1847	236	DAGGETT, Smith	E	1840	75,137
BINGHAM, Jeremiah	E	1837	26	DANIELS, Munson H.	E	1845	171
BIRD, Asher E.	W	1844	142	DAVIS, Eleazor B.	E	1842	92
BISSELL, Jerusha	W	1849	317	DAVIS, Francis	E	1838	12,34
BLINKO, John	E	1839	67	DAVIS, I. Baron	W	1843	131
BLODGETT, Henry C.	E	1847	214	DEAPER, John	E	1844	145
BLUBAUGH, Solomon	E	1848	253	DeMOTT, Samuel	E	1846	206
BOEDET, Job	E	1839	45	DICKSON, Salathiel	E	1846	198
BOWERS, Salter	E	1850	358	DONALSON, James	E	1845	163
BOWMAN, Baxter	W	1838	15,86	DONNELLY, James	E	1837	21
BOWSER, John	W	1844	160	DOOLITTLE, David	E	1841	76
BRADFORD, Harvey S.	E	1842	94	DORLAN, George	E	1835	1
BRIGGS, Elkanah	E	1840	70,79	DOTY, Horatio	E	1843	127
BRIGGS, Erastus	E	1839	63	DOUGLAS, Gustavus	E	1838	19
BROGAN, Patrick	E	1849	326	DUNLAP, Ann	E	1839	44
BUCKFIELD, John	E	1846	192	ECKLEY, John	E	1849	299
BURKHOLDER, Samuel	W	1843	130	ECKOLS, Charles H.	E	1839	56
BURNES, John	E	1836	23	ENGLISH, Joseph	E	1842	105
BURTIS, John	E	1837-8	25	EVANS, Alvin	E	1847	215
			177	FARNSWORTH, Ralph	E	1842	109
BYRNES, Matthew	E	1846	202	FARRELL, James	E	1837	61
CALDWELL, Aaron	E	1842	101	FLAGG, Junius	E	1847	224

Name	Type	Date	Case #	Name	Type	Date	Case #
FLEMING, John	W	1847	241	KEGAN, John	E	1848	276
FORBES, Erastus K.	E	1847	220	KELLOGG, Joseph E.	E	1839	53
FOURMAN, Eleazer				KEMP, Ulrick	E	1845	170
(Eleazun?)	E	1839	57	KEPLAK, Frederick	E	1842	104
FRENCH, John P. of				KITT, Eli	E	1843	265
Licking Co. Oh.	W	1847	219	KNAGG, John	E	1846.	191
FROBES, Henry Ernst	E	1849	298	KNAGGS, Matilda	W	1847	243
FULIS, John	E	1847	246	KNAPP, Ezra	E	1838	36
GALE, Electa	E	1840	80	KNOWLTON, Hiram	E	1838	34,(35)
GEER, Smith	E	1846	207	KOHTZ, John	E	1850	348
GOETTEL, John	E	1848	262	KUHN, Abraham	E.	1846	204
GORDINEER, John A.	W	1846	185	KUNCIE, Conrod	W	1850	353
GREASER, Christian	W	1847	235	LABOURNE, John	E	1838	39
GREEN, Alexander	E	1839	49	LAKE, Henry	E	1845	167
GREEN, Horace	E	1849	305	LANE, Thomas M.	E	1847	223
GREEN, Simion C.	E	1842	117	LASHER, Frederick	E	1840	81
GRIFFIN, William	E	1843	193	LATHAM, Chester	E	1842	106
GRUSSAM, James	E	1848	275	LEONARDSON, John Jr.	W	1845	168
HADLEY, Abraham	E	1842	91	LEWIS, Abram	E	1844	140
HALL, David	W	1847	217	LEWIS, Lyma n	E	1849	300
HALLOM, Edward				LOMBAR, Peter	E	1836	4
of New London, Ct.	W	1847	245	LONGINTIEFER, Stephen	E	1843	134
HAMILTON, Wiley	W	1841	77	MAHL, Reinhardt	E.	1849	314
HANCOCK, David	E	1848	250	MAH NEY, Bartholomew	E	1849	301
HARE, Henry I.	E	1841	88	MA ER, William	E	1843	126
HARRINATON, George M.	E	1850	351	MANLEY, Orwin	E	1849	292
HARRISON, Talmon	E	18471	240	MANN, Hirum	E	1843	223½
HARROUN, John	E	1843	128	MANON, Peter	E.	1848	247
HAWLEY, David W.	E	1844	224½	MARSH, Coleman	E	1846	190
HAYES, James	W	1846	201	MARTIN, William	E	1845	174
HAYNES, Jacob	E	1843	197	MASON, Luke of			
HEFFLEBOWER, John	W	1846	211	Wayne Co., N.Y.	W	1844	152
HIBBARD, Eliona	W	1847	242	MATHEWS, Chauncey	W	1847	227
HICKS, David	E	1849	295	MATTOON, Jacob	E	1850	331
HOLCOMB, Charles H.	E	1847	213	MAY, Alonzo	E	1848	271
HOLDER, Emanuel	E	1844	147,181	McMILLEN, Wm.	E	1849	309
HOLLOWAY, Alpheus S.	E	1848	259	MEECH, Reinhard	E	1849	294
HOLLOWAY, Cyrus	E	1842	115	MEEK (MERK?), Lucas	E	1848	255
HOLMES, John	E	1843	225½	MERCEREAN, Henry	E	1848	257
HOUSE, Conrad	E	1846	195	MERCK, Anthony	E	1845	175
HUBBELL, Hezekiah	E	1846	203	METZHER, William	E	1842	125
HUGHES, Jane	E	2848	261	MICKEUS, Peter	E	1842	123
HULCE, John	E.	1837	7	MILLER, John	E	1850	327
HUTCHISON, Joseph	E	1848	258	MILLER, Samuel	E	1850	350
JACKSON, James	W	1838	14	MILLS, Reuben	E	1847	233
JEMISON, George	E	1842	108	MINTON, Nancy	E	1847	216
JOHNSON, Enoch	E	1842	97	MOONEY, David B.	E	1849	302
JOHNSON, Jeremiah	E	1837	27	MORGON, George B.	E	1848	264
JONES, Eleazer	E	1847	212	MORRIS, James	E	1839	46
JONES, William	W	1847	228	NOBLE, Alonzo M.	E	1849	285
KEELER, Coleman I. Jr.	E	1846	178	NORTH, Isaac	E	1848	252

41

Name	Type	Date	Case #	Name	Type	Date	Case #
NORTON, Hiram	E.	1839?	41	STILWELL, Elisha	E	1849	286
O'BRIEN, Patrick	E	1840	82	SUTTON, Thomas P.	E	1842	103
PAGE, James S.	E	1838	10,32	SWIFT, Daniel	E	1849	308
			42	THOMAS, Hiram	E	1840	68
PARKER, Simeon	E	1847	230	THOMAS, Levi	E	1836	2, 120
PETER(?), Rufus S. of				TITUS, Israel	E.	1849	303
Ottego Co., N.Y.	E	1844	151	TITUS, James J.	E	1849	304
PETERS, Eshan	E	1844	146	TITUS, John Avery	E.	1841	84
PHILLIPS, Henry*	E	1838	9, 31	TRAPP, Andrew	E	1842	102
PHILLIPS, Henry*	J	1839	43	TREMAIN, Calvin	E	1845	169
POND, John P.	E	1847	229	TYRRELL, Cyrus	E.	1847	232
PRAY, Hannah	W	1850	335	VAN DERLISS, Hugh	E1	1878	263
PRAY, Parris	E	1850	332	VAN GUNTEN, John	W.	1848	279
PRENTIS, Joseph	E	1845	172	VAUGHN, Alexander	W	1847	225
PRESTON, Samuel	E	1839	40	VOGLESONG, John J.	E	1846	188
QUADE, Christopher	E	1842	99	VEN ALSTINE, Abraham	E	1842	111
CYNEY(?), Richard	E	1842	107	WAITE, Horace	E	1850	345
RAKESTRAW, Joseph	E	1845	164	WALDIN (WALDEN), David	E	1839	55
REED, Richard	E	1845	176,194	WALKER, Thomas W.	E	1850	336
REYNOLDS, Caleb	E	1841	89	WATERBURY, Hiram	E	1844	158
RICHARDSON, Oliver	E	1836	6	WEAST, Christopher	E	1842	114
RICH, Abram	E	1845	165	WEBBER, Noah	E	1849	310
ROEDER, John C.	E	1838	24	WHITE, David	W	1839	51
ROETWICK, Manley	E	1849	297	WHITE, Elvina C.	E	1850	334
ROREBACK, David	E	1839	48	WHITE, Ira	E	1842	95
RUMSEY, Lewis	E	1846	189	WHITE, Joseph	W	1848	280
SABIN, William H. of				WHITE, Thomas	W	1848	277,278
Onondago Co. N.Y.	W	1844	222½	WHITNEY, Michael T.	E	1840	74
SALESBURY, Peter	W	1844	159	WHITNEY, Milton D.	E	1839	54
SALSBURY, Runel	E	1849	291	WILKISON, James	W	1850	333,338
SAWYER, Stephen	E	1841	87	Alice Wilkinson, executrix, lost on			
SCHRAGG, Benedict	E	1844	144	board Steamer Griffith 6-17-1850			
SCRAFFENBERGER, Daniel	E	1841	83	WILKISON, William	E	1849	288
SHANK, Thomas	E	1844	149	WILLARD, Anthony L.	E	1846	200
SHORT, David	E	1845	173	WILLIAMS, Peter	E	1844	148,180
SIBLEY, William	W	1836	5	WILSON, Nathan	E	1841	78
SMITH, Benj. F.	E	1842	93	WILSON, William	E	1836	3
SMITH, Patrick	E	1847	222	WINSLOW, Martin	E	1848	282
SMITH, Willard	E	1838	8, 30	UNSCK(?), John	E	1847	239
SMITH, Wm. M.	E	1849	313				
SNEAD, Benjamin F.	E	1842	98				
SOUDER, John	E	1845	221				
STAIR, William	E	1848	248				
STEELE, Hiram	E	1838	38				
STEELE, Lee	W	1848	269				
STERLING, Micah of							
Watertown, N.Y.	W	1848	268				

MADISON COUNTY, OHIO
Deaths 1867-1870

Persons 50 years of age or over

Name	Date of Death	Age	Place of Death
ADAMS, Betsy	6-21-1868	78 y	- - - - - - - - -
ALLEN, Annie	3-20-1869	75 y	Darby Twp.
ALLEN, Calvin Sr.	9-17-1868	86 y	Caxton, Ill.
ARMSTRONG, Elizabeth	9-3-1867	72 y	Madison Co.
ALLEN, Harriet ·	2-8-1868	52 y	Plain City
ANDERSON, Gertrude	Oct. 1870	65 y	Fairfield Twp.
ARMATROUT, Jacob	9-15-1869	83 y	Amity
ABERNATHY, Nancy	4-10-1868	59 y	Mt. Sterling
BROWN, Sarah	10-15-1869	56 y	Midway
BURNS, Benjamin F.	4-5-1869	71 y	Pleasant Twp.
BURLEY, David	12-23-1868	70 y	Union
BELL, Daniel	12-8-1868	69 y	Lafayette
BATES, Dorcas	11-1-1869	68 y	Pike Twp.
BASKERVILLE, James	8-4-1868	66 y	Madison Co.
BLAIR, Jennie	8-25-1868	77 y	Madison Co.
BADLEY, Joseph	12-22-1869	53 y	Madison Co.
BALDWIN, L. S.	8-3-1869	50 y	Range Twp.
BUXENBURG, Peter	9-30-1867	84 y	Madison Co.
BUSICK, Sarah	5-6-1868	64 y	Pleasant Twp.
BROWN, Sarah	10-18-1869	56 y	Range Twp.
BASKERVILLE, William	8-2-1867	74 y	Madison Co.
CREATH, Catharine A.	4-15-1869	60 y	Pleasant Twp.
COWLING, Edward	12-19-1868	66 y	Madison Co.
CORDER, Elizabeth	10-29-1870	86 y	Fairfield Twp.
COLUMBER, E. S.	9-29-1870	55 y	Fairfield Twp.
CROUCH, George	9-11-1867	36 y	Lafayette
COLLENS, Ira	2-23-1868	50 y	W. Jefferson
CALHOUN, James	12-31-1869	67 y	Madison Co.
CALHOUN, James	12-30-1869	60 y	Canaan Twp.
CALENDER, John	6-14-1870	81 y	Fairfield Twp.
COBERLY, Mary	9-23-1868	78 y	Madison Co.

43

Name	Date	Age	Location
CARTER, Matilda	10-8-1868	55 y	Jefferson Twp.
COIN, Thomas	10-28-1868	65 y	Clark Co.
DAVIS, Elizabeth	7-27-1867	79 y	Madison Co.
DEVAULT, Levina	10-26-1867	70 y	Union
DAVIDSON, Patrick	12-8-1870	64 y	Fairfield Twp.
DELONG, Sarah	1-26-1868	67 y	Madison Co.
DELANEY, Sarah	6-22-1868	66 y	Monroe
DAVIDSON, Sarah	8-13-1870	90 y	Union
ECKELS, Daniel	12-21-1869	53 y	Madison Co.
FURROW, John	10-15-1867	53 y	Madison Co.
FISHER, John	4-7-1869	92 y	Range Twp.
FITROW, Joseph	4-14-1870	55 y	Jefferson Twp.
FOSSETT, Jadiah	12-8-1870	57 y	Range Twp.
FULTON, Phebe Low	7-13-1868	52 y	Plain City
GRIM, Barbara	10-11-1867	52 y	Madison Co.
GARDNER, Abner	4-10-1870	66 y	Fairfield Twp.
GOLDSBURY, Humphrey	8-5-1870	50 y	Range Twp.
GREGARY, James	10-23-1868	60 y	London
GALLIGHER, John	4-25-1869	86 y	Cannan Twp.
GUY, Polly	11-15-1869	83 y	Madison Co.
GUY, Mary	11-14-1869	87 y	Oak Run
GOSLEE, Thomas	7-7-1867	55 y	Madison Co.
GREGORY, William	10-22-1868	60 y	London
GREEN, William	6-2-1869	50 y	London
HASTINGS, . .(not given)	7-30-1867	54 y	Madison Co.
HUFFMAN, Amos	1-12-1869	64 y	Stokes Twp.
HULL, David	2-23-1869	65 y	Madison Co.
HARNESS, Cenia	2-11-1870	72 y	Pike Twp.
HICKS, Frances	4-6-1869	78 y	Pleasant Twp.
HARRIS, Hannah	12-4-1868	72 y	Somerford Twp.
HORNBECK, James	8-12-1869	59 y	Stokes Twp.
HILL, Polly	3-27-1868	78 y	Madison Co.
HAGER, Simeon	3-8-1870	75 y	Madison Co.
HEFLIN, William	9-9-1870	59 y	Fairfield Twp.
JONES, John	8-17-1868	78 y	Madison Co.
JACKSON, Nancy	3-27-1869	83 y	Fairfield Twp.
JACKSON, Thomas	8-26-1870	65 y	Fairfield Twp.
KEENE, Daniel	4-5-1869	75 y	Madison Co.
KING, Henry	11-9-1869	63 y	Madison Co.
KNAPP, Phebe	6-26-1869	67 y	Canaan Twp.
LEWIS, Catharine	1-22-1870	100 y	Oak Run
LYNCH, Ellen	3-17-1870	72 y	Canaan Twp.
LEWIS, Solomon	5-2-1870	75 y	Oak Run
LESTER, Sarah	7-5-1870	81 y	Fairfield Twp.
MIDDLETON, Anna S.	7-24-1867	72 y	London
MOORE, George	11-15-1867	60 y	West Jefferson
MARSH, John	11-25-1867	55 y	Madison Co.
MENSHALL, Jonathan	9-30-1868	85 y	Range Twp.
MILLIKIN, James	10-2-1868	87 y	Madison Co.
MAN, Lorenz D.	7-14-1868	66 y	Madison Co.
MINTER, Mary	8-5-1869	89 y	Deer Creek Twp.
MOUNT, Lenford	3-11-1870	52 y	London
MARK, Washington	9-21-1868	58 y	Deer Creek Twp.

McMURRAY, Alexander	10-26-1867	94 y	Madison Co.
McDONALD, Sarah	6-12-1869	63 y	Lafayette
McDONALD, . .(not given)	6-14-1869	62 y	Deer Creek Twp.
McCLELAND, William	1-15-1868	81 y	Jefferson Twp.
McCONN, William	5-30-1868	60 y	Madison Co.
McCOY, William	9-3-1869	84 y	Deer Creek Twp.
OWENS, William T.	12-20-1869	50 y	Lafayette
PHILLIPS, Andrew	10-27-1869	70 y	Union Twp.
POTER, Hannah	2-8-1868	78 y	Madison Co.
PUTNAM, Horace	5-12-1869	52 y	W. Jefferson
PETERS, John	8-20-1867	56 y	Madison Co.
PAINTER, Jemima	6-6-1868	71 y	Madison Co.
POWERS, Margaret	10-16-1868	67 y	Clark Co.
PANCAKE, Mary	Dec. 1869	73 y	Stokes Twp.
QUOUGH, Benjamin	3-5-1869	60 y	Madison Co.
RUBERT, Elizabeth	10-6-1870	77 y	Union Twp.
RAFFERTY, Isabell	6-14-1869	76 y	Tralesville
ROBERTS, Margaret	2-6-1868	68 y	Jefferson
SHEPHERD, Nancy	3-13-1868	60 y	W. Jefferson
SMITH, Anna	Apr. 1869	72 y	Pike Twp.
STEPHENS, Eliza	7-28-1868	61 y	Plain City
SAFFLEY, Mary	3-8-1869	75 y	Union Twp.
SHEPHERD, Nancy	3-13-1868	60 y	W. Jefferson
SIDNER, Nancy	7-10-1869	60 y	Paint Twp.
SAURRES, William H.	1-15-1870	60 y	London
THOMPSON, Jacob	3-3-1869	82 y	Union Twp.
TERRY, Mary	3-10-1869	56 y	Madison Co.
TYLER, Mary	3-10-1869	52 y	Madison Co.
TIRE, Mary	3-9-1869	53 y	Oak Run
TRAY, Nathaniel	9-30-1867	72 y	Madison Co.
THORNBURGH, Uriah	7-14-1867	78 y	Madison Co.
THOMPSON, Thomas	2-26-1870	65 y	Ross Co.
WILLIAMS, Betsy	6-17-1868	78 y	Madison Co.
WHEATLY, Charles	10-28-1869	78 y	Stokes Twp.
WHITTECAR, E. D.	2-26-1868	56 y	London.
WARNER, Frances	6-10-1869	72 y	London
WILSON, John	12-30-1868	56 y	Union Twp.
WILLOUGHBY, Margaret	9-12-1867	80 y	Madison Co.
WILSON, Nancy	11-30-1870	65 y	Union Twp.

R0201173442

Persons 50 years of age or over.

Name	Date of Death	Age	Place of Death	Place of Birth
ALLEN, Aseph	7-14-1874	84y 10m	Darby Twp.	Mass.
ADAIR, Borthier(?)	4-7-1875	77-1-19	London	Va.
ALDER, Elizabeth	1-1-1874	61-10-12	Canaan Twp.	Washington Co. Pa.
ARMUNTROUT, Elias	5-6-1875	58-11-6	Monroe Twp.	Va.
ALLEN, Luceus	11-29-1873	66-8-11	Darby Twp.	Vermont
ALLEN, Martha	5-6-1873	62 yr.	London	Ross Co.
ALKIRE, Sarah	3-13-1873	76 yr.	Pleasant Twp.	- - - - - -
ANDERSON, Ruben	12-12-1875	65-11-2	Oak Run	London, Ohio
BATES, Archabald L.	5-9-1873	79yr. 7d.	Pike Twp.	Rhode Id.
BUSICK, Arthur A.	12-27-1873	85 yr.	Pleasant Twp.	Md.
BOWER, George W.	12-9-1872	62 yr.	Fairfield Twp.	- - - - - - -
BIDWELL, Isaac	2-6-1874	61yr. 7m.	Canaan Twp.	Franklin Co., O.
BAKER, John	Aug. 1872	72 yr.	Monroe Twp.	- - - - - - -
BROWN, James	3-13-1875	79-10-17	Somerford Twp.	New York
BLACK, Mary	4-13-1875	93 yr.3d.	Madison Co.	Hampshire Co. Va.
BURRIS, Samuel	3-17-1872	73 yr.	Range Twp.	- - - - - - -
BOWERS, Rushama	9-29-1871	52 yr.	Darby Twp.	- - - - - - -
BASKERVILLE, Samuel	12-4-1873	75-5-27	Paint Twp.	Va.
BRANNON, Thomas	1-10-1875	70 yr.	Deer Creek Twp.	Ireland
BROWN, William	4-28-1875	55 yr.28d	Range Twp.	Fayette Co., Ohio
COMFORT, Bridget	4-20-1873	65 yr.	London	London
CHAMBERS, Catharine	6-17-1871	54 yr.	Darby Twp.	- - - - - - -
COUNTS, Daniel Sr.	6-29-1873	93 yr.	Range Twp.	- - - - - - -
CREATH, Elizabeth	11-21-1873	79-2-2	Fairfield Twp.	Hardy Co. Virginia
CASSADY, Hannah	6-8-1873	56 yr.	Madison Co.	Ohio
COOK, John J.	3-28-1872	72yr.	Pleasant Twp.	- - - - - - -
CANDLER, Jesse J.	1-13-1871	67 yr.	Sommerford Twp.	- - - - - - -
CONKLING, John	10-26-1873	73-10-1	Jefferson Twp.	Penna.
CORSON, John	8-30-1875	65 yr.	Range Twp.	Va.
CORRELL, Mag.	1-20-1871	60 yr.	Paint Twp.	- - - - - - -
CURTIN, Mary	12-11-1871	54 yr.	Deer Creek Twp.	- - - - - - -
CAMMON, Mary	2-27-1872	55 yr.	Paint Twp.	- - - - - - -
CAMPBELL, Peter	6-20-1871	57 yr.	Union Twp.	- - - - - - -
COOK, Nancy	2-20-1873	72 yr.	Pleasant Twp.	- - - - - - -
COUPLES, Samuel	3-25-1871	58 yr.	Jefferson Twp.	- - - - - - -
CLARK, Raphael	2-8-1872	77 yr.	Union Twp.	- - - - - - -
CHENOWETH, S. D.	4-20-1873	50 yr.	Union Twp.	- - - - - - -
CREGO, Rachel	3-17-1874	56-3-16	Canaan Twp.	- - - - - - -
COWLING, Richard	10-3-1873	75 yr.	London	England
CHENOWETH, S. D.	4-24-1873	50 yr.	Union Twp.	Madison Co.
CALLENDER, Rachel	2-16-1875	85-1-10	Fairfield Twp.	S. Charleston
CORNWELL, Tabitha A.	3-2-1873	52yr.	Union Twp.	- - - - - - -
CANFIELD, Thomas	11-3-1873	72 yr.	Union Twp.	Ireland
CRATH, William	1-14-1871	69 yr.	Pleasant Twp.	- - - - - - -
CREIGHTON, William H.	3-3-1871	59 yr.	Range Twp.	- - - - - - -
CHAPPELL, William	5-23-1871	67 yr.	Range Two.	- - - - - - -
CORRAN, William C.	3-16-1875	56-1-2	Somerford Twp.	New York

46

CRAWFORD, William H.	2-4-1875	75-11-18	London	Va.
CARTMELL, William	11-17-1875	96-4-17	Pike Twp.	Va.
DOMINEY, Alvin H.	3-31-1875	57yr.	Canaan Twp.	Clark Co.
DOUNTZ, Frederick	11-22-1871	82 yr.	Pleasant Twp.	- - - - - - -
DATCH, Elendor	1-8-1874	73-11-15	Xenia, Ohio	Va.
DAVIDSON, Jane	3-21-1873	64 yr.	Fairfield Twp.	- - - - - - -
DARLEY, Joanna	3-31-1875	64 yr.	Canaan Twp.	Ireland
DAVIDSON, Martha	5-15-1875	72 yr.	Fairfield Twp.	Penna.
DAVIS, Nancy Ann	Mar. 1875	83 yr.	London	- - - - - - -
DUNGAN, Sarah	12-23-1872	62 yr.	Union Twp.	- - - - - - -
EVANS, Amos	9-26-1871	68 yr.	Paint Twp.	- - - - - - -
ELLARS, Carty	7-20-1875	68-3-4	Range Twp.	Delaware
EVANS, Joseph	1-20-1874	.90 yr. 9d	Union Twp.	Va.
ELKINS, William	1-20-1874	74 yr.	Jefferson Twp.	England
FRANCIS, Chrispen	2-7-1873	81-5-1	Range Twp.	New Jersey
FEARING, Christina	5-27-1874	53-3-7	Jefferson Twp.	New Jersey
FLETCHER, Jacob	1-5-1872	84 yr.	Range Twp.	- - - - - - -
FOSTER, John	11-25-1873	71-8-21	Range Twp.	Ross Co.
FARRAR, Jonathan	7-22-1874	83-11-4	London	England
FISHER, Martha A.	12-21-1873	56-4-23	Monroe Twp.	Va.
FRANCIS, Samuel	5-1-1873	76 yrs.	Fairfield Twp.	Loudon Co. Va.
GARDNER, Abner	4-10-1870	66 yr.	Fairfield Twp.	- - - - - - -
GEER, Anna Viola	2-26-1873	90 yr.	Somerford Twp.	- - - - - - -
GIBBLIN, Ann	1-19-1875	70 yr.	Range Twp.	Ireland
GRAREN, Daniel	2-7-1875	76-1-19	Jefferson Twp.	Ireland
GREGORY, Joseph	3-18-1871	60 yr.	London	- - - - - - -
GRAHAM, John	8-20-1871	82 yr.	London	- - - - - - -
GRAY, Lemuel	12-13-1871	52 yr.	Union Twp.	- - - - - - -
GOREY, Michael	9-24-1873	50 yr.	Range Twp.	Ireland
GLAZE, Rebecca	5-30-1874	53 yr.	Fayette	- - - - - - -
GREEN, Thomas	July 1871	85 yr.	Range Twp.	- - - - - - -
GUY, Wilkinson	4-21-1872	59 yr.	Darby. Twp.	- - - - - - -
HERON, Barbara	1-6-1872	76 yr.	Range Twp.	- - - - - - -
HANSON, Daniel	6-30-1874	69-6-23	Union Twp.	Tenn.
HOWSMAN, Frances	2-21-1873	76 yr.	Union Twp.	- - - - - - -
HUGHS, Ellen	2-15-1874	65 yr.	London	Ireland
HARKNESS, John	1-12-1871	71 yr.	- - - - - -	- - - - - - -
HUTSON, John K.	10-26-1872	73 yr.	Stokes Twp.	- - - - - - -
HERRAD, J. H.	9-13-1874	60-4-15	Stokes Twp.	Stokes Twp.
HEATH, Matilda	12-8-1872	69 yr.	Monroe Twp.	- - - - - - -
HARNAHAN, Patrick	10-23-1873	68 yr.	Union Twp.	Ireland
HASKET, Orren	2-11-1874	52 yr.	Paint Twp.	Paint Twp.
HUTCHISON, Robert M.	11-12-1872	83-yr.	Union Twp.	- - - - - - -
HUMPHREY, Royal	8-2-1873	90 yr.	Canaan Two.	Ireland
JOHNSON, Abraham	1-14-1874	65-3-15	Jefferson Twp.	Madison Co.
JACKSON, Andrew J.	2-27-1874	54 yr.	London	Madison Co.
JONES, Isaac	4-26-1875	58-6-3	London	London
JACKSON, John	7-11-1873	54-1-25	Fairfield Twp.	Madison Co.
JOHNSON, Jesse	8-19-1874	75-3-5	Stokes Twp.	Penna.
		Father:-	Baley Johnson	
JONES, M. C.	1-5-1873	55 yr.	Union Twp.	- - - - - - -

JOHNSON, T. W.	2-12-1874	53-8-22	Fairfield Twp.	Montgomery Co. Md.
	Father:- Thomas B. Johnson			
KEEN, Mary	9-4-1871	65 yr.	Jefferson Twp.	- - - - - -
KILE, Nancy	3-17-1874	64 yr.24d.	Range Twp.	Highland Co.
KILGORE, Sarah	11-3-1872	82 yr.	Union Twp.	- - - - - -
KILGORE, Samuel	9-20-1875	52 yr.	Range Twp.	Fayette Co.
KNOTT, Zachariah	11-31-1872	55 yr.	Union Twp.	- - - - - -
LINCH, Isabella	2-6-1875	66 yr.	So. Salem(?)	Stokes Twp.
LANE, Junea(?)	5-9-1872	62 yr.	Oak Run	- - - - - -
LEWIS, James	3-21-1873	67 yr.	Fairfield Twp.	- - - - - -
LOMBARD, Jesse	1-21-1875	71-8-29	Plain City	Vermont
LILLY, James	10-10-1874	58 yr.6d.	London	Ross Co.
LOTSPEECER,James Quincy	2-26-1875	65-8-26	London	Fairfield County
LATHAM, Nancy	2-14-1873	65 yr.	Paint Twp.	- - - - - -
LESTER, Sarah	7-5-1870	81 yr.	Fairfield Twp.	- - - - - -
LYNN, Samuel	9-15-1874	69-3-4	Stokes Twp.	England
LOHR, Sarah	12-3-1875	57-6-23	London	Clark Co.
LANGAN, Thomas	12-25-1873	60 yr.	Union Twp.	Ireland
LELLARD, Thomas	12-9-1875	56-7-24	Paint Twp.	Va.
MILLER, Abraham	3-2-1875	56-8-17	Oak Run	Ohio
MORSE, Caleb(?)	1-29-1872	76 yr.	Pike Twp.	- - - - - -
MASTERSON, Frank	3-23-1873	73 yr.	Union Twp.	- - - - - -
MULFORD, Elizabeth	12-20-1875	57 yr.	London	Guernsey Co.
MURPHY, Isaac	9-22-1875	73 yr.	Pleasant Twp.	Va.
MITCHELL, Joseph	12-11-1871	55 yr.	Range Twp.	- - - - - -
MELVIN, Josep V.	4-15-1871	74 yr.	Somerford Twp.	- - - - - -
MARTH, Jonas	7-3-1871	54 yr.	Pleasant Twp.	- - - - - -
MILLER, John H.	1-16-1874	56 yr.	Pleasant Twp.	Va.
MAGRAUGH, James	1-8-1874	80 yr.	Union Twp.	Md.
MITCHELL, Matilda	3-12-1871	69 yr.	Union Twp.	- - - - - -
MARSHALL, James	3-27-1871	70 yr.	Pleasant Twp.	- - - - - -
MITCHELL, Magill	8-10-1874	76yr.6m.	Mt. Sterling	Kentucky
MOHAR, Patsy	July 1873	63 yr.	Darby Twp.	Ireland
MARTIN, Phoeba Ann	7-20-1875	52-8-20	La Fayette	Madison Co.
MORGRIDGE, Sally	1-29-1872	91 yr.	Darby Twp.	- - - - - -
MINSHALL, Walter W.	10-18-1874	63-8-17	London	London
McCLIMANS, David	3-11-1874	65-2-23	Range Twp.	Ross Co.
McCORMACK, Edward	3-21-1875	56yr.21d.	London	London
McGRAW, Joseph	1-8-1875	80 yr.	Union Twp.	- - - - - -
McCLINTOCK, William	11-20-1871	55 yr.	Range Twp.	- - - - - -
ORCUTT, B.	5-29-1871	76 yr.	Union Twp.	- - - - - -
OBOILS, Cornelius	8-30-1875	63 yr.	Fairfield Twp.	Ireland
OGLESBEE, Margaret	2-3-1873	65 yr.	Pleasant Twp.	- - - - - -
PFIFER, Abraham	4-11-1871	83 yr.	Paint Twp.	- - - - - -
PUCKET, Catharine	6-24-1872	70 yr.	Pleasant Twp.	- - - - - -
PELTON, David M.	4-8-1872	67 yr.	Union Twp.	- - - - - -
PANCAKE, Cephas	10-7-1874	55-7-21	Oak Run	- - - - - -
PRICE, Ester	6-2-1874	89-7-10	Franklin	Md.
PAYTON, Harry	5-1-1873	65 yr.	Pleasant Twp.	Va.
PAINTER, Joel	9-12-1873	86-9-2	Fairfield Twp.	Penna.
PELTON, Sallie	2-8-1871	64 yr.	- - - - - -	- - - - - -

48

PETERSON, Susan	1-29-1873	84 yr.	Union Twp.	- - - - - -
POSTAL, Solomon	6-16-1875	86 yr.	Somerford Twp.	Maryland
PETERSON, William	8-12-1871	83 yr.	Paint Twp.	- - - - - -
RAYBURN, Creighton M.	8-10-1871	52 yr.	Union Twp.	- - - - - -
RIGGIN, J. W.	12-23-1874	83 yr.2m.	Mt. Sterling	Pickaway
REA, Mathew	9-22-1873	81 yr.3m.	Fairfield Twp.	Rockbridge Co. Va.
REA, Pernelia	12-10-1871	66 yr.	Union Twp.	- - - - - -
ROWLEN, Rebecca	9-2-1872	80 yr.	Pleasant Twp.	- - - - - —
REEVES, Thomas	9-5-1871	83 yr.	Range Twp.	- - - - - -
ROUSE, Thomas	2-8-1874	76 yr.	Union Twp.	New York
SHEPHARD, Andrew	1-21-1873	78y 10m	Range Twp.	Va.
SLAUGHTER, Anna	3-17-1874	85-2-17	Stokes Twp.	Frederick Co. Va.
SPEASMAKE, Cssner	4-21-1873	79 yr.1mo.	Union Twp.	Germany
STOOKEY, Eli	11-23-1875	63 yr.	Calif.	Va.
SUVER, Elizabeth	12-28-1874	59-6-13	Range Twp.	Madison Co.
SOLOMON, Elehow Wm.	3-15-1875	65-10-7	Jefferson Twp.	New Jersey
SCHRYACK, Isaiah	1-2-1874	52-4-28	London	Urbana
SELF, Mariah	3-23-1873	64 yr.	Pleasant	- - - - - -
SMITH, Maud	10-31-1872	61 yr.	Stokes Twp.	- - - - - -
STATLER, Mary	2-11-1874	89 yr.	Somerford Twp.	Virginia
STONER, Samuel	1-2-1872	57 yr.	Jefferson Twp.	- - - - - -
SMITH, Richard	6-6-1872	76 yr.	Darby Twp.	- - - - - -
TIMMONS, Jane	3-30-1874	76-8-22	Range Twp.	Va.
TRUETT, James D.	10-15-1875	70-10-8	London	Md.
THRASHER, Nancy	7-30-1874	80 yr.	Union Twp.	Mass.
THOMPSON, Nancy	Mar. 1875	86 yr.	Union Twp.	Ky.
THOMAS, Scott	8-17-1873	83y	Fairfield Twp.	Virginia
TROWBRIDGE, William	6-17-1873	80-11-3	Union Twp.	Va.
VICKERS, William Smith	1-9-1873	76 yr.	Jefferson Twp.	- - - - - -
WILSON, Andrew	10-10-1871	65 yr.	Union Twp.	- - - - - -
WILLARD, Abner S.	12-16-1872	81 yr.	Somerford Twp.	- - - - - -
WILLIAMS, Eli	6-17-1873	87 yr.	Somerford Twp.	Canada
WORTHINGTON, Israel	9-3-1875	55 yr.	Canaan Twp.	Conn.
WATSON, Jessie	9-15-1871	58 yr.	London	- - - - - -
WILLIS, James Franklin	2-23-1875	65-7-3	London	N. Hampshire
WASHINGTON, Jennie	3-24-1875	70 yr.	London	Tenn.
WEST, Margaret	9-16-1871	89 yr.	Somerford Twp.	- - - - - -
WILLOUGHBY, Nancy	3-22-1874	76 yr.	Somerford Twp.	Ross Co.
WELSH, Sarah	10-9-1872	85 yr.	Canaan Twp.	- - - - - -
WILSON, William D.	3-25-1873	66 yr.	- - - - -	- - - - - -
YOAKUM, John	10-22-1871	83 yr.	Pleasant Twp.	- - - - - -
YEOWMANS, Louis	6-11-1875	75 yr.	Union Twp.	Delaware

The following will abstracts were taken from Will Record No. I. The page on which
each will is located is given in parenthesis at the end of each will.

"July Term 1810 - (Common) Pleas held at the House of Thomas Gwynne temporary Seat
of Justice for Madison County on the 31st of July in the year of our Lord one
thousand eight hundred and ten."

BLAIR, John - dated 7-21-1810 - recorded 7-31-1810 - wife, Susannah to have land
obtained from James McNUTT, deceased, and land obtained from James GALLOWAY, Junr.
- children, mentioned but not named except for son, Samuel; each to be given $2.00
in cash to buy a Bible with - Executors: son, Samuel Blair and Samuel McNUTT -
Signed: J. Blair - Witnesses: Michael DICKEY, Andrew SHIELDS & Robt. SHIELDS (1)

ROSS, Daniel - dated 9-26-1812 - recorded 11-2-1812 - Wife, Mary Ross - 5 sons:
William, Angus, John, Alexander and David; David not of age - Daughters: mentioned,
but not named - Signed: Daniel (mark) Ross - Witnesses: John SHIELDS, Andrew
SHIELDS and Simon HERDER   (3)

GREEN, Joseph - Pike Twp. - dated 10-9-1814 - recorded 2-28-1815 - Wife: Etthrine
Green, "all property she was possessed of previous to the solemnization of marriage
between her and myself" - Daughter: Experunie Green, not of age, to have all prop-
erty left to her by her mother at her death - Sons: James, Samuel and Lorenzo
Green; may not all be of age - Executors: David MITCHELL, Sen. and Robert NELSON -
Signed: Joseph Green - Witnesses: Jacob FAIRFIELD and John HAMMOND   (4)

MITCHELL, Samuel, Sen. - Darby Twp., Franklin Co. - dated 7-20-1808 - recorded
10-16-1816 - wife, mentioned but not named - sons: David and Samuel Mitchell, also
to serve as executors - Mentions: that balance of personal estate is to be divided
equally between Jean KIRKPATRICK and Elizabeth TAYLOR with half of Elizabeth TAYLOR's
share to her two sons, grandsons of testator, Alexander and Samuel McCULLOUGH; Alexander and Samuel not of age - Signed: Samuel Mitchell, Sen. - Witnesses: Moses
MITCHELL, John ROBINSON, Samuel MITCHELL and Elizabeth ROBINSON   (6)

WALTON, Peres - Pike Twp. - Dated 7-13-1815 - recorded 8-1-1817 - wife; Hannah Walton,
also to serve as Executrix - sons; John and Joseph Walton, John not of age -
Daughters: Polly, Hannah, Sally and Maria Walton - Signed: Peres Walton - Witnesses:
James GRAY, Moses PATRICK and John IRWIN   (8)

POOL, Robert - dated 5-25-1817 - recorded 8-1-1817 - wife, Nancy Pool - brother,
George Pool - mentions, child his wife is now with - mentions: money due from
Richard SHORT to be paid to John BRIANT and Charles STARRET; money due from Henry
Pool and also $100 left to testator by his father's will - Mentions: that Henry and
Asbery Pool are to share in real estate with above mentioned unborn child -
Executors: brother, George Pool and friend, Isaac DAVISON, Jun.- Signed: Robert
Pool - Witnesses: Jeremiah BODKIN and Isaac DAVISON, Sen.   (10)

PEYTON, John - Fluvanna Co., Va. - dated 10-9-1801 - recorded Fluvanna Co., Va.
10-26-1801 - recorded Madison Co., Ohio 8-1-1817 - Mentions: Mrs. Mary DUNCAN,
"with whom I now live", and her children: Robert Peyton DUNCAN, Lewis Langhorn DUNCAN,
John Duncan HOWEL, Nancy DUNCAN, Patty DUNCAN, Sally DUNCAN and Betsey DUNCAN -
Nephew, John PEYTON - Mentions land in Prince Wm. Co. and several thousand acres in
the western country - Executors: John Duncan son of Mrs. Mary Duncan; nephew, John
Peyton of Milton & friend, John Quarles of Fluvanna, Signed: John Peyton, Witnesses:
James DANIEL, John CHANDLER and William N. PEYTON   (12)

(Note:- The following two wills for William ALKIRE, appear to be for the same person, although they were recorded separately. As there was a difference in the wording, both are being abstracted here---The Editors)

ALKIRE, William - Deer Creek - dated 7-28-1818 - recorded May 1822 - wife, Temperance - sons: Robert, Jacob, Isaac, Abraham, Harmones, John, William, Joseph and Henry Green Alkire - Daughters: Mary Ann, Margaret and Elizabeth Alkire - Mentions: Liddea GRAHAM and Phebe Alkire - Mentions estate of Phoebe CLAY, deceased - Executors: Abraham Alkire - Mentions estate of Phoebe CLAY, deceased - Executors: Abraham Alkire and John GRAHAM - Signed: William Alkire - Witnesses: William CREATH and Abraham ALKIRE   (15)

ALKIRE, William - dated 7-30-1818 - recorded May 1822 - wife, Temperance - Daughters: Mary Ann Tanner; Margaret, Elizabeth and Phebe Alkire: Liddia GRAHAM - Sons: Robert, Jacob, Isaac, Abraham and Harmonas Alkire to have "money in hands of John DONALSTON my attorney in the state of Kentucky from Charles CLAY'S estate"; Joseph and Green Alkire, not of age, to have "all their grandfather Charles CLAY'S estate in hands of John DONALSTON, my attorney" - Executors: Abraham Alkire and John GRAYHAM - Signed: William Alkire - Witnesses: William CREATH, Robert DENTION and John J. SMITH   (19)

ERWIN, Mary - dated 2-3-1815 - recorded (?) May 1822 - Son : William Erwin - Mentions Sally, daughter of son William Erwin - Daughters: Jane BERGUS and Peggy Campbell - Mentions: son, William's wife Amelia and son, Joseph's wife Peggy - Executor: son, William Erwin - Signed: Mary (mark) Erwin - Witnesses: Benjamin MELVIN, James WRIGHT and James S. CAMPBELL   (21)

GREEN, Charles - dated 1-14-1820 - recorded (?) May 1822 - Son-in-law: George CHAPPELL - 3 youngest sons: Moses, Samuel and Henry - Mentions children, possibly more than named above - Executors: George CHAPPELL and Jonathan MINSHALL - Signed: Charles (mark) Green - Witnesses: James WITHROW and Ellis MINSHALL : (22)

GAGE, Alden - London - dated 10-1-1821 - recorded (?) May 1822 - Wife: Nancy M. Gage, also to serve as executrix - 2 sons, Alden A. and Horace M. Gage - Signed: Alden Gage - Witnesses: John THOMPSON and Anna (mark) MORES   (23)

ROBERTS, Abel - dated 7-12-1821 - recorded (not given) - Wife: Elizabeth Roberts - Son: William Roberts - Mentions: Mary ASHER and Elizabeth BYARD, to share equally in estate with son, William and wife, Elizabeth - Mentions: house and lot and rents since '72 in Pennsylvania; also money in hands of David RICE and Samuel KENNEDY - Mentions judgements against estate of William BELL, Samuel WEAVER and a claim against estate of Jane ROBERTS - 20 shillings to Susannah ASHER - Executor; John MOON - Signed: Abel Roberts - Witnesses: John ASHER and Mary ASHER   (26)

BARROW, James - Pleasant Twp., Clark County - dated 7-20-1822 - recorded (not given) - Children: mentioned but not named - Administrator: Solomon PORTER - Signed: James Barrow - Witnesses: Gibson SAVAGE and Daniel COLVER   (27)

DUNGAN, Jesse - dated 8-10-1822 - recorded (not given) - wife: Jane Dungan, to have land on Deer Creek patented to Jesse Dungan by President of United States, Warrant #5494, survey #6167 - Signed: Jesse Dungan - Witnesses: Burton BLIZZARD, William VINSON and Joseph PANCAKE   (28)

51

WATSON, Walter Senr. - Union Twp. - dated 1-16-1817 - recorded 8-5-1822 - Sons:
Abraham, William, James, Walter, David and Samuel - Daughters: Elenor MINSHALL,
Polly CHAPMAN and Delila HARVEY - Step-son: Marshall STONE and Elizabeth HELPHEN-
STINE - Mentions that sons Abraham and William are to carry out agreement to buy
58 acres of land from Col. Elias LANGHAM - Executors: son, William Watson and
Jonathan MINSHALL - Signed: Walter Watson - Witnesses: Thomas COBERLY and James
WITHROW   (29)

OGDEN, Albert - dated 3-31-1823 - recorded (not given) - wife: Margaret Ogden -
Children: Polly DAVISON (or DAWSON); Abner, Jonathan, Benjamin, Deborah, John,
Susan and Samuel Ogden - Executors: 2 eldest sons, Abner and Jonathan Ogden - Signed:
Albert Ogden - Witnesses: John J. SMITH, John READLE and David MARTIN   (31)

STEER, Simon - dated 9-10-1821 - recorded (not given) - Sons: eldest, Simon Berdsall
Steer: 2nd son, Alphus Green Steer - 2 daughters: Angella and Clinla - Executor:
friend, Patrick McLENE - Signed: Simon Steer - Witnesses: H. WARNER & P. LEWIS (33)

D'LASHMUTT, Elias - dated 7-28-1823 - recorded (not given) - Present wife: Anne,
mentions that she might removed to Kentucky - Daughter: Anne Maria D'Lashmutt -
Sons: Edmund Lyne D'Lashmutt, Walter Collen D'Lashmutt and Francis Alexander D'Lashmutt - Brother-in-law: William WALLING - Sister: Elizabeth WALLING - Nephews:
D'Lashmutt WALLING, son of William Walling; Nelson D. Walling - Mentions land: Black-
lick, Licking Co., Ohio; lot in town of New Freedom, Frederick Co., Maryland; town
of Jackson and other land in Cape Girardeau Co., Missouri- Mentions land on Deer
Creek conveyed to testator of James McNUTT by deed dated 2-31-1809 adjoining land
formerly conveyed to testator and Van D. D'Lashmutt by Henry COON -   :cutors.
friends, Ralph OSBORN, Arthur OHARA and Samuel G. FLENAGAN - Witnesses: J. R.
PARRISH, John F. CHENOWETH, John (mark) SPAIN and Aquela TOLAND   (34)

NORTON, James - Darby Twp. - dated 9-17-1823 - recorded 12-9-1823 - Wife: Deabory
Norton - Sons: Solomon and John Norton - Daughters: oldest, Cloe WOW; 2nd Sarepta
KING; 3rd Abigal DORNING; 4th, Kiziah KNAP; 5th, Phebe CONVERSE - Signed; James
Norton - Witnesses: Titus DART and Elisha HARD   (41)

COEBERLY, Thomas - dated 9-25-1823 - recorded 11-7-1823 - Wife: Juda - Sons: William,
Andrew, Job and James Cobberly O Daughters : Eve WATSON and Hannah SUTTON - Executor
- son, James Cobberlin - Signed: Thomas (mark) Cobberly - Witnesses: George
CHAPPELL and Marshal (mark) STONE   (43)

WALLING, D'Lashmutt - Clark Co., Ohio - dated 7-31-1822 - recorded (not given) -
Wife: Mary Walling - son-in-law; James MATHEWS - Sons: William, James, John, Jacob
and Thomas Walling - Daughters: Suckey BIDE, Betsey WILLIAMS, Polly MATHEWS and
Casear HUMBLE - Executor: Ezra MARKLE - Signed: D'Lashmutt (mark) Walling - Witnesses: George W. PEARCE, Asahel CLEAVELAND and Mary PEARCE   (45)

FRESHOUR, Abraham - dated 8-19-1824 - recorded 11-1-1824 - Wife: Elizabeth Freshour
- 3 sons: John, Abraham and Henry Freshour - Daughter: Margaret Freshour -
Executors: wife, Elizabeth Freshour and John FERNOVER of Highland Co., Ohio —
Signed: Abraham Freshour - Witnesses: John MOORE and John ARMSTRONG   (47)

52

ADAIR, John Sen. - dated November 1820 - recorded 11-3-1824 - Wife: Elizabeth Adair - Sons: Robert McNigh, John, Robert, William, Joseph, Samuel and Edward K. - Daughters: Elizabeth and Nancy - Executors: sons, John and Samuel and wife, Elizabeth - Signed: Jno. Adair Senr. Witnesses: John DAVIDSON, Adam COON and Wm. T. DAVIDSON   (49)

MARKLE, Gabriel Sen. - dated 6-26-1825 - recorded 10-20-1825 - Wife: ˙Catherine Markle - Sons: Gabriel, Jonathan and Samuel - Daughters: Hanna, Susan, Elinor, Hesther, Rachel, Catharine and Ezra - Grand-daughters: Lavina CLAMS (or CLAMO) and Catharine Markle - Executors: son, Jonathan Markle and son-in-law, George PRUGH - Signed: Gabriel Markle - Witnesses: John ARBUCKLE, Henry (mark) GROVES and Charles ATCHESON   (51)

The following Will Abstracts were taken from Will Record 1, page on which each will be located is given in parenthesis at the end of the will.

SPRINGER, Benjamin - dated 10-15-1823 - recorded 2-14-1826 - Wife: Elizabeth Springer - Sons: Robert, Thomas and Silas Springer - Daughter: Deborah Springe wife of Usual OSBORN - Executors: Friends, John MOORE and Abraham SHEPHERD - Witnesses: Reason FRANCIS, Jacob FRANCIS and Silas OSBORN   (54)

ALLEN, Ananias - dated 7-15-1823 - recorded 2-15-1826 - Wife: Rachel also to serve as Executrix - Sons: John, George, Elijah, David, James, Jeremiah, Ananias and heirs of son Daniel, deceased - Daughters: Mary, Margaret and Elizabeth - Signed: Ananias Allen - Witnesses: Joseph PANCAKE, Hugh BOWLAND and Wm. RABURN(56)

HUTSON, Skinner - dated 3-24-1824 - recorded 2-13-1826 - Wife: Jane Hutson - 2 sons: Austin and John Hutson - Executors: James KELGORE, Samuel HORNBACK and wife, Jane Hutson - Signed: Skinner (mark) Hutson - Witnesses: Benjamin BURLEY and Abraham (mark) BOSH   (58)

MELVIN, Phebe - dated 7-17-1821 - recorded 2-15-1826 - Daughters: Sarah TAYLOR; Jane H. Melvin, not of age, to sign her right of real estate to John, Joseph and Thomas Melvin legal representatives of Joseph Melvin, deceased - Executor: Son, John Melvin - Signed: Phebe (mark) Melvin - Witnesses: Wm. ERWIN, Wm. EAKINS and James TAYLOR (59)

MELVIN, John - dated 3-15-1825 - recorded 6-7-1826 - Wife: Jane Melvin - Sons: Jehu J., Charles, Joseph B. and Samuel Melvin - Daughter - Abigail LEWIS - Grand-daughter: Phebe Melvin - Mentions: Land adjoining John ADAIR and entry #5046 adjoining James McDONALD - Signed: John Melvin - Witnesses: Samuel ADAIR, Joseph B. MELVIN and Bartholomew S. MELVIN (62)

NOTEMAN, William - dated 1-27-1827 - recorded 2-20-1827 - Sons: Charles and William Willshire Noteman - Daughters: Ann and Betsey Noteman - Stepchildren: Rachel DAVIDSON, James SMITH and Samuel Littler SMITH - Mentions "silver watch left by Laban LITTLER in his last will and testament to my stepson John Smith" - Executors: William JONES and John MOORE - Signed: William Noteman - Witnesses: John DAVIDSON and Jesse STOUT - Codicil: Executors to obtain title for 50 acres of land from Charles ATCHISON and to sell same. (65)

GARNETT, Ann - Queen Anne Co., Maryland - dated 6-29-1822 - recorded Philadelphia, Pa. 5-17-1824 - recorded Madison Co., Ohio, Feb. 1827 - Bequesths all real estate to Henry D. SELLERS, Esq. of Queen Anne Co., Md., who is also to serve as executor - Relations: Maria WILLIAM, Ann G. BURRIS and Elizabeth DAVIDSON - Mentions: Caroline BAYARD of the city of Philadelphia; Sarah Maria BURRIS and Anne Garnett BURRIS - Signed: Ann Garnett - Witnesses: Ann WRIGHT, Rich'd H. BAYARD and Hugh L. HODGE (69)

(Note:- The following will is not recorded in its entire length in Madison
County, but is listed as an extract.)

WHITE, William (Extract of will) - Orange County (state not given - Virginia?)
recorded Madison County, Ohio 11-29-1828 - Son: Henry White; 2 tracts of land in
Ohio being 650 acres #3642 Fayette County and 180 acres #438 in Highland County -
Son: Jeremiah White; 150 acres #4367 in Clinton Co., Ohio and 150 acres #4258
in the same county along with 160 acres #4362 in Highland Co. Ohio. (72)

RAY, Andrew - dated 3-30-1827 - recorded 9-15-1828 - Wife: Hannah Ray also to
serve as executrix - Sons: James, Jesse, William and Thomas; also mentions
Robert Ray who may be a son - Daughter: B etsey - Sons-in-law: Lot BOZARTH,
Obediah JOHNSON and David STROUP - Mentions: Land in Green County - Signed:
Andrew Ray - Witnesses: Samuel HARROD and Richard ERWIN   (73)

BYERS, James - dated 1-25-1828 - recorded 9-15-1828 - Sons: John and Moses W.
Byers - Daughters: Jane STODGDON and Susanna Ann Byers - other children mention-
ed but not named - Executor: Moses W. Byers - Signed: James (mark) Byers -
Witnesses: Thomas McDONALD, Jonas BRADLEY and Adgines McDONALD (76)

COREY, John - dated 9-5-1829 - recorded 12-1-1829 - Wife: Sally Corey, to serve
as guardian of sons John, Henry & Addison - Sons: Henry, Joshua, John, Henry
and Addison - Daughters: Sophronia, Mahala, Rebecca and Joanna; may be another
daughter not named - Executor: Richard BALDWIN - Signed: John Corey -
Witnesses: John CLEMEN and Jemima (mark) OSBURN (78)

BLAGROVE, Charles - dated 7-30-1814 - recorded Henrico Co. Va. 6-23-1819 - recorded Madison Co., Ohio 9-21-1831 - Sister: Charlotte - Niece: Catharine E.
Blagrove - Brother: William Blagrove, mentions his daughter Parthenia Blagrove -
Executor: Friend, John TOMPKINS - Witnesses: John DEVENPORT and Henry B. Blagrove - Codicil dated 8-6-1814 names brother, Henry B. Glagrove. (80)

BASKERVILLE, Samuel - Union Twp. - dated 11-21-1828 - recorded 11-15-1830 - Wife:
Stateia Baskerville - Sons: William B., Richard A., Samuel B. and James M. P.
Baskerville - Daughters: Mary R. Baskerville, Martha EASTMAN, Judith Rebecca
Baskerville and Nancy M. Baskerville - Executors: Sons, William B. and Samuel B.
- Signed: S. Baskerville - Witnesses: Robert HUME, John MOORE and P. M.
(?) NENE   (83)

LANE, Dennis - dated 3-24-1828 - recorded 4-12-1830 - mentions a son who may not
be named - Daughter: Lilly WARD wife of Joseph WARD - 6 youngest children: John,
Suckey, Reynolds, Noble, Hooper and Mitchell Lane - Executor: Son-in-law, Joseph
Ward - Signed: Dennis Lane - Witnesses: John MOORE and Joseph McKELFISH (86)

LINSON, Edward - Greenbrier Co., Va. - dated 3-18-1824 - recorded Greenbrier Co.,
Va. 5-25-1831 - recorded Madison Co., Ohio 6-10-1831 - Wife: Anna - Daughters:
Betsey, Nancy, Sally and Polly - Sons: Jacob, John and George - Son Jacob's
wife, Dolly LINSON - Executors: John and George Linson - Signed: Edward T.
(mark) Linson - Witnesses: Ephraim T. SILVERS, Thomas DOTSON and Peter SEVESAY (89)

McCAFFERTY, Jonathan – dated 3–10–1830 – recorded 7–2–1831 – wife: Rebecca McCafferty – Eldest son: Matthias McCafferty – Daughters: Eldest, Ellen; Susannah and Mary – Executor: Burton BLIZZARD – Signed: Jonathan McCafferty – Witnesses: Peter COUNTS and Andrew JOHNSTON (94)

ANDREW, Josiah B. – dated 10–1–1831 – recorded 11–28–1831 – Wife: Jane K. Andrew – Sister: Anne HOYT – Niece: Eunice HOYT – Nephew: Isaac C. BEEMER – Children: Hannah E., Susan P. and Jane W. – Bequeaths to: Patience G. WITHINGTON, Andrew HOYT, Josiah B. A. HOYT, Elizabeth BEEMER and Henry SAVAGE – Executor: Henry JOHNSTON – Signed: J. B. Andrew – Witnesses: Sally (mark) SMITH and Adeline P. STILL (96)

ERWIN, John – dated 3–7–1830 – recorded 5–11–1832 – Wife: Rhoda S. Erwin to have "her furniture she brought here and all her sister Phebe brought", also the Family Bible – Sons: Smzeys(?), James and Benjamin – Brother: Samuel – Bequeath to Reuben and Sophia PLUMMER – Executors: Son, James Erwin and Reuben Plummer – Signed: John Erwin – Witnesses: William B. Erwin and Herman STOKES (99)

WATTS, John – Bedford Co., Va. – dated 8–27–1829 – recorded Bedford Co., Va. 7–27–1830 – recorded Ross Co., Ohio 4–1–1831 – recorded Madison Co., Ohio 9–21–1832 – Wife Betsey Watts – Sons: William and Arthur Watts – Daughter: Elizabeth R. Scott wife of Joseph M. Scott – Nephew: Edward Watts – Sarah and John daughter and son of son, William – Mentions land in Bedford Co., Va.; Senaca and Mollys Creek, Campbell Co. (state not given) and Chillicothe lands – Mentions Bank Stock at Chillicothe, Ohio – Signed: John Watts – Codicil dated 5–2–1830 names executors: William and Arthur Watts and nephew, Edward Watts – Witnesses: Wm. RADFORD, Gerard ALEXANDER and Joel YANCEY (102)

MUNFORD, William – Richmond, Virginia – dated 11–19–1822 – recorded Richmond, Va. 5–24–1834 – Wife: Sarah Munford also to serve as executrix – Son: George Wythe Munford to have law library – Daughter: Anna Rebecca SHERRARD – possibly more children not named – Signed: Wm. Munford (108)

The following records were taken from "Will Book 1" located in an attic storeroom under the jurisdiction of the Probate Court at the Court House at London. Page on which record may be found in original book is given in parenthesis.

GREENUP, Christopher of Frankfort, Ky. - dated (no month and day) 1817; recorded Franklin Co., Ky. 1-22-1833; recorded Madison Co. 5-24-1836. Sons: Wilson and Christopher. Daughters: Nancy wife of John G. Gamble, Susan wife of Craven P. Tuckett, Charlotte V.C. Greenup and Lucetta P. Greenup. States that all real and personal estate in Kentucky, Virginia and Ohio is to be sold (numerous land descriptions given on Kentucky land). Confirms having emancipated his negro man Gilbert and a negro woman Sally. Executors: John G. Gamble, Esq. of Richmond, Va., John Pope and Wm Hunter, Esqrs. of Frankfort and his son, Wilson P. Greenup. Signed: Christ. Greenup. Wit.: Gab'l Slaughter and Achillis Sneed. (128)

WEAVER, George - dated 12-21-1835; recorded 4-4-1836. Wife, Elizabeth. Sons: Jacob Weaver (eldest), Solomon Weaver (2nd son), John Weaver (3rd son) and George Weaver. Four daughters: Elizabeth, Margaret, Sarah and Mary Weaver. Grandsons: Ward Weaver a minor son of David Weaver, dec'd and John Weaver a minor son of Joseph Weaver, dec'd. Executors: son, Solomon Weaver and Fletcher W. Pratt. Signed: George (his mark) Weaver. Wit: John S. Sharp and William Beasly. (135)

THOMAS, John - dated 4-27-1836; recorded 6-30-1836. Wife, Sabra. Executors Ansel Bates Jr. Signed: John Thomas. Wit: John Nagley, Abner Cheney and Richard Baldwin. (139)

DULY, Alexander of Scott Co., Ky - dated 8-15-1833; recorded Scott Co., Ky 11-21-1835; recorded Madison Co. 6-30-1836. Wife, Sarah also to serve as executrix. Father, James Duly (living at time will was written). Bequeath to Rosian Ford. Mentions three negros--Tebitha, Levina and Sally who are to serve wife until they are 28 yrs. of age and then be emancipated. After death of wife Sarah, half of remaining estate to go to testator's brothers and sisters (not named) and other half to brothers and sisters (not named) of wife Sarah. Signed: Alexander Duly. Wit: Richard Quinn and Cynthia Quinn. (141)

SIMMS, Charles of Alexandria, District of Columbia - dated 7-10-1786; recorded District of Columbia 5-6-1820; recorded Madison Co. 10-14-1836. Wife, Nancy. Son, William Douglas Simms. Daughter, Catharine Simms. Mentions "any other children living at time of my death to share equally in estate." Mentions "land in western country." Signed: Charles Simms. Codicil dated 1-27-1799. Daughter Catharine wife of Buthbert Powell. Executors to be wife, Nancy; son, William Douglas Simms and son-in-law, Cuthbert Powell. Codicil dated 12-16-1811. Son, John D. Simms also to serve with above named executors. Codicil dated 2-11-1817. Son Wm D. Simms to have 150 acres land on Monteus(?) Island in Pa. and lands on Raccoon Creek in Pa. to be sold. (144)

FISH, Stephen of Jefferson twp. - dated 20th of 8th month 1836; recorded 11-19-1836. Wife, Elizabeth. Sons, David Fish. Daughters: Lydia Gregory, Rachel Downing, Eliza Fullington and Sarah Fairchild (last two named being youngest daus.). Executor, Daniel Osborn. Signed: Stephen Fish. Wit: Israel Wood, Rueben Wood and Selah Gregory. (150)

PHIFER, John - dated 2-23-1837; recorded 7-29-1837. Sons: George Phifer and Abraham Phifer. Daughters: Maria, Sarah, Elizabeth, Margarett, Duletha, Clarissa and Nancy. Grandchildren: Davis Phifer and Catharine Phifer children of John Phifer, dec'd; William, Gustavus, Lewis, Clarissa, Joseph and John Foos and Susanna Rader. Executors: Robinson Florence and son-in-law, John Moore. Signed: John Phifer. Wit: James M. Reeder and Washington Williams. (152)

PHEBUS, James of Pickaway Co., Ohio - dated 1-18-1837; recorded Madison Co. 5-29-1837. Wife, Sarah, also to serve as executrix. Son, Samuel. Wife, Sarah also to serve as guardian of children (not named except Samuel) during their minority. Signed: James Phebus. Wit: Edward Fitzgerald and William Garvin. (155)

MACE, Elizabeth - dated 6-19-1837; recorded 3-31-1838. Brother, Isaac Mace. Sister, Sarah Corbit. She also to have all legacy coming to testatrix from father's (not named) estate. Sister's son and daughter, Andrew and Sarah Corbit. Signed: Elizabeth Mace. Wit: Burton Blizard and Christian Selsor.(157)

WALLACE, Elenor - dated 8-15-1837; recorded 3-31-1838. (note: the following sons and daughters are named in the will in two groups). Group 1--Son, Stephen Wallace. Daughters: Harriet Humble, Nancy Wallace and Eliza Dugan. Group 2-- Sons: Michael Tullis, Jonathan Tullis and John W. Tullis. Daughters: Sarah Dockum, Mary Afton, Eliza Dungan and Rozetta Smith. Heir, Nancy Tullis. Signed: Elenor (her mark) Wallace. Wit: Peter Sewell, Nathan P. Sanford and Horace Sanford. (159)

WINKLEY, Ann - dated 10-1-1837; recorded 5-17-1838. Son, Edward Winkley, not of age. Bequeath to Joel Winkley, an orphan boy. Executor, William Easton. Signed: Ann Winkley. Wit: Joseph Chrisman, A. A. Hume. (162)

BIDWELL, Russel - dated (not given); recorded 10-30-1838. Personal estate to be divided among widow and children (not named). Executors: James Guy and Isaac Bidwell. Signed: Rusel Bidwell. Wit: James Millikin and Urial Bidwell. (164)

HUTCHEN, David W. - dated 8-9-1838; recorded 11-3-1838. Wife, Louisa to have tract of land Allen Co., Ohio being 160 acres W½ Section 25, Township 5 South, Range 6 East being patent No. 2536 patented to John Hutchin. Signed: David W. Hutchen. Wit: George L. Noland, D. Thompson and James Garner. (166)

GRAHAM, John of Richmond, Virginia - dated July (no day given) 1820; recorded
Henrico Co., Va. 10-6-1820; recorded Frankfort, Ky. 9-24-1821; recorded Madison
Co. (date not given-1838?). Bequeaths to: Mrs. Deen of State of Ohio, wife
of nephew, Walter Deen; John Brown son of John Brown; Robert Cappell son of
the late Robert Chappell of Lunenburg Co.; Amy Williams; Thomas Mack age near
3 years residing with Mrs. Smith widow of Wm. Smith in Orange Co.; Margaret Glenn
aged about 4 months old residing with Mrs. Eliza Glenn of Orange Co. in whose
care she was put by Mrs. Smith; nephew, Walter Deen; nephew, John McMurtee son
of sister, Christiann Graham widow of Hugh McMurtee of Glasgow, Scotland; sister,
Elizabeth Graham widow of James Deen of Kelsyth, Scotland; sister Jane (or Jean)
Graham widow of Robert Wilson of Banton near Kelsyth, Scotland; issue of dec'd
sister of Helen Graham widow of Patrick Hutchinson of Paisley, Scotland. Real
estate in Virginia and Ohio to Walter Deen and his heirs. Slaves to be emancipated
are Jasper after 1820 and Mary wife of Jasper. Freed man, Reuben Price. Slaves,
Lucy the Cook and her five daughers Aggy, Jenny, Betsey, Fanny and Mariann and
their children to be sold to persons of their choosing. Mentions that passage
of law that forbids emancipated negroes to stay in Virginia may effect where
emancipated slaves can live. Executors: Walter Deen and Robert Deen. Signed:
John Graham. Wit: A. P. Upshur, Joseph Mayo Jr. and J. Monor. Codicil dated
9-21-1820 states that slave, William, son of Aggy to be taught house carpenter
trade under slave, Nat and that he be sold to person of his choice or to whom
his father, Jasper reccomends. (168)

DEEN, Walter of Fayette Co., Ky. - dated 7-24-1837; recorded Fayette Co., Ky.
11-22-1838; recorded Madison Co. (date not given--1839?). Requests to be buried
on land where now resides with stone laid over grave with name, age and time
of death engraved. Wife, mentioned but not named. Brother, George W. Deen.
Five children: Mary Anderson Deen wife of George R. Tompkins; eldest son, John
Graham Deen; 2nd son, James Deen; Walter Myers (or Angus) Deen; and Robert
George Deen. Mentions land in Madison Co. Executors: brothers, George W. and
John Dean; and two eldest sons, John Graham Deen and James Deen. Signed: Walter
Deen. Wit: M. T. Scott and James A. Gunstead. (181)

BEDINGER, Daniel of Jefferson Co., Va. - dated 9-16-1838; Recorded Jefferson Co.,
Va. 2-18-1839; recorded Madison Co. (not given--1839?). Wife, Catharine H.,
all land in State of Ohio allotted me in distribution of brother, Edwin S.
Bedingers property in that state. Executor, William Lucas, Esq. Signed: Dan'l
Bedinger. Wit: M. A. Foster, Geo. W. Brown, Henry Bedinger. (188)

SELSOR, William - Oral Will - given 11-2-1838; recorded Greene Co., Wisconsin
5-4-1839; recorded Madison Co. 1839. Jacob Andrick of Greene Co., Wisconsin
deposes that William Selsor of Ohio died at his house on 11-2-1838 and did
on death bed declare he wanted his mother, Mary Selsor to have all property
at his death. Signed: Jacob Andrick and Mada Andrick. Joseph Kelly, J.P. (190)

BAKER, Joshua (John) - dated 12-19-1838; recorded (not given--1838 or 1839?).
Present wife, Matilda Baker. Daughter, Harriett Baker. Executors: Matilda Baker
and Alexander G. Simmerman. Signed: Joshua Baker. Wit: James Jones, Amos Evans
and Isaac N. Jones. (193)

SIDNER, John T. - dated 3-29-1839; recorded 1839. Wife, Margaret. Son, Marquis Sidner. Daughter, Eliza wife of Ganer P. Simpkins to be paid equally to her issue. Grand-daughter, Nancy Sidner daugher of son, Marquis Sidner. Mentions that other children (not named) to share equally in division of rest of estate. Executors: wife, Margaret and friend, Isaac Jones. Signed: John T. Sidner. Wit: Samuel Sexton, William Gardner and David Sidner. (191)

BRETTINGHAM, Solomon of Canaan twp. - dated 11-5-1835; recorded (not given). Wife, Leah. Sons: Abner, James Hampton, Enoch and George Riley. Daughters: Seley, Hetty, Nancy, Polly, Martha. Betsey and Sally. Executors: Ira Finch and Thomas Kilgore. Signed: Solomon Brettingham. Wit: William Walker, Thomas Kilgore and Charles McCloud. (194)

BIGELOW, Israel of Darby twp. - dated 5-15-1838; recorded (not given). Wife, Polly. Sons: Israel, Isaac, Lebben L., Daniel K., Eliphas, Timothy, Hosea and Chamberlin Bigelow; the last three named are not of age. Daughters: Dolly Larimer, Polly Daughterty, Almy Martin and Dianna Bigelow, Diana not of age. Daniel K. Bigelow to serve as guardian of three youngest children--Dianna, Hosea and Chamberlin. Executors: Isaac Bigelow and Daniel K. Bigelow. Signed: Israel Bigelow. Wit: Daniel Custard and James Goldsberry. (196)

ARCHABALD, Andrew - dated 11-1-1838; recorded (not given). Wife, Jane. Children are mentioned but not named. Executor: Randal Black. Signed: Andrew (his mark) Archabald. Wit: Daniel Wilson and John Norbeck. (198)

VANDERMAN, E. - dated 11-22-1839; recorded (not given). Wife, mentioned but not named, to have all real and personal property. Also mentions that he re-leases Presbyterian congregation from debt due him. Signed: E. Vanderman. Wit: A. Toland and Nath'l M. Miller. (199)

HAYS, John of Rockbridge Co., Va. - dated 5-29-1808; recorded Rockbridge Co., Va. 1-2-1839; recorded Madison Co. (not given). Wife, Anne and her three youngest sons, Andrew, John and Campbell. Son, Michael, all property in Ohio. Mentions that lands are to be sold if family wants to go to western country or anywhere else. Mentions house and lot near Lexington. Executors: wife, Anne and son, Michael. Signed: John Hays. Wit: James McCampbell, Robert Dixon and Alexander Shields. (199)

FETTERMAN, Washington Welssed, Attorney at law, of Pittsburgh, Pa. - dated 7-1-1837; recorded Allegheny Co., Pa. 2-4-1839; recorded Madison Co. (not given). Wife, Sarah, also to serve as guardian of children. Children: Gilbert, George, Gertrude, Alfred and Frances. Bequeaths to: his mother (not named) $1000.00 and to friend, William Shurty (or Shurly). Signed: W. W. Fetterman. Wit: H. Masterson(?) and George W. Hollandship. Codicil dated 6-27-1838 bequeaths to Belinda Remington $500.00. (203)

MELVIN, Charles - dated 12-17-1841; recorded 2-2-1842. Wife, Elizabeth. Sons: Joseph, who is to serve as sole executor; and Martin. Daughters: Abigail, Eliza Catharine; and Ann Robison Melvin; the last two named are not of age. Signed: Charles Melvin. Wit: James McDonald, Samuel Adair and William Winders. (207)

DAUGHERTY, William - dated (not given); recorded 7-23-1841. Three sons; John, Charles and William Daughterty, also to serve as executors. Daughter, Lavina Clark. Grand-daughters: (one not named) daughter of Mary E. Houser; Sarah Daugherty, not of age. Signed: William Daugherty. Wit: Thomas Briggs and Thomas Reeves. (209)

STUCKEY, David - dated 9-20-1837; recorded 1842. Wife, Mary. Sons: Archibald, Aaron and Eli Stuckey. Daughters: Elizabeth Lane, Susan Skiles and Mary Ann. Mentions lands owned in Virginia to be sold and money divided between all children. Signed; David (his mark) Stuckey. Wit: Edward Fitzgerald and Joseph (his mark) Wena(?). (211)

McDOWELL, Andrew - dated 12-12-1841; recorded 3-29-1842. Wife, Lucy J., also to serve as guardian of son and unborn child.. Son, Austin Fay McDowell, and the unborn child wife is now enciente. Executors: Benjamin A. Fay and Henry McCracken. Signed: Andrew McDowell. Wit: Eber. McDowell and Michael Sager. (213)

ADAIR, Anderson - dated 3-18-1842; recorded 6-7-1842. Wife, Margaret Jane, also to serve as guardian of son. Son, William Bruce Adair, a minor. Mentions brothers and sisters but does not name. Executors: wife, Margaret Jane and Joseph Powers. Signed: Anderson Adair. Wit: John McMullan and John McDonald. (217)

TIMMONS, Thomas - dated 5-17-1843; recorded 1843. Sons: John Timmons and Isby Timmons. Grandsons: John Wesley Timmons Jr. and William H. H. Timmons, Wm. H. H. being brother of John W. Jr. Bequeaths to Rebecca and Mary Ellen Timmons daughters of John Timmons. Signed: Thomas (his mark) Timmons. Wit: Samuel Gilliland, John Smith and James Sheets. (219)

CHAPMAN, Thomas - dated 6-15-1843; recorded 1843. Wife, Margarett. Daughter, Delilah Higgins, her orphan children--Isaac N. and Elizabeth Higgins. Step-daughters: Ellen and Ester Ridgway. Mentions that real estate is to be divided between children (may be additional children not named). Executors: David Watson Sr. and his son, Jesse Watson. Signed: Thomas Chapman Sr. Wit: Jacob Young and Jonathan Minshall. (220)

KENTON, Simon of Madison Co., Ohio - dated 1-23-1838; recorded 1844. Wife, mentioned but not named, not clear if she is living or not. Daughters: Ann wife of David Heiskell, Claricy Kenton and Sarah W. Kenton. Three sisters: Lucy wife of Duff Green, Martha wife of Oron North and Elizabeth wife of John Neff. Mentions children of three sisters, but does not name. Requests that son-in-law or any other persons kin to deceased or family to be appointed adms. with will annexed. Signed: Simon Kenton. Wit: G. N. Kerr and John Moore. (227)

61

BELL, Joseph now of Madison Co., Ohio, formerly of Berkley Co., Va. - dated 5-5-1842; recorded Clark Co., Ky. 5-22-1843; recorded Madison Co. (not given). Three children, William Bell, Daniel Bell and daughter, Rebecca Rafferty of Kentucky to have all land in Madison Co. to be divided agreeable to division testator made before he left Madison Co. to return to Virginia. Son, John R. Bell and son-in-law, Levi Heite to have land in Clark Co., Va. Grandchildren: Martha, Benjamin and Rebecca Miller. Executors: son, John R. Bell and son-in-law, Levi Heite. Signed: Joseph Bell. Codicil dated 5-5-1842. Son-in-law is Joseph Rafferty. Son, John R. Bell is at Winchester P.O., Frederick Co., Va. Codicil dated 11-10-1842. Son, John R. Bell in State of Ohio where he was badly crippled and returned to Virginia. (222)

WITHROW, Mary of Union twp. - dated 5-9-1840; recorded 11-6-1844. Sons, Washington and Samuel Withrow all right to land in Survey Nos. 12730, 12733 and 12734 which was deeded to Washington Withrow and testatrix, Mary Withrow by John Stroop and Isabella his wife by deed dated 1-26-1835 and recorded in Deed Book 9, page 208. Signed: Mary Withrow. Wit: William Coberly and James Sifrit. (230)

WORTHINGTON, Thomas of Ross Co., Ohio - dated 3-15-1827; recorded Ross Co. 10-8-1827; recorded Madison Co. (1844-45?). Wife, Eleanor, during lifetime to have dwelling house and farm where now live on hill called Adena. Sons: James, Albert, Thomas, William and Francis. Daughters: Mary Macomb; Sarah King, her son Thomas King, not of age; Eleanor; Margaret; and Elizabeth. Grandson, Thomas McComb. Will includes schedule of land owned in Hocking, Franklin, Ross, Clinton and Delaware Cos. Executors: wife and sons, James G., Albert G. and Thomas Worthington. Signed: T. Worthington. Wit: John Renshaw, James G. Harrison and George S. Milligan. (232)

CULLUMBER, John of Fairfield twp. - dated 2-1-1845; recorded 4-17-1845. Wife, mentioned but not named, to have all furniture and property she had when testator married her and to pay for two tombstones out of her share given her under law. Rest of heirs are to have equal share of estate as they come of age except Allen and Thomas who have had their part (other heirs not named). Appoints George G. McDonald to administer estate. Signed: John (his mark) Cullumber. Wit: George J. Archer and Armiger Lelly. (240)

PAUGH, Mary - dated 6-9-1838; recorded (1842?). Sons: William Guy, Charles Guy and James Guy. Daughter, Jane Mann. Bequeaths to Heirs of Moses Fullington. Executor, Charles Guy, who is also to serve as guardian of James Guy. Signed: Mary (her mark) Paugh. Wit: Nathan P. Sanford and Horace Sanford. (241)

MARTIN, Zenas - dated 2-28-1845; recorded 5-24-1845. Wife, Almira. Mentions his brothers and sisters (but not named). Step-son, his wife's son, David Henry Brooks, not of age. Executors: wife, Almira and neighbor, Peter E. Gettner. Signed: Zenas Martin. Wit: John W. Gray, and William Sager. (242)

MONTGOMERY, Hugh - dated 2-20-1845; recorded 7-1-1845. Wife, Katharine, also to serve as executrix. Sons: Robert and James. Signed: Hugh Mt Gomery. Wit: Thomas S. Robison and C. Honell (or Hanell). (244)

ARBUCKLE, John - dated 5-25-1845; recorded 12-15-1845. Wife, mentioned but not named. Sons: William, Matthew, Charles, James and Jacob Lockhart Arbuckle. Daughters: Susan; Rebecca; Elizabeth, married, now dec'd; and Sarah, married. Mentions a saw mill. Executor: son, Matthew Arbuckle. Signed: John Arbuckle. Wit: John M. Smith, Henry Warner, A. A. Hume. (245)

READ, Sarah of Jefferson - dated 3-15-1845; recorded (not given). Daughters: Rebecca Wook, Mary Read and Elizabeth Read. Executor: Jacob Ware of Champaign Co. Signed: Sarah (mark) Read. Wit: James Burnham and George Parrish. (248)

RAYBURN, John aged 73 years - dated 3-9-1846; recorded March term 1846. Wife, Mentioned but not named. "Four of my children" David Rayburn, Martha Rayburn, Creighton Mead Mayburn and Joseph Rayburn "having advanced and provided for my other children." "To seven grandchildren of my two deceased sons William Rayburn and John Rayburn, two (three are named) of the former and five of the latter, viz.: Rebecca Jane, John, Clinton, Albert, and James Rayburn, children of John; Margaret Blue formerly Rayburn, Margaret Rayburn, and William John Rayburn, children of William." Executors: wife and son, Creighton M. Rayburn. Signed John Rayburn. Wit: H. Brush and R. C. McComb. (250)

MARK, James - dated 11-30-1845; recorded 3-17-1846. Wife, Nancy. Sons: James W., Matthias and Washington Mark. Daughters and sons-in-law: John Taylor and Eliza his wife formerly Mark, James L. Bradley and Elizabeth his wife formerly Mark, William Foos and Sarah his wife formerly Mark and Jesse B. Ferguson and Lucinda V. his wife formerly Mark. Mentions land in Van Wert Co., Ohio. Signed: James Mark. Wit: Washington Bradley and David L. Bradley. (252)

YOUNG, Peter A. of Pleasant twp. - dated 9-25-1846; recorded 3-20-1846. Nephew, Frederick Young, also to serve as executor. Signed: Peter A. Young. Wit: William Kerkendall and John Murray. (254)

LINSON, Jacob - dated 1-20-1846; recorded 3-19-1846. Wife, Dolly. Sons: John, Washington, Edward, George and Jacob. Daughters: Nancy, Ruth, Catharine and Polly. Signed: Jacob Linson. Wit: Robert (his mark) McBride and John (his mark) McBride. (256)

JONES, Joseph - dated 5-21-1846; recorded 9-24-1846. Wife, Mary. Sons: William Jones; and Hardy Jones, an idiot. Daughters: Nancy Jones, Mary Thomas and Matilda Jones. Step-son, John Richard, an idiot. Grandson, William Fairfield. Executor: son, William. Signed: Joseph (his mark) Jones. Wit: Thomas Jones and Gilbert Webb. (257)

STUBBLEFIELD, Edward of Barry Co., Missouri - dated 2-1-1844; recorded Barry Co., Mo. 11-5-1845; recorded Madison Co. (not given). Wife, Sarah. Youngest son, David. Mentions that Ohio lands are to be sold and divided equally among children (not named except David and Robert). Executors: wife, Sarah; oldest son Robert Stubblefield; and George W .King. Signed. Edward Stubblefield. Wit: John Wright and Samuel Stonberry. (259)

ALKIRE, Jacob - dated 4-27-1844; recorded (not given). Only son, Gabriel Alkire to have farm where now live on west side of Deer Creek in Balors Survey No. 464. Mentions that he has deeded land also to other and "only child." (daughter?). Signed: Jacob (his mark) Alkire. Wit: John R. Robison and Reuben Redden. (264)

HAGER, Simion of Darby twp. - dated 10-8-1842; recorded (not given). Wife, mentioned but not named. Two sons: William B. and Aurelius Hager. Signed: Simion Hager. Wit: Jeremiah Doming (Downey?) and Josiah Marshall. Following will is an agreement dated 10-8-1842 by Wm B. and Aurelius Hager to keep Simion Hager and Polly his wife. (265)

CYPRESS, Andrew of Union twp. - dated 6-30-1827; recorded 1847. Wife, Hannah. Two daughters: Nancy Cypress and Rebecca Cypress. Son, John. Cypress. Mentions "children of both first and present wife" (not named except for above) and that estate should be divided between them both dead and living, share alike. Executors: wife, Hannah and son, John. Signed: Andrew (his mark) Cypress. Wit: E. Langham, S. Baskerville and Thomas Chapman Sr. (267)

SAYLE, David - dated 8-31-1844; recorded 11-16-1847. To Phebe Smith "woman I now live with all kitchen and household furniture so long as she lives and does not marry." Two sons: Seneca Sayle and David Sayle. Daughters: Phebe Moore, Mary Cole, Amy Rice and Lydia Sale. Grandson, Nathan Rice. Requests to reserve one-fourth acre of land on east-west line of tract where lives, east of the Blooming Burg Road for a burying ground. Executors: Phebe Smith and Job Coberly. Signed: David Sayle. Wit: Job Coberly and John Blancher. (270)

MANSFIELD, Hannah E. of Warehan Co., Mass, a married woman - dated 1-18-1847; recorded Mass. 5-1-1847; recorded Union Co., Ohio 9-18-1847; recorded Madison Co. (not given). Mother, Jane K. Bowers. Sisters: Jane W. Andrew and Helen MarBown(?). Husband, Richard S. Mansfield, to have all personal and real estate in Ohio and also to serve as executor. Signed: Hannah E. Mansfield. Wit: Sylvanus Bourne, A. Bourn and Alishia Burrows. (272)

TIMMONS, John W. of Pleasant twp. - dated 10-29-1845; recorded 1848. Wife, Charlotte. Sons: William A., Thomas W., John W., Henry Clay and Cotman Timmons; the last three named are not of age. Daughters: Drucilla Clarige, Mary Adams, Christiana A. Hyde, Charlotte Timmons, Catharine Timmons, Martha Timmons and Dorthea Timmons; the last two name are not of age. Executor: Henry W. Smith, who is also to serve as guardian of daughters, Dorthea and Martha and sons, Cotman, John W. and Henry Clay. Signed: John W. Timmons. Wit: William H. Squires and James McLain. (277)

For MADISON COUNTY, OHIO WILL ABSTRACTS 1810-1825 see Vol. 1, Issue 3 (July 1968 issue) of GATEWAY TO THE WEST and for MADISON COUNTY, OHIO WILL ABSTRACTS 1826-1835 see Vol. 2, Issue 3 (July 1970 issue).

Lydia BENNET to James GOODING - 3-18-1826 - Lydia Bennet late wife of Andrew Bennet late of Pleasant township and guardian of his minor children James and Sarah Bennet gives power of attorney to James Gooding to use personal property left by the deceased for the benefit of the children. (Bk. 1, P. 338)

Samuel SCRIBNER and others to Amos WILSON - 4-2-1827 - $200. - E½ NW¼ Section 20, Township 6, Range 16S. Samuel Scribner and Alvira his wife, James Brown and Lucy his wife, John Vanmeter and Sophy his wife, Chauncy Clark and Sarah his wife, heirs of the estate of Israel Clark, Jr., dec'd of Marion County, Ohio. (Bk. 1 P. 342)

Harvy CLARK and Nancy his wife of Delaware Co., Ohio to Samuel Scribner - 4-6-1827 - $65. - 80 acres E½ NW¼ Section 20, Township 6, Range 16S; also 40 acres S½ E½ SW¼ & 40 acres S½ W½ NE¼ Section 36, Township 4, Range 16. Bk. 1 P. 341)

James BROWN and Sarah his wife, Robert CROSKY and Mary his wife, Jacob DETRICK and Jane his wife, Joseph BRELSFORD and Eleanor his wife, all of Muskingum Co., Ohio and John M. SHAFER and Emely his wife of Marion Co., Ohio to Nathan PETERS - 12-25-1826 - $125. - 95.87 acres W½ SW¼ Section 7, Township 6S, Range 16 in Delaware district. (Bk. 1 P. 349)

Thomas GARTHROP aged 16 yrs. 6 months and 24 days, son of Richard GAWTHROP of Big Island twp. indentured to Isaac E. JAMES, Tanner and Currier for term of 4 years 5 months and 6 days until 6-29-1832 - dated 1-2-1828. Bk. 1 P. 431)

John TORRENCE Jr. son of John TORRENCE of Fairfield Co., Ohio aged 15 yrs. apprenticed to Nathan Peters of Marion Co. as cabinet maker for term of 6 years. (Bk. 1 P. 475)

Betsey BRINE and others to William BRANDLE - 12-20-1827 - $80. - 20 acres E½ NE¼ Section 2, Township 5, Range 13 in Delaware land district. - Betsey Brine widow of Luke Brine, dec'd, William Gaston, Jonathan Brine and Betsey his wife, William Larue and Cyntha his wife, Simon (or Luman) Brine and Almon Brine, heirs of Luke Brine, dec'd, all of Marion County. (Bk. 1 P. 509)

Sophia BOUNDS of Pleasant twp. binds her son Edmon BERRY aged 8 years 2 months and 23 days to Simon Hyatt of same to the occupation of farming until he is 17 years of age. (Bk. 1 P. 709)

Isaac WOODRUFF and Eliza his wife and Lyman Fields and Selina his wife of Waterloo, Litchfield Co., Ct. to Ransum LEWIS of Medina Co., Ohio 8-21-1824, all lands in Ohio which are by descent from Abraham Scott father of said Eliza and Selina or from Mary Scott wife of said Abraham who have died within the last two years in Ohio.(Bk 1 P272)

Hiram WILCOX and Mary his wife, Thomas VANHORN and Mary his wife, Nathan WYATT Jr. and Sarah his wife, Samuel D. WYATT and Lavinah his wife, Nathaniel HULL and Nancy his wife, Jacob PHIPPS and Elizabeth his wife and Timothy ALDREDGE and Temperance his wife of Delaware Co., Ohio to William WYATT of Marion County - 10-28-1824 - $260 - 80 acres W½ NE¼ Section 9, Township 6, Range 16 Delaware land district. (Bk. 1 P. 184)

John ALCOTT of Galena, Jo Davies Co., Illinois to John THOMPSON of Marion Co. - 3-3-1835 - Power of Attorney to receive of the adms. or executor of the will (if any) of John Alcott's father, Josiah Alcott late of Marion Co., his distributive share. (Deed Book 9, page 71)

Benjamin FISH, guardian to Pliny DUTTON - 4-11-1835 - Benjamin Fish guardian of Charles, Maria, Stephen, William, Harriet, Erastus, Abigail and Laura Gordin. Petition to sell land filed in Marion County Common Pleas Nov. 1834. Land, S½ E½ NE¼ Section 34, Township 4, Range 17. (Deed Book 9, page 171)

Nancy Ann ROBBINS, et al. to Peter CASNER - 3-8-1836 - $3000. - 80 acres e½ SE¼ Section 24 and 96 acres W½ NW¼ Section 30, Township 4S, Range 14 in Delaware land district - Nancy Ann Robbins, Frederick Robbins and Lawrence Robbins and Margaret his wife of Marion Co., Edward Robbins, John Robbins, Isaac Robbins, Elizabeth Robbins, Catharine Robbins and Eppaah Robbins, all of Lagrange County, Indiana. (Deed Book 9, page 116)

Eliza ROBERTS and Nathan CLARK adms. of John ROBERTS, dec'd to Andrew GEYER - 3-29-1837 - Petition filed in Marion County Common Pleas Court Sept. 1837 with adms. as petitioner and Charles, Mary, Cynthia, Russel, William and Harlon Roberts as respondents for petition to sell real estate described as E½ NW¼ Section 18, Township 5S, Range 17 in Delaware land district. (Deed Book 10, page 83)

Jacob SAVAGE and Catharine his wife of Fairfield Co., Ohio to Jacob B. ALSPACH - 12-15-1834 - $30. - their undivided part E½ NW¼ & W½ NE¼ Section 3, Township 6S, Range 16, 12 acres part of original 160 acres formerly owned by Aaron R. Hyrod, dec'd. (Deed Book 10, page 265

Jacob B. ALSPACH and Mary his wife of Fairfield Co., Ohio to Michael ALSPACH of Marion Co. - 11-21-1835 - $30. - 1/13th undivided part NE¼ NW¼ & E½ Section 3, Township 6S, Range 16, 12 acres of original tract of 160 acres formerly belonging to Aaron R. Heymrod, dec'd. (Deed Book 10, page 266)

George HYMROD and Hester his wife and Henry BORGER and Leah his wife of Fairfield Co., Ohio to Michael ALSPACH of Marion Co. - 10-16-1835 - $60. - part undivided E½ NW¼ & W½ NE¼ Section 3, Township 6S, Range 16 formerly owned by Aaron Hymrod. (Deed Book 10, page 267)

Isaac CHRISTY and Alas his wife to Michael ALSPACH, all of Marion Co. - 12-28-1835 - $35. - undivided 13th part E½ NW¼ & W½ NE¼ Section 3, Township 6S, Range 16 being 160 acres formerly owned by Aaron R. Hymrod, dec'd. (Deed Book 10, page 268)

Jacob SNYDER and Margaret his wife of Franklin Co., Ohio to Michael ALSPACH of Marion Co. - 10-23-1835 - $30. - one undivided thirteenth part E½ NW¼ & W½ NE¼ Section 3, Township 6S, Range 16 being 160 acres formerly owned by Aaron R. Hymrod, dec'd. (Deed Book 10, page 269)

Michael ALSPACH and Magdalena his wife to Isaac CHRISTY, all of Marion Co. - 6-20-1835 - $30. - undivided thirteenth part E½ NW¼& W½ NE¼ Section 3, Township 6S, Range 16 being 160 acres formerly owned by Aaron R. Hymrod, dec'd. (Deed Book 10, page 270)

N. BENEDICT and others to Eli BENEDICT - 3-24-1835 - Quit Claim $150. - 110 acres W½ & 30 acres off W side E½ SE¼ Section 19, Township 6S, Range 17 in. Delaware land district - Silvester Benedict and Susannah his wife, Nicholas Benedict and Lydia his wife, all of Marion Co. and John Longshore and Clarinda his wife of Delaware Co., Ohio. (Deed Book 10, page 398)

Daniel BENEDICT and Content his wife to Eli BENEDICT, all of Marion Co. - 6-15-1835 - $50. - Quit Claim W½ & 30 acres of W side E½ SE¼ Section 19, Township 6S, Range 17 in Delaware land district. (Deed Book 10, page 397)

Isaac BOWYER and Rebecca his wife to Eli BENEDICT, all of Marion Co. - 6-16-1837 - Quit Claim W part NE¼ fractional Section 30, Township tS, Range 17 in Delaware land district. (Deed Book 10, page 399)

Isaac THOMAS and others to James THOMAS - 3-24-1837 - Quit Claim - That Samuel Thomas, Esq. late of the state of Ohio died intestate leaving certain lands and goods and the following heirs: son, James Thomas, also adms. of estate; son, Isaac Thomas and Peggy his wife; daughter, Elizabeth formerly Thomas, wife of Charles Wilson; daughter, Peggy formerly Thomas, wife of Robert Moore, all of Huntingdon Co., Pa. (note: land not described). (Deed Book 10, page 403)

S. CAMPBELL and others to John CAMPBELL, William CAMPBELL and Joseph CAMPBELL, all of Marion Co. - 9-30-1837. - 110 acres off N part SW¼ Section 35, Township 5, Range 17 - Andrew Campbell and Susannah his wife, Samuel Eccles and Mary his wife, John Moriarty and Margery his wife, Johnston CAMPBELL and Bethany his wife, Abijah Crawford and Sarah his wife. (Deed Book 10, page 509)

George ROWE and others to Joel and Jesse MYERS - 9-2-1837 - $1000. - Quit Claim E½ SE¼ Section 22 and W½ NE¼ Section 27, Township 15, Range 21 in Wooster land district - Rachel Myers, Benjamin Myers and Elizabeth his wife, Isaac Myers and Margaret his wife, George Rowe and Susannah his wife, Philip Hubbart and Catharine his wife, Elizabeth Myers and Leah Myers, all of Marion Co. (Deed Book 11, page 203)

Joel MYERS, Jesse MYERS and Mary Ann his wife to Rachel MYERS, all of Marion Co. - 9-2-1830 - E½ SE¼ Section 22, Township 15, Range 21. (Deed Book 11, page 201)

Moses MYERS and Elizabeth his wife of Adams Co., Pa. to Jesse and Joel MYERS - 10-20-1837 - $100. - E½ SE¼ Section 22 & W½ NE¼ Section 27, Township 15, Range 21 in Wooster land district. (Deed Book 10, page 204)

Joel MYERS, Jesse MYERS and Mary Ann his wife to Elizabeth MYERS, all of Marion Co. - 9-2-1837 - $200. - in-lot #1 in town of Iberia. (Deed Book 10, page 205)

Lewis R. CARPENTER and Nancy HARDMAN executors of Daniel HARDMAN to John MORRISON - 7-22-1837 - Petition filed March Term 1837 in Marion County Common Pleas Court for sale of real estate N½ S¼ SE¼ Section 33, Township 5S, Range 17 subject to dower of Nancy Hardman, whereby the aforesaid executors were the petitioners and Henry Hardman, John Hardman, Eleanor Hardman, David Hardman, Abin (or Abner) Hardman, Naomia Hardman, Nancy Hardman, Elizabeth Hardman, John Foust and Sally his wife, heirs at law of deceased, were the respondents. (Deed Book 11, page 323)

James LIKINS and others to John HILL - 11-21-1835 - $100. - 16 acres N part NE¼ SE¼ Section 21, Township 4S, Range 16 - James Likins and Frances his wife, Elias Spurgeon and Jane his wife, John E. Likins, Elizabeth Likins and Nancy Likins, all of Marion Co.; the last three being minors by John Hill their guardian. (Deed Book 11, page 381)

James RHOADS and others to Jesse RHOADS of Pickaway Co., Ohio - 6-19-1838 - $600. - 91.66 acres E½ NW¼ Section 6, Township 5S, Range 14 - James Rhoads and Susannah his wife, Alexander Gillaspie and Sarah his wife, Franklin Hannaman and Dorothea his wife, all of Marion Co., Ohio and William Cockron and Nancy his wife of Lagrange Co., Indiana. (Deed Book 11, page 399)

Peter CASNER, et al. to David HOLDERMAN and Abraham HOLDERMAN - 4-3-1838 - $100. - 690 acres in Marion Co. being lands conveyed by Christopher Holderman Jr. and wife to Christopher Holderman, being E½ SE¼ Section 13, NE¼ Fractional Section 13 lot 1, E pt. NE¼ Fractional Section 13 lot 2, W pt. NE¼ Fractional Section 13, S½ S½ E½ SE¼ Section 12, S½ NE¼ Section <u>2</u>, all in Township 4S, Range <u>4</u> and W½ Fractional Section 18 lot 3, E pt. NW¼ Fractional section 18, lot 4, W pt. NW¼ fractional section 18 and S½ S½ SW¼ Section 7, all in Township 4S, Range 15. Peter Casner and Anna his wife of Marion Co., David Patrick and Magdalene his wife of Ross Co., Ohio, Jesse Rhoads and Elizabeth his wife of Marion Co., John Holderman and Julian his wife of Marion Co., Christopher Holderman and Susannah his wife of Ross Co., Ohio, George Holderman and Mary his wife of Ross Co., Ohio, Lemuel Steely and Gionea (Guynea) his wife of Ross Co., Ohio, Isaac Holderman of Ross Co., Ohio, and Mary Holderman of Ross Co., Ohio; with the said Anna Casner, Magdalene Patrick, Elizabeth Rhoads, John Holderman, Christopher Holderman, George Holderman, <u>Guinnia</u> Steely, Isaac Holderman, Mary Holderman, David Holderman and Abraham Holderman being the children and heirs of Christopher Holderman late of Pickaway Co., Ohio, dec'd, their being 13 heirs in all. (note: only 11 heirs named in this deed). (Deed Book 11, page 456)

The following records were abstracted from Common Pleas Record L. Page on which original record may be found is given in parenthesis. Only suits of a genealogical nature were copied. Suits for debt, trespass, ejectment, etc. were not copied.

6-5-1843 - Alexander TURNER adms. of Jacob BURKMAN (BURGHMAN), dec'd vs. Elias BURKMAN (BURGHMAN), etal. In Chancery. Filed 6-5-1843. Jacob BURKMAN (BURGHMAN), dec'd, late of Wadsworth twp, died 8-20-1842 and in his lifetime contracted to sell William Simcox what was known as the "Ely tract", but died without executing said deed. Widow, Betsey Burkman (Burghman). Heirs: Elias, Polly, Susan, Peggy, Jacob, Amanda, Abraham, Fritt, Isaac and George Burkman (Burghman). (1 & 444)

6-5-1843 - Rachel ROOT vs. James BERDON, et al. Petition for Partition. Filed 1-24-1843. David Berdon, dec'd, late of New York, N.Y., let will in Surogates Office New York. Land in Bedford twp., Cuyahoga Co., Ohio; Bristol twp., Trumbull Co., Ohio; Pierpont twp., Ashtabula Co., Ohio; Amherst twp., Lorain Co., Ohio and Brunswick twp., Medina Co., Ohio. Children: Peter Berdon, dec'd, his children--David S. and William Berdon, minors of Medina Co., Ohio; David Berdon, Jr., dec'd, without heirs; Margaret A. Berdon, dec'd, without heirs; Abraham Berdon; James Berdon of Jacksonville, Illinois; Rachel late Berdon, now Rachel Root; John Berdon, dec'd, his children--Rachel, Wife of Valantine A. Ketchan, Peter F. Berdon, John Berdon, Mary M. Berdon and George T. Berdon, all of Toledo, Ohio and the last four being minors; and George S. S. Berdon of New York, N.Y., he being youngest son of David Berdon, dec'd. (3 & 9)

6-5-1843 - Alford S. WRIGHT and Charlott WRIGHT vs. William A. MINER and Marcus MINER. Petition for Dower. Filed March Term 1843. Land, 79 acres Lot 1, Tract 1 in York twp.; also Lots 63 & 64, tract #3 of 14th Range Connecticut Western Reserve in Medina twp. Joseph Miner, dec'd, late of Medina twp., died 10-10-1842. Widow, Charlott now wife of Alford S. Wright of Medina twp. Heirs: William A. Miner and Marcus Miner. (16)

6-5-1843 - John POE and Polly POE vs. Elizabeth MUNSON, et al. Petition for Partition. Filed 1-14-1843. Land, Pt. lot 72, pt Lot 82 and pt Lot 93 except 1 acre of land in SW corner of said lot conveyed by Samuel R. Munson for a graveyard, all in Harrisville twp. Samuel B. Munson, dec'd, late of Harrisville twp. Widow, Maria Munson. Children: Polly wife of John Poe, Elizabeth Munson, Flora Munson, Perry Munson, Francis Munson, Lucius B. Munson, Lucy M. Munson and Demtt C. Munson, all of Harrisville twp., the last seven named being minors and all entitled to 1/8th part. (21)

10-12-1843 - John GREISINGER vs. Susanna GREISINGER. Petition for Divorce. Filed 7-11-1843. John now of Guilford twp. married Susanna on 2-7-1809 in Millfort twp., Leheigh Co., Penna. John lived with Susanna until 1837 and in 1837 or 1838 he came to Ohio, but then returned to Northampton Co., Penna. where Susanna then and still resides to move Susannah to Ohio, but that she refused and still refuses to move to Ohio. (149)

10-12-1843 - Phebe RUSSELL vs. William M. RUSSELL. Petition for Divorce. Filed 8-8-1843. Phebe now of Medina married William M. in April 1830 in Aswigatchie, St. Samnoin Co., New York and that they lived together until June of 1842 when William H. moved to Adrian, Michigan. Children: William A. aged 11 yrs., James H. aged 8 yrs., Susan J. aged 5 yrs., George aged 3 yrs. and Hiram N. aged 5 months. (152)

10-12-1843 - Ebenezer M. NORTON adms. of Jonas DIRRDOFF, dec'd vs Dorothy DIRRDOFF. Petition to sell land. Filed 3-3-1843. Jonas Dirrdoff, dec'd, late of Westfield twp. held lease for 27 acres land from Jonathan Sloan for 5 yrs. from 4-1-1842, he also owned 69 acres part Lots 18 & 19 in Westfield twp. Widow, Dorothy Dirrdorff. Heirs: Elizabeth wife of Robert Moon of Michigan; Mary wife of Luman Aldridge of Canaan twp., Wayne Co., Ohio; Henry Deirdorff; Jane Deirdorff; Rebecca Deirdorff; Joseph Deirdorff; Jonas (or John) Deirdorff; Susan Deirdorff and Martha Ann Deirdorff; the last seven named all of Westfield twp. (154)

10-12-1843 - Austin BADGER adms. of Jas. BADGER vs. Ann BADGER, et al. Petition to sell land. Filed 4-14-1843. Land, 100 acres of W side NW¼ Section 13, Township 2 North, Range 8 East being in Putnam Co., Ohio. Widow, Ann Badger. Children: Ward, Edmund, Almina, Van Buren A., Norton and Flora Badger, all minors and all of Seneca Co., Michigan except Van Buren A. who resides in Medina Co., Ohio. (166)

10-12-1843 - Curtis BATES guardian vs. Hortentia M. BATES and Talcott BATES, minor heirs of Talcott BATES, dec'd. Petition to sell land. Filed 3-7-1837. Land, Lot 96 in Norton twp. Talcott Bates, dec'd late of Norton. Widow, Elizabeth P. Brown late Elizabeth Bates. Heirs: Hortentia M. Bates, Abagail N. Bates and Talcott Bates, all minors and each entitled to 1/3rd part. (170)

10-12-1843 - Daniel G. BRIGGS adms. of Norton MILLER vs. Dorcas MILLER and Frederick W. MILLER. Petition to sell land. Filed 5-31-1842. Land 25 acres NE¼ Lot 25 Sharon twp. Norton Miller, dec'd, late of Sharon twp. Widow, Dorcas Miller. Child, Frederic Wales Miller, a minor. (176)

10-12-1843 - Delezon E. HAYNES and Pamelia HASTINGS adms. of Wartstill HASTINGS, dec'd vs Simon (or Lunin) DENING, etal. Petition to sell land. Filed 5-16-1843. Land, 25 acres pt Lot 3 in Section 13, also W part Lot 3 in Section 11, all in Township 4, Range 15, Liverpool twp., Connecticut Western Reserve. Wartstill Hastings, dec'd, late of Liverpool twp. Widow, Pamelia Hastings. Children: Sally L. wife of Simon (or Lunin) Deming, Alvi Hastings, Robert Hastings, Nathan Hastings, Justus Hastings, Wartstill Hastings and Lucius Hastings, all of Medina Co. (181)

10-12-1843 - Aaron PARDEE adms. of Josiah JAQUITH, dec'd vs. Miranda JAQUITH, et al. Petition to sell land. Filed 5-16-1843. Land, 100 acres part Lot 7, Tract 5 of Wadsworth twp. Widow, Miranda Jaquith. Children: Lucy wife of Josiah Brown; Sibil Jaquith, an idiot and township pauper; Thomas Jaquith, a minor; Josiah Jaquith Jr., dec'd, his children--William Henry, Abigail Rebecca and Charles Wesley Jaquith, all minors. (186)

3-11-1844 - Isaac T. WELTON and Semtary RAWSON, guardians of Samuel BUEL vs.
Lovina BUEL, et al. Petition to sell land. Filed 6-13-1844. Land, part Lot 9,
Township 4, Range 13, Hinckley twp., Connecticut Western Reserve. Samuel Buel,
an insane person. Wife, Lovina Buel, Children: Sidney K.. Lyman C., Samuel M.,
George M., Eliza A., Martha E. and Eliza M. Buel. (310)

3-11-1844 - Simon METZGAR and Stephen FRYMAN adms. of Reuben BILLMAN vs. Heirs.
Petition to sell land. Filed 9-2-1843. Land, 71.61 acres Small lot 5 in Large
Lot or Section 24 of Homer twp. Widow, Catharine Billman. Children: Charles W.
and Eliza Ann Billman, both minors. (344)

3-11-1844 - John NESMITH serving adms. of Mills RICHARDS vs. Elizatt RICHARDS,
et al. Petition to sell land. Filed 10-12-1843. Mills Richards, dec'd, died
seized of one undivided ninth part of 46½ acres part Lot 4 in Wadsworth twp.
Widow, Aurilla Richards, since dec'd. Heirs: Elizaett Richards, Marshall Richards,
Lois Richards, Sally Ann Richards and Mills Richards, all minors by Eliza
Humphrey their guardian. (348)

3-11-1844 - Harrison DAMEN vs. Hannah DAMEN, etal. Petition for Partition.
Filed March Term 1844. Land, 178.74 acres part Lots 32 & 33 of Hincley twp.
Nathan Damen, dec'd, died 9-16-1843. Widow, Hannah Damen. Children: Harrison,
Maria, Julius, Jane, Roxy, Nathan, Emily and Almira Damen, the last six named
being minors. (352)

3-11-1844 - Seymon PARDEE of Litchfield twp. vs. Eliphalet SANDERS, etal.
Petition for Partition. Filed 1-20-1844. Land, 110 acres NW corner Lot 49
Litchfield twp.; W½ Lot 20 and E½ Lot 22 Montville twp.; part Lot 17 in large
lot 1, Tract 1 called Hubbard Tract in Lafayette twp. Nathan Pardee left will
with Abner Ray and James Bachtel as executors. Partition: 1/3rd part, Seymon
Pardee; 1/3rd part, Tamma wife of Eliphalet Sanders of Montville twp.; 1/3rd
part, Sarah Ann, Elizabeth, James and Rose Ann Battle of Chatham twp. by John
Battle their guardian. (358)

3-11-1844 - Betsey LINDSLEY vs. Aaron K. LINDSLEY, et al. Petition for Dower.
Filed 3-11-1844. Benjamin Lindsley, late of Montville twp., dec'd, died on
8-20-1843 seized of an estate of inheritance in 41 acres part Lot 3 and 60 acres
lot 2; both in Montville twp. and Lot 24 Medina. Widow, Betsey Lindsley of Montville twp. Heirs: Aaron K. Lindsley, Zenas C. Lindsley, Amanda Barnes, Emily S.
wife of John Curtis, Phebe wife of Henry D. Bradly and Henry B. Lindsley. (366 &
451)

5-23-1844 - Orpha VAN DUSEN vs June A. WEST, et al. Petition to sell land.
Filed 10-14-1844 (1843?). Land, 37 acres Lot 46, Hinckley twp. Andrew Van Dusen,
dec'd late of Hinckley twp., left Orpha Van Dusen and Roe G. Van Dusen as the
adms. of his estate. Widow, Orpha Van Dusen. Children: June wife of Wm. K.
West, Rush L. Van Dusen, Ralph H. Van Dusen, Esther A. Van Dusen, Ray L. Van Dusen,
Martin B. Van Dusen and Don C. Van Dusen. (435)

5-23-1844 - John PARDEE adms. of Estate of John F. LONG vs. Katharine LONG, et al. Petition to sell land. Filed 9-2-1843. Land, 50 acres SW corner Lot 18 and 163.47 acres N½ or Subdivision of Lot 7, both in Guilford twp. Widow, Katharine Long. Children: John Long, Mary Long, Katharine Long 2nd, Daniel Long, Able Long and David Long. (439)

5-23-1844 - Urial H. PEAK adms. of Lewis R. PEAK, dec'd, late of Medina vs. Horatio PEAK. Petition to sell land. Filed 10-17-1843. Land, Lot 40 &n original town plat of Medina in Medina twp., Township 3, Range 14 of Connecticut Western Reserve. Son, Horatio Peak. (448)

5-23-1844 - Joseph OVERHOLT and Samuel MILLER adms. of David DESHLER vs. Catharine DESHLER. Petition to sell land. Filed 3-11-1844. Land, 50.41 acres part Lot 80, Township 2, Range 13, Sharon twp.; also 1 acre Lot 1, Tract 9 and 4 acres part Lot 1 Tract 9 in Wadsworth twp. Widow, Catharine Deshler. Heirs: Thomas, Sally, Amelia and Caty Ann Deshler, all minors. (455)

5-23-1844- Henry HESMER of Guilford twp., guardian vs. Alice KING. Petition to sell land. Filed 3-8-1844. Land, 97.31 acres part Section 12 of Guilford twp. except .31 (31/100ths) of an acre conveyed to the Methodist Society. Leavitt H. King, dec'd, late of Medina. Heir: Alice King, a minor. (466)

5-23-1844 - Dennis G. WESTEN vs. Thomas H. WESTEN. Petition for Partition. Filed 5-25-1844 (1843?). Land 100 acres part Lots 18 & 24 in Wadsworth twp. Austin Westen, dec'd Partition: 1/2 part, Dennis G. Westen of Granger twp.; 1/2 part, Thomas Hawley Westen of Granger twp., a minor. (470)

10-7-1844 - David TOD of Warren, Trumbull Co., Ohio, guardian vs. William McCURDY, et al. Petition to sell land. Filed 7-12-1841. Land, 85.98 acres part Lot 14 and 45.18 acres E part Lot 15, Tract 3, Township 4, Range 14, Brunswick twp. Connecticut Western Reserve. John S. McCurdy, dec'd. Heirs: William Jr., George T. and Sarah A. McCurdy, minors. (575)

10-7-1844 - Sally HILL vs. Benjamin HILL, et al. Petition for Dower. Filed 7-15-1842. Benjamin Hill, dec'd, late of Spender two., died 10-1-1841. Widow, Sally Hill of Spencer twp. Heirs: Benjamin Hill Jr.; Welcome Hill, Sally Davis, Lida Rayner (Ryner), Anna Allen, Omilla Hill, all of New York and Mary Smith of Spencer twp., Medina co. (581)

10-7-1844 - John BURGAN vs Maryette BURGAN. Divorce. Filed 7-25-1844. John Burgan now of Lafayette twp. married in March 1840 to Maryette Hawkins. Lived together until 5-5-1841. Have one female child (no name given). (599)

10-7-1844 - Almon FILKINS vs. Mary FILKINS. Divorce. Filed 8-3-1844. Almon now of Medina married 10-9-1834 in Livingston Co., New York to Mary McLaine. Mary now of Livingston Co , New York. Children: Lydia Filkins aged 8 yrs. 10 mos., Jane Filkins aged 7 yrs. 11 mos., David Filkins aged 5 yrs. 9 mos and Martin Van Buren Filkins aged 3 yrs. 9 mos. (602)

72

10-7-1844 - Maryette BURNHAM vs Milton BURNHAM. Divorce. Filed 7-9-1844
Maryette now of Wadsworth twp. married Milton on 1-16-1840, his residence unknown.
Maryette had no children by Burnham or otherwise. (605)

10-7-1844 - Harrison G. BLAKE and Maria GILBERT adms. of Wm. R. GILBERT vs. Emily J.
GILBERT, etal. Petition to sell land and for dower. Filed 3-16-1844. In 1839
dec'd agreed with James Warner that dec'd exchange farm he then owned in state of
New York for 100 acres land S part Lot 66 and part lot 67 in Montville twp., the
last in Lot 67 being 40 acres purchased from adms. of Samuel P. Chadwick, dec'd.
Heirs: Emily J., William H., Alixes M., Elma A., Hannah M. and Carcus G. Gilbert.
(614)

10-7-1844 - Dolly WILSON vs Samuel WILSON. Divorce. Filed 10-19-1843. Married
12-27-1827 at Otis, Berks Co., Mass. Samuel now of Medina Co., Ohio. No children.
(619)

The following records were copied from Death Record 1, pages on which record may be found in this book are given in parenthesis. Only persons 40 years of age and over were copied. Abbreviations used: d=died; m=married; s=single; w=widow or widower; pb=place of birth; pd=place of death; r=residence. Residence is same as place of death unless stated otherwise.

NISELY, Jacob - d 8-25-1867; a 77y; m; pd Montville twp.; pb York Co., Pa.   (1)
DEWEY, Reuben - d 8-7-1867; a 68y; m; pd Wadsworth; pb Ohio.   (1)
BIGELOW, _____(not given) - d 8-19-1867; a 70y; w; pd Wadsworth; pb Mass.   (1)
DANIELS, Fredrick - d 8-4-1867; a 71y; m; pd Westfield; pb Conn.   (1)
HOUSE, Elizabeth - d 8-4-1867; a 62y; m; pd Homer; pb------(1)
BIGELOW, Mrs. - d 9-19-1867; a 72y; w; pd Wadsworth; pb------- (1)
RICHARDS, Mrs. Celia - d 7-4-1867; a 77y; w; pd Chatham; pb------   (1)
SHAW, John - d 7-26-1867; a 86y; m; pd Chatham; pb Bridgewater, Plymouth Co.,
    Mass.   (1)
BOLEN, Ellewine - d 9-28-1867; a 61y; m; pd Seville; pb ------   (1)
FISHER, Martha Maria - d 9-14-1867; a 64y; w; pd Medina; pb Northampton, Mass.   (1)
WALTERS, Marten - d 10-15-1867; a 65y; m; pd Spencer; pb-------- (1)
UGER, Johann Jacob - d 11-10-1867; a 75y; m; pd Grafton, Lorain Co., Ohio;
    pb Dillinger, Baden, Germany.   (1)
BOLEHIMER, Paul - d 11-17-1867; a 56y; w; pd Liverpool; pb Liverpool.   (2)
ANDREAS, George - d 11-16-1867; a 81y; w; pd Harrisville; pb Vermont.   (2)
TERRILL, Betsey - d 10-8-1867; a 67y; w; pd Liverpool; pb------- (2)
DICKEY, John - d 10-17-1867; m; pd Guilford; pb-------- (2)
LEWIS, Mary - d 11-1-1867; a 40y; s; pd Lafayette; pb------   (2)
SHANK, Mrs. - d 5-10-1867; a 72y; w; pd Wadsworth; pb------   (2)
MILLS, Harry A. - d 12-4-1867; a 73y; m; pd Wadsworth; pb Conn.   (2)
MILLER, Rebecca - d 12-26-1867; a 61y; m; pd Akron, Summit Co.; pb Wisenburg,
    Lehigh Co., Pa.   (2)
NORTON, Alweda - d 1-26-1868; a 66y; m; pd Medina; pb Mass. Parents: _____
    Powers and Sally Powers.   (2)
INMAN, Elizabeth - d 1-18-1868; a 89y; pd Spencer; pb------   (2)
HAVEN, Mrs. - d 2-21-1868; a 61y; pd Penfield, Lorain Co.; pb------   (2)
WELLS, Marietta - d 4-17-1868; a 58y; w; pd Lafayette; pb Lafayette; parents,
    Robert and Mary Houston.   (2)
HOLBEN, David D. - d 5-10-1868; a 43y; m; pd Wadsworth; pb------   (2)
PRENTICE, William W. - d 5-26-1868; a 54y; m; pd Lodi; pb-----; parents, John B.
    and Anna Prentice.   (2)
SPACE, Philip - d 2-13-1870; a ??(adult); m; pd Spencer; pb Pennsylvania.   (3)
CLARK, Naham - d 6-25-1869; a 56y; m; pd Spencer; pb Becket, Berkshire Co.,
    Mass.   (3)
OVERHOLT, Elizabeth - d 2-16-1870; a 50y; pd Guilford; pb Plumsted, Bucks Co.,
    Pa.   (3)
FARNSWORTH, Charlotte - d 6-22-1869; a 78y; w; pd Guilford; pb Stockholm,
    St. Lawrence Co., New York.   (3)
WILSON, Mary - d 9-9-1869; a 48y; m; pd Guilford; pb New York.   (3)
LOCKER, Susan - d 1-12-1870; a ??(adult); m; pd Guilford; pb New York.   (3)
MARTIN, Margaret - d 2-28-1870; a 73y; w; pd Guilford; pb Switzerland.   (3)
GUIRES, Sherman S. - d 7-24-1869; a 73y; pd Guilford; pb Winsor, Hartford Co.,
    Conn.   (3)
HALDERMAN, John - d 9-16-1869; a 62y; m; pd Sharon twp.; pb Bethlehem, Northampton
    Co., Pa.; father, John Halderman. (3)

CASE, Wm. - d 8-22-1869; a 81y; s; pd Sharon twp.; pb Somerset, N. Jersey.   (3)
CASH, Rebecca - d 12-16-1869; m; pd Sharon twp.; pb Penna.   (3)
LYTLE, Elizabeth - d 2-2-1870; a 72y; m; pd Sharon twp.; pb Bloom, Columbia
    Co., Pa.   (3)
WAIT, E. - (male); d 3-4-1869; a 77y; m; pd Hinckley; pb Mass.   (3)
CARPENTER, Lydia - d Feb.____(1869 or 1870--not given); 70y; w; pd (not given);
    pb (not given).   (3)
MARGUT, Daniel - d 4-1-1869; a 88y; m; pd------; pb--------.   (3)
SAILSBURY, Mrs. - d 4-4-1869; a 69y; m; pd-------; pb--------.   (3)
WORLLEY, Rebecka - d 3-10-1869; a 72y; w; pd Hinckley; pb Schoharie Co., N. Y.   (3)
PUTNAM, Calvin - d May(?) 14, 1869; a 75y; m; pd Vermont; pb--------.   (3.)
FRUCH, Vaslita - d 11-1-1869; a 72y; m; pd-------; pb--------.   (3)
SEELEY, H. E. - d 9-18-1869; a 53y; m; pd Medina; pb Charlton, Saratoga Co.,
    N. Y.   (3)
HORTON, Seth - d 11-18-1869; a 74y; m; pd Medina; pb Walcott, New Haven Co.,
    Conn.   (3)
FEATHERLY, Henry - d 8-4-1869; a 76y; m; pd Medina; pb New York.   (4)
THAYER, Mary - d 3-4-1870; a 70y; w; pd Medina; pb New York.   (4)
LAMPHEAR, Abner - d 7-4-1869; a 53y; m; pd Brunswick; pb Franklin, Vermont.   (4)
WARNOCK, Robt (or Rolt) - d 1-19-1870; a 70y; m; pd Brunswick; pb Ireland.   (4)
MORTON, Harriet A. - d 3-3-1870; a 45y; m; pd Brunswick; pb Brunswick.   (4)
LINNELL, J. P. - d 3-21-1869; a 60y; m; pd Pittston, Luzerne Co., Pa.; pb
    Licking Co., Ohio.   (4)
CHAPMAN, William - d 2-4-1870; a 68y; m; pd Seville; pb Lowville, Jefferson Co.,
    N. York.   (4)
SMITH, John - d 4-5-1870; a 78y; w; pd Homer; pb Linksheir, England.   (4)
WITTIERSTINE, Abraham - 7-17-1869; a 66y; m; pd Homer; pb Northampton Co. Pa.   (4)
VANDERHOOF, Isaac - d 7-15-1869; a 64y; m; pd Homer; pb Dryden twp., Thompkins
    Co., N. Y.   (4)
PALMER, Rebecca - d 3-12-1870; a 42y; m; pd Homer; pb unknown.   (4)
CHAPMAN, Levi - d 1-8-1870; a 85y; m; pd Harrisville; pb Vermont.   (4)
LEE, Elizabeth - d 4-23-1869; a 69y; m; pd Lafayette; pb Crosscreek, Jefferson
    Co., Ohio; parents, Thos. and Margrette Elliott.   (4)
BARRETT, Lewis - d 1-28-1870; a 74y; m; pd Lafayette; pb New Jersey; parents,
    James and Ann Barrett.   (4)
NEEHAM, Hannah G. - d 3-25-1870; a 69y; w; pd Lafayette; pb Millford, Hillsborough
    Co., N. H.; parents, Eligah and Mehitable Averill.   (4)
AVERIL, Amand - (female); d 3-14-1870; a 72y; w; pd Lafayette; pb Tineborogh,
    Hillsborough, N. H.; father, Thos. Tawn.   (4)
RANDALL, Nathan - d 6-4-1869; a 98y; w; pd Lafayette; pb-------.   (4)
BARRETT, Hiram - d 9-18-1869; a 64y; s; pd Lafayette; pb-------.   (4)
NICKERSON, Sidney B. - d 10-28-1869; a 61y; w; pd Lafayette; pb Mass.   (4)
GRAVES, William B. - d 2-2-1870; a 82y; w; pd Lafayette; pb Mass.   (4)
BECKWITH, Sally - d 2-13-1870; a 82y; w; pd Lafayette; pb------.   (4)
THOMPSON, William - d 2-14-1870; a 84y; w; pd Lafayette; pb New York.   (4)
TILLOTSON, Sally - d 2-16-1869; a 65y; w; pd Medina; pb Mass.   (4)
MACK, Florinda - d Mar. 1870; a 63y; m; pd Westfield; pb Canandagern Co.,
    Ontario; parents, Wm. and Huldah Hickox.   (4)
MINER, Priscilla - d 9-15-1869; a 69y; pd Medina; pb Kalioo, N. H.   (4)

The following marriages were taken from Marriage Record 1 as found in the Probate Court.

ABBOT, Joel to Mary Spencer	4-25-1820
ADAMS, William to Martha Pickens	1-1-1825
ALESHIRE, Jacob to Matilda King	8-14-1823
ALESHIRE, James to Sarah King	1-16-1823
ALKIRE, Ellexander to Margaret Coleman	2-1-1825
ANDERSON, Luke to Catherine Collins	9-22-1822
ANDERSON, Michel to Jane Dorset	5-21-1823
ASHWORTH, James to Cathrin Albert	4-23-1821
ASHWORTH, Thomas to Nancy Blain	7-1-1824
AUMILLER, Jacob to Sarah Sayre	2-27-1820
BAILEY, Buryman to Sally Townsend	12-15-1825
BAILEY, John to Jean (Jane) Pickens	6-30-1825
BAILEY, William to Wealthy Ralph	6-17-1819
BAILEY, William to Rachel Bradshaw	9-22-1825
BARKLEY, Shedrack to Pemelia Pilcher	6-27-1823
BARTON, John to Laodicea Eddy	5-4-1820
BESTOW, John C. to Harriet Hutchins	12-7-1825
BICKLE, Leonard to Lucy Bolton	4-28-1822
BINGHAM, Silas to Mary Guthrey	10-6-1822
BLACK, Hamilton to Esther Gilbert	4-11-1822
BOLTON, Andrew to Elizabeth Bickle	1-23-1825
BOSWORTH, Marcus to Laurilla Reed	12-11-1825
BOTKIN, James to Mary Brooks	12-21-1820
BRADSHAW, James to Mary Harrington	3-20-1823
BRADSHAW, Jesse to Anna Meeke(r)	3-20-1823
BRADSHAW, Stephen to Almira Johnson	1-18-1821
BRADSHAW, William to Betsey Davis	12-27-1825
BRANCH, Harry to Elenor Shel (Shields)	8-24-1819
BRANCH, Josiah to Mary Davis	8-3-1819
BRANCH, Wm. to Anna Norris	8-7-1823
BROOCKS, John to Jane Erwin	10-11-1821
BROOKS, Andrew to Mrs. Rosanna Morrow	9-24-1822
BROWN, Marshall to Hannah McBride	12-5-1820
BUFFINGTON, Wm. H. to Mary Rowley	7-31-1821
BURNASS, Silas A. to Sally Newell	2-25-1821
BURROUGHS, Joseph to Mary Conwell	7-3-1825
BUZZARD, Eli to Nancy Sims	4-23-1820
CALDER, James to Phebe Osborn (no day given)	July 1823
CALDWELL, Henry to Elizabeth Martin	12-6-1821
CALDWELL, James E. to Sarah Hubbel	5-14-1820
CALDWELL, John to Betsey McCloskey	11-22-1821
CARR, Chase to Mary Tubbs	8-12-1823
CASTLE, Junia to Betsey Burroughs	6-25-1824
CASTLE, Junia to Jane Daines	4-20-1822
CASTLE, Philander to Abigail Harper	3-18-1824
CHAPMAN, Levi to Nancy Sayre	1-23-1823
CHASE, Archibald to Elizabeth Price	3-21-1824
CHASE, Charles to Mrs. Polly Holt	9-24-1822

76

CIRCLE, Michael to Elizabeth Circle   9-9-1819
COLEMAN, Thomas to Sarah Roush   12-23-1823
COOK, Russell G. to Polly (Sally) O. Miles   12-19-1822
COOPER, Samuel to Catharine Schiblaire   11-2-1825
CORN, William to Elizabeth Aleshire   5-2-1822
COWDERY, Jacob to Arian Pilcher   10-11-1821
COWDERY, Jacob to Harriet Jones   11-13-1823
COWDERY, Joel to Polly Branch   6-12-1821
COWDERY, Joel to Louis Stevens   12-11-1824
COWDERY, Roswell to Mercy Hoyt   6-20-1822
COWDERY, Squire to Abigail Adams   9-25-1822
DARBY, Daniel to Phebe Evans   9-12-1822
DAVIS, John Jr. to Evelina Hoit   7-14-1825
DAY, James to Minerva Smith (no day given)   Sept. 1825
DISNEY, Samuel to Sylvia Vining   3-14-1824
DIXON, William to Olive Ingals   11-4-1821
DONALLY, Andrew to Adrianne B. Vanduyne   2-12-1824
DOWNING, George to Harriet Chase   7-25-1822
DOWNING, Radner to Maria Black   4-23-1824
DURST, Abraham to Nancy Reed   12-15-1825
DURST, Henry to Hannah Alkire   3-25-1824
DURST, Michael to Susan Roler   7-29-1820
DUSKEY, Geo. to Catharine Wolf   6-26-1825
DYE, Martin to Margaret Brafield   4-6-1823
EDWARD, David to Hannah Sayre   10-8-1822
EVINS, George to Lucinda Price   3-18-1824
FORKNER, James to Catherine Rawsaw   9-22-1822
GANDEE, Levi T. to Margaret Handshaw   2-25-1820
GARDINER, Charles to Lucy Stedman   8-29-1821
GARDINER, Charles to Nancy G. Elliot   6-27-1825
GARDNER, Joshua to Nancy Caldwell   4-29-1819
GASTON, Jared to Diolama Coffman   4-10-1823
GASTON, John to Semilla Brine   4-11-1822
GASTON, John to Lydia Larue   11-2-1824
GENDEE, Uriah to Anna Newton   5-23-1823
GIBBS, Miles H. to Elizabeth Law   12-8-1822
GILES, Joseph Jr. to Elizabeth Townsend   9-5-1822
GILL, Gundy to Deborah Tubbs   8-19-1824
GRAHAM, James R. to Polly Brown   8-17-1820
GRAHAM, Samuel to Elizabeth Brooks(no date given)   -----(1823)
GRANT, Landress to Thirza Owen Baker (Barker)   5-5-1823
GREGORY, David to Charity Comans   6-19-1822
GRIFFIN, Joseph to Elizabeth Haden   4-5-1820
GUTHREY, Charles to Nancy Cowdery   6-5-1821
GUTHRIE, Elias to Mary Davis   5-28-1820
GUTHRIE, Herman (Herman) to Rhoda Birrell   5-11-1823
GUTHRIE, Stephen to Anna Harper   12-23-1824
GUYMON, Noah to Sarah Molden   7-17-1823
HALEY, John to Mary Shirkley   5-11-1824
HALL, James to Leah Ford   9-16-1821
HALLIDAY, Samuel to Eliza Parker   4-7-1822

HALSEY, Mark to Nabby Hull	7-30-1821
HAMILTON, Jude to Sally Gilmore	8-9-1821
HANNA, William to Elizabeth Jackson	5-8-1822
HARDING, Ransom to Eliza Simpson	5-14-1823
HARPER, Amos to Rachel Smith	12-1-1825
HARPER, Andrew to Elica Sawyer	3-13-1825
HASKINS, Harris H. to Elizabeth Coleman	1-13-1825
HECOX, Truman to Martha R. Quimby	12-4-1822
HIGLEY, Elam to Susan Clark	2-13-1825
HIGLEY, Lucius to Nancy Shepard	12-13-1821
HILZET, George to Matilda Gilman	12-26-1824
HOLT, Horace to Melinda Bellows	1-1-1824
HOWARD, Lewis to Nancy Stone	12-25-1822
HOWEL, John to Eliza Dye	6-26-1825
HOWEL, Joseph to Mary Ann Bradfield	8-25-1825
HUFF, Thomas to Phebe Aleshire	7-10-1823
HULL, Leicester to Rhoda Cooper	1-30-1823
HULL, Wm. to Eliza Oliver	4-2-1823
HUMPHREY, Wm. to Hannah Bailey	3-20-1823
HUTCHINS, Cyrus to Harriet Stedman	4-14-1822
HYSEL, Boswell to Christiana Hysell	11-20-1823
HYSEL, Owen to Sophia Archer	4-24-1823
HYSELL, John C. to Jane Bailey	11-17-1825
HYSLE, Smith to Elizabeth Hunter	4-28-1825
INGLES, George to Sarah Dixon	10-14-1824
INGLES, James to Catharine Wolfe	8-16-1824
IRWIN, John to Nancy Saxton	12-16-1825
JOHNSON, Aretemus to Palmira Chase	5-14-1820
JOHNSON, David to Mrs. Sarah Peden	6-30-1825
JOHNSON, John to Hannah Bradshaw	5-18-1823
KARR, Hamilton to Margaret Karr	4-25-1824
KELLY, Charles to Hannah Worthen	3-31-1825
KELLY, John L. to Mrs. Johamiah Pierce	4-19-1823
KERR, William to Jane Murray	3-19-1820
KING, Thomas to Mary Maloon	11-8-1825
KNAPP, Abraham to Mary Scott	2-19-1825
LALLANCE, Adam to Catherine Baker	12-26-1822
LARUE, William to Snythia Brine	11-10-1820
LATHROP, Hazael to Catharine Wright	5-10-1819
LEE, Wm. to Elizabeth Crowsaw	1-27-1823
LITTLETON, James to Milley Buffington	8-14-1825
LOGAN, James to Lovina Savage	2-15-1822
LUELLEN, Philip to Hannah Birch	1-4-1823
LYONS, John to Lydia Bennet	12-7-1822
McBRICE, Jacob to Catharine Watkins	4-29-1819
McCLASKEY, Thomas to Hetty Caldwell	2-20-1822
McGEORGE, Sam'l P. to Lydia Nolton	9-27-1821
McHENRY, Bartholomew to Christiana Brooks	2-26-1824
MADISON, John P. to Almira H. Wheeler	4-24-1823
MALOON, Josiah to Frances King	10-6-1825
MARICK, John to Mary Knapp	2-22-1824

MARTIN, James to Ruth Gibson	4-27-1820
MARTINDALE, David to Mary Davist (Darist)	2-24-1820
MAYHEN, Fielding to Mary Parson	1-21-1825
MAYNARD, Levy to Calesta Cleavland	1-7-1823
MERRILL, Cornelius to Euretta Benedick	2-15-1821
MONROE, George H. to Sally Eblen	8-23-1820
MURPHY, John to Peggy Bickle	7-10-1825
MURRAY, Archibald to Anna Gardner	1-13-1820
MURRAY, Wm. to Anna Crowell	10-8-1823
NEAS, John to Margaret Hayden	11-5-1822
NESSLERODE, Elias to Betsey Rowley	6-12-1823
OLIVER, Samuel to Mary Munson	6-14-1821
OSBORN, Henry L. to Mary Ann Post	4-6-1825
OSBORN, John to Polly Love	3-20-1823
PARKER, Ebenezer to Mary Sivett	11-15-1821
PARKER, Hiram to Charlot Scott	11-22-1821
PEARCE, Samuel to Sarah Mason	5-1-1823
PERKINS, Ezra to Olive Soule	12-26-1822
PHILLIPS, Daniel to Polly Sharp	7-5-1821
PHILLIPS, John to Betsey Sharp	12-20-1824
PHILLIPS, Justus B. to Eliza Holt	10-31-1819
PICKENS, John to Easther Lasley	7-3-1822
PILCHER, Abraham to Rebecca Johnson	8-18-1825
POWEL, James to Lydia Sayre	5-16-1824
POWEL, Wm. to Eleanor Hilman	5-14-1824
PRICE, David to Semilla Jencks	9-16-1821
PRICE, Meredith to Catharine Baringer	6-16-1825
QUIMBEY, Jonathan to Sally Ryther	12-22-1825
QUIMBY, Enos to Prudence Kelton	10-3-1824
RAILBACK, Daniel to Eunice Woodward	10-15-1822
RALPH, Obediah to Sally Smith	9-19-1822
RATHBURN, Alvan to Selenda Harding	10-21-1819
RATHBURN, Elisha to Polly Giles	9-23-1819
RATHBURN, Sereno to Sally Braley	7-2-1822
RAYNLAS, James to Eliza Ann Folsom	4-16-1823
REED, Samuel to Sally Landon	11-22-1821
REEVES, Richard Jr. to Mary Douglas	9-9-1824
RICE, Wm. to Sophronia Robinson	10-6-1825
RIGGS, James to Philena Dye	5-20-1824
ROBERTS, Pryor to Rachel Ebulin	3-15-1821
ROBERTS, Sam'l G. to Eliza Roush	5-6-1824
ROBINSON, Noah to Sinthe Swope	7-6-1819
ROUSH, Jacob to Margaret Weaver	4-20-1824
RUSSELL, William to Fanny Bailey	3-28-1822
SAFFORD, John H. to Nancy H. Booten	4-11-1820
SANS, Erastus to Elizabeth Hysell	4-22-1819
SAVAGE, Adam to Polly Hubbell	3-15-1821
SAVAGE, John to Jane Shepard	12-23-1819
SAXTON, Michael to Martha Write (Wright)	7-30-1822
SAYRE, Daniel to Hepziba Chapman	1-2-1820
SAYRE, Daniel to Sally Standford	2-14-1823

SAYRE, John G. to Elenor Blatchley   1-21-1823
SAYRE, Jonathan to Louisa Powel   12-18-1823
SAYRE, Uriah to Lurania Hughs   4-19-1825
SENTON, Samuel to Hannah Eddy   8-22-1822
SERVICE, Samuel to Esther Dixon   8-6-1820
SHARKY, John to Nancy Nelson   9-26-1825
SHEPARD, Charles to Polly Carpenter   4-22-1824
SHIELDS, John to Nancy Martin   1-25-1821
SHIELDS, William to Barsheba Fesler   5-17-1821
SIGLER, Eli to Melinda Phelps   1-30-1820
SIMS, Emanuel to Minerva Ledore   10-24-1824
SIMS, Rees W. to Rhoda King   12-19-1822
SISSELL, John to Sarah Batey   12-19-1819
SISSON, Wm. to Almira Chase   5-13-1824
SKINNER, Daniel to Nany Wynn   11-3-1825
SKINNER, Joseph to Polly Gaston   9-9-1824
SMITH, Hylam to Lidy Bailey   8-31-1825
SMITH, John to Julia Cummins   12-16-1819
SMITH, Livingston to Eliza Case   2-2-1823
SMITH, Thomas to Osia Slack   3-10-1822
SPICER, Moses to Nancy Collins   8-14-1821
STAATS, Elijah to Nancy Anderson   8-2-1826
STAATS, Isaac to Betsey Standley   1-25-1823
STANLEY, Jchn to Betsey Forrest   6-8-1824
STARCHER, Abraham to Margaret Evans   11-29-1821
STEADMAN, Alex to Lydia Winn   2-13-1823
STEITH, David to Cathrin Jackson   3-8-1821
STEVENS, Amos to Lydia Page   3-27-1823
STEVENS, Jesse to Nancy Everton   4-30-1820
STEVENSON, Joseph D. to Eliza Thoms   1-13-1820
STOUT, Abner to Sarah Hale   11-23-1820
STOUT, Abner to Polly Stedman   2-27-1825
STOW, James to Polly Everton   8-26-1819
SWEET, Benjamin to Eleanor Conner   11-21-1824
SYLVESTER, Joseph to Amelia Filkins   11-7-1825
TAYLOR, Luther to Lydia Townsend   10-6-1825
THORN, Lemuel to Almeria Branch   5-31-1820
TORRENCE, Albert to Christiann Sims   1-24-1823
TOWNSEN, Daniel to Peggy McClaskey   12-11-1823
TOWNSEN(D), Allen to Sally McCaskey   11-4-1819
TOWNSEND, Solomon to Caty Ann Townsend   3-15-1821
TOWNSEND, Thos. S. to Rebecka Riggs   10-18-1821
TUBBS, Ransler to Martha Atkins   3-25-1822
TUBBS,,Reuben to Elizabeth Buffington   6-13-1819
TUBBS, Russell to Sophia Cowdery   1-13-1823
TUBBS, William to Laura Cleveland   2-11-1820
TURNER, Robert to Elizabeth Bradfield   5-12-1822
TWICHELL, Ephraim to Phebe M. Knight   3-1-1824
TWITCHELL, William to Maria Davis(no date given) (1823-1824)
VANDUYN, William B. to Elizabeth Smith   11-10-1825
WAGNER, John to Elizabeth Hemmelrich   8-28-1819

80

WARNER, John to Barbara Watkins 5 /. 1817
WARREN, Charles to Tamer Wiley 11-9-1820
WATERS, Henry B. to Sarah King 10-5-1824
WELBERAGE, Henry to Catharine Roush 3-17-1823
WELDON, John to Mary Elliot 3-18-182(4)
WELLS, Henery R. to Sarah Howard 11-2-1819
WEAVER, Daniel to Hanah Sayre 11-17-1824
WELCH, William of Carthage twp., Athens Co. to
    Rebecca Worthen of Orange twp., Meigs Co. 12-7-1825
WHITE, John S. to Lucinda Bailey 9-25-1825
WHITNEY, Michel J. to Harriet Smith 6-28-1823
WILDER, Lemuel L. to Maranda Archer 12-4-1821
WILSON, Robert G. to Laura Burns 3-24-1822
WILSON, William to Harriet Collins 3-14-1822
WINKLEY, John to Matilda Smith 4-25-1820
WINN, Armstrong to Julia Nobles 3-1-1821
WOLFE, Joseph to Clarissa Chace 2-21-1822
WOODRUFF, David to Oliva Chase 1-23-1825
WOODRUFF, John to Mary Anderson 12-2-1823
WRIGHT, Eli to Abigal Ralph 8-27-1822
WRIGHT, Joseph to Tabitha Evans 1-13-1820

ADAMS, Charles to Mary Sims	10-26-1826
AREBAUGH, George to Jane Shirky	1-24-1828
ATKERSON, John to Brittany Holt	9-21--1826
AUBRIGHT, John Jr. to Julian Hunter	2-9-1826
AUSTIN, George to Mary Wright	6-19-1828
BAILEY, Ruel to Cynthia Rathburn	7-6-1828
BAILEY, William Jr. to Phebe Jasper	8-7-1828
BAKER, Nicholas to Lenory Cleaveland	1-27-1828
BARBER, David to Lydia N. Stanley	6-14-1827
BARNUM, Mathew to Susan Colmer	9-11-1828
BECKNAL, Nehemiah to Julia Larkin	3-16-1826
BENEDICT, Elisha H. to Maria Simpson	1-11-1826
BING, John to Salencia Gaston	2-15-1827
BISSELL, Alden to _____(not given) Atkins	6-20-1827
BISSELL, Hiram to Elizabeth Tubbs	5-8-1828
BOSWORTH, Alva to Ruth Tilsen	10-21-1827
BRADBURY, Joseph to Eliza Strong	1-11-1828
BRANCH, Samuel Jr. to Lucy Thorn	1-15-1827
BROOKS, James to Polly Casterson	9-7-1826
BROOKS, Mathew to Lydia Reeves	3-27-1828
BROWN, Benjamin to Melinda Bolton	11-4-1827
BUFFINGTON, Philip T. to Mary Sheath	1-1-1826
CABLE, George to Susan Johnson	10-16-1828
CAHOON, James D. to Hannah Shaw	12-7-1828
CARTWRIGHT, John to Thankful Whitney	4-29-1827
CASE, Thomas J. to Rebecca Romine	1-29-1826
CASTLE, Philander to Lydia Whitney	5-10-1827
CHASE, Abel to Esther Noble	5-1-1828
CHASE, Hyram to Nancy Meeker	6-28-1827
CHITWOOD, George R. to Sarah Stowell	8-30-1827
CHURCH, William to Patty Gardner	7-17-1827
COTTRELL, Andrew to Eliza Dailey	4-10-1828
COUNTER (KOUNTZ on lic.), John to Esther Jones	2-27-1826
CROOKS, Oratio N. to Eliza Anderson	4-23-1826
CROWSAUR, John to Nancy Smith	2-7-1828
DAILEY, Robert to Phebe Davis	8-30-1827
DAVIS, Eliakim to Mariam Gillaland	11-23-1826
DEVORE, Jesse to Harriet Cullums	4-15-1828
DILL, Josiah to Martha Chadwick	3-7-1826
DODDERER, Andrew to Nancy Davis	12-7-1826
DOGHERTY, James to Elizabeth Sleeth	12-27-1827
DOUGHERTY, David M. of Alex'r twp., Athen Co. to Rebecca Gibson	10-26-1826
DOWNING, Franklin to Nancy Black	11-16-1826
DUST (DURST?), Samuel to Mary Taylor	1-18-1827
ELLIOT, Fuller to Elizabeth Chase	9-7-1828
ENTSMINGER, John Lewis to Jane Kerr	3-2-1826
ERWIN, John to Mrs. Polly Brooks	9-4-1826
FLEMING, Barthalomew to Elizabeth Sealey	3-8-1827

```
FRAZIER, John to Clarissa Meeker
FRY, Timothy to Louisa Pierce                           7-12-1827
GARDNER, Alfred to Mercy Paine                          1-15-1827
GILES, Charles to Emily Tyler                           6-6-1827
GILL, James to Sarah Buffington                         7-27-1826
GILLELAND, Abrham P. to Polly Chapin                    8-15-1827
GILLELAND, Reuben to Lucy Frast                         7-23-1826
GRAY, James to Elizabeth Forrest                        7-4-1826
GREEN, Daniel to Anna M. Hovey                          8-5-1828
GRIM, Jacob to Mary Dust (Durst on lic.)                1-25-1827
HADEN, John to Jane Baird                               11-22-1827
HALL, Elle to Polley Lasley                             3-25-1828
HALL, Joab H. to Catherine Smith                        5-28-1826
HARDEN, Alven to Saly S. Pane                           8-2-1827
HARRISE (HORRISE), Aaron to Pamelia J. Ray              12-26-1828
HAWK, Isaac to Jane Reed                                7-17-1826
HAYMAN, Jeptha to Orphania Jones                        2-16-1826
HAYMAN, John H. to Catharine Grim                       2-21-1827
HAYSE, Jesse to Eliza Gipson                            7-25-1826
HAYWARD, Solomon to Mary Reed                           4-25-1827
HIBBARD, Alanson to Becca Grow                          11-18-1828
HIGLEY, Cyrus to Miriam Clough                          6-1-1828
HILL, Simeon to Hannah Saxton                           10-2-1828
HISLE (HYSELL), Robert to Mary Hisle (Hysell)           7-19-1827
HOIT, James to Jane McKim                               7-17-1826
HOIT, Joseph to Mariah Townsend                         12-4-1828
HOLT, Hiram to Matilda Murray                           2-22-1827
HOWELL, William to Jane Irwing                          4-3-1828
HUBBELL, Barailla                                       9-20-1827
HUGHS, James to Susan Price                             10-9-1828
HUTCHINS, Alexander to Polly Hull                       10-25-1828
INGLES, Anson to Deberah Meccum                         7-22-1827
INGOLS, George to Lucy Hussey                           3-6-1828
IRWIN, Benjamin to Margaret McHenry                     1-12-1826
JACKSON, Daniel to Elizabeth Pickens                    1-10-1826
JOHNSON, Isaac to Chloe Baker                           9-1-1827
JOHNSON, Thomas to Sarah Cowdery                        8-7-1828
JONES, Charles to Betsey M. Knight                      2-9-1826
KIBBLE, John to Hannah McIntyre                         5-3-1826
KIMES, John to Elizabeth Wilbarger                      12-5-1827
KIMES, Samuel to Sophiah Hovey                          12-18-1828
KINGSBERRY, Harley to Rhoda Castle                      5-14-1826
KLIENFELTER, Jacob to Margaret Osborn                   4-6-1828
KNIGHT, Silas W. to Maria Higley                        5-4-1826
LALLANCE, Jacob to Mary Redding                         7-2-1827
LANDON, Levin to Sally Barstow                          2-2-1826
LANE, Houlbur to Jenett Chase                           8-17-1826
LANE, William to Avaline Seely                          10-4-1827
LOTT, Daniel A. to Lavina Harper                        10-2-1827
                                                        9-16-1827
```

83

```
LOVET, William to Mary Smith                              9-15-1826
LUCKY, Joseph to Mary Hudson                             2-1-1827
McAVOY, Thomas to Polly Stow                             7-29-1826
McCLUER, James to Jane Ogle                              5-15-1828
McCORMICK, James to Rachel Clark                         6-5-1827
McHENRY (McHENDRY), Samuel to Sally Stedman              11-30-1826
McINTIRE, William to Elizabeth Williams                  9-11-1828
McLAIN, Charles to Lydia Roush                           3-7-1827
MAITLAND, William H. to Polly Torrence                   8-6-1828
MARTIN, Isaac to Mary Irwin                             10-29-1828
MARTINDELL, Andrew L. To Susannah Durst                  2-23-1826
MASTIN, James to Harriet Hull                           11-5-1827
MATISON, David C. to Margaret Purchase                   1-11--1827
MECUM, John to Catharine Howdyshelt                      2-7-1828
MURPHY, Isaac to Lucena Sylvester                       10-31-1827
MURRAY, Alexander H. to Catharine Smith                 12-18-1828
MURRAY, William to Louisa Robinson                       9-2-1827
NICHOL, Thomas to Maria Haly                             3-28-1828
NICHOLS, James to Jane McLaughlin                        1-17-1828
O'NEIL, Cain to Elizabeth McMahon (McMann on lic.)       6-29-1826
PARKER, Edwin W. to Ann C. Stout                        10-11-1827
PARSONS, Joab to Sinthy Larance                          1-17-1828
PARTLOW, Morgan to Lucy Erwin                            8-24-1827
PAULK, Cyrus A. to Hannah Jones                         10-30-1828
PECK, Samuel to Susan Shidler                            3-6-1828
PERSONS, Joseph to Mary Lovell                           5-3-1827
PETTY, Jesse to Asenth Secoy                             4-16-1826
PICKENS, John to Mary Ann Lawrence                       5-3-1827
PICKENS, Thompson to Mary Blake                          9-10-1826
PICKINS, James to Elanor Bailey                          6-8-1826
PILCHARD, Peter to Martha Richey                         6-14-1827
POND, Norman to Elizabeth Morgan                        12-7-1828
PRATT, Dr. Seth to Mrs. Nancy G. Gardner                11-5-1828
PRICE, Barnet to Phoebe Purinton                         7-29-1827
PRICE, Charles to Sarah Sissel                           5-22-1828
QUEEN, William to Rebecca Brooks                         7-10-1828
RARDON, David to Elizabeth Barringer                     7-5-1827
REED, Willard to Abagail Hoyt                            1-20-1828
REEVES, Solomon to Elizabeth Irwine                      1-17-1828
RICHARDSON, Charles W. to Sally Everton                  7-29-1826
RICKARD, John to Rebecca Wolfe                           1-10-1828
ROSS, Isaac to Margery Hussa                             3-2-1828
ROULEY, Joseph to Cloe Buffington                        3-11-1827
ROUSH, Jonas to Susannah Weaver                          5-21-1826
ROUSH, Wm to Dolly Wolf                                  5-8-1826
RUSSEL, James to Lydia Crowell                          10-15-1826
RUSSELL, Robert to Nancy Hoppers                         2-23-1826
SAYRE, Jonathan to Polly Walker                          4-12-1827
SAYRE, Robt. to Deborah Bebe                             6-2-1826
SCHEBLAINE, Eli to Rebecca Calahan                       1-11-1826
```

84

SCOTT, Numa P. to Elizabeth Stanford   4-10-1828
SCOTT, Samuel to Nancy Shirkee   8-20-1826
SEALEY, Orcon to Sara Pickins   7-11-1826
SEIKS, Henry to Rachel Brooks   10-18-1827
DHAFER, Charles to Matilda Holl   6-7-1827
SHEETS, William to Darcas Williams   1-18-1827
SHIM, Charles to Rebecca Miller   9-25-1828
SHIRKY, James to Sarah Haley   1-23-1828
SHUNWAY, Pearly to Mary Jencks   4-27-1826
SICKS, William to Athens Co. to Catherine Brooks of Scipio twp.   6-21-1827
SIMPSON, Josiah Jr. to Theressa Higley   7-24-1828
SLEEPER, Parker to Lydia Munrow   8-25-1828
SLOAN, Joseph to Elizabeth Thomas   12-4-1828
SMITH, John M. to Rachel B. Barton   2-9-1826
STICKNEY, Nathaniel to Jane Conant   7-3-1828
TARR, David to Elizabeth King   6-1-1826
THORNTON, John to Susannah Durst   12-19-1826
TINKHAM, Seth to Martha A. Melana   1-18-1827
TORRENCE, William to Maria Elliott   7-19-1827
TUBBS, Ezra to Annis D. Stone   5-29-1828
VINING, Timothy B. to Sina Jones   5-3-1826
WALBURN, William to Mary Brooks   12-11-1828
WALKER, Daniel to Mary Ryther   1-31-1827
WATSON, James to Sarah Sallow   10-21-1828
WELLS, Agrippa to Polly Howlet   11-23-1828
WHEATLEY, Henry to Nancy Simpson   6-22-1828
WILLIAMS, Jesse to Belinda King   9-21-1828
WILLIAMS, John to Mary King   9-13-1827
WILSON, Benjamin E. to Sally German   6-3-1828
WILSON, James to Patty Duncan   8-4-1827
WOLBURN, John to Nancy Brooks   12-20-1827
WOLF, George to Kassy Rice   3-23-1827
WOODWARD, Oliver to Saray Byard   2-24-1827
WRIGHT, Jesse to Lydia Smith   4-8-1828
WRIGHT, Josiah to Rachel Bickle   2-14-1828

Name	Date	Page
BAYHAM, Thomas	1827	24
BENEDICT, Felix	1828	41
BROWN, James	1837	140
of Providence Co., R. I.		
BROWN, Nicholas	1843	251
of Providence Co., R. I.		
BURNS, George	1830	50
CARTER, Benjamin Bowen	1840	214
of New York, formerly of		
Providence, R. I.		
CHAPEN, Benjamin	1843	247
CHILD, John	1827	26
of Bristol Co. R. I.		
COLEMAN, John	1843	239
COLEMAN, Thomas	1830	46
CONNER, James	1836	123
CUTTER, William	1831	64
of Rockingham Co. N. H.		
DABNEY, Abigail Mason	1835	94
of Salem, Mass.		
DILL, Josiah	1828	36
DOWNING, Samuel	1834	78
DUDLEY, Charles E.	1844	276
of Albany, New York		
ELLIOT, Joseph F.	1834	91
EVANS, Richard'	1844	288
GILES, Joseph	1839	176
GOFF, James C.	1837	144
GRAHAM, James	1834	89
GRIGSBY, Elias	1839	173
GROVER, Ezra	1835	160
GROW, Peter	1837	190
HALL, John	1824	80
HARDY, Farnum	1830	48
HARRIS, Edward Sr.	1839	178
of Washington Co., Ky.		
HARPER, Daniel	1738	183
HASKINS, Joel	1841	228
HOPPES, George	1833	285
HORTON, Amos	1840	203
of Providence Co. R. I.		
HUBBELL, Abijah	1841	235
HUDSON, David	1836	121
HULL, William	1824	7
HUPP, John	1834	92
HYSELL, James B.	1840	194
JENCKS, Rebecca Carter	1840	218
of Providence Co., R. I.		
JOHNSON, Joshua	1822	1
JONES, Seth	1824	8
JOY, Benjamin	1831	52
of Suffolk Co., Mass		
KELTON, Elias	1843	249
KERR, Hamilton Sr.	1825	13
KIMES, Abraham	1840	212
LAWRENCE, John McDougal	1837	131
of New York City		

Name	Date	Page
LIEPER, Thomas	1838	146
of Philadelphia Co. Pa.		
MURPHY, John	1824	6
MURRAY, William	1838	165
PEARCE, Fanny	1839	172
PICKERING, John Jr.	1840	200
of Bucks Co., Pa.		
PICKERING, Phineas	1840	197
of New Hanover Co., N. C.		
PIERCE, Mary	1844	295
PITMAN, John H.	1827	14
of Providence Co. R. I.		
PITMAN, Saunders	1840	207
of Providence, R. I.		
PUGH, Peter	1844	292
RICE, Adam	1837	138
RICE, Charles	1836	128
RIGGS, Jeremiah	1836	121
ROBERTS, Isaac	1827	30
ROBISON, Joseph	1841	231
SAFFORD, John	1827	18
of Essex Co., Mass.		
SAYRE, John H.	1832	67
SAYRE, Robert	1827	32
SCHIEFELIN, Jacob	1835	110
of New York City		
SIMS, Barnett	1839	185
SLEETH, David	1836	125
SOUTHWARD, Samuel	1839	168
of Watertown, New York		
SPENCER, Daniel S.	1843	245
STEDMAN, Levi	1823	2
STEDMAN, Lyman	1829	37
STEVENS, Benjamin	1841	230
STRONG, Stephen	1834	82
STURGIS, Russell	1831	71
of Suffolk Co., Mass.		
TREADWELL, John Dexter	1836	117
of Essex Co., Mass.		
TUBBS, Daniel	1838	170
WADSWORTH, Benjamin	1827	20
of Essex Co., Mass.		
WHALEY, James	1841	236
of Wood Co., Va.		
WHITLOCK, Benjamin	1841	233
WILKES, Charles of New York	1835	103
WILLIAMS, John	1839	186
WILLIAMSON, James	1844	280
WINN, Timothy	1828	43
WOLFE, George	1824	10
WOODS, Sarah	1844	289
of Allegheny Co., Pa.		
WYLLYS, Samuel	1844	297
YOUNG, Hugh	1831	70

The following records were copied from "Death Record 1" located in the Probate
Court at the court house at Pomeroy. This listing includes on persons 40 years
of age and over. Residence is same as place of death unless stated. Page on
which record may be found in original record is given in parenthesis. Abbreviations:
d=died; a=age; s=single; m=married; w=widow or widower; pd=place of death;
pb=place of birth; res=residence.

RASP, George - d 11-23-1867; a 48-1-6; m; pd Pomeroy; pb Henehelheim; occupation,
    coal digger. (2)
CALLAWAY, Abigail - d 10-29-1867; a 66y; m; pd Carthage, Athens Co., O.; pb New
    Jersey. (2)
WOOGERT, Hannah - d 11-3-1867; a 47-5-3; m; pd Scipio twp.; pb Washington Co.,
    Pa.; parents, Levi and Ruth Lindley. (2)
WEISENBACH, Henry - 11-26-1867; a 65y; w; pd Pomeroy; pb Bavaria. (2)
COY, Cristopher - d 11-7-1867; a 73y; m; pd Salem twp.; pb Pennsylvania. (2)
HECOX, Adaline - d 11-9-1867; a 41y; s; pd Meigs Co.; pb Chester twp.; parents,
    Jertha and Marilla Hecox; res. Chester twp. (2)
HOYT, Cyriel - d 1-16-1868; a 59y 1m; m; pd Meigs Co.; pb New Hampshire; parents,
    Robert and Susannah Hoyt; res. Chester twp. (2)
SMEHEY, Emily J. - d 3-5-1868; a 42-2-13; s; pd Meigs Co.; pb Loudon Co., Va.;
    parents, John and Elizabeth Smehey; res. Chester twp. (2)
WICKAM, Elizabeth - d 3-23-1868; a 47y 8m; m; pd Meigs Co.; pb Harrison Co., Va.;
    parents, Vincent and Lydia Glover; res. Bedford twp. (2)
ADAMS, Susan - d 5-16-1868; a 47y 5m; m; pd Middleport; pb W. Va. (2)
SMARR, Daniel B. - d 5-30-1868; a 43y; m; pd Salisbury twp.; pb W. Va. (2)
STEWART, Joseph P. - d 2-19-1868; a 72y; w; pd Salem O.; pb Penna. (2)
FELTON, Mrs. - d 3-28-1868; a 46y; m; pd McArthur O.; pb Salem. (2)
FLETCHER, Edward - d Apr 1868; a 90y; m; pd Wilkerville O.; pb Ireland. (2)
STRONG, Lucy - d Apr. 1868; a 73y; w; pd Salem; pb Massachusetts. (2)
JOACHIM, Henry - d 5-1-1868; a 46-2-2; m; pd Pomeroy; pb Edegheim. (2)
JOACHIM, Henry - d 5-1-1868; a 46-2-4; m; pd Pomeroy; pb Bavaria. (4)
GLOECKNER, George - d 5-3-1868; a 72y 3d; m; pd Pomeroy; pb Bavaria. (4)
COZART, Susan Rilla - d 7-27-1868; a 44-6-13; m; pd Lebanon twp.; pb Meigs Co. (4)
MEANOR, Benjamin - d 11-3-1868; a 71y; m; pd Salem twp.; pb Pennsylvania. (4)
BREWSTER, Eleanor - d 12-20-1868; a 60y; m; pd Salem twp.; pb New Lisbon, O. (4)
WERLY, Elizabetha - d 11-2-1868; a 71y; w; pd Chester twp.; pb Lambsheim. (4)
SCHRUBE, Anna Maria - d 12-25-1868; a 50-7-7; m; pd Salisbury twp.; pb Hemhelheim.(4)
BRAMBLE, Mary - d 12-24-1868; a 80-4-22; w; pd Farmers Run; pb New York. (4)
SCHRUBE, Anna Maria - d 12-26-1868; a 50y; m; pd Salisbury; pb Germany. (4)
COLE, Mesach - d 7-15-1867; a 75-3-28; s; pd Orange twp.; pb Maryland. (4)
CALDWELL, John W. - d 9-15-1867; a 57-2-26; m; pd Olive twp.; pb Penna. (4)
BOYD, Daniel - d 8-20-1867; a 72-aa-14; m; pd Carthage, O.; pb Ireland. (6)
GIBSON, Cyrus - d 9-7-1867; a 62y; m; pd Pomeroy; pb------. (6)
ROSES, Mary - d 8-31-1867; a 40y; m; pd Pomeroy; pb Portugul. (6)
FOOSE, Mary - d -----1867; a 52y; --; pd------; pb------; res. Syracuse. (6)
PARKER, James - d 7-28-1867; a 50y; m; pd Salisbury; pb W. Va. (6)
McKENZIE, John - d 1-23-1869; a 72-9-13; m; pd Bashan; pb Penna. (6)
DOUGHERTY, William - d 2-25-1869; a 48-10-19; m; pd Letart; pb Jackson Co.,
    W. Va. (6)

COOLEY, Malon - d 3-21-1869; a 48-7-7; m; pd Jackson Co., W. Va.; pb Indiana. (6)
FRUNGOTT, Susannah - d 1-14-1869; a 68-5-1; w; pd Pomeroy; pb Darmstadt. (6)
SLOAN, Deborah - d 12-26-1868; a 71y; m; pd Bedford twp.; pb Ohio. (8)
WELDER (WILDER), Moranda - d 3-30-1869; a 74y; m; pd Salisbury twp.; pb New York. (8)
McBRIDE, Catherine - d 1-3-1869; a 66y; s; pd Syracuse; pb Virginia. (8)
THOMAS, Edmund - d-----1869; a 50y; m; pd Minersville; pd Wales. (8)
McPHETER, John - d 1-20-1869; a 72y; w; pd Salem twp.; pb Penna. (8)
ERNST, Catherine - d May 1869; a 59-7-8; m; pd Pomeroy; pb Lambsheim. (8)
FISHER, Nikolaus - d May 1869; a 69y 4m; w; pd Pomeroy; pb Oppun. (8)
DURST, Sophia - d June 1869; a 89-5-27; m; pd Olive twp.; pb Oppan. (8)
FORENIGER. Julia Ann - d 3-31-1869; a 55-2-28; m; pd Syracuse; pb----- (10)
BRICKER, Benjamin - d 7-7-1869; a 78y; s; pd Syracuse; pb------. (10)
BALES, George - d 2-14-1869; a 56-1-11; m; pd Syracuse; pb Wales. (10)
BARTELS, Carl Gotlieb - d 5-1-1868; a 75-3-2; m; pd Syracuse; pb Germany. (10)
JONES, William - d 1-10-1869; a 69-5-19; m; pd Syracuse; pb Wales. (10)
DAVIS, Rachel - d 7-30-1868; a 40y; m; pd Minersville; pb Wales. (10)
EVANS, David - d 7-29-1868; a 74y; w; pd Minersville; pb Wales. (10)
THOMAS, Mary - d 7-20-1868; a 40y; m; pd Minersville; pb Wales. (10)
HARDEN. Wm - d 3-4-1869; a 63y; s; pd Minersville; pb Va. (10)
THOMAS, Edmond - d 12-25-1868; a 50y; --; pd Minersville; pb Wales. (12)
DAVIS, Wm J. - d 3-20-1869; a 61y; m; pd Minersville; pb Wales. (12)
WOLF, Mary - d 1-31-1869; a 60y; m; pd Sutton twp.; pb--------. (12)
McELROY, John - d March 1869; a 85y; m; pd Racine; pb Maryland. (12)
McKINSEY, John - d 1-24-1869; a 72-9-14; m; pd Sutton twp.; pb Penna. (12)
WILLIAMSON, Flora - d 7-30-1869; a 56-7-3; m; pd Great Bend, Va.; pb------;
     res. Jackson Co. W. Va. (12)
BEBOUT, Anna - d 90201869; a 59-8-19; m; pd near Basan; pb Pennsylvania. (12)
KELLING, Jacob - d 3-4-1870; a 90y; w; pd Pomeroy; pb Germany. (12)
ALLEN, William - d 7-26-1870; a 42y; m; pd Pomeroy; pb Wales. (12)
OLINGER, Anna M. - d 4-16-1870; a 76-9-4; w; pd Pomeroy; pb Pomeroy. (12)
SINCLAIR, Betsey - d 3-9-1870; a 50y; w; pd Pomeroy; pb South Carolina. (14)
DAVIS, Sarah - d 7-17-1869; a 65y; w; pd Pomeroy; pb England. (14)
JONES, Eliza - d 12-13-1869; a 40y; m; pd Pomeroy; pb Wales. (14)
FINDLEY, Margaret - d 3-7-1870; a 86y; w; pd Pomeroy; pb Germany. (14)
HITE (HILE), Abraham - d 1-3-1870; a 66-9-26; s; pd Pomeroy; pb Germany. (14)
NASH, Jonah - d 7-11-1869; a 53-5-29; m; pd Pomeroy; pb England. (16)
HIGLEY, Ransom B. - d 1-22-1871; a 41y 16d; m; pd Rutland; pb Rutland. (16)
SAVAGE, Dorothy - d 3-31-1870; a 74y; w; pd Rutland; pb Litchfield, Mass. (16)
VINING, Joseph - d 3-16-1870; a 89-11-24; m; pd Rutland; pb Hartford, Conn. (16)
RATHBURN, Elisha - d 8-8-1869; a 80-1-8; m; pd Rutland; pb Hartford, Conn. (16)
RUPE, Joshua - d 2-3-1870; a 50-10-12; m; pd Rutland; pb unknown. (16)
BALL, James W. - d 5-8-1870; a 58y; m pd Sutton; pb Louden Co., Va. (16)
CROOKS, Alexander - d 5-9-1870; a 46-2-5; --; pd Syracuse; pb--------. (16)
CARLETON, Isaac - d 3-24-1870; a 66y; --; pd Syracuse; pb-------. (16)
CREU, Joseph - d 12-23-1869; a 45y; --; pd Syracuse; pb------. (16)
DeWOLF, Nancy - d 4-6-1870; a 76y; --; pd Syracuse; pb--------. (16)
TAYLOR, Thomas - d 7-18-1869; a 56-11-25; --; pd Syracuse; pb W. Va. (18)
KALB, Michael - d 2-2-1869; a 46-3-9; m; pd Chester; pb Germany. (18)
WARNER, William - d 8-29-1869; a 48y 15d; m; pd Chester; pb unknown. (18)

RICE, Josiah - d 12-30-1869; a 89-4-15; m; pd Chester; pb Mass. (18)
RIDENOUR, Elizabeth - d 3-14-1869; a 74-8-8; m; pd Chester; pb-----. (18)
ATKINSON, John - d 3-18-1870; a 64-10-28; m; pd Bedford; pb Va. (18)
ERWIN, Elizabeth - d 4-9-1869; a 58-7-7; m; pd Bedford; pb Salisbury. (18)
HULL, Henry - d 8-3-1869; a 83-7-8; m; pd Bedford; pb New Jersey. (18)
SARGENT, George - d 8-3-1867; a 76-7-26; m; pd Bedford; pb Penn. (18)
WISE, Daniel Sr. - d 6-15-1867; a 72-9-26; m; pd Bedford; pb Penn. (18)
VALE, Ann - d 3-3-1870; a 83y; s; pd Columbia; pb--------. (18)
THROCKMORTON, James - d 4-25-1870; a 43-7-5; m; pd Columbia; pb-------. (18)
COTTRELL, Andrew - d 4-1-1870; a 65y 6m; m; pd Columbia; pb---------. (18)
RUTHERFORD, Moses - d 9-23-1869; a 76-11-21; m; pd Columbia; pb-------. (18)
RUTHERFORD, M. S. - d 9-23-1869; a 56-11-21; m; pd Columbia; pb--------. (18)
COTTRELL, A. W. - d 4-1-1870; a 65y 6m; m; pd Columbia; pb----------. (18)
RUTHERFORD, M. S. - d 9-23-1869; a 56-11-21; m; pd Columbia; pb-------. (18)
THROCKMORTON, J. S. - d 4-5-1870; a 43-7-5; pd Columbia; pb Tenn. (20)
VALE, Ann - d 3-3-1870; a 83y; s; pd Columbia; pb Columbia. (20)
CROWELL, Benj. - d 5-15-1869; a 72-1-8; m; pd Salem; pb Ohio. (20)
NELSON, Benj. - d 10-6-1870; a 68-2-10; m; pd Salem; pb Ohio. (20)
STRONG, W. R. - d 7-26-1869; a 42y; m; pd Salem; pb Ohio. (20)
DOUGHERTY, Wm - d 2-25-1869; a 48-9-12; --; pd Letart; pb Va. (20)
HARPOLD, Adam - d 10-24-1869; a 79y 14d; ---; pd Letart; pb Va. (20)
BETTY. Martin - d Feb. 1869; a 73y; w; pd Orange; pb Ireland. (20)
ROUSH, George B. - d 2-28-1870; a 49-11-25; w; pd Sutton twp.; pb Ohio. (20)
COOPER, George W. - d 2-19-1870; a 54y 5m; m; pd Sutton twp.; pb Ohio. (20)
AUMILLER, Jonathan - d 12-16-1869; a 41-2-4; m; pd Sutton twp.; pb Ohio. (20)
HASELTON, James - d 1-4-1870; a 90-8-24; --; pd Sutton twp.; pb Ohio. (20)
MALLORY, Elizabeth - d 8-12-1869; a 40-3-24; m; pd Sutton twp.; pb Ohio. (20)
JORDAN, Elizabeth - d 4-22-1870; a 69-3-38; s; pd Scipio; pb Scipio. (20)
HERRIS, Mary - d 2-26-1870; a 82-7-9; s; pd Scipio; pb Scipio. (20)
HEDRICH, Elizabeth - d 11-4-1870; a 84y 1m; s; pd Scipio; pb Scipio. (20)
BEBOUT, Ann - d 9-2-1869; a 59-9-19; m; pd Lebanon; pb Penn. (20)
WILLIAMSON, Florence - d 7-30-1869; a 57-5-9; m; pd Lebanon; pb W. Va. (22)
FOSTER, Edwin - d 5-19-1869; a 83y 10d; m; pd Pomeroy; pb Ireland. (22)
ALLENSWORTH, John - d 2-22-1870; a 80y; m; pd Pomeroy; pb Va. (22)
HAZLEWOOD, Eliza - d 11-26-1869; a 56y 2m; m; pd Pomeroy; pb Va. (22)
BUCK, Capt. - d 3-10-1870; a 65y; m; pd Pomeroy; pb Va. (22)
RAMSEY, Mary - d 7-1-1870; a 40y; m; pd Pomeroy; pb Va. (22)
SKIMER, David - d 12-15-1869; a 55y; w; pd Pomeroy; pb Rulten. (22)
BEMIS, John - d 5-2-1870; a 49y; m; pd Pomeroy; pb Ohio. (22)
FRY, Thomas - d 4-19-1869; a 65y; w; pd Pomeroy; pb Penn. (22)
DAVIS, Polly - d 12-31-1869; a 54y; m; pd Pomeroy; pb Ohio. (22)
RADFORD, Billy - d 7-14-1869; a 82y; m; pd Pomeroy; pb Penn. (22)
KAW, Charles C. - d 3-8-1870; a 40y; s; pd Middleport; pb Middleport. (22)
THOMPSON, Dafeney - d 4-1-1870; a 40y; m; pd Middleport; pb Mason Co. (W.Va.) (24)
PRESTON, Pheb - d 3-9-1870; a 90y; --; pd Middleport; pb-------. (24)
MORTEN, Cassandra - d 3-11-1870; a 67y 6m; w; pd Middleport; pb Middleport. (24)
ARCHER, Sarah A. - d 3-2-1871; a 59-9-21; m; pd Sutton twp.; pb Va. (24)
BLAIN, Matthew - d 8-31-1871; a 64-2-23; m; pd Sutton; pb Pa. (24)
CARSON, Robert - d 7-30-1871; a 66-5-20; m; pd Sutton; pb Pa. (24)

HAZLET, Jane - d 4-6-1871; a 54y; s; pd Sutton; pb Ireland. (24)
PETREL, Peter M. - d 6-17-1871; a 72-2-17; m; pd Sutton; pb France. (24)
SHOLTZ, Valentine - d 5-19-1871; a 69-3-13; m; pd Sutton; pb Germany. (24)
SPURCE, Zellah - d 2-11-1871; a 44-11-16; m; pd Sutton; pb Pa. (24)
TRIPP, Abigail - d 11-13-1870; a 61-7-13; m; pd Sutton; pb Pa. (24)
OURS, Mary - d 3-18-1871; a 65-1-9; m; pd Lebanon; pb W. Va. (26)
SMITH, John M. - d 5-15-1870; a 59y m; pd Lebanon; pb Va. (26)
SCHOLLER, Wm - d June 1870; a 45y; m; pd Lebanon; pb Pa. (26)
WILLIAMSON, Sam'l M. -d 11-21-18-70; a 61-8-17; m; pd Kansas City, Mo.; pb Ohio; res. Lebanon twp. (26)
BELL, William - d 3-28-1871; a 82-11-22; m; pd Lebanon; pb Ireland. (26)
APPLEGATE, Catherine - d 10-5-1870; a 69y 9m; m; pd Olive twp.; pb Pa. (26)
BARRETT, Caroline - d 2-20-1871; a 41-2-10; m; pd Olive; pb Ohio. (26)
CONGREVE, William - d 1-30-1871; a 67-11-3; m; pd Olive; pb W. Va. (26)
GREEN, Ourns - d 5-22-1870; a 59-11-5; m; pd Olive; pb New York. (26)
HETZER, Philip - d 5-19-1870; a 76-4-13; m; pd Olive; pb Penn. (26)
SUTHERLAND, Elmer - d 8-21-1870; a 46-a-9; m; pd Olive; pb Va. (26)
WILSON, Henry - d 8-22-1870; a 62-10-9; m; pd Olive; pb New York. (26)
CONAUT, Olive - d 9-4-1870; a 82-8-9; w; pd Orange twp.; pb Mass. (26)
HALSEY, Sidney - d 3-16-1871; a 46-8-15; m; pd Orange twp.; pb Pa. (26)
HEWELL, Sally - d 2-13-1871; a 88-9-5; w; pd Orange twp.; pb Mass. (26)
PILCHARD, John Sr. - d 3-29-1871; a 63-1-22; m; pd Letart; pb Maryland. (28)
SAERFORD, Thos. H. - d 5-11-1870; a 56-2-10; m; pd Letart; pb------. (28)
BAICKLE, Jane - d 5-13-1870; a 70y; m; pd Pomeroy; pb Scotland. (28)
HOUFLECH, John - d 6-9-1870; a 45-1-12; m; pd Pomeroy; pb Bavaria. (28)
KIRSTINE, John - d 1-2-1871; a 76y 24d; w; pd Pomeroy; pb Bavaria. (28)
WALTER, Barbara - d 1-9-1871; a 42-3-3; m; pd Pomeroy; pb Bavaria. (28)
BAILEY, Elizabeth - d 7-2-1870; a 71y; s; pd Salisbury; pb Va. (28)
GRUESER, Mary E. - d 12-3-1871; a 66y 2m; m; pd Salisbury; pb Germany. (28)
MARTIN, Elizabeth - d 6-12-1870; a 87y; s; pd Salisbury; pb Ireland. (28)
SCHREEHER, Henry - d 10-12-1870; a 53y; m; pd Salisbury; pb Germany. (28)
WINKLER, Peter - d 4-5-1871; a 62-9-1; m; pd Salisbury; pb Germany. (30)
MILLER, Abigail - d 2-12-1871; a 56y; m; pd Chester; pb Ohio. (30)
MONTGOMERY, Laura - d 8-5-1870; a 46-8-15; m; pd Salem; pb New York. (30)
STRONG, Ozias - d 3-3-1871; a 84-11-15; m; pd Salem; pb Mass. (30)
CHAPMAN, Orton - d 10-30-1870; a 64y 2m; m; pd Salem; pb Mass. (30)
NELSON, John - d 3-27-1871; a 93y; s; pd Salem; pb Ohio. (30)
LUTZ, John - d 4-7-1871; a 72-11-16; m; pd Salem; pb Germany. (30)
LYNCH, William - d 1-25-1871; a 52y; s; pd Salem; pb Penn. (30)
KNAPP, Sarah - d 3-22-1871; a 74-10-22; s; pd Salem; pb Vermont. (30)
LUTZ, Mary C. - d 4-25-1871; a 75-3-4; m; pd Salem; pb Germany. (30)
BALL, James W. - d 5-8-1870; a 58-5-8; m; pd Sutton; pb E. Va. (30)
BUCY, Mary Jane - d 6-1-1870; a 42-2-10; m; pd Sutton; pb Ohio. (30)
CARSON, Mary - d 5-19-1870; a 70-2-10; s; pd Pomeroy; pb Penn. (30)
CROOKS, Alexander - d 5-9-1870; a 46-3-5; m; pd Sutton; pb Chio. (30)
JENKINS, Mary Jane - d 9-1-1870; a 50-7-5; s; pd Sutton; pb Illinois. (30)
HALTER, Hannah - d 4-2-1871; a 50-1-10; m; pd Sutton; pb W.Va. (30)
SIMPSON, Sophia - d 7-25-1870; a 41-8-5; w; pd Sutton, pb Ohio. (30)
SCANLIN, Bridget - d 12-7-1870; a 44y; w; pd Sutton; pb Ireland. (30)

THOMAS, Anna - d 7-27-1870; a 56y; m; pd Sutton; pb Wales. (30)
THOMAS, David F. - d 8-31-1870; a 68-11-4; m; pd Sutton; pb Wales. (32)
WILLIAMS, William - d 12-19-1870; a 47-10-17; m; pd Sutton; pb Wales. (32)
WILLIAMS, Margaret - d 11-26-1870; a 69y; w; pd Sutton; pb----. (32)
ATKINSON, Gair - d 3-13-1871; a 42y 17d; m; pd Middleport; pb England. (32)
CURTWRIGHT, Wm E. - d 11-20-1870; a 61y 7m; s; pd Middleport; pb Ohio. (32)
DUNE, Thomas - d 3-30-1871; a 55y; m; pd Middleport; pb Ohio. (32)
DAVIS, Evan - d 10-9-1870; a 64y; m; pd Middleport; pb Ohio
JONES, Philip - d 10-6-1870; a 82-6-3; s; pd Middleport; pb Mass. (32)
LOWES, Hendley - d 12-1-1870; a 60-2-21; m; pd Middleport; pb England. (32)
ROUSH, Francis - d 2-3-1871; a 46-10-3; m; pd Middleport; pb Ohio. (32)
SAUSHING, Sarah - d 3-12-1871; a 74-2-12; w; pd Middleport; pb New Jersey. (32)
SMITH, John - d 2-25-1871; a 82y 10m; w; pd Middleport; pb unknown. (32)
WILDER, Samuel (or Lemuel) - d 1-20-1871; a---; s; pd Middleport; pb Vermont. (34)
WILLOCKS, Sarah - d 1-4-1871; a 85y; s; pd Middleport; pb New Jersey. (34)
WHITTEN, Jonathan - d 6-4-1870; a 67y; s; pd Middleport; pb New Jersey. (34)
WILSON, Eliza - d 6-12-1870; a 60-2-12; m; pd Middleport; pb Virginia. (34)
EVANS, Asher - d 1-2-1870; a 79-5-24; m; pd Columbia; pb Penn. (34)
NICHOL, James - d 1-25-1871; a 66-4-7; m; pd Columbia; pb Virginia. (34)
NOBLES, Charles F. - d 12-25-1870; a 75-4-5; m; pd Rutland; pb Vermont. (34)
CHURCH, Clement - d 1-4-1871; a 66-10-15; m; pd Rutland; pb Maine. (34)
HUMPHREY, Wm - d 7-9-1870; a 88-4-1; m; pd Rutland; pb England. (34)
JOHNSON, Joshua - d 2-5-1871; a 53-6-5; m; pd Scipio; pb Ohio. (34)
FRENCH, Russell - d Feb. 1871; a 80y; w; pd Scipio; pb Mass. (34)
ALKIRE, Catherine - d 4-5-1870; a 42y; w; pd Scipio; pb Ohio. (34)
CASEY, David - d 4-18-1871; a 49y; w; pd Scipio; pb Ohio. (34)
HARRIS, Susannah - d 3-18-1871; a 78-8-17; w; pd Scipio; pb Penn. (34)
COOK, Wm - d 1-1-1871; a 77y; s; pd Bedford; pb England. (34)
WELLS, Minerva - d 12-8-1870; a 74y 8m; s; pd Bedford; pb Virginia. (36)
GILLILAND, Elizabeth - d 9-12-1870; a 84-4-6; w; pd Bedford; pb Virginia. (36)
MOLER, Anne - d 1-9-1871; a 77y; m; pd Bedford; pb Penn. (36)
GREEN, Jesse - d 9-2-1870; a 80y 21d; m; pd Bedford; pb N. Hampshire! (36)
SPEARS, Mary - d 2-14-1871; a 51-11-4; m; pd Pomeroy; pb W. Va. (36)
BARTLETT, Samuel - d 6-24-1870; a 65y; w; pd Pomeroy; pb Wales. (36)
CURTIS, Peter - d 3-1-1871; a 87y; w; pd Pomeroy; pb Ireland. (36)
EVANS, David - d 2-15-1871; a 61y; s; pd Pomeroy; pb Wales. (36)
GREASER, Maria E. - d 12-3-1870; a 67y; m; pd Pomeroy; pb Wales. (36)
PROBST, George - d 7-17-1871; a 69y; m; pd Pomeroy; pb Penn. (36)
SCHAFFER, Valentine - d 6-26-1870; a 59y; m; pd Pomeroy; pb Germany. (36)
THOMPSON, Daphney - d 4-1-1870; a 50y; m; pd Pomeroy; pb Virginia. (36)
THOMPSON, Lydia - d 11-19-1870; a 80y; w; pd Pomeroy; pb Virginia. (36)
BACHLET, George - d 8-4-1870; a 68y; m; pd Pomeroy; pb Germany. (36)
BELL, Betsey - d 4-15-1870; a 40y; w; pd near Cincinnati; pb Virginia. (36)
EBERSBACH, Philip - d 1-14-1871; a 67-6-12; m; pd Pomeroy; pb Germany. (36)
JONES, Mary - d 12-5-1870; a 70y; m; pd Pomeroy; pb Wales. (36)
KEIFER, John - d 1-11-1871; a 78y; m; pd Pomeroy; pb Penn. (36)
ENOCHS, Joseph - d 8-5-1871; a 65y 4m; m; pd Pomeroy; pb Fishing C. Va.; parents,
    Enoch Enochs and Sarah Phocia. (38)
JOACHIM, Barbara - d 1-9-1872; a 43y; m; pd Pomeroy; pb Pomeroy. (38)

91

CURTIS, Peter - d 4-30-1871; a 88y; w; pd Pomeroy; pb Ireland. (38)
GRESSEL, Franz - d 7-17-1871; a 40y; s; pd Pomeroy; pb Saxonia. (38)
GLOCKNER, Anna M. - d 3-11-1872; a 62y; w; pd Pomeroy; pb Germany. (38)
HUFFMAN, John - d 10-7-1871; a 81y; w; pd Pomeroy; pb Germany. (38)
MASAR, Catharina - d 11-5-1871; a 62y; pd Pomeroy; pb Germany. (38)
JONES, Mary - d 3-22-1872; a 61y; w; pd Pomeroy; pb Wales. (40)
THOMAS, Joseph - d 11-16-1871; a 61y; m; pd Pomeroy; pb Virginia. (40)
ANDERSON, Margaret - d 8-31-1871; a 51-11-9; m; pd Middleport; pb England. (40)
BANINGER, Joseph - d 9-3-1871; a 54y 4m; m; pd Mt. Sterling; pb Meigs co. (40)
CURTIS, Atlanta - d 2-1-1872; a 60; w; pd Middleport; pb East Va. (40)
MURRAY, Scanda - 11-8-1871; a 42y; m; pd Middleport; pb Salisbury twp. (42)
RUSSELL, Rhoda - d 2-16-1872; a 51-10-2; m; pd Middleport; pb Rutland twp. (42)
STEPHENSON, Mary E. - d 3-26-1872; a 40-8-3; m; pd Middleport; pb Kanawha, W. Va.(42)
SOWERS, Philip - d 11-16-1871; a 52y 5m; m; pd Middleport; pb Berlin, Germany. (42)
VANCE, Isaac - d 7-1-1871; a 71y 4m; m; pd Middleport; pb Allegheny Co., Pa. (42)
AUSTIN, Susan - d 2-21-1871; a 60y; m; pd Rutland; pb Chester. (42)
CHASE, Francis - d 12-15-1871; a 61-5-15; m; pd Rutland; pb Kennebec Co., Maine.(42)
GILES, Maria E. - d 6-25-1871; a 44-8-5; m; pd Rutland; pb Rutland. (42)
KERS (or KENIS?), Nancy - d 10-21-1871; a 50y 5d; m; pd Rutland; pb Berkley, W.Va.(42)
LAME, Clanend - d 2-19-1871; a 62-5-14; s; pd Rutland; pb Washington Co., O. (42)
NOBLES, Osmin - d 3-26-1872; a 72-10-5; s; pd Rutland; pb Vermont. (42)
TITUS, Steven - d 9-13-1871; a 75-2-23; m; pd Rutland; pb Dutches Co., N.Y. (42)
STANSBURY, Eliza W. - d 8-27-1871; a 67-10-3; m; pd Rutland; pb Penn. (42)
STOW, Jane - d 5-20-1871; a 91-11-7; w; pd Rutland; pb Bedford, Mass. (42)
HUGG, John - d 9-6-1871; a 56-1-7; m; pd Salem twp.; pb Salem. (44)
HILL, Aaron - d 11-6-1871; a 48y 8m; m; pd Salem twp.; pb Ohio. (44)
BUSKIRK, Elem V. - d 8-13-1871; a 40-5-3- s; pd Salem twp.; pb Penn. (44)
STEEL, Elizabeth - d 1-23-1872; a 77-3-4; w; pd Salem twp.; pb Penn. (44)
STANDISH, Ellen - d 10-22-1871; a 63-4-20; m; pd Salem twp.; pb Penn. (44)
HOYDE, John - d 2-17-1872; a 62-8-2; pd Columbia twp.; pb unknown. (44)
STARKY, Perlia - d 10-7-1871; a 69-2-22; w; pd Columbia twp.; pb Virginia. (44)
STEVENS, Lydia - d 3-14-1872; a 71y; m; pd Scipio twp.; pb Maine. (44)
HOWELL, Wm - d 9-3-1871; a 82y; m; pd Scipio twp.; pb Canada. (44)
TEWKSBURY, Elizabeth - d 4-12-1871; a 88y; s; pd Scipio twp.; pb Vermont. (44)
HAYES, John - d 2-8-1872; a 72y 8d; m; pd Bedford twp.; pb Penn. (44)
CLARK, Catharine - d 7-22-1871; a 77-7-22; m; pd Bedford twp.; pb East Va. (44)
SANBORN, Jno. W. - d 9-13-1871; a 69y 11m; m; pd Bedford twp.; pb Va. (44)
MERCER, David - d 6-16-1871; a 87-6-1; s; pd Bedford twp.; pb New Hampshire. (44)
GREEN, Mary - d 4-19-1871; a 73-1-10; s; pd Bedford twp.; pb Penn. (44)
HEATON, Jane M. - d 1-12-1872; a 54-1-12; m; pd Bedford twp.; pb Monroe Co. (44)
FRISBIE, Nathaniel K. - d 10-9-1871; a 68y 20d; m; pd Chester twp.; pb Salisbury.(44)
SMITH, Sarah C. - d 9-24-1871; a 54-10-12; m; pd Chester twp.; pb Chester twp. (44)
GAVEN, Nancy - d 11-7-1871; a 77-3-28; w; pd Chester twp.; pb Penn. (44)
EICHINGER, John J. - d 2-22-1872; s; pd Chester twp.; pb Germany. (46)
KNIGHT, Benjamin - d 2-16-1872; a 65-11-13; m; pd Chester twp.; pb Garland, Me.(46)
BURCH, Sarah - d 3-24-1872; a 75y 4d; w; pd Olive twp.; pb New Jersey. (46)
COLEMAN, Wm - d 5-18-1871; a 51-7-27; m; pd Olive twp.; pb Olive. (46)
HETZER, George - d 5-16-1871; a 80-8-24; m; pd Olive twp.; pb Maryland. (46)
JAY, Elizabeth - d 10-18-1871; a 78-5-25; w; pd Olive twp.; pb New Jersey. (46)

PACKARD, Lucretia - d 10-8-1871; a 86y 18d; w; pd Olive twp.; pb Mass. (46)
STILL, John - d 1-8-1872; a 101y 2m 20d; m; pd Olive twp.; pb Penn. (46)
STILL, James H. - d 7-15-1871; a 47-1-1; m; pd Olive twp.; pb Ohio. (46)
MIDDLESWART, Tunis - d 1-12-1872; a 69-2-4; w; pd Lebanon twp.; pb Penn. (46)
COONEY, Lucinda - d 10-20-1871; a 66y; m; pd Lebanon twp.; pb Charleston, Va. (46)
TAYLOR, Isaac - d 11-28-1871; a------; m; pd Lebanon twp; pb Letart twp. (48)
TORENCE, Lucy - d 3-8-1872; a 66-7-25; m; pd Lebanon twp.; pb Maine. (48)
RINGLIN, Eliza - d 8-18-1871; a 87y; w; pd Lebanon twp.; pb Ireland. (48)
LOVETT, William - d 12-4-1871; a 67y 6m; m; pd Lebanon twp.; pb Marietta. (48)
SCHRICKER, Catharine - d 5-3-1871; a 68-6-3; --; pd Orange twp.; pb Germany. (48)
THOMAS, Bridget - d 4-4-1871; a 88-7-25; w; pd Sutton twp.; pb Penn. (48)
CROWSER, Nancy - d 2-4-1872; a 63-5-1; m;pd Racine; pb Virginia. (48)
McELWY, Catherine - d 8-27-1871; a 83y 14d; w; pd Racine; pb Germany. (48)
MILES, Mary - d 1-22-1872; a 68-1-17; w; pd Racine; pb Penn. (48)
WILCOXTON, Thomas - d 12-25-1871; a 71-8-9; w; pd Racine; pb Ohio. (48)
WOLF, Rebecca - d 5-20-1871; a 71-9-25; m; pd Sutton; pb E. Va. (48)
HUGHES, Margaret - d 1-6-1872; a 63y; m; pd Syracuse; pb Wales. (50)
KRAFT, Conrad - d 10-28-1871; a 84y; m; pd Sutton; pb Germany. (50)
QUINN, Peter - d 11-2-1871; a 57y; m; pd Syracuse - pb Ireland. (50)
REA, Robert - d 8-2-1871; a 50y; m; pd Minersville; pb Wales. (50)
CONRAD, Thomas - d 9-16-1871; a 66y; pd Salisbury twp.; pb Salisbury twp. (50)
HYSELL, Sally - d 6-22-1871; a 59y; pd Salisbury twp.; pb Salisbury twp. (50)
STEVENS, Catharine - d 12-23-1871; a 42y; s; pd Salisbury twp.; pb Salisbury twp. (50)
MISNER, Margaret - d 2-15-1872; a 81y; w; pd Salisbury twp.; pb Salisbury twp.(50)
CALE (or COLE?), Francis - d 7-24-1872; a 40y; pd Salisbury twp.; pb Salisbury twp. (50)
EARLY, Patsy - d 2-15-1872; a 90y; w; pd Salisbury twp.; pb Salisbury twp. (50)

The following cemetery is a contribution of Mr. Roy E. Lacy, Anna, Ohio.
Inscriptions recorded October 11, 1967.

BURNTWOOS CEMETERY

Located in Mercer County, Ohio, two miles east and one mile north of Coldwater.
This was the cemetery for the United (Liberal) Brethren Church, which has been
gone for about forty-five years. Many stones are down, but collected and placed
on cement cover of a grave. Other stones are in good shape.

JOHNSTON, Charles C. born 9-23-1876; died 2-27-1902
        Mary J. 1833-1914
        Gratz M. born 8-7-1824; died 12-8-1890
        Alvira A. dau of G. M. and M. S. died 9-19-1892; age 39-9-12
HAY, Gloria L. died 9-29-1906; age 7-6-2
GREEN, Infant dau of J. M. and E. died 6-7-1883
. . . . . (stone could not be moved)
. . . . . Samuel son of G. and Barba---- (Stone in pieces)
BEYER, Mary died 2-9-1884; ae 53-11-24; John d. 3-24-1890 ae 71-6-19(same stone)
YANEY, Elizabeth wife of Jacob Yaney d. 9-15-1854; age 24-10-20
        Barbara wife of George Yaney d. 3-30-1862; age 57-4-22
        John C. died 7-1-1887; age 85-2-16
COATE, Lydia wife of Joseph Coate died 1-10-1852; age 55 years
JOHNSTON, Mary E. dau of G. M. & M. J. Johnston died 3-16-1887 ae 3-6-14
        John E. died 2-10-1888; age 15y 4d (same stone as Mary E. Johnston)
MONROE, Henry died 2-26-1867; ae 56-9-10
. . . . . Mary E. dau of D - - - - (broken)
MONROE, George son of Henry and Mary J. Monroe died 3-21-1876; ae 23-2-29
YANEY, Hannah dau of J. & M. Yaney d. 11-4-1860; ae 2-5-16
(At this point there are a lot of broken stones placed on cement base, some I
have listed, others I could not move.)
. . . . David (not readable)
YANEY, Barbatha dau of G. and M. I. Yaney died 10-3-1857; age 1y 1d
JOHNSTON, Nancy dau of G. M. & M. I. Johnston died 9-15-1870; ae 1m 29d
KINDEL, Joseph son of Wm. J. & June died 2-19-1860; age 5-1-16
        Charles died 10-8-1860; age 3m 2d
HOLE, Rebecca dau of War---- and ---- Hole died 1-2-1850; age 28-5-12
KERNS, Job son of W. S. & Phebe died 12-8-188- ; age 12 days
YANEY, Sarah E. dau of H. & A. Yaney died 8-13-1865; age 9-6-23
BEAM, John J. died 2-23-1885; age 73-11-29
SHIVELY, Esther wife of D. Shively died 2-9-1888; age 73-11-2
BEAM, David died 7-3-1883; age 79-8-10
        David M. son of O. & H. died 9-9-1862; age 20-10-20
SNYDER, Mary A. wife of N. Snyder died 2-5-1881; age 53-8-29 (nee SHIVELY)
SHIVELY, Hettie O. dau of J. C. & A. died 12-1-1891; ae 10m 2d
LANE; Benjamin D. V. son of B. D. & S. died 3-10-1887; ae 18-8-17
COLE, Hannah wife of N. W. Cole died 3-28-187-; age 58-7-10
ROSABORN, William died 3-10-1887; age 78-8-8
CHRISTIAN, Abraham born 6-4-1844 died 4-10-1870
STEVENS, Xula R. dau ef J. A. & T. died 11-7-1885; ae 17-9-10
KINDEL, Pricilla (Mother) died 4-19-1876; ae 35-5-4
        Ima (Daughter) died 7-30-1881; ae 13-11-20
WYATT, Sarah Elizabeth dau of John T. & Nancy died 7-16-1882; age 37-10-17
KINDEL, Rev. William A. died 3-5-1893; ae 62-1-22
COATE, John son of B. & M. died 9-17-1852; age 23 days

WYATT, James E. son of J. T. & V. A. died 3-20-1882; age 2m 23d
    Mary C. wife of J. W. Wyatt died 5-27-1893; age 50-1-11
    James H. died 1-3-1872; age 31-7-29 CIVIL WAR Veteran
    Minnie A. his daughter died 9-22-1870; age 8m 12d
BEHM, Elizabeth Jane wife of C. Behm born 3-22-1840; died 12-21-1873
COATE, Joseph died 5-7-1857; age 56 years
KINDEL, Ammeta wife of Rev. Wm. Kindel died 9-13-1899; age 63-2-11
GRUNDEN, Nellie wife of J. F. 1893-1911
WYATT, James H. died 1-3-1872; age 31-7-29

ZIMMERMAN CEMETERY - BLACK CREEK TWP. - MERCER COUNTY, OHIO

Contributed by: Wilbur J. Miller Jr., 613 Rockford Rd., Box 292, Willshire, Ohio.
Cemetery is located right off of U.S. Route 33 on the Erastus-Durbin Road in the
Labadie Reserve of Sec. 2. All inscriptions taken.
HESSONG, Eliza J. dau. of L.&E.S. Hessong died Mar.. 4, 1891 Aged 13y 11m & 20d
_____(Note: Stone with no date, inscribed "Mother")
ZIMMERMAN, Jane wife of Isaac Zimmerman died Jan. 8, 1881 Aged 51y & 6m
ZIMERMON, Isaac died Mar. 23, 1875 Aged 48 yrs. & 16 ds.
ZIMMERMAN, Eli C. son of Isaac & Jane died Feb. 18, 1857 aged 5y 3m 15d
ZIMERMAN, Infant son of Isaac & Jane died (A)ug 24(?), 1860
DELLINGER, Margaret wife of Wm Dellinger died Sept. 1, 1864 Aged 38y 7m 18d
CROGHAN, Nathaniel died May 15, 1880 Aged 71y 1m 4d
BIENZ, Mary J. died Sept. 5, 1876 Aged 60y 11m 10d
    John B. died Mar. 28. 1875. Aged 59y 1m 4d
(Note: Piles of broken stones)
CROGHAN, Nancy wife of Nathaniel Croghan died Feb. 2, 1868 in her 59th year of
                                  her life
AMRINE(?), Infant dau. of S(?) & L. died Feb. 18, 18(81?)
HUCHER(?), Catharine wife of Jonathan(?) Hucher died Dec. 27, 1865 aged 63y
_____(Note: Stone with no marking left)

COATS-GRAY CEMETERY - BLACK CREEK TOWNSHIP - MERCER COUNTY, OHIO

Contributed by: Wilbur J. Miller Jr., 613 Rockford Rd., Willshire, Ohio 45898
Located on a small hill on Wabash Road in Section 15 between Rockford West Road
and Manley Road. All inscriptions taken.
COATS, James J. died Apr. 10, 1873 aged 18y & 11d
    David L. died Apr. 31, 1878 aged 43y 10m 28d
    Infant son of T. & S. A. Coats, Mar. 19, 1871 aged 5 ds.
GRAY, Ida J. dau. of T. & S. Gray died Apr. 4, 1864 aged 1m 12d
    Herbert W. son of Truman & S. Gray died Sept. 11, 1860 aged 3y 6m 2d
COATS, Joseph died Mar. 15, 1876 aged 83 years

95

ROEBUCK CEMETERY - MERCER COUNTY, OHIO

Contributed and copied by: Mr. and Mrs. Kenneth K. Ketring, Fairborn, Ohio

Cemetery is located in Dublin township, on Frysinger road one mile north of Route 33, on a knoll overlooking the St. Marys River, between Mercer and Rockford.

VANHORN, Christian died Feb. 7, 1877 age 73 yrs. 1 mo. 3 days
     Christian son of Christian Vanhorn died June 2, 1858 age 1 yr. 8 mo. 8 days
     David died Sept. 29, 1852 age 62 yrs. 8 mo. 14 days

BLACK, William, soldier, Co. H, 9th Ohio Inf.; Mahala 1843-1918

PUTNAM, William, soldier, Co. H, 4th Ohio Cav.

WELLS, Justus died June 18, 1893 age 66 yrs. 9 mo. 25 days

ROEBUCK, Ishmael died Jan. 15, 1853 age 43 yrs. 5 mo. (ss as Margaret Wells)

WELLS, Margaret died April 17, 1901 age 79 yrs. 6 mo. 28 days (ss Ishmael Roebuck)

ROEBUCK, Elizabeth C. (or G.) dau. of I. & M. died Feb. 16, 1853 age 11m 3d
     Henry N. son of I. & M. died Mar. 10, 1853 age _____ (?)

SANFT, In memory of Eliza wife of W. H. H. Sanft died June 17, 1845 age 30 yrs.

DULL, Susan wife of John Dull died Aug. 9, 1863 (or 1868?) age 23 yrs. 10 mo. 5 ds.

ROEBUCK, Warren, soldier, Co. K, 45th Ohio Inf.
     Garrison died April 10, 1852 age 40 yrs. 9 mo. 17 days
     George died Jan. 26, 1846 age 38 yrs. 2 mo. 27 days
     Catharine A. wife of Geo. Roebuck died March 11, 1875 age 68 yrs. 11 mo. 8 ds.
     Rewel died Oct. 29, 1841 age 63 yrs.
     Sarah wife of Rewel Roebuck died Dec. 12, 1842 age 53 yrs.
     John 1851-1929
     Branson 1813-1904 (note: following three inscriptioons on same stone)
        Phebe A., wife, died_____(?) age 29 yrs.
        Mary, wife, died 1815(?? or 1845??) age 27 yr.
        Albert, son, died 1853 age 12 yr. 8 m. 4 days
     John died July 10, 1889 (or 1869?) age 23 yrs.

DYSERT, Sarah E. ROEBUCK wife of Geo. W. Dysert died Spt. 13, 1874 age 24 yrs.
                                     5 mo. 8 days

        Two small children:
        Ida Bell died Sept. 17, 1874 age 4 mos.
        Infant died Jan. 1873 age 1 day
     Ellen dau of G. W. Dysert died Nov. 14, 1898 age 21y 9m 19d
     Margaret dau. of G. W. & S. E. Dysert died Sept. 26, 1873 age 1 yr.7m 11d

LAMOREAUX, John L. died Nov. 25, 1882 age 71 yrs. 2m 28d (ss as Rebecca)
     Rebecca died Spet. 5, 1878 age 68 yrs. 6 m. 20 d.

SAVEY(?), Elizabeth wife of W. M. Savey(?) died Nov. 4, 1879 age 60 yrs. 3 mo.

DYSERT, John H. died Feb. 12, 1900 age 89 yrs. 3 m. 12 d.
     Mary, wife, died April 2, 1876 aae 61 yrs. 23 days

ROEBUCK, Ruel died Sept. 20, 1888 age 57 yrs. 3 m. 15 d.
     Catharine wife of Ruel Roebuck died Feb. 16, 1883 age 42 yrs. 9m. 28d.

SMITH, James F. died Feb. 7, 1877 age 46 yrs. 9 m. 11 d.
     Charlie son of J. F. & A. (?) B. Smith died Oct. 22, 2869 age 2 yrs. 1m 5d
     Phebe A. wife of J. F. Smith died 1863 age 27 yrs.

HARRUF, (note: two small children's stones--can't be read)

(note; there were several stones which were not readable, cemetery is well kept).

96

ANDERSON CEMETERY
MERCER COUNTY, OHIO

Informant of location of cemetery: Mr. Charles A. Grover, 424 Tuller Ave.,
Big Rapids, Michigan 49307
Mr. Grover's grandmother on his paternal line was a "Scott". He also states the
cemetery is situated on land which formerly belonged to Nels ANDERSON, a very early
settler of the area whose wife was Mary Scott.

The Anderson Cemetery is located on the north borderline of Section 18, Recovery
Township. From Fort Recovery take State Route 49 north to Park Road, then west
one-fourth mile to east bank Wabash River. Cemetery located in field one-fourth
mile north. It is not fenced, but has posts marking corners. It is mowed. Nine
markers standing and the rest piled up. No doubt many markers are missing.

ISENHART, Eliza dau of Jac & C. Isenhart died Mar. 1840 in her 4th yr.
Elizabeth dau't of Jac & C. Isenhart died Apr. 6, 1851 AE 20y 3m 17d
Jane wife of Henry Isenhart died Oct. 14, 1851 Aged 21 y's 8 mo 8 ds
Jacob died Sep. 23, 1847 AE 40y 11m 25d (Note: Stone is broken and
this bottom with age seems to fit.)
SCOTT, Alexander died Sept. 2, 1836 Aged 75 years.
Richard died July 18, 1854 aged 68 yrs 6 mo.
Mary wife of Richard Scott died July 2, 1858 aged 65 yrs 7 mos & 6 d's.
Richard died April 15, 1860 aged 25 y's 6 mos & 9 D.
William H. son of B. & H. J. Scott died Feb. 12, 1875 aged 9 mos 12 D's.
Mandy wife of Alexander Scott died Aug. 24, 1852 (Broken)
Hannah wife of John Scott died Dec. 1, 1880 aged 46 ys 7 mo ? 17 das.
Marion, H. Co. K 51 Ohio Inf.
Samuel son of J. & H. Scott died April 11, 1863 aged 6 y's 20D.
Nancy daughter of Richard & Mary Scott died Aug. 29, 1835 aged 7 years.
Roderig A. son of W. & C. Scott died Feb. 15, 1870. AE 23 yrs 8 m 19 d.
RUNKLES, Samuel S. died Aug. 1, 1872 aged 49 ys & 5 m.
____ died Dec. 9, 1872 aged 16 ys 8 mo & 7 ds.
Mary J. dau of S. S. & A. Runkles died June 6, 1860 aged 10 ys & 26 D.
Martha M. dau of S. & A. Runkles died June 22, 1855 AE 1y 5m 7d.
DENNEY, Infant dau of J. & C. F. Denney died Oct. 11, 1859
Azariah son of J. & C. F. Denney died Dec. 7, 1851 Aged 2 ys 8 m & 29 Ds
ANDERSON, David died Oct. 5, 1843 Aged 44 yrs.
KNAUSE, Lucy daughter of George & Isabel Knause died Oct. 16, 1855 aged 8 yrs 1 mo
9d.
____, Margaret B. dau of S. S. & __(?) Broken, only middle of stone left.
Marlle__der(?) son of ____vy(?) 13th_____(Y)ears ____mo
(Note: Scaled off)

(Note:- Marker) "H.S."
(Note:- Foot Markers) "SR" "JI" "MR"

97

PIONEER CEMETERY - MERCER COUNTY, OHIO

Located in Fort Recovery, Ohio on street directly behind Catholic Church and school. The majority of the stones have been re-set in cement bases with part of the inscriptions quite often being in base.

(Plaque) "In 1851 the people of Fort Recovery discovered the bones of the soldiers of the Indian Wars 1791-1794 in their burial place along the banks of the Wabash.

"On this site September 10, 1851, known as bone burying day, the bones were re-interred with a ceremony which 5000 people attended.

"Found in 1872 when excavating for a building, the bones of Major General Richard Butler were interred with a celebration July 4, 1876. In 1891, the Centennial Year, the bones were taken up and lay in state for three days of celebration in the Disciple Church and on October 16, 1891 were placed in the park east of the present monument. When the monument was being erected in 1912, two boxes containing all that was mortal of the soldiers who fell in 1791-1794 were placed in a crypt in the foundation. (Placed in 1951 by the Fort Recovery Historical Society)"

(Plaque) "Placed in 1951 in memory of Samuel McDowell 1770-1847. Soldier. General St. Clair's Army 1791. General Wilkinson's Army 1792. General Wayne's Army 1793-1794. Pioneer Settler 1838. (By his descendants and the Fort Recovery Historical Soc. Inc.)"

Cemetery Inscriptions

WRIGHT, Rachel wife of Acre Wright died Sept. 16, 1873 aged 42 Y. 3M. 18D
GIMER, Perry U. son of Wm. M. Gimer died Mar. 18, 1860 aged 1 yr. 1 m. 1 d.
CARSON, John died July 22, 1843 (note: cemented in base)
NICKERSON, Nancy C. dau. of J. & A. (note: cemented in base)
DEHAYS, Christena wife of John Dehays died Sept. 17, 1861 aged 25 yrs. 4m 12d
McDOWELL, Samuel died May 4th, 1847 aged 77 years
    Mary wife of Samuel McDowell died Oct. 3, 1853 AE. 75 yrs. 6m 15d
    Margaret wife of John McDowell died Sept 29, 1845 aged 33 years & 2m
    Rachel dau. of John S. & Rachael died May 7, 1849 aged 11 yrs. 27 ds.
BEARDSLEE, Pheby dau of O. & L. (note: cemented in base)
McDOWELL, Elizabeth wife of John McDowell died Oct 26, 1831 aged 38 yrs. & 3d
SNYDER, Anthony W. son of W. & M. J. died July 28, 1861 aged 3 ys. 7 mo. 21 ds.
EDMISTON, Catharine wife of Jacob Edmiston died Mar. 4, 1852 aged 42 yrs.
DOWNS, Rachel died Aug. 29, 1871 (note: cemented in base)
SMITH, Rebecca J. dau. of A. H. & S. M. (note: cemented in base)
WRIGHT, Nathan son of Acre & Rachel died May 10, 1868 aged 12y 10m & 5d
EDMISTON, Abraham son of J. & C. died July 1850 aged 6 ys.(note: no day or mo.)
DOWNS, Wm. died Aug. 14, 1847 aged 54y 11m 9d
____CHUTT, Elizabeth died Oct. 11, 1859 aged 27 yrs. 6 mos. (note: stone broken)
McDANIEL, Wm. died March 4, 1857 (note: cemented in base)
JOHNSTON, George W. died Nov. 27, 1838 aged 24y 1m & 2d
THOMPSON, William died Mar. 12, 1853 aged about 73 ys.
SNYDER, Margaret dau. of W. & M. J. died Dec. 4, 1857 aged 8 y's 1 mo. 26 ds.
JONES, William S. son of Daniel & Sarah (note: cemented in base)
(JONES), George W. son of Daniel & Sarah (note: cemented in base)

SMALLWOOD, Marion wife of Branson Smallwood died July 19, 1847 aged 16y 3m & 7d
_____, Matilda D. (note: cemented in base)
HOFFMAN , Enoch son of D. & C. (note: cemented in base)
BEARDSLEE, Lucinda infant dau of D. & E. died Mar. 15, 1838
AINSWORTH, David son of Jos. & A. (note: cemented in base)
(D)EHAYS, Fredrick son of C. D. & E. died (note: cemented in base)
WALLINGFORD, Nancy daughter of Absalom & Martha Ann (note: cemented in base)
DUNW(OODY?), Wm. died Jan. 10, 1869 aged 36y 1m 14d (note: top of stone gone)
HOUSER, Wm. T. died June 15, 1848 aged 28y 8m 11d
McCRARY, Tower died Mar. 18, 1857 AE. 47y 9m 15d
GIBSON, William died Apr. 5, 1839 aged 50
McDANIEL, In memory of Elizabeth McDaniel died June 14, 1838 aged 23yr 6mo & 3day
BEARDLEE, Elanor died May 20, 1845 aged 2 mo 15 day
FISHER, Marcia wife of Clark Fisher died July 19, 1847 aged 45 y. 9 mo. & 17 d.
WOODBRIDGE, In memory of Joseph Egbert son of Ebenezer & Eliza S. who died
Aug. 22nd 1845 aged 13 mo. & 15 d.

THOMAS SCOTT - Will Book 1, page 1
Dated 12-1-1825 - recorded 3-4-1826 St. Marys - Transcribed 12-31-1832
Sons - Seybert and Samuel
Daughters - Eleanor, Ann, Mary and Eliza
Executors - sons-in-law, John Murdock and John Pickrel
Signed - Thomas Scott
Witnesses - John Armstrong, Robert Bigger and Nancy (mark) Murdock
Codicil - dated 12-3-1825
States that sons Seybert and Samuel are not of age
Signed - Thomas Scott
Witnesses - John Armstrong, Robert Bigger and Christian Benner

JOSEPH D. WEBB - Will Book 1, page 4
Dated 11-16-1831 - Recorded 11-2-1852
Wife - Margaret - also to serve as Executrix
Sons - John, Rezin, William, Thomas and Elisha (none are of age)
Daughters - Elizabeth, Sally Ann, Tirzah and Amanda Ann
Signed - Joseph D. Webb
Witnesses - Timothy Green and John Webb

JOHN HENRY SCHARDELMANN - Will Book 1, page 6 (Will in German)
Dated 1-30-1834 - Recorded 4-20-1854
Wife - mentioned, but not named
Gives money to "my William at Cincinnati"
Signed - John Henry Schardelman
Witnesses - John Henry Henning, William Meines, Katharine Veichers,
                                              Margaretta Cladden

NANCY CARTER - Will Book 1, page 8
Dated 10-31-1825 - Recorded 5-10-1834
Half-brother - Simeon Lucas of Rockingham Co., Virginia
Second cousin - Anne Woods of Miami County, Ohio
Executor - Richard R. Barrington
Signed - Nancy (mark) Carter
Witnesses - John Armstrong, Martin (mark) Cleland and Sarah(mark)Cleland

JOANNA BISHOP - Will Book 1, page 10
Dated 11-21-1833 - Recorded 2-5-1835
Mentions Richard Bishop - no relationship given
Brothers - Jonathan Forbes, Eli Forbes and Asahel Forbes
               Bible to be given to brother, Asahel Forbes
Mentions orphan girl, Nancy and her children which was raised by Joanna
Signed - Joanna Bishop   Bishop
Witnesses - Joseph Rider and Elizabeth Hurlin

JACOBUS J. VAN NUYS - St. Marys - Will Book 1, page 13
Dated 3-28-1834 - Recorded 2-14-1835
Wife - Rachel Van Nuys
Sons - John, James and Peter
Daughter - Margaret, deceased
Grandsons - Stephen Armstrong, George Major and James Willis Major being
               heirs at law of Margaret, late daughter, deceased.
Executors - James Watson Riley and Peter M. Van Nuys
Signed - Jacobus J. Van Nuys

Witnesses - William M. Murdock and Caleb Major
Verbal Codicil dated 11-9-1834 - Deposition given 11-17-1834
    by Peter M. Van Nuys, further bequest regarding son, John
    Van Nuys - Witness: Obadiah Valentine

ALEXANDER SCOTT - Recovery Twp. - Will Book 1, page 21
Dated 8-13-1835 - Recorded 1-9-1836
Wife - Nancy
Nephew - Alexander Scott, Jr.
Signed - Alexander Scott
Witnesses - Ebenezer R. Grover, Richard Scott and Jesse Freeman

JONATHAN LONGWORTH - Will Book 1, page 23
Dated 12-26-1835 - Recorded 1-9-1836
Children - Thomas (eldest son), Margery, Jonathan, Samuel, Eliza, Jackson.
            All, except Thomas, are not of age
Executor and Guardian of Children - son, Thomas Longworth
Signed - J. Longworth
Witnesses - A. V. Medbery and Belitha Wilkins

WILLIAM FRISINGER - Oral Will - Will Book 1, page 26
Deposition dated 4-15-1836 - Recorded 10-8-1837
William Frisinger died 4-8-1836
Wife - mentioned, not named
Executor - Jacob Frisinger
Signed - John P. Davis and Joseph Sidenbender
Witnesses - Joseph Greer and B. F. Stroöder

JOHN S. ARBAUGH - Oral Will - Will Book 1, page 28
Dated 9-19-1836 - Recorded 5-6-1837
Mentions - Susan Simens and Rebecca Whitman of Pocahontas County, Va.
Mother - Susan Keenan
Brothers - Jacob Arbaugh and George Arbaugh
Deposition signed - James (mark) Schoonover and Samuel Arbaugh

CHARLES FREDERICK NEITER - Town of Branen - Will Book 1, page 30
Dated 10-7-1836 - Recorded 8-9-1837
Wife - Katharine Louisa
Children - mentioned, but not named
Executor - wife, Katharine Louisa Neiter and John Henry Nunan
Signed - Charles Frederick Neiter
Witnesses - David Catterlin and Johnn Bern'd Neunan

JONAS RICHARDSON - Will Book 1, page 32
Dated 12-8-1836 - Recorded 5-6-1837
Wife - Parmela - also to serve as Executrix
Mentions lawful heirs but does not name
Signed - Jonas Richardson
Witnesses - James Grant, John Sineson and Alexander Grant

JOSEPH TAUBELING (TABELING) - Will Book 1, page 35
Dated 12-23-1837 - Recorded 4-23-1838
Wife - Anna Katherine Elizabeth - also to serve as Executrix
Mentions land adjoining Frederick
Signed - Joseph (mark) Taubeling
Witnesses: C. H. Low and B. H. Kramer

JESSIE MILLS - Van Wert County - Will Book 1, page 37
Dated 5-14-1838 - Recorded 6-8-1838
Brothers - Siles Mills, Squire Mills and Isaac Mills
Sisters - Delila - also mentions her son Nathan Koon
          Betsey Allender - mentions her son James Mills
Executor - Michael Tippie
Signed - Jesse Mills
Witnesses - Peter Harter and Jacob Ross

A. F. WILLIAM BULLMAN - German Twp. - Will Book 1, page 39
Dated 8-1-1838 - Recorded 8-10-1838
Wife - Caroline, to arrive from Germany October next
Mentions 5 children, but does not name
Executor - Henry Hehemann
Guardian of Children - Henry Steinmyer
Signed - A. F. William (mark) Bullman
Witnesses - Franz Jos. Holzgrave, Johann Heinrich Kramer and Lucus
                                                      Henry Meyer

ABRAHAM LONG - Will Book 1, page 42
Dated 8-13-1838 - Recorded 9-1-1838
Father - Jacob Long - also to serve as Executor
Mother - Elizabeth Long
Mentions land in Allen County, Ohio
Signed - Abraham Long
Witnesses - Rich'd K. Barrington, Aaron C. Badgly and Ephram Mekoy

JOHN ARMSTRONG - Will Book 1, page 44
Dated 3-18-1838 - Recorded 9-1-1838
Wife - mentioned, but not named
Sons - David (deceased), John and Samuel
Daughters - Jane, Mary, Nancy, Sarah and Rebecca
Grandsons - John and David Armstrong, sons of David Armstrong, dec'd
Executors - sons, John and Samuel
Signed - John Armstrong
Witnesses - Samuel McKee, Sabert Scott and Thomas McKee

JOHN DEDERICK HERMAN UHLHORN - Minster - Will Book 1, page 47
Dated 8-28-1838 - Recorded 10-29-1838
Wife - mentioned, but not named
Mentions first children and last children, but does not name
Signed - John Dederick Herman Uhlhorn
Witnesses - Z. Gerd. Enkmann, I. H. Pelster, J. Henry Feldmann,
           John Rud. Tancke and John Bernd. Feldman

The following wills were abstracted from Will Book 1, found in the Probate Court at the court house at Celina. Pages on which the original record may be found are given in parenthesis. For the Mercer County, Ohio Will Abstracts 1832-1838 see the September 1967 issue of GATEWAY.

WRIGHT, David - dated 11-20-1839; recorded 4-13-1840. Wife, Elizabeth. Sons: Ethan, Aaron, William and Cyrus; the first three named are not of age. Daughters: Mary, Elizabeth, Abigail, Ann and Peggy Jane Wright; all are not of age. Mentions Owen Wright; David Wright; Ajolin(?) Wright; Rachel Wright, now Rachel Purdy; Sally Wright, now Sally Chaney; no relationship stated, but appear to be children-- see codicil. Mentions legacy coming from father's estate, father being late of Franklin Co., Ohio. Executor, David Work. Signed: David Wright. Witnesses: I. H. Banks and Wm. B. Hedges. Codicil dated 11-20-1839 mentions son, Owen Wright. Witnesses: Wm. B. Hedges and I. H. Banks. (52)

McCRISTY, Jesse - dated 9-23-1839; recorded 11-6-1839. Sons: oldest son, David J.; Charles T.; John M.; George W.; Moses L. and Elisha D.; states "if son Charles T. should return home." Daughters: Phebe Ann, Martha Jane, Polly L. (note: probably same as Mary, who is named in another place in will) and Nancy. Executor, Robert Wiley. Signed: Jesse McCristy. Witnesses: J. A. Godard and Wm. B. Hedges. (55)

RIEGAL, J. Michael and wife Elizabeth, born Gernert - dated 8-2-1838; recorded 12-1-1838. This is a double will, where everything was willed to each other. Signed: J. Michael (his mark) Riegal and Elizabeth (her mark) Riegal. Witnesses: Lewis Henry Meyer, John Berned Kirmann and John Henry Neuman. (note: in the recording of the will it states "Elizabeth widow of Michael Riegal, late of this county."). (59)

PENGEL, Henry - dated 8-1-1839; recorded 6-13-1840. Wife, Henryetta, also to serve as executrix. Signed: Henry Pengle. (62)

SCHEMMELL, Theodore Herman - dated 8-27-1839; recorded 11-5-1839. Sons: Edward Henry, oldest son; John Henry; Christopher; Antany; and Joseph. Daughter, Eliza- beth. Signed: Theodore Herman Schemmel. Witnesses: Clerment Herchfelt, H. Bucher, Gerherd H. Kizer and Henry Patle. (64)

HERKENSCOFF (HERCANCHOFF, HERKENSCHOFF), John Henry of Minster - dated 8-17-1839; recorded 11-4-1839. Wife, Harred Engel Sperker. Mentions mother-in-law, but does not name. Mentions children by first wife and children by present wife, but does not name. Signed: John Henry (his mark) Herkenschoff. Witnesses: Herman Henry Busch and Herman Henry Stives (or Stines). (66)

HOLDHEID, Bernard - dated (not given); recorded 11-6-1839. Sons: Oldest son, Bernard; and Gerherd. Daughter, Elizabeth Holdheide. Signed: Bernard Holdheide. Witnesses: Bernard Post, J. H. Niehting, John Schlamann, Geret Francis Billman.(68)

KRAMER, Bernard Henry of Minster - dated 2-12-1840; recorded 4-15-1840. Wife, Engel Kramer formerly Bordaging. Children, mentioned but not named. Signed: B. H. Kramer. Witnesses: Francis Holtgraven and Carl H. Low. (73)

HUTT, Ludwick of Minster - dated (month not given)-6-1839; recorded 4-15-1840. Wife, Adel Heit Hutt formerly Brent. Children, mentioned but not named. Signed: Ludwick Hutt. Witnesses: John M. Drees, Elard Albers and Francis Sprake. (75)

HICKMAN, John Frederick of Statlow Town - dated 11-2-1835; recorded 5-10-1840. Wife, Mary Elizabeth Herbey. Signed: John Frederick Hickman. Witnesses: John W. Roof and And. Luas. (77)

HOHTT, Margaretta of Minster - dated 9-3-1839; recorded 4-15-1840. Sons: Eldest son, John Henry; and Werner, not married. Daughters: Sally Alexandria and Sophia; both not married. Signed: Margaretta (her mark) Hohtt. Witnesses: John Fangman, Henry Hemesaeth(?) and Henry Pohlmeyer. (79)

SPROCK, John Bernard - dated 3-19-1840; recorded 11-12-1840. Present wife, Anna Maria Sprock, before marriage named Elsen. Children: Bern'd Henry; Hellen Mary; Margaretta Maria; Mary Elizabeth; Anna Maria; Gesina Maria, in Germany; Mary Engle, in Germany. Signed: J. B. Sprock. Witnesses: Charles H. Dickman, John M. Drees and Joseph Wendell. (81)

LUEHMAN (LUHMANN), Henry - dated (not given); recorded 4-15-1840. Wife, mentioned but not named. Brother-in-law, George F. Tichmann. Signed: Henry L. Luhmann. Witnesses: J. F. Knop and F. Ludewick Pohlman. (83)

SCHROEDER, Frederick of St. John - dated 8-22-1840; recorded 11-10-1840. Wife, mentioned but not named. Sons: Francis, Frederick and Clements. Daughters: Catharine Maria and Maria Anna Schroeder. Signed: John Frederick (his mark) Schroeder. Witnesses: Gerhard Holsen and Anton Sweinfroot. (85)

LEONARD, Patrick - dated (not given); recorded 11-13-1840. Mentions money due from Peter Erving, Esq. of Richmond, Wayne Co., Indiana. Mentions parents, but does not name. Cousin, Owein Magoverin. Sister, Anne, of Richmond. Signed: Patrick Leonard. Witnesses: John Brady, Michael McGive(?), Archbard Richardson.(87)

GOKE (GOCKE), Herman - dated 2-10-1840; recorded 11-11-1840. Sons: Gerd. Henery, Johann Dirk and Bernd Herman Goke. Signed: Herman Goke. Witnesses: John D. Ahlerge and Henry Schiper. (89)

ELDER, William of Wilshire twp., Van Wert County - dated 5-18-1841; recorded 7-20-1841. Brother, Samuel Elder. Mentions Frederick Roop. Signed: William Elder. Witnesses: Frederick Roop and John W. Pearce. (91)

DICKMAN, Carl H. - dated 7-12-1841; recorded 9-11-1841. Wife, Maria Angela, also to serve as executrix. Signed: C. H. Dickman. Witnesses: John M. Drees, Antone Wendln and Bernerd Bungelman. (92)

WELLMANN, Henrietta - (German will) - dated 9-17-1841; recorded 11-20-1841. Refers to herself as Henrietta Dobbeling widow(?) of Herman Fredrick Wellman. Daughter, Sophia Margaret Wellman. Mentions Herman Fredrick Wellman and Heinrich Tengel. Signed: Henrietta Dobbeling (her mark) Wellmann. Witnesses: C. F. Tolgenkearst and John Masloh. (93)

SMART, Francis - dated 9-28-1841; recorded 11-24-1841. Wife, Judith, also to serve as Executrix. Son, Charles Smart. Daughters: Judith Wilbin and Almura Cannin. Signed: Francis Smart. Witnesses: Ebenezer Hull and Robert Linzee. (94)

BEVINGTON, Henry - Oral Will - dated 9-11-1841; recorded 11-24-1841. Wife, Rachael. Witnesses: W. B. Hedtles, Robt. Wiley and I. K. Evans. (96)

FRIBLEY, Jerome - dated 11-10-1841; recorded 11-18-1841. All of estate to Phebe Everet. to whom testator is engaged in a marriage contract. Executor, Doctor Lawrence Fulton. Signed: Jerome (his mark) Bribley. Witnesses: Joseph Greer, Evan Gilespie. (97)

DELANY, Isaac - dated 6-11-1841; recorded 9-7-1841. Wife and two sons, mentioned but not named. Signed: Isaac (his mark) Delany. Witnesses: Duke Hill, Benjamin Hill and Thomas Dison. (99)

ROSS, John - dated 2-11-1842; recorded 3-2-1842. Wife, Polly Ross, to have farm where now live for natural life, being 160 acres lying in Mercer and Van Wert Counties. Children, mentioned but not named. Executors: wife, Polly and John F. Torulinder(?). Wife, Polly to serve as guardian of minor children unless she marries again. Signed: John (his mark) Ross. Witnesses: Cyrenus Elliott and George W. Shelden. (100)

ROEBUCK, Greenley - dated 12-7-1841; recorded 3-2-1842. Wife, Parley Ann, also to serve as executrix. Signed: Greenley (his mark) Roebuck. Witnesses: Asa Presher (or Presho), James Harner and William Hamilton. (103)

LOW, Carl H. of Minster - dated 1-4-1842; recorded 6-22-1842. Wife, Mary Elizabeth Post. Two children: Ann Maria Elizabeth and Katharine Louisa. Signed: C. H. Low. Witnesses: John H. Schemmel and I. B. Fredericks. (104)

STROEFER, William - dated 11-3-1842 Minster; recorded 6-23-1842. Will made at house of Diedrick Wessels. All property to Diedrick and Theadore Wessel. Money to church for mass. Money to brother and sister (not named). Power of Attorney to Theadore Wessel. Signed: William (his mark) Stroefer. Witnesses: Henry Klavalage, Theadore Wessel and John Diederick Ahlaz. (106)

EICH, John of Minster - dated 10-18-1841; recorded 6-23-1842. Wife, Anna Maria Eich born Fleckenstein. Mentions house and lot 44 St. Marys. Signed: Jonnes Eich. Witnesses: Atono Haverback and Francis Schreder. (107)

SCHROEDER, Antone - dated (not given); recorded 9-6-1842. Wife (not named) of brother, Francis Wm. Schroeder and her children to have lot 9 in Minster. Sister, Maria and brother-in-law, Henry Kuostman. Signed: Antone (his mark) Schroeder. Witnesses: Wm. Henry Sprake, Henry Wilson, Eilard Albers. (108)

KIERTSCHHOFF, John Arnt of German twp. - dated (not given); recorded 10-1-1842. To friend, John Herman, Fernhold, also to serve as executor and administrator of estate. To sister, Greel Aeleheit Egeborn Kierchhoff and her heirs. Signed: John Arn (his mark) Kierchhoff. Witness: William Finke. Johann Gerhard Simmerman. (109)

SCHUMÖLLER, Henry of German twp. - dated 7-3-1842; recorded 9-6-1842. Wife, Mary Alice. Child, Bernadiner Elisabeth Schumöller, not of age. Father-in-law, John B. Stahman. Executor and guardian of daughter; father-in-law, John Bernard Stokman. Signed: Henry (his mark) Schumöller. Witnesses: J. H. Steinman, Christap Henry Richler and Bernard Brugen Schriut. (110)

WATKINS, Charles - dated 12-12-1842; recorded 4-14-1843. Wife, Jane. Daughter, Jane Anna. Signed; Charles (his mark) Watkins. Witnesses: Charles Route and Pe. Smith. (112)

VINSON, Curthbert - dated 5-12-1841; recorded 4-14-1843. Sister of testator's departed wife, Esther Lewis, to have farm and lot in St. Marys. Sons: James S., William A. and Malachi Vinson. Mentions "watch testator's deceased son (not named) gave to estator's daughter, Clarissa, should be given to her according to said gift." Money to missions of M. E. Church. Mentions unmarried daughters, but names no daughters except Clarissa. Executors: son, Malachi Vinson and son-in-law, Wm. Hollingsworth. Signed: Curthbert (his mark) Vinson. Witnesses: Franklin Linzee and Stacy Taylor. (113)

COLLINS, Andrew - dated (not given) recorded 4-14-1843. Mentions that his farm is nearly useless to his heirs by the reservoir bank passing through it. Wife, Martha. Sons: Charles Otto Collins; Alfred Collins, now absent; Lewis Collins, not of age; and John Collins, not of age. Daughter, Rachael Anne Collins. To John Nottingham for labor he performed, small sum. Witnesses: Aaron C. Badgeley and George (his mark) Crow. (115)

WATTS, James - dated 1-22-1843; recorded 5-31-1843. Wife, Charity. Mentions minor children, but does not name except for son, John S. Watts who may or may not be a minor. Nicholas P. Watts to receive east fractional land being 77 acres owned by testator in Section 25, Township 4 South, Range 3 East owned by testator, to discharge claim he holds against testator as his guardian. Executor, William Hamilton. Guardian of minor children, Justin Hamilton. Signed: James Watts. Witnesses: John M. Toland and William Hussey. (117)

HANSON, Samuel - dated 3-2-1843; recorded 5-5-1843. Wife, Catharine. Children: Fletcher Hanson, Sanford Hanson, Newton Hanson, Harriet Hanson, Raper Hanson, Maria Hanson, Rufus Hanson and any children born hereafter. Son, Wesley Hanson, dec'd. Mentions other children, but does not name. Executor, Justin Hamilton. Signed: Samuel Hanson. Witnesses: George W. Shepherd, and Michael Harmer. (119)

ROEBUCK, Benjamin - dated 2-11-1842; recorded (month and day not given) 1843. Wife, Elizabeth. Mentions minor children, daughter and all my children; but does not name except for sons serving as executors. Executors: wife, Elizabeth and sons, Lorenzo and James. Signed: Benjamin Roebuck. Witnesses: William Hamilton, William A. Johns and Samuel C. Barber. (121)

ELLIS, William - dated 7-25-1844; recorded 12-22-1844. Wife, Hannah, also to serve as executrix. Children mentioned but not named; four youngest to be made equal with what given older ones. Signed: William Ellis. Witnesses: William Beauchamp and John Green. (125)

BOWLTON, John - dated 9-19-1844; recorded 5-9-1845. Wife, Magdelina Boulton. Sons: Philip, James, John and Lewis Bolton. Daughters: Esther Reder, Christina Bowlton, Sally Bolton, Lydia Boulton and Anna Bolton. Mentions money coming from estate of testator's deceased father (not named). Executor; son, Lewis Boulton. Signed: John (hismark) Bolton. Witnesses: Wm. Hamilton and John Milner. (127)

TOMLINSON, John of Union twp. - dated 10-7-1839; recorded (not given-1845 or 1846). Wife, Rebecca, land in Mercer and Van Wert Counties. Sons: Joseph Foster, James, John F., Lewis F. and Jesse. Daughters: Mary Ross; Nancy Thomas, dec'd, her heirs; Rachel Smith, dec'd, her heirs. Son, John F. to serve as guardian of testator's sons, James and Joseph F. Executors: son, John F. Tomlinson and William Hamilton. Signed: John Tomlinson. Witnesses: William Hamilton and John Heath. Deposition given 11-25-1879 by John F. Tomlinson stating that all personal property in estate was exhausted in settlement of estate before death of widow. (129)

FOGALSANG, Fredrick Henry - dated 9-4-1836; recorded 9-23-1846. Wife, Sophia Margarette, also to serve as executrix. Grandson, Fredrick Henry Fogalsang, a minor with Lewis Henry Meyer to serve as his guardian. Signed: Fredrick H. Fogalsang. Witnesses: Bernard Koop and John Fredrick Soller. (130)

STEPHENSON, Samuel - dated 2-3-1845; recorded Sept. 1845. Wife, Catharine. Daughter, Charlotte Johnston. Bequeaths to John and Elizabeth Tilton, minor heirs of Sylvester and Catharine Tilton; to Elizabeth Herchel; to Ann Brown; no relation-ships, if any, stated. Silas Stephenson to have Family Bible. Balance of money from estate to be divided between John, Philip, Silas and Hiram Stephenson. Executors: Philip and Silas Stephenson. Signed: Samuel Stephenson. Witnesses: John S. Houston and John Stephenson. (133)

UPHOUSE, Henry of German twp. - dated 4-1-1839; recorded Sept. 1845. Wife, Mary Elizabeth, also to serve as executrix. Signed: Henry Uphouse. Witnesses: John B. Behmer and David Catterlin. (135)

FISHER, John of Liberty twp. - dated 12-25-1843; recorded Sept. 1845. Wife, Ann. Sons: William, Peter and Anthony More. Daughters(?): Matilda, Mary Jane and Sarah Ellen. Mentions child yet unborn. Signed: John Fisher. Witnesses: Isaac M. Price and Peter Fisher. (137)

SPROCK, Ann Maria born Elsen of Minster - dated 3-19-1840; recorded Sept. 1845. Step-daughter, Margaretta Maria Böhner born Sprock, who lives with testatrix to pay to her brothers and sisters: brother, Bernard Henry Sprock; sister, Hellen Maria Kruse born Sprock; sister, Maria Elizabeth Wehlman born Sprock; half-sister, Ann Maria Sprock; and to Martha Maria Bahmer born Sprock. Signed: Ann Maria (her mark) Sprock. Witnesses: John M. Drees, John Henry Uendler and Carl H. Dickman.(138)

CAMMON (CAMMON), John C. Wm. of New Bremen - dated 9-23-1840; recorded Sept. 1846. Wife, mentioned but not named. Son, Fredrick August. Daughter, Mary Louise. Signed: John C. W. Cammon. Witnesses: I. F. Bösche and G. Kleforth. (139)

BACHER, Philip of German twp. - dated 10-23-1843; recorded Sept. 1846. Wife, mentioned but not named, at her death farm to go to Jacob Bacher and his heirs. Executor, Jacob Bacher. Signed: Philip Bacher. Witnesses: Charles Böesel and August Wagner. (141)

BROUN, Margaret - dated 7-24-1845; recorded Sept. 1846. Sons: Joseph and Abram Broun. Daughter, Elizabeth Beech. Personal property to Amos and Margaret Harp. Signed: Margaret (her mark) Broun. Witnesses: Wm. B. Hedges and David Work. (143)

KING, Josias of Blackcreek twp. - dated (not given); recorded Sept. 1846. Wife, Elizabeth. Children, mentioned but not named. Executors: Absalom Brey and Jesse King. Signed: Josias King. Witnesses: William R. Shlater and Peter Shlater.(145)

WEICHMAN, Joseph of German twp. - dated 4-16-1842; recorded Nov. 1846. Wife, Elizabeth Weichman maiden name Sprock, also to serve as executrix. Testator owned land in Michigan. Signed: Joseph Weichman. Witnesses: I. H. Stenman and Clennus Fralling. (146)

CAMPBELL, Jesse Jr. - dated 10-6-1843; recorded 6-1-1847. Wife, Mary Campbell, also to serve as executrix. Signed: Jesse Campbell Jr. Witnesses: John G. Blake and John Miller. (148)

GANNON, Fredrick - dated 3-26-1846; recorded 6-1-1847. Wife, Elizabeth. Son, Romanias. Daughters: Mary. Sarah Eliza and Emily. Executors: wife, Elizabeth and son, Romanias. Signed: Frederick Gannon. Witnesses: Isaac M. Price, Michael Helworth and William Fetters. (150)

UPDUYKE, Smith - dated 3-6-1847; recorded 6-1-1847. Wife, Sarah. Sons: Jacob W., Isaac and Green. Signed: S. G. Updike. Witnesses: John R. Webb, Wm. Tullis and George Randaburgh. (151)

PERKINS, Simon of Warren, Trumbull Co., Ohio - dated 4-20-1844; recorded Trumbull Co. 10-27-1846; recorded Mercer Co. 7-14-1847. Wife, Nancy. All children except son, Henry have already received $5000.00 each and Henry when he reaches 24 years is to receive same. Owned land in Warren and Howland in Trumbull Co. and in Cleveland, Cuyahoga Co., Ohio. Executors: sons, Simon, Joseph and Jacob Perkins and nephew, Frederick Kinsman. Signed: Simon Perkins. Witnesses: Thomas D. Webb, Henry Lane and Charles White. (153)

SEWALL, Frederick - dated 6-29-1841; recorded 10-12-1848. Wife, Mary. Sons, Frederick and Henry. Executor, Barnard Romar. Signed: Fréderick (his mark) Sewall. Witnesses: Wm. Nichols and Richard (his mark) Byerly. (159)

MONEY, William - dated 7-10-1847; recorded 9-28-1847. Wife, Anna, also to serve as executrix. Signed: William (his mark) Money. Witnesses: Jacob I. Herrol and Robert Scott. (161)

COIL, John - dated 8-18-1848; recorded 10-11-1848. Wife, Hester Ann. Son, Jeremiah, not of age. Five daughters, Caroline, Martha Jane, Lusinda, Susan and Elizabeth. Executor; brother-in-law, Thomas Parrott. Signed: John (his mark) Coil. Witnesses: Jeremiah Coil, James T. Heath and Isaac H. Freyer. (163)

COIL, Andrew - dated 8-10-1848; recorded 10-11-1848. Wife, mentioned but not named. Son, John. Daughters: Nancy; 2nd dau., Elizabet, land in Van Wert Co.; 3rd dau., Amelia. Signed: Andrew (his mark) Coil. Witnesses: Justin Hamilton, James T. Heath and Thomas Parrott. (165)

HUIT, Nathaniel - dated 11-21-1847; recorded 11-12-1848. Wife, Elizabeth. Daughters: Mary McCoy (Mecoy) and Deborah Huit. Son, Smith Huit. Mentions Elisha and John Huit, possibly sons. Mentions Levi Huit, Elizabeth Potts, Jefferson Huit and Nathan Huit, possibly children. Signed: Nathaniel (his mark) Huit. Witnesses: James Gray, Joseph H. Robbins and Joseph H. Robbins Jr. (167)

POTTER, Thomas - native of Great Britian but resident of United States - dated 9-22-1845; recorded 6-6-1848. Wife, Esther. Sons: Henry and William Potter. Daughter, Hannah. Mentions children of his first wife, but does not name. Executors: Joshua D. Wright and son, William Potter. Signed: Thomas Potter. Witnesses: Joshua D. Wright and Miles V. Lance. (169)

BROWN, James H. - dated 10-27-1848; recorded 1-17-1849. Wife, Jane. Children, mentioned but not named except for son, James Thomas who is a cripple. Grandson, Caleb, son of daughter, Elizabeth P. Signed: James H. (his mark) Brown. Witnesses: Justin Hamilton and John H. Harbison. (172)

LINZEE, Robert of Jefferson twp. - dated 11-23-1848; recorded 3-15-1849. Children: Caroline, Ruth and Andrew Jackson Linzee. Nephew, Robert Linzee, who resides with family. Signed: Robert Linzee. Witnesses: Wm. Hunter and Lyman Dibble. (175)

LONG, John - dated 3-10-1848; recorded 6-16-1849. Wife, Susan. Sons: eldest, Jacob Long; 2nd son, Johnathan Long; 3rd son, David Long; 4th son, Aaron Long. To five heirs of Aliscander Piper, 87 acres Section 22 Liberty twp. Also mentions Mairum Iltere(?) and Charles Kelley. Executor; son, Jacob. Signed: John Long. Witnesses: Charles Hammel, John Hammel and Philip Waltman. (177)

VAN GUNDY, John - dated 1-24-1847; recorded 7-6-1849. Wife, Margaret. Heirs: Samuel Van Gundy, Jane Shepherd, Washington Van Gundy, Branson Van Gundy, Joshua Van Gundy, Elizabeth Van Gundy, Huldah Van Gundy, Elbe Van Gundy, Elmore Van Gundy, and John Jefferson Van Gundy. Executors: Wife, Margaret and son Washington. Signed: John (his mark) Van Gundy. Witnesses: Michael Marner and Daniel Murlin. (180)

GRAY (GREY), David - dated 10-9-1848; recorded 7-6-1849. Wife, Sarah. Children: Deborah Munsell, Catharine Faulkner, Samuel T. Gray, Joseph Gray, Elizabeth Gray, Mary Richardson, Ann Gray and Collins Gray; Collins not of age. Two grandchildren: Caroline and Philina Gray. Executors: wife, Sarah and son, Joseph. Signed: David Gray. Witnesses: Jacob Frank and Hiram Frank. (182)

COLLINS, Solomon of Gibson twp. - dated 5-12-1849; recorded 10-15-1849. Wife, Nancy. Oldest son, Major R. Collins. Daughter, Elner Hastings. To Phelise Jane, F. Bekora and Sara Ann E. W. Collins, relationship not stated, may be daughters. Sons, John F. and Solomon J. Collins. Executors: wife, Nancy and Waitman Hastings. Signed: Solomon Collins. Witnesses: David Hays and Robert Hunter. (184)

HEMMELGARD, John Henry - dated 4-28-1849; recorded 10-15-1849. Wife, mentioned but not named. Eldest son, John Theodore, also to serve as executor and to provide for his minor brothers and sisters, not named. Signed: John Henry Hemmelgard. Witnesses: Henry Beckman and Bernard Knapke. (186)

WESBROOK, Joseph of Minster - German will - dated 2-10-1842; recorded Nov. 1849. Wife, Maria Anna. Signed: Joseph Wesbrook. Witnesses: John B. Fredericks and B. H. Mese. (187)

The following records were taken from Death Record 1 located in the Probate Court of the court house at Celina. Page on which original record may be found is given in parenthesis. Residence is the same as place of death unless stated. This list contains only those persons 40 years of age and over. Abbreviations used: d=died; a=age; m=married; s=single; w=widow or widower; pd=place of death; pb=place of birth; r=residence.

BRANDSTELLER, Annie C. - d 7-5-1867; a 51-2-19; m; pd Mercer Co.; pb Hermersdorf G(ermany). (2)

KEITH, Edward - d July 1867; a 88y; m; pd Carthagena; pb Georgia. (2)

KEMPER, Henry - d 7-21-1867; a 63-5-7;m; pd Carthagena; pb Melle, Han. (2)

HERING, Judith - d 7-28-1867; a 43; s; pd Grunwald, Con.; pb Wurtunburg. (2)

KALKHOFF, Henry - d 7-8-1867; a 61y; s; pd St Johns; pb Prussia. (2)

LANFERSNEILER, Mary - d 8-10-1867; a 59y; m; pd St Johns; pb Switzerland. (2)

DURINGER, Anthony - d 8-28-1867; a 86y; w; pd St Wendelin; pb Europe. (2)

RICHARDS, Doran - d 9-6-1867; a 54y; m; pc Dublin twp.; pb Ireland. (2)

TANNER, Thomas - d 10-2-1867; a 73-5-20; m; pd Mercer Co.; pb S. Carolina; r Butler twp. (2)

PETRO, Asa J. - d 10-18-1867; a 59-6-8; m; pd Dublin twp.; pb Greene Co., O. (2)

STUDER, Joseph - d 10-27-1867; a 52y 10m; m; pd St Peterburg; pb France. (2)

SCHOSTER, Herman - d 10-9-1867; a 42y; m; pd Philothia; pb Alrenburg. (2)

RAMSSING, Adel - 11-3-1867; a 42y; m; pd St Johns; pb Holland. (2)

MÖLLERS, Franz Anton - d 12-30-1867; a 75y; m; pd St Rose; pb Prussia. (2)

WIENERS, Mary - d 12-13-1867; a 63-3-5; m; pd Philothia; pb Alrenburg. (2)

OVERMAN, Maria - d 12-17-1867; a 47y; m; pd Carthagena; pb-------. (2)

BORAFF, Michael - d 1-16-1868; a 88-7-27; w; pd Dublin twp.; pb Virginia. (2)

HAMPTON, Betsy - d 1-14-1868; a 100y; w; pd Granville twp.; pb----. (4)

WRIGHT, Eber - d 2-15-1868; a 56y; m; pd Cartagena; pb S. Carolina; parents, Geo P. and Sarah Wright. (4)

DEAL, Elizabeth - d 2-13-1868; a 71y 20m; w; pd Dublin twp.; pb Penn. (4)

WRIGHT, Sylva - d 2-16-1868; a 55-11-22; m; pd Liberty twp.; pb Maine. (4)

FELDHEISER, Johan - d 2-29-1868; a 47y; 2m; w; pd Celina; pb Germany. (4)

STEINLAGE, Mary - d 3-18-1868; a 55y; w; pd St Henry; pb Germany. (4)

STUCKE, Francesca - d 12-11-1867; a 40y; m; pd St Johns; pb Germany. (4)

SPALLMAN, Mary - d 9-5-1867; a 42; m; pd Philothia; pb Prussia. (4)

KEUTCH, Jacob - d 6-21-1868; a 44-5-1; m; pd Liberty twp.; pb France. (4)

RHEIDLER, Charles - d 5-16-1868; a 65y 3m; m; pd Butler twp.; pb Germany. (4)

DOCK, Frederick - d 6-29-1868; a 75y; m; pd Washington twp.; pb Germany. (4)

WEBBER, John - d 6-7-1868; a 56y; w; pd St Johns; pb Bavaria. (4)

BERGEMAN, Henry - d 7-3-1868; a 95y; w; pd St Johns; pb Hanover. (4)

STUDER, Joseph - d 10-28-1867; a 53y; m; pd Recovery twp.; pb France; father, Joseph Studer. (4)

BETZ, John - d 1-20-1868; a 82y; m; pd Washington twp.; pb-----. (4)

DIEBOLD, John - d 3-12-1868; a 45y; m; pd Recovery twp.; pb Germany. (4)

SCRANTON, Laura - d 4-24-1868; a 84y; w; pd Gibson twp.; pb Connecticut. (4)

ISHER, David - d 5-20-1868; a 69-9-6; m; pc Jefferson twp.; pb-----. (6)

MAYER, Jacob - d 11-25-1868; a 57-5-10; m; pd Hopewell twp.; pb Obenscheffhusen, Baden. (6)

ININGER, John - d 12-1-1868; a 67y 10d; m; pd Washington twp; pb Midesheim, France. (6)

HILLER, John - d 3-10-1869; a 63-10-2; m; pd Adams Co., Ind.; pb Germany. (6)
FELDHAUS, Frederick - d 4-24-1869; a 54-8-8; m; pd Mercer Co.; pb Germany. (6)
MAUSER, Abraham - d 6-25-1869; a 67y; m; pd Jay Co., Ind.; pb Penn. (6)
WUNDERLE, Anna M. - d 3-26-1869; a 40y; m; pd St. Henry; pb-----. (6)
KÜHNE, Bernard - d 10-10-1868; a 48y;m; pd St Henry; pb Europe. (6)
DESS, Joseph - d 12-5-1868; a 58y; m; pd St Henry; pb Europe. (6)
HEMELGARN, Anna M. - 3 12-8-1868; a 61y; m; pd St Henry; pb England. (6)
KNOX, Samuel - d 5-13-1869; a 40y; m; pd Mercer Co., O.; pb Starke Co. (6)
BERGMAN, Henry - 8-3-1868; a 49y; m; pd St Henry; pb Germany. (6)
KNOX, Squire - d 3-11-1869; a 69y; m; pd Mercer Co.; pb Tenn.; r Carthagena. (6)
AKERS, Anna E. - d 11-15-1868; a 67-9-1; w; pd Carthagena; pb Tenn. (6)
WEBER, John - d 6-7-1868; a 56y; w; pd St Johns; pb Europe. (6)
BERGMAN, Henry - d 7-3-1868; a 95y; w; pd St Johns; pb Hanover. (6)
DEPPEN, Joseph - d 10-1-1868; a 42y; m; pd St Johns; pb Hanover. (6)
SCHROEDER, Francis - d 11-9-1868; a 47y; m; pd St Johns; pb Hanover. (6)
SCHWIEDERMAN, Mary - d 12-23-1868; a 55y; w; pd St Sebastian; pb Hanover. (6)
MEYER, Catharine - d 11-13-1868; a 69-10-7; pd Blackcreek twp.; pb Germany. (8)
RECKER, Elizabeth - d 11-2-1868; a 68y; pd Jefferson twp.; pb Germany. (8)
BERG, John - d 8-21-1869; a 51y; m pd Dublin twp.; pb Dublin twp.; parents,
    Elijah and Mary Birg. (8)
HAUZER, William - d 12-7-1869; a 89-2-22; m; pd Union twp.; pb Delaware. (8)
ROSABONE, Nancy - d 1-10-1870; a 44-4-8-; m; pd Union twp.; pb Mercer Co. (8)
ROSS, A. L. - d 8-17-1869; a 45y; s; pd Union twp.; pb Ky. (8)
SHEARER, Jacob - d 11-17-1869; a 69y; m; pd Union twp.; pb Penn. (8)
KEISER, Rebecca - d 9-9-1869; a 79y; w; pd Marion twp.; pb Germany. (8)
REICHERL, Kelleau - d 10-6-1869; a 42y 7m; s; pd Marion twp.; pb Germany. (8)
SMITH, Breggton - d 10-7-1869; a 40y; s; pd Marion twp.; pb Germany. (8)
LECHEITER, Joseph - d 9-10-1869; a 63y 3m; w; pd Marion twp.; pb Germany. (8)
PAPPENBROCK, Henry - d 8-28-1869; a 49y 6m; m; pd Marion twp.; pb Germany. (8)
HALLERMAN, Henry - d 4-17-1870; a 79y; pd Marion twp.; pb Germany. (8)
SCHWEGMAN, Elizabeth - d 1-10-1869; a 70y; w; pd Marion twp.; pb Germany. (10)
ORDING, Gerherd - d 1-15-1870; a 60y 1m; m; pd Marion twp.; pb Germany; parents,
    Herman and Mary Myer. (10)
GARLACH, Feith - d 11-12-1869; a 60y 2m; m; pd Marion twp.; pb Germany. (10)
SEITZ, Max - d 11-17-1869; a 44y 1m; w; pd Marion twp.; pb Germany; parents,
    Matthias and mary Seitz. (10)
RAUBY, Catherine - d 4-1-1870; a 67y; m; pd Marion twp.; pb Germany; parents,
    Henry and Catherine Anthony. (10)
STAMMAN, Wilhelm - d 3-1-1870 a 80y; m; pd Marion twp.; pb Germany. (10)
STICKLEBROOK, John - 3 Sept. 1869; a 65y; s; pd Marion twp.; pb Germany. (10)
DEDICK, Clarke -d5-6-1869; a 67y; m; pd Recovery twp.; pb Germany. (10)
PATENT, James - d 2-23-1870; a 55y; m; pd Recovery twp.; pb Ireland. (10)
CAROLL, Laura - d 11-22-1869; a 48-3-13; m;; pd Center twp.; pb Hardin Co., Ky.;
    parents, James and Sybil Drury. (10)
CAROLL, William - d 3-11-1870; a 49y m; m; pd Center twp.; pb Miami Co., O.;
    mother, Rosetta Caroll. (10)
DIBBLE, Lyman - d 7-4-1869; a 65-4-22; m; pd Center twp.; pb Essex Co., N.Y.;
    parents, Levi and Rebecca Dibble.
GARWICK, Daniel - d 2-5-1870; a 58y 8m; m; pd Center twp.; pb York Co., Penn.;
    parents, M. and E. Garwick. (10)

MAY, Jacob - d 9-4-1869; a 60-7-3; m; pd Blackcreek twp.; pb same. (10)
SLOSSER, Jacob - d 9-12-1869; a 90-8-18; m; pd Blackcreek twp.; pb same.
        parents, E. and Elizabeth Slosser. (10)
MOLFE, Henry - d 1-15-1870; a 54-9-10; m; pd Blackcreek twp.; pb same. (10)
JACOBS, Annie M. - d 11-23-1870; a 53y 11m; m; pd Granville twp.; pb Germany. (12)
REUGERS, Mary A. - d 12-13-1869; a 65-1-1; m; pd Granville twp.; pb Germany, (12)
SEIFERMAN, Caroline - d 8-21-1869; a 67-1-1; m; pd Granville twp.; pb Germany. (12)
TOBE, Anna - d 10-10-1869; a 45y 3m; m; pd Granville twp.; pb Germany. (12)
CARDIER, Christian - d 1-23-1870 a 51y 12d; w; pd Washington twp.; pb Europe. (12)
TUERWERK, Christian - d 2-13-1870; a 53-3-23; m; pd Washington twp.; pb Europe.(12)
GIBSON, Mary - d 2-13-1870; a 40y; m; pd Washington twp.; pb Gallia Co. O. (12)
KENNARD, Ezra - d 9-17-1869; a 41-8-9; m; pd Washington twp.; pb Perry Co., O. (12)
PORTERFIELD, William - d 5-8-1870; a 73y 4m; m; pd Washington twp.; pb Ireland.(12)
ROUH, Ignathus - d 5-2-1869; a 54-3-1; m; pd Washington twp.; pb Ireland. (12)
WISHON, phebe - d 10-19-1879; a 64-5-18; w; pd Washington twp.; pb Virginia. (12)
BALLINGER, John - d----1869; a 60y; s; pd Infirmry; pb-----. (12)
BALLINGER, Henry - d----1869; a 70y; s; pd Infirmry; pb------. (12)
BALLOWMEYER, Cath. - d Jan 1870; a 95y; s; pd Infirmry; pb------. (12)
CONNER, Rebecca - d Apr 1869; a 70y; w; pd Infirmry; pb--------. (12)
CRAIG, Samuel - d 2-12-1870; a 46y 7m; m; pd Jefferson twp.; pb Darke Co., O.;
        parents Seymour and Sarah Craig. (12)
CRAIG, Merinda - d 2-23-1870; a 40-2-21; w; pd Jefferson twp.; pb Darke Co., O.;
        parents, Joseph and Catharine Brandon. (12)
CRAIG, Elizabeth - d 8-20-1869; a 62-1-8; w; pd Jefferson twp.; pb Virginia;
        parents, Daniel_____ and Patience_____. (12)
HUNTER, Annie - d 3-21-1870; a 40y; s; pd Infirmry; pb Penn. (12)
ELLIOT, Bernard - d 3-3-1870; a 43y 24d; w; pd Jefferson twp.; pb Darke Co., O.(12)
ELLIOT, Sophia A. - d 2-19-1870; a 43y 24d; m; pd Jefferson twp.; pb Miami Co., O.
        (12)
MORGAN, James - d 6-23-1869; a 50y; s; pd Jefferson twp.; pb Ireland. (14)
ORR, Jackson - d 12-28-1869; a 52y; m; pd Celina, O.; pb-------. (14)
RILEY, James Watson - d 1-1-1870; a 66y 10m; m; pd Jefferson twp.; pb Middletown,
        Ct.; parents, James and Phebe Riley. (14)
SIMMONS, Mary - d 12-5-1869; a 65y; m; pd Celina; pb N.J.; father, John A. ___. (14)
GARVER, Mary - d 12-7-1869; a 67y 7m; m; pd Franklin twp.; pb Germany. (14)
MUTER, Sarah - d 3-7-1870; a 78y; w; pd Franklin twp.; pb England. (14)
WIRE, Maria - d 4-5-1870; a 57y 4m; m; pd Hopewell twp.; pb same. (14)
FREITMAN, Geo. - d 7-31-1869; a 75y; m; pd Gibson twp.; pb Germany. (14)
HAYS, Catharine - d 3-4-1870; a 69y;m; pd Gibson twp.; pb Penn. (14)
JACKSON, John - d 12-30-1869; a 69y; m; pd Gibson twp.; pb Ky.; parents, John
        Jackson and Bethany Ragan. (14)
KELLER, S. R. - d 9-13-1869; a 52y; m; pd Gibson twp.; pb Penn.; parents, John
        and Sarah Keller. (14)
REOMEOR. Sarah Ann - d 4-24-1870; a 66y; m; pd Gibson twp.; pb Penn. (14)

113

The following records were found in the office of the Probate Court at the court house in Celina. Abbreviations are as follows: Civil Docket:A=cdA; Administration Docket (not numbered or lettered)=ad; page=p.

ADNEY, Barbary - 1849, ad-p421
BARRETT, Bridget aged 13 years on 23 Dec. 1846 - 1847. ad-p183
BEDDINGHOUSE, Henry, Anna M., Mary K., and Bernard - 1841, cdA-p114
BECKWITH, Emily - 1845. cdA-p167
BERNER, John Herman and Dorathy, heirs of Christian Berner - 1838. ad-p24; cdA-p70
BERNHARD, Catharine and Jacob - 1850. ad-p478
BIGGER, Maria Jane - 1841. cdA-p113
BLOCK, Carl aged 18 yrs., Henry aged 14 yrs., Herman aged 6 yrs., heirs of Henry
     Block - 1847. ad-p123
BOLTON, Lydia and Anna - 1846. ad-p170
BONEFIELD, Abel aged 17 yrs., Eliza aged 15 yrs. and Caroline aged 13 yrs. - 1850
     ad-p486
BRIO, Maria and George - 1846. ad-p178
BUCKER, Heirs of J. Dederick - 1842. ad-p68
BULLENBAUGH, Heirs of Peter - 1843. ad-p79
BURRIS, Alexander Walker, heir of Martin and Charity Burris - 1849. ad-p421
CATTERLIN, Hamilton, solomon and John, heirs and children of David Catterlin - 1839.
     ad-p28,49
CHAPMAN, Calvin Alpheus, Maria aged 14 yrs. on 15 March 1847, heirs of Reeve
     Chapman - 1847. ad-p182
COIL, William and Elizabeth Jane - 1848. ad-p189,387
COUNTERMAN, Derastus - 1844. ad-p159
COX, Nancy aged 14 yrs. - 1849. ad-p418
CROCKET, James R., Mary Anne and John W. - 1845. ad-p162, 164
EICHAR, John Alexander, Geo. W. and Henry - 1850. ad-p476
ELLIS, Phillip - 1850. ad-p477
FEOTER. Mocjp;as - 1849. ad-p194,402
FISHER, Silas, Anthony, John H., Mary Jane and Sarah Ellen - 1844. ad-p158
GAGLE, Matthias and William - 1844. ad-p156
GREY, Caroline Lovisa and Sarah Philena - 1850. ad-p488
GREY, Wm Collins - 1849. ad-p195,405
GUY, Harrison and Martha - 1840. ad-p155; cdA-p85
HALL, Isreal - 1850. ad-p476
HAMMEN, Michael and others - 1849. ad-p460
HARKENHOFF, Heirs of - 1841. ad-p59; cdA-p367
HEATH, Levina aged 6 yrs., Nancy T. aged 4 yrs., Anna Jane and John - 1849.
     ad-p195,196,406,407,486
HENRICH (HEINRICH), Paul, Gertrude, Dorothy, Catharine and John - 1849. ad-p197,411
HINES, Phillip aged 18 yrs., Anna aged 8 yrs. and Peter aged 4 yrs. - 1850.ad-p483
HOESCHEL, William & P. - 1846. ad-p170,191,394.487
HOTTZGAVER, Charles, Caroline and August - 1845. ad-p175
HOUSTON, Robert and John - 1840. cdA-p87,104,128
JACKSON, Clarinda Jane - 1845. ad-p164,474
JOHNS, Hannah aged 3 yrs. - 1847. ad-p184
KING, Amos aged 14 yrs., Noah aged 11 yrs., Almira aged 7 yrs., Andrew aged 9 yrs.,
     Martha aged 5 yrs., children of Josias King - 1846. ad-p176,187,382
KIZER, Granville - 1845. ad-p176
KOKEMILLER, Frederick, Caroline, Eliza and Wilhelmina - 1840. ad-p48,132

LAMB, Ance and others heirs of D.G. Lamb - 1840.   ad-p45; cdA-p104, 171f,202
LAMPING, Justina Wilhelmina aged 6 yrs. - 1847.   ad-p185
LEHORN, William and Margaret V. - 1845.   ad-p162
LEIKART, Battea - 1841.   ad-p55
LEIKART, Gabriel, son of John & Catharine Leikart - 1841.   ad-p55
LIPPS, Henry - 1850.   ad-p482
McCHRISTE, Francis and Lucinda - 1849.   ad-p458
McCRIESTER, Joseph and two others - 1842.   cdA-118
McINTYRE, Ephraim, Sarah E., William and Edward - 1844.   ad-p159
MADDEN, William aged 14 yrs., son of Charley Madden - 1847.   ad-p186
MEDBERY, Allen V. aged 3 yrs. on 20 Nov. 1846, heir of Allen V. Medbery - 1847.
    ad-p123
MERRILL, Jacob - 1850.   ad-p476
MERRILL, Sally - 1850   ad-477
MEYERS, Heirs of - 1840.   cdA-p66
MOORE, Oliver aged 18 yrs., Francis aged 16 yrs. and Ozias aged 15 yrs., children
    of Ozias Moore - 1847.   ad-p184
MUKER (MOEKER), Heirs of Herman F. - 1841.   ad-p60
NEWCOMB, Mary Jane aged 14 months - 1845.   ad-p173
NOBLE, Justin and John C. - 1846.   ad-p169
NOLAND, William aged 7 yrs. and Mary aged 4 yrs., heirs of Thomas Noland - 1849.
    ad-p416
OZENBAUGH, Minerva - 1850.   ad-p483
PICKREL, Andrew Jackson and Caroline - 1845.   adp174
PIERCE, Jacob, heir of Thomas Pierce Sr. - 1849.   ad-p422
ROEBUCK, Benjamin and John, heirs of John Roebuck - 1848.   ad-p191,392
ROEBUCK, Joseph aged 13 yrs. - 1845.   ad-p176
ROESNER, Margaret and Elizabeth - 1849.   ad-p197,410
RUSHAU, Mary Theresa Caroline and John Theodore - 1850.   ad-p482
RUTAN, Arsula - 1846.   ad-p120
SANAFT, Sarah Jane and Rhoda - 1850.   ad-p488
SCHROEDER, B. F. - 1840.   cdA-p64
SIMMONS, Mary - 1850.   ad-p484
SMITH, Litty Ann aged 6 yrs., Henry M. aged 4 yrs. and Mary E. aged 2 yrs. - 1850.
    ad-p485
SNEDOKER, Louisa - 1846.   ad-p116
STAGER, Sarah E. and William - 1846.   ad-p172,180
STATLER, Nancy and others, heirs of Samuel Statler - 1839.   ad-p29; cdA-p318
STEVENS, W. A. aged 10 yrs., John A. aged 8 yrs., Lorenzo D. aged 6 yrs. and Virgil
    aged 4 yrs., heirs of Peter and Rebecca Stevens - 1849.   ad-p417
STRICKER, Clements and Mary, children of Anthony Stricker - 1847.   ad-p183
STUKEY, Eve, Mary, Catharine, and Anthony - 1845.   ad-p165
TILTON, John and Elizabeth, heirs of Sylvester Tilton - 1844.   ad-p156,189,385
TOBE, Joseph, Agnes and two other boys, names not known - 1840.   ad-p52
WATKINS, Amy aged 6 yrs., heir of Joshua Watkins - 1847.   ad-p182
WATTS, Nicholas P. - 1844.   ad-p92; cdA-p148
WELLS, Justus, William and Roswell, heirs of Roswell and Elizabeth Wells - 1840.
    ad-p47,50
WHALLEN, James - 1850.   ad-p477
WHITLEY, C. B. - 1840.   cdA-p84
WHITMORE, Isaiah - 1849.   ad-p468
WILLIAMS, Jonas - 1844.   ad-p155
WIRTS, John, Maria and Joseph - 1837.   ad-p17

ARNOLD, David to Sally EMBRA   12-30-1810
BACON, Henry to Maria TENERY   11-2-1810
BARBEE, William to Margaret MARSHALL   11-2-1809
BARBER, Thomas to Elizabeth MACKEY   1-14-1812
BARRETT, Abner to Mary PEMBERTON   12-23-1810
BASSELL, William to Martha MELLENDER   10-20-1809
BAYMAN, Charles to Patsy HILL   10-16-1808
BEDLE, Abram to Nancy Riffle   12-24-1812
BENBOW, Barclay to Mary McCLURE   7-9-1807
        Barclay of Warren Co., Ohio
BENNET, Benjamin to Lucy HINKLE   10-20-1812
BIRELY, William to Elizabeth KEYSER   7-1-1810
BLAW, Joseph to Mary JUSHMAN   1-20-1808
BLUE, Barnabas to Francis DAVOR   2-19-1811
BLUE, Uriah to Charity KISER   10-11-1808
BRANDON, Armstrong to Eliza McCORKLE   10-12-1807
BROWN, William to Catharine SIMMONS   3-30-1809
BUMBARDNER, Daniel to Mary SHEETS   8-2-1812
COAT, John to Sally WRIGHT   1-7-1808
COATS, Jesse to Mary JOHNSTON   7-23-1809
COPPOCK, John to Nancy LITTLEJOHN   8-13-1808
COPPOCK, William to Unes COUGHREN   7-16-1809
COTHRAN, Jesse to Hannah EDDINGS   12-20-1810
COX, Absalon to Phoby SUMNERS   9-4-1808
CUNNINGHAM, Wm. to Barbara LEVENGOOD   11-26-1812
CURTIS, James to Elizabeth DYRK   12-8-1811
DINGMAN, James to Fanny WELKS   3-22-1811
DuBOIS, Francis to Elizabeth OLLIVER   7-1-1810
DYE, John to Mary LENON   7-6-1809
ELLEMON, John to Tabitha JAY   10-18-1812
ELLER, John to Sally BURKET   2-14-1811
EMBRES, James to Polly JEFFRIES   7-27-1809
FINCHER, William to Susannah FRIEND   4-8-1810
FLINN, John to Haggy PRIEST   9-5-1811
FREEMAN, Samuel, Jr. to Margaret REED   1-13-1808
        Lic. granted Mont. Co., Ohio
FRENCH, James to Hannah DEEM   9-16-1807
FRIEND, James to Susannah SHEET   4-11-1808*
FURROW, John to Sarah WIMANS   12-12-1812
GALBRETH, John to Harriot FAKES   12-17-1812
GARARD, Abner to Charlota GOBLE   11-11-1810
GARRARD, Isaac to Phoebe CARTER   8-26-1810
GESS, Joseph to Jane WILSON   10-31-1812
GOBLE, Joseph to Ruth BLUE   3-21-1811
GREEN, George W. to Nacy KNIGHT   10-18-1812
GREENE, Zechariah to Ruth NEAL   11-14-1810
GUARD, Elias to Esther BURNS   7-9-1810
HAMLET, Benjamin to Cloe THIMBLE   1-1-1812
HANKS, Thomas to Martha MACKOOL   2-7-1811
HARRIS, Richard to Hannah JENKINS   12-27-1810
HARTER, Benjamin to Mary RAWSER   12-21-1808
HATHAWAY, Abraham to Bethsheba COX   4-17-1810
HATHAWAY, Eleazer to Elizabeth FLINN   8-27-1810

*no date given; date recorded

HATHAWAY, Richard to Polly FLINN	3-25-1812
ILAY, James to Catharine SIMMS	2-28-1810
HAY, Joseph to Nancy JOHNSTON	3-22-1810
HENDERSPOTT, David to Catharine BENHAM	6-10-1809
HILL, Nathan to Fanny WILLIAMS	6-29-1809
HILLIARD, Daniel to Nancy MANNING	2-15-1809
HILLIARD, Joseph to Sally REED	11-26-1807
HOLENSWORTH, Carter to Charity RAMSEY	10-4-1810
HOLLINGSWORTH, John to Elizabeth RANSCO	11-21-1811
HOOVER, Henry to Sarah Curtis	11-12-1807
INGLE, John to Patty JENKINS	3-26-1812
JAY, Charles to Elizabeth MOTE	2-2-1811
JAY, Denny to Mary MACY	2-8-1810
JEFFRETH, William to Rebecca EMBRA	11-22-1810
JENKINS, Issacher to Esther PERSON	2-14-1811
JINKANS, Phineas to Mary FURMAS	1-3-1811
JOHNSTON, William to Catharine HALE	7-3-1811
JONES, Benjamin to Rachel MARSH	12-23-1808
JONES, Joseph to Priscilia MOONEY	4-25-1809
JONES, Samuel to Prudence MOONEY	10-4-1810
JULIAN, Stephen to Margary McCLURE	6-25-1810
KEELY, Albner to Jenny DICKSON	9-10-1807
KEESEMAN, George to Elizabeth BLACK	5-31-1810
KELLY, Solomon to Polly CORY	6-20-1811
KENSER, Jacob to Nelly AUDLER	7-1-1807
KINSER, John to Barbara SIMMONS	10-17-1809
KISER, Thomas to Sally JACKSON	5-22-1812
LALAN, John to Sally RAWSER	8-19-1809
LASNER, John H. to Anne LENAN	10-19-1809
LeTUMO, Francis to Rhoda COOPER	12-29-1807
LEVEL, Benjamin to Patsy McCORKLE	7-14-1807
LITTLEJOHN, Henry to Sarah Ann DUNCAN	10-8-1808
LOW, Herry to Sarah SUMPTION	4-12-1812
LULTON, John to Nancy MADDEN	10-21-1808
McCLURE, John to Abigal BUFFING	3-27-1811
McCLURE, Thomas to Sarah NELLY	1-13-1812
McCLURG, John to Elizabeth WEAKS	4-23-1812
McCLURG, John to Jane MOFFETT	10-29-1812
McCONNELL, Robert to Margaret VERNON	10-20-1809
McCOOL, Gabriel to Susannah RAMSEY	11-22-1807
McCOOL, Wells to Anne COATS	3-29-1810
McCOY, William to Nancy FEALDON	9-15-1807
McDONALD, Joseph to Temperence ELLEMON	10-18-1812
McDOWELL, Betsy to Thomas PHILLIPS	8-10-1809
McINTIRE, Robert to Pattey WILLIAMS	8-13-1812
McINTOSH, James to Margaret LINDSLEY	11-4-1811
McINTYRE, John to Susanna RENICK	8-7-1808
McJINSEY, William to Ruth MOONEY	4-25-1811
McKINNEY, John to Jane SCOTT	1-7-1810
MACK, Frederick to Barsheba PRIEST	12-19-1811
MANN, Augusteen to Elizabeth PRICE	9-15-1808
MANNING, John to Elizabeth HARTLEY	1-5-1810
MANNING, John to Jane BERRY	10-10-1811
MANSON, David to Sally CORNWELL	9-11-1810
MICHELS, Solomon to Sally JACOBS	3-11-1812

117

MILLER, Jonathan D. to Betsey H. MORRISON	2-27-1811
MOONEY, John to Nancy TERRY	12-31-1811
MORROW, James to Phebe BEEDLE	2-28-1811
MOTE, William to Elizabeth SHEETS	2-11-1810
MURRY, Charles to Peggy CRUMER	10-17-1811
NORTH, Thomas to Elizabeth ALLEN(ELLERS?)	9-4-1807**
	9-21-1807**
OFFIL, William to Polly McKINNEY	2-10-1808
ORDISON, Henry to Polly TELFORD	11-23-1809
ORR, James to Elizabeth KYLE	9-15-1810
OVERFIELD, Benjamin to Rebecca SUMPTION	7-5-1812
Greenville - Newton Twp.	
PEMBERTON, Isaah to Elizabeth ELIMON	1-15-1811
PEMBERTON, Isaah to Mary DUNKIN	2-17-1811
PERSON, William to Anna MILES	10-28-1810
PHILLIPS, Thomas to Betsy McDOWELL	8-10-1809
PRIEST, Elijah to Hannah MOCK	4-30-1812
RAGAN, Zadock to Sarah JOHNSTON	12-9-1810
RAMSEY, William to Rachel COATS	2-24-1811
RENCH, Joseph to Rhoda COATS	8-27-1811
REIPER, Samuel to Sally PRILAMAN	3-5-1812
RICHARDSON, George to Prudence PRILLEMAN	12-20-1808
RICHARDSON, William to Catharine MILLHOUSE	12-1-1812
RIDDLE, John to Sally McCLUN	2-23-1808
ROSS, William to A . . . ? COLEMAN	7-30-1808
RUKER, William to Pheby IDDINGS	10-11-1808
RUSH, Jesse to Mary SUMPTION	4-12-1812
SHAW, Thomas to Mary COX	1-3-1811
SHIDAKER, John to Caty BOOHER	9-13-1809
SIMMONS, John to Susannah MILLHOUSE	3-25-1808
SMALLEY, Freeman to Catharine FRADER	7-31-1808
SMITH, Jonathan to Elizabeth DEWEES	8-26-1810
SMITH, Philip to Elizabeth BATES	7-7-1811
STATLER, Christly to Fanny WINANS	5-31-1810
STATLER, John to Nelly DYE	5-20-1812
STINCHCOMB, David to Sarah DYE	3-17-1811
SUMPTION, Charles, Jr. to Mary EMRY	8-25-1811
SUMPTION, George to Elizabeth RUSH	6-18-1812
SUNDERLAND, Daniel to Polly PRILEMAN	5-28-1811
SUVELL, John R. to Polly HAY	10-19-1809
TENTUS, George to Ann PEARSON	10-27-1808
TULLIS, William to Sally BARBEE	9-3-1810
UNDERWOOD, William to Susannah WINANS	1-4-1810
VENAMAN, James to Polly MARSHALL	6-4-1812
VIRGIN, William to Roan BURNS	2-4-1808
WALLACE, John to Polly INDACUT	8-2-1810
WALLACE, John to Marjory HUSTON	3-27-1811
WALLACE, Ross to Elizabeth NEELY	1-19-1808
WEATHERHEAD, John to Rachel FRIEND	8-2-1812
WEAVER, Peter to Winney ROSS	8-19-1812
WESTFALL, Cornelius to Rachel DYE	4-25-1809
WESTFALL, Joel to Anna McGIMTSEY	6-4-1811
WESTFALL, Levi to Peggy PETTIT	4-4-1811
WILSON, Solomon to Lydia EMBRA	8-3-1810
WINANS, Benjamin to Betsy ROSS	12-29-1807

118

ABBOT, John to Abigail JOHNSON	6-6-1813
BALLENGER, James to Mary LARGE (LURGE?)	11-24-1816
BALLENGER, Daniel to Rachel HARRISON	12-25-1814
BEDLE, Daniel to Elizabeth LINDLEY	4-16-1813
BEEDLE, Simon to Sarah HATHAWAY	8-3-1815
BEERS, John to Polly THOMPSON	12-12-1816
BELEW, Joseph to Susanna PEARSON	9-12-1816
BENNET, Joshua to Rachael TULLE	12-5-1816
BERRY, William to Polly MOFFETT	7-1-1813
BOYER, Jacob to Betsey McCLERG	3-7-1816
BRIER, George to Letetia MITCHELL	4-28-1814
BROALS, John to Patience BURRASS	5-29-1815
BROWN, Isaac to Mary MENDENHALL	12-26-1815
BROWN, James to Nancy BARBEE	12-20-1814
BURGRAM, John to Rebecca CECIL	8-18-1814
BURKET, Andrew to Susannah BUMGARDNER	3-3-1816
BYRKET, Joseph to Sally ELLER	3-20-1814
CARROLL, Daniel to Jane DONELY	4-18-1815
CARY, Cephae to Rhoda GARARD	11-1-1815
CARY, David to Betsy WINANS	5-13-1815
CAVENDISH, William to Caty FRANTNER	8-5-1815
CECIL, John G. to Elizabeth WYGATE	3-16-1815
CHEVALIER, Charles to Mary HAMLET	1-25-1816
CLOYD, James to Betsy NESSONGER	10-13-1814
COATS, Joseph to Elizabeth COPPOCK	11-6-1816
COE, Joseph to Sarah WINANS	5-28-1815
CORY, John to Polly KNIGHT	7-6-1815
CURESTONE, Henry to Sally BURNEM	3-7-1816
DAVIS, Abraham to Nancy MORRIS	5-3-1814
DAVIS, Samuel D. to Nancy TULLES	11-26-1816
DEFREES, Archibald to Betsey BERRY	12-24-1816
DICKON, Nicholas to Sarah HITTLE	9-19-1816
DOUGLASS, Robert to Betsy STUDABAKER	4-21-1814
DUNKAN, Amos to Rachel UOATS	6-2-1813
DUNKIN, Isaac to Anna PEMBERTON	10-31-1816
DYE, Andrew, Jr. to Elizabeth MARTIN	7-7-1814
ELDOR, Charles to Susanna LONG	4-6-1815
ELLER, Henry to Molly RENCH	11-24-1816
ELLER, Joseph to Rachel CASSY	3-13-1813
ELLOR, Henry to Sally JEFFRIES	7-10-1814
EVANS, Edward J. to Susannah SIMMONS	6-16-1815
FINCHER, Lemuel to Jane JEFFRIES	5-21-1815
FLINN, William to Mary HUSTON	1-25-1816
FRIEND, Jesse to Susanna HOOVER	5-9-1813
GARARD, John to Rebecca EARLS	8-30-1813
GARARD, Joseph to Hanna DOLLISON	6-26-1816
GARRARD, Nathaniel to Polly KIMBLE	3-3-1813
GARREARD, John to Margaret DEWEESE	1-4-1816
GARVEY, John to Anne MARSHALL	2-16-1815
GILBERT, John to Edney COPPOCK	12-29-1814
GOHAGAN, William to Sally TENNERY	6-13-1813

```
HASTON, William to Margaret Flinn           3-12-1816
HIATT, Eby to Elizabeth Cory                8-24-1813
HIGGINS, Johnathan to Betsy Boyd            10-21-1813
HILL, John to Nancy Thompson                8-26-1813
HOOVER, Noah to Sarah Byrket                4-18-1813
HOOVER, Noah to Michel Yount                2-4-1815
HOOVER, Solomon to Mary Jones               9-7-1813
HUBBLE, Asa to Jane Montonney               12-22-1814
HUNTER, Thomas to Ann Blain                 2-27-1816
HUSTON, William to Elizabeth Hardesty       12-19-1816
INGLE, Michael to Rachal Hanks              1-22-1815
JACKSON, Alexander to Polly Jackson         7-30-1814
JACKSON, Giles to Mary Garard               8-2-1815
JACKSON, Henry to Rachel Jackson            10-19-1815
JERROME, William to Elizabeth Shook         7-24-1815
JOHNS, John to Sarah Northcut               11-10-1813
JOHNSON, Giles to Any Pear                  11-24-1814
JOHNSTON, Andrew to Hetty Cox               11-26-1815
JOHNSTON, John to Sally Case                11-28-1815
JONES, Francis to Polly Jones               5-14-1813
JONES, Thomas to Sarah Jones                1-19-1815
JONES, William to Catharine Kessler         8-10-1815
JULIAN, Isaac to Pleasant Jackson           1-2-1813
LAMME, James to Sally Mitchell              4-13-1815
LAURIGNOUR, Francis to Mary Frantner        8-5-1815
LAYTON, James to Edith Sweet                5-2-1816
LEFAVER, Daniel to Sally Mann               9-13-1814
LESSCENA, John to Sally Rudy                3-14-1816
LINDLEY, Denias to Susanna Simmons          5-6-1813
LONG, James to Betsey Ulery                 5-26-1816
McCLARY, John to Eliza Brandon              2-16-1815
McCLINTOCK, Adam to Marjoran Clingan        11-22-1815
McCLINTOCK, John to Mary Bay                12-5-1816
McCLURE, John to Jane Miller                1-18-1815
McCLURE, Robert to Esther Garard            10-26-1816
McCOOLE, John to Mary Hanes                 3-14-1813
McQUILLEN, Robert to Jane Childers          7-18-1815
MACKEY, Robert to Sah Hatfield              6-22-1815
MANER, Isaac to Catharine Williama (no mo. or da.)1813
MANGIN, John to Polly Richardson            2-24-1814
MANN, Barnabas to Sally Prillman            6-21-1816
MANN, George to Margaret Pearson            5-23-1816
MANN, Jacob to Elizabeth Shell              12-20-1814
MANNING, Enos to Griessal Cox               5-16-1816
MANNING, William to Ruth Julian             2-10-1814
MANSAN, James to Rachel Carter              11-16-1813
MARSH, Griffin to Sarah Mathews             4-3-1816
MARTIN, Merrick to Lavina Freeman           10-12-1815
MERRIT, William to Mary Batterel            8-20-1814
MILLER, Jacob to Catharine Connit (?)       12-19-1816
MILLER, Robert to Sarah Madden              5-12-1814
MILLHOUSE, John, Jr. to Margaret Boyour     1-14-1813
MILLINGER, John to Ellener Lenox            10-12-1815
MITCHELL, Moses Grant to Magdelen Brandon   12-19-1816
MOORE, Henry to Susannah Deeter             9-26-1816
```

GREEN, William to Lavina COPPOCK   5-19-1814
HANCE (HAND?), Willis to Sarah JOHN   11-19-1816
HANN, Robert to Polly McCORKLE (no month given)   (?)-9-1813
MUNN, James to Mary MANSON   6-20-1816
MURPHY, John to Jane DANNIELS   1-17-1816
MYERS, James to Catharine BLACK   4-20-1815
NUTT, Henry K. to Rosanna FINCHER   4-16-1815
OSBAN, John to Sally JOHNSON   8-12-1814
PEARSON, James to Tamer JAY   12-5-1816
PEARSON, William to Mary ANDERSON   12-1-1816
PECK, John to Barbary FRENCH   6-24-1815
PEPPERMAN, Samuel to Jane WILLIAMS   9-8-1814
PLATTAR, James to Hannah COX (2 dates) 1-15-1815   1-20-1815
PRESTEN, John to Sophia EWING   10-13-1814
PRICE, Henry to Peggy GARNER   1-20-1814
PRICE, Israel to Peggy GORDEN   2-24-1814
PRICE, Michael to Betsy PRICE   8-19-1814
PRIER, Andrew D. to Elizabeth THERBY   6-13-1814
RECTOR, John to Catharine PRICE   12-2-1813
RIGGANS, Robert to Polly BOYER   11-24-1814
ROBERSON, William to Susanna CANAN   11-2-1815
ROBERTS, Isaac to Jane LUCAS   12-2-1814
RUSH, James to Elizabeth WESTFALL   6-29-1816
SHELL, Christian to Grizzey LOUTHAIN   5-25-1815
SLAGAL, George to Sarah WYATTE   10-2-1814
SONGER, John to Elizabeth KEELING   12-6-1814
STATLER, Abraham to Sarah DYE   5-27-1813
STEENBARGER, Lewis to Susanna CIBLINGER   12-4-1815
STEVENS, William to Polly DEFREES   10-25-1815
STEWARD, William to Jeminah MANNING   10-29-1815
SUEL, Peter to Polly TULLIS   1-10-1814
TELFORD, John G. to Lucy KYLE   11-7-1816
TERRY, Nathan to Delilah WESTFALL   8-17-1815
TULLIS, David R. to Susana BARLEW   11-28-1815
TULLIS, John T. to Margaret MURRY   8-5-1816
UNDERWOOD, John to Mary SCUDDER   1-20-1813
VERNON, Thomas to Jane HOLLINGSWORTH   5-26-1816
WALKER, George to Martha NORTH   2-3-1814
WALKER, John to Betsy McCLURE   5-26-1814
WEAKS, Charles to Betsey MATTHEWS   2-4-1813
WEBB, John to Precilla KNIGHT   12-14-1815
WESTFALL, Job to Betsy TERRY   7-20-1815
WETHERHEAD, James to Margaret WEAVER   11-9-1814
WEVER, John to Betsey LONG   4-23-1816
WHALEN, John to Polly KENNEIR   12-19-1816
WHITE, Robert to Sally DICKSON   1-7-1813
WHITIONS, Richard to Polly MANNING   11-10-1816
WHITMON, David to Polly BAYMON   12-21-1815
WILLES(?), John to Delilah YOUNT   5-20-1813
WILLIAMS, Lewis to Sarah ROLLINS   7-24-1814
WILSON, Joseph to Perthena WOODS   8-15-1816

121

```
WOLLISON, George to Elizabeth YOUNG          1-10-1815
WOODRUFF, Hampton to Hannah BLUE             3-25-1813
WOODS, Thomas to Edith CASEY                 3-10-1816
WOODS, William to Jane MANSON                7-6-1813
WORLY, Caleb to Elizabeth ADAMS              10-28-1816
YOUNT, Henry to Elizabeth HOOVER             4-16-1815
```

ABBOT, John to Mary McCool	2-5-1820
ADAMS, Joseph to Jane Johnston	9-16-1819
ADAMSON, Joseph to Rachel Knight	10-7-1819
ALDRICH, Collin to Rebecca Furnis	11-4-1819
AMMONS, Jacob to Marcice Harmon	4-26-1820
ANDERSON, John to Mary Smith	1-10-1819
ANTHONY, Daniel to Susan Mendenhall	10-29-1820
ARCHER, Allen to Rachael Rogers	10-16-1817
ATKINS, Henry to Margaret Fielding	8-26-1819
BALLINGER, Jesse to Elizabeth Fetters	8-31-1820
BEENBLOSOM, George to Mary Cotes	9-4-1817
BEAZLEY, Peter to Hannah Smith	1-31-1819
BEENBLOSSOM, John to Peggy Kerns	10-11-1817
BEGGS, Thomas to Catherine Yontes	10-29-1819
BELLOW, Peter to Catherine Emmick	11-8-1820
BIGGER, Robert to Elizabeth Montgomery	6-8-1819
BIRLEY, Noah to Martha Rudy	8-10-1818
BLACK, Adam to Elizabeth Farmer	7-8-1819
BLACK, Samuel of Champaign Co. to Linney Mitchell	11-30-1817
BLACKMAN, Ebeneser to Susan Stockbridge	11-13-1818
BLUE, John to Amy Murphey	3-18-1819
BLUE, John B. to Rachael Sayers	12-10-1818
BLUE, Uriah to Margaret Gerard	10-20-1820
BOUSMAN, William to Nancy Shell	2-28-1820
BOYD, Andred to Ann Vernon	5-17-1817
BOYER, John to Polly Jamison	12-28-1819
BRADFORD, James G. to Caty Ann Conover	1-27-1820
BRIER, David to Elizabeth Jacobs	1-27-1820
BROWN, James to Sarah Coats	2-6-1820
BROWN, John to Turza Brandon	10-14-1819
BROWN, Robert to Elizabeth McKinney	1-20-1820
BROWN, Thomas to Jane Moffet	11-19-1818
BUKELS, James to Margaritt Norcutt	9-11-1818
CALDWELL, James to Elizabeth Ann Martin	5-1-1820
CAMPBELL, John to Elizabeth Hughey	11-11-1819
CANE, James to Sarah Thompson	12-31-1818
CANNON, Moses to Martha Bennet	8-11-1818
CANNON, Richard to Mary Brawdreck	6-3-1817
CAPRON, Welcome to Delany North	6-6-1819
CARLL, John to Margaret Coppock	11-7-1819
CARY, Isac to Abby Hudson	1-20-1820
CARY, Thomas to Mary Winons	2-3-1819
CAVEN, James to Catherine Platter	4-22-1819
CAVENDER, Thomas to Amy Tical	2-28-1820
CHAMBERS, Thomas to Mary Lennox	2-11-1819
CHAPPEZE, Henry to Elizabeth Morrow	1-12-1820
CHILDRES, Thomas to Phebe Perry	2-17-1820
CLARK, Culbertson to Sally Wallace	1-27-1820
CLARK, John to Harriott Jenkins	3-12-1818
CLARK, John G. to Mary Gohagan	2-6-1817
CLOYD, John to Rachael Jester	7-1-1817
COATS, Henry to Jane Fincher	10-26-1820

```
COLEMAN, Nathan V. to Mary Silbery                          12-31-1818
COMPTON, Runion to Mary Murphey - both of Elizabeth twp. 7-23-1818
COX, Benjamin S. to Millenet Sminth                        6-9-1817
CULBERTSON, Henry W. to Maria Coleman                      2-25-1819
CURTIS, Hiron to Jane Sheets                               8-1-1819
CURTIS, William Wiley to Lorena Inman                      2-12-1818
DAVIS, James to Hannah McKaig                              4-17-1817
DEWEESE, Joshua to Mary Garrard                            4-9-1818
DINGMAN, Abraham to Jemina Bobo                            2-18-1818
DOUGHERTY, Thomas to Lucinda Williams                      9-26-1818
DUMAND (DUMMAND), Joseph to Jemima Hendershott             12-20-1819
DUNHAM, Asa to Elizabeth Scott                             2-24-1818
DYE, Benjamin to Precila Dye                               6-26-1817
DYE, James to Elizabeth Dye                                12-18-1817
DYE, Stephen to Mary Meek                                  9-30-1819
DYE, Vincent to Rebecca Swails                             11-12-1820
EDWARDS, Wm. to Sophia Carson                              3-11-1819
EELY, Peter to Betsy Sunderland                            7-10-1817
EGENBROAD, Lewis to Mary McKenne                           6-29-1820
ELLEMON, David to Betsey Haworth                           5-4-1817
ELMORE, Joseph to Rachael Pemberton                        3-13-1817
ELSWORTH, William to Sarah Mesberis                        1-21-1819
EMBREE, Isaac to Ruth Pearsen                              2-12-1818
ENGLASH, Thomas E. to Matilda Trader                       10-24-1820
FARE, George to Polly Favorite                             7-4-1819
FEES, Henry to Sarah Coats                                 8-24-1820
FILLERRY, John to Susannah Riley                           7-24-1817
FLINN, William to Mary Rollings                            8-19-1819
FOLAND, Daniel to Hannah Crawford                          9-29-1818
FRENCH, Asa to Hannah Davis                                8-31-1820
GARARD, Johnathan to Elizabeth Winans                      9-10-1818
GEARHART, John Y. to Elizabeth Todd                        2-28-1820
GERRARD, John to Hannah Royal                              3-23-1820
GILLEN, William Bails to Peggy Moffett                     8-30-1819
GREEN, John to Sarah Clark                                 9-29-1817
GREENHAM, N. to Maria Carson                               4-9-1820
GUMP, Daniel to Paggy Studebaker                           9-16-1819
HACKLY, James to Rebecca Wells                             3-21-1817
HALE, Thomas to Jane Hurly                                 10-15-1818
HALL, Samuel to Fanny Alexander                            4-13-1820
HALLAND(?), James to Fanny Williams                        9-7-1820
HALLOWAY, Daylon to Barbara Smith                          4-24-1819
HANCE, William to Sarah Counts                             1-22-1818
HANNARD (KANNARD), John to Nancy McKenzy                   7-19-1818
HANSON, Bayille(?) to Rebecha Coats                        6-7-1818
HANY(?), Jacob to Elizabeth Smith                          11-7-1817
HARP, Jacob R. to Abijah Dunn                              9-24-1820
HAY, John A. to Mary Smith          (1818?)                12-24-1819
HEEKMAN, Joseph to Mary Mote                               7-27-1817
HELMECK, William to Elizabeth Pharrow                      9-3-1820
HENDRIX, William H. to Ann Pearson                         1-14-1819
HENSLEY, Simon to Polly Arnold                             2-23-1820
```

124

HOLLINGSWORTH, Ely to Rachael Neel(?)	6-12-1817
HOOVER, Jesse to Rebecah Yount	4-18-1819
HOOVER, Solomon to Barbary Phouts	7-5-1818
HOOVER, William to Sophia Young	3-25-1819
HOWARD, Lewis to Christene Snell	10-16-1818
HOWE, Martin to Sarah North	3-12-1817
HUHN, Joseph to Sarah Johnston	7-11-1820
HUMBERT, Lewis to Susan Landry	12-23-1819
HURLY, Cornelius to Sally Goble	10-1-1818
HURLY, Henry to Mary S. Kimble	8-7-1817
HUSTON, Joseph to Nancy Martin	9-4-1817
HUTCHENS, Jonathan to Catharine Carter	9-28-1820
IMLAY, Caleb to Mary Johnston	5-26-1817
INGLE, Abraham to Elizabeth Jenkins	9-4-1817
INGLE, Philip to Betsy Fease	9-18-1817
INMAN, George to Judy Burns	9-21-1820
INMON, Eli to Jane Coppock	11-29-1818
IRWIN, David to Elizabeth Davis	1-18-1817
JACKSON, James to Amelia Runnel	3-4-1819
JACOBS, Cadwalder to Jane coerter(?)	3-30-1820
JAY, William to Stasey Bosier	2-7-1819
JENTRY, Ephraim to Elizabeth Foland	12-21-1819
JESTER, John to Jemima Gofarth	8-21-1820
JOHNSON, William to Jemima Patter	2-18-1819
JONES, E. W. To Lydia Bollins	1-6-1820
JONES, Matrimor Allen to Ann Archer	10--8-1818
JONES, Nathan to Nancy Good	11-11-1817
JONES, Oliver to Nancy Flinn	1-17-1818
JULIN, Jesse to Sarah Brooks	10-9-1820
KELLY, Samuel to Mahala Yount	6-7-1819
KEYT, John to Margaret Widney	2-11-1818
KIMBLE, Edward to Nancy Cox	11-25-1819
KISER, Daniel H. to Nancy Young	4-1-1819
KNIGHT, John to Abigail Green	6-28-1818
KNOOP, Michael to Nancy Sheets	10-12-1818
LANDES, Jacob to Martha McCollom	4-2-1818
LARGE, Nathaniel to Fanny Miller	7-9-1818
LAWRENCE, Rice B. to Mary Garrett	11-22-1817
LENOX, James to Sally Wilson	2-12-1818
LENNOX, John to Nancy Mellinger	12-30-1817
LOCKHARD, Phillip to Rebecca Evans	9-8-1818
LODGE, Jacob to Nancy North	4-9-1820
LONG, John to Susannah Rench	1-1-1818
LORTON, John to Barbary _____(not given)	10-26-1820
LOWE, John to Jane Wyatt	12-19-1819
LOYD, John to Anna Dewese	2-26-1818
LYONS, Henry to Elizabeth Millhouse	2-12-1818
McCool, Elisha to Sarah Haworth	5-28-1817
McCRAY, James to Ruth Blue	6-24-1819
McDONALD, Archibald to Nancy Culbertson	9-21-1819
McKENZIE, William to Isabel Kimble	5-21-1820
MALOY, John L. to Anna Boils	12-25-1817

```
MANEAR, John to Mary Jackson                              9-16-1819
MANNING, Benjamin to Harriet Dunnen                       8-22-1818
MARKLEY, Moses to Mary Dinnan                             3-25-1819
MARSHALL, James to Margaret Hardisty                     2-20-1817
MATTOX, Thomas to Rebecca Mote                            2-21-1818
MEIGS, Ansel to Mary Davis                               9-17-1818
MELINGER, William to Rebecca Hurly                       12-17-1818
MELLING, Peter to Eleanor Hurley                         9-16-1819
MELLINGER, William to Jane Hughy                          3-18-1819
MENDENHALL, Richard to Sarah Pearson                     8-14-1817
MENDENHALL, Thadius to Precilla Stronger                 6-13-1820
MESSENGER, Peter to Joanna Platter                       12-21-1820
MICHAEL, Henry to Elizabeth Stewart                      9-26-1817
MILLER, Creslly to Hannah Wright                         7-20-1820
MITCHELL, George to Catherine Geerhart                    4-4-1819
MITSHER, Samuel H. to Elizabeth Nil(?)                   9-26-1818
MOOR, Henry to Barbary Rench                              3-9-1819
MOORE, Samuel to Elizabeth G. Mooney                     12-21-1820
MORGAN, James to Lucretia Bliss
     Deposition given Montgomery Co., Ohio before John Folkerth, J.P. by
     Mathew Teas who being sworn deposeth and saith that he was a quainted
     with James S. Morgan in the Town of Lincey, Ontario Co., New York, for
     between two and three years immediately preceeding the year 1812 and that
     the said James S. Morgan and Lucretia the daughter of one____(left blank)
     Bliss were living together as husband and wife during the said time and
     had two children during said time, that he always viewed them as legally
     married and never heard contrary surmised by any person.  Sworn and sub-
     scribed 11th day August 1819.  Signed Mathew Teas.  Witnessed John
     Folkerth, J.P.
MOTE, Jonathan to Cathrine Stacy                          5-4-1820
MOTE, William to Mary Byrkit                              6-19-1817
MYERS, Henry to Molly Dale                               10-19-1819
MYRES, Abram to Susanah Pence                            10-9-1817
NICHOLSON, Samuel to Fanny Brandon                       2-10-1820
NORRIS, _____(not given) to Susannah Miller             6-21-1818
NORTH, Samuel to Elizabeth Brooks                        2-11-1819
ORBESON, John to Susanah Kimble                           1-9-1817
PALMER, John to Margaret Hance              (1819?)      12-19-1818
PEARSON, Abel to Polly Buffington                        12-25-1817
PEARSON, Enoch to Rosanna McClure                        5-22-1817
PEARSON, Jacob to Nancy Hammons                          12-6-1818
PEARSON, Joseph to Delphia Patty                         2-5-1817
PEARSON, Moses to Sarah Mills                             5-4-1819
PEMBERTON, William to Hannah Pearson                     2-12-1817
PENNY, Elijah to Nancy Forguson                          8-18-1819
PETIGRUE, James to Elizabeth Hains                       1-23-1817
PETTIT, John to Elizabeth Dye                           12-30-1817
PHILIPS, James of Montgomery Co. to E. Delilah Price    10-29-1818
PINGREE, John to Emily Bratsher                          9-16-1819
POTTORF, Henry to Mary Pence                             8-13-1818
PRELIAMON, William to Margaret Williams                  1-23-1817
PRINCEHOUSE, Henry to Winford Griffen                    1-28-1819
```

126

```
RAYMOND, John to _____(not given) Livengood          3-10-1817
RECTER, John to Sophia Fare                          8-13-1820
REDENBAUGH, John to Susanna Evans                    1-20-1820
REES, Jeremiah to Mary Gump                          8-31-1820
RENCH, David to Sally Studibacher                    12-24-1818
RENCH, Jacob to Anne Burns                           1-17-1820
RIFFLE, John to Mary Bedle                           8-14-1817
ROBERTS, John to Catharine Julin                     8-29-1820
ROBERTS, John to Polly Shryock                       12-6--1820
ROGERS, Thomas to Jain Campbell                      4-8-1817
ROLLINS, Myhow to Lydia Murphey                      12-31-1818
ROYAL, Charles to Polly Gearhart                     3-14-1820
RUCH, Aaron to Catharine Rush                        2-16-1817
RUGGELS, George to Margaret Plummer                  9-11-1817
RUSSEL, John to Peggy Piler                          12-9-1820
SANDERS, Amsea to Nancy Lindly                       7-29-1819
SAYRS, James to Eleanor Godden                       11-5-1819
SCOTT, Hugh to Nancy Landon                          2-4-1819
SCOTT, William L. to Elizabeth Youtes                9-24-1819
SCUDDOR, Thomas to Nancy Blue                        11-30-1820
SHACKELFORD, James to Susannah Morrow                12-31-1818
SHACKELFORD, William to Frances Shackelford          10-23-1819
SHAGLY, Jacob to Sally Hurly                         8-3-1818
SHELL, Joseph H. to Elizabeth Williams               5-2-1820
SHELL, William to Sarah Sayres                       2-25-1820
SIMMONS, Jacob to Mehitable Rollings                 3-19-1818
SKELINGS, John to Sally Songer                       3-16-1819
SKINNER, Joseph to Lydia Stillwell                   9--28-1820
SKINNER, Samuel to Nancy Sheeling                    9-23-1819
SKINNER, William to Willey Wells                     9-28-1819
SLAGLE, John to Elizabeth Slagle                     7-31-1819
SMITH, Philip to Phebe Whiting                       4-20-1820
SNIDER, Thomas to Mary Boils                         1-8-1818
SONDERS, John to Sally Grumble                       1-3-1820
SONGER, Adam to Polly Keeling                        1-27-1818
SPENCER, John to Sarah Jones                         11-12-1818
SPILLERS, Peter to Susan Coats                       5-4-1820
STALEY, David to Priscilla Morrison                  1-26-1820
STEWARD, Ishmael to Sally Pearson                    12-2-1820
TEAGUE, Moses to Jane Coppock                        1-31-1817
TEBUGDIN, Zacheriah to Mary King                     2-12-1819
THAYER, Davis W. to Elizabeth Macy                   12-30-1820
THOMPSON, Matthew to Nancy Craig                     7-13-1820
THOMPSON, Samuel to Charlotte Jay                    3-2-1817
THORNBERRY, Richard to Clarisce Weeks                1-17-1820
ULLERY, John to Betsey Deter                         1-9-1817
VANSCOIK, Aaron to Sarah Green                       12-15-1820
WALLACE, Moses to Jane Hay                           1-30-1817
WALLACE, Reuben . to Barbara Cecil                   11-4-1819
WEST, Jeremiah to Matilda Wilson                     4-4-1820
WEVER, Peter Senr. to Jane Powersock                 7-3-1817
WHEELOCK, Lymon to Mary Fouts                        4-10-1820
WHITE, William to Elizabeth Jay                      11-26-1818
WILLIAMS, Henry to Sally Fellers (Fetters?)          2-27-1817
WISE, John to Polly Dennen                           8-27-1818
```

MIAMI COUNTY, OHIO - DIVORCES 1818-1831

The following records were taken from "Supreme Court Order Book 1808-1831" located in the Common Pleas (Clerk of Court's Office) storage room in the court house basement at Troy. Pages on which record may be found are given in parenthesis.

June 1818 - Jane BOWERSOCK vs. John BOWERSOCK. Petition for Divorce. Filed 2-25-1817. Jane Bowersock formerly Jane Ross married John Bowersock at Franklin, Warren County, Ohio in the winter of 1805. Lived together until March 1818. They had child (not named) born May 1810. John not presently a resident of Ohio. (54)

July 1818 - Andrew CULBERTSON vs. Mary CULBERTSON. Petition for Divorce. Filed 2-21-1817. Andrew married Mary in February 1806. Suit for divorce discontinued. *78)

7-10-1820 - William GUTWRIDGE vs. Hester GUTRIDGE. Petition for Divorce Filed 10-15-1817. William now a resident of Champaign County, Ohio married 6-1-1813 to Hester Masterson, then a resident of Troy, now a resident of Indiana. At time of marriage he was an ensign in the 26 Regt. U. S. Infantry. He was ordered to join the northern army commanded by General Brown and was unable to return home for 18 months. Hester was delivered of a child 12 months after he left that could not be his and after that Hester had an additional child by a Mr. Evans. (101)

7-1-1823 - John WEATHERHEAD vs. Rachel WEATHERHEAD. Petition for Divorce. Filed 1-4-1823. John married 8-1-1812 in Miami County, Ohio to Rachel Friend. Rachel on 11-13-1822 left petition, going with a man named David Jones. Petitioner has six children by Rachel, the youngest of which she took with her. (266)

7-1-1823 - Richard HUGHS vs. Margaret HUGHS. Petition for Divorce. Filed 11-16-1822. Richard married Margaret Brown on 10-19-1815 in Muskingum Co., Ohio. They lived together until 7-8-1818 when Margaret left petitioner. No children by marriage. Case dismissed.

7-9-1827 - Mary CULBERTSON vs. Andrew CULBERTSON. Petition for Divorce. Filed 11-24-1829. Mary Culbertson late Mary Danley married Andrew in February 1806 in Mifflin County, Pennsylvania. They lived together until September 1815, since which Andrew has been absent more than ten years. Three children by marriage. That Andrew returned to Pennsylvania and there married a Margaret Clark. (398)

7-9-1827 - Thomas W. MANSFIELD vs. Hannah MANSFIELD. Petition for Divorce. Filed 2-8-1826. Thomas married 1-21-1818 in Athens County, Ohio to Hannah Wilson. Hannah Left petitioner on 9-1-1822. (400)

7-7-1828 - Barbara LORTON vs. John LORTON. Petition for Divorce. Filed 3-26-1828. Married 10-25-1820 in Miami Co., Ohio. John left petitioner on 11-15-1824, she being left with an infant 11 months old. (414)

7-13-1831 - Samuel COPPOCK vs. Mary COPPOCK. Petition for Divorce. Filed 1-28-1831. Samuel married August 1826 in Darke County, Ohio to Mary Sumner. Mary on 8-4-1827 left petitioner and refused to reside with him. (415)

7-13-1831 - Henry LOY vs. Errilla LOY. Petition for Divorce. Filed 3-26-1829.
Henry married 12-23-1824 in Greene Co., Ohio to Errilla Burns. On 9-4-1828
Erilla left petitioner, with a man named David Wright. (419)

7-9-1831 - Richard HUGHS vs. Margaret HUGHS. Petition for Divorce. Filed
3-22-1828. Richard married Margaret Brown in 1815 in Muskingum Co., Ohio.
Lived together until July 1818 when Margaret left petitioner. (420)

7-13-1831 - Elizabeth DUNHAM vs. Asa DUNHAM. Petition for Divorce. Filed 1-25-1831.
Married 2-24-1818 in Miami Co., Ohio, lived together until 11-16-1825 when Asa
left petitioner with his three children. She is now compelled to support herself
and four children. (422)

7-13-1831 - Elizabeth LOGUE vs. Benjamin LOGUE. Petition for Divorce. Filed
3-14-1829. Married 11-25-1823 in Miami County, Ohio. Benjamin left Elizabeth
on 8-20-1825. (424)

The following abstracts were taken from Will Book A-1, Will Book A-2, Will Book A-3. Number of Will Book and number of page on which will may be found in original record is given in parenthesis.

MILES, William - dated 3-14-1807; recorded (not given); Union twp. late of Montgomery Co. Ohio. Wife, Rachel. Sons: David, Jonathan, William, Samuel and John. William, Samuel and John not of age. Daughters: Catharine Coat, Rhoda Hendricks, Elizabeth Coat, Sally Brown, Anne Miles and Abigail Miles. Anne and Abigail not of age. Mentions, Abner Barret. Executors: wife, Rachel and son (son-in-law?) William Coat. Signed: William Miles. Witnesses: Henry Coate, Samuel Littlejohn and Samuel Coate. (1-1)

SURFACE, John - dated 10-16-1808; recorded (not given). Sons: Andrew and John. Daughter: Elizabeth Surface (not of age). Mentions land lying on branch of Lees Creek, the water of Paint Creek. Executors: friends, Samuel Black and Ralph Stafford. Witnesses: John Williams, Christiopher Stafford and George (mark) Richison. Codicil: 10-24-1808, no additional information, only additional bequests to same parties. Witnesses: John Williams and George (mark) Overpeck. (1-6)

SHAKLEFORD (SHAKELFORD), Reuben - dated 8-26-1808; recorded (not given). Wife, Rebecca. Sons: William and James (to be bound out to trades). Daughter: Peggy. Signed: Reuben (mark) Shakleford. Witnesses: James Orr, John Todd and James Marshall. (1-9)

JENKINS, David - Elizabeth twp. Montgomery Co. Ohio. Dated: 8-20-1806, recorded (not given). Sons: William, David, Thomas, Jesse, Amos and Enoch. Daughters: Mary Jenkins and Elizabeth Crussel(?). Executors: David and Jesse Jenkins. Signed: David Jenkins. Witnesses: Jesse Gerrard and James Knight. (1-10)

FARR, Michael - Concord twp. Dated 2-18-1809; recorded (not given). Wife, Elizabeth. Children: Susannah Farr, George Farr, John Clark (Farr?), Sophia Farr and Catharine Farr (not of age). Executors: Wife, Elizabeth Farr and Samuel Pearson. Signed: Michal (mark) Farr. Witnesses: Richard Clegg, Samuel Freeman and Jacob Pearson. (1-12)

SHEETS, Andrew - Dated 5-29-1809. Recorded (not given). Wife, Catharine. Two eldest sons: Jacob and Martin Sheets. Mentions other children, not of age, but does not name. Executors: Catharine Sheets and son, Jacob Sheets. Signed: Andrew (mark) Sheets. Witnesses: David Hoover, Daniel Hoover, Jr. and John Mote. (1-14)

SUMME(SUMMA), Mikel - Rowen Co. N. Car. now of Miami Co. Ohio. Dated 7-18-1809. Recorded (not given). Only son: Peter Summe. Daughters: Margaret Pirelan (oldest dau.), Mary Carn (2nd dau.), Genny Pirelin (3rd dau.) and Kitran Summe (youngest dau.). Executors: Michael Williams, Jr. and Thomas Hill. Signed: Mikel (mark) Summa. Witnesses: James Youart, Peter (mark) Carn and James Hays. (1-16)

SIMPSON, John - Union twp. Dated: 4-18-1811. Recorded (not given). Wife: mentioned, but not named. Sons: David, John and James. Daughters: Hannah Shin and Ruth Hilburn. Mentions land in Pa. Bucks(?) Co. Salisbury twp. Also mentions 50 acres of land between John Simpson and William Neely's land; also lot in Falls Twp. (note: none of these land descriptions are very specific). Executors: Wife, not named; David and John Simpson. Signed: John Simpson. Witnesses: David Mote and Francis Jones. (1-18)

SUNDERLAND, Peter - Bethel twp. Dated 12-22-1812. Recorded (not given). Wife: mentioned, but not named. Children: Christenhen, Edward, Catharine, Emaline and William. Executors: Samuel Black of Champaign Co. Ohio and Peter Sunderland, Sr. Signed: Peter (mark) Sunderland. Witnesses: John Grayson Cecil and Thomas Stafford. (2-18)

JAY, Layton - Union twp. Dated: 10-23-1812. Recorded (not given). Wife: Elizabeth. Sons: William, John, James, David and Elijah. Daughters: Patience, Lotty, Abigail, Mary and Anna. Executor: William Jay. Signed: Layton Jay. Witnesses: Benjamin Coppock and Robert Pemberton. (2-19)

JOHNSTON, Abner - dated 11-25-1813. Recorded (not given). Wife: Sarah. Mentions 3 sons and 3 daughters, but does not name. Executor: Daniel Cory. Signed: Abner (mark) Johnston. Witnesses: John H. Crawford and Jonathan Johnston. (2-20)

THOMPSON, Joseph - Dated 9-1-1813. Recorded (not given). Sons: Joseph Thompson Jr., deceased and Richard Thompson. Daughters: Mary Jenkens and her husband William Jenkens, Jane Hilbum (or Hilburn) and her husband Levi Hilbum/Hilburn. Granddaughters: Sarah Miles formerly Sarah McKensey; Ann, Mary and Sary Thompson, daughters of Joseph Thompson, Jr., deceased. Mentions land conveyed to deceased by John Eleman, 182 acres in Newberry District, South Carolina; also tract of land containing 10 acres conveyed to deceased by Abijah O'Neal and Hugh O'Neal in Newberry District, South Carolina. Mentions money Hugh O'Neal collected from James Shepherd. Executors: William Jenkins and Mary Jenkins. Signed: Joseph Thompson. Witnesses: M.W.(?) Furnas, Robert Pearson and Thomas Pearson, Jr. (2-53)

GREEN, Thomas - Oral Will. Deposition dated 6-19-1813. Recorded 5-13-1814. Thomas Green departed life 6-17-1813. Wife: Abigail Green, if she ceases to be widow by death or marriage, estate is to be distributed by law. Witnesses: George Green and Clementine (mark) Shepherd. (2-55)

KYLE, Samuel, Sen. - Concord twp. Dated: 3-20-1814. Recorded: (not given). Wife: Mary, mentions money coming to her from her father's estate. Son: Samuel. Daughters: Lucy Kyle, Betsey Orr, and Ann Kirkley. Executors: son, Samuel Kyle and James Orr. Signed: Samuel (mark) Kyle. Witnesses: Cornelius Westfall, Reuben Westfall and James Youart. (2-56_

LOUTHAIN, John - Dated 4-7-1813. Recorded (not given). Sons: Samuel D., John, George and Absalom. Daughters: Tabitha, Sally, Milly, Nancy, Grissey, Polly, and Juley (last 5 daughters were unmarried). Executor: friend, Samuel Black. Signed: John Louthain. Witnesses: William Mitchell and George Louthain. (2-61)

LONG, William - dated 5-11-1813. Recorded (not given). Wife: Rachel. Sons: Robert (eldest son), William (2nd son), John and Stephen (2 youngest sons). Daughters: Elizabeth (married woman), Polly and youngest daughter Rachel. Executors: sons, William and James. Signed: William Long. Witnesses: James Long and Robt. Long. (2-64)

JENKINS, Enoch - Oral Will. Recorded (not given). Will given 2nd day, 2nd month, 1815. Deposition dated 4-24-1815. Brothers: David; Jesse; Amos; William, deceased; Isaac, deceased; and Thomas, deceased. Nephews: Robert and Isaac Jenkins sons of David Jenkins; Phineas, Joseph and William Jenkins, sons of William Jenkins, dec'd; David Jenkins son of Isaac Jenkins, dec'd; Ely and Isachac Jenkins sons of Thomas Jenkins, dec'd; Samuel Jenkins son of Amos Jenkins; Phineas Jenkins son of Jesse Jenkins. Executor: Jesse Jenkins. Witness: Jesse Jenkins and Amos Jenkins.(2-72)

CHILDERS, Henry - Oral Will. Recorded (not given). Will given on 1-13-1815. Deposition given 4-3-1815. Wife: Jane. 2 youngest sons: Henry and Elisha. Witnesses: James Blue and William (mark) Henarix. (2-74)

CARSON, John - Dated 12-24-1814. Recorded 1816. Wife, Sally. Sons: Samuel, John, Benjamin, William and James. Daughters: Sophia and Hannah. Executor: son, Benjamin. Signed: John Carson. Witnesses: John H. Crawford and Robert Morrison. (2-78)

SMITH, Agnes - Scott County, Kentucky. Dated 9-3-1800. Recorded 1816. 4 children of John Herson, deceased, does not name. Mentions Nancy Henderson and John Henderson. Executors: John A. Miller and William Berry. Signed: Agness Smith. Witnesses: Robert Miller and Wm. Berry. (2-83)

TRACE, Andrew - Dated 6-1-1816. Recorded, 1816. Sons: Adam and Andrew Trace. Daughter: Christiana Bowers. Grand-daughter: Sarah Bowers. Executors: Robert McConnell and John Cox. Signed: Andrew Trace. Witnesses: Robert Finney, Thomas Brown and Thomas Vernon. (2-91)

HAYS, Francis - Union twp. Dated 7-12-1811. Recorded 1817. Son: James Hays, also to serve as Executor. Signed: Francis Hays. Witnesses: Robert (mark) Dickson and James Youart. (2-94)

MOTE, David - Dated 9-26-1816. Recorded, 1817. Wife, Dorcas Mote. Mentions lawful heirs, does not name. Executor: James Patty. Signed: David Mote. Witnesses: Isaac Hasket and Elisha Jones. (2-95)

SMITH, Josiah - Dated 4-25-1817. Recorded 1817. Wife, Betsey. Sons: John (eldest son), Thomas Cory, Aron and Elnathan William Smith. Daughters: Jane, Salla, Fanny, Phebe, Caty and Harriett. Executor: Elnathan Cory. Signed: Josiah Smith. Witnesses: John H. Crawford, John A. Hays and David J. Cory. (2-99)

CRAWFORD, Robert - Dated 5-19-1817. Recorded 1817. Wife: Hannah C. Sons: Robert, James Lee and John H. Daughter: Charlotte Morrison. Grandson Andrew Crawford. Mentions land adjoining Daniel Fielding on north side of State Road for meeting house and burying place. Signed: Robert Crawford. Witnesses: William and Lewis Gearheard. (2-99)

HEARTLESS(HARLESS), Richard Wardrobe - Oral Will. Will given 6-13-1817. Deposition dated 6-18-1817. Newphew, George Clark a minor, son of John Clark. Witnesses: Barnahas (mark) Blue, Sen.; Barnabas Blue, Jr. and Bennet W. Langley. (2-102)

SMITH, Daniel - Concord twp. Dated 5-2-1817. Recorded 1819. Son, James Smith. Grandsons: Daniel and Abner Smith, not of age; Jacob Smith. Granddaughter: Elizabeth Smith. Step-granddaughter: Elizabeth Adams. Bible to grandson, Daniel Smith; 3 vol. of History of Holy Scripture to grandson, Abner Smith. Executors: friends, David Jenkins, Jr. and Benjamin Pearson. Signed: Daniel Smith. Witnesses: Isaac and Noah Pearson, Phineas Jenkins. (2-118)

GRIESMAN, Catharine - Dated 10-11-1813. Recorded 1819. Children: George, Catherine Shaffer, John William Greseman, John Giesman, Magdalene Rohn, Curella Bellaman, Susanna Werts and Anne Maria Giesaman. Executrix, daughter, Maria Giesaman. Signed: Catharine (mark) Giesaman. Witnesses: John Folkerth of Montgomery Co., Ohio and Addison Smith. On 2-19-1819 at Tulpehocken Twp. Bucks Co. Pa., Anna Maria Giesaman renounced right to executor the estate. (2-120)

JACOBS, Mark - Bethel Twp. Dated 5-16-1819. Recorded 1819. Wife, Margaret. Children mentioned, not named. Executors, Lewis Gearhard and Margaret Jacobs. Signed: Mark (mark) Jacobs. Witnesses: Andrew D. Brier and Cad. W. Jacobs. (2-127)

REES, David - Dated 2-1-1820 - Recorded 7-12-1820. Wife, Sophia. Sons: Jeremiah, Samuel, Cyrus, David and John. Daughters: Miria Steel, Polly Thomas, Elizabeth, Nancy, Sally, Catharine and Hariet Rees. (3 youngest children: David, John and Hariet). Executors: sons, Jeremiah and Samuel; Robert Morrison; David Jenkins. Signed: David Rees. Witnesses: John Snider, Isaac Russell, Alexander P. Ward. (2-135)

SKINNER, Anderson - Monroe Twp. Dated 1-3-1820. Recorded 8-14-1820. Wife, Nancy. Mentions children, does not name, youngest child not of age. Brother, Thomas Skinner. Signed: Anderson (mark) Skinner. Witnesses: Isaac Mahnin(?), Thomas Skinner and William McWanson(?). (2-138)

FADLER, George - Will in German. Not dated. Recorded 8-14-1820. Mentions wife and children, also mentions Wentel and Catharina as full heirs, not specific if they are same. Signed: George Fadler. Witnesses: David Deeter and Henry Born. (2-139)

SHIDEAKER, John - Dated 10-4-1815. Recorded 3-31-1821. Wife: Eve. Son: Michael. Daughter: Eve. Son-in-law: Matthias Long. Grandsons: John Shideaker, John Rouzer, Volentine Shideaker. Executor: son, Michael Shideaker. Signed: John Shidecker. Witnesses: Samuel Kyle and John Pettet. (2-149)

THERECK, Jacob - Newberry twp. Dated 8-13-1820. Recorded 3-31-1821. Wife: Elizabeth. Mentions children not of age, does not name. Mentions money coming from Pa. Executor: John Cable. Signed: Jacob Thereck (German signature). Witnesses: Johann(?) ....? and Emanuel Miller. (2-151)

133

HILL, Thomas - Dated 5-4-1818. Recorded 8-20-1821. Wife: Sarah. Sons: Nathan (eldest son) and John Hill. Daughters: Elizabeth now wife of Joseph Miller (eldest daughter) and Sally Hill (youngest daughter). Executors: sons, Nathan and John Hill. Mentions land in Darke County, Ohio. Signed: Thomas (mark) Hill. Witnesses: James Haworth, Noah Hanks and Elisha McCool. (2-159)

PEIRCE, Gainer - Dated: 5-9-1818. Recorded 4-8-1822. Wife, Ruth. Sons: Samuel (eldest), John, James, George and Benjamin D. Daughters: Mary Parham and Ruth Embree. Executors: wife, Ruth and son, Samuel. Signed: Gainer Peirce. Witnesses: Benjamin Pickering and Joseph Iddings. (3-1)

COATE(COAT-COTE), Marmaduke - Dated 10-2-1817. Recorded 1822. Wife, Mary. Sons: Moses, Henry, Samuel, James, William, John and Jesse. Daughter: Sarah Hall. Mentions meeting house lot. Executors: sons, Samuel and James Cote. Signed: Marmaduk (mark) Coat. Witnesses: Samuel Teague, Isaac Embree and William Ellemon. (3-2)

YOUNT, John - Dated 8-1-1821. Recorded 12-13-1822. Wife, Mary. Sons: Henry (eldest son), Solomon (next eldest) and Frederick (third and last son). Daughters: Delilah Werts and Rebeccah Hoover. Mentions land in Montgomery County, Ohio. Signed: John Yount. Witnesses: Thomas Macy and Walter D. Jay. (3-4)

CHAPEZE, Henry - Town of Piqua. Dated 3-17-1823. Recorded 4-14-1823. Practioner of Medicine. Mother, not named, of State of Kentucky; also, mentions a farm in Nelson Co., Ky. Wife, Elizabeth. Daughter Rossetta, also mentions unborn child. Signed: H. Chapeze. Executors: Robert Houston, Sr. and John McClory. Witnesses: John McCorkle and John Johnston. Codicil dated 3-19-1823 - names additional executor John McCorkle of Piqua; also, that monies are to be paid to John Johnston for safekeeping. Signed: H. Chapeze. Witnesses: John Johnston, Benj. Cox and Hugh Scott. (3-8)

FOUTS, Henry - Dated 12-23-1822. Recorded 1823. Wife, Susanna. Only son, John. Daughters: Barbara Hoover (eldest), Mary Wheelook (2nd), Rebecca Fouts (3rd dau. a single woman), Matilda Fouts (4th daughter-a minor) and Elizabeth Fouts (5th daughter-aminor). Executor: Frederick Yount. Signed: Henry Fouts. Witnesses: Henry Hoover and John Hoover. (3-10)

CECIL, Thomas - Dated 8-5-1823. Recorded 1823-4. Wife, Milley. Sons: William, John and James - mentions that son James is intending to intermarry with Catharine Carver daughter of Benjamin Carver. Daughters: Eleanor, Letey, Rebecca Cecil, Polly Woggle(Noggle?), Barbara Wallon and Nancy Earley. Executor: son, James if he does not marry Catharine Carver, if so, then son-in-law, Reuben Wallon of Clark County, Ohio is to serve as Executor. Signed: Thomas (mark) Cecil. Witnesses: Joseph R. John and Joseph Culbertson. (3-15)

YATES, Thomas - Dated 5-12-1823. Recorded 1823-4. Wife, Phebe Yates. Children: Jonathan L. Yates, Artis S. Yates, Edmund S. Yates, Elizabeth L. Liming (mar. woman) and Nezer S. Yates. Son-in-law, Warren Leming. Executor: son, Nezer S. Yates and friendly neighbor Matthew Dinsmore. Signed: Thomas Yates. Witnesses: Joseph and Myhew Rollins; Robert and John Dinsmore. (3-19)

134

WESTFALL, Rachel - Dated 5-1-1823. Recorded 1823-4. Step-mother, Ann Eye. Brothers: Stephen Dye, John M. Dye, Andrew Dye and Benjamin Dye. Sisters: Mary Dye w/o Samuel Dye, deceased and Betsy Dye. Also mentions Elizabeth wife of John Dye, Elizabeth wife of William Dye, deceased, Eleanor Love wife of Joseph Love, Mrs. Gray wife of Thomas B. Gray. Executor: brother, John M. Dye. Signed: Rachel (mark) Westfall. Witnesses: Samuel Kyle and George Louthain. Codicil dated 8-1-1823. Sister, Fanny Sayers. Niece, Rachel. Signed: Rachel (mark) Westfall. Witnesses: Samuel Kyle and Ezekiel Kirtley. (3-22)

STATLER, Christley - Dated 1-27-1824. Recorded 1824. Wife, Christena. Sons: John and Jacob, also to serve as Executors. Daughter: Polly. Signed: Christley Statler. Witnesses: George Statler and Christopher (no other name given). (3-24)

BROWN, Thomas - Dated 2-27-1823. Recorded June 1824. Wife and children, mentioned but not named. Executors: Robert McConnell and William Davidson. Signed: Thomas Brown. Witnesses: Samuel Jones, Francis Jones and John Davis. (3-26)

MILES, David - Dated 3-28-1820. Recorded 4-4-1825. Wife, Rebeca. Sons: William (eldest) and David (youngest). Daughter: Anna Cole formerly wife of Elijah Jones (eldest daughter). Executors: sons, William and David Miles. Signed: David (mark) Miles. Witnesses: James Haworth and Jonathan Miles. (3-27_

KNIFE, Michael - Dated 9-28-1825. Filed 9-28-1825. Wife, Elizabeth. Five children: Hannah, Nancy, John, Jonathan and Amy(or Aney). Executors: wife, Elizabeth and son-in-law, John Roderick. Signed: Michal (mark) Knife. Witnesses: Phillip(mark) Youc, Robert Pearson and Enoch Pearson. (3-31)

JENKINS, Jesse - Dated 2-28-1825. Recorded 11-26-1825. Sons: Jesse (not of age) and Phinehos. Daughters: Elizabeth Pearson, Rosanna Jenkins and (youngest) Hannah Jenkins. Executors: Samuel Teague, Ely Jenkins and John F. Pearson. Signed: Jesse Jenkins. Witnesses: David Jenkins, Jr., Benj. Smalley and Amos Jenkins. (3-35)

McCOOLE, Gabriel - 8-14-1825. Recorded 1-23-1826. Sons: Elisha and his present wife Sally McCoole; James; Thomas; Gabriel; Wells and John (John being deceased) Daughters: Rachel Evans; Martha Hanks; Nancy Wright, deceased; and Elizabeth M. Dorman. Mentions, Heirs of Nancy Wright, deceased, as Gabriel and John Wright. Heirs of John McCoole, deceased, as Hester, Pickering, Mack Alexander and Thomas McCoole. Executor: friend, Oliver Benton. Signed: Gabriel McCoole. Witnesses: James Haworth, Asa Inmon and Samuel Kelley. (3-39)

McCLURE, Robert - Dated 2-3-1826. Recorded 2-23-1826. Wife, Margaret. Three children: Mary, William and Elizabeth. Mentions land in Shelby County, Ohio. Executors: Richard Morrow and David Clark. Signed: Robert McClure. Witnesses: Henry Kitchen, J. Jenkinson and Hugh Scott. (3-42)

PALMER, Robert - Dated 7-11-1826. Recorded 7-12-1826(?). Wife, Martha also to serve as Executrix. Signed: Robert Palmer. Witnesses: John H. Woolcut, David Knight and Thomas J. Garrard. (3-45)

IDDINGS, Benjamin - Dated 4-19-1826. Recorded 7-25-1826. Wife, Ruth. Sons: Joseph and Talbott. Daughters: Ruth Green, Mary Ballinger, Phebe Rooker, Milley Pierce and Hannah Cothron. Grandsons: Benjamin and William Neal. Executors: son, Talbert Iddings and son-in-law Samuel Pierce. Signed: Benjamin Iddings. Witnesses: Benjamin Pearson and Joseph Pearson. (3-47)

CONCANNON, William - Dated 3-3-1826. Recorded 7-24-1826. Wife, Ann. Children: William; Polly; mentions seven youngest children of which only Sally and Catharine are named. Signed: William Concannon. Witnesses: Wm. McKinney and J. Concannon. (3-51)

WEAVER, Peter - Dated 6-20-1826. Recorded 11-7-1826. Wife, Jane. Children: Robert, Susan and Daniel. Executors: Casper Young and Jane Weaver. Signed: Peter (mark) Weaver. Witnesses: Mathew Neucomb, George Young and Peter Segler. (3-53)

Guardianship	Date	Case	Guardianship	Date	Case
ALEXANDER, Levi	1830	521	CALDWELL, Samuel, Davis &	1811	49
ALLEN, Archibald	1820	256	Sally		52
Kirby	1840	1041	CARSON, John	1833	629
ANTHONY, Sally	1838	908	Nancy	1824	356
AYERS, John R., Insau,Jane,	1840	1072	CARTER, Aaron	1817	186
Richard F., Mary A. &			William	1817	184
Rebecca			CASEY, Eli	1814	103
BAILY, Wm C.	1836	869	CASSEL, Michael & David	1839	996
BANNING, Jacob	1838	914	CATON, John	1837	837
BARBER, Melinda	1814	108	CAVEN, John & Samuel M.	1828	476
Susan	1814	107	CAVE NDER, Ruth Blackford	1830	523
BARBOUR, Stephen, Jane, Mary	1833	634	Thomas	1828	464
Ann & Chas.			CECIL, Nancy, Thomas &	1839	941
BARRINGTON, Thomas Pierce	1837	861	Barbara		
BEEDLE, Mary	1837	829	CHAPPEZE, Rosetta Henrietta	1826	418
BEER, James	1833	615	CHEVALIN, Sally Ann, Eliza-	1831	550
BELLUE, Isaac	1811	50	beth, Charlotte &		
BLUE, Jno. L, Abner, Mahet-	1822	301	Mary J.		
able, Mary, James W.			CHILDERS, Elisha	1825	393
and Blackford			James	1833	654
BLUE, Francis, Ruth, Mahet-	1834	668	CLARK, Jon Q., Foster T. &	1834	685
able & Wm S.			Henry G.		
BOSSON, David	1840	1073	Sally Ann & Wm G.	1833	655
BOTTSELL, Catherine Nancy,	1825	407	Samuel	1819	176
Mary Ann, Sarah			CLEMMAN, Benjamin	1810	38
Rebeca & Esther			CLINGANφ Edward, Susanna &	1823	351
BRAND, Esther, Anna & Sarah	1832	587	John		
BRANDON, Wm E. & Mary J.	1835	728	Elsey	1817	190
BROWN, Joseph	1836	802	Mary	1818	197
Nancy, Elizabeth,	1823	349	CLINGHAN, Dorcas	1836	771
Joseph, Mary & Jane			Jesse, Edward &	1836	770
BRUMBAUGH, Jacob	1824	364	Josiah		
BRYAN, George	1829	497	Nancy	1836	772
BUFFINGTON, Elenor & Hiram	1830	516	CLYNE, William, Isaac &	1834	709
BURGMAN, Elizabeth, Jacob,	1839	969	Ingram		
John P. & Charistian			COATE, Isaac	1821	273
BURROWS, Jos., Matilda A. &	1834	653	COLE, David M.	1837	842
Susanna			COLEMAN, Darwin	1839	991
BUZETT, Edward F., Melissa,	1840	1020	Lydia, Jasen, &	1807	9
Margaret A., Wm H.			Westley		
& Rachel			COPPOCK, Barbara, Mary Eliz-	1839	987
CALDWELL, Eliza, Gray & Mary	1840	1028	beth, Thomas &		
Jane			Sarah J.		
Rebecca Davis	1840	1034	John, Samuel & Nancy	1839	940
John W., Pemberton,	1828	477	CORY, Jane M.	1832	602
Mary J. & Stephen			COTHRAN, Jesse's Heirs	1830	536
Matthew, James &	1811	46	John	1831	574
Joseph		47	COTTRAN, Alexander	1818	206
		48	David Steaman	1818	205

Guardianship	Date	Case
COX, Unice, Hannah & Nancy	1811	.54
		55
		56
CREGAN, Mary, James, Nancy,	1820	237
Dan'l, Sarah & Cath.		
CREW, Casper, Wester &	1834	681
Mannalius S.		
CROCKETT, Chas, Marmoduk &	1829	507
Mordecai		
CROMER, Isa Mayo	1837	815
John	1832	586
CRUE, Casper W. & Menalcus S.	1840	1060
CULBERTSON, Samuel	1818	198
DAVIDSON, Douglas N.	1839	964
DAVIS, George G.	1831	557
Geo, Grove , Chas G.	1825	403
DEETER, Daniel, Susan, Emanuel	1834	666
& Catharine		
DELONG, Jacob	1822	309
DEMAN, Benejah, Abner,Susannah,	1835	758
and Olive		
DEPRAY, Jacob	1821	269
DEPRA, Jonathan,Betsy,Daniel	1821	272
Molly, John & David		
Henry	1821	268
DEWEESE, Ann & Sally	1822	312
Samuel, Peggy & Polly	1822	313
John, Mary, Elizabeth	1839	961
Andrew, David, Melissa & Thos. L.		
John G., Katharine	1837	853
Mary J., Tracy, Wm & Hannah		
DILBONE, Wm H., Margaret,	1814	110
Priscilla & John		
DIPPRA, Daniel	1823	329
DOLLISON, Mary A.	1835	732
William	1832	597
DORMAN, Elenor	1834	675
John B, Christian &	1833	647
David		
DRAKE, Jeremiah & Isabella	1825	410
DUNKIN, Isaiah, Richard & John	1828	480
Samuel, Sally, Amos &	1828	479
Richard		
DUNLAP, Alexander	1814	116
DUNN, Stephen	1824	385
DYE, Belinda & Mary	1823	332

Guardianship	Date	Cas
DYE, Marshall A, Mary A. &	1838	8
Margaret M.		
Wm H.H., Sarah A., Samuel,	1832	5
& John E		
EDWARDS, Olive	1824	3
ELLEMAN, Joseph & Margaret	1825	3
Jane, James & Wm	1836	7
FAGER, Catharine	1837	8
FALKNER, Joseph	1826	4
FINDLEY, John P.,Wm M,Sam'l P,	1827	4
James W, Elvira H. &		
Eliz. P.		
FOLKNER, Bailary and Mary	1835	7
FOSTER, Zeptha	1821	2
FOX, Archabald	1808	
FRAZEE, Moses	1840	10
FRAZIER, John	1839	9
David & Matilda	1830	5
Isreal	1830	5
FREEMAN, Caleb & Robert	1822	3
Mary	1815	1
Matilda	1815	1
Priscilla	1815	1
FRENCH, James	1812	
Johannah	1812	
John	1812	
Rachel	1812	
William	1812	
FRIEND, Andrew, John, Rebecca	1821	2
& Wm		
Elizabeth,Hester,Sarah	1831	5
Catharine, Jesse and		
Henry		
FRIZZLE, Jacob	1839	9
FRIZZELL, Elizabeth, Harriet E,	1839	9
Mary A. and Alice J.		
FULLER, Mary	1840	10
FURNAS, Robert W. & Rachel	1834	6
GAHAGAN, Maria	1839	9
GARARD, Elizabeth & Mary	1822	2
GARRETT, John C.	1819	2
GATES, Wm A, Timothy G., Abbott	1829	4
G, et al.		
GERARD, Abner	1815	1
GIBSON, Jonathan	1833	6
GIBBS, John	1824	3
GLENN, Charles	1829	4
GRAHAM, William	1839	9

Guardianship	Date	Case	Guardianship	Date	Case
GREEN, Wilkerson	1839	959	JENKINS, Hannah	1826	415
HAIN, James, Hester & Rosannah	1837	824	Jesse	1826	414
GRUBB, John, Elizabeth	1824	388	JOHNSON, James, Martha &	1821	259
HANNA, Harriet N.	1830	525	Elizabeth		
HARMON, Caroline	1840	1037	JOHNSTON, Daniel A.	1817	188
HAY, Jean	1808	20	David	1814	114
Joseph	1808	19	Eliza & Stephen	1821	263
HAYWORTH, Mary	1831	566	Eliza & Stephen	1823	334
Sampson	1831	565	James	1814	112
Wade & Joseph	1831	569	Jane	1817	185
HEDGES, William	1831	573	John, Stephen, Wm	1823	327
HELMICK, Jacob, Elizabeth,	1835	753	F.W. & Caroline		
Alexander, Mary Ann,			William	1817	189
et al.			Harriet	1833	612
John Harrison	1840	1031	Randall	1833	620
HENDERSHOTT, Addison, Wash-	1824	371	Seth S. & Jane P.	1840	1066
ington, John F. &			Wm and Mary F.	1840	1046
David			JONES, Elihu G, Isabella &	1833	617
HENDRICKS, Catharine	1814	86	Salem		
Polly	1814	85	Lindley M. & Elenor C.	1833	630
William	1809	28	Owen	1837	830
HICKMAN, Jonathan, Nancy,	1838	875	Susannah, Prudence &	1836	792
Oliver, Elizabeth,			Elanor C.		
& Jeremiah			Zelpha, Martha and	1840	1065
HILLIARD, Fielding and	1831	562	Rebecca		
Patterson			Joseph	1829	506
HIRT, Almira	1819	216	Mary & Phebe Ann	1830	529
HITCHEN, Wm	1840	1003	KERR, Martha, James, Wm J.	1836	807
HOLLEPETER, Rudolph, Mary &	1834	671	Mary and Harvey		
Elizabeth			KNIFE, Samuel	1840	897
HOOVER, William P.	1839	942	KNIGHT, Eliz, Priscilla	1822	315
HOUSER, Christian, Abraham,	1824	363	Corbly, Wm, Stephen,		
Eliza, Anna, Susanna,			Paul & Mary A.		
& Jacob			Jonathan, Hugh, Mar-	1830	522
Jonah	1835	736	aret & Clarissa		
HOWE, Sam'l M. & John D.	1831	571	KNIZA, Sarah, Jane, Susan,	1840	1017
HOWEL, George W.	1838	880	Caroline & Isaac		
HOWSER, Polly, Catharine,	1833	636	KNOX, John G. & James A.	1827	444
Isaac & John			Margaret, Miles & Eliz.	1827	439
HUTTSELL, John W.	1831	559	KRING, Philip & Catharine	1824	387
IDDINGS, Sarah and Hannah	1839	943	LANDRE, Richard	1829	486
INGLE, David, Lydia, Sally &	1839	975	LANDREE, Daniel	1813	73
Abraham			LANDRY, John	1827	455
JACKSON, William C.	1839	997	LOVE, Lewis	1834	706
JAY, Thomas	1816	163	LOVETT, Stephen C.	1838	871
JEFFRIES, Hannah, Alexander,	1839	949	LOW, George	1829	509
Sarah J. & Jones			MADDEN, Margaret, Henry & Wm	1816	151

Guardianship	Date	Case	Guardianship	Date	Case
MAHURIN, Anna and Catharine	1832	590	McCLURE, Andrew	1826	427
Belinda	1832	588	McCOOL, Mark Alexander	1817	180
MANHEIN, Rachel and Levinia	1832	589	McCOOLE, Hester	1817	192
MANN, Barnabass	1807	10	Thomas W.	1816	162
John & Molly	1808	15	McCORKLE, Mary J, Nancy, Jos,	1829	500
Ruth and Able	1833	656	et al.		
MANNING, John, Sarah A. Eliza-	1832	591	McCOY, Gilbert	1839	967
beth, Mary, Nancy, Wm,			Joseph G.	1832	585
and Azriah			McCULLOUGH, Eliza, Mary & Sam'l	1840	1021
MANSON, Wm	1826	417	McGrahan, Daniel	1815	129
MAPES, Thomas	1825	406	McJEMPSEY, Wm, Susannah, et al.	1826	429
MAPS, Elenor	1821	278	McKINNEY, James M., Samuel S.,	1835	761
MARSHALL, Lucilla	1823	320	et al.		
Margaret	1837	822	McKNIGHT, Rebecca	1833	622
Thomas and Shab	1838	892	Sarah J. & Catharine	1832	592
MART, Elizabeth, Peter, Polly,	1838	900	McLUNG, George Heber	1840	1059
Jacob and Andrew			McMAKEN, George, Caleb, James,	1839	999
MARTIN, Abijah and Wm	1834	665	et al.		
Delila, Eliz., John,	1834	652	William	1839	1000
Levi, Louis & Green			McMULLIN, Rebecca & Chas. H.	1838	894
Hannah	1833	657	McKNIGHT, William	1830	532
Levi	1834	708	NEAL, Hester, Rachel & Eliz'th	1824	374
MARTIN, Samuel	1827	453	John, Sarah, Mahlond and	1824	375
MATHEW, John	1840	1013	Thos. C.		
MEAGUIANS, Thram	1818	215	Rachel	1813	78
MEEKER, Abagail	1835	737	NEALE, Harriet, Lucinda, etal.	1826	435
MIKESELL, Wm, Katherine & Jacob	1839	970	NEALY, Benjamin	1816	165
MILLER, Anna, Maria, Mary Co.,	1840	1070	NEEPER, Margaret	1824	377
Geo. M. & David M.			NOLAN, James, et al.	1831	556
Dan'l, Martha, Nancy,	1827	452	NORTH, Allen, Lavina, et al.	1839	968
David & Eliz			OADEWALT, Margaret, Sarah and	1840	1052
John	1821	266	Mary E.		
MILLS, Peggy	1818	196	ODLE, Mary Cornhammah	1810	34
MINNICH, Barbara, Eliz. & David	1840	1015	ORR, Thomas K, Martha and	1826	416
MITCHELL, Moses G., Catharine	1826	419	PATTY, Elizabeth, Lot and Hugh	1834	669
& Mary Ann			PEARSON, Abigail	1830	520
MORELAND, Alex, Byers & James	1825	396	Benjamin	1815	171
MORGAN, Andrew Jackson	1833	613	Enoch	1809	33
MORROW, Elizabeth & Watson	1827	441	John	1809	32
Jane & Adams	1827	438	Mary	1809	31
MOTE, Carolina M, Hannah, John	1840	1104	Noah	1815	170
and Rhoda			Isaac	1838	876
Elias et al.	1839	968	Sarah,Abegail E., &	1840	1077
Mary M, Sally C, & David	1831	558	Milton		
MURPHY, Delilah	1820	242	PATTERSON, Catharine & Marg't	1837	825
Edward	1815	128	Mary Ellen & And'w	1837	826
James	1818	211	PECK, Anne	1815	136
John	1821	267	Joshua	1815	147

Guardianship	Date	Case	Guardianship	Date	Case
PEMBERTON, Joseph	1810	39	SEAS, Abraham and Jacob	1836	788
Lydia	1824	357	SEWELL, David and Sally Ann	1820	243
Richard	1819	219	SHEALY, Peggy & Elizabeth	1838	883
Robert, Mary and	1835	762			884
Prudence			SHEETS, Barbary	1818	202
PERSONETT, Leona	1837	833	Nancy	1818	207
POTT, James	1837	852	Wm	1818	203
POTTS, John, Sylvester and	1838	887	SHELL, Wm	1829	493
Richard			SILER, Jacob, Abner, Sarah	1827	449
PRENTISS, David	1839	993	A., et al.		
RARICK, Elizabeth, Catharine	1826	428	SKINNER, Archebald	1828	484
and Lydia			SMALLY, Nancy E., Abagail D.,	1837	817
REED, Elizabeth, Sarah, Frede-	1824	378	and Prudence		
rick, and John			SMELTZER, Reuben	1839	977
RENCH, Daniel	1819	226	SMITH, David	1828	465
REPLOGLE, Sarah	1839	948	Elizabeth and Henry	1827	460
RERICK, Christina	1824	360	John	1814	93
David & Barbary	1824	361	John Alfred	1829	492
RHINEHART, Jonathan	1840	1078	Lewis	1817	175
RINARD, Nancy	1829	505	SNIDER, Jacob	1839	988
ROBBINS, Amos, Bersheba,	1839	945	SPEAR, John and Mary	1824	355
et al.			SPENCER, John, James & Chas.	1835	836
ROBINS, David	1838	918	SPICER, Hiram	1836	790
Roswell, Samuel and	1838	919	SPOER, Jesse and Robert	1823	354
Sezelda Ann			STALEY, Catharine, David,	1834	679
ROBISON, Joseph	1836	796	et al.		
ROGERS, Thomas O.B.	1837	843	Joseph	1822	300
ROLLINS, Jonathan, Mary and	1825	397	STATLER, Camillus W.	1836	781
Esther			STEELE, James E.	1823	324
Myhew and Mary Jane	1827	457	STEPHENS, Harriet, Austin	1830	538
Wm F.	1830	519	and Eliz.		
ROSS, James H, Mary E., et al.	1840	1071	STEPHENSON, Wm. & Thomas	1822	295
Wm, John W. & Lewis	1836	804	STEWART, Ann	1828	475
Juda and Joseph	1819	229	Wm, John, Nancy and	1824	386
RUDY, Elizabeth, Susann,	1838	886	Chas.		
Andrew J. & Cath.			James L, Eliza and	1835	749
James, John & Mary Ann	1838	878	James		
John	1831	551	Wm, Eliz. G, et al.	1835	747
RUMSEY, Milow	1821	275	STUDEBAKER, Eliz., Jacob,	1826	432
RUSH, Lemuel	1816	156	Sam'l, et al.		
Maria	1816	155	STURGEON, Levi and George	1824	389
Thomas	1816	153	SUNDERLAND, Samuel G.	1828	468
William	1816	154	SYPE, Eliza and Semantha	1822	308
RUSSELL, Isaac	1815	132	TAYLOR, Ed	1837	828
SAY, Rebecca	1818	208	TEMPLETON, Mariah, Bulah, etal.	1837	816
SANDERS, Aaron	1808	18	THOMPSON, Joel	1835	733
Moses	1808	17	TINKLE, Priscilla	1837	840
SCOTT, Calvin	1825	400	TODD, John	1830	530

141

Guardianship	Date	Case
TODD, Sarah J. and James C.	1834	678
TOLAND, Rachel C. & Isabella J	1840	1033
TUCKER, Abraham	1815	123
Jacob	1815	124
Jonathan	1815	125
Joseph	1815	121
Matibaner	1815	126
Nathaniel	1816	150
Nicholas	1815	122
Susan	1816	152
TURNER, Elizabeth	1830	548
ULLERY, Catharine, Wm, Jacob and Elizabeth	1819	221
VANCE, Elisha	1824	367
VANHORN, James, Ann, John & Betsy	1821	271
Julia Ann	1826	426
Wilkinson	1821	274
VANSCOYAC, Henry, Abraham Harvey, Jane & David	1838	881
VORE, Rebecca, Peter & Sally	1826	791
WADSWORTH, Hosea	1820	249
WARNER, Rosanah	1833	614
WATKINS, Ebenezer	1834	702
Thos.J,Jonathan et al.	1834	711
WEAVER, Robert, Susannah & Daniel	1832	596
Robert, Susan & Daniel	1836	775

Guardianship	Date	Ca
WEEKS, Mary & James M.	1827	4
WELLS, Mary R.	1834	6
WESLER, Jacob	1836	7
WESTFALL, Mary	1835	7
WHARTON, John	1830	5
WHITAKER, David N., Jonathan, et al.	1839	9
WILLIAMS, Samuel K.	1835	7
Samuel	1830	5
WILSON, David	1836	8
WINANS, Samuel	1819	2
WOOD, Jonathan P.	1831	5
WORRELL, Amanda and Susan	1837	8
WRIGHT, John and Gabriel	1817	1
YATES, Sophrania, Rebecca and Mary	1838	8
YINGER, Sarah Ann, Dennis and Elizabeth	1839	9
YOUART, William T.	1823	3
YOUC, Abraham	1831	5
Larkin, Samuel, et al.	1830	5
Philip, Alexander & Eliz.	1830	5
YOUNG, George W.	1829	4
George W.	1840	10
YOURTY, Mary and John	1824	3

Guardianship	Date	Case
ALEXANDER, Martha & John	1849	1815
ANDERSON, Robert B.	1844	1337
ARMSTRONG, Nancy M, Wm H,	1845	1444
Freeman B, Henry,		
Francis, Martin &		
Fidelia		
BARLOW, Geo. W. & Carl E.	1850	1881
BARRINGTON, John, Sherman and		
James		
Wm & Alexander		
BATES, Harriet L. & Eliza	1850	1873
BECK, Sarah and Henry	1848	1695
BIRD, Malinda	1844	1307
Mortmer	1844	1305
BLACKMORE, Martha and Benj.	1848	1712
Sarah Ann H.	1846	1457
BLUE, Lewis D, Margaret, Anna,	1841	1114
Jane and Rebecca		
BOGART, George W.	1841	1108
BOOKER, Levi	1841	1167
BRANDON, Julia, Elizabeth C,	1846	1489
Mary J., Julia A,		
Priscilla, Sarah &		
Abel A.		
Mary A., Margaret J,	1842	1229
and Eliza A.		
BRANSON, Levi, DeWitt, John	1846	1518
and Abigail		
BRELSFORD, Sarah, Hiram, Wm P.	1847	1559
and Caroline		
BRENNER, Elizabeth	1844	1348
BREVARD, Lucinda, Samantha	1841	1120
and James		
BROWN, Fanny	1850	1856
Isabella, Phillip	1843	1258
Matilda, Phoebe		
and Francis		
James R, Mary T, Henry	1848	1675
C., and Miles K.		
Martin H.	1843	1280
Sarah A. and John M.	1848	1673
BRUCE, Elias M. and Louisa	1849	1809
BURKMAN, Susannah C. & John P.	1841	1109
CALDWELL, Samuel Newton	1841	1130
CAMPBELL, Elizabeth	1847	1567
John D.	1847	1602
Margaret & Jackson	1850	1846
CARRINGTON, Lavina, Wm H.,	1849	1816
Julia, Susan and		
Ephrain		

Guardianship	Date	Case
CARROLL, James, Oliver, Sophia	1846	1490
and John		
CAVEN, Nicholas I, W.W., and	1842	1228
Sarah G.		
CAVENET Henry and Rachel	1842	1249
Rachel and John	1850	1847
CHAMBERS, Harriet, Julia, Henry	1847	1628
P. and Louis H.		
Henry B. and Martia L.	1847	1562
CHEWELL, Laura W.	1846	1470
CLARK, Enoch S.	1841	1093
John A. & James G.	1841	1144
Ruth Ann	1841	1169
CLAY, Hiram, Susan A., Geo.,	1847	1590
Hack and John		
COATE, Thos E, Mary & Esther	1841	1115
CODDINGTON, Louisa & Henrietta	1850	1928
COLLINS, John S, James H. and	1842	1221
Geo. W.		
CONNER, Robert, James & Matilda	1844	1340
COPPOCK, Benjamin	1841	1111
Wm, Allen and Henry	1843	1284
COVAULT, Alexander	1850	1859
Margaret E. & Eliz.	1847	1555
Timothy H, Wm S. Rob't	1847	1545
J, and Israel		
Watkins, Alex, & Lewis	1847	1592
COX, John, Nancy and Sarah	1834	1390
William	1845	1389
CROY, Amy	1844	1304
CUTLER, Lavina, Emily & Mary D.	1849	1812
DEACON, Elizabeth Jane and	1850	1913
Margaret		
DEWEESE, James	1847	1626
Olive and Wm	1841	1158
Sylvester E, Jas. A.,	1850	1843
Malinda I, David M,		
and Sarah E.		
DUNKIN, Amos W.	1849	1730
Eli, Abigail, Isaac	1847	1618
and Elizabeth		
Elizabeth	1846	1454
Elizabeth	1847	1589
Saul, David & Amos E.	1847	1617
DYE, Benj. L. and Sarah Ann	1841	1092
Letitia	1844	1309
Sarah, John, Ellen,	1844	1319
Elizabeth and Wm		
EAKIN, Martha Ann	1847	1647
EATON, Helen M., Roene and	1849	1784
Ivers		

EDWARDS, Sarah	1849	1777
EKINS, Benj. F. and Clementine	1847	1702
ELLER, John	1846	1485
John, Henry, Daniel and Samuel	1841	1140
Philip, Enoch & Eliz.	1841	1112
Susan an Henry	1846	1487
ELMORE, Rachel	1847	1586
ENYEART, John, Sarah, Jane and Margaret	1845	1403
ESKEW, Wm W.	1850	1837
ETTER, Lydia, Eve, Mary, Eliz. and Fanny	1844	1347
EVETT, John G.	1847	1651
FALDER, Rebecca A.	1847	1626
FALKNER, Levi	1841	116D
FARVER, George and William	1845	1381
FAVORITE, Henry F. Rebecca Geo., Margaret and Abram	1848	1677
FETTERS, Catharine, Caroline, and Mary	1847	1615
Nancy, Catherine, Hannah & John	1850	1829
FIELDING, Maria, Jeremiah Danual & Harrietta	1841	1118
FLOCK, Isaac, Joshua & Lydia	1843	1242
FRAZEE, Sarah, Morris, Priscilla, John W. Jeresha, Dulcina P., and Moses	1846	1452
FRAZIER, Nathan	1845	1409
FRENCH, Moses F, Wm, James, Michael, Jos. W, and Philas	1850	1884
GARHAGAN, Maria	1850	1931
GILBALL, Louisa and Aaron	1846	1495
GODMAN, Julia H. Aulena Cornelia & Eliz. B.	1843	1250
GREEN, Daniel and John	1841	1151
Joseph, Elenor and Christopher	1844	1324
GROW, Catharine and Mary	1841	1164
GUMP, Levi, Wm, Mary & George	1849	1813
Lucy and Lavina	1849	1807
HAGAN, Edward B.	1849	1802
Henry B.	1849	1801
HALL, Olivia M.	1850	1919
HARKER, Adelaid and John F.	1849	1804
Caroline	1850	1839

HARSHBARGER, George	1850	186
Mary, Benj., Abigail, Hester, and Samuel	1845	137
HARTER, Louisa	1842	123
HAWORTH, James	1843	128
HAY, Noah	1845	144
HAYS, George Philip	1845	139
Martha J. & Wm D.	1845	140
Samuel	1845	138
HAYWOOD, Thos. P, Wm H, and Alex H.	1841	108
HELMICK, Isiah	1843	124
HENDLEY, William	1846	152
HENDRICKS, John, Samuel, Sara and Isaac	1850	188
HERRICKS, Samuel	1849	173
HEYWOOD, Isa E, Wm, Esther and Elliott A.	1850	192
HICKMAN, Benjamin	1842	119
Elizabeth	1842	120
HOLLIS, Edmund, Mary, Allen, and John B.	1850	188
HOOVER, Alonzo H.	1850	187
Henry, David & Mary E.	1846	147
Jacob, David & Daniel	1849	180
John L.	1847	161
Levi, Sarah E, & Geo.	1849	177
Louisa Jane	1849	179
HOPKINS, Mary J, David O. WmK. and Robt R.	1846	151
HUGHEL, Cynthia	1850	191
HUTCHINS, Alice	1841	111
IDDINGS, Elizabeth, Susan M. James P, & Martha H.	1848	164
INMAN, William and Noah	1849	173
JAY, Charity, Jane, Elisha, Rebecca, Martha & Mary(?)	1849	175
Lot B.	1846	151
Martha C.	1841	113
JEROME, William	1841	111
JOHNSON, Cornelia	1843	134
JOHNSTON, James A. and Margret	1850	192
James J., Margarett J	1849	181
Robt E, Wm & Mary		
JONES, Martha J, Jasper & Mary	1847	162
JULIEN, Elza	1848	170
KERR, Mary and Wm J.	1843	124
William H.	1847	160
KESSLER, An Eliza	1846	145

Guardianship	Date	Case
KEYTE, James, WmJ, Mary and Margaret J.	1850	1855
KINDLE, Hiram	1841	1119
KING, Mary Jane	1843	1271
KINSEY, Samuel, Lydia & Noah	1845	1380
KIRK, James J & Margaret A.	1849	1818
Mary	1850	1852
LANDIS, David	1846	1507
LEE, F.A. Harrison, Howard H, and John H.	1847	1636
Francis H, David L, Geo. E. and Mary C.	1850	1891
Julia Ann	1841	1107
LENHART, John W.	1850	1828
LOGAN, Geo. H. Emerette, John A, and James A.	1844	1330
LOGUE, John	1843	1241
LONG, Lucinda, Henry F. and Geo. W.	1847	1584
LONGANECKER, Sarah, Jeremiah Samuel, Joe & Henry	1849	1789
MACY, Samuel, Enoch, Moses, Thomas and Phebe	1841	1136
MANGEN, David K. and Mary A.	1847	1620
MANNING, William	1845	1360
MANSFIELD, Charles W.	1845	1374
MARR, John, Marion. Amanda and Jane	1848	1703
MARTIN, Levi	1843	1272
Sarah and Martin	1841	1096
William	1845	1387
MAX, Jeremiah	1844	1355
Solomon	1844	1356
MENDENHALL, Joseph & Rachel	1847	1582
Priscilla, Angeline, et al	1847	1591
MILES, Isreal, Elizabeth, Enoch P, and Ann O.	1842	1208
MILLER, Charlotte	1850	1882
Michael	1848	1649
MOCK, Leander	1849	1758
MOFFETT, Robert & Eliz.	1847	1613
MOUCH, Eve Dorothy	1848	1652
MONTGOMERY, John W, Mary A. and Nancy J.	1845	1416
MOODY, Mariah	1843	1251

Guardianship	Date	Case
MORRIS, Joseph P.	1843	1255
Martha Jane	1843	1256
MOSS, Aaron and Jacob	1847	1598
MUNSELL, Ward, Howard, Sarah, Jane, Caroline, Leander & Thos.	1841	1094
McCAMPBELL, Wm B, Sarah E. James R, et al	1850	1861
McCARY, Benj and John	1847	1604
McCLURE, John B.	1845	1431
Wm C.	1848	1693
McCOOL, Elisha, Nathaniel and Sarah	1843	1240
McCONNAUGHEY, Thomas H.	1848	1670
McCORKLE, Jas A, Eliz J. Mary E, Zelpha, Chas & David	1843	1267
McDONALD, Aaron and Mahala	1849	1729
McDOWELL, Lucinda I.	1850	1857
McINTIRE, John A. & Rebecca A.	1847	1594
McJILTON, Wm F, John F, Sarah F, et al.	1846	1478
McMAKEN, Charlotte, Joseph and George	1845	1423
McMILLEN, Lucinda, Angeline and Eresbia	1841	1138
McNABB, Margaret	1848	1664
McPHERSON, Lydia, James and John	1848	1716
Martha Ann	1849	1749
NELSON, Ruth A, Wm & Catharine	1850	1878
OAKS, John, Eliz., Mary, Priscilla and Margaret	1844	1359
PANABAKER, John, Chas. Stephen, et al	1844	1313
PATTERSON, Robert	1841	1141
Sam'l, David & John	1841	1163
PATTY, Joseph and David	1842	1196
PEARSON, Alpha, Dan'l, Sarah and Rachel	1850	1901
Enos, David Wesley, Mary J. and James	1849	1750
John M, Geo W, Eli Christopher et al.	1843	1290
John M.	1847	1599
Paul and Rachel	1845	1429
Rachel	1849	1731
Robert V.	1850	1853
PERRY, Andrew, Amos & Horatio	1843	1283

Guardianship	Date	Case
PERRY, Eliza A.	1844	1323
PETERSON, Sandferd	1849	1803
RAMSEY, Leander	1848	1701
Rob't, Lucinda etal.	1847	1596
RATHAAS, Mary Louisa	1841	1137
REDDICK, Elizabeth, Sarah J.	1847	1583
et al.		
REXFORD, Eugene and Hortensia	1849	1755
RICKER, Anna, Julia and Geo.	1850	1926
RIDDLE, Manning R, Nancy J.,	1844	1342
et al.		
ROBISON, Alexander, et al.	1841	1147
RODKEY, John, Jos., and Josiah	1842	1231
ROOT, Sarah	1847	1561
ROSS, Rachel and Clarissa	1845	1383
ROSS, Thomas S.	1847	1597
Virginia S. & Georganna	1845	1382
ROUTZON, Mary E. Albert M.	1844	1325
and Jemima		
RUBBLE, Susannah, Jos., Marg-	1848	1657
aret & Michael		
RUDY, Harman, Elias & Nancy	1845	1362
RUSSELL, Mahala, Hannah & Wm	1850	1923
SABIN, Charles & Lorenzo	1842	1183
SHAFFER, Mary, Wm & Rachel	1850	1915
SHEETS, Wm, Susannah, Robert	1841	1095
etal.		
SHELLEBARGER, Eliz. et al.	1846	1473
SHOAFF, Miles F.	1846	1463
SIMMONS, Henry & Philip	1845	1368
SLUSSER, Henry H., Sarah and	1848	1715
John		
SMITH, Gabriel V.	1846	1464
Hiram C.	1847	1619
John, Peter, Otilda,	1849	1744
et al.		
Stephen	1850	1867
STAFFORD, Mary, John W, and	1849	1806
Martha		
STEPHENS, Harry & Elizabeth	1844	1349
STEPHENSON, Wm W.	1846	1450
STEWART, Elizabeth	1847	1549
STILLWELL, Barnett	1847	1553
STILWELL, Francis M, et al.	1847	1595
STUDEBAKER, Sarah & Mariah	1850	1885
SWAGER, Elizabeth & Wm	1841	1105
Mary J. John, Sarah	1841	1098
A, and Susan		
TEMPLETON, James G. & Malinda	1843	1293

Guardianship	Date	Case
THOMPSON, James, Jeremiah,	1846	1475
et al.		
Rebecca and David	1846	1476
Sarah A.	1845	1410
VALENTINE, George	1845	1375
VAN HORN, Elizabeth, Mary	1842	1226
and Catharine		
Martha J.	1844	1322
VENAMAN, Mary J, James H,	1841	1145
Wm G, etal.		
WAGONER, Ellen, Eliz., Elisa,	1843	1244
Mahala, John W. Alvin		
WALLACE, Asa A.	1846	1458
WARD, Frank M.	1847	1568
WARNER, David, Joseph, Daniel	1842	1199
and Lydia		
WEATHERHEAD, Jacob, Rachel and	1848	1656
Eunice		
Jos. R. & James A.	1847	1593
WEBSTER, Wm C, Benj. H, Lewis	1850	1844
H, Rhoda A, et al.		
WELBAUUM, Chas, David, Sarah	1845	1393
and John		
WELLS, Elizabeth et al.	1841	1090
WERTZ, Emeline	1848	1658
WHITAKER, Robert S. & David H.	1847	1601
Sarah A.	1847	1548
Wm H, Mary J, & MaryE	1847	1538
WHITE, Mary	1849	1814
WIDNEY, John W.	1850	1877
WILEY, John O.	1849	1719
John O'Ferrell	1845	1440
WEILHELM, Saleza	1850	1845
WILLIAMS, Henry H.	1846	1477
WIMANS, Anna M, Anthony Hannah	1850	1830
E, Cory & Mary F.		
WOOD, George J.	1845	1442
Sarah J.	1845	1443
WOODWARD, John R. & Wm. W.	1850	1908
WOOLEY, Charles and Deborah	1842	1198
WOOLWINE, Wm F. & Ephraim A.	1841	1150
WORTHINGTON, Ester	1847	1568
WRIGHT, John Q., Warren, Harriet	1842	1223
and Wm		
WYATT, Naomi	1847	1581
YOUART, Andrew S. and Phebe	1848	1676
YOUNG, Andrew S, et al.	1845	1370

-20-1829 - Richard LANDREE aged 16 yrs. on 11 Aug. 1829, son of Simon Landre eceased, with consent of Joseph R. John his guardian and of his own free will s bound as an apprentice to James Cottingham, blacksmith, of Troy, to serve as lacksmith until 11 August 1834. (Deed Book 7, page 181)

-4-1830 - William McKEE aged 16 yrs. 1 mo. 20 ds., son of William McKEE Sr. of ost Creek Twp., of his own free will and with consent of his father is bound as an pprentice to Daniel Brown, blacksmith, of Concord twp. to learn trade of blacksmith or term of 4 yrs. 7 mos. and 10 ds. (Deed Book 7, page 343)

-18-1829 - Samuel STATLER aged 16 yrs. 4 mos. 6 ds., son of Christian STATLER of ashington twp., of his own free will and with consent of his father is bound as an pprentice to Joshua Wells, blacksmith, of Piqua, to learn trade of blacksmith for erm of 4 yrs. from 16 March 1829. (Deed Book 7, page 244)

-3-1829 - Frazee M. WINANS aged 15 yrs. 1 mo. 23 ds., son of Stephen WINANS, by onsent of his father and of his own will is bound as an apprentice to Azel Skinner f Troy, sadler and harness maker to learn trade for term of 5 yrs. 10 mos 7 ds ntil age of 21. (Deed Book 7, page 149)

-20-1828 - Amos Jenkins and Joseph Shepherd overseers of the poor of Monroe twp., iami Co. with consent of Davis Jenkins, Justice of the Peace of said twp. bind esse CLEGG a poor boy aged 16 yrs. 5 mo. & 28 ds. whose parents are unable to upport him, as apprentice to Samuel Rees of same twp. to be taught art of husbandry or term of 4 yrs. 6 mos. & 2 ds. until 21 years of age. (Deed Book 7, page 74)

-20-1828 - Amos Jenkins and Joseph Shepherd overseers of poor of Monroe twp., iami County with consent of Davis Jenkins, Justice of the Peace of said twp., nd George W. CLEGG a poor boy aged 8 yrs. 5 mos. & 21 ds., an illegitimate child s apprentice to Phinias Jenkins of same twp. to be taught husbandry for term of yrs. 6 mos. 9 ds. until 21 yrs. of age. (Deed Book 7, page 78)

-11-1830 - John Waggoner and Caleb Mendenhall overseers of poor of Union twp. and th consent of Oliver Benton, Justice of the Peace of said twp., bind John HANNAH NES, a poor boy aged 4 yrs. 3 mos. & 9 ds. a son of Jane HANNAH whose residence is known, as apprentice to David JONES in the art of farming for a term of 16 yrs., mos. 21 ds. until 21 yrs. of age. (Deed Book 7, page 385)

-11-1830 - John Waggoner and Caleb Mendenhall overseers of poor of Union twp., th consent of Oliver Benton, Justice of the Peace of said twp. bind Eliza Ann JAY, poor girl aged 9 yrs. 2 mos. & 26 ds., daughter of Charles JAY a poor person of id twp. who is unable to support said child, as apprentice to Jeremiah Mote, to e art of Housekeeping for a term of 8 yrs. 9 mos. 4 ds. until she is 18 yrs. of e. (Deed Book 7, page 405)

13-1830 - John LANSTON aged 15 yrs. 5 mos. 15 ds., son of Joseph LANSTON OF ncord twp., of his own will and with his father's consent to serve as apprentice D. W. Wallace, house carpenter and joiner, of Concord twp. to learn said trade, r period of four years from present date. (Deed Book 8, page 136)

2-9-1831 - Robert LOGAN father and guardian of Samuel M. LOGAN aged 8 yrs. on 17 Nov. 1830 and with consent of said minor, both bind said Sam'l M. Logan as apprentice to Joseph Davis of Staunton, Miami County as tailor until said Samuel is of full age of 21 years on 17 Nov. 1843. (Deed Book 8, page 330)

8-31-1830 - George SANDS does bind out his son George SANDS aged 13 yrs. 5 mos. & 14 ds. to Jacob Rench to be taught the art of farming for a term of 7 yrs. 8 mos. & 17 ds. from date until said George is 21 yrs. 10 mos. which will be 17 May 1838. (Deed Book 8, page 105)

7-16-1830 - Joseph R. John guardian of John WHARTIN doth bind, with voluntary consent of said John Whartin, as apprentice to Jacob Writter, Tinner. of Troy, to learn said trade and to serve Jacobe Riter from date until 10 June 1831. (Deed Book 8, page 62)

8-6-1831 - Simon HUSTLER, aged 15 yrs. on 3 Oct. 1831, son of George HUSTLER, with consent of his father and of his own will has bound himself as apprentice to Sam'l Mercer of Troy, shoe and boot maker. to learn trade for term of 6 yrs. 1 mo. & 27 ds until of full age of 21 yrs. (Deed Book 8, page 543)

11-27-1830 - David CARPENTER of Newberry twp. binds his daughter Julian CARPENTER aged 3 yrs. 10 mos to Isaac Statler of Washington twp. until said Julian is 18 yrs. of age. (Deed Book 8, page 295)

11-22-1830 - Henry Yount guardian of Edward FENTRESS as appointed by the Court of Common Pleas of Montgomery County, Ohio, said Edward Fentress being 7 yrs. 2 mos. & 8 ds., son of George FENTRESS, late of Montgomery County, dec'd, is bound to Caleb Mendenhall for 13 yrs. 9 mos. 22 ds until 21 yrs. of age to learn the occupation of farming. (Deed Book 8, page 389)

1-29-1831 - Matilda FRAZIER aged 8 yrs. 8 mos. 21 ds., daughter of Israel FRAZIER, with consent of William J. Thomas her guardian and of her own will is bound to Peter Kerns to learn the art of housewifery from date until she is 18 yrs. on 8 May 1840. (Deed Book 8, page 319)

3-19-1831- Harvey JULIEN aged 19 yrs. on 10 December last, with consent of Lewis Humbert his guardian and of his own will is bound to Samuel Mercer of Troy to learn shoemaker trade until 21 yrs. of age on 10 Sept. 1832. (Deed Book 8, page 390)

9-14-1830 - Mary V. JONES aged 5 yrs. 10 ds., daughter of Joseph JONES of Troy of her own free will and with consent of Henry W. Culbertson her guardian is bound to Asa Mayo of Troy to the art of housewifery, sewing, knitting, etc. for the term of 12 yrs. 11 mos. 20 ds. (Deed Book 8, page 129)

9-14-1830 - Phoebe Ann F. JONES aged 2 yrs. 10 mos. & 14 ds., daughter of Joseph JONES of Troy, of her own will and with consent of Henry W. Culbertson her guardian is bound to Isaac Roll for term of 15 yrs. 2 mos. & 6 ds. to learn art of housewifery, knitting, sewing, etc. (Deed Book 8, page 130)

5-22-1833 - Norvel D. MEREDITH of Troy binds his son, John L. MEREDITH aged 14 yrs. 9 mos. 14 ds. to William Barbee of Troy until he is of full age of 21 on 4 Aug. 1829 to be taught mercantile business. (Deed Book 10, page 317)

OLD LEATHERWOOD CEMETERY - MIAMI COUNTY, OHIO

Located in Section 1, Brown Township; on east side of the Lena-Palestine Road
about a mile north of the village of Lena and State Route 36. Inscriptions
taken 1969. A complete listing of all inscriptions in cemetery. Cemetery is
well kept and fenced.

BROWN, Augustus G. died Nov. 22, 1855 aged 40 yrs. 8 mo. & 16 d's.
LOOKER, Edgar son of G. R. & E. J. died June 3, 1867 aged 12 yrs. 3 mo.
PEARCE, In memory of Hannah consort of Doctor W. H. Pearce who departed this
    life Sept. 26th A.D. 1845 aged 23 years 8 mo. & 18 da.
NEEDLES, Joseph died Apr. 12, 1855 aged 48 yrs.
    David son of Jac. Needles died Dec. 31, 1854 aged 16 yrs. & 23 ds.
    Catharine wife of Joseph Needles died July 17, 1882 aged 75 ys. 4mo.15da.
    Eliza Jane daughter of Joseph & Catharine died August 18, 1862 aged 15yrs.
                                    2 mos. & 8 days.
    William, Co. C, 94 Ohio Inf. (GAR)
    Sarah daughter of J. & C. died Apr. 16, 1855 aged 1 yr. 8 mo. & 16 d's.
    Adam died Nov. 25, 1873 aged 37 yrs. 11 ms. 13 d.
    Clara G. dau. of A. & M. died May 5, 1871 aged 1 yr. 3 ms. 5 d.
HENNINGSHOT, Elizabeth wife of J. T. died Aug. 31, 1855 aged 27 y's. 8 Mo.
               & ____d (Note:- Cemented in base)
"Little Faran's Grave" (Note:- (Note:- Large Stone, but this is all that is
                        inscribed)
ADAMS, In Memory of Dr. M. D. Adams who died Sept. 8th 1846 aged 42 yrs. & 26 days
NOE, William died Oct. 1, 1847 aged about 46 years.
    Lysander F. son of W. & P. died Sept. 1, 1850 aged ___(Cemented in base)
McKINLEY, William died Aug. 29th, 1845 aged 49 yrs. 11 mo. 13 days.
    Nancy B. died Mar. 12, 1842 aged 19 yrs. 2 mo. 20 days.
    Mary wife of Wm. McKinley died Mar. 10th 1881 aged 85 yrs. 2 mo. 21 days
    (Note:- McKinleys all on same stone)
_____"In memory of Jane" (Note:- Slate stone effaced - unreadable)
DRAKE, William A. son of Wm. S. & Mary died Sept. 24, 1840 aged 23 y'rs.
                5 mo. & 4 dy.
    Elmira A. daughter of Wm. A. & Elsy A. died Mar. 24, 1843 aged 2y 12d
ALEXANDER, In memory of Ann Eliza daut. of Alexander M. and Sarrahan who de-
    parted this life Feb. 1840 aged 5 years & 2 mo.
FRENCH, In memory of Eliza wife of Hiram French who died Dec. 17 A.D. 1844
    aged 30 years & 4 mo.
BOWERSOCK, Elizabeth daughter of S. & S. died Feb. 12, 1856 aged 9 yrs. 13 ds.
    Peter H. son of Samuel & Sarah died dec. 2, 1841 aged 1 yea 11 mo 26 da
_____(Note:- Effaced stone)
EVERITT, Levi died Feb. 12, 1839 aged 47 years, a native of New Jersey.
    Epenetus was born in Bucks Co., Pa., died Aug. 19, 1838 aged 64 years.
    Elizabeth wife of Epenetus Everitt Sr. was born in Bucks Co., Pa.
               died April 23, 1835 aged 67 years.
    Rebecca died Feb. 17, 1864 aged 26(?) yrs. 8 mo. 8 ds.
    E. N. 1800-1885   Susannah his wife 1820-1896 (same stone)
CORY, Phebe wife of Ezra Cory died Dec. 31, 1852 aged 49 yrs. & 14 ds.
WILLIAMS, In memory of Miles Williams who died Jan. 19th 1837 aged 72 years
         & 13 days (REVOLUTIONARY SOLDIER)
_____(Note:- Child's stone completely effaced)

EVERITT, Jeremiah A. son of E. & J. S. died June 10, 1859 aged 8 mos.
    Van Buren E. son of E. & A. died Spet. 6, 1845 aged 5 years 6 mo. 27 ds.
    Sarah daughter of E. & A. died Mar. 23, 1844 aged 18 d's.
ROSS, In memory of Samuel A. Ross who departed this life Sept. 1st 1835 in the
    49th year of his age.
    In memory of John W. son of Samuel & Rachel Ross who died May 2, 1838
        aged 18 years 5 mo. & 3 days.
    In memory of Robert son of Samuel A. and Rachel who departed this life
        Dec. 6, 1845 aged 21 years 7 months and 19 days
    In memory of George D. son of Sam'l A. & Rachel Ross who died Jan.
        19, 1848 aged 32 years & 9 mo.
JOSEPH, Alonzo H. son of H. J. & M. died Jan. 27, 1851 AE. 5 n's. 23 d's.
BOYD, Archibald G. died Feb. 21, 1857 aged 31 y's. 11 ms. 5 ds.
WHITSIT, In memory of John Wm. son of Alexander & Ann Whitsit who died April
    4th A.D. 1843 aged 5 years 1 mo. & 10
    In memory of Wm. Whitsit a native of Ireland who died March 29th A.D.
    1835 aged 72 years
ATHERS, In memory of Sarah daughter of David & Margaret who died Aug. 31st
    1843 aged 14 years & 24 days.
    David died Sep. 11, 1850 aged 52 y's 9m. 26 d.
    James died Sept. 23, 1853 aged 61y 8m 20d
MOOR, William A. son of Isaac & Mary died Aug. 20, 1837 aged 3 y's & 3 d's
    Infant daughter of Isaac & Mary died Mar. 2, 1847
MERRI. In memory of Margaret daughter of Isaac & Margaret died July 29th A.D.
    1841 aged 8 years 8 mo. & 3 days
MERRITT, Rachel daughter of A. & F. (?) died July 7, 1845 aged 9 mo. & 26 d's.
BENHAM, Richard born Mar. 15, 1791 died Mar. 1, 1870, Corp. 2nd (Findlay's)
    Reg. Ohio Mil. WAR OF 1812, Apr. 25, 1812 to Apr. 24, 1813,
    married Mary Nutt 1813
    Abial Baltzell 1852 (Note:- New type stone, back to back with old
        stone. See below.)
BENHAM, Richard died Mar. 23, 1870 aged 79 yrs. & 8 ds.
    Moriah wife of Richard Benham died May 8, 1849 aged 51y 8m 26d
WOOLLEY, In memo- of Mary N. consort of Thomas C. Woolley who departed this
    life the 4th day of August A.D. 1843 aged 21 years 10 months and 6 days
    Infant daughter of T. C. & Mary N. died Dec. 8th 1838.
KELLY, Joseph B. son of J. W. & C. died Sep. 3, 1848 AE. 3y 8m 2d
    William son of J. W. & C. died Sep. 21, 1846 AE. 8m 27d
    Samuel died Mar. 8, 1860 aged 86y 3m & 22d
BLACKFORD, David died June 8, 1868 aged 52 years
    Mary wife of Lemuel Blackford died Feb. 1, 1851 aged 70 yrs 7 m 23ds.
    Lemuel died Sept. 24, 1856 aged 63 yrs. 5 mo. & 9d. (stone broken)
VENARD, Jerusha wife of James Vernard died Mar. 14, 1862 aged 63 y's. 5 m's. 5d.
    Jas. died Aug. 3, 1851 aged 49 y's. 2 mo. 15d.
    Jane K. daughter of J. & J. died April 25, 1850 aged 18 years 6 mo. 21d
SIMS, Mary wife of Chesley K. Sims died July 5, 1850 aged 28 y's. 4 mo. 9 ds.
ANDERSON, Mary E. daughter of J. D. & H. died Oct. 12, 1850 aged 17ys 11mo 8ds.
GILLES, Thomas died Dec. 13, 1868 aged 83 yrs. 3 ms. 21 ds.
    Ruth died May 26, 1831 aged 90 yrs. 1 day

150

CARTER, Elliot F. son of John & Sarah died Mar. 1, 1854 aged 1 yr. 2 mo. 27 d's.
       Martha A. daugher of John & Sarah died Sept. 7, 1851 aged 1y 7m 10ds.
HOLLOWAY, Lucy J. dau. of G. P. & E. died Mar. 22, 1854 aged 8 mos. & 21 ds.
SLUSSER, Peter died June 13, 1851 in his 61st yr.
       Mary died June 27, 1891 aged 89y 7m 26d (same stone as Peter)
WHITE, Mary Jane daughter of J.C.&E.M. died Sep. 5, 1854 aged 1yr. 11 ms. 2r ds.
WILLIAMS, Patience wife of J. Williams died Mar. 28, 1846 in her 57 year.
       In memory of Israel Williams died September 25th A.D. 1842 aged
              83 years & 4 days
BOYD, Emily G. dau. of J. J. & H. died July 6, 1851 aged 13y 4m 4d
       Huldah wife of J. J. Boyd died Nov. 24, 1845 aged 45y 5m 11d
       John J. died May 22, 1867 aged 68 ys. 6m ___ds.(Cemented over crack)
EVERITT, Charles E. son of Geo. J. & A.A. died Sept. 17, 1853 aged 1yr 1mo 26ds.
_____(Stone completely effaced)
LEMON, William son of T. & J. died Jan. 21, 1849 aged 76 y's.

WHITMER-WITMER CEMETERY - NEWBERRY TOWNSHIP - MIAMI COUNTY, OHIO

Cemetery located on south side Highway #36, west of Covington, Ohio.

GILBERT, In memory of H. J. Gilbert who died Nov. 14, 1845 aged 13 yrs. 7 months
              & 9 days
_____(Note: footstone) J. W. (?)
OLEWINE, Michael T. son of Abraham & Elizabeth died March 7th 1844 aged 2 mo.
              & 7 days.
GRAN (GRIN or GRUN?), Joseph son of J. & E. died July 28, 1847 aged 2 years
            8 months 16 days
_____(footstones) E.E.   E.W.   S.B.W.
WITMER, Joseph son of S. B. Witmer died Sept. 17th 1840 aged 11 ys. 11 ms. & 9 days
ERISMAN, Elizabeth wife of Jacob Erisman, daughter of _. B. & E. WITMER, died
           May 23, 1850 (or 1854?)
WHITMER, Elizabeth wife of Samuel B. Whitmer died Sept. 22, 1843 aged 40 ys.
          6 ms. & 2 d.
       Samuel B. died July 24, 1863 aged 66 yrs. 10 ms. 25 ds.
       Rozyann daughter of S. H. & S. died July 27, 1863 aged 2y 4m 11d

In the court house fire of 1840, the deed books which covered the period from the organization of the county to the date of the fire were badly burned around the edges. The remaining portion of these deeds were transcribed in 1858 into what is now known as Deed Book C (Burned Records). In many instances, a good portion of the right or left side, the top or bottom of the deeds was burned. Thus, there will be more blank spaces in these records than would be usual under normal circumstances. Because the information given here is intended as a finding aid and also due to the condition of the deeds, the land descriptions have not been included. The page on which the record may be found in Deed Book C, is given in parenthesis.

Washington ATKINS (no co-signer) to John HOLAWELL; (no date); attested to
  4-6-1836. (1)
Citzen BELL (BEALL) and Elizabeth wife to Isaac WISENER; (no date); attested to
  11-12-1835. (1)
Woodman OKEY and Catherine wife to Jacob LINDWOOD; (no date); attested to
  3-18-1839. (2)
Henry OKEY and Mine___wife to Woodman OKEY;(no date); attested to 1-6-1838. (2)
William MANTLE and Eleanor wife to Isaac WILLSON; (no dates). (3)
Elizabeth (her mark) ICE to Frederick ICE; Aug. ___ , 1833; attested to 8-12-1833.(4)
Levi (his mark) CORN and Elizabeth wife to James DUNN; (no date); attested to
  3-12-1839.   (5)
Jacob (his mark) HUFFMAN and Nancy wife to _____ _____;(no date); attested to
  2-22-1836. (5)
Seth B. DUSTAN and Maria A. wife to Conrad SNAILER (SCHNELLI):; (no date);
  attested to 8-1-1837.   (6)
John HURD and Sarah (her mark) wife to Adam MYERS; (no date); attested to 7-3-1837.(7)
Isaiah BARKER and Hannah (her mark) wife to___ AFFLICK; 6-15-1837. (7)
Crawford GLOVER and Jemina (her mark) wife to Cadwalder S. DUNGAN; 12-15-1835. (8)
Reuben YOHO and Elen wife to James SMITH; 9-12-1835. (9)
John SMITH (no co-signer) to Jonathan THOMPSON; (no date); attested to 3-16-1837.(9)
Thomas MARTIN and Mary (her mark) wife to John MAIDENS; 2-28-1838. (10)
Susannah (her mark) BRYSON of Belmont Co., Ohio to Valentine GETZ (also given as
  Felty GATZ in deed) of Monroe Co.; (no date); attested to 11-5-1830. (10)
Samuel WRIGHT and Mary wife to Stephen MELOTT; (no date); attested to 10-11-183_;
  recorded 11-15-1833. (11)
United States to Andrew PARKER of Harrison Co., Ohio; 3-20-1837. (12)
DAVID DYE and Dicy (her mark) wife to Aniel DYE; 7-30-1832. (12)
Benjamin BAKER and Sarah (her mark) wife to Simon DRUM; 10-20-1832. (13)
James CREE and Isabela (her mark) wife to _____ _____;(mp date_; attested to
  3-15-1837. (14)
James NOFFSINGER and _____ wife to William McCOMAS; (no date); attested to Aug.___,
  1838. (14)
Archibald WOOD and Am(n) wife of Ohio Co., Virginia to James PEARSON of Ohio Co.,
  Virginia; 11-6-1827. (15)
Richard CONNER and Priscilla wife to Benj. HAMILTON and Jemima BURCH;
  11-22-182_. (16)
Benjamin RUGGLES and Clarissa wife of Belmont Co., Ohio to John PATTERSON of same;
  11-20-1828. (17)
United States to Emanuel CISSNA assignee of Stephen CISSNER; 12-1-1829. (18)

152

Thos. BURNSIDES, Esq. and Elen wife of Centre Co., Penna. to William D. Henthorn;
7-12-1824; Whereas James (Burnsides?) of Philadelphia, dec'd, died seized of
patent dated 3-17-1788 of Lot 24, Township __, Range 3 on Sunfish Creek on
Ohio River...Burnsides died intestate without issue and estate descended to
his brother _____ Burnsides father of Thomas Burnsides and two sisters Isabella Wilson wife of _____ Wilson and Jane Phillips wife of Alexander Phillips
...Isabell Willson and Jane Phillips by deed dated 3-17-1806 Washington County,
Ohio deeded to William and Thos. Burnsides and said William by will recorded
Montgomery Co., Penna. 3-13-1807 devised his interest to his two sons Thomas
and Francis Burnsides. (16)

Thomas SMITH and Nancy wife of Somersett twp., Belmont Co., Ohio to David PEARSON;
3-18-18 9. (18)

Ahijah EATON and Jane his wife of Monroe Co. to Thompson MASON of Belmont Co., Ohio;
0-7-1829. (19)

William YOUNG and Dorcus wife to _____ _____; (no date); attested to 7-1-1830.(19)

Benjamin RUGGLES and Clarissa wife of Belmont Co., Ohio to Nolly HAYS of same;
11-21-1828. (19)

Andrew WALTERS and Esther wife to David GREENLEE of Belmont Co., Ohio; (no date);
attested to 10-14-1837. (20)

Henry FRESH (FRUSH) and Mary wife to Elijah HUDSON; 4-27-1835. (21)

David EATON and Hannah (her mark) wife to Leonard CHALK; 6-20-1835. (22)

Samuel BAKER 9 no co-signer) to James BAKER; 11-11-1825. (22)

Thomas (his mark) MORRIS and Mary (her mark) wife to John HECK; 1-22-1825. (23)

Thomas HENDERSHOT and Mary (her mark) wife to George GATES; (no dates); attested
to in Belmont Co., Ohio. (24)

Hesekiah (his mark) SHAW (no co-signer) to Zachariah SHAW; 11-11-1837. (25)

Rathey INGRAM and Mary (her mark) wife to Thomas MARTIN; 2-15-1834. (25)

William BUCHANAN and Mary Ann (her mark) wife to Robert MILLER; 3-28-1835. (26)

Citzen BEALL and Elizabeth wife to William TRUEX; 3-3-1826. (27)

John MELOTT and Mary wife to Daniel PATERSON; (no date); attested to June ___,
1835. (28)

Elliot HOLLAND, Sheriff Monroe Co., Ohio to William MASON; 6-23-1831; Whereas Leven
OKEY filed petition in Common Pleas Court 5-11-1830....Elizabeth MOWDER
relict of _____, dec'd. (28)

Benjamin RUGGLES and Clarissa wife to William CRAWFORD; 7-10-1826. (29)

Abner MARTIN and Sarah (her mark) wife to Isaac BALDWIN; 9-8-1825. (30)

Uriah HIGINBOTTOM and Elizabeth wife to _____; (no dates). (30)

Elizabeth LEIPER, Joseph REED, George Gray LEIPER and Paul BECK, executors of will
of _____ mas LEIPER (SEIPER), dec'd to Saraford CLARK; (no date); attested
to Philadelphia (Pa.?) 11-1-1826. (31)

John CLINGAN and Mary wife to Alexander FERRELL; 4-27-_____; (no other dates).(32)

Nathaniel McNICHOLS of Goshen twp.,_____ Co. to John McNICHOLS of same place. (32)

Humphry FINCH and Elizabeth wife of Montgomery Co., Indiana to James WA_____; no
date; attested to 1-26-1826. (33)

Adam HENTHORN and Susannah wife to Isaac BALDWIN; 3-30-1829. (34)

Jacob RUSH and Prudence wife to Jesse WARD; 10-20-18(28). (34)

Osaac BALDWIN and Mary wife to Samuel GREEN; 3-28-1829. (35)

Richard GRUAX and Mary (her mark) wife to Jacob FRANCE (FRANCES) and Ruth wife;
11-22-18(28). (35)

John MINDER and ____ wife to Nicholas FAUKHOUSER, 9-15-1829. (36)

153

United States to John MINDER; 5-1-1826. (36)
United States to John REED of Monroe Co.; (no date). (37)
James STERRET (his mark) to Margaret STERRET, now Margaret GOLDEN, daughter of
_____(James Sterret?); 7-29-1825; consideration of natural love
and affection. (37)
Leven OKEY and Hester wife to John HOLLISTER; 7-10-1827. (38)
Jeremiah HULLISTER of Monroe Co. to Reddick McKEE of Wheeling, Virginia; (no dates)
(38)
Edward FUGATE of Washington Co., ____ and Nancy (mark) wife to ____us POOL of Monroe
Co.; 5-22-1826. (39)
Stephen MELOTT and Jane (her mark) wife to _____; (no dates). (39)
Asail BOOTH and Bethiah wife to S. H. ARMSTRONG; 8-18-1831. (39)
George REMLY and Eleanor wife to ____ _____; (no date); attested to 8-18-1828.
(40)
John WINDLAND and Elizabeth (her mark) wife to Elias CONGER; 5-3-18__; (no other
dates). (40)
George GATEZ and M. Civil wife to Mary YOHO; (no date); attested to ___-31-1826.(41)
Edward GRIZZLE (GRIZZEL) and Hannah (her mark) wife to Thomas GREY; 12-27-1828.(41)
Archibald C. STUBING and Catharine (her mark) wife of Belmont Co., Ohio to Thos. A.
BENTING; (no date); attested to 5-8-1827. (42)
Elias PITMAN Jr. and Katharine wife to Elias PITTMAN Sr.; 8-6-1827. (42)
George CROW to Elias ALLEN; 1-22-1828. (43)
United States to James FOGGIN assignee of Mathew GILMORE; 7-19-1824. (43)
Notley HAYS and Sarah (her mark) wife of Belmont Co., Ohio to Wm. CRAWFORD of
Monroe Co.; 4-15-1830. (44)
John HENDERSHOT and Susannah (her mark) wife to James SMITH; 5-22-1824. (44)
Noble RAYER, Sheriff Monroe Co., Ohio to James ATKINSON; 2-22-1822. (45)
Thomas MACKEY (no co-signer) to Abraham MACKEY; 1-11-1828. (46)
Giles GADD and Elizabeth wife to Stephen POTTS; 6-7-1831. (46)
Richard TRUEX and Mary (mark) wife of Monroe Co. to William D. ROSE of Belmont
Co., Ohio; 12-8-1826. (47)
Jacob Moore and Ann (her mark) wife of Ohio Co., Virginia to John HENTHORN of
Monroe Co.; 5-31-1828. (48)
Jacob Miller and Nancy wife to William COCHRAN and Thomas COCHRAN; 3-9-1829. (49)
John LINN and Susannah (her mark) wife to John CLINE; 5-2-1826. (49)
Isaac JONES and Abigail wife to Samuel P. JONES; 9-18-1830. (50)
George ROUSH and Elizabeth (her mark) wife to Isaac JONES; 4-10-1824. (51)
Thomas WOOD and Laticia wife of Harrison Co., Ohio to Henry H. MOTT of Monroe
Co.; 9-3-1824. (51)
Daniel WILSON and Mary wife of Windsor twp., Morgan Co., Ohio to Thos. SMITH of
Sommersett twp., Belmont Co., Ohip; 3-17-1829. (52)
JOHNSTON's adms. to Richard CAIN; 3-16-1830; Whereas in the June term last past
Common Pleas Court of Monroe County, Archibald Johnston and Ann Johnston adms.
of Elijah Johnston dec'd filed petition to complete deed which said Johnston in
his lifetime agreed to sell land in Section 9, Township 3, Range 7 to Cain.
Signed: Archibald Johnston and Anna (her mark) Johnston. (53)
Gidion CHAPMAN and Sally (her mark) wife of Monroe Co. to Theopolis MURDOCK of
Belmont Co., Ohio; 9-16-1834. (54)
United States to Alexander BURUS of Washington Co., Penna.; 12-4-1821. (55)
Thomas WOOD and Laticia wife of Harrison Co., Ohio to Arthur McKEWN of same;
11-18-1824. (56)

Thomas HOLLINGSHEAD and Susanah (her mark) wife of Smith twp., Belmont Co., Ohio to John SHEPHERD;(no dates). (57)

Jeremiah RUSH and Mary (her mark0 wife to Abraham DAVIS; 11-30-1830. (57)

Elliott HOLLAND and Urania wife to Jeremiah RUSH; 12-5-1824. (58)

William IRWIN and Catherine wife to Thomas CARRICK; 4-1-1828. (59)

William COCHRAN and Frances wife to Jeremiah RUSH; 11-20-1827. (60)

United States to Ebenezer TINGLEY of Belmont Co., Ohio; 3-1-1832. (61)

Citizin BEALL and Elizabeth wife to George SPALDING; 8-17-1829. (61)

Peter MANN and Elizabeth wife to Stilwell TRUEX; 7-5-1824. (62)

Elias PITTMAN Jr. and Catherine (her mark) wife to Elias PITMAN Sr.; 8-6-1827. (63)

James BRYAN, James DANFORD and Mary wife to Samuel GILMORE; 8-26-1828. (64)

Richard CONNER and Priscilla (her mark) wife to Benjamin HAMILTON and Jemina BURCH; 11-22-1829. (65)

Aaron HARTLEY and Phoeba wife of Belmont Co., Ohio to James AYRES of Monroe Co.; 1-18-1828. (65)

John JONES and Martha (her mark) wife to Morgan JONES; 9-27-1831. (66)

Oswald SILL and Mary wife to Michael SILL 6-9-1823. (67)

Jesse WELLS and Betsey wife to Kane DAILEY; 12-13-1827. (68)

William DEMENT 9no co-signer) to John STRAKE Jr.; 3-7-1831. (70)

Rachel (her mark) CROW to Isaac CROW; 12-5-1828. (71)

Thomas FORSHEY and Catherine (her mark) wife to James HARKUM; 4-15-1824. (72)

John MINNEY and Eve (her mark) wife of Monroe Co. to Lewis BROOKS of Belmont Co., Ohio; 10-2-1826. (73)

John STRAHL Jr. (no co-signer) to Daniel GRAY; 7-8-1826. (74)

Rachel (her mark) CROW, widow of the late George Frederick CROW of Monroe Co. to Woodman OKEY and Edward REED of Monroe Co.; 8-31-1825. (74)

David (his mark) SUTTON and Sarah wife to Amos SUTTON; 3-25-1828. (75)

Harton HOWARD (no co-signer) of Marion Co., Ohio to his son, Henry HOWARD of Belmont Co., Ohio; 20th day, 12th mo. 1825; Wit.--Mary Howard and Ann Howard. (76)

Citizen BEALL and Elizabeth wife to George SPALDING; 5-11-1828. (76)

James FREEMAN (no co-signer) to Joseph FERRILL; 6-10-1824. (77)

Rachel (her mark) CROW to Woodman OKEY; 12-10-1827. (78)

Daniel GRAY and Deborah wife to Oswald SILL; 5-31-1830. (79)

Citizen BEALL and Elizabeth wife to Daniel EVANS and Ephraim EVANS; 1-29-1829. (80)

John HENDERSHOT and Susanna (her mark) wife to George WEAVER; 8-14-1824. (80)

John HENDERSHOT and Susanna (her mark) wife to Daniel GRAY; 10-27-1828. (81)

Citizn BEALL and Elizabeth wife to George SPALDING; 5-11-1828. (82)

John HENDERSHOT and Susanna wife to John MINNEY; 5-21-1823. (83)

Zenophon PERKINS (no co-signer) to Woodman OKEY; 8-15-1834. (83)

David SOUTHERLAND and Margaret wife to Jacob CROW; 3-24-1827. (84)

William LAWRENCE and Mary wife to James SMITH; 5-15-1824. (84)

David SUTHERLAND and Margaret (her mark) wife to Rachel CROW; 3-24-1827. (85)

United States to Ebenezer TINGLEY of Belmont Co., Ohio; (no dates) (86)

Jonathan WILLIAMS to Daniel WILLIAMS; _____ 1818. (86)

Levin OKEY and Esther wife to Woodman OKEY; _____ 1818. (86)

Levin OKEY and Esther wife to Arthur OKEY; (no dates). (87)

Hamel BUSKIRK to John JONES; _____ 1818. (87)

United States to Levin OKEY of Belmont Co., Ohio; _____ 1814. (88)

William D. HENTHORN and Susy wife to Reuben STURGEON; (no dates). (89)

155

William D. HENTHORN and Susy wife to Ephraim Dotey of._____Virginia;
    2-15-_____; (no other dates). (89)
Frederick FOGLE Sr., yeoman and Catharine (her mark) wife to Frederick FOGLE, Jr.;
    ____6,_____; (no other dates). (90)
Ambrose RUCKER and Sally wife to Lemuel RUCKER; 3-1-_____; (no other dates);
    consideration of natural love and affection. (90)
Ephraim DOTY to Isaac BALDWIN; 9-1-1819. (90)
Benjamin RUGGLES to Joseph_____; Apr.___,18__;(no other dates given). (91)
Joseph DRIGGS and Dolly wife to Theophilus MINOR; 4-26-1819. (91)
Notley HAYS and Sarah wife of Belmont Co., Ohio to David_____; June __, ____;
    (no other dates given). (92)
John HENDERSHOT and Susannah wife to Clem WALTERS; 11-26-1830. (92)
David CAGGARD and Anne wife to John RUTTER: Dec.__, 1819. (93)
United States to Archibald WOODS of Ohio Co., Virginia; 12-10-18__;(no other dates
    given). (93)
United States to James CREE of Belmont Co., Ohio; (no dates). (93)
Archibald WOODS and Ann wife to James JOHNSTON; 12-15-1819. (94)
John HECK and Mary (her mark) wife to John MADINS; 12-15-1819. (94)
John HENDERSHOT and Susannah wife to Horton HOWARD; 9-11-18__; (no other dates given).
    (95)
George ROUSH and _____ wife of Ohio Co., Virginia to James WALTON of Monroe Co.;
    Oct.__;.1819. (95)
David CONGER and Sarah wife of Greene Co., Penna. to son, Gershom CONGER;
    1-20-1820. (96)
Stilwell TRUAX and Mary wife to Richard TRUAX; 5-1-1819. (96)
William RAPER to Alexander MAYERS; 4-5-1820. (97)
George DUNLEVEY of Washington Co., Ohio to Zadok WEST; 2-18-____; (no other dates
    given). (97)
William D. HENTHORN and Susannah wife to Thomas HOWELL; 2-14-1820. (98)
George KINNY and Elizabeth (her mark) wife to Roger FOLEY; Feb. __, 18(20). (98)
John HENDERSHOT and Susannah wife to Robert WILSON Sr.; 6-2-____;·(no other dates
    given). (99)
John MAIN to William DRAPER of Washington _____; _____-1820; (99)
United States to Amos BRINTON of Chester Co., Penna.; 5-30-18__. (99)
_____WINLAND and Catharine wife to John BARRET; June __, ____; (no other dates
    given). (100)
United States to Elias JEFFRIES assignee of Levin OKEY; (no dates). (100)
United States to Elias JEFFRIES of Fayette Co., Penna.; 1-3-18__; (no other dates
    given). (101)
United States to William CUNNINGHAM assignee of Archibalc WOOD; Aug. __, 18__;
    (no other dates given). (102)
United States to Uriah HICKENBOTTON of Pennsylvania; 3-14-1818. (102)
Henry KIRKBRIDE and Catharine (her mark) wife to Amos WILLSON; 3-17-1828. (102)
_____ to Andrew SPROWL; Feb. __, 1820. (103)
John YOUNG of Greene Co. Commonwealth of _____ to Amos WEAVER of Washington
    _____; 3-20-___; (no other· dates given).   (103)
Earl SPROAT and James JOHNSTON to James HEPBURN; (no dates). (104)
Arthur CARTER and Bethann wife of Ohio Co., Virginia to Citizen BEALL of Monroe
    Co.; ____ 12,_____; (no other dates given). (104)

John VANDEVENTER and Ruth wife to John JONES; Apr. __, ____; (no other dates given). (105)

William D. HENTHORN and Susan wife to Elam PATTERSON; 4-17-1820. (105)

John LINN and Sarah wife to Abner_____; July __, ____; (no other date given).(106)

Earl SPROAT to John FRAIL; Jan. __, 1821. (106)

Elam PATTERSON and Ann wife to Benjamin HINCHMAN of Philadelphia, Penna.; 10-9-1820. (107)

James JOHNSTON to James S. SMITH; 11-5-(1820?). (107)

United States to James McMAHON; 4-7-18__; (no other dates given). (108)

John HENDERSHOT and Susanah wife to Thomas A. BURTING; 5-31-____; (no other dates given). (108)

John HENDERSHOT and Susana wife to John N. POWERS, Jan. __,____; (no other dates given). (109)

Ephraim DOTY and Mary wife to Isaac BALDWIN; 6-25-1821. (109)

John YOUNG of Greene Co., (Penna.?) and Susanna wife to John STARK(?) of Washington Co., _____; 3-20-1821. (109)

Elisha LIPPINCOMB and Mary wife to Gilbert McCOY; May __, 182_; (no other dates given). (110)

John STRAHL to Abraham BLANWELT; 7-21-1821. (111)

Jacob YOUNG of Belmont Co., Ohio and Ruth wife to Thomas McCLARY; (no dates). (111)

Christian STALEY to Humphrey FINCH; 7-6-1821. (112)

Zadok WEST and Rosana wife of Monroe Co. to Joseph BOONE of Washington Co., Ohio, May __,____; (no other dates given). (112)

United States to George DUNLAVEY of Marietta; 1-3-18__; (no other dates given). (113)

United States to Amos JONES assignee of Amos Buell JONES; 9-8-1820. (113)

Michael HESS and Jane wife to William HENTHORN; 6-2-1821. (113)

Casper MALLORY of Belmont Co., Ohio to John LONG of Virginia; July __, ____; recorded 8-14-1820. (114)

Martin BAKER and Sarah wife to Henry KIRKBRIDE; May __, 1820; recorded 9120-1821. (114)

Noble RAYL, Sheriff of Monroe Co., Ohio to William R. DICKERSON; recorded 11-15-1821. (115)

John HENDERSHOT and Susana wife to David HENDERSHOT; 6-16-1821. (115)

John HENDERSHOT and Susana wife to David HENDERSHOT; June __, ____; recorded 11-15-1821. (116)

Elias PITMAN and Sarah wife to Richard Truex; 8-29-18__; (no other dates given). (116)

Joseph SEAL and Charity wife to Richard TRUEX; 8-25-1821. (117)

Henry FOGLE and Elizabeth (her mark) wife to Thomas _____ick; 10-2-____! (no other dates given). (117)

Richard TRUEX and Mary wife to Samuel TRUEX; 8-29-1821. (118)

William D. HENTHORN and Susy wife to Cornelius ATKINSON; Dec. __, ____; recorded Feb. 1822. (118)

United States to John HENDERSHOT of Washington Co.; 5-24-1819. (119)

Joseph FERREL Sr. and Jane wife of Ohio Co., (Virginia) to Joseph FERREL Jr. of Monroe Co.; Oct. __, ____; (no other dates given). (119)

Joseph FERREL and Jane wife of Oh(io Co., Va.) to Joseph FERREL Jr.; Oct. 27, ____; (no other dates given). (119)

United States to Joseph FERREL of Virginia; 10-7-1816. (120)

157

Israel SAYRES of Washington Co., Penna. to Wm. SMITH and John HENDERSHOT of Monroe Co.; recorded 2-25-1822. (120)

William KENT to Robert HOPPER; 10-19-18__; recorded 3-1-1822. (121)

John HECK and Mary wife to Frederick FOGLE; 7-31-___; (no other dates given). (121)

Frederick FOGLE Sr. and Catharine wife to Henry FOGLE; Sept. __, 1819. (121)

John MECHEN and Sarah wife of Belmont Co., Ohio to Stilwell TRUEX;_____-1821; (no other dates given. (122)

John HENDERSHOT and Susanna wife of Monroe Co. to Jacob SMITH of Belmont Co., Ohio; 1-13-18_2; (no other dates given). (122)

James CARROTHERS and Susannah wife to David O'CONNER; Mar __, ____; recorded Apr. 1822. (123)

Nathan HOLLISTER and Abigail wife to Levin OKEY; 12-30-1820. (123)

Levin OKEY and Esther (her mark) wife to Nathan HOLLISTER; Dec.__, ____; (no other dates given). (124)

John BARRETT and Jane wife to Michael HESS; 2-9-___; (no other dates given). (124)

John CLINGAN and Mary wife to John TIDD; (no dates given). (125)

John BROWN to Elias CONGER Sr.; 9-23-___; (no other dates given). (125)

Robert WILSON and Mary (her mark) wife to Oswalt SILL; attested to 1822. (126)

David COPELAND and Ann wife to James BONCIL of Delaware Co.,____; 4-30-1822. (126)

George GEOTS and Seville (her mark) wife to Molly YOHO; Feb. __, ____; (no other dates given). (127)

Samuel STEEL and Nancy wife of Monroe Co. to George SHELL of Dauphin Co., Penna.; 5-25-1822. (127)

John HENDERSHOT and Susannah (her mark) wife to Peter MANN; recorded 7-27-1822. (127)

George GEOTZ and Seville wife to Solomon GEOTZ; attested to 3-20-___; (no other dates given). (128)

JASPER MALLERY and Harriet wife of Belmont Co., Ohio to Philip GRUNER of Penna.; ___ __, 182_; (no other dates given. (128)

George GEOTZ Sr. and Seville wife of Belmont Co., Ohio to George GEOTZ Jr. of same; Nov. __, 182_; recorded 9-22-1822. (129)

Philip GREENER (GRIENER) of Pennsylvania to John HENDERSHOT; attested to 9-10-1822. (129)

United States to Nathan HOLLISTER; (no dates). (130)

Elias PITTMAN Sr. and Sarah wife to Elias PITTMAN Jr.; 3-28-1828. (130)

Henry BAKER and Mary (her mark) wife of Ohio Co., Virginia to John BAKER of Monroe Co.; (no dates). (131)

United States to Henry BAKER of Belmont Co., Ohio; 12-10-1817. (131)

Samuel MORE and Mary (her mark) wife of Short Creek twp., (Harrison Co., Ohio?) to Arthur MAGONE of Same; Sept. __, ____; (no dates given). (131)

Zadok WEST to ____ _____; (no dates given). (132)

Joseph FERRIL and Esther wife of Monroe Co. to Thomas ALLIN of Ohio Co., Virginia; 5-1-18_2; (no other dates given). (132)

Samuel WELLS and Hannah wife of Belmont Co., Ohio to George McNICHOLS; 9-12-1822. (133)

Abraham BLANWELT and Sarah wife to David H. CRAIG, Schoolmaster of Center twp., Monroe Co.; Apr. __, 1818; (no other dates given). (133)

William D. HENTHORN and Susannah wife to Jacob MOORE: 9-16-1822. (134)
John HENDERSHOT and Susanna wife to Samuel JUMPS; Sept. __, ___; (no other dates given). (134)
Jacob YOUNG and Ruth wife of Belmont Co., Ohio to John Graham of Harrison Co., Ohio; 9-25-____; (no other dates given). (235)
John STRAHL and Ann wife to Thomas A. BUNTING; _____ 1822; recorded Mar. 1823. (135)
William GREEN and Abigail wife to Stephen MELOTT; 11-19-____; (no other dates given). (135)
Richard TRUEX and Mary wife to Jacob FRANCIS and Ruth wife; July __, _____; recorded Mar. 1823. (136)
William TRUEX and Rachel wife to Peter MANN; 8-20-1822. (136)
Robert MORRIS and Polly (her mark) wife to William BURTON; 4-26-____; (no other dates given). (137)
United States to Hiram DANFORD and Michael DANFORD; 7-27-1822. (137)
Benjamin RUGLES of Belmont Co., Ohio to Jeremiah HOLLISTER; 6-13-1823. (138)
Aaron KINSY of Jefferson Co., Ohio to John BUTLER of Belmont Co., Ohio; Apr. __, ___; (no other dates given). (138)
John FERREL and Jane wife of Ohio Co., Virginia to Joseph FERREL; 10-9-18__; (no other dates given). (138)
Jonathan CURTIS and Sibel wife to Asa BARTON; 12-11-18_2; (no other dates given). (139)
Richard KENNEY (KINNEY) of Chester Co., Penna. to Stilwell TRUEX; _____ 1819; recorded Aug. 1823. (139)
John MAIDENS and Mary wife to Stillwell TRUEX; 3-26-1820. (140)
Lemuel RUCKER Sr. to Lemuel RUCKER Jr., son of Lemuel Sr.; consideration of love and affection; 3-27-____; (no other dates given). (140)
John HENDERSHOT and Susanah (her mark) wife to Henry BOLDING (BALDING); _____1820; (no other dates given). (131)
Archabald WOODS and Ann wife of Sterling JOHNSTON of Belmont Co., Ohio; 6-22-1822. (141)
Azeriah SMALLEY, assignee for Cornelius VANDERVENTER to Stilwell MELOTT; May 1823. (142)
Henry (his mark) KIRKBRIDE and Catharine (her mark) wife to John SMITH; _____1820; (no other dates given). (143)
Jacob COLEMAN and Polly wife to _____; (no dates); recorded 9-7-1823. (143)
Robert WILSON and Mary wife to James CANARY; 6-10-____; (no other dates). (144)
John HENDERSHOTT and Susana (her mark) wife of Monroe Co. to Daniel BELFORD of Guernsey Co., Ohio; _____1823; (no other dates). (144)
Sarah WINLAND adms. of estate of Jacob WINLAND, dec'd to Hugh BROWN; ___20, 1822; (no other dates). (145)
Lemuel RUCKER and Ann wife to Garland RUCKER; 1-13-____; (no other dates. (145)
Lemuel RUCKER and ___ wife to Pascal RUCKER; (no dates). (146)
Benjamin RUGGLES to Joseph DRIGGS; 10-3-1823. (146)
George KISOR and _____wife to _____ _____IDE guardian of minor children of Jacob WINLAND, dec'd; (no dates); recorded 12-24-1823. (147)
PETER McGOLDRICK and Hannah wife of Belmont Co., Ohio to _____; 2-21-____; recorded 12-26-1823. (147)
Robert WILSON (Jr.?) to Gideon MASON; 3-22-1822. (148)

159

Thomas HOWELL of Monroe Co. to Charles WELLS of Tyler Co., Virginia; _____ 1823; recorded 11-26-1823. (148)

Thomas MORRIS to Samuel ECCORD; July __, _____; (no other dates). (149)

Benjamin RUGGLES to John KING; 9-30-1823. (149)

John COX and Elizabeth wife to David SAMSON; (no dates). (150)

Robinson SANFORD and _____ wife to James ROLANDS; _____ 1823; (no other dates). (150)

Noble RAYL to William RAYL of Manallin twp., Fayette Co., Pa.; _____ 1824; (no other dates). (151)

William ASKEW of Belmont Co., Ohio to Samuel WILSON, 12-17-1823. (151)

John McBRIDE to Mary McBRIDE; 6-5-____; (no other dates). (152)

Josiah DILLON and Daugherty (her mark) wife to Benjamin POWELL; 6-25-1823. (152)

Josiah FERREL and Esther wife of Monroe Co. to Thomas ALLEN of Penna.; 4-20-____; (no other dates). (152)

Ephraim JONES to Elliott HOLLAND; _____ 1823; (no other dates). (153)

James WALTON and Ruth wife to George ROUSH at Belmont Co., Ohio; 4-10-1824. (153)

Isaac JONES and Abigail wife to James WALTON; (no dates). (154)

Robert BALDWIN to James WALTON; 4-10-____; (no other dates). (154)

Gershom CONGER and Mahala wife to George ROUSH; _____ 1824; (no other dates). (155)

Jacob COLEMAN and Katharine wife of Belmont Co., Ohio to John GILMORE of Monroe Co.; 2-17-____; (no other dates). (155)

John N. POWERS and Sarah wife of Belmont Co., Ohio to Peter MANN; (no dates). (156)

Henry BAKER of Ohio Co., Virginia to Stephen BAKER; 10-11-1823. (156)

Michael HESS and Jane wife to Abraham LANDIS; Mar. __, ____; (no other dates). (157)

Robert STEWART to William STEWART (STUART) of Virginia; mortgage; 1-13-____; (no other dates). (157)

Frederick HAYS and Elizabeth (her mark) wife to Jacob SMITH; _____ 1824; (no other dates). (157)

George PAUL and Eliza wife of Ohio Co., Va. to Messor SAYRE; 3-26-____; (no other dates). (158)

David COPELAND (COMLIN) and Ann wife to John BARKER, Nov. __, ____; (no other dates). (158)

Stephen BAKER and Sally wife to Samuel BAKER of Ohio Co., Virginia; J__ 15, 18 4; (no other dates). (159)

_____ WHITE to _____ LIPPINCOUT; _____ 1823; recorded _____ 1824. (159)

Wm. DEMENT to Vincent DEMENT, son of William; consideration of natural love and affection; _____ 1824; (no other dates). (160)

Bethany PITTMAN to William PITTMAN; 1-3-____;(no other dates). (160)

Thomas PRIBBLE to James PRIBBLE; _____ 1824; (no other dates). (161)

John DAILY to ___ INSURANCE TRUST CO.; mortgage 9-12-____; (no other dates). (161)

Daniel (his mark) HICKMAN and Martha (her mark) wife to Wm. W. SATTERTHWAIT; _____ 1833; attested to in Belmont Co., Ohio. (162)

Joseph (his mark) BEAVER of Monroe Co. to John THOMPSON of Belmont Co., Ohio; attested to 1-27-1838. (163)

Wm. W. SATTERTHWAIT and Mary wife to Josiah BRYAN; _____ 1837; attested to in Belmont Co., Ohio. (163)

Daniel (his mark) HICKMAN and Martha (her mark) wife of Monroe Co. to Wm. W. SATTERTHWAIT of Belmont Co., Ohio; attested to 4-14-1835. (164)

George CROW to Edward SALISBERRY; Mortgage; 3-10-1838. (165)

John P. BEVON and Mary wife to Thomas MATTACK of Guernsey & Ohio; 1-11-1837.(166)

Samuel WRIGHT and Mary wife of Monroe Co. to Stephen Melott of same; 10-11-1833.(166)

John FERREL to _____ _____; Nov. 1829. (167)

Thomas ROUSH and Mariah wife to Samuel STOKELY; 2-2-1835; Whereas Earl Sproat and James Johnston were seized jointly of land in Twp. 1, Range 3 and that Earl Sproat devised and bequeathed one undivided sixth part of lands unsold by him at time of his death to Mariah who afterwards married Thomas Roush. Attested to Meigs Co., Ohio. (167)

John HIGGINS and Elizabeth wife of Monroe Co. to William MOOR; 2-17-1835. (168)

John FERREL of Tyler Co., Va. to Alexander FERREL of Monroe Co.; 11-3-1829. (169)

Baldwin (Baulden) BIDDLE and Mary wife of Ohio Co., Va. to William RUSSELL of Tyler Co., Va.; 4-16-1834; All right, title and claim of said Baulden Biddle and wife through last will and testament of Baulden Biddle's grandfather, Henry Dickinson to a certain tract lying in Jackson twp., Monroe Co. in fractional Section 30, Township 1, Range 4(?). (169)

Henry S. BARNES of Belmont Co., Ohio to Levin MAROBA of Monroe Co.; 8-26-1834.(170)

Jeremiah HOWELL to Isaac and George THOMPSON; land conveyed to Howell by John Houk and to Houk by Jeremiah Williams; attested to 7-8-1837. (171)

Jeremiah HOWELL to George and Isaac THOMPSON; attested to attested to 7-8-1827. (172)

David DYE to Peter EDDY; attested to 8-1-1837. (172)

Mary MARTIN to Thomas E. KINNEY; attested to 5-22-1837. (173)

Benedict KREBBS and Elizabeth wife to Ludwig EGER; attested to 9-10-1838. (173)

Gottleib WISEMAN of Monroe Co. to Benedict KREBS of same; 8-28-1838. (174)

Wm. J. CARRUTHERS and Margaret wife of Allegheny Co., Pa. to Daniel GRAY; attested to ___-5-1837; (no other dates). (175)

Michael FLOYD and Elizabeth wife of Monroe Co. to James WINLAND; 1-8-1834.(176)

Thomas A. BUNTING and Catharine wife to Adam THURTHAVER; attested to 11-14-1837. (176)

Jacob HAWILLER and Mary wife to Conrod VOLL (or WAHL); attested to 5-4-1837.(177)

John Shul LAWRENCE and Catharine (her mark) wife to Earhart MAST; attested to ___-26-1834; (no other dates). (178)

Samuel H. GUTHRIE and Rebecca G. wife to Joseph DRIGGS; attested to 11-20-___; (no other dates). (179)

Rufus MURRY and Sally wife to Rouse MURRY, all Monroe Co.; attested to 3-30-1832. (179)

Anders MUHLEMAN and Barbary wife to John MINDER; 7-20-1835. (180)

James McCOMAS and Elizabeth Anne wife to Leonard CHACK, all Monroe Co.; attested to 12-5-1835. (180)

Jonathan HENDERSHOTT and Elizabeth (her mark) wife to OHIO LIFE INSURANCE CO.: mortgage; attested to _____ 1835; recorded 11-26-1835. (182)

David TRIMBLY and John WALKER, executors of William GREEN to Colbert HARRIS; ___-28-1835; recorded 11-27-1835. (182)

Thomas CARRICK and Rachel wife of Belmont Co., Ohio to Philo BALDING of Monroe Co.; 5-26-1834. (183)

William MORRIS and Elizabeth wife to John CLINGAN; attested to 4-8-1834. (184)

Alfred CAIN and Mary (her mark) wife of Job ENGLE; attested to 8-__-1834; recorded 8-12-1834. (185)

Benjamin THOMAS and Rebecca (her mark) wife to David EATON Jr.; (no dates). (186)

John SMITH Jr. and Sarah wife to Michael LEIPER and Michael HISSEBINGER, all of Monroe Co.; 10-21-1833. (187)

Abraham LANDIS and Sarah wife of Monroe Co. to George WEAVER of same; 7-25-1833. (188)

Alexander FALSAN and Eleanor wife to _____; attested to 5-1-1833. (188)
United States to Benjamin SPRAGUE; 1-5-1831. (189)
Benjamin (his mark) SPRAGUE and Susannah (her mark) wife to Paul RUSH; all of
    Monroe Co.; 12-25-1833. (189)
David PALMER and Phoebe wife to Joseph PITTMAN, all of Monroe Co.; 1-5-1834. (190)
John MINDEN and Anna wife to Jasper MALLARY, all of Monroe Co.; 12-14-1833. (190)
John SMITH and Mariah wife to Christian RESSEIKER; 3-16-1833. (192)
Edward (his mark) MAGINESS and Jane (her mark) wife to Alexander FALSON, all of
    Monroe Co.; 5-1-1833. (192)
Henry HOOVER and Anna Mariah wife of Belmont Co., Ohio to William Powell of Monroe
    Co.; 2-2-1833. (193)
Thomas (his mark) Balis Sr. and Lamantha (her mark) wife to Thomas BALIS Jr.;
    (No dates). (193)
Richard FISHER and Hannah (her mark) wife to George BAKER and Joseph BOWER;
    attested to 9-25-1837. (193)
A draft of a Survey for Robert MILLER, containing 1 acre in center Section 18
    (no other description given); 4-12-1834. (194)
John KYGER and Mary wife to Thomas WESTON, all of Monroe Co.; SE¼ Section 22,
    Township __, Range 3 except 1 acre on NW bank of Opossom Creek occupied for a
    meeting house and burying ground on which now stands a small log cabin for use
    of Baptist Church; attested to 11-3-1832. (194)
David EATON and Hannah (her mark) wife to George WATERS, all Monroe Co.;
    9-6-1830. (195)
John TRIMBLY and Jemima wife to OHIO LIFE INSURANCE CO.; mortgage; 7-7-1835. (196)
Benjamin BAKER to _____; attested to 1-26-1833. (197)
_____ PASCHAL to _____; recorded 7-17-1838; (no other dates). (197)
William (his mark) SUTTON and Catharine (her mark) wife to James CARMICHAEL, all
    of Monroe Co.; 9-12-1835. (198)
Thomas COCHRAN Jr. and Mary wife of Washington Co., Ohio to William COCHRAN of
    Monroe Co.; 2-30-1834; attested to 2-13-1834; recorded 2-19-1834. (198)
William MANTLE and Eleanor wife to _____; attested to 9-6-1833. (200)
Thomas COCHRAN Jr. and Mary wife of Washington Co., Ohio to William COCHRAN;
    2-13-1830. (200)
John STRAHL Jr. and Hannah J. wife of Harrison Co., Ohio to James B. SMITH;
    attested to 11-10-1832. (200)
Reuben YOHO of Monroe Co. to Samuel H. GUTHRIE; attested to 2-7-1838. (201)
John HOWALT and Mary (her mark) wife of Monroe Co. to John BREKER; attested to
    1-12-1838. (201)
Jacob LAYMAN and Mary Ann wife of Belmont Co., Ohio to Wentesty Piglar FUNKHAUSER
    and _____ HOUBOUGHER; 1-7-1829. (202 & 204)
John SMITH and Mariah (her mark) wife to Christian BESECKER (or RESUKER); attested
    to 3-16-1833. (203)
Levi LINN heir of estate of Caleb LINN, dec'd to Benjamin TRUAX of Monroe Co.;
    2-17-1831; interest in NE¼ Section 5, Township 5, Range 5. Wit: John Linn
    and Joshua Linn. (204)
Benjamin TRUAX and Phoebe wife to Henry BROWN of Belmont Co., Ohio; 10-2-1833. (205)
Thomas PRIBBLE and Debby wife of Vermilion Co., Illinois to_____; attested
    to 9-23-1833. (205)
Stillwel MELOTT and Sarah wife to John CLETHERO, all of Monroe Co.; 4-1-1833. (205)

162

Isaac JANES and Abigail wife to Samuel GREEN of Monroe Co.; attested to 3-29-1833. (206)

John BEEVER and Nancy wife to Samuel PAYTON, all Monroe Co.; 4-10-1833. (207)

Matthew BALL and Elizabeth (her mark) wife of Benjamin STREET; attested to 10-18-1833. (208)

_____STARKEY to_____ _____; recorded 10-22-1838; (no other dates). (208)

Joshua DAVIS to Thomas ARMSTRONG; attested to 9-20-1838. (208)

Isaac BEARDMORE and Susannah wife to Robert GRAHAM; attested to _____ 1837. (209)

Samuel H. GUTHRIE and Rebecca wife to William D. BETT; 9-15-1832. (210)

Willis P. COLEMAN of Salem twp., Monroe Co., but now in St. Geneva Co., Missouri to John JONES; 7-17-1832. (211)

John (his mark) DUNN and Casander (her mark) wife of Monroe Co. to Jesse JACKSON of same; 9-13-1832. (212)

Alexander McMULLIN and Mary (her mark) wife of Ohio Co., Virginia to____ _____; attested to 8-23-1837. (212)

Urias MARTIN and Margaret wife to Samuel MARTIN, all of Monroe Co.; 3-14-1833.(213)

Robert WOOD and Mary wife of Penn twp., Morgan Co., Ohio formerly of (Monroe Co.?) to Robert LESSLIE of Monroe Co.; 10-12-1832. (214)

Samuel GREEN and Mary wife of Monroe Co. to Joel YOST of Belmont Co., Ohio; attested to 3-12-1833. (215)

Jacob PITTMAN and Ide (her mark) wife, William PITTMAN and Jemima (her mark) wife, Elias PITTMAN and Sarah wife, Samuel HENDERSHOTT and Ruth (her mark) wife, Benjamin PITTMAN and Catharine (her mark) wife, John PALMOR and Sarah (her mark) wife, heirs of the estate of Bethena _____ to _____ _____; (no dates); recorded 3-8-1833. (216-217)

John (his mark) WINLAND and Catharine (her mark) wife of Monroe Co. to Abner GREGG of Belmont Co., Ohio; 2-11-1833. (217)

Dugal C. MARTIN and Sarah wife of Jefferson Co., Ohio to Joseph SEALS; attested to 9-25-1832. (218)

John CONGER and Elizabeth wife of Monroe Co. to John and Alexander SINCLAIR; attested to 12-29-1837. (219)

John RUDY and George BRUNER to William SHALLI; attested to 10-2-1837 Allegheny Co., Penna. (220)

William ENOCHS and Lavisa (her mark) wife, James (his mark) SWANEY and Rebecca (her mark) wife, Henry (his mark) PRYOR and Ann (her mark) wife, Nathaniel DAVIS and Ann (her mark) wife, John HUPP and Susan wife to Kiney DAVIS; attested to 1-26-1836. (220)

James LUCUS and Margaret (her mark) wife to Francis MILLER; attested to 9-26-1837 (221)

Alexander McMULLIN and Mar_____ wife of Ohio Co., Virginia to Allen WAITS; 8-23-1837. (222)

Thomas SCANTLIN to Richard WARFIELD; Power of Attorney to sell Scantlin's land to Enoch Grandan; 10-__-1837; recorded 12-4-1827. (222)

Daniel GETZ and Nancy (her mark) wife to Joseph STOOKEY; attested to __-13-1833; recorded 12-1-1837. (223)

Robert MILLER and Mary wife to George BAKER and Joseph BOWER of Monroe Co.; attested to 9-25-1837. (223)

Robert MILLER and Mary wife to George BAKER and Joseph BOWER; attested to 9-25-1837. (224)

163

Robert (his mark) MORRIS and Isabella (her mark) wife to John CREE; 10-16-1837. (225)
Owen DEWAS and Mary wife to _____; (recorded 1-26-1838). (225
Joseph (his mark) SCOTT and Elizabeth wife to John CREE; attested to 10-14-1837.(226)
Elijah MORRIS of Bedford Co., Penna. to Elias PITTMAN of Monroe Co.; 8-7-1826.(226)
Joseph GIBSON to Nicholas COLEMAN of Belmont Co., Ohio; 10-29-1839. (227)
United States to Jeremiah LAZIER of Monroe Co.; (no dates given). (228)
John HENDERSHOT and Susannah (her mark) wife of Monroe Co. to Daniel GRAY; 2-27-1828.
    (228)
Israel HARRIS and Mary wife of Guernsey Co., Ohio to Ebenezer MAYBERRY of same;
    (no dates); recorded 7-7-1828. (229)
Joshua MAYBERRY to Ebenezer MAYBERRY of Guernsey Co., Ohio; 1-6-1838. (230)
Samuel LINDSEY and Margaret (her mark) wife to George W. GRIFFITH of Monroe Co.;
    attested to 10-25-18(38). (230)
Benjamin THOMAS and Rebecca (her mark) wife of Belmont Co., Ohio to James RIGG;
    attested to 8-15-1838. (231)
Jesse JACKSON and Jane wife to John DUNN; attested to 9-13-1832. (232)
Edward MERCER and Mary wife of Belmont Co., Ohio to William COCHRAN of Monroe Co.;
    8-6-1832. (233)
Benjamin RUGGLES and Clarissa wife to Elijah ANDREWS; attested to 9-16-1833. (233)
Elijah ANDREWS and Rachel wife to David DYE; attested to __-15-1839; recorded
    3-16-1839. (234)
Thomas FLOYD and D___illa wife to Thomas FARLEY; 6-20-1834. (235 & 236)
Gabriel STARKEY and Mary (mark) wife to William PREKENS, all of Monroe Co.;
    12-9-1834. (235)
Richard TRUAX and Rebecca (mark) wife to John MASON, all Monroe Co.; 2-17-1834.(236)
Gabriel STARKEY and Mary wife to William PREKENS; 12-9-1834. (237)
John FRAIL to Stephen_____; mortgage;_____1824; (no other dates). (237)
_____BARKES and Mary wife of Monroe Co. to_____McFARLAND; (no dates); recorded
    10-1-1838. (238)
Daniel O'CONNER of Woodsfield, Monroe Co. to Crawford RANDOLPH & CO.; mortgage;
    1-7-1829. (238)
Caleb DILLE and Rebecca wife now residing in Indiana to William TRUEX of Monroe
    Co.; 3-30-1829. (239)
Charles ATKINSON and Nancy wife of Monroe Co. to William C. WALTON; 3-9-1833. (239)
George WEAVER and Elizabeth (mark) wife to Abraham LANDIS;-- -29-1835; attested to
    8-31-1835. (240)
Abner CARLETON to Abram LANDIS; mortgage; 8-29-1835. (240)
James DUNWOODY and Elizabeth (mark) wife to Mary CARTER; attested to 10-25-1833.(241)
William TRUAX and Jane wife of Richland Co., Ohio to Thomas DAKEN; 10-22-1833.
    Wit.: Benj. P. Truax. (241)
John PORTER (PARTER) of Monroe Co. to Benjamin THOMAS of Belmont Co., Ohio;
    1-20-1835. (242)
Josiah BRYAN(T) and Mary wife to Jacob BINCE, all Monroe Co.; 2-1-1838. (243)
Ulrich KELLER to John REATH, both Monroe Co.; attested to 1-31-1838. (244)
Daniel GILMORE to Thomas GILMORE; attested to 9-20-1837. (244)
John SLOAN and Susannah (mark) wife of Monroe Co. to Joseph BAUCH of Allegheny Co.,
    Penna.; 8-25-1837. (245)

164

Jeremiah HOLLISTER and Sally wife to Thomas McMAHON and Elijah McMAHON, all Monroe Co.; 3-31-18_4; (no other dates). (246)

Martin (his mark) LEE and Susannah (her mark) wife to Lewis MORRIS, all of Monroe Co.; 6-1-1827. (246)

Arch'd WOODS of Ohio Co., Virginia to Isaac JONES of Monroe Co.; 9-10-1830. (246)

Thomas (his mark) SMITH and Huldah (her mark wife of Monroe Co. to James BLARE; 10-11-1830. (247)

Citizen BEALL to Elias RUSH; attested to 5-22-1830. (247)

Avery WEST and Elizabeth wife to Henry TITTLE; attested to 4-3-1830 Belmont Co., Ohio. (247)

Mary McBRIDE of Monroe Co. to William DUNN; _____ 1830; (no other dates given),(248)

Elliott HOLLAND, Sheriff Monroe Co., Ohio to Henry HARTER and John HARTER; Henry Harter at Sept. Term (no year) Common Pleas Court filed his petition against the widow and heirs of Matthias Harter, dec'd; (no dates given). (248)

Henry DECKER and Mary (mark) wife of Monroe Co. to Joshua LINN (LYNN); 3-21-1829.(249)

Citizen BEALL and Elizabeth wife to Joshua LINN, all of Monroe Co.; 12-3-1825.(250)

Theophilus MINOR of Monroe Co. to John MINOR of Natchez (Mississippi Territory); 3-10-1829. (250)

Leonard LIKENS and Ruth wife of Frederick Co., Virginia to Jacob HAWEILLER of Monroe Co.; 10-4-1833; being land conveyed to Likens by Province McCormick, trustee on 9-8-1832. (250)

William DELANEY and ___ wifr to _____ _____; attested to 10-3-1844. (252)

David SUTHERLAND, John BEVAN and _____ BLAKE, Trustee Section 16, Township 6, Range 7 to Thomas MARKEY of Monroe Co.; 99 year lease; 4-7-1823. (252)

David SAMSON and Susanna (mark) wife to Daniel COOK, all of Monroe Co.; 7-4-1833. (252 & 254)

Robert CARPENTER and Mary (mark) wife to John DAILY; attested to 11-18-1834. (253)

Thomas (his mark) BALIS Sr. and Susanna (her mark) wife to Thomas BALIS Jr.; attested to 5-10-1837. (254)

Robert MILLER and Mary (her mark) wife to George BAKER and Joseph BOWER; attested to 9-25-1837. (255)

Joshua WOODS and Sally (mark) wife to Jacob OGLE; attested to 4-15-1834. (256)

John DEVAUL to Christian HARTLINE; That Conrad Devaul on 10-25-1831 made his last will and testament stating land to go to his son John; attested to 6-4-1834. (256)

Ezer ELLIS to Samuel DANFORD; 3-10-1829. (257)

Citizen BEALL and Elizabeth wife to Elias RUSH, all Monroe Co.; 1-8-1830. (258)

George PAULL of Ohio Co., Virginia to Jeremiah WILLIAMS; attested to Dec. 1827; recorded 10-9-1830. (258)

Citizen BEALL and Elizabeth wife of Monroe Co. to Sus'ah HENTHORN; 7-31-1829.(258)

Jeremiah RUSH and Mary (her mark) wife to William COCHRAN; (no dates given.(259)

Elizabeth WINELAND admerx of Estate of John WINELAND Jr. late of Monroe Co., dec'd to John HUGGINS; Elizabeth Wineland filed petition in Common Pleas Court dated 8-28-1834 stating John Wineland Jr. departed leaving children and minor heirs; Jacob Winland, Margaret Winland and Mahala Winland; attested to 9-27-1834.(260)

Baltzer MELLINE of Stark Co., Ohio to Frederick Jacob BENTZ of Monroe Co.; (no dates given). (261)

_____ McVICKER and Martha wife to _____ _____; recorded 4-10-1835. (261)

John RUDY and George BRUNER of Pittsburgh, Penna. to William SHALLI; 10-2-1837. (262)

165

Philip NOLAND and Martha (mark) wife to John and Alexander SINCLAIR; attested to
    12-7-1837. (262)
John TRUAX and Margaret (mark) wife to Samuel MELOTT, all of Monroe Co.; 8-17-1829.
    (263)
Oswald SILL to William G. SHANKLAND; 5-1-1835. (264)
Andrew COWELL and Mary wife to Benjamin STINE of Monroe Co.; 10-22-1834. (264)
Michael FALSCROFF and Elizabeth (mark) wife to Godfrey STAGNER; recorded 12-2-1834.
    (265)
Daniel BRUSH and Nancy wife of Muskingum Co., Ohio to William WILSON of Monroe Co.;
    (no dates given). (266)
James LAVETT and Lavina wife to Rebecca CHAMBERLAIN; attested to 7-15-1838. (266)
William PHILPOT and Ruth wife to Wm. WILSON;   1838; recorded 1-29-1839.(267)
Daniel GRAY and Deborah wife to James CUNNINGHAM; 1-7-1839. (267)
John ANTOL and Elizabeth wife to Mary FOOT now wife of Moses JEFFERS; attested to
    1-2-1838. (268)
Peter MANN and Elizabeth (mark) wife to Joshua WOOD; attested to 6-24-1837. (269)
Joshua WOOD and Sally (mark) wife to Frederick FOGLE; attested to 1-29-1839.(269)
William GIVENS and Elizabeth (mark) wife to Jacob WYSENT; attested to July 1833.(270)
John MARSHAL and Elizabeth (mark) wife to Nicholas FELLURE; attested to 1-26-1839.
    (270)
Moses JEFFERS and Mary wife to Nicholas FELLURE; attested to 1-26-1839.(271)
Joshua RUSH and Mary (mark) wife to Jasper MALLORY; 12-__-1838; attested to 1-12-1839.
    (272)
Nimrod E. Henthorn and _____wife to John MARTIN, all Monroe Co.; 2-4-1837.(272)
Dennis (his mark) MOSENEY and Rachel (her mark) wife to John MARTIN; 4-9-1838.(273)
John ALTOP and Sarah (mark) wife to Jacob MOOSE; attested to 9-4-1833. (273)
James R. HUTCHINSON of Belmont Co., Ohio to John BROWN of same; 8-24-1833. (274)
John HUGGINS and Elizabeth (mark) wife to Thomas ALLEN; attested to 2-17-1834.(275)
Joseph JANES and Margaret wife to John COFFEE; attested to 6-20-1838. (275)
Mordeica DERTH and Susanna wife to Jacob LINDEMOOD; attested to 1-22-1839. (276)
Hiram FORSHEY and Catharine (mark) wife to William WILSON; 4-12-1838; Wit: John
    Forshey and Rachel (her mark) Forshey. (277)
William CRAIG and Rosana wife to William Wilson; (no dates given). (277)
Jacob WEYSANT and Margaret wife to_____ _____; attested to 1-21-1839. (278)
Jacob WEYSANT and Margaret wife to George SWALLEE; attested to 1-21-1839. (278)
John ULLOM and Margaret wife to Frederick MYERS; attested to 10-18-1838;
    Wit: William Myers and Hannah (her mark) Myers. (279)
James McVICKER and Elizabeth (mark) wife to Isaac PASCHAL; attested to Jan. 1839;
    (no other dates given). Wit: Thomas D. McVicker and Eleanor (mark) McVicker.
    (280)
George WEAVER to Daniel HICKMAN; 1-29-1839; mortgage. (280)
Susanna JANES to James JANES; attested to 11-23-1838. (280)
Alexander SINCLAIR and Jane wife to Richard TRUEX; 1-17-1838. (281)
John HUGGINS and Elizabeth (mark) wife to Edward COULTER, all of Monroe Co.;
    2-18-1835. (281)
Elizabeth ACE to Thomas EVANS and Catharine wife, all Monroe Co.; attested to
    9-20-1834. (282)
Issachar SCHOLFIELD and Edith wife of Belmont Co., Ohio to Thomas COCHRAN;
    attested to 10-9-1833. (283)

Daniel M. LAUGHLIN of Philadelphia, Penna., Attorney at Law to William NEPTUNE of
   Monroe Co., farmer; 2-3-1834.   (283)
Levi BARBER and Elizabeth wife of Washington Co., Ohio to Patrick ADAMS; attested to
   Mar. 1828; (no other dates); Wit.: David Barber, Austin Barber.   (284)
Benjamin THOMAS and Martha wife to Woodman OKEY and Edward REED, all of Monroe Co.;
   4-3-1828.   (285)
John BURTON and Elizabeth (mark) wife to Lewis STARKEY; attested to 6-28-1837.(285)
Daniel GRAY and Deborah wife to _____ _____; attested to 5-3-1830.   (286)
George HENDERSHOT and Elizabeth wife to Thomas MARTIN, all of Monroe Co.; 5-26-1828.
   (287)
David SLACK and Catharine wife to John HILL; (no dates; recorded 6-1-1839.(287)
Jonson LESLIE to Samuel CARLTON of Monroe Co.; 5-7-____;(no other dates). 288)
Gideon MASON and Hannah wife to Joel STRAHL; (no dates); recorded 11-8-1839. (288)
John MADINS and ____wife to _____; recorded 11-6-1839.   (289)
James BRACY and Gracy (mark) wife of Belmont Co., Ohio to Henry MEEK; attested to
   _____1838; (no other dates).   (289)
Samuel JANES and Cisne wife to ____es GORDON; (no dates given).   (290)
Joseph JANES and Margaret wife to Benjamin MORRIS; _____18_9; (no other dates
   given).   (291)
Charles (his mark) WILLIAMS and Salinah (mark) wife to John GRAY; 7-17-1839. (292)
Joseph DRIGGS of Monroe Co. to Samuel H. GUTHRIE; (no dates given). (292)
James TAYLOR and Anna wife of Monroe Co. to Benjamin McBURNEY of Guernsey Co., Ohio;
   8-15-1838.   (292 & 295)
Jacob OGLE and _____wife to _____ _____; 4-21-____; recorded Aug. 1838. (293)
Abraham JANES and Mary wife to Moses GORDON of Belmont Co., Ohio; attested to
   4-7-__ 8; (no other dates given).   (293)
Augustus S. ALDERMAN and Julia wife to James JANES; attested to 8-6-1838. (294)
Joseph FORSHEY and ___wife to William EARLY; attested to 5-8-1839.   (295)
James EARLY and Nancy wife to William EARLY of Harrison Co., Ohio; attested to
   5-17-1839.   (295)
Vance JOHNSTON and Caroline G. wife to Adam BEIGHT; attested to Sept. 1838. (296)
John W. HARTSHORN and ____wife to _____ _____; attested to 12-14-1836.   (297)
_____ _____to John McCAMMON; (no dates given).   (297)
Liberty CURTIS and Elizabeth (mark) wife to Hiram CURTIS; (no dates given).   (298)
David KING and Elizabeth wife to Iram CURTIS; attested to 12-21-1837.   (298)
John B. MOBLEY to Levi MOBLEY; (no dates given).   (299 & 300)
_____CANEAR (note: not enough of record left to show if Canear was grantor or
   grantee); Feb. 1837.   (300)
Aaron (his mark) MEDDERS and Esther (her mark) wife to_____ _____; _____1838;
   (no other dates given).   (300)
Ambrose H. MERRY and Margaret wife to Benson M_____; (no dates given).   (301)
United States to Moses T. SPENCER of Monroe Co.; (no dates); certificate #787,
   granted through Marietta Land Office.   (301)
Philip AULT of Belmont Co., Ohio to Alexander SINCLAIR; mortgage; 8-18-1835. (302)
Robert STEWART and Isabella (mark) wife to Barick FISHER, all of Monroe Co.;
   -11-1834; (no other dates given).   (303)
Jacob BALSIGER and Barbara wife of Monroe Co. to Christian WINZIRED; 3-22-1834.(303)
Isael BOOTH and Bethina wife to Isaac BALDWIN; 4-23-1834.   (304)
Anthony STINGLE and Elizabeth (mark) wife to Henry LONG; attested to 8-8-1836
   Pittsburgh, Allegheny Co., Penna.   (304)

Benjamin WHITE of Belmont Co., Ohio to Daniel TOMLINSON of Monroe Co.; 4-16-1838.
   (305)
David WEST and Rebecca wife to John H. BRIDGEMAN, all of Monroe Co.; 4-10-18__;
   (no other dates given). (306)
Mary MARTIN of Belmont Co., Ohio to _____ WHITE; attested to 4-4-183_; (no other
   dates given). (306)
Abraham STULL and Barbary (mark) wife to Andrew MATTHEWS; 3-1-1836. (307)
Stephen RATLIFF and Mary wife and Benjamin Ratliff of Wheeling, Virginia to Richard
   CORNEL of same; 3-20-____; (no other dates). (307)
John (his mark) ROBERTSON and Mary (mark) wife to John GIBSON; _____1838;
   recorded 12-12-1838. (308)
John McELROY and Nancy (mark) wife to Jonathan STACKHOUSE, all of Monroe Co.;
   10-17-1836. (308)
William ORN and Mary wife to Jonathan STACKHOUSE; 12-28-1837. (309)
William WILLIAMS and Margaret wife to Luke DILLE; (no dates); recorded 12-7-1838.(309)
Elliott HOLLAND, Sheriff of Monroe Co., Ohio to William COCHRAN; (no dates given).(310)
Robert CARPENTER and mary (mark) wife to Henry P. HUGHS; July 1834. (311)
Levin McCROLA and Jane Elizabeth wife of Monroe Co. to Leanhart MILLER of Ohio Co.,
   Virginia; attested to Nov. 1834; recorded 11-13-1834. (312)
John REED and Mary (mark) wife of Belmont Co., Ohio to William ALEXANDER of Monroe
   Co.; 10-17-1834. (313)
Benjamin PIATT and Lucinda (mark) wife of Monroe Co. to Thomas PIATT; 9-26-18__;
   (no other dates given). (314)
Jesse (his mark) DAVIS Sr. and Sarah (her mark) wife of Monroe Co. to Jesse DAVIS
   Jr.; 6-14-1834. (315)
Robert FERGUSON and Martha (her mark) wife to John FERGUSON, all of Monroe Co.;
   11-6-1834. (316)
Elijah STEPHEN and Margara (her mark) wife of John STEPHEN, all of Monroe Co.;
   12-4-1829. (317)
Samuel H. GUTHRIE and Rebecca G. wife of Monroe Co. to Achbold WOODS of Ohio Co.,
   Virginia; 6-4-1838. (318)
John CARMICHAEL and Mary wife to H. H. MOTT; 2-18-1833. (319)
George REMLEY and Eleanor (her mark) wife to Jacob GIMBERMAN, all of Monroe Co.;
   1-13-1834. (320)
Daniel KYGER and Anne (mark) wife of Monroe Co. to Mary DURKEE; 10-19-1832. (321)
Robert FERGUSON to Thomas ROBISON, both of Monroe Co.; 4-6-1833. (322)
Cornelius ATKINSON and Mary (mark) wife to Isaac JANES; (no dates) recorded
   3-16-1834. (323)
Mary MARTIN to Benjamin WHITE; 3-3-1834; Wit: Citizen Beall, Sarah White. (323)
Thomas COCHRAN and Mary Ann wife to Henry KIRKBRIDE of Monroe Co.; __-25-18__;
   (no other dates given). (324)
Jacob O. PITTMAN and Ide (mark) wife to George STEWARD; attested to 2-22-1833.(325)
Daniel DYE and Vincent DYE executors of Will of Daniel DYE, dec'd, late of Monroe Co.
   to Reuben DYE; 5-9-1829; Whereas Daniel Dye by will bequeathed to Reuben Dye of
   Monroe Co. all legal right to farm where Reuben lived at time of decease of said
   Daniel being NW¼ Section 4, Township __, Range 5, conveyed to Reuben by heirs of
   estate of Daniel Dye, dec'd (note: not named). (315
David HENDERSHOT and Eleanor wife to Elias SLOAN, all of Monroe Co.; 12-10-1832.(316)
Peter MELOTT and Easter wife to Jacob MELOTT, all of Monroe Co.; __ary 9, 1832.(327)

Henry FRUST and Mary (mark) wife to _____ _____; _____ 1834 (only date given).(327)
John GILMORE and Margaret wife to Cornelius N. JANES; (no dates); recorded 3-10-1834. (328)

Cornelius ATKINSON of Monroe Co. to Isaac JANES; 4-15-1833. (329)
Jacob TSHAPPAT and Susannah wife to _____ _____; (no dates given). (329)
John GILMORE and Margaret wife to Cornelius N. JANES, all of Monroe Co.; 2-27-1834. (329)

James RADCLIFF of Ohio Co., Virginia to William MOTT; 10-5-1829. (330)
Joseph VARNER and Lucy (mark) wife of Belmont Co., Ohio to Emmanuel MANN and Hugh HENDERSON of Monroe Co.; attested to 12-15-1835. (330)
Isaac MITCHEL to William OLLOM, both of Monroe Co.; 8-16-1833. (331)
Thomas LANAM and Mary (mark) wife to Caltan MERRY; attested to 6-7-1838. (332)
Abner MUNDEL and Delila wife of Green Co., Penna. to Apolo STEPHENS of Monroe Co. (333 & 352)

Jasper MALLORY and Harriet wife to William STRAHL, all of Monroe Co.; _____ 1839; (no other dates given). (333)
William BERT to _____ _____; (no dates); recorded 11-29-1839. (334)
George SULLIVAN and Sarah wife to Adam HELLEM; 7-15-1839. (334)
Mathew SMITH of Belmont Co., Ohio to James KENNEDY of Monroe Co.; 2-28-1834. (335)
Stephen ATKINSON and Elizabeth (mark) wife to Jno. B. GRADHOUSE; attested to 3-24-1838. (336)

Jacob TSCHAPPAT and Susannah wife to George GRADHOUSE; attested to 6-2-1838. (336)
Adam (his mark) MYERS and Mary wife to Jno. HURD; Jan. 1834. (337 & 404)
Geo. PAUL and Eliza wife to Joseph MORRIS and David JENNINGS; 6-13-1826. (338)
John OLLOM and Susanna (her mark) wife to Alexander DAVIS and Nathaniel STEENROD; attested to 11-23-1833. (338)

Richard BARRETT and Ann wife, Morris CARRICK and Eliza Ann wife, Nathaniel SPURGIN and Sarah (mark) wife, Samuel DARNON and Kethura wife, John CARRICK and Jane wife, heirs of George CARRICK, dec'd. to _____ _____; 3-3-1838; mentions widow's dower; signatures attested to in Belmont Co., Ohio. (340)
Jesse RICH and Mary wife to Edward R. LANE, all of Monroe Co.; 8-17-18__; (no other dates given). (341)
_____ DRUM and Mary wife to _____ _____; Aug. 1832. (341)
Stephen ATKINSON and Elizabeth wife to _____ _____; (no dates); recorded 10-29-1838. (341)
John DUNFEE and Sarah (mark) wife to William McCARTY, all of Monroe Co.; attested to 7-3-1838. (341)

Michael PHOLSEGRAVE and Elizabeth wife to _____ _____; attested to 8-15-1838.(342)
Stephen ATKINSON and Eliz____ wife to John DUNFEE; 7-13-____; (no other dates).(343)
William H. BELL and Rebecca wife to David DYE; attested to 2-17-1838. (343)
Joseph JANES and Margaret wife to Stephen BROWN; attested to 4-21-1838. (344)
Richard SANDS and Rebecca wife to William EVANS; attested to 8-16-1834. (345)
William MASON and Margaret (mark) wife to Thomas LITTLE, all of Monroe Co.; 6-23-1834. (346)

David CRAWFORD and Mary (mark) wife to Robert W. OGG, all of Monroe Co.; 10-17-1834. (346)
John WINLAND of Monroe Co. to James WINLAND; bond; 2-5-1833. (347)
Thomas WOOD and Leticia wife to Henry H. MOTT; attested to 9-3-1829. (348)
William G. SHANKLAND and Harrie wife and John L. SMITH and Elizabeth wife, all of Belmont Co., Ohio to Oswald SILL; 11-2-1829. (349)

Jeremiah HICKS and Mary Ann (mark) wife ot Jesse HARRISON; attested to 6-28-1833 (34
Edward MERSER and Mary wife of Belmont Co., Ohio to Jacob HADLEE of Monroe Co.;
    8-4-1833. (349)
Jabez OSBORN, Gideon OSBORN and Elizabeth wife to Christian VINIKI, all of Monroe
    Co.; 9-23-1833. (350)
William SMITH and Elizabeth (mark) wife to Benjamin STEPHENS, all of Monroe Co.;
    11-18-1833. (351)
Baker BOTT and Barbary wife to David SAMSON; attested to 11-2-18__; recorded
    12-3-1833. (352)
Thomas (his mark) MORRIS and Mary (her mark) wife of Monroe Co. to John HAYDEN
    of Belmont Co., Ohio; 11-15-1833. (353)
Thomas STEPHEN and Nancy (mark) wife to James KENNEDY; attested to 8-23-___;
    recorded 8-29-1834. (354)
Jesse MORRIS and Emily P. wife to Samuel SMITH; attested to 4-10-1834. (355)
James McMILLEN and Margaret wife to Alexander SINCLAIR; 3-18-1834. (356)
Isaac JONES and Abigail wife to Thomas CUMMINS; (no dates); recorded 2-21-1833.(357)
Daniel KYGER and Anne wife to Sebastian BAURY; 10-19-18_2;(no other dates). (357)
Sheriffs Deed to SHAW, Tifany & Cos.; (no date); Israel F. Randolph, Joel F.
    Randolph and William Crawford; suit filed in June Term 1830 of Common Pleas
    Court. (358)
Henry SMITH and Effamay wife of Monroe Co. to Stephen RATCLIFF of Ohio Co.,
    Virginia; 7-17-1832. (359)
Henry KIRKBRIDE and Catharine wife to David KIRKBRIDE Jr.; 8-1-1832. (360)
John LLOYD of Knox Co., Ohio to Wm. BROWN; (no dates); recorded 6-10-1839. (361)
John TRUEX and Bethenia wife to Benjamin_____; attested to 10-3-1833. (361)
Philip (his mark) ALLEN Jr. and Christena (her mark) wife to James W. SHANKLAND &
    Co.; (no dates given). (362)
Alexander FERREL and Rebecca (mark) wife to Thomas CARRICK; attested to 6-4-1833.(36
Alexander MASSIE and Mary (mark) wife to Thomas CARRICK, all of Monroe Co.;
    8-9-183_; (no other dates given). (363)
David KIRKBRIDE to Enoch GRANDON; attested to 1-24-1829. (364)
John R. DYE and Priscilla wife of Washington Co., Ohio to Elizabeth DYE of
    Monroe Co.;-(no dates given); land patented to John R. Dye by United States
    1-13-1828. (364)
Daniel (his mark) HARRIS to Elizabeth, Edey, Hetta, Sarah, Rebecca and Lovey LAW;
    Mansion House with Stable, barn pasture ground near St. Clairsville in
    Belmont Co., Ohio, also two quarter sections of Seneca Fork of Wi_____
    in Township 6, Range 7 in Monroe Co.; attested to 11-27-1826. (365)
Joseph DILLE and Elizabeth (mark) wife of Monroe Co. to James RATCLIFF; attested
    to 3-8-1828. (366)
Jacob MILLER and Nancy wife to William COCHRAN and Thomas COCHRAN, all of Monroe
    Co.; 3-9-1829. (367)
John FERREL and Nancy wife of Ohio Co., Virginia to James KENNEDY of Pittsburgh,
    Allegheny Co., Penna.; 3-25-1829. (367)
Isaac JONES and Abigail wife to ___uel GREEN; attested to 4-16-1829. (368)
David HENDERSHOT of Vermilion Co., Illinois to William LAFLEN of Monroe Co.;
    1-24-1835. (368)

ames REESE and Hannah (mark) wife to Henry STINE, all of Monroe Co.; 4-4-1835.(369)

oshua WOOD and Sally (mark) wife to Daniel MICHAEL of Monroe Co.; 4-9-1835. (370)

ichard SHEPHERD Sr. of Belmont Co., Ohio to Michael STINE of Monroe Co.; 12-23-1834. (371)

amuel SLUSHER to ____ _____; attested to 8-31-1826. (371)

itizen BEALL and Elizabeth wife of Monroe Co. to Stilwell MELOTT; 8-2-____; (no other dates given). (372)

ABRIEL STARKEY and Mary wife to William PICKINS, all of Monroe Co.; 1-9-1836.(373)

ohn BELL and Sarah wife to Russell STARKLEY, all of Monre Co.; (no dates). (373)

homas (his mark) EVANS to Michael BEAVER; 3-3-1833. (374)

ohn (his mark) WINLAND and Catharine (mark) wife to Samuel WATTERS; (no dates); recorded 9-6-1834. (374)

enjamin S. COWEN adms. of Estate of William CRAWFORD, dec'd to John SM_____p attested to___-27-1839; (no other dates given). (375)

___ BARNS and Jane wife to _____; (no dates given). (376)

lat of town of Calais; (no date given). (376)

elson HOGUE and Lucy Ann wife of Monroe Co. to John LASHURE of Belmont Co., Ohio 11-26-1838. (376)

eremiah LASHER to Joseph FORESHEY, both of Monroe Co.; July 18__; (no other dates given). (377)

aniel BRUSH and Nancy wife to John DAVIS; (no dates); recorded 4-24-1839. (378)

saac BEARMORE to John McELVAIN; (no dates); recorded 4-23-1839. (378)

ohn HUGGINS and Elizabeth wife to John DAVIS 2nd of Monroe Co.; 4-23-18_7; (no other dates given). (378)

oseph YEAZLE and Barbara wife of Ohio Co., Virginia to ____ _____; attested to 2-23-1839. (378)

lexander McWILLIAMS to John GIBSON; (no dates); recorded 4-24-1839 (379)

as. L. HENTHORN to Jas. ALEXANDER; mortgage; (no dates); recorded 4-26-1839 (379)

aniel KYGER and Anne (mark) wife of Monroe Co. to Henry KOCH; 10-19-1832. (380 & 384)

ornelius OKEY and Hannah (mark) wife to James OKEY; 1-1-1838. (380)

ames WARD to Balding COX; "I James Ward on behalf of myself and other heirs of Seth Ward, dec'd..."; (note: other heirs not named); attested to 6-17-1837. (381)

onah GERARD (GARRARD) and Mary (her mark) wife of Monroe Co. to John HAYDEN of Belmont Co., Ohio; 11-7-1832. (381 & 382)

ames BAILEY and Elizabeth (her E mark) wife to Jacob WALTER, late of Guernsey Co., Ohio; 8-22-1832. (381)

amuel GREEN and Mary A. wife of Moses WARD; attested to 4-1-1838; (note: written along margin is "see Vol. E, page 453"). (383)

ohn McNICHOLS and Mariah wife of Belmont Co., Ohio to Thomas NELSON of Monroe Co.; 9-1-1832. (385)

acob PITTMAN and Ide wife of Monroe Co. to Jabez STARR; 6-27-____; (no other dates given). (385)

ohn McNICHOLS and Maria wife to ____ _____; attested to 9-1-1832. (386)

gh MILLIGAN and Ruth wife of Ohio Co., Virginia to Valentine MOUHART of Monroe Co.; 10-13-1832. (386)

aiah F. MORRIS and Phebe (mark) wife to Thomas GRAY, all of Belmont Co., Ohio; 6-1-1832. (387)

David HENDERSHOT and Eleanor (mark) wife to Elias PICKEN; attested to 3-9-1831.(388)
Lewis BALDING and Sarah (mark) wife to William LAWRENCE; attested to 8-10-1832.(389)
Henry BALDING to William LAWRENCE; 6-11-1832. (390)
Godfrey STAGNER and Julianne (mark) wife to Michael FALSCROFF; -------1833; (no
    other date given). (391)
John CANNELL and Elizabeth (mark) wife of Belmont Co., Ohio to George MYERS Sr.
    of same; attested to 12-30-1837. (391)
Owen DEWEES and Mary wife to James AYRES; 1-10-1838. (392)
Charles POWEL and Rebecca (mark) wife to Elizabeth POWEL; attested to Oct. 1838;
    (no other dates given). (392)
Joshua DAVIS to Jasper MALLORY; mortgage; attested to 1-18-1838. (393)
William B. BAILEY and Mary wife of Washington Co., Ohio to Jacob MOTTS;
    12-18-1837. (394)
United States to John WINK; _-13-1819; (no other dates given). (394)
Cornelius STKINSON and Mary (mark) wife to Asael BOOTH; (no dates given). (395)
Benjamin TRUAX and Phebe wife to _____; (no dates); recorded 6-1-1839.(395)
Christian HARTLINE to Samuel HURD; 6-23-18__; (no other dates given). (395)
Robert W. OGG and Rebecca wife to George BUCK; attested to 7-7-1838 Belmont
    Co., Ohio. (396)
Stephen ULLOM and Eleanor wife to ____ _____; attested to May 1838. (396)
David LASHURE and Mary (mark) wife to Daniel GRAY; attested to 3-15-1838. (397)
Samuel KINCAIDE and Nancy (mark) wife to John ST(I)LES; 3-17-1837. (398)
John STILES to John A. WEST; 4-20-1837. (399)
George HENDERSHOT and Elizabeth wife to David KIRKBRIDE; 9-6-1838. (399)
Thomas DUNFEE and Elizabeth wife to Henry SHUTTS; 8-8-1836. (400 & 403)
Plat of town believed to be part of Miltonsburg. (401)
John MADENS and Mary Ann wife of Monroe Co. to Christian SNIDER of Virginia;
    3-16-1838. (402)
William JOHNSON and Lucinda wife of Washington Co., Ohio to Washington DUNN of
    Tayler Co., Virginia. (402)
William THORNTON to Elijah THORNTON; 3-29-1839. (403)
John (his mark) OSBORN to Gideon OSBORN; 5-13-1835. (404)
William HENTHORN and Fanny wife to Israeil BROWN Sr.; (no dates given). (405)
Jacob W. WATTS to John GRIFFETH; attested to Oct. 1834. (406)
United States to Henry LAMP of Belmont Co., Ohio; 2-10-1819. (406)
James YOUNG and Hes___ wife to Jacob OGLE; (no dates); recorded 6-29-1837. (407)
Jesse RICH and Mary (mark) wife to William MYERS; 5-25-1837. (407)
John HECK and Mary wife to William G. SHANKLAND; 9-21-1834. (408)
John F. RANDOLPH (Special Master Commissioner) to William G. SHANKLAND; attested
    to Feb. 1834; recorded 3-20-1834. (409)
Woodman OKEY and Catharine (mark) wife to Frederick WAGONER; attested to 4-27-1837.
    (409)
Israel HERST to_____; attested to May 1837; recorded 5-23-1837. (410)
Joel F. RANDOLPH, Sheriff Monroe Co., Ohio to John WINLAND; Feb. 1834. (410)
Adam MYERS to_____; (no dates given). (412)
William SMITH and Sarah wife to John ROBERTSON; 1-15-1834. (413 & 415)
George (his mark) HIGINBOTHOM and Delila (her mark) wife to Otho PORTER; attested
    to 11-19-1838. (413)
James SMITH and Mahala wife to Jacob HANES, all of Monroe Co.; (no dates given).
    (414)

172

Henry BAKER and Nancy wife to _____ _____; (no dates) recorded 4-11-1839. (414)

Barak FISHER and Jane (mark) wife to Francis ALLEN; (no dates); recorded 8-8-1837. (415)

Sampson GREEN and Amy wife to Robert WINCHESTER; (no dates); Greens' attested to deed 3-17-1837 Belmont Co., Ohio. (416)

Benjamin RUGGLES to Levi BARBER; (no dates); Ruggles attested to deed-----1823, Washington Co., Ohio. (416)

United States to Jacob OLLOM; ____10, 182_; (no other dates). (417)

Benjamin RUGGLES of Belmont Co., Ohio to Levi BARBER of Washington Co., Ohio; (no dates). (417)

Joseph STOCKEY Sr. and Rebecca wife of Monroe Co. to David GAITZ of same; 5-10-1833. (418)

Richard TRUAX and Mary (mark) wife of Monroe Co. to George STEWARD; 2-24-1830.(418)

Bethuel RUSH and Sarah (mark) wife to Thomas KELLY; (no dates); attested to 9-7-1832. (419)

William McKRACKEN and Jane wife of Belmont Co., Oho to _____ __HITE of Monroe Co.; (no date); attested to 2-20-1833. (419)

Richard TRUAX and Mary (mark) wife of Monroe Co. to Joshua LINN; 3-2_-1830; attested to 3-20-1830. (420)

Citizen BEALL and Elizabeth wife to Warren THORNBERRY; (no date); attested to 5-30-1832. (421)

Robert F. NAYLOR and Mary B. wife of Monroe Co. to Warren THORNBERRY; 11-27-1831.(422)

Barnet BETFORD and Drusilla (mark) wife to Shadrack MITCHELL; (no date); attested to Aug. 1839. (423)

John George AUTENREED and Maria wife of Monroe Co. to Benedict BERGUNTHAL; 4-12-1831. (423)

Jonathan (mark) MORRIS and Sarah wife to Benjamin STINE; (no date); attested to 4-12-____ (no other dates given). (424)

Benedict RESIGER and Ann (mark) wife to Peter RIESEGER; 12-2-1831. (424)

Emmanuel HUPP and Mary wife to Thomas STEWART; (no date); recorded 6-10-18__.(425)

Abraham ENOCHS and Sarah wife to Thomas STEWART; (no dates). (425)

John HUPP and Sar(ah) wife to _____ STEWART; (no date); recorded 6-10-1837. (426)

Jacob WILLIAMS to Michael STINE; 11-12-____; (no other dates). (426)

Elijah TIPPINS and Charlotte (mark) wife to ____ ____; (no date) recorded 6-7-1839. (426)

Caleb SICICUM (LINCICUM?) to Thomas YOUNG; (no date); recorded 6-7-1839. (428)

Nich___GASSAWAY and Amelia wife to _____; 4-10-1826. (428)

Michael CROW to _____ _____; (no dates). (421)

James CUMMINS and Mary wife to John GOODHUE; 8-21-1833. (429)

Paul (mark) RUSH and Darcas (mark) wife of Monroe Co. to Joshua MORRIS of Monroe Co.; 10-19-1833. (430 & 432)

Alexander FALSON and Eleanor wife of Monroe Co. to John PORTER; 11-4-1833. (430)

Messer SAYRE and Margaret (mark) wife to ____ _____; (no date); recorded 1-17-1834. (431)

William JOHNSTON to ____ _____; Jan. __, 1834; recorded 1-31-1834. (432)

James TUTTLE Jr. and Esther wife to _____ _____; (no date); attested to 12-7-1833; recorded 2-3-1834. (433)

Elias PITTMAN and Catharine (mark) wife to George MAKINSON, all of Monroe Co.; 4-20-1832. (433 & 435)

173

William JOHNSTON and Esther wife to William STEELE; (no dates). (433)

Jonas SAMS and Ann (mark) wife of Monroe Co. to James R. HUTCHINSON of Belmont
Co., Ohio; -------1833; attested to 8-7-1833; recorded 1-25-1834. (434)

William YOUNG and Dorcas wife of Monroe Co. to Thomas YOUNG, William YOUNG Jr.
and John WYBEAUT in trust; 5-3-_____; (no other dates.) (435)

Samuel BUSKIRK to _____; attested to 2-__-183_; (no other dates). (436)

William JARVIS and Elizabeth (mark) wife of Guernsey Co., Ohio to Peter JOHNSTON;
1-25-1832. (436)

Isaac RUSH to John PALMER; (no date); recorded 7-4-1832. (436)

Asa (mark) FORSHEY and Sarah (mark) wife to Joseph POWERS; (no date); attested to
10-3-1838; recorded 12-1-1838. (437)

George OKEY and Elizabeth (mark) wife to Asa FORSHEY; (no date); attested to
8-8-1838; recorded 12-1-1838. (438)

Woodman OKEY and Katharine (mark) wife to Asa FORSHEY; (no date); attested to
8-8-1838; recorded 12-1-1838. (438)

William JARVIS and Elizabeth (mark) wife to Benjamin STINE; (no date); attested
to 8-12-1839. (439)

Jacob BAKER and Mary (mark) wife to John BAKER (no date); attested to 10-1-1832;
recorded 12-30-1832. (440)

Jacob BAKER and Mary (mark) wife of Monroe Co. to Henry BAKER; 9-25-1832. (440)

Asael BOOTH and Bethia wife of Monroe Co. to George Ph. ILLIGE of Monroe Co.;
11-2-1832. (441-443)

Edward MERCER and Mary (mark) wife of Belmont Co., Ohio to Henry KIRKBRIDE; 8-6-1832.
(441 & 444)

Jonathan HARRIS and Sarah wife to Richard SMITH; 6-17-1832. (443)

John BUTLER of Belmont Co., Ohio to Edward GRIZZLE; 3-6-1829; patented to Aaron
Kinsey and conveyed to Butler by Kinsey 4-28-1823. (443)

Joseph BOON and Asena wife of Monroe Co. to David HUMMEL; 4-19-___; (no other
dates); granted to Geo. Dunlavy by patent and by Dunlavy to Boon. (444)

Daniel GRAY to _____; attested to ------1838; (no other dates). (445)

John HUFFMAN and Elizabeth wife to William C. BEVAN; attested to 6-23-1838;
recorded 7-6-1838. (445)

Christian (mark) HARTLINE and Mary (mark) wife to Samuel HURD; attested to
6-23-1833; recorded 9-2-1833. (446)

Vincent DEMENT of Monroe Co. to Frederick REINERS of Allegheny Co. (Pa.?);
--------(183_(?); (no other dates). (447)

Hanna and McCarty of Washington Co., Pa. to Edward R. LANE of Monroe Co.;
12-29-1832. (447)

James M. ROWND of Belmont Co., Ohio to John GIBSON; attested to 4-8-1833; recorded
4-27-1833. (448)

William STEWART and Nancy wife of Washington, Co., Pa. to Richard FISHER of Monroe
Co.; 4-8-1833. (449)

Amos WILLSON and Elizabeth wife to John WINLAND, all of Monroe Co.; 3-21-1833.(449)

Hanton H. TAYLOR and Charlotte (mark) wife of Monroe Co. to George EWERS of
Belmont Co., Ohio; 4-18-1839. (450)

Henry FRUSH and _____ wife to _____; (no date); recorded 4-18-1833. (450)

John BUSKIRK and Mary (mark) wife of Monroe Co. to Jeremiah WALTON; 9-29-1832.(450)

Jacob O. PITMAN and Ide wife of Monroe Co. to George STEWART of Monroe Co.;
2-19-1833. (452)

Henry KIRKBRIDE and Catharine wife to David KIRKBRIDE; attested to 8-31-1832; recorded 1-10-1833. (452)

Citizen BEALL and Elizabeth wife of Monroe Co. to John PALMOR; M___29, 1826; (no other dates). (453)

John and Jacob OLLOM and Susana (mark) and Mary their wives to Jonah F. RANDOLPH; attested to 12-22-1831. (453)

United States to John Ollom; 5-10-1827. (454)

Archibold WOODS to George STEED; attested to 5-16-1831. (455)

Isaac (mark) CROW to Zopper PERKINS; 7-9-1831. (455)

William TRACY and Patience wife of Monroe Co. to Mathew STEWART of Belmont Co., Ohio; 7-13-1831. (456)

James ELSON and Harriet wife of Monroe Co. to Washington DUNN of Tyler (Co., Va.); recorded 4-12-1839. (456)

Francis GRAY, Elizabeth GRAY widow of Samuel GRAY late of Belmont Co., Ohio dec'd, Maria Gray, James Gray, Richard Gray, _____Gray, Alexander McCANDLESS and Ann wife late Ann Gray, heirs under will of Samuel GRAY, dec'd; Agreement; 11-3-_____(no other dates; prior 1844); James Gray executor of will of Samuel Gray, dec'd. (457)

Peter WEVER and Margaret wife to William BUCHANAN; attested to 3-19-1839; recorded 4-15-1839. (457)

John CARMICHAEL and Mary wife to Edward SALISBURY; attested to 2-18-1833. (458)

Benjamin DESELMS and Alice (mark) wife to Jacob TRUAX; (no date); attested to 2-15-183_; recorded 2-20-1833. (458)

Gersham WRIGHT and Rhoda wife of Monroe Co. to Andrew WALTERS of Belmont Co., Ohio; 3-27-1833. (459)

Stephen POTTS to _____; (no dates); recorded 8-5-1833. (460)

John SMITH Jr. of Franklin Co., Ohio to George STEED of Monroe Co.; 4-4-1833. (460)

Edward R. LANE of Monroe Co. to William McCARTY of Washington Co._____; 2-5-1833. (461)

Samuel H. GUTHRIE and Rebecca wife to Isaac JAMES; attested to April 1839; recorded 4-18-1839. (462)

John MORRISON Sr. and Elizabeth wife of Monroe Co. to John MORRISON; 5-31-1832; "John Sr. and wife Elizabeth to have premises....during natural life."(462)

Samuel BUSKIRK and Carity wife of Monroe Co. to James ATKINSON; 2-3-1830. (462)

United States to Joseph CALLAND; 6-1-1827. (463)

Daniel KYGER and Anne (mark) wife to Adam HENTHORN; attested to __-23-1832; (no other dates). (463)

William WILLEY and Sarah (mark) wife to John M. GARRY; attested to 12-17-18_1; (no other dates). (465)

James ATKINSON and Rhoda wife to Jeremiah WALTON, all of Monroe Co.; 4-7-1832.(465)

United States to James ATKINSON of Monroe Co.; (no dates). (466)

James CAROTHERS and Susannah wife to William COCHRAN, all of Monroe Co.; 4-5-1833. (466)

John STRAHL Jr. and Hannah Jane wife of Harrison Co., Ohio to James B. SMITH of Monroe Co.; 11-10-1832. (467)

James CREE and Isabella wife of Thomas MORRIS, all of Monroe Co.; 4-21-1828. (467 & 469)

Philip ALLEN and Anne wife to Joseph CLINE, all of Monroe Co.; 2-16-18_8; (no other dates). (468)

175

James SMITH and Nancy wife of Belmont Co., Ohio to Thomas MORRIS of Monroe Co.;
    attested to 4-21-18_8; (no other dates). (468)
John TRUAX and Susanna wife to Thomas ELLIOTT, all of Monroe Co.; 4-8-1829. (469)
Elias PITTMAN Sr. and Sarah (mark) wife to Elias PITTMAN Jr., all of Monroe Co.;
    12-28-1827. (470)
Michael CROW to OKEY and REED; attested to 12-5-1828; "Michael Crow one of heirs
    of _____ _____"...."the said G. F. Crow died seized." (470)
William ATKINSON and Mary wife of Monroe Co. to John REDMAN; 7-14-1825. (471)
Levi BARBER and Elizabeth wife of Washington (Co.,_____) to Stephen BARNES of
    Monroe Co.; 12-2-1825. (472)
Robert HILL and Hannah wife to Nathaniel CASSELL; attested to 3-28-1839; recorded
    4-12-1839. (472)
Elias ALLEN and Mary (mark) wife to Owen HALE; attested to 9-28-1831. (473)
David HENDERSHOT and Eleanor (mark) wife to James CREE; (no date) attested to
    3-19-1839; recorded 7-25-1837. (474)
Ephraim STEENROD and Mary wife of ____Co., Virginia to Samuel STEEL; 3-12-1834.(474
Nelson HOGUE to_____; recorded 4-27-1839. (475)
George HEDGES and Elizabeth (mark) wife to_____ _____; attested to __-26-1833;
    recorded 6-16-1834. (475)
Crawford GLOVER and Jemima wife of Monroe Co. to AFFLICK and HICKS of Malaga;
    11-9-1833. (476)
Wm. G. SHANKLAND and Harriet wife to Esther WOOD, all of Belmont Co., Ohio;
    4-3-1834. (476)
George REMLEY and Eleanor (mark) Wife of Monroe Co. to John B. WATSON; 4-13-1833.(4
Joseph DRIGGS of Richland Co., Ohio and Phebe wife of Samuel H. GUTHRIE of Monroe
    Co.; 12-11-1832. (478)
Daniel KYGER to _____ _____; recorded 9-23-1833. (479)
William (mark) SUTTON and Catharine (mark) wife of Monroe Co. to Joseph W.
    SATTERTHWAIT of Belmont Co., Ohio; 8-7-18__; recorded 8-26-1833. (479)
David MASON and Haseey wife of Monroe Co. to David ERLEWINE; 5-9-1833.(480,484-5)
Samuel JONES and Cisner wife of Monroe Co. to Abraham JONES; attested to 8-17-1833;
    recorded 8-26-1833. (480)
William MORRIS and Elizabeth wife to _____ _____; 7-27-1837. (482)
James (mark) EDWARDS and Catharine (mark) wife to Equilles THOMAS; attested to
    2-21-1837; recorded 7-25-1837. (482)
Alpheus W. COULTER and Margaret (mark) wife to John BRACK, all of Monroe Co.;
    attested to 12-17-1837; recorded 12-21-1837. (483)
Isaac (mark) CLAYNE of Monroe Co. to Peter WEAVER; 8-28-1833. (483)
Samuel TRUAX and Rebecca wife to William GREEN, all of Sunsbury twp., Monroe Co.;
    8-29-1821. (485)
William GREEN to David TRIMBLEY, all of Monroe Co.; 3-23-1830 "32 acres of land
    is a s____ from William Green to his daughter". (485)
Joshua MORRIS and Charity wife of Monroe Co. to Elijah HUDSON of Belmont Co.;
    8-23-1833. (486)
Lewis MORRIS and Rebecca wife of Belmont Co., Ohio to David TRIMBLEY of Monroe
    Co.; 4-2-1833. (486)
John YOST and Margaret (mark) wife to George HOELZEL, all of Monroe Co.; 8-29-1833.
    (488)

William WALTERS and Elizabeth (mark) wife of Malaga twp., Monroe Co. to Peter GREOSSER; attested to Aug. 1833; recorded 9-19-1833. (489)

James CALDWELL to Andrew MORRIS; Caldwell attested to Belmont Co. 1-17-1837; recorded 6-28-1837. (490)

James TAYLOR and Ann wife to Samuel WRIGHT; (no date); attested to April 1837; recorded 6-27-1837. (491)

Oddey A. BRACK and Sarah (mark) wife to Isaac A. BRACK; attested to 10-14-1836; recorded 7-11-1837. (491)

John LINN and Sarah wife to Lewis WOOL_____; attested to July 1837; recorded 7-11-1837. (492)

Thomas FORSHEY and Catharine (mark) wife to Benjamin McVAY Jr.; attested to 1-11-1834; recorded 5-5-1834. (493)

William WHITE and Sarah wife to John CLITHEROW; 3-17-183_(no other dates). (494)

Isaac EDDY and Nancy (mark) wife of Monroe Co. to Jesse RIGGS; 1-4-1834. (494)

Seymour KING and Amy wife to Joseph ADDIS; attested to 2-5-1837; recorded 7-5-1838. (495)

John BOLIN and Mary wife and Leah CALENDER to Nathan P. GRISSELL; (no date); attested to 10-24-___; recorded 7-3-____. (496)

Silas SEVERANCE and Mary (mark) wife to James ELLIS; 4-4-1838. (497)

Samuel HUTCHINSON to Jasper MAL(LARY); recorded 7-3-1838. (497)

Citizen BEALL and Elizabeth wife to Jasper MALLARY; attested to 5-2-1838; recorded 7-3-1838. (498)

Richard SMITH and Henrietta wife to Thomas MITCHELL; attested to 6-12-1838; recorded 7-5-1838. (498)

William ULLOM and Judah wife to Robert MILLS; attested to 9-11-1837. (499)

John BOLIN and Mary wife and Leah CALENDER to John STRAHL; attested to 10-24-1837. (499)

James (mark) STARRET to Jacob BARE; attested to Vermillion Co., Indiana 5-25-183_; recorded 7-3-1838. (500)

Samuel GUTHRIE and Rebecca G. wife and Nelson DRIGGS to Jno. GIBSON and Wm STEEL; attested to 2-4-18__; recorded 2-11-1834. (501)

Daniel NICHOLSON and Martha wife to Jacob BACHER; attested to 3-29-1838; recorded 7-4-1838. (501)

Fawcet CRAIG to John HAGUE, both of Monroe Co.; attested to Sept. 1838; recorded 12-18-1838. (502)

Levi HART and Jane wife of _____ Pa. to William HOPTON; 4-5-1832. (503)

Abraham FORSHEY and Sally (mark) wife to Arthur DRIM (DUNN or DUM?); attested to 7-5-1838; recorded 12-17-1838. (504)

Eli HOOPES and Eliza wife of Monroe Co. to Joseph ROGERS of Belmont Co., Ohio; 4-1-1834. (504)

William (mark) HENTHORN, John (mark) HENTHORN and Mary (mark) wife to Andrew WALTERS, all of Monroe Co.; 3-29-1834. (505)

James L. (mark) HENTHRON and Rachel (mark) wife of Monroe Co. to James ALEXANDER of Belmont Co., Ohio; 3-26-1834. (505)

William WILLARD and Sarah wife of Monroe Co. to Isaac WILLARD of (Guernsey Co., Ohio?); 6-10-1834. (507)

Robert F. NAYLOR and Mary wife of Woodsfield, Monroe Co. to Michael RUTTER of Monroe Co.; 6-19-1834. (508)

Robert BRAMHALL and Mary (mark) wife to _____; recorded 4-9-1833. (508)

Elizabeth (mark) HENTHORN to Jasper MALLORY, both of Monroe Co.; 10-13-1832. (508)

Stilwell MELOTT and Sarah (mark) wife to John CLITHERO, attested to 4-1-1833; recorded 4-18-1833. (509)

177

Stephen McTEAGUE (McTAIGUE) to Mathew DAUGHERTY; attested to 7-15-1837; recorded
7-25-1839. (509)

Eli CURTIS and Elizabeth wife to Joseph CURTIS; attested to 6-12-1837; recorded
7-25-1837. (510)

William MOOR and Elizabeth wife of Monroe Co. to Daniel NICHOLSON of Belmont Co.,
Ohio; 1-24-1833 . (511)

Abijah EATON and Jane wife of Monroe Co. to Edward SLAY of Harrison Co., Ohio;
5-26-1831. (512)

Joseph MORRISON and Elizabeth wife (in deed, signed Margaret) to Josiah M. Dillon;
6-24-1831. (512)

Martha WILLIAMS to Joseph WILLIAMS; (no dates); release of Martha Williams "....
my late husband Daniel Williams at his deceased possessed of SW¼ Section
30, Township __, Range 5, left me by law possessed of third part of land
during my natural life...."; Quit Claim. (513)

James TAYLOR and Ann wife to John B. MALLORY; attested to 4-7-1837; recorded
6-22-1837. (513)

Paul RI___ and Darcas wife to ____ ____; recorded 6-22-1837. (513)

David EATON and Rachel (mark) wife of Monroe Co. to Samuel CARLTON of Belmont
Co., Ohio; 2-3-1834. (514)

John (mark) MOOSE and Rachel (mark) wife to John GIBSON; attested to 12-21-1838;
recorded 1-27-1829. (515)

Hezekiah DEVAUGHN to Dan ULLOM, both of Monroe Co.; 2-10-1837. (515)

Hezekiah (mark) HUTCHINSON to Thomas MARTIN; recorded 1-22-1839. (516)

John HENDERSHOT and Susanna (mark) wife to George DEMENT; -------1824 (no other
dates). (516)

Stephen MELOTT and Jane wife of Monroe Co. to Katharine TRUAX; __-26-____(no
other dates). (517)

George BOYD and Emily wife to Thomas AYRES; attested to 3-13-____; recorded
4-20-1839. (517)

David EATON and Hannah (mark) wife to ____ ____; attested to 10-23-____;
recorded 4-22-1839. (518)

Patrick ADAMS and Elizabeth wife to James SMITH and Ann SMITH of Monroe Co.;
attested to 3-9-1837; recorded 1-13-1838. (518)

James SMITH and Nancy wife and Ann SMITH to Benjamin KEEN; attested to 9-25-1838.(5

Francis COOPER and Margaret (mark) wife to William BLAINE; attested to 5-13-1831;
patented to Cooper in 1828. (520)

Elihu MORRIS and Mary wife to Thomas MITCHELL; (no dates). (521)

JOB S. MORRIS and Harriet wife to Thomas MITCHELL; attested to 6-12-1838; recorded
7-5-1838. (521)

Master Commissioners to Richard SIMMONS, etal.; (no dates). (522)

Messer SAYRE to William SMITH; 1-15-1___ (no other dates). (523)

John ROBERTSON to Messer SAYRE; 1-15-1834. (524)

Asahel BOOTH and Bethiah wife of Monroe Co. to Abby HEDGE of Wheeling, Ohio Co.,
Va.; attested to 1-22-1833; recorded 1-23-1833. (525)

Henry KIRKBRIDE and Catharine wife of Monroe Co. to Stephen CONGER; 8-31-1832.(526)

James CARMICHAEL and Mary (mark) wife to ____ ____; attested to 4-26-1832. (527)

John ROOD and Catharine (mark) wife to Adam FREDERICK and George SHAFER; attested
to 6-3-1835; recorded 10-7-1835. (527)

Arthur PORTER to William H. HEADLY; recorded 12-1-1838. (528)

Richard (mark) FORSHEY and Nancy L. wife to Peter CROW of Franklin twp.;7-2-1838.(5

Mathew ROGERS and Jane (mark) wife to William THORNBERRY of Washington Co. ____;
9-10-1838 . (529-30)

Harrison LUCAS and Barbary (mark) wife to Zimery OSBIN, all of Monroe Co.;
7-24-18_8; attested to July 1838; recorded 11-28-1838. (529)

Casper WALTER and Barbara wife to _____DETERICK; attested to 4-28-1838; recorded
11-28-1838. (530)

Stephen MELOTT and Jane (mark) wife to John EVANS of Belmont Co., Ohio; attested
to 8-12-1833; recorded 1-3-1834. (531)

Amos L. SPENCER and Elizabeth wife to Henry HUPP; A___ 26, 183_ (no other dates).(532)

Job SMITH and Mahala (mark) wife of Belmont Co., Ohio to Alexander FERRIL of
Monroe Co.; 8-4-1829; Quit Claim; $10.00; undivided interest in part W½
Section 31, Township 5, Range __. (533)

Matilda FERRIL to Alexander FERRIL, both of Monroe Co.; 12-15-1830; Quit Claim;
$10.00; undivided interest in part W½ SE¼ Section 31, Township 5, Range __.
Recorded 11-8-1833. (533)

Hiram FERRIL to _____; (no date); recorded 11-8-1833. (534)

S.S. SALISBURY and Sally wife to William GRIFFITH, all Monroe Co.; 8-27-1831. (534)

Asael BOOTH and Bethia wife to Joseph OLLOM; 6-5-183_ (no other dates). (535)

James BAKER and Nancy wife to Elijah DUNN; 6-11-1831. (535)

_____McNICHOLS and Maria wife of Belmont Co., Ohio to Isaiah ELY of Monroe
Co.; 9-1-1832. (536)

William SMITH and Elizabeth wife of Monroe Co. to John GARRISON of Belmont Co.,
Ohio; 2-27-1832. (537)

Henry BALDING to Lewis BALDING, both of Monroe Co.; 4-23-1832. (538)

Brooks LANUNN to___hael ARCHER; recorded 4-17-1834. (538)

Stephen HENTHORN to Samuel MARTIN, both of Monroe Co.; 4-5-1834. (538)

William ENOCHS, Joseph ENOCHS, Abraham (mark) ENOCHS, Catharine (mark) ENOCHS,
and Sarah ENOCHS all of Monroe Co. to Wrathey INGRAHAM of Monroe Co.;
$50.00, part Section 26, Township 5, Range __, East side Duck Creek,
known by name of Camp Run. (539)

William STURGEON to Randolph WITTENBROOK; attested to 12-16-1833; recorded
12-25-1833. (540)

Charles CECIL executor of will of Earl SPROAT, late Monroe Co., dec'd to James
PATTON; will presented June Term 1830; Thomas Weston guardian of Elisa Harwitt,
James and Sarah the natural children and heirs of Earl Sproat, dec'd;
Publication notice given in Marietta Gazette; deed attested to March 1831
(no other dates). (540 & 551)

James HEPBURN and Elizabeth wife of Monroe Co. to Edward BOOTH of Ohio Co., Va.;
12-2-1830. (541)

James HEPBURN and Elizabeth wife of Edward Booth; attested to 12-2-(1830?). (541)

John BURTON and Elizabeth wife to Francis ALLEN; attested to A___ 29, 1837 (no
other dates). (541)

John HARBIN and Rachel (mark) wife to Francis ALLEN; attested to 4-20-1837;
recorded 8-7-1837. (542)

Martin BAKER and Sarah (mark) wife to James WINLAND; (no dates). (543)

William TRACY and Patience wife to Mathew STEWART; attested to 7-30-18__ (no other
dates). (544)

William McKACHEN and Jane wife to Andrew ARMSTRONG, all of Monroe Co.; 4-14-1831.(544)

William MATLE to James McCOMAS, both of Monroe Co.; 1-3-1832. (545)

Jacob RUSH and Prudence wife to Bethuel RUSH, all of Monroe Co.; 3-29-1828. (545)

Adam MYERS and Mary wife to William MYERS, all of Monroe Co.; 1-11-1832. (545)

John N. POWERS and Sarah wife to John NEP_____; 4-3-1832. (546)

John SHEPHERD and Sarah (mark) wife to Richard SHEPHERD, all of Belmont Co., Ohio;
4-16-1832. (547)

Joshua CRAIG and Ann wife to Crumlin (or Erunlin) FEAMS, all of Monroe Co.;
2-14-1831. (548)
Isaac BALDWIN and Polly wife to _____; (no dates). (548)
Samuel H. GUTHRIE and Rebecca wife of Monroe Co. to Isaac BAKER; 11-12-1831. (548)
John BURTON and Elizabeth wife to James ALLEN; recorded 6-4-1838. (549)
Thomas GRAY and Catharine wife of Harrison Co., Ohio to Mary and Leah CAVENDER
of Monroe Co.; 11-13-1832. (550 & 557)
David HENDERSHOT and Eleaner wife of Monroe Co. to Elias PICKERING of Belmont Co.,
Ohio; 3-9-1831. (550)
Thomas REA to _____; recorded 12-3-1832. (551)
Ephraim POLLOCK and Abigale H. wife to _____; attested to Ohio Co., Va.
7-5-1837; recorded 7-29-1837. (552)
Henry SELACH and Margaret wife to George KELZOR and Jacob KELZOR; 12-22-1838.(553)
William JARVIS and Elizabeth wife of Monroe Co. to Mary WILLIAMS; recorded
12-24-1838. (554)
James (mark) WILLIAMSON and Mary wife of Monroe Co. to Joseph ALLEN; 12-1-1837.(554)
Joseph CLINE and Sarah (mark) wife of Monroe Co. to Joseph ALLEN; 1-15-18_8 (no
other dates). (555)
James HODGE and Agness (mark) wife to Thomas WILSON; attested to 2-27-1838;
recorded 6-6-1838. (556)
Elizabeth (mark) BRYSON to Robert F. NAYLOR; attested to 1-19-1838 Belmont Co.,
Ohio; recorded 6-4-1838. (557)
Thomas (mark) FLOID Jr. and Lydia wife to George W. BAKER; recorded 9-16-1837.(558)
Drusilla (mark) BLAKE and Joseph Blake her husband to Edmond HAYS; attested to
--------1837 (note: surname given as BLACK in attesting to deed); recorded
9-15-1837. (558)
Jacob HEADLEY and Cynthia wife to _____; recorded 1-7-1839. (559)
Joshua (mark) SANDS and Sarah wife of Monroe Co. to Elijah GRAY of Guernsey Co.,
Ohio; attested to 3-8-1838; recorded 1-8-1839. (559)
James (mark) LOYD and Sarah wife to Joseph RICHARDS; __-29-1830; attested to
3-29-1830 Ohio Co., Va. (560)
Samuel STEEL and Nancy (mark) wife to Christopher SHOUP; 8-23-1830; attested to
8-23-1830 Ohio Co., Va. (561)
James PRIBBLE and Flora wife of Monroe Co. to Levi HART of Green Co., Pa.;
4-2-1830. (561)
Woodman OKEY and Catharine wife of Center twp., Monroe Co. to William CRAWFORD
of Monroe Co.; 1-26-1827. (562)
Richard SIMMS and Dorcas wife, George DULTY and Mary wife, Zachariah JACOB and
Nancy wife all of Ohio Co., Va. to Thomas POLLOCK and Ephraim POLLOCK;
6-26-___; attested to Ohio Co., Va. 6-26-1837. (562)
Charles WELLS to Asael BOOTH; recorded 4-16-1837; Booth gave mortgage to Wells
of Marshall Co., Va. in Jan. 1833. (563)
Mary CARTER of (Belm)ont Co., Ohio to John GRAY; (no dates). (564)
Robert (mark) MILLER and Mary (mark) wife to Balzer BOTT; 11-30-183_; recorded
1-14-1834. (565)
New MEREDITH and Dorcas (mark) wife to Balzer BOTT; attested to 11-30-1833. (566)
John BRUCE and Catharine (mark) wife to _____; attested to 9-25-1829. (566)
Samuel ECCORD and Susanna (mark) wife to Oswald SILL; 8-18-1829. (567)
John HECK and Mary (mark) wife to Samuel ECCORD, all of Monroe Co.; 4-13-1829.
(568 & 570)
William MORRIS and Susannah (mark) wife of Morgan Co., Ohio to David EATON of
Monroe Co.; 3-13-1833. (568)

Alexander FOLSON and Eleanor wife to John SNYDER, all of Monroe Co.; 5-1-1833.(569)

John STRAHL Sr. and Ann wife of Monroe Co. to Samuel ECCORD; 4-13-1829. (570)

Levi BARBER and Elizabeth wife to Henry MASON; attested to 8-27-____, Marietta, Washington Co., Ohio (no other dates). (571)

Nancy (mark) PHILLIPS late Nancy OKEY to Arthur OKEY, both of Monroe Co.; Quit Claim; $70.00; 62 acres NW¼ Section 30, Township 4, Range __; attested to 10-24-1829. (571)

John GRAY and Hannah (mark) wife late Hannah OKEY to Arthur OKEY, all of Monroe Co.; Quit Claim; 62 acres part NW¼ Section 30, Township 4, Range __: "all interest in effects of L3vin Okey, dec'd late of said county;" 10-31-1829.(572)

Levi WOOD and Phebe (mark) wife to Daniel GIVENS; attested to Ma·___ 2, 1837 (no other dates). (573)

Daniel MICHAEL and Margaret (mark) wife to Daniel GIVENS; attested to 3-2-1837. (573)

David PIRSON and Elizabeth (mark) wife to Lewis KLIPNER; attested to 2-10-1836.(574)

William MYERS and Hannah (mark) wife to ____ ____; recorded 1-15-1839. (575)

Benjamin McBERNEY and Martha (mark) wife to Isaac McBERNEY, all of Guernsey Co., Ohio; attested to 1-13-1839; recorded 1-15-1839. (575)

Henry H. MOTT and Mary wife to Martin BAKER, all of Monroe Co.; 9-20-1838. (576)

John GIBSON and Catharine wife to John DAVENPORT, all of Belmont Co., Ohio; attested to 12-26-1837; recorded 1-16-1838. (576)

Michael RUTTER and Mary wife to William STEEL of Monroe Co.; attested to 1-8-1838. (577)

Philip NOLAND and Martha (mark) wife of Monroe Co. to Cyrus NOLAND; attested to 10-29-1834. (578)

William D. PATTON and Margaret Ann (mark) wife to John ARN; recorded 1-28-1835.(579)

Oswald SILL and Mary Wright Sill his wife to William G. SHANKLAND and John L. SMITH; recorded 12-17-1835. (580)

Conrad DEVAUL Jr. to John DEVAUL, both of Monroe Co.; 10-12-1835; Conrad Devaul late of Monroe Co., dec'd in his lifetime seized of land Green twp. W½ NW¼ Section 33, Township 3, Range 4; Will of Conrad Devaul dated Oct. 1831, at decease of his wife Mary above described premises equally divided among children, one half to son Conrad Devaul; recorded 12-18-1835. (581)

David WATSON and Kesiah wife to John DEVAUL, all of Monroe Co., Ohio; 5-5-18(3)4; Conrad Devaul late of Monroe Co., dec'd died seized of W½ NW¼ Section 3_, Township 3, Range 4; Conrad Devaul made will Oct. 25, ___, at decease of his wife Mary lands to be divided among his children, half share of his daughter Kesiah Watson goes to her ____ James Hannel, thereby leaving Kesiah a half. (582)

Robert MARSHALL of Ohio Co., Va. and Lucinda wife to John TINGLEY of Monroe Co.; recorded 4-13-1839. (583)

John TINGLEY to John MOOSE Jr. both of Monroe Co.; attested to 4-6-18__; recorded 4-15-1839. (583)

Gideon MASON and Hannah wife of Monroe Co. to Richard WHEELER of Belmont Co., Ohio; 10-26-1835. (584)

James WATSON and Elizabeth (mark) wife to James WILSON, all of Monroe Co.; 4-4-1837. (584)

The following records were copied from Docket A-1. Pages are given in parenthesis (). The case number (#) is also being given as sometimes the packet of vouchers, receipts, etc. will give additional information.

COPPOCK, Thomas guardian of five orphan children - 3-13-1804 - #3½ - (6)

ADAMS, Thomas and Nancy, orphan children who lately lived with Ralph French - Daniel C. Cooper guardian - 8-13-1804 - #4 - (6)

COCHRAN, Richard alias SLOAN - John Gerard, guardian - 8-13-1804 - #5 - (6)

PALMER, John orphan under the care of Andrew Lock and Susanna Donohoo - William Snodgrass, guardian - 8-13-1804 - #6 - (6)

ELLIOTT, William in care of Paul D. Butler - John Miller of Wolf Creek, guardian - 8-13-1804 - #7 - (6)

THOMSON, Samuel who is unable to handle his affairs - George Newcom and William Vancleve, guardians - 8-13-1804 - #8 - (7)

TAYLOR, Nelly and Lewis orphans in care of George Newcom - Col. Robert Patterson guardian - 2-8-1805 - #14 - (10)

PAGE, Abraham and MAULSTON, James orphan children in care of Col. Robert Patterson - George Newcom, guardian - 2-8-1805 - #15 - (10)

ABBOT, Polly - Daniel C. Cooper, guardian - 8-30-1805 - #20½ - (33)

MAYER (MOYER), Jacob aged 17 yrs., Peter aged 15 yrs., John aged 18 yrs., Daniel aged 13 yrs., Elizabeth aged 10 yrs. and Michael aged 12 yrs. heirs of the late Henry Mayer (Moyer), deceased - John Brower and Christian Brower, guardians - 12-25-1805 - #22 - (37)

DAVIS, Mary aged 8 yrs. and Esther aged 6 yrs. heirs of Thomas Davis, deceased - Mary Davis and John McCabe guardians - 12-25-1805 - #23 - (38)

SWINEHART, Anna aged 4 yrs., Elizabeth aged 2 yrs. and Gabriel aged 1 yr. heirs of Gabriel Swinehart, deceased - Salome Swinehart and Adam Swinehart, guardians - 12-24-1805 - #24 - (38)

JACKSON, William aged 12 yrs. and Giles aged 9 yrs. heirs of William Jackson late of Warren County - John Edwards, guardian - 8-26-1806 - #28 - (41)

GEPHART, Elizabeth aged 8 yrs. and John aged 5 yrs. heirs of Peter Gephart, deceased - Valentine Gephart and Matthias Rigal, guardians - 8-26-1806 - #29 - (41)

DAVIS, Lewis aged 18 yrs. - John McCabe, guardian - 8-27-1806 - #30 - (42)

KIRKWOOD, Joseph aged 11 yrs. heir of David Kirkwood - Robert Edger, guardian - 4-28-1807 - #41 - (64)

LUCAS, David an insolvent debtor - John Coppock, trustee with William Madden as security - 4-29-1807 - #42 - (64)

FRITZ, Christian of Dayton, unable to handle affairs - David Squier and John Miller, guardians - 7-18-1807 and 9-7-1807 - #45 & #48 - (65 & 71)

FRITZ, Christian, given the right to handle his own affairs - 1-6-1808 - #50 (75)

McCLURE, Alexander aged 14 yrs. minor heir of Robert Elliott, deceased - William McClure, guardian - 4-26-1808 - #51 - (76)

HUEY, Nancy and Robert heirs of Robert Huey - Henry Disbrow, guardian - 1-7-1809 - $58 - (89)

ROGERS, James L. under 14 yrs. of age, heir of Alexander Rogers late of Pennsylvania - James Hanna, guardian - 5-10-1811 - #71½ - (133)

SWARTZEL, John aged 10 yrs. and Frederick aged 6 yrs. - Susannah Swartzel widow of the late Matthias Swartzel, guardian - 5-10-1811 -

DAVIS, Daniel aged 18 yrs. heir of Lewis Davis - William Van Cleve, guardian - 1-6-1812 - #79 - (142)

STUMP, George aged 11 yrs. heir of Leonard Stump – William Emrick, guardian –
    1-7-1812 – #80 (142)

LOWRY, David aged 4 yrs. heir of Archibald Lowry – James Steel and Horasho G.
    Philips, guardian – #81 – (147)

SATHAM, John – David Reed, guardian – 1-9-1812 – #83 – (148)

GRIMES, John aged 14 yrs. – Christopher Curtner, guardian – 1-9-1812 – #84 – (148)

FISHER, Abijah aged 10 yrs. – William Sourbray, guardian – 1-9-1812 – #85 – (148)

Contributed by: Mrs. Clyde Shilt, Rt. 3, Westbrook, Brookville, Ohio 45309.
The following records are found in the Probate Court of the court house at Dayton.
The docket and page number under which the original record may be found are given in
parenthesis. The case number under which the original papers are filed is also given
and it should be noted that a little additional information such as when a minor
became of age, might be found under the case number.

5-4-1812 - Robert Edger appointed guardian of Rachel GRAY aged 4 yrs. and Robert
Gray aged 1 yr. Case #88. (Doc. B-1, p.1)

9-8-1812 - Philip Gunckel appointed guardian of Elizabeth STUMP aged 14 yrs.
Case #92. (Doc. B-1, p.13)

9-8-1812 - Ephraim GENTRY aged 15 yrs., heir of John Gentry chose Hannah Gentry as
his guardian. Case #93. Hannah Gentry also to serve as guardian of Samuel
GENTRY aged 13 yrs., John GENTRY aged 11 yrs., Margaret GENTRY aged 7 yrs.,
and Abigail GENTRY aged 5 yrs., heirs of John Gentry. Case #94. (Doc. B-1,p13)

1-4-1813 - Silas RICE aged 17 yrs., son of Henry Rice, dec'd, chose Henry Marquest
as his guardian. Case #99. (Doc. B-1, p. 15)

1-4-1813 - Lewis NEFF aged 19 yrs., Daniel NEFF aged 17 yrs. and Polly NEFF aged
13 yrs., heirs of Henry Neff, dec'd, chose John Kerr as their guardian.
Case #102. (Doc. B-1, page 16)

1-4-1813 - James DAVIS aged 18 yrs., Hannah DAVIS aged 14 yrs. and Levi DAVIS aged
12 yrs., heirs of Thomas Davis, dec'd, chose Levin Hatfield as their guardian.
Case #103. (Doc. B-1, p. 16)

5-3-1813 - John D. Campbell appointed guardian of Samuel SUNDERLAND aged 1 yr.,
heir of Daniel Sunderland, dec'd. Case #111. (Doc. B-1, p. 31)

5-3-1813 - John DAVIS aged 17 yrs., heir of Lewis Davis, dec'd, chose his mother,
Mary Davis as his guardian. Case #112. (Doc. B-1, p.31)

5-3-1813 - John WILSON aged 16 yrs., son of John Wilson chose Christopher Curtner
as his guardian. Case #113. (Doc. B-1, p.31)

5-4-1813 - Francis INNES aged 15 yrs., heir of Francis Innes, dec'd, chose
Nathaniel Innes of Kentucky as his guardian. Case #115. (Doc. B-1, p.35)

9-6-1813 - Henry WORMAN aged 16 yrs., heir of George Worman, dec'd, chose Henry
Worman as his guardian. Case #118. (Doc. B-1, p. 56)

9-6-1813 - Charlotte Newcom appointed guardian of Mary NEWCOM aged 4 yrs. and
Robert NEWCOM aged 1 yr., heirs of William Newcom, dec'd. Case #119. (Doc.
B-1, p. 56)

9-6-1813 - Jacob MILLER aged 16 yrs., heir of John Miller, dec'd chose William
Browne (Brower) as his guardian Case #122&123. (Doc. B-1, p. 56

4-14-1814 - John HOLE aged 15 yrs., Matilda HOLE aged 14 yrs. and Phebe HOLE
aged 12 yrs., heirs of Doctor John Hole, chose Richard Mason as their
guardian. Case #150. (Doc. B-1, p. 98)

Sept 1814 - Philip Wagner and Joseph Rohrer appointed guardians of David MILLER
AGED 11 YRS., John MILLER aged 9 yrs., and Abraham MILLER aged 6 yrs.
heirs of John Miller, dec'd. Case #156. (Doc. B-1, p. 129)

Sept 1814 - Samuel THRALL aged 15 yrs., heir of Jos. Thrall, dec'd, chose Joseph
Brown as his guardian. Case #157. (Doc. B-1, p. 129)

Sept 1814 - Enos Miles appointed guardian of Isaac RENTFREW aged 11 yrs., Jacob
RENTFREW aged 9 yrs. and John RENTFREW aged 6 yrs., heirs of Turpin Rentfrew,
dec'd. Case #158. (Doc. B-1, p. 129)

Sept 1814 - James RENTFREW aged 14 yrs. chose Enos Miles as his guardian. Case #159. (Doc. B-1, p. 130)

Sept.1814 - John Schenck appointed guardian of Daniel SCHENCK aged 13 yrs., heir of Wm. Schenck. Case #164. (Doc. B-1, p.131)

9-7-1814 - Jeremiah WOOD aged 17 yrs., heir of Samuel Wood, dec'd, chose Jonas Wood as his guardian. Case #166. (Doc. B-1, p. 131)

Jan 1815 - Joseph BUTCHER aged 15 yrs., heir of Matthias Butcher chose Peter Lehman as his guardian. Case #171. (Doc. B-1, p. 146)

Jan 1815 - Peter YOUNT aged 19 yrs., heir of Jacob Yount, chose Frederick Nuttz as his guardian. Case #174. (Doc. B-1, p. 147)

Mar 1815 - David Simmons appointed guardian of Scott SHAW aged 10 yrs., heir of Freeman Shaw. Case #177. (Doc. B-1, p. 152)

5-1-1815 - Joseph PARK Jr. aged 18 yrs., heir of Robert Park, chose Joseph Park as his guardian. Case #183. (Doc. C-1, p7)

5-1-1815 - Joseph Park appointed guardian of Elizabeth D. PARK aged 3 yrs., heir of Robert Park. Case #186. James Park appointed guardian of Thomas B. PARK aged 8 yrs., heir of Robert Park. Case #187. (Doc. C-1, p.7)

Sept 1815 - William King appointed guardian of Andrew PARK aged 10 yrs. and Isabella PARK aged 6 yrs., heirs of Robert Park. Case #188. (Doc. G-1,p.8)

Sept 1815 - Sally G. Squire appointed guardian of Phebe SQUIRE aged 8 yrs., Eliza SQUIRE aged 6 yrs., Juliet SQUIRE aged 4 yrs. and Rebecca SQUIRE aged 9 months, heirs of David Squire. Case #189. (Doc. C-a, p.8)

Sept 1815 - William WILSON aged 18 yrs., heir of Joseph Wilson, chose Horatio G. Phillips as his guardian. Case #190. (Doc. C-1, p.8)

(May) 1815 - James MORROW aged 16 yrs., son of James Morrow, chose Jerome Mote as his guardian. Case #192. (Doc. C-1, p.9)

9-4-1815 - Jacob HOOVER aged 18 yrs., heir of Daniel Hoover chose Andrew Hoover as his guardian. Case #197. Frederic HOOVER aged 16 yrs. heir of Daniel Hoover chose Daniel Yount as his guardian. Case #198. (Doc. C-1, p.23)

9-4-1815 - Edward FORD aged 16 yrs., heir of Stephen Ford, chose James Whitfield as his guardian. Case #199. (Doc. C-1, p.23)

9-4-1815 - James COTTINGHAM aged 16 yrs., heir of William Cottingham chose Thomas Cottons as his guardian. Case #200. (Doc. C-1, p.23)

9-4-1815 - Nathaniel TAYLOR aged 17 yrs., heir of William Taylor chose Sally Wilson as his guardian. Case #201. Sally Wilson also to serve as guardian of Richard TAYLOR aged 13 yrs., William TAYLOR aged 12 yrs., heirs of William Taylor and of Jane WILSON aged 2 yrs., heir of Joseph Wilson. Case #202. (Doc. C-1, p.24)

9-6-1815 - Powell JOHN aged 20 yrs., Bouch JOHN aged 18 yrs., Mary JOHN aged 16 yrs., Samuel JOHN aged 14 yrs. and Anna JOHN aged 12 yrs., heirs of David John chose Eleanor John as their guardian with Eleanor also to serve as guardian of Daniel JOHN aged 10 yrs., Sally JOHN aged 8 yrs. and Eleanor JOHN aged 5 yrs., heirs of David John. Case #204 (Doc. C-1, p.25)

9-6-1815 - Sarah MAST aged 12 yrs., heir of Jacob Most, chose Leonard Eller as her guardian with Leonard also to serve as guardian of Rebecca MAST aged 10 yrs., heir of Jacob Most. Case #206. John Waggoner appointed guardian of Susanna MAST aged 8 yrs. and Nancy MAST aged 6 yrs., heirs of Jacob Most. Case #207. (Doc. C-1, p.25)

9-6-1815 - John Regans appointed guardian of Chloe LETURNO aged 5 yrs., heir of Francis Leturno. Case #208. (Doc. C-1, p.26)

10-13-1815 - John McCOLLOM aged 14 yrs. and Parry McCOLLOM aged 13 yrs., heirs of Hugh McCOLLOM, chose George Newcom as their guardian. Case #213. Rachel McCollom appointed guardian of Maria McCOLLOM aged 11 yrs., Lucinda McCOLLOM aged 6 yrs. and Ethan McCOLLOM aged 4 yrs., heirs of Hugh McCollom. Case #214. (Doc. C-1, p.34)

11-7-1815 - John SHOUB aged 17 yrs., heir of Martin Shoub chose Daniel Stetler as his guardian. Case 219. Barbara SHOUB aged 15 yrs., her of Martin Shoub, chose William Stetler as her guardian. Case #220. Martin Shuey appointed guardian of Henry SHOUB aged 13 yrs., Martin SHOUB aged 12 yrs. and Lydia SHOUB, minor heirs of John Shoub. Case #221. Daniel Stetler appointed guardian of Catherine SHOUB aged 8 yrs. and Elizabeth SHOUB aged 6 yrs., heirs of Martin Shoub. Case #222. (Doc. C-1, p.34)

Jan 1816 - Henry SHOUP aged 14 yrs, son of Martin shoup, chose Martin Shuey as his guardian, Case 225. (Doc. C-1, p. 48)

Jan 1816 - Mary COGLER aged 17 yrs., daughter of Adam Cogler, chose Andrew Reid as her guardian. Case #228. (Doc. C-1, p.49)

Jan 1816 - David WHETON aged 14 yrs., minor of John Wheton, dec'd, chose Robert Patterson as his guardian. Case #229½. (Doc. C-1, p.49)

Jan 1816 - Michael Myers and Aron Miller appointed guardians of John ROARER aged 7 yrs., Catharine ROARER aged 5 yrs., Jacob ROARER Jr. aged 4 yrs. and Mary ROARER aged 2 yrs., minors of Jacob Roarer. Case #230. (Doc. C-1, p.50)

Apr 1816 - Joseph Fouts and Jenny Fouts appointed guardians of James SMITH aged 9 yrs. and Sarah SMITH aged 6 yrs., heirs of Peter Smith. Case #236. (Doc. C-1, p. 84)

Apr 1816 - Samuel CARVER aged 16 yrs., heir of John Carver, chose John Ritter his guardian. Case #237. (Doc. C-1, p.84)

Apr 1816 - John WILSON aged 16 yrs. heir of Joseph Wilson, chose Joseph Pence as his guardian. Case #238. (Doc. C-1, p.84)

Aug 1816 - Betsy GEPHART aged 10 yrs. and John GEPHART aged 15 yrs., heirs of Peter Gephart chose Peter Banta as their guardian. Case #241. (Doc. C-1, p.98)

Aug. 1816 - Margaret KOCH aged 15 yrs. and Betsy KOCH aged 13 yrs., heirs of Christian Koch, chose Frederick Staver as their guardian. Case #242. Henry KOCH aged 14 yrs., heir of Christian Koch, chose Ulrich Sailer as his guardian. Case #243. (Doc. C-1, p.98)

Aug. 1816 - Casper Staver Jr. appointed guardian of Polly KOCH aged 10 yrs. and Frederick KOCH aged 8 yrs. Case #244. Philip Gunckel appointed guardian of Sally KOCH aged 6 yrs., Christiana KOCH aged 4 yrs. and Michael KOCH aged 2 yrs., heirs of Christian Koch. Case #245. (Doc. C-1, p. 99)

Aug. 1816 - Samuel Heain appointed guardian of Isabella DODD aged 8 yrs. and William DODD aged 5 yrs., heirs of Joseph Dodd, Jr. Case 246. (Doc. C-1, p.99)

12-23-1816 - John Huston appointed guardian of Mary BSXTER aged 11 yrs., Peggy BAXTER aged 8 yrs., Anna BAXTER aged 5 yrs. and Daniel BAXTER aged 3 yrs., heirs of Daniel Baxter. Case #253. (Doc. C-1, p.115)

12-23-1816 - George FOGELSONG aged 15 yrs., Jacob FOGELSONG aged 14 yrs. chose John Hizer as their guardian with Hizer to also serve as guardian of Christian Fogelsong aged 13 yrs., all heirs of Christian Fogelsong. Case #254. (Doc. C-1, p.115)

12-23-1816 - David JOHNSON aged 16 yrs. and Polly JOHNSON aged 14 yrs., heirs of David Johnson chose John Johnson as their guardian. Case #256. (Doc. C-1, p.115)

12-15-1816 - Isaac MIDDLETON an orphan aged 14 yrs. chose Aaron Nutt as his guardian. Case #257. (Doc. C-1, p. 116)

12-17-1816 - Russel RICE aged 18 yrs. chose John Lehman as his guardian. Case #261. (Doc. C-a, p. 116)

5-19-1817 - James CRAIG aged 17 yrs., heir of John Craig, chose Seymour Craig as his guardian. Case #266. Nancy CRAIG aged 17 yrs. and Jeremiah S. CRAIG aged 15 yrs., heirs of John Craig, chose William Dodd as their guardian. Case #267. Enos Terry appointed guardian of Alexander CRAIG aged 12 yrs., David CRAIG aged 12 yrs. and Phebe CRAIG aged 10 yrs., minor heirs of John Craig. Case #268. (Doc. C-1, p. 132)

5-19-1817 - Stephen JONES aged 15 yrs., heir of Moses Jones, chose John Huston as his guardian. Case #269. (Doc. C-1, p. 132)

5-19-1817 - Nathaniel Bloomfield appointed guardian of ?Alexander WILSON, heir of Joseph Wilson. Case #270. (Doc. C-1, p. 132)

5-19-1817 - Daniel GEPHART aged 16 yrs., heir of John Gephart, chose Henry Gephart as his guardian. Case #271. (Doc. C-1, p. 132)

5-19-1817 - Moses CAN aged 16 yrs., heir of James Can, chose Henry Clark as his guardian. Case #276. (Doc. C-1, p.133)

5-19-1817 - Jacob Hershberger appointed guardian of Elizabeth PHILLIPS aged 6 yrs. and William PHILLIPS aged 7 yrs., heirs of George Phillips. Case #277. (Doc. C-1, p. 133)

5-22-1817 - Jacob YOUNT aged 17 yrs., heir of Jacob Yount, chose Frederic Nutt as his guardian. Case 279. (Doc. C-1, p. 133)

10-11-1817 - Charity CROWEL aged 15 yrs. and Phebe CROWELL aged 12 yrs., heirs of Samuel Crowel, chose Elizabeth Crowel as their guardian. Case #291. Elizabeth Crowel also to serve as guardian of Mary CROWEL aged 6 yrs., heir of Samuel Crowel. Case #292. (Doc. C-a, p.154)

10-13-1817 - Samuel Martindale appointed guardian of Insco JAY aged 4 yrs. and Joanna JAY aged 2 yrs., heirs of Thomas Jay. Case #294. (Doc. C-1, p. 157)

10-13-1817 - George Gephart appointed guardian of Jacob GEBHART aged 11 yrs. and Abraham GEBHART aged 2 yrs.; Michael Hoobler appointed guardian of Catherine GEBHART aged 9 yrs., Barbara GEBHART aged 7 yrs. and Margaret GEBHART aged 4 yrs.; all heirs of John Gebhart. Case #294½ & #562. (Doc. C-1, p. 157)

1-26-1818 - John C. LANE aged 18 yrs., heir of George Lane chose Sidney Denise as his guardian. Case #298. (Doc. C-1, p. 172)

1-26-1818 - Nancy HARDMAN aged 16 yrs. and Elizabeth HARDMAN aged 13 yrs. chose Elizabeth Hardman and Solomon Hardman as their guardians, with Elizabeth and Solomon to also serve as guardian of Sarah HARDMAN aged 10 yrs., Susaa HARDMAN aged 8 yrs., Mary HARDMAN aged 6 yrs., Joseph HARDMAN aged 4 yrs. and William HARDMAN aged 2 yrs.; all heirs of Joseph Hardman. Case #299. (Doc. C-1, p. 173)

1-26-1818 - Jacob Ruby appointed guardian of Jacob HAY aged 8 yrs., George HAY aged 6 yrs. and Michael HAY aged 2 yrs. Case #300. (Doc. C-1, p. 173)

1-27-1818 - John CULBERTSON aged 16 yrs. and Acenith CULBERTSON aged 14 yrs., heirs of John Culbertson chose Robert Culbertson as their guardian. Case #301. (Doc. C-1, p. 173)

187

1-28-1818 - Nathan BAYLESS aged 14 yrs., heir of Samuel Bayless chose Benjamin
    Bayliss as his guardian. Case #302. (Doc. C-1, p. 173)
1-28-1818 - George Parsons appointed guardian of Aaron TAFF aged 6 yrs., heir of
    Abraham Taff. Case #303. (Doc. C-1, p. 173)
1-30-1818 - Jesse BRACKEN aged 15 yrs., heir of Jesse Bracken chose Alexander
    Hughey as his guardian. Case #304. (Doc. C-1, p. 174)
4-21-1818 - John EWING aged 16 yrs., heir of John Ewing chose William Gardner
    Ewing as his guardian. Case #314. (Doc. C-1, p. 202)
4-21-1818 - Daniel Heistand appointed guardian of Jacob HAY aged 9 yrs., George
    HAY aged 6 yrs. and Michael HAY aged 2 yrs., children of Jacob Hay who appear
    in court and agreed to appointment of said Daniel Heistand. Case #315.
    (Doc. C-1, p.202)
4-21-1818 - Elizabeth Becher appointed guardian of Barbary BECHER aged 10 yrs.,
    Eliza BECHER aged 8 yrs. and 5 months. John BECHER aged 6 yrs. and Peter
    BECHER aged 3 months, heirs of Peter Becher. Case #316. (Doc. C-1, p.202)
4-25-1818 - Terris Simpson aged 13 yrs. chose William Bomberger has her guardian.
    Case #318. (Doc. C-1, p.203)
4-27-1818 - Elizabeth Galahan appointed guardian of John GALLAHAN aged 8 yrs.,
    Polly GALLAHAN aged 5 yrs. and Eliza GALLAHAN aged 8 months, heirs of Edward
    Gallahan. Case #320. (Doc. C-1, p.203)
4-28-1818 - James Reeder appointed guardian of Campbell BOWMAN aged 6 yrs.
    heir of Gilbert Bowman. Case #325. (Doc. C-1, p.207)
8-4-1818 - Jacob SHEIDLER aged 19 yrs., Elias SHEIDLER aged 16 yrs. and Sarah
    SHEIDLER aged 13 yrs., heirs of George Sheidler chose their mother Mary
    Sheidler as their guardian. Case #340. (Doc. D-1,p.3)
8-4-1818 - George Washington CASSADY aged 15 yrs. heir of Peter Cassady chose
    John Cassady as his guardian. Case #341. (Doc. D-1, p.3)
11-3-1818 - George HIMES aged 19 yrs., Martin HIMES aged 17 yrs., Francis HIMES
    aged 15 yrs. and Nancy HIMES aged 13 yrs. chose Joseph Coleman as their
    guardian and Coleman also to serve as guardian of Thomas HIMES aged 11 yrs.
    and Rachel HIMES aged 4 yrs.; all heirs of John Himes. Case #347. (Doc.
    D-1, p.39)
11-3-1818 - John H. Schenck and Sidney Denise appointed guardians of Zebulon
    BARCALOW aged 7 yrs., George BARCALOW aged 6 yrs., Derrick BARCALOW aged
    5 yrs., Eleanor BARCALOW aged 3 yrs., John BARCALOW aged 1 yr. and Ann
    BARCALOW aged 4 months, minor heirs of Benjamin Barcalow. Case #349. (Doc.
    D-1, p.40)
11-4-1818 - Catharine SHOUP aged 12 yrs., minor heir of Martin Shoup. chose
    Abraham Pontius as her guardian. Case #350. (Doc. D-1, p.40)
11-5-1818 - Jacob Dehl and John Heistand appointed guardian of Peter HEISTAND,
    a person unable to handle his own affairs. Case #351 & #352) (Doc. D-1,
    p.40)
11-4-1818- John MILLER aged 14 yrs., heir of John Miller, chose Joel Fouts as
    his guardian. Case #353. (Doc. D-1, p. 41)
11-9-1818 - Abraham Troxel appointed guardian of Elizabeth ARNOLD aged 10 yrs.,
    Mary ARNOLD aged 9 yrs., Sarah ARNOLD aged 7 yrs., Jacob ARNOLD aged 6 yrs.,
    and Catharine ARNOLD aged 3 yrs., children of Christian Arnold, to take care
    of estate which descends to them from their grandfather George Sheidler and
    from John Sheidler, dec'd. Case #354. (Doc. D-1, p.41)

4-19-1819 - William MANLOVE aged 17 yrs., son of William Manlove, dec'd, chose Alexander McConnel as his guardian. Case #364. (Doc. D-1, p.71)

4-19-1819 - Ninrod HADDIX aged 14 yrs., son of Ninrod HADDIX, dec'd chose John Haddix as his guardian. Case #365. (Doc. D-1, p.71)

4-19-1819 - Lemuel James EDWARDS aged 14 yrs., son of John Edwards chose William Dodds Sr. as his guardian. Case #366. (Doc. D-1, p.71)

4-19-1819 - Susanna SNIDER aged 15 yrs., chose Henry Brombaugh as her guardian and court appointed Samuel Folkerth guardian of Henry SNIDER aged 13 yrs., Jacob SNIDER aged 11 yrsl., Catharine SNIDER aged 9 yrs. and Daniel SNIDER aged 7 yrs., all heirs of William Snider. Case #367 & #368. (Doc. D-1, p.71)

4-19-1819 - Fanny STONER aged 17 yrs., chose George Stump her guardian with Stump also to serve as guardian of John STONER aged 13 yrs., Polly STONER aged 11 yrs., Anna STONER aged 9 yrs. and Jacob STONER aged 5 yrs., all heirs of Jacob Stoner. Case #369. (Doc. D-1, p.71)

4-19-1819 - Martin HOOVER aged 16 yrs. chose Jonas Hoover as her guardian with Jonas also to serve as guardian of Peggy HOOVER aged 8 yrs. Case #370. (Doc. D-1, p. 72)

4-19-1819 - Daniel Heistand appointed guardian of Abraham HOOVER aged 12 yrs. and Esther Hoover aged 10 yrs; Catherine Hoover, widow of Martin Hoover relinquishes her right to be appointed guardian. Case #371. (Doc. D-1, p.72)

4-21-1819 - Catherine EMRICK aged 15 yrs. chose Christopher Emrick as her guardian. Elizabeth EMRICK aged 14 yrs. chose Christopher Taylor as her guardian, with Taylor also to serve as guardian of Samuel EMRICK aged 11 yrs. George Emrick appointed guardian of John EMRICK aged 9 yrs. and Polly EMRICK aged 6 yrs. Lewis Shuey appointed guardian of Peter EMRICK aged 4 yrs. and Andrew EMRICK AGED 1 YR.: ALL HEIRS OF Andrew Emrick, dec'd. Elizabeth Emrick, widow relinquishes her right to serve as guardian of her children. Case #374 375, 376 & 377. (Doc. D-1, p. 73)

4-26-1819 - James HANNA appointed guardian of Amos Thompson HANNA aged 8 yrs., and Harriet Newel HANNA aged 2 yrs., children of James Hanna, who are entitled to a dividend of estate of their dec'd mother under the will of their grandfather, John McLean, dec'd. Case #378. (Doc. D-1, p.74)

4-26-1819 - John Williams appointed guardian of his children, John WILLIAMS aged 12 yrs., Nathaniel WILLIAMS aged 10 yrs., William WILLIAMS aged 9 yrs , Matilda WILLIAMS aged 5 yrs. and Ellis WILLIAMS aged 3 yrs.; who are to receive a legacy from their grandfather (not named). Case #379. (Doc. D-1, p.74)

4-26-1819 - John GIEL aged 17 yrs., minor of John Giel, dec'd, chose Samuel Archer as his guardian. Case #380. (Doc. D-1, p.74)

5-16-1819 - Joseph EVANS aged 16 yrs., heir of Lewis Evans, dec'd, chose Martin Sprague as his guardian. Case #393. (Doc. D-1, p. 133)

5-18-1819 - Daniel RUSE aged 16 yrs., heir of Nicholas Ruse, dec'd, chose Nathaniel Stutsman as his guardian. Case #395. (Doc. D-1, p.134)

6-23-1819 - Peter CASTAR aged 19 yrs., heir of Conrad Castar, dec'd, chose Samuel Bringham as his guardian. Case #398. (Doc. D-1, p. 135)

6-23-1819 - Thomas CASTAR aged 18 yrs. and John CASTAR aged 10 yrs., heirs of Conrad Castor, dec'd, chose Benjamin Waggoner as their guardian, Case #399. James Johnson appointed guardian of Elizabeth CASTOR aged 10 yrs., Barsheba CASTOR aged 7 yrs. and Rebecca CASTOR aged 5 yrs. Case #400. (Doc. D-1, p.137)

189

8-23-1819 - Michael Nager appointed guardian of John CLARK aged 6 yrs. and Rebecca
CLARK aged 3 yrs., minor heirs of Henry Clark, dec'd; widow (not named) of
Henry Clark Jr., dec'd relinquishes right to be appointed guardian. Case #401.
(Doc. D-1, p. 137)

11-15-1819 - Daniel SHIVELY aged 19 yrs. chose Susanna Shively widow of Daniel
Shively as his guardian and said Susanna relinquishes her right as guardian
of all other heirs. David SHIVELY aged 17 yrs. chose David Shively as his
guardian. John Shively aged 15 yrs. chose Jacob Shively as his gardian.
All being heirs of Daniel Shively, dec'd. Case #408, 409 & 410.
(Doc. D-1, p.165)

3-6-1820 - Susannah Sheibly appointed guardian of Christopher SHEIBLY aged 13 yrs.
and Susannah SHEIBLY aged 9 yrs., heirs of Daniel Sheibly, dec'd. Case #417.
(Doc. D-1, p.192)

3-6-1820 - Frederick Holsople appointed guardian of Jacob RUSE aged 13 yrs.,
Nancy RUSE aged 9 yrs., Mary RUSE aged 6 yrs., George RUSE aged 4 yrs. and
Phebe RUSE aged 1 yr., heirs of Nicholas RUSE, dec'd. Case #418. (Doc.
D-1, p.192)

3-7-1820 - Wilson CLARK aged 15 yrs., heir of Henry Clark, dec'd, chose Solomon
Clark as his guardian. Case #419. (Doc. D-1, p.192)

3-10-1820 - Aaron Baker appointed guardian of Mary NEWKIRK aged 8 yrs., minor
child of Catharine Reed wife of Abraham Reed. Case #421. (Doc. D-1, p. 198)

3-10-1820 - Elizabeth Burkhard appointed guardian of Isaac BERKHARD aged 10 yrs.,
Martin BERKHARD aged 8 yrs., Barbara BERKHARD aged 5 yrs., heirs of Henry
Berkhard. Case #422. (Doc. D-1, p. 202)

3-10-1820 - Alexander CRAIG and David CRAIG aged 16 yrs., heirs of John Craig,
dec'd, chose Seymour Craig as their guardian. Case #423. (Doc. D-1, p.202)

7-24-1820 - Julia Ann NOLAN aged 12 yrs., heir of James Nolan, dec'd, chose
William Patterson as her guardian. Case #426. (Doc. D-1, p.234)

7-24-1820 - Rosanna BENNET aged 15 yrs., heir of Thomas Bennet, dec'd, chose
Jacob Overholser as her guardian, Case #427. (Doc. D-1, p. 234)

7-24-1820 - John Shively appointed guardian of Catharine BLICENSTAFFER aged 10
yrs., Leonard BLICKENSTAFFER aged 9 yrs., Elizabeth BLICKENSTAFFER aged 8
yrs., Hannah BLICKENSTAFFER aged 6 yrs., Jacob BLICKENSTAFFER aged 4 yrs.
and Joseph BLICKENSTAFFER aged 2 yrs.; all heirs of Joseph Blickenstaffer,
dec'd. Case #428. (Doc. D-1, p.234)

7-27-1820 - George LIGHTY aged 17 yrs., heir of Conrad Lighty, dec'd, chose
William Long as his guardian. Case #433. (Doc. D-1, p. 235)

7-31-1820 - James Catham appointed guardian of John H. WAGGONER aged 11 yrs.
and Fariba WAGGONER aged 9 yrs., heirs of Reuben Waggoner, dec'd. Case
#435. (Doc. D-1, p.236)

10-30-1820 - George YOUNG aged 15 yrs., heir of George Young, dec'd, chose George
WOLLATON as his guardian. Case #440. (Doc. D-1, p. 256)

10-31-1820 - William HATFIELD aged 20 yrs. and Benjamin HATFIELD aged 16 yrs.,
heirs of William Hatfield, dec'd, chose John Bower as their guardian, Case
#442. Mary HATFIELD aged 18yrs., heir of William Hatfield, dec'd, chose
Jonathan Hatfield as her guardian. Case #443. (Doc. D-1, p. 257

10-31-1820 - Henry DEAL aged 20 yrs., heir of Philip Deal, dec'd, chose John
Stoneberger as his guardian. Case #444. (Doc. D-1, p.257)

11-6-1820 - Joseph SHOLLEY aged 16 yrs., heir of John Sholley, chose John Sholley
as his guardian. Case #448. (Doc. D-1, p.264)

MONTGOMERY COUNTY, OHIO - GUARDIANSHIPS 1821-1825

Contributed by: Mrs. Clyde Shilt, Rt. 3, Westbrook, Brookville, Ohio 45309

The following records are found in the Probate Court of the court house at Dayton.
The docket and page number under which the original record may be found are given
in parenthesis. The case number under which the original papers are filed is also
given and it should be noted that a little additional information such as when
minor became of age, might be found under the case number.

3-6-1821 - Ruhamah Lechlider appointed guardian of Mary Ann LECHLIDER aged 3 yrs.
and Adam LECHLIDER aged 11 months, heirs of Conrad Lechlider. Case #455.
(Doc. D-1, p. 295)

3-10-1821 - David D. BRADFORD aged 15 yrs. chose James G. Bradford as his guardian.
Case 458. (Doc. D-1, page 296)

3-10-1821 - John Bradford appointed guardian of Allen BRADFORD aged 8 yrs., heir
of John Bradford, dec'd. Case #459. (Doc. D-1, p. 296)

3-10-1821 - John Bonner appointed guardian of Ebenezer Wead Boner aged 8 yrs.,
heir of John Boner. Case #460. (Doc. D-1, p. 460)

3-12-1821 - Joseph REED aged 14 yrs., Chose George L. Houston as his guardian.
Case #462. Sarah REED aged 13 yrs. chose James Hannah her guardian and Hanna
also to serve as guardian of Adget M. REED aged 8 yrs., Elizabeth REED aged
6 yrs., Matilda REED aged 3 yrs. and Abraham REED aged 2 yrs. Case #463.
All heirs of Abraham Reed, dec'd. (Doc. D-1, p. 297)

3-12-1821 - Catharine BOWSER aged 14 yrs. and Sarah BOWSER aged 12 yrs. chose
Henry Bowser as their guardian and Henry to also serve as guardian of Henry
BOWSER aged 11 yrs., David BOWSER aged 9 yrs. and Daniel BOWSER aged 7 yrs.;
all heirs of Daniel Bowser, dec'd. Case #464. (Doc. D-1, p. 297)

3-13-1821 - Christian Shively appointed guardian of Jacob HAY aged 12 yrs.,
George HAY aged 9 yrs. and Michael HAY aged 5 yrs., heirs and Jacob Hay.
Case #465. (Doc. D-1, p. 306)

3-16-1821 - Andrew SHAW aged 15 yrs., heir of Freeman Shaw, dec'd, chose Abraham
Darst as his guardian. Case #466. (Doc. D-1, p. 306)

7-24-1821 - Abraham HOOVER aged 15 yrs. and Esther HOOVER aged 13 yrs., heirs
of Martin Hoover, chose John Hoser as their guardian. Case #476. (Doc. E-1
p. 27)

7-24-1821 - William YOUNT aged 15 yrs., heir of George Yount, chose Henry Yount
Jr. as his guardian. Case #477. Lucy YOUNT aged 13 yrs., chose William
Fincher as her guardian and Fincher to also serve as guardian of Sarah Yount
aged 11 yrs. Case #478. John Yount appointed guardian of George Yount
aged 9 yrs. Case #479. (Doc. E-1, p. 27)

7-30-1821 - Henry SHOUP aged 19 yrs. and Elizabeth SHOUP aged 12 yrs., heirs of
Martin Shoup, chose Adam Shuey as their guardian. Case #482. (Doc. E-1,
p. 28)

7-30-1821 - William Bowser appointed guardian of William RICHARDSON aged 12 yrs.
and John RICHARDSON aged 10 yrs., heirs of Daniel Richardson. Case #483.
(Doc. E-1, p. 28)

7-30-1821 - Lorinda MARSHALL aged 14 yrs. chose Abraham Darst as her guardian and
Darst also to serve as guardian of Washington MARSHALL aged 12 yrs. and
Zephaniah MARSHALL aged 10 yrs.; all heirs of William Marshall. Case #484.
(Doc. E-1, p. 28)

7-31-1821 - Conrad Kauffman appointed guardian of George HORNER, an idiot aged
15 yrs. and John HORNER aged 10 yrs., heirs of John Horner, dec'd. Case
#485. (Doc. E-1, p. 36)
7-31-1821 - Thomas CARPENTER aged 18 yrs., heir of Hopkins Carpenter, dec'd,
chose Joseph Peirce as his guardian. Case #486. (Doc. E-a, p. 36)
10-30-1821 - Margaret Stiver and Adam Swinehart appointed guardians of Solomon
STIVER aged 5 yrs., Absalom STIVER aged 4 yrs., Anna Maria STIVER aged 2
yrs. and Catherine STIVER aged 9 months, children and heirs of John Stiver,
dec'd. Case #495. (Doc. E-1, p. 59)
10-30-1821 - Jacob GEPHART aged 16 yrs., heir of John Gephart, dec'd, chose John
Snepp as his guardian. Case #496. (Doc. E-1, p. 59)
10-31-1821 - Abraham WELBAUM aged 18 yrs. heir of Charles Wellbaum, dec'd
chose Peter Fetter as his guardian. Case #499. (Doc. E-1, p. 74)
11-5-1821 - Catharine GEPHART aged 13 yrs., heir of Elizabeth Gephart, dec'd,
chose Abraham Troxell as her guardian. Case #507. (Doc. E-1, p. 90)
11-5-1821 - David WOODROW aged 18 yrs., son of James Woodrow, dec'd, chose
Obadiah Conover as his guardian. Case #508. (Doc. E-1, p. 90)
11-5-1821 - William Van Cleve appointed guardian of his daughter, Catharine
VAN CLEVE, heir of Wiley, dec'd. (note: only names given). Case #509.
(Doc. E-a, p. 90)
11-6-1821 - Thomas King appointed guardian of Elizabeth Dovey PARKS aged 10
yrs., heir of Robert Parks, dec'd. Case #510. (Doc. E-1, p. 97)
2-26-1822 - Jacob KINSEY aged 17 yrs. and Joseph KINSEY aged 15 yrs. chose
Jacob Mullendore as their guardian and Mullendore to also serve as guardian
of Lewis KINSEY aged 13 yrs., Noah KINSEY aged 11 yrs., Polly KINSEY aged
8 yrs., David KINSEY aged 6 yrs., Jonas KINSEY aged 5 yrs. and Susanna
KINSEY aged 2 yrs., all heirs of John Kinsey, dec'd. Case 523. (Doc. E-1,
p. 161)
3-4-1822 - Henrietta Maria VAN CLEVE aged 16 yrs., Mary Cornelia VAN CLEVE aged
14 yrs. and Sarah Sophia VAN CLEVE aged 12 yrs., heirs of Benjamin Van Cleve,
dec'd, chose William Van Cleve as their guardian. Case #527. (Doc. E-1,
p. 163)
3-5-1822 - Henrietta E. Peirce, widow, guardian to Mary PEIRCE aged 10 yrs.,
David Zeigler PEIRCE aged 8 yrs., Jeremiah Hunt PEIRCE aged 3 yrs. and
Joseph PEIRCE aged 1 yr., heirs of Joseph Peirce, dec'd. Case #528.
(Doc. E-1, p. 171)
3-5-1822 - Henry Brown appointed guardian of Chloe LATERNO (Leturno) aged 11 yrs.,
heir of Francis Laterno, dec'd. Henry Brown has money now in hand as the
adms. of John Regan, dec'd who was former guardian. Case #529. (Doc. E-1,
p. 171)
9-23-1822 - Eli SHUMAN aged 16 yrs., heir of Isaac Shuman (Suman), dec'd, chose
Jacob Suman as his guardian. Case #537. (Doc. E-1, p. 228)
9-23-1822 - Sally EAGLE aged 15 yrs., heir of Peter Eagle, dec'd, chose Daniel
Gephart as her guardian. Case #542. (Doc. E-1, p. 229(
9-23-1822 - Edward COLEMAN aged 16 yrs. chose George C. Davis as his guardian.
Case #543. (Doc. E-1, p. 229)
9-23-1822 - William Cox appointed guardian of Jacob COX aged 2 yrs., heir of John
Cox, dec'd. Case #546. (Doc. E-1, p. 230)
9-24-1822 - George SCHOERER aged 17 yrs. chose Abraham Darst as his guardian.
(note: no case number given and not indexed). (Doc. E-1, p. 231)

9-23-1822 - Henry ZEARING aged 15 yrs. chose Jacob Gephart as his guardian and Gephart to also serve as guardian of Samuel Zearing aged 12 yrs., heirs of Henry Zearing, dec'd. Case #548. Fanny Zearing appointed guardian of Catharine ZEARING aged 9 yrs., Maria ZEARING aged 8 yrs., Elizabeth ZEARING aged 7 yrs., David ZEARING aged 5 yrs., Susannah ZEARING aged 3 yrs. and Hannah ZEARING aged 9 months, heirs of Henry Zearing, dec'd. Case #549. (Doc. E-1, p. 238)

9-23-1822 - Sarah MORGAN aged 15 yrs., heir of Charles Morgan, dec'd, chose David Huston as her guardian. Case #550. (Doc. E-1, p. 238)

6-3-1822 - Elizabeth SHAFFER aged 18 yrs., heir of Jacob Shaffer, dec'd, chose Henry Shaffer as her guardian. Case #558. (Doc. E-1, p. 209)

2-24-1823 - Hannah GRIPE aged 16 yrs. chose Stephen Ullery as her guardian and Ullery also to serve as guardian of Stephen GRIPE aged 9 yrs., heirs of John Gripe, dec'd. Case #563. Henry Netsker appointed guardian of David GRIPE aged 7 yrs. and Elizabeth GRIPE aged 11 yrs., heirs of John Gripe, dec'd. Case #564. (Doc. E-1, p. 292)

2-24-1823 - Daniel WELDY aged 15 yrs. chose George Gephart as his guardian and Gephart also to serve as guardian of Jacob WELDY aged 11 yrs., heirs of Christian Weldy, dec'd. Case #567. Henry McGraw appointed guardian of Mary Ann WELDY aged 8 yrs., Rebecca WELDY aged 5 yrs. and Henry WELDY aged 2 yrs., heirs of Christian Weldy, dec'd. Case #568. (Doc. E-1, p.292)

2-24-1823 - James Miles appointed guardian of Aaron MIKESELL aged 12 yrs. and Abraham MIKESELL aged 10 yrs., heirs of John B. MIKESELL, dec'd. Case #570. (Doc. E-1, p. 294)

2-27-1823 - Fountain Scott CONNELLY aged 16 yrs. chose his mother, Pamela Connelly as his guardian. Case #571. (Doc. E-1, p. 313)

2-28-1823 - Sally McWhinney appointed guardian of James McWHINNEY aged 11 yrs. and William McWHINNEY aged 9 yrs., heirs of John McWhinney, dec'd. Case #572. (Doc. E-1, p. 313)

5-19-1823 - George Washington KENNADY aged 15 yrs. chose William M. Smith as his guardian. Case #375. (Doc. E-1, p. 334)

5-19-1823 - Mary HOOVER aged 15 yrs., heir of Daniel Hoover Jr., dec'd, chose John Hoover as her guardian. Case #577. (Doc. E-1, p. 334)

5-19-1823 - John Hoover appointed guardian of Sally HOOVER aged 12 yrs. and Susannah HOOVER aged 9 yrs., heirs of Daniel Hoover Jr., dec'd. Case #578. (Doc. E-a, p. 334)

5-20-1823 - Daniel KELSEY aged 17 yrs., heir of Thomas Kelsey, dec'd, chose Wm. Watkins as his guardian. Case #579. (Doc. E-1, p. 334)

5-20-1823 - George WOLF aged 14 yrs., heir of George Wolf, dec'd who died in Cumberland Co., Pa., chose Peter Treon as his guardian. Case #580. (Doc. E-1, p. 335)

10-13-1823 - Joseph Kepler appointed guardian of Allen MOTE aged 8 yrs., Ginsey MOTE aged 6 yrs., Ely MOTE aged 4 yrs. and David MOTE aged 2 yrs., minor heirs of David Mote. Case #590. (Doc. F-1, p. 29)

10-15-1823 - Elizabeth Owen widow of William Owen, dec'd, appointed guardian of John OWEN aged 7 yrs. and William OWEN aged 3 yrs., minor heirs of William Owen, dec'd. Case #602. (Doc. F-1, p. 33)

10-15-1823 - John Jininger appointed guardian of Michael SWANK aged 11 yrs., minor heir of Jacob Swank, dec'd. Case #604. Catharine Swank appointed guardian of Susannah SWANK aged 8 yrs. and John SWANK aged 6 yrs., minor heirs of Jacob Swank, dec'd. Case #605. Peter SWANK aged 19 yrs. and Daniel SWANK aged 15 yrs., minor heirs of Jacob Swank, dec'd, chose Jacob Henning as their guardian. Case #606. (Doc. F-1, p. 33)

10-15-1823 - Sally SHIVELY aged 14 yrs., heir of Isaac Shively chose Samuel
    Ulery as her guardian. Case #607. (Doc. F-1, p. 33)
10-15-1823 - John Stump appointed guardian of Solomon ZEARING aged 5 yrs.,
    heir of Jacob Zearing, dec'd. Case #608. (Doc. F-1, p. 34)
10-16-1823 - John BLAKE aged 14 yrs. chose James Henderson as his guardian. Case
    #609. (Doc. F-1, p. 34)
10-17-1823 - James MOTE aged 15 yrs. chose John Mote as his guardian and John
    also to serve as guardian of Jesse MOTE aged 9 yrs. Case #611. (Doc. F-1, p.3
10-27-1823 - Joseph H. Conover appointed guardian of Alexander G. CONOVER aged
    4 yrs., minor heir of Garret Conover, dec'd. Case #613. (Doc. F-1, p. 42)
10-27-1823 - David EAGLE aged 14 yrs., heir of Peter Eagle, dec'd, chose Jacob
    Eagle as his guardian. Case #614. (Doc. F-1, p. 43)
10-27-1823 - David SHIVELY aged 20 yrs., heir of Jacob Shively, dec'd, chose
    Thomas Patton as his guardian. Case #615. (Doc. F-1, p. 44)
10-27-1823 - John McMEANS aged 16 yrs., heir of John McMeans, dec'd, chose
    Thomas Patton as his guardian. Case #616. (Doc. F-1, p. 44)
3-1-1824 - Elizabeth WELDY aged 15 yrs., heir of Christian Weldy, chose George
    Gephart as her guardian, Case #627. (Doc. F-1, p. 127)
3-1-1824 - Lydia SHOUP aged 12 yrs., heir of Martin SHOUP, dec'd, chose Chris-
    topher Shupert as her guardian. Case #628. (Doc. F-1, p. 128)
3-1-1824 - Chloe LATERNA aged 16 yrs., heir of Francis Latterna, dec'd, chose
    Francis Patterson as her guardian. Case #630. (Doc. F-1, p. 128)
3-1-1824 - Solomon HYER aged 19 yrs., David HYER aged 17 yrs. and Isaac HYER
    aged 15 yrs., heirs of Isaac Hyer, dec'd, chose Nathaniel Burket as their
    guardian. Case #631. John Ehrstine appointed guardian of Nancy HYER aged
    11 yrs., Absalom HYER aged 9 yrs., Belinda HYER aged 7 yrs., Moses HYER
    aged 4 yrs. and Abraham HYER aged 2 yrs., heirs of Isaac Hyer, dec'd. Case
    #632. (Doc. F-1, p. 129)
3-2-1824 - Samuel Becker appointed guardian of Henry BECKER aged 12 yrs., heir
    of John Baker, dec'd. Case #636. (Doc. F-1, p. 130)
3-2-1824 - Adam Zeller appointed guardian of Henry ZELLER aged 12 yrs. and
    Adam ZELLER aged 10 yrs., heirs of Henry Zeller, dec'd. Case #637. Lewis
    Shuey appointed guardian of Catharine ZELLER aged 7 yrs. and Daniel ZELLER
    aged 2 yrs., heirs of Henry Zeller. Case #638. (Doc. F-1, p. 130)
3-3-1824 - John Olinger appointed guardian of Michael Flora aged 12 yrs., heir
    of Joseph Flora, dec'd. Case #640. Emanuel Flora appointed guardian of
    Mary FLORA aged 10 yrs. Case #641. (Doc. F-1, p. 130)
3-3-1824 - George Washington WRIGHT aged 14 yrs., heir of Josiah Wright, dec'd
    chose Thomas Coke Wright as his guardian. Case #642. (Doc. F-1, p. 130)
3-8-1824 - Elizabeth Bowen appointed guardian of David W. BOWEN aged 14 yrs.,
    Nathaniel W. BOWEN aged 12 yrs., Abraham H. BOWEN aged 9 yrs. and Robert
    H. BOWEN aged 6 yrs., heirs of Enoch Bowen, dec'd. Case #644. (Doc. F-1,
    p. 140)
3-8-1824 - Andrew BECKER aged 19 yrs., heir of David Becker, dec'd, chose John
    Becker as his guardian. Case #645. (Doc. F-1, p. 140)
3-9-1824 - David Ludy appointed guardian of Lovina BECKER aged 4 yrs., Andrew
    Becker aged 3 yrs. and David BECKER an infant, heirs of David Becker.
    Case #648. (Doc. F-1, p. 149)

3-9-1824 - Adam Bolander and Rinehart Schnep appointed guardians of William SCHNEP aged 13 yrs., John SCHNEP aged 10 yrs., Daniel SCHNEP aged 8 yrs., Catharine SCHNEP aged 7 yrs., Lewis SCHNEP aged 5 yrs. and Peter SCHNEP aged 3 yrs., heirs of Daniel SCHNEP, dec'd. Case #649. (Doc. F-1, p. 149)

6-7-1824 - William ENNIS aged 17 yrs. and Rebecca ENNIS aged 13 yrs. chose Joseph Shank their guardian and Shank also to serve as guardian of Absalom ENNIS aged 10 yrs., all heirs of John Ennis, dec'd. Case #651. (Doc. F-1, p. 183)

6-8-1824 - John Hissong appointed guardian of William HART aged 12 yrs., John HART aged 10 yrs., Henry HART aged 8 yrs., Jacob HART aged 6 yrs. and David HART aged 4 yrs. Case #653. (Doc. F-1, p. 183)

6-16-1824 - Mary SHAW aged 17 yrs. and Sarah SHAW aged 13 yrs. chose Joseph Johnson as their guardian. Case #655. Thomas SHAW aged 15 yrs. chose Samuel Archer as his guardian; heirs of James Shaw, dec'd. Case #656. (Doc. F-1, p. 186)

6-17-1824 - Christian SCHIVELY appointed guardian of Hannah CRIPE aged 9 yrs. and Catharine CRIPE aged 15 yrs. chose Schively as her guardian; heirs of Joseph Cripe. Case #657. (Doc. F-1, p. 186)

6-18-1824 - Daniel Deeter Sr. Appointed guardian of Samuel DEETER an insane person, Case #658. (Doc. F-1, p. 187)

11-8-1824 - Jacob Weaver appointed guardian of Lydia and Louisa TOMAN, heirs of Valentine Toman, dec'd. Case #669. (Doc. F-1, p. 217)

11-8-1824 - James VANKIRK aged 18 yrs., Sarah VANKIRK aged 14 yrs. and Jane VANKIRK aged 12 yrs. chose Hannah Vankirk their mother as their guardian and Hannah also to serve as guardian of Anna VANKIRK aged 10 yrs. and Hannah VANKIRK aged 7 yrs., all heirs of James Vankirk, dec'd. Case #671. (Doc. F-1, p. 217)

11-8-1824 - John Yount appointed guardian of George YOUNT aged 12 yrs., son of George Yount, dec'd. Case #672. (Doc. F-1, p. 217)

11-9-1824 - Jesse Hutchens appointed guardian of his son, Daniel Hutchens aged 4 yrs. Case #673. (Doc. F-1, p. 218)

11-10-1824 - John Bradford appointed guardian of Mary BRADFORD aged 6 yrs., heir of William Bradford, dec'd. Case #675. (Doc. F-1, p. 218)

11-11-1824 - Samuel MILLER aged 19 yrs. and Henry MILLER aged 15 yrs., heirs of Michael Miller, dec'd, chose Henry Hipple as their guardian. Case #676. (Doc. F-1, p. 218)

11-12-1824 - Lewis A. HILDRETH aged 18 yrs. on the 13th day of Dec. next, heir of Jonathan Hildreth, dec'd, chose Henry Stoddard as his guardian. Case #677. (Doc. F-1, p. 218)

11-13-1824 - John ANDERSON, aged 15 yrs., heir of John Anderson, dec'd, chose George W. Smith as his guardian. Case #678. (Doc. F-1, p. 219)

11-20-1824 - Joseph GRIFFITH aged 17 yrs., heir of Eleazer Griffith, dec'd, chose Isaac Griffith as his guardian. Case #679. (Doc. F-1, p. 222)

11-20-1824 - Jacob Zook appointed guardian of his children, Samuel ZOOK aged 10 yrs., John ZOOK aged 9 yrs., William ZOOK aged 8 yrs., Eve ZOOK aged 7 yrs., Esther ZOOK aged 6 yrs., Catharine ZOOK aged 5 yrs. and Jacob ZOOK aged 4 yrs. Case #681. (Doc. F-1, p. 223)

2-1-1825 - Henry SHEPHARD aged 15 yrs. chose Lewis McNight as his guardian. Case #683. (Doc. F-1, p. 224)

6-7-1824 - Samuel Heistand appointed guardian of Peter HEISTAND an insane
person. Case #684. (Doc. F-1, p. 164)

2-28-1825 - Sarah UMBARGER aged 16 yrs., heir of George Umbarger, dec'd, chose
Daniel Noffsinger as her guardian. Case #686. (Doc. F-1, p. 225)

2-28-1825 - Jacob STETLER aged 17 yrs., heir of Henry Stetler, dec'd, chose Daniel
Stetler as his guardian. Case #688. (Doc. F-1, p. 225)

3-1-1825 - Catharine CARROLL aged 13 yrs. chose John Oblinger as her guardian
and Oblinger also to serve as guardian of William CARROLL aged 11 yrs.
Case #689. (Doc. F-1, p. 225)

3-7-1825 - Sarah Davis appointed guardian of George DAVIS aged 5 yrs., John
DAVIS aged 3 yrs. and Sarah DAVIS aged 1 yr., heirs of Lewis Davis, dec'd.
Case #693. (Doc. F-1, p. 226)

3-7-1825 - James Hannah guardian of Sarah, Adgit, Elizabeth, Matilda and Abraham
REID, heirs of Abraham Reid, dec'd, is released as guardian and Aaron Baker
is appointed guardian of Adget Reid aged 12 yrs., Elizabeth Reid aged 10 yrs.,
Matilda Reid aged 7 yrs. and Abraham Reid aged 6 yrs. Case #468. (Doc.
F-1, p. 230)

3-7-1825 - Henry STETLER aged 16 yrs., heir of Henry Stetler, chose William
Stetler as his guardian. Case #695. (Doc. F-1, p. 236)

5-30-1825 - Tena JENKINS aged 17 yrs. chose Frederick Nutts as her guardian.
Case #697. (Doc. F-1, p. 305)

5-30-1825 - William SCHNEPP aged 15 yrs., heir of Daniel Schnepp, dec'd, chose
Philip Schnepp as his guardian. Case #698. (Doc. F-1, p. 305)

5-30-1825 - George DENISE aged 16 yrs. and Elenor DENISE aged 14 yrs. chose John
H. Schenck as their guardian and Schenck also to serve as guardian of Sarah
Ann DENISE aged 11 yrs., Margaret DENISE aged 9 yrs. and Sidney DENISE aged
6 yrs., all heirs of John Denise, dec'd. Case #701. (Doc. F-1, p. 306)

5-31-1825 - Amos PIERSON aged 16 yrs. heir of Joseph Pierson, dec'd, chose
Samuel Martindale as his guardian. Case #704. (Doc. F-1, p. 306)

6-4-1825 - Abigail RYON, heir of Joseph Ryon, dec'd, chose Geo. C. Davis as
her guardian. Case #705. (Doc. F-1, p. 306)

10-12-1825 - Frederick COOK aged 17 yrs., heir of Christian Cook chose Lewis
Shuey as his guardian. Case #715. (Doc. G-1, p. 46)

10-12-1825 - John FETTER aged 20 yrs., heir of Peter Fetter, chose Charles
Welbaum as his guardian. Case #717. (Doc. G-1, p. 46)

10-13-1825 - William Dodson appointed guardian of Jacob, Polly and Catharine
FETTER, heirs of Peter Fetter, dec'd. Case #718. (Doc. G-1, p. 47)

10-15-1825 - Elizabeth WITHEROW aged 17 yrs. on 7 day of Nov. next, James WITHEROW
aged 15 yrs. on 29 Dec. next and Mary P. WITHEROW aged 12 yrs. on 17 Feb.
last past chose Nathaniel Wilson as their guardian and Wilson to also serve
as guardian of Jane WITHEROW aged 9 yrs. on 12 Apr. last past, Sarah T.
WITHEROW aged 7 yrs. on 13 Sept. last past and Samuel T. W. WITHEROW aged 2
yrs. on 10 Aug. last past, all children and heirs of Samuel Witherow, dec'd,
late of Franklin Co., Pa. Case #719. (Doc. G-1, p. 47)

10-15-1825 - John FLORA aged 15 yrs. chose Emanuel Flora his guardian and Emanuel
also to serve as guardian of Jonathan FLORA aged 7 yrs., heirs of Henry Flora,
dec'd. Case #720. (Doc. G-1, p. 47)

10-15-1825 - John Kimmel appointed guardian of Rachel FLORA aged 10 yrs. and
David FLORA aged 7 yrs., heirs of Henry Flora, dec'd. Case #721. Martin
Weybright appointed guardian of Nathaniel FLORA aged 2 yrs., heir of Henry
Flora, dec'd. Case #722. John Oblinger appointed guardian of Henry FLORA
aged 12 yrs., heir of Henry Flora, dec'd. Case #723. (Doc. G-1, p. 48)

10-17-1825 - Polly ROWYER aged 16 yrs. and Elizabeth ROWYER aged 15 yrs. chose
Emanuel Flora their guardian with Flora also to serve as guardian of
Abraham ROWYER aged 13 yrs., John ROWYER aged 11 yrs., Henry ROWYER aged
9 yrs. and George Rowyer aged 7 yrs., heirs of Henry Rowyer, dec'd.
Case #724. (Doc. G-1, p. 48)
10-17-1825 - Samuel Hagar appointed guardian of Julia Anna MARTIN aged 2 yrs.,
heir of Margaret Taylor, dec'd. Case #725. (Doc. G-1, p. 48)
10-17-1825 - John Stump appointed guardian of Rebecca MOSES 17 yrs., heir of
michael Moses late of Penn. Case #729. (Doc. G-1, p. 55)

Contributed by: Mrs. Clyde Shilt, Rt. 3, Westbrook, Brookville, Ohio 45309

The following records are found in the Probate Court of the court house at Dayton.
The docket and page number under which the original record may be found are given
in parenthesis. The case number under which the original papers are filed is also
given and it should be noted that a little additional information such as when the
minor became of age, might be found under the case number.

2-28-1826 - Elizabeth FLORA aged 13 yrs. (June 1825), heir of Henry Flora, dec'd,
     chose John Olinger as her guardian. Case #738. (Doc. G-1, p. 116)
2-27-1826 - John DEPREY, heir of Daniel Deprey, dec'd, chose Andrew Yount as
     his guardian. Case #741. (Doc. G-1, p. 117)
2-27-1826 - Campbell BOWMAN aged 14 yrs., son of Gilbert Bowman, dec'd, chose
     William Reeder as his guardian. Case #742. (Doc. G-1, p. 117)
2-27-1826 - John Hagan appointed guardian of Livinia BAKER aged 6 yrs., Andrew
     BAKER aged 4 yrs. and David BAKER aged 3 yrs., children and heirs of
     David Baker, dec'd. Case #743. (Doc. G-1, p. 118)
2-27-1826 - William Hipple appointed guardian of Susannah SELL aged 11 yrs.,
     heir of Christian Sell, dec'd. Case #747. (Doc. G-1, p. 118)
3-7-1826 - Chloe LATURNO aged 17 yrs., heir of Francis Laturno, chose Andrew
     Irwin as her guardian. Case #750. (Doc. G-1, p. 121)
5-29-1826 - Rebecca INSCO aged 17 yrs., heir of James Insco, chose Isaac Campbell
     as her guardian. Case #756. (Doc. G-1, p. 223)
5-29-1826 - Jesse Lowe appointed guardian of Jane BREWSTER aged 3 yrs. on 7 Apr.
     1826. Case #757. (Doc. G-1, p. 224)
5-29-1826 - Eli SUMAN aged 19 yrs. in Sept. 1825, Sarah SUMAN aged 16 yrs. and James
     SUMAN aged 14 yrs. on May 1, 1826, children and heirs of Manes and Catherine
     Suman, dec'd, chose Henry Stoddard as their guardian. Case #758. (Doc.
     G-1, p. 224)
5-30-1826 - Barbara GEPHART aged 15 yrs. and Margaret GEPHART aged 13 yrs. chose
     John Snep as their guardian with Snep also to serve as guardian of Abraham
     GEPHART aged 11 yrs., all heirs of John Gephart, dec'd. Case #759. (Doc.
     G-1, p. 224)
5-30-1826 - Joseph COOPER aged 17 yrs. on Feb. 1, 1826, Mary COOPER aged 15 yrs.
     on July 11, 1826 and Rhoda COOPER aged 13 yrs. on Feb. 1826 chose Joseph
     Cooper and Benjamin Owens as their guardians and Cooper and Owens to also
     serve as guardians of Allen COOPER aged 11 yrs. and Abijah COOPER aged 9 yrs.,
     all heirs of Isaac Cooper. Case #761. (Doc. G-1, p. 225)
5-31-1826 - Caroline SIMONTON aged 14 yrs. on Apr. 1, 1826 chose Joshua Worley
     as her guardian. Case #762. (Doc. G-1, p. 225)
6-2-1826 - John KNIFE aged 19 yrs. on May 25, 1826, Charles KNIFE aged 17 yrs.
     on Mar. 6, 1826 and Susannah KNIFE aged 12 yrs. chose Joshua Mills as their
     guardian. Case #763. (Doc. G-1, p. 225)
6-2-1826 - David Waggoner appointed guardian of Mary KNIFE aged 10 yrs., Catherine
     KNIFE aged 8 yrs., and Conrad KNIFE aged 5 yrs., children and heirs of
     Conrad Knife, dec'd. Case #764. (Doc. G-1, p. 225)
6-5-1826 - Catherine SEARING aged 13 yrs., heir of Henry Searing, chose Philip
     Searing as her guardian. Case #765. (Doc. G-1, p. 226)
6-5-1826 - Lewis DILL aged 18 yrs. and Amy DILL aged 14 yrs., heirs of John C.
     Dill, chose George Stump as their guardian. Case #766. (Doc. G-1, p. 226)

6-5-1826 - Mary Dill appointed guardian of Augustus DILL aged 12 yrs., heir of
     John C. Dill, dec'd. Case #767. (Doc. G-1, p. 226)
6-5-1826 - John BECKER aged 14 yrs. in Jan. 1826, heir of Peter Becker, dec'd,
     chose Jacob Oblinger as his guardian. Case #768. (Doc. G-1, p. 229)
9-25-1826 - Lydia KARGES aged 12 yrs. in June 1826 chose Samuel Himes as her
     guardian. Case #775. (Doc. G-1, p. 258)
9-25-1826 - John SHEPPERD, aged 14 yrs., son of John Shepperd, dec'd, dec'd, chose
     Anna Shepperd as his guardian. Case #777. (Doc. G-1, p. 258)
9-25-1826 - Idia Ann SCHENCK, aged 17 yrs., daughter of Garret Schenck of New
     Jersey, chose Sidney Denise as her guardian. Case #778. (Doc. G-1, p. 258)
9-25-1826 - Frederick Waggoner appointed guardian of Henry WEAVER aged 12 yrs.,
     David WEAVER aged 9 yrs. and Sarah WEAVER aged 6 yrs., heirs of Henry Weaver,
     dec'd. Case #781. Peter Weaver appointed guardian of Daniel WEAVER aged 5
     yrs. and Mary WEAVER aged 3 yrs., heirs of Henry Weaver, dec'd. Case #782.
     (Doc. G-1, p. 259)
9-25-1826 - Henry Hipple appointed guardian of Samuel KINNAMAN born Aug. 5, 1813,
     Washington KINNAMAN born June 17, 1816 and Walter KINNAMAN born May 27, 1818,
     heirs of Samuel J. Kinnaman, dec'd. Case #783. (Doc. G-1, p. 259)
9-26-1826 - Anna CLARK aged 13 yrs. daughter of Jesse Clark, dec'd, chose George
     Beardshire as her guardian. Case #785. (Doc. G-1, p. 260)
9-28-1826 - Catherine KEPLER aged 14 yrs. in July 1826, daughter of George Kepler,
     dec'd, chose Peter Fouts her guardian. Case #786. (Doc. G-1, p. 260)
10-2-1826 - James T. Snodgrass appointed guardian of Neal HART aged 11 yrs., John
     HART aged 9 yrs., Sarah HART aged 7 yrs. and Hugh Peter HART an infant,
     heirs of Peter Hart. Case #788. (Doc. G-1, p. 260)
10-2-1826 - Henry LIGHTER aged 20 yrs. and John LIGHTER aged 17 yrs. chose
     Elizabeth Lighter their guardian and Elizabeth to also serve as guardian
     of Frederick LIGHTER aged 14 yrs., Elizabeth LIGHTER aged 12 yrs., Catharine
     LIGHTER aged 9 yrs., Christianna LIGHTER aged 7 yrs., Daniel LIGHTER
     aged 5 yrs., Mary LIGHTER aged 3 yrs. and George LIGHTER aged 4 months,
     children of John Lighter, dec'd. Case #790. (Doc. G-1, p. 261)
10-2-1826 - Catherine ARCHER aged 12 yrs. chose George Favorite and Elias Matthews
     as her guardians with Favorite and Matthews to also serve as guardians of
     John P. Archer, both children of Zachariah Archer, dec'd. Case #792. (Doc.
     G-1, p. 264)
10-2-1826 - Anna Pettigrew appointed guardian of David and Armstrong Pettigrew,
     heirs of James Pettigrew, dec'd. Case #793. (Doc. G-1, p. 269)
10-2-1826 - Thomas Conover appointed guardian of Thomas WILLIAMSON aged 12 yrs.,
     son of Wm. Williamson. Case #794. (Doc. G-1, p. 269)
10-3-1826 - Fielding Lowry appointed guardian of his son, Fielding Lowry Jr.
     Case #796. (Doc. G-1, p. 275)
3-5-1827 - Leonard Hier appointed guardian of Phebe CAYLOR aged 8 yrs. in June
     1826, daughter of Joseph Caylor and one of the heirs at law under will of John
     Burkhard, dec'd, in right of her mother who was entitled to a legacy. Case
     #800. (Doc. G-1, p. 321)
3-5-1827 - Rudy HIER aged 20 yrs. chose Leonard Hier as her guardian. Case #801.
     (Doc. G-1, p. 321)
3-5-1827 - Nathaniel MAXWELL aged 18 yrs. and Phebe MAXWELL aged 16 yrs. chose
     Thomas Maxwell as their guardian and Thomas Maxwell also to serve as guardian
     of George MAXWELL aged 13 yrs., all heirs of Thomas Maxwell. Case #802.
     (Doc. G-1, p. 321)

3-5-1827 - Jonathan D. Rouk appointed guardian of Abraham SHOWER aged 13 yrs.,
Polly Ann SHOWER aged 10 yrs. and Delia SHOWER aged 8 yrs., children and heirs
of David Shower, dec'd. Case #803. (Doc. G-1, p. 322)

3-5-1827 - Daniel WAREHAM aged 16 yrs., son of Philip Wareham, chose William Mc-
Creary as his guardian. Case #805. (Doc. G-1, p. 322)

3-5-1827 - Mary Rodes appointed guardian of Jefferson RODES ages 11 yrs., Delilah
RODES aged 8 yrs., Henry RODES aged 6 yrs., Eden RODES aged 4 yrs. and Maria
RODES aged 3 yrs., children of Jacob Rodes. Case #806. (Doc. G-1, p. 322)

3-9-1827 - Mary GEPHART aged 15 yrs., Elizabeth GEPHART aged 15 yrs. and Rebecca
GEPHART aged 12 yrs. chose Chreistopher Schuppert as their guardian with
Schuppert also to serve as guardian of George GEPHART aged 9 yrs. and Sarah
GEPHART aged 6 yrs., heirs of George Gephart, dec'd. Case #807. (Doc. G-1,
p. 323)

3-13-1827 - Thomas BROWN aged 15 yrs., son of Joseph Brown, dec'd, chose Elisha
Brabham as his guardian. Case #808. (Doc. G-1, p. 324)

3-13-1827 - Barbara PAINTER aged 15 yrs. and Ann PAINTER aged 14 yrs. chose John
T. Kinnaman as their guardian and Kinnaman also to serve as guardian of David
PAINTER aged 10 yrs., all heirs of Mathias Painter, dec'd. Case #809.
(Doc. G-1, p. 332)

7-23-1827 - Benjamin Hutchins appointed guardian of Joseph TOMLINSON aged 12 yrs.
Case #819. (Doc. G-1, p. 372)

7-23-1827 - Elizabeth HUFFMAN aged 15 yrs. chose John Steele as her guardian.
Case #821. Mary HUFFMAN aged 14 yrs. chose Samuel Rohrer as her guardian.
Case #822. (Doc. G-1, p. 372)

7-25-1827 - Samuel HEISTAND appointed guardian of Rosannah HEISTAND aged 9 yrs.,
sole heir of Peter Heistand, dec'd. Case #825. (Doc. G-1, p. 373)

7-25-1827 - John Duncan CAMPBELL aged 20 yrs. and William CAMPBELL aged 17 yrs.,
heirs of John D. Campbell, dec'd, chose Robert C. Crawford as their guardian.
Case #826. (Doc. G-1, p. 373)

7-30-1827 - George HARTSEL aged 14 yrs. chose Joseph Watson as his guardian.
Case #828. (Doc. G-1, p. 377)

7-30-1827 - Charles CARPENTER aged 16 yrs., son of Hopkins Carpenter, dec'd, chose
James Steele as his guardian. Case #829. (Doc. G-1, p. 382)

7-30-1827 - Daniel CROY aged 15 yrs. and James CROY aged 14 yrs., heirs of John
Croy, chose John Croy as their guardian. Case #830. (Doc. G-1, p. 383)

10-22-1827 - John WEAD aged 20 yrs. and Mary Jane WEAD aged 18 yrs. children of
Jane Wead late Jane Gibson, dec'd, chose Robert Wead, their father as their
guardian. Case #834. (Doc. H-1, p. 17)

10-29-1827 - James CAMPBELL aged 16 yrs., heir of John D. Campbell, dec'd, chose
Robert C. Crawford as his guardian. Case #843. (Doc. H-1, p. 25)

10-29-1827 - Margaret Campbell appointed guardian of Shach Bazar Bently CAMPBELL
aged 10 yrs. and Samuel A. Campbell aged 7 yrs., heirs of John D. Campbell.
Case #844. (Doc. H-1, p. 25)

10-29-1827 - George Olinger appointed guardian of John HUFFMAN aged 13 yrs.,
Lydia HUFFMAN aged 9 yrs., Sarah HUFFMAN aged 16 yrs. and Fanny HUFFMAN aged
5 yrs., heirs of George Huffman, dec'd. Case #846. (Doc. H-1, p. 28)

10-30-1827 - William PHILLIPS aged 18 yrs. chose William Brown as his guardian.
Case #848. (Doc. H-1, p. 33)

10-30-1827 - Enos KELLER aged 16 yrs. chose Joseph Kessler as his guardian. Case
#849. (Doc. H-1, p. 33)

3-3-1828 - Felix THOMPKINS aged 18 yrs. chose Obadiah B. Conover as his guardian. Case #860. (Doc. H-1, p. 157)

3-3-1828 - Susannah WARNER aged 14 yrs. chose Henry Brombaugh as her guardian, with Henry to also serve as guardian of Elizabeth WARNER aged 11 yrs. and Christian WARNER aged 5 yrs., all heirs of Andrew Warner. Case #863. (Doc. H-1, p. 158)

3-3-1828 - Huldah WAYMIRE aged 18 yrs., Andrew WAYMIRE aged 17 yrs., Elizabeth WAYMIRE aged 15 yrs. and Rebecca WAYMIRE aged 13 yrs. chose Abraham Huffman as their guardian with Abraham to also serve as guardian of John WAYMIRE aged 11 yrs., Enoch WAYMIRE aged 8 yrs. and Lydia WAYMIRE aged 6 yrs., all heirs of Frederick Waymire. Case #864. (Doc. H-1, p. 159). 9-29-1829 - Huldah mar. John Staley and Elizabeth mar. Eli Hoffman. (Doc. H-1, p. 463)

3-5-1828 - Ebenezer B. BRODWELL aged 20 yrs. and Mary L. BROADWELL aged 16 yrs. chose Silas Broadwell as their guardian with Silas to also serve as guardian of Josiah BROADWELL aged 13 yrs., Ann BROADWELL aged 7 yrs., Silas BROADWELL aged 5 yrs. and Susan BROADWELL aged 8 months, all children of said Silas Broadwell. Case #866. (Dod. H-1, p. 160)

3-6-1828 - Joseph BROWN aged 17 yrs., son of James Brown, dec'd, chose William Haney as his guardian. Case #868. (Doc. H-1, p. 160)

3-7-1828 - Osins MUSSLEMAN aged 15 yrs., son of David Mussleman, dec'd, chose John Mussleman as his guardian. Case #869. (Doc. H-1, p. 161)

3-10-1828 - David WAGONER aged 14 yrs. and Susannah WAGONER aged 13 yrs. chose John Wagoner as their guardian with John to also serve as guardian of Elizabeth WAGONER aged 11 yrs., Esther WAGONER aged 10 yrs. and Benjamin WAGONER aged 9 yrs., all heirs of Martin Waybright Sr., dec'd. Case #871. (Doc. H-1, p.163)

3-10-1828 - John MURRAY aged 20 yrs., Jacob MURRAY aged 18 yrs., Daniel MURRAY aged 15 yrs. and Catharine MURRAY aged 14 yrs. chose their mother, Elizabeth Murray as their guardian with said Elizabeth to also serve as guardian of Elizabeth MURRAY aged 9 yrs., all heirs of John Murray, dec'd. Case #872. (Doc. H-1, p. 164)

3-10-1828 - Ethan L. McCOLLOM aged 16 yrs., heir of Hugh McCollom, dec'd, chose Elisha Brabham as his guardian. Case #873. (Doc. H-1, p. 164)

3-10-1828 - James COLLINS aged 14 yrs., son of John Collins, dec'd, chose Obadiah B. Conover his guardian. Case #874. (Doc. H-1, p. 165)

3-10-1828 - George Swank appointed guardian of his son, Jacob SWANK aged 13 yrs. Case #875. (Doc. H-1, p. 168)

3-10-1828 - Samuel KELLY aged 14 yrs., an illegitmate child by Catharine Kelly, chose Abraham Durst as his guardian. Case #876. (Doc. H-1, p. 169)

3-11-1828 - Christian G. Espich appointed guardian of Philip HOLLER, an insane person of German twp. Case #879. (Doc. H-1, p. 174)

3-12-1828 - John BUCKWALTER aged 16 yrs. and Mary BUCKWALTER aged 14 yrs. chose Michael Moyer as their guardian and court appointed P. Moyer guardian of Benjamin BUCKWALTER aged 8 yrs. and Daniel BUCKWALTER aged 4 yrs., all heirs of John Buckwalter, dec'd. Case #881. (Doc. H-1, p. 175)

3-12-1828- Horatio REY aged 13 yrs., son of James REY, dec'd, chose H. G. Phillips as his guardian. Case #882. (Doc. H-1, p. 175)

7-21-1828 - Mary Kelly appointed guardian of Emerline KELLY aged 6 yrs., Clinton KELLY aged 4 yrs. and Hannah Ann KELLY aged 2 yrs., heirs of John Kelly. Case #888. (Doc. H-1, p. 235)

7-21-1828 - Jacob Gripe appointed guardian of Henry GRIPE aged 11 yrs., Samuel
GRIPE aged 10 yrs., Mary GRIPE aged 8 yrs. and Catharine GRIPE aged 7 yrs.,
heirs of___(left blank) Gripe. Case #890. (Doc. H-1, p. 235)

7-21-1828 - Elizabeth WARNER aged 14 yrs. chose Henry Brombaugh as her guardian.
Case #891. (Doc. H-1, p. 235)

7-21-1828 - John TAPSCOT aged 14 yrs. chose Wm M. Smith as his guardian. Case
#892. (Doc. H-1, p. 235)

7-21-1828 - Jerry Caldwell appointed guardian of Mary Jane IRWIN aged 5 yrs., minor
daughter of James Irwin and heir of Agnes and Jno. McKee, dec'd of Pennsylvania. Case #895. (Doc. H-1, p. 236)

7-21-1828 - Christian Winebrenner appointed guardian of John MOSSEY aged 13 yrs.,
minor heir of Henry MASSEY, dec'd. Case #896. (Doc. H-1, p. 236)

7-21-1828 - Obadiah B. Conover appointed guardian of Brainard SMITH, an insane
person, court refused appointment on 7-26-1828 and appointed Ira I. Fenn
guardian. Case # 897. (Doc. H-1, p. 236-240)

7-24-1828 - Betsy SWANK aged 15 yrs. chose George Swank as her guardian. Case
#899. (Doc. H-1, p. 239)

7-25-1828 - Michael SWANK aged 16 yrs., son of Jacob Swank, dec'd, chose John
Stump as his guardian. Case #902. (Doc. H-1, p. 240)

7-28-1828 - Joseph DAVID aged 14 yrs. chose Stephen David as his guardian. Case
#903. (Doc. H-1, p. 241)

7-28-1828 - Samuel HARSHBERGER aged 14 yrs., heir of Jacob Harshberger, chose
Jonas Harshberger as his guardian. Case #906. (Doc. H-1, p. 246)

7-28-1828 - Jacob Dininger appointed guardian of Elizabeth DININGER aged 8 yrs.,
Catharine Dininger aged 6 yrs., John Dininger aged 4 yrs., heirs of John
Dininger, dec'd. Case #907. (Doc. H-1, p. 249)

7-29-1828 - Daniel AZEWALT (OSWALT?) aged 16 yrs., heir of Daniel Azewalt, chose
Elizabeth Azewalt, his mother as his guardian. Case #908. (Doc. H-1, p. 258)

8-1-1828 - Mary Ann HART aged 16 yrs., heir of Peter Hart, dec'd, chose James
Snodgrass as her guardian. Case #910. (Doc. H-1, p. 258)

10-20-1828 - Frederick Gundner appointed guardian of Charles Frederick GUNDNER
and Henry Theodore GUNDNER, children of said Frederick Gundner and Catharine
his late wife. Case #919. (Doc. H-a, p. 301)

10-20-1828 - Joseph McCREIGHT aged 16 yrs., son of Thomas McCreight chose Lat
Cooper as his guardian. Case #920. (Doc. H-1, p. 301)

10-20-1828 - William BOURNE aged 15 yrs., son of Jas. Bourne, chose John W. Van
Cleve as his guardian. Case #921. (Doc. H-1, p. 301)

10-21-1828 - Jane SHEARER aged 15 yrs., chose her father, Christian Shearer as
her guardian. Case #923. (Doc. H-1, p. 302)

10-27-1828 - Catherine P. Irwin appointed guardian of Andrew Barr IRWIN aged 19
months, heir of Andrew Irwin, dec'd. Case #927. (Doc. H-1, p. 311)

10-28-1828 - Elias Murray appointed guardian of Ann Maria Murray aged 12 yrs.,
Julius Abbott Murray aged 10 yrs., Julian Huntington Murray aged 8 yrs. and
Lucius Junius Murray aged 5 yrs., heirs of Moses Bigsby. Case #929. (Doc.
H-1, p. 318)

3-9-1829 - Jacob Methard appointed guardian of his son, James METHARD aged 12 yrs.
Case #931. (Doc. H-1, p. 380)

3-9-1829 - John GALLAHAN aged 19 yrs. and Mary GALLAHAN aged 16 yrs., children of
Edward Gallahan, dec'd, chose Edward Coblentz and John Johnson as their
guardians. Case #937. (Doc. H-1, p. 381)

3-9-1829 - Samuel Robbins appointed guardian of Amos H. ROBBINS aged 9 yrs.,
Bathshebe ROBBINS aged 8 yrs., Deborah ROBBINS aged 6 yrs. and Elenor H.
ROBBINS aged 4 yrs., heirs of Aaron Robbins. Case #940. (Doc. H-1, p. 382)

3-9-1829 - Benjamin BENHAM aged 17 yrs. chose James Russell as his guardian.
Case #942. (Doc. H-1, p. 382)

3-9-1829 - Henry Shiedler appointed guardian of Samuel STONER aged 12 yrs., Sarah
STONER aged 9 yrs., Susan STONER aged 8 yrs., Jacob STONER aged 6 yrs., Aaron
STONER aged 5 yrs. and Elizabeth STONER aged 2 yrs., heirs of Abraham Stoner,
dec'd. Case #942. (Doc. H-1, p. 382)

3-10-1829- Rachel FLORA aged 12 yrs., daughter and heir of Henry Flora, dec'd, chose
Christian Shively as her guardian. Case #945. (Doc. H-1, p. 383)

3-31-1829 - Josiah Broadwell appointed guardian of Thomas VORE, Rebecca VORE,
Peter VORE and Mary VORE, heirs of Rebecca Vore, dec'd. Case #948. (Doc.
H-a, p. 400)

6-1-1829 - John Snowbarger appointed guardian of Susannah ZOOK aged 3 yrs., heir
of Samuel Zook, dec'd. Case #951. (Doc. H-1, p. 430)

6-3-1829 - Daniel Young appointed guardian of Jefferson A. YOUNG a minor illegitmate
child born Oct. last of whom Daniel AGENBROAD is the reputed father. Case
#954. (Doc. H-1, p. 431)

6-8-1829 - Albert A. McCLURE aged 14 yrs., son of Wm McClure, dec'd, chose Joshua
Greer as his guardian. Case #956. (Doc. H-1, p. 431)

6-8-1829 - James Russell appointed guardian of Thoas. WATKINS aged 12 yrs., heir
of Jonathan Watkins, dec'd. Case #957. (Doc. H-1, p. 432)

6-9-1829 - Abraham Kinsey appointed guardian of Abraham, Lewis, Margaret, Anna
and Philip KINSEY aged 13, 12, 10, 8 and 6 yrs., children of Abraham Kinsie.
6-11-1829 - Mary KINSIE aged 15 yrs., daughter of Abraham Kinsie chose her
father as her guardian. Case #959. (Doc. H-1, p. 442)

6-11-1829 - John WODEMAN aged 19 yrs., Elizabeth WODEMAN aged 17 yrs. and Jacob
WODEMAN aged 15 yrs., heirs of Jno. Wodeman, dec'd, chose John Folkerth as
their guardian. Case #960. (Doc. H-1, p. 442)

6-11-1829 - Henry Hipple appointed guardian of Barbary LESHER aged 11 months on
17 June last, minor child of Jacob Lesher. Case #963. (Doc. H-1, p. 444)

6-11-1829 - Henry REGANS aged 18 yrs., heir of John Regans, dec'd, chose John W.
Vancleve as his guardian. Case #964. (Doc. H-1, p. 444)

9-21-1829 - Abraham STONER aged 19 yrs., Henry STONER aged 17 yrs., heirs of
Abraham Stoner, dec'd, chose Peter Creager as their guardian. Case #967.
(Doc. H-1, p. 445)

9-21-1829 - Daniel STONER aged 16 yrs., heir of Abraham Stoner, chose Henry
Shidler as his guardian. Case #968. (Doc. H-1, p. 445)

9-21-1829 - Samuel Noffsinger appointed guardian of Susan Noffsinger aged 11 yrs.,
Daniel NOFFSINGER aged 10 yrs. and Henry NOFFSINGER aged 8 yrs., children and
heirs of Catharine Noffsinger, dec'd. Case #969. (Doc. H-1, p. 445)

9-21-1829 - Elizabeth MILLER aged 14 yrs. chose her father, abraham Miller as
her guardian with Abraham to also serve as guardian of Jacob MILLER aged
13 yrs., Anna MILLER aged 11 yrs., Sally MILLER aged 10 yrs., Julia Ann
MILLER aged 9 yrs., Margaret MILLER aged 7 yrs. and Christiana MILLER aged
5 yrs., heirs of Christian Miller, dec'd. Case #970. (Doc. H-1, p. 445)

9-21-1829 - Daniel SNYDER aged 17 yrs., heir of William Snyder, dec'd, chose John
Mast as his guardian. Case #972. (Doc. H-1, p. 446)

9-21-1829 - George R. STURGEON aged 18 yrs. and Susannah STURGEON aged 15 yrs. chose Moses Greer as their guardian. Case #973. (Doc. H-1, p. 446)

9-24-1829 - Elizabeth VORE aged 13 yrs., heir of Joseph Vore, dec'd chose Josiah Broadwell as her guardian. Case #980. (Doc. H-1, p. 448)

9-28-1829 - Henry ZELLER aged 18 yrs. and Adam ZELLER aged 14 yrs., heirs of Henry Zeller, chose Michael Gunckel as their guardian. Case #982. (Doc. H-1, p. 451)

9-30-1829- John Canfield SMITH aged 15 yrs., chose Norman Fenn as his guardian. Case #983. (Doc. H-1, p. 463)

10-3-1829 - Nancy T. HENDERSON aged 14 yrs. chose Luther Bruen as her guardian with Luther to also serve as guardian of Jane HENDERSON aged 11 yrs., William C. HENDERSON aged 8 yrs. and Martha W. HENDERSON aged 6 yrs., heirs of James Henderson. Case #984. (Doc. H-1, p. 464)

7-22-1828 - Benjamin Owens and Joseph Cooper guardians of minor heirs of Isaac Cooper, dec'd appeared in court and made it known that Benjamin Owens is to remove from state of Ohio and asked to be removed as guardian, whereupon cour removed both guardians and Mary Cooper aged 17 yrs., Rhoda Cooper aged 15 yrs heirs of said Isaac Cooper, dec'd, chose Joseph Cooper and Denny Jay as their guardians with said Cooper and Jay to also serve as guardians of Allen Cooper aged 13 yrs. and Abijah Cooper aged 11 yrs., also heirs of Isaac Cooper, dec Case #992. (Doc. H-1, p. 238)

Contributed by: Mrs. Clyde Shilt, Rt. 3, Westbrook, Brookville, Ohio 45309

The following records were found in the Probate Court of the court house at Dayton. The docket and page number under which the original record may be found are given in parenthesis. The case number under which the original papers are filed is also given and it should be noted that a little additional information such as when the minor became of age, might be found under the case number.

3-1-1830 - Josiah Broadwell appointed guardian of Andrew HALL aged 9 yrs., William HALL aged 7 yrs. and James Madison HALL aged 5 yrs., children of Joseph Hall, dec'd. Case #993. (Doc. H-1, p. 478)

3-1-1830 - On affidavit of Phillip Weaver it is ordered that Frederick Waggoner be removed as guardian of David WEAVER and Sally WEAVER, minor heirs of Henry Weaver, dec'd and court appointed Michael Weaver guardian of the said David Weaver aged 12 yrs. and Jacob Weaver appointed guardian of Sally Weaver (no age given). Case #994½. (Doc. H-1, page 479)

3-1-1830 - John Oldfather appointed guardian of Jacob GOOD aged 7 yrs. and Susannah GOOD aged 2 yrs., heirs of John Good, dec'd. Case #995. (Doc. H-1, p. 479)

3-1-1830 - Daniel Stetler appointed guardian of Betsy GOOD aged 4 yrs., heir of John Good, dec'd. Case #996. (Doc. H-1, p. 479)

3-1-1830 - Elizabeth Long appointed guardian of William LONG aged 11 yrs., Elizabeth LONG aged 10 yrs., Susannah LONG aged 6 yrs. and Martha LONG aged 5 yrs., heirs of Wm. Long, dec'd. Case #997. (Doc. H-1, p. 479)

3-8-1830 - Thomas Rowan McELHANY aged 15 yrs., heir of Robert McElheny, dec'd, chose Jane McElhaney as his guardian. Case #999. (Doc. H-1, p. 484)

3-8-1830 - George Olinger appointed guardian of Hannah KIMMEL aged 6 yrs., heir of Jonas Kimmel, dec'd. Case #1000. (Doc. H-1, p. 484)

3-8-1830 - Henry AYRES aged 16 yrs., son of Stephen C. Ayres, dec'd, chose Samuel King as his guardian. Case #1001. (Doc. H-1, p. 487)

3-13-1830 - James LONG aged 19 yrs. and Jane LONG aged 17 yrs., heirs of William Long, dec'd, chose Elizabeth Long as their guardian, with said Elizabeth to also serve as guardian of Sarah Long aged 14 yrs. Case #1003 (Doc. H-1, p. 494)

3-13-1830 - Thomas Neal appointed guardian of Matilda SIDELER aged 10 yrs. on 19 of Aug. 1829 and Eliza SIDELER aged 8 yrs. on 1st of Jan. 1830, said children have no property. Case #1004. (Doc. H-1, p. 494)

6-15-1830 - Joseph H. Conover guardian of Alexander G. CONOVER requests removal from guardianship as unable to care for him because of body infirmities. Peter P. Lowe appointed guardian of said Alexander G. Conover. Case #1008. (Doc. H-1, p. 499)

6-15-1830 - Rhoda Clark appointed guardian of Jesse Findlay CLARK and Benjamin Franklin CLARK aged 4 yrs., children of Jesse Clark, dec'd. Case #1010. (Doc. H-1, p. 499)

6-21-1830 - George Olinger appointed guardian of Daniel KIMMEL aged 3 months, heir of Jonas Kimmel, dec'd. Case #1011. (Doc. H-1, p. 502)

6-21-1830 - Henry GEPHART aged 19 yrs., Elizabeth GEPHART aged 16 yrs., Daniel GEPHART aged 13 yrs., heirs of Henry Gephart, dec'd, chose Daniel Monbeck as their guardian. Case #1012. (Doc. H-1, p. 503)

6-21-1830 - Jacob STOKER aged 20 yrs., George W. STOKER aged 18 yrs. and Lucy Ann
STOKER aged 13 yrs., heirs of William Stoker, dec'd, chose Sarah Stoker, thei
mother as their guardian with said Sarah to also serve as guardian of John
STOKER aged 9 yrs., Elizabeth STOKER aged 7 yrs. and Sarah STOKER aged 4 yrs.
also heirs of William Stoker. Case #1013. (Doc. H-1, p. 506)

6-21-1830 - Overseers of the poor of Dayton twp. ask that guardian be appointed
for Mary WAMPLER and Nancy WAMPLER, idiots. Court appointed Ira J. Fenn
guardian. Case #1014. (Doc. I-1, p. 4)

9-21-1830 - John Snep appointed guardian of Sarah SNEP aged 3 yrs. and Maria SNEP
aged 2 yrs., heirs of Leonard Snep, dec'd. Case #1021. (Doc. I-1, p. 9)

9-21-1830 - Mary FENTRESS aged 16 yrs. and Ann FENTRESS aged 14 yrs., heirs of
George Fentress, chose Solomon Yount as their guardian. Case #1023. (Doc.
I-1, p. 9)

9-21-1830 - Joseph FENTRESS aged 16 yrs., heir of George Fentress, dec'd chose
Henry Hoover as his guardian. Case #1024. (Doc. I-1, p. 9)

9-21-1830 - Henry Yount appointed guardian of George FENTRESS aged 10 yrs., Elizabeth FENTRESS aged 8 yrs., Edward FENTRESS aged 6 yrs. and Rosannah FENTRESS
aged 5 yrs., heirs of George FENTRESS, dec'd. Case #1025. (Doc. I-1, p. 9)

9-21-1830 - William Clark appointed guardian of Betsy McCABE aged 11 yrs. Case
#1027. (Doc. I-1, p. 10)

9-21-1830 - William SISSON aged 17 yrs. chose Henry Stoddard as his guardian.
Case #1028. (Doc. I-1, p. 10)

9-24-1830 - Henry Hipple guardian of Geo. HORNER an insane person. No papers
in packet. Case #1030½. (Doc. I-1, p. 10). Sept term 1838 Hipple ordered
to settle estate. (Doc. K-1, p. 5)

9-25-1830 - Henry Hipple appointed guardian of William SHIVELY aged 7 yrs.,
Hariot SHIVELY aged 5 yrs., Sarah SHIVELY aged 3 yrs. and Mary SHIVELY
aged 5 months, heirs of Adam Shively, dec'd. Case #1031. (Doc. I-1, p. 11)

9-27-1830 - George Rowe appointed guardian of Samuel ANDREW aged 16 yrs. Case
#1033. (Doc. I-1, p. 13)

9-27-1830 - John Matthias CATROW aged 16 yrs., heir of Charles Catrow, dec'd,
chose Tobias Vanscoyck as his guardian. Case #1034. (Doc. I-1, p. 13)

9-27-1830 - Elizabeth Watkins appointed guardian of Jonathan WATKINS aged 10 yrs.
Clarissa WATKINS aged 8 yrs., Phebe WATKINS aged 6 yrs. and William WATKINS
aged 4 yrs., heirs of William Watkins, dec'd. Case #1035. (Doc. I-1, p. 14)

9-29-1830 - James Harvey McGREW aged 20 yrs., one of the heirs of James Mc Grew,
dec'd, chose Jacob Leedis as his guardian. Case #1037. (Doc. I-4, p. 23)

9-30-1830 - Sarah McGrew appointed guardian of Mary Ann McGREW aged 13 yrs.,
George W. McGREW aged 15 yrs. and John Steele McGREW (no age given), heirs
of James McGrew, dec'd. Case 1038. (Doc. I-1, p. 23)

10-2-1830 - James SISSON aged 16 yrs., son of James Sisson, dec'd, chose William
Kirk as his guardian. Case #1039. (Doc. I-1, p. 23)

10-2-1830 - Elvira SMITH aged 14 yrs. chose Martin Smith as her guardian, with
said Martin to also serve as guardian of Julia SMITH aged 13 yrs., Holland
SMITH aged 10 yrs., Hannah SMITH aged 6 yrs. and Amelius SMITH aged 4 yrs.,
heirs of Josiah Smith. Case #1040. (Doc. I-1, p. 23)

3-17-1831 - Jacob Whitsel appointed guardian of James WHITSEL. Case #1048.
(Doc. I-1, p. 26)

3-21-1831 - George Schaeffer appointed guardian of William SCHAEFFER aged 13 yrs.
and Samuel SCHAEFFER aged 10 yrs., children of Jacob Schaeffer, dec'd. Case
#1049. (Doc. I-1, p. 27)

3-2/-1831 - Joseph Kennedy appointed guardian of Caroline BROWN aged 10 yrs.
Case #1052. (Doc. I-1, p. 28)

3-2/-1831 - Horace RAY aged 15 yrs. chose Horatio G. Phillips as his guardian.
Case #1053. (Doc. I-1, p. 28)

3-26-1831 - Elizabeth MAHUSIN, heir of Isaac Mahusin, dec'd, chose John Martindale
as her guardian. Case #105/. (Doc. I-1, p. 32)

3-26-1831 - Aaron SNIDER aged 17 yrs., heir of Henry Snider, chose Ira J. Fenn
as his guardian. Case #1056. (Doc. I-1, p. 38)

6-7-1831 - Christian Winebrenner appointed guardian of Henry Frederick GRUNDNER
aged 8 yrs., heir of Frederick Grundner, dec'd. Case #1063. (Doc. I-1, p. 41)

6-13-1831 - William Creager appointed guardian of Abraham CREAGER, aged 16 months,
heir of Catharine Creager, dec'd, who was one of the heirs of Abram STONER,
dec'd. Case #1064. (Doc. I-1, p. 41)

6-13-1831 - Caleb GREEMEN aged 16 yrs. and 6 months, chose Abraham Darst as his
guardian. Case #1065. (Doc. I-1, p. 42)

6-13-1831 - Thomas McWHINNEY aged 17 yrs., heir of John McWhinney, chose Wm. Hamiel
as his guardian. Case #1066. (Doc. I-1, p. 42)

6-13-1831 - Barbara SCHAEFFER aged 12 yrs., heir of Jacob Schaeffer chose George
Schaeffer as her guardian. Case #1067. (Doc. I-1, p. 44)

6-13-1831 - Hannah Maria McCLEAN chose Peter P. Lowe as her guardian. Case #1068.
(Doc. I-1, p. 44)

3-16-1831 - Mary R. Rigby appointed guardian of Phebe RIGBY aged 4 yrs. and George
RIGBY aged 3 yrs., children of Richard Rigby, dec'd. Case #1071. (Doc. I-1,
p. 34)

9-19-1831 - Daniel ZEHRING aged 14 yrs., son of Henry Zehring, dec'd, chose
Emanuel Gephart as his guardian. Case #1074. (Doc. I-4, p. 59)

9-19-1831 - Elizabeth LANDES aged 19 yrs. and Mary LANDES aged 15 yrs., heirs of
Jesse Landes, dec'd, chose George Brower as their guardian. Case #1075.
(Doc. I-1, p. 59)

9-19-1831 - Catharine KEENER aged 15 yrs., heir of John Kenner, dec'd, chose Henry
Hipple as her guardian. Case #1076. (Doc. I-1, p. 59)

9-27-1831 - Elizabeth ELDER aged 16 yrs. and Benedict ELDER aged 14 yrs., chose
William A. Hopkins as their guardian, with said Hopkins also to serve as
guardian of Eve ELDER aged 10 yrs., all children of Charles Elder, dec'd.
Case #1082. (Doc. I-1, p. 73)

10-1-1831 - Mary B. LOWRY aged 18 yrs., Harriet S. LOWRY aged 15 yrs. and Ann E. P.
LOWRY aged 13 yrs., heirs of John SMITH, dec'd, chose their father, Fielding
LOWRY as their guardian. Case #1083. (Doc. I-1, p. 76)

11-21-1831 - William H. HARRISON aged 18 yrs. and Leonard B. HARRISON aged 17 yrs.
chose Edmon Harrison as their guardian, with said Leonard to also serve as
guardian of Caroline HARRISON aged 12 yrs. and Charles HARRISON aged 9 yrs.
Case #1088. (Doc. I-1, p. 78)

3-5-1832 - Mary Ann Roberts appointed guardian of John Wesley ROBERTS aged 11 yrs.,
heir of John Roberts, dec'd. Case #1094. (Doc. I-1, p. 81)

3-5-1832 - Phebe MILLER aged 17 yrs., heir of Moses Miller, dec'd, chose John Bower
as her guardian. Case #1097. (Doc. I-1, p. 81)

3-5-1832 - Catharine MILLER aged 15 yrs., heir of Moses Miller, chose Samuel
McFadden as her guardian. Case #1098. (Doc. I-1, p. 82)

3-5-1832 - Elizabeth McCORMICK aged 14 yrs., heir of William McCOMMACK, dec'd,
chose John A. Short as her guardian. Case #1099. (Doc. I-1, p. 82)

3-6-1832 - Wm H. Hopkins appointed guardian of heirs of Charles Elder, failed to give bond and appointment vacated. Elizabeth ELDER aged 16 yrs. and Benedict ELDER aged 14 yrs. chose Mathias Long as their guardian with Long to also serve as guardian of Eve ELDER aged 10 yrs., heirs of said Charles Elder. Case #1100. (Doc. I-1, p. 82)

3-7-1832 - Angeline HESS aged 18 yrs. and Frances HESS aged 15 yrs., heirs of John Hess chose Charles M. Varian as their guardian. Case #1101. (Doc. I-1, p. 82)

3-8-1832 - Joseph B. JOHN aged 19 yrs., heir of Benjamin John, dec'd, chose Leonard Miller as his guardian. Case #1102. (Doc. I-1, p. 83)

3-10-1832- George W. Smith appointed guardian of John MILLER aged 3 yrs., heir of John Miller, dec'd. Case #1103. (Doc. I-1, p. 83)

3-12-1832 - Amos Grey appointed guardian of Phebe Ann TURNBAUGH aged 11 yrs., heir of John Turnbaugh. Case #1104. (Doc. L-1, p. 82)

3-12-1832 - Levina BAKER aged 12 yrs., heir of David Baker, chose John Turner as her guardian. Case #1107. (Doc. I-1, p. 96)

3-12-1832 - George Warner appointed guardian of Susannah WARNER aged 10 yrs., Catharine WARNER aged 8 yrs., Mary Ann WARNER aged 6 yrs. and David WARNER aged 3 yrs., heirs of David Warner, dec'd. Case #1108. (Doc. I-1, p. 97)

3-13-1832 - William Graham appointed guardian of George SNIDER aged 13 yrs. and Mary SNIDER aged 10 yrs., heirs of Henry Snider, dec'd. Case #1109. (Doc. I-1, p. 106)

3-13-1832 - George MORGAN aged 15 yrs., son of John J. Morgan dec'd, chose James Wilson as his guardian. Case #1110. (Doc. I-1, p. 106)

3-16-1832 - Mary McMAKEN aged 14 yrs. and Joseph G. McMAKEN aged 17 yrs. chose Joseph H. McMaken as their guardian with Joseph also to serve as guardian of Ezekiel McMAKEN aged 13 yrs., heirs of Robert MOORE, dec'd. Case #1111. (Doc. I-1, p. 111)

3-16-1832 - Joseph H. Maken appointed guardian of Maria C. McMAKEN aged 5 yrs., heir of Joseph MEAD. Case #1112. (Doc. I-1, p. 111)

5-29-1832 - William John appointed guardian of Abraham JOHN aged 4 yrs., Mary JOHN aged 2 yrs. and Elizabeth JOHN aged 1 yr., children of William John, and heirs of Catharine John. Case #1118. (Doc. I-1, p. 115)

6-4-1832 - James Riddle appointed guardian of Isabella RIDDLE aged 11 yrs and 11 months and Abigal RIDDLE aged 9 yrs, children of said guardian and heirs of their late grandfather, James Riddle. Case #1119. (Doc. I-1, p. 117)

9-3-1832 - William Compton appointed guardian of Patty MORGAN aged 9 yrs., heir of Samuel Morgan. Case #1126. (Doc. I-1, p. 132)

9-3-1832 - Samuel SPENCE aged 20 yrs., Thomas SPENCE aged 17 yrs. and Mary Ann SPENCE aged 13 yrs., heirs of Andrew Spence, chose David Jenkins as their guardian. Case #1128. (Doc. I-1, p. 132)

9-4-1832 - Levi WALLASTON aged 16 yrs. and Susan WALLASTON aged 14 yrs., heirs of George WALLASTON, chose Levi Wallaston as their guardian. Case #1133. (Doc. I-1, p. 134)

9-5-1832 - Rachel Waggamon appointed guardian of Samuel WAGGAMON aged 10 yrs., Anna WAGGAMON aged 9 yrs., Elizabeth WAGGAMON aged 6 yrs. and Catharine WAGGAMAN aged 3 yrs., heirs of Joel Waggamon. Case #1134. (Doc. I-1, p. 134)

9-10-1832 - Nelson Donallan and David Hoover, overseers of the poor of Randolph twp. found Samuel MILLER to be an idiot and court appointed Jacob Miller, brother of said Samuel as his guardian. Case #1138. (Doc. I-1, p. 136)

9-10-1832 - Samuel STONER aged 15 yrs., son of Abraham Stoner, chose Henry Stoner as his guardian. Case #1139. (Doc. I-1, p. 136).

9-10-1832 - Elizabeth IZOR aged 14 yrs. and Mariah IZOR aged 12 yrs., heirs of Joshua D. Izor, chose Henry Shideler ad their guardian with Shideler also to serve as guardian of Daniel IZOR aged 9 yrs., Lewis IZOR aged 7 yrs. and Margaret IZOR aged 4 yrs., all heirs of said Joshua D. Izor, dec'd. Case #1140. (Doc. I-4, p. 136)

9-11-1832 - John William RIKE aged 16 yrs. and Daniel RIKE aged 11 yrs. chose Jno. Prugh as their guardian with Prugh to also serve as guardian of Henry RIKE aged 12 yrs., Adam RIKE aged 10 yrs., Catharine RIKE aged 8 yrs. and Philip RIKE aged 4 yrs., all heirs of Philip Rike, dec'd. Case #1141. (Doc. I-1, p. 145)

9-11-1832 - John CLARK aged 20 yrs. and Rebecca CLARK aged 16 yrs., heirs of Jesse Clark. chose Samuel Hager as their guardian. Case #1142. (Doc. I-1, p. 146)

9-11-1832 - Nathaniel Willson appointed guardian of Elizabeth WILLSON aged 11 yrs., and David WILLSON aged 8 yrs., heirs of James Willson. Case #1144. (Doc. I-1, p. 146)

9-11-1832 - Salmon Sanford appointed guardian of Peter SHENEFIELD aged 13 yrs., Jacob SHENEFIELD aged 10 yrs. and Christiana SHENEFIELD aged 7 yrs., heirs of William Shenefield. Case #1146. (Doc. I-1, p. 147)

9-11-1832 - Thomas COEN aged 16 yrs., son of Thomas Coen, dec'd, chose John Cline as his guardian. Case #1147. (Doc. I-1, p. 147)

9-11-1832 - Daniel BAXTER aged 19 yrs., heir of Daniel Baxter, chose Levi Jennings Sr. as his guardian. Case #1148. (Doc. I-1, p. 148)

3-11-1833 - Mary MARTIN aged 17 yrs., heir of George Martin, chose William C. Patterson as her guardian. Case #1150. (Doc. I-1, p. 153)

3-11-1833 - Calvin TEAGARDEN aged 19 yrs. and Henry TEAGARDEN aged 17 yrs., heirs of Abraham Teagarden, chose Thomas Crook as their guardian. Case #1152. (Doc. I-1, p. 154)

3-11-1833 - Abraham SHOWERS aged 18 yrs., Polly Ann SHOWERS aged 16 yrs. and Delilah SHOWERS aged 14 yrs., children of David Showers, chose Abraham Troxell as their guardian. Case #1153. (Doc. I-1, p. 156)

3-11-1833 - Tunis SCHENCK aged 15 yrs. and Sarah SCHENCK aged 13 yrs., children of Cryonce Schenck, chose John G. Lane as their guardian. Case #1154. (Doc. I-1, p. 160)

3-11-1833 - Gilbert Lane appointed guardian of Mariah SCHENCK aged 11 yrs., Daniel SCHENCK aged 9 yrs. and William SCHENCK aged 7 yrs., children of Cryonce Schenck, dec'd. Case #1155. (Doc. I-1, p. 160)

3-11-1833 - William CARLE aged 19 yrs., Charles CARLE aged 18 yrs. and David CARLE aged 16 yrs., children of David Carle, dec'd, chose Nathaniel Evey as their guardian. Case #1156. (Doc. I-1, p. 160)

3-12-1833 - Johnson CANFIELD, heir of Tunis Canfield, chose William Raymond as his guardian. Case #1157. (Doc. I-1, p. 167)

3-15-1833 - Peter CLOTTIS aged 16 yrs. chose James Brown as his guardian. Case #1158. (Doc. I-1, p. 167)

3-16-1833 - George Cullum appointed guardian of his son, James CULLUM aged 14 yrs. Case #1159. (Doc. I-1, p. 169)

5-28-1833 - John A. Deem appointed guardian of his children, James Argus DEEM aged 11 yrs., Willson DEEM aged 9 yrs. and Elizabeth DEEM aged 7 yrs., heirs of Moses MILLER, dec'd. Case #1168. (Doc. I-1, p. 179)

5-28-1833 - Eliza Ann GALLAHAN aged 15 yrs., heir of Edward Gallahan, chose John
Gallahan as her guardian. Case #1169. (Doc. I-1, p. 179)

5-28-1833 - Phebe HECKMAN aged 20 yrs., Abraham HECKMAN aged 19 yrs. and Catharine
HECKMAN aged 17 yrs., heirs of Peter Heckman and Mary Heckman, dec'd, chose
John I. Greybill as their guardian. Case #1170. (Doc. I-1, p. 179)

5-28-1833 - Isaac Hasket appointed guardian of Lemuel ENNIS aged 11 yrs., heir
of Thompson Ennis, dec'd. Case #1171. (Doc. I-1, p. 188)

5-28-1833 - Mary ENSEY aged 17 yrs., heir of Dennis Ensey, chose Elizabeth Ensey
as her guardian. Case #1173. (Doc. I-1, p. 194)

5-28-1833 - James CARL aged 15 yrs. and John CARL aged 14 yrs., children of David
Carl, chose Benjamin Wagganer as their guardian. Case #1174. (Doc. I-1, p. 19

5-28-1833 - Samuel GOODLICK aged 16 yrs., son of Samuel Goodlick, chose Thomas
Weakley as his guardian. Case #1175. (Doc. I-1, p. 195)

9-2-1833 - Magdalene OVERHOLSER aged 13 yrs., daughter of Abraham Overhalser, dec'd
chose David Hoover as her guardian. Case #1177. (Doc. I-1, p. 197)

9-2-1833 - Stephen Grove appointed guardian of Phillip GROVE aged 11 yrs., son of
Henry Grove. Case #1179. (Doc. I-1, p. 197)

9-2-1833 - Abraham ROBINSON aged 14 yrs. chose Christian Shearer and Richard
Taylor as his guardians with Shearer and Taylor to also serve as guardians
of Sarah Jane ROBINSON aged 6 yrs., both being heirs of John Robinson.
Case #1186. (Doc. I-1, p. 199)

9-3-1833 - Lewis RECHER aged 16 yrs., son of Peter Recher, dec'd, chose John
Recher as his guardian. Case #1190. (Doc. I-1, p. 201)

9-12-1833 - Magdalena MARTIN aged 19 yrs., Mary MARTIN aged 17 yrs. and Daniel
MARTIN aged 15 yrs. chose Absolem Mast as their guardian with Mast to also
serve as guardian of Rosa MARTIN aged 11 yrs., Jacob MARTIN aged 9 yrs.,
David MARTIN aged 7 yrs., Catherine MARTIN aged 5 yrs. and Barbara MARTIN
aged 3 yrs., all heirs of David Martin, dec'd. Case #1204. (Doc. I-1, p. 224)

10-7-1833 - David RODEBAUGH appointed guardian of Susanna SWARTZEL aged 3 yrs., sol
heir of Philip Swartzel. Case #1316. (Doc. I-1, p. 228)

10-28-1833 - Samuel STONER aged 17 yrs., heir of Abraham Stoner, dec'd, chose
Abraham Stoner as his guardian. Case #1219. (Doc. I-1, p. 230)

11-13-1833 - On application of Catharine Edgar, court appointed Benjamin Iddings
guardian of George B. Edgar aged 2 yrs., heir of Robert A. Edgar. Case
#1222. (Doc. I-1, p. 231)

11-13-1833 - John STANSEL aged 20 yrs. on 2 Dec. next, chose Samuel Broadaway as
his guardian. Case #1223. (Doc. I-1, p. 231)

12-5-1833 - John MILLER aged 17 yrs., Hannah MILLER aged 16 yrs. and Sarah MILLER
aged 15 yrs. chose Samuel Maxwell as their guardian with Maxwell also to
serve as guardian of William MILLER aged 15 yrs., Samuel MILLER Aged 12 yrs.,
Martha MILLER aged 11 yrs., Ephraim MILLER aged 10 yrs., Henry MILLER aged 8
yrs. and Emily MILLER aged 7 yrs., all heirs of Mary Miller, dec'd. Case
#1225. (Doc. I-1, p. 232)

9-13-1833 - Thomas GRIFFY aged 14 yrs. in August last, one of the heirs of Thomas
Griffy late of Darke Co., chose George Puterbaugh as his guardian. Case
#1233. (Doc. I-1, p. 222)

MONTGOMERY COUNTY, OHIO— GUARDIANSHIPS 1834-1837

Contributed by: Mrs. Clyde Shilt, Rt. 3, Westbrook, Ohio 45309

The following records are found in the Probate Court of the court house at Dayton.
The docket and page number under which the original record may be found are given
in parenthesis. The case number under which the original papers are filed is also
given and it should be noted that a little additional information such as when the
minor became of age, might be found under the case number.

3-17-1834 - Jonas FLORY aged 16 yrs., heir of Henry Flory, chose Abraham Weaver
    as his guardian. Case #1239. (Doc. I-1, p. 241)
3-17-1834 - Daniel W. KEILER aged 16 yrs., heir of Daniel Keiler, chose Elijah
    Gorsuch as his guardian. Case #1242. (Doc. I-1, p. 244)
3-17-1834 - Andrew Colhoun appointed guardian of his daughter, Mary COLHOUN
    aged 2 yrs. Case #1243. (Doc. I-1, p. 246)
3-18-1834 - John LESLIE aged 16 yrs., son of David Leslie, chose George Olinger
    as his guardian. Case #1344. (Doc. I-1, p. 247)
3-25-1834 - Alexander CONOVER aged 14 yrs., heir of Joseph H. Conover, chose
    Susan T. Conover, his mother, as his guardian. Case #1246. (Doc. I-1, p.250)
3-26-1834 - Mary NEWMAN aged 19 yrs., Eve NEWMAN aged 17 yrs., Ruth NEWMAN aged
    14 yrs., heirs of Thomas Newman, chose William Newman as their guardian with
    William also to serve as guardian of Mark A. NEWMAN aged 13 yrs. Case #1247.
    (Doc. I-1, p. 250)
3-26-1834 - Massa STOCKER aged 15 yrs., heir of Jacob Stoker, chose Adam Deam as
    her guardian with said Adam to also serve as guardian of Sarah Jane STOKER
    aged 10 yrs., both heirs of Jacob Stoker. Case #1248. (Doc. I-1, p. 250)
3-28-1834 - Susannah STOKER aged 14 yrs., heir of Abraham Stoner, chose Peter
    Creager as her guardian. Case #1250. (Doc. I-1, p. 251)
3-28-1834 - Cornelius MORGAN aged 15 yrs., heir of Cornelius Morgan, dec'd,
    chose David Emick as his guardian with Emick to also serve as guardian of
    Elizabeth MORGAN 11 yrs., also heir of said Cornelius Morgan. Case #1251.
    (Doc. I-1, p. 251)
4-7-1834 - Abram Overleese appointed guardian of Mary HISER aged 7 yrs. and
    Cyntha HISER aged 5 yrs., heirs of Peter Hiser. Case #1254. (Doc. I-1,
    p. 262)
7-21-1834 - Noah ARNETT aged 16 yrs. in Feb. 1834 and Philip ARNETT aged 14 yrs.
    in Oct. 1833 chose Adam Shuey as their guardian with said Shuey to also serve
    as guardian of Delilah ARNETT aged 9 yrs. on 1 Jan. 1834, all heirs of Philip
    Arnett, dec'd. Case #1255. (Doc. I-1, p. 263)
7-25-1834 - Henry WAYMIRE aged 18 yrs. in July 1834, Sally WAYMIRE aged 16 yrs.
    in June 1834, Rebecca WAYMIRE aged 14 yrs. in March 1834 and Rosanna WAYMIRE
    aged 13 yrs. in Oct. 1834 chose Charles Patty as their guardian. Case #1259.
    (Doc. I-1, p. 264)
7-26-1834 - David Lamme appointed guardian of David ETTER aged 6 yrs., heir of
    William Etter. Case #1261. (Doc. I-1, p. 266)
7-26-1834 - William G. Ewing appointed guardian of Joseph ETTER aged 3 yrs. in
    fall of 1833, heir of William Etter. Case #1262. (Doc. I-1, p. 267)
10-3-1834 - John S. Parsons appointed guardian of Richard M. PARSONS aged 6 yrs.
    in Oct. 1834 and George L. PARSONS aged 4 yrs. in Oct. 1834, children of
    Frances Parsons, dec'd, who was one of the heirs of Richard MASON, dec'd.
    Case #1274. (Doc. I-1, p. 299)
10-6-1834 - Lucy Ann Teigler GREENE aged 15 yrs. in Jan. 1834 and Eliza J. GREENE
    aged 14 yrs. in Sept. 1834 chose their mother, Mrs. Achsah Green as their

guardian with Mrs. Greene to also serve as guardian of Mary Sophia GREENE aged
10 yrs. in Jan. 1834, Harriet C. GREENE aged 5 yrs. in Dec. 1834 and Charles
Henry GREENE aged 2 yrs. in May 1834, all children of Charles R. Greene, Case
#1276. (Doc. I-1, p. 300)

2-23-1835 - Daniel YOUNKEY aged 17 in April next chose William N.C. Worley as
his guardian with Worley to also serve as guardian of John YOUNKEY aged 13
Yrs. in April next and Joseph YOUNKEY 11 yrs. in June next, heirs of John
Jonkey. Case #1285. (Doc. J-a, p. 1)

2-23-1835 - Elsey WILSON aged 14 yrs., heir of Hannah Wilson late Hannah BARRETT,
chose Simeon Wilson as her guardian. Case #1286. (Doc. J-1, p. 1)

2-23-1835 - On request of widow of John Clayton, court appointed William McCormick
guardian of Elizabeth CLAYTON aged 1 yr., Noah CLAYTON aged 3 yrs., John
CLAYTON aged 4 yrs., Harvey CLAYTON aged 6 yrs. and William CLAYTON aged 8
yrs., all heirs of John Clayton, dec'd. Case #1288. (Doc. J-1, p. 2)

2-24-1835 - Henry Stoddard appointed guardian of his son, Asa P. STODDARD aged
12 yrs. on 21st of Sept. 1834. Case #1289. (Doc. J-1, p. 2)

2-27-1835 - Allen COOPER aged 19 yrs. on 27 Mar. 1834 and Abijah COOPER aged 18
yrs. on 21 Feb. 1835, heirs of Isaac Cooper, chose Joseph C. Cooper as their
guardian. Case #1290. (Doc. J-1, p. 3)

3-2-1835 - William K. McELHENY aged 16 yrs. in April 1835 chose Robert Karr as
his guardian with Karr also to serve as guardian of Samuel McELHENY aged 12 yrs.
in May 1835, both heirs of Robert McElheby Sr. Case #1292. (Doc. J-1, P.4)

3-4-1835 - Jacob GROVE aged 17 yrs., son of Henry Grove chose Samuel Boyer as his
guardian with Boyer also to serve as guardian of Philip GROVE aged 12 yrs.,
also a son of Henry Grove. Case #1294. (Doc. J-1, p. 5)

3-13-1835 - Morgan HATFIELD aged 19 yrs. and John HATFIELD aged 14 yrs., chose
their mother, Elizabeth Hatfield as their guardian with Elizabeth also to
serve as guardian of Sarah HATFIELD aged 12 yrs., Alfred HATFIELD aged 10 yrs.
and Mary E. HATFIELD aged 6 yrs., all heirs of Jeremiah Hatfield. Case
#1298. (Doc. J-1, p. 10)

3-13-1835 - Amy Jane JOHNSON aged 12 yrs. in Jan. 1835 chose her mother, Mary E.
Johnson as her guardian with Mary E. to also serve as guardian of Henrietta
JOHNSON aged 9 yrs. in Aug. 1834, Caroline JOHNSON aged 6 yrs. in Dec. 1834
and Dennis C. JOHNSON aged 4 yrs. in Feb. 1834, all heirs of Joseph Johnson.
Case #1299. (Doc. J-1, p. 11)

3-11-1835 - Bathshebe THURSTON widow of Otho Thurston appointed guardian of
Durinda THURSTON aged 7 yrs. 6 June 1834, Mary Valentine THURSTON aged 3 yrs.
7 Aug. 1834, Isaac THURSTON aged 2 yrs. 8 Feb. 1835 and Charlotte Temple
THURSTON aged 1 yr. 7 Apr. 1835, children and heirs of Otho Thurston. Case
#1300. (Doc. J-1, p. 11)

3-17-1835 - Elizabeth Smith appointed guardian of Catherine SMITH aged 10 yrs.,
John SMITH aged 7 yrs., Isaac SMITH aged 5 yrs. and Henry Augustus SMITH
aged 2 yrs., heirs of Henry Smith. Case #1301. (Doc. J-1, p. 27)

3-17-1835 - George MUCK aged 18 yrs. in Aug. 1834 chose his mother, Margaret Muck
as his guardian with Margaret also to serve as guardian of Catherine MUCK
aged 11 yrs. in May 1834, both heirs of Johh Muck, dec'd. Case #1302. (Doc.
J-1, p. 27)

3-19-1835 - Valentine BUTT aged 14 yrs. and 2 mos., heir of Jacob Butt, chose his
brother, Solomon Butt as his guardian. Case #1303. (Doc. J-1, p. 28)

3-24-1835 - Samuel Bowman appointed guardian of Charity STOKER aged 4 yrs. 10 Sept.
1834 and Elizabeth STOKER aged 1 yr. 13 Mar. 1835. Case #1305. (Doc. J-1,
p. 29)

3-26-1835 - Jacob GARLOCK aged 14 yrs., 3 mos. 14 ds., son of Henry Garlock chose
Luther Bruen as his guardian. Case #1306. (Doc. J-1, p. 39)

3-27-1835 - Andrew BECKER aged 14 yrs. 23 Nov. 1834 chose Jacob Weybrighter as his
guardian with Jacob also to serve as guardian of David BECKER aged 12 yrs.,
both heirs of David Becker. Case #1307. (Doc. J-1, p. 39)

7-13-1835 - Jacob Ulery appointed guardian of Samuel SOLLEBARGER born 26 May 1832
and Anna SOLLEBERGER bor 1 Feb. 1834, heirs of Abraham Sollebarger. Case
#1315. (Doc. J-1, p. 45)

7-13-1835 - Elizabeth ARNETT aged 13 yrs. and 10 mos., daughter of Philip Arnett,
chose Adam Shuey as her guardian. Case #1317. (Doc. J-1, p. 46)

7-13-1835 - Daniel CRICKBAUM aged 10 yrs. 6 Feb. 1835, grandson of Susannah Holler,
chose George Arnett as his guardian. Case #1318. (Doc. J-1, P. 46)

7-13-1835 - George MACY aged 17 yrs. and Thomas MACY aged 15 yrs. chose their father,
John Macy as their guardian with John to also serve as guardian of his other
children, Isaac MACY aged 12 yrs., Mary MACY aged 9 yrs., Alexander MACY aged
7 yrs., William MACY aged 5 yrs. and Nancy MACY aged 3 yrs., all heirs of
Nancy Macy. Case #1319. (Doc. J-1, p. 46)

7-13-1835 - Leonard Miller appointed guardian of Benjamin F. CLARK and Jesse
Findley CLARK, twin brothers aged 9 yrs. on 8 Mar. 1835, children and heirs
of Jesse Clark, dec'd, the mother and guardian of said children, Rhoda Parsons
appointed as guardian by the name of Rhoda Clark having lately dec'd. Case
#1320. (Doc. J-1, p. 47)

7--20-1835 - James Deen appointed guardian of his children, Mary Elizabeth DEEN
aged 6 yrs., John Thomas DEEN aged 4 yrs. and Nancy DEEN aged 15 yrs., heirs
of Nancy Deen. Case #1325. (Doc. J-1, p.49)

7-20-1835 - Margery B. STILES aged 15 yrs. on 5 July 1835, daughter of Sarah REEDER
late Sarah Stiles, chose Samuel Wilson as her guardian. Case #1326. (Doc.
J-1, p.49)

7-20-1835 - Hiram DUNWIDDIE aged 16 yrs. in Mar. 1836, child of John Dunwiddie,
chose James Russell as his guardian. Case #1327. (Doc. J-1, p. 49)

7-20-1835 - Jane H. HENDERSON aged 16 yrs., William C. HENDERSON aged 14 yrs. and
Martha W. HENDERSON aged 12 yrs., heirs of James Henderson chose their mother,
Elizabeth as their guardian. Case #1332. (Doc. J-1, p. 51)

7-22-1835 - Solomon STIVER aged 19 yrs. in March last and Mary Ann STIVER aged
16 yrs., heirs of John Stiver, chose John Apple as their guardian. Case
#1334. (Doc. J-1, p. 81)

7-22-1835 - Absolem STIVER aged 18 yrs. and Catherine STIVER aged 15 yrs., heirs
of John Stiver, chose John Crider as their guardian. Case #1335. (Doc. J-1,
p. 81)

7-22-1835 - Jacob Weybright appointed guardian of Nathaniel FLORY aged 12 yrs.,
heir of Henry Flory. Case #1336. (Doc. J-1, p. 81)

7-28-1835 - Nancy Bridgeman appointed guardian of her children, John BRIDGEMAN
aged 7 yrs. on 7 Aug. and Mary L. BRIDGEMAN aged 6 yrs. on 1 Nov. 1835,
children of John Bridgeman. Case #1337. (Doc. J-1, p. 83)

9-21-1835 - William Bradford appointed guardian of Thomas L. ALLEN aged 16 yrs.
on 25 April 1835, minor of John Allen, dec'd. Case #1342. (Doc. J-1, p. 92)

9-21-1835 - Mary Keiser, their mother appointed guardian of Daniel KEISER aged 14
yrs. on 14 Jan. 1835, George KEISER aged 13 yrs. on 14 Apr. 1835, John Q.
KEISER aged 9 yrs. on 13 Oct. 1835, William KEISER aged 7 yrs. on 17 July
1835 and Mary Ann Elizabeth KEISER aged 4 yrs. on 29 Apr. 1835, heirs of
John Keiser. Case #1343. (Doc. J-1, p. 92)

9-22-1835 - Samuel Broadaway appointed guardian of Johon A. BROADAWAY aged 8 yrs.
on 23 Aug. 1835, child of Ambrose Broadaway. Case #1344. (Doc. J-1, p. 93)

9-25-1835 - Daniel RECKER aged 15 yrs. chose Samuel Noffsinger as his guardian
with Noffsinger to also serve as guardian of Fanny BECKER aged 12 yrs. and
Samuel BECKER aged 10 yrs., children of Samuel Becker. Case #1345. (Doc. J-1,
p. 93)

9-30-1835 - Allis SCHENCK aged 16 yrs. chose Obediah Schenck as her guardian with
Obediah to also serve as guardian of David Schenck aged 11 yrs. and Phebe
Schenck aged 9 yrs., all heirs of David Schenck. Case #1348. (Doc. J-1,
p. 131)

10-3-1835 - Elias W. Spinning appointed guardian of Benjamin McLEAN (no age given)
heir of John McLean. Case #1350. (Doc. J-1, p. 136)

10-5-1835 - John Fetters appointed guardian of his children, Jacob FETTERS aged
5 yrs. in Oct. 1835 and George FETTERS aged 2 yrs. in Aug. 1835, heirs of
Julia Am Fetters. Case #1352. (Doc. J-1, p. 137)

10-5-1835 - Margaret Reichard appointed guardian of her children, David REICHARD
aged 12 yrs. in Mar. 1836, Samuel REICHARD aged 10 yrs. in Mar. 1836, Mary
Magdalena REICHARD aged 6 yrs. in Nov. 1835 and Elizabeth REICHARD aged 2 yrs.
in Jan. 1836, children of Samuel Reichard, Case #1353. (Doc. J-1, p. 137)

10-6-1835 - Jesse Parsons appointed guardian of Richard M. PARSONS aged 7 yrs.
and George M. PARSONS aged 5 yrs., heirs and John A. Parsons. Case #1354.
(Doc. J-1, p. 138)

11-20-1835(?) - Jacob H. Catterline appointed guardian of Percival H. CATTERLINE,
minor of Jacob Catterline. Case #1357. (Doc. J-a, p. 101)

11-20-1835(?) - Andrew McElheney appointed guardian of Jane McELHENEY aged 4 yrs.
Case #1358. (Doc. J-1, p. 135)

2-5-1836 - Jesse MICHAEL aged 19 yrs. and 1 month, son of Leah Michael, chose
Stephen Jones as his guardian. Case #1362. (Doc. J-1, p. 144)

4-25-1836 - Joseph Hauvermale appointed guardian of Mary SLIFER aged 11 yrs. and
Mahala SLIFER aged 9 yrs., heirs of Jacob Slifer. Case #1369. (Doc. J-1,
p. 149).

425-1836 - Abraham Voorheis appointed guardian of Rachel SLIFER aged 5 yrs. heir
of Jacob Slifer. Case #1370. (Doc. J-1, p. 149)

4-29-1836 - Almus E. VINTON aged 15 yrs. and Malvina VINTON aged 12 yrs. chose
Joseph Hubler as their guardian with Hubler to also serve as guardian of
David P. VINTON aged 7 yrs., all children of Rosewell M. Vinton. Case #1374.
(Doc. J-1, p. 150)

5-3-1836 - David MASON aged 14 yrs., heir of Richard Mason, chose his mother,
Frances Mason as his guardian. Case #1375. (Doc. J-1, p. 150)

5-6-1836 - Catherine S. HAINES aged 15 yrs. chose her father, Job Haines as her
guardian with Job also to serve as guardian of Charles Beatty HAINES aged 13
yrs., Harriet S. HAINES aged 11 yrs. and Job HAINES aged 9 yrs., also childre
of said Job Haines. Case #1377. (Doc. J-1, p. 151)

5-6-1836 - Jacob POORMAN aged 14 yrs., son of Daniel Poorman, chose John Stump as
his guardian. Case #1378. (Doc. J-1, p. 151)

5-9-1836 - Seymour YEAZEL aged 18 yrs. in July 1836, heir of Christian Yeazel,
chose John Yeazel as his guardian. Case #1382. (Doc. J-1, p. 153)

5-9-1836 - William Stoner appointed guardian of Lydia KUNS aged 11 yrs. in Dec.
last, heir of Jacob Kuns, dec'd. Case #1383. (Doc. J-1, p. 153)

5--9-1836 - Joseph KEISER aged 18 yrs. on 26 July 1836, chose his mother, Mary Keiser as his guardian with Mary also serve as guardian of her son, Jacob KEISER aged 12 yrs. on 25 May 1836, both heirs of John Keiser. Case #1384. (Doc. J-1, p. 153)

5-9-1836 - Jacob Waybright appointed guardian of Abraham STUTSMAN aged 4 yrs. on 18 Aug. last, son and heir of Abraham Stutsman. Case #1389. (Doc. J-1, p. 155)

5-9-1836 - George DAVIS aged 17 yrs., son of Lewis Davis, chose David Davis as his guardian, Case #1390. (Doc. J-1, p. 158)

5-9-1836 - Daniel DAVIS aged 15yrs., son of Daniel Davis, chose James Elliott as his guardian. Case #1391. (Doc. J-1, p. 173)

5-13-1836 - Henry Foutz appointed guardian of Enos YOUNT aged 10 yrs. in Nov. 1835, son of Enos Young. Case #1393. (Doc. J-1, p. 175)

5-16-1836 - George Parsons appointed guardian of Richard M. Parsons, child of John S. Parsons. Case #1394. (Doc. J-1, p. 175)

5-17-1836 - John STOKER aged 15 yrs. on 28 Jan. 1836 and Betsy Ann STOKER aged 13 yrs. in May 1836 chose Jacob Stoker their guardian with Jacob to also serve as guardian of Isaac STOKER aged 9 yrs. in Jan. 1836, all children of William Stoker. Case #1395. (Doc. J-1, p. 175)

8-23-1836 - Catherine LOURY aged 16 yrs. in May 1836, William LOURY Jr. aged 14 yrs. in Jan. 1836 and Sarah Ann LOURY aged 12 yrs. in Mar. 1836 chose their mother, Nancy Loury as their guardian with Nancy also to serve as guardian of George Maley LOURY aged 10 yrs. in Oct. 1836, Rosanna LOURY aged 7 yrs. in Feb. 1836, James LOURY aged 5 yrs. in June 1836 and David LOURY aged 5 yrs. in Jan. 1836, all children and heirs of James Loury. Case #1401. (Doc. J-1, p. 187)

8-23-1836 - Mary SHANEFELDT aged 16 yrs., child of William Shanefeldt, chose John Heck as her guardian. Case #1402. (Doc. J-1, p. 187)

8-29-1836 - Margaret BARKALOW aged 12 yrs. on 14 July 1834 chose Benjamin Vandevere and Benjamin Dubois as her guardians with Vandevere and Dubois to also serve as guardian of Eliza Ann BARKALOW aged 10 yrs. on 3 May 1836, Rebecca BARKALOW aged 8 yrs. on 4 Nov. 1836, Tobias P. BARKALOW aged 6 yrs. on 9 Jan. 1836, Phebe Jane BARKALOW aged 2 yrs. on 28 Mar. 1834 and James V. BARKALOW aged 6 months on 12 Aug. 1836, all children and heirs of James Barkalow, dec'd. Case #1403. (Doc. J-1, p. 220). (note: in Guardians Docket this is marked as Case #3341 & 3351)

9-1-1836 - Joseph Reichard appointed guardian of Catherine ARNETT aged 7 yrs. on Aug. 1836 and Benjamin ARNETT aged 6 yrs. on Jan. 1837, heirs of Philip Arnett. Case #1405. (Doc. J-1, p. 223)

9-1-1836 - Jesse Ware appointed guardian of Harrison GRIMES aged 13 yrs. William GRIMES aged 12 yrs., Lucinda GRIMES aged 8 yrs., Cornelius GRIMES aged 6 yrs. and Manerva GRIMES aged 4 yrs., children and heirs of Jeremiah Grimes and Barbara Grimes, both dec'd. Case #1406. (Doc. J-1, p. 224)

9-1-1836 - George W. DRILL aged 19 yrs. in May 1836, Jacob A. DRILL aged 17 yrs. in May 1836 chose Jemima Drill as their guardian with Jemima to also serve as guardian of John Wm. DRILL aged 9 yrs. and Amy Rebecca DRILL aged 5 yrs., all heirs of George Drill. Case #1407. (Doc. J-1, p. 224)

9-9-1836 - Joseph VANOSTRAN aged 17 yrs., heir of Joseph Vanostran, chose James Vanostran his guardian. Case #1411. (Doc. J-1, p. 228)

9-12-1836 - Andrew WALDEN a mulatto boy age 14 yrs., chose Jefferson Patterson as his guardian. Case #1412. (Doc. J-1, P. 228)

9-12-1836 - Samuel Boogher appointed guardian of Maria BOOGHER aged 9 yrs., George
BOOGHER aged 7 yrs., Elizabeth BOOGHER about 5 yrs., Mary BOOGHER aged 3 yrs.
and Catherine BOOGHER aged 2 yrs., children of Samuel and Mary Booher and
heirs of George BEARDSHIRE, dec'd. Case #1413. (Doc. J-1, p. 240)
9-13-1836 - Rosanna TROXELL appointed guardian of Mary TROXELL aged 10 yrs. in
1836, Lewis TROXELL aged 9 yrs. and Abraham TROXELL aged 5 yrs., children and
heirs of Samuel Troxell. Case #1414. (Doc. J-1, p. 244)
9-16-1836 - Christopher Folkerth appointed guardian of George W. SHOUP aged 9 yrs.,
Elizabeth M. Shoup aged 7 yrs. and Mary Ann Shoup aged 4 yrs., heirs of David
Shoup. Case #1415. (Doc. J-1, p. 245)
9-17-1836 - Holland SMITH aged 16 yrs. and Hannah SMITH aged 12 yrs., chose their
mother, Chloe Smith as their guardian with Chloe also to serve as guardian of
Aurilius SMITH aged 9 yrs., all heirs of Josiah Smith. Case #1416. (Doc.
J-1, p. 252)
11-15-1836 - Godfrey KESSLER aged 15 yrs. on 12 Aug. 1836, heir of Charles Kessler,
chose John Hale as his guardian, Case #1420. (Doc. J-1, p. 257)
11-25-1836 - Daniel WHIP aged 16 yrs. in June 1836, child of Daniel Whip and heir
of Christ. EASTERDAY, dec'd, of Maryland, chose George Shortz as his guardian.
Case #1422. (Doc. J-1, p. 264)
12-12-1836 - Jonas KINSEY aged 19 yrs. and 6 mos. and Susannah KINSEY aged 17 yrs.
and 2 mos., children of John Kinsey, chose Jacob Myers as their guardian.
Case #1427. (Doc. J-1, p. 284)
12-13-1836 - Luther B. HUSTON aged 17 yrs. on 19 Jan. 1837, child of David Huston
and heir of Abraham BARNETT, chose David Huston as his guardian. Case #1428.
(Doc. J-1, p. 287)
12-15-1836 - John A. IRWIN aged 19 yrs. in Apr. last, Minerva IRWIN aged 17 yrs.
in Mar. last and Eliza IRWIN aged 15 yrs. this month chose James Wilson as
their guardian and on application of Martha Miller late Martha Irwin court
appointed said Willson to also serve as guardian of Samuel IRWIN aged 12 yrs.
in May last, Isaac Irwin aged 8 yrs. in Aug. last, Mary Jane IRWIN aged 7ᵢyrs.
in Nov. last and Elizab th IRWIN aged 2 yrs. in May last, being children of
William Irwin, dec'd. Case #1429. (Doc. J-1, p. 289) Samuel Irwin indentured
to Aaron Sunderland. (Doc. K-1, p. 5)
12-17-1836 - Farlander MIKEE born March 24, 1834, daughter of Leah Mikee, chose
Abraham Darst as her guardian. Case #1432. (Doc. J-1, p. 264)
3-25-1837 - Harriet HARRIS aged 13 yrs., heir of Geo. Harris, chose David H.
Bruen as her guardian. Case #1447. (Doc. J-1, p. 318)
3-27-1837 - Christian LESLEY aged 15 yrs., heir of David Lesley, chose Jacob
Halderman as his guardian. Case #1448. (Doc. J-1, p. 318)
3-27-1837 - Elizabeth FULTZ aged 15 yrs. chose Samuel Rodeheffer as her guardian
with Rodeheffer to also serve as guardian of John FULTZ aged 14 yrs. in June
next, Catharine FULTZ aged 12 yrs. in Nov. next, William FULTZ aged 10 yrs.
in Nov. next, Samuel FULTZ aged 7 yrs. on 20 March instant, Isaac FULTZ.
Case #1449. (Doc. J-1, p. 318)
7-17-1837 - Eli MOTE aged 19 yrs. in Nov. 1837 and David MOTE aged 17 yrs. in
Dec. 1837, children and heirs of David Mote, chose Jonathan Mote as their
guardian. Case #1461. (Doc. J-1, p. 332)
7-17-1837 - Zenuah Kniesly appointed guardian of Benjamin KNIESLY aged 3 yrs.,
heir of Benjamin Kniesly. Case #1462. (Doc. J-1, p. 334)
7-20--1837 - Joseph BRENNER aged 20 yrs. in Nov. 1837, Elizabeth BRENNER Aged 18
yrs. in Nov. 1837, Elias BRENNER aged 16 yrs. in Sept. 1837 and David BRENNER
aged 14 yrs. in May 1837 chose George Kellenberger as their guardian. Case
#1463. (Doc. J-1, p. 334)

7-24--1837 - Philip EMERICK aged 17 yrs. in Dec. 1837 and Leah EMERICK aged 15 yrs. in July 1837 chose Thomas Emerick as their guardian with Thomas also to serve as guardian of Charles EMERICK aged 14 yrs. in Nov. 1837, all heirs of John C. Emerick. Case #1465. (Doc. J-1, p. 339)

7-24-1837 - Christian Rohrer appointed guardian of John EMERICK aged 12 yrs. in July 1837, Caroline EMERICK aged 7 yrs. in Sept. 1837, Aaron EMERICK aged 5 yrs. in April 1837 and Rachael EMERICK aged 1 yr. in May 1837, Heirs of John C. Emerick. Case #1466. (Doc. J-1, p. 339)

7-24-1837 - Daniel McCLURE aged 15 yrs. in Mar. 1837 chose Simon Eby as his guardian with Eby also to serve as guardian of Catharine McCLURE aged 10 yrs. in June 1837, heirs of Randall McClure. Case #1467. (Doc. J-1, p. 340)

7-24-1837 - Henry Gunckel appointed guardian of Jeremiah McCLURE aged 13 yrs. in April 1837 and William McCLURE aged 8 yrs. in May 1837, heirs of Randall McClure. Case #1468. (Doc. J-1, p. 340)

7-24-1837 - Henry TREON aged 18 yrs. in Oct. 1837 chose Christopher C. Emerick as his guardian. Case #1469. (Doc. J-1, p. 340)

7-26-1837 - Henry G. Markey appointed guardian of his children, Joseph MARKEY aged 8 yrs. in Nov. 1837, David MARKEY aged 5 yrs. in Nov. 1837 and John MARKEY aged 3 yrs. in Dec. 1837, heirs of Catherine Markey. Case #1472. (Doc. J-1, p. 354)

7-26-1837 - Daniel Hawvermake appointed guardian of Samuel WIRRICK aged 12 yrs. in Mar. 1837, Jacob WIRRICK aged 10 yrs. in Jan. 1837, Mary WIRRICK aged 7 yrs. in Jan. 1837 and Martin WIRRICK aged 5 yrs. in Aug. 1837, children and heirs of William Wirrick. Case #1473. (Doc. J-1, p. 355)

7-26-1837 - William SHEWEY aged 15 yrs. on 1 Aug. 1837, heir of Henry Shewey, chose John Zeller as his guardian. Case #1474. (Doc. J-1, p. 355)

7-26-1837 - Noah NACE aged 16 yrs. in Sept. 1837, heir of Jacob Nace, chose James Brown as his guardian. Case #1475. (Doc. J-1, p. 355)

7-28-1837 - David Martin appointed guardian of Christian MARTIN aged 12 yrs. in May 1837, John MARTIN aged 9 yrs. in Jan. 1837 and David MARTIN aged 8 yrs. in May 1837, children of Christena Martin, dec'd, and heirs of John GARBER, dec'd. Case #1476. (Doc. J-1, p. 357)

7-29-1837 - Joseph BRANNAMAN aged 18 yrs. in Sept. 1837, heir of Abraham Brannaham chose Daniel Booher as his guardian. Case #1478. (Doc. J-1, p. 358)

7-29-1837 - Finley BRANAMAN aged 19 yrs. in Jan. 1837, heir of Abraham Branaham chose Jacob Snyder as his guardian. Case #1479. (Doc. J-1, p. 359)

7-29-1837 - Eli Noffsinger appointed guardian of David PRESSELL an insane person of Jefferson twp. Case #1480. (Doc. J-1, p. 360

7-31-1837 - Benjamin Iddings who was appointed guardian of George B. EDGAR, minor son of Robert A. Edgar, dec'd appeared in court on 13 Nov. 1833 and asked to be discharged and court appointed James W. Kerr guardian of George B. EDGAR aged 5 yrs. on 8 July 1837. Case #1481. (Doc. J-1, p. 360)

7-31-1837 - Samuel Fetters appointed guardian of John PHILLIPS aged 8 yrs. and Homer PHILLIPS aged 10 yrs., heirs of Richard Phillips. Case #1482. (Doc. J-1, p. 360)

8-2-1837 - Christian Kauffman appointed guardian of David BRANAMAN aged 13 yrs. Jacob and Rosannah H. BRENAMAN aged 10 yrs., heirs of Abraham Branaman. Case #1484. (Doc. J-1, p. 363)

8-4-1837 - John Shroyer appointed guardian of Susan BRANAMAN aged 10 yrs. heir of Abraham Branaman. Case #1486. (Doc. J-1, p. 365)

8-4-1837 - David BALDWIN aged 14 yrs., son of Ellis S. Baldwin, chose John Robbins as his guardian. Case #1487. (Doc. J-1, p. 365)

8-5-1837 - Mary Marshall appointed guardian of her child, Mary MARSHALL aged 2 yrs. Case #1489. (Doc. J-1, p. 367)

9-18-1837 - Josiah SHIDELER aged 16 yrs. on 10 March 1837, heir of Joseph SHIDELER, chose Henry Shideler as his guardian. Case #1491. (Doc. J-1, p. 373)

9-18-1837 - Jonathan SHIDELER aged 14 yrs. on 28 Nov. 1836 chose George Brower as his guardian with Brower to also serve as guardian of Gabriel SHIDELER aged 11 yrs. on 28 Feb. 1837, both heirs of Joseph Shideler. Case #1492. (Doc. J-1, p. 373)

9-29-1837 - Jacob Holdermon appointed guardian of Absalom LESLIE aged 14 yrs. in fall of 1837, heir of David Leslie. Case #1493. (Doc. J-1, p. 373)

9-29-1837 - Fanny Neiswanger appointed guardian of George NEISWANGER aged 12 yrs. on Oct. 1837, Mary NEISWANGER aged 9 yrs. in Nov. 1837, John NEISWANGER aged 7 yrs. in Mar. 1837, Fanny NEISWANGER aged 5 yrs. in Aug. 1837 and Susannah NEISWANGER aged 3 yrs. in Oct. 1837, all children and heirs of George Neiswanger. Case #1494. (Doc. J-1, p. 374)

9-29-1837 - Eliza DILTZ aged 17 yrs. on 5 Oct. 1837, Susan DILTZ aged 15 yrs. in Oct. 1837 and Catharine DILTZ aged 13 yrs. on 1 Sept. 1837 chose Peter Long as their guardian with Long to also serve as guardian of John DILTZ aged 9 yrs. in Oct. 1837 and Cornelius DILTZ aged 5 yrs. in 1838, all heirs of Cornelius Diltz. Case #1495. (Doc. J-1, p. 374)

9-29-1837 - Mary SHAW aged 15 yrs. in Aug. 1837, daughter of Andrew Shaw and heir of Richard Shaw, dec'd, chose Sarah Neil as her guardian. Case #1496. (Doc. J-1, p. 374)

9-29-1837 - Eli Noffsinger previously appointed guardian of David PRESSEL an insane person asks to be removed and court appointed James A. Shedd as guardian. Case #1498. (Doc. J-1, p. 375)

10-6-1837 - Martha Jane OBLINGER aged 15 yrs. on 29 Jan. 1838, daughter and heir of Christian Oblinger, chose James Perrine as her guardian. Case #1503. (Doc. J-1, p. 401)

10-6-1837 - William John OBLINGER aged 17 yrs. on 14 Jan. 1837 chose George A. Hatfield as his guardian with Hatfield to also serve as guardian of Charles W. OBLINGER aged 13 yrs. on 8 Sept. 1837 and Horatio OBLINGER aged 11 yrs. on 8 May 1837, all heirs of Christian Oblinger. Case #1504. (Doc. J-1, p. 402)

EARLY DEATH RECORDS of MONTGOMERY COUNTY, OHIO
Book No. 1 - 1866-1875

The following is submitted by Mrs. Thelma Hinkle, 2709 Loris Drive, Dayton, Ohio
45449

Date submitted:
February 1968

MONTGOMERY COUNTY, OHIO
Probate Records, Dayton

These are adult deaths and small children were not copied. These were reported
in groups that occurred over periods of weeks or even sometimes months, and very
often, the same death was reported by more than one person, since both Doctors
and Ministers might have made a report of the same death at different times.
Therefore you will see duplications, but may find added data in these duplications.

Pages 2 & 3 - Reported by Wm. Lane, Sexton
Oct. 4, 1867 #10 - JACOB WONDERLY, b. Lebanon Co., Pa., ae 85-0-0 single, white,
died 7-12-1867 Ohio, Montgomery Co., Dayton.
Oct. 4, 1867 #12 - JAMES HARTLAN, b. Huntingdon Co., Pa., ae 54-9-0, laborer,
single, died 7-11-1867, Montgomery Co., Dayton; res. Mad River Twp.
Oct. - 1867 #37 - JNO. PERRINE, b. New Jersey, ae 94-0-0, married, white, died
1867, July 29, Ohio, Montgomery Co., Dayton; res. Dayton, Ohio
Oct. 4, 1867 #39 - HENRY GLENN, b. Scotland, ae 56-0-0, carpet weaver, married
died 7-30-1867, Montgomery Co., Miami City; res. Miami City.

Pages 4 & 5 - Reported by Wm. Lane, Sexton
Oct. 4, 1867 #45 - JNO BRADLEY, b. Morgan Co., ae 42-0-0, Steamboat Capt., married,
white, died 8-7-1867 Ohio, Montgomery Co., res. Montgomery Co.
Oct. 4, 1867 #52 - JOSEPH S. SWAYNIE b. Montgomery Co., ae 34, occup. Hotel,
single, white, died 8-15-1867, Tennessee,·Davidson Co., Nashville;
res. Nashville, Tenn.
Oct. 4, 1867 #56 - ELIZABETH DEL(R)AN, b. Germany ae 62-0-0, single, white died
8-22-1867, Ohio, Montgomery Co., Harrison Twp; Res. Harrison Twp.
Oct. 4, 1869 #61 - JNO. MATCACK, b. Virginia, ae 70, married, white, died 8-25-
1867 Indiana, Ft. Wayne; res. Ft. Wayne, Ind.
Oct. 4. 1867 #66 PETER BUNCH, b. Penn., ae 89-8-, shoemaker, single, died 8-28-
1867 Montgomery Co., Dayton; res. Dayton, Ohio
Oct. 4, 1867 - #73 - LEWISA BOWERS, b. Germany, ae 77-   , widow, d 9-8-1867 Ohio
Montgomery Co., Dayton; res. Dayton, Ohio
Oct. 4, 1867 #76 - THO. WESTROW, b. England, ae 35--, white, died 9-11-1867 Ohio,
Montgomery Co., Dayton, drowning; res. Piqua
Oct. 4, 1867 #79 - REBECCA WHITTON, b. Indiana ae 83-4-   , widow, d. 8-14-1867
Ohio, Montgomery Co., Dayton; res. Dayton, Ohio
Oct. 4, 1867 #83 - MRS. MANN, b. Kentucky, ae 33, widow, white, d. 9-20-1867
Ohio, Montgomery Co., Osborn; res. Dayton, Ohio
Oct. 4, 1867, #85 - MARTIN WILKIE, b. Scotland, ae 76, widow, white d. 8-21-1867
Ohio, Montgomery Co., Dayton; res. Dayton, Ohio
Oct. 4, 1867, #86 - JOHNSON V. PERRINE, b. New Jersey, ae 65, single, white,
d. 9-26-1867, Ohio, Montgomery Co., Dayton; res. Dayton, Ohio.
Oct. 4, 1867, #87 - SCYNTHIA E. HALTEMAN b. Zanesville, Ohio, ae 33, married,
white, died 1867, Sept. 27, Ohio, Montgomery Co., Dayton; res. Dayton

Book 1, 1866–1875   Pages 6 & 7
(The following were incorrectly dated 186(8) at top of page, followed by "ditto
  marks". The correct date is "1867")
Oct. 17, 186(8), #143 – BARBY GRIMES, b. Frederick Co., Md., ae 69-5-15, farmer,
            widow, white, d. 7-23-1867 Montgomery Co., Germantown; res. German-
            town. Father, Conrad. Mother, Elizabeth Spencer. Rept by Stierwalt,
                                                                                M.D.
Oct. 17, 186(8), #144 – JNO C. WEAVER – b. Butler Co., Ohio ae 29-7-21, farmer,
            married, white, d. 8-2-1867, Ohio, Butler Co.; res. Jacksonburg.
            Father, Jno. Mother, Esther Weaver. Rept. by Stierwalt, M.D.
Aug. 30, 186(8), #146 – WM. PAULEY, b. Lebanon, Warren Co., (Ohio), ae 31-10-20,
            Occup. Milling, married, white, d. 8-26-1867 Ohio, Butler Co.,
            Germantown; res. Germantown, Father, Jno. Mother, Mary M. Pauley.
            Reported by Steirwalt, M.D.
Sept. 30, 186(8), #149 – CORA PHILLIPS, b. Maryland, ae 36, single white, d. 7-18-
            1867, Montgomery Co., Dayton; res. Fourth St. Rep. by Dr. Clements
Oct. 7, 186(8), #157 – HENRY COX – b. Ala. (Alabama?), ae 36-1-1, laborer, single
            white, d. 7-30-1867, Ohio, Montgomery Co. Res. Clermont Co., Ohio.
            Reported Dr. Conndy.
Oct. 7, 186(8), #158 – WM. SKEEN, b. Ohio, ae 23, farmer, single, white, d.8-30-
            1867 Ohio, Butler Co. Res. Highland Co., Ohio. Rept. by Dr. Conndy
Oct. 12, 1867, #96 – THOS. WILKEE, b. unknown, ae 75— no occup., widowed, white,
            no date of death, died Ohio, Montgomery Co., Dayton; res. Dayton.
            (reported by Henry K. Steel, M.D.,-this is possibly same as #85)
Oct. 12, 1867 – #98, PHILLIP LEASOR, b. Germany, ae 48, occup. not known, white,
            d. 1867 Aug., 6 Ohio, Montgomery Co., Germantown; res. Germantown,
            reported by Henry K. Steel, M.D.
Oct. 12, 1867 – #99, ELIZABETH HOUSER, b. Maryland, ae 69—, occup. not known,
            white, d. 9-4-1867 Ohio, Montgomery Co., Germantown; res. Dayton.
            Reported by Henry K. Steel, M.D.
Oct. 7, 1867 – #103, SHOOGART WILKIE, b. Scotland, ae 76 —, widowed, white,
            d. 9-22-1867, Ohio, Montgomery Co., Dayton; res. Dayton.
            Father: Wm. Craig, Mother – Craig, reported by E. Kock, M.D.
Oct. 7, 1867, #104 – CHARLOTTE VELDER, b. Butler Co., Ohio, ae 60-0-24, no occup.
            married, white, d. 9-24-1867 Ohio, Montgomery Co., Dayton; res
            Dayton. Father:- Jno Sinkey; mother – don't know. Reported by
            E. Kock, M.D.
Oct. 12, 1867, #110 – MARY HOOK – b. Rockingham, Va., ae 80-7-16, housekeeper,
            single, white, d. 9-6-1867 Ohio, Montgomery Co., Perry Twp.
            res. South East Piermont

Pages 6 & 7
Oct. 9, 1867 #92 – CATH. FENSTEMACHER, b. Penn., ae 71-1-15, widow, white, d
            7-24-1867 Ohio, Montgomery Co., Alexandersville; res. Alexanders-
            ville. Father: . . Hock, mother . . reported by: David Winter,
                                                                    Minister
Oct. 12, 1867 – # – JOHN C. TORRENCE b. Mass. ae 55 – day laborer, widower, white
            d. 9-20-1867 Ohio, Montgomery Co., Perry Twp. res. Joel Wogerman's.
Oct. 1, 1867, #115 – D. J. KELLY, b. Ireland, ae 47 – Catholic Priest, single,
            white, d. 9-17-1867 – no place of death; res. East Second St.
Oct. 2, 1867 – #116, JACOB G. KING, b. Virginia, ae 59-2-2, Mechanic, married,
            white, d. 8-1-1867 Ohio, Montgomery Co.; res. Pyrmont, reported by
            Dr. Josiah Conner.

Oct. 2, 1867 - #118, MARY HOOK, b. Virginia, ae 89-7-16, single, white, d.9-6-
1867, Montgomery Co., Pyrmont; res. near Pyrmont. (same as #110
Sept. 28, 1867 - #119, ISAAC ANDERSON. b. Gr. Britain, ae 42 - Saddler, married,
white, d. 7-4-1867, Montgomery Co., Dayton; res. #6 Vanburen St.
Oct. 5, 1867 #123 - MARY GRINER (in different in in brackets is "BRINKLE")
b. France, ae 54, widow, white, d. 7-27-1867, Ohio, Montgomery Co.,
Dayton; res. Bline St., Dayton. (In column of Father & Mother is
BERKEL, could be the name of person reporting death, as from this
point this column is used for this when father & mother are not known)
Oct. 5, 1867 #124 - CAPT. JNO BRADLEY, b. France, ae 54, Steamboat Capt., single,
white, d. 8-7-1867, Ohio, Montgomery Co., Mad River Twp.; res.
Mad River Twp. Reported by Jacob Bosler, M.D. (same as #45?)
Oct. 5, 1867 #125, - MRS. HATTERMAN b. (ditto marks used - France or Ohio?) ae 54,
Ohio, Montgomery Co., Dayton, d. 9-27-1867; res. Franklin St.
Reported by Jacob Bosler, M.D.
Oct. 21, 1867, #131 - ELIZA VORHEES, b. Clay Twp., ae 46-7-23, single, white,
d. 9-21-1867, Montgomery Co., Ohio; res. Clay Township. Reported
by Rev. W. J. Emerson

Pages 8 & 9 (note year date at top of entry column is "1868" and ditto marks used
throughout page, but believe this should be "1867")
Sept. 30, 186(8) #134 - CARL CLAWORM, b. Prussia, ae 44-6-2, carpenter, married
white, d. 7-7-1867 Ohio, Montgomery Co., Dayton; res. Dayton.
Reported by Rev. Fred Groth.
Sept. 30, 186(8) #138 - L. R. BAIRER (BAUER), b. Germany, ae 77-9-22, widow, d.
9-8-1867 Ohio, Montgomery Co., Dayton. Rept. by Rev. Fred Groth
Oct. 17, 186(8), #139 - JNO BRADLY - b. Morgon Co., Ohio - no date - Capt. Steam-
boat, married, white, d. 9-6-1867, Ohio, Green Co.; res. Montgomery
Co. Rept. by Rev. W. D. Hykes? (Same as #45 and #124?)
Oct. 17, 186(8), #140 - LENA BRADLEY, b. Montgomery Do., ae 20, white, d. 9-3(or 8)
-1867, Ohio, Montgomery Co., Dayton; Res. Dayton - Father, Jno Bradley; mother, Sarah Bradley.
Oct. 18, 186(8), #141 - CHRISTIAN FORRER, B. Penn., Dauphn Co. ae 72-7--, farmer,
single, white, died 1867, Aug. 12, Ohio, Montg. Co. Dayton; res.
Dayton. ("Single" may also mean "widowed")

Contributed by: Thelma A. Hinkle, 2709 Loris Drive, Dayton, Ohio 45449
Abstracted from the "Miamisburg Bulletin", published weekly on Friday.

12-6-1872 - DIED Monday Nov. 2nd, Mrs. Sophia BROUGH, relict of John BROUGH aged 83yrs. 10mos. 5ds. Services Lutheran Church by Rev. Shultz. Mrs. Brough was born 27 January 1789 Dauphin Co., Pennsylvania. Moved to Ohio in the fall of 1831 and resided Miamisburg ever since. Confirmed in Evang. Lutheran Church in youth.

12-27-1872 - DIED, John Peter REICHARD, formerly of this place, committed suicide in Huntington, Indiana.

1-3-1873 - DIED, Friday 3d, Mrs. Mary Malinda ZIMMER wife of Jacob ZIMMER, Esq. Aged 44 yrs. 11 mos. 26 ds. Services Reformed Church by Rev. I. H. Reiter. Interment Miamisburg Cemetery. Mrs. Mary Malinda Zimmer's maiden name was KLINCK, born at Hagerstown, Maryland January 8, 1818, about the year 1830 with parents came to Cincinnati, Ohio and 1833 to Miamisburg. Married Jacob Zimmer on 4 April 1839 by Rev. Henry Heincke. Had seven children, four sons and three daughters, one son preceded her in death.

1-3-1873 - DIED, Mrs. Elias COTTERMAN of Bradford, Miami County, Ohio formerly of Miamisburg.

1-24-1873 - DIED, January 19, Henry BALLENBAUGH, aged 78 yrs. 9 mos. 4 ds. Services Reformed Church by Rev. I. H. Reiter. Burial in Private Graveyard on farm of Mr. Ungerer. Mr. Ballenbaugh was born in Wertemberg, Germany April 15, 1794, came to America in 1816, a few years later settled in Miamisburg. Married March 8, 1821 to Hannah UNGERER who preceded him in death March 3, 1872.

2-28-1873 - DIED, James M. CASKEY of this city, Saturday 22, aged 58 yrs. 4 mos. Services M. E. Church. Burial Union Cemetery. Born Rockbridge County, Virginia, October, 1814. To Ohio in 1829. Married Sarah McCALLAY on May 16, 1844. Leaves his wife, two daughters, mother, one brother and three sisters.

3-7-1873 - DIED, on the 2nd, Lydia wife of Isaac MOYER aged 47 yrs 11 mos. 10 ds. Member of Lutheran Church. Born Pennsylvania and immigrated with parents at an early date to this vicinity.

4-4-1873 - DIED, Catharine P. URSCHEL on March 30, wife of Lewis URSCHEL, aged 34 yrs. 8 mos. 3 ds. Born Pittsburgh, Pennsylvania. Member of the Evan. Lutheran Church. Immigrated first Cincinnati, Ohio in 1852. Married Mr. Urschell in Newport, Kentucky 1854 and immigrated with him to Miamisburg.

4-18-1873 - DIED, Henry STETTLER, April 12, aged 63 yrs. 7 mos. 13 ds. Native of Maryland. Married 18 July 1830 to Mahala SHARRITS. Member of Stettler Reformed Church since 1823. Interment Stettlers Church Cemetery.

4-25-1873 - DIED, Bernard REGAN, Monday 21, aged 44 yrs. 6 mos. 17 ds. Born Lower Canada, Oct. 4, 1828, to Miamisburg in 1855. Leaves wife, three children, mother, three brothers and two sisters.

6-6-1873 - DIED, Henry GEBHARDT, Monday 2d., aged 82 yrs. 2 mos. 11 ds. Native of Berks County, Pennsylvania. Immigrated in 1828. Interment Evangelical Lutheran Church Cemetery of Gettysburg.

The following records were copied from DOCKET A-1. Pages are given in parenthesis (). The case number (#) is also being given as quite often the estate packet of vouchers, receipts, etc. will give additional information.

DAVIS, Thomas of the State of Delaware - Adms., Hannah Davis, widow -
    11-22-1803 - #1 - (1)

BIGGER, Joseph of Washington Twp. - Adms., Abigail Bigger and James Bigger -
    11-22-1803 - #2 - (1)

MAULSBY, William of Dayton - Adms., Maria Maulsby and George Newcom -
    6-7-1804 - #3 - (5)

MAYER (MOYER), Henry of German Twp. - Adms., Elizabeth Mayer and Christian Mayer
    - Securities, Michael Mayer and John Mikesell - 11-6-1804 - #9 - (8)

COX, Daniel of Elizabeth Twp. - Adms., Joseph Coe and Elizabeth his wife - Securities, John Gerard and Jerom Holt - 11-6-1804 - #10 - (9)

SWINEHART, Gabriel of German Twp. - Adms., Salome Swinehart and Adam Swinehart -
    Securities, Jacob Fouts and Jesse Davenport - 11-17-1804 - #11 - (9)

GEPHART, Peter of German Twp. - Adms., Catharine Gephart and Daniel Miller -
    Securities, John Bowman and Zachariah Hole - 1-4-1805 - #12 - (9)

MITCHEL, Edward of Washington Twp. - Adms. Edward Mitchel and Sarah Mitchel -
    Securities, Benj. Robins and Thompson Ennes - 2-5-1805 - #13 - (13)

TAYLOR, William of Pennsylvania - Adms., Nathaniel Lyon of German Twp. -
    Securities, James Porter and Zachariah Hole - 8-27-1805 - #16 - (31)

BARNET, John of Dayton Twp. - Adms., Elizabeth Barnet and Abraham Barnet -
    Securities, David Riffle and Andrew Hays. - 8-27-1805 - #17 - (31)

SMITH, Josiah of German Twp. - Adms., Lettitia Smith - Securities, Andrew Tharp
    and Boaz Tharp - 8-28-1807 - #18 - (32)

CULBERTSON, John of Dayton Twp. - Adms., Ignatius Ross - Securities, Jerom Holt
    and Paul D. Butler - 8-30-1805 - #20 - (33)

DAVIS, Thomas of Dayton Twp. - Adms., Mary Davis - Securities, David Reid and
    Daniel C. Cooper - 9-28-1805 - #21 - (33)

BANTA, Abraham - Adms., Peter Banta - Securities, Jacob Long and John Vanausdale
    - 4-22-1806 - #25 - (38)

NEWCOM, Matthew of Dayton - Adms., George Newcom - Securities, John Folkerth and
    Jerom Holt - 8-28-1806 - #31 - (42)

KNOTTS, Nathaniel of Washington Twp. - Adms., Lydia Knotts - Security, John
    Price - 12-23-1806 - Deceased left four children - #32 - (46)

OLWINE, Jacob of German Twp. - Adms., Daniel Kemp - Securities, Martin Shuey
    and Christopher Emrick - 12-23-1806 - #33 - (46)

AIKEN, John of Dayton - Adms., John Driscol - Securities, John Grimes and
    George Newcom - 12-24-1806 - #34 - (46)

HAY, William of Dayton Twp. - Adms., Ann Hay - Securities, James Hay and Alex-
    ander Telford - 12-24-1806 - #35 - (47)

WOODS, Samuel of Dayton - Adms., Rhoda Wood and John Robb - Securities, David
    Squier and Robert Newcom - 2-4-1807 - #36 - (55)

YOST, Jacob - Adms., Casper Young - Securities, Stephen Jay and George Grove -
    2-4-1807 - #37 - (55)

SAUNDERS, Elihy of Elizabeth Twp. - Adms., Mary Saunders - Securities, Hezekiah
    Hubbel and Joseph Whitten - 2-4-1807 - #38 - (55)

HUEY, Robert Jr. of Dayton Twp. - Adms., John Folkerth and Albert R. Huey -
    Securities, James Miller and Christopher Curtner - 4-28-1807 - #40 -
    (64)

FOGELSONG, Christian of Jefferson Twp. - Adms., Barbara Fogelsong and Christopher
        Mason - Securities, Henry Hepner and Peter Weaver - 5-12-1807 - #44 (65)
GENTLE, John of Jefferson Twp. - Adms., William Newman and Hannah Gentle -
        Securities, Richard Cox and John Cox - 8-25-1807 - #46 - (68)
PLUMBER, Philemon of Jefferson Twp. - Adms., Sophia Plummer and George Sinks, Jr.
        - Securities, Thomas Newman and Jacob Byrket - 8-25-1807 - #47 - (68)
TRINE, Christian of Dayton Twp. - Adms. Peter Suman - Securities, George Grove
        and Francis Dilts - 4-29-1808 - #52 - (77)
STUART, John of Dayton Twp. - Adms., Peggy Stuart and James Millegan - Securities,
        James Patterson and John Patterson - 9-6-1808 - #54 - (78)
MURPHY, Doctor William of Dayton - Adms., Henry Disbrow - Securities, Matthew
        Patton and Henry Marquast - 1-3-1809 - #56 - (88)
ELLIOT, Doctor John of Dayton - Adms., Horatio G. Phillips - Securities, Joseph
        H. Crane and Isaac G. Barnet - 5-6-1809 - #59 - (95)
SCHWARTZEL, Matthias of German Twp. - Adms., Henry Crist and Jacob Colman - Sec-
        urities, Philip Schwartzel and Henry Sheidler - 10-28-1809 - #60 - (99)
BUCHES, Daniel - Adms., Samuel Buches - Securities, Peter Lehman and John Brad-
        ford - 5-1-1810 - #61 - (106)
KIRKWOOD, Robert of Dayton Twp. - Adms., Anna Kirkwood and Samuel Grimes - Secur-
        ities, Hugh Andrews and Jacob Long - 5-1-1810 - #62 - (106)
YOUNT, George of Randolph Twp. - Adms., George Yount, Jr. and Andrew Sinks -
        Securities, Daniel Hoover, Jr. and Thomas Newman - 9-4-1810 - #67 (119)
DAVIS, Lewis of Dayton Twp. - Adms., Mary Davis, widow - Securities, Jerom Holt
        and George Grove - 9-4-1810 - #68 - (119)
MILLER, John of Jefferson Twp. - Adms., Susanna Miller, widow - Securities,
        Daniel Miller and John Mikesell - 9-4-1810 - #69 - (119)
HATFIELD, Jonathan - Adms., Amey Hatfield and John Archer, Jr. - Securities,
        Benjamin Archer and Edward Mitchel - 5-7-1811 - #71 - (131)
DAVIS, Thomas - 5-9-1811 - Motion of Levin Hatfield and Sarah his wife late Sarah
        Davis one of the heirs of Thomas Davis, deceased; citation against John
        Price and Hannah his wife late Hannah Davis admarx. of the estate of
        Thomas Davis, deceased - #1 - (131)
NEFF, John of Dayton Twp. - Estate with will annexed - Adms., Henry Neff and Dan-
        iel Neff - Securities, Christian Neff and Abraham Neff - 9-10-1811 -
        #73 - (134)
STUMP, Leonard - Adms., Julianna Stump and George Stump - Securities, Philip
        Gunckel and William Emrich - 9-10-1811 - #74 - (134)
McCANN, James of Dayton Twp. - Adms., Nancy McCann - Securities, James Hanna
        and James Bay - 11-9-1811 - #76 - (138)
WILSON, William of Dayton Twp. - Adms., Thomas Ramsay and John Ritchie - Securi-
        ties, David Reed and William McClure - 11-16-1811 - #77 - (138)
MASON, Simon - Adms., Daniel Fetters - Securities, Daniel Martin and Robert
        Woods - 1-8-1812 - #82 - (147)
GRAY, Richard of Dayton Twp. - Adms., Jane Gray - Securities, John Devor and
        Jerom Holt - 3-21-1812 - #86 - (149)

MONTGOMERY COUNTY, OHIO - NATURALIZATIONS, 1818-1833

Contributed and prepared by Stephen E. Haller and Robert H. Smith
Archives and Special Collections, Wright State University, Dayton, Ohio 45431

In the first half of the nineteenth century, clerks of courts recorded all naturalization papers and proceedings (declarations of intent and final certificates) in
the Minutes/Journals of the Common Pleas Court. Thereafter, the Probate Court
assumed jurisdiction over naturalizations. A separate docket exists in Montgomery
County for the years 1834-1855, but all earlier naturalizations are scattered entries
in the unindexed Minute Books. All naturalization records for the county are being
preserved at the Archives and Special Collections of Wright State University. In
response to the need for an index to the pre-1834 naturalizations, the authors prepared this abstract of all information given.

AMAN, Joseph; certificate Mar. 11, 1833, Vol. H-1
    Aged 27 and from Stunweiler, France
BECK, James; certificate July 22, 1828, Vol. F-1
    From Ireland and resided in Montgomery County for previous 19 years
BIERLE, Henry; declaration Feb. 27, 1823, Vol. D-1
    Aged 35 and born in village of Aldorf, county of Edenkoben, Bavaria
BOECKING, Christian Tibald; certificate Mar. 6, 1833, Vol. H-1
    Aged 22, born in Bayern, Germany, and arrived at Wilmington, Delaware on Sept.
    4, 1831
BOETHE, John C.; certificate Mar. 6, 1833, Vol. H-1
    Aged 25, born in Magdebergh, Prussia, and arrived at New York City on Nov. 13,
    1831
BUECHNER, Frederic Christopher; declaration Sept. 23, 1822, Vol. D-1
    Born in Circle of Palitine, District of Falkenstein, Germany and resided in
    Stokes County, North Carolina in 1817
BYERS, Robert; declaration Oct. 15, 1823, Vol. D-1
    Born in Ireland and resided in Philadelphia in June, 1816
BYERS, William; declaration Sept. 23, 1822, Vol. D-1
    Aged 25 and born in Ireland
CLAPP, Peter; declaration June 16, 1830, Vol. G-1
    Aged 28, a farmer, and born in Wertemberg, Germany
CLASS, Jacob; certificate Mar. 5, 1833, Vol. H-1
    Born in Stutgard, Wertemberg, Germany and resided in Stark County, Ohio in
    April, 1826
CUNNINGHAM, William; declaration Sept. 30, 1829, Vol. G-1
    Aged 33, a cooper, and born in Fermanagh County, Ireland
DAVIDSON, William; certificate Sept. 30, 1830, Vol. G-1
    Aged 30, a shoemaker, and born in Norway
DECHANT, George Frederick; declaration Apr. 22, 1818, Vol. B-1
    Aged 37 and born in Appenheim, Prussia
DECHANT, John Peter; declaration Apr. 22, 1818, Vol. B-1
    Aged 35 and born in Appenheim, Prussia
DEHL, Justus; certificate Mar. 7, 1833, Vol. H-1
    Aged 53, born in Hesse-Darmstadt, Germany, and arrived at Baltimore, Maryland
    on Mar. 7, 1832
DETTMER, Ernst Justice; declaration Sept. 5, 1833, Vol. H-1 & certificate
    Feb. 12, 1835, a marginal notation in Vol. H-1
    Aged 40, a farmer, and born in Diepholtz, Hanover

DETTMER, Justus; certificate June 5, 1833, Vol. H-1
 Aged 32 and born in Hanover
DIEBINE, William; certificate Mar. 11, 1833, Vol. H-1
 Aged 33 and born in Hesse-Darmstadt, Germany
DININGER, John; declaration Oct. 15, 1823, Vol. D-1
 Aged 25 and born in Wertemberg, Germany
DUNKERLY, Ann; Mar. 4, 1822, Vol. D-1
 Aged 8, daughter of James Dunkerly, and born in Great Britain
_____, Enoch; Mar. 4, 1822, Vol. D-1
 Aged 14, son of James Dunkerly, and born in Great Britain
_____, George; Mar. 4, 1822, Vol. D-1
 Aged 2, son of James Dunkerly, and born in United States
_____, James; declaration Mar. 4, 1822, Vol. D-1 & certificate Mar. 17,
 1829, Vol. F-1
 Aged 45 in 1822 and born in Great Britain
_____, James; Mar. 4, 1822, Vol. D-1
 Aged 5, son of James Dunkerly, and born in Great Britain
_____, Joseph; declaration Mar. 4, 1822, Vol. D-1 and certificate
 Mar. 17, 1829, Vol. F-1
 Aged 18 in Oct., 1821, son of James Dunkerly, and born in Great Britain
_____, Luke; Mar. 4, 1822, Vol. D-1
 Aged 16, son of James Dunkerly, and born in Great Britain
_____, Mary; Mar. 4, 1822, Vol. D-1
 Aged 10, daughter of James Dunkerly, and born in Great Britain
_____, Susannah; Mar. 4, 1822, Vol. D-1
 Aged 12, daughter of James Dunkerly, and born in Great Britain
EVANS, William; declaration Oct. 25, 1828, Vol. F-1
 Aged 32, a weaver, and born in Ireland
FATE, George A.; declaration June 18, 1830, Vol. G-1
 Aged 25 and born in Wertemberg, Germany
FRISHE, Gered Henry; certificate Sept. 5, 1833, Vol. H-1
 Aged 29, a laborer, and born in Venne, Hanover
GANS, Daniel; certificate Mar. 6, 1833, Vol. H-1
 Aged 24, born in Telle, Hanover, and arrived at Baltimore, Maryland
 on Aug. 1, 1832
GARRAT, John; declaration Oct. 15, 1823, Vol. D-1
 Aged 24 and born in Ballyknocken, County of Down, Ireland
GLECKLER, Gotlieb; declaration Mar. 4, 1830, Vol. G-1
 Aged 34, a tailor, and born in Duirmenz, Germany
GOUTER, Nicholas; certificate Mar. 5, 1833, Vol. H-1
 Born in Breinlingen, Hartzog of Baden, Germany and resided in Berks
 County, Pennsylvania in Vovember, 1830
HANDER, Thomas; certificate Mar. 9, 1833, Vol. H-1
 Aged 60, born in Combwell, England, and arrived in the United States
 on August 17, 1831
HEYSER, Abraham; declaration Mar. 11, 1829, Vol. F-1
 Aged 36, a silversmith, and born in Lilly, Brabant, Prussia
HIENCKE, Henry; declaration May 21, 1823, Vol. D-1
 Born in Grunswick, Germany and resided in Philadelphia, Pennsylvania
 in November, 1817

HOFFMEISTER, Henry Rudolph; declaration Sept. 5, 1833, Vol. H-1 and
    certificate June 10, 1835, marginal notation in Vol. H-1
    Aged 37 in 1833, a farmer, and born in Osnabruck, Hanover
HURD, Robert; declaration Mar. 1829, Vol. F-1 and certificate Mar. 8,
    1832, Vol. H-1
    Aged 42 in 1829 and born in Lincolnshire, England
KERNER, Lewis; certificate Sept. 25, 1830, Vol. G-1
    Born in Bowendaugh, Germany and resided in Muskingum County, Ohio
    in August, 1828
KETZER, John; declaration Apr. 19, 1819, Vol. C-1
    Born in Hanover
KOEHNER, Jacob; certificate June 5, 1833, Vol. H-1
    Aged 32, born in Hanover, and resided in Owen County, Kentucky
    in May, 1830
KOOK, John; certificate Mar. 7, 1833, Vol. H-1
    Aged 47, born in Alsfeld, Hesse, Germany, and arrived at Baltimore,
    Maryland on August 1, 1832
KNEPSLY, Lawrence; certificate Sept. 25, 1830, Vol. G-1
    Aged 26, born in Baden, Germany, and resided in Muskingum County,
    Ohio in August, 1828
LANE, George; certificate June 3, 1833, Vol. H-1
    Aged 30 and born in Oxfordshire, England
LANE, Richard; certificate Sept. 10, 1833, Vol. H-1
    Aged 24, a hair dresser, and born in Oxfordshire, England
LEIDLER, Jacob; certificate Sept. 3, 1833, Vol. H-1
    Aged 41, a butcher, and born in Turkheim, Bavaria
LESHER, Adam; declaration Sept. 14, 1832, Vol. H-1
    Aged 33, a day laborer, born in Bavaria, and arrived in the United
    States in September, 1825
LINDSEY, Robert; declaration Mar. 4, 1822, Vol. D-1
    Aged 28 and born in Great Britian
LORENTZ, Peter; certificate Sept. 3, 1833, Vol. H-1
    Aged 32, a weaver, and born in Esekborough, France
McCOY, Samuel; declaration Mar. 4, 1822, Vol. D-1
    Aged 26 and born in Great Britain
McMUNAH, Robert; certificate Mar. 6, 1833, Vol. H-1
    Aged 37, born in Cumberland County, England, and arrived at New York
    City on Sept. 6, 1827
METTOUS, Francis; certificate June 4, 1832, Vol. H-1
    Aged 30, a miller, born in Canton of Uri, Switzerland, left there in 1817,
    and arrived in the United States in 1818
MEYER, John George; certificate Sept. 6, 1833, Vol. H-1
    Aged 30, a distiller, and born in Stutgard, Wertemberg, Germany
MILLER, Aaron; declaration Mar. 9, 1821, Vol. C-1
    Aged 57 and born in parish of Ashton-under-Lyne, county of Lancaster, Ireland
MILLER, John; declaration Mar. 4, 1822, Vol. D-1
    Aged 28 and born in Great Britain
NEWTON, James; declaration Sept. 23, 1822, Vol. D-1 and certificate Sept. 3,
    1833, Vol. H-1
    Born in Lancashire, England
OWENS, William; declaration Feb. 26, 1822, Vol. D-1
    Born in South Whales, Great Britain and resided in New Jersey in 1797

PLATE, John F.; declaration Mar. 12, 1829, Vol. F-1 and certificate Mar. 8, 1832, Vol. H-1
    Aged 32 in 1829 and born in Leson, Hanover
REGENATT, Ambrose; certificate Mar. 19, 1831, Vol. G-1
    Aged 36 and born in Baden, Germany
RESSLER, Andrew; declaration July 6, 1824, Vol. E-1 and certificate July 25, 1828, Vol. F-1
    Aged 40 in 1828 and born in Walberg, Wurtemberg, Germany
RONDEFELT, Jacob; declaration Mar. 9, 1829, Vol. F-1
    Aged 51, a physician, and born in Saxony, Germany
RUEGGER, Jacob; certificate Sept. 29, 1831, Vol. G-1
    Aged 60 and born in Switzerland
SAMBAUCH, George; declaration Sept. 25, 1830, Vol. G-1 and certificate November 24, 1830, Vol. G-1
    Aged 47, a farmer, and born in Saxony, Germany
SANDHAM, Richard; certificate June 4, 1832, Vol. H-1
    Born in Liverpool, England
SCHEURICK, Sebastion; certificate Sept. 10, 1833, Vol. H-1
    Aged 24, a coach maker, and born in Wirtheim, Baden, Germany
SCHINK, Philip; declaration Mar. 2, 1830, Vol. G-1
    Aged 30 and born in Buckinghiem, France
SCHUYCH, Lewis; certificate June 5, 1833, Vol. H-1
    Aged 28 and born in France
SHAFFER, John; declaration Mar. 7, 1823, Vol. D-1
    Aged 51 and born in village of Bergen, Hanover near Frankfort on the Main
SHEPPERD, John; declaration Mar. 5, 1832, Vol. H-1
    Aged 55, a farmer, and born in Devonshire, England
SNYDER, Jacob; declaration May 28, 1833, Vol. H-1
    Aged 64 and born in Basle, Switzerland
STANFIELD, George; certificate Sept. 27, 1830, Vol. G-1
    Aged 30, a woolen weaver, and born in Cheshire, England
STRUGLE, Christian; certificate Sept. 5, 1833, Vol. H-1
    Aged 22 and born in Wertemburg, Germany
SWEARER, John; certificate Mar. 11, 1833, Vol. H-1
    Aged 27 and born in Breidnan, Baden, Germany
VANNAWALD, John; certificate Sept. 14, 1832, Vol. H-1
    Aged 34, a miller, born in Saxony, Germany, and arrived in the United States in November, 1825
WEITZEL, Frederick; certificate Mar. 6, 1833, Vol. H-1
    Aged 28, born in Hesse-Darmstadt, Germany, and arrived at New York City on Sept. 3, 1831
WHITWORTH, Emma; Oct. 1, 1831, Vol. G-1
    Aged 11, daughter of Mathew Whitworth, and born in Lincoln County, England
    _____, George Frederick; Oct. 1, 1831, Vol. G-1
    Son of Mathew Whitworth and born in Lincoln County, England
    _____, Mathew; certificate Oct. 1, 1831, Vol. G-1
    Aged 40, born in parish of Saibeck, England, sailed from Liverpool on May 5, 1830 aboard the <u>Washington</u> (Capt. Parsons), and arrived at New York City on June 22, 1830
    _____, Susannah; Oct. 1, 1831, Vol. G-1
    Wife of Mathew Whitworth and born in parish of Swineshead, England

Jacob AREHART by Heirs to Abraham AREHART 10-25-1853 - John WILHELM and Elizabeth WILHELM his wife formerly Elizabeth AREHART widow of Jacob AREHART of Montgomery County, Ohio for consideration of $300. paid by Abraham AREHART of Henry County, Iowa one of the heirs at law of said Jacob AREHART, deceased; one undivided 1/5th part of SW¼ Section 22, Twp. 3, Range 6 and one undivided 1/5th part being 20 acres SW corner SE¼ Section 22, Twp. 3, Range 6 - Volume W-2, page 568

John CLYMER by Heirs of Christina SCHEVETZ 12-1-1853 - Elizabeth Clymer widow of John Clymer, deceased; John Clymer, Jr. and Mary Jane his wife; Andrew J. HUBLER and Mary his wife of Montgomery County, Ohio and Henry CLYMER and Mary his wife of Richland County, Ohio heirs of John Clymer, deceased - $86. - Lot 80 in town of Liberty, Montgomery County, Ohio - Volume W-2, page 653

Cornelius CHRISTOPHER by heirs to Joseph STUDYBAKER and Henry Clippert 2-24-1854 - $3750. - SE¼ Section 32, Twp. 6, Range 4 - 160 acres. Signed: John Christopher and Margaret his wife; Joseph Christopher and Elizabeth his wife; Peter Christopher and Elizabeth his wife; Cornelius Christopher and Leah his wife of Jersey Co. Illinois - Volume W-2., page 805

John BARNET by Heirs to Abraham and James BARNET 7-1-1816 - 133 acres which John Barnet late of Montgomery County purchased of the United States in fraction Section 14 and north end of fraction section 13 and north end of NW¼ Section 7, Township 1, Range 7. - John Barned died intestate leaving heirs, to-wit: Sons, Abraham and James; daughters, Mary wife of David HUSTON of Greene County, Ohio; Elizabeth wife of George HARRIS; Susan wife of Luther BRUEN and Rachel wife of William WALTON - consideration of $800. - Volume E-1, page 159

SOLOMAN HARTMAN by Heirs to Benjamin HARTMAN 3-27-1818 - SW¼ Section 26, Township 5, Range 4 - Mary Hartman widow of Soloman Hartman, deceased; Elizabeth MILLER and Aaron MILLER her husband; Sarah MILLER and David MILLER her husband; Joshua Hartman heirs of Soloman Hartman, deceased of Montgomery County, Ohio - Benjamin Hartman of Montgomery County, Ohio also one of the heirs of Solomon Hartman, deceased - Volume F-1, page 351

HENRY APPLE, etal. to Philip STOCKSLAGER 4-1-1848 - $1500. - W½ SW¼ Section 20, Township 4, Range 4, 80 acres - Signed: Henry APPLE and Sarah his wife, Samuel STIVER and Mary his wife, Jacob GEISWEIT and Abigail his wife, John STROUP and Eliza his wife, and Samuel STROUP of Montgomery County, Ohio - Volume R-2, p. 242

FREDERICK WOLF heirs to Christian TAYLOR 7-1-1832 - $80. - Lot 70 in Germantown - Signed: Barbary Wolf widow of Fred. Wolf, deceased; George Wolf, Margareth Wolf, Elizabeth Wolf, Jacob Wolf and Mary his wife of Wayne County, Indiana; Daniel Wolf, Catharine FOUST wife of Daniel FOUST of Tippecanoe County, Indiana; heirs of Frederick Wolf, deceased - Volume T-1, Page 465

Christopher W. EMRICK, et al. to Jacob EMMINGER 10-16-1844 - $1498. - 45 acres part of W½ Section 13, Township 3, Range 4, German Twp. Signed: Christopher W. Emrick and Catharine his wife of St. Joseph County, Indiana; Samuel BOWER and Elizabeth his wife, John BEACHLER and Magdalene his wife, Jacob Emerick and Lavina his wife, Jacob GRUBER and Susannah his wife of Preble County, Ohio; Daniel KERSNER and Mary his wife of Fayette County, Indiana; William R. Emrick and Catherine his wife, John Emrick and Mary his wife, Samuel BECHTOL and Christiana his wife of Montgomery County, Ohio; heirs at law of the estate of William EMRICK, deceased, late of Montgomery Co., Ohio - Volume A-3, page 113

Abner GERARD by heirs to Richard STEPHENS 11-2-1825 - $500. - part of N½ Section 34, Township 3, Range 5 - Signed: John SHANKS and Elizabeth his wife, Benjamin LUCE and Ann Ohio Luce his wife of Miami County, Ohio; Edward MITCHEL and Margaret his wife, Jonathan GARRARD and Elizabeth his wife, Abner GERARD and Ann his wife, William H. CAMPBELL and Judith his wife, Abednigo STEPHENS and Hetabel his wife, Henry GARARD, Thomas I. (orJ.) GERARD, Richard BOLIN and Martha his wife, and Milton GARRARD heirs at law of Abner GERARD, deceased - Volume K-1, page 312 - (Note: Surname was spelled GERARD, GARRARD and GARARD as given above in various places within deed)

George BICKEL, et al. to Henry BICKEL 10-21-1815 - Quit Claim - $1.00 161 acres NE¼ Section 6, Township 2, Range 5 - Tobias BICKEL and Susan, wife; Simeon BICKEL and Rosina, wife of Preble County, Ohio; John BICKEL and Catharine, wife; Andrew ABEL and Catharine, wife of Clermong County, Ohio; George BICKEL; Thomas BICKEL and Barbara, wife; George SHAFER and Barbara, wife of Montgomery County, Ohio, heirs of John BICKEL deceased, late of Montgomery County, Ohio - Henry BICKEL one of the heirs at law of John BICKEL, deceased - Volume D-1, pages 438-441

David ULRICH, Sr. to Daniel SHIVELY 5-11-1814 - David Ulrich, Sr. and Barbara (mark) Ulrich for consideration of parental love and regard for Daniel Shively and Susannah his wife their son-in-law and daughter - part of Section 34, Township 4, Range 5 - Volume D-1, page 133

Catharine GEBHART, et al. to William HOLE 2-7-1817 - $200. - E½ Section 25, Township 1, Range 6 - Catharine GEBHART widow of Valentine GEBHART, deceased; George GEBHART and Margaret, wife, John GABHART and Marier, wife; Andrew GABHART and Catharine, wife; Daniel GABHART and Polly, wife; Jacob KERGER and Margaret, wife; Philip GABHART and Elizabeth, wife, heirs and assigns of Valentine GABHART, deceased - Volume F-1, page 22

Abraham NEFF and others to Daniel NEFF 12-27-1813 - Deed of Gift - Quit Claim - 99 acres part of fractional Sections 14 and 15, Township 2, Range 6 - "bordered on the north by lands of Henry NEFF, deceased" - Abraham Neff and others along with Daniel Neff heirs of John NEFF, deceased late of Montgomery County, Ohio - Signed: Abraham NEFF; Adam NEFF; Lewis (mark) NEFF; Martin HOUSER and Barbara (mark) Houser, wife; Jesse CLARK and Dolly (mark) Clark, wife; George SHOUP and Elizabeth (mark) Shoup; Abraham BRENNEMAN and Anna (mark) Brenneman, wife, George BEARDSHIRE and Mary (mark) BARSHERER, wife; David BRIGGS and Ester BRIGGS, wife of Montgomery Co. Ohio; John MILLER and Catharine (mark) Miller, wife of Monongalia Co. Virginia - Volume D-1, pages 181-188

Enos TERRY, et al., adms. to Peter DIXON - 12-(no day given)-1818 - Enos Terry adms. and Elizabeth Terry admsrx. of the estate of John CRAIG, deceased, late of Montgomery County, Ohio - John Craig left the following issue: Mary ATCHESON, late Mary Craig; Sarah LANG, late Sarah Craig; Martha THOMPSON, late Martha Craig; Seymour CRAIG; Elizabeth CRAIG; Nancy CRAIG; James CRAIG; Jeremiah CRAIG; Alexander CRAIG: David CRAIG and Phebe CRAIG, some of which are minors - Agreement to grant 3/4 acres of land (description?) - Signed: Enos TERRY and Elizabeth (mark) TERRY - Witnesses: John McFARLAND and John BEERS - Volume G-1, page 179

MYERS (MOYERS), George et al from President U. S. A. - 10-30-1809 part of Sections 9 and 10, Township 2, Range 5. George Myers (Moyers) for one undivided moiety and Elizabeth GEPHART and John GEPHART heirs of Peter GEPHART, deceased, for the other moiety. Volume B-1, Page 276

CONNELLY, Deborah and Rebecca; Enoch CARTER and Sarah CARTER, wife; of the City of Philadelphia by Henry STODDARD of Dayton, Ohio; their attorney; to Jonathan MARSH 9-29-1827 -N½ of Sec. 25, Twp. 1, Range 6. Elisabeth CONNELLY of Miamisburg, Montgomery Co. Ohio to Jonathan MARSH - N½ Sec. 25, Twp. 1, Range 6 - Signed: Elizabeth CONNELLY. Evan DAVIS and Leticia DAVIS, wife, and Elizabeth CONNELLY of Montgomery County, Ohio to Jonathan MARSH - 133 acres N½ Sec. 25, Twp. 1, Range 6 - tract of land which Charles CONNELLY, late of Montgomery Co. Ohio died seized of - three undivided fifth parts which Deborah and Rebecca CONNELLY, Enoch CARTER and Sarah CARTER, wife, of the city of Philadelphia conveyed to said MARSH along with the dower right of Elizabeth CONNELLY, widow of Charles CONNELLY, deceased. - Signed: Evan DAVIS and Letiicia DAVIS, wife, and Elizabeth CONNELLY. Volume Z-1, pages 185-186-437

GEPHART, Peter by Daniel and Catharine MILLER, adms., David MILLER, George MOYER and wife Elizabeth to David MANBECK - 5-12-1810 - Pt. Sec. 9 and fractional Sec. 10, Twp. 2, Range 5 - Petition to sell real estate filed by Daniel MILLER and Catharine MILLER, wife, late Catharine GEPHART by and with Daniel MILLER, administrator of the estate of Peter GEPHART, late of Montgomery County, Ohio, deceased - land purchased by Peter GEPHART with George MOYER - that Peter GEPHART, deceased, left minor children - Signed: Daniel MILLER and Catharine (mark) MILLER, wife; David MILLER; George MOYER and Elizabeth (mark) MOYER, wife. Volume B-1, pages 284-286

AYERS, Isaac et al to Samuel Ayers. Rec'd 10-20-1827; Recorded 12-28-1827 Estate of Amsey Ayers, deceased, Elizabeth Ayers, Butler County, Ohio. Signed: Isaac Ayers and Betsy, wife, John Ayers and Charity, wife, Simon S. Ayers empowered Samuel Ayers, executor of estate. Book L-1, Page 175

FRYBARGER, Valentine et al to George Frybarger - 3-16-1837 - So. pt. NW¼ Sec. 2, Twp 2, Range 7 - 93 acres - George Frybarger (Friberger) of Fayette Co. Indiana and his heirs to undivided two-thirds of the foregoing tract - said tract being a part of same land given by the late George Frybarger, deceased, to his son Martin Frybarger from whence the grantors inherited as brother and heirs-at-law. The said George FRIBERGER being entitled to one-third of above tract as heir of Martin Frybarger, deceased - Signed: Valentine Frybarger and Elizabeth Frybarger, wife; Daniel ECKMAN and Ann ECKMAN, wife, all of Montgomery Co. Ohio. Witnesses: John GARNER and Jacob WIGGINS Volume Z-1, page 249

HOSTETTER, David et al to Christian Hostetter. Rec'd 12-5-1828; Recorded 1-20-1829. Estate of Christian Hostetter, State of Ohio. 100 acres Montgomery Co. O. SE pt. Sec. 36, Twp. 6, Range 4E. Abraham Hostetter, Attorney for Thomas SNIDER and Anna, wife, (d/o Christian Hostetter). David Hostetter s/o Adam Hostetter, deceased, who was s/o Christian Hostetter; Jacob HENLEY and Catharine, wife, (d/o Adam); Daniel BOWER, Elizabeth, wife, (d/o Adam), Daniel Hostetter s/o Adam. John Hostetter and Hannah Hostetter, son and daughter of Adam, who was one of the heirs of Christian Hostetter. Power of Atty. Christian Hostetter, Orange Co. Indiana Book L-1, Page 660

231

HOSTETTER, Christian to Christian ARNOLD. Rec'd 3-9-1829; Rec'd 3-24-1829. Made
Dec. 6th, 1828 between Christian H. Hostetter of County of Orange, Ind. and also
as Attorney-in-Fact for Jonas SNIDER and Anna, wife, of Shelby Co. Ky., David
Hostetter, Jacob HENLEY and Caty, wife, and Daniel BOWERS and Elizabeth, wife,
Daniel Hostetter and Hannah Hostetter, Clark Co. Ind. and Barbara HOSTER, Abraham
Hostetter, James Hostetter and Ulila, wife, Christian LEATHERMAN and Barbara, wife,
Jacob Leatherman and Elizabeth, wife, of Orange Co., Ind, heirs-at-law of Christian Hostetter, deceased of Montgomery County, Ohio.
Book L-1, Page 741

RASER, Daniel et al to John Raser, Rec'd 6-4-1827; Recorded 9-27-1827
Land taken off north Sec. 25, Twp. 6, Range 4. Montgomery Co., Ohio
Signed: Daniel Raser and Elizabeth (wife), Peter WILES and Barbara (wife), Martin
WEYBRIGHT and Christeny (wife), John RORER (ROHRER elsewhere) and Catherine (wife),
George NISWONGER and Frances (wife), Joseph WILLIAMSON and Ann (wife), Henry SHANK
and Elizabeth (wife), Jacob SHANK and Sarah (wife).
Book L-1, Page 563

NEFF, Christian – Estate of: William Cox, Exc. to George Beacher
Rec'd 10-1-1828; Recorded 12-8-1828 Land Sec. 11, Twp. 2, Range 6E Mont. Co. Ohio
Signed: William Cox and Polly (wife), Elijah Cox and Barbara (wife), Stephen
BRANAMAN, Abraham Branaman and Sara Branaman, heirs.
Book L-1, Page 44

LINDENMUTH & EMRICK to John Stump. Rec'd 6-5-1827; Recorded 10-11-1827
Quit-claim deed for 50 and 46/100 acres in German Township (Montgomery Co.)
E half of Sec. 11, Twp. 3, Range 4 E. Signed: Jonathan Lindermuth and Susannah
(wife, William Emrick and Magdaline (wife), Abraham Emrick and Hannah (wife),
Henry Emrich and Elizabeth (wife), John Stiver, Junior and Cristina (wife).

WIRICK, Rebecca et al to William Wirick. Rec'd 2-27-1829; Rec. 2-27-1829
Parcel of land: Lot No. 12, on plat of the Town of Dayton, containing ten acres.
Signed: Rebekah Wirick, widow of Jacob Wirick, deceased, John Wirick and Catherine Wirick (wife), John Weaver and Barbara Weaver (wife), Jacob Wirick and
Margaret Wirick (wife).
Book L-1, Page 247

ANDREWS, John et al to James Guthery. Rec'd 1-30-1828; Recorded 1-31-1828
Hugh Andrews d. 5-17-1811 in Greene County, Ohio leaving several tracts of land
lying in county of Greene and county of Montgomery. Mont. Co.: SE qt Sec 15,
Twp 2, Range 8. Greene Co.: NW qt, Sec. 8 in same range Twp. containing 115
acres, were set off to Elizabeth Andrews, widow of Hugh Andrews. Elizabeth has
since married James Guthrie of County of Greene. Release made by John Andrews and
Susan (wife), James Andrews and Mary C. (wife), Alexander Stephens and Eliza
Stephens.
Book L-1, Page 422

DAVIS, George C. to Ephraim P. Davis. Rec'd 5-29-1828; Recorded 8-13-1828
CHRISTOPHER CURTNER, deceased, late of Montgomery County. George C. Davis, adm.
of estate of Ephraim P. Davis of Miami County. Lot No. 41 in town of Dayton,
Ohio, subdivided. Signed: Jacob Curtner, Elizabeth Clark, John Reed, William
Reed, James Reed, Alvin Reed, Elizabeth Ingles, wife of Boon Ingles, Polly Blackenburgh, wife of John Blackenburgh, John Curtner, Henry Curtner, Mary Sourbray,
wife of George Sourbray – heirs-at-law of Christopher Curtner.

The following record was contributed by:- Mrs. Anne Hinton, 603 Rockford Ave., Apt. 3, Dayton, Ohio 45405

THIS IS A RECORD FOUND IN THE RECORDERS OFC MONTGOMERY COUNTY COURT HOUSE, DAYTON, OHIO.

VOL B PG 18   DEEDS RECORDS

This indenture made this second day of August in the year of our Lord one thousand eight hundred and six Witnesseth that James Hannah and Thos. John, overseers of the poor in the township of Dayton and County of Montgomery by and with the advise and consent of Christopher Curtner one of the Justices of the Peace of the said county have placed and by these presents do place and bind out an orphan child named Robert CULBERTSON, son of John Culbertson deceased, with Robert Culbertson of the Town and County aforesaid. Whereas the said Overseers of the Poor witnesseth that the said Robert is eleven years eleven months and twenty-five days and that the said Robert shall faithfully obey the said Robert Culbertson's lawful commands, his secrets keep, shall not waste or damage willingly or suffer any to be done but in all things shall behave himself in a becoming manner unto the said Culbertson, his heirs or assigns and the said Robert Culbertson on his part doth promise and agree to instruct or cause to be instructed, the said Robert in the art of making hats in a good and workman-like manner, to teach or cause to be taught in reading, writing and arithmetic to the rule of three if capable of being taught, and the said Robt. Culbertson doth obligate himself to find him, the said Robert, in boarding, lodging and clothing and to furnish him with two suits of clothes at the expiration of his time; one for every day and one for Sunday. And the Overseers doth bind the said Robt. to serve the said Culbertson until he shall become of the age of twenty-one yrs which will be in the yr of our Lord one thousand eight hundred and fifteen on the seventh day of Aug.

In Testimony whereof we have unto set our hands and seals the day and date above written.

Witness present: Signed - James Hanna
Dale Cooper   Thos John
Entered for record 8-211806   Christopher Curtner
               Robert Culbertson

(Mrs. Hinton states: "The names are similar because this is in reality Uncle and Nephew and I understand there were three of these brothers bound out and all made a wonderful mark in and on the world as men.").

CHILD, BIRTH & BAPTISM	PARENTS	SPONSOR-WITNESS
GOTTSCHALK, Jacob b. 3-30-1837; bapt. 5-19-1837	Johannes Gottschalk and wife Sara	Parents
NISCHWITZ, Susanna b. 1-7-1837; bapt. 6-11-1837	Jacob Nischwitz and wife Elizabeth	Parents
ARWEN, (not given) b. 4-12-1837; bapt. 6-11-1837	Thomas Arwen and wife Susanna	Parents
TRUMF, Elisabeth b. 10-6-1836; bapt. 6-11-1837	Fridrich Trumf and wife Maria	Parents
MEYER, Ely Henrich b. 6-27-1837; bapt. 7-16-1837	Johannes Meyer and wife Rebeka	Lydia Klazz
BEKER, Anna b. 5-9?-1831; bapt. 7-20-1837	Andreas Beker and wife Augusta	Jacob Radefeld and wife Christiana
BOESHAR, Sarah Anna b. 1-1-1837; bapt. 7-20-1837	Samuel Boesher and wife Lidia	Emma Radefeld
EHRHART, Susana b. 1-26-1834; bapt. 2-9-1834	Abraham Ehrhart and wife Rebeke	Rebeke Ehrhart
EHRHART, William b. 3-16-1835; bapt. soon after	Abraham Ehrhart and wife Rebeke	Parents
EHRHART, Anna Maria b. 2-18-1837; bapt. 8020-1837	Abraham Ehrhart and wife Rebeke	Parents
KIRSCHNER, Willhelm Jacob b. 2-8-1834; bapt. 8-20-1837	Michael Kirschner and wife Magdalena	Parents
McDERNY, Christofel Collumbus b. 7-10-1837; bapt. 8-20-1837	Bernie McDerny and wife Elizabeth	--------
MOHR, Barbara Anna b. 3-7-1837; bapt. 8-20-1837	Jacob Mohr and wife Maria	Parents
LENTZ, John Hennrich b. 9-19-1836; bpt. 8-25-1837	Johan Lentz and wife Chatarina	Parents
McDARGH, John b. 4-27-183_; bapt. 9-17-1837	John McDargh and wife Susana	Parents
McDARGH, Georg Waschington b. 8-3-1837; bapt. 9-17-1837	John McDargh and wife Susana	Parents
EHRHART, Maria b. 4-13-1827; bapt. 10-1-1837	William Ehrhart and wife Sara	Parents
EHRHART, Susanna b. 3-9-1829; bapt. 10-1-1837	William Ehrhart and wife Sara	Parents
EHRHART, Elisabeth b. 6-5-1831; bapt. 10-1-1837	William Ehrhart and wife Sara	Parents
EHRHART, Nancy b. 1-9-1833; bapt. 10-1-1837	William Ehrhart and wife Sara	Parents
EHRHART, Daniel b. 1-13-1835; bapt. 10_____	William Ehrhart and wife Sara	Parents
EHRHART, 11y (hole in paper) b. 4-11-1837; bapt. 10-1-1837	William Ehrhart and wife Sara	Parents
GOSCHERT, Johannes Frenkling b. 2-9-1837; bapt. 10-1-1837	Samuel Goschert and wife Maria	Parents
FISEL, Lessa b. 9-17-1837; bapt. 11-5-1837	Johannes Fisel and wife Rebeka	Catherina Fisel

CHILD, BIRTH & BAPTISM	PARENTS	SPONSOR-WITNESS
TERRELL, Johan William b. 5-14-1836; bapt. 11-6-1837	Jacobus Terrell and wife Barbara	his mother
TERREL, Heinrich Marty b. 5-14-1836; bapt. 11-6-1837	Jacobus Terrel and wife Barbara	his mother
KRATZER, Emanuel b. 1-28-1829; bapt. 12-25-1837	Georg Kratzer and wife Catherina	Parents
MERKER, Martin b. 3-6-1837; bapt. 5-10-1838	Eli Marker Catherina	Johannes Meyer Marceta
KRANEMILLER, Catherina b. 1-8-1838; bapt. 7-19-1838	Jacob Kranemiller and wife Marcreta	Parents
SEYBOLD, Anna Maria b. 9-17-1836; bapt. 5-12-1838	Georg Seybold wife Jacobbina	Parents
EHRHART, Anna Elisabeth b. 9-24-1838; bapt. 10-26-1838	Abraham Ehrhart and wife Rebeka	Parents
SEYBOLD, Johannes Georg b. 8-4-1837; bapt. 10-27-1838	Johannes Seybold and wife Anna Magtalena	Parents
STUTZ, David b. 12-14-1837; bapt. 10-27-1838	Johannes Stutz and wife Anna	Parents
GUNKEL, Barbary Anna b. 8-5-1838; bapt. 10-30-1838	Christian Gunkel and wife Maria	Conrath Meyer and wife Elisabeth
GUNKEL, Maria Catherina b. 11-5-1837; bapt. 10-30-1838	Christian Gunkel and wife Maria	Georg Klazz and wife Lydia
LENTZ, Maria Elisabeth b. 7-25-1838; bapt. 11-22-1838	Johannes Lentz wife Catherina	the mother
EBERT, William b. 4-24-1825; bapt. 12-25-1838	William Ebert Maria	Jacob Merker
EBERT, Mehely b. 1-31-1829; bapt. 12-25-1838	William Ebert Maria	Heinrich Erbe wife Elisabeth
EBERT, Carloim b. 6-17-1832; bapt. 12-25-1838	William Ebert Maria	Ely Merker wife Catherina
EBERT, Lydia b. 4-17-1835; bapt. 12-25-1838	William Ebert Maria	Lydia Klazz
EBERT, _____ (hole in page) b. 3-__-1837; bapt. 12-_5-1838	William Ebert Maria	Maria Anna Klazz
PFISTERER, Jacob b. 10-21-1838; bapt. 4-13-1839	Philip Pfisterer Magdalena	Parents
GOTTSCHALK, Lusinda b. 1-20-1839; bapt. 4-14-1839	Johan Gottschalk Sara	Parents
MICHEL, Marcreta b. 2-25-1839; bapt. 4-14-1839	Johan Michel Maria	Parents
KRANEMILLER, Jacob b. 3-16-1839; bapt. 4-14-1839	Jacob Kranemiller Marcreda	Parents
MOR, David b. 3-1-1839; bapt. 4-14-1839	Jacob Mor Maria	Parents
BOLL, Sara and Elisabeth b. 1-17-1839; bapt. 4-15-1839	Siman Boll Magdalena	Parents

The above baptisms were all by George Klazz.

CHILD	PARENTS	BORN	BAPTIZED
EVERLING, Jacob	Adam and Margaritta	6-12-1838	4-25-1841
EVERLING, Frederick	Adam and Margaritta	1-19-1840	4-25-1841
MAUS, David	Andrias and Susana	1-28-1841	6-20-1841
WEBER, Elisabeth	Heinrich and Sarah	4-15-1838	7-17-1841
WEBER, Maria	Heinrich and Sarah	1-27-1840	7-17-1841
GOTSCHALD, Sahra	Jacob and Christina	1-17-1841	7-18-1841
FIESTER, Peter	Pfilip and Magdalena	3-6-1841	8-14-1841
SCHERP, David	Jacob and Sarah	8-6-1841	8-14-1841
SCHLENKER, David and Cornelius	Salomon and Susana	10-1-1840	3-27-1842
MILLER, Johannes	Michel and Maria	10-27-1841	3-27-1842
SCHEFER, Henrich	Jacob and Elisabet	10-5-1841	3-27-1842
TAUFER, Susene	Henrich and Elisabet	11-8-1835	4-23-1842
TAUFER, Elisabet	Henrich and Elisabet	2-8-1838	4-23-1842
TAUFER, David	Henrich and Elisabet	4-7-1840	4-23-1842
MOHR, Bernhard	Jacob and Maria	8-14-1841	4-23-1842
CUPPERT, Catherina	Peter and Sara	2-13-1842	4-23-1842
BOLD, John	Simon and Magdalina	4-12-1842	11-5-1842
ERBE, Susanna	Henry and Elisabeth	1-15-1842	11-5-1842
KLEIN, James Vallentein	Henrich and Luesa	12-19-1842	3-11-1843
KEIDER, Maria	David and Catarina	7-28-1837	4-9-1843
KEIDER, Michel	David and Catharina	2-24-1840	4-9-1843
KEIDER (REIDER), David	David and Catharina	3-5-1842	4-9-1843
SCHLENKER, David Rosenmiller	Salomon and Susane	11-2-1842	3-7-1843
GOTTSCHALK, George	Johan and Sara	11-2-1842	--------
GOTTSCHALK, Michael	Jacob and Christina	11-7-1842	--------
PISEL, Elyser	Johan and Rebeke	1-2-1843	6-3-1843
TAUFER, Henrich	Henrich and Elisabeth	3-8-1843	6-4-1843
BRENDENBURG, Joseph Vaschenton	Jacob and Sara	10-1-1836	9-24-1843
EVERLING, Wilhelm	Adam and Margareta	10-15-1842	9-24-1843
SCHEFFER, Elisabeth	Henrich and Elisabet	3-7-1839	10-22-1843
SCHEFFER, Marien	Henrich and Elisabet	4-8-1841	10-22-1843
MICHEL, Jacob	-------(adult?)		10-22-1843
MILLER, Magdalena	Michel and Maria	12-6-1843	2-11-1844
WEIT (WHITE), Daniel Theodore	James and Maria	7-23-1843	2-11-1844
PRUSMAN, Jacob Nathaniel	Daniel Prusman	12-11-1843	2-11-1844
SCHEFER, Johannes	Jacob and Elisabeth	2-4-1844	3-9-1844
KRONMILLER, Barbara	Jacob and Markertta	11-18-1840	5-4-1844
KRONMILLER, Susanna	Jacob and Markereta	1-21-1843	5-4-1844
CAUDON, William Henry	Waschenton and Cadarina	8-10-1838	5-4-1844
CAJDON, Metta Elisabet	Waschenton and Catharina	5-18-1841	5-4-1844
COUDEN, Markeret Em	Waschenton and Catharina	11-16-1843	5-4-1844
MOHR, Daniel	Jacob and Maria	3-15-1844	5-4-1844
KLEIN, Adam	Henrich and Suse	4-13-1844	5-4-1844

CHILD	PARENTS	BORN	BAPTIZED
MAUS, Markaret Elisabet	Andreas and Susana	8-7-1844	4-5-1845
GOTTSCHALK, Johannes	Jacob and Christina	8-27-1844	4-5-1845
ECKERT, Jacob	Gottlieb and Maria	10-18-1844	6-15-1845
ECKERT, Daniel	Gottlieb and Maria	2-13-1846	2-16-1846
STAUFFER, Mary Ann	Henry and Elisabth	10-1-1845	4-11-1846
GOTTSCHALL, Mary Ann	John and Sarah	2-20-1845	10-10-1846
_____, Henrich Adam	(parents not given)	6-12-1846	8-23-1846
RIDER, Johanes	David and Catharina	10-21-1846	5-29-1847
MILLER, Ana Maria	Michael and Ana Maria	11-15-1846	5-29-1847
WERNER, David	Wilhelm and Chatarina	8-5-1847	12-12-1847
BERNHART, Soffia Regina Eliesa	Herman Bernhart and Wilhelmina Rott	12-20-1847	2-5-1848
LANG (LONG), Johan Friderick	Johan and Susana	10-15-1848	9-10-1848
CAUDING, Mery Loweine	Wachenton and Catarina	12-15-1848	7-22-1849
REIDER, Emeleia	David and Catharina	3-4-1849	7-22-1849
NISHWITZ, Theodore Augustus	David and Rebecca Ann	2-10-1849	8-19-1849
RIDER, Anna	David and Catharina	1-24-1836	----------
RIDER, Maria	David and Catharina	7-28-1837	----------
RIDER, Michael	David and Catharina	2-24-1840	----------
RIDER, David	David and Catharine	3-5-1842	----------
RIDER, Jacob	David and Catharine	6-4-1844	----------
RIDER, John	David and Catharine	10-21-1846	----------
RIDER, Emeline	David and Catharine	3-4-1849	----------
RIDER, Henry	David and Catharine	12-28-1852	----------

Baptisms listed above were by D. P. Rosenmiller.

MONTGOMERY COUNTY, OHIO - STILLWATER LUTHERAN CHURCH CEMETERY

The cemetery is located on the site of the original Stillwater Lutheran Church in Section 13, Township 5, Range 5 of Butler township. The church and cemetery were on what was known as Old Church Road (now vacated) which laid between Dog Leg Road and Frederick Pike just south of Route 440 (Old National Road).

RYDER, Sarah wife of Michael Ryder died Aug. 3, 1867 aged 23 yrs. & 7 mos.
    Michael died Mar. 28, 1871 aged 31 yrs. 1 mo. & 4 d's.
BOLL, John G. son of Simon & Magdelena died June 16, 1854 aged 23y 6m 20d
WEISSENBORN, Christopher son of C. & Cathrine S. died July 4, 1851 a. 30y & 2d
(Footstones) C.S.W.   J.   G.B.
RYDER, Catharine Anna dau. of D. & C. died Nov. 14, 1859 aged 3y 11m & 1d
(note: broken stone) died June 10,____aged 33 yrs. 1mo. & 5d.
WEISSENBORN, Catharina Sophia wife of Christopher Weissenborn, dau. of F. & S.
    Schlotteludever, died April 20, 1851 aged 21 yrs. 1 mo. & no days
(note: empty base with stone gone; also footstones) M.W.   C.W.   A.M.
WISE, Mary wife of Jacob Wise died April 10, 1847 age 68 yrs.
(note: another empty base with stone gone)

CROWEL, Elizabeth wife of Henry Crowel died Oct. 3, 1853 aged 75 yrs.
      Henry died Aug. 22, 1846 aged __yrs. 8 mo. & 16 d's (stone effaced)
(footstones) S.C.   M.C.   N.N. (note: large empty base with stone gone)
POUND, David M. son of P. & D. died Jany 8, 1851 aged 11 days
(footstones) L.K.   S.O.   S.O.S.
WEAVER, Elizabeth, dau. of Michael & Barbara Caylor born Nov. 14, 1779 died
           May 7, 1842 aged 69 yrs. 6 mo. & 7 d.
WEBER, Conrad died Oct. 1851 aged 62 yrs.
SHAFER, John who was born Aug. 17, 1821 and departed this life Sept. 7th 1812
      aged 21 years & 21 days (note: no line shows which would make this 1842
      rather than 1812, but date apparently should be 1842.)
(note: empty base with stone gone; also footstones) A.M.   E.M.
WARNER, Joellen wife of Amos Warner died Oct. 5, 1858 aged 27 yrs. 3 mo. 25 ds.
CROWEL, Sophia died Aug 3, 1850 aged 24 yrs. 14 ds.
CROWELL, Mary died Sept. 7, 1853 aged 51 yrs. 2 mo. & 12 ds.
MAUS, Mary wife of Elias Maus, dau. of Richard & Mary Sandham died Jan. 7, 1844
           aged 21 yrs. 11 mo. & 7 ds.
SANDHAM, Richard died Feb. 13, 1857 aged 72 yrs. 6 mo. & 26 d's. A native of England
      Mary wife of Richard Sandham, a native of England, who died May 3, 1842
           aged 56 years & 3 months
HALE, Here lies the mortal remains of John Hale, a native of England, died Oct.
           28, 1841 age 43 yrs. (Signed) Ann Hale
(note: next two stones are broken)
SCHEAFFER, Sarah A. dau. of J. & S. (died) Dec. 27, 1849 Ag. 5m. & 1d.
      Infant son of John & Susannah _____1846
KELLER, Lewis died Sept. 11, 1861 aged 62 yrs. 6 mo. & 9 ds.
      Jerome died Oct. 16, 1853 aged 85 yrs.
      Lewis died Jan. 25, 1842 aged 37 yrs.
SMITH, Lovinan dau. of D. & E. died Apr. 4, 1843 aged 7 years
(footstone) A.M.M.(?)
FRYBARGER, Jacob son of Jacob & Anna died Sept. 30, 1848 aged 30 yrs. 6 mos.
SAHEE, Elizabeth wife of Michael Sahee died Nov. 9, 1865 aged 62 yrs. 11 mo. 18 ds.
(footstones) L.K.   J.W.
WARNER, Elizabeth dau of G. & S. died May 29, 1835 aged 4 yrs. 11 mo. & 6 d's.
      Margaret wife of George Warner died May 3, 1855 aged 59 yrs. 8 mos.
(footstones) E.W.   S.W.
WARNER, Susanna wife of George Warner died Nov. 2, 1851 aged 58yrs.
      George Sr. died Oct. 17, 1858 aged 60 yrs. & 6 mos.
(note: broken stone)_____3 mo. & 11 ds.
HARDAR, John son of John & Sophia died June 1871 aged 7 yrs. 2 m. & 17 d's
ERHART, Jacob husband of Elizabeth Erhart born Apr. 18, 1793 died Aug. 6, 1837
EHRHERT, Susannah dau. of Jacob Ehrhert born April 26, 1823 died June 9, 1855
      John son of Jacob Ehrhert born April 2nd, 1830 died Jan. 31, 1831
MICHAEL, Anna Mary, a native of York Co., Pa., died Dec. 10, 1844 aged 98 years
           & 3 months
FRYBARGER, Anna M. wife of Jacob Frybarger died Feb. 25, 1865 aged 86 yrs. & 4 mos.
      Jacob died Feb. 15, 1842 aged 66 yrs. 6 mos.
FISSEL, Henry born June 5, 1768 died June 3, 1844
      Magdelena wife of Henry Fissel born Aug. 30, 1744 died Dec. 23, 1838

ALEXANDER, G. died Feb. 19, 1838 aged 77 years
(footstones)   G.K.   M.K.
KLINE, Louisa wife of Henry Kline died Apr. 22, 1844 aged 24 yrs. & 7 mos.
    Catharine wife of Mathias Kline died Sept. 6, 1876 aged 76 yrs. 3m 21 ds.
DICKENSHEETS, Samuel A. son of Frederick & Sarah died March 22, 1865 a. 3y & 22d
PALMER, David died Apr. 5, 1872 aged 43 yrs. 10 mos. & 20 ds.
FISHEL, Daniel died Sept. 22, 1859 aged 55 yrs. & 4 mo2.
BALMER, Emma dau. of Elizabeth Balmer died Sept. 10, 1866 aged 13y 8m & 11d
    Margaret dau. of Andrew & Margaret died Feb. 16, 1848 aged 2y 2m & 15d
    Infant son of David & Leah Balmer (note: no dates)
    Mandilla dau. of Andrew & Margaret died Aug. 12, 1822 aged 3 (or 8) years
        5 months & 12 d's
    Jacob son of Matthew & Mary born May 5, 1831 died Feb. 20, 1881 aged
        49 yea. 3 (or 8) mos. & 15 d's (note: stone broken)
    John son of Andrew & Margaret born Aug. 10, 1829 died Feb. 27, 1850
        aged 20 yrs. 6 mos. & 17 d's.
    Andrew died Apr. 28, 1874 aged 72 yrs. & 7 mos.
    Margaret wife of Andrew Balmer died Oct. 10, 1870 aged 66 yrs. & 2 mos.
WARNER, David born Mar. 12, 1796 died June 7, 1830
    Elizabeth wife of David Warner born Mar. 4, 1798 died July 9, 1869
    David son of D. & E. born Dec. 14, 1828 died Sept. 24, 1840
NISHWITZ, Margaret Jane dau. of Geo. & Catherine M. d. Sept. 4, 1839 a. 4m & 6d
    Catharine A. M. wife of Geo. Nishwitz died Mar. 15, 1854 aged 36y 6m 19d
KUNKLE, Infant of Henry & Elizabeth Kunkle (note: no dates)
SCHEAFER, Jacob (died)_____aged 41 yrs. 11 m. & 7 d's (stone broken)
COBLE, John died Aug. 10, 1835 aged 23 yrs. & 10 mos.
SHAEFER, Frederick died Aug. 31, 1880 aged 80 yrs. 9 mo. & 24 ds.
SMITH, Elizabeth wife of David Smith died April 13, 1859 aged 38y 5m & 20d
(note: broken stone) _____ died Feb. 10, 1837
SMITH, Elizabeth dau. of D. & E. died Oct. 10, 1837 aged 3 yrs. 4 mo. & 15 d's
BASSRE, Sarah died June 13, 1869 aged 58 years
    Benjamin died Apri. 22, 1863 aged 85 years
BOSCHOR, Maria born Oct. 12, 1783 died May 5, 1855
DOOLEY, Henry died Oct. 20, 1829 aged 23 yrs. 8mos. & 18 days
NEWMAN, Naomi wife of William Newman died Oct. 5, 1868 aged 91 years
QUILLIN, Absalom son of J. & O. died Jan. 1820 aged 17 years & 9 mos. (no day given)
ACHLENKER, David Carmellias son of Solomon & Susan, who died Jany 18, 1844
        aged 8 years 8 months & 18 days
    Mary Elizabeth dau. of Solomon & Susan d. Sept. 9, 1839 a. 3y 4m 27d
    George Henry son of Solomon & Susan D. Dec. 20, 1839 a. 4y 2m 26d
    Elizabeth wife of George Schlenker died Oct. 5, 1850 aged 69y 6m 1d
    George died Jan. 2, 1844 aged 67 yrs. & 6 mos.
WAYMIRE, Solomon born Feb. 23, 1791 died Apr. 18, 1837
ROOF, Sarah J. died Sept. 29, 1842 aged 2 yrs. & 22 ds.
(note: the following inscriptions were found in the 1930's, but were not found in
                                     1972)
KNOPP, George born Feb. 22, 1851 died Dec. 1, 1875
BALMER, Jacob son of Andrew & Margaret born May 5, 1831 died Feb. 20, 1850
HALE, Anna wife of John Hale born Dec. 28, 1808 died Jan. 14, 1862

WEAVER, Richard son of Henry & Sarah born May 16, 1843 died Nov. 12, 1844
    Sarah dau. of Henry & Sarah died July 7, 1846 aged 1 year
CRESS, Elizabeth died Aug. 24, 1841 aged 79 yrs.
MAST, Elizabeth died Mar. 25, 1822 aged 13 yrs.
    Austin died Apr. 23, 1840 aged 3 mo.
COBLE, Anthony died Nov. 8, 1820 aged 2 yrs.
NEWMAN, William died May 13, 1852 age 75 yrs. 5 mos.
RANKA, John died Feb. 1, 1868 aged 64 yrs.
    Minnie wife of John Ranka died Mar. 20, 1871 age 36 yrs.
The church records for the Stillwater Lutheran Church are now kept at the Luthera
Church in Vandalia; many of these records are in German. The cemetery inscriptio
for the graveyard were transcribed by Lois Baker, Mrs. Andrew Mazak and Irene For
The cemetery is in very poor condition and there is little doubt that there have
more stones than what is there in 1972.

PONTIUS CEMETERY - GERMAN TOWNSHIP - MONTGOMERY COUNTY, OHIO

Contributed by: Rose Shilt, Westbrook Rd., Brookville, Ohio. Located Sec. 6.
Inscriptions taken August 1971 by Mr. and Mrs. Clyde Shilt.
MOSES, Elizabeth died Nov. 27, 1882 aged 51 y. 3 m. 9 d.
    Robert K. died April 11, 1869 aged 40 y. 3 m. 25 d.
    Aaron son of Robert & Elizabeth died April 6, 1862 aged 4 y. 9 m. 8 d.
SHELIMAN, Sarah A. dau. of John & Margaret died Jan. 7, 1845 aged 2 days
PONTIUS, Peter, Born in Pa. Jan. 10, 1823 died April 25, 1850 aged 27 y 3 m. 15 d
    Catharine wife of Frederic Pontius & dau. of Anthony Miller born in Berks
        Co. Pa. Sep. 30, 1794 died Oct. 3, 1843 aged 43 ys. 3 ds.
    Frederick died July 7, 1868 aged 78 yr. 10 m. 19 ds.

HOOK CEMETERY - PERRY TOWNSHIP - MONTGOMERY COUNTY, OHIO

Contributed by: Rose Shilt, Westbrook Rd., Brookville, Ohio. Cemetery located in
Sec. 8 on farm of Earl Rhodes, Providence Rd., first house east of Crawford Rd.
Cemetery formerly fenced, only post remains. Inscriptions taken 1971.
HOOK, Mary born Jan. 20, 1778 died Sept. 6, 1867
    Elizabeth born Oct. 20, 1775 died May 1, 1871
    James died Sept. 14, 1848 aged 62 yrs. 8 mo. 20 ds.
    Mary d. 12-2-1844 aged 95 yrs. 6 mo. 21 ds.

SWANK CEMETERY - PERRY TOWNSHIP - MONTGOMERY COUNTY, OHIO

Contributed by: Rose Shilt, Westbrook Rd., Brookville, Ohio. Cemetery located in
Sec. 11, west side Wolf Creek Rd. north of Providence on creek edge behind home of
Amos Towe. Fence enclosed. Inscriptions taken 1971.
SWANK, Catharine died March 27, 1859, 57 yrs. 4 mo. 20 ds.
    Mahala wife of Aaron Swank died July 16, 1866 aged 27 yrs. 6 mo. 22 ds.
P. S. - died Aug. 29, 1837 aged 74 yr. 1 mo. 1 d.
C. S. (foot stone)
M. S. (foot stone)
(Note: There are 3 bases beside Mahala's tombstone, but markers are gone.)

MULLENDORE CEMETERY - JACKSON TOWNSHIP - MONTGOMERY COUNTY, OHIO

Contributed by:- Mrs. Clyde Shilt, Rt. 3, Westbrook Rd., Brookville, Ohio 45309

Cemetery is located in the SW¼ Section 31 Jackson twp. It is located on the Mowen farm, on County Line Road, past the pond on the right side.

SWINEHEART, Elizabeth wife of P. Swineheart died ____ 20, 1870
COOVER, Laura wife of S. H. Coover died Jan. 15, 1879 age 26 yrs. 6m. 22 ds.
MULLENDORE, Daniel died Feb. 11, 1851 age 33 yrs. 10 m. 20 ds.
BEAR, Marcus son of H. & Ellen died Oct. 1, 1850 age 5m. 16 ds.
MULLENDORE, John Wesley son of Jacob & Harriet died Jan. 27, 1854 age 6 yrs. 5m. 19ds.
BEAR, Sarah Ann dau. of H. & L. died May 6, 1839 aged 1 yr. 8 m. 19 ds.
MULLENDORE, Ozro son of David & Hannah died Apr. 16, 1850 age 1 yr.. & 5 ds.
    Josiah son of David & Hannah died April 18, 1850 aged 3 yrs. 8 m. 25 ds.
    Catharine dau. of David & Hannah died Nov. 9, 1848 age 5 yr. 3 m 27 ds.
    Joseph son of Jacob & Maria died Oct. 4, 1853 age 7 yr. 5 m. 14 ds.
BEAR, Josiah son of H. & L. died Nov. 24, 1841 age 21 ds.
    Lydia wife of Henry Bear died Nov. 20, 1841 age 21 yrs.
GILBERT, Alice Roselle Jane dau. of Jesse & Hannah died July 4, 1856 age 4 m. 10 ds.

MUNGER-BUTT CEMETERY - MIAMI TOWNSHIP - MONTGOMERY COUNTY, OHIO

Contributed by: Robert C. Kennedy, 1524 Laird Ave., Dayton, Ohio 45420

Cemetery is located on what was once Solomon Butt's land in SE¼ Section 8 of Miami township (originally a part of Washington twp.) a short distance from the Washington twp. line. Cemetery is located about 40 yards from the first jog in Munger Road which comes from Mad River Road, this road then takes a circuitous route around a heavily forested area, then heads due north into the Alexandersville-Bellbrook Road. The cemetery is in a stand of trees surrounded by a section of new homes being built by Zengel Construction Company.

BUTT, Esther wife of Jacob Butt, born Penna. 1775 or 1777, died July 1, 1857 aged 21 years 8 days (?) (note: broken stone lying flat)
BUTT, Jacob born April 30, 1770 died (?) aged 64 years (intact stone lying flat)
MUNGER, Nancy died Feb. 28, 1863 (note: stone lying flat)
WHISLER, Daniel L. died Dec. 18, (?) aged 34
SAUM, Children of Joseph and Martha Saum (broken monument with just base remaining)

(Editor's note: In 1968 we visited this cemetery which at that time was in a completely overgrown state. Essentially the inscriptions we copied were the same as Mr. Kennedy's; however since there were a few additions, we will include our listing. Anita Short)

BUTT, Jacob born Apr. 30, 1770, died (?), aged 64 yrs. 2 mo. & 15 ds.
(note: did not find the stone of Esther Butt, but it may have been covered)
WHISLER, Daniel died Dec. 1_, 18__ aged 3_ yrs. & 6 days
_____, (note: probably SAUM children), John H. died Apr. 12, 1872 aged 3 yrs. & 19 ds.
    Cora Ann died Apr. 6, 1872 aged 20 years
    Evaline died Mar. --, 1872 aged 6 yrs.
    (note: John H., Cora Ann and Evaline all on same stone)
KIBLINGER, Nancy died Feb. 28, 1863 aged 63 yrs. 4 mos.
_____, Our Babe Adazilla died Jan. 17, 1862 aged 9 mo. & 19 ds. (note: no surname given)

STETTLER CHURCH CEMETERY - MIAMI TOWNSHIP - MONTGOMERY COUNTY, OHIO

Contributed by: Rose Shilt, Westbrook Rd., Brookville, Ohio 45309.
Cemetery is located on east side of Union Rd. past its intersection with Zeck Rd.
Inscriptions taken Sept. 1971.

STETTLER, J. William died Feb. 11, 1836 aged 58 yrs. 10 mo. 11 da.
 Mary wife of J. W. Stettler died May 18, 1859 aged 82 yrs. 8 mo. __ ds.
 George died Mar. 20, 1836 aged 19 yrs. 4 mos. 3 ds.
 D. D. died Sept. 19, 1848 aged 37 yrs. 11 mo. 8 ds.
 Daniel died May 15, 1858 aged 78 yrs. 10 mo. 15 ds.
 Catharine wife of Daniel Stettler died Nov. 27, 1863 aged 78 yrs. 1 mo. 16 ds.
 George V. born Aug. 31, 1739 died Apr. 23, 1815.
 Eva Catharine wife of George V. Stettler born Feb. 16, 1742 died June 9, 1838
 Henry died Jan. 26, 179 (?) age 55 yrs. 10 mo. 18 da.
 Thomas died Spet. 4, 1881 aged 78 yrs. 3 mo. 11 ds.
 Elizabeth died Aug. 9, 1877 aged 71 yrs.
 John George son of Philip & Mary died June 19, 1860 age 19 yrs. 7 mo. 27 ds.
 Henry Jr. died Apr. 12, 1873 aged 63 yrs. 3 mo. 18 ds.
 Mahala 1811-1893
RIEGEL, Mathias died May 25, 1834 age 73 yrs. 8 mo. 10 ds.
 Margaret wife of Mathias Riegel died Dec. 31, 1825 age 65 yrs.
 George died Aug. 19, 1845 age 58 yrs. 8 mo.
ROCKEY, Barbara wife of Jacob Rockey died Dec. 18, 1849 age 32 yrs. 1 mo. 18ds.
 Catharine wife of Jacob Rockey died July 30, 1858 age 37 yrs.
 Charles son of J. H. & C. died April 19, 1873 age 4 mo. 1 d.
FOCHT, Ann wife of Peter Focht died Sept. 26, 1837 age 21 yrs. 1 mo. 23 ds.
HELLERMAN, Adam, died Apr. 7, 1836 age 33 yrs. 1 mo.
GEBHART, Peter died Oct. 13, 1856 age 35 yrs.
 Florence M. dau. of Wm. & Mary died Aug. 1, 1858.
 John A. son of Wm. & Mary died July 26, 185_(?) age 3 yr.
 Henry D. son of Wm. & Mary died ____185_(?) age 1 yr. 11 m. 12 d.
 Julia Ann dau. of Wm. & Mary died Oct. 30, 1858 age 7 yrs. 2 mo. 12 ds.
 Wm. Henry son of John & Elizabeth died Oct. 30, 1861 age 4 yrs. 3 mo. 18 da.
 Peter died Aug. 12, 1856 aged 25 yrs. 11 mo. 2 ds.
 Wm. F. son of P. & S. died Mar. 11, 1856 aged 15 yrs. 6 mo. 14 ds.
CAMP, Augusta dau. of Peter & Mary A. died June 28, 1855 aged 26 yrs. 2 mo. 2 ds.
KUHN, Manorva wife of Charles Kuhn died Feb. 11, 1880 age 29 yrs. 9 mo. 13 ds.
 Mary dau. of C. & M. died Nov. 29, 1877 aged 3 yrs. 8 mo. 20 ds. (ss as Manor
HOFFMAN, Adolph 1834-1916 Charlotte Agnes 1836-1879 (same stone)
JOHNSON, Our baby, son of Mr. & Mrs. Letcher Johnson - May 18, 1931
RIDINGER, Paul 1909-1939
LIBCAP, Michael died Dec. 21, 1836 age 33 yrs.
 Catharine wife of Jacob Libcap died June 19, 1861 age 18 yrs. 2 mo. 15 ds.
               (48 yrs.?)

 Sarah S. 1854-1914
 Louis B. son of J. & C. died May 7, 1859 aged 2 mo. 16 ds.
 Sarah C. dau. of J. & C. died June 25, 1861 aged 11 yrs. 2 mo. 1 d.
 Charles 1888-1890   Thomas 1874-1877

SHUPERT, Sarah M. Wife of Peter R. Shupert died May 12, 1859 age 20 yrs. 1 mo. 12 ds.
John Peter son of Geo. & Mary died Nov. 13, 1861 age 5 yrs. 5 ds.
Mary M. dau. of Geo. & Mary died Nov. 23, 1861 aged 2 yrs. 1 mo. 20 ds.
Carl M. son of Mr. & Mrs. Nelson Shupert. (Note: No dates.)
Edna F. dau. of Mr. & Mrs. Nelson Shupert. (Note: No dates.)
Sarah dau. of Geo. & Mary died Nov. 19, 1849 aged 3 yr. 19 ds.
John son of Geo. & Mary died Oct. 10, 1849 aged 4 yrs.
(Note:- Large stone inscribed, "Children of P. & H. Shupert" with three
small markers inscribed each, "Infant" nearby.)
PONTIUS, Elizabeth died July 7, 1862 age 55 yrs. 9 mo. 13 ds.
John died Nov. 14, 1900 age 81 yrs. 9 mo. 5 ds. (ss Mary M.)
Father & Mother
Mary M. wife of John Pontius died Jan. 9, 1885 age 68 yrs. 5 mo. 15 ds.
Abraham died Dec. 16, 1862. (Note: No age given.)
Eve Catharine wife of Abraham Pontius died Nov. 3, 1862 age 84 yrs. 1 mo.
15 ds.
Elizabeth wife of D. Pontius _____(Note: Stone broken - no dates.)
Sarah Ann dau. of Daniel & Sarah died July 2, 1861 aged 8 yrs. 7 mo. 11 ds.
Daniel son of D. & S. died July 9, 1861 aged 3 yrs. 20 ds.
John son of D. & S. died July 19, 1861 aged 11 yrs. 1 mo.
Samuel son of D. & S. died July 9, 1861 aged 2 yrs. 27 ds.
Henry son of D. & S. died Jan. 27, 1847 aged 2 yr. 8 m. 20 ds.
Infant dau. of D. & S. died Jan. 26, 1847 aged 21 ds.
PONTIOUS, Emma dau. of J. & M. died Oct. 18, 1865 aged 7 yrs. 28 ds.
Malinda dau. of J. & M. died Oct. 17, 1865 aged 18 yr. 1 m. 12 d.
Andrew son of J. & M. died Oct. 5, 1865 aged 8 yrs. 8 m. 11 ds.
Clement Vallaningham son of J. & M. died Oct. 15, 188_(?) aged 8 yrs. _(?)
mo. 1 d.
SHARITS, Clara Augusta dau. of John & Rodia born Dec. 3, 1855 died Oct. 18, 1861
SHARRET, Charles W. son of H . & E. died Oct. 11, 1856 aged 11 mo. 14 ds.
Infant son of H. & E. (Note: No dates.)
Laura A. dau. of H. & E. died July 8, 1857 aged 11 yrs. 3 mo. 11 ds.
Wm. A. son of Z & C. died Nov. 28, 1863 aged 3 yr. 6 m. 7 ds.
HIPPLE, Adam M. Feb. 10, 1894 - Aug. 16, 1895.
Mary & Daniel - Mother & Father. (Note: No dates.)
Peter James son of John W. & Elizabeth died May 16, 1848 age 2 yr. 7 mo. 2 ds.
Charles E. son of J. & M. born Oct. 11, 1874 died Nov. 11, 1877.
(Note: Broken marker with only inscrip. left.) _____11 mo. 12 ds.
(Note: Unreadable marker near marker of George RIEGEL, footstone reads) G.R.
(Note: Two unmarked graves with Civil War metal markers marking graves.)

WELBAUM CEMETERY - PERRY TOWNSHIP - MONTGOMERY COUNTY, OHIO

Cemetery located in NE¼ Section 1. It is on the south side of Westbrook Rd., 1/8th
mile west of its intersection with Diamond Mill Rd. Cemetery is fenced in and no
longer active. Inscriptions taken September 1968 by Rose Shilt and Anita Short.

RASOR, Infant son of Earl & Dora - Nov. 4, 1904
HOLSAPPLE, Sarah daughter of John & Mary died July 20, 1856 aged 4 yrs. & 12 d's
HOLSAPPEL, Adam died Sept. 29, 1843 aged 39 yrs. 10 mo. 16 ds.
    Samuel died July 20, 1856 aged 32 yrs. 3 mos. 24 ds.
    (Note: Effaced stone, no longer readable)
TIPNER, Lear daug. of D. & C. died Apr. 7, 1850 aged 16 d.
DITMORE, Frederick died Feb. 27, 1850 aged 66 yrs. 5 mo. & 10 ds.
    Daniel died Oct. 12, 1875 aged 54 ys. 8 mo. & 28 ds.
ARNOLD, John son of J. & B. died Nov. 1820 aged 3 ys. 3 m. (Note: No death day
                                     given)

    John died Apr. 19, 1837 aged 55 yrs. 18 d.
    Barbary wife of John Arnold died Mar. 7, 1872 aged 72y. 10 m. & 6 d.
WELLBAUM, Sarah wife of C. Wellbaum died Dec. 11, 1851 aged 51 ys. 4 ms. & 19 d.
    Christian died Jan. 19, 1880 aged 84 ys. 1 m. & 28 ds.
CURK, Sarah dau. of M. & P. died Mar. 17, 1872 aged 13 y's. 6m. 8 d's.
    Joseph son of M. & P. died Apr. 12, 1884 aged 28 y. 8 m. 14 ds. (ss Sarah)
    Mary wife of Michael Curk born April 16, 1823 died June 15, 1887 aged 64y.
                               2m 1d
    Michael died Dec. 11, 1887 aged 70 y. 11 m. 16 d.
FRYMAN, Jacob 1834-1914
    Joseph born Nov. 8, 1820 died april 21, 1892 (Note: ss Elizabeth - "Father
                                  and Mother")
    Elizabeth born Oct. 26, 1818 died Oct. 20, 1900
    John 1856-19__(Note: not engraved); Elizabeth his wife 1866-1899; Joseph E
                                  1891-1899
ARNOLD, Henry Sr. (Note: No dates inscribed)
    Elizabeth wife of H. Arnold Sr. (Note: No dates inscribed)
TOBIAS, Paul - Dec. 12, 1812 - Mar. 8, 1899, Father (Note: ss as Sarah)
    Sarah wife of P. Tobias - Mar. 23, 1818 - Oct. 15, 1892, Mother
ARNOLD, Nicholas died Dec. 1, 1844 aged 22 y's. 6m. 16 d.
TOBIAS, Sarina daughter of Paul & Sarah died Oct. 30, 1854 aged 2 yrs.
    Talitha daughter of Paul & Sarah died Nov. 16, 1853 aged 5 yrs. 9 mo. 5 d'
    Children of Paul & Sarah (Note: Same stone as follows)
        Laura Ellen died Sept. 6, 1860 aged 1 yr. 9 mo. 5 ds.
        Henry Arnold died Sept. 21, 1860 aged 1 yr. 9 mo. 20 ds.
KINSEY, Enos son of M. & E. died May 24, 1854 aged 16 y's. 1 m. 20 d.
ARNOLD, Arthur son of Henry H. & Elizabeth died Mar. 11, 1858 aged 3 yrs. 6 mos.
        8 (note: Word "days" not given)
TOBIAS, Joseph Anson son of Paul & Sarah died Oct. 8, 1860 aged 5 yrs. 1 mo.____;
        (Note: Rest cemented in base)
ARNOLD, Catharine wife of Joseph Arnold died Nov. 11, 1861 aged 71 y's & 6 mo.
    Joseph died Nov. 2, 1863 aged 75 yrs. 7 mos. & 14 ds.
SWANK, Clement son of S. & C. died Sept. 16, 1864 aged 1 yr. 5 mo. 26 ds.
ARNOLD, Henry W. died June 10, 1874 aged 49 ys. 2 ms. 20 ds.

WEAVER, Elizabeth 1832-1904
MARSH, Mary born apr. 29, 1837 died July 25, 1918 (ss as Emanuel Arnold)
ARNOLD, Emanuel born Aug. 22, 1830 died May 27, 1886
     Mary wife of Christian Arnold born July 15, 1790 died Jan. 13, 1875 aged
                84 yrs. 5 mo. & 28 d.
     Christian born Mar. 5, 1786 died June 29, 1855 aged 69 yrs. 3 mo. 24 d.
     Henry son of C. & M. died Aug. 1816
     Francis dau. of A. & C. died Dec. 18, 1874 aged 1 yr. 7 mo. & 14 da.
     Martha J. dau. of A. & C. died Nov. 26, 1874 aged 9 yrs. 7 mo. & 10 ds.
     Dora A. dau. of A. & C. died Dec. 16, 1874 aged 6 yrs. & 4 ds.
     (Note: Francis, Martha J. and Dora A. all on same stone.)
     Amelia dau. of Aaron & Catharine died Jan. 16, 1863 aged 4 yrs. 6 mo. 26 dys.
     Lavina dau. of Aaron & Catharine died July 4, 18__ (Note: Cemented in base.)

BACHMAN CEMETERY - CLAY TOWNSHIP - MONTGOMERY COUNTY, OHIO

Located at Bachman on south side of Route 440 (Old National Rd.) behind vacant
house. Cemetery is fenced, but unkept—most of the stones are no longer upright.
Inscriptions were taken fall 1968 by Rose Shilt and Anita Short.

BACHMAN, John E. died June 4, 1853 aged 50 y'r. 10 mo. & 2 ds.
     Polly S. wife of John E. Bachman died May 23, 1863 aged 44 y'rs. 8 m. & 7d.
     Enoch son of John E. & Polly died Jan. 31, 1836 aged 1 day
     Loami son of John E. & Polly died Jan. 31, 1836 aged 1 day (ss as Enoch)
GARARD, Esther A. daughter of J. & R. died Aug. 5, 1855 aged 2 yrs. 1 mo. & 2 ds.
PIATT, James died Nov. 10, 1857 aged 53 y's.
ARNOLD, Catharine wife of Henry Arnold died Feb. 5, 1859 aged 41 ys. 8 ms. & 26 ds.
HOMAN, Martha dau. of Wm. & E. died Jan. 11, 1858 ag'd 3 m'o & 29 d's.
     Mary O. dau. of Wm. & E. died Sept. 19, 1859 ag'd 10 m. 28 d's.
     John H. son of W. L. & E. died Feb. 27, 1870 aged 2 y'rs. & 9 d's.
     Wm. L. 1816-1895
     Wm. H. 1858-1908
     Elizabeth 1835-1909
BACHMAN, Enoch died Oct. 14, 1855 aged 70 yr's. 4 mo. & 2 d's.
     Barbara wife of Enoch Bachman died May 17, 1849 aged 62 y's. 9 m's & 20 d.
     (Note: Stone with top gone)_____ aged 11 yr. 3 mo. & 14 ds.
ASHLEY, Elder Loami died Sept. 25, 1855 aged 71 yrs. 1 mo. 16 ds.

MARSHALL CEMETERY - CLAY TOWNSHIP - MONTGOMERY COUNTY, OHIO

Cemetery located in Section 32 on Roy Snyder farm, north side of Westbrook Rd.,
west of Crawford Rd. Cemetery on west side of house back in middle of field, all
but one stone gone. Inscription taken 1971 and contributed by Rose Shilt.

MARSHALL, I. - Sept. 1, 1842 - 68 yr. 2 mo. 5 ds.

245

MONTGOMERY COUNTY, OHIO, CLAY TOWNSHIP - SWANK CEMETERY

Contributed by: Mrs. Clyde Shilt, Westbrooke Rd., Brookville, Ohio.
This cemetery is located in the NW¼ Section 24, Township 6, Range 4E, on the south side of Wengerlawn Road, about a block east of Welbaum Road. Inscriptions taken in October, 1977.

SWANK, Jacob died May 6, 1875, aged 79 yrs. 5 mos. 24 ds.
        Sarah died Aug. 4, 1851, aged 52 yrs. 11 mos. 26 ds. (ss as Jacob)
        Mary died Apr. 20, 1876, aged 76 yrs. 8 mos. 11 ds. (ss as Jacob)
SWANK, Sarah wife of Jacob Swank died Aug. 4, 1851, aged 52 yrs. 11 mos. 26 ds.
        (note: Sarah has individual stone and also inscription on same stone
            with Jacob)
RASER, Daniel - Pvt. Pa. Mil. Arty., Rev. War. (died) 1816
        Barbara (died) 1821
        (note: inscriptions for Daniel and Barbara are on same stone which
         is a later stone and not contemporary with their death dates)
SWANK, Mary Etta dau. of Jacob & Lydia A., died Feb. 15, 1857, aged 1 mo. & 12 ds.
        Alvin son of S.&E., died Sept. 16, 1854, aged 11 yrs. 1 mo. 3 ds.
        Alvin son of George D. & (?) Waitman, died Oct. 1851 aged 16 weeks
        Augustus son of George D. & (?) Waitman, died May 21, 1857, aged 3 yrs.
                        6 mos. 20 ds.

Footstones found: A.S.; A.W.; S.W.

MONTGOMERY COUNTY, OHIO - REVOLUTIONARY SOLDIER'S GRAVE MARKED

Contributed by: Mrs. Clyde Shilt, R#2, Westbrooke, Brookville, Ohio

LEWISBURG LEADER, Thursday, June 27, 1935. Dayton's Richard Montgomery Chapter of the SAR will mark the grave of Mr. Sebastian Heeter at the Providence Lutheran Church Cemetery southwest of Brookville, near Pymont next Sunday June 30. Mr. Sebastian Heeter who fought in the War of American Independence, was born in Huntington Co., Pa. His wife Elizabeth, dau. of Mr. and Mrs. Henry Rarick was born in Philadelphia Co., Pa. They were married Aug. 11, 1795. To them were born 11 children: Henry, Frederick, Catherine, Abraham, Daniel, Polly, Jacob, Samuel, Sebastian and David. They located in Madison twp., Montgomery County about the cl of the War of 1812. He contributed liberally to the erection of the first church of Ellerton.

Clipping from the Dayton paper (not dated--July 1935) gives additional information as follows: Services were held at New Providence Lutheran Church in Perry tqp., Montgomery Co. near New Lebanon. Mr. Heeter settled in Perry twp. in 1815. He was born in 1760 in Hopewell twp., Bedford Co., Pa. now known as Huntingdon Co., was married twice and had 15 children. At the services, two gransons were present Joseph Heeter 81, former Lewisburg Postmaster and Dean Ridley of Dayton. Dick Heeter, son of Otto of Lewisburg and gr-gr-grandson of Sebastian unveiled the marker. Six year old Kenneth Weaver was the youngest descendant present.

MORGAN COUNTY, OHIO - GUARDIANSHIPS 1836-1843

The following records consist of guardianship bonds which have been bound together into a book (no cover). They have been wrapped in a paper wrapper and are located in the Archives Room on the third floor (attic) of the Morgan County Court House. Pages are not numbered, but are given below in the order they appear in the book.

6-27-1836 - Zachariah CADDINGTON guardian of Eliza FULLER aged 16 years.

6-27-1836 - Alexander SIMPSON guardian of Joseph S., Phoebe Ann, Robert and Rachel WILLIAMS, children of Jacob WILLIAMS, dec'd.

6-27-1836 - Alexander SIMSON guardian of Anna PLUMMER.

7-1-1836 - Eliza M. WOOD guardian of Sarah, Frederick Mary, Eliza, Georgena, Harriet, John and Charles WOOD.

7-2-1836 - Nathan MOODY guardian of Lydia, Pracilla, Florence, Eliza Ann, John, William and Dianna (note: no surname given).

9-30-1836 - James OGIE guardian of John M. and Samuel D. GIBSON, children of Samuel D. GIBSON, dec'd.

9-30-1836 - Samuel AIKINS guardian of Jacob T. LAMB aged 17 years.

9-30-1836 - James MITCHEL guardian of Jesse WEBBER son of Jonas WEBBER.

10-1-1836 - James HAMMOND guardian of Wm. HAMMOND aged 10 years and Eliza Ellen HAMMOND aged 7 years, children of Jas. HAMMOND, dec'd.

3-18-1837 - John SIBERT guardian of Mary Jane MOLER aged 20 months.

3-7-1838 - Sam'l ALLARD guardian of Catharine PLETCHER aged 9 years, Washington PLETCHER aged 6 years and Phoebe PLETCHER aged 4 years, heirs of Jacob PLETCHER, dec'd.

3-9-1838 - Caleb W. FOUTS guardian of Emerson STILLMAN.

6-25-1838 - James DAVIS guardian of Nancy HARRIS aged 16 years, Rachel HARRIS aged 14 years and Isaac HARRIS aged 11 years.

6-29-1838 - William ANGUISH guardian of James M. ANGUISH aged 10 years and David ANGUISH aged 5 years, as heirs of John TWEEDY grandfather of said James M. and David.

10-27-1838 - James NEWLON guardian of William NEWLON aged 19 years and Mary NEWLON aged 14 years, children of David NEWLON, dec'd.

10-27-1838 - James NEWLON guardian of John NEWLON aged 9 years, heir of David NEWLON, dec'd.

12-26-1838 - John THOMPSON guardian of Mordecai THOMPSON an insane son of William THOMPSON late of Chester County, Pennsylvania, dec'd.

247

4-8-1839 - Joshua DAVIS guardian of Eliza DAVIS aged 16 years.

4-8-1839 - James KADELL guardian of Susannah THOMPSON.

4-11-1839 - Jacob R. PRICE guardian of Rece PRICE aged 16 years, Jane Eliza PRICE aged 13 years, Elijah PRICE aged 12 years, Jefferson Jackson PRICE aged 9 years and Sarah Ann PRICE aged 5 years, heirs of Andrew HEART, dec'd.

4-11-1839 - Jacob W. STANBERRY guardian of Nathan BANCUS.

4-12-1839 - Caleb W. FOUTS guardian of Nancy HOLBROOK aged 13 years past and Malissa HOLBROOK aged 11 years past, heirs of Jonathan HOLBROOK, dec'd.

4-13-1839 - Jacob KRAPPS guardian of John JOHNSON aged 17 years past, William JOHNSON aged 15 years past, Abraham JOHNSON aged 13 years past and George W. JOHNSON aged 6 years past, children of Jas. JOHNSON, dec'd.

4-13-1839 - John WALPOLE guardian of Rebecca BECKWITH aged 16 years past, daughter of Tobias BECKWITH, dec'd.

7-10-1839 - Isaac HARRIS guardian of Lydia Ann HARRIS aged near 16 years, Isaac D. HARRIS aged near 4 years and Christena HARRIS aged near 2 years, children of Smith HARRIS, dec'd.

7-13-1839 - Alexander SIMPSON guardian of Samuel SCOTT aged 16 years and Lowly SCOTT aged 14 years, children of Obediah SCOTT, dec'd.

7-13-1839 - Jane SCOTT guardian of Justus SCOTT aged 8 years, Louisa SCOTT aged 6 years and Obediah SCOTT aged 5 months, heirs of Obediah SCOTT, dec'd.

11-6-1839 - William AIKINS guardian of Henry W. NEWMAN aged about 19 years, son of Allen NEWMAN, dec'd.

11-6-1839 - John AIKINS guardian of William M. EVANS aged 20 years past, son of Joseph EVANS, dec'd.

3-31-1840 - Conway GARLINGTON guardian of Elizabeth PADGET aged 11 years, heir of Aquilla PADGET.

7-2-1841 - Catharine APPLEMAN guardian of Margaret APPLEMAN, daughter of Jacob APPLEMAN, dec'd.

4-2-1840 - Alexander BROWN guardian of Cashing DeGARMO aged 14 years last Oct.

4-4-1840 - William HADLEY guardian of Geo. THISTEL aged about 11 years, son of Ezra THISTIL, dec'd.

4-4-1840 - William HADLEY guardian of Benjamin F. THISTELL aged 14 years, son of Ezra THISTELL.

7-20-1840 - Wm. HENDERSON guardian of Mary Ann ROBERTS aged about 17 years, daughter of Abraham ROBERTS.

7-24-1840 – James DOSTER guardian of Thomas ODELL aged 16 years, son of Henry ODELL, dec'd.

7-25-1840 – Harman SEAMAN guardian of David SEAMAN aged 14 years past, son of John SEAMAN, dec'd.

7-25-1840 – Alexander SIMPSON guardian of Robert LINKENS aged 13 years October last, son of Henry LINKINS, dec'd.

7-25-1840 – John KIRBY guardian of Jesse SEAMAN aged 12 years and Perley J. SEAMAN aged 10 years, children of Jas. SEAMAN, dec'd.

10-5-1840 – William COMER (or CORNER) guardian of Hannah Matilda ADY aged 9 years and Frances Mary ADY aged 6 years, children of Jas. T. ADY, dec'd.

10-10-1840 – George HENDERSON Sr. guardian of Joseph SAWYER aged 16 years, James Hughs SAWYER aged 14 years and Mary Eunice SAWYER aged 12 years, children of Thomas SAWYER, dec'd.

10-14-1840 – Elijah HELLYER guardian of Robert CHILCOAT aged 14 years May 28, 1840.

10-14-1840 – Elijah HELLYER guardian of Elizabeth CHILCOAT aged 11 years and Thomas CHILCOAT aged 9 years.

3-30-1842 – Catharine APPLEMAN guardian of Margaret, John, Sally, Elizabeth, Eli and Jane APPLEMAN, children of Jacob APPLEMAN, dec'd.

3-31-1841 – David AYERS guardian of Nathaniel AYERS aged 15 years last May, son of Nathaniel AYERS, dec'd.

4-2-1841 – Richard SANDS guardian of Anne WOLF aged 9 years, daughter of John WOLF, dec'd.

4-3-1841 – Alexander SIMPSON guardian of James Wesley LINKINS aged 16 years last October, son of Henry LINKINS, dec'd.

5-31-1841 – Sarah STOUT guardian of Moses STOUT aged 19 years, Rebecca STOUT aged 17 years, Elizabeth STOUT aged 15 years and Sarah STOUT aged 12 years, children of John STOUT, dec'd.

6-28-1841 – Elijah HELLYER guardian of DAVIS aged 12 years and Wm. DAVIS aged 10 years, children of John DAVIS, dec'd.

6-28-1841 – Joseph P. NAYLOR guardian of George W. CANE aged 16 years past and Anna Maria CANE aged 14 years past, children of Walter CAIN, dec'd.

6-30-1841 – Robert BELL guardian of Thomas BELL aged 15 years last past, son of Jno. BELL, dec'd.

6-30-1841 – William CORNER guardian of Hannah ADY aged 9 years past and Frances Mary ADY aged 6 years past, children of James T. ADY, dec'd.

* 7-3-1841 - John McINTYRE appointed guardian by will of James McDOWELL, dec'd late of Morgan County of Elizabeth McDOWELL aged 11 years, Ann McDOWELL aged 9 years, William McDOWELL aged 7 years, John McDOWELL aged 6 years, Samuel McDOWELL aged 4 years and James McDOWELL aged 2 years, heirs of said James McDOWELL, dec'd.

8-30-1841 - Robert CUNNINGHAM guardian of Henry CHUFFY aged 18 years October next and Ephraim CHUFFY aged 16 years October Next, sons of Jesse S. CHUFFY, dec'd.

8-30-1841 - Ellen CHUFFY guardian of Eliza Jane CHUFFY aged 10 years, Nancy CHUFFY aged 8 years, Patrick CHUFFY aged 7 years and Charlotte CHUFFY aged 4 years, children of Jesse CHUFFY, dec'd.

10-5-1841 - Richard PENROSE guardian of Edwin GRIFFITH aged 2 years old last May.

11-8-1841 - William FARRA guardian of Sally Ann HAMMOND aged 17 years May last, William C. HAMMOND aged 14 years November 1841 and Eliza Ellen HAMMOND aged 11 years last Feby.

11-8-1841 - Alexander ADAMS guardian of Sarah Ann McCONNELL and Caroline A. McCONNELL.

12-14-1841 - Abraham ROBERTS guardian of Mary Jane ROBERTS aged 19 years next March and Rebecca Ann ROBERTS aged 17 years April next, children of Lydia ROBERTS dec'd and Heirs-at-Law of Henry SMITH, dec'd.

12-14-1841 - Abraham ROBERTS guardian of Fergus ROBERTS aged 13 years March next. child of Lydia ROBERTS, dec'd and Heir of Henry SMITH, dec'd.

3-1-1842 - Elijah STEVENS guardian of John A. C. LELAN aged 17 years, heir of Baldwin LELAN, dec'd.

3-5-1842 - Leicester G. CONVERS guardian of Benjamin G. CONVERSE aged 7 years on 7th August 1841, heir of Sophah CONVERSE, dec'd.

3-5-1842 - John SAMMONS guardian of Eliza Ann SAMMONS aged 16 years past, a legetee of John VANASDALL, dec'd.

3-5-1842 - John SAMMONS guardian of Walter SAMMONS aged 13 years past, Roseanna SAMMONS aged 12 years past, Sarah Ellen SAMMONS aged 9 years past and Elizabeth SAMMONS aged 5 years past, legatees of John VANASDAL, dec'd.

3-8-1842 - David BALDRIDGE guardian of Jonathan H., Elijah D., Sarah Ann, Mary E. and Abraham BLAZIER, children of Abraham BLAZIER, dec'd.

8-11-1842 - Sidney MASON guardian of Wm., Alazan, Hanabal, Isabel, Eleanor B. and Matilda McCLAIN, children of William McCLAIN, dec'd.

8-12-1842 - Henry B. DEARBORN guardian of Josephus B. BUKLEY.

8-19-1842 - William T. BASCOM guardian of Hannah N. STRAHL.

*The contents of this page were inadvertently duplicated in the original and are here repeated on p. 251 and the first line of p. 252.

7-3-1841 - John McINTYRE appointed guardian by will of James McDOWELL, dec'd late of Morgan County of Elizabeth McDOWELL aged 11 years, Ann McDOWELL aged 9 years, William McDOWELL aged 7 years, John McDOWELL aged 6 years, Samuel McDOWELL aged 4 years and James McDOWELL aged 2 years, heirs of said James McDOWELL, dec'd.

8-30-1841 - Robert CUNNINGHAM guardian of Henry CHUFFY aged 18 years Octcher next and Ephraim CHUFFY aged 16 years October next, sons of Jesse S. CHUFFY, dec'd.

8-30-1841 - Ellen CHUFFY guardian of Eliza Jane CHUFFY aged 10 years, Nancy CHUFFY aged 8 years, Patrick CHUFFY aged 7 years and Charlotte CHUFFY aged 4 years, children of Jesse CHUFFY, dec'd.

10-5-1841 - Richard PENROSE guardian of Edwin GRIFFITH aged 2 years old last May.

11-8-1841 - William FARRA guardian of Sally Ann HAMMOND aged 17 years May last, William C. HAMMOND aged 14 years November 1841 and Eliza Ellen HAMMOND aged 11 years last Feby.

11-8-1841 - Alexander ADAMS guardian of Sarah Ann McCONNELL and Caroline A. McCONNELL.

12-14-1841 - Abraham ROBERTS guardian of Mary Jane ROBERTS aged 19 years next March and Rebecca Ann ROBERTS aged 17 years April next, children of Lydia ROBERTS, dec'd and heirs at law of Henry SMITH, dec'd.

12-14-1841 - Abraham ROBERTS guardian of Fergus ROBERTS aged 13 years March next, child of Lydia ROBERTS, dec'd and heir of Henry SMITH, dec'd.

3-1-1842 - Elijah STEVENS guardian of John A. C. LELAN aged 17 years, heir of Baldwin LELAN, dec'd.

3-5-1842 - Leicester G. CONVERS guardian of Benjamin G. CONVERSE aged 7 years on 7th August 1841, heir of Sophah CONVERSE, dec'd.

3-5-1842 - John SAMMONS guardian of Eliza Ann SAMMONS aged 16 years past, a legetee of John VANASDALL, dec'd.

3-5-1842 - John SAMMONS guardian of Walter SAMMONS aged 13 years past, Roseanna SAMMONS aged 12 years past, Sarah Ellen SAMMONS aged 9 years past and Elizabeth SAMMONS aged 5 years past, legatees of John VANASDAL, dec'd.

3-8-1842 - David BALDRIDGE guardian of Jonathan H., Elijah D., Sarah Ann, Mary E. and Abraham BLAZIER, children of Abraham BLAZIER, dec'd.

8-11-1842 - Sidney MASON guardian of Wm., Alazan, Hanabal, Isabel, Eleanor B. and Matilda McCLAIN, children of William McCLAIN, dec'd.

8-12-1842 - Henry B. DEARBORN guardian of Josephus B. BUKLEY.

8-19-1842 - William T. BASCOM guardian of Hannah N. STRAHL.

11-21-1842 - George SLUSSER guardian of Hannah DURLIN aged 15 years, daughter of William DURLIN.

11-24-1842 - Samuel HARRIS guardian of Nancy Jane ACKLES aged 2 months, daughter of Jas. H. ACKLES.

11-25-1842 - Rachel NIXON guardian of Eliza Ann NIXON aged 16 years July 20, 1842, daughter of Hugh NIXON, dec'd.

11-28-1842 - Martin WALPOLE guardian of Charles McGOVERN and Matthew McGOVERN, sons of Charles McGOVERN, dec'd.

11-28-1842 - Martin WALPOLE guardian of Patrick McGOVERN, Elizabeth McGOVERN and James McGOVERN, children of Charles McGOVERN, dec'd.

3-13-1843 - George A. VINCENT guardian of Absolem WELLS aged 19 years, Flora WELLS aged 17 years and Benjamin F. WELLS aged 14 years, children of Amon WELLS, dec'd.

3-13-1843 - George A. VINCENT guardian of John WELLS aged 10 years and Alexander S. WELLS, heirs of Amon WELLS, dec'd.

3-13-1843 - Israel PARSONS guardian of James, Ellen and Mary Jane BLAZIER, 'rs of Jacob BLAZIER, dec'd.

3-13-1843 - Arnold SHEPARD guardian of Morris Kelly SHEPARD aged 17 years, 2 months and 9 days, son of said Arnold SHEPARD.

3-14-1843 - James LEGGETT guardian of Eli J. HAGAMAN.

3-14-1843 - Jacob RUTLEDGE guardian of Samuel HOOVER aged 16 years.

3-17-1843 - Alexander SIMPSON guardian of John J. and Rachel SMITH.

3-18-1843 - Andrew BRIGGS guardian of Robert and Rebecca BRIGGS, children of William BRIGGS, dec'd.

3-18-1843 - Andrew BRIGGS guardian of Charlotte BRIGGS aged 10 years and Nancy BRIGGS aged 8 years, children of William BRIGGS, dec'd.

3-18-1843 - Enoch POLAND guardian of his son Samuel POLAND.

3-18-1843 - Solomon PLETCHER guardian of Washington PLETCHER aged 12 years and Phoebe PLETCHER aged 10 years.

The following records consist of guardianship bonds which have been bound together into a book (no cover). They have been wrapped in a paper wrapper and are located in the Archives Room on the third floor (attic) of the Morgan County Court House. Pages are not numbered.

7-3-1843 - Jacob BALDERSON guardian of Horatio GEDDIS and Hamilton GEDDIS, heirs of William GEDDIS, dec'd and legatees of John GEDDIS, dec'd.

7-3-1843 - Jacob BALDERSON guardian of James GEDDIS aged 1 year, heir of Wm. GEDDIS, dec'd and legatee of John GEDDIS, dec'd.

8-14-1843 - Joseph STRAHL guardian of Hannah Ann STRAHL aged 12 years, daughter of Jas. STRAHL, dec'd.

8-14-1843 - Caleb HITCHCOCK guardian of Peter ROSE aged 16 years last March, son of Robt. ROSE, dec'd.

8-14-1843 - Joseph ROBERTS guardian of Nathan BANKUS aged 19 years and John BANKUS aged 16 years.

8-16-1843 - James NEWLON guardian of John NEWLON aged 14 years July last, son of David NEWLON, dec'd.

8-17-1843 - John B. STONE, guardian of John SIMONS aged 14 years January last, son of John SIMONS, dec'd.

11-20-1843 - Caleb HITCHCOCK guardian of Nancy ROSE aged 13 years 16th June last.

11-29-1843 - George RICHARDSON guardian of Susanna GRIST under 12 years.

3-16-1844 - Samuel BONE guardian of John HARPER aged 18 years 29th next April, Margaret HARPER aged 15 years next February and Mary HARPER aged 13 years 11 December next.

3-16-1844 - Samuel BONE guardian of Rhoda HARPER aged 10 years, Rachel HARPER aged 8 years, Betsey HARPER aged 6 years, Fenton HARPER aged 4 years, Daniel(?) HARPER aged 2 years and Samuel D. HARPER aged 7 months.

5-7-1844 - Phinias KEYS guardian of Luther, Patience and Emeline VANCLIEF, children of Peter VANCLIEF, dec'd.

5-10-1844 - Richard MILLER guardian of James Miller son of Chas. MILLER, dec'd.

5-10-1844 - Richard MILLER guardian of Nicholas MILLER.

5-7-1844 - Susannah SMITH guardian of Rebecca HOWARD an insane daughter of David HOWARD, dec'd.

5-7-1844 - Solomon PLETCHER guardian of Catharine Pletcher, daughter of Jacob Pletcher, dec'd.

5-7--1844 - William PETTET guardian of Jonathan, Eli and Ellis PETTET, heirs of Plummer PETTET, dec'd.

5-9-1844 - Daniel CHANDLER guardian of James F. SIMON, son of Fortner Simon.

5-10-1844 - Isaac PEACE guardian of Rebecca, Charity and Louisa SMITH, daughters wf Nathan SMITH, dec'd.

5-10-1844 - Samuel McCUNE guardian of David H., Joshua D. and William H. H. SMITH.

5-11-1844 - John CLYMER guardian of Thomas William and Barah Ann MORRIS, children of Thomas MORRIS, dec'd.

11-4-1844 - William NEISWANGER guardian of James VANHORN aged 20 years, Margaret VANHORN aged 16 years and Elizabeth VANHORN aged 17 years, children of Thomas VANHORN.

11-4-1844 - William NEISWANGER guardian of Mary Elvina VANHORN aged 11 years and John T. Burk VANHORN aged 7 years.

11-9-1844 - Edwin CORNER guardian of Joseph CHAMBERS aged 6 years and Elizabeth CHAMBERS aged 3 years, children of Jos. CHAMBERS, dec'd.

4-28-1845 - John W. BOSWORTH guardian of George BRADY aged 15 years past, son of David BRADY, dec'd.

5-19-1845 - Jacob BINGMAN guardian of Barah THOMPSON aged 13 years, daughter of Joshua THOMPSON, dec'd.

5-19-1845 - Jacob BINGMAN guardian of Franklin THOMPSON aged 11 years and Ann THOMPSON aged 9 years.

5-20-1845 - James AIKINS guardian of Elizabeth E. AIKINS aged 5 years, daughter of said guardian and heir of Alexander FOSTER.

5-20-1845 - Philip BROOKS guardian of Margaret and Ruth BROOKS.

5-20-1845 - Philip BROOKS guardian of John R. and Sarah BROOKS.

5-22-1845 - William HENDERSON guardian of John, Benj. and Mary Ann BRADLEY.

5-22-1845 - William HENDERSON guardian of William BRADLEY aged 11 years and Cyrus BRADLEY aged 6 years.

5-24-1845 - William AIKIN guardian of David RAMSEY aged 20 years next August.

5-24-1845 - Mathew BIGGER guardian of Nancy COLLINS aged 10 years and Lewis COLLINS aged 11 years, heirs of Isaac COLLINS, dec'd.

5-24-1845 - Daniel E. CHANDLER guardian of Georgiana CHANDLER aged 8 years, Araminta CHANDLER aged 7 years and Robert F. CHANDLER aged 5 years, heirs of Jacob KAHLER, dec'd.

7-28-1845 - Samuel SAILOR Jr. guardian of Caroline COOPER aged 8 years past, John COOPER aged 7 years past, David COOPER aged 4 years past, Thomas COOPER aged 3 years past and James COOPER aged 1 year past.

8-2-1845 - Amon WELLS guardian of Mary Wells aged 16 years and Laura Jane WELLS aged 14 years.

8-2-1845 - Amon WELLS guardian of Harriet Wells aged 11 years and Nancy WELLS aged 9 years.

11-3-1845 - Jacob BINGMAN guardian of Henry THOMPSON aged 15 years past, son of Joshua THOMPSON, dec'd.

11-4-1845 - Philip BROOKS guardian of Eliza HARWARD aged 3 years past and Madeson HARWARD aged 21 months past, heirs of Henry HARWARD, dec'd.

11-5-1845 - Jacob FOWLER guardian of Wm. S. FOWLER aged 12 years, Nathan FOWLER aged 10 years and James FOWLER aged 7 years, heirs of Nathan SMITH, dec'd.

11-5-1845 - Isaac KEYSER guardian of Joseph GREER.

11-10-1845 - Daniel C. WALKER guardian of John, Mary Ann and Geo. W. SANBORN, children of Geo. W. SANBORN, dec'd.

11-12-1845 - Steward HOPKINS guardian of Isaac MELVIN aged 7 years, son of Chas. MELVIN, dec'd.

12-31-1845 - Joshua DAVIS guardian of William SPRAGUE aged 18 years and Margaret SPRAGUE aged 15 years, heirs of Nathan SPRAGUE, dec'd.

12-31-1845 - Joshua DAVIS guardian of Samuel, Eliza, Martha and Susan SPRAGUE, heirs of Nathaniel SPRAGUE, dec'd.

2-11-1846 - George BELL guardian of James H. BELL, son of James BELL, dec'd.

3-3-1846 - Reuben McVAY guardian of James PORTER aged 9 years, son of Joseph PORTER.

3-3-1846 - Henry DOUDNA guardian of Rachel PICKET aged 17 years and Hannah PICKET aged 15 years.

3-3-1846 - Henry DOUDNA guardian of Sarah PICKET aged 10 years, Thomas PICKET aged 6 years and Matilda PICKET aged 3 years.

3-3-1846 - Oliver KEYSER guardian of John M. COLLINS aged 20 years and Margaret J. COLLINS aged 14 years, children of Sam'l COLLINS, dec'd.

3-4-1846 - Ellen CHEFFEY guardian of Eliza Jane CHEFFEY aged 14 years and Nancy CHEFFEY aged 13 years, children of Jesse CHEFFEY, dec'd.

3-4-1846 Robert McONNEL guardian of James FARRA Jr. aged 5 years October last.

3-5-1846 - Josiah WRIGHT guardian of Olive EDDINGTON aged 8 years October last and Susan EDDINGTON aged 5 years December last, heirs of Jonathan EDDINGTON, dec'd.

3-5-1846 - Josiah WRIGHT guardian of Ursula EDDINGTON aged 14 years past, daughter of Jonathan EDDINGTON, dec'd.

3-5-1846 - Eskridge TORBERT guardian of Mary PUGH aged 19 years, heir at law of Samuel PUGH late of the State of Virginia.

3-6-1846 - Ezra E. EVANS guardian of Morris MARTIN aged 20 years, son of Thos. MARTIN, dec'd.

3-7-1846 - John W. SANDS guardian of James J. NELSON aged 15 years, son of John NELSON, dec'd.

3-7-1846 - John W. SANDS guardian of Isaac, Seth, Henry, Robert and John NELSON, sons of John NELSON, dec'd

3-7-1846 - Samuel WILSON guardian of William, Whitney, James and Mary MARTIN, heirs of Thomas MARTIN, dec'd.

3-7-1846 - James MURRAY guardian of Robert, Joseph and Thomas MARTIN, children of Thos. MARTIN, dec'd.

6-11-1846 - William HANN guardian of Elizabeth TORBERT aged 13 years, daughter of Wm. TORBERT, dec'd.

6-11-1846 - John HENDERSON guardian of Catherine HENDERSON aged 2 years and Drusilla HENDERSON aged 4 months, children of Chas. HENDERSON, dec'd.

6-12-1846 - Owen MARIS guardian of Marshall J. MARIS aged 18 years and Mary Anna MARIS aged 15 years, heirs at law of Owen MARIS.

6-12-1846 - Owen MARIS guardian of Rebecca MARIS aged 9 years, Clark MARIS aged 7 years and George MARIS aged 5 years.

6-13-1846 - Wm. PATTON guardian of Mahlon PATTON aged 20 years, Jared PATTON aged 18 years, Merrick PATTON aged 16 years and Esther PATTON aged 12 years, children of Wm. PATTON.
6-13-1846 - Wm. PATTON guardian of Lydia PATTON aged 10 years, daughter of Wm. PATTO

6-13-1846 - Ephraim JOHNSON (JOHNSTON) guardian of Ephraim JOHNSON aged 9 years, Joh JOHNSON aged 7 years, Jane JOHNSON aged 6 years and Elizabeth JOHNSON aged 4 years, heirs of Andrew JOHNSON, dec'd.

6-16-1846 - William COPE guardian of Elias COPE, son of James COPE, dec'd.

6-16-1846 - Ann E. COPE guardian of Emalina, James and Lucretia COPE minor children
of James COPE, dec'd.

6-16-1846 - Nicholas COBURN Jr. guardian of America McVEIGH aged 17 years, Stacy
McVEIGH aged 15 years and Orsemus McVEIGH aged 14 years, children of Stacy McVEIGH,
dec'd.

6-16-1846 - Nicholas COBURN Jr. guardian of Silas McVEIGH aged 12 years and Catherine
McVEIGH aged 10 years, heirs of Stacey McVEIGH, dec'd.

6-19-1846 - Alexander SIMPSON guardian of Robert WILLIAMS aged 15 years, son of
Jacob WILLIAMS.

7-21-1846 - Jacob M. SMITH guardian of Sion CRAMBLET aged 18 years past, heir of
P. I. ATKESON, dec'd.

9-8-1846 - David LONG guardian of Mary Jane STEWART, daughter of James STEWART, dec'd.

9-8-1846 - William HENDERSON guardian of Emily Jane HEDGE aged 7 years, Cecelia HEDGE
aged 6 years and Mary Ellen HEDGE aged 6 months.

9-8-1846 - Oliver KEYSER guardian of Francis A . GALLATIN aged 3 years and Susannah
G. GALLATIN aged 1 year, children of Susannah GALLATIN.

9-8-1846 - William MARQUIS guardian of Gallatin S. MARQUIS aged 2 years and Francis
A. MARQUIS aged 3 months.

9-9-1846 - John B. STONE guardian of George KERR, aged 18 years past.

9-10-1846 - Peter KEITH guardian of Perry ROLAND aged 16 years and 11 months, son
of Edward ROLAND, dec'd.

9-17-1846 - Ralph PORTER guardian of Seth S. PORTER aged 12 years, Jonathan C. PORTER
aged 10 years and Ruby B. PORTER aged 6 years, children of said Ralph PORTER.

9-19-1846 - Benjamin WELLS guardian of John WELLS, aged 14 years, son of Amon WELLS.

2-25-1847 - Susannah SMITH guardian of Rebecca HOWARD an insane daughter of David
HOWARD.

3-1-1847 - Joseph PENROSE guardian of Mary Elvira PENROSE aged 7 years past and
Albert PENROSE aged 6 years past, heirs at law of Abel GILBERT.

3-1-1847 - James HAMMOND guardian of Thos. M., Austin, Mary, Kalista, Lewis and
George WHITE, children of Wm. WHITE, dec'd.

MORGAN COUNTY, OHIO - COMMON PLEAS MINUTE BOOK A

Contributed by: Maydell Alderman, 79 North Eighth St., McConnelsville, Ohio 43756

The following records were copied from "Minute Book A" located in the Archives at
the court house in McConnelsville. Page on which record may be found in original
book is given in parenthesis.

4-5-1819 - William RANNELS produced commissions as Presiding Judge, Sherebiah CLARK
    and William B. YOUNG produced comissions as Associate Judges, said commissions
    granted by Ethan Allen BROWN, Governor of Ohio Apr. 5, 1819.   (1)
4-6-1819 - Samuel Augustus BARKER appointed Clerk until next term. John DOLAND
    appointed prosecuting attorney for state. Timothy GAYLORD appointed Recorder
    for county. William DAVIS appointed Surveyor for county.   (1)
4-6-1819 - John DODDS by his attorney John DOLAND acknowledged indebtedness to Isaac
    VAN HORN of Muskingum County in amount of $114.34½.   (2)
5-21-1819 - Samuel MARTIN appointed adms. of estate of his brother, Thomas MARTIN,
    dec'd late of Morgan twp. Appraisers: Wm MONTGOMERY & Timothy M. GATES. (2)
7-5-1819 - Grand Jury summoned: William M. DAWES, foreman; Sylvanus NEWTON, Joseph
    DEVEREAUX, Archibald McCOLLUM, Richard CHEADLE, Arphaxad DUVOL, Zadoc DICKER-
    SON, Gilbert OLNEY, Isaac HEDGES, Simeon MUGRIDGE, Samuel HENRY, Asa EMERSON,
    Nathaniel SHEPARD, Rufus P. STONE, Alexander McCONNEL.   (3)
7-5-1819 - James YOUNG granted license to keep tavern at his residence in McConnel-
    ville by paying County Treasury $7.00.   (3)
7-5-1819 - William ALOWAY discharge his recongnizance for breach of peace on body
    of John HULL.   (3)
7-5-1819 - Timothy M. GATES brought into court. Bond, Daniel COLEMAN and Enoch
    LOPER.   (3)
7-5-1819 - David STEVENS granted license to keep tavern at his house in Megsville. (3)
7-5-1819 - Jacob P. SPRINGER granted license to keep tavern at his residence in
    McConnelsville.   (3)
7-6-1819 - Centre Township struck off and qualified electors authorized to elect
    two Justices of the Peace.   (4)
7-6-1819 - Olive Green Township. to call an election to elect two Justices of the
    Peace.   (4)
7-6-1819 - Enoch LOPER for assault & battery on James FRISBY. Not Guilty plea. (4)
7-6-1819 - State of Ohio vs. Enoch LOPER, found guilty and fined $3.00 and costs.
    Jury: Timothy M. GATES, Benjamin JOHNSON, William MURPHY, Wm LEWIS, Micah
    ADAMS, Philip KAHLER, Benjamin WITHAM, Elisha WITHAM, Abraham HEWS, John
    SEAMAN, Samuel WHITE and Benjamin W. TALBOT.   (5)
7-6-1819 - Cornelius P. FINCH granted license to vend goods in Lexington.   (5)
7-6-1819 - Jacob ADAMS granted license to vend goods in McConnelsville.   (5)
7-6-1819 - Enoch LOPER for assault & battery on body of Ezekiel HYETTE, guilty. (5)
7-6-1819 - Enoch LOPER for assault & battery on Job ARMSTRONG, Constable.
    Indictment quashed.   (5)
7-7-1819 - George MELLOER license to keep tavern at his residence in Malta.   (7)
7-7-1819 - Daniel COLEMAN for Petit Larceny, pled not guilty but verdict of guilty
    ordered, imprisoned two hours and fine of $20.00 and costs.   (5-6)
7-7-1819 - Bloom Township set off and ordered that two Justices of Peace be elected
    at house of James WHITAKER.   (7)
7-7-1819 - George MELLOER acknowledged to owe Wm HEWS for use of Simeon POOL $240.00
    Wm HEWS for use of Simeon POOL vs. John LUCAS, Assumpsit(?), Damages $120.00.
    (7-8)

258

7-7-1819 - James LARISON license to keep tavern at his residence in McConnelsville.(8)
7-7-1819 - York Township established, ordered that two Justices of the Peace be
elected at house of John STONEBURNER. Olive Township established. Brookfield Township established. Windsor Township established with electors
to meet at house of John HARRIS. Bristol Township established with electors
to meet at house of Mr. (Simon) MERVIN. (8,9,10)
10-4-1819 - Lovet BISHOP vs. John DAVIS. Davis to await final judgment. (11)
10-4-1819 - Ezekiel (MOORE) vs. Philip MOORE. Slander. Jury: Levi DAVIS, John B.
PERRY, Phineas COBURN, Simeon BLAKE, James WHITAKER, Wm SILVEY, James HARRIS,
Jared ANDREWS, Levi ELLIS, Levi DEAVER, John SHUTT, Johnathan PORTER. (11)
10-4-1819 - James REED brings certificate from Commonwealth of Pennsylvana wherein
he applied for citizenship. Was born County Antrim Ireland, was 24 years old
at time of application (March 3, 1813), emigrated from Belfast, in 1807 and
arrived in Penna. in June of same year. Certificate issued by Clerk. (12-13)
(note: Morgan Co. History p. 253 states "- he was an Irishman, residing on
Duck Creek, now in Noble County.")
10-4-1819 - Bill of Indictment against Robert WELCH for assault and battery on Thos.
MURY (MURRAY). (13)
10-5-1819 - Ezekiel HYATT vs. Philip MOORE. Verdict for pltff of $17.00 & costs.(13)
10-5-1819 - Samuel W. CULBERTSON vs. Daniel BEAN. Trespass. Judgment by default.
Damages $360.00 and costs. (14)
10-5-1819 - John BECKWITH vs. Levi DEVER. Debt $85.00. Judgment by default. (14)
10-5-1819 - John BRADY vs. Benjamin W. TALBOT. Debt $100.00. Jdgt. by default. (14)
10-5-1819 - Isaiah ALLEN for use of Vachel HALL vs. Absalom BRODERICK. Judgment
by default. Damages $126.50. (15)
10-5-1819 - Jacob P. SPRINGER vs. James YOUNG. Covenant. Case cont. (15)
10-5-1819 - Samuel THOMPSON vs. James YOUNG. Debt. $79.20. (15)
10-5-1819 - Wm HUGHS for use of Simeon POOL vs. John LUCAS. Trespass. $103.32. (15)
10-5-1819 - John HULL vs. William ALLOWAY and Mary his wife. Pltf came not. (15-16)
10-5-1819 - Wilber SPRAGUE vs. Aaron HEWS. Suit dismissed. (16)
10-5-1819 - John LUCAS vs. Patrick CHEADLE. Parties consent to final arbitration
of Thomas WHITE, Sylvanus NEWTON and Wm DAVIS. (Appeal 7-10-1820). (17)
10-5-1819 - State of Ohio vs. Polly MOORE. Deft. discharged. (17)
10-5-1819 - John CARLOW vs. James YOUNG and Barney T. PRATT. Case dismissed. (17)
10-5-1819 - State of Ohio vs. Abraham HEWS. Assault and Battery on Wm LEWIS.
Pled guilty and asked for mercy. Fined $1.00. (18)
10-5-1819 - Timothy GAYLORD licensed to keep a ferry across the Muskingum River
at McConnelsville for one year. (18)
10-5-1819 - David LAPAN produced a certificate from Adriel HERSEY certifying that
he was a minister of the Free Willed Baptists. License granted. (18)
3-27-1820 - Ezra OSBORN, President of Court. Grand Jurors named: Dennis GIBBS,
foreman; Joseph SMITH, talesman; Daniel DUVAL, John NOBLE, Joseph CHEADLE,
Simeon MORGAREIDGE, Phineas COBURN, Robert P. HILLIARD (summoned but did not
appear), Zecheriah CUDDINGTON, Timothy M. GATES, Solomon BROWN, Henry AWMILLER,
Joseph McCONNEL, John BELL, Lenoard ST CLAIR, Simeon MERVIN. (19)
3-27-1820 - Oman OLNEY arraigned for assault and battery on Catharine OLNEY.
Asa EMERSON Jr. a witness. Plead guilty and fined $5.00 and costs. (20)
3-27-1820 - Nathaniel SHEPERD granted license to keep tavern at his house in Morgan
twp. (21)
3-27-1820 - B.W. TALBOT, Joseph LIPPITT and Samuel T. ROBERTS granted licenses to
keep tavern at their respective dwellings. (21)
3-27-1820 - Will of James SPENCER produced and proven. (21)
3-27-1820 - David EMERSON vs. Thomas TUFT. Appeal dismissed. (21)

3-27-1820 - David McGARRY and Ann his wife vs. James REED. Slander. Case cont.(22)
3-27-1820 - Jacob FOGAL vs. John REED. Appeal entered. (22)
3-28-1820 - Enoch LOPER for assault and battery on John HULL. Guilty. $1.00 & costs.
   (22)
3-28-1820 - James YOUNG acknowledges to owe Samuel GATES $800.00 to be levied on
   his goods, chattels, tenements and real estate. (23)
3-28-1820 - Edwin CORNER license to vend goods in McConnelsville. (24)
3-28-1820 - James YOUNG vs. Wm JANES. In Chancery. Appeal to Supreme Court. (24)
3-28-1820 - State of Ohio vs. John MOORE. Deft. discharged. (25)
3-28-1820 - Jacob P. SPRINGER elected Sheriff. John BELL contested election and
   was overruled. (25)
2-29-1820 - Benjamin W. TALBOT vs. John BRADY. In Chancery. (26)
7-10-1820 - Ezra OSBORN, President of Court. Grand Jurors: Timothy M. GATES,
   foreman; Levi LITTLE, Josiah WRIGHT, Elijah BALL, John SNIFF, Jobe WEST,
   Daniel LAWRENCE, James McELROY, James DYE, Joseph MILLS. Talesmen: Richard
   DOOR, John McKEE, Peter BURGOON, Jacob SWOB, Andrew WHARTON. (27)
7-10-1820 - Sam'l GAZAWAY vs. John BELL. Case cont. (27)
7-10-1820 - Aaron HANESWORTH vs. Jacob SEREL, alias Jacob JACOBS. Slander. Case
   dismissed. (29)
7-11-1820 - Jurors elected: Joseph DEVEREAUX, Stephen HUTCHENS, Foster (Forster)
   EDWARDS, John HARRIS, Wm OLIPHANT, Robt. McCUNE, Henry HUNTER, John N.
   GIBSON, Richard JENKINS, Luther DEARBORN, Wm BRIGGS, Jacob KAHLER. (30)
7-11-1820 - Nicholas COBURN granted license to keep ferry across Muskingum River
   at or near his house for one year. (30)
7-11-1820 - Philip MOORE and Mary his wife vs. John GARLAND and Ann CARLAND minors
   under 21 years by J. P. SPRINGER, guardian. (31)
7-11-1820 - Catharine BOND, widow of Richard E. BOND elects not to take estate as
   willed and devised by her late husband. She is appointed admsrs. under bond
   of $1000.00 with Caleb WELLS and John MARTIN, sureties. Appraisers: Henry
   HAMILTON, Francis SCOTT and Mr. CHARLOTTE. (31)
7-11-1820 - Timothy PEACEABLE possessee of Michael DEVER vs. Thomas TROUBLESOME
   with notice to Simeon MORGAREIDGE, tenant in possession. Ejectment.
   Discont. on false clamor. (32)
7-11-1820 - Elijah DAY vs. Erasmus ROSE. In Attachment - case cont. (32)
7-11-1820 - Benjamin W. TALBOT vs. John BRADY. In Chancery. Brady is not a resident of this state and suit to be advertized for nine weeks in Zanesville
   paper. (32)
7-11-1820 - William LAMMA indicted for assault and battery. (35)
7-11-1820 - Robert WINTERS license to vend goods in McConnelsville. (35)
7-11-1820 - Court having power to fine and imprison Hananiah NEWTON, aged 58 years,
   resident of Windsor, who declares he served in Revolutionary War as follows:
   Entered July 10, 1778, Massachusetts line, served three years, honorably
   discharged as set forth in his Pension Allication made June 2, 1818 in
   Pennsylvania and transferred to Ohio. All his property consists of two
   acres of Indian corn growing, 1/4th acre of rye, 8 bushels wheat in the
   stalk, 1 Kettle, 1 pot, 1 Tea Kettle, 1 Dutch oven, 2 axes, 6 cups and
   saucers, 4 knives and forks, 4 plates, 2 sows with 7 pigs. $30.00 owed to
   John Cheadle, applicant in debt $30.00 to Zebulon Boardman and $9.92 to Thos.
   Sills. Family consists of wife aged fifty-four, twins aged fourteen in good
   health and a son aged ten of a weak constitution. (36)

7-12-1820 - Pension Declaration. Augustine ANDERSON, aged 70 years, resident of Deerfield Township. Served in Revolutionary war from New Jersey. Schedule of Property: Lands, none; Personal Property, none except 2 Beds and necessary clothing for the family, 2 pots, 1 kettle worth $4.00. Occupation: Taylor - unable to pursue for want of eyesight. Four in family, viz.. my wife aged 61 years; one daughter Matilda aged 16 able to support herself; one grandson named Joseph Blain aged 10 years, able to support himself.   (37)
(note: Matilda married Jeremie Weston Nov. 28, 1821. Joseph Blain married Elizabeth Chalf May 7, 1836.)

7-12-1820 - Wm MURPHY indicted for resisting a police officer.   (39)

7-12-1820 - Benjamin WIMER vs. Jane YOUNG. Declared a non-suit.   (39)

7-12-1820 - Nathaniel AYERS vs. Thomas WALLS.   cont'd.   (40)

7-12-1820 - Pension Declaration. Hugh OSBOURN, aged 60 yrs., resident of Bristol Twp. Served in Revolutionary War in the Naval Service 1781 on board Aliance Frigate. Schedule of property: 2 blankets, 1 cow, 1 heafer, 1 calf, 1 large kettle, 1 spider, 2 tin cups, 2 spoons. Debts due me, note of $4.00. Family: Wife about 57 yrs. old and one son aged 19 yrs. and unable to perform any kind of labor.   (40)

10-29-1820 - Grand Jurors: Wm M. DAINES, foreman, Alex. McCONNEL, Rufus P. STONE, John HASKET, Hollis HUTCHINS, Benj. W. TALBOT, Zepheniah TYSON, Jno. D. RUTLEDGE, Robt. ROWLAND, James LONGSTRETH, Barsilla COBURN, Stephen CHARLOTTE.

10-31-1820 - James BURGOON indicted for maiming and pleads not guilty.   (42)

10-31-1820 - Jacob ADAMS granted license to keep tavern at his residence in McCONNELSVILLE.   (42)

10-31-1820 - Naturalization: Richard CAMPBELL makes declaration. Born in Ireland; arrived in New York sometime in the year 1801; about 44 years of age; resides in Salem Twp., Washington County; has two sons, John CAMPBELL aged 18 years and Robert CAMPBELL aged 14 years born in Ireland. Certificate issued to him and his sons.   (46)

10-31-1820 - Naturalization: Joseph REID makes declaration. Bor in Ireland, arrived Norfolk, Va. September 26, 1801; about 43 years of age; resides in Noble Twp. (46)

10-31-1820 - Naturalization: William NIXON, born in Ireland, arrived at Philadelphia in 1792, now 35 years old and resides in Deerfield Twp. Certificate issued. (47)

10-31-1820 - Naturalization: Hugh NIXON, born Ireland, arrived at Philadelphia in 1792, now 38 years old and resides in Deerfield Twp. Certificate issued.(47)

10-31-1820 - Edward MELLOER fined $15.00 and cost for affray.   (48)

10-31-1820 - Will of Jonathan FRISBEY produced for Probate. Wm MONTGOMERY and James GRISBEY gave bond for executor and executrix (not named) 500.00. (48)

10-31-1820 - William ALLISON pleads guilty to assault and battery against John BRUEN.   (48)

10-31-1820 - Barna SUTTIFF pleads not guilty to assault and battery against John EVANS.   (48)

10-31-1820 - Samuel EVANS pleads not guilty to assault and battery against John EVANS.   (49)

10-31-1820 - David MILLER vs. Samuel SHATTUCK. Appeal from Judgment of Simeon Meriven, J.P. & constable of Bristol Twp. denied.   (50)

10-31-1820 - William B. YOUNG granted license to keep tavern at his house in Matta. (50)

10-31-1820 - Samuel A. BARKER appointed Master Commissioner in Chancery.   (51)

10-31-1820 - False Imprisonment. John McKEE vs. John REED Jun., slander. Robert
McKEE vs. John REED Jun., slander. John REED Jun. vs. John McKEE, David
McGARRY and Elijah DAY.   (52)
11-1-1820 - Naturalization: John COLISON (COLLISON) declares intention of becoming
a citizen, etc. as per paper on file. (Certificate issued 9-27-1824).   (54)
11-1-1820 - Pension declaration: John SPRINGUM, aged abt. 65 years, served in Virginia line.. States he has no income nor any property other than one suit of
wearing apparel. Occupation, farmer but injured and unable to labor.
(signs with his mark.)   (55)
11-1-1820 - Pension declaration: Mathew WILSON, aged 65 years, enlisted May 10,
1776; joined his Regiment at Hatbush, L.I. and in battles of Long Island,
White Plains, Newton, Princeton and Brandy Wine; at the massacre of Pioli
(sic.)and Germantown Battle and took up winter quarters at Valley Forge.
Discharged June 1, 1778, but served on frontiers of Northumberland County,
Penna. as a spie to the end of the War. Trade formerly follwed was coopering. One son at home 14 years old, one boy and girl put out on service.   (55)
11-1-1820 - Jacob ADAMS indicted vs. Timoth M. GATES.   (57)
11-1-1820 - Caleb WELLS indicted vs. Wm. E. JOHNSTON.   (57)
11-1-1820 - Report of John BROWNING (Evidently refers to Naturalization). Birthplace, Westmoreland, age 48, English, residence, Morgan County, Ohio.   (60)
11-1-1820 - Timoth GAYLORD indicted for Extortion.   (60)
12-20-1820 - Sarah FRISBEY qualified as Executor of estate of Jonathan FRISBEY,
dec'd.   (61)
12-10-1820 - Hennetta KNOX, widow, and John Whaley KNOX, son, granted Letters of
Administration to the Estate of Tilman KNOX, dec'd. Appraisers: Thomas
Murray, Isaac Council and Joseph Kidd.   (61)
3-27-1821 - Grand Jurors: Daniel CHANDLER, Foreman, Jared ANDREWS, John PRICE,
Garret JORDAN, Adam KECK (KEITH), Thomas DYE, Samuel McCLINTOCK, Nathan
NEWTON, Asher ALLEN, Samuel WHITE, Nathan SMITH. Talesman: Michael DENEN,
Israel REDMAN, Samuel HENRY and Isaac WALBRIDGE.   (62)
3-27-1821 - Charles David appointed guardian to Irana BARTLET, John BARTLET and
James BARTLET with Simeon Montgomery and Wm. Davis, sureties.   (63)
3-28-1821 - George RUSSEL, minister licensed,as ordained minister of the Baptist
Church, to solemnize marriages.   (64)
3-28-1821 - Robert OLIVER declared not guilty for maiming, assault & battery.   (66)
3-28-1821 - Nehemiah BLAKE indicted for assault and battery.   (66)
3-28-1821 - William WOODS indicted for assault and battery.   (67)
3-28-1821 - Letters of Administration granted to James Burgoon and Cornelius Farrel
on Estate of Peter BURGOON, dec'd, with Bartholomew Longstreth and John
Murphy, sureties. Appraisers: George Smith, Bartholomew Longstreth and
Wm. Foreacre.   (68)
3-28-1821 - Asa EMERSON granted tavern license.   (68)
3-29-1821 - George KNOX and orphan child of Tilman KNOX, dec'd, chooses Zepheneah
Tyson his guardian and Thomas Jenkins his security.   (73)
3-29-1821 - Jacob P. Springer chosen guardian by Rettay B. KNOX with George Mellor
his surety.   (73)
3-29-1821 - John W. Knox chosen guardian by Bethnel KNOX with Thomas Jenkins his
surety.   (73)
3-29-1821 - Hennitta Knox appointed guardian of Charles and Sally KNOX orphan children of Tilman KNOX with Andrew Welch their surety.   (74)
3-29-1821 - Thomas BYERS indicted for perjury and pleads not guilty.   (74)

262

3-29-1821 - Pension Declaration: John KIRK, aged 67 years a resident in Bristol twp., enlisted in 1776 and served in Maryland line for six months and taken prisoner at Fort Washington and let off on parole of honor. Family consists of wife aged 78 years and infirm, and a grand-daughter aged 12 years in good health. Property valued at $8.00. (75)

3-29-1821 - Richard GILLWELL, Alexander BROWN, Job KENISON, Thomas JENKINS, county payroll. (76)

3-30-1821 - Julia DEARBORN widow of Luther DEARBORN appointed administratrix of his estate with Timothy M. Gates and Barna Sutleff sureties. Appraisers: Sylvenus Newton, Samuel Henry and Ephraim Ellis. (77)

3-30-1821 - Jeremy Weston granted Letters of Adminstration on Estate of Jonathan CHANAY, late of Morgan twp. Sureties: Timothy M. Gates and Alexander McConnel. Appraisers: Wm. M. Daines, Nathionel Shepherd and Amasa Piper.(77)

7-10-1821 - Grand Jurors: Enoch McIntosh, Foreman, Joseph Davis, Henry Moore, John Sniff, Jacob Kahler, John Brown, Nicholas Coburn, Wm. Scoggen, Isaac Hedges, Shubiah Smith, Andrew Bridge. Talesman: Benj. Thorla, Wm. Silvey (replaced by Hugh Riley), John Seaman, John Williams. (78)

7-10-1821 - Samuel S. ROBERTS granted license to keep tavern at his house in Deerfield twp. (78)

7-10-1821 - Joseph BELL indicted for assault and battery and found guilty. (80)

7-11-1821 - Samuel BARKER appointed Clerk of the Court. (81-83?)

7-11-1821 - Charlotte Green, widow of Oliver W. GREEN, late of Brookfield twp. appointed admix. with Wm. Rannells and Andrew Wharton, sureties. Appraisers: Daniel Whitamore, Findla Collins and John Draper. (84)

7-11-1821 - Will of Joseph SMITH, late of Bloom twp. Executors: Wm. Montgomery, James Whitaker. Witnesses: Micah Adams, Jeremiah Conaway. (84)

7-12-1821 - Highman (Hyman) LAZARUS granted license to vend goods in town of Malta. (87)

7-12-1821 - Estate of Jonathan FRISHEY. Land located NE¼ Sec. 10 Twp 11 R12 Dist. Zanesville. To pay widow Sarah Frishey one-third of proceeds. (87)

7-13-1821 - Appl. granted to Wm. B. YOUNG for ferry across Muskingum at Malta. Former lease by Timoth GAYLORD abandoned. (89)

7-13-1821 - Thurman RANSOM vs. James YOUNG. Trial next term. (90)

7-13-1821 - Mary WALTER by next friend Samuel Walter vs. John HULL. Slander. (90)

7-13-1821 - Alexander R. PINKERTON vs. Lewis REMEY. Slander. (93)

7-13-1821 - Benjamin NOTT, Windsor twp. chooses Richard Cheadle his guardian with Alexander McCONNEL his surity. (95)

7-25-1821 - Samuel A. BARKER, Clerk of Ct. Augustus BARKER, depty clerk. (97)

10-29-1821 - Grand Jurors: Nathan Dearborn, Wm. Massey, Ebenezer Barchus, Sam'l Wickam, Jonathan Hews, Henry Carrol, Wm. Foreacre, Wm. Ogle, Isaac James, Nathan Smith (of Bloom), Joseph McConnel, Sam'l M. Dike. Talesmen: Wm. Hawkins, Timothy Gaylord, Samuel Walker. (98)

10-29-1821 - David STEVENS indicted selling liquor without license. (98)

10-29-1821 - Samuel Walker appointed guardian for Mary WALKER, a minor, to prosecute the suit of Mary Walker vs. Reuben Porter for slander. (98)

10-30-1821 - Union Township formed. (102)

10-30-1821 - Will of William NIXON proven. Executor, Hugh Nixon. Sureties: Mills Hall, Elijah Ball. Appraisers: Mills Hall, Elijah Ball, James Nelson. (101)

10-31-1821 - William Davis appt. Administrator Estate of Titus B. HINMAN, late of Windsor twp. Sureties, David Emerson, John Cheadle. (105)

10-31-1821 - William DAVIS appt. Administrator of estate of his brother Joshua
DAVIS, late of Windsor twp. upon widow's request. Appraisers: Samuel
Henry, Nathan Dearborn, Asa Emerson, Junr.   (106)
10-31-1821 - Elisha HAND, Nathan DEARBORN, Richard Cheadle apptd. appraisers
of personal property of Titus B. HENMAN.   (106)
10-31-1821 - Abagail Godrey, widow of Prince GODFREY, late of Windsor twp. apptd.
Administratrix. Sureties: Nathan Dearborn, Samuel Henry.   (106)
11-1-1821 - William Free apptd. Administrator of estate of Joseph MATHENEY, late of
Olive twp. Sureties: Jacob P. Springer, Robt. McKee. Appraisers: Robt.
McKee, Gilman Dudley, David Wells.   (111)
3-25-1822 - Grand Jurors: Saml Henry, Ezekiel Dye, Jacob Fogle, Aaron Hanesworth,
John Waller, Wm. Warren, Alexander Martin, Wm. Jacobs, Michael Shriver, John
Jones, Matthew Grimes, Wm. Free, Joseph Blackburn. Talesmen: Geo. Newman,
Jonathan Porter.   (112)
3-25-1822 - Joseph DEVEREAUX granted license to keep a tavern at his house in
Bristol twp.   (113)
3-25-1822 - Naturalization: John MURPHY born in County of Cork sometime in the
year 1781, as he believes. Arrived in New York City April 3, 1807.   (114)
3-25-1822 - Naturalization: Andrew GOSMAN, born in County of Parin, Germany sometime in the year 1785. Arrived in Philadelphia August 25, 1817 with his
children Agnes aged about three years and Frederick aged about four, born in
County of Parin. Renounces allegiance to Francis first, Emperor of Austria.
Declares his declaration of intention to become citizen of United States.(11
3-25-1822 - Gilman Dudley apptd guardian of Sidney and John GLIDDEN, heirs of John
GLIDDEN, late of Olive twp. Sureties: Wm. Free, Dennis Gibbs.   (115)
3-25-1822 - Naturalization: David McGARRY makes declaration of intention to become
citizen. Born County of Antrim, Ireland February 25, 1795. Arxived Amboy,
New Jersey September 23, 1815. Renounces allegiance to George IV.   (119)
3-25-1822 - Timoth GAYLORD appointed Recorder Morgan County.   (119)
7-15-1822 - Grand Jurors: Jeremiah Conaway, Uriah Harris, Wm. Benis, Geo. Crow,
Geo. Dye, Ephrain Wight, Wm. Brown, Wilkes Bozman, Stephen Roe, David Proutz
Bartholomew Longstreth, Sam'l Moody, Joseph Anderson. Talesman: James
Grubb, Nathanel Shepherd.   (120)
7-15-1822 - Natralization: James CLEMENTS, native of Ireland. Declaration made in
Penna. three years since Certificate issued.   (122)
7-15-1822 - John Mellor proved affidavits of George MELLOR and John QUIGLEY stating
he had resided in U.S. between 18th day of June 1798 and 14th day of April
1802 and was of good moral character. Certificate issues.   (122)
7-15-1822 - Naturalization: Samuel MELLOR a native of England, upon affidavit of
John Quigley. Certificate issued.   (123)
7-15-1822 - Naturalization: Samuel MELLOR 3rd, native of England upon affidavit of
John Quigley. Certificate issued.   (124)
7-15-1822 - John SPEEDMAN indicted for stealing a mare.   (124)
7-15-1822 - Naturalization: George MELLOR, native of England, on oath of John
Quigley. Certificate issued.   (125)
7-16-1822 - Naturalization: Declaration of John SMITH, born in County of Corin,
Ireland sometime in the year 1788, believes he arrived at Sockets Harbor
in New York about August 20, 1819 with his child Ann aged about 6 weeks
born in Montreal, Lower Canada.   (128)
7-16-1822 - Declaration of Mathew WALPOLE, born in County of Leitrim, Ireland, in
Europe sometime in the year 1762 and arrived in City of New York Sept. 18,
1817.   (129)

7-16-1822 - Naturalization: Declaration of Matthew WALPOLE, Junr., born in County of Cavan, Ireland sometime in year of 1788 as he believes and arrived at Sackets Harbour with his child Patrick aged about 4 years, born County Cavan, August 20, 1819. (129)

7-16-1822 - Naturalization: Martin WALPOLE, born in County Cavan, Ireland 1778 and arrived in City of New York in the month of August 1816. Certificate issued. (130)

7-16-1822 - Naturalization: Patrick LAFFEN(LAFFAND) born in County of Carlow, Ireland about year 1782and believes he arrived in Boston August 6, 1818. Certificate issued. (130)

7-16-1822 - Naturalization: Andrew DEWGAN(DUGAN), born in County Monnon(Monaghan), Ireland; is 65 years of age and arrived in Jersey City July 14, 1806. Application filed March 20, 1822. (131)

7-17-1822 - John SPEELMAN found guilty of stealing a mare. Sentenced to Penitentuary in Columbus for three years. (135)

11-7-1822 - Grand Jurors: Timoth Gaylord, Simeon Morgareidge, Richard McElhaney, Wm. Fouts, Casper Tront, John Quigley, James Stones, Hugh Nickerson, Henry McElroy, Wm. C. Johnson, Erastus Hoskins, John Shutt. Talesmen: John McGarry, Wm. Massey, James Briggs. (137)

11-7-1822 - Will of Enos HEDDEN, late of Morgan twp. proven with James A. Gilespey and Phoebe Hedden executors. Appraisers: John Seaman, Wm. Palmer and Isaac James. (139)

11-7-1822 - Jane YOUNG, widow, appointed Administratrix of estate of William B. YOUNG with Rufus P. Stone and Jacob R. Price, sureties. Appraisers: Wm. Fouts, Jacob P. Springer and Jonathan Porter. (140)

11-7-1822 - Naturalization: Daniel PETTAY, born in County of Lincoln, District of Niagara of Upper Canada on June 8, 1796. Arrived at Buffalo, N.Y. Sept. 22, 1819 with his daughter Rebecca aged two years. Renounces allegiance to George IV. Certificate issued. (140)

11-7-1822 - Bradbury Hutchens, assignee of George DUNLEVY vs. William OLIVER. From Docket of Esqr. Stansbery. cont'd. (140)

11-7-1822 - Doctor Jonas DAVIS vs. Nathan ROBERTS. Debt. (141)

5-1-1823 - Grand Jurors: Gilbert Olney, David Smith, Michael Wiseman, Asabel Tompkins, Wm. Chappelear, Joseph Merrit, Peter Bond, Mills Hall, Geo. Herring, Linus Moore, Robt. Henry, John Swank. Talesman: Simon Merevin, James Briggs. (145)

5-1-1823 - William and Robert Silvey appointed Administrators of estate of James SILVEY, late of Bloom twp. Sureties: Jacob Adams, Thos. Campbell. Appraisers: wm. Montgomery, Abel Larison, Jos. Stones. (145)

5-1-1823 - Joel HAINES, an orphan, son of Thos. HAINES, chooses Nimrod Williams of Penn twp. as his guardian. Sureties: John White, Wm. Hawkins. (146)

5-1-1823 - Wm. C. JOHNSON indicted for murder in the first degree. (Reads not guilty and removed to jail. (146-147)

5-2-1823 - Daniel Hutchens appointed Administrator estate of Hollis HUTCHINS, late of Olive twp. Sureties: James Archebald, Joseph L. Clark. Appraisers: Sherebiah Clark, Simeon Blake, James Webber. (149)

5-2-1823 - James Archibald and Elisha Spencer, executors of estate of James SPENCER, filed account. (Will recorded Dec. 11, 1819). (149)

5-2-1823 - Naturalization: James ANDERSON born in County Tyrone, Ireland in year 1790, arrive in City of New York about June 20, 1816. (149)

5-2-1823 - Catharine Williams, widow of Jonathan WILLIAMS appt'd Administratrix.
    Sureties: James Larison, Wm. Montgomery. Appraisers: Wm. Montgomery,
    Wm. Silvey, Jno. Patterson.   (150)
5-2-1823 - Samuel S. ROBERTS indicted for selling liquor without license.   (151)
5-3-1823 - Richard STILWELL resigns as Prosecuting Attorney.   (153)
5-3-1823 - Wm. C. JOHNSON sent to Penetentary for life for murder.   (153)
7-17-1823 - Grand Jury: Sylvenus Piper, Sam'l Henry, John Dutrow, Andrew Dutrow,
    Joseph Pettit, Peter Stoveburner, Wm. Willey, James Weber, Jonas Ball, James
    Buller, Ephraim C. Ellis, Wm. Montgomery, John Shutt, Isaac James, Theophilus
    Caton.   (156)
7-17-1823 - Isabella Turner and Jacob R. Price apptd. administrators estate of
    Samuel TURNER. Sureties: Edwin Corner, Wm. Hawkins. Appraisers: Alex
    McConnel, Jonathan Porter, John D. Rutledge.   (156)
7-17-1823 - Will of Silas THURLO proven by Nathan Smith and Erastus Hoskins, witness
    Susannah Thurlo and Robt. McKee, executors. Appraisers: Erastus Hoskins,
    John Noble, Sherebrat Clark.   (156)
7-17-1823 - Rebecca Murray and Ami Lawrence apptd. administrators of estate of Thom.
    MURRAY. Sureties: Enoch McIntosh, John Laughrey. Appraisers: B. W. Talbot
    Isaac Coaneil, Sam'l Murray.   (156)
7-17-1823 - Jane YOUNG, widow of Wm. B. YOUNG granted Ferry license at present
    landing.   (156)
7-17-1823 - Store license granted Shepherd and McIntosh.   (157)
7-17-1823 - Lester G. CONVERSE vs. Gilbert OLNEY. Became a non-suit.   (157)
7-17-1823 - Naturalization: Samuel MARTIN born Trowbridge, Wiltshire, England
    March 3, 1796, arrived New York City July 27, 1817.   (158)
7-17-1823 - Naturalization: George Pinkney MARTIN born Trowbridge, Wiltshire,
    England February 26, 1793; arrived Philadelphia Sept. 17, 1819.   (158)
7-17-1823 - James Larison apptd. guardian of Thomas WILLIAMS aged 2 years 2nd
    December last.   (159)
7-18-1823 - Catharine Williams authorized to sell Jonathan WILLIAMS land - E½ of NW
    Quar. of Sec. 2 T10 R12 of SW Quar. Sec 35 T11 R12 Zanesville lands.   (161)
7-18-1823 - Reuben PORTER. vs. James SCOTT as husband of Mary Walter.   (163)
7-18-1823 - Zecheriah LAWRENCE. Insolvency Petition presented.   (164)
7-18-1823 - Naturalization: Edward MELLOR. Resided in state 28 years. Certificate
    given him.   (164)
7-18-1823 - Naturalization: Jacob GOODLEAF (or WOOLAP) born Canton of Bern, Switzer
    land March 30, 1783, married Maria RYE June 1805. Children born Switzerland
    Abraham March 23, 1806; Henry July 31, 1808; Jacob August 4, 1811. Family to
    Philadelphia sometime in year 1818.   (164)
7-11-1823 - Charlotte Green appointed guardian Mary GREEN aged under 2 years, daugh
    ter of Oliver W. Green, late of Brookfield twp. Sureties: Andrew Whorton,
    Thomas Deven.   (166)
8-16-1823 - Jonathan Hughs appointed adminstrator of estate of Coonrod HARMAN, late
    of Centre twp. Sureties: Garet Jordan, Wm. Corle. Appraisers: Jacob Jord
    Abraham Jordan, Wm. Oliphant.   (166)
8-16-1823 - John W. Taylor appointed administrator estate of Henry TAYLOR, late of
    Meigsville twp. Sureties: John Taylor, John Patterson of Meigsville twp.
    Appraisers: Wm. Horner, John Patterson, Henry Nichols, Phineas Coburn.
11-17-1823 - Michael King appointed administrator of Joel HAINER, dec'd, of Penn tw
    Appraisers: Asahel Tompkins, Thomas Nash, Nathan Jennings.   (169)
11-17-1823 - ADAMS & SHUGERT granted store license in McConnsville.   (169)
11-17-1823 - Wm. DAWES granted store license in McConnsville.   (169)

11-17-1823 - Will of Peter GORE late of Olive twp. John Taylor administrator. Sureties: Aaron Hughs, Jonathan Hughs. Appraisers, Aaron & Jonathan Hughs, Peter Cadwell. (170)

11-17-1823 - Will of George CARREL. No executor named, widow relinquishes, wishes Jonathan Hughs apptd. administrator. Appraisers: John Taylor, Aaron Hughs, Jacob Jordan. (170)

11-17-1823 - Will of John REED. John Noble reuses, Wm. P. Willey to serve alone. Sureties: George Dye, Erastus Hoskins. (171)

11-17-1823 - Naturalization: Declaration of William HARMAN born County Yorkshire, England 1774. Arrived Philadelphia Aug. 26, 1818. (172)

11-17-1823 - John HUNT ordained minister Presbyterian Church. License granted.(173)

11-17-1823 - Thomas BYERS, insolvent debtor, files petition. (173)

11-18-1823 - Will of Henry TETERS. Rosanna TETERS, widow surrenders to son Henry TETERS adms. Sureties: Philip Swank, Jonathan Rex. Appraisers: Thos Dye, Sam'l McClintock, Jno. Swank. (175)

11-18-1823 - Timothy M. Gates apptd. Adm. of Stephen GATES, dec'd. Appraisers: Israel Redman, Jno. T. Ferrel, Edwin Corner. (175)

11-18-1823 - Sarah Cheadle appt. adms. John CHEADLE with Richard and Asa Cheadle adms. Sureties: Barzella Coburn, Elisha Hand. Appraisers: Sylvenus Newton, Timothy Blackburn, Elisha Hand. (175)

11-18-1823 - Margaret Pettit appt. admsx. estate of Samuel PETTIT. Sureties: John Sneff, Wm Massey. Appraisers: Wm. Massey, John Sniff, Isaac James. (176)

11-18-1813 - Richard Cheadle and Barzella Coburn appt. adms. estate of Benjamin CURRINGTON. Sureties: Zechariah Caddington, Edwin Corner. (176)

11-18-1823 - Eunice White admsx. of late husband Samuel WHITE. Sureties: Asa Emerson, Richard Cheadle. (178)

12-9-1823 - Jacob R. PRICE appointed Corner pro-tem. (180)

3-22-1824 - Jurors: Rufus P. Stone, James McAdoo, James Grubb, Wm. Montgomery, Dexter Brown, Amos Bates, Sam'l Hally, Simeon Blaker(?), Henry Moler, Wm. Horner, Jno. Archibald, Ambrose Elliott. Talesmen: Jno. Patterson, Hath. Shepherd, Asa Emerson - Shepherd replaced by James Woodington. (183)

3-22-1824 - Will of Thomas BRANNON. Mary Brannon, widow, exetrix., Sam'l McClintock Extor. Sureties: Zecheriah Blackburn, George Dye. Appraisers: Thos. Dye, Nathan Smith, John Sears. (184)

3-22-1824 - Robt. McKEE license to vend goods in Olive twp. (184)

3-22-1824 - John PERRY indicted for killing a steer. Pleads not guilty. (185)

3-23-1824 - Mary Akins apptd. admsx., Sam'l Akins adms. estate of Robert AKINS.(188)

3-23-1824 - John P. Anderson to show cause why Ambrose Schott should not be apptd. adms. of David ANDERSON, late of Centre twp. (190)

3-24-1824 - Naturalization: Declaration of William LUCK, born in County of East Kent, England 1791. Arrived New York City in July, 1816. (193)

5-3-1824 - Will of James LYON proven by Erastus Hoskens, John George, witnesses.(196)

5-3-1824 - Will of Nicholas CLINGENSMITH proven by David Fulton, Robt. Caldwell, witnesses. (196)

5-3-1824 - Pension Declaration: John MAHANA aged about 64 years. Enlisted in town of Holden, Mass. in fore part of year 1781 as a private and served 3 years. Discharge has been distroyed. Was in battle at Valentine Hill and at Terry Town when it was burned by the British. Original Declaration dated May 18, 1818. (198)

5-4-1824 - John SMITH granted license to keep tavern in town of New Market. (200)

5-4-1824 - Samuel MOODY ordained minister Baptist Society, granted license. (201)

6-4-1824 - Samuel FERREL indicted for larceny. Indictment quashed 6-5-1824. (201)

6-4-1824 - Rhoda Wight apptd. guardian of Frances, Edward R. and Royal C. WIGHT children of Ephraim C. WIGHT. Sureties: Pheneas Coburn & Adin Waterman. (201)

6-4-1824 - Mrs. Phoe Sprague apptd. guardian of Edward HEDDEN aged 12 yrs.; Susan aged 8; Emmet aged 6; James aged 4 and Mary 3, orphan children of Enos HEDDEN late of Morgan twp. (Phoebe Hedden married Isaac Sprague Dec. 26, 1823.)(202)

9-27-1824 - Jurors: James Young, Marvin Gifford, Joseph Blackburn, Daniel F. Harper, Alex. Greenlee, John McKees, Joseph Hutchens, Parley Chapman, Michael Stoneburner, John Stoneburner, Jason Andrews, Jacob Fouts. Talesman: Arphaxad Duvol, Jno. D. Rutledge, Sylvenus Piper. (208)

9-27-1824 - Catharine, widow of Nicholas CLENGENSMITH, elects to take under(?) the Will Letters Testamentary granted to David Clengensmith and Duncan Anderson. Appraisers: Nathan Essex, Samuel Sailor and John Gragg. (210)

9-27-1824 - Robt. Hanesworth apptd. guardian of Marinda Kent. Sureties: Andrew Vest and Aaron Hanesworth. (210)

9-27-1824 - Will of Wilber SPRAGUE (widow Gartry (sp.) proven by Benjamin and Peter Keith, witnesses. Letters Testamentary granted Thomas Sealey, Wm. Sprague and Wm. Boon. (211)

9-27-1824 - Samuel McClintick apptd. Administrator, with Will annexed of estate of James LYONS late of Brookfield twp. (211)

9-27-1824 - Wm. HEALEY indicted for assault and battery vs. Sophia HUGHS. (211)

9-27-1824 - Naturalization: John COLISON(COLLISON) native of England. Certificate issued 9-27-1824. (212)

9-27-1824 - George(?) RUSSEL native of England granted certificate. (first name unclear) (212)

9-28-1824 - Estate of Bartholomew LONGSTRETH. Administrators: Philip Longstreth and Michael George by wish of widow (her name not given). Sureties: Wm. M. Dawes and Jacob Ehert. (216)

9-28-1824 - Wm. MONTGOMERY - County Surveyor. (216)

9-28-1824 - Daniel PETTAY ordained minister of the Methodist Episcopal Church. Granted license. (216)

9-28-1824 - George, John W., Thomas, Bethnel and John KNOX indicted for assault and battery. (217)

9-29-1824 - William MURPHY granted license to keep tavern in town of Malta. (221)

9-29-1824 - Edwin Corner, Sheriff, sold land of Nathan ROBERTS. (222)

3-14-1825 - Gilman Dudley appt'd. guardian to Nathan MATHENA aged 20; Cyrus MATHENA aged 18; Martha MATHENA. Sureties: Andrew Mathena, James Kyle. (226)

3-14-1825 - Agnes Boyd apptd. Admtris. and James Kyle admins. of estate of Thomas BOYD. Sureties: James Archibald, Michael Morrison. Appraisers: Jno. Archibald, Edward Parrish, Alex. Greenlee. (226)

3-14-1823 - Case of John LENON, Charlotte LENON, Michael LENON - cont'd. (226)

3-14-1825 - Dan McGUNNEGAL chooses John Henry as his guardian. (228)

3-14-1825 - Estate of Theophilus CATON. Theophilus Caton (Jr.?), Abel Larrison apptd. Admines. Appraisers: Wm Montgomery, Wm Silvey, James Stones. (229)

3-14-1825 - Perley B. JOHNSON appointed Deputy Clerk of Courts. (229)

3-15-1825 - Will of Elisha HARRIS proven by John Caldwell and Isaac Hill, Witnesses. Letters Testimentary granted Morgan Harris; the widow. Margaret Harris, declining to serve. (229)

3-16-1825 - Will of Wm. HUTCHESON proved by George Russel and Sam'l T. Gates,witness Letters granted to James Hutchenson, executor and Aaron Harkless - Aaron refused to administor. (241)

3-16-1825 - Estate of Samuel TURNER. Lands to be sold. Edwin Corner apptd. guardian to Eliza, Adaline and John Turner, heirs-at-law.   (242)

3-17-1825 - Rebecca Graham admtrix. and Calvin Conant, Adm. of goods, chattels of George GRAHAM for the use of Thos. Wilson vs. Henry Moore, Edwin Corner. (246)

3-17-1825 - Jane Young apptd. guardian of Jane, Joseph, Emeline, Alexander YOUNG; and Wm. Young chooses said Jane YOUNG his guardian; all minor children and heirs of Wm. B. YOUNG, dec'd.   (249)

3-17-1825 - Andrew GOSMAN admitted a citzen of the United States.   (249)

5-30-1825 - Jorors: Rufus P. Stone, Joseph Bell, Asher Allen, Samuel Fara, Jno. Sevall, Dan'l Chandler, Joseph Tilton Junr., Wm. Roland. James Nelson, Wilks Bosman, Jno. Raney, Benj. David.   (251)

5-30-1825 - Joseph L. CLERK(CLARK) an ordained minister of Baptist Church allowed to solemnize the rites of matrimony.   (252)

5-30-1825 - Wm. WELLS indicted for assault and battery on Edward MILLER(MELLOR), Edward MILLER, Jnr.   (253)

5-30-1825 - Wm. SHERMAN indicted for assault and battery on Abraham DAVIS.   (255)

5-31-1825 - Certificate of his discharged issued to John KELSEY an insolvent debtor.   (260)

5-31-1825 - Certificate of his discharged issued to Benj. ATWELL, an insolvent debtor.   (260)

5-31-1825 - Examiners of Common Schools: Rev. John HUNT, Francis A. BARKER, Perley B. JOHNSON appointed for one year.   (262)

5-31-1825 - Luther D. BARKER granted license to sell goods in McConnelsville. (262)

5-31-1825 - Thomas and James Picket apptd. adms. of estate of Moses PICKET. Surities: Michael King, Gideon Mills. Appraisers: Jno. Simpson, Jno. Hodgin, Robt. Todd.   (263)

5-31-1825 - Naturalization: George MORRIS, a native of England. granted certificate having given intention three years since.   (265)

5-31-1825 - Naturalization: Declaration of Thomas JENKINS born in Princepatch (or Prinerpatch) of Wales in Europe in 1795, arrived New York City July 1801. (266)

5-31-1824 - Naturalization: Declaration of John RODGERS, born County Tyrone, Ireland August 1790 and arrived City of Baltimore November 2, 1810.   (267)

6-1-1825 - License granted to Thomas DEVIN to vend goods in McConnelsville. (267)

8-15-1825 - Jailer discharged Wm. MILLER and Wm. CAIN by orders.   (268)

10-28-1825 - James A. Gillespie apptd. admin. of estate of Matthew LUTTON. Sureties: Sam'l McCune, Benj. W. Talbot.   (271)

10-28-1825 - Andrew Briggs apptd. adms. of estate of James BRIGGS, the widow relinquishing her rights.   (271)

11-21-1825 - Jurors: Jas. A. Gillespie, Joseph Hutchens, Senr., Sam'l S. Roberts, Thos. Hellyer, Jacob Rogers, Richard Cheadle, Elijah Ball, Jno. Hammond, Wm. Stevens, Jno. Smith, Calvin Franklin.   (273)

11-21-1825 - Enoch S. McINTOSH granted license to vend goods in store Centre twp. (274)

11-21-1825 - Naturalization: Application Clement PINE born Bridgewater, Somerset, England in 1793, arrived New York City Dec. 17, 1819.   (276)

11-21-1825 - Naturalization: Application of Alfred MARTIN born Trowbridge, Wiltshire England Nov. 9, 1787. Arrived Norfolk, Va. May 18, 1818.   (276)

11-21-1825 - Naturalization: Dr. Samuel MARTIN granted certificate.   (277)

11-21-1825 - Naturalization: Matthew WALPOLE granted certificate.   (277)

11-21-1825 - Naturalization: Application of Archibald McCOLLUM born in Province of Nova Scotia March 22, 1790. Arrived Philadelphia April, 1796.   (280)

11-21-1825 - Naturalization: Andrew DUGAN granted certificate.   (281)

269

11-22-1825 - Joseph C. Linn apptd. admins. estate of Jeffrey BLISS with Pheness
    COBURN and Job Armstrong security. Appraisers: David Scott, Philander
    Andrews and Patrick Sherlock.   (289)
11-22-1825 - David Waller apptd. admin. estate of John WALLER with Wm. Carrell and
    John Farley security. Appraisers: Wm. Ellison, Wm. Sheckle, David Wilson.(28
11-22-1825 - Naturalization: Application John PIDCOCK born Derbyshire, Parish of
    Worleswith Dec. 18, 1797. Arrived City of Baltimore Nov. 6, 1818.   (291)
11-22-1825 - Naturalization: Application Alexander CONN born Downs, County Tyrone,
    Ireland in 1797. Arrived City of Baltimore in Sept. 1820.   (291)
11-22-1825 - George Pinkney MARTIN granted certificate of citizenship.   (292)
11-22-1825 - Wm. Laughead vs. Sylvanus Newton etal.: Betsey WALBRIDGE, mother of the
    minor children defendants, Eliza, Sylvanus, Ira, Elvira and Roinena WALBRIDGE,
    apptd. guardian to defend for them in the suit.   (293)
11-22-1825 - Samuel MORRISON indicted assault and battery on Martin TROHEE.   (294)
11-22-1825 - John M. Ward apptd. guardian to Elizabeth CHAMBERLAIN, aged 6 years with
    Alex. McConnel and Abraham Ward his security.   (294-295)
11-22-1825 - John BRIGGS aged 19, chooses Wm. Montgomery as his guardian.   (295)
11-22-1825 - Phebe Nixon apptd. guardian to Jeremiah, Ann, Edward NIXON, minors.(295
11-22-1825 - Will of Vachel OGG - witnesses: Alexander Brown, Samuel Moody.   (195)
11-22-1825 - John COLLISON indicted for assault and battery on James GAYLORD.   (295)
11-23-1825 - Thomas Devin apptd. guardian to Wm. DAVIS aged 15.   (301)
11-23-1825 - Insolvent debtors: John P. FERREL, Simeon POOL Senr., John FRAKES.(303
11-23-1825 - Joshua BREEZE ordained minister of the gospel of the Regular Baptist
    Church allowed to solemnize marriage rites in this state.   (304)
2, 1826   - Grand Jurors: Chas. McCarty, Benj. Blake, Jno. Dodds, Levi Davis, Wm.
    McElroy, Jas. Ogle, Frances Pettay, Israel Blake, Wm. P. Willey, Jas. A.
    Gillespe, Wm. Massey, Geo. Mellor. Talesman: Sam'l Henry, Geo. Duman. (307)
2-20-1826 - Naturalization: Certificate of Citizenship to John TAYLOR, of England.(
2-20-1826 - Josiah Wright apptd. admin. estate of Samuel STANBERY. Surities: John
    Raney, Geo. Pidcock. Widow declined to act.   (308)
2-20-1826 - Josiah Wright apptd. admin. on estate of Huldah BREWSTER.   (308)
2-20-1826 - Elijah SMITH assault and battery vs. David EMERSON. Guilty.   (309)
2-20-1826 - Casper HOLENBECK vs. Wm. BEMIS. Verdict - non-suit.   (310)
2-20-1826 - Ashberry S. PENNINGTON vs. John PATTERSON. Default.   (311)
2-21-1826 - Joseph Cheadle apptd. guardian to Lovisa CURRINGTON aged 4 years. (317)
2-21-1826 - Ahel Larrison apptd. guardian to Mary and Greenberry CATON minors under
    age of 14. Surities: Wm. Montgomery, Timothy M. Gates.   (317)
2-21-1826 - Neophilus Catron apptd. guardian to John, Catharine, Andrew and Sarah
    CATON, minors.   (318)
2-21-1826 - Naturalization: Martin WALPOLE issued Certificate.   (319)
5-8-1826 - Grand Jurors: John B. Stone, Thos. Atkerson, Wm. McMurray Jnr., Michael
    Wiseman, Isaac Jordan, Peter Hand, Richard Thorls, Robt. Jackson, Nathan
    Essex, Sam'l Marquis, Henry Moore, John Patten.   (321)
5-8-1826 - Hugh Riley apptd admin. estate of Vachel OGG. Surities: Joshua Breeze,
    Wm. Daives. Widow relinquishes right. Appraisers: Samuel Moody, Josiah
    Wright, Joseph Pettit.   (323)
5-8-1826 - Eliza Davis apptd. adms. of estate of Ezekiel DAVIS. Surities: Wm. Davi
    Joseph Springer. Appraisers: Elisha Hand, Alex. McMillen,Henry Blackmore.(32
5-8-1826 - Theophilus CATON, Junr. aged 14, December 25th last chooses Theophilus
    Caton as his guardian.   (323)
5-8-1826 - Nicholas LONGWORTH vs. Frederic ENELAND. Debt.   (325)

5-8-1826 - Naturalization: Certificate issued to William HARMON. (326)
5-8-1826 - Simeon POOL, Jr., Guy W. POOL indicted for assault and battery vs. Hannah
   POOL. (Guy W. Pool found not guilty.)   (327)
5-9-1826 - George OGLE vs. Mary OGLE - Breaking the peace.   (329)
5-9-1826 - Jacob BROWN vs. Nathanel CHAPMAN - assault and battery.   (330)
5-9-1826 - Will of James NELSON proven by Wm MASSEY and John Sniff, witnesses.
   L/t granted to Priscilla NELSON the extrx.   (331)
5-10-1826 - James HUNTER vs. Stephen CHARLOTTE. Slander.   (335)
5-10-1826 - Johez UTTER indicted for horse stealing. Verdict, imprisonment. (337)
5-18-1826 - Wm. G. DOORE jailed for rape of Sarah DOORE. Mrs. Sarah Doore and
   Thos. McGroth sureties.   (339)
8-24-1826 - Jane Perry and Robt. Welch, 2nd, apptd. adminrs. estate of Wm. PERRY
   late of Meigsville. Surities: Benj. W. Talbot, Zephanrah Tyson. Appraisers:
   Sylvanus Olney, Nicholas Dearbin, James Buller.   (341)
8-24-1826 - Hugh Niley apptd. admin. of estate of David HELMICK. Sureties: Sam'l
   Aikens, Amos Conaway. Appraisers: Josiah Wright,James Reed,Jno. Shutt. (341)
9-28-1826 - Asahel Tompkins apptd. admin. estate of Henry JENNINGS. Widow Mary refused to serve. Appraisers: Jno. Simpson, John Harris, Isaac Davis. (342)
12-4-1826 - Benjamin THORLA aged 17, Daniel THORLA aged 20 choose Erastus Hoskins as
   guardian and court apptd. same as guardian to Silas THORLA aged 6, Wesley
   THORLA aged 4. Sureties: Francis Scott, John Archibald.   (344)
12-4-1826 - Margaret BOYD aged 14, Nancy BOYD aged 12 choose John Archibald as
   guardian and court apptd. him guardian to Anna, John, Wiley, Robert BOYD
   minors under age of 12.   (345)
12-5-1826 - Forris BELKNAP vs. Jesse SCOTT. Trespass.   (348)
12-6-1826 - Simeon POOL Junr. indicted for assault and battery vs. Bains SUTTIFF.(354)
12-6-1826 - Parnell GANNETT indicted for assault & battery Richard McELHENEY. (355)
12-6-1826 - Russel PROUTZ granted license to vend goods store in Brookfield twp.(358)
12-6-1826 - Alexander SIMPSON & Co. granted license to vend in McConnelsville. (358)
12-7-1826 - Partition of Hiram L.J. BROWN, tenant in common with James, Mary W.,
   Sarah R. and Robert BROWN of SW Quar. of Sec30 T6 R10 and portions Secs. 31
   and 32 agreed to.   (362)
12-7-1826 - Nancy CLEMONS indicted for assault and battery vs. Hyman Lazarus and
   Fanny Lazarus.   (366)
12-8-1826 - John Gragg apptd admin. estate Wm. ALLISON, wife Betsey relinquishing.(371)
12-8-1826 - Wilks Bosman chosen guardian by John R. BOSMAN aged 18, Frances S. BOSMAN
   aged 13, Ruth R. BOSMAN aged 15, Wm. H. BOSMAN aged 13, ElizabethBOSMAN 10.(372)
12-8-1826 - Thos. Pettit apptd. admin. estate of Andrew DUGAN. Sureties: James
   Forsyth, Wm. Dawes. Appraisers: John W. Johnson, Sylvanius Piper, Henry
   Dawes.   (372)
12-8-1826 - Edward Nichols apptd. admin. estate of John BOLTON with Sam'l McCune and
   Wm. Gibson, security. Appraisers: John Gibson, Jas. Whitaker, Richard
   McElhana.   (373)
12-8-1826 - Wm. DAWES chosen Deputy Clerk by Parley B. JOHNSON, Clerk.   (373)
12-8-1826 - Naturalization: Declaration of William FORDICE born near Patridge Island,
   County of Parsborough, Nova Scotia, May 11, 1786. Arrived Fairfax, Vermont
   October, 1812 and brought with him one son, Nelson FORDICE aged 1 year.(376)
4-3-1827 - Wm. WELLS guilty assault & battery against James & Arthur ALLOWAY. (378)
4-3-1827 - Jurors: Jonathan Pyle, Geo. Harward, Andrew Scott, Asahel Tompkins, Job
   Armstrong, Sam'l McClintock, Elijah Davis, Joshua Clarke;Davis Tilton, Geo.
   Crow, Isaac Baker, Sam'l Allord.   (378)

4-3-1827 - Asa Cheadle saith he was well acquainted with Isaac B. HERSEY, late of
Washington County, Ohio, and that he died without issue, and that Franklin
HERSEY; Achsey DAVIS, wife of Joshua Davis late Achsah HERSEY; and Betsey
SMITH, wife of Elijah Smith, late Betsey HERSEY, are the heirs and only heirs
(379)
4-3-1827 - Elijah ATKENS granted license to keep tavern in New Market.   (381)
4-3-1827 - John Jacob BROCK vs. Henry FREBIS and Anna, his wife. Mortgage.   (381)
4-3-1827 - John GEORGE indicted petit larceny.   (383)
4-4-1827 - Joseph Chalk apptd. guardian to Palmira CHALK, aged 10, Ransom CHALK, age
8; and Patience CHALK, aged 5.   (388)
4-5-1827 - John W. Taylor adms. of Henry TAYLOR, dec'd, to show cause why he should
not be removed. (Removed by the court July 16, 1827)   (397)
4-6-1827 - Matthew HARMISTON indicted for larceny and guilty.   (399)
4-6-1827 - Adam KEITH vs. Peter SHACKLEE.. Trespass.   (399)
4-6-1827 - John MAXWELL aged 17 years chose David Fulton as his guardian. Court al.
apptd. him guardian of William aged 13, Mary aged 12, Eliza aged 11, Basel
aged 9 and Thomas aged 6 years.   (400)
4-6-1827 - Fanny HARMESTON indicted for larceny. Not guilty.   (401)
4-7-1827 - Edward HEDDEN aged 14, chose Isaac Sprague as his guardian and court
named him guardian to Emmet HEDDEN aged 9, Susan aged 11, James 7 and Mary
aged 6 years.   (406)
4-7-1827 - Robert Welsh, Senr. appnt. guardian of James WELCH aged 13, Jane aged 9,
Robert aged 7 and Margaret aged 5 years.   (407)
4-7-1827 - Will of George SHIRLEY proven. Witnesses: Wm. H. Shacklee, Sherebrah
Clark. Letters Testamentory granted to Joseph Shirley, executor. Sureties:
Adam Keith, Lewis Sherley.   (407).
4-7-1827 - Naturalization: Lenhart BLESSING, native of Germany made application to
to County of Frederick, Maryland, March 16, 1822 for himself and his children
Lenhard then aged 15, Jacob 13, Ann Maria 7, Samuel 1.   (409)
7-16-1827 - Grand Jurors: James Reed, Benj. Berry, Robt. Fulton, Jno. Wiley, Asa
White, Enoch S. McIntosh, Jonathan Eddington, Wm. Horner, Geo. Newman,
Anselm Taylor, Andrew Tevault, Jno. Raney.   (416)
7-18-1827 - Case of Hannah ANDERSON for assault and battery, cont'd.   (419)
7-18-1827 - Samuel WORK declared Insolvent.   (421)
7-18-1827 - Joseph BLANE indicted for Larceny. Found guilty.   (421)
7-19-1827 - Complaint of Mary PATTERSON, an unmarried woman, bastard child born
August 14, 1826 and that Israel LUCAS is the father. (Case dismissed by
agreement of parties October 16, 1827)   (426)
7-19-1827 - Isaac BARKER granted tavern license at his house in Malta.   (427)
10-5-1827 - Grand Jurors: James Young, Geo. Shaver, Uriah Harris, Nathan Smith,
James Whitaker, Geo. Herring, Jesse Waller, Hugh Nickerson, Sylvester Westco
Peter Cadwell, Wm. Boon, Wm. Brewster, Nathan Dearborn, Geo. Harword, Thos.
Campbell.   (429)
10-5-1827 - Will of Matthew DIMMICK proven by James Gragg and John Needham, witness
Letters granted to Mahlon Wilson, executor. Appraisers: John Sears, John
Gragg and John W. Starr.   (432)
10-15-1827 - Jacob ADAMS vs. Lewit H. Vannelzer. In Chancery. Case refers to titl
to Lot No. 6 in McConnelsville.   (432)
10-15-1827 - Lewis WALLER and wife Phoebe vs. Joseph KEITH. Slander.   (434)
10-15-1827 - James GREATHOUSE vs. Alex. McMILLEN. Case dismissed.   (435)
10-15-1827 - Thos. CAMPBELL vs. Charles BURGOON. Slander. Case dismissed. (435)

10-15-1827 - Naturalization: Declaration of James CONN, born County Tyrone 1780
       and arrived Baltimore July 1826.   (436)
10-16-1827 - Ann Ray apptd administrix estate of Richard RAY. Sureties: Wm.
       Harmon, Geo. Johnson.   (439)
10-16-1827 - Levi CULVER(CULNER) ordained minister of the gospel of the regular
       Baptist Church granted license to solemnize marriages.   (439)
10-16-1827 - Isaac PARRISH granted license to vend goods at store in Olive twp.(444)
10-17-1827 - Naturalization: Declaration of George JOHNSON born Brenchley, County of
       Kent, England, Dec. 6, 1790; arrived in New York May 26, 1825, with two sons,
       viz. John aged eleven, and George aged two years.   (445)
10-17-1827 - Thomas TAYLOR applied for benefit as Insolvent Debtor.   (446)
10-17-1827 - Will of Thomas HAMPTON proven on oaths of Jno. Hampton, Rebecca Thomas,
       witnesses. Letters Testementory granted to Isaac Hanes and Jno. H.
       Livezy, executors named.   (446)
10-17-1827 - Naturalization: Certificate issued to Adam YOUNMON, a native of Germany,
       he having produced evidence of his application three years past.   (448)
10-17-1827 - Joseph Chalk apptd. guardian to Eliza CHALK aged 17 years and Isbella
       CHALK aged 15 years.   (448)
12-24-1827 - Criminal Case: George BEARD charged with murdering David RICE.   (449)
2-11-1828 - Rebecca Harris apptd. admtix. estate of David HARRIS. Sureties: John
       Collison, Jno. E. Hanna. Appraisers: Sam'l McCune, Wm. Irvin. Isaac Hanes.
       (450)
4-7-1828 - Will of Nathan SMITH proved on oaths of Andrew Warton, Benj. Hardin,
       John Draper, witnesses. L/t granted Rosanna SMITH, executrix. Appraisers:
       John Sears, Charles Harinard and Vincent Dye.   (451)
4-7-1828 - James FULLER vs. Samuel WALTERS etal. Jno. E. Hanna apptd. guardian to
       defend the infant defendents. (note: widow was Betsey WALTERS).   (451)
4-8-1828 - Michael ARCHER vs. John DILLE. Debt.   (454)
4-8-1828 - Naturalization: Declaration of John Gotlip (sic.) BAZLER, born Wurtten-
       berg, Germany, March 17, 1780, arrived Philadelphia August 25, 1820.
       Renounces allegiance to Nederick V.   (454)
4-8-1828 - Naturalization: Declaration of David MILHAM, born Breeds, Sussex, England
       Dec. 18, 1796. Arrived New York City October 1817.   (455)
4-8-1828 - James W. HOLLAND. Case dismissed.   (456)
4-8-1828 - Augustine ANDERSON vs. John RAINEY. Trespass.   (457)
4-9-1828 - Andres BLINN vs. Wm. SWANK. Case dismissed.   (462)
4-9-1828 - James WOODINGTON took Insolvent Debts Act.   (463)
4-9-1828 - Will of Peleg LINCOLN proved. Witnesses: Wm. M. Daines, Jno. Sidwell.
       Letters granted to Betsey Lincoln, Sylvanus Piper, Executors named.   (463)
4-10-1828 - George BEARD, guilty of murder second degree.   (466)
4-11-1828 - Benjamin HARDING license to keep tavern-former house of Edwin Corner.(467)
4-11-1828 - Stephen FITSIMMONS(sic.) appointed assistant deputy.   (468)
4-11-1828 - Will of Jesse WILSON proved. John Hunt, Charles Robinson, witnesses.
       Letters granted John Wilson, Francis A. Barker, executors named.   (468)
4-11-1828 - James L. Gage replaces John W. Taylor admin. estate of Henry TAYLOR.(469)
4-11-1828 - John Collison apptd. guardian to John HARRIS age 13 years and Cyrus
       HARRIS age 10 years.   (468)
4-11-1828 - John WORK aged 20 years, Sarah WORK aged 17, Elizabeth WORK aged 16 choose
       Robert Todd as their guardian and same apptd. by court as guardian to Robert
       WORK aged 13 years, Nancy WORK aged 11 years, David WORK aged 6 years.   (467)
4-11-1828 - David SPANGLER allowed 40.00 as Prosecuting Attorney this term.   (467)

4-11-1828 - John Shutt apptd. guardian to Letitia H. STANBERY aged 3 years the 11th
day of next June. Securities: Wm. Dawes, Forster Edwards. (470)
4-11-1828 - From Sheriff to Joseph ANDERSON Lot No. 64. (470)
4-11-1828 - School Examiners: John HUNT, Benoni ALLEN, James L. GAGE. (470)
7-21-1828 - Geo. Desman(?), Sam'l Baker, Wm. Ball, Isaac Hedges, Joseph Morris,
Samuel Long, James Marshall, Garret Cavener, Wm. Scott, John Dedham, Ephraim
Eikman, John Jordan, Mahlon Wilson, Thos. Campbell, Aaron B. Lott. (471)
7-21-1828 - John PICKINGPAUGH indicted for assault and battery against Robt. Jackson.
(472)
7-21-1828 - Rev. Benoni ALLEN, minister of the gospel Baptist Church licensed. (473)
7-21-1828 - John HAMPSHIRE, late of Deerfield, died intestate. Elizabeth, his widow
granted Letters of Administration. Martin Price, Philip Stout, security.(473
7-21-1828 - John CLEMENS vs. Jesse GAUSE. Attachment. (474)
7-21-1828 - Eliza EAKMAN vs. Nancy MAXWELL. Damage. (477)
7-21-1828 - John MILLIGAN indicted for assault and battery against Rhoda GROVES.(477
7-22-1828 - Naturalization: Certificate issued to David McGARRY. (479)
7-22-1828 - Sam'l W. CULBERTSON vs. Zuriel and Raymond SHERWOOD. Case settled. (481
7-23-1828 - Hannah Pool, widow, relict of Simeon POOL, petition in Chancery for
dower. Land description given. (484)
7-23-1828 - Rachel and Rebecca HARPER above 12 years of age, choose Wm. Patterson
as their guardian. (486)
7-23-1828 - Naturalization: Declaration of John O'FLINN, born County of Galway
1783, arrived New York August 8 about ten years ago. (486)
7-23-1828 - Will of Caleb OSBORN proven by Geo. & Harriet Osborn, Widow Eliza Osborn
(488)
7-23-1828 - Thomas Campbell apptd. guardian of John STANBERY aged 12 years Oct. 5,
next; Joel STANBERY aged 10 years May 18 last; Ira STANBERY 8 years March 29
last; Ezra STANBERY aged 6 years January 2 last, children of Samuel STANBERRY
dec'd, with Wm. Oliver security. (489)
7-23-1828 - Sarah Stanbery apptd. guardian Harriet STANBERY aged 5 years on 21st
day of November next; Martha STANBERY aged 2 years the 21st November last.(48
8-16-1828 - Mary DICKERSON aged 20 years 25th March last; Harriet DICKERSON aged 18
years 12th March 1828; Gulana DICKERSON (twin) aged 16 years 31st December
1827; Zadock,Jnr. DICKERSON (twin) aged 16 years 31st December 1827; Rhoda
DICKERSON aged 14 years 31st March 1828 chose David Dickerson, their brother,
as their guardian. Securities: Zodock Dickerson, Senr. and Jacob R. Price.
(491)
10-15-1828 - Grand Jurors: James Young, Joseph Blackburn, James Kyle, Wm. Bowen,
Henry Roberts, Geo. Pellorten, Zechariah Carrington, Dennis Gibbs, Israel
Wilkerson, Wm. Eneland, Jno. Taylor Senr., Jno B. Jones, Chas. Harword,
Arphasad Devol, Sam'l Henry. (492)
10-15-1828 - Jefferson Glidden, James S. Warren, Wm. Tilton granted license to vend
goods in Olive twp. (492)
10-15-1828 - Rebecca LUAS vs. Amery KEYES. Bastardy Complaint. (494)
10-15-1828 - Joseph CHALK indicted for larceny - guilty. (495)
10-16-1828 - Thomas PERRY aged 17 years and John PERRY 14 chose Samuel Fouts as thei
guardian. Security: Andrew Fouts and David Miller. (497)
10-16-1828 - Edward BOSMAN, late of Brookfield twp, died intestate. Wilks Bosman,
father of deceased, appointed administrator. (498)
10-16-1828 - Naturalization: Declaration of William HEMPFIELD, born County of Cumberland and arrived New York City July 3, 1818. (498)

274

10-16-1828 - Josphus STEVENS indicted for larceny.   (499)

10-16-1828 - Naturalization: Declaration of Wm. CLARK, arrived in this country in
the year 1818 from County of Londonderry, a minor, and is now 21 years of age.
(500)

10-16-1828 - Ann Minerva QUIGLEY aged 17 years and George C. QUIGLEY aged 16 years
chose Geo. L.Corner their guardian and said Corner apptd. by court as guardian for Columbus QUIGLEY aged 12 years; Isabel QUIGLEY 8 years; Wm. M.
QUIGLEY aged 6 years and Lucretia QUIGLEY aged 4 years.   (500)

10-16-1828 - Samuel BAGLEY granted license to keep tavern his house in New Market.(501)

10-16-1828 - Zachariah NASH vs. Benj. and Nathan JENNINGS. Case dismissed. (501)

10-17-1828 - George Pidecock entered as next friend of Kiturah PIDCOCK to prosecute
her suit vs. Joseph ROBERTS.   (502)

10-17-1828 - Jacob HAMLER of Deerfield died intestate. Widow, Rachel Hamler
granted administratrix.   (502)

10-17-1828 - James M. GAYLORD aged 17 years and Mary Jane GAYLORD aged 15 years
chose Timothy Gaylord their guardian and court apptd. same as guardian to
Harriet W. GAYLORD aged 9 years.   (504)

10-17-1828 - Naturalization: John RODGERS issued certificate.   (504)

10-17-1828 - Petitions of John SEAMAN, Israel REDMOND and Robt. McCONNEL for ferries
across the Muskingum. Cont'd until next term.   (504)

10-17-1828 - Benjamin HARDING and Nancy MAXWELL - Insolvent debtors.   (504)
(note: This completes Minute Book A)

Contributed by: Mary Louise Rizor, 410 Cherry St., Galion, ohio 44833

This church was formerly known as the BORTNER GERMANDE REFORMED CHURCH. It is
located in North Bloomfield township of Morrow County.

NAME OF CHILD	DATE OF BIRTH	BAPTISED	SPONSORS
Peter son of Michael & Rebecca WILMAN	Oct. 20, 1840	Jan. 3, 1841	John & Lena Peterman
Henry son of John & Hannah SHEFFER	Apr. 2, 1840	Jan. 3, 1841	Parents
John son of Henry & Amy Mulvina SOWERS	June 5, 1841	July 18, 1841	Parents
Lucinda dau. of Ulrich & Hannah SMITH	Mar. 28, 1841	July 18, 1841	George & Margarette Smith
Susana dau. of John CERNAIN and Litia	Apr. 22, 1841	July 18, 1841	Peter & Catarin Wilhalm
John Christian son of Joseph & Catrin LONG	Apr. 10, 1839	July 18, 1841	Parents
Charles son of Jacob & Catarin TISHER	Aug. 17, 1841	Oct. 10, 1841	Parents
Catrin dau. of Charles & Eve TISHER	June 31, 1841	Oct. 10, 1841	Parents
Mary dau. of John & Laky TOSIN	(not given)	Oct. 10, 1841	Mary Sneyder
Jacob HENNY dau. Margaretha_____?	(not given)	(not given)	(not given)
Friedrich BACK son of Peter	June 14, 1843	(not given)	(not given)
Adam SELL son of Amos	(not given)	(not given)	(not given)
Michael WILLOUER son of Jacob	Oct. 23, 1842	(not given)	(not given)
Peter WILLOUER son of _____?	Dec. 31, 1842	(not given)	(not given)
Johana dau. of Levi GERBERICH	(not given)	(not given)	(not given)
Andrew WILLAUER son of Heinrich	June 24, 1842	(not given)	(not given)
Anna Maria dau. of Fridrich BACK & Catarina	Dec. 27, 1844	Aug. 11, 1845	Parents
Anne Carlina dau. of George & Sarea BORTNER	Nov. 3, 1844	Jan. 6, 1845	Sarea Henney
Eli son of Henry & Margrat BORTNER	Mar. 7, 1829	(not given)	George & Elisbat Ruhl
Jacob son of Henry & Margrat BORTNER	May 10, 1831	(not given)	Parents
John son of Henry & Margrat BORTNER	Dec. 4, 1833	(not given)	Henry Snyder
Margrat dau. of Henry & Margrat BORTNER	Feb. 6, 1837	(not given)	George & Margrat Smith

NAME OF CHILD	DATE OF BIRTH	BAPTISED	SPONSORS
Heinrich SCHMITT	Mar. 22, 1846	(not given)	(not given)
J_____ SCHMITT	Nov. 25, 1849	June 7, 1850	(not given)
William MILLER son of Wilhelm MILLER	Apr. 1, 1850	(not given)	(not given)
Anna Jane dau. of Carl BORTNER	May 10, 1856	June 7, 1856	(not given)
Jerome BORTNER Bapt. by Christian Wiler	Sept. 15, 1852	May 13, 1855	Henry Bortner
Jasua BORTNER Bapt. by Christian Wiler	Sept. 20, 1855	Oct. 28, 1855	Levi Warner

Note: Morrow County was erected and organized judically in 1848 from Marion, Delaware, Knox and Richland Counties

277

MORROW COUNTY, OHIO - DEATH RECORDS 1867-1870

The following records were copied from "Death Record 1." They include only
persons 40 years of age and over. Abbreviations used are: d-died; a-age;
m-married; w-widow or widower; s-single; pd-place of death; pb-place of birth;
r-residence. If both are not given, place of death and residence are same.
Page on which record may be found is given in parenthesis.

STILLEY, Rachel - d 11-7-1867; a 73-9-7; pd Chesterville; pb Brownsville, Pa.(2)
LEE, John C. - d 9-11-1867; a 69y 25d; m; pd Caledonia; pb------(2)
SILVERTHORN, Ellen G. - d 10-10-1867; a 43-6-6; pd Cardington; pb------(2)
PLOTNER, Hannah - d 9-7-1867; a 65y 9m; pd Richland twp.; pb------(4)
FIELDS, Charles - d 10-8-1867; a 67y pd Cardington; pb Morrow Co. (4)
COLLINS, Margaret - d 7-14-1867; a 60y; m; pd Bennington twp.; pd------(4)
BRIDE, Amanda - d 7-27-1867; a 43-3-13; s; pd N. Bloomfield; pb------(6)
CATON, Ann - d 8-28-1867; a 47y 3m; s; pd Blooming Grove; pb------(6)
BRODBECK, Mrs. Elizabeth - d 8-29-1867; a 67y 4m; m; pd Perry twp.; pb Pa. (8)
LENTZ, Mrs. Elizabeth - 8-29-1867; a 66-1-13; pd Perry twp.; pb Pa. (8)
BENNETT, Phebe - d 7-20-1867; a 74-7-21; m; pd Perry twp.; pb Addison Co. Vt.(10)
MOSIER, Nancy - d 7-31-1867; a 52-10-5; w; pd Perry twp.; pb Belmont, Ohio (10)
REESE, David - d 7-4-1867; a 55y; m; pd Cardington; pb Granville, S.C. (12)
CRAMER, William S. - d 7-14-1867; a 46y; m; pd Chesterville; pb------(14)
BURCK, Alvira(/) d 7-24-1867; a 51y; pd Delaware Co.; pb------ (16)
JEFFREY, Robert F. - d 11-3-1867; ae 47-2-24; m; pd Morrow Co.; pb------(20)
WARNER, Ruth - d 9-26-1867; a 84-6-24; w; pd Harmony twp.; pb Pa. (22)
SYLVESTER, Ellen G. - d 10-10-1867; a 42y; m; pd Canaan twp.; pb Marion Co. Ohio(24)
TALMAGE, James M. - d 9-29-1867; a 51-1-21; m; pd Gilead twp.; pb Ohio. (26)
McKEE, Hannah - d 11-24-1867; a 40-9-27; m; pd Gilead twp.; pb Ohio. (26)
OVERLY, James S. - d 12-8-1867; a 43-10-4; m; pd N. Bloomfield; pb------(28)
KERR, James - d 12-6-1867; a 63y; m; pd N. Bloomfield; pb------(28)
BRATTON, Mary - d 7-13-1867; a 63-8-10; w; pd Morrow Co.; pb------(30)
LOWE, John Bishop - d 10-18-1867; a 53-11-29; m; pd Tully twp.; pb Baden,
                                                Germany. (34)
ARMSTRONG, Ann B. - d 12-16-1867; a 53y; pd Tully twp.; pb Harrison Co. Va. (34)
BROWN, Isaac - d 9-24-1867; a 68y; pd Mt. Gilead; pb Va. (36),
CRANER, Christian - d 10-10-1867; a 64y 9d; m; pd Crawford Co.; pb Germany. (38)
WILLHOUS, Andrew - d 9-16-1867; a 74-11-16; m; pd N. Bloomfield; pb Germany. (40)
FLINT, Daniel - d 9-23-1867; a 64-10-4; m; pd Washington twp.; pb York State. (40)
RULE, Jacob - d 10-5-1867; a 54-3-24; m; pd West Point; pb Pa. (40)
McCONICA, James d 1-20-1868; a 85y; pd Lincoln twp.; pb Ireland. (2)
POTTER, Thomas - d 2-27-1868; a 75y; m; pd Gilead twp.; pb Yorkshire, England.(2)
STRUBLE, Nancy - d 2-6-1868; a 48-1-19; pd Franklin twp.; pb Warren Co., N.J.;
                                                r. Chester. (2)
CAMPBELL, Sarah - d 2-26-1868; a 69-3-27; m; pd Franklin twp.; pb Northumberland
                                                Co. Pa. (2)
BOWEN, John - d 1-3-1868; a 87y 11m; pd Chester twp.; pb Wales; r Chesterville. (2)
MADDEN, Rebecca - d 4-9-1868; a 70-10-10; pd Harmony twp.; pb Philadelphia, Pa.(2)
EMLEN, Susan - d 2-19-1868; a 65y; s; pd Chester twp.; pb Montgomery Co.(2)
BAKER, Morris - d 1-20-1868; a 62y; pd Harmony twp.; pb Knox Co. (2)
SUETLAND, Fuller M. - d 3-2-1868; a 66-5-23; m; pd S. Bloomfield twp.; pb Pa.;
                                                r. Sparta, Ohio. (2)
FERNSLER, Mary - d 2-13-1868; ae 67-11-4; pd Troy twp.; pb------(2)

278

McCONNELL, John - d 3-12-1868; a 89-1-3; pd North Bloomfield; pb-------(2)
NORTON, Sarah C. - d 3-17-1868; ae 44-11-17; m; pd North Bloomfield; pb-----(2)
WILLITTS, Ellis - d 6-2-1868; ae 70y; m; pd Bennington twp.; pb Morrow Co. (4)
MYERS, Joel - d 5-2-1868; ae 56-1-17; m; pd Iberia; pb Adams Co., Pa. (4)
McCLELLAN, Mary - d 5-7-1868; a 47-10-8; m; pd Iberia; pb Warren Co., N. J. (4)
PAGE, Polly - d 6-3-1868; a 60y; m; pd Pagetown; pb ------- (4)
MORRIS, Joseph - d 7-1-1868; a 72y; pd Bennington; pb-----(4)
McNAY, Samuel - d 4-26-1868; a 71-2-13; m; pd Chester twp.; pb Adams Co., Pa. (4)
WHITE, Orpha - d 5-2-1868; a 53-4-15; m; pd N. Bloomfield; pb Herkimer Co. N.Y. (4)
ROBERTS, Solomon - d 6-28-1868; a 72y 3m; m; pd Sparta; pb western Va.; parents,
          Nathan and Ruth Roberts (4)
GALE, James - d 9-8-1868; a 63y; m; pd Franklin twp.; pb------(4)
STEPHENS, Joseph - d 9-27-1868; a 42-7-3; m; pd N. Bloomfield; pb Morrow Co. (4)
WOOD, Daniel - d 9-24-1868; a 79-8-5; m; pd Peru twp.; pb Vermont. (4)
ANDERSON, Amsa W. - d 6-20-1868; a 55-1-6; m; pd S. Bloomfield; pb Manchester, Vt.;
          parents, David and Elizabeth Anderson. (6)
MANVILLE, John - d 5-4-1868; a 75-2-22; m; pd Sparta; pb Pa. (6)
BALLARD, Fredrick - d 11-6-1868; a 88-3-19; pd Sparta; pb Hartford, Ct. (6)
BEARD, Comodore R. - d. 10-8-1868; a 57y; m; pd S. Bloomfield; pb New York State;
          parents, Vietor and Mary E. Beard. (6)
EMLIN, Susan - d 2-19-1868; a 65y; m; pd Chesterville; pb Pa. (6)
SMITH, Jeremiah - d 10-28-1868; a 72y; m; pd Harmony twp.; pb Ct. (6)
SMITH, Sarah A. - d 11-28-1868; a 57-6-22; m; pd Morrow Co.; pb Washington Co.,N.Y.(6)
FRANCIS, Alfred P. - d 12-28-1868; a 64-4-10; m; pd Morrow Co.; pb Stockbridge,N.Y.(6)
THOMAS, Lucretia M. - d 7-14-1868; a 47-10-14; m; pd Morrow Co.; pb Licking Co., O.;
          r. Perry twp. (6)
RICE, John - d. 10-7-1868; a 74-2-5; m; pd Morrow Co.; pb Pa.; r. near Caledonia.(6)
DAVIS, John - d 10-1-1868; a 58-11-28; m; pd N. Bloomfield; pb-------(6)
DICKERSON, Asa - d 12-16-1868; a 71-4-16; m; pd-------; pb-----; r. Sanduck twp. (6)
JENKINS, Tryphania Y. - d 1-14-1869; a 45-2-14; m; pd Chester; pb Chester, N.C.(6)
HULL, Charles - d 2-19-1869; a 77y; m; pd Congress twp.; pb------- (6)
MOODY, Ezemiah - d 1-4-1869; a 48y; m; pd Tully twp.; pb Cumberland, Pa.(6)
GARDNER, Mrs. - d 3-22-1869; a 54y; m; pd Chesterville; pb York State. (6)
NILEY, Hannah - d 6-15-1869; a 46-9-15; pd Springfield twp., Richland Co.; pb--(6)
MILLER, Isaac - d 6-21-1869; a 77-4-19; pd N. Bloomfield; pb Washington Co., Pa.(6)
WELSH, William - d 9-16-1869; a 75y; pd Gilead twp.; pb Gilead twp. (42)
HARRIS, James - d 11-19-1869; a 61-5-23; m; pd Harmont twp.; pb Perry Co., Pa. (42)
BUTLERS, Margarett - d 10-26-1869; a 84y; pd Bennington; pb Maine. (42)
DAVIDSON, Ann - d 9-3-1869; a 60y; pd Woodbury twp.; pb-----(42)
JAMES, Charlotte - d 9-12-1869; a 85y 19d; w; pd Woodbury twp.; pb------(42)
PRATT, Ezekiel - 10-20-1869; a 78-5-20; w; pd Peru twp.; pb-------(42)
CARPENTER, Chester - d 10-8-1869; a 43y 11m; m; pd Westfield; pb Ohio. (42)
BREMOZER, Jacob - d 10-21-1869; a 76-3-23; m; pd Westfield; pb Md. (42)
BRENIZER, Adam - d 12-7-1869; a 71y; m; pd Westfield; pb Md. (42)
TOAST, Emily - d 10-2-1869; a 47-2-7; m; pd Westfield; pb Ohio. (42)
BURKET, Micheal - d 9-18-1869; a 87-6-13; w; pd Perry twp.; pb Pa. (44)
CONE (CAVE), Asa H. - d 9-9-1869; a 82y; m; pd Perry twp.; pb Vermont. (44)
CACE, Jacob - d 10-13-1869; a 75-11-12; m; pd Lincoln twp.; pb N.Y. (44)
VAUGHN, Phebe - d 11-15-1869; a 84-9-4; m; pd Lincoln twp.; pb Chester Co.,Pa.(44)
VINN (WINE), George - d 8-5-1869; a 48-2-10; w; pd Lincoln twp.; pb Pa. (44)

MEAD, Samuel - d 11-9-1869; a 82-5-5; m; pd S. Bloomfield; pb Ct. (44)
BARR, James - d 10-18-1869; a 73y 4m; m; pd Bloomfield; pb Pa. (44)
COLMARY, John - d 5-10-1869; a 74-7-3; m; pd Washington twp.; pb Washington Co.Pa.(46)
FOLTZ, Barbara - d 11-5-1869; a 73-8-11; m; pd Congress; pb Germany. (46)
McCAMMON, John - d 4-16-1869; a 82y 7m; pd Congress; pb Pa. (46)
NIMSIK, Solomon - d 11-28-1869; a 67-6-20; w; pd Congress; pb N. Y. (46)
SCHWARTZ, Henry - d 9-15-1869: a 57-6-6; m; pd Congress; pb Pa. (46)
KINSEL, D. B. - d 9-8-1869; a 50-6-4; m; pd Chesterville; pb Md. (46)
ROBY, Catherine - d 3-12-1870; a 74-7-9; w; pd---; pb Westmorland Co., Pa.;
r. Harmony twp. (42)
BEARD, Reuben - d 1-13-1870; a 64-7-11; m; pd Bennington; pb N.Y. (42)
BUNKER, Reuben - d 1-5-1870; a 59y; m; pd Woodbury twp.; pb----- (42)
KENZIE, John - d 4-25-1870; a 73-10-21; m; pd N. Bloomfield; pb Germany. (42)
CROTHERS, Andrew - d 2-21-1870; a 87y; m; pd N. Bloomfield; pb Pa. (42)
WINDBIGLER, Wm. - d 3-28-1870; a 68-11-2; m; pd Troy twp.; pb Lancaster Co., Pa.;
Parents, Wm. Windbigler. (42)
CLAYPOOL, John - d 4-7-1870; a 63-4-2; m; pd Cardington; pb Va. (44)
BLAIR, John - d 3-1-1870; a 52y 7m; m; pd Cardington; pd Richland. (44)
LENETT, Stephen - d 3-20-1870; a 77-5-11; m; pd Cardington; pb Va. (44)
SMITH, Anna - d 3-1-1870 a 77-7-5; w; pd Cardington; pb Ct. (44)
BLAKELY, Rosanna - d 1-26-1870; a 80-1-2; w; pd Lincoln twp.; pb Pa. (44)
DARBY, Rufus - d 1-7-1870; a 85-10-27; m; pd S. Bloomfield; pb N. Y. (44)
HULSE, Mariah - d 3-8-1870; a 58y; m; pd S. Bloomfield; pb N.Y. (44)
BLISS, Caroline N.C. - d 1-8-1870 a 48-1-29; m; pd S. Bloomfield; pb S. Bloomfield.(44
CRISWELL, Larkin - d 3-28-1870; a 72-2-3; w; pd Franklin twp.; pb Baltimore Co. P.(46)
FAUX, Charlotte - d 3-18-1870; a 68-8-3; w; pd Congress; pb Congress. (46)
HENDERSON, Mary - d 3-27-1870; a 84y; w; pd Congress; pb Pa. (46)
PIERSON, Amianih - d 4-6-1870; a 69-5-6; m; pd Congress; pb Pa. (46)
WILLIAMS, Rachel - d 2-11-1870; a 73-1-18; m; pd Congress; pb Pa. (46)
WILHELM, Peter - d 1-8-1870; a 89y 7m; w; pd Congress; pb Pa. (46)
BROWN, George - d 4-18-1870; a 79y; s; pd Chester twp.; pb R. I. (46)
COLEMAN, Deborah - d 1-22-1870 a 75-2-7; m; pd---; pb N.J.; r. Chester twp. (46)
SHOEWALTER, Wm - d 2-20-1870; a 52y; m; pd Chester twp.; pb Pa. (46)
WILLETS, Jane - d 5-2-1870; a 55y; m; pd Chesterville; pb Ohio. (46)
BLISS, Mason - d 12-5-1870; a 57y; m; pd S. Bloomfield; pb-----(48)
DUSTAN, Lydia - d 12-30-1870; a 76y; m; pd S. Bloomfield; pb Boston, Mass. (48)
HARRIS, Jane - d 6-4-1870; a 67-10-14; pd S. Bloomfield; pb Md. (48)
JENKINSON, Martha - d 9-6-1870; a 75-6-25; m; pd-----; pb-----(48)
LYNDER, Sarah - d 9-25-1870; a 42-7-1; m; pd Canaan twp.; pb Muskingum Co., Ohio.(48)
ASHBAUGH, Matilda - d 10-20-1870; a 49-7-17; m; pd Canaan twp.; pb Delaware Co., Ohio
(48)
RICHARDSON, Margaret - d 3-26-1870; a 58y; w; pd Canaan twp.; pb Morrow Co. (48)
SMITH, M.C. - d 6-8-1870; a 76y; w; pd Canaan twp.; pb Morrow Co. (48)
HUNT, Margaret - d 7-7-1870; a 70y 9m; w; pd Lincoln; pb-----(48)
JONES, Hannah - d 12-4-1870; a 66-1-13; m; pd Lincoln; pb Ohio. (48)
SAGE, Alvin R. - d 5-22-1870; a 48y 6m; m; pd Lincoln; pb N.Y. (48)
ROGERS, S.S. - d 11-23-1870; a 60410-2; m; pd Bennington; pb N.Y. (48)
COOK, David - d 11-4-1870; a 68-10-9; m; pd-----; pb Vermont. (48)
BOSTON, William - d 11-6-1870; a 70y; m; pd Westfield; pb New Castle, England. (48)
VANSICKLE, Elizabeth - d 10-30-1870; a 51-10-10; m; pd Peru twp.; pb Bennington
twp. (50)

BOYER, Isaac - d 10-9-1870; a 83-6-20; m; pd Cardington; pb Va. (50)
JENKINS, Eda J. - d 8-12-1870; a 62-7-26; w; pd Cardington; pb Va. (50)
MYERS, Mary - d 8-10-1870; a 58-5-10; m; pd Cardington; pb Pa. (50)
EARLEY, John - d Dec. 1870; a 83y; s; pd Washington twp.; pb Ireland. (50)
FURGUSON, Mary - d 10-19-1870; a 55y; m; pd Troy twp.; pb——(50)
BINGHAM, Sarah - d 6-17-1870; a 72-6-6; w; pd Gilead twp.; pb Morrow Co. (50)
JOYA, Job - d 12-13-1870; a 55y 11m; m; pd Mt. Gilead; pb Pa. (52)
HULL, Sarah - d 1-26-1870; a 74-3-2; w; pd Congress; pb Pa. (52)
PARKS, John - d 9-14-1870; a 58-11-7; m; pd Congress; pb Pa. (52)
WIRICK, Sarah J. - d 4-23-1870; a 47y; m; pd Congress; pb Richland Co. (52)
HEPPES, Jacobpiennie - d 12-26-1870; a 75-9-8; m; pd Congress; pb Germany. (52)
WATKINS, James - d 3-20-1870; a 85-3-24; m; pd Morrow Co.; pb Wales. (52)
HOTCHKISS, Titus - d 11-15-1870; a 62-4-15; m; pd Harmony; pb N.Y. (52)
MORRIS, Matilda - d. 6-12-1870; a 61-5-5; w; pd Harmony; pb Ohio. (52)
ULERY, Jacob - d 6-4-1870; a 72-1-18; m; pd Harmony; pb Pa. (52)
GEORGE, Jane - d 6-23-1870; a 74y 10m; m; pd——; pb Wales; r. Harmony. (52)
DAILY, Rebecca - d 3-15-1870; a 53-1-21; m; pd Chester; pb Ireland Co. Ver. (52)
HOWARD, David R. - d 4-7-1870; a 49y 6m; pd Chester twp.; pb Chester twp. (52)
PRUDY, Fannie - d 10-25-1870; a 66-5-10; m; pd Perry twp.; pb——— (52)
BURGABILL, Peter - d 6-30-1870; a 78-8-9; w; pd Perry twp.; pb Perry twp. (52)

It should be explained that Transcript A (Tr-A) is the earliest volume of deeds and is a transcript from WASHINGTON COUNTY, Ohio. Letters and numbers given at end of deed refer to the volume and page in which the deeds are recorded in Muskingum County, Ohio. Abbreviations:- ¼ = quarter; T = township; R = range; S = section.

SHUSTER, Martin - Military service - 7-5-1803 - Guernsey Co., 100 acres, Lot 5, 2nd ¼, T10, R2 - Tr-A/68 and A/18.

SMITH, Sarah - Heir at law of Arthur Smith, Corporal in late army; Military Service - 11-17-1802 - Tuscarawas Co., 100 acres, Lot 6, 4th ¼, T7, R2 - Tr-A/248 and A/222

BEYMER, George assignee of William WALTON a Captain in Army, Military Service - 5-6-1805 - Guernsey Co., Lots 15, 16, & 17; 3rd ¼; T2, R2 - Tr-A/234 and A/208

BEAHAM, James - Soldier, Military Service - 9-21-1801 - Guernsey Co., 100 acres, Lot 38, 3rd ¼, T2, R2 - Tr-A/89 and A/156

WOODBRIDGE, Dudley - Military Service - 4-22-1800 - 4000 acres, 1st ¼, T3, R8 - Tr-A/182 and A/150

McLANE, Allen - Captain, Military Service - 5-7-1800 - Lots 4,5, & 6; 1st ¼; T2, R3, 300 acres - Tr-A/167 and A/136

VANCE, Samuel C. and Solomon SILBEY - Military Service - 3-29-1800 - 4000 acres, 1st ¼, T1, R8 - Tr-A/1

RATHBONE, John - Military Service - 5-23-1800 - 4000 acres, 3rd ¼, T1, R8 - Tr-A/10

BLUNDEN, William - Drum Major, Military Service - 10-28-1801 - 100 acres, Lot 29, 3rd ¼, T1, R9 - Tr-A/23

PUTNAM, Rufus and William DUSENBERRY - 2-21-1803 - S19, T15, R14 - Tr-A/40

MATTHEWS, Increase; Levi WHIPPLE and Rufus PUTNAM - (date?) - S1-12, T16, R14 - Tr-A/40

MATTHEWS, Increase; Levi WHIPPLE and Rufus PUTNAM - (date?) - west fractional S5 & S6, T12, R13 - Tr-A/40

BEGGS, Zaccheus - Rolf POMEROY's Military Service - 6-27-1804 - Guernsey Co., 100 acres, Lots 1 & 2, 4th ¼ T3, R2 - B/165

PEASLEE, Zaccheus - Burlington, Chittenden Co., Vermont, Lieut., Army - 2-20-1805 - 200 acres, S20 & 21, 3rd ¼, T2, R8 - B/57

BOYD, James assignee of Hugh SWEENY - Military Service - 2-15-1806 - Tuscarawas Co., 100 acres, Lot 7, 3rd ¼, T8, R1 - B/96

RASLY (RASSELLY), John - Military Service - 2-15-1806 - Tuscarawas Co., 100 acres, Lot 9, 3rd ¼. T8, R1 - B/96

EVERY, George - Military Service - 12-26-1805 - Tuscarawas Co., 100 acres, Lot 18, 4th ¼. T7, R2 - B/117

HECHEWELDER, John assignee of William and Benjamin MILLS heirs ofJames Mills, dec'd, a Capt. in Army, Military Service - 3-26-1806 - Tuscarawas Co., Lots 1 & 2, 3rd ¼. T7, R2 and Lot 2, 1st ¼, T6, R2 - 100 acres B/145

GERNON, Richard assignee of Amassa SHIRTLIFF, Sgt., Military Service - 2-1-1805 - Tuscarawas Co., Lot 3, 1st ¼, T6, R2 - B/147

GERNON, Richard assignee of David MORRISON, soldier, Military Service - 2-1-1805 - Tuscarawas Co., 100 acres, Lot 4, 1st ¼, T6, R2 - B/148

GERNON, Richard assignee of Andrew BATSTON, soldier, Military Service - 2-1-1805 - Tuscarawas Co., 100 acres, Lot 6, 1st ¼. T6, R2 - B/149

ADAMS, George assignee of George PAINTER - 12-16-1808 - SE¼ S18, T3, R7 - B/418
ENFANT, Peter Charles L. - 1-13-1803 - 300 acres, Lots 23, 24 & 25; 3rd ¼, T2,
    R8 - B/426
NORTON, Carlos A.assignee of Robert ROBINSON, Drumer, Military Service - 3-5-
    1806 - 100 acres, Lot 7, 3rd ¼, T1, R9 - B/428
NORTON, Carlos A. assignee of Samuel COWDERY, Dragoon, Military Service - 3-5-
    1806 - 100 acres, Lot 8, 3rd ¼. T1, R9 - B/430
SPEAR, Stewart of Adams Co., Penna. - 11-10-1807 - Guernsey Co., NE¼ S20, T2, R4
    - B/433
McBRIDE, Richard and Andrew assignees of James FLAHERTY - 12-20-1808 - SE¼ S 13;
    T16, R14 - B/473
SCHNIDER, Adam of Washington Co., Maryland - 2-10-1809 - SE¼ S20, T9, R3 - B/496
ST. CLAIR, Daniel - Lieut., Military Service - 3-28-1805 - 200 acres, Lots 1 & 2,
    3rd ¼ T1, R9 - B/504
BLACK, James assignee of Luke DEVORE, soldier, Military Service - 1-4-1806 -
    Guernsey Co., 100 acres, Lot 25, 3rd ¼, T1, R1 - B/522
BICKHAM, Elizabeth admrx. of estate of John BICKHAM, dec'd and in trust for heirs
    and devisees of John Bickham a Lieut. Military Service - 9-14-1805 -
    Guernsey Co., 100 acres each Lots 8 & 9, 3rd ¼, T2, R2 - B/559

GILMAN, Benj. Ives assignee of Peleg MASON - 1-4-1810 - West fractional S30 & 32;
    whole S32, T13, R12 - C/11
KEAN, Edward - Military Service - 2-24-1806 - 100 acres, Lot 35, 1st ¼, T2, R8 -
    C/159
HAMMER, Jacob of Fairfield Co., Ohio - 8-3-1810 - NE¼ S32, T17, R15 - C/160
STOCKTON, John Cox assignee of Thomas MITCHELL, fifer, Military Service - 1-16-
    1811 - 100 acres, Lot 17, 3rd ¼, T3, R5 - C/220
RESSLAR, Isaac assignee of Jacob SWOMLEY assignee of William GITLING, Cornet, Mil-
    itary Service - 2-4-1811 - 100 acres, Lot 40 3rd ¼, T1, R9 - C/300
HULL, Nathan - 12-15-1810 - NE¼, S28, T17, R15 - C/307
ASHCRAFT, Daniel - 4-24-1809 - SW¼. S22, T4, R9 - C/320
FRAZER, Benj. - Military Service - 1-16-1811 - 100 acres, Lot 21, 1st ¼, T2, R6
    - C/254
CREVASTER, Jacob - Military Service - 1-6-1811 - 100 acres, Lot 22, 1st ¼, T2;
    R6 - C/255
WAY, Samuel - Military Service - 1-16-1811 - 100 acres, 1st ¼, T2, R6 - C/255
BEEMAN, Moses - Military Service - 1-16-1811 - 100 acres, Lot 27, 1st ¼, T2, R6
    - C/156
GILMAN, Nicholas - Military Service - 3-20-1800 - 3809.70 acres, 1st ¼ T3, R7
    - C/256
PRICE, Jeffrey and Lewis DENT - 12-7-1811 - SW¼ S7, T12, R13 - C/375
HUNMELL, Charles assignee of Alexander McCOY - 12-23-1811 - SW¼, S23, T17, R15
    - C/387
SHERG, Jacob assignee of Joseph FICKLE - (date?) - SE¼ S30, T17, R15 - C/428
ROBINSON, John assignee of Robert McCONNELL - 2-3-1812 - West fraction of S24,
    T10, R12 - C/451
TOPKIN, Gerard assignee of William ROBERTS - 4-10-1809 - NW¼ S10, T1, R5 - C/479
TOPKIN, Gerard assignee of Thomas McKEE - 11-25-1811 - NE¼ S12, T1, R5 - C/479
TOPKIN, Gerard assignee of Robert HARDISTY - 11-25-1811 - SE¼ S9, T1, R5 - C/480
WILSON, John assignee of Robert LOVE - 12-23-1811 - NW¼ S30, T17, R5 - C/481
ZANE, Isaac assignee of John ZANE - 8-19-1812 - SE¼ S2, T16, R14 - C/524

WOOD, Jonathan - 11-19-1812 - SE$\frac{1}{4}$ S25, T3, R9 - D/26
CALHOON, David of Allegany Co., Penna - 4-20-1812 - NW$\frac{1}{4}$ S23, T1, R5 - D/28
FLUCKY, George assignee of Isaac SELLERS - 12-14-1812 - SW$\frac{1}{4}$ S6, T15, R16 - D/35
TADROW (TADRON), John - 3-19-1811 - SW$\frac{1}{4}$ S7, T15, R14 - D/51
WHITAKER, Lewis of Ohio Co., Virginia - 8-19-1812 - NE$\frac{1}{4}$ S24, T11, R13, - D/59
McLEAN, Wm. of Fayette Co., Penna. - 12-23-1811 - SW$\frac{1}{4}$ S17, T13, R12 - D/75
FIELDS, David of Bedford Co., Penna - 4-20-1812 - SW$\frac{1}{4}$ S8, T3, R8 - D/76
SMITH, James of Belmont Co., Ohio - 12-4-1812 - SW$\frac{1}{4}$ S18, T18, R15 - D/85
COUZENS, Elizabeth heir at law of John WICKHAM, dec'd, Lieut., Military Service -
    3-5-1804 - 200 acres, Lots 9 & 10, 3rd $\frac{1}{4}$, T1, R9 - D/123
WYNN, - 2-10-1813 - SW$\frac{1}{4}$ S9, T1, R6 - D/132
WOODRUFE, Silas assignee of Robert LEVICK, soldier, Military Service - 12-8-1805
    - 100 acres, Lot 31, 1st $\frac{1}{4}$, T2, R8 - D/145
COOPER, Jacob assignee of William WILSON - 8-19-1812 - NE$\frac{1}{4}$ S1, T15, R15 - D/192
SHROYER, Philip Jr. and Henry BENTER assignees of George DYCE alias DINS, Pvt. in
    Maryland Line - 9-1-1813 - 100 acres, Lot 14, 3rd $\frac{1}{4}$, T3, R5 - D/218
CLARK, Wm. assignee of Isaac SMITH, soldier, Military Service - 3-28-1805 -
    100 acres, Lot 40,1st $\frac{1}{4}$, T2, R8 - D/309
ELLIOTT, Samuel assignee of Henry RESONER - 3-17-1814 - SW$\frac{1}{4}$ S3, T1, R9 - D/310
WYLIE, John of Allaganey Co.; Penna. - 4-20-1812 - SW$\frac{1}{4}$ S14, T1; R5 - D/321
WYLIE, John of Allaganey Co., Penna. - 4-20-1812 - NE$\frac{1}{4}$ S15, T1, R5 - D/322
JACKSON, John George assignee of George P. RANSOM adms. of Samuel RANSOM, dec'd,
    late Capt. in Connecticut line - 6-24-1838(?) - 200 acres, Lots 26 & 36,
    3rd $\frac{1}{4}$, T4, R8 - D/389
DETRICK, Baker assignee of Godfrey WEYMER - 8-19-1812 - SW$\frac{1}{4}$ S14, T16, R14 - D/416
BAKER, Philip Sr. assignee of Jacob AYRES - 4-10-1811 - east fractional S8, T12,
    R12 - D/408
WHEELER, Thomothy - 8-19-1812 - NW$\frac{1}{4}$ S14, T16, R15 - D/433
ANSPACH, John of Franklin Co., Penna. - 4-7-1810 - SE$\frac{1}{4}$ S3, T1, R7 - D/483
LIVENGOOD, Peter - 3-27-1812 - NW$\frac{1}{4}$ S15, T1, R6 - D/498
COLE, Andrew - Military service - 7-24-1810 - 100 acres, Lot 15, 4th $\frac{1}{4}$, T8, R1
    - D/500
SMITH, Thomas - 10-8-1814 - SW$\frac{1}{4}$ S3, T13, R12 - D/561
WORKMAN, Benj. of Westmoreland Co., Penna. - 12-2-1814 - SW$\frac{1}{4}$ S7, T1, R5 - D/569
GALIHER, Peter of Westmoreland Co., Penna. - 12-1-1814 - SW$\frac{1}{4}$ S4, T1, R5 - D/595
ROSWELL, Zachariah - Serg't., Military Service - 5-20-1806 - 100 acres, Lot 17,
    1st $\frac{1}{4}$, T2, R8 - D/613
LIVENGOOD, Jacob - 4-20-1812 - SE$\frac{1}{4}$ S12, T1, R6 - D/655
LEVINGOOD, Jacob - 3-22-1813 - SW$\frac{1}{4}$ S12, T1, R6 - D/656
FULTON, Robert and James KIRKER - 10-10-1814 - SE$\frac{1}{4}$ S23, T2, R8 - D/717

DANHAUR, Elias of Philadelphia - 4-29-1814 - NE$\frac{1}{4}$ S17, T11, R13 - E/15
COOPER, Jacob of Loudon Co., Virginia - 10-10-1814 - SW$\frac{1}{4}$ S31, T15, R14 - E/59
PRICE, Jeffrey and Isaac VAN HORN, Jr. - 6-17-1815 - NE$\frac{1}{4}$ S22, T1, R9 - E/60
CUSAC, Andrew of Fairfield Co., Ohio - 2-11-1814 - NE$\frac{1}{4}$ S14, T16, R15 - E/73
SMITH, Jacob - 8-30-1815 - SE$\frac{1}{4}$ S21, T4, R5 - E/105
CRANE, George - 8-19-1812 - NE$\frac{1}{4}$ S5, T13, R12 - E/122
LINN, Robert - 12-28-1814 - NE$\frac{1}{4}$ S15, T13, R12 - E/128
CONWAY, Samuel assignee of Robert McCONNELL - 12-23-1811 - NW$\frac{1}{4}$ S4, T1, R6 - E/136
WORTMAN, Lot of Westmoreland Co., Penna. - 12-11-1815 - NE$\frac{1}{4}$ S16, T2, R5 - E/224
VARNER, Martin assignee of Isaac HARRIS - 4-6-1815 - NW$\frac{1}{4}$ S5, T1, R9 - E/284

MILLAR, William and Nicholas RIBBLE (or REBBLE) - 10-10-1814 - NW¼ S35, T17,
    R15 - E/321
BARND, Christian - 2-3-1817 - SW¼ S 32, T16, R15 - E/394
WATSON, Alex. assignee of Edward Smith - 3-8-1817 - SE¼ Se, T18, R15 - E/414
GORDON, Charles and John PHILLIPS assignees of Henry GORDON and John GYSINGER
    - 3-8-1817 - NE¼ S19, T17, R15 - E/414
MATHEWS, Increase - 2-4-1817 - NW¼ S3, T14, R14 - E/432
BEARD, William H. - 12-19-1816 - NW¼ S31, T17, R15 - E/438
THOMPSON, Daniel assignee of William CLAYPOOL - 9-30-1815 - NE¼ S24, T3, R9 -
    E/443
PARKER, John - Military Service - 1-18-1804 - 100 acres, Lot 27, 3rd ¼, T1, R9
    - E/460
BECKWITH, Tobias - 3-8-1817 - SW¼ S2, T8, R13 - E/466

SLACK, Abel - 2-23-1814 - NW¼ S8, T2, R6 - F/21
SPENCER, James and George - 5-3-1817 - NE¼ S5, T15, R15 - F/22
VERNON, Joseph - 1-30-1813 - NE¼ S5, T1, R6 - F/73
SARCHET, Thomas assignee of Charles MARQUAND - 3-8-1817 - NW¼ S24, T13, R12 - F/81
FINDLEY, James and David DUTRO - 5-10-1816 - east fractional S5, T12, R12 - F/95
WISECARVER, Abraham of Coshocton Co., Ohio - 3-14-1818 - NW¼ S18, T3, R6 - F/159
CRAWFORD, William of Washington Co., Penna. - 3-16-1818 - NW¼ S34, T13, R11 -
    F/192
NORTHUP, Henry assignee of the legal heirs of George DOHERTY, dec'd, a Major in
    the North Carolina line - 9-2-1815 - 400 acres, Lots 26, 29, 34 & 37;
    1st ¼, T2, R6 - F/231
REMSON, Isaac Jr. assignee of Thomas FISHER - 9-18-1817 - NW¼ S12, T17, R15, -
    F/242
DAVIS, Amasa - 3-27-1812 - NE¼ S23, T1, R6 - F/256
DAVIS, Amasa assignee of Thomas KINNEY - 5-13-1817 - NW¼ S22, T1, R6 - F/255
WIRTS, Peter - 3-12-1817 - SW¼ S7, T2, R5 - F/260
GEORGE, Alexander of Washington Co., Penna. - 12-19-1816 - SW¼ S10, T2, R5 -
    F/286
RICHEY, George - 6-25-1817 - SE¼ S4, T1, R5 - F/288
NORTHUP, Henry assignee of Martha MELVIN admrx. of the estate of George MELVIN,
    dec'd a Captain in the Georgia Line - 300 acres, Lot 25, 1st ¼, T2, R6;
    Lot 28, 3rd ¼, T8, R6 and Lot 27, 3rd ¼, T10, R5 - F/314
RICHARDSON, David assignee of George STOWNER - 12-10-1817 - SE¼ S13, T3, R5 -
    F/342
REED, Ellis assignee of Daniel CONVERSE - 6-30-1818 - NW¼ S36, T13, R12 - F/343
ROBINSON, William assignee of George BEYMER - 12-14-1812 - NW¼ S16, T1, R5 -
    F/371
PARKER, James - 6-25-1817 - SE¼ S24, T15, R14 - F/386
HOGSEED, Jacob of Washington Co., Penna - 1-23-1819 - NE¼ S12, T2, R5, - F/389
SELF, William assignee of George JAY - 3-16-1818 - SW¼ S11, T1, R6 - F/409
DAVIS, Jno. of Lancaster Co.,Penna. - 7-6-1819 - NE¼ S13, T12, R12 - F/455
POMPEY, Jno. assignee of David SMITH - 4-10-1819 - SW¼ S1, T3, R5 - F/459
RICKETTS, Benjamin assignee of William SPENCER - 5-10-1816 - NE¼ S15, T3, R8 -
    F/462

ROBINSON, Kennedy assignee of John ANTRIM, soldier, Military Service - 3-23-1807
    - 100 acres, Lot 24, 3rd ¼, T1, R15 - G/7
DULTY, John of Ohio Co., Virginia - 6-3-1819 - 295 acres, "½ S3, T11, R13 - G/52
BOLIN, Robert and Thomas SAVAGE assignees of Levi PRIEST and John PRIEST, Jr. -
    8-8-1818 - NW¼ S21, T1, R9 - G/24
RICHARDSON, Rufus assignee of Henry NORTHUP - 12-10-1817 - NW¼ S10, T3, R5 - G/24
ARMSTRONG, Alexander - 6-3-1819 - SE¼ S12, T2, R6 - G/74
SPEER, Thomas assignee of Robert SPEER - 2-26-1811 - SE¼ S1, T1, R5 - G/102
HOGSEED, Walter assignee of James HOGSEED - 1-21-1820 - NW¼ S11, T2, R5 - G/174
YAUGER, Wm. of Allegheny Co., Penna. - 2-11-1819 - SW¼ S20, T12, R11 - G/174
DERNER, Jacob Sr. assignee of Jacob DERNER - 2-3-1817 - SW¼ S22, T2, R6 - G/154
GORDEN, James assignee of Peter LANDERMAN - 5-30-1820 - SW¼ S31, T12, R11 - G/212
CRAWFORD, William of Washington Co., Penna. - 4-13-1820 - 141 acres, NW¼ S3, T12,
    R11 - G/213
CAMPBELL, Jno. - 10-26-1820 - NE¼ S18, &3, R6 - G/249
VAN HORNE, Isaac - 3-10-1817 - NE¼ S21, T11, R13 - G/399
FICKLE, Benjamin assignee of Benjamin TURNER - 11-18-1812 - NW¼ S17, T15, R14 -
    G/443
LAWRENCE, William - 7-14-1817 - NE¼ S26, T15, R14 - G/477
BARRETT, John - 9-8-1820 - SW¼ S19, T3, R6 - G/481
ROCHELL, John - Capt. in North Carolina Line, Military Service. 300 acres, Lots
    9, 10 & 23; 1st ¼, T2, R6 - G/486
HADDEN, John of Belmont Co., Ohio - 4-20-1812 - SW¼ S8, T1, R5 - G/503
LATTA, Thomas of Jefferson Co., Ohio - 3-17-1814 - SE¼ S8, T1, R5 - G/504
GEORGE, William in his own right and Alexander CULBERTSON assignee of Con's.
    SPRINGER - 2-18-1817 - SE¼ S9, T16, R14 - G/539
McCOMAS, Daniel of Washington Co., Penna - 3-22-1813 - SW¼ S14, T13, R11 - G/580
GREEN, Elias assignee of David BROWN a Private in Revolutionary War - 7-8-1812
    - 100 acres, Lot 17, S3, T3, R5 - G/599
UNDERWOOD, Robert - Military Service - 3-29-1800 - 4000 acres, 2nd ¼. T1, R7 -
    G/624
OFFICER, James of Washington Co., Penna. - 11-18-1812 - NE¼ S1, T13, R12 - G/650

STEVENSON, Thomas - 8-20-1823 - 160.34 acres, NW¼ S25, T1, R5 - H/73
KEENE, Samuel Y. - Surgeon's mate, Military Service - 2-27-1808 - 300 acres,
    Lots 13, 16 & 23; 3rd ¼, T3, R5 - H/117
BOLLER, Frederick - Military Service - 3-28-1800 - 3995.80 acres, 4th ¼, T3, R8
    - H/148
SPICER, John of Butler Co., Penna - 10-1-1824 - 152 acres, SE¼ S23, T2, R6 -
    H/225
BAKER, Jacob - 7-6-1819 - SE¼ S20, T11, R13 - H/225
ST. CLAIR, John - 4-10-1819 - NW¼ S23, T13, R11 - H/279
GREEN, Joseph of Stubenville, Ohio - 10-1-1824 - 156 acres, SW¼ S6, T6, R5 -
    H/345
WORTMAN, Benjamin - 3-10-1825 - 90.58 acres, W½ SE¼ S25, T11, R11 - H/380
BELL, George assignee of Samuel THOMPSON - 3-8-1817 - NE¼ S10, T16, R14 - H/385
KELLY, Thomas of Chambersburgh, Penna. - 7-24-1811 - SE¼ S9, T1, R7 - H/505
KELLY, Thomas of Chambersburgh, Penna. - 7-24-1811 - NE¼ S9, T1, R7 - H/506
HOOKER, Richard in his own right and as assignee of William McCLUNG(?) -
    6-20-1809 - Sections 19 & 30, T13, R12, - H/616

CARR, Hezekiah - Drummer, 3rd Regt., Maryland Line - 3-1-1814 - 100 acres,
    Lot 35, 1st ¼, T2, R6 - I/48
ZANE, Thomas - 9-8-1821 - W½ SE¼ S14, T12, R12 - I/101
FULTON, Robert assignee of John McMAHON - 10-20-1825 - 160 acres, NW¼ S14, T3,
    R8 - I/110
CHRISTIE, George - 6-23-1825 - 176.82 acres, NW¼ S2, T14, R14 - I/114
ELLIOTT, Thomas of Washington Co., Ohio - 7-26-1825 - NW¼ S21, T1, R6 - I/135
DUFF, Daniel of Gurnsey Co., Ohio - 10-1-1824 - NE¼ S3, T2, R5 - I/206
GEORGE, Jacob of Washington Co., Penna. - 11-29-1819 - 155.32 acres, NE¼ S23, T3,
    R5 - I/208
TAYLOR, Samuel of Westmoreland Co., Penna. - 12-23-1811 - SW¼ S21, T2, R8 - I/228
GLADMAN, Thomas of Licking Co., Ohio - 11-1-1826 - NW¼ S4, T1, R9 - I/251
HAMMOND, George - 6-1-1827 - 80.81 acres, E½ SE¼ S22, T13, R12 - I/523
HORNE, Daniel - 11-19-1812 - NW¼ S36, T17, R15, - I/566
FINNEY, Heirs of William - 6-23-1825 - 159.18 acres, SE¼ S33, T12, R12 - I/599
WIMP, James and Sally, Ann, George, Mary Ann, Aviey and John R. LENHART heirs at
    law of John LENHARD, dec'd assignee of John FORD - 5-20-1828 - 161 acres,
    SE¼ S17, T15, R14 - I/632
WORSTALL, John - 7-30-1827 - 161.56 acres, NE¼ S16, T11, R13 - I/642
BOYLE, John assignee of Moses DILLON - 5-20-1828 - SE¼ S22, T1, R9 - I/703

MYERS, Nathaniel - 3-10-1825 E½ SW¼ S15, T13, R11 - K/69
STANBERRY, Jonas assignee of Thomas MOOREHEAD and Jonathan CLARK - 5-20-1828 -
    165.98 acres, NW¼ S13, T15, R14 - K/102
REED, Heirs of Samuel assignee of James McCOID - 6-10-1825 - 159.40 acres, SW¼
    S14, T12, R12 - K/179
FRAZIER, Daniel - 11-5-1819 - 158 acres, SW¼ S34, T13, R12 - K/559
CARLISLE, Jonathan Jr. assignee of David J. MARPLE - 12-30-1810 - fractional
    sections 7 & 8, T11, R13 - K/743

ZIMMERMAN, Jacob assignee of James MOORE - 10-26-1820 - 160 acres, NE¼ S15, T2,
    R6 - L/82
JORDAN, Joseph - 8-20-1823 - E½ NE¼ S25, T12, R11 - L/589
WALKER, Samuel assignee of William BALDWIN - 5-20-1828 - NW¼ S15, T2, R8 - L/485
McCONNELL, William assignee of Robert McCONNELL - 11-18-1812 - SE¼ S2, T1, R7
    - L/622
CASS, Jonathan - Military Service - 5-12-1800 - 4000 acres, 2nd ¼, T3, R7 - L/648

287

SPICER, Daniel - 4-7-1820 - 160 acres, SE¼ S20, T2, R6 - M/25
WHEELER; Hanson of Brooks Co., Virginia - 2-10-1831 - 77 acres, W½ NE¼ S18, T3,
    R5 - M/133
MACK, Jacob assignee of Balser TITERACK - 8-19-1812 - NE¼ S11, T18, R15 - M/167
TETARICK, Nicholas assignee of Balser TITARICK - 7-15-1813 - SE¼ S17, T11, R13 -
    M/442
TETARICK, Nicholas - 9-18-1817 - SW¼ S17, T11, R13 - M/442
BARTON, William assignee of Valentine SHIREY - 5-3-1831 - 165.38 acres, SE¼ S15,
    T3, R6 - M/512
DULTY, John of Ohio Co., Virginia - 6-3-1819 - 317 acres, W½ S3, T11, R13 - N/346
DRUM, Samuel - 6-7-1814 - NE¼ S15, T1, R9 - 0/74
DRUM, Samuel - 5-20-1828 - 160 acres, NW¼ S14, T1, R9 - 0/74
NORMAN, George - 3-14-1818 - NE¼ S1, T18, R15 - 0/624
STURGES, Solomon of Putnam, Ohio - 2-20-1831 - 160 acres NE¼ S19, T12, R12 -
    P/278
MITCHELL, Thomas of Allegheny Co., Penna. - 8-13-1825 - NW¼ S29, T12, R11 -
    P/314
MITCHELL, Thomas of Allegheny Co., Penna. - 11-2-1830 - 94 acres, NE¼ S 13,
    T12, R11 - P/315
SMITH, William Lane - 4-17-1833 - 94 acres, NW¼ S30, T12, R11 - P/345
MOORE, John - 6-25-1817 - NW¼ S19, T13, R11 - P/387
MOORE, John assignee of Lewis PEIRCE - 4-7-1820 - 157 acres, SW¼ S19, T13, R11 -
    P/387
TOMLINSON, Thomas - 4-17-1833 - 159 acres, SE¼ S4, T12, R12 - P/408
GRANDSTAFF, John - 7-26-1825 - 155 acres, NE¼ S11, T12, R12 - P/414
MATHEWS, John - 9-14-1814 - SW¼ S5, T11, R13 - P/417
MATHEWS, John assignee of James JEFFRIES - 3-5-1813 - NW¼ S12, T14, R15 - P/416
MATHEWS, John assignee of Robert NYE - 8-19-1812 - SW¼ S1, T15, R14 - P/417
MATHEWS, John assignee of James FLAHERTY, Richard and Andrew McBRIDE - 3-8-1817 -
    NW¼ S6, T11, R13 - P/418
MATHEWS, John - 12-16-1812 - NW¼ S1, T15, R14 - P/418
MATHEWS, John - 8-19-1812 - SE¼ S1, T15, R14 - P/419
ONSTOTT, Peter - 10-2-1826 - 77 acres, NE¼ S6, T12, R11 - P/419
MUNROE, Daniel - 5-5-1823 - 157 acres, NE¼ S24, T13, R12 - P/439
CHANDIER, John - 10-10-1806 - S14, T13, R12- P/436
SHIELDS, Joseph of Allegheny Co., Penna. - 10-10-1814 - SW¼ S17, T13, R11 -
    P/436
GRANSTAFF, Adam of Ohio Co., Virginia - 6-16-1826 - 141 acres, NW¼ S4, T12, R11
    - P/491
LABAN, Elizabeth and Thaddeus IEMERT, executors of Lewis IEMERT, dec'd, assignees
    of Zachariah FOWIR - 7-18-1820 - 160 acres, NW¼ S7, T3, R8 - P/492

JOHN, Jesse assignee of Daniel FRAZIER - 11-5-1819 - NW¼ S35, T12, R12 - P/508
BROWN, James Sr. - 1-30-1810 - SW¼ S19, T1, R6 - P/523
DOSER, George of Morgan Co., Ohio - 4-2-1832 - 79 acres, SE¼ S9, T10, R13 - P/552
DOSER, George - 2-10-1831 - 79 acres, SE¼ S9, T10, R13 - P/552
BORDER, George - 7-2-1832 - 80 acres, NW¼ S9, T3, R6 - P/553
BORDER, George - 12-1-1830 - 80 acres, NW¼ S9, T3, R6 - P/554
BEAN, David - 6-6-1826 - 80 acres, SW¼ S9, T12, R12 - P/586
CLAPPER, Joseph - 12-1-1826 - SE¼ S9, T12, R12 - P/598
HARTFORD, John - 8-13-1825 - 155 acres, SW¼ S4, T3, R8 - P/607
BLUNT, William - 12-19-1814 - SW¼ S3, T2, R8 - P/611
BLUNT, William - 3-22-1813 - SE¼ S4, T2, R8 - P/611
WEST, William - 6-1-1831 - 82 acres, SW¼ S17, T12, R11 - P/641
REED, David - 8-21-1823 - 82 acres, SW¼ S17, T12, R11 - P/641

289

The following wills were abstracted from Will Book C. Page on which Will may be found is given in parenthesis.

SULLIVAN, Charles - dated 2-22-1832; recorded 3-7-1832. Wife, Clarisa. Son, Charles. Two youngest daughters: Lucy Beamer and Nancy. Executor: friend, James Even. Signed: Charles Sullivan. Witnesses: Peter Holmes and Spencer Brown. (1)

JAMES, David of Meigs twp. - dated 1-16-1830; recorded 4-5-1832. Wife, Nancy. Sons: Isaac, John, Thomas, David, Rufus and Griffith. Daughters: Mary Ann, Eliza, Hannah and Nancy. Executors: wife, Nancy and John Hammond. Signed: David James. Witnesses: Caleb Woodard and Thomas Green. (2)

FLETCHER, William Sr. - dated 3-9-1832; recorded 7-14-1832. Wife, Catharine. Son, William. Daughter, Tene Fletcher. Mentions other children but does not name. Executors: wife, Catharine and son, William. Signed: William (his mark) Fletcher Sr. Witnesses: Geo. N. Flood, Joseph P. Huston and Isabella (her mark) Cunningham. (3)

DUGAN, Andrew of Newton twp. - dated 2-25-1832; recorded 4-14-1832. Wife, Betsey. Five children: Benjamin, John, Jane, Andrew and Martha Dugan, all not of age. Executor: Milton B. Cushing of Putnam. Signed: Andrew Dugan. Witnesses: William Lawrence and Alexander Work. (5)

HAMMILL, Samuel - dated 8-4-1831; recorded 4-16-1832. Wife, Margaret, also to serve as executrix. Sister, Martha Wilson. Nephew, Samuel Beatty. Signed; Samuel Hammell. Witnesses: Appleton Douner and John Hough. (8)

McCLEARY, John of Zanesville - dated 6-27-1832; recorded 7-3-1832. Wife, Susan. Children: Mary Ellen, Jane, James and Catharine McCleary. Executor: David Maginnis of Zanesville. Signed: John McCleary. Witnesses: David Spangler and David Reed. (10)

GRAPES, David - dated 8-21-1828; recorded 7-7-1832. Wife, Catharine, also to serve as executrix. Sons: Jacob, George, John and Henry. Daughter, Sarah Russell. Witnesses: Grafton Duval, Wm. F. (his mark) Ryley and Mary (her mark) Ryley. (11)

McALISTER, Elizabeth - dated 5-28-1832; recorded 7-6-1832. Mother, Nancy Rogers. Executor, Connel Rodgers. Signed: Elizabeth (her mark) McAllister. Witnesses: Thomas Flood and William Davis. (13)

BUCKINGHAM, Ebenezer - dated 1-25-1822; recorded 9-3-1832. Wife, Eunice. Son, CatharinesPutnens to have legacy from his grandfather. Mentions other children but does not name. Mentions first wife but does not name. Mentions his aged parents but does not name. Sisters: Sarah Sprague, Matilda Cooly and Esther Lamb. Executors: wife, Eunice; brother, Alvah Buckingham; and brother-in-law, Solomon Georges. Witnesses: M. B. Cusing and A. A. Guthrie. (14)

WELLS, John of Zanesville twp. - dated 4-11-1830; recorded 12-27-1832. Wife, Sarah also to serve as executrix. Signed: John Wells. Witnesses: Thomas Moorehead and Richard Brookover. (15)

HARTFORD, John - dated 1-7-1833; recorded 1-26-1833. Wife, Jane. Sons, William G. and John. Daughters: Jane wife of Joseph Wright, Mary Hartford and Ann. Mentions unborn child. Executors: son, John and Robert Wilson, Esq. Signed: John Hartford. Witnesses: John Barron and Mathew Wilson. (15)

HOWDEN, Andrew Jr. of Zanesville - dated (not given); recorded 2-11-1833. Wife, Ann B. Son, Theophilus, not of age. Brothers: William and Thomas. Testator owned house in Hillsborough, Penna. Executors: Ann B. and Thomas Howden. Signed: A. Howden Jr. Witnesses: Alex'r Harper and Chas. B. Goddard. (16)

ROSS, John of Highland twp. - dated 9-5-1832; recorded 11-23-1832. Wife, Jane to have S½ SW¼ Section 4, Township 2, Range 5. Sons: James, Thomas and Samuel. Daughters: Rebecca McCluskey, Mary White, Hannah Ramsey, Isabella Ross and Mary Ross. Executors: James Hunter and brother-in-law, John Acheson. Signed: John Ross. Witnesses: Robert McCall and Samuel Ross. (18)

HOLETON, Nicholas C. of Falls twp. - dated (not given); recorded 11-23-1832. Wife, Rebecca. Six sons: John, Samuel, Francis, Washington, Silas and Gomailial, Five daughters: Mary Ann, Tabitha, Eliza, Christeena and Elizabeth. Executors: wife, Rebecca and son, John. Signed: N. L. Holeton. Witnesses: Reuben Savidge and Edward Smith. (20)

BOYER, Peter of Hopewell twp. - dated 9-7-1832; recorded 11-23-1832. Wife, Catharine. Sons: Jacob, John, Peter, Bardsley, David, William and Andrew. Daughters: Betsey Rundle, Sally Kiler, Peggy Weekley and fourth daughter mentioned but not named. Executors: Jacob and John Boyer. Signed: Peter (his mark) Boyer. Witnesses: Elmar Wheaton, Thomas (his mark) Bounds and Samuel Frey. (21)

KARNS, Lewis - dated 5-24-1832; recorded 11-24-1832. Wife, Eleanor, to have 79 acres NE¼ Section 1, Township 12, Range 13 in Wayne twp. Children: Henry Karns; Lewis Karns Jr., dec'd, his children--Michael, Eleanor, Cassia, Henry, Sanford, John, William and Lewis Karns; Susannah Carlisle; Mary Mercer; Ruth Amy Joseph; Abigail Curtis; John Karns; Jacob Karns; and Stephen D. Karns. Executors: wife, Eleanor and son, Henry. Signed: Lewis (his mark) Karns. Witnesses: Jno. Burwell, Mathias Spangler Jr. and J. W. Spry. (22)

CONRAD, Rebecca - dated 1-3-1828; recorded 11-24-1832. Son, Jacob Crawford. Daughters: Sarah Jefferies and Rebecca wife of Jacob Miller. Mentions estate at Pittsburgh being part of Jacob Conrad's pension. Executor: James Jefferies. Signed: Rebecca (her mark) Conrad. Witnesses: Grafton Duval and W. Jefferies.(24)

THORNBURGH, Thomas of Meigs twp. - Noncupative will - dated 11-17-1832; recorded 4-22-1833. Wife, Nancy. Mentions children but does not name, not all of age. Guardian of children to be John B. Taylor and James Starrett. Witnesses: Thomas Morrison and Jacob Onstot. (25)

McCULLY, Patrick of Blue Rock twp. - dated 3-9-1833; recorded 4-24-1833. Wife, Sarah. After death of wife Sarah, estate to go to Sarah Roberts, daughter of Thomas Roberts. Executors: wife, Sarah and Jeremiah Argo. Signed: Patrick McCully. Witnesses: John Coverdill and John Grandstaff. (26)

BOGGS, Moses - dated 2-1-1832; recorded 5-3-1833. Wife, Margaret. Sons: Robert & James. Daughters: Hannah Robertson, Agnes and Margaret. Executors: son, Robert; friends, John Robertson and Thomas Flood. Signed: Moses Boggs. Witnesses: Chas. C. Gilbert, Geo. W. Flood and William Blackson. (27)

BENTLEY, Mary - dated 9-19-1832; recorded 5-3-1833. Brother, Anthony Mauk, also to serve as executor. Children: Harriet, Eliza and William; not of age. Signed: Mary (her mark) Bentley. Witnesses: Wm. M. Ilree(?) Jr. and Jacob Mauk. (30)

PALMER, Eliakim - dated 7-17-1833; recorded 8-9-1833. Wife, Sarah. Sons: Howard and Otho Palmer. Daughter, Mary Boring. Grandchildren: Elizabeth, William H., Mary Ann and John N. Palmer. Mentions owning lot in Washington D.C. Brother-in-law, John Ellis living in Washington D.C. Executors: son-in-law, Edward Boring and son, Otho Palmer. Signed: Eliakim Palmer and Sarah (her mark) Palmer. Witnesses: Joseph C. Huston and James (his mark) McGuire. (31)

HENRY, Jacob - dated 5-15-1833; recorded 8-10-1833. Wife, Margaret, also to serve as executrix. Wife is to enter two half quarter sections of land in the name of his two children. Signed: Jacob Henry. Witnesses: Robert Aikins and James Vanderwit. (33)

SPEER, William of Union twp. - dated 6-11-1833; recorded 8-9-1833. Wife, Rebecca, Two sons: Robert and William Speer. Daughters: Sarah wife of Patterson Proudfit, Jane Spear, Polly Speer, Margaret Speer, Eliza Speer, Martha Speer and Nancy Ann Speer. Brothers: Thomas Speer and Stuart Speer. Executors: son, Robert and brother, Stuart. Signed: William Speer. Witnesses: John Jamison and John Hull.(35)

MILLER, Phillip - dated 5-22-1832; recorded 8-10-1833. Sons: Christopher; Noah; Mikiel; Jacob; Abraham and Isaac, dec'd, his heirs being four in number (not named). Executor: son, Abraham. Signed: Phillip (his mark) Miller. Witnesses: Geo. Johnson and Henry Richards. (36)

HOPKINS, James of Brushcreek twp. - dated 6-20-1833; recorded 8-9-1833. Wife, Sarah. Children mentioned but not named. Executors: wife, Sarah and John Worstal. Signed: James (his mark) Hopkins. Witnesses: Samuel stover and Robert Boyd.(37)

FLESHER, Balsar - dated 10-21-1830; recorded 8-10-1833. Wife, Mary. Children: Catharine Aldridge, Sarah Daugherty, Ann Drum, Mary Shaw, Matilda Baird, Henry Flesher, John Flesher and Peter Flesher. Grand-daughter, Margaret Lamb. Mentions land part second half Township 1, Range 8 and also land that Isaac Drum lives on. Executor, David Sherrard. Signed: Balser (his mark) Flesher. Witnesses: John Roberts, Robert J. Smith and David Sherrard. (38)

CARRON, Michael of Springfield twp. - dated 11-2-1828; recorded 8-24-1833. Son, James to have 52 3/4 acres SW¼ Section 15, Township 16, Range 14 where testator now lives. Daughters: Mary Callehan, Rosannah Holdridge, Nancy Russell and Peggy Ward. Brother, John Carron. Executors: son, James and Alanson Holdridge. Signed: Michael (his mark) Carron. Witnesses: Wm. H. Mair(?), George Relland and Hannah McCormick. (40)

REAGER, John of Licking twp. - dated 6-22-1831; recorded 10-9-1833. Step-son, Leonard Stump. Brother, Anthony Reager. Heirs of late brother, Jacob Reager. Heirs of brother-in-law, John Roerbaugh. Heirs of brother-in-law, John Ulerick Spear (Spore). Heirs of brother-in-law, Joseph Scott. Brother, Henry Reager, his daughter Anne Reager. Wife, mentioned but not named. Wife's grandson, John Reager Stump. Executor: step-son, Leonard Stump. Signed: John (his IR mark) Reager. Witnesses: Horatio J. Cox and Thomas Bealmear. (41)

COE, Nathan - dated 8-1-1833; recorded 10-9-1833. Two sons, Joshua and Isaac. Daughters: Elizabeth Hawk, Rebeccah McCammert, Mary Perrygoy, Anna Conn, Sarah Meeks, Harriet Nut and Ally Nut. Wife, Darcuss Coe. Executor: son-in-law, Samuel McCammart. Signed: Nathan Coe. Witnesses: Henry Buller and Stephen (his mark) Piatt. (42)

MENDENHALL, Hannah - dated 7-27-1833; recorded 10-9-1833. Grand-daughters: Hannah Griffee and Hannah Bennett. Mentions: Margaret Drake, Lydia Wimmer, Esther Shepherd, Hannah Reed, Samuel son of R. C. Mendenhall and Samuel son of Uriah Parke; relationship, if any, not stated. Executor: Jared Brush of Zanesville. Signed: H. Mendenhall. Witnesses: David Vanderbark and John Lovet. (43)

LOVE, Lettuce - dated 8-5-1828; recorded 10-22-1833. Daughters: Jane Marshall and Margaret. Sons: Thomas, Alexander and James. Executrix; daughter, Margaret. Signed: Lettuce (her mark) Love. Witnesses: Andrew Wharton and Elizabeth Wharton. (44)

RICHEY, George of Union twp. - dated 6-24-1830; recorded 11-16-1833. Wife, Mary. Three sons: William E., George and Thomas Richey. Three daughters: Jane, Prudence and Catherine Richey. Executors: son, William E. Richey and Archibald Campbell. Signed: George (his mark) Richey. Witnesses: Samuel Cabeer, A. Campbell and Thomas Richey. (45)

OLIVER, Jane of Zanesville - dated 9-27-1833; recorded 11-22-1833. Sons: William, Alexander and Thomas. Daughters: Precilla Carpenter and Hetty. Executor, James Doster. Signed: Jane Oliver. (47)

ROBERTS, Wm. R. of Newton twp. - dated 1-17-1829; recorded 11-23-1833. Wife, Frances. Signed: William R. Roberts. Witnesses: M. Gillespie and Em. Anderson. (48)

ELLIS, Elias - dated 7-30-1833; recorded 11-23-1833. Daughters: Hannah Dorsey and Eliza Ellis. Sons: Elias and Thomas Ellis, also to serve as executors. Signed: Elias (his EE mark) Ellis. Witnesses: John Vanvoorhes and James Taggert Jr. (49)

The following records were abstracted from Will Book A. Pages on which record may be found are given in parenthesis.

W I L L S

AMORY, Edward - dated 8-24-1804; recorded 11-21-1804. Wife, Elizabeth. Sons:- George and Van. Executors:- Wife, Elizabeth and Isaac Evans. Signed:- Edward Amory. Witnesses:- James Robinson, Jacob Jackson and Barbara Miller. (1)

McMORDEE, Adam - dated 1-24-1806; recorded 11-22-1806. Brothers:- Francis, John and Robert. Sisters:- Jean Armstrong and Nancy Speer. Mentions land in Lycoming County (no date given), also land lately sold to Avon Huse. Executors:- Thomas Speer and David Enlaw. Signed:- Adam McMordee. Witnesses:- Penhord Marshall and Avon Hughs. (5)

FULTON, Samuel of Tuskarawa - dated 8-15-1804; recorded Dec. 1806. Wife, Jane. Sons:- Samuel, William and John. Mentions other children but does not name. Executors:- Sons, William and John. Signed:- Sam'l Fulton. Witnesses:- Ebenezer Buckingham Jr., Charles Williams and William Whitton. (10)

HAUCK, George of Zanesville - dated 9-9-1808; recorded Apr. 1809. Father, Jacob Hauck, also to serve as executor. Brothers:- Frederick and William. Sister, Margaret. Signed:- George Hauck. Witnesses:- W. Selliman, Daniel McClane and W. Raynolds. (132)

WILLIAMSON, William - dated 8-1-1809; recorded 12-19-1809. Wife, Jane Williamson, being with an expected heir. Son, Robert. Daughter, Jane. Brother, John Crassan (or Crasson). Executors:- Wife, Jane and Joseph Scarborugh. Signed:- William (mark) Williamson. Witnesses:- Francis Bowen and Elijah Havens. (134)

OLINGER, George of Madison twp. - dated 2-13-1810; recorded 4-16-1810. Wife, Susanna. Children:- Samuel, Isaac, Barbara, Mary and George Olinger. Executors:- Wife, Susanna; Thomas Nesbet and John Hendricks. Signed:- George Olinger. Witnesses:- James Ware and Jacob Henricks. (137)

BAIRD, Hugh of Madison twp. - dated 3-13-1810; recorded 4-16-1810. Wife, Sarah. Children:- Joseph, Samuel, Mary, James and Jane. Executors:- Wife, Sarah and sons, Joseph and John. Signed:- Hugh Baird. Witnesses:- James Baird, Thomas Nisbet and John Baird. (140)

RANDOLF, John of Newton twp. - dated 7-15-1811; recorded 12-16-1811. Wife, Jane. Sons:- James and David, not of age. Daughters:- Mary, Neomy, Jane and Mariah. Executor:- Wife, Jane. Signed:- John Randolf. Witnesses:- Jeremiah Spurgin, Walter Williams and Eleanor (mark) Calhoun. (197)

BAIRD, John of Madison twp. - dated 3-8-1812; recorded 8-12-1812. Wife, Mary Beard. Sons:- Alexander, Samuel and John. Daughters:- Martha Baird, Jane Beard and Agnes Baird. Executors:- Brother-in-law, Thomas Nisbet and friend, Joseph Boyle. Signed:- John Baird. Witnesses:- Joseph Baird, James Barr and Thomas Nesbet. Codicil dated 3-11-1812, mentions Reformed Church at Jonathan Creek which is to have one acre of land for a meeting house and grave yard. Witnesses:- James Baird, Thomas Nesbit and Joseph Boyle.   (211)

DERWATER, John - dated 7-19-1812; recorded 12-14-1812. Wife, Naomia. Sons, John and Jacob. Daughters:- Eve wife of Frederick Wyant, Fanny wife of John Starner, Elizabeth wife of John Blacher, Catharine wife of John Lermore, Barbara wife of Jacob Lermore and Anna wife of Jacob Scofield. Mentions Margaret Earlart and John Blecker, daughter and son of testator's daughter Fanny Starner. Executors:- Richard Brockover and Wyllis Silliman. Signed:- John (mark) Derwater. Witnesses:- Jacob Brockover, Thomas Morehead, Rich'd Brockover and W. Silliman. Codicil dated 10-2-1812, gives no additional information. Witnesses:- Rich'd Brookover, Alex'd D. Tucker and Mary Brockover.   (218)

HAMILTON, William of Hopewell twp. - dated 2-11-1813; recorded 6-8-1814. Wife, Susanna. Sons:- Benjamin of Monongalia Co., Va.; William and Samuel. Daughters:- Cassandrea Harrison of Monongalia Co., Va.; Rachel Smith, dec'd; Elizabeth wife of Robert Manley; Rebecca Dent; and Susanna Heath. Grandchildren:- Children of daughter, Rachel Smith, dec'd—Stephen, William, John, Darias, Cassandra and Susanna Smith. Mentions money to be collected from John C. Jackson of Virginia; also mentionsland in Licking Co., Ohio; black girl, Mary Chadwick who is to remain with family. Executors:- Sons, Benjamin, William and Samuel; with son Benj. to attend to business in Virginia. Signed:- William Hamilton. Witnesses:- Thomas Nesbit, George Dils and Eve B. Morgan.   (222)

CLAYTON, Thomas - dated 6-14-1811; recorded Apr. 1813. Wife, Mary. Children:- Samuel, Martha wife of Isaac Milleson, John, Joseph, William, Mary, Betsy and Rachael. Executors:- Sons, John, Joseph and William. Signed:- Thomas Clayton. Witnesses:- James Nanpur(?) and Wyllis Silliman.   (224)

BUCKINGHAM, Stephen - verbal will - recorded 10-19-1813. Brother, Ebenezer to serve as executor and to care for wife and children (not named). Witnesses:- Esther McColly and Ann Hunt.   (227)

LANE, Richard - dated 9-10-1813; recorded 12-20-1813. Wife, Catharine. Sons:- Samuel, Richard and Dutton. Daughters:- Jamiana, Elizabeth, Charity, Nancy and Catharine. Executors:- Samuel Baxter and Henry Butler. Signed:- Richard Lane. Witnesses:- Samuel Giel, Wm. Baxter and Abrm. Lane.   (229)

KIRKER, James of Pennsylvania - dated 10-16-1013; recorded 10-19-1813.
Wife, Martha. Son, William C. Brother, Thomas; also to serve as guardian
of son, William C. Sister, Mary Kean. Mentions:- Nephew, Joseph Kean and
niece, Margaret Kean orphan children of Jacob Kean, dec'd; also mentions
nephew, James McCaig. Signed:- James Kirker. Witnesses:- All. Laughlin
and S. W. Culbertson. Codicil dated 10-16-1813, mentions mother, but does
not name.   (227)

STEENSON, James of Madison twp. - dated 7-24-1813; recorded 12-22-1813.
Wife, Jane. Children:- Mary, William, John, Sarah and Peggy Ann Steenson.
Executors:- Wife, Jane and brother-in-law, Robert Ardry. Signed:- James
Steenson. Witnesses:- Thomas Nesbit and Wm. Mitchell.   (231)

WELLS, William of Springfield - dated 1-24-1814; recorded 2-11-1814.
Daughter, Betsy Reed. Brother, Elisha Wells. Nephews and Niece:- Arman,
Laura and William Wells to have 1000 acres of land on which brother Elisha
Wells lives. Nephew, Joseph Wells. Niece, Jane Kean. Bequeaths to:-
Eliza Whipple daughter of Levi Whipple; Heirs of Doctor Abner Mosley;
Levi Whipple who is also to serve as executor. Signed:- William Wells.
Witnesses:- Benj. Tupper, Robert Moore and Arius Nye. Codicil dated
1-25-1814, mentions Doctor Richard Allison; same witnesses.   (235)

TUPPER, Benjamin of Springfield - dated 2-1-1814; recorded 2-11-1814.
Wife, Polly. Mentions children but does not name except for son, Edward
W. Tupper. Mentions stock in trade with E. Buckingham Jr. Executors:-
Wife, Patty; brother, Edward W. Tupper; Edwin Putnam Esq. and Ebenezer
Buckingham Jr. Signed:- Benj. Tupper. Witnesses:- Ebenezer Buckingham,
Increase Matthews and Levi Whipple.   (238)

E S T A T E S

STULL, Martin - dated 1-1-1807. Adms.:- Hannah Stull, widow. Sureties:-
Martin Stull, Joseph Derrah and James Beeham.   (13)

CARHART, Seth - dated 4-23-1806. Adms., Joseph Scott and Margaret Carhart.
Sureties:- Valentine Johnston and Abel Lewis.   (15)

BAINTER, Godfrey - Sale bill. (not dated 1804-1807?).   (22)

WHEELAND, Peter - dated 11-19-1804. Adms., Godfrey Haga and Barbara
Wheeland. Sureties:- James Clark and Conrad Bremer.   (26)

OLIVE, David - dated 11-19-1804. Adms., Levi Whipple and Cessley Olive.
Sureties:- Increase Mathews and John Chandler.   (33)

TASWELL, Newcum - dated 4-29-1806. Adms, Daniel Converse. Sureties:-
Richard McBride and Joseph Williams.   (45)

ROUNSIFER, Quick of Tusharawa twp. - dated Dec. 1806. Adms., Benjamin Brison. James Milford and Christianna, his wife, who appear to be nearest of kin to deceased relinquish their right to administer the estate. Sureties, Henry Sills and Isaac Evans.   (38)

SINCLAIRE (ST. CLAIR), Robert of Springfield - dated Apr. 1807. Adms., Increase Mathews. Sureties, Wylys Selliman and Henry Crook.   (48)

FINLEY, James - dated Apr. 1807. Adms., Ely Sherman. Sureties, Zachariah Chancler and Samuel Beech.   (55)

ROLLENS, John - dated 6-4-1807. Adms., Joseph F. Mumo and Daniel Converse. Sureties, Robert Speer and Christian Spangler.   (59)

URY, David - dated 9-8-1807. Adms., Robert Bay. Sureties, Isaac Van Horn and Isaac Zane.   (64)

MORSE, Joseph - dated 12-3-1807. Adms., Edmond Morse and Charles Williams. Sureties, William Whitten and Daniel Converse. Account dated Aug. 1811 lists $5.00 for boarding Edmond Morse brother of deceased; Also expenses for trips to Armandage Co., New York and Lebanon, Ohio to collect money due from estate of Cashpaia (?) Wyllys Selliman.   (69)

CARPENTER, John - dated 9-30-1806. Adms., George Carpenter. Sureties, Jesse Fulton and William Morrison.   (75)

HART, Elijah - dated Apr. 1807. Adms., Robert Speer. Sureties, Joseph F. Mumo and Robert Taylor. Large Bible is listed among personal property.(80)

LIVENGOOD, Jacob - dated Apr. 1808. Adms., John Walters and Catherine Livengood. Sureties, John Bowers and Robert McConnell. Among persons purchasing items at public sale were Catherine Livengood and daughter, Mary, Jacob Livengood and Peter Livengood.   (86)

BUZZAWAY (BUZAWAY), Isaac of Marietta - dated 8-17-1802; recorded 1808. Inventory of estate. Mentions widow (not named). Heirs:- Michael Remel and wife Catharine; Abraham Romich and wife Hannah, Hannah not of age; Elizabeth, a minor; Mary, a minor and Michael, a minor 19 years of age. (93)

STIVERS, Ralph - dated 12-20-1808. Adms., Joseph Stivers. Sureties, James Fair and Joseph Williams. Mentions widow but does not name.   (105)

MONTGOMERY, William - dated 12-19-1809. Adms., Elizabeth Montgomery. Sureties, William Talbert and Stephen Rud (or Reed?).   (116)

CASSETTE, Dennis - dated 4-8-1808. Adms., Charles Hammond. Sureties, John McIntire and George Beymer.   (125)

297

LEBART, John - dated 4-29-1807. Adms. Adam Dash and Eleanor Dahr.
Sureties, Martin Lawden Slago and Benjamin Richards.   (129)

DEAVER, John T. - dated 8-27-1810. Adms., Ebenezer Granger. Sureties,
Increase Mathews and Levi Whipple. Mentions partnership of Deaver and
Relfe.   (143)

PAINTER, Major George of Zanesville - dated 4-25-1809. Adms., Isaac Van
Horne Sr. Security, William Wells. Among purchasers of items at public
sale was Mary Painter.   (164)

RICHARDSON, John - dated 8-20-1810. Adms., John K. McCune and Elizabeth
Richardson. Sureties, David Findley and John Raynolds.   (183)

MANLEY, Robert - dated Dec. 1811. Adms.:- Elizabeth Manley, widow.
Sureties, William Hamilton and John E. Dent.   (194)

BLYTHE, Benj. - dated Apr. 1811. Adms., Samuel Culbertson. Sureties,
Wyllis Selliman and Alexander Culbertson.   (203)

GARDNER, Edward T. - dated May 1812. Adms., James Perry. Sureties, Robt.
Mitchell and Robert Fulton. (206)

SHAW, William of Jefferson township - dated 1-16-1811. Inventory of
estate. (208)

DONNER, Solomon - dated Apr. 1812. Adms., Jeffrey Price. Sureties,
Richard Brookover and James Reever.   (209)

DOUGHTY, Richard - dated Aug. 1812. Adms., John Adams and Joseph Robins.
Sureties, Christian Spangler and Thos. Moreheart.   (215)

PIERCE, Benoni - dated 2-12-1812. Adms., Elizabeth Pierce and Wyllis
Selliman.   (220)

SINCLAIR, Thos. - dated 4-1-1813. Adms., James Senclair and Robert
Mitchell. Sureties:- Wm. Craig, John McKenney, Dan'l Converse and Andrew
Miller.   (220)

McKEE, Thomas - dated Apr. 1813. Adms., Jos. McKee.   (221)

COOKERY, Josiah - dated Aug. 1813. Adms., Sam'l Thompson.   (225)

LANE, Richard - dated 10-19-1813. Adms. Frederick Guier and Polly Lane.
(225)

SLOAN, Benj. - dated 10-19-1813. Adms. Isaac Van Horn and Agnis Sloan.
(226)

WILLIAMS, Walter - dated 10-19-1813. Adms., John Bromage and Joseph Wiley.
(226)

BROWN, John - dated 11-15-1813. Adms., Wm. Brown and Nancy Brown. (229)

PATTERSON, Robert - dated 12-23-1813. Adms., Charles Roberts and Elizabeth Patterson. (233)

CHANDLER, Jesse - dated 2-11-1814. Adms., Abel Perrin and Henrietta Chandler. (234)

JONES, John - dated 2-11-1814. Adms., Nathan Fleming and Sarah Jones. (237)

G U A R D I A N S H I P S

OLIVE, James - minor son of David Olive. Dated 8-15-1808. Abel Lewis guardian. (102)

MINGUS, Charles - dated 8-18-1808. Daniel Stilwell, guardian. (104)

HART, Andrew, John, Martin, Peggy, Hartel, Mary and Jane - minor children of Elijah Hart, dec'd. Dated Dec. 1809. Robert McConnel and Daniel Stilwell, guardians. (121)

PRIOR, Joseph, Mary and Barbara - minor children of Timothy Prior, dec'd. Dated Dec. 1809. Isaac Prior and Barbara Prior, guardians. (123)

SMOTE, John B. - a minor aged 15 yrs. Dated Dec. 1811. Mary Smote, guardian. (201)

OLLIVE, Joseph - a minor. Dated Dec. 1811. William Scofield, guardian. (202)

BARTLETT, Charles - a minor aged 14 yrs. Dated Apr. 1812. William Burnham, guardian. (204)

ASHBROOK, Elias and Thomas - minors. Dated Apr. 1812. Jonathan Carrell, guardian. (204)

HILLEAR, Benjamin Franklin - aged 15 yrs. Dated 8-1-1812. Ann Hilliar, widow appointed guardian of her son. (207)

BREWSTER, Gunston - unable to handle own affairs. Dated Apr. 1813. John Raynolds, guardian. (221)

JUNIPHER, George - a minor. Dated 5-4-1813. Dollie McDonald, guardian. (224)

McCONNELL, Jane - dated Apr. 1813. Robert McConnell, guardian. (225)

REED, James - a minor aged 14 yrs. Dated Aug. 1813. Levi Whipple, guardian. (225)

CARHART, Nancy, John and Teracy – minor children of Seth Carhart, dec'd. Dated 7-13-1814. James Scott, guardian. (230).

LANE, Catharine – dated 12-22-1813. Dotton Lane, guardian. (231)

SLOAN, Ann – a minor aged 14 yrs. Dated 12-25-1813. James Culbertson, guardian. Alex and Sam. Culbertson, security. (234)

NOBLE COUNTY, OHIO – DEATH RECORDS 1867-1869

The following death records are for persons <u>40 years of age and over only</u>.
They have been taken from Death Record Book #1. Place of residence is the same as
place of death unless stated otherwise. Page on which record may be found is given
in parenthesis. ABBREVIATIONS: d–died; a–age; pd–place of death; pb–place of birth;
res–residence; oc–occupation.

KIRK, William – d 8-1-1867; a 67-1-26; pd Sarahsville; pb Pennsylvania; married;
    oc blacksmith; parents, John and Jane Kirk (2)

STEVENS, Vernon – d 7-27-1867; a 53-3-26; pd Noble Co.; pb Washington Co. Ohio;
    married; oc farmer (2)

CASSELL, James F. – d 12-1-1867; a 56y; pd Olive twp.; pb Belmont Co. Ohio; married;
    oc Physician; Father, Nathaniel Cassell   (4)

FRANKLIN, Alexander – d 10-29-1867; a 70-6-7; pd Marion twp.; pb Ireland; married;
    oc farmer   (4)

JORDAN, Jacob – d 10-25-1867; a 67-7-5; a 67-7-5; pd Jackson twp.; pb Green Co
    Penna; widower; oc farmer   (4)

KULENTZ, John – d 12-9-1867; a 67y; pd Sharon twp.; pb Sharon twp.; oc farme.,
    father, John Kulentz   (4)

MERRILL, Elizabeth d 11-9-1867; a 97y; pd County Infirmary; widow   (4)

SIX, Nancy – d 11-30-1867; a 70y; pd Adams twp; pb Green Co Penna.; widow; father,
    James Goodin

ARMSTRONG, James – d 2-20-2868; a 62y; pd Enoch twp.; pb Virginia; oc farmer (6)

ANDERSON, James – d 2-27-1868; a 40y; pd Beaver twp.; married; oc farmer (6)

CASSELL, Sarah – d 3-18-1868; a 47y; pd Olive twp.; pb Noble twp.; widow   (6)

CONNER, Eliza J. – d 3-5-1868; a 40y; pd Olive twp.; married   (6)

CAFFEE, John – d 1-17-1868; a 85-7-17; pd Jackson twp.; married; oc farmer (6)

DEVALLD, Clark – d 3-17-1868; a 40y; pd Center twp; married; oc farmer (6)

FINLEY, John – d 3-20-1868; a 80y 5d; pd Center twp; married; oc farmer (6)

GARRETTSON, J. – d 4-10-1868; a 65y pd Elk twp.; married; oc farmer; res Iowa (6)

MANTEL, Jacob – d 3-14-1868; a 65y; pd Jefferson twp; pb German; married; oc shoe-
    maker   (6)

NORRIS, William – d 2-27-1868; a 88y 27d; pd Infirmery; pb Louden Co va; single (6)

PETTERY, Francis – d 3-20-1868; a 77y 2m; pd Center twp.; pb Canada; married; oc
    farmer (6)

PITZER, Jacob – d 1-24-1868; a 60y; pd Elk twp.; pb German; married; oc farmer;
    parents, Johann Pitzer and Catharina Danner   (6)

WILSON, William – d 1-16-1868; a 74-9-27; pd Sharon twp.; pb Louden Co Va;
    married; oc farmer (8)

YOUNG, Robert – d 3-3-1868; a 43y 9m; pd Center twp.; pb Stark(?) twp.; married;
    oc farmer (8)

BARNES, Lucinda – d 4-28-1868; a 44y; pd Olive twp.; pb Belmont Co Ohio; single;
    parents, Peter and Margaret Barnes. (10)

BARLOW, James – d 6-8-1868; a 58y; pd Monroe Co Ohio; pb Maryland; single; res Monroe
    Co Ohio; oc farmer; parents, Z. and Susan Barlow (10)

DELONG, John – d 5-29-1868; a 81-6-13; pd Sharon twp.; pb Maryland; married; oc
    farmer (10)

DANFORD, James – d 5-28-1868; a 70-5-5; married.; pd Sharon twp; pb Virginia (10)

ELDER, Stewart – d 5-20-1868; a 50y; pd Brookfield twp; pb Pennsylvania; married;
    oc farmer (10)

McADAMS, John – d 6-15-1868; a 74y; pd Ohio twp.; pb Pennsylvania; married;
    oc farmer   (10)

REIS, Elizabeth Anna - d 6-5-1868; a 58-2-5; pd Elk twp; pb German; married (10)
RAYNER, Nancy S. - d 9-7-1868; a 70y 5m; pd Ohio twp; pb Pennsylvania (10)
STILGENBAUER, Andreas - d 4-9-1868; a 75y; pd Elk twp.; pb German; married oc farmer
                                                                    (10)
ARCHER, Simon - d 8-1-1868; a 75-1-1; pd Stock twp; pb Virginia; married; oc farmer
                                                                    (12)
ARCHIBALD, Margaret - d 11-27-1868; a 66-3-12; pd Sharon twp; pb Pennsylvania;
                married (12)
LINDSEY, Mary Ann · d 7-12-1868; a 67y; pd Williamsburg; pb England; widow (12)
LAWHEAD, Mary - d 12-2-1868; a 52y; pd Beaver twp; single
MORRISON, Peggy - d 10-13-1868; a 79y; pd Noble Co; pb Maryland (12)
ROSS, Jane - d Sept 1868; a 72y; pd Sharon twp; pb Pennsylvania (12)
CALDWELL, Samuel - d 2-27-1869; a 69y; pd Caldwell; pb Pennsylvania; married; oc
                farmer; res Olive tsp. (14)
GOODWELL, John - d 1-1-1869; a 60y; pd Noble Co.; pb Vermont; married; oc farmer (14)
RAINY, Edward - d 2-25-1869; a 52y; pd Sharon twp.; pb Jackson twp.; single; oc
                mail carrier (14)
WILY, Thomas - d 2-17-1869; a 59y; pd Olive twp; pb Washington Co Ohio; married;
                oc farmer (14)
YOUNTZ, Mary - d 3-24-1869; a 54y; pd Ohio; married (14)
HARTMAN, Margaret - d 7-14-1869; a 80-3-3; pd Enoch twp.; pb Bavaria; widow (16)
JAMES, Luke - d 4-11-1869; a 77y; pd Jefferson twp; married; oc farmer (16)
WILD, George - d 5-30-1869; a 40-2-9; pd Stock twp; pb Bavaria; married; oc
                stone mason (16)
DUMING, James - d 9-29-1869; a 61y; pd Noble Co; pb Allegheny Co. Pa; married;
                oc farmer (18)
PARRISH, William - d 12-5-1869; a 62y; pd Noble Co; married; oc Notary Public (18)
WALTERS, John - d 11-18-1869; a 43y; pd Noble Co; pb Noble Co; married; oc farmer(18
WALTERS, George - d Aug 1869; a 79y; pd Noble Co; pb Noble Co; widower; oc farmer(18
STAATS, Anna - d 9-20-1869; a 70y; pd Noble Co; married (18)
ROUSE, Mary - d 10-8-1869;. a 67y; pd Center twp; married (20)
STEWART, John - d 11-6-1869; a 94y; pd Center twp.; pb Ireland; widower; oc farmer(20
OGIE, Lucinda - d 12-31-1869; a 56y; pd Plive twp; pb Noble Co; married (20)
STITT, John - d 9-23-1869; a 56y; pd Olive twp; pb Washington Co; married; oc farmer
                                                                    (20)
COOPPER, Eli B. - d 11-2-1869; a 57y; pd Olive twp.; pb Maryland; married (20)
TILTON, Benjamin - d 7-20-1869; a 73y; pd Olive twp.; pb Mass.; married (20)
CRUM, Agnes - d 3-22-1869; a 60y; pd Elk twp.; pb Monroe Center; married (22)
CRUM, David - d 6-16-1869; a 69y; pd Elk twp; pb Noble Co.; married; oc farmer (22)
PITZER, Margaret - d 3-3-1869; a 64y; pd Elk Twp.; pb Noble Co.; married (22)
HELM, Margaret - d 5-5-1869; a 81y; pd Elk twp.; pb Germany (22)
PARMER, Mary - d 5-25-1869; a 77y; pd Noble Co; pb Pennsylvania; widow (22)
hUPP, Margaret - d 8-16-1869; a 40y; married (22)
McVEY, Renson(?) - d 7-10-1869; a 76y; pd Noble Co.; pb Green Co. Penna; married;
                oc farmer (26)
DEPEN(?), Margaret - d 12-12-1869; a 93y; pd Noble Co.; pb New York; widow (26)

The following wills are found in Will Book 1. Date given is date will was recorded.
If date of recording was not given, the date is the date will was made and is designated as such by a "d" following date.

Name	Date	Page			
ANDERSON, Duncan	1861	176	HARRAH, James	1861	190
ATKINSON, Isaac	1853	30	HOSKIN, Wait	1857	100
BAILEY, Jesse	1855	91	HUTCHINS, Roxalina	1858	104
BALL, Moses	1855	56	IAMS, Isaac	1852	2
BLAKE, Benjamin	1855d	73	JACKSON, Thomas	1859	159
BOND, Peter of	1855	68	JAMES, Thomas	1855	78
Muskingum Co., Ohio			JOHNSON, David	1853	40
BOON, John	1854	48	JORDEN, Adam	1861	191
BRINTON, William	1857	72	KARNES, Peter	1853	10
BROWER, Lewis	1857	126	KECKLEY (KACKLEY),		
BROWN, John	1858	122	Samuel Sr.	1861	197
BROWNING, John	1856	71	KEITH, Benjamin	1859	145
BURSON, Phebe	1859	128	KENNADY, Irwin	1852	8
CALDWELL, John	1855	64	KERRIGAN, Henry	1852	17
CARNEG, Willes	1858	115	LEMIX (LUMAX), James Sr.	1859	153
CLARK, Andrew W.	1852	13	LOWREY, William	1861	186
CLEVENGER, Charlotte	1855	60	McCAIN, Jacob	1859	151
COLLINS, Findlay	1854	51	McDONALD, Ronald	1857	101
COPE, Thomas	1858	124	McGARRY, John Sr.	1858	167
CRAIG, William	1856	65	McGEE, Andrew	1859	163
DAILEY, Eliza	1859	143	McWILLIAMS, Philip	1857	108
DOOLEY, John	1856	87	MARKS, Mason	1858	136
DOWNEY, Ephraim	1855	63	MARTIN, John	1858	160
DYSON, John B.	1852	7	MASTERS, Catharine	1859	121
EBBERT, Peter	1856	75	MAYHEW, Frederick	1854	54
ESSEX, Nathan Sr.	1853	36	MILHORN, John	1857	92
FARLEY, James	1855	61	MILLER, Frederick	1858	102
FEAMS, Letitia	1858	134	MORRIS, Henry Sr.	1855	79
alias KILROY, alias WEAKFIELD			MORRIS, James	1857	113
(signed Weakfield) of Monroe			MULLEN, Ann	1854	55
Co., Ohio.)			OGLE, Alfred	1858	98
FINLEY, James	1861	195	OLIVER, Daniel	1853	39
FITZGERALD, Reuben	1854	49	PALMER, Daniel	1859	156
FLOOD, Anna	1858	130	PRIOR, Isaac	1860	165
FLOOD, John	1856	76	PROUTZ, Russel	1855	80
FORMISH, William	1852	18	RACEY, Lander	1855	83
GALASPIE, George	1861	175	RANNELLS, William	1855	58
GALLAGHER, Edmund	1860	171	REED, John	1853	32
GALLATIN, Jerusha	1859	158	REAVES, Joseph	1856	81
GANT, Joel	1856	77	REEVES, Joseph	1856	96
GOULD, James	1852	11	(rec. twice)		
GREGG, Uriah	1861	188	RHODES, Sanford	1860	173
GREEN, Susan	1858	112	RICHEY, Thomas of	1860	169
HAFT, Isabella	1857	84	Guernsey Co., Ohio		
HAGA, Jacob	1857	105	ROSS, John B.	1861	178

Name	Date	Page	Name	Date	Page
ROUND, James M. Sr.	1858	107	THORLEE, Richard	1859	138
SCHAFFER, Valentine	1856	85	TILTON, Helron	1859	147
SCHOFIELD, Joseph	1857	109	VORHIS, Aaron Sr.	1861	182
SCOTT, Francis	1852	4	WAKEFIELD, Letitia	1856	90
SHAMHART, Henry	1858	119	(see Letitia Feams)		
SHANNON, Jane	1852	1	WALLACE, Charity	1854	53
SHARROCK, Tenty of	1854	43	WALLER, Lewis	1856	89
Morrow Co., Ohio			WARD, Sutton	1859	149
SIMON, Aaron	1854	47	WHEALDON, Nathan	1858	117
SMITH, Joseph James	1859	140	WICKHAM, Benjamin	1852	15
SMITH, William Sr.	1855	125	WILSON, William	1855	70
SMOOT, John	1852	19	WINSTANLEY, Peter	1861	192
SNODE, William	1861	180	WOOD, Henry	1859	155
STRANATHAN, Thomas	1855	86	WORK, Samuel	1853	34
STRONG, Albert Sr.	1854	45	WYBRANT, Hugh	1853	37
TAYLOR, Edward Heuit	1853	42	YARNALL, Benjamin	1852	20
TAYLOR, John	1852	24	YOHO, Jacob	1852	26
TAYLOR, Peter	1855	22	YOUNG, Holesworth	1852	8
THORLA, Benjamin	1861	184			

NOBLE COUNTY, OHIO - COMMON PLEAS COURT RECORDS 1854-1859

The following records were copied from Petition Books located in the Clerk of Court's Office at the court house at Caldwell. Civil suits for debt were not copied, but all records of genealogical importance were copied. The book in which the record may be found is given in the underlined heading. Page on which record may be found is given in parenthesis at the end of each individual record.

Petition Record 1

4-10-1854 - John BAIRD vs. Henry MUSSER, George SALLADAY, adms., et al. Petition. Filed 12-14-1854 (1853?). Joseph Salladay, dec'd, died in August 1852, with administrator appointed 8-23-1852. Salladay in his lifetime on 4-3-1850 contracted to sell Baird land where he lived located in Salladay's tract of 100 acres and 44 sw. perches SW cor. NWP Section 2, Township 7, Range 9. Widow, Sarah Salladay. Children: Eliza Ann intermarried with William Stewart, who has since deceased and Thomas Salladay, a minor. (36)

9-28-1854 - Mary E. BEVAN vs. John M. HUFFMAN. Bastardy. Filed 5-30-1854. Mary Ellen Bevan an unmarrird woman and resident of Marion twp., now expectant with child. Huffman found responssble. (180)

6-7-1855 - Elizabeth McVICKER's adms. vs. Alexander McVICKERS. Filed 2-17-1855. On 10-1-1853 Alexander McVickers had in his possession $50.00 previously given to him by Elizabeth McVickers, dec'd, whoch money was to be paid for lands for children of Isaac Pascoll they being grandchildren of Elizabeth McVickers, dec'd. (270)

4-8-1856 - Thomas BAILES vs. Mary WICKUM, et al. Filed 12-17-1855. Thomas Bailes father of Thomas Bailes on 5-10-1837 was seized of S½ SW¼ Section 32, Township 7, Range 8 being land sold in Zanesville land district, said land formerly lying in Monroe Co. now in Noble Co. consisting of 82.40 acres. Said father, Thomas Bailes with wife Susannah did sell said land to son, Thomas Bailes and made deed, but a mistake was made in the description of land. Said petition is now filed to correct mistake. Thomas Bailes (Sr.) died in 1843. Children: petitioner, son, Thomas Bailes; Mary late Balis of Iowa widow of Bernard R. Wickhum, who is now dead; Sarah late Balis wife of Henry Rauser of Kansas Territory; Susanna late Balis of Iowa widow of George Hursey, who is now dead; Desire late Balis wife of John Browning, residence unknown; Margaret late Balis wife of Charles Hoggins (or Haggins); Elmyra late Balis wife of Morgan Wickman; Lucinda late Balis, now dec'd, in her lifetime wife of Cyrus Metheney, her children--Andrew, Thomas, Rachel and Cyrus Metheney, Nancy Ann late Metheney wife of Frederick Lemum and Samantha late Metheney wife of William Alltop. (379)

10-8-1856 - Jeremiah RICH vs Rolly (or Polly) RICH, et al. Filed 12-5-1855. George Rich late of Guernsey County, Ohio, dec'd, died seized of 336 acres N½ Section 35, Township 8, Range 9 formerly in Guernsey County now in Noble County. Widow, Jane Rich, now dec'd. Children and heirs: Rolly (or Polly) Rich; Jane Rich; and Ann late Rich, now dec'd, late wife of Wm W. Rhodes, her children-- Elizabeth Jane late Rhodes wife of Madison Secrist, George Rhodes, Lydia Ann late Rhodes wife of Levi Lyons, John Rhodes, Henry Rhodes, Mary Rhodes, Jeremiah Rhodes and Mariah Rhodes, the last four named being minors. (432)

10-9-1856 - Margaret ANDERSON vs. Joshua SHOTTO. Bastardy. Filed 6-14-1856.
Margaret an unmarried woman of Center twp. became pregnant Oct. 1855. Shotto
acknowledges he is father of child. (479)

10-9-1856 - Melissa FOGLE vs. Clark DEVOLLD. Bastardy. Filed 9-19-1856.
Melissa Ann Fogle an unmarried woman of Enoch twp. has resided in Noble County
for 18 years. Child born 5-7-1856. Cornelius Wells appointed guardian of
child for purpose of this suit. Defendant is married. Defendant found guilty.(499)

10-9-1856 - Ann MASTERS vs. John RAY. Bastardy. Filed 4-1-1856. Ann an
unmarried woman of Noble County. Defendant acknowledges being father of child.(516)

Petition Record 2

10-6-1857 - Alfred LIPPITT vs. J. K. KNOWLTON, et al. In Partition. Filed
4-27-1857. Land, 40 acres SW¼ SW¼ and 40 acres SE¼ SW¼ Section 13, Township
8, Range 10. Malinda Lippitt, dec'd, died 1857. Children and grandchildren:
1/7th part, son, Alfred Lippitt of Noble Co.; 1/7th part, daughter, Sarah wife
of J. K. Knowlton of Guernsey Co., Ohio; 1/7th part, son, Benjamin Lippitt, dec'd,
his son--Otis Lippitt, a minor of Noble Co.; 1/7th part, daughter, Mariah wife
of John S. Conner of Noble Co.; 1/7th part, son, Christopher Lippitt of Noble
Co.; 1/7th part, son, Elihu Lippitt of Noble Co.; 1/7th part, son, Joseph W.
Lippitt of Noble Co. (50)

6-12-1858 - Ruth Ellen ARCHER vs. Solomon ARCHER. Petition for Divorce. Filed
4-12-1858. Married 1-11-1855 in Noble County. Defendant's place of residence
is not known. Plaintiff asks restoration of her former name of Ruth Ellen
Berry. (120)

9-8-1858 - John BARCLAY Sr. vs. Margaret BARCLAY. Petition for Divorce. Filed
6-17-1857. John married in April 1843 in Olive township, Morgan County, Ohio
(now Noble County) to Margaret Mitchell. Issue of the marriage was John Barclay
aged 13 years on 3-3-1857. Plaintiff states Margaret has been gone from his
home more than three years. Margaret filed cross petition in which she states
that they were separated and that she did not desert. (153)

12-9-1857 - Philip JARVIS vs William JARVIS, et al. Petition for Partition.
Filed 8-8-1856. John Jarvis, late of Noble Co., dec'd in his lifetime by deed
conveyed land to his minor children issue of his late marriage with Mary Jarvis
who is his present widow, said children being--James W. Jarvis, Joseph A. Jarvis
and Miriam Jarvis. Land deeded was 77 acres W½ SE¼ and 60 acres S end E½ SW¼
Section 21, Township 8, Range 7. That James W. and Joseph A. Jarvis died in
about April of 1856 leaving no heirs and that their 2/3rds interest is to be
inherited by all the children and grandchildren of John Jarvis, dec'd. Children
and grandchildren of John Jarvis, dec'd: 1/9th part, son, Philip Jarvis; 1/9th
part, daughter, Sarah wife of Brice Lucas of Guernsey Co., Ohio; 1/9th part
jointly or 1/63rd part each, son, Bazel Jarvis, dec'd, his children--Maranda
wife of____(left blank) Hutton, Mary Jarvis of Guernsey Co., Ohio, John L.
Jarvis, residence unknown, Rebecca wife of ____(left blank) Smith, Ruth A. Jarvis,
Nancy Jarvis, a minor all of Guernsey Co., Ohio and Nancy wife of Daniel Speers
of Owen Co., Indiana; 1/9th part jointly or 1/27th part each, son Heed Jarvis,

(Philip Jarvis vs. William Jarvis, et al. cont.)
dec'd, his children--Wm V. Nancy, and Ezekiel Jarvis, all minors of Noble Co.;
1/9th part, son, Andrew Jarvis of Vinton Co., Ohio; 1/9th part, son, William
Jarvis of Noble Co.; 1/9th part, daughter, Ruth A. wife of Hamilton Carter of
Belmont Co., Ohio; 1/9th part, daughter, Miriam Jarvis, a minor of Noble Co.
Widow, Mary Jarvis entitled to dower. (171)

4-11-1857 - Catharine SANDS vs. James B. SANDS. Petition for Divorce. Filed
1-10-1857. Catharine married James on 9-1-1834 in Caledonia, Livingston Co.,
New yor. James is now a resident of Canandaigna, Ontario Co., N.Y. Separated
6-15-1854. (184)

6-24-1857 - Samuel HARTLINE vs. Elizabeth EARLEY. Petition for Divorce. Filed
4-8-1857. Samuel married 10-31-1820 in Monroe Co., Ohio to Elizabeth Runion.
That Samuel left home and was gone for four years and when he returned he found
Elizabeth living with Joseph Wiggins with which she continued to live and have
seven children by him. That Joseph Wiggins died on 30 November 1848 and that
Elizabeth then began living with Benoni Earley of Monroe County and were married
in Monroe County by Rev. A. G. Ewing. (186)

4-11-1857 - Susan KENT vs. James KENT, et al. Petition for Dower. Filed
4-22-1856. That Susan married in 1849 to William Kent and that he died in
January 1856 in Noble County seized of W½ NW¼ and SE¼ NW¼ Section 23, Township
7, Range 7 in Monroe Co. and E½, also 2 acres off E side SW¼ both in Section 29,
Township 7, Range 7 and 1.33 acres NE cor. E½ NE¼ Section 28, Township 7, Range
7 all in Noble Co. and that Susan Kent is entitled to dower in said land. Heirs
by next right to estate inheritance are: James Kent; John Kent; William Kent;
Rebecca Kent; Mary Ann Kent; Josiah Kent; Sarah wife of James Reed; Maria wife
of George W. Brown; and Elizabeth Rucker, dec'd, her children--George, Robert
and Sarah Ann Rucker. (188)

4-11-1857 - Joseph BURSON vs. Sarah STARR, et al. Petition for Partition.
Filed 2-13-1856. That Joseph Burson by purchase is entitled to undivided
7/12th parts of 74 acres NE¼ Section 33, Township 8, Range 7. Samuel Starr,
dec'd. Widow, Mary Starr, entitled to dower. Partition: 1/12th part jointly
or each (note: not specified, but probably 1/12th each): Sarah, Samuel, Hannah,
William and Elizabeth Starr, all minors and all of Noble Co. (215)

5-11-1858 - Emily Jane POOL vs. Robert W. POOL. Petition for Divorce. Filed
1-19-1857. Married 7-17-1853 in Noble Co. (245)

9-9-1858 - John C. Wernecke vs. Lizitta BENNINGHOUS, et al. Petition for
Partition. Filed 7-27-1858. Land, Lots 11,12 & 13 in Harrietsville, also
W½ NW¼ and E½ NW¼ Section 26, Township 5, Range 7 except town plat of Harriets-
ville and 7 acres where mill stands, in which petitioner John C. Wernecke owns
one half, with other half being owned at his decease by Theodore F. Bennington.
Widow, Mary. Children: Lizetta, Arthur and Anne Bennington all of Monroe Co.,
Ohio. (257

-25-1859 - Rachel HOOVER vs. Isaac L. HOOVER. Petition for Divorce. Filed
-6-1858. Married 6-4-1854 in Noble Co., Ohio. Isaac L. Hoover now of the
tate of Illinois. (261)

3-25-1859 - George KACKLEY vs. Mary KACKLEY. Petition for Divorce. Filed 10-25-1858. George married 8-18-1853 in Buffalow twp., Noble County to Mary Secrist. That Mary has been absent for three years. (295)

3-25-1859 - John WATSON vs. Mary WATSON. Petition for Divorce. Filed 12-20-1858. John married 8-12-1855 in Noble County to Mary Runnels. Mary has been absent for about 3 years and now lives in Clinton Co., Illinois. (298)

3-26-1859 - Casaline THOMAS vs. Isaac ARCHER, minor son of James ARCHER, Jr. Bastardy. Filed 2-14-1859. Casaline unmarried woman of Stock twp. and resident of Noble Co. for 10 years. Archers are also of Stock twp. Casaline six months pregnant on 12-3-1858. Deft. to pay support. (329)

3-23-1859 - Jacob CLEARY vs. Mary A. CLEARY, et al. Petition for Partition. Filed 4-7-1858. Land, 40.17 acres SW¼ NE¼ Section 35, Township 8, Range 8 as sold in Zanesville land district. Partition: 1/6th part, Jacob Cleary of Noble Co.; 1/6th part, Mary Ann Clary; 1/6th part, William Clary; 1/6th part, Edward Clary, 1/6th part, Thomas Cleary; 1/6th part, Joseh Clary; all of Noble Co. (375)

9-1-1859 - John BONEY (or BOUEY) vs. George STONEKING, et al. Petition for Partition. Filed 12-21-1858. Land, a;; W½ NW¼ Section 26, Township 8, Range 10, except 7 acres in SW corner owned by Aaron Gould. Partition: 1/10th part, Julia Ann wife of John Boney; 1/10th part, Avy wife of George Stoneking; 1/10th part, Elizabeth Hipsley; 1/20th part, Nancy Jane McPheters; 1/10th part, Lydia Ann wife of Steward Elder; 1/20th part, Sarah Hipsley; 1/10th part, Harriet Hipsley; 1/10th part, Andrew Hipsley; 1/10th part, Josephus Hipsley; all of Noble Co., Ohio. (398)

12-9-1857 - Abraham LARRICK vs. Benjamin LARRICK, et al. Petition for Partition. File 5-4-1857. Land, NE¼ Section 17, Township 8, Range 9 as sold in Zanesville land district. Casper Larrick, dec'd. Children, each entitled to 1/6th part: Abraham Larrick of Noble Co.; Jacob Larrick of Noble Co.; Benjamin Larrick of Noble Co.; John Larrick of Guernsey Co., Ohio; Catharine widow of Benjamin Hardesty who is now dec'd, of Noble Co.; Rachel wife of Elijah Thompson of Noble Co. (515)

3-25-1859 - Henry WILLEY vs. Wm W. WILLEY, et al. Petition for Partition. Filed 7-5-1858. Land, 65 acres W part NW¼ Section 30, 35 acres E pt NE¼ and 7 acres SW cor. NE¼ Section 25, all in Township 7, Range 9. Also, 40 acres SE¼ SE¼ and 10 acres S end SW¼ SE¼ Section 26 and 2½ acres SE cor. E½ NW¼ Section 25, all in Township 8, Range 10. Also lot 19 in Hoskinsville, all in Noble Co. George Willey, dec'd. Widow, Nancy Willey, entitled to dower. Partition: 1/7th part each, Henry Willey of Noble Co., William W. Willey of Iowa, Sylvester Willey, Abigail Fulkreth, George E. Willey, Sarah Willey, and Austin Willey, all of Noble Co. and the last three named being minors. (522)

3-25-1859 - Samuel C. CARPENTER vs. Alexander CARPENTER, et al. Petition for Partition. Filed 1-18-1858. Land, 40.16 acres NW¼ SW¼ and 40.16 acres SE¼ SW¼ Section 7, also SE¼ SE¼ Section 13 being 39.70 acres, all in Township 8, Range 4, being in Marietta Land district. Thomas Carpenter, dec'd, died in forepart of

(Samuel C. Carpenter vs. Alexander Carpenter, et al. cont.)
year 1857. Sons of dec'd each entitled to 1/5th part: Samuel C. Carpenter,
Alexander Carpenter, Vincent Carpenter, Richard Carpenter and Thomas Carpenter,
all of Noble Co. and the last two named being minors. Widow, Lavina Carpenter is
entitled to dower in said land. (528)

9-3-1859 - Mary HISER vs. Charles HISER. Petition for Divorce. Filed 3-22-1859.
Mary's maiden name was Wissen of Wipen, that she was formerly married to Adam
Shank and had seven children by Shank who are all under 15 years of age at the
present time. That said Adam Shank died in Oct. 1857 in Noble Co. leaving Mary
100 acres of land and $2025.00 in personal property. That Mary married Charles
Hiser on 11-19-1857 in Noble County. (note: surname at different places is
also spelled "Hyser".) (548)

9-3-1859 - Susannah BARNHOUSE vs. Joseph McCUNE. Bastardy. Filed 3-10-1859.
Susannah an unmarried woman gave birth to child on 10-3-1858 by Joseph McCune
of Sharon twp. Joseph required to pay support. (566)

9-3-1859 - Elizabeth BENNET vs. William MATHENY. Bastardy. Filed 8-3-1859.
Elizabeth an unmarried woman testified before Justice of the Peace that she
gave birth of May 9th, said statement or deposition by Elizabeth taken on
5-13-1859 at residence of William Bennet. Wm Matheny charged with support
of said child. (568)

Noble County was formed on March 11, 1851 from Guernsey, Monroe, Morgan and
Washington Counties in the following manner: Beaver, Wayne, Seneca and Buffalo
townships from Guernsey County; Marion, Stock and Enoch townships and nearly
2/3rds of the eastern side of Center twp. and all of Elk except 4 sw miles of
its south end from Monroe County; Olive, Jackson, Sharon, Noble and Brookfield
townships and the western part of Center from Morgan County; the 4 sw miles
that form the southern part of Elk and that part of Jefferson lying directly west
from Washington County. (Information from the Recorder's Office at the Court
House in Caldwell, Noble County).

NOBLE COUNTY, OHIO - COMMON PLEAS COURT RECORDS 1859-1864

The following records were copied from Petition Books located in the Clerk of
Court's Office at the court house at Caldwell. Civil Suits for debt were not
copied, but all records of genealogical importance were copied. The book in which
the record may be found is given in the underlined heading. Page on which record
may be found is given in parenthesis at the end of each individual record.

Petition Record 3

11-8-1859 - Henry MORRIS guardian of Sarah E. and Hannah J. MORRIS vs Robert
LEEK, et al. Petition for Partition. Filed 2-7-1859. Land, 80 acres E½ NE¼
and 40 acres SE¼ NW¼ Section 1, Township 8, Range 7 in Marietta land district.
Resin Leek, dec'd, late of Noble Co. Widow, Barbara Leek, entitled to dower.
Partition: 1/8th part, Robert Leek of Noble Co.; 1/8th part each to Sarah E.
and Hannah J. Morris, minors of Noble Co. (12)

3-22-1859 - Edward SALISBURY vs. Roland BEVAN, et al. Petition for Partition.
Filed 5-3-1856. Land, NW¼ Section 34, Township 6, Range 7 except 15 acres off
west end. John Bevan, dec'd. Widow, Mary Bevan. Children each entitled to
1/8th part: Findley Bevan, who sold his interest to Edward Salisbury of Monroe
Co., Ohio; Rolland Bevan; Sarah wife of David Maxwell; Jesse L. Bevan; Thomas
W. Bevan; Elener wife of Richard Barnett; Mary Ann wife of Sam'l Holms; and
William C. Bevan; all of Noble Co. (91)

9-8-1858 - James DOBBINS vs. Sarah M. DOBBINS, et al. Petition for Partition.
Filed 1-26-1858. Land, 20 acres part NW cor NE¼ NW¼ Section 20, Township 6,
Range 7 in Marietta Land District. Partition 1/3rd part, Barbara wife of
James Dobbins; 1/3 part, Sarah M. Dobbins, a minor; 1/3rd part, Charlotte
C. Dobbins, a minor. (174)

11-9-1859 - Susanna MILLER vs. Francis MILLER. Petition for Dower. Filed
12-30-1858. Land, 50 acres N½ Section 29, Township 5, Range 7. Frederick
Miller, dec'd. Widow, Susanna Miller. That Susanna married Frederick on
4-10-1832 and that Frederick died on 11-30-1857. That Susanna has right to
dower in above mentioned land, but that Francis Miller claims to hold estate. (209)

11-12-1859 - Mary A. SMITH vs. John SMITH. Petition for Divorce. Filed
9-1-1859. Married 3-25-1852 in Noble Co., Ohio. Issue of Marriage is James
Smith aged 6 years. (250)

3-10-1860 - James KENT vs. James P. REED, et al. Petition for Partition.
Filed 5-2-1857. Land, E½ Section 29 and 2 acres E side SW¼ Section 29, both
in Township 7, Range 7, also 1.33 acres NE cor. E½ NE¼ Section 28, Township 7,
Range 7 in Noble Co. Also W½ NW¼ and SE¼ NW¼ Section 33, Township 7, Range 7
in Monroe Co., Ohio. William Kent, dec'd, died 1-1-1856. Widow, Susan Kent,
entitled to dower. Children and grandchildren: 1/9th part, son, James Kent of
Noble Co.; 1/9th part, daughter, Sarah wife of James. Reed of Noble Co.; 1/9th
part, daughter, Mariah wife of George W. Brown of Noble Co.; 1/9th part, daughter,
Rebecca Kent of Noble Co.; 1/9th part, son, Josiah Kent of California; 1/9th part
son John Kent of Noble Co.; 1/9th part, daughter, Mary Ann Kent of Noble Co.; 1/9
th part, son William T. Kent of Noble Co.; 1/9th part jointly or 1/27th part each,
daughter, Eliza Rucker, dec'd, her children--Robert, George W. and Sarah A.
Rucker, all minors of Noble Co. (308)

3-8-1860 - Nancy TILTON vs. Smith TILTON and Rufus TILTON. Petition for Dower.
Filed 8-24-1859. Hebron Tilton, dec'd, died 5-5-1859 seized of an estate of
inheritance in NE¼ Section 28, Township 6, Range 9 except 3 acres in NW corner
owned by Wm Gouchnour. That Hebron Tilton left will dated 11-12-1858 devising
E½ of land to Rufus Tilton and W½ of land to Smith Tilton and in which said,
Nancy as widow claims dower interest. (365)

3-9-1860 - Sarah A. McPHERSON vs. Wm McPHERSON. Petition for divorce and
alimoney. Filed 11-30-1859. Sarah married 12-8-1845 at Summerfield, Monroe
Co., Ohio to Wm McPherson of Monroe Co. Issue of marriages is one child now
living, John W. H. McPherson aged about 9 months. William is now in parts
unknown. Defendant to pay plaintiff $1500.00 and then $1000.00. (381)

8-2-1860 - Sarah Jane GIBSON vs. Margaret GIBSON and elmira BAILES. Petition
for Partition. Filed 6-22-1859. Land, lots 5 and 6 in Perryopolis. Partition:
1/3rd part, Sarah Jane Gibson of Noble Co.; 1/3 part, Margaret Gibson, a minor
of Noble Co.; 1/3rd part, Elmire Bailis, a minor of Noble Co. (394)

8-2-1860 - Mary E. HOOK vs Cyrus HICKMAN. Bastardy. Filed 2-5-1860. Mary
Elizabeth an unmarried woman, now expecting child. Deft. to pay support. (463)

11-15-1860 - Wm L. JONES vs. James JONES, et al. In Partition. Filed 5-21-1860.
Land, NW¼ and SW¼ Section 9, E½ SE¼ Section 15, E½ NE¼ Section 14, E½ SW¼
W½ SE¼ except 4¼ acres owned by John Delong W½ NE¼ and N½ E½ NE¼ all in Section
8, 15 acres NW¼ Section 7 and 3½ acres part W½ SE¼ Section 9, with all above
described land being in Township 8, Range 7 and all in Marietta land district.
Thomas Jones, dec'd, late of Noble Co. Children, 1/9th part each: William L.
Jones; James Jones; John Jones, Samuel Jones; Jarred Jones, a minor; Elizabeth
Jones; Mary Jones, a minor; Sabrah Jones, a minor; and Sarah B. Formerly Jones
wife of Joshua Douglas; all of Noble Co. (465)

11-16-1860 - Elizabeth KEITH vs. George GRAHAM. Petition for Dower. Filed
11-4-1859. Benjamin Keith, dec'd of Noble Co., Ohio d əd in 1859 leaving widow,
Elizabeth Keith. Said Benjamin died seized by estate of inheritance, 80 acres
W½ SE¼ Section 33, Township 6, Range 9 and 53 acres NW part fractional Section
4, Township 5, Range 9 of which George Graham now claims to hold title and in
which Elizabeth Keith claims dower. (505)

11-16-1860 - Elizabeth KEITH vs. Andrew KEITH and Balser KEITH. Petition for
Dower. Filed 11-4-1859. Benjamin Keith died in 1859 leaving Elizabeth Keith
as widow. Benjamin Keith died seized of estate of inheritance in land (note:
described as in above petition). That Balser and Andrew Keith claim to hold
estate in land and that Elizabeth Keith claims dower interest. (508)

11-14-1860 - Priscilla CARNEY vs. John CARNEY and Thomas CARNEY, Petition for
Dower. Filed 3-6-1860. That Priscilla married 12-22-1850 in Guernsey Co., Ohio
to Willis Carney who died 2-12-1857 seized of NW¼ SW¼ and SW¼ NW¼ Section 10,
Township 5, Range 8 in Zanesville land district and in which Priscilla claims
dower interest. Priscilla also has son, Thomas Carney, a minor who is entitled
to a 1/3rd interest in said land. (535)

11-14-1860 - Elnora HOSKINS vs. Henry HOSKINS and Lewis HOSKINS. Petition for Dower. Filed 3-6-1860. Wait Hoskins, dec'd, died 4-20-1857 leaving widow Elnora who he married 12-23-1855 and he died seized of 81 acres E½ SE¼ Section 27 and 40 acres SW¼ SW¼ Section 26, both in Township 10, Range 8 in Brookfield twp. That defts. now occupy land and refuses to set off dower to said Elnora.(538)

3-7-1861 - Maryann LANAM and Caroline LANAM by Henry LANAM, guardian vs. Nancy HUPP, et al. Petition for Partition. Filed 6-12-1860. Land, E½ SW¼ except 11 acres NE corner owned by John Hupp and W½ SW¼ except 20 acres N end owned by John Hupp, Jackson Hupp, John D. Gross and Daniel Hupp Jr., all said land being in Section 21, Township 6, Range 8. Daniel Hupp dec'd. Widow, Nancy Hupp, entitled to dower. Children: 1/11th part jointly or 1/27th part each, Eloner Lanam, dec'd, her children--Mary Ann and Caroline Lanam; 1/11th part, Silas Hupp; 1/11th part, Jackson Hupp; 1/11th part, Samuel Hupp; 1/11th part, John Hupp; 1/11th part, Eveline wife of Henry Archer; 1/11th part, Sarah wife of Richard Poling; 1/11th part, Mary Ann wife of Simon Archer; 1/11th part, Margaret wife of George Craig; 1/11th part, Nancy wife of Samuel Templeton; 1/11th part, Lucinda wife of John C. Smith. (551)

Petition Record 4

4-12-1861 - Sarah A. WAGONER vs. Isaac WAGONER, et al. Petition for Partition. Filed 5-21-1860. Land, 41.43 acres N½ E½ SW¼ and 5 acres part NW Corner S½ SW¼, all in section 2, Township 8, Range 7 in Marietta land district. Barney Wagoner, dec'd. Children, 1/6th part each: Sarah Ann Wagoner, Isaac Wagoner, Elizabeth Wagoner, William Wagoner, Richard Wagoner and John W. Wagoner, all of Noble Co. and the last five named being minors. (15)

4-11-1861 - Ann McGUIRE vs. James McGUIRE, et al. Petition for Alimony. Filed 8-29-1860. Ann married 10-23-1856 at Steubenville, Ohio to James McQuire and they separated 8-28-1859. Issue of Marriages are: Ann Eliza (note: no age given). John aged 16 yrs., William aged 14 yrs., Mary E. aged 12 yrs. and James Francis aged 10 yrs. That said James abandoned her and that he is now in business and can provide for her and family. (54)

6-5-1861 - William A. MORRIS vs. Mary J. MORRIS. Petition for Divorce. Filed 4-20-1861. Married 1-27-1854 in Sunbury twp., Monroe Co., Ohio. That Mary's place of residence is not known. (138)

6-6-1861 - Alfred B. LEEPER vs. Charles HARLAN, et al. Petition for partition. Filed 9-25-1860. Land, 54 acres W end S½ NE¼ and 4 acres NW corner SE¼ all in Section 2, Township 7, Range 8 and also town lots 19,20,21 & 22 in town of Freedom, William Leeper, dec'd. Children: son, Alfred B. Leeper; daughter, Virginia wife of Lorenzo Currence of Virginia; daughter, Jerusha wife of Charles Harlan of Noble Co.; daughter, Sarah A. Leeper of Missouri; daughter, Mary E. Leeper, a minor of Noble Co.; son, William P. Leeper, a minor of Missouri. (150)

11-14-1861 - Rachel OSBORN vs. Isaac OSBORN. Petition for Divorce. Filed 11-16-1860. Rachel married in 1840 in Monroe Co., Ohio to Isaac Osborn and they separated in October 1860. That Isaac owns 10 acres SW corner Section 4, Township 5, Range 8. That Rachel has resided in Ohio for more than 40 years and has resided the last year with her father in Monroe Co., Ohio. (205)

312

11-15-1861 - John V. WATSON vs. Henry KELLER, etal. Petition for ,Partition.
Filed 12-27-1860. Land, NE¼ Section 21 and 5 acres fraction 4 in NW cor. SW¼
NW¼ Section 22, all in Township 8, Range 8. Abraham Moser, dec'd. Widow, Hannah
now Hannah Keller. Heirs: Catharine wife of John V. Watson of Noble Co.; Henry
Keller of Noble Co.; Levi J. Freel of Noble Co.; Mary Freal of Noble Co.;
Sarah J. Moser of Noble Co.; Samson Moser, a minor of Noble Co.; John Moser of
Kansas territory; and Morris Moser of California. (282)

6-6-1862 - Isaac WAGONER vs. Isaiah WAGONER, et al. Petition for Partition.
Filed 10-2-1862. Isaac Wagoner received from United States on 9-28-1850 for
service as Private in War with Great Britain 6-18-1812 a bounty land warrant for
80 acres #55,239 dated 4-5-1854 and dec'd died leaving warrant not disposed of
and in the hands of his administrator. Isaac Wagoner, dec'd. Children: Isaac
Wagoner; Isaiah Wagoner; Mary Huntsman formerly Wagoner; Nancy Wagoner; John
Wagoner, dec'd, his children--Isaac Wagoner, Elizabeth Wagoner, Mary C. Wagoner,
Mary Wagoner, John Wagoner, B.J. Wagoner and N.W. wife of Vernon Mercer; Barney
Wagoner, dec'd, his children--Isaac Wagoner, Sarah A. Wagoner, Mary E. Wagoner,
William W. Wagoner, Richard Wagoner and John W. Wagoner; all of the aforementioned
being of Beaver twp., Noble Co.; Ruth Elliott formerly Ruth Waggoner, dec'd,
her children--Isaac Elliott, John W. Elliott, Jesse Elliott, Ann formerly Elliott
wife of Hagre Donley, Mary formerly Elliott wife of Selathiel Ray and Elizabeth
formerly Elliott wife of Robert Ray, all of Elk twp., Noble Co. (406)

10-8-1862 - Marshall WILLEY vs. Filetus FOWLER, et al. In Partition. Filed
4-19-1862. Land, E½ SW¼ Section22, Township 7, Range 9. Lemuel Fowler, dec'd,
died intestate in 1861. Widow, Deborah Fowler of Noble Co. Children and grandchildren: 1/6th part, daughter, Olla wife of Marshall Willey of Noble Co.;
1/6th part, son, Filetus Fowler of Noble Co.; 1/6th part, daughter, Fidelia
wife of Enos Glover of Noble Co.; 1/6th part, daughter, Caroline Fowler of Noble
Co.; 1/6th part, son, Lemuel Fowler of Noble Co.; 1/6th part, daughter, Margaret
Willey, dec'd, her daughter--Margaret Willey of Noble Co. (505)

3-13-1863 - William GUILER vs. Mary A. GUILER. Petition for Divorce. Filed
12-12-1862. William married 11-20-1856 in Noble Co. to Mary A. Ray. Mary A.
filed cross petition stating William owned land: 80 acres S½ SW¼ Section 15,
80 acres E½ NE¼ Section 21, 40.48 acres NW¼ NW¼ and 5 acres both part Section
22 and 2 acres pt NW¼ SW¼ Section 15, all in Township 7, Range 8. (516

3-11-1863 - James J. SQUIER vs. Squire McCANN, et al. Petition for Partition.
Filed 8-6-1862. Land, 28 acres NW part W½ SE¼ and 25 acres SE cor. W½ NE¼
Section 7, Township 7, Range 8. Partition: 1/9th part, James J. Squier of Iowa;
1/9th part, Squire McCann; 1/9th part, Mary wife of James Stevens; 1/9th part,
Jane wife of William J. Young; 1/9th part, Sarah wife of William Danford; 1/9th
part, Hannah wife of Edward Bates; all of Noble Co.; 1/9th part, Anna wife of
William Tracy of Iowa; 1/9th part, Thomas McCann of Iowa; 1/9th part, Elizabeth
wife of Bazel Tracy of Missouri. (542)

3-11-1863 - John C. SHAFER vs. George SHAFER, et al. Petition for Petition.
Filed 4-22-1862. Land, W½ SE¼ & SE¼ SE¼ Section 28, Township 8, Range 8.
Conrad Shafer, dec'd. Widow, Mary Shafer entitled to dower. Children: 1/9th
part, John C. Shafer of Noble Co.; 1/9th part, George Shafer of Noble Co.; 1/9th
part, William Shafer of Noble Co.; 1/9th part, Nelson Shafer of Noble Co.; 1/9th

part, Elizabeth wife of Levi Keller of Noble Co.; 1/9th part, Mary Ann of Noble Co. wife of George W. Brown whose residence is not known; 1/9th part, Samuel Shafer of Lawrence Co., Ohio; 1/9th part, James Shafer of Iowa; 1/9th part jointly, Margaret Needham, dec'd of Iowa, her children--John Needham, Mary Ann wife of John Y. Hopkins, Samuel Needham, Elizabeth Needham now married but husband's name not known, Mariam Needham now married but husband's name not known, Heirs of Margaret Needham whose names are not known as is her married name not known, William Needham, David Leander Needham and Athelia Belle Needham all of Iowa.(566)

6-3-1863 - Baldwin M. LEELAND vs. Rebecca LEELAND. Petition for Divorce. Filed 4-11-1863. Married 3-5-1859 in Sharon twp. Noble Co. (581)

6-3-1863 - Elizabeth PARSONS vs. Zadock PARSONS. Petition for Divorce. Filed 4-11-1863. Married 2-15-1854 in Middleburgh, Noble Co. Issue of marriage: Rachel M. Parsons aged 2 yrs. and Nancy Jane Parsons aged 1 yr. (600)

Petition Record 5
6-4-1863 - Mary WOODARD vs. Joseph HUTCHENS, et al. Petition for Partition. Filed 8-20-1862. Land, 30 acres SW part NE¼ Section 15 and fractional 3 of Section 15, all in Township 6, Range 9 in Zanesville land district. Partition: 1/8 part, Mary Woodard of Noble Co.; 2/8ths part, Joseph Hutchins; 1/8th part, Jefferson Hutchins; 1/8th part, Lucena Hutchins; 1/8 part, Elizabeth wife of Wilson F. McIntyre; all of Noble Co.; 1/8th part, Bartlett Hutchens of Morgan Co., Ohio; 1/8th part, Lydia wife of John Bartlett of Washington Co., Ohio. (30)

6-2-1863 - William ROSS vs. Jane ROSS, et al. Petition for Partition. Filed 1-11-1862. Land, SE¼ and 63 acres SW¼ Section 18, Township 6, Range 9. Clement Ross, dec'd, died about 11 years ago. Widow, Jane Ross, entitled to dower. Children: Randall Ross; John B. Ross, now dec'd; Mary wife of William Long; Elizabeth wife of Samuel Milligan; and William Ross. (34)

10-7-1863 - Hannah McINTOSH vs. Stewart GORDON. Petition for Dower. Filed 6-3-1863. Hannah McIntosh of Washington Co., Ohio married William McIntish who died seized of NE¼ NE¼ Section 8 and SE¼ Section 5, all in Township 5, Range 8 in which Hannah is entitled to dower and in which Stewart Gordon claims to hold estate. (100)

10-7-1863 - Lorinda FOWLER vs. James BIRD. Bastardy. Filed 4-27-1863. Lorinda an unmarried woman gave birth to child 7-7-1862 and claims James Bird to be the father of said child. Deft. to pay support. (105)

4-7-1864 - Andrew KUNTZ vs. Ann CALDWELL, etal. Petition for Partition. Filed 8-22-1863. Andrew Kuntz of Morgan Co., Ohio is seized of 10/13ths parts of W½ NW¼ Section 27, Township 7, Range 10 in Noble Co. in Zanesville Land District and tenants in common are: Ann Caldwell of Noble Co.; Elzy Caldwell of Morgan Co., Ohio and Heirs of Abraham Shuster, dec'd, late of Iowa whose names are not known. (108)

4-7-1864 - Wm S. FARRELL vs. Martha L. ADDIS, et al. In Partition. Filed 5-12-1863. Land, 40 acres SE¼ NW¼ Section 30, Township 5, Range 9 in Jackson twp., in Zanesville land district. Thomas Farrell, dec'd. Widow, Martha, entitled to dower. Partition: 1/2 part, Wm S. Farrell of Noble Co.; 1/2 part Martha L. wife of John Addis. (141)

314

4-6-1864 - Sarah E. DEAVER vs. Frederick ROACH Jr. Bastardy. Filed 6-1-1863.
Both are of Beaver twp. Sarah an unmarried woman expecting a child of whom
Roach is claimed to be father. (209)

4-5-1864 - J.H.B. LARRICK vs. Asa LARRICK, et al. Petition for Partition.
Filed 8-14-1863. Land, 40 acres SE¼ SE¼ Ssction 19, 40 acres NE¼ NE¼ and 40
acres SE¼ NW¼ both in Section 30, 39 acres SW¼ SW¼, 39 acres NE¼ SW¼ and part
NW¼ SE¼ all in Section 20, and 40 acres NW¼ SW¼ Section 29, all in Township 8,
Range 9. James V. Larrick, dec'd, died in 1863 intestate. Widow, Mary Larrick
of Noble Co., entitled to dower. Children: son, Moses Larrick; son, J.H.B.
Larrick; son, Asa Larrick; son, William T. Larrick; son, Mordecai B. Larrick;
son, Levi E. Larrick; and daughter, Rosanna Larrick; the last four named being
minors. (218)

4-9-1864 - Sarah A. MENDENHALL vs. Oliver P. DILLEY. Bastardy. Filed 3-10-1864.
Sarah an unmarried woman has given birth to child (no date given). Oliver
adjudged to be father. (251)

7-6-1864 - Levina ARNOLD vs James Sherb. Breach of marriage contract. Filed
2-4-1862. Deft. promised to marry plaintiff on 10-5-1860. Plaintiff awarded
$500.00. (342)

7-6-1864 - Patterson F. YOHO vs. Charlotte J. YOHO. Petition for Divorce.
Filed 6-2-1863. Married in August 1851 in Marshall Co., Virginia. Lived
together until May 10, 1852. Charlotte now resides in Marshall Co., Virginia.(346)

10-5-1864 - James McCUNE 2nd vs. Michael McCUNE, etal. In partition. Filed
2-6-1864. Land, 81 acres W½ SE¼, fractional No. 1 in w part NE¼ being 114 acres
and fractional No. 3 in E side NE¼ being 17 acres, all in Section 29 and fractional No. 3 in W part NW¼ Section 28 being 7½ acres, all in Township 7, Range 9.
Charles McCune, dec'd. Widow, Sebrah McCune entitled to dower. Heirs: 1/7th
part jointly or 1/28th part each, John McCune, dec'd, his children--James McCune 2nd,
George McCune, Isaac E. McCune and William McCune 2nd, the last three being minors;
1/7th part, Michael McCune of Missouri; 1/7th part, James McCune of Missouri; 1/7th
part, Rosannah Barnhorse; 1/7th part, William McCune; 1/7th part, Joseph McCune;
1/7th part, Franklin McCune; the last four named all being of Noble Co. (363)

10-5-1864 - Jacob GREGG vs. Hannah LAW, et al. Petition for Partition. Filed
8-14-1863. Land, 177 acres SW¼ Section 19, Township 8, Range 8 in Zanesville land
district. James Stevens, dec'd, died 2-19-1863. Widow, Mary Stevens of Noble Co.
entitled to dower. Children: daughter, Emmy wife of Jacob Gregg of Noble Co.;
daughter, Hannah widow of Ada Law, dec'd; daughter, Rachel wife of Charles W.
Gipson; daughter, Sarah wife of Joseph Johnston; daughter, Anna Mariah Stevens,
a minor; son, James Bascom Stevens, a minor, all of afore mentioned of Noble Co.;
son, Thomas M. Stevens of Tuscarawas Co., Ohio; son, Jonathan Stevens of Guthrie
Co., Iowa; son, William Stevens; son, John Stevens, dec'd, his children--Jane,
William S., James F. and Daniel L. Stevens, Minors. (373)

PAULDING COUNTY, OHIO – COMMON PLEAS COURT RECORDS
JOURNALS 1, 2, 3 – 1842-1855

The following records were taken from "Journal 1,2,3" ~~ found in the Common Pleas
Court (Clerk of Court's Office) at the court house at Paulding. Page on which
record may be found in original book is given in parenthesis.

4-25-1842 - Will of Charles COLLINS, dec'd presented to court. John Kingery
appointed adms. with will annexed (5)
4-25-1842 - Tavern license granted to Wm W. BURLEY to keep tavern at his residence
in town of New Rochester. (8)
4-25-1842 - William N. Snook appointed guardian of Joseph BANKS aged 17 yrs. Hiram
BANKS aged 15 yrs. and Matilda BANKS aged 7 yrs. children and heirs of Samuel
BANKS, dec'd. (8)
4-26-1842 - Tavern license granted to Isaac WOODCOX to keep tavern at his residence
in Antwerp. (9)
4-26-1842 - Tavern license granted to Richard BANKS to keep tavern at his residence
in Carryall township. (9)
4-26-1842 - Gilman C. Mudgett and Wm Richmond appo8nted adms. of the estate of
David W. CHILDS, dec'd late of Carryall twp. (10)
4-26-1842 - Tavern license granted to Samuel S. HANKINS to keep tavern at his
residence in Charloe. (10)
4-26-1842 - James Taylor and Samuel Hankins sureties of George W. Williams adms.
of the estate of Jedediah Austin, dec'd, are to show cause. (12,33)
9-26-1842 - Joseph MILLER minister of the United Brethren church granted license
to solemnize marriages. (15)
9-26-1842 - Tavern license granted to George H. PHILLIPS to keep tavern at his
residence in Charlote. (17)
9-26-1842 - Will of David L. CURTIS, dec'd presented to court. Herman J. Curtis
appointed adms. with the will annexed. (22)
4-17-1843 - John KIMMELL granted license to keep Ferry across Flat Rock Creek in
Auglaize township. Rate: 6½ cents for ferrying a man and 12½ cents for a man
and horse. (30)
4-18-1843 - John Kingry adms. of William HANNA, dec'd vs. S. E. J. HANNA, heirs of
dec'd. Petition to sell real estate of said dec'd. (32,57,174)
4-18-1843 - Samuel S. HANKINS granted license to keep a Temperance tavern at his
residence in Charlote. (32)
4-18-1843 - Tavern license granted to Isaac WOODCOX to keep tavern at his residence
in Antwerp. (32)
4-18-1843 - Sarah D. Applegate widow of dec'd appointed admsx. of the estate of
Oliver S. APPLEGATE, dec'd. (33,35)
4-18-1843 - John Mason, etal vs. John Hudson, etal. Whereas the Abraham HUDSON
the purchaser of land of Shadrack HUDSON, dec'd has paid to the sheriff the
consideration money for said land it is ordered that the sheriff mke deed
and to pay the consideration money as follows: to John MASON $19.49½; to
Robert SHIRLEY and Sarah his wife $19.49½; to Elias SHIRLEY and Phebe his wife
$19.49½ to John HUDSON $19.49½; to Abraham HUDSON. $19.49½; to Elizabeth HUDSON
$19.49½ to Samuel HUDSON $19.49½; to Shadrack HUDSON $19.49½; to James HUDSON
$19.49½. (33)
4-18-1843 - Ferry license granted to Pierce TAYLOR to keep a ferry at the mouth of
Little Auglaize River in Brown township. (36)
9-25-1843 - Thomas POWERS, native of Ireland makes his declaration of intention to
become citizen. (42)

-25-1843 - John S. McLEAN granted license to keep ferry across Flat Rock Creek in Auglaize township. (44)

-25-1843 - Tavern license granted to George H. PHILLIPS to keep tavern at his residence in Charlote. (44)

-30-1844 - Tavern license granted to Isaac WOODCOX to keep tavern at his residence in the town of Antwerp. (57)

-30-1844 - Tavern license granted to Andrew E. and George S. SCHOOLEY to keep tavern at their residence in the town of Junction. (57)

-30-1844 - Tavern license granted to Joseph GUIVER to keep tavern at his residence in Charlote. (57)

-30-1844 - Tavern license granted to Samuel S. HANKINS to keep tavern at his residence in Charlote. (57)

-30-1844 - Naturalization. Joseph SINGER a native of Prussia made his declaration of intention 10-6-1840 in Williams County, Ohio; now makes application and is naturalized. (57)

-30-1844 - Naturalization. Timothy TOOLE (note: no further information given).(58)

-26-1844 - Tavern license granted to William SMITH to keep tavern at his residence in Charloe. (69)

-26-1844 - Tavern license granted to Isaac WOODCOX to keep tavern in the town of Antwerp. (70)

-27-1844 - Ann Murphy widow of Robert MURPHY, dec'd vs. the administrators. That she be paid her allowance of $100.00. (73)

-27-1844 - Robert HAKES vs. Caroline HAKES, petition for divorce, granted. (73)

-27-1844 - Harriet McCLELLAND vs. James McCLELLAND, petition for divorce, granted. Harriet to have custody of children, issue of said marriage being, Francis McClelland, Melissa McClelland and Henry McClelland. (73)

-27-1844 - Tavern license granted to Henry BRUBACHER to keep tavern at his house in town of Junction. (79)

-27-1844 - Tavern license granted to William K. DAGGETT to keep tavern at his house in town of Junction. (79)

-27-1844 - Naturalization. Barney MELMON (note: no other information given).(79)

-27-1844 - Naturalization. John MANSFIELD(note: no other information given). (79)

-27-1844 - Naturalization. Patrick LANE (note; no other information given). (80)

-27-1844 - Naturalization. James O'BRIEN (note;no other information given). (80)

-28-1844 - Naturalization. John FATEY(Latty?) (note: no other info. given). (83)

-28-1844 - Naturalization. Dennis FEE (note: no other information given). (84)

-28-1844 - Naturalization. James MALLEN (note; no other information given). (84)

-28-1844 - Naturalization. Thomas WHALEN (note; no other info. given.) (84)

note: record jumps from court of May 28, 1844 to court of Oct. 10, 1845; if there are records for terms of court in between, they are not given in this book)

)-10-1745 - Naturalization. Thomas POWERS (note; no other info. given. (89)

)-10-1845 - Naturalization. Joseph M. O'CONNER (note: no other info. given). (89)

)-11-1845 - Naturalization. Adam MAST (note: no other information given). (94)

)-11-1845 - John GALLAGHER, native of Ireland now residing in Paulding County makes his declaration of intention to become citizen. (100)

)-11-1845 - William McCULLOUGH, native of Ireland makes his declaration of intention to become citizen. (101)

)-11-1845 - Matthew DUFFE, native of Ireland makes his declaration of intention to become citizen. (101)

)-11-1845 - Samuel S. Hankins adms. devonis non of the estate of Jedediah AUSTIN, dec'd tendered his resignation as adms. (101)

10-22-1845 - Naturalization. Lyle TATE (no vurther information given). (101)
11-22-1745 - John W. Ayres appointed adms. of the estate of Jedeiah Austin, dec'd.
   (103)
5-24-1846 - Alfred Gower HALL vs. Phoebe Hall, petition for divorce granted. (104)
5-25-1846 - Charles Badger adms. of estate of Benjamin F. SHELDON, dec'd vs.
   Nathan G. Sales, to confirm sale of land.   (105)
5-25-1846 - Tavern license granted to Isaac WOODCOX to retail spiritous liquors at
   the Antwerp House in Antwerp.   (105)
5-25-1846 - Tavern license granted to Henry BRUBACHER to retail spiritous liquors
   at the American House in Junction.   (106)
5-25-1846 - Tavern license granted to William SMYTH to retail spiritous liquors at
   the Junction House in Junction.   (106)
5-25-1846 - Henry APPLEGATE aged 14 yrs. on 11 July last chose Zachariah Graves
   as his guardian with Zachariah also to serve as guardian of Tabitha Ann APPLE-
   GATE aged 9 yrs. on 11 Sept. last past, Sarah Ann APPLEGATE aged 11 yrs. on 13
   Dec. last past, Kezziah APPLEGATE aged 7 yrs. on 3 April last past, Nancy APPLE-
   GATE aged 5 yrs. on 15 August last past, and Oliver S. APPLEGATE aged 4 yrs. on
   17 Dec. last past, all children of Oliver S. Applegate, dec'd.   (107)
5-25-1846 - Barnabas D. Blue appointed adms. of the estate of William BLUE, dec'd
   (108)
5-25-1846 - Naturalization, Nicholas BAKER (Note: no further information given).(11
5-26-1846 - Tavern license granted to Samuel S. HANKINS to keep tavern at his
   present stand in Charloe.   (113)
5-27-1846 - Tavern license granted to Zra J. SMITH to keep tavern at his residence
   in Charloe.   (114)
5-27-1846 - Tavern license granted to Richard BANKS to keep tavern at his residence
   in Carryall twp.   (114)
11-2-1846 - John W. Ayres adms. debonis non of estate of Jedediah AUSTIN vs. Esther
   B. AUSTIN and other heirs, petition to sell real estate being W½ NW¼ Section 15,
   Township 1 North, Range 2 East.   (121)
11-2-1846 - Naturalization. Frederick GENSHAW (note: no other info. given).   (121)
11-2-1846 - Naturalization, Andrew FELONY (note: no other info. given). (121)
11-2-1846 - Naturalization, William Finney (note: no other info. given). (121)
11-3-1846 - Ferry license granted to Alfred THOMPSON to run ferry across Little
   Auglaize River where the Lima and Defiance Free Turnpike Road crosses river.(126
5-3-1847 - Tavern license granted to Samuel S. HANKINS to keep tavern at his residence in Charloe.   (134)
5-4-1847 - Tavern license granted to Henry BRUBACHER to keep tavern at the American
   House in the town of Junction.   (140)
5-4-1847 - Oliver Jeffery appointed adms. of the estate of Gilbert JEFFREY, dec'd.
   (144, 153)
9-18-1847 - Tavern license granted to Richard BANKS to keep tavern at his residence
   in Carryall township.   (154)
9-18-1847 - Tavern license granted to Frederick LYON to keep tavern in the village
   of Junction.   (154)
11-29-1847 - John Mussulman appointed adms. of the estate of Peter E. ALLEBAUGH,
   dec'd.   (157)

318

5-2-1848 - Naturalization. Wm McCULLOUGH (no further information given). (161)
5-2-1848 - Naturalization. Robert McCULLOUGH (no further information given). (161)
5-2-1848 - Naturalization. Matthew DUFFEE (no further information given). (161)
5-2-1848 - Naturalization. John GALLAHER (no further information given). (161)
5-2-1848 - Naturalization. Dennis McLAUGHLIN (no further info. given). (161)
5-2-1848 - John Fahee appointed guardian of Sarah WALLACE aged 8 yrs. and Edward
    WALLACE aged 13 yrs. children of James WALLACE, dec'd. (163)
5-3-1848 - Wm Porter adms. of estate of Margaret MOSS, dec'd vs. William MOSS, to
    collect debt. (164)
5-3-1848 - William RODGERS granted license to keep ferry at crossing of Maumee
    River near where State Road leading from Hicksville to Antwerp crosses river.
    Rates: man on foot, five cents; man and horse, ten cents; each additional
    horse, five cents; waggon or carriage drawn by one horse, 15 cents; wagon or
    carriage drawn by two horses or oxen, twenty cents; each extra horse in addition,
    five cents; Head of cattle, horses, mules or jacks, three cents; each head of
    hogs or sheep, one cent. (166)
5-4-1848 - Ferry license granted to Alfred THOMPSON across Little Auglaize where
    Lima and Defiance Free Turnpike crosses. (167)
5-5-1848 - Samuel W. Hudson appointed adms. of the estate of William BARTLETT, dec'd
    (169)
5-8-1848 - Tavern License granted to E. H. WEST to keep tavern at his residence in
    Charloe. (173)
5-8-1848 - Tavern license granted to Henry BRUBACHER to keep tavern at his residence
    in Junction. (174)
5-8-1848 - Tavern license granted to Allen PARKER to keep tavern at his residence
    in Antwerp. (174)
5-8-1848 - Tavern license granted to Richard S. BANKS to keep tavern at his resi-
    dence in Paulding County. (174)
5-8-1848 - Samuel Hudson appointed guardian of Oliver JEFFREY aged 12 yrs.,
    Sylvester JEFFREY aged 8 yrs., Charlotte JEFFREY aged 6 yrs., Gilbert JEFFREY
    aged 4 yrs. and Amy Ann JEFFREY aged 1 year, also Hannah JEFFREY aged 14 yrs.
    chose said Samuel W. Hudson as her guardian, all children of Gilbert JEFFREY,
    dec'd. (174)
5-8-1848 - Daniel Malott appointed guardian of Mary Ann BALL aged 11 yrs., Jane
    BALL aged 13 yrs., Aaron BALL aged 9 yrs. and Harrison BALL aged 8 yrs.,
    children of David BALL, dec'd. (178)
10-24-1848 - Naturalization. Consard HENRY; oath--James H. Barr and Richard Strout.
    (183)
10-24-1848 - Sarah Ann APPLEGATE aged 15 yrs., child of Oliver S. APPLEGATE, dec'd,
    chose Zachariah Graves as her guardian. (183)
10-25-1848 - Eli H. Day appointed adms. of the estate of Isaac DAY, dec'd. Eli H.
    being son of dec'd. (189)
10-25-1848 - Final settlemen in the estate of Charles COLLINS, dec'd, made by
    John Kingery, adms. (192)
2-24-1849 - Royal B. Cooper appointed adms. of the estate of James WILSON, dec'd
    (193)
2-24-1849 - Royal B. Cooper and Robert McCullough appointed adms. of the estate of
    William McCULLOUGH, dec'd. (193)
2-24-1849 - Richard Strout appointed adms. of the estate of Frederick LYON, dec'd.
    (193)

2-24-1849 - Richard Strout appointed adms. of the estate of Donald CAMEEON, dec'd. (193)

4-2-1849 - John S. ALEXANDER, native of Ireland, makes his declaration of intention to become citizen. (194)

5-2 -1849 - Joseph REEB, native of France makes his declaration of intention to become citizen. (194)

5-31-1849 - George MAGER, native of France makes his declaration of intention to become citizen. (194)

4-24-1849 - John Finley appointed adms. of the estate of Jane M. ALLEN, dec'd.(195)

4-24-1849 - Mary COX aged 16 yrs. and Michael COX aged 14 yrs., daughter and son of James COX, dec'd, chose Thomas Powers as their guardian. (200)

4-24-1849 - Harrison Mellinger appointed guardian of William MELLINGER aged 12 yrs., David MELLINGER aged 9 yrs. and Joseph MELLINGER aged 6 yrs. (200)

4-25-1849 - Thomas Powers appointed guardian of Jane MALLON aged 2 yrs. (201)

4-25-1849 - John Mussulman adms of estate of Peter EARABAUGH, dec'd files account. (201)

4-25-1849 - Ferry license granted to William RODGERS to run ferry in Carryall twp. across Mumee River where Hicksville Turnpike crosses river. (201)

4-25-1849 - Ferry license granted to Robert HAKES to run ferry across Big Auglaize River at Charloe at place of his residence where Henry County State Road crosses river. (205)

4-25-1849 - Tavern license granted to Samuel S. HANKINS to keep tavern at his house at Charloe. (205)

4-25-1849 - Tavern license granted to Isaac WOODCOX to keep tavern without privilege of retailing liquors at his house in Antwerp. (205)

8-11-1849 - Shadrack R. Hudson appointed adms. of the estate of Samuel W. HUDSON, dec'd. (213)

8-11-1849 - Robert Shirley appointed guardian of Rolla C. HUDSON aged 6 yrs., Mary Anna HUDSON aged 4 yrs. and youngest infant daughter (name not given) aged 1 year, all children of Samuel W. HUDSON, dec'd. (213)

11-10-1849 - John Mason appointed adms. debonis non of the estate of William BARTLETT, dec'd, in place of Samuel W. Hudson the former adms. (214)

5-6-1850 - Naturalization. Abraham LATTY, native of Ireland. Oath: Horatio N. Curtis and Wm Feeling. (221)

5-6-1850 - Naturalization. Richard COBE, native of Ireland. (221)

5-6-1850 - Naturalization. William NICHOLLS, native of Ireland. (121)

5-6-1850 - Tavern license granted to Henry BRUBACHER to keep tavern at his residence in Junction. (222)

5-6-1850 - Tavern license granted to Isaac WOODCOX without spiritous liquors at his house in Antwerp. (222)

5-6-1850 - Tavern license granted to Samuel S. HANKINS to keep tavern without spiritous liquors at his house in Charloe. (222)

5-6-1850 - Tavern license granted to Dana COLUMBIA to keep tavern without spiritous liquors at his residence in Junction. (222)

5-6-1850 - Estate of Samuel BANKS, dec'd. Former adms. removed and Peter Snook appointed adms. (222)

5-6-1850 - Estate of Frederick LYON, dec'd. Former adms. resigned and Sidney S. Sprague appointed adms. debonis non with final settlement filed. (222)

5-6-1850 - James and Shadrack R. Hudson adms. of estate of Shadrack HUDSON, dec'd, filed final settlement. (223)

5-6-1850 - Edward WALLACE aged 15 yrs., son of James Wallace, dec'd chose Henry Marcellus as his guardian and Marcellus also to serve as guardian of Sarah WALLACE aged 8 yrs., daughter of said James Wallace, dec'd. (224)

5-6-1850 - Ferry licence to William RODGERS for ferry across Maumee River in Carryall twp. where Hicksville Turnpike crosses. (224)

5--6-1850 - Solomon M. PRENTICE vs. Dorcas PRENTICE, petition for divorce, case continued. (226)

5-6-1850 - Robert Murphy and Joseph K. Murphy adms. of the estate of Robert MURPHY, dec'd file final settlement of accounts. (226)

5-7-1850 - Thomas Powers as guardian of Michael Cox and Jane Mallen and others, minor children of Jane Mallen dec'd vs. John Fahy adms. of estate of Jane MALLEN, dec'd, to increase allowance of said children. (231)

5-7-1850 - Ferry license granted to Jacob SWITZER to keep ferry across the Little Auglaize River where Defiance Free Turnpike crosses river. (233)

8-2-1850 - Ezra J. Smith appointed adms. of the estate of William RODGEES, dec'd. (237)

8-22--1850 - Henry Marcellus appointed adms. of the estate of William SHERLOCK, dec'd. (237)

10-8-1850 - Edward JONES, native of England makes his declaration of intention to become citizen. (238)

11-16-1850 - Shadrack M. Carey appointed adms. of the estate of Isaac CAREY, dec'd. (238)

11-16-1850 - Horace Sessions appointed guardian of Merina A. CAREY, child of Isaac Carey, dec'd. David C. Carey appointed guardian of William S. CAREY and Cornelia C. Carey, children of Isaac Carey, dec'd, (238)

3-25-1851 - Harriet Nicholl appointed admsx. of estate of William NICHOLL, dec'd. (239)

4-9-1851 - Abigail Ganshaw appointed admsx. of estate of Frederick GANSHAW, dec'd. (239)

5-19-1851 - Will of Sanford MAIN presented to the court. A. A. Cole and Samuel Durand, executors. (240)

6-30-1851 - W. N. Snook appointed adms. of the estate of Joseph T. BANKS, dec'd.(240)

9-2-1851 - Will of John M. PHELPS, dec'd presented to the court. Abraham Glassmire, executor. (241)

9-2-1851 - Abraham Glassmire appointed guardian of Richard PHELPS, Sham PHELPS and Phebe PHELPS, children of John M. Phelps, dec'd. (241)

9-23-1851 - Silas W. Clish and Seneca Dimmock appointed adms. of the estate of Sarah Ann AXTLE, dec'd.

2-3-1852 - Oliver T. Jeffrey appointed adms. of the estate of Oliver JEFFREY Sr., dec'd. (242)

2-3-1852 - John Crosson appointed guardian of Catharine King born July 8, 1842 and James King born Sept. 1844, children of James King, dec'd. (243)

2-3-1852 - John Crosson appointed guardian of Sylvester Wilson Jeffrey (no birth date given), Charlotte JEFFREY born May 1842, Gilbert JEFFREY born Sept. 1844 and Amy Ann JEFFREY born Feb. 5, 1847. (243)

2-3-1852 - Robert Hakes appointed adms. debonis non of the estate of Gilbert L. Jeffrey, dec'd. (243)

4-20-1852 - Tavern license granted to Ann P. HANKINS to keep tavern at her residence in Charloe. (255)
12-7-1852 - Tavern license granted to Dana COLUMBIA to keep tavern at his house in Junction. (259)
12-7-1852 - Tavern license granted to James THOMPSON to keep tavern at his house in Paulding. (259)
12-7-1852 - Huldah HOLDRIGE vs. James C. HOLDRIGE, petition for divorce, granted. Custody of George W. Holdridge minor child of said marriaged granted to Huldah. (263)
12-7-1852 - Naturalization. George SHARP, native of England. (264)
4-26-1853 - Ansel CAREY vs. Shadrack H. CARY, petition for assignment of dower. Being 1/3rd of 76.22 acres S½ SE fractional quarter of Section 19 and 79.33 acres NE fractional quarter of Section 30, all in township 3 North, Range 4 East. (268)
4-26-1853 - Naturalization. Joseph REEB, native of France. (269)
4-26-1853 - Tavern license granted to Isaac WOODCOX to keep tavern at his residence in Antwerp. (269)
4-26-1853 - Ferry license granted to Jabez MEAD across Auglaize River near his residence. (269)
4-26-1853 - Tavern license granted to E. J. SMITH to keep tavern at his residence in Paulding. (269)
4-26-1853 - Auctioneer license granted to John W. AYRES. (269)
4-26-1853 - Naturalization. Duncan CLARK, native of Great Brittain and Ireland.(270)
4-26-1853 - Ferry license granted to Luther LOVELAND across Maumee near Antwerp.(270)
7-13-1853 - William MELIA, native of Ireland makes his declaration of intention to become citizen. (281)
11-9-1853 - Frederick HUFFNER, native of Switzerland makes his declaration of intention to become citizen. (281)
10-4-1853 - Eliza RIDENOUR vs. Jacob RIDENOUR, petition for divorce, granted. Eliza restored all property both real and personal that she had prior to marriage. (286)
10-4-1853 - Mary McCOY vs. Jonathan McCOY, petition for divorce. Case dismissed. (287)
10-5-1853 - Tavern license granted to John BARNHART to keep tavern at the Brubacher stand in Junction. (293)
10-5-1853 - Tavern license granted to Dana COLUMBIA to keep tavern at Junction House in Junction. (293)
12-7-1853 - August TASTLEBEE, native of Prussia makes his declaration of intention to become citizen. (294)
2-6-1854 - Henry TUGER, native of Bavaria makes his declaration of intention to become citizen. (294)
5-30-1854 - Naturalization. Timothy HAYES, native of Ireland. (296)
5-30-1854 - Naturalization. Francis SHELLET, native of France. (296)
6-1-1854 - Tavern license granted to Ezra J. SMITH to keep tavern at his home in Paulding. (308)
6-1-1854 - Ferry license granted to Truman TERRY across Maumee River in Carryall twp. where Hicksville Turnpike intersects. (308)
10-3-1854 - Naturalization. Noble ALEXANDER, native of Ireland. (310)
10-3-1854 - Tavern license granted to John CROSSON to keep tavern at his residence in Paulding. (310)

10-3-1854 - Auctioneer license granted to Jacob SWITZER. (310)
10-4-1854 - Naturalization. Henry Bodinas, native of Saxe Schwartzburg, Germany. (314)
10-4-1854 - Naturalization. John Philip RIDENBAUGH, native of Bavaria. (314)
3-6-1855 - Naturalization. Christian DUTTERER, native of Germany. (323)
3-6-1855 - Naturalization. Christian GAMMANTHALLER, native of Canton, Berne. (324)
3-7-1855 - Naturalization. Frederick RAROOL, native of Rhein Berne, Germany. (328)
3-8-1855 - Charles REEB, native of France makes his declaration of intention to become citizen. (333)
10-2-1855 - Naturalization. George MAJAR, native of France. (335)

PAULDING COUNTY, OHIO - COMMON PLEAS COURT RECORDS
COURT RECORD A & C - 1840-1853

The following records were taken from "Court Record A & C" which is a Supreme Court Record found in the Common Pleas Court (Clerk of Court's Office) at the court house at Paulding. The page on which the record may be found in the original book is given in parenthesis.

7-12-1843 - Peter F. CLARK vs. Mary Ann CLARK, Petition for Divorce. Filed 5-11-1843. Peter married Mary Ann on 6-10-1839 in Brown township, Paulding Co., Ohio by Pierce Taylor, J.P. That Mary Ann left Peter on July 15, 1839. Divorce granted. (24)

7-12-1843 - Delila CHAMBERLAIN vs. William CHAMBERLAIN. Petition for Divorce. Filed 5-10-1843. That Delila married William on 8-15-1835 in Indiana by Judge Seeley. That William has been absent for some time. Divorce granted. (25)

4-17-1842 - John MASON, et al. vs. John HUDSON et al. Partition. Filed 3-15-1842. Land, 60 acres E fractional SE¼ Section 30, Township 3 North, Range 4 East. Partition: 1/9th part, John Mason of Paulding Co., Ohio; 1/9th part, Robert Shirley and Sarah his wife late Sarah Hudson of Paulding Co., Ohio; 1/9th part, Elias Shirley and Phebe his wife late Phebe Hudson of Williams Co., Ohio; 1/9th part, John Hudson of Paulding Co.; 1/9th part, Abram Hudson of Paulding Co ; 1/9th part, Elizabeth Hudson of Paulding Co.; 1/9th part, Samuel Hudson of Paulding Co.; 1/9th part, Shadrack Hudson of Paulding Co.; 1/9th part, James Hudson of Williams Co. (145)

4-29-1844 - John KINGERY adms. of Wm HANNA, dec'd vs. Sarah HANNA, widow, et al. Petition to sell real estate. Filed 4-26-1841. Land, 66.61 acres NW fractional S½ Section 22, Township 2 North, Range 4 East. William Hanna, dec'd. Widow, Sarah Hanna of Seneca Co., Ohio. Heir, James Hanna of Seneca Co., Ohio. (183)

4-25-1840 - Wm BANKS adms. of the estate of Samuel BANKS vs. Martha BANKS, etal. Petition to complete real contract. Filed 4-22-1840. That Samuel Banks in his lifetime on 1-22-1835 contracted to sell to Joel Munson 103.17 acres SE fractional N½ Section 27 Township 3 North, Range 1 East. Heirs of Samuel Banks: Martha Banks, Joseph Banks, Hiram Banks, and Matilda Banks. (313)

323

9-26-1843 - John HUDSON et al. vs. Elizx SHIRLEY, et al. In Chancery. Filed
9-28-1841. That John Hudson and Abram Hudson of Paulding county in 1820 purchased
undivided half SE fractional Section 19 Township 3 North, Range 4 in Paulding County
containing 153.84 acres and that half of land being 76.92 acres was held separately
by Shadrack Hudson grantee of said orators. That Shadrack was the father of orators
and was to reside andy occupy said land as a tenant and that he improved land and
on 10-13-1836 John Hudson deeded and conveyed to his father Shadrack for $100.00
his portion of said land. That said Shadrack Hudson died in May 1841 leaving
children: John Hudson, Abram Hudson, Phebe wife of Elias Shirley, Abigail wife of
Isaac Carey, Sarah wife of Robert Shirley, Samuel Hudson, Shadrack Hudson and
Elizabeth Hudson all of Paulding County and James Hudson of Williams County, Ohio.
Mentions that Hudsons apparently had interests also in Miami County (Ohio). 339

5-27-1845 - Robert HAKES vs. Caroline HAKES, Petition for Divorce. Filed 2-20-1845.
That Robert married Caroline Dresser on 2-23-1833 in Cayuga County, New York. That
Caroline is now a resident of Indiana having eloped with Robert Foster on 3-6-1844.
(387)

5-25-1846 - Alfred Gowan HALL vs. Phoebe HALL. Petition for Divorce. Filed
3-24-1846. That Alfred Gowan Hall has for the last two years last past resided
in Oberlin, Lorain County, Ohio and did so until September 1844 when he came to
Paulding County. That he married on 6-17-1839 in Morristown, St. Lawrence County,
New York to said Phoebe. That after marriage petitioner removed from St. Lawrence
County to Rochester, New York and that in that place Phoebe deserted him and went
to Canada. (395)

5-4-1847 - Barnabas D. BLUE vs. James BLUE, et al. In Chancery. Filed 7-3-1846.
That William K. Blue in his lifetime contracted to sell to Barnabas D. Blue the
undivided half of 40 acres SW¼ SW¼ and 10 acres being undivided half NW corner
SW¼ all in Section 36, Township 2 North, Range 1 East, but that William K. Blue
died before contract could be completed. That William K. Blue died 2-5-1846 leaving
the following heirs: James Blue, Mary wife of James D. McAnally, Sarah wife of
James Kellog, John Blue and George Blue, the last two being minors and all parties
of Defiance Co., Ohio. (401)

12-7-1852 - Huldah HOLDRIDGE vs. James HOLDRIDGE. Petition for Divorce. Filed
5-8-1852. That Huldah married James on 1-24-1850 in Crane township of Paulding
County, Ohio by Bernard B. Woodcock, J.P. Divorce granted with child of said
marriage, George W. Holdridge born Oct. 13, 1850 to Huldah. (461)

12-7-1852 - John MASON adms. de bonis non of estate of William BARTLETT, dec'd vs.
Thomas BARTLETT, et al. Petition to sell land. Filed 11-10-1849. Land 80 acres
E½ SW¼ Section 30, Township 3 North, Range 4 East. That dec'd left no widow sur-
viving him and left the following heirs: Son, Thomas Bartlett of Indiana; Daughter,
Sarah wife of James Turhune; daughter, Frances wife of John Clouser; daughter,
Harriet wife of William Nicoll, daughter, Mary wife of Samuel W. Hudson--they both
being dec'd, their children--Rolla C., Ella and Frances Elizabeth Hudson, all
minors. (464)

5-26-1853 - Robert HAWKINS vs. Henry HAWKINS, et al. Bill in chancery. Filed
11-27-1852. That Robert Hawkins now of Paulding County was previously a resident
of Franklin County, Indiana and that in Nov. of 1851 he came to Paulding County
and chose to purchase NW¼ NE¼ and SE¼ Section 35, Township 3 North, Range 1
East containing 80 acres and entered same at the land office in Defiance in the
name of his brother, Reuben, but that he paid for same and Reuben was supposed to
deed said land to him, but never did so before his death. That Reuben Hawkins
died 11-4-1852 in Paulding Co., Ohio leaving no widow but survived by the following
minor children: Henry Hawkins aged 12 yrs., Nancy Hawkins aged 10 yrs., Rachel
Hawkins aged 8 yrs., Huldah Hawkins aged 6 yrs. and Mary Hawkins aged 3 yrs., all
of Paulding Co., Ohio. (473)

10-3-1853 - Aurel CAREY vs. S. H. CAREY, et al. Petition for Partition. Filed
3-28-1851. That Aurel Carey now a resident of Painesville, Ohio on 11-17-1847
in Paulding County, Ohio married Isaac Carey and that Isaac died 10-25-1850 in
Paulding County, Ohio leaving as his widow, Aurel Carey and the following heirs
by next estate of inheritance: Shadrack Hudson Carey, David C. Carey, Lydia Ann
Carey William Carey, Caroline Carey, Wirona H. Carey and Eliza Jane wife of William
Allen. That at death of Isaac he owned S½ SE fractional quarter Section 19 containing 76.92 acres and NE fractional quarter Section 30 containing 79.30 acres, all
in Township 3 North Range 4 East Paulding County, Ohio in which Aurel holds dower
interest. (489)

ANKNEY CEMETERY - PAULDING COUNTY, OHIO

Contributed by: Mrs. Mary Ellen Bowman, R. R. 5, Columbia City, Ind. 46725

This cemetery is located north of County Road 180 and is on County Road 127, about midway, in Emerald Township, Paulding County, Ohio.

ANKNEY, Alvin son of J. & M. Ankney died 1 Aug. 1877 aged 3y 1m 8d
    Christian born 13 Sept. 1809 died 22 Aug. 1894
    David died 2 Feb. 1895 aged 72y 9m 6d Father (note: this stone is
      toppled over and could well have inscription on the underside.)
    E. B. born 2 Aug. 1897 died 15 Aug. 1898 aged 1 y & 13d
    E. H. 1869-1911 (very large stone, toppled over)
    Elizabeth wife of Christian Ankney born 11 Feb. 1826 died 6 Spet. 1906
    Elsie M. daughter of D. H. & E. 1895-1895
    Emanul A. 1867-1937
    Emma 1870-1930
    Fredric A. 1870-1924
    George died 28 Feb. 1923 aged 77y 11m 25d GAR
    Gideon son of D. & E. died 29 June 1864 aged 3 days
    James A. son of D. H. & E. 1903-1903
    James H. son of D. & N. Ankney died 11 May 1859 aged 1m & 1d
    Mabel A. Daughter of J. H. & Nettie Ankney died 14 Oct. 1901 aged 1y 1m & 11d
    Mabria died 12 Nov. 1887 aged 10y 8m __(?)d
    Margaret died 19 June 1887 aged 65y & 4d (note: see Mumford)
    Mary A. daughter of D. & E. died 4 June 1877 aged 1y & 1d
    Mary Ann daughter of J. & E. Ankney died 29 Aug. 1873 aged 4m & 7d
    Nancy A. died 15 June 1859 aged 30y 9m 2d Mother
    Virgel I. daughter of J. H. & N. died 24 Aug. 1908 aged 4m & 26d
    William son of D. & N. A. died 10 Oct. 1853 aged 1y 11m 1d
BROWN, Infant son of S. & I. A. Brown died 2 September 1897
    Ada daughter of S. L. & C. Brown died 27 July 1871 aged 11m & 7d
    Catherine wife of S. L. Brown died 12 February 1879 aged 52y & 3d (note:
      this is another large stone which is toppled over and could very
      well have an inscription on the underside.)
    Elmer C. son of S. & I. A. Brown died 6 Aug. 1896 aged 1y & 14d
    Emett R. 1910-1911; Isadore 1892-1895; Lola M. 1906-1906; Roy J. 1908-1908
    _____(?) (note: this could be S. L., husband of Catherine Brown. There
      is a GAR standard in the ground by this stone and it is logical
      to assume that the husband may be buried here.)
    Susan F. 1898-1900; William 1896-1898
BOLIER, Julia A. 1852-1900   Martin 1843-1902
CHIPPI, Martha A. born 30 Nov. 1932 died 1 Dec. 1932 1/2 day (note: this is a
    handmade stone.)
FACKLER, Amanda daughter of W. & E. Fackler died __(?) May 1877 aged 7 years
GOOD, Anna E. wife of D. C. Good died 16 Mar. 1888 aged 30y 6m __(?)d
    Sarah J. died 27 Aug. 1888 aged 11m & 1d
GEROD, Emma daughter of S. & A. Gerod died 6 Oct. 1878(?) aged 9y 8m 3d
LEVEY, John son of J. & S. 1876-1887 (note: another large stone which has toppled
    over)
    Susan 1849-1887
MUMFORD, Marget died 17 Oct. 1888 aged 30y 6m 2d (note: this name is inscribed on
    same stone with that of Margaret Ankney).

MYERS, John died 20 Feb. 1882 aged 81y 5m & 3d (note another stone toppled over.)
SHANKS, Mary A. wife of Christopher Shanks died 19 July 1905 aged 17y 2m & 9d
SHAWVER, Emma wife of S. D. Shawver 1876-1900
STEINMAN, Jacob born 28 Feb. 1786 died 21 Nov. 1875
WOLF, Lizzie M. daughter of Rachel Wolf died 7 May 1889 aged 1y 11m & 9d
       Infant son of J. W. & E. J. Wolf died 8 Jan. 1880
       John W. 1857-1917, Father   Eliva J. 1857-1897, Mother
- - - - - - - --

ANKNEY FARM CEMETERY - PAULDING COUNTY, OHIO

This cemetery is located in Emerals Township, Paulding County, Ohio, on County
Road 121.

ANKNEY, Martha J. daughter of H. & L. (?). Ankney died 21 Jan. 1864 aged 15y 5m 18d
       Michel died 16 Feb. 1861 (or 1864) aged 56y 11m 16d
       Mikel died 9 Dec. 1876 aged 33y & 11d, GAR
       Susana A. wife of M. Ankney died 20 Dec. 1861 (or 1864) aged 7_(?)y
          11(?)m--(?)d
CHEMIN, Emmanuel D. son of E. & E. Chemin died 30 Sept. 1864 aged 1y 3(or 8)m 2d
       Franklin son of E. & E. Chemin died 1877 aged 2m & 10 (or 18)d
       Leory died 21 March 1887 aged 1 (?)y & 8m
HANENKRAT, Anna E. born 17 Oct. 1845 died 20 Sept. 1873
JENKINS, Infant son of J. M. & R. Jenkins - 26 Apr. 1879
STALL, Sarah E. daughter of C. & E. Stall died 10 Mar. 1854 aged 1y & 11m
WOLF, Elizabeth wife of Simon Wolf died 5 Oct. 1865 aged 25y 7m 17d
WOODCOCK, Hannah J. wife of Dr. B. B. Woodcock died 2 July 1870 aged 61y 7m 21d
(note: also in this abandoned cemetery were foot markers with initials:)
          H.J.W.   F.C.
- - - - - - - - -

GORDON CEMETERY - PAULDING COUNTY, OHIO

Contributed by: Mrs. Mary Ellen Bowman, R. R. 5, Columbia City, Ind. 46725

BAKER, Ethan F. 1891-1899 (Brother)   Gladys D. 1894-1899 (Sister)
BREECE, Elizabeth died 2 Nov. 1893 aged 76y 10m & 13 (or 18)d
       P. C. died 13 Mar. 1891 aged 77y & 16d (apparently a soldier)
       Elizabeth died 29 Nov. 1892 aged 76y 8m & 13d
       Betsey A. 1857-1887
       Hannah M. wife of Henry C. Breece born 10 June 1861 died 15 Feb. 1893
       Milton son of H. H. & H. M. Breece died 30 Aug. 1891 aged 2y 6m & 19d
       Infant daughter of H. G. & H. M. Breece born 15 Dec. 1885 died 25 Dec. 1885
          aged 9 days
       _____(?) - "In remembrance of H. C. & H. M. Breece born 30 April 1884 died
          30 April 1884"
BREININGER, Irene died 9 June 1908 (note: no further inscription)
DURFEY, Iloe M. daughter of E.L.&M.A. Durfey died 15 Dec. 1897 aged 7 (or 8) y
       3m & 5d
GORDPM, Anna wife of Samuel Gordon died 22 Mar. 1866 aged 63y 1m & 6d
       Samuel died 9 Jan. 1873 aged 78y 9m & 22d
       Sarah wife of Samuel Gordon died 29 Jan. 1849 aged 52y 10m & 8d

GORDON, Martha C. wife of Coe Gordon born 29 May 1827 died 24 May 1873
    Alice G. 1871-1943   Samuel 1854-1923
    Infant daughter of S.E.&A.G. died 21 Feb. 1895 aged 1 day
    Malinda died 19 Feb. 1904 aged 63y 10m 13d
    William died 11 May 1874 aged 49y 9m & 11d
    Harry son of L. _.(?) & M. Gordon died 8 Feb. 1896 aged 8y 1m & 28d
HUGHES, Elizabeth wife of A.L. Hughes died 21 June 1852 (or 1854) aged 21y & 25d
HEAZLIT, Caroline M. wife of D.W. Heazlit died 5 July 1897 aged 70y 8m & 11d
HOWEY, Robert H. 1851-1924; Mary M. 1860-1933; William A. 1847-1920
    Mary J. 1810-1895
HUTCHINS, Jemina 1861-1929   Albert 1859-1934
    Dessie F. daughter of A. & M. Hutchins died 19 Aug. 1895 aged 6m & 16d
JACKSON, Albert M. died 22 Sept. 1875 aged 23y 5m & 2d
    Cora M. 1863-1931   Stephen O. 1851-1918
KOPP, Infant son of Jacob and Liza (note: no other inscription)
KLENDER, Dora 1854-1935   Frederick 1844-1925
    Carl son of F. & D. Klender 1891-1893
LEICHTY, William - Company G (or C), 14th Ohio Infantry
LANDIS, G. Frances daughter of J. & S. Landis died 12 Sept. 1863 aged 1y 8m & 9d
MILLER, Olive Durfey 1888-1911
MORLEY, Hannah wife of Alexander Morley 1871-1896
    Alexander died 1894 aged 3m & 7d (note: this is assumed to also be a
        Morley, since it is in the Morley family area.)
    Joel died 1896 aged 5m & 26d (note: same assumption as above.)
    James H. son of J.& (?). Morley died 18 (or 19) March 1886 aged 5y 5m & 18d
    Amelia E. 1849-1890, (Mother)   William 1851-1923, (Father)
    Harry C. - 1890 aged 5m & 2d   W. Nelson 1880-1916
MEADS, Elma L. daughter of M.A.&S.J. Meads died 18 Feb. 1910 aged 13d
OURS, Charles 1828-1899
    Emma wife of Charles Ours died 7 Apr. 1901 aged 73y 2m & 27d
ROBERTSON, Samuel G. son of S.G.& Eva died 21 June 1877 aged 7y & 8d
SNELL, Andrew J. 1857-1923
    William M. died 11 Apr. 1902 aged 17y 2m & 22d
SHEETS, Dora H. 1882-1914
THOMPSON, Alexander 1868-1926 (Son); Laura A. 1837-1909 (Mother)
    Katie A. 1868-1920

- - - - - - -- - - - -

HASH CEMETERY - PAULDING COUNTY, OHIO

Contributed by: Mrs. Mary Ellen Bowman, R. R. 5, Columbia City, Ind. 46725

This little cemetery is on a dirt road in Emerald Township, Paulding County, Ohio.
Although the surname is found as Hasch in the cemetery, the official name seems to
be Hash Cemetery.

ANKNEY, John H. 1846-1914, GAR
    Mary A. wife of John H. Ankney 1846-1912
BANDY, Anna E. daughter of J.&S.L. Bandy died 14 Sept. 1873 aged 1y 1m & 1d (*x)
    Charline wife of Peter Bandy 1852-_____(Mother)
    Clara V. daughter of J. & S. L. Bandy died 4 Feb. 1879 aged 1y & 16d (*x)

BANDY, J. Hazen son of J. & S. L. Bandy died 10 May 1888 aged 9m & 3d   (*x)
        John died 3 Oct. 1930 aged 84y 7m & 5d (*)
        Peter 1850-1915 (Father)
        In memory of Submit L. wife of John Bandy died 20 Feb. 1896 aged 41y 1m
                            & 5d (*)
COMADOLL, Dennis son of P. & C. Comadoll died 14 Mar. 1898 aged 16y & 4d
HASCH, Betty Lou - 1922
        Caroline wife of John Hasch 1845-1905   John 1848-1925
        Cleo - 1904 aged 4m   Leo A. 1902-1903
        Clifford H. - 1918
        Floyd J. 1906-1920
KINKLE, Conrad died 9 Oct. 1868 (note: balance of information buried underground)
        Susanna wife of C. Kinkle died 22 Mar. 1866 aged 37y 11m & 17d
KINZER, Anna M. wife of John D. Kinzer died 22 Apr. 1894 aged 72y 9m & 18d
        Gottlop son of J. D. & A. M. Kinzer died 3 Sept. 1860 aged 1y & 4m
        J. C. died 14 Feb. 1887 aged 42y 3m & 14d
        Jacob 1861-1909, aged 48y
        John D. died 29 Oct. 1858 aged 5y 8m & 12
        John D. died 1 Mar. 1895 aged 77y & 8d
        Mary wife of Jacob Kinzer 1866-1958
NEDROW, Anna L. died 24 Oct. 1888 aged 19y 1m & 12d
        John died 28 Oct. 1871 aged 31y 7m & 18d GAR
WEINMANN, Mary A. wife of George Weinmann 1879-1946   George 1878-1957
WEIPPERT, Infant daughter of J. J. & Nettie (or Hettie) born 1900 died 1901 aged
                            10d
        Dorothy M. died 26 May 1914 (note: balance of stone is buried)
        Mildred L. daughter of J. J. & Nettie (or Hettie) born 1902 died 1906
                        aged 4y 1m & 10d
YEARLING, Tomy - 1904   Kattie - 1904
WEIPPERT, Glades R. born Nov. 20, 1910 died 17 June 1912

* = All names on one stone

x = Each of these names has separate stones also, all weathered, not totally
    legible, and the stones are piled along the fence.

Contributed by:- Mrs. Mary Ellen Bowman, R. R. 5, Columbia City, Indiana 46725

This cemetery is located on the east side of State Route 49, south of the Defiance-Paulding County line (Ohio), in Paulding County; back a lane, ine the woods on the Clark farm.

BRUSH, Mary A. wife of G. H. Brush died 10 Feb. 1861 aged 20y 1m 17d
 Mariet G. died 2 Mar. 1849 aged 8m & 9d
 Luella P. born 29 Nov. 1861 died 27 Dec. 1861
 Marriett M. born 19 Mar. 1859 died 1 Dec. 1865
BARNAND (or BARNARD), Oliver died 4 Mar. 1872 aged 33y 11m 11d
BANKS, Jedediah died 13 Dec. 1872 aged 16y 3m 27d, Copl. Co. A, 132 Ohio Infantry
 Caroline D. died 31 July 1884 aged 38y 1m (?)d
 Sarah J. wife of J. T. Banks died 6 (or 8) Aug. 1872 aged 27y 1m 1d
 Richard son of ____(?) Banks died 10 Sept. 1874 aged 11m & 18d
BRUSH, William H. born 17 Sept. 1855.died 6 Mar. 1879
 Zachry son of M. W. & L. C. Brush died 7 Jan. 1883 aged 18y 9m 26d
 Louisa C. wife of M. W. Brush died 30 Nov. 1891 aged 59y 7m 25d
COLLINS, John died 6 Sept. 1887 aged 20y 7m & 10d
 Harriet died 11 June 1879 aged 60y 10m & 17d
CLARK, Joseph died 2 May 1873 aged 58y 2m & 17d
COBY, J. S. died 3 May 1860 aged 38 (or 88) plus years
COTTRELL, Emma C. daughter of N. ___(?) & M. A. Cottrell died ___(?) 1897 aged 4m 13
CHAMPION, Julia M. born 15 Apr. 1878 died 22 Apr. 1878
 George W. born 23 Dec. 1842 died 17 June 1901, Coprl. Co. I, 100O Ohio Inf.
 Charles Bruce 1873-1931
DONAT, John son of J. & P. Donat died 21 Sept. 1867 aged 29y 6m
 Polly daughter of J. Donat died 20 Feb. 186_(?) aged 15y & 8m(?)
 Jonathan died 11 Aug. 1879 aged 75y & 1m
DUNKIN, David died 4 Dec. 1882 aged 84y 3m 16d
 Carolina wife of David Dunkin born 27 Jan. 1821 died 3 Mar. 1911
 George H. son of D. & C. Dunkin died 5 December 1882 aged 18y 4m & 28d
 (Note: Even though the inscription on the last stone would indicate
  father and son. the inscription clearly states "father" and "brother".)
ELY, Francis M. ___(?) of N. H. & J. A. Ely died 20 Dec. 1866 aged 4y 7m & 17d
FRIEND, Margaret died 14 March 1878 aged 48y 7m & 8d
 George died 5 Nov. 1894 (aged 73y 9m & 4d)
FITZPATRICK, Mary Rosa (Note: Nb dates legible) aged 3y & 15d
GORDON, Sarah M. C. born 6 May 1808 died 10 Oct. 1880
GRAM, John W. died 12(?) Nov. 18__(?)
 Harriet wife of S.(?) Gram died 26 Oct. 1876 aged 39 years
GROSE, Ida M. 1881-1964
GLADWIN, Mary died 15 Aug. 1883 aged 38y 10m & 3d
HOOK, Margaret wife Frank Oswalt died 27 May 1882 aged 22y & 19d
 Levi son of John and Mary Hook died 6 Mar. 1861 aged 2y 1m & 6d
 ____(?) daughter of J. M. (J.&M.?) Hook died 30 Jan. 1876(?) aged 11m 20d
HALL, James died 11 May 1866 aged 35y & 11m
HIGGENS, Robert (Note: Nothing else visible on stone.)
HART, Mary Brill (note: Nothing else visible on stone.)

HOPPER, Laton (?) A. died 10 Dec. 1871 aged 6y 7m

HARRIS, Winnie B. daughter of J. & F. Harris died 22 Sept. 1880 aged 3y & 12d

HOOVER, George H. 1830-1899

JOHNSTON, Simmion D. son of A. W. & C. E. Johnston died 11 Jan. 1900 aged 21y 4m 10d
     Wilson V. son of A. W. & C. E. Johnston died 6 Jan. 1899 aged 18y 4m & 18d

KEMMERER, Becca A.*; Manda*; Lydia* (*Note: Separate stones for each, but no dates
                          on any of the three.)

KEMMER, William J. died 6 May 1894 aged 37y 8m 8d

LAYMON, Eli 1839-1894

MIDDAUGH, Lovey L. daughter of A. & E. Middaugh died 15 (or 17) Aug. <u>1820</u> aged
                                   1y(?)m (could be 11) 2d
     Alfred died 6 June 1897 aged 65y

MUNGER, John D. born 15 July 1812 died 8 Feb. 1880, Father
     Sophia born 27 Nov. 1814 died 30 Apr. 1885, Mother
     Trifena R. born 12 June 1844 died 20 Apr. 1853
     Zenith N. died 25 Jan. 1889 aged 376 & 28d
     Luther W. son of Z. N. & F.(?) Munger died 23 Aug. 1892 aged 8y 3m & 16d
     Edmond died 1 Sept. 1899 aged 21y 9m & 5d

McALLA, Thomas 1803-1865 Catherine wife of Thomas McAlla 1814-1855
     David son of Thomas & Catherine McAlla 1835-1855
     Martha daughter of Thomas & Catherine McAlla 1843-1880
     Rebecca daughter of Thomas & Catherine McAlla 1847-1849
     Hester daughter of Thomas & Catherine McAlla 1855-1855
     Isaac(?) Co. I. 1000 Ohio Infantry

McCORMICK, J. (Note: No dates)
     Harriet wife of J. McCormick 1834-1859
     William F. 1854-1857
     Infant son of J. & P. - 1873

OSWALT, Margaret Hook wife of Frank Oswalt died 27 May 1882 aged 22y & 19d
     Roy H. 1880-1902 aged 21y 8m & 15d, Co. F, 30 USU (or USV)
     Minerva A. daughter of J. & C. (or G.) Oswalt died 26 Apr. 1871 aged
                                   11m & 22d
     O. W. born 20 Mar. 1852 died 14 Sept. 1853
     Sarah born 28 June 1841 died 12 Dec. 1854
     Henry born 8 Nov. 1811 died 12 Oct. 1892
     Emily wife of Henry Oswalt; daughter of John Tomilson; granddaughter of
               Andrew Huston of Cumberland, Maryland, born 3 Mar. 1811 died 21
               Dec. 1883 aged 72y 8m & 20d
     Florus born 17 May 1878 died 15 Jan. 1913
     John born 20 Sept. 1837 died 22 June 1917
     E. A. wife of John Oswalt born 8 May 1841 died 24 June 1909
     Corpl. John, Co. C, 14th Ohio Infantry
     Eva Dell (Note: No stone; recent burial with marker from Perkins & Reeb
                  Funeral Home, Hicksville, Ohio.)
     Rozetta died 1898 (Note: Marker same as above)
     C. 1858-1958 (Note: Marker same as above)

PURDY, Joseph M. died 5 July 1870 aged 41y 8m & 29d
     Sarah Jane wife of Joseph Purdy born 9 Aug. 1832(?) died 16 June 1902
     Nathaniel son of J. & S. born and died 28 Dec. 1839

PERRY, Esther O. daughter of N. J. & C. A. died 10 Feb. 1865 aged 5(or 6)y 8m & 12d
     Charlotte A. wife of N. J. Perry died 23 Mar. 1895 aged 51y 11m & 19d
     Cpl. Newton J., Co. I, 1000 Ohio Infantry
     Herbert S. son of W. S. & E̅. J. Perry died 29 Jan. 1898 aged 9m & 6d
     Ethelinda L. daughter of G. S. & L.(?) Perry born 12 Apr. 1906 died 15 Apr.
                                                                              1906
PARRY, Robert died 22 Feb. 1893 aged 5y & 11d
SE̅ELY, A. R. died 12 July 1837 (or 1857) aged 15y __(?)m & __(?)d
SAVAGE, Daniel died 1 Apr. 1869 aged 23 (or 25)y & 18d, Co. G̅. 14th Ohio Infantry
SCHOOLEY, Infant son of O. F. & O. B. Schooley died 18 Mar. 1898 aged 1y 5m & 12d
SMITH, Rhuville V. 1847-1885
TEEGARDIN, Viola L. born 2 Feb. 1908 died 31 July 1951
WENTWORTH, Rachael wife of T. Wentworth, Esq. died 5 June 1858 aged 66y 9m & 29d
ZUBER, Joseph died 19 May 1856 aged 42y & 3m
     Elizabeth wife of Joseph Zuber died 16 May 1856 aged 39y & 10m
     Rozeta daughter of J. & E. Zuber died 24 Aug. 1852 aged 10m &__(?)d

The following records were taken from "Death Record 1" located in the Probate Court at the court house at Paulding. Page on which record may be found in the original book is given in parenthesis. Only persons over 40 years of age have been included in this record. Abbreviations: d=died; a=age; m=married; m=married; w=widow or widower; s=single; pd=place of death; pb=place of birth; res=residence. Residence is same as place of death unless stated otherwise.

BUDD, Eli - d 7-6-1867; a 46y; m; pd Brown twp.; pb Delaware Co., Ohio. (2)
LICHTY, Ann - d 7-22-1867; a 57-5-11; w; pd Crane twp.; pb Maryland. (2)
MALLETT, Henry - d 9-3-1867; a 53-5-25; m; pd Brown twp.; pb Brown twp. (2)
CREARY, Robert M. - d 9-30-1867; a 55y; m; pd Paulding twp.; pb Penn. (2)
EDDYBURN, Anna - d 9-10-1867; a 59y; m; pd Paulding twp.; pb Trumbull Co., Ohio. (2)
SHEPARD, Catharine - d 11-26-1867; a 45y; m; pd Carryall twp.; pb Ireland. (2)
BURT, Lot - d 5-13-1868; a 51-3-19; m; pd Brown twp.; pb Morro Co., Ohio. (2)
BARNHOUSE, E.S. - d 5-20-1868; a87y 4m; m; pd Brown twp.; pb (not given). (2)
MOORE, Alexander - d 4-26-1868; a 62y; m; pd Carryall twp.; pb (not given). (2)
SLOUGH, Nancy Ann - d 8-10-1868; a 52y; m; pd Carryall twp.; pb (not given). (2)
ZELOFF, Peter - d 9-10-1868; a 64y; m; pd Carryall twp.; pb (not given). (4)
WOODCOX, Isaac - d 9-21-1868; a 65-7-25; m; pd Carryall twp.; pb (not given). (4)
ZELLOFF, Peter - d 9-12-1868; a 55y; m; pd Carryall twp.; pb unknown. (4)
BAYARD, George - d 10-2-1868; a 50y; m; pd Carryall twp.; pb unknown. (4)
LANDIS, John - d 12-31-1868; a 61-8-24; m; pd Auglaize twp.; pb Penn. (4)
BABLE, Jane - d 2-7-1869; a 58y 16d; m; pd Auglaize twp.; pb Ohio. (4)
WARREN, Lucrecia - d 12-28 a 55y; m; pd Crane twp.; pb Va. (4)
FORNASH (FOMASH), William - d 11-22-1868; a 45-2-20; m; pd Crane twp.; pb Va.;
          father, William Fornash or Fomash; mother, Ann Formash or Fomash. (4)
BARNHOUSE, Thos. - d 3-16-1869; a 80y 8m; w; pd Brown twp.; pb Penn. (4)
GREEN, Sarah - d 1-12-1869; a 67y 9m; m; pd Brown twp.; pb Penn. (4)
WILLIAMS, Lysander - d 10-5-1868; a 52-10-15; m; pd Auglaize twp.; pb N.Y. (4)
FRENCH, Harriet Amanda - d 3-29-1869; a 49y; m; pd Auglaize twp.; pb New York. (6)
BROWN, Elizabeth - d 2-29-1868; a 43-3-9; m; pd Washington twp.; pb Ohio. (6)
HUTCHINS, Joshua - d 2-20-1869; a 67-3-19; m; pd Washington twp.; pb New York. (6)
HOIT, Betsy - d 2-28-1868; a 70y; w; pd Washington twp.; pb Kentucky. (6)
CRAWFORD, William - d 11-24-1868; a 55 (or 35)y; m; pd Washington twp.; pb Ky. (6)
BELLIS, William - d 2-23-1869; a 68y; m; pd Benton twp.; pb Ohio. (6)
SHEPHERD, John - d 9-22-1867; a 80y; m; pd Harrison twp.; pb Kentucky. (6)
SHEPHERD, Mary - d 4-15-1868; a 68-10-7; w; pd Harrison twp.; pb Kentucky. (6)
RODENBAUGH, Philip - d 4-22-1868; a 62-3-28; m; pd Harrison twp.; pb Germany. (6)
HOWELL, Catherine - d 11-18-1868; a 54y; m; pd Harrison twp.; pb Penn. (6)
COUGHLIN, Sarah Jane - d 10-20-1868; a 40y; m; pd Jackson twp.; pb Ireland. (6)
COUGHLIN, Dennis - d 10-29-1868; a 63y; m; pd Jackson twp.; pb Ireland;
          father, Michael Coughlin. (6)
McPHERSON, Wealthy - d 4-4-1869; a 55y; w; pd Paulding Co. Inf.; pb Penn. (6)
KINKLE, Konrad - d 10-9-1868; a 54-9-11; w; pd Emerald twp.; pb German. (6)
HARTZELL, Verina - d 1-24-1869; a 49y 10m; w; pd Emerald twp.; pb Switzerland;
          father, John Rey; mother, Elizabeth Rey. (6)
McNAMARA, James - d 7-13-1868; a 48y; m; pd Emerald twp.; pb Co. Clar. Ireland. (6)
LAMBERT, Joseph C. - d 8-7-1868; a (born) 5-3-1820; m; pd Latty twp.; pb Ohio. (6)
STALL, Christopher - d 11-8-1869; a 58y; m; pd Carryall twp.; pb Ohio. (6)
MAJOR, George - d 7-22-1869; a 60y 22d; m; pd Carryall twp.; pb Germany. (8)
WORDEN, Ira - d 12-6-1869; a 73y; w; pd Carryall twp.; pb New York. (8)

JONES, Catherine - d 4-11-1870; a 73y 6m; s; pd Brown twp.; pb Penn. (8)
HARBAUGH, Frederick G. - d 2-12-1870; a 72-4-10; m; pd Brown twp.; pb Penn. (8)
FREDERICK, Peter - d 2-10-1870; a 55-3-5; m; pd Brown twp.; pb Ohio. (8)
KLRICK, P.H. - d 2-12-1870; a 67y; m; pd Washington twp.; pb unknown. (8)
LUCAS, Nathaniel - d 2-13-1869; a 56-2-3; m; pd Washington twp.; pb Ohio. (8)
STERN, Aaron - d 9-6-1870; a 40y; m; pd Washington twp.; pb Tenn. (8)
CATTELL, Tabitha - d 2-20-1870; a 55-1-15; s; pd Washington twp.; pb Ohio. (8)
HARGER(?), Mary - d 11-5-1869; a 67y; m; pd Washington twp.; pb Ohio. (8)
YOUNG (or FOURNY), Mary - d 9-11-1869; a 80y; w; pd Jackson twp.; pb Ireland. (8)
DOBSON, Kesiah - d 2-15-1870; a 40y; pd Jackson twp.; pb unknown. (8)
BONE, Charlotte - d 2-17-1870; a 50y; pd Jackson twp.; pb Unknown. (8)
CARLE, Mary - d 9-15-1869; a 80-11-6; w; pd Emerald twp.; pb Maryland. (8)
DUTTERER, Francis C.-d 11-3-1869;a 62-11-23; m; pd Emerald twp.; pb Germany. (10)
CHANEY, Margaret - d July 1869; a 65y; s; pd Paulding tw.; pb Ohio. (10)
WALKER, Theodoreck - d 3-26-1870; a 67y; m; pd Blue Creek twp.; pb Virginia. (10)
MURFREY(?), Fanny - d 8-27-1869; a 71 years; m; Latty twp.; pb Virginia. (10)
SCHOOLEY, Olivia S. - d 9-4-1870; a 49-11-10; m; pd Auglaize twp.; pb Ohio. (10)
MAY, Jacob - d 9-25-1870; a 80y 28d; pd Brown twp.; pb Penn.; w. (10)
STARR, Susannah - d 2-23-1871; a 61-9-20; m; pd Brown twp.; pb Ohio. (12)
SHISLER, Samuel - d 9-17-1870; a 77y 1m; m; pd Brown twp.; pb Virginia. (12)
PURDY, Joseph Miller - d 7-6-1870; a 41y 9m; m; d Carryall twp.; b Holmes Co. Oh.(12)
ROCK, Jeanette - d 8-11-1870; a 64y; m; pd Crane twp.; pb Prussia. (12)
BRUDLE, David - d 6-7-1870; a 69y; m; pd Crane twp.; pb Genessee Co., N.Y. (12)
NEWTON, Caroline E. - d 3-3-1871; a 42y; m; pd Crane twp.; pb Ft. Ann, N.Y. (12)
ASHLEY, John - d 4-3-1871; a 45y; s; pd Crane twp.; pb Canada. (12)
EATON, Betsy - d 11-27-1870; a 73y; w; Crane twp.; b N.Y. (12)
NOBLE, Alexander - d Oct. 1870; a 73y; w; d Emerald twp.; b Ireland. (12)
WHELAN, Thomas - d 3-10-1871; a 72-9-3; m; pd Emerald twp.; pb Ireland. (12)
CHANEY, Sophia - d 9-25-1870; a 52-11-16; m; pd Harrison twp.; pb Franklin Co. (14)
RYAN, John - d 2-17-1871; a 48y; m; pd Jackson twp.; pb Jackson. (14)
MORRISON, James - d 11-15-1870; a 63y; m; pd Jackson twp.; pb Scotland. (14)
POINER, Thomas C. - d 7-20-1870; a 61-3-20; m; pd Jackson twp.; pb Ohio. (14)
PLUMB, Elizabeth W. - d 3-8-1871; a 59-7-20; m; pd Washington; pb Dutchess Co., N.Y.
(14)
GROSSENBANDUR, Samuel - d 7-23-1871; a 71y; m; pd Auglaize twp.; pb Germany. (16)
LANDIS, Solomon - d 2-1-1872; a 51-5-13; m; pd Paulding Co.; pb Tuscarawas Co. O.(16
NEPHUS, George - d 2-2-1872; a 55y; w; pd Auglaize twp.; pb Delaware Co., Ohio. (16
ECKERT, Fidelia - d 3-17-1872; a 67y; m; pd Auglaize twp.; pb Germany. (16)
MANSFIELD, Rosana - d 3-15-1872; a 55-1-11; __; pd Auglaize twp.; pb unknown. (16)
BYNDS, James - d Sept. 1871; a 69y 9m; w; pd Brown twp.; pb Brown twp. Blacksmith.(1
GREEN, David - d 12-30-1871; a 73y; --; pd Brown twp.; pb Vermont. Farmer. (16)
BIDLACK, James F. - d 7-24-1871; a 47y; --; pd Brown twp.; pb Penn. Farmer. (16)
BIDLACK, Mary - d 7-9-1871; a 51-2-22; --; pd Brown twp.; pb Vermont. (16)
AYRES, Sarah - d 10-4-1871; a 86y; --; pd Brown twp.; pb Fayette Co., Penn. (16)
DEALY, Henry - d 10-23-1871; a 59-5-11; m; pd Bruton; pb Virginia. Farmer. (16)
SNOOK, Annie - d 1-3-1872; a 59-3-25; w; pd Carryall twp.; pb Penn. (16)
LYSHER, Matilda - d 2-10-1872; a 72y 15d; m; Carryall twp.; pb Carryall twp. (18)
FISHER, Mary R. - d 3-5-1872; a 45y; m; pd Antwerp; pb N.Y. (18)
DUNDERMAN, Philip - d 7-18-1871; a 62y; w; pd Carryall twp.; pb Germany. (18)
SHIRLEY, John J. d 3-4-1872; a 46-5-26; m; pd Antwerp; pb Ross Co., Ohio. (18)
GORDON, George F.R. - d 6-3-1871; a 58-9-20; m; pd Crane twp.; pb N.Y. (18)
WOLFF, John - d 9-18-1871; a 47-1-7; m; pd Crane twp.; pb Bavaria. (18)

334

HUNT, Klune - d 11-17-1871; a 46-2-4; m; pd Crane twp.; pb Bavaria. (18)
CHANEY, Emily - d 3-24-1872; a 42-3-27; m; pd Crane twp.; pb Clarmont Co. (18)
HALL, William - d 8-14-1871; a 74-6-14; w; pd _____ N.Y.; former res Crane twp. (18)
GEARY, Michael - d 3-6-1872; a 42y; s; pd Emerald twp.; pb Ireland. Laborer. (18)
WHETSEL, Margaret - d 7-21-1871; a 54y; m; pd Emerald twp.; pb Africa. Colored. (18)
ANDERSON, Rebecca - d 5-9-1871; a 44y 10m; m; pd Jackson twp.; pb Logan Co., Ohio.(20)
MERLIN, Peter N. -d9-16-1871; a 70-1-15; w; pd Jackson twp.; pb unknown. Farmer. (20)
MILLER, John - d 2-7-1872; a 72y10m; w; pd Paulding twp.; b Shenandoa, Va. (20)
MILLER, Rebecca - d 1-26-1872; a 65-11-9; m; pd Paulding; pb Belmont Co., Ohio. (20)
BEVILHIMER, Corod - d 11-12-1871; a 43-2-9; m; pd Latty twp.; pb Penn. (20)
BIGLER, Jonathan - d 12-14-1871; a 60-5-13; m; pd Washington; pb N.Y. Farmer. (20)

PAULDING COUNTY, OHIO - MARRIAGES 1839-1845

The following records were taken from "Marriage Record 1" as found in the court
house (Probate Court) at Paulding. "Marriage Record 1" contains marriages for the
period 1839-1860. It is a transcript and a very poor one at that, made about 1871.
Whether by accident or because they were never recorded, the marriages (other than
a few) from 1845 through 1851 are not included in this book. On page 8 the marriages jump from 1843 to the 1852-1853 period. A few marriages for the year 1844
are recorded in the back of the book with a section of ministers licenses, but the
missing period is not covered anywhere in this book. With the hope that this
missing period of marriages will eventually be found, we will give the marriages
in two separate lists--the first list covering the 1839 to 1845 period and the
second list covering the 1852-1853 period. We might add that at this time the
transcribed "Marriage Record 1" is the only book available for this period--
what happened to the original book is not now known. Page on which the record may
be found is given in parenthesis.

ADAMS, Armstrong C. to Sarah Damsheath	6-6-1841	(4)
ADAMS, Charles to Mary Ann Plummer	10-30-1844	(56)
BAILY, Joseph to Christena Vogelly	5-21-1840	(1)
BANKS, Richard C. to Caroline Slate (or Slute)	9-21-1843	(54)
BARNWILL, John to Ann King	2-25-1845	(57)
BILLIN, John to Mary Hurst	9-28-1842	(7)
CAMPBELL, John to Lydia Harrell	5-1-1845	(57)
CAREY, Shadrach Hudson to Rachel Shirley	11-11-1842	(7)
CARTER, Calvin H. to Elmaretta Sales	9-13-1841	(4)
CLARK, George to Caroline Kimmel	3-16-(1843?)	(54)
CLARK, Joseph to Eliza Jane Hughes	11-9-1843	(54)
CLARK, Peter F. to Nancy Quinn	12-22-1844	(57)
CLEMMER, Eli to Deborah Mason	9-16-1841	(3)
COOPER, Royal D. to Nancy Caims	1-6-1841	(3)
DELONG, Solomon to Maria Landis	8-26-1841	(4)
DODD, William to Mary Thompson	10-3-1841	(5)
DONOVAN, Dennis to Julia Ann Donovan	12-20-1840	(3)
EARTABOUGH, Peter to Louisa Thomas	12-13-1840	(2)
EMERSON, John to Susan S. Taylor	3-22-1842	(5)

FLEMING, Matthew to Mary Ann Champion   10-15-1840   (2)
GAMBLE, George P. T. to Nancy Glassmire   11-16-1839   (1)
GARDNER, Charles to Mary Shaw   1-18-1844   (54)
GRICE, John F. to Elizabeth Lanea(?)   11-16-1840   (2)
GROVES, William S. to Elizabeth Wilson   7-27-1843   (8)
HAUSHER(?), Jacob to Eliza White   7-10-1841   (4)
HELMICK, John R. to Cordelia Jane Hurd   12-24-1839   (1)
HUDSON, Samuel W. to Mary Ann Bartlett   4-19-1842   (7)
INMAN, Theodore to Sarah Sigler   1-17-1842   (5)
JEFFREY, Oliver T. to Parthena Herriman   1-26-1844   (55)
JOHNSON, Alexander to Matraly Wells   9-13-1843   (7)
LEMAN, Gabrill to Elizabeth Backman   (no day given)   3- -1842   (6)
                                                                   rec. 3-13-1842
McANULLY, John to Margret Doherty   6-28-1842   (6)
McGILLIGUTHY (or McGILLIENDDY), Daniel to   10-10-1843   (54)
                                   Julian Harley (or Hurly)
MURPHA, David to Lucy L. Srouf   4-29-1840   (1)
MURPHY, David to Elizabeth Grove   3-4-1844   (55)
MARCELLAS, Hugh J. to Nancy Elkins   11-20-1840   (3)
MILLER, Lewis to Sara Murphy   (no year given-1843?) 7-11-   (8)
NICHOLL, William to Harriet Bartlett   10-27-1844   (56)
OLIVER, David L. of Williams Co. to Elizabeth Teats   12-27-1840   (3)
                            of Paulding Co.
PHELPS, Edward to Emily R. Eaton   (no date--1842 or 1843?)   (8)
REEKWITH, John to Maheilia Chafell   1-6-1842   (6)
RENNER, Christian to Elizabeth Kline   9-4-1843   (54)
RUNYON, Martin S. to Sarah Ann Banks   12-19-1839   (1)
RUNYON, Martin S. to Eliza Porket   11-25-1941   (5)
SCHOOLEY, Andrew E. to Olivia Romine   5-2-1844   (55)
SNOOK, William N. to Martha Banks   10-1-1840   (2)
SPURRIER, Louis to Elizabeth Spurrier   6-26-1842   (6)
STOHRS, John to Anna Maria Elizabeth Beatty   11-28-1841   (5)
STORES, Hur to Elizabeth Kimmel   9-24-1844   (56)
STROUT, Sunford to Mary Platter   2-5-1842   (6)
TATE, William to Mary Thomas   (no month given)   -23-1844   (55)
TAYLOR, John to Lucretia Bell   11-8-1841   (7)
THOMAS, John to Martha Taylor, both of Brown twp.   7-3-1840   (2)
TRAVIS, John to Mary Platter   9-8-1842   (6)
WENTWORTH, Chare E. to Rebecca Ann Sisson   10-16-1844   (56)
WEST, Calvin Benjamin to Elizabeth L. Hudson   4-19-1842   (7)
WHITE, George to Rebecca _____ (surname not given)   12-27-1840   (3)
WILLIAMSON, George W. to Cynthia Austin   3-1-1841   (3)
                            - - - - -

PAULDING COUNTY, OHIO - MARRIAGES 1852-1853

ASHTON, Zachariah to Elizabeth Bummer (Brunner?)   6-26-1852   (10)
BALL, Jonathan to Catharine Daniels   12-15-1853   (14)
BANKS, Thomas J. to Eliza Ann Spaicer   9-9-1852   (10)
BARCUS, Eli to Eliza Jane Bigley   5-31-1853   (9)
BARTLESON, John Eaton to Melissa Kirkpatrick   9-2-1852   (10)
BEAVER, Henry to Margret Ann Loffelt   10-9-1853   (14)
BENNET, John to Marrilla Hoots   5-5-1853   (12)
BIDLACK, Benjamin to Barbary Miller   (no other date given)   8-   (8)
                                                                  rec. 7-6-1853

336

BLAKLEY, William to Nancy Hank	3-20-1852	(9)
BOGERT, George W. to Sarah Ann Sichty	4-25-1852	(9)
BOLSELL, John to Mary Stephens	3-22-1852	(8)
BRICELECER, Isaac to Harriet James	7-3-1853	(13)
BROWN, David to Sarah Savage	3-21-1852	(9)
BROWN, Henry A. to Sarah M. Slade	4-10-1853	(12)
CAMPBELL, Hamilton to Mary Anderson	10-15-1852	(11)
CARNEY, Isaac to Samantha Harris	7-28-1853	(9)
CHUMPION, Andrew to Nancy Hughes	10-2-1853	(14)
CLINE, Adam to Hulda Holdridge	1-11-1853	(11)
CURTIS, Frederick to Francis Boues	10-27-1853	(14)
GEFFERY, Oliver T. to Mary Amanda Jenkins	7-28-1852	(10)
GOODWIN, Noab (or Noah) to Hannah Suliven	8-24-1852	(11)
HART, Lyman to Hester T. Kingery	3-13-1853	(12)
HARDY, Henry to M. A. Platter	9-23-1852	(10)
HARVIS (HARRIS?), Squire to Margret Barnhill	5-24-1853	(12)
HUGHES, Andre S. to Elizabeth Mathers	11-7-1852	(10)
HUTCHINS, George to Sarah Chester	12-10-1853	(17)
INMAN, David to Sarah Gester	8-16-1853	(13)
KAKE (HAKE), Andrew to E. Geffery	8-25-1853	(13)
KEEFER, Samuel to Sarah Spitsnoggle	10-12-1853	(14)
KINGERY, John to Sarah Bidlack	2-22-1853	(11)
KINGERY, John E. to Sarah A. Green	4-30-1853	(12)
MELLINGER, Freeborn to Jane Mather	2-23-1853	(12)
MELLINGER, Harrison to Catharine Lars	10-21-1853	(15)
MURPHY, Daniel to Hannah Allen	10-16-1853	(15)
NOGGLE, John H. to Rebecca Julian	8-11-1852	(11)
NORTHRUP, William to Rebecca Wilmason	9-16-1852	(11)
PEEUS(?), William to Martha Kimmel	5-18-1853	(16)
PIERCE, Joshua to Matilda Hoover	7-30-1853	(8)
PLUM, Adam to Susan Hank	6-3-1852	(9)
PLUMMER, Joseph to Charlotta Swift	8-8-1853	(13)
RAMBURGH (RUMBAUGH?), Daniel to Tabitha Applegate	12-8-1853	(14)
RUFFNER, Frederick to Catharine McClalin	11-14-1853	(14)
RUMBAUGH, Nathaniel to Hester Murphy	11-20-1853	(15)
RUTH, James to Mary Grundy	1-24-1853	(12)
SAYLOR, Jacob to Eliza Jane Curtis	1-1-1852	(8)
SHIRLEY, Nathan to Mrs. Ann Hankins	5-5-1853	(13)
SHIRLEY, William H. to Julia Burt	12-25-1852	(9)
SHUBERT, Andrew to Mariah Kempt	1-25-1853	(11)
SNELLABARGER, George to Elfinda Durt	8-9-1853	(15)
STURR, Jacob to Loiza Hart	2-6-1853	(12)
WARD, Charles to Neoma McKeul	8-18-1853	(13)
WENTWORTH, David to Mary Ann Eaton (rec. with 1852-53 mar.)	6-26-1856?	(9)
WIMAN, Henry to Leah Mellenger	8-20-1852	(10)
WREN, John to Mary A. Harris	12-31-1853	(16)

PERRY COUNTY, OHIO - UNITED STATES LAND GRANTS

Name	Date	Description	Section Twp. & Range	Named Twp.	Acres	Volume & Page
BUXTON, Thomas	7-7-1816	ne¼	32-18-17	Thorn		A-41
assignee of Peter KINSON						
SAUM, Mathias	9-20-1815	se¼	5-16-16	Reading		A-104
assignee of Philip DUPLER adms. of Fred'k DUPLER, dec'd.						
KING, Christian	3-24-1812	ne¼	17-16-16	Reading		A-234
assignee of Robert ROBINSON						
LANDIS, Henry	8-20-1808	w½	8-16-16	Reading		A-297
assignee of Henry KALLBACK						
McDONALD, Mitchal	9-16-1819	se¼	23-15-16	Jackson		A-553
assignee of James DUTTON						
McDONALD, Mitchal	9-16-1819	ne¼	26-15-16	Jackson		A554
assignee of James DUTTON						
MILLER, Isaac	8-20-1823	w½ sw¼	19-13-14	Bearfield	79	B-105
of Green Co., Pennsylvania						
KLINGER, Adam	10-12-1823	nw¼	21-15-16	Jackson	161	B-304
of Fairfield Co., Ohio						
CALL, James	8-20-1823	ne¼	36-16-15	Harrison	156	B-324
and Peter EARLY						
STRAIT, Jacob	10-26-1820	nw¼	6-15-15	Pike	122	B-336
of Licking Co., Ohio						
SMITH, Samuel	8-26-1824	se¼	29-15-15	Pike	160	B-360
of Guernsey Co., Ohio						
STURGEON, John	7-22-1817	ne¼	23-17-16	Hopewell		B-365
of Fairfield Co., Ohio						
STURGEON, John	6-9-1814	se¼	23-17-16	Hopewell		B-365
assignee of Daniel AINEY						
BEERY, Samuel	9-1-1824	w½ nw¼	6-14-16	Monday Creek	139	B-388
CUSAC, Daniel	8-6-1825	e½ ne¼	21-16-15	Clayton	77	C-96
MARTIN, William	5-5-1823	nw¼	33-14-14	Harrison	160	C-159
of Muskingum Co., Ohio						
NOON, John	5-20-1828	w½ sw¼	23-16-15	Clayton	77	D-259
of Muskingum Co., Ohio						
REAM, Christian	9-16-1819	ne¼	11-15-16	Jackson		D-274
of Fairfield Co., Ohio						
KRATZER, Samuel	9-3-1817	nw¼	15-16-16	Reading	100	D-500
of Fairfield Co., Ohio						
JOHNSON, Simon	5-23-1825	sw¼	36-16-16	Reading	100	E-84
a colored man of Fairfield Co., Ohio						
MITCHELL, Robert	2-10-1812	sw¼	31-15-16	Jackson	100	E-222
of Fairfield Co., Ohio						
CLAYTON, Samuel	7-13-1831	nw¼	8-14-15	Salt Lick	152	E-471
assignee of Isaiah RUSH						
DUTTON, James	10-1-1816	sw¼	21-15-16	Jackson	160	E-512
of Fairfield Co., Ohio						
DUTTON, James	10-1-1816	nw¼	28-15-16	Jackson		E-513
of Fairfield Co., Ohio						
SNYDER, Daniel	5-10-1811	nw¼	33-1817	Thorn		F-313
of Fairfield Co., Ohio						
TEAL, Lawson (index)	5-20-1828	w½ sw¼	1-15-15	Pike	78	F-398
TELL, Osson (deed) assignee of George OGG						

338

Name	Date	Description	Section Twp. & Range	Named Twp.	Acres	Volume & Page
KITCHEN, Daniel	6-9-1818	ne$\frac{1}{4}$	24-15-16	Jackson		F-414
of Fairfield Co., Ohio						
GARDNER, John	2-27-1813	nw$\frac{1}{4}$	34-16-15	Clayton		F-474
assignee of Joseph BABB						
HENTHORN, James	11-8-1812	ne$\frac{1}{4}$	5-18-15	Thorn		F-502
assignee of Nathan Henthorn						
DITTOE, Jacob	12-11-1812	ne$\frac{1}{4}$	21-16-16	Reading		F-544
of Fairfield Co., Ohio						
GALAGHER, Patrick	10-21-1824	ne$\frac{1}{4}$	23-16-15	Clayton	155	F572
and Patrick Cullanghand assignees of James CHIDISTER						
WHIPS, Ezekiel	4-2-1832	w$\frac{1}{2}$ nw$\frac{1}{4}$	1-14-15	Pleasant	80	F-631
CRISLEY, Lawrence	7-8-1814	se$\frac{1}{4}$	11-15-16	Jackson		G-289
of Fairfield Co., Ohio						
STURGES, Solomon	10-5-1835	ne$\frac{1}{4}$ nw$\frac{1}{4}$	5-14-15	Salt Lick	38	G-335
assignee of Nathaniel SKINNER						
STURGES, Solomon	10-5-1835	w$\frac{1}{2}$ nw$\frac{1}{4}$	5-14-15	Salt Lick	76	G-336
of Putnam Co., Ohio						
ROBERTS, John	8-4-1835	nw$\frac{1}{4}$	8-14-14	Harrison		G-339
of Muskingum Co., Ohio						
STANSBERRY, Jonas	10-5-1835	nw$\frac{1}{4}$ nw$\frac{1}{4}$	30-14-14	Harrison	50	G-390
assignee of Patrick NUGENT						
STANSBERRY, Jonas	4-30-1835	sw$\frac{1}{4}$ nw$\frac{1}{4}$	30-14-14	Harrison	50	G-391
of Muskingum Co., Ohio						
WEISZ, George	12-1-1830	w$\frac{1}{2}$ nw$\frac{1}{4}$	34-14-15	Coal	76	G-507
of Fairfield Co., Ohio						
WILSON, Thomas	3-8-1817	sw$\frac{1}{4}$	5-15-15	Pike		G-612
assignee of Michael WILSON						
GEORGE, Isaac	7-2-1832	e$\frac{1}{2}$ sw$\frac{1}{4}$	9-13-14	Bearfield	80	G-625
of Morgan Co., Ohio						
SMITH, Andrew	2-19-1806	n$\frac{1}{2}$	20-17-16	Hopewell	320	H-2
of Fairfield Co., Ohio						
CONOWAY, Jeremiah	2-3-1807	e$\frac{1}{2}$	19-16-16	Reading	320	H-11
and Jacob COFMAN						
COOPER, Joseph	11-16-1806	e$\frac{1}{2}$	2-18-17	Thorn	320	H-12
assignee of Jacob COOPER						
REAM, William	3-20-1809	se$\frac{1}{4}$	14-18-17	Thorn		H-56
of Fairfield Co., Ohio						
LASLEY, David	2-20-1809	se$\frac{1}{4}$	34-17-16	Hopewell		H-59
assignee of Joseph BABB						
HENDRICKS, Peter	6-13-1811	ne$\frac{1}{4}$	33-17-16	Hopewell		H-76
of Fairfield Co., Ohio						
POORMAN, Bernard	3-5-1809	w$\frac{1}{4}$	32-17-16	Hopewell		H-76
assignee of John WAGGONER						
AUNSPAUGH, Adam	10-8-1805	whole	1-17-17	Reading	640	H-76
assignee of Michael NEYLAND						
AUNSBAUGH, Adam	10-13-1807	w$\frac{1}{2}$	25-17-17	Reading		H-77
assignee of Michael SENFF						
FISHER, John	3-3-1807	whole	36-18-17	Thorn	640	H-77
of Fairfield Co., Ohio						

Name	Date	Description	Section Twp. & Range	Named Twp.	Acres	Volume & Page
AUNSBAUGH, Adam	11-10-1807	whole	12-17-17	Reading	640	H-78
of Fairfield Co., Ohio						
FLUCKEY, George	12-14-1812	sw¼	6-16-15	Clayton		H-91
assignee of Isaac SELLERS						
DILLS, George	7-15-1811	ne¼	4-17-15	Madison		H-92
of Muskingum Co., Ohio						
SHERG, Jacob	12-3-1811	se¼	30-17-15	Madison		H-109
assignee of Joseph FICKLE						
HALL, Nathan	12-15-1810	ne¼	28-17-15	Madison		H-110
of Muskingum Co., Ohio						
WILSON, John	12-23-1811	nw¼	30-17-15	Madison		H-110
assignee of Robert LOVE						
CUSAC, Andrew	2-11-1814	ne¼	14-16-15	Clayton		H-146
of Fairfield Co., Ohio						
COOPER, Jacob	8-19-1812	ne¼	1-16-15	Clayton		H-209
assignee of William WILSON						
PHILLIPS, John	3-18-1817	ne¼	19-17-15	Madison		H-251
and Charge GORDON assignees of Henry GORDON and John GUISINGER						
BARND, Christian	2-3-1817	sw¼	32-16-15	Clayton		H-253
of Muskingum Co., Ohio						
ADAMS, Evi	8-1-1835	ne¼	9-15-16	Jackson	159	H-352
assignee of John SIDEY and Edward ADAMS						
HUSH , Peter	2-10-1812	ne¼	5-18-17	Thorn		H-368
in his own right as assignee of Nathaniel TEAL						
HEDRICK, Peter	4-10-1810	se¼	18-17-16	Hopewell		H-371
of Fairfield Co., Ohio						
SMITH, Andrew	3-27-1812	sw¼	4-17-16	Hopewell		H-372
of Fairfield Co., Ohio						
CLARK, Daniel	5-30-1833	e½ sw¼	24-15-16	Jackson	80	H-415
MARTIN, William	10-5-1835	ne¼ nw¼	29-14-14	Harrison	40	H-421
MUNYON, John	4-21-1835	sw¼ nw¼	7-14-15	Salt Lick	40	H-440
MUNYON, George	9-23-1835	ne¼ sw¼	7-14-15	Salt Lick	40	H-440
MUNYON, John	9-23-1835	nw¼ sw¼	7-14-15	Salt Lick	40	H-441
SKINNER, Richard	10-5-1835	nw¼ sw¼	18-14-15	Salt Lick		H-515
SHREEVE, James	2-22-1814	nw¼	28-16-15	Clayton	157	H-538
of Muskingum Co., Ohio						
SPARE, Thomas	9-30-1835	se¼ nw¼	13-12-14	Monroe		H-548
assignee of Ferdinand MALLEN						
SELLERS, Henry	3-7-1812	ne¼	35-17-16	Hopewell		J-25
assignee of Henry NAGLE						
KING, John	4-20-1811	w½	35-18-17	Thorn		J-98
of Fairfield Co., Ohio						
LONG, George	3-27-1813	se¼	26-18-17	Thorn		J-108
assignee of Oliver SIMPSON						
KELLY, Joseph	7-1-1831	w½ nw¼	18-14-14	Harrison	99	J-124
ZARTMAN, Peter	12-11-1812	se¼	24-18-17	Thorn		J-147
of Fairfield Co., Ohio						
STRAWN, Thomas	4-20-1812	sw¼	35-17-16	Hopewell		J-159
assignee of Joseph BABB						

Name	Date	Description	Section Twp. & Range	Named Twp.	Acres	Volume & Page
SHERLOCK, Abraham	12-4-1823	e½ nw¼	35-15-16	Jackson	80	J-187
assignee of John BECK						
BECK, John	8-12-1828	w½ ne¼	34-15-16	Jackson	81	J-187
BECK, John	1-4-1831	e½ ne¼	34-15-16	Jackson	81	J-188
BECK, John	3-5-1834	sw¼ nw¼	35-15-16	Jackson	40	J-188
BECK, John	11-25-1835	ne¼ sw¼	35-15-16	Jackson	40	J-189
HUDSON, Thomas	9-10-1834	nw¼ nw¼	35-15-16	Jackson	40	J-190
BROWN, Mathew	12-1-1830	e½ sw¼	15-15-15	Pike	80	J-399
HENTHORN, James	6-16-1817	ne¼	22-18-17	Thorn		J-439
of Fairfield Co., Ohio						
McFARLAND, William Jr.	9-30-1835	sw¼ ne¼	24-15-15	Pike		J-440
of Licking Co., Ohio						
McGONIGLE, Richard	9-14-1835	nw¼ nw¼	31-13-15	Pleasant	39	J-441
SWINEHART, John	3-3-1812	se¼	2-17-16	Hopewell	100	J-518
of Fairfield Co., Ohio						
STANBERRY, Jonas	8-5-1827	se¼ sw¼	19-14-14	Harrison	50	J-530
assignee of John PROBY						
MOORE, Littleton Jr.	4-2-1835	e½ se¼	17-13-14	Bearfield	78	J-551
of Muskingum Co., Ohio						
MOORE, Littleton Jr.	4-2-1835	w½ se¼	17-13-14	Bearfield	78	J-552
of Muskingum Co., Ohio						
GREEN, Joshua	1-4-1831	w½ ne¼	35-16-16	Reading		J-553
LANDIS, David	8-20-1808	ne¼	7-16-16	Reading		J-576
assignee of Henry KOLBOCK						
SWINEHART, John	8-30-1813	sw¼	9-17-16	Hopewell		J-582
of Fairfield Co., Ohio						
RIDENOUR, David	9-27-1814	sw¼	29-17-16	Hopewell		J-582
and John RIDENOUR of Fairfield Co., Ohio						
TUCKER, John Wesley	10-5-1835	sw¼ sw¼	31-14-14	Harrison	51	J-641
NOON, James	2-10-1830	e½ sw¼	23-16-15	Clayton	77	J-641
WAGGONER, John	11-26-1813	se¼	29-16-16	Reading		K-87
of Fairfield Co., Ohio						
JONAS, Samuel	4-30-1835	nw¼ sw¼	3-14-15	Salt Lick		K-121
BASHORE, John	9-21-1815	ne¼	29-17-16	Hopewell		K-153
of Fairfield Co., Ohio						
BASHORE, John	1-20-1809	ne¼	28-17-16	Hopewell		K-154
of Fairfield Co., Ohio						
RITER, Lawrence	6-20-1809	w¼	7-18-17	Thorn		K-158
of Fairfield Co., Ohio						
STURGES, Solomon	10-5-1835	e½ sw¼	26-15-15	Pike		K-189
of Putnam Co., Ohio						
MILLER, John	2-16-1809	ne¼	25-17-17	Reading		K-242
of Fairfield Co., Ohio						
REAM, Christian	1-26-1809	sw¼	17-16-16	Reading		K-262
assignee of William ROBINSON						
KING, Christian	3-15-1817	nw¼	11-15-16	Jackson		K-311
and William KING assignees of Joseph PETTY and John CASTLE						
POE, Benjamin D.	2-10-1831	e½ ne¼	21-14-14	Harrison	80	K-352

HOPEWELL BAPTIST CEMETERY - PERRY COUNTY, OHIO

Contributed by: Catharine Fedochak, 647 Moraine Rd., Chesterton, Ind. 46304

Cemetery located one mile east of Somerset, Ohio. Inscriptions copied for Mrs. Fedorchak by her aunt, Mrs. C. C. Burkhart.

GOODIN, Sarah daughter of Susanah and Moses died Sept. 26, 1836 aged 12 yrs., 2 months, 6 days
GOODIN, Jane wife of Samuel Goodin died July 5, 1826 aged 33 years (May be 83 or 88 yrs. rather than 33)
GOODIN, Jane - our age to 70 years is set, how short the turn, how frail the state, and if to 80 we arrive, we rather sigh and groan than live. (note: not known if there are two Jane Goddins or if this is epitaph for the first mentioned Jane)
SKINNER, Jane died Aug. 1, 1825 aged 16 yrs 4 months
        Elizabeth died Dec. 25, 1824 aged 20 years, 1 month
        Fany died Oct. 15, 1818 aged 15 years
        Mary wife of Robert Skinner died Oct. 24, 1846 aged 39 years, 1 mo. 6 days
        Robert died Feb. 23, 1856
        Elizabeth, daughter, died Feb. 13, 1850
        William died May 3, 1850, aged 40 years, 5 months, 27 days
        Sarah died Mar. 23, 1832 aged 93 years
CURRY, George H. died Oct. 20, 1854 aged 62 years, __(?) mos. 18 days
        Rachel wife of George Curry died Feb. 22, 1841 aged 39 yrs. 4 mos. 27 days
HULL, Rebecca wife of Daniel Hull died June 15, 1814 aged 36 years
        Reuel S. died July 28, 1823 aged 1 month
        Hannah wife of Benjamin Hull died May 28, 1850 aged 91 years, 10 months
        Benjamin died Aug. 17, 1823 aged 78 years
        Joel died May 25, 1825 aged 17 years
RUTLEDGE, Margaret wife of William Ruthledge died July 8, 1832 aged 73 years
JOHNSON, Rachel died April 1, 1840 aged 86 years
GOBEL, Sarah died Sept. 25, 1875 aged 91 years 4 mos. 16 days
BENNETT, Abraham died Mar. 26, 1862 aged 81 years, 6 months, 16 days
        Martha wife of Abraham Bennett died Sept. 14, 1858 aged 77 yrs., 4 mos., 10 days

STRAWN, Thomas died Feb. 16, 1854 aged 83 years, 11 months, 6 days
        Hannah, first wife, died Feb. 25, 1811 aged 39 years
        Sarah, second wife, died Nov. 7, 1841
        (note: Three Strawn inscriptions all on same stone)
THOMPSON, Nancy wife of John Thompson died Dec. 5, 1812 aged 81 years
        John died May 1855 aged 84 years
YOST, Martha dau. of Wm & Eleanor died Oct. 13, 1853 aged 3 yrs. 1 mo. 24 days
        Eleanor (note: only epitaph readable)
SPENCER, Thomas died Sept. 4, 1815 aged 50 years
        Margaret, consort of Thomas Spencer died July 27, 1840 aged 69 years,
            3m. 14 days
KELLY, Mary consort of Joseph Kelly who departed this life this day Aug. 31, 1833,
        aged 26 years, 6 months, 20 days, with an infant in her arms.
SPENCER, James died Dec. 9, 1825 Revolutionary War Veteran
HARTSEL, John died Oct. 17, 1841 aged 65 years, 4 months, 28 days
MELICK, Eleanor died May 7, 1827 aged 72 years, 22 days (Note: OHIO DAR ROSTER III
        states John Melick is supposed to be buried in this cemetery, roster
        gives birth date which matches this inscription; however, roster gives
        her death date of 1828)
REAM, Horace died May 20, 1835 aged 11 years 5 mos. 27 days
        James died Jan. 30, 1839 aged 2 years 5 mos. 23 days
SAYRE, Reuel died June 8, 1841 aged 86 years 5 months, 19 days (note: Rev. soldier)
        John, infant son of Reuel and Rebecca died Sept. 7, 1831 aged 5 years,
            9 days
        Hope, consort of Reuel Sayre died May 24, 1840 aged 76 years, 3 months
            24 days
RITCHEY, Jane A. wife of Gideon Ritchey died Dec. 8, 1839 aged 27 years, 2 months,
            7 days.

CATHOLIC CEMETERY - SOMERSET - PERRY COUNTY, OHIO

Contributed by Catharine Fedochak, 647 Moraine Rd., Chesterton, Ind. 46304

The Catholic Cemetery adjoins the Catholic Church in the town of Somerset.
Not all inscriptions were copied, but a fair representation of the names in
this cemetery is given.

BURSHUS, Michael died Nov. 11, 1833 aged 52 years
BRADLEY, Eneas departed this life Nov. 1, 1840 aged 48 years, a native of
        Co. of Donegal, parish of Moville, Ireland
BURSHUW, Mary Ann consort of Menroth Burshu died Aug. 21, 1845 aged 34 years
            4 mos. 10 d.
BOUR, Frances wife of Joseph Bour died Mar. 29, 1868 aged 70 years
CREIGHTON, James, native of County Monaghan, parish of Cleninbush, departed
        this life Mar. 5, 1843 aged 60 years.
        John born Dec. 25, 1793 died Sept. 14, 1865
CLUNEY, Margaret departed this life 1833, aged 52 years
CUSAK, Catharine consort of E. C. Cusak departed this life Feb. 8, 1837,
            aged 20 years

343

COSTIGAN, Michael son of Jacob & Cecilia died Nov. 22, 1844 aged 5 yrs. 1 mo. 22 ds.
    Mary A. dau. of Jacob & Cecilia died Jan. 8, 1838 aged 3 yrs.___?mo.___?ds.
CORDON, Wm M. son of Wm. & Lydia died Feb. 25, 1841 aged 1 mo.
CULL, Mary wife of Michael Cull died Sept. 1, 1839 aged about 40 years, a native
    of County of Monaughen, Ireland.
COLLINS, Rosannah consort of John Collins departed this life Feb. 19, 1842 aged
    42 years, a native of the parish of Girvahy, County Down, Ireland
    John died Aug. 9, 1846 aged 52 years, a native of parish of Girvahy,
    Co. Down, Ireland
COONY, Charles Frederick son of Patrick and Mary departed this life Aug. 26,
    1845 aged 1 year, 2 mos. and 15 hours
DOWNHOUR, Margaret consort of John Downhour died Sept. 20, 1828, aged 68 years
    John died May 18, 1837 aged 78 years
DeLONG, Joseph departed this life Aug.___?, 1842 aged 52 years
    Elizabeth consort of Joseph DeLong died 1848, aged ____?
DENNIS, David son of N. & R. died Aug. 30, 1830 aged 1 yr. 2 mos. 11 days
DITTOE, Clara dau. of Peter S. and Ann Dittoe died May 22, 1835 aged 11 weeks
DONLEY, Nancy consort of James Donley died Jan. 16, 1841 aged 76 years, native
    of County Tyrone, parish of Drumore, Ireland
    James died Oct. 20, 1846 aged 82 years, native of Tyrone Co., Parish
    of Drumore, Ireland.
DEAN, Mary Ann consort of James Dean died Jan. 8, 1847 aged 54y 7m 13d
DOUDLE, Peter died Jan. 23, 1848 aged 39 years, native of Ireland
FOOTMAN, Margaret consort of Wm. Footman departed this life Oct. 25, 1835,
    aged 25 years 10 days
FINK, Anthony born Mar. 11, 1795 died Mar. 4, 1864
FINCK, Mary Spurck born Oct. 17, 1802 died Jan. 19, 1878
    John born Nov. 27, 1757, died Dec. 13, 1833 aged 76 years, 16 days
    Mary consort of John Finck Sr. born Mar. 1767 died Dec. 1841 aged 74y 9m
FINK, Mary E. dau. of Adam and Alice born Mar. 30, 1833 died Jan 9, 1835 aged
    21 months, 10 days
FINCK, Edmund Thadeus, son of Anthony & Mary departed this life Jan. 30, 1839,
    aged 11 yrs.
    John Jr. born April 4, 1790, died Oct. 26, 1842, aged 52 yrs. 6 mos. 22ds.
    George son of David P. & E. died Mar. 22, 1841 aged 4 yrs. 4 m. 22 d.
    George_____(very old stone rest not readable)
FLOWERS, Nickalas Dominic son of Henry & Susannah departed this life July 11,
    1844 aged 20 years 3 mos. 24 days.
GALLAGHER, Francis died Mar. 25, 1881 aged about 77
    Anne wife of Francis Gallagher died June 26, 1882 aged about 73
    Charles died Jan. 29, 1881 aged 44 yrs. 6m 1 day.
GOOD, Eliza Anjelus died Aug. 9, 1829 aged 2 years 7 m. 9 d
GUISINGER, Emily J. dau. of Jacob & Mary died Oct. 3, 1838, aged 1 yr. 11 m. 18 d.
GORDON, Wm died Nov. 4, 1849 aged 77 years
    Mary wife of William Gordon died August 18, 1867 aged 78 yrs. 10 months.
HAMILTON, James died Sept. 26, 1836 aged 43 years
    Margaret consort of James Hamilton died Sept. 27, 1836, natives of
    Ireland, Co. of Armaugh (note: James and Margaret on same stone)
HAUGHRAN, John son of Patrick & Eliz. departed this life Sept. 5, 1838 aged
    13 years, 6 mos. 6 d.

HARPER, William 1793-1864, War of 1812
    Elizabeth died Sept. 12, 1839 aged 97 years
HODGE, Rachel C. wife of Joseph Hodge died Aug. 17, 1849 in the 52nd year of
                  her age
    Joseph died Sept.___?, 1855 aged 70 years, --? m.__? d.
HINTELANG, Casperdied Aug. 31, 1842, aged 48 years
HEARHOLTZEN, John B. died July 4, 1845 aged 38 years, 3 mos.
    Joseph died Jan. 26, 1839 aged 64.
JOHNSON, Isabelle dau. of James & Sara died Mar. 8, 1833 aged 7 yrs. 9 mos. 19 d.
    Elizabeth dau. of James & Sara died Aug. 6, 1833 aged 11 mos. 25 days
    Sara Jane dau. of Jacob & Sarah departed this life Oct. 25, 1840,
              aged 13 years, 4 mos. 13 d.
    Mary Ann dau. of James of Sara died June 24, 1828 aged 10 mos. 14 days
JACKSON, Elizabeth dau. of J.J. & S.H. departed this life Mar. 28, 1842 aged
              22 years, 2 mos. 23 days.
KENNEDY, Bridget died Mar. 25, 1870 aged 78 yrs. 2m. 21 d.
KINNEDY, Phillip departed this life April 13, 1852 aged 76 yrs.
KENADY, Michael died Apr. 2, 1850 aged 33 years.
KUNKLER, Christian died July 12, 1833 aged 60 yrs. 7 mos. 16 days.
LITZINGER, Elen wife of Jacob Litzinger, and dau. of Miles CLUNEY died June 22,
              1855 aged 42 years
McDONALD, Susan departed this life Oct. 28, 1831 aged 66 years
    Felix departed this life Sept. 7, 1828 aged 44 years
    Ellen Maria dau. of Patrick & Elizabeth born Mar. 1, 1829, died Mar.
              22, 1843
McGOWEN, Mary consort of Jesse G. McGowen departed this life Aug. 6, 1838,
           aged 40 yrs. 2 mos. 29 days. (note: This stone in row with
           all other Finck markers)
MUSSELMAN, Sara died May 18, 1833 aged 55 years 8 mos . 26 days.
    Elizabeth wife of Wm Musselman died Jan. 30, 1852 aged 52 yrs.
MORIS, Rose died July 22, 1841 aged 50 years 2 mos.
MILLER, John died April 24, 1847 aged 74 years
    Hannah consort of John Miller died Sept. 3, 1842 aged 72y 9m. 3d.
MAUGHRAN, John departed this life May 11, 1839 aged 65 years, 23 days, native
           of King Co. Ireland
OVERMYER, Mary M. died Mar. 11, 1864 aged 65 years. 4 mos.
O'NEIL, Francis died Nov. 2, 1886 aged about 86
    Bridget wife of Francis O'Neil died Jan. 1, 1884 aged about 93 yrs.
PERRUNG, Sarah consort of Jacob Perrung died April 27, 1845 aged 29 yrs. 5 m. 9 d.
RYAN, Rody departed this life June 14, 1837 aged 47 yrs.
    Mary consort of Rody Ryan died Feb. 22, 1848 aged 42 yrs., native of Co.
           Tyrone, Ireland
    John D. died May 2, 1849 in the 24th year of his age
    James son of Rody & Mary died Jan. 23, 1846 age 19 years
ROBY, Margaret consort of John Roby died April 1, 1835 aged 24 years 9 mos.
SLEVIN, Jane consort of James Slevin died April 12, 1832 aged 23 years
    Barbara consort of John Slevin departed this life June 11, 1845 aged
           28 years
SCOTT, Elizabeth born in Co. of Wicklow, Ireland in 1773, departed this life
    Fryday 2nd Nov. 1838 at 7 o'clock am, aged 65 yrs.

SWARTZ, Anthony died Oct. 4, 1840 aged 50 years

SPURCK, Mary consort of Peter Spurck, died Feb. 18, 1839 aged 64 yrs. 4 mos.
        Peter died July 31, 1839 aged 75 years

SHARKEY, Hugh, native of Co. Tyrone Ireland, died Mar. 15, 1839 aged 39 yrs.
        10 m. 11 days.

TRUNNEL, Silas died May 10, 1849 aged 66 years

WEIR, George K - W. Va. Vol. Cav., killed in action at Fayetteville, W. Va.
        Sept. 10, 1862 aged 22 years 14 days
        Eliza born Dublin, Ireland Aug. 2, 1799, died Jan. 28, 1871

WISEMAN, Wm H. son of Wm and Catharine died Sept. 5, 1838 aged 10 years
        Ellen dau. of Wm & Cath. died Sept. 9, 1838 aged 4 yrs.
        Lewis T. son of Wm & Catharine departed this life Sept. 19, 1838
        aged 6 years.
        Wm. died Feb. 2, 1854 aged 84 years
        Rebecca consort of Wm Wiseman ·Sr. departed this life July 22, 1839
        aged 63 years.

WAGNER, Magdalena wife of M. Wagner died Mar. 22, 1880, aged 8 years.

The following records were abstracted from "Partition Record Book A", which is located in the Common Pleas Court (Clerk of Courts Office). Pages on which records may be found are given in parenthesis.

7-19-1821 - Jacob LONG vs. Heirs of George LONG, dec'd. Filed Nov. 1820. Partition: son, Jaclb Long, SW¼ Section 11, Township 18, Range 17; son, George Long, SW¼ Section 11, Township 18, Range 17; dau., Elizabeth Rarick formerly Long, E½ Section 11, Township 18, Range 17; dau., Margaret Parkison formerly Long, E½ Section 11, Township 18, Range 17; dau., Christianna Haverling formerly Long, part SW¼ Section 13, Township 17, Range 17; dau., Susannah Dennis, dec'd formerly Long, her children—John, Samuel and Sarah Dennis, minors, SW¼ Section 13, Township 17, Range 17. (1)

11-20-1821 - Charles C. HOOD guardian of Joel BECKWITH a minor over 14 years. Petition to sell land. Filed July 1821. Joel and John Beckworth tenants in common of NW¼ Section 1, Township 13, Range 14. (4)

3-12-1822 - John MIDDAUGH adms. of Aaron VANNATTA, dec'd. Petition to sell land. Filed Apr. 1821. Land described NW¼ Section 22, Township 16, Range 16. Widow mentioned but not named. (5)

7-17-1821 - Adam SNIDER vendee of Jacob HAINES vs. Henry SALTZGAVER and Mary his wife, et al. Filed 5-26-1821. Petition for Partition. John HAINES, dec'd died intestate. Land described as NW¼ and SW¼Section 34, Township 18, Range 17. Children and heirs: son, John Haines; son, Jacob Haines of Chambersburg, Franklin Co., Pa.; dau., Christiana wife of Anthony Clippenger; dau., Susanna wife of Abraham Frey; dau., Catharine, dec'd wife cf George Croft, her children—John Croft and GeorgeCroft, minors of Cumberland Co., Pa. and Mary wife of Henry Saltzgaver of Adams Co., Pa.; son, Peter Haines, died intestate leaving no children. Adam Snider purchased irterest of some of heirs. (7)

6-10-1822 - Mary WAIT. Petition for Dower. Filed 3-12-1822. Land, lot #4 in town of Somerset. Mary widow of Benjamin Wait, dec'd. (10)

11-6-1822 - Robert BLACK adms. with will annexed of William BLACK, dec'd. Petition to sell land according to former contract. Part Section 32, Township 15, Range 16 contract to sell to Caleb North of Muskingum Co., Ohio. Robert Black son of William Black, dec'd. (11)

9-16-1823 - Matthias Losier and Rosannah his wife, et al, Heirs. Petition for Partition. Filed 4-28-1823. Land part Section 6, Township 17, Range 16. Peter TUMBOLD, dec'd, left no lineal heirs but the following collateral heirs: sister, Rosannah Losier; sister, Elizabeth McInturf, dec'd, her children—Frederick, John, Daniel, Christiana, Susannah and Polly McInturf all of Ohio; brother, Abraham Tombold of Fayette Co., Pa.; sister, Barbara Robinson, dec'd, her children—John, Polly and Elizabeth Robinson of Fayette Co., Pa; sister,

347

(Matthias Losier - continued)

Nancy Hays of Westmoreland Co., Pa.; sister, Sarah Stockberger, dec'd, her three sons—Mathias Stockberger of Pa., George Stockberger of Perry Co. and Michael Stockberger, dec'd, his children—Frederick, Elizabeth, Michael, Mathias, John, Catharine and Christiana Stockberger of Ohio. (12)

10-2-1823 - Evi ADAMS adms. of Edward ADAMS, dec'd. Petition to sell land. Filed Apr. 1823. Land described as W½ NW¼ Section 9, Township 15, Range 16. (15)

6-17-1823 - Samuel HOOPER, Jacob HOOPER, et al. Petition for Partition. Filed Apr. 1823. Land SE¼ Section 19, Township 17, Range 18. Jacob HOOPER, Sr., dec'd. Widow, Lititia Hooper. Children:- Samuel and Jacob Hooper of Fairfield Co., Ohio; Philip Hooper of Franklin Co., Ohio; James and Ezekiel Hooper of Perry Co. and John Hooper of Fairfield Co., Ohio. (16)

6-7-1824 - Catharine DEARMONT. Petition for Dower. Filed Mar. 1824. Land lots 110 and 111 town of Somerset. Catharine widow of William Dearmont, dec'd. (18)

6-7-1824 - Peter KEINAN and Belinda his wife vs. Heirs of Solomon BROWN, dec'd. Petition for Dower. Filed 2-21-1824. Land SW¼ Section 24, Township 18, Range 17. Belinda widow of Solomon Brown, dec'd and now wife of Peter KEENAN. (19)

9-29-1824 - Alexander MORRISON and Adam BROWN adms. of Solomon BROWN, dec'd. Petition to sell land. Filed 3-1-1824. Land SW¼ Section 24, Township 18, Range 17. (20)

9-29-1824 - George FLUCKEY adms. of Joseph PARSON, dec'd. Petition to sell land. Land 160 acres SW¼ Section 11, Township 14, Range 16. Two children, George and Joshua PARSON, minors. (21)

10-3-1823 - Jacob STOKER vs. Heirs of Michael STOKER, dec'd. Petition for PARTITION. Filed Nov. 1822. Land, in-lots 60 and 143 town of Somerset. Sons: Jacob, John and Michael Stoker. Daughters: Margaret Adams, Saloma Reynolds, Catharine Hidlebaugh, Charlotte Stoker, Maria Stoker, Barbara Burdoon, Magdalena Stimmel, dec'd, her children—Michael Stimmel, Polly Plum, Peter Stimmel, Daniel Stimmel, Catharine Johnson, Jacob Stimmel, Betsey Lane and Mary Ann Stimmel. (22)

3-22-1825 - Jacob MILLER vs. Heirs of Jacob MILLER, dec'd. Petition for Partition. Filed Mar. 1824. Land 160 acres NW¼ Section 3, Township 16, Range 16. Widow, Margaret Miller. Children: Jacob and John Miller of Perry Co.; Henry and Joseph Miller of Fairfield Co., Ohio; Elizabeth wife of Peter Eversole of New Albany, Indiana; Susan wife of Jacob Webster of Fairfield Co., Ohio; Christena wife of Rola Rison of Wolf Creek, Muskingum Co., Ohio; Margaret wife of Tobias Dershom of Perry Co.; Catharine wife of Jesse Griffey of Perry Co.; Magdalene widow of Daniel Shearer, dec'd of Perry Co. (24)

3-22-1825 - William STALL and Henry BOYER adms. of Michael BOYER, dec'd vs.
Heirs. Petition to sell land. Land (not described) to John Brubaker as by
agreement of 1819. (26)

6-14-1825 - Peter BARB adms. of John BLIZZARD, dec'd. Petition to sell land.
Filed Mar. 1825. Land being a house and lot in Thornbille. Four children;
Edy, Phebe, John and Mervin, all minors. · (27)

3-21-1825 - Magdelene BOWMAN, widow vs. Heirs of Joseph BOWMAN, dec'd.
Petition for Dower. Filed 3-29-1824. Land 40 acres NE¼ Section 25, Township
17, Range 17. (28)

10-8-1825 - Sarah PEMBERTON, Thomas PEMBERTON, Rebecca PEMBERTON and others.
Petition for Partition. Filed 3-21-1824. On 1-3-1816, Sarah, Thomas and
Rebecca together with Lucy Ann and Elizabeth Pemberton purchased from William
Ware and Elizabeth his wife of Muskingum Co., Ohio the SE¼ Section 9, Township
14, Range 14 situated in Muskingum County now Perry Co. Lucy Ann Pemberton
died intestate in the latter part of 1821 with out marriage leaving mother
Sarah Pemberton entitled to one-fifth part; brother, Thomas O. entitled to
one-third part; sister, Rebecca entitled to one-third part; and sister,
Elizabeth who married on 3-19-1820 Alexander Wilson Brumage with said Elizabeth having died in November 1824 leaving children, John in his fourth year,
Lucy Ann three years and Henry Wilson Brumage aged 6 months. (29)

10-8-1825 - William McCORMACK and Joseph GILLISPIE adms. of John McCORMACK,
dec'd vs. Heirs. Petition to sell land. Land, lot 81 in Somerset sold to
Benjamin Huff as by agreement of 5-5-1821. (31)

3-3-1826 - Hannah SKINNER adms. of Nathaniel SKINNER, dec'd. Petition to
sell land. · Land S½ SW¼ Section 29, Township 16, Range 15 sold to John Philips.
Nathaniel Skinner left minors (not named) under 21 yrs. of age. (32)

3-3-1826 - Henry STATLER Jr. adms. of Joseph STATLER, dec'd vs. Henry, Hiram,
Nicholas, Julian, Jerome, Rachel and William STATLER. Petition to sell land.
Land being part of E½ Section 9, Township 16, Range 16, adjoining Somerset.
Joseph Statler left the following brothers and sisters as heirs; Henry,
Nicholas, Hiram aged 17 yrs., Jule Ann aged 12 or 14 yrs., Jerome aged 10 yrs.,
Rachel aged 8 yrs. and William aged 6 yrs. (32)

3-3-1829 - George BOWMAN adms. of Joseph BOWMAN, dec'd vs. Heirs. Petition
to sell land. Filed 3-19-1825. Joseph Bowman died Sept. 1822 intestate.
Children: Thomas Bowman; Mary wife of John Waggoner Jr.; Magdalene, dec'd,
wife of Joseph Civits, her children—Charles, Thomas, Joseph, James and
Jacob Civits. Land described as 40 acres part NE¼ Section 25, Township 17.
(34)

6-6-1826 - Nathan BENJAMIN and Edith A. his wife vs. Heirs of Nathan SHAW. Petition for Partition. Filed 1-3-1826. Land E½ SE¼ Section 21, Township 16, Range 15 being 77 acres which was received by patent from United States. Nathan Shaw died intestate leaving no children and the following brothers and sisters as heirs: Mary and Elizabeth Shaw, both of age; Catharine, John, Margaret and Stephen Shaw, minors; Nancy Kelly, dec'd, her children— John, Betsey and Mary Kelly, minors. (37)

6-6-1826 - Joseph S. BROWN and Sarah BENJAMIN executors of James BENJAMIN, dec'd vs. Heirs, Petition to sell land. Land described as part of NE¼ and SW¼ SWP Section 25, Township 17, Range 6, sold to David Miller. James Benjamin left minor heirs, not named. (39)

6-7-1826 - William GREEN vs. Heirs of Thomas GREEN, dec'd. Petition for Partition. Filed Mar. 1825. Land being lot 64 in town of Somerset formerly called town of Middle Town. Children: William Green; Nancy Gray, dec'd, her children—Ellen, Jonas and Eliza Gray, minors; John Green; Rebecca Green; Samuel Green, all of Perry Co.; Richard Green and Robert Green of Muskingum Co., Ohio. (40)

6-10-1826 - Alexander TENANT and Ann his wife vs. Margaret BROOKS. Petition for Partition. Filed 6-13-1825. Land, SE¼ Section 22, Township 17, Range 16. Francis Brooks, dec'd. Children: David Brooks, died without issue; Sarah Brooks, died without issue; Ann Tenant; Margaret Brooks of Perry Co. (42)

6-12-1826 - Anthony DITTOE and Michael DITTOE executors of Jacob KITTOE, dec'd vs. Heirs. Petition to sell land. Land, NE¼ Section 32, Township 16, Range 16 sold by agreement of 2-23-1825 to John Hull. (44)

9-27-1826 - John NEEL and Mary SLAUGHTER adms. of John SLAUGHTER, dec'd vs. Heirs. Petition to sell land. Land, east quarter of half section 1, Township 18, Range 16 being 174 acres, sold as by agreement of 12-9-1823 to Samuel Parr. (45)

10-3-1827 - John WISWELL and Sarah WISWELL vs. Jonas ENFIELD and Jacob CATTERLIN his guardian. Petition for Partition. Filed Feb. 1827. James SPENCER, dec'd. Land, N½ NW¼ Section 12, Township 16, Range 16, devised by James Spencer in his will to Sarah Wiswell and Jonas Enfield. (46)

10-4-1827 - Rachel MILLS vs. Daniel LIDEY, David PARDEE, John B. ORTON and Solomon BARNET. Petition for Dower. Filed 12-11-1826. Land, part of NE¼ Section 3, Township 16, Range 16. On September 1811 Rachel married Roswell Mills of Perry Co., now deceased and he died 18 July 1826. (47)

10-8-1827 - George STOCKBERGER guardian of Michael STOCKBERGER, eta. Petition to sell land. Michael, Mathias, John, Catharine and Christiann Stockberger heirs of Michael Stockberger, dec'd; their right to four-ninths part of 18½ acres Section 1, Township 17, Range 16 by right of their ancestor Michael Stockberger. (51)

350

2-19-1828 - Barbara McNUTT vs. Eliza Ann and John McNUTT. Petition for Dower. Filed Feb. 1827. Joseph McNutt, dec'd. Widow, Barbara McNutt. Two minor heirs, John and Eliza McNutt. Land, NW¼ Section 12 Township 4 north, Range 15 of U.S. lands sold in Delaware district, also E½ NE¼ Section 17, Township 16, Range 16 sold in Chilicothe district and part NW¼ Section 15, Township 16, Range 16. (52)

5-28-1828 - Christian KING vs. John KING and Alexander COSTONIAN and wife. Petition for Partition. Filed 12-5-1827. Land W½ Section 35 and part E½ Section 35, Township 18, Range 17. John KING, dec'd. Henry King; Christian King; John King of Pike Co., Ohio; Alexander Costonian and Marillas his wife formerly King of Perry Co.; Adam Spohr and wife; John J. Brock and wife tenants in common set off by deed of Peter King dated 12-16-1823 excepting portion alloted to Peter King and Christian King. (54)

5-28-1828 - Alexander BAIRD vs. Samuel, John, Thomas, Martha, Jane and Agnes Baird. Petition for Partition. Filed 2-6-1828. John Baird, dec'd. Sons:- Alexander, Samuel, John and Thomas BAIRD, last two are minors. Daughters:- Martha formerly Baird wife of Samuel Baird, Jane Baird and Agnes Baird. Land SW¼ Section 5 and NW¼ Section 8½ Township 17, Range 15. (57)

9-30-1830 - Eleanor HENTHORN adms. of Jesse HENTHORN, dec'd vs. John C. HENTHORN. Petition to sell land. Filed 2-11-1828. Land part NW¼ Section 22, Township 17, Range 18, Thorn Twp. Jesse THENTHORN died Nov. 1827 intestate. Widow, Eleanor Henthorn. One child, John C. Henthorn aged 1 year. (61)

9-13-1830 - James CAIN and wife vs. Nathan BENJAMIN, et al. Petition for Partition. Filed 1-28-1828. Hannah formerly Benjamin wife of James Cain was married in 1820 in New York and moved to Perry Co. in 1820. In June 1825 James Benjamin, father of said Hannah Cain, died at Somerset, Perry Co. Land SW¼ Section 25, Township 17, Range 16 excepting 9 acres sold in deceased lifetime to Nathan Benjamin. Widow of James Benjamin, dec'd (not named) married in the spring of 1826 to John Bowers and now resides in Licking Co., Ohio. Nine heirs:- Nathan Benjamin, James Benjamin, Samuel Benjamin, John Benjamin, Hannah wife of James Crain, Mary Hutchins a widow, Emeline wife of Edward Forguson, Elsee Benjamin, all of Perry Co. and Sarah Benjamin of Licking Co., Ohio. Guardian of Sarah Benjamin is Mary Bowers, her mother-in-law. (62)

2-18-1829 - William STALL and Henry BOYER adms. of Michael BOYER, dec'd vs. Daniel RANKIN, et al. Petition to sell land. Filed 2-20-1828. Land SW¼ Section 22, Township 18, Range 17. Widow, Hannah Boyer now the wife of Daniel Rankin. Children: Elizabeth, Henry, Mary, Catharine and John Boyer. (65)

2-18-1829 - Eliza Ann VANNATTA adms. of Elijah VANNATTA, dec'd vs. Heirs. Petition to complete real contract. Contract dated 11-9-1826 to sell SW¼ Section 32, Township 16, Range 16 to William Elder. Elijah left one or more minor heirs (not named). (68)

351

2-20-1829 - David KAUDERMAN and Lewis KAUDERMAN adms. of George KAUDERMAN, dec'd vs. Eve KAUDERMAN and others. Petition to sell land. Filed 9-6-1828. Land, lot 90 in town of New Reading. Widow, Eve Kauderman. Children: Lewis Kauderman, David Kauderman, Mary wife of John Wollaver, Henry, Eliza and Susan Kauderman, minors. (69)

5-27-1829 - John B. ORTON and George ZIEGLER adms. of James JARVIS, dec'd vs. Heirs. Petition to sell land. Filed May 1827. Land, NE¼ Section 27, Township 16, Range 16. Children: Thomas, Moses, William, Jesse, Philip and Sarah JARVIS, Rebecca wife of George Taylor, Mary Jarvis and Elizabeth wife of John H. Burroughs. (70)

9-30-1829 - John WEEDMAN and Rachel WEEDMAN vs. Thomas Wilson, et al heirs of Asa WILSON, dec'd. Petition for Partition. Filed 12-15-1828. Land, 100 acres SW¼ and 41 acres NW¼, Section 14, Township 17, Range 16. Deceased left a widow (not named) who is now deceased. Children: Rachel wife of John Weedman; Thomas, Edward, Isaiah, Eliza and Sarah Wilson. (72)

9-30-1829 - John P. BAKER and George CLAPPER executors of John Philip BAKER, dec'd of Muskingum Co., Ohio. Petition to sell land. Land 142 acres NW corner Section 7, Township 17, Range 5, sold to Edward Ward. (74)

10-1-1829 - Jacob CATTERLIN vs. Timothy LYNCH, et al. heirs of William LYNCH, late of Perry Co. Petition for Partition. Filed 4-3-1829. Land S½ NE¼ Section 32, Township 18, Range 17. Widow, mentioned but not named. Eight children: Willimina wife of Barton James of Butler Co., Ohio; Timothy Lynch thought to be in Louisiana; Samuel Lynch of Indiana; John Lynch of Maryland; Walter Lynch; Eleanor wife of_____(blank) Virtue; Mary wife of___(blank) Lane; and Susanna Lynch; all of Baltimore, Maryland. (75)

2-17-1830 - William DEAL vs. David DEAL, et al. Petition for Partition. Filed 4-16-1829. Christian Deal, dec'd of Reading Twp. Widow, Susanna Deal. Children: William, David, John, Sophia and Anna Deal, Sarah wife of Jacob Ream, all of Perry Co. Land N½ Section 4, Township 16, Range 16, (77)

2-18-1830 - William LASHLEY vs. Margery LASHLEY, et al. heirs of William LASHLEY, dec'd. Petition for Partition. Filed 4-16-1829. Land; lots 36 and 96 in town of Somerset. William LASHLEY, dec'd late of Reading Twp. Widow, Margery Lashley. Children: William LASHLEY, Alexander Lashley, Aaron Lashley, Rebecca wife of John Brumage, Teresa wife of John McLane, Mary wife of John Brandt, all of Perry Co. and Elizabeth wife of_____ (blank) Hekimer, residence unknown. (79)

2-19-1830 - David ILES and wife vs. Peter J. RUFFNER. Petition for Partition. Filed 7-10-1824. Land, NE¼ Section 19, Township 17. Peter RUFFNER, dec'd. Children:- Savillah wife of David Iles of Fairfield Co., Ohio and Peter J. Ruffner of Cincinnati, Ohio. (81)

PERRY COUNTY, OHIO - WILL ABSTRACTS 1818-1851

Contributed by:- Mrs. Rosalie Hartinger, 3208 Chandler Ct., Dayton, Ohio 45420

Copied from what is now known as Volume A-B, originally abstracted by the late
Calvin L. McClintock of New Lexington. Pages on which record may be found are
given in parenthesis.

ATWATER, Christopher - dated 8-7-1822. Wife, Betsy. Executrix, Betsy Atwater.
Witnesses: Thomas Moore, Wm. Southall and Wash. Dodd. (24)

ANDERSON, Joseph - dated 1-20-1831. Wife, Levina. Brother, Isaac Anderson.
Half Brother, John Anderson. Half Sister, Hannah Anderson. Executrix, Levina
Anderson. Witnesses: Daniel Kemper, Elijah Kemper and Wesley Kemper. (79)

ALLEN, John - dated 2-5-1835. Wife, Margaret. Jasper Allen only child named,
other children not named. Witnesses: Benj. Humphrey and Richard Allen. (98)

ANGLE, John P. - dated 3-13-1834. Wife, Polly. Children: Isaiah Angle, Eliz-
abeth Kelsey, Joseph Angle, Jacob B. Angle, Mary Angle, John Angle, Aaron Angle,
Abram Angle, Paul Angle, Catherine Angle and Jemima Angle. Executrix: Wife,
Polly Angle. Witnesses: Geo. B. Page, John Vanatta and Bernard Grimes. (117)

ANDERSON, John - dated 11-29-1834. No wife named. Sons: John and Isaac Anderson. Daughter, Susan Kennard. Grand-daughter, Levinah Anderson. Executor,
Isaac Anderson. Witnesses: Daniel Kemper and Jacob Kemper. (118)

AMRINE, Frederick - dated 11-21-1836. Wife, Catherine. Grand-daughter, Mary
Amrine. Witnesses: Sam. Curran and Thos. Traner. (129)

AUSPACH, Adam - dated 4-10-1833. Wife not named. Sons: Jacob, Benjamin,
Christian, John, Adam and David. Daughters: Elizabeth Dupler (Philip), Magdalena Binckley (Adam), Catherine Ridenour (Ludwick), Barbara Spohn (Jacob).
Executor, Christian Auspach. Witnesses: Michael Fisher and Jacob Shirder
(both in German). (135)

BECKWITH, David - dated 4-11-1818. Wife, Catherine. Sons: George, John and Joel.
Daughters: Susanna McClain (McCaslin?) and Elizabeth Beckwith. Executor, John
Beckwith. Witnesses: John B. Orton and Benj. Wait. (2)

BUGH, Peter Sr. - dated 10-5-1819. Wife, Catherine. Sons: William, John,
Michael, Jacob, Peter and Israel. Daughters: Charlotta Chidester (James) and
Susanna Jones (John). Executors: William and Peter Bugh, Jr. Witnesses:
Geo. Trout and John B. Orton. (11)

BOGLE, Joseph - dated 5-30-1817. Wife, Elizabeth. Children: James Bogle and
Elizabeth Harner. Executor, James Bogle. Witnesses: Thos Nesbit and Wm.
Mitchell. (18)

BROOKS, Francis - dated 5-6-1822. Son, David. Daughters: Mary, Anna, Sarah
and Margaret. Executors: David and Anna. Witnesses: Joel Strawn and Jacob
Hinebaugh. (21)

353

BLACK, Robert - dated 4-9-1817; proved 9-24-1822. Wife and children not named. Caleb North is named. (Oral will made after receiving a fatal wound) Witnesses: Christian Barnd, Caleb Shreeve and David Carroll. (24)

BURKEY, John - dated 3-27-1823. Wife, Susana. Children: John, David, Daniel, Samuel, Henry, Martin, Michael, Rachel and Lydia. Executors: Sam. Ream and Thos. King. Witnesses: David Ream and Wm. Barrington. (28)

BAESHORE, Jacob - dated 8-16-1823. Wife not named. Mentions Graveyard at Binckley School house. Bequeaths to: John Binckley, Mary Begher, Nancy Leach, Henry Binckley, Elizabeth Binckley and Geo. Binckley heirs of Jacob Binckley, dec'd (grand-children?). Executor, Adam Binckley. Witnesses: Adam Binckley, Geo. Witner and Peter Baker. (31)

BRANDT, Lodwick - dated 7-26-1822. Wife not named. Daughter, Elizabeth and her children—Mary, Eliza, Louis, James, John and Isaiah. Son, Lodwick Brandt. Grandsons: John Brandt, Martin and Jacob Mohler. Son-in-law, John Kane. Executors: John Hammon and David Brandt. Witnesses: Jacob Brandt and Adam Brandt.(32)

BRADSHAW, David - dated 2-28-1824. No wife named. Nephew; Geo. Bradshaw, son of Robert. Sister, Nancy Guisinger. Executor, Roswell Mills. Witnesses: Jacob Binckley and Michael Rugh. (38)

BEARD, Joseph - dated 10-15-1823. Wife, Mary. Sons: William, Thomas and Alfred. Daughters: Mary Ramsey, Eliza Cowden, Elizabeth Beard and Rebecca Beard. Executors: wife, Mary; sons, Wm. and Alfred Beard. Witnesses: Thomas Nesbit, Joseph McGarlin and Samuel Kelley. (39)

BINCKLEY, Henry - dated 1-5-1825. Wife, Catherine. Daughters: Elizabeth Downhour, Mary, Milla Bugh, and Nancy. Sons: Adam and Emanuel. Executors: Roswell Mills and Peter Humberger. Witnesses: Roswell Mills, Philip Spohn and Christian Ream. (40)

BYRNE, Edward of Brownsville, Fayette County, Penna. - dated 5-29-1821. Wife, Editha Ann, also to serve as executrix. Witnesses: Felix Cull and Thos. McKeown. (43)

BENJAMIN, James - dated 5-13-1825. Wife, Sarah. Sons: Nathan, James and Samuel. Daughter, Sarah Josling. Grandson, James Hutcher. Executors: Wife, Sarah and Joseph Brown. Witnesses: Samuel Binckley and E. Rechman. (44)

BOYER, Henry - dated 11-30-1825. Wife, Catherine. Nephew, Henry Capman, son of John. Judge George Trout to administer property until Henry is of age. Executor, George Trout. Witnesses: Wm. P. Darst, Sam. Binckley and Geo. Morris. (47)

BRADLEY, John - dated 7-30-1826. Wife, Mary. Children: Patrick, William, Ann and John. Executors: Patrick Largey and Levi Burgoon. Witnesses: Owen Martin, James Hanlon and Patrick McCristal. (53)

BOGLE, William - dated 6-5-1828. Wife, Rebecca. Sons: Samuel and Holmes. Daughters: Elizabeth and Rebecca. Executors: Sons, Samuel and Holmes Bogle. Witnesses: Thomas Nesbit and M. G. lligher. (74)

BEVERAGE, Tracy – dated 8-26-1831. No wife. Children: John, Sarah, Susan, William, Samuel, Noble, Mary, Ann, Thos. H., Keziah and Chas. C. Executor, Henry Roberts. Witnesses: Henry Roberts and Thomas Taylor. (84)

BINCKLEY, Christian – dated 1-5-1831. No wife. Children: Catherine Spohn (Philip), Christiana Musser (Theabold), Elizabeth Fye (Jacob), and Adam Binckley. Daughter-in-law, Freny widow of John Binckley. Mentions graveyard at Binckley Schoolhouse. Executors: Adam Binckley and Jacob Fye. Witnesses: Peter Bugh and David Long. (90)

BEAN, Paul – dated 5-14-1834. Wife, Mary Magdalene. Son, Peter. Son-in-law, Adam Troup. Daughters: Elizabeth Smith and Christiana Foster. Executor, Alexander Zartman. Witnesses: Peter Hetrick and Jacob Foght. (104)

BAIRD, Mary – dated 6-17-1834. Daughters: Jane Baird and Nancy Sabin (David). Son, Alexander Baird. Executors: Robert Wiley and Alexander Baird. Witnesses: Samuel and Daniel Baird; Thomas Nesbit. (120)

BOWERS, George D. – dated 4-1-1838. Wife, Margaret. No children named. Executor, Thos. Hammond, Jr. Witnesses: Wm. Mechling and Martin Ridenour. (141)

BERKHIMER, John – dated 1-1-1839. Wife, Catherine. Children: Nathan, Edward, Keziah and James. Grandson, Nathan Spitler. Executors: Nathan and Edward Berkhimer. Witnesses: Charles C. Hood, Geo. B. Page and B. Stone. (149)

BOGLE, Holmes – dated 3-23-1849. Wife, Mary. Sons: William, James, Mitchell and Erastus. Daughter?, Sally Ann McCurdy. Executors: Wife, Mary and Samuel Bogle. Witnesses: Thomas C. Armstrong, John Stewart and John Wilson. (151)

BURKET, Michael – dated 10-1-1838. Wife, Mary. Children: Mary, Catherine, Martha, Michael, Joseph, Margaret, Ann, Rose Ann, Geo. Ammon and John Marks. No executor named. Witnesses: Wm. Dempsey and Henry Hare. (159)

BRUMAGE, Alexander Wilson – dated 10-5-1840. Wife, Comfort. Children not named. Executor, John James. Witnesses: James Weaver and Jacob Holcomb. (169)

BEAVER, George – dated 3-25-1842. Wife, Elizabeth. Children: Margaret, Nancy, Rachel and Thomas. Executors: Thomas Beaver and Wm. T. Johnson. Witnesses: David Fulton and John Flanigan. (174)

BENNETT, Robert – dated 8-11-1842. Wife, Cecily. Children not named. Executor not named. Witnesses: J. Brown, B. Brison and Henry Walker. (179)

BALL, James – dated 10-26-1842. Wife, Eliza. Children not named. Mentions Father and Mother Vail. Executors: Stephen Barnes and John Ball (Bell?). Witnesses: Robert Regester and W. B. Lyons. (183)

BAIRD, Eleanor – dated 8-21-1844. Son, Thos. Warren Baird. Daughters: Mary Baird, Eliza Ann and Tabitha. No executor named. Witnesses: E. B. Calderhead and Andrew Walker. (195)

BELL, John - dated 5-10-1838. Wife, Jane. Children: Samuel, Joseph, Elizabeth, Martha Jane and Mary. Grandson, Washington Hitchcock. Executors: Israel Hitchcock and John Greene. Witnesses: James and Eleanor Greene. (197)

BURGOON, Francis - dated 4-24-1839. Wife, Elizabeth. Sons: Jacob, David, Peter and William. Daughters: Mary Carl (Joshua), Edith Ingle (David), and Rachel. Grand-daughter, Maria Fisher, daughter of Teressa Burgoon. Executor: Son, Jacob Burgoon. Witnesses: Elias and John Vanatta. (209)

BURTON, Isaac - dated 9-29-1845. Wife, Jarver. Children not named. Executors: John Rambo and C. S. McQueen. Witnesses: Geo. Lowery and J. E. Mann. (210)

BEAMER, Henry - dated 7-9-1845. Wife, Salome. Son, Jacob, only child named. Executors: James Culbertson and Solomon Witmer. Witnesses: W. D. Brake and Wm. Dempsey. (216)

BASORE, John - dated 6-19-1845. Wife not named. Children: David Basore, Thos. Basore and Elizabeth Statler. Executor, Isaac Zartman. Witnesses: S. S. Rickley and Alex. Zartman. (244)

BARNES, Isaac - dated 8-5-1847. Wife not named. Sons: Stephen, Isaac and Amzi. Daughters: Cynthia, Lois Strait, Susanna Sater and Esther Ketcham. Executors: William McCullough and Amzi Barnes. Witnesses: Sam. Work and Wm. McCullough. (268)

BRECKBILL, Jacob - dated 10-29-1848 at Ottumwa, Iowa. Wife, Mary Ann. Children: James, Abraham and Patience. Executrix: Wife, Mary Ann. Trustees: John D. Deven and John Baldwin. Witnesses: W. H. Baldwin, A. B. Galinger and James C. Talman. Codicil dated 10-30-1848 names Abraham B. Galinger to act as trustee with wife, Mary Ann and John D. Devin. Witnesses: James C. Talman and A. S. Gebhart. Will proved 4-5-1849 in Warren Co., Iowa. (269)

BIGGAM, James - dated 9-28-1849. Wife, Eliza. Mother-in-law, Elizabeth Pence. Son, Jonathan only child named; wife Eliza to act as his guardian. No executor named. Witnesses: Levi Williams, Jacob Hearing and Edward Minshell. (281)

BUCHANAN, James - dated 4-6-1847; proved 6-14-1847 Greene Co., Ohio. Mother, Phebe Buchanan. Brother, James H . Buchanan. Requests to be buried in lead coffin in Rush Creek burial ground of the Associated Reformed Church in Fairfield Co., Ohio. Bequeaths library for Associated Ref. Church at Cedarville, Ohio and residue to be invested with proceeds of interest to be used for religious papers and periodicals for above named congregation. Executors: Thomas A Read and Joseph Kyle. Witnesses: Sam. Kyle and Junius Townsley. (286)

BRUMAGE, John - dated 9-24-1850; proved 11-6-1850. Brothers: Henry and Joseph. Sisters: Rebecca, Mariah, Hannah, Lucy and Elizabeth. Executor, Thos Iliff. Witnesses: Joshua Tracey and Janard Tracey. (303)

CRIST, Philip - dated 1-17-1817. Wife, Christiana. Children: Jacob, John, Betsey Crull (John), William, Daniel, Catherine Sutton (Levi), Sarah Drumm, Frederick and Philip. Executor not named. Witnesses: Hugh Boyle, Christian King and Thos. Ewing. (3)

356

COWEN, Walter – dated 1-8-1822. No wife. Brothers: Thomas and Robert. Nieces: Frances and Susanna Cowan. Nephew, Robert. Executor, Thomas Cowan. Witnesses: John Sturgeon and Andrew Henkel. (29)

CAIN, John – dated 1-4-1824. Wife, Pheby. Daughters: Eliza Farier, Ellenor, Nancy, Priscilla, Phebey, Joana and Melinda. Sons: Daniel G., Nathaniel C., Nehemiah C., Chas. C. and John B. Executors: Wife, Phebey and James Ritchey. Witnesses: Thos. King and Geo. Crossan. (37)

COEN, Samuel – dated 4-26-1829. Wife, Margaret. Sons: John, William and Samuel. Daughters: Mary, Nancy, Sarah Ray, Martha, Malinda, and Jane T. Executors: Wife, Margaret and James Ross. Witnesses: James Ross and Mary Cowen. (67)

CALKINS, Samuel G. – dated 1-5-1830. Wife, Hester. Son, Daniel. Daughter, Hester Johnson (Benj.). No executor named. Witnesses: Peter Cochran and Joseph Osborn. (71)

COVER, Jacob – dated 4-1-1830. Wife, Catherine. Children: Jacob, John, Michael, Samuel, Henry, Mary, Lawrence and Catherine. Executors: Joseph Good and Daniel Helser. Witnesses: John Humbarger and Wm. P. Darst. (73)

CAMPBELL, Philip – dated 3-4-1829. Wife, Mary. Children: Bernard, Mathew and Elizabeth. Executors: Wife, Mary and Bernard Cull. Witnesses: Felix and Bernard Cull. (74)

CAMPBLE, Mary – dated 3-25-1832. Children: Elizabeth, Mathew and Bernard. Mentions St. Joseph's Catholic Church. Executors: John Beckwith and Wm. McClure. Witnesses: Geo. Jackson and Jacob Swinehart. (87)

CHILCOTE, Elizabeth – dated 6-30-1829. Son, Joshua. Daughters: Ann Curran and Margaret Miller. Executor: Grandson, Sam. Curran. Witnesses: H. W. Davis and John Shaw. (91)

COWEN, Thomas – dated 8-30-1833. Wife, Elizabeth. Daughters: Frances, Mariah, Harriet, Martha and Elizabeth. Sons: Robert, Charles, John, George and Horatio. Son-in-law, Jesse Bough (Bugh). Grandchildren: Elizabeth and Mary Bough (Bugh). Daughter-in-law, Jane Cowen. Executors: George and Horatio. Witnesses: Geo. Higgins and Michael Bosserman. (97)

CROSBY, James – dated 3-10-1828. Wife, Hannah. Heirs: John Crosby; Rebecca Carnet, dec'd; Isaac Denny; Elizabeth wife of John Morrow; Margaret, dec'd, wife of John Leisure; Ed Crosbie; Polly wife of Basil Conaway; Katherine wife of Benj. Nelson; Sarah Crosbie; Hannah wife of Wm. Martin; and Nancy Crosbie. Executors: Wm. Martin and Ed. Crosbie. Witnesses: Barnhart Olwine and John Gardner.(115)

COMLY, Joshua – dated 8-10-1835. Verbal will at point of death. Bequeaths all to his mother, Catherine Comly. Witnesses: John Comly, Ira Carroll and Asa Brown. (118)

CASSELL, Margaret – dated 5-8-1837. Mother, Catharine Cassell. Brother, Abraham. Witnesses: B. Stone and John Beckwith. (138)

COCHRAN, John - dated 2-23-1839. Wife, Mary. Children: John, James, Joseph, Robert, Thomas, Sarah, Agnes McGreevy wife of Aaron Petty. Executors: Son, Thos. Cochran and John Banatta. Witnesses: Peter Middaugh, Samuel and Thos. L. Forsyth. (148)

CHAPPELEAR, Zacharia - dated 8-23-1838. Wife, Liney. Daughters: Nancy and Catherine. Executor: Hedgeman B. Chappelear. Witnesses: Chas. Henkel and Jacob Fye. (152)

CLARK, Alexander - dated 2-12-1839. Wife, Mary. Children: Margaret, Allen, Daniel, Alexander and other children not named. Executors: Wife, Mary and son, Allen. Witnesses: John Crossen and Hugh Sharkey. (153)

CAIN, James - dated 12-26-1839. No wife. Children: Priscilla, William, Jasper, James and Joseph. Executors: David Ream and Wm. Williams, Jr. Witnesses: Robert Stewart and Andrew Ream. (158)

CARROL, David - dated 11-27-1834. Wife, Elizabeth. Sister, Hannah Carroll. Children not named. Executors: Wife, Elizabeth and Benj. Carroll. Witnesses: Stephen Barnes and Sam. Skinner. (162)

CODY, Michael - dated 6-9-1842. Wife, Bridget Tobin. Children: John, James, Patrick, William, Martin, Bridget, Elizabeth, Ellen, Thomas and Michael. Executors: Thomas Beath and brother, Pat. Cody. Overseer, John Clark. Guardian of children, John Moore. Witnesses: Thomas Beath, John Burns and Wm. Ryan.(175)

CHILCOTE, Joshua - dated 11-29-1839. Wife and children mentioned but not named. Executor mentioned but not named. Witnesses: Sam. Curran and Nathan Chilcote.(204)

CANNON, Isaac - dated 10-10-1845. Wife, Catherine. Children: Catherine Weaver, William, Wesley, Hester Primrose, Alsa, John and George. Grandson, E. Neal Howell. Executor, James Curran. Witnesses: James Porter and Jesse E. Porter. (208)

COMBS, John - dated 6-9-1845. No wife. Children: James, William, Mary Spencer, Eleanor Stevenson, and John. Executors: John and James Combs. Witnesses: Wm. B. Davis and Peter McMullen. (212)

COLLINS, John - dated 8-8-1846. No wife. Children: Henry, John, Edward and daughters not named. Brother, Arthur Collins. Executors: Son, Henry and John Lidey. Witnesses: Arthur Collins and Mannes S. D'Arco. (218)

CROSSEN, Cornelius - dated 3-27-1840. No wife. Nephews, John and Cornelius Crossen. Nieces: Frances, Catherine, Ann and Margaret Crossen. Executors: Cornelius and John. Witnesses: Owen Martin and Sam. Crossen. (222)

CRITCHETT, Michael - dated 4-10-1846. Wife, Ann. Children not named. Executors: Wife, Ann and Chas. Carter. Witnesses: Andrew Barton and Thos. B. Ayers. (229)

CASTANIAN, Alexander - dated 6-22-1833; proved 9-18-1849. Wife, Marylis. Sons: John Serenus and David. Executrix, wife. Witnesses: Jacob and Geo. Long. (274)

CHALFANT, Robert - dated 8-15-1848; proved 4-14-1851. Wife, Mercy. Sons: Robert, Wm. H., and Samuel. Grandson, Robert. Daughter, Margaret Cochran (Thos.). Son, Charles, Daughter, Lydia Strawn. Daughter, Sarah Melick. Grand-daughter, Sarah. Grand-daughter, Jane Cochran. Daughter, Comfort Bear. Executor, Robert Chalfant. Witnesses: John and Uzziah Wilson. (313)

COMBS, James - dated 11-4-1851; proved 11-29-1851. Wife, Mary. Children: Lewis, George, Levi, John, Thomas, Wm. Henry, Charles, Rebecca, Elenora and Christena Catherine. Executors: Lewis and George. Witnesses: Daniel Baker and Hugh Love. (325)

DITTOE, Jacob - dated 3-2-1825. Wife, Anne Catherine. Children: Sarah, Henry, Jacob, Michael, John, Peter, and Rachel Hodge. Grand-daughter, Eleanora M. C. Dittoe, daughter of Jacob. Executors: brother, Anthony and son, Michael. Witnesses: Ed. Keenin, Thos. Martin and Anne Dayler. (49)

DEAN, Masson - dated 6-16-1825. No wife. Children: Masson, Catherine, Mary Ann and James. Grand-daughter, Elizabeth Quinch. Executors: son, Masson and daughter, Mary Ann. Witnesses: Thos. Curran and Michael Bosserman. (52)

DELONG, Joseph - dated 7-16-1831. No wife. Nine children: William, Lydia, Joseph Edward, Augustine, Mary, Elizabeth, Sarah, Cecelia and Lucinda. Executors: Isaac and David Delong. Witnesses: Sam. Curran and Isaac Delong. (83)

DAVISON, John - dated 3-31-1836. No wife. Children: Edward, Absolom, Artist, Sally Ramsey, Lucy Graham, Zeruah, Isaac W. and Darkey. No executor named. Witnesses: Andrew Walker and Agnes Walker. (122)

DILLS, John - dated 11-21-1835. Wife not named. Wm. Swackhammer to have everything for keeping John and his wife. Executors: Jacob Richards and Wm. H. Herron. Witnesses: Joseph Watt, Jacob Richards and Wm. H. Herron. (124)

DOWNHOUR, John - dated 5-5-1837; codicil 5-21-1837. Wife, Naomi. Children: Jacob, Peter, George, Stephen Polly, Magdalene, Betsey and John; the last named is deceased. Executors: Henry Dittoe and Havier Batch. Witnesses: Philip Harvey and Geo. Minnich. Codicil mentions youngest daughter, Elizabeth. Witnesses: M. D. Brock and Geo. Stinchcomb. (130)

DOWNHOUR, Peter - dated 6-2-1838. Wife, Catherine. Children not named. Executors: Wife, Catherine and Jacob Binckley. Witnesses: Daniel Fry and Thornton Taylor. (155)

DONALDSON, Ebenezer R. - dated 11-30-1840. Wife not named. Children: Mathew, Martha Shreeve, Sarah, Mary, James, Elizabeth Goodin, Rebecca Bennet and John. Grandson, John Shreeve. Executor, Mathew Donaldson. Witnesses: Joseph James and David P. Shreeve. (164)

DELONG, Isaac - dated 4-4-1842. Wife, Nancy. Children: William, Mary, John, George and Philip. Executor: son, William. Witnesses: Ira E. Lyons and Wm. B. Lyons. (170)

DUSENBERRY, William - dated 6-13-1840. Wife, Catherine. Heirs: John Dusenberry, Henry Dusenberry, Benjamin Dusenberry, John Hummel, Elizabeth Henderson, Benjamin Fickle, Catherine Wise, Jacob Hummel and Joseph Fickle. Grandson, Wm. Dusenberry. Executor: son, John Dusenberry. Witnesses: John and Barnet Hammer. (217)

DOLAN, Charles - dated 9-7-1846. Verbal will at point of death. Heirs not named. Executor and Guardian of children: Rev. Mathew O'Brien. Witnesses: Rev. Mathew O'Brien and Pat. W. Sweeney. (218)

DARSHAM, Christian - dated 6-21-1844. Wife, Catherine. Children: Tobias, Jacob, Catherine Miller, and Christian, Jr. Grandson, Christian son of Tobias. Executors: son, Jacob and Jacob Focht. Witnesses: Anthony Fink and Christian L. Griner. (236)

ELLIS, Henry - dated 3-17-1828. Wife not named. Son, Stephen, only child named. Witnesses: Wm. B. Martin and Wm. Henry Herron. (60)

EBY, John - dated 12-19-1829. Wife, Eve. Children: John, Magdaline, Andrew, Peter, David, Jacob, Abraham, Barbara Kepler, Eve Fink, Catherine Fickle. Executors: son, Andrew and Henry Kelley. Witnesses: John Schofield and Joseph G. Fickle. (75)

ELLIS, Michael - dated 9-20-1824. Wife not named. Children: William, Ira, Benjamin, Patsey, Reuben, Michael, Wesley, Betsey, Susannah, Francis and George. Executors: sons, Reuben and Michael. Witnesses: Jesse and Abraham Carlick. (83)

ENSMINGER, Henry - dated 10-1-1832. Wife, Rachel. Children: Ann Maria, Rebecca, Mary, Elizabeth, Lawrence, Henry, Andrew, Daniel, John, Philip, Cornelius and Samuel. Executrix: wife, Rachel. Witnesses: Lyle Fulton, Benjamin Rutter and John Schofield. (93)

ECKLES, Richard - dated 10-9-1829. Wife, Margaret. Children: William, Julia Barnd and Sally Brant. Grandson, Samuel Skinner. Executrix: wife, Margaret. Witnesses: John Comley and Robert Stewart. (111)

ECKLES, Margaret - dated 2-2-1847. Son-in-law, Jacob Barnd to have lots in village of Selreesport, Allegheny Co., Maryland with all personal property for maintaining said Margaret for the past 10 or 12 years. No executor named. Witnesses: Eli Montgomery, Jesse Skinner and Elizabeth Vanwey. (328)

FINCK, Daniel - dated 2-17-1818; proved 4-26-1819. Wife not named. Children: Joseph, William, Mary, Sarah and Philip. Executors: son, William and John Hendricks. Witnesses: James Ward and Jacob Hendricks. (1)

FATE, Thomas – dated 5-1-1823. Wife, Leah. Children: John, Martin, George and Shadrack. Executor, Hugh Riley of Morgan Co., Ohio. Witnesses: R. Sanborne, John Courtney and Thomas Pettit. (36)

FISHER, John – dated 2-14-1823. Wife, Susannah. Children: John, Adam, Michael, Jacob, Magdalene, Catharine Zartman (Samuel), Barbara Zartman (Henry), and Eva Maria. Executors: son, John and John Humbarger. Witnesses: J. Fisher and Adam Auspach (both in German). (57)

FULLERTON, Samuel – dated 1-10-1824. No wife. Sons: James, Robert, John and Samuel. Daughters: Jane, Mary and Catherine. Executors: sons, James and Samuel. Witnesses: Wm. and Homes Bogle. (59)

FORQUER, Michael – dated 11-5-1830. No wife. Brother, William and Rosanna his wife. Mentions Wm. Forquer Jr. and John Forquer Sr.; Wm. Forquer to collect all debts. Witnesses: Wm. Fowler and Wm. Biddison. (77)

FATE, Martin – dated 5-14-1828. No wife. Brothers: John and George Fate. Executor: brother, George. Witnesses: Robert Sanborn and Jane Stoughton. (78)

FUNDERBURG, Noah – dated 3-17-1826. Wife, Barbara. Children: Jacob, Sarah, Catherine, Hetty, Mary, Samuel, Eliza and Rachel. Executors: wife, Barbara and son, Jacob. Witnesses: Wm. P. Darst and Daniel Parkinson. (82)

FINK (FINCK), John – dated 11-21-1833. Wife, Mary. Children: Jacob, John, Joseph, Anthony, Mary McGowen, Adam, Elizabeth McDonald, Sarah Johnson, Frances Hewit, and David. Executors: wife, Mary and sons, Jacob and Adam. Witnesses: John B. Orton and Edmond C. Cusack. (100)

FISHER, William – dated 3-19-1836. No wife. Brothers: Philip. Samuel, Joseph and George. Sisters: Mary, Hannah, Margaret and Eliza. Executor: brother, Philip. Witnesses: John Knitz and John Lidey. (123)

FORGUSON, Elizabeth – dated 2-13-1843. No husband. Daughter, Rebecca Oats. Grand-daughters: Harriet and Rebecca Forguson. Witnesses: Elijah Helser and Philip Harvey. (179)

FINK, John – dated 10-25-1842. Wife, Elizabeth. Children: Mary Ann and James; only children named. Executors: brother, Adam and son-in-law, Ed. Droge. Witnesses: Nicholas D. Young and Jacob Finck. (181)

FISHER, Leonard – dated 9-29-1840. Wife, Maria. Children and step-child: Anthony Fisher, Jacob Fritz, Andrew Fisher, Magdalene Smith (George, Maria, Sophia Lash (Michael), Genevieve Fisher and Gunan Fisher. Witnesses: Jacob Dittoe and Isaac Lefever. (189)

FLING, Sarah – dated 3-30-1844. Husband, James. Brothers and Sisters mentioned but not named. Executor, husband, James. Witnesses: Samuel Curran and Ruel Cooper. (193)

FORQUER, William – not dated. Wife, Cecily. Children: Michael D., Charles, and Sarah Elizabeth; only ones named. Executor: son, Michael D. Witnesses: Samuel H. Gordon and John O'Connor. (228)

FEALTY, Bernard – dated 6-25-1836. Wife, Ann. Children: David and Morgan; only ones named. Executors: wife, Ann and Wm. McGargle. Witnesses: John and Myles Green. (240)

FRANKS, Jonathan – dated 5-6-1851; proved 6-23-1851. Wife not named. Son, Peter land in Hardin Co., Ohio. Son, Jacob to have home farm. Daughter, Sarah land in Logan Co., Ohio. Executor: son, Jacob. Witnesses: Barnard Daugherty and Henry Sprankle. (320)

GOOD, John Sr. – dated 10-2-1818. Wife, Susannah. Sons: Joseph, Christian, John Jr., and Benjamin. Daughters: Barbara Bisecker (David); Hannah Carr, dec'd (Wm.); Susannah Rehm (Jacob Ream); Elizabeth; Catherine and Rachel. Owned quarter section in Richland County adjoining Greenstown. Executors: son, Joseph and son-in-law, Jacob Rehm (Ream). Witnesses: Henry Statler and Peter Bugh Sr. Codicil dated 3-27-1819 mentions timber on daughter, Barbara's land. Witnesses: Peter Miller and Peter Bugh. (14)

GROVES, John – dated 10-1-1826. Wife, Nancy. Children: Mary, Abraham, James, George and Rebecca. Executors: son, Abraham and Henry Nesmith. Witnesses: Henry Nesmith, Wm. Karr and Henry Bowman (in German). (54)

GORDON, Charles – dated 8-8-1821. Wife, Nancy. Children: Henry, George, John, Jeremiah, Charles, Hester Warner (John), Mary, William and Nancy Gordon. Executors: son, Henry and Wm. Williams. Witnesses: John and Samuel Henricks.(60)

GOODEN (GOODIN), Moses Sr. – dated 4-17-1831. No wife. Children: Jane Ogg; Phebe Oatley; Smith Gooden, dec'd; David Gooden, dec'd; Moses Gooden Jr.; Asa Gooden; Polly Gooden; Elizabeth Hartzell; Samuel Gooden; and Martha Gooden. Executors: Stephen Barnes and Daniel Hull. Witnesses: Stephen Barnes and Smith Riley. (99)

GINTER, Henry – dated 2-18-1839. Wife, Mary Eve. Children: Henry, Frederick and Jacob; only ones named. No executor named. Witnesses: John E. Linn, John Wolf and Jacob Overmeyer. (108)

GORDON, James – dated 7-13-1840. Wife, Sarah. Son, Bazzel, only child named. Executors: wife, Sarah and son, Bazel. Witnesses: Isaac Brown and Wm. Johnson. (160)

GOBLE, Isaac – dated 3-24-1843. Wife, Sarah. Children: Evi (or Eve), Simeon, Enos, Robert, Hannah Forsythe (John), Elizabeth Williams (George) and Sarah. Executors: wife, Sarah and George Williams. Witnesses: John Vanatta and Barnet Hammers. (184)

362

ARLINGER, John - dated 11-22-1836. Wife, Elizabeth. Children: George; Jacob; Magdalena Wilson (James); Elizabeth Dirst (Martin); Joseph; Sarah Barnd (John): and Mary Foncannon, dec'd. Grand-daughter, Elizabeth Foncannon. Executors: wife, Elizabeth and Peter A. Vansickle. Witnesses: John Vanatta and Samuel Miller.(186)

RIGSBY, Moses - dated 3-5-1836. Wife, Lucy C. Children: Moses B. Jr.; Cassey Daniels; Moses A. Smoot, son of Stephen and Susannah Smoot; and Benjamin A. Humphrey. Executrix; wife, Lucy. Witnesses: J. McDonald and Richard Williams. (193)

RATTON, Mary - dated 8-9-1845. Legatees: Charles Beaths, Mary Beaths, Elizabeth Beaths, William Beaths, John Beaths, Thomas Beaths Jr. and Euphemia Beaths; share equally. Executor, Thomas Beaths Sr. Witnesses: John J. Clark and Hugh Murphy. 206)

ORDON, George - dated 1-14-1846. No wife. Children: Abraham, George, Peggy Franks, Sally Franks, Betsey Crosby, Charles, Hannah Armstrong and Nancy. Executors: John Wilson and Abisha Davison. Witnesses: Frederick and Abisha Davison. (214)

ORDON, William - dated 10-2-1849; proved 11-10-1849. Wife, Mary. Children: Sarah Johnson, Margaret Hoy, Elizabeth Wiseman, Mary Clark, Eleanor Clark, Nancy Pragg, Jane Guyton, Susanna Hewit, Cassandra Cochran, Lucy Heffley, Mark Gordon, George W. Gordon, and William Gordon, dec'd, his son (testator's grandson), adm. Executors: John J. Jackson and Mark Gordon. Witnesses: Peter Witmer and Daniel Baker. (278)

RAY, Jonas H. - dated 7-20-1850; proved 10-1-1850. Wife, Achsah M. P. No children named. Executrix; wife, Achsah. Witnesses: Robert F. Brook and Edward S. Spencer. 297)

ORDON, Samuel H. - dated 2-10-1851; proved 4-1-1851. Wife not named. Children: John, Sarah E., Robert F. and Emma C. Executor, Isaac Yost. Witnesses: J. J. Wilson and John S. Manly. (315)

RIGGS, Samuel - dated 10-14-1850; proved 7-19-1851. Wife, Deborah. Children: John and Elizabeth Johnston (David). Executors: wife, Deborah and son, John. Witnesses: W. E. Finck, John Elder and Jonathan K. Jay. (321)

OOPER, Jacob - dated 7-9-1815. No wife. Children: Philip, James, Jacob, Ezekiel, John, Samuel, Polly and Rebecca. No executor named. Witnessess: James Allen, Sam. Wiseman and Philip Hooper. (6)

AMMER, Jacob - dated 1-8-1816. Wife not named. Children: George, Mary, Barbara, Jn, Barnet, Catherine, Esther, Martha and John. Executors: son, John and Geo. Ousley. Witnesses: Geo. Fluckey and Joseph Beard. (8)

ULL, Benjamin - dated 9-8-1822. Wife, Hannah. Children: John, Jacob, Samuel, Daniel, Elizabeth and Catherine. Executor; son, John. Witnesses: Thomas King and Ruel Sayre Jr. (33)

363

HESLER, John - dated 7-27-1825. No wife. Children by 1st wife: Sarah, Jenny, Catherine, Elizabeth and Hannah. Children by 2nd wife: Jacob, Nancy, Susanna and Rebecca. Executor; son, Jacob. Witnesses: Thos. King and Thos. Wilson. (45)

HENRICKS, Elizabeth - dated 2-22-1826. Children: Jacob, Margaret, John, George, Samuel, Daniel, Peter, Elijah and Elizabeth. Executors: Michael Foght and Robert Wiley. Witnesses: Elijah Scofield and James Ward. (49)

HARDIN, Ignatius - dated 1-29-1827. Wife, Rachel. Children: Polly, Elizabeth, Sarah, Rebecca, Rachel, Nancy, dec'd, her daughter—Lydia; John, James; Joseph; Even; David; Benjamin; and Polly, dec'd, her son—Isaiah. Executors: wife, Rachel and sons, Joseph, Even and David. Witnesses: Geo. and Jacob Zeigler. (55)

HINES, Martin - dated 2-20-1826. Wife, Elizabeth. Daughter, Amy McLaughlin. Executors: wife and daughter. Witnesses: Wm. and Robert Spencer. (58)

HAMISFAR, Abraham - dated 9-12-1828. Wife, Hannah. Children: Hannah Gordon and Charles. Executor; son, Charles. Witnesses: Thomas Cowen and Katherine Hamisfar. (61)

HAMMOND, Rebecca of Brook County, Virginia - dated 11-13-1828. Nieces: Margaret and Temperance Hood. Sisters: Catherine Meryman, Eliza Viers and Frances Hood. Mentions that negro slave girl Kitt, is to be freed in two years. No executor named. Witnesses: Wm. McClay Awl and Margaret M. Trout. (62)

HUMPHREY, Benjamin - dated 6-8-1832. Wife, Betty. Son, Benjamin Jr. Executors: son, Benjamin and David Humphrey. Witnesses: John Iliff and John Reed. (92)

HUMBARGER, John - dated 6-23-1833. Wife, Margaret. Heirs: Wilson Crissel alias Wilson McClelland, Hannah Miller and Sarah Dupler wife of Wm. Sheeler. Executor, Adam Binckley, Esq. Witnesses: Geo. Brunner and John Lidey. (96)

HAZELTON, John - dated 10-6-1834. Wife, Barbara. Children: Catherine Skinner, Samuel, William, Henry, Sarah, Elizabeth Skinner, John, Joseph, Mary Sain, James and Lot Hazelton. Executors: sons, John and James. Witnesses: Benj. Good and Edwin Huff. (107)

HELSER, David - dated 3-9-1835. Wife not named. Children: John, Elizabeth, Margaret, David, Sally, George, Solomon, Samuel and Jacob. Executors: John and Daniel Helser Jr. Witnesses: Wm. Karr, Daniel Kelser and Adam Fisher (in German). (112)

HUMBARGER, Peter - dated 12-23-1837. Wife not named. Children: Peter, John, Adam, Benjamin, Henry, Jacob, Susanna, Catherine, Rebecca, Hannah and Mary. Executors: sons, Peter and John. Witnesses: Daniel Helser and Alexander Castanian. (139)

HUSTON, Archibald - dated 11-16-1837. Wife not named. Children: John, Robert, Mary, Jane, Hannah and Archibald. Daughter, Ellener, dec'd, her children— Rebecca, Sarah Jane and Ann Elizabeth. Executors: sons, John and Robert. Witnesses: James Kelley and Daniel Crosby. (140)

HELSER, Daniel - dated 9-10-1838. Wife, Elizabeth. Children: Catherine, Susanna, Elizabeth, Hannah, Polly, Sally, Anna, John, Liza and Ameline. Executor, mentioned but not named. Witnesses: Jacob Snider and John Shrider. (145)

HEARHOLZER, Joseph - dated 2-24-1836. Wife, Helena. Children: John; Elizabeth, Magdalena; and Mariana, dec'd, her daughter—Mariana. Executrix: wife, Helena. Witnesses: Anthony Fink and Christian L. Griner. (146)

HART, John - dated 5-9-1839. Wife, Elizabeth. Children: William, Joseph, Susan and Elizabeth. Executor, Charles Lamb. Witnesses: Hugh Taylor and Benjamin Brown. (152)

HARPER, Samuel - dated 7-24-1842. Wife, Margaret. Brother, Thomas Harper. Executor, Thomas Whitaker. Witnesses: Thos. Whitaker and Eli Montgomery. (174)

HANBY, John - dated 12-1-1842. Wife, Sarah. Children: William, Samuel, George, Eliza Ann Tabler and Martha Miliness. Executors: wife, Sarah and Joseph Walmire. Witnesses: George Grubb and George Hanbey. (180)

HOLLENBACK, Jacob Sr. - dated 9-15-1834. Wife, Susannah. Children: daughter, Susana, only one named. No executor or witnesses given. (202)

HEARHOLZER, John B. - dated 6-25-1842. No wife. Sons, John. Mentions four daughters, does not name. Mother, Helena Hearholzer. Executors: Jacob Castigan and Charles Elder. Witnesses: John Elder and John Lentz (in German) (205)

HAMILTON, Frances - dated July 1845. Father, James Hamilton, dec'd. Guardian, Emanuel Crossen. Entire estate to Sisters of St. Mary's for their care of said Frances. Executor, Jacob Castigan. Witnesses: E. R. Magruder and Patrick McDonald. (206)

HAMISFAR, Thomas - dated 8-20-1844. No wife. Half-brothers; David L. and Charles W. Hamisfar. Executor, James B. Ritchey. Witnesses: John Wilson and Isaac Hamisfar. (207)

HOLCOMB, John B. - dated 10-17-1845. Wife, Rachel. Sons: John B., Elijah, Buris(?). and Thomas. Sons-in-law: Conrad Whitlock, John Parker, Joseph Parker, and Nathan Moody. Executor; son, John B. Holcomb. Witnesses: Robert Lyle and B. Longstreth. (211)

HOLLENBACK, Susannah - dated 4-20-1846. Children: John, Daniel, Jacob, Hamsen, Nancy McClelland, Sarah Black and Susanna McKeever. No executor named. Witnesses: Robert McClelland and Samuel Skinner. (230)

HAMMER, John - dated 4-3-1849; proved 5-15-1849. Wife, Charlotte, Children: Jacob, George and Sarah. Executors: sons, Jacob and George. Witnesses: Nicholas H. Taylor, Barnet Hammer and Jacob W. Hammer. (264)

HUNDSUCKER, Samuel - dated 8-13-1848; proved 1-30-1849. Brother, Jackson Clark, testators claim against U. S. Gov't for service in 2nd Reg't Ohio Volunteers, Capt. Wm. A. Latham Comd'g. Sister, Jane Clark. Also to brother, Jackson Clark, all land due from Gov't for service in A Co. of Dragoons, Capt. James West Comd'g., made up in Mexico in the town of Tampico after testator's first years service had expired. Executor, Joseph Lenville. Witnesses: Robert Martin and James Hutchins. (256)

HARDY, John - dated 3-12-1849; proved 9-11-1849. Wife, Mary. No children named. Executor, John Cowen. Witnesses: Geo. Boylan, C. P. Hackney and Robert Thrush. (275)

HAMAND, Elijah - dated 6-3-1850; proved 2-27-1851. No wife. Brother, Wm. Hamand. Sisters: Nancy and Rebocca Hamand, everything including deceased's land in Tipp-ecanoe Co., Indiana. Executor, Thos. Hamand Sr. Witnesses: R. W. McMahon and E. S. Spencer. (307)

HENDERSON, Elizabeth - dated 7-6-1850; proved 7-1-1851. Children: James C., John P., Samuel R., Eliza Jane, Thomas L., William F., Alva W., Ebenezer B. Grand-daughter, Elizabeth Rebecca Pee. Executor: brother, James H. Ramsey. Witnesses: R. M. Brown, James Culbertson and Jacob Thomas. (319)

HOUGH, John - dated 6-23-1851; proved 1-10-1852. Wife, Nancy. Wife's daughter, Mary. Nine children, not named. Executor, Benjamin Moore. Witnesses: Samuel Curran and Samuel Axline. (329)

IIAMS (IJAMS), Isaac H. - dated 9-12-1845. Wife, Elizabeth. Wife's son, Ephraim Koons. Brother, F. R. Iiams. Sisters: Comfort Stevenson and Sarah Jackson. Niece, Caroline Elizabeth Iiams. Nephews: Isaac Turner, Isaac H. Iliff, Wm. E. Iiams and Joseph Henry Harrison Iams. Executors: Ephriam Koons and John J. Jack-son. Witnesses: Isaac Larimer and J. F. Dollison. (215)

JONES, Thomas - dated 4-14-1820. Wife not named. Children: John, Sarah Ann and Harrison. Executors: John Melick and John Rose. Witnesses: Jacob Reed and John Melick. (18)

JACKSON, George - dated 11-26-1846. Wife, Mary. Children: William, George and Mary Bruner (Geo. Jr.). Executors: wife, Mary and Geo. Brunner Sr. Witnesses: Jacob Noles and Thos. Hood. (224)

KRUMRYNE, Christian - dated 3-1-1821. Wife, Catharine. Children by wife Cath-arine: Malena, Henry, Susanna, Margaret, Martin, John, Jacob and Eliza. Other children: Philip, Michael, Elizabeth Fore, Mary Wilson and Peter. Executors: wife, Catharine and George Trout Sr. Witnesses: Peter Adlin, Leonard Ream and Joseph Wheatcraft. (20)

KENNEDY, Dennis - dated 10-4-1824. Wife, Ruth. Children: John, Prucy, Ruth, Sally, Abigail, Seth and James. Executors: sons, John and Seath. Witnesses: Hugh L. Hankinson, Samuel Clayton and Robert Chriswell. (41)

KING, Rachel - dated 5-18-1818. Heirs: daughter, Jane Wilson (Thomas); Rachel and Catherine Tedrow daughters of Michael and Catherine Tedrow, both deceased, late of Somerset Co., Pa.; son, Moses King; daughter, Rachel Ream (Samuel). Executors: David King of Somerset Co., Pa. and son, Thomas. Witnesses: Henry Shaner and James Wilson. (56)

KELLY, John - dated 2-17-1830. No wife. James Johnson to have all land and everything for kindness and favors shown testator. No executor named. Witnesses: Wm. McClure and Adam Finck. (88)

KOVER, Adam - dated 3-20-1830. Wife, Elizabeth. Children: Samuel, John, Katherine Shenefield, Mary Dixson, Adam, Sally Hart, Elizabeth Snatterly and Henry H. Executors: George Shelley Tanner and Jacob Kefover. Witnesses: Holmes Beagle and Daniel Griffith. (110)

KING, Thomas - dated 1-2-1839. Wife, Nancy; to have land in Monticello Co., Indiana. Adopted son, Wm. Harrison Skinner, who was raised from an infant. Martha Skinner, a young woman raised from childhood to have land in Delaware Co., Indiana. Executors: son, W. Harrison Skinner and Aaron Johnson. Witnesses: Aaron and Robert Johnson. (156)

KLINGLER, Adam - dated 11-2-1831. No wife. Children: Adam and David. Sons-in-law: George Waggoner and Henry Bashore. Executors: Fred'k From and David Klingler. Witnesses: Wm. Kerr and David Helzer. (172)

KIRCHER, Michael - dated 2-2-1839. Wife, Christiana. Children not named. Executors: Myles Green and Anthony Fritch. Witnesses: P. Franklin and John J. Greene. (191)

KUNS (KUNCE), George - dated 5-23-1844. Wife, Susanna. Children: Catherine; Samuel; Sally, dec'd, her son--Sam'l Henderson; only ones named. Executor: Wm. Yost. Witnesses: Jacob Fisher and John Stockbarger. (196)

KEMPER, Amos R. - dated 7-2-1845. Verbal Will at point of death. Wife not named. Children not named. Executor, Jacob Hooper. Witnesses: John A. Smith and Benj. Ellis. (205)

KETCHAM, Holmes - dated 8-29-1842. Wife, Mary. Children: Obadiah. John H., Andrew, Hiram, Alice, Esther Jane, Cynthia Mariah, Keturah Ann and Nancy. Executrix: wife, Nancy. Witnesses: Philip Bidison and Alvah Tharp. (237)

KIM, Adolphus - dated 8-27-1846; proved 5-15-1849. Christian L. Griner of Somersett, Attorney for estate. Wife, Maria Ann. Son, Augustin, only child named. Executor, Christian L. Griner. Witnesses: Anthony Finck and Christian L. Griner. (266)

KURETH, Frantz - dated 1-13-1850; proved 4-24-1850. Translated from German by Christian L. Griner. Wife not named. Children: Martin, Elizabeth and Maria Ann. Executor: son, Martin. Witnesses: George and Joseph Schmitt (in German). (285)

KINTZ, Mary - dated 2-24-1842; proved 7-25-1849. Mother, Eleanor Dittoe.
Children: Mary Jane, Frederick, George, Charles, Anthony, Nancy Stine, Polly
Welsh (Brice B.). Grandchildren: Mary Ann, Jacob, James and Wm. Welsh.
Executors: Joseph Fink and Michael Dittoe. Witnesses: Henry and Jacob
Dittoe. (272)

KEENAN, Patrick - dated 8-11-1850; proved 10-1-1850. Wife, Mary. Children:
Eleanor, Elizabeth and John, only ones named. Executors: wife, Mary and son,
John. Witnesses: John Clark Jr. and Alex. McClain. (292)

KAYLOR, Frederick - dated 9-14-1836; proved 9-30-1850. No wife. Children:
Jacob, Margaret Boerstler (Daniel), Sally Fling and Christiana. Grand-daughter,
Polly Pence. Executor: son, Jacob. Witnesses: Samuel Curran and Joshua
Chilcote. (293)

KING, Thomas S. - dated 4-10-1850; proved 10-1-1850. Wife, Sarah. Children:
William L., David S., and Martha J. No executor named. Witnesses: Daniel
Springer and John McDonald. (301)

LONG, Catharine - dated 2-9-1821 (in German). No husband. Children: George,
Jacob, Elizabeth Kohrig, Catherine Overmeyer, Christiana Heberling and
Margaretha Parkinson. Executors: son, Jacob and son-in-law, Johannes Obermeyer.
Witnesses: John M. Mullon and Wm. Fullerton. (26)

LOTT, Charles - dated 3-12-1830. No wife. Children: Peter, Abraham, Charl
William and Sally Crossen (Wm. R.). Executor; son, Peter. Witnesses: John
Crook and John Miller. (72)

LOOFBORROW, Jonathan - dated 11-22-1831. Wife, Barbara. Daughter, Mary Coleburn; only child named. Executors; wife, Barbara and George Morris. Witnesses:
George Mains and John Barnd. (127)

LOVE, Mary - dated 10-7-1841. Daughter, Anna Jane Cain (William). Grandchildren: Thomas and Sarah Cain. No executor named. Witnesses: John Crook,
James Love and James Sherlock. (194)

LITZINGER, Jacob - dated 1-30-1845. Wife not named. Sons, John and Jacob.
No executor named. Witnesses: John H. Dittoe, James Dillon and John Eckenrode.
(200)

LOY, Jacob O., M.D. - dated 5-30-1845. Wife not named. Children: Margaret
Susanna and George William Washington Loy. Partner Dr. Samuel H. Gordon.
Guardian of children, Otto H. Moeller. Executors: Otto H. Mueller and John
Fressler. Witnesses: P. S. Greene and Wm. F. Lehman (201)

LACY, Manuel - dated 1-15-1829. Wife, Mary. Children: Maria; Joseph; Benjamin; and James, dec'd. Grandchildren: John Thomas and Manuel, sons of James.
Administrators: don, Joseph and Henry D. Cochran. Witnesses: Stephen Wise
and George Kishler. (203)

LATIMER, Alexander - dated 6-25-1846. Wife not named. Four children, not named. Witnesses: John Wilson and Ebenezer B. Calderhead. (219)

LAIRD, Davis - dated 6-4-1846. Wife, Eliza. Children: Rees D. and Mary Ann Laird. No executor named and no appraisement. Witnesses: Henry Kelley and Wm. F. Dilts. (220)

LAIRD, William - dated 2-23-1847. Wife, Mary. Children: William D., John, James, Moses, Elijah, Susan Huston, Mary Laughman, Rebecca Hunt, Sarah Jane Pierce, Eliza and Rachel. Executor: Wm. D. Laird. Witnesses: Henry Kelley and Wm. Simpson. (228)

LEHMAN, Jacob A. - dated 3-14-1848. No wife. Daughter, Ann B. Son, Christian. Executor, John Stoltz. Witnesses: John Stoltz and Jacob Sain. (251)

LECKEY, Elizabeth - dated 10-13-1846; proved 1-28-1850. Children: Thomas, Ruth and Hannah. No executor named. Witnesses: Joseph Hodges and Nelson Rogers. (283)

LACEY, Mahlon - dated 6-26-1848; proved 10-1-1850. Wife, Anna. Son, Mahlon Albert Lacey. Executor, John Lidey. Witnesses: Wm. Johnston and Wm. Neeley.(295)

LENHART, David - dated 6-18-1850; proved 9-30-1850. Verbal will at point of death. Wife, Harriet. Children not named. Witnesses: John W. Baird and David A. Lenhart. (296)

LECKRONE, John - dated 4-27-1849; proved 1-10-1852. No wife. Children not named. Executors: David Helser, Isaac Zartman and Solomon Helser. Witnesses: Joseph Ridenour and Isaac Zartman. (330)

MYERS, John - dated 2-18-1819. Wife, Margaret. Children: Caty, Peggy, Mary, Elizabeth, Peter, Martin, Henry, Jacob and Samuel. Executors: wife, Margaret and William Keith. Witnesses: Jacob Sines, Lydia J. Murdock and Jacob Sines Jr. Codicil dated 3-30-1819 gives wife more of estate. Same witnesses. (7)

MILLER, John - dated 9-3-1822. (In German). Gives his place of birth and parents. No wife. Only child, Maria Ann. Executors: George Baumann (Bowman) and Rev. Andrew Henkel. Witnesses: Barnhart Bowman and Peter Bowman. (27)

MURRAY, Hugh - dated 8-20-1823. No wife. Sister, Catherine Margaret. All to friend, John McBride; who is also to serve as executor. Witnesses: Roswell Mills and Daniel Lidey. (35)

McNUTT, Joseph - dated 6-3-1825. No wife. Children: John and Eliza Ann; land at Sandusky, Ohio and near Somerset, Ohio, 80 acres. Executors: Charles C. Hood and John Beckwith. Witnesses: Charles Waddell, Jacob Mains and Gottlieb Shue. (43)

MILLER, Jacob - dated 7-7-1825. Wife, Catherine. Wife's father, Wm. Reagel (or Rail). Daughter, Polly Hill (George), only child named. Executors: wife, Catherine; George Brunner and Rosswell Mills, Witnesses: Edward Simpson, Richard J. Lilley and Roswell Mills. (46)

MOORE, William - dated 11-17-1830. Wife, Nancy. Daughter, Mary Delong only child named. Executors: wife, Nancy and James McFarlin. Witnesses: Samuel Curran and Robert Bradshaw. (77)

McMULLEN, James - dated 11-26-1830. Wife, Jane. Sons: Annanias and Alonzo. Executor: son Annanias. Witnesses: Jonathan Babb and Henry Wilson. (78)

MECHLING, Jacob - dated 4-26-1831. Wife, Mary. Heirs: children of daughter, Esther, dec'd—Joshua, Jacob M., Lovey M. and Samuel Mechling; daughter, Mary Ilief (Fredrick), land in Allegheny twp., Armstrong Co., Pa.; daughter, Hannah Cooperider (Peter); son, Jacob; son, Peter, dec'd, his seven children—Sally, Catherine, Jacob, John, Peter, Eliza and Magdalene; son, Frederick; son, John; son, George; daughter, Elizabeth Smith (Jacob); son, Samuel; Samuel son of Wulliam Mechling. Executors: sons, Jacob and Frederick; John Stockbarger. Witnesses: Jacob Foght and John Daniel (both in German). (79)

MOORE, John - dated 12-22-1814 (note: recorded ca 1832-33). Wife, Mary. Children: Mary, Robert, Agnes, Martha, Jane, James and John. Executors: son, Robert and James Patterson. Witnesses: John Sharp, John McCarel and James Patterson. (86)

McDONALD, Michael - dated 9-2-1833. No wife. Children: Elenor, Daniel, Michael, John, Mary and Nancy. Executors: sons, Daniel and Robert. Witnesses: Joshua Brown and Robert McDonald. (109)

MOORE, Joseph - dated 6-19-1833. Wife Chloe. Five sons: John, James G., Benjamin, Elijah and Robert Moore. Executor: son. Benjamin. Witnesses: Lyle Fulton and Peter Harney. (109)

McDONALD, Robert - dated 3-24-1835. Wife not named. Children: Robert, John, Mary and Rosanna. Executor: son, Robert. Witness: Jacob Strohl. (113)

McCORMICK, Thomas - dated 5-5-1835. No wife. Children: John; Anna; Elizabeth; Mary; William, dec'd; and James. Grand-daughter, Sarah Ann Daughter of William, dec'd. Executors: son, John and Wm. Chamberlain. Witnesses: John Lidey and Peter Zeigler. (114)

MOYER, John - dated 4-15-1823. No wife. Children: Barbara, Elizabeth, Ann Maria, Catherine, John Jr. and Michael. Grandchildren: Peter, Martin and Jacob Overmeyer, children of Barbara; Solomon Moyer son of Michael; Catherine and Sally Moyer daughers of Michael. Sally Moyer widow of Michael. Executor, John Waggoner Sr. Witnesses: Rosewell Mills, Adam Klingler and Edward Keenin. (124)

MARTIN, Jacob - dated 4-24-1837 with codicil dated 5-3-1837. No wife. Son, George, only child named; codicil gives George more land. Executor: son, George. Witnesses: Wm. Coffman and Hezekiah Franklin. Witnesses to codicil: Hezekiah Franklin and Rowland Shiplett. (132)

McKERNAN, Daniel - dated 6-22-1840. No wife. Brother, James, sole heir. Executor: brother, James. Witnesses: Henry Sherlock and Daniel O'Hara. (165)

MITCHELL, William - dated 11-15-1844. No wife. Children: William F.; John F., dec'd; Violet Mitchell (Mathew); Susan Bessant (John), and George. Grand-daughter, Mary Cain. Executor: son, George. Witnesses: James S. and Wm. McClary. (219)

MAUTZ, Conrad - dated 1-23-1847. No wife. Grand-daughter, Maria, daughter of Gohn George, dec'd; Elizabeth Staubus (William). Executor, Geo. Kisler. Witnesses: Geo. Kishler and John Palmer. (225)

McCORMICK, Adah - dated 3-9-1847. Daughter, Rebecca Defenbaugh (Isaiah). No executor named. Witnesses: Samuel Cassel, Thos. S. Keyes and John Lidey. (230)

MILLER, John - dated 12-9-1840. Wife, Hannah. Children: Jacob; Anna Grubb, dec'd; and Elizabeth Hutchinson. Executor, John Lidey. Witnesses: John Folk and Robert M. Martin. (231)

MITCHELL, Randolph - dated 5-1-1847. Wife, Lydia. No children mentioned. Executors; Peter Witmer and Solomon C. Mitchell. Witnesses: Peter Shrider and Rev. Chas. H. Hood. (232)

McCANDLISH, William - dated 10-2-1847. Wife, Rebecca. Children not named. No executor named. Witnesses: James Sherlock and James Ross. (241)

MATHERS, John - dated 11-17-1847. Wife, Mary Ann. Children not named. Overseers of estate; John Statler and Henry McAnelly. Witnesses: Myer Hines and Christopher Staley. (241)

McCORMICK, James - dated 9-21-1843. Wife, Jane. Children: James, Johnson, Robert, Hugh, Mary Ann and Rebecca Jane. Executors: son, Johnson and John Lidey. Witnesses: David and John Hutchinson. (250)

MUMFORD, James - dated 4-2-1845. Wife, Elizabeth. Sons, Levi and Thomas. Daughter, Mary Babcock. Grandson, Benjamin Mumford. Step-daughter, Delia West. Executor, Isaac Carter. Witnesses: John I. Cunningham and Isaac Jones. (252)

MARTIN, Owen - dated 7-12-1848; proved 1-30-1849. Wife, Sarah, Children: Henry Martin and Mary McCristal. Executors: son, Henry and Henry McAnelly. Witnesses: Thos. J. Maginnis and Samuel Barker. (254)

MOORE, Mary - dated 1-9-1844; proved 5-15-1849. Brother and Sister, Robert and Nancy Moore. Executors: brother Robert; two nephews, John and Wm. C. Moore. Witnesses: John S., Robert and Wm. C. Moore. (262)

McGINLEY, John - dated 6-24-1851; proved 9-29-1851. Wife, Bridget. Sister, Ellen Galigher. Executor of this estate, Patrick McMullen; Arch Bishop of Cincinnati executor after death of wife and sister. Witnesses: Ignatius Groff and Arthur Taggart. (324)

NIXON, Robert - dated 12-5-1828. Wife, Catherine. Children: John, Levi, Isaac, Jonathan, Elijah, Elizabeth, Mary Ann, Susannah, Sarah and 2 younger sons not named. Executors; wife, Catharine and son, Levi. Witnesses: Joshua Hankinson; Joseph and Sarah Johnson. (64)

NESBIT, Thomas - dated 2-24-1843. No wife. HEIRS: Julia M. Baird; Margaret Nesbit; Thomas and Nancy Nesbit, son and daughter of James Baird; Thomas Baird son of Alexander; John Baird. Executor, John Baird. Witnesses: Andrew Walker, Rees Davis and George Fullerton. (181)

NOLES, Jacob - dated 2-25-1846. Wife, Barbara. Children: Leroy, Henry, Clara, Almeda, Matilda, Harriet, Emeline, Asbury Fletcher and Ann Maria. Executor, John Beckwith. Witnesses: Ensor Chilcote and George Brunner. Codicil dated 4-4-1847 makes wife, Barbara, sole and only executrix. Same witnesses. (239)

NULL, Conrad - dated 9-18-1848. Wife, Catherine. Mentions deceased wife, Margaret. Children: Anna Catherine, Susannah and Lucinda. Executors: John and Samuel Cupp. Witnesses: Emanuel Fisher and Wm. Dempsey. (257)

OWENS, Stephen - dated 12-16-1836. Wife, Nancy. Children: George Washington; Nancy; Margaret; Susannah; Permelier; Rebecca Wilkins; Sarah Ann Rider; Stephen William, dec'd. No executor named. Witnesses: Wm. Combs and Geo. Wolf. (131)

ORNDORFF, Henry - dated 1-13-1848. No wife. Mother, Eve. Children: Margaret, William and George. Executor, Henry D. Cochran. Witnesses: Geo. Kishler and Henry D. Cochran. (245)

O'HARA, Patrick - dated 7-10-1848. Wife not named. Children: Daniel; Margaret; John, dec'd. Grandchildren: David and Anna Maria children of John, dec'd. Executor: son, Daniel. Witnesses: John J. Clark and Arthur McCortney. (253)

PARGIN, James - dated 6-4-1829. Wife, Margaret. Children: James, Nancy Stultz (Samuel), Elizabeth Vanatta (James) and Sarah Brown (Loyd). Executor: wife, Margaret. Witnesses: Rev. Thos L. Forsythe, Stephen Vanatta and Joseph Petty. (72)

PACE, Jacob - dated 4-20-1836. Wife, Margaret. Children: David, Chester, Priscilla, Amy, Joseph, Joanna, Hannah, Jacob, Michael, Mary and Elizabeth. Executors; wife, Margaret and James Kelley. Witnesses: Daniel G. Ellis, Jacob Pace Jr. and Allen Oliver. (126)

PARROT, Samuel - dated 4-2-1835. Wife, Ellen. Children: George and Philip, only ones named. Executor; son-in-law, Joseph Linville. Witnesses: John B. Orton, Patrick McDonald and Edmund C. Cusack. (187)

POTTER, William - dated 11-15-1845. Wife, Abigail. No children named. Witnesses: F. L. Flowers and Kelita Potter. (213)

PHERSON, George - dated 1-5-1847. Wife, Margaret. Children: William, George, John, Jonathan, Jane, Rebecca and Martha. Grand-daughter, Margaret Lucinda. Executors: Samuel Curran and James S. Sellars. (227)

372

PLANK, Adam - dated 4-13-1835. Wife, Christena. Children: Adam, Joseph, Elizabeth, Hubbard, Hannah Kober and Mary Hartzog. Executors: Michael Bosserman and Jacob Kefover. Witnesses: ____? Baultzer and John Eversole. (233)

PACE, Noah - dated 5-3-1849; proved 9-13-1849. No wife. Sister, Almira Higgins. Brothers, William and Charles. Nephew; John, son of Charles. Mother Elizabeth Chappelear. Executor, John C. Chappelear. Witnesses: Ira Carroll and Miner Pace. (276)

RIDENOUR, Ludwick - dated 1-27-1820. Wife not named. Children: Martin, Ludwick, Jacob, Isaac, Mathias, David, John, Evy and Mottelene. Executor, Jacob Mechling. Witnesses: Thomas Cowen and Paul Beam. (19)

RAIL, William - dated 1-1-1816. No wife. Children: Susannah George; Mary Magdalena Souslin; Mary Poorman; Catherine Miller; Esther Brown; Hannah Rail; Eve Dittoe; and Elizabeth Swank, dec'd, her daughter--Susannah Sahm. Grand-daughters, Catherine and Elizabeth Swank. Executors: sons-in-law, John Poorman and John Dittoe. Witnesses: Michael and Henry Dittoe. (30)

REYCUP, Catharine - dated 5-10-1826. Husband; John, dec'd. Sons, Joseph house and lot in Bainbridge, Ross co. Ohio. Bequeaths to Barbara Funderberg house and lot in town of Liberty, Frederick Co., Maryland. Executor, Noah Funderburg. Witnesses: Wm. P. Darst and E. Richman. (53)

RUNNELS, James - dated 1-19-1829. Wife, Ann. Heirs: Ellen Love, Nancy, Joseph, Benjamin, Mary, Elizabeth, Sarah and Jane. Executor, Isaac Delong. Witnesses: Samuel Curran and Joseph Delong. (64)

REESE, George - dated 1-29-1836. Wife, Emeline. Children: Nicholas J.Y., Angeline, Francis D., Elizabeth and Jacob. Executors: Abraham Ward and Isaiah Shepard. Witnesses: Stephen Ward and Thomas Clemens. (121)

REED, Jeremiah - dated Mar. 1833. Wife not named. Two sons and six daughters, not named. Executors: John Reed and John Melick. Witnesses: Samuel Curran, Isaac Delong and Ethan Allen Reed. (138)

RUSK, James - dated 3-4-1839. No wife. Daughter, Margaret Rusk, only one named. Witnesses: Samuel Curran and John Sellars. (155)

REED, George - dated 3-2-1842. No wife. Children: John M., Mary Thrapp and Margaret Holcomb. Executor; son, John. Witnesses: Leonard Strait and Mary Foreaker. (171)

ROBINSON, Andrew - dated 11-7-1843. Wife not named. Children: James, Richard and Rose Fitzgerald. Executor: Patrick McMullen. Witnesses: (Judge) John McGinley and Philip Deime. (190)

ROUSCULP, Philip - dated 11-21-1835. Wife, Anna Mary. Children: Jacob, Daniel, George, Peter, John, Sally, Philip and Samuel. Executors: son, Jacob and Andrew Smith. Witnesses: Lewis Bateson and John F. Randolph. (198)

RYAN, William - datéd 10-16-1847. Wife, Mary Elizabeth. Children not named.
Executrix; wife, Mary Elizabeth. Witnesses: Allen Clark and Arthur McCartney.
(242)

ROBERTS, Joseph - dated 9-25-1847. Wife, Sarah. Children: William and John.
Mentions Margaret wife of John. Grandsons, George and James. Executor; son,
William. Witnesses: Nicholas H. and David S. Taylor. (249)

RUTLEDGE, Susan - dated 8-8-1845; proved 5-16-1849. Nephews; Jacob Rockhold,
Elisha John Rockhold and Ephraim Rockhold. Nieces: Hannah Sites and Ellen
Rockhold. Executor: nephew, Jacob Rockhold. Witnesses: John T. Cuningham and
Nicholas Hitchcock. (258)

RYAN, John - dated 4-12-1849; proved 5-15-1849. Wife, Rose. Children not named.
Executrix; wife, Rose. Witnesses: T. J. Maginnis, E. R. Magruder and A. McElwee.
(261)

RUSK, John - dated 8-10-1849; proved 1-28-1850. Wife, Mary Ann. Daughters;
Margaret Ann and Ann Maria. Executor, Jacob Hermon. Witnesses: Robert Lyle
and Samuel Hearing. (280)

ROBISON, Robert of East Finley twp., Washington Co., Penna. - dated 4-18-1833;
proved 10-9-1837. Wife, Nancy. Children: Philip, William, Mary Canin (Michael)
and Gresoll Lyel (David). Grandson, Robert Canin. Executor: son, Philip.
Witnesses: J. Henderson and Wm. J. Haines. (304)

RIDENOUR, Ludwick - dated 6-9-1849; proved 3-27-1851. Wife, Catherine.
Children: Christian, Noah, Diannah, Nancy, Juleyan, Sophia, Samuel, Elizabeth
Helser, and Hannah Poorman. Executors: Bernard Bouman and Jacob Poorman.
Witnesses: Samuel Auspach, Abraham Wolf and Bernard Bouman. (316)

STOKER, Michael - dated 5-10-1818. Wife, Mary. Children: Jacob, Mary,
Charlotte, Catherine, Barbara, Michael, John, Margaret, Salome and Magdalene.
Executrix; wife, Mary. Witnesses: Roswell Mills and Leonard Ream. (5)

SHUNK, Isaac - dated 10-11-1819. Wife, Elizabeth. Children: Henry, his
daughter—Elizabeth; Isaac; and Polly Brown (John). Executors: wife, Elizabeth
and Barney Poorman. Witnesses: John B. Orton and Leonard Ream. (9)

SULLIVAN, Cornelius - dated ——-1818. Wife, Christena. Children: Mary Cornell
(James), Sarah King (William), Margaret McConnel (John), Susanna, Cornelius, And-
rew, Elizabeth and David; last five named by wife Christena. Executors: wife,
Christena and son, Cornelius. Witnesses: Daniel Nunemaker, Wm. Wilson and C. W.
Harrington. (23)

SANDERSON, Alexander - dated 2-4-1825. Wife, Elizabeth. Children: George,
Robert, William and Peggy Heck. Executors: George and Robert. Witnesses:
Christopher Huston, Joseph Shaver and John Meres. (42)

PENCER, James - dated 10-7-1825. No wife. Daughter, Sarah Wiswell, her son--onas Enfield. Executors: Thos. King and Samuel Ream. Witnesses: David M. ellers, Samuel Riggs and Jonathan Fickle. (48)

PRINGER, Charles - dated 10-19-1826. No wife. No children. Peter Dittoe rustee of estate in trust. Executor, Peter Dittoe. Witnesses: George Spurch nd Joel Beckwith. (56)

PIES, Philip - dated 8-3-1828. Wife, Susannah. Children: Adam, Jacob, Philip, braham S., Peter and David. Executors: sons, Peter and David. Witnesses: oseph Shaver and Peter Witmer. (62)

ELBY, John - dated 7-17-1829. No wife. No children. Father and Mother, Eli nd Ruby Selby. Nephew, John Selby Groves. Executors: brothers, Thomas and oshua Selby, Witnesses: George Gardner, John H. Ijams and Joel North. (70)

KINNER, John Sr. - dated 4-15-1828. No wife. Children: William, George, ohn Jr., Cornelius, Elizabeth Green, Nancy Goodin, Rebecca Barndt and Eleanor rout. Executors: George Skinner and Christian Barnd. Witnesses: William nd Robert Spencer. (92)

POHN, Philip - dated 3-16-1831. Wife, Catrina. Son, John, only child named nd he is to serve as executor. Witnesses (not given). (95)

HAVER, Joseph - dated 7-30-1834. Wife, Margaret. Children: Alexander, lizabeth, Lidey, Margaret Heck, George, Joseph, James and Samuel. Grand-aughters; Margaret and Rachel Linville. Executors: son, Alexander and John idey. Witnesses: Mary Fisher and John B. Orton. (105)

CHOFIELD, Elijah - dated 1-27-1836. Wife, Dorcas. Children: Elias, Benjamin, hoda, John, Elizabeth, Daniel, Dorcas, Elijah, Jesse, Polly and Susanna. Grand-aughters: Adia and Martha Bush. Executors: Elias and Benjamin Schofield. itnesses: John and Balultzer Eversole. (128)

CALLAN, James - not dated, ca. 1835 or 1836. Wife, Mary. Children: Thomas nd Mary Ann. Witnesses: John Moore and Robert Redmond. (129)

HELLEY, George - dated 10-21-1837. Wife, Margaret. Children: Michael, Daniel, lizabeth Cooperider (Manuel) and Sally Welty (Peter). Executors: George Shelly nd George Defenbaugh. Witnesses: John Wilson and George Trout. (134)

WINEHART, John - dated 2-21-1838. Wife, Christina. Children: Peter, Sally usbaugh, Elizabeth Cooperider, Catherine, Jacob, Jonas, Samuel, Julid, Daniel, eorge and Andrew. Executors: son, Peter and George Shelly. Witnesses: eter King and Andrew Smith. (137)

ANDERS, George - dated 3-6-1838. Wife, Charlotte. No children. Witnesses: has. C. Hood and John Law. (143)

AFFLE, Orlando - dated 4-13-1837. Wife, Deborah. Nephew, David Saffle. iece, Martha Saffle. Witnesses: Thomas Whitaker and Robert McClung. (143)

STIERS, Benjamin - dated Jan. 1831. Wife, Maglin. Children: George, Henry, Samuel, Benjamin Jr., Jacob, Catherine, Ann and Elizabeth Smith. Executor: son, Henry. Witnesses: Henry Shaner and Robert Clark. (144)

SHICK, John - dated 8-28-1838. Wife, Mary Ann. Children: Margaret, Rosannah, Mary Ann, John Andrew, Frederick and Catherine. Executors: wife, Mary Ann and Wm. McCaslin. Witnesses (not given.) (144)

SENFT (SINIFT), Philip - dated 11-6-1830. No wife. Children: Adam, Henry, John, Christena Householder (Adam), Katy Davis (James M.), Barbara Shore (John), Polly Miller (Peter) and Nancy Freeman (John). Grand-daughter, Susan Senft. Executors: Wm. Davis and Peter Sain. Witnesses: T. Odling and George Zeigler. (147)

SHARKEY, Hugh - dated 3-6-1839. No wife. No children named. Executor: mother, Barbara Sharkey. Witnesses: Henry Dittoe and Adam Fink. (154)

SKINNER, James - dated 9-8-1840. Wife, Eve. Son, James Jr. Executors: wife, Eve and Samuel Skinner, Esq. Witnesses: Charles McCloskey and James Wilson. (157

SMITH, John - dated 10-13-1839. Wife, Margaret. Children: John, Elizabeth and Mary. Executrix: wife, Margaret. Witnesses: John Beckwith and Benjamin Huff. (160)

SAYRE, Ruel - dated 5-19-1834. Wife, Hope. Children: Reuben, Phebey, Rachel, Ruel Jr. and Hope. Executors: wife, Hope and son, Ruel. Witnesses: John Ansel John Gibson and Thos. King. (166)

STOKER, Mary - dated 8-7-1839. Heirs: Allen O., George W., Philander H. A., and John Milton Binckley children of Charlotte Binckley; George Hidlebaugh son of Cathrine Croskey; Jacob Stoker; balance of estate to Charlotte Binckley. Executor John W. Davis. Witnesses: Harriet D. Davis and Roxanna N. Hamond. (168)

SHERLOCK, Abraham - dated 4-10-1842. Wife not named. Children: John O. P., Nancy McLain (Charles), Sarah Nixon, Henry, James, Margaret Harden, George, and Jane Cochran. Executor, Henry Sherlock. Witnesses: Arthur McCortney and Andrew M. Cubbison. (177)

STOLTZ, Lewis - dated 11-9-1842. Wife, Rebecca. Children not named. Executors: John Klingler and Robert Sanderson. Witnesses: John Spohn and George Hays. (180

SCHOLFIELD, John - dated 3-22-1842. Wife, Mahala. Children: Jane Mariah, Joseph Elizabeth, Rebecca, Lemuel, Margaret Amrine, Mary Ann Cannon, John, and Susannah Burgess. Executor, Wm. Cannon. Witnesses: Benjamin Moore, Robert Moore and Joseph Hough. (182)

STEWART, Robert - dated 1-14-1843. Wife Sarah. Children: Eliza Ann Elder only one named. Executrix: wife, Sarah. Witnesses: Jesse Skinner and Robert E. Huston. (188)

SHARKEY, Barbara - dated 8-26-1844. Only child, Elizabeth Sharkey. Sister, Teres Dean. Executor, Dr. E.R. Magruder. Witnesses: Hugh Dean and Peter Snider. (192)

STOCKBERGER, George - dated 5-19-1842. Wife, Christena. Children: John; George; Solomon; Elizabeth Waggoner, dec'd; Nancy; Polly Cooperider, dec'd; Christena Loy, dec'd; Susana; Katharine; Hannah; and Meina. Executor: brother, John Stockberger. Witnesses: P. W. Dumbauld and P. C. Dumbauld. (221)

STROCKLINE, Joseph - dated 9-23-1846. Wife, Frances. Children: John, Joseph, Catherine, Elizabeth, Mary Ann and Martha. Executors: son, John and Lewis Stoltz. Witnesses: Isaac Pence and John Lidey. (226)

STRAIT, William - dated 12-18-1847. Wife, Sophia. Children: Margaret, Catherine, Christopher, Henry, William, Samuel, Sarah, Betsy, Barbara and Mary, Executors; son, Christopher and Samuel Barker. Witnesses: John McGinley and Israel Hitchcock. (243)

SAHM, Jacob - dated 4-24-1849; proved 9-11-1849. Wife, Elizabeth. No children named. Executor, Wm. Mechling. Witnesses: Thomas Randolph and Solomon Moyer. (277)

SAIN, Jacob - dated 3-14-1850; proved 4-23-1850. Wife, Sarah. Children: Philip Sain, Christian Kiser Sain, Levi Sain, Luertisha Stewart (John N.), Samuel Manley Sain, Matilda MdFadden Sain, Wm. Reynolds Sain, Margaret Ann Whitmer Sain, Jacob Sain Jr., and David Wilson Sain. Executor, George Stoltz. Witnesses: Daniel Baker and Wm. B. Black. (284)

SCOTT, Mathew - dated 4-2-1849; proved 8-3-1850. Wife, Susan. Children: Martin F., Barnaby and Julia Whitehead. Nephew, Henry H. Scott. Executors; son, Martin and nephew, Henry H. Scott of Des Moines Co., Iowa. Witnesses: Wm. Hart and Jacob Costigan. (288)

SELLARS, Margaret - dated 12-4-1849; proved 10-1-1850. Children: James Alva Sellars, Naomi Sellars, Mahala Sellars, Margaret Sellars, Reuben Sellars, Louisa Sellars, Elizabeth Sellars, Mary Sellars, Jacob Sellars and one not named. Executor: son, Jacob. Witnesses: Samuel Curran and Andrew Law. (300)

SANDERS, John - dated 8-15-1845; proved 1-18-1851. Wife, Mary. Children: George, John, Mary and William. Executor; son, William. Witnesses: Jacob Castigan and Abraham Hamisfar. (306)

STURGEON, Simpson - dated 12-20-1850; proved 4-1-1851. No wife. Niece, Eliza Jane Cowen. Nephew, Robert Cowen. Brothers; Mitchel and John. Sister, Eliza Manning. Executor, Dixon Brown. Witnesses: Elizabeth Sturgeon and John Wilson. (312)

STURGEON, John - dated 8-18-1846; proved 4-2-1851. Wife, Elizabeth. Children: Mitchell; Moses; John P.; Mary; Simpson; Harriet Cowen, dec'd; and Eliza Manning (edgar). Executors: son, John P. and Wm. Love. Witnesses: Dixon Brown and Wm. Spencer. Codicil dated 6-20-1850 gives to daughter Mary and grand-daughter Eliza Jane Cowen gets residue of estate and to live on it six years. Also changes John P. as executor to Moses Sturgeon. Same witnesses. (309)

SHAFER, Alexander - dated 9-9-1850; proved 3-31-1851. Wife, Sarah. Children: James, John, Joseph, Peter, Alexander R., Margaret, Mary, Matilda and Samuel H. Executors: wife, Sarah; John Heck and Peter Middaugh. Witnesses: Henry, John and Alexander Heck. (318)

SNIDER, Jacob - dated 8-30-1851; proved 9-30-1851. Wife, Susan, Children not named. No executor named. Witnesses: Chas. H. Hood and Michael Bosserman. (323)

TOMBOLD, Mary - dated 4-6-1819. No husband. Legatees: John Slaughter; Wm. Dodds; Rebecca Everly; sister, Barbara Boyer; and George Baster. Executor, Joel Strawn. Witnesses: Daniel Kemper; Joel and Sarah Strawn. (22)

TROUT, George Sr. - dated 5-21-1821. Wife, Margaret. Children: Jacob, John, Elizabeth, Polly, Margaret, George Jr., Sophia, Juliana S., Michael, Henry and Philip. Grandson, Ephraim son of John. Executors; Geo. Beckwith and Geo. Trout. Witnesses: John Beckwith, Chas. Henkel and S. Swinehart. (68)

TEEL, Noah - not dated. Wife, Ann. Son, Asa, only child named. Executors; Lossor Teel and John Chappelear. Witnesses: Samuel Ogborn and Wm. McCaslin. (76)

THOMAS, Aaron - dated 12-29-1831. Wife, Rosanna. Children: Jacob, Elizabeth Morrow (Andrew), David, Jesse, Samuel and Evan. Executors: sons, Jesse and Evan. Witnesses: Daniel Spohn, Peter Witmer and John Liday. (85)

THOMPSON, David W. - dated 6-3-1832. No wife. Children: Polly Ann, Esther, Elizabeth, Mahala and David Moore Thompson. Executor, M. D. Brooks. Witnesses: M. D. Brooks and Israel Penrod. (89)

THOMPSON, John - dated 6-12-1824. Wife, Nancy. Children: Samuel, William, John Jr., Isaac, Ann Fickle and Jane McBride. Executors: William Spencer and William Forsythe. Witnesses: William and Robert Spencer. (94)

Thompson, William - dated 5-18-1837. Wife, Mary. Children: Thomas, Mariah, Margaret, Andrew and John. Executors; wife, Mary and William McBride. Witnesses: Thos. King and Isaac Brown. (133)

THRALL, Samuel - dated 9-5-1836. Wife not named. Children: James, Sophia and Patience Thrall, Eliza Hollenback, Mary Babb, Charlotte Comley, Martha Hollenback, Ellenor Babb, Ann Teal and Juliana Hammond. Executor, James Thrall. Witnesses: Chas. C. Hood and Thos. Hood. (150)

THARP, Job - dated 1-25-1847. Wife, Lucy. Children not named. Executor; son, James. Witnesses: Levi Williams and Isaiah Conoway. (224)

TAGUE, Peter - dated 1-6-1847. Wife, Ellenor. Children: John, Patrick, Edward, and Rose. Executor; son, John. Witnesses: Peter and Patrick Tague. (235)

TROUT, Henry - dated 1-15-1849; proved 5-16-1849. Wife, Harriet. Children: Elizabeth Yest, Ann Margaret Trout, Zeddig and Wilson Trout. Executrix; wife, Harriet. Witnesses: James Manning and Nicholas S. Zeigler. (260)

TERRELL, Jesse - dated 1-26-1850; proved 4-23-1850. Wife, Rebecca. Children: James, Asa, Lucinda and Arminda. Executrix; wife, Rebecca. Witnesses: Robert Ralson and Barney Entley. (282)

THARP, Reuben - dated 7-26-1850; proved 10-1-1850. Wife, Sarah. Children: Margaret, Lavina, Huldah, Sarah, Rhoda, Emily, James, Elijah and Elisha. Executors; sons, James and Elisha. Witnesses: Jacob R. White and William Spencer. (293)

VANHORN, Isaac - dated 12-16-1822. Wife, Sarah. No children named. Executrix; wife, Sarah. Witnesses: Samuel Bigelow, James Allen and James Hooper. (29)

WALKER, William - dated 8-20-1821. Wife, Mary. Children: Henry, Elizabeth Fink, Joseph and Joanna. Executors: Henry Walker and John Fink. Witnesses: Thos. Cady, Andrew Trumbo and Elizabeth Ann Fink. (25)

WILSON, John - dated 1-17-1823. Wife, Jane. Children: Samuel, Sara, John, James and other children not named. Executors: James, John and Samuel. Witnesses: Asbury Elder and Samuel Baird. (34)

WILSON, Asa - dated 1-2-1825. Verbal will at point of death. Wife not named. Children not named. Witnesses: Daniel Griggs, Esiah Wilson, Juley and Edward Ward. (39)

WILSON, Sarah - dated 11-7-1828. Children: Thomas, Amos, Edward, Isiah, Rachel Weedman, Liza and Sarah. Executors; sons, Thomas and Amos. Witnesses: Jeremiah Ward and Thomas Cowen. (61)

WISEMAN, Jacob - dated 8-7-1828. Wife, Mary. Children: Jacob, Henry, Betsy, Barbara Rinebold (Henry), Catherine and Polly Runkle (Samuel). Executors; wife, Mary and son, Jacob. Witnesses: P. Odlin and James Henderson. (65)

WEBB, Michael - dated 4-12-1834. Wife, Rebecca. No children named. Executrix; wife, Rebecca. Witnesses: John May and Geo. B. Fury. (106)

WHITMER, Peter - dated 9-24-1831. Wife, Magdalene. Children: Jacob, Sarah, Mary, Lydia, Peter, Solomon, John, Daniel, Susanna and George. Executors: sons, Peter and Solomon. Witnesses: C. Skinner and James Brown. (119)

WARD, Edward - dated 11-27-1834. Wife, Lucy. Children: Isaac, living in Maryland, to receive farm he lives on there; John; James; Jeremiah; Amos; William; and Ann Burgess (Joseph). Executors: William Ward and Joseph Burgess. Witnesses: John and Esther Wilson. (163)

WILSON, Thomas - dated 12-7-1841. Wife, Polly. Mentions two sons but does not name Executrix; wife, Polly. Witnesses: Samuel Skinner, Samuel Rusk and Samuel Grosendyke. (170)

WISEMAN, John - dated ------1838. Wife, Sarah. Children: Elizabeth, Jacob G., Joseph G., Philip S., John R., Isaac, Ann Stinchcomb, Sarah Bratton and Margaret Morgan. Executor, Joseph G. Wiseman. Witnesses: Jacob Hooper and Benjamin Linville. (173)

WHEATCRAFT, Rachel - dated 4-14-1843. Chilcren: Nancy, Catherine Canaday, Rachel LaRue, Harmon, Edward, Joseph and Malachi. Grand-daughter, Rachel daughter of Edward. Witnesses: John Beckwith and Elizabeth Purcel. (185)

WISEMAN, Adam - dated 1-13-1844. Wife, Susannah. Children: Peter, John, George, Elizabeth and Jacob. Mentions Joel son of Jacob. Executors: Isaac Zartman and Peter Bowman. Witnesses: Alexander Zartman and Peter Bowman. (223)

WARD, Lucy - dated 4-18-1845. Wife of Edward, dec'd. Niece, Sarah Wilson, for care of testatrix since 1827 to have entire estate. Witnesses: Henry Kelley and Edward Davison. (234)

WILLISON, William - dated 4-23-1847. Wife, Easter. Children: Harrison and John. Executor, Bartholomew Tatman. Witnesses: Benjamin and Bartholomew Tatman. (238)

WEBSTER, Joseph - dated 3-27-1848; proved 9-18-1849. Wife, Permelia. Children: Dickinson, Judith Browning (Oliver), and Even. Executors: Oliver Browning and Chas. H. Hood. Witnesses: Jacob Nider and Chas. H. Hood. (246)

WHEATCRAFT, Edward - dated 4-10-1848. Wife. Deborah. Children: Samuel, Joseph, Daniel, James Finley and Rachel. Executor, James Sherlock. Witnesses: T. W. Evans and M. Fry. (247)

WILSON, William - dated 12-18-1848. No wife. Children: Archibald, Robert B., Milton, Morrison, Sarah Powell, Mary Vanvey and Jane Forquer. Witnesses: Wm. Meloy and John Riley. (255)

WOLF, John - dated 10-25-1842; proved 8-10-1850. No wife. Children: John, Peter, George, William, Abraham, Philip, Eliza and Maria. Executors; sons, John and William. Witnesses: John Dennis and Henry Sherlock. (291)

WHEATCRAFT, Joseph - dated 5-31-1838. Wife, Rachel. Children: Nancy, Rachel, Catherine, Edward, Joseph, David H., Malachi, Harmon and Daniel. Executors: Chas. C. Hood and John Beckwith. Witnesses: John B. Orton and Matilda Orton. (331)

YOUNG, Willis S. - dated 11-28-1845. Wife, Catherine. Legatees: Gilbert and Catherine Brooks, son and daughter of M. D. Brooks and Eliza his wife; Gilbert to get tanyard and Catherine everything else. Executors: wife, Catherine; C. M. Young and M. D. Brooks. Witnesses: R. H. Peters, Robert Forgrave and John H. Mitchell. (248)

380

ZEIGLER, George - dated 7-23-1835. Wife, Mary. Children: Peter, Jacob, Susanna; George, John, Mary, Magdalena, David and Nicholas. Executors: son, Peter and Daniel Poorman. Witnesses: Daniel Griggs, John Beckwith and Chas. Henkel. (116)

ZARTMAN, Henry - dated (not given); proved 2-17-1840. Wife, Barbara. No children named. Executor, Isaac Zartman. Witnesses: Isaiah Lovell and Charles Henkel.(157)

ZEIGLER, Peter - dated 4-15-1845. Verbal will at point of death. Wife, Sarah. No children named. Executor, William Wirick. Witnesses: George Henry and Valentine Wirick. (195)

ZARTMAN, Alexander - dated 7-24-1847; proved 1-10-1852. Wife, Saloma. Children: Levi, Sarah, Israel, Isaac, Joshua, Henry, Margaret and Magdalene. Executors: sons, Isaac and Israel. Witnesses: Andrew Smith and Jacob Weimer. (327)

ALEXANDER, David to Pency RECTOR	4-21-1811
ALKERE, Samuel to Dolly ALKIRE	12-29-1813
ALKIRE, Jacob to Polly PHOEBUS	3-28-1812
ALKIRE, Michael to Polly BARTON	12-18-1814
ANDERSON, Abraham to Mary RELEY	7-26-1810
ARROWHOOD, Job to Rebecca MICAEL	1-26-1812
ATCHISON, John to Ruth CORWIN	11-3-1811
ATCHISON, William to Nancy GRATTON	12-25-1814
ATER, William to Margaret COLDSON	12-20-1814
BALLAH, James to Caty HITLER	12-19-1812
BARNES, William to Sarah MARGUISS	9-2-1813
BAUDER, Anthony to Christiana STROUSER	11-12-1810
BAUGH, Jacob to Ann JUSTICE	11-26-1812
BEAR, John to Ann MAGNESS	12-15-1811
BECKETT, James to Elizabeth BECKETT	5-31-1812
BELL, Abner to Merzy SMITH	3-26-1812
BELL, Isaiah to Phebe BOWMAN	3-22-1814
BELL, Thomas to Ruth FREEMAN	12-14-1813
BIERLY, Darick to Mary COLE	12-23-1813
BIRBRIDGE, James to Elizabeth REEVES	5-30-1811
BLOXION, Jeremiah to Susannah JUSTICE	11-24-1811
BLUE, Frederick to Elizabeth REDDIN	4-25-1814
BOGART, George to Martha BLUE	2-11-1813
BOWEN, David to Sarah WOOLERY	8-27-1811
BOWEN, William to Peggy KERR	8-2-1810
BOWIN, Truman to Nancy LEWIS	6-8-1810
BOWSHER, Daniel to Polly FREES	10-20-1811
BOYER, Samuel to Elizabeth HUT	10-25-1811
BRASKETT, William to Polly HEATER	12-30-1811
BRINER, John to Marah ROADE	6-12-1810
BROWN, Henry to Jane GORMLY	11-22-1814
BROWN, Joshua to Actious HALL	1-3-1811
BROWN, Moses to Margaret STEWART	8-18-1812
BURTON, William to Polly COLE	3-21-1811
BUSACK, Benjamin to Polly GOUTY lic.	2-26-1811
CALDWELL, James to Polly BAUGH	3-24-1812
CAMBLE, Ishable to Drusille WILLIAMSON	9-16-1810
CAMPBELL, Archibald to Prescella WILLIAMSON lic.	9-14-1810
(Note: Above two could be same)	
CARR, John to M. SCOTHERN	10-20-1814
CASLER, James to Mary WHITESIDES	6-25-1812
CASSNER, Martin to Bitsey WITNER	4-12-1814
CASSNER, Matthias to Sally HORN	12-8-1812
CHAMP, Abraham to Rose WALSTON	3-10-1814
CIATH, Caleb to Mary SHAFER	7-28-1814
CLARK, William to Anna CLARK	1-3-1813
CODY, Jeremiah to Dolly MARTIN	3-17-1814
COLE, Joshua to Susannah RYNIAR	2-7-1811
COMLY, John to Elizabeth PITCHER	7-17-1814

```
COOK, Henry to Catharine GROVES                            4-18-1813
COON, George to Sarah CUTLER                               3-10-1812
CORWIN, Oliver to Polly McCONNELL                          1-21-1812
CORY, Abija to Anna MARTIN                                 2-17-1811
CREVISTON, John to Polly SMOCK                             8-25-1814
CROSE, Philip to Prescella BECKS                  lic.     4-23-1810
CROW, David to Mary CONELLY                                9-1-1814
CURREY, William to Atsey GREEN                            12-23-1810
CURTS, Hector to Margaret PONTIOUS                         1-19-1813
CUTLER, John to Caty JEE                                   8-2-1810
DALBY, John to Mary CAAN                                   4-14-1811
DAVIS, Benjamin to Elizabeth STULY                       12-30-1813
DAVIS, Enos to Elenor CARNAHAN                           10-31-1811
DAVIS, George to Rachael GLAZE                            12-1-1813
DAVIS, John to Nancy DAVIS                                 7-7-1814
DAVIS, William to Mary CRAIG                               6-1-1812
DECKER, Isaac to Caty BISHOP                               5-23-1814
DECKER, Joseph to Mary Fruchey                            4-3-1814
DEHAVEN, Peter to Mary CURRELL                            4-22-1812
DELESHMOT, Van B. to Margaret BAUGH                        1-4-1813
DEWITT, Martin to Hullday BURGETT                          2-6-1814
DICKISON, William to Elenor FITZGERALD                     3-2-1811
DICKSON, Alexander to Mary WASH                           11-13-1814
DICKSON, Robert Spence to Hannah MILLER                   11-23-1812
DISERD, Joseph to Sally DRIVER                            2-10-1814
DORUM, George to Sally CLINE                              12-1-1811
DOUGLAS, Andrew to Elizabeth CASADAY                       2-4-1811
DOWNING, John to Polly CHAMP                               3-4-1814
DRESBACH, Henry to Mary HEDGES                            6-13-1811
DUNNACK, Joshua to Dinah TOOLMAN                          12-26-1811
DYE, A. to P. HARRISON                                   12-15-1814
EARL, Mathew to Phebe TIFFIN                              5-24-1814
EARNEST, Michael to Mary KINNEAR                         11-24-1811
EARNHEART (ARNHART), William to Jane PATTERSON            6-12-1810
EDWARDS, William to Mary VALENTINE                        4-10-1814
EVANS, George to Phoebe SHORT                     lic.    6-16-1810
EVANS, Jona to Elizabeth FLORY                           12-10-1811
EWING, William to Sally GILES                             8-12-1813
FETHEROFF, Samuel to Susanna RECKELDAFFER                 4-5-1814
FIELDS, Robert to Susan WILLETS                          10-13-1814
FINCH, Solomon to Rachael JUSTICE                         9-21-1810
FLEEHARTY, John to Margaret REED                         11-23-1814
FLEMING, Ferguson to Susannah GREHAM                      5-1-1810
FLEMING, Robert to Eleanor MORROW                         8-4-1811
FOGLER, Henry to Barbara CLINE                           12-2-1812
FOLTZ, John to Sophia VALENTINE                           8-2-1814
FORSEMAN, Henry to Jane FORSEMAN                          3-17-1814
FRAZER, Alexander, Jr. to Hannah SWISHER                  7-29-1814
FRAZIER, James, Jr. to Elizabeth CASE                     8-2-1810
```

383

```
FREEMAN, Benj'n to Nelly WEBB                              10-14-1814
FREEMAN, Isaac to Nelly WILSON                            12-20-1812
FUNSTON, Wm. to Precilla LAPERRY                           3-12-1813
GATEWOOD, Phillip to Lettitia DENNY                        2-9-1813
GIFFORD, Joseph to Polly DILLAHA                           2-7-1811
GIBSON, Robert to Emelia REED                             8-9-1810
GLASS (GLAZIER-lic.), Joseph to Eva RAGER                  9-13-1810
GLAZE, John to Rachel BALL                                 7-30-1812
GLICK, Solomon to Polly SPANGLER                           8-6-1814
GOINGS, Joseph to Hannah CARY                             12-11-1811
GOODMAN, John to Eve HOSSELTON                             5-5-1813
GRAHAM, John to Lydia ALKERE                               5-4-1812
GRALLE, Phillip to Sally BAUM                             11-14-1813
GRANT, Peter to Casey MARTIN                               6-6-1812
GRIER, James to Mary Ann HAYES                             8-2-1813
GRIM, David to Susan WANAMACHER                            5-23-1811
GROOM, Job to Polly BLOOM                                  3-17-1814
GROOM, Wm. to Nancy MOORE                                  3-3-1814
GROVES, Luis to Elizabeth WILSON                          12-23-1813
HALL, William to Barbara WEST                              7-3-1814
HARDEN, Isaac to Catharine SPANGLER                        8-28-1810
        at home of Benjamin CLARK, her brother-in-law
HARMAN, George to Betsey SEASHOTTS                        11-26-1812
HARTLE, Jacob to Caty SPADE                                8-10-1811
HARVY, James to Nancy OXFORD                               3-14-1814
HASELTON, Jacob to Betsey LONG                             8-9-1811
HAYS, George to Mary GREER                                 3-10-1812
HEATER, Solomon to Sally ELSEY                            10-16-1812
HEDGES, John to Susanna MILLER                             7-27-1812
HEDGES, Joseph to Mary NEVILL                              9-3-1810
HEETER, David to Polly REEDER                             10-29-1811
HELM, Jacob to Peggy COON                                  8-16-1811
HEMPHILL, Johnston to Mary CROWDER                        12-19-1811
HENDERSON, James of Ross Co. to Rachel HENDERSON           4-25-1811
HENDERSON, James to Rebecca KYLES                          6-2-1814
HENRY, Enoch to Maria PURCE                    lic.        3-11-1813
HERDER, Simeon to Barbara WASH                             8-16-1810
HIBBS, John to Polly PHEBUS                                2-17-1811
HIGGINS, Robert to Sarah RAWLINGS              LIC.        7-16-1810
HILLERY, John to Rachael KOONCE                           12-16-1813
HOBBS, Richard to Rachael ROSS                            6-12-1813
HORNBACK, John to Jane CAMPBELL                           8-10-1811
HOSSELTON, Jacob to Elizabeth SLEGAR                      11-18-1811
HOWARD, Vetchel to Rachel SWANK                            4-26-1812
HULSE, James R. to Rebecca VAN METRE                       5-7-1812
HUSTON, John to Elizabeth Baum                             6-28-1812
IMBERSON (EMBERSON), James to Catharine FRYBACK            1-31-1811
JACKSON, John to Anna FRYBACK                              4-10-1812
JENKINS, William to Margaret Ann PURL                      4-11-1813
```

```
JOHNSTON, Samuel to Elizabeth KERR                          5-23-1812
JONES, James to Anna DURBIN                                 4-2-1812
JONES, Robert to Agness JOHNSTON                            9-13-1810
JUSTICE, Daniel to Caty BAUGH                               7-24-1813
JUSTICE, Jessee to Caty BOWSHER                             1-30-1812
JUSTICE, Jessee to Sarah TEETERS                            7-30-1812
KELLY, Joseph to Elizabeth SHAFER                    lic.   4-28-1810
KERR, Gideon to Elizabeth PECK                             6-22-1814
KEYS, Horation R. to Frances MAUPPIN                       12-16-1813
KIMBLE, Jonathan to Nancey RILER                           5-17-1811
KINSER, George to Dullene TUNESS                           4-26-1810
KLINE, Jacob to Catharine LUDWIG                          10-24-1813
KUDER, Robert to Elizabeth DILMAN                          9-13-1812
KYLE, John to Susannah VANMETER                            7-31-1810
LAMB, James to Margaret REED                               9-26-1811
LARKINS, Edward to Elizabeth BUCK                         12-25-1810
LAWRENCE, Wm. to Mary HOBBS                                 3-7-1813
LAYTON, David to Polly BEVANS                             11-19-1814
LEEPER, Thomas to Kitty BAUM                               1-12-1813
LEGGIT, Daniel to Rachael HUFFMAN                          5-19-1814
LEONARD, Charles to Anna DECKER                            6-30-1814
LEWIN, John to Selome CLUTTER                        lic.   5-24-1810
LIST, George to Barbara MOYER                             11-2-1811
LOCK, John to Nancy DAVISON                                4-1-1812
LUCAS, Willerby to Rose McCONNAL                          10-31-1813
LUTZ, Jacob D. to Polly BROUGHER                           1-27-1813
LUTZ, John H. to Mary SAYLOR                               2-5-1811
McCLEAN, Elexander to Mariah DUNCAN                       10-23-1810
McCONNEL, John of Highland Co. to Betsey COONROD          3-15-1814
McKENNEY, John to Lear MARTIN                             12-12-1811
McKENNEY, John to Betsey SOUTHWARD                         9-1-1814
McKENNY, H. to Sarah LEWIS                                11-3-1814
McKENZIE, Jas. to Rebecca GEORGE                          11-24-1814
McNAMER, Brian to Anne MOORE                              11-4-1810
MADDEN, Dennis to Catharine MICHAEL                        7-19-1812
MARSH, David to Susannah BARNS                            12-2-1813
MARTIN, Adam to Caty PONTIOUS                              6-3-1811
MARTIN, Jacob to Manday ROADS                              9-11-1810
MARTIN, John to Catharine DEREAU                           9-25-1814
MARTIN, Tulman to Nancy WEST                               2-4-1813
MAY, Henry of Ross Co. to Susan McCUTCHIN                 5-26-1814
MEDSKER, George to Nancy MORRIS                            7-5-1812
MESSICK, George to Jane ROLAND                             2-28-1811
MEWHORTER, John to Rebecca WILDBAHN                        2-22-1814
MICHAEL, Cornelias to Mary BAYLEY                          1-6-1811
MILLER, Adam to Polly FITZGERALD                           3-6-1814
MILLER, William to Enor TOWN                               4-11-1811
MILLER, William to Margaret FORSMAN                        3-17-1814
```

MILLS, Adam to Catharine DAVIS	3-24-1811
MOORE, Fergus to Leno QUICK	2-28-1813
MOORE, Isaac to Ruth EVANS	8-29-1811
MOORE, James to Precella DUNAHOE	11-8-1810
MOORE, Rubal to Elizabeth STUMP	12-21-1813
MORGAN, John E. to Betsey MONTGOMERY	11-15-1812
MORRELL, Jesse to Mary HERROLD	5-15-1810
MORRIS, Thomas to Nancy WOLVERTON	3-24-1814
MORRISS, Benedick to Lydia MORRISS	5-4-1812
MORRISS, Henry to Charity SHELBY	3-28-1811
MORRISS, Joseph to Peggy DEWIT	9-10-1811
MORSE, John to Kitty HILLER	4-10-1814
MOYERS, Abraham to Precilla ANGLES	4-1-1813
MUSKINGS, John to Nancy COLESTON	3-26-1812
NEIL, Jacob to Margaret GRAHAM	9-24-1811
NIGHT, William to Polly HUBARD	7-27-1814
NYE, George to Sarah PASCHAL	6-18-1811
OSBORN, Ralph to Catharine RENICK	4-26-1812
OUTAN, Jesse to Nelly MORE	2-14-1814
OXFORD, Abel to Rachel CALLAHAN	11-20-1814
PAINE, John to Sarah LAWRENCE	3-17-1811
PANCAKE, Isaac to Susannah BAUGH	3-11-1813
PARISH, Meredith to Sarah GALBREATH	12-22-1814
PAUL, Zachariah to Sally THOMPSON	2-27-1814
PELTY, Ebenezer to Susannah SLAGEL	11-30-1812
PETERS, Tunis to Mary Eve GLAZE	2-28-1811
PETTY, Absalom to Luzen BALEY	12-1-1814
PHEBUS, Samuel to Polly CRABLE	2-21-1813
PLATTER, George to Polley HYATT	8-19-1811
PLUM, Henry to Caty CRAYBILL	10-17=1813
PONTIOUS, Daniel to Polly METGER	3-22-1814
PONTIOUS, Samuel to Milly EVANS	6-30-1811
PONTIUS, George to Dorothy MOYER	6-16-1811
POTTS, Anthony to Cloe SMITH	6-2-1814
POULSON, Elisha to Nancy THOMPSON	2-11-1813
POWLSON, William to Elizabeth ENGLAND	7-25-1811
PEPPERS, Abel C. to Margret LAUNES	8-14-1814
POWERS, John to Theodocia MENELEY	2-12-1811
RADCLEFF, Isaac to Polley McKINSEY	2-2-1812
RAWLING, David to Jane MARTIN	9-16-1810
REASON, Samuel to Phebe HOWARD	1-16-1812
REED, James to Hannah KELLY	4-20-1813
REED, John to Elizabeth VICARS	7-26-1810
REED, John to Delilah HARVEY	9-22-1814
RELEY, John to Nancy WATERMAN	9-29-1813
RENICK, Jonathan to Lucender SUDDETH	3-22-1812
RETTER, Henry to Mary SHUCK	11-16-1813
ROBINS, Matthias to Catharine McCONNAL	4-10-1814
ROBINSON, James T. to Mary MORRIS	10-12-1813

ROSS, Thomas to Nancy BAKER	6-12-1812
RUSH, Jacob to Amelia DAVIS	3-25-1813
RUSH, Moses to Margaret EAKER	7-24-1814
RUSH, Peter to Peggy CREVISTON	8-22-1811
SAGE, Harlehigh to Lucinda PRATT	1-18-1812
SEARFAUSE, Philip to Sarah SMITH	7-28-1814
SHELBY, Joseph to Sarah STEELY	6-18-1811
SHOAP, Thomas to Sarah MARTIN	7-21-1811
SMITH, Jeremiah to Rhoda HEDGES	2-20-1814
SMITH, Phillip to Polly STROUD	12-27-1812
SOCKRIDER, John to Catharine ROADS	8-30-1812
SPYKER, Henry to Elizabeth TODD	8-19-1810
STAGE, Richard to Elizabeth GLAZE	8-3-1811
STALL, Hugh to Mary NEWHOUSE	10-2-1810
STANLEY, Robert (Thomas-lic.) to Betsey CENTIR	3-8-1814
STEPHENSON, Zachariah to Polly GLAZE	7-27-1812
STEVENSON, David to Mary Magdaline BARNES	11-10-1811
STONEROCK, George to Margaret LEWIS	1-14-1813
STROUSE, Philip to Deborah GREEN	9-2-1813
STULTZ, Henry to Rachel HANSHAW	7-24-1814
SUTHERLAND, John to Sarah BAKER	11-3-1811
SWANK, Isaac to Sarah MADDEN	6-28-1812
SWANK, Peter to Nancy McMAHAN	8-29-1811
SWANK, Rich'd to Mary FRICKLE	4-5-1812
SWANK, William to Polly LOYD	6-12-1814
SWIGART, John to Eliza WHITE	4-7-1814
TAYLOR, Mathine to Lydia WILSON	4-22-1811
TETTSWORTH, J. to M. CLEFTON	11-20-1814
THOMPSON, John to Jane MILLER	11-26-1811
THUCLY(?), Simon to Caty FOUGLAR	12-22-1812
TIFFIN, John to Sarah Hall MADDOX	1-11-1814
TIPTON, Thomas to Elizabeth TOMLINSON	12-26-1813
TODD, Jonah to Amanda WILLIAMS	8-23-1810
TOOTLE, John to Olly ARMSTRONG	4-20-1813
TOWERS, Thomas to Deborah ROSS	7-18-1814
TRULLINGER, Abraham to Margaret TRULLINGER	9-11-1814
TRULLINGER, Jacob to Polly GORDY	4-19-1812
TRULLINGER, Phillip to Caty WEST	10-20-1814
VAN BUSKIRK, Michael to Juretta CLEVINGER lic.	9-8-1810
VANCE, Elisha to Anne GORDY	4-8-1813
VANDERVORT, James to Rachel PETERS	8-23-1810
VANDORAN, William to Molly GAY	5-2-1811
VANHOOK, Thomas to Nancy REDDIN	11-22-1814
VANHORN, Walter to H ope WHITE	11-25-1810
VANWICKLE, Dan'l to Christiana HOLT	7-27-1812
VERLINE, Henry to Catherine CLINE lic.	12-10-1810
VEZE, Samuel to Esther OHARRO	8-6-1811
WADDAL, Joseph to Sarah RILEY	12-5-1811

387

```
WADDLE, James L. to Barbara FRESE               10-12-1811
WALKER, John to Rachel MARTIN                   9-9-1812
WARD, George to Mary HECKERTHORN                1-3-1811
WARTS, Christian to Caty WHISTLER               4-11-1814
WEBB, Robert to Nancy FITZGARALD                1-29-1813
WEBB, Wm. to Massy HIBBS                         4-30-1813
WARNER, Silas to Sarah RILEY                    1-28-1813
WEST, Samuel to Elizabeth SCOTT                 12-31-1810
WHITE, Charles to Polly HINTON                  4-12-1812
WHITMAN, George to Rebecca HATH (HEATH)         6-26-1810
WILLETS, Isaiah to Henrietta ALLESON            12-30-1813
WILLEY, Amos to Elizabeth ROBISON               9-23-1813
WILLIAMS, David to Sarah McKENZEE               12-9-1813
WILLIAMS, Edward to Rebeckah WILSON             7-23-1811
WILLIAMS, Enoch to Mary WEAVER both of Walnut Twp. 8-20-1810
WILLIAMS, John to Hannah JOHNSTON               9-16-1810
WILSON, Daniel to Sally GORDY                   2-23-1814
WOLLINGTON, Thomas to Nithie STOKES             6-15-1810
ZERING, John to Catharine SPENGLER              12-9-1810
```

PICKAWAY COUNTY, OHIO
Declarations of Intention for Naturalization
Taken from records found in Probate Court, Court House at Circleville, Ohio

KELLENBERGER, George - 2-23-1860 - age 32 - native of Wurtemburg, Germany - Emigrated 2-15-1853 from Monheim - Arrived at Philadelphia 3-22-1853

ROHT, Leonard - 3-30-1860 - age 57 - Native of Hesse Darmstadt, Germany - Emigrated 4-15-1852 from Havre - Arrived New York June 1852

MOORE, Edmund - 4-2-1860 - age 35 - Native of Ireland - Emigrated 8-2-1851 from Cork - Arrived New York 10-17-1851

LEIST, George - not dated, between 4-2-1860 and 8-18-1860 - age 26- Native of Hesse Darmestadt, Germany - Emigrated 6-29-1854 from Havre de Grasse - Arrived New York 9-14-1854

ROESZ, Henry - 8-18-1860 - age 55 - Native of Kurhessen, Germany - Emigrated 10-15-1855 from Bremen - Arrived Baltimore 12-31-1855

HAUSE, John Gottleib - 8-29-1860 - age 33 - Native of Saxe Weimer - Emigrated 7-10-1857 from Hamburg - Arrived New York 9-9-1857

KELLY, John - 9-17-1860 - age 21 - Native of Ireland - Emigrated 9-7-1856 from Liverpool - Arrived New York 10-7-1856

SARMON, Robert - 9-17-1860 - age 31 - Native of Ireland - Emigrated 3-28-1849 from Belfast - Arrived New York 5-3-1849

HOFFMAN, Jacob - 9-27-1860 - age 31 - Native of Baden, Germany - Emigrated 2-21-1857 from Havre - Arrived New York 4-14-1857

GEIGER, Henry - 10-6-1860 - Native of Wirtemburg, Germany - Emigrated 9-5-1854 from Breman - Arrived New York 11-25-1854

SKEHAN, Patrick - 10-6-1860 - age 26 - Native of Ireland - Emigrated 6-21-1860 from Queenstown - Arrived New York 7-4-1860.

MONARTY, Edward - 10-6-1860 - age 35 - Native of Ireland - Emigrated May 1846 from Liverpool - Arrived Boston July 1846

SIDELL, Gotlieb - 10-8-1860 - age 55 - Native of Saxony, Germany - Emigrated 11-5-1854 from Bologna - Arrived New York 12-20-1854

COULTER, John - Oct. 1860 - age 29 - Native of Canada - Emigrated July 1851
    from Hamilton - Arrived Buffalo July 1851
DASRING, Arnold - 10-9-1860 - age 25 - Native of Hessen, Germany - Emigrated
    5-1-1853 from Hessen Cassel - Arrived New York 6-3-1853
ROGAN, Patrick - 10-9-1860 - age 30 - Native of Ireland - Emigrated 6-22-1849
    from Liverpool - Arrived New York 8-7-1849
IVELT, Nicholas - 10-10-1860 - age 36 - Native of Bion, Germany - Emigrated
    3-1-1857 from Bremen - Arrived New Orleans 5-25-1857
MILT, John - 10-13-1860 - age 33 - Native of Hesse Darmstadt, Germany - Emigrated
    4-12-1846 from Rotterdam - Arrived New York 5-30-1846
GREENFIELD, Thomas - 10-16-1860 - age 23 - Native of England - Emigrated
    3-18-1855 from London - Arrived New York 4-30-1855
LIEBING, John - 10-20-1860 - age 31 - Native of Wirtenburg, Germany - Emigrated
    5-24-1854 from London - Arrived New York 7-5-1854
RYAN, Lawrence - 11-2-1860 - age 37 - Native of Ireland - Emigrated August 1849
    from Dublin - Arrived New York Oct. 1849
WINEHART, Jacob - 11-24-1860 - age 23 - Native of Prussia, Germany - Emigrated
    9-24-1858 from Hamburg - Arrived New York 11-10-1858
ROBERTS, Edward - 12-7-1860 - age 26 - Native of England - Emigrated 5-11-1858
    from Liverpool - Arrived New York 7-4-1858
KERRIGAN, Terrence - 12-29-1860 - age 41 - Native of Ireland - Emigrated 7-12-1849
    from Londonderry - Arrived New York 12-22-1849
TURTON, Richard - (not dated) - age 25 - Native of England - Emigrated 4-29-1857
    from Liverpool - Arrived New York 5-30-1857
CARROLL, Daniel - 4-1-1861 - age 31 - Native of Ireland - Emigrated 6-20-1848
    from Liverpool - Arrived Philadelphia 7-30-1848
NEEDHAM, Michael 4-12-1861 - age 30 - Native of Ireland - Emigrated 2-8-1846
    from Liverpool - Arrived New York 3-15-1846
MITCHELL, John - 3-21-1862 - age 38 - Native of England - Emigrated 3-7-1853
    from London - Arrived New York 5-1-1853
GRANT, John - 4-29-1860 - age 46 - Native of Canada - Emigrated 2-27-1860 from
    Kingston Canada West - Arrived Ogdensburg, New York 3-1-1860

It should be noted that the date wills were filed or recorded is not given in the record. Therefore all wills are given in the order that they appeared in the record.

MILLER, Nicholas - Will Book 1, page 1 - dated 4-26-1810 - wife: Elizabeth - children: mentioned but not named, were not of age - Executor: Samuel Hill - Signed: Nicholas Miller - Witnesses: Seth Watson, Sam'l Hill and Peter (mark) Clyne.

DRESBACH, John - Will Book 1, page 2 - dated 4-28-1810 - wife: Catherine - brother: Daniel - children: mentioned but not named - Executors: brother, Daniel Dresbach and brother-in-law, John Ely - Signed: John Dresbach - Witnesses: Charles Botkin, And'w Ensworth and James Denny.

CLOSE, William - Pickaway Twp. - Will Book 1, page 5 - Verbal Will - Will given 6-20-1810 - William Close died 6-20-1810 - children: mentioned but not named - Executor: William Rush - Deposition named 6-22-1810 by witnesses: Andrew Rush, John Rush, Truman Bowen and George (mark) Vance.

MORRIS, Mary - Pickaway Twp. - Will Book 1, page 6 - dated 2-6-1811 - sons: Ignatious, Benadict and Jessy - daughter: Hannah - Signed: Mary (mark) Moress - Witnesses: John Gay and Zachariah R. Clary.

BLOXOM, William - Washington Twp. - Will Book 1, page 8 - dated 4-25-1808; (recorded 1810 or after) - wife: Mary Bloxem - sons: Jeremiah, Moses, John and William - daughters: Margaret and Pheroby Bloxum - Executor: wife, Mary and son, William - Signed: William (mark) Bloxum - Witnesses: John McNeal, William Bealy and Peter(?) Conyser.

WINSHIP, WINN - Will Book 1, page 9 - wife: Hetty - sister: Elizabeth Parcels - sons: Winn, Thomas Jefferson, William Henry and Edwin - daughters: Mary, Harriott and Nancy; Nancy's share in trust of Jesse Spencer - states that wife Hetty may wish to go to Chillicothe to live with her children - will gives several land descriptions - Executors: friend, Jesse Spencer of Chillicothe and David Kinnear of Pickaway Co. - dated 12-24-1812 - Signed: Winn Winship - Witnesses: Samuel McAdow, Tho. North, John Parcels and Ben. Mowbray.

CHANEY, James C. - Will Book 1, page 14 - dated 1-24-1811 - wife: Elizabeth - children: mentions but does not name - Signed: James Chaney - Witnesses: Henry Ross, David Cook and Ruth (mark) Cook.

CROW, Thomas - Will Book 1, page 14 - dated 1-24-1812 - Wife: Elizabeth - sons: Joseph, David, John, Robert, Samuel, Thomas and William - daughters: Susannah wife of Charles Fielder; Mary Rush wife of Runnel Rush to have large Bible - Mentions wife Elizabeth Crow's children but does not name - Gives several land descriptions - Executors: wife, Mary and friend, Samuel Harvey - Signed: Thomas Crow - Witnesses: David Kinnear, Henry Haller and Daniel Smith.

*For *John* read *Job*. GATEWAY TO THE WEST, Vol. 2: No. 3 (July-Sept. 1969).

RENICK, John - Will Book 1, page 17 - (not dated) - Wife: Mary - sons: Jonathan, Abel and Ashel - daughters: Polly Renick, Rachael Van Meter, Marget Van Meter, Ann McNeal, Kitty Osborn and Polly Renick - Executors: James and Asahel Renick - Signed: John Renick - Witnesses: Daniel Turney and Wm. Seymore - Codicil dated 1-10-1814 - son: James Renick to have land on Buck Creek in Shampain (Champaign) Co. - Signed: John Renick - Same witnesses.

ATCHISON, Pfielding - Will Book 1, page 19 - dated 1-24-1814 - wife: Hannah - brother: Samuel Atchison - orphan boy: Levi James - Executor: Aron Sullivan - Signed: Phielden Atchison - Witnesses: Thomas (mark) McDanal, John Pancake and Isaac Pankake.

WADDLE, James - Will Book 1, page 21 - dated 3-28-1814 - Sons: Joseph and William; Joseph to have s½ and William to have n½ sec. 5, twp. 11, range 21 Worthington Survey - Daughters: Sally and Polly - Executor: son, Thomas Waddle - Signed: James Waddell - Witnesses: James Martin, Charles Shubridge and Benjamin Pontious.

LOOFBOURROW, John W. - Ross Co., Ohio - Will Book 1, page 22 - dated 12-15-1808 (recorded 1810 or after) - wife: mentioned but not named - sons: Jacob, John, Benjamin, Wade, Ebenezer, Thomas and Nathan - daughters: Abigail Harbert, Sarah Harbert, Rebecca Barkley and Mary Barkley - Mentions that Elizabeth Thompson is to be given her freedom when of age - Executors: Nathan Cory and son, Benjamin Loofbourrow - Signed: John Wade Loofbourrow - Witnesses: Peter Jackson and Mary (mark) Jackson.

COONROD, Woollery, Sr. - Will Book 1, page 25 - dated 2-15-1814 - sons: Peter, deceased; John, Jacob, Adam, George, Woollery and Henry - daughters: Barbary Harpole, Elizabeth Merrel and Catharine Lowther - grand-daughter: Barbary Coonrod daughter of son Peter, deceased - Daughter-in-law: Elizabeth Coonrod wife of son Peter - Executor: son, Henry Coonrod - Signed: Woollery (mark) Coonrod - Witnesses: James Casler and John Rusk.

FORSMAN, Philip - Upper Mountbethel Twp., Northampton Co., Penna. - Will Book 1, page 26 - dated 1-19-1814 - brothers: Heirs of brother Hugh Forsman, deceased; Alexander, Samuel, Joseph, Robert, George and William - Sister: Jane wife of Lewis Woolverton - children of brother William: George, Philip, Hugh, William and Jane - Executors: brothers, Robert and William Forsman - Signed: Philip Forsman - Witnesses: Robert Butts, John(?) Masey and Henry Wiedman - Recorded Northampton Co., Penna. 4-27-1814.

PENNYWELL, George - Will Book 1, page 30 - dated 8-20-1814 - Bequeath to Job Clifton; Bridget Bradford and Polly Downey daughter of Summerset Downey - Executor: Purnal H. Baker - Signed: George (mark) Pennywell - Witnesses: Cram(?) (mark) Boner and Benjamin Clifton.

ATCHISON, Samuel - Will Book 1, page 31 - dated 11-16-1813 - wife: Nancy, also to serve as executrix - Signed: Samuel (mark) Atchison - Witnesses: Francis Nicholas and Theodoius Seasbourn.

JOHNSON; Robert – Washington Twp. – Will Book 1, page 32 – dated 10-19-1814 – Wife: Frances, also to serve as Executrix – children: mentioned but not named – Signed: Robert (mark) Johnson – Witnesses: John Griffeth and Nathaniel Ross.

CAMPBELL, Joseph – Will Book 1, page 33 – dated 1-3-1815 – wife: Mary, also to serve as Executrix – sons: Robert, William, John, Joseph and Thomas – daughters: Mary and Nancy Campbell – Signed: Joseph Campbell – Witnesses: Aaron Sullivan and Elizabeth (mark) Galbreath.

RUSH, Henry – Will Book 1, page 39 – dated 12-17-1815 – children: Catherine, John, Mary, Andrew, George, James, Henry, Peter, Susannah, Moses and Aaron – Mentions, "all my children yet living and I wish heirs of those that are dead to draw their parents share as fast as they come of age" – Mentions land near Greenville entered in Peter and Andrew's name to be paid for from John Hiller's share – Executors: sons, George and Peter – Signed: Henry Rush – Witnesses: John Rawls and Westley Rush.

HAMMON, Mark – (surname also given as HAMMOND, HAMMONS) – Will Book 1, page 41 – dated 11-12-1815 – Wife: Nancy, also to serve as Executrix – Sons: William, Mark and Allen – Daughters: Betsey Landis, Lucy Brown and Nancy Hammons – Signed: Mark Hammon – Witnesses: John McLain, Joseph Brown and Lucy Brown.

SMITH, Jacob H. – Will Book 1, page 42 – dated 4-29-1815 – Mentions, "all my children" but names only daughter Sarah as she remained single – Executors: Martin Smith and James Smith – Signed: Jacob H. (mark) Smith – Witnesses: Alex'r Rowen and Joseph Baker.

FORSMAN, Robert – Mountbethel Twp., Northampton Co., Penna. – Will Book 1, page 44 – dated 8-17-1793 – wife: Jane – Sons: Hugh, Alexander, Samuel, Joseph, Robert, George, Philip and William – daughters: Agness and Jane – Mentions four grandsons each named Robert Forsman – Executors: sons, Hugh and William – Signed: Robert Forsman – Witnesses: Abraham(?) Defner, Anne Scott and John Scott – Filed 8-21-1809, recorded 6-24-1815 Northampton Co., Penna.

SHORT, James – Harrison Twp. – Will Book 1, page 49 – dated 8-5-1816 – wife: Sarah – son: Stephen Short, also to serve as executor – daughters: Mary wife of John Robinson, Rachel wife of Jonathan Holmes and Phebe wife of George Evans – Grandson Abraham Holmes son of daughter Elizabeth, deceased, and Joshua Holmes – Signed: James Short – Witnesses: Harleleigh Sage and Simon Hadley.

RECTOR, JOHN – Will Book 1, page 53 – dated 11-15-1818 – wife: Starling – childre Polly, Edward, Sanford and an infant – Executor and guardian of the children: brother, Calvard(?) Rector – Signed: John Rector – Witnesses: Philip Minniar and Solomon Minniar.

VAN KIRK, Mary – Will Book 1, page 55 – dated 12-21-1818 – Bequeaths to: Rachel Heavelo, Polly McCraken, Barnac Van Kirk, Polly Abbott, William Heaveto, Mary Van Kirk, Ruben Abbott, Grace Van Kirk, Sally Abbott, Barnard Abbott and William Abbot – Grand-daughter: Mary Abbott – Signed: Mary (mark) Van Kirk – Witnesses: William Fowler, James Collins and Benjamin Cox.

MILLER, Joash – Will Book 1, page 57 – Verbal Will – wife: Nancy – Four married daughters: Catharine Paulsgrove, Rebecca Westenhaver, Mary Hedges and Susannah Hedges – Two unmarried daughters: Nancy and Betsey – Sons: Peter and Joseph Miller – Son-in-law: Jacob Westenhaver – Mentions daughter Rebecca's son, Edward Kennady – Administrators: sons; Peter and Joseph and son-in-law, John Hedges – Will given 2-16-1819 – Witnesses: John Fisher, William Wilson and John Buntlinger.

MATTHIAS, Henry Sr. – Salt Creek Twp. – Will Book 1, page 60 – dated 12-23-1817 – Wife: Doratia – son: Henry – daughters: Barbary, Catherine (Caty) and Mary – Signed: Henry Mathias – Witnesses: Jacob Landis and Benjamin Kessner.

HOGEN, Elizabeth – Will Book 1, page 63 – Bequeaths to: William Hill, Jr.; Eleanor Hill and William Hill – Mentions negro woman, Lettice which Francis Hill is authorized to sell in Virginia – Executor: William Hill – will dated 10-16-1816 – Signed: Elisabeth Hogen – Witnesses: Wm. Florence, Margaret Hill and Fanny Florence.

HITLER, George – Will Book 1, page 64 – dated 11-16-1817 – wife: Susannah also to serve as Executrix – Sons: Jacob, George, Abraham and Joseph – Daughters: Elizabeth, Susannah, Sarah and Polly – son-in-law: James Ballah – Mentions a tract of land purchased from Anthony and Elizabeth Bole, formerly Elizabeth Miller – Signed: George Hitler – Witnesses: John Hunter, John Ely and Thos. Herbert.

HADLEY, Simon – Stanton Village, Mill Creek Hundred, New Castle Co., Delaware – Will Book 1, page 68 – dated 7th day, 11th month, 1803 – Sisters: eldest, Elisabeth wife of Henry Dixon; Emey wife of Isaac Dixon; Mary wife of Samuel Pennock – Nephews: John and Samuel Hadley sons of brother Samuel Hadley, dec'd – Nieces: Rebecca Thomson daughter of sister Hannah Thompson, deceased; Phobe and Sarah Hadley daughters of brother Samuel Hadley, deceased – Executor: brother-in-law, Isaac Dixon of Wilmington, New Castle Co., Del. – Signed: Simon Hadley – Witnesses: Moses Rea, John Dixon and Isaac Dixon – Codicil dated 8-20-1818 Simon Hadley, Harrison Twp., Pickaway Co., Ohio formerly of Delaware – requests that nephew John Dickson be executor in place of Isaac Dixon, deceased, and further appoints Stephen Short of Harrison Twp., Pickaway Co. as co-executor – Witnesses: Harleleigh Sage and Isaac Southworth, Jr.

CALDWELL, Catharine – Will Book 1, page 76 – dated 9-12-1817 – Son: Alexander, also to serve as executor – Daughters: Sidney; Catherine Hunter – Grandchildren: Henry White; Eliza Swigart – Sons-in-law: Johnson Hemphill and Peter White – Signed: Catharine (mark) Caldwell – Witnesses: Henry Cook, Allston Phillips and Jasper (mark) Jacobs.

PICKAWAY COUNTY, OHIO - PARTITION RECORDS 1836-1840

The following records were taken from Partition Record 1 (1836-1845) located in the Common Pleas Court (Clerk of the Courts Office) at the court house at Circleville. Page on which record may be found in the original book is given in parenthesis.

4-25-1836 - Nathan REED vs. Heirs of Nathan REED. Petition for Partition. Filed 4-20-1835. Land, 400 acres survey dated 11-20-1807; 100 acres Military Warrant 2964 in name Wm Bredant and 200 acres Military Warrant 3087 name John Kenedy on Mill Creek, Union Co., Ohio; Entry 5249 in Delaware Co., Ohio...(other numerous descriptions). Nathan REID of Bedford Co., Va., dec'd. Widow, has died since death of Nathan. Children: Nathan Reid of Bedford Co., Va.; John Reid, dec'd, his three children--Sophia T. late Reid wife of Lafayette Searcey, William Reid and John Reid, the last two not of age and all of Henry Co., Tennessee; Elizabeth formerly Reid, dec'd, late wife of Robert T. Cabell, her son--Samuel I. Cabell of Kanawha County, Virginia; Pamelia Reid, died without issue; Patsey formerly Reid, wife of Greenville Penn of Patrick Co., Virginia; Maria Reid, died without issue; Francis Reid; Catharine Reid, died without issue; Mary Ann formerly Reid, dec'd, late wife of Edmund Penn of Edgefield, South Carolina, her child--Mary Ann Penn, a minor of Patrick County, Virginia. (1)

4-26-1836 - George S. BINKLEY vs. George and Maria BINKLEY. Petition to sell land. Filed 11-5-1835. Land, 30 acres Lot 6, N½ Section 26, Township 15, Range 19 as divided by Common Pleas Court of Fairfield Co., Ohio between Heirs of Henry Abrams on petition of Ann Harper one of said heirs and subject to dower of Ruth Abrams, widow of Henry Abrams. That Orphia Binkley, dec'd, late wife of petitioner, George Binkley was orphia Abrams one of the children of Henry Abrams, dec'd, late of Franklin Co., Ohio. That petitioner, George Binkley is guardian of his children by Orphia--George H. and Maria L. Binkley. (7)

4-27-1836 - James GREENE guardian of Harriet GREENE, etal. Petition to sell land. Filed 4-27-1836. Land, 12 acres and 79½ poles part NE¼ Section 30, Township 11, Range 21. John WRIGHT Sr., dec'd. Widow, Polly Wright, entitled to dower. 1/10th share to Harriet, Martha, John and William Henry Greene by right of their mother, Elizabeth Greene, late Elizabeth Wright. That James Greene is guardian of his said minor children by said Elizabeth Wright Greene. (9)

4-27-1836 - Margaret WILLIAMS and Abrm. J. WILLIAMS adms. of David WILLIAMS, dec'd vs. Heirs. Petition to execute contract real estate. Filed 4-4-1836. That David Williams in his lifetime on 8-6-1828 contracted to convey to Peter Parcels before 5-1-1832 undivided 1/3rd part W½ Section 22, Township 11, Range 20 (W.S.) being about 100 acres. David Williams, dec'd. Children: Mary Williams, Abner Williams, Rebecca Williams, David Williams, William Williams, Benjamin Williams, Isaac Williams, and Sarah Williams; all of Franklin County, Ohio; the last five being named being minors. (13)

4-27-1836 - Andrew HUSTON vs George MATZLER, etal. Petition for Partition. Filed 7-21-1835. Land, 100 acres west bank Scioto River in Lawrence Butler survey being same land which division among devisees of George WEST late of Pickaway Co., Ohio, dec'd was set apart to Margaret wife of John MATZLER and on which the Matzler resided prior to their death. John and Margaret MATZLER, dec'd. (Cont. next page)

394

Heirs: 1/6th part, Elizabeth March and husband, her share being sold to Andrew Huston; 1/6th part, George Matzler a minor, John West guardian; 1/6th part, Derissa Matzler; 1/6th part, David Matzler; 1/6th part, Keturah Matzler; 1/6th part, John Matzler; the last four named being minors by John Olds, guardian. (15)

4-27-1836 - Truston P. BROWN and wife vs. Margaret CANNON, et al. Petition for Partition. Filed 6-3-1835. Land, 35½ acres conveyed to Jesse Cannon now dec'd by Henry Rector and wife by deed dated 12-29-1823 and recorded in Book G, pages 254-5; also 99 acres and 109 poles adjoining above tract, conveyed to Jesse Cannon by Jacob Hotsonpillen by deed dated 8-21-1813 and recorded in Book A, pages 602-3. Jesse CANNON, dec'd. Widow, Margaret Cannon entitled to dower. Heirs: 1/4th part, Tabitha wife of Truston P. Brown of Pickaway Co., Ohio; 1/4th part, Matthew W. Cannon of Indiana; 1/4th part, Sarah wife of Coonrad Peck of Indiana; 1/4th part, Jesse Cannon of Pickaway Co., Ohio. (19)

4-26-1836 - Wm D. WOOD, adms. vs. Widow and Heirs of Mitchel PRITCHARD, dec'd. Petition to sell land. Filed 7-17-1834. Land, lots 6 & 7 in Palestine. Mitchell Pritchard, dec'd, late of Darby township. Widow, Anne Pritchard. Children: Elizabeth, Edward and Thomas Pritchard, all minors.   (23)

8-9-1836 - Augustus L. PERRILL adms. of Joseph WRIGHT, dec'd vs. Heirs. Petition to sell land. Filed 8-22-1835. Joseph Wright, dec'd was a minor under 21 years at time of his death and left no personal property or money except real estate being part NE¼ Section 30, Township 11, Range 21, 11 acres and 84½ poles adjoining town of Circleville; that Polly Anderson was guardian of Joseph Wright and had settled account with court. Joseph Wright, dec'd. Brothers and sisters: Thomas Wright, dec'd, his children--Mary Ann, William and Catherine Wright, all minors; Elizabeth Greene, late Wright, dec'd, her children--Harriet, Martha, John and William Greene, all minors; John Wright, dec'd, his son, John Wright, a minor; Barbara late Wright wife of Joshua McClary; Mary late Wright wife of William Cangrow; Hugh Wright; Sarah Wright; Lucinda Wright; July Ann Wright; the last three named being minors. Also, that William Wright who left Pickaway County in the spring of 1827 or 1828 and has not been heard from since was a brother of said Joseph Wright, dec'd. (28)

8-9-1836 - Lydia GROCE vs. Heirs of John GROCE, dec'd. Petition for Partition. Filed 11-7-1835. Land, in-lot 179 Circleville. John Groce, dec'd. Widow, Margaret Groce entitled to dower. Children: 1/5th part, Lydia Groce; 1/5th part, Bentley Groce; 1/5th part, John Groce; 1/5th part, Mahlon Groce; 1/5th part, Betsey Ann Groce; all of Pickaway Co., the last four named being minors.   (32

8-9-1836 - Mary Magdelene YATES vs. Andrew HUSTON. Petition for Dower. Filed 4-23-1836. Land, NW¼ Section 6, Township 11, Range 2 (W.S.); part fractional Sections 1 & 2, Township 4, Range 22 (W.S.), totaling 235 acres. Joseph Yates, dec'd late of Pickaway Co. Widow, Mary Magdelene Yates entitled to dower. Andrew Huston owner of land by conveyance from heirs to him subject to dower. (35)

11-1-1836 - Joseph JOHNSON of Hancock Co., Ohio guardian of Sarah ALBRIGHT, a minor vs. His Ward. Petition to sell land. Filed 8-5-1836. Land, 14¼ acres pt NE¼ Section 2, Township 9, Range 21 Matthews Survey. Sarah Albright aged about 14 years. (38)

11-1-1836 - Edward S. DAVISSON, et al, vs. Ann M. BALDWIN, et al. Petition for Partition. Filed 6-10-1836. Land, Survey of 500 acres in favor of Cornelius Baldwin (Surgeon 6 months more than 6 years) to United States in Virginia Line, Cont'l Establishment, Military Warrant 4248 on waters Deer Creek and Yellow Bud, granted by patent to Baldwin on 9-29-1818. Cornelius Baldwin, dec'd, late of Frederick Co., Virginia. Widow, has since died. Partition: 1/7th part, Elenor C. late Baldwin wife of Edward S. Davisson; 1/7th part, Mary Briscoe Baldwin; 1/7th part, Isaac Hite Baldwin; 1/7th part, Cornelius E. Baldwin; 1/7th part, Ann M. Baldwin; 1/7th part, James M. Baldwin; 1/7th part, Robert S. Baldwin; the first four of Frederick Co., Va. and the last three being minors. (41)

11-1-1836 - Nathaniel COOLEY vs. Isaac BECHTEL, et al. Petition for Partition. Filed 9-9-1836. Land, NE¼ Section 34, Township 9, Range 21 (M.S.) Samuel BETCHTELL, dec'd. Heirs: John Betchtell, Samuel Betchtell, Henry Betchtell, David Betchtell, Andrew Betchtell, Nancy late Betchtell wife of E. Skinner, Isaac Betchtell, and Christine late Betchtell wife of George Lape (or Lasse); the last two named being minors and of Fairfield Co., Ohio and the first six named having sold their 6/8ths (jointly--1/8th singularly) interest to Nathaniel Cooley. (45)

11-1-1836 - Joseph OLDS vs. Peter STAHL, etal. Petition for Partition. Filed 2-18-1836. Land, 233 acres part Section 36, Township 11, Range 21 (M.S.). James MORRIS Sr., dec'd. by will devised land to three youngest children, of which 2/3res was decreed by the last Supreme Court of Pickaway County, Ohio to be the property of all heirs at law of deceased subject to dower. Widow, Molly Morris, who has since married Peter Stahl of Pickaway Co., Ohio and is entitled to dower. Heirs: John Morris; Joseph Morris; James Morris; Moses Morris; Thomas Wadell and his wife; George Metzger and his wife; Jacob Frazier and his wife; Louisa late Morris wife of William North of Fairfield Co., Ohio; Matilda Smith late Morris, dec'd, her children--Permelia, Zilleman, Belinda and Martha Smith, all minors of Pickaway Co.; Benjamin Morris, dec'd, his children--Jacob Morris of Louisiana, Benjamin Morris, James Morris and Elizabeth Stephenson all of Indiana; Thomas Morris, dec'd, his children--Thomas, James and Joseph Morris all of Pickaway Co.; William Harvey Morris, a minor, Samuel Lybrand his guardian; Henry Morris, a minor, Samuel Lybrand his guardian. The first seven named sold their interest to Joseph Olds. (48)

11-3-1836 - Joseph HURST adms. of William THOMAS, dec'd vs. Widow and Heirs. Petition to sell land. Filed 4-14-1836. Land, in-lots 2,7, & 8 and also N½ lot 9 (town not stated). Widow, Mary Thomas. Child, Jane late Thomas wife of James Davis. (54)

11-8-1836 - John M. ALKIRE vs. Edward TANNER. Petition for Partition. Filed 4-26-1836. Land: Tract 1--90 acres, 2 rods and 20 poles, lines--Robert Alkire, Deer Creek; Tract 2--115 acres, lines--Deer Creek, Elias Langhan, Wm. Scott and part Baylor tract. Courtney Tanner, dec'd, late of Pickaway Co., Ohio. Widow, departed life since decease of husband. Seven children, six of who sold their interests to John M. Alkire and are not named and Edward Tanner, son of Courtney Tanner, dec'd, who is a minor by George Alkire his guardian. (57)

396

10-5-1836 - Heirs of Isaac WILLIAMS vs. Heirs of Edward WILLIAMS. Petition for Partition. Filed 5-21-1832. Land, Survey of William Heth part Military Warrant 2162 on waters of Scioto River, lines--Wm Heth's No. 1194; Heirs of Isaac Williams entitled to one-half and Heir of Edward Williams entitled to one-half. Isaac WILLIAMS, dec'd. Widow, Mary Williams entitled to dower of one-half of said land (being 1/3rd of 1/2). Children: Joseph, Isaac, Eliza Ann, Sarah, John, James, Vincent and Rebecca Williams; the last seven named being minors. Edward WILLIAMS, dec'd. Children: Vincent, Edward, Sarah, Mary, Wm S., Josephine and Elizabeth Williams; the last six name being minors. (60 & 68)

11-8-1836 - Gershom M. PETERS, guardian vs. His Ward. Petition to sell land. Filed 4-28-1836. Land, E½ lot 2 and whole lot 3 in eight blocks of lots surveyed by Licking Canal Company in town of Granville, Licking Co., Ohio. James BERRY, dec'd, late of Licking County, Ohio. Widow, Mirander Berry, now wife of Gershom M. Peters. Children: James W. and Lydia E. Berry by Gershom M. Peters their guardian. (65)

3-18-1837 - Widow and Heirs of Daniel HANSON, dec'd vs. Jeremiah BROWN, etal. (note: this is heading of case as given). Petition for Partition. Filed 3-10-1836. Land, 110 acres Deer Creek township, lines--Geo. Mathews and Edward Rector. Daniel Hanson entitled to 3/7ths part. Jeremiah Brown, George Smith, Mary Smith and Rachel Smith, the last two named being minors are tenants in common with Hanson by right from Polly Landon late Smith widow of Jones Smith, with said Polly being entitled to dower. (75)

7-1-1837 - John CHRISTY vs. Catharine CHRISTY, et al. Petition for Partition. Filed 3-13-1837. Land: NE¼ Section 25, Township 9, Range 21 Pickaway Co.; in-lots 8 & 25 town of Amanda and 94 acres part Section 30, Township 13, Range 20 conveyed to Abraham Christy (in name of Crist) by deed dated 9-17-1829 by Christian Whiteman and wife as recorded Book R, page 527, Fairfield Co., Ohio. Abraham CHRISTY, dec'd, late of Pickaway Co. Widow, Catharine Christy, entitled to dower. Children: Abraham Christy of Pickaway Co.; Elizabeth late Christy wife of George Stout Jr. of Pickaway Co.; Nancy late Christy wife of Jonathan Stout of Fairfield Co., Ohio; John Christy; Margaret late Christy wife of John Court- wright; Christina formerly Christy, dec'd wife of Jacob Courtwright, her daughter- Isabella Courtwright of Fairfield Co., Ohio a minor, with her father, Jacob Court- wright her guardian; Catharine Christy; Susannah Christy; Sarah Christy; and Isabella Christy; the last four named all of Pickaway Co. and the last three named being minors with their mother, Catharine Christy as their guardian. (79)

9-28-1837 - Catharine SEYMOUR vs. Adam SEYMOUR and Corilla L. SEYMOUR. In Chancery for Dower. Filed 3-2-1837. Land, one equal one half of tract of 800 acres part John Nevills Survey No. 767 conveyed to Richard Seymour and Adam Seymour by James D. Caldwell by deed dated 4-28-1836. Richard SEYMOUR, dec'd, died in January 1837. Widow, Catharine Seymour, entitled to dower. Child, Corilla L. Seymour. (83 & 110)

9-8-1837 - Claris HORNBACK vs. Elsey LISTER, et al. Petition for Partition. Filed 3-9-183(6). Land, 75 acres on Clarks Run a branch of Deer Creek part 1000 acre survey of Adam Shepherd #4289, lines--Henry Resten, John Steen, Shepherds original line. Michael HORNBACK, dec'd, died intestate on 11-8-1835. Children: James Hornback; Curtis Hornback; Lydia Hornback; Claris Hornback; Robison Hornback; George Hornback; Dorothy Hornback (last three named sold interest to Elecy Lister); Marinda Hornback; Joseph B. Hornback; the last two named being minors. (88)

3-24-1838 - Hervey ORR and wife vs. Widow and Heirs of James SMITH, dec'd. Petition for Partition. Filed 5-15-1837. Land, 125 acres part Survey 4721 in name of Frederick Segles representatives, and 100 acres part entry 4721 on waters of Yellow Bud. James Smith, dec'd, left will by which he devised tracts to four daughters. Widow, not named. Children: Alexander Smith, Pencey wife of Hervey Orr, Elizabeth wife of John H. Ater, Maria Smith, Margaret Smith and James Smith. The last named James Smith was born after father's death and posthumous child not named in will. (92)

7-3-1838 - William SOUTHARD and wife vs. Heirs of George DARR, dec'd. Petition for Partition. Filed 4-7-1837. Land, 96 acres Hay Run branch of Deer Creek in Survey 7898 in name of Henry Massie, lines--Thomas Jones Survey 7745 now owned by Joseph Scott; and 19 acres Survey 9333 entered and patented by Cadawallader Wallace, lines--Ann B. West, line of Henry Massie Survey 7898. George Darr, dec'd, late of Pickaway Co. Widow, Sarah now the wife of Jacob Funk of Pickaway Co., Ohio. Children: Ann late Darr wife of William Southard; Peter Darr of Indiana; David Darr; Elizabeth late Darr wife of Frederick Funk; Margaret late Darr wife of ____(not given) Hines; all of Indiana; William Darr of Kentucky; John Darr of Kentucky; Sarah late Darr wife of ____(not given) Flurry of Virginia; Catharine Guy, late Darr, dec'd, her children--Willis, John, George, Hezekiah, Samuel, Nelson, Ann, Margaret, Catharine and Mary Guy, residents of Ohio but exact residence unknown. (97)

7-3-1838 - Benjamin HALL vs. John W. EASTERDAY, et al. Petition for Partition. Filed 2-1-1838. Land, 99 acres and 137 poles part NW¼ Section 36, Township 2, Range 22 (Mathews Survey), Walnut twp. Christian Easterday, dec'd. Heirs: Thomas Nelson Easterday, Mary late Easterday wife of Robert Elgee, John W. Easterday, Sarah Ellen Easterday and Noah Easterday; the first two named sold their interest to Benjamin Hall. (104)

7-3-1838 - Solomon T. LOFFER vs. Daniel P. LOFFER, et al. Petition for Partition. Filed 4-9-1838. Land, NW¼ Section 23, Township 10, Range 21 (M.S.). Christian Loffer, dec'd, died intestate. Children: Solomon T. Loffer, Sarah Loffer, Henry Loffer, Christian Loffer, Ellen Loffer, Daniel Loffer and Simon P. Loffer; the last two named being minors. (108)

9-15-1838 - Robert HAYS guardian of Isaac HAYS vs. His Ward. Petition to sell land. Filed 6-30-1838. Land, lot 146 Circleville. Robert Hays guardian of his son Isaac Hays. (note: no further information given). (120)

398

9-15-1838 - John HOLDERMAN, etal. Heirs of Christopher Holderman, dec'd vs. Lemuel STEELEY and others. Petition for Partition. Filed 9-11-1838. 1180 acres in Sections 34,33,28,27 & 29, Township 11, Range 20 Worthington Survey, Marion Co., Ohio; 930 acres in Sections 12,13 & 2, Township 4S Range 14; Section 7 & 18, Township 4S, Range 15; Section 23, Township 4, Range 14 and Section 22, Township 5, Range 14. Christopher Holdermfn Sr., dec'd. Widow, Eleanor Holderman, entitled to dower. Heirs: John Holderman; Gwana (or Gwinna) wife of Lemuel Steeley; Anna wife of Peter Coshner; Magdalene wife of David Patrick; Elizabeth wife of Jesse Rhodes; Christopher Holderman Jr.; George Holderman; David Holderman Jr.; Abraham Holderman; Isaac Holderman; Mary Holderman; Eleanor Holderman, a minor with John Holderman her guardian; Jacob Holderman, a minor with Lemuel Steeley his guardian. (114)

4-9-1839 - Archibald LYBRAND adms. of Peter ZEHRING, dec'd vs Catharine ZEHRING, et al. Petition to sell land. Filed 6-26-1838. Land, S½ lot 8 in Square 8 in town of Tarlton. Widow, Catharine Zehring of Tarlton, entitled to dower. Five children: Joseph, William, John, Sephas and Peter Zehring, all minors. (122)

5-9-1839 - Nicholas McNEMOR, et al. Petition for Partition. Filed 5-6-1839. Land in Pickaway and Ross Counties. Philip McNemor, dec'd left will by which he devised his land to children--Nicholas McNemor, Philip McNemor, Noah McNemor, William McNemor and Harriet wife of Frederick Bush. That since death of Philip, his son William has died intestate leaving as his only heirs--Elizabeth and Sarah McNemor. (126)

5-8-1839 - Charles R. BYE and wife vs. Widow and Heirs of Jonathan HOLMES, dec'd. Petition for Partition. Filed 5-15-1837. Land, 317 acres S½ Section 22, 100 acres part Section 34 and fractional Section 33, 160 acres SW¼ Section 23, all in Township 3, Range 22 (M.S.) and also undivided 1/2 Lot 24 in Bloomfield. Widow, Rachel Holmes. Children: Mary late Holmes wife of Charles R. Bye of Pickaway Co.; James Holmes of Pickaway Co.; Elizabeth Musser (or Mercer) of Pickaway Co.; Isaac Holmes of Pickaway Co.; Juliann wife of David Spangler of Franklin Co., Ohio; and Jane Holmes of Pickaway Co. (130)

8-14-1839 - Michael ROW vs. Widow and Heirs of John ROW, dec'd. Petition for Partition. Filed 11-21-1838. Land, lot 20 in Philip Yeger Jr. addition to Circleville. Widow, Catharine Row of Pickaway Co., entitled to dower. Children: Michael Row of Putnam Co., Ohio; John Row of Scioto Co., Ohio; Catharine late Row wife of Solomon Cooder of Wood Co., Ohio; Anna late Row wife of Ely Todd of Putnam Co., Ohio; Jacob Row of Pike Co., Ohio; Elizabeth Tomlinson late Row of Pickaway Co.; Margaret Galbreath late Row, dec'd, her children--Catharine, Jane, William, John and Henry Galbreath, of Seneca Co., Ohio. (136)

8-14-1839 - James BALLAH and wife vs. Jacob HILLER (HITLER), etal. Petition for Partition. Filed 1-29-1839. Land, 152 acres and 88 poles part Section 33, Township 11, Range 21 (W.S.). George Hitler, dec'd. Widow, Susannah Hitler, entitled to dower. Heirs: Catharine wife of James Ballah, Elizabeth wife of Samuel Evans, John Hitler, Jacob Hitler, Sally Lane, Abraham Hitler, George Hitler, Mary Earnhart and Joseph Hitler. (141)

8-14-1839 - Jacob WELTER adms. of Peter WELTER, dec'd vs. Heirs. Petition to sell real estate. Filed 9-14-1838. Land, in-lot 181 Circleville. Widow, Sophia Welter. Children: Molly, Jacob, Peter, Margaret and William Welter. (146 & 149)

8-14-1839 - Joseph OLDS adms. of Amasa M. OLDS, dec'd vs. Heirs. Petition to convey real estate. Filed 8-13-1839. Land, Amasa Olds in his lifetime in 1837 or 1838 contracted to sell lots 19,22,25,26, etc. in Circleville to William R. Rhinehart, Philip Zegar and others. Amasa M. Olds left two minor children, Sarah and Joseph Olds, both of Fayette Co., Ohio. Joseph Olds administrator of estate is brother of Amasa M. Olds, dec'd. (152)

8-15-1839 - Ann K. HOGE, guardian. Petition to sell land. Filed 6-25-1831. Land, 535 acres Highland Co., Ohio part Entry 1831 in names of Reddick, Hardin, Gray and Mercer being lot 6 in Partition Record in Ross Co., Ohio conveyed by Moses Hoge to John B. Hoge; also 1/3rd part 200 acres Pickaway Co. part entry 582 in name of Robert White who patented in trust for John B. Hoge. John B. Hoge, dec'd. Children: John Blair Hoge and Elizabeth Ann Hoge, minors by Ann K. Hoge their guardian. 2/3rds part, Thomas D. Hoge and Danuel D. Hoge, dec'd, his widow, Elizabeth K. Hoge and minor children--Moses Duery Hoge, Ann Lacy Hoge, Elizabeth P. Hoge and William James Hoge. (154)

4-8-1839 - William BOGGS guardian of Mary Jane SISCO vs. Mary Jane SISCO. Petition to sell land. FILED 4-13-1839. Land, part Section 12 and fractional Section 16, Township 3, Range 22 (W.S.), lines--bank of Scioto, Sisco Creek. 1/4th part, Mary Ann Sisco, late Buttain wife of John Sisco, her daughter--Mary Jane Sisco a minor with Wm Boggs as guardian, of Logan Co., Ohio. That Mary Ann late Buttain wife of John Sisco was the daughter of William Buttain, dec'd, late of Pickaway Co. (163)

11-19-1839 - Hugh FORESMAN guardian of William JACKSON vs. His Ward. Petition to sell land. Filed 5-4-1839. Land, lot 32, Circleville. James Jackson, dec'd, late of Pickaway Co. Widow, Mary Jackson. Child: William Jackson, a minor. (166)

11-19-1839 - Wm K. ARTHUR guardian of Margaret and Charles D. BOTKIN. Petition to sell land. Filed 3-6-1839. Land, part lot 11 in Hustons addition to Circleville. George Botkin, dec'd. Children: Margaret and Charles D. Botkin. (169)

11-19-1839 - Rachel DAVIS vs. Asahel RENICK. Petition for Dower. Filed 5-4-1839. Land, 100 acres conveyed by Wm Marquis part of Survey in name of David Mirewrather. Thomas Glaze, dec'd, late of Pickaway Co. Widow, Rachel Glaze now Rachel Davis.(17

4-18-1840 - Jeremiah RAY vs. Jonn RAY, et al. Petition for Partition. Filed 8-13-1839. Land, part W½ Section 8, Township 10, Range 21 (W.S.). George RAY, dec'd. Heirs: John Ray of Vermillion Co., Illinois; George Ray of Illinois; Jeremiah Ray; Sarah late Ray wife of Noah Messick; Hannah late Ray wife of William Shank; Margaret McGeady late Ray; Benjamin Ray; Reuben Ray; Elias Ray; all of Pickaway Co. the last three being minors by____(not given) Swisher their guardian. (185)

-18-1840 - Charles SHOEMAKER and others vs. Catharine MARTZ and others. Petition
or Partition. Filed 1-5-1839. Land, NE¼ Section 5, Township 11, Range 20 (W.S.),
also 102 acres and 49½ poles NWP same Section, Twp. and Range. Abraham MARTZ,
ec'd, died intestate. Widow, Catharine Martz, entitled to dower. Children:
ohn Martz of Indiana; Polly wife of Samuel Spangler of Fairfield Co., Ohio;
amuel Martz of Pickaway Co.; Susannah Martz of Pickaway Co.; Catharine, dec'd,
ate wife of Abraham Casner, her children--Leah, Elizabeth and Catharine Casner
ll of Indiana;----(first name not given) Shoemaker, dec'd, her children--Charles,
ophia, Joseph, Jacob and Molly Shoemaker, minors of Pickaway Co. by Daniel
hoemaker their guardian. (176)

-18-1840 - Eleazer MYERS and Sarah wife vs. heirs of David SLOAN, dec'd.
etition for Dower. Filed 8-13-1839. Land, 160 acres NW¼ Section 23 and 160
cres NE¼ Section 22, Township 3, Range 22 (M.S.). David Sloan, dec'd, died
ntestate. Widow, Sarah now wife of Eleazer Myers. Children: Charles, Richard,
annah and Sarah Sloan, all minors and of Pickaway Co. (192)

-18-1840 - Jonathan PETERS guardian Jacob HAMORS Heirs vs. Heirs. Petition to
ell land. Filed 11-5-1839. Land, 84 acres W½ SW¼ Section 5, Township 11, Range 21
W.S.). Jacob Hamor, dec'd, late of Pickaway Co. Widow, Rebecca Hammon, entitled
o dower. Children: Henrietta Hamor and Amos Theobald Hamor. (196)

-8-1840 - James MITCHEL and Elizabeth his wife vs. John GILLOLAND, et al. Petition
or Partition. Filed 11-12-1839. Land, lots 23 & 24 Darbyville. David Thomas,
ec'd, late of Pickaway Co. died 6-29-1837. Widow, Elizabeth now the wife of James
itchel of Madison Co., Ohio. Brothers and Sisters: Elizabeth late Thomas wife
f John Gilloland, residence not known; John Thomas, dec'd; Nancy, dec'd, wife of
ohn Clark, her children--David, Samuel, Elizabeth, Henry and John Clark, all minors
f Pickaway Co.; Dolly late Thomas wife of David (or Daniel) Thompson; and Robert
homas. (199)

0-26-1840 - Robert COURTNEY and Priscilla COURTNEY vs. James CAMPBELL and others.
etition for Partition. Filed 6-2-1840. Land, 361½ acres whole of entry 8758;
ines--Jesse McKays survey 6149, Hay Run, John Hoffman survey 8753, Ann B. West
urvey 6226, Wm Rulor Survey 6431, David Mills survey 8379, John McCormick survey
076 & 7078. Jane CAMPBELL, dec'd, who was one of the heirs of Thomas HILL.
artition to devisees of Jane Campbell: Priscilla wife of Robert Courtney of King
nd Queen Co., Va.; Mary Carolton who died intestate, her son Benous Callton, and
er grandchildren--Artemelia wife of John Segar, Hermon Coulton, Betsy Molly Coulton,
ane Esther Coulton, Hanis Coulton, Ellen Coulton, Ann Coulton, last six all child-
en of Hannis Coulton son of Mary, Mary Ann Jones, Ellen Jones, Susan Jones children
f Keturah Jones, dec'd late Coulton daughter of Mary, James Parks, Mary Mills late
arks wife of Laswell Fogg, William Parks, Alexander Parks, John H. Parks, Cornelius
arks children of Mary Parks late Carlton daughter of Mary, all of King and Queen Co.,
a.; William Campbell of King and Queen Co., Va.; Robert and Achillis Campbell; Mary
nn Rousey late Campbell wife of Wm. B. Rousey of King William Co., Va.; George
ampbell of Joe Davison Co., Illinois; Alexander Campbell, dec'd, his children--
mily Fox late Campbell and Alexander Campbell of King and Queen Co., Va.; Hannah
effries, dec'd, her children--James J.C. Jeffries and Juliet Pollard late Jeffries
ife of Smith John Pollard of King and Queen Co., Va.; Whitaker Campbell, dec'd, his
hildren--Mary Jane, Sarah B., Thomas W., Pempey and Lucy A. Campbell all of King

(COURTNEY vs. CAMPBELL, cont.)
and Queen Co., Va.; Jane Jones of Caroline Co., Va.; James Campbell of Mercer
Co., Kentucky; Benjamin Campbell of Christian Co., Kentucky. (201)

10-28-1840 - Harriet L. RENICK vs. Thomas RENICK, et al. Petition for Dower.
Filed 4-17-1840. Land, 72 acres Darby Creek in Survey 512 in name of William
Wilson; 75 acres adjacent being Survey 6376 in name of A. Renick; 130 acres
immediately on west and adjoining tract 1 part Survey 501; 268 acres David Merrweathers Survey 549 and various other descriptions. Asahel RENICK, dec'd late
of Pickaway Co., Ohio died intestate. Widow, Harriet L. Renick. Brothers and
Sisters: Thomas Renick of Pickaway Co.; Jonathan Renick of Pickaway Co.; James
Renick of Pickaway Co.; Abel Renick of Marion Co., Ohio; Rachel Vanmeter, dec'd,
her children--Sidney wife of Benjamin Huckle of Indiana, Sarah wife of John F.
Huckle of Hardin Co., Ohio, James W. Vanmeter of Ill., Daniel T. Vanmeter of Pick
way Co., Thomas Vanmeter of Ind. or Ill., Cecelia B. Vanmeter of Ind., Rebecca
Vanmeter of Pickaway Co., Mary (or Murry) Vanmeter of Ill., and Joseph Vanmeter
of Pickaway Co.; Ann Claypool, dec'd, her children--Benjamin McNeal, Catharine wi
of Wesley Claypool, Sarah wife of Lewis Sifford, John R. McNeal, Reese McNeal,
Samuel McNeal and Ashel C. McNeal all of Ross Co., Ohio, the last three named
being minors; Catharine Osborn, dec'd, her children--John R. Osborn of Huron Co.,
Ohio, James D. Osborn of Franklin Co., Ohio, Mary wife of Josiah Renick of Pickaw
Co., Jane wife of Alexander Renick of Pickaway Co., Ann Osborn of Pickaway Co.,
William Renick Osborn of Athens Co., Ohio, Henry Osborn of Franklin Co., Ohio and
Lucy Osborn of Pickaway Co., the last three named being minors; Margaret wife of
Henry Vanmeter of Champaign Co., Ohio; --_ _____ (not given--sister of Asahe
dec'd, her daughter--Margaret wife of Samuel McMasters of Scioto Co., Ohio. (207

Deaths for period ending on 1st day of March 1857. It should be noted that probably death dated March 1st through December 31st took place in 1856. Unless otherwise stated, place of death and residence was in the township under which deaths are listed.

SALT CREEK TOWNSHIP

CAMPBELL, Jane Francus - d. Aug. 30 at Stringtown, Residence: Tarlton, Born: Tarlton - Parents: Jacob Campbell and Maria Rose.

BUSHERD, Jesse d. June 6 at Tarlton; age 51; married; Residence Tarlton; born; Tarlton.

BITLER, Dan'l. - d. Oct. 20 at Tarlton; age 6 months; Residence and Born Tarlton; Parents C. F. Bitler and Sarah Hickman.

MERGAN, George - d. ----1857 at Tarlton; age 87; Singe; Residence Tarleton; born Virginia

DRUH, Infant - d. Feb. 16; Parents William Drum and Sarah Bowman.

THOMAS, Mary A. - d. Mar. 16; age 42; married; b. Salt Creek Twp.; Parents: James and Mary Anderson.

SPANGLER, Jacob - d. Oct. 23; age 23; Single; b. Salt Creek Twp.; Parents J. and Cath. Spangler.

ROOT, Sylvester - d. Feb. 7; age 1 year; b. Salt Creek Twp.; Parents: Wm. and M. Root.

STIEN, Polly W. - d. Dec. 11; age 19; married; b. Salt Creek Twp.; Parents: James and Ann Koof.

REICHERDERFER, Vinus - d. Sept. 19; age 37- married; b. Tennessee. Parents: J. and Rebecca Reichelderfer.

REICHELDERFER, Rebecca - d. Nov. 20; age 63; married; b. Tennessee; Father: H. Lumhart.

TODD, Geo. - d. July 2; age 19; single; Residence: Stringtown; b. Tarlton; Parents: Joel and Maria Todd.

NYE, Adam - d. Jan. 5 at Tarlton; age 67; married; Residence Tarlton; b. Maryland.

LEIGHNER, Elias - d. ----1857 at Camp Charlotte; age 21; single; Residence Camp Charlotte; Parents: James Leighner and Mary Frease.

HALDERMAN, Eleaner - d. ----1857; age 76; married; Parents: C. Halderman and Eleanor Black.

HALDERMAN, Nelson - d. ----1857; age 18; single; b. Salt Creek Twp.; Parents: Geo. Halderman and Mary (?) Jenes.

GOSSINE, Edward - d. July 8 at Musquito Gulf; age 39; married; Residence Tarlton.

PICKAWAY TOWNSHIP

HURDLE, Mary Catharine - d. Aug. 1; age 20; single; b. Pickaway Twp.; Father: R. Hurdle.

LOCIER, Jacob - d. Jan. 14; (no age given); widower; b. New York.

WEIDER, Mary A. - d. Jan. 5; age 21 yrs. 8 mos.; single; b. Pickaway Twp.; Parents: D. and E. J. Weider.

STEVENS, Elizabeth Jane - d. Dec. 12; age 21; single; b. Pickaway Twp.; Parents: Sam'l and M. Stevens.

RODE, Cath. - d. December (no day given); age 50, married; b. Germany

WASHINGTON TOWNSHIP

MARTIN, Edson B. - d. Sept. 1; age 3 mos.; b. Washington Twp.; Parents: Jacob
and Elizabeth Martin.
SAUNAN, Hannah - d. Dec. (No day given); age 3 mos.; b. Washington Twp.; Parents:
R. and Hannah Saunan.
HOFFMAN, David - d. Jan. (no day given); age 19; single; b. Washington Twp.
Parents John and Julia Ann Hoffman.
BORKERT, Henry - d. Apr. (no day given); age 1 yr.; b. Washington Twp.; -
Parents: Jonas and Rachel Borket.
SCHOCK, Henry - d. Dec. (no day given); age 90; widower; b. Penna.; Father:
H. Schock.
SEAL, Mary - d. Mar. (No day given); age 20; single; b. Pickaway Twp.; Parents
Samuel and Mary Seal.

1st Ward, CIRCLEVILLE

VAN DEMARK, Mary E. - d. Feb. 21; age 7 yrs. 10 mos.; b. Walnut Twp.; Parents:
E. and Margaret Van Demark.
JUSTUS, Aquilla - d. Aug. 1; age 32; married; b. Walnut Twp.; Parents: Aquilla
and Phebe Justis.
SMITH, Wm. D. - d. Oct. 2; age 53; married; b. Virginia; Parents Jno. and Margare
Smith.
MEAD, Elizabeth B. - d. Jan. 21; age 37; b. Pickaway County; Parents: Jno. and
Cath. Dehert.
KINNEAR, Nancy - d. Jan. 1; age 64, married.
BAHT, Edward - d. Dec. 29; age 3 mos.; b. Pickaway Co.; Father Adam W. Baht.
ALLISON, Edw'd C. - d. July 8; age 3 mos. b. Pickaway Co.; Parents:
Henry and Mary Allison.
BROWN, Levi B. - d. Sept. 26; age 1 yr.; b. Pickaway Co.; Parents: Jacob and
Lucinda Brown.
LINN, John - d. (no date given); age 23; b. Lancaster, Penna.; Parents Wm. and
Susan Linn.
DONEY, Barton - d. Dec. 28; age 1 yr.; b. Circleville; Parents Jas. B. and
Rachel Doney.
BEARD, Harriet - d. Sept. 4; (no age given) b. Circleville; Parents B. F. and
Martha Beard.
SCOTT, Ann - d. Apr. 29; age 84; widow; b. Virginia; Parents Jno. and Margaret
Howard.

2nd Ward, CIRCLEVILLE

BARNHILL, Jacob - d. Aug. 12; age 35; married; b. Ohio; Parents: Jno. Barnhill
and Charity Foust.
KETSTADT, Mary - d. May 13; married; b. Germany; Father: Geo. Tirgman.
KETSTADT, John M. - d. Mar. 26; age 1yr.; b. Circleville; Father: M. Ketstadt.
BRUNNER, Lydia - d. Dec. 29; age 65; married; b. Virginia.
HEATER, Elizabeth - d. Aug. 26; age 1 yr.; b. Circleville; Parents Jno. and E.
Heater.

3rd Ward, CIRCLEVILLE

DRAKELY, Thos. - d. Aug. 27; age 63; single; Residence Wheeling, Va.; b. New
England.

3rd Ward, CIRCLEVILLE

HASWELL, Mary C. - d. Nov. 2; age 26; married; b. Adelphia, Ohio.
HASWELL, Henry - d. Dec. 1; age 4 mos.; b. Circleville; Parents A. J. Haswell and Mary Campbell.
KEMP, John - d. Mar. 5; age 52; married; b. Virginia.
BLAKE, James - d. Dec. 7; age 57; married; b. Virginia.
WILKES, Ann - d. Dec. 4; age 72; widow; b. England.
HIMROD, Ann - d. Feb. 14; age 10 mos.; b. Circleville; Parents Elijah Himrod and M. Littleton.
SAGE, Harry - d. Jan. 21; age 9 mos.; b. Circleville; Parents H. H. Sage and Nancy Campbell.
COOPER, Lucinda - d. Dec. 8; age 13; b. Pickaway Co.; Parents Jacob H. Cooper and Eliza Beard.

WALNUT TOWNSHIP

GLICK, John - d. Jan. 26; age 42; married; b. Fairfield Co.; Father Philip Glick.
O'HARRA, Hugh - d. Sept. 8; age 58; married.
FLAGEL, Mary L. - d. Aug. 1; age 15 days; b. Pickaway Co.; Father E. J. Flagal.
ABBOTT, Mary - d. Apr. 5; age 75; widow: b. Pickaway Co.
MORRISON, Sarah A. - d. Sept. 9; age 9; b. Pickaway Co.; Father Wm. Morrison.
NUTTER, Sarah - d. Sept. 20; age 4; b. Pickaway Co.; Father L. L. Nutter.

HARRISON TOWNSHIP

GRIFFEY, Geo. - d. July 18; age 1 yr.; Residence: S. Bloomfield; b. Harrison Twp.; Parents S. and E. Griffey.
WINN, John - d. Apr. 12; age 19; single; b. Licking Co., Ohio; Parents S. and S. Winn.
DAWSON, Wm. - d. Oct. 14; age 65; single.
JOHNSTON, Hugh - d. Sept. 22; age 7 mos. 4 days; Residence Circleville Twp.; b. Circleville; Parents James Johnston and Jane Maxwell.
DAWSON, Parthenia - d. Nov. 25; age 54; married; Parents James and Mary Dawson.
NEWTON, Isaac - d. Nov. 2; age 63; married; b. Maryland.
WEST, Sarah - d. August (no day given); age 19; single; Residence S. Bloomfield; Parents David and Mary West.
TERRENCE, Joshua M. - d. Sept. 27; at Ashville; age 6 weeks; Residence and born Ashville; Parents Caleb and A. A. Terrence.
WILKINS, Nat. - d. Oct. 18; age 77; widower; Residence Millport; born Maryland.

WAYNE TOWNSHIP

SMITH, George - d. Sept. 10; age 45; married; b. Ross Co., Ohio; Parents Jonas and Mary Smith.
ANDERSON, Isaac - d. Apr. 13; age 40; married; Parents Thos. and L. Anderson.
HURST, Sophia O. - d. Sept. 27; age 1 yr.; b. Wayne Twp.; Parents Geo. W. and Cath. Hurst.
COLLINS, Charles - d. Aug. 11; age 2 yrs.; b. Wayne Twp.; Parents Tarlton and Mary Collins.
CAMPBELL, Virginia - d. Mar. 23; age 2 yrs.; b. Wayne Twp.; Parents Joseph and Sarah Campbell.

JACKSON TOWNSHIP

WHITESIDE, Sarah - d. Sept. 26; age 34; married; Parents Wm. and Sarah Littleton.
DUVALL, William - d. Sept. 27; age 38; Father Marcam Duvall.
PAPWATER, Infant son - d. Sept. 1; age 3 days; Parents Isaac and Eliza Papwater.
BENSYL, L. W. - d. Aug. 14; age 7 yrs.; Parents Balser and Rebecca Bensyl.
STONEROCK, Jacob - d. Aug. 24; age 3 yrs. Parents Henry and Julia Stonerock.
REYNOLDS, Infant son - d. Nov. 26; age 1 day; Parents James and Martha Reynolds.
CALDWELL, Alex - d. Aug. 1; age 9 yrs.; Parents Henry and Nancy Caldwell.
HAWKS, Frances - d. Sept. 16; age 29 days; Mother Martha D. Hawks.
MACHIER, Henry d. Feb. 22; (no age given); single; b. Virginia; Parents James
    and Elizabeth Machier.
CALDWELL, John C. - d. Dec. 19; age 6 mos.; Parents W. B. and Elizabeth Caldwell.
BOWSHIER, Mary - d. Aug. 2; (no age given); married; Father F. Harman.
JOHNSON, Joseph - d. Sept. 6; age 67: widower; b. Maryland.

SCIOTO TOWNSHIP

JOHNSON, Mary - d. June 30; age 6 yrs; Parents Rich'd and Levina Johnson.
REED, Mary Elizabeth - d. Oct. 18; age 13; Place of Death, Franklin Co. Ohio;
    Parents E. M. and Mary Reed.
FLING, Nathan W. - d. Nov. 6; age 29; single; Parents Wm. and Nacy Fling.
RUSSEL, Benj. - d. Nov. 25; age 30; married.
CLIFTON, Jeremiah - d. July 31; age 1 mo.; Parents Noah and Prescilla Clifton.
DANAH, Joshua - d. Feb. 27; (no age or other info. given).

DARBY TOWNSHIP

WILSON, Anna - d. Sept. 8; age 33; married; b. Ohio; Parents Sam'l and Ann White.
CORY, Elisha - d. Jan. 30; age 77; married; b. Maryland; Parents Solomon and
    Edy Cory.
WALTERS, James - d. Jan. 31; age 19; single; b. Ohio; Parents Levi and Mary Walters.
GILLILAN, Andrew - d. June 7 at Muhlenbert; age 21; single; b. Ohio; Parents
    Sam'l and Elizabeth Gillilan.
DAVIS, Martha - d. May 24; age 24; married; Parents Jno. and Elizabeth Davis.
ADKINS, Wm. - d. Feb. 14; age 31; married; b. Ohio; Parents Reuben and M. Adkins.
BROWN, William - d. Feb. 28; age 11; b. Ohio; Parents Wm. & Rachel Brown.
RIDGWAY, Thorbley - d. Jan. 22; age 20; b. Ohio; Parents Thos. and Eliza Ridgway.
DARST, Jacob - d. Jan. 21; age 71; married; b. Penna.; Parents Henry and Mary
    Darst.

MONROE TOWNSHIP

STEEL, Wm. Franklin - d. Sept. 2; age 8 mos.; Parents J. A. & Julia Steel.
ABERNATHY, Rhoda - d. May 1; (no age or other info given)
RILEY, Infant son - d. May 9; Parents Bryan and Bridget Riley.
BARLOW, James - d. Jan. 28; age 75; married.
CLEVENGER, Emaline - d. Jan. 24; age 33; married; b. Perry Twp.; Father Peter
    Lewis.
CLEVENGER, Ruth - d. Feb. 13, age 61; married
RICHEY, Cath. - d. Jan. 17; age 75; widow; b. Ireland; Father Jno. Porter.
DAVIS, Wm. - d. May 11; age 8 mos.; Residence Darby Twp.; b. Darby Twp.;
    Father Ebenezer Davis.

MONROE TOWNSHIP

PORTER, Rosa Ann - d. Sept. 1; age 8 mos.; Parents James and Mary Ann Porter.
SMITH, William J. - d. June 14; (no age given); Parents Merril and Nancy Smith.
MOUSER, John A. - d. Jan. 5; age 18; single; Father Jacob P. Mouser.
DOWNS, Mary F. - d. Feb. 19; age 2 days - Father John Downs.

MUHLENBERG TOWNSHIP

PARKERSON, Nancy - d. Jan. 25; age 77; widow.
O'NEIL, Joseph - d. Aug. 26; age 44; married; b. Franklin Co.; ParentsC. & F. Oniel.
JAMES, Dan'l. - d. Dec. 20; age 5 yrs.; Parents Jno. & S. James.
JAMES, John - Feb. 1; age 3 yrs.; Parents Jno. & S. James.
JAMES, Sarah - Feb. 13; age 24; widow; b. Franklin Twp.; Parents H. & L. Bailey.
STUFFLEBEAN, Sarah - d. July 9; age 22; single; Parents W. & E. Stufflebean.
ROWE, Dudley - d. Nov. 14; age 11; Parents Jno. & D. Rowe.
ROWE, Adison - d. Nov. 26; age 7; Parents Jno. & D. Rowe.
FRANCE, John W. - d. Feb. 6; age 9 mos.; Parents W. & M. France.
WHITESIDE, Baxter - d. Apr. 1 at Darbyville; age 3 mos.; Parents J. and M.
    Whiteside.
YATES, David - d. July 31 Darbysville; age 41; b. Deer Creek; Parents David
    and C. Yates.
PHEBUS, Chas. - d. Sept. 14 at Darbysville; age 5 mos. b. Deer Creek; Parents
    G. and S. (or L.) A. Phebus.

DEER CREEK TOWNSHIP

JOHNSON, Infant daughter - d. Sept. 5; Parents Wm. and Margaret Ann Johnson.
CHERRY, Benj. - d. Mar. 18; (no age given) Parents Sam'l and Christena Cherry.
DOWNING, John - d. Feb. 13; age 71.
VENT, Sarah - d. Dec. 5; (no age or other info. given)
STONEROCK, Infant of H. and E. Stonerock.
HARRIS, Mary - d. Oct. 16; (no age given); Parents Jno. and Mahala Harris.
GRAHAM, Mary A. - d. May 17; age 44.
O'NEIL, Margaret - d. Aug. 20; age 87.

PERRY TOWNSHIP

KONE, Lucretia C. - d. Nov. 18; age 44; married; b. Ross Co.; Parents Stephen
    and Milly Simmons.
LEWIS, William R. - d. Jan. 3; age 27 days; b. Perry Twp.; Parents Jno. and
    Mary Lewis.
DICK, Sarah - d. Mar. 17; age 14; married; b. Virginia; Parents T. & M. McEntire.
AMSPAUGH, Alfred B. - d. May 9; age 5 yrs.; b. Ross Co.; Parents J. _ M. Amspaugh.
LUKINS, Margaret E. - d. Oct. 21 Deer Creek Twp.; age 28 days; b. Deer Creek Twp.;
    Parents A. & M. Lukins.
LUKINS, Thos. E. - d. Sept. 14 Deer Creek Twp.; age 18 mos.; b. Deer Creek Twp.;
    Parents A. & M. Lukins.
ENGLISH, Infant son - d. July 25 at New Holland; age 8 days; Parents J. & E.
    English.
BAGGS, Thomas - d. Oct. 14; age 2 yrs.; Parents D. _ H. Baggs.
BENNETT, Infant son - d. Dec. 10; Parents G. & M. Bennett.
KIMMEY, Infant son - d. Nov. 1; Parents A. & M. Kimmey.
EVANS, Martha J. - d. June 25; age 2 yrs.; Parents John and Amanda Evans.
LONG, Alex. - d. March (no day given); age 65; married.
PENNWELL, Infant son - d. March (no day given); Parents James and Clara Pennwell.

407

PIKE COUNTY, OHIO - FUNERAL RECORDS 1913-1917

Copied and contributed by Mrs. Loraine Panico, 2260 Ashley Drive,
Columbus, Ohio 43229

From the "RECORD OF FUNERAL" at the HAMMERSTEIN FUNERAL HOME of Beaver, Ohio.
Pages on which record may be found are given in parenthesis. The records
are given as found with the exception that the following abbreviations have
been used:- a = aged, y = years, n = months, d = days, Int. = Interment.
It should be stressed that on some records not all the information was filled
in; thus, some records will not be as complete as others.

JAMES, Cynthia - place of death Orient, Ohio; date of funeral Jan. 6, 1913;
   a. 99y 11m 21d; Int. Beaver Chapel Cemetery. (1)
CONKEL, Mrs. John - date of funeral Jan. 6, 1913; date of death Jan. 4, 1913;
   a. 51y; Int. Lucasville Cemetery. (2)
ADAMS, John - date of death Jan. 27, 1913; date of birth Aug. 26, 1835;
   a. 77y 5m 1d. (3)
DOUGLASS, George - date of death Jan. 29, 1913; a. 55y.; Int. Meadow Run
   Cemetery. (4)
RAPP, Mrs. Michael - date of death Feb. 1, 1913; a. 80y; Int. Bethel
   Cemetery. (5)
PFLEGER, Mrs. Magdalena - date of death, Feb. 19, 1913; a 80y. (7)
HUNTER, Mary - date of death Feb. 28, 1913; date of birth Jan. 1, 1832;
   a. 81y 2m; Int. Bethel Cemetery. (8)
TOPE, John Nelson - date of death March 4, 1913; date of birth Nov. 25, 1854;
   a. 58y 3m 9d; Int. Beaver Cemetery. (9)
BAXTER, Cornelius - date of death March 13, 1913; a 66y. (10)
McCARTNEY, Mrs. J. D. - date of death March 16, 1913; a 42y. (11)
CRABTREE, Mrs. - (formerly Wooten) - date of death March 18, 1913. (12)
GILLILAND, Abigal Allard - date of death Apr. 7, 1913; date of birth June 1,
   1865; a. 47y 10m 18d; Int. Beaver Cemetery. (17)
LEVISAY, Nancy - date of death May 4, 1913; date of birth May 4, 1820;
   a. 93y. (18)
DOBYNS, Geroge Washington - date of death May 8, 1913; date of birth Feb.
   22, 1913. (19)
MINNIX, Mrs. - date of death May 10, 1913; a. 73 about; Int. Bethel Cemetery.
WISEMAN, Eliza Crabtree - date of death May 28, 1913; date of birth (20)
   Oct. 1877; Int. Beaver Cemetery. (22)
VANFOSSAN, Samuel - date of death June 21, 1913; date of birth 1845;
   a. 68y; Int. Buckeye Cemetery. (24)
BLAKEMAN, James - date of death June 21, 1913; a. 76y 2m 10d; Int Camp
   Creek Cemetery. (25)
KESINGER, Cynthia Jane - date of death June 24, 1913; a 80y; Int. Pleasant
   Grove Cemetery. (26)
BROWN, David Tiplon - date of death July 1, 1913; a 64y; Int. Stockdale
   Cemetery. (27)
ALLARD, Harriett Anne - date of death July 23, 1913; date of birth June
   1834; a. 79y; Int. Stockdale Cemetery. (27)

CARTNEY, Lucinda M. C. - date of death Aug. 6, 1913; date of birth 1836;
    a. 76y; Int. Bethel Cemetery. (32)
LETT, Eliza Jane - date of death Aug. 12, 1913; a. 27 y. (33)
FRICK, Jacob - date of death Dec. 5, 1913; a. 62y; Int. Beaver Cemetery. (40)
HOOVER, Permelia Keys - date of death Jan. 3, 1914; date of birth Aug. 3,
    1821; a. 92y 5m. (42)
KEAIRNES, John W. - date of death Feb. 1, 1914; a 47y; Int. Jenkins Cemetery.
PARRIL, Stafford - date of death Feb. 14, 1914; a. 58y. (45)   (43)
ALBERT, John - date of death Feb. 25, 1914; a. 58y 1m 5d. (46)
POLLY, Henry - funeral Feb. 25, 1914; a 42y. (47)
OPP, Catheryne - date of death March 6, 1914; a 66y; Int. Beaver Cemetery.(48)
SPOHN, Margaret - date of death April 1, 1914; date of birth 1830; a. 83y
    1m 15d; Int. Germany cemetery. (50)
YOUNG, Catharine - date of death April 4, 1914; date of birth 1830; a. 83y
    7m 3d. (51)
SCHWARTZ, Martin - date of death April 27, 1914; a. 45y 1m; Int. Gravel
    Hill Cemetery. (52)
SCHRADER, Henry Frederick - date of death May 13, 1914; a. 18y; Int. Beaver
    Cemetery; (son of Philip P. & Lean Schrader). (54)
WALKER, Edith A. - date of death July 4, 1914; date of birth 1841; a. 72;
    Int. Walker Cemetery; colored. (57)
BANDY, Patterson - date of death Aug. 6, 1914; a. 68y; Int. Beaver Chapel
    Cemetery. (60)
FOUT, Dova Beatrice - date of death Sept. 24, 1914; a. 22y. (63)
REISINGER, Rhoda Ellen - date of death Nov. 6, 1914; a 65y; Int. Allen
    Cemetery. (66)
SCHILLING, George - date or death Nov. 30, 1914; a. 20y 5m; Int. Given
    Chapel Cemetery. (68)
POLLY, Elizabeth - date of birth 1837; date of death Jan. 5, 1915;
    a. 77y 10m 20d (72)
SHOEMAKER, Isabelle Flack - date of funeral Jan. 19, 1915; a. 37y. (73)
WESE, Bertha - date of funeral Jan. 24, 1915; a 27y. (74)
HOLCOMB, Mary Ann - date of death Jan. 27, 1915; a 78y. (75)
GROW, Herbert - date of death March 23, 1915; a 24y; Int. Bethel Cemetery.(79)
GORDON, D. A. - date of death March 28, 1915; Int. Scioto Cemetery. (80)
BURNS, Ora - date of death April 11, 1915; a. 24y; Int. McCune Cemetery. (81)
STEWART, James Doliver - date of death April 18, 1915; Int. near Gallipolis.
HIATT, William - date of death April 22, 1915; Int. Beaver Cemetery;   (83)
    (was married and a carpenter). (85)
PALMER, Zua James - date of death May 3, 1915; a. 35y; Int. Beaver Chapel
    Cemetery. (86)
HIATT, Mrs. Wm. - date of funeral May 12, 1915. (87)
SHERIDAN, Mrs. James - funeral May 13, 1915; a. 50y. (88)
FOUT, George - date of funeral May 23, 1915; (married). (89)
ALESHIRE, Mahala - date of death July 6, 1915; a. 80y; (widow). (90)
BRAME, John - date of death July 17, 1915; date of birth 1836; a. 79y 10m;
    Int. Mt. Carmel cemetery. (91)

409

TOPE, James Jefferson - date of death Aug. 4, 1915, midnight; a. 58y. (93)
BLAKEMAN, Mary - date of funeral Aug. 9, 1915; a. nearly 15y. (94)
DAVIS, Martin Van Buren - date of death Aug. 20, 1915; date of birth June
    20, 1844; a. 71y 1m 20d. (95)
ADUDDELL, Huldah - date of death Nov. 21, 1915 (4:30 P.M.); date of birth
    Feb. 9, 1832; a. 83y 9m 12d; Int. Beaver Cem. (97)
BROWN, Winnie Grace - date of death Nov. 24, 1915; date of birth Aug. 15,
    1899; a. 16y 3m 15d; Int. Stockdale Com. (98)
ADUDDELL, Huldah - date of death Nov. 21, 1915; date of birth Feb. 9, 1832;
    a. 83y 9m 12d; Int. Beaver Cemetery. (99)
BROWN, Matilda Mossbarger Canoel - date of death Nov. 28, 1915; a. 72y. (101)
HINES, Elizabeth Ellen - date of death Dec. 7, 1915; date of birth Jan. 7,
    1857; a. 58y 11m; Int. Beaver Cem. (102)
PFLEGER, Philip Lewis - date of death Dec. 9, 1915; date of birth Oct. 13,
    1886; a. 29y 1m 26d. (103)
LYONS, John W. - date of death, Dec. 18, 1915; date of birth Feb. 7, 1841;
    a. 74 y. 10m 11d; Int. Beaver Cemetery. (104)
McLAUGHLIN, Samuel - date of death Dec. 31, 1915; date of birth Aug. 20,
    1848; a. 67y 4m 11d; Int. Limerick Cem. (105)
BROWN, Viola Clements - funeral Jan. 22, 1916; a. 30y. (108)
CRAWFORD, Mattie - date of death Feb. 8, 1916; date of birth July 23, 1890;
    a. 25y 6m 10d; Int. Atlanta, Georgia. (111)
BUTCHER, Emily Scurlock - date of death Feb. 21, 1916; date of birth 1836;
    a. 79y 1m 10d; Int. Beaver Cemetery. (112)
DEEMER, Jane - date of death March 2, 1916; date of birth, unknown;
    a. about 70y; Int. Mt. Carmel Cemetery. (113)
RHINEFRANK, Jacb - date of death March 13, 1916; a. 66y; Int. Mound Cemetery. (114)
GAHM, Katheryne Meldick - date of death March 23, 1916; a. 64y. (115)
CRABTREE, Madison - funeral March 30, 1916; a. 86y. (117)
EVANS, Elizabeth - date of death April 13, 1916; date of birth March 1, 1818;
    a. 98y 1m 13d; Int. Mountain Ridge Cemetery; (widow). (118)
PLUMB, John A. - date of death May 4, 1916 (6 A.M.) date of birth Oct. 4,
    1871; a. 44y 7m. (120)
FRASIER, Sarah Crabtree- date of death May 15, 1916; date of birth 1861;
    a. 54y. (121)
FOUT, John - date of death July 19, 1916; date of birth Feb. 2, 1882; a 33y
    5m 11d. (124)
BRAME, Hariett - date of death Aug. 14, 1916; a 76y 19d; Int. Mt. Carmel
    Cemetery. (125)
POWERS, Chas. - date of death Aug. 30; funeral Sept. 1, 1916. (127)
RUSSELL, Lydia - date of death Sept. 1916; cause (old age). (131)
BRUST, Elizabeth - date of death Oct. 7, 1916; a 66y; Int. Beaver Cemetery. (133)
WHALEY, Job - date of death Oct. 13, 1916; a. 56y. (134)
FOUT, Mrs. George - date of death October 29, 1916. (138)
ALLISON, Lucy J. - date of death Nov. 5, 1916; a. 55y; Int. Mt. Carmel
    Cemetery. (140)
NUMPLEBY, Jackson H. - date of death Nov. 2, 1916; (married). (142)
RAPP, Jacob Sr. - date of death Nov. 26, 1916; date of birth 1840; a. 76y. (144)

410

OBER, William Sr. - date of death Nov. 27, 1916; birth 1832; a. 84y 6m 7d; Int. Beaver Cemetery. (145)

BUTLER, Mason Randall - date of death Dec. 18, 1916; birth Aug. 27, 1872; a. 44y 3m 21d; Int. Bethesda Cemetery. (146)

BAPST, Jacob Sr. - date of death Jan. 2, 1917; date of birth Nov. 2, 1842; a. 74y 2m. (148)

ADAMS, Martha - date of death Jan. 5, 1917; date of birth Oct. 10, 1870; a. 46y 2m 25d; name of mother Margaret Hammond; name of father George Schilling; Int. Givens Givens Chapel (from death certificate in book)

ADAMS, Martha Schilling - date of death Jan. 5, 1917; date of birth Oct. 10, 1870; a. 46y 2m 25d; Int. Givens chapel. (149)

SCHAFER, Eva Christena - date of death Jan. 19, 1917; date of birth Jan. 29, 1849; a. 67y 11m 20d; Int. Beaver Cemetery. (150)

RAPP, Dicy Melinda - date of death Jan. 28, 1917; date of birth Oct. 4, 1838; a. 77y 3m 24d. (151)

PFLEGER, Henry - funeral Jan. 31, 1917; a. 34y. (154)

SIEMON, Anna Catherina - date of death Feb. 11, 1917; a. 85y 6m 25d.

LEIST, Edward - date of death March 7, 1917; a. 27y; Int. Beaver Cemetery; (Clara Leist, his widow). (157)

LEIST, Alice - adopted child of Coon & Catharine Leist; date of death March 15, 1917; date of birth Dec. 29, 1874; a. 42y 2m 16d; Int. Beaver Cemetery. (158)

SLAUGHTER, Annie J. - date of death March 16, 1917; date of birth Jan. 9, 1834; a. 83y 2m 6d; Int. Beaver Cem. (159)

SLAUGHTER, Annie Jos. - date of death Mar. 6, 1917; birth Jan. 9, 1834; a. 83y 2m 6d; (name of father Wm. J. Jackson, birth place Virginia; name of mother Susanna Pruitt, birth place Virginia; from certificate of death in book)

CLAAR, William E. - date of death March 19, 1917; date of birth Aug. 16, 1861; a. 55y 7m 3d. (160)

CLAAR, William E. - died 4-16-1917; born Oct. 18, 1846; a. 70y 5m 29d (father Samuel Claar, birthplace Ohio; mother Elizabeth Masters, birthplace Ohio)

GORDON, William B. - date of death April 16, 1917; date of birth Oct. 18, 1846; a. 70y 5m 29d; Int. Scioto Cem. (161)

BROWN, Nancy Colis - date of death April 25, 1917; date of birth Aug. 22, 1848; a. 68y 8m 3d; Int. Stockdale Cemetery. (162)

NELSON, C. J. - date of death March 25, 1917; a. old. (163)

PLUMB, Samuel - date of death May 15, 1917; birth April 30, 1841; a. 76y 15d.

STROPEN(?), Ellen Polly - funeral May 28, 1917, Int. Beaver Chapel; (165) (married). (166)

FOUT, Mary Anne - date of death May 27, 1917; date of birth Jan. 23, 1836; a. 81y 4m 4d; Int. Beaver Cem.; (name of father James Schwartz; name of mother E. Stoll). (167)

FLACK, Sarah Carter - date of death May 13, 1917; a. about 80; Int. Flack Cemetery. (168)

411

THOMPSON, Amy "Pool" - date of death July 4, 1917; date of birth Dec. 4, 1880; a. 36 y 7 m. (170)
BUTCHER, Mrs. - date of death Sept. 30, 1917; a. abt. 65; Int. Beaver Chapel Cem. (175)
FOUT, Adam - date of death Oct. 27, 1917; birth Dec. 24, 1863; a. 53y 10m 3d; Int. Beaver Cem. (176)

CABLEMAN, Kate - date of death Oct. 29, 1917; a. 73y 1m; Int. Bethel Cem. (177)
PFLEGER, Mrs. Chas. - date of death Nov. 22, 1917, a 60y. (179)
FERRELL, James - date of death Nov. 22, 1917; a 83y 7m. (180)
SCOTT, Geo. W.- date of death Nov. 29, 1917; date of birth April 12, 1864; a. 53y 7m 17d. (181)
BALZER. Katharyne - date of death Dec. 3, 1917; date of birth July 10, 1869; a. 48y 4m 23d (182)
BROWN, Jefferson D. - date of death Dec. 7, 1917; date of birth June 5, 1855; a 62y 6m 1d. (183)

PREBLE COUNTY, OHIO - 1860 Mortality Schedule

Taken 1859. Children under 10 years of age were given but not listed here.
Columns are: Name, age, sex, place of birth, when died and marital status.
There were no lists designated for Jefferson and Dixon townships.

WASHINGTON TOWNSHIP

NEARON, Mary	73	f	Ky.	Dec.	m
CLEAR, John J.	15	m	Oh.	Mar.	
ROBESON, Samuel H.	56	m	Va.	May	m
EDSON, John	82	m	Va.	May	m
CLEAR, Elizabeth	75	f	N.C.	Apr.	m
JELLISON, Samuel	69	m	Me.	Sept.	w
AKERMAN, Mary	79	f	Ky.	Sept.	m
MAY, Martin	26	m	Oh.	Jan.	
SHIDLER, Jacob	82	m	Pa.	July	w
CAMPBELL, Mary C.	14	f	Oh.	Sept.	
LOCKWOOD, Eliz'th	31	f	Oh.	Mar.	m
MINOR, Rossalie	17	f	Oh.	Aug.	
MINSHALL, Ellis	54	m	Oh.	Apr.	m
RILEY, George	27	m	Gy.	May	
CUNNINGHAM, E. A.	36	f	Oh.	Dec.	m
BONER, Eveline	59	f	Pa.	Aug.	m
SHAW, Nancy	73	f	Ky.	Nov.	w
TOWN, Susan	58	f	Pa.	June	m
WAGONERY, Sarah	31	f	Oh.	June	m

LANIER TOWNSHIP

FISHER, Catharine	41	f	Oh.	Feb.	
EARLEY, Demariaus	16	f	Oh.	June	
BUNNELL, Thos. J.	49	m	Oh.	Oct.	m
BLACK, Barbara	77	f	Va.	Aug.	w
ZITZER, Catharine	67	f	Sw.	Jan.	m
RINEHART, Mary	67	f	Va.	July	w
NAEFF, Abraham	76	m	Pa.	June	w
SHIDELER, Henry B.	19	m	Oh.	May	
REYNOLDS, Isiah	23	m	Oh.	Sept.	
MIKESELL, Eliz'th	14	f	Oh.	May	
KAYLER, Arthur	24	m	Oh.	Feb.	m

GASPER TOWNSHIP

KUCHENBECKER, Mary	26	f	Oh.	Aug.	m
CAMPBELL, William	67	m	Del.	Sept.	m
KAYLER, Jacob	61	m	Oh.	Mar.	w
DENISTON, Seges	57	f	Va.	Oct.	m
KINCAID, John	75	m	Va.	May	m
COSBEY, Rebecca	34	f	Ind.	Sept.	m
DAVIS, Currella	12	f	Oh.	July	
JONES, Wileber	56	f	S.C.	Feb.	m
JONES, Rachel	81	f	N.C.	Nov.	w
BAILEY, William	85	m	Pa.	Apr.	
WILKINSON, Charles	72	m	Va.	May	

JACKSON TOWNSHIP

HAYNES, Barbara	77	f	Va.	Sept.	
KINDIG, Francis	16	m	Oh.	May	
BRUMBAUGH, Franklin	42	m	Oh.	Feb.	
GEPHART, Jane	33	f	Oh.	Oct.	m
CAMPBELL, Mary A.	22	f	Ind.	Aug.	m
BERRY, Manda	28	f	Oh.	June	m
SWAIN, Elizabeth	76	f	N.Y.	July	w
LANIER, Henry	22	m	Oh.	June	
McCORD, Jane	65	f	Pa.	Nov.	m

ISRAEL TOWNSHIP

KINDAL, Enoch	29	m	N.J.	Sept.	
McRACIN, Saml. N.	59	m	Ky.	Sept.	
McQUISTON, Archable	54	m	S.C.	Oct.	m
RIDENHOUR, Lott	16	m	Oh.	Mar.	
McQUISTON, Eliza	26	f	Ind.	Sept.	m
GILLMORE, Martha	20	f	Oh.	July	m
SWAN, Ann	35	f	Ind.	Apr.	m
GARD, Levi	81	m	Pa.	Jan.	m
FOSTER, James	21	m	Oh.	July	
JONES, Ann	16	f	Oh.	May	

SOMERS TOWNSHIP

McDERMIT, Parney	45	m	Ire.	Jan.	m
ROBERTSON, John	55	m	Del.	Aug.	m
HELLER, Eliz'th	36	f	Va.	Mar.	m
WALKER, C. C.	61	m	N.Y.	May	m
BARNETT, Alex	35	m	Oh.	Sept.	m
McCRISTY, Levina	34	f	Oh.	July	m
KENTWORTH, David	47	m	Oh.	Nov.	m
YOUNG, Nancy	24	f	Oh.	Apr.	m
MACEY, John	64	m	Va.	July	m
WILKINS, Joseph	14	m	Oh.	June	

TWIN TOWNSHIP

SHIELDS, Marg't	30	f	Oh.	Oct.	
SOWERS, Mary	59	f	Oh.	Nov.	
PETERS, Susan	36	f	Oh.	July	
WHERLEY, Elizah	21	f	Oh.	Aug.	
OZIAS, Nancy	25	f	Oh.	Nov.	
WYSONG, Valentine	83	m	Pa.	July	
WESTERFIELD, Hannah E.	15	f	Oh.	Feb.	
DANS, Priscilla	19	f	Oh.	June	

413

HARRISON TOWNSHIP

LEAS, Catharine	72 f	Pa.	Oct.	
EARHART, Catharine	42 f	Pa.	Oct.	
WITTERS, George W.	26 m	Oh.	Aug.	
BAMTHISEL, Cath.	93 f	Pa.	May	
WRIGHT, William	26 m	Oh.	Apr.	
WRIGHT, Sarah	17 f	Oh.	Dec.	
HOMAN, Peter	66 m	Pa.	Jan.	m
HOMAN, Nelson	22 m	Oh.	Mar.	
COTTERMAN, Randolph	11 m	Oh.	Nov.	
EMMONS, Ann	22 f	Oh.	Aug.	
McGRUY(?), James	71 m	Pa.	Apr.	m
SHELLERS, Cath.	47 f	N.J.	Mar.	m
ETZLER, Mary C.	16 f	Oh.	Sept.	
BOYD, Joseph	26 m	Oh.	May	
ENOCH, Jane	81 f	Va.	May	
PATTON, Wm. H.	18 m	Pa.	Oct.	
PHILLIPS, Hezekiah	69 m	Tenn.	Aug.	
COX, Mary	31 f	Oh.	July	

MONROE TOWNSHIP

HAPNER, John	53 m	Va.	Oct.	
HORN, George L.	14 m	Oh.	- -	
JELLISON, Sarah	80 f	N.J.	Sept.	
RICHARDS, Susan E.	32 f	Oh.	June	
WHERLEY, Polly	63 f	Va.	Feb.	
WALKER, Nancy	45 f	Va.	Apr.	
JUDY, Margaret	22 f	Oh.	July	
McCOWN, Banner	70 m	N.J.	June	
SHELLY, Mary	60 f	Va.	July	
SHUMAN, Allen	14 m	Oh.	Feb.	
DENNY, Rebecca Jane	41 f	Oh.	Jan.	
THOMPSON, Robert	56 m	Va.	Feb.	
BOLENS, Samuel H.	24 m	Oh.	Feb.	
REID, Margaret	55 f	Va.	Aug.	
SPARKS, Nancy	71 f	Md.	May	
SMITH, Mary R.	48 f	Pa.	May	
HAWLEY, Eri	55 m	N.Y.	Nov.	

GRATIS TOWNSHIP

YINGLING, John	25 m	Oh.	July	
FERRY, Julyann	81 f	Md.	Sept.	w
PHILIPS, Henry	71 m	Va.	June	m
TAYLOR, Jane	32 f	Oh.	Aug.	m
GREGG, Druzela	53 f	Va.	June	m
GREGG, Rhoda	12 f	Oh.	Oct.	
ESLINGER, Kaziah	15 f	Oh.	July	
BROWN, Henry	37 m	Md.	Sept.	m

414

From a book in Common Pleas Court entitled, "Supreme Court Record A".
Pages are given in parenthesis.

HENDRICKS, David E. vs. Rosannah HENDRICKS - Petition for Divorce 6-18-1819 -
David in his petition states that he married Rosannah in April 1799 and that they
are the parents of eleven children, 5 boys and 6 girls as follows: David, George,
William and James, all under 21 years; Rachel, Jane, Scynthia, Nancy, Elizabeth,
and Julia, the last two are of age and married.   (79)

PRICE, Nancy vs. Christian PRICE - Petition for Divorce - filed 6-29-1818 -
Nancy in her petition states that she married 5-6-1795 in Montgomery Co. Virginia
to Christian Price who is now living in Indiana; that they had two children, -
son and a daughter. She further states that she has land in Preble Co. and in
Indiana and also has a small amount coming from her father as one of his heirs.
- Recorded 6-18-1819 -   (82)

SELLERS, Catherine vs. Nathan SELLERS, Jr. and Nathan SELLERS, Sr. - Petition for
alimony - Catherine Sellers, late Catherine Moffet, was married in November 1817
to Nathan Sellers, Jr. - That Nathan now owns property in the name of his father,
Nathan Sellers, Sr.   (102)

EIKMAN, John vs. Sally EIKMAN - Petition for Divorce - 6-30-1820 - John in his
petition states that on 6-10-1819 he married Sally STACY. That Sally is and was
the wife of John SPENCER.   (136)

BYRES, Isaac vs. Polly BYRES - Petition for Divorce - filed 4-5-1822 Isaac in
his petition states that about 24 years ago he married Polly KENNEDAY in Montgomery Co., Virginia. That about two years after their marriage they removed to
Galliapolis. That they were the parents of five children, whom Isaac brought to
Preble County with him as Polly was living at the home of her father. Petition
discontinued 6-20-1823.   (201)

GREEN, John vs. Elizabeth GREEN - Petition for Divorce - filed 6-30-1821 - John
Green states that he was married in June 1807 to Elizabeth his wife. - Recorded
6-30-1823 -   (203)

WITTER, Mary vs. Samuel WITTER and Christopher WITTER - Petition for alimony -
6-20-1823 - Mary Witter late Mary Brown was married 9-26-1820 to Samuel Witter (204)

SHAFFER, Michael vs. Mary SHAFFER - Petition for Divorce - 7-12-1824 - Michael in
his petition states that he married Mary on 8-7-1814 -   (22)

PHILLIPS, Urania vs. James PHILLIPS - Petition for Divorce - 7-3-1826 - Petition
Dismissed -   (281)

ROSS, Charles vs. Sarah ROSS - Petition for Divorce - 7-3-1826 - Charles in his
petition stated that he was married 8-10-1821 to Sarah STUART, Recorded July
Term 1827 -   (281)

415

The following records were abstracted from a small, old volume which is kept in the Recorder's Office. The volume is not marked by number nor letter. The page on which record may be found is given in parenthesis.

1-1-1825 - Samuel H. Smith aged 15 yrs. 8 mos. by John J. Hawkins his guardian as designated by will of Samuel Hawkins, dec'd grandfather of said Samuel H. Smith; to be bound unto John Acton until Samuel is 21 yrs. of age ending 5-1-1830. (1)

3-18-1825 - Chatrain Ellis places her son, Silas Stanback born 11-7-1822 as apprentice to Robert Brown until said Silas is 21 yrs. of age. (3)

5-14-1825 - Patrick Graham of Gratis Twp., a poor boy aged 12 yrs. 3 mos. 14 days apprenticed to John Peters for term of 5 yrs. 8 mos. and 16 days. (5)

9-21-1825 - Rebecca Bowers and Stephen Taylor of Warren Co., Ohio indenture Daniel Murphy aged 14 yrs. 3 mos. and 26 ds., son of Rebecca and brother-in-law of Stephen Taylor, to James M. Grimes for 3 yrs. and 6 mos. (7)

1-14-1826 - Mary Jane Gillispie an orphan girl of Israel Twp., aged 9 yrs. 9 mos. and 4 days bound to Ebenezer Elliott to serve 8 yrs. 2 mos. and 27 days. Witnesses: Wm. Gilmore and Martha T. Gillispie. (10)

10-17-1825 - John Davis aged 9 yrs. 5 mos. and 7 ds., son of Moses Davis of Israel Twp. by consent of father to serve John Pinkerton until 21 yrs. of age on 5-10-1837. (12)

10-10-1826 - Ebenezer McGuffin Gillispie a poor boy of Israel Twp. aged 5 yrs. 11 mos. and 25 ds. indentured to John Caldwell until 21 yrs. on 10-15-1841. (14)

10-10-1826 - Fanny Johnson aged 7 yrs. 5 mos. 16 ds. daughter of James Johnson of Israel Twp. who is unable to support his child, is bound to James Buck until 18 yrs of age on 4-24-1837. (17)

7-14-1827 - Wm. Man a destitute child aged 2 yrs. and 1 mo. of Somers Twp. is bound to John C. Page of said township to serve until of full age. (20)

7-14-1827 - Hannah Lane a destitute girl of Somers Twp. aged 5 yrs. and 3 mos. is bound to John C. Page of Somers twp. until of full age. (22)

8-22-1827 - William Reynolds a poor boy of Gratis Twp. aged 1 yr. 9 mo. and 10 ds. son of Margaret Reynolds of said township who can not support her child is bound to Thomas Stubbs until he is 21 years. on 11-12-1846. (25)

11-2-1827 - William Bryant a poor boy of Washington Twp. aged 3 yrs. 10 mos. and 29 ds. son of Betsy Bryant of Washington Twp. who is unable to support her child, is bound to George Harter of Twin Twp. until he is 21 yrs. of age on 12-4-1844. (28)

4-22-1828 - Jane Hubble placed her son William Hubbell who on 12 May next will be 18 yrs. with Samuel P. Wilson to learn the trade of Cooper until 4-22-1830.(31)

3-22-1828 - James Monroe Green a poor boy of Jefferson Twp. aged 4 yrs. 4 mos and 14 days son of Sarah Blancher of Jefferson Twp. who can not support her child is apprenticed to George Mills of said township until 21 years of age. (33)

8-1-1828 - Nimrod Sallee who will be 18 yrs. on the 15th day of present month, of his own will and with consent of William Salee his father has bound himself as apprentice in the trace of coopering to Samuel P. Wilson of Eaton until 21 yrs. of age. (35)

10-11-1828 - George Show who will be 21 yrs. on 7 June next by his own free will and with consent of John J. Hawkins his guardian has bound himself as apprentice in the trade of tailor unto Hiram Orum of Eaton until 21 yrs. of age. (37)

10-16-1829 - Henry Atchason aged 18 yrs. 7 mos. and 19 ds. of his own free will and with consent of Anthony Atchason his guardian, binds himself to learn the trade of hatter to William Longnecker of Eaton until 21 yrs. of age. (40)

11-15-1828 - Ephrain Mikesell who on the 9th day of this month was 17½ yrs. with consent of Valentine B. Mikesell his father, binds himself as apprentice to Hiram Orum of Eaton to serve until 5-15-1831 when aged 20 yrs. and 6 days. (42)

1-10-1829 - John Marsh who on 22 Aug. next will be 18 yrs., of his own free will and by consent of his father Timothy Marsh has bound himself as apprentice to learn the trade of hatter, to James Gardner of Eaton to serve until 21 yrs. on 8-22-1832. (44)

3-14-1829 - Josiah Muntz a destitute child of Jefferson Twp. aged 9 yrs. 3 mos. and 17 ds. is bound to learn the trade of clothier to John Horseman until 12-25-1840. (45)

5-22-1829 - John M. Milligan an orphan child aged 5 yrs. 6 mos. and 29 ds. by Nathan Brown Jr. his guardian isbound unto James Boyse a farmer of Israel Twp. until 21 yrs. of age. (47)

6-12-1829 - Joseph Rehard aged about 17 yrs. son of Anthoney Rehard of Gratis Twp. of his own free will and with consent of his father is to serve as apprentice in trade of tanner to Nathan Sayler of Gratis Twp. for three years. (49)

7-4-1829 - William Washington Scott an orphan boy of Washington Twp. aged 6 yrs. 10 mos. and 12 days son of William Scott, dec'd is bound as an apprentice as clerk in store to John G. Jamison, until 21 yrs. on 8-23-1843. (51)

10-4-1829 - Jacob Christman who will be 17 yrs. on 7 January next with consent of his father David Christman is apprenticed as carpenter and house joiner to John Haltrey until 21 yrs. on 1-7-1834. (54)

2-27-1830 - Margaret Kane of Israel Twp. a poor girl aged 11 yrs. daughter of Sarah Davis who is unable to support her child is bound unto Hugh McQuiston until 18 yrs. of age. (56)

417

9-10-1829 - Michael Lower aged 14 yrs. 6 mos. and 4 ds. son of William and Nancy Lower of Harrison Twp. of his own free will and by consent of his guardian Jacob Werts is apprenticed as a farmer to Joseph Black of said township until 21 yrs. of age on 11-18-1835. (58)

2-27-1830 - Alexander Kane a poor boy of Israel Twp. aged 9 yrs. and 6 ms. son of Sarah Davis of said township who is unable to support her child, is bound to William Magaw Jr. until 21 yrs. of age on 8-27-1841. (60)

6-10-1830 - John Neff Jr. who will be 19 yrs. on 4 March next of his own will and by consent of his father John Neff Sr. is apprenticed in the trade of printing to Enoch Edmonson of Eaton until 21 yrs. on 3-1-1833. (62)

6-23-1830 - Samuel Morris aged 15 yrs. 4 mos. and 27 ds. son of Isaac Morris late of the state of Indiana, dec'd, by his free will and with the consent of James McClung his guardian is apprenticed in the trade of tailor to Richard Slone Jr. of Israel Twp. for 4 yrs. 5 mos. and 23 ds. (64)

7-3-1830 - George Strickler a poor boy of Lanier Twp. aged 16 yrs. 8 mos. son of John Strickler, dec'd apprenticed as a farmer to Jacob Fudge until 21 yrs. on 11-3-1834. (66)

7-3-1830 - Daniel F. Francis a poor boy of Lanier Twp. aged 15 yrs. 6 mos. and 20 ds. son of Amelia Francis of North Carolina who is unable to support her child is bound to the occupation of farmer to Jacob Fudge until 21 yrs. on 12-14-1835. (69)

10-13-1830 - Emiline Ewen a poor girl of Somers Twp. aged 8 yrs. 11 mos. and 29 ds. daughter of Polly Ewen who is unable to support her child is bound to housework to Jonathan Casto until 18 yrs. on 11-1-1839. (72)

9-12-1829 - Warren Ashley a poor boy of Lanier Twp. aged 15 yrs. and 10 mos. to serve as apprentice as farmer to Joseph Dillman of said township until 21 yrs. of age on 11-12-1834. (78)

4-23-1831 - Alfred Wolf a poor boy of Harrison Twp. aged 8 yrs. and 6 ds. son of John Wolf, dec'd to serve as apprentice as farmer to Christian Shellers until 21 yrs of age on 3-18-1844. (81)

5-9-1831 - Joshua Jaqua aged 17 yrs. and 9 ds. son of Darius Jaqua of Jefferson Twp. of his own free will and by consent of his father is bound to James Paul until 21 yrs. of age on 5-1-1834. (83)

The following records were taken from consent slips which are filed in a packet in the file boxes located in the Probate Court. Dates given are not marriage dates, but date consent was written.

4-15-1848 - Mary HAVENS gives consent for her daughter, Margaret STEPHENS to marry Peter MORRICKS.
3-7-1848 - James YOUNG gives consent for his son, John Henry Young under 21 years to marry Miss Elizabeth EMERICK.
4-5-1848 - Jonas HATFIELD gives consent for his son, Moses HATFIELD to marry.
3-8-1848 - John and Susan EMRICK gives consent for daughter, Elizabeth EMERICK to marry John M. YOUNG.
5-1-1848 - Jarod E. DOUGLAS gives consent for Mary E. L. DOUGLAS to marry William L. STUTES.
12-9-1849 - Wm. AILES gives consent for Sarah AILES to marry John C. DEEM.
9-29-1849 - Joseph STEWART gives consent for Mary Ann Stewart to marry.
12-4-1849 - Amos WRIGHT gives consent for his son, Peter WRIGHT to marry Mary WILLIAMS who is more than 18 years of age.
11-27-1849 - Andrew (his mark) IRICK gives consent for Joseph IRICK to marry. Attest: David IRICK.
12-19-1849 - Eaton - Mary A. BLACK gives consent for her daughter, Mildred Ann Black to marry Thomas W. WILEY.
11-30-1849 - Spartansburg, Ia. - John LEWIS gives consent for his son, Stephen G. LEWIS to marry.
1-28-1850 - New Paris - Lewis S. DAVIS gives consent for his sister, Ellen R. DAVIS, she being 18 on 7 July last; to marry A. G. STEPHEN.
1-7-1850 - William PENCE gives consent for his daughter, Mahala PENCE to Mary Charles COPPOQ.
10-2-1851 - Nathaniel ELLIOTT, consent for daughter, Margaret to marry Thomas F. LAMB.
5-3-1852 - Joseph H. MAUZY gives consent for his son, James L. MAUZY to marry Mary THOMPSON.
10-20-1852 - Ann Mc. (her mark) SPANGLER gives consent for Lydia Ann SPANGLER of Preble Co., Ohio to marry Lewis E. DILL of Butler Co.
7-24-1852 - John L. DUVALL of Darke Co., Ohio gives consent for his daughter, Jane DUVALL to marry Dr. Daniel J. SHERER.
8-6-1852 - On oath of John LONG, John SHILT father of Barbara Ann SHILT states that she is more than 17 years old and gives consent for her to marry Daniel K. LONG.
7-31-1852 - On oath of Samuel B. MANN, Amanda CRIGER daughter of John CRIGER has consent to marry George W. YEAGER.
8-9-1852 - Margaret ATEN gives consent for her son, Austin C. ATEN marry Catharine E. DUNLAP.
12-21-1852 - Thomas CHILDERS gives consent for his adopted daughter, Francis CHILDERS to marry Henry CLAWSON.
9-4-1852 - On oath of Jacob PRICE, Sophia LOCK gives consent for her son, Adam LOCK to marry Mary REDMAN.
10-25-1852 - James Y.(?) FRANCIS gives consent for daughter, Lydia Ann FRANCIS to marry Wm. R. PATTERSON.

12-22-1852 - Harrison twp. - Margaret GEBHART relic of David GEBHART, dec'd gives
consent for her daughter, Maria GEBHEART to marry John L.
WILLSON. Witness: William (his mark) GEBHART.

11-10-1852 - Robert C. PATTERSON guardian of Andrew PATTERSON gives consent for
Andrew to marry Margaret WISONG.

7-25-1852 - David and Margaret Ann WARNER give consent for daughter, Luvina
WARNER to marry William C. ROBERTS.

6-5-1852 - Mary GARBER mother and only surviving parent gives consent for
Henry GARBER to marry Amanda FALENSTINE.

4-8-1853 - Hagerstown - Elizabeth UTZ gives consent for her daughter, Louisa F.
UTZ to marry Sylvester A. CLEVENGER.

12-2-1853 - Euphemia - Jacob DIEHL gives consent for his daughter to marry Wm.
CAMPBELL.

10-10-1853 - Isabella DOYAL gives consent for her daughter, Mary DOYAL to marry
John WILT.

2-21-1853 - John and Elizabeth SAYLER give consent for their daughter, Rebecca
Sayler to marry Noah SWIHART. Witnesses: Solomon SAYLER,
Catharine SAYLER.

8-27-1853 - John and Mary BROWN give consent for daughter, Mary BROWN to marry
Samuel SOUDERS.

2-27-1853 - David EIKENBARY gives consent for his son, Reuben EIKENBARY to
marry Mary C. GEYER, daughter of George GEYER.

5-31-1853 - Robert RAPER gives consent for Elizabeth KILLEM to marry.

4-8-1853 - Hillery GREEN gives consent for his son, William GREEN to marry.

9-3-1853 - On oath of Cornelius S. SACKMAN, Samuel SACKMAN gives consent for his
daughter, Helen Alice SACKMAN to marry James D. MORRISON.

2-19-1853 - Cincinnati, Ohio (telegram) - Moses NELSON gives consent for Lucinda
NELSON to marry John EARL.

11-18-1853 - M. AKER gives consent for son, William W. AKER to marry Harriet N.
STEPHENS.

12-27-1853 - On oath of Samuel COX, Elizabeth COX gives consent for her daughter
Alvina COX who is more than 17 yrs. to marry James SNODGRASS
who is more than 21 years.

9-27-1853 - On oath of Jacob STERSENBACH, Caroline MEGELY gives consent for her
daughter, Catharine C. MEGELYmore than 16 years to marry
ELKANNAH H. BATES who is more than 21 years.

10-3-1853 - On oath of Daniel DISHER, George HORN gives consent for his son,
George M. HORN who is more than 20 years to marry.

10-3-1853 - On oath of Alfred LOY, Adam LOY gives consent for his daughter, Mary
Ann LOY who is more than 16 yrs. to marry William J. WIKLE
who is more than 21 years.

7-26-1853 - B. DARRAH gives consent for his daughter, Rebecca DARRAH to marry
Thomas ST JOHN. Witness: Benjamin DARRAH, Jr.

9-2-1856 - On oath of uncle, Jesse Smith; Harriet GREEN gives consent for her
son William W. GREEN to marry Magdalene HOFFMAN.

1-31-1863 - Maria GREEN gives consent for Isaac N. GREENE to marry.

420

PREBLE COUNTY, OHIO - NEWSPAPER OBITUARIES AND DEATH NOTICES 1850-1856

From the EATON DEMOCRAT published in Eaton, Ohio on Thursday.

6-20-1850 - DIED, Mrs. MARSH of Union County (Indiana?) on 19th ult., left several small children.

6-27-1850 - DIED on Sun. last near Eaton, Sarah Jane daughter of Micajah L. & Mary A WHITE, aged 2 years, 9 months and 25 days.

7-11-1850 - DIED in Eaton on Tues. last after a long illness, Mr. Joseph BROWN, aged 75 years.

7-25-1850 - DIED near Fair Haven on Monday morning last, Mr. B. C. HAWTHORN, aged about 28 years. Also, at the same time and place a sister of the above deceased.

8-22-1850 - DIED Thursday morning week, in Dixon township, Mrs. Euphemia EVANS consort of Karn Evans in the 43rd year of her age. The deceased was a native of Bucks County, Pennsylvania, but had been a number of years a resident of Dixon township.

8-29-1850 - DIED Tuesday afternoon last in New Westville this county, James FIELDS killed by fall into a well.

9-19-1850 - DIED on Monday last, Mr. Aaron MONFORT at an advanced age. DIED on Saturday morning last, Henry Chambers only child and son of W. C. and M. C. GOULD, aged 1 year 4 months and 2 days.

9-26-1850 - DIED on Monday night last, Mrs. Jane wife of Mr. David HAWK, aged about 35 years.

10-3-1850 - DIED on the 29th ult., Elizabeth MONFORT aged 61 years and 5 months.

10-10-1850 - DIED on Wednesday last, Rev. P. A. MUTCHNER for about nine years a member of the Ohio Conference of the M. E. Church and at the time of his death, minister in charge of the Camden Circuit in this county.

12-5-1850 - DIED on the 26th ult., Mrs. Mary consort of Mr. Valentine B. MIKESILL. The deceased was one of the oldest inhabitants of Preble County. DIED on the 1st inst., Miss Susan eldest daughter of Dr. John STURR, aged about 19 years. DIED on the 29th ult. on the 29th ult. in Cincinnati after 4 days illness, Holly son of Rev. William RAPGER, and one of the firm of Raper and Brothers. The deceased had friends in this county. Left a wife and child. DIED on the 27th ult., Joseph A. son of Mr. Jesse WARE, aged about 25 years.

2-20-1851 - DIED in Eaton, Monday on the 10th inst., Elizabeth TIZZARD mother of the editor of the Eaton Register, aged 61 years 1 month and 18 days.

4-17-1851 - DIED in this place Monday evening last, Mrs. Clarissa consort of Mr. Samuel L. TINGLE leaving husband and four children. She was a member of the M. E. Church. DIED, Theodore McCLELLAN son of Samuel and Catharine McClellan at the residence of his father in Dixon township on Friday the 11th inst., aged 31 years and 14 days.

421

5-15-1851 - DIED on Saturday last in Twin township, Mr. Jacob STOTLER, aged about 55 years. He was a Mason.

6-5-1851 - DIED in Eaton on the 28th ult., Miss Mary TOWN in the 17th year of her age.

7-3-1851 - DIED on the 26th ult. in Eaton, Margaret M. infant daughter of John and Mary Ann MARSH, aged about 6 months. DIED in West Alexandria on the 28th ult., Miss Frances HUTSON, aged about 18 years.

8-14-1851 - DIED on the 6th inst., Elizabeth A. daughter of John P. and M. B. ACTON, aged 6 months. DIED on Monday last, White Cloud, infant son of T. J. and Margaret LARSH, aged about 4 weeks.

8-21-1851 - DIED on the 13th inst., Francis X. A. son of Thomas and Mary Ann FORD, aged 2 years, 8 months and 6 days.

9-4-1851 - DIED in West Alexandria on the 27th ult., Joseph N. son of Josiah and Harriet DAVIS, aged 7 months.

9-11-1851 - DIED on Saturday evening 30th Ult., Mrs. Martha Ann McCLELLAN consort of John L. McClellan, aged 30 years 6 months and 27 days. Mrs. McClellan was a native of Rockbridge County, Virginia from whence she emigraged to this county with her father, Mr. John GORE, about 14 years ago. She leaves husband and three small children.

10-9-1851 - DIED in Washington township on Friday last, Francis L. son of Valentine and Susannah SNYDER.

11-6-1851 - DIED at his residence in Eaton on Saturday evening the 1st inst. at 9 o'clock, James GARDNER one of the Associate Judges of the Common Pleas of Preble County. Judge Gardner was in the 50th year of his age. He was a member of the Presbyterian Church. DIED in Eaton on the 30th ult., Mr. Archibald STEWART, age 28 years. A native of Scotland, he came to this country four years ago, part of which time was spent in Cincinnati

1-8-1852 - DIED on the 29th ult, Mrs. Elizabeth COOPER, aged 69 years.

2-5-1852 - DIED in Eaton on the 27th ult., Mrs. Elizabeth F. LANIUS mother of· Richard Y. Lanius of this place, aged about 83 years. DIED in ths county on the 29th ult., N. M. BIXSY. The deceased was born in Concord, New Hampshire on the 26th day May 1819. Emigrated to Ohio in the fall of 1837. His father is still living in Warren, Grafton Co. N. H. (Boston and N. H. papers please copy.)

5-27-1852 - DIED in Jefferson township, Preble County, on 23d inst., Mr. William HAWLEY in the 23d year of his age. He left a wife and 1 child.

.6-3-1852 - DIED at his residence in Gratis township on the 29th ult., Mr. John HALSEY in the 25th year of his age. He leaves a wife and two children.

422

7-15-1852 - DIED at his residence two miles west of Eaton on Tuesday the 6th inst., Mr. William B. ACTON, in the 36th year of his age. He leaves a wife and children. I.O.O.F.

8-12-1852 - At a meeting of the members of the Bar held at the Court House in Eaton on the 5th day August A.D. 1852 members testified as to their respect of the Hon. Joseph S. HAWKINS, late a member of said Bar. DIED in West Alexandria on the 7th inst., Seward H. only child of Dr. F. J. and Hester A. STRATTEN, aged 1 year, 8 months and 11 days.

8-19-1852 - DIED at his residence in Springfield, Missouri on the 3d ult., Mr. Lewis STEPHENS, late a citizen of this county, in the 58th year of his age.

9-9-1852 - DIED on Monday morning last in Eaton after a short illness, Francis H. REVEL, an old and highly esteemed citizen. The deceased resided in Eaton for the last eight years, previous to that time he resided some thirty years in Hamilton County. He was about 70 years of age.

11-18-1852 - DIED in Fair Haven on the 4th inst., Alonzo son of George and Rebecca A. HOOVER, aged 3 years, 6 months and 5 days.

1-13-1853 - DIED at his residence in Jackson township on the 29th of December 1852, John C. McMANUS, Esq. in the 66th year of his age. He received a classic education, studied law in the office of his relative, Wm. McManus, Esq. in Troy, New York. At the commencement of the War of 1812, he emigrated to Ohio, attached himself to the American army where he honorably and faithfully served his country, first in the Adjutant General's and afterwards the paymasters department. At the close of the war in 1815, he settled in Butler County, Ohio; soon after assisted in the original surveys in western Indiana and Illinois, again returned to Butler County, where he was associated at the Bar with Coblets, Benham and others, then the most eminent lawyers in Ohio. About the year 1820, he removed to this county where he acted as Prosecuting attorney and finally retired to his homestead. He was a Justice of the Peace for many years and a member of the M. E. Church. (Dayton, Ohio and Memphis, Tenn. papers please copy.)

2-10-1853 - DIED in Eaton on Friday morning last, Mrs. Mary wife of Dr. J. H. HELM, aged about 27 years.

3-17-1853 - DIED at the residence of her father in Dixon township on the 1st inst., Mary Ann LEWELLEN youngest daughter of John L. LEWELLEN, aged 19 years, 9 months and 15 days.

5-26-1853 - DIED in Eaton on Friday 13th inst., Mrs. Juletta SIMPSON consort of Mr. James Simpson of this place, aged 55 years. A devoted wife and mother. Member of the Presbyterian Church. DIED at his late residence two miles west of Eaton 9n 7th inst., James B. TAYLOR aged 49 years. He left a widow and several small children.

423

8-18-1853 - DIED in Eaton on the 14th inst., Mr. William D. HOLMS, aged about 20 years. Printer by trade, nine months ago he went to Memphis, Tennessee to persue his trade, but took sick and returned home in June.

9-8-1853 - DIED in Germantown, Ohio at the residence of her grandparents on the 30th ult., Mary only daughter of Dr. J. H. HELM of this place aged 8 months.

9-29-1853 - DIED on Monday last about 12 o'clock m., John M. GRAY, Esq., cashier of the Eaton Bank.

1-19-1854 - DIED on the 12th January 1854, Mary Jerusha CHADWICK, daughter of Marcus B. and Mary Eliza Chadwick, aged 3 years, 5 months and 4 days.

2-9-1854 - DIED on Monday morning last, Mrs. Elizabeth consort of Mr. Frederick HERBEST. DIED on Saturday last in Connersville, Indiana, Edwin only son of Isaac and Elizabeth LYNCH, aged 10 months. Interment Eaton.

3-2-1854 - DIED on the 23rd of Feb., Asa MELOY, esq. in the 54th year of his age.

4-13-1854 - DIED at the residence of her brother, Mr. Patterson Purviance in Jefferson township, on the 5th inst., Miss Jane PURVIANCE in the 46th year of her age.

4-29-1854 - DIED Monday last, Miss Elizabeth McGRIFF, aged about 25 years. DIED in Eaton April 21, 1854, Mrs. Mary SELLERS aged 55 years. The deceased was born August 29, 1799 and has resided many years in Preble County. A wife and mother.

5-11-1854 - DIED on Saturday last near Eaton, Mr. Isaac SMILEY, aged about 28 years. I.O.O.F.

6-8-1854 - DIED near Camden on Thursday last, Capt. J. WEBB one of the oldest and most respectable citizens of Preble County. DIED on Thursday morning at the residence of Dr. John Sturr, Jane daughter of the late Robert STAUNTON, aged 11 years and 5 months.

6-15-1854 - DIED on the 7th inst. in Dixon township, David HINKLE, aged 42 years. (Carlisle, Pa. and Greenville papers please copy.)

7-20-1854 - DIED on the 12th inst., Lucy Ann, second daughter of John MARSH, Esq., in the 11th year of her age.

8-17-1854 - DIED on the 2d inst., William H. CHRISTMAN, aged 15 years and 3 months. DIED on Saturday 12th inst., Amanda Jane wife of Jefferson CLAWSON in the 26th year of her age. Sermon by Rev. Elihu Moore in the Universalist Meeting house in Monroe township. TRIBUTE to Thomas P. QUINN, lawyer who attended Farmers College near Cincinnati and law school in that city; member of Preble County Bar.

8-21-1854 - DIED Friday evening last, Mrs. Lavina consort of R. Y. LANIUS in the 35th year of her age.

9-14-1854 – DIED on the 7th inst., Frederick H. son of Col. G. D. and Elmira Hendricks, aged 2 years.

10-19-1854 – DIED on the 7th inst., Mr. James K. FORD, aged 21 years. DIED on Wednesday last, Mr. Byrd HAWKINS, aged about 47 years. Masonic Honors.

11-2-1854 – DIED on the 17th ult. at New Westville, Mrs. Mary consort of James McWHINNY, aged 36 years. Wife and mother.

1-4-1855 – DIED Saturday December 30th at 4 o'clock P.M., Mrs. Sarah L. wife of Dr. A. C. McDILL of Fairhaven, Preble County.

1-12-1855 – DIED in Eaton, January 3d, Mrs. Elizabeth ALBRIGHT in the 30th year of her age. She left an aged mother, a husband and four small children. She was a member of the M.E. Church. DIED 9th December, John PIERCE at his late residence in Preble County, aged 69 years. At the same place on 25th December, Mary wife of John PIERCE, aged 59 years.

2-25-1855 – DIED on the 19th December 1854 in Israel township, Preble County, Mrs. Jane GAMBLE, aged one hundred and five years. DIED on the 11th inst., Mr. David TRUAX, aged ninety-nine years, eleven months and three weeks, for many years a resident of Dixon township, Preble County.

5-17-1855 – DIED Sunday morning last, John Thomas eldest son of John P. and Bethenia ACTON, aged about 14 years.

5-24-1855 – DIED at the residence of his father on the Sabbath morning, May 13, 1855, eldest son of John P. and Berthenia M. ACTON in the 14th year of his age. (Note: Repeat of above.)

5-31-1855 – DIED on the 24th day of May at his father's residence two miles south of Eaton, Jacob S. HOLDERMAN, aged 18 years and 4 months.

8-2-1855 – DIED at her late residence in Eaton, Mrs. Mary CRUME wife of Dr. P. M. Crume. She was born July 1, 1808 and died July 27, 1855 aged 47 years and 27 days. In August of 1821 when 13 years, she and her brother, Rev. J. C. DEEM of Cincinnati Conference joined the M.E. Church under the ministry of Rev. W. A. Raver.

9-6-1855 – DIED at her residence in Dixon township, Preble County on 31st ult., Mrs. Charity LEWELLAND consort of Lewis Lewelland, aged 63 years, 10 months and 13 days. She came to Preble County in the year 1826 and in 1827 married Lewis Lewelland. She leaves a husband and family of children.

9-13-1844 – DIED in Eaton on 8th September 1855, Mr. James B. EPPLEY, aged 23 years, 9 months and 28 days. Educated at Wittenburg College, Springfield, Ohio.

10-11-1855 – DIED in Eaton on 8th inst., Miss Hannah WALKER, in the 72nd year of her age.

11-15-1855 – DIED in Eaton on 5th inst., Mr. David HAUK, aged about 44 years.

11-22-1855 - DIED near Eaton on 19th inst., Mr. Robert A. BLOOMFIELD, aged about
26 yrs. DIED in Eaton on 19th, Miss Hulda HICE. DIED at the residence of her
son-in-law, John Leedy near Largo, Indiana on 30 October 1855, Mrs. Mary FALL in
the 74th year of her age. The deceased emigrated from North Carolina in 1806 with
her husband Daniel Fall and settled near Eaton, Preble County, Ohio. In 1822 she
was left a widow with seven children, most of them small. She was a member of the
Christian church.

12-6-1855 - DIED in Twin township on 6th ult., Mrs. Sarah KITSON consort of Mr.
Geo. Kitson in the 55th year of her age.

12-11-1855 - DIED in Cincinnati on 3d inst., Mr. Pierson SMITH of Eaton aged
about 40 years.

3-6-1856 - OBITUARY, Robert MARTIN born September 18, 1794 in the state of Maryland
and died February 26th, 1856, aged 61 years, 5 months and 25 days. In his 8th
year he emigrated to Cincinnati, Ohio with his parents with whom he settled in
Butler County in 1812 (or 1822--ink blot), he married Miss Rebecca Richardson.
He came to Eaton in 1829. Served term as Judge of Circuit Court. In the War of
1812-13, he served one campaign under Capt. Spencer of Hamilton. He was a member
of the M. E. church.

4-3-1856 - OBITUARY, Mary STEPHENS consort of John Stephens died in Gasper township. She was born December 31, 1824 and died March 23, 1855, aged 31 years, 2
months and 31 days. She was a member of the M.E. CHURCH.

5-1-1856 - DIED, Eaton on 28th ult., Dr. H. J. STURR, aged about 27 years.
Dr. Henry Sturr leaves a wife.

5-22-1856 - OBITUARY, Mary Ann STREET was born July 2, 1814 and died May 16, 1856,
aged 41 years, 10 months and 17 days. She married December 19, 1836 to James L.
Street. She leaves a husband and six children. Member M.E. Church.

5-29-1856 - DIED 12th May 1856, John Van Winkle ADAMSON, infant son of Eld. Enos
and Sara Louisa Adamson, aged 1 year 10 months and 16 days.

6-12-1856 - DIED at his residence adjacent to Eaton on 29th ult., Mr. Charles BRUCE,
aged 60 years and 5 months. Resident of Preble Count all his life.

9-11-1856 - DIED 29th August 1856, Sarah WILSON consort of James Wilson in the 59th
year of her age. DIED on 7th September 1856, James WILSON in the 65th year of his
age. He was 38 years a resident of Lanier township this county. DIED in Eaton
8th inst., John B. C. infant son of Dr. J. H. and Margaret HELM.

10-2-1856 - DIED in Eaton on Saturday, September 27th inst. at the residence of
Daniel Lesh, Clara HUBBARD daughter of Benjamin and Minerva Hubbard in the 4th
year of her age.

10-9-1856 - DIED in Eaton the 7th inst., Bird B. infant son of Helen M. LAMB,
aged 14 months and 24 days.

United States Land Patents Granted in MONROE TOWNSHIP - PREBLE COUNTY, OHIO
(Township 9 - Range 2)

Name	Sect.	Area	Acres	Date	Vol. & Page
TANNER, James	1	NE¼		8-1-1814	34/287
THATCHER, Jesse of Kentucky	1	SW¼		5-6-1815	101/109
PHILLIPS, Thomas J. assignee of William Neithercut	2	E½ NE¼	79	9-9-1824	40/393
BANTA, John assignee of David Williams	2	SE¼		5-6-1819	142/199
CAMPBELL, John of Butler Countym Ohio	2	SW¼	159	5-20-1825	145/507
COLLINS, John of Warren County, Ohio	3	E½ NE¼	80	4-2-1831	75/55
WILLIAMS, William	3	NW¼	160	10-22-1825	56/205
McCASH, Ann	3	SE¼		4-8-1819	48/325
COOPER, Alexander	4	W½ NE¼	79	8-14-1834	80/63
BAKER, George	4	E½ SE¼	79	3-5-1832	54/44
DOYAL, Edward assignee of Ralph Voris	4	SW¼		9-20-1825	73/508
MILLS, John	5	NE¼		3-11-1825	9/212
MILLS, John	5	NW¼		5-16-1819	4/274
KYLE, James of Butler County, Ohio	6	N½	239	8-14-1834	20/269
McCOY, Chas. S.	7	E½ SE¼	59	8-14-1834	85/282
PETRY, Jacob	7	SW¼	118	8-14-1834	27/104
WEIDNER, Jacob of Butler County, Ohio	8	NE¼	160	10-2-1825	98/118
YOUNG, David of Butler County, Ohio	8	NW¼	161	8-14-1834	94/540
JUDAY, John, Jr. & Jacob assignee of Valentine Eversolt	9	SW¼	159	4-1-1825	68/204
COSSAIRT, Peter assignee of Amos Thatcher	11	NE¼	156	3-3-1821	105/187
TAYLOR, William of Butler County, Ohio	11	S½	320	7-28-1844	136/475
BROWN, Michael	12	NE¼	159	8-12-1825	166/397
NEITHERCUTT, William	12	E½ NW¼	80	4-15-1822	142/170
COSSIART, Francis Of Warren County, Ohio	12	W½ NW¼	80	1-17-1828	142/171
PAINTER, John of Warren County, Ohio	12	SE¼	160		
DAVISSON, Josiah of Warren County, Ohio	14	Whole		5-14-1816	73/516
FUDGE, Jacob	15	SE¼	159	4-2-1829	73/509
JUDY, John Sr.	15	E½ NW¼	80	9-30-1825	116/495
ADAMS, Isaiah	17	E½	321	7-19-1824	75/481) 75/492)
WEHRLEY, Jonathan	17	E½ SW¼	80	3-5-1832	38/481
SHURLEY, Jonathan	17	W½ NW¼	80	5-17-1833	145/390
WEARLY, John H.	17	E½ NW¼	80	5-17-1833	145/391
McGREW, John of Montgomery County, Ohio	19	NE¼	122	1-3-1831	22/289
BROCK (BROOKS?), Moses James Maguire assignees in part of James McGuire	20	W½ NE¼	80	10-20-1827	94/33

Name	Sect.	Area	Acres	Date	Vol. & Page
RUNYAN, John	20	SE¼	160	9-16-1819	142/218
of Hamilton County, Ohio					
McDONAL, William	20	E½ SW¼	80	11-2-1830	52/6
assignee of Samuel Woodward					
HAVNER, Jacob	20	W½ SW¼	80	8-2-1833	17/361
assignee of Peter Harsh					
WHRLEY, Samuel J.	22	W½ SE¼	79	1-3-1831	68/600
ROUSE, Jacob of Kentucky	22	E½ SW¼	79	4-2-1829	136/4
HAPNER, Jacob	23	E½ SE¼	78	4-2-1829	121/150
CHRISLER, Wm. of Virginia	24	SE¼		3-17-1818	71/42
SHIELDS, Isaac	24	SW¼	159	4-1-1825	71/28
CHRISLEY, Aaron	26	NE¼	159	9-18-1820	79/97
LOUCKS, Adam	26	SE¼	159	11-2-1830	75/360
assignee of Abraham Icasnogh					
BICKEL, Jacob Jr.	26	SW¼	159	1-7-1826	35/393
ZELLER, Adam	27	W½ NE¼	82	11-10-1831	22/157
of Montgomery County, Ohio					
BOWMAN, Martin	27	SE¼	163	9-20-1827	121/153
assignee of Adam Louck					
TULLY, James	27	W½ SW¼	82	8-1-1823	111/152
HENDRICKS, George Drummond	28	E½ NE¼	80	3-5-1832	75/440
BYRNE, Charles of Cincinnati	29	NE¼	160	7-19-1824	75/430
MONROE TOWNSHIP SCHOOLS	29	NW¼		9-8-1843	91/131
BROWN, William	29	SE¼	160	8-12-1826	75/431
Of Montgomery County, Ohio					
CURRY, John Jr.	30	NE¼	124	7-19-1824	23/405
WESCO, Henry	31	W½		5-2-1827	52/576
of Pennsylvania					
KEEVER, Adam	32	NE¼	161	5-27-1824	75/426
of Warren County, Ohio					
DONNEL, Patrick of Pennsylvania	32	SW¼		7-28-1819	89/268
FUDGE, Daniel	33	E½ SW¼	80	3-20-1828	116/381
GREGORY, Henry	34	E½ SW¼	475	7-19-1824	103/275
of Hamilton County, Ohio					
REVEL, Francis Henry	35	W½	316	12-6-1823	39/113
REVEL, Francis Henry	36	SE¼	162	9-4-1823	36/447

* *

Guardianship	Year	Case No.
ACRE, Jacob, Michael, Elizabeth and John	1825	231
BANTA, Cornelius V.	1830	405
BARE, Peggy and Nancy	1826	301
BENNETT, Samuel, William and Benjamin	1827	328
BICKLE, Sally and Christina	1832	467
BLACK, Alexander S.	1825	238
BLACK, Peter and Mary	1821	145
BLOOMFIELD, Reuben	1823	179
BROCK, Jonathan	1828	349
BROWN, Hannah, Clayton and Samuel	1825	240
BRYANT, Jacob	1825	265
CAMPBELL, Susan Jane	1831	456
CARR, Harry H.	1825	230
CLAPP, George	1826	295
CLAPP, Jno.	1829	388
CLEMENTS, Hiram, Stephen and Emily	1816	50
COOPER, William, Hannah, Sarah, Felix, Rachel and Hulda	1831	461
CURRY, John and Mary Jane	1831	457
CURTIS, William	1821	123
DAVIS, Daniel, Moses, Aaron, Luther and Doctor	1832	474
DAVISSON, Margaret	1832	498
DeCAMP, Gavin and Melissa Janie	1829	373
DECORSEY, Seth, Anna and Samuel	1831	440
DEMOTT, John and Aaron	1831	458
DOOLEY, Martin L., Silas, Agness, Samuel, Rachel	1826	284
EBERSOLE, Harman, Jacob, Eliza and Mary	1828	362
ELLIOT, Melison, Rachel and Mary	1829	384
ELLIOTT, William	1825	255
ERLOUGHER, John, Australia and Catherine	1824	217
ETZLER, Abdel and Mary Magdelean	1820	106
FALL, Anna, Jacob, John, Elizabeth, Andrew, Mary and Sarah	1826	283
FERGUSON, Margaret, Clements, and Mary Timanda	1831	443
FLEMING, James	1829	369
FLEMING, John C.	1825	259
FLEMING, Sally and Eliza	1818	72
FOSE, Anna, John and Elizabeth	1830	427
FRAME, Rachel, William and Levi	1830	413
FREEMAN, Lauretta, Ervin, Henry and Daniel	1830	412
GARBER, John, Elizabeth, Henry and Mary	1817	68
GARBER, Mary	1825	237
GARVER, John, Henry and Elizabeth	1831	444
GIFFORD, Jesse	1830	428
GIFFORD, Nathan	1817	64
GIMES, Cornelius	1825	232
GLINES, John	1831	452
HALDEMAN, Allen	1822	160
HARBISON, Mariah, Henry and Amanda	1826	296
HARRIS, John, Nancy, Robert, Anna and Phoebe	1816	56
HARSHMAN, Peter, John, Barbara, Christina and Moses	1831	450
HART, Matilda	1832	486

Guardianship	Year	Case No.
HAYNES, William, Frederick and John	1830	430
HELL, Jacob	1832	479
HELL, John and Polly	1832	499
HENDERSON, Elizabeth	1823	198
HENDERSON, Samuel	1824	209
HENDRISSON, Hanah	1831	458
HEWSTON, Rachel and Caty	1816	57
HILL, Cyntha, Eliza, Selina and James	1826	281
HILL, Harvey	1826	269
HOBSON, Sarah, Charles, Mary, Isaac and Rachel	1829	372
INMAN, Benjamin, Samuel, Jacob, Job, Brazilla and Joseph	1828	336
IRELAND, Samuel	1825	244
JENKINS, Henry and Jas. H.	1826	285
JONES, Mary Ann, Susan and George W.	1829	390
JUDY, John and Catherine	1830	420
KESTER, Samuel, Jacob, Andrew and Diana	1832	470
KING, Samuel, Jacob, John, Mary, James and Anna	1825	262
LANDIS, Elizabeth and Henry	1818	74
LANDIS, Rebecca	1816	59
LINK, Betsy, Mary U., Athanon, Mary, Barbara, Eve, Susannah	1827	323
LIONS, Tabitha and Isaac	1821	124
LOUGH, Levi	1819	89
LOUGH, Levi	1826	290
LOWER, Sarah Ann, Margaret and William	1832	482
McCALLIE, Mariah and John C.	1828	365
McCOY, Nathan, Sally, Nelly and John	1826	300
McGREW, John, Washington, James and Samuel	1832	471
McGUIRE, Hetty, Mehala and Nathan	1823	186
McGUIRE, Nathan, Joseph, Hetty and Matilda	1819	95
McKINSTER, Matilda and James	1824	208
MARSHALL, Joseph and Jane	1830	414
MENDENHALL, Elijah, Hannah, Mary, Eliza Ann and Grace	1831	438
MENDENHALL, Marmaduke and Jos. E.	1829	379
MIKESELL, Aaron	1825	235
MILLIGAN, Grizzel, Samuel and John	1829	378
MOORE, Levi A.	1822	151
MORRIS, John	1822	161
MORRIS, Samuel	1830	404
NEAL, John and Mary	1824	225
NEFF, North, Josephus and Sarah	1831	454
NEWTON, James H., Charles H. and Wm. H.	1819	92
NICKOM, Nancy, John, Curtland, Jesse and Abigal	1819	88
NISBET, Caroline and Walter	1823	181
NISBET, John	1823	185
NISBET, Margaret Jane, Elizabeth, Thomas James and Mary	1823	184
NISBET, William	1823	183
NISBET, William	1825	254
PARHAM, Benajah	1818	73

Guardianship	Year	Case No.
PARHAM, Deliah and Elizabeth	1829	368
PAUL, James	1823	195
PENCE, Catherine and Thomas	1832	476
PENETT, Henry, Felix and Samuel	1831	441
PHILLIPS, Parker	1819	103
PICKLE, Elizabeth, Sarah, Mary, Jacob, George, Henry, Simon	1828	346
PILSEN, Hugh - an insane person	1820	104
POORMAN, Barbara	1829	383
POTTERF, Jefferson	1831	451
RAMSEY, Preston B.	1828	363
REED, Mary	1832	488
REED, William, Josiah, Sarah Jane and James I.	1832	483
ROSS, Henry C., Perris B., Robert E., Absalom and Jas. B.	1826	303
SAWYERS, Joseph C.	1823	176
SCOTT, Abner	1821	134
SHIVELY, Anny and Leah	1829	370
SHIVELY, Jacob	1829	371
SHOEMAN, Jacob	1823	193
SPACHT, Fanny E.	1832	475
STERETT, Maria	1831	463
STETLER, John	1825	260
STONER, Elizabeth and Henry	1828	337
STONER, Frederick and Barbara	1831	469
STRATTEN, Abigal	1823	196
CYTTE (LYTLE?), Hetty, Andrew J., Susan, Joseph, Margaret	1831	455
TALBERT; Elijah and Nathan	1828	339
TAYLOR, Salam	1832	472
TEAL, Catherine	1820	109
TEAL, Joseph	1829	108
THOMPSON, Dennis Whalen	1819	91
Truax, Isaac Jr.	1821	135
TRUNER, William	1817	63
UTTZ, Nancy, Mary Ann, Wirenda, Susannah and William	1827	314
WASHBURN, Heirs of Matthew	1815	45
WEAST, Andrew S., John H., Hannah, Jacob ,and Henry R.	1825	233
WESTERFIELD, Isaac, Caroline and Johannah	1832	481
WIBLE, Betsey and Nicholas	1825	257
WIKLE, Andrew and Phebe	1830	418
WILSON, Alexander and Joseph	1822	152
WILSON, James H., Robert W. and John L.	1832	480
WOODWARD, Nathan and Mahlon	1830	416
ZELLERS, Sarah, Reuben and Lucinda	1820	117
ZIMMERMAN, Eli A. K., John B., William J. and Elizabeth	1823	187

The foregoing guardianships can be found in the office of the Probate Court in the court house at Eaton under the listed case numbers.

The following guardianships are found in packets under the case number given, in the Probate Court at the court house in Eaton.

Guardianship	Date	Case No.
ACKER, Jacob	1834	541
ACKER, Michael	1834	540
AILES, Caroline S.	1846	1144
Marilda Ann		
Wm U.		
ALEXANDER, Enoch	1849	1360
Sarah Leah		
Rachel Jane		
Mary Catharine		
ALLEN, Lorinda	1849	1408
AMMERMAN, Lorinda Jane	1847	1204
Wm Martin		
AMPY, Nancy, Hezekiah,	1845	1106
Elizabeth & Harvey		
ANDERSON, Rebecca	1833	525
Sarah Adaline		
BAGGS, James W., Thomas A.,	1833	507
Wm P. & Hugh H.		
BALLINGER, Jacob	1850	1477
BANTA, Hannah & Isaac	1847	1272
BANTA, James	1848	1294
BARR, Alexander	1839	776
Nancy Eliza		
BEACHLER, Wm Henry	1850	1478
BEALL, Joseph	1838	734
BECK, Elizabeth & William	1845	1114
BEECH, Lewis	1847	1208
BEEZLY, Tenperance Ophelia	1839	811
BELL, Henry, Lucinda	1846	1127
Martha, Josiah,		
Sarah, Maria &		
John		
BIGGS, Sarah, Ephraim,	1834	578
Joshua & Margaret		
BLACK, David, Abraham,	1841	877
Henry, Foster & Uri		
BLACK, Wm H., Henry &	1846	1188
Sarah Ann		
BLOUNT, Ambrose Alexander	1840	903
BLUNT, Ambrose	1835	589
BOBLET, Jacob H.	1842	941
BORDEN, Susan, Wm & Geo.	1849	1428
BOYSE, Alexander P.	1848	1329
BPYSE, Ananias	1848	1328
BRADSHAW, Ann	1837	690
BRANSON, Amos & Thomas	1844	1056

Guardianship	Date	Case No.
BRAWLEY, Thos. F. & Levi P.	1842	979
BROWN, Adam, Jacob & David	1841	910
BROWN, George	1845	1085
BROWN, Hiram	1850	1537
BROWN, Jonas, Sarah, John	1833	524
Jonathan & Richard		
BROWN, Joseph	1846	1182
BROWN, Mary Ann	1842	967
BROWN, Nathan	1845	1086
BROWN, Nehemiah & Charles	1841	869
BROWN, Samuel S.	1844	1031
BROWN, Wm D. &Martha Ann	1844	1028
BURSON, Eden	1839	804
BUTT, Harriet & Jonathan	1839	826
CALDWELL, Andrew M. & Mary	1839	795
CALDWELL, Henry Poindexter	1839	770
& John		
CALDWELL, Jas. C.	1850	1533
CAMPBELL, Baloner	1839	771
CAMPBELL, Wm D., Mary,	1846	1165
Henrietta & Juliett		
CAMPBELL, Wm H., H. Susannah	1846	1153
F., Alzina H.,		
Sarah Ann & John D.		
CARTER, Jos. Milton	1847	1237
CARTWELL, Nancy Ann	1838	736
CAUGHEY, George W. & John	1846	1175
CHILDERS, Thomas D.	1833	510
CLARK, Magdalena	1841	858
CLEVENGER, Caroline & Shubal	1848	1311
CLEVENGER, Sarah Ann	1848	1317
CLEVENGER, William	1842	955
CLINGENPEEL, Joseph, Allen	1839	814
Andrew & Geo.		
COOMBS, Joseph	1850	1479
CRAIG, Harriet Jane &	1838	737
Joseph Seymore		
CRAMPTON, Letta Charlotte	1849	1417
Margaret Cath.		
CRAMPTON, Rebecca C. &	1838	726
Margaret C.		
CRAMPTON, Smith, Margaret,	1837	715
Mallissa, John,		
Jesse & Sarah		
CRIST, Henry C.	1849	1374
CRUME, Thos. M., Martha Jane	1847	1226
Geo. F.M. & Pliny		
McConnel		

432

Guardianship	Date	Case No.	Guardianship	Date	Case No.
UME, Wm Wallace	1849	1361	EMERICK, Joel	1847	1216
RRY, John & Mary Jane	1836	644	EMMONS, Abraham	1835	628
ILY, Joseph Wm Henry,	1845	1077	EMMONS, Isaac & John	1840	843
Anna Katharine &			ENGLISH, Isabel C., Martha E.,	1850	1459
John Edmund			Rebecca, Sam'l B., &		
VIS, John	1834	542	Andrew F.		
ARDORF, Geo. Washington	1839	819	EVERLY, Daniel, Peter, John &	1847	1263
RUMPLE, Peter S. &	1848	1285	Wm Eli		
Mary Catharine			FANSLER, Absolom	1849	1367
VELIN, Elizabeth, Jemima,	1834	577	FELLER, Maria	1840	841
& Eunice Louisa			FLEMING, Juliett & Jane	1838	752
FFENDALL, Elizabeth S.	1838	745	FLEMING, Madison, Aveline &	1834	551
FFENDALL, Sarah	1847	1202	Desin		
FFENDALL, Susannah & Mary	1847	1235	FOSTER, Hugh	1839	806
LL, Julia Ann, John	1841	878	FOSTER, James B. & Thomas H.	1846	1141
Wesley, Tiresa,			FOSTER, James B. & Thomas H.	1850	1535
Lucinda Jane, Cath-			FOX, Mary Ann, Wm & Henrietta	1847	1253
arine & Francis			FRAZIER, Rebecca Jane	1847	1258
LLMAN, Joseph, Mary,	1839	813	FUDGE, Mary Ann, Rebecca Jane,	1849	1424
John & David			& Sarah Elizabeth		
OLEY, Elvina &	1850	1536	GARD, Aaron, Lydia, Simeon &	1849	1449
Catharine Jane			Stephen		
OLEY, Kirtland & Martha	1838	731	GARD. Lewis	184.	575
OLEY, Martha	1837	692	GARD, Mary Ann	1842	959
OLEY, Richard, Selisa,	1850	1531	GARDNER, Elizabeth Ann, John	1846	1155
Orpha, Caleb W.,			Franklin, Emeline		
Levi P. & Samuel			Mary, & Perry V.		
ORMAN, Solomon	1849	1369	GARDNER, Gilbert Lafayette &	1847	1198
ORMAN, Susan	1849	1368	Edwin W.		
FFIELD, Susan Elizabeth	1850	1490	GILLESPIE, John & Wm	1842	962
NNUCH, Margaret	1849	1340	GILLESPIE, Ebenezer H.	1839	772
NWIDDIE, Almira	1847	1250	GILPIN, Mary Agnes & Enos	1840	892
NWIDDIE, Debotah & Ruth	1839	769	GLINES, James	1835	596
RHART, Elizabeth, Nancy	1847	1241	GLUNT, John Samuel & Susannah	1850	1484
Daniel, Mary &			GOODWIN, Lavina, Mary & Abigail	1848	1292
Michael			GRAY, Abner	1842	985
WIN, Hiram	1843	1013	GREEN, Henry	1849	1415
BERT. Nancy, Delilah &	1836	651	GREGG, Harman	1847	1239
James			GRUBER, Mary Elizabeth	1846	1187
BERT, Nancy, James &	1850	1503	HAMMEL, John, Sophia & Samuel	1835	607
Delilah			HAFNER, Nelson	1850	1495
KENBERRY, Lydia, Eliza-	1840	894	HARDY, John, Joseph, Henry	1833	519
beth, Christi-			Sarah & Elizabeth		
ana, Joseph,			HARDY, Sarah Ann & Melinda	1836	679
John, Mary &			HARLAN, John G. & Nancy E.	1840	831
Peter			HARRIS, Mos, Robert, Jonathan	1836	637
DER, William	1840	893	& Margaret Elizabeth		
LER. Daniel	1844	1050	HARSHMAN, Isaac, Daniel, Anna,	1840	906
LIOTT, Horance & Martha	1847	1248	John, James, Harvey,		
Ann			& Eliza		

433

Guardianship	Date	Case No.
HARSHMAN, John W.	1844	1038
HART, David	1844	1033
HART, George	1844	1032
HARVEY, Mary Jane & Athelia	1837	702
HASTY, Ezra Franklin	1850	1500
HASTY, Hester Ann & Ezra F.	1839	802
HAWKINS, Jos. Campbel	1850	1468
HAYS, Rebecca, Polly, John, Wm Robt. & Thomas	1837	703
HILL, Elizabeth Ann & Thos.	1849	1414
HILEMAN, Henry, Philip, David, Peter, Mary Jane, Elizabeth & Daniel	1840	901
HILL, Patrick	1846	1183
HOCKS, Samuel	1850	1457
HOLDERMAN, John	1845	1090
HOLMES, Hannah, Margaret & Janett	1838	751
HOLSOPPLE, Moses	1850	1515
HOOVER, Geo., Wm, Louise, Sarah & Caroline	1836	666
HORNADAY, Ezra	1839	805
HOUP, John	1844	1036
HUBBEL, John R.	1836	646
HUFFMAN, Margaret E.	1839	825
HUNT, Samuel	1848	1306
HUNTER, John, David, Maria, Ione, Robert & Catherine	1834	549
HUSTON, Wm Riley & John	1845	1078
IMLAY, Lydia Ann & Geo. T.	1848	1293
INGERSOL, Ezra, Elizabeth, Hannah, Jane, & Nancy Ann	1837	696
IRWIN, Betsy & Abigail	1837	689
IRWIN, John B.	1839	820
JACKSON, James	1842	970
JACKSON, Martha, James Belinda A. Elizabeth H. & Nancy	1848	1324
JEFFRIES, James	1839	803
JENNINGS, John P., Sarah M., Elizabeth Jane & Mary F.	1846	1181
JOHNSON, Alexander	1850	1485
JOHNSON, Geo. Ferguson, Thos. Maxwell, & Eliza	1838	758

Guardianship	Date	Case No.
JOHNSON, Thomas F., Maxwell & Eliza	1838	748
JOHNSON, Wm Henry Harrison	1838	756
JONES, Deborah Ann, Keziah & Susanna	1838	761
JONES, Macy B., Elizabeth Ann & Henry Newton	1844	1057
JONES, Sarah Jane	1834	545
KELTNER, Sarah, Emeline, Henry Martin & Catharine	1843	1006
KELLY, John, Cornelius, Keziah & Jeremiah	1842	949
KENNY, George, Wm, Jefferson, Elizabeth & Susan	1836	648
KESLER, Amanda Mariah	1845	1092
KING, Jephthat	1833	534
KIRKPATRICK, David & John	1842	977
KIRKPATRICK, John & Esther Ann	1847	1251
KLINGENPEEL, Margaret & Benj.	1847	1233
KLINGER, Daniel, Joseph, Peter, Elizabeth, Jackson & Samuel	1836	674
LAMB, Pen the Mon, Benj. & Daniel	1844	1034
LAMM, Henry & Aaron	1850	1532
LANTIS, Samuel & Asenith	1838	727
LEAS, Julius E.	1845	1105
LINCOLN, Henry, Lucy Ann, Elizabeth, David & Mary Jane	1846	1147
LINTNER, David M.	1850	1458
LINTNER, Wm Henry	1849	1450
LOCK, Adam	1844	1055
LOCK, Jacob, Abram, Isaac, Christina, Sally, Elizabeth, Solomon & Rosannah Margaret	1837	711
LOCKWOOD, Wm & Geo.	1840	899
LOY, Christopher & Jane	1836	672
LOY, Susannah & Matilda Jane	1842	991
McBRIDE, Heirs of Jas.	1835	590
McCAMPBELL, Phebe Ann & Elmyra	1839	807
McCHRISTY, John & Mary	1845	1113
McCLUNG, Margaret	1846	1166
McCLUNG, Wm B.	1846	1167
McCOY, Heirs of Archibald	1840	832
McCOY, Jas. Irvin	1846	1192

Guardianship	Date	Case No.
McDANIELS, John, Mary Abigail, Olinda, Samuel, Wm, & Lucinda	1838	735
McGHEE, Catherine	1849	1443
McGHEE, James, Mary Jane, Geo. H. & Thomas Allen	1849	1444
cHUTT, Joseph G.	1840	897
cQUISTON, David & Martha Jane	1845	1111
cWHINNEY, Eli, Sarah, Mary, Cynthia & Rachel	1846	1170
cWHINNEY, Newton	1839	779
cWHINNEY, Samuel	1839	780
cWHINNEY, Wm H.	1846	1136
AHAFFEY, John	1834	562
ARSH, Hetty	1839	794
ETTERT, David G., Martin C. Wm G., Lydia A., Christena, Rachel & Amanda	1847	1230
ILLER, Katherine R.	1835	598
ILLER, Mary C. & Huldah	1835	516
ILLER, Mary Susan, Martha Jane & John A.	1849	1370
ILLIKEN, John	1838	730
ILLS, Mary Ann & Reuben	1838	732
ILLS, Wm, Amos, John, Elizabeth, Rebecca Henry, Joseph & George	1836	642
ILLS, Wm, John & Jane	1840	844
INOR, Phinias	1837	695
ITCHELL, Franklin & Samuel	1847	1256
ITCHELL, Sarah, Harrison, Velinda, Lavina, Louisa & Milton	1844	1053
OON, Rebecca & Thomas H.G.	1834	558
OORE, Isaac S.	1835	630
OORE, Samuel	1834	559
OORE, Thomas	1835	594
ORTON, Hannah & Thomas	1841	861
OSES, Robert, Martha & Wm	1847	1209
OSES, Wm & James	1850	1463

Guardianship	Date	Case No.
MUCKLEWAIN, Andres, Naomy & Moses	1839	784
MULLENDORE, George, Jos., Aaron & Noah	1847	1207
MURPHY, Mary Ann, Elizabeth I., Martin P., James, Hannah & Rebecca	1837	691
NEWTON, Thos.	1846	1160
NICCUM, Thos. D.	1838	733
NICOL, John & Joanna	1839	799
O'KANE, Peter & Margaret Ellen	1847	1266
ORR, Alexander P., Mary Jane, James M. & John C.	1844	1026
OVERHOLSER, Joel, Christian, Henry & Mary	1837	694
OVERHOLTZ, John, Daniel, Jos., Isaac, Julia Ann, Lewis, Wm, Jonathan, Jacob, Elizabeth & Mary Ann	1842	943
OVERHOLTZ, Lewis & Phebe Ann	1835	591
OZIAS, David Franklin & Amanda Emeline Weekly	1850	1486
PARKER, Christina	1845	1112
PARSEL, Cyrus	1844	1059
PATTY, Eli Alexander	1845	1097
PAXTON, Jonathan	1839	782
PEIRCE, Squeir Little	1850	1524
PETRY, Catharine, Michael, Nancy, Sarah, Magdalena, & Susannah	1847	1229
PHILIPS, Jerman & John	1840	900
PINKERTON, Jos. L.	1849	1427
POTTENGER, Mary F., Hiram, Margaretta, Granville, Hester & Cecilia	1846	1190
POTTENGER, Wm K.	1848	1314
POTTER, Levi & Carlton	1849	1384
POTTINGER, Prudence	1847	1228
POTERF, Gasper & Squire James	1845	1118
POTTERF, Nancy Jane	1845	1081
PREBLE, Barnet & Scynthia	1839	775
PRIBBLE, Amelia & Oliver O.H.	1838	738
PRICE, George	1839	785
PRUGH, Hester	1841	927

Guardianship	Date	Case No.
PURSELL, Hannah	1838	724
PURVIANCE, Patterson James	1835	626
QUINN, John B.	1842	986
RAMSEY, Wm Gilmore, Martha Agnes, Thomas Lacy, & Sam'l Rutherford	1841	922
RANDALL, Rebecca, Jis, Nancy, Phebe, Martha, & Nathan	1836	671
REDMAN, John	1842	945
REEVES, Josephine	1849	1387
REEVES, Louisa & Diploma L.	1849	1390
REYNOLDS, Almedia	1849	1420
RHEA, John Wm. Harmonius, Elizabeth & Elias B.	1836	641
RIDENOUR, Levi N.	1840	847
RIGGS, Asahel, Arthur, Margaret, Eli, Pamela, Cyrus & Benj.	1850	1523
RINER, Elizabeth & Rebecca	1842	950
BISOZ, Milton & Francis	1849	1446
ROBERTS, John	1849	1378
ROBERTS, Mary Chloe	1833	527
ROBERTSON, Ezra, Mary Ann, Rachel, Catharine, Huldah, Eleanor & Harriet	1833	511
ROBERTSON, Rhoda & Wm	1850	1513
ROBESON, Rhoda Ann, Sarah Elizabeth, Mary Jane & Abigail M.	1842	962
RODMAN, John Abel, Gertrude, Isaac & Benj.	1848	1288
RODGERS, Isaac, Emily, Keziah & Lydia Ann	1850	1498
ROUTZSONG, Lucinda & Daniel	1849	1354
ROW, Milton	1849	1372
RUNYON, Beall, Martin, John, Elizabeth, Massa, & Jacob	1838	739
SACKMAN, John Michael & Henry Wm	1836	660
SACKMAN, Mary Elizabeth & Chas. Soloman	1839	824
SACKMAN, Oliver, Samantha & Agnes Elizabeth	1848	1298

Guardianship	Date	Case No.
SAMPLE, Levi T. & Isaac N.W.	1850	1512
SAYLOR, Abraham, Polly, Philip & Rebecca	1833	518
SCOTT, John Wesley	1845	1110
SELLARS, Susan E. E.	1834	561
SELLARS, John Harvey	1850	1517
SEMPLE, Elizabeth, Lattin, Mary Rebecca, Sarah Jane & James	1841	921
SEWARD, Mary Maria	1848	1316
SHAFFER, Elizabeth	1846	1152
SHAFFER, John Henry	1845	1096
SHANK, Polly, Sally Ann & Daniel	1839	778
SHANK, Wm, Jacob, George & John	1836	673
SHEARER, Hannah Sophia	1837	710
SHEILDS, Eliza Margaret	1850	1496
SHEILDS, Maria Elizabeth John A. Wilson, Mary Catharine & Sarah Jane	1850	1497
SHERER, Doanah, Geo. H., Perminia & Mary Elizabeth	1845	1076
SHIVE (SHINE), Conrad	1844	1030
SHUMAKER, George, Eliazer, Solomon	1837	700
SLOANE, Lafayette	1837	704
SMITH, Ann Eliza	1849	1432
SMITH, Eliza Jane, Lucy Ann, John, Wm & Abraham	1847	1227
SMITH, Martha Ellen, George, Wm, Mary & Samuel	1845	1080
SMITH, Mary Amanda, Adella Virginia, Geo. Jackson	1848	1326
SMITH, Samuel	1838	744
SMITH, Samuel	1840	889
SMITH, William Harvey	1850	1530
SNODGRASS, James, Sarah Jane and Andrew H.	1839	810
SOLOMON, John	1834	539
STEPHENS, Dewitt C. & Laura	1844	1024
STEPHENS, John B., Richard, Eliza & Fanny	1838	762
STEPHENS, Wm D. Nathaniel B., Martin F.	1839	809
STERRET, Eleanor	1834	536

436

Guardianship	Date	Case No.
STETLER, Celia Jane & Elizabeth Melvina	1849	1377
STEWART, Mary W. & Ezra H.	1849	1350
STOVER, David Pendleton, Sarah Jane, Geo. Washington, & Benj. Clinton	1850	1473
SWAIN, John Lindsay, Jos. B., Jacob, Martin Van Buren, Elizabeth Jane & Schlinda	1850	1499
SWIHART, Heirs of Jacob	1840	838
SWIHART, Wm Adam, Nancy Margaret, Francis, Marion & Sarah Cath.	1844	1029
SWISHER, Heirs of Robt	1846	1132
SWISHER, Sarah Catharine Eliza Caroline, & Nancy Maria	1846	1131
TAMMAN, Priscilla	1835	617
TAYLOR, Lydia & John Williams	1843	999
TAYLOR, Michael B., Susan E., James Lee, & Squire T.	1838	759
THOMPSON, Isaac, Wm, Nancy, Zinni & Elijah	1839	822
THOMPSON, John Benj. & Elizabeth	1839	818
THRALLS, Margaret Ann	1834	547
TODD, James, Gavin, Wm & John	1836	635
TUCKER, Thomas V.	1846	1150
UNGER, Aaron Andrew	1849	1356
VANDOREN, Cornelius Abraham, Frances	1850	1521
VANTZ, Jonas	1833	526
VANWINKLE, Robert	1834	575
WATERS, James	1836	652

Guardianship	Date	Case No.
WATT, David P., John B., Elizabeth M., Jas. A., Mary P., & Martha E.	1848	1318
WATT, James H. & Sarah E.	1846	1280
WATT, L.P., Margaret Nancy Jane, Louisa, Levi & Milton	1835	616
WEED, Jonathan P.	1844	1044
WESCO, Theodore	1842	953
WESTERFIELD, Stephen	1833	522
WHITE, John, Calvin & Jane	1836	636
WHITRIDGE, Almira, Louisa, Eveline & Lorenzo	1847	1228
WHITRIDGE. Ann Eliza, Chas. J., Wm F., & Milcah E.	1848	1305
WHITRIDGE, Wm E., Lydia R., John H., Henry C., & Ruth J.	1848	1287
WILLIAMS, Mary Jane & Elizabeth	1847	1242
WILLIAMS, Wm H. H. & Susannah J.	1846	859
WILSON, David	1842	958
WILSON, Martha Ann, Wm Joseph, Mary Jane, Elizabeth Margaret & Suffrona J.	1838	754
WINCE, Peter, Philip, Mary, Daniel & Elizabeth	1836	645
WINDSOR, Heirs of Enos	1839	823
WINKLEY, Louis, Irena & Eliza	1843	1018
WINNIGER, John & Geo.	1842	980
WOLLARD, Robert, Elizabeth, Frances Jane & Patrick Marcus	1846	1139
YORK, Diadema	1835	597
YOUNG, Eliza Ann, Sarah Jane, & Christina	1846	1151
ZELLERS, Sarah	1835	595

RICHLAND COUNTY, OHIO - COMMON PLEAS COURT MINUTES 1822-1825

The following records were copied from "Journal 2", located in the Clerk of Court's Storage Room, Weights and Measures, Second Floor of the Richland County Court House. The records are under the jurisdiction of the Clerk of Court's Office. Pages on which record may be found are given in parenthesis.

4-1-1822 - Henry KEITH appointed adms. of the estate of Michael KEITH. (1) Will of Mary ARMSTRONG presented. (2)

4-2-1822 - John KINNEY appointed adms. of the estate of Lewis KINNEY, dec'd. (4) Account filed by adms. of Abraham CUPPY late of Brook County, Virginia; Abraham Cuppy in his lifetime owned SE¼ Section 31, Township 23, Range 16 in Richland County. (4)

4-2-1822 - John HENDLY now aged 18 years and 4 months chose Isaac OSBURN as his guardian. (5)

4-2-1822 - James CLINGAN born County Craven, Ireland, aged 40 years; resided in United States before 1-29-1795 makes application to become citizen. (6)

4-3-1822 - Francis MITCHELL and Joseph MITCHELL appointed adms. of the estate of George MITCHELL, dec'd. (9) Will of James MAHAN presented. (9)

4-4-1822 - John STEWART appointed guardian of William CUNNINGHAM aged 13 yrs., John CUNNINGHAM aged 12 yrs. and James Duncan CUNNINGHAM aged 10 yrs. heirs of Hugh CUNNINGHAM, dec'd. (12)

4-5-1822 - John CROSTHWAIT aged 16 yrs. and Sarah CROSTHWAITE aged 13 yrs., son and daughter of Robert CROSTHWAIT chose Robert CROSTHWAIT as their guardian with said Robert to also serve as guardian of Bertha CROSTHWAIT aged 10 yrs. (13)

7-29-1822 - George COFFENBERRY and Eleanor POLLOCK appointed adms. of the estate of Hugh POLLOCK, dec'd. (24)

7-29-1822 - James HALL aged 16 yrs. in October 1821 chose Bartholomew WILLIAMSON as his guardian. (28)

7-30-1822 - Will of George BURGET presented. (31)

7-30-1822 - William BEACH aged 16 yrs. in Nov. next, heir of Charles BEACH, dec'd, chose Jonathan BEACH as his guardian. (36)

7-30-1822 - Doranda ROCK (ROCKWELL?) aged 16 yrs., heir of Frederick ROCK chose James SMITH as her guardian. (37)

8-18-1822 - Minister license granted to Rev. James JOHNSTON a minister of the Presbyterian church. (40)

8-18-1822 - George SWARINGEN aged 16 yrs., heir of Samuel SWARINGEN late of Brooke County, Virginia, dec'd, chose Henry W. WILCOXON as his guardian. (41)

8-18-1822 - Michael DOUGLAS, native of Ireland, Naturalization. (43)

11-11-1822 - Will of Joseph ARCHER Sr. presented. (51) Matilda CLINE appointed adms. of the estate of Joseph CLINE, dec'd. (51)

11-11-1822 - Joseph CLINE under 14 yrs. of age, heir of Joseph CLINE, dec'd had James POWELL appointed his guardian. (51)

11-11-1822 - Roger MOSS (or MOSES?) over 21 yrs. of age, native of Ireland and Britain, makes his application to become citizen. (53)

11-12-1822 - Joseph STAFEL, over 21 yrs., native of Switzerland, makes his application to become citizen. (57)

11-14-1822 - John H. ROCKWELL aged 17 yrs., heir of Joseph ROCKWELL chose James ROCKWELL as his guardian, Dorinda ROCKWELL aged 16 yrs., heir of Frederick ROCKWELL chose James ROCKWELL as her guardian. (68)

11-15-1822 - William KEYS over 21 yrs. of age, native of Great Britain and Ireland makes his application to become citizen. (70)

1-25-1823 - Robert JOHNSTON appointed adms. of the estate of James JOHNSTON, dec'd. (74)

3-31-1823 - Abel COOK appointed adms. of the estate of Noah B. COOK, dec'd. (75) Will of James STAFFORD presented. (75) Nathan WALKER minister of the Episcopal Church granted ministers license. (76)

3-31-1823 - Solomon COOK appointed guardian of Zeba COOK aged 17 yrs. last Nov., Martha COOK aged 5 yrs. last Sept., Peggy COOK aged 3 yrs. last April and Mathew Bryant COOK aged 1 year last April or May, heirs of Noah B. COOK, dec'd. (76)

3-31-1823 - Daniel PROSSER a Revolutionary soldier having filed his Declaration and the Court having heard his Testimony and said Daniel Prosser having sworn to and subscribed to his said Declaration and shedule in Order to obtain his pension under the Law of Congress are of opinion that the total amount of value of the property in the schedule annexed to his declaration is forty one Dollars and thirty five cents. (79)

3-31-1823 - Stephen BUTLER and John EMERICK appointed adms. of the estate of John LAUGHLIN, dec'd. (83) Abraham D. W. BODLY appointed adms. of the estate of Jasper M. SMALLY, dec'd. (91)

7-21-1823 - David COULTER and James H. DAY appointed adms. of the estate of Jabex PARKER, dec'd. (99) John COX minister of the Baptist Church granted ministers license. (100) Will of George BURGETT presented. (105)

7-21-1823 - Peter SHAW aged 16 yrs. chose John STEWART as his guardian. (107)

7-23-1823 - Hannah PERRY aged 18 yrs., William PERRY aged 16 yrs., Samuel PERRY aged 14 yrs. and Elizabeth PERRY aged 13 yrs. chose Jane PERRY as their guardian. (115)

7-23-1823 - Jane PERRY appointed guardian of Margaret PERRY aged 9 yrs. and Mary PERRY aged 6 yrs. (116)

7-23-1823 - George ROCKWELL aged 14 yrs., son of Frederick ROCKWELL chose James ROCKWELL as his guardian. (188)

7-23-1823 - Jane PERRY adms. of the estate of Samuel PERRY, dec'd, presented account. (120)

8-15-1823 - Isaac HITCHCOCK and John DICKSON appointed adms. of the estate of Thomas ELLIS, dec'd. (122)

9-20-1823 - Margaret SHRADER and Daniel CARTER appointed adms. of the estate of Jabez SHRADER, dec'd. (122)

11-4-1823 - On motion, It appeared to the Court by Satisfactory Evidence that Hannah CAFFEE late Hannah HENDERSON now wife of Amos H. CAFFEE, Elizabeth ROOT late Elizabeth HENDERSON now wife of Abner ROOT & Sarah Henderson are daughters and heirs at law of David HENDERSON, dec'd, late soldier in Lee's Legion in the Revolutionary War who died at Alexandria within the District of Columbia in May 1805. It is thereupon ordered by the Court that the same be duly certified with the seal of the Court for the benefit of said Heirs at Law in procuring certain lands claimed from the United States on account of the Revolutionary Services of the said David Henderson, dec'd. (128)

11-4-1823 - William HUFF and Ezra WILLIAMS appointed adms. of the estate of Gamaiel HUFF, dec'd. (128) John E. PAGE appointed adms. of the Estate of Ebenezer PAGE, dec'd. (128) Ephraim VAIL and John D. BEVEIR appointed adms. of the estate of Peter RUCKMAN, dec'd. (133)

11-4-1823 - John ELLIS aged 15 yrs., heir of Thomas ELLIS, dec'd, chose Jacob OSBURNhis guardian. Sarah ELLIS aged 12 yrs., heir of Thomas ELLIS, dec'd chose Isaac HITCHCOCK her guardian. James FORGESON appointed guardian of Martha ELLIS aged 9 yrs., daughter of Thomas ELLIS, dec'd. (134)

11-4-1823 - Aaron BEARD adms. of Dan MURDOCK filed account. (134) Silas ENSIGN minister of the New Jerusalem Church granted minister's license. (135)

11-5-1823 - Joseph PARK (or PASK?), native of Great Britain and Ireland makes his application to become citizen. (141) George CRAWFORD and John OLIVER appointed adms. of the estate of Stephen H. MORY, dec'd. (141)

5-17-1824 - Catharine HUNTSMAN appointed adms. of the estate of Jonathan HUNTSMAN, dec'd. (151) Alexander McBRIDE, III and Samuel RICHEY appointed adms. of the estate of Thomas McBRIDE. (152)

440

5-17-1824 - John DALLY appointed guardian of Vincent DALLY aged 12 yrs. Sept. last and Hannah DALLY aged 9 yrs. 16 last Sept., son and daughter of Charles DALLY (DAELY), dec'd. (153)

5-17-1823 - Duncan McBRIDE aged 17 yrs. June next, heir of Thomas McBRIDE, chose John STEWART, Esq. as his guardian. (153)

5-17-1823 - Robert LULTER(?) aged 16 yrs. 11 June next chose Solomon CAR as his guardian. (154)

5-17-1823 - Phebe LOCY aged 14 yrs. chose Jeptha DEEN as her guardian. (154)

5-17-1823 - Will of William MAHIGAN presented. (154) Will of John MAUN presented. (156)

5-18-1824 - Susan BURGETT aged 12 yrs., heir of George BURGETT chose Thomas BURGETT as her guardian. (161)

5-19-1824 - Jeremiah COPELAND, native of Great Britain, to United States 5-22-1822 makes his application to become citizen. (164)

5-20-1824 - Julia NEWELL and Robert BENTLEY appointed adms. of the estate of David NEWELL, dec'd. (166)

5-21-1824 - Will of Alexander CURRAN presented. (169) John WILER, a foreigner reported himself with one John U. TANNER, a minor in his service to Court and state that they have resided in Ohio more than 4 yrs.; and make application to become citizens. (170)

8-4-1824 - Will of Benjamin LOUIRH(?) presented. (182)

8-4-1824 - Clark H. RICE aged 19 yrs., Orson W. RICE aged 10 yrs. and Abigail RICE aged 14 yrs., heirs of Ebenezer Rice, dec'd, chose Alexander RICE as their guardian. (182) Alexander RICE appointed guardian of Levi A. RICE aged 9 yrs. and Samuel B. RICE aged 6 yrs., heirs of Ebenezer RICE, dec'd. (183)

8-6-1824 - Jonathan COULTER appointed adms. of the estate of John THOMAS, dec'd (197) Ruth LEE appointed adms. of the estate of William C. LEE, dec'd. (203)

8-7-1824 - John STEWART appointed adms. with the will annexed of John MANN, dec'd. (205)

8-7-1824 - Ellzey HEDGES appointed guardian of Andrew and Joseph NEWMAN aged 14 yrs., heirs of Jacob NEWMAN, dec'd. (205)

10-6-1824 - Jacob KUYKENDOLL appointed adms. of William KUYKENDOLL, dec'd, late of Aubern twp. (209) Will of Francis MORRISON presented. (210) Will of David ROSS presented. (211) Will of Abraham WILLIAMS presented. (211) Ruth WOODWARD appointed adms. of the estate of John WOODWARD, dec'd. (212) Ruth CHOLCOATE appointed adms. of the estate of Mordecai CHILCOATE, dec'd. (213)

441

10-6-1824 - Rachel SHRIVER aged 17 yrs. 11 mos. & 11 ds. chose Nathaniel BAILY as her guardian. (213)

10-6-1824 - Will of Phillip MAINS presented. (217) James McKELVEY minister of the Baptist Church granted ministers license. (213) Margaret AMES widow of Ephraim S. AMES relinquishes her right to adms. estate and requests that Abraham Dewit BODLEY and Elias J. AMES be appointed adms. (221)

10-6-1824 - Patrick LYNCH, native of Great Britain and Ireland, makes his application to become citizen. (225)

11-30-1824 - Jonathan HUNTSMAN appointed adms. of the estate of Catharine HUNTSMAN late of Perry twp. dec'd. (241)

1-8-1825 - William CLEMENTS appointed adms. of the estate of James CLEMENTS, dec'd. (241)

3-7-1825 - James POWELL appointed guardian of Joseph CLINE son of Joseph CLINE, dec'd. (246)

3-7-1825 - David BODLEY and Henry BODLEY appointed adms. of the estate of Abraham J. BEVEAR, late of Plymouth, dec'd. (246)

3-7-1825 - John EDINGTON appointed guardian of James McCALLY aged 6 yrs. & 7 mos. (247)

3-7-1825 - James FINNEY aged 14 yrs. chose Daniel COOK as his guardian. (247) Daniel Cook appointed guardian of William FINNEY aged 14 yrs., heir of Robert FINNEY, dec'd. (248) Will of Robert FINNEY presented. (248)

3-7-1825 - Lemuel BOULTER a Revolutionary Soldier having filed his Declaration, and the Court having heard the testimony and said Lemuel Boulter having sworn to and subscribed to his declaration in order to obtain a pension under the Law of Congress, are of opinion that the total amount in value of the property in the schedule annexed to his declaration is sixty eight Dollars and forty three cents. (249)

3-8-1825 - John COON appointed guardian of Margaret HUNTSMAN aged 8 yrs. & 10 mos. (251)

3-8-1825 - John EMERICK appointed guardian of Elizabeth, Christian, Rebecca Ann, Lucinda and Catharine Ann LAUGHLIN. (251)

3-8-1825 - John COON guardian of Margaret HUNTSMAN, heir of James HUNTSMAN, dec'd produced an indenture binding said Margaret to John SHANCK. (252)

3-8-1825 - John G. PETERSON guardian of Robert SMITH, an insane person, filed account. (253)

3-8-1825 - John EMERICK guardian of Christiana LAUGHLIN, orphan of John LAUGHLIN produced and indenture binding said Christiana to Henry B. CURTIS and Elizabeth his wife of Knox Co., Ohio, said Christiana to serve as a servant girl until 18 yrs. of age. (255)

3-9-1825 - Isaac GREBEN appointed adms. of the estate of John GREBEN, dec'd. (259)

3-9-1825 - Isaac HANDLY aged 17 yrs. on 19 August 1824 and James HANDLY aged 15 yrs. on 15 July 1824 chose Isaac Osburn as their guardian. (259) Will of John HANDLEY presented. (262)

5-2-1825 - Edward MURRY and Catharine YOUNGBLOOD appointed adms. of the estate of John C. YOUNGBLOOD, dec'd, late of Orange twp. (278) William YOUNG appointed adms. of the estate of Henry THOMPSON, dec'd. (278)

5-2-1825 - John WILLIAMS appointed guardian of Mary THOMPSON aged 4 yrs., heir of Henry THOMPSON. (279)

5-2-1825 - James STEEL appointed guardian of Catharine HUNTSMAN aged 11 yrs., heir of James HUNTSMAN. (279)

5-3-1825 - Will of James FORD presented, Nicholas Ford, executor. (285)

5-3-1825 - Peter HUFF aged 19 yrs. August next, heir of Gamiel HUFF, dec'd, chose Robert HUFF as his guardian. (287)

5-3-1825 - Ebenezer McDONNALD aged 14 yrs. 11 mos. 10 days chose Robert SORRELS as his guardian. (287)

5-6-1825 - James PARKER appointed guardian of ____(not given) DULING, heir of Zachariah DULING, dec'd.

8-22-1825 - Catharine LOW and Benjamin HARTMAN appointed adms. of the estate of Joseph LOW late of Monroe twp.

9-14-1825 - Will of George OSWALT late of Green twp. presented. (306)

10-10-1825 - John G. PETTERSON appointed adms. of the estate of James VAIL, dec'd late of Monroe twp. (308)

10-10-1825 - William A. JOHNSTON aged 14 yrs. 14 April last, heir of James JOHNSTON chose Daniel JOHNSTON his guardian. (309)

10-10-1825 - Catharine HUNTSMAN aged 13 yrs., heir of James HUNTSMAN, dec'd, chose Jacob MYERS her guardian. Samuel HUNTSMAN aged 16 yrs., heir of James HUNTSMAN, dec'd chose Peter WEYRICK his guardian. (310)

10-10-1825 - Elizabeth PARK appointed adms. of the estate of Matthew PARK late of Bloomingrove twp., dec'd. (310)

10-10-1825 - Will of Francis ANDREWS late of Miflin twp. presented. (311)

10-10-1825 - Charity HUFF aged 16 yrs. 31 July last, heir of Gameal HUFF chose Robert HUFF her guardian. (310)

10-10-1825 - David KENNEDY appointed guardian of Mary, Eliza and Jane McCALMON, heirs of Samuel McCALMON, dec'd. (311)

10-10-1825 - Williamson CARROTHERS appointed guardian of Samuel McCALMON and Martha McCALMON, heirs of Samuel McCALMON, dec'd. (312)

10-10-1825 - James STEWART appointed adms. of the estate of James BALLENTEIN, dec'd late of Madison twp. (312) Benjamin OGDON and John OGDON appointed adms. of the estate of Henry OGDON, dec'd. (313) Will of Joseph MARKLEY late of Montgomery twp. presented. (313) Will of Sarah BULL late of Loudenville presented. (314) Will of Catharine HUFF late of Sandusky twp. presented. (315) Will of John GRIMES(?) presented. (315)

10-11-1825 - Jane BEVIER appointed guardian of William BEVIER aged 3 yrs. and Jacob BEVIER aged 1 yr. heirs of Abraham J. BEVIER, dec'd. (324)

10-12-1825 - Will of John SNIDER late of Auburn twp. presented. (325)

10-12-1825 - Martha ELLIS aged 12 yrs., heir of Thomas ELLIS chose Levi STEPHENSON as her guardian. (326)

10-12-1825 - Levi BODLEY appointed adms. of the estate of John OUSTER late of Plymouth, dec'd. (327)

10-12-1825 - Elias SLOCUM appointed guardian of Elizabeth STAFFORD aged 4 yrs. and Jemima STAFFORD aged 6 yrs., heirs of James STAFFORD, dec'd. (328)

10-12-1825 - Will of James CHAMBERS presented. (328)

10-13-1825 - In the mater of Jeremiah CONINE a Revolutionary Soldier. In the said matter and declaration aforesaid it appears to the satisfaction of the Court that the said Jeremiah Conine did serve in the Revolutionary War as stated in the preceding declaration against the common enemy for the term of nine months under one engagement on the continental establishment and it is the opinion of the Court that the total amount in value of the property exhibited in the aforesaid schedule is sixty five dollars and one cent. (331)

10-13-1825 - Elizabeth OUSTERHOUT appointed guardian of James OUSTERHOUT aged 2 yrs. & 2 mos., heir of John OUSTERHOUT, dec'd. (332)

10-13-1825 - Martin NEAL and John EVERETT appointed adms. of the estate of Adam CASE of Washington twp. (334) Will of Thomas MOOR of Tropy twp. presented. (335)

10-14-1825 - James ROBINSON aged 16 yrs. 2 Nov. next chose John ROBINSON as his guardian. (339)

10-15-1825 - John Agner ARMSTRONG, native of Great Britain and Ireland makes his application to become citizen. (347)

The following records were copied from "Chancery Record 1", located in the Clerk of Court's Storage Records Weights and Measures, Second Floor of the Richland County Court House. The Records are under the jurisdiction of the Clerk of Court's Office. Pages on which record may be found are given in parenthesis.

Ruth PRESTON and others by Henry St. John their guardian vs. David MITCHELL In Chancery. Filed July 1823. William Preston, dec'd died intestate in Wayne County, Ohio on 8-20-1820. Children: Ruth, William, Sarah, Hannah, John and Theodocea Preston, all minors. That William Preston, dec'd and David Mitchel had entered into an article of agreement during said Preston's lifetime. (63)

Elizabeth McCALMON vs. Mary McCALMON, et al. In Chancery. Filed 2-23-1826. Land, SW¼ Section 6, Township 20, Range 18. Samuel McCalmon, dec'd, late of Washington twp. Widow, Elizabeth McCalmon. Children: Mary, Elizabeth, Jane, Samuel and Martha McCalmon. (164)

Michael TIERMAN Jr. vs. Jacob BEAM and others. In Chancery. Filed 9-27-1824. That Michael Tierman recovered two judgements against Jacob Beam, then and noe of Richland County, Ohio in the Common Pleas Court of Belmont Co., Ohio in the August Term 1817. That Beams land in Richland County consisting of the NE¼ Section 36 and SE¼ Section 25, Township 21, Range 18 was purchased 5-31-1811 from Jacob Newman. That Jacob Newman died in 1813 leaving Andrew Coffenbury and James McClure as his executors. Widow, Susannah Newman of Richland Co.; Children: Jacob Newman, and Catharine wife of John Free of Franklin Co., Pa.; Henry Newman, Andrew Newman and Joseph Newman of Richland County, the last two named being minors. (169)

James H. DAY and David COULTER adms. of the Estate of Jabez PARKER vs. Heirs of Jabez PARKER. Filed March 1825. Petition to sell certificate for E½ SW¼ Section 35, Township 21, Range 16. Administrators state that they do not know the names of the heirs of Jabez Parker. (198)

James RAMSEY and David WALLACE executors of William WALLACE, dec'd vs. Luke McGUIRE adms. of James McGUIRE, dec'd, et al. In Chancery. Filed Oct. 1826. William Walace late of Brooke Co., Va. James McGuire Sr., died on 3-20-1819 at Brooke Co., Va.; in his lifetime borrowed $450.00 from William Wallace, dec'd with mortgage on SW¼ Section 13, Township 23, Range 19 and E½ Section 20, Township 22, Range19 of lands sold at Wooster, being situated in Richland Co. Heirs of James McGuire, Luke McGuire, James Brown and Jane his wife, George Baxter and Ruth his wife, all of Brooke Co. Va., Edison McGuire, Nicholas McGuire, George Davis and Margaret his wife, William Davis and Mary his wife, Thomas Thorley and Patience his wife, Ebenezer Davis, Edward Davis, Catharine Davis, Patience Davis and Ruth Davis, all of Tuscarawas Co., Ohio; the last four named being minors. (203)

Margaret JAQUES vs Jeremiah JAQUES, et al. In Chancery. Filed Feb. 1829. Land, SW¼ Section 17, Township 21, Range 18. Samuel Jaques, dec'd. Widow, Margaret Jaques. Children: Jeremiah Jaques, Sanford Jaques, David Jaques, And wife of Richard Condon, Samuel Jaques, Nancy Jaques, Warren Jaques, John Jaques and Jesse Jaques. (304)

Samuel PHIPPS vs. Mary PHIPPS et al. In Chancery. Filed 5-17-1826. Samuel Phipps of Jefferson twp., Richland County formerly of Westmoreland Co., Pa. in 1815 gave money to Robert Phipps to buy land in Ohio; said Robert bought land in Jefferson twp. being 160 acres SW¼ and 160 acres NW¼ Section 17, Township 21, Range 17 which he retained entirely in his own name. Robert Phipps died in January 1826. Widow, Sarah Phipps. _Four_ children: Mary, Isabella, Margaret, Sarah and Samuel Phipps Jr. (note: five children are named, but it states specifically that there were four.) (221)

Joseph CURRAN and Matthias HIMES adms. with will annexed of the estate of Alexander CURRAN, dec'd vs. Stephen B. CURRAN, et al. Petition to sell land. Filed May 1826. Land, deceased possessed two undivided third parts of 90 acres of Virginia Military District school land in E part SE¼ Section 15, Township 21, Range 18. Children: John, Alexander, William F., Cartmell, Hamilton and Eliza Curran, minors by Jacob Parker their guardian; and Stephen B. Curran. (240)

Sarah PHIPPS vs. Henry CLAPPER, et al. In Chancery. Filed 9-22-1826. Sarah Phipps of Richland County states that on about 7-15-1824 she was married to Robert Phipps late of Richland County, now deceased and that said Robert died about 1-11-1826 leaving Henry Clapper executor of his will. That said Robert Phipps, dec'd had five children by his former wife as follows: Polly Phipps aged 13 yrs., Margaret Phipps aged 12 yrs., Isabella Phipps aged 11 yrs., Sarah Phipps aged 9 yrs. and Samuel Phipps (note: age not given), all residents of Richland County except Margaret who resides in Pennsylvania. (278)

Adms. of Nathaniel ATWOOD. Petition to make deed. Filed 2-19-1828. John Edsall, Samuel Edsall and Hannah Curran late Atwood, adms. of estate of Nathaniel Atwood, dec'd petition to make deed to SE¼ Section 24, Township 21, Range 19 to Silas Pearce as contracted in 1819 by said deceased. (281)

John HENLEY and Margaret WELCH executors of the will of John WELCH, dec'd vs. Jane WELCH. Petition to sell land. Filed 2-20-1827. Land, NW¼ Section 22, Township 24, Range 17 sold in Canton land district. John Welch late of Washington Co., Pa. died there. Widow, Margaret. Daughter, Jane. (313)

Isaac CHARLES and Anna CHARLES adms. of the estate of Elijah CHARLES, dec'd. Petition to make deed. Filed March 1829. Elijah Charles in his lifetime on 6-21-1819 at Mansfield contracted to John Dickson of same place 160 acres NE¼ Section 19, Township 24, Range 17. Children: Isaac, Charles, Sarah wife of John Dickson, Nancy wife of William Taggart, John Charles, Mary Charles, Samuel Charles, Elijah Charles, Elizabeth Charles, Stephenson Charles and Esther Charles; the last four named being minors. (330)

Elizabeth TAYLOR and Isaac CHARLES adms. of the estate of Samuel TAYLOR, dec'd. Petition to make deed. Filed March 1829. Land, 40 acres E side NE¼ Section 18, Township 24, Range 17. Samuel Taylor in his lifetime on Oct. 1826 contracted said land to James Porter. Heirs of Samuel Taylor, dec'd; John Taylor, Isaac Taylor, William Taylor, Francis Taylor, Abraham Taylor, Benjamin Taylor, Mary Woodmansee, Hannah Bayard, Nancy Taylor, Mary Young, John Young, Rebecca Young, Abraham Young, Elizabeth Young and William Young and Hannah Young. (339)

William STOUDT and Mary his wife vs. William Monroe SANDERSON. Petition for Dower.
Filed May 1828. Land, part NW¼ Section 7, Township 21, Range 18. Henry Sanderson,
dec'd. Widow, Mary now the wife of William Stoudt. Son, William Monroe Sanderson,
a minor. (333)

James N. AYERS adms. of the estate of John B. TAYLOR. Petition to make deed.
Filed May 1829. Land, SW¼ Section 14, Township 22, Range 19 in Canton land district.
John B. Taylor on 10-30-1821 in his lifetime contracted at Sharon said land to Henry
Taylor. John P. Taylor died August 12th last at Sharon. Children: John, Charles,
Elener, Evelina and Bennet Taylor; minors. Also that John B. Taylor and Henry Taylor
jointly owned NE¼ Section 13, Township 22, Range 19 late the property of Walter Tay-
lor their deceased brother. (347)

Jacob VAN HOUTON and Levi GUNSAULIES adms. of the estate of Ephraim S. AMES vs. Elias
J. AMES. Petition to sell land. Filed 9-20-1828. Land, 50 acres East end SE¼ Section 9, Township 23, Range 19 possessed by Ames by title bond given by Abraham Bevin
who died intestate leaving William and Jacob Bevin his minor heirs. Ephraim S. Ames
left widow Mary Ames and son Elias J. Ames as his only heirs. (355)

Elizabeth TAYLOR vs. John TAYLOR, et al. In Chancery for Dower. Filed 8-27-1828.
Land, 160 acres NE¼ Section 18, Township 24, Range 17 in Wooster land district.
Samuel Taylor, dec'd. Widow, Elizabeth, That Samuel Taylor died without issue leav-
ing the following brothers and sisters and their children, to-wit: John Taylor;
Isaac Taylor; William Taylor; Francis Taylor; Abraham Taylor; Benjamin Taylor; Mary
wife of Thomas Woodmansee; Hannah wife of George Bayard; Nancy Taylor; Sarah Young,
dec'd, her children—Mary, John, Rebecca, Abraham, Elizabeth, Hannah and William
Young. (371)

Charles SAVERS (SAVIERS) adms. of the estate of George ULLERY, dec'd. Petition to
make deed. Filed May 1829. George Ullery in his lifetime in 1825 at Milton, Richland Co. contracted to James Grimes the SE¼ Section 1, Township 22, Range 18. George
Ullery departed this life 8-7-1827 at Franklin, Richland Co. Children: Henry, Polly,
Aaron, Rebecca, George, Ephraim, John and Samuel Ullery, all minors except Henry.
(378)

Jacob PARKER adms. of the estate of John HINDMAN, dec'd vs. Harriet HINDMAN, et al.
Petition to sell land. Filed 3-14-1829. Land, quarter section of land in Sandusky Co.,
Ohio NE¼ Section 9, Township 5, Range 16 being 160 acres sold in Delaware land dis-
trict. John Hindman, dec'd, died in 1822. Four children: Harriet, Susan, John and
Elizabeth Hindman, all minors of Bedford Co., Pennsylvania. (414)

John BAILEY adms. of the estate of Nathaniel BAILEY, dec'd vs. Nancy BAILEY, et al.
Petition to sell land. Filed 3-10-1829. Land, NE¼ Section 33, Township 25, Range 17.
Widow, Mary Bailey. Heirs: Nancy, Mary, Nathaniel, Elias and John Bailey. (420)

Benjamin L. BROWN adms. of the estate of Richard ROBERTS vs. Sarah ROBERTS, et al.
Petition to sell real estate. Filed March 1829. Land, 160 acres SW¼ Section 29,
Township 19, Range 18. Widow, Sarah Roberts. Children: Rachel and Ann Roberts.
(437)

Henry FORGESON et al. vs. Alfred LINCOLN. In Chancery. Filed March 1830. John Forgeson in his lifetime held certificate from Wooster land district for 160 acres SE¼ Section 13, Township 22, Range 19 in Richland County of which he sold 100 acres to Lincoln in exchange for 320 acres in Illinois. John Forgeson, dec'd. Widow, Jane Forgeson. Children: Henry Forgeson, Elizabeth Forgeson, Eleanor wife of Abraham Pittenger, Margaret wife of William Porter, Ruth Forgeson, John Forgeson, William Forgeson, Nimrod Forgeson, James Forgeson and Jane Forgeson Jr.; the last five named being minors by Jane Forgeson their guardian. (448)

John STEWART adms. of the estate of William McCONAHEY vs. William McCONAHEY. Petition to sell land. Filed 5-22-1829. Land, 160 acres SE¼ Section 34, Township 21, Range 18. William McConahey died intestate in 1825. Heirs: William and Isabella McConahey, both minors of Belmont County, Ohio. (461)

Mariah MURPHY and Edward TRECKLE adms. of the estate of James MURPHY, dec'd vs. Juliann MURPHY, et al. Petition to sell land. Filed 10-20-1829. Land, part SW¼ Section 30, Township 23, Range 16. Widow, Mariah Murphy. Heirs: Julia Ann Murphy, Eliza Jane Murphy and Mary Ann Murphy. (468)

William LOCKHART adms. of estate of John PUGH vs. Mary PUGH. Petition to sell lands Filed 10-19-1829. Land, Lot 24 in 1st quarter Township 5, Range 18 of Salt Reserve of U. S. Military District being 110.88 acres sold at Delaware, Ohio. One child and heir, Mary Pugh, a minor of Hampshire Co., Virginia. (473)

John GRAHAM and Ruth GRAHAM vs. Lydia S. WOODWARD. In Chancery for Dower. Filed 10-8-1829. John Woodward, dec'd contracted 12-25-1822 to Charles Spooner W½ SW¼ Section 9, Township 19, Range 19. Heirs: Lydia Woodward, Malvina Woodward, Ezra S. Woodward and Drusilla Woodward. (480)

Matthew PECKEN (PICKEN) adms. Petition to make deed. Filed March 1831. Matthew Pecken contracted in his lifetime on 7-28-1830 to sell NE¼ Section 8, Township 22, Range 17 to Fredrick Switzer. Matthew Pecken (Picken) died intestate in Harrison Co., Ohio. Brothers and Sisters: Jane wife of James English. Elizabeth wife of Thomas Fisher, Sarah wife of John Donaghey, Matilda wife of George Barton, Susannah wife of Hamilton McFadden, Alphas Pecken, Alexander Picken and William Picken; all of Harrison Co., Ohip; the last two named being minors. (497)

John FINCH and Elizabeth HALFERTY adms. of the estate of William HALFERTY, dec'd vs. James HALFERTY et al. Petition to sell land. Filed March 1830. Land, N½ NE¼ & NW¼ Section 17, Township 19, Range 19. William Halferty died intestate in 1828. Widow, Elizabeth Halferty. Children: James, Edward, Margaret, Isabella, John, William, Mary, Robert and Jane Halferty, all minors of Richland Co. (561)

Andrew PERKINS adms. of the Estate of Thomas McQUOWN vs. David McQUOWN, et al. Petition to sell land. Filed 5-4-1830. Land, 80 acres SE corner SW¼ Section 30 and 63 acres part NE corner NW¼ Section 31, Township 20, Range 18. Widow, Margaret. Children: David, Andrew, Allsworth, Peggy Jane, Mary Eliza, Thomas and Harrison McQuown. (571)

James PURDY and Cunningham HAZELETT adms. of the estate of Patrick B. PURDY, dec'd vs. Archibald PURDY, et al. Petition to sell land. Filed 2-18-1831. Land, W½ SW¼ Section 4, Township 21, Range 19, Widow, Jane Purdy Sr. Heirs: James Purdy, Archibald Purdy, Alexander W. Purdy, Jane Purdy, Esther wife of Seth Hull, Sarah wife of Cunningham Hazlett, and Mary wife of John B. Craighed.   (579)

James DOUGHERTY adms. of the estate of Abraham GLOSSER, dec'd vs. Henry GLOSSER, et al. Petition to sell land. Filed 6-14-1831. Land, Lot 60 in Bellville. Widow, Ann Glosser. Children: Henry Glosser, Margaret Ann Glosser and Gillman Glosser.   (589)

Charlotte SAMS adms. of the estate of Miles J. VANORMAN, dec'd vs. Elizabeth VANORMAN, et al. Petition to sell land. Filed 10-19-1829. Land, 40 acres SW corner NW¼ Section 25, Township 18, Range 20(?). Widow, Charlotte Vandorman now Charlotte Sams. Heirs: Elizabeth, Sophia, Jasper, Clarissa, Jerusha, Nancy, Amanda, Rachel and Ira Vannorman.   (613)

Gideon BIGELOW and Mary BIGELOW vs. John McCART et al. In Chancery for Dower. Filed 2-15-1831. Land, SE¼ Section 25, Township 23, Range 19. Henry McCART, dec'd. Widow, Mary now the wife of Gideon Bigelow; Mary married Henry McCart in 1801. Children: Henry McCart of Richland Co., John McCart, Jesse McCart both of Fairfield Co. Ohio, Martha McCart, Esther McCart, Sarah McCart, Mary McCart, Rachel McCart, Amy McCart and Abraham Perry McCart; the last seven named being minors and all of Richland County.   (630)

Polly SMITH vs. Tunis(?) SMITH, et al. In Chancery for Dower. Filed 10-13-1830. That Gasper Smith now deceased became seized on 8-21-1826 of 80 acres part of Section 17, Township 22, Range 20; that Gasper died on 9-15-1829 leaving as his widow Polly Smith. That Gasper Smith married Polly on 7-24-1814 in Huntington Co., Pennsylvania. Seven children: Tunis(?) Smith aged about 15 yrs., Hannah Smith aged about 12 yrs., Jacob Smith aged about 10 yrs., Sarah Smith aged about 8 yrs., Catharine Smith aged about 6 yrs., Hester Smith aged about 3 yrs. and Mary Smith aged about 2 yrs.   (641)

Joseph CELLAR and Agness CELLAR executors of Joseph CELLAR, dec'd vs. John CELLAR, et al. Petition in Chancery. Filed 5-4-1832. Land, SW¼ Section 20, Township 20, Range 16 in Canton land district. Widow, Agness. Sons: John and Joseph Cellar. Daughters: Mary former Cellar wife of Thomas Wright; Eliza formerly Cellar wife of John Gault, Martha Cellar; and Sarah Cellar.   (665)

William CHURCH and Samuel JOHNSTON adms. of the estate of Daniel JOHNSTON, dec'd vs. Eliza JOHNSTON, et al. Petition to sell land. Filed 5-23-1832. Land, SE¼ Section 34, Township 21, Range 19. Widow Rachel Johnston. Heirs: Eliza, William D., Thomas S., Augustus T., Amasa, James J., Samuel S., Sally Ann and Matilda Johnston. (671)

Jacob FLACK adms. of the estate of William HALL, dec'd vs Melinda HALL, et al. Petition to sell land. Filed 6-15-1831. Land, W½ SW¼ Section 12, Township 19, Range 20. Widow, Mary Hall. Children: Melinda, Sarah, Isaac, Lydia, John, Elizabeth and Charlista Ann Hall.   (675)

2-18-1833 - Orlando METCALF and Jefferson REYNOLDS guardians of the Heirs of William REYNOLDS, dec'd. Petition to sell land. Filed 5-21-1832. Land, SE¼ Section 17 and NW¼ Section 20, Township 21, Range 18. Heirs: George, Rebekah, John, William, Harris and Carolina Reynolds. (690)

6-17-1833 - Arthur RUARK executor of will of William RORICK, dec'd. vs. Margaret RORICK, et al. Petition to sell land. Filed 10-31-1832. Land, NE¼ Section 15, Township 21, Range 18 Virginia Military School lands. Widow, Margaret Rorick. Heirs: Henry, Jonas, Rowland P., William and Jesse Rorick. (735)

John L. COULTER adms. of the estate of Herny ROOP, dec'd vs. Eliza ROOP, et al. To Complete Contract. Filed 6-15-1833. Henry Roope in his lifetime on 3-20-1830 contracted to Edwin Grant one undivided half of in-lots 256, 257, & 258 in Mansfield. Children of Henry Roop: Eliza and William M. Roop, not of age. (737)

William DOWNEY vs. Joseph CAIRNS, et al. In Chancery to correct error. Filed 5-11-1830. On 9-1-1819 Joseph Cairns then of Mansfield, now of Columbus, Franklin Co., Ohio sold in-lot 128 Mansfield to John McLINCHY, late of Mansfield who died 11-27-1826 leaving as his heirs: John, William, Michael and Nancy McLinchey, all of Richland Co. and all minors. (740)

450

The following marriages are from Marriage Record A-B. It should be noted that no returns appear to have been recorded for the years 1801 and 1802

BATES, Emer to Mary GREENLEE - Paxton Twp.	4-12-1804
BEATY, Adam to Polly REED	8-30-1798
BECK, Alexander to Mary McKENNEY	11-28-1804
BENSON, Rozen to Jane JOAT	3-8-1804
BLAIR, James to Hannah KARTER	11-24-1799
BOLTEN, James to Nancy COX	6-23-1803
BOOTS, Martin to Eve ARAHOOD	6-18-1804
BOWERS, Adam to Betsey FLOOD	1-5-1804
BOYD, Jonathan to Elizabeth HEART	7-7-1803
BRITTON, Nathan to Ketty STEVENS	2-28-1800
BROWN, Andrew to Jane GALLASPIE	2-22-1804
CAMBRIDGE, James to Polly NICKINS	8-14-1804
CHERRY, Andrew to Elizabeth REDDING	9-12-1803
CLARK, Jonathan to . . . . GUTHREY (no name given)	9-29-1800
CLARK, William to Martha CLARK	12-12-1799
CMAM (McMANN?), Joseph to Elizabeth McCARTNEY	3-12-1799
COBLER, David to Ann Freeman	9-4-1804
COCHRAN, James to Rachel KERR	8-30-1804
COGHRAN (COCHRAN), William to Betsey McNAIRY	1-3-1799
COMER, John to Sarah BARBEE	12-22-1803
COMER, William to Nancy BARBEE(both of Jefferson Twp.)	7-5-1804
CONNER, William to Sarah BRADLY	7-20-1800
COONE, Adam to Hannah MARQUIS	6-??-1804
COOPER, John to Rebeccah MOORE	1-3-1804
COUGLE, Alexander to Mary CROW	1-12-1804
COUNTS, Joseph to Betsey McCAFFERTY	4-3-1800
CRABB, Reuben to Polly CLEVENGER	3-24-1804
CRAWFORD, Hugh to Margaret KLYNE	12-27-1799
CROOK, Joseph to Susannah GIBLAR	10-13-1803
CROUCH, Andrew to Eleoner CROUSH	8-7-1800
CROUCH, Joseph to Margaret McCALL	1-31-1804
DAVIS, Benjamin to Patty REDING	4-14-1803
DAVIS, Isaac to Mary RECTOR	3-18-1800
DELAY, Jonathan to Deborah HOLLINSHEAD - Green Twp.	6-5-1804
DEVORE, Josias to Catherine WHETSONE	5-17-1803
DICKISON, Isaac to Peggy MARTIN	4-5-1804
DINES, James to Leah LITTLETON	1-2-1804
DOWNING, Francis to Elizabeth FOSTER	4-19-1804
DOWNING, Meshair to Sarah DOWNING	12-27-1799
DUNLAP, Robert to Rebecah TAYLOR - Paxton Twp.	3-29-1804
EATORS, Jacob to Nancy SOLLARS	4-13-1804
ENGLAND, John to Anna BURK	9-24-1804
FINLEY, John P. to Sarah STRAIN	2-7-1803
FLEATH, John to Nancy TOMLIN	8-2-1804
FLENEGEN, Samuel to Betsey MOORHEAD	12-5-1798
FOSTER, Jacob to Sarah CLARK	4-3-1804
FRANKLIN, Sam'l to Rebecca CARPENTER	7-2-1803
FREELAND, Luke to Ruth THOMPSON	2-29-1804
FUNK, Abraham to Elizabeth FEALHER	5-27-1800

```
GASKINS, James to Mary McCOLLUM                                    9-22-1803
GLAZE, Richard to Nancy VANMICKLE (VANWICKLE)                      9-27-1804
GRAMBEL, Daniel to Sally JONES                                     1-1-1804
GRAVES, Elexander to Rebeccah COMER                               11-28-1803
GREEN, Allen to Nelly FITSCHARLES                                 12-11-1800
GREEN, William to Hannah Anderson - Scioto Twp.                    2-27-1804
GRIMES, Thomas to Elenor MOUNTS - TeTe Twp.                        7-16-1804
GRUBB, Daniel to Barbary STREVY                                   12-13-1803
GUTHREY, George to Sarah HOWARD                                    7-20-1799
GUTHREY, John to Eliner HOWARD                                    12-27-1799
HALL, James to Abey STACHER                                       10-11-1804
HARBERT, Richard to Catren VANDASON                                1-5-1804
HARVEY, Richard Esq. to Elizabeth DUVOIS                           4-22-1800
HAYNES, William to Sarah DICKSON                                   9-11-1798
HENRY, Samuel to Letitia BELL                                     10-7-1800
HILL, Henry to Eve NICKIUS                                         6-22-1803
HODDY, William to Elizabeth COREY                                  8-27-1799
HOWARD, Lewis to Marion BURNS                                     12-29-1803
HOWARD, Lida to Sarah BODKIN                                      10-6-1803
HUBBARD, Jacob to Elizabeth STACKHOUSE                             9-8-1804
HUBBARD, Titus to Elizabeth GREENWOOD    (No date given  -  1804?)
HUFF, Joseph to Hanna FINLEY                                       4-7-1803
JAMISON, George to Jean DAVIS                                      5-10-1804
JENES, Frederick to Catharine TREESUM(?)                         12-20-1804
JOHNSTON, James to Eleanor TIMMONS                                 9-20-1804
KELLER, George to Betsey TELBILL                                 10-15-1803
KELLY, Andrew to Ann CATING                                        3-22-1804
KILGORE, James to Anna FOLTEN - PAXTON TWp.                        4-15-1804
KUHNS, John to Metilda DESBORD                                     5-22-1800
LATON, Elias to Abigail WILLIAMS (dau. of Ann WILLIAMS)            1-10-1804
LOCKARD, Elijah to Betsey FLEMING                                 9-11-1798
LOCKHARD, William to Mary DOLL                                     1-16-1804
LONG, Robert to Catharine GOWENS - Scioto Twp.                    7-15-1803
LOVELAND, Joseph to Nancy SHALLENBERGER                           5-20-1800
LOWTHER, George to Becky SNYDER                                    6-3-1800
McCAFFERTY, James to Elizabeth RICHARDSON                          1-25-1804
McCAULES, John to Nancy FLEEMIN - Peakasin Twp.                    4-21-1800
McCONNELL, William to Susannah PANCAKE                             3-22-1804
McCOY, Joseph to Jenny McNAIRY                                     6-20-1799
McCULLOUGH, John to Catherine MYERS                              10-11-1804
McDONALD, John to Catherine CUTRIGHT                               2-5-1799
McDOUGAL, James to Elinor BRITTAIN                                 2-9-1804
McDOUGAL, John to Margaret STOCKDON                               11-12-1799
McGILL, Hugh to Sarah EAKINS                                       6-1-1803
McGUIRE, Robert to Rescilla CLARK                                 8-29-1804
McGUIRE, Thomas to Nancy McGUIRE - Scioto Twp.                     6-7-1804
McKEE, John to Jane ALEXANDER                                      8-22-1803
McLEAN, Jeremiah to Sally SHEARER                                  2-17-1800
McMACHLAM(?), Benjamin to Nancy BOGGS                              Nov. 1804
MACHES, . . . . to Jennie SKIDMORE (SKIEMORE)                      1-9-1800
        (no name given)    of Franklinton, Ross Co.
MALONE, Haatley to Margarete JOHNSON                               7-28-1803
```

```
MARGER, John to Catherine CALDWELL                              4-20-1800
MARIM, Richard to Ruth CORWIN                                   9-7-1800
MILLER, John to Betsey CAILES                                   8-24-1804
MILLER, Robert to Fanny MOONEY                                  6-14-1804
MINER, Philip to Elizabeth RICHARD                              3-24-1803
MONTGOMERY, William to Mary CROUCH                              1-17-1804
MOUNTAIN, James to Rebeccah CAMPBELL                            6-28-1804
MURPHY, William to Deborey FLOUSON                              8-24-1804
NIBLACH, William to Sidney CLARK                                1-25-1804
NORTON, Moses to Polly WHITECOTTON - Pipe Twp.                  2-12-1804
NOTEMAN, Andrew to Catty WEEKS                                  4-1-1800
NOTEMAN, Andrew to Betsey McCUNE                                8-30-1804
OBRIAN, John to Polly FOSTER                                    1-22-1804
PAGE, John to Margaret EMMERY                                   7-19-1804
PARKER, William to Elizabeth DAVIS                              8-2-1803
PEDICK, Joshua to Temer COMBER                                  4-7-1800
PEERCE, Thomas to Betsey FRANCIS                                8-21-1804
PETTY, Joseph to Ave MARE (WARE?)                              11-24-1799
RAGOI, Thomas John to Catherine VALENTINE                       5-5-1804
RICHARDS, Jacob to Rosey NOULEN                                 4-29-1800
RICHARDSON, Samuel to Mary COMER                                6-2-1803
RIDDON, John to Nancy SHEFUS                                   11-14-1804
RIESTINE, Barnett to Jane WRIGHT                                6-5-1800
RIGHT, David to Polly COOK                                      5-15-1800
ROBERTS, Daniel to Rebeccah HINTON                             3-6-1804
ROBERTSON, Alexander to Rebecca STEVENSON                       2-1-1799
ROGERS, Benjamin to Betsey JACKSON                             1-3-1799
ROULT, James to Abigail WILLET - Scioto Twp.                   11-11-1803
RUDIE, William to Rachel COX                                    4-7-1803
RUSH, Henry to Rachel CREVISTON                                1-29-1804
RUSH, James to Polly CREVISTON                                 3-20-1804
RUSH, William to Nelly GRAVES                                  1-24-1804
SHANTEN, Abraham to Hanah JACKSON                              5-3-1800
SHAW, Samuel to Elizabeth KIRKPATRICK                          3-31-1800
SHEPHERD, David to Elizabeth BETZ                              7-19-1803
SHEPHERD, James to Francis DAILY                               12-2-1804
SHERLOCK, Edward to Margaret FAULKNER                          1-12-1799
SHOCK, Michael to Sally SOLLERS                                3-15-1804
SMITH, (AARASMITH), John Arra to Rebecca CROUCH                8-21-1804
SMITH, Robert to Dinah NICOLSON                                12-30-1799
SMITH, (ARRONSMITH), Samuel Arron to Elizabeth THILLER         11-27-1804
SNEL, Thomas to Nancy ABET                                     2-13-1804
SNYDER, Isaac to Polly LOWTHER                                 4-15-1800
STAGGS, William to Betsey CLAWSON                              4-5-1804
STITT, James to Sally HILL                                     1-12-1804
STOCKEY, Abraham to Eve BUSH                                   6-2-1803
STRONS (STROUS), MICH'L to Mary WALKER                         3-31-1803
TARCUSON, George to Rebecca ROSS                               10-18-1803
TAYLOR, Drake to Sarah FITSCHARLES                            4-9-1800
TEMPLIN, Solmon to Agnes WILSON                                5-5-1803
THOMAS, John to Catherine PUTMAN                               10-13-1803
THOMPSON, Mathew to Polly HENDERSON                            5-6-1800
```

453

```
TIFFIN, Joseph to Nancy WOOD                                    10-20-1803
TIGER, Samuel to Elizabeth SAMMAS                               4-3-1804
TINLOW, William to Jean RODYWAS                                 2-2-1804
TOMLIN, John to Rebeccah Foster                                 1-1-1804
TOMLIN, Richard to Catherine TOMLIN                             12-6-1804
TOUJON (TOUJOU), Andrew to Elizabeth YONSTON                    11-27-1798
VANCE, William of Belmont Co. to Mary KIRK, Scioto Twp.         3-22-1804
                                           Ross Co.
WASHBURN, James to Elizabeth CONTRIMAN                          7-20-1803
WEBB, Elisha to Mary TOMLIN                                     12-4-1804
WEBSTER, James Brice to Millia DAWSON                           3(?)-24-1804
WESTFALL, Cornelius to Sarah RUMSVNERS                          1-12-1804
WHETZELL, Daniel to Martha SMITH                                1-11-1804
WHITNEY, Thomas to Marcia EMMORY                                7-12-1804
WILFONG, David to Susannah CHAP                                 7-19-1804
WILKINSON, Thomas to Kitty LINKSYLLER                           4-16-1799
WILLIAMS, Elias to Christian CONTRMAN                           9-24-1804
WILLIAMS, George to Elizabeth DELAY                             2-26-1799
WILLIAMS, George to Sarah CAVENDER                             11-15-1804
```

———————————

ROSS COUNTY, OHIO - MARRIAGES 1803-1807

Contributed by: Mrs. Patrick Clark, Route 10, Box 76, Chillicothe, Ohio 45601

Explanation: The following marriages were copies from Marriage Record A-B, which is a book now located in the Probate Court of this county. Dates and names have been given exactly as found in this original record. However, in surveying these records in their original form before they were alphabetized, it would appear that a number of these marriages actually took place in 1806, although the date given is 1805. These marriages have been designated by an (*) asterisk. It is emphasized and it should be taken into consideration that the person making, or transcribing this record, was an exceptionally poor in spelling.

                        Also, in aiding the genealogical researcher to reconcile these records with Bible and other records he may have; it should be explained that in the July, 1903 issue of the OLD NORTHWEST GENEALOGICAL QUARTERLY a list of Ross County, Ohio marriages was published. At that time the source from which the records were copies was stated as, "copied from the original deerskin bound folio, Book A, May 21, 1903". This article further stated that "the entries are nearly all in the handwriting of the different justices....no records can be found previous to April, 1803". At the present time (1970), nothing is known of the deerskin bound folio, Book A; and the present Marriage Record A-B does contain marriages for as early as 1798 (Note-see July, 1969 issues of GATEWAY, Ross County, Ohio Marriages 1798-1804). * Marie Clark and Anita Short, C.G.

*Pages 451-453, this volume.

Notes in parenthesis - by transcriber, Marie Clark
Notes in parenthesis preceded by "NW" - denotes differences found in article
of July, 1903 in OLD NORTHWEST GENEALOGICAL QUARTERLY.

ADAMSON, Isaac to Anna McCune   1-8-1807
ALEXANDER, James to Polly Hatton - Jefferson twp.   2-1-1805*
ANDERSON, William to Lida Hopkins   6-20-1805
ATCHISON, Phielden to Hannah Pancake   7-3-1806
ATER, Isaac to Betsey Smith (NW - 3-21-1804)   3-21-1805
ATERS, Geo. to Mary Branmick   3-29-1805*
AUSTRILL, Wm. to Rebecca Warren - Franklin twp.   3-27-1807
BAKER, John to Mary Johnston   (NW - 2-18-1806)   2-18-1805*
BAKER, Joseph to Martha Jackson   (NW - 1-28-1806   1-28-1805*
BAKER, Wm. to Sarah Jackson   11-6-1806
BALDWIN, Francis to Margaret Mealhouse -Scioto twp.(NW-Meachouse)5-23-1805
BARKER, Wm. to Sarah Hubbard   3-26-1807
BARNES, James to Elizabeth Sergent   (NW - 1-20-1806)   1-20-1805*
BARR, Amos to Margaret Anderson   1-22-1807
BATES, Samuel to Jane Hankins (NW - Daniel Bates)   10-3-1805
BEACHER, Frederick to Christian Larkings   1-24-1805
BERRY, James to Nancy Smith (NW - Benny - 1-9-1805)   11-14-1805
BERRY, Stephen to Jenny Greelee - Paxton twp.   11-13-1806
BLAZIER, Phinias to Mary _____ (not given)   5-5-1805
BLUNIER, Benjamin to Sarah Paverman (NW - Oaverman)   2-14-1805
BONNER, Abraham to Elizabeth Bryan - Concord twp.   1-6-1807
BOOTS, Martin to Mary Odle.- Jefferson twp.   (NW - 9-1-1805)   8-31-1805
BOWDLE, Joseph to Lucretia Brown   2-21-1807
BRADLEY, Isaac to Eleanor Scott   10-3-1805
BRIGGS, Walter to Morgan Reeves   4-24-1805*
BRINEY, John to Elsy Blue   5-8-1806*
BROWN, Edward to Lesly Brown   12-5-1806
BROWN, John to Ann Sollars (NW - 1-5-1806)   1-5-1805*
BROWN, Thos. to Elizabeth Bowdle   2-12-1807
BROWN, Wm. to Dianna Brown   1-8-1807
BUCK, Joseph to Ann Buck   6-5-1805
BURGAN, Wm. to Catherine_____(name or date not given)   (1805-6?)
BUSKIRK, John to Juda Clifton   2-12-1807
CARREE, Wm. to Ann Beever (NW - Bureer - 12-10-1805)   12-19-1805
CARPENTER, Elisha to Elizabeth Odle (NW - 2-5-1806)   2-5-1805*
CARTER, Thomas to Barbara Given (NW - 1-12-1806)   1-12-1805*
CASEY, John to Hannah Bush   6-5-1805
CASTT, _____(not given) to Deborah Purtee   6-9-1805*
CHERRY, Zachariah A. to Elizabeth McCune (mo. & da. not given)   -----1806
CLARAGE, William to Mary Cox   2-3-1805
CLARK, Abraham to Sarah Jamison   5-8-1805
CLARK, Wm. to Pheby Elzy - Jefferson twp.   7-19-1805*
CLARK, Wm. to Kitty Brown   12-2-1806
COLLINS, Wm. of Adams Co. to Percila Guthrie of Ross Co.   2-19-1807
COOK, John to Letitia Ross (NW - 11-16-1805)   11-15-1805
COOPER, Joel to June McMullin - Jefferson twp.(NW-Jane-3-5-1806) 2-7-1805*
CORDER, George to Jennie Ross (NW - Carder - 2-19-1804)   2-16-1805
COX, Nathan to Ann Dixon - Jefferson twp.   12-1-1806

CREERFIELD, Moses to Sally Whitecotten - Tick twp.(NW - Overfield)5-9-1805
CRABB, Edward to Nancy Smith (NW - 3-20-1806)   3-20-1805*
CRABB, Henry to Nancy Driver (no date given)   (1805-6?)
CRABB, Jacob to Nancy Champ   8-8-1805
CRABB, Jeremiah to Annabella Anderson (NW - 1-28-1806)   1-30-1805*
CRABB, Ozmond to Mary Hubb   (year not given)   12-16-(1806)
CRAGO, Jonathan to Susannah Moss (mo. & da. not given)   ----1806
CRIDER, Jacob to Rebecca Downs   9-4-1805*
CRIDER, Michael to Elizabeth Smith (NW - 3-10-1804)   3-10-1805
CRISPIN, John to Rachel Postogate   8-13-1805*
CROUSE, David to Elizabeth Boggs   1-13-1807
CUTTER, John to Mary Wilbourn   2-8-1807
CUTRIGHT, Andrew to Phebe Angle - Jefferson twp.   8-13-1806
DAVIDSON, Samuel to Elizabeth Muckelhany   11-13-1806
DAVIS, David W. to Elizabeth Braninburgh (NW - Bramonburgh)   1-27-1805
DAY, Peter to Elizabeth Day   red. 12-18-1805*
DELANY, Isaac to Patty Jones - Jefferson twp.   6-4-1805
DEVALT, Nicholas to Frankey Popejoy   2-12-1807
DEVORSE, Joseph to Catherine Miller   4-18-1807
DICKISON, Isaac to Peggy Martin   4-5-1805
DILCEVER, Michael to Hannah Coon (NW - Delcever - 4-13-1805) 4-11-1805
DIX, John to Elizabeth Boyers of Chillicothe (NW - Dise)   7-14-1805
DIXON, Joseph to Ann Radliff - Jefferson twp.   1-8-1807
DONOUGH, Robt. to Precilla Stephens   6-27-1805
DORSEN, Zadock to Ann Oneal   8-11-1805
DOWNS, David to Sarah Murphy (NW - 10-17-1805)   10-27-1805
DOWNS, John to Caroline Holder   9-3-1805*
DOWNS, Thos. to Susannah Figart   3-12-1807
DUGAN, Thos. to Nancy Hewitt (NW - 2-24-1806)   2-24-1805*
EAMINS, John to Nancy Moss (NW - 4-16-1805)   4-16-(1805?)
EARL, Granthem to Margaret Funston   8-8-1805
ELLIOTT, David to Betsy Svarts (1806 written in pencil)   3-13-1805*
EMMERY, Geo. to Ann Francis (NW - 2-7-1806)   2-7-1805*
ESSEY, Jonathan to Elizabeth Evans   2-17-1805*
EVANS, Gilbert to Mary Crage (no mo. & da. given)   ----1806
EWING, Thomas to Peggy Edward   6-26-1805*
FLEMING, Robt. to Polly Ferin   11-23-1805*
FLINT, Joseph to Elizabeth Montgomery (NW - 2-5-1806)   1-5-1805*
FREDERICK, Henry to Catherine Weeder   2-14-1805
FRIEND, Wm. to Elizabeth Grimes - Jefferson twp.   12-2-1806
GIBBONS, Wm. to Betsy McClintock - Jefferson twp.   4-24-1805*
GIBBS, James to Nancy Bramble - Scioto twp.   5-23-1805
GIBSON, William to Sarah Semard - Scioto twp.(NW - Givson-Samard,
                                        2-3-1804)   2-3-1805
GIFFORD, Timothy to Elizabeth McDonald (NW - 12-25-1805)   12-24-1805
GOLDSBERRY, Benjamin to Hannah Doyly   rec.2-12-1807
GROVE, William to Elizabeth Stinson (NW - Graves)   1-8-1805
HADDICK, Wm. to Catherine Monier   6-20-1805*
HAINES, Benj. to Sarah Huston   4-2-1807
HALL, Anthony to Mary Ward   4-29-1806
HARBER, Wm. to Ann R. Smith   10-28-1805*
HARR, David to Nancy Shegley - Scioto twp.   3-22-1805
HEATH, Wm. to Elizabeth Taylor (2 dates given, 10-30-1807) 10-30-1806

456

```
HINES, John to Caty Jones                                              1-1-1805
HINKLE, Jacob to Nancy Kennedy  (NW - 9-24-1805)                       4-24-1805
HINTON, Thomas to Margaret Furman                                      6-28-1805
HIXSON, Daniel to Margaret Cunningham                                  2-17-1807
HODGES, Daniel to Hannah Miller - Jefferson twp.(NW - 8-29-1805)       8-28-1805
HODGES, Thomas to Elizabeth England - Jefferson twp.                   6-12-1805*
HOLDERMAN, Abraham to Charlotte Oneal                                  1-13-1807
HUBBARD, John to Anna Bowdle (note: this mar. given in NW only)        3-28-1805
HUBBARD, Phielden to Betsey Stuthard                                   7-18-1805
HUGHS, John to Unis Wicks                                              1-1-1807
HUFLINES, Adam to Rebecca Driver  (no date given)                      (1805-o?)
IREDICK, Andrew to Polly Barton                                        6-17-1805*
JAMES, Thomas to Charlotte Massie  (NW - 1-1-1806)                     1-1-1805*
JOHNSTON, William to Peggy McClilman                                   5-9-1805
JOLLY, Wm. to Elizabeth Cating - Jefferson twp.                        4-25-1805
JUSTICE, John to Barbary Creviston                                     4-8-1807
KEAN, Huffman to Precilla Wheaton                                      3-24-1807
KENNER, John to Catherine Gossard - Concord twp.                       7-15-1805*
KILLOUGH, John to Elizabeth McConnell                                  5-1-1805*
KING, Freeman to Easter Smith                                          1-9-1805*
KINGERY, Samuel to Eve Spong                                           10-11-1805*
KITE, John to Catherine Gunday                                         5-14-1805
KRUSON, Geo. to June Glove (NW - Kinser, George-Jane Glove)            8-4-1805
LAMB, Maxwell to Susannah Hollyday (NW - 2-25-1806)                    2-25-1805*
LANE, Dannis to Elizabeth Harris                                       10-10-1805
LATON, Asher to Rebecca Davis                                          12-25-1805*
LENES, Fredrick to Catharine Trusam (this mar. given in NW only)       12-20-1805
LIGEN, Samuel to Elizabeth Sammas (this mar. given in NW only)         4-3-1805
LITTLE, Jacob to Rachel Kenedy                                         8-1-1805
LONG, John to Catherine Boderick (NW - Raderick 12-21-1805)            12-5-1805
LONGSHORE, James to Peggy Martin (NW - 3-7-1806)                       2-6-1805*
LOVELAND, Joseph to Dolly Rodgers                                      7-1-1805*
LOVELESS, John to Rebecca McCall                                       2-12-1807
LOWE, Abraham to Catherine Hill                                        11-22-1806
McCABE, Isaiah to Jean McCune (NW - 4-7-1804)                          4-7-1805
McCAFFERTY, Thomas to Rachel Johnston                                  4-4-1805
McCARTNEY, John to Elinor Dorhady (no date given)                      (1805-5?)
McCARTNEY, John to Margaret Mills (or Wills) - Concord twp.            3-27-1807
McCLAIN, James to Mary Osburn                                          9-4-1805*
McCRACKEN, Thomas to Deby Andrew                                       11-1-1806
McCUN, John to Margaret Neil                                           8-7-1805*
McFADGEN, John to Catherine Henderson                                  10-23-1805
McCLAUGHLIN, Cornelius to Nancy Quinbey - Lick twp.                    5-4-1805*
MAHON, James to Catherine Shern (NW - Kerr, 2-26-1806)                 1-25-1805*
MARTIN, James to Margaret Phillips                                     4-30-1805*
MENSON, John to Grace Kingem (NW - Monson-Kingam)                      4-29-1805
MILLEHAN, John to Mary Wyatt (NW - Millikan, 12-19-1806)              12-19-1805
MILLER, Isaac to Rebeccah Malone (NW - 1-2-1806)                       1-2-1805*
MILLER, Samuel to Hannah Pursell                                       7-4-1805
MILLER, Warmack to Polly Hodges - Jefferson twp.                       6-17-1805*
MILS, Richard to Mary Bowdle                                           9-1-1805*
MITCHELL, Frederick to Lucy Land                                       10-24-1805
MITHELL, Robt. to Rhoda Hancock (NW - Handycock, 1-23-1806)            1-23-1805*
```

MOFFETT, Nathan to Charrity Coss - Jefferson twp. (NW -
                 Charrety Cox, 8-1-1805)   7-27-1805
MONTGOMERY, WM. to Mary Roveland (1806 written in pencil) 5-1-1805*
MOODY, Simon to Rebecca Hill   rec. 2-15-1807
MOOTS, Phillip to Catherine Goodman   9-23-1805*
MORGON, William to Polly Wolf (NW - Morgan, 3-6-1805) 3-5-1805
MORRIS, Benamin to Mary Weider   4-17-1805*
MORRISON, Robt. to Sally Dunlap - Paxton twp.   8-10-1806
MOUNTS, Asa to Jane McMULLIN   12-4-1806
MUSSELMAN, Daniel to Christina Weider (NW - 10-6-1805 10-5-1805
NAPP, Thomas to Letty Beading - Scioto twp.   8-1-1805*
NEFF, Corneluis to Catherine Cooc - Jefferson twp.(NW-Cox,3-31-1806)3-31-1805*
NICHOLS, Balace to Milinda Gibbs of Chillicothe (NW-Melinda,12-3-1806)12-8-1805
NICHOLSON, Abner to Phebe Rommie - Concord twp.   7-14-1806
NOPP, John to Rachel Richee (NW - Richie, 2-13-1806)   2-13-1805*
ODLE, Wm. to Sarah Carpenter - Jefferson twp.   8-7-1806
OLDAKER, Jesse to Charity Wycoff   2-18-1807
PANCAKE, Leaven to Elizabeth Reed (NW - Pancason, Senon, 8-15-1805)6-10-1805
PANCAKE, Valentine to Polly L. Moons (NW - Polly G. Rooks) 4-4-1805
PARISH, Jolly to Elizabeth Smith   8-1-1805
PARKER, Prentice to Polly Moore   4-3-1805*
        married at house of Girgie(?) Moore, Wayne twp.
PATERSON, Jacob to Jane Sample .   rec. 12-18-1805*
PHILLIPS, James to Margaret Woodfield (NW - 3-21-1806) 2-13-1805*
PICKENS, John to Nancy Carlisle (NW - 3-25-1805)   3-14-1805
PIPER, Philip to Betsy Manner   2-1-1805
PIPLER, David to Elizabeth White   9-30-1806
PHWEBB, Peter to Rebecca Gripp   3-21-1807
PE, Thomas to Polly H utchins   8-30-1806
RAINS, Isaac to Sarah Dixon - Jefferson twp.   1-13-1807
REED, Thomas to Nancy Hustone - Scioto twp. (NW - 4-16-1805) 4-15-1805
RHEAS,, Abraham to Margaret McCarty   2-19-1805
RICHARDSON, John to Polly McCafferty   6-5-1805*
RICEE, Wm. to Betsey Galbreth (this mar. given in NW only) 1-1-1805
RICETS, Chas. to Catherine Clark   12-23-1806
RICETS, Chane of Fairfield Co. to Margaret Colair of Ross Co. 12-23-1806
RIDLN, John to Nancy Phebus   11-28-1805
ROBIN, Daniel to Mary Harper (no date given)   (1805-6?)
RODES James to Susannah Keloy   2-9-1807
RODGER, Thomas to Polly McCoy (1806 written in pencil) 3-6-1805*
ROEBUC. Rose(?) to Sarah Jones   10-15-1805*
ROSS, ames to Lory Williams(no yr. given—NW gives Lery,10-17-1805)10-17-
                                     ·(1805?)
ROSS, an to Rachel Trigger   1-29-1807
ROSS, Nhaniel to Charlett Reed   12-16-1806
RUSH, Go, to Mary Rush (no mo. & da. given)   ———1806
RUSSELL John to Elizabeth Humphrey - Jefferson twp. 8-9-1805
SCOTT, oseph to Martha Finley - Scioto twp.   1-31-1805
SHARTEL. Philip to Elizabeth Markel (no date given) ——(1807?)
SHEELER James to Jane Miller (no date given)   (1805-6?)
SHELBY, ohn to Elinor Morris (no day given)   July 1806
SHEPHER Jonathan to Betsey Daly   1-17-1807

458

SHETLY, atthew to Nancy Shahoon (no date given—NW gives Kelly,
    Mathew to Nancy Cahoon)   (1805-6?)
SMITH, Anhy to Sarah Pillars.   4-13-1805*
SMITH, Sixn to Sarah Sharp   4-14-1807
SMITH, Wm. to Mary Shields (NW - 2-17-1806)   2-17-1805*
SNAP, John w Catherine Myers   2-19-1807
STEEL, Ro'bt. to Mary Williamson (NW - 5-23-1805)   5-20-1805
STEWART, John to Elizabeth Kinkaid   5-23-1805
STIDMAN, James to Mary Currants   7-22-1806
STONEROCK, William to Rebecca Jones   3-1-1805
STRADER, Michael to Elizabeth Wise - Concord twp.   3-21-1807
STRAIN, Samuel to _____ (no name given)   12-18-1805*
STREVEY, Peter to Tibitha Thoms (NW - Thomas, 2-20-1806) 2-20-1805*
STEWART, Jermiah to Anna Corns   4-25-1807
SULL, Thos. to Nancy Abel (this mar. given in NW only) 2-13-1804
SULLIVAN, Aaron to Sarah Barr   rec. 2-12-1807
TATE, Robt. to Jane Harper (no date given)   (1805-6?)
TAVERS, Asa to Susannah Roderick   4-9-1807
TAYLOR, George to Mary Thomas   7-25-1805
TAYLOR, James to Susannah Cating (NW - 1-23-1806)   1-23-1805*
THOMPSON, Abraham to Polly McColovey   9-9-1805*
THORP, Allen to Milley Asher - Jefferson twp.   12-30-1806
THROUP, Wm. to Catherine Long (NW - 12-2-1805)   11-8-1805
TIMMONS, John to Ann Brittam   6-19-1805*
TOOPS, Henry to Sally Habb(?) (NW - Hall, 12-30-1805) 12-26-1805
TURNEY, Henry to Peggy Webster   8-21-1805*
    "by candlelight and all parties present appeared well satisfied"
TURPIN, James to Sofiat Thurman   2-5-1807
TUTTLE, James to Elizabeth Greenlee (NW - 12-4-1806) 12-27-1805
ULM, Edward to Sarah Nathan   4-30-1805*
VANDERFORD, Eli to Susannah Ratcliff - Jefferson twp. 2-12-1807
VANMETER, Joseph to Rachel Menick (no date given-NW-Renick,
                   3-25-1805)   ——(1805?)
VINSON, William to Sarah Well (NW - Sarah Willoughby) 3-28-1805
WADDLE, Francis to Jane Baird   12-10-1806
WADDLE, John to Nancy Mann   11-18-1806
WADDLE, John to Polly Blain   1-20-1807
WALKER, Horatio to Susannah Sadler   12-4-1806
WALLACE, Wm. to Ellinor Dill   10-23-1805*
WARIGH, Lemon to Rachel Hotton   2-3-1807
WARNER, Levi to Massee Windon (NW - Massie Winder, 4-10-1804) 4-10-1805
WASHBURN, James to Nancy Cutright (NW - 11-22-1806) 11-22-1805
WEBSTER, John to Elizabeth Winder   5-2-1805
WHITE, John to Rody Palmer (1806 written in pencil)   5-8-1805*
WHITSEL, Samuel to Ruth Crouse   1-18-1807
WILLVAN, George to Barbara Meetz   4-27-1805*
WILFONG, Christain to Hannah Sheby   7-17-1806
WILKINS, Thos. to _____ Calver (not given)   2-18-1807
WILLIAMS, George to Sarah Cavender (NW - 11-16-1805) 11-15-1805
WILLIAMS, Godfrey to Catherine Lance (NW - Wilkins, Godfrey) 1-3-1805
WILLIAMS, Wm. to Nancy Noble   10-31-1805
WILLOUGHBY, Andrew to Levina Scott   10-10-1805

```
WILLS, John to Keziah McCune                                    8-14-1805*
WILSON, Alexander to Eddy Graham - Lic twp.                     2-20-1805*
WILSON, John to Margaret Tomlinson                              4-14-1803
WILSON, John to Polly Finch                                     9-25-1805*
WILSON, Joseph, a blackman to Sarah, a black woman-Jefferson twp. 8-5-1806
WILSON, Josiah to Elizabeth Provabb (NW - Provatt, 5-15-1805)   5-9-1805
WOLF, Philip to Rebecca Phillips   (no mo. & da. given)         ----1805*
WOODS, Zachariah to Mary Bruff - Scioto twp.                    5-9-1805
WYCOFF, Wm. to Sophia Wilfrong - Jefferson twp.                 2-19-1807
```

(Note:- .The following record was included with the marriages between that of
Balace Nicholas and Daniel Robins. It is not dated, but appears to be recorded
in 1805-1806)
"The following is a true record of all Black and mulatto persons, recorded in
the Clerk's office of the Court of Common Pleas, according to 'Act of Assembly
entitled an 'Act to regulate black and Mulatto Persons. David-a blackman other-
wise called David Hector Adam Griffin Ch-Adam-Jacob-Dinah-Reesy-Dennis-Annis-
Eelzey J.-Alex-Elijah Brown-Nathan Stansbury-Patty Carmon-Daniel J. Reesy-Will
Brown A.B.
May 24 and June 1

Contributed by: Mrs. Patrick Clark, Route #10, Box 76, Chillicothe, Ohio 45601

The following marriages were copied from Marriage Register Volume A (Black book)
April 1803-July 1809 and also from Marriage Volume A-B (White book) 1798-1825.
Differences from the white book will be found in parenthesis.

ACTON, Richard to Ruth Baker	1-1-1807
ADKERSON, Charles to Sukey White	6-16-1808
ALKINE, George to Catherine Rush	11-26-1807
ANDERSON, Haza to Elicabeth Rains	1-14-1808
ANDERSON, John to Peggy Norman (Newman)	11-22-1807
ANDERSON, William to Mary Reynolds	7-19-1808
ARMSTRONG, William to Jane (June) Cawson (Caourson)	3-17-1808
ATER, Henry to Polly Dilliha	4-11-1809.
ATER, Samuel to Margaret Hines	3-1-1809
BAILEY, James to Eve Pontius	10-6-1807
BALEY, Thomas to Catherine Arrowhood	8-8-1808
BAKER, Martin to Catherine Simpson	3-29-1808
BALDWIN, Michael to Catherine Braiden (Brandew) - both of Chill.	4-3-1808
BEACH, John to Barbara England (Engle)	5-22-1808
BEAL, Philip to Mary Pryor	3-23-1809
BECKLEY, Philip to Haley McSherry rec. 3-3-1809	(no date given)
(note: groom's name also given as BURKLEY, Harley)	
BEECHAM (BUCHAM), Henry to Marry Arrowsmith	11-10-1808
BEEVER, Baudle to Betsey Green	3-5-1807
BEEVER, Isaac to Sally Cox	11-17-1808
BENNETT, John to Negomi (Megomi) Howard	2-19-1807
BENNIT, Joseph to Catherine Strader	2-12-1808
BENTLEY, John to Susanna Pigman	11-5-1808
BENTLEY, Joseph to Sarah Price	3-28-1808
BERRY, Richard to Elizabeth Dolly (2 dates - 6-27-1807)	6-28-1807
BIRT, Abraham to Elizabeth Young	11-18-1808
BISHONG, George to Liddie Rush	2-16-1809
BISHOP, David to Mary Long	1-15-1809
BISHOP, Robert to Sally Hill	7-16-1807
BLACK, John to Martha Sheet or Street	4-21-1808
BLIZZARD, Burton to Anilla Williba	10-18-1808
BLUE, John to Pensela Reeves	7-7-1808
BODKIN, John to Elizabeth Coons	1-15-1809
BONEHAM, Warford to Rebecca Mayson	4-30-1809
BOWEN, Isaac to Rody Smith	3-31-1808
BCWERS, Solomon to Deborah Lalon	10-22-1807
BOWLER, Henry to Margaret MCrary	1-19-1809
BRADES, John to Mary Williams	6-16-1809
BRAMBLE, Charles to Polly Messick	11-7-1808
BRIGGS, Joseph to Violette (Hislette) McClish	6-25-1807
BROTHERLIN, Christian to Sarah MClure	9-18-1807
BROWN, Benjamin to Julia Westfall	11-13-1808
BROWN, Daniel to Margaret Miller	6-25-1807
BROWN, James to Slashey Sollars - both of Chillicothe	5-10-1807

461

```
BROWN, Thomas to Betsey Little (no mar. date given)        rec.  3-3-1809
BROWN, William to Mary Odle                                      10-6-1808
BRYAN, William to Peggy Lowder                                   8-20-1807
BURKLEY, Harley - see BECKLEY, Philip
BURNS, Joseph to Delilah Tipton                                  8-25-1808
BURREL, Francis to Elizabeth Hazal - both of Lick twp.           3-17-1808
CAMPBELL, Robert to Nancy Atchison                               4-21-1808
CAMPBELL, Solomon to Elenor Wilkinson                            6-17-1807
CARDER, Amsted to Elizabeth Bragg                                1-20-1808
CASEY, John to Hannah Bush  (mar. not recorded in white book)    6-5-1806
CAUSLEY (CREASLEY), John to Elizabeth Stachard                   10-20-1807
CAVETT, Richard to Margaret Baum - both of Chillicothe           6-30-1808
CHAMP, John to Mary Shanton                (3-26-1807)           3-20-1807
CHANDLER, William to Sarah Harrison                              4-14-1809
CHENEWORTH, John to Betsey Foster                                9-6-1807
CHIEHESTER, Wm. to Margaret McConnamicher (mar. not in white book) 1-29-1807
CHIPMAN, John to Lookey Kain (Rain)                              1-28-1808
CILAS (SILAS), Alkier to Rebecchah Davis                         6-23-1808
CILE (PYLE), Oliver to Nancy Jones                               2-29-1808
CLARKE, Daniel to Catherine Foster                              4-12-1807
CLARKE, Noah to Esther Miller or Mills                          6-24-1808
CLAYTON, William to Elizabeth Carter                            8-25-1808
CLEVINGER, Bazil to Margaret Wolf                               9-20-1808
CLIFFIN, Benjamin to Lucy Williams                             8-10-1808
CLIFTON, Charles to Elizabeth Brown                            8-23-1808
CLIFTON, George to Fanny Smith                                 9-9-1808
CLIFTON, Job to Ann Vanbuskirk                                 4-25-1808
COCHRAN, David to Rhody Demint                                 4-11-1809
COMEAN, Smith to Polly Dillan                                  12-24-1807
COMER, John to Polly Baker                                     7-14-1808
CONLEY, Barton to Jene Eyestone (Iston)                        12-29-1807
      (note:  groom's surname also given as OVERLY, Boston)
COOK, William to Anne Sull                                     11-5-1807
COOPER, Spencer to Mary Elmore                                 8-2-1808
CDOVER, Samuel to Nancy MClue                                  5-23-1809
CORWIN, John to Mary sindenbender (Lidenbender) (no date given) -----1808?
CORWIN, Pheanus to Mary Hall - mar. at house of W. Halls,      3-10-1808
                        Miller, Wayne twp.
CORWINE, Samuel to Mary Wilson                                 8-9-1808
COUNTZ, Daniel to Elizabeth Walker                            10-28-1808
COX, Joseph to Amey Baker                                     9-5-1808
CRABB, Henderson to Jemimah Downing                          3-23-1809
CREASLEY, John - see CAUSLEY, John
CRIDER, Emanuel to Eve_____(surname not given)              11-15-1807
CROOKHAW (CROCKHAW), George L. to Salley Lake - both of Lick twp.; 1-19-1808
                 married at Scioto Salt Works
CROUCH, John to Betty Reystone                               1-28-1808
CURRY, James to Dalia Kain                                   12-3-1807
DANIELS, James to Rebecca Guthery                            5-21-1808
```

462

```
DARBY, William to Hannah Andrew                                    2-17-1809
DAUGHERTY, Michael to Peggy McLaughlin                             3-7-1808
DAVENPORT, Abraham to Epienis Griffith (no mar. date given)   rec.7-20-1809
DAVIS, John to Polly Parish                                       1-26-1809
DAWSON, David to Nancy Mullet                                    12-6-1808
DEARDUFF, Daniel to Ealdon King                                   6-10-1807
DEHAVEN, Abraham to Polly Buele(?) (Bunn)                         3-8-1808
DEVON (DEVORS), John to Margaret Matthes                          4-18-1809
DEWITT, John to Mary Barker                                       4-11-1808
DIXON, William to Malinda Arthur - mar. at house of Wm Arthurs,  3-25-1808
                                   Wayne twp.
DIXON, William to Betsey Parish                                   2-9-1809
DRUREY, Edward to Jane Burns (Bains)                             11-10-1808
DUFFEE, Samuel to Nancy Kilbreth                                 1-12-1809
DULEY, Charles to Hannah Gooding                                 3-31-1808
EARLY, Peter to Elizabeth McNemer                                1-28-1808
ELLIOTT, John to Jennie Rodgers                                 11-12-1807
EMETT, John to Margaret Rush                    (5-12-1808)       6-9-1808
ENGLAND, Jacob to Nancy Ona(?) England                          12-17-1807
ENGLES, Valentine to Polly Stroup                                1-12-1809
EVANS, Robert to Sally Steen                                     4-17-1808
EVANS, Thomas to Jenna Steen                                    10-13-1807
FITSWORTH, Isaac to Jenna Lingree                               11-13-1808
FLEMING, John to Elizabeth Moore - mar. at Widow Moore's         2-22-1808
                                   house, Wayne twp.
FOLEY, James to Polly Marsh                                       2-1-1808
FOSTER, Lawrence to Eliz. Loman                                 12-24-1807
FOY, Jacob to Mary V. Gundy                                      1-21-1808
FRAIN, Daniel to Martha H. Baker                               10-30-1807
FRANKLIN, James to Sarah Rush                                  12-31-1807
FREDRICK, Daniel to Christiana Strawser                        10-6-1808
FREEMAN, James to Sally Anthony                                 3-25-1809
GAY, Jacob to Auug(?) Harbor                                   11-10-1808
GEEHEART, Samuel to Deborah Crago                              2-16-1808
GIBB, James to Mary Shepherd                                   8-20-1807
GIVEN, William to Jean Mahon                                  10-20-1808
GOODMAN, William to Betsey Conner                             10-18-1808
GOSLEE, Samuel to Polly Mitchell                               3-9-1809
GOSSARD, Phillip to Treesy Plummer                            8-27-1807
GRADY, John to Letty Swan                                      8-6-1808
GRAHAM, Robert to Sarah Pancake                               5-28-1808
GROVE, Fredrick to Nancy More        (note: no day given)     May 1808
HAND, George to Barbary Crose                                  6-7-1808
HANKINS, David to Jean Clevenger                              6-16-1808
HARDEN, Hiram to Elsy Keys                                     9-17-1807
HARRISON, Eli to Rachel Woolcut                                7-7-1808
HATTON, William to Jemima Botckin                             5-21-1809
HEALTH, Jonathan to Huldah Nicholson                         11-8-1807
HENDERSON, David to Abigail Henderson                         3-17-1808
```

463

```
HENDERSON, James to Mary White                                           12-31-1807
HERREL, Daniel to Mary James                                             6-29-1807
HESS, Babzer to Sarah Emmele                                             4-11-1809
HIER, Jacob to Mary Teeter (Fuller)                                      1-14-1808
HILL, James V. or O. to Phillis Bowan                                    11-24-1808
HILL, John to Catrona Brodley (Broadley)                                 7-13-1809
HITCHENS, George to Sally England                                        8-11-1808
HINES, Philip to Sally Mattox                                            7-26-1808
HINSHAW, John to Margaret Ratcliff                                       1-19-1809
HINTON, David to Susannah Rogers                                         2-22-1807
HIXON, John to Nancy Stephens                                            9-24-(1807?)
HOLLWAY, William to Phebe Crispin (note: with 1809 marriages)            1-26-1804
HOLTON, Benjamin to Nancy Fleming                                        4-27-1809
HOPKIN, Joseph to Elizabeth Stinon                                       5-12-1808
HOPKINS, William to Elizabeth Hornback                                   1-28-1807
HORN, Daniel to Polly Mores (Hover?                                      6-5-1807
HOSTENTON, Jacob to Anna Murray                                          10-27-1807
HOWSHOUR, John to Priscella Wolf                                         10-11-1808
HUBBARD, Jacob to Sarah Elmore                                           11-18-1808
HUDSON, George to Mary Butenhall    (note:  no day given)               Feb. 1808
HUDSON, Robert to Nancy Taylor                                           5-15-1808
HUSTON, James to Mary Botts (Ball)                                       1-8-1807
HUTINGTER, Christian to Mary Crabb                                       12-25-1807
HYATE, John - see WYATE, John
JACKSON, Edward to Phillis Bradley                                       6-5-1807
JAMISON, Jacob to Cty. (Cloy) Hopkins                                    6-23-1808
JEANS, Isaac to Dolley Balley                                            9-20-1808
JEFFREYS, Joseph to Hetty Nicholas                                       3-29-1808
JOHNSON, James to Betsey Carson                                          4-28-1808
JONES, James to Pheby Stonerock                                          2-30-1808
JONES, Samuel to Rachel Minshall                                         2-7-1808
JONES, Thomas to Polly Cessna                                            1-1-1809
KEENER, Adam to Hetty Commer                                             2-16-1808
KELLEY, Wm. to Susannah McPherson                                        6-4-1807
KERR, James to Dolly Hornback  (no mar. date given)          rec.  7-20-1809
KERR, John to Polly Donahoe                                              2-4-1808
KILLISON, Moses to Catherine Bonnete  (Bennebb)                          6-23-1808
KING, John to Rachel Hixon                                               2-25-1808
KIRKBRIGHT, John to Ann Williams                                         9-22-1808
KIZER, Peter to Sukey Johnston                                           1-12-1809
KNOWLY, (KNOWLES), Adam to Rachel Culver (Calver)                        6-6-1808
LITTLE, John to Abba Cozad                                               8-4-1809
LINTON, Zacheriah to Jean Locaud                                         11-24-1808
LISTER, William to Sally Hurt                                            8-11-1808
LITTLETON, Matthew to Sophia Harper                                      9-6-1808
LOCHARD, Joseph to Magdalen Doll (Dell)                                  3-8-1808
LONG, Edward to Rebecca Taylor                (4-16-1807)               4-5-1807
LONG, John to Elizabeth Taylor                                          7-2-1807
LOVELYS (LOVELESS), Wm. to Elizabeth Watkins                            6-13-1807
```

```
LOWELL, Joseph M. of Scioto Co. to Jane Cutliff (Gatliff)        6-16-1808
McCAFFERTY, Jonathan to Rebecca Crisoin                          4-7-1808
McCAFFERTY, Richard to Lydia Dickenson                           7-3-1807
McCAFFERTY, Samuel to Jean McCartney                             8-20-1807
McCORKEL, Wm to Nancy Smith                                      8-26-1807
McCOY, John to Jane MCraden                                      8-23-1808
McDONALD, William to Mary Ann Willis                             4-26-1808
McFARLAND, John to Margaret Rockford (Rochard)                   10-29-1807
McMULLIN, John to Margaret Stewart                               6-16-1808
MACE, Jacob to Becky Dillin                                      8-28-1808
MACKEY, Robert to Mary Ann Wilson                                4-17-1809
MAHAN, William to Betsey Young                                   2-18-1808
MASON, Thomas to Seley (Sally) Tom (date 3-18-1809 also given;   1-29-1809
    marriage recorded three times--date 1-29-1809 appear to be correct)
MASSIE, Wingate to Polly Compton                                 9-13-1808
MEADEN, Alfred to Polly Mitchel                                  6-21-1808
MELONE, William to Elizabeth Melone                              1-24-1809
MICKER, Wheeler to Sally Kilborn          (10-5-1808)            11-5-1808
MIERS, John to Lucy Plummer                                      8-25-1808
MOFFITT, Nathan to Catherine Rains                               12-9-1807
MONNETT, William to Mary Smith                                   3-25-1809
MONTGOMERY, Hugh to Catherine Cyphers                            3-17-1808
MONTGOMERY, Humphrey to Elizabeth Wilson (3-3-1805--rec. 3-4-1808)  3-3-1808
MONTGOMERY, John to Catherine Perrill                            9-22-1808
MOOTS, George to Christana Goodman (mar. not in white book)      7-28-1806
MORRIS, Benjamin to Anna Thompson                                2-9-1808
MORRIS, Davied to Polly Logue                                    7-16-1807
MORRIS, Jessie to Elizabeth Stingley                             10-25-1807
MYARS, George to Sally Harbar                                    1-12-1809
MYERS, Abraham to Catherine Solsgarven                           5-28-1807
MYERS, Jacob to Mary Harbut (Harber)                             5-25-1809
NASHEE, George to Sally MClean                                   11-24-1808
NEBINCALL, Jacob to Widow Buck (Bark)                            3-23-1809
NELSON, Thomas to Agga Nikens                                    11-13-1808
NEWMAN, Michael to Elizabeth Copsy                               12-31-1807
NIKENS, James to Rachel Simpson                                  12-22-1808
NICHOLSON, Henry to Nancy Durgens                                10-20-1807
NICHOLSON, Robert to Mary Dungan                                 2-5-1807
OVERLY, Boston to Jene Eyestone (Iston)                          12-29-1807
        (note:  groom's name given also as CONLEY, Barton)
PARCELS, Peter to Hannah Kerns                                   2-4-1808
PARISH, John to Elsey Oliver                                     1-5-1808
PARISH, Reuben to Sarah Lewis                                    3-28-1809
PARKER, Silas to Sally Wells (Walls) - Both of Lick twp.         3-30-1808
PEARCE, Samuel to Elinor Francis (note; no month and year given)  __-19-(1807?)
PEPPERS, John to Sophia Peppers (mar. not in white book)         4-1-1806
PERR, William to Elizabeth Vandeman                              2-18-1808
PONTIUS, Benjamin to Rosanna Myers                               4-24-1808
PYLE, Oliver - see CILE, Oliver
```

465

```
RAGAÑ, John to Leamon Southwards                                    8-4-1809
RAINS, Isaac to Rebecca Barkwood (Backwood)                         12-1-1808
RAINS, Lawren to Hannah Dixon                                       2-15-1809
RAMEY, Caleb to Sarah Stuthard                                      4-6-1809
RANKEN, John to Polly Ayers                                         1-15-1809
RANKIN, Hugh to Nancy Rankin                                        2-28-1806
RATCLIFF, John to Susannah Pore                                     6-18-1807
RATCLIFF, John to Mary Cowber (Comber)                              3-16-1808
RECTOR, Edward to Peggy Brown                                       12-29-1808
REDFEARN, John to Elizabeth Vestal (Virtal)                        6-5-1808
REED (READ), Solomon to Polly Beaker                               7-9-1807
REED, Thomas to Matilda Dawson                                     10-22-1807
REED, William to Polly Harper                                      2-16-1808
RENICK, Adam to Catherine Pontius                                  4-4-1809
RICHARDSON, Robert to Sarah Willis                                12-4-1808
RICHEY, Thomas to Jane Tong (Young-Yong)                          7-5-1808
ROBERTS, Charles to Margaret Kendel                               7-30-1807
ROBERTS, Isaac to Dinah (Cuiah) Corsey                            11-10-1808
ROBINSON, Robt to Susie Brown                                     6-25-1807
ROBINSON, William to Sarah Lane                                   1-21-1808
ROCKHOLD, John to Rebecca Combs                                   7-26-1807
ROEBUCK, Benj. to Elizabeth Russell                              7-6-1807
ROGERS, James to Elizabeth Strain                                12-29-1807
ROMINE, Thomas to Lucy(?) Emery                                  1-28-1808
ROOK, John to Nancy Wills - both of Lick twp                     6-29-1808
ROSS, James to Margaret McCune (mar. not in white book)          2-1-1807
RUMNALDS, Benjamin to Nicey Reed                                 3-5-1809
RUSELL (RUPEL), Thomas to Margaret Young                         8-10-1807
RUSH, Andrew to Isebella Earnhart                                12-18-1808
RYAN, Benj. to Nancy Callender                                   5-27-1807
SAARY, Solomon to Matty Gundy                                    11-26-1808
SADLER, William to Nancy Porter                                  2-2-1809
SCOOT (SCOTT), John to Ruth Dickason                            10-29-1809
SCOTT, Elijhu to Mahala Witters                                 7-7-1807
SCOTT, Moses (Norris) to Rhoda Creig                            6-25-1807
SHEELY, Lawrence to Betsey Haynes                               5-25-1808
SHEPHERD, Jacob to Isabella Jones                               4-4-1809
SHEPHERD, John to Betsey Vanmeter (no mar. date given)    rec.  3-3-1809
SHEPHERD, Joseph to Polly Betz                                  4-21-1809
Shields, John to Elizabeth Worthington                         12-29-1808
SIGLER, John to Mahala Rogard (Bogan)                          8-7-1808
SLAVENS, Reuben to Nancy Blair                                 11-29-1808
SMITH, Jacob to Eliza (Liza) Fute                              6-24-1808
SMITH, James to Phebe Trussum                                  11-24-1808
SMITH, Nicholas to Elizabeth Ewing                             9-27-1807
SMITH, Robert to Phebe Rankin of Pickaway twp.                6-21-1807
SOLLARS, John to Cetty Stothard (Southland)                   6-2-1808
SOUTHARD, Hudson to Jane MKeen                                 2-16-1809
STEEL, John to Nancy Little                                    9-10-1807
```

```
STEEL, Thomas to Betsy Phillips                                              10-26-1807
STEELY, John to Margaret Emmerson                                            9-30-1808
STEINER, Abraham to Betsey Lewis                                             3-5-1809
STEPHEN, John to Nancy Bowin   (no mar. date given)           rec.          7-20-1809
STEWART, Abraham to Peggy M. Mullen                                         2-18-1808
STIPP, Abraham to Rebecca Kuykendall (Rykendall)                            5-7-1807
STIPP, John to Rebecca Kuykendall                                         12-22-1808
STOCKTON, David to Betsy Anderson                                           7-7-1808
STOCTON, William to Ann Rebekah Dungan                                    12-29-1807
STOOKEY, Jacob to Susannah Hyre (mar. recorded twice-2dates given)        4-3-1808
                                                                           3-20-1808
STREEBY (STREELY), Daniel to Betsey Thomas                                 6-29-1809
TABB, John L. to Hannah Betz                                                8-3-1808
TAYLOR, John to Catherine Juda                                             2-9-1808
THOMAS, Aaron to Sarah Westfall                                          10-22-(1807?)
THOMAS, Jacob to Eliza Gay                                               12-24-1807
THOMPSON, Ezekiel to Diney (Viney) Davis                                  439-1809
TIFFIN, Edward Esq. to Polly Porter                                        4-16-1809
TIMMONS, Anmanias to Ellenor Rotten                                      12-23-1807
TIMMONS, Stephen to Mary Corkwell                                          6-25-1807
TOD, Samuel to May Ballard (Balleb)                                        5-22-1808
TODD, Samuel to Rhenmia Frow                                              12-5-1807
TOOPS, John to Nancy Stauley                                             10-30-1808
TRISS, Morris A. to Milly Jacobs                                           3-29-1809
TROUTNER, George to Betsy Crawford                                        4-12-1808
TURMOR, William to Susannah Bradley                                       4-28-1807
TWEFORD, Clement to Milcah Hicks                                           9-1-1808
VANMETER, James to Rebecca Roberts                                        12-4-1808
VINDEN, Isaac to Amelia (Alexander) Sadler                                 4-9-1809
WADDLE, Samuel to Eliz. M. Lane                                            6-7-1808
WALTER, Michael of Fairfield Co. to
        Elizabeth Anderson of Washington twp. Ross Co.                     12-8-1808
WARRING, Humphrey to Nancy Gossom                                          2-21-1809
WHEELAND, George to Jane McRoberts                                       10-29-1807
WHEELER, Robert to Polly Clevenger                                        3-26-1808
WHETLOW, Francis to Margarett Blue                                       12-24-1808
WIER, Obed to Catherine Nathan                                             7-7-1807
WILEY, Jessie to Polly Die                                                11-3-1808
WILKINSON, John to Delila Ceistal (Oustat)                                1-14-1808
WILKISON, Richard to Rachel Ratcliff                                       3-9-1809
WILLIAMS, Amos to Anna Warren                                             4-24-1809
WILLIAMS, Isaac to Mary Hendricks                                         1-21-1808
WILLIAMS, John to Polly Cox                                                9-5-1808
WILLIAMS, Zedikiah to Peggy Hillery                                      10-14-1808
WILLS, Absolom to Fanny Gess - both of Lick twp.                          6-2-1808
WILSON, _____(not given) to Polly Downdride                              11-26-1807
WILSON, William Esq. to Rachel Dixon                                      11-8-1808
WOLF, George to Sarah Cuierson (Camuson)                                  1-19-1808
WOODS, Zachariah to Mary Waters                                           7-16-1809
```

```
WOODWARD, Lewis to Elizabeth Huston                             8-16-1807
WRIGHT, John to Anna Colen                                      2-29-1808
WYATE (HYATE), Joseph to Hannah Cox                             3-16-1808
WYCOFF, Nicholas to Margaret Tweed                             3-14-1809
YATES, Morris to Polly Gundy                                    2-21-1809
YOUNG, Joseph to Elizabeth Pigmon         (6-7-1808)           6-5-1808
YOUNG, Silas to Margaret Young                                 3-22-1808
_____, (note: no names given for bride or groom) - Pickaway twp.)4-10-1807
```

ROSS COUNTY, OHIO - TERRITORIAL COURT ORDER BOOK - 1798-1799

Contributed by: Mrs. Patrick Clark, Route #10, Box 76, Chillicothe, Ohio 45601

Note: The following records were taken from Order Book-Territorial Court 1798-1800
located in the Clerk of Court's Office. The majority of the cases were civil cases
and have been abstracted for genealogical data and as a finding aid only.
(ages on which original record may be found are given in parenthesis.)

Cincinnati, bearing date of 11 Oct. 1798, by order of Gov. Arthur St. Clair of the
establishment of Common Pleas of Ross Co., of the territory of the United States
North West of the Ohio River. (1)

Thomas Worthington, James Scott, Samuel Finley, William Patton and Elias Longham,
squires. Edward Tiffin, to keep seal and records; Jeremiah McClain Esq. appointed
Sheriff of Ross Co. 11 Oct. 1798. (2)

Court held 4th Tuesday of Dec. 1798

BEDFORD & MOWRY vs. William WYLIE. Damage. Case dis.--deft. could not be found. (2)
BEAL, Will vs. William WYLE. Damage. Case dis.--deft. could not be found. (2)
HUNTER, Margaret vs. Joseph HUNTER. Damage. Suit discont. (3)
SMITH, Samuel vs. David WARREN. debt. (3)
LAMB, William vs. David WARREN. Damage. Suit discont. (3)
POLLOCK, John vs. John KENNEDY & John COLLINS. Debt. Plff. to recover. (3-4)
NICHOLSON, William vs. Joseph DICKSON. Debt. Plff. to recover. (4)
MOORHEAD, Thomas vs. Samuel FLANNAGEN. Damage. Suit dismissed. (4)
LEWIS, Tilman vs. Samuel HUSHOR. Damage. Suit dismissed. (4)
LEWIS, Tilman vs. George HASHER. Suit discont. (4)
McCLURE, John vs. Joseph WILSON. Trespassing, assault, and battery, Discont. (5)
ONER, James vs. Samuel STOOPS. Damage. Suit discont. (5)
McNICKLE, Alexander vs. Samuel STOOPS. Damage. Suit discont. (5)
LDER, Samuel vs. Samuel STOOPS. Damage. John S. Wills, atty. for plff. Suit
                                                              discont. (5)
WESBROW, Henry vs. Montgomery SHERRY. Damages. John S. WILL atty. for plff.
        Sherry made promissory note 12-30-1797 in Ross Co. John Doe and Richard
        Roe pledges. Plff. to recover from deft. (6-7)

Court held 4th Tuesday of March 1799 Same officers present.

McCENE, Jeremiah vs. James ROGERS. Damages. R. F. SLAUGHTER atty. for plff. Rogers
        made promissory note 9-12-1797 at Chillicothe. Plff. to recover. (8-10)
ALDWIN, Francis vs. Joseph POTTER. Damages. Plff. to recover. (10)
MAYER, John vs. William PORT. Damages. John S. Will plff. atty. Plff. to recover.
                                                                            (10)
FERR, Richard vs. John DERR. Ejectment from out-lot containing 4 acres in town of
        Chillicothe, on the demise of Elias Langham. John Derr late of Ross Co.
        breaking and entering with force and arms and ejectment of Ferr from
        premises. Wm. Sprigg atty for plff. Claim title is in possession of James
        Hayes who was made deft in place of Derr. Jury called--Isaac Davis, James
        Johnston, James McClene, William Lamb, John Beaty, Stephen Cisma. John
        Turner, Wm. Jenkins, Joseph Johnston, John Clemens, Joseph Tiffin & Thomas
        Dick. Case found in favor of deft. (11-13)

469

PHELPS, John vs. James BLAIR. Damages. R. F. Slaugher atty. Plff. to recover.(14)
JOHNSTON, William vs. Noble CRAWFORD. Damages. Suit discont. (14)
LANGHAM & JAMES vs. Robert McMAHAN. Suit discont. (14)
KEYS, William vs. William COCKREN, R. F. Slaughter atty. Suit discont. (15)
COOPER, William vs. William COCKRAN. Damages. R. F. Slaughter, atty. Suit discont. (15)
BRINEY, Daniel vs. Robt. M. MAHAN. Damages. Plff. obtained attachment against lands goods & Chattels of deft. John S. Will, atty. Suit discont. (15)
BONER, William vs. Daniel HAMILTON. Damages. Suit discont. (16)
BONER, William vs. Daniel HAMILTON. Damages. Suit discont. (16)
JOHNSTON, William vs. Abraham DEAN & James DEAN. Damages. Wm. Sprigg. atty. Suit discont. (16)
JOHNSON, William vs. Charles JOHNSON. $50. Suit discont. (17)
KELLY, Ezekiel & John HAMPSON vs. John WILFONG & Samuel HUSHOR. $500. Suit discont. (17)
BROWN, Joseph vs. Daniel M. FARLIN. $40. Suit discont. (17)
FWINCHEN, James vs. Joseph DIXON. $20. John S. Wills, atty. Suit discont. (18)
BATES, John vs. Benjamin MILLER. $50. John S. Will, atty, Deft to recover against plff. for default. (18)
SLAUGHTER, Robert F. esq. licensed to practice as an attorney. (18)

Court held 4th Tuesday June 1799 Officers present except James Scott
CREIGHTON, Will esq. granted a license as an attorney. (18)
MONTGOMERY, James Esq. granted a license as an attorney. (18)
BOTTS, Moses vs. Wm. THOMPSON. $150. John S. Wills atty. William Thompson of Bourbon Co. Ky & Ross Co. Ohio. Plff. to recover. Thompson was indebted 1 Sept. 1798. (19-22)
POTTER, Joseph vs. John JOHNSON. $50. R. F. Slaughter atty. Note made 5 June 1799. Plff. to recover. (22-23)
LANGHAM & JAMES vs. James HAYS. $40. Plffs. to recover. (24)

Court held 4th Wednesday June 1799 All Esquires present.
EDWARDS, John vs. Charles MUTES. $80 for purchase of hemp and sugar 21 July 1798. Plff. to recover. (24-26)
DUFFIN, Hugh vs. Robert BALLENTINE. $100. Note made 9 June 1798 at Chillicothe. Wm. Creighton, atty. John Doe & Richard Roe pledges for prosecution. John S. Wills atty for deft. Jury called consisting of:

Fergus MOORE	James GRUBB	James HEWITT	Thomas WHITE
Elias BOOTMAN	George HETH	Bazel ABRAMS	Henry SHAW
John BESHONG	George KILLGORE	Robert EVANS	David HAYS(27-30

THOMAS, Michael vs. William & John BISWELL. $50. Abner Meeker surity to note made 9 Aug. 1798. Plff. to recover. (31-34
HUSTON, Paul vs. Samuel STOOPS. $50. R. F. Slaughter, atty. Plff. to recover interest & money from 2 Dec. 1798. (35)
LANGHAM & JAMES vs. Joseph LEMMON. Plff. to recover $35.47. from deft. (35-36_

470

HARRIS, Samuel vs. Matthew STOKES. $50 on 2 April 1798 at Chillicothe. Jury called
    consisting of:

John CLEMMONS	William HUTT	Joseph TIFRIN	John McDONALD
Thomas WHITE	Robert EVANS	Anthony S. DAVENPORT	William COOPER
Uriah POLLIN	Hugh MOORE	Tilmen LEWIS	James GRUBB
			(36-40)

BOYLE, John & Hugh vs. James ROGERS. Debt. Plff. to recover $54.70. (41)
McDONALD, William vs. James ROGERS. $200. Thomas McDonald security for plff.,
    Daniel Hambleton security for deft. Debt made 6 August 1798. Plff
    to recover. (41-45)
HUNTER, Joseph vs. Lucas SULIVANT. Plff rendered to Sullivant 69 lbs. Kentucky
    Currency equal to $230. Debt made 2-3-1798 at Washington, Ky. Deft.
    says he paid note. Jury called consisting of:

Thomas DICK	John EVANS	Alexander CRAIG	Lucas NEBUCKAS(?)
Elias BOATMAN	John BESHONZ	Thomas McDONALD	Gasper CORE
John JOHNSTONE	Oliver BROWN	James LOGAN	Aaron STEPHENSON
Jury found for plff.	(45-48)		

ROBERTSON, John vs. Charles JAMISON. $50. note made 4-13-1798 at Chillicothe.
    Plff. to recover $20.45. (48-51)
CHAPMAN, John vs. George HUSHER. $20., Plff. to recover. (51)
STEEL, John vs. Samuel HARRIS. $51., note made 7-10-1798 Ross Co.; Plff to recover.
    (52-54)

All officers present but William PATTON.
HORNER, James vs. Caleb STOCKDON. 153 lbs. 3 schillings, Penn. currency equal
    to $408.50. Plff. to recover. (54-55)
FINLEY, Samuel vs. Samuel HARRIS. James Rogers surity for deft. Note made Jan.
    1799 for $30. worth of goods, wares and merchandise. Plff. to recover.
    (55-57)
McINTIRE, John vs. James ROGERS & Joseph POTTER. Note made Chillicothe 11-6-1799
    for 19 spanish mill dollars. Plff. to recover. (57-67)
DUNCAN, Daniel vs. Abner MEEKER. John Biswell suriety for deft. 114 lbs.
    14 shillings of Kentucky equal $382.66 2/3 by not made 2-22-1797.
    Plff. to recover. (67-71)
LANGHAM & JAMES vs. James ROGERS. Plffs. to recover. (71)
EVANS, John vs. James ROGERS. Plff. to recover. (71)
CRAIG, Alexander vs. James McGENE. Plff. to recover. (72)
CRAIGUE, Alexander vs. James McCENE. Plff. to recover. (73)

All officers present but William Patton.
WALLACE, Thomas vs. Archabald Rupell. James Boner suriety for deft. Plff paid
    on 6-1-1795 defts passage from Ireland to America and found him necessaries
    for two yrs. from date of note. Deft was to pay plff. within 6 days after
    arrival in Phila. 8 gineas British equal to $37.30 and then to serve plff.
    Since deft. did not serve, he was liable for passage etc. Jury found in
    favor of plff. Jury called consisting of:

John ADAMS	James LOGAN	John MONTGOMERY	John McCARDBURGH
Joseph JEFFRIES	Robert EVAN	John TURNER	Thomas ROGERS
Jacob SHELPHERD	Lucas NEBUKER	Abraham STEPS	Samuel WILSON
			(73-78)

BISWELL, John vs. Isaac OWENS & Elijah WILSON. Filed Dec. 4th Tues. 1798. On 9-1-1798 Owens and Wilson were to build roof for house in Chillicothe of Biswell, but did not do job in substantial manner. Jury found in favor of plff. for $38.86. Jury called consisting of:

Joseph JEFFRIES	John MONTGOMERY	Robert EVANS	Thomas DAVIDSON
William HURTT	David HAYS	James LOGAN	John McCANBURGH
William KEYS	Caleb STOCKEN	Joseph GIFFORD	Lucas NEBUKER
			(78-81)

MILLEGAN, James vs. Wm. JOHNSTONE. Filed 4th Tues. Dec. 1798. Johnstone was to deliver 70 bushels of corn by 4-24-1798, he refused and was indebted $100. Jury found in favor of plff. Jury called consisting of:

John KIRKPATRICK	Isaac OWENS	James GRUBB	William HODDY
John BISHONG	Samuel STOOPS	Samuel WITHROW	Richard HODDY
David STOCKON	Daniel BRINEY	Alexander CRAIG	George HEATH
			(81-84)

DRENNEN, Thomas vs. Thomas WHITE. Slanderous Words. Damage $300. Jury found for deft. Jury called consisting of:

William CREIGHTON	James CARRY	Hugh WARDS	Isaac DAVIS
James BONER	Joseph LANE	Samuel WILSON	Abraham STIP
John JOHNSTONE	Jas. WEBSTER	John COLLET	John ADAMS(84-88)

Court held 4th Saturday June 1799 Wm. Patton absent

FINLY, Samuel vs. Daniel HAMILTON. $150. Note made 6-11-1798. Plff. to recover(89)

BLAIR, John vs. James BLAIR. Filed 4th Tues. Dec. 1798. Note made 5-25-1797 Ross Co. 3 lbs. 15 shillings & 6 pence of Kentucky equals $12.58, also beef steer at house of said John Blair at Bourbon price. Judgement for plff on condition deft. to appear next term court. (91-93)

BEWELL, Walter vs. James HERRIOTT. $60. James S. Webster suriety for deft. Plff. to recover. (93-94)

WILKEN, John & Charles Jr., merchants vs. David DUNCAN. Debt. $272.75. Andrew Tybout on 7-14-1796 at Phila. made bill of exchange to Duncan. (94-97)

ABRAMS, Reuben vs. Caleb STOCKDON. $100 due by acct. Suit dismissed. (97)

LANGHAM & JAMES vs. Samuel HARRIS. $27.39 with interest. Plffs favor. (98)

JAMISON, Charles vs. Samuel MCLWAIN. Case dismissed. (98)

HARRIS, Samuel vs. Henry SHEELY. Case dismissed. (98)

HENDERSON, David vs. Charles JAMISON. Case dismissed. (99)

FINLEY, Robert W. vs. Negro Joe & Negro Sarah. Slander. Case dismissed. (99)

GREGG, Thomas vs. William W. CNAHAN. Deft to recover 4 shillings. (99)

LAMB, William vs. Peter RICKABAUGH. Case dismissed. (99-100)

LANGHAM & JAMES vs. Isaac EATON. Case dismissed. (100)

SMITH, Samuel vs. Caleb STOCKTON. Case dismissed. (100)

URNSTON, Benjamin vs. Thomas DAVISON. Case dismissed. (100-101)

JACKSON, Samuel vs. Em. ROE, W. JOHNSTONE & David JOHNSTONE. Case dismissed. (101)

STEWART, John vs. Furgus MOORE. Note made 7-26-1798 in Ross Co. Was bound unto John Stewart of Huntington Co. Penn. $240 confirmed by general warrantee known as No. 258 lying between John Biswell, etc. Case dismissed.(101-103)

472

June 1799 - cont.
DONALDSON, John vs. Daniel BRINEY. $74. by note of 2-29-1799. Plffs. favof.(103-105)
LANGHAM & JAMES vs. Peter RICKABAUGH. Debt. Plffs. favor. (105-107)
LANGHAM & JAMES vs. Isaac WARNER. Debt. Plffs. favor. (107-108)
LANGHAM & JAMES vs. Charles CRQUE. Debt. of $17. made 1-1-1790 Chillicothe.
Case dismissed. (108-110)
McDONGAL, John vs. William PORT. debt made 9-11-1798 for $33.51. Case discont.(110-114)
McGANARD, Henry vs. Daniel HAMILTON. Debt of $38. Suit settled out of court.(114-117)
HURST, Abraham vs. William POST. Debt $35. made 2-14-1798. Plff. to recover.(117-120)

Court held 4th Wednesday September 1799
BALDWIN, Michael granted license to practice as attorney. (121)
THOMPSON, James vs. Samuel STOOPS. Filed 10-22-1798. Note made 8-11-1798 of $1000.
Plff. rented for 1 yr. a dwelling house, kitchen and stable. Deft to do
work, which he did not do. Jury found $100. plffs. favor. Jury called
consisting of:

John McDONALD	Hygett LOWNES	John MEALHOUSE	John CHENWORTH
John HADDY	Benj. KILPATRICK	Daniel HAMILTON	Philip WORLEY
John BISHONG	Richard SEDWICK	Thomas DICK	William COOPER
			(121-124)

RUSSELL, James vs. Daniel HAMILTON. Filed 4th Dec. 1798 for $1000. damages. Deft
on 12-13-1797 made not in Penn. money equal to $901.85. Plff. to recover.
(125-129)
McDOUGAL, John vs. Edward PATCHELL. Assault & Battery. Suit dismissed.(129-130)

Court held 1st Thursday September 1799
James Scott, James Dunlap and James Furguson, Esq. - Justices.
McDONALD, William Jr. vs. Joseph POTTER. Debt $131.50 made on 3-6-1799. Thomas
Greg surety. Plff. to recover. (131-134)
McDONGAL, John vs Robert McMAHAN. Note of $18.52 made 6-12-1798. Plff. to recover.
(134-137)
KENNETT, Pressly vs. Samuel STOOPS. Debt. deft made not 9-19-1798 at Chillicothe
equal to $19.90. Plff. to recover. (137-140)
REEVES, Jessee vs. Joseph DIXTON. Debt. Note made 5-6-1798 for $42. Plff. to recover.
(140-143)

Court held 1st Fri. after 4th Tues. September 1799
James Scott, James Ferguson, John Guthry and Wm. Patton, Esq. - Justices.
WOLFE, Phillip vs. John Collet. Filed Dec. 1798. Trespass. Litigation over a
mare with plff. asking $250. Deft. to pay plff. $96.23. Jury:

James FURGUSON	David HAYS	John JOHNSTONE	Samuel STOOPS
Anthony S. DEVENPORT	Robert COOPER	William HUTT	James WEBSTER
Jose LANE	Isaac DAVIS	James GRUBB	John McCOY

(Note: The following may have been transcribed out of place in the record.)
Depositions to be taken of Abraham Wetstone and James Woods. Evidence for plff.
of Beford Co. Pa. Samuel Dixon to take deposition of Col. Charles Campbell
_____ Wright and Docter Simon Hovey of Westmoreland Co. Penn. at house of
Dixon on 15 Apr., Also that Matthew Cary Esq. of Alexandia in Huntington Co.
Penn to take deposition of John Richards on 26 Apr. at the house of said Gray.
Deposition of Thomas Province to be taken before James Scott Esq. Also de-
position to be taken of Abraham Whetstone Jr. next Monday before Elias Langham
also order to take deposition Betsey Wood which shall be read at trial.
Cont. to Sept. term. Jury called:

William LAMB	Robert GREG	Wm. COOPER	Thomas DICK
Hugh BOYLE	Benjamin FITZPATRICK	James McGILL	Lucas NEBUCCAR
Caleb STOCKTON	James HENDERSON	John BERSHONG	Adam TURNER
			(144-150)

TURNER, Richard vs. John GOFSET. Filed 4th Tues. Mar. 1799. Gofset on 13 Feb. 1797
at Chillicothe made note for Kentucky money equals to $14.50.
Plff. to recover. (150-152)

McDONALD, William Jr. vs. Daniel BRINEY. Filed Mar. term 1799. Note made 3-6-1799
for $41 on demand. Plff. to recover. (153-155)

CAMPBELL, William vs. James JOHNSTON. Filed Mar. term 1799. On 11-15-1797 at
Chillicothe-one watch to be turned safe or 60 bushes of corn. Plff. to
recover. (155-158)

McDONALD, William vs. John BISWELL. Filed Mar. 1799. Note made 3-9-1799 at
Chillicothe for $35.50. Plff. to recover. (159-161)

CHESERANE, Adam vs. Robt. McMAHAN. File Mar. 1799. On 12-2-1797 note made for
$20. Plff. to recover. (161-164)

BESHONG, John vs. Wm. CRACK (CRAIG?). Filed Dec. term 1798 in Adams Co. presently
Ross. On 2-20-1798, Craig sold a keel boat to load in the amount of 8 ton
from mouth of Scioto River to Chillicothe for which Bishong is to pay $1
per hundred which Bishong is to collect from owners of loading. Craig also
to bring 100 bushes of corn from the Pee Pee town to Chillicothe for Bishong.
Craig did not perform his agreements. Bishong asks $250 damages. Cont.
June term. Jury called:

John CLEMMENS	William HALL	Joseph TIFFIN	John McDONALD
Thomas WHITE	Robert EVANS	Anthony S. DAVENPORT	Em. COOPER
Uriah POLLIN	Hugh MOORE	Tiliman LEWIS	James GRUBB

John Clemons is withdrawn and rest of jury is discharged. Case cont. to
Sept. term 1799. Jury called:

Benjamin McCLURE	John WELLS	John HARGUS	Philip WORLEY
John McDONALD	David GATES	John HODDY	Thomas ROGERS
John BROWN	Joseph GIFFORD	John GALLOWAY	John KIMBLE

Plff. to recover $151.91 and costs. Deft. motion to give him till Sat. next
to file errors in arrest of judgement. Next day, errors found good by law
to preclude plff. to obtain judgement. Case dismissed. (164-167)

SIBBIT, James vs. Robert McMAHAN. Filed mar. 1799. In Jan. 1799 Daniel Briney and
McMahan purchased a certain boat of a W. Samuel Teters which Sibbit, Briney
and McMahan were to pay $180 each and each was to have right to dispose of
his third provided it does not interfere with others. McMahan sold his interest to Joseph Vance, but did not has his $180. Suit abated. (168-170)

DRENNEN, Thomas vs. Robert GREGG. Mathew Stokes suriety. Filed Mar. 1799. Deft.
to recover. (170-172)

McDONALD, William vs. Matthew STOKES. Filed June 1799. $60 sometime in year 1790
for the occupation and use of room upon art of an inlot in Chillicothe.
Stokes was to build a chimney of stone for use of room. Stokes not only
left premises but removed part of the house itself. Plff. to recover.
(172-173)

WILLS, John S. vs. Edward PATCHEL. Suit discontinued. (174)

McCOY, William vs. Benjamin McCLURE. $65. Plff. to recover. (174)

KELLEY, William & Co. vs. John GOSSETT. Wm. Kelly and John Cowens merchants and co-partners. Note made 2-7-1797 in Kentucky money equal to $43.22. Plff. to recover. (175-176)

WALLER, John vs. James ROGERS. Thomas Dick surity. Filed June term 1799. On 2-10-1799 $30 for goods and merchandise. Plff. to recover. (177-178)

McCOY, John vs. John THOS. Debt of $61. and 4 shillings and 4-1-1799. Plff. to recover. (178-179)

McCOURTNEY, Alexander vs. Charles MOOT and Conrad MOOT. Filed June 1799. Case cont. to Sept. Term 1799. On 6-5-1798 bill of 180 lbs. Penn. currence with 49 lbs. 17 shillings 4 pence to be paid before 7-5-1798. Penn. currency equal to $398.30. Plff to recover. (181-182)

MUTES, Charles vs. John GUTHREE. June 1799. Note made 7-28-1798 in Penn. currency equal to $177. Plff. to recover. (182-184)

THOMPSON, William vs. Barnabas LAMBAT. Case dismissed. (184)

BATES, Emphraim vs. Wm. WARNER. Case dismissed. (184)

HARR, Everrard vs. James McCLANE, Case dismissed. (184)

GREGG, Thomas vs Robert COOPER. Case dismissed. (185)

BOYLE, John and Hugh vs. David WRIGHT. Case dismissed. (185)

WILLS, John S. vs. Robert BALENTINE. Case discontinued. (185)

TEMPLETON, John vs. James PHILLIPS. Case dismissed. (185)

BROWN, John vs. Robert SIMPSON and Reuben ABRAMS. Case discontinued. (186)

BOYLE, John and Hugh vs. John McCLURE. Suit dismissed. (186)

GARDNER, Absolem vs. William WALLACE. Suit discontinued. (186)

ROOK, William vs. David DUNCAN. Case dismissed. (186)

STEPENSON, Marcus vs. Aaron STEPENSON. Filed Mar. 1799. $60. Case cont. till June term. the cont. till Sept. term and dismissed. (187-188)

LANGHAM, Elias and Thomas JAMES, Firm vs. Uriah POLLIN. Filed June 1799. Pollin bought store goods amounting to $35. Case cont. till Sept. and then dismissed. (189-190)

LANGHAM & JAMES vs. Samuel STOOPS. Debt $54.50. Case cont. to Sept. term and then dismissed. (191-192)

475

ROSS COUNTY, OHIO - TERRITORIAL COURT ORDER BOOK 1799-1800

Contributed by: Mrs. Patrick Clark, Route #10, Box 76, Chillicothe, Ohio 45601

The following records were taken from "Order Book Territorial Court 1798-1800" located in the Clerk of Court's office at the court house at Chillicothe. These cases are generally civil in nature and have been abstract only for names and genealogical data as a finding aid. Pages on which record may be found in the original book are given in parenthesis.

Court held 1st Fri after 4th Tues of Dec. 1799

KENNET, Pressly(?) vs. Daniel HAMILTON. Filed Nov. 2, 1798. To collect debt for goods and wares purchased by Hamilton. Cont. to March term, cont to June term, cont to Sept term where plff did not appear with deft to recover costs from plff. Jury: Isaac DAVIS, Isaac OWENS, John BISHONG, James HAYS, John WILKINSON, Benj. MILLER, Joseph TIFFIN, Robt W. FINLEY, James KILGORE, Wm McCLENEHAM, Elias BOATMAN and John PATTON. (193-196)

BROOKS, Benj. and wife vs James RAMSEY. Filed March term 1799. Case for words. Benj. Brooks Sr. and wife Agnes complain that Ramsey accused said Agnes of hogstealing. That words were stated by Ramsey in Ross Co. on Sept 1, 1798 Cont to June term 1799 at which court it was ordered that deposition be taken from Henry Stucker and wife Lydia of Fayette Co., Pa. Cont to Dec. term where jury found Agnes, guilty of offense and in favor of deft to recover costs. Jury: Samuel THOMAS, Wm LAPPER, Jas. S. WEBSTER, John McLANDBURG, Thos. McDONALD, Daniel BRINEY, Phillip STRIDER, John CLEMMONS, Jacob WIDNER, Samuel SARGENT, Benj. UMSTONE, John GOFSETT. (196-199)

BASTER, Reuben vs. John JOHNSTON, plff to recover from deft $40. and costs. (199)

Court held 1st Sat after 4th Tues of Dec. 1799

BRINEY, Daniel vs. Robt McMAHAN. Filed March term 1799. On May 10, 1798 Briney, McMahan and James Sibbet purchased a boat of Sam'l Teters and to pay $60 each, 1/3 liable to Briney for $80. Briney and Sibbet purchased another boat of Teters which became joint property with McMahan selling his 1/3 part of boat to Joseph Vance. Cont to June term 1799, cont to Sept term, cont to Dec. term where plff to recover $40 and costs. Jury: Sam'l THOMAS, Wm FRIEGHTON, Thos. McDONALD, Adam GILFILLIN, John KIRKENDOL, Abraham DEARDUFF, Sam'l SARGENT, Fergus MOORE, Benj. URMSTONE, James McCLURE, Michael THOMAS and John GOSSET. (200-202)

GILFILLEN, Adam vs. James ROGERS. Filed Sept term 1799. To collect on note Cont to Dec term 1799 with plff to recover. (202-204)

JENKS, John vs. James KER and Thos. LONG. Filed Dec term 1798, cont to March term 1799. To collect note for 100 bushels of corn. Cont. to June term, cont. to Sept term, cont to Dec. term 1799. Jury found for plff. Jury: Jeremiah WHITE, John CLEMONS, David SHEPHERD, James PHILIPS, James FULTON, Philip STREIDER, Jacob WYDNER, David HAYS, Wm RHEY, Thos. McDONALD, Nicholas JAMES and John TETERS. (204-206)

476

Court held 1st Mon after 4th Tues Dec 1799

Present: Sam'l FINDLEY, Elias LANGHAM, James FERGUS and John GUTHRIE, Esq., Justices. (206)

BEASLEY, John and Andrew ALLISON vs. Robt McMAHAN and Jonathan ROADS, To collect debt. Cont to June term, cont to Dec. term where plff found to recover. (206-208)

JOHNSTONE, Wm vs. Sam'l HOWARD. Johnstone charges Howard entered his property and took cattle and damaged tree. Filed March term, cont. to June term, cont to Dec. term with jury found deft not guilty and plff to pay costs. Jury: John McLANBURG, John LUSH, Isaac DAVIS, Adam McMURDY, Wm CREIGHTON, Edward PATCHEL, David SHEPHERD, Jas. FULTON, Hugh WOODS, Wm TONG (or LONG) and James RAMSEY. (208-210)

FEN, Richard vs. John Den. Ejectment. Plff claims deft with force dentered tract of 550 acres being part of larger tract of 166 acres which E. Tiffin demised for term of years not yet expired. Deft asks that John Blackmore be made deft in suit. Dec term defts found guilty with plff to recover. Jury: John McLANBURG, Wm B. YOUNG, Jas. BONER, James LOGAN, Thos. ROGERS, Reuben ABRAMS, David SHEPHERD, Adam McMURDIE, James FULTON, Hugh WOODS, Nicholas JAMES and Daniel HAMILTON. (210-214)

Court held 1st Tues. 4th Thurs. Dec. 1799

Present: Sam'l FINDLEY, Elias LANGHAM, James FARGUS, Esqs., Justices. (214)

BLAIR, Thomas F. vs. Dan ROTRICK. Filed Dec. term 1798, cont to March term, on June 24, 1798 Blair purchased of Thomas Lewis of Kentucky nine acfes in name of Williams on west side of Scioto River above mouth of PeePee including Parriria(?) near same for $3000, with $2000 to pay on July 20, 1798, Rotrick on July 10, 1789 bought 300 acres for $1500 from Thomas Blair being part of said land with $100 paid to Blair on July 18, 1798. Blair lost his purchase of land, so brings suit. Cont to June term, cont to Sept term, cont to Dec. term with habeas corpus issued for seizure of deft. (214-126)

URMSTONE, Benj. vs. Thos. DAVIDSON and John COLLET. Filed June term 1799. Urmstone late of Adams Co. but now of Ross Co. complains that Davidson late of Pa. and Collett of Territory NW ohio owe $160 from note of Aug. 29, 1798. Cont to Sept term, cont to Dec. term where suit dismissed and deft to pay plff. (216-218)

BROOKS, Benj. Jr. by next friend Benj. BROOKS Sr. vs James RAMSEY. Case for words. Filed Mar. term 1798. Deft accused plff of being thief. Cont to June term, cont to Dec term where jury found for plff to recover. Jury: Jos. JOHNSTONE, Jas. KIRKPATRICK, David HAYS, Adam TURNER, Wm RHEA, Wm THOMPSON, Michael THOMAS, Wm HUNT, Saml D. JACKSON, Jas. THOMPSON, Wm COOPER, and Benj. KIRKPATRICK. (219-221)

HUTT, Wm vs. T hos. JAMES. Filed June 1799. To collect money due for work and labor. Cont to Sept term, jury: Isaac DAVIS, Jas. PHILLIPS, John McDONALD, Thos. McDONALD, Jas. MILLER, Harry WORLEY, Gabriel COYLE, John BROWN, Adam GILFELLIN, Jos. BLACK and Philip WORLEY. Jury found for plff in amount of $15. Deft asks new trial and jury verdict set aside, jury: David HAYS, Reuben BAXTER, Jacob MILLER, Nicholas JAMES, Wm B. YOUNG, John CLEMANS, James RAMSEY, Hugh WOODS, Adam McMURDY, David T. HUFFMAN, Harding CRAUCH, and Wm JOHNSTONE. Jury found in favor of deft and he to recover costs. (221-224)

Present: Sam'l FINLEY, Elias LANGHAM, James FURGUSON, Esqs., Justices. (224)
EDGAR, Andrew vs. James RAMSEY. Case for words. Filed June term 1799. Deft
called Edgar a thief. Cont to Sept term. Cont to Dec. term, Jury: Joseph
JOHNSTON, Alex JENKINS, Jacob MILLER, Thos McDONALD, Wm COOPER, Jacob WYDNER,
David SHEPHERD, Reuben BAXTER, Philip STRYDER, Christian RICHARDS, Nicholas
JAMES and Nathan KENNEDY. Plff to recover. (224-226)
ACKENBERGER, Stephen vs. Jacob WIDNER. Filed June term 1799. To collect debt.
Cont to Sept term, cont to Dec term, Jury: Jos, JOHNSTONE, Philip STRYDER,
David BELCHER, Alex JENKINS, Benj KIRKPATRICK, Jas. PHILIP, David SHEPHERD,
Reuben BAXTER, Jas LOGAN, David HAYS, Edwd PATCHEL and Jacob MILLER. Plff
to recover. (227-229)
GISONS, George vs. William POST. Filed March term 1799. To collect debt made
Mar. 20, 1798 at Chillicothe than in Adams Co., now in Ross Co. Cont to
June term 1799, cont to Sept term, cont to Dec term, Jury: John McLANBURGH,
Wm WARREN, John CLEMENS, Jacob WYDNER, Dan BRINEY, Wm NORTON, Nicholas JAMES,
Adam McMURDIE, Wm RUTLEDGE, Wm STEWART, Robt McMAHAN, and Stephen ACKENBEERGER.
Plff to recover. (229-231)
KERN, Wm vs. John WOOLCOAT. Filed June 1799. To collect note for corn. Cont.
Sept term, cont to Dec. term, Jury: Wm HUTT, John M(c)CLURE, James BONER,
Jos. JOHNSTONE, David HUGHMAN, George HAINS, Dan BRINEY, Jacob MILLER,
Johnstone HEMPHILL, Robt McMAHAN, Harding CROUCH, Ben. BROOKS. Plff to
recover. (232-233)
HIGHLANDS, John vs. James M(c)CLUNE. Filed June term 1799. To collect debt
for work and labor. Cont to Sept term, cont to Dec. term, Jury: (same as
listed above). Plff to recover. (234-236)
HANCE, Elisha vs. Jas. McLANE. Filed June term 1799. To collect for work, labor
and material. Cont to Sept term, cont to Dec term, jury: (same as above except
name of Jos. Hemphill omitted). Plff to recover. (236-238)
LANGHAM, Elias and Thomas JAMES vs Sam'l TAYLOR. Filed June term 1799. To
collect for goods and wares purchased under firm of Langham and James. Cont to
Sept term, cont to Dec term, plff to recover. (238-240)

Present: Jas SCOTT, Sam'l FINLEY, James FERGUSON, Elias LANGHAM and Jas. DUNLAP,
Esqs., Justices. (240) Court received information that Gen'l George Washing-
ton hath departed this life and showed their respect by giving a resolution.
(241)
BLOOM, Christian vs Benj. WHITE. Plff & deft agree to $40 and costs. Plff agrees
to stay of execution and Judgement until June term next. (241)
BAITS, Ephraim vs. Thos. BRIGGS. Filed Apr. 1799. On attachment against Thos.
Briggs estate for possession of personal property found in possession of
Jas Forges, left there by Jas. Warren. Sheriff to sell attached effects
to pay judgement. (241-242)
POTTER, Jos. vs. Johnstone HEMPHILL. Filed June term 1799. To collect debt.
Cont to sept term, cont to Dec. term with plff to recover. (242-243)
BRINEY, Daniel vs. Joseph POTTER, judgement for plff to recover in debt of
money with stay of execution until June term next. (243)

478

Sheriff to receive out of treasury, monies to cover expenses and costs paid to: Bedford and Mowy vs Wylie, Deal vs Wylie, Greeg vs. Rupell (Russell), Givins vs, Rupell, Bayle vs Rupell, Potter vs. Rupell, Johnstone vs. Rupell. (243)

CLEMENS, John to receive $9.75 out of treasury for record and maintaining certain prisoners. (244)

LANGHAM, Elias and Thomas JAMES vs. Robert FINLEY. Filed Sept 1799. To collect debt for purchase by Finley of goods and wares, cont to Dec. term with plff to recover. (244-245)

MOORS, Furges vs. Samuel TAYLOR and Samuel WILSON. Filed June term 1799. To collect on note. Cont to sept term, cont to Dec. term, plff to recover. (246-247)

BONER, James vs. David DUNCAN. Filed June term 1799. To collect on note. Cont to Sept term, cont to Dec. term, plff to recover. (247-249)

WILSON, Samuel vs. Henry RICKSUCKER. Filed Oct. 1798. Wilson obtained attachment against lands, goods and chattels. Cont to Dec term 1798, cont to March 1799, cont to June, cont to Sept, cont to Dec, when sheriff ordered to sell attached effects to satisfy judgement. (249-251)

BEDFORD and MOWRY vs. Wm WYLIE. Filed June term 1799. Nathaniel Bedford and Peter Mowry, physicians to collect debt of ?50 for labor and medicine for Wm Wylie and family. Cont to Sept term, sheriff ordered to produce Wylie but did not comply and sheriff fined $27.56 with Judgement overruled by sheriff and his atty. cont to Dec. term when sheriff still did not comply and sheriff again fined $27.56 and ordered that sheriff be taken. (251-253)

DEAL, Wm vs Wm WYLIE. Filed June term 1799. To collect debt for beef, veal, mutton and other meats. Cont to Sept 1799 when sheriff failed to produce Wylie, cont to Dec term with sheriff fined $53.08 and ordered to be taken. (253-255)

GREGG, Thos. vs Arche RUPELL. Filed June term 1799. To collect note. Sheriff to produce Rupell at Sept term, but failed to do so and fined $77.25.(255-257)

POTTER, Joseph vs. Arche RUPEL. Filed June 1799. To collect note (note: proceedings against sheriff as above, Dec. term, plff to recover. (257-259)

BOYLE, John and Hugh vs. Arche RUPPELL. Filed June term 1799. To collect debt. Cont to Sept, cont to Dec. (259-260)

JOHNSTON, James vs. Arche RUPEL. Filed June term 1799. Cont to Sept term $55. and costs, Sheriff to pay. (260-261)

GIVENS, George vs. Arche RUPEL. Filed June term 1799. Sheriff returned on writ of Capias ad Repondendum. Sheriff to produce deft in Sept term, cont to Dec. term with sheriff to ,pay $60 and costs. (261-262)

CULP, George vs. Daniel HAMELTON. Filed June term 1799. To collect debt. Culp of Bourbon Co., Ky and Hamilton of Chillicothe. On Mar 27, 1798 Hamilton sold Culp bear skins, deer skins, etc. and to be delivered at Limestone by Hamilton to Culp to be stored at John Taylor's warehouse and Culp to pay storage and to pay Hamilton in whiskey to be purchased in Ky...Hamilton's brother John Hamilton of Bourbon Co., Ky to judge whiskey to be good proof and to be received at Limestone. Culp delivered whiskey but Hamilton didn't deliver. Cont to Sept term, cont to Dec. term, suit discontinued. (262-265)

WILSON, John vs. John CLARKE. Filed June term 1799. To collect debt. About
May 1, 1799 William Clarke son of John Clark being under age, request of
father shot at and beat horse property of Wilson. Cont to Sept term, cont.
to Dec. term, plff failed to appear and deft to receive costs. (265-267)

McCLENE, James vs. Elisha HANCE. Filed June 1799, cont to Sept term, cont to
Dec. term, deft to receive cost from plff. (268)

SHARP, John vs. Matthew STOKES. Filed June term 1799, cont to Sept term, to Dec.
term, deft failed to appear and plff to recover. (268-270)

URMSTONE, Benj. vs. John CLEMENS. Filed Sept term 1799, cont Dec. term, suit
discont. (270)

PHILLIPS, James vs. Joseph TEMPLETON, Filed Sept 1799, cont to Dec. term, deft
to recover from plff. (271)

CRAIGSEN, Wm vs Polly BROWN, Sept 1799, deft to recover from plff. (271-272)

BONER, James vs. Joseph HUNTER, plff defaulted with deft to receive costs. (272)

CRAWFORD, James vs. John TUTTLE, plff defaulted, deft to receive costs. (272)

JOHNSTON, Wm vs. Wm MORTON, plff defaulted, deft to receive costs. (273)

McELWAIN, Samuel vs. W. LAFFIN. Filed June term 1799. To collect note. Cont
to Sept term, cont to Dec term. with plff to recover. (273-275)

STOCKTEN, David vs. Jeremiah M(c)CIEN, plff defaulted, deft to recover costs.(275).

MOUNTS, Abner vs. John BISWELL. Filed June term 1799. To collect debt. Cont to
Sept. cont to Dec. term. plff to recover. (276-278)

MORTON, Wm vs. Wm JOHNSTON, plff defaulted, deft to receive costs. (278)

HOLLER, Adam vs. Peter RICKABAUGH, case dismissed, costs to each. (278)

McDONALD, Wm vs James CARR. Filed Dec. 1798, cont to Mar. term, cont to June
term. To collect debt for beef purchased by Car. Cont to Sept term, cont
to Dec. term with plff to recover. (279-281

KEYS, William vs. James HANLEN, suit dismissed by mutual consent at cost of
sheriff. (281

MOORE, Furgus vs John STEWART. Note of 7-3-1798 for $65. June term 1799 cont. to
Sept., deft pleads not guilty. Dec Term, plff to recover $65. (281-283)

REED, Samuel vs. James THOMPSON, June term 1799 for $300 case damages. 9-24-1798,
$128 to be paid 4-1-1799 and another note for $100. cont. to Sept, deft pleads
not guilty. Dec term, deft relinquishes former plea and pff to recover $228
and 5% interest 4-1-1799. (284-286)

HUSTON, Paul vs. Joseph POTTER and William JOHNSTON, June term 1799. Note of
9-24-1798 at Chillicothe of $99 to be paid 3-1-1799. (286-288)

(note: pages 289-290 are blank)

HUSTON, Paul vs. Joseph POTTER and William JOHNSTON, case cont., $294 with $400
damages, cont to Sept., cont. to Dec. Dec Term, deft relinquishes former
plea, plff to recover damages and costs. (291-92)

SLAUGHER, Robert F. vs. James MAY, suit dismissed by mutual consent. (293)

HUSTON, Paul vs. James BONER. June term 1799. To collect promissary note. Deft.
relinquishes plea. (292-297)

BOYCE, Robert vs. John McClure. Filed Sept. term 1799. Damages of $50.; Dec.
term 1799 suit dismissed. (297-298)

POWEL, David vs. James SCOTT and John BISHONG. Filed June term 1799. To collect
promissory note. Deft. relinquishes to plff. (298-300)

ROBINS, John vs. Caleb STOCKTON. Filed June term 1799. To collect promissory note dated Dec. 25 1798. Case cont. to Sept 1799. Case cont. to Dec 1799 when deft relinquishes plea. (301-304)

ROBINS, Daniel vs. Caleb STOCKTON. Filed June term 1799. To collect promissory note dated Feb. 14, 1799. Cont. to Sept term. Cont. to Dec. term when deft relinquishes former plea. (304-307)

LANGHAM, Elias vs. John CLEMENS. Filed June term 1799. To collect debt. Plff. to recover damages of $20.16. (307-309)

LANGHAM, Elias vs. James DELAY. Suit dismissed. Deft. to pay cost to plff. (309)

RINGLAND, John vs. John GOSSETT. Filed Dec. term 1799. To collect note. Plff. to recover. (309-310)

ABRAMS, Henry vs. James TEMPLANE. Filed June term 1799. To collect note. That Abrams cultivated tract of land not far from house of Templane and raised crop of corn, building crib for corn and placed said corn in crib and that Templane set fire in neglegent manner which burned corn and crib. Cont. to Sept 1799 term. Cont to Dec. term when deft relinquishes plea. (311-313)

MOORE, Furgus vs. James ROGERS. Filed June term 1799. To collect debt. Cont. to Sept term, cont. to Dec. term when deft relinquishes plea. (313-315)

WALLER, John vs, George SKIDMORE. Filed June term 1799. Note dated Aug. 26, 1797 in state of Kentucky, that is to say at Chillicothe, Ross Co. Deft. relinquishes plea at Dec. term. (315-317)

VIGO, Frances vs. James DYER. Filed June term 1799. James Dyer with Jonathan Frewill(?) and Jacob Hull note dated June 21, 1796 of $1000 with condition payable of 100 lbs. currant money of Virginia to be paid by May 1, 1799. Dec term deft. relinquishes plea. (317-319)

KEBB(?), Hugh W. vs Caleb STOCKEN. Filed June term 1799. Debt. Cont. to Sept. term, cont to Dec. term when deft relinquishes plea. (320-322)

POTTER, Joseph vs. James BONNER. Filed June term 1799. Damages. Cont. to Dec. term when deft relinquishes plea. (322-324)

LANGHAM, Elias and Thomas JAMES vs. Elias HANCE. Filed June term 1799. To collect note. Cont to Sept. term, cont. to Dec. term when deft relinquishes plea. (324-326)

LANGHAM, Elias and Thomas JAMES vs. John CLEMENS. Filed June 1799. To collect debt. Cont. to Sept. term, cont. to Dec. term when deft relinquishes plea. (326-328)

Court held 4th Tuesday of March 1800

Present: Samuel FINDLEY, William PATTON, James DUNLAP, Esqs., Justices. (328)

BROOKS, Linch vs. John ANDERSON. Plff to recover and costs. (328)

McMICKEL, James vs. Joseph JEFFERIES. Trespass for false imprisonment filed Sept. 1799. McMickel asks damages of $1000. against Jefferies. Cont. to Dec. 1799 term. Deft states he committed battery complained of in plff declaration but avows it was justifiable. March term, deft relinquishes plea. Suit dismissed with deft to pay plff his costs expended. (328-330)

McDOUGAL, John vs. John BEATTY. Filed Mar. term 1800. To collect debt of goods, wares and merchandise received. (330-332)

Court of first day after 4th Tues. in March 1800

Present: Samuel FINLEY, William PATTON, James DUNLAP, Esqs., Justices. (332)
HUTT, William S. vs. Thomas GREGG. Filed Sept. term 1799. Asst. and battery.
On Aug. 6, 1799 at Chillicothe Gregg did assult and beat Hutt. Cont.
to Dec. 1799 term, cont to March 1800 term when deft relinquishes plea.
(332-324--pages misnumbered--should be 332-334)

Court held Thurs after 4th Tues in March 1800

Present: Samuel FINLEY, William PATTON, James DUNLAP, Esq., Justices. (324)
RIDGLEY, Frederick vs. Azel ALDREDGE. Filed March 1800. To collect note.
(324-326)
ROGERS, James vs. Samuel STOOPS. Filed Sept. term 1799. Cont. to next term.
To collect for goods, wares and merchandize. Cont. to March term 1800,
when deft relinquishes former plea. (326-329)
McDOUGAL, John vs. Nicholas MILLER. Filed March term $800. To collect note.
Plff. to recover. (330-331)
HUNTER, Joseph vs Lucas SULLIVANT. Filed Dec. 1798, cont to March term 1799
That on 9-28-1798 deft did deceive and defraud said Joseph Hunter of $150.
Cont to June term, cont to Sept term, cont to Dec. term. Jury: Joseph
JOHNSTON, William B. YOUNG, Nicholas JAMES, John CLEMENTS. Reuben BAXTER,
David HAUGHMAN, Jacob WYDNER, James RAMSEY, Adam McMURDIE, Harding CROUSE,
James MILLER and Hugh WOODS ruled plff to be assessed damages of $117.87.
Verdit set aside. Deft to pay cost of trial and new one cont to March term.
Jury: Thomas DAVIDSON, John BATY, Furgus MOORE, Joseph JEFFERIES, David HAYS,
John BROWN, John BAYLESS, Mathew THOMPSON, Henry HUSTON, Isaac DAWSON, Samuel
SHAW and Joseph McCOY. Deft did assume assess plff damages of $188. with
plff to recover against deft. (331-334)
McDOUGAL, John vs. John CLEMENS. Filed March 1800 term. To collect note.
Plff to recover. (335-336)
HUSTON, Paul vs. John BISWELL and William BISWELL. Filed June 1799. To collect
debt. Cont to Dec. term, cont. to March 1800 term. Deft relinquishes plea.
(336-338)
HAGGIN, John vs. William LAPPIN (or SAPPIN). Filed June 1799. To collect
damages. Cont. Dec. term, cont March term 1800. Jury: Abraham MILLER,
George KILGORE, Samuel DAVIS, William HUTT, Thomas HEROD, John McLENE,
Zach. TAYLOR, John McCLURE, John WILSON, David HAUGHMAN, John CLEMENS
and Azel ALRIDGE. Plff to recover. (339-340)
ATCHESON, Ailas vs. Robert TEMPLANE. Filed Sept term 1799. To collect note.
Cont Dec. term 1799, cont March term 1800 when deft relinquishes plea and
plff to recover. (341-343)
BROOKS, Linch vs. Caleb STOCKTON. Filed Sept term 1799. To collect note.
Mar. term 1800 deft relinquishes plea and plff to recover (343-346)
SMITH, Samuel vs. Martin MYERS. Filed Sept term 1799. To collect note. Cont.
to Mar. term 1800. Plff to recover. (346-348)
FINLEY, Samuel vs. Joseph LEMON. Petition that sometime in March 1799 various
articles and goods were sold to Lemon at Chillicothe. At March term 1800
found that plff to recover with judgement executed at next term. (348-350)

482

Present: Samuel FINLEY, James DUNLAP, John GUTHREE, William PATTON, Esq., Justices. (350)

BUSKIRK, Lewis vs. John HARGUS and John EVANS. Filed Sept. term 1799. Collect debt for cattle sold to defts. Cont next term, cont. to Mar. term 1801 when deft relinquishes plea. (350-353)

MEEKER COCHRAN & CO. vs. Barton EWELL and James EWELL. Filed March term 1799, cont. June term, cont. Sept. term, cont. Dec. Term. Ewells were merchants and partners in company which on Apr. 30, 1799 at Philadelphia, Pa. became indebted for $432 in goods, wares and merch'd. Cont March term with defts not present, plffs to recover. (353-356)

BATES, John vs. Benj. MILLER. Filed June term 1799. Debt for 1200 shingles, 50 clapboards, quanity of lathes and 8 joists delivered by Bates to Miller. He also hewed 10 logs, laid foundation of house of 24 sw feet and other work. Cont. to next term, cont. to Dec term, cont. to March term. Jury: Joseph HUNTER, Benj. SELLS, John BROWN, James DUNGAN, Ezekiel MITCHELL, John COOR (or COX), Jacob WYDENER, Fred HANK (or HAUK), Henry BOWMAN, Samuel JACKSON, John CLEMENS and James LOGAN. Plff and deft to pay costs. (356-358)

BOYLES, John and Hugh vs. Kindrey DAVIS. Filed March 1800 term. Boyles as merchants and carpenters for debt for goods and wares bought by deft Dec. 26, 1799 at Chillicothe. Plff to recover. (359-360)

PATCHELL, Edward vs. Daniel HAMILTON. Filed Sept term 1799. To collect debt. Cont to Dec. term, cont. to March term with plff. to recover costs. (360-361)

BOYLES, John and Hugh vs. Samuel CAMPBELL. Filed March term 1800. To collect debt. Plffs. to recover. (362-363)

NICELY, Abraham vs. John DERUSH. Filed March term 1800. To collect $13. for hire and use of occupational set of tools which were property of Abraham. Court found in favor of deft. (364-366)

BOYLES, John and Hugh vs. John Graham. Filed Dec. term 1800(1799?). Boyles as merchants and carpenters to recover debt for goods and wares. Plff to recover. (366-368)

ABRAMS, Reuben vs. Josiah PRICE. Filed Sept term 1799. To collect $50. for work and labour. Cont. to Dec. term, cont. to March term. Jury: Humphrey MONTGOMERY, Lucas NEBAKER, Philip WOLF, Abraham STIP, Samuel C. FLANNAKERR, John BOYLE, William NIBPACK, Ezekiel MITCHELL, James PHILLIPS, Alexander JENKINS, D. HARESMAN(?) and John BROWN. Plff. to recover $52. and costs. (368-371)

McMAHAN, William vs. Bennett LODSDAN and James MARTIN Sr. Filed March term 1800. To collect debt as executed before Robert Armstrong, J.P. of Alleghany Co., Maryland vs Bennett Logsdan and James Martin. Plff to recover. (371-372)

REED, David vs. Samuel STOOPS. Filed Sept term 1799. To collect note. Cont. Dec. term, cont. March term with plff to recover. (372-374)

CROSS, William vs. Samuel STOOPS. Filed Sept. term 1799. To collect note. Cont. to Dec. 1799, cont to March term 1800 with plff to recover. (374-377)

ELDER, Samuel vs. Samuel STOOPS. Filed Sept term 1799, cont. to Dec. term. Cont. to March term with plff to recover. (377-378)

DAVIS, David vs. William McCANDES. Filed March term 1800. To collect note dated Oct 28, 1797 in amount of 6 lbs. 6 shillings 9 pence in currency of Kentucky with interest. Plff to recover. (378)

483

BROWN, John vs. Samuel SMITH. Filed Dec. term 1799. Note by Reuben Addams made
   to order of Samuel Smith Esq. on Sept. 24, 1799 at Chillicothe in favor of
   John Brown "to bearer 164 gallons & 3 quarts of whiskey on Reuben's account".
   Not delivered so plff asking $200. value. Case discontinued. Costs paid
   by Reuben Abrams. (379-380)
BOYLES, John and Hugh vs. Wm JAMIESON. Filed Dec term 1799. Boyles as merchants
   to collect debt. Plff to recover. (380-382)
SMITH, Samuel vs. William JOHNSTON. To collect debt. Case cont. to next term,
   At March term 1800 deft relinquishes plea and plff to recover. (383-385)
CARLISLE, John vs. John S. Wills. Assault and battery. Case cont. to March term
   when plff did not prosecute and suit dismissed. (384-385)
GREGG, Nathan and Robert vs. John GUTHERY. Filed March term 1800. Greggs as
   merchants and co-partners to collect note. Plff to recover. (385-387)
JAMIESON, Charles vs Ezekiel MITCHELL. To collect note. Deft. defaulted
   and plff to recover. (387-388)
BEATTY, John C. vs. James MARTIN Sr. Filed March term 1800. To collect debt.
   Deft defaulted and plff to recover. (388-389)
RINGLAND, John vs. Benj. URMSTON. To collect debt of note witnessed by James
   Ferguson. Deft defaulted and plff to recover. (389-390)
BOYLES, John and Hugh vs. Samuel McADAM. Filed March term 1800. To collect debt
   for goods. Deft. defaulted and plff to recover. (391-392)

Court held June term 1800

Court held before Thomas Worthington, Esq. and his associate Justices. (392)
LAWSON, James vs. Robert ADAMS. Filed Dec term 1799. Lawson, late of Hamilton
   Co. but now of Adams County complains of Robert Adams late of Hamilton Co.
   but now of Ross Co. amount of 1000 lbs ($3,333). Case cont. to June term,
   cont. to Sept term, cont to Dec. term, cont. to March term. June term, jury:
   James GOODIN(G?), Thomas DICK, Eli SARGART, Samuel SARGENT, James May,
   Daniel BRINEY, Francis CREMOR, William WILSON, James LOGAN, Jared DAVIS,
   William JOHNSTONE and Thomas LONGWITH. Deft. acquitted and pff to pay costs.
   392-394)
BESHONG, John vs. William CRAIG. Filed Dec term 1799. Beshong to collect debt.
   Debt made Feb. 20, 1798 at Chillicothe in Adams Co., at present in Ross Co.
   by Beshong and Craig both of Chillicothe. Beshong sold Craig a keel boat to
   bring load of 8 ton from mouth of Scioto River to Chillicothe, load included
   180 bushels of corn from Pee Pee to Chillicothe. Cont. to March term, cont.
   to June term, jury: Eli SARGENT, Samuel HILL, Daniel SARGENT, John STEWART,
   Adam RICE, Ezekiel MITCHELL, James S. WEBSTER, John MONTGOMERY, James WALLEN,
   James LOGAN, Charles CRAIG and Samuel SHAW. Pff to recover $67.60 after which
   he ask that verdict set aside and new trial. Second jury: James S. WEBSTER,
   James KILPATRICK, Eli SARGENT, Charles JOHNSTON, Robert SMITH, William McDONALD,
   Samuel McADOW, Reuben ABRAMS, Francis CREMOR, Isaac WARNER, James GOODIN and
   Thomas LONG. Plff to receive $150. (394-397)
LEE, William vs. Walter BEWELL (BURL). Filed Dec. term 1799. At Chillicothe on
   Oct. 20, 1798 Lee bought certain Continental Virginia land Warrent for 200
   acres No. 2531 given by Commonwealth of Virginia to Bernard Rogers a sargent
   in the Continental Line for 3 years service performed by said Rogers in late
   American Revolution. Lee claims siad warrant is not genuine and asks $150.

484

from Buell who sold warrant to him. Cont to March term, cont to June term
Jury: William RECTOR, John McCULLOCK, Joseph TOMLINSON, Abel PURSLEY, James S.
WEBSTER, Hugh WOODS, Lot MATHEWS, Joseph PIERCE, John GIBSON, James McCONNEL,
James PHILLIPS and Charles CHESNUTT. Jury found in favor of deft and plff
to pay costs. (398-399)

GREGG, Thomas vs. Hugh Woods. Filed Dec. term 1799. To collect note. Case
cont to March term, cont to June term. Samuel Finley surety for Hugh Woods.
Plff to recover (400-401)

LANGHAM, Elias and Thomas JAMES vs. John RUTHERFORD. To collect for goods
delivered. Cont to March term, cont to June term with plff to recover.
(402-403)

McCLURE, John vs. Joseph WILSON. Filed Sept term 1799, cont to Dec. term. Case
for words. MClure charges that Wilson called him a thief and he asks damages.
Cont to March term when deft answers, cont to June term. Jury: Reuben ABRAMS,
Wm HUTT, John McCOY, Jacob AUL(?), William WALLACE, David HAYS, Samuel McADOW,
John McLANDBURG, Benj. URMSTON, Thomas McDONALD, Francis CREEMER, and William
JOHNSTON. Plff to recover. (403-405)

McCLURE, William by John McCLURE his next friend vs. William WILSON. Filed Sept
term 1799, cont to Dec. term. Assault. Case cont to March when jury called:
Samuel SARGENT, Samuel WALKER, John STEWART, James LOGAN, Adam GILFILLIN
James WALLERR(?), James GOODING, John MONTGOMERY, Charles CRAIG, Nicholas
SEBRELL (or LEBRELL), james S. WEBSTER and Walter JOHNSTON. Plff to recover.
(405-407)

CREEMOR, Frances vs Samuel WALKER. Case for words. Filed Dec. term 1799. Creemor
accuses Walker was instigated by the devil, not having the peace of God
before his eyes did in 1799 at Chillicothe maliciously call him a thief.
Cont to March term, cont. to June term, jury: Isaac WARNER, Benjamin URMSTONE,
William RECTOR, Samuel SARGENT, James GOODING, Charles JOHNSTON, Jos.
KIRKPATRICK, John BESHONG, Robert SMITH, James ?S. WEBSTER, Samuel McADOW
and Reuben ABRAMS. Plff received $2.00 damages. (407-409)

JOHNSTONE, James vs. Abraham DEERDUFF. Filed Dec term 1799. To collect note
made Apr. 23, 1799 for 80 Spanish Mill. Case cont to next term. June term
deft relinquishes plea and plff to recover. (409-411)

WOODS, John vs. Samuel COATS. Filed June term 1800. To collect note. Deft.
defaulted and plff to recover. (411-412)

VERTNER, Daniel vs. Abram STIPP. To collect debt of 6 lbs. 3 shillings 3 pence
Kentucky currency. Deft defaulted and plff to recover. (412-413)

TAYLOR, Joseph vs. Thomas DAVIDSON. Filed June term 1800. To collect note of
11 lbs 19 shillings 6 pence Kentucky Currency. Deft defaulted and plff
to recover. (413-414)

GREGG, Thomas vs. Hugh WOODS. Filed Dec. term 1799. To collect debt of note
made Oct. 28, 1799. Cont to March term, cont to June term where deft
relinquishes plea and plff to recover. (415-416)

JAMES, Thomas vs. Thomas McDONALD. Filed June term 1800. To collect note of
order of corn and pork. Deft defaulted and plff to recover. (416-418)

DONOUGHE, Robert vs Joseph COWGILL. Filed June term 1799. To collect note.
Case cont to Sept, case cont to Dec. term, cont to March 1800, cont to June
1800 when jury called: Eli SARGEN T, John NOLAND, William JOHNSTON, Abraham
DEAN, James BLAIR, William MUSTARD, Samuel SARGENT, James S. WEBSTER, Daniel
ROTUCK, James KIRKPATRICK, Adam GILFILLIN and Robert SMITH. Plff to recover.
(418-422)

485

HORNER, John vs. Archibald McDonald. Filed March term 1800. To collect note of 18 gallons of good merchantable whiskey. Deft defaulted and plff to recover. (422-423)

RODGERS, James vs. John BLAIR. Filed June term 1800. Article of Agreement made July 25, 1799 between James Rogers of Franklinton and John Blair of Chillicothe by which James sold John one lot in Franklinton at south end Main St. leading to Chillicothe, Plat No. 200 with note for amount. Deft defaulted and plff to recover. (424-425)

STEWART, Arthur vs. Robert DAVIS. For goods and wares sold Robert Davis. Deft defaulted and plff. to recover. (425-426)

PEYTON, Stephen and Abrm. DEAN vs William THOMPSON. To collect debt for work and labor. Cont to Sept term, cont to Dec. term, cont to March term 1800, cont. to June term at which plff has not prosecuted suit and deft to recover costs. (427-429)

EDGAR, John vs. Lucas NEBUKER. Plea of trespass. Nebuker on June 6, 1798 in Westmorland Co., Penn. gave note to Edgar for two stills entered in his name in Salem twp. of said county as will appear in revenue officers books of 1797 and 1798. Samuel Wilson appeared in court for deft. Case cont to March term 1800, cont June term with plff to recover. (429-431)

EVANS, John vs. Samuel STOOPS and Jesse WILLITS. Filed Dec. term 1799. To collect note. Cont to March term, cont to June term with plff to recover. (432-435)

EVANS, John vs. Alex. DENISTON and Jacob GUNDY. Filed Dec. term 1799. To collect note. Cont to March term, cont to June term with plff to recover. (435-437)

DURBIN, Thomas vs. Martin MYERS. Filed Dec. 1799 term. To collect debt. Cont. to March term, cont to June term with plff to recover. (437-439)

HUNTER, Joseph vs. Thomas RANKINS. Filed Dec. term 1799. To collect note. Cont to March term, cont to June term with plff to recover. (439-441)

KHOAR, Casper vs John Brown. Filed Sept term 1799. To collect money due for work and labor. Cont to Dec term, cont to March term, cont to June term Jury: John McCULLY, John McCLURE, William RECTOR, Fredk. HOUK, John PETERS, James ROBINSON, Daniel BRINEY, Henry SHEELY, Thomas McDONALD, William JOHNSTONE, John CLEMENS and Charles JOHNSTONE. Deft. to recover from plff the costs. (441-444)

DUFFIN, Hugh vs. John RUTHERFORD. Filed Dec term 1799. To collect note. Cont to March term, cont to June term when deft relinquishes plea in favor with plff to recover. (444-446)

McDOWELL, James, William STEWART and Sarah his wife and Andrew RAYBOUNE, adms. of Joseph McCUNE, dec'd vs William RANKIN. Filed June term 1800. To collect debt. Plffs in Nov. 1796 in Court of Quarter Sessions of Bourbon Co., Ky. ob tained judgement from deft. Plffs to recover 40 lbs. with interest from Dec. 26, 1795. (447-448)

HENDERSON, Samuel vs. John McCLURE. Filed June term 1800. Samuel Henderson Sr. to collect note. Deft defaulted and plff to recover. (448-449)

(note: following written on the back page) William McDonald, Esq. of City of Urbana. Charles O'Neil of Chillicothe. Charles O. Neil Brank Bank of the U. S. City of Urbana. Miss S. S. Gregg to E. T. Langham.

ROSS COUNTY, OHIO
Index to Estates and Guardianships
1797-1814

Ross County was the sixth county formed from the Northwest Territory. Nine counties:- Franklin, Fayette, Highland, Greene, Hocking, Montgomery, Pickaway, Pike and Vinton were formed, or partially formed, from Ross county. Therefore, the early records of this county play a very important part in Ohio history and genealogical research. Although we prefer to print as complete records as possible, it is thought, that at this time, the following material may be of immediate assistance and interest to researchers. The Case Number, referring to the estate packet, has been given to assist those who may desire to have further research or photocopy work performed.

Year	NAME	Case No.	Year	NAME	Case No.
1801	APWRIGHT, Catharine	1	1806	BARR, John	436
1803	ANDREW, David	5	1809	BRYANT, John	446
1805	APPLEGATE, Eleanor	9	1809	BISHOP, John	448
1805	AFFLEGATE, Elizabeth	10	1811	BAKER, John	450
1803	ALEXANDER, Francis	3	1814	BAKER, Josiah	458
1805	AUGUSTINE, Gasper	234	1803	BOGGS, Moses	431
1801	ANDERSON, John	2	1804	BAKER, Mesheeh	433
1803	ATHISON, John	4	1811	BENCH, Phebe	451
1804	APPLEGATE, John	6	1813	BURR, Peter	454
1808	ANDERSON, Joseph etal.	17	1800	BROWN, Rachel	428
1814	ADAMS, Hugh	20	1808	BROWN, Rebecca	442
1811	ADAIR, James	18	1810	BROWN, Richard	449
1814	ANDERSON, John	19	1813	BEARD, Robert	455
1805	APPLEGATE, Lucy	12	1805	BARNES, Simon	434
1805	APPLEGATE, Mary	8	1804	BELL, William	432
----	AMBLER, Owen	13	1807	BARLOW, William	441
1804	ARMSTRONG, Robert	7	1808	BETZ, William	443
1807	ABRAMS, Reuben	14	----	CARNAHAN, Adam	1240
1808	AMBLER, Shelly	16	1805	CREANOR, Aaron	1250
1805	APPLEGATE, William	11	1807	COON, Adam	1256
1807	ARMSTRONG, William	15	1813	CARROLL, Clement	1279
1808	BACK, Abraham	444	1807	CURN, David J.	1254
1800	BOGART, Cornelius	427	1810	COREY, David	1266
1803	BLUNT, Cyrus	430	1814	CONNER, David etal	----
1806	BELL, Charles etal.	439	1809	CONNER, Esther etal.	1263
1806	BAKER, Charles & James	440	1813	CREAMOR, Francis	1278
1809	BROWN, Clement	447	1813	CUTLISS, George	1273
1812	BLOCHER, Christian	452	1814	CLIFFORD, George	1280
1814	BOGART, Cornelius	456	1813	COOLEY, Henry	1277
1814	BENCH, Cristian	460	1801	CRUSIN, Isaac	1864
1812	BENCH, Daniel	453	1802	CONNER, Isaac	1241
----	BAZIL, Ezekiel	429	1798	COOK, Joseph	1237
1806	BELL, Elizabeth	437	1800	CROUCH, John	1238
1806	BAKER, Francis etal.	438	1803	CLARK, Joshua	1245
1814	BYERS, Isaac	457	1803	CORBETT, James	1246
1798	BROWN, James	424	1805	COMPTON, James	1248
1800	BUZZARD, John	425	1805	CRAWFORD, James	1249
1803	BARNES, John	426	1806	CONNERS, Jacob	1253
1805	BUCHANNAN, James	435	1807	CORBETT, James	1257

Year	NAME	No.	Year	NAME	No.
1808	CASEY, John	1258	1805	EYSTONE, Casper	234
1810	COMBS, John	1265	1811	ENGLE, Henry	238
1811	CLARK, John	1267	1812	EVANS, Horasio etal	240
1813	CROW, Jacob W.	1276	1803	EYRE, John	232
1814	CAMPBELL, John P.	1281	1806	ELLIOTT, Joseph, dec'd.	235
1814	CORBETT, Jane	1284	1807	ELLIOTT, Jos. W., minor	237
1808	CANNON, Lowder	1259	1807	ELLIOTT, Margaret	236
1809	CONNER, Madelina etal.	1264	1805	ERHART, Nicholas	233
1803	CREVISTON, Nicholas	1244	1814	ENGLAND, Titus	239
1811	COX, Rush etal.	1269	1814	EDMISTON, Thomas	242
1801	CHAFFIN, Solomon	1239	1814	FLINN, Bazel etal.	2292
1803	CONNER, Samuel	1247	1806	FRANCIS, Cornelius	2285
1805	CLIFTON, Samuel	1251	1807	FRAME, Elon	2287
1807	CARDER, Sarah	1255	1813	FLINN, Hugh	2288
1808	COX, Samuel	1261	1800	FOSTER, John	2281
1809	COREY, Simeon	1262	1801	FULTON, James	2282
1811	COX, Samuel	1268	1806	FERGUSON, James	2284
1811	COX, Solomon	1260(8)	1813	FULTON, John S.	2289
1806	CRAIG, Samuel	1270	1814	FLINN, Nancy	2291
1811	COX, Samuel etal	1271	1815	FERNEAN(U), Philip	2294
1812	COX, Solomon, dec'd	1272	1807	FRAME, Sarah B.	2286
1803	CAMPBELL, William	1242	1813	FREDERICK, Solomon	2290
1801	CARDER, William	1243	1804	FRANCIS, William	2283
1805	CRAIG, William	1252	1808	GRIFFIN, Alexand.	2572
1808	COX, William	1260	1814	GREEN, Charles Jr.	2577
1813	CAREY, William	1274	1806	GRUBB, James	2570
1813	CORBETT, William	1275	1811	GREGG, Jacob	2574
1814	COHOON, Wm. & Elizabeth	1282	1814	GRUBB, Jacob	2576
1814	CORBETT, Wm., minor	1285	1812	GOSSARD, Philip	2575
1806	DEAN, Abraham	1879	1808	GREGG, Robert	2571
1801	DENNY, David	1874	1809	GRIFFITH, Sally etal.	2573
1813	DAWSON, David	1889	1805	GREGG, Thomas	2569
1809	DEAN, Elizabeth etal.	1884	1814	GRIMES, Thomas	2578
1812	DEABLER, George	1887	1805	HEAD, Asa	3668
1812	DIXON, Hale	1888	1808	HOPKINS, Arch. etal.	2923
1805	DOWNS, John	1876	1811	HIGGINS, Archibald	2929
1808	DINES, Jeremiah	1882	1814	HAYES, Andrew	2937
1810	DIXON, Jesse	1885	1805	HOLLAND, Betsy etal	2914
1813	DREES, Michael	2277	1807	HARE, Catharine	2918
1813	DEMMIT, Moses, dec'd	1890	1810	HAINS, Christian	2925
1813	DEMMIT, Moses	1891	1808	HAYES, David	2922
1810	DUNBAR, Nancy etal.	1886	1813	HOTZEBULER, David	2935
1801	DUGAN, Patrick	1875	1798	HOBBS, Ephraim	2907
1805	DEHAVEN, Peter	1878	1812	HULL, Ezekiel	2930
1806	DONOUGH, Robert	1880	1812	HUST, Elizabeth	2932
1806	DICKINSON, Thomas	1881	1814	HOSHOUR, Elizabeth	2939
1800	DAILEY, William	1873	1800	HELSEY, Henry	2908
1805	DUNBAR, William	1877	1805	HOWARD, Henry	2911
1809	DURHAM, William	1883	1813	HOLTZENBULER, Henry	2934
1814	ESSEY, Abner	241	1813	HOSHOUR, Henry	2936

488

Year	NAME	No.	Year	NAME	No.
1813	HEATON, Isaac	2933	1806	LEWIS, David	4266
1804	HOUSE, Joseph	3669	1807	LEBOURN, David	4267
1806	HUGHES, John	2909	————	LARRICK, Elizabeth	4264
1803	HUME, John	2910	1810	LOVESS, Elias	4270
1805	HUBBARD, John	2912	1805	LYNN, Hugh	4265
1805	HARVEY, Jonathan etal.	2913	1814	LIPSCOMB, Isaac	4271
1806	HOPKINS, John	2917	1808	LOVELESS, John	4268
1811	HUBBARD, Jacob	2926	1809	LAMON, Joseph	4269
1811	HAINES, Jacob	2927	1814	LEONARD, Sylva	4272
1807	HALL, Margaret	2921	1806	MILLER, Abraham	5007
1811	HAINES, Mary	2928	1809	MORRIS, Alexander	5017
1805	HOWARD, Samuel	2916	1814	MEEKER, Abner	5030
1807	HALL, Thomas	2919	1805	McROBERTS, Alexander	5662
1807	HODGES, Thomas	2920	1812	McCLINTOCK, Alexander	5679
1809	HURST, Thomas	2924	1814	McMULLEN, Alexander	5681
1804	HOLLAND, William	2915	1808	MILLER, Benjamin	5014
1813	HOWARD, William	2931	1814	MARKLE, Benjamin etal.	5034
1814	HADDIX, William	2938	1808	McNEAL, Benjamin	5674
1803	IMMEL, John	3670	1814	MERKLE, Catharine	5029
1804	ISTONE, Jasper	3671	1814	MARAH, Cornelius	5397
1810	ILIFF, Joseph	3672	1814	McCOY, Cynthia etal	5683
1805	JOLLY, David	3719	1805	MARKLE, Daniel	5004
1806	JUVENAL, David	3721	1802	McCUNE, David	5661
1810	JAMES, Henry	3727	1806	McLAIN, Duncan	5667
1813	JEFFERSON, Henry	3730	1811	McFARLAND, Daniel	5676
1803	JOHNSTON, John	3718	1813	McILROY, Daniel	5680
1806	JOHNSTON, Jesse	3722	1812	MILLER, Elizabeth etal.	5022
1809	JUVENAL, Jacob	3725	1813	MASSIE, Elizabeth etal.	5027
1810	JONES, Joseph	3726	1814	MEEKER, Evalena	5032
1813	JEFFERSON, John	3732	1806	MOORE, Fergus	5006
1808	JUMBLE, Michael	3724	1801	MERCER, George	4998
1812	JOHNSTON, Margaret	3729	1808	MOORE, Hugh	5012
1812	JOHNSTON, Patrick	3728	1809	MILLER, Henry etal.	5018
1808	JAMISON, Samuel	3723	1814	MEEKER, Harvey	5033
1814	JONES, Samuel	3731	1801	McGOMERY, Humphrey	5664
1805	JAMISON, William	3720	1810	McGOMERY, Humphrey	5672
1812	KERR, David	3923	1803	MOOTS, John	4999
1805	KIRKENDALL, Henry	3919	1804	MILLER, Jacob	5000
1801	KRUSON, Isaac	3915	1805	MITCHELL, Jean	5001
1805	KENT, Jesse	3917	1805	MARKLE, John	5003
1801	KENNEDY, John	3918	1806	MARTIN, Joseph	5005
1810	KERR, James	3921	1807	MITCHELL, James	5008
1803	KIRKENDALL, John	3933	1807	MARKLE, James	5010
1810	KERR, Mary	3920	1807	MOYER, Jacob	5013
1814	KELLY, Nicholas	3924	1808	MARKLE, Joseph etal.	5015
1800	KIRK, Samuel	3914	1810	MILLER, John	5019
1803	KRUSON, Sally	3916	1812	MOONEY, John	5020
1811	KELLEY, William	3922	1813	MOUNTS, Jesse	5024
1814	KILGORE, William	3925	1814	MARKLE, John etal.	5041
1802	LARRICK, Benjamin	4263	1804	McCUNE, Joseph	5666

Year	NAME	No.	Year	NAME	No.
1810	McQUALITY, Jane	5671	1813	PAINTER, Jacob	5998
1811	McCOY, Joseph	5675	1802	POTTER, Martha	5978
1811	McQUALITY, James etal.	5677	1804	PATTON, Margaret	5982
1814	McGUIRE, John	5682	1807	POWERS, Michael	5989
1810	McCLEAN, Moses	5673	1808	PHILIPPS, Major	5991
1811	McCLEAN, Margaret	5678	1806	PARK, Robert	5987
1813	MASSIE, Nathaniel	5025	1806	PATTON, Rebecca	5988
1807	McCLAIN, Polly etal.	5669	1804	PATTON, Sarah etal	5984
1809	McFARLAND, Robert	5670	1810	POSTGATE, Thomas	5993
1813	MOUNTS, Sarah	5023	1800	PORT, William	5976
1801	McCULLOCH, Samuel	5665	1805	PATTON, William	5986
1813	MOUNTS, Thomas etal.	5026	1814	PRICE, William Jr.	6000
1814	MEEKER, Tandy	5031	1814	QUGLEY, Jonathan	4896
1806	MORGAN, William	5002	1807	RUSH, Abner etal	6603
1807	MOORE, William	5009	1807	RICHARDS, Christian	6648
1809	MARTIN, William Jr.	5016	1807	RUSH, Catharine etal	6649
1812	MILLER, William	5021	1814	ROWE, Conny	6650
1814	MORROW, William	5028	1807	RADCLIFF, Ezekiel etal.	6694
1799	McELROY, William	5663	1807	RODGERS, Hamilton	6777
1811	NOBLE, Caleb	4628	1801	RODGERS, James	6810
1811	NOBLE, Charity	4630	1801	ROSS, John	6811
1811	NIXON, John	4626	1801	RIDDLE, John	6812
1805	NOBLE, Levin Sr.	4623	1807	RUSH, John	6813
1811	NOBLE, Levin Jr.	4627	1807	RADCLIFF, John	6814
1804	NOLIN, Matthew	4621	1807	RADCLIFF, Jesse	6815
1804	NATHAN, Nicholas	4622	1807	RECTOR, John etal.	6816
1811	NOBLE, Nathan	4629	1803	RODGERS, Lewis	6945
1801	NOLIN, Richard	4620	1810	RHINEHART, Motelene etal.	6957
1809	NOBLE, Summers	4625	1813	ROSS, Philip	7017
1806	NOBLE, Tamey	8605	1803	ROSS, Robert	7032
1806	NOBLE, William	4624	1805	RALSTON, Robert	7031
1813	NIBLACK, William	4631	1805	ROSS, Robert	7033
1809	OVERLY, Eve	4757	1807	RATCLIFF, Rachael	7034
1806	OBRIANT, John	446	1808	REED, Richard	7035
1804	OVERLY, Martin	4756	1807	RATCLIFF, Simon	7055
1814	OSBURN, Richard	4759	1807	RUSH, Samuel	7050
1806	OLERY, Samuel	4758	1813	ROWE, Sandridge	7057
1809	PETERS, Abraham	5992	1813	REYNOLDS, William	7152
1813	PEPPLE, Abraham	5997	1813	STRAWSER, Abraham	7705
1804	PATTON, Esther	5981	1813	SHOPE, Bernard	7775
1804	PATTON, Esther	5983	1813	STRAWSER, Christian	7792
1802	PORTER, George	5980	1807	STOCKTON, David	7860
1805	PIERCE, Griffith	5985	1807	SEABOURN, David	7861
1814	PORTER, Henry	5999	1813	STREEVEY, Daniel	7862
1802	POTTER, Joseph	5977	1801	SMITH, Elizabeth	7899
1804	PATTON, John	5979	1802	SCOTT, Elizabeth	7900
1807	PARRISH, Jolly	5990	1809	SARGEANT, Elizabeth etal.	7901
1811	PHILIPS, John	5994	1813	STAFFORD, Elizabeth	7902
1812	PHILIPS, Joseph	5995	1800	STEELE, George	7907
1813	PETTYJOHN, James	5996	1806	SHANER, George	7968

490

Year	NAME	No.	Year	NAME	No.
1807	SPENCER, Gustavus	7969	1813	TURNEY, Elizabeth	6320
1799	SIBBELS, James	8072	1803	TAYLOR, Henry J.	6305
1800	SAILOR, Jacob	8073	1812	TURNEY, Henry	6317
1803	SAMPLE, James	8074	1812	TUTTLE, Isaiah etal.	6319
1805	SMITH, Jeremiah	8075	1803	TIMMONS, John	6306
1805	SAMPLE, James	8076	1805	TAYLOR, John	6308
1808	STOCKTON, John	8077	1810	TRIMBLE, John	6314
1810	STRAWSER, John	8078	1810	THOMPSON, Joseph	6315
1810	SQUIRE, James	8079	1808	TREES, Michael	6310
1812	STOCKTON, John	8080	1809	THOMPSON, Matthew	6312
1813	SHAGELY, Jacob	8081	1810	THOMPSON, Oswald	6313
1814	SNAPP, John	8082	1802	THOMAS, Samuel	6304
1814	STALLCUP, John	8083	1804	TYLER, Walter	6307
1814	STUTHART, John	8084	1810	THOMPSON, William	6316
1808	SODDERS, Lawrence	8300	1813	ULREY, Henry	4876
1813	SIDWELL, Levi	8301	1813	VANGUNDY, Chris.	4897
1809	SMITH, Martha	8330	1801	WILSON, Charles	7200
1804	STEELE, Peggy etal.	8413	1802	WRIGHT, Edward	7234
1814	SMITH, Peter	8414	1803	WRIGHT, Gabriel	7281
1805	STINSON, Robert	8593	1814	WATTMAN, Isaac	7335
1805	STEPHENSON, Robert	8445	1797	WILSON, James	7337
1805	SMITH, Richard	8446	1805	WILLIAMS, John	7338
1813	SIDWELL, Rebecca etal.	8447	1806	WRIGHT, Jonathan	7339
1810	SURFUS, Samuel etal	8474	1807	WILKINSON, John	7240
1811	STOCKTON, Samuel	8475	1813	WATT, John	7343
1814	SARGENT, Snowder	8476	1814	WRIGHT, John	7344
1804	STOCKTON, Thomas	8509	1814	WILEY, Jared	7345
1805	SMITH, Thomas	8510	1814	WILLIAMS, John	7346
1807	STOCKTON, Thomas	8511	1809	WICK, Moses	7504
1810	SMITH, Thompson	8513	1814	WRIGHT, Moses	7506
1804	STOCKTON, William	8535	1803	WILLIAMS, Nathan	7551
1804	SMITH, William	8534	1808	WRIGHT, Phenius etal.	7563
1807	SARGENT, William	8536	1805	WALLACE, Samuel	7593
1814	STURGEON, William	8537	1806	WELCH, Samuel	7594
1812	TIMMONS, Abraham	6318	1802	WEBSTER, Taylor	7625
1807	TATE, David	6309	1807	YATES, Benjamin	4971
1809	TETERS, Daniel	6311	1810	YATES, Delilah etal.	4972

Year	Name	Case No.	Year	Name	Case No.
.820	AMSWORTHY, Abraham	29	1816	CRUSEN, Sarah	1296
1819	AMSWORTHY, Bennet	26	1817	COGAN, Samuel	1300
1918	AULT, Elizabeth	23	1819	COON, Samuel	1303
1817	ADAMS, Isaac H.	22	1816	COCHRAN, William	1292
1818	ARNET, Jonathan	25	1817	COGAN, William	1299
1820	AMSWORTHY, Lewis	28	1816	DARST, Daniel	1894
1818	ADAMS, Robert	21	1820	DEHAVEN, Herman	1902
1818	ALLEN, William	24	1815	DOUGLAS, James	1892
1819	ASKEW, William	27	1816	DAVID, James	1895
-----	BUCHANNAN, Adam	1233	1818	DEVAN, Jacob etal.	1899
1815	BAIRD, Alexander	462	1819	DUNLAP, John	1900
1818	BURNSIDES, Alexander	469	1815	DALBY, Peter	1893
1820	BROWN, Adam	479	1820	DAY, Peter	1903
1817	BOGART, Ezekiel etal.	468	1817	DINES, Rebecca	1896
1819	BOGART, Ezekiel & Mary	475	1820	DAY, Samuel, dec'd	1901
1820	BENNETT, Edward	477	1820	DAY, Samuel, minor	1904
1815	BURNS, Francis	464	1817	DICKEY, William	1898
1819	BISHOP, Frederick	473	1818	DICKEY, Washington	1898
1815	BOGART, Gasper	466	1817	EMMITT, James	243
1715	BALEY, John	463	1820	FARNOW, Archa	2301
1816	BROWN, James, Jr.	467	1820	FARLOW, Benjamin	2302
1818	BLOUCHER, John	470	1816	FERGUSON, Charles	2295
1818	BEARD, Joseph M. etal	471	1815	FRY, Henry	2293
1819	BEACH, John	472	1818	FARDING, James	2298
1819	BEATH, Joseph	474	1818	FERNEAN (U), John etal.	2299
1820	BRIGGS, Joseph	476	1820	FREW, McKnight	2300
1820	BRYANT, John	478	1817	FREDERICK, Peter	2296
1815	BARNHOUSE, Magnus	465	1817	FAIL, Samuel etal.	2297
1815	BARNHOUSE, Richard	465	1817	GREGG, Amor	2587
1815	BRIGGS, Walter	461	1815	GOLDSBERRY, Benj.	2579
1815	CLARK, Alexander etal.	1290	1820	GRIEVE, David L.	2599
1817	CRAIG, Alexander	1298	1816	GRAHAM, Felix	2586
1820	CHURCHILL, Alexander	1306	1816	GRUBB, Henry etal.	2584
1815	COBB, Christian B.	1291	1815	GRIMES, John	2580
1820	CREMEEN, Curtis	1307	1815	GRANT, Jonathan	2581
1820	COON, Charles	1309	1817	GRUBB, James	2588
1815	COZAD, Daniel	1288	1817	GODFREY, Joseph	2589
1820	CRYDER, Diana etal.	1310	1818	GRIBBIN, John	2591
1819	COPE, Eve & Daniel	1304	1818	GILLFILLAN, John etal.	2592
1817	COCHRAN, Isaac	1301	1820	GRAHAM, John	2593
1820	CLAYPOOL, Isaac	1308	1817	GOTHARD, Maria	2590
1815	CALDWELL, Joseph	1287	1816	GREGG, Nathan	2583
1815	COZAD, John	1289	1816	GILLGILLAN, Thomas	2582
1816	COLLINS, Joseph	1294	1816	GREGG, Wesley	2585
1817	CUMMINS, John	1297	1815	HOLE, Allen	2942
1819	COCHRAN, John	1302	1819	HOUGH, Benjamin	2948
1816	CRYDER, Michael	1203	1815	HENDRICK, Edward	2940

Year	Name	Case No.	Year	Name	Case No.
1820	CRYDER, Michael	1305	1816	HARR, Everard etal.	2949
1816	CHESNUT, Patrick	----	1819	HOUGH, Ellen M. etal.	2952
1820	HELLINGS, John	2953	1818	MILLER, Mary A.	5049
1820	HOLLAND, John etal	2954	1818	MYERS, Polly	5048
1815	HEMPHILL, Matthew	2943	1819	MILLER, Robert	5051
1818	HOUSER, Michael	2947	1819	MILLER, Susan etal	5052
1817	HALL, Peggy	2951	1815	McGUIRE, Sarah etal	5684
1816	HOLMES, Robert	2945	1816	McPHERIN, Samuel	5686
1817	HICKS, Thomas	2946	1820	McMUNN, Samuel	5695
1815	HADDIX, Winny	2944	1816	McMUNN, William	5688
1816	HOLMAN, Wm. etal.	2950	1819	McINTOSH, William	5692
1818	JANNEY, Carter	3738	1819	McCLEAN, William	5694
1815	JONES, Edwin etal.	3734	1820	McCOY, William Jr.	5697
1817	JOHNSTON, James	3735	1816	NEAR, David	4632
1817	JANNEY, Joseph	3736	1818	NORWOOD, Joshua	4634
1815	JOHNSTON, Matilda	3733	1817	NEAR, William etal.	4633
1820	JONES, Samuel	3740	1819	OTT, Joseph	4761
1815	KELLOUGH, Allen	3928	1818	OTT, Philip	4760
1817	KNIGHT, Fielding	3931	1817	PAINTER, George	6001
1818	KUYKENDALL, Henry	3932	1818	PRICKETT, Isaac	6007
1815	KIRKENDALL, John	3926	1816	PURSELL, John	6004
1818	KILBOURN, Lemuel	3934	1818	PICKENS, John	6006
1815	KIRKENDALL, Noah	3927	1816	PIERCE, Polly etal.	6005
1816	KIZER, Peter	3930	1815	PEARCE, Samuel	6002
1815	KING, Robert	3929	1815	PEARCE, Samuel etal	6003
1820	LEGG, George etal.	4277	1819	ROSS, Ann etal.	6604
1818	LUNBECK, Henry	4275	1820	REED, Allen	6605
1818	LUNBECK, Mary etal.	4276	1818	RALSTON, Benjamin	6643
1817	LITTLE, Peter	4273	1815	ROWE, Elizabeth etal.	6695
1818	LYONS, Thomas	4274	1815	RICE, John	6817
1817	MINSHALL, Amos	5044	1816	ROBINSON, James H.	6818
1820	MACE, Andrew	5054	1816	ROBINSON, John J.	6819
1817	McMUNN, Ann etal	5689	1820	REEVES, John D.	6820
1815	McGUIRE, Christianna	5685	1815	RUSH, Lewis	6946
1816	McREA, Charles	5687	1816	RICE, Mary A. etal.	6958
1819	McFARLAND, Calender	5693	1815	RALSTON, Nancy etal.	7005
1817	MOSES, Elizabeth	5043	1818	ROCK, Samuel	7058
1818	MINSHALL, Ellis	5045	1820	RUSH, Samuel	7059
1815	MEAD, Hezekiah	5036	1815	RAKES, William	7115
1816	MAINES, Henry	5037	1815	ROWE, William etal.	7116
1817	McCLURE, Hugh etal.	5690	1816	SMITH, Benjamin	7776
1815	MARKLE, John	5035	1815	SMITH, Christianna	7793
1816	MARKLE, Jacob	5038	1815	SLOW, Clarissa	7794
1816	MILLER, Joseph	5039	1815	SHAGELY, Joseph etal.	8085
1816	MARTIN, John	5040	1816	SHOBE, Jacob	8086
1817	MAHON, John	5042	1817	STEWART, James	8087
1819	MOFFITT, Joshua	5050	1819	SCHAFFER, Jacob	8088

Year	Name	Case No.	Year	Name	Case No
1820	MACAN, John G.	5053	1819	SCOTT, John	8089
1820	McCAFFERTY, John	5696	1819	SIMPSON, Robert	8448
1818	McQUALiTY, Kiturah	5691	1815	SMITH, Samuel	8477
1815	MOSS, Mary etal.	5037	1817	STRAWSER, Solomon	8478
1818	MOSS, Mary etal.	5047	1818	SCOTT, Samuel	8479
1816	SKID, Thomas	8512	1820	WILEY, George et al.	7284
1820	STEEL, Thomas	8514	1815	WILLIAMS, John	7341
1820	SHACKLEFORD, Wm. et al.	8538	1815	WILLIAMS, John	7342
1814	TIMMONS, Eli	6321	1815	WITZEL, John	7347
1819	TIMMONS, Elizabeth et al.	6327	1816	WINDER, James	7348
1819	TOOPS, John	6326	1818	WINDER, John Jr.	7349
1820	TURNEY, James	6329	1819	WILSON, John	7351
1816	TAYLOR, Mary	6322	1819	WALKER, John	7352
1820	TUCKER, Mary et al.	6330	1820	WALKER, John	7353
1820	THOMPSON, Nathan	6328	1819	WINDER, John	7350
1816	TIMMONS, Polly	6324	1819	WEBSTER, Letty	7484
1816	TIMMONS, Thos. J. et al.	6323	----	WELMOUTH, Lemuel et al.	7485
1817	THOMAS, William	6325	1819	WHITESIDE, Margaret	7505
1815	ULREY, Hiram et al.	4879	1820	WILEY, Marcissa et al.	7552
1814	ULREY, Jesse	4877	1820	WILSON, Robert R. et al.	7575
1816	VANMETER, Henry	4898	1820	WILEY, Robert	7576
1816	VANMETER, Lydia	4900	1816	WRIGHT, Sarah	7595
1817	VANDERVART, Nathaniel	4901	1815	WILLIAMS, Thomas	7626
1817	WOLF, David	7223	1815	WINSHIP, Thomas et al.	7627
1817	WILLIAMS, Elizabeth et al.	1235	1816	WILLIAMS, Thomas	7628
1817	WATT, George et al.	7282	1816	WILLIAMSON, Thomas	7629
1820	WILEY, George	7283	1815	WILLIAMS, William	7654
			1815	WEBSTER, William B.	7655

The following marriages were copied from Volume A. Two ministers and one justice of the peace used the title "Mrs." in front of the bride's name, more than is normally found. This title has been copied as found, but caution should be used as it is possible that some of these ladies may have been "Miss" rather than "Mrs."

ADAMS, Lucius to Electy Phelps	2-15-1830
ALDRICH, David to Elizabeth Bixler	2-16-1831
ALDRICK, William to Elizabeth Collins	3-11-1827
AMSDEN, Thomas to Lydia Chapman - both of York twp.	9-8-1824
ANDERSON, Wesley to Loiza Harkness - mar. return from Tiffin	4-15-1829
BAKER, Jacob to Catharine Sharp	11-24-1831
BAKER, Samuel to Elizabeth Cleaveland	9-30-1827
BARNES, Benjamin to Catharine Curtis	9-3-1825
BARNEY, Benjamin to Minerva Harris - both of Seneca twp.	3-20-1821
BARNEY, Consider C. to Hannah Frees	7-28-1828
BARNHEAD, Jacob to Sarah Highlund	3-8-1832
BARNY, West to Sophrona Willson	10-17-1820
BATCHFORD, John to Mrs. Euice Davenport	10-24-1830
BATES, John to Selome Brown	5-29-1831
BEBO, Charles to Josettee Mitchell	2-19-1823
BELLAIR, Augustin to Mary Lafleur	2-19-1823
BENTON, Burr to Lucinda Blackman	7-30-1828
BENTON, Jesse to Mary Drumb	11-27-1831
BIGGERSTAFF, Samuel to Eliza Leezer	6-30-1828
BIRDSEY, Nathan D. to Mary Ann Christie	4-8-1832
BISNETT, Thomas to Catharine Ganuge	6-26-1831
BIXLER, George to Susan Foster	2-16-1831
BIXLER, Henry to Susan Burnet	2-18-1830
BOWLES, David to Nancy Hollaway - both of Sandusky twp.	6-6-1823
BOWLES, W. K. to Sarah West	10-13-1830
BRISH, W. M. to Delila Snook	4-6-1830
BRISTAL, Elbridge A. to Sarah Whitenger	11-6-1825
BROWN, A. L. to Eliza Duncan	5-2-1830
BROWN, David J.(?) to Sarah Ann Baker	11-11-1829
BROWN, Jeremiah P. to Sally Walker	12-22-1825
BROWN, Jeremiah P. to Evae Parish	1-5-1832
BROWN, Luther to Jane Castlelow	6-1-1830
BROWN, Stanton H. to Elizabeth Whitinger	10-17-1832
BUEL, Elijah to Sarah Guinall	4-3-1831
BULLARD, William to Sally Coffin	4-20-1826
BURNET, Joseph to Betsy Enter (Euter)	1-9-1825
CALVIN, John to Harriet Mugg	1-23-1828
CARPENTER, Samuel B. to Wealthly Barnes	3-20-1825
CARR, David to Sally Stultz	11-14-1830
CARTER, John G. to Ann Upcott	8-18-1827
CAVALLIER, Albert to Eliza Mowery	11-24-1818
CHAMBERS, Benjamin to Lydia Bowles	11-24-1825
CHAPEL, Peter C. to Laura Ann Babcock	7-21-1826
CHAPMAN, Joseph to Mrs. Mary Ann Walker	4-5-1831

```
CHARD, David to Rachel B. Burnett                                    8-13-1824
CHARD, William Jr. to Susan Burnet                                   2-16-1825
CLEVELAND, Clark to Elize Graves                                     10-6-1831
COCHRAN, David to Polly Cole                                         11-5-1825
COLE, Eber to Catharine McCormick                                    1-10-1831
COLEMAN, Jos. to Laura Ann Chapel                                    12-20-1830
COOPER, John to Hannah Cadwallader                                   2-1-1832
CORNELL, Joel to Sally Hawk                                          2-6-1828
CRANE, Amos to Esther Glick                                          1-16-1831
CURTIS, Benjamin to Sally Cleaveland - both of Green Creek twp.      10-10-1824
CURTIS, Joseph H. to Cintha Gibbs                                    12-27-1824
DAVENPORT, Edson to Jane Sidoras                                     5-19-1831
DAVIS, John of Huron Co. to Hannah SUTTON of Corghan twp., SCO       11-17-1821
DAY, Schugler to Mrs. Emily Brown                                    5-2-1830
DEAN, Matthias to Breadison Gibbs                                    2-18-1832
DEMOSS, Thomas to Margarett Bisinett                                 8-29-1821
DESELIN, Jacob to Margaret Stewart                                   8-9-1827
DESELMS, Jonathan to Sarah Gallant                                   1-5-1832
DESHETER, Joseph to Orilla Purina                                    8-2-1829
DEW, James H. to Elizabeth Westor (Weston)                           3-25-1832
DOLLISON, Daniel to Mrs. Amy Bond                                    9-20-1829
DRAKE, J. C. to Charlotte Gibbs                                      4-4-1830
DRUM, Levi to Almira Pratt                                           5-6-1830
DRUMO, William to Margarett Richards                                 7-8-1829
DUKES, Andrew to Gitty Swim                                          8-8-1823
DUNHAM, Eli to Abigail Sprague                                       4-9-1823
EATON, John to Polly Orr - both of Seneca twp.                       2-25-1821
EMERSON, Jesse to Mrs. Jemima Blinn                                  2-18-1829
EMERSON, Thomas to Elizabeth Glick                                   8-15-1830
EVERETT, Jeremiah to Eunice Woolley                                  10-28-1832
EVERETT, Joel to Maria Grimes                                        1-1-1831
FINTON, Vanranssalaer to Matilda Wilson                              2-27-1831
FOLLETT, Abel D. to Laura Smith                                      12-12-1829
FONCANNON, William to Rebecca Gordon                                 3-13-1823
FOOT, M. D. to Mrs. Susan Campbell                                   -----1829
FORGERSON, Holsy to Caroline Camp                                    1-20-1830
FORGUSON, Thomas to Mary Ann Hull                                    7-5-1827
FULLER, John to Rhody Powers                                         7-21-1826
GALE, Benjamin to Margaret Martin                                    2-12-1824
GALLANT, John to Elenor Deselmno                                     7-6-1825
GAVIT, Asa B. to Jemima Strawn                                       12-23-1824
GERMAN, Anthony to Jane Tebo                                         10-13-1822
GRANT, Zachariah to Mary Putnam                                      4-11-1822
GRAVES, Asa to Mary Alexander                                        3-10-1831
GRAVES, Inerean (Inerear) to Amelia Harrington                       7-18-1824
GRAVES, Tyler to Lavina Smoke                                        12-28-1824
GREEN, Lewther F. to Reioth Right                                    12-9-1831
GREGNON, John B. to Archange Lafleur                                 2-19-1823
GROVER, Oliver to Margaret Alexander                                 12-6-1832
```

HARKNESS, Doct. Lamon G. to Julia Follett	8-2-1829
HARRINGTON, Wesley to Malinda Wilson	10-31-1830
HAWKINS, John to Milly Starens (mar. return from Portage)	1-2-1831
HENINGER, Jacob to Susanah Reed	2-15-1831
HOLLINSHEAD, Samuel to Mary Whitinger	6-5-1822
HOUTS, William to Mrs. Mary McCune	12-19-1830
HOWARD, Simeon B. to Phebe Maria Thompson	4-5-1829
HOWARD, Simon B. to Mrs. Harriet Weaver	11-15-1831
HOWELL, Silas of Harris twp to Louisa Coone of York twp.	5-21-1831
HREN, George R. to Hannah Young	7-10-1832
HUBBARD, Cyrus to Nancy Chipman	3-10-1822
HUBBEL, Samuel B. to Elizabeth Shannon	5-30-1830
HUNTER, John J. to Mrs. Rhoda George	2-24-1831
JOHNSON, Levi to Abegel M. Stults	10-25-1832
JONES, George to Jane Ginnall	2-17-1828
JUDD, Alvin to Lucy Pogue	3-18-1828
KEPHART, Daniel to Kathran Ried	9-23-1832
KETRICK, George to Rathieme Henricks	6-15-1832
KETTLE, Samuel to Ann Winters	5-21-1829
KINNEY, Uri to Unice Calvin	10-17-1827
KNAPP, John to Prudence Tharp	12-18-1828
KNIGHT, Willard to Olive Trask - both of Thompson twp.	5-12-1823
KRIDLER, Frederick to Ellen Creger	10-25-1832
LAD, Hampton to Ann Williams	11-15-1832
LAFONTAIN, Alexander to Elizabeth Pinay	2-9-1828
LAFORCE, Archibald S. to Rebecca Misner	12-9-1830
LAFOUR, Bezry to Eliza Jemison	1-24-1831
LAKE, Joseph L. to Elener Eichur (Eichen)	4-18-1822
LASHWARE, Joseph to Malinda Deshetter - both of Riley twp.	10-30-1830
LATHROP, Daniel to Cyrena M. Bristal	12-10-1826
LATHROP, George to Fanny Courtright	1-20-1831
LATHROP, Henry to Hannah Harvey	12-1-1831
LATHROP, Isaac to Sylva Harvey	12-20-1829
LAY, John to Aurora L. Evans	7-22-1830
LEE, James to Marinda Brayton	7-23-1829
LEMMON, William to Lovica Barber	5-11-1828
LOUCKS, Abraham to Rebecca Townsend	3-19-1829
LOVELAND, Aaron to Miss G. M. Vandoren	8-29-1830
LUTHER, Eli to Mrs. Catharine Fistler	2-25-1830
LYTLE, Hugh to Anvilley Hopkins	3-24-1831
McCLELLAND, William to Mary Wallon	12-14-(1823)
McCOLLEY, Samuel to Elizabeth Camear	4-3-1823
McCORD, Carnahan to Almira Bebe	1-10-1828
McNUTT, Alexander to Sarah Demun	3-7-1822
McNUTT, John to Mary Ann Stults	11-29-1827
MARTIN, Richard to Sally Tuller (Fuller?)	4-27-1826
MATHERS, James to Sarah Clark	11-30-1821
MAY, Isaac to Nancy McMillan	1-13-1830
MILLER, Oliver to Mary Ann Rosman	7-16-1825

```
MILLER, Thomas to Harriet Cochran                                    10-25-1827
MILLS, Eber to Eliza Rollins                                         1-10-1823
MISNER, William L. to Susann Sutton                                  2-23-1826
MIXTON, Samuel to Harriet Comwell                                    7-8-1827
MOMINA, Anthony to Sally Deomoss                                     8-29-1821
MOORE, James to Harriet Patterson                                    1-20-1831
MOORE, Nathaniel B. to Phidelia Develly                             2-11-1830
MORROW, Daniel to Clarissa Leezer                                   5-30-1831
MUNGER, Gains to Celia Smith                                         2-22-1826
MURRY, Seth W. to Catharine Forbes                                   9-11-1826
MYERS, William to Mrs. Amy Thompson                                  7-10-1829
NELSON, Benjamin to Thankful Hoff - both of Townsend twp.          10-12-1830
NEWMAN, Samuel P. to Elizabeth Veecher (Vetcher)                   11-29-1828
NICHOLS, Moses to Altie F. Hubbard                                   6-3-1821
NITCHER, John to Eleanor Guinall                                    10-3-1830
OGBURN, Robert J. to Elizabeth Nial                                 3-22-1832
OLDS, Ezra to Mrs. Polly Hardy                                       1-5-1828
OLMSTED, Geo. G. to Jane Whitinger                                   5-8-1828
OLMSTED, Jesse S. to Julia Ferguson                                  1-1-1821
PARISH, Levi to Polly Bixler                                         4-8-1832
PARK, George to Mary Daugherty                                       1-5-1824
PARKER, Ackley to Roxy Thompson                                    12-26-1831
PARKS, Ebenezer W. of Oxford twp., Huron Co. to
             Mary Bears of Townsend, Sandusky Co.                    8-3-1831
PHELPS, Seth to Elizabeth Hopkins                                    3-8-1829
PLIMPTON, Dwight to Paulina Emerson - mar. return from Tiffin       8-11-1829
PONYARD, Francis to Rosy Wright                                      7-22-1826
POWERS, Isaac to Hannah Foster                                       3-15-1825
PRESTON, John to Cathrin Smith                                     12-29-1831
PRIOR, John to Mary Bixler                                           6-19-1824
PULFORD, Severett to Mrs. Eleanor Roth                             10-25-1829
PUTNAM, Ira H. to Mary Garst                                         9-11-1823
PUTNAM, Urzel to Anna Gordon - both of York twp.                   11-11-1822
REED, Jacob to Nancy Rollins                                         1-8-1824
RICE, Daniel to Ann Barney - Ann of Seneca twp.                    12-14-1820
RICE, Ezekiel to Elizabeth Fletcher                                 5-13-1830
RICE, Russel to Margaret McBeath                                     7-16-1826
RICHARDS, Peter to Mary Mony                                         2-20-1826
ROACH, Price to Catharine Barnes                                     9-6-1827
RODGER, Linas to Clarissa Brown                                     3-13-1832
ROGERS, Eliphalet to Hannah Jackson                                 4-8-1822
ROSS, James to Kathran Spoon                                        5-13-1832
SCOTHORN, Benjamin to Evaline E. Ogle                               5-8-1831
SCOTHORN, William to Betsy Harris                                  8-15-1830
SCRANTON, James A. to Rachel Whitaker - both of Sandusky           4-21-1823
SHALL, Michael to Eleanor Bawley                                    7-26-1825
SHANNON, George to Mary Johnston                                   12-26-1827
SHAWL, Benjamin to Elizabeth Cinque                                 1-12-1831
SHEPARDSON, James P. to Mrs. Nancy Ausburne                         2-10-1828
SHERWOOD, William D. to Loris Emerson                              10-1-1822
```

```
SMITH, Elisha to Mrs. Nancy Hubbard                              1-11-1830
SMITH, George to Rebecca Shawl                                  12-16-1830
SMITH, Jason W. to Margarett Tibballs                           10-18-1829
SNOW, Henry to (Mrs.?) Diadema Ward                              3-26-1829
SPRINGER, Peter to Elizabeth Braty                             12-23-1823
STANLEY, Thomas W. to Amanda Newman                             1-3-1829
STEPHENSON, Ebenezer to Hannah Coal                            12-11-1828
STINSON, Seth to Betsy Stull                                    2-15-1832
STONE, Christopher to Mrs. Polly Eaton                          1-6-1829
STONER, George to Elizabeth Bowles                              5-6-1824
STULL, Michael to Diana Baker                                   3-10-1829
STULTZ, John to Jamimah Overmire                                3-29-1832
TAYLOR, James to Elizabeth Upcott                               1-13-1828
TEW, Paul to Elizabeth B. McIntyre                             12-25-1832
THORN, Garret to Caroline Austin                                6-1-1830
TILLOTSON, Reuben to Ann Hilton (or Hitton)                    12-7-1826
TINDALL, John to Laure Frasy                                    6-27-1832
TOPPING, Flavel to Matilda Nash                                11-24-1831
TUTTLE, Walbet to Ann Hoskins                                  11-27-1831
TUTTLE, William W. to Sally M. Knox                             1-1-1827
TYLER, Morris to Elta Bristol                                   1-2-1822
TYLER, Morris to Sophia Bristol                                 1-8-1832
UTLEY, Samuel to Sarah Smith                                    6-3-1827
VANDOREN, Abraham to Polly Bates                                7-1-1828
VERDICATE, Allsain to Nelly Mushell                            2-17-1829
VERDICATE, John to Mary Ann Musshel                           12-31-1828
WALTERS, Ephraim to Elizabeth Kline                            3-20-1831
WANNELL, Isaac to Margrat Shook                                2-23-1832
WEGEMAN, George to Christina Murre                             3-22-1832
WHITE, David of Oxford twp., Huron Co. to
              Rebecca Stull of Riley twp., Sandusky Co.        10-20-1829
WHITE, David to Mrs. Eliza Wallace                             3-17-1831
WHITE, Thomas to Susanna Bowlus                               12-12-1822
WIDENER, Michael to Nancy Benjamin                             2-5-1827
WILDER, Levi to Helen Topping                                  3-21-1830
WILLIAMS, Ezra to Mrs. Sallina Williams                       11-25-1827
WILLIAMS, Jacob to Mary Smith                                  10-1-1826
WILLS, Roswell to Elizabeth Sutton - Eliz. of Portage twp.    12-7-1820
WILSON, C. C. to Mary Chambers                                 1-15-1829
WILSON, Fredinand to Amelia Graves                             7-19-1829
WOOLCUTT, John to Hannah Stults                               12-9-1824
WRIGHT, Cyrenus to Diana Cole                                  2-8-1824
```

SCIOTO COUNTY, OHIO - WILL ABSTRACTS 1809-1836

The following records were taken from Will Book A, found in the Probate Court.
Portsmouth is the county seat. Pages on which record may be found are given in
parenthesis. The index is numbered; thus, wills begin on page 40. None have been
omitted.

BRUBAKER, John - dated 1-1-1610; recorded (not given). Brother, Abraham Brubaker to
have all lands and estate and to pay other brothers and sisters (not named) $300. in
six years. Executor, John Stover. Signed: John (his mark) Brubaker. Witnesses:
Peter Lionbarger Jr. and Peter Lionbarger Sr. (40)

DUGAN, Thomas - dated 1-22-1809; recorded (not given). Wife, Nancy, also to serve as
executrix. Eldest son, Adison Dugan born 15 Feb. 1804. Youngest son, James Dugan
born 22 Nov. 1806. Signed: Thomas Dugan. Witnesses: Wm. Collings, William Talbott
and Dan'l Bolinghouse. (41)

McKINNEY, Daniel - dated 4-13-1812; recorded (not given). Wife, Mary to have 50 acres
testator purchased from Samuel Vanhook. Sons: Solomon, William Thomas Berry, Theo-
dore and Daniel McKinney. First wife's two children: Tishe and Seleh McKinney.
Second wife's daughter, Cynthia. Brother, William's widow (not named) 3 acres west
fork of Limestone Creek in Kentucky bounded by lands of Edward Martin and others.
Bequeath to Hir um Devowe (no relationship if any is stated). Owned land in Ohio and
Kentucky. Executor: Duncan McArthur. Signed: Daniel McKinney. Witnesses: James
Edison, John Collison and Hiram (his mark) Devowe. (42)

SCARBOROUGH, John of Alexandria - dated 12-29-1812; recorded (not given). Mother,
Mary Scarborough to have 565½ acres in Madison Co. on waters of Deer Creek part of
entry #6781 entered by John Scarborough containing 1111 acres on part of military
warrant #3414; she is also to serve as executrix. Signed: John Scarborough.
Witnesses: Silas Cole, Ezra Bradford, and John Brooks. (43)

SALLADAY, Philip - dated 3-19-1813; recorded (not given). Wife, Christena. Sons:
George, John, Samuel and David. Daughters: Elizabeth, Mary, Nancy, Neely and Sally.
Executors; son, George Salladay and Mathew Curran. Signed: Philip Salladay.
Witnesses: Alex'r Curran, Thompson Sebring and Elizabeth (her mark) Sebring. (44)

BOYDSTONE, Presley - dated 6-10-1812; recorded (not given). Daughters: Catharine
Mustard, her children--Lydia and Elizabeth; Elizabeth Barns; and Ann Talbot wife of
William Talbot. Executors: sons-in-law; William Talbot, Samuel Mustard and John
Barnes. Signed: Presley Boydstone. Witnesses: Isaac Evans, John Pickens and John
Hull. Codicil dated 8-27-1812 gives additional bequeath to daughter, Elizabeth Barns
Witnesses: Jas. Parrell and Asa (his mark) Fulkmore. (45)

LUCAS, William Sr. - dated 6-4-1813; recorded (not given). Sons: William Lucas,
dec'd, his heirs; Samuel Lucas, dec'd, his heirs; Joseph Lucas, dec'd, his heirs;
Robert Lucas; and John Lucas. Daughters; Susannah Buckles. Lavise Stienburger,
Abigail Clark and Rebeccah Reed. Executors: sons, John and Robert Lucas; and friend
William Kendal. Signed: William Lucas, Sen. Witnesses: Ezra Osborne, John R.
Turner and Nathan Glover. (47)

500

SHEWARD, John - dated 5-19-1814; recorded (not given). Wife, Phebe, also to
serve as executrix. Children: Ruth McCoy; Sally Wees; Tace Kinkead; eldest son
Isaiah Sheward; Rebeckah Boher (or Baker); Nathan Sheward; two youngest sons,
Ezekiel and James Sheward; Phebe Sheward, not of age; David Sheward, not of age
(note: only those children stated as eldest son, etc. were specifically named;
however, it is inferred that the rest were children). Signed: James Sheward.
Witnesses: Emanuel Trexler, Samuel Trexler and John (his mark) Clammons. (50)

STOCKHAM, William - dated 9-28-1812; recorded (not given). Wife, Susanah.
Son, William. Two youngest sons: David and Daniel Paine; both not of age.
Signed: William Stockham. Witnesses: Samuel Crull and Jane Crull. (51)

BARNES, Thomas of Porter twp. - dated 1-1-1819; recorded (not given). Wife, Sarah,
also to serve as executrix. Eldest son, Robert Barnes. Second son, Henry Barnes,
to have 50 acres in Robert Barnes legacy adjoining east end of where testator now
resides. Youngest son, William Barnes, not of age. Eldest daughter, Nancy Barnes,
Youngest daughter, Mary Dever. Signed: Thomas (his mark) Barnes. Witnesses:
Jacob Poole, James B. Goodrich and Richard G. Swezeey(?). (52)

SPANGLER, Henry of Jefferson twp. - dated 9-15-1818; recorded (not given). Wife,
Susannah. Sons: eldest, Jacob; 2nd, Henry; youngest, George. Daughters: eldest,
Elizabeth Irwin; 2nd, Polly Huse; 3rd, Susannah Rodger; 4th, Sarah Simmons; 5th,
Nancy Spangle; 6th, Lydia Spangle; 7th, Caty Spangle; 8th and youngest, Rachel.
Executors: John Lucas and Jesse Cockerel. Signed: Henry Spangle. Witnesses:
Charles Crull and Charles Green. (54)

(note: pages 55 and 56 are missing from book)

MONROE, Moses - dated 1-2-1816; recorded (not given). Wife, Bridget, also to serve
as executrix. Children: Barnabus Monrow, Daniel Monrow, Solloman Monrow, Lida
Shoomaker, Phebe Stroud, Jesse Monrow, Aaron Monrow, Cizy Monrow, and John Monroe.
Signed: Moses (his mark) Monrow. Witnesses: Samuel Crull and Thomas (his mark)
Luis. (57)

PATTON, Thomas of Green twp. - dated 7-16-1817; recorded (not given). Wife, Mary.
Sons: eldest son, Thomas, land where he lives known as #27 in French Grant; James;
Samuel, land where he lives except 2 acres adjoining mill; four youngest sons,
Jeremiah, John, Uriah and Abner, Abner is not of age, to have lots testator now
lives on known as #30 & #31 and 2 saw mills on Pine Creek. Five daughters: Ruth,
Rachel, Nancy, Rebecca and Jenny. Requests that Mills be repaired and rented.
Executors: wife, Mary; son, Thomas Patton; and Francis Duliel. Signed: Thos.
Patton. Witnesses: Wm. M. Burke, Francis Duliel and Peter Duliel. (58)

HARDIN, Thomas - dated 9-23-1817; recorded (not given). Wife, Elender. Sons:
Daniel, Thomas, John and James Hardin. Daughters: Elizabeth Morgin, Jane Coleman,
Ellanor Bradshaw, Sally Stewart and Rachel Rardin. (note: not signed.) Witnesses:
Perry Liston and John Liston. (60)

501

CORSON, Henry - Verbal Will given 19th inst.; deposition given 5-21-1816; recorded (not given). Only child, a daughter (not named) living in Cape May Co., New Jersey. Requests that John Colten, Esq. and Silas Cole take out adms. papers on estate. Witnesses: Thomas Collins and John Welch. (60)

MOUK, Samuel of Vernon twp. - dated 8-5-1819; recorded (not given). Wife, Caty (?) Two sons, Joseph and Peter Mouk. Wife to keep sons for 11 years and then to put them to trades. Other children implied, but not named. Executor and guardian, Thompson Sebring. Witnesses: Frederick Mouk. William Hoppès. Codicil 8-5-1819, no additional information. (61)

CLARK, James - dated 7-30-1818; recorded (not given). Sons: James Clark, land on Turkey Creek; William Clark; Samuel Clark; youngest son, Thomas Clark, property in Jefferson twp. Daughters: Nancy, 1 lot in town of Frankfort, Hampshire Co., Virginia; Jane Johnson; Rachel Clark; Hester Clark; and Susan Clark, Susan not of age. Grandchild, James Clark to have 65 acres of upper survey on Turkey Creek one of branches of Scioto Brush Creek. Executors: son, James Clark and Isaac Johnson. Signed: James Clark. Witnesses: William McDonald, Jacob Johnson and David Murphey. (62)

WILKINSON, Samuel Scott - dated 10-8-1821; recorded (got given). All estate to mother, brothers and sisters (not named). Executor, Aaron Kinney. Signed: Samuel Scott Wilkinson. Witnesses: Jacob Clonymon(?), J. Kendal and Ezra Osborn. (63)

CHENEY, John of Porter twp. - dated 9-3-1821; recorded (not given). Wife, Rachel, also to serve as executrix. Sons; Trestram, John Rufus and Roswell Cheney. Two only daughters; Hannah Kendal and Abigal C. Drury. Signed: John Cheeney. Witnesses: John Young, Barna Wickson. Wm. Colegrove, Sarah (her mark) Colegrove and Sarah Cheney. (64)

WORLEY, Anthony - dated 7-6-1822; recorded August 1822. Wife, Jane. Sons: Moses, Elijah and Anthony. Daughters: Nancy Welch, Betsy Perry, Patience Crouch, Polly and Margaret. Signed: Anthony (his mark) Worley. Witnesses; Henry Burris, Sen., John Worley and Jas. Eidson. (65)

SMITH, John - dated (not given--ca. 1822); recorded (not given). Wife, Mercy. Friend, Eskridge Hall. Executors: wife, Mercy and Eskridge Hall. Witnesses: Charles Stratton, Nathan Wheeler and Saunders Darby. (66)

HERSEY, Nathan of Portsmouth - dated 1-23-1822; recorded August 1822. Son, Doctor Thomas Hersey, also to serve as executor. Grandson, Elmer Wilson Hersey with Doctor Thomas Hersey to serve as his guardian. Mentions land in town of Perryoppolis, Washington twp., Fayette Co., Pennsylvania. Signed: Nathan Hersey. Witnesses: James B. Prescott, Luke Coon Jr., Marth E. Hersey, Louisia Porter and Samuel M. Tracy. (67)

BROWN, John - dated 10-23-1823; recorded 12-10-1823. Wife, Hannah. Only son, John Brown Jr. Daughter, Rachel Hendall. Grandchild, Minerva E. B. Lucas, only child of daughter Betsey Lucas. Executors: wife, Hannah and Robert Lucas. Signed: John Brown. Witnesses: Henry Kirkendall and Ezra Osborn. (68)

WILLIAMS· Isaac of Portsmouth - dated 6-3-1812; recorded December 1822. Testator states that he is now leaving for army and he leaves his lot in Portsmouth to John Brown Jr. and his heirs, said lot noe being leased to Brown. Signed: Isaac (his mark) Williams. Witnesses: Ezra Osborn and Wm. Huston. (68)

WILSON, James Sr. - dated 8-29-1823; recorded (not given). Sons: John and James Wilson. Daughters: Susana wife of John Callaman, Elizabeth wife of Jeremiah Armstrong and Patsey wife of Jessey Nelson. Bequeath to Joseph (or Josiah) Nelson, son of Jesse Nelson. Signed: James (his mark) Wilson Sr. Witnesses: Thos. Brown and John (his mark) Brown. (69)

FEURT, Gabriel Sr. - dated 1-28-1824; recorded July 1824. Nephew, Gabriel Feurt Jr. Mentions cooper tools. Signed: Gabriel Fourt. Witnesses: Jesse Hitchcock and Isabella (her mark) Feurt. (70)

REEVE, Gabriel of Porter twp. - dated 2-19-1824; recorded July 1824. Wife, Hannah, also to serve as executrix. ¯Four children; Volney, Tracy, Elijah Barton and Fanny Ann Reeve. Signed; Gabriel Reeve. Witnesses: John D. Miller and William Burk. (70)

BROWN, Hannah widow of John Brown - dated 2-16-1825; recorded (not given). Son, David Jones. Grand-daughter, Minerva E. B. Lucas, only child of daughter Elizabeth Lucas, dec d. Son, John Brown, Daughter, Rachel Hendal, dec d. Executors: Robbert Lucas and David Jones. Signed: Hannah (her mark) Brown. Witnesses: Noah Graves and William (his mark) Trimer. (71)

DAWSON, Edward of Madison twp. - dated 12-10-1824; recorded (not given). Wife, Katharine, also to serve as executrix. "Heirs of Edward Dawson--Elizabeth Dawson, John Dawson and Catharine Baker." Signed: Edward (his mark) Dawsen. Witnesses: Caleb Bennet, Absalom Nye and Henry Nye. (72 & 77)

NAILER, Mrs. Louisa - verbal will 8-25-1825; recorded 9-22-1825. All estate to Sally Bennet. "George" mentioned, but no surname or relationship, if any, is given. Witnesses: Henry Fierney and Jane Fierney. (73)

CAMFIELD, Ebenezer of Green twp. - dated 3-17-1819; recorded October 1825. Wife, Mary, Step-son, Ezra Harel. Daughters; Sary Olds, Rachel Grant, Sibble Ransom, Anna Morgan and Subrution(?) Morgen. Bequeath to George and Mary Eare, Both not of age (no relationship if any is stated). Executors: friend, Asa Boyington and step-son, Ezra Harel, Signed: Ebenezer Camfield. Witnesses: Asa Boyinton and Benjamin Locke. (74)

DARBY, Sander of Portsmouth - dated 11-16-1818; recorded (not given). Sister, Mary wife of James Green of Philadelphia. Signed: Sander Darby. Witnesses: James Zinn, James Marsh and Wm. Peck. (76)

GILRUTH, Thomas - dated 2-16-1826 French Grant; recorded 4-5-1826. Wife, mentioned but not named. also to serve as execitrox/ Sons: William and James. Daughter, Mary wife of William S. Thomas. Bequeaths one-fourth acre ground around Hanorah Gilruth's grave for a burial ground. Signed: Thomas Gilruth. Witnesses: John B. Rowel and William Paver(?). (77)

503

RICHMOND, Peter of Green twp. - dated 2-10-1826; recorded April 1826. To Joseph Bonsor, also to serve as executor, all real estate being 217 acres in French Grant known as No. 64. Signed: Peter (his mark) Richmond. Witnesses: Jonathan Mead and John H. Patten. (78)

SALLADAY, David - dated 2-2-1826; recorded April 1826. Wife, Mary, also to serve as executrix. Three sons: Alonzo, Josfus and Octavius; none are of age. Three daughters: Emeline, Minerva and Sarah Salladay; none are of age. Signed: David Salladay. Witnesses: Levi Sikes and William (his mark) Smith. (78)

McINTIRE, Elijah of Portsmouth - Verbal Will - will given 8-20-1827 with testator dying the next morning; recorded August 1827. Father, Henry McIntire of Stafford Co., Virginia. Witnesses: Jacob Offner and Edward Hamilton. (79)

DEVER, John - dated 3-4-1819; recorded 11-26-1827. Wife, Hannah. Sons: James, William and John. Daughters: Polly Feurl, Sarah McDowel, Betsey Detsey Willcockson (Willcoxon), Hannah Guthery and Rachel. Executors: son, William and Benjamin Feurl. Signed: John Deaver. Witnesses: John Lucas, David Murphy and James Williams. (81)

EIDSON, James of Nile twp. - dated 1-11-1828; recorded 3-3-1828. Wife, Sarah. Sons-in-law; Aaron Hall to have Nile twp. tract and Isaac Worley to have Washington twp. tract. Daughters: Elizabeth wife of Isaac Worley and Margaret wife of Aron Hall. Executors: John Corn, Isaac Worly and Aron Hall. Signed: Jas. Edison. Witnesses; Foreman Wavre(?) and Thos. Coabe. (83)

COLE, Edmund - dated 11-17-1827; recorded 6-16-1828. Wife, Phebe. Son, Ira. Daughters: Fanny Adams, Laura Cole and Alzina. Executors: wife, Phebe and Abijiah Bullersen. Signed: Edmund Cole. Witnesses: Benjamin Fair and Hester Sharp. (85)

COLE, Silas of Alexandria - dated ___-27-1827 (note: no month given); recorded 9-20-1828. Wife. Louisa. Sons: Lucas Cole, dec'd, his children (not named); Marcus Cole; and Amos Cole. Daughters: Polly wife of Reuben Weil; Louisa Smith, now dec'd, her children and testator's grandchildren (not named); Minene Cole and Philomela Cole. Executor: son, Amos Cole. Signed: Silas Cole. Witnesses: Ezra Osborn and Henry Ballentine. (86)

VIRGIN, Rachel - dated 8-2- 1828; recorded 9-11-1828. Sons: George O., Abraham, Resin and Kinzey Virgin. Daughters: 2nd dau., Jemima Cikes (Sikes); 3rd dau., Rachel Cikes (Sikes); 4th and youngest dau., Charity Virgin. Executor, Luther Wheeler. Signed: Rachel Virgin. Witnesses: Luther Wheeler and Rebecha Wheller. (90)

GROVER, Isaiah of Vernon twp. - dated 4-24-1;829; recorded 7-9-1829. Wife, Sarah, also to serve as executrix. Sons: eldest, Isaiah Grover; and youngest, Leonard Grover, both not of age. Signed: Isaiah Grover. Witnesses: Miranda Searl, Jeremiah White and Tompkins Chamberlain. (92)

PEEBLES, William of Portsmouth - dated 7-11-1829; recorded 10-1-1829. Brothers and Sisters: Rachel Rodgers Pebbless, Betsy Hamstead, Jane Finley Wood, Richard Rodgers Pebless, John Geddis Pebless, and Joseph Scott Pebless. Executors: father, John Pebless and mother, Margaret Pebless. Signed: Wm. Peebles. Witnesses: Thomas Irvin, Elizann Brainard and J. A. Binghan. Codicil dated same day, no additional information. (94)

SHACKFORD, Josiah of Portsmouth - dated 4-7-1808; recorded 10-2-1829. All estate to nephews and nieces (not named). If any of the heirs bring suit against estate, their share is to go to the poor of the town they reside in. Signed: Josiah Shackford. Witnesses: Jacob Offnere, Aaron Kinney and George W. Clingman. (97)

MASSIE, Henry of Jefferson Co., Kentucky - dated 2-16-1830; recorded 9-13-1830. Wife, Hellen Massie, also to serve as executrix. Nieces: Constance Massie and Elizabeth Thompson. Nephews: Heeth (or Huth) Jones of Louisville; Nathaniel Massie of Ohio, son of testator's dec'd brother, Nathaniel Massie; Henry Bullett son of Catherine Bullett; and Alexander Scott Bullett son of Wm. C. Bullett. Brother, Thomas Massie. (note: will contains many land descriptions for land in Kentucky and Ohio). Signed: H. Massie. Witnesses: W. C. Gett, N. Bullett and Edward Johnson. (102)

GLOVER, Elijah of Portsmouth - dated 3-25-1826; recorded 3-10-1830. Wife, Catherine, also to serve as executrix. Three sons: John, Eli and Samuel Glover. Two daughters: Elizabeth B. and Ann Massie Glover. Signed: Elijah Glover. Witnesses: C. McCoy and Ezra Osborn. (105)

ROUSE, Reason - dated 3-21-1831; recorded 6-15-1831. Wife, Martha, also to serve as executrix. Signed: Reason Rouse. Witnesses: David Jones. David Vannest, Thomas Rouse and John Rouse. (108)

BELOTE, Gesrge - dated (not given); recorded 6-16-1831. Eldest son, James Beloat. Bequeath to Polly Stewart and John Stewart. Bequeath to Nancy Montgomery late Nancy Beloat. Bequeath to Edward Beloat and William Montgomery. Wife, Mary Beloat and her children--George Beloat, Joseph Beloat, Wm. Tuine (or Quine) Beloat, Menervy Beloat Syder, Jacob Beloat and Caroline Beloate. Testator appoints wife, Mary Beloat admsrx. and Walter Beloat, adms. Witnesses: A. W. Lucas and John J. Colins. (109

WELLS, Timothy of Madison twp. - dated 9-23--1831; recorded 3-10-1832. Brothers: Richard and James. Sisters: Martha; Mary; and Deborah Wells, her daughter--Evangely (called Emily elsewhere in will). Father and Mother, Richard Wells and Deborah Wells. Executor: brother, Richard Wells. Signed: Thimothy Wells. Witnesses: Ebe Corwin, James Corwin and Peter Wikoff. (112)

WOODRING, John of Porter twp. - dated 8-17-1829; recorded 9=17-1832. Wife, Christina. Son, Jacob Woodring and his daughter, Mary now wife of Michael Butt. Grandson, Joseph Shoemaker. "My two blind children"--Joseph Woodring and Christiana--two blind children not to become a public charge and Joseph Shoemaker is to give security to Overseers of Poor of Porter twp. to assure same. Executors: son, Jacob and grandson, Jacob Shoemaker. Signed: Joseph Woodring. Witnesses: Isaac Price, John Tuschler and John Bensen. (114)

LAWSON, John Sr. of Greenup Co., Kentucky - dated 7-30-1831; recorded 3-18-1833. Wife, Catharine, also to serve as executrix; to have plantation and negroes-- Dan, Clem, Sam, Joseph, Polly, Hagar and Jane. Eldest daughter, Hannah Lawson now McKay. Six youngest children: Elizabeth, Mary An, Rebecca Jane, John Taylor, Thomas and Catharine; all not of age. Mentions land in Kentucky and Ohio; also that negro, Moses is to be sold. Signed: John Lawson. Witnesses: James Lawson and Clarkson Z. Smith. (115)

ARMSTRONG, John, formerly of Cincinnati - Verbal Will - deposition given 5-12-1833; recorded 9-19-1833. Brother, Joshua Armstrong, also to serve as executor. Sister, Druscilla Walker. Witnesses: H. Ingram and David McCall. (118)

BISSELL (BYSELL), Rufus - da ed 7-25-1833; recorded 9-20-1833. Wife, Sarah. Signed: Rufus Bissell. Witnesses: William Story and Jesse Young. (120)

CONKLIN, Joseph - dated 6-8-1833; recorded 2-26-1834. Wife, Hannah. To Joseph Conklin son of William Conklin, part of lot in French grant except one acre which is a burial ground which testator bequeaths to the public. Mentions children but does not name. Signed: Joseph (his mark) Conklin. Witnesses: John Montgomery and Harrison Morrison. (122)

LACROIX, Michael - dated 3-5-1834; recorded 7-21-1834. Two children, Katherine and William; not of age. Two brothers: Andrew and Alexander Lucrois. Three sisters: Cecilla Wait, Zera (or Zeru) Dieluwit and Emily Baby. Executor: Peter F. Serroll. Children to live with William Montgomery and wife Hannah until they are of age. Signed: Michael Lacroix. Witnesses: William (or Milton) Montgomery and John McKee. (123)

WILLIAMSON, Martha - dated 9-11-1826; recorded 9-1-1834. Children: James, Peter, Frances, Thomas, Joseph, Margaret Ann and Sally Williamson. Executors: sons, James and Peter. Signed: Martha (her mark) Williamson. Witnesses: Elijah Reeves, Thomas Reeves, James Andrews and Joseph Oarel. (124)

BENNETT, Thaddeus of Porter twp. - dated 5-15-1833; recorded 9-11-1834. Wife, Rachel. Sons: Benjamin, Joseph, Ira G., Jesse and Thomas. Daughter, Sarah. Mentions Rhoda wife of son, Ira G. Grandson and grand-daughter; Gushum and Mahitable Bennett, Bequeaths $1.00 each to: Mary Squires, Rhoda Crawford, Mahitable Dodge, Eunice Gaston, Catharine Taubut and Betsy Ann Lindsey (note: may be daughters, but not stated). Executors: wife; and son, Joseph Bennett. Signed: Thadeus Bennett. Witnesses: Moses Bennett, Betsy Bennett and Esther Mead. (125)

HARRET, William - dated 8-2-1833; recorded 4-20-1835. Wife, Maragarett. Three sons, John, Henry and Samuel Harbet. Two daughters: Elizabeth Ishmael and Susanna Royse. Grandson, William Harbert, also to serve as executor. Signed: William (his mark) Harbet. Witnesses: John Nichols, Otho Dawsen and Thos. Caul. (128)

MASTERS, John, late of Chillicothe, Ross Co., Ohio, now of Scioto Co., Ohio - dated 2-12-1831; recorded (not given). Brothers: Benjamin, George and Ezekiel Masters. Sisters: Elizabeth Spaulding, dec'd, her children (not named), Nancy Wedding; and Melissa Mitchel. Mentions land in Chillicothe now occupied by Samuel Deonnl as an inn keeper; lots in Portsmouth and lots in Piketon, Pike Co. Executor: brother, Benjamin Masters. Signed: John Masters. Witnesses: John R. Turner and Henry Jeffories. (129)

DEVER, William of Morgan twp. - dated 11-21-1834; recorded 4-25-1835. Wife, mentioned but not named. Children: eldest son, John; eldest dau., Hanna; son, Joseph; dau., Louisa; 3rd and youngest dau. Mary Alvira (or Malvina). Executors: wife; and son, John. Signed: William Dever. Witnesses: A. B. Bemes. George McDougal and David Noel. (131)

DARLINGTON, Robert - dated 9-3-1835; recorded 12-10-1835. Wife. Belinda. Nephews: Joseph and Daniel Darlington, sons of brother, Samuel Darlington. Nieces: Louisa Collins and Julia Darlington. Bequeath to Joseph Buekels Rankin (no relationship if any, is stated). Executors: John Cramer and Clark Meller. Signed: Robert Darlington. Witnesses: John C. Clemmons and Charles Cox. (134)

CRULL, William - dated 1-28-1836; recorded 4-30-1836. Wife, Mary. Step-son, William P. Cuttey(?). Daughters: Susannah, Rachel, Anna, Asseneth, Jemima, Martha and Mary. Executors: brother, Charles Crull and nephew, Wm. M. Crull. Signed: William Crull. Witnesses: Samuel Crull and Daniel P. Stockham. (136)

DUDUIT, William of Granstown - dated 8-7-1835; recorded 4-28-1836. Wife, Zaire. Children, mentioned but not named except oldest son, William; youngest children are not of age. Signed: W. Duduit. Witnesses: M. White, Ezra Heird and Daniel D. F. Heird. (137)

OVERMAN, Enlice - dated 5-6-1836; recorded 6-9-1836. Wife, Polly. Children: Abraham, Mary Ann, Margaret, John, George and Amanda. Mentions outstanding money in Virginia. Executor: Isaac P. Cunningham. Signed: Enlice (his mark) Overman. Witnesses: William S. Rennick, Aaron Clark and Abram H. Albertson. (139)

VASTINE, John - dated 4-10-1834; recorded 11-14-1836. Sons: John Vastine Jr., William Vastine, Frederic Vastine, Gabriel Vastine, and Abraham Vastine, Daughter, Mary wife of David Smith, Mentions land in Pike Co., Ohio; also 45 acres on Brush Creek purchased from General William Kendall. Executor; son, John. Signed: John Vastine. Witnesses: Wilson Gatis, C. S. Smith and Charles Tracy. (140)

SQUIRES, Samuel - dated 9-20-1836; recorded 11-14-1836. Wife, Mary. Mentions "all children........children by last woman as well as first". Bequeath to John Stiles, "his mother's part." Mentions "my two little boys" Samuel and Phineas. Executor - brother, Nathaniel Squires. Signed: Samuel (his mark) Squires. Witnesses: A. Batterson and H. Taylor. (142)

CRULL, David - dated 9-20-1836; recorded 11-14-1836. Wife, Mary. Sons: Thomas, Caleb, Joshua and David. Daughters: Nancy, Mary, Elinor and Maryann. Signed: David (his mark) Crull. Witnesses: David Jones, Charles Crull and Tanday Taylor. (143)

The following records have been abstracted from Will Book A, located in the Probate Court at the court house at Portsmouth. Page on which record may be found is given in parenthesis

HULL, Isaac of Bloom twp. - dated 11-12-1830; recorded May 1837. Wife, Ann, also to serve as executrix. Daughter, Rebecca. States "have provided for other children." Signed: Isaac (mark) Hull. Witnesses: N.S. Daniel and Pheba Daniel. (144)

WELCH, John of Porter twp. - dated 11-14-1836; recorded 5-3-1837. Wife, Elizabeth, also to serve as executrix. Children: Hénrietta, Mary, Dilly (Dilla), Louise and Henry Welch. Signed: John Welch. Witnesses: Wm Re. Louther, Wm Morford and Jefferson Boyer. (146)

HUNPHREY, Morris - dated 7-7-1836; recorded 5-4-1837. Sons: John (eldest son), Thomas, Henry, Morris and William Hunphrey. Daughters: Sally Hunphry now Sally Seinbeck, Rachel Hunphry now Rachel Sprouse, and Elizabeth Hunphry now Elizabeth Rupell (or Russell). Signed: Morris Hunphrey. Witnesses: Philip S. Heyward, John Rueff and Gabriel Hunphrey. (147)

LUCAS, William Jr. - Oral Will - given 10-23-1837; recorded 11-18-1837. Wife, Annie. Son, John Lucas, a minor. Mother, Elizabeth Lucas Sr.; Mentions: Levi Lucas, Adrian and his wife Betsey, no relationship stated. Adms.: wife, Annie and brother, Adrian Lucas. (149)

OVERMAN, Mary - dated 12-2-1837; recorded 4-12-1838. Sons: John and George Overman, not of age. Daughters: Mary Ann, lately deceased; Margaret Overman; and Amanda Overman, not of age. Executor: James L. Eakin. Witnesses: James Lambert and John Lambert. (150)

PILES, Rachel - widow and relict of John Piles, dec'd - dated 1-6-1838; recorded 4-3-1838. "My children": Joseph Piles, Eliza Ann Piles, Lucinda and Matilda. $1.00 each to Sally Blower, Betsy Heely, Jeremiah Piles, Ruhama Mitchell, Cynthia More and William Piles; no relationship stated. Signed: Rachel (mark) Piles. Witnesses: J. R. Turner, Andrew Crichton. (152)

GWATHNEY, George S. - dated 5-9-1838; recorded (not given--Aug. 1838). Wife, Anna. Mentions money coming from uncle, Joseph Fox's estate, Fox beint testator's agent. Executor, David Pollock. Signed: George S. Gwathney. Witnesses: John Vastine, Thomas Pollock and A. B. Banes. (153)

LEWIS, Jacob M. late of Philadelphia, Pa., now of Portsmouth, Ohio. - dated 4-23-1838; recorded 8-16-1838. Brothers: James O. Lewis, his six or seven children (not named); John F. Lewis; and George A. Lewis. Nephew, Thomas B. Lewis, son of dec'd brother, Wm A. Lewis. Niece, Anna Maria Lewis, sister of Thos. B. Owned store in Portsmouth. Executors: friends, Wilson Gates and Enos Gunn. Signed: J. M. Lewis. Witnesses: W. Kinney, Lorezo C. Goff and W. Barbar. (154)

LEONARD, Elizabeth of Portsmouth - dated 9-27-1837; recorded (not given--Nov. 1838). Children: Polly Leonard, Adam Leonard, Nancy Baker, Jacob Leonard, Elizabeth Huston, Susan Davis and Sarah Caldwell. Executor: G.S.B. Hemstead. Signed: Elizabeth(mark) Leonard. Witnesses: M. Gregory and G.S.B. Hempstead. (156)

FUNK, Martin of Clay twp. - dated 10-4-1838; recorded 11-8-1838. Children: John Funk, Polly Sill, Jacob Funk, Catharine Timmonds, Barbara Micklewait and Betsy Jamison. One acre land to be set apart for public burying ground and to include burying ground on farm I now live on. Executor: Joseph Micklewait. Signed: Martin (mark) Funk. Witnesses: Wm Kendall and Manassa Lawson. (157)

NOLDER, William - dated 9-20-1838; recorded 11-9-1838. Sons: John, William, Lemuel (or Samuel--both given but believe same) and James. Daughters: Elizabeth Balinger, Marget Finney, Sarah, Mary, Jane and Matilda. Executors: John F. Smith and Zina Gunn. Signed: Wm (mark) Nolder. Witnesses: Zina Gunn and John F. Smith. (158)

JONES, David - dated 1-19-1839; recorded (not given--Feb. 1839). Wife, Rachel, also to administer estate. Sons: Thomas C. Jones, George O. Jones, Wm Kendall Jones, and John Lucas Jones. Daughters: Eliza widow of Elijah Weaver, Rebecca a single woman, Rachel a single woman, Hanna Travis a married woman, and Abigail Cramer a married woman. Signed: David Jones. Witnesses: Charles Crull and Thomas J. Crull. Codicil dated 1-19-1838. Money bequeathed to son, John Lucas Jones not to be paid if he at any time marries Mary Rankins daughter of Wm. Rankins. Wit: Charles Crull and Thomas J. Crull. (159)

GRAVES, George of Washington twp. - dated 12-13-1832; recorded 5-21-1839. Sons: John Graves, George Graves and William Graves; listed in order of age. Daughters: Susanna Stanly, Amy Lawrence, Eleanor Shaver, Harriet Garrison, Lovena Graves, Mary Graves, Sarah Graves and Caroline Graves; Lovena, Mary and Sarah are not of age. Executor: William Hull. Signed: George Graves. Witnesses: Ezra Osborn and Havillah Gunn. Deposition of witness, Havillah Gunn states he had known Graves for about 20 years and would judge him to be about 50 years of age. (162)

WORLEY, Isaac of Washington twp. - dated 2-27-1839; recorded 5-25-1839. Wife, Elizabeth. Three oldest sons: James E., John and Wm S. Worley. Three youngest sons, Samuel F., Jesse P. and Richard M. Worley. Daughters: Matilda Bowman and Mary Ann Truet. "To John Worley a tract or parcel of land now used as a burying ground agreeable to plat of survey intended for use of public". Executors: Jacob Worley and Forman Moore. Signed: Isaac Worly. Witnesses: Sam'l Nixon and Joseph Worley. (167)

BIBBY, Abraham - dated 4-21-1838; recorded 5-25-1839. Wife, Sarah, also to serve as executrix. Sons: Isaac, Abraham, George W. and John Bibby. Daughters: Elizabeth, Eathalinda and Almira Bibby. Signed: Abraham (mark) Bibby. Witnesses: Otho Dawson and Middleton Hutton (or Huston?). (170)

DEWEY, Joseph of Madison twp. - dated 3-22-1839; recorded 8-12-1839. Wife, Rosanna. Brother, Erastus H. Dewey. Children, mentioned but not named. Mentions that land is to be purchased in Ross Co., Ohio. Signed: Joseph Dewey. Witnesses: Daniel Clemmons and Levi Linsey. (171)

BACCUS, Peter - dated 5-30-1836; recorded August 1839. Wife, Barbara, to have 2 half quarter sections of land in Section 5, Township 6, Range 2 in Pike Co., Illinois. Sons: eldest son, Jacob; son, Enoch; 3rd son Michael; son(?), Larcus Short; son, Thomas Jefferson; 5th son, John Smith; youngest son, Ezra. Daughter, Sene. Signed: Peter Baccus. Witnesses: Wm Power and Rebecca Power. (173)

BROWN, Mary - dated (not dated); recorded 11-12-1839. Sons: Joseph Belout; 2nd son, Joseph Belout; 3rd son, William Quinn Belout. Daughters: eldest daughter, Minerva Kikendall; two youngest daughers, Lydia and Caroline Jayne Belout. Brother, J. R. Turner. Executor: brother-in-law, Walter Belout. Signed: Mary (mark) Brown. Witnesses: William Shields and Bridget L. Payton. (174)

BELOUT, Smith - dated 10-10-1839; recorded 11-8-1839. Brothers: George and John. Sisters: Margaret McNeal, Mary Fullerton, Lidia Pattengill and Ann Belout. Executor, George Belout. Signed: Smith Belout. Witnesses: Luther Wheeler and Walter Belout. (175)

HELM(S), Abraham - dated 12-7-1839; recorded May 1840. Wife, Catharine, also to serve as executrix. Signed: A. Helm. Witnesses: M. Gregory and Thomas Morgan. (176)

OSBORNE, Ezra of Portsmouth - dated 1-17-1839; recorded 5-25-1840. Adopted daughters: Hannah O. Gamaye (or Gamage?) and Jane A. Osborn. Executors: William Hull of Portsmouth, merchant; and Hannah O. Gamaye (Gamage). Signed: Ezra Osborn. Witnesses: Jacob Offnere and Samuel J. McCloud. (177)

WORLEY, John of Nile twp. - dated 12-29-1839; recorded 5-26-1840. Wife, Patience. Children: Jacob; Joseph; John M; Susan Truet; Nancy Burrows; Anna Moore; Heirs of Patience Walker, dec'd; Heirs of Isaac Worley, dec'd; and Sally Allen. Executors: Levi Moore and Joshua Nurse. Signed: John Worley. Witnesses: Samuel Nixon and Forman Moore. (179)

REEVE, Volney of Wheelersburg - dated 4-20-1834; recorded 5-29-1840. Wife, Theresa, also to serve as executrix. Signed: Volney Reeve. Witnesses: Horatio Caswell and Lucy Caswell. (180)

EDGER, Joseph of Washington twp. - dated (not dated); recorded 9-12-1840. Wife, Mary. Brother, John. Wife to care for aged parents should they survive testator. Executors: wife, Mary and neighbor, Francis Cleveland. Signed: Joseph Edger. Witnesses: John McCachlun, Hugh Stewart and William Stewart. (184)

HAMMETT, George of Clay twp. - dated 4-13-1831; recorded 11-28-1840. Wife, Elizabeth. Grand-daughter, Desdemona Medkirk. Executors: son-in-law, John North and friend, G.S.B. Hemstead. Signed: George (mark) Hammett. Witnesses: G.S.B. Hemstead and R.R. Peebles. Codicil dated 6-1-1836 states that Wm Hull is to replace John Noel as one of esecutors. Witnesses: G.S.B. Hemstead and W. Hull. (185)

SCIOTO COUNTY, OHIO - MARRIAGES 1804-1815

The following records were copied from "Marriage Record A" as found in the Probate Court at the court house in Portsmouth. Marriage Record A consists of three books bound as one. The majority of the book is large in size and covers the marriages from 1815-1840. However, bound in the back of this book are two books, the one small in size and the other medium in size which cover the marriages from 1804-1815. Some marriages are cuplicated in both books.

ABBOT, James to Dolly Chamberlain	8-18-1812
ABBOTT, Samuel to Aurellas Chamber	10-1-1812
ADKIN, David to Anna Stewart	12-14-1814
AIKEN, John to Hannah Wright	12-19-1805
ANDERSON, Jacob to Julia Huston	8-11-1814
ANDREWS, James to Esther Powers	12-29-1814
ARDOE (ARDOR), Lewis to Patsy Carpenter - Upper twp.	6-5-1809
BAKER, Isaac to Rebecah Sherward	2-3-1814
BALLENGER, Asa to Amanda Swan	9-28-1815
BARBER, Uriah to Rachel Beard	10-7-1806
BARKELOW, Edward to Ruth Patton of Green twp.	9-24-1806
BARTON, Joseph to Elizabeth Rector	10-1-1805
BASSET, Amos to Susannah Colgin	9-11-1811
BASSETE, Alexander to Ann Mickey	3-1-1805
BELOAT, George to Mary Turner	4-22-1812
BENEMAN, Thomas to Sally Vanost	4-12-1807
BENNET, Benjamin to Mary Rollins	11-8-1814
BENNET, Thomas to Francis Lawer	6-10-1810
BENNETT, Amos to Deany Lee	11-8-1814
BENNETT, Henry to Nancy Lower	11-4-1814
BENNETT, John to Rebecca Bennett	12-9-1815
BENNETT, William to Rebeckah Jones	5-9-1805
BERRY, John to Elizabeth Glaze	6-28-1812
BEVER, Thomas to Sarey Hickman	4-17-1804
BIRT, Joseph to Peggy Munn	1-16-1812
BIVINS, John to Matilda Barton	11-25-1814
BLYTHE, Thomas to Unice Chaffin	9-9-1814
BOEN, William to Susannah Triggs	1-29-1814
BOLDSTON (BOELSTON), Joshua to Winney -?- (not given)	4-10-1806
BORN, Edward to Nancy Scott	5-6-1813
BOULTENHOUS, Daniel to Susannah Graves	3-7-1805
BOWEN, John to Rachell Feurt	2-2-1815
BOYNTON, Charles to Rhoda Sumner	3-3-1814
BOYNTON, Joseph E. to Elizabeth Wheeler	1-18-1813
BRADSHAW, George to Jane Gilkison	3-21-1805
BRADSHAW, Isaac to Nancy Saladay	3-1-1812
BRADSHAW, Robert to Susannah Baccus	9-5-1811
BRADSHAW, William to Elliner Rardon	3-18-1809
BREWER, Jacob to Mary Rinely	10-29-1807
BREWER, Stephen to Lucinda Bowyer	8-2-1807
BROOM, Edward to Susannah Baker - Upper twp.	3-19-1809
BROWN, Aaron to Catherine Yingling - Upper twp.	3-29-1808
BROWN, George to Anna Higgins	6-14-1808
BRUER, John to Margery Ferguson	3-19-1811

511

```
BURK, John to Catherine Stewart                                    7-17-1815
BURT, Christopher to Elizabeth Brittenham                          7-28-1810
BURT, William to Mary Boen                                         7-15-1810
BYERS, William Jr. to/Bunnel(mar. by Wm Byers Sr., J.P.)           5-25-1815
BYERS, William Sr. to Hannah Bunnel (mar. by Robert Lucas, J.P.)   8-25-1815
BYERS, Wm Jr. to Margaret Tucker                                   1-4-1811
CANADA, Thomas to Nancy Stout                                      11-27-1814
CARPENTER, Wm to Hannah Clark                                      12-22-1814
CARTER, Aquilla to Nancy Dillan                                    1-18-1822
CARTRON, Francis to Mary Saro                                      1-13-1806
CHAMBERLAIN, Anson (or Andrew) to Mary Morty (Mortz)               4-5-1814
CHAMBERLAIN, Wiate to Polly White                                  10-14-1813
CHAPMAN, John to Polly Reeve                                       9-10-1815
CHAPMAN, Josiah to Isabel Hitchcock                                11-26-1815
CHAPMAN, Reuben to Nancy Feurquay                                  8-2-1809
CLARK, John to Abigail Lucas                                       3-15-1810
CLARK, John to Hester(?) Coal                                      6-28-1814
CLARK, Richard to Katharine Olbert                                 3-24-1814
COLEGROVE, Peleg to Anne Johnston                                  5-23-1811
COLLINS, Thomas to Susy Carey                                      12-17-1812
COLLINS, Martin to Elizabeth Shoulwiler                            8-7-1815
COLVIN, John to Margaret Davisson                                  5-27-1807
COMAWAY, Simon to Rachel McAuley                                   2-25-1808
CONKLIN, Gideon to Rachel Patton                                   7-9-1807
CONKLIN, William to Mary Conklin                                   8-15-1808
CONNEL, Alexander to Aidy Martin, a widow                          3-16-1810
COUNEE, Philip to Elizabeth Short - Upper twp.                     12-7-1809
CRABTREE, Thomas to Phebe Graham                                   12-16-1813
CRACRAFT, Charles to Sarah Stephenson                              12-20-1809
CRAIG, William to Mary Bennet                                      1-12-1815
CROSS, Joseph to Elizabeth Helmer                                  12-9-1815
CROW, Abraham to Elizabeth Harris                                  2-15-1814
CRULL, Charles to Elizabeth Cramer                                 9-26-1809
CRULL, William to Ruth Stockham                                    4-11-1811
CULP, Jacob to Nancy Bowen                                         2-3-1814
CURCH, Joel to Nancy Cook                                          1-25-1811
CURRY,HENDERSON to Arcade Walls                                    11-23-1809
CURY, Ezra to Elizabeth Leeth                                      11-22-1814
CUSTICE, Thomas to Catherine Smith                                 10-19-1815
CUSTICE, William to Nancy Beloat                                   6-29-1815
DARLINGTON, Elisha to Eve Cramer                                   3-4-1813
DAVIS, Benjamon to Jane Wooley                                     3-27-1811
DAVIS, Elnathan to Mary Kniff                                      11-4-1810
DAVIS, Wm to Rachel Poss                                           1-7-1810
DAWSON, Abijah to Anna Shoemaker                                   8-20-1810
DAWXON, James to Anna Birt(?)                                      4-28-1812
DAY, Ezekiel of Upper twp. to Rebecca Bowen of Bloom twp.          12-30-1813
DEEN, William to Hannah Peyton                                     7-16-1808
DIXON, Eli to Elizabeth Graham                                     6-16-1814
DOD, Isaac to Nancy Hannaman - Seal twp.                           2-18-1808
DYSART, Stephen to Susannah Hannaman                               11-23-1809
```

512

```
EALLADAY, David to Polly Sikes                              3-24-1814
EASTBURN, Philip to Mary Aldridge                           5-21-1812
ELDRED, Samuel to Mary Walker                               9-16-1813
ELINTON, Pleasant to Mary Holland - Upper twp.             10-5-1809
FERGUSON, Samuel to Jane Bouser                             6-7-1809
FEURT, Benjamin to Mary Dever                              1-26-1812
PEURT, Gabriel to Lydia Hitchcock                          2-13-1812
FOXTER, Luke to Sarah Reed                                 12-9-1805
FRY, Daniel to Polly Hale                                 11-27-1815
FUERT, Anderson to Elizabeth Pumel                         3-23-1815
FULLAR, Alphonso to Mary Swain                             9-11-1814
FUNK, John to Margaret Glover                               6-1-1815
GALLANT, John to Sarah Travis                             10-29-1807
GALLHER, Manfield to Hannah Ullem                         11-29-1812
GARRET, Russell to Elizabeth Randall                       1-6-1814
GILLAN, Presley to Agalitha Duduit                        12-6-1810
GINATT, John B. to Barbara Smith - Upper twp.             8-29-1806
GIVANS, William to Rachel Stackham                        10-24-1810
GIVENS, Wm to Susanna Anderson                            7-13-1809
GLAZE, Abraham to Sary Owens                               6-24-1815
GLAZE, Airhart to Ruth Marret                              6-16-1811
GLAZE, Andrew Jr. to Susanna Cockbell                      3-19-1812
GLAZE, John to Elizabeth Marret                            2-12-1807
GLOVER, Nathan to Polly Jones                              7-11-1808
GODARE, James to Mary Godare                              10-6-1815
GOODEN, Daniel to Sarah Buck                               9-9-1810
GRAHAN, James to Polly Louderback - Green twp.           11-15-1807
GRAHAM, John to Catharine Richaback                        1-2-1810
GRAHAM, Seth to Susannah Noel                            10-10-1811
GRAVES, William to Lyddy Dugan                            3-18-1806
GREEN, Clarke to Eliza Logan                               9-8-1810
GREEN, James to Polly Ritchie                             5-16-1815
GUTHRIE, Joseph to Hannah Devor                            3-2-1815
HALEY, Carter to Hana Gililan - Upper twp.               10-5-1810
HALL, Aaron to Margaret Edison                            2-15-1815
HAMILTON, Ruben to Elizabeth  Kahal                        1-9-1812
HARRIS, William to Jane Clark                             3-25-1811
HATTAN, John to Elinar Colgan                             2-24-1814
HICE, Philip to Hannah Louderback                         9-11-1814
HIGGINS, John to Patsy Bennett                            2-22-1806
HOLAND, William to Susannah Buck                           6-16-1808
HOLLAND, Francis to Margaret Buck                         10-29-1804
HOWARD, Nathan to Nancy McDougal                          11-9-1813
HUGHES, William to Elizabeth Young                        7-13-1811
HULL, Isaac to Anna Burt                                   3-21-1809
JACKSON, James to Martha Harmon of Nile twp.              9-13-1804
JACOBS, Jacob to Hannah Utt                              10-18-1810
JACOBS, John to Susannah Trexler                          4-25-1809
JONES, Ande to Lucinda Harley                             7-18-1815
KELLY, John to Abigail Lambert                             9-1-1804
KELLY, Joseph to Kitty Dollarhide - Upper twp.            4-17-1808
```

KICHENBOTTON, James to Susanna Cheffren(?)	7-29-1814
KINDALL, William to Rachel Brown	5-29-1806
KING, John to Nancy Dungan	9-19-1813
KIRKENDALL, David to Polly Campbell	10-7-1813
KNIFF, George to Eleanor Bigham	12-23-1814
KNIGHT, George to Arrenda P. Simmon	9-8-1810
LAMBERT, Richard to Nancy Carpenter	10-11-1804
LAMBERT, Rochard to Barbary Hepler (Heasler) - Upper twp.	8-13-1811
LAVY, William to Rebeckah Beatty	4-7-1810
LECLEREG, Francis to Mary Louis Cadot	10-21-1809
LEE, Oliver to Eleanor Welch	4-2-1812
LEFORGE, John to Elliner Moore	6-18-1807
LEWIS, David to Rebecca Thorne	10-19-1815
LEWIS (orLOWERS), Griffin to Rachel McLees	7-4-1805
LEWIS, Philip Sr. to Elizabeth McBride	2-19-1805
LINDSEY, William to Rhoda Wilson	6-21-1814
LITTLEJOHN, Vallentine to Polly Foster	12-14-1809
LOCKE, Benjamin to Cynthia Poynton	12-22-1814
LONG, Robert to Elizabeth Dunlap	8-5-1813
LONG, William to Elizabeth Maldrick	9-10-1815
LOVE, John to Loran Green	1-4-1814
LOVELL, John to Mary McKenney	1-8-1813
LOWDERBACK, Michael to Ellie Munyon	12-14-1813
LUCAS, Robert to Eliza Brown	4-3-1810
LUMBARGER, Peter to Sarah Lambert	2-24-1812
McAULEY, James to Anna Hughes	2-11-1808
McCRERY, Nathan to Mary Dix	11-10-1814
McCUN, Daniel to Sally Fletcher	1-30-1812
McDONALD, David to Nancy Munn	1-5-1815
McDONALD, William to Nancy Barker	10-28-1808
McDOWEL, Wm to Sarah Dever	11-28-1809
McFADGIN, William to Priscilla Hammett	1-24-1814
McKINEY (McKINSEY), Daniel Jr. to Caty Sampson	6-24-1808
McKINNEY, George Jr. to Harriett Buress (Burness)	2-11-1813
McKINNEY, Solomon to Elizabeth Green	7-11-1811
McKINZEY, John to Mary Crow	8-28-1808
McWHORTER, Hugh to Polly Smith	4-12-1815
MAG(UIRE?), Lewis to Elizabeth Coleman	9-25-1804
MANLEY, Isaac to Esther Colvin	11-27-1814
MARSHALL, Jesse to Hannah Kirkendoll	2-2-1809
MARTIN, Jesse to Mary Ann Bowen	11-4-1813
MEEK, James to Mary Sallady	2-25-1807
MELONE, John to Lydia Janye (Payne?)	3-30-1809
MERCER, Nottingham to Hannah Trexler	12-1-1814
MIDKINS, James to Lucinda Hammett	8-30-1808
MITCHEL, William to Sarah Myers	3-22-1810
MONROE, Charles to Patty Jacobs	2-8-1810
MOORE , Allen to Naomi Carey	9-8-1810
MOORE, Allen to Hanah Bouser - Wayne twp.	----1812
MOORE, David to Cela Shelpman	3-12-1807
MOORE, Forman to Anna Worley	2-15-1815

```
MOORE, Foster of Adams Co. to Delila Moore of Scioto Co.    2-23-1809
MOORE, Jacob to Lucinda Bacom                               6-25-1804
MOORE, John to Nancy Jackson                                7-12-1806
MOORE, Joseph to Dolly Lawson                               1-15-1812
MOORE, Levi to Amanda Gunn                                  12-29-1814
MOORE, Philip to Amelia Collins                             3-15-1811
MOORE, Philip to Cynthia Belli                              1-10-1812
MOORE, William to Kathrine Hammet                           8-12-1812
MOORE, William to Elizabeth Snook                           5-4-1813
MUNN, David to Tabitha Frizell                              12-17-1807
MUNN, William to Joanna Hitchcock                           2-14-1811
MUNROW, Daniel to Martha Stroud                             6-26-1806
MUSTARD, George to Elenor Delia                             6-28-1810
MUSTARD, Joseph to Sarah Carter - Seal twp.                 11-29-1808
MUSTARD, William to Jean Delea - Seal twp.                  2-15-1810
NEICE, William to Lydia Weaver                              11-15-1812
NELSON, Thomas to Elizabeth Martin                          7-18-1815
NICHOLS, Thomas to Eliza McNomar                            4-9-1807
NICOLS, William to Esebeth Harmon                           8-3-1814
NICOLES, David to Nancy Hutton                              8-11-1808
NICOLES, Joseph to Rachel Dysart                            2-22-1809
NICOLES, William to Nancy Hughes                            6-6-1809
NOEL, Abraham G. to Mary Gaze                               10-5-1815
NOEL, Jacob to Lucretia Hitchcock                           4-7-1807
NOEL, Jacob to Anna Glover                                  9-5-1815
NOEL, John to Margaret Lowery                               4-2-1815
NOEL, Nicholas to Nancy Frisel                              9-24-1812
NOEL, Peter to Susannah Feurt                               10-23-1806
OLIVER, John to Anna Kirkendall                             7-18-1815
PARISH, Joshua to Elizabeth Marshall                        7-10-1805
PARISH, Joshua to Catharine Willas (Millas)                 11-3-1807
PARTEE, James to Elizabeth Carter - Seal twp.               7-7-1808
PATTON, Samuel to Elizabeth Patton                          12-4-1813
PATTON, Thos. to Jane Lowry                                 2-10-1808
PAYNE, Isaac to Polly Meline                                12-20-1808
PAYNE, Olney to Marian Bartley                              12-11-1808
PERRY, Isaac to Catherine Lowderback                        10-12-1815
PERRY, John to Drusilla Nuel (Noel)                         10-18-1805
PERRY, Samuel to Margaret Lindsey                           4-24-1813
PETERSON, William to Mary Holland                           10-17-1805
PEWTERS, John to Jinny McDowell - Green twp.                1-28-1808
PEWTERS, John to Betsey Price                               9-10-1812
PEYTON, William to Bridget Turner                           10-21-1813
PHILIPS, Samuel M. to Mary Brewer                           2-12-1809
PILES, Absalom to Abina Marshal                             10-27-1812
PLUMB, William to Elizabeth Marshall                        7-21-1808
POLLOCK, John to Mary Noel                                  11-13-1806
POLOCK, David to Nancy Mustard                              12-11-1806
POWEL, Veneen to Mary Kelly                                 5-30-1813
PRESCOTT, James B. to Lydia C. Boynton                      11-12-1815
PRICE, Wm to Mary Ann Hammet                                8-4-1812
```

515

```
RAGSDALE, BERRY TO Sarah Chapman                          6-30-1815
RANKIN, William to Elizabeth Groninger                    7-28-1814
RAREDON, James to Mary Noel                               12-20-1812
RARDON, Daniel to Rebeckah Duey                           6-26-1807
RARDON, James to Mary Stump                               7-6-1809
RAWLLING, Charles to Elizabeth Parry                      12-9-1813
RECTOR, Frederick to Naomi Barton                         9-18-1805
RICE, Jeremiah to Sarah Winn                              10-25-1812
RIDGELY, William to Hannah Simmons                        12-20-1810
RITTER, Frederick to Sarah Campbel                        5-16-1811
ROBINSON, Abraham to Rebeccah Logan                       3-22-1814
ROBY, William to Mary Collins                             10-9-1807  1807
ROLAND, John Richard to Mary Kelly both of virginia       6-23-1807
ROUSH, Cornelius to Elizabeth Millmon                     5-16-1813
RUSLEY, James to Nancy Leth                               10-22-1814
RUTTER, William to Rachel Weeks                           9-4-1806
SALLADAY, George to Phebe Cheffen                         5-9-1812
SALLADAY, Samuel to Sarah Gilkison                        7-1-1806
SALISBURY, John to Mary Liston                            9-14-1811
SALSBURY, William to Ruth Myers                           9-3-1812
SANFORD, Enoch to Margaret Blundet                        12-11-1814
SAPPINGTON, Thomas to Jane Taylor                         6-4-1812
SCOTT, Robert to Elizabeth Burt - Green twp.              9-12-1810
SCOTT, William to Hannah Baker                            1-15-1807
SHAFFER, George to Mary Lewis                             12-15-1814
SHELPMAN, Jacob to Peggy Daley                            7-12-1814
SHEWARD, Isaiah to Rachel Trexler                         2-23-1815
SHOOT, Richard to Hannah Maoarty                          3-31-1814
SIMPSON, John to Mary Noel                                1-3-1805
SMITH, Isaac to Elizabeth Turner                          6-8-1815
SMITH, James to Louisa Cole                               2-13-1812
SMITH, John to Mary Stratton                              9-28-1812
SMITH, John to Nancy Compton                              2-10-1814
SMITH, William to Lydia Mustard                           2-2-1815
SMYERS, Frederick to Susannah Crull                       1-9-1812
SNOOK (SNUKE), Jeremiah to Nancy Pitthoue                 12-12-1805
STACKHAM, Joseph to Hannah Bennett                        3-25-1808
St. CLAIR, Perry to Mary Mills - Upper twp                2-7-1809
STEENNBERGAR, Charles to Levise Lucas                     9-7-1809
STEWART, Stephen to Caroline Duduit                       3-23-1815
STOCKHAN, Aaron to Rhuamy Sikes                           5-6-1811
SURELEY, Rezen to Sally Mustard                           11-17-1814
SWOPE, William to Margaret Call                           5-11-1815
TAYLOR, John to Mary Moore                                4-16-1812
THOMPSON, Daddy(?) to Cynthia Thomas                      11-3-1810
THOMPSON, James to Susannah Maloe  (Malone?)              5-24-1812
THOMPSON, John to Sally Malone                            10-13-1814
THOMPSON, Robert to Rebecca Baccus                        7-20-1815
THOMPSON, William to Elizabeth Gibbs                      1-1-1809
THORNTON, John H. to Sarah Glover                         9-18-1809
THRONE, Conrod to Rebeckah Norman                         12-11-1806
```

```
TIRVY, George to Miriam Sutton                                  3-18-1809
TRAVIS, Joseph to Rachel Cramer                                 3-30-1809
TRAVIS, Noah to Elizabeth Spangler                              1-21-1815
TURNER, William to Elizabeth Fleming                            12-13-1814
UTT, Adam to Priscilla Bennett                                  9-29-1809
UTT, Jacob to Jemima Crull                                      8-17-1809
UTT, Jacob to Peggy Utt                                         5-17-1812
VALADAY, Francis to Nancy Slater - Upper twp.                   8-12-1808
VANBERON (VANBEBLOW), John to Polly Tregs (Triggs?)             1-23-1812
VAREN, Detter to Dolly Rinner                                   6-25-1811
VIOLET, Sampson to Sarah Boydston                               -----1811
WADDILL, Charles to Eleanor Moore                               7-27-1813
WALLS, Joshua to Sarah Bowers                                   4-10-1806
WALSINGER, John to Rachel Lovel                                 10-1-1804
WARD, Robert to Polly McKinsey                                  7-10-1808
WARDEN, Barnet to Francis Biegle of Greenup Co., Ky.            5-16-1807
WARNOCK, Wm to Polly Forster                                    7-31-1806
WARREN, Clement to Mary Barton                                  10-17-1805
WATT, James to Elizabeth Call                                   4-23-1815
WAUGH, John to Augustine Didaway (Dudwit)                       2-15-1813
WEBB, James to Sarah Broom                                      2-12-1808
WEST, William to Sally Worley                                   4-19-1814
WHEATON, Uriah to Margaret Mackey - Seal twp.                   4-11-1809
WHEELER, Nathan 3d to Nancy Chamberlin                          5-13-1812
WHITE, John to Sylva Wyman                                      11-13-1814
WHITE, Mathew to Naomi Barton                                   2-16-1812
WHITE, Tapley to Prudence Martin - Madison twp.                 5-23-1811
WHITE, Uriah to Mary Huston                                     7-5-1808
WILCOXEN, Loyd to Elizabeth Trewet(?)                           6-29-1815
WILCOXON, Levin to Margaret Williamson                          3-23-1809
WILCOXON, Walter to Elizabeth Deaver                            12-27-1810
WILLCOXEN, George D. H. to Anna Hokinson                        8-30-1815
WILLCOXEN, Thomas to Sally Willcoxen                            10-19-1815
WILLIAMS, Eli to Sarah Davis of Green twp.                      4-23-1806
WILLIAMS, Frank to Eve Mackeltree                               5-6-1813
WILLIAMS, Jesse to Ledea Shores                                 4-11-1810
WILLIAMS, Jessy to Ann Daley - Seal twp.                        3-21-1806
WILLIAMS, Robert to Comfort Lewis                               8-7-1811
WILSON, Samuel to Esther Lee                                    4-13-1815
WOLF, David to Elizabeth Ghopes                                 8-22-1814
WOLF, Jesse to Nancy Horner                                     12-28-1815
WORLEY, Isaac to Elizabeth Eddison                              11-2-1811
WRAY, James to Ellener Peyton                                   2-9-1809
WRIGHT, Isaac to Rebecah Noel                                   7-2-1812
WRIGHT, John to Mary Fletcher                                   7-11-1806
WRIGHT, William to Caty Noel                                    5-21-1807
YINGLING, Christian to Patsey Lee                               10-20-1814
ZORNS (ZORUS), Thomas to Prudende Pettit                        11-1-1813
```

517

The following records were taken from Marriage Record Book Two.

ADAMS, James to Matilda Sampson	lic.	6-5-1842
ADELSPERGER, John to Cindrilla Ricketts	lic.	8-30-1841
ALLEN, Gideon to Barbara Bowser		1-28-1842

"Gideon Allen says that he about five years since obtained a license to marry with above Barbara Bowser and that they were married unlawfully by a Preacher named Fry who was not legally authorized to perform marriages and therefore has now applied for license to be lawfully intermarried with said Barbara Bowser."

ALLEN, Simon to Mary Ann Rollins		11-13-1842
ALLISON, Richard to Elizabeth E. Lee		12-24-1842
ANWAY, Harrison to Elizabeth Hillis		9-16-1841
ARNEY, Jacob to Mary McNutt		10-23-1842
ARNEY, Samuel to Heulda McNutt		10-23-1842
ASH, Upton to Barbara Ann Bower		8-21-1842
BAKER, William to Margaret Mull		6-26-1841
BALDWIN, Absalam C. to Mary Jane Hedges		3-4-1841
BALDWIN, Peter S. to Merilla McDimick		3-9-1842
BARE, Benjamin to Mary Enick		9-1-1841
BARNHART, Michael to Harriet Bobe - both of Bloom twp.		3-24-1842
BARTULT, Henry to Mary Ann Rieter		2-13-1842
BATTENFIELD, Solomon to Olive Metcalf	lic.	12-3-1842
BEARD, Joseph to Louisa Baker		4-14-1842
BEARD, Samuel to Polly Ainsly		12-27-1842
BEAVER, George to Catherine Lightner		10-25-1842
BECKMAN, Solomon to Barbara Souter		9-8-1842
BENNER, Daniel E. to Sarah Chamberlin		12-12-1841
BENNETT, Eli to Margaret Pennock		9-9-1841
BERGSTRESER, William to Margaret Lover		9-29-1842
BERNARD, Isaiah to Ann Engles		10-2-1841
BERRY, George of Crawford Co. to Elizabeth Hannan		10-9-1842
BIBLER, Jacob to Elizabeth Curtis		2-24-1842
BLAIR, Thomas to Mary Sailor		1-20-1842
BOGART, Martin V. to Achea Sloat		11-21-1842
BOLIN, Even Howe to Eliza Harkey		6-16-1842
BOSIER, David to Eliza J. Heartly		8-12-1841
BOWDLE, John to Maria Goetschins		5-29-1842
BOWE, Erastus G. to Mary E. Hart		9-25-1842
BOWSER, Michael to Magdaline Kuntz		6-3-1842
BOYER, John to Margaret Morris		2-9-1842
BROMLY, Richard to Ann Parsons		5-18-1841
BROWN, Chester to Elizabeth Chester		11-3-1841
BROWN, Jeptha to Sally Holmes		4-20-1842
BURNS, George to Sarah Ann Chamberlin		6-22-1842
BUTMAN, Benjamin F. to Mary Butterfield		11-10-1842
CADY, John to Mary A. McKinan (McKimer)		9-11-1842
CARPENTER, Daniel to Malvina Summerlin		9-19-1842

```
CARR, Jacob to Hannah Decker                              12-15-1842
CASSITY, Franklin to Charity Gilbert                      11-9-1842
CHAMBERLIN, David to Pamelia Tarner                       10-21-1841
CHAMBERLIN, Levi to Mary Ann Griswold                     4-14-1842
CHANY, John to Catherine Feasle                           12-5-1841
CHAPIN, Lorin to Catherine Roof                           10-22-1842
CLARK, John to Hannah Maria Berry                         12-16-1841
CLAY, John to Helen Heate(r)                              4-13-1842
CLINE, William to Maria H. Stafford                       10-21-1841
COE, David E. to Margaret Hyter                           3-24-1842
COLE, Lewis P. to Ann Scothern                            11-27-1842
COLE, Nathan Jr. to Laura Jane Walker                     3-17-1842
COOK, Leonard to Susannah Battenfield                     12-8-1842
COOK, Peter to Sally Bixler                               3-30-1842
COOLEY, William to Betsey Roberts                         12-15-1842
COOLY, Alvin to Sarah Warner                              12-29-1841
COTTER, Philip to Margaret Cotter                   lic.  5-21-1842
CREEGER, Lawrence to Susannah Mussetter                   10-30-1842
CROCKETT, Oliver A. to Laura N. Scofille                  8-11-1842
CULLMAN, George to Mary Nagel                       lic.  8-22-1842
CUMMINGS, James to Mary M. Strickling                     5-19-1842
DECKER, Rudolphus to Eleanor Smith                        11-10-1842
DELDINE, John H. to Lydia G. Riggs                        12-30-1841
DELDINE, William M. to Christina Berger                   1-11-1842
DeWITT, Paul to Mary Reed                           lic.  6-25-1842
DEWITTE, Joseph to Mary Ann Eby (Ely?)                    7-13-1841
DILLON, John J. to Hannah Whiteman                        6-9-1842
DILLON, Thomas to Roda Adams                              11-24-1842
DITTO, Solomon to Mary Jane Dever                         4-3-1842
DOW, Alvin to Olive Brayton                               12-29-1841
DOWNY, Noah to Margaret Fuce                        lic.  8-7-1841
DURFY, Delectus to Dianna D. Green                        7-4-1841
EBY, (Ely), Noah to Laura Merryman                        3-13-1842
ECKMAN, George to Margaret Sisty                          6-27-1841
EDWARDS, Martin to Elizabeth Hiett                        8-7-1842
ENNIS, William to Mary Kelley                             10-23-1842
EYLER, Elias to Mary Ann Bunkerhoff                       5-14-1842
FEEFIELD(?), Daniel to Mahetable Sellen (Seller)          4-12-1842
FISHER, Henry to Catharine Heck                     lic.  5-7-1842
FISHER, James to Hannah Royer                             6-9-1841
FISHER, John to Catherine Colp                            4-4-1842
FISHER, Peter to Sarah Hulit                              8-28-1841
FISHER, Stephen to Barbara Hinselman                      10-29-1842
FLEET, William to Eliza Ogden                             10-6-1842
FREEMAN, B. N. to Martha Ellen Lemon                      11-22-1842
GALE, Harrison to Mary Ann Bradt                          5-5-1842
GARDNER, Stephen D. to Catherine Han                .lic. 2-10-1842
GARN, John to Fanny Ash                                   10-28-1841
GASS, John to Angeline Rollins                            .9-15-1842
```

519

```
GEE, Henry to Eliza Williams                                     5-30-1841
GERK, William N. to Laura Lewis                                 10-14-1841
GIBBONS, Abraham to Elizabeth Shively                           4-21-1842
GRIFFIN, Hezekiah to Jumma (Jemima?) Heousmen                   3-13-1842
GROVE, Michael to Mary Ann Croan                                 1-4-1842
HAIGHT, Victory to Elizabeth Battenfield                   lic. 12-5-1842
HAINES, David R. to Jenima Hartsock                            9-16-1841
HALES, Joel to Mary Vandyke                                   12-22-1842
HALL, Arad to Hannah Lake                                      9-23-1841
HALL, Luther A. to Cynthia Ann Hedges (Note: Date as given) 4-7-1835
HALLGEN, Frederick to Emily Weller                             8-21-1842
HANFORD, James to Catherine Catlin                             1-30-1842
HANNAM, Perry to Margaret Carraus                             10-20-1841
HARBAUGH, Uriah to Susannah Boyer                              7-28-1842
HARDENBURG, Aaron to Elizabeth Grimes                          4-21-1841
HARFESTER, David to Mary Nafe                                  3-31-1842
HARPSTER, Solomon to Hannah Bowerman                          12-14-1842
HAYER, William Robinson to Ann Grimes                          7-17-1841
HAYES, Joseph to Elizabeth Staub                              10-23-1842
HECK, George to Sarah Carr                                      7-8-1841
HENRICH, Christian to Magdalin Strawbecker                     11-2-1842
HIGH, David to Mary Witmer                                    10-31-1841
HILL, John to Elizabeth Lesher                                11-11-1841
HILL, Welcome to Ann Steel                                     2-23-1842
HITE, Isaac to Lucinda Jackson                                3-10-1842
HITESMAN, Frederick to Magdalena Grist                         6-5-1842
HIVELY, Jacob to Catherine Whitsel                            8-10-1841
HOFFMAN, George to Eve Flisher                                11-5-1842
HOLCOMBE, Charles Ogden to Anne Rebecca Barber                8-29-1842
HOLOPETER, Isaiah to Sarah McWilliams                          2-3-1842
HOLMES, John Sr. to Sarah Hanna                               8-26-1841
HOMEER, Alexander to Catherine Louer                          3-25-1842
HOOVER, Jacob to Margaret E. Daylong                          7-31-1842
HOOVER, Joseph to Hannah Karn                                10-21-1842
HOPKINS, Samuel to Artimetia Iumister(?)                      1-13-1842
HOUCK, Isaac to Mary Ann Harholtcer                       lic. 5-25-1842
HUETT, Solomon to Ellen E. Bowee                              9-29-1842
HUNTER, William to Clarinda Hedges                           11-28-1830
INGRAHAM, Mason to Esther Mallett                             5-19-1842
KAELHLE, John to Rosa Leanhart                                 4-7-1842
KAGY, Henry to Phebe Miller                                    4-3-1842
KEEFER, Charles to Margaret Wise                              1-12-1842
KEIFFE, Edmund to Mary Cotter                                10-30-1842
KELLEY, Owen to Emily Jane Cole                               4-22-1842
KEMP, Thomas to Elizabeth E. Moore                             9-9-1841
KEPPEL, George to Mary E. Rosenberger                        11-10-1842
KIDDER, Amos M. to Mary Ann Brown                             8-14-1842
KIEHOLTZ, William to Mary Ann Sneath                           4-7-1842
KING, George to Elizabeth Kissabeth                           10-9-1842
```

520

KING, Ignatius to Susan Brown   9-15-1842
KINGSEER, Endney to Keddy Bower   lic.10-17-1842
KIRKENDALL, Daniel D. To Polly Welch   11-11-1842
KISLER, William to Ann Keppel   3-20-1842
KISSABETH, Philip to Elizabeth Dowman   8-30-1842
KISSLER, John to Rebecca Ann Kime   10-28-1841
KLEINFELTER, Henry to Cathrine Haefner   lic.2-14-1842
KNAPP, Sylvester to Sophia Ann Thompson   9-4-1842
KRITES, Jonas to Mary Walter   7-5-1842
KYLE, George H. to Margaret Porter   10-27-1842
LADD, Henry to Rebecca Chamberlin   8-21-1842
LAKY, Nelson to Sarah Robertson   10-14-1841
LANG, William to Mary P. Owen   12-14-1841
LANGEWAINE, Joseph to Sarah Ann Julian   1-9-1842
LANGEWAINE, Peter to Amelia F. Hendall   7-14-1842
LAUGHERY, Charles to Hannah Banks   11-1-1842
LAWRENCE, John to Eleanor Jones   12-30-1841
LEITNER (SEITNER), David to Margaret Sohn   8-4-1842
LEWIS, George to Catharine Heming   5-13-1841
LEY, Andrew to Mary Stancity(?)   lic.11-30-1841
LIGHTCAP, Levi to Mary Smith   1-26-1842
LITENER, Paul to Margaret Shuemaker   4-7-1842
LIVSENEY, John to Ann R. Bell   10-17-1841
LOUDENSLAGER, William to Ann Royer   10-21-1842
McCARLEY, Alexander to Susan ?S. Childs   1-20-1842
McCUTCHEN, Warren to Ann Rogers   11-23-1842
MACKRILL, Robert to Leanah Beare   3-20-1842
MARK, John to Appellonia Gase   lic.2-5-1842
MATHEWSON, William B. to Charlotte W. Houk   5-16-1841
MATTISON, Darias to Mary Jane Witter   10-3-1841
MEASLE, John to Sarah Finch   9-1-1841
MERCHANT, John to Rachel Edwards   6-13-1841
MEYERS, Ferdinand to Julian Arholtzer   lic.2-5-1842
MILLER, James to Susan Meook   lic.2-3-1842
MILLER, Jeremiah to Hannah Rebecca School   6-21-1842
MILLER, Jesse to Sally Berzstuser   8-5-1841
MILLER, John to Julian Stover   11-24-1841
MOYER, Adams to Margaret Leuser   8-23-1841
MUNDAY, George to Margaret Kimball - both of Reed twp.   2-10-1842
MYER, Daniel to Catharine Shidly   9-20-1841
MYERS, Elias to Sarah Sprecher   10-26-1842
NOEL, Nicholas to Catherine Rineholt   4-10-1842
NORTON, Cyrus G. to Ann R. Snook   3-24-1842
OGDEN, Gilbert M. to Sarah Jops   11-18-1841
OGDEN, Stephen M. to Polly Clark   9-1-1842
OGLE, Thomas to Mary Jane Bentley   5-10-1842
OPT, John to Rebecca Seitz   11-11-1841
PACKWOOD (PACKARD), Alonzo to Jane E. Alexander   12-4-1842
PAINE, James to Maria Ann Kline   1-23-1842
PANE, John W. to Susan Rule   9-12-1841
PARKHURST, Jeremiah to Lucy Ann McDougle   11-11-1841
PATTERSON, Daniel H. to Catharine Seitz   3-31-1842

521

```
PATTERSON, William M. to Kezia Montgomery                        12-26-1841
PENNINGTON, Robert to Caroline Antonia Kuhn                      2-23-1842
PENSE, David to Eleanor Bowland                                 2-10-1842
PERKINS, Alva to Lavina Squires                                 9-1-1841
PERRY, Abraham H. to Nancy L. Wilson                            11-3-1842
PIERCE, Thomas F. to Lovina Grant                               9-11-1842
PLANTS, Jacob to Elizabeth Eastep                               9-18-1842
POPPLETON, L. W. to Caroline Ogden                              1-27-1842
PORTZ, John to Mary Hut                                         6-2-1842
READ, Seth to Emily Benschoter                                 10-26-1842
REITZ, Joseph to Eve Wagner                                    10-8-1841
RHINE, Jacob to Anna Potes - divorced wife of Havey Steel       7-7-1842
RINEHOLT, Francis to Catharine Hatt                            11-11-1841
ROBINSON, Isaac H. to Mary Hahn                                10-1-1842
ROCKWELL, William H. to Polly Clark                             7-27-1842
ROGERS, William to Mary Preble                                 5-5-1842
ROSENBERGER, David to Hannah Stafford                          4-7-1842
ROSENBERGER, Nicholas to Hannah Keppel                        11-17-1842
ROUGRANT, E. X. to Caroline Brown                             12-23-1841
ROWELL, William to Mary Bartlett                               3-20-1842
RUMPLE, John to Mary Fisher                                   10-18-1842
RUTEAGER, Valentine to Margaret Zroirline             lic.6-27-1842
SAUNDERS, Anthony J. to Magdalena Bistner                     11-3-1842
SCHALK, Frederick to Mary Wonderly                            12-27-1842
SCHER, Valentine to Ann Maria Diem                            9-1-1842
SCOTT, Robert to Sarah Ann Norris                             7-29-1841
SEAGCHRIST, Christian to Christina Souder                     5-19-1842
SELLERS, Frederick to Hannah Shideler                        12-22-1842
SENN, John to Catharine Waggoner                              8-23-1841
SHAEFER, Adam to Frances Camp - both of Venice twp.           7-10-1842
SHAW, Silas W. to Sarah L. Ogden                              9-22-1841
SHEDENHELNN, Henry to Elizabeth Hoyerware                     9-13-1841
SHEFFERTY, John to Anna Houanstein                           11-11-1841
SHELBURT, John to Aolina Shunburger                   lic.8-7-1841
SHIPPY, Jonathan to Mary Kemp                                 1-2-1842
SHOUF, John to Catherine Hendrix                             10-24-1841
SHRIVER, William to Harriet Car                              11-16-1842
SINTO, Anthony to Magdalena Wella                      lic. 2-3-1842
SITES, William to Eve Leatherman                              3-27-1842
SLAGMAKER, Francis to Magdalena Adams                         6-24-1841
SMITH, Daniel to Mary Bell                      (1842?)      12-13-1843
SMITH, John to Christina Berger                              8-23-1841
SMITH, Joseph to Elizabeth Heann (hearn)                     8-24-1841
SNACK, Henry to Catherine Starkey                     lic.  7-6-1842
SNIDER, Jacob to Elizabeth Bloom                             12-27-1842
SOUDER, John Wesley to Elizabeth Abeville                     8-16-1842
SPANGLE, John H. to Sabina Ganon                             11-11-1841
SPEILMAN, Philip to Celarista Plumb                          11-5-1842
SPRINGER, Charles R. to Margaret Bussick                     5-4-1842
SRUON(?), Valentine to Mary Waggoner                  lic.  11-21-1842
```

522

```
STAHL, William to Rebecca Foster                              3-25-1841
STAIB, Lewis to Catharine Amick                             10-20-1842
STANLEY, William H. to Tabatha Culver                        9-19-1841
STRAUSBAUGH, George to Susannah (Hanna) Noel                11-1-1842
STEPHENS, Amos to Meribeah Swope                             1-13-1842
STEPHENSON, James D. to Mary Sayres                          1-1-1842
STEVENS, Wm. C. to Mary Dean                                 9-21-1842
STOUT, Bartholomew to Catharine Camp                        10-28-1841
STOUT, George to Elizabeth Camp - both of Venice twp.        7-17-1842
STRICKLING, George to Sarah Egbert                          12-13-1842
STUBORN, Daniel to Mary Ann Powell                           9-20-1841
SULLIVAN, Jeremiah to Joanna King                           11-2-1841
SWARM, John to Barbara Henger                               10-6-1842
TAMBERT(LAMBERT?), John to Elizabeth Gentzer                 7-12-1841
THOMAS, Martin to Mary Dicken                               11-3-1842
TIBBETS, Lanson to Nancy Sheller                            10-28-1841
TINDALL, Hendrixson to Smantha Dodge                         8-31-1841
TRUE, Haynes to Lucinda Stivers                             11-20-1842
TWISS, Russell to Sally Ann Hall                             2-10-1842
UNSER, John to Regina Shalk                      lic.        8-2-1842
VANDYKE, Samuel to Ann Hales                                 4-28-1842
VANNATTE, Peter to Mary Ann Harris                           8-5-1841
WAGGONER, Christian to Betsy Waggoner                        9-11-1842
WAGGONER, Daniel to Martha Jane Davis                       10-26-1841
WALLENSIEGLE, George to Regina Brandal                       5-15-1842
WARK, JOhn to Evy Laser                                     11-2-1842
WARRINGTON, John to Catherine Fisher                        11-1-1841
WATSON, Sylvester to Elizabeth McClung                       8-18-1841
WEAVER, George to Barbara Weaver                            11-22-1842
WEHR, Levi to Elizabeth Wehr                                10-25-1842
WELCH, James to Elizabeth Hollopeter                        12-23-1841
WELCH, Martin to Mary Lawrence                               9-18-1842
WELKER, William N. to Aszubia McNutte                        6-13-1841
WHITE, George W. to Catherine Josephs                        4-19-1841
WHITE, Gilbert to Julia Lemmon                               5-8-1842
WHITEMAN, Absalam to Nancy Paine                             9-18-1842
WHITEMAN, Jacob to Mary McNutt                               4-28-1842
WHITSEL, Jacob to Hanrietta Grell                           11-3-1842
WILBER, Henry to Rachel Smith                               12-15-1842
WILLIAMS, Henry to Zilpha Botsford                           6-24-1841
WILLIAMS, John to Henrietta Ragon                            1-20-1842
WILLIAMS, Lorenzo Dow to Rebecca Stewart                     2-12-1842
WITMER, Christian to Harriet Hilterbrack                     8-28-1842
WOLF, Joseph to Mary Goess                                   6-7-1842
WOOD, Garrett V. to Elizabeth Painter                       11-24-1842
WOOLET, Joseph to Jemima Mulbourn                            3-27-1842
WYANT, Benjamin to Martha Drake                             11-6-1841
ZAHM, Lewis to Ellen Lemmon                                 10-6-1842
ZANGLER, Joseph to Ragina Myres                             11-28-1841
ZEPERICK, David to Sarah Soward                             11-4-1841
ZEPHART, Peter to Elizabeth Miller                          10-26-1841
ZWIRLEIN, John to Theressa Klesthlic                         4-23-1842
```

The following abstracts were taken from Will Book 1, pages on which record may be found are given in parenthesis.

HOPKINS, Eppenetus of Scipio twp; dated 3-8-1828; filed 5-19-1828; recorded 1-4-1830. Wife, Polly. Adopted daughter, Mary Ann. Signed: Eppenetus Hopkins. Witnesses: George Spangle, Michael Neikirk and Joshua Maynard.   (5)

CRAWMER, John - dated 6-30-1829; filed 11-3-1829; recorded 1-4-1830. Wife, Mary Cramer, also to serve as executrix. Signed: John (mark) Crawmer. Witnesses: Henry C. Bush, E. Dresbach and W. Bush. (6)

CULVER, David - dated 9-9-1829; filed 11-9-1829; recorded 1-4-1830. Wife, Frances Culver. Sons: Chester, David and Carpenter; Carpenter not of age. Only daughter; Diana. Executor: John Tingler. Signed: David Culver. Witnesses: Wm. S. Nafus and Cornelius Nafus.   (7)

CLARK, Samuel of Eden twp. - dated 11-6-1829; filed 11-25-1829; recorded 1-4-1830. Mentions his late wife who is now deceased. Father and Mother-in-law: Josiah Lock and wife, to have piece of land in Covington, Genesee Co., New York which was deeded to Clark 2-9-1827 by Ira Lock. Brothers-in-law: Ira, Elam, Milo and Myron Lock. Mentions William Roberts Lock and Sidney Erie Lock the two eldest sons of brother-in-law, Ira Lock. Sisters-in-law: Phebe Pratt, Hannah Pamerly and Catharine Lock. Brothers: William Clark and John Clark. Sisters: Polly Stevens, Rebecca Brooks, Anna Clark and Sarah Calvert. Mentions Samuel C., Elijah and James M. Brooks sons of sister, Rebecca Brooks. Nieces: Margaret dau of brother, William Clark; Polly dau. of brother, John Clark; Betsy, youngest dau. of sister Anna; Polly dau. of sister Sarah. Mentions Sally Jane dau. of nephew Matthew Clark. Friend, Doctor James McClung. Money to Associate Reformed Church. Executors: brothers, William and John Clark and brother William's second son, Mathew Clark. Signed: Samuel Clark. Witnesses: James Robinson, Ezra Brown and Montgomery H. Fitch.   (9)

CRUM, George - dated 3-27-1829; filed 4-26-1830; recorded 10-30-1830. Brother, Abraham Crum, also to serve as executor. Mentions: money and share of property due from his father's estate. Signed: George (mark) Crum. Witnesses: Isaac Dumond, Wm. Sebrel and John Sonder.   (11)

MONTGOMERY, William - dated 1-21-1830; filed 12-7-1831; recorded 2-17-1831. Wife, Christiney. Wife's son, Samuel Themle. Two youngest children: William and Isabella Montgomery. Mentions: "as I have already given unto the remainder of my children". Executors: John Sonder and George Stoner. Signed: William Montgomery. Witnesses: John Cunn (or Crum?) and Lorenzo Abbot.   (12)

DOUGHERTY, Peter - dated (not given); recorded 9-24-1831. Wife, Mary. Sons: Dennis, Charles and John. Mentions: Money due for 80 acres of land in Pennsylvania. Executors: Wife, Mary and son, Dennis. Signed: Peter (mark) Dougherty. Witnesses: James Gordon and David A. Craft.   (14)

McKEE, Sarah - dated 5-28-1832; recorded March 1833. Sisters: Elizabeth McKee, Isabella Long and Rebecca Keen. Executrix: sister, Elizabeth McKee. Signed: Sarah (mark) McKee. Witnesses: Geo. W. Gist, M. Bush and Samuel Long.   (18)

FOX, Rhodolphus of New Berlin, Chenango Co., New York. Dated 8-9-1829; recorded 10-30-1829 Oxford, Chenango Co., N. Y.; Recorded 3-20-1832 Seneca Co., Ohio. Sister, Delight Fox to have land in Seneca Co., Ohio. Executor: Amasa Fox of Sherburn, Chenango Co., N. Y. Signed: Rhodolphus Fox. Witnesses: Alva Babcock, Oran Taylor and Mathew Calkins. (15)

FREAS, John the Elder of Clinton Twp., Yeoman. Dated 6-16-1832; recorded 2-8-1834. Sons: William; John; Martin; Jacob, dec'd, his heirs and his widow, Rachel; Peter, Daughters: Mary; Elizabeth Oman; Susanna Rees, dec'd, her heirs; Ann Hickethorn; Catharine Detterich. Executors: James Herin and Peter Marsh. Witnesses: Jacob Bogart, Peter Marsh and David E. Owen. (20)

STINEBOUGH, Philip - dated 1-9-1833; recorded 2-8-1834. Wife, Catharine, also to serve as executrix. Children: Mentioned but not named—youngest is not of age. Signed: Philip (mark) Stinebough. Witnesses: Moses Spencer and Jonathan Talbott. (22)

FLACK, George - dated 6-30-1832; recorded 9-25-1834. Children: Lewis W., Magdelana, Delila, George Dixon, Hiram, Henry Jeremiah, John Jackson, Josiah and Analiza Flack; last six named are not of age. Mentions that part of children are by first wife. Executor: Henry Cronice. Signed: George Flack. Witnesses: E. Dresbach, Geo. W. Gist and David Smith. (23)

RICHIE, Maria B. of town of Fort Ball. Dated 2-26-1834; recorded 10-2-1834. Youngest son: George Gilmon Reichie. Youngest daughter: Frances Maria Richie. Daughter-in-law: Mary Cary of Green Brier Co., Va. to have "Canne's Bible" in two separate volumes. Mentions: "other children already provided for". Executor: Son, Robert C. J. Cary of town of Ft. Ball. Signed: Maria B. Richie. Witnesses: Abel Rawson, Milton McNeal and David Beck. (26)

FREEMAN, Stephen - dated 9-14-1834; recorded 10-2-1834. Wife, Magdalena. Adopted son: Joseph Slinger. Mentions: Six notes held on persons residing in Perry County, Ohio. Signed: Stephen (mark) Freeman. Witnesses: David Bishop, A. Dick and Jno. J. Steiner. (28)

BATSON, Edward - dated 9-19-1834; recorded 11-14-1834. Wife, Eleanor, also to serve as executrix. Signed: Edward (mark) Batson. Witnesses: Jacob Nicewarner and Andrew Love. (30)

WISE, John of Reed Twp. - dated 11-24-1834; recorded 1-31-1835. Wife, Sophia, also to serve as executrix. Children: Catharine wife of Daniel Craighton, Solomon, Adam, John, Margaret, Jacob, Elizabeth, Susannah, Sophia and George. Mentions: Blacksmith shop and tools. Signed: John (mark) Wise. Witnesses: John C. Lemmon and B. Lemmon. (31)

BRINKERHOOFF, James - dated 7-14-1835; recorded 9-21-1835. Wife, Elizabeth. Brother, H. Brinkerhoff, also to serve as executor. Signed: James Brinkerhoff. Witnesses: Jacob C. Magoffin and Peter Lott. (33)

BOYER, Thomas - dated 3-1-1835; recorded 12-29-1835. Wife, Hannah, also to serve as executrix. Signed: Thos. Boyer. Witnesses: Benj. Pittenger and Marcus Z. Graft. (35)

BRUNER, Peter - dated 10-20-1835; recorded 1-11-1836. Wife, Nancy, also to serve as executrix. Signed: Peter (mark) Bruner. Witnesses: Lorenzo Abbot, Milton Frary and George Wiseman. (37)

RANDELL, Thomas - dated 3-10-1836; recorded 6-25-1836. Wife, Margarett. Children: Mentioned, but not named. Signed: Thomas Randell. Witnesses: John Crockett and Thomas Choate. (38)

FOX, Michael - Dated (not given); recorded 7-20-1836. Wife, Elizabeth. Son, Michael Fox. Oldest daughter, Sarah Fox. Executors: Wife, Elizabeth; John Wallenslagh and Jonas Goodforth. Signed Michael Fox. Witnesses: Stephen Fisher and Samuel Arnold. (40)

OSWALTS, Jacob - Dated 8-29-1836; recorded 9-26-1836. Sons: Michael, John, Samuel, Jacob and Joseph. Eight Daughters; mentions, but does not name. Owned land in Big Spring Twp. and lot in Springville. Executors: Erastus H. Cook and son, Michael Oswalts. Signed: Jacob Oswalts. Witnesses: Benjamin Bower and Peter Weimer. (42)

INGLE, Isaac - dated 6-13-1836; recorded 1-24-1837. Son, Isaac Ingle. Executor: Reubin J. Cary. Signed: Isaac (mark) Ingle. Witnesses: Timothy Green and Miner Green. (44)

CORY, Jemima - dated 6-10-1836; recorded 3-27-1837. Chilcren: Samuel, Orin, Uzel, Julia, Arbitty and Polly. Two sisters: Phebe and Polly. Grandson: Alanson W. Cory. Executor: Son-in-law, George Dennison and son, Orin J. Cory. Signed: Jemima Cory. Witnesses: John Gibson and William Cornell. (45)

FOX, David - Dated 2-6-1837; recorded 3-27-1837. Wife: Mentioned, but not named. Eldest Son, Isaac Fox. Mentions other children, but does not name, not all of age. Executors: Son, Isaac Fox and neighbor, Christian Mussetter. Signed: David Fox. Witnesses: Michael Twoney and Peter Wagner Jr. (47)

MITTOWER, Andrew - Dated 8-25-1837; recorded 9-25-1837. Wife, Mary. Mentions: "my kinsman John Mittower of Scripio". Mentions: Heirs of his father and heirs of his wife Mary's father, but does not name. Executors: Andrew Mittower of Reed township. Signed: Andrew (mark) Mittower. Witnesses: Michael Noe and Joshua Maynard. (49)

BOWSER, John - Dated 1-2-1824; recorded 6-17-1837. Wife, Modlena Bowser. Children: Catherin wife of Philip Stinebough; Sarah; Elizabeth wife of George Neikirk; Jacob; Modlena; Susana; Barbara; Nancy Reator, dec'd, her three sons—Eli Benjamin, Otho and David. Executor: Oldest son, Jacob Bowser. Signed: John Bowser. Witnesses: Samuel Workman and Dewault (mark) Kandal. Witnesses testified by deposition to their signatures from Hagerstown, Washington County, Maryland; and stated that at the time John Bowser made his will, he was upwards of 40 years of age. (50)

ZEPERNICH, Daniel - dated 8-29-1837; recorded 4-3-1838. Wife, Elizabeth. Sons: John, David, Frederick, Daniel and Joseph; last three not of age. Daughters: Sarah, Mary Sepernich and Elizabeth Zepernich. Brother Frederick. Mentions land in Wood Co., Ohio. Executors: Wife, Elizabeth and sons, John and David. Signed: Daniel (mark) Zepernich. Witnesses: H. B. Dean and Stephen Chapman. (55)

WAGGONER, George - dated 3-21-1838; recorded 5-5-1838. Wife, Mary Ann Waggner. Four sons: Frederick, George, Nicols and John Waggner. Two daughters: Mary Ann Jonson and Elizabeth Hine. Executors: wife, Mary Ann and son, George. Signed: George Waggner. Witnesses: Abraham Eyestone and John Elarton. (58)

JENKINS, Benjamin - dated 1-9-1839; recorded 2-4-1839. Son: John Jenkins. Only daughter: Margaret Jenkins. Adopted son: Chester Mathews. Mentions property in town of Springville and also in Big Spring twp. Executor: brother, John Jenkins and Israel Harmus. Signed: Benj. Jenkins. Witnesses: Leonard Cook and Anderson (mark) Jenkins. (60)

HILL, James W. of town of Tiffin - Verbal Will - will made 1-26-1839; deposition given 2-4-1839; recorded 2-4-1839. Everything to Josiah Hedges for paying debts and giving a decent burial. Witnesses: Joseph Walker and Jacob Karns. (63)

THATCHER, James of Reed twp. - dated 6-26-1838; recorded 5-7-1839. Wife, Lydia. Three sons: John, Orin and Calvin. Daughters: Clarinda (also given as Caroline), Almeda, Mariah and Romelia Thatcher. Executors: Wife, Lydia and John Clark. Signed: James (mark) Thatcher. Witnesses: Elijah Read and John Clark. (64)

BLOOM, John - dated 1-19-1839; recorded 5-8-1839. Wife, Elizabeth, also to serve as executrix. Four children: Anne, Mariah, John and Elizabeth. Signed: John Bloom (German signature). Witnesses: Uriah Egbert, Enoch Fry and John Hubert (German signature). (66)

MORTON, John of Tiffin, Clinton twp. - Dated 2-8-1839; recorded 5-9-1839. Everything to Evan L. Morton and Matilda his wife, with Evan also to serve as executor; relationship, if any, not stated. Signed: John Morton. Witnesses: Joshua Seney and Gabriel J. Run(?). (66)

STARKEY, Jesse - dated 7-8-1839; Recorded 9-18-1839. Wife, Katherine. Sons: Levi, Simon Peter, David and Jesse. Daughters: Elizabeth, Sally, Maliny and Rebecca J. Starkey. Executors: Wife, Katherine and Thomas Hues. Signed: Jesse (mark) Starkey. Witnesses: Henry Feasel and John Bishop. (68)

DOWSE, William - dated 10-14-1839; recorded 11-4-1839. Brother: John Dowse. Sister: Mary Haltbey formerly Mary Dowse, living in Old England, county of Linkinghere, town of Guadring. Executor: Chauncey Rendall and Henry McCarney. Signed: William Dowse. Witnesses: Witnesses: William L. Hamilton and J. L. McClung. (70)

FLACK, John L. - dated 6-6-1839; recorded 1-4-1840. Wife, Barbara. Sons: Jacob and Lewis L., also to serve as executors. Daughters: Lydia wife of William Gault and Barbara wife of John Turner. Numerous land descriptions given. Signed: John L. Flack. Witnesses: Henry C. Brish and H. Kuhn. (71)

LIVERS? (Liners?), John A. - dated 6-1-1840; recorded 6-16-1840. Wife, Caroline, also to serve as executrix. Children: Mentioned, but not named; specifies that they are to be raised in the Catholic Church. Witnesses: Samuel Nolen and Jos. Elder. (75)

LYON, Reuben D. of Scipio - dated 6-4-1840; recorded 6-16-1840. Wife, mentioned but not named. Sons: Chester, Charles M. and Reuben D. Jr. Daughters: Ruth Ann, Sarah, Elizabeth and Mary. Daniel Brown to serve as guardian of two youngest children, Reuben D. and Mary. Executors: Daniel Brown and Timothy P. Roberts. Signed: Reuben D. Lyon. Witnesses: Edson Stickney and Wm. L. Hamilton. (76)

B RENEMAN, William of Loudon twp. - dated 5-6-1840; recorded 6-30-1840. Two brothers: Isaac and Joseph Brenaman. Mentions: Other brothers and sister but does not name. Signed: William Breneman. Witnesses: Henry Ebersole and Jacob Grove. (77)

DECKER, Henry - dated 12-28-1839; recorded 5-12-1840. Father: Henry Decker, now living in Mifflin Co., Pennsylvania, the W½ SW¼ Section 22, Township 27N, Range 12 subject to sale at Ft. Wayne, Indiana. To children of sister Catherine now deceased, to-wit: David, Linah, Henry and Solomon. Signed: Henry Decker. Witnesses: John Royer and George Horner. (79)

MYERS, George Sr. - dated 6-18-1839; recorded 5-12-1840. Wife, Agnes. Seven children: Phebe, Elizabeth, John, Isaac, Philip, George and Jacob Myers. Executor: Lorenzo Abbott. Signed: George Myers, Sen. Witnesses: Abraham Anderson and Peter Been. (80)

CASALE, Joseph - dated 2-5-1839 recorded 5-12-1840. Brothers: David and John Casale. Mentions rights in estate of deceased father; also mentions mother who is living, but does not name. Sister (?) Catherine Stannard and Mary Casale. Mentions note of John Stannard. Mentions farm in Putnam County, Ohio. Executor: friend, John Terry. Signed: Joseph Casale. Witnesses: David Beard and Maria L. Stoke. (81)

VELLNAGLE, Julius - dated 9-7-1840; recorded 9-29-1840. Wife, Nanetta, also to serve as executrix. Signed: Julius Vellnagle. Witnesses: J. Seney and Philip Wenty. (83)

WYCOFF, Henry - dated 4-2-1839; recorded 9-29-1840. Wife, Mariah. Mother, Mary Wyceff. Two sisters: Hannah Fergason and Susanna Stillwell. Sisters son, John Stillwell. Executors: Wife, Maria and Elisha Jones. Signed Henry (mark) Wycoff. Witnesses: John Holms and Samuel Wyant. (84)

CLAY, Mathias of Loudon twp. - dated 6-29-1840; recorded 11-26-1840. Wife, mentioned, but not named. Daughter: Margaret. Signed: Mathias Clay (German signature). Witnesses: Henry Ebersole and Jacob Croan. (86)

KONRAD, Adam A. of Tiffin - Will written in German - dated 3-22-1841; recorded 4-2-1841. Wife, Caroline, also to serve as executrix, guardian and tudor of children. Two children: Emilia and Wilhilmina. Signed; Adam A. Conrad (German). Witnesses: John Krauss and William Long. (89)

CULVER, Benjamin – dated 12-4-1840; recorded 1-25-1841. Wife, Tabatha, also to serve as executrix. Mentions: "to the inhabitants of Pleasant twp., one acre of land for the purpose of having the same used as a burying ground known at present by being called 'Culvers Burying Ground' and being on the farm on which I now reside...The said graveyard is near the bank of the Sandusky River and nearly north from the dwelling house which I now occupy and the said one acre of land includes all the graves now made thereon agreeably to a survey thereof heretofore made by Samuel T. Wright." Mentions: That no part or portion is to go to my brothers or sisters and their heirs. Signed: Benjamin (mark) Colver. Witnesses: Eli Snook and Abel Rawson. (87)

UMSTED, Enoch – dated 9-30-1837; recorded 5-5-1841. Wife, Sarah. Children: Deliah Sonder, Rebecca Bernard, Nancy Huss, Susanna Cramer, Eliza Umsted, Aaron Umsted, Elisha Umsted and Eli Umsted. Executor: Son, Elisha Umsted. Signed; Enoch Umsted. Witnesses: F. W. Shinn and Jacob Crager. (91)

SIMMONS, Peter – dated 4-17-1841; recorded 5-26-1841. Wife, Mary Ann. Sons: John, Adam and Peter. Daughters: Margaret Bokey, Catherine Courdate (Kourdate), Magdalena Simons, Elizabeth Casner (Comer), Eve Fathus and Elizabeth Struser. Mentions: Money coming from Germany. Executor: Son, Peter Simons. Signed: Peter (mark) Simons. Witnesses: Frederick Cleaggoner and John Peter Courtode. (93)

BRUSH, John T. of Sandusky Co., Ohio – dated 9-1-1840; recorded 7-1-1841. Wife, Susan Albina Brush, also to serve as executrix. Signed: John T. Brush. Witnesses: John M. Smith and Isaac Norton. (95)

MORGENTHALER, Jacob – dated 8-8-1841; recorded 11-5-1841. Wife: Christana. Sons: Jacob, Godgred, Gotlape and John. Daughters: Christine, Doretha, Katherine, and Margaretta. Executor: Son, Jacob. Signed: John Morgenthaler. Witnesses: Peter (mark) Ebersole and A. W. Ulex. (96)

CALLAMON, John of Tiffin – Dated 8-19-1841; recorded 11-6-1841. Children of sister, Catharine formerly Catherine Callanon of Laughred Co., Galway, Ireland. Bequeath to Rev. Jaseph Macnemu(?). Executors: Robert Montgomery and Patrick Kinney. Signed: John Callanon. Witnesses: Rich'd Williams and James Cahill.(100)

GALT, William – dated 11-1-1841; recorded 11-11-1841. Eli Norris, who is also to serve as executor; no relationship, if any, is given. Signed: William Galt. Witnesses: Joel Stone and Levi Davis. (101)

LOVE, Andrew – dated 10-12-1841; recorded 11-11-1841. Wife, Magdalena. Children: William, Sarah, James W., Prudence and Abigail. Executor: Friend, Levi Keller, Signed: Andrew Love. Witnesses: Warren Buel and G. J. Keen. (102)

CUMMINS, Mathias – dated 10-2-1841; recorded 12-11-1841. Wife, Phebe, to have household furniture she had in her possession at time of marriage. Mentions seven heirs, names only five oldest sons: James, David, William, George and Jacob. Mentions: Land in both Seneca and Williams County, Ohio. Executor: John Hall. Signed: Mathias Cummins. Witnesses: Abraham Smith and Reuben Mallison. (104)

McCARTNEY, Henry of Scipio - dated (not given); recorded 2-8-1842. Sons: Charles, Henry, Reuben, Robert, Rufus and John. Daughters: Ann wife of Johnson Chittenden and Jane McCartney. Executors: Daniel Brown and Samuel McClung. Signed: Henry McCartney. Witnesses: Gilbert J. Ogden and James A. Stewart. (107)

TEARE, Thomas of town of Tiffin - dated 12-11-1841; recorded 3-1-1842. Brother: Caesar Tear of Isle of Man, Great Britian. Sisters: Ester & Jane. Executor: Joseph Gibson of Tiffin. Signed: Thomas Teare. Witnesses: Luther M. Frank and Abel Rawson. (110)

WRIGHT, Eli of Seneca twp. - dated 1-12-1841; recorded 3-18-1842. Sons: Hamilton Tr., Eli and Josiah. Daughters: Delilah wife of Ebenezer Hubbard, Anna wife of Joseph Saxton and Martha wife of Michael Saxton. Executor: Benjamin Depue. Signed: Ely Wright. Witnesses: Abel Rawson, John K. Gibson and William McClung. (112)

McDANIEL, James W. - dated 7-20-1841; recorded 3-18-1842. Wife, Theresa M., also to serve as executrix. Signed: James W. McDaniel. Witnesses: Lorenzo Abbott and Samuel R. Swope. (114)

CRONKITE, Tunis - dated 11-22-1841; recorded 3-18-1842. Wife: Nancy. Sons: Soloman, Seth, Wilhelmus and James. Daughters: Mary E. and Martha Ellen Cronkite. Executors: Sons, Wilhelmus and James. Signed: Tunis (mark) Cronkite. Witnesses: Ananias Ashley and Samuel Cassety. (116)

MARVIN, Hannah of Scipio - dated 8-28-1841; recorded 6-4-1842. Husband, Zacharia Marvin, also to serve as executor. Mother, mentioned, but not named. Sister: Margaret Finch. Adopted daughter: Elen. Brothers: Ira, Samuel, Lewis, John and Solomon. Mentions: Brother Ira's wife Margaret. Land Hannah owned was purchased from Nathaniel Owen and George Morehart. Signed: Hannah Marvin. Witnesses: Daniel Brown and Sally Ann Brown. Deposition dated 5-13-1833 attached to will states: "Zachariah Marvin and Hannah Finch both of Scipio have agreed to join in a marriage covenant.....that Hannah shall provide money for Zachariah to improve farm she now owns..." Signed: Hannah Finch and Zachariah Marvin. (118)

HEDGES, Isaac - dated 8-28-1842; recorded 9-9-1842. Sons: Charles, Isaac, Alexander, and John. Daughters: Hannah Stull; Dorcas Bloom; Susannah Stull, deceased, her children—Lavina, Henson and Edward Stull; Emelia. Executor: John Galbreath. Signed: Isaac Hedges. Witnesses: Andrew Eley, Lyman Forbush and Richard Conner. (121)

KIRCHNER, Henry of Tiffin - dated 8-19-1842; recorded 9-9-1842. Wife, Eva Barbara, also to serve as executrix. Children: Catherine, John Michael, Eva Barbara, and Mary Margaret Kirchner. Signed: Henry Kirchner. Witnesses: John Snider and Joseph Rouker. (123)

BIGHAM, William - dated 8-7-1840; recorded 9-10-1842. Wife, Jane. Son: John. Youngest daughter: Mary Bigham. Executors: Wife, Jane and son, John. Signed: William Bigham. Witnesses: T. B. Willoughby and Diana Willoughby. (125)

BERGER, George - dated (not given); recorded 9-10-1842. Wife, Margaret. Children: Samuel and Andrew; may be more. Executors: Sons, Samuel and Andrew Berger and Daniel Loudenslager. Signed: George Berger. (126)

530

FREE, Frederick - dated 8-30-1842; recorded 11-12-1842. Wife, Elizabeth, also to serve as executrix. Children, mentioned but not named, not of age. Mentions: That he owns claims and property in Virginia and in the east. Requests that John Zimmerman brother of his wife, now living in Pennsylvania is to control and manage business affairs in Virginia. Signed: Frederick Free. Witnesses: Andrew Lugenbul and Jesse Stine. (128)

BAKER, John of Big Spring twp. - dated 10-26-1842; recorded 11-21-1842. Wife, Clarissa. Sons: James and John. Daughters: Delilah Baker and Mary Battenfelt. Signed: John Baker. Witnesses: H. L. Kirkham and Lawrence Courtaell. (130)

CRABILL, Christian of Big Spring twp. - dated 10-13-1842; recorded 12-1-1842. Wife: Elmina. Four children, three sons and one daughter: Isaac, Phianna, George and David Crabill. Executors: Wife, Elmina and Benjamin Boure. Signed: Christian Crabill. Witnesses: Charles Henderson and William Pressler. (131)

SENECA COUNTY, OHIO - MINISTERS' LICENCES

(As found recorded in the first book of marriages.)

Minister	Church	Date Issued	Place Issued	Date Recorded Seneca County
BURGESS, Oliver	- - - -	3-30-1840	Lucas County	--------1841
CHUBB, Rolla H.	M. E.	10-19-1840	Wood County	--------1841
SPRAKLIN, Rev. Alfred	". B.	July 1839	Richland County	--------1841
KEATING, John	Baptist	11-2-1829	Seneca County	--------1841
PARKER, Seth C.	Free Will Baptist	12-15-1841	Seneca County	12-15-1841
SPICER, Rev. Jabiah	Presbyterian	10-18-1839	Trumbull County	------1841
FERRIS, John L.	M. E.	Mar. 1839	Huron County	1-6-1842
TURNER, William	----------	7-28-1841	Columbiana Co.	1-26-1842
PETTIT, Rev. John	Independant Congregational	Mar. 1833	Ashtabula Co.	5-9-1842
GAMBERT, Rev. Henry	Evangelical	7-1-1829	Fairfield Co.	5-31-1842
PECK, Rev. Simeon	Presbyterian	4-12-1842	Crawford County	6-20-1842
SAMPSON, Hamilton	Baptist	5-24-1841	Wayne County	7-5-1842
HILL, Leonard	---------	10-10-1842	Huron County	10-10-1842
CAMPBELL, Rev. David	Baptist	6-1-1838	Allen County	10-12-1842

531

SHELBY COUNTY, OHIO   LENFOX CEMETERY
Franklin Twp.   North of Sidney, Ohio
       Inscriptions copied 1967

Submitted by:- Mr. Roy E. Lacy, Anna, Ohio-45302

Located north of Sidney on Route #25 (Sidney-Wapakoneta Rd.) on
east side of road. This is an old cemetery donated by Lennox.
The stones are all down and some covered by litter and ground.
I may have missed some because of this and undergrowth of trees.

DEVER, Loyd died 4-28-1865; ae 70-7-19
YINGER, Debora w/o H. died 11-2-1875; ae 70-1-7
Large stone - no marking
BINKLEY, Jacob born 11-29-1867; ae 80-11-7
COHEN, Hugh died 9-30-1873; ae 18-2-6
McVAY, Thomas died 12-26-1884; ae 79-5-1
    Inf. child of G.W. & Lizzie McVay - no dates
    Little Tarry s/o G.W. & Lizzie McVay d. 9-22-1878;ae 3m. 23
LAPHAM, Thomas E. s/o E.J. & S.J. died 9-8-1870; ae 2-10-2
McVAY, Hemlie W. s/o G.W. & Lizzie died 10-9-1882; ae 22-5-16
ALBRIGHT, Mathias died 4-11-1889 ae 75 years
    Sarah w/o Mathias died 4-14- 1879 ae 64yrs. 17da.
    4 children ss as Mathias and Sarah
    . . . . died 3-10-1838; ae 2yr. 16da.
    John L. died 1-13-1842; ae 3mo 4da.
    Peter M. died 10-23-1856; ae 3 mo.
    Lydia A. died 5-4-1880; ae 40-8-1
BLUE, Michael died 2-7-1875; ae 60-4-6--next stone unreadable
. . . . died 1-7-1861; ae 8-6-1
LIMES, ... died 1-?-1861; ae (unreadable)
B. . . . ., Michael - unreadable
MYERS, Jos . .(?) . . . . ae 15-5-5
LENOX, John died 11-20-1852; ae 62 years
McCULLOUGH, William died 3-3-1858; ae 63-3-12
          Cynthia w/o William d. 11-18-1860; ae 39yr. 4mo.
LENOX, Richard M. died 3-15-1869; ae 45yr. 5mo.
McDONALD, William S. died 4-20-1863; ae 77-5-11   )
        Mary died 8-22-1860; ae 66 years) ss
. . . . Stone probably "Kelley"
KELLEY, Nancy w/o G. Kelley died 4-3-1845; ae 60 years
. . .FEE, Sarah Gre. . died 9-22-1840; ae 2yr. 2mo.
McVAY, Eliza A s/o I.T. and J. died 7-11-1850; ae 21-6-11
DYE, Inf. s/o J.J. and Elizabeth died 9-7-1852; ae 6da.
DEWEESE, James s/o Elder Joshua died 6-3-1852; ae 74-9-25
BONHAM, Inf. s/o D.W. and L. died 7-18-1863
WOODS, d/o William and E. A. died 8-6-1862; ae 8mo.)
        Willie died 9-25-1875; ae 4mo.   ) ss
LAWHEAD, Mary L. died 1-18-1887; ae 68-9-13
BENNETT, Tobias s/o N. and S. died 10-17-1839; ae 19 years
    Stephen s/o N. & S. died 9-13-1839; ae 21
    (?) Probably "Bennett" d. 10-11-1866; ae. 17-2-(?)
BENNETT, Sarah w/o Nehemiah d. 9-5-1879; ae 80-5-9
. . . . . . Unreadable stone (near Bennett)
DEWEESE, Meme w/o David died 3-9-1865; ae 49-1-10
    David died 3-13-1866; ae 54-2-22

McVAY, Alice d/o A. and J. A. died 9-29-1882; ae 8-6-24
     John died 4-2-1853; ae 7-7-26
     Henry died 8-23-1869; ae 53yr. 9mo.
     Mellie died 4-8-1864; ae 77-11-1
GRIT, Mary w/o William died 9-19-1861; ae 67-5-27
WOLF, Maggie A. d/o H. and M.E. died 12-6-1873; ae 1-5-3
     Josie E. s/o H. & M.E. died 12-2-1877; ae 4mo 24da.
McVAY, John M. s/o of M. and M. L. died 8-20-1852; ae 20 months
     Edward s/o M. & M.L. died 6-14-1852; ae 2 months
MALO, Edward s/o C. and P. died 9-3-1856; ae 24-11-9

There are no stones for the following VETERANS listed:-
WAR of 1812, Jacob LEAPLEY, lot 15-25- born 6-3-1790 Cook Co., Va.
     died 6-7-1860, buried 6-10-1860
WAR of 1812, Jacob SHANK lot 11-1-31 born 11-8-1784 Va.
     died 11-10-1851, buried 11-13-1851

This cemetery was listed 10-2-1967 by Roy E. Lacy, Anna, Ohio

     *

     SHELBY COUNTY, OHIO   LONG CEMETERY
     Dinsmore Twp. NW qt. Sec. 14

This is not as old nor as large as some cemeteries. The Needmore
Church of Christ was built just west of the cemetery in 1881, but
has been closed and moved years ago. Mr. William Wiford was the
main Layman at the time the church closed and his descendants live
in and near Sidney. Many of these graves have no markers so I
will first list those which have markers. Mr. E. C. Long lives
across the road from the plot and having many relatives buried in
the cemetery, advised me of many other burials.

WICAL, Carrie H. d/o W. and I. died 5-14-1902; ae 7-7-6
     Catherine w/o Shepard born 6-6-1865; died 10-26-1908
     Shepard died 6-26-1918; ae 83-9-25
ROBINSON, Ella WICAL 1880-1950
BEERS, Gerty Viola d. 3-13-1896; ae 7 yrs. d/o Thomas BEERS
GILLIMORE, U. M. died 2-4-1899; ae 24-1-18
     Mrs. U. M. Gillmore and baby . . . no marker
WADE, J. d. 3-18-1882; ae 60yrs. 1da. Grandfather of Ed Long
                     (Father of Mr. Long's mother)
BECK, James - no stone
     Margaret w/o James d. 11-26-1897; ae 54 years
     Four children of James and Margaret - no stones
LONG, Ed. C. 1878-
     Edna R. KIES Long (2nd wife) 1901-
     Sophia WADE Long (1st wife) 1878-1915
     Louella C. 1899-1899 (Daughter)
     Ethel I. 1900-1900 (daughter)
     Charles - no marker
     Mary L. w/o Charles died 3-18-1900; ae 53
WICAL, John b. 2-13-1828; d. 7-5-1906 CIVIL WAR VETERAN
     Elizabeth w/o John b. 1-28-1838; d. 3-7-1923; dau. no marker

BOYER, Mahalia w/o Ed. died 7-28-1889; ae 32-2-27
REEVES, Mary J. 1828-1897
WIFORD, L. F. father of Wm. Wiford, b. 1-16-1820; d. 7-28-1896
     Ed. L. 1863-1910 s/o L. F. Wiford
DOWNS, Martha M. b. 3-30-1827; died 10-22-1891
     Henry b. 2-27-1818; d. 8-20-1889; CIVIL WAR VETERAN

The following are other people buried in this cemetery with no
markers and the names were given by memory by Ed. Long:-

Lon DAVIS and four or five of his children. Harry DAVIS
Dave DAVIS, inf. child. Cal BUCK, inf. child. Miss CLAYTON
Al WICAL, wife and two children. Joe WOODELL and two children.
Emma DAVIS, wife of Henry Davis.
There probably are a couple more graves here of which Mr. Long
has no knowledge.
          * * * * * * * * * * * * * * * * * * *

       SHELBY COUNTY, OHIO   OLD LORAMIE CEMETERY
       Dinsmore Twp. NW¼ Sec. 9   Copied 1965
       By: Mr. Roy E. Lacy, Anna, Ohio

Located one mile south of Botkins, Ohio. In the early days it
probably was called "Curts Cemetery". I have added the Veterans
names as recorded in the Recorder's Office, where no stones were
erected.
BLAKLEY, Morenos s/o J. and E. died 12-27-1853; ae 7-2-13
     Samuel died 7-12-1857; ae 78 years
BRUCE, Jackson H. CIVIL WAR (no marker) b.11-16-1845 Pa.;d.11-21-1
BORLIN, James K. s/o P. and C. died 1-1-1847; ae 2yr 6da.
BOYER, Edith d/o S.F. and C. died 12-1-1895; ae 12-1-1
     Emma w/o C. died 10-21-1876; ae 24-8-26
BOTKIN, Russel died 11-3-1868; ae 35-9-2
     Catherine w/o Russel died 4-10-1862; ae 30-1-5
     Erastes s/o B. and E. died 12-28-1831; ae 10mo. 21da.
     Eliza w/o B. died 7-18-1839; ae 30yrs.-?-?
     . . . . not readable
     Elizabeth d/o D. and S. M. - not readable
     Paul E. s/o A. and R. born 9-17-1895; died 5- 25-1900
     Silvenes born 6-11-1851; died 9-26-1899
BUPP, Emily J. w/o John d. 8-11-1882; ae 29-10-3
BOTKIN, Charles died 6-19-1885; ae 28-3-13
CAMPBELL, Margaret died 11-19-1896; ae 63 years
COLLINS, Franklin - CIVIL WAR (no marker)
        Frankie s/o Dr. S. M. and Sophia died 8-5-1875; ae 7m. 5d
        Carrie E. d/o Dr. S. M. & Sophia died 9-18-1879; ae 5m27d
COCKLIN, Michael s/o Macheal and Caroline - date not readable
     Three graves but not readable
COTTRELL, Elam died 11-13-1856; ae 34yr. 4mo.
COOK, Sarah M. w/o Abraham died 5-12-1874; ae 50 years
CROSS, Nancy w/o Oliver died 1-16-1879; ae 69-11-16
CURTS, Pricella w/o Thomas Curts, Jr. died 7-7-1860; ae not readab
     William P. died 6-2-1862; ae 26-11- 2
     Mary w/o William died 3-18-1857; ae 20-2-21
     Joseph died 3-8-1817 WAR of 1812

CURTS, Julia Ann d/o Joseph died 12-24-1919; ae 50-(?)-(?)
        Thomas born 1-16-1755; died 5-28-1842 WAR of 1812
        Lawrence - REVOLUTIONARY WAR - no marker
DANNER, Clarisa V. d/o E.H. & L.C. d. 1-12-1865; ae 10-9-2
ELLIOTT, Samuel b. 7-12-1833; d.8-22-1868;ae 37-7-17 CIVIL WAR
        William A. s/o ? & C. died 3-12-1862; ae 1-9-7
        William died 4-17-1857; ae 52-5-2
        Bertha d/o Wm. & Margaret d. 4-11-1813; ae 11yr. 9mo.
        Rebecca w/o Richard died 10-15-1838
        R. C. died 12-7-1884; ae 78-5-27
        Elizabeth died 7-22-1875; ae 49-1-27
        Wm. Joseph s/o Joseph & ? died 9-7-1868; ae unreaeable
        Sarah d/o F. & S. died 3-24-1856; ae 11mo 11da.
. . . . Emnit s/o (?) & Caroline died (?); ae 2-1-6
GARTLEY, George W. b. 10-2-1827 Pa.; d. 3-17-1871 CIVIL WAR
GLICK, Jacob died 3-9-1854; ae 15yr. 6da.
GRAY, Damuel died 7-5-1882; ae 71-3-0
        Elizabeth w/o Samuel d. 4-23-1879; ae 63-8-15
        Joseph M. s/o Samuel & Elizabeth d. 2-18-1861; ae 12-2-21
GILMORE, Lewis C. b. 3-6-1791; d.4-4-1870; CIVIL WAR (No marker)
        Isaac A. b. 10-14-1839; d. 9-20-1863 CIVIL WAR No marker
GILLIMORE, Esabell d/o E. died 8-11-1873; ae 3mo. 11da.
        Esabell d/o S. & E. died 5-8-1873; ae 15-9-11
GILIMORE, Samuel died 5-20-1878; ae 74-2-1
        Margaret w/o Mark d. 9-27-188(?); ae unreadable
        Mark b. 1-11-1824; d. 7-24-1894 CIVIL WAR (No marker)
HASTINGS, Wm. B. b. 4-1-1831; d.2-28-1878;ae47-1-14 CIVIL WAR
HILDEBRAND, Irvan hus./E.J. b.6-4-1840; d.7-1-1902 CIVIL WAR
                                              (no marker)
HILBRANT, Mary w/o Joseph d. 12-17-1866; ae 48-2-13
        Joseph b. 3-4-1836; d. 1-17-1873 ae 60 yrs CIVIL WAR
        Henry E. s/o I. & E.J. d. 12-9-1884; ae 15yr. 5mo.
        Ferdinand s/o Joseph & Mary d. 6-14-1865; ae 22yr 3da.
                                         CIVIL WAR
HINSKY, Adam b. 6-6-1847; d. 9-7-1889 CIVIL WAR (no marker)
        (It is possible that Ida May Misky is Ida May Hinsky)
HOWELL, Mandy d/o D. and Sarah d. 5-2-18?? (Stone broken)
        David died ? ? 1857; ae. 2(?)-5-5
HUNT, Harley E. s/o P. & Mary d. 2-23-1884; ae 1-10-28
        Dora 1867-1891
        Byron d. 2-23-1878; ae 23da.
JACKSON, Amanda died 7-31-1855; ae 9mo. 1da.
        Mahala died 10-31-1895; ae 87-8-25
        Thomas died 5-21-1847; ae 2yr. 2mo.
        Richard s/o B. & E. died 2-9-1846; ae 11 da.
        Sarah I. d/o B. & E. died 3-1-1810; ae 9mo. 1da.
KILLIAN, Philip died 1-28-1866; ae 51-6-24
        Mary d/o B. & Me died 8-19-1867; ae 1-4-16
LONGSTRETCH, John H. s/o John & E. d. 8-21-1856;.ae (?)-11-23
        Estella d/o John H. & E. d.12-14-1865;ae 2mo. 3da.
        John died 1-10-1840; ae 26 years
McMANNANCY, James b.11-15-1811 Botkins;d.8-17-1871 CIVIL WAR
                                          no marker

535

McMANNANCY, Geo. b. 11-5-1843;d.2-11-1864 CIVIL WAR (No marker)
MALAHAM, Mary w/o C. W. died 8-8-1874 ae 33-0-1
MINSKY, Ida May d/o Adam & Ada d. 7-28-1873; ae 34-6-1
                (This could be "Hinsky" instead of "Minsky")
PARR, Samuel died 7-25-1848 ae 38 yrs.
      Samuel died 10-1-1885 ae 25-10-5
      Samuel H. b. 6-3-1829 Pa.; d. 10-1-1868 CIVIL WAR (No marker)
      Robert E. s/o W.A. & E. d.(unreadable); ae 1mo. 16da.
PRICE, Peter - CIVIL WAR (No marker)
ROBBINS, Cerelda L. d/o David & I.E. d. 11-27-1876; ae 10-5-28
      . . . . d. 1-7-1862 ae 21-4-13
      Mary E. d/o David & I.E. d. 1-13-1862; ae 1-5-12
      Benjamin s/o David and I.E. d. 5-19-18?? no ae
      Charles Alonzo s/o W.E. & E.A. d. 12-15-1878 ae 2-3-5
SCHNIPPEL, Herman b. 6-2-1840 Germ. d. 7-4-1902 CIVIL WAR (no mark)
SMITH, William s/o M. & M. died 6th year of life
      Thomas W. d. 5-21-1862 ae 21yr. 5mo.
      John J. s/o M.&J. died 4-25-1848 ae 3mo. 5da.
      Mathias d. 7-21-1869 ae 60-10-12
STYLES, Jonathan died 2-27-1887 ae 57yr. 1da.
STOCKER, Susannah d/o John D. & Marie d. 3-18-1878 ae 17yr. 10mo.
TROUT, Lucinda w/o W. d. 5-6-1876; ae 34-1-26
WALTZ, Sarah A d/o Wm. & M.C. d. 9-18-1865; ae 1yr. 7mo.
      Wm. b. 4-2-1834 Shelby Co.;d.2-6-1878;ae 48-11-21 CIVIL WAR
WIFORD, Catherine w/o Jacob d. 10-26-1867; ae 70-10-8
WILLIAMS, Alexander s/o J. & S.R. d. 1-18-1873 ae unreadable
      Jerome B. s/o C.B. & E. d. 1-13-18?? ae 7mo. 15da.
WOODELL, Martha M. w/o Ira H. d. 12-27-1878; ae 20-3-11
. . . . . John H. d. 8-2-187(?) ae 83-7-19
. . . . . Amanda d/o David & Annie d. 1-8-1880 ae 22-1-10
. . . . . Charles (unreadable)
. . . . . Lavina d/o (?) and H. (?) d. 3-22-1810 ae ?? 12 da

                The inscriptions in this cemetery
                    were taken 3-17-1965
                           by
                Mr. Roy E. Lacy, Anna, Ohio

536

MILLS CEMETERY - SHELBY COUNTY, OHIO

Located in Cynthian Township, Section 31, Township 10, Range 5; at end of Mills
Road (no-outlet) off of Rangeline Road just north of its intersection with State
Route 66. Cemetery is no longer active. Inscriptions taken Sept. 1968 by Lois
Baker, Jac Baker and Anita Short.

HALE, Samuel son of G. & M. died May 8, 1845 aged 13 y's. 5m's. & 13 d's.
    Eliza dau of G. & M. died May 10, 1847 aged 14 y's. 5 m. & 7d's.
    Maria wife of George Hale died Feb. 3, 1845 in the 37th y'r of her age
SHORT, Isaac (die)d Aug.__, 1843 aged 2 years
    Sarah Jane died July 28, 1843 (aged) __year and 10 mo., son and daut of
        Geo. and (Eli)zabeth Short (Note: Isaac and Sarah on same stone, stone
            broken in several places.)
SMITH, In memory of John B. Smith deceast June the 23rd 1837 aged fifty two years
            seven months and 23 days
MILLS, In memory of Betsey wife of Wm. Mills died March 1st 1831 aged 41 years
            6 mo. & 17 ds.
    Sally Amarintha daughter of W. & J. died March 22nd 1836 aged 3 years 4 mo.
            & 12 ds.
URBN, Phillip son of I. & M. died Apr. 13, 1852 aged 9 ds.
MILLS, William son of D. & E. R. died May 23, 1853 ag'd 3 ys. 3 ms. & 21 ds.
HALE, Henry son of G. & M. died Jan. 20, 1852 aged 21 y's. 6 m's. & 22 d's.
    Betsy mother of Geo. Hale died March 14, 1839 aged 84 yrs.
    Martin son of G. & M. died July 29, 1856 aged 13 y'rs. 4 m. & 28 d.
    George died Mar. 28, 1855 aged 55 y's. 10 m's. & 24 d's.
HOUSER, Infant dau. of Jacob & Charlotte died May 1, 1855 aged 13 d.
MEYERS, Joseph son of H. H. & C. die(d) Aug. 1 _____ (broken)
DAY, In memory of Minerva daughter of Noah & Mary Day born May 20th 1845 aged 1Yr.
    In memory of Martha J. daughter of Noah & Mary born Jan. 3rd 1837; aged
            about 5 years.
    In memory of Mary wife of Noah Day__6__(rest of inscription effaced)
    Corpl. Thos., Co. B, 50 Ohio Inf.
MEYERS, Christena wife of H.H.Meyers died Nov. 20, 1849 aged 24 y'rs. 11 ms 20 ds.
MILLER, Dinah, wife of Jas. Mille(r) died Dec. 5, 1854 aged 32 ys. 5 ms. & 13 ds.
    In memory of Polly Ann Miller died Feb. 26, 1843 aged 23 yrs. 10 mo. 23 ds.
    Joseph M. son of James & Dinah died Aug. 28, 1850 aged 1 yr. 9 mo. & 15 ds.
    John died Jan. 11, 1853 ag'd 70 y. 10 m. 24 d.
    Sarah wife of John Miller died Nov. 30, 1851 aged 63y. 11m. & _3d.(broken)
    Sarah Jane dau. of John & Sarah died Aug. 9, 1854 aged 28 yrs. 2 ms. 17 ds.
CHAMBERS, Margaret departed this life Aprile 2, 1823 aged 17 y 13 d lived a mild
          & tender wife to R. Chambers 1 y 3 m 8 d (Note: Hand-carved)
MEYERS, _____ died Jan. 17, 1851 aged 7 y'rs. & 25 d's. (Top of stone gone)
BUTT, Barbary wife of Jacob Butt, died Oct. 30, 1852 aged 37 yrs. 2 mo. 10 ds.
_____, Barbara Elen_____(died) (J)an. 13, 1849 aged 3 m. & 24 ds.
    (Stone broken into three pieces, one piece gone.)
CRUSE, John son of Peter and Martha Ann M. died July 13, 1863 aged 30 yrs.9m 14ds.
    Ruth Ann Daughter of Peter & Martha Ann died Mar. 15, 1857 aged 26 yrs.
            4 mos. 17 ds.
    Peter died June 30, 1873 aged 74y & 14d (same stone as Martha A.)
    Martha A. wife of Peter Cruse died Nov. 24, 1857 aged 54y 11m & 2d
Note: 2 unmarked GAR graves. Footstones: G.S.-H.D.-J.C.-_.D.-HH-G.H.-M.H.

SHELBY COUNTY, OHIO - MONTRA METHODIST CEMETERY

Contributed by:- Roy E. Lacy, Anna, Ohio.

This cemetery is located one mile east of the village. The Church is no longer
there and probably the last burial was about 1900. The cemetery is well-kept
and clean; however, some stones are in bad shape. Transcribed 5-26-1970

Catherine Parent died 8-11-1884 aged 74y 1m 21d
Mary C. daughter of Gibson and Irene Nedey died 4-15-1852 age 10y 11m 1d
Margaret wife of Jefferson Baker d. 1-2-1882 age 55y 10m 11d
Jefferson Baker died 11-7-1873 age 45y 2m 8d
Infant Baker died   6-1-1867
Plazzie (?) dau W. L. and A. J. Howell d. 6-17-1867 age 13y 8m 10d
Amanda L. wife of A. R. Howell d. 3-20-1900 age 72y 6m 2d
A. R. W. Howell d. 1-4-1906 age 80y 7m 2d
Edgar O. Howell d. 1-9-1882 age 27-10-0
Simeon N. Howell d. 6-20-1900 age 2m 10d
Samantha dau of T. R. E. Howell d. 8-30-1854 age 61y 7m 13d
Not readable   3-26-1851 age ?-9-18 Probably a Howell
Barbara A. Blakely dau of Franklin and E.
Not readable d. 4-6-18— (Next to Barbra)
Nancy (?) dau. of Reben and Vitale (?) Staley d. 12-7-1832 age 28yrs 6m 10d
Not readable James son of M. and R. died 1860
Elizabeth Howell wife of Jonathan d. 1-31-1881 age 88 yrs. 2mo. 27das.
Jonathan Howell Civil War Vet d. 7-27-1871 age 82yrs. 2 mos. 3 das.
Eveline wife of Jonathan Hanna d.1-5-1881 age 32 yrs 10 mos 12 das.
Brooks Akers d. 7-14-1867 age 51yrs. 2mo. 4das.
Marie N. Akers d. 9-12-1889 age 13yrs. 1mo. 6das.
              Elijah Holmes Children
Mary E. d. 10-3-1861 age 4yrs. 8 mos. 13 das.
Levi E. d. 3-14-1863 age 5y 29d
Anna E. M. d. 3-7-1863 age 2y 2m 18d
Elijah Holmes father d. 1-30-1861 age 39y 10m 23d
Rebecca dau of - - - - Howell d. 6-6-1838 - Stone partly buried.
Sarah E. Dau of Jonathan and Elizabeth Howell d. 9-10-1847 age 10y 9m 27d
Mariam dau. of J. and E. Howell d. 7-2-1854 age 16y 6m 1d
Not readable probably Howell as full row are Howell
Not readable dau. of J. and M. Baker d. 5-17-1861 age 3y 9m 6d.
John Shellenbarger Civil War Vet died 2-12-1892 no age given,
Susanna his wife d. 3-7-1881
Mary B. dau of W. S. and M. Foster d. 8-9-1878 age 20y 9m 25d
William S. Foster d. 9-8-1873 age 57y 10m 10d.
Mary E. dau. of J. M. and M. A. Blakeley d. 8-7-1872 age 1y 6m 16das.
William son of J. M. and M. A. Blakeley d. 7-6-1878 - no age given.

538

MEDARIS CEMETERY - PERRY TOWNSHIP - SHELBY COUNTY, OHIO

Contributed by Mrs. R. J. Adams, Route 5, Sidney, Ohio 45365

Cemetery is located on Dingman-Slagle Rd. between Pasco-Montra and Jackson Rds.

COBLE, John d. Nov. 23, 1879 a. 83y 9m 11d
MEDARIS, Elizabell W. consort of Washington Medaris ____(note: rest unreadable;
    Sutton SHELBY COUNTY HISTORY states...Elizabeth Salters Medaris, wife of
    Washington--died 1843.)
SHINN, Elizabeth wife of Clement I. Shinn d. April 11, 1852 a. 22
MATHIOUS, Sarah C., d. Jan. 21, 1861 a. 9y
LINE, Oscar E., son of D. M. & S. A. Line d. Dec. 13, 1854 a. 3y
    O. Belle, dau of D. M. & S. A. Line d. Jan. 25, 1855 a 11m(?)
RINEHART, Barbara wife of Peter Rinehart d. _____ 1847 a. 75y
    Peter d. Aug. 27, 1855 a. 82y
LINE, Henry C. d. May 18, 1851 a. 55y
          Elizabeth wife of H. C. Line d. July ____(note: stone broken)
          John d. April 2, 1846 a 42y
          George son of J. & A. Line d. Aug. 7, 1864 a. 25y 5m 23d. Member Co.
              K, 134 Reg. O.V.G.
          Martin son of J. & A. Line d. Sept. 30, 1866 a.____(note: stone broken)
          Ann 1811-1880; Johnathan 1841-1870; Amanda 1844-1873
DODSON, Mary wife of J. C. Dodson d. Jan. 13, 1868 a. 46y
HARRITT(?), Robert son of S. & C. Harritt(?) d.____1817 (or 1847?) a 13y
        (note: questionable, very hard to read)
BALL, Susannah wife of Harrison Ball d. Nov. 30, 1865 a.____(note; stone broken)
        Harrison_____(note; stone illegible)
MILLER, Daniel d. June 13, 1858 in the 83rd year of his age
REDENBO, Eliza Jane dau. of ____(?) Redenbo died____185_, a 11 years

SMALL CEMETERY - PERRY TOWNSHIP - SHELBY COUNTY, OHIO

Contributed by:- Mrs. D. J. Adams, Route 5, Sidney, Ohio 45365

Cemetery is located on Thompson Rd., southeast of Port Jefferson. Name of cemetery
may be Ward(?).
CARGILL, Mary A. wife of D. Cargill d. Aug. 25, 1866 a. 63y 6m 1d
PENCE, Allie A. dau. of A. I. & M. J. Pence d. May 20, 1866 a. 1y 1m 14d
DeWEESE, Benjamin son of J. D. & L. DeWeese d. Sept. 12, 1868 a. 14y 6m 24d
COX, Mary A. wife of Enogh Cox d. Mar. 12, 1881 a 59y 28d
CONNET, B. P. d. Feb. 6, 1862 a 62y(?)
BUCKINGHAM, Alexander d. October 28, 1865 a 50y 4m 28d (Masonic emblem
        Maria wife of Alexander Buckingham d. Dec. 10, 1866 a 50y 9m 21d
COX, Jessee b. April 8, 1812 d. Oct. 22, 1878
    Mary wife of Jessee Cox b. Jan. 4, 1820 (note: no other date)

Located in Perry Township, Section 19 & 20 lines, on Pence Road. Inscriptions taken by Barbara A. Adams, R.5, Sidney, O. Contributed by Roy Lacy, Anna, O.

LINE, Elizabeth dau of S. and E. died 9-16-1860 age 22 yr 7 mo
    Solomon died 12-8-1865 age 51 yr 8 da
WEST, Mary A. dau of S. and L. A. died 5-3-1855 age 12 yr 8 mo 15 da
JACKSON, Ruth wife of H. L. Jackson died 1-11-1859 age 80 yr 1 mo 22 da
    Henry L. died 2-25-2866 age 85 yr 21 da
BARCUS, Moses died 3-17-1863 age 89 yr 14 da
    Nancy, wife of Moses Barcus died 3-16-1863 age 88 yr 11 mo 6 da
SPARLING, Elizabeth dau. of J. M. and N. died June 1851 aged 12 yr.
DEWEESE, John M. 1801-1841 Susannah his wife 1807-1874 (same stone)
    Sons of J. H. Deweese; 1824 R.J.; ___1841; J.E . 1843 (same stone)
    In Memory of John Runyan son of John M. and Susannah Deweese died
      4-12-1843 aged 1 yr 7 mo 7 da (Note:- Same as J. B.)
COX, Rosannah dau. of N. and M. E. died 3-22-1861 age 8 yr 5 mo 12 da
    John son of N. and M. E. died 10-13-1866 age 6 yr 7 mo 4 da
THOMPSON, Martha died 9-2-1849 age 4 yr
WAGONER, Margaret Adelna dau of Thomas and B.E. died 1-24-1855 age 1y 2m 17d
BLUE, Infant son of M. and M. K. died 9-8-1855 age 6 mo.
THOMPSON, Smallwood died 3-31-1875 age 84 yr 1 mo 8 da
    Margaret wife of Smallwood Thompson died 8-13-1895 age 94y 9m 4da.
HILLIARD, Amanda dau of E. and H. died 1855 age 8 mo.
    Nancy died Apr. 1843 age 84 yr
    Martha K. dau of E. and H. died 1852 aged 15 da.
    Infant dau. of E. and H. Infant son of E. and H. (No dates)
MANNING, Nathaniel died 5-4-1853 age 51 yr 2 mo 6 da.
    Sarah wife of Nathaniel Manning died 4-2-1860 age 59 yr 3 mo 28 da.
    Thomas son of N. and Sarah died 9-19-1847 age 11 yr 11 mo 18 da.
ROBINSON, Solomon died 11-19-1818 (1848?) age 72 yr 11 mo S. of 2-1849(?)
    Hannah died 9-22-1853 age 52yr 1mo 25da.

OLD DUNKARD CEMETERY - SHELBY COUNTY, OHIO - PERRY TOWNSHIP

Contributed by: Mrs. D. J. Adams, Route 5, Sidney, Ohio 45365

Cemetery is located on State Route 29, one mile east of Pasco. Copied April, 19

BLACK, James C., d. March 23, 1852 aged 22y 4m 10d
GARBER, Catherine, wife of Joseph Garber d. Aug. 24, 1851 aged 73y 10m 5d
    Rev. Joseph d. Oct. 5, 1854 aged 81y
    Martin b. Apr. 28, 1798 d. Aug. 30, 1851
MARRS, Samuel b. July 16, 1789 d. Nov. 11, 1876 age 88y 3m 16d
JACKSON, Catherine d. March 3, 1844 aged 42y 11m 11d, Our Mother
    Henry, _____(note: stone broken), Our Father
MILLER, Catherine, wife of Henry R. Miller d. Dec. 16, 1871 aged 43y 7m 11d
    Franklin, son of H. & C. Miller d. Feb. 4, 1858 aged 11d(?)
    Henry d. Feb. 12, 1889 aged 83y 6m 1d
PEPPER, Betsy, wife of William Pepper d. May 5, 1876 aged 74y 4m 16d
    Chas. AX., son of M. & E. Pepper d. Aug. 14, 1860 aged 1 y
REDENBO, Elizabeth, wife of Samuel Redenbo d. Aug. 12, 1883 aged 75y 4m 11d
    Infant son of S. & E. Redenbo d. Mar. 25, 1858
    Samuel d. June 27, 1878 aged 79y 3m 2d
    Sarah, wife of Lewis P. Redenbo d. Mar. 18, 1884 aged 25y 1m 8d

SHELBY COUNTY, OHIO - ELLIOTT CEMETERY

Contributed by Roy E. Lacy, Anna, Ohio

This cemetery is located one mile north and one mile west of Jackson Center, in Jackson township. It is an old cemetery with many graves without markers and no doubt some are gone. Cemetery is in good condition. Transcribed 5-27-1970.

George Bowden Civil War Vet. Plot 4-1 born 3-2-1840 Harrisburg, Pa.
         died 4-22-1872
Sarah Jane dau of R. and S. Glick died 7-7-1861 age 8-11-26
         Glick died 10-24-1861 age 26-1-12
Mary Glick wife of Joad died 4-10-1869 age 41-2-21
Four infant Glick - dates not given
Infant - not readable
         Elliott wife of John C. died 6-3-1860 age 40-3-20
John C. Elliott born 10-6-1811 died 1-8-1902
Termitha wife of L. ?. Elliott died 9-1-1861 age 23-3-17
Margaret J. wife of L. F. Glick age 21-10-24— Stone broken
stone broken - died 9-3-1861 age 1-3-12
Mattie dau of P. C. and S. Lawhead died 1-20-1878 age 70
Nettie May Egbert 1889-1933
         added as by Military records
Archie De Frague lot 12-1 born 8-3-1883 Belguem died 10-14-1936 War I Vet.
William Wills Civil War Vet. 10t 2-18- Born 7-16-1839 Athens, Ohio
         died 2-17-1880 — Sons George and Henry
Unknown —— Civil War lot 3-13
Unknown —— Civil War lot 3-12

GALLEY CEMETERY - CYNTHIAN TOWNSHIP - SHELBY COUNTY, OHIO

Located NW¼ Sec. 29, Twp. 10, Range 5, North side Cardo-Roman Rd, 1/8th mile west of intersection with Galley Rd. All inscriptions taken. All on same stone.
DINGLER, Henry died Apr. 30, 1874 aged 57y 7m & 25d
        Susanna wife of H. Dingler died May 1, 1881 aged 66y 5m 14d
        Isaac son of H. & S. Dingler died Mar. 4, 1855 aged 5y & 10m
(Note: base for a stone, but stone is gone)

It should be noted that there are no separate will books in this county. All original copies of wills are filed in estate packets or files and are listed as estates, thus there is no designation as to which estates contain wills.
First column = name; second column = year; third column = "E" for Estate and "G" for Guardianship; fourth column = file number. Estates or guardianships which contain no papers are designated "np".

ADAMS, Elijah	1850	E	A578	BOTKIN, S. H. etal.	1821	G	A3
ADAMS, Samuel W.	1848	E	A459	BOWE, John	1843	E	A299
ALBRIGHT, John B.	1849	E	A506	BOWE, Judy etal.	1841	G	A239
ALEXANDER, James T.	1840	E	A207	BRADING, James	1845	E	A374
ALKENBERG, Henrich etal.	1849	G	A545	BRANDENBURG, Samuel	1845	E	A371
ALLEN, Silas D.	1850	E	A553	BROWN, Caroline L.	1849	G	A544
ALLEN, William	1846	E	A384	BRYAN, Henry etal.	1842	G	A264
AMAN, Charles	1841	E	A230	BRYAN, James	1842	E	A296
ANDERSON, William	1832	E	A74	BRYAN, James D.	1849	E	A489
ANDREWS, John	1842	E	A285	BRYAN, Jesse	1832	E	A75
ARKENBURG, Bernard	1849	E	A514	BURDETT, Booth	1843	E	A297
ARLING, Bernard etal.	1847	G	A450	BURNETT, Ralph	1846	E	A389
ARLING, John H.	1849	E	A519	BUSHMAN, H. H.	1847	E	A429
AYERS, Caleb etal.	1847	G	A449	BYERLEY, Richard	1842	E	A270
				BYERS, Rachel etal	1842	G	A265
BABCOCK, Azariah	1848	G	A477	BYERS, Samuel	1840	E	A219
BABCOCK, William	1847	E	A435				
BAKER, Moses	1848	E	A451	CAIN, David	1847	G	A440
BALMER, George	1846	E	A383	CAIN, Henry J.	1843	G	A335
BARBEE, Elias	1842	E	A257	CAIN, James	1841	E	A245
BARBER, Edwin	1847	E	A421	CALDWELL, Robert M.	1840	E	A210
BARNER, Charles	1843	E	A312	CALDWELL, Thomas	1847	E	A414
BAUMER, Henry	1849	E	A496	CAMPBELL, Andrew	1840	E	A217
BEDELL, John etal.	1835	G	A115	CAMPBELL, Jackson etal.	1846	G	A408
BECK, John	1839	E	A173	CAMPBELL, John	1842	E	A292
BEDIN, Benjamin	1843	E	A311	CAMPBELL, Pleasant	1843	E	A313
BELL, Lavina etal	1846	G	A402	CANNON, Joseph	1825	E	A36
BELL, William	1845	E	A370	CAREY, Sarah A.	1842	G	A278
BENDER, John	1840	E	A195	CAREY, Sarah J.	1843	G	A324
BENNETT, John	1820	E	A6	CARPER, Henry etal.	1837	G	A140
BERNING, Henry	1850	E	A556	CARROLL, William	1840	E	A220
BIRD, Samuel	1846	E	A397	CARTER, David	1848	E	A453
BLAKE, John	1836	Enp	B39	CASSEL, Thomas	1823	E	A22
BLAKELY, Atchison	1828	E	A45	CATHCART, Thomas M.	1845	E	A375
BLAKELY, Mary B.	1828	E	A48	CATTERLIN, Hamilton	1847	G	A447
BLAKELY, Robert	1842	E	A259	CECIL, Boston etal.	1837	G	A136
BLAKELY, Robert	1849	G	A543	CECIL, Julia	1828	G	A49
BLOCK, Henry D.	1849	G	A527	CECIL, Lydia	1829	E	A53
BLUE, Barnabas	1842	E	A295	CECIL, William	1825	E	A32
BOCKRATH, Mathias	1850	E	A574	CECIL, Zachariah	1823	E	A24
BOLMER, Solomon etal.	1847	G	A448	CHAMBERS, Robert	1826	E	A37
BOSEL, John G.	1842	E	A289	CISCO, Henry	1846	E	A390
BOTHEL, William	1849	E	A490	CLARK, Daniel Z.	1849	E	A508
BOTKIN, Charles	1820	E	A40	CLARK, Elizabeth	1849	E	A501
BOTKIN, George	1833	E	A79	CLARK, Mary etal	1849	G	A525

CLATON, Lewis	1847 E	A424	EGBERT, John H.	1849 E	A517
CLAWSON, Frederick	1845 E	A361	ELLIOTT, Robert	1849 E	A507
CLAWSON, Josiah	1847 E	A420	ELLSWORTH, John	1824 E	A29
CLAWSON, Peter	1836 E	A121	ELSWORTH, Aquilla	1839 E	A170
CLAWSON, Peter	1842 E	A273	ENOCH, Francis	1847 E	A412
COLBY, Joseph	1841 E	A244	EVERLY, Jacob	1839 E	A169
COLBY, Wm. H.	1848 E	A464	EVERLY, Jacob	1850 E	A575
COLEMAN, Philip	1839 E	At?74	EVERLY, Rachael etal.	1840 G	A194
CONANT, Rufus	1845 E	A373			
CONKLIN, Jacob	1839 E	A177	FARNUM, Samuel	1841 E	A226
CONROY, Edward	1842 E	A283	FEERER, Hannah E. etal	1850 G	A594
CONROY, Isaac etal	1845 G	A354	FELDWISCH, William	1843 E	A302
COOK, Augustus	1847 G	A441	FERGUS, John	1837 E	A132
COON, David	1850 E	A564	FERREE, Peter	1842 E	A262
COUNTS, Adam	1848 E	A457	FLINN, James	1822 E	A14
COVILL, William	1843 E	A298	FLINT, Ariel	1849 E	A494
COX, Joshua	1847 E	A432	FOOTE, Henry B.	1824 E	A30
CRAMER, John	1846 E	A391	FOOTE, John B.	1828 G	A47
CROY, Jacob	1840 E	A190	FOOTE, Wm. McLean	1824 G	A27
CROZIER, Robert etal	1841 G	A240	FORSYTHE, James	1838 E	A148
CURTISS, Joshua	1839 E	A178	FOSNIGHT, George	1849 E	A487
CURRYER, Joseph C. etal.	1848 G	A472	FOSNIGHT, Henry	1850 E	A568
CURTNER, Peter	1844 E	A341	FOSNIGHT, Martin	1849 E	A486
			FOX, John	1841 E	A228
DAVENPORT, Abraham	1838 E	A149	FOX, Thomas	1839 E	A179
DAVENPORT, Elizabeth etal.	1839 G	A185	FOX, Thomas	1840 G	A114
DAVIDSON, Ephrain	1835 E	A99	FRANCIS, Jemima	1849 G	A540
DAVIDSON, John	1843 E	A423	FRANKEBERGER, Joel	1842 E	A293
DAVIS, Dalinda etal.	1846 G	A407	FRY, Christian	1846 E	A392
DAVIS, Mary	1836 E	A120	FULTON, Benjamin	1847 E	A415
DAVIS, Mary	1836 G	A127	FURMAN, Joel	1849 E	A502
DAVIS, Oliver P.	1837 G	A134	FURROW, James G.	1842 E	A284
DAVIS, Tobiatha	1822 G	A12	FURROW, John P.	1849 E	A498
DAY, Henry	1841 E	A231	FUSON, Jane	1849 G	A526
DAY, Lewis	1831 E	A63			
DAY, Lewis etal.	1835 G	A113	GAMBLE, Elizabeth etal	1843 Gnp	B306
DEFREES, Joseph	1826 E	A38	GAMBLE, Samuel	1850 E	A584
DENNY, Samuel S.	1836 E	A117	GEARHEART, James F.	1847 G	A446
DEPPE, Charles etal	1850 G	A595	GEISIER, Philip	1842 E	A290
DEPPE, Julius	1850 E	A577	GERRARD, David W.	1832 G	A68
DEVER, Henry	1850 E	A573	GILHAUS, John H.	1849 E	A493
DEWEESE, Jethro etal.	1849 G	A542	GILLESPIE, John	1849 E	A478
DEWEESE, John M.	1849 E	A512	GOBLE, Clarinda	1839 G	A184
DOAK, Patrick	1849 E	A513	GOCKEMEYER, Henry M.	1847 E	A430
DOBBINS, Joseph	1836 E	A119	GOINGS, George	1848 E	A458
DONSTON, Abraham	1839 E	A166	GOINGS, Samuel W. etal	1848 G	A475
DOWNING, William	1850 E	A576	GOUGE, Robert	1834 E	A92
DRAKE, Abraham etal.	1837 G	A138	GRAHAM, John	1848 E	A466
DRAKE, William	1828 E	A46	GREER, Jacob W.	1841 E	A225
DRAKE, William	1837 E	A144	GROSVENOR, Launson	1849 E	A485
DREES, Tobias etal	1848 G	A476	GROTTENTHALER, George M.	1849 E	A504
DRESSMAN, Herman H.	1849 G	A520	GUMP, John etal	1835 G	A107

543

GUTHRIE, James G.	1844 E	A343
GUTHRIE, Louisa etal	1846 G	A401
HAGELBARGER, Peter etal.	1838 G	A157
HAGELBARGER, Philip J.	1837 E	A137
HALL, Peter L.	1841 E	A229
HALL, William	1846 E	A399
HARDESTY, Benjamin	1840 E	A20
HARDESTY, Robert	1819 E	A2
HARMES, Henry	1841 E	A243
HARMS, Lena etal.	1840 G	A213
HARRISON, Nancy etal.	1831 G	A67
HARTMAN, Peter	1834 E	A82
HARTMAN, Susannah etal.	1835 G	A111
HATHAWAY, Albert K.	1843 E	A301
HATHAWAY, Florence E.	1843 G	A321
HATHAWAY, Mary	1845 G	A368
HATHAWAY, Mary	1847 E	A425
HELSCHER, Barney W.	1850 E	A569
HENRY, David	1834 E	A84
HENRY, William	1843 E	A314
HICKS, Moses	1822 E	A16
HIGGINS, John V.	1840 E	A221
HIGGINS, Nelly	1840 E	A227
HIGGINS, Thomas etal	1840 G	A212
HILBRENK, Francis	1849 G	A539
HILL, William	1842 E	A286
HOLMES, Thomas	1831 E	A64
HOLMES, Thos. & Fanny	1831 G	A66
HORNER, George	1845 G	A369
HOUSER, Daniel	1837 E	A143
HOWE, Morris	1844 E	A336
HUBBLE, Asa	1832 E	A73
HUBBLE, Hezekiah	1838 E	A162
HUGHES, Samuel	1837 E	A139
HUNT, Enoch	1842 E	A274
HUNT, George W.	1843 G	A320
HUNT, Ira	1845 E	A367
HUNTINGTON, William H.	1845 E	A380
HUNTSMAN, Catharine	1834 G	A93
HURLEY, Thomas	1821 E	A9
HURST, Drewey	1845 E	A376
IIAMS, William	1845 E	A366
IKE, William etal.	1834 G	A97
IKE, William	1850 E	A580
IMBUSH, John Gerard	1841 E	A224
IRWIN, Francis	1850 E	A570

JACKSON, Mary Ann etal.	1849 G	A537
JOHNSON, William S.	1846 E	A381
JOHNSTON, Deborah	1847 E	A413
JOHNSTON, Henry etal	1847 G	A442
JOHNSTON, Henry	1849 E	A479
JOHNSTON, John	1846 E	A385
JOHNSTON, Robert	1844 E	A337
JOHNSTON, Samuel R. etal.	1849 G	A538
JOHNSTON, Thomas	1842 E	A291
JOHNSTON, William	1850 Enp	B556
JULIAN, Isaac	1838 E	A158
JULIAN, Jesse etal.	1838 G	A156
JULIAN, Oliver N. P.	1844 G	A348
JULIAN, Pleasant	1842 E	A287
JULIAN, Sarah A. etal.	1842 G	A263
JULIAN, Stephen	1829 E	A55
KNISE, John	1837 E	A141
KELLER, Samuel etal	1835 G	A108
KELLY, Mary Ann	1840 G	A211
KELSEY, Calvin	1843 E	4315
KENNARD, A. C.	1836 E	4118
KENNARD, George etal.	1850 G	4590
KENNARD, Isaac	1841 E	A247
KENNEY, David	1840 E	A202
KENNEY, Nancy	1847 E	A411
KEFLINGER, Jacob	1849 E	A492
KERSHNER, David	1833 G	A81
KINDLE, William V.	1849 E	A481
KING, B. Harrison	1839 E	A176
KING, David	1838 E	A160
KINNEY, George W. etal.	1848 G	A474
KIPLINGER, Elizabeth	1849 G	A524
KIPLINGER, Jas. H. etal.	1849 G	A536
KIRTLEY, John	1834 E	A85
KIRTLEY, William H.	1834 G	A96
KISER, Huldah	1840 G	A198
KIZER, Nicholas	1844 E	A339
KOBERLEIN, Nicholas etal.	1834 G	A95
KOEBERLEIN, N.	1834 E	A91
LAMBERT, Amos	1849 E	A488
LAUGHLIN, Robert	1850 E	A581
LAW, John H.	1849 E	A515
LAWLER, Michael	1850 E	A558
LAYMAN, John	1833 E	A80
LEACH, Nathaniel	1839 E	A165
LEAPLEY, Otho	1839 E	A175
LECKEY, William M.	1850 G	A593
Le FEVRE, Henry J.	1848 E	A455
Le FEVRE, John	1840 E	A203
LEMASTER, Lemuel Q.	1843 E	A303

LEMASTERS, Sally etal.	1843	G	A319
LEMING, Hugh	1850	E	A571
LINE, Levi S.	1835	E	A100
LINN, John	1850	E	A557
LOCHARD, Thomas	1834	G	A94
LOGAN, John	1843	G	A316
LORTON, William	1850	E	A565
LOUTHAIN, Bicy etal.	1835	G	A109
LUTTRELL, Lewis	1837	E	A142
McCASHEN, Absalom etal.	1845	G	A353
McCASHEN, Nancy etal.	1837	G	A129
McCLOSKEY, Michael	1845	E	A372
McCLOSKEY, William N.	1846	G	A409
McCLURE, Enoch etal.	1841	G	A238
McCLURE, Joseph M.	1847	G	A443
McCLURE, Robert	1831	E	A65
McCLURE, Robert	1841	E	A254
McCOLLAM, Robert etal.	1835	G	A110
McCOLLUM, Jacob M.	1832	E	A70
McCORMICK, James	1842	E	A262
McCORMICK, James etal.	1844	G	A349
McCULLOUGH, John	1841	E	A250
McCULLOUGH, Mary etal.	1841	G	A237
McDERMOT, Martin	1850	E	A559
McDONALD, James	1848	E	A454
McDONALD, John	1842	E	A260
McGINTRY, E. B.	1840	E	A205
McKEE, James	1849	E	A497
McKEE, James etal	1849	G	A522
McKEE, John	1848	E	A460
McKEE, John etal.	1848	G	A473
McKEE, Maria etal.	1849	G	A535
McKEE, Sarah	1847	E	A427
McKEE, Thomas M.	1838	E	A150
McLAUGHLIN, James etal	1840	G	A196
McMACKEN, Andrew	1833	E	A77
McMAKEN, Andrew	1845	G	A355
McMULLEN, Daniel	1842	E	A269
McNAMER, Philip	1844	E	A334
McVEY, James M.	1838	E	A152
MANGAN, John	1821	E	A11
MANGAN, Reuben	1826	G	A39
MANN, John	1833	E	A78
MANNING, James	1826	E	A44
MARRS, William	1844	E	A342
MARSHALL, James A.	1838	G	A155
MARSHALL, Samuel	1838	E	A154
MAETIN, Jacob	1835	E	A101
MARTZ, George	1850	E	A555
MARTZ, Mary A. etal.	1850	G	A592

MARTZ, Michael	1849	E	A505
MASON, Charles	1844	E	A340
MAXSON, Simon	1842	E	A275
MELLINGER, B. F.	1850	E	A554
MELLINGER, Jane etal.	1832	G	A69&B68
MELLINGER, Jasper etal.	1850	G	A591
MELLINGER, John	1831	E	A62
MELLINGER, John	1836	E	A122
MELLINGER, John	1849	E	A491
MELLINGER, Joseph	1840	E	A206
MELLINGER, Louisa etal.	1847	G	A439
MELLINGER, Margaret	1849	E	A511
MELTER, August etal.	1849	G	A523
MELTER, Gerhard H.	1850	E	A579
MENDENHALL, Mary E. etal.	1843	G	A326
MENDENHALL, Mordecai	1836	E	A123
MENDENHALL, William	1841	E	A249
MERANDA, Newland	1846	E	A207
MERANDA, Samuel etal.	1850	G	A589
MEYER, John B.	1849	E	A503
MILES, John	1850	G	A588
MILHOLLIN, Edward J. etal.	1837	G	A126
	&	1839	
MILHOLLIN, Jonathan	1834	E	A89
MILLER, Elizabeth etal	1845	G	A356
MILLER, George	1836	E	A124
MILLER, John	1834	E	A73
MILLER, Robert	1839	E	A171
MILLS, Philemon	1847	E	A426
MOORE, Richard H.	1840	E	A215
MORGAN, Aaron	1849	G	A534
MOOTHART, Andrew	1844	E	A338
MOOTHART, Mary A. etal	1843	G	A318
MOYER, George	1822	E	A15
MOYER, George	1850	E	A582
MULVEY, Arthur	1839	E	A181
MUNCH, Eli	1838	E	A161
MUNCH, Mary Jane	1840	G	A197
MUNSEY, Albert S. etal	1848	G	A471
MUNSEY, John	1847	E	A417
MUSSELMAN, Jane	1844	G	A347
MUSSELMAN, Peter	1840	E	A199
MUSSELMAN, Samuel etal.	1837	G	A133
MYERS, David	1842	E	A256
NELSON, John	1850	E	A560
NICHOLAS, Jonathan	1850	E	A572
NISWONGER, Thomas	1838	E	A147
OGLE, Rebecca etal.	1846	G	A400
OGLE, Willis	1849	E	A480
ORBISON, John	1838	E	A153

PACKER, John P.	1839 E	A167		RUGGLES, Elizabeth	1823 E	A21
PARKER, William etal	1841 G	A236		RUGGLES, John	1823 E	A20
PARKS, Isaac	1822 E	A13		RUSH, Jesse	1846 E	A395
PARR, Samuel	1849 E	A509		RUSSELL, Andrew	1822 E	A17
PARTINGTCN, Joseph	1844 E	A335		RUSSELL, Andrew	a842 E	A271
PARTINGTON, Richard	1841 E	A223		RUSSELL, Andrew	1843 G	A333
PATRICK, David	1850 E	A567		RUSSELL, Joseph etal.	1827 G	A42
PATTERSON, Jane	1848 G	A470		RUSSELL, Sarah etal.	1843 G	A322
PATTERSON, Thomas	1847 E	A410				
PEARSON, John J.	1849 E	A499		SARVER, Samuel	1842 E	A281
PENROD, Michael	1840 E	A216		SAVAGE, George P.	1847 E	A431
PENROD, Samuel etal.	1844 G	A346		SCHAPPER, Christian	1849 E	A516
PEPOIT, John etal.	1849 G	A533		SCHAPPER, Henry etal.	1849 Gnp	B483
PERRINE, Urias B.	1846 E	A386		SCHNELLE, Christopher etal.	1838 G	A164
PERSINGER, Jacob	1850 E	A562		SCHNELLE, J. D. Victor	1838 E	A146
PERSINGER, Madison	1829 E	A54		SCHULZ, Dinah etal.	1849 G	A530
PERSINGER, Sarah	1829 G	A57		SCHUMAN, John W.	1848 E	A455
PHILIPS, Elizabeth etal.	1819 G	A1		SCHUPEL, John F.	1846 E	A394
PILSON, Esther	1837 E	A135		SCHWARTZ, Benjamin	1847 E	A434
PONTIOUS, Conrad	1821 E	A10		SCOTT, George	1841 E	A232
POOL, George	1848 E	A462		SCOTT, George L.	1845 E	A365
POOL, Robert	1827 G	A41		SEATON, Ebenezer	1839 E	A183
POST, Isreal	1850 E	A552		SHAFFER, Anton	1848 E	A452
POWELL, Samuel	1842 E	A279		SHAFFER, Benedict	1850 E	A563
PRATT, William	1823 E	A25		SHAFFER, Francis	1850 E	A550
PRILLEMAN, Christian	1840 E	A201		SHAW, Alexander	1841 E	A252
PUTHOFF, G. H.	1842 E	A280		SHAW, Jane L. etal.	1844 G	A550
				SHAW, John	1841 E	A246
Quinn, Ellen etal	1849 G	A532		SHAW, John	1845 E	A351
QUINN, Michael	1849 E	A546		SHAW, Thomas	1849 E	A500
				SHEABLE, Bartholomew	1842 E	A258
REDENBOUGH, John	1847 E	A418		SHEARBAUGH, Michael	1842 E	A276
REDMAN, George	1846 E	A382		SKILLEN, William	1841 E	A251
REED, Hugh M.	1844 G	A345		SKILLEN, William	1843 E	A317
REHLING, Bernard	1845 E	A363		SMITH, Adam	1841 E	A248
RICHARDSON, Zebediah	1823 E	A19		SMITH, George etal.	1847 G	A438
RILEY, Edward	1825 E	A35		SMITH, John	1837 E	A131
RINEHART, Barbara etal	1845 G	A358		SOMMERS, Jacob	1839 E	A182
ROBBINS, Thomas	1845 E	A378		SPRAY, Benjamin	1834 E	A98
ROBERTS, Anderson	1842 E	A288		SPRAY, James etal.	1835 G	A114
ROBERTS, John L.	1845 G	A357		STALEY, Levi	1850 E	A585
ROBINSON, Thos. R. etal	1820 G	A3		STARRETT, Charles	1830 E	A58
ROBINSON, William	1841 E	A222		STARRETT, Elizabeth	1830 G	A59
ROBY, Ruel	1820 E	A5		STARRETT, J. D. M. etal.	1831 G	A60
ROBY, Ruel A. etal.	1823 G	A18		STARRETT, J. D. M.	1846 G	A405
RODGERS, John	1840 E	A204		STARRETT, James etal.	1829 G	A50
ROTCHER, Christian	1840 E	A218		STEELEY, James	1843 E	A305
ROTT, Joseph	1844 G	A344		STEEN, Robert	1823 E	A23
ROTT, Joseph	1850 E	A663		STEEN, Thomas etal.	1824 G	A26
ROTTINGHAUS, Elizabeth	1849 E	4518		STEPHENS, Eliza etal.	1841 G	A242
ROTTINGHOUSE, John F.	1847 E	A433		STEPHENSON, Robert W.	1850 E	A566
ROUTH, John	1845 E	4362		STEPHENSON, Thomas	1840 E	A208

546

STEVENS, Lydia A.	1849	G	A531
STEWART, Elizah	1841	E	A235
STEWART, Evie etal	1836	G	A125
STEWART, Mary	1843	E	A304
STEWART, Moses B.	1832	E	A71
STEWART, Sarah Ann etal.	1843	G	A332
STOKER, Cornelius	1849	E	A547
STONER, William	1843	E	A306
STONEROCK, Samuel	1846	E	A393
STRALHAM, Henry	1850	E	A548
STURGEON, Moses	1849	E	A495
STURM, Henry	1832	E	A72
STURM, Peggy Ann etal.	1824	G	A28
SULLENBARGER, Sam'l etal.	1836	G	A128
SULLIVAN, Burton	1843	G	A331
SULLIVAN, George	1842	E	A294
SULLIVAN, Wiley etal	1843	G	A330
SUMMERS, George	1841	E	A252
SUMMERS, John etal	1839	G	A189
SUNDERLAN D, Joseph	1833	E	A76
SWEENEY, William	1850	E	A583
TAYLOR, Abraham	1849	E	A482
TAYLOR, Ann etal	1834	G	A88
TAYLOR, David	1834	E	A86
TAYLOR, David etal	1835	G	A104
TAYLOR, Margaret	1846	G	A404
TAYLOR, Mary etal.	1835	G	A105
TERSTERGE, Joseph etal.	1842	G	A267
TERSTIEGE, Bernard	1843	E	A307
TERSTIEGE, Henry	1843	E	A308
TERWILLEGAR, Cornelius	1842	E	A277
TERWILLIGER, Nathan etal.	1849	G	A521
THIEMANN, George F.	1849	E	A510
THOKE, John H.	1849	E	A483
THOMPSON, Freeborn	1839	E	A172
THOMPSON, John	1825	E	A33
THOMPSON, Robert P. etal.	1841	G	A241
TILLBERY, Thomas	1849	E	A484
TINAN, Patrick	1845	E	A377
TODD, John	1847	E	A422
TOLBERT, Ruth	1845	E	A364
TRAIN, Christopher	1850	E	A549
TRUBY, Obediah	1840	G	A193
TUCKER, William B.	1843	E	A309
TUNIS, Lindley	1837	E	A130
TUNKS, Philip	1845	E	A352
UNDERWOOD, John etal.	1849	G	A528
UPDEGRAFF, Joseph S.	1847	E	A379

VALENTINE, Daniel	1842	E	A268
VANDEMARK, Catherine	1848	E	A456
VANEMARK, Daniel	1840	E	A209
VANOTE, Rhoda	1846	G	A403
WABBY, Isaac	1824	E	A31
WALTERS, Charles etal	1849	G	A541
WARNACKLEY, David	1847	G	A437
WEBB, James	1848	E	A463
WELCH, John	1842	E	A282
WELLS, William	1838	E	A151
WELLS, William	1842	G	A266
WEST, James	1838	E	A163
WIBBLING, Hiram etal	1840	G	A192
WICKS, John	1846	E	A388
WIDNEY, John	1827	G	A40
WIERBRINK, John	1847	E	A439
WIKOFF, Isaac	1848	E	A468
WILKIN, Sarah j. etal.	1850	G	A587
WILKIN, Stephen	1850	E	A551
WILKINSON, Booth B. etal.	1850	G	A586
WILKINSON, Samuel	1820	E	A7
WILKINSON, Thomas	1828	E	A56
WILLIAM, Matthew	1835	E	A102
WILLIAMS, David B.	1839	E	A180
WILLIAMS, David L.	1829	G	A
WILLIAMS, Walter	1841	E	A233
WILLIAMS, William	1847	E	A416
WILLIAMS, William	1847	G	A444
WILSON, Anna	1847	E	A428
WILSON, Esther	1836	E	A116
WILSON, Cyrus	1831	E	A61
WILSON, Hugh	1841	E	A255
WILSON, Jane E. etal.	1843	G	A329
WILSON, John	1841	E	A234
WILSON, Robert	1829	E	A52
WILSON, Robert S.	1843	G	A328
WILSON, Robert S. etal.	1839	G	A188
WINANS, Louisa etal.	1834	G	A87
WINGET, Louisa etal.	1845	G	A359
WINGET, William	1842	E	A272
WINNANS, Mary E. etal	1847	G	A436
WIPLING, Ann Margaret	1839	G	A187
WIPLING, Herman	1839	E	A168
WISE, Jacob	1829	E	A51
WOMKLDORF, George	1848	E	A467
WOOLERY, Henry	1848	E	A469
WUEBBLING, Anna M.	1843	E	A310
WUEBBLING, Anna M.	1843	G	A327
WYATT, Martha etal.	1837	G	A145
YINGER, Daniel etal.	1845	G	A360
YOUNG, Aaron	1843	E	A300
YOUNG, Michael	1825	E	A34
YOUNG, Samuel	1835	G	A103

There are an unusual number of licenses issued for which no marriage returns were filed. It is possible that a number of these people were married, but the minister or justice of the peace neglected to file the marriage return.

ANDERSON, Joseph D. to Hannah Lareau	lic. 11-7-1831
ARSTINGSTULL, Barnurd to Nancy Pegg	lic. 8-22-1832
BAKER, Clark to Sarah Lawrence	2-23-1832
BAKER, John to Lucinda Flinn	4-15-1833
BARKER, Caleb to Julian Rush	6-24-1830
BARNETT, James H. to Lydia Cane	7-7-1833
BEERS, Thomas to Lucinda Kelly	11-7-1833
BERRY, James to Sarah Ann Winans	11-28-1833
BIRD, John to Phebe Ellsworth	7-9-1833
BOYER, Lewis to Mary Day	9-4-1833
BRACKIN, Isaac H. to Elizabeth Todd	10-28-1830
BRODRICK, Mark A. to Margaret Taylor	11-26-1831
BRODRICK, Nehemiah F. to Margaret L. Henry	8-18-1831
BRYAN, William to Mary Hartman	10-24-1833
BULL, Jacob to Barbary Houser	10-4-1832
BYERS, Samuel to Ann Wilson	7-14-1831
BYRLEY, William to Anne Hardesty	2-18-1830
CANNON, James to Mary Jackson	12-23-1830
CARY, David to Isabella Garard	1-24-1832
CARY, Thomas to Catharine Cole	7-18-1831
CARY, Wm. A. to Catharine Vandemark	5-14-1833
CASPER, John to Susannah Wyett	5-16-1833
CECIL, Bazel to Mary Plummer	10-20-1831
CECIL, Shelby to Sarah Cane	8-25-1831
CECIL, Stewart to Lydia Casper	lic.11-12-1833
CECIL, Wm. W. to Alidza Mellinger	7-18-1833
CHILDERS, Thos. to Sarah Hopkins	1-20-1831
CHILES, George to Elizabeth McVey	9-12-1833
CLARK, Samuel to Sarah Crozier	8-31-1831
CLAWSON, Andrew to Mary Kiggins (Higgins)	lic. 3-15-1830
CLAWSON, Henry to Sarah Bryan	8-22-1833
CLAWSON, Ichabod to Allis King	1-27-1833
CLAWSON, Israel to Nancy Boyer	3-20-1830
CLAWSON, John to Anna Keness	7-21-1833
COLE, Samuel to Mary McVay	3-26-1833
COLEMAN, Thomas to Katharine Bogart	7-31-1831
COLLETT, Lemuel G. to Elizabeth Donoven	5-18-1830
COON, Joseph to Margaret Jeffers	10-30-1831
CORUS, Silas to Polly Austin	11-14-1833
CORY, John to Martha Ellsworth	2-17-1833
CRAIG, James to Delila Jackson	10-18-1832
CROY, James to Mary Ann Young	8-15-1833
CROZIER, John to Jane Patterson	lic. 10-4-1831
CROZIER, Richard J. to Susan McCane	3-28-1833
DAVENPORT, John to Clarinda Brodrick	4-17-1833

```
DAVIS, Daniel to Margaret Stout                              9-25-1832
DAVIS, James to Pressocy Young                               2-9-1832
DAVIS, Tubal C. to Catherine Mellinger                      12-16-1830
DAY, John W. to Rosanna Stoker                               5-23-1832
DEEDS, John R. to Sarah Ditto                                9-20-1832
DEFREES, Thomas J. to Nancy Blankenship                      6-6-1831
DOUK, William to Eliza Jane Sturgeon                         2-17-1831
DUNN, Robert to Sarah Day                                   12-11-1832
EDWARDS, John S. to Sophia Mills                            11-6-1831
ELDRIDGE, Elijah to Elizabeth Gibson                         6-10-1830
EVANS, Walter to Mary Staley                                11-24-1831
FOX, Daniel L. to Rosannah Christman                         9-17-1833
FRANCIS, Jonathan to Elizabeth Baker                         4-1-1832
FRANCIS, Richard to Minerva Moore                           11-8-1832
GATES, David to Sarah Tice                             lic. 3-13-1832
GINN, John to Mary Ann Johnston                              1-5-1833
HARDIN, Taylor to Eliza Danner                              10-21-1831
HARRIER, Samuel to Hannah Austin                             2-27-1830
HATHAWAY, Silas D. to Sarah Hathaway                         3-24-1832
HEATH, Jesse to Eliza Redinbaugh                             7-1-1830
HENDERSHOTT, David to Mahitabel Gerard                       5-6-1830
HENDERSON, John to Ann Clawson                         lic. 3-29-1830
HIGGINS, Francis to Mary Doak                                1-3-1833
HIGGINS, William to Clarissa Boyer                           9-26-1833
HOLLY, Manning to Jerusha Hubbell                            5-30-1831
HOUSTON, David to Cynthian Ellis                             6-7-1832
HOWELL, Jefferson to Martha Barker                    lic. 12-21-1831
HUBBLE, Hezekiah to Mary Flinn                               2-21-1831
HUNT, Doran T. to Sarah Franklin                             7-25-1833
HUNT, Enoch S. to Ruth A. Franklin                          12-25-1832
IKE, Paul to Sarah Reynolds                                 10-25-1832
IKE, Samuel to Rebecca Mangen                                2-28-1833
IRWIN, James to Christena Sturrett                           3-31-1831
JACKSON, Morris W. to Elizabeth Gilbert                lic. 2-19-1832
JOHNSTON, John B. to Jane Castle                       lic. 4-25-1832
JOHNSTON, John to Christena Rinehart                   lic. 5-31-1832
JOHNSTON, William to Mary Drake                              5-22-1832
JONES, Zacariah to Lucy lee Clayton                          1-31-1833
JUSTINE, Michael of Seneca Co. to Sarah Smith                9-12-1833
KELLY, Dan to Emoline Coleman                                3-13-1830
KENDALL, Benjamin to Mary Boggs                        lic. 12-15-1832
KENNARD, A.D. to Rebecca Blake                               1-24-1832
KINDALL, John to Jane Long                                  11-28-1833
KINNARD, William to Nancy Cole                               4-25-1833
KIRTLAN, William to Sarah Bryan                              8-30-1832
LANE, Joseph K. to Lucinda Underwood                         3-22-1832
LAYMAN, John to Margret Steele                         lic. 1-4-1831
LEADLY, John to Minerva Hubble                         lic. 3-12-1833
LEFAVORS, David to Eliza Mellinger                           1-3-1830
```

549

```
LEMASTERS, Lemuel to Hannah Albright                      lic. 5-24-1832
LEMASTERS, Luman W. to Nancy Young                             1-19-1832
LENOX, John to Hetty Stephens                                 2-10-1831
LUCAS, John to Mary Fullen                                    11-4-1830
LUCAS, Joshua to Jane Parke                                   4-29-1830
LUNG(?), Jacob to Sarah Beckman                               4-15-1833
LYONS, Jacob to Mary Barber                                   2-14-1832
McCLURE, Samuel to Susannah Farrow                            1-10-1833
McCOLLOUGH, Robert to Amanda Lenox                            2-18-1830
McCULLOCH, Samuel H. to Mary Spray                            6-21-1831
McDANIEL, Wm. to Sally Williams                          lic. 3-11-1833
McFARLAND, John Q. to Frances M. McFarland                    1-15-1832
McKINNEY, Jesse to Elizabeth Carter                           8-15-1832
McLEAN, James to Ann Debo                                     1-22-1833
McVAY, Thomas to Jane Lemasters                               3-15-1831
MADDEN, Henry to Matilda Williams                             8-14-1832
MANN, John to Rachel Berry                                    9-23-1832
MAPES, Benjamin to Sophia Clawson - consent: Ichabod Clawson3-3-1831
MARSHALL, Jacob to Lusinda Moore                              3-26-1833
MARTIN, Timothy to Hannah Tilberry                       lic. 4-2-1833
MAULT, Charles to Elizabeth Hubble                       lic. 9-8-1831
MEDARIS, Jonathan H. to Demaris Lucas                        12-12-1831
MILLER, Abraham to Mary Ellis                                10-25-1830
MILLS, Joseph to Mary Harmond                                 4-10-1831
MOUNTS, William to Susan C. Green                            10-6-1833
MURPHEY, Thomas to Eliza Jane Stout                           8-28-1832
MURPHEY, William to Celia N. Harris                           5-8-1831
MUSSLEMAN, John to Sarah Robinson                            12-3-1831
MYRES, Jacob F. to Jane Flinn                                 7-11-1833
NEAL, John to Jane Wilson                                    10-25-1831
NEAL, Richard A. of Champaign Co. to Charlotte Chiles         8-25-1831
NEWCOMB, Matthew to Mary Cary                                10-6-1831
NOGGLE, Thomas I. to Katharine Danelson                       1-20-1831
PATTEN, Thomas to Rachel Randall                              3-4-1832
PEARSON, Charles M. to Margaret Zemer                        11-20-1831
PEER, Thomas to Sophia Ike                                    5-2-1832
PERDU, Eli G. to Milly Risor                                 10-31-1830
PIERSON, Sampson to Nancy McClure                             8-1-1832
PLUMMER, Joseph to Hulday Mann                                4-22-1830
RARIDAN, Saml. to Sarah Gerard                           lic. 2-16-1833
RECTOR, Joseph to Elizabeth McDaniel                     lic. July 1833
REDENBAUGH, David to Peggy Lucas                              3-30-1830
REED, Richard to Elizabeth Van Bluricum                  lic. 6-23-1831
RICHARDSON, Erie to Marjary Stewart                           6-10-1832
RICHARDSON, Thomas to Phebe Carter                            3-3-1831
ROBERTS, Anderson to Sarah Louthin                            9-11-1832
ROBERTS, Andrew to Jane Skillen                               4-20-1830
ROBERTS, James M. to Terresa Armstrong                        9-8-1832
ROBERTSON, William to Sarah Medaris                           2-15-1831
```

```
RODGERS, Richard to Catharine E. Johnston               5-2-1833
RUCKMAN, Thomas W. to Mary Roberts                      6-28-1833
SCOTT, Theopilus to Betsey Beden - consent: Benj. Beden  2-20-1831
SHAW, Samuel to Mary Stephenson                    lic. 10-20-1831
SHIPLEY, John to Nancy Hashan (Hushan)                  9-9-1832
SIMMONS, Charles to Rachel Wilkinson                    1-30-1831
SPEACE, Henry to Elizabeth Conroy                       4-4-1833
SPIECE, John to Hannah Mere                             1-28-1830
SPRAGUE, John to Margaret Baggs                         4-29-1830
SPUR, John to Nancy Richardson                          8-4-1831
SROUFE (SROUSSE), George to Isabel Grimes               9-16-1830
STALEY, Reuben to Nancy Ann Richardson                  2-18-1830
STEWART, Daniel to Catharine Savage                     3-30-1833
STEWART, Richard to Arlinda McCabe                 lic. 6-9-1831
STOKER, Elijah to Lydia Day                            12-6-1831
STOKER, Jacob to Sophia Whisman                         3-21-1830
STOKER, Jno. W. to Margaret Hoshan                      6-9-1833
STONE, Daniel to Elizabeth Cecil                        3-8-1831
STURM, George to Mary Ann Stout                         3-14-1833
STURM, Henry S. to Elizabeth Osborn                     3-13-1831
SULLEVAN, Newton M. to Elizabeth Thompson               8-8-1833
SWAN, Lauson to Elizabeth Kinman                   lic. 3-3-1832
THATCHER, Jacob to Nancy Goodin                         4-1-1830
THOMAS, Ezekiel to Adeline Safford                     12-8-1831
THOMPSON, Stephen of Miami Co. to Phebe Hardesty       12-6-1832
TILBERRY, Abraham to Margaret Flinn                     9-30-1830
TILBURY, Thomas to Serina Boston                        2-26-1833
TULEY, William to Mary Houston                     lic. 4-20-1832
VANBLICOME, John to Nancy McNamer                       6-3-1830
VANCAMP, Thomas to Nancy Rector                         8-14-1831
VANDEGRIFT, Jesse to Eliza Carroll                      2-19-1833
WATTS, Benjamin to Elizabeth Dunlap                lic. 9-14-1831
WILEY, John to Isabella Sturgeon                        4-28-1831
WILEY, William H. to Margaret Sturgeon                  8-29-1833
WILFONG, Hiram to Hannah Shapley                       11-10-1831
WILLIAMS, Daniel P. to Mary Shaw                       11-29-1833
WILLSON, Robert to Sarah Sharr                          2-5-1833
WILSON, James to Prudence Eldridge                     10-13-1831
WILSON, William to Lucy Willson                         1-22-1833
WOOLOET, Saml. to Eliza Fugate                          4-15-1830
WORLEY, Stephen G. to Anna D. McClenehan               10-28-1830
WRIGHT, John to Rebecca Shaw                            2-5-1833
WRIGHT, William to Caroline Widney                      6-29-1830
YOUNG, Aaron to Elizabeth S. Layman                     9-13-1832
YOUNG, Isaac to Wilmoth Lucas                           7-28-1833
ZEMER, George to Elizabeth Day                          8-29-1833
ZUMER, Abraham to Mary Flumer (Plummer)                 1-21-1830
```

Page on which record may be found is given in parenthesis. Deed Book A can be found in the Recorder's Office at the court house at Sidney.

ROBY, Ruel of Turtle Creek twp.; Inventory and account 4-24-1821; recorded 7-25-1821. (102)

BOTKIN, Charles, Inventory 5-25-1820. (129

BENNETT, John of Cinthiana twp.; Inventory 10-11-1820

MANGAN (MAUGAN), John; Account 2-9-1822; recorded 7-25-1822. (143)

PONTIOUS, Conrod of Loramie twp.; 11-28-1821; recorded 7-25-1822; Property set off of widow, Susana Pontious and account filed. (143)

HULSLY, Thomas of Loramie twp.; Inventory 1-5-1822; recorded 7-27-1822. (151)

MANGAN (MAUGAN), John; Inventory 5-18-1822; recorded 7-30-1822; one quarter section land on Swifts Run in Miami County with a house and improvements on it; one half quarter on Lormies Creek in Shelby County with one payment paid on it with a small improvement on it; 320 acres in Arkansas Territory and $53.81½ cash. Snow Richardson, adms. (156)

ROBY, Ruel; account 5-20-1822; recorded 7-30-1822. (157)

HURLEY, Thomas of Loramie twp.; bill of sale of goods 1-10-1822; Mary Hurley, adms. (159)

MOYERS, George; inventory 10-18-1822; recorded 3-18-1823. (186)

HICKS, Moses of Cynthian twp.; inventory 10-5-1822; recorded 3-22-1823. (189)

FLINN, James Sr.; will; dated 7-1-1822; filed 11-11-1823; recorded 4-24-1823. Wife, Mary and her children to have two half quarter sections of land whereon we now live. To Daniel C. Flinn, James Flinn and George N. Flinn, three quarter sections of land in Illinois State being N½ Section 30, Township 13 North, Range 9 and also quarter of Section 12, Township 6 South, Range 3 West as appropriated for military bountys in state of Illinois. Three dollars each to Mary McCinne, William Flinn and Margaret Houston. (note: no relationships on above are stated). Executors: wife Mary Flinn and son, Daniel C. Flinn. Signed: James Flinn. Wit;Wm Gibson and Alexander Miller. Signed and attested to in Shelby Co. (191) Inventory of James Flinn of Cynthian twp. (229). Accounty filed on estate 4-19-1823. (237)

MORRIS, George Sr. of Cynthian twp.; inventory 10-17-1822; recorded 4-24-1823.(192)

RUSSELL, Andrew of Turtle Creek twp.; inventory 11-11-1822; recorded 4-24-1823; sale bill of estate 10-10-1822. (194 & 236)

PUNCHUS (PONTIOUS), Conrod; list of debts due estate 11-11-1822 recorded 6-4-1823. (109)

PARKS, Isaac; inventory 12-27-1822; recorded 6-4-1823 (217-291)

WILKINSON, Samuel; appraisement of estate 11-27-2823. (185)

RUGGLES, Elizabeth; inventory 10-29-1823. (286) sale bill. (289)

552

The following records were abstracted from Will Book A, pages on which record may be found have been given in parenthesis. Dates on which wills were
recorded were not given. Wills have been listed as they appear, thus, in
some instances it may be possible to determine fairly accurately the approx-
imate date of recording by checking the dates of the surrounding wills.

STANTON, William - dated 13th day, 1st month, 1811. Sons:- William, James,
Latham, Laccheus (or Zaccheus) and Aaron Stanton. Daughters:- Sarah Gardner,
Hephzibah Holloway, and Deborah Stanton. Executors:- Sons, James, Laccheus
and Aaron; Amos Holloway, and Micajh Macy Joynt. Signed: William Stanton.
Witnesses: William Hamlin, John Hamlin, Timothy Grumell, Ely Johnston and
Britain Johnston. (1)

EDGINGTON, John - dated 8-21-1812. Wife, mentioned but not named. Sons:-
Isaac, Aaron, John and Noah. Daughters:- Rebecah, Sally, Peggy and Nancy.
Executors:- George Alben and his son, William Alben. Signed: John Edginton.
Witnesses:- Matthew Rowland, Abraham Stephens and James Barber. (1)

SHIVELY, Jacob of Osnaburg township - dated 2-3-1814. Wife, Elizabeth. Sons:
Jacob and Uly Shively. Daughters:- Susan Thomas, Mary Thomas and Elizabeth
Weller. Executors:- Jacob Shively and Uly Shively. Signed: Jacob Shively
(German signature). Witnesses: John Studybaker, Jacob Bowers and Robert
Huston. (2)

BEACHTLE, Jacob of Canton township - dated 12-20-1813. Wife, Catharine.
Sons:- David, John, George, Jacob, Martin, Frederick, Daniel and Thomas
Beachtle; David was not of age. Daughters:- Magdalena Flora, Barbara
Brothers and Mary Beachtle. Executor:- Son, John Beachtle. Signed:-
Jacob (his mark) Beachtle. Witnesses:- David Silver, John Richards and
Leonard Mowan. (4)

SHORB, Peter - dated 3-28-1814. Wife, Mary. Five brothers:- John, Jacob,
Stephen, Andrew and Adam. Executor:- Brother, John Shorb. Signed:- Peter
(his mark) Shorb. Witnesses:- Andrew Rappe, Judith Leaky and Joseph (his
mark) Croninger. (5)

WESHLER, Henry of Plain township - dated 4-15-1811. Son-in-law, George
Snyder and Catharine his wife. Son, Christian, his children—Nancy, Henry
and Catharine. Son, Henry. Son, George. Son, Jacob. Daughter, Barbara,
dec'd late of Huntington County, Pennsylvania, her children (not named).
Daughter, Margaret Hermon. Executors: Friends, Jacob Shumbarger and Simon
Essig. Signed: Henry Weshler (German signature). Witnesses: James
Campbell and Dan'l McClure. (5)

JOHNSTON, Britan - dated 20th day, 3rd month, 1815. Children: Drusilla,
Hordah, John and Robert. Executor: Son, Robert Johnston. Signed: Britan
(his mark) Johnston. Witnesses: Jesse Fetts and Shadrah Fetts. (7)

SHIVELY, Jacob of Nimiskillen township - dated 11-23-1814. Wife, mentioned but not named. Mentions sons and daughters but only names sons, Jacob and Daniel. Executors:- John Bower and John Studybaker. Signed: Jacob Shively. Witnesses:- Henry Boughman, Jr. and James McFaddin. (7)

CAMPBELL, William - dated 7-10-1815. Wife, Ruth. Children: James Campbell, Ephraim Campbell, William Campbell, Margaret Campbell, Ruth Campbell, Dugal Campbell, Rachael Campbell, Able Campbell, Benjamin Campbell and Mary McCoy. Executor: Son, James Campbell, Jr., also, James Campbell, Sr. of Fayette County, Pennsylvania. Signed:- William Campbell. Witnesses:- James F. Leonard and Richard Hardgrove. (9)

ELDREDGE, James of Tuscarawas township - dated 3-5-1816. Wife, Sarah, Sons: Nathan, William, Stephen and Thomas. Daughters:- Polly Vial, Abigail Wood and Sarah Austin. Executor:- Son, William Eldredg. Signed: James (his mark) Eldredg. Witnesses: John Meacon, Edward Otis and Lucy Wood. (10)

HALL, Parnel of the town of Osnaburgh - dated 7-18-1816. Niece, Francys Collins daughter of John Collins. Bequeath to: Lititia daughter of Isaac Hall, Francys Erel daughter of Gilberthorp Erel, Parnel Hall son of Able Hall and Parnel Kineer son of Thomas Kineer; relationships if any, not stated. Executors:- Bilberthorp Erel and John Sluss, Esq. Signed:- Parnel Hall. Witnesses:- John Sturdybaker, George Gregory and Henry Tawney. (10)

CROFFERT, Joseph of Osnaburgh township - dated 5-23-1816. Wife, Margaret. Sons:- John and Jacob Croffert. Daughters:- Magdalena, Catharine, An Mary and Christina. Mentions money coming from his sister. Executor:- Son, John Croffert. Signed:- Joseph Croffert (German signature). Witnesses:- John Sturdybaker, John Bower and Jacob Leonal. (11)

PAUELLUS, Daniel of Addison township, Yeoman. - dated 6-17-1816. Wife, Hanney. Children:- Mentions children but only names son, Jacob. Mentions money in Woodbary township, Huntingdon County (Pa.). Executors:- Wife, Hanney and Abraham Lezer. Signed: Daniel Paules. Witnesses:- Johannes --?-- and Simon Spitler. (12)

DEWALT, Valentine of Oznaburg township - dated 10-28-1816. Wife, Magdalen. Sons:- Valentine and Philip. Daughter:- Magdalena. May be other children not named. Executors:- Son, Philip and wife, Magdalena. Signed:- Valentine Dewalt (German signature). Witnesses:- John Surdybaker, John Dungan and Henry Tawney. (13)

THOMPSON, John of Dierfield, Portage County, Ohio - dated 9-25-1813. Wife, Rebeccah, also to serve as Executrix. Signed:- John Thompson. Witnesses:- Wm. Reed and Elizabeth (her mark) Hazen. (14)

HEWITT, John of Sandy township - dated 1-30-1817. Brothers: William and James Hewitt. Sisters:- Margaret Creighton, Catharine Mayes, Fanny, Nancy and Mary Ann. Niece, Anna Creighton. Newphews:- John Creighton, Jr., James Creighton son of John Creighton, Sr., and Robert Creighton. Bequeath to Mary Ann Faulk, relationship, if any, not stated. Executors:- Peter Mottice and James Creighton. Signed:- John Hewitt, Witnesses:- Peter Mottice and Alpheus Brown. Codicil dated 2-5-1817 mentions brother-in-law, John Creighton, Sr. Same witnesses. (15)

CHIDESTER, Ephraim - dated 2-3-1817. Wife, Mary. Sons:- James, Ephraim, Thomas and Samuel. Daughter:- Elenor. Step-daughter:- Margaret M. Common. Grandchildren:- Maria Samuel, Jacob Jennings and Elenor Harris. Executors:- Wife, Mary; sons, Samuel and Ephraim Chidester; and Wm. Henry. Signed:- Ephraim Chidester. Witnesses:- Amon (or Amos) Hart, Jane Manmant and Thos. Rotch. (17)

MILLER, Michael of Nimiskilling township - dated 8-5-1817. Wife, Mary. Children:- Catharine, Mary, Jacob, Jonathan, David, Michael and Joseph. Executors:- Son-in-law, Samuel Bosserman and son, Jacob Miller. Signed:- Michael Miller. Witnesses:- John Sturdybaker, Daniel Mathias and Ezekiel Marsh. (18)

RIDER, Chrisdana of Sugar Creek township - dated 8-13-1816. Sister, Mary. Brother, Jacob, he is to have bond and divide between his three brothers and one sister. Signed:- Chrisdena (her mark) Rider. Witnesses:- William Nicholas, Conrad (his mark) Eagler and Valentine Wagoner. (19)

GREEN, Freelove of Charleston, Brooke County, Virginia - dated (no month and day given) 1815. Brother, Samuel Tillinghast. Nephew, Samuel Tillinghast. Niece, Sarah Collins widow of Holdon Collins. Niece, Sarah Hammond wife of Charles Hammond. Niece, Eliza T. Vilette daughter of my beloved niece, Mrs. Patience T. McWilliams. Friends, Mrs. Stevens, Sally Stevens and Eliza Stevens of Rhode Island. Bequeath to John Fling of Charleston the perceptor of niece, Eliza T. Vilette. Executrix:- Eliza T. Vilette of Charleston. Signed:- Freelove Green. Witnesses:- Jesse Edgington, W. Dewalt and S. R. Bakewell. (20)

SNIDER, Nicholas - dated 1-24-1816. Sons: George, Jacob, Michael and Peter Snider. Daughter, Susanna wife of David Wiley. Daughter, Elizabeth Snider now Row. Daughter, Magdalena, dec'd, late wife of George Row, her heirs-- John, Sally, Elizabeth, Magdalena, Catharine, Jacob and Lydia Row. Daughter, Christina Snyder. Executor: Benjamin Bryfogle. Signed: Nicholas Snyder (German signature). Witnesses:- John Kryder and George Roin(?). Codicil dated 1-24-1816 names wife, Barbara. Same witnesses. (21)

SAPPINGTON, Thomas of Pike township - dated 2-3-1818. Wife, Mary. Daughter, Mary to have Big Bibbol. Sisters: Mary Cocks, Racheal Sagere and Marththree Sappington. Executors: Wife, Mary and John Shott. Signed:- Thomas Sappington. Witness:- Pitney Guest. (22)

555

WORLEY, John of Sandy township - dated 12-16-1817. Wife, Mary. Sons:-
Thomas, Michael, Daniel, Eaky (also given as Akey), Joseph and Jacob.
Daughters:- Mary, Rebecca, Catharine and Nancy. Not all children were of
age. Executors:- Daniel and Peter Shafer. Signed: John (his mark) Worley.
Witnesses:- James McElroy, Henry Shane and John Shane. (23)

FLICKINGER, Christian of Canton - dated 12-17-1817. Friend and nurse, Mrs.
Pryscilla Petit. Brothers:- Jacob, Michael and John Fleckinger. Sisters:-
Peggy Cline and Polly; mentions their children, but does not name. Deceased
wife's brothers and sisters:- George Cribs, Jno Kroft, Frederick Kroft, and
Phillip Kroft (Note: George Cribs appears to be husband of deceased wife's
sister). Executors: Jacob Ropp, and John Shorb. Signed:- Christian
Flickinger. Witnesses:- Anthoney Weyer, George Fogle and Wm. Raynolds.
Codicil dated 12-18-1817 gives no additional information. (24)

WARDEN, Robert - dated 4-30-1818. Wife, Ruth, who is now expecting a child.
Bequeath to Mary Jean, one of two daughters of first wife Margaret, the other
daughter being deceased. Bequeath to brother, John Warden's two daughters,
Mary and Martha Warden; also mentions that John has two additional daughters
but does not name. Requests to be buried in Graveyard near first wife.
Mentions land in Wayne County, Ohio. Executors:- John Warden, Robert Lytle
and Andrew Lytle. Signed:- Robert Warden. Witnesses:- Ebenezer Shaw and
Jacob Jemim(?). Codicil dated 5-3-1818 mentions Mary Jean's two cousins,
Margareta Lytle and Polly Rendols. Lytle daughters of Robert Lytle,
Same witnesses. (26)

FULTON, Benjamin - dated 6-13-1818. Sons:- William, John and George Fulton.
Daughters:- Isabella, Rachael and Elizabeth Fulton. Executors: Peter
Johnson and Stephen Harris. Signed:- Benjamin Fulton. Witnesses:- Peter
Johnson, James Ervins and William Walker.

PORTER, Moses - dated 8-31-1817. Wife, Mary, also to serve as executrix.
Nephew, Moses Porter, son of Isaac Porter. Signed: Moses Porter,
Witnesses:- James Reed and William Hardesty. (28)

HATTON, Aquilla of Baltimore County, Maryland - dated 11-19-1811; recorded
Baltimore County, Maryland 9-23-1818. Wife, Ann. to have land called,
"Thompson's Choice" and lot in Baltimore. Sons:- Zachariah, Aquilla,
Caleb, John, Wesley, Joshua and Francis Asbury Hatton. Daughters:- Ann
Weaver, Elizabeth Greenfield, and Mary Stansbury. Mentions land in Ohio.
Executors:- Wife, Ann and son, Aquilla. Signed: Aquil Hatton.
Witnesses:- Philip Chamberlain, Henry Guyton and John Guyton. (28)

MARKLEY, Christopher of Green township - dated 2-12-1816. Wife, mentioned
but not named. Sons:- Daniel and John. Daughters:- Catharine, Christina,
Elizabeth, Susana, Mary and Esther. Executors:- Sons, Daniel and John.
Signed:- Christopher (his mark) Markly. Witnesses:- Henry K. Burg and
Michael Young. (30)

556

OPPERT, Andrew - dated 4-7-1819. Wife, Susannah, also to serve as executrix. Daughter, Elizabeth Dayhoff. Signed:- Andrew Oppert. Witnesses:- Jesse Stewart, James Baxter and Jacob McGish. (31)

BAIR, Rudolph - dated 8-13-1819. Wife, Barbara. Sons:- George, Christopher, John and Daniel Bair. Daughters:- Susana wife of John Smith and Elizabeth Bair a single woman. Mentions land in Section 8, Township 17, Range 6 which includes a sawmill. Executors:- George Bair, Christopher Bair and Daniel Bair. Signed:- Rudolph Bair. Witnesses:- Jacob Miller and D. Burget. (32)

HERDMAN, Jacob of Osnaburg township - dated 12-25-1819. Wife, mentioned but not named. Children:- Christian, Jacob, Magdaleen, George, Catharine, Daniel and Susana; not all children are of age. Executors:- Sons, Christian and Jacob. Signed:- Jacob Hardman, (German signature). Witness:- John Studybaker. (33)

WARE, Tobias - dated 11-18-1819. Wife, Catharine. Children: John Ware, Peter Ware, Elizabeth Ware, Hannah Ware, Catharine Moetz and Polly Spangler. Executors:- Son, Peter Ware and Henry Butterbaugh. Signed:- Tobias Ware. Witness:- Jacob Bachtel. (34)

FAULKS, Mary Ann of Sandy township - dated 7-18-1820. Father, Andrew, also to serve as executor. Mother, Anna. Sister, Sophia. Brothers, John and Andrew. Requests that a head-stone be put on her grave and also on grave of Nancy Ann. Signed:- Mary A. Faulks. Witnesses:- Alpheus Brown and Alexander Cameron. (35)

SCHLOSSER, Henry of Canton township - dated 6-24-1818. Wife, Mary. Children, mentioned but not named. Executors:- Jacob Schlosser and John Sluss. Signed:- Henry Schlosser. Witnesses:- John (his mark) Zerbe and --?-- Young. (36)

PENIX (PENICK), William of Bethehem township - dated 11-2-1820. Wife, Sally, to have cow brought from Pennsylvania. Sons:- John, James, Jacob, Caleb and William Penix. Daughters: Nancy, Hannah and Nelly Penix. Requests that he be buried in Mathias Shepler's Graveyard. Executor:- Nicholas Stump. Signed: William (his mark) Penix. Witnesses:- Abraham Shepler and Matthias Shepler. (37)

ARMSTRONG, Robert - dated 10-30-1820. Wife, Ezebella. Sons:- Robert, William, John, George and James. Daughters:- Elizabeth Shepherd, Mary Adaway, Ann Henderson and Ezabella. Executor:- Joseph Shepherd. Signed:- Robert Armstrong. Witnesses:- Charles Patch, George Armstrong and Harvy Shoemaker. (38)

PATTIT, Pessella - dated 3-16-1820 - Son, George Fogle. Son, Peter Prince.
Administrators:- Jacob Rob and George Cribbs. Signed: Prissili (her mark)
Pattit. Witnesses:- Gersham Norris and George Cribbs. (39)

BULL, Hezekiah of Mount Stanhope - dated 18th day, 2nd month, 1820. Son,
George Washington Bull of Loudonville, Richland County, Ohio. Daughters:-
Maria, Louisa W., and Emmele C. Bull. May be more children. Mentions shares
in Hartford Bank. Executor:- Thomas Taylor of Loudonville, Richland County,
Ohio. Signed:- Hezekiah Bull. Witnesses:- Aaron Chapman, Mayhew Folger,
Mary Folger and James Duncan. (39)

WISE, Peter of Plain township - dated 10-2-1821. Wife, mentioned but not
named. Sons:- Adam; Abraham; Daniel, dec'd, his children—Peter, George,
Elias, Sarah and Aney Wise; Andrew and his wife Hannah, to have land testator purchased from Jacob Painter of Stark County; Peter; and Jacob.
Daughters:- Catharine Shidelar; Susannah Tombough; Hannah Zoller, to have
claim on plantation in Washington County, Pennsylvania which testator sold
to his son Andrew; Molly Bricker; Elizabeth Wise; and Rebecca Wise.
Mention mills. Executors:- Anthony Hausel and John Hoover. Signed:-
Peter Wise. Witnesses:- John Staly, Samuel Bander and John Shenebarger.(39)

THOMAS, Samuel of Plain township - dated 12-23-1821. Wife, mentioned but not
named. Son, John Thomas. Executor: John Hoover. Signed:- Samuel Thomas.
Witnesses:- Peter Wise, Philip Goerges and Joseph (his mark) Ebie. (41)

MACEUTERFER, George - dated 4-22-1820. Sons:- George Jr., dec'd, his heirs
(not named); John; William; Jacob; and Christian. Daughters:- Susana Seiner;
Mary Bair; Catharine Hidigh, dec'd, her children (not named); Christina
Livingston, dec'd, her children not named except for her oldest son, George
Firestone. Executors:- Son, John and John Augustine. Signed:- George
(his mark) Maceuterfer. Witnesses:- John Augustine, Samuel Dewese and
Jasper Daniel. (42)

STEWART, Jesse - dated 1-2-1822 1-2-1822 - Wife, Elenor. Five children:-
Thomas, Isabel, Charity, Charles and Edward. Administrators:- Wife,
Elenor and Wm. Elson. Signed:- Jesse Stewart. Witnesses:- Wm. Elson
and John Baxter. (43)

SHAW, John of Tuscarawas township - dated 3-19-1819. Wife, Rachel. Son,
Ebenezer Shaw. . Daughter, Rachel Pirkins. Grand-daughter, Rachel Fulton.
Executors:- Ebenezer Shaw and John Warden. Signed:- John Shaw.
Witnesses:- Daniel Hoy and Charles Hoy. (43)

BROWN, Henry of Nimishillen township, Yeoman - dated 10-5-1816. Wife,
Christina. Daughter, Christina. Executors:- Martin Houpes and Christian
Hoover. Signed:- Henry Brown (German signature). Witnesses:- Henry
Bachman, Frederick Obenouer and David Hoover. (44)

BURDEN, Job - dated 18th day, 3rd month, 1822. Wife, Mary. Sons:-
David, Levi, Reuben and Job Burden. Daughters:- Sarah Stanley, Hannah
Hutton, Mary Elliot, Lidia Burden, Anna Burden and Rachel Burden.
Executors:- William Hutton and Francis Elliot. Signed: Job Burden.
Witnesses:- Nathan Gaskill, Daniel Gaskill and Job Holloway. (45)

KOUHLMAN, Jacob of Canton township - dated 3-16-1822 - Wife, Machderline.
Children:- Jacob, John, George, Jonas, William, Machtalena and Catherine.
Executors:- Sons, Jacob and John. Signed:- Jacob Kohlman.
Witness:- John Trump. (45)

McNAMARA, Hugh - dated 4-22-1822. Wife, Sarah, also to serve as executrix.
Children:- Robert, James. Mag, John and Jane. Mentions money coming from
tract of land sold in Crawford County, Pennsylvania by testator to Hezekiah
Segur. Signed:- Hugh McNamara. Witnesses:- John Reed, Alex'd Snodgrass
and Thomas Latta. (46)

The following records were taken from "Will Record 1-2-3-4" located in the Probate Court at the court house in New Philadelphia. Page on which record may be found in the original volume is given in parenthesis.

KELLER, Martin Sr. - Estate filed 4-24-1809, "...that whereas Martin Keller Senior late of said county deceased, died intestate, and that at the time of his decease was seised of Divers goods and chattles to the value of hundred dollars and upwards.." David Peter and Henry Keller appointed adms. on petition 6o have adms. appointed filed by Henry Keller, Martin Keller and Verona Keller. Inventory filed 6-16-1809. Account filed 4-24-181-, names widow, Eva Keller. (1-3)

MOSSER, Samuel of Lawrence twp. - dated 1-14-1811; recorded April 1811. Wife, Catrena, "150 acres where I now live", house and lot in Lawrenceville to be sold. Mentions children but does not name, not all are of age as mentions that "all sons to learn trades as soon as they become fourteen years of age or sooner." Mentions that Timothy Lamperson to be raised by wife Catrena until he is fourteen years of age. Executors: wife, Catrena and Abraham Mosser. Signed: Samuel Mosser. Witnesses: Abraham Mosser and Catrena Mosser. (3)

KNESTRICK Frederick - dated 8-1-1811; recorded Nov. 1811. Wife, Margaret. Eleven children: John, William, Jacob, Elizabeth, Henry, Jeremiah, Mary, Catharine, Nancy, Margaret and Sally. Executors: son, John Knestrick and Richard Burrel. Signed: Frederick (his K mark) Knestrick. Witnesses: Christian Deardorff and John Burress. (4)

YOUNG, Jacob of New Philadelphia - dated 8-20-1812; recorded Dec. 1812. "Am Drafted in the Militia of Ohio and is going to the Army." Appoints brother, John Young as agent or attorney for him to take all property and estate in his care and Jacob Young. Witnesses: Abraham Knisely and James Clark. (4)

ITZEN, Philip of New Philadelphia - dated 7-2-1813; recorded August 1813. Wife, Frances. Children: Elizabeth wife of Jacob Knisely, Lewis Itzken, William Itzken, Ann Mareah Itzken, John Itzken, Phillip Itzken and Christopher Itzken, not all are of age. Executors: son-in-law, Jacob Knisely and friend, Abraham Knisely. Signed: Philip (his X mark) Itzken. Witnesses: John Knisely, Peter Williams and James Clark. Codicil dated 7-2-1813 gives additional references to land only. Signed: Philip (his mark) Itzken. Witnesses: same as above. (4-5)

KASEBERR, John Jr. - dated 7-24-1813; recorded August 1813. Sons: John, David and Jacob. Daughters: Mary; Agnes; Catherine; Hannah; Elizabeth Riply. Executors: Matthias Burtzfield and Conrad Roth. Signed: John Kasebeer. Witnesses: Michaek Kore and Nathan (mark) Peticord. (5-6)

RATEKIN, James - dated 6th day, 4th month, 1813; recorded 10-5-1813. Daughter, Jane Ball to have land in Section 6, Township 14, Range 7. Daughter, Sarah Gregg to have SW¼ & NW¼ Section 10, Township 11, Range 4. Grandson, James R. Haigg to have 107 acres SW¼ Section 30, Township 13, Range 6 with tanyard thereon. Grand-daughter Sarah Hutts to have NE¼ Section 8, Township 15, Range 7. Rest of property to be divided among all grandchildren when youngest grandchild now living becomes of age. Executors: Samuel Barber, Isaac Parker, Peter Thomas and Morgan Lewis. Signed: James Ratekin. Witnesses: Curtis Grumble, William Judkins, James Judkins and Mervick Starr. (6)

GINTER, Peter Sr. - dated 1-9-1814; recorded 4-28-1814. Wife, Elizabeth. Eight children: Catherine, Christian, Susan, Peter, Mary, Justina, John and Abraham. Friend, Jacob Winch to be guardian of two youngest sons, John and Abraham. Executors: wife, Elizabeth and friend, Jacob Winch. Signed: Peter Ginter. Witnesses: Christian Blickendorffer and John Blickendorffer. (6-7)

O'DONNOLD, Cornelius of Salem twp. - dated 4-6-1814; recorded 4-28-1814. Wife, Rachel O'Donnold, maiden name of Webb. Sons (in order of age): James O'Donnold, Cornelius O'Donnold, William O'Donnold and Daniel O'Donnold. Daughters (in order of age): Patty O'Donnold, Elisabeth O'Donnold, Emelie O'Donnold and Eleanore O'Donnold. Executors: wife, Rachel and friend, Boaz Walton, Esq. Signed: Cornelius (his x mark) O'Donnold. Witnesses: Henery Davis, Casper Engler and George G. Miller. (7)

COLVER, John of New Philadelphia - dated 12-30-1813; recorded 4-28-1814. Names oldest daughter, Polly, not of age; mentions other children but does not name. Owned house and lot no. 535 in New Philadelphia, also other lots in same place and also land near Coshocton. Executors: Nathaniel Colver and Godfry Westheaver. Signed: John Colver. Witnesses: Peter Andreas and John Romig. (7-8)

EVERT, Thomas - noncupative will with deposition given 4-28-1814; recorded April 1814. Boaz Walton and Peter Edmonds Jr. say that Thomas Evert of Salem twp. a single man about three or four weeks ago in his last sickness made a verbal will giving his youngest brother, Charles Everet all property. Executor, brother, John Everet. Witnesses: Boaz Walton and Peter Edmonds. (8)

WARNER, Jonathan of Gnadenhutten, Washington County, Northwest Territory, yeoman- dated 6-10-1802; recorded April 1814. Wife, Sarah and brother-in-law and friend, Joseph Everett of Washington Co. Signed: Jonathan Warner. Witnesses: Nathan Warner, Joseph Everett and John Heckwelder. (8)

JINNINGS, Simeon of Oxford twp. - dated 3-15-1814; recorded August 1814. Children: Hetebel Jinnings, Mary Jinnings and Washington Jinnings. Bequeaths sorrell horse, saddle and briddle to Conrad Westhaver. Executors: Boaz Walton, Esq. and Conrad Westhaver. Signed: Simeon Jinnings. Witnesses: Henry Everett, Alexander Hubbard and Christian (his mark) Westhoever. Codicil dated 3-16-1814 "positively and absolutely disinherit my wife Elenor". Signed: Simeon Jinnings. Witnesses: same as above. (9)

GLENN, John of New Philadelphia - dated 6-29-1813; recorded August 1814. "...and whereas I am resolved to go out and serve my country in this present war as an enlisted soldier". Bequeaths lots 95 and 96 in New Philadelphia to Henry Shuller and his heirs. Signed: John Glenn. Witnesses: Christian Espich, John Williams. (9)

GRAM, Henry - dated 2-1-1815 (1813?); recorded August 1814. - Wife, Hester. Mentions children not of age but does not name. Executor, Jacob Urich. Signed: Henry Gram. Witnesses: Thomas Williams, Boaz Walton Sr. Codicil dated 2-1-1815 (1813?) states wife is to receive one one third should she remarry. Signed: Henery Gram. Witnesses: same as above. (9-10)

BEST, Samuel of Goshen twp. - verbal will dated 5-25-1816; deposition given 6-4-1816; recorded 8-29-1816. Wife, Agnes Best. Children mentioned but not named, some are still living at home. Witnesses: Doctor Jacob Benoss, Jacob Casebeer, David Casebeer. Widow, Agnes Best appointed adms. of estate with will annexed. (10)

FOUCKLER, Godlieb of Goshen twp. - dated 10-15-1816; recorded Dec. 1816. Wife, Maria Barbara. Children: Phillip, Jacob, Adam, Godlieb, Henery, Magdaline, Daniel, Eve and Catharine. Mentions money coming from twelve bonds from Jacob Opp of York Co., Pennsylvania and money due from William Griffeth of Bedford Co. (Penna.). Executors: son, Henery and son-in-law, Frederick Shull. Signed: Godlieb Fouckler. Witnesses: Christian Espich and Jacob How. (10-11)

UHRICH, Michael - dated 7-31-1817; recorded August 1817. Sons: Michael, Jacob, to keep grist and saw mill; John. Daughters: Hannah and Catherine. Step-son, John Huber. Mentions "all my children" so is questionable if more children or not. Executors: sons, Jacob and Michael. Signed: Michael (his x mark) Uhrich. Witnesses: John Roming, Nathan McGrue. (11)

SHUSTER, Daniel - dated 6-5-1818; recorded Sept. 1818. Wife, Margaret Shuster to have one thousand dollars. Bequeaths to: George Study, quarter of Section 33, George Tressel quarter of Section 36, George Horninger quarter of Section 6, Michael Smith quarter of Section 12, Henery Macamon quarter of Section 23, Adam Macamon quarter of Section 17, Samuel Shuster quarter of Section 27, all in Township 15, Range 7; also to--John Welsh quarter of Section 25 and to Thomas McCrerry quarter of Section 25, both in Township 16, Range 7. Bequeaths to: John Shuster a quarter of a section of land (not stated or described), clock, silver watch, etc.; Sarah Shuster three lots being 400 & 42, 400 & 43, 400 & 83 in New Philadelphia. "If they all keep house together until John is of age, kitchen furniture to be divided equal between widdow, Samuel, John and Sarah Shuster". Executor: Thos. McCreery. Signed: Daniel Shuster. Witnesses: Lewis (mark) Macamon, George Trassal. (12)

BLICKENSDERFER, Christian Sr. of Warick twp. - dated (not given); recorded 6-10-1820. Wife, Barbara, interest of $2000.00 bank stock owned in Farmers Bank of Lancaster, Pa. and house where now live. Children: Maria wife of Abraham Ricksecker, Christiana Elizabeth, John, George, Christian, Elizabeth. Executors: son, Christian and son-in-law, Abraham Ricksecker. Signed: Christian Blickensderfer Sr. Witnesses: Jacob Blickensderfer and William Blickensderfer. (12-13)

CRITZ, Jacob of Dover twp. - dated 6-14-1820; recorded 3-31-1821. Wife, Elizabeth Critz. Sons: Andrew, Harry, George, John and Peter Critz; Andrew to learn trade of tanner. Daughters: Susan Overholt, Elizabeth Critz, Margaret, Katy and Sarah. Executors: Frederick Swinehart and Abraham Overhalt. Signed: Jacob Critz. Wit_ nesses: Isaac Thomas and Josinnus Crillery. (13)

SHANNON, Thomas - dated (not given); recorded (not given-1821). Wife, Rebecca, also to serve as sole executrix. Children: (five oldest) Temperance, Enos, Rebecca, Nancy and Eliza (Eliza not of age), (youngest daughter) Charlotte, (youngest son) Joseph. Signed: Thomas (his mark) Shannon. Witnesses: William Sharon and Joseph Huff. (14)

PIERPOINT, Elenor of Oxford twp. - dated 11-17-1820; recorded (not given-1821). Daughter, Sarah wife of Daniel Booth, to have all personal estate. Executors: friends, George Harris and William Harris. Signed: Elenor (mark) Pierpoint. Witnesses: Nicholas Neighbour and Jesse Hill. (14)

MOSSER, Abraham - dated 1-14-1822; recorded Jan. 1822. Wife, Mary. Daughters: Mary Taylor, Elizabeth Hormish and Eve Good. Grandchildren, Mary Good now Mary Stout to have two lots in Lawrenceville. Granschild, Susanna Blosser. Three sons-in-law, John Taylor, Christly Hormish and Jacob Good. Executors: John Macham and John Taylor. Signed: Abraham (his x mark) Mosser. Witnesses: George Brantingham and Henry Hidegrass. (14-15)

GLASS, Jacob - dated 1-19-1822; recorded April 1822. Wife, Eve Glass, income from SE¼ Section 17, Township 14, Range 7 until youngest child is of age. Daughter, Catharine Stoneman. My heirs: Matthias, Sarah, Elizabeth, Marton, John, Solomon and Mary Glass. Executors: Henry Snider and Matthias Glass. Signed: Jacob (his x mark) Glass. Witnesses: Benjamin Price and John (mark) Stoneman. (15)

GARMIRE, Francis - dated 12-24-1821; recorded 1-17-1822. Wife, Elizabeth Garmire. Sons: William (eldest), John and Christopher Garmire. Mentions 84 acres S½ SW¼ Section 3, Township 14, Range 7. Executor: son, John Garmire. Signed: Francis Garmire. Witnesses: William (mark) Gamble, Abraham Barnerd. (15-16)

FACKLER, Barbara, widow of Goshen twp. - dated 2-6-1822; recorded 4-15--1822. Son, Godlieb Fackler, also to serve as sole executor. Signed: Barbara Fackler. Witnesses: Michael Redinger and William Butt. (16)

WARNER, Mary of Oxford twp. - dated 5-7-1818; recorded April 1822. Niece, Mary Brook daughter of Benjamin Brook. Sister, Lidy Brook wife of Benjamin Brook. Mentions sister, Liddy Brook's children but doesn't name except for Mary. Executors: friends, Jesse Walton and Adam Stocker. Signed: Mary (her x mark) Warner. Witnesses: Andrew Creter, John Hogland and Nicholas Neighbour. (16)

GIMLINS, George of Dover twp. - dated 9-12-1821; recorded August 1822. Wife, Catharine. Sons: Bernhart, Joab, John. Daughters: Margaret wife of George Kuhn, Barbara wife of Henry Fackler, Elizabeth, Sarah. Executors: sons, John and Bernhart. Signed: George Gimlins. Witnesses: George W. Canfield, Abraham Snyder. Codicil dated 7-6-1822 gives no additional information. Witnesses: same as above. (16-17)

WALTER, Peter of Dover twp. - dated 2-8-1822; recorded August 1822. Wife, Elizabeth Walter. Mentions brother, George Walter, dec'd, who bequeathed legacy to testator. Son: Martin. Executors: Abraham Overholt and Martin Walter. Signed: Peter Walter. Witnesses: John Weibel, Michael Welty. (18)

GILPIN, Samuel - dated 10-27-1821; recorded April 1822. Wife, Sarah Gilpin, land being SW¼ Section 17, Township 5, Range 1 as sold at Zanesville and also she is to serve as sole executrix. Mentions "my children" but does not name. Signed: Samuel Gilpin. Witnesses: Ephraim Sears and Jane Sears. (18)

SELDENRIGHT, David Sr. of Sugarcreek twp. - dated 11-8-1822; recorded April 1823. Wife, Mary. use of place where now live during her natural life being NE¼ Section 18, Township 8, Range 4. Son, David Seldenright. Daughters: Catharine wife of Charles Still, Elizabeth wife of Michael Frock, Rebecca wife of Supple Kurns, Catharine Seldenright, Mary wife of George Mary, Modena wife of George Conter, Christiana. Executor: George Conter. Signed: David (his x mark) Seldenright Sr. Witnesses: Allen Richardson, George Richardson, Thomas Richardson. (18-19)

HOUCK, Jacob - dated (no month and day given) 1821; recorded 4-3-1823. Wife, Margaret, land where now live being SE¼ Section 23, Township 13, Range 6, during her natural life. Sons: Jacob and Henry. Daughters: Elizabeth and Catharine. States that wife is now pregnant and should the heir be male, property is not to be sold until he is 21 years. Witnesses: William Perkins, Joseph Rutter and lot Jeming. (19)

VAN LEHM (VAN LEHR), Henry of Warwick twp. - dated 4-1-1820; recorded Feb. 1823. Wife, Mary, also to serve as sole executrix. Two sons: Henry and Benjamin. Signed: Henry Van Lehn. Witnesses: Jacob Blickensderfer and John Blickenaderfer. (19-20)

BLICKENSDERFER, George of Warwick twp. - dated 7-29-1823 recorded August 1823. Wife, Susanna use of all personal property and house where not live until youngest child is of age. Children: Sally, Thomas, Catharine, Rosanna and Mary. That testator recently seized as tenant in common with brothers John and Christian Blickensderfer and sister Maria Rickseker to two tracts of land adjoining land of sister Maria Rickseker and lately owned by testator's sister, Christiana Elizabeth now dec'd and whereas by verified contract with Gabriel Romig husband of dec'd sister, he is to have one of tracts as soon as deed can be made. Executor: cousin, Benjamin Blickenaderfer, Esq. Signed: George Blickensderfer. Witnesses: John Blickensderfer and Christian Blickensderfer. (20)

HARBAUGH, John Sr. of Sandy twp.- dated Sept 1823 (no day given); recorded 10-11-1823. Wife, Elizabeth Harbaugh. Deed to be made to NE¼ Section 4, Township 10, Range 1 in U. S. Military District to three stepchildren: Philip Woodring, Elizabeth wife of Isaac Harbaugh and Luisa Wilhelmena wife of James Reanes (Reaves). Testator's children: John Harbaugh Jr., Samuel Harbaugh, David Harbaugh, Benjamin Harbaugh Jr., Isaac Harbaugh, Amos Harbaugh and Amalia wife of Philip Swanck. Executor: son, Isaac Harbaugh. Signed: John Harbaugh. Witnesses: Henry Laffer and Peter Shaffer. (21)

THOMPSON, John of Warren twp. - dated 11-18-1822; recorded March 1824. Wife, Susanna. Mentions that moveable property is to be equally divided between Frederick Thompson, Jacob Thompson and Michael Thompson (relationship if any is not stated). Daughter, Mary, to haver her portion at time of her marriage. Mentions "H.B." but does not state any relationship if any. Executor, Adam Sherod of Warren twp. Signed: John (his x mark) Thompson. Witnesses: Samuel Knight, John Ramsberger. (22)
WORFORD, William - dated 28 day, 1st month, 1824; recorded March 1824. Wife, mentioned but not named. Sons: William and John. Daughters, mentioned but not named. Signed: William Worford. Witnesses: Isaac Skeets, Isaac Masters, Nicholas Aldridge (21-22)
MOONINGER, George - dated 7-6-1823; recorded March 1824. Wife, Elizabeth. Children mentioned but not named, not all of age. If wife remarries, Adam Mackaman to be guardian of children. Signed: George Mooninger. Witnesses: Jacob Shaffer, George Trussell. (22)

ANDRESS, Peter to Nancy Miller	9-28-1811
ARNOLD, John to Elizabeth Judy	3-27-1810
BARR, Joseph to Christeena Peffer	4-22-1812
BARRAT, Arthur to Elizabeth Wolf	11-13-1817
BEAM, Joseph to Jane Wares	1-30-1814
BEAMER, Peter to Ruth Kelly	8-21-1817
BEAUGHER, George to Sarah Shull	2-17-1817
BEAVER, Jacob to Lovey Norris	1-16-1810
BENELL, William to Catharine Laughbaugh	12-17-1816
BEST, Isaac to Catharine Knable	7-30-1811
BLAUCH, Christian to Elizabeth Weldy	11-2-1817
BLICKENSTUFFER, George to Susannah Bickle	11-19-1811
BOYLES, Thomas to Susannah Cazier	1-23-1816
BRENIZER, Henry to Nancy Wallic	10-20-1814
BUNTREGER, John to Magdalena Rensberger	12-26-1816
BURROWAY, Michael to Mary Miller	2-17-1813
BUTLER, Absolom to Jane Lene	3-21-1811
BUTT, William to Susanah Wimer	8-22-1815
CAPLES, Robert to Eloner Tracy	2-21-1813
CAPLES, Robert F. to Charlotte Laffer	2-23-1812
CARR, Aquilla to Drusilla Trimplin	3-8-1809
CARR, Benjamin to Mary Jennings	3-23-1809
CARR, William to Catharine Good	10-5-1808
CASEBEER, John to Sarah Smiley	6-19-1817
CASEBIER, Jacob to Elizabeth Knisely	4-4-1809
CASEY, Benjamin to Lydia Demuth	10-19-1815
CASTLEMAN, David to Ann Crawford	2-16-1815
CHERYHOLMES, Jacob to Mary Itzken	4-1-1813
CLINE, Jacob to Elizabeth Stall	11-21-1813
COGAN, Jacob to Lydia Sell	6-6-1813
COLLET, William to Sarah Hill	2-18-1813
CORDERY, Noble to Margart Smith	11-17-1811
CORRELL, Jacob to Eloner Porter	3-25-1817
CRAIGE, John to Hannah McCune	3-2-1809
CREEMER, Henry to Elizabeth Speck	1-30-1812
CREITS, George to Catharine Herbaugh	3-24-1814
CREITZ, Andrew to Mary Herbaugh	2-7-1811
CRIPLIVER, Jacob to Catharine Bloom	11-12-1811
CRITS, Nicholas to Susana Humel	9-19-1816
CROSS, Isaac to Sophia Pedycoart	2-5-1815
CROWEL, Henry to Elizabeth Amick	5-10-1816
DALY, William A. R. to Ann Pedycoart (no date given)	—-(1815?)
DEARDORFF, Christian to Peggy Butt	12-18-1817
DEEDS, Daniel to Catharina Noll	10-6-1816
DICKEY, John to Mary Deetz	10-5-1817
DOWDS, Martin to Mary McEntire	4-21-1811
EDMONDS, David to Elizabeth Knaus	9-12-1809
EDMONDS, Edward to Susana Rhoads	12-17-1816
EDMONDS, Nathaniel to Mary Smith	6-14-1810

```
EDMONS, Peter Jr. to Hannah Walton                                    4-14-1818
EDWARDS, John to Charlotte Trumbs                                     12-22-1812
ELLES, Richard to Agnes Best                                         9-4-1817
ESPICH, Jacob to Catharine Tarr                                      1010-1814
ESPICK, John to Elizabeth Young                                      2-8-1816
EVERETT, Henry to Elizabeth ODonnell                                 5-25-1815
EVERETT, John to Rebeccah Taylor                                     12-7-1809
EVERETT, Joseph to Barbara Miller                                    2-21-1811
EVERETT, Joseph, Sr. to Rachel ODonnald                              9-15-1814
EVERETT, Moses to Mary Burroway                                      4-3-1810
EVERHEART, George to Catharine Buntriger                             9-10-1816
FACKLER, Godfove to Hannah Hemminger                                 1-1-1816
FELLERS, Abraham to Susanah Mack                                     10-3-1815
FIREBAUGH, John to Elizabeth Friend                                  5-10-1812
FLICKENGER, John to Margaret Demuth                                  4-7-1812
FRANTZ, David to Rachel Collet                                       4-27-1813
FREDERICK, Peter to Verone Keller                                    2-22-1813
FRY, Samuel to Sarah Simmers                                         11-8-1814
GARDNER, Joshua to Catharine Neighbour                               11-16-1816
GOHEN, Hugh to Sarah Richardson                                      3-3-1812
GOUSER, David to _____ Miller(her given name not stated)             8-22-1813
GOUTER, George to Magdalena Seldonwright                             9-6-1814
GOVETER, Jacob to Mary Miller                                        5-4-1817
HALL, Samuel to Carroline Painter                                    7-8-1817
HARGRAVE, Richard to Susanna Byerly                                  10-21-1817
HEARTLINE, Peter to Christena Palmer                                 4-6-1817
HEARTLY, John to Mary ODonnell                                       5-7-1811
HEMINGER, Andrew to Barbara Philips                                  10-21-1817
HENDERSON, James to Sarah Cordra                                     6-9-1816
HENELY, Samuel to Elizabeth Flickenger                               11-1-1814
HENRY, Abraham to Lucy Ayres                                         9-29-1811
HERBACH, Benjamin to Judith Knaus                                    9-18-1817
HERBAUGH, Daniel to Catherine Stickle                                5-3-1809
HERBAUGH, David to Margaret Becher                                   3-6-1810
HERBAUGH, Frederick to Rhody Smily                                   10-3-1815
HERBAUGH, Isaac to Elizabeth Woodring                                12-8-1812
HERBAUGH, Samuel to Jane Gibbs                                       9-19-1809
HERMAN, Levi to Mary Wilson                 (1815?)                   12-27-1816(?)
HOOPENGARDEN, Jacob to Sarah Baltzley                                11-28-1816
HOVERSTOCK, Conrad to Martha Bowers                                  9-12-1816
HOVERSTOCK, Tobias to Peggy Kollar                                   5-1-1817
HUFF, Samuel to Caty Streavy                                         10-4-1817
HYMES, George to Catharine Mosser                                    10-30-1814
ISENAGLE, John to Ann Beamer            (no date given)              1812-1813(?)
ISENOGLE, David to Eliza Muncy                                       7-11-1816
JAMES, Thomas to Nancy Meeks                                         4-7-1812
JENNINGS, Amos to Hannah Patterson                                   Aug. 1810
JININGS, Belly to Alesebeth Collet                                   10-21-1817
JOHNSON, Amos to Euphema Heston                                      3-3-1814
```

```
JOHNSON, Joseph to Christenah Lambe                              1-4-1810
JOHNSON, William to Sarah Delong                                12-3-1812
JOHNSON, William to Sarah Heckerthorn                           10-9-1817
KASEBEER, Samuel to Mary Shull                                  3-10-1817
KASSBER, David to Agness Woods                                  1-4-1817
KELLER, Henry to Mary Frederick                                 6-3-1816
KELLY, James to Ann Kent                                        12-20-1810
KISER, Daniel to Mary Dormer                                    3-11-1810
KLINE, Henry to Becky Flickinger                                11-15-1809
KLINE, John to Mary Giering                                     12-27-1810
KLINE, Philip to Margaret Caken                                 7-20-1817
KLINGLESMITH, Peter to Sarah Gard                               4-16-1815
KNAUS, Thomas to Susan Reichman                                 9-4-1817
KNIESTER, Jacob to Mary Magdalene Knaus                         6-18-1811
KNISELY, Jacob to Elizabeth Itzken                              6-10-1813
KUHN, George William to Margaret Gimling                        3-20-1810
LACEY, William to Nancy Bockman                                 1-25-1810
LAFFER, Bartholow to Catharine Mosser                           11-30-1815
LAFFER, Philip to Mary Caples                                   6-11-1816
LAMBERSON, Timothy to Elizabeth Mosser                          2-22-1809
LANEHART, Daniel to Elizabeth Shanks                            1-12-1817
LAPPIN, Samuel Jr. to Comfort Hillery                           10-23-1817
LAUGHLIN, John C. to Nancy Boyd                                 1-30-1816
LEMOUYON, Stephen to Elided Norris                              3-7-1808
LONG, Joseph to Catharine Winclepleck                           5-18-1817
LUCKENBAUGH, Abraham to Rosannah Herkedron                      9-8-1813
LUKE, George to Eve Bickle                                      2-4-1812
LYNN, Adam to Ibby Williams                                     7-21-1814
McCLASH, Robert to Catharine Walters                            6-16-1815
McCREARY, John to Peggy Slute                                   10-28-1810
McCREERY, Thomas to Christena Shuster                           8-15-1815
McGREW, Nathan to Mary Huston                                   3-6-1817
M_____, William to Mary Delong (rest of surname not given)      3-5-1812
MADDEN, Joseph to Drusilla Richardson                           7-24-1817
MARKS, James to Rebecca Mills                                   7-10-1817
MARRY, George to Mary Sullenwright                              6-7-1814
MILLER, George to Margaret Leininger                            8-26-1813
MILLER, Henry to Magtilena Showalter                            5-23-1816
MILLS, Samuel to Catharine Willard                              2-19-1811
MISER, Frederick to Elizabeth Bickle                            2-18-1812
MOONEY, John to Rachel McCleery                                 2-14-1815
NEEL, George to Mary Crist                                      7-8-1817
NEIGHBOUR, John to Margaret Neighbour                           11-16-1816
NELSON, James to Ann Swoveland                                  11-7-1816
NEWPORT, Henry to Hannah Sell                                   10-11-1810
NORES, Charles to Catharine Baker                               3-2-1817
ODONNALD, James to Catharena Dustimer                           5-6-1813
OMY, Aantony to Elizabeth Write            (1816?)              12-21-1817
OTIS, Jesse to Charlotte Davy                                   4-17-1817
```

OVERHOLE, Joseph to Barbara Kline	4-13-1817
OVERHOLT, Abraham to Susannah Creitz	5-3-1814
PATEES, Isaac to Cactrena Kyser	11-13-1808
PATTERSON, Aaron to Amelia Rubert	10-20-1811
PATTERSON, William to Catharine Snider	1-15-1811
PEDYCOURT, John S. to Nancy Good	6-7-1814
PENCE, John to Eve Baughman	10-16-1814
PEPPERS, John to Catharine Reardon	4-3-1817
PRICE, Christopher to Elizabeth Guygar	4-3-1817
REBSTOCK, George to Sarah Hymes	5-13-1813
REEVES, Joseph to Sarah Ane Kraus	9-18-1817
REGHERT, Conrad to Elizabeth Good	7-17-1808
RICE, Joseph to Salome Heckewelder	9-29-1808
ROBINETT, James to Sarah Mith	10-19-1813
RUSSEL, Samuel to Rebeccah Neal	2-8-1814
SADDERIS, Frederick to Mary Best	9-17-1815
SCHOOLY, Richard to Rachel Wilson	3-15-1812
SCOTT, Thomas to Isabella Carlile	2-13-1817
SELL, Jonathan to Margaret Douglass	5-20-1812
SELL, Peter to Peggy Lucas	2-21-1811
SHALENBERGER, Jacob to Catharine Miller	1-23-1812
SHAMEL, George to Sarah Demuth	12-18-1810
SHANKS, James to Christeena Helwig	9-5-1813
SHENMAN, Henry to Julianna Bickel	10-22-1811
SHOUP, John Jacob to Barbara Muma	6-12-1814
SHULL, Frederick to Catharine Fauekler	9-24-1814
SHULL, Isaac to Hannah Shenk	9-10-1811
SIMMERS, Jesse to Mary Ginther	9-16-1817
SLUTHOWER, George to Mary Stiffler	2-9-1815
SLUTS, John to Catharine Kollar	3-1-1816
SNELBAKER, John to Elizabeth Kline	1-22-1809
SNIDER, Adam to Sarah Frantz	3-24-1811
SPRINGER, Mathias to Susanah Curry	11-15-1817
STEEFE, Jacob to Rachel Ruebart	2-13-1817
STEELSMITH, John to Catharine Flickenger	11-12-1815
STEPHENS, Zacheriah to Elizabeth Schooly	6-12-1817
STIFFLER, John to Hetty Funk	2-27-1817
STOUGH, Samuel to Susanah Knisely	1-2-1817
STOUT, George to Christina Fagy	12-8-1816
SUTHERLAND, Vachel to Mary Williams	2-6-1817
SWARTZ, John to Mary Baker	3-6-1817
SWENK, Philip to Amelia Herbaugh	4-18-1815
SWITZER, John to Catharena Waltman	3-24-1812
TAILOR, John to Catharine Ginther	5-2-1811
THOMAS, George to Rebeccah Wallick	1-19-1815
UHRICH, Jacob to Anna Maria Demuth	1-17-1809
UHRICH, Michael to Mary Balsly	3-19-1812
VANPELT, Daniel to Catharine Huston	2-20-1812
VARANDE, Aaron to Mary Collet	12-26-1811

568

```
VENAMON, Edmond to Margaret McIntire        3-8-1815
WADE, John to Sarah Jennings                8-3-1813
WAGGONER, Mathias to Nancy Delong           1-27-1814
WALLICK, Jacob to Elizabeth Hoverstock      5-6-1817
WATTLE, Joseph to Elizabeth Tanner          8-27-1817
WEAVER, Frederick to Mary Beamer            9-18-1810
WELDY, George to Sarah Altman               12-24-1816
WELDY, Jacob to Elizabeth Butt              11-7-1810
WELDY, John to Hannah Allman                7-22-1812
WELDY, Philip to Sarah Overholt             5-13-1816
WEST, Morris to Sarah Lacey                 4-2-1812
WHITEHEAD, David H. to Elinor Young         12-11-1817
WIELAND, Peter to Lydia Srimplin            7-13-1812
WILLARD, Henry to Susan Giegler             1-15-1811
WILLARD, Lewy to Catherine Wilcock          11-27-1817
WILLIAMS, Benjamin to Mary Jennings         12-12-1816
WILLIAMS, Levy to Nancy Tracy               9-25-1817
WILLIAMS, Peter to Mary Knisely             2-25-1813
WILLIAMS, Thomas to Drusilla Jennings       5-9-1816
WILSON, Joseph to Martha Holmes             11-2-1815
WINCKLEPLECH, Philip to Rosannah Kyser      7-10-1813
WINCKLEPLECK, Jacob to Catharine Kyser      10-22-1811
WOLF, Edward to Catharine Kasebeer          4-23-1815
WOLF, John to Mary Cram                     4-2-1817
WOLF, William to Catharine Ripley           10-16-1812
WORTH, James to Charity Kent                11-26-1810
WYNING, Jacob to Elizabeth Baker            8-29-1813
YANT, Henry to Margaret Stucty              8-22-1816
YOUNG, Henry to Barbara Rank                9-16-1817
YOUNG, John to Sarah Albright               10-1-1811
```

TUSCARAWAS COUNTY, OHIO - MARRIAGES 1818-1823

The following marriages were taken from "Book 1-2-3" found in the Probate Court at the court house at New Philadelphia. This book, the only one available is a transcription.

ADAMS, Joseph to Jane Ayres	6-28-1821
ALBAUGH, Eli to Hannah Pearch	1-1-1822
ALBERT, Abraham to Catharine Hoopingarner	7-9-1820
ALDMAN, Jess to Mary Spencer	10-5-1823
ALLISON, Wm. to Martha Keller	1-26-1819
ALLWOOD, Christopher to Elizabeth Witman	11-12-1823
ALTMAN, Isaac to Nancy Wallick	7-10-1821
ANTROBOSS, Geo. to Salethy French	9-18-1820
ARCHIBOLD, Thomas to Linny Berry Andrews	6-14-1821
AULT, Mathias to Eliza Ann Harbough	4-15-1821
AX, Geo. to Elizabeth Snyder	4-25-1822
AX, John to Nancy Collins	4-13-1820
BACHLER, John Martin Middaugh	4-17-1823
BAKER, Abraham to Eve Kline	9-16-1819
BALTZLY, John to Elizabeth Baker	11-29-1819
BALTZLY, Peter to Catharine Ridinger	10-24-1822
BARR, Alexander H. to Bridget D. Dome	9-29-1818
BARRICK, Abraham to Hannah Beamer	4-8-1821
BARRICK, Isaac to Mary Swaley	3-14-1822
BARRON, Jacob to Magdalene Formey	3-8-1821
BARTON, Joseph to Elizabeth Butt	2-1-1821
BAUMAN, John to Susanna Noles	11-10-1822
BAYES, Peter to Mary Morgin	9-14-1823
BEAMER, Adam to Catharine Study	7-5-1821
BEAMER, Geo. to Elizabeth Study	2-11-1819
BEAMER, Isaac to Mary Yant	9-23-1819
BEAVERES, Geo. to Catharine Best	5-23-1822
BEER, Rev. Joshua to Susanna Mcfolurene(McFarland?)	4-15-1823
BELLMAN, Andrew to Elizabeth Ginther	12-29-1822
BENELL, Andrew to Barbara Hostetter	4-6-1819
BENFER, Philip to Sarah Humerichouse	7-8-1821
BENINGER, John to Elizabeth Rager	1-9-1821
BENNER, John to Sarah Mills	12-24-1818
BENNETT, Michael J. to Caroline Benepe	1-30-1823
BEST, Adam to Mary Moore	4-18-1822
BEST, John to Tresse Buel	1-9-1821
BEST, Solomon to Margret Bevene	11-25-1819
BLICKENSDERFER, Abraham to Elizabeth Tachudy	12-9-1821
BLICKENSDERFER, Benjamin to Barbara Frederick	10-22-1818
BOODRIFF, Nathan to Mary Knisely	1-14-1821
BOUGHMAN, Jacob to Sally Ritter	3-29-1818
BOWERS, David to Susann Harman	4-16-1818
BOYD, Robt to Catherine Crege	12-4-1823
BRAND, Conrad to Magdeline Rhinehart	5-14-1820
BRAND, Henry to Barbara Benell	5-2-1820
BRANNT, Samuel to Mary Forney	2-24-1820

BREWER, John to Rachel Harsman   3-30-1821
BROWN, Barnard to Emley Trumbow   1-9-1823
BROWN, Jonas to Betsy Miller   8-9-1818
BROWN, Samuel to Susanna McGaw   4-8-1819
BURREL, Richard to Margaret Kenestirck   9-9-1823
BUTT, Chas to Mary Ann McKee   12-27-1821
BUZKIRK, Chas. to Mary Ann McKee   12-27-1821
BUZZARD, Peter to Elizabeth Deity   5-16-1819
BUZZARD, Malicha to Barbary Neff   9-23-1823
CARLILE, James to Mary Whitcraft   7-21-1818
CARMINGHAM, Adam to Mary Hill   11-5-1822
CARIS, Manach to Elizabeth Shevoe   9-21-1820
CARR, Hugh to Mary Casebeer   8-27-1822
CARR, Richard B. to Elizabeth Good   6-18-1822
CARRY, John to Pleasant Casebeer   3-16-1821
CASEBEER, John to Nancy Smiley   1-11-1821
CASEY, Benjamin to Rebecca Shaller   1-9-1823
CASIER, Thomas to Mary Laffer   7-29-1819
CASSIES, Charles(?) to Matilda Tracy   6-28-1819
CISEL, Philip to Mary Logan   4-18-1822
CISSIL, Emon to Jane Niblock   5-30-1822
COINS (CORNS), Chas. To Catharine Minnich   1-2-1823
COLLETTE, Abraham to Stary Durn   10-9-1823
CONN, Geo. to Sarah Carlisle   3-25-1819
CONRAD, Jacob to Mary Finkle   11-10-1818
COOK, Joseph to Elizabeth Wilson   10-30-1823
COMBS, John to Susanna Rammage   7-13-1823
CRAWFORD, Eli to Sary Boyd   4-29-1819
CREATER, Andrew to Elizabeth Neighbor   5-18-1818
CRIPLEAVOR, John to Elisa Myres   6-13-1822
CRITZ, John to Mary Waters   3-19-1822
CROSS, Daniel to Hannah Silley   3-20-1823
CUNNINGHAM, Wm. to Rebecca Johnson   1-25-1821
CUNNING, Richard to Nancy Swagler   10-24-1822
CUNNINGS, Thomas to Mary Moore   12-28-1820
DAVIS, Jacob to Hannah C. Daniel   3-28-1820
DAVY, Wm to Pheby Gordon   6-3-1819
DEETZ, Wm to Elizabeth Lester   3-31-1820
DEITZ, Henry to Susanna Domer   9-8-1822
DEMING, Mathias to Eliza Tracy   1-7-1822
DEMUTH, Christopher to Elisabeth Gunther   4-16-1818
DIVER, Samuel to Caroline Walton   12-8-1819
DUCK, Philip to Jane Ervin   2-26-1822
DUNLAP, James to Crissy Newton   4-15-1818
DUNLAP, Wm to Ann Newton   12-10-1818
ECKARD, Peter to Mary Frantz   5-13-1823
EDGERLY, Daniel W. to Anna Mariah Itzkin   10-22-1820
EMERY, Van to Martha Williams   2-19-1820
ENGLISH, James W. to Nancy Pritchard   6-3-1823

```
ESPICH, Chas. F. to Rebecca Thomas                      12-27-1821
EVERETT, Chas. to Susana French                         6-27-1822
EVERETT, Jacob to Catherine Collince                    5-20-1823
FAKER, Havir to Anne Marie Nadel                        9-14-1818
FASHBAUGH, John to Elizabeth Engal                      12-17-1822
FINTON, James to Sarah Wolfe                            4-28-1818
FISHER, Henry to Elizabeth Kritz                        3-12-1822
FLETCHER, Francis to Barbery Slone                      4-2-1818
FOREMAN, Philip to Lavina Porter                        9-16-1822
FORNEY, Christian to Christianna Hoftsinger             2-24-1820
FORNEY, Peter to Magdalena Noftsinger                   2-22-1820
FOSTER, Benjamin to Nancy Shewrnan                      3-30-1819
FOSTER, Moses to Mary Kail                              8-14-1823
FOSTER, Samuel to Martha Johnson                        3-26-1818
FRANCE, Christian to Elizabeth Jones                    11-6-1823
FREDERICK, Abraham to Juda Ax                           11-14-1822
FREDERICK, Joseph to Mary Spiker                        5-16-1822
FROM, Henry to Salome Rebstock                          12-13-1823
FRONE, Chas. Tobias to Elizabeth Barbara Relstock       10-18-1821
FRY, Thos. to Juliann Prong                             2-6-1823
GAMBLE, Robt to Sarah Shull                             5-1-1823
GARABANT, Zachariah to Elener Rearen                    1-18-1821
GARMORE, John to Caty Eddleman                          1-29-1819
GASEUGH, Thos. to Elizabeth Wilt                        9-18-1823
GERMY, Jacob to Dorothea Widdle                         10-12-1818
GINLINA, Jacob to Mary Wallick                          10-26-1819
GINTHER, Daniel to Adah Simmers                         4-3-1823
GLASS, Mathias to Sarah Rowe                            11-15-1821
GOOD, Jacob to Mary Carr                                12-8-1818
GOODRICH, Geo. to Abigail Farden                        5-9-1820.
GRAHAM, John to Anne Cahill                             2-2-1819
GRAM, Henery to Rachel Prindle                          7-13-1820
GRIFFITH, Nathan to Friszilla Wordle                    7-20-1820
GREWELL, John to Sarah Brewell                          1-20-1821
GRUMRINE, John to Catharine Bowers                      7-7-1818
GUNTHER, John to Lydia Demuth                           2-20-1821
HARBAUGH, Frederick to Susan Thomas                     12-10-1818
HARBAUGH, Peter to Patty Stickle                        10-4-1818
HARFER, Wm to Mary Hatery                               6-20-1822
HARMAN, Geo. to Elizabeth Thomas                        4-22-1819
HARMAN, Michael to Elizabeth Thomas                     11-11-1822
HARRIS, John to Mary Keller                             8-24-1820
HARRIS, Wm. to Elizabeth Tufford                        5-5-1818
HATON, Nathaniel to Mehala Davis                        7-6-1820
HAYS, David to Susannah Hizer                           1-27-1820
HEDLY, Gabriel to Elizabeth Graham                      2-8-1821
HEMINGER, Geo. to Susan Philips                         7-23-1820
HENRY, Wm to Elizabeth Riley                            6-4-1818
HERLESS, Geo. to Susanna Leatherman                     3-11-1823
```

```
HERRIS, Isarel to Elisabeth Wisegerver          10-10-1819
HERRON, Isaiah to Sarah Glass                   10-27-1822
HEZLER, Abraham to Susan Menjard                3-20-1820
HILL, Chas. Jr. to Susan Carr                   4-1-1823
HILL, Daniel to Mary Frants                     12-24-1822
HILL, Robt to Hannah Buskirk                    1-15-1822
HILL, Wm to Mary Kitwiler                        12-11-1823
HIMES, Peter to Mary Bush                        1-20-1818
HINES, Wm. to Mary Engal                         6-13-1820
HIXON, Samuel to Elizabeth Cotem                12-26-1822
HOCKSTETLER, Jacob to Francey Miller            7-28-1822
HOGLAND, Henry to Jane(?) Maefild               7-12-1821
HOGLAND, John to Anne Neighbour                 7-6-1822
HOLMES, Samuel to Sarah Butter                  8-8-1822
HOOPENGARENER, John to Elizabeth Walter         12-26-1819
HOOPENGARNER, Daniel to Rachel Miller           9-23-1821
HOSTETTER, Jeremiah to Elizabeth Brand          11-21-1819
HOYER, John to Peggy Crits                      11-13--1823
HUES, Richard to Rebecca Reeves.                4-16-1823
HUFF, Henry to Margret Smith                    11-1-1821
INGLE, Peter to Charlotte Seward                10-20-1818
ITZKIN, Lewis to Charlotte Young                12-4-1820
JENNINGS, Lewis to Martha Moor                  4-19-1821
JIMMESON, Andrew to Juliann Taylor              2-26-1822
JOHNSON, James to Jane Heblock                  12-1-1818
JOHNSTON, Wm Geo. to Nancy Richards             8-3-1821
KELLER, John to Elizabeth Fashbough             2-4-1823
KELLER, Martin Jr. to Elizabeth Riclenger       4-17-1823
KENT, Frederick to Nancy Ax                     11-24-1822
KIBY, Jonathan to Sarah Salyers                 4-19-1821
KILGORE, Robert M. to Sarah Baught              10-13-1821
KING, Thomas to Elizabeth Benninger             7-11-1819
KISER, Isaac to Sally Biddinger                 1-27-1822
KITCH, David to Rebecca Landes                  7-5-1821
KLINE, David to Elizabeth Kore                  9-11-1821
KLINE, Jonas to Elizabeth Bear                  7-10-1821
KNACE, Abraham to Susannah Sees                 7-1-1823
KNAHT, James to Hariet Garmore                  6-23-1820
KNEEGER, Peter to Elizabeth Buickman            11-16-1820
KUHN, John Geo. to Polly Homerichouse           11-30-1820
LANGEREGE, Robt to Jane Boyd                    9-27-1821
LAUBAUGH, John to Margaret Sharp                1-7-1823
LAUGHLIN, James to Elizabeth McCleary           6-5-1821
LAWES, Henry to Catty Herman                    8-25-1818
LEATHERMAN, Daniel to Sophia Suelley            a0-27-1822
LEGHTY, John to Catherine Bacher                8-3-1823
LEGIT, Benjamin to Mary Alexander               9-27-1821
LENHART, Peter to Nancy Thomas                  9-18-1823
LENHERST, David to Sally Shoup                  9-2-1823
```

573

```
LEUES, John to Margret Crem                             11-2-1820
LIMBOTH, Frederick, to Elizabeth Dearidoff              12-2-1819
LOWE, Jacob to Hanah Rider                              7-3-1823
LOWER, Geo. to Margret Harbough                         4-10-1821
LUKE, John to Magelan Shutt                             3-18-1821
LYRON, James R. to Elizabeth Simmers                    8-29-1822
MCADUE, James to Jane Delong                            9-16-1823
McCERY, Benjamin to Caty Haraman                        6-14-1821
McCRERY, James to Catherine Custer                      9-4-1823
McFARSAN, Robert to Cathrine Foster                     1-29-1818
McFERSON, Geo. to Mary Durn                             10-9-1823
McFERSON, Robert to Mary Fleek                          10-31-1819
McPHERRIN, Thos. to Elizabeth Martin                    11-11-1823
McWUESTON, Wm. to Eve Frantce                           8-21-1823
MAGNY, Forgy to Eloner  Coulter                         11-6-1823
MASON, John to Catharine Gushen                         11-25-1819
MASTERS, Joseph to Susanah Homes                        4-24-1823
MAYSE, James to Amelia German                           1-29-1822
MELLISEEK, Jacob to Sarah Holmes                        6-20-1821
MERRIM, John to Marian Wilcoby                          8-18-1821
MIDDLETON, Jacob to Mary Cahill                         3-11-1819
MILLAR, Joseph to Margaret Noel                         6-23-1822
MILLER, David to Ann Misfer (Mishler)                   9-7-1823
MILLER, Henry to Elizabeth Herron                       2-14-1822
MILLER, Jacob to Elizabeth Bellman                      10-21-1823
MILLER, Jacob J. to Anna Neighbour                      12-31-1818
MILLER, John J. to Catherine Mills                      7-27-1823
MILLS, Thos. to Peggy Muncey                            10-23-1823
MILLS, Wm. to Catherine Strawn                          12-4-1823
MISHLER, Abraham to Ann Cuarr                           12-7-1823
MISOR, Frederick to Catharine Mackaman                  3-28-1820
MOCK, Frederick to Barbara Howman                       6-13-1820
MOCK, Michael to Catharine Bixler                       2-7-1823
MONEY, Thomas to Rebecca McClery                        6-14-1821
MOOR, Thomas to Catherine Best                          6-7-1821
MORGIN, Lewis to Catherine Bidinger                     11-20-1823
MYERS, James to Mary Dorothy Bornig                     1-31-1822
MYERS, John to Lurany Ross                              4-6-1819
NEIGHBOUR, Nicholas Esquire to Hannah Uhrich            5-21-1818
NELL, James to Margaret Carlile                         1-13-1820
NIBLACK, Robt. to Lidey Vallentine        2 dates       (9-5-1822
                                                        (9-19-1822
NIEGEMAN, John to Abigail Demuth                        12-10-1819
NORIS, Geo. to Elizabeth Hinton                         5-20-1821
O'DONALD, Cornelius to Lydia Walton                     6-13-1822
OLESHOUSE, David to Estren Barchfield                   2-10-1820
PALMER, James to Hannah Shane                           6-19-1818
PARKER, Richard to Christena Davis (note: no day given)7-?-1823
PATRICK, James to Catharine Westfale                    7-30-1821
PEARCE, Isaac to Mary Riley                             5-8-1823
PATTARS, Geo. to Mary Ann Vale                          12-23-1823
```

574

```
PEARCH, Joseph to Sarah Close                           10-24-1822
PENROD, John to Mary Kiser                               4-10-1821
PENROD, Peter to Elizabeth Sharp                         2-13-1820
PENROD, Solomon to Catharine Olinger                     12-1-1822
PETERSON, Geo. Esq. to Ausila Huff                       4-12-1821
PFOUTZ, Michael to Mary Heastand                         5-11-1823
PHILLIPS, Adam to Caty Huff                              10-20-1818
PHILIPS, John to Catharine Heminger                      2-20-1820
POCOCK, Eli to Catharine Knistrick                       7-5-1819
PORTER, Reison to Catherine French                       12-4-1823
PRESTOCK, Martin to Hanah Weeland                        6-15-1820
PRICE, James to Mary -?- (no surname given)              6-14-1821
PRICE, James to Polly Stoneman                           1-1-1822
PRICE, Wm to Martha Foster                               12-11-1823
PRICHARD, Resin to Susanne Laffer                        12-12-1822
PRIDER, James to Catharine Cadwill                       6-11-1820
QUEYERE, Geo. to Susana Knaus                            4-25-1822
RAGER, Jacob Jr. to Lovina Engler                        2-25-1823
RAM, John to Nancy Myers                                 7-15-1821
RANK, Philip to Lydia Dodge                              9-11-1821
RANNEY, Doc. Orange to Elizabeth Jacobs                  4-3-1823
RAVER, Henry to Rossannah Sinter                         2-12-1822
RAWLEY, Luther to Jane Dunlap                            4-6-1819
RAYMOR, Geo. to Susanah Miller                           5-2-1822
REVEL, Thos. C. to Eve Hipple                            8-19-1821
REVESE, James to Lucy Woodring                           9-17-1818
RHOADS, Samuel to Hanah Simers                           4-4-1820
RIGEL, John to Sarah Leatherman                          8-13-1822
RILEY, John A. B. to Eliza Riley                         2-6-1821
RINEHART, Adam to Barbara Marvel                         4-27-1819
RINEHART, John to Rebecca Carrel                         4-27-1819
RINEHART, Philip to Rosina Brant                         10-12-1819
ROBY, Horatio to Precious R. Roby                        1-4-1821
ROBY, Horatio to Jane H. Roby                            4-10-1823
ROMIG, Gabriel to Christine Elicabeth Blickensdorfer     11-7-1822
ROSEBERRY, Michael to Drusilla Peterson                  7-8-1823
ROSHONG (BUSHONG?), Daniel to Elizabeth Barnhouse        5-2-1822
ROULTON, Chas. to Sarah Pickett                          9-25-1818
ROUSH, Frederick to Christina Roush                      8-12-1819
ROUSH, John to Magilina Roush                            1-24-1820
RUSSELL, Isaac to Charlotte Kelly                        2-28-1822
BUTLER, Joseph to Susannah Bacon                         11-7-1822
SANDERS, Dennis to Julyann Murry                         6-24-1819
SARGENT, Robt. to Mary Best                              6-15-1819
SCOTT, Mathew to Susanah Swally                          4-29-1823
SELS, Israel to Catharine Smith                          10-1-1818
SERGENT, Lawrence to Elizabeth Benfort                   8-5-1823
SEWELL, Abner to Mary Johnston                           9-26-1822
```

```
SHANK, Jacob to Magdalena France                        6-3-1819
SHANKS, Joseph to Susarina Blosser                      7-10-1823
SHAHON, Amon to Lucreid Runes                           8-9-1821
SHATTOCK, Joseph to Aggy Stiffler                       1-9-1823
SHEPHER, Jeremiah R. to Elizabeth Smith                 11-12-1822
SHEWMAKER, Jacob to Elizabeth Eamis                     9-2-1821
SHISLER, Henry to Mary Hammel                           12-15-1818
SHISLER, Samuel to Elizabeth Hillery                    3-4-1819
SHOWALTER, John to Elizabeth Thomas                     12-15-1818
SHOWALTER, Peter to Phebe Robert                        11-18-1821
SHUSTER, John to Elizabeth Winegate  2 dates            (12-14-1820
                                                        (12-19-1822
SIGLER, Geo. to Mary Gosage                             2-22-1820
SIMERS, Henry to Martha Davis                           10-8-1821
SIMERS, Isaac to Ruth Davis                             5-22-1819
SIMMERS, Wm to Mary Walton                              6-3-1819
SMILEY, Wm to Elizabeth Swinehart                       8-14-1823
SMITH, Daniel to Catharine Swinhart                     4-29-1819
SMITH, Henry W. to Sarah Price                          5-30-1819
SMITH, Jacob to Susan Baker                             11-28-1819
SMITH, James R. to Anna Masters                         8-24-1823
SMITH, Wm G. to Mary Price                              12-26-1822
SNIDER, Philip to Hannah Rubert                         10-31-1820
SNITKER, Jacob to Ruthnita                              1-26-1819
SNYDER, Henry to Elizabeth Michael                      2-4-1819
SPICKER, Christian to Susan Foreman                     9-14-1819
SPVE, Jonathan to Harriet Dys                           4-9-1823
STEMPLE, Daniel to Susanna Smith                        2-17-1820
STIFFLER, David to Martha Smith                         6-10-1821
STIFFLER, David to Lydia Baltzly                        10-4-1821
STIFFLER, Geo. to Nancy Dust                            8-28-1821
STOCKER, John to Elizabeth Stocker                      10-24-1820
STONEHAUER, John to Mary Gard                           6-27-1819
STONEMAN, Benjamin to Elizabeth Rippith                 9-30-1821
STONEMAN, John Jr. to Catharine Glass                   1-15-1818
STOODY, John to Susanna Yant                            3-27-1823
STRAKER, Albert to Lewis(?) Putt                        2-1-1822
STURN, Mathias to Ann Tiernel                           4-19-1819
SWALLEY, Chas. to Ledy Beamer                           12-11-1823
SWIHART, Isarel to Catharine Letherman                  6-15-1820
SWINEHART, Daniel to Voste (Vaste) Hoagland             7-9-1823
SWINEHEART, Gabriel to Margret Fry                      2-15-1821
SWINEHEART, John to Elizabeth Cline                     4-5-1821
THARLEY, Thomas to Putura McGuire                       1-15-1818
THOMAS, Jacob to Barbara Harman                         10-29-1822
TOLBERT, John to Mary Maefild                           8-2-1821
TOMAS, John D. to Martha Snyder                         12-30-1819
TSHUDY, Martin to Dorcas Elis/t Peter                   4-23-1821
```

TUCKER, John to Ruth Sparks	12-13-1818
TUCKER, Samuel to Mary Sells	3-16-1820
TUNLIN, James to Margret Collet	12-28-1819
TWALLO, Jacob to Margaret Uties	6-29-1823
UTTER, Jabes to Ann Trusel	8-14-1823
VANATOR, Benjamin to Sarah Foster	9-28-1819
WADE, Elias to Mary Wimer	3-15-1819
WAGNER, John to Mary Farmer	11-19-1818
WALICK, Geo. to Polly Kenestrick	7-6-1820
WALLACK, Phillip to Elizabeth Showalter	2-2-1819
WALTER, John to Sarah Giraga	2-10-1822
WALTON, Boaz Esquire to CatharineRhoades	3-26-1818
WALTZ, Daniel to Elizabeth Swinehart	11-21-1822
WARNER, Amassa to Cynthia Walton	3-30-1819
WARNER, Daniel to Mary Simmers	2-26-1818
WATKINS, (WALKINS), Wm to Elizabeth Shield	5-7-1823
WEAVER, James to Patty Wingate	9-2-1818
WEST, Levi to Sarah Johnson	3-18-1819
WHITACRE, Thornton to Elizabeth Espich	9-18-1821
WHITE, John to Elizabeth Stiffler	1-9-1823
WIANT, Jacob to Christene Sherrets	6-26-1821
WILLIAMS, Henry to Sarah Gray	11-21-1822
WILLIAMS, James to Magdalena Cosbindas	9-18-1820
WILLIAMS, Mathew to Nancy Ensely	6-10-1822
WILLIAMS, Silas to Sally Laffin	7-15-1819
WILLIAMS, Thos. to Amelia O'Donnell	1-13-1822
WILLOBY, Farlington B. to Diana Caldwell	9-17-1822
WILSON, Amos to Mary Osler	11-27-1823
WILSON, Andrew to Patty Woodrow	10-3-1818
WILSON, John to Mary Hays	1-2-1823
WINGATE, Cyrus to Elizabeth Finton	7-17-1823
WINGATE, Isaac to Urselah Crist	6--11-1818
MOTTS, David to Sarah Combs	4-13-1823
YANT, John Jr. to Ann Hillery	4-4-1822
YANT, Michael to Mary Beamer	6-8-1820

Addenda to earlier marriages:

LAMBERSON, Samuel to Elisabeth Early	7-18-1816
(recorded with 1819 marriages0	
McGREW, Nathan to Mary Huston	3-6-1817
WOLF, John to Mary Crame	4-2-1817
(recorded with 1822 marriages)	

CEMETERIES IN TUSCARAWAS COUNTY and HOLMES COUNTY, OHIO - submitted by
Mrs. Dion Morrison, 3331 LeRoy St., San Bernardino, California-92404
(Partial Listings)

UNION HILL E.U.B. CEMETERY

BAKER, Ephraim A. - - Aug. 12, 1834 - Sept. 16, 1905
    Catharine M. (BYERS) Mar. 18, 1843 - Aug. 18, 1909
    Franklin W. - - Dec. 25, 1871 - May 8, 1907
    William C. - - June 2, 1838 - July 26, 1917
    Anna w/o Wm. - - Nov. 27, 1842 - Jan. 14, 1934
    Iola - - - Jan. 14, 1873 - Jan. 27, 1934
    Elnora - - 1874-1952
    Henry - - June 24, 1833 - Aug. 24, 1915 -
DIETZ, Catherine C. - Mar. 6, 1840 - Aug. 7, 1905 w/o Henry
MILLER, Abner - - May 12, 1862 - Nov. 6, 1935
    Leah - - April 14, 1861 - Jan 3, 1939
    Elizabeth - - 1890 - 1949
    Victor M. - - ____ 22, 1890 - 12y 5m 9d
    Sarah Ann, - Mar. 18, 1891 - 22y w/o J. C. Miller
    Silvius - 1837 - 1911
HATTERY, Emeliné - 1841 - 1919
MILLER, Moses A. - Sept. 6, 1860 - May 14, 1937
    Malinda - April 28, 1864 - July 3, 1920
HATTERY, Isaiah - Jan. 30, 1850 - 2y 1m 12d s/o E. & M. Hattery
    Infant - Feb. 2, 1850 - 20d child of E. & M. Hattery
    Noah - Nov. 15, 1853 - Nov. 12, 1859 - 6y 10m 2d
    Ephraim - Jan. 13, 1814 - Nov. 28, 1899
    Mary - - May 13, 1821 - April 13, 1879
    Allen - - Feb. 1, 1889 - 50y 23d
MILLER, Ruby KNECHT - - 1895-1943 (near grave of Victor M. Miller)
HERSHEY, John A. - - 1877-1958
    John - - 1845-1910
    Magdalina - 1848-1920 wife of John

- - - - - - - - - - - -

CEMETERY off Highway 39E, by Hillcrest Farm Sign, Walnut Creek, Holmes C
MIDDAUGH, Jesse M. - - May 18, 1897 - 73y 1m 21d
MILLER, Drusilla - - Mar. 5, 1851 - 21y 11m 21d w/o Andrew Miller
MIDDAUGH, Sarah - - 1860 - 1935
    Daniel - - 1849 - 1931
    Ester V. - May 28, 1890, 1m 4d - d/o D. & S. Middaugh
    Benjamin - Feb. 19, 1896, 69y 10m 20d, Vet. 1861-1865
    Susan - May 21, 1906 - 77y 10m 22d w/o Benjamin Middaugh

- - - - - - - - - - - -

TOWNSHIP 163 - HOLMES COUNTY, OHIO Cemetery off 39E on hill; Church
        below; Walnut Creek Menonite Church 1896
MILLER, Malinda - - - 1866-1952 w/o Samuel H.
    Samuel H. - - 1862-1928
    Annie R. - - - 1892-1955
    Abraham R. 1888-1950; Roy F. 1898-1947 (brothers)
    Lydia - - 1860-1941 w/o Benedict B.
    Benedict B. 1857 - 1944
    William J. - Dec. 27, 1856 - Jan. 16, 1946
    Frances J. - Aug. 12, 1859 - Apr. 10, 1911 w/o William J.
    Rev. Alvin - 1892-1966
    Elizabéth - - Nov. 11, 1904; 44y 10m 26d w/o John H.
    John H. - June 8, 1902, 48y 22d
    Lillie - 1882-1966 w/o Seth
    Seth - 1879-1957   578

CEMETERIES IN TUSCARAWAS COUNTY and HOLMES COUNTY, OHIO - submitted by
Mrs. Dion Morrison, 3331 LeRoy St., San Bernardino, California-92404
(Partial Listings) TOWNSHIP 163 - HOMES COUNTY, OHIO
CEMETERY off 39E on hill by Walnut Creek Menonite Church 1896. Cont.
MILLER, Anna D. - - - Mar. 3, 1879 - Aug. 14, 1957
        Jemima -   - Jan. 5, 1876 - May 31, 1928
        Moses, -   - Jan. 18, 1877 - 74y 11m 20d
        Catherine - - Jan. 31, 1871 - 76y 5m 26d
        Moses M. - - - Sept. 5, 1915 - 80y 11m 26d
        Henry H. - - - Aug. 22, 1853 - May 23, 1903
        Sarah - - - - March 18, 1900 - 71y 10d
        Percy -   1885-1961
        Catherine - Dec. 26, 1886 - 47y 1m 11d w/o Isaac A. Miller
        John E. -   Feb. 18, 1906 - 88y 9m 11d
        Sarah -   - March 3, 1897 - 77y 6m 7d, w/o John E. Miller
WEAVER, John J. - - Jan. 3, 1870 - 59y 9m
        Moses -   Dec. 13, 1887 - 38y 6m 18d
        Elnora - Oct. 13, 1896 - 19y 11m 13d
        Elizabeth - June 18, 1901 - 81y 1m 24d
        Emma -   1875 - 1932 w/o Emery Weaver
        Emery - 1875 - 1930
        - - - - - - - - - - - - - - - - - -

SHANESVILLE, TUSCARAWAS COUNTY, OHIO - CEMETERY on hill at Main and
                                       Hillcrest Drive
BAKER, John H. - - 1857-1928
        Louisa -   - 1849 - 1926
FORNEY__? -   - - Feb. 28, 1800 - Jan. 31, 1887
BAKER, ANNA - - Apr. 26, 1872 - 66y 1m 4d w/o Henry Baker, Jr.
        Henry, Jr. - May 25, 1870 - 75y 4m 12d
MILLER, Lydia - - Jan. 25, 1870 - 79y 2m 30d w/o Henry J. Miller
        ____?___ - - July 10, 1838 - May 14, 1888
        Charles A. - March 22, 1858 - May 10, 1882, 24y 1m 18d
BAKER, Henry -   Sept. 4, 1897 - 74y 7m 10d
              "This stone got by Henry Baker, Junior".
        Margaret (FUNK) - Oct. 6, 1825 - 64y (b. 1761 in Ireland)
              "This stone got by Elizabeth Vining"
HATTERY, Susan - - Aug. 29, 1843 - 26y 5m 7d w/o John Hattery
BAKER, Barbara - Nov. 16, 1881 - 47y 6m 21d w/o Henry Baker

The death records listed below are from "Death Record 1" found in the Probate Court at the court house at Marysville. This listing pertains primarily to persons 40 years of age and over. Residence is same as place of death unless stated otherwise. Abbreviations used: d=died; a=age; m=married; w=widow or widower; s=single; pd=place of death; pb=place of birth; res=residence. Page on which record may be found in original book is given in parenthesis.

PRISE, Eva Margaret - d 8-4-1867; a 81y 7d; w; pd Paris twp.; pb Europe. (2)
SHOPE, Elianor - d 9-2-1867 or 9-21-1867 (two dates given); a 65y 3m 27d; pd Paris twp.; pb Greene Co., Pa. (2)
SOUTHARD, Sarah - d 9-24-1867; a 40y 1m 10d; m; pd Marysville twp.; pb Fayette Co., Pa. (2)
BARNES, Susannah - d 10-3-1867; a 63y 1m;/pd Paris twp.; pb Harrison Co., Ohio. (2)
LOCK, Louisa - d 9-3-1867; a 61y; w; pd Union twp.; pb-----. (2)
BROWN, Jane - d 8-31-1867; a 77y; w; pd Infirmary; pb unknown. (2)
HOOVER, Joshua - d 9-14-1867; a 71y; m; pd Infirmary; pb unknown. (2)
SCOTT, Nancy - d 8-29-1867; a 62y; w; pd Leesburg two; pb---------(2)
SCOTT, Frances - d Sept 1867; a 61y 1m 13d; w; pd Leesburg twp.; pb Belmont Co., Ohio; parents, Samuel & M. A. Barkherst. (2)
ELLIS, David C. - d 10-3-1867; a 58y; m; pd Union Co., Ohio; pb New York. (2)
PATRICK, John - d 10-26-1867; a 45; m; pd Dover twp.; pb Virginia. (2)
GOFF, Samuel - d 3-2-1868; a 81y; m; pd Taylor twp.; pb Maine. (4)
GOFF, Betsey - d 3-6-1868; a 78y; w; pd Taylor twp.; pb Maine. (4)
JAKEWAY, David - d 2-22-1868; a 76y 4m 2d; m; pd Taylor twp.; pb Oswego, N.Y. (4)
LAUK, Samuel - d 2-13-1868; a about 60y; m; pd Paris twp.; pb------(4)
RYAN, James - d 3-15-1868; a 74y; w; pd Marysville; pb-------. (4)
KELSEY, Cyrus - d 3-8-1868; a 60y; m; ps Marysville; pb----- (4)
FELL, Ann - d 1-15-1868; a 70y; m; pd North Lewisburg; pb Pa. (4)
LOUCK, Samuel - d 2-12-1868; s; pd Paris twp.; pb--------. (4)
MIDDLETON, Timothy - d Aug. 1867; w; pd Liberty twp.; pb-------. (4)
SKIDMORE, William - d 11-23-1867; a 65y; m; pd Liberty twp.; pb-------. (4)
BRAKE, Mrs. - d 1-26-1868; a 65y; w; pd Liberty twp.; pb-------. (4)
HILDEBRAND, Ann M. - d 6-18-1868; a 41y 3m 19d; s; pd Leesburg twp.; pb-------. (4)
SKEELS, Harvey - d 10-28-1867; a 67y; m; pd Leesburg twp.; pb--------. (4)
GUNDERMAN, George - d 6-17-1868; a 74y 10m; m; pd Germany; pb-------; res. Marysville. (4)
HUME, Mary E. - d 6-7-1868; a 54y; w; pd-----; pb---------. (4)
DIXON, John - d (no date given--1867-8); a42y 6m 19d; m; pd Liberty twp.; pb Va. (4)
BERNS, Mary M. - d 8-27-1868; a 76; w; pd Paris twp.; pb Frederick Co., Md.; parents, Fred and Catharine Bachman. (6)
NEBELL, Augustus - d 9-27-1868; a 59y; m; pd Marysville; pb Germany. (6)
TURNER, Thomas - d 10-13-1868; a 63y; m; pd Marysville; pb don't know. (6)
RICHEY, Mrs. Philip - d 8-24-1868; a 65y; m; pd Dover twp.; pb don't know. (6)
BENTON, Matilda - d 9-27-1868; a 68y; w; pd Marysville; pb Maryland. (6)
JENKINS, John - d 9-25-1868; a 50y; m; pd Union twp.; pb-----. (6)
MACHLING, Philip P. - d 11-4-1868; a 72y 10m 3d; m; pd Taylor twp.; pb Pa. (6)
TURNER, Thomas - d 10-13-1868; a 60y; m; pd Marysville; pb Maryland; parents, Thomas and Jemima Turner. (6)

COE, Martha E. - d 11-25-1868; a 39y 9m 14d; m; pd Marysville; pb Darby twp.;
    parents, Jas. and Margaret Boal. (6)
OWEN, Godfrey - d 11-10-1868; a 72y; w; pd Paris twp.; pb unknown. (6)
BROWN, C. M. - d 12-4-1868; a 45y; s; pd Paris twp.; pb unknown. (6)
MARSH, Mrs. Mary - d 12-23-1868; a 60y; s; pd Allen twp.; pb unknown. (6)
ROSE, Lucy - d 2-6-1869; a 67y 11m 20d; m; pd Milford twp.; pb Windham, Conn. (6)
TURNER, Robert - d 3-13-1869; a 87y 6m 11d; m; pd Marysville; pb Hartford, Me. (6)
COE, Moses - d 3-18-1869; a 42y 3m 8d; m; pd near Marysville; pb near Canonsburg,
    Pa. (6)
FLECKENGER, Stephen - d 1-22-1869; a 45y; m; pd York twp.; pb---------. (6)
DAWSON, Mrs. John - d 3-14-1869; a 75y; m; pd near Allen Center; pb unknown. (8)
SPAIN, Mrs. Aaron - d 4-5-1869; a unknown; m; pd near Lewisburg; pb Canada. (8)
COE, Moses - d 3-18-1869; a 43y; w; pd Paris twp.; pb Paris twp. (8)
WATKINS, John W. - d 5-14-1869; a 51y 4m 7d; m; pd Milford Center; pb Pa. (8)
CLARK, Caleb - d 5-7-1869; a 56y; m; pd Allen twp.; pb------. (8)
BALLON (BALLOU), Martin - d 11-25-1869; a 89y; w; pd Union twp.; pb Rhode Island;
    parents, David and Lucy Ballon (Ballou). (10)
BORGER, Elizabeth - d 9-11-1869; a 72y; m; pd Union twp.; pb Germany; parents,
    Schury and Barbary Borger. (10)
EDGAR, Daniel - 12-19-1869; a 40y; m; pd Milford Center; pb Ireland; parents,
    John and Hannah Edgar. (10)
HOPKINS, John W. - d 5-14-1869; a 51y; m; pd Milford Center; pb Pa.; parents,
    father, Benjamin Hopkins, mother--Elizabeth Williams. (10)
MITCHELL, Dixon - d 5-6-1869; a 64y; m; pd Milford Center; pb Ohio; parents,
    David and Martha Mitchell. (10)
NEAL, Catharine - d 5-6-1869; a 69y; m; pd Milford Center; pb Vermont; parents,
    Isaac and Lucy Bigelow. (10)
PAYNE, John R. - d 2-9-1870; a 38y; m; pd Union twp.; pb Union twp.; father,
    Sumner Payne; mother, Aurilla Burnham. (10)
PORTER, Alvin - d 12-31-1869; a 31y; s; pd Union twp.; pb Union twp.; father,
    Wm Porter; mother, Hannah Snodgrass. (10)
SMITH, Anna - d 4-22-1869; a 72y; w; pd Union twp.; pb Vermont; parents, John
    and Experience Foster. (10)
SNODGRASS, Samuel - d 2-23-1870; a 66y; m; pd Milford Center; pb Pa.; parents,
    Robert and Jane Snodgrass. (10)
MAPES, Delight - d 7-14-1869; a 74y 4m 10d; w; pd Jerome twp.; pb------. (10)
RUDOLPH, Julia Ann - d 3-9-1870; a 66y 10m 28d; w; pd Jerome twp.; pb-----(10)
WAGNER, Ann - d 7-11-1869; a 82y; w; pd Jerome twp.; pb Maryland. (10)
HILL, Isarael - d (no date given 1869-70); a 56y 1m 11d; m; pd Jerome twp.;
    pb-------. (10)
BELL, Sarah - d 10-31-1869; a 90y 3m 3d; w; pd Mill Creek twp.; pb Carlisle, Pa.(10)
ROHTSEN, David - d 10-2-1869; a 92y 8m; w; pd Mill Creek twp.; pb------(10)
LIGGETT, Sarah - d 3-28-1870; a 50y 11m 8d; m; pd Mill Creek twp.; pb-------. (10)
MYERS, Hannah - d 2-8-1870; a 58y; m; pd Dover twp.; pb-----. (10)
CLARK, Elizabeth - d 2-2-1870; a 77y 19d; w; pd Dover twp.; pb-----. (10)
SHIRK, Sarah - d 9-25-1869; a 78y 8m 22d; m; pd Liberty twp.; pb Virginia. (10)
GRIFFIN, Charlotte - d 5-10-1869; a 60y 3m 10d; s; pd Liberty twp.; pb Md. (10)
KELSEY, M.D. - d 9-17-1869; a 70y; w; pd Liberty twp.; pb Vermont. (10)
TAYLOR, Washington - d 3-12-1870; a 47y 7d; m; pd Liberty twp.; pb Ohio. (10)

DEAN, George - d 5-25-1869; a 47y 4m 23d; m; pd Liberty twp.; pb Ohio. (10)
GREEN, Amos H. - d 5-21-1869; a 43y; m; pd Leesburg twp.; pb Pa. (10)
LANGSTAFF, James H. - d 8-11-1869; a 60y; pd Granville, Ohio; pb New Jersey. (12)
CLEVENGER, Hannah - d 3-15-1870; a 56y 5m 16d; m; pd Leesburgh twp.; pb Ohio. (12)
TATMAN, Abigail - d 4-17-1869; a 65y 1m 6d; m; pd Leesburgh twp.; pb West Va. (12)
LEE, Anna - d 3-30-1870; a 73y 4m 7d Leesburgh twp.; pb Virginia; widow. (12)
CRYDER, Joseph - d 4-21-1870; a 55y; m; pd Leesburgh twp.; pb Virginia. (12)
WILBER, Christopher - d 10-13-1869; a 55y 9m 26d; m; pd Allen twp.; pb New York. (12)
DAWSON, Kesiah - d 4-20-1870; a 51y; m; pd Allen twp.; pb Licking Co., Ohio. (12)
CLARK, Caleb - d 5-7-1869; a 56y; m; pd Allen twp.; pb West Virginia. (12)
THOMPSON, Nancy - d 5-22-1869; a 57y; m; pd Allen twp.; pb Belmont Co., Ohio. (12)
CRESWELL, William - d 11-18-1869; a 68y 9m 18d; m; pd Jackson twp.; pb Pa. (12)
SHAFFER, William - d 3-25-1870; a 59y 7m 11d; m; pd Jackson twp.; pb Pa. (12)
ANDREWS, Azubah - d 5-19-1869; a 78y 2m 8d; w; pd Jackson twp.; pb Jerico,
    Vermont. (12)
STORMS, Rebecca - d 9-11-1869; a 43y 6m 7d; m; pd York twp.; pb Harrison Co.,
    Ohio. (14)
IRWIN, Eliza B. - d 3-31-1870; a 61y 10m 27d; m; pd Claibourne twp.; pb-------(14)
STEPHENS, Oliver G. - d 4-15-1869; a 46y 5m; m; pd Richwood, Ohio; pb New Jersey.(14)
WALLACE, William - d 1-3-1869; a 49y 1m 20d; m; pd Claiborne twp.; pb Harrison
    Co., Ohio. (14)
WILLIAMS, Minervia - d 2-18-1870; a 45y 11m 21d; pd Washington twp.; pb Logan
    Co., Ohio. (14)
GREEN, Henry H. - d 1-28-1870; a 55y 8m 7d; m; pd Washington twp.; pb Logan Co.,
    Ohio. (14)
BIRD, Mary - d 3-6-1870; a 69y 1m 16d; m; pd Washington twp.; pb Maine. (14)
McADOW, Rebecca d 11-12-1869; a 74y 2m 28d; m; pd Taylor twp.; pb---- (14)
PICKET, Mary - d May 1869; a 72y; w; pd Marysville; pb Connecticut. (14)
PIERSON, Abel S. - d Sept. 1869; a 75y; w; pd Marysville; pb New York. (14)
BARBOUR, Electa - d Dec. 1869; a 69y; w; pd Marysville; pb New York. (14)
TURNER, Malinda - d Feb. 1870; a 40y; pd Marysville; pb Marysville. (16)
MELCHING, F. C. - d May 1870; m; pd Marysville; pb Bavaria. (16)
MARSHALL, Charity - d Feb. 1870; a 89y; w; pd Paris twsp.; pb Kentucky. (16)
ORAHOOD, Anna - d Aug. 1869; a 53y; m; pd Paris twp.; pb---------. (16)
NICOL, John L. - d Mar. 1870; a 49y; m; pd Paris twp.; pb Bavaria. (16)
BLAND, Peter - d 12-14-1870; a 46y 9m 14d; m; pd Union twp.; pb Union twp.;
    parents, Saul and Abigal Bland. (18)
BURROWS, Mary - d 2-11-1871; a 65y; w; pd Milford Center; pb------. (18)
BOWEN, Nancy - d 4-14-1870; a 81y 7m 11d; pd Milford Center; pb Vermont;
    parents, Obidiah and Hannah Rice. (18)
GABRIEL, Richard - d 5-15-1870; a 90y 3m 10d; w; pd Union twp.; pb Maryland. (18)
HARRINGTON, Elizabeth - d 8-15-1870; a 86y 8m 26d; w; pd Union twp.; pb Rhode
    Island; parents, George and Sarah Rice. (18)
MOODIE, George - d 12-25-1870; a 69y 8m 1d; w; pd Milford Center; pb Virginia;
    father, Roger Moodie. (18)
PARTHEMOR, Frederick - d 11-14-1870; a 63y 5m 20d; m; pd Union twp.; pb Pa.;
    parents, John and Catharine Parthemor. (18)
WATSON, Wm M. - d 7-1-1870; a 67y 7m 29d; m; pd Union twp.; pb Pa.; parents,
    John and Margaret Watson. (18)

582

BROWN, Isaac - d 6-22-1870; a 40y 2m 13d; m; pd Darby twp.; pb Ohio. (18)
BROWN, Catharine - d 1-8-1871; a 67y 6m 24d; m; pd Darby twp.; pb Ohio. (18)
REED, Jane - d 2-20-1871; a 58y 23d; w; pd Darby twp.; pb Ohio.. (18)
FAIRBANKS, Lewis - d 5-8-1870; a 66y 11m 3d; w; pd Jerome twp.; pb Vermont. (18)
FREDERICK, Martha - d 8-15-1870; a 58y 10m 5d; m; pd Jerome twp.; pb Virginia;
    parents, Joseph and Sarah Wells. (18)
HARRIOTT, E. M. - d 10-14-1870; a 41y 24d; m; pd Jerome twp.; pb Ohio; father,
    J. S. Norris. (18)
McCULLAUGH, Samuel - d 4-7-1871; a 70y 5m 27d; m; pd Jerome twp.; pb Union Co.,
    Ohio. (18)
BOWIC, Rebecca - d 12-23-1870; 1 72y 8m 5d; w; pd Millcreek twp.; pb Maryland. (18)
FISH, James H. - d 1-19-1871; a 77y; m; pd Millcreek twp.; pb Maryland. (18)
BLACK, Henry - d 2-1-1871; a 53y 2m 4d; m; pd Dover twp.; pb Ohio. (18)
MYERS, Adam - d 2-21-1871; a 62y 3m 10d; m; pd Dover twp.; pb Virginia. (18)
MYERS, John - d 2-21-1871; a 58y 4m 20d; w; pd Dover twp.; pb Virginia. (18)
ARYO, Sarah - d 7-22-1870; a 43y 8m; m; pd Liberty twp.; pb Ohio. (20)
CARTER, Francis - d 7-23-1870; a 63y 2m; m; pd Liberty twp.; pb Ohio. (20)
DEAN, Lucinda d 7-27-1870; a 56y; m; pd Liberty twp.; pb New York. (20)
ORAHOOD, Noah - d 12-15-1870; a 43y; m; pd Liberty twp.; pb Ohio. (20)
KINDLE, Sarah - d 12-1-1870; a 92y; w; pd Leesburg twp.; pb Virginia. (20)
FLEMMING, Elizabeth - d 7-17-1870; a 73y; s; pd Leesburg twp.; pb W. Va. (20)
HOSKINS, Richard - d 11-19-1870; a 67y; w; pd Leesburg twp.; pb Ohio. (20)
LOCKHART, Elizabeth J. - d 4-10-1871; a 41y 6m 10d; m; pd Leesburg twp.; pb Ohio.(20)
MONTGOMERY, Mary M. - d 2-26-1871; a 53y 5m 20d; m; pd Leesburg twp.; pb Ohio. (20)
DONAHUE, Winifred - d 6-1-1870; a 49y; m; pd Allen twp.; pb Ireland. (20)
IRVINE, Nancy - d 2-2-1871; a 47y 5m 17d; m; pd Allen twp.; pb Ireland. (20)
POLING, Samuel - d 2-7-1871; a 68y; w; pd Allen twp.; pb Maryland. (20)
STOKES, Delilah - d 5-7-1870; a 44y 4m 13d; m; pd Allen twp.; pb Ohio. (20)
STOKES, Phebe - d 10-2-1870; a 84y 1m 15d; w; pd Allen twp.; pb Ohio. (20)
GODFREY, Isaac - d 8-18-1870; a 81y; w.; pd Jackson twp.; pb Maryland. (20)
JARRARD, Phebe C. - d 7-7-1870; a44y 3m 12d; m; pd Jackson twp.; pb Ohio. (20)
ATKINSON, Ralph - d 10-2-1870; a 66y 2m 4d; w; pd York twp.; pb Pennsylvania. (22)
FIGLEY, Mary - d 3-13-1871; a 56y 3m 13d; m; pd York twp.; pb Virginia. (22)
MIDDLETON, Anna - d 11-21-1870; a 75y 4m 5d; m; pd Paris twp.; pb Virginia. (22)
NICOL, John L. - d 3-23-1870; a 49y 2m 17d; pd Paris twp.; pb Germany. (22)
MITCHELL, Leonard - d 4-1-1870; a 43y 7m; s; pd Paris twp.; pb Ohio. (22)
SEARS, Allison - d 8-5-1870; a 82y 5m; m; pd Paris twp.; pb Ohio. (22)
TURNER, Aquilla - d 1-6-1871; a 69y 10m; m; pd Paris twp.; pb Ohio. (22)
BROOKS, William - d 10-16-1870; a 85y; w; pd Paris twp.; pb Pennsylvania. (22)
BAILEY, Jane - d 3-6-1870; a 88y9m 7d; s; pd Paris twp.; pb-----. (22)
HUFFINE, Mary J. - d 3-11-1871 - a 56y 7m 11d; m; pd Marysville; pb Ohio. (22)
JEWELL, John - d 12-26-1870; a 58y 11m 10d; m; pd Marysville; pb Ohio. (22)
LANSDOWN, Hester H. - d 3-26-1871; a 53y 6m 9d; w; pd Marysville; pb Ohio. (22)
BARNETT, Mary - d 9-28-1870; a 74y 6m 26d; w; pd Taylor twp.; pb Pennsylvania. (22)
CORNELL, Sarah - d 9-17-1870; a 85y 6m 8d; w; pd Taylor twp.; pb Pennsylvania. (22)
GREEN, Eliza A. - d 12-12-1870; a 40y 3m 13d; m; pd Taylor twp.; pb Ohio. (22)
McCARTY, Henry - d 2-5-1871; a 69y 11m 14d; m; pd Taylor twp.; pb New York. (22)
PATRICK, Thomas J. - d 9-28-1870; a 74y 6m 26d; w; pd Taylor twp.; pb Pa. (24)
SIPSON, Joseph - d 4-20-1870; a 61y 3m 2d; m; pd Taylor twp.; pb England. (24)

583

WELCH, Fidelia - d 6-5-1870; a 44y 11m 12d; s; pd Taylor twp.; pb Vermont. (24)
YEARSLEY, Mary H. - d 7-18-1870; a 65y 3m 21d; w; pd Broadway twp.; pb Pa. (24)
SNEDEKER, John F. - d Feb. 1871; a 52y; m; pd Claibourne twp.; pb Virginia. (24)
DAVIS, Michael - d 7-2-1871; a 83y 5m; m; pd Union twp.; pb Virginia. (26)
HOPKINS, Elizabeth - d 10-12-1871; a 77y 2m 1d; w; pd Union twp.; pb England. (26)
DALE, John - d 5-30-1871; a 75y 11m 16d; m; pd Jerome twp.; pb Ohio. (26)
LATIMER, Dimmis - d 9-19-1871; a 73y 11m 19d; w; pd Dublin; pb Pennsylvania. (26)
SCOTT, Peter B. - d 5-20-1871; a 54y; m; pd Jerome twp.; pb Virginia. (26)
GREEN, Margaret - d 11-20-1871; a 58y 2m 4d; m; Dover twp.; pb Pennsylvania. (26)
HERRIOTT, Samuel - d 7-29-1871; a 74y; m; pd New Dover; pb New Jersey. (26)
RICHEY, Adam - d 9-24-1871; a 65y 1m 4d; m; pd New Dover; pb Pennsylvania. (26)
SAID, Susan - d Oct. 1871; a 58y; m; pd Dover twp.; pb Ohio. (26)
WORLEY, David W. - d 12-24-1871; a 74y 6m 15d; m; pd New Dover; pb Ohio. (26)
CLEMENT, Anna - d 2-8-1871; a 64y 9m 20d; m; pd Marysville; pb Vermont. (26)
ORAHOOD, Samuel - d 9-7-1871; a 80y 4m; w; pd Paris twp.; pb Virginia. (26)
CARTER, Sarah J. - d 12-18-1871; a 50y 8m 8d; m; pd Liberty twp.; pb Pa. (28)
TWIFORD, Nancy M. - d July 1871; a 63y; pd Liberty twp.; pb Ohio. (28)
CAREY, Henry H. - d 9-21-1871; a 41y 6m 19d; m; pd Leesburg twp.; pb Ohio. (28)
GANDY, Lucinda - d 11-14-1871; a 64y 3m; w; pd Leesburg twp.; pb Ohio. (28)
DIXON, John - d 8-9-1871; a 81y 4m 9d; w; pd Jackson twp.; pb Virginia. (28)
DYSERT, Mary - d 6-23-1871; a 77y 2m; w; pd Jackson twp.; pb Kentucky. (28)
HENDERSON, Charles - d 5-17-1871; a 86y 1m 10d; w; pd Franklin Co.; pb Virginia.(28)
SHAFFER, Miram M. - d 12-28-1871; a 74y 2m 11d; m; pd Jackson twp; pb Ohio. (28)
KINPLE, Lena A. - d 6-30-1871; a 45y 10m 10d; m; pd Jackson twp.; pb Ohio. (28)
FIGLEY, Mary - d 3-13-1871; a 56y 6m 13d; m; pd York twp.; pb Virginia. (28)
LATSON, Sarah - d 10-1-1871; a 73y 6m; w; pd Claiborne twp.; pb New York. (28)
McMELLEN, Mathew - d 8-18-1871; a 52y; s; pd Claiborne twp.; pb Ohio. (28)
McPHERSON, George - d 9-19-1871; a 60y 10m; w; pd Claiborne twp.; pb Ohio. (28)
ROSS, Hugh - d 7-27-1871; a 49y; m; pd Claiborne twp.; pb Ohio. (28)
RUHL, Michael - d 10-28-1871; a 76y 9m; w; pd Claiborne twp.; pb Germany. (28)
WALLACE, Samuel - d 10-25-1871; a 51y; m; pd Claiborne twp.; pb Ohio. (28)
WELLS, John D. - 5-5-1871; a 63y 5m 15d; m; pd Washington twp.; pb Md. (28)
STYER, Joseph T. - d 7-28-1871; a 45y 2m 26d; m; pd Taylor twp.; pb Ohio. (28)

Taken from Marriage Record 1.

AMRINE, Abraham Sugr. to Anancy Adams	5-30-1824
AMRINE, Abraham Jr. to Polly Wolford	5-17-1824
BARTHALMEW, John to Rosanah Sagar	10-22-1822
BAUGHAN, Jeremiah to Elizabeth Brake	12-28-1823
BORAM, Wm. to Urana Willson	4-3-1824
BROOKS, Charles to Polly Hanahman	9-1-1821
BROOKS, Jonathan to Mary Gates	4-26-1822
BROWN, William A. to Mary Bagley	5-29-1821
BURDICK, Reuben to Elizabeth Dunwiddie	2-22-1825
BURDICK, Silas to Margaret Richey	4-14-1825
BURNAM, Elba to Lorinda Burnam	12-7-1820
BURNAM, Jacob to Eliza Mecuham	3-20-1823
BURNHAM, David to Nancy Gabriel	5-17-1825
BURNHAM, Harvy to Eliza Hovey	11-17-1825
BURROWS, Jonathan to Elizabeth Laid (Said?)	6-1-1823
CHANDLER, Winthrop to Lucy Hammond	10-23-1820
COLVER, Handish to Betsy McCloud	2-15-1821
CONCLETON, Wm. to Martha Thompson	5-10-1821
CONNER, James to Debby Dewit	8-20-1822
CRAIG, Andrew to Betsy Vandrevander	10-3-1822
CRATTY, Robert to Elenor Porter	9-3-1822
DAVISON, Abraham to Jane Martin	2-25-1821
DEAKENS, John to Peggy News	5-22-1820
DINWIDDIE, Robert to Susan Bradley	2-6-1823
DODDS, Andrew to Hannah Kukman (Kerkman)	1-27-1822
DODGE, Hiram to Clarinda Parminter	3-7-1822
DONALLY, John to Betsy Milter (Miller-Milton)	7-11-1822
ELIFRITS, George to Martha Haris	2-4-1823
FOSTER, Benjamin to Amanda Cone	6-1-1820
GARRISON, Josiah to Caroline Calver	5-9-1822
GEERS, Joseph to Jane Churchil	4-6-1823
GILL, David to Elenor Piper	6-6-1822
GORTON, Benjamin to Maryaan Coollidge	12-15-1825
GRAHAM, Thomas to Gimmima Conkilton	4-24-1823
GRAHAM, William to Elizabeth Bell	12-17-1823
GREEN, Moses to Sarah Stickle	10-9-1823
HAGAR, Simeon to Rhoda Taylor	2-12-1824
HANNAHMAN, Robert L. to Hannah Plummer	3-16-1823
HARIS, Garret to Sarah Orr	12-26-1822
HARTSON, Moses to Polly Lucabill	9-23-1824
HARRIS, Daniel to Sybbil Lothrop	1-14-1824
HARRINGTON, David to Fanny Lane	12-18-1823
HATHAWAY, Nicholas to Elizabeth Morton	4-15-1824
HILL, Stephen to Susannah Lucanbill	9-23-1824
HOLYCROSS, Edmond to Jane Andrew	4-7-1825
HOVEY, Harden to Eliza Brown	5-1-1824

```
HOVEY, Samuel to Rachel Comer                                    1-10-1825
HULSE, Henry to Polly Willson                                    9-23-1825
JOHNSON, Jotham to Polly Marquess                          lic. 2-10-1824
JOHNSON, Stephen to Hannah N. Patch                        lic. 6-3-1824
KENADY, Hezekiah to Martha Saunders                             4-24-1823
KENADY, John to Betsey Morse                                    5-30-1824
KNIGHT, Westbrook to Catharine Cramer                           5-2-1823
LAMEN, Joseph to Mary Cochran                                   8-22-1823
LIPPETS (TIBBELLS), Fayette to Matilda Ann McGown               7-12-1824
LOCKWOOD, Israel to Angeline Calver                             8-15-1822
LOOKINGBILL, George to Margaret Sager                          12-26-1824
McCUNE, John to Polly Hagers                                    9-28-1820
McDONALD, John to Philomela Miller                         lic. 12-20-1825
MATHERS, Southard of Champaign Co. to Phelemie Rice of
                                            Union Co.           8-17-1823
MAYS, Robert to Sarah D. Mitchel                               11-20-1823
MILES, Jonathan to Susanah Porter                          lic. 1-23-1822
MITCHEL, Jesse to Eliza W. Robinson                            12-26-1823
MITCHELL, David Seign. to Hannah Calwell                       10-6-1825
MORROW, John to Polly Parthimore                              12-14-1820
NEWHOUN (NEWHOUS), Wm. to Ann Richey                            6-5-1823
ORAHOOD, Caleb to Elizabeth Sherk                             12-1-1825
ORRAHOOD, Elijah to Sarah Carter                               1-6-1825
OSBORN, Thomas to Elizabeth Price                             11-27-1820
PATHEMORE, Jacob to Sarah C. Thornton                          3-31-1825
PARMENTER, Asahel to Elenor Doge                               3-13-1822
PARMENTER, George to Nancy Marquess                       lic. 8-14-1821
PAYNE, Sumner to Aurelia Burnham                          lic. 2-1-1825
PORTER, John to Hannah Dodds                                  11-25-1824
PORTER, John Jr. to Jane Crawford                             12-30-1824
PORTER, William to Hannah Snodgrass                            1-20-1825
PRICE, John to _____(not given) Saunders                lic. 4-19-1824
REDFORD, Moses to Betsy Southward                              9-6-1820
REED, James to Elizabeth Johnston (mo. and day not given)  -----1822
REED, John to Jane Ann Snodgrass                               6-30-1825
REED, Samuel 4th to Joanna C. Hathaway                         4-8-1824
REED, Thomas to Jean (Jane) Snodgrass                          4-20-1820
RESE, Warren to Lucy Hibard (Hubbert)                          2-22-1822
RICHEY, William to Massey Bodley                           lic. 11-20-1820
RIPLEY, David of Champaign Co. to Phebe Coolidge of Union Co.4-7-1824
ROBINSON, John W. to Betsey Mitchel                            8-28-1823
ROBINSON, Reaves to Hannah Willson                             8-1-1823
SAGAR, Bengamin to Debby Rossel                                6-12-1823
SAUNDERS, Thomas to Mariah Geer                                4-29-1822
SMITH, Richard of Darby twp., Madison Co. to
            Betsy McCloud of Darby twp., Union Co.            12-5-1822
SNODGRASS, James to Polly McDowell                        lic. 5-15-1820
TAYLOR, John to Jane Noteman                                   3-7-1822
```

```
THOMPSON, Wm. to Sally Sherman                    8-14-1823
TILBY (SILBY), Benjamin to Lydia Hillard          3-22-1821
WHITE, Elisha to Sarah Colver                     10-14-1821
WILLMETH, Lemuel to Lydia Gibson                  5-30-1824
WINGET, Calvin to Cynthia Irwin                   9-26-1822
WOOD, Michael S. to Eliza Thayer                  7-15-1822
WOODS, Thomas F. to Sarah Shelpman                6-30-1825
```

The following marriages are all from "Marriage Record 1" with the exception of
a few for the year 1836 which are from "Marriage Record 2". All marriages are
from the first mentioned book unless they are marked "Book 2". Both records are
found in the Probate Court at the cour house in Marysville.

AMERINE, Andrew to Ruth Wells		4-28-1829
AMRINE, John to Catharine Shearer		11-30-1831
AMRINE, Josiah to Sarah Reed	lic.	(no date-1832?
AMRINE, Wesley to Elizabeth Westlake		12-20-1832
ANDERS, Miram to Catharine Shisler		8-13-1836
ANDERS, Randal to Sophia Almona Thomas		6-3-1833
ANDERSON, Wm to Mary Argo		10-13-1835
ANDREWS, Peter to Delilah Dewit		11-6-1828
ANTHONY, John to Mary Elifrits		2-12-1832
BADLEY, Martin (Edward M. on lic.) to Elizabeth Wilmeth		1-6-1831
BANCROFT, Thomas to Eliza Thompson		10-29-1832
BATES, Cranston to Mary Gorton	lic.	10-9-1826
BAUGH, Wm M. to Nancy Dixon		12-19-1835
BAUGHN, Mordica to Ozillye Orahood		11-16-1826
BAY, Joseph R. to Mary Dysert		9-4-1836
BAYLOR, Frederick to Emelia Sage		2-12-1834
BEAGLER, Tobias to Sarah Amrine		1-4-1827
BEARD, Amos to Rebecca Duval		1-11-1832
BEBE, Samuel to Lucy Ann Rogers (1827? recorded with		12-31-1829
Jan. 1828 marriages)		
BECK, Abraham to Mary Doty		1-16-1834
BEGGS, Andrew to Nancy Mullen		12-22-1831
BELL, Silas to Abigal Sherman		2-22-1826
BENNET, Ira to Betsy Scott	lic.	8-12-1829
BETHARD, Alex'r to Diana Clark		12-26-1833
BIGGS, James to Angeline M. Robinson		12-8-1833
BIRGE, Josiah to Martha Cowgill		7-5-1832
BISHOP, Daniel of Logan Co. to Margaret Milligan of Union Co.		4-8-1830
BOWEN, Abram (Abraham on lic.) to Sarah Badley		2-7-1833
BOWEN, Edward to Julian Dysert		11-13-1834
BOWEN, Jesse to Susanna Spergin		6-4-1829
BOYCE, Lemuel to Rebecca Fleming (Flemmor on lic.)		1-13-1833
BRAKE, Adam to Eve Baughan		1-19-1826
BRANNEN, Joseph to Nancy Ann Bacon		4-21-1835
BREAK, Michael to Polly Shirke		1-15-1829
BROOKS, Elmana to Fidelia Plummer		10-8-1835
BROWN, Adam to Mary Jolly		12-11-1834
BROWN, Christian to Huldah McNear		2-26-1835
BROWN, Jonathan to Mahaly Clark		1-17-1828
BROWN, Mannual to Lydia Crouse		11-20-1829
BROWN, Martin to Dorothy Lookingbill		9-14-1835
BUCKMAN, Jehial P. to Clarinda A. Plummer		1-10-1828
CAMPBELL, Wm to Ann Colbert		5-31-1829
CARPENTER, E. to Betsey Ann Allen		7-9-1835
CARR, Alson to Rebeca Davis	lic.	12-31-1834
CARTER, Daniel to Hannah Thompson		5-14-1835

```
CARTER, Lemual to Jemima Orahood                                    4-14-1831
CARTER, Levi to Elizabeth Orrahood                                 10-6-1831
CARTER, Thomas to Aaiy Chapman                                      7-1-1835
CHAPMAN, Abner to Mary Chapman                    (Book 2)          9-6-1836
CHENY, John to Sarah Brannon                                       7-28-1831
CHERRY, Ralph to Rachel Comer                            lic.  4-4-1827
CLARK, James to Sarah Willson                                      8-21-1827
CLAYTON, Wm to Rebecca Westlake                                   11-22-1833
COCHRAN, James to Elizabeth Reece                                11-21-1826
COFFMAN, William to Mary Brake                                    6-28-1829
COLLINS, Mathias to Prudence Gates                       lic. 12-7-1826
COLVIN, William P. to Eliza Hibberd                              11-22-1831
CONCKRIGHT, Hollis to Betsey Brown                               9-14-1834
COHE, Nelson to Louisa Curry                                     11-22-1831
CORTRIGHT, John to Martha Mitchell                               7-23-1829
CRAWFORD, James H. to Deliverance A. Huffman                      9-5-1834
CULLER, Gideon B. to Lovina Marquis                             10-11-1835
CULVER, Asahel to Emline Chapman                                10-12-1836
CULVER, Russell to Mary F. Culver                                7-4-1832
CURRY, Otway to Mary Noteman                                    12-17-1828
CURRY, Stephenson to Sarah Robinson                             12-8-1830
DALE, John to Betsey Smith                               lic.3-25-1834
DANIELS, James to Sarah Spurgen                                 12-27-1835
DANT, Calvin to Mary Clark                                      10-28-1835
DAVIS, Wm to Sarah Paver                                         2-18-1830
DEATH, Asahel to Rebecca Cummins                                3-30-1836
DICKSON (DIXON on lic.), John to Elizabeth Duval                 2-8-1832
DILLSEIVER, John to Sally Jane Bridge                           7-14-1833
DODD, Samuel H. to Mahaly Clarke                                1-1-1833
DODD, Thomas to Mary Comer                                     10-14-1830
DOLBIER, Benjamin to Eliza Woods   (note: no year given)        9-22-(1831?)
DOST, Titus to Catharine Green            (Book 2               8-14-1836
DUVAL, David to Elizabeth Culeshine                      lic.9-9-1826
DYSERT, John to Mary Longbtake                                 10-10-1833
EDGAR, John W. to Permela Johnson                               4-6-1826
EDGAR, William to Rachael Kiger                                 3-11-1829
EASTMAN, Apples to Barbary Markius                              6-1-1829
ELFRITS, Abraham to Polly Doram                                4-15-1827
ELLIOTT, Harrison P. to Elma Gandy                             9-30-1836
ELLIOTT, John to Louisa Wood                                   1-26-1832
ELYFRITS, David to Sarah Burwell                               7-29-1830
EPPAS, Wm to Laura Hutchison                                  11-15-1833
EVANS, David to Levenia Price                                  2-24-1834
EVANS, James W. to Mary McWilliams                       lic. 9-2-1833
EWING, Thomas M. to Nancy G. Robinson                         1-19-1832
FENNER, Benj. to Sarah Bennet                                 1-12-1828
FLEMOR, John to Silicia Elifritz                              3-31-1832
FORD, James to Martha Marcuss                     (Book 2)     9-15-1836
FRANKEBERGER, Eli to Caroline Rice                       lic.  4-5-1827
```

589

```
FURROW, Daniel to Polly Baty                                          lic. Oct. 1826
GALLOWAY, John to (not given) Coe                                     lic. (no date-1932)
GAMBAL, John to Sarah McEntire                                        2-5-1832
GANDY, Isaac to Eliza Maskill                                         9-29-1836
GANDY, Jacob to Lucinda Elliott                                       12-18-1834
GATES, Robens to Phebe Shepherd                                       6-9-1832
GIBSON, Joseph to Polly Anderson                                      1-4-1827
GOULDSBURY, John to Elizabeth Impson                                  3-14-1833
GRAGG, Edward to Maria Campbell                                       7-8-1830
GRAY, John to July Ann Sherman                                        5-26-1832
GRAYHAM, Robert to Judeth Bell                                        12-22-1829
GREGG, James to Eliza Bear                           (Book 2)         9-7-1836
GRIFFETH, John to Flavilla Reed                                       11-14-1835
GRIFFIN, Levin to Emily Hand                                          3-15-1832
HALE, Leonard to Sarah Crawford                      (Book 2)         12-29-1836
HALLOCK, Wesley to Mary Stone                                         7-4-1834
HAMILTON, John to Hannah Hill                        (Book 2)         8-28-1836
HARRINGTON, Nelson to Hannah Kigar (1830?) - recorded with           8-1-1831
                                   August 1830 marriages)
HARRISON, Aaron to Margaret Lookenbill                               1-14-1827
HARRISON, Alexander to Elizabeth Rowe                               1-2-1830
HARRISON, William to America Harrison                               3-20-1828
HERRIMAN, Adron to Mary Ann Sagar                              lic. 12-27-1826
HIBBARD, Lorenzo D. to Hannah Rice                                 12-11-1830
HILL, Sanford W. to Margaret McCawley                              2-23-1831
HINTON, Levi to Amina (Mina) Ann Harrington                        9-11-1828
HOLYCROSS, Benj. to Malinay Impson                                 6-29-1831
HOLYCROSS, David to Phebe Fenner                                   10-23-1834
HOLYCROSS, James to Meranda Impson                                 1-8-1829
HOLYCROSS, William to Amy Anders                                   2-9-1826
HOSKINS, Richard to Ann H. Martin (1827? - marriage return         10-25-1828
                                   filed 1-25-1828)
HUFFMAN, Wm to Phebe Bordon                                        11-6-1834
HUGHBANKS, Perry to Sarah White                                    6-18-1829
HULSE, Joseph to Acksah Gandy                                      7-5-1832
IRWIN, James P. to Polly Reynolds                                  11-7-1826
IRWIN, John of Maison (Madison?) Co. to Rhoda Stokes of Union Co.  1-4-1827
JOLLY, Joel to Drucilla Brown                                      11-27-1834
KAZAR (KARAR on lic.), Nelson to Sally McLoud                      12-26-1833
KELLY, Galader A. to Nancy Hays                                    3-5-1836
KENT, Hiram to Merandy Harrington                                  4-16-1829
KENT, John to Eleanor Clark                                        3-2-1834
KEYES, Andrew to Rebecca Sabins                               lic. 1-24-1829
KIMBLE, Hiram D. to Catharine Culver                              10-10-1836
KIGAR, Isaac to Ruth King                                         10-6-1831
KING, John to Polly Porter                                        6-29-1826
KINGRY, John to Sophia Carter                                     12-20-1828
KNAP, Porter to Mary Taylor                                       12-2-1830
KONHRIGHT, Lymon to Sarah Culver                                  2-15-1827
```

590

```
KONKLIN, Joseph to Eliza Gamble                              4-10-1832
LANE, John to Mary Dysart                                   11-24-1829
LEE, Cyprian to Mary Irwin                                  11-11-1830
LOCK, Benjamin to Elizabeth Lyon                      lic.   3-14-1829
LOCK, John S. to Loiza Harrington                           1-28-1826
LOCK, Jonathan to Charetta McCunber (?)                     6-9-1831
LONGBRAKE, Jacob to Susan Farnum                           12-12-1833
LOOKINBIL, Peter to Mary Ann Dixon          (Book2)         9-14-1836
LOW, John to Mary Jackson                                   2-17-1831
LOW, Lucas to Margaret Sager                          lic.   3-6-1828
LUCKENBILL, John to Elizabeth Andrus                        9-10-1828
McCAWKEY, John to Eleanor Laughlin                          2-12-1835
McCLOUD, James to Adaline Stewart                           1-23-1834
McDONALD, Samuel to Rachael Corner                         10-23-1834
McLOUD, Wm to Sophia Smith                                  1-11-1834
MASTELLER, Thos. to Matilda Brannen                         2-18-1836
MATHER, Increase to Sarah Dilseiver                   lic.9-20-1832
MATHERS, Wm to Phebe Allen                                  3-26-1832
MERSHAWN, John to Hester Garwood                            4-24-1834
MIDDLETON, John to Mrs. Anna Cobumber       (Book 2)       12-29-1836
MIDDLINGTON, Lansing to Polly Andrews                       6-14-1832
MILLIGAN, Benj'n to Lydia Sayman                            4-10-1834
MITCHELL, William to Mary W. Reed                           4-13-1826
MOODY, Elias to Ann Impson                                  8-26-1830
MOODY, George to Margaret Stackhous                        12-23-1830
MOODY, Henry to Elizabeth Moody                             7-7-1831
MORE, Daniel to Mary Coder                                  8-28-1834
MORROW, James to Jane McWilliams                            4-1-1833
MORROW, Wm to Louisa Alexander                             10-1-1832
MORSE, Rha to Sarah Portemon                              12-16-1830
MULLEN, Joseph to Sarah Gibson                             6-7-1832
MILLIN, Stephen D. to Latitia Shelpman                     7-4-1833
MYERS, Christopher to Hannah Graham                       12-11-1828
MYERS, Michael to Catharine Johnson                        7-28-1836
ORANOODT, Jacob to Prescella Garret                        1-14-1830
PARKER, John to Clarinda Carter                            7-17-1834
PARKINSON, Wm to Jane Reed                                 10-2-1828
PARMENTER, Sylvester to Elizabeth R. Spencer               8-2-1834
PATCH, Stephen to Sarah Ann Howard                    lic.(no date-1832)
PATRICK, Ira to Laura Tarpring                             2-9-1826
PHELPS, Horrace to Harriet Dickinson                      11-30-1834
PHELPS, Levi to Sarah Cooper                              10-3-1826
PLUMMER, John Westley to Matilda Randal                   12-27-1827
POLLOCK, George to Sarah Jane Ribinson                    10-19-1832
PORTER, Jesse to Eleanor R. Reed                      lic.   3-26-1828
PORTHEMORE, Frederick to Permelia Morse                   1-12-1832
PORTHEMORE, George to Mary Wood                           10-21-1829
POTTER, Edward to Elizabeth Reynolds                      8-2-1832
PRICE, Wm to Hannah Carney                                1-21-1830
RANDAL, Tabor to Elizabeth Cheny                          1-2-1832
RANDALL, Thomas to Mary Stewart                           2-6-1827
```

```
RATHBORN, Charles to Elizabeth Russell                              11-25-1830
REAMES, Edward to Huldah Impson                                     3-26-1833
REED, David to Mary Allen                                          2-12-1829
REED, Jacob to Ann Shesler                                         3-9-1835
REED, James to Asenath McWilliams                                 10-16-1834
REED, John P. to Melinda Asher                       lic.          4-11-1826
REED, Joseph to Nancy Rice                                        10-10-1833
REED, Samuel to Sarah Davis                                       2-12-1829
REED, Samuel to Susan Amrine                                      8-29-1833
REED, Thos. to Jane Robenson                                      8-19-1830
REED, Wm to Mary Amrine                              (Book 2)      8-28-1836
REYNOLDS, James to Elizabeth Russell                              12-4-1834
REYBIKDS (MUTTEN on lic.), Thomas to Jane Reynolds               10-25-1832
RICE, Harvey to Susan Thomas                         (Book 2)      9-15-1836
RICE, Jason to Julia Lathrop                                      10-11-1826
RIDDLE, Abner to Clarrissa R. Gooding                lic.          (no date-1831)
ROBINSON, Joseph to Sarah D. Gooding                             10-16-1833
ROBINSON, Patterson to Nancy Marshall                (Book2)      12-6-1836
ROBINSON, William to Hannah Coe                                  10-4-1826
ROBINSON, Wm M. to Hannah H. Crawford                            2-12-1829
ROSEBERRY, Joseph to Margaret Carter                             1-29-1829
ROYEL, Merrall to Elizabeth Kerew                    (Book 2)     11-27-1836
RUSSELL, James to Charity Smith                                  2-10-1828
SAGAR, Abraham to Evaline Smith                                  2-26-1835
SAGER, Adam to Elizabeth Smith                                   1-13-1833
SAGER, Christian to Elizabeth Russell                            11-9-1835
SUGAR, Fayette to Theresa Clark                                  9-20-1832
SAGAR, Henry to Naomi Carney                                     5-26-1830
SAGAR, Levi to Margaret Low                          lic.         11-8-1828
SCOTT, Lewis to Mahala A. Bennett                    Book 2)      8-25-1836
SEAMIN, Jacob to Caroline Saunders                               5-6-1830
SENNET, Gideon to Lucy Alley                                     10-2-1828
SHAFER, Daniel to Elizabeth Leaver                               4-7-1835
SHELPMAN, Cornelius to Mary Mullen                               2-16-1832
SHIRK, Levi to Patsey Taylor                                     9-9-1832
SIMPSON, Samuel to Mary Vorannon                                 10-23-1828
SINNET, Jacob to Eve King                                        2-15-1826
SMART, John S. to Mary Robinson                                  5-23-1833
SMITH, Edward to Hannah Elliott                                  3-12-1833
SMITH, Henry to Belinda Bennit                                   3-6-1836
SMITH, James to Mary Ann (Margaret on lic.) Grayham             2-27-1831
SMITH, Job to Mary Moore                             (Book 2)     7-21-1836
SMITH, John to Malinda Scott                                     8-14-1834
SMITH, Robny to Delila Reynolds (1828? - recorded with Dec.     12-18-1829
                     1828 marriages)
SMITH, Samuel to Mary E. Marquis                                12-30-1830
SNODGRASS, James R. to Elizabeth Worthington                    8-28-1832
SNODGRASS, Robert to Eleanor Robinson                           1-1-1828
```

```
SNODGRASS, Samuel to Nancy Morrison                              7-9-1835
SNODGRASS, William to Sarah Robinson                             3-19-1829
SOMER, Jacob to (not given) Griddinger                           4-10-1834
SOUT (LOUT?), Aaron to Elizabeth Harrison                        9-9-1833
SOUTHARD, William to Phebe Burwell                               5-14-1831
SPAIN, Edward to Mary Gabriel                                    10-24-1833
SPAIN, Hezekiah of Champaign Co. to Susanna(h) Epp(e)s           (8-11-1829)
         Of Union Co.                        2 dates  (9-3-1829 )
SPAIN, Paschael to Milly Spain                                   12-30-1835
SPENCER, Levi to Rachael E. Tunks                                2-28-1833
SPERGIN, Jesse to Susan Willson                                  4-9-1829
STARWAT, Mervin to Lucinda Comely                                5-3-1835
STEWART, John to Adaline Robert                                  3-2-1830
STINER, Christian to Ruth Gibson (note: probably same as         7-9-1829
         Christopher Stoner; if so, recorded twice0
STMY, Hollis to Prudence S. Williams                      lic. 3-16-1829
STOKES, Joseph to Logan Co. to Mary Austin of Union Co.          4-23-1829
STONER(?), Christopher to Ruth Gibson                            7-9-1829
STRONG, Eri to Elizabeth Baldwin                                 3-10-1831
SYMPSON, Oliver to Maria Wood                                    1-23-1830
TARBERT (HARBERT on lic.) Eligah to Elnor Reed                   10-24-1833
TARPARING, Lawrence to Mary Davis                                2-14-1826
TAYLOR, Asa to Elizabeth Comer                                   1-20-1831
TAYLOR, Levi to Margaret Sagar                                   2-4-1830
TAYLOR, Moses to Susan Marshall                                  7-9-1828
TAYLOR, Wm to Elizabeth Burdick                                  11-28-1830
THOMPSON, James to Catharine Gamble                              1-5-1832
THOMPSON, Wm to Matilda Gambal                                   3-26-1832
TONGET, Larkin to Mary Bennett                                   2-7-1833
TUCKER, Lemuel to Maria Walton                                   1-18-1828
TURNER, William to Etitille Ervin                                7-13-1834
TWIFORD, Thomas to Nancy Irvin                            lic. (no date-1832)
WALKER, Daniel D. to Sarah Cralinger                             2-5-1835
Wells, Absolem to Mary Galland                                   9-18-1833
WELLS, David to Keziah Amrine                                    2-21-1830
WELLS, James to Sarah Hicks                                      1-11-1832
WEST, John to Caroline Palch (Patch?)                     lic. 1-2-1829
WESTLAKE, George to Tamer Lundy                                  11-12-1835
WESTLAKE, Welling to Sophia Elliot                               9-7-1828
WESTLAKE, Zephaniah to Isabella Gragg                            11-11-1829
WHITE, George to Maria Newell                                    6-15-1832
WILCOX, Jonathan to Charity Patch                                2-20-1834
WILLER, Christopher to Mina Allen                                3-19-1834
WILLER (WITTER on lic.), Elijah to Mary Ann Ballow               4-4-1830
WILLIAMS, Amos A. to Eleanor Stewart                      lic. 3-31-1828
WILLARD, James to Sarah Lockwood                                 5-30-1830
WILSON, Joseph to Lousa Atwood                                   10-6-1836
WILSON, Robert to Rachel Culver                                  3-5-1833
WILSON, William to Hannah Sagar                                  7-7-1831
WILSON, William to Sarah Ann Williams                            6-1-1833
```

WINGET, Stephen to Matilda W. Marshall		10-26-1829
WOODS, Thomas F. to Lucy Palmer		11-22-1831
WOOLCOTT, Minor to Clarinda Butler	lic.	7-13-1826
WOOLFORD, Elijah to Elizabeth Amrine		6-24-1830
WORLEY, William to Jane Golder		10-12-1834
WYNENT, Jas. to Eliza Bates		10-8-1835

UNION COUNTY, OHIO - MINSTERS' LICENSES 1826-1836

MINISTER	CHURCH	DATE ISSUED	COUNTY ISSUED	RECORDED UNION CO.
LAURENCE, Rev. Benj'n	M.E.	2-26-1828	Butler Co., O.	3-6-1829
CARNEY, Rev. John	Baptist	11-13-1817	Pike Co., Ohio	6-6-1829
DAVISON, Daniel	M.E.	9-15-1815	Champaign Co.,O.	7-1-1830
JONES, Isaac	Baptist	7-9-1830	Madison, Ohio	11-22-1831
BIGELOW, Rev. Russel	Methodist	9-5-1818	Butler Co. Ohio	------1831
ASHLEY, Harry	Christian	4-12--1831	Darke Co. Ohio	12-25-1831
DUDLEY, Rev. David	Free-Will Baptist	7-16-1822	Delaware Co., O.	------1831
BURGE, Christian	Christian	7-15-1821	-----------	4-6-1832
CAMP, Rev. Harvey	M. E.	10-22-1832	Richland Co. O.	11-10-1833
JOHNSON, Rev. John	M. E.	10-12-1830	Monroe Co., O.	------1834
CENVERN, Jeremiah	M. E.	11-27-1813	Madison Co. O.	10-24-1834
WESTLAKE, William	M. E.	3-17-1831	Fayette Co. O.	11-17-1834
FRAZELL, Warren	M. E.	11-5-1830	Madison Co. O.	------1855
RAPER, William H.	M. E.	1-1-1822	Hamilton Co.O.	------1835
REYNOLDS, Thomas	Presbyterian	3-11-1835	Delaware Co.O.	------1835
MINEAR, Adam	N. E.	10-22-1829	Pickaway Co.O.	------1835
SOUS, Rev. Benjamín	M. E.	8-11-1818	Warren Co. Oh.	------1835

(note: the following two licenses are on slips of paper in book with not all information given)

| MARVIN, Samuel B. | | 10-14-1824 |
| BARBER, Hallet | | 4-25-1834 |

UNION COUNTY, OHI(- WILL, ESTATE AND GUARDIANSHIP RECORDS 1821-1828

The following records were copied from "Record of Wills 1821-1829" located in the Probate Court. Pages on which record may be found are given in parenthesis.

Joshua EWING of Jerome twp. - Will - dated 4-24-1821; recorded (not given). Wife, Margaret. Eight children: Polly J. Chapman, Eliza Mitchale, George Jamison, Joshua Green, Peggy Jamison, Cynthia Annes, Martha Ramsey and Harriet Newel. Mentions possibility of wife bearing another child. Executors: wife, Margaret and brother, James Ewing. Signed: Joshuah Ewing. Witnesses: James E. Donalson, Calvin Winget and Elizabeth Gill. (1)

Samuel MITCHELL - Nuncupative Will - will given 5-28-1821; recorded 6-16-1821. Wife, mentioned but not named. Three sons: Samuel, James and David. Daughters: Sarah, Margaret, Jean, Elizabeth and Eleanor. Not all children were of age. Executors: wife and her brother, Alexander Robinson. Witnesses: Samuel Kirkpatrick and Jane Kirkpatrick. (3)

Eliphaz BURNAM of Union twp. - Will - dated 9-6-1821; recorded 1-10-1822. Wife, Lydia. Two sons, Jacob and Eliphaz; also to serve as executors. Daughters: Zelinda H. Lerce, Orvilla, Julliett, Lydia Smith and Nancy. Signed: Eliphaz Durnam. Witnesses: Anson Howard, Nicholas Hathaway and Harden Harvey. (4)

James COCHRAN - Will - dated 9-20-1822; recorded 12-15-1822. Son, James. Daughters: Susanah, Elener, Mary, Rosannah and Jane; three youngest daughters not married. Executors: Andrew Gill and Alexander Reed. Signed: James Cochran. Witnesses: Charlot Haver (or Hover), Sarah Haver (or Hover) and William Ware. (5)

George BROWN of Union twp. - Verbal Will - will given 8-30-1823; recorded 11-8-1823. Wife, mentioned but not named. Son, George. Mentions that farm testator purchased from William Burnam is to go back to him. Witnesses: John Reed and Elizabeth McDonald. (6)

Samuel GALLOWAY - Estate - Adms. Achsy Galloway. Letters issued 11-13-1821; recorded April Term 1824. (31)

Orlando BAGLEY - Estate - Adms., Jesse Bagley. Letters issued 11-13-1821; recorded April Term 1824. (36)

Joseph STEWART - Estate - Adms. Eleanor Stewart and Joan F. Gabriel. Letters issued 9-14-1821; recorded April Term 1824. (42)

Abraham SAGER – Appraisal of personal property; 4-29-1823. (58)

Augustus COOLIDGE – Estate – Adms., John Coolidge. Letters issued 8-19-1823. (59)

George ORR – Estate – Adms., Susannah Orr and William Orr. Letters issued 8-19-1823. (60)

Samuel TEETERS – Estate – Adms., Thomas McDaniel. Letters issued 11-3-1823. (63)

James ROBINSON – Estate – Adms., Jane Robinson, widow. Letters issued 11-4-1823.(66)

William MUNGER – Estate – Adms., Asa Plumer. Letters issued 11-3-1823. (73)

James CONNER – Estate – Adms., James Buck. Deborah Conner, widow declined adms. Letters issued 11-12-1823. (74)

Reuben KERR – Estate – Adms., Michael Kerr (Carr). Letters issued 4-19-1824. (79)

Lancelot MAZE (MAYS) – Estate – Adms., Mary Maze and Robert Maze. Letters issued 4-19-1824. (81)

Betsey ORR – Estate – Adms., William Orr. Letters issued 4-19-1824. (85)

David REED – Verbal Will – recorded 6-25-1824. Wife, Margaret. Eldest son, Thomas Reed; two youngest sons, Samuel and Seppas Reed. Four daughters, Betsy, Jane, Synthia and Lydia Reed. Witnesses: Alex'r Reed and James Curry. Alex'r Reed appointed adms. (88)

Benjamin BEDLACK – Estate – Adms., Richard Gabriel. Letters issued 4-19-1824. (98)

Eleanor COCHRAN of Union twp. – Will – dated 4-2-1822; recorded 4-22-1824. Oldest daughter, Rosanna Porter; daughter, Susannah Porter. Two sons, Thomas and James Cochran. Grandson, William Piper. Executor: son-in-law, John Porter. Signed: Eleanor (her mark) Cochran. Witnesses: Andrew Gill and Robert Snodgrass. (101)

George BROWN – Estate – Adms., David Conner. Letters issued 6-16-1824. (104)

Harden HOVEY of Union twp. – Estate – Adms., Edmond Hovey and Samuel T. Hovey. Letters issued 6-16-1824. (118)

James COCHRAN – Estate – Adms., Ezra Winget and Joseph Lawrence. Letters issue 9-27-1824. (123)

Samuel KIRKPATRICK of Darby twp. – dated 4-13-1822; recorded 9-27-1824. Wife, Jane Daughter, Elizabeth Irwin. Executors: wife, Jane and Samuel Robinson. Signed: Samuel Kirkpatrick. Witnesses: Samuel Leeper and James M. Crawford. (125)

John SHERMAN – Estate – Adms., William Thompson. Letters issued 9-27-1824. (131)

Balsor KING - Estate - Adms., John King. Eve King, widow, declined adms. Letters issued 9-27-1824. (140)

Andrew BURNHAM - Estate - Adms., Nathaniel Kazan. Letters issued 9-27-1824. (147)

John COOLIDGE appointed guardian of Lucy COOLIDGE an insane person, daughter of Augustus COOLIDGE, dec'd; 8-18-1823. (163)

James SNODGRASS - Estate - Adms., Agnes Snodgrass and Alex Robinson. Letters issued 2-26-1825. (168)

Guardianship of Eleanor STEWART for William and Adaline STEWART vacated, with James STEWART being appointed guardian of William and Adaline and also, John STEWART; 2-25-1825. (171)

David BURNHAM appointed guardian of George and Jedediah B. FULLER; 2-25-1825. (173)

David COMER appointed guardian of George Washington COOLIDGE: 2-25-1825. (174)

James A. CURRY appointed guardian of Julian SHERMAN aged 9 yrs. and John SHERMAN aged 7 yrs., heirs of John SHERMAN, dec'd.; 2-25-1825. (176)

George BROWN - Estate - Adms., Harvey Burnham. Eliza HOVEY relinquishes right to adms. estate; Letters issued 6-27-1827. (180)

David COMER of Uniob twp. - Will - dated 5-21-1825; recorded 6-27-1825. Wife, mentioned but not named. Two daughters, Eliza and Rachel to have land in Deer Creek twp. of Madison County. Son, Samuel Bear and daughter Polly to have homestead where testator lives and lot 40 in Marysville. Bequest to the Heirs of Joshua Bogard (not named) who are not of age, to be handled by Robert Carnell their uncle. Executors: Nicholas Hathaway and Anson Howard. Signed: David Comer. Witnesses: Edmond Hovey, James Willber and Reuben Plummer. (184)

James ANDERSON - Estate - Adms., Samuel Mitchell. Letters issued 10-3-1825. (192)

David BURNHAM appointed guardian of Samuel SHEROWWD aged 18 yrs.; 10-3-1825. (195)

James F. COOLIDGE appointed guardian of George W. COOLIDGE aged 18 yrs; 10-3-1825. (197)

James BOAL appointed guardian of Abraham SAGAR aged 2 yrs. heir of Abraham SAGAR, dec'd; 10-3-1825. (199)

James BOAL appointed guardian of Martha KING aged 7 yrs., George KING aged 4 yrs. and David B. KING aged 2 yrs., heirs of Balsor KING, dec'd.; 10-3-1825. (201)

Daniel BOWEN - Estate - Adms., Richard Gabriel. Widow, Nancy Bowen declined right to adms. estate. Letters issued 2-17-1826. (210)

Pierce LANPHIN appointed guardian of Juliann SHERMAN aged 9 yrs. and John SHERMAN aged 7 yrs., heirs of John SHERMAN, dec'd.; 2-27-1826. (213)

Margaret REED appointed guardian of Cynthia and Lydia REED, heirs of David REED, dec'd; 2-17-1826. (214)

Samuel REED appointed guardian of Samuel REED aged 18 yrs., Cephas REED aged 16 yrs. and Jane REED aged 14 yrs.; heirs of David REED, dec'd; 2-17-1826. (214)

Jeremiah GARNER - Estate - Adms., Cyprean Lee. Letters issued 11-13-1826. (233)

Uriah WOOD - Estate - Adms., Ira Wood and Michael Wood. Letters issued 11-13-1826. (236)

James McDOWELL - Verbal Will - will given 10-15-1826; recorded 11-13-1826. Wife, mentioned but not named. Mentions four children but only names youngest child, Hannah who was not of age. Executor, Robert Nelson. Witnesses: Robert Nelson and Thomas Reed. James Snodgrass was appointed adms. (240)

Nancy BOWEN appointed guardian of Jane BOWEN aged 10 yrs. 28 Feb. 1827, Daniel BOWEN, aged 7 yrs. 8 July 1827 and Peleg BOWEN aged 3 yrs. 15 April 1827; (not dated-1827?). (266)

Josias MILLER - Estate - Adms., Silas G. Strong. Letters issued 10-8-1827. (273)

George WOODWARD - Estate - Adms., Benjamin Hopkins. Widow, Lydia Woodward relinquishes right to adms. estate. Letters issued 1-15-1828. (286)

James STEWART attested to the death of his father, James STEWART, who while living was guardian of Eleanor, William and Adaline STEWART, heirs of Joseph STEWART, dec'd. Harvey BURNHAM is now appointed their guardian; 2-22-1828. (292)

Deposition that James SNODGRASS, dec'd, left a widow Agnes Snodgrass and the following children—William Snodgrass, Jane late Snodgrass now the wife of John Reed, James R. Snodgrass, Samuel Snodgrass, Polly Snodgrass and Agnes Snodgrass Jr.; 2-28-1828. (293)

UNION COUNTY, Ohio was formed in 1820 from parts of FRANKLIN, MADISON and LOGAN Counties.

VAN WERT COUNTY, OHIO - COMMON PLEAS COURT RECORDS
JOURNAL A - 1837-1847

The following records were taken from "Journal A" located in the vault of the
Common Pleas Court (Clerk of Court's Office) at the court house at Van Wert. Page
on which record may be found in original book is given in parenthesis.

10-3-1837 - First session of court held at Willshire.
5-11-1838 - Grans Jury: Daniel P. CROSS, James MAJOR, Peter FISINGER, Jacob W.
   HARPER, Robert GILLELAND, Washington MARK, Peter BULLENBAUGH, John KEETH, David
   KING, John F. DODDS, Ezra F. PARRET, Eli COMPTON, John POOL, Thomas C. MILLER,
   Henry MEYERS. (3)
5-11-1838 - William CASE granted license to keep tavern at his house in Willshire.(4)
5-11-1838 - Thomas C. MILLER granted license to keep tavern at his house in
   Willshire. (4)
5-11-1838 - Henry REICHARD vs. Rachel McMANAS and others. Petition for Partition.
   Widow, Rachel McManus entitled to dower, Partition: 2/7ths part, Henry REICHARD;
   1/7th part William McMANAS; 1/7 part, Henry McMANAS; 1/7th part, Jacob McMANAS;
   1/7th part, Philip McMANAS; 1/7th part, unknown heirs of John McMANAS Jr., dec'd.
   (5)
5-11-1838 - Petit Jurors: Joseph JOHNSON, Charles MOUNT, Asahel BURRIGHT, Daniel
   COOK, Joseph GLEASON, Daniel STETLER, Stephen GLEASON, William MARRS, Levi
   SAWYER and James YOUNG. (8)
11-16-1838 - Grand Jury: Thomas C. MILLER, Abraham PONTIUS, Daniel STETLER, David
   KING, Ezra F. GERARD, John KEATH, Joshua CHILCOAT, Sam'l FOSTER, Owen BURRIGHT,
   William H. PURDY, John KEITH, Jacob M. HARPER, Martin W. KEMP, Quinton REED,
   George LESLIE. (10)
11-16-1838 - Peter Bolenbaugher appointed guardian of Isaac AYERS aged 12 yrs. on
   13 March past, Sarah Anny AYERS aged 10 yrs. on 20 March past, and George WASH-
   INGTON AYERS aged 8 yrs. on 4 July past, minor children of George AYERS, dec'd.
   (14)
11-16-1838 - Samuel CLARK granted license to keep tavern in Van Wert. (14)
4-19-1839 - William CASE granted license to keep tavern at his houss in Willshire.(19)
4-19-1839 - Thomas C. MILLER granted license to keep tavern at his house in Willshire township. (19)
4-19-1839 - James Q. GRAVES granted license to keep tavern at his house in Van
   Wert. (19)
4-19-1839 - Will of Henry MYERS, dec'd produced and recorded by court. (24)
9-20-1839 - William H. PURDY granted license to keep tavern at his house in Willshire. (28)
9-20-1839 - John ALSAP granted license to keep tavern at his house in Willshire
   township. (29)
9-20-1839 - Will of Abiah COOK, dec'd produced and recorded in court. (29)
9-29-1839 - Thomas Mott appointed adms. of the estate of Gideon MOTT, dec'd, late
   of Van Wert County. (30)
5-1-1840 - Joseph GLEASON granted license to keep tavern at house formerly kept by
   James Q. GREAVES in Van Wert. (33)
5-1-1840 - Samuel M. CLARK granted license to keep tavern at house occupied as
   tavern by him in Van Wert. (34)
5-1-1840 - State of Ohio vs. TAWOHESUCH (TZWOHESUGH) alias George SOLOMON. Indictment for Murder. Found "Found "Guilty of manslaughter" and given five years
   hard labor in solitary confinement in penitentary of Ohio. (36 & 37)
7-1-1840 - Thomas R. KEAR appointed auctioneer and gave bond. (42)

599

9-25-1840 - Jonathan MAJOR granted license to keep tavern at house lately occupied by Mr. Alsap in Willshire. (46)

9-25-1840 - William H. PURDY granted license to keep tavern at his house in Willshire. (47)

5-3-1841 - John HART a native of Germany made his declaration of intention to become citizen. (51)

5-3-1841 - S.M. CLARK granted license to keep tavern at house now occupied by him. (51)

5-3-1841 - Joseph GLEASON granted license to keep tavern at house now occupied by him. (51)

5-3-1841 - John K. Hunter appointed guardian of Peterson WILSON aged 2 yrs., child of Isaac WILSON, dec'd. (52)

5-4-1841 - Thomas R. KEAR appointed auctioneer. (60)

10-4-1841 - Jonathan W. MAJOR granted license to keep tavern at his house in Willshire. (65)

10-4-1841 - Martin SHOWALTER aged 23 years, native of Bavaria makes his declaration of intention to become citizen. (67)

10-4-1841 - Even B. Jones appointed adms. of the estate of John BEVINGTON, dec'd late of Van Wert County. (70)

10-4-1841 - Elias Evers appointed adms. of the estate of Joseph CLARK, dec'd late of Van Wert County. (70)

10-4-1841 - Elizabeth Bevington appointed guardian of Henry BEVINGTON, Nancy Ann BEVINGTON, Rebecca Jane BEVINGTON, James BEVINGTON and Mary BEVINGTON all children of John BEVINGTON, dec'd. (72)

10-4-1841 - Thomas R. Kear appointed adms. of the estate of Noah FRISINGER, dec'd, late of Van Wert County. (73)

10-5-1841 - William H. PURDY granted license to keep tavern at his house at Willshire. (76)

10-5-1841 - Henry GERMANN and Jacob GERMANN made oath of Renunciation and allegiance and were admitted to all rights and privileges of citizens of the United States of America. (76)

5-2-1842 - Samuel M. CLARK granted license to keep tavern at his house in Van Wert. (83)

5-2-1842 - Joseph GLEASON granted license to keep tavern at his residence in Van Wert. (83)

5-3-1842 - Henry KAZER, a native of Switzerland makes his declaration of intention to become citizen. (89)

5-4-1842 - John Myers executor of the estate of Henry MEYERS, dec'd filed final settlement. (94)

5-4-1842 - Thomas R. Mott adms. of the estate of Gideon MOTT, dec'd filed final settlement. (94)

10-3-1842 - Jonathan MAJORS granted license to keep tavern at house occupied by him in Willshire. (100)

10-3-1842 - Evan B. JONES a native of Wales. Naturalization. Declaration of intention made in Common Pleas Court of Butler County, Ohio on 10-6-1840. (101)

10-4-1842 - William H. PURDY granted license to keep tavern at house occupied by him in Willshire. (104)

10-4-1842 - Peter GERMAN a native of Hesse Hamburgh Germany makes his declaration of intention to become citizen. (108)

10-4-1842 - Charles P. GERMAN a native of Hesse Hamburgh Germany makes his declaration of intention to become citizen. (108)

600

10-4-1842 - Peter HEWITT a native of Hesse Hamburgh Germany. Naturalization.
Oath by Jacob German and Charles German. (110)
10-4-1842 - Sylvester Woolery appointed guardian of Levi KNOX aged 12 yrs., Susan
KNOX aged 10 yrs., George KNOX aged 8 yrs., Lydia KNOX aged 6 yrs., Norman
KNOX aged 4 yrs., and Martha KNOX aged 1 yr. & 6 mos., children of George KNOX,
dec'd. (110)
10-4-1842 - Jacob KREISHER a native of Prussia. Naturalization. Oath by Jacob
German and Charles German. (111)
10-4-1842 - Philip Michael KREISHER a native of Prussia. Naturalization. Declaration of intention made in Common Pleas Court of Holmes County, Ohio on 6-17-
1840. Oath by Charles German and Jacob German. (112)
10-4-1842 - Mary Ann CLARK aged 12 yrs. chose Lewis Culver as her guardian and he
appointed to also serve as guardian of Rachel CLARK aged 9 yrs. (118)
10-4-1842 - Elizabeth CLARK aged 13 yrs. chose John Arnold as her guardian and he
appointed to also serve as guardian of Nathan CLARK aged 9 yrs. (118)
11-12-1842 - Jacob M. Harper appointed adms. of the estate of Joshua WATKINS,
dec'd. (120)
11-12-1842 - Esther Eliza BRONSON aged 17 yrs. daughter of Augustus BRONSON, dec'd
chose George W. Angevim as her guardian and he appointed to also serve as guardian of Hannah C. BRONSON aged 10 yrs., and Aaron A. BRONSON aged 6 yrs., children of Augustus Bronson, dec'd. (120)
5-1-1843 - Baltis BIENTZ a native of Germany. Naturalization. Oath by Christian
Auker and John W. Conn. (132)
5-1-1843 - Rev. John HILL a minister of the United Brethren church granted license
to solemnize marriages. (133)
5-2-1843 - Morgan SAVIDGE granted license to keep tavern at his house in Van Wert.
(136)
5-3-1843 - John HARTZ a native of Germany. Naturalization. Oath by Charles German
and Daniel Cook. (145)
10-2-1843 - Jonathan JAJOR granted license to keep tavern at house occupied by him
in Willshire. (152)
10-2-1843 - Jared Gates appointed adms. of the estate of James HEMPHILL, dec'd.
Widow, Fanny GATES relinquishes right to adms. estate. (153)
10-2-1843 - Solomon FURMAN appointed guardian of Stephen COOK an idiot aged 45
years. (154)
10-2-1843 - Frederick SCHUMM a native of Wurtemburgh, Germany. Naturalization.
Oath by Henry Reichard and Thomas R. Kear. (159)
10-2-1843 - John SCHUMM, Jacob SCHUMM and George SCHUMM, natives of Germany.
Naturalization. Oath by Henry Reichard and Thomas R. Kear. (159)
10-3-1843 - William H. PURDY granted license to keep tavern at his house in Willshire. (161)
10-3-1843 - James Reed appointed adms. of the estate of George W. HARTER, dec'd.
Late widow, Rachel REED relinquishes right to adms. (162)
10-3-1843 - John BRENNER a native of Germany makes his declaration of intention to
become citizen. (164)
10-3-1843 - Lewis SCHUMM a native of Wurtenburgh, Germany. Naturalization. Oath
by John Tumbleson and Henry Schumm. (166)
5-8-1844 - Frederick William HONSTETT a native of Prussia now a resident of Van Wert
County makes his declaration of intention to become citizen. (175)

5-9-1844 - Elizabeth SHULTZ aged 14 yrs. and Sarah SHULTZ aged 12 yrs., children of
Eve SHULTZ, dec'd chose Amos Roop as their guardian. (178)

5-9-1844 - Adam Woolford appointed guardian of Sarah Jane HARTER aged 11 yrs.,
Elizabeth HARTER aged 9 yrs. and George Ann HARTER aged 2 yrs., children of
George W. HARTER, dec'd. (181)

5-9-1844 - Frederick PFEIL a native of Germany. Naturalization. Declaration of
intention filed in Common Pleas court of Columbiana Co., Ohio on 5-30-1833.(182)

5-9-1844 - Henry KAZER a native of Switzerland. Naturalization. Declaration of
intention made 5-3-1842 in this court. Oath by John G. Morse and Samuel Maddux.
(182)

5-11-1844 - Joseph GLEASON granted license to keep tavern selling spiritous liquors
at his house in Van Wert. (194)

5-11-1844 - Morgan SAVIDGE granted license to keep tavern selling spiritous liquors
at his house in Van Wert. (195)

5-11-1844 - Robert BURROWS vs. Susan BURROWS, petition for divorce. (196)

7-8-1844 - Crenus Elliott Jr. appointed adms. of the estate of Francis ELLIOTT,
dec'd. Widow, Laura Elliott relinquishes right to adms. (198)

9-25-1844 - James Walters appointed adms. of the estate of David WALTERS, dec'd.
Widow, Mary Walter relinquishes her right to adms. (204)

9-25-1844 - Bernard ESCH a native of Hanover now of Van Wert County makes his
declaration of intention to become citizen. (209)

9-25-1844 - Henry ZENTMAN a native of Hanover now of Van Wert County makes his
declaration of intention to become citizen. (209)

9-25-1844 - Conrad LAUDRICK a native of Prussia now of Van Wert County makes his
declaration of intention to become citizen. (209)

9-25-1844 - Abiah FURMAN vs. Jacob THORN (or THOM). Bastardy. Jacob found guilty
of being father of said child of Abiah and fined $200.00 for support of child.(211)

9-26-1844 - William MEYER a native of Hanover. Naturalization. Declaration of
intention made in common pleas court of Mercer Co., Ohio on 11-10-1840. Oath
by John Lewis and Henry Powel. (212)

9-26-1844 - Jonathan MAJOR granted license to keep temperance tavern at house
occupied by him at Willshire. (212)

9-26-1844 - Peter Brubaker appointed adms. de bonis non of the estate of James
HEMPHILL, dec'd. (214)

9-27-1844 - George Reese appointed adms. of the estate of Philip REESE, dec'd.
Widow, Maria Reese relinquishes right to adms. (222)

5-12-1845 - Catherine WALTERS aged 16 yrs. on 20th day of Feb. last past, daughter
of David Walters, dec'd chose Alexander Walters as her guardian. (227)

5-12-1845 - Jacob W. Johns appointed guardian of Lucinda J. ELLER aged 9 yrs. on
30 January last past, child of Frederick ELLER, dec'd. (228)

5-12-1845 - Michael Anderson appointed adms. of the estate of Thomas ANDERSON, dec'd.
Widow, Susannah Anderson relinquishes her right to adms. (228)

5-12-1845 - George P. GERMAN a native of Hesse Hamburgh Germany now a resident of
Van Wert County makes his declaration of intention to become citizen. (231)

5-12-1845 - Charles P. GERMAN a native of Hessan Hamburg Germany. Naturalization.
Declaration of intention made in common pleas court of this county 10-4-1842.
Oath by Peter German and Jacob German. (231)

5-12-1845 - Peter GERMAN a native of Hesse Hamburg Germany. Naturalization.
Declaration of intention made in common pleas court this county 10-4-1842.
Oath by Jacob German and Peter German. (232)

5-12-1845 - Henry SHOWALTER a native of Bavaria Germany. Naturalization. Came
to United States at under 16 years of age. Oath by Peter Heart and Martin
Showalter. (233)

5-12-1845 - George P. RIDEBAUGH a native of Hesse Hamburgh Germany. Naturalization. Came to United States at under 16 yrs. of age. Oath by Peter German and Jacob German. (233)

5-12-1845 - John GIESLER a native of Hessen Hamburgh Germany. Naturalization. Declaration of intention made in common pleas court of Holmes County, Ohio on 11-12-1841. Oath by Peter German and Jacob German. (234)

5-13-1845 - Thomas C. MILLER granted license to keep temperance tavern at his house in Willshire township. (240)

5-13-1845 - David MAJOR granted license to keep a tavern at his house in Willshire township. (241)

5-15-1845 - Joseph GLEASON granted license to keep tavern with privilege of retailing at his residence in Pleasant township. (250)

5-16-1845 - Thomas THORN granted license to keep temperance tavern at his house.(256)

5-17-1845 - Samuel ENGLERIGHT appointed auctioneer. (263)

8-5-1845 - Coonrod HENRY a native of Bavaria Germany now of Van Wert County makes his declaration of intention to become citizen. (272)

9-29-1845 - Morgan SAVIDGE granted license to keep a tavern at his residence in Broedike. (274)

9-29-1845 - Robert MAJOR granted license to keep tavern at his house in Willshire. (275)

9-29-1845 - Benjamin FISHER granted license to keep tavern at his house in Van Wert. (275)

9-29-1845 - Jacob LEITRICK a native of Hessen Hamburgh Germany. Naturalization. Declaration of intention made in common pleas court of this county 10-2-1843, (276)

9-29-1845 - Andrew ROEHM a native of Wurtemburgh Germany. Naturalization. Declaration of intention made in common pleas court of this county 9-12-1840. (276)

9-29-1845 - Absalom Brey appointed adms. of the estate of John SHAFFER, dec'd. Widow, Christena Shaffer relinquishes her right to adms. (277)

9-29-1845 - Absalom Brey appointed adms. of estate of John SHLATER, dec'd. Widow, Phebe Shlater relinquishes her right to adms. (278)

9-29-1845 - Robert BURROWS vs. Susan BURROWS, in petition for divorce--case dismissed. (282)

9-30-1845 - Benjamin D. STROTHER vs. Mary Ann STROTHER. Petition for divorce. Divorce granted with custody of children (not named) granted to petitioner.(294)

10-2-1845 - Solomon Furman removed as guardian of Stephen COOK and Daniel Cook appointed his guardian. (301)

11-15-1845 - Robert GILLILAND appointed adms. of the estate of William HILL, dec'd. (303)

3-14-1846 - Elizabeth Bredeick and Bernard Esch appointed adms. of the estate of Ferdinand BREDEICK, dec'd. (305)

3-14-1846 - Hannah C. BRONSON aged 13 yrs. on 14 January last past, daughter of Augustus Bronson, dec'd chose John F. Woodruff as her guardian. (306)

5-12-1846 - Joseph GLEASON granted license to keep tavern in town of Van Wert.(308)

5-12-1846 - Samuel ENGLERIGHT appointed auctioneer. (309)

5-12-1846 - Charles SCHMIT a native of Baden Germany. Naturalization. Declaration of intention made in common pleas cour of this county on 10-2-1843. (309)

5-12-1846 - David MAJOR granted license to keep temperance tavern at his house in Willshire. (313)

5-12-1846 - Josiah DELONG granted license to keep tavern at his house in Section 10 of this county. (313)

5-13-1846 - Henry Rohleous appointed adms. of the estate of Clemmens ROHLEOUS, dec'd. (316)
5-13-1846 - Conrod Housted appointed adms. of the estate of Philip REESE, dec'd. Former adms., George Reese resigned. (317)
5-16-1846 - Robert Miller appointed guardian of Samuel MILLER aged 17 yrs., David MILLER aged 15 yrs., Elizabeth MILLER aged 11 yrs., Delilah MILLER aged 10 yrs., Anderson J. MILLER aged 8 yrs., George and John MILLER aged 6 yrs., minor heirs of William HILL late of Van Wert County, dec'd. (339)
5-16-1846 - John F. Woodruff appointed guardian of Aaron A. BRONSON aged 10 yrs.(339)
7-30-1846 - Jacob Hageman appointed adms. of the estate of Isaac HAGEMAN, dec'd. Widow, Elizabeth Hageman relinquishes her right to adms. (346)
9-17-1846 - Charles P. Edson appointed adms. of the estate of James BURSON, dec'd. Widow, Fian Burson relinquishes her right to adms. (347)
10-20-1846 - Mary HARZOG aged 16 yrs. chose Solomon Harzog as her guardian and court appointed him to also serve as guardian of Jesse HARZOG aged 13 yrs., Leo HARZOG aged 11 yrs., King HARZOG aged 10 yrs., Eliza HARZOG aged 7 yrs. and Benjamin HARZOG aged 5 yrs., children of Susannah HARZOG, dec'd. (348)
10-20-1846 - John Bowen Sr. appointed adms. of the estate of John BOWEN Jr., dec'd. Widow, Nancy Bowen relinquishes her right to adms. (349)
10-21-1846 - William J. COCHRAN a minister of the United Brethren church granted license to solemnize marriages. (363)
10-21-1846 - Casper GEISE a native of Hanover Germany makes his declaration of intention to become citizen. (365)
10-21-1846 - T. F. CLARK granted license to keep a tavern in his house in Section ten of said county. (365)
10-22-1846 - Jane VANHORNE vs. George VANHORNE, petition for divorce. (368)
10-22-1846 - William Moorman appointed guardian of Elizabeth MOORMAN aged 12 yrs., minor child of agnes MOORMAN, dec'd. (368)
10-22-1846 - Benjamin FISHER granted license to keep a tavern at his house in Section Ten. (369)
1-11-1847 - GREIFE (GREISSE) appointed adms. of the estate of Casper LIPPOLD, dec'd late of Van Wert County. (386)
4-26-1847 - George M. Brickner appointed adms. of the estate of John BREDEICK, dec'd (390)
4-26-1847 - Sarah E. Redman appointed admsx. of the estate of Thomas J. REDMAN, dec'd. (390)
4-26-1847 - Joseph GLEASON granted license to keep tavern without retailing liquors at his house in Van Wert. (390)
4-26-1847 - George WITTE a native of Hanover Germany now of Van Wert County makes his declaration of intention to become citizen. (393)
4-26-1847 - Martin SHOWALTER a native of Bavaria now of Van Wert County. Naturalization. Declaration of intention made in this court 10-4-1841. (393)
4-26-1847 - John N. BENTLER a native of Baden Germany now of Putnam County, Ohio. Naturalization. Declaration of intention made in common pleas court of Sandusky County, Ohio 10-5-1841. Oath by George M. Brickner and H. Joseph Boehmer. (394)
4-27-1847 - Frederick W. HONNSTETT a native of Prussia now of Van Wert County. Naturalization. Declaration of intention made in this county. 5-8-1844. (409)
4-27-1847 - David MAJOR granted license to keep tavern with out retailing liquors at his house in Willshire. (423)
4-27-1847 - Jacob M. HARPER granted license to keep tavern without retailing liquors at his house in Willshire. (423)

604

5-17-1847 - David Major appointed guardian of Mary Elizabeth BLOOM aged 11 yrs. on 4 July past, William Jesse BLOOM aged 5 yrs. on 19 Sept. past and Eliza L. Ann BLOOM aged 2 yrs. on 2nd July past, children of John BLOOM, dec'd. (426)

VAN WERT COUNTY, OHIO — Ministers' License Recorded

Name	Church	Date Issued	County Issued	Recorded Van Wert County
BROCK, Rev. Wesly	ME	Nov. 1834	Hardin	8-16-1842
KELLUM, Rev. John P.	ME	12-30-1837	Lorain	1-11-1844
KERNS, Rev. Daniel	Evang.	4-21-1843	Seneca	4-15-1844
FUSON, William	Baptist	12-19-1820	Lawrence	5-13-1844
VAN VALKINBURG, J. G.	Zoar Bapt.	3-23-1839	Stark	7-15-1846
BURGER, George	Luth.	12-19-1844	Hancock	7-17-1846
KALB, John S.	ME	11-10-1845	Hancock	9-17-1846
RILEY, Daniel	Methodist	5-20-1845	Putnam	(not given-1847)
WILLIAMS, Rev. Edward	ME	5-19-1831	Greene	3-26-1847
HARMOUNT, Rev. Alexander	Methodist	8-26-1845	Logan	1-6-1849
HOOK, Rev. Elisha	ME	11-18-1846	Logan	4-10-1849
THURMAN, Frederick William	Luth.	7-13-1838	Union	4-17-1849
DONER, Abraham Ger.	Evan. Luth.	5-5-1842	Allen	6-21-1849
OLDFIELD, Reuben	ME	10-12-1848	Mercer	9-7-1849
LAY, James M.	U.B.	4-20-1849	Auglaize	11-13-1849
WARD, Lafayette	ME	8-20-1846	Ashland	11-16-1849
BONHAM, Moses	—	7-20-1839	Logan	10-18-1844
CAMERON, Rev. James	Presb.	10-29-1844	Harrison	6-25-1849

ADAMS, Moses R. to Elizabeth Ann Kennear	10-7-1847
AGLER, William to Hannah Dull	3-21-1847
ANDERSON, William to Phobe Morse	6-11-1843
ANTHONY, Abraham to Lydia Ann Bower	3-8-1849
BACKUS, Walley to Rachel Zimmerman	4-16-1846
BAWZELL, John to Sarah Gaskill	4-4-1844
BAXTER, George to Jane Sprowl	3-8-1849
BELL, James to Mary F. Johnson	6-26-1842
BENSON, William to Lydia Kuzsen	1-14-1849
BIENZ, John to Loisa Billman	12-1-1848
BLOSSOM, John to Sarah Hartzog	4-12-1849
BOLENBAUGHER, Abraham to Elizabeth Stetler	11-16-1845
BOLENBAUGHER, David to Lavina Counterman	8-15-1844
BOLENBAUGHER, George to Sarah Pontius	5-16-1844
BOROFF, Samuel to Lear Snyder	12-27-1846
BOROUGHS, Morris to Eliza Braham	5-15-1849
BOWEN, Cyrus to Mary McQueen	7-7-1840
BOWER, John to Margaret McQueen	10-31-1844
BOWYER, John to Catharine Purdy	11-16-1843
BRENNER, John to Elizabeth Harzogg	1-14-1840
BRITTSON, Isaac to Elizabeth Pring	11-26-1840
BROWN, Alexander W. to Margaret Bevington	10-18-1849
BRUBAKER, Peter to Catharine Dull	11-26-1844
BUGES(?), Daniel to Margaret Bullenbaugher	6-22-1841
BULLENBAUGH, Peter to Catharine Middleton	11-15-1840
BURRIDGE, Alden L. to Mary Jane Spear	Iss. 10-16-1844
BURTCH, William J. to Hetty Sands	1-21-1841
BUSSING, John to Mary Christena Blename (or Blemee?)	4-28-1848
BYER (BOYER), Jacob to Lydia Allspach	1-11-1849
CASTEEL, John to Elizabeth Harter	3-25-1849
CAVETT, John to Abby C. Williams	4-14-1842
CHILCOTE, William to Eliza Walter	8-31-1847
CLINE, John to Sarah Brees	9-24-1849
CLINK, Josiah to (not given) Keeth	12-26-1840
COWEN, Jacob P. to Amy Edgecomb	7-1-1847
CREEK, Samuel to Lydia Dull	11-30-1848
CREMEAN, Jas. to Susan Somersett	12-16-1841
CREMEAN, Smith, Jr. to Sarah Ann Bowersock	6-19-1844
CROSS, Alonzo to Mary Boenbaugher	Iss. 8-7-1844
CROSS, Bolivar to Mary Z. Counterman	9-30-1849
CROSS, Edmond to Mary Ann Gause	Iss. 3-27-1846
CURL, Jesse C. to Mary Baldridge	2-22-1848
DAILY, James T. to Mary Johnson	10-14-1841
DAUGHERTY, Isaac to Lydia McDonald	3-22-1846
DAVIS, James Oliver to Rebecca Miller	4-20-1846
DAVIS, John to Sophia Benner	10-29-1848
DCAMP, John to Lydia Williams	3-8-1842
DENMON, John to Nancy Jane Claton	8-12-1849
DULL, Jacob to Harriet Ream	11-18-1845

```
DUNCAN, Joseph to Sarah Hipsheer                              6-30-1840
ENGLISHMAN, John Charles Adam to Anna Margaret Buttner        4-12-1849
ESCH, Bernard to Teresa Hackman                         Iss. 1-11-1847
EVERS, Darias to Emily Gleason                               11-1-1846
EVERS, Perry to Nancy Davis                                  5-17-1846
FINFROCK, Jonathan to Elizabeth Anne Pobl                    2-3-1842
FISHER, Benjamin to Lodemia Smith                            9-26-1847
FORTNEY, Adam to Sarah Shaffer                               10-17-1847
FOSNAUGHT, Elias to Mary Fender                              7-5-1849
FOSTER, Henry to Mary Maddux                                 5-7-1840
FOSTER, Jesse to Elizabeth Bower                             2-1-1844
FRONTFIELD, William to Christena Cless                       11-20-1846
GALEY (GAGEBY?), David to Lucinda Johnson                    1-18-1849
GATES, Jared to Fanny Hemphill                               7-31-1841
GEISER, Casper to Catherine M. Hanker                        10-20-1847
GERARD, E. F. to Matilda Agler                               7-30-1846
GERMAN, Charles to Elizabeth Schmitt                         3-23-1845
GERMANN, Peter to Katharine Dietrick                         7-5-1849
GERMANN, Philip C. to Anne E. Germann                        3-8-1842
GILLILAND, Charles to Rachael Mees                           7-8-1849
GILLILAND, Hugh to Nancy King                                10-28-1841
GILLILAND, Robert to Henrietta C. Marsh                      6-25-1849
GILLILAND, Thomas to Eliza Spears                            7-10-1847
GLENN, Solon J. to Rebecca A. Tullis                         11-8-1849
GOLLIVER, William to Margaret Taylor                         3-26-1846
GOODWIN, Jacob to Martha Ann Rice                            1-2-1848
GOODRICH, Nelson to Polly Duncan                             12-10-1840
GUNSET, Henry to Matty Stam                                  3-28-1847
GUTHRIE, George N. to Sarah Jane Moore                       3-20-1845
GUTHRIE, John to Nancy Duncan                                8-16-1844
GUY, George to Sarah Gilliland                               3-29-1840
GUY, George to Margaret Clapper                              10-23-1841
GUY, George to Sarah Welch                                   12-9-1849
HALTERY, Edward to Mary Ann Hagerman                         5-16-1848
HAMKER, Mathias to Catharine Staffin                         12-18-1849
HARP, Jonas to Mary Putman                                   6-4-1848
HARP, Reuben to Elenor Rowland                               1-31-1843
HART, Peter to Mary Germann                                  1-17-1840
HARVEY, Obadiah to Roszillah Hoaglin                         12-24-1846
HARZOG, Soloman to Mary Blossom                              6-27-1844
HARTZOG, George W. to Elizabeth Bolenbaugher                 12-21-1843
HENKLE, Isaac to Jane Agler                                  3-29-1849
HIGH, Edward to Sarah Ann Densell                            8-27-1848
HIGH, Jacob to Catharine Wilt                                1-7-1849
HINES, Doctor Philip J. To Relief Morse                      3-6-1842
HIPSHIRE, John to Susan Taylor                               11-28-1844
HIPSHIRE, Jonathan to Elizabeth Myers                        10-30-1849
HIRE, Elijah to Sarah Wortman                                9-7-1845
HIRE, Jeremiah to Sarah Summersett                           9-12-1843
```

```
HIRE, John to Mary Pollock                          6-10-1841
HIRE, John to Mary Wortman                          3-29-1849
HOUBER, Christian to Fredenker Blankenhorn     Iss. 11-17-1849
HOUSTEAD, Frederick W. to Elizabeth Stoup          11-11-1847
HOWARD, Basha to Eliza Johnson                      8-9-1849
HUDSPETH, John to Sarah Hattery                     3-31-1846
HUDSPETH, Thomas to Roda Copper                     4-19-1849
HUMY(?), Joseph to Elizabeth Bowen                  5-5-1840
IMMILL, Isaih to Rosanna Jones                      6-20-1847
IRELAND, Robert to Melinda H. Maddux               7-2-1848
JAQUE, Alford to Maria Snider                       10-4-1849
JONES, Albert W. to Betsy Tibbury                   5-24-1849
JONES, Evan to Lucinda Ayres                        4-6-1843
JONES, Joseph to Jane M. Miller                     2-10-1848
KEATH, Johnzee to Priscilla Arnold                  6-22-1841
KEVER, James to Susan Hudspeth                      9-25-1842
KEIHL, Charles to Ann Elizabeth Klein              10-25-1849
KENTNER, George to Rebecca Welch                    4-24-1849
KING, T. W. to Jane E. Gilliland                    4-21-1842
KINGSLEY, Manning to Jane Savidge                   7-8-1847
KREISHER, Peter to Catharine German                4-13-1846
LENOX, John W. to Susan Ann Short                  12-25-1849
LEWIS, William to Sarah Myers                       9-15-1842
LIHEHART, Casemer to Catharine Holler              11-5-1846
LILLY, John to Elizabeth Wright                     8-8-1841
LINTEMAN, Frederick to Mary Blumas                  4-4-1849
LINTERMUTH, Solomon to Sarah Harzog                 4-15-1843
McCAMPBELL, Andrew J. to Mary J. Tisdale            7-26-1849
McCOY, Moses to Mary Penabaker                      8-17-1843
McKIM, Thomas S. to Calinda Major                   8-23-1846
McMANNIMA, Danl. L. to Mary Ann Taylor             10-6-1842
McMILLEN, John to Mary Ann Elder                    8-5-1847
McQUEEN, Adam J. to Sabria I. Furman                2-25-1846
McQUEEN, Anthony to Elanor Pring                    8-2-1849
MAJOR, David to Sarah Squire                        2-13-1847
MANLY, Robert to Rachael Morehead                   9-24-1848
MARTIN, Silas to Susan Irvin                        8-16-1842
METCALF, Z. to Susan Jameson                        8-15-1847
MEWHISTER, Frederick to Elizabeth Scott            12-12-1844
MEWHISTER, James to Sarah Jane Harter               9-27-1846
MEWHISTER, William to Elizabeth Walters             6-25-1848
MILLER, Israel to Nancy F. Maddux                   2-14-1847
MILLER, James to Charlotte Miller                  10-17-1844
MILLER, James to Louisa Boroff                     12-28-1848
MILLER, Joshua to Lydia Mix                        10-27-1842
MILLER, Robert to Elizabeth Maddux                  8-9-1846
MIRES, John to Sarah Parcher                        9-30-1847
MOONEY, Peter to Sarah Scott                        8-20-1848
MOORE, Joseph D. to Nancy Ross                      8-8-1844
```

```
MOORE, Peter to Elizabeth Brown                        3-25-1849
MOREHEAD, Emanuel to Sarah C. Heller                   6-11-1843
MURPHY, James to Elizabeth Grimes                      4-5-1849
MYERS, John to Elizabeth Gilliland                     1-2-1842
ORTENDORF, Joseph to Agnes Paul                        10-24-1848
OSBURN, Joseph H. to Barbary E. Heath                  8-6-1848
PALMER, John to Polly Benson                           10-5-1848
PARKINSON, Jacob to Rhoda Morse                        9-11-1846
PAUL, Henry H. to Catharine Reed                       2-20-1849
POLLOCH, William to Drusilla Reed                      4-30-1843
PONTIUS, William to Elizabeth Heath                    8-23-1849
PRESTON, Norman C. to Sarah Cook                       9-10-1846
PRIDDY, John N. to Mary Jane Maddux                    2-25-1846
PRIDDY, Thomas D. to Caroline Dcamp                    4-15-1843
PRING, Jeremiah to Elizabeth Shultz                    4-11-1847
PRING, John to Caroline Minard                         2-11-1844
PUTMAN, Alexander to Mary Temple                       3-22-1849
RATLIFF, Moses C. to Sarah Ann Toliver                 2-23-1845
REDMAN, Thomas J. to Sarah E. Miller                   10-28-1844
REED, James to Rachel Harter                           12-27-1842
RICHY, David to Laura Wells                            11-12-1840
RIDENOUR, Amicy to Elmira Atkinson                     3-22-1848
RIGBY, Isaac to Jane Crothers                          3-4-1848
ROBERTS, John W. to Lydia Swigart                      12-16-1849
ROBINSON, William L. to Emily Stacy                    11-2-1845
ROEHM, Andrew to Catharine Bientz                      8-16-1840
BOICE, Austin to Sarah Jane Gleason                    3-18-1847
ROSE, Obadiah to Nancy Sheater                         1-11-1849
RUSH, Jonas to Elizabeth Smith                         8-10-1848
RUSH, Jonas to Elizabeth Dull                          9-19-1844
SANDERSON, Foster M. to Mary Heath                     11-5-1848
SANDS, Christian to Mary Manley                        12-14-1848
SANDS, David to Mary Underwood                         4-27-1848
SCHARRER, John Rudolph to Elizabeth Bury               6-10-1842
SHAFFER, Joshua to Catharine Hageman                   12-23-1842
SHEETS, Adam to Sarah Ann Davis                        1-14-1847
SHEETS, John to Susanna Runnels                        1-20-1849
SHOWALTER, Henry to Mary Hartz                         9-16-1841
SHOWALTER, Martin to Anna Aucker                       7-2-1843
SHOWALTER, Martin to Elizabeth McGarvy                 10-16-1848
SLEMMER, Peter to Catharine Youse(?)                   1-3-1843
SLEMNER, George to Mary E. Redebaugh          Iss. 2-28-1844
SLYTER, Richard to Catharine Fritz                     5-22-1842
SMITH, Benjamin C. to Lodemia Royce                    3-19-1846
SMITH, Charles to Sarah E. Redman             Iss. 5-9-1849
SMITH, David to Mary Hartzog                           2-8-1849
SPEARS, Richard C. to Louiza Spear                     4-27-1845
SPEARS, Samuel I. to Susanna Crothers         Iss. 3-1-1849
SPICER, Stephen to Elizabeth Evans                     10-26-1848
STABAUGH, George to Susan Snider                       10-16-1849
```

STABAUGH, John to Mary Ann McManinea	3-12-1848
STAMS, Jesse to Sylvia Ann Furnam	7-6-1848
STANSBERY, William C. to Eliza Jane Stetler	1-4-1846
STSTFIELD, Francis M. to Polly Harter	8-18-1840
STETLER, Jacob to Rosana Bolenbaugher	Iss. 3-15-1848
STEWART, Joseph to Roxana Van Valkinburgh	6-25-1846
STREEKFOOT, George to Margaretha Blasseneck	May 1847
STRIPE, Jacob to Elizabeth Harvey	10-23-1845
STRIPE, William to Lydia Royce	5-7-1843
STROTHER, Alexander to Hannah Arnold	1-27-1848
STROTHERS, Benjamin D. to Elizabeth Thomas	12-7-1845
SUMMERSETT, William F. to Leah Samm	1-4-1849
SWANK, John to Julia Ann Stetler	3-5-1843
SYKES, George S. to Hannah DeCamp	11-9-1847
TAYLOR, Henry to Amy Kever	8-11-1842
THORN, Benjamin to Elvina Davis	1-17-1848
THORN, Jacob to Mary Gleason	5-24-1846
THORN, Thomas to Lodusky Royce	5-9-1847
TODD, Andrew R. to Susan Baldrige	1-18-1846
TODD, William to Mary Hire	3-25-1841
TOMLINSON, Joseph to Mary Arnold	11-9-1845
TROOP, Andrew I. to Hannah E. Cobb	3-2-1848
WAGNER, Azariah to Susan Baker	3-9-1841
WAGONER, Henry P. to Margaret M. Martin	11-8-1849
WALTER, John to Margaret Meeker	6-19-1849
WALTERS, Alexander to Jane Harter	9-28-1843
WALTERS, George to Dorothea Cless	4-10-1845
WALTERS, James to Amanda Harter	2-3-1842
WALTERS, James to Margaret White	4-23-1848
WEGESIN, Hennan(?) H. to Mary Baumgarter	4-28-1848
WEIBLE, Henry to Mary Wills	8-29-1849
WELLS, Edward R. to Sarah Thorn	6-11-1843
WILEY, Isaac to Mary Wright	8-4-1840
WILT, Jacob to Elizabeth Heney (Haney)	10-25-1849
WOODRUFF, John F. to Nancy Bronson	10-17-1842
WOOTEN, Caleb W. to Delilah Duncan	8-24-1843
YOUNG, William H. to Amanda Armitage	1-29-1844
ZIMMERMAN, Jacob to Fanny Anthony	7-9-1848

610

Contributed by: Mr. Wilbur J. Miller, Jr., R.R.1, Box 87, Willshire, Ohio 45898

This is the older section of the Willshire Cemetery which dates back to 1834.
It is along U.S. Rt. 33 on the town limits in Willshire twp., Section 32.

ROSS, Daniel d Nov. 10, 1862 age 27 yrs.
ROSS, _____(Stone fell down) d Dec. 31, 1891 age 81 yrs. 8 mo.
ROSS, Mary C. wife of Dr. J. K. Ross d. Sept. 25, 1899 age 51 yrs. 7 mo. 13 ds.
_____, (Base for stone)
ROSS, Griffin son of John & Eliza A. Ross d. Sept. 4, 1849 age 10 mo. 26 d.
ROSS, William R. son of John & Eliza A. Ross d July 29, 1845 age 5 yrs. 8 mos. 15 ds.
ROSS, Sarah Ann wife of John Ross d Sept. 23, 1841 age 20 yrs. 10 mos. 28 ds.
ROSS, James d June 15, 1845 aged 15 years
ROSS, William d Mar. 12, 1850 age 27 years
ROSS, John d Dec. 24, 1854 age 75 years - Soldier of the War of 1812
ROSS, Margaret d Apr. 12, 1863 age 75 years
_____, (Base for stone)
ROSS, Wm. d Oct. 16, 1848 age 82 years - Soldier of the War of 1812
_____, My Dear Mother (stone - must be C. Hill)
HILL, Philip d May 12, 1846 age 55 yrs. 5 mos.
HILL, Philip son of P. and C. Hill d Mar. 14, 1841 age 7 yrs. 1 mo.
REECE, Rebecca d June 28, 1864 aged 37 yrs.
ROSS, Sarah Ann D. dau of W. and Rebecca Ross d Oct. 10, 1852 (stone broken off)
ROSS, Jane wife of J. H. Ross d Mar. 27, 1871 age 40 yrs. 6 mo. 18 ds.
ROSS, Joseph d Aug. 16, 1899 age 75 yrs. 7 mo. 8 ds. (note: stone fallen over)
ROOP, Clara O. dau of S. & M.Roop (note: stone bur. in ground)
_____, (note: stone broken off) d Mar. 6, 1869 age 12 yrs. 4 mo 18 ds.
ROOP, William Elden son of S. and M. Roop d Nov. 25, 1874 (note: stone bur.)
NICHOLS, James son of F. and K. Nichols d (note: stone bur.)
NICHOLS, Fredrick Nichols, Sr. (note: stone is bur.)
NICHOLS, David d Aug. 1, 1854 age 34 yrs. 5mo. 13 ds
NICHOLS, Catharine wife of F. Nichols d Nov. 27, 1874 age 73 yrs. 11 mos. 24 ds.
HENDERSON, Bushrod H. d Oct. 27, 1845 age 27 yrs. 8 mo. 19 ds.
HENDERSON, Charles d Nov. 18, 1838 age 65 yrs. 10 mos. 22 ds.
HENDERSON, Amelia wife of Chas. Henderson d Apr. 17, 1855 age 64 yrs. 2 mos. 3 ds.
HENDERSON, Inf. children of B. M. and M. Henderson
CASE, Elisabeth dau of Wm. and E. Case d Aug. 20, 1872 age 8 mo. 29 ds.
CASE, Susanna wife of William Case d Oct. 7, 1866 aged 50 yrs. 11 mo. 1 ds.
CASE, Scottie son of Wm. and S. Case d Jan. 8, 1862 aged 1 yr. 11 mo. 14 ds.
CLATON, Sarah Jane wife of Samuel Claton d Nov. 7, 1857 age 21 yrs. 10 mos. 27 ds.
JOHNSON, Isadoria dau of J.F. and E. Johnson d Sept. 22, 1860 age 1 yr. 1 mo. 7 ds.
JOHNSON, James F. (note: stone bur.)
BOLANBAUCH, Levina wife of David Bolanbauch d Aug. 16, 1854 age 25 yrs. 7 mo. 20 ds.
CASE, Clement L. V. 1863-1864
CASE, Catherine wife of W. Case 1835-1867
CASE, Washington 1833-1905
WOLLET, Elizabeth wife of John Wollet (note: stone broken off)
STREET, Benjamin M. son of Thomas and Martha J. Street d Oct. 29, 1870
                          age 22 yrs. 11 mos. 12 ds.
STREET, Ephriam B. son of T. and M.J. Street d Apr. 1, 1857 age 3 yrs. 11 mo. 24 ds.
STREET, Thomas M. son of T. and M.J. Street d Apr. 2, 1857 age 5 yrs. 1 mo. 19 ds.

STREET, John A. son of T. and M. J. Street d Sept. 17, 1844 age 10 mos. 25 ds.
STREET, Caroline A. Street d Aug. 15, 1875 (note: stone bur.)
NICHOLS, Minerva wife of C. C. Nichols d Feb. 23, 1875 age 38 yrs. 3 mos. 17 ds.
JORDAN, Louisa Ann dau of S. and S. Jordan d July 25, 1851 age 10 yrs. 7 mos. 25 ds.
JORDAN, Sarah Jane dau of S. and S. Jordan d Oct. 11, 1844 (note: stone bur.)
JORDAN, Silas d Apr. 2, 1875 age 62 yrs. 3 mos. 4 ds. "Father and Mother"
JORDAN, Sarah wife of S. Jordan d Sept. 27, 1879 age 67 yrs. 11 mos. 21 ds.
STREET, Thomas d Aug. 21, 1876 age 61 yrs. 4 mos. 25 ds.
STREET, Elijah F. d Nov. 9, 1876 age 20 yrs. 8 mos. 4 ds.
STREET, Martha J. wife of Thos. Street d Sept. 26, 1881 aged 57 yrs. 5 mos. 2 ds.
STREET, Inf. son of C. H. and Elizabeth Street d Dec. 9, 1873
HOPE, Anna M. d Apr. 18, 1879 age 71 yrs. 5 mos. 20 ds.
HOPE, John d Apr. 15, 1864 age 54 yrs. 9 mos.
MANCHE, Anna Catharine dau of John and Barbara Manche d Aug. 7, 1862 age 2 mos. 24ds.
MANCHE, Ceorc(Loeorc?) son of J. and B. Manche d Sept. 16, 1858 aged 7 mos. 12 ds.
PRICE, Zoie dau of J. M. and E. T. Price d July 26, 1876 aged 2 yrs, 11 nis, 24 ds,
SWARTS, Henry S. son of William and Elizabeth Swarts d Dec. 20, 1851 age 17 yrs.
                                                            11 mos. 25 ds.
DURBIN, Theresa R. 1844-1875
RUSSELL, Lois wife of Phineas S. Russell d Aug. 16, 1855 age 33 yrs. 11 mos. 2 ds.
WINKLER, Martin d Jan. 12, 1863 age 74 yrs. 2 mos. 1 da.
WINKLER, Rosina wife of Martin Winkler d Sept. 9, 1861 age 57 years
WINKLER, Pauline dau of Martin and Rosina Winkler (note: stone bur.)
WINKLER, Theresa dau of M. and E. Winkler Mar. 13, 1867--Mar. 25, 1867
WATKINS, Caler d Dec. 25, 1866 age 58 yrs. 3 mos.
WATKINS, Amy dau of J. and M. Watkins d Aug. 11, 1854 age 13 yrs. 8 mos. 3 ds.
WATKINS, Joshua d Oct. 30, 1842 age 61 yrs. 2 mos. 1 ds.
WATKINS, Nancy wife of Joshua Watkins d Jan. 15, 1837 age 52 yrs. 9 mos. 4 ds.
HARPER, Jacob M. d May 19, 1847 age 42 yrs. 4 mos.
DELLINGER, Emma dau of W. and N. Dellinger d July 14, 1874 age 6 yrs. 1 mos. 28 ds.
DELLINGER, Nancy wife of Wm. Dellinger d Mar. 30, 1874 age 41 yrs. 5 mos. 11 ds.
DELLINGER, Joseph Kemy son of W. and M. Dellinger d (note: stone bur.)
DELLINGER, Lucinda J. dau of W. and M.(N?) Dellinger d Nov 15, 1852 age 1yr 10m 10ds.
_____, (note: no stone)
PURDY, George W. d Sept. 11, 1864 age 61 yrs. 8 mos. __ ds.
_____, (note: stone broken and bur. Perhaps wife of George Purdy?)
CRONINGER, Carl W. son of Dr. M. and A.E. Croninger d Feb. 16, 1875 age 6y 9m 19ds.
CRIST, Cyrus son of J. and E. Crist d Mar. 5, 1863 age 12 yrs. 1 mo. 23 ds.
                                                (note: stone bur. in ground)
_____, (note: another stone bur.)
WHITE, Charles d Sept. 4, 1862 age 1 yr. 11 mo.) Children of John and
WHITE, Mary Rosetta d Sept. 3, 1862 age 3 yr 18ds) Sarah Ellen White
STOVE, Edwin A. d Sept. 23, 1863 age 3 yrs. 5 mos. 13 ds.
STOVE, Alfred d Aug. 30, 1869 age 1 mo. 5 ds.
STOVE, Kate A. d Nov. 27, 1867 age 5 yrs. 5 mos. 7 ds.
STOVE, Ida I. d Aug. 27, 1859 age 1 mos. 2 ds.
STOVE, Frederick W. d Sept. 10, 1871 age 6 yrs. 5 mos. 8 ds.
STOVE, Monroe d Apr. 3, 1868 age 5 ds.
WHITE, John d Mar. 5, 1863 age 30 yrs. (note: rest is bur.)
STETLER, Levi d Oct. 1, AD 1868 age 12 yrs. 6 mos.
_____, (note: stone unreadable)

BUSH, Nancy dau of John and Elizabeth Bush d Oct. 15, 1843 in the 10 years of her
age. She was born in Shelby Co. Ohio
BLOSSOM, Henry A. son of Edward P. and Nancy Blossom d Jan. 25, 1842 age 4 yrs.
5 mos. 2 ds.
BLOSSOM, Elizabeth M. dau of E. P. and Nancy Blossom d Aug. 21, 1841 age 6 yrs.
7 mos. 6 ds.
BLOSSOM, Edward P. d Feb. 3, 1859 age 50 yrs. 11 mos. and 11 ds.
TICKLE, Idna V. dau of J. and I. Tickle d Aug. 30, 1876 age 8 mos. 24 ds.
CRIST, (note: name missing. Joseph?) d Mar. 3, 1865 age 40 yrs. 2 mos. 17ds.
CRIST, Eliza wife of Joseph Crist d Feb. 26, 1863 age 36 yrs. 3 mos. 12 ds.
CRIST, Jobes son of Joseph and Eliza Crist d Feb. 2, 1863 age 10 yrs. 5 mos. 17 ds.
CRIST, Daniel son of J. and E. Crist d Feb. 9, 1863 age 10 yrs. 5 mos. 17 ds.
CRIST, Laura Jane dau of J. and E. Crist d Feb. 25, 1863 age 2 yrs. 11 mos. 28 ds.
CRIST, Medora Ellen dau of J. and E. Crist d Mar. 1, 1863 age 11 mos. 6 ds.
TROUTNER, Elizabeth wife of Peter Troutner (note: stone bur.)
CHASE, Benj. Co. E., 46 Ohio Inf.
HEATH, Rebecca Elizabeth dau of James C. and Nancey Heath d Oct. 25, 1841
age 1 yr. 10 mos. 29 ds.
JEWEL, George d Sept. 17, 1875 age 34 yrs. 2 mos. 26 ds.
JEWEL, Ida M. dau of G. and M. Jewel d Jan. 6, 1873 age 3 yrs. 11 mos. 15 ds.
BLOSSOM, Henry C. d May 24, 1856(66?) age 5 yrs. 25 ds.) Children of I. A. and
BLOSSOM, Geo. W. d May 25, 1856(66?) age 2 yrs. 3 mos.) R. D. Blossom
BLOSSOM, Ansel d Oct. 24, 1850 age 72 years
BLOSSOM, Mercy Ladd wife of Ansel Blossom d Jan. 9, 1848 age 65 years
MILLER, Bithicah Catharine wife of Daniel Miller d June 5, 1834 age 22 yrs. 8 mos.
HILL, W. d Oct. 8, 1889 age 39 yrs. 1 mo. 23 ds.
JOHNSON, David son of Grif'n and Jamina Johnson d July 26, 1844 age 3 yrs. 9 mos.
22 ds.
JOHNSON, Willis H. son of Grif'n and Jamima Johnson d Dec. 12, 1838 age 1 mo. 20 ds.
HEATH, Hanah dau of George and Rachel Janie d Nov. 6, 1838 age 18 ds.
ROOP, John d Mar. 20, 1850 age 43 yrs. 11 mos. 14 ds.
ROOP, Simon P. son of Amos(?) and Rachel Roop d July 7, 1849 age 5 mos. 15 ds.
ROOP, Amos d Mar. 25, 1858 age 43 yrs. 4 mos. 19 ds.
FRISINGER, Rebecca Ann wife of David Frisinger and dau of A. and R. Roop
d Nov. 16, A.D. 1869 age 29 yrs. 11 mos. 5 ds.
FRISINGER, Rachel E. dau of D. and R.A. Frisinger d Jan. 23, 1875 age 7 yrs. 4 mos.15d
STETLER, Phebe wife of John Stetler (note: stone bur.)
STETLER, Alonzo son of J. and P. Stetler d Mar. 12, 1858 age 4 yrs. 4 mos. 25 ds.
STETLER, Harvey son of J. and P. Stetler d Mar. 9, (age 2mo? stone bur.)
STETLER, Angeline dau of J. and P. Stetler d July 28, 1854 age 5 yrs. 3 mos. 28 ds.
McINTIRE, William d July 26, 1854 age 12 yrs. 8 mos. 4 ds.
_____, (note: stone broken off - Stetler?)
HUSTON, Inf dau of Henry and Sarrah E. Huston d Feb. 8, 1887
EVANS, Roy A. son of William M. and Effie M. Evans b Oct. 13, 1898 d Oct. 22, 1898
EVANS, Infant - 1902
CROSS, Jane wife of D. D. Cross d June 3, 1854 age 52y 4m 22 ds.
CROSS, Alford son of R.D. and M.Z. Cross d Apr. 23, 1851 age 1 yr. 3 mos. 20 ds.
STETLER, James Dewey son of J. and P. Stetler d May 4, 1844 age 5 mos. (stone bur.)
CROSS, Daniel D. son of E. & B. Cross d Oct. 14, 1844 age 5 mos.
CROSS, Inf dau of E. and M. Cross d Oct. 15, 1850
CROSS, Betsey wife of E. Cross d Sept. 24, 1845 "In her 22 years of her age."

CROSS, Marenda dau of E. and B. Cross d Sept. 14, 1851 "in her 9 years of her age."
CROSS, Mary Ann wife of E. Cross d July 29, 1854 "In the 26 year of her age."
CROSS, Cotilda dau of E. and M.A. Cross d Sept. 23, 1854 age 1 yr. 5 mos. 15 ds.
GAUSE, Sarah A. dau of D. and Mary Ann Gause d May 15, 1857 age 1 mo. 2 ds.
FORD, Roxana B. dau of J.L. and A. Ford d July 28, 1889 aged 1 yr. 6 mo. 24 ds.
CROSS, Daniel D. son of A. and M.Z. Cross d Apr. 27, 1869 age 1 yr. 10 mos. 27 ds.
CROSS, Inf. dau. of A. and M.Z. Cross
CROSS, George D. son of A. and M.Z. Cross d Apr. 13, 1881 age 11 yrs. 9 mos. 29 ds.
CROSS, Mary Z. wife of Alonzo CROSS d May 2, 1881 age 42 yrs. 7 mos. 17 ds.
CROSS, Mary M. wife of Alonzo Cross d Dec. 17, 1858 age 27 yrs. 10 mos. 14 ds.
CROSS, Iver(?) (note: stone broken and bur.)
CROSS, D. D. d Apr. 15, 1876 age 76 yrs. 4 mos. 24 ds.
CROSS, Mary A. d May 18, 1890 age 83 yrs. 5 mos. 5 ds.
WILLEY, John F. son of E. and M. Willey d July 21, 1871 age 5 mos. 15 ds.
WILLEY, William F. son of E. and M. Willey d Mar. 7, 1869 age 1 mo. 15 ds.
PARK, Wm. Co. C., 74th Ind. Inf. - GAR Vetern 1861-1865 U.S. flag
_____, (note: stone broken) aged 24 yrs. 5 mos. 30 ds.
_____, (note: stone bur.)
THOMAS, Thos. Co. C., 41st Ohio Inf. - GAR 1861-1865 - U.S. flag
_____, (note: stone bur.)
HEATH, Nancy wife of James C. Heath d Mar. 18, 1856 age 38 yrs. 5 mos. 3 ds.
DETTMER, Frankie son of G.A. and R. Dettmer d Mar. 1, 1874 age 5 yrs. 10 mos. 13 ds.
DETTMER, Nancy E. wife of G.A. Dettmer d July 21, 1869 age 32 yrs. 1 mo. 4 ds.
DETTMER, Rachel wife of G.A. Dettmer (note: stone bur.)
DETTMER, Ernest J. (note: stone bur.)
DETTMER, M. M. Wilhelmine wife of E. J. Dettmer d (note: stone bur.)
DETTMER, John W. son of G.A. and Rachel Dettmer d Oct. 29, 1861 age 1 yr. 10 mos.
                                                                                    16 ds
MILLER, Charles L. d Aug. 13, 1874 age 1 yr. 2 mos. 27 ds.) Children of A. W. and
MILLER, Jonnie W. d Sept. 15, 1882 age 1 yr. 24 ds.   )   S. E. Miller
DETTMER, Inf. son of G.A. and R. Dettmer d Feb. 20, 1865 age 2 mos. 26 ds.
DETTMER, Jacob E. son of G.A. and Rachel Dettmer d Nov. 4, 1861 age 4yr 7mo 22ds
DETTMER, Mahala A. dau of G.A. and Rachel Dettmer d Dec. 30, 1862 age 7yr 2mo 3ds
WILLEY, Elizabeth wife of E. Willey d Oct. 28, 1857 age 25 yrs. 1 mo. 8 ds.
_____, Inf. dau. of A.M. and M. (note: stone bur.)
STETLER, Rhoda d Jan. 7, 1877 age 74 yrs. 13 ds.
HELLER, Francis E. dau of J.L. and P. Heller d Jan. 15, 1865 age 1 yr 10 mos 19 ds
HELLER, Mary A. dau of J.L. and P. Heller d Feb. 9, 1865 age 3 yrs 10 mos 9 ds
SOPT, (Herman?) Gufane Sron von Wr. Sopt Gof Sept.(Dec.) 1,3,1859Wlt 21 Falyro
                                                             (German)
_____, (note: stone bur. in tree)
STETLER(?), Samuel son of D. and R. Stetler d 1849 age 5 yrs.
STETLER, Jeffry son of I. and R. Stetler d Aug. 4, 1849 age 11 mos. 27 ds.
STETLER, Margaret dau of ___ and ___ Stetler d Sept. 25, 1849 age ___ (?)
STETLER, Lucinda wife of Levi Stetler d Jan. 18, 1861 age 36 years
LAMB, Martha J. b Mar. 1, 1835 d Oct. 14, 1913   ) ss (note: stone on
MAJOR, James W. d Mar. 6, 1863 age 3lyrs 11mos 28ds)   ground)
MAJOR, Wm. d Jan. 15, 1853 age 71 yrs. 5 mos. 17 ds
MAJOR, Rachel wife of William Major d Aug. 20, 1846 age 53 yrs. 4 mos. 20 ds.

614

STETLER, Emaline dau of J. and R. Stetler age 14 ds.
STETLER, Abraham son of J. and R. Stetler age 1 yr. 6 mos.
BOLLENBAUCHER, Peter d Dec. 7, 1847 age 28 yrs.
BOLLENBAUGHER, Elizabeth dau of P. and R. Bollenbaugher age 7 mos.
STETLER, Catharine dau of J. and R. Stetler d (note: unreadable)
TICKEL, Margaret wife of Jacob Tickel d May 25, 1844 age 47 yrs. 1 mo. 10 ds.
STETLER, Margaret wife of Henry Stetler d Jan. 31, 1846 age 16 yrs.
STETLER, Lewis son of Geo. and Lydia Stetler d Jan. 31, 1846 age 16 yrs. 6 mos. 26ds.
SWANK, Emaline dau of J. and J. Swank d May 11, 1848 age 4 yrs. 1 mos. 21 ds.
STETLER, Harrod son of_____Stetler d May 27, 1865 age 4 yrs. 3 mos. 19 ds.
TICKLE, Pheby J. dau of J. and E. Tickle d Aug. 16, 1855 age 4 yrs. 4 mos. 20 ds.
STETLER, John W. son of J. and M.A. Stetler d Apr. 7, 1853 (note: stone bur.)
STETLER, inf. dau. of J. and M.A. Stetler d Jan. 22, 1840-----------
STETLER, Threse E. dau of J. and M.A. Stetler d Dec. 22, 1852 age 3 yrs. 4 mos. 20ds.
MAJOR, George d Nov. 4, 1847 age 30 yrs. (note: stone bur.)
MAJOR, Laura E. dau of J.M. and W. Major d May 6, 1855 age 1 mo. 17 ds.
BOLANEAUCHER, Pheby A. dau of P. and R. Bolanbaugher d Feb. 5, 1864 age 22 yrs.
BOLLANBAUGHER, Jacob son of L. and R. BOLLANBAUGHER (note: stone broken)
MAJOR, _____ (note: top stone broken) d Sept. 12, 1842 age 8 mo. 10 ds.
MAJOR, Jonathan W. d Apr. 6, 1843 age 33 yrs. (note: stone bur.)
MAJOR, William d Sept. 10, 1847 age 39 yrs. 11 mos. 5 ds.
MAJOR, Elizabeth wife of Wm. Major d Nov. 15, 18__ (note: stone bur.)
_____, (note: stone bur. in ground)
MAJOR, Hannan J. dau of James and Nancy Major d Aug. 3, 1848 age 10 mos. 13 ds.
MAJOR, Nancy wife of James Major, Jr. d Sept. 7th, 1844 age 21 yrs. 3 mos. 24 ds.
DAILEY, Nimrod son of E. and M.A. Dailey d May 5, 1855 age 19 yrs. 29 ds.
DAILEY, Esaias d Oct. 14, 1869 age 63 yrs. 10 mos. 5 ds. GAR1861-1865) U.S. flag
                                                    "Our Father"
DAILEY, Mary Ann wife of Esias Dailey d July 22, 1854 age 43 yrs. 8 mos. 5 ds.
                                                    "Our Mother"
ALTHON, Karl F. son of H. and A.E. Althon d Sept. 14, 1873 age 1 yr. 2 mos. 8 ds.
ALTHON, Lissetta dau of H. and A.E. Althon d Sept. 18, 1873 age 6 yrs. 4 mos. 26 ds.
SMITH, Malinda J. wife of D.M. Smith d Feb. 6, 1861 age 22 yrs. 4 mos. 24 ds.
_____, (note: stone bur. and broken)
_____, "In memory of Catharine" (note: unreadable)
DAILEY, Mary Susan dau of A.T. and E.J. Dailey d Aug. 10, 1859 age 1 yr. 8 ds.
DAILEY, Orainiewind son of A.T. and L.J. Dailey d Feb. 3, 1864 age 8 yrs. 9mos. 22ds
LEARD, Lucy P. d Nov. 12, 1859 age 16 yrs. 23 ds.
LEARD, Mary C. (note: stone bur.)
MAJOR, David Sen. d Nov. 4, 1847 age 68 yrs. 10 mos. 1 da.
STETLER, Emanuel son of_____Stetler D Sept. 17, 1862age 4 yrs. 3 mos. 19 ds
STETLER, Inf dau of J. and R. Stetler (note: unreadable)
STETLER, Daniel d Jan. 25, 1854 age 53(59)) yrs. 4 mos. 4 ds.
STETLER, Dewey F. son of O. & G. Stetler d Feb. 22, 1883 age 2 mos. 3 ds.
DELLINGER, Inf son of Wm. and M. (N?) Dellinger d Sept. 3, 1854
PASSWATERS, Michael C. son of T.B. and N. Passwaters d Feb. 23, 1866 age 12 yrs.
                                                                        10 ds.

SIMMS, Wm. R. d Feb. 27, 1872 age 18 yrs. 1 mo. 27 ds.
SYPHERS, William d Mar. 13, 1853 age 68 yrs. 10 mos. 11 ds.

_____, (note: stone unreadable - must be one of the Godard)
GODARD, Th____ M. (note: stone broken) son of E.A. and Hannah Godard
b June 4, 1833 age 2 yrs. 2 mos.
GODARD, Susan dau of E.A. and Hannah Godard b Aug. 2, 1828 age 5 yrs. 7 mos.
GODARD, Rachel D. dau of E.A. and Hannah Godard b Apr. 18, 1836 age 6 yrs. 5 mos.
_____, (note: Pile of broken stones - unreadable. One by tree unreadable)
GODARD, William son of E.A. and Hannah Godard b Jan. 1835 age 4 ds.
PETERMAN, Inf dau of H. and R. Peterman d Sept. 1, 1858 age 10 ds.
PETERMAN, Rachel wife of H. Peterman d (note: stone bur.)
McMANNIS, Mary dau of R. and E. McManis d (note: stone bur.)
McMANNIS, Inf son of R. and E. McMannis d July 27, 1851
McMANNIS, Elizabeth wife of Robert McManis d July 27, 1851 age 33 yrs. 9 mos. 23 ds.
McMANNIS, William son of Robert and Elizabeth McMannis d Apr 2, 1864 age 24 yrs.
7 mos. 18 ds.

_____, Sarah (note: All illegible)
_____, (note: Stone bur.)
MOREHEAD, Charles E. son of C. and H.M. Morehead d Mar. 23, 1876 age 1 yr. 2mos.
18 ds.
MOREHEAD, Hannah M. wife of Calvin Morehead d July 7, 1877 age 34 yrs. 4 mos. 13 ds.
MOREHEAD, Carrie dau of C. and H.M. Morehead b Jan. 8, 1873 d Aug. 9, 1890
SHAUNDING, Henry b ca 1841 - Co. E., 46th Ohio Inf., GAR 1861-65 - U.S. Flag
GAUSE, Missouri(?) - Enoch Gause d July 13, 1886 aged 37 yrs. 1 mo. 22 ds.
GAR 1861-1865 - U.S. Flag
NEPTUNE, Lydia wife of Wm Neptune d Nov. 8, 1855 age 66yrs. 7 mo. 3 ds.
NEPTUNE, Wm d Nov. 10, 1846 age 67 yrs. 1 da.
KISAER, Rollo M. son of T.J. and S.S. Kisaer d Mar. 8, 1863 age 18 yrs. 11 ds.
U.S. War Veteran
PURDY, Rachael wife of William M.H. Purdy d Feb 18, 1855 age 38 yrs. 9 mos. 13 ds.
_____, (note: stone bur.)
PURDY, Inf son to T.H. and S. Purdy d Apr 6, 1852
MELSHEIMER, Charles Edwin son of C.A. and E.A.M. Melsheimer d Sep 7, 1858
age 1 mo 17 ds
PEARCE, Mary Ann FRANK wife of L.D. Pearce d Feb. 11, 1860 age 37 yrs. 2 mos. 15 ds.
PEARCE, Thomas A. son of L.D. and Catharine I. Pearce d Mar 13, 1863 age 13 mos.
17 ds.
MILLER, Jacob son of James and Lavisa Miller d Aug. 25, 1850 age 1 mo.
IWICOLULC(?), Isaac N. son of I. and R. Iwicolulc(?) d Oct. 16, 18__ age 1 yr.
6 mos.-----(Note: stone bur.)
PEARCE, Sarah wife of L.D. Pearce - (note: stone bur.)
PEARCE, Affalander S. dau of L.D. and C.I. Pearce d Oct. 13, 1847 age 1 (or 4) yrs.
2 mos. 23 ds.
PEARCE,_____, wife of L.D. Pearce (note: stone broken)
_____, "Our Orlando d Oct. 17, 1851
PEARCE, Inf son of I.J. and M.E. Pearce d July 6, 1852
_____, - (note: small stone bur.)
HAYES, Theresa B. wife of Samuel Hayes d Sept. 7, 1866 age 22 yrs. 7 mos. 3 ds.
PEARCE, Theresa V. wife of J.W. Pearce d in child bed Mar 11, 1844 18 yrs.
(note: stone bur.)

616

ARCE, Emaline W. wife of J.W. Pearce d with cholera July 21, 1854 age 34 yrs.
(note: stone bur.)
_____, Byron d Mar 11, 1867 age 14 years
ARCE, Kittie dau of J.W. and R. Pearce d Apr 6, 1869 age 6 yrs. 7 mos. 6 ds.
_____, Henry son (note: stone bur.) (both stones same size as
_____, Inf. (note: stone bur.) (Bertha E. Wood
OD, Bertha E. dau of A.J. and C.E. Wood d Sept. 25, 1875 (note: stone bur.)
REMAN, India Pearce 1858-1936 - GAR 1861-1865? U.S. Flag
LLS, D. B. Co. e, 71st Ohio Inf. U.S. Flag 1861-1865
ARCE, Dr. J. W. Pearce d Feb 4, 1892 age 75 years. 3 mos. 26 ds. Asst. Surgeon
51st Ind. Inf.
ARCE, Rebecca 1833-1911
HNSON, Nancy M. - May 18, 1825-Aug. 8, 1874)
HNSON, George W. - Apr. 5, 1834-Nov. 22, 1906) ss
NSWORTH, Susan wife of W.S. Ainsworth d Feb. 5, 1854 age 45 yrs. 7(2?) mos. 6 ds.
NSWORTH, Lydia Ann dau of W.S. and S. Ainsworth d Aug. 15, 1864 age 11 yrs.
6 mos. 23 ds.
NSWORTH, Emma L. dau of W. S. and Susan Ainsworth (note: stone bur.)
NES(?), _____(note: top of stone broken off) d Dec. 6, 1855 age 45 yrs. 6 mos.
16 ds.
NES, Catharine wife of Even Jones (note: stone bur.)
NES, John son of M.C. and M. Jones d Oct. 18, 1867 age 26 days
NES, Emma L. dau of M.C. and M. Jones d Aug. 7, 1872 age 13 yrs. 7 mos. 8 ds.
NES, Miles C. Jones d July 30, 1876 age 43 yrs. 5 mos. 18 ds. GAR marker U.S. flag
ONINGER, Dr. M. d Aug. 24, 1878 age 56 yrs. 6 mos. 18 ds.
ONINGER, Lydia A. wife of Dr. M. Croninger d Oct. 22, 1865 age 35 yrs. 8 mos. 16 ds.
ONINGER, Calvin son of Dr. M. and L.A. Croninger b Oct. d Aug. 29, 1865 age 2 yrs.
11 mos. 10 ds.
GNER, Annie Catharine consort of Michael H. Wagner d Sept. 17, 1862 age 30 yrs.
1 mo. 4 ds.
LENBAUGHER, Elizabeth wife of John Bolenbaugher d Sept. 16, 1847 age 16 yrs.
7 mos. 7 ds.
LENBAUGHER, John d (note: stone bur.)
LENBAUGHER, James W. son of A. and E. Bolenbaugher d Aug. 3, 1861 (stone bur.)
_____, 1 yr. 11 mos. 14 ds. (May belong to Fristoe - below)
ISTOE, Mary V. dau of Wm H. and N. Fristoe d Nov. 5, 1850 (note: stone bur.)
JOR, Martha wife of Robert Major d April 10, 1846 age 26 yrs. 4 mos. 27 ds.
JOR, Sarah wife of David Major d Sept. 17, 1843 age 43 yrs. 5 mos. 13 ds.
JOR, In memory of Evalina consort of David Major d Aug. 19, 1845 age 30 yrs. 9 mos.
5 ds.
LICK, Anna d Sept. 9, 1845 age 19 yrs. 5 mos.
JOR, Evelinah wife of David Major d Aug. 19, 1845 age 30 yrs. 9 mos. 5 ds.
JOR, David d Jan. 15, 1854 age 43 yrs. 2 mos. - GAR 1861-65(?) U.S. Flag
JOR, Hannah E. d June 30, 1855 age 20 yrs. and _ ds.
NTA, Two Infant Children of Henry and Lydia Banta
NTA, Lydia wife of Henry Banta d Mar. 10, 1859 age 23 yrs. 10 ds.
LER, George d Feb. 3, 1862 age 74 yrs. 9 mos. 29 ds.
LER, Sarah wife of Geo. Eyler d July 10, 1855 age 48 yrs. 15 ds.
LER, George W. son of G. and S. Eyler d Jan. 17, 1857 age 14 yrs. 11 mos. 7 ds.
LER, William H. d Mar. 17, 1861 age 26 yrs. 3 ds.
_____. (note: stone unreadable)

MOSURE, James O. son of D. and R.A. Mosure d Jan. 8, 1866 age 1 yr. (stone broken)
GULICK, George W. son of A. and S. M. Gulick d Aug. 18, 1850 age 18 yrs. 5 mos. 24 ds.
GULICK, Sarah M. wife of Amos Gulick d Aug. 13, 1850 age 46 yrs. 4 mos. 2 ds.
OLNEY, Lucy wife of Ithamar Olney d July 17, 1850 age 55 yrs. and 14 ds.
PIERCY, John A. son of J. and M. Piercy (note: stone bur.)
ROSS, Oliver S. son of O. and A. Ross d Mar. 31, 1803(06?) age 1 yr. 6 mos. 16 ds.
_____, Calvin and Amos sons of J. and E.A. - twin stone   (?)
PATRICK, Louisa J. wife of Lyman Y. Patrick d Dec. 2, 1873 age 20 yrs. 1 mo. 5 ds.
PATRICK, James W. son of L.S. and J. Patrick d Aug. 15, 1876 age 1 yr. 6 ds.
DETTER, George son of _____ and Mary A. Detter_____ 5 yrs.
MYERS. Anna D. b Aug. 19, 1815 d Feb. 7, 1888 age 72 yrs. 5 mos. 18 ds.
MYERS, Jonathan d Oct. 21, 1871 age 63 yrs. 8 8 mos. 20 ds.
THOMAS, Lucinda wife of Charles Thomas d Dec. 29, 1861 age 21 yrs. 4 ds.
HARB, Birdie dau of W.B. and Carolina Herb d Feb. 9, 1871 age 16 ds.
HARB, Infant son of Wm B. and C. Harb d Mar. 20, 1858
HARB, Little Jimmy son of Wm B. and Carolina Harb d Feb. 23, 1863 age 6 mos. 12 ds.
HARB, Little Frankie son of M. L. and A. C. Harb d Apr. 14, 1863 age 5 mos. 14 ds.
MILTON, Sarah wife of John Milton d Dec. 6, 1850 age 73 years
TUTTLE, Isabell former wife of John DEWPEW b Nov. 19, 1836 d Mar. 16, 1898
DEWPEW, John husband of Isabell DEPEW b Sept. 25, 1832 d Mar. 25, 1869
COUNTERMAN, Jno. Co. C., 11th Ind. Cart. GAR 1861-65 U.S. Flag
CHILCOAT, Joshua - Co. C., 11th Ind. GAR 1861-1865
HAMRICK, Mary wife of Albert Hamrick d. Aug. 29, 1859 age 60 yrs. 2 mos.
HAMRICK, Rachel wife of Albert Hamrick d Jue 12, 1873 age 29 yrs. 4 mos. 26 ds.
ARRON(?), B. W. (note: illegible)
TICKLE, Thompson d Feb. 13, 1875 age 26 yrs. 1 mo. 13 ds.
TICKLE, Peter d April 1, 1869 age .42 yrs. 20 ds.
TICKLE, Inf child of Peter and Anna Tickle b Jan. 18, 1862 age 1 da.
STETLER, Mahala dau of J. and R. Stetler d Oct. 22, 1857
TICKLE, Emaline wife of John Tickle d bur. 1858
TICKLE, Rachel A. dau of J. and E. Tickle d Oct. 11, 1859 age 7 yrs. 3 mos. 21 ds.
STETLER(?), Mathda V. (note: broken stone)
TICKLE, Elizabeth wife of John Tickle d Dec. 17, 1872 age 53 yrs. 8 mos. 21 ds.
TICKLE, William son of J. and E. Tickle d Apr. (?) 1851 age 6yrs. 11 mos. 21 ds.
STETLER, Nelson son of J. and R. Stetler d Sept. 6, 1851 age 6 yrs. 11 mos. 29 ds.
STETLER, Sarah Ida dau of Thomason and Nancy Stetler (note: stone bur.)
SWANK, John d Mar. 3, 1856 age 35 yrs. 11 mos. 19 ds.
SWANK, Louisa dau of J. and J. Swank d Sept. 3, 1857 age 2 yrs. 3 mos. 6 ds.
STETLER, Julia H. wife of Jeffry Stetler d Oct. 10, 1870 age 50 yrs. 5 mos. 27 ds.
_____, (note: broken stone) d Mar. 7, 1872 age 2 yrs. 1 mo. 27 ds.
TROUTNER, Inf son of C. W. and C. Troutner d Mar. 12, 1874
PASSWATER, Jesse C. son of R. and E. Passwater d Sept. 18, 1874 age 1 yr. 7 mos. 23d.
M'KIM, Celestina dau of T. S. and R. P. M'Kim d May 8, 1847 age 5 yrs. 8 mos. 21 ds.
M'KIM, Inf son of T. S. and C. M'Kim
M'KIM, Celinda wife of Thomas S. M'Kim d Sept. 1, 1850 age 25 yrs. 10 mos. 29 ds.
_____, (note: small stone) GAR 1861-1865 marker. U.S. Flag
WATRED, Marion W. son of J.R. and E. Watred d Feb. 21, 1873 age 5 mos. 20 ds.
PHILBEE, James d Aug. 2, 1875 age 85 years
PHILBEE, Jane wife of J. Philbee d May 28, 1877 age 80 years

618

LLER, Mary J. d July 3, 1879 age 56 yrs. 2 mos. 10 ds.

ETLER, _____ d Feb. 12, 1875 age 69 yrs. and 7 mos.

ETLER(?), Lydia wife of_____ (note: stone bur.)

ETLER, Iona F. dau of W. L. & C. Stetler d May 14, 1875 age 1 yr. 28 ds.

ETLER, Jacob d Nov. 26, 1872 age 65 yrs. 4 mos. 17 ds.

ETLER, Alfred d Dec. 16, 1863 age 32 yrs. 6 mos. 28 ds.

RICKLER, Effam dau of Wm and Lydia Strickler d Sept. 28, 1876(0?) age 1 yr. 20 ds.

ERY, Corp'l Dan'l Co. C., 47th Ind. Inf.

GUST, Henry F. son of W. and M.G. August d Mar. 6, 1872)

GUST, John A. son of W. and M.G. August d_____1869   ) (note: stones bur.)

ANDT, John W. son of Charles and Amanda Brandt d Jan. 27, 1863 age 5 yrs. 5mos.16ds.

ANDT, Rosana May dau of C. and A. Brandt d May 17, 1869 age 2 yrs. 1 mo.

ANDT, Inf dau of C. and A. Brandt   Apr. 2, 1871

ANDT, Inf son of C. and A. Brandt d Feb. 19, 1873 age 4 days

ANDT, Amanda 1840-1927

ANDT, Charles d May 3, 1876 age 42 yrs. 8 mos. 7 ds.

ANDT, Chas. Co. K, 110 Ohio Inf. (marker) GAR 1861-65 U.S. Flag

KER, Lafayette 1832-1919 and Eliza 1836-1871 Co. C. 47th Reg. I.V.I.
                          (marker) GAR 1861-65 U.S. Flag

KER, Eliza wife of L. Riker d Nov. 12, 1871 age 35 yrs. 8 mos. and 3 ds.

ERY, William d Aug. 6, 1874 age 69 yrs. 7 mos. 1 da.

ERY, Barbara wife of William Avery d Sept. 11, 1867 age 60 yrs. 1 mos. and 10 ds.

ERY, L.D. husband of_____ (note: stone bur)(marker) GAR 1861-65 U.S. Flag

ERY, James F. d Nov. 22, 1875 age 3 yrs. 3 mos. 11 ds.

ERY, Nancy E. dau of L. and M.J. Avery d Jan. 18, 1851 age 10 ds.

ERY, John C. son of J. and E.J. Avery d Sep. 11, 1863 age 1 yr. 11 mos. 25 ds.

ERY, William M. son of J. and E.J. Avery d Oct. 10, 1863 (note: stone bur.)

SS, James son of J. and C. Ross d July 25, 1845 age 2 yrs. 2 mos. and 19 ds.

SS, Willis son of J. and C. Ross d Oct. 17, 1845 age 1 yr. 3 mos. 13 ds.

SS, Sarah J. dau of J. and C. Ross d Dec. 10, 1870 age 22 yrs. 10 mos. 4 ds.

SS, Kelita son of J. and C. Ross d Jan. 1, 1972 age 19 yrs. 10 mos. 4 ds.

SS, Catharine wife of J. B. Ross b Nov. 10, 1813 d Aug. 9, 1879

SS, Joseph B. Ross b Feb. 25, 1815 d Dec. 18, 1877

SS,_____(note: stone fell over) d Aug. 18, 1901 age 60 yrs. 7 mos. 27 ds.

LLER, Thos C. d. Oct. 2, 1853 age 63 yrs. 6 mos. 15 ds.

LLER, Rachel wife of Thos. C. Miller d Oct. 30, 1851 age 60 yrs. 6 mos. 18 ds.

OMAN, (note: stone broken) _ancis son of Thomas J. and Sarah E. Redman
                          d Aug. 26, 1846 age 1 yr. 4 ds.

OMAN, Thomas J. d Mar. 12, 1847 age 28 yrs. 6 mos. 28 ds. "In Memory of"

ILSBERY, Wm H. d Feb. 25, 1847 age 27 years

HNSON, Elizabeth wife of Thos. Johnson d. May 25, 1908 age 61 yrs. 14 ds.

_____, (note: stone broken) d May 5, 1875 age 5 yrs. 6 mos. 1 ds.

_____, (note: a line of bases but no stones)

_____, (note: two small stones but no marking)

ICHARD, Sarah wife of Henry R. Reichard d Sept. 28, 1874 age 74 yrs. 5 mos. 16 ds.

ICHARD, Calvin d Apr. 30, 1871 age 28 yrs. 7 mos. 12 ds. (marker) GAR 1864-65
                                                          U.S. Flag

ICHARD, Henry b Nov. 10, 1797 d (note: stone bur.)

_____, (note: small stone)

_____, (note: stones broken off and bur.)

United States Land Patents Granted In
VAN WERT COUNTY, OHIO

Although many deeds and land patents (grants or entries) were dated earlier, the
first deed in Van Wert County was not recorded until January 17, 1838. The majo
ity of the land was granted through the land offices at Lima, Wapakoneta and Pic
The following is **not** a complete listing of all land patents in Van Wert County,
is a complete listing of patents recorded in Deed Volumes A, B, C & D.
Abbreviations: N,S,E,W-North, South, East, West - f-fractional - ¼-quarter -
½-half (Example: NW¼ SW f¼ - North West quarter of the South West Fraction quart

Name	Section, Twp. & Range	Area	Acres	Date	Vol.& Page
ALEXANDER, Isaac	29-3S-1E	E½ NW¼	160	10-7-1835	A/40!
of Muskingum Co., Ohio		W½ NE¼			
ANDERSON, John	23-3S-1E	W½ NE¼	80	10-10-1840	B/39(
of Holmes Co., Ohio					
ASDEL, James	29-2S-3E	E½ NW¼ &	160	9-4-1838	A/33:
of Columbiana Co., Ohio		W½ NE¼			
BAILEY, Amaziah	27-3S-2E	SW¼	160	10-10-1840	B/41(
of Richland Co., Ohio					
BARTON, Henry	28-2S-2E	N½	320	8-21-1837	A/33
of Columbiana Co., Ohio					
BAUSERMAN, Jacob	3-2S-1E	NE¼	160	10-10-1840	C/30
of Portage Co., Ohio					
BEAMER, Henry	35-1S1E	W½ NE¼	80	10-10-1840	D/51
of Carroll Co., Ohio					
	26-1S-1E	SW¼ SE¼	40	10-10-1840	D/51
BEBB, William	30-2S-4E	SE¼	160	3-18-1837	D/14
of Butler Co., Ohio					
	31-2S-4E	NE¼	160	3-18-1837	D/14
	19-1S-4E	E½ SW¼	80	8-1-1844	D/14
	30-1S-4E	E½ NW¼	87	8-1-1844	D/14
	8-2S-4E	E½ NW¼	80	8-1-1844	D/15
	2-1S-3E	N f½	331	6-1-1845	D/15
	25-1S-3E	E½	320	6-1-1845	D/15
	17-1S-4E	NW¼	160	6-1-1845	D/15
	18-1S-4E	E½ SW¼ &	206	6-1-1845	D/15
		W½ SW¼ & SE¼ NE¼			
	10-1S-2E	E½ SE¼	80	6-1-1845	D/15
	1-1S-3E	E½ & SW¼	483	6-1-1845	D/15
	6-1S-4E	whole	638	6-1-1845	D/15
	18-1S-4E	NWf¼·½NE¼NE¼NE¼	288	9-10-1844	D/15
BEBEHYMIR, Peter	10-3-3E1		160	8-21-1837	B/21
of Franklin Co., Ohio					
BOLENBAUCHER, Peter	3-3S-1E	NW f¼ E½	38	8-9-1824	A/1:
of Montgomery Co., Ohio					
BRONSON, Nancy	6-2S-2E	W½ NE¼	80	3-16-1837	C/2:
of Portage Co., Ohio					
BURRAWS, Robert	28-2S3E	SW¼ &	280	3-20-1837	C/5:
of Trumbull Co., Ohio		E½ NW¼ & SW¼ NW¼			
BURRIGHT, Orin	19-2S-4E	W½ NE¼	80	9-4-1838	B/1.
of Mercer Co., Ohio					

Name	Section Twp. & Range	Area	Acres	Date	Vol.& Page
CASSELS(CAPLES), Charles of Tuscarawas Co., Ohio	2-2S-2E	SE¼	160	3-18-1837	C/216
CAVETT, Joseph of Licking Co., Ohio	19-2S-4E	NW¼ SW f¼	44	9-4-1838	D/169
	19-2S-4E	SW¼ SW f¼	44	9-4-1838	D/170
COLEMAN, Guilford D. of Mason Co., Ky.	13-2S-4E	E½ SE¼	80	1-7-1845	D/139
COLEMAN, Henry of Crawford Co., Ohio	27-2S-1E	E½ NE¼	80	10-10-1840	B/432
COLEMAN, John of Richland Co., Ohio	2-3S-1E	W½ NW f¼	77	10-10-1840	B/431
COLEMAN, Valentine of Crawford Co., Ohio	26-2S-1E	W½ NW¼	80	10-10-1840	B/430
CRAFTS, Samuel S. of Otsego Co., New York	15-2S-2E	S½ & NW¼	480	3-20-1837	C/82
	14-2S-2E	S½ & N¼	480	3-20-1837	C/83
CULVER, Lewis	24-2S-2E	W½ SW¼ & SW¼ NW f¼	119	3-20-1837	B/73
CUMMINGS, Emanuel of Carroll Co., Ohio	32-3S-2E	W½ SE¼ SE¼	120	9-4-1838	B/242
	13-1S-1E	SW¼ NW¼	40	10-10-1840	B/243
CUSH, Daniel D. of Licking Co., Ohio	20-2S-1E	N½ NW¼	80	8-1-1844	C/468
DAVIS, William of Richland Co., Ohio	20-2S-2E	S½ NE¼	--	8-21-1837	A/234
DEANER(DEAVER), Joseph of Fairfield Co., Ohio	6-2S-4E	E½ SE¼	80	10-10-1840	C/360
DELONG, Isaac of Union Co., Ohio	29?-2S-4E	W½ SE¼	80	9-4-1838	B/218
DEVER, Evan of Greene Co., Ohio	20-2S-2E	N½ NE¼	80	3-20-1837	C/316
DIX, Peres Main of Delaware Co., Ohio	9-2S-2E	N½ NW¼	80	3-20-1837	B/244
	12-2S-2E	NE¼ SW¼	40	3-20-1837	D/496
FAUCHER, Samuel ef Delaware Co., Ohio	10-3S-3E	NW¼	160	8-21-1837	B/214
FAUSNOUGHT, David of Franklin Co., Ohio	12-2S-1E	E½ SE¼	80	8-21-1837	C/445
FREEMAN, John A. of Greene Co., Ohio	23-3S-3E	NW¼	160	8-21-1837	D/546
Gleason, Abigail	31-2S-2E	W½ SE¼	80	10-10-1840	B/328
GLEASON, Clarissa	9-3S-2E	W½ ?E¼(torn)	80	8-1-1844	D/1
GLEASON, Joseph	31-2S-2E	NE¼ NE¼ NW f¼	280	10-10-1840	B/302
of Lorain Co. O.	31-2S-2E	SW f¼ S½ NW f¼	291	8-1-1844	D/190
GLEASON, Mary	30-2S-2E	E½ SE¼	80	8-1-1844	D/1
GLEASON, Stephen of Lorain Co., Ohio	7-24-N11E	SE¼	160	8-20-1838	A/254
GILLILAND, Adam	21-2S-3E	W½ SW¼ W½ NW¼	160	8-21-1837	C/121
	20-2S-3E	E½ SE¼ E½ NE¼	160	8-21-1837	C/122

621

Name	Section, Twp. & Range	Area		Acres Date	Vol. Page
GILLAND, James Gordon	9-2S-3E	SE¼ & S½ NE¼	240	2-25-1836	A/189
of Adams Co., Pa.					
HALL, Daniel	33-3S-2E	E½ SE¼	80	9-4-1838	C/77
of Delaware Co., Ohio					
HAYDEN, Joseph	18-3S-4E	SE¼ SW¼	47	3-16-1837	D/513
HERBERT, Joseph	26-2S-2E	NW¼	160	8-21-1837	A/334
of Columbiana Co., Ohio					
HILL, William	14-2S-3E	N½ SE¼	80	3-20-1837	B/473
HILL, William	14-2S-3E	S½ NE¼	80	2-15-1836	B/474
of Putnam Co., Ohio					
HOAGLIN, Enoch M.	19-1S-3E	W½ NW ¼	86	6-1-1845	D/263
of Richland Co., Ohio					
HOLCOMB, Johnathan B.	6-3S-1E	N½ SE¼ & S½ NE¼	157	3-20-1837	B/170
of Warren Co., Ohio					
JACOBS, Thomas K.	6-3S-4E	NE¼	162	8-21-1837	B/239
of Richland Co., Ohio					
JOHNSON, Benjamin	28-2S-1E	SW¼ & S½ NW¼	240	8-1-1844	D/491
of Brooke Co., Va.					
JOHNSON, Julius	19-3S-2E	E½ NW ¼	104	10-10-1840	C/322
of Medina Co., Ohio					
JONES, Lucinda A.	24-3S-1E	E½ NE¼ & NW¼ NE¼	120	10-10-1840	C/388
of Lorain Co., Ohio					
JORDAN, Henry	17-1S-2E	W½ NE¼	80	9-10-1844	D/536
of Stark Co., Ohio					
KEEFER, Henry	12-1S- 2E	W½ NE¼	80	10-1-1846	D/514
of Richland Co., Ohio					
KEITH, John	25-3S-?E	S½ NE¼ & E½ SW¼	160	. . . . .(?)	D/4
of Madison Co., Ohio				(paper torn & pages gone)	
KESSLER, Abraham	13-2S-3E	N½ SW¼	.80	3-18-1837	B/197
of Fairfield Co., Ohio					
KETCHEM, Philip	31-3S-1E	SE¼ NW¼ & SW¼ NE¼	73	3-20-1837	A/378
of Licking Co., Ohio 31-3S-1E		W½ SE¼	80	3-20-1837	A/379
KILMER, Philip	2-2S-1E	E½	316	8-1-1844	C/541
of Muskingum Co., Ohio 1-2S-1E		W½	320	8-1-1844	D/262
KING, David	17-2S-4E	W½NW¼	80	3-15-1837	C/589
of Clark Co., Ohio 18-2S-4E		NE¼ NE¼	40	3-15-1837	C/590
KLINKER, Joseph	3-3S-1E	NE ¼	155	10-10-1840	C/267
of Crawford Co., Ohio					
KRAMER, D. T.	17-3S-2E	E½ NE¼	80	10-9-1841	C/460
assignee of John B. DAVIDSON					
LAKE, William	34-3S-3E	W½ NW¼ & NE¼ NW¼	120	9-4-1838	D/271
of Licking Co., Ohio					
McCLURE, Samuel	27-3S-3E	NW¼	160	8-21-1837	B/180
of Beaver Co., Pa.26-3S-3E		W½	320	8-21-1837	B/184
McCLURE, William	27-3S-3E	S½ & NE¼	480	8-21-1837	B/182
of Beaver Co., Pa.22-3S-3E		SE¼ SE¼	40	8-21-1837	B/183
McCOY, Andrew	27-2S-3E	SW¼ SE¼	40	8-21-1837	B/307
of Madison Co., Ohio					
McCULLOUGH, John	32-2S-4E	NE¼	160	3-20-1837	C/367
of Adams Co., Ohio					

Name	Section, Twp. & Range	Area	Acres	Date	Vol. Page
McDONOUGH, Hugh	26-3S-1E	NE¼	160	10-10-1840	D/16
•f Tuscarawas C•., Ohi•					
McKEE, Henry	32-3S-2E	NE¼ & NE¼ SE¼	200	9-4-1838	C/543
of Westmoreland C•., Pa.					
MAJORS, William	31-3S-1E	W½ NW¼	67	10-9-1835	A/314
MALTBIE, Hiram	31-3S-4E	SE¼	160	3-20-1837	D/577
of Montgomery Co., Ohio					
MARK, Washington	25-3S-3E	NW¼ NE¼	40	11-27-1833	D/528
of Madison Co., Ohio	25-3S-3E	NE¼ NW¼	40	11-27-1833	D/529
	25-3S-3E	NE¼ NE¼	40	8-24-1837	D/512
MATTOX, James L.	9-2S-2E	W½ NE¼ & E½ NW¼	160	3-18-1837	D/226
MILLIGAN, Hugh	32-2S-3E	E½ NE¼	80	9-4-1838	D/161
of Ross Co., Ohi•					
MORSE, John G.	15-1S-1E	SE¼ NE¼ & NE¼ NW¼	80	10-10-1840	D/470
•f Onondago Co., New Y•rk					
MYERS, George	35-2S-1E	E½ NW¼	80	10-10-1840	C/284
of Richland Co., Ohi•					
NEISWANGER, David	23-3S-1E	E½ NE¼	80	10-10-1840	B/391
of Holmes Co., Ohi•					
PERKINS, Simon	12-2S-2E	W½ NW¼	80	3-15-1837	B/437
•f Trumbull C•., Ohi•					
PHELPS, Edward M.	31-3S-1E	SE¼ NE¼	40	9-4-1838	B/122
of Mercer Co., Ohio					
POLLOCK, Thomas	31-2S-4E	W½ NW¼ & SE¼ NW f¼	132	8-21-1837	B/447
•f Columbiana Co., Ohi•					
POLOCK, Thomas	36-2S-3E	SE¼	160	8-21-1837	B/448
of Columbiana Co., Ohi•					
PONTIUS, John	9-2S-1E	S½ NW¼	80	11-10-1840	C/314
•f Stark Co., Ohio	9-2S-1E	N½ NW¼	80	10-10-1840	C/315
PRICE, David M.	21-3S-1E	W½ NW¼ & SE¼ NW¼	120	9-4-1838	A/179
PUTNAM, Peter	30-3S-2E	SE¼	160	10-10-1840	D/208
of Stark Co., Ohio					
REDMAN, William	33-38-2E	W½ NW¼	80	9-4-1838	C/602
of Carroll C•., Ohio					
ROSS, Mary L.	7-2S-3E	W½ NWf¼	95	10-10-1840	B/326
•f Allen C•., Ohio					
ROSS, Milton J.	6-3S-4E	W½ SW f¼	95	10-10-1840	B/322
of Allen Co., Ohio	7-2S-2E	E½ NW f¼	95	10-10-1840	B/325
ROWLAND, Levi	11-3S-2E	SW¼	160	9-4-1838	B/272
•f Harrison Co., Ohio					
SHANNON, Lanty	23-3S-3E	SW¼	160	9-4-1838	B/256
of Licking C•., Ohi•					
SMITH, Ge•rge	29-3S-2E	NE¼	160	9-4-1838	A/342
•f Columbiana Co., Ohi•					
SMITH, Jesse	7-2S-2E	SW¼ SW f¼	48	9-10-1844	D/261
SMITH, John	26-3S-3E	E½	320	8-21-1837	B/181
of Beaver Co., Pa.	7-2S-2E	E½ NE¼ & SW¼NE¼&NW¼SW¼	160 9-10-1844		D/240
SMITH, William G.	29-3S-2E	NW¼	160	9-4-1838	A/336
•f Columbiana Co., Ohio					

Name	Section Twp. & Range	Area	Acres	Date	Vol. Page
STEPHENS, Joseph	30-1S-3E	W½ SW f¼	80	11-10-1840	D/550
of Fairfield Co., Ohio					
STODDART, John	24-2S-3E	SW¼	160	8-21-1837	B/232
of Miami Co., Ohio					
STRIPE, Jacob, Jr.	31-1S-3E	W½	339	8-21-1837	A/305
of Fairfield Co., Ohio	27-1S-3E	NW¼	160	8-21-1837	A/306
	30-1S-3E	E½ SW f¼	86	11-10-1840	B/287
STRIPE, Jacob, Sr.	36-1S-2E	W½ SW¼ & E½ SW¼	160	11-10-1840	B/395
of Fairfield Co., Ohio					
STRIPE, Warner	28-1S-3E	E½ NE¼	80	8-21-1837	A/307
of Fairfield Co., Ohio	8-1S-3E	W½SE¼&E½SW¼	80	11-10-1840	B/393
	28-1S-3E	E½ SE¼	80	6-1-1845	D/551
STRIPE, William	32-1S-3E	NW¼	160	8-21-1837	B/76
of Fairfield Co., Ohio	36-1S-2E	E½ SE¼	80	8-21-1837	B/77
	30-1S-3E	SE¼	160	8-21-1837	B/78
	32-1S-3E	SW¼	160	8-21-1837	B/79
STROHM, Isaac	36-3S-2E	NW¼	160	9-10-1844	D/482
of Greene Co., Ohio					
STROTHER, Benjamin	14-3S-3E	NW¼ & NW¼SW¼&W½NE¼	320	3-20-1837	D/591
of Hancock Co., Ohio					
TAYLOR, Henry	4-3S-1E	E½ SE¼	80	10-10-1840	C/254
of Highland Co., Ohio					
THOMPSON, John	28-2S-2E	SE¼	160	8-21-1837	C/277
of Carroll Co., Ohio					
THOMPSON, Joseph	32-2S-2E	NW¼	160	8-21-1837	C/106
of Columbiana Co., Ohio					
THOMPSON, Robert M.	32-2S-2E	SW¼	160	8-21-1837	B/175
of Columbiana Co., Ohio					
THOMPSON, Sarah	29-2S-2E	SW¼	160	8-21-1837	C/312
of Columbiana Co., Ohio					
THORN, Benjamin	34-2S-2E	E½ NE¼	80	8-21-1837	A/252
of Trumbull Co., Ohio					
THORN, Thomas	34-2S-2E	SW¼ NE¼	40	10-10-1840	B/355
of Hardin Co., Ohio					
TIMNEY(?), Daniel	19-3S-2E	W½ NE¼	80	10-10-1840	D/90
of Clark Co., Ohio					
TINDALL, Zachariah	17-3S-1E	E½ SW¼	80	9-4-1838	D/187
of Beaver Co., Pa.	7-2S-1E	NW¼ NE¼	40	8-1-1844	D/188
TODD, Michael	1-3S-3E	W½ NE¼	80	8-21-1837	B/446
of Columbiana Co., Ohio					
TUMBLESON, John	8-2S-2E	SE¼	60	10-10-1840	C/105
of Tuscarawas Co., Ohio					
VANEMON, Robert	18-2S-1E	E½ NW¼	80	6-1-1845	D/128
of Beaver Co., Pa.	6-2S-1E	W½ SE¼	80	6-1-1845	D/128
WELLS, Elisha	21-2S-2E	NW¼ & W½ NE¼	--	8-21-1837	B/6
of Richland Co., Ohio					
WELLS, Lyman S.	5-1S-1E	NW¼ NW f¼	40	11-10-1840	B/301
WILLIAMS, John	6-2S-4E	SW¼	160	3-18-1837	D/614
of Fairfield Co., Ohio					

624

Name	Section Twp. & Range	Area	Acres	Date	Vol. Page
WILLIAMS, Samuel O. of Licking Co., Ohio	22-2S-3E	NE¼ SW¼ &NW¼ SE¼	80	8-1-1844	D/629
WILLS, Peter of Seneca Co., Ohio	9-2S-3E	E½ NW¼	80	3-16-1837	B/165
WILSON, Joseph of Butler Co., Ohio	18-3S-4E	W½ SW¼	94	2-15-1836	B/202
WILSON, Joseph of Montgomery Co., Ohio	12-2S-2E	E½ NW¼	80	9-15-1835	B/210
WOOD, Otis M. of Geauga Co., Ohio	2-2S-2E	SE¼ SW¼	40	3-20-1837	C/123
WOODS, Christian of Carroll Co., Ohio	14-3S-3E	S½ SW¼	80	10-10-1840	D/357
WRIGHT, Thomas of Hamilton Co., Ohio	36-3S-1E	SE¼	160	10-10-1840	D/437

=====================

Names of Townships - 1968

HARRISON - Sections 1-36, Township 2 South, Range 1 East
HOAGLIN   - Sections 2-11, 14-23, 25-36; Township 1 South Range 3 East
JACKSON   - Sections 1, 12, 13, & 24; Township 1 South; Range 3 East and
            Sections 4-9, 16-21, 28-33; Township 1 South; Range 4 East
JENNINGS - Sections 4-9, 16-21, 28-33; Township 3 South; Range 4 East and
            Section 4-9, 16-18; Township 4 South; Range 4 East
LIBERTY   - Sections 1-36, Township 3 South, Range 2 East
PLEASANT - Sections 1-36, Township 2 South, Range 2 East
RIDGE   - Sections 1-36, Township 2 South, Range 3 East
TULLY   - Sections 1-36, Township 1 South, Range 1 East
UNION   - Sections 1-36, Township 1 South, Range 2 East
WASHINGTON - Sections 1-36, Township 2 South, Range 4 East
WILLSHIRE - Sections 1-36, Township 3 South, Range 1 East
YORK   - Sections 1-36, Township 3 South, Range 3 East

=================

VAN WERT COUNTY, OHIO - WILL ABSTRACTS 1840-1850

The following abstracts were taken from Will Book 1, pages on which record may be found are given in parenthesis.

MADDUX, James - dated 5-20-1840; recorded (not given) - Sons: Charles, deceased; Thomas H.; Peter; John and Samuel. Daughters: Minerva Jennings; Rachel, deceased; Rosanna Hill wife of John Hill and Mary Jane Foster. Grandchildren: David and Sarah Jane Maddux residing in Fayette Co., Ohio, children of son, Charles Maddux, deceased; Sarah Jane Buzzard heir of daughter Rachel, deceased. Executor: William Priddy. Signed: James (mark) Maddux. Witnesses: Joseph Gleason and Edward R. Wells.   (1)

625

BOLENBAUGHER, Jacob - dated 8-15-1843; recorded 10-2-1843. Brothers: John, Peter and Michael. Mentions: Elizabeth, but does not state relationship. Executor: Henry Reichard. Signed: Jacob (mark) Bolenbaugher. Witnesses: J. W. Pearce, Ansel Blossom and Joshua Miller. (3)

DAVIS, William - dated 5-11-1843; recorded 10-2-1843. Wife: Mentioned, but not named. Children: Dau., Jane Glenn and son, James Oliver Davis; possibly more children not named. Executor: Stephen Gleason. Signed: William (mark) Davis. Witnesses: W. Buckingham, Jacob W. Johns and R. Gilliland. (5)

LUTZ, Henry - Verbal Will - Deposition 2-21-1846. Recorded 5-12-1846. Son: Abraham Lutz. Brother: Abraham Lutz. Witnesses: Henry Lutz, Hiram Sharitt and Martin Winkler. (7)

ERNEST, Gottfried - Verbal Will.- Deposition 5-15-1846. Recorded 5-15-1846. Father: Mentioned, but not named. Names: George Bentz and states that he is to have his father's name. Witnesses: John George Bentz, T. J. Leg, Dr. J. N. Bentler, G. M. Brickner, H. Hegnerman and Dr. H. M. Wentz. (6)

FOSTER, Samuel - dated 1-29-1844. Recorded (not given—1846?). Children by 1st wife Marth Foster: Henry Foster, Jesse Foster, William H. Foster, Macinda Foster and Sarah Meek. Children by present wife (not named): Joel Foster, Elizabeth Foster, Mary Foster and Rachel Foster. Requests: To be interred in the graveyard of Richard Pring's. Executor: Davis Johnson. Signed: Samuel (mark) Foster. Witnesses: Richard Pring and Joseph Johnson. (8)

MARK, James of Madison Co., Ohio - dated 11-30-1845. Recorded 3-28-1846. Wife: Nancy. Sons: James W., Matthias and Washington. Sons-in-law and daughters: John Taylor and Eliza his wife formerly Eliza Mark; James L. Bradley and Elizabeth his wife formerly Elizabeth Mark; William Foos and Sarah his wife, formerly Sarah Mark; Jesse B. Ferguson and Lucind his wife formerly Lucind Mark. Signed: James Mark. Witnesses: Washington Bradley and David L. Bradley. (9)

HARTZOG, George - dated 12-27-1846. Recorded 6-22-1847. Wife: Mentioned, but not named. Children: Son, Eli Hartzog and dau., Catharine Harrison, other children not named, youngest not of age. Executor: Eli Hartzog. Signed: George (mark) Hartzog. Witnesses: George Burdy (or Bundy) and Israel Hartzog. (12)

PERKINS, Simon of Warren, Trumbull Co., Ohio - dated 4-20-1844. Recorded 9-23-1847. Wife: Nancy. Children: Simon, Joseph, Jacob and Henry B.; possibly more not named. Mentions: Land in Warren and Howlan, Trumbull Co., Ohio; land in Cleveland, Cuyahoga Co., Ohio. Executors: Sons; Simon, Joseph and Jacob with nephew, Frederick Kinsmin. Signed: Simon Perkins. Witnesses: Thomas D. Webb, Henry Lane and Charles White. (13)

HAGAMAN (HAGERMAN), William - dated 9-2-1847; recorded 9-28-1847. Wife: Mary Ann. Infant son: John. Daughters: Elizabeth and Sarah Jane. Brother: Jacob, to enter land near sisters in Pulaski Co., Ind. Executor: Jacob Hageman. Signed: William (mark) Hagerman. Witnesses: E. M. Hoaglin and Jacob Stripe. (18)

626

MORSE, John G. of Tully Twp. - dated 7-21-1847; recorded 9-21-1847. Wife: Mercy A. Brother: William W. Morse. Sister: Maria Morse. Mentions: American Bible Society. Signed: John G. Morse. Witnesses: James Wortman, William Henney and Michael Anderson.   (20)

WROCKLAGE, Christian Matthias of Washington Twp. - dated 4-8-1846; recorded 3-2-1847. Wife: Maria Elisabeth, born Gerdemann Chief (?) - Children by 1st marriage: Theodore, Elisabeth and Gertrude Wrocklage. Children by 2nd marriage: Anna Mariah, Gerhard Matthias, Maria Agnes, Maria Catharine, Bernardina and Maria Elisabeth Wrocklage. Mentions: Land in Jennings Twp., Putnam Co., Ohio - Signed: Christian M. (mark) Wrocklage - Witnesses:- J. O. Brederick and H. J. Boehmer. (22)

LONGSWORTH, Solomon of Washington Twp. - dated 8-4-1847; recorded 9-22-1847. Sons: Solomon Reexe (Reece?) and Enoch George. Executors: Son, Enoch G. Longsworth. Signed: Solomon Longsworth. Witnesses: Thomas W. Bondell and John Summersett.   (24)

GOODWIN, Joshua of York Twp. - dated 10-31-1846; recorded 4-26-1847. Wife: Sarah, also to serve as Executrix and guardian of children. Children: John, Amos, Joshua, Sarah Ann, Benjamin, Jehu and Angeline. Signed: Joshua Goodwin. Witnesses: Giles J. Sheldon, George W. Griffin, Jacob Goodwin and John Frisner.   (25)

MYERS, John - dated 6-15-1848;-recorded 6-27-1848. Wife, mentioned but not named. Son: Thomas, not of age. Two daughters: Ann Eliza and Melissa Jane, not of age. Requests: That wife be guardian of children. Executor: Robert Gilliland. Signed: John (mark) Myers. Witnesses:- Luther Dodge and Robt. Gilliland.   (26)

REES, Christopher of Union Twp. - Dated 11-23-1848; recorded 12-7-1848. Wife: Mentioned, but not named. Children: Frederick, Henry, Wilmina and Carolina. Signed: Christopher Rees. Witnesses: E. M. Hoaglin and Elizabeth Spealer.   (28)

BOWERSOCK, Jacob - dated 7-15-1844;-recorded 4-11-1849 - Wife: Nancy, also to serve as Executrix - Sons: Henry, eldest son; Valentine and James - Mentions: Four eldest daughters, not named - Witnesses: John PALMER, Edward (mark) SUNDERLAND and Geo. MILLER. (30)

MORRISON, William - late of Orange Twp. Hancock Co., Ohio. Wife: Mentioned but not named. Father: John Morrison. Sons: James, oldest; John and William B., two youngest sons. Friend: Wm. Parks guardian of father's land in Van Wert Co. Mentions land in Hancock Co and also a lot to public for burying ground in Hancock Co. Executors: James Morrison and William Parks - Signed: William Morrison - Witnesses: John CUMMAN and John SHEW - Codicil: No additional information. (31)

The following records were taken from "Final Record 1". The page on which the record may be found is given in parenthesis. Only records of a genealogical nature have been included, ones for the collection of promissary notes and debts were not copied.

8-13-1850 - Amos CHAPMAN guardian of Patten and Martha LOVING vs. Catharine CHAPMAN. Petition to sell land. Filed 5-15-1850. Land, 80 acres W½ NW¼ Section 23, Township 9, Range 18 and part E½ NE¼ Section 22, Township 9, Range 18 being 20 acres. Thomas Loving, dec'd. Widow, Catharine formerly Loving, now wife of Amos Chapman, entitled to dower, Children: Patten Loving and Martha Loving, minors by Amos Chapman their guardian. (14)

8-13-1850 - Sylvanus BARTLETT adms. of Sylvanus BARTLETT, dec'd vs. Amanda BARTLETT, et al. Petition to sell land. Filed 4-25-1850. Land, 15 acres adjoining New Plymouth, also 3/4 acre adjoining meeting house lot in New Plymouth, , both part NW¼ Section 36, Township 11, Range 16. Widow, Amanda Bartlett, Children: Sylvanus, John, Julia, Samuel, William and Mary Bartlett; the last five named being minors.(17)

8-13-1850 - Margurett MUNROE vs. James L. MUNROE. Petition for Divorce. Filed 6-7-1850. Married in November 1843 in Jackson Co., Ohio. James L. Munroe now a resident of Perry Co., Ohio. One son, Richard, a minor. Margurett has right to real estate being part of Section 12 & 13, Township 9, Range 18 containing 100 acres, which came to her by descent from her father, Richard McDougal, as described in Petition for Partition on record in Common Pleas Court of Jackson Co., Ohio. (21)

3-18-1851 - John DUFFIELD vs Lusina DUFFIELD. Petition for Divorce. Filed 12-12-1850. Married 12-26-1848, her maiden name was Lusina Carr. That at time of marriage Lusina had a former husband still living by the name of Asa Thorp. That she married Thorp five or six years ago in Athens Co., Ohio and said marriage has never been disolved. (38)

5-27-1851 - John C. P. BROWN vs. James FURY, et al. Petition for Partition. Filed 12-31-1850. Land, 80 acres W½ SE¼ Section 35, Township 12, Range 17. John JOHNSON, dec'd, late of Vinton Co. Widow, Eleanor Johnson. Heirs: Elizabeth wife of James M. Fury of Porter Co., Indiana; John Johnson of Porter Co., Indiana; Polly G. wife of Jonathan Bussard. Elizabeth Fury and widow, Eleanor sold their interests to Lucian Chapin who sold said interest to Brown. (note: there may be more heirs than named in this petition). (73)

5-27-1851 - David JOHNSON vs. Earl GRADY, et al. In Partition. Filed 5-13-1850. Land, part SE corner Section 20, Township 8, Range 16 in Ohio Co. purchase, except 1/2 acre where graveyard is located on said premises and 24 acres previously deeded to Ann Wale; leaving 56 acres. That Earl Grady and two others whose names are unknown to petitioner, of Gallia County, children and heirs of Maxamilla Grady late Maxamilla Geer, now dec'd, who was daughter and heir at law of Earl P. Geer, who died intestate seized of the above premises and who are tenents in common with petitioner, said petitioner holding three undivided fourth interests. (97)

9-15-1851 - Samuel S. MURRY, et al. vs Minerva ZINN, et al. Filed 3-18-1851. William Zinn, dec;d. That on 9-8-1848, William Zinn then in full life agreed to sell 148 acres part NW corner Sections 19 & 25, Township 9, Range 16, now in Vinton twp., Vinton Co., but formerly in Athens Co. to Samuel Howdesheldt and Peter Starr, but died before deed was made; that Howdesheldt and Starr assigned their interest to Samuel S. Murry. Children: Minerva, Elizabeth, John and George Zinn, all minors.   (116)

9-15-1851 - G. W. SHOCKEY adms. of the Estate of Joseph MARTIN, dec'd vs. Widow and Heirs. Petition to sell land. Filed 8-21-1850. Land, 50 acres off NW¼ Section 26, Township 10, Range 16 in Brown twp. Widow, Elizabeth Martin. Heirs: William Martin, Nancy Martin, David Martin, Charles Martin and Laura Martin.   (129)

3-29-1852 - Andrew WOLF vs. Mahala COLVIN, et al.   In Chancery. Filed 5-29-1851. Land, 41.06 acres NW¼ NE¼ Section 5, Township 11, Range 17, Elk twp., now in Vinton Co., formerly in Athens Co.; mortgaged by William Colvin to August C. Schaal who assigned mortgage to Andrew Wolf. William Colvin, dec'd, died about October 1849. Widow, Mahala Colvin, entitled to dower. Children: Jacob, Acklin, Martin, Martha and Polly Colvin, all minors.   (141)

3-29-1852 - James WALKER vs. Betsey SMITH, etal. In Chancery. Filed 6-21-1851. Land, 40 acres SW¼ SW¼ Section 11, Township 10, Range 17, now in Vinton Co., formerly in Jackson County; William Smith Jr. agreed to sell to James Walker but did not complete deed before he died. William Smith Jr., dec'd, formerly of Guernsey Co., but removed to and died in Illinois. Widow, Betsey Smith. Children: Hiram H., Robert Mc., William H., John Y. and George Smith, all minors and all of Illinois.(144)

3-23-1852 - James WALKER vs. John CUNNINGHAM, et al. In Chancery. Filed 5-21-1851. Land, 40 acres NW¼ SW¼ Section 11, Township 10, Range 17, now in Vinton Co., formerly in Jackson Co. Nicholas Cunningham, late of Ross Co., Ohio, dec'd. Heirs: John Cunningham of Illinois; Elizabeth wife of David Alexander of Illinois; Maria wife of Alffed White of Illinois; Thomas Cunningham of Lake Co., Indiana; Nicholas Cunningham of Lake Co., Indiana; Edward Cunningham of Lake Co., Indiana; Luke Cunningham of Iowa, Calvin Cunningham of Texas; and David Cunningham of Ross Co., Ohio. Nicholas Cunningham before his decease assigned his interest in above land to Wm. Smith of Guernsey Co., Ohio who assigned said interest to Walker.   (147)

3-29-1852 - Josephine KEATON vs. Calvin Keaton. Petition for Divorce. Filed 11-5-1851. Married 12-12-1844; her maiden name was Josephine Arnold. Owns land in Vinton County, formerly in Athens Co. Calvin's residence is unknown, he left Josephine in June of 1848. One son, John A. Keaton aged 3 yrs. last December. (152)

3-29-1852 - Esther MORRISON vs. John MORRISON. Petition for Divorce. Filed 12-30-1851. Married 9-17-1816 in Essex Co., New Jersey. Her maiden anem was Esther Johnson, Own 23 acres land in Vinton County.   (154)

3-29-1852 - John GRAVES adms. of John LEFFLER, dec'd vs. Frances LEFFLER and John LEFFLER. Petition to sell lands. Filed 4-28-1851. Land. 120 acres W½ MW¼ Section 25 and SW¼ SW¼ Section 24, Township 9, Range 19. Widow, Frances Leffler of Stark Co., Illinois, entitled to dower. Child: John Leffler, a minor.   (179)

3-29-1852 - Edward SALTS adms. of William LIVELY, dec'd vs Mary LIVELY, et al.
Petition to sell land. Filed 8-13-1851. Land, 80 acres W½ NE¼ Section 12, Township
10, Range 18. William Lively, dec'd, left estate with will annexed. Widow, Mary
Lively of Vinton Co., entitled to dower. Legatees named under will: Matilda wife of
Edwards Salts of Vinton Co.; Cottrell Lively of Vinton Co.; Sarah Lively of Vinton
Co.; Clarinda formerly Lively wife of John Goodrich of Jackson, Ohio; Wilson Lively;
Mary Lively; David Lively; Elizabeth Lively; Neoma Lively; Rebecca Lively; and Will-
iam Lively; the last seven named of Vinton Co. and the last five named are minors and
specified as the "five youngest children of testator". (157)

3-29-1852 - William CATLIN adms. of Cyrus MAN, dec'd vs. Margarett MAN, et al.
Petition to sell land. Filed 6-20-1851. Land, 80 acres SE¼ NW¼ & NE¼ SW¼ Section
21, Township 12, Range 17. Cyrus Man, dec'd, late of Vinton Co. Widow, Margarett
Man, entitl4d to dower. Heirs: Thomas Man; Elizabeth Burgess of New York State;
Sarah Wademan formerly Man; Temperance formerly Man wife of Henry Hoover; Charlott
formerly Man wife of Abner Jackson; Mary Hoover, her heirs, names unknown, supposed
to reside in Pennsylvania; Sena formerly Man wife of Michael Hoover of Perry Co.,
Ohio; Heirs of Abeah and Abner Dickin, whose names are unknown, supposed to reside
in Delaware Co., Ohio; and Jeremiah Man of Indiana.   (162)

3-29-1852 - Amos ROBERTS guardian of Amos Martin, et al. Petition to sell land.
Filed 5-26-1851. 107 acres (no section or lot number given) Township 8, Range 11,
also 27 acres off 160 acres Lot 1105 and 80 acres Lot 1104, Township 8, Range 11.
William Martin, dec'd. Widow, M. T. Martin. Children: Amos, Rebecca, Alexander,
William and Amanda Martin, all minors and all of Vinton Co.; the children named are
jointly entitled to 4/11ths parts of said land.   (184)

3-29-1852 - Stephen DARBY guardian of John, Nancy and William SWAIM. Petition to
sell land. Filed 5-29-1851. Land, 80 acres SW¼ NE¼ and SE¼ NW¼ Section 20, Township 9, Range 18. Moses Swaim, dec'd, late of Vinton Co. Widow, Lydia Fox formerly
Swaim. Children: John D. Swaim aged 11 years, Nancy Swaim aged 10 yrs. and William
Swaim aged 8 yrs.   (189)

3-29-1852 - Joseph DIXON vs. Jacob COX, et al. Petition for Partition. Filed
7-28-1851. Land, 66½ acres South part NW¼ and 160 acres SW¼ Section 32, Township
10, Ra ge 19. Jacob Cox, dec'd/ heirs: Jacob Cox; Rebecca wife of Joseph Dixon of
Ross Co., Ohio; Ann wife of Samuel Timmons; Nicholas Cox; Malon Cox; Elizabeth Cox,
Hannah Cox and Matilda Cox; the last two named being minors.   (193)

3-30-1852 - Humphrey CLARK adms. of Abraham COZAD, dec'd vs. Charity COZAD, et al.
Petition to sell lands. Filed 5-26-1851. Land, 40 acres NE¼ NE¼ Section 29
(except 17 acres conveyed 12-11-1847 by Cozad and wife to Wm. Lewis) and 40 acres
SE¼ SE¼ Section 20, Township 9, Range 18. Widow, Charity Cozad. Heirs: Susan
late Cozad wife of Nathan Dickson; Elizabeth late Cozad wife of Humphrey Clark;
Catharine late Cozad wife of Charles Hobson; Levi Cozad; Job Cozad; Mary late Cozad
wife of John Lewis; Henry Cozad; and John Cozad; all of Vinton Co., the last two
named being minors.   (201)

630

6-28-1852 - Rebecca Ann MORRIS vs. Lewis MORRIS, et al. In Partition. Filed 11-22-1851. Land, 40 acres NW¼ NE¼ Section 17, Township 9, Range 18. John Morris, dec'd, late of Guernsey Co., Ohio. Widow, Phebe late Morris, now wife of Hazel Barbee of Vinton Co. Heirs: Caroline formerly Morris wife of David Barbee of Indiana; Rebecca Ann Morris, Lewis Morris; Lucinda Morris; Elizabeth Morris; Maria Morris; and William H. Morris. (235)

6-28-1852 - Frederick FRICK vs. Christiana FRICK, et al. Filed 2-10-18 1. Land, 40 acres SW¼ NE¼ Section 20, Township 20, Range 17 in which Jacob F. Frick and August Shall were tenents in common with Frick dying seized of one undivided half interest. Jacob F. Frick, dec'd. Widow, Christiana Frick. Heirs: Frederick Frick, Catharine wife of Charles Haines, Christiana formerly Frick wife of Godleib Faber, Mary frick and Caroline Frick; the last name being a minor. (241)

3-28-1853 - James ADAMS vs. Myra ADAMS. Petition for Divorce. Filed (not given). Married 12-25-1848 in Hocking Co., Ohio. (264)

3-28-1853. Martin GROFF vs. David GROFF, et al. In Partition. Filed 2-1-1853. Land, 262 acres Lot #2, Sections 9 & 15, Township 11, Range 16, Brown twp. Christian Groff, dec'd, late of Jefferson Co., Ohio. Heirs-each entitled to 1/10th part: Martin Groff of Jefferson Co., Ohio; David Groff of Defiance Co., Ohio; Susan Groff of Hamilton Co., Ohio; Catharine Groff of Jefferson Co., Ohio; Jacob Groff; Elizabeth Groff; Mary Groff; the last three named all of Lancaster Co., Pennsylvania, Richard Groff of Iowa; Samuel Groff, residence unknown; and Heirs of Benjamin Groff, dec'd of Illinois. (273)

3-28-1853 - Jacob L. CURRIER vs. Thomas O"NEAL, et al. Petition for Partition. Filed 2-9-1853. Land, 480 acres S½ & NW¼ Section 11, Township 11, Range 16. Partition: 1/36th part earch or 1/6th part jointly: Henry son of Charles O'Neal, Henry son of James O'Neal, Henry son of James Hathaway, Henry son of Peggy Donaly, Henry son of Nancy Donally and Henry O'Neal; 1/7th part, Martha Lee; 1/7th part James O'Neal; 1/7th par, Thomas O'Neal; 1/7th part, Charles O'Neal; 1/7th part, Peggy Donaly; 1/7th part, John O'Neal. Resicendes are given as follows, no further distinction given: Thomas O'Neal of Hocking Co., Ohio; Heirs of Charles O'Neal, residence and names unknown; Henry O'Neal of California; Henry Hathaway, residence unknown; Heirs of Peggy Donally of Indiana; Henry Donally of Indiana; Heirs of Nancy Conally, names and residence unknown; Henry Donally, residence unknown; John O'Neal of Portage Co., Ohio; Henry O'Neal, residence unknown. (276)

3-28-1853- Sarah SNOOK vs. George SNOOK, et al. In Partition. Filed 12-22-1851. Land, 3.02 acres off SE corner E½ SW¼; 10 acres SW corner W½ SE¼; and 42 rods SW cprmer W½ SE¼, all in Section 8, Township 10, Range 17. John Snook, dec'd. late of Vinton Co. Widow (mentioned, not named). Partition: 1/6th part, Sarah Snook of Vinton Co.; 1/6th part, George Snook of Missouri; 1/yth part, Henry Snook of Missouri; 1/6th part, Perlina Snook of Illinois; 1/6th part, William Snook of Illinois; 1/6th part, Catharine Crow of Illinois. (301)

6-6-1853 - Henry EUTSLER, Jr. vs. Susan JONES, et al. In Chancery. Filed 9-16-1851. Land, 40 acres NW corner NE¼ Section 25, Township 9, Range 16 contracted to be sold to Henry Eutsler and Joseph C. Kirkendall. William ZIN, dec'd died in spring of 1849 or 1850. Widow, Susan late Zin, now wife of Andrew Jones. Children: Minerva, Elizabeth, John and George Zin, all minors. (330)

631

6-6-1853 - Philemon BUTTON vs. Sarah M. BUTTON. Petition for Divorce. Filed 4-4-1853. Married in November 1845; her maiden ane was Sarah M. Myrick. Sarah's residence unknown, was residing in Lake Co., Indiana until October of 1851. (341)

6-6-1853 - Mary BURNS vs. John BURNS. Petition for Divorce. Filed 3-28-1853. Married 4-14-1844. Two children (not named). (343)

6-6-1853 - Ruth THORPE admsrx. of Estate of Wm. THORPE, dec'd vs. Thomas JOHNSON, et al. Filed 9-17-1851. Land, 170.60 acres East part Section 30, Township 10, Range 16. Wm. Thorpe died without issue leaving as his only heir, his widow, Ruth. That Thomas Johnson is not an heir, but claims to have interest in said land. (355)

10-4-1853 - Catharine RUSSELL vs Samuel RUSSELL, Petition for Divorce. Filed 8-3-1853. Married 1-30-1850 in Athens Co., Ohio. Samuel's residence unknown. (380)

10-4-1853 - William H. TRIPP vs. Nancy N. TRIPP, et al. In Chancery. Filed 11-5-1852. Land, NE¼ SWP; SE¼ NW¼; and SW: NE: all in Section 1, Township 8, Range 18, each containing 39.31 acres, being in Jackson Co., Ohio; purchased jointly by Wm. H. A. Tripp, Wm. H. Tripp and William Colvin in 1847. William H. A. Tripp, dec;d. Widow, Nancy N. Tripp. Children: William H. Tripp, Lovina wife of Robert F. Jones, Jesse Tripp, Stephen Tripp, John Tripp, Oliver Tripp, Joseph Tripp, Leonidas Tripp, Louisa Tripp, David Tripp, Holden Tripp, Betsy wife of Alexander Livingston, Mary Ann wife of Eli Livingston, and Rebecca Tripp. (406)

3-27-1854 - David REMY vs. Harriet SHRICK, et al. In Partition. Filed 12-24-1853. Land, SWP SEP and NWP SEP Section 27, Township 9, Range 18, deeded by Lewis Remy, dec'd in his lifetime to his son, Alexander Remy, now dec'd as a deed of gift. Lewis Remy, dec'd, died prior to 1851. Children: Alexander Remy, dec'd, died January 1851 leaving widow, Sarah Ann now wife of William Shield of Vinton Co. and only son and heir--Alexander Remy, who died as a minor in July 1853; David Remy; James Remy; Hiram Remy; Ibie Remy; Emily late Remy wife of Elihua Gardner; Harriet late Remy wife of Philip Shrick of Iowa; Julia Ann late Remy wife of Henry Shuster of Morgan Co., Ohio; Lewis Remy of Fulton Co., Illinois; John Remy, dec'd. his children --Letitia, John W., Eleanor and James Remy, all minors of Vinton Co.; Elias Remy, dec'd, his children--Eliza Ann late Remy wife of Andrew Eutzler, Jane late Remy wife of William Soller of Ross Co. Ohio, Isabel Remy of Morgan Co. Ohio, Margaret Remy, Marian Remy, Ealinor Remy and Harriet Remy, all of Vinton Co. (557)

60501854 - John YEAGER vs Harvey YEAGER, et al. In Partition. Filed 12-28-1853. George Yeager, dec'd and Christian Yeager, dec'd in their lifetime were each seized of undivided one half of In-lots 10&11 in town of Hamden. George YEAGER, dec'd, died in April 1850 leaving widow, Mahala Yeager and children--John Yeager, Harvey Yeager, Lavinia F. Yeager and Emarillis Yeager, all of Vinton Co., the last three named being minors. Christian YEAGER, dec'd, died in August 1852 leaving widow, Mary Yeager of Jackson Co., Ohio and children--Mary, Eliza Ann, Sally Ann, Rebecca, Margaret A. and Ladora Yeager, the first four of Vinton Co. and the last two of Jackson Co., Ohio and the last five named being minors. (579)

6-5-1854 - Sarah WINES vs. William WINES. Petition for Divorce. Filed (not given). Married 8-24-1837 in Hocking Co., Ohio; lived together until 9-1-1844. (588)

The following wills were abstracted from "Will Book 1" located in the probate Court of the court house at McArthur. Page on which record may be found is given in parenthesis.

MORRISON, Isaac - dated 4-15-1853; recorded 7-25-1853. Wife, Sarah, SW¼ Section 29, Township 11, Range 17 during her natural life. Sons: John, previously mentioned land after Sarah's death; Calvin of the State of Illinois, already given land; Persey, residence unknown, already given land but also to have in-lot 30 in McArthur and if he does not return in one year after testator's death lot is to be sold and money divided between his children he had by Hannah Morrison, dec'd formerly Hannah Barnes. Daughter, Belinda Arthur, part SW¼ Section 29, Township 11, Range 17. Executor: Lemuel Payne. Signed: Isaac (his mark) Morrison. Witnesses: E. F. Bingham, Theodore Morrison and Geo. Lantz. (1)

COTTON, Luther of Wilkesville - dated 11-17-1852; recorded 7-27-1853. Adopted son, Richard Brooks to have all estate and also to serve as executor. Signed: Luther Cotton. Witnesses: W.P. Rathburn, Wm L. Haley and George W. Thompson. (3)

LISTON, Ebenezer of Wilkesville twp. - dated 4-16-1853; recorded 7-27-1853. Wife, Mary all estate and also to be sole executrix. Signed: Ebenezer Liston. Witnesses: W. P. Rathburn and Wm L. Haley. (5)

BOOTH, David - dated 5-22-1850; recorded 8-9-1853. Wife, Elizabeth. Two sons, David H. Booth and Hiram Booth to have farm and tract of land where testator now lives in Willkesville twp. being 180 acres South part Section 2, Township 8, Range 16 of Ohio Company land. Daughters: Sophia Wells, Lydia Ann Wells and Polly

Lee. Grandson, Charles Purington. Esecutor: Zimry Wells. Signed: David (his mark) Booth. Witnesses: Hiram Wilcox and William Davis. (6)

SAVELY, George - dated 6-24-1853; recorded 8-23-1853. Sons in order of age: John, Henry, Edward, James and Jeptha Savely. Jeptha is to have farm where he now resides being 80 acres E½ NE¼ Section 18, Township 11, Range 17. Executor: son, Jeptha Savely. Signed: George Savely. Witnesses: Robert Aikin and James Hays. (8)

CASSILL, Abraham - dated 5-28-1853; recorded 8-31-1853. Wife, Maria. Two sons: Anthony and Allen Cassill. Daughters: Elizabeth wife of Henry Hofkins, Catherine wife of Hiram Ranney and Sarah Cassill. Grandchildren, Abraham Hoffkins and Sarah Mariah Hoffkins son and daughter of Voss and Polly Hofkins. Owned 240 acres in NE¼ and SE¼ Section 36, Township 9, Range 18 and 100 acres W½ SW¼ Section 6, Township 10, Range 17. Executor: son, Anthony Cassill. Signed Abraham Cassill. Witnesses: George Lantz, John Dodds and James Remy. (9)

LYLE, Mary - dated 1-22-1853; recorded 8-31-1853. Sons: Butler Lyle, Jackson Lyle, James Lyle, Robert Lyle, George Lyle, Harrison Lyle, Foster Lyle, John Lyle and William Lyle. Daughters: Sarah Hook, Mary Ann Garrett; also, daughter, Jane Williams, dec'd, her son--Alexander Williams, not of age. Mentions money due testator from descent to her from estate of Hans Wilson and Jane Wilson his wife. Executors: Cornelius Bamborough and John Kenney. Signed: Mary (her mark) Lyle. Witnesses: John Kenney and Levi Starr. (12)

FREEMAN, Daniel - dated 10-27-1853; recorded 2-1-1854. Wife, Mahala, to have use of 40 acres SE¼ SE¼ Section 27, Township 10, range 19 during natural life. Sons: John W. Freeman and George W. Freeman. Remainder of my heirs: Stephen S. Freeman, Clark C. Freeman, John K. Freeman, Philip Freeman, Sarah Ann Freeman and Eliza Freeman. Executors: wife, Mahala and son, John W. Signed: Daniel (his mark) Freeman. Witnesses: James McGee and Joseph Heskett. (14)

BINGHAM, Ralph of Swan twp. - dated 9-30-1853; recorded 4-13-1854. Wife Lucy. Daughter, Patty Irena. Signed: Ralph Bingham. Witnesses: Andres Shurtz and Benjamin Edwards. (16)

EVANS, David - dated 5-25-1854; recorded 5-31-1854. Wife, Abigail. Children: Solomon Evans, Alexander Evans, Richard Evans, Daniel Evans, David Evans, Elizabeth Allen, Christenia Catlin, Isaac Evans, Charles Evans and Issabella Evans. Four youngest children are minors and two youngest children are twins. Executor: A. W. Bothwell. Signed: David (his mark) Evans. Witnesses: A. W. Bothwell, Henry T. Bray and Amanda M. Myers. (17)

MEANS, James W. of Ironton, Lawrence Co., Ohio - dated 10-10-1853; recorded Lawrence Co., Ohio 5-20-1854; recorded Vinton Co. (not given-August 1854?). Wife, mentioned but not named to have $8000.00 along with household goods and furniture. Sons: John William Means and James Means. Brother, Hugh Means to be guardian of testators two above named sons until they are 21 years. Sister, Elizabeth W. Burgess. Testator owned lots in Ironton, property in Vinton Co. and interest in business of Lawrence Furnace. Executors: John E. Clark and Samuel Richards. Signed: James W. Means. Witnesses: John Campbell and John Kelly. (20)

SALMONS, Levi - dated 4-8-1854; recorded 8-8-1854. Wife, Sarah. Sons: James Salmons, William Salmons and Levi Reed Salmons. Daughters: Mary wife of Benjamin Powers and Elizabeth Messer. Executor, Henry E. Ewing. Signed: Levi (his mark) Salmons. Witnesses: Henry E. Ewing and John Frazee Jr. (22)

JOHNSON, Jacob H. of Elk township - dated 7-5-1854; recorded 8-12-1854. Mentions his deceased wife. Mother, Rebecca Johnson. Brothers: James Johnson to have mill property known as Johnsons Mill being about 2 acres and saw mill; john Johnson; Aaron M. Johnson; Willson D. Johnson. Sisters: Rachel Dunkle, Elizabeth McDougal, Nancy Howe and Rebecca Ann Johnston. Executor: brother, James Johnson. Signed: J. H. Johnson. Wotnesses: E. F. Bingham and John Huhn. Codicil dated 7-7-1854 gives no additional information. Witnesses: Andrew Wolf and James Bothwell. (24)

CASSILL, Henry - dated 8-12-1854; recorded 10-2-1854. Son, William Cassill, all real estate including mill. Daughter, Margaret Cassill. Grandson, John Salts, not of age. If Eleanor Massy shall stay with testator until his death she is to live in his house as long as she wishes. Executors: Jacob Cassill, William Cassill and William Martindill. Signed: Henry (his mark) Cassill. Witnesses: Samuel Darby and John Redfearn. (26)

KARR, John - dated 7-23-1854; recorded 10-7-1854. Wife, Rebecca, one third of farm where now live in Elk twp. being SE¼ NW¼ NE¼ Section 17, Township 11, Range 17, 81 acres. Son, William Karr to have two thirds of above mentioned farm and when he is 24 years of age to pay $50.00 to each of testator's two daughters, Elizabeth Jane and Mary Maria. Executor: John L. Dillon. Signed: John (his mark) Karr. Witnesses: Jeptha (his mark) Savely and William Dillon. (27)

BAKER, Joseph - dated 9-26-1854; recorded 11-15-1854. Daughter, Elizabeth wife of Abraham Byres and her husband said Abraham to have all estate. Mentions other family but that they have no claim on estate. Signed: Joseph Baker. Witnesses: Francis McCraw and Jacob Dixon. Codicil dated 9-26-1854 names executors: Peter Smallwood, James Baker and Josiah Baker. Witnesses: Joseph Brewer, Willis (his mark) Brewer and Joshua Costlow. (28)

BROWN, Samuel H. of Meigs County, Ohio - dated 4-27-1854; recorded Meigs Co., Ohio 10-27-1854 recorded Vinton Co. (not stated). Wife, Mary D. Son, John M. Brown, not of age. Daughter, Mary Lucy Brown. Executors: H. S. Bundy of Jackson County and Melzer Nye Jr. of Meigs County. Signed: Samuel H. Brown. Witnesses: B. P. Hewitt, Hiram Hulbert and Pearly Brown. Codicil dated 9-30-1854 states that if son, John should die before reaching majority brother, Pearly Brown; brother, Lemuel G. Brown, Mary G. Bussard (no relationship if any given); and Harvey Brown minor son of Ephraim C. Brown (no relationship given) are to share in estate. Witnesses; Stephen Titus, Margaretta L. Titus and Pearly G. Brown. (30)

DILLEN, Mary W. - dated 1-20-1855; recorded 4-21-1855. Husband (not named) to have all property she received from her father Samuel Hamilton, dec'd whose will is recorded in Muskingum County, Ohio. Mentions that she is entitled to part of father's home farm in Hopewell twp. to which her father's widow, Mary H,. Hamilton is entitled to dower. Signed: Mary W. Dillen. Witnesses: Elizabeth Smith and Isaiah Smith.(33)

SINCLAIR, William of Elk township - dated 4-30-1855; recorded 5-7-1855. Wife, Jane. Sons: Thomas Sinclair and William Sinclair. Daughters: Elizabeth Cassel, Martha Snook, Katharine Nixon, Sarah Ann Sinclair and Nancy Margaret Sinclair. Grandson, Andrew Sinclair. Executor: son, Thomas Sinclair. Signed: William Sinclair. Witnesses: John Sirely, George Foster and Samuel Dempsey. (34)

McCONNELL, James - dated 6-9-1855; recorded 7-5-1855. Mother (not named) to have $1000.00. Sister, Elizabeth. Brothers: William and John. Executor, Patrick Murdock. Signed: James McConnel. Witnesses: Covington Murdock and Jacob Hill. (36)

BAY, Robert - dated 6-28-1855; recorded 10-8-185. Daughter, Eliza Bay to have farm where testator resides of 358 acres. Daughter, Ann wife of Simon Morgan to have 277 acres already set off to her. 360 acres in Grant County, Indiana to be divided between three children: Harrison Bay, Cynthia Longstreth and Thomas M. Bay. Executor: son, Thomas M. Bay. Signed: Robert Bay. Witnesses: Sam J. Rannell and Thomas Bay. (37)

COLLINS, Levi of Harrison twp. - dated 9-29-1855; recorded 10-16-1855. Wife mentioned but not named to have 40 acres in Section 13, Township 9, Range 19. Five daughters: Elizabeth, dec'd, her children (no named), Catharine; Mary; Manda; and Leticia; the last two are not of age and wife is to serve as guardian of them. Two sons: John and William. Executors: John Collins and John Alder. Signed: Levi (his mark) Collins. Witnesses: John Graves, Eli Graves and William (his mark) Huit. (38)

YEAGER, John of Clinton township - dated 5-31-1853; recorded 3-8-1856. Wife, Mary Eliza. $1.00 to Estate of George Yeager, dec'd. $1.00 to Estate of Christian Yeager, dec'd. $1.00 to Heirs of Sophia Trip, only heirs of her body. Son, John Yeager, one-third of property. To Rachel Catlin, one-third of property. To Mary Crow one-third of property. Wife's wearing apparel after her death to go to her four daughters: Cathrine, Elizabeth, Rachel and Mary who are the wives of John Critsswister, Patric Reed, Rial Catlin and Mathias Crow. Executor: Benjamin Diel. Signed: John (his mark) Yeager. Witnesses: Samuel Tarr and Thos. Scantlen. (40)

GRAHAM, Cathrine - dated 1-11-1856; recirded 3-24-1856. Requests that She be buried in burying ground on David Johnson's farm beside her deceased husband, William Graham according to the rites of the United Brethren Church and that tombstones be placed at her grave and that of her deceased husband. Grand-daughter, Elizabeth Pyle wife of William Pyle. Grand-daughter, Annie Engle. Sister, Mary McMannas. Grand-daughter, Isabel wife of Daniel Evans. Grandsons: Joseph H. Engle and William Engle, not of age. Signed: Cathrine (her mark) Graham. Witnesses: Joseph Grandstaff, Joseph McMannas and Henry McMannas. (42)

DOLAN, Simon of Wilkesville twp. - dated 4-10-1856; recorded 4-28-1856. Aged mother-in-law, Mrs. Alice Dunn. Sister, Ellen O. Lily. Bequeaths to John Karr (no relationship if any given). Executors: John Karr. Signed: Simon Dolan. Witnesses: David Kelly, Patrick Kelly and James Murphy. (44)

VANDERFORD, William - dated 2-21-1856; recorded 6-9-1856. Sons: Eli, William, Joel, Richard, Austin and Alexander. Alexander to have farm where testator resides being 110 acres part NE¼ Section 23, Township 10, Range 19. Grandson, William Vanderford, son of son, Jesse. Daughters: Nancy and Mary. Executors; sons, William and Alexander. Signed: William Vanderford. Witnesses: James McGee and Solomon Nichols. (45)

CATLIN, William - dated 7-31-1856; recorded 9-16-1856. Wife, Catharine also to serve as executrix. Brother, James Catlin. Sister, Jane Fox. Signed: William (his mark) Catlin. Witnesses: I. S. Hawk and Charles Brown. (46)

ATKINSON, Joseph - dated 9-13-1856; record d 10-10-1856. Wife, mentioned but not named , to have farm where reside during her natural life being 88 acres Section 24, Township 11, Range 16, part of NE¼. Sons: Thomas and Samuel. Daughters: Nancy Margaret Axa Ann (note: no commas use, so undertain if four daughters or less). Signed: Joseph Atchison. Witnesses: T. O. Hill and B. J. Atchison. (48)

PUTMAN, David of Marietta, Washington Co., Ohio - dated 6-13-1853; recorded Washington Co., Ohio 4-10-1856; recorded Vinton Co. 11-27-1856. Wife, Betsy to occupy during her natural life two town lots 39 & 40 in Harman with stone dwelling house (except office). Two grandchildren, William and Elizabeth P. Gardner to have lot 32 in Marietta and $1500.00 for their education. Mentions other grandchildren but does not name. Four sons: Charles March Putnam, Douglas Putnam, David Putnam Jr. and George Putnam. Son, Douglas to have part of dwelling house used and called "my land office". Executor: son, Douglas. Signed: David Putman. Witnesses: Henry Fearing and Stephen Newton. (49)

636

LLAWAY, Joseph - dated 11-7-1856; recorded 12-6-1856. Sons: Daniel Allaways
nd Thomas Allaways. Daughters: Malinda Murray and Sarah Allaways. Executor:
on, Daniel Signed: Joseph Allaway. Witnesses: John Cain and William Smallwood.
53)

LAPP, David of Starr twp., Hocking County, Ohio - dated 6-4-1856; recorded
ocking Co., Ohio 6-21-1856; recorded Vinton Co. 3-23-1857. Wife, mentioned
ut not named. Bequeath to (no relationship if any stated): Matilda Johnson;
ichard Ludlow (or Sudsow) 38 acres Section 19, Township 12, Range 16; George
udlow or Sudeow 24 acres Section 24, Township 11, Range 16; Jerome B. Sillibridge
W½ NE¼ Section 24, Township 11, Range 16; Robert Crawford E½ NW¼ NE¼ Section
4, Township 11, Range 16. Also mentions heirs of Joseph Ludlow (or Sudeow) not
erein named. Executors: Zina Ferris and E. B. Weed. Signed: David Clap.
itnesses: T. R. Mill and B. A. Weed. (54)

ALDRON, Philip - dated 10-14-1856; recorded 3-25-1857. Wife, Elizabeth. Leaves
earing apparel to Daniel Boots. Executor: neighbor, James Hearkless. Signed:
hilip Waldron. Witnesses: James Harkless and James R. Anderson. (56)

ISSON, William P. - dated 3-28-1857; recorded 5-6-1857. Mother, Hope Sisson of
ristol County, Mass. to have lot 426 in first addition to Ironton, Lawrence
ounty, Ohio and SE¼ Section 16, Township 3, Range 7 in Wayne Co., Illinois.
xecutor: William M. Boles of Lawrence Co., Ohio. Signed: Wm P. Sisson. Witnesses:
ohn P. Plyley and Henry Payne. (58)

ENNINGS, Enos - dated 3-25-1857; recorded 5-18-1857. Wife, Catherine to have
ll south end of farm where now live. Testator died serving as treasurer of
linton twp. Executor: Thomas G. Vaughters. Signed: Enox Jennings. Witnesses:
. S. Bundy and Caroline Bundy. (60)

ANE, Lemuel - dated 5-8-1857; recorded 10-13-1857. Wife, Orpha. Five sons and
hree daughters: Lorenzo Lane, Austin Lane, Permius Lane, Abraham Vinton Lane,
oyal Hastings Lane, Electa Prate, Clarissa Lane and Louanna Varner. Executors:
on, Royal Hasting Lane and friend, John S. Hawk. Signed: Lemuel Lane. Wit-
esses: Bryr Huggins and Susannah Lane. (62)

cMANNIS, Henry - dated 1-29-1857: recorded 12-30-1857. Wife, Mary to serve as
xecutrix and to have 64 acres where now live during her natural life. Children:
lizabeth wife of Thomas Falkerer, Jacob McMannis, William McMannis, Louisa wife
f Isaac Hass, Joseph McMannis and Samuel McMannis. Signed: Henry McMannis. Wit-
esses: Jacob Binkley and Andrew Shurts. (64)

HOMPSON, Rees of Scioto County, Ohio - dated 5-13-1856; recorded Scioto Co.,
hio 8-4-1856; recorded Vinton Co. (not given). Wife, Lydia. Wife's sister,
aceretia McCray. Infant son, Joseph Rees Thompson. Executors: Joseph L.
hompson of Scioto County and Levi Dungan of Jackson Co., Ohio. Testator owned
ne fourth of Iron Valley Furnace known as firm of Thompson, Lasley & Co. George
urress Jr. to be guardian of minor son. Signed: Rees Thompson. Witnesses:
enderson Harper and Daniel (his mark) Malone. (66)

Contributed by: Mrs. Clyde O. Shilt, R#3, Westbrook Rd., Brookville, Ohio 4509

The following records are found in the Probate Court at the court house at Lebanon,
Ohio. References as to where record may be found are given in parenthesis. Abbreviations used are as follows: p-page; prl-Probate Record 1 (Special Sessions);
ed-Estate Docket (note: gives only reference to box and case number); bx-box number
and case number; wr-Will Record; np-no papers; op-Overseer of Poor. It should
be noted that the Probate Record 1 (Special Sessions and Will Record are the primary
sources giving childrens' ages and essential information.

Oct. 1804 - John COWAN chose Mechailth Reeder as his guardian. (prl-p4; ed0-p2;
    bx1-#6 np)

Oct. 1804 - Abigail COWAN chose John Shaw Jr. as her guardian. (prl-p4; ed0-p3;
    bx1-#7 np)

1-22-1805 - John WICHERHAM chose Joseph Corwin as his guardian. (prl-p6; ed0-p4;
    bx1-#11 np)

May 1805 - Cyrus BONE chose Frances Dice as his guardian. (prl-p7; ed0-p5; bx1-#15)

Sept 1805 - Moses COREY and Mary COREY, children of Jeremiah COREY chose Joseph
    Lamb as their guardian. (prl-p8; ed0-p6; bx9-#18 np)

Sept 1805 - Jeremiah COREY, son of Jeremiah COREY chose Silas Hurin, Esq. as his
    guardian. (prl-p9; ed0-p7; bx9-#19 np)

Sept 1805 - Elnathan COREY, Uriah COREY and James COREY chose Jodrph Lamb as their
    guardian. (prl-p9; ed0-p7; bx1-#20)

Sept 1806 - Samuel COBURN chose Moses Richard Cunningham as his guardian. (prl-p13;
    ed0-p10; bx1-#29 np)

Sept 1808 - Elias LITTLE chose Wm Mason as his guardian. (prl-p14; ed0-p11;
    bx2-#3 np)

9-19-1806 - Sarah HIGGINS AND Archibald HIGGINS heirs of Judiah HIGGINS, dec'd
    with Jeremiah Lawson appointed their guardian. (prl-p14; ed0-p12; bx2-#5
    np)

1-24-1807 - Wm BROWN chose James Brown as his guardian. (prl-p16; ed0-p13;
    bx2-#8 np)

5-19-1807 - James BROWN 17 yrs. and Jane BROWN 14 yrs. chose James Johnson as
    their guardian. (prl-p17; ed0-p14; bx2-#12 np)

May 1807 - Phebe Loller and Joseph Dunham appointed guardian of Elizabeth LOLLER
    aged 11 yrs, Moses LOLLER 8 yrs., Nancy LOLLER 7 yrs., Joseph LOLLER 6 yrs.,
    Elisha LOLLER 4 yrs., Polly LOLLER 2 yrs. and Phebe LOLLER 10 mos. (prl-
    p18; ed0-p15; bx2-#15 np)

9-22-1807 - James Johnson appointed guardian of Margaret JOHNSON aged 9 mos., minor
    child of John JOHNSON. (prl-p19; ed0-p16; bx2-#18 np)

9-23-1807 - Cornelius VOORHIS chose Luke Voorhis as his guardian. (prl-p20; ed0-p17;
    bx2-#19 np)

9-23-1807 - Elizabeth ROSS aged 4 yrs. with John C. Death appointed guardian.
    (prl-p20; ed0-p17; bx2-#20)

9-24-1807 - Martha BROWN, Joseph BROWN, Mary BROWN, Elenor BROWN and William
    BROWN, all minors under 11 yrs., children of Charles BROWN, with Joseph
    Sawyer and James McCashen appointed guardians. (prl-p20; ed0-p17;
    bx2-#21 np)

9-24-1807 - Henry Lee and Zephemiah Lee appointed guardians of William LEE 8 yrs.
    and David LEE 6 yrs. (prl-p20; ed0-p18; bx2-#22 np)

1-23-1808 - John HANNAH aged 17 yrs. and Betsy HANNAH aged 15 yrs., heirs of John
    HANNAH chose James Morrison as their guardian. (prl-p24; ed0-p20; bx3-#5 np)

8-13-1808 - Peter DRAKE 18 yrs., Elizabeth DRAKE 15 yrs., and Jane DRAKE 14 yrs., children of Peter DRAKE chose Edward Drake as their guardian. (prl-p24; ed0-p21; bx3-#7 np)

5-27-1808 - Elizabeth relict of Peter Sellers and Henry King appointed guardians of William SELLERS 10 yrs., Elizabeth SELLERS 8 yrs., Adams SELLERS 5 yrs. 6 mos. and Joseph SELLERS 3 yrs., minors of Peter SELLERS. (prl-p25; ed0-p21; bx3-#8)

5-31-1808 - Clarissa VANHORN 15 yrs. chose Thomas B. Vanborne as her guardian. (prl-p26; ed0-p22; bx3-#11 np)

6-1-1808 - Samuel PERRY 17 yrs. chose John McLean as his guardian, on oath of Miss Gaddis who states she heard the mother of Perry say that she had no objection. (prl-p26; ed0-p23; bx3-#12 np)

10-17-1808 - Rachel BRIGHT 5 yrs. and Goodwin BRIGHT 2 yrs. children and heirs of Goodwin BRIGHT, with William Martindale appointed guardian. (prl-p28; ed0-p24; bx3-#15 np)

2-13-1809 - Rhoda LEE 14 yrs., daughter of William Lee chose William M. Christy as her guardian. (prl-p31; ed0-p26; bx3-#22 np)

2-21-1809 - John DUCKWORTH 19 yrs., son of Robert DUCKWORTH, dec'd, chose Ichabode Corwin his guardian. (prl-p31; ed0-p26; bx3-#23 np)

6-6-1809 - Elizabeth LEE 5 yrs. and Keziah LEE 3 yrs. children of Wm Lee, dec'd with William McCristy appointed guardian. (pr!-p36; ed0-p27; bx3-#26)

6-7-1809 - Jemima VESTAL 14 yrs. chose Elizabeth Vestal and Joseph Leas as her guardians and court appointed same to serve as guardians of Samuel VESTAL 12 YRS., Mary VESTAL 10 yrs., Elizabeth VESTAL 7 yrs., Rachel VESTAL 4 yrs., children and heirs of John VESTAL, dec'd (prl-p36; ed0-p28; bx3-#27 npP

1-7-1809 - Joseph Scofield appointed guardian of Peggy BRADFORD 16 yrs., Robert BRADFORD 14 yrs., John BRADFORD 12 yrs., Polly BRADFORD 10 yrs., James BRADFORD 7 yrs. and William BRADFORD 2 yrs., children and heirs of John BRADFORD. (prl-p36; ed0-p28; bx3-#28 np)

6-16-1809 - Joseph BENHAM 14 yrs., son and heir of Robert BENHAM, dec'd chose Matthias Corwin as his guardian. (prl-p37; ed0-p29; bx3-#29)

6-19-1809 - Jane Adams appointed guardian of John ADAMS 13 yrs,, David ADAMS 11 yrs., Elijah ADAMS 9 yrs., children and heirs of David ADAMS, dec'd. (prl-p37; ed0-p29; bx3-#30 np)

June 1809 - Walter Dickinson and David Randolph appointed guardian of Prudence THURSTON 11 yrs., Charles THURSTON 8 yrs. and Betsy THURSTON 6 yrs., children and heirs of Joseph THURSTON. (prl-p38; ed0-p29; bx3-#31)

Oct. 1809 - George YARGER 15 yrs. son and heir of Albright YARGER, dec'd chose Martin Earhart Sr. as his guardian. (prl-p40; ed0-p30; bx3-#35 np)

11-6-1809 - William M. Wiles and John Shaw appointed guardians of Aikens WILES 12 yrs., Polly WILES 9 yrs., John WILES 7 yrs., Thompson WILES 5 yrs. and Martha WILES 2 yrs. (prl-p41; ed0-p32; bx4-#4 np)

2-16-1810 - James WILES 17 yrs. son of John WILES, dec'd chose William M. Wiles as his guardian. (prl-p45; ed0-p33; bx4-#8 np)

2-17-1810 - Elizabeth TUTTLE 15 yrs., daughter of John TUTTLE, dec'd chose David Morris as her guardian. (prl-p45; ed0-p33; bx4-#9 np).

4-6-1810 - Solomon CHRISTMAN 20 yrs. chose Henry King as his guardian. (prl-p46; ed0-p34; bx-#11 np)

6-15-1810 - Joseph KIRKWOOD 14 yrs. chose Samuel Dick as his guardian. (prl-p47; ed0-p35; bx4-#13 np)

Oct. 1809 - Isaac BRITTON, Steddom BRITTON, Maurice BRITTON, Murdock BRITTON, Richard BRITTON and Levinia BRITTON, children and heirs of Richard BRITTON dec'd with Elisha Taber of Champaign Co., Ohio appointed guardian by that court. Said children entitled to lot 21 in Lebanon Warren Co. (prl-p39; ed0-p30; bx3-#33 np)

6-7-1810 - Elizabeth SEWARD 15 yrs., daughter of Richard SEWARD dec'd chose Peter Teez as her guardian. (prl-p48; ed0-p35; bx4-#15 np)

10-3-1810 - Isabel GILLESPIE 14 yrs. heir of _____(left blank) GILLESPIE chose Thomas Irwin of Butler Co. as her guardian. (prl-p49; ed0-p36; bx4-#18 np)

10-10-1810 - Lemuel NEWMAN 15 yrs. chose Charles West as his guardian. (prl-p50; ed0-p37; bx4-#19 np)

10-16-1810 - John FALTZ 16 yrs. chose Cornelius Voorhis as his guardian. (prl-p50; ed0-p37; bx-4#20 np)

2-15-1811 - Noah BUNNEL 17 yrs. on April next and Daniel BUNNEL 14 yrs. 25 Oct. chose George Harrisbarger as their guardian and court also appointed him guardian of Catharine BUNNEL 12 yrs. Mar. 25 next. (prl-p52; ed0-p38; bx5-#1 np)

2-15-1811 - Samuel BUNNEL 14 yrs. on Oct. 25 last chose Adam Keever as his guardian (prl-p52; ed0-p38; bx5-#2 np)

2-15-1811 - Polly NULL 17 yrs. and Sally NULL 10 yrs. chose Adam Surface their guardian. (prl-p53; ed0-p38; bx5-#3 np)

2-15-1811 - Anna NULL 16 yrs. and Catharine NULL 14 yrs. chose Peter Kesling as their guardian (prl-p53; ed0-p39; bx5-#4 np)

2-15-1811 - George WAY(T) 10 yrs. and Mary WAY(T) 8 yrs. children of Benjamin WAY(T) dec'd, with George Cowgall appointed guardian. (prl-p53; ed0-p39; bx5-#5 np)

2-16-1811 - Elijah PHILLIPS 15 yrs. chose Ichabod Corwin as his guardian. (prl-p54; ed0-p39; bx5-#6 np)

6-10-1811 - Samuel Yeoman appointed guardian of Jonathan MEEKER 6 yrs. and Nancy MEEKER 2 yrs. (prl-56; ed0-p40; bx5-#9 np)

10-24-1811 - Daniel VOORHIS 17 yrs. son of John VOORHIS dec'd chose Francis Dill as his guardian. (prl-p58; ed0-p44; bx5-#19 np)

Oct. 1811 - Isaac Muller and Wm M. Wiles appointed guardian of Catharine MOON daughter of Phineas MOON dec'd. (prl-p58; ed0-44; bx5-p21 np)

Feb. 1812 - John Frederick KERN. Peter Crist provided certificate from register of wills of Frederick Co., Md. showing that said Peter Crist was appointed guardian of John Frederick CARN only heir of Frederick KERN late of Frederick Co. Md, dec'd, Crist having presented to the court that he is now a citizen of Warren Co.--granted. (prl-p58; ed0-p45; bx5-#22; wr3-p7)

2-19-1812 - John Halsey appointed guardian of Jemima WILLIAMS 12 yrs, Elizabeth WILLIAMS 11 yrs., Rachel WILLIAMS 9 yrs., John WILLIAMS 7 yrs. and Mary WILLIAMS 2 yrs., children of Noah WILLIAMS dec'd. (prl-p59; ed0-p45; bx5-#24 np; wr8-p158)

2-19-1812 - Alexander CRAWFORD son of Thomas CRAWFORD dec'd chose Samuel Crawford as his guardian. (prl-p59; ed0-p46; bx5-#25 np)

2-19-1812 - Samuel Crawford appointed guardian of Andrew CRAWFORD 13 yrs., John CRAWFORD 7 yrs., children of Thomas CRAWFORD dec'd. (prl-p60; ed0-p46; bx5-#26 np)

2-20-1812 - Francis CRANE 16 yrs. daughter of George CRAIN late of Daughfin(Dauphin) Co., Pa. chose Thomas Boal as her guardian. (prl-p61; ed0-p47; bx5-#28 np)

6-11-1811 - John BURNS 16 yrs. on 28 Apr. 1811 and Matthew BURNS 14 yrs. chose Peter Peas as their guardian. (prl-p62; ed0-p41; bx5-#12 np)

Apr. 1812 - Samuel Caldwell appointed guardian of Sally McCASHEN 4 yrs. and John McCASHEN 2 yrs., children of John McCASHEN dec'd. (prl-p63; ed0-p47; bx5-#29 np)

Apr. 1812 - Samuel Coldwell appointed guardian of Mary Ann McCASHEN 7 yrs. and Abigail McCASHEN 9 yrs., daughters of John McCASHEN dec'd. (prl-p63; ed0-p47; bx5-#30 np)

Apr. 1812 - James McCASHEN son of John McCASHEN dec'd chose Matthias Corwin as his guardian. (prl-p62; ed0-47; bx5-#29 np)

6-15-1812 - Paul Lewis appointed guardian of Sarah CLEVENGER 3 yrs. next Sept. (prl-p64; ed0-p48; bx6-#1; wr3-p223)

6-19-1812 - Peter Perlee appointed guardian of Debarough STEPHENSON 15 yrs., Caroline STEPHENSON 13 yrs., May STEPHENSON 11 yrs. and Susanna STEPHENSON 9 yrs., daughters of Robert STEPHENSON. (prl-p65; ed0-p49; bx6-#6 np)

6-22-1812 - Mary Simpson appointed guardian of her children, William D. SIMPSON 9 yrs. and Thomas I. SIMPSON 6 yrs. (prl-p65; ed0-p50; bx6-#8 np)

June 1812 - Court ordered notice to be given Wm Patten and Christianna his wife to have guardian appointed of children of Calvin BALL, dec'd. 6-17-1813 - Olinda BALL 13 yrs. chose her mother, Christianna PATTEN as her guardian with Christianna to also serve as guardian of Seneca BALL 14 yrs., a son both children of Calvin BALL. (prl-p65; ed0-p50; bx6-#9 np)

10-26-1812 - Rebecca LIGGET 14 yrs., daughter of Alexander LIGGET dec'd chose Joseph Munts as her guardian. (prl-p66; ed0-p51; bx6-#12 np)

10-27-1812 - Thomas CLEVENGER 15 yrs., son of Zachariah CLEVENGER dec'd chose Samuel Chamberlin as his guardian. (prl-p66; ed0-p52; bx6-#13 np)

10-27-1812 - Joseph Kirby Sr. appointed guardian of Joseph CLEVENGER 12 yrs. son of Zachariah CLEVENGER. (prl-p67; ed0-p52; bx6-#14 np)

Feb. 1813 - James Armstrong appointed guardian of James ARMSTRONG 10 yrs., Mary ARMSTRONG 8 yrs. and Samuel ARMSTRONG 6 yrs., children of Samuel ARMSTRONG of Hamilton Co., Ohio, dec'd. (prl-p69; ed0-p54; bx6-#20)

2-17-1813 - Elizabeth BURNTRIGER, Mary BURNTRIGER, Daniel BURNTRIGER, Andrew BURNTRIGER and Sarah BURNTRIGER children of David BURNTRIGER dec'd are entitled to personal and real estate of their father and that Elizabeth and Mary are between 12 and 18 yrs. and unmarried, that the other three are under 12 yrs. and have no guardian although their father has been dead for several years. Order that Mary and Elizabeth come to court and choose a guardian and notice be served to Thomas FITSGERALD and Elizabeth his wife late BURNTRIGER. (prl-p71; ed0-p55; bx6-#24 np). (note: see court of 8-7-1820 for further data)

2-18-1813 - Albert VOORHIS son of John VOORHIS dec'd chose Matthias Corwin as his guardian. (prl-p72; ed0-p56; bx6-#25 np)

10-21--1813 - Aaron WILES 15 yrs. chose Silas Hurin as his guardian. (prl-p77; ed0-58; bx 7-#3 np)

10-21-1813 - Mary WILES 13 yrs. chose Henry Montfort as her guardian. (prl-p77; ed0-p59; bx7-#4 np)

10-13-1813 - Robert Gill appointed guardian of Edward BRAZILTTON 11 yrs. and William BRAZITTON 7yrs., sons and heirs of William BRAZETTON. (prl-p80; ed0-p63; bx7-#16 np)

10-14-1813 - Thomas CURRY 14 yrs. chose Henry Miller as his guardian. (prl-p81; ed0-p63; bx7-#17 np)

10-14-1813 - Frederick SNYDER 16 yrs. chose Coonrod Snider as his guardian. (prl-p81; ed0-p63; bx7-#18 np)

10-14-1813 - Matthias BAKER 13 yrs. and Moses BAKER 16 yrs. chose Percy Kitchell as their guardian. (prl-p81; edO-p64; bx7-#19 np).

Feb. 1814 - Samuel BRADY chose Samuel Pope as his guardian. (prl-p83; edO-p64; bx7-#21 np)

Feb. 1814 - Luther LAIRD 15 yrs. chose Percy Kitchell as his guardian, (prl-p84; edO-p65; bx7-#22 np)

Jan. 1814 - Jesse PHILLIPS 15 yrs. chose Icabod Corwin as his guardian. (prl-p84; edO-p65; bx7-p23 np)

Feb. 1814 - Thomas LAMBSON 19 yrs. and Hannah LAMBSON 15 yrs. chose Daniel Skinner as their guardian. (prl-p85; edO-p66; bx7-#26 np)

June 1814 - Eli CUSTER (CRISTER) 15 yrs. son of George CRISTER dec'd chose George I. Isham as his guardian. (prl-p94; edO-p94; edO-p73; bx8-#18 np)

6-18-1814 - Joseph HICKS 16 yrs. son of David HICKS chose Samuel Sergeant as his guardian. (prl-p96; edO-p76; bx8-#27 np)

6-14-1814 - Samuel MORTON 16 yrs. son of Thomas MORTON dec'd chose Samuel Sergeant as his guardian. (prl-p97; edO-p77; bx8-#26 np)

6-18-1814 - Abigal Lamson appointed guardian of Amos LAMSON 2 yrs. son and heir of Eleaser LAMSON. (prl-p97; bx8-#29 np)

6-18-1814 - Ann HURIN 17 yrs. and Experience HURIN 15 yrs. children of Otherie HURIN dec'd chose John St John as their guardian. (prl-p105; edO-p86; bx10-#8 np)

6-18-1814 - Hannah HURIN 14 yrs. chose John Tharp as her guardian. (prl-p106; edO-p86; bx10-#9 np)

6-18-1814 - Rebecca HURIN 12 yrs. chose John St John as her guardian. (prl-p106; edO-p86; bx10-#10 np)

6-18-1814 - Bethiel Hurin and Jno. St John appointed guardian of Seth HURIN 11 yrs., Thallia HURIN 8 yrs., Phebe HURIN 6 yrs., Berthia HURIN 4 yrs and Benjamin A. HURIN 2 yrs. (prl-p106; edO-p87; bx10-#11 np)

10-10-1814 - William JAMES 10 yrs. chose Nathan Richardson as his guardian. (pri-p.109; edO-p88; bx11-#3)

10-14-1814 - William JAMES 17 yrs. son of Joseph JAMES chose William Lowry as his guardian. (prl-p111; edO-p91; bx11-#11 np)

10-18-1814 - Peter COSOT chose Noah Cory as his guardian. (prl-p112; edO-p91; bx11-#13 np)

10-18-1814 - Noah Cory appointed guardian of Francis CASSOT 13 yrs., Dumis CASSOT 10 yrs., Bernard CASSOT 7 yrs., Maria CASSOT 3 yrs. and Elizabeth CASSOT 12 mos. (prl-p112; edO-p92; bx11-#14 np)

2-14-1815 - Samuel HICKS 19 yrs. chose Sampson Sergeant as his guardian. (prl-p115; edO-p92; bx11-#16 np)

2-14-1815 - Abraham Lowry appointed guardian of Elizabeth HICKS 11 yrs. (prl-p115; edO-p93; bx11-#17 np)

2-16-1815 - Ezra HICKS 14 yrs. chose Ezra Robinson as his guardian. (prl-p116; edO-p94; bx11-#21 np)

2-20-1815 - Woodruff FLAY (FLAG?) 15 yrs. chose Anna Flay (Flag?) as his guardian. (prl-p117; edO-p95; bx11-#23 np)

2-22-1815 - Samuel BRADY 14 yrs. chose Francis Davis as his guardian. (prl-p117; edO-p95; bx11-#24 np)

2-21-1815 - Eben Shaw FREEMAN 14 yrs. chose Archibald Shaw his guardian. (prl-p117; edO-p95; bx11-#25 np)

6-16-1815 - Nancy WILSON daughter of West WILSON dec'd chose Oliver Crawford as her guardian. (prl-p122; edO-p96; bx11-#27 np)

6-16-1815 - John WILSON 10 yrs. chose James Todd as his guardian. (prl-p122; edO-p96; bx11-#28 np)

6-22-1815 - William MINER 17 yrs., heir of Henry MINER dec'd chose David Sutton as his guardian. (prl-p124; edO-p97; bxll-#31 np)

6-12-1815 - William PARRISH 14 yrs. son of Stephen PARRISH dec'd chose Thomas Anderson as his guardian. (prl-p125; edO-p98; bxl2-#3 np)

6-14-1815 - John Lowry TROUSDALE son of Samuel TRAUSDALE chose John Robeson as his guardian. (prl-p126; edO-p100; bxl2-#8)

6-17-1815 - Samuel JAMES 14 yrs. son of Samuel JAMES dec'd chose Daniel F. Rieder as his guardian. (prl-p127; edO-p101; bxl2-#11 np)

10-14-1815 - Isaac Ward appointed guardian of Rebecca CUSHING 17 yrs., Mary Ward CUSHING 9 yrs., Elizabeth CUSHING 7 yrs. and Rowland Owen CUSHING 5 yrs. (prl-p131; edO-p104; bxl2-#19 np)

10-17-1815 - Hannah Stout appointed guardian of Henry STOUT 8 yrs. and Rachel STOUT 5 yrs. (prl-p131; edO-p104; bxl2-#21 np)

10-18-1815 - Jeptha F. Moore appointed guardian of Westly JAMES 17 yrs., Elizabeth JAMES 5 yrs., Susan JAMES 11 yrs. and Saran JAMES 13 yrs. (prl-p131; edO-p105; bxl2-#22 np)

10-21--1815 - William N. Wiles appointed guardian of James CANIER. (prl-p132; edO-p105; bxl2-#24 np)

10-18-1815 - Daniel Morgan appointed guardian of David MORGAN 14 yrs. and Felix MORGAN 16 yrs. children of Gabriel MORGAN dec'd. (prl-p132; edO-p106; bxl2-#25 np)

10-23-1815 - Daniel Morgan appointed guardian of his brother, John MORGAN 19 yrs. Jacob Morgan appointed guardian of Abraham MORGAN 17 yrs. Ester Morgan appointed guardian of Joseph MORGAN 11 yrs. (prl-p132; edO-p106;bxl2-#26 np)

10-23-1815 - Daniel WINTROAD 16 yrs. chose Peter Wintroad as his guardian. (prl-p133; edO-p107; bxl2-#30 np)

2-13-1816 - Sampson Sargent appointed guardian of Meeker Squire MORTON 15 yrs. (prl-p138; edO-p110; bxl3-#8 np)

2-19-1816 - John Vandike of Butler Co., Ohio appointed guardian of Henry VANDIKE 1 yr. and Jane VANDIKE 14 yrs., children of Henry VANDIKE dec'd. (prl-p138; edO-p111; bxl3-#9 np)

2-21-1816 - Jacob HELMICK 17 yrs. chose Theophilus Simonton as his guardian. (prl-p139; edO-p111; bxl3-#10 np)

2-24-1816 - William FRIEND 17 yrs., son of Joseph FRIEND late of Kentucky, dec'd chose Owen Todd as his guardian. (prl-p139; edO-p111; bxl3-#11 no)

8-21-1816 - Mary McGINNIS chose Joseph Berry as her guardian. (prl-p141; edO-p112; bxl3-#13 npP)

July 1816 - John MITCHELL 17 yrs. chose Wm Gray as his guardian. (prl-p145; edO-p114; bxl3-#19 np)

7-8-1816 - Hiram KIMBLE 16 yrs. chose Francis Bedle as his guardian. (prl-p146; edO-p1141 bxl3-#20 np)

7-8-1816 - John K. WATZ 14 yrs. chose Ashbel Kitchel as his guardian. (prl-p146; edO-p115; bxl3-#21 np)

7-8-1816 - Daniel F. Reeder appointed guardian of David GRIFFIN 13 yrs. (prl-p146; edO-p115; bxl3-#22 np)

1-25-1817 - Hiram BARKER 16 yrs. on 20 July 1816 son of William BARKER dec'd chose John Wallace as his guardian. (prl-p149; edO-p116; bxl3-#25 np)

11-11-1816 - Jonathan Newman appointed guardian of Lucretia CLOUD 8 yrs. (prl-p151; edO-p117; bxl3-#28 np)

11-11-1816- Caleb Crane appointed guardian of Isaac COLLY 6 yrs. and Samuel COLLY
    3 yrs., children of Samuel COLLY dec'd. (prl-p151; ed0-p117; bx13-#29 np)
11-11-1816 - Hiram ROOD 14 yrs. son of John ROOD dec'd chose Peter Pease as his
    guardian. (prl-p151; ed0-p118; bx14-#1)
11-11-1816 - Hannah CLARK 14 yrs. chose Peter Pease as her guardian. (prl-p152;
    ed0-p118; bx14-#3 np)
11-11-1816 - Amos Harris appointed guardian of Catharine EVERHEART 4 yrs. and Lydia
    EVERHEART 1 yr. children and heirs of Samuel EVERHEART. (prl-p152; ed0-
    p119; bx14-#4 np)
11-11-1816 - Rebecca Murphy appointed guardian of James MURPHY 10 yrs., son of
    Edward MURPHY. (prl-p152; ed0-p119; bx14-#5 np)
11-11-1816 - Nancy WARMAN 14 yrs., daughter of Joshua WARMAN dec'd chose David
    Hawk as her guardian. (prl-p152; ed0-p119; bx14-#6 np)
11-11-1816 - David Hawk appointed guardian of Juliet WARMAN 11 yrs., Catharine
    WARMAN 9 yrs. and Sally WARMAN 3 yrs., children of Joshua WARMAN dec'd.
    (prl-p153; ed0-p120; bx14-#7 np)
11-11-1816 - Margaret MARSH 16 yrs., Nancy MARSH 14 yrs. and Mariah MARSH 12 yrs.,
    heirs of William MARSH chose George Folglesong as their guardian. (prl-
    p153; ed0-p120; bx14-#8 np)
11-11-1816 - George Foglesong appointed guardian of Elizabeth MARSH 10 yrs. and
    James Johnson MARSH 8 yrs., children of William MARSH. (prl-p153; ed0-p120;
    bx14-#9 np)
Nov. 1816 - Archibald HILL 18 yrs. son of David HILL chose Eli Huston as his
    guardian. (prl-p154; ed0-p121; bx14-#11 np)
Nov. 1816 - Alexander EDY 18 yrs. son of David EDY chose Eli Huston as his guardian
    (prl-p154; ed0-p121; bx 14-#12 np)
11-23-1816 - Lemuel LINDSAY 14 yrs. son of Oliver LINDSAY chose Eli Huston as his
    guardian. (prl-p154; ed0-p122; bx14-#13 np)
11-23-1816 - Samuel HILL 16rs. and Thomas HILL 14 yrs. minor heirs of David HILL
    chose Eli Huston as their guardian. (prl-p154; ed0-p122; bx14-#14 np)
11-23-1816 - David PEGG 15 yrs. son of Nathan PEGG chose Eli Huston as his guardian.
    (prl-p154; ed0-p122; bx14-#15 np)
11-23-1816 - Jane EDY 14 yrs. daughter of David EDY dec'd chose Stephen Spinning
    as her guardian. (prl-p154; ed0-p123; bx14-#16 np)
11-25-1816 - Jacob Hawn appointed guardian of Sally HAWN 5 yrs. child of Daniel
    HAWN. (prl-p155; ed0-p123; bx14-#17 np)
11-25-1816 - Sarah WATSON 13 yrs. daughter of John WATSON chose Thomas Gibbs as
    her guardian. (prl-p155; ed0-p123; bx14-#18)
4-14-1817 - Isaac BLACKFORD a black boy 19 yrs. chose James Freeman as his guardian.
    (prl-p157; ed0-p124; bx14-#21)
4-16-1817 - Abraham VanMATRE 16 yrs. chose Nathan Kelly as his guardian. (prl-p158;
    ed0-p125; bx14-#22 npP
4-14-1817 - Eli HELMICK 14 yrs., son of Jacob HELMICK dec'd chose Joseph Bennet
    as his guardian. (prl-p158; ed0-p125; bx14-#23 np)
4-16-1817 - Nathan Kelly appointed guardian of Margaret VanMATRE 11 yrs., Lewis D.
    VanMATRE 10 yrs., Thomas I. VanMATRE 8 yrs. and Melissa VanMATRE 6 yrs.,
    children of Morgan VanMATRE. (prl-p158; ed0-p125; bx14-#24 np)
4-16-1817 - William WILLIAMS 18 yrs. chose Margaret Williams as his guardian.
    (prl-p158; ed0-p126; bx14-#25 np)
4-16-1817 - Isaac Death appointed guardian of Sarah MURPHY 16 yrs., daughter of
    Samuel MURPHY. (prl-p158; ed0-p126; bx14-#26 np)

4-19-1817 - Abraham FLAGG 14 yrs. son of Jacob FLAGG dec'd chose Anne Flagg as his guardian. (prl-p158; ed0-p126; bx14-#27 np)

4-19-1817 - John Johnson VanMATRE 14 yrs. son of Morgan VanMATRE dec'd chose Nathan Kelly as his guardian. (prl-p159; ed0-p127; bx14-#28 np)

4-19-1817 - Samuel WEST a black boy 11 yrs. with James Smith appointed his guardian. (prl-1159; ed0-p127; bx14-#29 np)

4-21-1817 - Jesse FLORA 14 yrs. son of John FLORA dec'd chose Sylvanus Cornel as his guardian. (prl-p159; ed0-p128; bx14-#32 np)

4-21-1817 - Samuel Shepley appointed guardian of Mary SNIDER 11 yrs., Elizabeth SNIDER 9 yrs., Esther SNIDER 7 yrs., David SNIDER 5 yrs. and William SNIDER 4 yrs., heirs of Arnold Snider. (prl-p159; ed0-p128; bx14-#33 np)

4-25-1817 - George Kesling appointed guardian of Elizabeth EDWARDS 7 yrs., Joseph EDWARDS 6 yrs., John EDWARDS 4 yrs. and Nancy EDWARDS 2 yrs., children of Josias EDWARDS. (prl-p160; ed0-p129; bx14-#34 np)

4-29-1817 - Margaret Farner (or Farver) appointed guardian of Feorge FARNER (or FARVER) 2 yrs., son of Michael FARNER (or FARVER) dec'd. (prl-p161; ed0-p130; bx14-#37 np)

9-1-1817 - John Reeves appointed guardian of John BRADY 13 yrs. and William BRADY 7 yrs., children of William BRADY dec'd. (prl-p164; ed0-p131; bx14-#40 np)

9-2-1817 - George AINSWORTH 17 yrs., son of Laza AINSWORTH dec'd chose James Death as his guardian. (prl-p165; ed0-p131; bx14-#42 np)

9-2-1817 - Samuel AINSWORTH 14 yrs., heir of Lazarus AINSWORTH dec'd chose Johnson Robb as his guardian. (prl-p165; ed0-p132; bx14-#44)

9-4-1817 - William REED 17 yrs., son of Joseph REED dec'd chose Nicholas Vandervert as his guardian. (prl-p165; ed0-p132; bx14-#45 np)

9-4-1817 - John Patterson appointed guardian of Hugh HERBISON son of James HERBISON, dec'd. (prl-p165; ed0-133; bx14-#46 np)

9-8-1817 - Hariet SKINNER 17yrs. daughter of Cornelius SKINNER dec'd chose Thomas Kephart as her guardian. (prl-p166; ed0-p133; bx14-#47 np)

9-8-1817 - John Patterson appointed guardian of Jane HERBISON 9 yrs., John HERBISON 3 yrs. and Ruth HERBISON 1 yr., children of James Herbison. (prl-p166; ed0-p133; bx14-#48 np)

9-11-1817 - David Jennings appointed guardian of James M. BAILEY 8 yrs., John R. BAILEY 7 yrs. and Thomas Z. BAILEY 5 yrs., sons of Thomas Z. BAILEY dec'd. (prl-p166; ed0-p134; bx15-#1 np)

9-13--1817 - John BRADY 15 Yrs. chose Thomas Covenhoven as his guardian. (prl-p134; ed0-p134; bx15-#2 np)

12-30-1817 - James HEATH 17 yrs. chose George Hansbarger as his guardian. (prl-p170; ed0-p135; bx15-#6 np)

12-30-1817 - Abram VanVleet appointed guardian of SQUIRE a black boy 12 yrs. (prl-p170; ed0-p136; bx15-#7 np)

12-5-1817 - Joab Snook appointed guardian of Johnson SNOOK 10 yrs. with consent of mother. (prl-p171; ed0-p137; bx15-#10 np)

5-2-1817 - William COCHRAN 15 yrs., son of John COCHRAN dec'd chose Abram VanVleet as his guardian. (prl-p171; ed0-137; bx15-#12 np)

Contributed by: Mrs. Clyde O. Shilt, R.R.3, Westbrook Rd., Brookville, Ohio 45309

The following records are found in the Probate Court at the court house at Lebanon, Ohio. Reference as to where record may be found is given in parenthesis. Abbreviations used are as follows: p-page; prl-Probate Record 1 (Special Sessions); ed-Estate Docket (note: gives only reference to box and case number); bx-box number and case number; wr-Will Record; np-no papers; op-Overseer of Poor. It should be noted that the Probate Record 1 (Special Sessions and Will Record are the primary sources giving children's ages and essential information.)

1-1-1818- Ephraim McCLEARY 14 yrs. chose Peter Pease as his guardian. (pra-p170; edO-p136; bx15-#9 np)

1-5-1817(8) - Lewis ROSE son of Stephen ROSE, dec'd, chose William Ferguson as his guardian. (prl-p171; edO-p137; bx15-#11 np)

1-5-1818 - John McLean appointed guardian of Samuel ROADS son of Samuel ROADS. (prl-171; prl-p175; edO-p138; bx15#13; wr3-p126)

3-24-1818 - Betsy CRITZER 14 yrs. daughter of George CRITZER chose Abraham Haney as his guardian. (prl-p175; edO-p139; bx15-#16 np)

3-27-1818 - Thomas CLAYTON 19 yrs. son of Thomas CLAYTON dec'd, chose Sampson Sergent as his guardian. (prl-p176; edO-p140; bx15-#19np)

Mar. 1818 - John ST. JOHN 14 yrs. and Job ST. JOHN 16 yrs. sons of Noah ST. JOHN chose Francis Dunlavy as their guardian. (prl-p176; edO-p140; bx15-#20np)

3-30-1818 - William Snook appointed guardian of Henry STOUT 10 yrs. and Rachel Ann STOUT 7 yrs. children of George STOUT, dec'd. (prl-p177; edO-p140; bx15-#21 np)

3-31-1818 - Andrew ROLSTON 17 yrs. and Margaret ROLSTON 14 yrs. chose Martha Rolston as their guardian and court appointed her to also serve as guardian of Robert ROLSTON 11 yrs., Martha ROLSTON 8 yrs., Mary ROLSTON 7 yrs. and Eleanor ROLSTON 5 yrs., all children of Edward ROLSTON dec'd. (prl-p177; edO-p141; box 15-#22 np)

4-2-1818 - John WILES 16 yrs. child of John WILES dec'd chose John Welton as his guardian. (prl-p177; edO-p141; bx15-#23 np)

4-2-1818 - Samuel Stewart appointed guardian of David STEWART 9 yrs., Warren STEWART 1 yr. and Joseph S. STEWART 5 yrs., children of Samuel STEWART. (prl-p178; edO-p141; bx15-#24 np)

4-6-1818 - James THOMPSON 16 yrs. chose Wyllis Pierson as his guardian. (prl-p178; edO-p142; bx15-#25 np)

4-10-1818 - Watson MOUNTS 17 yrs. son of William MOUNTS, dec'd, chose Nathan Kelley as his guardian. (prl-p178; edO-p143; bx15-#28 np)

4-11-1818 - Albert M. CAYWOOD son of Thomas CAYWOOD chose Jacob D. Lowe as his guardian. (prl-p179; edO-p143; bx15-#29 np)

4-13-1818 - Margaret VOORHISE 15 yrs. daughter of Cornelius VOORHISE, dec'd, chose Daniel Vorhise as her guardian and court appointed him to also serve as guardian of Magdalene VOORHISE 11 yrs. (prl-p179; edO-p143; bx15-#30 np)

4-14-1818 - George Hamsberger appointed as guardian of John LAFFERTY 12 yrs. son of Richard LAFFERTY, dec'd. (prl-p180; edO-p144; bx15-#31 np)

8-11-1818 - Caleb Thompson appointed guardian of Sary MURPHY 17 yrs. daughter of Samuel MURPHY, dec'd. (prl-p182; edO-p144; bx15-#32 np)

8-11-1818 - Bedent Baird appointed guardian of Hiram BAIRD 11 yrs., son of John BAIRD, dec'd. (prl-p182; edO-p144; bx15-#33 np)

Aug. 1818 - Kindall DAVIS 17 yrs. chose Benoni Haskins as his guardian. (prl-p183; edO-p145; bx15-#35 np)

Aug. 1818 - LEWIS, a black boy 16 yrs. chose Thomas Freeman his guardian.
(prl-p185; edO-p146; bxl5-#38 npP

Aug. 1818 - William ELY 18 yrs., Jane ELY 17 yrs., Sally ELY 15 yrs., Mary ELY,
13 yrs., children of Joseph ELY, dec'd, chose Derrich Barkalow as guardian.
(prl-p184; edO-p146; bxl5-#39 np) also guardian of John ELY 9 yrs.

Aug. 1818 - Thomas CUNNINGHAM 14 yrs. son of Francis CUNNINGHAM, dec'd, chose George
Kesling as guardian. (prl-p185; edO-p147; bsl5-#42)

Aug. 1818 - Thompson WILES 14 yrs. son of John WILES, dec'd, chose John Welton as
guardian. (prl-p185; edO-p148; bxl5-#43 np)

Aug. 1818 - William HOPKINS 14 yrs. son of James HOPKINS, dec'd, chose John Hopkins,
Esq. as guardian. (prl-p186; edO-p149; bxl6-#1 np)

Aug. 1818 - Thomas BLACK 17 yrs. son of James BLACK, dec'd, chose Robert Wood as
guardian. (prl-p186; edO-p149; bxl6-#2 np)

8-26-1818 - George FARNER 12 yrs., Peter FARNER 10 yrs., Margaret FARNER 7 yrs.
children of Michael FARNER. Guardian Matthew B. Upton.
(prl-p187; edO-p149 np; bxl6-#6)

Aug. 1818 - Martha McDONALD 16 yrs., Rachel McDONALD 12 yrs., Samuel McDONALD 15 yrs.,
Sarah McDONALD 10 yrs. children of William McDONALD. Guardian William
McDonald, guardian of Sarah, George Keever guardian of others.
(prl-p187; edO-p150; bxl6-#4 & 5 np)

11-17-1818 - Ezra CRANE 17 yrs. son of Amos CRANE, dec'd, chose Hulda Crane and
she was appointed guardian of Phebe 11 yrs. (prl-p189; edO-p151; bxl6-#7)

Nov. 1818 - Hannah HOMAN 16 yrs., Polly HOMAN 14 yrs., Samuel HOMAN 19 yrs. children
of Fredrick HOMAN, dec'd, chose Thomas Venard as guardian. Samuel HOMAN
chose Abraham Merrit. (prl-p190; edO-p152; bxl6-#10 & 11 np)

Nov. 1818 - John FARRIS 17 yrs. son of David FARRIS, dec'd, chose James Farris as
guardian. (prl-p190; edO-p153; bxl6-#14 np)

Nov. 1818 - Daniel BINKLEY 19 yrs. son of Joseph BINKLEY, dec'd, chose Adam Leaver
as guardian. (prl-p191; edO-p154; bxl6-#16 np)

Nov. 1818 - Andrew ROBINSON 16yrs., Jane ROBINSON 15 yrs., James H. ROBINSON 13 yrs.,
Thomas B. ROBINSON 10 yrs., John H. ROBINSON 8 yrs., Milton G. ROBINSON 6 yrs.
children of James H. ROBINSON, dec'd. Guardian, Elizabeth Robinson.
(prl-p191; edO-p154; bxl6-#17 np)

Nov. 1818 - Joseph ROBINSON 19 yrs. son of James H. ROBINSON, dec'd, chose James
Parks, his guardian. (prl-p191; bxl6-#18 np)

Nov. 1818 - William ROLSTON 17 yrs., David ROLSTON 13 yrs., John ROLSTON 11 yrs.,
James ROLSTON 7 yrs., Margaret ROLSTON 6 yrs., children of William ROLSTON,
dec'd, chose Elenor Rolston as guardian. (prl-p192; edO-p155; bxl6#19&20 np)

Oct. 1818 - Jonathan Elmore SIMPSON 9 yrs. son of John SIMPSON, dec'd. Guardian.
John Reeves. (prl-p195; edO-p157; bxl7-#1 np)

3-29-1819 - Mary HAWN 8 yrs., Harriet HAWN 6 yrs., George HAWN 4 yrs., Sally HAWN
2 yrs., Jacob HAWN 4 mon. children of Jacob HAWN, dec'd. Guardian, Lewis
Davis. (prl-p199; edO-159; bxl7-#6)

3-29-1819 - Joel HUTCHINSON 14 yrs. son of (blank), dec'd, chose Jesse Hutchinson
as guardian. (prl-p200; edO-p159; bxl7-#7 np)

3-30-1819 - Prudence HELMICK, Prudence 12 yrs. dau. of Jacob HELMICK, dec'd, chose
John V. Collins as guardian. (prl-p200; edO-p160; bxl7-#8 np)

3-30-1819 - Nathan HELMICK 14 yrs. son of Jacob HELMICK, dec'd, chose John Martin as
guardian. (prl-p200; edo-p160; bxl7-#9 np)

4-1-1819 - David FARQUER 14 yrs. son of Hugh FARQUER, dec'd, chose John Farquer his
guardian. (prl-p200; edO-p161; bxl7-#11 np)

647

4-2-1819 - John HINKLEY 18 yrs., and Ophiah HINKLEY 6 yrs. heirs of John HINKLEY, dec'd. Guardian, Moses Dudley. (prl-p201; edO-p161; bx17-#12 np)

4-3-1819 - David JOHNSON 17 yrs. son of John JOHNSON, dec'd, chose Joseph Quirs, guardian. (prl-p201; edO-p161; bx17-#13 np)

4-6-1819 - Lewis LINDSLY 14 yrs. son of Jonathan LINDSLEY, dec'd, chose Hannah Lindsly, guardian. (prl-p201; edO-p162; bx17-#15 np)

4-9-1819 - Charlotte HIBBS 10 yrs., dau. of Easton HIBBS, dec'd. Guardian, George Kesling at request of mother. (prl-p202; edO-p163; bx17-#19 np)

4-10-1819 - Abraham COON 18 yrs. son of Stephen COON chose Thomas Graham his guardian. (prl-p202; edO-p164; bx18-#1 np)

4-10-1819 - Noah OXLEY 18 yrs. son of Lewis OXLEY, dec'd, chose William Oxley his guardian. (prl-p203; edO-p164; bx18-#2 np.

4-10-1819 - Adam SELLERS 16 yrs., Joseph SELLERS 14 yrs. chose Elizabeth Swift and William Sellers as guardians. (prl-p203; edO-p164; bx18-#3 np)
(note - see bx3-#8-5-27-1808--minors of Peter Sellers--GATEWAY Vol.X No.II page 54)

4-1-1819 - Joseph HOGAN 15 yrs., Jacob HOGAN 14 yrs. chose Enos Williams, Esq. as guardian. (prl-p203; edO-p165; bx18-#4 np)

5-15-1819 - Jeremiah MAY 16 yrs. and Hannah MAY 15 yrs. heirs of Henry MAY, dec'd, chose Agnes May guardian. (prl-p204; edO-p166; bx18-#7 np)

4-15-1819 - Eliza MAY 10 yrs., John MAY 9 yrs., Jane MAY 7 yrs., Margaret MAY 5 yrs., James MAY 3 yrs., heirs of Henry MAY. Guardian, Agnes May.
(prl-p205; edO-p166; bx18-#8 np)

3-1-1819 - Eliza HAWN 7 yrs., Sarah HAWN 9 yrs. daus. of Daniel HAWN. Guardians, Christian Hawn and John G. Mounts. (prl-p205; edO-p166; bx18-#9; wr2-p394; wr3-p232)

7-12-1819 - SARAH ANNE 12 yrs. black girl and dau. of George a black man chose John C. Winans guardian. (prl-p207; edO-p167; bx18-#10 np)

7-12-1819 - Elias STONE 13 yrs. son of Francis STONE, dec'd. Guardian Abiah Miner. (prl-p207; edO-p167; bx18-#11 np)

7-15-1819 - John NEILY 14 yrs. son of John NEILEY, dec'd, chose Benjamin N. Fall his guardian. (prl-p208; edO-p168; bx18-#14 np)

7-15-1819 - Aaron JAMES 15 yrs. heir of Samuel JAMES, dec'd, chose William Lowry his guardian. (prl-p208; edO-p168; bx18-#15 np)

7-15-1819 - William JAMES 16 yrs. heir of Samuel JAMES, dec'd, chose Nathan Richardson as guardian. (prl-p208; edO-___-not listed or box no.)

7-17-1819 - Miriah FLAGG 13 yrs. heir of Jacob FLAY(FLAG), dec'd, chose Peter Parles guardian. (prl-p208; edO-p169; bx18-#16 np)

7-17-1819 - William STEWART 19 yrs. heir of James STEWART, chose Joseph Lamb as guardian. (prl-p209; edO-p169; bx18-#18 np)

7-17-1819 - John STEWART 17 yrs. heir of James STEWART, chose Miciah Reeder as guardian. (prl-p209; edO-p170; bx18-#19)

7-26-1819 - Angelina MIRANDA heir of George MIRANDA, dec'd. Guardian Joab Madison at request of widow. Age 4 yrs. (prl-p210; edO-p170; bx18-#21 np)

7-29-1819 - William CUSHING 16 yrs., Anne CUSHING 13 yrs., Cortland CUSHING 10 yrs., Hannah CUSHING 7 yrs., Clarisa CUSHING 4 yrs. heirs of Daniel CUSHING. Guardian, Thomas B. VanHorne. (prl-p210; edO-p171; bx18-#22 np)

7-16-1819 - Jonathan CUSHING infant and heir of Jonathan CUSHING, dec'd. Guardian, John Reeves. (prl-p211; edO-p171; bx18-#23 no)

10-1-1819 - Narcissa Cloe ANDERSON 11 yrs., Ellenor Clarissa ANDERSON 11 yrs., Gelia
Elizabeth ANDERSON 9 yrs. heirs of Archibald ANDERSON, dec'd. Guardian,
Samuel Serring. (prl-p213; ed0-p172; bx18-#25 np)
10-1819 - Martha HUNT 14 yrs. daughter of Aaron HUNT, dec'd, chose John Hunt for
her guardian. (prl-p214; ed0-p172; bx18-#26 np)
11-1-1819 - James WILLSON, an insane person; court appointed guardian John Bigger,
Thomas Irwin. (prl-p215&216; ed0-p173; bx18-#28)
11-9-1819 - Samuel WELCH 17 yrs. heir of Samuel WELCH, dec'd, chose George Harnsberger as guardian. (prl-p217; ed0-p174; bx19-#5 np)
11-10-1819 - Nancy WILLSON 16 yrs. daughter of West WILSON, dec'd. chose Elijah
Epperson as guardian. (prl-p217; ed0-p175; bx19-#4 np)
11-11-1819 - John DAWSON 14 yrs. heir of Malon DAWSON, dec'd, chose Matthias Corwin
as guardian. (prl-p217; ed0-p175; bx19-#6 np)
11-12-1819 - John JACK 16 yrs. heir of James JACK, chose Robert Lee as guardian.
(prl-p217; ed0-p176; bx19-#7 np)
11-12-1819 - Phebe STEWARD 14 yrs. dau. of John STEWAT, dec'd, chose Nathan Sharp,
as guardian. (prl-p218; ed0-p177; bx19-#8 np)
1-6-1820 - Washington DUDLEY 10 yrs. son of Peter DUDLEY. Guardian, Moses Dudley at
request of mother, Ruby Dudley. (prl-p221; ed0-p178; bx19-#12 np)
3-18-1820 - Sarah GILCHRIST 17 yrs., Jane GILCHRIST 14 yrs. daughters of Robert
GILCHRIST late of Montgomery County, Ohio chose Mary Gilchrist as guardian.
She was also appointed guardian of Miriah GILCHRIST 11 yrs., Robert Willson
GILCHRIST 10 yrs., Margaret Anne GILCHRIST 9 yrs., James Parks GILCHRIST
7 yrs. children of Robert GILCHRIST, dec'd. (prl-p226; ed0-p180;bx19-#19 np)
8-7-1820 - Robert WHITACRE 12 yrs., Nancy WHITACRE 8 yrs., Frances WHITACRE 5 yrs.
John M. WHITACRE 3 yrs., Sarah R. WHITACRE 1 yr., Price WHITACRE 6 yrs.
children of Jonas WHITACRE, dec'd. Guardian, Samuel Nixon.
(prl-p229; ed0-p182; bx20-#1; wr4-p16; wr5-p124)
_____Sarah HILL, John HILL, Jane HILL, Joshua HILL, minors. (ed0-p175; bx19-#5.
Half brother and sister of Levin Constable. (estate-1817-)
8-7-1820 - Susan BURNTRIGGER 7 yrs., Daniel BURNTRIGGER 16 yrs., Sarah BURNTRIGGER
15 yrs. heirs of David BURNTRIGGER, dec'd, chose Elizabeth Fitzgerald as
guardian and court appointed same for Elizabeth BURNTRIGGER 9 yrs.
(prl-p230; ed0-p55-_____) (2-17-1813-repeat)
8-10-1820 - Cephas GASKILL a black boy 5 yrs. Guardian Robert Whitacre.
(prl-p231; ed0-p183; bx20-#5 np)
8-12-1820 - William CRANE 12 yrs. son of Noah CRANE, dec'd. Guardian, Icabod Corwin.
(prl-p231; ed0-p184; bx20-#6 np)
8-19-1820 - Catharine LYTLE daughter of David LYTLE, dec'd, 11 yrs. Guardian,
Alexandria Crawford. (prl-p252; ed0-p185; bx20-#9 np)
8-19-1820 - Emeline DUDLEY 11 yrs. daughter of Daniel DUDLEY, dec'd. Guardian,
Jonathan Hopkins. (prl-p232; ed0-p185; bx20-#10 np)
8-19-1820 - Stephen WEBB. George Hornsberger, guardian. Relinquish rights.
(prl-p233)
8-26-1820 - Daniel SNYDER 16 yrs. son of Henry SNIDER, dec'd, chose Coonrad Snider
as guardian. (prl-p233; ed0-p185; bx20-#11 np)
8-25-1820 - Catharine HARPER, an insane person. Guardians, Patrick Maloy and
Coulson Payne. (prl-p234; ed0-p186; bx20-#13)
10-8-1820 - Maria HEATH 14 yrs. July 14, 1820, heir of Levi HEATH, dec'd, chose
Joseph Heath her guardian. Alcina HEATH 11 yrs. Mar. 1820- guardian,
William Heath. (prl-p237; ed0-p187; bx20-#16 np)

11-16-1820 - Juliann SWARTHOUT 8 yrs. Guardian, James Parks. (prl-p239; ed0-p188; bx20-#20 np)

11-8-1820 - Hannah CONOVER 16 yrs. daughter of Peter CONOVER, dec'd, chose Benjamin J. Dubois as guardian. (prl-p240; ed0-p150; bx21-#1 np)

11-8-1820 - Sophia CONOVER 13 yrs., Elizabeth CONOVER 5 yrs. daughters of Peter CONOVER. Guardian, Daniel Dubois. (prl-p240; ed0-p190; bx21-#2 np)

11-8-1820 - Mary CONOVER 2 yrs. and Peter CONOVER 9 yrs. heirs of Peter CONOVER. Guardian, Benjamin Dubois. (prl-p241; ed0-p190; bx21-#3 np)

11-10-1820 - John WILSON 13 yrs., Hugh WILSON 6 yrs. heirs of William WILSON, dec'd. Guardian, William Hopkins. (prl-p241; ed0-p191; bx21-#4 np)

11-10-1820 - Polly WILSON 15 yrs. daughter of William WILSON, dec'd, chose William Hopkins as guardian. (prl-p241; (not indexed in ed0)

11-15-1820 - Richard HATHAWAY 14 yrs. son of Richard HATHAWAY, dec'd, chose Enos Williams as guardian. (prl-p245; bx21-#6 np)

11-15-1820 - Polly HATHAWAY 8 yrs. dau. of Richard HATHAWAY. Guardian Joseph Dunham. (prl-p245; ed0-p192; bx21-#7 np)

11-15-1820 - Elizabeth HARPER 14 yrs. chose Joseph Dunham as guardian and court appointed Patrick Meloy and Coulson Payne guardian of John HARPER 13 yrs. and Catharine HARPER 7 yrs. (prl-p243; ed0-p192, bx21-#8 & 9 np)

11-17-1820 - Charles KAY 7 yrs., Rebecca KAY 11 yrs., John S. KAY 16 yrs., Mary Ann KAY 14 yrs. heirs of Matthias KAY. Guardian John Satterthwate. (prl-p244; ed0-p193; bx21-#11)

11-17-1820 - Mariah MASON 15 yrs. daughter of James MASON, dec'd, chose John Leonard as guardian. (prl-p244, ed0-p193; bx21-#12 np)

11-18-1820 - William SMITH 13 yrs. heir of Thomas SMITH, dec'd. Guardian, James Frazier. (prl-p246; ed0-p194; bx21#15 np)

11-21-1820 - James WILSON, an insane person. Court appointed Allen Wright, guardian. Request of overseer of poor of Franklin twp. (prl-p249; ed0-p195; bx18-#28) (Note - see 11-1-1819 - James WILLSON, an insane person, court appointed guardiansJohn Bigger, Thomas Irwin. (prl-p215&216; ed0-p173; bx18#28)

3-1-1821 - Charles DAVIS 16 yrs. son of Francis DAVIS, dec'd, chose John Adams as guardian. (prl-p249; ed0-p196; bx21#19 np)

Mar. 1821 - John DAWSON 14 yrs. son of Mahlon DAWSON, dec'd, chose Matthias Corwin, Esq. as guardian. (prl-p251; ed0-p175; bx19-#6) (Note: see 11-11-1819 - John DAWSON 14 yrs. heir of Malon DAWSON, dec'd, chose Matthias Corwin as guardian. (prl-p217; ed0-p175; bx19-#6 np)

8-7-1821 - Jeremiah STIBBINS 16 yrs. and Levi STIBBINS 14 yrs. sons of Elijah STIBBINS chose Amos Kelsey guardian. (prl-p257; ed0-p199; bx22-#3)

8-7-1821 - Peggy HAWK 13 yrs. daughter of David HAWK chose Henry How guardian. (prl-p258; ed0-p201; bx22-#9 np)

8-7-1821 - Hosea SMITH 17 yrs. son of Abner SMITH, dec'd, chose Nathaniel Parshall guardian. (prl-p259; ed0-p202; bx22-#11 np)

8-7-1821 - William POTTER 9 yrs. Guardian, William Sinnard. (prl-p259;ed)-p203; bx22-#15 np)

8-17-1821 - George CHANCE, an insane person. Guardian, Caleb Chance. Request of Turtle Creek twp. OP. (prl-p260; ed0-p204; bx22-#16)

8-22-1821 - Thomas Jefferson HELMIC, a black boy 11 yrs. Guardian, Israel T. Gibson. (prl-p261; ed0-p204; bx22-#17 np)

8-23-1821 - William COLEMAN 8 yrs. son of William COLEMAN. Guardian, Anne Fox. (prl-p261; ed0-p205; bx22-#19 np)

8-23-1821 - Mary McCULLOUGH 6 yrs. Emily McCULLOUGH 4 yrs. Guardian John J. Jack.
  (prl-p261; ed0-p205; bx22-#20 np)
9-5-1821 - Jesse MOUNT 10 mon. heir of Elijah MOUNT, dec'd. Guardian, Elias
  Cowenhooven. (prl-p264; ed0-p206; bx23-#2 np & bx24-#3; ed0-p212)
11-13-1821 - William SIMPSON 18 yrs. son of John SIMPSON, chose Matthias Corwin,
  guardian. (prl-p268; ed0-p208; bx23-#9 np)
11-15-1821 - Theophilus STONE 15 yrs. son of Francis STONE, dec'd, chose Abiah
  Miner as guardian. (prl-p268; ed0-p209; bx23-#11 np)
11-17-1821 - Joseph POTTER 14 yrs. son of Joseph POTTER, dec'd, chose William
  Sinnard, guardian. (prl-p268; ed0-p209; bx#25-#12 np)
11-19-1821 - George KINDER, an insane person. Guardian, John Gallagher at request
  of Turtle Creek twp. OP. (prl-p268; ed0-p210; bx23-#13)
11-21-1821 - Samuel HOPKINS 15 yrs. son of James HOPKINS, dec'd chose William
  HOPKINS as guardian. (prl-p269; ed0-p210; bx23-#15 np)
11-21-1821 - Cynthia HOLLIDAY 17 yrs., Samuel HOLLIDAY 15 yrs. and Anne HOLLIDAY
  12 yrs., children of Samuel HOLLIDAY, dec'd, chose John T. Jack as guardian
  and court appointed guardian of Lititia HOLLIDAY 7 yrs.
  (prl-p269; ed0-p211; bx23-#16 np)
11-22-1821 - Richard HARMAN, an insane person, who has no estate. Guardian, John
  Sinnard at request of Turtle Creek twp. OP. (prl-p269; ed0-p211; bx23-#18)
11-22-1821 - Cornelius VORHEES, an insane person, having no estate. Guardian,
  Wyllis Pierson at request of Turtle Creek twp. OP.(prl-270;ed0-p212;bx24#1np)
11-23-1821 - John MARTINDALE/son of John MARTINDALE, dec'd, chose Allen Wright as
  guardian. (prl-p270; ed0-p212; bx24-#2 np)
3-4-1822 - Joseph ROSS 15 yrs., Robert ROSS 18 yrs. heirs of John ROSS, dec'd,
  chose John Bingham their guardian. (prl-p274; ed0-p213; bx24-#6 np)
3-9-1822 - James P. SCHENCK 14 yrs. son of William C. SCHENCK, dec'd, chose James
  Findley, guardian. (prl-p276; ed0-p215; bx24-#10 np)
3-12-1822 - Sarah HAMILTON 11 yrs., Job HAMILTON 9 yrs., Isaac HAMILTON 7 yrs.,
  Jacob HAMILTON 5 yrs., James HAMILTON 3 yrs. children of James HAMILTON,
  dec'd. Guardian, Elizabeth Hamilton. (prl-p276; ed0-p215; bx24-#12 np)
3-12-1822 - Cephus GUTTERY 19 yrs., William GUTTERY 17 yrs. chose William Guttrey ,
  guardian. (prl-p276; ed0-p216; bx24-#13 np)
6-4-1822 - Hester COMPTON 17 yrs., Rebecca COMPTON 14 yrs. children of Matthew
  COMPTON, dec'd, chose Stephen Compton, guardian.(pr!-p279;ed0-p216;bx24-#15)
6-4-1822 - Elizabeth COMPTON 15 yrs., John COMPTON 13 yrs., and Rachael COMPTON
  6 yrs. heirs of Matthew COMPTON. Guardian, Samuel Campbell.
  (prl-p279;280; ed0-p217; bx24-#16 np)
6-4-1822 - Amos COMPTON 12 yrs., Obediah COMPTON 9 yrs. children of Matthew
  COMPTON, dec'd. Guardian Stephen Compton. (prl-p280; ed0-p217; bx24-#17)
6-7-1822 - Abraham NICHOLSON 16 yrs. son of William NICHOLSON, dec'd, chose John
  Bartlet, guardian. (prl-p280; ed0-p217; bx24-#18 np)
6-12-1822 - John MARTIN 16 yrs., Anne MARTIN 14 yrs. and Samuel MARTIN 11 yrs.
  son of Robert MARTIN, dec'd, chose Jepthah Lightfoot guardian.
  (prl-p281; ed0-p218; bx24-#19 np)
6-14-1822 - William FARRIS 10 yrs. son of Daniel FARIS, dec'd. Guardian, Robert
  L. Jack. (prl-p281; ed0-p218; bx24-#20 np)
6-15-1822 - James BONER 17 yrs. son of John BONER, dec'd, chose William Miner,
  guardian. (prl-p282; ed0-p219; bx24-#22 np)
Oct. 1822 - Zimri STRATTON 15 yrs., Letitia STRATTON 5 yrs. children of Job
  STRATTON, dec'd, chose Jonathan Hains, guardian.(prl-p285;ed0-p221;bx25-#6)

Oct. 1822 - John THOMAS 14 yrs. son of Joseph THOMAS chose Edward Thomas, guardian. (prl-p285; edO-p221; bx25-#7)

Oct. 1822 - NATHAN, a black boy 12 yrs. son of (blank), dec'd. Guardian, William Gray. (prl-p285; edO-p222; bx25-#8 np)

Oct. 1822 - Huston CASIDAY 9 yrs., Logan CASIDAY 6 yrs. sons of James CASIDAY, dec'd. Guardian, William Casiday. (prl-p286; edO-p223; bx25-#10)

Oct. 1822 - Belinda GUTTERY 14 yrs. daughter of Andrew GUTHREY chose Joab Madison as guardian. (prl-p287; edO-p223; bx25-#13 np)

Oct. 1822 - James R. DUGAN 20 yrs. son of James DUGAN, dec'd, chose Nathan Kelly, guardian. (prl-p287; edO-p224; bx25-#14 np)

Oct. 1822 - David STEWART 13 yrs., Warren STEWART 11 yrs., James STEWART 9 yrs. Guardian, Samuel Stuart. (prl-p287; (4-2-18-prl-p178; bxl5-#24) (repeat--date 4-2-1818)

Oct. 1822 - Robert McKNIGHT 17 yrs. son of William McKNIGHT chose Zebulon Beard as guardian. (prl-p287; edO-p225; bx25-#16)

11-30-1822 - Joel KELSY 17 yrs., Daniel KELSY 15 yrs., Elmira KELSY 12 yrs., children of Daniel KELSY chose John Kelsy as guardian, also Levina KELSY 10 yrs., Rebecca KELSY 7 yrs., Israel KELSY Israel 5 yrs. (prl-p289; edO-p226; bx26-#1)

2-12-1823 - Samuel C. FINDLY 14 yrs., Robert P. FINDLY 13 yrs., Rebecca FINDLY 11 yrs., Hannah FINDLY 8 yrs., Levina FINDLY 6 yrs., Hiram Merrick FINDLY 4 yrs., and Mary Thompson FINDLY 2 yrs. children of William P. FINDLEY, dec'd. prl-p290; edO-p226; bx26-#3)

Mar. 1823 - Cornelius BALL 17 yrs. and Cyrus BALL 18 yrs. children of Calvin BALL, dec'd. Guardian Seneca Ball. (prl-p291; edO-p227; bx26-#6 np)

Mar. 1823 - James BAILEY 14 yrs. son of Thomas Israel BAILEY chose Robert Lee, guardian. (prl-p291; edO-p228; bx26-#9 np)

Mar. 1823 - William B. SPENCE son of Isaac SPENCE, dec'd, 17 yrs., chose Samuel B. Walker, guardian. (prl-p291; edO-p229; bx26-#10-np)

Mar. 1823 - Delila McFARLAN 16 mon. daughter of Daniel McFARLAN. Guardian, Elizabeth McFarlan. (prl-p292; edO-p229; bx26-#12 np)

Mar. 1823 - Elizabeth PHILLIPS daughter of Thomas PHILLIPS, dec'd. Guardian, Charles Fye. (prl-p292; edO-p250; bx26-#23 np)

Mar. 1823 - Rebecca McELVINE 17 yrs. daughter of Moses McELVINE, chose John Meloy, guardian. (prl-p292; edO-p230; bx26-#14 np)

Mar. 1823 - Abraham DUNHAM 17 yrs. son of James DUNHAM, dec'd, chose William Ferguson, guardian. (edO-p231; bx26-#26 np)

May 1823 - Mahala WILSON daughter of Sylvester WILSON. Guardian, Rachael Wilson. (prl-p296; edO-p232; bx26#21 np)

5-28-1823 - Mary GILLESPIE 17 yrs. daughter of John GILLESPIE, dec'd, chose Jacob D. Lowe as guardian. (prl-p296; edO-p233; bx27-#2 np)

May 1823 - John CREAMER 14 yrs., Alexander CREAMER 12 yrs., Nancy CREAMER 20 yrs., Eliza CREAMER 9 yrs. children of John CREAMER. Guardian, John Shawhan. (prl-p296; edO-p234; bx27-#4)

May 1823 - Robert BENHAM 15 yrs. son of Absalom BENHAM, dec, chose William N. Wiles as guardian. (prl-p296; edO-p234; bx27-#5 np)

May 1823 - Nancy AULD 14 yrs., John AULD 4 yrs. children of Michael AULD, dec'd. Guardian, Sarah Auld. (prl-p297; edO-p234; bx27-#6 np)

May 1823 - Catharine WOOD 8 yrs., Silas WOOD 6 yrs., Joseph WOOD 4 yrs., Martha Jane WOOD 2 yrs. children of Robert WOOD. Guardian, John Reeves. (prl-p298; edO-p235; bx27-#7)

9-9-1823 - Isaac THOMAS 15 yrs. child of Edward THOMAS. (prl-p300;edO-p237; bx27#15np)

9-11-1823 - Richard MURPHY 15 yrs. son of Edward MURPHY chose John Graft guardian. (prl-p301; edO-p238; bx27-#16 np)

9-13-1823 - Lydia EARNHART 8 yrs. Guardian Daniel Crane.(prl-p301;edO-p238;bx27#17np)

9-16-1823 - Elmira GRIGGS 9 yrs. daughter of Ebenezer GRIGGS. Guardian, Joseph Canby. (prl-p301; edO-p239; bx28#2 np)

9-16-1823 - Edward Young GRIBBS 4 yrs. son of Ebenezer GRIGGS. Guardian, William Gray. (prl-p301; edO-p239; bx28-#3)

9-23-1823 - Mary Ann DEATH 13 yrs., Daniel DEATH 15 yrs., Elizabeth DEATH 11 yrs. Hugh DEATH 7 yrs., Hannah DEATH 4 yrs. children of James DEATH. Guardian, Sarah Death. (prl-p303; edO-p240; bx28-#6 np)

9-23-1825 - Harman SHRADER 15 yrs. son of Harman SHRADER, dec'd, chose Robert Lee, guardian. (prl-p304; edO-p241; bx28-#7 np)

9-23-1823 - William GUTTERY 13 yrs., Aseneth GUTTERY 11 yrs., Demos GUTTERY 9 yrs., Samuel GUTTERY 6 yrs., heirs of Andrew GUTTERY, dec'd. Guardian, William and Sarah Guttery. (prl-p304; edO-p242; bx28-#10 np)

10-30-1823 - Elisha CAST 13 yrs., Alfred CAST 11 yrs,, William Riely CAST 6 yrs. Guardian, John Cast. (prl-p306; edO-p244; bx29-#5 np)

3-29-1824 - Agnes LAFORCE 17 yrs., Archibald LAFORCE 15 yrs., Margaret LAFORCE 12 yrs., William LAFORCE 13 yrs,, Robinson LAFORCE 11 yrs. heirs of Robinson LAFORCE. Guardian, Solomon Shaw. (prl-p309; edO-p247; bx29-#14 np)

4-12-1824 - Chalkly THOMAS 5 yrs., Mary THOMAS 3 yrs. heirs of Jesse THOMAS, dec'd. Guardian, Jesse Willson. (prl-p310; edO-p247; bx29-#15)

4-26-1824 - Joshua WILLSON 15 yrs. son of John WILLSON, dec'd, chose Ichabod Corwin, Guardian. (prl-p310; edO-p248; bx30-#3 np)

4-26-1824 - Benjamin SIBBIT 18 yrs. son of Aaron SIBBIT chose James Perrine, Guardian. (prl-p310; edO-p249; bx30-#4)

5-26-1824 - Joseph CORWIN 2 mon. son of Joseph CORWIN. Guardian, Joseph Corwin, Sr. (prl-p310; edO-p249; bx30-#6)

4-27-1824 - Alfred BUNNEL 18 yrs. son of David BUNNEL, dec'd, chose John Bunnel, Guardian. (prl-p311; edO-p250; bx30-#7 np)

4-27-1824 - David STODDARD 18 yrs. son of George STODDARD, dec'd, chose Garret A. Schenck, Guardian. (prl-p311; edO-p250; bx30-#8 np)

4-27-1824 - Eliza Jane McKY 2 yrs. Guardian, William McKy. (prl-p311; edO-p250; bx30-#9 np)

4-30-1824 - William STEWART, an insane person. Guardian, Ichabod Corwin. prl-p312; edO-p252; bx30-#13)

April 1824 - Harriet N. WILEY 4 yrs. daughter of John WILEY late of Butler Co., dec'd. Guardian, Israel Woodrull. (prl-p312; edO-p252; bx30-#15 np)

5-4-1824 - Sarah Jane CUMMINS 11 mon. daughter of Thomas CUMMINS. Guardian, Jeals(?) Cummins. (prl-p312; edO-p253; bx30-#16 np)

5-5-1824 - Beza BUNNEL 16 yrs. son of David BUNNEL, dec'd, chose George Lowry, Guardian. (prl-p312; edO-p253; bx30-#17 np)

5-5-1824 - Seth CROWELL 19 yrs., Moses CROWELL 15 yrs. sons of Moses CROWELL, dec'd, chose Caleb Bond, Guardian. (prl-p312; edO-p254; bx30-#19 np)

5-11-1824 - Franklin CORWIN 7 yrs., Emeline Amelia CORWIN 2 yrs. children of Matthias CORWIN, dec'd. Guardian, Matthias Corwin. (prl-p313; edO-p254; bx30-#20 np)

5-12-1824 - Sarah HOPKINS 14 yrs. heir of James HOPKINS chose Abraham Haney, Guardian. (prl-p314; edO-p255; bx30-#22 np)

5-17-1824 - David HOPKINS 11 yrs. son of James HOPKINS, dec'd. Guardian, William Hopkins. (prl-p314; edO-p255; bx30-#23 np)

5-5-1824 - William McKNIGHT 13 yrs., Sarah Jane McKNIGHT 8 yrs., Catharine McKNIGHT
7 yrs., Rebecca McKNIGHT 4 yrs., children of William McKNIGHT. Guardian,
Lewis Davis. (prl-p315; ed0-p255; bx30-#24)

5-13-1824 - William THOMAS 17 yrs. son of William THOMAS chose Absolom Fox,
Guardian. prl-p315; ed0-p256; bx30-#25 np)

8-23-1824 - Henry COMPTON 17 yrs., Matilda COMPTON 16 yrs., children of Joseph
COMPTON chose John Steddom, guardian and Samuel COMPTON 17 yrs. and Patty
COMPTON 13 yrs. chose John Cook, Guardian and Phares COMPTON 10 yrs., Ann
COMPTON 8 yrs., Clarissa COMPTON 1 yr. Guardian, Robert Farmon.
prl-p315; ed0-p256; wr3-p51; wr4-p87; bx30-#26)

8-24-1824 - Edward MURPHY 14 yrs. son of Edward MURPHY chose William Ferguson,
Guardian. (prl-p316; ed0-p259; bx31-#6 np)

8-24-1824 - Benjamin BITMORE 16 yrs. son of Sedate BITMORE, dec'd, chose Robert Lee,
Guardian. (prl-p316; ed0-p260; bx31-#8 np)

8-31-1824 - Catherine WILLSON 2 yrs. daughter of George WILLSON, dec'd. Guardian,
Jesse Flora. (prl-p317; ed0-p261; bx31-#12 np)

8-4-1824 - Elizabeth BAKER 13 yrs. daughter of Jacob BAKER, dec'd, chose Abraham
Thomas her guardian and court appointed him guardian of William BAKER 11 yrs.,
Joseph BAKER 10 yrs. (prl-p318; ed0-p262; bx31-#15.)

9-4-1824 - Samuel ARMSTRONG 17 yrs. son of Samuel ARMSTRONG, dec'd, chose James
Armstrong, Guardian. (prl-p318; ed0-p263; bx31-#16 np)

9-6-1824 - John TURK 15 yrs. son of John TURK chose Theophulus Simonton, Guardian.
prl-p318; ed0-p264; bx32-#1 np)

9-8-1824 - Lydia CLOUD 15 yrs. and Mary Earl CLOUD 14 yrs. daughters of Mordecai
CLOUD, dec'd, chose Thomas Evans, Guardian. prl-p319; ed0-p265; bx32-#4 np)

9-9-1824 - Simon SEDAM 10 yrs. Guardian, Thomas Corwin; Ann Eliza SEDAM 9 yrs.
Guardian Lydia SEDAM, children of Simon SEDAM. (prl-p319; ed0-p265;
bx32-#5&6 np)

11-18-1824 - Ephraim BLACKFORD 14 yrs. son of Ephraim BLACKFORD chose Nathaniel
Blackford, Guardian. (prl-p322; ed0-p268; bx32-#15 np)

11-18-1824 - Maria HENDRICKSON 1 yr. daughter of Peter HENDRICKSON her guardian.
(prl-p322; ed0-p269; bx32-#17 np)

11-20-1824 - Nelly SCHENCK 13 yrs., William SCHENCK 11 yrs., Hannah SCHENCK 9 yrs.,
Sarah SCHENCK 3 yrs. chose Andrew Robb as Guardian. Jonathan SCHENCK 6 yrs.
chose Peter Schenck Guardian. All heirs of John SCHENCK, dec'd.
(ed0-p269; bx32#18&19)

5-17-1825 - Soloman McCAIN 14 yrs. son of John McCAIN, dec'd, chose Absalom McCain
his Guardian. (ed0-p273; bx33-#8 np)

5-19-1825 - Mary BRINEY 16 yrs. daughter of Frederick BRINEY, dec'd, chose Mason
Seward, Guardian. (ed0-p274; bx33-#11 np)

5-24-1825 - Mevilla EDDY 18 yrs., Phebe EDDY 16 yrs. daughters of Joseph EDDY, dec'd
chose Phebe Eddy their Guardian.

5-27-1825 - Emily LATHROP 8 yrs. daughter of Martin LATHROP, dec'd. Guardian,
Rebecca Lathrop. (ed0-p275; bx33-#12 np)

5-30-1825 - Thomas HUET 15 yrs. son of John HUET, dec'd, chose Joseph Coles his
Guardian. (ed0-p275; bx33-#13 np)

9-12-1825 - Washington F. ADAMS son of John ADAMS, age 14 yrs. Guardian, William
McLean. (ed0-p280; bx34-#6; wr2-p63)

9-12-1825 - Louisa BLACKFORD 11 yrs. daughter of Ephraim BLACKFORD. Guardian, Jame
R. Blackford. (ed0-p282; bx34-#9 np; wr2-p64)

9-12-1825 - Sarah TRIMBLE, insane. Guardian, Joseph Halsey. (edO-p283; bx34-#11; wr2-p64)

9-12-1825 - Sally C. GREGORY 13 yrs., William S. GREGORY 17 yrs., Emma M. GREGORY 11 yrs. children of Benedict GREGORY. Guardian John N. C. Schenck. (edO-p283; bx34-#12 np; wr2-p64)

9-12-1825 - Daniel BRINEY 14 yrs. son of Frederick BRINEY. Guardian, Mason Leonard. (edO-p285; bx35-#1 np; wr2-p65)

9-12-1825 - Catharine BLACKFORD 16 yrs., Mahlon BLACKFORD 15 yrs. children of John BLACKFORD, Guardian, Susan Blackford. (edO-p286; bx35#3 np; wr2-p66)

9-12-1825 - Drew WALDEN 6 yrs., Martha WALDEN 4 yrs., Margaret WALDEN 2 yrs. Guardian, Mary Drew. (edO-287; bx35-#6; wr2-p67)

12-12-1825 - John TULLIS 15 yrs. son of Joel TULLIS chose David Tullis, Guardian. (edO-p292; bx36-#3 np; wr2-p92)

12-12-1825 - Andrew BAIRD 14 yrs., son of James BAIRD, dec'd, chose Lewis Davis, Guardian. (edO-p292; bx36-4 np; wr2-p92)

12-12-1825 - Mary Ann COWAN 3 mon. daughter of William COWAN, dec'd. Guardian, Thomas Smith. (edO-p293; bx36-#5 np; wr2-p92)

12-12-1825 - Hiram BAIRD 19 yrs., son of John BAIRD. Guardian, John S. Haller. (edO-p294; wr2-p93; bx36-#8 np)

12-12-1825 - James MOON 15 yrs., son of Mary MOON, dec'd, chose James Moon, Guardian. edO-p295; bx36-#9 np; wr2-p94)

12-12-1825 - William H. BATY 6 yrs., Jane BATY 14 yrs. children of Samuel BATY, dec'd. Guardian, Daniel Voorhis. (edO-p295; bx36-#10 np; wr2-p94)

4-10-1826 - Tena HARMAN 13 yrs. daughter of Adam HARMAN chose Philip Fry, Guardian. (edO-p300; bx37-#1 np; wr2-p202)

4-10-1826 - James M. PRICE 17 yrs. son of James PRICE. Guardian, John Gerrard. edO-p300; bx37-#2 np; wr2-p202)

4-10-1826 - John R. BAILEY 15 yrs. son of Thomas J. BAILY. Guardian, Cyrenius Jennings. (edO-p301; bx37-#4 np; wr2-p203)

4-10-1826 - Abner BUNNELL, insane, Joseph Mulford appointed Guardian of estate-1/8 part E½ S21 T4 R3 from estate of Father, Abner BUNNELL and share of mother Ann BUNNELL estate. Order of OP of Turtle Creek twp.(edO-p302;bx37#6;wr2-204)

4-10-1826 - David TICHENOR 12 yrs., Ann Eliza TICHENOR 8 yrs., Thomas Miranda TICHE-NOR 5 yrs. children of Nathaniel TICHENOR. Guardian Abagail Tichenor. (edO-p303; bx37-#7; wr2-p204)

April 1826 - Elizabeth WILKINSON 7 yrs., Rebecca WILKINSON 6 yrs., Aaron H. WILKERSON 4 yrs. children of Mahlon WILKINSON, dec'd. Guardian, Keziah Wilkinson. (edO-p304; bx37-#9 np; wr2-p213)

April 1826 - David H. TULLIS 13 yrs. son of Jonathan TULLIS, dec'd. Guardian, Francis Dunlevy. (edO-p304; bx37-#10 np; wr2-p213--see bx55-#18)

April 1826 - Sarah Jane CUMMINS 2 yrs. daughter of Thomas CUMMINS. Guardian, David Nichols. (edO-p305; bx37-#11 np; wr2-p214)

8-14-1826 - James VAN HORN 17 yrs. son of Robert VAN HORN. Guardian Jesse Coat. (edO-p307; bx38-#2 np; wr2-p263)

8-24-1826 - John VAN EATON 15 yrs. son of John VAN EATON. Guardian, Silas Davis. (edO-p309; bx38-#6 np; wr2-p264)

8-14-1826 - Aaron TAFF 14 yrs. son of Abram TAFF. Guardian. Samuel Gustin. (edO-p310; bx38-#7 np; wr2-p264)

8-14-1826 Maria GUTTERY 16 yrs. Guard. Samuel Bowman.(edO-p310;bx38#8;wr2-p264)

8-14-1826 - Phebe McCOWAN 14 yrs. daughter of John McCOWAN. Guardian, Alva Scofield. (edO-p311; bx38-#10 np; wr2-;p265)

8-14-1826 - Sedate BICKMORE 15 yrs. son of Sedate BICKMORE. Guardian, John Burke.
    ed0-p312; bx38#11 np; wr2-p265)
8-14-1826 - William POTTER 14 yrs. son of Joseph POTTER chose Wyllis Pierson as
    Guardian. (ed0-p312; bx38-#12 np; wr2-p265)
8-14-1826 - John AMMONS 16 yrs., William AMMONS 14 yrs., Sarah AMMONS 12 yrs., David
    AMMONS 8 yrs., Miley AMMONS 10 yrs., Samuel S.W. AMMONS 1 yr. children of
    William AMMONS, dec'd. Guardian, Peter VanDyke and John Monfort.
    (ed0-p313; bx38-#13 np; wr2-p266)
8-14-1826 - Warren ANDERSON 17 yrs. son of James ANDERSON, dec'd, chose David
    Coddington as guardian. (ed0-313; bx38-#14 np; wr2-p266)
8-14-1826 - Letty LINDSLEY 19 yrs. daughter of Jonathan LINDSLEY, dec'd, chose
    Lewis Lindsley as Guardian. (ed0-p314; bx38-#15 np; wr2-p266)
10-30-1826 - Sarah CHADBURN 9 yrs. daughter of Ivory H. CHADBURN, dec'd. Guardian,
    Joseph Marsh. (ed0-p314; bx38-#16 np; wr2-p303)
10-30-1826 - Lewis CHIVINGTON 10 yrs., Sarah CHIVINGTON 6 yrs., John CHIVINGTON
    4 yrs., Isaac CHIVINGTON 1 yr. children of Isaac CHIVINGTON, dec'd. Guardian,
    James Hill. (ed0-p316; bx38-#19 np; wr2-p303)
10-30-1826 - Joseph BRANDENBURG 20 yrs., Sarah BRANDENBURG 18 yrs., Israel BRANDEN-
    BURG 15 yrs. children of Aaron BRANDENBURG. Guardian, Thomas Gibbs.
    (ed0-p318; bx38-#24; wr2-p320)

ABLE, Alexander to Mary LINDLEY · 10-29-1807
ADAMS, John to Polly CUNNINGHAM · 1-21-1810
ADAMS, Mathew C. to Mary PIERCE · 5-11-1806
ALEXANDER, Daniel to Sarah FRY · 4-1-1806
ALLEN, Bethuel to Clarcy GEE · 8-29-1809
ALLEN, Joseph to . . . . KITCHEL · 5-11-1805
ANDERSON, William to Jane KELLY · 2-26-1804
BABCOCK, William to Mary REEDER · 2-16-1808
BACON(?), Joseph to Rebecca MASON · 12-18-1806
BAKER, Jacob to Nancy MOUNTS · 12-7-1809
BAKER, John to Mary BILLER (BELLER) · 7-20-1807
BALDWIN, Jonas to Elizabeth REED · 12-14-1809
BANTY, Edward to Jane DAVISSON · 7-10-1808
BASEY, Lismun to Elizabeth THARP · 7-1-1807
BEDLE, Jacob to Elizabeth BENHAM · 4-23-1805
BEEDLE, Joseph to Sarah Riffle · 6-28-1809
BELL, John to Elizabeth DUNAWAY · 9-22-1807
BENHAM, Robert to Polly PRICE · 7-3-1806
BENHAM, Robert, Jr. to Nancy PRICE · 8-17-1808
BENNET, Janes to Anne CLARK · 1-20-1807
BENSON, Wm. to Mary STEWART · 1-14-1808
BISHOP, David W. to Mary CORY · 8-23-1810
BLACKFORD, John to Elizabeth BUCKLES · 7-24-1804
BLACKFORD, Reuben to Abigail ROLL · 2-14-1809
BLAKE, John to Elizabeth LOVE · 11-15-1804
BLOSE, George to Elizabeth DETEROW · 10-11-1810-
BONTA, Albert to Elizabeth VOORHIS · 1-16-1809
BOTKIN, Richard to Elizabeth HESTER · 12-25-1808
BOWERSOCK, John to Jane ROSS · 1-7-1806
BOWSER, John to Elizabeth MARTIN · 1-12-1809
BOWYER, John to Jane SHIPLER · 1-11-1810
BRADLEY, Patrick to Rachel LEE · 3-29-1810
BRADSTREET, Daniel to Sarah MARCH · 9-13-1803
BRANDERBERRY, Henry to Rhoda GOBLE · 5-25-1809
BRANDSTRETTER, Andrew to Frances WILKINSON 1-19-1808
BRIDGES, Joseph to Rebecca MILLS · 1-1-1805
BRINEY, John to Hannah DEMOSS · 8-28-1804
BROWN, Asa to Sarah SWANGER · 8-4-1808
BROWN, Joseph to Dinah COOKE · 10-24-1809
BRYANT, John to Elizabeth SWANK · 3-31-1807
BUNDLE, William to Christiana NIGH · 12-13-1810
BURK, Samuel to Sarah SMITH · 1-23-1808
BURNS, Thomas P. to Amelia CAIN · 7-30-1807
BUSH, Abraham to Mary CARTER · 3-15-1807
CACHEL, Daniel to Lydia WATSON · 9-26-1805
CAMPBELL, John to Ruth PURKINS · 11-6-1806
CAMPELE, Jonathan to Rach BURNS · 5-30-1805
CARTER, James to Sarah FREEL · 2-23-1804
CASE, Ebenezer to Nancy BALBRIDGE · 12-22-1808
CASE, Joseph to Sarah PHILLIPS · 8-30-1810
CASE, Thomas to Jane SIMONTON · 8-31-1809
CASSLE, John to Patsey CASSEL · 10-19-1808
CHAMSLY, Antoney to Martha THOMAS · 6-17-1810
CHENOWORTH, Joseph to Nancy JAMES · 6-15-1806

```
CLARK, Jonathan to Ruth ELMORE          9-11-1810
CLARK, Stepanes to Phebe HOLE           7-29-1804
CLARK, Thomas to Rachel MARTINDALE      9-10-1807
CLEVENGER, Daniel to Susanna FRY        5-30-1809
CLOUD, Abner to Mary HUSSEY             7-2-1807
CLOUD, Mordecai to Rebecca THORNTON     8-28-1808
COBURN, Francis to Rhoda SHAWHAN        11-2-1808
COCHRON, James to Peggy WATSON          3-18-1806
COCHRON, Robert to Polly SMITH          11-10-1808
COLLETT, Joshua to Elizabeth VAN HORN   10-18-1808
CONAWAY, Moses to Anne MILLS            6-6-1809
CORY, Jeremiah to Theodorin SERRING     3-31-1808
COX, William to Lydia BARALOW           6-4-1808
CRAFT, John to Sarah WARD               12-6-1810
CRAFT, Timothy to Sarah RAY             12-25-1809
CRITCHFIELD, John to Catharine BRANDSTRETTER 3-10-1807
CUMMINS, James to Sarah NUTT            1-11-1810
CUNNINGHAM, Richard to Rahel CUNNINGHAM 1-3-1810
CURL, Thomas to Tolly FAREL             9-25-1806
CURTIS, John to Nancy FLEMING           5-13-1810
DAVIS, George to Rebecca GARRETSON      3-10-1808
DAVIS, John to Elizabeth SERRING        6-4-1805
DAVIS, Jonathan to Anne CHADWICK        12-24-1805
DAVIS, Lewis to Sarah HARMON            8-23-1804
DAVIS, William to Sarah LAMB            4-25-1805
DAVISSON, Isaac to Sarah CARL           10-4-1808
DEATH, James to Sarah DEATH             2-20-1806
DEATH, John C. to Anne AINSWORTH        9-23-1809
DEHAYSE, William to Betsey EVERMAN      9-25-1810
DEMITT, William to Susanna ELLIOTT      11-12-1809
DENNY, George to Sarah HIGGINS          4-13-1810
DICKERSON, Caleb to Elizabeth BOWYER    3-26-1807
DILE, Aron to Anne RAY                  11-15-1809
DILL, Henry H. to Nelly SHAW            5-12-1807
DILLON, Thomas to Betsey WILLIAMS       1-18-1810
DOAN, John to Charlotte ODELL           12-30-1809
DODS, Benjamin to Tatty DRAKE           10-2-1803
DOUGLAS, David to Elizabeth . . .       May 1806
DRAKE, Henry to Hannah STENNING         4-5-1610
DRAKE, John to Sarah STOUT              5-14-1809
DRAPER, William to Rachel SKYLES        9-11-1807
DROULARD, John to Rebecca DRAPER        3-16-1809
DUCKWORTH, George to Sarah CORWIN       7-14-1805
DUNHAM, Edward to Betsy WATSON          3-17-1808
DYNIS, William to Martha BLACKFORD      11-5-1805
EARHART, Peter to Prudence LEVISTON     6-30-1808
EDWARDS, James to Martha MANNING        4-26-1810
ELWELL, Josiah to Hannah JEFFRES        2-5-1809
ENARD, Benjamin to Mary COWAN           5-5-1808
ESTEL, Levi to Hannah GRIMES            6-11-1807
EULLAS, Jacob to Thebe KELSEY           6-17-1804
EVERHART, George to Sarah MARTIN        4-21-1808
FERGUSON, William to Catharine RUE      8-24-1806
FLEMING, John to Jemima HATHAWAY        9-20-1810
```

```
FLETCHER, Henry to Sarah TAYLOR            9-10-1809
FORDYCE, David to Jane M. TORLAND          5-12-1810
FORDYCE, William to Susanna TRIMBLE        6-23-1809
FOSNUTT, Jacob to Caty OZIAS               7-5-1808
FOX, Joseph to Betsey UNGRY                3-21-1809.
FRY, Jonathan to Anne SEWARD               11-10-1808
FUDGE, Adam to Elizabeth WILLIAMS          11-20-1805
FUGE, David to Elizabeth HUNTER            8-9-1804
GARRARD, John to Mary KIRBY                2-20-1806
GARRARD, Moses to Mary Adamson             2-2-1809
GARRISON, John to Rebecca SILLAS           1-23-1810
GARWOOD, Hosia to Masey HESTER             8-7-1806
GILBREATH, Joseph to Mary BUCKHANNON       June 1806
GILLESPIE, James to Mary Johnson           9-20-1803
GILLIM, Thomas to Jane SPRAY               10-15-1807
GLEN, Aaron to Peggy PRICE                 4-10-1806
GOLLEHER, John to Elizabeth NYE            4-16-1809
GOODE, Burwell to Elizabeth SMITH          1-9-1807
GOODPASTURE, James to Mary RUNYAN          9-24-1807
GORDEN, William to Phebe DANE              12-22-1804
GORDIN, John to Ketsey WARD                10-24-1803
HAIL, Thomas to Elizabeth YATES            9-24-1805
HAINS, Joseph to Ruth DOAN                 9-24-1807
HAINS, Joshua to Mary SILVERS              1-17-1807
HALL, Richard to Elenor FOSTER             2-6-1810
HALL, Samuel to Abigal DOWNS               8-4-1807
HARLAN, Jonathan to Hannah MORRISON        9-1-1809
HARRIS, John to Hester HOWE                9-22-1808
HARRIS, John to Jane MILLER                11-13-1809
HARSHMAN, Peter to Christena SELLERS       3-26-1807
HATHAWAY, Abraham to Margaret MALOY        5-8-1806
HATHAWAY, Ebenezer to Enne MALOY           12-25-1810
HATHAWAY, Ephrain to Betsey CLARK          11-1-1807
HAWN, Daniel to Betsey FOX                 10-2-1808
HAWN, Jacob to Peggy HUNTER                12-29-1808
HAWORTH, William to Ruth WRIGHT            10-20-1808
HAYNES, Charles to Hannah McCLOUD          2-12-1810
HAYS, David to Peggy HESTER                6-21-1810
HEATON, Samuel to Magdalane BAKER          8-27-1805
HEATON, Samuel to Enneny EDDY              1-12-1809
HEATON, William to Mary HART               6-14-1810
HELFIELD, Clark to Abigail TREMBLE         11-30-1804
HENDRIX, Wm. to Catharine RYNARD-2 dates 9-20-1809-9-22-09
HESTER, Abraham to Elizabeth MORROW        5-24-1804
HORSBROOK, Daniel to Eunice BATES          8-14-1808
HUDGEL, Thomas to Elizabeth COWGEL         2-3-1807
HUNT, Isaac to Hannah CARPENTER            2-16-1808
HURLEY, Leven to Mary PRICE                4-12-1808
HURLEY, Zadock to Lellis CAMPBEL           12-6-1805
HUSTON, Eli to Mary STEDDOM                2-23-1809
HUTCHINSON, Jonathan to Catharine REED     4-14-1808
HUTCHINSON, Joseph to Ann BIGHAM           3-17-1808
JAMES, Jonathan to Mehetable GASSARD(?)    6-27-1805
JAY, William to Lydia McMILLAN             10-2-1806
```

659

```
JAY, William to Rachel MILLS                    2-26-1809
JOHNSON, James to Mary SAWYER                   1-7-1806
JOHNSON, James to Darcus Clark                  7-27-1809
JOHNSON, John to Polly CRAIN-2 dates  9-10-1805--9-17-05
JOHNSTON, Benjamin to Charity FARRIS.           9-5-1809
JOHNSTON, Guian to Anne TODD                    10-3-1805
JONES, Benjamin to Hannah JULYON                8-30-1803
JONES, Israel to Caty McGRIFF                   12-3-1807
JONES, John to Betsey STEWART                   11-23-1804
JONES, William to Patty MARTINDALE              1-14-1808
JORDEN, James to Sarah SEMMONS                  12-29-1803
KEES, James to Mary BIGGS                       9-4-1809
KEEVER, Adam to Mary HUNTER                     9-20-1804
KEEVER, Martin to Polly STANFORD                8-20-1806
KELLEY, Ezra to Rhoda BLACKFORD                 2-18-1810
KELLY, James to Rebecca LUDLUM                  2-14-1904
KENNADY, Robert to Lydia LAWRENCE               4-12-1810
KESLING, Henry to Elizabeth NULL                10-11-1810
KEVER, George to Abigail BUNNEL                 3-25-1808
KIRBY, Benjamin to Mary EACHUS(?)               10-24-1805
KIRBY, James to Sarah THARIS                    2-8-1810
KIRBY, Joseph to Sarah MULLIN                   3-9-1807
LAFFERTY, Richard to Rebecca HORMELL            11-22-1810
LARRISON, Amos to Hannah SLEASMAN               3-29 -1806
LAW, William to Nancy BLAIR                     3-1-1810
LAYMON, Abraham to Elizabeth GOODPASTURE 2-5-1807
LEE, John to Rebecca WRIGHT                     4-13-1809
LEE, Robert to Mary JACK                        12-17-1806
LEE, Zepheniah to Elizabeth COLE                5-9-1809
LEFAVOUR, Christian to Geals MALOY              3-17-1808
LEFORCE, Robinson to Sally SHAW                 4-3-1806
LEONARD, Caleb to Catherine McINTOSH            8-15-1807
LEWIS, Paul to Hosea CLEVENGER                  3-4-1810
LITTLE, Elias to Rebecca MULFORD                3-8-1810
LITTLE, Joseph to Mary CLARK                    11-17-1805
LITTLE, Levi to Betsey CURRAIN                  12-25-1810
LITTLE, William to Darnis LIGGITT               7-9-1809
LIVINGSTON, William to Elizabeth TAPPAN 1-15-1809
LOUDERBOUGH, John to Rhoda SHANE                2-22-1810
LOWE, Abraham D. to Hetty STEVENSON             3-12-1806
LOWRY, William to Eliza FOX                     8-20-1809
LUCAS, Caleb to Sarah SEWELL                    11-14-1809
LUDLOW, Cooper to Elizabeth REEDER              10-4-1804
LUDLUM, Ephrain to Mary KELLY                   8-14-1809
McBRIDE, William to Debora MILLS                2-2-1807
McCARTY, William to Sarah PHILLIPS              7-17-1806
McCASHEN, James to Jane KENNEDY                 4-20-1809
McCOLLESTER, Michael to Hannah HICKS            11-5-1806
McCOLOUGH, Samuel to Mary LEONARD               9-8-1803
McCRAY, John to Sarah DILL                      3-17-1808
McDONNOLD, James to Barbara EVERMAN             4-21-1806
```

```
McDONNOLD, James to Peggy SERRING          9-28-1806
McDONNOLD, John to Phebe RICHARDSON        9-21-1803
McDONNOLD, John to Sarah STUBBS            7-3-1806
McGRIFF, A. to N. VANSCOYK                 5-31-1810
McLEAN, Nathaniel to Hester NUTT           12-20-1809
McNEELY, George to Sissey KELLY            8-13-1803
MACY, Seth to Mary BAINBRIDGE              10-8-1807
MADDEN, Eli to Hannah HARLAN               3-15-1810
MADDOX, John to Susanna EVERRAN            5-15-1804
MALLOW (MALLON), Peter to Barbary PRICE    8-20-1807
MANSON, John to Elizabeth YOUNG (no date)1807-08?
MARTIN, James to Sarah WALKER              4-18-1809
MARTINDALE, James to Betsey ADINGTON       10-1-1807
MARTINDALE, Martin to Elizabeth PEARSEN    12-27-1810
MATSON, John to Mary ANDERSON              10-18-1808
MERANDA, Thomas to Elizabeth STEWART       9-28-1809
MILES, William to Sarah ELMORE             8-10-1809
MILLER, David to Catharine KEILART         12-17-1805
MILLER, George to Elizabeth TODD           6-26-1807
MILLER, Isaac to Mary STEWART              1-1-1805
MILLER, John to Hannah MELOY               4-15-1810
MILLS, Thomas to . . . CACHEL              3-12-1806
MITCHEL, John to Mary LINE                 12-15-1809
MONGRAM, John to Rebecca KNOWLS            1-19-1809
MOODY, John to Polly BALDWIN               3-13-1806
MOON, Phinehas to Elenor WILES             9-13-1810
MOON, Phinias to Jane MULLIN               3-7-1808
MORFORD, Cornelius to Margaret RAY         5-24-1810
MORGAN, Thomas to Margaret FOSLER          7-28-1810
MORROW, James to Rhoda BOWING              3-18-1804
MOSS, Nathaniel to Nancy HOLE              5-5-1808
MOUNTS, Joseph to Elizabeth LIGGET         10-2-1804
MULLIN, James to Polley CARTER             11-9-1809
MURPHY, Samuel to Betsey MILLER            7-12-1810
NERON, John to Mary Everman                5-22-1808
NEWMAN, Joseph to Rachel ROBB              6-12-1806
NIXON, Samuel to Elizabeth BALDWIN         12-20-1807
NULL, Adam to Kezia REGGS                  7-1-1805
OLIVER, Allen to Nancy BROWN               ----1806
ORSBORN, Absalom to Lucreca JOSLEN         1-30-1810
ORSBORN, Daniel to Elizabeth Hi ghday      8-9-1808
ORSDORN, Morris to Hester BENNET           12-24-1808
PAINTEER, James to Susannah MURPHY         7-28-1803
PAINTER, George to Magdalene BANTA         6-1-1808
PARKES, Jonathan to Fanny FITSGARRET       11-2-1809
PETERSON, Garret to Lenah MONTFORT         12-15-1806
PHILLIPS, John to Polley COLE              3-22-1810
POLK, William to Hannah HOLSON             3-30-1809
PORTER, Nathaniel to Dorcas FALLENASH      2-1-1805
PORTER, Robert to Thalia THARP             6-30-1810
POWERS, Edward to Mary WRIGHT              9-22-1810
PRATT, Elisha to Hester PARNEL             9-22-1808
```

```
PRILL, John to Sarah BEST                          12-31-1809
PUGH, Abel to Rachel LAMBERT                        12-4-1806
PUGH, Job to Nancy SWIFT                            10-25-1808
RAGEN, Wright to Sally CASSLE                       8-11-1808
REED, Allen to Margaret McGRIFF                     1-16-1806
REEDER, Benjamin to Mary McKENNEY                   11-2-1808
REEDER, Daniel F. to Rebecca RICE                   7-24-1806
REEDER, Jonathan to Sarah McKenney MORRIS 6-4-1808
REES, Robert to Sarah LEONARD                       1-1-1810
REESE, Thomas to Sarah HAWORTH                      5-7-1807
REYNARD, John to Sarah HATHAWAY                     9-13-1810
RHONAMAR(?), Jacob to Rachel BEGGS                  3-22-1810
RICHARDSON, Aaron to Polly ERHART                   4-17-1808
RITRMON, Peter to Abigail LEONARD                   7-7-1808
ROBB, Andrew to Ann DEARTH                          9-1-1803
ROBB, John to Elizabeth FOX                         6-15-1805
ROBERTS, Isaac to Sarah PORTER                      1-10-1805
ROBERTS, Phinias to Sarah ADDINGTON                 11-6-1806
ROBINSON, Henson to Polly COBURN                    12-18-1804
RODE, John to Hester LEWIS                          9-3-1807
ROFF, Edward to Ame BRINEY                          4-26-1804
ROLSTON, William to Cloner BUCKHANON                10-23-1804
ROSS, David to Jane LIVINGSTON                      10-10-1809
RUNYAN, Benhan to Rachel JONES                      2-25-1807
RUNYAN, John to Catharine WILLIAMS                  2-25-1808
RUNYON, Benjamin to Mary STEEL                      5-4-1807
RUNYON, Joseph to Elizabeth AURL                    11-10-1806
RUSK, James to Sarah FRENCH                         8-14-1805(?)
RUSSELL, Luther to Sally THORN                      4-1-1810
SALLEE, William to Rachel PRICE                     3-25-1806
SANDERS, Hezekiah to Mary SUFFERINS                 12-24-1807
SARES, Peter to Elsa Hester BUNTON                  12-5-1810
SCOT, Thomas to Mary KIRBEY                         12-15-1809
SEAMAN, Wn. B. to Nancy BALDWIN                     2-8-1810
SEAMON, Henry to Hester SMITH                       9-10-1807
SERRING, Ezekiel to Patience BURROWS               10-26-1810
SEWART, Alexander to Rebecca CLARK                  10-15-1807
SHAUL, Mathew to Mary BOTKIN                        3-7-1808
SHAW, James to Polly COWAN                          3-4-1803
SHAW, John to Jane COWEN                            8-14-1804
SHAW, Patrick to Hester SEWELL                      3-22-1804
SHAWHEN, David to Elizabeth MOUNTS                  12-18-1806
SHERMIN, Thomas to Rachel SMITH                     7-26-1810
SHINN, George to Anne BERRY                         6-12-1808
SINARD, William to Mary CHATBOURN                   12-21-1809
SLEASMAN, Christopher to Sarah FIELDS               12-12-1807
SMALLY, Benjamin to Mary LIGGET                     7-28-1807
SMITH, David to Mary THOMAS                         12-15-1809
SMITH, Jonathan to Nancy LUDLUM                     7-19-1809
SMITH, William to Polly WILLIAMS                    8-6-1809
SNELL, John to Mary SHIVELY                         2-26-1807
SNOOK, John M. to Julian KIBBY                      1-19-1809
SNOOK, William to Abia FIELDS                       4-8-1803
SNUFF, Abram to Polly BRANCH                        12-20-1809
```

```
SPENCER, John to Margaret HEATON            3-17-1808
SPRAY, James to Phebe ROBERTS               4-19-1810
STEWART, Samuel to Rhoda MILLS              4-19-1808
STEWART, William S. to Rachel ROLL          5-5-1810
ST. JOHN, James to Elizabeth . . .          9-25-1809
ST. JOHN, John to Rhoda WOODS               1-31-1805
STONER, John to Polly FRONIE                2-10-1807
STORMS, Daniel to Mary WARD                 12-3-1806
STUDABAKER, Abraham to Mary TOWNSEND        3-24-1806
SUTTON, Cornelius to Judith BABCOCK         12-9-1806
SUTTON, David, Jr. to Charlotte SMOOK       4-1-1807
SWANGER, Isaac to Elizabeth DOUGHERTY       9-11-1806
SWIFT, Malahi to Elizabeth SELLERS          2-23-1809
SWIFT, Thomas to Valinda PUGH               7-7-1808
TABOR, Elisha to Elenor BRITTON             5-1-1806
TAFF, Abraham to Jane GUSTIN                11-1-1810
TAFTEN, Thomas to Sarah DIKE                1-20-1810
THOMAS, Edward to Pernelia WRIGHT           7-2-1805
THOMAS, Samuel to Mary ST. JOHN Issued      6-8-1808
THOMPSON, Charles to Rachel VANDAN          9-29-1810
THOMPSON, George to Sarah WOOLF             4-3-1807
THOMPSON, William to Peggy LEONARD          5-21-1806
TICER, Austen to Susanna WRIGHT             11-30-1809
TICHANOR, Aaron to Rachel SMITH             6-29-1809
TICHANOR, Jonathan to Sarah TAYLOR          2-20-1810
TODD, James to Jane NEELY                   9-31-1805
TOMSET, Samuel to Sarah CLARK               6-14-1809
TOWNSEND, John to Mary EASTERLAND           7-23-1807
TOWNSEND, Joseph to Barbara STUDEBAKER      5-29-1806
TRIMBLE, Daniel to Rachel SMITH             7-12-1804
TULLIS, Ezra to Mary BLUE                   2-13-1806
TULLIS, Stephen to Dorothy BARBER           8-23-1804
TURELL, John to Sarah BLACKFORD             4-3-1806
VANBRIKE, Barnard to Rebecca HALL           4-6-1807
VANDINE, Mathew to Sarah NICKLES            2-21-1805
VANNILL, John to Elizabeth NUTT             2-19-1804
VANOTE, Ezekiel to Sally ROBBINS            12-3-1808
VANOY, John to Eloner LEE                   11-22-1807
VANSCHOYCH, John to Nancy GOLDEN            5-3-1810
VARNER, Joseph to Sarah DOUTHET            7-18-1810
VENARD, Francis to Rachel HUDGEL           8-15-1805
WAGGONER, Michael to Sally ARMSTRONG       5-14-1809
WALDROP, Isaac to Kitty CAMPBLE            1-30-1806
WALKER, John to Elizabeth VANSELL          12-27-1810
WARD, Joseph to Rach STITES                4-13-1805
WARD, Joseph to Lucinda MACY               12-22-1808
WARMAN, Stephen to Harriet KITCHEL         6-20-1809
WATKINS, Robert to Elizabeth ELLIOTT       8-31-1809
WATS, Samuel to Elizabeth McINTOSH         8-30-1804
WESTERFIELD, James to Mary DOWING          12-5-1806
WHISLER, Edward to Joanna KNIGHT           1-7-1805
WHITACRE, Jonas to Sarah BALDWIN           8-26-1806
WHITACRE, Oliver to Elizabeth KIBBY        9-16-1807
```

663

```
WHITSON, Jorden to Mary STRAY                  2-28-1805
WHITE, Jacob to Polly FRENCH                   1-15-1805
WICOFF, Garret D. to Thebe COX                 12-17-1810
WILES, William R. to Nancy ARMS                8-22-1809
WILLIAMS, Soloman to Elizabeth HAYS            9-20-1808
WILLIAMSON, George to Jane MORRESON            9-6-1810
WILLIS, Joseph to Mary Ann POTTS               3-25-1806
WILLS, Charles to Mary THATCHER                7-25-1810
WILSON, Alexander to Rozetta FIELD             1-19-1808
WILSON, Cylvester to Rachel ROSS               5-10-1808
WILSON, Isaac to Ruth JONES                    10-1-1807
WILSON, John to Jane DILL                      12-30-1804
WILSON, John to Charity BOWMAN                 6-4-1810
WINGET, Daniel to Ruth BLACKBURN               1-15-1807
WINTEROW, Adam to Polly CLAYTON                2-18-1808
WOLF, John to Elizabeth WELCH                  1-5-1809
WORLEY, Mahon to Peggy Montfort                10-8-1804
WRIGHT, Thomas to Elizabeth REESE              2-17-1809
YOUNG, David to Sarah Pearson                  3-4-1805
```

WARREN COUNTY, OHIO - MARRIAGES 1810-1812

The following marriages were taken from Marriage Record 1
(1803-1852) located in the Probate Court.

```
ALLINGER, Joseph to Sarah Compton              12-14-1811
AYER (OYER), Francis to Mary Surface           4-5-1812
BACTRSLER(?), Thomas to Mariah Cambell         5-11-1812
BADLEY, Daniel(?) to Easter Black              4-9-1812
BALDWIN, Jonathan to Harriet Blanset           1-8-1811
BALDWIN, Sam'l to Elizabeth Varner             3-22-1812
BALL, Luther to Elizabeth Fry                  1-4-1811
BANNON, Michael to Nancy Clark                 12-31-1812
BARTA (BANTA?), John to Hannah Newport         11-12-1812
BEDLE, Solomon to Mary Tingle                  8-16-1811
BENSON, Henry to Elizabeth Walker              2-14-1811
BERRY, Samuel to Mary Dunlap                   5-8-1811
BOLIN, Enoch to Sarah Morris                   12-24-1811
BONE, David to Prudence Jeffirs                2-20-1812
BONE, Thomas to Elizabeth Murphy               6-2-1812
BANTA, Albert to Nancy Johns                   5-26-1811
BOWEN, Henry to Jemima Yeaman                  11-19-1812
BROGAN, John to Margaret Dunlap                6-11-1812
BURNS, Adam to Rhoda Lee                    (No date-1812?)
CARTER, James to Elizabeth Curtis              6-27-1811
CARPENTER, George to Susannah Currard          12-26-1811
CASON, Thomas to Mary Pearson                  11-21-1811
CLARK, Jacob to Pacience Wright                2-27-1812
CLARK, John to Mary Powell                     1-1-1811
CLARK, Thomas to Elizabeth Bone                4-11-1811
CLAY, Squire to Fanny Brandbury                12-26-1811
CLEMANS, John to Catharine Dutterow            4-30-1812
```

CLEVENGER, Zechariah to Nancy Boyd	5-28-1812
COBAUM, Samuel to Roda Carroll	12-31-1812
CORWIN, Benjamin to Rebecca Howell	5-14-1811
CORWIN, Moses B. to Margaret Fox	6-5-1811
CORY, Moses to Elizabeth Manning	6-30-1811
COVENHOVEN, Isaac to Elizabeth Deardoff	9-29-1812
COVERT, Robert B. to Patsey Kimble	1-13-1811
COX, David to Esther Lytle	10-22-1811
CRAWFORD, Oliver to Peggy Nealy	5-9-1811
CREAMER, David to Ann Carvall	7-30-1811
CREAMER, Jacob to Mary Crassen	12-31-1812
CROCKET, Andrew to Sarah Mullin	12-19-1812
CUMMINS, Robert to Polly Oharo	8-22-1811
CUMMINS, William to Mary McCarty	5-2-1811
CURTIS, Joseph to Hannah Horner	3-26-1811
DELORAR(?), Alse to Mary Thompson	3-17-1812
DIE, Andrew to Catharine Riffle	11-17-1812
DILL, William to Olitta Nevius	10-23-1811
DILLON, Jesse to Hannah Pugh	1-9-1811
DOOFMAN, John to Barbara Creamer	10-8-1812
DYKE, George to Racheal Tullis	7-16-1812
EAKAN, James to Anna Fox	7-7-1812
ELDER, William to Elizabeth Morris	10-27-1812
ELTZROTH, Valentine to Patience Mount	10-29-1812
EVANS, Wm. to Rebecca Herly	1-1-1812
EVEMAN, Philip to Ann Kelly	8-8-1811
FALKNER, David to Mary Galaspy	(no date-1811?)
FAULKNER, Thomas to Polley McGuire	1-31-1811
FAULKNOR, Thomas to Elizabeth McGuire	7-10-1812
FELLOWS, Jacob to Elizabeth Kesler	10-17-1812
FITSGERAEL, Thomas to Elizabeth Burntriger	2-6-1812
FORD, Elijah to Jarusha Kibby	8-8-1811
FOX, Absalam to Jane McFarland	2-23-1812
FYE, Nicholas to Peggy Ozias	11-28-1811
GALEENER, Peter to Christianna Shepherd	12-20-1811
GASSAWAY, Henry to Polly Teabott	3-7-1811
GILLAS, Reubin to Permillia Blancett	4-19-1812
GLASFORD, William to Nancy Bell	6-27-1811
GODWIN, Nathan to Elizabeth Wirt	6-1-1812
GOLDON, Thomas to Elizabeth Linch	3-5-1811
GRAY, Amos to Sophia Christman	3-14-1811
GREEN, Randolph to Priscilla Death	2-24-1811
HALL, Thomas to Sacale Ann Wilcoff	9-10-1811
HART, Sam'l to Jane Bigham	12-10-1811
HASHMAN (KASHMAN?), Elijah to Nancy Alexander	8-15-1812
HATHAWAY, Abraham to Pricilla Dollarson	6-1-1812
HATHAWAY, Sam'l to Mary Morris	2-4-1812
HAYS, David to Mary Kelsey	3-14-1811
HAYS, John to Betsey Kelsey	9-6-1810
HIGHWAY, Samuel to Mary Quinnians	1-23-1811
HILL, John to Catherine Burton	6-14-1812
HOBSON, William to Welthy Dill	10-31-1811
HOLMES, Thomas to Mary Vosnight	8-4-1812

HOPKINS, John to Susannah Branstrator	7-20-1812	
HORMAL, John to Phebe Hathaway	2-13-1812	
HUFMAN, Stephen to Catharine Leaf	7-1-1812	
HULING, William to Elizabeth Burder	7-5-1811	
JEDKINS, Joel to Rebekah Drake	12-5-1812	
JEFFERS, George to Sinthy McGuire	10-10-1811	
JOHNSTON, Charles F. to Elizabeth Trimble	12-12-1811	
KEENAN, Joseph to Anna Spencer	2-13-1812	
KELL (HELL), Samuel to Peggy Haney (Harvey)	10-10-1811	
KELSEY, Jessey to Hetty Marek	12-12-1812	
KISLING, Peter to Laury Griffy	12-3-1812	
LAWSON (LAMSON?), Eleaser to Abigail Eddy	2-10-1811	
LEONARD, James to Jane Beggs	2-13-1812	
LITTLE, Levi to Betsey Surrain	12-25-1810	
McCAIN, John to Elizabeth Goldwin	(no date-1811?)	
McCARDY, James to Mary Gibson	8-22-1812	
McCHORD, John to Jane Sawyer	8-13-1812	
McDONNAL, John to Nancy Day	8-10-1812	
McKINSEY, Samuel to Rebeca Spray	10-29-1812	
MARGRAW, John to Polly Kennedy	6-13-1811	
MATHER, Ebenezer to Elizabeth Reed	8-3-1811	
MERPHY, Nathaniel to Elizabeth Jones	11-21-1811	
MERRIT, Joseph to Nancy Carter	8-30-1811	
MIERS, Bolsom to Mary Receses	8-3-1811	
MILLARD, Timothy to Elizabeth Heaton	8-22-1812	
MOORE, Lewis to Nancy McCashion	12-28-1812	
MORRIS, Isaac to Polley Bran	1-1-1811	
MORRIS, Isah to Rachel Carpenter	5-10-1812	
MORRISON, Arthur to Lucy Emily	10-13-1812	
MUNGER, Harvy to Catherine Grey	2-16-1812	
MURPHEY, John to Margaret Marshall	7-19-1811	
NEWCUM, Samuel to Susannah Price	9-30-1812	
OSBOURN, James to Elizabeth Tuttle	11-4-1812	
OSTIN, Joel to Hannah Williams	12-17-1812	
PAINTER, John to Rachel Banta	6-30-1811	
PATTEN, William to Christian Ball	4-20-1811	
PELEFISCH(?), Christian to Frances Baldwin	4-2-1812	
PETERSON, William to Sarah Caine	12-18-1812	
PETRO, Michael to Ivy Sutton	7-4-1811	
PUGH, Azariah to Susannah Coppock	3-3-1811	
RAGAN, Wilks to Buy Gant	8-6-1812	
RAGEM, Elijah to Sarah Wiees	6-27-1812	
REEVES, John to Nancy Thompson	8-24-1812	
RICHARDSON, Elijah to Dilly Bishop	7-23-1811	
ROBERTSON, David to Sophia Painter	4-16-1811	
ROHR, Christian to Polly Howard	6-17-1812	
ROSS, John to Saly Barne	3-22-1811	
ROSS, Joseph to Sara Kelly	8-26-1812	
ROSS, Phineas to Mary Hunt	12-20-1812	
ROSS, Thomas to Elizabeth Boraugh	6-30-1812	
ROSS, Thomas A. to Harriet Van Horn	7-16-1811	
RUNION, Absalam to Sarah Hart	3-5-1812	
RYNEARSON, Minney to Sarah Carel	3-7-1811	

666

```
SHEPHERD, Jonathan to Ann Rinearson          8-1-1811
SINERD, BENJ. to Abigail Hster              (no date-1812?)
STEVENSON, Thomas to Detsey Newport          2-21-1811
STITES, Benjamine to Mary Drake             11-5-1811
ST JOHN, Seth to Sarah Halleday              4-6-1811
STOUT, Raliph P. to Sarah Shaw              12-1-1812
SUELL, Thomas to Elizabeth Stark             9-8-1811
SUMMERS, John to Beannah Conley              7-3-1812
SWANGER, Jacob to Mary Marshall              4-2-1812
TAYLOR, John to Margaret Robb                1-31-1811
TEST, Banj'm to Mary West                    7-16-1812
THOMAS, Joseph to Elizabeth Silvers         12-28-1812
THOMPSON, Thomas to Peggy Goodpasture        1-8-1811
TINSLEY, Joseph to Sarah Bowyer              7-25-1811
TUFF, James to Sarah Snow                    6-6-1811
ULERY, John to Jane Drake                    4-23-1812
VANDERVEST, Jonas to Elizabeth Reed          9-5-1811
VOORHIS, James to Martha Maloy              12-4-1812
WATKINS, John to Rachael Hunt                3-14-1811
WESTERFIELD, John M. to Nancy Downing       12-28-1812
WEYRE, John to Polly Phillips                1-17-1811
WICKOFF, Garret P. to Phebe Cox              3-10-1811
WILKER(?), Samuel to Hannah West             8-1-1812
WILLIAM, Fegary to Ann Anderson              7-18-1811
WILLIAMS, Andrew to Jemima Roba              7-13-1812
WILLIAS, William to Nancy Flora              6-13-1811
WILSON, John to Elizabeth Stanford           9-5-1811
WOODINGTON, John to Martha Bloomer           3-12-1812
WRIGHT, Allen to Sarah Chadbourn             1-17-1811
WRIGHT, Thomas to Elizabeth Harramon         1-18-1812
ZEGLER, Peter to Anna Harshman               3-22-1812
```

Abstracts of wills for 1805 were previously published in the September 1967 issue of GATEWAY TO THE WEST. The following records are from Will Book 1, pages on which record may be found are given in parenthesis.

MINNIR, Levin late of Gilford Co., North Carolina, now of Warren Co. - dated 12-6-1805; recorded 1-21-1806. Wife, Mary. Three sons; Benston, Noah and Levin, the last two not of age. Mentions seven daughters who were not of age, does not name. Mentions; Blacksmith tools. Executors: Wife, Mary and Joshua Holland. Signed: Levin Minnir. Witnesses: John Shaw and Enos Williams. (16)

STEEL, Hugh of Duck Creek - dated 10-29-1805; recorded 6-28-1806. Heir: James Long, Esq.; also to serve as executor. Signed: Hugh Steel. Witnesses: John Bigger Sr. and William Stitt. (17)

YOUNG, James of Franklin Twp. - dated 3-8-1806; recorded 9-12-1807. Brother; John Young of Franklin Twp. Executors: Robert Young, son of aforesaid John Young and Joseph Parks. Signed: James Young. Witnesses: John C. Death, John Clarke and James Death Jr. (18)

Bigham, Hugh - dated 8-8-1804; recorded 9-14-1807. Wife, Sarah. Sons, Alexander and John. Daughters; Anne, Polly and Jane. Executors: Wife, Sarah and son, John. Signed: Hugh (mark) Bigham. Witnesses: Jeremiah Morrow and John Bigham. (19)

McMILLAN, William of Wayne Twp. - Dated 16th day, 6th month, 1806; recorded 9-16-1807. Sons: Thomas, William, Henry, David and Jonathan; with David to receive the Bible. Daughters: Mary, wife of Joseph Baxter and Lydia McMillan. Mentions: Land purchased by son, David from the executors of Peter Arnold, dec'd. Executor: Son, Jonathan. Signed: William McMillan. Witnesses: John Woolman and Enock Wickersham. (21)

LANDERS, George - Dated 8-1-1807; recorded 12-8-1807. Heir: Friend, William R. Goodwin, Executors: William R. Goodwin and Ephraim Kibby. Signed: George (mark) Landers. Witnesses: John A. Cook and R. J. Hutchinson. (23)

RIPPEL, Jacob - Dated 11-9-1808; recorded 10-19-1809. Wife; mentioned but not named, also to serve as executrix. Mentions two sons, but does not name. Mentions daughters, but does not name. Signed: Jacob (mark) Riffel. Witnesses: Joseph Case, Elizabeth (mark) Case and Joshua Surng(?). (24)

TAYLOR, Nathan - Oral will - Deposition dated 12-17-1808; recorded 2-7-1809. Heir: Aron Ward. Nathan Taylor died December 16th, 1808. Witnesses: Stephen Bowyer and Bazella Clarke. (24)

KINDER, Abraham - Bated 8-2-1809; recorded 10-24-1809. Wife, Margaret. Sons, John and George. Daughters, Nancy and Polly. Signed: Abrm. Kinder. Witnesses: Wm. C. Schenck, Ithamer Drake and John McCashen. (25)

BENHAM, Robert - Dated 2-6-1809; recorded 10-25-1809. Wife, Elizabeth. Sons, Joseph and Peter. Executor: Friend, Enos Williams. Signed: Robert Benham. Witnesses: Benjamin Wiggins, Aron Siblet and Ansin Tennant. (27)

WILES, John of Turtle Creek Twp. - Dated 10-14-1809; recorded 11-25-1809. Sons, James and William. Daughter, Elenor. Mentions, younger children, but does not name. Father-in-law, Rodger McKinley. Executors: Adam Nutt and Joseph Camb. Signed: John (mark) Wiles. Witnesses: Caleb Mulford and John Shaw. (29)

EDWARDS, John - dated 20th day, 1st month, 1810; recorded 7-16-1810. Brothers: Nathaniel, Archabald and William. Sister, Ruth Carter. Executors: Brothers, Nathaniel and Archabald Edwards. Signed: John Edwards. Witnesses: Levi Cook and Jonathan Newman. (30)

PAINTER, George - Dated 10-21-1809; recorded 2-6-1810. Wife, Sophia. Sons, John and George. Daughters: Sophia Price, Margaret Haney and Mary Thatcher. Executors: Wife, Sophia and son, John. Signed: George (mark) Painter. Witnesses: Peter Bonta and Jacob Tremble. (31)

DECAN, Thomas - Dated 5-25-1811; recorded 6-10-1811. Wife, Peggy. Sons: William, James and John. Mentions an unborn child; there are possibly other children not named. Executors: James Wilkeson and James Miranda. Signed: Thomas (mark) Decan. Witnesses: Andrew Brandstater, John Wilkerson and Stephanus Clark. (33)

THOMPSON, William of Deerfield - Dated 4-1-1811; recorded 6-18-1811. Wife, Catharine, also to serve as executrix. Signed: William Thompson. Witnesses: Andrew Lytle, John Snook and Benjamin Stites. (35)

MOON, Phineas of the town of Lebanon. - Dated 8-30-1811; recorded 10-14-1811. Wife, Elenor. Daughter, Catharine. Executor, George Foglesong. Signed: Phineas Moon. Witnesses: Enos Williams and William M. Wiles. (36)

TULLIS, Michael of Deerfield Twp. - Dated 11-7-1811; recorded 2-20-1812. Wife, Elenor, also to serve as executrix. Mentions children, the youngest not of age, but does not name. Signed: Michael (mark) Tullis. Witnesses: Edward Rolf and David Briney. (38)

EDIE, David of Knox Co., Indiana Territory - Dated 7-16-1812; recorded 2-9-1813. Wife, Margret. Children, mentioned but not named. Executors: Henry Miller and John McCombs. Signed: David Edie. Witnesses: William Gallagher, John Edington and Adam Gallagher. (39)

WORTHINGTON, Joseph of Knox Co., Indiana Territory - Dated 7-15-1812; recorded 2-9-1813. Wife, Elizabeth. Children, mentioned but not named. Executors: Henry Miller and John McCombs. Signed: Joseph (mark) Worthington. Witnesses: John McCombs, John Haven(?)Jr., Enoch Davis and Wm. Galloher. (41)

HOPKINS, James Sr. - Dated 7-11-1813; recorded 9-15-1813. Wife, Rachel. Sons: John, James, William, Samuel, Alexander and David. Daughter, Sarah. Executors: friend, Michael H. Johnson and son, Jno. Hopkins. Signed: James Hopkins. Witnesses: Michael H. Johnson, James Hart and Martha Hopkins. (44)

DANIELS, Nathan of Turtle Creek Twp. - Dated 5-24-1814; recorded 6-17-1814. Wife, Hannah. Son, James. Executors: Son, James and John Sellers. Signed: Nathan (mark) Daniels. Witnesses: Elijah Stites and David Jay. (47)

BUNNELL, Stephen Sr. - dated 10-13-1812; recorded 2-16-1813. Sons: James, Stephen, Jonas, David and Nathaniel. Daughters: Rhoda and Mary. Executors: Son, Nathaniel and Ephraim Blackford, husband of daughter Mary. Signed: Stephen Bunnell. Witnesses: Luther Russel, Tergus McLean and John Blair. (42)

McCLEARY, Mary of Franklin Twp. - Dated 6-13-1813; recorded 10-20-1813. Son, Thomas. Daughters: Elizabeth Sawyer, Dorcas McCleary and Nancy Young. Executors: Robert Robison and Joseph Parks, Jr. Signed: Mary (mark) McCleary. Witnesses: Michael Auld, Joseph Parks and Robert Young. (50)

BRINEY, Frederick, Private in Capt. Shaw's Company of Ohio Militia. Dated, Camp Meigs 7-14-1812; recorded 10-11-1813. Wife, Anna. Children, mentioned but not named. Executors: Wife, Anne and friend, Edward Roff. Signed: Frederick Briney. Witnesses: James Kennedy and Samuel Harris. (52)

HAWN, David of Franklin - Dated 7-29-1813; recorded 10-11-1813. Wife, Elizabeth. Daughters, Sally and Elizabeth. Executors: Brother, Jacob Hawn and wife's father, John Fox. Signed: Daniel Hawn. Witnesses: James McEwen, Martin Earhart and Lewis Davis. (54)

SMITH, David B. - Oral Will - Deposition dated 11-16-1813; recorded (not given), Heir: Sister, Mary Earhart, wife of George Earhart. David B. Smith died October 27th, 1813. Witnesses: Jacob Ambrose and John Roads. (55)

BEEDLE, William - Dated 3-9-1812; recorded 2-14-1814. Wife, Esther, Son, James, Daughters: Susanna Davis, Lydia Davis, Phebe Mulford and Mary Holle (Hole). Grandsons: John Davis, son of Jonathan Davis, and John Beedle. Executors: Grandson, John Davis and Dr. Davis Morris. Signed: William Beedle. Witnesses: Joseph Reynolds, Adam Nutland(?) and David Sutton. (57)

KIRBY, Richard - Dated 7-1-1813; recorded 4-2-1814. Wife, Mary. Son, Samuel, not of age. Daughters: Mary, Rebecah and Anne (Anna) Kirby. Mentions a graveyard on land designated to son Samuel, situated in Section 1 or 2, Township 3, Range 4. Executors: Wife, Mary, and Thomas Scott. Signed: Richard Kirby. Witnesses: Wm. Lowry, Jesse Palmer and Robert Porter. Codicil dated 7-31-1813, no additional information and same witnesses. (61)

FARRIS, David - Dated 3-11-1814; recorded 6-16-1814. Wife, Elizabeth. Sons: David, John, William and James. Daughters: Polly, Charity, Elizabeth, Rebecca, Jane, Nancy, Dolly and Priscilla. Executors: Eli Harvey and Caleb Harvey. Signed: David Farris. Witnesses: Stephen McKinny and Dan'l Freestone. (66)

McKANE, John - Dated 5-7-1812; recorded 2-14-1815. Sons: Richard, John, Daniel, Robert, William and James. Daughters: Mary Cummins and Elizabeth Ramsy. Executors William Lytle and Matthias Corwin. Signed: John McKane. Witnesses: David Bone and Enos Williams. (68)

HOLLIDAY, Samuel - Dated 1-28-1815; recorded 6-19-1815. Wife, Betsy, also to serve as executrix. Children, mentioned but not named. Signed: Samuel Holiday. Witnesses: Owen Todd, John T. Jack and James Jack. (72)

PARKS, Joseph of Turtle Creek Twp. - Dated 3-19-1813; recorded 6-13-1814. Wife, Jane. Sons: Robert, John, Joseph and James. Daughters: Betsy wife of James H. Robison and Isabella wife of John Clark. Executors: Wife, Jane; Sons, Robert and John. Signed: Joseph Parks. Witnesses: John Bigger, Moses D. Karn and Robert Young. (70)

WARREN COUNTY, OHIO - WILL ABSTRACTS

ROBERT ROSS - Bk. 1, P. 7; dated 9-24-1803; Recorded 9-11-1805
Wife - Elizabeth. Sons - Benjamin, John and Asten
Daughters - Sarah, Jean, Winnie and Elizabeth (last 2 not of age)
Mentions a sawmill and grist mill.   Signed - Robert Ross
Witnesses - John C. Death and James Death, Jr.

JOHN COWAN - Bk. 1, P. 9; dated 9-15-1804; Recorded 9-12-1805
Wife - Mary (Mary stepmother of Mary and Abigail); Son - John, Jr.
Daughters - Jane, Mary and Abigail
Executors - wife, Mary and brother, James Cowan
Signed - John Cowan. Witnesses - Timothy Sewel and Maleom Worley

WILLIAM JAMES - Hamilton Co., Ohio Bk. 1, P. 11; Dated 2-25-1803
Recorded 9-12-1805; Wife - mentioned but not named
Sons - John, Richard, Jonathan and David (David not of age)
Daughters - Rachel, Ann, Sarah and Jane
Mentions aged mother, but does not name
Mentions money due from Virginia and Hamilton County, Ohio
Executrix, wife - not named. Signed - William James
Witnesses - David Faulknor and Absalom Thomas
Codicil dated 9-29-1804 - no additional information - witnesses:
                    Jonah Vandevart and John Vandevart

JOHN VESTAL - Bk. 1, P. 14; dated 7-10-1804; Recorded 9-13-1805
Wife - Elizabeth. Mentions daughter, does not name; also mentions
           unborn child.   Signed - John Vestal
      Witnesses - Isaac Perkins and Layton Jay

RHOLAN KINDLE - Bk 1, P. 15; dated 3-12-1804; Recorded 9-13-1805
Wife - Agnes. Son - William
Daughters - Amelia, Mary, Charity, Elenor and Susannah
Signed - Rholan (mark) Kindle. Witnesses - David Fox, Evan Stephens

671

Note:- This book is located in the Clerk of Courts office, Common Pleas Court Records at the court house, Lebanon, Ohio. Pages on which the record may be found are given in parenthesis.

4-14-1817 - Will of James BERRYHILL proven. (Note: This Will is not found recorded in Will Book 1 of the Probate records which includes Wills for this year.) (7)

4-14-1817 - Isaac BLACKFORD, a black boy aged 19 yrs., chose James FREEMAN as his guardian. (8)

4-14-1817 - Eli HELMICK aged 14 yrs., son of Jacob Helmick, dec'd, chose Joseph BENNETT as his guardian. (8)

4-14-1817 - Petition brought by the householders of the town of Lebanon for the incorporation of said town, Names subscribed:

Matthias Ross	Ezekiel Creetors	David Baker
William McLeem	G. Hansberger	George Johnston
Samuel Nixon	Nathaniel McLean	Francis Davis
Robert Woods	Wm. M. Wiles	Wallace Bratton
James Frazier	William McMaster	William Heaton
John Hathaway	Christopher Eanenfight	Absalom Runnion
Charles Howel	Benjamin Weleler	John Reeves
Charles C. Root	James Clark	George Foglesong Potter
Joseph Roll	Abbott Godard	Tobias Breting
Thomas Farquer	Jacob Short	John Prill
John B. Cole	Ivory H. Chadbourne	Joseph Foot
Henry C. Jones	Wm. Coleman	Oaky Vanhise
David V. Williamson	James Edwards	Henry Adams Jr.
Caldwell Sample	Richard Parsall	Wm. Sinnard
John Snook	John H. Kean	D. M. Mitchel
Robert Chess(?)	Amzy Ayres	William Grey
Daniel Skinner	George Rutter	Daniel Manning
Jacob Dutterow	D F. Heaton	Richard Skinner
Stephen Gard	Jeddiah Gulick	Abram Van Vleet
Jacob Beller	Wm. Lowry	Thomas Freeman
Peter Beller	William Lytle	Geo. Kesling
James Brown	William Rokhill	Eli Truitt
Recompense Stansberry	John State	Richard H. Bowyer
Jesse Hardisty	Joshua Hollingsworth	Matthias Corwin Jr.
Gustavus Everts	Wm. Woodard	Wm. Johnston
Stacy Taylor	John Connery	Elizabeth Laird
John G. Stiles	William Stone	Ann Dover
George Smith	Alanso Hill	Joseph Keenan
Frederick Rook	Ephraim Hathaway	Rebecca McCreey
Benjamin Painter	Benjamin Inyard	Jonathan Marquant
Henry Adams	Roderick Noll	Margaret Abbott
Anthony Georghegan	Joseph Berry	Henry Breting
John D. Bowers	Jonas Seaman	Daniel Morris
Thomas Best	T. W. Colliett	Benjamin Sayre
Josephus Denham	James Hill	Elizabeth Boyer

672

Samuel Chamberlain	James DeCamp	John Willson
Sarah Lytle	Ashur Wolley	Henry Miller
Abet Kelly	Amos Smith	(8)

4-16-1817 - Abraham VAN MATRE aged 16 yrs. chose Nathan KELLY as his guardian and court appointed Kelly as guardian of Margaret Van Matre aged 11 yrs., Lewis D. Van Matre aged 10 yrs., Thomas J. Van Matre aged 8 yrs., and Malissa Van Matre aged 6 yrs., children and heirs of Morgan Van Matre, dec'd. (26)

4-16-1817 - William WILLIAMS aged 18 yrs. chose Margaret Williams as his guardian (27)

4-16-1817 - Court appointed Isaac DEATH guardian of Sarah MURPHY aged 17 yrs., daughter of Samuel Murphy, dec'd. (27)

4-19-1817 - Abraham FLAG aged 14 yrs., son and heir of Jacob Flag, dec'd, chose Anne Flagg as her guardian. (41)

4-19-1817 - Court appointed James SMITH guardian of Samuel WEST, a black boy aged 11 yrs. (41)

4-19-1817 - John Johnson VAN MATRE aged 14 yrs., son and heir of Morgan Van Matre, chose Nathan Kelly as his guardian. (41)

4-19-1817 - Letters of administration granted to Robert WHITACRE and Fanny MIRANDA to adms. estate of George MIRANDA, dec'd. (41)

4-21-1817 - Letters of adms. granted to William HILL to adms, estate of Levin CONSTANCE, dec'd. (46)

4-21-1817 - Jesse FLORA aged 17 yrs., son of John Flora, dec'd, chose Sylvanus CORNEL his guardian. (46)

4-21-1817 - Court appointed Samuel SHEPLEY guardian of Mary SNIDER aged 11 yrs., Elizabeth Snider aged 9 yrs., Esther Snider aged 7 yrs., Daniel (or David?) Snider aged 5 yrs. and William Snider aged 4 yrs., heirs of Arnold Snyder, dec'd. (46)

4-25-1817 - Court Appointed George KESLING guardian of Elizabeth EDWARDS aged 7 yrs., Joseph Edwards aged 6 yrs., John Edwards aged 4 yrs. and Nancy Edwards aged 2 yrs., children and heirs of Josias Edwards, dec'd. (70)

4-26-1817 - Letters of administration granted to John BIGGER to adms. estate of Henry MAY, dec'd; widow (not named) relinquishes her right to adms. estate. (88)

4-29-1817 - Letters of adms. granted to John BARLOW to adms. estate of Wm. A. Barlow, dec'd. (89)

4-29-1817 - Court appointed Margaret FARNER guardian of George Farner aged 10 yrs., son of Michael Farner, dec'd. (89)

9-1-1817 - Letters of adms. granted to George EARHART and Nicholas EARHART to adms. estate of Martin Earhart, dec'd. (98)

9-1-1817 - Court appointed John REEVES guardian of John BRADY aged 13 yrs. and William Brady aged 7 yrs., children and heirs of William Brady, dec'd. (98)

9-2-1817 - Letters of adms. granted to Benjamin PAINTER to adms. estate of Ezekiel Painter, dec'd. (103)

9-2-1817 - George AINSWORTH aged 17 yrs., son of Lazarus Ainsworth, dec'd, chose James DEATH as his guardian. (103)

9-2-1817 - On relinquishment of Ann DEATH, mother of Margaret AINSWORTH, court appointed Johnson ROBB fuardian of Margaret aged 11 yrs. (103)

9-2-1817 - Samuel AINSWORTH aged 14 yrs., son of Lazarus Ainsworth, chose Johnson ROBB as his guardian. (103)

9-8-1817 - Harriet SKINNER aged 17 yrs., daughter of Cornelius Skinner, dec'd, chose Thomas KEPHART as her guardian. (124)

9-8-1817 - Court appointed John PATTERSON guardian of Jane HERBISON aged 9 yrs., John Herbison aged 3 yrs. and Ruth Herbison aged 1 yr. children of James Herbison, dec'd. (124)

9-11-1817 - Court appointed David JENNINGS guardian of James M. BAILEY aged 8 yrs., John N. Bailey aged 7 yrs, and Thomas Z. Bailey aged 5 yrs., sons of Thomas Z. Bailey, dec'd. (138)

9-13-1817 - John BRADY aged 15 yrs., chose Thomas COVENHOVEN as his guardian. (158)

12-22-1817 - Letters of adms. granted to John Sellars to adms. estate of Leonard KRATCH, dec'd. (169)

1-5-1818 - Court appointed Joab SNOOK guardian of Johnson Snook aged 10 yrs., with consent of mother (not named). (244)

1-5-1818 - Lewis ROSE aged 16 yrs., son of Stephen ROSE, dec'd, chose William FERGUSON as his guardian. (244)

1-5-1818 - William COCHRAN aged 15 yrs., son of John COCHRAN, dec'd, chose Abram VAN VLEET as his guardian. (244)

3-24-1818 - Court appointed John McKEAN guardian of Samuel ROADS aged ___ (not given), son of Samuel ROADS, dec'd. (251)

3-24-1818 - Betsy CRITZER aged 14 yrs., daughter of George Critzer, dec'd, chose Abraham HANEY as her guardian. (251)

3-26-1818 - Letters of Adms. granted to Joseph TAPSCOTT and John N. C. SCHENCK to adms. estate of Joseph ELY, dec'd. (259)

3-27-1818 - Thomas CLAYTON aged 19 yrs., son of Thomas CLAYTON, dec'd, chose Sampson SERGEANT as his guardian. (267)

3-30-1818 - Court appointed William SNOOK guardian of Henry STOUT aged 10 yrs. and Rachel Ann Stout aged 7 yrs., children of George W. STOUT, dec'd. (276)

674

3-31-1818 - Andrew ROLSTON aged 17 yrs. and Margaret Rolston aged 14 yrs. chose Martha Rolston their guardian and court appointed Martha to also serve as guardian of Robert Rolston aged 11 yrs., Martha Rolston aged 8 yrs., Mary Rolston aged 7 yrs. and Elenor Rolston aged 5 yrs., all children of Edward Rolston, dec'd. (281)

4-2-1818 - John WILES aged 16 yrs., child of John Wiles, dec'd, chose John WALTON as his guardian. (287)

4-2-1818 - Court appointed Samuel STEWART guardian of David Stewart aged 9 yrs., Warner Stewart aged 7 yrs. and Joseph S. Stewart aged 5 yrs., children of said Samuel Stewart. (287)

4-6-1818 - James THOMPSON aged 16 yrs., chose Wyllis PIERSON as his guardian. (300)

4-9-1818 - Letters of adms. granted to Providence MOUNTS to adms. estate of Catherine MOUNTS, dec'd. (318)

4-10-1818 - Letters of adms. granted to John D. LOWE to adms. the estate of John Crone, dec'd. (323)

4-10-1818 - Watson MOUNT aged 17 yrs., son of William Mount, chose Nathan Kelly as his guardian. (323)

4-13-1818 - Margaret VOORHIS aged 15 yrs., chose Daniel VOORHIS as her guardian and court appointed said Daniel to also serve as guardian of Magdalene VOORHIS aged 11 yrs., both children of Cornelius VOORHIS. (343)

4-14-1818 - Court appointed George HANSBERGER guardian of John LAFFERTY aged 12 yrs., son of Richard Lafferty, dec'd. (344)

675

Note: Pages on which original record may be found is given in parenthesis. These records were abstracted for genealogical data only. In the case of debts, mortgages or suits of this nature, only the names were abstracted. This book may be found in the office of the Clerk of Court at the court house in Lebanon.

2-28-1831 - John WHITE vs. James MORROW, et al. Debt. (1)

2-28-1831 - Arthur BROWN vs. Joseph CANBY and James HUSTON. Debt. (7)

2-28-1831 - John RHINE and Joshua W. RHINE vs. Henry CLARK, et al. Filed 4-9-1827. That Joshua Wilson Rhine is a minor under 21 and the son of John Rhine. That four years ago John Rhine and West Burgess moved from Maryland and that John Rhine purchased land with said Burgess being part fractional Section 17, Township 4, of 2nd Range. That West Burgess returned to Maryland where he died in 1825 leaving a will in Maryland with George Fox as executor. That West Burgess left the following children and heirs--Elizabeth, of full age; Thompson; Mary Ann; Nancy Lyons; Rebecca Burgess; and Price Burgess; the last two named being minors. That said Burgess bequeathed to Joshua Wilson Rhine one half of the Warren County tract, which is now contracted to said Henry Clark. (12)

2-28-1831 - Mary FREEMAN vs. Michael BROWN and Daniel BOYD. Debt. (23)

2-28-1831 - Edmund ROBINSON, guardian. Filed 11-1-1830. Edmund Robinson guardian of Samuel, Jane, Lydia Ann, Elizabeth, Joseph and Lucinda Robinson, minor heirs and children of Nancy Robinson, dec'd. That on 1st May last, Nancy Robinson, dec'd, wife of Petitioner, Edmund Robinson, died seized of undivided one-eighth interest in Section 28, Township 4, Range 4 and that Jane Brelsford is entitled to dower in said land. (27)

2-28-1831 - Benjamin DUBOIS, guardian. Filed 11-1-1830. Benjamin Dubois guardian of Aaron, George, David, Lucy Ann, Jane, Lydia Margaret, Samuel, William, John and Joseph Pittman, minor heirs of Joseph Pittman and Edith his wife, along with David Webb and Rachel his wife late Pittman and Moore Pittman, all of age, who are also heirs of Joseph Pittman and Edith his wife. That on 8-1-1815 Nathaniel Everinger was seized of 50 acres part Section 32, 2nd township, 5th range and by will of said Everinger partition was made with N½ being assigned to Lucy Hall and S½ assigned to Edith Pittman. That on or about 10-1-1825 Edith Pittman died intestate leaving petitioners as her heirs, and that Joseph Pittman is also deceased. (31)

5-23-1831 - John N. C. SCHENCK vs. John D. SWALLOW, et al. Debt. (39)

5-23-1831 - David MILLS, adms. vs. Patience JESSOP and others. Filed 4-12-1830. Petition to make contract. Land, part Military Warrant No. 1048. That David Mills is the adms. of the estate of Jonathan JESSOP who died intestate in Wayne twp. in November 1829 leaving widow, Patience Jessop and four minor children-- Charles, William, Daniel and Thomas Jessop. (57)

5-23-1831 - William WILKERSON, adms. vs. Mary TITUS and others. Filed 11-1-1830.
Land, original survey of Tucker and Woodson 1525 part Military Survey 2226. Timothy
Titus, dec'd died intestate leaving widow, Mary Titus; and children: Phillip, Jacob,
Ann, Mary, Zellah, Edith and Timothy Titus; the last three named being minors. (63)

5-23-1831 - John JENNINGS vs. Joshua WARD and Paul LEWIS. Concerning grist and
saw mill. (73)

5-23-1831 - John N. C. SCHENCK vs. Daniel BRADLEY and Joseph CADY. Debt. (80)

5-23-1831 - John SNYDER, et al. Petition for Partition. Filed 11-15-1830.
That Thomas Gustin of Warren Co., Ohio is adms. of estate of John GUSTIN, dec'd,
who died 7-5-1829 seized of pt. SE¼ Section 9 and NE¼ Section 8, Township 3,
Range 4. That Gustin left widow, Jane Gustin and children--Cynthia wife of John
Snider, Bethana, Mary, Naomi and Renee Jane Gustin; the last four named being
minors. (82)

9-19-1831 - Charles FARQUHER et al. vs. James HAMILTON, et al. Filed 4-19-1824.
William Wilson, dec'd. That on Oct. 1810 William Wilson contracted with Alexander
Hamilton to purchase 100 acres part Military Survey No. 1333¼ in Hamilton twp.
William Wilson left the following children: Hannah late Wilson wife of Charles
Farquehar, Robert Wilson, Mary late Wilson wife of William Williamson, John Wilson
and Hugh Wilson; the last two named being minors by Wm. Hopkins their guardian. (93)

9-19-1831 - John N. C. SCHENCK vs. James W. LANIER, et al. Mortgage. (113)

9-19-1831 - William MURRAY, executor vs. Robert YOUNG and wife, adms. Debt.
Robert Young and Mary his wife, late Mary Gassaway, adms. of estate of Henry
Gassaway, dec'd. (119)

9-19-1831 - John LEOPOLD, etal. Filed 2-25-1830. Land, part fraction Section
1, 1st township, 5th range. John Leopold, dec'd, late of Franklin. Children:
John Leopold; Valentine Leopold now living near Morgantown, Virginia; Catharine
Richards afterwards Grintner, dec'd, her children--Mary Ann late Grintner wife
of Thomas Hays, Henry Grintner a minor by Frederick Grintner his guardian, a
brother of Mary Ann, and John Richard son of said Catharine by her first husband,
a minor by Isaac Wimmer his guardian. (121)

9-19-1831 - William WILKERSON, adms. of Timothy TITUS. (note: see page 63). (132)

9-19-1831 - Andrew WHITACRE and John WHITACRE, executors. Dispute over land title.
Andrew Whitacre and John Whitacre, executors of Robert Whitacre, dec'd, who died
Oct. 1828. (133)

9-19-1831 - James HIPKINS Jr. Concerning land. Mentions will of William Hopkins.
(135)

9-19-1831 - Edmund P. MATTHEWS, guardian. Filed May 1831. John Boyd, dec'd, late of Mason County, Kentucky. Land in Salem and Hamilton twps., Warren Co. Heirs of John Boyd--John N. and Amsy(?) P. Boyd, minors by Matthews their guardian. Other heirs of said Boyd being of full age have sold their interests. (137)

2-27-1832 - William COX vs John Hall guardian of Martha Jane COX. Debt. (143)

2-27-1832 - Peter FEERER vs. William McKNIGHT, et al. Filed 7-26-1831. Land, pt. Section 28, Township 2, Range 4 in Franklin twp. William McKnight, dec'd, died in 1820. Children: Robert McKnight; William McKnight, a minor under 21 yrs.; Sarah Jane McKnight aged 16 yrs.; Catharine McKnight aged 14 yrs.; Rebecca McKnight aged 12 yrs.; said minors all of Montgomery Co., Ohio. Joseph Robb late of this county now of Wabash Co. (Indiana?) was guardian of minors. Robert McKnight being of full age has sold his interest to petitioner. (143)

2-27-1832 - Rebecca CARTER, guardian. Filed May 1831. Fenton Carter, dec'd. Widow, Rebecca Carter. Children, Elizabeth and Joshua Carter, both minors. Fenton Carter, dec'd inherited from his father, Joshua Carter, dec'd, late of Warren Co., Ohio and undivided one-eighth part of 55 acres Section 34, 4th Township, 4th Range. (147)

5-7-1832 - Warren SABIN vs. Benjamin Cox, et al. Debt. (153)

5-7-1832 - David WELLS and Nicholas LONGWORTH vs. Zerubabel WELLS. Concerning title to land. David and Zerubabel are brothers. (168)

5-7-1832 - Daniel SWALLOW, et al vs. John SATTERTHWAITE, et al. Debt. (190

5-7-1832 - Anthony H. DUNLEVY and Thomas CORWIN adms. of estate of Henry SHARE vs. Mary SHARE and others. Lot 58 in Lebanon. Widow, Mary Share. Children: Mary wife of Peter Bowman of Hamilton Co., Ohio; Catharine wife of Charles Feight of Montgomery Co., Ohio; Ephraim Share of Warren Co.; Barbara Share; Peter Levi Share and Letitia Hortensia Share; the last three named being minors and all of Warren Co. (197)

5-7-1832 - Simon HAGERMAN vs. James MURPHY of New Jersey. Debt. (206)

5-7-1832 - Horace G. PHILLIPS, et al. vs. John Satterthwaite. Debt. (210)

5-7-1832 - Mary FERGUSON vs. George BUNDY. Filed 2-7-1832. William Ferguson, dec'd died intestate 11-30-1831 leaving widow Mary Ferguson who he married in 1814. While and during their marriage they became possessed of two 4 acre plots of out-lots in town of Lebanon. (212)

5-7-1832 - James GRAY, executor of the Will of John GRAY vs. Hannah GRAY and others. Filed 2-27-1832. John Gray late of Fountain County, Indiana, dec'd, died in Aug. 1830 leaving widow, Hannah Gray and children: Phebe late Gray wife of Silas Davis, James Gray, Anna late Gray wife of George J. Cowgill and Hannah Gray, a minor. Petition to complete contract on land. (213)

5-7-1832 - John N. C. SCHENCK vs. Mary PLUM. Mortgage. (215)

5-7-1832 - John T. HALL, Petition concerning land. (226)

5-7-1832 - Joseph CORWIN, guardian. Joseph Corwin is guardian of David B. Corwin a minor aged 8 yrs., who is entitled by descent to 35 acres NW¼ Section 25, Township 3, Range 4, said land belonged to mother of David B. Corwin; who was one of the heirs of David Bumtrager late of Warren Co., Ohio, dec'd. (230)

5-7-1832 - Anthony H. DUNLEVY, guardian. Filed 2-27-1832. Anthony H. Dunlevy guardian of Amos Samson a minor aged 19 yrs. who is possessed of 33 3/4 acres which descended to him from his father and grandfather (not named), late of Warren Co., Ohio, dec'd; said land being part SW corner Section 18, Township 4, Range 3. (233)

5-7-1832 - Abigail TICHENOR, guardian. Abigail guardian of David, Ann Eliza and Hannah M. Tichenor, all minors, children of Nathaniel Tichenor, dec'd, late of Warren Co., who died seized of NW¼ Section 6, Township 9, Range 2 in Preble Co., Ohio. (237)

5-7-1832 - John BURNET, etal. Filed 5-7-1832. Land, Section 13, Township 4, Range 4. Isaac Hawkins, dec'd, who died intestate about Oct. 1831 leaving widow, Mary Hawkins and children: Elizabeth late Hawkins wife of John Burnet; Nathan Jones and Margaret his wife, late Hawkins; Abraham Hawkins; Sarah late Hawkins wife of Reuben Garrison; Ruth Hawkins; Isaac Hawkins; and Seth Hawkins; the last three named being minors by Robert Furnas their guardian. (238)

9-24-1832 - James PARKS and James H. McMEEN executors of will of John McMEEN vs. Mary McMEEN and others. Filed 8-9-1830. John McMeen, dec'd died in Feb. 1828 leaving widow Mary McMeen and two children and heirs Elizabeth Robinson and William McMeen. William H. Hamilton husband of Mariah McMeen, dec'd who died since her father, who is tenant by curtesy of the child of said Mariah, dec'd, without issue--James McMeen, John B. McMeen, Joseph A. McMeen, Grisella McMean the wife of petitioner James and petitioner James McMean. (note: wording in this is as given--). (267)

9-24-1832 - William Cox, et al. vs. David TEMPLETON, et al. Land West end S½ Section 27 Township 3 of 4th Range. John Cox, dec'd late of Warren Co., died 1-2-1829 leaving widow, Jane Cox who afterward on 10-26-1830 married Joseph Mats, said widow entitled to dower. John left an infant child who died in August 1830 aged about 2 yrs. John left the following brothers and sisters: William Cox of Greene Co., Ohio; Joseph Cox of Montgomery Co., Ohio; Ellen late Cox wife of John Templeton of Clark Co., Ohio; Margaret Cox of Greene Co., Ohio; and Hannah Templeton late Cox, dec'd, late wife of William Templeton, her children-- James and David Templeton, both minors. (249)

9-24-1832 - Elizabeth BLACKFORD vs. Jarvis STOKES, guardian. Filed 5023-1831. David BLACKFORD, dec'd. Widow, Elizabeth Blackford. Petition to have Stokes removed as guardian of David Nelson, Sarah Ann and Emily Blackford. (256)

679

9-24-1832 - Robert SMITH vs. Timothy SMITH, et al. Filed Sept. 1831. John
Smith Jr. dec'd late of Warren Co., Ohio died leaving a will and children--
Robert Smith and John H. Smith who under will shared in land. Said John H.
Smith died intestate with Conrad Smith as adms. of his estate, leaving children--
Timothy Smith, George Smith, Mariah Smith and Rachel Smith--the last two named
being minors. (257)

9-24-1832 - Mary RUE vs Henry HYSER. Filed Feb. 1832. Benjamin Rue late of
Warren Co., dec'd, died 9-2-1823 leaving widow Mary Rue who he married 8-9-1793.
During marriage they became possessed of 200 acres part fractional Section 4,
5th Township, 3rd Range in Union township except small piece of ground conveyed
by said Rue to Baptist Church for meeting house and burying ground. Said land
is now in possession of Hyser. (260)

9-24-1832 - John GOWDY executor of will of George FOGLESONG vs. William ROBINSON,
et al. Filed 5-7-1832. George Foglesong dec'd, died in July 1831 leaving children:
Prudence late Fogelesong wife of John Gowdy; Sarah late Foglesong wife of William
Robinson; John S. Foglesong; William G. Foglesong; and Margaret C. Foglesong, the
last three named being minors and all of Greene Co., Ohio. Said George Foglesong
died seized of parts of lots 4 and 5, part of Section 5, Township 4, Range 3,
part of which land he had conveyed to James Liddle, and part of which was alloted
to George and Sarah Martin as two of the heirs of Barbara Martin who was the
daughter of Martin Earhart, as was made in the division of lands among his heirs.
(264)

9-24-1832 - Daniel GROSVENOR, guardian vs. Lewis DAVIS late guardian of the
McKnight Heirs. (267)

9-24-1832 - Daniel CRANE and Sarah his wife vs Cephas GRITTERY. Filed 5-7-1832.
Andrew Grittery, dec'd, late of Warren Co. died leaving widow, Sarah now the wife
of Daniel Crain, married in Feb. last. Andrew died seized of 100 acres Section
10, Township 5, Range 3, with dower in same previously set off to said Sarah
in partition suit filed by children of Andrew and Sarah. Only child named
is Cephas Grittery. (268)

9-24-1832 - Ballard SMITH and wife vs. Samuel MASON and others. Filed 9-24-1832.
Petition to complete land contract. Ballard Smith and Susannah his wife about
Feb. 1829 by their agent John Carter purchased lands near Palmyra being one acre
in land owned by William Mason of Deerfield township, but for which Mason died
without making deed. Children of William Mason, dec'd: Sam'l Mason, Maria wife
of Lucas D. Leonard, Cynthia Mason and Sally Mason; the last two named being minors
by James McCowen their guardian. (270)

680

The following records were taken from "Minute Book 9" as found in the Common Pleas Court (Clerk of Court's Office) at the court house in Lebanon. Page on which record may be found in the original book is given in parenthesis.

3-29-1841 - Tavern licenses granted: Samuel EGBERT at his residence in Mason, Joseph HURST at his residence in Franklin, Edmund ROBINSON at his residence in this county, George KINDER at his residence in Franklin, Abraham B. BUTLER at his residence in Butlersville. (1 & 2)

3-29-1841 - Will of Robert HAMILTON presented to court and proven. (2)

3-29-1841 - Tavern licenses granted: Asab 1 C. BATES at his residence in this county, Noah SALSBURY at his residence in Roachester, Andrew SWAN(?) at his residence in Hopkinsville, John C. KINNEY at his residence in Springboro. (3)

3-30-1841 - George W. EVANS aged 19 yrs and Elizabeth EVANS aged 16 yrs., children of Joseph Evans chose said Joseph Evans as their guardian. (8)

3-30-1841 - Estate of Richard BORDEN, dec'd. Widow, Sarah Ann BORDEN relinquishes right to adms. estate. (9)

3-31-1841 - Martha Clark appointed guardian of Rebecca Ann CLARK aged 8 yrs., Susan CLARK aged 6 yrs. and Enos W. CLARK aged 4 yrs., children of Jonathan Clark, dec'd late of the state of Indiana. (12)

4-2-1841 - Estate of John ADAMS dec'd. Wm. Adams appointed adms. (15)

4-3-1841 - Jesse Spray appointed guardian of Joseph FURNAS aged 4 yrs. and Isaac FURNAS aged 18months, children of Isaac Furnas, dec'd. (18)

4-3-1841 - Vinson DOAN aged 15 yrs. and Margaret DOAN aged 13 yrs. chose John SHAWHAN as their guardian and court appointed him to also serve as guardian of Isaac DOAN aged 10 yrs., Jemima DOAN aged 8 yrs., Joseph C. DOAN aged 4 yrs. and Elizabeth DOAN aged 2 yrs., all children of Hannah Doan, dec'd. (18)

4-6-1841 - License granted to William HENRY and John HENRY to vend goods, wares and merchandise throughout Ohio for term of three months. (23)

4-7-1841 - Jonathan TRIBLY granted license to keep tavern at his residence this county. (30)

4-7-1841 - Will of Jacob NIGGLE presented to court and proven. (30)

4-7-1841 - Samuel W. Harrington appointed guardian of his son, Nelson HARRINGTON aged 3 yrs. (31)

4-12-1841 - Will of John R. DUNN presented to court and proven. (43)

4-13-1841 - Estate of Philip OLINGER, dec'd. John S. Todd appointed adms. (48)

4-14-1841 - Estate of Isaac P. Compton, dec'd. Elias Fisher appointed adms. (54)

4-14-1841 - William S. MICKLE granted license to keep tavern at his residence in Roachester. (54)

4-14-1841 - Thomas SMITH aged 14 yrs., son of Thomas Smith, dec'd chose Henry Smith as his guardian. (54)

4-16-1841 - Jefferson KING aged 14 yrs., son of George King, dec'd, chose John King as his guardian. (72)

8-2-1841 - Tavern licenses granted: James GREER at his residence in Franklin, Benjamin KEMP at his residence in Waynesville, Robert BILLET at his residence in this county. (87)

8-2-1841 - Tavern licenses granted; Aaron MINTLE at his residence in Ridgeville, John WELTON at his residence in Mason, William MORRIS at his residence in Oceola. (88)

8-2-1841 - Will of Mitchell McCONNELL(?) presented to court and proven. (88)

8-2-1841 - Estate of Charles JOHNSON dec'd. Anne Johnson and Henry Houk appointed adms. (88)

8-2-1841 - Estate of Jonathan SCOTT, dec'd. Thompson Lamb appointed adms. (88)

8-2-1841 - Estate of Culbut WATSON, dec'd. Culbut A. Watson and John Watson appointed adms. (89)

8-2-1841 - Will of Asher PLACE presented to court and proven. (89)

8-2-1841 - Ezra Plummer appointed guardian of Joseph PLACE aged 17 yrs., Mary PLACE
aged 14 yrs., David PLACE aged 11 yrs. and Sarah Ann PLACE aged 4 yrs., children
of Asher Place, dec'd. (89)

8-2-1841 - Estate of Eli CRAIG, dec'd. James Craig appointed adms. (90)

8-2-1841 - Rev. Samuel NEWELL a minister of the Presbyterian Church granted license
to solemnize marriages. (90)

8-4-1841 - Tavern licenses granted to: Levi WILLIAMS at his residence in Genn Town,
David CODDINGTON at his residence in Hopkinsville. (104)

8-5-1841 - William N. SCHAEFFER granted license to keep tavern at his residence
in Lebanon. (111)

8-5-1841 - David MATTHEWS aged 16 yrs. and Catharine MATTHEWS aged 13 yrs. chose
Wm Crossan as their guardian and court appointed him to also serve as guardian
of Eliza Jane MATTHEWS aged 9 yrs., Alexander MATTHEWS aged 7 yrs. and Isaac
MATTHEWS aged 5 yrs., all children of Jonathan Matthews, dec'd. (111)

8-9-1841 - Benjamin BARNHART granted license to keep tavern at his residence in
Waynesville. (124)

8-10-1841 - Will of Susannah COON presented to court and proven. (127)

8-10-1841 - Will of Sally OGDEN presented to court and proven. (127)

8-12-1841 - Jacob BILMIRE granted license to keep tavern at his residence in
Lebanon. (135)

8-13-1841 - James JEFFERY aged 19 yrs. and Mary JEFFERY aged 17 yrs. chose Eleanor
Jeffery and Henry Sherwood as their guardians and court appointed them to also
serve as guardians of William JEFFERY aged 12 yrs. and Jacob JEFFERY aged 13
yrs., all children of Francis Jeffery, dec'd. (138)

8-13-1841 - Martha Ann PARKS aged 16 yrs. and Grizella PARKS aged 14 yrs. chose
Hiram McCreary as their guardian and court appointed him to also serve as
guardian of Rebecca PARKS aged 9 yrs. and Joseph PARKS aged 8 yrs., all children
of James Parks, dec'd. (138)

8-13-1841 - James GORDON granted license to keep tavern at his residence in Springboro. (138)

8-13-1841 - Samuel Kelly appointed guardian of Margaret KELLY aged 10 yrs., Isaac
KELLY aged 8 yrs., Anne KELLY aged 6 yrs. and Hannah KELLY aged 1 yr., all
children of Achsah Kelly, dec'd. (138-9)

8-14-1841 - David R. DYCHE aged 14 yrs. and Nancy DYCHE aged 12 yrs. chose Mary
Dyche as their guardian and court appointed her to also serve as guardian of
George DYCHE aged 9 yrs. and Ruth DYCHE aged 6 yrs., all children of William
Dyche, dec'd. (143)

8-17-1841 - Sarah JENNINGS vs. James S. ONEALL. Bastardy. (149)

8-17-1841 - Will of Elizabeth STAUTON presented to court and proven. (150)

8-17-1841 - Mary PHILLIPS aged 15 yrs. chose John Jones as her guardian and court
also appointed him to serve as guardian of Sarah PHILLIPS aged 10 yrs and
Thomas PHILLIPS aged 4 yrs., all children of Joseph PHILLIPS, dec'd. (150)

8-18-1841 - Rachel OSBORN aged 16 yrs. and Sarah OSBORN aged 13 yrs., children of
Squier Osborn, dec'd chose Anna Osborn as their guardian. (155)

8-18-1841 - John OSBORN granted license to keep tavern at his residence in this
county. (155)

8-19-1841 - Samuel JAMES granted license to keep tavern at his residence in this
county. (159)

11-1-1841 Tavern Licenses granted to: Peter W. WIKOFF, Ben CLARK in Raysville, Alexander CALLAHAN in Ridgeville, James GREER in Franklin, Stephen COOK in Mountholly, James T. SHARP, James FUGATE in Mason and Calvin BRADLEY in Lebanon. (170)

11-1-1841 - William Hufford appointed guardian of Huston SHURTS aged 2 yrs. and Ruben(?) SHURTS aged 8 yrs., children of John Shurts, dec'd. (170)

11-1-1841 - Amanda EDWARDS aged 16 yrs., child of Eden Edwards chose Samuel Mason as her guardian. (170)

11-1-1841 - Will of David BROWN presented to court and proven. (170)

11-1-1841 - William HINES aged 18 yrs. and Nancy HINES aged 15 yrs., children of Hugh Hines chose Abram Hines as their guardian. (171)

11-1-1841 - Estate of Morman BUTTERWORTH, dec'd. Henry Butterworth appointed adms (171)

11-1-1841 - Nuncapative will of John WALDRON presented to court and proven. (171)

11-1-1841 - Samuel VAIL aged 14 yrs., child of Aaron Vail, dec'd, chose David Evans as his guardian. (172)

11-2-1841 - Jonah Cadwallader appointed guardian of William L. DOCTOR aged 13 yrs., Elizabeth V. DOCYOR aged 8 yrs., James St. DOCTOR aged 6 yrs. and John K. DOCTOR aged 3 yrs., children of John Doctor, dec'd. (176)

11-3-1841 - William CROSLEY granted license to keep tavern at his residence in this county. (178)

11-3-1841 - Will of Isaac WATSON presented to court and proven. (179)

11-3-1841 - James TOTTEN granted license to keep tavern at his residence in Deerfield. (179)

11-4-1841 - Estate of Thomas STEVENSON, dec'd. Robert Stevenson appointed adms. (180)

11-4-1841 - Enoch HAMELL granted license to keep tavern at his residence in Waynesville. (180)

11-5-1841 - Eliza Jane SELLERS aged 17 yrs. and Cynthia Ann SELLERS aged 15 yrs., children of Parthena Sellers, dec'd, chose William Sellers as their guardian. (188)

11-8-1841 - Estate of Sarah ANDERSON, dec'd. Enos Williams appointed adms. (195)

11-9-1841 - Nancy Scott appointed guardian of Levi E. SCOTT aged 10 yrs., Susan SCOTT aged 5 yrs. and George W. SCOTT aged 3 yrs., children of Jonathan Scott, dec'd. (196)

11-9-1841 - Clarissa A. BROWN aged 14 yrs., child of Stacy Brown, dec'd, chose Joseph Edwards as her guardian. (196)

11-9-1841 - John Bone appointed guardian of Mary Jane BROWN aged 11 yrs. child of Stacy Brown, dec'd. (197)

11-9-1841 - Samuel SCOTT aged 19 yrs. and Joseph SCOTT aged 18 yrs., children of Jonathan Scott, dec'd, chose Isaac Bennet as their guardian. (197)

11-9-1841 - Thomas SCOTT aged 14 yrs. and Eliza Jane SCOTT aged 12 yrs., children of Jonathan Scott, dec'd, chose Jacob Todhunter as their guardian. (197)

11-10-1841 - Auctioneer license tranted to Joseph L. Hatfield. (199)

11-10-1841 - Estate of Garet P. WIKOFF, dec'd. Peter W. Wikoff appointed adms. (199)

11-10-1841 - Estate of Joshua HOLLINGSWORTH, dec'd. Lydia Hollingsworth appointed adms. (200)

11-11-1841 - Thomas Biggs appointed guardian of John HAMILTON aged 9 yrs., a colored boy. (201)

11-13-1841 - William GAB granted license to keep tavern at his residence in Franklin. (207)

11-15-1841 - Mary HOLLINGSWORTH granted license to keep tavern at her residence in Lebanon. (213)

11-15-1841 - Joseph WILLIAMS granted license to keep tavern at his residence in Roachester. (229)

11-16-1841 - Authenticated copy of will of Alethia RUSSELL presented to the court and recorded. (219)

11-17-1841 - Estate of Peter CANON, dec'd. John Maple appointed adms. (227)

11-17-1841 - Ann PENDERY aged 15 yrs. chose Eliza Pendery as her guardian and court appointed her to also serve as the guardian of Mary PENDERY aged 11 yrs., Jeremiah PENDERY aged 11 yrs., John G. PENDERY aged 8 yrs., Thomas PENDERY aged 6 yrs. and Deborah Jane PENDERY aged 3 yrs., all children of Thomas Pendery, dec'd. (227)

11-18-1841 - Thomas Riggs guardian of John HAMILTON a colored boy has by indenture dated this day bound to Mary Hollingsworth, the said John Hamilton. (230)

11-20-1841 - William Russell appointed guardian of Corydon SPINNING aged 12 yrs. child of John Spinning, dec'd. (238)

11-20-1841 - Auctioneer license granted to Benjamin SELLERS. (238)

11-20-1841 - Jeremiah Stansel appointed guardian of Alexander J. GREGG aged 6 Yrs. and Ann B. GREGG aged 3 yrs., children of Israel Gregg, dec'd. (240)

3-28-1842 - Estate of John YOUNG, dec'd. William R. Collett appointed adms. Widow, Sarah Young relinquishes right to adms. (244)

3-28-1842 - Thomas KELSEY aged 14 yrs., son of David Kelsey, dec'd, chose James Hollingsworth as his guardian. (245)

3-28-1842 - Authenticated copy of will of John LEE of Kentucky presented to court and recorded. (245)

3-28-1842 - Barney CROSSON files his declaration of intention o become citizen, he is a native of Ireland. (245)

3-28-1842 - Jeremiah McCARTY, native of Ireland. Naturalization. He filed his declaration of intention 11-30-1835 in Jefferson County, Ohio. (246)

3-28-1842 - Will of Thomas NEWPORT presented to the court and proven. (246)

3-28-1842 - Estate of Jacob FRYBERGER, dec'd. Amassa Sawyer appointed adms.; widow, Hannah Fryberger having relinquished right to adms. (246)

3-28-1842 - Lavina E. GREELY aged 12 years, daughter of Daniel Greely, dec'd, chose Samuel Brown as her guardian. (247)

3-28-1842 - Letitia Haines appointed guardian of Deborah W. HAINES aged 7 yrs., Bethuel HAINES aged 6 yrs., Mary Ann HAINES aged 4 yrs., Rachel W. HAINES aged 3 yrs. and Samuel H. HAINES aged 1 yr., children of Wilkins Haines, dec'd.(247)

3-28-1842 - Tavern licenses granted to: John ROARK at his residence in Roachester, Abraham B. BUTLER at his residence in Butlersville, Price S. WHITACRE at his residence in Middleton. (249)

3-29-1842 - Estate of John McDONALD, dec'd. Joseph Thompson appointed adms. (249)

3-30-1842 - Joseph HURST granted license to keep tavern at his residence in Franklin. (254)

3-30-1842 - Adaline DEARDORFF otherwise called Adaline STOUTENBOROUGH aged 14 yrs., daughter of Catharine Shepherd, chose Eleanor Stoutenborough as her guardian. (254)

3-31-1842 - Estate of Rebecca DRAKE, dec'd. Peter Drake appointed adms. (256)

3-31-1842 - William Butterworth appointed guardian of Joseph C. JOHNSON aged 13 yrs. and 11 months, child of Joseph Johnson, late of Laporte County, Indiana, dec'd. (256)

3-31-1842 - William H. GOODWIN aged 16 yrs. and Alexander GOODWIN aged 14 yrs., Children of William Goodwin, dec'd, chose William Crosson as their guardian. (256)

4-1-1842 - Estate of Garret SCHENCK, dec'd with will annexed. John J. Walters and Peter Schenck appointed adms. (260)

4-4-1842 - Elmira GREEN aged 17 yrs. and Joseph GREEN aged 15 yrs. chose Lydia Green as their guardian and she appointed by court to also serve as guardian of John GREEN aged 13 yrs., Hannah GREEN aged 11 yrs., Elizabeth GREEN aged 9 yrs. and Frederick GREEN aged 7 yrs., all children of Benjamin Green, dec'd. (272)

4-6-1842 - Timothy Wharton appointed guardian of Elizabeth WHARTON aged 4 yrs., child of said Timothy, and Rebecca Wharton, dec'd. (279)

4-6-1842 - Jonathan TRIBLY granted license to keep tavern at his residence in Warren county. (279)

4-7-1842 - Estate of Isaac M. WOODARD, dec'd. Jesse Harvey appointed adms.; widow, Jane Woodard relinquishes right to adms. (293)

4-7-1842 - James Lindsey appointed guardian of William WOODARD aged 12 yrs., child of Isaac M. Woodard, dec'd. (293)

4-7-1842 - David BAKER granted license to keep tavern at his residence in Lebanon. (295)

4-8-1842 - Estate of William G. TAYLOR, dec'd. Daniel McCray appointed adms.; widow, Ann Maria Taylor relinquishes right to adms. (295)

4-9-1842 - Estate of John ROSS, dec'd. Thomas Ross appointed adms.; widow, Clarissa Ross relinquishes right to adms. (302)

4-9-1842 - Jabish PHILLIPS granted license to keep tavern at his residence in Lebanon. (304)

8-15-1842 - Will of John KESLER presented to the court and proven. (311)

8-15-1842 - William BASSET, native of England makes his declaration of intention to become citizen. (312)

8-15-1842 - Tavern licenses granted to: John C. KINNEY at his residence in Springboro; jacob MILLER at his residence (not stated); James B. GRAHAM at his residence in Lebanon. (312)

8-15-1842 - Will of Thomas DAUGHERTY presented in court and proven. (312)

8-15-1842 - Abraham STORMS and Rachel STORMS, application for arrearages of pension due them as heirs of Abraham Storms. The court after examination do find from the most satisfactory evidence exhibited to them, that Abraham Storms, dec'd was a pensioner of the United States at the rate of eight dollars per month, that he was a resident of the county of Warren in the state of Ohio, and died therein on the fourth day of May 1842--that he left no widow, but left a son and daughter the before named Abraham Storms and Rachel Storms as his only children and heirs at law. And the Court order these facts to be entered upon their Journal and certificate by clerk in due form of law. (313)

8-15-1842 - George ARCHDEACON, native of Ireland makes his declaration of intention to become citizen. (313)

8-15-1842 - Will of Robert KINCAID presented to court and proven. (314)

8-15-1842 - Estate of Jonathan CLARK dec'd. Milton Clark appointed adms.; widow, Henrietta Clark relinquishes her right to adms. (314)

8-15-1842 - Lemuel Hadden appointed guardian of William W. SCHENCK aged 8 yrs. and Phebe Ann Schenck aged 6 yrs., children of Obadiah Schenck, dec'd. (314)

8-15-1842 - Estate of Elijah C. FOOT, dec'd. Amos B. Foot appoineed adms. (315)

8-15-1842 - Mary Ann ANISON vs. Elliott TRUMP. Bastardy. (315)

8-16-1842 - Richard HEATON granted license to keep tavern at his residence in Mountholly. (324)

8-16-1842 - Richard LASHLEY, native of England makes his declaration of intention to become citizen. (324)

8--17-1842 - Thomas SCOTT, native of Ireland makes his declaration of intention to
became citizen. (334)

8-17-1842 - James McFISHER, native of Nova Scotia. Naturalization. Declaration
of intention made at March term 1840. Oath by George J. Smith and William
Sellers. (334)

8-17-1842 - David DAVIS, native of England. Naturalization. Declaration of
intention made at court of 8-3-1840. Oath by William Woodruff and Benjamin
Sellers. (335)

8-17-1842 - Alfred LEE granted license to keep tavern at his residence in Waynesville. (335)

8-17-1842 - Leopold GOEPPER aged 15 yrs. chose Mary M. Goepper his guardian and
court appointed her to above serve as the guardian of Maxamillian GOEPPER
aged 11 yrs. and Willhemina GOEPPER aged 4 yrs., all children of Michael
goepper, dec'd. (336)

8-17-1842 - Amos St. ROGERS a minister of the Presbyterian church granted license
to solemnize marriages. (336)

8-18-1842 - John WALTERS, native of England files his declaration of intention
to become citizen. (338)

8-18-1842 - Thomas HICKS aged 17 yrs., Sarah HICKS aged 15 yrs. and Hannah HICKS
aged 12 yrs., children of Samuel Hicks, dec'd chose Thomas Ireland as their
guardian. (338)

8-18-1842 - John McMULLEN, native of Ireland files his declaration of intention to
become citizen. (339)

8-19-1842 - Richard ARCHDEACON, native of Ireland. Naturalization. Declaration
of intention made 4-13-1840 in Common Pleas Court of Columbiana Co., Ohio.
Oath, Robert M. Hull and Samuel Perrott. (340)

8-19-1842 - James GLASGOW native of Ireland. Naturalization. Declaration of intention made 8-19-1840. Oath, Moses Miller and Francis Phillips. (341)

8-20-1842 - Philip KLAMON native of Berne. Naturalization. Declaration of intention made 8-18-1840 before this court. Oath, Henry King and George Kesling.
(346)

8-23-1842 - William E. HART aged 14 yrs. and Margaret HART aged 12 yrs., children
of James Hart, dec'd, chose Robert Irwin as their guardian. (354)

8-23-1842 - Will of George SHINN presented to court and proven. (355)

8-23-1842 - Estate of William HART, dec'd. Peter Monfort appointed adms. (365)

8-27-1842 - James McFisher appointed guardian of Sarah Catharine LOGAN aged 2 yrs.,
child of William Logan, dec'd. (369)

8-29-1842 - William BUNSTON Sr., native of England. Naturalization. Declaration
of intention made 8-6-1840. Oath by William M. Charters and Jacob Morris.(374)

8-29-1842 - William BUNSTON Jr., native of England. Naturalization. Oath by
William BUNSTON Sr. and Jacob Morris. (375)

8-30-1842 - John FINNEGAN native of Ireland makes his declaration of intention to
become citizen. (375)

9-2-1842 - Richard CAMPBELL native of Ireland makes his declaration of intention to
become citizen. (396)

9-2-1842 - Remembrance W. DAVIS aged 17 yrs., child of Rembrance W. Davis, dec'd,
chose Joel A. Stokes as his guardian. (396)

9-5-1842 - Joseph JAMISON granted license to keep tavern at his residence in
Franklin. (405)

9-5-1842 - Joshua BORDEN, applt. for arrearages of pension. The court orders the
clerk to certify that satisfactory evidence has been exhibited to this court
that Job Borden was a pensioner of the United States at the rate of seventy
three dollars and thirty three cents per annum--that he was a resident of the
county of Warren in the State of Ohio and died in said county in the year
1839 on 30th or 31st January of said year, that he left no widow and that he
left a child whose name is Joshua Borden who is the only child of Job Borden
now living. (406)
9-5-1842 - Allen BARBER, native of England. Naturalization. (408)
10-20-1842 - John TOMPKINS, native of England makes declaration of intention to
became citizen. (411)
11-14-1842 - Will of Hartshorn WHITE presented to court and proven. (413)
11-14-1842 - James BALDWIN aged 20 years and Sarah Jane BALDWIN aged 17 yrs. chose
Calvin Kitchel as their guardian and court appointed him to also serve as
guardian of Catharine BALDWIN aged 11 yrs., all children of Jacob Baldwin,
dec'd. (413)
11-14-1842 - Estate of Anthony BRANDENBURG, dec'd. Joel A. Stokes appointed adms.
(414)
11-14-1842 - Tavern licenses granted to: Wm W. SCHAEFFER at his residence in Lebanon,
Aaron MINTLO at his residence in Ridgeville, James FUGATE at his residence in
Mason. (414)
11-14-1842 - Estate of Robert SLACK, dec'd. Absalom Chenoweth appointed adms. (415)
11-14-1842 - Estate of John BRELSFORD, dec'd. Thomas Brelsford appointed adms.;
widow, Elizabeth Brelsford relinquishes right to adms. (415)
11-14-1842 - Will of George W. STINE presented to court and proven. (415)
11-15-1842 - Tavern license granted to: Enoch HAMMEL at his residence in Waynesville,
Calvin BRADLEY at his residence in Lebanon. (426)
11-16-1842 - Samuel McDONALD native of Ireland. Naturalization. Declaration of
intention made 11-13-1840. Oath by Robert M. Hull and Samuel Perrott. (433)
11-16-1842 - Estate of Okey McCABE, dec'd. Derrick Barkalow appointed adms.;
widow, Deborah McCabe relinquishes right to adms. (437)
11-16-1842 - Samuel CRAIG aged 16 yrs. and Jesse CRAIG aged 14 yrs. chose John
Shawhan as their guardian and court appointed him to also serve as guardian of
Martin CRAIG aged 11 yrs., Minerva CRAIG aged 9 yrs. and Eli CRAIG aged 4 yrs.
all children of all Craig, dec'd. (437)
11-21-1842 - Estate of George MILTENBERGER, dec'd. John Miltenberger and Adam
Miltenberger appointed adms.; widow, Catherine Miltenberger relinquishes right
to adms. (456)
11-23-1842 - Thomas COLLETT native of England. Naturalization. Declaration of
of intention made 1-29-1833 in Prothonotary of District Court of city and
County of Philadelphia. Oath by Elias Fisher and John Lloyd. (462)
11-26-1842 - Smith Conklin appointed guardian of Julia WALDRON aged 5 yrs., child
of John Waldron, dec'd. (468)
11-26-1842 - Robert CARTER aged 16 yrs., child of James Carter, dec'd, chose
Henry I. Ross as his guardian. (468)
12-1-1842 - James Coe appointed guardian of Rebecca PARKS aged 11 yrs. and Joseph
PARKS aged 10 yrs., children of James Parks, dec'd. (481)
12-1-1842 - Delilah Stephenson appointed guardian of Minerva STEPHENSON aged
11 yrs., David A. R. STEPHENSON aged 10 yrs., Mary Ann STEPHESON aged 6 yrs.
and Thomas St. STEPHENSON aged 2 yrs., children of Robert STEPHENSON, dec'd.
(481)

12-1-1842 - William WOODWARD aged 17 yrs., child of William Woodard chose John
    Woodward as his guardian. (482)
12-1-1842 - Garret PATTERSON native of Ireland makes his declaration of intention
    to become citizen. (482)
12-2-1842 - Frederick WEISSENBERGER native of Wurtemburgh makes his declaration of
    intention to become citizen. (483)
12-3-1842 - David P. EGBERT granted license to keep tavern at his residence in
    Lebanon. (484)
12-5-1842 - Henry HOLEMAN native of Prussia makes his declaration of intention to
    become citizen. (486)
12-10-1842 - Estate of Henry LASHLEY, dec'd. John Lashley appointed adms. (504)
3-27-1843 - Estate of Edward L. KENRICH, dec'd. David Montgomery and William
    Barton appointed adms.; widow, Patience Kenrich relinquishes right to adms.
    (508)
3-27-1843 - Estate of David LEER, dec'd. Robert Wilson appointed adms.; widow,
    Mary Lear relinquishes right to adm. (508)
3-27-1843 - Joshua McDONAL aged 20 yrs., child of James McDonald chose Joel A.
    Stokes as his guardian. (508)
3-27-1843 - Sullivan F. STERNS granted license to keep tavern at his residence in
    Butlersville. (508)
3-27-1843 - Will of Moses CROSLEY presented to court and proven. (509)
3-27-1843 - John W. DOUGHERTY aged 17 yrs. chose John Vandervort as his guardian and
    court appointed him to also serve as the guardian of James F. DOUGHERTY aged
    12 yrs., William K. Dougherty aged 8 yrs., Martha A. DOUGHERTY aged 6 yrs.,
    Sarah E. DOUGHERTY aged 4 yrs. and Elizabeth A. DOUGHERTY aged 2 yrs., all
    children of Thomas Dougherty, dec'd. (509)
3-29-1843 - Elisha COZART granted license to keep tavern at his residence in this
    county. (525)
3-29-1843 - Estate of Peter SMITH, dec'd. David H. Smith appointed adms.; widow,
    Elizabeth Smith relinquishes right to adms. (525)
3-29-1843 - Estate of Daniel DOUGHMAN, dec'd. William Crosson appointed adms.;
    widow, Eve Doughman relinquishes right to adms. (526)
3-29-1843 - Joseph HURST granted license to keep tavern at his residence in Franklin.
    (526)
3-29-1843 - Sarah COVERT aged 17 yrs., child of Joseph Covert, dec'd, chose Cath-
    arine Covert as her guardian. (526)
3-30-1843 - John Eltaroth appointed guardian of John SHEATHNER an insane person.(534)
4-5-1843 - Estate of Martha STEDDOM, dec'd. Edward Noble appointed adms. (556)
4-5-1843 - James Brown appointed guardian of Mary Jane BROWN aged 10 months, child
    of David Brown, dec'd. (557)
4-5-1843 - John R. MULFORD aged 15 yrs., child of Joseph Mulford, dec'd, chose Jehu
    Mulford as his guardian. (557)
4-5-1843 - Estate of Richard ROACH, dec'd. Lewis Fairchild appointed adms; widow,
    Ann Roach relinquishes her right to adms. (557)
4-5-1843 - Will of John S. ROBINSON presented in court and proven. (557)
4-6-1843 - James GREER granted license to keep tavern at his residence in Franklin;
    Jonathan TRIBLY granted license to keep tavern at his residence in county.
    (562-3)
4-7-1843 - Estate of Cyrus SIMINTON, dec'd. Wm B. Strout appointed adms.; widow,
    Nancy Siminton relinquishes right to adms. (564)

4-7-1843 - Ross TARNPRET(?) aged 18 yrs., child of Daniel TARNPRET(?), chose
William Mills as his guardian. (564)
4-7-1843 - Will of Beriah WOOD presented to court and proven. (565)
4-7-1843 - Will of Isaac PHILLIPS presented to court and proven. (565a)
4-7-1843 - Charles LEWIS aged 16 yrs. chose William Lewis as his guardian and court
appointed him to also serve as the guardian of John LEWIS aged 10 yrs., both
children of Paul LEWIS Jr., dec'd. (565a)
4-8-1843 - Will of Isaac JOHN presented to court and proven. (568)
4-8-1843 - Rebecca WILSON aged 12 yrs., child of David Wilson chose Eliza Wilson
as her guardian. (568)
4-10-1843 - Adonjah Francis appointed guardian of his children, Tobias FRANCIS
aged 6 yrs. and Lydia Ann FRANCIS aged 2 yrs. (573)
4-10-1843 - Estate of Mordcai TAYLOR Sr., dec'd. Mordecai Taylor appointed adms.
(573)
4-10-1843 - Authenticated copy of will of William PENQUITE of Fanquier Co., Virginia
produced to court and recorded. (573)
4-10-1843 - Estate of James HILL, dec'd. William Crosson appointed adms.; widow,
Deborah Hill relinquishes right to adms. (575)
4-10-1843 - Estate of Nathan HARLAN, dec'd. Rezin B. Edwards appointed adms.;
widow, Sarah Harlan relinquishes right to adms. (575)
4-10-1843 - Estate of Isaiah M. CORBLEY, dec'd. James C. Sabin appointed adms.;
widow, Mary Ann Corbley relinquishes right to adms. (576)
4-10-1843 - Tavern licenses granted: Jabish PHILLIPS at his residence in Lebanon;
John OSBORN at his residence in this county. (577)
4-11-1843 - Price S. WHITACRE granted license to keep tavern at his residence in
Middleboro. (578)
4-11-1843 - Estate of Joseph I. CLAYTON, dec'd. Bradford Chase appointed adms. (578)
4-11-1843 - William L. Schenck appointed guardian of Ann Elizabeth CLAYTON aged
9 yrs., child of Joseph I. Clayton, dec'd. (578)
4-11-1843 - John McCARTY aged 19 yrs., child of David McCarty, dec'd, chose John
McCarty Sr. as his guardian. (579)
8-21-1843 - Peter DeHAVEN granted license to keep tavern in Mount Holly. (589)
8-21-1843 - Tavern licenses granted: Henry and Elias L. RUNYON in Oceola, Casper
MILLER in Franklin, Amos SHAWHAN (place not stated), Harman STRADER in Roach-
chester, Rhew CLARK in Raysville, Richard LACKEY in Harveysburg, Michael D.
BOWSER in Waynesville, John KING in Mason, Isaac HUMES in Mason. (590)
8-21-1843 - Frederick MURPHY aged 16 yrs. and Labin MURPHY aged 14 yrs. chose Mary
Murphy as their guardian and court appointed her to also serve as guardian of
Stephen MURPHY aged 12 yrs., all children of Stephen Murphy, dec'd. (590)
8-21-1843 - William BEARD aged 20 yrs. and Joseph BEARD aged 17 yrs. chose Derrick
Barkalow as their guardian and court appointed him to also serve as guardian of
Mary Ann BEARD aged 10 yrs., all children of James Beard, dec'd. (591)
8-21-1843 - Lewis Kendall appointed guardian of Ellen KENDALL aged 11 yrs., Connie
KENDALL aged 9 yrs., Mary KENDALL aged 7 yrs., Lewis KENDALL aged 4 yrs. and
Sarah Ann KENDALL aged 2 yrs., all children of said Lewis Kendall. (591)
7-21-1843 - Estate of William GILLESPIE, dec'd. John Gillespie and Wm M. Corwin
appointed adms.; widow, Catharine Gillespie relinquishes right to adms. (591)
8-21-1843 - Catharine Gillespie appointed guardian of John GILLESPIE aged 8 yrs.,
William H. GILLESPIE aged 7 yrs., Sarah Ann GILLESPIE aged 4 yrs., Catharine
GILLESPIE aged 3 yrs. and Elizabeth GILLESPIE aged 1 yr., all children of
William Gillespie, dec'd. (591)

8-21-1843 - Caroline LIND aged 13 yrs., child of John M. Lind, chose said John
M. Lind as her guardian. (592)
8-21-1843 - Will of Jehu JACOBS presented in court and proven. (592)
8-21-1843 - Estate of Solomon GOODPASTER, dec'd. Wm Crosson appointed adms.;
widow, Susannah Goodpaster relinquishes right to adms. (593)
8-21-1843 - Estate of Isaac DUNN, dec'd. George F. Longstreth appointed adms. (593)
8-21-1843 - Samuel W. Throp appointed guardian of John H. DENISE aged 9 yrs. and
Rhoda Jane DENISE aged 7 yrs., children of Obadiah Denise aged 9 yrs. and
8-22-1843 - Rebecca Jane MILLER vs. Alfred MARTIN. Bastardy. (608)
8-22-1843 - James O. FOSTER granted license to keep tavern at his residence in
this county. (608)
8-22-1843 - Wm N. SCHAEFFER granted license to keep tavern at his residence in
Lebanon. (610)
8-23-1843 - Geo. P. WILLIAMSON granted license to keep tavern at his residence in
Lebanon. (611)
8-24-1843 - Auctioneer license granted to James D. BLACKBURN. (614)
8-24-1843 - Patrick FINNEY, native of Ireland. Naturalization. (615)
3-28-1843 - Estate of Christopher HORNADAY, dec'd. Henry Sherwood appointed adms.;
widow, Lucinda Hornaday relinquishes right to adms. (633)
8-30-1843 - Will of Mary ROHRIS presented to court and proven. (645)
8-30-1843 - Frederick WEISENBERGER, native of Wurtenburgh. Naturalization. (646)
8-31-1843 - David Ralston appointed guardian of Sarah Ann HARKRADER aged 8 yrs.
and Elizabeth HARKRADER aged 4 yrs., children of David Harkrader, dec'd.(648)
8-31-1843 - Mary Ann ROBISON aged 16 yrs. and Hannah Maria ROBISON aged 14 yrs.
chose Samuel Long as their guardian and court appointed him to also serve as
guardian of Eliza ROBISON aged 7 yrs., call children of John L. Robison,
dec'd. (648)
8-31-1843 - James POWELL native of England. Naturalization. Declaration of
intention made 10-22-1839. (649)
8-31-1843 - Rosa ma WUKKUANS vs. David THOMPSON. Bastardy. (650 & 654)
8-31-1843 - Susannah RUCH vs. John R. SPENCER. Bastardy. (651)
9-1-1843 - Joseph Voorhees appointed guardian of Emaline PINDLE aged 9 yrs.,
Elizabeth PINDLE aged 7 yrs., Joseph Thomas PINDLE aged 5 yrs. and Charles
Angus PINDLE aged 3 yrs., all children of Adolphus Pindle and his wife
Rebecca (now dec'd). (652)
9-4-1843 - Estate of Jehu JACOBS, dec'd. Levi Bouzer appointed adms. (655)
9-4-1843 - Will of Sanuel PASTON presented to court and proven. (656)
9-4-1843 - James SIMONTON aged 18 yrs. and Sarah Jane SIMONTON aged 16 yrs. chose
Elizabeth Simonton as their guardian and court also appointed her to serve
as guardian of Susan SIMONTON aged 11 yrs., Richard H. SIMONTON aged 10 yrs.,
Rebecca SIMONTON aged 8 yrs. and Eliza Ellen SIMONTON aged 6 yrs., all children
of Cyrus Simonton, dec'd. (656)
9-4-1843 - Will of Joseph J. NEWMAN presented to the court and proven. (658)
9-5-1843 - Theophilus S. Farquer appointed guardian of George W. MIRANDA aged 9
yrs. child of Franklin Miranda. (665)
9-5-1843 - Estate of Joseph WILKINSON, dec'd. Isaac Peacock appointed adms. (665)
9-7-1843 - Estate of Abram BREWER, dec'd. John Williamson appointed adms.; widow,
Ann Brewer relinquishes right to adms. (672)
9-7-1843 - David BAKER granted license to keep tavern at his residence in Lebanon.
(675)
9-8-1843 - Will of Abigail SMITH presented to the court and proven. (676)

9-8-1843 - William H.P. Denny appointed guardian of his son, George B. DENNY aged 11 yrs. (677)

9-8-1843 - Estate of Thomas HUMPHREYS, dec'd. Thomas Humphreys appointed adms.; widow, Sarah Humphreys relinquishes right to adms. (677)

9-8-1843 - Phebe WOOD vs. Samuel SPIER. Bastardy. (677)

9-9-1843 - Jarvis Stokes appointed guardian of Martha Jane SATTERTHWAITE aged 5 yrs. and Mary Elizabeth SATERTHWAITE aged 3 yrs., children of Samuel Satterthwaite, dec'd. (682)

OLIVE BRANCH CEMETERY
Warren County, Ohio

Contributed by:- Mrs. Herret W. Everitt, R. R. 1, Lebanon, Ohio   45036
Inscriptions recorded by:- Mrs. Everitt and Mrs. Ralph Giehls
Date -April 3, 1968
Location:- Seven miles east of Lebanon, Ohio on Wilmington Road (or County
Road No. 7), Washington Township, Warren County.

ANDREWS, Joseph son of G. E. & M. d. June 30, 1870; age 1 y. 10 m. 20 da.
AUSTIN, Rebecca wife of Rev. S. S. d. Oct. 1869; age 60 y. 10 m.
BARKLEY, John d. June 30, 1864; age 70 y. 8 m. 12 da.
        Elizabeth wife of John d. Nov. 1, 1872; age 75 y. 5 da.
        John W. d. Feb. 11, 1863; age 21 y 5 m. 11 da.
        Clara Lizzie dau of J. W. & M. T. d. Apr. 22, 1863; age 5 m. 10 da.
        (Foot markers: E.B.; J.W.B.; G.W.B.)
CAMPBELL, Lizzie wife of Elih d. Apr. 11, 1875; age 23 y. 5 m. 21 da.
        James d. Aug. 12, 1867; age 87 y. 4 m. 24 das.
        Temperance wife of James d. Aug. 20, 1872; age 74 y.6 m. 6 da.
CUMMINS, Francis M. b. Jan 5, 1840; d. Oct. 27, 1888
        Little Eva b. Jan. 18, 1870; d. Sept. 3, 1873
        Charlie G. b. Nov. 9, 1879; d. June 9, 1886
        Chloe died Jan. 10, 1859
COOPER, Jakie son of J. & E. d. Aug. 9, 1880; age 10 m. 5 das.
DRAKE, Rev. Joel 1765-1840 "Here sleeps within this grave the body of Rev. Joel
        Drake who was born in the year of our Lord, 1765 and departed this life
        July 8, 1840."
        Sarah wife of Rev. Joel Drake born 1765; died Aug. 6, 1852
        Matilda dau of Daniel & Julia J. d. Apr. 22, 1856; age 15 yrs. 11 m. 6 da.
        John W. died July 14, 1880; ae 74 y. 5 m. 8 da.
        (Enclosed by iron fence are the following Drake graves:)
        Mary V. dau of J. W. & E. E. d. Apr. 17, 1863; age 19 y. 9 m. 12 da.
        Amanda I. dau of J. W. & E. E. d. Aug. 5, 1852; age 1 y. 7 m.
        William B. son of J. W. & E. E. d. Aug 23, 1851; age 10 y. 6m. 27 da.
        Martha J. dau of J. W. & E. E. d. Aug. 8, 1851; age 15 y 8 da.
        Isaih E. son of J. W. & E. E. d. June 7, 1849; age 13 y 5 m. 11 da.
        Elizabeth E. wife of J. W. d. Dec. 6, 1891; age 81 y. 6 m. 11 da.
        (The following poen is on the tombstone of Matilda Drake:)
        "Farewell vain world and thy delights, I'll see no more of thee. I rest
        in hope that God will show a bright World to me."
DOUGAL, Johnm d. Feb. 2, 1873; age 68 years
FRAZEE, Nancy A. dau of Dr. W. T. & R. A. d. Aug. 6, 1852; age 10 m. 25 da.
FIRES, Almond A d. Aug. 5, 1880; age 66y. 11 m. 9da.
FRYER, Sarah wife of W. d. Feb. 19, 1866; age 66 y. 5 m. 10 da.
        Thomas son of W. & S. died July 12, 1851; age 30 years
        Henry W. b. Aug. 24, 1860; d. Sept. 25, 1895
        Margaret wife of James M. died Oct. 14, 1866; age 42 y. 6 m.
GREY, W. H. d. 1870 - 187 Ohio Infantry - CIVIL WAR
GRAY, Ivy d. Oct. 2, 1859; age 72 y 2 m.
. . . . (Large stone - writing not readable)
GARNER, Ben J. d. Oct 30, 1870; age 44 y. 2 m. 13 d.
HATHAWAY, Francis M. son of E. & S. d. Sept 4, 1858; age 10 m. 28 da.
HINKINS, George S. son of J. & R. died August . . . 1851
        David son of Jacob & Rachel d. Sept 17, 1845; age 4 days
        Van Buren son of Jacob & Rachel died Mar. 4, 1841; age 7 y. 4 m. 29 da.
        John W. son of Jacob & Rachel d. Mar. 3, 1844; age 1 y. 3 m. 3 da.

HINKINS, Jacob d. Aug. 7, 1851; age 46 y. 1 m. 2 da.
      Rachel wife of Jacob d. Nov. 25, 1868; age 57 y 2 m 15 da.
. . . . .(Large stone - no marking) (Foot stone = T.B.H.)
HARNER, Lucina dau of R. & M. d. Dec. 18, 1853; age 21 y. 1 m. 20 da.
HUSTEN, Levicy - (no dates on marker - only name)
KING, Catherine wife of A. W. d. Oct. 27, 1868; age 42 y. 2 m. 27 da.
JEFFERY, Sarah wife of Francis d. Feb. 28, 1887; age 45 y. 8 m. 11 da.
MADDOX, Stephen d. April 16, 1839; age 27 y. 9 m. 19 da
MILLS, John d. Oct 6, 1846; age 56 years
      Laura A. dau of H. & M. d. Oct 31, 1864; age 7 y. 9 m.
      Mary J. dau of H. & M. d. Oct 24, 1864; age 4 y. 7 m.
McDONALD, Phebea dau of Richard & Jane B. d. Nov. 13, 1864; age 20 y 6 m. 3 da.
      Samantha dau of Richard & Jane B. d. Nov. 15, 1864; age 18 y. 6 m. 8 da.
PILCHER, Rosalie dau of J. M. M. d. Nov. 16, 1859; age 3 y. 8 m.
      (Foot markers: E.T.P. & R.E.P.)
PARIS, Lewis D. b. Aug. 20, 1796; d. Mar. 15, 1881
PIDGEON, Isaac d. Jan. 20, 1871; age 76 y. 4 m. 17 d.
      Rhoda d. May 4, 1853; age 61 years
ROBERTSON, Caroline wife of Ezra R.; died Mar. 30, 1864
SMITH, Martha I. dau of John & Margareta L. d. Jan 1848; ae 22 mos. 15 da.
      ("Now Lord we give our child to Thee. To Thee we do resign.
      We hope again to see its face and in Thy Kingdom shine.")
WILSON, James C. b. July 8, 1827 d. Apr. 20, 1886; age 58 y 9 m. 12 das.
      Andrew J. son of William & R. d. Jan 29, 1851; age 17 y 2 m. 15 da.
      William d. July 1, 1865; age 37 y. 6 m. 1 d.
      Rachel d. May 29, 1861; age 5 y. 7 m. 27 da.) daus of David & Wanda
      Margaret d. May 23, 1861; age 2 y 3 m. 8 da.)   Wilson
WEEKS, Victory E. wife of James d. Mar 29, 1866; age 29 y. 9 m. 2 da.
      Eddy son of J. & V. E. d. Sept. 14, 1866; age 6 y. 9 m.
WARWICK, Aby wife of Albert d. Apr. 6, 1863; age 19 y. 3 m. 13 da.
ZENTMEYERS, Elizabeth wife of George, Sr. d. Feb. 18, 1854; age 77 y. 3 m. 9 da.
      George d. May 20, 1836; age 66 y 8 m 7 da.
      David son of Dal died Sept 3, 1853; age 1 y 4 m 13 da.

(The following initials on markers: "T.G" "L.R." "D.K." "M.H.D." "S.J.L."
  "R.P." "J.S.H." "A.G.W.")

ALSO JUST PLAIN FIELD STONES WITH NO MARKINGS ON THEM.

"OLD FRANKLIN CEMETERY", FRANKLIN, OHIO
WARREN COUNTY

Contributed by: Lois Baker, 330 E. Main St., Versailles, Ohio 45380
and Marsha Fitzgerald.

From 1796 until 1870 early residents of Franklin and Franklin Township, Warren County were interred in the "Old Franklin" Cemetery located on Fourth Street between the Canal and the "Hill". Today this area houses the railroad line, the "new" library, and other business places. The 1875 plat map of Franklin shows the "Old Franklin" Cemetery in two sections. Shortly before 1871 a portion of the "Old Franklin" Cemetery was condemned for railroad right-of-way. These bodies were removed to a new resting place. Four removals were made from the "Old Cemetery" in 1915. After nearly half a century of controversy to abandon the "Old Cemetery" on the "Hill", the major removal of the forgotten dead was completed in the 1930's. All of these bodies have been interred in the Woodhill Cemetery at the edge of Franklin. The interment of these bodies were placed in several areas of the cemetery. Local descendants had their ancestors interred in small groups throughout the cemetery. Those whose descendants were not traced, were buried in groups situated in many sections of Woodhill Cemetery.

There is no complete listing of the bodies that were removed from the "Old Franklin" Cemetery. Nor are these removal lists recorded in the alphabetical indexes of the cemetery books. Two lists were accidently found while researching for ancestors. A notation made in one of the books that four bodies were removed from the "Old Franklin" Cemetery in 1915. Another list was found in a cemetery deed book which listed approximately 70 graves that were removed from the old cemetery and a revision which shows that the graves were renumbered. In several of the books one sexton did make his own index to burials that were not in the regular index at the beginning of the book. Unfortunately this practice was not continued.

This compiler copied the lists as found recorded in the books. Numbers and dashes were used in the book list to designate ages in years, months, and days. Other times no ages nor dates were given. The list showing the graves were first numbered in black ink and the revised list is numbered in red ink. Both numbered lists were copied as found. Beginning with 28 on the first list and as 25 on the second list, the graves are double numbered 25/28. Some numbers were left blank on the first list. On the second list the numbers do not follow in consecutive order.

Removal from Franklin Cemetery, Sept. 11, 1915:
1. Samuel Funk
2. Elias Brandon
3. William McLain
4. Bennett Raines
Bodies removed from Old Franklin Cemetery to Woodhill found on pages 3, 4, 5 of Cemetery Deed Book 2. Avenue 21-9
1. Amos Maxwell 23-3-18   Feb. 2. 1845
2. Elizabeth Rossman 73   - - July 11, 1814
3. Maud Ann Schneck 6 - 24   Aug. 14, 1834
4. Obediah Schnecl 1 4 4   Jan. 22 1841
5. Obediah Schnecl 25 11 8   June 9 1840
6. Phoebe Hudaon 48 3 12   Oct. 1 1834
7. David Schneck 47 1 3   Jan 22 1827

694

```
8.  Daniel Hankins    June 9 1791      Nov 12 1831
9.  Susannah Fox    75  1   2    May 1 1836
10. Michael Fox    77  7  17    Aug 23 1837
11. John Fox                     Mch  1816
12. Anne Fox                     June  1840
13. George Gillespie    82 - 7    Oct 14 1882
14. Jane Gillespie    76  -    -   Sept 7 1814
15. George Gillespie, Jr.    53  - -   Oct 18 1820
16. Jane Rabb        70  -  -    Aug 23 1822
17. Samuel Rabb    78  7  -     Sept 14  1829
18. John Rabb                    Feb 9 1813
19. Henry C Knipple   Jan 19 1820    Jan 31 1840
20. Louis Knipple    May 28  1789    Apr 20 1833
21. Infant Marlatt
22. Infant Marlatt  - Twins        Dec 14 1830
23. William Marlatt    -    7   1    Apr 1 1829
24. Jacob
25. Infant daughter
26.
27.
25/28  Jonathan Robbins    65  -  -  Aug 18 1824
26/29  Effie Robbins  59  -  12 Aug 31 1822
27/30  Wilhomina Mesler   1  5  9   July 23 1839
28/31  Sarah Jane Morrow    1  9  2   Feb 5 1842
29/32  Daniel H Frees    -  2  22   Jan 20 1842
30/33  Sarah Jane Baird    Sept 30 1837  · Sept 24  1840
31/34  John Lick   26  5  12    Apr 2 1831
32/35  William Barkalow   Jan 27 1791    Sept 28 1807
33/36  William Centik    1  -  27   Sept 1 1836  (Clutch)
34/37  Phoebe Centik   5  5  2   May 28 1833  (Clutch)
35/38  George Kinder   67  6  14    Nov 28 1834
36/39  Abraham Kinder   June 17 1773    Aug 2 1809
37/40  Mary C Finney   1  -  3    May 23 1844
38/41  Ann Akin   56  4  13   July 15 1850
39/42  Jos H Tipton            Sept 10 1834
40/43  Sarah Tipton   July 23 1809    July 23 1834
41/44  Helena Lanier   58  9  29    Aug 1 1847
42/45  John Cume   27  2  20   Dec 23 1832
43/46  Francis McGilliard  -  -  14    Dec 20 1837
44/47  Robert McGilliard  -  -  10 Aug 25 1843
45/48  Mary Annah McGilliard   Mch 13 1833    Aug 17 1834
46/49  William V McGilliard  -  -  17    Oct 4 1835
47/30  Daniel Hon   39  -  -    Aug 25 1813
48/51  Nancy Hilt   13  4  22    Aug 8 1842
49/52  Mary Ann Rogers   3  5  29    Dec 14 1841
50/53  Mrs Aaron Rogers (Abigail)   45 - -    June 22 1842
51/54  Aaron Rogers  57  2  18    Mch 24 1855
52/55  Columbus Parkhurst   5  -  -    Sept 4 1836
59/56  Archer Ainsworth   23  -  -    Dec 23 1825
53/57  Esther Ball   32  3  6    Apr 6 1840
54/58  Elizabeth Sansel   30  1  6    Apr 14 1838
```

695

```
55/59   Henry G. Share   -   1    3      Nov 7 1827
56/60   Simon L Share    -   2    5      Dec 27 1828
57/61   Chloe Allen    25  11    -       Mach 24 1823
  62
  63
  64
  65
60/66   Anna Francis
62/67   George L Davis     Feb 13 1818       Aug 18 1822
63/68   William McKnight    50   -   21      Sept 4 1821
66/69   Samuel B Hunter    2   3   14        April 12 1841
61/70   Margaret Hunter    17 9 21        Oct 17 1839
67/71   Louiza McKee    25   7   14       Oct 22 1810
64/72   Mellen Henry     36       July 2 1824
           & Aaron    same grave    Oct 4 1824
65/73   Elizabeth McCandles     31       Dec 6 1813
68/74   David Van Schork         Apr 22 1839
69/75   Noah Pottor    67 8 24       Oct 5 1830
70/76   William Famil    Feb 14 1784       Feb 14 1845
```

CAESARS CREEK (FRIENDS) CEMETERY
WARREN COUNTY, OHIO

The location of this cemetery is the northeast corner of Survey #2382 in Wayne Township. It is located on the "No Outlet" portion of the New Burlington Road, one-fourth mile from its intersection with the Compton Road. As is true with most Friends cemeteries, there are a number of small stones with no inscriptions. The graveyard is enclosed with a four foot stone fence. Inscriptions were taken in the summer of 1964 by Anita Short.

STEWART, Thomas d. 8-2-1885 a 72y
        Elizabeth w/o Wm. T. Stewart d. 11-21-1883 a. 21-9-3
HOLLINGSWORTH, David d. 1-9-1859 a. 53y
SLEEPER, E. - no dates
ENKINS, Cary J. d. 6-7-1859 a. 29-1-24
EASTERD, Charissa d/o C. & C. Easterd d. 9-17-1853 a 18-6-13
STEWART, G. W. d 4-2-1861 a 34y 15d
EASTERD, Nomona A. d/o N. & M. Easterd d. 10-5-1859 a 5-10-15
SPRAY, Samuel dec. 3d-20th-1836 a 77-11-27
        Mary w/o S. Spray dec. 6th mo-18th-1843 a 82y 6m
FURNAS, Solomon s/o R. & N. Furnas d. 11 of 11 mo-1833 a. 2-11-20
        John d 9 of 3 mo-1830 a. 64-7-4
        Ruth d. 21 of 9 mo-1824 a. 48y 22d
COOK, Charity dec. 13 of 11 mo-1822 a. 76-11-11
SPRAY, Martin d. 6-5-1845 a. 23-5-26
        John s/o Jesse & Eunice d. 6-18-1842 ae 2-5-24
COLLETT, Sarah R. c/o M. & R. Collet d. 12-11-1854 a 33-4-11
        Daniel Pvt. of Va. Regt - Rev. War - 2-10-1752 = 6-28-1835
SPRAY, Charles F. s/o A. & E. E. Spray d. 12d-1m-1863 a. 3m 16d
        Elizabeth w/o Amos Spray d. 14 of 3 mo-1863 a. 25-10-4
        Dinah d/o J. & M. Spray d. 5th mo. - 18th-1864 a. 20-10-29
        Rebecca w/o Jesse Spray d. 9th mo. - 8th-1871 a. 66-7-15
        Jesse d. 1st mo - 1st-1881 a. 79-10-26
COMPTON, Nancy d. 3rd mo - 9th-1876 a. 66-1-12) Same type stone as
        Phares d. 6th mo -1st-1877 a. 63-6-22)   James Spray
        Joseph 1834-1914; Ann R. 1834-1879 (ss)
        Joel T. b 6th mo - 7-1837 d. 9th mo - 15-1885
        Susannah D. w/o J. T. b. 8th mo-14-1838 d. 2nd mo-11-1889 (ss Joel T.)
MILLS, W. Elmer 1864-1935; Nannie D. C. 1867-1897
WILSON, Walter T. 1863-1946; Jennie HAINES 1866-1939; Edgar J. their son
                                   1892-1896 (all ss)
        Edgar J. s/o W. T. & J. M. Wilson d. 12-16-1896 a. 4-6-1
HAINES, Eli b. 8m-12d-1827 d. 6-18-1897 a. 69-10-6
        Emily S. w/o Eli Haines b. 2-7-1837 d 9-24-1909 a. 72-7-17 (ss Eli)
        Zimri F. 1868-1935; Ella C. 1870-1946 (ss)
HAWKINS, Nancy W. 1853-1944; Jesse 1846-1928; Jehu S. 1842-1922
McPHERSON, George W. d. 2-5-1908 a. 34-2-14
SPRAY, Jesse 1815-1891; Eunice, his wife, 1815-1895 (ss)
HAWKINS, Amos b 5-23-1813 d 7-19-1896; Massie b. 8-29-1824 d. 9-27-1891 (ss)
SPRAY, Alva G. s/o Amos & Sarah A. Spray d. 2-5-1883 a 17-4-17
HAWKINS, James b. 1-6-1841 d. 1-18-1898; Mary M., his wife, b. 9-3-1839
                                 d. 3-13-1877 (ss James)

HAWKINS, Morris J. s/o James & Mary M. d. 7-20-1872 a. 3-7-29
          Willie S. s/o James & Mary M. d. 7-6-1866 a 2y 12d
MILLS, Jonathan d. 2-24-1864 a 45-2-28
COOK, John d. 9-22-1861 a. 80-7-24
SPRAY, Mary Ann d/o J. & M. d. 9-25-1860 a. 20-2-26
MILLS, Charity d. 22 of 8mo-1860 a 40-6-1
SPRAY, John d. 6-6-1853 a 63-3-21
WALKER, Lewis d. 1-1-1844 a 24-4-20
          Dinah w/o Lewis Walker d. 5-18-1843 a. 24-2-26
SPRAY, Sarah w/o John Spray d. 7-31-1840 a 44-1-7
          Mary w/o Jesse Spray d. 5-4-1844 a. 41-1-28
COOK, Dinah d. 12 of 7m-1844 a 59-9-2
          Samuel d. 19 of 2mo-1855 a 46-11-24
MILLS, Dinah d/o J. & M. Mills d. 10 of 6m-1855 a 4-11-23
JAY, Rebecca d/o John & L. Jay d. 3 of 12m-1855 a 31-11-1
COOK, William s/o S. & K. Cook d. 30 of 3m-1858 a. 5-9-16
          Mary A. d/o J. & D. (?) Cook d. 1-18-1859 a 2-7-22
JAY, Layton d. 3 of 8m-1860 a 31-3-4
MILLS, Lizzie d/o J. & Mary Mills d. 5-28-1863 a 6-4-5
ROMINE, Emily d/o Jesse & A. Romine b. 9-20-1813 d. 10-15-1886
COMPTON, Martha b. 4-13-1852 d. 1-1-1914
HILL, Joseph H. d. 4-20-1896 a. 40-7-16
COMPTON, Jesse b. 1-12-1825 d. 4-16-1908; Esther b. 7-16-1831 d. 3-10-1919 (ss)
MENDENHALL, Hazel E. d/o Chas. & Nettie d. 12-18-1894 a. 5d
SHEPHERD, Charles R. 1859-1952; Lydia E. 1854-1933 (ss)
          Ernest 1893-1963; Cora L. 1891-19-- (ss)
PAINTER, Gladys Sprain 1896-1941
          Elva Hinshaw 1869-1946
          Joseph Henry 1865-1939
MILLS, Charles F. 1858-1922; Hannah P. 1862-1945
JOHNSON, Margaret 1845-1931
PAINTER, Joseph C. d. 9-28-1906 a 86-4-7
          Hannah S. w/o J. C. Painter d. 7-29-1892 a. 70-4-8
MILLS, Job b. 9-1-1816 d. 12-10-1902
          Lydia w/o Stephen Mills d. 12-23-1879 a 37y 7d
          Allie R. d/o Stephen & Lydia d. 7-16-1879 a 10-11-9
          Charley A. s/o Stephen & Lydia d. 9-29-1876 a. 2y 12d
COMPTON, William d. 3-6-1894 a. 65-11-5; Ruth w/o Wm. Compton d. 2-12-1882
                                        a. 73-2-13 (ss)
HAWKINS, Sarah w/o J. H. d. 3-26-1871 a 97-10-7
COMNTON, Amos s/o Wm. & D. Comnton d. 12-15-1865 a 33-3-10
COMPTON, Phebe d. 31 of 8m-1860 a 20-1-25
WILSON, Ann 1800-1867
COMPTON, Christopher d. 22 of 8m-1860 a 12-6-25
(Stone initialed "P. H.")
WILSON, Sara d/o E. & R. B. Wilson d. 23 of 9m-1853 a 5-4-9
          Spencer s/o J. & M. Wilson d. 29 of 9m-1853 a 1-2-1
COMPTON, Samuel b. 9-16-1796 d. 3-12-1861 a 64-6-26
          Ally b. 3-10-1804 d. 8-14-1884 a. 80-5-4
          Nancy b. 10-12-1828 d. 5-2-1898
          Rebecca b. 10-8-1826 d. 8-20-1902

698

COMPTON, Rhesa A. s/o Amos & Ann d. 10-20-1865 a. 1-8-13
        Mary d/o Amos & Ann d. 4-5-1874 a. 19-6-18
        Amos 1830-1880; Ann, his wife, 1830-1904 (ss)
SHEPHERD, Emma A. w/o Albert Shepherd b. 4-12-1858 d. 9-28-1885
SEXTON, Hannah 1840-1917; Sarah 1837-1927 (ss)
        Elizabeth b. 12-14-1823 d. 1-3-1833; Rebecca b. 1-14-1827 d. 12-6-1832;
        Ann b. 11-13-1829 d. 1-19-1832 (ss) Daus of John & Mary Sexton. Son:-
        Samuel, M.D. b. 12-31-1833 near Xenia,O. d. 7-11-1896 New York City.
PENN, George S. b. Bottetourte Co. Virginia; d. 12-29-1929 near Xenia, O. a 76y
COMPTON, William Foster 1823-1896; Catharine 1819-1906 (ss)
ELLIS, Indiana Lindley 1856-1924
COMPTON, J. Orville 1862-1925; Ella S. 1863-1930 (ss) Louisa J. 1864-1949
STEEDOM, Edward R. 1860 R. 1860-1929; Martha E. 1861-1932 (ss)
WILSON, Samuel 1858-1936; Ella 1861- (unengraved)
        Enos B. b. 2-27-1861 d. 10-26-1949
        John 1869-1951; Ellanora 1872-1917 (ss)
        W. Gilbert b. 8-8-1905 d. 11-3-1905
        Amos b. 3-26-1821 d. 11-29-1907; Mary w/o Amos Wilson b. 7-27-1822
                                              d. 2-17-1899 (ss)
        Enos d. 4-7-1900 a 78-4-5; Rebecca B. w/o E. Wilson d. 5-18-1879 a.60-4-4
GENETHAN, Dear Little Philip (no dates)
FARQUHAR, William Henry (no dates)
JAY, Rebecca d. 10-9-1854 a. 52-2-14
WHITSON, Jordan d. 1 of 4m-1847 a 70y 27d
        Mary w/o Jordan Whitson d. 5-6-1862 a 73y 16d
FARQUHAR, Linden son of P. & S. E. d. 8-24-1867 a. 1-4-16
        Iradel d. 8-17-1861 a. 5m 10d
(Stone underground)
WYNTER, Little Lynn d. 8-14-1872 a. 1m 8d
FARQUHAR, Willie A s/o P. & S. E. d. 10-16-1873 a. 1m 4d
COMPTON, John d. 16 of 1m-1860 a. 886 17d; Ann d. 8 of 8m-1861 a. 78-3-13
FURNAS, Robert d. 2-16-1863 a. 90-7-19
        Hannah w/o Robert Furnas d. 2-17-1864 a. 85-6-19
MILLS, Sarah W. 1836-1863; John L. s/o Henry F. & Sarah W. 1861-1863 (ss)
. . . . .(?), Matilda (no dates or surname)
FARQUHAR, Philip b. 2-16-1828 d. 2-16-1912 a. 84y; Sarah E., his wife,
        b. 7-9-1840 d. 2-11-1873 a. 32-5-3 (ss)
MORGAN, William 1816-1897; Matilda 1808-1864; Ruth J. 1827-(unengraved) (ss)
COOK, Hannah w/o Samuel Cook; d/o John & Ann COMPTON b.3-10-1814 d. 2-28-1895
                                              a. 80-11-18
COMPTON, Maria d/o John & Ann d. 11-12-1886 a. 66-10-25
COOK, Maria d/o Samuel & Hannah b. 2-1-1844 d. 4-9-1921
BALLARD, John 1808-1898; Lydia 1816-1900
MILLS, George 1834-1918; Ann P. 1837-1911 (ss)
HOWE, Charles E. 1865-1917; Jessie B. 1867-1956 (ss)
HAWKINS, Noah 1827-1905; Henry d. 8-18-1877 a. 79y; Charles d. 7-20-1858 a.28-7-14
        William s/o A. & R. Hawkins d. 1 of 10m-1857 a. (unengraved)
        Amos d. 20 of 9m-1852 a. 36-5-24
FURNAS, Rebecca d. 5 of 10m-1844 a. 77-1-24
COMPTON, John d. 9-6-1843 a. 27y 27d; Judith d. 11-9-1869 a. 33(?)y-5-9
HAWKINS, Benjamin H. d. 10-7-1852 a 44-6-6

                              699

COMPTON, Dinah d. 15th-11m-1852 a. 75-2-16
        Stephen d. 7-14-1862 a. 87-10-15
        Henry d. 11-18-1880 a. 82-1-2
CHENOWETH, Walter s/o A. W. & S. A. d. 1-6-1889 a. 1m 23d
        Hazel d/o Mr. & Mrs. Fred d. 1-7-1931 a 4y 9m
        Earl F. d. 9-6-19--(?) s/o Frances & Ethel (Painted metal)
        John W. s/o William & Mary T. b. 9-5-1859 d. 10-14-1935
        Horace 1869-1917
ROBISON, Harold 1894-1954; Mary 1900------(ss)
DAMICO, Dortha M. Ohio Captain Army Nurse Corps WWII 6-19-1918=5-18-1965
JACKSON, Ella Blanche 1887-1943; Clinton W. 1872-19-- (ss)
        Andrew 1869-1930; Zenobin, his wife, 1869-1911 (ss)
STEWART, Mathew M. 1845-1916; Edith Ellen, his wife, 1837-1902 .
SPRADLING, Wm. 1906------; Eva 1907------
SHUPERT, Wanda L. 1908------
MOON, William B. 1864-1950; Emma C. 1885-1924; Mary A. 1838-1922
        Neri 1838-1920; Eunice E. 1867-1918
        Lonnie s/o N. & M. A. Moon b. 10-11-1870 d. 4-9-1871
        Jemima d/o N. & M. A. Moon b. 9-6-1860 d. 2-27-1864
JACKSON, Infant s/o Uriah & Ann d. 2-15-1879
COMPTON, Amos d. 14 of 9m-1824 a. 54-2-5
JOHNSON, (Ch. of Robert & Sarah CRAFT Johnson): Orlistis R. d. 3-8-1849 a.9-4-11;
        Margaret d. 4-2-1849 a. 12-1-1; Robert d. 8-17-1853 a 1y 2m (end)
        Robert T. d. 10-4-1852 a 44-8-4
WALTON, Rachel d/o M. & D. d. 20 of 1m-1855 a. 2-6-2; Mary d. 22 of 1m-1855
        a. 4-6-11 (also d/o M. & D.) (ss)
MENDENHALL, William s/o J. & R. d. 16 of 4m-1853 a 53-5-21 (33y?)
WALTON, Edward T. s/o M. & D. d. 10 of 9m-1856 a. 1-4-1
        Allie d/o M. & D. Walton d. 30th-12m-1869 a. 1-6-28·
        John s/o S. & C. Walton d. 11-5-1860 a. 25-1-27
        Catharine w/o Samuel Walton d. 4-15-1864 a. 62-6-26
BOND, Susley d/o Isaac & Lydia Bond d. 3-29-1880 a 81-11-8
STANFIELD, Ruth d. 2-1-1882 a 86-9-20
CAROTHERS, Jennie F. d/o Josiah & Alice T. b. 9-26-1875 d. 1-19-1879
        Willie A. s/o Josiah & Alice T. b. 1-15-1877 d. 1-29-1879
WALTON, Anna E. d/o E. R. & A. Walton b. 9-11-1876 d. 12-20-1878
        Ruthetta d/o E. R. & A. Walton b. 4-10-1872 d. 12-26-1878
        Rebecca Catharine d/o E. R. & A. Walton b. 5-14-1874 d. 12-29-1878
MIARS, Infant d/o C. W. & Hetty Miars 9-15-1919·
COMPTON, Amos S. 1837-1904 a. 67-2-19; Catherine M. 1842-1909 a. 67-7-28 (ss)
        John d. 3-26-1895 a. 86y 26d; Rebecca w/o John d. 10-14-1895/82-7-24(ss)
WALTON, Edward R. b. 1-5-1832 d. 8-14-1906 a. 74-7-9
        Alice, his wife, b. 7-7-1836 d. 4-2-1918 a. 82-2-26 (ss)
BURNETT, Roy W. s/o F. M. & M. Burnett b. 5-28-1880 d. 7-12-1880
JAY, John d. 1-27-1884 a 85-8-28; Lydia w/o John d. 8-31-1886 a. 83-7-11
SHEPHERD, Maud d. 11-5-1889 a. 5-8-13
PARTINGTON, Eliezer 1877-1951; Flora H. 1883-19-- (ss)
STANRIELD, Wm. M. 1832-1906; Charity A., His wife, 1840 - unengraved - (ss)
        Neva 1816-1923; Evan J. 1860-1906
HARNER, (Gray stone - unreadable)
        Clement L. b. 8-15-1866; d. 5-16-1888

700

LUMPKIN, Elmer T. s/o W. H. & Amy B. d. 8-30-1893 a. 1-9-8
    Children of W. H. & A. B. Lumpkin: Mabe d. 9-25-1895 a 1-4-12
                                Wayne E. d. 1-18-1904 a. 9m 19d
MENDENHALL, Morris D. s/o Allen & Ida d. 9-6-1877 a 9m 21d
    Walter E. s/o Wm. A. & Ida A. d. 5-31-1880 a 18m 6d
    Wm. Allen s/o Wm. & Betty d. 3-6-1884 a 36-9-6
    Ida A. 1856-1927
    Ruth d/o Wm. B. d. 5-26-1886 a. 46-3-25
    Samuel s/o Wm. & Bette d. 4-7-1879 a. 42-4-7
    Mary Catharine d/o John & Eunice d. 2-15-1879 a. 10-5-17
    Anna R. d/o John & Eunice d. 2-2-1876 a 12-6-18
    Bettie w/o Wm. Mendenhall d. 3-1-1869 a. 63-4-16
WALTON, Edward d. 4-10-1867 a. 90-4-7
SPEER, Lydia M. d/o J. & M. Speer d. 21 of 7m-1857 a. 14-7-14
WALTON, Rachel w/o M. Walton d. 26 of 4m-1848 a 23-2-4
    Samuel d. 3-9-1844 a 39-11-13
    Mary w/o M. Walton d. 15 of 3m-1844 a. 28-2-20
    Rebecca w/o Edward Walton d. 11 of 9m-1842 a 67-5-1
HUFF, M. 7-20-1846
STILES, Celestia d/o I. & N. Stiles d. 3-29-1856 a. 5-9-9
REAGAN, Mary d. 3-17-1852 a. 53-8-17
STANFIELD, Massey Kennedy 1801-1873; Samuel d. 9-11-1854 a. 60-7-15
STILES, Victory d/o I. & N. Stiles d. 8-28-1855 a 11d
STANFIELD, Elizabeth d/o S. & M. d. 9-9-1856 a 16-10-9
ANDERSON, James d. 8-27-1858 a. 71-9-24
BEACH, Sarah Ellen d/o Harrison & Mary A. d. 1-1-1873 a. 23-2-15
COMPTON, Elijah 1844-1923; Adelaide 1856-1948 (ss)
BEACH, Etta Lorena d/o Harrison & Mary A. d. 6-30-1879 a 5-7-23
LOYD, Michael d. 4-3-1882 a. 68-3-10;Phebe d. 9-12-1888 a. 71-7-28 (ss)
    John W. s/o M. & P Loyd d. 1-2-1893 a 53-9-14
COMPTON, Samuel B. b. 8-18-1839 d. 12-15-1904
    Mary E., his wife, b. 3-22-1843 d. 10-31-19
BEACH, Mary A. 1825-1910; Harrison 1827-1905 (ss)
COMPTON, Anna Elle 1876-1945
    Mary A. d/o Phebe E. d. 10-8-1894 a 13-11-4
    Eli d. 12-18-1884 a 42y
    Theresa w/o Elijah Compton d. 4-15-1878 a. 32-3-6
    Seth d. 1-24-1887 a 72-6-7
    Mary w/o S. Compton d. 7-19-1863 a. 50-4-7
MILLS, John Linley s/o H. F. & S. W. Mills d. 9-10-1863 a. ---(underground)
COMPTON, Ruth d. 12-of 2m-1882 a 73-2-13
(Foot stones: "M.A.S."   "JS.")
COMPTON, Eli s/o Samuel & Phebe d. 8-17-1883 a 73-9-28
    Eunice d/o of Edward & Deborah WALTON w/o Eli Compton d.30th-9m-1879
                                a. 67-10-3
    Sarah Jane d/o E. & E. d. 28d-9-m-1862 a. 2y 9d
HAINES, (Ch. of E. & E. S. Haines): Stephen A. d. 29th-6m-1866 a 6-9-21
                        Mary E. d. 28th-6m-1866 a. 4-9-20 (ss)

NOTE: The following additional inscription from Caesar's Creek Cemetery appeared in GATEWAY TO THE
WEST, Vol. 6: No. 3 (July-Sept. 1973): Cary S. Jenkins died 3rd month, 6th day, 1859, aged 23 yrs., 10 months,
24 days.

701

Contributed by: Mrs. Gordon M. Hower, 5743 S. 99th Court, Apt. 3B, Omaha, Neb.
Note: The following inscriptions were obtained by Mrs. Hower while working on her
family history. It is not known that the inscriptions for each cemetery are complete or if there are additional inscriptions for other families which were not
taken.

Rosebud Acres Cemetery is located outside of Loveland, Ohio.
HENRY, Lucinda A. wife of J. D. Henry b 9-15-1822 d 1-18-1873 a 50y 4m 3d
    James D. 8-20-1813 - 1-22-1875 61y 5m 2d
HILL, William d 5-12-1878 a 76y 6m 6d ....friend...husband...father
    James d 6-5-1863 a 68y 4m 5d "To our parents" (note: wife's inscription
                                                                   not given)
CLINTON, Joseph d 2-13-1878 a 78y 4m 19d (note: same stone as Mattie)
    Mattie wife of Joseph Clinton d 4-10-1865 a 70y 6m, ...wife...mother
    Ellen b 2-14-1796 d 2-24-1882
    Rachael d 1-30-1846 (no age given) Elizabeth d 11-21-1858 (no age given)
    James, son of Isaac & Elizabeth Clinton, who emigrated to Ohio from Co.
        Armaugh, Ireland, 1792, b 9-24-1806 d 2-27-1890 88y 5m 3d
    Isaac - (note: stone unreadable)
    Elizabeth - (note: stone unreadable)
SIMONTON, Alonzo L. b 8-22-1845 d 7-10-1869 a 23y 10m 18d
    Infant daughter b Oct 1842 d Oct 1842 ae 1d
    Peggy b 1798 d 8-29-1845   Ellen b 1766 d 9-29-1848 ae 82y
RAMSEY, Mary E. b Jan. 1850 d Feb. 1852
GIRTON, _____ daughter of M. & S. A. d. 4-18-1855 a 13y 4m 2d
SIMONTON, Jno., Co. C, 1st Ohio Cav. (Civil War)
HILL, Elizabeth wife of Hilip Hill d 1-16-1831 a 77y 1m 10d
    Philip b 2-3-1769 d 1-10-1818 (1848?) ae 78y 11m 7d
    Amelia wife of P. W. Hill d 9-4-1854 a 25y 4m 19d
    Benjamin son of Philip & Elizabeth Hill d 2-6-1841 a 36y 10m 22d
DONIELS, Mary (note: no further record given)
Stone marked S.E.P.
HILL, Eliza wife of William Hill d 3-31-1862 (no age given)
    Julia Ann daughter of William and Eliza Hill d. 3-22-1855 (no age given)
Stone marked E.M.
HENRY, Sarah Jane daughter of James D. and Lucinda A. Henry d 11-8-1861 a 20y 2m 26d

      WAGONER ESTATE CEMETERY - WARREN COUNTY, OHIO - HAMILTON TOWNSHIP

Located close to Clermont County line near Loveland, Ohio.
GORHAM, Richmond Holmes son of Amos T. and Mary E. d 7-5-1863 ae 4y 2m 7d
DEERWERTER, John S. d 8-10-1836 ae 10m 7d
RAMSEY, Frances V. wife of H. C. (note: no fur inscription given)
HALL, William A. son of A. & M. J. d 10-19-1852 a 8m 11d
MICHAELS, Jacob b 2-4-1822 d 7-16-1873
    Sallie A. (no further inscription given)
    Sallie L. b 6-8-1868 d 10-16-1874
RADCLIFF, C. F., Co. D, 36th Ind. Inf.
Stone marked G.E.S.

DONNELL, John d 3-6-1870 a 58y 1m 21d
HALL, Alexander d 6-3-1838 ae 71y 6m 7d
  Molly wife of Alexander Hall d 9-4-1811(?) a 50y
One stone each marked: M.H. J.H. E.H.
HILL, Sacred to the memory of John Hill who died 1-6-1803 a 68
  Sacred to the memory of Elizabeth, consort of John Hill who died 9-15-1800
        a 56y

The following records were copied from records in the Clerk of Court's Office at the court house in Marietta. The heading gives the book that the record may be found in. Page on which record may be found is given in parenthesis.

Journal Common Pleas 5

3-6-1826 - William McKAY born in County Caettness, Scotland in June 1782. Sailed from Greenock on 6-15-1823 and landed in New York on 8-28-1823. Shortly after he came to Washington Co., Ohio and has resided here since. (25-26)

5-19-1826 - Richard PARKER born Skillington, Lincolnshire, Great Britain on 6-28-1790. Sailed from London on 8-7-1820 and arrived in Philadelphia on 10-7-1820. Came to Marietta in November of the same year and has resided here since. (49)

4-12-1827 - James MORRIS born in Isle of Wight on 8-15-1796, emigrated to Ohio and resided since. (129-130)

April 1828 - Patrick GARRY now of Watertown, born County of West Meath, Ireland on 6-1-1819. Sailed from port of Dublin in Ireland on board British Merchant Brig called "The Margaret" and on September 4th of same year arrived in Quebec, Lower Canada and departed to Ohio on November 4th of same year and arrived in Washington Co. where has since resided. (239)

April 1828 - Henry JOHNSTON born in County of Antrin in Ireland in middle of May 1783. Sailed from Londonderry in ship "perseverance" of New York on 5-25-1806 and landed in New York on August 1 of same year. Resided in New York and New Jersey from that time until 6-20-1816 when came to Ohio. (246)

April 1828 - James FRASER now of Warren twp., was born in County of Lanackshire in Scotland on 8-19-1803. Sailed from Greenock on the ship "Friends" of New York on 4-6-1823 and landed in New York on 6-5-1823 and left for Ohio on 6-10-1823 where has resided since. (247)

7-31-1828 - James BESWICK born Lancashire, England in 1767. Sailed from Liverpool on ship "Robert Fulton" on 8-12-1819 and arrived in New York in September of the same year after which in three or four days departed for Marietta, Washington Co. (287)

7-31-1828 - Samuel BESWICK now of Watertown twp., born Cheshire, Great Britain on 9-22-1819. Sailed from Liverpool, England on ship "Robert Fulton" and arrived in New York City in middle of September of same year and departed to Washington County. Also attested to by oath of James Beswick, father of Samuel Beswick. (28-29)

10-24-1828 - David DOW now of Salem, born in County of Perth in North Britain on 7-15-1770. On 5-20-1820 embarked for Quebeck on ship "Dow Lomond" and arrived there in seven weeks and on about 11-22-1820 arrived in Washington Co.(325

10-24-1828 - Thomas HALL now of Fearing twp., born in Lincolnshire, England in 1776. In June of 1818 sailed from Liverpool, England on board American Brig "Isabella" and arrived about September 1st of same year at Philadelphia and immediately came to Washington County where arrived in November. (327)

7-29-1829 - John SCOTT now of Salem twp., born Roxbury County in Scotland on 2-4-1807. On 7-2-1818 sailed from Leath, Scotland on board Brithis Merchantman called "British Queen" and arrived in Hallifax in middle of August the same year, then to Philadelphia on last day of September the same year and then immediately to Marietta in company with his father and family where arrived in September 1819 and has resided since. (384)

Journal Common Pleas 6

4-27-1830 - John NESBET now of Fearing twp., born County Down in Ireland on or about 1798 and is now about 32 years. Sailed from Belfast, Ireland about 5-12-1817 bound for Norfolk, Va. where arrived July 25th of same year. For last nine years has resided in Fearing twp. (12)

4-30-1830 - Thomas RIDGWAY, born Nova Scotia on 1-22-1796 and emigrated from Nova Scotia to United States about 1820 and has resided about 7 years in Union twp. (35-36)

8-2-1830 - John BRACKENRIDGE now of Watertown twp., born Argyllshire, Scotland about 7-19-1799 and sailed from Campbellstown on about 7-25-1820, landed in Philadelphia about Sept. 20 of same year and from 10-4-1820 has resided in Ohio. (51)

8-2-1830 - Hugh BRACKENRIDGE now of Watertown twp., born Argylshire, Scotland on 7-19-1799 and sailed from Campbellstown about 7-25-1820, landed Philadelphia September 20th of same year and has resided in Ohio since 10-4-1820. (51)

8-3-1830 - John LEEDHAM now of Fearing twp., born County of Lincoln in Great Britain on 9-7-1790 and is now 40 years old. Sailed from Liverpool, England on 6-6-1818 and landed Philadelphia, Pa. on August 2nd of same year and came immediately to Washington Co. (55)

5-17-1831 - Hugh WILCOX now of Salem twp., born County Down, Ireland in 1797 and is now 34 years old. Sailed from Belfast, Ireland and landed in Quebec, Canada and then came to Black Rock, New York on 8-2-1818 and has lived the last eleven years in Washington Co. (146)

5-17-1831 - William SCOTT, born in Scotland in the County of Roxburgh, Parish of Morebattle in 1776 where he resided until 7-2-1818 when he and family sailed from Leith aboard merchant vessel "The British Queen" arriving in Hallifax on August 26 of same year and then took passage on the brig "Elizabeth" for Philadelphia where arrived September 29th and in September of 1819 came to Fearing twp. and in April of 1821 moved to Salem twp. (147)

705

5-17-1831 - Hugh WILCOX now of Salem twp., born in County Down, Ireland in 1758 and is now 73 years old. Sailed from Belfast, Ireland and landed in Quebeck, Canada, then came to Black Rock, New York in 1818 and has lived the last eleven years in Washington Co. (148-149)

8-16-1831 - James BELL now of Salem twp., born in Scotland in 1779, sailed from Leith on board ship "Delmarnock on 3-28-1818 and arrived in New York on May 22nd following and came directly to Ohio and Washington County and has resided here since. Now 51 years of age. (200-201)

8-17-1831 - Thomas MORRIS, now of Aurelius twp., born in County Lancashire, Great Britain on 4-25-1799 and is now 32 years old. Sailed from Liverpool, Great Britain on board the American Merchant Ship "Jefferson" on 5-20-1830 bound to Baltimore where arrived July 8th of same year and in a few days came to the Western Country and on December 25th last past together with his wife, Jane Morris who also emigrated with him, she now being 31 years of age and four children viz.--Andrew Morris aged 8 years, Margaret Morris aged about 6 years, John Morris aged 4 years and Jane Morris aged 2 years arrived at Aurelius in this county where he now resides. (207-208)

8-11-1831 - Dennis RYAN now of Watertown twp., born in County of Westmeath, Ireland on 12-20-1795 and is now 36 years old. On 5-30-1821 sailed from Dublin on British Merchant Ship "William" and arrived at Quebec on July 18th of same year, then removed to United States. (211)

10-27-1832 - William Fleming, born Argyle, Scotland 9-16-1782. Sailed from port of Cambleton, Scotland in ship "Telegraph" on 8-25-1821 and arrived in Philadelphia on Sept. 19th following, then to Warren twp., Washington County. Now 50 years of age (365)

10-27-1832 - James HARVEY, born County Argyle, Scotland in 1789 and is now 43 years old. Sailed from Cambletown, Scotland on 5-7-1817 for Philadelphia and arrived sometime in August of the same year. For the last fifteen years has lived in Wesley and Warren twp., Washington Co. (366)

5-24-1833 - Hans BREDAHL born in Oderise, Denmark on 7-26-1801. Sailed from Elsinore on 11-17-1825 and landed in Portsmouth, New Hampshire on 9-10-1826, having been in meantime cast away, then went to New York where resided until June of 1832 when came to Marietta on July 9th. (396)

5-24-1833 - Clef NEALSON otherwise known as Oliver NELSON, born in Edinburgh, Sweden on 2-22-1798. Sailed from Stockholm on 8-14-1831 and landed in New York on October 8th of same year. Resided in New York until March of 1832 and then to Marietta. (397)

5-24-1833 - Christian Frederick SIVERTSON, born in Copenhagen, Denmark on 2-20-1809. Sailed from Elsineur on 9-16-1831 and landed in New York on 1-10-1832 where resided until June 1832 when came to Washington Co. (399)

5-25-1833 - Owens MARTIN now of town of Warren, born 6-11-1810 in County of
Monaghon, Ireland. On May 25 (1831) shipped from Liverpool, England for Norfolk,
Virginia and arrived 6-30-(1831). Arrived 8-8-1831 in Marietta. (411)

WASHINGTON COUNTY, OHIO - DIVORCES 1800-1811

The following records were taken from "Record of Common Pleas 1" as found in
the Clerk of Court's Office at the court house at Marietta. Page on which
record may be found in original book is given in parenthesis.

5-5-18-5 - John DROWN vs. Nancy DROWN. Divorce. John married 5-29-1794 at
Marietta to Nancy Duval. That Nancy eloped from petitioner with Chester Howe.
Nancy is to have custody of two daughters, Delilah and Drusilla Drown. John
is to have custody of children Benjamin Drown, Notley Drown and John Drown Jr.(197)

Sept. 1800 - Esther GRAHAM vs. John GRAHAM. Petition for Divorce. Married in
1784. John is late of Athens Co., Ohio and he left petitioner about four years
ago. Esther to have custody of children (not named). (200)

Oct. 1808 - John CHEADLE vs. N. CHEADLE. Petition for Divorce. John Cheadle
now of Roxbury twp. married in 1793 to Naomah White then both of Barnard, Windsor
Co., Vermont. John had five children by Naomah of which five are now living:
Electa, Parmela, John, Arial and Gilman, the youngest being now 15 months old.
Naomah received personal property as alimony. (288)

Oct. 1809 - Mary WALKER vs John WALKER. Petition for Divorce. Filed 6-20-1809.
Mary married 1-20-1805 to John Walker alias John Wilson. John deswerted petitioner
and was last known to be in New Orleans. (359)

July 1811 - John TAYLOR vs Mary M. TAYLOR. Petition for Divorce. Filed
6-21-1810. John, a waggoner, married 5-10-1806 to Mary M. Harrison. Mary is
now of Marietta and she is to have custody of child (not named) born after her
marriage to John. (432)

July 1811 - John VINCENT vs. Rachel VINCENT. Petition for Divorce. Case
dismissed. (461)

July 1811 - Horace WOLCOTT vs. Lucy WOLCOTT. Petition for Divorce. Filed
3-25-1811. Horace now a resident of Licking Co., Ohio married 3-22-1788 to
Lucy Smith in Sandesfield, Berkshire Co., Miss. They came to the Northwest
Territory now Ohio in 1797 and Lucy is now a resident of Washington Co. (475)

July 1811 - Theophilus H. POWERS vs. Charlotte POWERS. Petition for Divorce.
Filed 11-29-1810. Theophilus married in the middle of May 1801 to Charlotte
Devol. (477)

The following death records include persons 40 years of age and over only. The records were taken from Death Record 1. Page on which record may be found is given in parenthesis. Abbreviations used:- d=died; a=age; m=married; w=widow or widower; s= single; pd=place of death; pb=place of birth; residence is same as place of death unless stated otherwise.

PALMER, David - d 3-22-1867; a. 89y 6m 11d; pd Adams twp.; pb New Jersey. (2)

WARD Mahala S. - d 8-2-1867; a. 50y 25d; pd Muskingum twp.; pb Lawrence Co., Ohio; parents, Peter Wakefield and Keziah Wakefield. (2)

ROSS, Gray - d 8-21-1867; a 59y 8m 3d; pd Newport twp.; pb Scotland; parents, _____ Ross and Mary Ross. (2)

HAYWARD, Wm. G. - d 8-26-1867; a 44y 8m 26; pd Waterford; pb Waterford; parents, Ed T.Hayward and Charlotte Hayward. (2)

SNIDER, Margaret - d 7-16-1867; w; a 57y 2m 14d; pd Marietta; pd Germany. (2)

OTIS, Anna - d 7-16-1867; w; a 85y 4m; pd Marietta; pb England. (2)

BRIGHAM, Asa - d 7-31-1867; s; a ;60y 4m ; pd Marietta; pb Germany. (2)

HAMBLETON, Samuel N. - d 7-5-1867; m; a 45y 4m 1d; pd Lower Salem, O.; pd Noble Co.; parents. Wm. Hambleton and Martha Hambleton. (2)

BAKER, John George - d 8-14-;857; w; a 79y 11d; pd Newport twp.; pb Germany. (2)

MILLER, Theobald - d 9-4-1867; w; a 73y 6m 7d; pd Fearing twp.; pb Germany. (4)

MILLER, Elizabeth - d 9-26-1867; m; a 50y 3m 24d; pd Newport twp.; pb Germany. (4)

BELL, Christian - d 9-12-1867; w; a 74y 9m; pd Grandview twp.; pb Ireland. (4)

CREW, William - d 7--29-1867; w; a 60y; pd Wesley twp.; pd N.C.; parents, Jacob Crew and Rachel Crew. (4)

CONGLETON, David - d 8-21-1867; m; a 65y; pd Liberty twp.; pb Belmont Co., Ohio; parents, William Congleton and Jane Congleton. (4)

BALTZ, Daniel - d 9-18-1867; m; a 71y; pd Aurelius twp.; pb Germany; parents, Adam Baltz and Margretha Klee. (4)

BECKER, Philippina - d 7-4-1867; m; a 48y; pd Salem twp.; pb Germany; parents, Theobald Becker and Katharina Morganstin. (4)

SANFORD, Mary - d 9-30-1867; a 77y; pd Marietta twp.; pb England. (4)

PLAFF, Margaret - d 1-27-1868; m; a 58y; pd Fearing twp.; pb Germany; parents, Peter Plaff and Margaret Wagner. (4)

McFARLAND, Elizabeth Bradley - d 10-22-1867; w; a 85y 4m 13d; pd Marietta; pb Mass.(4)

HART, Benjamin - d 12-24-1867; a 56y; pd Watertown twp.; pb New Cortland. (4)

WOOLFORD, John - d 11-28-1867; m; a 76y; pd Washington Co.; pb Belmont Co.; residence Adams twp.; parents, Adam Woolford and Margaret Woolford. (6)

HART, Benjamin - d 12-24-1867; m; a. 86y; pd Newport; pb ----. (6)

FORREST, Gilbert - d 10-13-1867; w; a 86y 9m 13d; pd Marietta; pb Baltimore Co., Md; parents, John Forrest and Rachel Forrest. (6)

JETT, Owen - d 10-17-1867; m; a 73y 1m 20d; pd Marietta; pb Faquier Co., Va.; parents, Thomas Jett and Lucina Jett. (6)

MOORE, Elsie - d. 11-5-1867; m; a 62y; pd Harmar; pd Wood Co., W.Va.; parents, Geo. Whiting and Lucy Whiting. (6)

SULIVAN, Charles - d 11-24-1867; w; a 73y 3m; pd Marietta; pb Frankfort, Pa. (6)

WARREN, Nancy - d 10-7-1867; m; a 47y pd Franklin, O.; pb Maryland; residence, Franklin Co., Ohio. (6)

FORREST, Gabriel - d 10-12-1867; m; a 87y; pd Marietta; pb Maryland. (6)

HARING, Dr. Joseph C. - d 10-13-1867; m; a 45y; pd Marietta; pb Germany. (6)

CRAM, Sarah A. - d 11-3-1867; w; a 53y; pd Marietta; pb Zanwacillw, O. (6)

WISEMAN, John - d 11-13-1867; m; a 80y; pd Marietta; pb Germany. (6)

KUNZ, Margreth - d. 5-25-1868; m; a 50y 5m; pd Marietta; pb Germany; parents, Christian Fish and Elizabeth Fish. (6)

PLUMMER, Fannie - d 3-12-1868; a 72y; pd Marietta; pb -----. (6)

EIDMULLET, Dorothea Margaretha - d 3-4-1868; m; a 62y; pd Liberty twp.; pb Germany; parents, Peter Bidemuller and Elizabeth Rockilhaub. (8)

BECK, Adam - d 6-21--1868; w; a 80y 7m 19d; pd Salem twp., pb Germany; parents, Adam Beck and Maria Wagner. (8)

HENEMAN, George - d 3-27-1868; a 67y 1m 25d; pd Marietta; pb -----. (8)

HOUKIMER, Eleanor; d 6-2-1868; m; a 58y 3m; pd Marietta; pb Connecticut. (8)

TAYLOR, Eliza - d 6-10-1868; a 55y 8m 27d; pd Marietta; pb Washington Co. (8)

LOVELL, Harriet - d 6-9-1868; m; a 50y; pd Zanesville; pb Marietta. (8)

HILDRETH, Rhoda C. - d 6-21-1868; w; a 82y 10m; pd Marietta; pb Mass. (8)

FERNLEY, Hannah - d 4-2-1868; m; a 75y; pd Marietta; pb Baltimore. (8)

SMITH, John - d 4-7-1868; m; a 74y; pd Marietta; pb Washington Co. (8)

ABEUSCHEON, Jacob Sr. - d 4-15-1868; m; a 66y 8m 9d; pd Marietta; pb Germany. (8)

TREVOR, Maria - d 5-3-1868; m; a 55y; pd Marietta; pb Marietta; father, Joseph Holden. (10)

ANDERSON, John - d 2-25-2868; s; a 64y 3m; pd Marietta; pb Marietta. (10)

SKINNER, Adaline - d 3-7-1868; m; a 42y 1m 11d; pd Harmar; pb Waterford twp. (10)

THEIS, Jacob Sr. - d. 3-10-1868; m; a 59y 7m 18d; pd Marietta; pb Germanyy. (10)

ABENSHEN, Frederick - d 3-11-1868; m; a 64y 11m; pd Marietta; pb Germany. (10)

HEATH, Bridget - d 3-10-1868; w; a 59y; pd Union twp.; pb Ireland. (10)

COLLINS, Anna Bell - d 4-16-1868; m; a 82y; pd Fearing twp. pb Ireland. (10)

CUNNINGHAM, Simon - d 4-21-1868; w; a 77y; pd Aurelius twp.; pb Maine. (10)

RUMMES(?), Sarah - d 7-29-1867; w; a 68y; pd Washington Co.; pb N.Y. State; Residence, Adams twp.; father, _____ Tillotson. (10)

KIGER, George - d 9-3-1867; m; a 48y; pd Aurelius twp.; pb -------. (10)

PRICE, Susannah - d 2-10-1868; w; a 75y; pd Noble Co.; pb -----. (10)

BRENAN, Hugh - d 6-29-1868; m; a 70y; pd Marietta; pb Ireland. (10)

HOFFMAN, Jacob M. - d 6-2-1868; m; a 72y; pd Union twp; pb Ohio. (10)

DETAMBEL, Elizabeth - d 4-24-1868; m; a 72y; pd Watertown; pb Germany. (10)

LOVEL, Harriet - d 1-8-1868; m; a 42y 11m 21d; pd Zanesville; pb Washington Co. (10)

BARTH, Katharine - d 9-1-1868 w; a 79y; pd Fearing twp.; pb Germany; parents, Theobald Barth and Elizabeth Drumm. (12)

WELDENKEN, Catharine - d 7-26-1868; m; a 55y; pd Marietta; pb Germany. (12)

SEILER, Ann Maria - d 11-11-1868; w; a 76y; pd Union; pb Wurtemburg. (12)

FINKEL, Peter - d 10-29-1868; m; a 68y; pd Union; pb Germany. (12)

SHIPMAN, Maria B. - d 7-15-1868; m; a 42y; pd Marietta; pb Marietta. (12)

SCHNEPF, Louisa - d 9020-2868; m; a 44y; pd Marietta; pb Marietta. (12)

FIELD, Richard - d 11-30-1868; m; a 45y; pd Marietta; pb England. (12)

HENNAMON, Henry - d 12-30-1868; a 79y; pd Salem twp.; pb Germany. (12)

RUCH (RRECH), Salome - d 12-30-1868; m; 55y; pd Liberty twp.; pb Germany; father, George Ruch. (14)

YOUNG, Jacob - d 9-30-1868; w; a 67y 5m 4d; pd Lawrence; pb Germany; parents, Jacob Young and Elis. Hinkelman. (14)

ALICHT, Regina Charlotte - d 10-10-1868; w; a 93y 5m 8d; pd Fearing; pb Germany; parents, Casper Alicht and Eva Weingard. (14)

CLOS, Peter - d 12-9-1868; m; a 53y 10m; pd Newport; pb Germany; parents, Adam Clos and Katharine Becker. (14)

THURLOW, Silas - d 11-4-1868; s; a 45y; pd Huntsville, Ala; pb Marietta; residence, Marietta. (14)

709

BUELL, Susan W. - d 11-14-1868; s; a 43y 7m 28d; pd Marietta; pb Marietta. (14)
LOVENZ, Henry - d 1-4w-1869; m; a 85y; pd Marietta; pb Bavaria. (12)
LANG, Nicholas - d 1-15-1869; m; a 63y; pd Union; pb Germany. (12)
HOPP, John - d 1-15-1869; a 78y; pd Muskingum twp.; pb Germany. (12)
SEILER, Maria Kath. - d 2-13-1869; a 77y; pd Fearing; pb Germany. (12)
YOUNG, Margaret - d 2-3-1869; m; a 66y; pd Liberty twp.; pb Germany. (14)
GEILDING, John - d 2-6-1869; w; a 63y; pd Decatur twp.; pb England; parents,
    John Giddings and Hannah _____. (14)
DUFUR, Abel - d 5-2-1869; m; a 66y; pd Decatur; pb N.Y. State; parents, Daniel Defur
    and Sarah _____. (14)
DECKER, Jacob - d 3-31-1869; m; a 40y; pd Marietta; pb Germany. (14)
WILKING, Daniel - d 7-2-1869; w; a 88y; pd Muskingum; pb Germany. (14)
DOURSON, Thomas - d 4-2-1869; m; a 60y; pd ----; pb Allegheny Co., Pa.; residence,
    Salem twp.; parents, Thomas Dourson and Mary ____. (14)
SCHRAMM, Michael - d 4-12-1869; w; a - near 53; pd Fearing; pb Germany; parents,
    Jacob Schramm and Katharine Laur. (14)
ZIMMER, Johannes - d 4-15-1869; m; a 67y 26d; pd Fearing pb Germany; parents,
    Johannes : Zimmer and Barbara Hollinger. (14)
KLEIN, Jacob - d 5-16-1869; m; a - near 53; pd Marietta twp.; pb Germany; parents,
    Jacob Klein and Margaretha Nun. (14)
FABER, John - d 1-1-1869; m; a 43y; pd Marietta; pb Germany. (14)
LAURENCE, Henry - d 1-5-1869; m; a 85y 26d; pd Marietta; pb Germany. (14)
TIBBITTS, Horace - d 1-17-1869; m; a 46y; pd Marietta; pb Mass. (14)
DETERLY, Mary - d 1-27-1869; w; a 80y 7m; pd Marietta; pb Va. (16)
SEEMAN, Anna M. - d 1-27-1869; m; a 46y 3m 4d; pd Marietta; pb Germany. (16)
TEISCHER, Henry - d 2-27-2869; m; a 61y 2m; pd Marietta; pb Germany. (16)
LANG, David - d 4-7-1869; m; a 41y; pd Marietta; pb Germany. (16)
HUFF, Eli- d 4-12-1869; m; a 52y; pd Marietta; pb Marietta. (16)
CRANDLE, Zedakiah - d 4-16-1869; m; a 98y; pd Marietta; pb-----. (16)
BONNEY, Elizabeth B. - d 4 18-1869; w; a 76y; pd Marietta; pb Pa. (16)
CHESS, James - d 6-1-1869; m; Aa 59y; pd Marietta; pb Marietta. (16)
BOSWORTH, Daniel P. - d 6-9-1869; m; a 68y; pd Marietta; pb Mass. (16)
TAYLOR, Elizabeth - d 6-14-1869; m; a 80y; pd Marietta twp.; pb-----. (16)
GOLDSMITH, James - d 6-15-1869; m; a 51y; pd Marietta; pb ------. (16)
STRATTON, Raymond - d 6-24-2869; m; a 58y; pd Harmer; pb --------. (16)
PLAFF, Peter - d 1-7-1869; w; a 74y; pd Fearing; pb Germany; parents, JacobPfaff
    and Katharine Muller. (18)
CHANDLER, Anna - d 7-7-1869; w; a 73y; pd Lowell, O.; pb West Chester, Pa. (18)
DAVIDSON, William - d 8-27-2869; m; a 73y; pd Aurelius twp.; pb England. (18)
KILE, John - d 8-14-1869; m; a 75y 2m 17d; pd Aurelius twp.; pb Va. (18)
SMITHSON, Rebecca - d 8-2-1869; w; a 89y 11m; pd Aurelius twp.; pb England. (18)
HENRY, John B. - d 11-12-1869; m; a 44y 2m 24d; pd Barlow twp.; pb Barlow twp. (28)
WHITFIELD, Ann - d 4-2-1869; m; a 60y; pd Bar low twp.; pb Va. (18)
CONKRIGHT, Sarah - d 5-5-1869; w; a 84y 1m 24d; pd Barlow twp.; pd Connecticut. (18)
FERNAL, Noah - d 12-22-1869; w; a 85y 10m 27d; pd Belpre; pb Maaine. (20)
TILTON, Phebe - d 11-20-1869; m; a 44y 8m 17d; pd Dunham twp.; pb unknown. (20)
STEVENS, George W. - d 9-8-1869; m; a 44y 11m 20d; pd Fairfield; pb Belpre. (20)
STOCKDALE, Thomas - d 1-12-1869; m; a 53y 11m 27d; pd Fairfield; pb ------- . (20)
SCOTT, John - d 12-26-1869; w; a 72y 1m 9d; pd Liberty twp.; pb New York; parents,
    Charles Scott and Mary _____. (20)
McAFEE, Nancy M. - d 8-4-1869; a 43y 8m 26; pd Liberty twp.; pb Guernsey Co.;
    parents, Joseph Masters and Sarah _____. (20)

710

BINEGAR, John - d 5-6-1869; m; a 44y; pd Liberty twp.; pb West Va.; father, Jonathan Benegar.   (20)
GERBER, Daniel - d 10-2-1869; w; a 77y 6m 19d; pd Fearing twp.; pb Germany.   (20)
ZUMBRO, Frans - d 10-1-1869; m; a 64y 4m 26d; pd Fearing twp.; pb Germany.   (20)
SPINDLER, Peter - d 10-18-1869; m; a 62y 5m 3d; pd Fearing twp.; pb Germany; parents, Peter Spindler and Magdalena Molter.   (20)
LAFABRE, Katharina - d 7-17-1869; s; a 48y 7m 5d; pd Fearing twp.; pb Fearing twp.; father, Leonhard Lafaber.   (20)
SCHRAMM, Michael - d 4-12-1869; w; a 64y 2m 2d; pd Fearing twp.; pb Germany: parents, Jacob Schramm and Katharina Lauren.   (20)
GRIMES, Lemuel - d 10-19-1869; m; a 586 10m 25d; pd Fearing twp.; pb Bellmont Co.(22)
SEEVERS, Anna - d 6-17-1869; w; a 65y 4m 23d; pd Fearing twp.; pb Bishber Co. Pa.(22)
ZIMMER, Johannes - d 4-15-1869; m; a 67y 26d; pd Fearing twp.; pb Germany; parents, Joannes Zimmer and Barbara Hollinger.   (22)
BAKER, Peter - d Dec. 1869; m; a 84y; pd Fearing twp.; pd Germany.   (22)
NEAN (NEAU), John - d 6-4-1869; m; a 70y 6m; pd Grandview twp.; pb Germany.   (22)
ROACH, Elizabeth - d 11-7-1869; w; a 83y; pd Grandview twp.; pb Germany.   (22)
BROWN, Sarah E. - d 11-13-1869; m; a 58y 1d; pd Grandview twp.; pb Hampshire Co. Va.   (22)
DUFER, Abel - d 5-2-1869; m; a 66y 7m 23d; pd Decatur twp.; pb New York.   (22)
GIDDINGS, John - d 2-6-1869; w; a 53y 1m 6d; pd Decatur twp.; pb England.   (22)
NELSON, Richard - d 7-28-1869; m; a 41y 6m 16d; pd Decatur twp.; pb Washington Co. O.   (22)
PLACE, Sarah - d 11-22-1869; w; a 76y 5m 18d; pd Decatur twp.; pb Va.   (22)
CARR, Lucinda - d 1-15-1869; w; a 80y; pd Decatur twp.; pb Va.   (22)
POWELL, Burk - d 3-15-1869; m; a 48y; pd Lawrence; pb -------.   (24)
TREADWAY, Mary - d 8-24-1869; m; a 61y 3m; pd Lawrence; pb Fearing.   (24)
GRAHAM, Amy - d 7-14-1869; w; a 63y 1m 13d; pd Lawrence; pb New Jersey.   (24)
BARNETT, Mary Ann - d 11-12-1869; m; a 47y; pd Lawrence; pb Guernsey Co. O.   (24)
HUNTSMAN, Mark E. - d 12-15-1869; m; a 54y; pd Lawrence; pb Belmont Co.   (24)
CLINE, Jacob - d 5-16-12869; m; a 53y; pd Marietta; pb Germany.   (24)
MILLER, Rachel - d Sept. 1869; w; a 75y; pd Marietta; pb Marietta.   (24)
DECKER, John - d 9-28-1869; m; a 78y 1m 12d; pd Muskingum; pb Germany.   (24)
WILKING, Daniel - d 7-2-1869; w; a 89y 2m; pd Muskingum; pb Germany.   (24)
KIGGINS, Lydia B. - d. 10-28-1869; w; a 69y 5m 14d; pd Newport twp.; pv Ohio Co., Va. (26)
BRECKENRIDGE, Martha - d 3-11-1869; w; a 63y; pd Palmer twp.; pb Scotland.   (26)
GUY, Cyrus - 10-24-1869; m; a 49y; pd Palmer twp; pb Columbiana Co., O.   (26)
FARRELL, Mary - d 11-28-1869; m; a 56y; pd Union twp.; pb Ireland.   (26)
McCULOUGH, Mary - d 6-8-1869; m; a 57y; pd Union twp.; pb Ireland.   (26)
ANDERSON, John H. - d 9-2-1869; s; a 79y 5m 3d; pd Warren twp.; pb Pa.   (26)
FRENCH, Isaac - d 4-25-1869; m; a 77y 20d; pd Warren two.; pb Pa.   (26)
FRENCH, Joseph - d 5-25-1869; a 75y; pd Warren twp.; pb Pa.   (26)
BOOTHBY, Robert - d 9-25-1869; m; a 87y 7m; pd Warren twp.; pb England.   (26)
TURNER, David - d 12-29-1869; m; a 45y; pd Warren twp.; pb Scotland.   (26)
DYE, Mrs. Samuel - d 12-4-1869; m; a 60y 3m 10d; pd Warren twp.; pb Ohio.   (26)
CORY, Charles S. - d 6-17-1869; a 77y 6m 20d; pd Waterford twp.; pb Waterford twp.   (28)
FISHER, Joshua - d 7-16-1868; m; a 61y; pd ---; pd ---; res. Waterford twp.   (28)
DODGE, P. O. - d 3-16-1869; m; a 44y 6m; pd Waterford twp.; pb Waterford twp.   (28)
LAURENCE, D.C. - 3-1-1869; m; a 70y; pd Waterford twp.; pb ---.   (28)
BUDY, Walter - d 8-31-1869; m; a 60y 8m; pd Waterford twp.; pb ----.   (28)

711

BEISH, Charles - d 3-17-1869; m; a 52y 3m 10d; pd Waterford twp.; pb---. (28)
POWERS, Polly - d 4-20-1869; a 75y; pd Waterford twp.; pb ------. (28)
ARNOLD, Jos. - d 8-21-1868; w; a 89y 4m 4d; pd Watertown twp.; pb Providence,R.I.(28)
JENKINS, Nancy - d 4-9-1869; s; a. (over 40); pd Watertown twp; pb Watertown. (28)
HUHL, Louisa - d 8-17-1869; m; a 48y; pd Wesley twp.; pb Westmoreland Co. Pa. (28)
STRANEL, Elmer - d Mar. 1869; s; a 56y; pd Wesley; pb Morgan Co. (30)
SKIPTON, William - d 12-23-1869; w; 83y 1m 14d; pd Harmar; pb Pa. (30)
STRATTON, Raymond - d 7-10-1869; m; a 58y 5m; pd Harmar; pb Ring. N.H. (30)
GOLDSMITH, James J. - d 6-13-1869; m; a 52y 5m 11d; pd Marietta 1st ward; pb Fearing (30)
BOSWORTH, Daniel P. - 6-9-1869; m; a 68y; pd Marietta 1st ward; pb Halifax, Mass.(30)
GUITTEAN, Annie I. - d 11-22-1869; s; a 77y 2m 7d; pd Marietta 1st Ward; pb Litchfield, Ct. (30)
MAXWELL, Mary D. - d 12-19-1869; w; a 58y 3m 4d; pd Marietta 1st Ward; pb near Brunswick, N.J. (30)
WOODBRIDGE, Maria M. - d 12-5-1869; w; a 82y 4m 2d; pd Marietta 1st Ward; pb Princetown, N.Y. (30)
BONNEY, Elizabeth - d 4-18-1869; w; a 73y 8m 10d; pd Marietta 1st Ward; pb Ithaca, N.Y. (30)
KEUCK, Matilda Jane - d 11-29-1869; m; a 40y 7m 7d; pd Marietta 3rd Ward; pb---(30)
SOYEZ, Louis - d 9-9-1869; m; a 73y; pd Marietta 3rd Ward; pb France. (30)
CRANDLE, Zederick - d 4-16-1869; m; a 98y 3m 16d; pd Marietta 3rd Ward; pb N.Y.(32)
LANG, David - d 4-7-1869; m; a 41y 5d; pd Marietta 3rd Ward; pb Germany; parents, Daniel Lang and Catharine Lang. (32)
BROOKOVER, Sarah - d 7-14-1869; m; a 77y 4m 2d; pd Independence; pb Pa. (32)
SIPPEL, Elizabeth - d 6-9-1869; m; a 64y 4m 15d; pd Independence; pb Germany. (32)
YOST, Anna C. - d 9-24-1869; m; a 69y 7m 28d; pd Independence; pb Germany. (32)

Washington County, Ohio was one of the four original counties of the Northwest
Territory.

ALLEN, Justus to Polly DEVOL of Waterford	6-23-1791
AMLIN, James to Nancy CAMPBELL	1-2-1798
BAILEY, Caleb to Anne JAMES - both of Belleprie	7-24-1791
BAKER, Benjamin to Sarah NEWTON	9-1-1791
BAKER, Samuel Jr. of Waterford to Margaret KELLY of Marietta	12-16-1795
BARNS, Samuel to Cynthia GOODALE - both of Belleprie	8-22-1793
BEAUDEAU (BANDEAU), Francis to Jeannette DEMIER	
both of Gallipolis	9-9-1791
BEAUDOT, Jean to Marqueritte MARGARET - both of Gallipolis	3-4-1794
BERNARD, Michael to Mary Magdelaine CHANDEVERT	
both of Marietta	5-20-1797
BIDDLE, Ben: to Abigail CONIUS	9-26-1791
BLAKE, Simeon to Lavina PECK	12-14-1797
BLIU, Francoise to Francis DAVOUS - both of Gallipolis	11-8-1795
BROWNING, William to Abigail PUTNAM - both of Marietta	4-10-1791
BUFFINGTON, William to Sarah HUGHES	12-25-1798
BURHAM, William to Christian OLIVER	8-27-1789
CASEY, Wanton to Elizabeth GOODAH - both of Marietta	10-25-1789
CHANDIVERT, Stephen to Madalane BRUNIER	2-15-1796
CHEZEAU, Auguste to Jeanne Francois DUSAILLE	
both of Gallipolis	3-27-1794
CLARK, John to Lorena SHEPARD	10-19-1798
COBERN, Phinehas to Patience OLNEY - both of Waterford	7-18-1796
COLVIN, Sam'l to Sarah DALY - both of Belleprie	5-10-1797
CONVERSE, James to Lois OLNEY - both of Waterford	10-18-1795
COREY, Thomas to Nancy WELLES	2-17-1791
COURTNEY, Neal to Polly McLEAN(E)	11-22-1796
CRAIGG, Joel to Betsey PUTNAM	12-7-1797
CUSHING, Samuel to Batheheba DEVOL - both of Waterford	2-5-1794
DANA, Benjamin to Sally SHAW	4-17-1798
DATHE, Charles Francis to Jean CADDOT - Gallipolis	12-9-1796
DAVIS, Daniel to Drusilla OLNEY	1-7-1795
DELANO, Cornelius to Sarah GOODALE - both of Bellepre	8-8-1792
DeLARGUILLON, Francis to Hannah HARRIS	
both of Gallipolis	7-10-1796
DENNY, John to Sally BOOTHBY - both of Marietta	7-3-1796
DEVOL, Gilbert to Mary COBERN	3-25-1790
DEVOL, Jonathan to Clarissa SHERMAN - both of Waterford	11-11-1794
D.NACHT, Joseph Winon to Jean PARMONTIER - Gallipolis	4-7-1797
DOUDE, Andrew to Abigail CARR	4-19-1791
BROWN, John to Nancy DEVOL - both of Marietta	5-29-1794
DUNHAM, Daniel to Keziah SEVETH (SWETH)	3-23-1797
DWELLERS (DEVELLERS), Jules Amane to Elisabeth BEUZELIN	
widow of John WONUTERN(?) - both of Gallipolis	6-6-1792
ELENWOOD, Daniel to Fanny INGALS	3-18-1798
EVELAND, Frederick to Nancy LEE	3-16-1797
FEARING, Paul Esq. of Marietta to Cynthia ROUSE of Belleprie	11-28-1795
FLETCHER, Joseph to Catherine WARTH - both of Marietta	8-29-1793

FORD, Phenas of Marietta to Mary BENJAMIN of Harrison Co. Va. 4-5-1798
FLORD, William to Sarah FORD - both of Waterford   11-26-1798
FULLER, Joseph to Susanna STACY   4-13-1796
FURING (FEERING), Noah to Rebecca RHEA   9-14-1790
GARDINER, John to Margaret Letete ROBINSON both ofGallipolis 2-14-1794
GRIFFING, Ebenezer to Grace ROBERTS - both of Belleville   6-19-1797
GUTHRIE, Trueman to Elizabeth STONE   7-21-1796
HALL, George to Mary JACKSON - both of Middletown   8-13-1798
HAMMOND, Michael to Nancy McDONOLD   12-19-1798
HAMMOND, Zoeth to Abigail DYE   8-15-1797
HART, Doc'r Josiah to Anna MOULTON   12-28-1797
HARVIY, Amos to Rebecca Jones   9-28-1797
HASKEL, Major Jonathan to Phebe GREENE   4-8-1792
HEART, Selah to Sally WATROUS (WATERS) - both of Marietta   10-30-1793
HENDERSON, Edward to Sally LOVEKIN   5-5-1791
HEWET, Moses to Sally HEWET   6-3-1790
HINCKLEY, Nath'l to Sally PERRY (TORRY) both of Waterford   10-13-1796
HOWE, Pearley to Persis (Paris) PUTNAM   5-2-1798
HUET, Moses to Pheebe COOKE   10-16-1797
HUTCHINSON, Thomas to Sally WELCH - both of Marietta   12-21-1792
ISHAM, Russell to Elisabeth NOTT   1-2-1797
JOHNSON, Benjamin to Hannah JAMES   10-9-1797
KENNE, Nathan to Mary WILLSON   9-26-1791
KERR, Hamilton to Suckey NYGHSWONGER - both of Marietta   1-10-1793
LaFERTE, Creatus to Lydia McINTIRE - both of Gallipolis   3-30-1794
LAKE, Andrew to Elizabeth GOSS - both of Adams   5-17-1798
LANE, Thomas to Mary DOUBLEDAY   9-17-1797
LARROW, Jacob to Sally GARDINER   10-3-1797
LECROIN, Andrew to Marry Catterine SAROT - Gallipolis   2-10-1797
LeTALLIUR, John Basstiste to Marie Francois Charlotte LeROI,
            widow of Pierre LeSEUSIOR - both of Gallipolis   2-1-1794
LINCOLN, Joseph to Francis LEVINS   11-14-1790
LINCOLN, Obediah to Peggy McCUNE   4-12-1797
LORD, Thomas Esq. to Elanor OLIVER - both of Marietta   4-20-1795
LOUVET, Daniel to Phebe WEST   1-1-1798
LUCAS, Samuel to Elizabeth ROBERTSON   4-19-1798
LUCAS, William to Peggy HARRIS   4-11-1796
LUCKEY, Samuel to Huldah WRIGHT (WHITE)   5-16-1798
McCLUER, Andrew to Polly ALLEN - both of Waterford   11-11-1794
McINTOSH, Nathan to Rhoda SHEPARD - both of Marietta   6-21-1792
MALDON, John Lewis to Hannah Mion BUTHE - Gallipolis   3-12-1797
MARIAN, Francois to Louise NEME widow of Pierre MORREL -
            both of Gallipolis   2-18-1794
MARTIN, Charles Honeywood to Mary GAYLORD   8-22-1797
MARVEN, Picket to Polly WARTH   7-21-1791
MASON, William to Susanna COBERN   7-14-1790
MAYO, Daniel to Polly PUTNAM   10-21-1798
MENTEL, Auguste Weldman to Victore Charlotte LUTERE   4-15-1794
MILLER, Jeseph to Betsy DIGGANS - both of Gallipolis   6-19-1797
MILLS, Charles to Sally NYSWONGER   3-29-1795
MUNSELL, Levi to Lucretia OLIVER   12-14-1789

714

NEWELL, William to Patty SEAMANS - both of Marietta   12-23-1792
NISWONGER, John to Mrs. Peggy COLEMAN   11-19-1797
NOVERS, William to Peggy BRADLEY   11-17-1798
OLIVER, William to Liza OLIVER   3-19-1795
PEAKSLEY, Elijah to Thamur SHERWOOD - both of Virginia   6-4-1791
PETIT, John G. to Lucy WOODBRIDGE   4-20-1795
PHILLIPEAU, Anthony to Editha FLAGG - both of Marietta   6-20-1796
PHILLIPS, Ezra to Polly SCOTT   10-12-1797
POTTS, Robert to Peggy OLIVER   7-3-1790
PRATT, Azariah to Sarah NYE   5-4-1797
PROCTER, Jacob to Elisabeth WELLS - both of Waterford   1-5-1797
PUTNAM, Aaron Waldo to Charlotte LORING both of Belleprie   6-23-1791
RIGHT, Simeon to Ruth DUNHAM - both of Belleprie   7-24-1791
ROGERS, John to Mariamne CAPRON - both of Marietta   7-9-1789
SEAMANS, Gilbert to Anna HAMMON - both of Adams   5-18-1797
SEAMANS, Joseph to Abigail NEAL   2-1-1798
SEAMANS, Samuel of town of Adams to Sarah LAW of Waterford   11-28-1797
SHERMAN, Josiah to Polly BROWN - both of Waterford   4-30-1798
SHOEMAN, John Conrad of Marietta toLucy SHEREMAN of Waterford 9-3-1795
SMITH, Benjamin to Almy BARKER   10-5-1797
SMITH, James to Prissilla PORTER   12-19-1797
SIMMONS, Samuel to Lydia TILLSON   4-4-1790
SPRAGUE, Jonathan to Tabra SEAMANS   9-18-1792
SPRAGUE, Samuel to Hannah DELONG - both of Waterford   5-15-1795
SPRAGUE, Wilber to Gratry HULLERAFF - both of Waterford   8-18-1796
SPRINGER, Peleg to Sally WELLES   2-17-1791
STAATS, Abraham to Elisabeth HUGHES   12-23-1798
STACY, William to Hannah SHEFFIELD   7-29-1790
STONE, Israel to Mary COMER   8-20-1796
STONE, Sardine of Rainbow Settlement to Polly SMITH of
                            Harrison County   12-6-1796
STROUD, William to Mary LINDSEY   1-1-1798
SUTTON, Robert to Elisabeth CLINE   12-29-1796
TALLAGE, Jean Baptist Nicholus of Gallipolis to Catherine
                            WARTH of Marietta   4-23-1795
THORNLY, Samuel to Sarah PUTNAM   11-2-1796
TILLTON, Joseph to Bathsheba DUNHAM - both of Belleprie   8-21-1797
TUTTLE, Joel to Huldah SANFORD   7-13-1790
TUTTLE, Linus to Mary TOLMON   11-8-1796
VALODIN, Francis to Maria Gaberiel LaFORGE both of Gallipolis 9-18-1798
VISINIER, Charles Nicholas to Sophia CARTERON
                            both of Gallipolis   6-30-1793
WARREN, Elijah to Peggy DAVENPORT - both of Marietta   12-8-1793
WARTH, Robert to Katherine LaLANU (LaLANCE)both of Marietta   1-31-1794
WEBSTER, Andrew to Sally BROWN - both of Waterford   4-3-1794
WELLES, David to Polly COREY   4-17-1791
WHITE, John to Presilla DEVOLL - both of Marietta   10-12-1789
WHITE, Pelatiah to Susanna WELLES   2-24-1791
WHITMORE, Francis to Rebecca STROUD   8-14-1798
WILLSON, David to Easter CONIUS - both of Waterford   9-26-1791
WRIGHT, Simeon to Mehitabel WHITHAM   10-5-1797

AMES, Cyrus to Azuba MORE — both of Belpre	5-3-1801
AMLEN, John Jr. to Jean CAMPBELL	10-22-1799
ATCHINSON; John to Elizabeth FULTON	4-24-1800
ATCHINSON, Reuben to Polly SEAMONS	1-20-1801
ATKINSON, William Dawson to Jean ARWIN — Gallipolis	8-29-1799
BAILY; John Jr. to Sarah FARMER — both of Middletown	1-29-1800
BAKER, William to Jane BIEBER — both of Salem Tower, Mcravian Town of Muskingum	2-19-1801
BARKER, Michael to Isabella HARPER	4-1-1801
BARROWS, Henry to Bethial HEWITT — both of Middletown	7-28-1799
BATTLE; Francis to Abigail WELCH — both of Marietta	5-21-1801
BEAVER, John to Catharine BAKER — Newton Twp.	10-3-1799
BENBEBBER, Jesse to Rachel GREENLEE both of Kanawha Co. Va.	7-9-1799
BENT, Abner of Belpre to Eliza WILLIAMS of Marietta	1-18-1802
BETHEL, Edward to Pamelia (Pemelia) SWANK	11-11-1802
BIGGERSTAFF, John to Mary LEWIS	11-9-1802
BOBO, Israel to Margaret GRAHAM	4-2-1801
BROOKS, John to Delany HEARVEY — Middletown	7-3-1801
BROWN; James to Isabella OLIVER — both of Waterford	10-28-1800
BROWN; John to Mrs. Elizabeth DEVOL — both of Adams	3-23-1802
BROWN, William of Middletown to Polly BROWN of Waterford	3-25-1800
BUCK, Titus to Betsey HART — both of Marietta	6-2-1799
BUCKINGHAM, Stephen to Easter COOLEY — both of Belpre	1-13-1802
BURFORD, James to Sally BIERS	7-8-1800
BUTLER, Isaac to Nancy BARRTHAM	6-24-1802
CHAPMAN; David to Peggy McCALL	2-28-1799
CHAPMAN; Ezra to Betsey JONES	11-13-1799
* CHEADLE, Geo. of Waterford to Mrs. Mercy HERSEY of Adams	1-20-1802
COBURN, Asa to town of Adams to Rhoda BAKER of Waterford	1-24-1799
COLEMAN; Daniel to Mary NOTT	8-2-1802
COLEMAN; Thomas to Jane RARIDIN	8-18-1800
CONVERSE, Daniel to Sally MUNRO	4-3-1800
CRAIG, Samuel to Fanny JOHNSON	2-17-1801
DANA; Luther to Grace STONE	3-17-1799
DANA; William of Newport to Polly FOSTER of Belprie	5-2-1802
DAVIS; Amsa to Clarissa BROWN	11-14-1802
DAVIS; Asa of Waterford to Mrs. Joanna OLNY of Marietta	3-25-1802
DAVIS; Daniel of Waterford to Sally OLNEY of Marietta	2-14-1799
DAVIS; Hezekiel to Elizabeth COLEMAN — both of Waterford	2-14-1799
DAY, Noah to Bittsa GATES — both of Waterford	9-6-1799
DAZET, Joseph to Constance DAVRANGE	7-13-1800
DePU, George to Mary COULTER — both of Waterford	1-6-1801
DEVOL; Presburry to Patience BROWNWELL — both of Waterford	4-27-1800
DEVOL, Wing to Clara HART	10-16-1800
DICKISON, Christopher to Francis LEWIS of Ohio Co., Va.	11-5-1800
DIXON; Thomas to Roesey MYERS	12-25-1801
DODGE; John of Waterford to Katharine Galand of Salem	7-10-1799
DODGE, Oliver to Mrs. Anna MANCHESTER	7-24-1800
DORR, Edmon to Anna FARMER — both of Middletown	2-17-1799
DURGEE. Silas to Eleanor WILLIAMS	7-20-1802

*For *Cheadle, Geo.* read *Cheadle, Asa Jr.*; for *Mercy Hersey* read *Mercey Hersey*. GATEWAY TO THE WEST, Vol. 2: No. 3 (July-Sept. 1969).

```
EVANS, Simeon to Elizabeth MILLER - both of Waterford          6-16-1799
FERRARD, Peter to Margaret VIOLET - both of Gallipolis        3-22-1799
FOLSOM, Samuel to Catharine SMITH                             11-27-1802
FORENARK, Charles to Sarah RUHARTS of Newton Twp.            4-12-1799
FORREST, Joseph to Moriban HAMMOND                            1-7-1801
FOUTS; Frederick to Nancy BIGERSTAFF - both of Middletown     1-22-1801
FROST, Stephen to Nancy ELLISON - both Adamstown              12-18-1800
FULLER, Joseph to Anna DAVIS - both of Adams                  3-51-1801
GALEN, Andrew to Ruth ALLEN - both of Waterford               12-17-1800
GALBRAITH, John to Sally PRIOR                                4-12-1801
GALER; Peter to Elizabeth ALLEN - both of Waterford          6-13-1801
GATES, Timothy to Margaret HUGHS - Waterford                  5-14-1800
GOODNO, Daniel to Sally CUSHING                  Middle of April 1802
GREER, Paul to Maria EVRITT - both of Gnadenhullen,
                         Middle Moravian on Muskingum         1-25-1801
GRIFFIN, Asael to Betsey CHAPMAN                             10-21-1800
HARDEN; James to Sarah PREZEL                                 8-17-1802
HARRIS; John to Elizabeth BINGHAM - both of Middletown       2-19-1801
HARVEY, Elijah to Margaret BARRACK of Newton                 12-22-1800
HIET; Jesse to Sarah BEALS                                   8-4-1800
HILL; Alexander to Sarah FOSTER - both of Marietta           12-30-1802
HILL, William to Rachael ROUSKINS (RAUKINS)                 4-1-1801
HOLLENKUK, Chasper to Lucy SHERMON - both of Waterford       6-2-1801
HOOK, John to Esbel McCLINANS                                12-14-1802
HOW (HOWE), George to Mary WHITEHOWN                          9-7-1802
HUET, Isarael to Betsey BOBO - both of Middletown            2-19-1799
HUGHS, William to Elizabeth LUCAS - both of Waterford        3-23-1800
JOHNSON; Joseph to Sarah WELL(S)                             5-29-1799
JOHNSON, Levi to Sally COOK(E)                               10-16-1799
JONES, Thomas to Mary HANES of Ohio Co., Va.                 5-14-1801
KAZY, William to Nancy HARDEN                                11-7-1800
KELLY , George to Nancy WILLIAMS                             2-17-1801
KEMLY, James to Nancy Taylor JOHNSON                         1-27-1801
KILGOR, Matthew Lesley to Elizabeth ARMSTRONG - Gallipolis   10-3-1799
KIRKPATRICK, James to Susanna MUNRO                          2-9-1801
LALANCE, Peter to Catharine ROUSE                            1-4-1799
LANGFORD, Dudley to Rebecca STAATS                           3-10-1799
LAURENT, James to Elizabeth BUZELEN - both of Gallipolis     1-3-1801
LEATH, John to Sally McKEE                                   10-18-1802
LEONARD, William B. to Lydia MILTON                          7-10-1802
LERUE, Jacob to Elizabeth RANDOLS - Newport Twp.             5-6-1802
McBRIDE, Richard of Marietta to Mrs. Hannah HAMMONS of
                                            Waterford        12-23-1802
McCOY, Alexander to Sabrina BEAH - both of Waterford        2-21-1799
McCULLOCK, George to Catharine SERITIHFIELD                 8-3-1802
McDANIEL, David to Betsey McCARLEY                          3-5-1801
McGARVY, Patrick to Anne KING - both of Gallipolis         3-20-1800
MANN, James of Newton to Lucena DAVIS of Waterford         2-14-1799
MIMAIN, Peter to Elizabeth PICKET of Middletown            5-12-1801
MONTGOMERY, John to Elizabeth JOHNSTON                     8-28-1800
MORRISON, Samuel to Nancy BURRILL                          6-24-1802
```

717

MULFORD, Daniel to Mary JULLY - both of Middletown	5-8-1800
NOGLE, Isaac to Nancy PATTEN	8-12-1800
NORTHUP, Lensy to Susannah PAINTER	5-27-1802
NYE, Ebenezer to Silena GARDNER of Adams Twp.	11-21-1802
OLIVER, John to Catharine MATHEWS - both of Adams	4-9-1801
OLNEY, Discovery to Sarah STUCK - both of Waterford	4-23-1801
OLNEY, Telvenus of Waterford to Anna STACK (STOCK) of Newton	5-15-1799
ORCHER (ARCHER), Joseph to Sarah WELLS of Ohio Co., Va.	9-8-1801
OWEN, James to Ajuleah BROWN - both of Adams	4-27-1800
PATTEN, William to Mary HARDEN	6-7-1800
PERKINS, Doct'r Eliphas of Middletown to Catharine GREENE	3-24-1802
POWERS, Theophelus Stanford to Charlotte DEVOL both of Waterford	5-16-1802
PUGSLEY, Joseph to Olive PUGSLEY	4-4-1802
PUTNAM, George of Belleprie to Lucinda OLIVER of Adams	3-31-1799
RAGON, Jacob to Jean McCLIMANS	5-17-1802
RARREDON, Thomas to Polly RAY	12-24-1800
RASOR, Dinnes to Mary HOLDEN	1-28-1802
REBURN, William to Jenny DANIEL	1-3-1800
REMEL (RIMEL), Michael to Maria Catharine BORROWY both of Gnadenhullen	11-8-1801
RICE, Ezekiel to Elizabeth MILLER of Kanawha Co., Va.	4-1-1800
RIGGS, Jeremiah to Rachel KELLER	2-13-1800
RIGGS, John to Sarah WILSON	7-7-1802
ROLLAND, Joseph to Mary DOYL	9-14-1802
ROMIG, Abraham to Johanna BORROWY - both of Gnadenhullen	4-18-1802
RYTHER, James to Lois PEIRCE	7-20-1802
SAFFORD, Robert Esq. to Catherine CAMERON both of Gallipolis	7-15-1801
SCOTT, Thomas to Betsey KELLER - both of Wood Co., Va.	9-24-1799
SHARP, Thomas to Unity MERRIL	3-24-1801
SHELDEN, Abrah to Ruth WOOD - Middletown	7-9-1801
SHEVININ, Nicholas to Hannah Mion MALDON	11-24-1800
SIBLEY, Solomon Esq. of Wayne Co. to Sally SPROAT	10-31-1802
SIMMONS, John to Rebeeke WOODS - Newport Twp.	4-1-1802
SMITH, Hezekiah of Fairfield Co. to Susan GOODALE of Belprie	6-7-1802
SMITH, James to Mary BEEL of Ohio Co., Va.	6-12-1800
STAATS, Joseph to Margery DOUGHERTY of Newton	4-14-1801
STADEN, John to Elizabeth GREEN of Newton	1-5-1801
STEWART, Falander B. to Sarah SCOTT of Ohio Co., Va.	5-28-1801
STEWART, Lemuel J. to Jane COLDWELL of Newton Twp.	5-2-1801
STILL, Ebenezer of Salem to Mary HUGHS of Waterford	2-6-1800
STOKELY, David of Newton to Abigail HULBERT of Waterford	7-3-1799
STONE, James to Ruth ASHCRAFT	10-4-1802
STONE, Jasper to Polly Lucens CONVERSE - both of Adamstown	10-11-1801
STONE, Noyes to Peggy HANSON of Adams	4-13-1801
STRAIT, Aron to Elizabeth RASSOR	11-11-1800
THOMAS, Francis to Nancy ANERUM - both of Ohio Co., Va.	8-14-1800
THOMPSON, Enus to Elizabeth HIGGINS	5-16-1801
TILLIMAN, Willis to Deborah W. CASS	2-3-1802
TROTTER, William to Polly COOPER	12-16-1800
TUPPER, Benjamin to Patty PUTNAM - both of Marietta	3-25-1802

718

VINCENT, Anthony Claudius to Florence BARTHILOT   1-23-1799
WALKER, John to Lydia SAWYER   3-14-1802
WARD, Israel of Virginia to Rhoda BARKER of Middletown 4-2-1800
WELLS, Daniel to Elizabeth ANERUM of Ohio Co., Va.   3-12-1801
WELLS, Thomas to Pegay PATTERSON - both of Adamstown   2-4-1801
WHITE, David to Rebecca PORTER   4-31-1802
WHITE, John to Matilda LEAVENS   12-19-1802
WHITE, Nathaniel to Nancy THORNTON both of Kenhawa Co. Va.   7-25-1799
WILLIAMSON, Moses of Ohio Co., Va. to Hanrah LINN of Newton Twp.3-1-1801
WILLIAMSON, Samuel Esq. to Deborah DICKERSON of Newport Twp. 6-10-1800
WINSON, Jacob to Cintia FLARNENAN   10-3-1802
WOODFORD, William to Diana FORD   10-13-1799
YATES, Samuel of Marietta to Pheby BRION of Kanawha Co., Va.   6-10-1799
YOUNG, Aaron to Mary PICKET - both of Middletown   1-27-1801

The following records were taken from Probate Record Book 1. The page on which the original record may be found is given in parenthesis.

12-22-1789 - Estate of Samuel Holden PARSON, Esq., dec'd. Letters of adms. to Enoch Parson, son of dec'd. (1)

2-2-1790 - Estate of Stephen CHUBB, late of Marietta, dec'd. Letters of adms. to Captain Josiah Monro, a creditor. (1)

2-10-1790 - Estate of Joshua CHEEVER, late of Marietta, dec'd. Letters of adms. to William Burnham, a creditor. (1)

3-22-1790 - Inventory of Estate of Samuel Holden PARSONS, dec'd. (1)

3-22-1790 - Account of Estate of Samuel Holden PARSONS, Esq., dec'd. Widow mentioned, but not named. (3)

4-8-1790 - Estate of Benjamin CONVERS, late of Marietta, dec'd. Letters of adms. to Esther Convers, widow of dec'd. Inventory of Estate of Benjamin Convers, dec'd, late of Wolf Creek settlement. (4)

5-3-1790 - Inventory and appraisement of Estate of Stephen CHUBB, dec'd. (4)

5-17-1790 - Inventory of Estate of Joshua CHEEVER, late of Marietta, dec'd. (4)

5-17-1790 - Estate of Thomas WELLS, late of Marietta, dec'd. Letters of adms. to Joseph Wells and David Wells, sons of dec'd. Clark Wells, eldest son declining. (4)

6-23-1790 - Estate of Jacob BERRY, late a soldier of United States service. Letters of adms. to James Cox, recommended by Capt. Zeigler. (4)

6-29-1790 - Estate of John BRYAN, late a soldier in the service of the Unite States. Letters of adms. to John Chambers, recommended by Capt. David Zeigler. (5)

6-29-1790 - Estate of Michael KNIGHT, late a soldier in the service of the United States. Letters of adms. to Mary Knight, widow of dec'd. (5)

7-1-1790 - Estate of Conrad KEYLER, late a soldier in the service of the United States. Letters of adms. to Capt. David Zeigler. (5)

7-11-1790 - Estate of James YORK, late a soldier in the service of the United States. Letters of adms. to Capt. David Zeigler. (5)

7-8-1790 - Estate of William SIMPSON, late a soldier in Hearts Co., dec'd Letters of adms. to Capt. Jonathan Heart. (5)

9-6-1790 - Estate of Nathaniel DAVIS, late of Marietta, dec'd. Letters of adms. to Benjamin Tupper, esq. (5)

3-28-1791 - Estate of Richard MELLEN, late a soldier in the service of the United States. Letters of adms. to Capt. David Zeigler. (5)

3-28-1791 - Estate of William GRUBB, late a soldier in the service of the United States. Letters of adms. to Capt. David Zeigler. (5)

6-4-1790 - Inventory and appraisement of Estate of Thomas WELLS, dec'd. (5)

4-6-1791 - Estate of Daniel DUNHAM, late of Bel-pre', dec'd. Letters of adms. to Bathsheba Dunham, widow, Inventory of Estate of Daniel Dunham, dec'd. (5)

4-6-1791 - Nuncupative Will of Charles RANSOM - dated 12-7-1790 Fort Harmer. Deposition of John Bartlet and Amos Seymore both of Capt. Hearts. Co. 1st U.S. Reg. stating that on 3 Oct. last past on their march against the Indian Towns, Charles Ransom of the same company, should he die or be killed, his personal estate, clothes, pay, etc. to go to David Chapman of the same company and said Chapman made his will in favor of Ransom. Recorded 4-6-1791. (6)

4-6-1791 - Nuncupative Will of Stephen WOODS - ated 2-24-1791. Deposition by
Samuel Drake and Lemuel Lane stating that on 1st Oct. on march to Miami
Villages about 20 miles from Ft. Washington, that they were with Stephen
Woods, dec'd, then a soldier in Capt. Hearts Co. and that in case he was
killed that Solomon Phelps a soldier in same company was to receive all
his estate. Recorded 4-6-1791. (6)

4-6-1791 - Nuncupative Will of Justice SQUIRES, dec'd - dated 12-6-1790 Fort
Harmar. Deposition by George Hooper and Simeon Brundewick stating that
Justice Squires of Capt. Heart's Co. of 1st U.S. Regt. bequeathed all
his estate to John Nelson. Recorded 4-6-1791. (6)

4-12-1791 - Nuncupative Will of Hezekiah PEASE, dec'd. - dated 4-6-1791. Deposition by John Kidd and Jedediah Armstrong stating that on 30 Sept. last
past at Fort Washington, Hamilton Co., Hezekiah Pease then a soldier in
Capt. Hearts Co., should he be killed going against the Miami Villages
stated that all his estates was to go to James Allen a soldier in same
company. Recorded 4-12-1791. (7)

4-22-1791 - Will of Ebn. FROTHINGHAM Jr. - dated 6-23-1790. Mentions "God
has been fit to remove by death my dear beloved wife." Brother, Peter,
two shares of land in Ohio purchased in my name. Brother, John, to see
that testator's children (not named) are schooled. Brother, Samuel.
Sisters: Hannah and Lydia. Sisters-in-law; Betsey and Sally Boarman to
have what testator's wife brought with her. Requests that Mr. Whitman
be paid for building testator's house in Marietta. Executors: father,
Eben. Frothingham and brother, Peter Frothingham. Signed: Ebn. Frothingham
Jr. Witnesses: Jacob Springer, C. Ormsby and Thos. Lane. (7)

4-30-1791 - Inventory of Estate of Ebenezer Frothingham Jr. of Marietta, dec'.(8)

4-22-1791 - Estate of Joseph ROGERS, late of Marietta, dec'd. Letters of adms.
to Ebenezer Sproat, Esq. (8)

8-19-1791 - Inventory of Estate of Nathaniel DAVIS, late of Marietta, dec'd. (8)

7-17-1792 - Inventory of Estate of Charles RANSON, soldier, 1st U.S. Regt. (8)

7-17-1792 - Adms. account of Estate of Stephen WOODS, 1st U.S. Regt. (8)

7-17-1792 - Adms. account of Estate of Justice SQUIRES, 1st U.S. Regt. (8.)

7-17-1792 - Adms. account of Estate of Hezekiah PEAS, 1st U.S. Regt. (8)

7-18-1792 - Will of Benjamin TUPPER, esq., dec'd, late of Marietta, Northwest
Territory - dated 5-27-1792. Wife, Huldah, also to serve as executrix,
to have house in Marietta, gardens and river gardens. Sons: Anselm, Edward
White and Benjamin Tupper, the last being a minor; each to have one share
in Ohio Company. Daughter, Minerva Nye, to have share in Ohio Co. drawn
in the name of Ichabod Nye. To Timothy Meigs. a minor and son of good
friend, Return Jonathan Meigs, to have 2/20th part of testator's interest
in Scioto Company. To good friend, Ebenezer Battelle, 1/20th part or share
in Scioto Company. To good friend, Nathaniel Cushing, 1/20th part or share
in Scioto Company. Signed: Benj'n Tupper. Witnesses: Joseph Wood, Christopher
Burlingame and Sukey Burlinggame. (9)

10-15-1790 - Estate of Zebulon THROOP, late of Marietta, dec'd. Letters of
adms. to Robert Oliver, Esq. (10)

11-30-1792 - Estate of Amos BLISS, late of Marietta, dec'd. Letters of adms. to
Phebe Bliss, widow. (10)

721

8-15-1792 - Inventory of Estate of Benjamin TUPPER. Lists 4 shares Ohio Co in
name of dec'd; 1 share each in name of Anselm, Benjamin Jr. and Edw. W. Tupper
and 1 share in partnership with Ichabod Nye. (10)
1-24-1793 - Estate of Turpin FAYLES, late of Marietta, dec'd. Letters of adms. to
William Chambers of Mason Co., Ky., a creditor. (11)
2-21-1793 - Estate of James LAWSON, dec'd, late of Gallipolis. Leters of adms.
to John Mathews of Gallipolis, a creditor. (11)
8-14-1793 - Inventory of Estate of James LAWSON. (11)
2-21-1793 - Estate of Elijah BODWELL, dec'd, late of Gallipolis. Letters of
adms. to John Mathews of same place, a partner in trade with dec'd.
8-14-1793. Inventory of Estate of Elijah Bodwell. (11)
4-6-1793 - Return Jonathan MEIGS appointed guardian of James FLAGG, a minor at
the request of Editha Flagg, his mother. (11)
8-9-1793 - Estate of Henry BAGLEY, late of Marietta, dec'd. Letters of adms. to
Doctor Jabez True. 12-3-1793 Inventory of Estate of Henry Bagley. (11)
11-16-1793 - Estate of John Lewis COUNTANT, late of Gallipolis, dec'd. Letters
of adms. to Francis D'Hebecourt of same place. Bond and appr. of John
Gilbert Petet, Esq. and John Lewis LeClerc. 3-7-1794 Inventory Estate
of John Lewis Countant. (12)
Jan. 1793 - Inventory of Estate of Amos BLISS, dec'd. Listed are 4 acres land
in Virgin's bottom and one donation lot in Bel-pre #12. (12)
9-21-1793 - Inventory of Estate of Zebulon THROUP, dec'd. (12)
5-13-1794 - Estate of Robert WARTH, late of Marietta, dec'd. Letters of adms.
to John Warth, brother of dec'd. Inventory of Estate of Robert Warth
includes lots in Meigs, 8 acre lot and Harris lot. (12)
7-6-1794 - Adms. account of Estate of Daniel Dunham, late of Bel-pre'. (13)
7-15-1794 - Estate of Samuel Holden PARSONS, dec'd. Letters of adms. de bonis non
to William Walter Parsons, son of dec'd. Letter of attorney by widow and
all heirs (not named). Mentions 5 shares in Ohio Co. and right to 5385 acres
land in State of Connecticut, held by said Parsons. (13)
7-16-1794 - Estate of Henry BAGLEY declared insolvent. (13)
8-6-1794 - Estate of Casar MAUPETIT, late of Gallipolis, dec'd. Letters of adms.
to John Gilbert Petit, Esq. Appraisors: Claude Menger and Francis
D'Hebecourt. (13)
9-3-1794 - Estate of Francis Abel SARRASIN, late of Gallipolis, dec'd. Letters
of adms. to John Lewis Violette of same place. Bond, Peter Magnier and
Michael Chanterelle. Appraisers, J. B. LeTailleur and John Gabriel Gervais.(14)
1-24-1795 - Estate of Prter DUCHALLARD, late of Gallipolis, dec'd. Letters of
adms. to John Gilbert Petit, Esq. who gave bond with Francis D'Hebecourt.
Appraisers, Francis D'Hebecourt and Lewis LeClerc. (14)
1-24-1795 - Estate of Jaques RENOUARD, late of Gallipolis, dec'd. Letters of
adms. to John Gilbert Petit, Esq. who gave bond with Francis D'Hebecourt.
Appraisers, Francis D'Hebecourt and Lewis LeClerc. (14)
1-27-1795 - Estate of Nicholas LeSURE, late of Gallipolis, dec'd. Letters of
adms. to John Gilbert Petit, Esq. who gave bond with Francis D'Hebecourt.
Appraisers, Francis D'Hebecourt and Lewis LeClerc. (14)
2-12-1795 - Estate of John GARDNER, late of Gallipolis, dec'd. Letters of adms.
to Margaret Little Gardner, widow. 8-25-1795 Inventory of Estate of John
Gardner. (14)

2-17-1795 - Estate of Peter DROZ, late of Gallipolis, dec'd. Letters of adms. to
Lewis Violette who gave bond with Claude Cadot. Appraisers, J. P. Romaine
Bureau and Lewis Leclerc. (14)
3-21-1795 - Estate of Jonas DAVIS, Yeoman, late of Bel-pre', dec'd. Letters of
adms. to Isaac Peirce. 9-5-1796 Inventory of estate of Jonas Davis. (15)
5-16-1795 - Will of William MOULTON of Hamstead, Rockingham Co., New Hampshire,
Yeoman, late of Marietta - dated 11-23-1787. Wife, Lydia, also to serve as
executrix. Sons: Joseph and Edmund Moulton. Daughters: Molley wife of
Doctor John Bond: Anna; Lydia; and Katharine. Mentions his Ohio Company
land, Signed: William Mouton. Witnesses: Nehemiah Kelly, Edward Greeley
and John Calfe. (15)
-----1792 - Appraisement of estate of William MOULTON, late of Marrietta, dec'd.(16)
6-11-1795 - Thomas STANLEY of Marietta appointed guardian of Lydia HURLBUT,
an orphan and minor. (16)
8-11-1795 - Estate of Julien PRADEL, late of Gallipolis, dec'd. Letters of adms.
to Nicholas Questel of same who gave bond with John Parmentier and Claude
Cadot. Appraisers, John B. LeTailleur and Peter Bureau. (16)
8-22-1795 - Estate of James PATTERSON, late of Marietta, dec'd. Leters of adms.
to Thomas Stanley. (17)
9-15-1795 - Inventory of estate of Francis Abel SARRASIN, dec'd, lists 1 four
acre lot, 3 city lots and 2 acres Scioto Co. (17)
10-1-1795 - Adms. account of Estate of Daniel DUNHAM, dec'd, late of Bel-pre.
Money paid to and received by Jno. Dunham in New England. Paid to son,
Daniel Dunham for journeying from Bel-pre to Conway, Mass. Said daughter,
_____(not given) Wright. (17)
10-1-1795 - Will of Major FAIRCHILD - dated 6-30-1795. To Christian Burnham
wife of William Burnham of Marietta (no relationship if any, stated), one
half testators share in Ohio Company Purchase. To nephew, William Fairchild
Magee, all real and personal estate in State of Rhode Island. To Abel
Rice (no relationship if any, statee), land in Ohio Company Purchase. To
sister, Ann Boler's children (not named). Executors: William Fairchild
Magee of Rhode Island and Return Jonathan Meigs Jr. of Marietta. Signed:
Major Fairchild. Witnesses: Josiah Munro, Abraham Whipple and Jesse Beach.(18)
10-31-1795 - Estate of Abel RICE, late of Marietta, dec'd. Letters of adms.
to Doctor Jabez True. (18)
12-10-1795 - Estate of Constant WELBER, late of Gallipolis, dec'd. Letters of
adms. to John Peter Romain Bureau of same place. (18)
12-22-1795 - Inventory and account of estate of Twipin FAYLES, late of Marietta,
dec'd. (18)
1-18-1796 - Estate of Major FAIRCHILD, dec'd. Letters of adms. to Doctor Jabez
True of Marietta. Return Jonathan Meigs Jr. declining. (18)
1-26-1796 - Inventory of Estate of Major FAIRCHILD, dec'd. (19)
2-1-1796 - Estate of Samuel FELLSHAN, late of Marietta, dec'd. Letters of adms.
to Daniel Davis of Waterford. (19)
2-5-1796 - Estate of Nathan GOODALE, late of Bel-pre', dec'd. Letters of adms.
to Isaac Pierce. 4-26-1796 Inventory of estate of Nathan Goodale lists
several lots in Bel-pre'. (19)

2-13-1796 - Adms. account of Estate of Major Fairchild; estate declared insolvent.(19

2-5-1796 - Estate of Timothy GOODALE, of Bel-pre', dec'd. Letters of adms.
to Isaac Peirce, esq. of same place. 4-26-1796 Inventory of Estate of
Timothy Goodale, dec'd. (20)

4-27-1796 - Adms. account of Estate of John Gardner, of Gallipolis, dec'd. (20)

8-30-1796 - Estate of Firmin BRUNIER, late of Gallipolis, dec'd. Letters of adms.
to Stephen Chandivert of same place with Nicholas Thevenin and Lewis Berthe
on bond. (20)

11-2-1796 - Estate of Remy Thiery QUIFFE, late of Gallipolis, dec'd. Letters of
adms. to Peter Robert Maquet of same place. Bond $1000. with Christopher
Etienne and Francis Joseph Winnocus Devacht of same as sureties. Apprqisers,
J. B. LeTailleur and J. P. R. Bureau. (20)

11-2-1796 - Estate of Anthony NIBERT, late of Gallipolis, dec'd. Letters of adms.
to Francis Joseph Winocus Devacht of same. Bond $1000. with Christopher
Etienne and John Peter Romain Bureau as sureties. Appraisers, John Baptist
LeTailleur and Marin Duport. (20)

11-3-1796 - Estate of Peter SERROT, late of Gallipolis, dec'd. Letters of adms.
to Maria Katharine Aveline Serrot, widow. Bond of $1000. with John Baptist
LeTaileur and Marin Duport as securities. Appraisers, John B .LeTailleur
and Marin Duport. (21)

11-4-1796 - Estate of Lewis BERTHE, late of Gallipolis, dec'd. Letters of adms.
to Hannah Mion Berthe, widow. Bond $1000. with John Lewis Maldan and John
Baptist Ginat as sureties. Appraisers, J. B. LeTailleur and Marin Duport (21)

11-10-1795 - First adms account of Estate of Francis Abel Sarrasin; 2nd adms.
account made 11-21-1796. (21)

12-15-1796 - Citation issued to next of kindred of John PARMENTIER, late of
Gallipolis to show cause why nuncupative will said to be made by dec'd
has not been proved and allowed. 12-30-1796 L. LeClerc, constable saith
no kindred of Parmentier found in bailwick. (21)

8-25-1795 - Inventory of Estate of Peter DROZ, late of Gallipolis, dec'd. Lists
2 city lots opposite the Island; 2 lots next to Doct'r Petit. (22)

11-21-1796 - Adms. account of Estate of Julien BRADEL, late of Gallipolis. (22)

12-27-1796 - Estate of Peter Thomas THOMAS, late of Gallipolis, dec'd. Letters
of adms. to Simon Subbil, a creditor of same place. Bond of $1000. with
John Peter Romaine Bureau and Francis Thierry of Marietta as sureties.
Appraisers, John Baptist LeTaileur and Marin Duport. (22)

12-27-1796 - Account of articles belonging to John GARDNER, dec'd. (22)

1-5-1797 - Estate of Claude CADOT, late of Gallipolis, dec'd. Letters of adms.
to Jane Cadot, widow. Bond of $1000. with Stephen Bastide and John Baptist
Ferraro both of Gallipolis as sureties. Appraisers, John Baptist LeTailleur
and John Peter Romaine Bureau. (22)

1-5-1797 - Will of Francis DUVERGER, native of Harfeuil, Parish du forest, Province
of France, late of Gallipolis, Washington Co., Northwest Territory - dated
9-4-1796. Brothers and Sister: Stephen Duverger, Anthony Duverger and
Martha Duverger; all of France. Executor: John Gilbert Petit, Esq. of
Gallipolis. Signed: F. Duvege. Witnesses: P. Bureau, (Nicholas) Prioux
and P. Ferard. (23)

12-13-1796 - Will of Joachim PIGNOLET of Gallipolis, Washington Co., Northwest Territory - dated 9-20-1796. Daughter, Jeanne Francoise Pignolet Parmentier, also to serve as executrix. Signed: Joachim (his mark) Pignolet. Witnesses: P. Bureau, (Nicholas) Prioux and J. W. Devacht. (23)

1-13-1797 - Noncupative Will of John PARMENTIER. Memorial and Petition of Jeanne Francoise Parmentier of Gallipolis, widow of John Parmentier, Turner, late of Gallipolis, Washington Co., showeth that John Parmentier died 16 September 1796 and that before his death before witnesses Francis Joseph Winocus Devacht and Nicholas Prioux of Gallipolis, he devised all his estate to his wife, dated 1-13-1797. Letters of adms. granted to Jeanne Francoise Parmentier, widow on 3-22-1797. (24)

3-22-1797 - Inventory of Estate of Francis DUVERGE, late of Gallipolis. Listed are 1 Congress Lot #27 of 217 acres on the Ohio; 1 seven acre lot #35 and 1 town lot. (25)

2-21-1797 - Inventory of Lewis BERTHE, late of Gallipolis. Included were 1 house and 2 town lots #152 & 157 Gallipolis; 2 town lots #283 & 284 Gallipolis; 1 seven acre lot #56 Gallipolis; 8 town lots in minsteral land situated Gallipolis; and 217 acres land patented by Congress #12. (25)

1-9-1797 - Inventory of Remy Thierry QUIFFE, late of Gallipolis. List includes shoemaker tools, 217 acres Congress land, town lot Gallipolis; and 7 acre lot Gallipolis. (25)

11-3-1796 - Inventory of Estate of Peter SERROT, late of Gallipolis. List includes 7 town lots #55,56,57,356,357,358,364. Gallipolis; and 1 seven acre lot #57.(26)

3-13-1797 - Inventory of Anthony VIBERT (NIBERT), late of Gallipolis. List includes house and 5 town lots in minsteral lands, Gallipolis, 1 town lot #444, Gallipolis; 1 seven acre lot #30, Gallipolis; and 217 acres Congress lands #82. (26)

4-5-1797 - Inventory of Estate of Claude CADOT, late of Gallipolis. List includes 3 town lots; four acre lot; 1 seven acre lot; 217 acres Congress lands #89 granted French Inhabitants of Gallipolis by Congress 4-1-1797. (26)

4-4-1797 - Inventory of Peter Thomas THOMAS, late of Gallipolis. List includes 4 town lots #413,414,415 & 416; 2 seven acre lots #40 & (not given); 217 acres Congress land granted to French Inhabitants. 4-25-1797 Adms. account of estate of Peter Thomas Thomas. (27)

Aug. 1797 - Estate of William WILLSON, late of Waterford, dec'd. Letters of Adms. granted to George Willson. (28)

8-29-1797 - Adms. account of Estate of Remmy Thierry QUIFFE, late of Gallipolis.(28)

8-29-1797 - Adms. account of Estate of Claude CADOT, late of Gallipolis. (28)

-----1797 - Will of John FULHAM late of Ireland, resident of Province of Rhode Island - dated 4-9-1791. Brother, Thomas Fulham of County of Eastmeath, Kingdom of Ireland; to study at College of Edinburgh. To Peter Turner of East Greenwich, Rhode Island. Phicisson and Wanton Casey of Bell Pre, Western banks of Ohio; also to serve as executors. Signed: John Fulham. Witnesses: Andrew Boyd, Lydia King and Jonathan Gray. (29)

10-30-1797 - Adms. account of Estate of Samuel Holden PARSONS. (30)

11-22-1797 - Estate of Asa COBURN, late of Waterford, dec'd. Letters of adms. to Robert Oliver, Esq. (31)

725

Jan. 1797 - Estate of Giles FORD, late of Waterford, dec'd. Letters of adms. to William Ford. (31)

1-10-1798 - Will of Peter FROTHINGHAM - dated Greenville 8-12-1795. Brothers: Samuel and John. Sisters: Hannah and Lydia. Executors: brother, Samuel and sister, Hannah. Signed: Peter Frothingham. Witnesses: Peircy Pape, Joseph G. Andrews and Geo. Strother. (31)

3-8-1798 - Estate of Nicholas PETIT, late of Gallipolis, dec'd. Letters of adms. to Stephen Willermy. Bond $300, with Claudius Barhelot and J. P. Bureau as securities. Appraisers, John B. LeTailleur and Lewis McClerc. (31)

3-13-1798 - Estate of Jesse BEACH, late of Waterford, dec'd. Letters of adms. to Asa Beach of same place. (32)

3-31-1798 - Inventory of Estate of James McDONALD, late of Bel-pre, dec'd. List includes 100 acres in town of Waterford granted by Ohio Company deed 4-19-1797, #21. (32)

4-26-1798 - Inventory of Estate of Jesse BEACH, late of Waterford, dec'd. (32)

3-3-1798 - Inventory of Estate of Giles FORD, late of Waterford, dec'd. (32)

5-26-1798 - Estate of Nicholas PRIEAU, late of Gallipolis, dec'd. Letters of adms. to John Peter Romain Bureau. Bond with Edward White Tupper and Benjamin Tupper as securities. Appraisers, Francis Joseph DeVacht and Francis LeClerg. (33)

5-26-1798 - Inventory of Estate of Nicholas PETIT. List includes two town lots #49 & 50 with 2 cabins in Gallipolis and 7 acre lot #63. (33)

6-19-1798 - Inventory of Estate of Nicholas PRIEAU, late of Gallipolis. List includes six town lots #233,234,250,253,264 & 267 planted with apple and peach trees; 1 small lot adjacent the above being #17; 1 small lot #11 and 1 four acre lot #306; all Gallipolis. (33)

7-26-1798 - Estate of Daniel QUIMEY, late of Marietta, dec'd. Letters of adms. to John Quimby. (33)

8-6-1798 - Adms. account of estate of Giles FORD, late of Waterford. Petition to orphans court for support of widow and child (not named). (33)

10-1-1798 - Inventory of Estate of Asa COBURN, late of Waterford. List includes several descriptions of land in Ohio Company. (33)

11-3-1798 - Estate of John LEVINS, late of Bel-Pre, dec'd. Letters of adms. to Easter Levins and Joseph Levins. (35)

11-27-1798 - Estate of James JOHNSON. Letters of adms. to George Johnson. (35)

12-22-1798 - Inventory of Estate of John Levins. (35)

9-5-1799 - Estate of Joshua REED, late of Salem, dec'd. Letters of adms. to Mary Reed, widow and Ephraim True. (36)

9-27-1799 - Estate of William ALCOCK, late of Marietta, dec'd. Letters of adms. to Sarah Alcock, widow. (36)

10-9-1799 - Estate of Ebenezer FELCH, dec'd. Letters of adms. to Dudley Woodbridge, Esq.; Sarah Felch, widow, relinquishing. (36)

The following records were taken from Probate Record Book 1. The page on which the original record may be found is given in parenthesis.

1-6-1800 - Inventory of the Estate of Joshua REED. (36)

1-8-1800 - Estate of Isaac EMMONS, dec'd. Letters of adms. to William Skinner, a creditor. (36)

1-13-1800 - Will of Gilbert SEAMONS - dated 11-23-1799. Wife, Martha. Daughters: usanna, Sabra, Martha and Polly. Sons: Samuel Benjamin and Bennajah, Grandson, William, son of daughter, Sabra, to have land south side Muskingum River. Administrators: 2 sons (not named, but in recording of will named as Gilbert and Preserved Seamons). Signed: Gilbert Seamons. Witnesses: Enoch Wing, William Davis and Stephen Frost. (36)

2-22-1800 - Estate of James JOHNSON, dec'd. Letters of adms. de bonis non to Valentine Johnson, one of the heirs of said estate. (37)

3-21-1800 - Estate of John HARMON, late of Waterford, dec'd. Letters of adms. to Nehemiah Sprague. (37)

3-21-1800 - Estate of Samuel BARNS, dec'd. Letters of adms. to Isaac Pierce, Esq. (37)

3-27-1800 - Dower set off to Mary REED widow of Joshua Reed, being land west side of Duck Creek. (37)

4-9-1800 - Estate of Nathan SMITH, late of Marietta, dec'd. Letters of adms. to Simion Demming. (37)

5-19-1800 - Will of Maria J. DALLIEZ, late of Gallipolis, Washington Co., Northwest Territory - dated 4-8-1800. To John Vandenbenden, son of Mertnias Vanderbenden, personal property and 2 town lots deeded to testatrix by R. J. Meigs and Paul Fearing. To Ange Mick and Alexandriens Maquet, single women. To Mrs. Davous wife of Francis Davous, one 7 acre lot. To Lydia Safford, child of Robert and Catherine Safford, 150 acres by patent granted by Congress #7. Executor, Robert Safford. Signed: Maria (her mark) Dalliez. Witnesses: LeTaileur, P. N. Maquet and Marian Duport. (37)

6-25-1800 - Estate of Archibald LAKE, dec'd. Letters of adms. to Andrew Lake. (38)

6-25-1800 - Inventory of Estate of James JOHNSON, dec'd. (38)

9-1-1800 - Inventory of Estate of Aaron ABBIT, dec'd. List includes 34 acres in school lands. (39)

9-4-1800 - Inventory of Estate of Nathan SMITH, dec'd, late of Marietta. (39)

9-3-1800 - Inventory of Estate of Maria Josephine DALLIEZ, late of Gallipolis, dec'd. (40)

9-10-1800 - Estate of John FRIEND, dec'd. Letters of adms. to Ephrain Cutler, Esq. widow, Hannah Friend relinquishes, 9-11-1800 Inventory of Estate of John Friend, late of Massachusets, who died in Washington Co., Northwest Territory. List includes 30 acres being #1292; 50 acres being #348; 320 acres Section 5 Township 7, Range 14; and 131 acres Section 10, Township 7, Range 14. (40)

10-7-1800 - Inventory of Estate of Archibald LAKE, late of town of Adams, dec'd.(41)

10-7-1800 - Adms. account estate of Nathan SMITH. (41)

10-17-1800 - Estate of Ebenezer TOLMAN, late of Salem, dec'd. Letters of adms. to Seth Tolman. (42)

10-21-1800 - Estate of William Pitt PUTMAN, dec'd. Letters of adms. to Bethiah Putman and William Putman. (42)

12-31-1800 - Estate of William ROBINSON, late of Marietta, dec'd. Letters of adms. to Jean Robinson. (42)

1-27-1801 - Estate of James SMITH, late of Adams twp. dec'd. Letters of adms. to Priscilla Smith. (42)

3-20-1801 - Inventory of Estate of William ALCOCK, late of Marietta. List includes 8 acres land and house; lease on 100 acres congress lands. (42)

4-6-1801 - Inventory of Estate of James SMITH, late of Adams twp., dec'd. (43)

4-6-1801 - Estate of Jonathan STONE, dec'd. Letters of adms. to Susanna Stone, widow and Benjamin Franklin Stone. (44)

7-31-1801 - Priscilla SMITH, widow of James Smith, dec'd, assigned dower in the homestead farm. (44)

9-2-1801 - Inventory of Estate of Jonathan STONE, late of Bel-pre, dec'd. List includes numerous land descriptions. (44)

9-12-1801 - Estate of Bennett ROGERS, a transient person. Letters of Adms. to Robert Safford. Inventory of estate taken same day. (45)

10-6-1801 - Estate of Josiah MUNRO, late of Marietta, dec'd. Letters of adms. to Jabez True. (45)

10-7-1801 - Estate of Jacob BUCKMAN, late of Marietta, dec'd. Letters of adms. to Joseph Buell. (45)

10-22-1801 - Will of Hannah COOPER of Belpre - dated 1-17-1799. Grandchildren: Abner, Lemuel, Frederick, Charles, Jacob and Hannah Cooper. Executor: son, Jeremiah Cooper. Signed: Hannah (her mark) Cooper. Witnesses: Daniel Ellenwood, Samuel Meek and D. Loring. (45)

10-23-1801 - Estate of Joseph THOMPSON, dec'd. Letters of adms. to Robert Oliver, Esq. (46)

10-30-1801 - Inventory of Estate of Samuel Barns, late of Middletown, dec'd. (46)

11-20-1801 - Estate of Robert TAYLOR, late of Marietta, dec'd. Letters of adms. to William Taylor. (48)

11-20-1801 - Estate of Edward HENDERSON, dec'd. Letters of adms. to Sally Henderson. (48)

11-23-1801 - Estate of Richard PATTEN, late of Marietta, dec'd. Letters of adms. to Ruth Patten and William Patten. (48)

1-23-1802 - Estate of Martin HERSEY, late of Adams, dec'd. Letters of adms. to Mary Hersey, widow. (48)

3-19-1802 - Estate of Matthew DORR, late of Middletown, dec'd. Letters of adms. to Edmund Dorr. 5-31-1802 - Inventory of Estate of Matthew Dorr. List includes 100 acres Donation Lands. (48)

6-2-1802 - Overseers of Poor of Middletown twp. charge Isaac BARKER with not supporting family. (48)

6-17-1802 - Estate of Jacob HIMMEL, dec'd. Letters of adms. to Thomas Himmel. (48)

6-18-1802 - Estate of John BRIGGS, late of Newtown, dec'd. Letters of adms. to John Briggs. (48)

6-23-1802 - Inventory of Estate of John FULHAM, late of New Orleans in Spanish Dominion lying in Washington County, Northwest Territory. List includes numerous land descriptions. (48)

6-23-1802 - Inventory of Estate of Hannah Cooper, late of Bel-Pre. (49)

7-5-1802 - Inventory of estate of Richard PATTEN, late of Marietta. (49)

7-12-1802 - Inventory of Estate of Martin HERSEY, late of Adams. List includes homestead; land on Shade River; land on Hocking Rover; land at LeTart Falls; 3 acre lot and one-half acre house lot. (49)

-12-1802 - Asa CHEADLE Jr. joint adms. of estate of Martin HERSEY with late Mary
Hersey now Mary Cheadle wife of said Asa, represent that estate is not suffic-
ient to pay debts and asks dower be set off to said Mary Cheadle late widow of
Martin Hersey, out of said estate. (50)
-20-1802 - Estate of Ebenezer BUELL, late of Marietta, dec'd. Letters of adms. to
Joseph Buell and Timothy Buell. (50)
-2-1802 - Inventory of Estate of Robert TAYLOR, late of Marietta. List includes
one-half share Ohio Co. purchase in name of Subal Barr; one-third of 160 acres
lot in name of Elias Hall; one-third of 8 acre lot and one-third of a 3 acre
lot, both in name of Elias Hall. (50)
-3-1802 - Inventory of Estate of Jacob BUEKMAN (BUCKMAN), dec'd. (50)
-17-1802 - Estate of Isaac BURROWAY, dec'd. Letters of adms. to John Hackenwelder.
(51)
-17-1802 - Request that dower be assigned to Susanna STONE, widow of Jonathan
STONE. (51)
-31-1802 - Estate of William STACEY, late of Marietta, dec'd. Letters of adms.
to his sons, William and Gideon Stacey. (51)
-31-1802 - Inventory of estate of James PATTERSON, dec'd. List includes one share
Ohio Co. land and 1 share in 5th division. (51)
-6-1802 - Estate of Zoeth HAMMON, late of Waterford, dec'd. Letters of adms. to
Wanton Devoll. (51)
6-1802 - Estate of John CASE, dec'd. Letters of adms. to Betsey Case and Brewster
Higby. (51)
8-1802 - Adms. account of Estate of Matthew DORR, late of Middletown. (51)
23-1802 - Adms. account of Estate of William Pitt PUTMAN. (51)
-4-1802 - Inventory of Estate of John BRIGGS. (52)
-4-1802 - Inventory of Estate of Jacob HUMMEL. (52)
-7-1802 - Estate of Eleazer CURTIS, late of Belpre, dec'd. Letters of adms. to
Eunice Curtis. (53)
-10-1802 - Estate of Ebenezer PEIRCE, dec'd. Letters of adms. to Levi Allen. (53)
18-1803 - Inventory of Estate of John CASE, late of Gallipolis. List includes
113 acre share land and 391 acres. (53)
26-1803 - Inventory of Estate of Eleazor CURTIS. (54)
29-1803 - Inventory of Estate of Zoath HAMMON. (55)
g. 1803 - Will of Jacob RAMBO of Waterford - dated 6-20-1803. Wife, Catharine.
Mentions: "one of my sons" Jackson Rambo. Grandson, Jacob Rambo, son of
Rebeckah Tenley. Signed: Jacob (his mark) Rambo. Witnesses: Ezekiel Deming.
William Williams and Jesse (his mark) McFarlin. 9-7-1803 Inventory of estate
of Jacob Rambo. (57)
c. 1803 - Estate of Anthony SPACHT, late of Belpre, dec'd. Letters of adms. to
Jacob Spacht, eldest son of dec'd. 4-2-1804 Inventory of Estate of Anthony
Spacht. (58)
-31-1803 - Inventory of Estate of Timothy PRIOUX (PRYER). (58)
g. 1804 - Adms. account of estate of Nicholas PRIOUX, late of Gallipolis. (58)
19-1804 - Inventory of Estate of Henry YOUNG, late of Marietta. (59)
g. 1804 - Adms. account of estate of Henry YOUNG, late of Marietta. (60)
r. 1804 - Will of Edward W. HOWARD of Marietta twp., farmer - dated 4-9-1804.
To Bridget Foree of Marietta twp. $100. To Edward Howard son of Henry Howard
$100. Son, Henry Howard, residue of estate. Executors: John Brough, Esq.
and Bridgart Foree of Marietta twp. Signed: Edward W. Howard. Witnesses:
Aaron Howe, Joseph Cummings and Thomas Ramsey. 12-17-1804 Inventory of estate

of Edward W. Howard, late of Marietta. (60) Adms. account of estate of
Edward W. Howard, 8-20-1805. (61)
-----(1804-5?) - Will of Coggshall OLNEY of Marietta - dated 2-16-1804. Wife, Sarah.
Sons: Washington Olney and Discovery Olney. Daughters: Joanna, now dec'd,
late wife of Asa Davis; Sally wife of Daniel Davis, her children--Joanna,
Edwin Olney and Saphrona. Mentions adopted daughter, Jenny, not married, who
was the girl given by her mother. Mentions and bequeaths 8 rods land west of
house for family Burying Ground. Mentions land in Gallia County. Executors:
wife, Sarah; Ebenezer Ney and Daniel Davis Jr. Signed: Coggeshall Olney.
Witnesses: Abraham Whipple, Joseph Babcock, Mary Babcock and Huldah Olney. (62)
12-12-1804 - Inventory of Estate of Coggshall OLNEY, late of Marietta. (63)
------1804 - Will of Peregrine FOSTER of Belpre - dated 4-29-1802. Wife, Mary.
Sons: Peregrine Pitt, Frederick Augustus and Theodore Sedgwick; lands in
Newark twp., Vermont. Brother, Dwight Foster, Esq.; land in French Grant,
1300 acres in Good Co., Virginia, and lands in Ohio Co in name of Dwight
Foster. Three daughters: Polly Putnam, Seraph Dwight and Betsy Marietta.
To John Creed for his faithful service, 100 acres land in Donation Tract
#63 Washington County. Executor, William Rufus Putnam, Esq. of Marietta.
Signed: Paegrine Foster. Witnesses: Eben'r Battelle Jr., Abner Bent and
Charles Stretton. Codicil dated 2-23-1803 gives no additional information.
(63) 12-12-1804 - Inventory of Estate of Peregrine FOSTER.   (64)
Dec. 1804 - Adms. account of estate of Zoath HAMMOND, late of Waterford.   (65)
8-22-1804 - Adms account of estate of James SMITH. List inclues cost of schooling
for one child (not named). Priscilla Culver wife of Ebenezer Culver, late
Priscilla Smith, adms. of estate.   (65)
Aug. 1804 - Estate of Griffin GREENE, late of Marietta, dec'd. Letters of adms.
to Philip Greene.   (66)
-----(1804-5?) - Will of William WILLIAMS of Waterford twp. - dated 8-24-1804.
Wife, Martha. Sons: Wm and Ahira. Executor, Simeon Deming. Signed:
William Williams, Witnesses: Simon Starlin and Simon Starlin Jr. 6-15-1805
Inventory of Estate of William Williams.   (66)
Sec. 1804 - Estate of John QUIGLEY, late of Waterford, dec'd. Letters of adms.
to Robert Oliver.   (67)
4-13-1805 - Inventory of Estate of William WILLIAMS, dec'd.   (67)
Aug. 1803 - Adms. account of estate of Jonathan STONE of Belpre.   (67)
11-20-1802 - Inventory of Estate of Ebnezer PEIRCE of Waterford.   (68)
8-23-1805 - Inventory of Estate of Edward HENDERSON of Belpre.   (68)
2-6-1805 - Adms. account of Estate of Ebenezer Felch.   (70)
1-17-1805 - Estate of Daniel STORY of Marietta. Letters of adms. to William
Burnham of Marietta. (70) Jan. 1805 Inventory of Estate of Reverend Daniel
Story of Marietta.   (71)
Apr. 1805 - Will of Ebenezer SPROAT, Esq. of Providence Plantations, Providence,
Rhode Island and late of Marietta - dated 5-17-1786. Wife, Katherine.
Daughter, Sarah Sproat. Signed: E. Sproat. Witnesses: Pelatiah Hitchcock,
Peregrine Foster and Theodore Foster.   (74)
7-2-1805 - Inventory of Estate of Ebenezer SPROAT, Esq. of Marrietta. (75)
Dec. 1804 - Adms. account of Estate of John Case of Gallipolis.   (77)
Dec. 1805 - Inventory of Estate of Richard Greene, late of Marietta.   (77)

WASHINGTON COUNTY, OHIO – INDEX TO LAND ENTRIES

The following is an index to all land entries found in the first forty-three Deed Books. First number following name is deed book in which record may be found, second number is the page. If more than one deed for same person is on a page the number "2" is given in parenthesis—(2). a/o denotes assignee of. Land deeded to the "DIRECTORS OF THE OHIO COMPANY" is recorded in Volume 1, pages 115, 117 and 122.

ACKLEY, Russell	39-373	BROUGHTON, Jno. &		DANA, Betsy H.	42-232
ALBERRY, Richard	41-290	WHISTON, Jesse	26-418	DANA, Betsy M.	42-232
ALLEN, David	41-597	BROUGHTON, John	43-50	DANA, George	19-53
ALLEN, Isaac	43-47	BRYAN, Joseph	41-434	DANA, William	37-166
ANDERSON, John	37-522	BUCKINGHAM, Alvah	29-399		37-182
ARCHER, James	32-279		41-526		37-482
ARCHER, Simeon &			42-55		37-483
WRIGHT, Jonathan	18-208	BURRIS, Benj.	25-249	DANA, Wm. W.	10-352
AREND, Christian	40-320	BURRIS, John	17-131	DANA, Wm. W.	41-162
AYERS, John C.	41-32		22-611(2)	DAVIS, John	34-25
AYLES, Elias	41-556		25-149	DAY, John	41-453
AYRES, John C.	36-90				41-454(2)
	41-625	CADY, James	30-435(2)	DELONG, David	31-363
		CALVERT, Francis	41-72		42-212
BACHELOR, John	21-266	CALVERT, Joel	36-578	DIXON, John	30-313
BADGELY, Wm.	30-3	CAMP, Samuel	30-465	DOAN, Argellous	17-190
BAILEY, Charles A.	33-59		30-466	DOWELL, John	42-335
	33-60	CARLE, Ephraim T.	41-589	DUGAN, Samuel	36-370
BANE, James	41-480		41-590	DUNHAM, Amos	26-219
BARKER, Joseph	20-155	CARTER, John	35-39	DUSTIN, Miahill	40-538
	42-15	CARVER, Rachel	38-501		40-539
BARNES, Lewis	33-294	CASSADY, George	30-266	DUTTON, Harison	32-136
BARRETT, Wilson	38-549	CASSADY, Morton	30-209	DUTTON, James	32-276
BARTHOLLOWMEW, S.M.	39-108	CAYWOOD,		DUTTON, Joseph	22-185
	39-109(2)	Joseph 2nd	29-168		32-275
BATCHELDER, Ebenezer	20-172	CHAMBERLAIN, Thos	35-24	DUVALL, Jas. A.	41-590
BATCHELOR, John	29-382	CLARK, Alexander	41-337	DYAR, Jos. B.	40-100
BATCHELOR, John Jr.	29-383	CLINE, Adam	31-303		40-101
BATTON, Jesse	35-122	CLINE, Andrew	32-48	DYE, Amos	38-335
BECK, Samuel	40-305	CLINE, David	22-207		38-366
BECK, Vivan B.	40-304	CLINE, Thomas	35-32		43-64
BELL, Samuel	16-476	COLER, John	20-318	DYE, Daniel H. &	
BELL, Samuel Jr.	26-281		20-319	Jno. G.	40-600
BENNETT, John	12-47	COLLINS, Samuel	24-61	DYE, Ezekiel	37-335
BENNETT, Wm. P.	40-306	COOPER, Elisha	42-576	DYE, John	23-438
BERRY, Daniel	31-498	COOPER, " Jr.	41-611	DYE, Jno. W.	40-601(2)
BIXLY, George E.	40-273	COOPER, John	42-575	DYE, Jonathan	26-418
BLACKINGHAM, Alvah	35-195	CORNER, William	18-407	DYE, Rob't & Dan.	36-559
BLACKMER, Jesse	38-478		36-155	DYE, Samuel	27-314
BOWZER, Jacob	14-82	COZENS, Hezekiah	25-292	DYER, Jos. B.	29-209
	14-83	CRAIG, Isaac	39-321		
BOYD, Andrew	39-550	CRAIG, William	36-435	EDWARDS, Isaac	23-218
BOYD, George	41-73	CRAWFORD, Edward	31-95	ELDER, James	17-89
BRECKENRIDGE, Dav'd	29-147	CROTHERS, John Wm	30-281	EILINWOOD, Sam'l	26-482
BROPHY, John	29-88	CULTER, D. C.	39-426	ELLIS, Silas	41-376

731

Name	Ref	Name	Ref	Name	Ref
EOFFE, Jacob	32-324	HUFF, Bushrod	38-22	McMAHON, James	19-433
EUTELBUSH, John	34-348		38-23	McMASTERS, Andrew	42-48
EWART, F. W.	36-296	HUFF, Jona	36-164	McWILLIAMS, Jas.	40-578
		HUFFMAN, Roven	40-305		
FAIRLEY, Andrew	39-374	HUMPHREYS, Isaac	29-490	MACKALL, John D.	42-545
FISHER, Abraham	35-315		35-394		42-547
FLACK, James	26-420			MALSTER, John	20-312
FORD, Amon	26-61	JAYNE, Henry	32-307	MASTER, Joseph	39-546
FRENCH, Otho	39-196		35-120	MASTERS, Jas.	41-75
FULLER, Elizabeth	40-125		35-121	MIDDLESWART, Jacob	29-377
FULLER, Moses	40-124	JAYNE, Nelson	40-171	MILLER, John	30-65(2)
FULLER, Russell	32-387	JAYNE, Robert F.	40-170	MINER, Mathew	11-11
FULLER, Samuel H.	40-302	JENNINGS, Zebulon	38-68	MITCHELL, James	21-512
FULLER, Solomon	39-86	JETT, Thos. Jr.	18-182	MOON, Abraham	36-128
		JONES, David	39-164	MOORE, Joseph	40-330
GAMBE, William	33-539	JONSON, Rensellear	21-19	MORGANSTERN, Adam	42-233
GAMBLE, Henry	40-614(2)			MORRISON, Morris	41-502
GARRETSON, Hannah	43-65	KARR, Nathan	14-47	MUNROE, Rassilas	40-307
GARVIN, Mathew	31-417		18-183(2)		
GERKIN, Gerd	38-477	KELLEY, Wm. Jr.	40-641	NEEDHAM, Jasper	18-97
GILPIN, Caleb C.	31-100	KEEN, Jesse	34-398	NIXON, William	11-324
GOULD, Benjamin	18-411	KERR, Charles	40-424	NYE, Arius	36-508
	21-120	KETCH, Benjamin	16-97	NYE, Icahabod	25-175
GRAY, William	26-140	KIDDER, Gideon	31-39		25-176
GREENE, Isaac	38-142	KINFALL, Jeremiah	11-289		
	38-143	KIRK, Geo. W.	33-593	ORMISTON, James	38-540
GROVER, Elijah	36-85(2)	KITTS, Christian	41-25	OTIS, Stephen	36-543
			41-26		
HALE, Stephen	43-147			PALMER, James	36-379
HANCH(?), John	39-598	LASHLEY, Caleb	42-572		36-633
HANLIN, Jas & Felix	18-474	LEE, Samuel	42-44	PALMER, Jewett	39-634
HANNOLD, Isaiah M.	37-684	LEWELLEN, James	41-171	PALMER, Joseph	36-378
HARLSHOM, Leonard	40-553	LEWIS, Daniel	40-277	PALMER, Polly	36-379
HARMON, William	38-576	LIVERMORE, Jonas	29-268	PATTON, Mahlon	31-219
HARVEY, James	32-301	LORING, Jesse	25-192	PATTON, Thomas	41-24
HAWES, Willia	31-113	LOW, John	25-243	PAYNE, Vincent	30-124
HAYWARD, E. J.(?)	32-204	LUNDY, James	42-288	PEDICORD, Thomas	31-325
HEARN, Daniel	14-449	LYONS, John	40-429	PICKLE, John	31-95
HELMES, James	40-408(2)	LYTLE, Henry	43-158		31-96
HENRY, John	37-187			PINNEY, Benj.	41-232
HILDERBRAND, John	32-75	McALLISTER, Heirs		PORTER, Abner	34-493
HILDRETH, Sam'l P.	16-461(2)	of Wm.	21-433	PORTER, Joseph	42-91(2)
HILL, John	39-452	McCOY, James	40-579		42-92
HOLDEN, Joseph	13-299	McELROY, John	36-589	PRICE, Aaron	34-425
HOLDRON, Colman	39-153	McINTOSH, Wm. W.	36-640	PRIEST, Stephen	35-644
	39-154		36-641		38-214
HOLLAND, Horace	36-534		36-642	PRIOR, Elijah	32-161
HOLLISTER, Nathan	43-328	McKIBBEN, David	15-190	PRUNLY(?), Samuel	37-137
HOLLISTER, Rich.D.	29-150	McKINSEY, Alex.	29-89	PUTNAM, Aaron W.	13-32
HOSKINSON, Ezekiel	31-88	McMAHON, Abraham	41-266		19-400
HOSKINSON, Geo. W.	29-393		41-267	PUTNAM, David	28-456
	35-394				32-127

732

TNAM, Doughlas 38-642
TNAM, L. & P. 25-174
TNAM, Wm. P. &
  LABAN,Vincent 20-265
TNAM, Wm. Pitt 37-527

ILLIN, Amos 40-273

KE, Jacob 39-485
CTOR, Enoch 22-63
ED, Elijah 34-121
ED, Ezekiel 36-556
  36-557
EVE, Joshua 36-116
YNOLDS, Caleb 33-289
YNOLDS, Thomas 17-389
GGS, Hezekiah 39-348
NARD, Isaac 24-114
NARD, John 24-113
NARD, Sam'l K. 41-332
SS, Daniel Sr. 34-394
WLAND, Wm. 40-426
  40-427(2)
  40-428(2)
  40-429(2)

THERFORD, Dan'l 37-612
AN, Ausman 42-421

HOFIELD, Henry 31-208
OTT, Theodore 30-422
OTT, Thos. A. 33-340
EETZ, Adam 32-42
OCKEY, Jacob 36-179(2)

SHOCKEY, Minerva 36-180
SPRAGUE, Fred'k 41-380
STACKHOUSE, Isaac 40-610
STANLEY,Amzi,etal 13-308
STANSBERRY, Jonas 31-42
STENCART, Alex. 35-112
STEVENS, Samuel 42-364
STEWART, Daniel 39-34
STONE, John 24-240
STONE, Rufus P. 15-464
STORY, Harrison 37-694
STUBBS, Jacob 33-630
STULTS, Noah 40-448
STURGIS, Sol.
  a/o H. COZENS 27-448
STURGIS, Solomon 40-746

TALBOTT, Chas. 42-73
TEMPLETON, Geo. 43-367
TICE, James 13-19
  17-55
  24-528
TICE, Selomon 21-539
TINGLEY, Ebenezer 31-345
TINGLEY, Isabella 31-346
TOLMAN, Chester 27-66
TOOL, Patrick 42-14
TROVE(?), John 41-243
  41-244
TRUE, Amlin 31-38
TUTTLE, Linus
  s/o A. DOAN 15-384

VALENTINE, Benj. 29-493
  32-407
VARD, Nahum 31-101
VINCENT, Laban &
  Wm. P. PUTNAM 20-265

WALKER, Aaron 39-395
WARD, Nahum 36-563
  36-564
WARUFF(?), Oliver 36-478
WELLINGTON, Geo. 11-266
WEST, Sam'l M. 39-546
WEST, Sidney 29-365
WHISTON, Jesse &
  Jno. BROUGHTON 26-418
WHITTESIY, Wm. A. 29-257
WHITTLESEY, Wm. A. 36-381
WILKINS &
  WOODBRIDGE 40-513
WILLIAMSON, Jas. 18-129
WILSON, Hugh 25-247
WILSON, John 31-46
WISE, Andrew 36-42
WISE, Jacob 36-154
WOODFORD, Oliver
  Jr. & Elihu 18-221
WOODWARD, Mary 29-359
WOODWARD, Oliver
  Jr. 29-102
WRIGHT, Charles 33-291
WRIGHT, Jonathan
  & Simeon ARCHER 18-208

Cemetery is located in the northeast corner of Route 30 and Jefferson-Southern Rd.

FISHBURN, Abraham son of F. & S. d. Apr. 18, 1864; ae 9y 9m 9d
COCKLIN, Martha dau of R. & M. d. Apr. 18, 1864; ae 13y 10m 17d
    Martha wife of Joseph Cocklin d. Mar. 3, 1865; ae 32y 8m 20d
 . . . . . (Note, large stone down - can not be moved)
KLINE, Catharine B. wife of Jacob Kline d. Oct. 31, 1854; ae 32y 1m 28d
    Jacob d. Aug. 1, 1885; ae 77 yrs.
WAGONER, Anna L. dau of W. H. & A. L. d. Jan. 23, 1864; ae 1y 3d
    Elizabeth wife of Wm. b. Feb. 5, 1811;d. Dec. 21, 1873;ae 62y 10m 16d
JOLLIFF, Thomas b. July 11, 1801; d. Jan. 16, 1879
    Mary wife of Thomas Jolliff d. Feb. 4, 1875; ae 69y 8m 15d
    Moses d. Feb. 2, 1845, ae 12y 2m 20d
ALLAMAN, Children of W. H. & R. (all same stone):-
    Jennie d. Aug. 17, 1862 ae 5d; Mary d. Feb. 24, 1864 ae 14d
    Adrin A. d. Feb. 25, 1861 ae 2y 6m 5d; Willie d. Aug. 15, 1860 ae 2d
SWARTZ, Harvey son of J.(? chipped) & C d. Sept. 23, 1848; ae 2y 5m 23d
FOLGATE, . . .(effaced) wife of John Folgate d. Jan. 29, 1849; ae 77y 4m
FOLGATE, John born Mar. 12, 1765; died Sept 15, 1870; aged 105 yr. 6 mo. 3 ds.
PALMER, John G. (C.?) d. Aug. 1, 1859 in the 84th year of his age
    Mary wife of John C. Palmer d. Dec. 15, 1855; ae 62 years
SWARTS, George W. d. Apr. 23, 1844; ae (effaced)
EDWARDS, Homer, Esq. d. Jan. 15, 1850; ae 48y & 5d
SWARTZ, Benwell - Feb. 22, 1821 - Mar. 3, 1898 (same stone as Lucetta)
    Lucetta Nov. 9, 1828 - Jan. 3, 1904
COCKLIN, Peter d. May 30, 1866; ae 59y 1m 15d
    Mary wife of P. Cocklin d. April 15, 1885; ae 68y 2m 16d
LICH (or LIGH), John d. Sept. 27, 1873; ae 81 years
FISHBURN, Nancy Jane dau of F. & S. d. Nov 10, 1867; ae 22 years
ZELLER, John son of G. & J. d. Dec. 13, 1856; ae 3m 22d
WALTER, Henry G. d. Dec. 11, 1898; ae 25y 8m 28d (Walter inscriptions all on
    William G. d. Nov. 10, 1890; ae 22y 16d   same stone)
    Charles F. d. Dec. 22, 1883; ae 1y 9m 11d
WHITEMYER, Adrian d. Sept. 18, 1885; ae 16y 9m 23d
SWARTS, Aug. - Co. E, 120th O.V.I. (This is a metal emblem)
WALTER, Jacob 1823-1901; Catharine his wife 1838-1914 (same stone)
    Edward their son 1877-1903 (same stone as above)
SWEETLAND, Robert A. d. 1955; Ellen M. d. 19--(not engraved - same stone)
CALDWELL, Ada M. 1885-1962
ALLAMAN, Henry Mar. 29, 1836 - May 12, 1902   (Allaman inscriptions all on
    Rebecca Dec. 10, 1834 - Feb. 6, 1898   same stone)
    Adrian Aug. 22, 1858;Feb. 27,1861; Willie Aug. 13,1860; Aug. 15,1860
    Jennie Aug. 12, 1862; Aug. 17, 1862; Harry Feb. 24, 1864
FISHBURN, Henry 1847-1898; Leah his wife 1845-1926; William H. 1869-1898(same stone)
 . . . . . (Two field stones, one inscribed "Will" and the other "Ida")
BAKER, Bertha V. 1875-1962; Lyman J. 1882-1932 (same stone)
GIBSON, Milo W. 1903-1948; Ester V. 1918 - - --- (same stone)
WEIRICK, David Co. B., 60 O.V.I. 1834-(unengraved); Mary his wife 1841-1900 (same s)
WALKER Sisters - Mabel, Martha, Viola (no dates or ages)
WRIGHT, Robert d. Mar. 24, 1860; ae 40y 1d
LANTZ, Sarah wife of Emanuel Lantz d. Jan 24, 1855 ae 54y 9m 20d
EDWARDS, Maria wife of Homer Edwards, Esq. d. May 25, 1849; ae 35y 10m 21d

ZARING, Ida L. d. Aug. 9, 1865; ae 7y 2m 8d (same stone as twins)
    Twins b. Jan. 15, 1885; children of E. & M. Zaring
CHRISTIAN, Nathan M. son of N. & L. d. June 22, 1870; ae 3y 6m 9d
GIPE, John son of LAH Gipe d. Feb. 18, 1860; ae 2m 10d (The inscrip. "LAH" as on)
GEIP, Rosana dau of J. & E. d. June 14, 1872; ae 53y 11m 15d   stone)
TEENEY, Wilson E. son of L. & M. d. Sept. 3, 1858; ae 1y & 25 d
GIPE, John d. Mar. 18, 1861; ae 71y 1m 8d
BAKER, A. 1800-1891; Samuel H. son of A. & H. died . . . (cemented in base)
    Hannah wife of A. Baker; b. Lancaster Co. Mar. 30-1797; d. May 9, 1871
FISHBURN, Cora Ellen dau of . . . Fishburn . . . . (weathered)
    Levi, Co. I, 16 O.V.I. 1837-1903 (same stone as Mary)
    Mary his wife 18__(not inscribed)-1933
MARKS, Emeline 1876-1899 (same stone as Levi & Mary Fishburn)
FISHBURN, Edward D. 1879-1908
DILCARD, Lizzie FISHBURN age 20 years (no date inscribed)
FISHBURN, Clementnie b. July 12, 1872 d. Feb. 6, 1884 (same stone as Mary)
    Mary b. Oct. 29, 1870 d. Sept. 18, 1885
BRIDENSTINE, Susan d. March 31, 1843 ae 2y 2m 11d
    Samuel d. May 9, 1843 ae 10m 27d
WEIRICK, Sarah wife of Henry Wierick d. Apr. 1, 1878; ae 79y 6m 7d
    Henry d. Nov. 24, 1868 ae 73y 7m 25d
. . . . . . (Large old type rose-slate stone - effaced)
ALLAMAN, Samuel b. Aug. 5, 1811 d. Mar. 10, 1844   (Allamans' all on
    Barbara b. Feb. 16, 1810 d. July 2, 1873   same stone)
    Rachael b. Aug. 1, 1833 d. Apr. 8, 1894
    Elizabeth b. Nov. 9, 1840 d. Feb. 19, 1844
HOUSER, Amelia wife of Jasoe(?) Houser d. Jan. 30, 1852; ae 28y 2. 29d
                                    (stone is very weathered)
BINGGELI, Anna 1833-1887
DERBY, Mary E. dau. of W. R. & H. A. d. Feb. 12, 1841; ae 5 m
    (Large old type rose-slate stone - effaced)
BAKER, Regeina dau of S. & E. d. Sept. 3, 1837; ae 1y 1m 28d
    Catharine A. dau. of A. & H. d. Sept. 25, 1837; ae 4m & 28d
UPHAM, Curtis Z. son of L. H. & Elizabeth d. Jan. 16, 1842; ae 2y 3m 18d
    Hannah L. dau of L. H. & Elizabeth d. March 6, 1841 (or 1844); 1y 4m 6d
    Myra E. dau. of L. H. & E. d. Aug. 2, 1844
BLACK, Peter son of P. & L. d. Oct. 8, 1848 ae 6m 12d
KETTERING, Barbara wife of Philip Kettering d. Sept. 5, 1847 ae 42y 5m 11d
    Moses son of P. & B. d. Aug. 18, 1840 ae 1y 6m (same stone as Barbara)
JOLLIFF, Peter d. Apr. 24, 1857; ae 63y 7m 23d
JOLIFF, Rebecca wife of Peter Joliff d. August 1864; age 75 years
JOLLIFF, Reuban d. Dec. 5, 1845; ae 7y 7m 21d
    Christian d. Dec. 11, 1845; ae 18y 8m & 10d
    Aaron d. Dec. 26, 1845; ae 13y 10m 13d
SWARTZ, Ann Jenette dau. of C. & E. d. May 3, 1869; ae 2y 9m 3d

Note:- The "F" on "FOLGATE" was postively plain, but no sign of there having
been a short horizonal mark on the "F" so this name may be incorrect. In the
name "COCKLIN" it was impossible to distinguish if a "C" or "G". Flour was
used to read all these "hard-to-cipher" inscriptions)

The following records were taken from Will Book 3 as found in the Probate Court at the court house at Wooster. Pages on which original record may be found are given in parenthesis.

HUFFNER, John - dated 9-4-1840; recorded 10-6-1840. Wife, Elizabeth, to have 77 acre plantation in Perry twp. during her natural life. Five children, mentioned but not named. Executors: wife, Elizabeth and John S. Meng. Signed: John Heffner. Witnesses: Henry Jackson, Philip Meng Sr. (1)

VAN NOSTREN, Margaret of Wayne twp. - dated 8-28-1839; recorded 9-21-1840. Requests that she be buried in the burying ground of Bethney Church at Wooster. Mother (not named), to have all estate which might have fallen to Margaret from her father's estate. Signed: Margaret Vannosetstren. Witnesses: James Van Nostren, J. H. Downing. (2)

OGDEN, Oliver - dated 5-21-1840; recorded 9-21-1840. Wife, Elizabeth, also to serve as executrix. Hugh Norton to be guardian of children until they are 21 yrs. of age (children not named). Signed: Oliver Ogden. Witnesses: Thomas Barton, Josiah Barton. (3)

BISHOP, John - dated 6-20-1840; recorded 8-12-1840. Wife (not named) and children (not named) to remain on farm testator now owns until youngest child is of age. Esecutor: brother, Christian Bishop. Signed: John (his mark) Bishop. Witnesses: Alexander Scott, John Miller. (4)

WILLYARD, George L. of Wooster - verbal will given 7-22-1840; deposition given 7-27-1840; recorded 8-12-1840. Leaves all estate to his mother (not named). Witnesses: Wm McMahon, James C. Miller. (5)

HARRISON, Mathew of Southwark, Moyamensing twp., Philadelphia Co., Penna. - dated 12-15-1831; recorded Wayne Co., Ohio 3-8-1841. Wife, Margaret. Executors: Andrew McFadden and High Dickson, both of Philadelphia. Signed: Mathew (his mark) Harrison. Witnesses: Thomas Dickson, James Black, Samuel McFadden Jr. (6)

ALEXANDER, John - dated 2-13-1842; recorded 3-8-1841. Wife, Mary, to have 1/3 of farm in Franklin twp. containing 188 acres. Son, Thomas W. Alexander, not of age. Mentions other children and specifically "unmarried daughters", but does not name. Executors: Aaron Franks and Jacob Nixon. Signed: John Alexander. Witnesses: James Wilson, Daniel Miller. Codicil dated 2-14-1841 gives no additional information. (7)

SERVICE, Hugh - dated 9-10-1840; recorded 3-8-1841. Wife, Phoebe, also to serve as executrix. Signed: Hugh Service. Witnesses: William Boles, Thomas Gabriel. (9)

MILLER, Christian of Wayne twp. - dated 4-16-1839; recorded 3-8-1841. Wife, Barbara. Son, Christian Miller. Daughters: Catharine Crybill and her heirs (not named); Magdalena Wanger, Meria Rhoads and Barbara Miller. Executor, Gideon Zook. Signed: Christian Miller (German signature). Witnesses: William Reiter, Amos Reiter. Codicil dated 2-17-1841 gives no additional data. (10)

KIRKENDALL, Christopher - dated 2-14-1837; recorded 5-4-1841. Wife, Elizabeth, plantation where now lives containing 80 acres during her natural life. Sons: Samuel, James, Christopher and Archibald Kirkendall. Daughters: Sarah, Phoebe, Eliza and Mary. Executors: wife, Elizabeth and son, Samuel. Signed; Christopher Kirkendall. Witnesses: Samuel K. Miller, John Scott, William Meeks. (12)

FINLEY, Michael - dated 5-3-1841; recorded 5-24-1841. Wife, Elizabeth. Brother, Ebenezer Finley, also to serve as executor. If wife dies or remarries, all estate is to fall to children of brother, Ebenezer. Signed: Michael Finley. Witnesses: Robert Hatfield, Nancy Hatfield. (14)

FOLMER, Jacob of Wooster twp. (Will in German) - dated 2-22-1841; recorded 5-24-1841. Wife, Catharine born Klotz; to have both legacy coming from his parents (not named) and testators own property. Children, mentioned but not named. Signed: Jacob Folmer (German signature). Witnesses: Conrod Strack, Ralph Funk, Frederick Svenchen. (15)

MEYER, Jacob of Mohecan - dated 12-27-1840; recorded 5-24-1841. Wife, Elizabeth. Mentions Myers Miller now living with testator, not of age. Executors: nephew, Jacob Miller and Samuel Montgomery. Signed: Jacob Meyer. Witnesses: Elzey Wilson, Isaac Baker. (17)

JAMISON, Stephen M. - dated 5-7-1841; recorded 5-24-1841. Wife, Nancy S. Jameson, to have house and lot in village of Dover. Three children: Rebecca Jane, Rodney Carr, and Stephen Rush; all not of age. Testator owns drug and grocery store; out-lot Dover; house and lot in Middletown; also lot in Lima, Allen Co., Ohio. Executor, John McFarland. Signed: Stephen M. Jameson. Witnesses: Arch'd Hanna, James Cuningham. (18)

BECK, Aaron - dated 3-31-1841; recorded 5-24-1841. Wife, Amy Beck. Two sons, Metcalf and Alford Beck, with Alford to have silver watch and 8 day marble clock, etc. Mentions log yard. Executors: son, Metcalf Beck and George Pfouts Jr. Signed: Aaron Beck. Witnesses: Frederick Shull, Jacob Beam. (20)

HOFF, Philip - dated 4-30-1840; recorded 7-13-1841. Farm in NW¼ Section 1, Township 15, Range 13 where testator now lives is to be sold with proceeds divided into nine shares with 8 shares to children (not named other than executors) and ninth share to children of son, Jacob Huff, dec'd so that his oldest daughter (not named) receives $100.00 and other children rest of said share. Executors: sons, George Huff, Peter Huff, and Henry Huff. Signed: Philip Huff. Witnesses: John H. Harris, Wm. McMahon. (22)

STIBBS, Joseph - dated 8-10-1841; recorded 8-25-1841. Estate to be divided into six shares, with shares to: son, Reasin B. Stibbs; son, Joseph Stibbs, his wife Mary and their children; son, Thomas Stibbs; grandchildren Henry and Rebecca M. Hamilton; daughter, Margaret, a minor; daughter, Henrietta, a minor. Margaret and Henrietta to be cared for as they have been in the past by Mrs. Elizabeth Hull until they are of age. Mentions several properties which appear to be leased, also "lower mills". Executors: son, Reasin B. Stibbs; David Robison; and Edward Avery. Signed: J. Stibbs. Witnesses: R. Beall, A. Hemphill, Cyrus Shink. (25)

EBERMAN, Jacob M. of Wooster - dated 9-3-1833; recorded 8-26-1841. Wife, Sarah, also to serve as executrix. Children, mentioned but not named. Signed: Jacob M. Eberman. Witnesses: I. W. Schuckers, Samuel Schuckers. (27)

YODER, Isaac of Green twp. - dated 4-9-1841; recorded 9-27-1841. Wife, Catharine, house and lot in Wooster. To David Yoder of Holmes Co., Ohio, "my sister Elizabeth's son" twenty dollars. To Jeptha Plank Sr. $2000.00 and to Catharine Miller daughter of Frederick Miller of Wayne Co. $200.00 (no relationship if any stated). Rest of estate to go for relief of the poor of the Omish Society or Church. Executors: friends, Jeptha Plank Sr. and Gideon Zook. Signed: Isaac Yoder. Witnesses: Jacob Erb, John Weidman, John Wyse.   (28)

METCALF, John H. - dated 7-23-1841; recorded 9-27-1841. Wife, Nancy, after her death farm to be divided between Edward Metcalf and Vachel Metcalf and they are to pay Hannah Metcalf fifty dollars and Margaret Metcalf one hundred dollars within two years time (no relationship if any stated--children?). Signed: John H. Metcalf. Witnesses: Daniel Pocock, John Metcalf.   (30)

SHOEMAKER, Christian - dated 9-30-1840; recorded 10-4-1841. Wife, Catharine, at her death all estate to go to John Stoner with whom testator and wife make their home. Executor, John Stoner. Signed; Christian Shoemaker. Witnesses: John Schrock, Simon Ruble. (31)

HATFIELD, Robert - dated 8-6-1839; recorded 9-27-1841. Wife, Nancy Hatfield. Sons: William, Aaron, George D. and Cyrus. Daughters: Margaret Dunham, Catharine A. Cunningham, Mary Hatfield now Johnston and Sarah Hatfield. Signed: Robert Hatfield. Witnesses: Adam Hatfield, Thomas Dunham.   (33)

SHAFFER, George of Plain twp. - dated 8-25-1840; recorded 9-27-1841. Wife, Elizabeth. Sons: George, Jacob, Abraham and John. Daughters: Elizabeth, Sarah, Mary, Hannah, Lidi, Mary or Mary Anna (sic) and Judia. Executors: son, Abraham and Jacob Solliday. Signed: George Shaffer. Witnesses: David Kauffman, George Ackerman.   (34)

DEARMAN, Samuel - dated 8-16-1841; recorded 9-27-1841. Wife, Margaret. Sons: Robert and James, also to serve as executors. Daughters: Mary, Ann McClelland and Elizabeth Gott. Signed: Samuel (his mark) Dearman. Witnesses: James Culbertson, Robert Reed, Leonard Richards. (35)

KAMPF, Anthony - dated 10-12-1841; recorded 10-25-1841. Wife, Sarah. Daughters: Elizabeth, Sarah Kampf, and Mariah Kampf. Grandson, John Kampf of John Kampf, not of age. Mentions "all children to share estate". Executors: JohnMcFarland and David Anderson. Signed: Anthony (his mark) Kampf. Witnesses: Charles McFadden, James Evans Jr. (37)

McCRACKEN, James - dated 1-23-1835; recorded 10-25-1841. Wife, Agnes. Sons: Thomas McCracken, his sons--William and Henry McCracken; John McCracken; Nathaniel McCracken, his son--James McCracken; James McCracken. Daughters: Ann Adair; Susan McCracken; Rachel McCracken; Nessy Moderwell; Elizabeth McCracken. Mentions two daughters (not named) of Maria Philips, also, Samuel and Valentine Wright sons of Rual Wright; but no relationship of any is given. Executors: son, James McCracken and Alexander McBride. Signed: James McCracken. Witnesses: John Q. Hutcheson, Thomas (his mark) Tate. (38)

DAY, Oliver of East Union twp. - dated 5-4-1840; recorded 3-14-1842. Wife, Margaret. Three sons, Elam Day, Oliver Day and David P. Day all of Hancock Co., Ohio. Three daughters: Diadema Goodal of Buffalo, New York; Clarissa Dame of Fort Defiance, Ohio; and Hannah Culling of Melan, Huron Co., Ohio. Stepson and son of beloved wife, David Morros, who has lived with testator from time he was eight years old until married and had family and yet a part of testators family. Executor, Samuel Orr, Esq. of East Union twp. Signed: Oliver Day. Witnesses: David Pechen, Smith Orr, Samuel Orr, Thomas Orr. (40)

COCKRELL, Robert of Canaan twp. - dated 1-15-1841; recorded 12-1-1841. Wife, Prudence. Oldes son, Hiram Cockrell, if he outlives present wife Ellen he is to share with rest of children in estate. Sons, John and Robert Mortimer Cockrell, to have land entered at Chillicothe land office by certificate of 11-15-1838; they are also to serve as executors. Signed: Robert (his mark) Cockrell. Witnesses: Christian Hower, George Brickman. (41)

HEISER, John - dated 9-21-1841; recorded 11-9-1841. Mentions his deceased wife. Sons: John Heiser and William Heiser; with son, John to keep William during William's natural life. Two daughters: Elizabeth Otto and Catharine Goudy. Nephew, Daniel M. Fletcher, not of age, to be in John Heisers care until he reaches 21 yrs. of age. Executors: son, John Heizer and Edmund Ingmand. Signed: John Heiser. Witnesses: Elijah Yocum, E. Ingmand. (43)

STILSON, George A. - dated 12-24-1841; recorded 3-14-1842. Wife, Louisa. Son, William. Daughter, Harriet Stilson. Executors: wife, Louisa and Richard Cahill. Signed: George A. Stilson. Witnesses: Ch's C. Parsons, Mary Moffit. (44)

SANDS, William of Paint twp. - dated 7-5-1841; recorded 3-14-1842. Wife, Sarah, house and lot in Ledrightsburg. Sons: William, James and John; John left home before 21 yrs. Daughters: Margaret Johnston, Jane Campbell, Elizabeth Bays and Mary McFadden. Executor, Isaac Goodin Sr. Signed: William (his mark) Sands. Witnesses: Thomas Ingram, David Goff and David Wisard Jr. (46)

ELLIOTT, Simeon - dated 4-7-1842; recorded 5-23-1842. Wife, Eleanor. Four sons; Thomas, John, William and Simeon Elliott. Four daughters; Margaret, Charity, Anne and Jane Elliott. Executor; brother, Thomas Elliott. Signed: Simeon Elliott. Witnesses: Jonas Denton, Henry Frank, Wm Lance (or Sance?). (47)

JOHNSTON, Robert of Chippewa twp. - oral will - will given 4-20-1842; deposition given 4-26-1842; recorded 5-23-1842. Requests payment be made on his land out of office of Virginia Military District School land. Witnesses: Isaac Kyle, David Keck. (49)

MENG, Philip of Perry twp. - dated 3-9-1842; recorded 5-23-1842. Wife, Mary Margaretha Meng. Daughter, Anna Snyder with her husband and child to live with Mary Margaretha. At death of wife rest of estate to be divided between "all my legal heirs". Executors: John S. Meng and George Buffermere. Signed: Philip Meng. Witnesses: John Snyder, Jacob Miller. (50)

NOBLE, James - dated 1-31-1842; recorded 3-14-1842. Wife, Elizabeth. Sons: William, John, Robert and James Noble. Daughter, Elizabeth Johnston. Executor: son, Robert Noble. Signed: James (his mark) Noble. Witnesses: Andrew Ault, David Bierer. (52)

SILBER, Christian - dated 3-21-1841; recorded 9-26-1842. Wife, Catharine. Five sons: Michael, Jacob, Christian, Daniel and John. Daughters: Elizabeth Deffendoffer, Catharine Core, Margaret Stonebreaker and Sophia Thomas. Executors: sons, Michael and Daniel. Signed: Christian Silber. Witnesses: Wm. Goodfellow, Frederick Mesner. (53)

TRAUGER, John - dated 8-19-1842; recorded 9-26-1842. Wife, Mary, plantation where now live in Congress twp. containing 200 acres. Son, Jacob H. Trauger, not of age. To Martha Catharine, Mary and Paul Trauger children of George Trauger, they are not of age. Executors: wife, Mary and George Trauger. Signed: John Trauger. Witnesses: Jacob Felger, M. Funk. (55)

STOOLMILLER, Lewis of Chippewa twp. - dated 9-17-1842; recorded 9-26-1842. Wife, Elizabeth. Children, mentioned but not named except for daughter, Louisa; all are not of age. Signed: Lewis (his mark) Stoolmiller. Witnesses: David Andrews, George Row. (57)

FOLTZ, John - dated 3-2-1842; recorded 9-26-1842. Wife, Mary. Sons: Gideon, Joseph, David, Jonathan, Samuel, John, William, Frederick and Eli Jackson Foltz; with first eight named to have legacy coming out of testator's father-in-law's estate. Five daughters: Elizabeth Shreve, Mary Spencer, Rebecca Foltz, Eliza Cameron and Julia A. Foltz; to have money coming from testator's father's estate. Executor: friend, William Sidle. Signed: John Foltz. Witnesses: William Bruce, Thomas McConkey.(58)

BEALL, Reasen - dated 2-18-1843; recorded 2-28-1843. Wife, Nancy, farm where now reside pt. Section 3, Township 15, Range 13, also my newest Bible. Daughters: Maria E. Euningham, Nancy C. Shenk, Harriet Christmas and Mary Jane Culbertson. Grand-children: Mary Jane, William H., Caroline, Rebecca B., Emma and Ednumd B. Christmas. Grandsons: Reasin Beall Shenk son of Cyrus Shenk; Reason Beall Stibbs; William Cox, t have watch; Julian Shenk; Thomas Stibbs, to have case of mathematical instruments. Grand-daughters: Ellen E. and Jane Cox daughters of William Cox; Rebecca Beall Christmas to have forto piano. Nephews: John Beall; Parker Campbell Beall to have Surveyors Compass and Chains. Bible to Nancy C. Spenk. $370.00 to each of children of Cyrust & Nancy C. Spenk: Rebecca B. McMillen, Julie Spenk, Martha Spenk, Sophrona Spenk, Reasin Beall Spenk, Amanda Spenk and Nancy Ann Beall Spenk. $370.00 to Reasin Beall Stibbs. $370.00 to Joseph Stibbs. $370.00 each to Reasin Beall Stibbs in trust for Thomas, Margaret and Henrietta Stibbs. $370.00 to Levi Cox in trust for grandchildren--William Cox, Maria E. Vanmetre, Joseph Cox, Cyrus Cox and Terressa Cox. $370.00 each to William Cox of Lancaster in trust for grandchildren Ellen E. and Jane Cox. $370.00 to daughter, Maria E. Cuningham. $370.00 each to John Cuningham in trust for grandchildren--Cushman and Rebecca B. Cuningham. $370.00 to daughter, Harriet Christmas. $370.00 each to Reasen Beall Stibbs in trust for William H., Mary Jane, Caroline, Rebecca Beall, Emma and Edmund Christmas. $370.00 to Mary Jane Culbertson. Mentions not of $7000.00 which testator holds on estate of Joseph Stibbs, dec'd. Bequeaths $50.00 each to John Fisht and Sophronia McAfee and $100.00 to Mary Ann Graham. Bequeaths to Rev. William McCandless the use of undivided half of house and lot he now occupies as long as he remains pastor of congregation he has charge of

740

(continued - Beall, Reasen)
in Wooster. Executors: Syres Spenk, Reasin Beall Stibbs and Levi Cox. Signed: R.
Beall. Witnesses: James A. Grant, S. N. Bissel, Wm H. Keys. (note: surname of
Shenk is given as Spenk is some places). (59)

OKELY, William - dated 10-1-1842; recorded 12-20-1842. Children: Mary Clark, Betsy
Meek, Abraham Okely, Rachel Bennet and Aaron Okely, dec'd, his two children (not
named). Grandsons: William Foster and Jacob Steiner. Grand-daughters: Rachel
Steiner and Mary Ann Meek. Mentions estate of William Clark, dec'd. Executors:
Adam Sheneman and George Emery. Signed: Wm Okely. Witnesses: A. H. Byers,
Benjamin C. Byers. (63)

SIKES, George - dated 10-5-1843; recorded 12-5-1843. Wife, Eve. Mentions sons and
daughters, but does not name. Executor, David Kauffman, Esq. Signed: George Seix.
Witnesses: Michael Ely, Lemuel Miller, John Berger, Jacob Lybarger. (64)

MILLER, George - dated 3-24-1842; recorded 5-22-1843. Wife, Mary. Sons: John, Gil-
bert, James, Joseph, William S., George and Samuel Miller. Daughters: Mary Saint,
Isabella Hogan and Jane Ensminger. Executors: son, Gilbert Miller and S. Wilkin.
Signed: George Miller. Witnesses: Thomas (his mark) Richey, John (his mark)
Richey. (65)

PEPPARD, Jonathan of Fredericksburg - dated 11-14-1842; recorded 3-6-1843. Sons:
William, Francis, David, John and Isaac. Daughters: Rebecca; Jane; Mary; and Phebe
Hatfield, dec'd, her children (not named). Executors: son, Francis Peppard and son-
in-law, Jimpsey Hucheson. Signed: Jonathan Peppard. Witnesses: Edward R. Geary,
James Hutcheson. (67)

HAGUE, William - dated 2-18-1843; recorded 3-6-1843. Wife (not named specifically,
but name be Margaret?), at her death or marriage, all estate to William Haines.
Executors: Margaret Hague and Gilbert Leech. Signed: William (his mark) Hague.
Witnesses: Samuel Spencer, Ebenezer (his mark) Martin. (68)

NOLD, John of Wooster - dated 12-12-1842; recorded 3-6-1843. Wife, Catharine.
Children mention but not named except for son, William. Son-in-law, Gotlieb Gasche.
Executors: wife, Catharine and son, William. Signed: John Nold. Witnesses: H. S.
Wolford, Charles Gashey. (69)

EARL, Mary of Franklin twp. - dated 10-6-1842; recorded 3-6-1843. Mother, Abigail
Smith. Brothers and Sisters; Samuel F. Smith, James O. Smith, Nicholas S. Smith,
Henry A. Smith, Rebecca Griffeth, Abigail Bristo(w), George P. Smith and Eleanor
Smith, "all my interest in homestead farm". Nieces: Mary Jane and Sarah Ann
Griffeth. Mentions Catharine wife of brother, Samuel Smit . Mentions $19.00 she is
to receive for school teaching. Mentions judgement against "Robert Earl my former
husband". Executor, John Orr. Signed: Mary Earl. Witnesses: James Wilson,
Samuel Buckmaster. (70)

COE, Margaret - dated 4-5-1842; recorded 3-6-1843. Sons: Ebenezer, James, Benjamin
and Stephen Coe. Daughter, Eunes Davis. Grandson, Stephen Williams Coe. Signed:
Margaret Coe. Witnesses: Samuel Brice, Henry Shield. (72)

AUSTEN, Ambrose of Jeromesville - dated 2-21-1837; recorded 3-6-1843. Wife, Susannah Austin. Sons: Eldest son, Charles Austin; Henry Austin, now living in Liverpool, Old England; John Austin; Ambrose Austen; and Joseph Austin. Daughters: eldest dau., Susannah Peirce living Pine Creek near Pittsburg, Penna.; youngest dau., Charlotte Austin. Executors: three sons; Charles, Ambrose and Joseph Austin. Signed: Ambrose Austin. Witnesses: John Winbigler, Mary (her mark) Winbigler, Sarah Ann Winbigler. (74)

SMITH, Eli B. - dated 1-24-1843; recorded 3-6-1843. Wife, Fanny, use of farm and Lot #3 in Fredericksburg. Children, mentioned but not named, not of age. Executor, Daniel Black. Signed: Eli B. Smith. Witnesses: Daniel Black, John Smith. (76)

SANSOM, Joseph of Chester twp. - dated 10-19-1842; recorded 11-21-1842. Wife, Isabella. Sons: William and Joseph Sansom. Daughters: Mary Shipley, Jane Sansom and Sarah Sansom. Executor, Jacob Miller of Perry twp. Signed: Joseph (his mark) Sansom. Witnesses: John A. Smilie, Joseph Gruey. (77)

NIXON, William Sr. - dated 10-1-1833; recorded 3-6-1843. Bequest ot Agnes Caldwell or State of Pennsylvania widow and relict of Samuel Caldwell, dec'd. To Jane, Mary, Robert, Margaret, Samuel and Isabella Caldwell, children of above mentioned Samuel and Agnes Caldwell. Rest of estate to Samuel Taggart of Wayne Co. with whom testator resides. Executors: George Gardner Sr. and David Morrow. Signed: William (his mark) Nixon. Witnesses: Smith Fenton, Robert Fenton. (79)

WOODS, Alexander of Chippewa twp. - dated 3-15-1843; recorded 3-29-1843. Wife, Mary, to have whole control and share of her father's estate coming in Pennsylvania. Oldest son, Reuben N. Woods. Oldest daughter, Mary Woods, received schooling at Granville. Second daughter, Martha Woods, expenses of foreign schooling. Youngest son, Harvey Woods. Five hundred dollars for religious purposes. Wife, Mary to be guardian of son Harvey and daughter Martha until of age. Executor; neighbor, John Brown of Chippewa twp. Signed: Alexander Woods by John Brown at his request. Witnesses: Ephraim Chidester, Daniel Huffman. (80)

SMITH, Thomas - dated 6-25-1842; recorded 4-13-1843. Sons; Isaac J. Smith; Samuel Smith to have books "Laws of Pennsylvania", "Blackstones Commentaries", also surveying compass and leveling instruments; Harvey Smith; and Joseph Smith. Daughters: Joanna Smith and Josephine Smith. Grand-daughters: Eleanor J. Smith daughter of Joseph Smith, dec'd and Elizabeth Smith daughter of William Smith. Bequest to Julia Allison. Rest of estate to be divided equally between: Isaac J. Smith, William Smith, Adison Smith, Rebecca Roberts wife of Leonard Roberts " my daughter", Hannah M. wife of Doctor Nathaniel Dusten, Mary Ann wife of Shibnah Shink, Harvey Smith, Samuel Smith, Joanna Smith, Thomas Smith, Charles Smith, Josephine Smith and Joseph Smith. Executor; friend, Charles McClure. Signed: Thomas Smith. Witnesses: Alexander McBride, John Q. Hutcheson. (83)

BAKER, John of Perry twp - dated 3-7-1842; recorded 3-6-1843. Heirs: son, David Baker; Polly Henish; Betsy Martin; son, John Baker; daughter, Peggy Shearer; daughter Anna Elson; daughter, Sally Ficke (Fike); and daughter, Susannah Detwiler. Executor, David Baker. Signed: John Baker. Witnesses: Samuel Luce, Andrew Kollar. (85)

GARDINER, George Sr. - dated 2-24-1843; recorded 5-22-1843. Wife, Elizabeth. Sons: James and George Gardiner. Daughters: Martha Foreman; Sally Robison, her children (not named); Sidna; Fanny Gardiner; Elizabeth Gardiner. Grandson, David Foreman son of Alexander and Sidna Foreman of Hancock Co., Ohio, land where they now live. Executors: Aaron Franks and Wilson Robeson. Signed: George Gardiner. Witnesses: F. Beecher, Daniel Hines. Codicil dated 3429-1843 names daughters Sidna Robeson and Martha Foreman. Same witnesses. (88)

SMITH, Elizabeth of Wooster twp. - dated 1-6-1841; recorded 7-13-1843. Mentions money due from estate of her deceased husband, Nicholas Smith which is to be paid to Valentine G. Smith. Bequeaths to Sarah Butterbaugh; Maria Smith daughter of Valentine G. Smith; Nicholas Smith son of Valentine G. Smith, to have family Bible; Rebecca Fleck; Valentine G. Smith, to have residue of estate, also to serve as executor; (note: specific relationships if any not given). Signed: Elizabeth (her mark) Smith. Witnesses: Isaac Burnett Jr., Isaac Burnett Sr. (90)

BARTOL, Mathias - dated 9-30-1843; recorded 9-28-1843. Wife, mentioned but not named. Sons: George, John and Abraham Bartol; the last two are unmarried. Mentions several "sons and daughters" and their heirs, some may be ceceased(?). Executors: son, George and son-in-law, William Taggart. Signed: Mathias (his mark) Bartol. Witnesses: William Taggart, J. W. Schucker. (91)

BIGHAM, John of Green twp. - dated 7-22-1843; recorded 9-28-1843. Wife, Catharine. Three sons: Robert, Michael and Hugh Bigham. Three daughters: Nancy, Jane and Mary; Mary not of age. Mentions money coming from his brother's estate in Pennsylvania. Executors: wife, Catharine and son, Robert. Signed: John (his mark) Bigham. Witnesses: Thomas Dorrough, George Speva. (93)

STEINER, Peter - dated 1-13-1843; recorded 9-28-1843. Wife, Barbary. Youngest son, Jacob Steiner. Mentions "all my children". Executors: two sons, Uley Steiner and Daniel Steiner. Signed: Peter Steiner. Witnesses: Andrew Ault, Peter Zimmerly.(95)

OWEN, Moses of Jeromeville - dated 3-28-1839; recorded 5-22-1843. Wife, Rhoda Ann Owens. Mentions brothers children, but does not name. Executors: wife, Rhoda Ann and friend, Daniel McDonald. Signed: Moses Owens. Witnesses: Thomas Dunham, John L. Skggs. (96)

BECKLEY, Daniel of Chester twp. - dated 2-7-1843; recorded 9-28-1843. Sons: Thomas, James, Conrod, Edward and Daniel Beckley. Daughters: Sarah wife of Henry Kauffman and Catharine wife of Henry Emery. Executor: son, Edward. Signed: Daniel (his mark) Beckly. Witnesses: John Craig, Peter Christy of Chippewa twp. (98)

HOCKENBERG, Michael - dated 6-16-1843; recorded 12-5-1843. Sons: Lazarus, George, Harmon, Peter and John Hockenberg; with Abraham Lantz to be guardian of son John until age of 21 years. Daughters: Sophia Baatlet, Christeena Bowman, and Mary Stull. Two grand-daughters: Sarah and Mary Fenstemaker daughters of daughter, Delila. Bequeaths to Susanna Cretzer (no relationship if any stated). Executor, Samuel Ferguson. Signed: Michael Hockenberg. Witnesses: John Barkhamer, Samuel Blair. (99)

ETZWELER, Frederick of Lake twp. - dated 9-26-1843; recorded 9-28-1843. Wife, Christena. Sons: George, Daniel, John, Jacob or his heirs, and Joseph: Joseph to have blacksmith tools. Daughters: Mary Elizabeth and Lydia Etswiler. Executor, David Kauffman. Signed: Frederick Etswiler. Witnesses: Jacob Long, George Bender. (104)

743

WILLIAMS COUNTY, OHIO - MARRIAGES 1824-1837

The following records were taken from "Marriage Record 1-2" located in the Probate Court of the court house at Bryan.

AUSTIN, James B. to Ruth Shirley	8-12-1830
BACK, John to Catherine Miers	10-26-1826
BACK, Samuel to Mary Doty	4-11-1830
BALL, Jared A. to Malind Stater	8-2-1836
BANKS, Richard to Nancy Murphy	3-10-1836
BARKER, John to Olive Martin	6-30-1833
BATES, Joseph to Phebe Ann Hagerman	3-23-1837
BEAVER, William to Susannah Brackbill	4-7-1836
BENDER, William to Sntha Fee	3-16-1837
BLUE, James H. to Mary Ellen Hill	9-20-1836
BOWERS, Samuel to Elizabeth Hunter	1-13-1825
BRIDENBAUGH, Frederick to Catherine Davis	2-19-1833
BRIDENBAUGH, John to Mary Hively	1-6-1833
BRIDENBAUGH, Peter to Evaline Lewis	11-20-1831
BUCKLIN, Albert to Mary Ann Gunn	9-15-1832
CALENDER, Caprel to Frances Byers	7-14-1836
CAREY, John to Rachel Harter	11-15-1826
CARR, Thomas to Leakit Belair	6-10-1827
CARROLL, William to Sary Evans	9-17-1837
CASAT, Henry to Mary Ann Acus	2-6-1834
CHAMBERS, William to Mary Hunter	12-21-1834
CLARK, Harvey to Polly Stubbs	1-31-1837
CLEMMER, John to Mary Glasmore	11-29-1835
COLLINS, John to Harriet Murphy	10-19-1837
COLVER, Joel to Phebe Ann Sales	8-14-1836
COMPARET, Joseph to Mary Blair	3-17-1834
COONROD, Honorable Woolsey to Mary Coy	1-23-1835
CRAIG, James to Maria Soloven	2-28-1827
CRAIG, James W. to Sarah Jolly	10-31-1825
CROW, Nicholas to Nancy Woodcox	8-9-1832
CURTIS, Horatio N. to Susannah Woodcox	5-16-1833
DAVISON, Jacob to Rachel Tittle	9-23-1828
DeLONG, Jefferson to Eliza Belair	4-19-1833
DEPO, Charles W. to Rosanna Donley	4-8-1836
DONLEY, Henry to Amelia Mason	12-25-1836
DONLEY, William to Belinda Fee	11-12-1836
DUNSCOMB, Gilbert to Nancy Donat	2-15-1837
DYCCAS, Jacob to Hannah Carey	11-29-1827
EVENS, Isaac to Katherine Shirt	6-8-1837
FEE, John to Mary Ann B. Holton	4-9-1833
GLEASON, Cahen to Sarah Luther	8-6-1835
GORDON, William to Elenor Spurier	7-7-1831
GRAVES, James D. to Eliza Jane Carvin	8-31-1837
GRIFFITH, Hiram to Elizabeth Wells	12-8-1836
GROVE, Abijah to Sarah Williams	5-30-1833
GROVE, Jeptha to Sarah Story	4-17-1834

744

```
GROVE, Lampson to Lunicia Shasteen                      6-23-1830
GUNN, Ausman to Elisa Ann Scribner                      7-31-1826
GUNN, Carver to Nancy Ann Scribner                      12-2-1824
GUNN, Carver to Eve DeLong                              6-1-1828
GUTHRIE, Thomas to Eliza Dawson                         4-27-1835
HALL, Horace to Eliza Hilton                            8-30-1835
HARMON, Samuel to Margaret Felming                      12-1-1833
HARRIS, Thomas to Ann Walling                           9-1-1829
HARTER, John to Eliza Herrall                           3-24-1833
HEADLEY, Samuel to Rebecca Woodcox                      8-31-1837
HECKOX, George L. to Charity Sanford                    1-11-1837
HENRY, William to Julia Holler                          1-1-1834
HILL, George W. to Sarah Ann Mullican                   3-17-1836
HILTON, Brice to Sophia Umbenhour                       11-24-1836
HILTON, Ezra to Catherine Blair                         1-8-1837
HILTON, Jesse to Cynthia Travis                         11-3-1831
HIVELY, Isaac to Magdalena Bible                        10-3-1836
HOLLINGSHEAD, John to Rachel Stubbs                     1-2-1837
HOLT, Justice to Susanna Reynolds                       2-28-1837
HOOD, Andrew to Mary Perkins                            12-12-1830
HOOD, Andrew to Elizabeth Reid                          1-1-1837
HOULTON, John to Sarah Fee                              2-5-1833
HOULTON, Samuel to Hannah Fee                           2-6-1833
HOUSER, Austen to Pernelia Blackman                     6-6-1837
HUGHS, Montreville to Harriet Ann Fuller                9-10-1837
HUNTER, Joseph to Nancy McCully                         6-5-1834
JOHNSON, George to _____ Dorrot                        10-25-1836
KENT, George to Elizabeth Kritzer                       6-13-1837
KILLAJOR, Hector to Mary Colganlog                      1-1-1835
KING, Lewis to Jane Prettyman                           10-24-1837
LADD, James Elison to Artemasa Sullivan                 7-23-1833
LANDON, Theron to Harriet Bates                         6-7-1836
LAUDAMAN, David to Catherine T. Traxler                 12-10-1837
LEONARD, Rueben to Elizabeth Dyce                       4-21-1836
LEWIS, William to Elizabeth Hively                      6-3-1832
LUCE, William to Catherine Platter                      8-4-1836
McANALLY, James D. to Mary Ann Blue                     9-19-1832
McCLISH, John to Abby Barker                            8-7-1830
McCULLY, Robert to Amirah Talbot                        3-19-1835
McHILL, Daniel to Parmelia Snook                        6-7-1832
MACANALLY, Uriah P. R. to Elizabeth Mullian             2-12-1831
MACATER, Charles to Susannah Leaf                       5-2-1833
MANLY, Asher Bruse to Clarissa Douglas                  11-21-1837
MARTIN, J. M. to Rosanna Auker                          3-15-1837
MERITHEW, Benjamin to Rebecca Byrode                    7-4-1831
MIEDON, Putnam to Jane Ann Sharp                        3-31-1836
MILLER, John to Samantha Harris                         9-20-1829
MILLER, Samuel to Diantha Harris                        9-28-1830
MORRIS, Dan to Lucretia Martin                          12-16-1832
```

```
MURPHY, David P. J. To Nancy Runyan                        10-21-1830
MURPHY, Joseph H. to Phebe Ann Carvin                      11-30-1837
MURPHY, Robert to Emeline Banks                             8-16-1836
MYERS, Samuel to Margaret Harden                           12-25-1833
MYSON, Frederick to Catherine Leonard                      12-31-1835
NICKLE, John B. to Hannah Foster                            2-7-1833
PACKARD, Honorable William B. to Mary Coy                  10-16-1834
PALMER, Soloman W. to Sarah D. Allen                       12-31-1837
PARTEE, Laurence to Rebecca Webb           2 dates (7-27-1829
                                                   (8-2-1829
PERKINS, Garret to Elizabeth Tittle                        8-17-1828
PERKINS, Isaac to Mary Tittle                              5-26-1825
PERRY, Adam to Catharine Ann Guthrie                       1-9-1836
PHILBRICK, Clark to Mary Hilton                            3-15-1827
PLATTER, Joseph to Mary Ann Sales                          9-15-1836
PLATTER, Lewis to Elizabeth Gordon                         2-29-1831
PLUMMER, John to Malinda Perkins                           6-27-1830
POOL, Frederick to Susannah Neil                           5-22-1834
PURTEE, James to Elizabeth Perkins                         4-26-1826
PURTEE, Lewis to Dianna Webb                               11-8-1827
QUICK, Thomas P. to Eliza Simpson                          6-21-1832
REED, Amos to Sarah Craig                                  5-1-1836
RHON, Samuel to Charity Hews                               7-11-1833
RIDENOUR, Michael to Margaret Harter                       3-10-1833
ROBINSON, Henry to Harriett Gordon                         12-14-1837
ROGERS, William to Elizabeth Platter                       5-20-1830
ROLEDSCO, Collier to Hannah Platter                        3-2-1837
ROTH, Solomon to Lottie Brown                              10-4-1832
ROWLEY, Ransom to Margaret Epley                           1-31-1837
RUNYAN, Christian to Nancy Graves                          11-24-1831
RUNYAN, Hugh E. to Sophia T. Bank                          9-26-1833
SAYTON, Ulrick to Rachel Mullican                          6-7-1836
SCRIBNER, Edwin to Lucinda Bucklin                         10-26-1831
SEELEY, Alexander P. to Sarah Ann Banks                    8-16-1836
SEMANS, William to Mrs. Mary W. Wells                      11-9-1834
SHIRLEY, Elias to Phoebe Hudson                            3-1-1827
SHIRLEY, Robert to Sarah Hudson                            9-15-1829
SLUSSER, Jones P. to Mary M. Prettyman                     4-30-1837
SNOOK, Jacob to Catherine Sampsel                          8-13-1837
SNOOK, Wilson H. to Anna Murphy                            10-16-1834
SPURRIER, Frederick to Mary Runyan                         4-7-1833
STEVENS, Frederick F. to Elizabeth Oliver                  7-13-1836
STINSON, Horace to Jane Sufficool                          11-9-1837
STUBBS, Joseph to Sodica Reynolds                          11-20-1836
TAYLOR, Jonathan B. to Polly H. Stubbs                     1-16-1836
THACKER, Martial to Jane Cary                              6-6-1833
THATCHER, Daniel to Mary Devall                            2-25-1830
TITTLE, George to Susannah Graves                          11-24-1831
TITTLE, Peter to Mary Rhone                                7-21-1829
```

746

```
TRAVIS, Ezra to Mary Hilton                              9-29-1830
TROOP, David C. to Julia Ann Sharp                      11-27-1836
VANCELL, Joseph to Sarah Butler                          7-2-1832
WASHBURN, Norman to Susan Miller                         3-3-1829
WAUN, Thomas to Mary Shirley                             8-11-1825
WAX, Anthony to Jane Shaw                               11-28-1837
WELCH, William to Anna Sutton                          11-12-1828
WELLS, Abraham to Elizabeth Fisher         (1833?)     12-12-1834
WHITE, Isaac G. To Rebecca Carey                        ·8-6-1829
WHITE, Jeremiah to Margaret Maretin                     3-30-1828
WILDER, Jacob G. to Jane Dawson                         1-18-1837
WILLIAMS, Henry F. to Mary Robinson                     2-26-1837
WILSON, St. John to Orpha Grove                          2-6-1834
WINANS, Matthias S. to Grizzy McCally                    6-6-1833
WOODCOX, Cornelius to Polly Saylor                      11-5-1835
WOODCOX, Isaac to Sally Irvin                            2-9-1837
WOODCOX, Solomon to Loucina E. Bartlett                11-10-1836
YOUNG, John to Margaret Shiny                           7-21-1827
ZELLER, John to Rebecca Brunier                         9-21-1834
```

The foregoing is a complete listing of all marriages taking place in Williams County from 1824-1837. Although its formation date was early (1824), it location in the very northwestern corner of Ohio was instrumental in its being thinly populated during its early years. Williams County is an important county to northwestern Ohio as the following counties were formed from at least a portion of its territory: Defiance in 1845, Fulton in 1850 and Henry in 1834.

WILLIAMS COUNTY, OHIO - DEATH RECORDS 1867-1871

The following records were taken from Death Record 1 located in the Probate Court at the court house in Bryan. Page on which record may be found is given in paren-thesis. Only death records for persons 40 years and over have been copied. Abbreviations used: d=died; a=age; m=married; w=widow; s=single; pd=place of death; pb=place of birth; res=residence; w=widower. Residence is same as place of death unless stated.

RANDOLPH, Rachel - d 8-12-1867; a 80y; s; pd Williams Co.; pb N.Y.(?).   (1)
GREAGUE, Susan M. - d 9-5-1867; a 73y; s; pd Williams Co.; pb France.   (1)
EVERHEART, Calvin - d 4-12-1868; a 40y; pd NW twp.; pb Masolin, Stark Co., O.   (1)
FARR, Elizabeth - d 9-25-1868; a 56y 19d; m; pd near Bryan; pb Crawford Co.,
      Ohio.   (1)
BROWN, Abraham - d 12-14-1868; a 65-8-24; pd Bryan; pb Fayette Co., Pa.   (1)
PERKINS, Garret - d 10-15-1868; a 63-7-20; w; pd near Bryan; pb Ross Co., O.   (1)
WILLIAMS, Fanny - d 10-25-1868; a 64-4-19; w; pd Bryan; pb Lancaster Co., Pa.   (1)
METZTER, Saloma - d 2-25-1869; a 57-4-25; m; pd Florence twp.; pb unknown.   (1)
DILLON, Asa - d Dec. 1868; a 93y 2m; w; pd West Unity; pb Virginia; parents,
      Jonathan and Mary Dillon.   (1)
YOUNG, Hannah - d 4-1-1869; a 55-3-27; m; pd----------; pb------------.   (1)
TRESSLER, Jonathan - d 4-3-1869; a 76-7-10; m; pd---------; pb-----------.   (1)
GARDNER, Mrs. - d 4-10-1869; a 76y; w; pd-------------- pb----------.   (1)
STUBBS, Phebe - d 5-17-1869; a 72y; w; pd------------ pb------------.   (1)
MAY, Jacob - d 5-21-1869; a 62y; m; pd Springfield twp.; pb France.   (2)
MALLORY, John - d 9-24-1869; a 40y; m; pd Springfield twp.; pb Pa.   (2)
PITZER, Margaret - d 10-14-1869; a 82y; w; pd Springfield twp.; pb Springfield
      twp.; parents, M. and Cath. Pitzer.   (2)
STOUGH, Lyman - d 12-23-1869; a 58y; m; pd Springfield twp.; pb Springfield twp. (2)
McREA, Joseph - d Sept. 1869; a 48y; m; pd Northwest twp.; pb--------.   (2)
MALCON, Thomas - d Nov. 1869; a 40y; m; pd Northwest twp.; pb--------.   (2)
WHALEY, Thomas - d Mar. 1870; a 83y; w; pd Northwest twp.; pb Rhode Island.   (2)
WHALEY, Susanna - d Aug. 1869; a 88y; m; pd Northwest twp.; pb New York.   (2)
      (note: there is a notation that Thomas and Susannah Whaley were husband
            and wife.)
OGDEN, William H. - d 12-27-1869; a 50y; w; pd Bryan; pb Conn.   (2)
GRISWOLD, Jared - d 6-16-1869; a 49y; m; pd Pulaski twp.; pb Mass.   (2)
GILBERT, J. T. - d 2-24-1870; a 76y; m; occupation, Physician; pd Bryan;
      pb Vermont.   (2)
PENNOCK, Ira - d 3-4-1870; a 58y; m; pd Bryan; pb Portage Co., Ohio; last
      place of res., Ill.   (2)
SCHAFFER, Samuel - d 4-21-1870; a 64y; m; pd Pioneer; pb Penn.   (2)
BURKHART, Peter - d 10-26-1869; a 81y; s; pd St. Joseph twp.; pb Germany.   (3)
POAL, Banister - d 9-10-1869; a 86y; m; pd Edgerton; pb Va.   (3)
MORRIS, Charles - d 7-34-1869; a 59y; m; pd Edgerton; pb N. Y.   (3)
BECK, Rachel - d 1-23-1870; a 81y; s; pd Edgerton; pb------.   (3)
LIND, Nancy - d 4-2-1870; a 68y; w; pd St. Joseph twp.; pb Penn.   (3)
MATER, Stephen - d 2-4-1870; a 73y; m; pd St. Joseph twp.; pb Switzerland.   (3)
PRESTON, Wm C. - d 8-16-1869; a 71y; w; pd St. Joseph twp.; pb Vermont.   (3)
GENTIT, Susan - d 1-21-1870; a 73y; w; pd Edgerton; pb France.   (3)

748

McREAN, Joseph - d 7-16-1869; a 81y; w; pd Edgerton; pb Penn.   (3)
RESHEL (RISHEL), Magdeline - d 11-24-(1869?); a 59y; w; pd Edgerton; pb Penn.   (3)
KOHENDORF, John M. - d 3-25-1870; a 76y; w; pd Edgerton; pb Wertenburg.   (3)
CASSEL, Sophia - d 3-11-1870; a 65y; m; pd Millcreek twp.; pb Maryland; remarks,
     Jacob Cassel.   (3)
GOWER, John S. - d 6-23-1869; a 68y; m; pd Millcreek twp.; pb York Co., Pa.;
     remarks, Jacob R. Gower.   (3)
SHULTZ, William - d 3-1-1870; a 69y; m; pd Millcreek twp.; pb Pa.; remarks,
     Sarah Shultz.   (3)
GEORGE, Weibly - d 10-15-1870; a 66y; w; pd Millcreek twp.; pb Cumberland Co.,
     Pa.; remarks Henry Srashel(?).   (3)
HARBAUGH, Harris B. - d Nov. 1869; a 42y; m; pd Florence twp.; pb Florence twp. (3)
CULLENBAUGH, Mary Ann - d Sept. 1869; a 72y; w; pd Florence twp.; pb Florence
     twp.   (3)
COLLER, Sarah - d July 1869; a 69y; w; pd Florence twp.; pb Florence twp.   (3)
ALTMAN, Joseph - d 3-5-1869; a 49y 10m; m; pd Center twp.; pb----------.   (4)
DILMAN, Jacob - d 3-7-1870; a 67y; m; pd Center twp.; pb---------.   (4)
DONER, Mary - d 3-20-1869; a 60y; m; pd Center twp.; pb---------.   (4)
KIMBLE, Eliza Jane - d 10-12-1869; a 48y; pd Center twp.; pb----------.   (4)
FRANK, Daniel - d 8-24-1869; a 59y; m; pd Center twp.; pb----------.   (4)
CRAWFORD, Eligah - d 8-5-1869; a 89y; m; pd Bridgwater twp.; pb Northumberland
     Co., Pa.   (4)
CRAWFORD, Rebecca - d 7-26-1869; a 78y; m; pd Bridgwater twp.; pb Northumberland
     Co., Pa.   (4)
HAWKINS, Joseph - d 2-2-1870; a 79y; m; pd Bridgwater twp.; pb N. Y.   (4)
HONNAH, Versilla - d 9-6-1870; a 61y; m; pd Bridgwater twp.; pb Veaver Co., Pa. (4)
KOLLAR, George - d 9-7-1869; a 74y; m; pd Superior twp.; pb--------.   (4)
YOUNG, Hannah - d 4-1-1869; a 55y; m; pd Superior twp.; pb----------,   (4)
ALTAFFER, Sarah - d 12-17-1869; a 66y; w; pd Jefferson twp.; pb--------.   (4)
NORTH, Nancy - d -------1870; a 58y; m; pd Jefferson twp.; pb--------.   (4)
ALTMAN, George - d 6-13-1869; a 68y; m; pd Brady twp.; pb Va.   (5)
ASHLEMAIN, John - d 12-10-1869; a 51y; m; pd Brady twp.; pb Switzerland.   (5)
KUNKLE, George Henry - d 2-12-1870; a 77y; m; pd Brady twp.; pb Berks Co., Va.   (5)
RICHIE, Drusilla - d 12-10-1869; a 76y; m; pd West Unity; pb Va.   (5)
ROUR, George - d 7-18-1869; a 52y; m; pd Stryker, O.; pb France.   (5)
VANANDA, William Collet - d 4-18-1870; a 43y; pd Brady twp.; pb Wane, Ohio.   (5)
RIGG, John - d 9-24-1870; a 66y; m; pd Northwest twp.; pb England.   (5)
CLAYTON, Joseph - d 11-3-1870; a 52y; s; pd Northwest twp.; pb England.   (5)
BRUNK, Sarah - d 12-19-1870; a 71y; w; pd Northwest twp.; pb New York.   (5)
OWEN, Sally - d 3-25-1871; a 43y; m; pd Northwest twp.; pb---------.   (5)
OWEN, Ira - d 3-26-1871; m; pd Northwest twp.; pb----------.   (5)
McLAIN, Melinda - d 3-7-1871; a 41y; m; Northwest twp.; pb Maine.   (5)

The following records were taken from Will Book 1 located in the Probate Court at the court house in Bryan. The page on which the record may be found in this book is given in parenthesis.

JOLLY, James of Highland Co., Ohio - dated 8-16-1809; recorded (not given). Wife, Agnes. Six children, not of age (mentioned but not named). Executors: wife, Agnes and nephew, John McConnel. Signed: James Jolly. Witnesses: Augustus Richards and Bigger Head. (1)

McCLURE, Alexander of Williams Co., late of Darke Co., Ohio - dated 9-18-1827; recorded 9-29-1827. Wife, Nancy. Only son, Samuel McClure aged 7 years or near, 110 acres on East fork Whitewater (Darke Co.). Four daughters, Elizabeth Ramsey, Jane McClure, Martha McClure and Rosana McClure, 116 acres on Auglaize River (Williams Co.) Executors: wife, Nancy and Jonathan Thomas. Signed: Alexander McClure. Witnesses: Christopher Sroufe and John Evans. (2)

WALLING, Elias - dated 3-7-1828; recorded (not given). Wife, Anna. Sons: eldest son, Robert, not of age, to be bound to Mr. Johnson of Piqua County; 2nd son, Daniel, not of age, to be bound to John Wilson of Shelby County; 3rd son, Isaac Tiffin, to be bound to James Johnston of Piqua County. Daughter, Margaret Ann Walling. Signed: Elias (mark) Walling. Witnesses: William Bowen and Joseph White. (3)

SCRIBNER, Elisha of Damascus twp. - dated 4-25-1829; recorded (not given). Wife, Nancy, Sons: Edwin, Zacheus Lewis, Elisha Husted, Uri and Abraham. Eldest daughter, Ann Eliza Gunn. Grandson, Carver S. Gunn. Mentions "my third wife and Edwin to take charge of the children." Executors: wife, Nancy and Payne C. Parker. Signed: Elisha Scribner. Witnesses: William C. Griffin and John Abbott. (4)

DeLONG, David of Damascus twp. - dated 1-22-1830; recorded (not given). Wife, Catharine. Children: oldest son, Jacob DeLong; 2nd son, Nicholas DeLong; oldest daughter, Eve Gunn; Jefferson DeLong; Columbus DeLong; and Eleanor DeLong. Wife, Catharine to be guardian of Columbus and Eleanor. Executors: wife, Catharine and Carver Gunn. Signed: David DeLong. Witnesses: Jacob DeLong and Charles Gunn. (5)

SROUFE, Sebastian - dated 12-2-1829; recorded (not given). Sons and daughters: Lewis Sroufe, Joseph Sroufe, Alfred Sroufe, Albert Sroufe, George Sroufe and Susan Sroufe. Mentions "That wife's three sons shall have living with my children ...and be clothed schooled as his own until of age." Executors: wife, Mary and oldest son, Lewis Sroufe. Signed: Sebastian Sroufe. Witnesses: John Kingery. Thomas D. Sroufe and Christopher Sroufe. (6)

HIVELEY, John - dated 1-2-1831; recorded 7-7-183_ (note: last number in year not given). Wife, Rebecca. Sons: Jacob, Michael, John, Joseph, Isaac, Thomas and Adam Hively. Daughters: Elizabeth and Polly. Executor, John Evans. Signed: John Hively (German signature). Witnesses: Samuel Washburn and Pay C. Parker. Codicil dated 1-2-1831, no additional information given, same witnesses. (11)

COLGAN, William - dated 1-25-1837; recorded 4-19-1838. Sons: eldest son, William Colgan; 2nd son, Daniel Colgan. Daughters: eldest, Hannah Hamilton widow of John Hamilton, dec'd; 2nd dau., Susannah Ford; 3rd dau., Eleanor Halton; 4th dau., Mary Major, one Bible and other items. Executor: William Leman (or Seman) of Defiance, Ohio. Signed: William (his C mark) Colgan. Witnesses: David Carpenter and Julia Ann Carpenter. (15)

COY, Adam - dated 1-1-1839; recorded 3-13-1839. Wife, Mary. Son and daughter, Henry Coy and Nancy Ann Coy, not of age. Executors: wife, Mary and brother, Jacob Coy. Woolery Coonrod to be guardian of son and daughter. Signed: Adam (his mark) Coy. Witnesses: Jacob Hall and Adam Sollinger. (16)

RIDER, James - dated 2-19-1839; recorded 4-19-1839. Wife, mentioned but not named, to have farm where reside W½ SW¼ S24, T6, R4E being 80 acres. Three children: Caroline, Mary and Reuben Rider, not of age. Daughter, Caroline will be 18 years of age on 7-8-1851. Wife to be guardian of three children. Executors: John Sellinger and R. B. Janes. Signed: James Rider. Witnesses: Jacob Smith and Jacob Coy. (18)

HILL, James - dated 2-16-1834; recorded (not given). All property to George W. Hill (no relationship if any stated) for testator's four children (not named). Executor: George W. Hill. Witnesses: John Evans and George Snook. (20)

HUNTER, Cyrus of Richland twp. - dated (not given); recorded (not given). Wife, Mary. Children: eldest son, Cyrus Robinson Hunter; William Addison Hunter; and Mary Jane Hunter; all not of age. Executrix; wife, Mary. Signed: Cyrus Hunter. Witnesses: John Evans and Thomas Brown. (21)

QUICK, Thomas P. - dated 8-14-1835; recorded (not given). Wife, Elizabeth formerly Elizabeth Simpson to have farm where now live formerly owned by Andrew Simpson and purchased from his estate at adms. sale being 2/3rds and after death of wife farm to go to Evans W. Simpson and Varsalion Simpson heirs of Andrew Simpson and upon their receiving land they are to pay to Rebecca, Hannah and Eliza Jane Simpson an equitable part of value of land they also being lineal heirs of Andrew Simpson; said farm being in Crane twp. Executrix: wife, Elizabeth. Signed: Thomas P. (his mark) Quick. Witnesses: Nathaniel L. Thomas and Schuyler Fisher. (22)

HALLER, John - dated 10-19-1835; recorded (not given). Wife, Mary. Seven children: Julia, Wesley Andrews, Mary Ann, Lucinda Collins, John Mitton (or Milton), Henry Raper and Luisa Gertrude Haller, all not of age. (note: probably other children). Wife, Mary and friend, William Dawson to be guardian of children and if wife marries then guardians to be Doctor Rufus Kibbe and William Dawson. Executors: son, William Haller and William Dawson. Signed: John Haller. Witnesses: James M. Gillespie and William Dawson. (24)

LEASURE, William - dated 12-24-1835; recorded (not given). Two children: John and Caroline, John not of age. Joseph Leasure of Westmoreland Co., Pa. to be guardian of children. Executors: Jesse Leasure and James Jennison. Signed: William Leasure. Witnesses: Isaac Evans and John Sullinger. (26)

751

FOSTER, Robert - dated 6-13-1836; recorded (not given . Wife, Nancy. Sons: Robert, John and Rainy Foster; Rainy not of age. Daughter, Mary Foster. Mentions: Nancy Jane girl now bound to testator as an apprentice. Signed: Robert (his mark) Foster. Witnesses: John Kingrey and Gilbert L. Jeffrey. (27)

SPRAGUE, Solomon of Delaware twp. - dated 12-25-1835; recorded (not given). One Son, William B. Sprague, also to serve as executor. Five Daughters: Betsy Brace, Sarah Gleason, Mary Sprague, Phebe Barber and Evaline Lindenberger. Owns land in Springfield twp. and Delaware twp., Williams Co., Ohio and also in Porter twp., Delaware Co., Ohio. Signed: Solomon Sprague. Witnesses: Wm Lemans I. Hoover. (28)

SHIRLEY, Robert Sr. - dated 1-25-1836; recorded (not given). Wife, Rachael. Six children: Nathan, James, Elias, Robert, Ruth and John. Executor: son, Nathan Shirley. Signed: Robert Shirley. Witnesses: Peter Sharp and Isaac Hall. (30)

BLAIR, James - dated 9-12-1839; recorded (not given). Wife, Nancy. Two sons now living at home: Wright Blair and Seth Blair to have farm where now live in Section 32 at St. Joseph twp. Daughters: Fanny Fowler, Rebeckah Snow and Nancy Blair. Four children of former wife: oldest daughter, Anna, a married woman; John Blair; Asa Blair; and James Blair. Executor: son, Wright Blair. Signed: James Blair. Witnesses: Elisha Clark, Thomas Olds, I.B. and William Dawson. (32)

STODARD, Israel - dated 12-30-1841; recorded 4-18-1842. Wife, Lois, also to serve as executrix. Four children: Dwite, Sarah, Israel and Dorcas Stodard. Witnesses: Daniel Coy, John Halley and Harriet (her mark) Halley. (34)

COON, James of Florence twp. - dated 5-29-1843; recorded 9-19-1843. Wife, mentioned but not named to have reside being 52.58 acres w½ fractional S28, T8N, R1E and other land. Son, Joel. Daughter, Betsey Jane. Mentions dower set off to testator's mother (not named) situated on Marcellus, Onondaga Co., New York which testator falls heir to at her decease. Bequeath to the M. E. Church for meeting house and burying ground 1½ acre in SW corner Section 10 Township 10S of Michigan Base line of Range 4 West. Executor: Moses Thomas, also to serve as guardian of two children until of age; if he should die then James Allman is to serve as guardian. Signed: James Coon. Witnesses: Levi Cunningham and Martin Perky. (36)

BARRONE, George of Millcreek twp. - dated 5-19-1844; recorded 6-15-1844. Wife, Margaret. Seven children: Bitsey wife of Joseph Hanes, Mary wife of James Black, Elias, Simon, Lydia, Susana and Hiram. Son, Hiram to be sent to Westmoreland Co., Pa. to be brought up by testator's connections there, if not, then court of William County to appoint a guardian. Executors: John Rings and George Ely. Signed: George (his mark) Barrone. Witnesses: Alanson Pike and David Angel. (39)

752

SEVERENCE, (David or Daniel) - dated 10-6-1844; recorded 11-23-1844. Wife, mentioned but not named. Sons: Alfred and Benjamin Severence; Benjamin not of age. Daughters: Hannah Packard, Mary Ann Dow, Elizabeth Severence, Nancy Severence, Lucinda Severence and Caroline Severence; last three named not of age. Executors: Calvin Ackley and John J. Hagerman. Signed: Daniel (his mark) Severence. Witnesses: Daniel Axtell and Alanson Pike. (43)

LEHMAN, Adam of Cumberland Co., Pa. - dat d 2-18-1845; recorded Cumberland Co., Pa. 5-31-1845; recorded Williams Co. (not given). Wife, Magdalena. Children: John, Adam, David, Daniel, Mary, Sarah, Margaret and Samuel. Mentions that land in Frankfort twp., Cumberland Co., Pa. and also land in Williams Co., Ohio to be sold. Brother, Jacob Lehman to be guardian of daughter, Margaret and son, Samuel. Cousin, Jacob Lehman to be guardian of daughters, Mary and Sarah. Executors: brother, Jacob Lehman and cousin, Jacob Lehman. Signed: Adam Lehman.(46)

SMITH, William S. - dated 12-7-1843; recorded 6-10-1846. Wife, Margarett, also to serve as executrix. Mentions children and their heirs, but does not name. Signed: William S. Smith. Witnesses: John Rings and Rachel C. Rings. (49)

SICKLES, Elias of Jefferson twp. - dated 4-27-1846; recorded 12-7-1846. Wife mentioned but not named, to have farm where now live in Section 10 of Jefferson twp. Son, Jacob. Daughter, Susannah. Signed: Elias (his mark) Sickles. Witnesses: George W. Mers, Thomas Reid and William Ferrier. (51)

SIMON, John - dated 8-11-1846; recorded (not given). Wife, mentioned but not named, to have farm where now reside in Florence twp. Son, John Simon, not of age. Guardian of son, John to be John Adam Simon. Executor: John Adam Simon. Signed: John Simon (German signature). Witnesses: George Castine and John Nauman. (53)

PERKINS, Simon of Warren, Trumbull Co., Ohio - dated 4-20-1844; recorded Trumbull Co., Ohio 12-3-1844; recorded William Co. 11-15-1847. Wife, Nancy. All children except Henry have already received $5000.00 each, Henry not of age. Mentions much property in various counties, stocks, bonds, etc. Executors: son, Simon Perkins; nephew, Frederick Kusman(?); sons, Joseph and Jacob Perkins. Signed: Simon Perkins. Witnesses: Thomas D. Webb, Henry Lane and Charles White. (54)

ROGERS, John - dated 4-23-1848; recorded 11-21-1848. Wife, Elizabeth, land now reside on in Jefferson twp., she also to serve as executrix. Children, mentioned but not named. Signed: John (mark) Rogers. Witnesses: Wm. H. McGrew and John Miller. (63)

DAUGHTER, Marmaduke of Pulaski twp. - dated 9-30-1848; recorded (not given). Wife, Mary M. Executors: wife, Mary M. and Stephen I.(or J.) Daughter. Signed: Marmaduke Daughter. Witnesses: James (mark) Jenkins, John Opdycke and L. M. Boothmas. (65)

DISBROW, Jacob - dated 3-26-1845: recorded (not given. Wife Anna, farm where now live in Superior twp. Executors: wife, Anna and William Crispey. Witnesses: William Crispey and Charles Duvall. (66)

FRITSCH, Lewis - dated 3-8-1849; recorded 12-7-1849. Sons: Lewis, Hirommus and John. Wife, mentioned but not named. Signed: Lewis Fritsch. Witnesses: Conrod Pfeifer and Philip Jocky (or Jacky). (68)

DOOLITTLE, Harmon of Springfield twp. - dated 9-23-1849; recorded (not given). Wife, mentioned but not named. Children: Sophia C., Phebe Ann, John S. and Horace H. Doolittle; wife to serve as their guardian. Signed: Harmon Doolittle. Witnesses: Nathaniel Lyon and Daniel Colgun. (69)

GIRTON, George of Springfield twp. - dated 1-2-1850; recorded (not given). Wife, mentioned but not named. Mentions that "if there should hereafter be a lawful heir of mine I bequeath one third." Executors: John Sloan and Joel Mackerel. Signed: George Girton. Witnesses: John Sloan and Joel Mackerell. (70)

BERKHOLDER, Peter - dated (not given); recorded (not given-1850?). Wife, Barbara, also to serve as executrix. Sons: Joseph, Abraham and Christian Berkholder. (note: probably other children not named.) Signed: Peter Berkholder. Witnesses: Henry Sheets and Frederick Sheets. (72)

EVANS, John (of Allen Co., Ind.?) - dated 8-10-1842; recorded Allen Co., Indiana 8-16-1842; recorded Williams Co., Ohio in 1929, many years after originally dated and recorded. Requests to be buried in Fort Wayne. Wife, mentioned but not named. Daughters: Merica (Evans?) and Elizabeth Hill. Sons: Carey and Rush. Executors: daughter, Merica: sons, Carey and Rush; Hugh McCulloch; Allen Hamilton; and Pierce Evans. Requests that children provide for Aley Cumberlin so long as she may live. Signed: John Evans. Witnesses: L. G. Thompson and W. G. Evans. (Will Book 16, page 465)

The following records were copied from "Final Chancery Record 2". Page on which record can be found is given in parenthesis. This book is located in the Common Pleas (Clerk of Court's Office) at the court house at Bowling Green. This book does not appear to be a complete recording of all transactions that took place during this period, although all of a genealogical nature found recorded in this book were copied.

3-8-1839 - Caleb NORTH adms. of Estate of James SMITH, dec'd vs. James T. BUGH, et al. Petition for Partition. Filed 4-17-1838. Land, 40 acres NW¼ NE¼ Section 31, Township 6N, Range 10E. Widow, Elizabeth Smith, now wife of Jesse T. Bugh. Heir: William Smith. (30)

10-5-1839 - Sarah LINSCOTT guardian of Heman W. LINSCOTT vs. Heman LINSCOTT, et al. Petition to sell land. Filed 1-10-1839. Land, N½ W½ SE¼ Section 36, Township 6, Range 9N. Heman Linscott, dec'd late of Wood Co. Heir: Heman H. Linscott, a minor. (49)

4-8-1840 - Ezra ROOD vs. Decius WADSWORTH, et al. Petition for Partition. Filed 11-28-1838. Land, one-third River Tract #64 in Reserve of 12 mi. square at foot of Rapids of Miami of Lake Erie held in tenary with Sylvester Day and Thomas Emerson; also one half of River tracts 54, 56, 57 of same held with Decius Wadsworth and other heirs of George Wadsworth, dec'd, Stephen Mark, Sylvester Day, Charles Townsend, George Coit and others, John ANDERSON, dec'd, late of Detroit, Michigan. Widow, mentioned but not named. Brother, Thomas Anderson and his wife Anna. That other brothers and sisters of John Anderson, dec'd are either dead or gone to parts unknown; that his father and mother are both dead. Ezra Rood is of Detroit, Michigan; no relationship if any, is stated. (65)

4-10-1840- James C. GLASGOW adms. of John GLASGOW vs. Mary GLASGOW, et al. Petition to sell lands. Filed 5-29-1838. Land, Holmes Co., Ohio part Lot 46, 1st Quarter, Township 9, Range 7 of Western Reserve, school lands sold at Millersburg. John Glasgow, dec'd, late of Wood Co. Widow, Mary Glasgow of Beaver Co., Pa. Heirs: James C. Glasgow and William W. Glasgow, a minor, William W. of Beaver Co., Pa. (77)

6-27-1840 - John G. WILLIARD adms. of Estate of Wm. DONALDSON, dec'd vs. Andrew DONALDSON, et al. Confirmation of Sale of Land. Land, 80 acres S part NE¼ Section 4, Township 3N, Range 12. Wm. Donaldson, dec'd, late of Wood Co., died intestate leaving no widow or children. Heirs: Eunice wife of James M. Charles of Michigan; Andrew Donaldson; John Donaldson; Ruth Anna wife of Benjamin Scott; Mary Ann Donaldson; Hiram Donaldson, a minor; the last named residence not stated, Wood Co.? (87)

10-20-1840 - Robert BLACK adms. of John GRABER vs. Heirs. Petition to sell land. Filed 10-22-1839. Land, 40 acres SE¼ NW¼ and 40 acres SW¼ NE¼ Section 31, fractional township 6N, Range 10. Heirs names and residences are unknown to petitioner. (116)

4-7-1841 - Rebecca KROTZER vs. Heirs of Joseph KROTZER. Petition for Dower.
Filed 3-14-1840. Joseph Krotzer late of Freadom, Wood Co., dec'd died in
1839 seized of an estate of inheritence in 160 acres NE¼ Section 12, Township
5, Range 12. Widow, Rebecca Krotzer of Freadom, Wood Co. Heirs: William,
Joseph, Peter, Rebecca and Isaac Krotzer, all minors by James M. Coffinberry,
their guardian. (132)

6-29-1841 - Samuel CARSON and Barbary his wife vs. Jonathan CROM, et al. Petition
for Partition. Filed 4-6-1841. Land, 80 acres W½ SE¼ and also NE¼ Section 21;
W½ ME¼ Section 22, all in Township 5N, Range 9E; also lot 7, Section 1 in town
of Gilead, Wood Co. John McKEE, late of Wood Co., dec'd, died several years
since, intestate. Widow, Barbara McKee, now wife of Samuel Carson. Heirs:
Hugh McKeen, sold his interest to Barbara Carson; Maria wife of Jonathan Crom;
Elizabeth wife of Edwin R. Howard; Nancy wife of Asa Smith; John McKee, a minor.
(144)

3-24-1842 - George M. BAIRD and Eunice S. BALLON adms. of Amasa BALLON, dec'd
vs. Julia and Charlotte BALLON. Petition to sell land. Filed 3-26-1839. Land,
50 acres part NW¼ Section 34 on Findley Road (no Township and Range given).
Widow, Eunice S. Ballon. Heirs: Julia and Charlotte Ballon, both of age. (163)

3-24-1842 - Robert McCORMICK adms. of James McCORMICK, dec'd vs. Joseph WADDLE,
etal. Petition to sell lands. Filed 3-8-1841. Land; 160 acres SW¼ Section 4
and 40 acres NE¼ SE¼ Section 5, both in Township 3, Range 12; also lots 13-20,
22,23,25-30, 35,36, 38-47 and out lots 2-9 (in West Millgrove?). Heirs:
Robert McCormick; Martha late McCormick wife of Joseph Waddle; George McCormick;
Margaret wife of David Adams; Christena McCormick; Elizabeth McCormick; Sarah
McCormick; and Thomas F. McCormick; the last two named being minors. (165,236,
237,239)

3-24-1842 - Christian HOUTZ adms. of Thomas COLLIER, dec'd vs. William CANFIELD,
et al. Petition to sell land. Filed 6-26-a841. Land, equal undivided one half
part of lot 75 in town of Parrysburg. Heirs: Sally wife of William Canfield;
Harriet Collier; Catharine Collier; _____(not given) wife of Christian Houtz.(172)

6-9-1842 - Dresden W. H. HOWARD vs. Angenette HOWARD. Petition for Partition.
Filed 10-24-1841. Land: 76 acres S12 T5, R8 Henry Co., Ohio; 40 acres SE¼ SE¼
and 40 acres NE¼ SE¼ Section 31, 40 acres NW¼ SW¼ Section 32, all Township 5N
Range 10N and 40 acres NW¼ SW¼ S5, T4N R1ON, all Wood Co., Ohio; 80 acres E½ NE¼,
80 acres SE¼ NW¼ and SW¼ NE¼ and 67 acres S fractional half, all in S9, T10, R3,
76 acres E½ NE¼ S32 T8 R8, E½ NE¼ NW¼ NE¼ S33 T8 R7, all in Lucas Co., Ohio.
Edward Howard, dec'd, late of Wood Co. Widow, mentioned but not named. Two
children: Dresden W. H. Howard of age and Anjenette Howard, a minor. (191)

10-24-1842 - Nathaniel D. BLINN vs. J. H. JEROME, et al. Petition for Partition.
Filed 9-14-1837. Land, 21.59 acres out-lot 282 town of Perrysburg, purchased
by Nathaniel D. Blinn together with Nathaniel Jenison in November 1832. Nathaniel
JENISON, dec'd, died sometime in May or June 1833 leaving no issue. Widow, Sally
Jenison, now wife of Jonathan H. Jerome. Brothers and Sisters: Martha wife of
Hiram P. Barlow; Mary wife of Leonard Whitmore; George Jenison; Charles V.
Jenison; Olive Jenison; Francis Jenison; Harriett Jenison; and Ralph Jenison;
the last three named being minors; and all named being of Wood and Lucas Cos., Ohio.
(205)

10-25-1842 - Adam RADABACH vs. Thomas RADABACH. Petition for Partition. Filed
4-27-1840. Land, 80 acres S½ NE¼ Section 8, Township 5N, Range 12 purchased
through Bucyrus land office. Peter Radabach, dec'd, late of Medina Co., Ohio.
Widow, Catharine Radabach of Medina Co., Ohio. Children: 1/9th part, Adam
Radabach of Medina Co., Ohio; 1/9th part, Thomas Radabach of Medina Co., Ohio;
1/9th part, John Radabach of Medina Co., Ohio; 1/9th part, Joseph Radabach of
Medina Co., Ohio; 1/9th part, Peter Radabach of Centre Co., Pa.; 1/9th part,
Rebecca wife of John Burrill of Northumberland Co., Pa.; 1/9th part, Elizabeth
wife of Carlisle Pember of Wood Co., Ohio; 1/9th part jointly, Daniel Radabach,
dec'd, his children--Christiana, Catharine, Daniel, Lydia and Betsey Radabach
of Stark Co., Ohio; 1/9th part jointly, Samuel Radabach, dec'd, his children--
John and Eliza Radabach of Armstrong Co., Pa.   (211)

10-26-1842 - Isaac VAN TASSELL adms. of H. TEABOO vs. Sophia TEABOO. Petition
to sell land. Filed 10-26-1841. Land, N½ NE¼ S6, T7N, R15; S½ SW fractional
S31, T8N, R15; SE¼ fractional S36, T8N, R14; 40 acres N½ NE¼ S1 T7N, R14.
Hiram TEABAULT, dec'd, late of Wood Co. died in 1837. Widow (not named) died
shortly after Hiram. One child, Sophia Teaboo, aged 11 yrs. of Wood Co. (232)

3-29-1844 - John WEBB, et al. executor of A. RICE, dec'd vs. A. RICE, 2nd, et al.
Petition to sell land. Filed 3-27-1843. Land, 80 acres S½ SE¼ Section 20,
Township 6N, Range 12. Ambrose Rice, dec'd. Widow, mentioned but not named.
Heirs: Ambrose Rice, 2nd of Indiana; Ambrose Rice Lee of Pennsylvania; Ambrose
Rice Eckler of Michigan; Ambrose Rice French residence unknown; Ambrose Rice
Gage of Morgan Co., Ohio; Ambrose Rice Pray of Lucas Co., Ohio; Oscar Hibbard
of Lucas Co., Ohio; Jason Hibbard of Lucas Co., Ohio; Robert A. Hibbard of
Lucas Co., Ohio; Edward Howard, dec'd, his heirs--Nancy Howard a widow, Dresden
Howard and Anjenette Howard, all of Wood Co., Ohio.   (241)

3-18-1843 - William M. TAGGART vs. Lucy TAGGART, et al. Petition for Partition.
Filed 7-16-1842. Land, in-lot 98 and out-lots 8, 108, 117 in Perrysburg.
Partition: 1/4th part, William M. Taggart of Kenton, Hardin Co., Ohio; 1/4th
part, Lucy Taggart of Richland Co., Ohio; 1/4th part, William M. Hoyt of Richland
Co., Ohio; 1/4th part, Mary Hoyt of Richland Co., Ohio.   (244)

10-24-1843 - Samuel WILES, guardian vs. Richard F. DONALDSON, et al. Petition
to sell lands. Filed 10-19-1836. Land, tract 75 of 152 acres E½ NW¼ Section 34,
Township 3 (no range given), being 80 acres at foot of Rapids of Miami of the Lake.
Thomas Donaldson, dec'd, late of Muskingum Co., Ohio. Widow, Nancy Donaldson
of Muskingum Co., Ohio. Children: Richard F. Donaldson aged 15 yrs.; Harriett
Catherine Donaldson aged 13 yrs.; Frances Amanda Donaldson aged 10 yrs. (9 yrs.
May 1835); Robert Safford Donaldson aged 6 yrs. (5 yrs. Oct. 1835); Aras Berkley
Donaldson aged 5 yrs. (4 yrs. Feb. 1835); and James H. Donaldson aged 2 yrs. (11
months in 1835), all of Muskingum Co., Ohio. In the year 1834 Samuel Wilds
was in Muskingum Co., Ohio appointed guardian of the following additional
children of the deceased: Hiram Alexander Donaldson aged 20 yrs. Feb. last (1834);
George Thomas Donaldson aged 16 yrs. 3 Feb. last (1834); and at that time
two of the children listed above were listed with ages as follows--Richard
Franklin Donaldson aged 14 yrs. March last (1834) and Harriet Catharine Donaldson
aged 12 yrs. May last (1834).   (249)

5-?-1845 - Edy DOLIVAR vs. Ira DOLIVAR. Divorce. Filed 2-10-1844. Married
1-1-1835 in Geauga Co., Ohio. That on 5-15-1841 Ira stated his intention to
move from Wisconsin to Geauga Co., but did not do so. That Edy removed to
Wood Co., Ohio in June 1844. One daughter, Sarah Jane Dolivar aged 8 yrs.
2 Dec. last. (324)

10-1-1846 - John EVERS vs. Celinda EVERS. Divorce. Filed 7-3-1845. That
John married on 3-30-1835 to Celinda White late of Wood County, but now of
parts unknown. Two sons (not named, one being 8 yrs and the other 4 yrs.
claimed by John. That Celinda took with her a child aged 5 months not claimed
by John. (335)

3-29-1847 - Henry SHIVELY vs. George SMITH, et al. Petition to sell land.
Filed 3-16-1843. Land, W½ NE¼ NW¼ Section 30, Township 5N, Range 11, Centre
twp. Jacob Smith, dec'd late of Wood Co. with Henry Shively as adms. of his
estate. Heirs: Brother, Thomas Smith, dec'd, his heirs--James Smith of Summit
Co., Ohio, Amanda wife of Joseph Arbuckle of Illinois, Mary wife of Cleerl(?)
Cleveland of Summit Co., Ohio, Rebecca wife of ____(left blank) Rhodes of Summit
Co., Ohio, Elizabeth Smith of Summit Co., Ohio and Margaret wife of Henry
Lundy of Wood Co., Ohio; (no relationship given for following heirs--possibly
brothers and sisters?) George Smith; Caleb Smith; Mary wife of Henry Hixon;
all of Summit Co., Ohio; John Smith of Union Co., Pa.; Anna wife of Stilwell
Stilwell of Union Co., Pa.; Elizabeth wife of David L. Hixon of Wood Co., Ohio;
James Smith of Summit Co., Ohio. (337)

10-25-1848 - Orlandhia Jane KEELER and James DONALDSON adms. of Ralph O. KEELER
vs. John HOLISTER and Olmsted KEELER, et al. Petition to sell land. Filed (not
given). Undivided one half SE¼ E½ SW¼ and W½ NE¼ S35, T5, R9; SW¼ S2, N½ SW¼
S3, N½ NW¼ S11, all in T4, R9; E part SW¼ S6, T4, R10, that John Hollister
of Buffalo, New York is owner of other undivided one half. Widow, Orlanthia Jane
Keeler. Heirs by next inheritance: William Olmsted, Ralph O., Electa Amelia
and Sarah Grace Keeler, all minors. (347, 354)

10-28-1847 - James DUNIFACE (DONIFACE), et al. vs. Robert H. KELLY. Petition
for Partition. Filed 2-10-1846. James Kelly died seized of in-lots 793, 208,
& 225 Perrysburg; Elizabeth Kelly died seized of NE¼ Section 34, Township 3
(no Range given) of U.S. Reserve at foot of Rapids of Miami of Lake Erie; John
R. Kelly died seized of E½ in-lot 317 and W½ E½ out-lot (note: number not given)
Perrysburg. James Kelly, dec'd; Elizabeth Kelly, dec'd; and John R. Kelly, dec'd.
Heirs: Margaret M. wife of John C. Robinson of Summit Co., Ohio; Sarah H. wife
of John Hutchinson of Huntington Co., Pa.; Robert H. Kelly; Susan wife of James
Doniface; Eliza H. wife of John Bates and James H. Kelly; all of Wood Co., Ohio.
(356)

10-23-1849 - AMOS vs. AMOS, et al. Petition for Partition. Filed 2-28-1848.
Land, 80 acres S½ NW¼ Section 1, Township 4N, Range 11E. Michael Amos Sr.,
dec'd, died 10-14-1838 intestate. Widow, Caroline Amos. Children: (ages given
are ages at time of death of father in 1838) Michael Amos Jr. age 20 yrs.; Catharine
now wife of Jacob Dauterman, aged 16 yrs.; Adam Amos aged 14 yrs; George Amos
aged 11 yrs.; Frederick Amos aged 5 yrs.; Jacob Amos aged 2 yrs.; Margaret Amos
aged 2 yrs. (359)

10-22-1849 - Sylvanus HATCH adms. of Estate of Samuel CLARKE, Jr. Petition to
sell lands. Filed 3-9-1849. Land, 60 acres N½ SW¼ Section 17, Township 5N,
Range 10E. Widow, Margaret Clarke. Heirs: Frances Clarke, Stebbins Clarke
and Adolphus Clark. (367)

10-29-1847 - James JONES, adms. vs. Mary CALLAHAN, et al. Petition to sell land.
Filed 4-10-1845. Land, S½ NW¼ Section 11, Township 3N, Range 12E, 80 acres.
Jesse P. BORTON, dec'd. Widow, Mary Borton, now wife of ____(left blank) Callahan.
Children: Benjamin F., Caleb, Eliza and Sarah Ann Borton, all of.Columbiana
Co., Ohio. (393)

10-23-1849 - Benjamin BROWN adms. of Peter PAINTER vs. Widow and Heirs. Petition
to sell land. Filed 3-1-1847. Land, S½ NE¼ Section 10, S½ NW¼, NEP NW¼, and
NW¼ NE¼ Section 11. All in Township 3N, Range 1, totaling 240 acres. Peter
Painter, dec'd, late of Wood Co. Widow, Elizabeth Painter. Heirs: Adam Painter,
Michael Painter, Henry Painter, Samuel Painter, John Painter, Peter Painter,
Zelotus Painter, Margaret Ann Pratt, Katharine Sarah Painter and Maria Painter.
(395)

April Term 1850 - John A. KELLY adms. of Estate of A. ROLLINS. vs. Heirs.
Petition to sell land. Filed 3-1-1847. Land, E½ NW¼ Section 32 and all
W½ NW¼ Section 33, Township 4N, Range 12E. Almon Rollins, dec'd, late of Wood
Co. Heirs: Martha wife of John Carroll, Julia Ann Rollins, Sophia Rollins,
Celesta Ann Rollins, William Rollins, Harriett Amanda Rollins and Mary E. Rollins.
(423)

April Term 1850 - Oris CROSLY vs. Charlotte M. BALLON and Lucy M. CROSLY.
Petition to sell land. Filed (not given). Land, 50 acres part of River
tract #46 Wood Co. Eunice S. Crosly, dec'd late of Lucas Co., Ohio. Heirs
to 1/3 part: Charlotte M. Ballon and Lucy M. Crosly, minor children of Eunice
S. Crosly by Oris Crosly their guardian, of Henry Co., Ohio. (426)

April Term 1850 - Samuel MOSS and Augustus MOSS vs. Abi FITCH, etal. In Chancery.
Filed 2-10-1847. Land, W½ SE¼ Section 33, Township 6N, Range 10, being 80 acres,
mortgaged to Samuel and Augustus Moss. Montgomery H. Fitch, dec'd, died 5-1-1846.
Widow, Abi Fitch. Eight minor children: James M., Mary S., Eliza J., Charlotte E.,
Amaza S., Lydia and William H. Fitch, all of Seneca Co., Ohio. (note: states
eight children, but only names seven). (429)

759

WOOD COUNTY, OHIO - WILL ABSTRACTS 1820-1850

The following wills were abstracted from Will Book A-1&2. Will Book A consists of two parts and the following records are from Part 1. Page on which the original record may be found is given in parenthesis. The will records are in the Probate Court at the court house in Bowling Green.

THURSTON, Samuel H. of Waynesfield twp. - verbal will; deposition dated 11-7-1820; recorded 12-6-1820. Samuel H. Thurston died on the morning of Nov. 5, 1820. Left 2/3 of estate to Lucius Thurston Carlin and 1/3 of estate to Masonic Lodge of Waynesfield twp. Deposition given by James Carlin and Susan (her mark) Carlin. Witnesses: James Carlin and Seneca Allen(?). (1)

SPAFFORD, Olive - widow of Amos Spafford of Fort Meigs, Wood Co., dec'd - dated 5-31-1822; recorded 2-12-1823. Sons: Aurora Spafford, to have Bible which contains family record; Samuel Spafford; both to serve as executors. Daughter, Clvey wife of Almon Gibbs. Four grandsons; John Craw, Richard Craw, Sarvis Gilbert and Lester Gilbert; all not of age. Signed: Olive Spafford. Witnesses: Thos. R. McKnight, Thos. W. Powell and Ambrose Rice. (2)

HOWARD, Thomas - dated 2-9-1825; recorded 12-12-1825. Sons: eldest, Edward Howard; Robert Howard; Richard M. W. Howard; Alexander Howard; William Howard. Daughter, Sidney wife of Joshua Nelson. Grandsons: John and David Howard, sons of Alexander Howard; Governor Howard Nelson, son of Joshua Nelson. Executors: son, Edward Howard and Thomas R. McKnight. Signed: Thos. Howard. Witnesses: T. W. Powell and Aurora Spafford. Codicil dated 3-28-1825. Grandsons: Dresden Winfield Huston Howard, son of Edward Howard; and Pike Moroe Howard, son of Edward Howard, Pike M. Howard is not of age. Signed: Thomas Howard. Same witnesses. (4)

NASON, Stephen - dated 4-21-1826; recorded 12-6-1826. Wife, Julia Ann. Sons: eldest, Alexander Nason; youngest, William Nason. Executor; friend and neighbor, Eber Wilson. Signed: Stephen Nason. Witnesses: T. W. Powell, Samuel F. Wilson and Sophronia Wilson. (10)

ROSEBERRY, Ebenezer of Marion Co., Ohio - dated 12-14-1825; recorded 1-23-1829. Three children: two daughters, Mary and Nancy Roseberry to have "all wife's wearing apparel"' son, John Roseberry. Owned land in Sandusky Co. Ohio; Marion Co., Ohio and Perrysburg, Wood Co., Ohio. Executors: John Green and David A. Beardsley. Signed: Ebenezer Roseberry. Witnesses: (not given). (12)

SAFFER, Jonas - dated 5-18-1832; recorded 9-24-1833. Land in Wood Co. to Thomas Donaldson. Horse to William Thomas Donaldson, son of William Donaldson, William Thomas not now living in Ohio. Executor: Thomas Donaldson of Muskingum Co., Ohio. Signed: Jonas Saffer. Witnesses: John E. Hanna and William Deverny. (16)

RICE, Daniel - dated 5-20-1834; recorded 6-23-1835. Son, Isaac Rice. Son (?), John Rice, dec'd, his heirs--Isaac, Mary, Elizabeth, Nancy and Anabela Rice. Daughters: Polly Simons, dec'd, her children--Susaan, Benjamin & Maria Simons; Anne Seltenright; Lydia Horne; Fany Simons; Margaret Steortes; Elizabeth Shong. Executors: Isaac Rice and John Shong of Crawford Co., Ohio. Signed: Daniel (his mark) Rice. Witnesses: John Crom Sr. and Daniel Bearly. (21)

760

WILKISON, Jacob - dated 8-26-1833; recorded 5-15-1834. Wife, Sally, also to serve as executrix. Signed: Jacob Wilkison. Witnesses: John J. Lovett and John Elder. (19)

KELLOGG, Daniel M. of Perrysburg - dated 8-20-1836; recorded Rensselaer Co., N. Y. 9-19-1836; recorded Wood Co. 12-1-1836. Sisters: Chloe Kellogg and Martha A. wife of George W. Francis. Brothers: John C. Kellogg, Christopher S. Kellogg and Giles C. Kellogg and his wife Adeline. Mentions children of brother, Christopher S. Kellogg, but does not name. Bequeaths to David C. Doan and Daniel R. Biddlecomb of Perrysburg. Mentions Illinois land and property in Ohio and Michigan. Executor: brother, Giles C. Kellogg of Troy. Signed: D. M. Kellogg. Witnesses: Justin Kellogg, Daniel T. Francis, H. Z. Hayper and Dillon Beebe all of Troy, Rensselaer Co., N. Y. (23)

HAYS, Henry of Perry twp. - dated (not given); recorded (not given-1836 or 1837). Wife, Jane. Sons: James, Andrew, Thomas, Marshal, David and John; John not of age. Daughter, Loas A. Wade. Executors: James Hays and James Hays Jr. Signed: Henry Hays. Witnesses: (not given). (31)

WILSON, Eber - dated 10-11-1836; recorded 12-18-1837. Wife, Rebecca Wilson. Sons: Samuel F. Wilson, Eber Wilson Jr. and Charles Wilson. Daughter, Fidelia Bull. Daughter(?), Eliza Reed. Executors: wife, Rebecca and son Eber Jr. Signed: Eber (his mark) Wilson. Witnesses: J. C. Spink and Tobias Rudesill. (32)

ALTMAN (ALLMAN), William of Columbiana Co., Ohio - dated 1-28-1839; recorded Columbiana Co. 3-26-1839; recorded Wood Co. 6-14-1839. Wife, mentioned but not named. Children: Mary Scates, David Altman, Elizabeth Candles, Susanna Rummell, Catharine Sidener, Hannah Roph, Sarah Glesser, Anne Altman, and Lydia Altman. Grandson, George Glosser. Owns farm in Wood Co. leased by Israel Stall; owns land in Hardin Co., Ohio. Executors: friend, Anthony Hardman and son-in-law, David Glesser. Signed: William Allman. Witnesses: Joseph Hisey and John Hicy.

RADUBACH, Peter of Guilford twp., Medina Co., Ohio - dated 4-10-1838; recorded Medina Co. 11-12-1838; recorded Wood Co. 11-15-1838. Wife, Katharine Radubach. Sons: oldest son, Daniel Radubach, dec'd, died Huron Co., Ohio, his heirs (not named); 2nd son, Peter Radubach, lives Center Co., Penna.; 3rd son, John Radubach lives Medina Co., Ohio; son, Thomas Radubach; son, Samuel Radubach, dec'd, died Armstrong Co., Penna., his heirs (not named); son, Joseph Radubach lives Armstrong Co., Penna.; son, Adam Radubach. Daughters: Rebecca wife of John Runnil, lives in south part of Ohio; and Elizabeth. Owned land in Meadville, Penna. Executors: Sons, Thomas Radubach, Adam Radubach and Thomas Radubach. Signed: Peter Radubach. Witnesses: Samuel McConnel and George K. Pardee. 1st Codicil dated 4-10-1838 and 2nd Codicil dated 6-14-1838; no additional information given. (35)

THOMPSON, Chaucy of Huron Co., Ohio; dated 9-1-1836; recorded Huron Co. 3-18-1837; recorded Wood Co. 1-22-1840. Wife, Eunice M. Thompson, also to serve as executrix. Signed: Chaucy Thompson. Witnesses: I. W. Brooks and Anson Fox. (40)

HOWARD, Edward of Weston twp. - dated 2-2-1841; recorded 2-14-1841. Wife, Nancy, farm where "now live formerly owned by Joseph Keith". Son, Dresden W. H. Howard. Daughter, Anjanett Howard, not of age. Executors: son, Dresden W. H. Howard and Francis Hinsdale. Signed: E. Howard. Witnesses: Wm. Pratt and Francis Hinsdale.

WARDSWORTH, Dacias born at Farmington, Conn., now residing in New Haven, Conn. - dated 9-24-1821; recorded New Haven, Conn. 11-14-1821; recorded Wood Co. 4-15-1841. Brother, Sidney Wardsworth of Farmington, "all lands which came to me by my late honored father, William Wardsworth of Farmington, lately deceased." Brother, Romeo (or Homeo) Wardsworth residing in New York. Brother, George Wardsworth, his children (not named). Friend, Eli Whitney, a legacy of $250.00. Nephew, Eli Blake, "my mechine for carrying on secret correspondance". Executor: brother, Romeo (or Homeo) Wardsworth. Signed: Dacius Wardsworth. Witnesses: Henry Edwards E. Lewis and Peley P. Lanford. (44)

TREMAN, Julius - dated 9-21-1841; recorded 1-29-1842. Wife, Nancy I. Treman, to have 63 acres land in Granger twp., Medina Co., Ohio, being land deeded to testator by his father, Jeremiah Treman of Granger twp., Medina Co., Ohio in the spring of 1841. Two sons; George Elmore Treman and Julius Derwin Treman. Executors: wife, Nancy J. and brother, John M. Treman. Signed: Julius Treman. Witnesses: Henry A. Harris and Peter P. Boyde. (46)

TRACY. Thomas R. of Plain twp. - dated 12-9-1841; recorded 2-10-1842. Wife, Lydia. Sons: Lyman, John, Thomas, Mercena R., William, Ebenezer, Mason, Joseph R. and Isaac Tracy. Daughters: Orsella Pike, Sofa Newton, Harriet Vincent, Abigal Tracy and Ruth A. Tracy. Grandson, John Tracy Jr., not of age. Executors: wife, Lydia and Joseph R. Tracy. Signed: Thos. R. Tracy. Witnesses: Henry Shively, David Maginnis and Isaac Van Tassel. Codicil (not dated), no additional information.(48)

SMITH, John of Perrysburg, "in the 78th year of my age" - dated 12-23-1841; recorded 4-12-1842. Wife, Caroline. Owned land in Lorain Co., Ohio. Signed: John Smith. Witnesses: John Brownsberger, E. N. Knight, Geo. W. Owen and Electa Blinn. (53)

RICE, Ambrose - dated 12-2-1840; recorded 5-10-1842. To Ambrose Rice, Second of Alleghany Co., Penna. To Ambrose Rice Gage of Morgan Co., Ohio. To Ambrose Rice Eckler of Catskill, New York. to have Eagle or Rice's Island in Sandusky Bay containing 134.42 acres. To Ambrose Rice, Second of Allen Co., Indiana. To Ambrose Rice Murry of Michigan, to have lot in Monroe, Michigan. To Ambrose Rice French of Cincinnati, Ohio. To Ambrose Rice Pray of Lucas Co., Ohio. To Oscar S. Hibbard, Jason R. Hibbard and Mortimer D. Hibbard, all of Lucas Co., Ohio. To Edward Howard of Wood Co. To Robert A. Howard of Lucas Co., Ohio. (note: will contains many land descriptions). Executors: James L. Gage of MorganCo., Ohio; John Webb of Wood Co.; and Jonathan H. Jerome of Lucas Co., Ohio. Signed: Ambrose Rice. Witnesses: Addison Smith and Hezekiah L. Hosmer. (55)

ROWAN, John of Louisville (Ky.) - dated 1-28-1840; recorded Jefferson Co., Ky. 8-28-1843; recorded Wood Co. (not given-1843-1844). Wife, mentioned but not named, to have interest in city wharf and ferry. Four children: Alice Shaw, Elizabeth Rowa and John Rowan (note: other children not named, but mentions "unmarried daughters"). Grandchildren: J. R. Steele, Eliza Harvey and Josephine Rowan; Josephine under 9 yrs of age. Sister, _____ Cooper (not named further). Namesake, John Rowan Perth. Frie Jas. Guthrie. Mentions "my law library". Owned Kentucky property, property on Maumee, Lower Sandusky and in Toledo; also Louisville property. His home is called "Federal Hill" and requests that if he dies within 50 miles of same that he be buried by his departed children and that no tombstone be placed at his grave, as no tombston have been or are to be placed at said children's graves. Friend, Mr. Lewis Tyler to act as agent for estate. Executors: James Guthrie and He ry Pirth, Esquires. Signe John Rowan. Witnesses: (not given). (61)

SNIDER, Daniel of Centre twp. - dated 9-1-1842; recorded 10-23-1843. Wife, Sarah, also to serve as executrix. Son, Samuel. Mentions "my family". Signed: Daniel (his mark) Snider. Witnesses: Joseph Ralston, Samuel Snider and Philip Condit.(72)

BIRDSALL, John O., Minister of the Gospel of Perrysburg - dated 6-5-1844; recorded 7-6-1844. Sons: oldest son, John A. Judson Birdsall; 2nd son, George Dana Boardman Birdsall; son, Wm. Lary Birdsall, to have "what was his mothers best arm chair"; infant son, Francis Mason Birdsall, to have Family Bible, Only daughter, Almira Elizabeth Birdsall, under 12 yrs. of age, to have property "formerly of her mother". Owned land in DeKalb Co., Indiana and Jackson Co., Michigan. Friend, Dr. Jeremiah Peck. Executors: Dr. John Geigler. Elijah Huntington, Esq. and "my brother", Nathan Birdsall, Esq. of Otsego Co., N. Y. Signed: John O. Birdsall. Witnesses: John Geigler and Jane Zeigler. (74)

BADGER, Joseph of Perrysburg, in the "87th year of my life" - dated 2-28-1844; recorded (not given-1844-1845). Wife, Abagail Badger. Executor, Tobias Rudersill. Signed: Joseph Badger. Witnesses: George Powers and Abner Brown. (81)

OBERDORF, Mathias of Weston twp. - dated 5-16-1839; recorded 5-2-1845. Wife, Eava Oberdorf. Sons: oldest son, Samuel Oberdorf; and 2nd son, Daniel Oberdorf. Daughters: Barberry May, Anna, Mary and Maugred. Executor: son, Samuel. Signed; Matthias Oberdorf. Witnesses: Henry Kimberlin and Joseph King. (83)

RAITT, Sally F. wife of James Raitt, formerly Sally Cobran of Richland Co., Ohio - dated 4-7-1845; recorded Richland Co., Ohio 5-2-1845; recorded Wood Co. (not given-1845-1846). Children: Elizabeth, Nancy and Sarah Jane Raitt. Executor: husband, James Raitt. Signed: Sally F. Raitt. Witnesses: Robert Larimer and James Cobran.

OSTRANDER, John - dated 1-20-1846; recorded 3-11-1846. Wife, Sarah. Children, mentioned but not named, may not be of age. Executors: wife, Sarah and Theodore G Frisbe. Signed: John (his mark) Ostrander. Witnesses: Thomas L. Bane and Skiff Bassett. (91)

WOODBURY, Benjamin of Plain twp. - dated 12-23-1845; recorded 3-11-1846. Wife, Mehitable, also to serve as admrx. Children, mentioned but not named. Signed: Benjamin Woodbury. Witnesses: Nathaniel T. Fay. Hez. L. Nosmer and J. W. Woodbury.(95)

DOUGLASS, Elizabeth of Delaware Co., Ohio formerly of Augusta Co., Virginia - dated 3-22-1843; recorded 3-13-1846. Son, John A. Douglass, dec'd, his widow, and his children--Ellen S., Sally H. (or W.?), Martha C. and John A. Douglass. Daughter, Mary G. McCutchen. Elizabeth owned farm known by name of "Sweet Home" in Augusta Co., Virginia. Executors: friends, Dr. Isaac Hall and Matthew F. Wilson, Signed: Elizabeth Douglass. Witnesses: Thomas Lewis, Robert B. Reeder, John A. Kelly and John G. Willard. (98)

COREY, Samuel P. - dated 4-6-1846; recorded 9-29-1846. Wife, mentioned but not named. Three sons: George D., Ambrose and Orrin I. Two daughters, Louisa C. Dana and Mary E. Corey. Executor, George D. Cory. Signed: Samuel P. Corey. Witnesses: Alfred Brown and Benjamin Brown. Codicil dated 4-6-1846 changing executor to Ambrose Corey. Same witnesses. (102)

BROWN, Alfred - verbal will; deposition dated 9-23-1846; recorded 9-29-1846. Brother, Benjamin, also to serve as adms. Mentions other brothers but does not name. Witnesses: Mordica. Chilcoat and Ambrose Cory. (107)

CROTHERS, Francis of Portage twp. - dated 1-21-1847; recorded 3-29-1847. Wife, Elizabeth. Sons (in order of age): James H., Wm. R., Samuel, David W. and Lewis Cass Crothers. Daughters (in order of age): Nancy Jane Crothers, Ellen Crothers and Mary Margaret. Executors: son, Wm. R. Crothers and friend, John McMahan. Signed: F. Crothers. Witnesses: George Mercer and J. B. Bostwick. (108)

COLNEY, James B. of Perrysburg - dated 4-3-1846; recorded (not given-1847). Wife, Clarissa B. Colney, also to serve as executrix. Signed: James B. Colney. Witnesses: E. Huntington and Seth C. Dean. (111)

STACY, George of Center twp. - dated 3-19-1846; recorded (not given 1847). Wife, mentioned but not named. Executors: wife and James Smith. Mentions "my family". Signed: George Stacy. Witnesses: Henry Shively and Alex. McMiller. (112)

WALTERS, Jacob of Weston twp. - dated 1-28-1847; recorded 3-30-1847. Wife, Elizabeth Walters. Youngest child, Sarah Catherine, not of age. Mentions "other children". Executors: wife, Elizabeth and son, John Walters. Signed: Jacob Walters. Witnesses: Wm. Martin, John Crom Jr. and Joseph Walters. (115)

WHITACRE, Mahlon of Bloom twp. - dated 7-26-1847; recorded 10-26-1847. Wife, mentioned but not named. Four surviving children: Edward M. Whitacre, Reason Whitacre, Isaac Whitacre and Lydian McCrory. To Martha Whitacre wife of Preston Whitacre, dec'd. To Alice and Phebe A. Stackhouse, Phebe A. not of age. Executors: Reason Whitacre and Moses Bunhon. Signed: Mahlon Whitacre. Witnesses: David Milbourn and William Alez. (116)

NEARING, Neptune of Plain twp. - dated 2-17-1844; recorded (not given). Wife, Stella Nearing, at her death to her heirs--Rosetta Nearing and Guy Nearing. To John S. Parsons and Geo. N. Parsons, not of age, $100.00 each as long as they remain with their mother or leave with her permission. To Stella M. Parsons, $50.00, as long as she remains with mother or leaves with her permission. Signed: Neptune (his mark) Nearing. Witnesses: D. Edgerton and J. W. Woodbury. Codicil dated 2-17-1844, no additional information. (119)

EDGERTON, Nathaniel of Plain twp. - dated 12-27-1842; recorded (not given). Wife, Lydia, Son, Abraham D. Wife's daughter, Susan G. Signed: Nathaniel Edgerton. Witnesses: Benjamin Woodbury, John Evers, Ezekiel McFerrin. (120)

KIGER, Jeremiah of Perry twp. - dated 11-12-1845; recorded 11-19-1845. Wife, mentioned but not named. Children, mentioned but not named. Executor: John A. Kelley. Signed: Jeremiah Kiger. Witnesses: Daniel Stone and Wm. Osman. (122)

STONE, Daniel - dated 3-1-1847; recorded 3-29-1847. Wife, Rosanna. Mentions "all the heirs". Executors: brother, Henry Stone and Erastus Ranger. Signed: Daniel Stone. Witnesses: Norman Russel and Emery B. Walcott. (124)

HUNTER, Stephen of Plain twp. - dated 5-21-1846; recorded 10-28-1847. Son, George Henry Hunter, not of age. Brother, Philander Hunter, to serve as executor and also guardian of son, George Henry. Mentions "my mother", but does not name. Signed: Stephen (his mark) Hunter. Witnesses: Loring Farras and Lydia Johnson. (125

WELLS, David of Perry twp. - dated 4-6-1847; recorded 10-29-1847. Wife, mentioned but not named. Son, Solomon Wells. Son-in-law, John Sharer. Daughters: Nancy Rice of Carroll Co., Ohio; Amelia Wells; and Sarah Jane Wells. Executor, James Jones. Signed: David (his mark) Wells. Witnesses: Samuel M. Chilcote and John Norris. (128)

SAGE, Roswell - dated 3-18-1848; recorded 6-3-1848. Sons: John Wesley and Seymore Norton. Daughters: Caroline Rhoda, Sarah Marietta, Eleanor Amanda and Emily (note: there may also be another daughter named Harriet, or this may be Emily's middle name). Executor, Levi Lock. Signed: Roswell Sage. Witnesses: George I. (or J.) Poe and Hollis Fay. (131)

St. CLAIR (SIN CLAIR), George of Montgomery twp. - dated 5-29-1843; recorded 8-4-1848. Wife, Hannah. Sons: Samuel, Columbus, Joseph, George Jr., Francis, James and Peter St. Clair. Daughters: Eunice, Elizabeth, Mariah, Sarah and Hannah St Clair. Executors: wife, Hannah and son, George Jr. Signed: George St Clair. Witnesses; Theodore G. Frisble and Theodonus H. C. Frisble. (132)

SMITH, Caroline of Perrysburg twp. - dated 8-30-1847; recorded 8-19-1848. Son, James J. Smith, also to serve as executor. Owns land in Lorain Co. Signed: Caroline Smith. Witnesses: George W. Owens and Joseph Brownsberger. (137)

HAYS, James - dated (not given); recorded 10-10-1848. Son, John Hays. Son, Henry, his son, James. Mentions "rest of my children"; also requests "all my baskets be divided among my girls". Executors: John Hays and Samuel M. Chilcote. Signed: James Hays. Witnesses: Ezra Brown and Henry Slaughterback. (138)

HOWARD, Orange - dated 4-7-1848; recorded 10-24-1848. Wife, mentioned but not named. Sons: Sanford Howard and Orange Howard Jr. Daughter, Philanda Winter. Executor; son, Sanford Howard. Signed: Orange Howard. Witnesses: Ransom Howard and Thomas Gorrill. (141)

VAN TASSEL, Isaac of Plain twp. - dated 11-7-1846; recorded 4-3-1849. Wife, L. B. Van Tassell. Requests tombstones. Signed: Isaac Van Tassel. Witnesses: Stephen St John as executor. (143)

JUSTICE, John of Montgomery - dated 1-11-1849; recorded 10-24-1849. Wife, Susan, Son, James Armstrong Justice. Daughters: Jane Justice, Elizabeth An Justice and Mary Justice. Mentions "children by present wife". Executors: wife, Susan and Ezra Morgan. Signed: John Justice. Witnesses: T. G. Frisbie and S. Morgan.(144)

SMITH, Van Ranslear of Center twp. - dated 7-24-1849; recorded 10-24-1849. Wife, Catharine, also to serve as executrix. Son, James Valentine Smith, under 24 years of age. Signed: V. R. Smith. Witnesses: S. W. St John and Nathan Moore. (145)

SPAFFORD, Aurora of Perrysburg - dated 4-7-1847; recorded 4-2-1850. Wife, Mary, to have farm known as "Spaffords Grant". Sons: oldest son, Alfred Jarvis Spafford; youngest son, James Aurora Spafford. Daughters: oldest daughter, Louisa Smith and her heirs; daughter, Miranda Crane; youngest daughter, Mary Olivia Hopkins and her heirs. Executors: wife, Mary; son, Alfred Jarvis Spafford; and son-in-law, William H. Hopkins. Signed: Aurora Spafford. Witnesses: John Webb and Daniel Lindsay. (148)

ROBY, Charles C. of Perrysburg - dated 4-18-1840; recorded 6-24-1850. Wife, Amelia R. Roby. Daughter, Abby Ameria Roby. Executor, David Ladd. Signed: Chs. C. Roby. Witnesses: Jos. Utley and E. D. Peck. (152)

MAYER, Francis - dated 2-3-1847; recorded 10-26-1847. Wife, Frances Mayer. Children, mentioned but not named. Executors: wife, Frances and Lorin Smith. Signed: Francis I. Mayer. Witnesses: Oliver Saunders and Eli W. Calvin. (Will Book A, Part 2, page 61)

--- A ---

Aarasmith, John 453
Abbit, Aaron 727
Abbot, Abby 31
Abbot, James 511
Abbot, Joel 76
Abbot, John 119, 123
Abbot, Julia 30
Abbot, Lorenzo 524, 526
Abbot, Polly 182
Abbott, Barnard 392
Abbott, John 750
Abbott, Justin 28
Abbott, Lorenzo 528, 530
Abbott, Margaret 672
Abbott, Mary 392, 405
Abbott, Polly 392
Abbott, Ruben 392
Abbott, Sally 392
Abbott, Samuel 511
Abbott, Weltha 31
Abbott, William 392
Abel, Andrew 230
Abel, Catharine 230
Abel, Nancy 459
Abenshen, Frederick 709
Abernathy, Rhoda 406
Abet, Nancy 453
Abeuscheon, Jacob (Sr.) 709
Abeville, Elizabeth 522
Able, Alexander 657
Abnernathy, Nancy 43
Abrahams, Reuben 477
Abrams, Bazel 470
Abrams, Henry 394, 481
Abrams, Orphia 394
Abrams, Reuben 472, 475, 483, 484, 485, 487
Abrams, Ruth 394
Ace, Elizabeth 166
Acheson, John 291
Achlenker, David Carmellias 239
Achlenker, Elizabeth 239
Achlenker, George 239
Achlenker, George Henry 239
Achlenker, Mary Elizabeth 239
Achlenker, Solomon 239
Achlenker, Susan 239

Ackenberger, Stephen 478
Ackengeerger, Stephen 478
Acker, Jacob 432
Acker, Michael 432
Ackerman, George 738
Ackles, Jas. H. 252
Ackles, Nancy Jane 252
Ackley, Calvin 753
Ackley, Russell 731
Acre, Elizabeth 429
Acre, Jacob 429
Acre, John 429
Acre, Michael 429
Acton, Berthenia M. 425
Acton, Bethenia 425
Acton, Elizabeth A. 422
Acton, John 416
Acton, John P. 422, 425
Acton, John Thomas 425
Acton, M. B. 422
Acton, Richard 461
Acton, William B. 423
Acus, Mary Ann 744
Adair, Anderson 61
Adair, Ann 738
Adair, Borthier 46
Adair, Charlotte 35
Adair, Edward K. 53
Adair, Elizabeth 53
Adair, James 487
Adair, Jno. (Sr.) 53
Adair, John 53, 54
Adair, John (Sr.) 53
Adair, Joseph 53
Adair, Margaret Jane 61
Adair, Nancy 53
Adair, Robert 53
Adair, Robert McNigh 53
Adair, Samuel 53, 54, 61
Adair, William 53
Adair, William Bruce 61
Adams, --- 266
Adams, Abigail 77
Adams, Alexander 250, 251
Adams, Anancy 585
Adams, Armstrong C. 335
Adams, Betsy 43
Adams, Calvin 28
Adams, Charles 82, 335
Adams, David 639, 756
Adams, Edward 340, 348
Adams, Elijah 542, 639

Adams, Elizabeth 122, 133
Adams, Evi 340, 348
Adams, Fanny 504
Adams, Flava 28
Adams, George 283
Adams, Henry 672
Adams, Henry (Jr.) 672
Adams, Hugh 487
Adams, Isaac H. 492
Adams, Isaac N. 28, 40
Adams, Isaiah 427
Adams, Jacob 258, 261, 262, 265, 272
Adams, James 518
Adams, Jane 639
Adams, John 298, 408, 472, 639, 650, 654, 657, 681
Adams, Joseph 123, 570
Adams, Lucius 495
Adams, M. D. (Dr.) 149
Adams, Magdalena 522
Adams, Margaret 348, 756
Adams, Martha 411
Adams, Mathew C. 657
Adams, Micah 258, 263
Adams, Milton M. 28
Adams, Moses R. 606
Adams, Myra 631
Adams, Nancy 182
Adams, Patrick 167
Adams, Rheuby 28
Adams, Robert 484, 492
Adams, Roda 519
Adams, Samuel 6
Adams, Samuel W. 542
Adams, Sarah Ann 30
Adams, Susan 87
Adams, Thomas 182
Adams, Washington F. 654
Adams, William 76
Adams, Wm. 681
Adamson, Elizabeth 5
Adamson, Enos (Elder) 426
Adamson, Isaac 455
Adamson, John Van Winkle 426
Adamson, Joseph 123
Adamson, Mary 659
Adamson, Sara Louisa 426
Adaway, Mary 557
Addams, Reuben 484

Addington, Sarah 662
Addis, John 314
Addis, Joseph 177
Addis, Martha L. 314
Adelsperger, John 518
Adington, Betsey 661
Adkerson, Charles 461
Adkin, David 511
Adkins, M. 406
Adkins, Reuben 406
Adkins, Wm. 406
Adlin, Peter 366
Adney, Barbary 114
Aduddell, Huldah 410
Ady, Frances Mary 249
Ady, Hannah 249
Ady, Hannah Matilda 249
Ady, James T. 249
Ady, Jas. T. 249
Ady, Mary 249
Afflick, --- 176
Afflick, . . . 152
Afton, Mary 58
Agee, Sarah 6
Agenbroad, Daniel 203
Agie, Sarah 6
Agler, Jane 607
Agler, Matilda 607
Agler, William 606
Ahlaz, John Diederick 105
Ahlerge, John D. 104
Aiken, John 223, 511
Aikens, Saml. 271
Aikin, Robert 633
Aikin, William 254
Aikins, Elizabeth E. 254
Aikins, James 254
Aikins, John 248
Aikins, Robert 292
Aikins, Samuel 247
Aikins, William 248
Ailes, Caroline S. 432
Ailes, Marilda Ann 432
Ailes, Sarah 419
Ailes, Wm. 419
Ailes, Wm. U. 432
Ainey, Daniel 338
Ainsly, Polly 518
Ainsworth, A. 99
Ainsworth, Anne 658
Ainsworth, Archer 695
Ainsworth, David 99
Ainsworth, Emma L. 617
Ainsworth, George 645, 674
Ainsworth, Jos. 99
Ainsworth, Laza 645
Ainsworth, Lazarus 645, 674
Ainsworth, Lydia Ann 617
Ainsworth, Margaret 674
Ainsworth, S. 617
Ainsworth, Samuel 645, 674
Ainsworth, Susan 617
Ainsworth, W. S. 617
Aker, M. 420
Aker, William W. 420

Akerman, Mary 413
Akers, Anna E. 112
Akers, Brooks 538
Akers, Marie N. 538
Akin, Ann 695
Akins, Mary 267
Akins, Robert 267
Akins, Saml. 267
Albaugh, Eli 570
Alben, George 553
Alben, William 553
Alberry, Richard 731
Albers, Eilard 105
Albers, Elard 104
Albert, Abraham 570
Albert, Cathrin 76
Albert, John 409
Albertson, Abram H. 507
Albright, Elizabeth 425
Albright, John B. 542
Albright, John L. 532
Albright, Lydia A. 532
Albright, Mathias 532
Albright, Pete M. 532
Albright, Sarah 395, 532, 569
Alcock, Sarah 726
Alcock, William 726, 728
Alcott, John 66
Alcott, Josiah 66
Alcott, Mahitable 30
Alder, Elizabeth 46
Alder, John 635
Alderman, Augustus S. 167
Alderman, Julia 167
Aldman, Jess 570
Aldredge, Azel 482
Aldredge, Temperance 65
Aldredge, Timothy 65
Aldrich, Collin 123
Aldrich, David 495
Aldrich, William 495
Aldridge, Catharine 292
Aldridge, Luman 70
Aldridge, Mary 513
Aldridge, Nicholas 564
Aleshire, Elizabeth 77
Aleshire, Jacob 76
Aleshire, James 76
Aleshire, Mahala 409
Aleshire, Phebe 78
Alexander, Alexander M. 149
Alexander, Ann Eliza 149
Alexander, Daniel 657
Alexander, David 382, 629
Alexander, Elizabeth 629
Alexander, Enoch 432
Alexander, Fanny 124
Alexander, Francis 487
Alexander, G. 239
Alexander, Gerard 56
Alexander, Isaac 620
Alexander, James 177, 455
Alexander, James T. 542
Alexander, Jane 452

Alexander, Jane E. 521
Alexander, Jas. 171
Alexander, John 143, 736
Alexander, John S. 320
Alexander, Joseph 11
Alexander, Levi 137
Alexander, Louisa 591
Alexander, Margaret 14, 496
Alexander, Martha 11, 143
Alexander, Mary 496, 573, 736
Alexander, Mary Catharine 432
Alexander, Nancy 665
Alexander, Noble 322
Alexander, Rachel 13
Alexander, Rachel Jane 432
Alexander, Sarah Leah 432
Alexander, Sarrahan 149
Alexander, Thomas W. 736
Alexander, William 168
Alez, William 764
Alicht, Casper 709
Alicht, Ragina Charlotte 709
Alkenberg, Henrich 542
Alkere, Lydia 384
Alkere, Samuel 382
Alkine, George 461
Alkire, Abraham 51
Alkire, Catherine 91
Alkire, Dolly 382
Alkire, Elizabeth 51
Alkire, Ellexander 76
Alkire, Gabriel 64
Alkire, George 396
Alkire, Green 51
Alkire, Hannah 77
Alkire, Harmonas 51
Alkire, Harmones 51
Alkire, Henry Green 51
Alkire, Isaac 51
Alkire, Jacob 51, 64, 382
Alkire, John 51
Alkire, John M. 396
Alkire, Joseph 51
Alkire, Margaret 51
Alkire, Mary Ann 51
Alkire, Michael 382
Alkire, Phebe 51
Alkire, Robert 51, 396
Alkire, Sarah 46
Alkire, Temperance 51
Alkire, William 51
Allaman, Adrian 734
Allaman, Adrin A. 734
Allaman, Barbara 735
Allaman, Elizabeth 735
Allaman, Harry 734
Allaman, Henry 734
Allaman, Jennie 734
Allaman, Mary 734
Allaman, R. 734
Allaman, Rachael 735

Allaman, Rebecca 734
Allaman, Samuel 735
Allaman, W. H. 734
Allaman, Willie 734
Allard, Abigal 408
Allard, Harriett Anne
408
Allard, Saml. 247
Allaway, Joseph 637
Allaways, Daniel 637
Allaways, Malinda 637
Allaways, Sarah 637
Allaways, Thomas 637
Allebaugh, Peter E. 318
Allen, Ananias 54
Allen, Anna 72
Allen, Anne 175
Allen, Annie 43
Allen, Archibald 137
Allen, Aseph 46
Allen, Asher 262, 269
Allen, Benoni 274
Allen, Benoni (Rev.) 274
Allen, Bethuel 657
Allen, Betsey Ann 588
Allen, Calvin (Sr.) 43
Allen, Chloe 696
Allen, Christena 170
Allen, Daniel 54
Allen, David 54, 731
Allen, Elias 154, 176
Allen, Elijah 54
Allen, Elizabeth 54,
118, 717
Allen, Francis 173, 179
Allen, George 54
Allen, Gideon 518
Allen, Hannah 337
Allen, Harriet 43
Allen, Irene 28
Allen, Isaac 731
Allen, Isaihah 259
Allen, James 54, 180,
363, 379, 721
Allen, Jane M. 320
Allen, Jasper 353
Allen, Jeremiah 54
Allen, John 54, 213, 353
Allen, Joseph 180, 657
Allen, Justus 713
Allen, Kirby 137
Allen, Levi 729
Allen, Lorinda 432
Allen, Luceus 46
Allen, Margaret 54, 353
Allen, Martha 46
Allen, Mary 15, 54,
176, 592
Allen, Mina 593
Allen, Phebe 591
Allen, Philip 175
Allen, Philip (Jr.) 170
Allen, Polly 714
Allen, Rachel 54
Allen, Richard 353
Allen, Ruth 717
Allen, Sally 510
Allen, Sarah D. 746
Allen, Seneca 760

Allen, Silas D. 542
Allen, Simon 518
Allen, Thomas 160, 166
Allen, Thomas L. 213
Allen, William 88, 325,
492, 542
Allender, Betsey 102
Allensworth, John 89
Alleson, Henrietta 388
Alley, Lucy 592
Allin, Thomas 158
Allinger, Joseph 664
Allis, Polly A. 33
Allison, Andrew 477
Allison, Betsey 271
Allison, Edwd. C. 404
Allison, Henry 404
Allison, Julia 742
Allison, Lucy J. 410
Allison, Mary 404
Allison, Richard 518
Allison, Richard (Dr.)
296
Allison, William 261
Allison, Wm. 271, 570
Allman, Catharine 761
Allman, Elizabeth 761
Allman, Hannah 569, 761
Allman, James 752
Allman, Mary 761
Allman, Sarah 761
Allman, Susanna 761
Allman, William 761
Allmon, Thomas 9
Allord, Saml. 271
Alloway, Arthur 271
Alloway, James 271
Alloway, William 259
Allspach, Lydia 606
Alltop, William 305
Allwood, Christopher 570
Allwood, William 40
Aloway, William 258
Alridge, Azel 482
Alsap, --- 600
Alsap, John 599
Alspach, Jacob B. 66
Alspach, Magdalena 67
Alspach, Mary 66
Alspach, Michael 66, 67
Altaffer, Sarah 749
Althon, A. E. 615
Althon, H. 615
Althon, Karl F. 615
Althon, Lissetta 615
Altman, Anne 761
Altman, Catharine 761
Altman, David 761
Altman, Elizabeth 761
Altman, George 749
Altman, Hannah 761
Altman, Isaac 570
Altman, Joseph 749
Altman, Lydia 761
Altman, Mary 761
Altman, Sarah 569, 761
Altman, Susanna 761
Altman, William 761
Altop, John 166

Altop, Sarah 166
Aman, Charles 542
Aman, Joseph 225
Ambler, Owen 487
Ambler, Shelly 487
Ambrose, Jacob 670
Amel, Catharine 15
Amerine, Andrew 588
Ames, Cyrus 716
Ames, Elias J. 442, 447
Ames, Ephraim S. 442,
447
Ames, Margaret 442
Ames, Mary 447
Ames, Nellie Gordon 37
Ames, Nelson O. 37
Ames, Orpheus Nelson 37
Amick, Catharine 523
Amick, Elizabeth 565
Amlen, John (Jr.) 716
Amlin, James 713
Ammerman, Lorinda Jane
432
Ammerman, Wm. Martin 432
Ammons, David 656
Ammons, Jacob 123
Ammons, John 656
Ammons, Miley 656
Ammons, Samuel S. W. 656
Ammons, Sarah 656
Ammons, William 656
Amory, Edward 294
Amory, Elizabeth 294
Amory, George 294
Amory, Van 294
Amos, Adam 758
Amos, Caroline 758
Amos, Catharine 758
Amos, Frederick 758
Amos, George 758
Amos, Jacob 758
Amos, Margaret 758
Amos, Michael (Jr.) 758
Amos, Michael (Sr.) 758
Ampy, Elizabeth 432
Ampy, Harvey 432
Ampy, Hezekiah 432
Ampy, Nancy 432
Amrine, Abraham (Jr.)
585
Amrine, Abraham Sugr.
585
Amrine, Catherine 353
Amrine, Elizabeth 594
Amrine, Frederick 353
Amrine, John 588
Amrine, Josiah 588
Amrine, Keziah 593
Amrine, L. 95
Amrine, Margaret 376
Amrine, Mary 353, 592
Amrine, S. 95
Amrine, Sarah 588
Amrine, Susan 592
Amrine, Wesley 588
Amsden, Thomas 495
Amspaugh, Alfred B. 407
Amspaugh, J. 407
Amspaugh, M. 407

Amsworthy, Abraham 492
Amsworthy, Bennet 492
Amsworthy, Lewis 492
Anders, Amy 590
Anders, Miram 588
Anders, Randal 588
Anderson, Abraham 382, 528
Anderson, Amsa W. 279
Anderson, Ann 667
Anderson, Anna 755
Anderson, Annabella 456
Anderson, Archibald 649
Anderson, Augustine 261, 273
Anderson, Betsy 467
Anderson, David 97, 267, 279, 738
Anderson, Duncan 268, 303
Anderson, E. 405
Anderson, Eliza 82
Anderson, Elizabeth 279, 467
Anderson, Ellenor Clarissa 649
Anderson, Em. 293
Anderson, Gelia Elizabeth 649
Anderson, Gertrude 43
Anderson, H. 150
Anderson, Hannah 272, 353, 452
Anderson, Haza 461
Anderson, Isaac 221, 353, 405
Anderson, J. D. 150
Anderson, Jacob 511
Anderson, James 265, 301, 403, 597, 656, 701
Anderson, James R. 637
Anderson, John 123, 195, 353, 461, 481, 487, 620, 709, 731, 755
Anderson, John H. 711
Anderson, John P. 267
Anderson, Joseph 264, 274, 353, 487
Anderson, Joseph D. 548
Anderson, Levina 353
Anderson, Levinah 353
Anderson, Luke 76
Anderson, Margaret 92, 306, 455
Anderson, Mary 81, 121, 337, 403, 661
Anderson, Mary A. 403
Anderson, Mary E. 150
Anderson, Matilda 261
Anderson, Michael 602, 627
Anderson, Michel 76
Anderson, Nancy 80
Anderson, Narcissa Cloe 649
Anderson, Nels 97
Anderson, Polly 395, 590
Anderson, Rebecca 335, 432

Anderson, Robert B. 143
Anderson, Ruben 46
Anderson, Sarah 683
Anderson, Sarah Adaline 432
Anderson, Susan 353
Anderson, Susanna 513
Anderson, Susannah 602
Anderson, Thomas 602, 643, 755
Anderson, Thos. 405
Anderson, Warren 656
Anderson, Wesley 495
Anderson, William 455, 461, 542, 606, 657
Anderson, Wm. 588
Andreas, George 74
Andreas, Peter 561
Andress, Peter 565
Andrew, Anne 56
Andrew, David 487
Andrew, Deby 457
Andrew, Hannah 463
Andrew, Hannah E. 56
Andrew, J. B. 56
Andrew, Jane 585
Andrew, Jane K. 56
Andrew, Jane W. 56, 64
Andrew, Josiah B. 56
Andrew, Samuel 206
Andrew, Susan P. 56
Andrews, Azubah 582
Andrews, David 740
Andrews, Elijah 164
Andrews, Elizabeth 232
Andrews, Francis 443
Andrews, G. E. 692
Andrews, Hugh 224, 232
Andrews, James 25, 232, 506, 511
Andrews, Jared 259, 262
Andrews, Jason 268
Andrews, John 16, 25, 232, 542
Andrews, Joseph 692
Andrews, Joseph G. 726
Andrews, Linny Berry 570
Andrews, M. 692
Andrews, Margaret 10
Andrews, Mary C. 232
Andrews, Peter 588
Andrews, Philander 270
Andrews, Polly 591
Andrews, Rachel 164
Andrews, Rodney 28
Andrews, Samuel 28
Andrews, Susan 232
Andrick, Jacob 59
Andrick, Mada 59
Andrus, Elizabeth 591
Anerum, Elizabeth 719
Anerum, Nancy 718
Angel, David 752
Angevim, George W. 601
Angle, Aaron 353
Angle, Abram 353
Angle, Catherine 353
Angle, Elizabeth 353
Angle, Isaiah 353

Angle, Jacob B. 353
Angle, Jemima 353
Angle, John 353
Angle, John P. 353
Angle, Joseph 353
Angle, Mary 353
Angle, Paul 353
Angle, Phebe 456
Angle, Polly 353
Angles, Precilla 386
Anguish, David 247
Anguish, James M. 247
Anguish, William 247
Anison, Mary Ann 685
Ankney, Alvin 326
Ankney, Christian 326
Ankney, D. 326
Ankney, D. H. 326
Ankney, David 326
Ankney, E. 326
Ankney, E. B. 326
Ankney, E. H. 326
Ankney, Elizabeth 326
Ankney, Elsie M. 326
Ankney, Emanul A. 326
Ankney, Emma 326
Ankney, Fredric A. 326
Ankney, George 326
Ankney, Gideon 326
Ankney, H. L. 327
Ankney, J. 326
Ankney, J. H. 326
Ankney, James A. 326
Ankney, James H. 326
Ankney, John H. 328
Ankney, M. 326, 327
Ankney, Mabel A. 326
Ankney, Mabria 326
Ankney, Margaret 326
Ankney, Martha J. 327
Ankney, Mary A. 326, 328
Ankney, Mary Ann 326
Ankney, Michel 327
Ankney, Mikel 327
Ankney, N. 326
Ankney, N. A. 326
Ankney, Nancy A. 326
Ankney, Nettie 326
Ankney, Susana A. 327
Ankney, Virgel I. 326
Ankney, William 326
Ansel, John 376
Anspach, John 284
Anthony, Abraham 606
Anthony, Catherine 112
Anthony, Daniel 123
Anthony, Fanny 610
Anthony, Henry 112
Anthony, John 588
Anthony, Sally 137, 463
Antol, Elizabeth 166
Antol, John 166
Antrim, Esther 26
Antrim, John 286
Antrim, Levi 27
Antrim, Thomas 26
Antroboss, Geo. 570
Anway, Harrison 518
Apple, Henry 229

770

Apple, John 213
Apple, Sarah 229
Applegate, Catherine 90
Applegate, Eleanor 487
Applegate, Elizabeth 487
Applegate, Henry 318
Applegate, John 487
Applegate, Kezziah 318
Applegate, Lucy 487
Applegate, Mary 487
Applegate, Nancy 318
Applegate, Oliver S.
 316, 318, 319
Applegate, Sarah Ann
 318, 319
Applegate, Sarah D. 316
Applegate, Tabitha 337
Applegate, Tabitha Ann
 318
Applegate, William 487
Appleman, Catharine 248,
 249
Appleman, Eli 249
Appleman, Elizabeth 249
Appleman, Jacob 248, 249
Appleman, Jane 249
Appleman, John 249
Appleman, Margaret 248,
 249
Appleman, Sally 249
Apwright, Catharine 487
Arahood, Eve 451
Arbaugh, George 101
Arbaugh, Jacob 101
Arbaugh, John S. 101
Arbaugh, Samuel 101
Arbuckle, Amanda 758
Arbuckle, Charles 63
Arbuckle, Elizabeth 63
Arbuckle, Jacob Lockhart
 63
Arbuckle, James 63
Arbuckle, John 53, 63
Arbuckle, Joseph 758
Arbuckle, Matthew 63
Arbuckle, Rebecca 63
Arbuckle, Sarah 63
Arbuckle, Susan 63
Arbuckle, William 63
Archabald, Andrew 60
Archabald, Jane 60
Archdeacon, George 685
Archdeacon, Richard 686
Archebald, James 265
Archer, . . . hael 179
Archer, Allen 123
Archer, Ann 125
Archer, Benjamin 224
Archer, Betsey 12
Archer, Catherine 199
Archer, David 16
Archer, Elizabeth 12, 16
Archer, George J. 62
Archer, Henry 312
Archer, Isaac 308
Archer, James 731
Archer, James (Jr.) 308
Archer, John (Jr.) 224
Archer, John P. 199

Archer, Joseph 718
Archer, Joseph (Sr.) 439
Archer, Maranda 81
Archer, Michael 273
Archer, Ruth Ellen 306
Archer, Samuel 189, 195
Archer, Sarah A. 89
Archer, Simeon 731, 733
Archer, Simon 302, 312
Archer, Solomon 306
Archer, Sophia 78
Archer, Zachariah 199
Archibald, James 265,
 268
Archibald, Jno. 267,
 268, 271
Archibald, Margaret 302
Archibold, Thomas 570
Ardoe, Lewis 511
Ardor, Lewis 511
Ardry, Robert 296
Arebaugh, George 82
Arehart, Abraham 229
Arehart, Elizabeth 229
Arehart, Jacob 229
Arend, Christian 731
Argo, Jeremiah 291
Argo, Mary 588
Arholtzer, Julian 521
Arins, Ellen 14
Arkenburg, Bernard 542
Arling, Bernard 542
Arling, John H. 542
Armatrout, Jacob 43
Armitage, Amanda 610
Arms, Nancy 664
Armstrong, Alexander 286
Armstrong, Andrew 179
Armstrong, Ann 557
Armstrong, Ann B. 278
Armstrong, David 102
Armstrong, Elizabeth 43,
 557, 717
Armstrong, Ezabella 557
Armstrong, Ezebella 557
Armstrong, Fidelia 143
Armstrong, Francis 143
Armstrong, Freeman B.
 143
Armstrong, George 557
Armstrong, Hannah 363
Armstrong, Henry 143
Armstrong, James 301,
 557, 641, 654
Armstrong, Jane 102
Armstrong, Jean 294
Armstrong, Jedediah 721
Armstrong, Jeremiah 503
Armstrong, Job 258, 270,
 271
Armstrong, John 52,
 100, 102, 506, 557
Armstrong, John Agner
 444
Armstrong, Joshua 506
Armstrong, Martin 143
Armstrong, Mary 102,
 438, 557, 641
Armstrong, Nancy 102

Armstrong, Nancy M. 143
Armstrong, Olly 387
Armstrong, Rebecca 102
Armstrong, Robert 483,
 487, 557
Armstrong, S. H. 154
Armstrong, Sally 663
Armstrong, Samuel 102,
 641, 654
Armstrong, Sarah 102
Armstrong, Stephen 100
Armstrong, Terresa 550
Armstrong, Thomas 163
Armstrong, Thomas C. 355
Armstrong, William 461,
 487, 557
Armstrong, Wm. H. 143
Armuntrout, Elias 46
Arn, John 181
Arnet, Jonathan 492
Arnett, Benjamin 215
Arnett, Catherine 215
Arnett, Delilah 211
Arnett, Elizabeth 213
Arnett, George 213
Arnett, Noah 211
Arnett, Philip 211, 213,
 215
Arney, Jacob 518
Arney, Samuel 518
Arnhart, William 383
Arnold, A. 245
Arnold, Aaron 245
Arnold, Amelia 245
Arnold, Arthur 244
Arnold, Barbary 244
Arnold, C. 245
Arnold, Catharine 188,
 244, 245
Arnold, Christian 188,
 232, 245
Arnold, David 116
Arnold, Dora A. 245
Arnold, Elizabeth 188,
 244
Arnold, Emanuel 245
Arnold, Francis 245
Arnold, H. (Sr.) 244
Arnold, Hannah 610
Arnold, Henry 245
Arnold, Henry (Sr.) 244
Arnold, Henry H. 244
Arnold, Henry W. 244
Arnold, J. B. 244
Arnold, Jacob 188
Arnold, John 244, 565,
 601
Arnold, Jos. 712
Arnold, Joseph 244
Arnold, Josephine 629
Arnold, Lavina 245
Arnold, Levina 315
Arnold, M. 245
Arnold, Martha J. 245
Arnold, Mary 36, 188,
 245, 610
Arnold, Nicholas 244
Arnold, Peter 668
Arnold, Polly 124

Arnold, Priscilla 608
Arnold, Samuel 526
Arnold, Sarah 188
Arron, B. W. 618
Arronsmith, Samuel 453
Arrowhood, Catherine 461
Arrowhood, Job 382
Arrowsmith, Marry 461
Arskin, John 11
Arskin, Polly 13
Arskins, Anne 13
Arstingstull, Barnurd
  548
Arthur, Belinda 633
Arthur, Mainda 463
Arthur, Wm. K. 400
Arthurs, Wm. 463
Artis, Jane 21
Arwen, Susanna 234
Arwen, Thomas 234
Arwin, Jean 716
Aryo, Sarah 583
Asdel, James 620
Ash, Fanny 519
Ash, Upton 518
Ashbaugh, Andrew 21
Ashbaugh, Matilda 280
Ashbrook, Elias 299
Ashbrook, Thomas 299
Ashcraft, Daniel 283
Ashcraft, Ruth 718
Asher, John 51
Asher, Mary 51
Asher, Melinda 592
Asher, Milley 459
Asher, Susannah 51
Ashlemain, John 749
Ashley, Ananias 530
Ashley, Harry 594
Ashley, John 334
Ashley, Loami (Elder)
  245
Ashley, Warren 418
Ashton, Zachariah 336
Ashworth, James 76
Ashworth, Thomas 76
Askew, William 160, 492
Atchason, Anthony 417
Atchason, Henry 417
Atcheson, Ailas 482
Atcheson, Charles 53
Atcheson, Mary 230
Atchinson, John 716
Atchinson, Reuben 716
Atchison, B. J. 636
Atchison, Charles 54
Atchison, Hannah 391
Atchison, John 382
Atchison, Joseph 636
Atchison, Nancy 391, 462
Atchison, Pfielding 391
Atchison, Phielden 391,
  455
Atchison, Samuel 391
Atchison, William 382
Aten, Austin C. 419
Aten, Margaret 419
Atephenson, Aaron 471
Ater, Henry 461

Ater, Isaac 455
Ater, John H. 398
Ater, Samuel 461
Ater, William 382
Aters, Geo. 455
Athison, John 487
Atkens, Elijah 272
Atkerson, John 82
Atkerson, Thos. 270
Atkeson, P. I. 257
Atkingson, Cornelius 172
Atkins, --- 82
Atkins, Henry 123
Atkins, Martha 80
Atkins, Washington 152
Atkinson, Ann 636
Atkinson, Axa 636
Atkinson, Charles 164
Atkinson, Cornelius 157,
  168, 169
Atkinson, Eliz . . . 169
Atkinson, Elizabeth 169
Atkinson, Elmira 609
Atkinson, Gair 91
Atkinson, Isaac 303
Atkinson, James 154, 175
Atkinson, John 89
Atkinson, Joseph 636
Atkinson, Margaret 636
Atkinson, Mary 30, 168,
  172, 176
Atkinson, Nancy 164, 636
Atkinson, Nancy Margaret
  Axa Ann 636
Atkinson, Ralph 583
Atkinson, Rhoda 175
Atkinson, Samuel 636
Atkinson, Stephen 169
Atkinson, Thomas 636
Atkinson, William 176
Atkinson, William Dawson
  716
Atwater, Betsy 353
Atwater, Christopher 353
Atwell, Benj. 269
Atwell, Phebe 29
Atwood, Hannah 446
Atwood, Lousa 593
Atwood, Nathaniel 446
Aubright, John (Jr.) 82
Aucker, Anna 609
Audler, Nelly 117
August, Henry F. 619
August, John A. 619
August, M. G. 619
August, W. 619
Augustine, Gasper 487
Augustine, John 558
Auker, Christian 601
Auker, Rosanna 745
Aul, Jacob 485
Auld, John 652
Auld, Michael 652, 670
Auld, Nancy 652
Auld, Sarah 652
Ault, Andrew 740, 743
Ault, Elizabeth 492
Ault, Mathias 570
Ault, Philip 167

Aumiller, Jacob 76
Aumiller, Jonathan 89
Aunsbaugh, Adam 339, 340
Aunspaugh, Adam 339
Aurl, Elizabeth 662
Ausbaugh, Sally 375
Ausburne, Nancy 498
Auspach, Adam 353, 361
Auspach, Barbara 353
Auspach, Benjamin 353
Auspach, Catherine 353
Auspach, Christian 353
Auspach, David 353
Auspach, Elizabeth 353
Auspach, Jacob 353
Auspach, John 353
Auspach, Magdalena 353
Auspach, Samuel 374
Austen, Ambrose 742
Austen, Mary 16
Austen, William 16
Austin, Ambrose 742
Austin, Carlisle H. 11
Austin, Caroline 499
Austin, Charles 742
Austin, Charlotte 742
Austin, Cynthia 336
Austin, Elsa 30
Austin, Esther B. 318
Austin, George 82
Austin, Hannah 549
Austin, Henry 28, 742
Austin, James B. 744
Austin, Jedediah 316,
  317, 318
Austin, John 742
Austin, Joseph 742
Austin, Mary 593
Austin, Polly 548
Austin, Rebecca 692
Austin, Renew 32
Austin, S. S. (Rev.) 692
Austin, Sarah 554
Austin, Susan 92
Austin, Susannah 742
Auston, Rebecca 21
Austrill, Wm. 455
Autenreed, John George
  173
Autenreed, Maria 173
Averil, Amand 75
Averill, Eligah 75
Averill, Hannah G. 75
Averill, Mehitable 75
Avery, Barbara 619
Avery, Danl. (Corpl.)
  619
Avery, E. J. 619
Avery, Edward 737
Avery, J. 619
Avery, James F. 619
Avery, John C. 619
Avery, L. 619
Avery, L. D. 619
Avery, M. J. 619
Avery, Nancy E. 619
Avery, William 619
Avery, William M. 619
Awl, Wm. McClay 364

Awmiller, Henry   259
Ax, Geo.   570
Ax, John   570
Ax, Juda   572
Ax, Nancy   573
Axline, Samuel   366
Axtell, Daniel   753
Axtell, Harriet   40
Axtle, Sarah Ann   321
Ayer, Francis   664
Ayers, Amsey   231
Ayers, Betsy   231
Ayers, Caleb   542
Ayers, Charity   231
Ayers, David   249
Ayers, Elizabeth   231
Ayers, George   599
Ayers, George Washington
   599
Ayers, Insau   137
Ayers, Isaac   231, 599
Ayers, James N.   447
Ayers, Jane   137
Ayers, John   231
Ayers, John C.   731
Ayers, John R.   137
Ayers, Mary A.   137
Ayers, Nathaniel   249,
   261
Ayers, Polly   466
Ayers, Rebecca   137
Ayers, Richard F.   137
Ayers, Samuel   231
Ayers, Sarah Anny   599
Ayers, Simon S.   231
Ayers, Thos. B.   358
Ayles, Elias   731
Ayres, Amzy   672
Ayres, Henry   205
Ayres, Jacob   284
Ayres, James   155, 172
Ayres, Jane   570
Ayres, John C.   731
Ayres, John W.   318, 322
Ayres, Lucinda   608
Ayres, Lucy   566
Ayres, Sarah   334
Ayres, Stephen C.   205
Ayres, Thomas   178
Azewalt, Daniel   202
Azewalt, Elizabeth   202

--- B ---

B. Dillane, Isaac   24
B . . . , Michael   532
Baatlet, Sophia   743
Babb, Ellenor   378
Babb, Jonathan   370
Babb, Joseph   339, 340
Babb, Mary   378
Babcock, Abraham F.   28
Babcock, Alva   525
Babcock, Azariah   542
Babcock, Joseph   730
Babcock, Judith   663
Babcock, Laura Ann   495

Babcock, Mary   371, 730
Babcock, William   542,
   657
Bable, Jane   333
Baby, Emily   506
Baccus, Barbara   510
Baccus, Enoch   510
Baccus, Ezra   510
Baccus, Jacob   510
Baccus, John Smith   510
Baccus, Larcus Short   510
Baccus, Michael   510
Baccus, Peter   510
Baccus, Rebecca   516
Baccus, Sene   510
Baccus, Susannah   511
Baccus, Thomas Jefferson
   510
Bachelor, John   731
Bacher, Catherine   573
Bacher, Jacob   108, 177
Bacher, Philip   108
Bachler, John Martin
   Middaugh   570
Bachlet, George   91
Bachman, Barbara   245
Bachman, Catharine   580
Bachman, Enoch   245
Bachman, Fred   580
Bachman, Henry   558
Bachman, John E.   245
Bachman, Loami   245
Bachman, Mary M.   580
Bachman, Polly   245
Bachman, Polly S.   245
Bachtel, Jacob   557
Bachtel, James   71
Back, Abraham   487
Back, Anna Maria   276
Back, Catarina   276
Back, Fridrich   276
Back, Friedrich   276
Back, John   744
Back, Peter   276
Back, Samuel   744
Backman, Elizabeth   336
Backus, Walley   606
Backwood, Rebecca   466
Bacom, Lucinda   515
Bacon, Benjamin   28, 35
Bacon, Harriet   30
Bacon, Henry   116
Bacon, Joseph   657
Bacon, Nancy Ann   588
Bacon, Samuel   35
Bacon, Susannah   575
Bactrsler, Thomas   664
Badgeley, Aaron C.   106
Badgely, Wm.   731
Badger, Abagail   763
Badger, Almina   70
Badger, Ann   70
Badger, Austin   70
Badger, Charles   318
Badger, Edmund   70
Badger, Flora   70
Badger, Jas.   70
Badger, Joseph   763
Badger, Norton   70

Badger, Van Buren A.   70
Badger, Ward   70
Badgly, Aaron C.   102
Badley, Daniel   664
Badley, Edward M.   588
Badley, Joseph   43
Badley, Martin   588
Badley, Sarah   588
Baehmer, Martha Maria
   107
Baeshore, Jacob   354
Baggs, D.   407
Baggs, H.   407
Baggs, Hugh H.   432
Baggs, James W.   432
Baggs, Margaret   551
Baggs, Thomas   407
Baggs, Thomas A.   432
Baggs, Wm. P.   432
Bagley, Henry   722
Bagley, Jesse   595
Bagley, Mary   585
Bagley, Orlando   595
Bagley, Samuel   275
Bahmer, Martha Maria 107
Baht, Adam W.   404
Baht, Edward   404
Baickle, Jane   90
Bailes, Elmira   311
Bailes, Susannah   305
Bailes, Thomas   305
Bailes, Thomas (Sr.)   305
Bailess, Delilah   12
Bailess, Josiah   11
Bailess, Louisa Ann   11
Bailey, Amaziah   620
Bailey, Buryman   76
Bailey, Caleb   713
Bailey, Charles   28
Bailey, Charles A.   731
Bailey, Elanor   84
Bailey, Elias   447
Bailey, Elizabeth   90,
   171
Bailey, Fanny   79
Bailey, H.   407
Bailey, Hannah   78
Bailey, James   171, 461,
   652
Bailey, James M.   645,
   674
Bailey, Jane   78, 583
Bailey, Jesse   303
Bailey, John   76, 447
Bailey, John N.   674
Bailey, John R.   645, 655
Bailey, L.   407
Bailey, Lidy   80
Bailey, Lucinda   81
Bailey, Mary   172, 447
Bailey, Nancy   447
Bailey, Nathaniel   447
Bailey, Ruel   82
Bailey, Sarah   407
Bailey, Thomas Israel
   652
Bailey, Thomas Z.   645,
   674
Bailey, William   76, 413

773

Bailey, William (Jr.) 82
Bailey, William B. 172
Bailis, Elmire 311
Bailor, Frederick 11
Baily, John (Jr.) 716
Baily, Joseph 335
Baily, Nathaniel 442
Baily, Thomas J. 655
Baily, Winney 11
Baily, Wm. C. 137
Bainbridge, Mary 661
Bains, Jane 463
Bainter, Godfrey 296
Bair, Barbara 557
Bair, Christopher 557
Bair, Daniel 557
Bair, Elizabeth 557
Bair, George 557
Bair, John 557
Bair, Mary 558
Bair, Rudolph 557
Bair, Susana 557
Baird, Agnes 295, 351
Baird, Alexander 295,
351, 355, 372, 492
Baird, Andrew 655
Baird, Bedent 646
Baird, Daniel 355
Baird, Eleanor 355
Baird, Eliza Ann 355
Baird, George M. 756
Baird, Hiram 646, 655
Baird, Hugh 294
Baird, James 294, 295,
372, 655
Baird, Jane 83, 294,
351, 355, 459
Baird, John 295, 305,
351, 372, 646, 655
Baird, John W. 369
Baird, Joseph 294, 295
Baird, Julia M. 372
Baird, Martha 295, 351
Baird, Mary 294, 355
Baird, Matilda 292
Baird, Nancy 355
Baird, Nancy Nesbit 372
Baird, Samuel 294, 295,
351, 355, 379
Baird, Sarah 294
Baird, Sarah Jane 695
Baird, Tabitha 355
Baird, Thomas 351, 372
Baird, Thos. Warren 355
Bairer, L. R. 221
Baits, Ephraim 478
Baker, A. 735
Baker, Aaron 190, 196
Baker, Abraham 570
Baker, Amey 462
Baker, Andrew 198
Baker, Anna 578, 579,
742
Baker, Barbara 579
Baker, Benjamin 152,
162, 713
Baker, Bertha V. 734
Baker, Catharine 503,
567, 716

Baker, Catharine A. 735
Baker, Catharine M. 578
Baker, Catherine 78
Baker, Charles 487
Baker, Chloe 83
Baker, Clarissa 531
Baker, Clark 548
Baker, Daniel 359, 363,
377
Baker, David 198, 208,
672, 685, 690, 742
Baker, Delilah 531
Baker, Diana 499
Baker, E. 735
Baker, Elizabeth 549,
569, 570, 635, 654
Baker, Elnora 578
Baker, Ephraim A. 578
Baker, Ethan F. 327
Baker, Francis 487
Baker, Franklin W. 578
Baker, George 36, 162,
163, 165, 427
Baker, George W. 180
Baker, Gladys D. 327
Baker, H. 735
Baker, Hannah 516, 735
Baker, Harriett 59
Baker, Henry 158, 160,
173, 174, 578, 579
Baker, Henry (Jr.) 579
Baker, Iola 578
Baker, Isaac 180, 271,
511, 737
Baker, J. 538
Baker, Jacob 174, 286,
495, 654, 657
Baker, James 153, 179,
487, 531, 635
Baker, Jefferson 538
Baker, John 46, 59, 158,
174, 194, 455, 487,
531, 548, 657, 742
Baker, John George 708
Baker, John H. 579
Baker, John P. 352
Baker, John Philip 352
Baker, Joseph 392, 455,
635, 654
Baker, Joshua 59
Baker, Josiah 40, 487,
635
Baker, Levina 208
Baker, Livinia 198
Baker, Louisa 518, 579
Baker, Lyman J. 734
Baker, M. 538
Baker, Magdalane 659
Baker, Margaret 538
Baker, Margaret Funk 579
Baker, Martha H. 463
Baker, Martin 157, 179,
181, 461
Baker, Mary 158, 174,
531, 568
Baker, Matilda 59
Baker, Matthias 642
Baker, Mesheeh 487
Baker, Morris 278

Baker, Moses 542, 642
Baker, Nancy 173, 179,
387, 509
Baker, Nicholas 82, 318
Baker, Peggy 742
Baker, Peter 354, 711
Baker, Philip (Sr.) 284
Baker, Polly 462
Baker, Purnal H. 391
Baker, Rebeckah 501
Baker, Regeina 735
Baker, Rhoda 716
Baker, Ruth 461
Baker, S. 735
Baker, Sally 160, 742
Baker, Saml. 274
Baker, Samuel 153, 160,
495
Baker, Samuel (Jr.) 713
Baker, Samuel H. 735
Baker, Sarah 152, 157,
179, 387
Baker, Sarah Ann 495
Baker, Stephen 160
Baker, Susan 576, 610
Baker, Susannah 511, 742
Baker, Thirza Owen 77
Baker, William 518,
654, 716
Baker, William C. 578
Baker, Wm. 455, 578
Bakewell, S. R. 555
Bal, James W. 88
Balbridge, Nancy 657
Balderson, Jacob 253
Balding, Henry 159,
172, 179
Balding, Lewis 172, 179
Balding, Philo 161
Balding, Sarah 172
Baldridge, David 250,
251
Baldridge, Mary 606
Baldrige, Susan 610
Baldwin, Absalam C. 518
Baldwin, Ann M. 396
Baldwin, Catharine 687
Baldwin, Cornelius 396
Baldwin, Cornelius E.
396
Baldwin, Cornell R. 38
Baldwin, David 218
Baldwin, Elenor C. 396
Baldwin, Eliza T. 38
Baldwin, Elizabeth 593,
661
Baldwin, Ellis S. 218
Baldwin, Frances 666
Baldwin, Francis 455,
469
Baldwin, Isaac 153,
156, 157, 167, 180
Baldwin, Isaac Hite 396
Baldwin, Jacob 687
Baldwin, James 687
Baldwin, James M. 396
Baldwin, James R. 8
Baldwin, Jesse 11
Baldwin, John 356

Baldwin, John N. 40
Baldwin, John T. 40
Baldwin, Jonas 657
Baldwin, Jonathan 664
Baldwin, L. S. 43
Baldwin, Mary 153
Baldwin, Mary Briscoe 396
Baldwin, Michael 461, 473
Baldwin, Nancy 662
Baldwin, Osaac 153
Baldwin, Peter S. 518
Baldwin, Phedima 30
Baldwin, Philander 8
Baldwin, Polly 180, 661
Baldwin, Richard 27, 55, 57
Baldwin, Robert 160
Baldwin, Robert S. 396
Baldwin, Saml. 664
Baldwin, Sarah 663
Baldwin, Sarah Jane 687
Baldwin, Urinia 38
Baldwin, W. H. 356
Baldwin, William 287
Balentine, Robert 475
Bales, George 88
Baley, Charles 28
Baley, John 492
Baley, Luzen 386
Baley, Thomas 461
Balinger, Elizabeth 509
Balis, Desire 305
Balis, Elmyra 305
Balis, Lamantha 162
Balis, Lucinda 305
Balis, Margaret 305
Balis, Mary 305
Balis, Sarah 305
Balis, Susanna 165, 305
Balis, Thomas (Jr.) 162, 165
Balis, Thomas (Sr.) 162, 165
Ball, Aaron 319
Ball, Calvin 641, 652
Ball, Christian 666
Ball, Cornelius 652
Ball, Cyrus 652
Ball, David 319
Ball, Elijah 260, 263, 269
Ball, Eliza 355
Ball, Elizabeth 163
Ball, Esther 695
Ball, Harrison 319, 539
Ball, James 355
Ball, James W. 90
Ball, Jane 319, 560
Ball, Jared A. 744
Ball, John 355
Ball, Jonas 266
Ball, Jonathan 336
Ball, Luther 664
Ball, Mary 464
Ball, Mary Ann 319
Ball, Matthew 163
Ball, Moses 303

Ball, Olinda 641
Ball, Rachel 384
Ball, Seneca 641, 652
Ball, Susannah 539
Ball, Wm. 274
Ballah, Catharine 399
Ballah, James 382, 393, 399
Ballard, Fredrick 279
Ballard, John 699
Ballard, Lydia 699
Ballard, May 467
Balleb, May 467
Ballenbaugh, Henry 222
Ballenger, Asa 511
Ballenger, Daniel 119
Ballenger, James 119
Ballenger, John 11
Ballenger, Martha 15
Ballenger, Samuel 17
Ballentein, James 444
Ballentine, Henry 504
Ballentine, Robert 470
Balley, Dolley 464
Ballinger, Henry 113
Ballinger, Jacob 432
Ballinger, Jesse 123
Ballinger, John 21, 113
Ballinger, Margaret 22
Ballinger, Mary 136
Ballon, Amasa 756
Ballon, Charlotte 756
Ballon, Charlotte M. 759
Ballon, David 581
Ballon, Eunice S. 756
Ballon, Julia 756
Ballon, Lucy 581
Ballon, Martin 581
Ballou, David 581
Ballou, Lucy 581
Ballou, Martin 581
Ballow, Mary Ann 593
Ballowmeyer, Cath. 113
Balmer, Andrew 239
Balmer, David 239
Balmer, Elizabeth 239
Balmer, Emma 239
Balmer, George 542
Balmer, Jacob 239
Balmer, John 239
Balmer, Leah 239
Balmer, Mandilla 239
Balmer, Margaret 239
Balmer, Mary 239
Balmer, Matthew 239
Balsiger, Barbara 167
Balsiger, Jacob 167
Balsly, Mary 568
Baltz, Adam 708
Baltz, Daniel 708
Baltzley, Sarah 566
Baltzly, John 570
Baltzly, Lydia 576
Baltzly, Peter 570
Balzer, Katharyne 412
Bamborough, Cornelius 633
Bamthisel, Cath. 414
Banatta, John 358

Bancroft, Thomas 588
Bancus, Nathan 248
Bandeau, Francis 713
Bander, Samuel 558
Bandy, Anna E. 328
Bandy, Charline 328
Bandy, Clara V. 328
Bandy, J. 328, 329
Bandy, J. Hazen 329
Bandy, John 329
Bandy, Patterson 409
Bandy, Peter 328, 329
Bandy, S. L. 328, 329
Bandy, Submit L. 329
Bane, James 731
Bane, Thomas L. 763
Banes, A. B. 508
Baninger, Joseph 92
Bank, Sophia T. 746
Banks, Caroline D. 330
Banks, Emeline 746
Banks, Hannah 521
Banks, Hiram 316, 323
Banks, I. H. 103
Banks, J. T. 330
Banks, Jedediah 330
Banks, Joseph 316, 323
Banks, Joseph T. 321
Banks, Martha 323, 336
Banks, Matilda 316, 323
Banks, Richard 316, 318, 330, 744
Banks, Richard C. 335
Banks, Richard S. 319
Banks, Samuel 316, 320, 323
Banks, Sarah Ann 336, 746
Banks, Sarah J. 330
Banks, Thomas J. 336
Banks, Wm. 323
Bankus, John 253
Bankus, Nathan 253
Banning, Jacob 137
Banning, Mary 31
Bannon, Michael 664
Banta, Abraham 223
Banta, Albert 664
Banta, Cornelius V. 429
Banta, Hannah 432
Banta, Henry 617
Banta, Isaac 432
Banta, James 432
Banta, John 427, 664
Banta, Lydia 617
Banta, Magdalene 661
Banta, Peter 186
Banta, Rachel 666
Banty, Edward 657
Bapst, Jacob (Sr.) 411
Baralow, Lydia 658
Barb, Peter 349
Barbar, W. 508
Barbee, David 631
Barbee, Elias 542
Barbee, Hazel 631
Barbee, Nancy 119, 451
Barbee, Sally 118
Barbee, Sarah 451

775

Barbee, William 116, 148
Barber, Allen 687
Barber, Anne Rebecca 520
Barber, Austin 167
Barber, David 82, 167
Barber, Dorothy 663
Barber, Edwin 542
Barber, Elizabeth 167, 176, 181
Barber, Hallet 594
Barber, James 553
Barber, Levi 167, 173, 176, 181
Barber, Lovica 497
Barber, Mary 550
Barber, Melinda 137
Barber, Phebe 752
Barber, Samuel 560
Barber, Samuel C. 106
Barber, Susan 137
Barber, Thomas 116
Barber, Uriah 511
Barbour, Ann 137
Barbour, Chas. 137
Barbour, Electa 582
Barbour, Jane 137
Barbour, Mary 137
Barbour, Stephen 137
Barcalow, Ann 188
Barcalow, Benjamin 188
Barcalow, Derrick 188
Barcalow, Eleanor 188
Barcalow, George 188
Barcalow, John 188
Barcalow, Zebulon 188
Barchfield, Estren 574
Barchus, Ebenezer 263
Barclane, Sally 38
Barclay, John 306
Barclay, John (Sr.) 306
Barclay, Margaret 306
Barcus, Eli 336
Barcus, Moses 540
Barcus, Nancy 540
Bare, Benjamin 518
Bare, Jacob 177
Bare, Nancy 429
Bare, Peggy 429
Barhelot, Claudius 726
Baringer, Catharine 79
Bark, --- 465
Barkalow, Derrich 647
Barkalow, Derrick 687, 689
Barkalow, Eliza Ann 215
Barkalow, James 215
Barkalow, James V. 215
Barkalow, Margaret 215
Barkalow, Phebe Jane 215
Barkalow, Rebecca 215
Barkalow, Tobias P. 215
Barkalow, William 695
Barkelow, Edward 511
Barker, Abby 745
Barker, Almy 715
Barker, Augustus 263
Barker, Caleb 548
Barker, Francis A. 269, 273

Barker, Hannah 152
Barker, Hiram 643
Barker, Isaac 272, 728
Barker, Isaiah 152
Barker, John 160, 744
Barker, Joseph 731
Barker, Luther D. 269
Barker, Martha 549
Barker, Mary 463
Barker, Michael 716
Barker, Nancy 514
Barker, Rhoda 719
Barker, Samuel 263, 371, 377
Barker, Samuel A. 261, 263
Barker, Samuel Augustus 258
Barker, William 643
Barker, Wm. 455
Barkes, Mary 164
Barkhamer, John 743
Barkheimer, Isaac 40
Barkheimer, Jacob 40
Barkherst, Frances 580
Barkherst, M. A. 580
Barkherst, Samuel 580
Barkley, Clara Lizzie 692
Barkley, Elizabeth 692
Barkley, J. W. 692
Barkley, John 692
Barkley, John W. 692
Barkley, M. I. 692
Barkley, Mary 391
Barkley, Rebecca 391
Barkley, Shedrack 76
Barkman, Elizabeth 21
Barkwood, Rebecca 466
Barlew, Susana 121
Barlow, Carl E. 143
Barlow, Geo. W. 143
Barlow, Hiram P. 756
Barlow, James 301, 406
Barlow, John 673
Barlow, Susan 301
Barlow, William 487
Barlow, Wm. A. 673
Barlow, Z. 301
Barnand, Oliver 330
Barnard, Oliver 330
Barnd, Christian 285, 340, 354, 375
Barnd, Jacob 360
Barnd, John 363, 368
Barnd, Julia 360
Barnd, Sarah 363
Barndt, Rebecca 375
Barne, Saly 666
Barned, Abraham 229
Barned, Elizabeth 229
Barned, James 229
Barned, John 229
Barned, Mary 229
Barned, Rachel 229
Barned, Susan 229
Barner, Charles 542
Barnerd, Abraham 563
Barnes, Amanda 71

Barnes, Amzi 356
Barnes, Benjamin 495
Barnes, Catharine 498
Barnes, Christian 38
Barnes, Cynthia 356
Barnes, Esther 356
Barnes, Gabriel H. 7
Barnes, Hannah 633
Barnes, Henry 501
Barnes, Henry S. 161
Barnes, Isaac 356
Barnes, James 455
Barnes, John 487, 500
Barnes, Lewis 731
Barnes, Lois 356
Barnes, Lucinda 301
Barnes, Margaret 301
Barnes, Mary 501
Barnes, Mary Magdaline 387
Barnes, Nancy 501
Barnes, Peter 301
Barnes, Robert 501
Barnes, Sarah 501
Barnes, Simon 487
Barnes, Stephen 176, 355, 356, 358, 362
Barnes, Susanna 356
Barnes, Susannah 580
Barnes, Thomas 501
Barnes, Wealthly 495
Barnes, William 382, 501
Barnet, Abraham 223, 229
Barnet, Elizabeth 223
Barnet, Isaac G. 224
Barnet, James 229
Barnet, John 223, 229
Barnet, Solomon 350
Barnett, Abraham 216
Barnett, Alex 413
Barnett, James H. 548
Barnett, Mary 583
Barnett, Mary Ann 711
Barnett, Richard 310
Barney, Ann 498
Barney, Benjamin 495
Barney, Consider C. 495
Barney, Philena 30
Barney, Royal (Jr.) 28
Barnhart, Benjamin 682
Barnhart, John 322
Barnhart, Michael 518
Barnhead, Jacob 495
Barnhill, Jacob 404
Barnhill, Jno. 404
Barnhill, Margret 337
Barnhouse, E. S. 333
Barnhouse, Elizabeth 575
Barnhouse, Magnus 492
Barnhouse, Richard 492
Barnhouse, Rosannah 315
Barnhouse, Susannah 309
Barnhouse, Thos. 333
Barns, Amanda 31
Barns, Elizabeth 500
Barns, Fanny 31
Barns, Jane 171
Barns, Samuel 713, 727, 728

Barns, Sardis G. 28
Barns, Susannah 385
Barnum, Harriet 31
Barnum, John 28
Barnum, Leman 28
Barnum, Mathew 82
Barnum, Pamela 28
Barnum, Sylvester 28
Barnwill, John 335
Barny, West 495
Barr, Alexander 432
Barr, Alexander H. 570
Barr, Amos 455
Barr, James 280, 295
Barr, James M. 319
Barr, John 487
Barr, Joseph 565
Barr, Nancy Eliza 432
Barr, Sarah 459
Barr, Subal 729
Barrack, Margaret 717
Barrat, Arthur 565
Barret, Abner 130
Barret, John 156
Barrett, --- 36
Barrett, Abner 116
Barrett, Ann 75, 169
Barrett, Beanzer 38
Barrett, Bridget 114
Barrett, Caroline 90
Barrett, Hannah 212
Barrett, Harrison 38
Barrett, Hiram 75
Barrett, James 75
Barrett, Jane 158
Barrett, John 158, 286
Barrett, Lewis 75
Barrett, Louiza 38
Barrett, Richard 169
Barrett, Wesley 38
Barrett, Wilson 731
Barrick, Abraham 570
Barrick, Isaac 570
Barringer, Elizabeth 84
Barrington, Alexander 143
Barrington, James 143
Barrington, John 143
Barrington, Richard R. 100
Barrington, Richd. K. 102
Barrington, Sherman 143
Barrington, Thomas Pierce 137
Barrington, Wm. 143, 354
Barron, Jacob 570
Barron, John 291
Barron, Lamard W. 40
Barrone, Bitsey 752
Barrone, Elias 752
Barrone, George 752
Barrone, Hiram 752
Barrone, Lydia 752
Barrone, Margaret 752
Barrone, Mary 752
Barrone, Simon 752
Barrone, Susana 752
Barrow, James 51
Barrow, Lamard W. 40
Barrows, Henry 716

Barrtham, Nancy 716
Barsherer, Mary 230
Barstow, Sally 83
Barta, John 664
Bartels, Carl Gotlieb 88
Barth, Katharine 709
Barth, Theobald 709
Barthalmew, John 585
Barthilot, Florence 719
Barthollowmew, S. M. 731
Bartleson, John Eaton 336
Bartlet, Irana 262
Bartlet, James 262
Bartlet, John 262, 651, 720
Bartlett, Amanda 628
Bartlett, Charles 299
Bartlett, Frances 324
Bartlett, Harriet 324, 336
Bartlett, John 314, 628
Bartlett, Julia 628
Bartlett, Loucina E. 747
Bartlett, Lydia 314
Bartlett, Mary 324, 522, 628
Bartlett, Mary Ann 336
Bartlett, Samuel 91, 628
Bartlett, Sarah 324, 743
Bartlett, Sylvanus 628
Bartlett, Thomas 324
Bartlett, William 319, 320, 324, 628
Bartley, Marian 515
Bartley, Simeon 40
Bartol, Abraham 743
Bartol, George 743
Bartol, John 743
Bartol, Mathias 743
Barton, Andrew 358
Barton, Asa 159
Barton, George 448
Barton, Henry 620
Barton, John 76
Barton, Joseph 511, 570
Barton, Josiah 736
Barton, Mary 517
Barton, Matilda 511
Barton, Naomi 516, 517
Barton, Polly 382, 457
Barton, Rachel B. 85
Barton, Thomas 736
Barton, William 288, 688
Bartult, Henry 518
Bascom, William T. 250, 252
Basey, Lismun 657
Bashore, Henry 367
Bashore, John 341
Baskerville, James 43
Baskerville, James M. P. 55
Baskerville, Judith Rebecca 55
Baskerville, Martha 55
Baskerville, Mary R. 55
Baskerville, Nancy M. 55
Baskerville, Richard A. 55

Baskerville, S. 55, 64
Baskerville, Samuel 46, 55
Baskerville, Samuel B. 55
Baskerville, Stateia 55
Baskerville, William 43
Baskerville, William B. 55
Basore, David 356
Basore, Elizabeth 356
Basore, John 356
Basore, Thos. 356
Bassart, Andrew 5
Bassell, William 116
Basset, Amos 511
Basset, William 685
Bassete, Alexander 511
Bassett, Skiff 763
Bassre, Benjamin 239
Bassre, Sarah 239
Baster, George 378
Baster, Reuben 476
Bastide, Stephen 724
Batch, Havier 359
Batchelder, Ebenezer 731
Batchelor, John 731
Batchelor, John (Jr.) 731
Batchford, John 495
Bateman, Asahel 40
Bates, Abagail N. 70
Bates, Amos 267
Bates, Ansel (Jr.) 57
Bates, Archabald L. 46
Bates, Asab . . . 1 C. 681
Bates, Cranston 588
Bates, Curtis 70
Bates, Daniel 455
Bates, Dorcas 43
Bates, Edward 313
Bates, Eliza 143, 594
Bates, Eliza H. 758
Bates, Elizabeth 118
Bates, Elkannah H. 420
Bates, Emer 451
Bates, Emphraim 475
Bates, Eunice 659
Bates, Hannah 313
Bates, Harriet 745
Bates, Harriet L. 143
Bates, Hortentia M. 70
Bates, John 470, 483, 495, 758
Bates, Joseph 744
Bates, Polly 499
Bates, Samuel 455
Bates, Talcott 70
Bateson, Lewis 373
Batey, Sarah 80
Batleis, Nathaniel 40
Batson, Edward 525
Batson, Eleanor 525
Batston, Andrew 282
Battelle, Ebenezer 721
Battelle, Ebenr. (Jr.) 730
Battenfelt, Mary 531

Battenfield, Elizabeth 520
Battenfield, Solomon 518
Battenfield, Susannah 519
Batterel, Mary 120
Batterson, A. 507
Battle, Elizabeth 71
Battle, Francis 716
Battle, Ithiel 33
Battle, James 71
Battle, John 71
Battle, Rose Ann 71
Battle, Sarah 33
Battle, Sarah Ann 71
Batton, Jesse 731
Baty, Jane 655
Baty, John 482
Baty, Polly 590
Baty, Samuel 655
Baty, William H. 655
Bauch, Joseph 164
Bauder, Anthony 382
Bauer, L. R. 221
Baugh, Caty 385
Baugh, Jacob 382
Baugh, Margaret 383
Baugh, Polly 382
Baugh, Susannah 386
Baugh, Wm. M. 588
Baughan, Eve 588
Baughan, Jeremiah 585
Baughman, Eve 568
Baughn, Mordica 588
Baught, Sarah 573
Baultzer, . . . 373
Baum, Elizabeth 384
Baum, Kitty 385
Baum, Margaret 462
Baum, Sally 384
Bauman, John 570
Baumann, George 369
Baumer, Henry 542
Baumgarter, Mary 610
Baury, Sebastian 170
Bauserman, Jacob 620
Bawley, Eleanor 498
Bawzell, John 606
Baxter, Anna 186
Baxter, Cornelius 408
Baxter, Daniel 186, 209
Baxter, George 445, 606
Baxter, James 557
Baxter, John 558
Baxter, Joseph 668
Baxter, Peggy 186
Baxter, Reuben 477, 478, 482
Baxter, Ruth 445
Baxter, Samuel 295
Baxter, Wm. 295
Bay, Ann 635
Bay, Cynthia 635
Bay, Eliza 635
Bay, Harrison 635
Bay, James 224
Bay, Joseph R. 588
Bay, Mary 120
Bay, Robert 297, 635

Bay, Thomas 635
Bay, Thomas M. 635
Bayard, Caroline 54
Bayard, George 333, 447
Bayard, Hannah 446
Bayard, Richd. H. 54
Bayes, Peter 570
Bayham, Thomas 86
Bayle, --- 479
Bayless, John 482
Bayless, Nathan 188
Bayless, Samuel 188
Bayley, Mary 385
Bayliss, Benjamin 188
Baylor, --- 396
Baylor, Frederick 588
Baylor, William 427
Baymon, Polly 121
Bays, Elizabeth 739
Bazil, Ezekiel 487
Bazler, John Gotlip 273
Beach, Asa 726
Beach, Charles 438
Beach, Etta Lorena 701
Beach, Harrison 701
Beach, Jesse 723, 726
Beach, John 461, 492
Beach, Jonathan 438
Beach, Mary 701
Beach, Mary A. 701
Beach, Sarah Ellen 701
Beach, William 438
Beacher, Frederick 455
Beacher, George 232
Beachler, John 229
Beachler, Magdalene 229
Beachler, Wm. Henry 432
Beachtle, Barbara 553
Beachtle, Catharine 553
Beachtle, Daniel 553
Beachtle, David 553
Beachtle, Frederick 553
Beachtle, George 553
Beachtle, Jacob 553
Beachtle, John 553
Beachtle, Magdalene 553
Beachtle, Martin 553
Beachtle, Mary 553
Beachtle, Thomas 553
Beagle, Holmes 367
Beagler, Tobias 588
Beah, Sabrina 717
Beaham, James 282
Beaker, Polly 466
Beal, Elizabeth 165
Beal, Jonathan 16
Beal, Philip 461
Beal, William 40
Beall, Beall 741
Beall, Citizen 155, 156, 165, 168, 171, 173, 175, 177
Beall, Citizin 155
Beall, Citzen 152, 153
Beall, Citzin 155
Beall, Elizabeth 152, 153, 155, 171, 173, 175, 177
Beall, Harriet 740

Beall, John 740
Beall, Joseph 432
Beall, Maria E. 740
Beall, Mary Jane 740
Beall, Nancy 740
Beall, Nancy C. 740
Beall, Parker Campbell 740
Beall, R. 737
Beall, Reasen 740
Bealmear, Thomas 293
Beals, Sarah 717
Bealy, William 390
Beam, David 94
Beam, David M. 94
Beam, H. 94
Beam, Jacob 445, 737
Beam, John J. 94
Beam, Joseph 565
Beam, Nancy 31
Beam, O. 94
Beam, Paul 373
Beamer, Adam 570
Beamer, Geo. 570
Beamer, Hannah 570
Beamer, Henry 356, 620
Beamer, Isaac 570
Beamer, Jacob 356
Beamer, Ledy 576
Beamer, Lucy 290
Beamer, Mary 569, 577
Beamer, Peter 565
Beamer, Salome 356
Bean, Christiana 355
Bean, Daniel 259
Bean, David 289
Bean, Elizabeth 355
Bean, Mary Magdalene 355
Bean, Paul 355
Bean, Peter 355
Bear, Comfort 359
Bear, Eliza 590
Bear, Elizabeth 573
Bear, Ellen 241
Bear, H. 241
Bear, Henry 241
Bear, John 382
Bear, Josiah 241
Bear, L. 241
Bear, Lydia 241
Bear, Marcus 241
Bear, Sarah Ann 241
Beard, Aaron 440
Beard, Alfred 354
Beard, Amos 588
Beard, B. F. 404
Beard, Comodore R. 279
Beard, David 528
Beard, Eliza 354, 405
Beard, Elizabeth 354
Beard, George 273, 273
Beard, Harriet 404
Beard, James 689
Beard, Jane 295
Beard, Joseph 354, 363, 518, 689
Beard, Joseph M. 492
Beard, Martha 404
Beard, Mary 295, 354

Beard, Mary Ann 689
Beard, Mary E. 279
Beard, Polly 11
Beard, Rachel 511
Beard, Rebecca 354
Beard, Reuben 280
Beard, Robert 487
Beard, Samuel 518
Beard, Thomas 354
Beard, Vietor 279
Beard, William 354, 689
Beard, William H. 285
Beard, Wm. 354
Beard, Zebulon 652
Beardlee, Elanor 99
Beardmore, Isaac 163
Beardmore, Susannah 163
Beardshire, George 199, 216, 230
Beardslee, D. 99
Beardslee, E. 99
Beardslee, L. 98
Beardslee, Lucinda 99
Beardslee, O. 98
Beardslee, Pheby 98
Beardsley, David A. 760
Beare, Leanah 521
Bearly, Daniel 760
Bearmore, Isaac 171
Bears, Mary 498
Beasley, John 477
Beasly, William 57
Beath, Joseph 492
Beath, Thomas 358
Beaths, Charles 363
Beaths, Elizabeth 363
Beaths, Euphemia 363
Beaths, John 363
Beaths, Mary 363
Beaths, Thomas (Jr.) 363
Beaths, Thomas (Sr.) 363
Beaths, William 363
Beatty, Anna Maria Elizabeth 336
Beatty, John 481
Beatty, John C. 484
Beatty, Rebeckah 514
Beatty, Samuel 290
Beaty, Adam 451
Beaty, John 469
Beauchamp, William 106
Beaudeau, Francis 713
Beaudot, Jean 713
Beaugher, George 565
Beaver, Elizabeth 355
Beaver, George 355, 518
Beaver, Henry 336
Beaver, Jacob 565
Beaver, John 716
Beaver, Joseph 160
Beaver, Margaret 355
Beaver, Michael 171
Beaver, Nancy 355
Beaver, Rachel 355
Beaver, Thomas 355
Beaver, William 744
Beaveres, Geo. 570
Beazley, Peter 123
Bebb, William 620

Bebe, Almira 497
Bebe, Deborah 84
Bebe, Samuel 588
Bebee, Levi 40
Bebehymir, Peter 620
Bebo, Charles 495
Bebout, Ann 89
Bebout, Anna 88
Becher, Barbary 188
Becher, Eliza 188
Becher, Elizabeth 188
Becher, John 188
Becher, Margaret 566
Becher, Peter 188
Bechtel, Isaac 396
Bechtol, Christiana 229
Bechtol, Samuel 229
Beck, Aaron 737
Beck, Abraham 588
Beck, Adam 709
Beck, Alexander 451
Beck, Alford 737
Beck, Amy 737
Beck, David 525
Beck, Elizabeth 432
Beck, Henry 143
Beck, James 225, 533
Beck, John 341, 542
Beck, Margaret 533
Beck, Metcalf 737
Beck, Paul 153
Beck, Rachel 748
Beck, Samuel 731
Beck, Sarah 143
Beck, Vivan B. 731
Beck, William 432
Becker, Andrew 194, 213
Becker, David 194, 213
Becker, Fanny 214
Becker, George 36
Becker, Henry 194
Becker, John 194, 199
Becker, Katharine 709
Becker, Lovina 194
Becker, Peter 199
Becker, Philippina 708
Becker, Samuel 194, 214
Becker, Theobald 708
Beckett, Elizabeth 382
Beckett, James 382
Beckilhaub, Elizabeth 709
Beckley, Catharine 743
Beckley, Conrod 743
Beckley, Daniel 743
Beckley, Edward 743
Beckley, James 743
Beckley, Philip 461, 462
Beckley, Sarah 743
Beckley, Thomas 743
Beckly, Daniel 743
Beckman, Henry 110
Beckman, Sarah 550
Beckman, Solomon 518
Becknal, Nehemiah 82
Becks, Prescella 383
Beckwith, Catherine 353
Beckwith, David 353
Beckwith, Elizabeth 353

Beckwith, Emily 114
Beckwith, Geo. 378
Beckwith, George 353
Beckwith, Joel 347, 353, 375
Beckwith, John 259, 353, 357, 369, 372, 376, 378, 380, 381
Beckwith, Rebecca 248
Beckwith, Sally 75
Beckwith, Susanna 353
Beckwith, Tobias 248, 285
Beckworth, John 347
Beddinghouse, Anna M. 114
Beddinghouse, Bernard 114
Beddinghouse, Henry 114
Beddinghouse, Mary K. 114
Bedell, John 542
Beden, Benj. 551
Beden, Betsey 551
Bedford, --- 469
Bedford, Nathaniel 479
Bedillan, Isaac 24
Bedillan, Osilla 24
Bedillin, Abraham 24
Bedillin, David Row 24
Bedillin, Frederick 24
Bedillin, Isaac 24
Bedin, Benjamin 542
Bedinger, Catharine H. 59
Bedinger, Daniel 59
Bedinger, Danl. 59
Bedinger, Edwin S. 59
Bedinger, Henry 59
Bedlack, Benjamin 596
Bedle, Abram 116
Bedle, Daniel 119
Bedle, Francis 643
Bedle, Jacob 657
Bedle, Mary 127
Bedle, Solomon 664
Bedortha, Theodore 28
Beebe, Almena 30
Beebe, Caroline 31
Beebe, Dillon 761
Beebe, Laurel 28
Beebe, Willis 28
Beech, Elizabeth 108
Beech, Lewis 432
Beech, Samuel 297
Beecham, Henry 461
Beecher, F. 743
Beedle, Esther 670
Beedle, James 670
Beedle, John 670
Beedle, Joseph 657
Beedle, Lydia 670
Beedle, Mary 137, 670
Beedle, Phebe 118, 670
Beedle, Simon 119
Beedle, Susanna 670
Beedle, William 670
Beeham, James 296
Beekham, Polly 14

779

Beekman, John C. 40
Beel, Mary 718
Beeman, Moses 283
Beemer, Elizabeth 56
Beemer, Isaac C. 56
Beemus, Jonas 28
Been, Peter 528
Beenblosom, George 123
Beenblossom, John 123
Beer, James 137
Beer, Joshua (Rev.) 570
Beers, Gerty Viola 533
Beers, John 119, 230
Beers, Thomas 533, 548
Beery, Samuel 338
Beever, Ann 455
Beever, Baudle 461
Beever, Isaac 461
Beever, John 163
Beever, Nancy 163
Beezly, Tenperance
  Ophelia 432
Beggs, Andrew 588
Beggs, Jane 666
Beggs, Rachel 662
Beggs, Thomas 123
Beggs, Zaccheus 282
Begher, Mary 354
Behm, C. 95
Behm, Elizabeth Jane 95
Behmer, John B. 107
Behrunes, John B. 40
Beight, Adam 167
Beish, Charles 712
Beker, Andreas 234
Beker, Anna 234
Beker, Augusta 234
Belair, Eliza 744
Belair, Leakit 744
Belcher, David 478
Belew, Joseph 119
Belford, Daniel 159
Belknap, Forris 271
Bell, Abner 382
Bell, Ann R. 521
Bell, Betsey 91
Bell, Charles 487
Bell, Christian 708
Bell, Citzen 152
Bell, Daniel 43, 62
Bell, Elizabeth 152,
  356, 487, 585
Bell, George 255, 286
Bell, Henry 432
Bell, Isaiah 382
Bell, James 255, 606,
  706
Bell, James H. 255
Bell, Jane 356
Bell, Jno. 249
Bell, John 171, 259,
  260, 355, 356, 432,
  657
Bell, John R. 62
Bell, Joseph 62, 263,
  269, 356
Bell, Josiah 432
Bell, Judeth 590
Bell, Lavina 542

Bell, Letitia 452
Bell, Lucinda 432
Bell, Lucretia 336
Bell, Maria 432
Bell, Martha 432
Bell, Martha Jane 356
Bell, Mary 356, 522
Bell, Nancy 665
Bell, Rebecca 62, 169
Bell, Robert 249
Bell, Samuel 356, 731
Bell, Samuel (Jr.) 731
Bell, Sarah 171, 432,
  581
Bell, Silas 588
Bell, Thomas 249, 382
Bell, William 51, 62,
  90, 487, 542
Bell, William H. 169
Bellair, Augustin 495
Bellaman, Curella 133
Beller, Jacob 672
Beller, Mary 657
Beller, Peter 672
Belli, Cynthia 515
Bellis, William 333
Bellman, Andrew 570
Bellman, Elizabeth 574
Bellow, Peter 123
Bellows, Melinda 78
Bellue, Isaac 137
Beloat, Edward 505
Beloat, George 505, 511
Beloat, Jacob 505
Beloat, James 505
Beloat, Joseph 505
Beloat, Mary 505
Beloat, Menervy 505
Beloat, Nancy 505, 512
Beloat, Walter 505
Beloat, Wm. Quine 505
Beloat, Wm. Tuine 505
Beloate, Caroline 505
Belote, Gesrge 505
Belout, Ann 510
Belout, Caroline Jayne
  510
Belout, George 510
Belout, John 510
Belout, Joseph 510
Belout, Lidia 510
Belout, Lydia 510
Belout, Margaret 510
Belout, Mary 510
Belout, Smith 510
Belout, Walter 510
Belout, William Quinn
  510
Bemes, A. B. 507
Bemis, John 89
Bemis, Wm. 270
Benbebber, Jesse 716
Benbow, Barclay 116
Bench, Cristian 487
Bench, Daniel 487
Bench, Phebe 487
Bender, George 743
Bender, John 542
Bender, William 744

Benedick, Euretta 79
Benedict, Content 67
Benedict, Daniel 67
Benedict, Eli 67
Benedict, Elisha H. 82
Benedict, Felix 86
Benedict, Lydia 67
Benedict, N. 67
Benedict, Nicholas 67
Benedict, Silvester 67
Benedict, Susannah 67
Benegar, Jonathan 711
Benell, Andrew 570
Benell, Barbara 570
Benell, William 565
Beneman, Thomas 511
Benepe, Caroline 570
Benett, Stephen 280
Benfer, Philip 570
Benfort, Elizabeth 575
Benham, --- 423
Benham, Abiel Baltzer
  150
Benham, Absalom 652
Benham, Benjamin 203
Benham, Elizabeth 657,
  668
Benham, Joseph 639, 668
Benham, Moriah 150
Benham, Peter 668
Benham, Richard 150
Benham, Robert 639,
  652, 657, 668
Benham, Robert (Jr.) 657
Beninger, John 570
Benis, Wm. 264
Benjamin, Edith A. 350
Benjamin, Elsee 351
Benjamin, Emeline 351
Benjamin, Hannah 351
Benjamin, James 350,
  351, 354
Benjamin, John 351
Benjamin, Mary 351, 714
Benjamin, Nancy 499
Benjamin, Nathan 350,
  351, 354
Benjamin, Samuel 351,
  354
Benjamin, Sarah 350,
  351, 354
Bennebb, Catherine 464
Bennell, Abner 655
Benner, Christian 100
Benner, Daniel E. 518
Benner, John 570
Benner, Sophia 606
Bennet, Andrew 65
Bennet, Benjamin 116,
  511
Bennet, Caleb 503
Bennet, Elizabeth 309
Bennet, Hester 661
Bennet, Ira 588
Bennet, Isaac 683
Bennet, James 65, 657
Bennet, John 336
Bennet, Joseph 644
Bennet, Joshua 119

Bennet, Lydia 65, 78
Bennet, Martha 123
Bennet, Mary 512
Bennet, Rachel 741
Bennet, Rebecca 359
Bennet, Rosanna 190
Bennet, Sally 503
Bennet, Sarah 65, 589
Bennet, Thomas 190, 511
Bennet, William 309
Bennett, Abraham 342
Bennett, Amos 511
Bennett, Benjamin 429, 506
Bennett, Betsy 506
Bennett, Cecily 355
Bennett, David (Jr.) 28
Bennett, Edward 492
Bennett, Eli 518
Bennett, G. 407
Bennett, Gushum 506
Bennett, Hannah 293, 516
Bennett, Henry 511
Bennett, Henry H. 11
Bennett, Ira G. 506
Bennett, Jesse 506
Bennett, John 461, 511, 542, 552, 731
Bennett, Joseph 506, 672
Bennett, M. 407
Bennett, Mahala A. 592
Bennett, Mahitable 506
Bennett, Martha 342
Bennett, Mary 593
Bennett, Michael J. 570
Bennett, Moses 506
Bennett, N. 532
Bennett, Nehemiah 532
Bennett, Patsy 513
Bennett, Phebe 278
Bennett, Philo 40
Bennett, Priscilla 517
Bennett, Rachel 506
Bennett, Rebecca 511
Bennett, Rhoda 506
Bennett, Robert 355
Bennett, S. 532
Bennett, Samuel 429
Bennett, Sarah 506, 532
Bennett, Stephen 532
Bennett, Thaddeus 506
Bennett, Thadeus 506
Bennett, Thomas 506
Bennett, Tobias 532
Bennett, William 429, 511
Bennett, Wm. P. 731
Benninger, Elizabeth 573
Benninghous, Lizitta 307
Bennington, Anne 307
Bennington, Arthur 307
Bennington, Lizetta 307
Bennington, Mary 307
Bennington, Theodore F. 307
Bennit, Belinda 592
Bennit, Joseph 461
Benoss, Jacob (Dr.) 562
Benschoter, Emily 522

Bensen, John 505
Benson, Henry 664
Benson, Polly 609
Benson, Rozen 451
Benson, William 606
Benson, Wm. 657
Bensyl, Balser 406
Bensyl, L. W. 406
Bensyl, Rebecca 406
Bent, Abner 716, 730
Benter, Henry 284
Benting, Thos. A. 154
Bentler, J. N. (Dr.) 626
Bentler, John N. 604
Bentley, Eliza 292
Bentley, Harriet 292
Bentley, John 461
Bentley, Joseph 461
Bentley, Mary 292
Bentley, Mary Jane 521
Bentley, Robert 441
Bentley, William 292
Bently, Simeon 5
Benton, Burr 495
Benton, Jesse 495
Benton, Matilda 580
Benton, Oliver 135, 147
Bentz, George 626
Bentz, Jacob 165
Bentz, John George 626
Berdan, George 38
Berdan, John 38, 40
Berdan, Mary Margaret 38
Berdan, Peter Frederick 38
Berdon, Abraham 69
Berdon, David 69
Berdon, David (Jr.) 69
Berdon, David S. 69
Berdon, George S. S. 69
Berdon, George T. 69
Berdon, James 69
Berdon, John 69
Berdon, Margaret A. 69
Berdon, Mary M. 69
Berdon, Peter 69
Berdon, Peter F. 69
Berdon, Rachel 69
Berdon, William 69
Berg, John 112
Berg, Maria Eva 35
Bergeman, Henry 111
Berger, Andrew 530
Berger, Christina 519, 522
Berger, George 530
Berger, John 741
Berger, Margaret 530
Berger, Samuel 530
Bergman, Henry 112
Bergstreser, William 518
Bergunthal, Benedict 173
Bergus, Jane 51
Berham, Catharine 117
Berkel, --- 221
Berkhard, Barbara 190
Berkhard, Henry 190
Berkhard, Isaac 190
Berkhard, Martin 190

Berkhimer, Catherine 355
Berkhimer, Edward 355
Berkhimer, James 355
Berkhimer, John 355
Berkhimer, Keziah 355
Berkhimer, Nathan 355
Berkholder, Abraham 754
Berkholder, Barbara 754
Berkholder, Christian 754
Berkholder, Jacob 38
Berkholder, Joseph 754
Berkholder, Moses 38
Berkholder, Peter 754
Berkholder, Salome 38
Bernard, Isaiah 518
Bernard, Michael 713
Bernard, Rebecca 529
Berner, Christian 114
Berner, Dorathy 114
Berner, John Herman 114
Bernhard, Catharine 114
Bernhard, Jacob 114
Bernhart, Herman 237
Bernhart, Soffia Regina Eliesa 237
Berning, Henry 542
Berns, Mary M. 580
Berry, Anne 662
Berry, Benj. 272
Berry, Betsey 119
Berry, Daniel 40, 731
Berry, Edmon 65
Berry, George 518
Berry, Hannah Maria 519
Berry, Isaac S. 38
Berry, Jacob 720
Berry, James 397, 455, 548
Berry, James W. 397
Berry, Jane 117
Berry, John 511
Berry, Joseph 643, 672
Berry, Lydia E. 397
Berry, Manda 413
Berry, Mary S. 38
Berry, Mirander 397
Berry, Rachel 550
Berry, Richard 461
Berry, Ruth Ellen 306
Berry, Samuel 664
Berry, Stephen 455
Berry, Thomas 4
Berry, William 119, 132
Berry, Wm. 132
Berryhill, James 672
Bershong, John 474
Bert, Nathaniel 25
Bert, William 169
Berthe, Hannah Mion 724
Berthe, Lewis 724, 725
Berzstuser, Sally 521
Besecker, Christian 162
Beshong, John 470, 474, 484, 485
Beshonz, John 471
Bessant, John 371
Bessant, Susan 371
Best, Adam 570

Best, Agnes 562, 566
Best, Catharine 570
Best, Catherine 574
Best, Isaac 565
Best, Jacob 40
Best, John 570
Best, Mary 568, 575
Best, Samuel 562
Best, Sarah 662
Best, Solomon 570
Best, Thomas 11, 672
Bestow, John C. 76
Beswick, James 704
Beswick, Samuel 704
Betchtell, Andrew 396
Betchtell, Christine 396
Betchtell, David 396
Betchtell, Henry 396
Betchtell, Isaac 396
Betchtell, John 396
Betchtell, Nancy 396
Betchtell, Samuel 396
Betford, Barnet 173
Betford, Drusilla 173
Bethard, Alexr. 588
Bethel, Edward 716
Bett, William D. 163
Betty, Martin 89
Betz, Elizabeth 453
Betz, Hannah 467
Betz, John 111
Betz, Polly 466
Betz, William 487
Beuzelin, Elisabeth 713
Bevan, Elener 310
Bevan, Findley 310
Bevan, Jesse L. 310
Bevan, John 165, 310
Bevan, Mary 310
Bevan, Mary Ann 310
Bevan, Mary E. 305
Bevan, Mary Ellen 305
Bevan, Roland 310
Bevan, Rolland 310
Bevan, Sarah 310
Bevan, Thomas W. 310
Bevan, William C. 174,
310
Bevans, Polly 385
Bevear, Abraham J. 442
Beveir, John D. 440
Bevene, Margret 570
Bever, Thomas 511
Beverage, Ann 355
Beverage, Chas. C. 355
Beverage, John 355
Beverage, Keziah 355
Beverage, Mary 355
Beverage, Noble 355
Beverage, Samuel 355
Beverage, Sarah 355
Beverage, Susan 355
Beverage, Thos. H. 355
Beverage, Tracy 355
Beverage, William 355
Bevier, Abraham J. 444
Bevier, Jacob 444
Bevier, Jane 444
Bevier, William 444

Bevilhimer, Corod 335
Bevin, Abraham 447
Bevin, Jacob 447
Bevin, William 447
Bevington, Elizabeth 600
Bevington, Henry 105,
600
Bevington, James 600
Bevington, John 600
Bevington, Margaret 606
Bevington, Mary 600
Bevington, Nancy Ann 600
Bevington, Rachael 105
Bevington, Rebecca Jane
600
Bevires, George 40
Bevon, John P. 160
Bevon, Mary 160
Bewell, Walter 472, 484
Beyer, John 94
Beyer, Mary 94
Beyers, Elizabeth 456
Beymer, George 282,
285, 297
Bibby, Abraham 509
Bibby, Almira 509
Bibby, Eathalinda 509
Bibby, Elizabeth 509
Bibby, George W. 509
Bibby, Isaac 509
Bibby, John 509
Bibby, Sarah 509
Bible, Magdalena 745
Bibler, Jacob 518
Bickel, Barbara 230
Bickel, Catharine 230
Bickel, George 230
Bickel, Henry 230
Bickel, Jacob (Jr.) 428
Bickel, John 230
Bickel, Julianna 568
Bickel, Rosina 230
Bickel, Simeon 230
Bickel, Susan 230
Bickel, Thomas 230
Bickel, Tobias 230
Bickham, Elizabeth 283
Bickham, John 283
Bickle, Christina 429
Bickle, Elizabeth 76,
567
Bickle, Eve 567
Bickle, Leonard 76
Bickle, Peggy 79
Bickle, Rachel 85
Bickle, Sally 429
Bickle, Susannah 565
Bickmore, Sedate 656
Biddinger, Sally 573
Biddison, Wm. 361
Biddle, Baldwin 161
Biddle, Baulden 161
Biddle, Ben. 713
Biddle, Mary 161
Biddlecomb, Daniel R. 761
Bide, Suckey 52
Bidinger, Catherine 574
Bidison, Philip 367
Bidlack, Benjamin 336

Bidlack, James F. 334
Bidlack, Mary 334
Bidlack, Sarah 337
Bidwell, Isaac 46, 58
Bidwell, Rusel 58
Bidwell, Russel 58
Bidwell, Urial 58
Bieber, Jane 716
Biegle, Francis 517
Bientz, Baltis 601
Bientz, Catharine 609
Bienz, John 606
Bienz, John B. 95
Bienz, Mary J. 95
Bierer, David 740
Bierle, Henry 225
Bierly, Darick 382
Biers, Sally 716
Bigelow, --- 74
Bigelow, Almy 60
Bigelow, Catharine 581
Bigelow, Chamberlin 60
Bigelow, Daniel K. 60
Bigelow, Diana 60
Bigelow, Dianna 60
Bigelow, Dolly 60
Bigelow, Eliphas 60
Bigelow, Gideon 449
Bigelow, Hosea 60
Bigelow, Isaac 60, 581
Bigelow, Israel 60
Bigelow, Lebben L. 60
Bigelow, Lucy 581
Bigelow, Mary 449
Bigelow, Polly 60
Bigelow, Russel (Rev.)
594
Bigelow, Samuel 379
Bigelow, Timothy 60
Bigerstaff, Nancy 717
Biggam, Eliza 356
Biggam, James 356
Biggam, Jonathan 356
Bigger, Abigail 223
Bigger, James 223
Bigger, John 649, 650,
671, 673
Bigger, John (Sr.) 668
Bigger, Joseph 223
Bigger, Maria Jane 114
Bigger, Mathew 254
Bigger, Robert 100, 123
Biggerstaff, John 716
Biggerstaff, Samuel 495
Biggs, Ephraim 432
Biggs, James 588
Biggs, Joshua 432
Biggs, Margaret 432
Biggs, Mary 660
Biggs, Sarah 432
Biggs, Thomas 683
Bigham, Alexander 668
Bigham, Ann 659
Bigham, Anne 668
Bigham, Catharine 743
Bigham, Eleanor 514
Bigham, Hugh 668, 743
Bigham, Jane 530, 665,
668, 743

782

Bigham, John 530, 668, 743
Bigham, Mary 530, 743
Bigham, Michael 743
Bigham, Nancy 743
Bigham, Polly 668
Bigham, Robert 743
Bigham, Sarah 668
Bigham, William 530
Bigler, Jonathan 335
Bigley, Eliza Jane 336
Bigsby, Moses 202
Biller, Mary 657
Billet, Robert 681
Billin, John 335
Billman, Catharine 71
Billman, Charles W. 71
Billman, Eliza Ann 71
Billman, Geret Francis 103
Billman, Reuben 71
Bilman, Loisa 606
Bilmire, Jacob 682
Bince, Jacob 164
Binckley, Adam 353, 354, 355, 364
Binckley, Catherine 354, 355
Binckley, Christian 355
Binckley, Christiana 355
Binckley, Elizabeth 354, 355
Binckley, Emanuel 354
Binckley, Freny 355
Binckley, Geo. 354
Binckley, Henry 354
Binckley, Jacob 354, 359
Binckley, John 354, 355
Binckley, Magdalena 353
Binckley, Mary 354
Binckley, Milla 354
Binckley, Nancy 354
Binckley, Sam. 354
Binckley, Samuel 354
Binder, Jacob 40
Binegar, John 711
Bing, John 82
Binggeli, Anna 735
Bingham, E. F. 633, 634
Bingham, Elizabeth 717
Bingham, Jeremiah 40
Bingham, John 651
Bingham, Lucy 634
Bingham, Patty Irena 634
Bingham, Ralph 634
Bingham, Sarah 281
Bingham, Silas 76
Binghan, J. A. 505
Bingman, Jacob 254, 255
Binkley, Daniel 647
Binkley, George 394
Binkley, George H. 394
Binkley, George S. 394
Binkley, Jacob 532, 637
Binkley, Joseph 647
Binkley, Maria 394
Binkley, Maria L. 394
Binkley, Orphia 394
Birbridge, James 382

Birch, Hannah 78
Bird, Asher E. 40
Bird, James 314
Bird, John 548
Bird, Malinda 143
Bird, Mary 582
Bird, Mortmer 143
Bird, Samuel 542
Birdsall, Almira Elizabeth 763
Birdsall, Francis Mason 763
Birdsall, George Dana Boardman 763
Birdsall, John A. Judson 763
Birdsall, John O. 763
Birdsall, Nathan 763
Birdsall, Wm. Lary 763
Birdsey, Nathan D. 495
Birely, William 116
Birg, Elijah 112
Birg, Mary 112
Birge, Josiah 588
Birley, Noah 123
Birrell, Rhoda 77
Birt, Abraham 461
Birt, Anna 512
Birt, Joseph 511
Bisecker, Barbara 362
Bisecker, David 362
Bishong, George 461
Bishong, John 472, 473, 474, 476, 480
Bishop, Caty 383
Bishop, Christian 736
Bishop, Daniel 588
Bishop, David 461, 525
Bishop, David W. 657
Bishop, Dilly 666
Bishop, Frederick 492
Bishop, James 11
Bishop, Joanna 100
Bishop, John 11, 487, 527, 736
Bishop, Lovet 259
Bishop, Minah 14
Bishop, Richard 100
Bishop, Robert 461
Bishop, William 11
Bisinett, Margarett 496
Bisnett, Thomas 495
Bisoz, Francis 436
Bisoz, Milton 436
Bissel, S. N. 741
Bissell, Alden 82
Bissell, Hiram 82
Bissell, Jerusha 40
Bissell, Rufus 506
Bissell, Sarah 506
Bisset, Margaret 29
Bistner, Magdalena 522
Biswell, John 470, 471, 472, 474, 480, 482
Biswell, William 470, 482
Bitler, C. F. 403
Bitler, Danl. 403
Bitmore, Benjamin 654

Bitmore, Sedate 654
Bivins, Benj. 34
Bivins, Benjn. 34
Bivins, John 511
Bixler, Catharrine 574
Bixler, Elizabeth 495
Bixler, George 495
Bixler, Henry 495
Bixler, Polly 498
Bixler, Sally 519
Bixly, George E. 731
Bixsy, N. M. 422
Blacher, John 295
Black, Abraham 432
Black, Adam 123
Black, Alexander 10
Black, Alexander S. 429
Black, Barbara 413
Black, Catharine 121
Black, Daniel 742
Black, David 432
Black, Drusilla 180
Black, Easter 664
Black, Eleanor 403
Black, Elizabeth 117
Black, Foster 432
Black, Hamilton 76
Black, Henry 432, 583
Black, James 283, 736, 752
Black, James C. 540
Black, Jane 21
Black, John 461
Black, Jos. 477
Black, Joseph 11, 180, 418
Black, L. 735
Black, Mahala 96
Black, Maria 77
Black, Mary 46, 429
Black, Mary A. 419
Black, Mildred Ann 419
Black, Nancy 82
Black, P. 735
Black, Peter 429, 735
Black, Randal 60
Black, Robert 347, 354, 755
Black, Samuel 123, 130, 131
Black, Sarah 365
Black, Sarah Ann 432
Black, Thomas 647
Black, Uri 432
Black, William 96, 347
Black, Wm. B. 377
Black, Wm. H. 432
Blackburn, James D. 690
Blackburn, Joseph 264, 268, 274
Blackburn, Ruth 664
Blackburn, Timothy 267
Blackburn, Zecheriah 267
Blackenburgh, John 232
Blackenburgh, Polly 232
Blackford, Catharine 655
Blackford, David 150, 679
Blackford, David Nelson 679

Blackford, Elizabeth 679
Blackford, Emily 679
Blackford, Ephraim 654, 670
Blackford, Isaac 644, 672
Blackford, James R. 654
Blackford, John 655, 657
Blackford, Lemuel 150
Blackford, Louisa 654
Blackford, Mahlon 655
Blackford, Martha 658
Blackford, Mary 150
Blackford, Nathaniel 654
Blackford, Reuben 657
Blackford, Rhoda 660
Blackford, Sarah 663
Blackford, Sarah Ann 679
Blackford, Susan 655
Blackingham, Alvah 731
Blackman, Ebeneser 123
Blackman, Lucinda 495
Blackman, Pernelia 745
Blackmer, Jesse 731
Blackmore, Benj. 143
Blackmore, Henry 270
Blackmore, John 477
Blackmore, Martha 143
Blackmore, Sarah Ann H. 143
Blackson, William 292
Blagg, Samuel 11
Blagrove, Catharine E. 55
Blagrove, Charles 55
Blagrove, Charlotte 55
Blagrove, Henry B. 55
Blagrove, Parthenia 55
Blagrove, William 55
Blain, Ann 120
Blain, Joseph 261
Blain, Matthew 89
Blain, Nancy 76
Blain, Polly 459
Blaine, William 178
Blair, Anna 752
Blair, Asa 752
Blair, Brice 11, 16
Blair, Catherine 745
Blair, Fanny 752
Blair, J. 50
Blair, James 20, 451, 470, 472, 485, 752
Blair, Jennie 43
Blair, John 50, 280, 472, 486, 670, 752
Blair, Mary 744
Blair, Mary E. 21
Blair, Nancy 466, 660, 752
Blair, Rebeckah 752
Blair, Samuel 50, 743
Blair, Seth 752
Blair, Susannah 50
Blair, Thomas 477, 518
Blair, Thomas F. 477
Blair, William 16
Blair, Wright 752
Blake, . . . 165

Blake, Benj. 270
Blake, Benjamin 303
Blake, Drusilla 180
Blake, Eli 762
Blake, Harrison G. 73
Blake, Israel 270
Blake, James 405
Blake, John 194, 542, 657
Blake, John G. 108
Blake, Joseph 180
Blake, Mary 84
Blake, Nehemiah 262
Blake, Rebecca 549
Blake, Simeon 259, 265, 713
Blakeley, J. M. 538
Blakeley, M. A. 538
Blakeley, Mary E. 538
Blakeley, William 538
Blakely, Atchison 542
Blakely, Barbara A. 538
Blakely, Barbra 538
Blakely, E. 538
Blakely, Franklin 538
Blakely, Mary B. 542
Blakely, Robert 542
Blakely, Rosanna 280
Blakeman, James 408
Blakeman, Mary 410
Blaker, Simeon 267
Blakeslee, James S. 28
Blakesly, Hannah 29
Blakley, E. 534
Blakley, J. 534
Blakley, Morenos 534
Blakley, Samuel 534
Blakley, William 337
Blancett, Permillia 665
Blancher, John 64
Blancher, Sarah 417
Bland, Abigal 582
Bland, Peter 582
Bland, Saul 582
Blane, Joseph 272
Blankenhorn, Fredenker 608
Blankenship, Nancy 549
Blanset, Harriet 664
Blanwelt, Abraham 157, 158
Blanwelt, Sarah 158
Blare, James 165
Blasseneck, Margaretha 610
Blatchley, Elenor 80
Blauch, Christian 565
Blaw, Joseph 116
Blaylock, Vachel 11
Blazier, Abraham 250, 251
Blazier, Elijah D. 250, 251
Blazier, Ellen 252
Blazier, Jacob 252
Blazier, James 252
Blazier, Jonathan H. 250, 251
Blazier, Mary 455

Blazier, Mary E. 250, 251
Blazier, Mary Jane 252
Blazier, Phinias 455
Blazier, Sarah Ann 250, 251
Blecker, John 295
Blemee, Mary Christena 606
Blename, Mary Christena 606
Blessing, Ann Maria 272
Blessing, Jacob 272
Blessing, Lenhard 272
Blessing, Lenhart 272
Blessing, Samuel 272
Blicenstaffer, Catharine 190
Blickenaderfer, Benjamin 564
Blickenaderfer, John 564
Blickendorffer, Christian 561
Blickendorffer, John 561
Blickensderfer, Abraham 570
Blickensderfer, Barbara 562
Blickensderfer, Benjamin 570
Blickensderfer, Catharine 564
Blickensderfer, Christian 562, 564
Blickensderfer, Christian (Sr.) 562
Blickensderfer, Christiana Elizabeth 562, 564
Blickensderfer, Elizabeth 562
Blickensderfer, George 562, 564
Blickensderfer, Jacob 562, 564
Blickensderfer, John 562, 564
Blickensderfer, Maria 562, 564
Blickensderfer, Mary 564
Blickensderfer, Rosanna 564
Blickensderfer, Sally 564
Blickensderfer, Susanna 564
Blickensderfer, Thomas 564
Blickensderfer, William 562
Blickensdorfer, Christine Elizabeth 575
Blickenstaffer, Elizabeth 190
Blickenstaffer, Hannah 190
Blickenstaffer, Jacob 190
Blickenstaffer, Joseph 190

784

Blickenstaffer, Leonard 190
Blickenstuffer, George 565
Blinko, John 40
Blinn, Andres 273
Blinn, Electa 762
Blinn, Jemima 496
Blinn, Nathaniel D. 756
Bliss, Amos 721, 722
Bliss, Caroline N. C. 280
Bliss, Jeffrey 270
Bliss, Lucretia 126
Bliss, Mason 280
Bliss, Phebe 721
Bliu, Francoise 713
Blizard, Burton 58
Blizzard, Burton 51, 56, 461
Blizzard, Edy 349
Blizzard, John 349
Blizzard, Mervin 349
Blizzard, Phebe 349
Blocher, Christian 487
Block, Carl 114
Block, Henry 114
Block, Henry D. 542
Block, Herman 114
Blodgett, Henry C. 40
Blog, Caty 25
Bloom, Anne 527
Bloom, Catharine 565
Bloom, Christian 478
Bloom, Dorcas 530
Bloom, Eliza L. Ann 605
Bloom, Elizabeth 522, 527
Bloom, John 527, 605
Bloom, Mariah 527
Bloom, Mary Elizabeth 605
Bloom, Polly 384
Bloom, William Jesse 605
Bloomer, Martha 667
Bloomfield, Nathaniel 187
Bloomfield, Reuben 429
Bloomfield, Robert A. 426
Blose, George 657
Blosser, Susanna 563
Blosser, Susarina 576
Blossom, Ansel 613, 626
Blossom, E. P. 613
Blossom, Edward P. 613
Blossom, Elizabeth M. 613
Blossom, Geo. W. 613
Blossom, Henry A. 613
Blossom, Henry C. 613
Blossom, I. A. 613
Blossom, John 606
Blossom, Mary 607
Blossom, Mercy Ladd 613
Blossom, Nancy 613
Blossom, R. D. 613
Bloucher, John 492
Blount, Ambrose Alexander 432

Blower, Sally 508
Bloxem, Mary 390
Bloxion, Jeremiah 382
Bloxom, Jeremiah 390
Bloxom, Job 390
Bloxom, John 390
Bloxom, Moses 390
Bloxom, William 390
Bloxum, Margaret 390
Bloxum, Pheroby 390
Bloxum, William 390
Blubaugh, Solomon 40
Blue, Abner 137
Blue, Anna 143
Blue, Barnabas 116, 542
Blue, Barnabas (Jr.) 133
Blue, Barnabas D. 318, 324
Blue, Barnahas (Sr.) 133
Blue, Blackford 137
Blue, Elsy 455
Blue, Francis 137
Blue, Frederick 382
Blue, George 324
Blue, Hannah 122
Blue, James 132, 324
Blue, James H. 744
Blue, James W. 137
Blue, Jane 143
Blue, Jno. L. 137
Blue, John 11, 123, 324, 461
Blue, John B. 123
Blue, Lewis D. 143
Blue, M. 540
Blue, M. M. 540
Blue, Mahetable 137
Blue, Margaret 63, 143
Blue, Margarett 467
Blue, Martha 382
Blue, Mary 137, 324, 663
Blue, Mary Ann 745
Blue, Michael 532
Blue, Nancy 127
Blue, Rebecca 143
Blue, Ruth 116, 125, 137
Blue, Sarah 324
Blue, Uriah 116, 123
Blue, William 11, 318
Blue, William K. 324
Blue, Wm. S. 137
Blumas, Mary 608
Blunden, William 282
Blundet, Margaret 516
Blunier, Benjamin 455
Blunt, Ambrose 432
Blunt, Cyrus 487
Blunt, William 289
Blythe, Benj. 298
Blythe, Thomas 511
Boal, James 597
Boal, Jas. 581
Boal, Margaret 581
Boal, Martha E. 581
Boal, Thomas 640
Boardman, Zebulon 260
Boarman, Betsey 721
Boarman, Sally 721
Boatman, Elias 471, 476

Bobe, Harriet 518
Boblet, Jacob H. 432
Bobo, Betsey 717
Bobo, Israel 716
Bobo, Jemina 124
Bockman, Nancy 567
Bockrath, Mathias 542
Boderick, Catherine 457
Bodinas, Henry 323
Bodkin, Jeremiah 50
Bodkin, John 461
Bodkin, Sarah 452
Bodley, Abraham Dewit 442
Bodley, David 442
Bodley, Henry 442
Bodley, Levi 444
Bodley, Massey 586
Bodly, Abraham D. W. 439
Bodwell, Elijah 722
Bodwin, Nathan 665
Boecking, Christian Tibald 225
Boedet, Job 40
Boehmer, H. J. 627
Boehmer, H. Joseph 604
Boehner, Margaretta Maria 107
Boelston, Joshua 511
Boelston, Winney 511
Boen, Mary 512
Boen, William 511
Boenbaugher, Mary 606
Boerstler, Daniel 368
Boerstler, Margaret 368
Boesche, I. F. 107
Boesel, Charles 108
Boeshar, Sarah Anna 234
Boesher, Lidia 234
Boesher, Samuel 234
Boethe, John C. 225
Bogan, Mahala 466
Bogard, Joshua 597
Bogart, Cornelius 487
Bogart, Ezekiel 492
Bogart, Gasper 492
Bogart, George 382
Bogart, George W. 143
Bogart, Jacob 525
Bogart, Katharine 548
Bogart, Martin V. 518
Boger, Hannah 14
Bogert, George W. 337
Boggs, Agnes 292
Boggs, Elizabeth 456
Boggs, Hannah 292
Boggs, James 292
Boggs, Margaret 292
Boggs, Mary 549
Boggs, Moses 292, 487
Boggs, Nancy 452
Boggs, Robert 292
Boggs, William 400
Boggs, Wm. 400
Bogle, Elizabeth 353, 354
Bogle, Erastus 355
Bogle, Holmes 354, 355
Bogle, Homes 361

Bogle, James 353, 355
Bogle, Joseph 353
Bogle, Mary 355
Bogle, Mitchell 355
Bogle, Rebecca 354
Bogle, Sally Ann 355
Bogle, Samuel 354, 355
Bogle, William 354, 355
Bogle, Wm. 361
Boher, Rebeckah 501
Bohner, Margaretta Maria 107
Boice, Austin 609
Boils, Anna 125
Boils, Mary 127
Bokey, Margaret 529
Bolanbauch, David 611
Bolanbauch, Levina 611
Bolanbaugher, P. 615
Bolanbaugher, R. 615
Bolander, Adam 195
Bold, John 236
Bold, Magdalina 236
Bold, Simon 236
Bolding, Henry 159
Boldston, Joshua 511
Boldston, Winney 511
Bole, Anthony 393
Bole, Elizabeth 393
Bolehimer, Paul 74
Bolen, Ellewine 74
Bolenbaucher, Peter 620
Bolenbaugher, A. 617
Bolenbaugher, Abraham 606
Bolenbaugher, David 606
Bolenbaugher, E. 617
Bolenbaugher, Elizabeth 607, 617, 626
Bolenbaugher, George 606
Bolenbaugher, Jacob 626
Bolenbaugher, James W. 617
Bolenbaugher, John 617, 626
Bolenbaugher, Michael 626
Bolenbaugher, Peter 599, 626
Bolenbaugher, Rosana 610
Bolens, Samuel H. 414
Boler, Ann 723
Boles, William 736
Boles, William M. 637
Bolier, Julia A. 326
Bolier, Martin 326
Bolin, Enoch 664
Bolin, Even Howe 518
Bolin, John 177
Bolin, Martha 230
Bolin, Mary 177
Bolin, Richard 230
Bolin, Robert 286
Bolinghouse, Danl. 500
Boll, Elisabeth 235
Boll, John G. 237
Boll, Magdalena 235, 237
Boll, Sara 235
Boll, Siman 235

Boll, Simon 237
Bollanbaugher, Jacob 615
Bollanbaugher, L. 615
Bollanbaugher, R. 615
Bollaneaucher, Pheby A. 615
Bollenbaucher, Peter 615
Bollenbaugher, Elizabeth 615
Bollenbaugher, P. 615
Bollenbaugher, R. 615
Boller, Frederick 286
Bollins, Lydia 125
Bolmer, Solomon 542
Bolsell, John 337
Bolten, James 451
Bolton, Andrew 76
Bolton, Anna 107, 114
Bolton, James 107
Bolton, John 107, 271
Bolton, Lewis 107
Bolton, Lucy 76
Bolton, Lydia 114
Bolton, Melinda 82
Bolton, Philip 107
Bolton, Sally 107
Bomberger, William 188
Boncil, James 158
Bond, Amy 496
Bond, Caleb 653
Bond, Catharine 260
Bond, Isaac 700
Bond, John (Dr.) 723
Bond, Lydia 700
Bond, Peter 265, 303
Bond, Richard E. 260
Bond, Susley 700
Bondell, Thomas W. 627
Bone, Charlotte 334
Bone, Cyrus 638
Bone, David 664, 670
Bone, Elizabeth 664
Bone, John 683
Bone, Samuel 253
Bone, Thomas 664
Bonefield, Abel 114
Bonefield, Caroline 114
Bonefield, Eliza 114
Boneham, Warford 461
Boner, Cram 391
Boner, Ebenezer Wead 191
Boner, Eveline 413
Boner, James 469, 471, 472, 478, 479, 480, 651
Boner, Jas. 477
Boner, John 191, 651
Boner, William 470
Boney, John 308
Boney, Julia Ann 308
Bonham, D. W. 532
Bonham, L. 532
Bonham, Moses 605
Bonner, Abraham 455
Bonner, James 481
Bonner, John 191
Bonnete, Catherine 464
Bonney, Elizabeth 712
Bonney, Elizabeth B. 710

Bonsor, Joseph 504
Bonta, Albert 657
Bonta, Peter 669
Boodriff, Nathan 570
Boogher, Catherine 216
Boogher, Elizabeth 216
Boogher, George 216
Boogher, Maria 216
Boogher, Mary 216
Boogher, Samuel 216
Booher, Caty 118
Booher, Daniel 217
Booker, Levi 143
Boon, Asena 174
Boon, John 303
Boon, Joseph 174
Boon, Wm. 268, 272
Boone, Joseph 157
Booten, Nancy H. 79
Booth, Asael 167, 172, 174, 179, 180
Booth, Asahel 178
Booth, Asail 154
Booth, Bethia 174, 179
Booth, Bethiah 154, 178
Booth, Bethina 167
Booth, Daniel 563
Booth, David 633
Booth, David H. 633
Booth, Edward 179
Booth, Elizabeth 633
Booth, Hiram 633
Booth, Lydia Ann 633
Booth, Polly 633
Booth, Sophia 633
Boothby, Robert 711
Boothby, Sally 713
Boothmas, L. M. 753
Bootman, Elias 470
Boots, Daniel 637
Boots, Martin 451, 455
Boraff, Michael 111
Boram, Polly 589
Boram, Wm. 585
Boraugh, Elizabeth 666
Borden, Geo. 432
Borden, Job 687
Borden, Joshua 687
Borden, Richard 681
Borden, Sarah Ann 681
Borden, Susan 432
Borden, Wm. 432
Border, George 289
Bordon, Phebe 590
Borger, Barbary 581
Borger, Elizabeth 581
Borger, Henry 66
Borger, Schury 581
Boring, Edward 292
Boring, Mary 292
Borkert, Henry 404
Borket, Jonas 404
Borket, Rachel 404
Borlin, C. 534
Borlin, James K. 534
Borlin, P. 534
Born, Edward 511
Born, Henry 133
Bornig, Mary Dorothy 574

786

Boroff, Louisa 608
Boroff, Samuel 606
Boroughs, Morris 606
Borrowy, Johanna 718
Borrowy, Maria Catharine
  718
Bortner, Anna Jane 277
Bortner, Anne Carlina
  276
Bortner, Carl 277
Bortner, Eli 276
Bortner, George 276
Bortner, Henry 276, 277
Bortner, Jacob 276
Bortner, Jasua 277
Bortner, Jerome 277
Bortner, John 276
Bortner, Margrat 276
Bortner, Sarea 276
Borton, Benjamin F. 759
Borton, Caleb 759
Borton, Eliza 759
Borton, Jesse P. 759
Borton, Mary 759
Borton, Sarah Ann 759
Bosche, I. F. 107
Boschor, Maria 239
Bosel, John G. 542
Bosh, Abraham 54
Bosier, David 518
Bosier, Stasey 125
Bosler, Jacob (Dr.) 221
Bosman, Edward 274
Bosman, Elizabeth 271
Bosman, Frances S. 271
Bosman, John R. 271
Bosman, Ruth R. 271
Bosman, Wilks 269, 271,
  274
Bosman, Wm. H. 271
Bosserman, Michael 357,
  359, 373, 378
Bosserman, Samuel 555
Bosson, David 137
Boston, Serina 551
Boston, William 280
Bostwick, J. B. 764
Bosworth, Alva 82
Bosworth, Daniel P. 710,
  712
Bosworth, John W. 254
Bosworth, Marcus 76
Botckin, Jemima 463
Bothel, William 542
Bothwell, A. W. 634
Bothwell, James 634
Botkin, A. 534
Botkin, B. 534
Botkin, Catherine 534
Botkin, Charles 390,
  534, 542, 552
Botkin, Charles D. 400
Botkin, D. 534
Botkin, E. 534
Botkin, Eliza 534
Botkin, Elizabeth 534
Botkin, Erastes 534
Botkin, George 400, 542
Botkin, James 76

Botkin, John 11
Botkin, Margaret 400
Botkin, Mary 662
Botkin, Paul E. 534
Botkin, R. 534
Botkin, Richard 657
Botkin, Russel 534
Botkin, S. H. 542
Botkin, S. M. 534
Botkin, Silvenes 534
Botsford, Zilpha 523
Bott, Baker 170
Bott, Balzer 180
Bott, Barbary 170
Botts, Mary 464
Botts, Moses 470
Bottsell, Catherine
  Nancy 137
Bottsell, Esther 137
Bottsell, Mary Ann 137
Bottsell, Sarah Rebeca
  137
Boues, Francis 337
Bouey, John 308
Bough, Elizabeth 357
Bough, Jesse 357
Bough, Mary 357
Boughman, Henry (Jr.)
  554
Boughman, Jacob 570
Boultenhous, Daniel 511
Boulter, Lemuel 442
Boulton, Lewis 107
Boulton, Lydia 107
Boulton, Magdelina 107
Bouman, Bernard 374
Bounds, Sophia 65
Bounds, Thomas 291
Boure, Benjamin 531
Bourn, A. 64
Bourne, Jas. 202
Bourne, Sylvanus 64
Bourne, William 202
Bouser, Hanah 514
Bouser, Jane 513
Bousman, Barbara 24
Bousman, Eleanor 24
Bousman, John 24
Bousman, Maria 24
Bousman, Maximilla 24
Bousman, Nicholdemus 24
Bousman, Sarah 24
Bousman, William 24, 123
Bouzer, Levi 690
Bowan, Phillis 464
Bowden, George 541
Bowdle, Anna 457
Bowdle, Elizabeth 455
Bowdle, John 518
Bowdle, Joseph 455
Bowdle, Mary 457
Bowe, Erastus G. 518
Bowe, John 542
Bowe, Judy 542
Bowee, Ellen E. 520
Bowen, Abraham H. 194
Bowen, Abram 588
Bowen, Cyrus 606
Bowen, Daniel 597, 598

Bowen, David 382
Bowen, David W. 194
Bowen, Edward 588
Bowen, Elizabeth 194,
  608
Bowen, Enoch 194
Bowen, Francis 294
Bowen, Henry 664
Bowen, Isaac 461
Bowen, Jane 598
Bowen, Jesse 588
Bowen, John 278, 511
Bowen, John (Jr.) 604
Bowen, John (Sr.) 604
Bowen, Mary Ann 514
Bowen, Nancy 512, 582,
  597, 598, 604
Bowen, Nathaniel W. 194
Bowen, Peleg 598
Bowen, Rebecca 512
Bowen, Robert H. 194
Bowen, Truman 390
Bowen, William 382, 750
Bowen, Wm. 274
Bower, Barbara Ann 518
Bower, Benjamin 526
Bower, Daniel 231
Bower, Elizabeth 229,
  231, 607
Bower, George W. 46
Bower, John 190, 207,
  554, 606
Bower, Joseph 162, 163,
  165
Bower, Keddy 521
Bower, Lydia Ann 606
Bower, Samuel 229
Bowerman, Hannah 520
Bowers, Adam 451
Bowers, Catharine 572
Bowers, Christiana 132
Bowers, Daniel 232
Bowers, David 570
Bowers, Elizabeth 232
Bowers, George D. 355
Bowers, Jacob 553
Bowers, Jane K. 64
Bowers, John 297, 351
Bowers, John D. 672
Bowers, Lewisa 219
Bowers, Martha 566
Bowers, Mary 351
Bowers, Rebecca 416
Bowers, Rushama 46
Bowers, Salter 40
Bowers, Samuel 744
Bowers, Sarah 132, 517
Bowers, Solomon 461
Bowersock, Elizabeth 149
Bowersock, Henry 627
Bowersock, Jacob 627
Bowersock, James 627
Bowersock, Jane 128
Bowersock, John 128, 657
Bowersock, Nancy 627
Bowersock, Peter H. 149
Bowersock, S. 149
Bowersock, Samuel 149
Bowersock, Sarah 149

Bowersock, Sarah Ann 606
Bowersock, Valentine 627
Bowic, Rebecca 583
Bowin, Nancy 467
Bowin, Truman 382
Bowing, Rhoda 661
Bowland, Eleanor 522
Bowland, Hugh 54
Bowler, Henry 461
Bowles, David 495
Bowles, Elizabeth 499
Bowles, Lydia 495
Bowles, W. K. 495
Bowlton, Christina 107
Bowlton, John 107
Bowlus, Susanna 499
Bowman, Barnhart 369
Bowman, Baxter 40
Bowman, Campbell 188, 198
Bowman, Charity 664
Bowman, Christeena 743
Bowman, George 349, 369
Bowman, Gilbert 188, 198
Bowman, Henry 362, 483
Bowman, John 223
Bowman, Joseph 349
Bowman, Magdalene 349
Bowman, Magdelene 349
Bowman, Martin 428
Bowman, Mary 349
Bowman, Matilda 509
Bowman, Peter 369, 380, 678
Bowman, Phebe 382
Bowman, Samuel 212, 655
Bowman, Sarah 403
Bowman, Thomas 349
Bowser, Barbara 518, 526
Bowser, Catharine 191
Bowser, Catherin 526
Bowser, Daniel 191
Bowser, David 191
Bowser, Elizabeth 526
Bowser, Henry 191
Bowser, Jacob 526
Bowser, John 40, 526, 657
Bowser, Michael 518
Bowser, Michael D. 689
Bowser, Modlena 526
Bowser, Nancy 526
Bowser, Sarah 191, 526
Bowser, Susana 526
Bowser, William 191
Bowsher, Caty 385
Bowsher, Daniel 382
Bowshier, Mary 406
Bowyer, Elizabeth 658
Bowyer, Isaac 67
Bowyer, John 606, 657
Bowyer, Lucinda 511
Bowyer, Rebecca 67
Bowyer, Richard H. 672
Bowyer, Sarah 667
Bowyer, Stephen 668
Bowzer, Jacob 731
Boxler, Mary 498
Boyce, John 6

Boyce, Lemuel 588
Boyce, Robert 480
Boyd, Agnes 268
Boyd, Amsy P. 678
Boyd, Andred 123
Boyd, Andrew 725, 731
Boyd, Anna 271
Boyd, Archibald G. 150
Boyd, Betsy 120
Boyd, Daniel 87, 676
Boyd, Emily 178
Boyd, Emily G. 151
Boyd, George 178, 731
Boyd, H. 151
Boyd, Huldah 151
Boyd, J. J. 151
Boyd, James 282
Boyd, Jane 573
Boyd, John 271, 678
Boyd, John J. 151
Boyd, John N. 678
Boyd, Jonathan 451
Boyd, Joseph 414
Boyd, Margaret 271
Boyd, Nancy 271, 567, 665
Boyd, Robert 21, 271, 292
Boyd, Robt. 570
Boyd, Sary 571
Boyd, Thomas 268
Boyd, Wiley 271
Boyde, Peter P. 762
Boydston, Sarah 517
Boydstone, Ann 500
Boydstone, Catharine 500
Boydstone, Elizabeth 500
Boydstone, Presley 500
Boyer, Andrew 291
Boyer, Barbara 378
Boyer, Bardsley 291
Boyer, Betsey 291
Boyer, C. 534
Boyer, Catharine 291, 351
Boyer, Catherine 354
Boyer, Clarissa 549
Boyer, David 291
Boyer, Ed. 534
Boyer, Edith 534
Boyer, Elizabeth 351, 672
Boyer, Emma 534
Boyer, Hannah 351, 525
Boyer, Henry 349, 351, 354
Boyer, Isaac 281
Boyer, Jacob 119, 291, 606
Boyer, Jefferson 508
Boyer, John 123, 291, 351, 518
Boyer, Lewis 548
Boyer, Mahalia 534
Boyer, Mary 351
Boyer, Michael 349, 351
Boyer, Nancy 548
Boyer, Peggy 291
Boyer, Peter 291

Boyer, Polly 121
Boyer, S. R. 534
Boyer, Sally 291
Boyer, Samuel 212, 382
Boyer, Susannah 520
Boyer, Thomas 525
Boyer, Thos. 525
Boyer, William 291
Boyington, Asa 503
Boyinton, Asa 503
Boylan, Geo. 366
Boyle, Hugh 356, 471, 474, 475, 479
Boyle, John 287, 471, 475, 479, 483
Boyle, Joseph 295
Boyles, Hugh 483, 484
Boyles, John 483, 484
Boyles, Thomas 565
Boynton, Charles 511
Boynton, Joseph E. 511
Boynton, Lydia C. 515
Boyour, Margaret 120
Boyse, Alexander P. 432
Boyse, James 417
Bozarth, Lot 55
Bozman, Wilkes 264
Bpyse, Ananias 432
Brabham, Elisha 200, 201
Brace, Betsy 752
Brack, Isaac A. 177
Brack, John 176
Brack, Oddey A. 177
Brack, Sarah 177
Brackbill, Susannah 744
Bracken, Jesse 188
Brackenridge, Hugh 705
Brackenridge, John 705
Brackin, Isaac H. 548
Bracy, Gracy 167
Bracy, James 167
Bradaway, Samuel 214
Bradbury, Joseph 82
Bradel, Julien 724
Braden, Robert 11
Bradenbury, Aaron 28
Brades, John 461
Bradfield, Elizabeth 80
Bradfield, Mary Ann 78
Bradford, Allen 191
Bradford, Bridget 391
Bradford, David D. 191
Bradford, Ezra 500
Bradford, Harvey S. 40
Bradford, James 639
Bradford, James G. 123, 191
Bradford, John 191, 195, 224, 639
Bradford, Lucy 36
Bradford, Mary 195
Bradford, Peggy 639
Bradford, Polly 639
Bradford, Robert 639
Bradford, William 195, 213, 639
Brading, James 542
Bradley, Ann 354
Bradley, Benj. 254

Bradley, Calvin 683, 687
Bradley, Cyrus 254
Bradley, Daniel 677
Bradley, David L. 63, 626
Bradley, Elizabeth 63
Bradley, Eneas 343
Bradley, Isaac 455
Bradley, James L. 63, 626
Bradley, Jason 28
Bradley, Jno. 219, 221
Bradley, Jno. (Capt.) 221
Bradley, John 254, 354
Bradley, Jonas 55
Bradley, Lena 221
Bradley, Mary 354
Bradley, Mary Ann 254
Bradley, Patrick 354, 657
Bradley, Peggy 715
Bradley, Phillis 464
Bradley, Sarah 221
Bradley, Susan 585
Bradley, Susannah 467
Bradley, Washington 63, 626
Bradley, William 254, 354
Bradly, Henry D. 71
Bradly, Jno. (Capt.) 221
Bradly, Phebe 71
Bradly, Sarah 451
Bradshaw, Ann 432
Bradshaw, David 354
Bradshaw, Ellanor 501
Bradshaw, Geo. 354
Bradshaw, George 511
Bradshaw, Hannah 78
Bradshaw, Isaac 511
Bradshaw, James 76
Bradshaw, Jesse 76
Bradshaw, Nancy 354
Bradshaw, Rachel 76
Bradshaw, Robert 354, 370, 511
Bradshaw, Stephen 76
Bradshaw, William 76, 511
Bradstreet, Daniel 657
Bradt, Mary Ann 519
Brady, David 254
Brady, George 254
Brady, John 104, 259, 260, 645, 673, 674
Brady, Samuel 642
Brady, William 645, 673
Brafield, Margaret 77
Bragg, Elizabeth 462
Braham, Eliza 606
Braiden, Catherine 461
Brainard, Elizann 505
Brake, --- 580
Brake, Adam 588
Brake, Elizabeth 585
Brake, Mary 589
Brake, W. D. 356
Braley, Sally 79

Braman, Silence 30
Bramble, Charles 461
Bramble, Mary 87
Bramble, Nancy 456
Brame, Hariett 410
Brame, John 409
Bramhall, Mary 177
Bramhall, Robert 177
Bramonburgh, Elizabeth 456
Bran, Polley 666
Branaham, Abraham 217
Branaman, Abraham 217, 232
Branaman, David 217
Branaman, Finley 217
Branaman, Sara 232
Branaman, Stephen 232
Branaman, Susan 217
Branch, Almeria 80
Branch, Harry 76
Branch, Josiah 76
Branch, Polly 77, 662
Branch, Samuel (Jr.) 82
Branch, Wm. 76
Brand, Anna 137
Brand, Conrad 570
Brand, Elizabeth 573
Brand, Esther 137
Brand, Henry 570
Brand, Sarah 137
Brandal, Regina 523
Brandbury, Fanny 664
Brandenburg, Aaron 656
Brandenburg, Anthony 687
Brandenburg, Israel 656
Brandenburg, Joseph 656
Brandenburg, Samuel 542
Brandenburg, Sarah 656
Branderberry, Henry 657
Brandew, Catherine 461
Brandle, William 65
Brandon, Abel A. 143
Brandon, Armstrong 116
Brandon, Catharine 113
Brandon, Elias 694
Brandon, Eliza 120
Brandon, Eliza A. 143
Brandon, Elizabeth C. 143
Brandon, Fanny 126
Brandon, Joseph 113
Brandon, Julia 143
Brandon, Julia A. 143
Brandon, Magdelen 120
Brandon, Margaret J. 143
Brandon, Mary A. 143
Brandon, Mary J. 137, 143
Brandon, Priscilla 143
Brandon, Sarah 143
Brandon, Turza 123
Brandon, Wm. E. 137
Brandstater, Andrew 669
Brandsteller, Annie C. 111
Brandstretter, Andrew 657
Brandstretter, Catharine 658

Brandt, A. 619
Brandt, Adam 354
Brandt, Amanda 619
Brandt, C. 619
Brandt, Charles 619
Brandt, Chas. 619
Brandt, David 354
Brandt, Elizabeth 354
Brandt, Jacob 354
Brandt, John 352, 354
Brandt, John W. 619
Brandt, Lodwick 354
Brandt, Rosana May 619
Braninburgh, Elizabeth 456
Brank, Charles O. Neil 486
Branmick, Mary 455
Brannaham, Abraham 217
Brannaman, Joseph 217
Brannen, Joseph 588
Brannen, Matilda 591
Brannon, Mary 267
Brannon, Sarah 589
Brannon, Thomas 46, 267
Brannt, Samuel 570
Bransen, Abram 11
Bransen, Rachel 11
Branson, Abigail 143
Branson, Amos 432
Branson, DeWitt 143
Branson, John 143
Branson, Levi 143
Branson, Thomas 432
Branstrator, Susannah 666
Brant, Rosina 575
Brant, Sally 360
Brantingham, George 563
Braskett, William 382
Bratsher, Emily 126
Brattain, Mary Ann 9
Brattain, Zimri 9
Brattin, Stephen 11
Bratton, Mary 278
Bratton, Sarah 380
Bratton, Wallace 672
Braty, Elizabeth 499
Brawdreck, Mary 123
Brawley, Levi P. 432
Brawley, Thos. F. 432
Bray, Henry T. 634
Brayton, Marinda 497
Brayton, Olive 519
Brazetton, William 641
Braziltton, Edward 641
Brazitton, William 641
Break, Michael 588
Breceick, Elizabeth 603
Breckbill, Abraham 356
Breckbill, Jacob 356
Breckbill, James 356
Breckbill, Mary Ann 356
Breckbill, Patience 356
Breckenridge, Davd. 731
Breckinridge, Martha 711
Bredahl, Hans 706
Bredant, Wm. 394
Bredeick, Ferdinand 603

Bredeick, John 604
Brederick, J. O. 627
Breece, Betsey A. 327
Breece, Elizabeth 327
Breece, H. G. 327
Breece, H. H. 327
Breece, H. M. 327
Breece, Hannah M. 327
Breece, Henry C. 327
Breece, Milton 327
Breece, P. C. 327
Brees, Sarah 606
Breeze, Joshua 270
Breininger, Irene 327
Breker, John 162
Brelsford, Caroline 143
Brelsford, Eleanor 65
Brelsford, Elizabeth 687
Brelsford, Hiram 143
Brelsford, Jane 676
Brelsford, John 687
Brelsford, Joseph 65
Brelsford, Sarah 143
Brelsford, Thomas 687
Brelsford, Wm. P. 143
Bremer, Conrad 296
Bremozer, Jacob 279
Brenaman, Isaac 528
Brenaman, Jacob 217
Brenaman, Joseph 528
Brenaman, Rosannah H. 217
Brenan, Hugh 709
Brendenburg, Jacob 236
Brendenburg, Joseph Vaschenton 236
Brendenburg, Sara 236
Breneman, William 528
Brenizer, Adam 279
Brenizer, Henry 565
Brenneman, Abraham 230
Brenneman, Anna 230
Brenner, David 216
Brenner, Elias 216
Brenner, Elizabeth 143, 216
Brenner, John 601, 606
Brenner, Joseph 216
Brent, Adel Heit 104
Breting, Henry 672
Breting, Tobias 672
Brettingham, Abner 60
Brettingham, Betsey 60
Brettingham, Enoch 60
Brettingham, George Riley 60
Brettingham, Hetty 60
Brettingham, James Hampton 60
Brettingham, Leah 60
Brettingham, Martha 60
Brettingham, Nancy 60
Brettingham, Polly 60
Brettingham, Sally 60
Brettingham, Seley 60
Brettingham, Solomon 60
Brevard, James 143
Brevard, Lucinda 143
Brevard, Samantha 143

Brewell, Sarah 572
Brewer, Abram 690
Brewer, Ann 690
Brewer, Jacob 511
Brewer, John 571
Brewer, Joseph 635
Brewer, Mary 515
Brewer, Stephen 511
Brewer, Willis 635
Brewster, Eleanor 87
Brewster, Gunston 299
Brewster, Huldah 270
Brewster, Jane 198
Brewster, Wm. 272
Brey, Absalom 108, 603
Briant, John 50
Bribley, Jerome 105
Brice, Samuel 741
Bricelecer, Isaac 337
Bricker, Benjamin 88
Bricker, Molly 558
Brickman, George 739
Brickner, G. M. 626
Brickner, George M. 604
Bride, Amanda 278
Bridenbaugh, Frederick 744
Bridenbaugh, John 744
Bridenbaugh, Peter 744
Bridenstine, Samuel 735
Bridenstine, Susan 735
Bridge, Andrew 263
Bridge, Sally Jane 589
Bridgeman, John 213
Bridgeman, John H. 168
Bridgeman, Mary L. 213
Bridgeman, Nancy 213
Bridges, Joseph 657
Brier, Andrew D. 133
Brier, David 123
Brier, George 119
Bries, John 16
Briese, Robert 16
Briggs, Amos 35
Briggs, Andrew 252, 269
Briggs, Charles 33
Briggs, Charlotte 252
Briggs, Daniel G. 70
Briggs, David 230
Briggs, Elkanah 40
Briggs, Erastus 40
Briggs, Ester 230
Briggs, James 265, 269
Briggs, John 270, 728, 729
Briggs, Joseph 461, 492
Briggs, Nancy 252
Briggs, Otis 28
Briggs, Rebecca 252
Briggs, Robert 252
Briggs, Thomas 61
Briggs, Thos. 478
Briggs, Walter 455, 492
Briggs, William 252
Briggs, Wm. 260
Brigham, Asa 708
Bright, Goodwin 639
Bright, Rachel 639
Brine, Almon 65

Brine, Betsey 65
Brine, Jonathan 65
Brine, Luke 65
Brine, Luman 65
Brine, Semilla 77
Brine, Simon 65
Brine, Snythia 78
Briner, Catharine 38
Briner, John 382
Briner, John Gotleit 38
Briney, Ame 662
Briney, Anna 670
Briney, Anne 670
Briney, Dan 478
Briney, Dan 478
Briney, Daniel 470, 472, 473, 474, 476, 478, 484, 486, 655, 669
Briney, Frederick 654, 655, 670
Briney, John 455, 657
Briney, Mary 654
Bringham, Samuel 189
Brinkerhoff, H. 525
Brinkerhoff, James 525
Brinkerhooff, Elizabeth 525
Brinkerhooff, James 525
Brinkle, Mary 221
Brinton, Amos 156
Brinton, William 303
Brio, George 114
Brio, Maria 114
Brion, Pheby 719
Brish, Henry C. 527
Brish, W. M. 495
Brison, B. 355
Brison, Benjamin 297
Bristal, Cyrena M. 497
Bristal, Elbridge A. 495
Bristo, Abigail 741
Bristol, Elta 499
Bristol, Sophia 499
Bristow, Abigail 741
Brittain, Elinor 452
Brittam, Ann 459
Brittenham, Elizabeth 512
Britton, Elenor 663
Britton, Isaac 640
Britton, Levinia 640
Britton, Maurice 640
Britton, Murdock 640
Britton, Nathan 451
Britton, Richard 640
Britton, Steddom 640
Brittson, Isaac 606
Broadaway, Ambrose 214
Broadaway, Johon A. 214
Broadaway, Samuel 210
Broadley, Catrona 464
Broadwell, Ann 201
Broadwell, Josiah 201, 203, 204, 205
Broadwell, Mary L. 201
Broadwell, Silas 201
Broadwell, Susan 201
Broals, John 119
Brock, John J. 351

Brock, John Jacob 272
Brock, Jonathan 429
Brock, M. D. 359
Brock, Moses 427
Brock, Wesly (Rev.) 605
Brockover, Jacob 295
Brockover, Mary 295
Brockover, Richard 295
Brockover, Richd. 295
Brodbeck, Elizabeth 278
Broderick, Absalom 259
Brodley, Catrona 464
Brodrick, Clarinda 548
Brodrick, Mark A. 548
Brodrick, Nehemiah F. 548
Brodwell, Ebenezer B. 201
Brogan, John 664
Brogan, Patrick 40
Bromage, John 298
Brombaugh, Henry 189, 201, 202
Bromly, Richard 518
Bronson, Aaron A. 601, 604
Bronson, Abraham 8
Bronson, Albert 28
Bronson, Augustus 601, 603
Bronson, C. P. (Rev.) 28
Bronson, Esther Eliza 601
Bronson, Eunice 28
Bronson, George W. 8
Bronson, Hannah C. 601, 603
Bronson, James H. 8
Bronson, John E. 8
Bronson, Mary 8
Bronson, Nancy 610, 620
Bronson, Philana Ann 8
Bronson, Rebecca B. 8
Bronson, Robert 8
Bronson, Sarah 8
Bronson, William 8
Broocks, John 76
Brook, Benjamin 563
Brook, Liddy 563
Brook, Lidy 563
Brook, Mary 563
Brook, Robert F. 363
Brookover, Richard 290, 298
Brookover, Richd. 295
Brookover, Sarah 712
Brooks, Agnes 476
Brooks, Andrew 76
Brooks, Ann 350
Brooks, Anna 353
Brooks, Ben. 478
Brooks, Benj. 476
Brooks, Benj. (Jr.) 477
Brooks, Benj. (Sr.) 476, 477
Brooks, Calvin W. 28
Brooks, Catherine 85, 380
Brooks, Charles 585

Brooks, Christiana 78
Brooks, David 350, 353
Brooks, David Henry 62
Brooks, Elijah 524
Brooks, Eliza 380
Brooks, Elizabeth 77, 126
Brooks, Elmana 588
Brooks, Francis 350, 353
Brooks, Gilbert 380
Brooks, I. W. 761
Brooks, James 82
Brooks, James M. 524
Brooks, John 500, 716
Brooks, John R. 254
Brooks, Jonathan 585
Brooks, Lewis 155
Brooks, Linch 481, 482
Brooks, M. D. 378, 380
Brooks, Margaret 254, 350, 353
Brooks, Mary 76, 85, 353
Brooks, Mathew 82
Brooks, Moses 427
Brooks, Nancy 85
Brooks, Philip 254, 255
Brooks, Polly 82
Brooks, Rachel 85
Brooks, Rebecca 84, 524
Brooks, Richard 633
Brooks, Ruth 254
Brooks, Samuel C. 524
Brooks, Sarah 28, 125, 254, 350, 353
Brooks, William 583
Broom, Edward 511
Broom, Sarah 517
Brophy, John 731
Brotherlin, Christian 461
Brothers, Barbara 553
Brough, John 222, 729
Brough, Sophia 222
Brougher, Polly 385
Broughton, Jno. 731, 733
Broughton, John 731
Broun, Abram 108
Broun, Elizabeth 108
Broun, Joseph 108
Broun, Margaret 108
Brower, Christian 182
Brower, George 207, 218
Brower, John 182
Brower, Lewis 303
Brower, William 184
Brown, --- (Gen.) 128
Brown, A. L. 495
Brown, Aaron 25, 511
Brown, Abner 763
Brown, Abraham 748
Brown, Ada 326
Brown, Adam 348, 432, 492, 588
Brown, Agusta 28
Brown, Ajuleah 718
Brown, Alexander 248, 263, 270
Brown, Alexander W. 606
Brown, Alfred 763, 764

Brown, Alpheus 557
Brown, Andrew 451
Brown, Ann 107
Brown, Arthur 676
Brown, Asa 357, 657
Brown, Augustus G. 149
Brown, Barnard 571
Brown, Belinda 348
Brown, Benjamin 82, 365, 461, 759, 763, 764
Brown, Benjamin L. 447
Brown, Benjamin S. 5
Brown, Betsey 12, 589
Brown, C. 326
Brown, C. M. 581
Brown, Caroline 207, 522
Brown, Caroline L. 542
Brown, Catharine 583
Brown, Catherine 326
Brown, Charles 432, 636, 638
Brown, Chester 518
Brown, Christian 588
Brown, Christina 558
Brown, Clarissa 498, 716
Brown, Clarissa A. 683
Brown, Clayton 429
Brown, Clement 487
Brown, Daniel 147, 461, 528, 530
Brown, David 286, 337, 432, 683, 688
Brown, David J. 495
Brown, David Tiplon 408
Brown, Dexter 267
Brown, Dianna 455
Brown, Dixon 377, 378
Brown, Drucilla 590
Brown, Edward 455
Brown, Elenor 638
Brown, Elijah 460
Brown, Eliza 514, 585
Brown, Elizabeth 21, 137, 333, 462, 609
Brown, Elizabeth P. 70, 109
Brown, Elmer C. 326
Brown, Emett R. 326
Brown, Emily 496
Brown, Emma J. 38
Brown, Ephraim C. 635
Brown, Esther 373
Brown, Ethan Allen 258
Brown, Ezra 524, 765
Brown, Fanny 143
Brown, Francis 143
Brown, Geo. W. 59
Brown, George 280, 432, 511, 595, 596, 597
Brown, George W. 307, 310, 314
Brown, Hannah 429, 502, 503
Brown, Harvey 635
Brown, Henry 162, 192, 382, 414, 558
Brown, Henry A. 337
Brown, Henry C. 143
Brown, Hiram 432

Brown, Hiram L. J.   271
Brown, Hugh   159
Brown, I. A.   326
Brown, Isaac   119, 278,
  362, 378, 583
Brown, Isabell   20
Brown, Isabella   143
Brown, Isadore   326
Brown, Israeil (Sr.)   172
Brown, J.   355
Brown, Jacob   271, 404,
  432
Brown, James   18, 46,
  65, 86, 119, 123,
  201, 209, 217, 271,
  379, 445, 461, 487,
  638, 672, 688, 716
Brown, James (Jr.)   492
Brown, James (Sr.)   289
Brown, James H.   109
Brown, James R.   143
Brown, James Thomas   109
Brown, Jane   109, 137,
  445, 580, 638
Brown, Jefferson D.   412
Brown, Jeptha   518
Brown, Jeremiah   397
Brown, Jeremiah P.   495
Brown, John   59, 123,
  158, 166, 263, 299,
  303, 374, 420, 432,
  455, 474, 475, 477,
  482, 483, 484, 486,
  502, 503, 635, 713,
  716, 742
Brown, John (Jr.)   502,
  503
Brown, John C. P.   628
Brown, John M.   143, 635
Brown, Jonas   432, 571
Brown, Jonathan   432, 588
Brown, Joseph   23, 137,
  184, 200, 201, 354,
  392, 421, 432, 470,
  638, 657
Brown, Joseph S.   350
Brown, Joshua   370, 382
Brown, Josiah   70
Brown, Kitty   455
Brown, Lemuel G.   635
Brown, Lesly   455
Brown, Levi B.   404
Brown, Lola M.   326
Brown, Lottie   746
Brown, Loyd   372
Brown, Lucinda   404
Brown, Lucretia   455
Brown, Lucy   65, 392, 392
Brown, Luther   495
Brown, Mannual   588
Brown, Margaret   128, 129
Brown, Maria   307
Brown, Marshall   76
Brown, Martha   638
Brown, Martha Ann   432
Brown, Martin   588
Brown, Martin H.   143
Brown, Mary   137, 415,
  420, 510, 638

Brown, Mary Ann   432, 520
Brown, Mary D.   635
Brown, Mary Jane   683,
  688
Brown, Mary Lucy   635
Brown, Mary T.   143
Brown, Mary W.   31, 271
Brown, Mathew   341
Brown, Matilda   143
Brown, Matilda
  Mossbarger Canoel   410
Brown, Michael   427, 676
Brown, Miles K.   143
Brown, Moses   382
Brown, Nancy   137, 299,
  661
Brown, Nancy Colis   411
Brown, Nathan   432
Brown, Nathan (Jr.)   417
Brown, Nehemiah   432
Brown, Nicholas   86
Brown, Oliver   471
Brown, Pearly   635
Brown, Pearly G.   635
Brown, Peggy   466
Brown, Phillip   143
Brown, Phoebe   143
Brown, Polly   77, 374,
  480, 715, 716
Brown, R. M.   366
Brown, Rachel   406, 487,
  514
Brown, Rebecca   487
Brown, Richard   432, 487
Brown, Robert   123, 271,
  416
Brown, Roy J.   326
Brown, Ruth   14
Brown, S.   326
Brown, S. L.   326
Brown, Sally   130, 715
Brown, Sally Ann   530
Brown, Samuel   429, 571,
  684
Brown, Samuel H.   635
Brown, Samuel S.   432
Brown, Sarah   43, 65,
  372, 432
Brown, Sarah A.   143
Brown, Sarah E.   711
Brown, Sarah R.   271
Brown, Selome   495
Brown, Solomon   259, 348
Brown, Spencer   290
Brown, Stacy   683
Brown, Stanton H.   495
Brown, Stephen   33, 34,
  169
Brown, Susan   521
Brown, Susan F.   326
Brown, Susie   466
Brown, Tabitha   395
Brown, Thomas   28, 123,
  132, 135, 200, 462,
  751
Brown, Thos.   455, 503
Brown, Truston P.   395
Brown, Viola Clements
  410

Brown, Will   460
Brown, William   16, 46,
  116, 200, 326, 406,
  428, 462, 638, 716
Brown, William A.   585
Brown, Winnie Grace   410
Brown, Wm.   170, 264,
  299, 406, 455, 638
Brown, Wm. D.   432
Browne, William   184
Browning, John   262,
  303, 305
Browning, Judith   380
Browning, Oliver   380
Browning, William   713
Brownsberger, John   762
Brownsberger, Joseph   765
Brownwell, Patience   716
Brubacher, Henry   317,
  318, 319, 320
Brubaker, Abraham   500
Brubaker, John   349, 500
Brubaker, Peter   602, 606
Bruce, Catharine   180
Bruce, Charles   426
Bruce, Elias M.   143
Bruce, Hannah   31
Bruce, Jackson H.   534
Bruce, John   180
Bruce, Louisa   143
Bruce, William   740
Brudle, David   334
Bruen, David H.   216
Bruen, John   261
Bruen, Luther   204, 213,
  229
Bruer, John   511
Bruff, Mary   460
Brumage, Alexander
  Wilson   349, 355
Brumage, Comfort   355
Brumage, Elizabeth   356
Brumage, Hannah   356
Brumage, Henry   356
Brumage, Henry Wilson
  349
Brumage, John   349, 352,
  356
Brumage, Joseph   356
Brumage, Lucy   356
Brumage, Lucy Ann   349
Brumage, Mariah   356
Brumage, Rebecca   356
Brumbaugh, Franklin   413
Brumbaugh, Jacob   137
Brundewick, Simeon   721
Bruner, Geo. (Jr.)   366
Bruner, George   163, 165
Bruner, Mary   366
Bruner, Nancy   526
Bruner, Peter   526
Brunier, Firmin   724
Brunier, Madalane   713
Brunier, Rebecca   747
Brunk, Sarah   749
Brunner, Elizabeth   336
Brunner, Geo.   364
Brunner, Geo. (Sr.)   366
Brunner, George   369, 372

Brunner, Lydia 404
Brunson, Sally M. 28
Brush, Daniel 166, 171
Brush, G. H. 330
Brush, H. 63
Brush, Jared 293
Brush, John T. 529
Brush, L. C. 330
Brush, Louisa C. 330
Brush, Luella P. 330
Brush, M. W. 330
Brush, Mariet G. 330
Brush, Marriett M. 330
Brush, Mary A. 330
Brush, Nancy 166, 171
Brush, Susan Albina 529
Brush, William H. 330
Brush, Zachry 330
Brust, Elizabeth 410
Bryan, Elizabeth 455
Bryan, George 137
Bryan, Henry 542
Bryan, James 155, 542
Bryan, James D. 542
Bryan, Jesse 542
Bryan, John 720
Bryan, Joseph 731
Bryan, Josiah 160, 164
Bryan, Mary 164
Bryan, Sarah 548, 549
Bryan, William 462, 548
Bryant, Betsey 35
Bryant, Betsy 416
Bryant, Jacob 429
Bryant, John 487, 492,
  657
Bryant, Josiah 164
Bryant, Mary 164
Bryant, William 416
Bryfogle, Benjamin 555
Bryson, Elizabeth 180
Bryson, Susannah 152
Bucham, Henry 461
Buchanan, James 356
Buchanan, James H. 356
Buchanan, Mary Ann 153
Buchanan, Phebe 356
Buchanan, William 153,
  175
Buchannan, Adam 492
Buchannan, James 487
Bucher, H. 103
Buches, Daniel 224
Buches, Samuel 224
Buck, --- 465
Buck, --- (Capt.) 89
Buck, Ann 455
Buck, Cal 534
Buck, Elizabeth 385
Buck, George 172
Buck, James 416, 596
Buck, Joseph 455
Buck, Margaret 513
Buck, Maria 30
Buck, Sarah 513
Buck, Susannah 513
Buck, Titus 716
Bucker, J. Dederick 114
Buckfield, John 40

Buckhannon, Mary 659
Buckhanon, Cloner 662
Buckingham, Alexander
  539
Buckingham, Alvah 290,
  731
Buckingham, Catharines
  Putnens 290
Buckingham, E. (Jr.) 296
Buckingham, Ebenezer
  290, 295, 296
Buckingham, Ebenezer
  (Jr.) 294, 296
Buckingham, Esther 290
Buckingham, Eunice 290
Buckingham, Maria 539
Buckingham, Matilda 290
Buckingham, Sarah 290
Buckingham, Stephen 295,
  716
Buckingham, W. 626
Buckland, Cynthia 30
Buckles, Elizabeth 657
Buckles, Susannah 500
Bucklin, Albert 744
Bucklin, Lucinda 746
Buckman, Jacob 728, 729
Buckman, Jehial P. 588
Buckmaster, Samuel 741
Buckwalter, Benjamin 201
Buckwalter, Daniel 201
Buckwalter, John 201
Buckwalter, Mary 201
Buckwater, Henry 21
Buckwater, Susannah 21
Bucy, Mary Jane 90
Budd, Eli 333
Budy, Walter 711
Buechner, Frederic
  Christopher 225
Buekman, Jacob 729
Buel, Elijah 495
Buel, Eliza A. 71
Buel, Eliza M. 71
Buel, George M. 71
Buel, Lovina 71
Buel, Lyman C. 71
Buel, Martha E. 71
Buel, Samuel 71
Buel, Samuel M. 71
Buel, Sidney K. 71
Buel, Tresse 570
Buel, Warren 529
Buele, Polly 463
Buell, Ebenezer 729
Buell, Joseph 728, 729
Buell, Susan W. 710
Buell, Timothy 729
Buell, Walter 485
Buffermere, George 739
Buffing, Abigal 117
Buffington, Cloe 84
Buffington, Elenor 137
Buffington, Elizabeth 80
Buffington, Hiram 137
Buffington, Milley 78
Buffington, Philip T. 82
Buffington, Polly 126
Buffington, Sarah 83

Buffington, William 713
Buffington, Wm. H. 76
Buges, Daniel 606
Bugh, Catherine 353
Bugh, Charlotta 353
Bugh, Elizabeth 357
Bugh, Israel 353
Bugh, Jacob 353
Bugh, James T. 755
Bugh, Jesse 357
Bugh, John 353
Bugh, Mary 357
Bugh, Michael 353
Bugh, Milla 354
Bugh, Peter 353, 355, 362
Bugh, Peter (Jr.) 353
Bugh, Peter (Sr.) 353,
  362
Bugh, Susanna 353
Bugh, William 353
Buickman, Elizabeth 573
Bukels, James 123
Bukley, Josephus B. 250,
  251
Bulkley, Emily 35
Bull, Emmele C. 558
Bull, Fidelia 761
Bull, George Washington
  558
Bull, Hezekiah 558
Bull, Jacob 548
Bull, Louisa W. 558
Bull, Maria 558
Bull, Sarah 444
Bullard, William 495
Bullenbaugh, Peter 114,
  599, 606
Bullenbaugher, Margaret
  606
Buller, Daniel 25
Buller, Henry 293
Buller, James 11, 266,
  271
Bullersen, Abijiah 504
Bullett, Alexander Scott
  505
Bullett, Catherine 505
Bullett, Henry 26, 505
Bullett, N. 505
Bullett, Wm. C. 505
Bullitt, Alexander Scott
  26
Bullitt, Cuthbert 26
Bullitt, N. 26
Bullitt, William C. 26
Bullman, A. F. William
  102
Bullman, Caroline 102
Bumbardner, Daniel 116
Bumgardner, Susannah 119
Bummer, Elizabeth 336
Bumtrager, David 679
Bunch, Peter 219
Bundle, William 657
Bundy, Caroline 637
Bundy, George 626, 678
Bundy, H. S. 635, 637
Bundy, Reuben 16
Bundy, Sally 16

Bungelman, Bernerd 104
Bunhon, Moses 764
Bunker, Reuben 280
Bunkerhoff, Mary Ann 519
Bunn, Polly 463
Bunnel, Abigail 660
Bunnel, Alfred 653
Bunnel, Beza 653
Bunnel, Catharine 640
Bunnel, Daniel 640
Bunnel, David 653
Bunnel, Hannah 512
Bunnel, John 653
Bunnel, Noah 640
Bunnel, Samuel 640
Bunnell, Abner 655
Bunnell, Ann 655
Bunnell, David 670
Bunnell, James 670
Bunnell, Jonas 670
Bunnell, Mary 670
Bunnell, Nathaniel 670
Bunnell, Rhoda 670
Bunnell, Stephen 670
Bunnell, Stephen (Sr.)
  670
Bunnell, Thos. J. 413
Bunston, William (Jr.)
  686
Bunston, William (Sr.)
  686
Bunting, Catharine 161
Bunting, Thomas A. 159,
  161
Buntlinger, John 393
Bunton, Elsa Hester 662
Buntreger, John 565
Buntriger, Catharine 566
Bupp, Emily J. 534
Bupp, John 534
Burch, Jemima 152
Burch, Jemina 155
Burch, Sarah 92
Burck, Alvira 278
Burden, Anna 559
Burden, David 559
Burden, Hannah 559
Burden, Job 559
Burden, Levi 559
Burden, Lidia 559
Burden, Mary 559
Burden, Rachel 559
Burden, Reuben 559
Burden, Sarah 559
Burder, Elizabeth 666
Burdett, Booth 542
Burdick, Elizabeth 593
Burdick, Reuben 585
Burdick, Sias 585
Burdoon, Barbara 348
Burdy, George 626
Bureau, J. P. 726
Bureau, J. P. R. 724
Bureau, J. P. Romaine
  723
Bureau, John Peter
  Romain 723, 724, 726
Bureau, John Peter
  Romaine 724

Bureau, P. 724, 725
Bureau, Peter 723
Bureer, Ann 455
Buress, Harriett 514
Burford, James 716
Burg, Henry K. 556
Burgabill, Peter 281
Burgan, Catherine 455
Burgan, John 72
Burgan, Maryette 72
Burgan, Wm. 455
Burge, Adams 28
Burge, Christian 594
Burger, George 605
Burgess, Ann 379
Burgess, Betsey 15
Burgess, Elizabeth 630,
  676
Burgess, Elizabeth W.
  634
Burgess, Joseph 379
Burgess, Mary Ann 676
Burgess, Nancy Lyons 676
Burgess, Oliver 531
Burgess, Price 676
Burgess, Rebecca 676
Burgess, Susannah 376
Burgess, Thompson 676
Burgess, West 676
Burget, D. 557
Burget, George 438
Burgett, George 439, 441
Burgett, Hullday 383
Burgett, Susan 441
Burgett, Thomas 441
Burghman, Abraham 69
Burghman, Amanda 69
Burghman, Betsey 69
Burghman, Elias 69
Burghman, Fritt 69
Burghman, George 69
Burghman, Isaac 69
Burghman, Jacob 69
Burghman, Peggy 69
Burghman, Polly 69
Burghman, Susan 69
Burgman, Charistian 137
Burgman, Elizabeth 137
Burgman, Jacob 137
Burgman, John P. 137
Burgoon, Charles 272
Burgoon, David 356
Burgoon, Edith 356
Burgoon, Elizabeth 356
Burgoon, Francis 356
Burgoon, Jacob 356
Burgoon, James 261, 262
Burgoon, Levi 354
Burgoon, Mary 356
Burgoon, Peter 260,
  262, 356
Burgoon, Rachel 356
Burgoon, Teressa 356
Burgoon, William 356
Burgram, John 119
Burham, William 713
Burill, Lavina 22
Burk, Anna 451
Burk, John 512

Burk, Samuel 657
Burk, Sophia 30
Burk, William 503
Burke, John 656
Burke, Wm. M. 501
Burket, Andrew 119
Burket, Ann 355
Burket, Catherine 355
Burket, Geo. Ammon 355
Burket, John Marks 355
Burket, Joseph 355
Burket, Margaret 355
Burket, Martha 355
Burket, Mary 355
Burket, Michael 355
Burket, Micheal 279
Burket, Nathaniel 194
Burket, Rose Ann 355
Burket, Sally 116
Burkey, Daniel 354
Burkey, David 354
Burkey, Henry 354
Burkey, John 354
Burkey, Lydia 354
Burkey, Martin 354
Burkey, Michael 354
Burkey, Rachel 354
Burkey, Samuel 354
Burkey, Susana 354
Burkhard, Elizabeth 190
Burkhard, John 199
Burkhart, Peter 748
Burkholder, Samuel 40
Burkley, Harley 461, 462
Burkman, Abraham 69
Burkman, Amanda 69
Burkman, Betsey 69
Burkman, Elias 69
Burkman, Fritt 69
Burkman, George 69
Burkman, Isaac 69
Burkman, Jacob 69
Burkman, John P. 143
Burkman, Peggy 69
Burkman, Polly 69
Burkman, Susan 69
Burkman, Susannah C. 143
Burl, Walter 484
Burley, Benjamin 54
Burley, David 43
Burley, Wm. W. 316
Burlingame, Christopher
  721
Burlinggame, Sukey 721
Burnam, Elba 585
Burnam, Eliphaz 595
Burnam, Jacob 585, 595
Burnam, Julliett 595
Burnam, Lorinda 585
Burnam, Lydia 595
Burnam, Nancy 595
Burnam, Orvilla 595
Burnam, William 595
Burnam, Zelinda H. 595
Burnass, Silas A. 76
Burnem, Sally 119
Burner, Hampson 4
Burnes, John 40
Burness, Harriett 514

Burnet, John 679
Burnet, Joseph 495
Burnet, Susan 495, 496
Burnett, F. M. 700
Burnett, Isaac (Jr.) 743
Burnett, Isaac (Sr.) 743
Burnett, M. 700
Burnett, Rachel B. 496
Burnett, Ralph 542
Burnett, Roy W. 700
Burnham, Andrew 597
Burnham, Aurelia 586
Burnham, Aurilla 581
Burnham, Christian 723
Burnham, David 585, 597
Burnham, Harvey 585, 597, 598
Burnham, James 63
Burnham, Maryette 73
Burnham, Milton 73
Burnham, William 299, 720, 723, 730
Burniel, Hannah 512
Burns, Adam 664
Burns, Anne 127
Burns, Benjamin F. 43
Burns, Errilla 129
Burns, Esther 116
Burns, Francis 492
Burns, George 86, 518
Burns, Jane 463
Burns, John 358, 632, 640
Burns, Joseph 462
Burns, Judy 125
Burns, Laura 81
Burns, Marion 452
Burns, Mary 632
Burns, Matthew 640
Burns, Ora 409
Burns, Rach 657
Burns, Roan 118
Burns, Thomas P. 657
Burnsides, Alexander 492
Burnsides, Elen 153
Burnsides, Francis 153
Burnsides, Isabella 153
Burnsides, James 153
Burnsides, Jane 153
Burnsides, John 11
Burnsides, Thomas 153
Burnsides, Thos. 153
Burnsides, William 153
Burntriger, Andrew 641
Burntriger, Daniel 641
Burntriger, David 641
Burntriger, Elizabeth 641, 665
Burntriger, Mary 641
Burntriger, Sarah 641
Burntrigger, Daniel 649
Burntrigger, David 649
Burntrigger, Elizabeth 649
Burntrigger, Sarah 649
Burntrigger, Susan 649
Burr, Peter 487
Burrass, Patience 119
Burraws, Robert 620

Burrel, Francis 462
Burrel, Richard 560, 571
Burrell, Abraham 36
Burrell, Daniel H. 36
Burrell, Eliza 32
Burrell, Eunice 29
Burrell, Isaac 28
Burrell, Sally 31
Burrell, Saloma 31
Burress, George (Jr.) 637
Burress, John 560
Burridge, Alden L. 606
Burright, Asahel 599
Burright, Orin 620
Burright, Owen 599
Burrill, John 757
Burrill, Nancy 717
Burris, Alexander Walker 114
Burris, Ann G. 54
Burris, Anne Garnett 54
Burris, Benj. 731
Burris, Charity 114
Burris, Henry (Sr.) 502
Burris, John 731
Burris, Martin 114
Burris, Samuel 46
Burris, Sarah Maria 54
Burroughs, Betsey 76
Burroughs, John H. 352
Burroughs, Joseph 76
Burroway, Isaac 729
Burroway, Mary 566
Burroway, Michael 565
Burrows, Alishia 64
Burrows, Jonathan 585
Burrows, Jos. 137
Burrows, Mary 582
Burrows, Matilda A. 137
Burrows, Nancy 510
Burrows, Patience 662
Burrows, Robert 602, 603
Burrows, Susan 602, 603
Burrows, Susanna 137
Burshu, Menroth 343
Burshus, Michael 343
Burshuw, Mary Ann 343
Burson, Eden 432
Burson, Fian 604
Burson, James 604
Burson, Joseph 307
Burson, Phebe 303
Burt, Anna 513
Burt, Christopher 512
Burt, Elizabeth 516
Burt, Julia 337
Burt, Lot 333
Burt, William 512
Burtch, William J. 606
Burting, Thomas 157
Burtis, John 40
Burton, Catherine 665
Burton, Elizabeth 167, 179, 180
Burton, Isaac 356
Burton, Jarver 356
Burton, John 167, 179, 180

Burton, William 159, 382
Burtzfield, Matthias 560
Burus, Alexander 154
Burwell, Jno. 291
Burwell, Phebe 593
Burwell, Sarah 589
Bury, Elizabeth 609
Busack, Benjamin 382
Busch, Herman Henry 103
Bush, Abraham 657
Bush, Adia 375
Bush, Elizabeth 613
Bush, Eve 453
Bush, Frederick 399
Bush, Hannah 455, 462
Bush, Henry C. 524
Bush, John 613
Bush, M. 524
Bush, Martha 375
Bush, Mary 573
Bush, Nancy 613
Bush, W. 524
Busheng, Delilee 24
Busheng, Gemima 24
Busheng, Jacob 24
Busheng, James 24
Busheng, John 24
Busheng, Nancy 24
Busherd, Jesse 403
Bushman, H. H. 542
Bushong, Daniel 575
Bushong, Nancy L. 21
Busick, Arthur A. 46
Busick, Sarah 43
Buskirk, Carity 175
Buskirk, Elem V. 92
Buskirk, Hamel 155
Buskirk, Hannah 573
Buskirk, John 174, 455
Buskirk, Lewis 483
Buskirk, Mary 174
Buskirk, Samuel 174, 175
Bussard, Jonathan 628
Bussard, Mary G. 635
Bussard, Polly G. 628
Bussick, Margaret 522
Bussing, John 606
Butcher, --- 412
Butcher, Emily Scurlock 410
Butcher, Joseph 185
Butcher, Matthias 185
Butenhall, Mary 464
Buthe, Hannah Mion 714
Butler, Abraham B. 681, 684
Butler, Absolom 565
Butler, Clarinda 594
Butler, Henry 295
Butler, Isaac 716
Butler, John 159, 174
Butler, Joseph 575
Butler, Justus 28
Butler, Lawrence 394
Butler, Mason Randall 411
Butler, Paul D. 182, 223
Butler, Richard (Maj. Gen.) 98

795

Butler, Sarah 747
Butler, Stephen 439
Butlers, Margarett 279
Butman, Benjamin F. 518
Butolph, Rachel 31
Butt, Barbary 537
Butt, Chas. 571
Butt, Elizabeth 569, 570
Butt, Esther 241
Butt, Harriet 432
Butt, Jacob 212, 241, 537
Butt, Jonathan 432
Butt, Michael 505
Butt, Peggy 565
Butt, Solomon 212, 241
Butt, Valentine 212
Butt, William 563, 565
Buttain, Mary Ann 400
Buttain, William 400
Butter, Sarah 573
Butterbaugh, Henry 557
Butterbaugh, Sarah 743
Butterfield, Mary 518
Butterworth, Henry 683
Butterworth, Norman 683
Butterworth, William 684
Buttner, Anna Margaret 607
Buttolph, George 28
Button, Philemon 632
Button, Sarah M. 632
Butts, Robert 391
Buxenburg, Peter 43
Buxton, Thomas 338
Buzaway, Isaac 297
Buzelen, Elizabeth 717
Buzett, Edward F. 137
Buzett, Margaret A. 137
Buzett, Melissa 137
Buzett, Rachel 137
Buzett, Wm. H. 137
Buzkirk, Chas. 571
Buzzard, Eli 76
Buzzard, John 487
Buzzard, Malicha 571
Buzzard, Peter 571
Buzzard, Sarah Jane 625
Buzzaway, Isaac 297
Byard, Elizabeth 51
Byard, Saray 85
Bye, Charles R. 399
Byer, Jacob 606
Byerley, Richard 542
Byerly, Richard 108
Byerly, Susanna 566
Byers, A. H. 741
Byers, Benjamin C. 741
Byers, Catharine M. 578
Byers, Frances 744
Byers, Isaac 487
Byers, James 55
Byers, Jane 55
Byers, John 55
Byers, Moses W. 55
Byers, Rachel 542
Byers, Robert 225
Byers, Samuel 542, 548
Byers, Susanna Ann 55

Byers, Thomas 262, 267
Byers, William 225
Byers, William (Jr.) 512
Byers, William (Sr.) 512
Byers, Wm. (Jr.) 512
Byers, Wm. (Sr.) 512
Bynds, Joseph 334
Byres, Abraham 635
Byres, Isaac 415
Byres, Polly 415
Byrk, Elizabeth 116
Byrket, Jacob 224
Byrket, Joseph 119
Byrket, Sarah 120
Byrkit, Mary 126
Byrley, William 548
Byrne, Charles 428
Byrne, Editha Ann 354
Byrne, Edward 354
Byrnes, Matthew 40
Byrode, Rebecca 745
Bysell, Rufus 506
Bysell, Sarah 506

--- C ---

Caan, Mary 383
Cabeer, Samuel 293
Cabell, Robert T. 394
Cabell, Samuel I. 394
Cable, George 82
Cable, John 133
Cableman, Kate 412
Cace, Jacob 279
Cachel, . . . 661
Cachel, Daniel 657
Caddington, Zachariah 247
Caddington, Zechariah 267
Caddot, Jean 713
Cadot, Claude 723, 724, 725
Cadot, Jane 724
Cadot, Mary Louis 514
Cadwallader, Hannah 496
Cadwallader, Jonah 683
Cadwell, Peter 267, 272
Cadwill, Catharine 575
Cady, James 731
Cady, John 518
Cady, Joseph 677
Cady, Thos. 379
Caffee, Amos H. 440
Caffee, Hannah 440
Caffee, John 301
Caggard, Anne 156
Caggard, David 156
Cahill, Anne 572
Cahill, James 529
Cahill, Mary 574
Cahill, Richard 739
Cahoon, James D. 82
Cahoon, Jesse S. 28
Cahoon, Nancy 459
Cahoon, Wilber (Jr.) 28
Cailes, Betsey 453

Caims, Nancy 335
Cain, Alfred 161
Cain, Amelia 657
Cain, Anna Jane 368
Cain, Chas. C. 357
Cain, Daniel G. 357
Cain, David 542
Cain, Eliza 357
Cain, Ellenor 357
Cain, Henry 11, 16
Cain, Henry J. 542
Cain, James 351, 358, 542
Cain, Jasper 358
Cain, Joana 357
Cain, John 357, 637
Cain, John B. 357
Cain, Joseph 358
Cain, Joshua 16
Cain, Mary 161, 371
Cain, Melinda 357
Cain, Nancy 357
Cain, Nathaniel C. 357
Cain, Nehemiah C. 357
Cain, Phebey 357
Cain, Pheby 357
Cain, Priscilla 357, 358
Cain, Richard 154
Cain, Sally 12
Cain, Sarah 368
Cain, Thomas 368
Cain, Walter 249
Cain, William 358, 368
Cain, Wm. 269
Caine, Sarah 666
Cairns, Joseph 450
Caken, Margaret 567
Calahan, Rebecca 84
Calder, James 76
Calderhead, E. B. 355
Calderhead, Ebenezer B. 369
Caldwell, Aaron 40
Caldwell, Ada M. 734
Caldwell, Agnes 742
Caldwell, Alex 406
Caldwell, Alexander 393
Caldwell, Andrew M. 432
Caldwell, Ann 314
Caldwell, Catharine 393
Caldwell, Catherine 393, 453
Caldwell, Davis 137
Caldwell, Diana 577
Caldwell, Eliza 137
Caldwell, Elizabeth 406
Caldwell, Elzy 314
Caldwell, Gray 137
Caldwell, Henry 76, 406
Caldwell, Henry Poindexter 432
Caldwell, Hetty 78
Caldwell, Isabella 742
Caldwell, James 123, 137, 177, 382
Caldwell, James D. 397
Caldwell, James E. 76
Caldwell, Jane 742
Caldwell, Jas. C. 432

Caldwell, Jerry 202
Caldwell, John 76, 268, 303, 416, 432
Caldwell, John C. 406
Caldwell, John W. 87, 137
Caldwell, Joseph 137, 492
Caldwell, Margaret 742
Caldwell, Mary 432, 742
Caldwell, Mary J. 137
Caldwell, Mary Jane 137
Caldwell, Matthew 137
Caldwell, Nancy 77, 406
Caldwell, Pemberton 137
Caldwell, Rebecca Davis 137
Caldwell, Robert 742
Caldwell, Robert M. 542
Caldwell, Robt. 267
Caldwell, Sally 137
Caldwell, Samuel 25, 137, 302, 641, 742
Caldwell, Samuel Newton 143
Caldwell, Sarah 509
Caldwell, Sidney 393
Caldwell, Stephen 137
Caldwell, Thomas 542
Caldwell, W. B. 406
Cale, Francis 93
Calender, Caprel 744
Calender, John 43
Calender, Leah 177
Calfe, John 723
Calhoon, David 284
Calhoun, Abner 11
Calhoun, Eleanor 294
Calhoun, James 43
Calkins, Daniel 357
Calkins, Hester 357
Calkins, Mathew 525
Calkins, Samuel G. 357
Call, Elizabeth 517
Call, James 338
Call, Margaret 516
Callahan, Alexander 683
Callahan, Mary 759
Callahan, Rachel 386
Callaman, John 503
Callamon, John 529
Calland, Joseph 175
Callanon, Catharine 529
Callanon, John 529
Callaway, Abigail 87
Callehan, Mary 292
Callender, Nancy 466
Callender, Rachel 46
Callton, Benous 401
Calver, --- 459
Calver, Angeline 586
Calver, Caroline 585
Calver, Rachel 464
Calvert, Francis 731
Calvert, Joel 731
Calvert, Polly 524
Calvert, Sarah 524
Calvin, Eli W. 766
Calvin, James 33

Calvin, John 495
Calvin, Unice 497
Calwell, Hannah 586
Camb, Joseph 669
Cambell, Mariah 664
Camble, Ishable 382
Cambridge, James 451
Camear, Elizabeth 497
Cameeon, Donald 320
Cameron, Alexander 557
Cameron, Catherine 718
Cameron, Eliza 740
Cameron, James (Rev.) 605
Camfield, Anna 503
Camfield, Ebenezer 503
Camfield, Mary 503
Camfield, Rachel 503
Camfield, Sary 503
Camfield, Sibble 503
Camfield, Subrution 503
Cammon, Fredrick August 107
Cammon, John C. W. 107
Cammon, John C. Wm. 107
Cammon, Mary 46
Cammon, Mary Louise 107
Camp, Augusta 242
Camp, Caroline 496
Camp, Catharine 523
Camp, Elizabeth 523
Camp, Frances 522
Camp, Harvey (Rev.) 594
Camp, Mary A. 242
Camp, Peter 242
Camp, Samuel 731
Campbel, Lellis 659
Campbel, Sarah 516
Campbell, A. 293
Campbell, Able 554
Campbell, Achillis 401
Campbell, Alexander 401
Campbell, Alzina H. 432
Campbell, Andrew 67, 542
Campbell, Archibald 293, 382
Campbell, Benjamin 402, 554
Campbell, Bernard 357
Campbell, Bethany 67
Campbell, Charles (Col.) 473
Campbell, David (Rev.) 531
Campbell, Dugal 554
Campbell, Ealoner 432
Campbell, Elih 692
Campbell, Elizabeth 143, 357
Campbell, Emily 401
Campbell, Ephraim 554
Campbell, George 11, 401
Campbell, Hamilton 337
Campbell, Henrietta 432
Campbell, Isaac 198
Campbell, Jackson 143, 542
Campbell, Jacob 403
Campbell, Jain 127

Campbell, James 11, 200, 401, 402, 553, 554, 692
Campbell, James (Jr.) 554
Campbell, James (Sr.) 554
Campbell, James S. 51
Campbell, Jane 384, 401, 739
Campbell, Jane Francus 403
Campbell, Jean 716
Campbell, Jesse (Jr.) 108
Campbell, Jno. 286
Campbell, John 67, 123, 261, 335, 392, 427, 542, 634, 657
Campbell, John D. 143, 184, 200, 432
Campbell, John Duncan 200
Campbell, John P. 488
Campbell, Johnston 67
Campbell, Joseph 67, 392, 405
Campbell, Judith 230
Campbell, Juliett 432
Campbell, Lizzie 692
Campbell, Lucy A. 401
Campbell, Margaret 143, 200, 534, 554
Campbell, Maria 590
Campbell, Mary 108, 357, 392, 405, 432, 554
Campbell, Mary A. 413
Campbell, Mary Ann 401
Campbell, Mary C. 413
Campbell, Mary Jane 401
Campbell, Mathew 357
Campbell, Nancy 392, 405, 713
Campbell, Peggy 51
Campbell, Pempey 401
Campbell, Peter 46
Campbell, Philip 357
Campbell, Pleasant 542
Campbell, Polly 514
Campbell, Rachael 554
Campbell, Rebeccah 453
Campbell, Richard 261, 686
Campbell, Robert 261, 392, 401, 462
Campbell, Ruth 554
Campbell, S. 67
Campbell, Samuel 483, 651
Campbell, Samuel A. 200
Campbell, Sarah 278, 405
Campbell, Sarah Ann 432
Campbell, Sarah B. 401
Campbell, Shach Bazar Bently 200
Campbell, Solomon 462
Campbell, Susan 496
Campbell, Susan Jane 429
Campbell, Susannah 67

Campbell, Susannah F. 432
Campbell, Temperance 692
Campbell, Thomas 274, 392
Campbell, Thomas W. 401
Campbell, Thos. 265, 272, 274
Campbell, Virginia 405
Campbell, Whitaker 401
Campbell, William 11, 67, 200, 392, 401, 413, 474, 488, 554
Campbell, William H. 230
Campbell, Wm. 420, 588
Campbell, Wm. D. 432
Campbell, Wm. H. H. 432
Campble, Bernard 357
Campble, Elizabeth 357
Campble, Jonathan 657
Campble, Kitty 663
Campble, Mary 357
Campble, Mathew 357
Camuson, Sarah 467
Can, James 187
Can, Moses 187
Canada, Thomas 512
Canaday, Catherine 380
Canahan, William W. 472
Canana, Susanna 121
Canary, James 159
Canby, Ann 8
Canby, Hannah 8
Canby, Israel 8
Canby, John 8
Canby, Joseph 8, 653, 676
Canby, Lydia 8
Canby, Margaret H. 8
Canby, Mary 8
Canby, Noah H. 8
Canby, Richard S. 8
Canby, Robert H. 8
Canby, Sarah B. 8
Candler, Jesse J. 46
Candles, Elizabeth 761
Cane, Anna Maria 249
Cane, George W. 249
Cane, James 123
Cane, Lydia 548
Cane, Sarah 548
Canear, . . . 167
Canfield, George W. 563
Canfield, Johnson 209
Canfield, Sally 756
Canfield, Thomas 46
Canfield, Tunis 209
Canfield, William 756
Cangrow, William 395
Canier, James 643
Canin, Mary 374
Canin, Michael 374
Canin, Robert 374
Cannell, Elizabeth 172
Cannell, John 172
Cannin, Almura 105
Cannon, Alsa 358
Cannon, Catherine 358
Cannon, George 358

Cannon, Hester 358
Cannon, Isaac 358
Cannon, James 548
Cannon, Jesse 395
Cannon, John 358
Cannon, Joseph 542
Cannon, Lowder 488
Cannon, Margaret 395
Cannon, Mary Ann 376
Cannon, Matthew W. 395
Cannon, Moses 123
Cannon, Richard 123
Cannon, Wesley 358
Cannon, William 358
Cannon, Wm. 376
Canoel, Matilda Mossbarger 410
Canon, Peter 684
Cantril, John 27
Caourson, June 461
Caples, Charles 621
Caples, Mary 567
Caples, Robert 565
Caples, Robert F. 565
Capman, Henry 354
Capman, John 354
Cappell, Robert 59
Capron, Mariamne 715
Capron, Welcome 123
Car, Harriet 522
Car, Solomon 441
Carbill, David 531
Carbill, Elmina 531
Carbill, George 531
Carbill, Isaac 531
Carbill, Phianna 531
Carder, Amsted 462
Carder, Sarah 488
Carder, William 488
Cardier, Christian 113
Carel, Sarah 666
Carey, Ansel 322
Carey, Aurel 325
Carey, Caroline 325
Carey, Cornelia C. 321
Carey, David C. 321, 325
Carey, Eliza Jane 325
Carey, Hannah 744
Carey, Henry H. 584
Carey, Isaac 321, 324, 325
Carey, John 744
Carey, Lydia Ann 325
Carey, Merina A. 321
Carey, Naomi 514
Carey, Rebecca 747
Carey, S. H. 325
Carey, Sarah A. 542
Carey, Sarah J. 542
Carey, Shadrach Hudson 335
Carey, Shadrack Hudson 325
Carey, Shadrack M. 321
Carey, Susy 512
Carey, William 325, 488
Carey, William S. 321
Carey, Wirona H. 325
Cargill, D. 539

Cargill, Mary A. 539
Carhart, John 300
Carhart, Margaret 296
Carhart, Nancy 300
Carhart, Seth 296, 300
Carhart, Teracy 300
Caris, Manach 571
Carl, David 210
Carl, James 210
Carl, John 210
Carl, Joshua 356
Carl, Mary 356
Carl, Sarah 658
Carland, Ann 260
Carland, John 260
Carle, Charles 209
Carle, David 209
Carle, Ephraim T. 731
Carle, Mary 334
Carle, William 209
Carleton, Abner 164
Carleton, Isaac 88
Carlick, Abraham 360
Carlick, Jesse 360
Carlile, Isabella 568
Carlile, James 571
Carlile, Leah 12
Carlile, Margaret 574
Carlin, James 760
Carlin, Lucius Thurston 760
Carlin, Susan 760
Carlisle, Archibald 20
Carlisle, John 484
Carlisle, Jonathan (Jr.) 287
Carlisle, Nancy 458
Carlisle, Sarah 571
Carlisle, Susannah 291
Carll, John 123
Carlow, John 259
Carlton, Mary 401
Carlton, Samuel 167, 178
Carmichael, James 162, 178
Carmichael, John 168, 175
Carmichael, Mary 168, 175, 178
Carmingham, Adam 571
Carmon, Patty 460
Carn, John Frederick 640
Carn, Mary 130
Carn, Peter 130
Carnahan, Adam 487
Carnahan, Elenor 383
Carneg, Willes 303
Carnell, Robert 597
Carner, Michael 11
Carnet, Rebecca 357
Carney, Hannah 591
Carney, Isaac 337
Carney, John 311
Carney, John (Rev.) 594
Carney, Naomi 592
Carney, Priscilla 311
Carney, Thomas 311
Carney, Willis 311
Caroll, Laura 112

Caroll, Rosetta 112
Caroll, William 112
Carolton, Mary 401
Carothers, Alice T. 700
Carothers, James 175
Carothers, Jennie F. 700
Carothers, Josiah 700
Carothers, Susannah 175
Carothers, Willie A. 700
Carpenter, Alexander 308, 309
Carpenter, B. G. 37
Carpenter, Barlow G. 36
Carpenter, Charles 200
Carpenter, Chester 279
Carpenter, Daniel 518
Carpenter, David 148, 751
Carpenter, E. 588
Carpenter, Elisha 455
Carpenter, Elizabeth 14
Carpenter, George 297, 664
Carpenter, Hannah 659
Carpenter, Hopkins 192, 200
Carpenter, John 297
Carpenter, Julia Ann 751
Carpenter, Julian 148
Carpenter, Lavina 309
Carpenter, Lewis R. 68
Carpenter, Lucinda 37
Carpenter, Lusenia 33
Carpenter, Lydia 75
Carpenter, Mariah 29
Carpenter, Mary 165, 168
Carpenter, Nancy 514
Carpenter, Patsy 511
Carpenter, Polly 80
Carpenter, Precilla 293
Carpenter, Rachel 666
Carpenter, Rebecca 451
Carpenter, Richard 309
Carpenter, Robert 165, 168
Carpenter, Sally 11
Carpenter, Samuel B. 495
Carpenter, Samuel C. 308, 309
Carpenter, Sarah 458
Carpenter, Susan 15
Carpenter, Thomas 192, 308, 309
Carpenter, Vincent 309
Carpenter, Wm. 512
Carper, Henry 542
Carr, Abigail 713
Carr, Alson 588
Carr, Aquilla 565
Carr, Benjamin 565
Carr, Chase 76
Carr, David 495
Carr, Hannah 362
Carr, Harry H. 429
Carr, Hezekiah 287
Carr, Hugh 571
Carr, Jacob 519
Carr, James 480
Carr, John 382

Carr, Lucinda 711
Carr, Lusina 628
Carr, Mary 572
Carr, Michael 596
Carr, Richard B. 571
Carr, Sarah 520
Carr, Susan 573
Carr, Thomas 744
Carr, William 565
Carr, Wm. 362
Carrago, Elenor 11
Carrago, Frances 15
Carraus, Margaret 520
Carree, Wm. 455
Carrel, George 267
Carrel, Rebecca 575
Carrell, Jonathan 299
Carrell, Wm. 270
Carrick, Eliza Ann 169
Carrick, George 169
Carrick, Jane 169
Carrick, John 169
Carrick, Morris 169
Carrick, Rachel 161
Carrick, Thomas 155, 161, 170
Carrington, Ephrain 143
Carrington, Julia 143
Carrington, Lavina 143
Carrington, Susan 143
Carrington, Wm. H. 143
Carrington, Zechariah 274
Carrol, David 358
Carrol, Elizabeth 358
Carrol, Henry 263
Carrol, William 11
Carroll, Benj. 358
Carroll, Catharine 196
Carroll, Clement 487
Carroll, Daniel 119, 389
Carroll, David 354
Carroll, Eliza 551
Carroll, Hannah 358
Carroll, Ira 357, 373
Carroll, James 143
Carroll, John 143, 759
Carroll, Martha 759
Carroll, Oliver 143
Carroll, Roda 665
Carroll, Sophia 143
Carroll, William 196, 542, 744
Carron, James 292
Carron, John 292
Carron, Mary 292
Carron, Michael 292
Carron, Nancy 292
Carron, Peggy 292
Carron, Rosannah 292
Carrothers, James 158
Carrothers, Susannah 158
Carrothers, Williamson 444
Carruthers, Margaret 161
Carruthers, Wm. J. 161
Carry, James 472
Carry, John 571
Carson, Barbara 756

Carson, Barbary 756
Carson, Benjamin 132
Carson, Betsey 464
Carson, Hannah 132
Carson, James 132
Carson, John 98, 132, 137
Carson, Maria 124
Carson, Mary 90
Carson, Nancy 137
Carson, Robert 89
Carson, Sally 132
Carson, Samuel 132, 756
Carson, Sophia 124, 132
Carson, William 132
Carter, Aaron 137
Carter, Aquilla 512
Carter, Arthur 156
Carter, Benjamin Bowen 86
Carter, Bethann 156
Carter, Calvin H. 335
Carter, Catharine 125
Carter, Chas. 358
Carter, Clarinda 591
Carter, Daniel 440, 588
Carter, David 542
Carter, Elizabeth 462, 515, 550, 678
Carter, Elliot F. 151
Carter, Enoch 231
Carter, Fenton 678
Carter, Francis 583
Carter, Isaac 371
Carter, James 657, 664, 687
Carter, Jerusha 31
Carter, John 151, 680, 731
Carter, John G. 495
Carter, Jonathan 11
Carter, Jos. Milton 432
Carter, Joshua 678
Carter, Kemp G. 9
Carter, Lemual 589
Carter, Levi 589
Carter, Margaret 592
Carter, Martha A. 151
Carter, Mary 164, 180, 657
Carter, Matilda 44
Carter, Nancy 100, 666
Carter, Patsey 15
Carter, Phebe 550
Carter, Phoebe 116
Carter, Polley 661
Carter, Polly 16
Carter, Rachel 120
Carter, Rebecca 678
Carter, Robert 687
Carter, Ruth 669
Carter, Samuel 16
Carter, Sarah 151, 231, 411, 515, 586
Carter, Sarah J. 584
Carter, Sophia 590
Carter, Thomas 455, 589
Carter, William 16, 28, 137

Carteron, Sophia 715
Cartmell, William 47
Cartney, Lucinda M. C.
    409
Cartron, Francis 512
Cartwell, Nancy Ann 432
Cartwright, John 82
Carvall, Ann 665
Carver, Benjamin 134
Carver, Catharine 134
Carver, John 186
Carver, Rachel 731
Carver, Samuel 186
Carvin, Eliza Jane 744
Carvin, Phebe Ann 746
Cary, Cephae 119
Cary, David 119, 548
Cary, Hannah 384
Cary, Isac 123
Cary, Jane 746
Cary, Mary 525, 550
Cary, Matthew 473
Cary, Reubin J. 526
Cary, Robert C. J. 525
Cary, Shadrack H. 322
Cary, Thomas 123, 548
Cary, Wm. A. 548
Casaday, Elizabeth 383
Casale, Catherine 528
Casale, David 528
Casale, John 528
Casale, Joseph 528
Casale, Mary 528
Casat, Henry 744
Casbier, Jacob 565
Case, Adaline 29
Case, Adam 444
Case, Albert 40
Case, Betsey 729
Case, Catherine 611
Case, Clement L. V. 611
Case, E. 611
Case, Ebenezer 657
Case, Elisabeth 611
Case, Eliza 80
Case, Elizabeth 383, 668
Case, John 729, 730
Case, Joseph 657, 668
Case, Moses 35
Case, Orra 30
Case, S. 611
Case, Sally 120
Case, Scottie 611
Case, Susanna 611
Case, Thomas 657
Case, Thomas J. 82
Case, W. 611
Case, Washington 611
Case, William 599, 611
Case, Wm. 75, 611
Casebeer, David 562
Casebeer, Jacob 562
Casebeer, John 565, 571
Casebeer, Mary 571
Casebeer, Pleasant 571
Caseboll, Robert 11
Casey, Benjamin 565, 571
Casey, David 91
Casey, Edith 122

Casey, Eli 137
Casey, John 455, 462,
    488
Casey, Phicisson 725
Casey, Wanton 713, 725
Cash, Israel 28
Cash, Rebecca 75
Cash, Sally 31
Casiday, Huston 652
Casiday, James 652
Casiday, Logan 652
Casiday, William 652
Casier, Thomas 571
Caskey, James M. 222
Casler, James 382, 391
Casner, Abraham 401
Casner, Anna 68
Casner, Catharine 401
Casner, Elizabeth 401,
    529
Casner, Leah 401
Casner, Peter 66, 68
Cason, Thomas 664
Casper, John 548
Casper, Lydia 548
Cass, Deborah W. 718
Cass, Jonathan 287
Cassady, George 731
Cassady, George
    Washington 188
Cassady, Hannah 46
Cassady, John 188
Cassady, Morton 731
Cassady, Peter 188
Cassel, David 137
Cassel, Elizabeth 635
Cassel, Jacob 749
Cassel, Michael 137
Cassel, Patsey 657
Cassel, Samuel 371
Cassel, Sophia 749
Cassel, Thomas 542
Cassell, Abraham 357
Cassell, Catharine 357
Cassell, James F. 301
Cassell, Margaret 357
Cassell, Nathaniel 176,
    301
Cassell, Sarah 301
Cassels, Charles 621
Cassette, Dennis 297
Cassety, Samuel 530
Cassies, Charles 571
Cassill, Abraham 633
Cassill, Allen 633
Cassill, Anthony 633
Cassill, Catherine 633
Cassill, Elizabeth 633
Cassill, Henry 634
Cassill, Jacob 634
Cassill, Margaret 634
Cassill, Maria 633
Cassill, Sarah 633
Cassill, William 634
Cassity, Franklin 519
Cassle, John 657
Cassle, Sally 662
Cassner, Martin 382
Cassner, Matthias 382

Cassot, Bernard 642
Cassot, Dumis 642
Cassot, Elizabeth 642
Cassot, Francis 642
Cassot, Maria 642
Cassy, Rachel 119
Cast, Alfred 653
Cast, Elisha 653
Cast, John 653
Cast, William Riely 653
Castanian, Alexander
    358, 364
Castanian, David 358
Castanian, John Serenus
    358
Castanian, Marylis 358
Castar, Conrad 189
Castar, John 189
Castar, Peter 189
Castar, Thomas 189
Casteel, John 606
Casterson, Polly 82
Castigan, Jacob 365, 377
Castine, George 753
Castle, Jane 549
Castle, John 341
Castle, Junia 76
Castle, Philander 76, 82
Castle, Rhoda 83
Castlelow, Jane 495
Castleman, David 565
Casto, Jonathan 418
Castor, Barsheba 189
Castor, Conrad 189
Castor, Elizabeth 189
Castor, Rebecca 189
Castt, Deborah 455
Caswell, Horatio 510
Caswell, Lucy 510
Catham, James 190
Cathcart, Thomas M. 542
Cating, Ann 452
Cating, Elizabeth 457
Cating, Susannah 459
Catlin, Catharine 636
Catlin, Catherine 520
Catlin, Christenia 634
Catlin, James 636
Catlin, Jane 636
Catlin, Rachel 636
Catlin, Rial 636
Catlin, William 630, 636
Caton, Andrew 270
Caton, Ann 278
Caton, Catharine 270
Caton, Greenberry 270
Caton, John 137, 270
Caton, Mary 270
Caton, Sarah 270
Caton, Theophilus 266,
    268, 270
Caton, Theophilus (Jr.)
    268, 270
Catron, Neophilus 270
Catrow, Charles 206
Catrow, John Matthias 206
Cattell, Tabitha 334
Catterlin, David 101,
    107, 114

800

Catterlin, Hamilton 114, 542
Catterlin, Jacob 350, 352
Catterlin, John 114
Catterlin, Solomon 114
Catterline, Jacob 214
Catterline, Jacob H. 214
Catterline, Percival H. 214
Cauding, Catarina 237
Cauding, Mery Loweine 237
Cauding, Wachenton 237
Caudon, Cadarina 236
Caudon, Catharina 236
Caudon, Metta Elisabet 236
Caudon, Waschenton 236
Caudon, William Henry 236
Caughey, George W. 432
Caughey, John 432
Caul, Thos. 506
Caushen, William 11
Causley, John 462
Cavallier, Albert 495
Cave, Asa H. 279
Caven, James 123
Caven, John 137
Caven, Nicholas I. 143
Caven, Samuel M. 137
Caven, Sarah G. 143
Caven, W. W. 143
Cavender, Henry 143
Cavender, John 143
Cavender, Leah 180
Cavender, Mary 180
Cavender, Rachel 143
Cavender, Ruth Blackford 137
Cavender, Sarah 454, 459
Cavender, Thomas 123, 137
Cavendish, William 119
Cavener, Garret 274
Cavett, John 606
Cavett, Joseph 621
Cavett, Riehard 462
Cavinac, Mary Ellen 38
Cavinac, Morgan 38, 40
Cavinac, Wm. 38
Cawson, Jane 461
Caylor, Barbara 238
Caylor, Elizabeth 238
Caylor, Joseph 199
Caylor, Michael 238
Caylor, Phebe 199
Caywood, Albert M. 646
Caywood, Joseph (II) 731
Caywood, Thomas 646
Cazier, Susannah 565
Cecil, Barbara 127, 134, 137
Cecil, Bazel 548
Cecil, Boston 542
Cecil, Charles 179
Cecil, Eleanor 134
Cecil, Elizabeth 551

Cecil, James 134
Cecil, John 134
Cecil, John G. 119
Cecil, John Grayson 131
Cecil, Julia 542
Cecil, Letey 134
Cecil, Lydia 542
Cecil, Milley 134
Cecil, Nancy 134, 137
Cecil, Polly 134
Cecil, Rebecca 119, 134
Cecil, Shelby 548
Cecil, Stewart 548
Cecil, Thomas 134, 137
Cecil, William 134, 542
Cecil, Wm. W. 548
Cecil, Zachariah 542
Ceistal, Delila 467
Cellar, Agness 449
Cellar, Eliza 449
Cellar, John 449
Cellar, Joseph 449
Cellar, Martha 449
Cellar, Mary 449
Cellar, Sarah 449
Centik, Phoebe 695
Centik, William 695
Centir, Betsey 387
Cenvern, Jeremiah 594
Cernain, John 276
Cernain, Litia 276
Cernain, Susana 276
Cessna, Polly 464
Chace, Clarissa 81
Chack, Leonard 161
Chadbourn, Sarah 667
Chadbourne, Ivory H. 672
Chadburn, Ivory H. 656
Chadburn, Sarah 656
Chadwick, Anne 658
Chadwick, Marcus B. 424
Chadwick, Martha 82
Chadwick, Mary 295
Chadwick, Mary Eliza 424
Chadwick, Mary Jerusha 424
Chadwick, Samuel P. 73
Chafell, Maheilia 336
Chaffin, Solomon 488
Chaffin, Unice 511
Chalf, Elizabeth 261
Chalfant, Charles 359
Chalfant, Comfort 359
Chalfant, Lydia 359
Chalfant, Margaret 359
Chalfant, Mercy 359
Chalfant, Robert 359
Chalfant, Samuel 359
Chalfant, Sarah 359
Chalfant, Wm. H. 359
Chalk, Eliza 273
Chalk, Isbella 273
Chalk, Joseph 272, 273, 274
Chalk, Leonard 153
Chalk, Palmira 272
Chalk, Patience 272
Chalk, Ransom 272
Chamber, Aurellas 511

Chamberlain, Andrew 512
Chamberlain, Anson 512
Chamberlain, Calvin 4
Chamberlain, Delila 323
Chamberlain, Dolly 511
Chamberlain, Elizabeth 270
Chamberlain, Harriet 4
Chamberlain, Judah 4
Chamberlain, Judith 4
Chamberlain, Lansing 4
Chamberlain, Moses 40
Chamberlain, Phebe 4
Chamberlain, Philip 556
Chamberlain, Rebecca 166
Chamberlain, Samuel 673
Chamberlain, Thos. 731
Chamberlain, Tompkins 504
Chamberlain, Vincent 4
Chamberlain, Warren 4
Chamberlain, Wiate 512
Chamberlain, William 323
Chamberlain, Wm. 370
Chamberlin, David 519
Chamberlin, Levi 519
Chamberlin, Nancy 517
Chamberlin, Rebecca 521
Chamberlin, Samuel 641
Chamberlin, Sarah 518
Chamberlin, Sarah Ann 518
Chambers, Absalom 21
Chambers, Benjamin 495
Chambers, Catharine 46
Chambers, Elizabeth 254
Chambers, Harriet 143
Chambers, Henry 421
Chambers, Henry B. 143
Chambers, Henry P. 143
Chambers, James 444
Chambers, John 720
Chambers, Jos. 254
Chambers, Joseph 40, 254
Chambers, Julia 143
Chambers, Louis N. 143
Chambers, Margaret 537
Chambers, Martia L. 143
Chambers, Mary 499
Chambers, R. 537
Chambers, Robert 40, 542
Chambers, Stephen 35
Chambers, Thomas 123
Chambers, William 722, 744
Champ, Abraham 382
Champ, John 462
Champ, Nancy 456
Champ, Polly 383
Champion, Charles Bruce 330
Champion, George W. 330
Champion, Julia M. 330
Champion, Mary Ann 336
Champion, Orlando 40
Chamsly, Antoney 657
Chanay, Jonathan 263
Chance, Caleb 650
Chance, George 650

Chancler, Zachariah 297
Chandevert, Mary
  Magdelaine 713
Chandivert, Stephen
  713, 724
Chandler, Anna 710
Chandler, Araminta 255
Chandler, Daniel 254,
  255, 262
Chandler, Danl. 269
Chandler, Eliza 6
Chandler, Georgiana 255
Chandler, Henrietta 299
Chandler, Jesse 299
Chandler, John 50, 288,
  296
Chandler, Robert F. 255
Chandler, Spencer 6
Chandler, William 462
Chandler, Winthrop 585
Chaney, Edward J. 1
Chaney, Elizabeth 390
Chaney, Emily 335
Chaney, Francis W. 1
Chaney, Hannah 1
Chaney, James 390
Chaney, James C. 390
Chaney, Jane 1
Chaney, Joanna 1
Chaney, John 1
Chaney, John McLease 1
Chaney, Margaret 334
Chaney, Marquis L. 1
Chaney, Mary Ann 1
Chaney, Nelson W. 1
Chaney, Perry M. 1
Chaney, Sally 103
Chaney, Sarah Ann 1
Chaney, Sophia 334
Chaney, William C. 1
Chaney, Wm. C. 1
Chanter, Martha 28
Chanter, Mary 30
Chanterelle, Michael 722
Chantler, Alfred 34
Chany, John 519
Chap, Susannah 454
Chapel, Laura Ann 496
Chapel, Peter C. 495
Chapen, Benjamin 86
Chapeze, Elizabeth 134
Chapeze, H. 134
Chapeze, Henry 134
Chapeze, Rossetta 134
Chapin, Lorin 519
Chapin, Lucian 628
Chapin, Norman 34
Chapin, Polly 83
Chapman, Aaiy 589
Chapman, Aaron 558
Chapman, Abner 589
Chapman, Alonzo R. 34
Chapman, Amos 628
Chapman, Betsey 717
Chapman, Calvin Alpheus
  114
Chapman, Catharine 628
Chapman, David 716, 720
Chapman, Delilah 61

Chapman, Emline 589
Chapman, Ezra 716
Chapman, Gidion 154
Chapman, Hannah 30
Chapman, Hepziba 79
Chapman, John 471, 512
Chapman, Joseph 495
Chapman, Josiah 512
Chapman, Levi 75, 76
Chapman, Lydia 495
Chapman, Margarett 61
Chapman, Maria 114
Chapman, Mary 589
Chapman, Milton 28
Chapman, Nathanel 271
Chapman, Orton 90
Chapman, Parley 268
Chapman, Polly 52
Chapman, Polly J. 595
Chapman, Reeve 114
Chapman, Reuben 512
Chapman, Sally 154
Chapman, Sarah 516
Chapman, Stephen 527
Chapman, Thomas 61
Chapman, Thomas (Sr.)
  61, 64
Chapman, William 75
Chappelear, Catherine
  358
Chappelear, Elizabeth
  373
Chappelear, Hedgeman B.
  358
Chappelear, John 378
Chappelear, John C. 373
Chappelear, Liney 358
Chappelear, Nancy 358
Chappelear, Wm. 265
Chappelear, Zacharia 358
Chappell, George 51, 52
Chappell, Joshua 11
Chappell, Robert 59
Chappell, William 46
Chappeze, Henry 123
Chappeze, Rosetta
  Henrietta 137
Chard, David 496
Chard, William (Jr.) 496
Charles, Anna 446
Charles, Charles 446
Charles, Elijah 446
Charles, Elizabeth 446
Charles, Esther 446
Charles, Eunice 755
Charles, Isaac 446
Charles, James M. 755
Charles, John 446
Charles, Mary 446
Charles, Nancy 446
Charles, Samuel 446
Charles, Sarah 446
Charles, Stephenson 446
Charlotte, --- 260
Charlotte, Stephen 261,
  271
Charter, Dennis 40
Charters, William M. 686
Chase, Abel 82

Chase, Almira 80
Chase, Archibald 76
Chase, Benj. 613
Chase, Bradford 689
Chase, Charles 76
Chase, Elizabeth 82
Chase, Francis 92
Chase, Harriet 77
Chase, Hyram 82
Chase, Jenett 83
Chase, Oliva 81
Chase, Palmira 78
Chatbourn, Mary 662
Chatfield, Albert A. 40
Cheadle, Arial 707
Cheadle, Asa 267, 272,
  716
Cheadle, Asa (Jr.) 716,
  729
Cheadle, Electa 707
Cheadle, Geo. 716
Cheadle, Gilman 707
Cheadle, John 260, 263,
  267, 707
Cheadle, Joseph 259, 270
Cheadle, Mary 729
Cheadle, N. 707
Cheadle, Naomah 707
Cheadle, Parmela 707
Cheadle, Patrick 259
Cheadle, Richard 258,
  263, 264, 267, 269
Cheadle, Sarah 267
Cheeney, John 502
Cheever, Joshua 720
Cheffen, Phebe 516
Cheffey, Eliza Jane 256
Cheffey, Ellen 256
Cheffey, Jesse 256
Cheffey, Nancy 256
Cheffren, Susanna 514
Chemin, E. 327
Chemin, Emmanuel D. 327
Chemin, Franklin 327
Chemin, Leory 327
Cheneworth, John 462
Cheney, Abigail C. 502
Cheney, Abner 57
Cheney, Hannah 502
Cheney, John 502
Cheney, Rachel 502
Cheney, Roswell 40, 502
Cheney, Sarah 502
Cheney, Trestram 502
Chenoweth, A. W. 700
Chenoweth, Absalom 687
Chenoweth, Earl F. 700
Chenoweth, Ethel 700
Chenoweth, Frances 700
Chenoweth, Fred 700
Chenoweth, Hazel 700
Chenoweth, Horace 700
Chenoweth, John F. 52
Chenoweth, John W. 700
Chenoweth, Mary T. 700
Chenoweth, S. A. 700
Chenoweth, S. D. 46
Chenoweth, Walter 700
Chenoweth, William 700

Chenoworth, Joseph 657
Chenworth, John 473
Cheny, Elizabeth 591
Cheny, John 589
Cherry, Andrew 451
Cherry, Andrew I. 9
Cherry, Benj. 407
Cherry, Christena 407
Cherry, Ralph 589
Cherry, Saml. 407
Cherry, Zachariah A. 455
Cheryholmes, Jacob 565
Cheserane, Adam 474
Chesnut, Patrick 493
Chesnutt, Charles 485
Chess, James 710
Chess, Robert 672
Chester, Elizabeth 518
Chester, Sarah 337
Chevalier, Charles 119
Chevalin, Charlotte 137
Chevalin, Elizabeth 137
Chevalin, Mary J. 137
Chevalin, Sally Ann 137
Chewell, Laura W. 143
Chezeau, Auguste 713
Chidester, Charlotta 353
Chidester, Elenor 555
Chidester, Ephraim 555, 742
Chidester, James 353, 555
Chidester, Mary 555
Chidester, Samuel 555
Chidester, Thomas 555
Chidister, James 339
Chiehester, Wm. 462
Chilcoat, Elizabeth 249
Chilcoat, Joshua 599, 618
Chilcoat, Mordica 764
Chilcoat, Robert 249
Chilcoat, Thomas 249
Chilcoate, Mordecai 441
Chilcote, Ann 357
Chilcote, Elizabeth 357
Chilcote, Ensor 372
Chilcote, Joshua 357, 358, 368
Chilcote, Margaret 357
Chilcote, Nathan 358
Chilcote, Samuel M. 765
Chilcote, William 606
Child, John 86
Childers, Elisha 132, 137
Childers, Francis 419
Childers, Henry 132
Childers, James 137
Childers, Jane 132
Childers, Thomas 419
Childers, Thomas D. 432
Childers, Thos. 548
Childres, Thomas 123
Childs, David W. 316
Childs, Susan S. 521
Chiles, Charlotte 550
Chiles, George 548
Chilsan, Lydia 13

Chipman, John 462
Chipman, Nancy 497
Chippi, Martha A. 326
Chittenden, Johnson 530
Chitwood, George R. 82
Chivington, Isaac 656
Chivington, John 656
Chivington, Lewis 656
Chivington, Sarah 656
Choate, Thomas 526
Cholcoate, Ruth 441
Chrisler, Wm. 428
Chrisley, Aaron 428
Chrisman, Joseph 58
Christian, Abraham 94
Christian, L. 735
Christian, N. 735
Christian, Nathan M. 735
Christie, George 287
Christie, Mary Ann 495
Christman, David 417
Christman, Jacob 417
Christman, Rebecca Beall 740
Christman, Rosannah 549
Christman, Solomon 639
Christman, Sophia 665
Christman, William H. 424
Christmas, Caroline 740
Christmas, Edmund 740
Christmas, Ednumd B. 740
Christmas, Emma 740
Christmas, Harriet 740
Christmas, Mary Jane 740
Christmas, Rebecca B. 740
Christmas, Rebecca Beall 740
Christmas, William H. 740
Christopher, Cornelius 229
Christopher, Elizabeth 229
Christopher, John 229
Christopher, Joseph 229
Christopher, Leah 229
Christopher, Margaret 229
Christopher, Peter 229
Christy, Abraham 397
Christy, Catharine 397
Christy, Christina 397
Christy, Elizabeth 397
Christy, Isaac 66, 67
Christy, Isabella 397
Christy, John 397
Christy, Margaret 397
Christy, Nancy 397
Christy, Peter 743
Christy, Sarah 397
Christy, Susannah 397
Christy, William M. 639
Chriswell, Robert 366
Chubb, Rolla H. 531
Chubb, Stephen 720
Chuffy, Charlotte 250, 251

Chuffy, Eliza Jane 250, 251
Chuffy, Ellen 250, 251
Chuffy, Ephraim 250, 251
Chuffy, Henry 250, 251
Chuffy, Jesse 250, 251
Chuffy, Jesse S. 250, 251
Chuffy, Nancy 250, 251
Chuffy, Patrick 250, 251
Chumpion, Andrew 337
Church, Clement 91
Church, William 82, 449
Churchil, Jane 585
Churchill, Alexander 492
Churchward, Mary 36
Chushing, Robert 34
Ciath, Caleb 382
Ciblinger, Susanna 121
Cikes, Jemima 504
Cikes, Rachel 504
Cilas, Alkier 462
Cile, Oliver 462, 465
Cinque, Elizabeth 498
Circle, Elizabeth 77
Circle, Michael 77
Cisco, Henry 542
Cisel, Philip 571
Cisma, Stephen 469
Cissil, Emon 571
Cissna, Emanuel 152
Cissner, Stephen 152
Civil, M. 154
Civits, Charles 349
Civits, Jacob 349
Civits, James 349
Civits, Joseph 349
Civits, Thomas 349
Claar, Samuel 411
Claar, William E. 411
Cladden, Margaretta 100
Clammons, John 501
Clamo, Lavina 53
Clams, Lavina 53
Clap, David 637
Clapp, David 637
Clapp, George 429
Clapp, Jno. 429
Clapp, Peter 225
Clapper, George 352
Clapper, Henry 446
Clapper, Joseph 289
Clapper, Margaret 607
Clarage, William 455
Clarige, Drucilla 64
Clark, Aaron 507
Clark, Abigail 500
Clark, Abraham 455
Clark, Adolphus 759
Clark, Alexander 358, 492, 731
Clark, Allen 358, 374
Clark, Andrew W. 303
Clark, Anna 23, 28, 199, 382, 524
Clark, Anne 657
Clark, Ben 683
Clark, Benjamin 384
Clark, Benjamin F. 213

Clark, Benjamin Franklin 205
Clark, Betsey 659
Clark, Betsy 524
Clark, Caleb 581, 582
Clark, Catharine 92
Clark, Catherine 458
Clark, Chauncy 65
Clark, Culbertson 123
Clark, Daniel 340, 358
Clark, Daniel Z. 542
Clark, Darcus 660
Clark, David 135, 401
Clark, Diana 588
Clark, Dolly 230
Clark, Dorothy 28
Clark, Duncan 322
Clark, Eleanor 363, 590
Clark, Elisha 752
Clark, Elizabeth 232, 401, 542, 581, 601
Clark, Enoch S. 143
Clark, Enos W. 681
Clark, Foster T. 137
Clark, George 133, 335
Clark, Hannah 512, 644
Clark, Harvey 744
Clark, Harvy 65
Clark, Henrietta 685
Clark, Henry 187, 190, 401, 676
Clark, Henry (Jr.) 190
Clark, Henry G. 137
Clark, Hester 502
Clark, Humphrey 630
Clark, Israel (Jr.) 65
Clark, Jackson 366
Clark, Jacob 664
Clark, James 28, 296, 502, 560, 589, 672
Clark, James G. 143
Clark, Jane 366, 502, 513
Clark, Jesse 199, 205, 209, 213, 230
Clark, Jesse Findlay 205
Clark, Jesse Findley 213
Clark, John 123, 133, 190, 209, 358, 401, 480, 488, 512, 519, 524, 527, 664, 671, 713
Clark, John (Jr.) 368
Clark, John A. 143
Clark, John B. 28
Clark, John E. 634
Clark, John G. 123
Clark, John J. 363, 372
Clark, Jon Q. 137
Clark, Jonathan 287, 451, 658, 681, 685
Clark, Joseph 330, 335, 600
Clark, Joseph L. 265, 269
Clark, Joshua 487
Clark, Lavina 61
Clark, Magdalena 432
Clark, Mahaly 588

Clark, Margaret 128, 358, 524
Clark, Martha 451, 681
Clark, Mary 358, 363, 542, 589, 660, 741
Clark, Mary Ann 323, 601
Clark, Mathew 524
Clark, Matthew 524
Clark, Milton 685
Clark, Miranda 30
Clark, Naham 74
Clark, Nancy 65, 502, 664
Clark, Nathan 66, 601
Clark, Peter F. 323, 335
Clark, Polly 521, 522, 524
Clark, Rachel 84, 502, 601
Clark, Raphael 46
Clark, Rebecca 190, 209, 524, 662
Clark, Rebecca Ann 681
Clark, Rescilla 452
Clark, Rhew 689
Clark, Rhoda 205, 213
Clark, Richard 512
Clark, Robert 376
Clark, Ruth Ann 143
Clark, S. M. 600
Clark, Sally Ann 137
Clark, Sally Jane 524
Clark, Samuel 137, 401, 502, 524, 548, 599
Clark, Samuel M. 599, 600
Clark, Saraford 153
Clark, Sarah 65, 124, 451, 497, 524, 663
Clark, Sherebiah 258, 265
Clark, Sherebrah 272
Clark, Sherebrat 266
Clark, Sidney 453
Clark, Solomon 190
Clark, Stepanes 658
Clark, Stephanus 669
Clark, Susan 78, 502, 681
Clark, T. F. 604
Clark, Theresa 592
Clark, Thomas 502, 658, 664
Clark, William 28, 206, 382, 451, 502, 524, 741
Clark, Wilson 190
Clark, Wm. 275, 284, 455
Clark, Wm. G. 137
Clarke, Bazella 668
Clarke, Daniel 462
Clarke, Frances 759
Clarke, John 480, 668
Clarke, Joshua 271
Clarke, Mahaly 589
Clarke, Margaret 759
Clarke, Noah 462
Clarke, Oren 28
Clarke, Samuel (Jr.) 759

Clarke, Stebbins 759
Clarke, William 480
Clary, Edward 308
Clary, Joseh 308
Clary, Mary Ann 308
Clary, William 308
Clary, Zachariah R. 390
Class, Jacob 225
Claton, Lewis 543
Claton, Nancy Jane 606
Claton, Samuel 611
Claton, Sarah Jane 611
Claworm, Carl 221
Clawson, Amanda Jane 424
Clawson, Andrew 548
Clawson, Ann 549
Clawson, Betsey 453
Clawson, Frederick 543
Clawson, Henry 419, 548
Clawson, Ichabod 548, 550
Clawson, Israel 548
Clawson, Jefferson 424
Clawson, John 548
Clawson, Josiah 543
Clawson, Peter 543
Clawson, Sophia 550
Clay, Charles 51
Clay, Geo. 143
Clay, Hiram 143
Clay, John 143, 519
Clay, John T. 28
Clay, Mack 143
Clay, Margaret 528
Clay, Mathias 528
Clay, Phoebe 51
Clay, Squire 664
Clay, Susan A. 143
Clayne, Isaac 176
Claypool, Ann 402
Claypool, Catharine 402
Claypool, Isaac 492
Claypool, John 280
Claypool, Wesley 402
Claypool, William 285
Clayton, --- 534
Clayton, Ann Elizabeth 689
Clayton, Betsy 295
Clayton, Elizabeth 212
Clayton, Harvey 212
Clayton, John 212, 295
Clayton, Joseph 295, 749
Clayton, Joseph I. 689
Clayton, Lucy Lee 549
Clayton, Martha 295
Clayton, Mary 295
Clayton, Noah 212
Clayton, Polly 664
Clayton, Rachael 295
Clayton, Samuel 295, 338, 366
Clayton, Thomas 295, 646, 674
Clayton, William 212, 295, 462
Clayton, Wm. 589
Cleaggoner, Frederick 529

Clear, Elizabeth 413
Clear, John J. 413
Cleary, Jacob 308
Cleary, Mary A. 308
Cleary, Thomas 308
Cleaveland, Asahel 52
Cleaveland, Elizabeth 495
Cleaveland, Lenory 82
Cleaveland, Sally 496
Cleavland, Calesta 79
Clefford, Luther L. 28
Clefford, Mary 28
Clefford, Theadocia 29
Clefton, M. 387
Clegg, George W. 147
Clegg, Jesse 147
Clegg, Richard 130
Cleland, Martin 100
Cleland, Sarah 100
Clemans, John 477, 664
Clemen, John 55
Clemens, Chesterfield W. 40
Clemens, John 274, 469, 478, 479, 480, 481, 482, 483, 486
Clemens, Thomas 373
Clement, Anna 584
Clements, --- (Dr.) 220
Clements, Emily 429
Clements, Hiram 429
Clements, James 264, 442
Clements, John 482
Clements, Stephen 429
Clements, William 442
Clemman, Benjamin 137
Clemmens, John 474
Clemmer, Eli 335
Clemmer, John 744
Clemmons, Daniel 509
Clemmons, John 471, 476
Clemmons, John C. 507
Clemons, John 474, 476
Clemons, Nancy 271
Clengensmith, Catharine 268
Clengensmith, David 268
Clengensmith, Nicholas 268
Clerk, Joseph L. 269
Cless, Christena 607
Cless, Dorothea 610
Clethero, John 162
Cleveland, Clark 496
Cleveland, Cleerl 758
Cleveland, Francis 510
Cleveland, Laura 80
Cleveland, Mary 758
Clevenger, Caroline 432
Clevenger, Charlotte 303
Clevenger, Daniel 658
Clevenger, Emaline 406
Clevenger, Hannah 582
Clevenger, Hosea 660
Clevenger, Jean 463
Clevenger, Joseph 641
Clevenger, Polly 451, 467

Clevenger, Ruth 406
Clevenger, Sarah 641
Clevenger, Sarah Ann 432
Clevenger, Shubal 432
Clevenger, Sylvester A. 420
Clevenger, Thomas 641
Clevenger, William 432
Clevenger, Zachariah 641
Clevenger, Zechariah 665
Clevinger, Bazil 462
Clevinger, Juretta 387
Cliffin, Benjamin 462
Clifford, George 487
Clifford, Martha 35
Clifton, Benjamin 391
Clifton, Charles 462
Clifton, George 462
Clifton, Jeremiah 406
Clifton, Job 391, 462
Clifton, Juda 455
Clifton, Noah 406
Clifton, Prescilla 406
Clifton, Samuel 488
Cline, Adam 337, 731
Cline, Andrew 731
Cline, Barbara 383
Cline, Catherine 387
Cline, David 731
Cline, Elisabeth 715
Cline, Elizabeth 576
Cline, Jacob 565, 711
Cline, John 154, 209, 606
Cline, Joseph 175, 180, 439, 442
Cline, Matilda 439
Cline, Peggy 556
Cline, Peter 11
Cline, Sally 383
Cline, Sarah 180
Cline, Thomas 731
Cline, William 519
Clingan, Edward 137
Clingan, Elsey 137
Clingan, James 438
Clingan, John 137, 153, 158, 161
Clingan, Marjoran 120
Clingan, Mary 137, 153, 158
Clingan, Susanna 137
Clingenpeel, Allen 432
Clingenpeel, Andrew 432
Clingenpeel, Geo. 432
Clingenpeel, Joseph 432
Clingensmith, Nicholas 267
Clinger, John 2
Clinghan, Dorcas 137
Clinghan, Edward 137
Clinghan, Jesse 137
Clinghan, Josiah 137
Clinghan, Nancy 137
Clingman, George W. 505
Clink, Josiah 606
Clinton, Elizabeth 702
Clinton, Ellen 702
Clinton, Isaac 702

Clinton, James 702
Clinton, Joseph 702
Clinton, Mattie 702
Clinton, Rachael 702
Clippenger, Anthony 347
Clippert, Henry 229
Clish, Silas W. 321
Clithero, John 177
Clitherow, John 177
Clonymon, Jacob 502
Clos, Adam 709
Clos, Peter 709
Close, Marinda 28
Close, Sarah 575
Close, William 390
Clottis, Peter 209
Cloud, Abner 658
Cloud, Lucretia 643
Cloud, Lydia 654
Cloud, Mary Earl 654
Cloud, Mordecai 654, 658
Clough, Miriam 83
Clouser, John 324
Cloyd, James 119
Cloyd, John 123
Cluney, Margaret 343
Cluney, Miles 345
Clutter, Selome 385
Clymer, Elizabeth 229
Clymer, Henry 229
Clymer, John 229, 254
Clymer, John (Jr.) 229
Clymer, Mary Jane 229
Clyne, Ingram 137
Clyne, Isaac 137
Clyne, Peter 390
Clyne, William 137
Cmam, Joseph 451
Cmith, Susanna 576
Cnahan, William W. 472
Coabe, Thos. 504
Coal, Hannah 499
Coal, Hester 512
Coaneil, Isaac 266
Coat, Catharine 130
Coat, Elizabeth 130
Coat, Henry 134
Coat, James 134
Coat, Jesse 134, 655
Coat, John 116, 134
Coat, Marmaduk 134
Coat, Marmaduke 134
Coat, Mary 134
Coat, Moses 134
Coat, Samuel 134
Coat, Sarah 134
Coat, William 130, 134
Coate, B. 94
Coate, Esther 143
Coate, Henry 130, 134
Coate, Isaac 137
Coate, James 134
Coate, Jesse 134
Coate, John 94, 134
Coate, Joseph 94, 95
Coate, Lydia 94
Coate, M. 94
Coate, Marmaduk 134
Coate, Marmaduke 134

Coate, Mary 134, 143
Coate, Moses 134
Coate, Samuel 130, 134
Coate, Sarah 134
Coate, Thos. E. 143
Coate, William 134
Coats, Anne 117
Coats, David L. 95
Coats, Henry 123
Coats, James J. 95
Coats, Jesse 116
Coats, Joseph 95, 119
Coats, Rachel 118, 119
Coats, Rebecha 124
Coats, Rhoda 118
Coats, S. A. 95
Coats, Samuel 485
Coats, Sarah 123, 124
Coats, Susan 127
Coats, T. 95
Cobaum, Samuel 665
Cobb, Christian B. 492
Cobb, Hannah E. 610
Cobberly, Andrew 52
Cobberly, Eve 52
Cobberly, Hannah 52
Cobberly, James 52
Cobberly, Job 52
Cobberly, Juda 52
Cobberly, Thomas 52
Cobberly, William 52
Cobe, Richard 320
Coberly, Job 64
Coberly, Mary 43
Coberly, Thomas 52
Coberly, William 62
Cobern, Mary 713
Cobern, Phinehas 713
Cobern, Susanna 714
Coble, Anthony 240
Coble, John 239, 539
Coblentz, Edward 202
Cobler, David 451
Coblets, --- 423
Cobran, James 763
Cobumber, Anna 591
Coburn, Asa 716, 725, 726
Coburn, Barsilla 261
Coburn, Barzella 267
Coburn, Francis 658
Coburn, Nicholas 260, 263
Coburn, Nicholas (Jr.) 257
Coburn, Pheneas 268
Coburn, Pheness 270
Coburn, Phineas 259, 266
Coburn, Polly 662
Coburn, Samuel 638
Coby, J. S. 330
Cochran, --- 483
Cochran, Agnes McGreevy 358
Cochran, Cassandra 363
Cochran, David 462, 496
Cochran, Eleanor 596
Cochran, Elener 595
Cochran, Frances 155

Cochran, Harriet 498
Cochran, Henry D. 368, 372
Cochran, Isaac 492
Cochran, James 358, 451, 589, 595, 596
Cochran, Jane 359, 376, 595
Cochran, John 358, 492, 645, 674
Cochran, Joseph 358
Cochran, Margaret 359
Cochran, Mary 162, 358, 586, 595
Cochran, Mary Ann 168
Cochran, Peter 357
Cochran, Phebe 21
Cochran, Richard 182
Cochran, Robert 358
Cochran, Rosanna 596
Cochran, Rosannah 595
Cochran, Sarah 358
Cochran, Susanah 595
Cochran, Susannah 596
Cochran, Thomas 154, 166, 168, 170, 358, 596
Cochran, Thomas (Jr.) 162
Cochran, Thos. 358, 359
Cochran, William 154, 155, 162, 164, 165, 168, 170, 175, 451, 492, 645, 674
Cochran, William J. 604
Cochron, James 658
Cochron, Robert 658
Cockbell, Susanna 513
Cockerel, Jesse 501
Cocklin, --- 735
Cocklin, Caroline 534
Cocklin, Macheal 534
Cocklin, Mary 734
Cocklin, Michael 534
Cocklin, P. 734
Cocklin, Peter 734
Cockran, William 470
Cockrell, Ellen 739
Cockrell, Hiram 739
Cockrell, John 739
Cockrell, Prudence 739
Cockrell, Robert 739
Cockrell, Robert Mortimer 739
Cockren, William 470
Cockron, Nancy 68
Cockron, William 68
Cocks, Mary 555
Codding, Oscar S. 34
Coddington, David 656, 682
Coddington, Henrietta 143
Coddington, Louisa 143
Coder, Mary 591
Cody, Bridget 358
Cody, Bridget Tobin 358
Cody, Elizabeth 358
Cody, Ellen 358

Cody, James 358
Cody, Jeremiah 382
Cody, John 358
Cody, Martin 358
Cody, Michael 358
Cody, Pat. 358
Cody, Patrick 358
Cody, Thomas 358
Cody, William 358
Coe, --- 590
Coe, Ally 293
Coe, Anna 293
Coe, Benjamin 741
Coe, Darcuss 293
Coe, David E. 519
Coe, Ebenezer 741
Coe, Elizabeth 223, 293
Coe, Hannah 592
Coe, Harriet 293
Coe, Isaac 293
Coe, James 687, 741
Coe, Joseph 119, 223
Coe, Joshua 293
Coe, Margaret 741
Coe, Martha E. 581
Coe, Mary 293
Coe, Moses 581
Coe, Nathan 293
Coe, Rebeccah 293
Coe, Sarah 293
Coe, Stephen 741
Coe, Stephen Williams 741
Coe, William 11
Coen, Jane T. 357
Coen, John 357
Coen, Malinda 357
Coen, Marrgaret 357
Coen, Martha 357
Coen, Mary 357
Coen, Nancy 357
Coen, Samuel 357
Coen, Sarah 357
Coen, Thomas 209
Coen, William 357
Coerter, Jane 125
Coffee, John 166
Coffenberry, George 438
Coffenbury, Andrew 445
Coffin, Benj. D. 40
Coffin, Sally 495
Coffinberry, James M. 756
Coffman, Diolama 77
Coffman, William 589
Coffman, Wm. 370
Cofman, Jacob 339
Cogan, Jacob 565
Cogan, Samuel 492
Cogan, William 492
Coghran, William 451
Cogler, Adam 186
Cogler, Mary 186
Cohen, Elizabeth 14
Cohen, Hugh 532
Cohoon, Elizabeth 488
Cohoon, Wm. 488
Coil, Amelia 109
Coil, Andrew 109

Coil, Caroline 108
Coil, Elizabet 109
Coil, Elizabeth 108
Coil, Elizabeth Jane 114
Coil, Hester Ann 108
Coil, Jeremiah 108
Coil, John 108, 109
Coil, Lusinda 108
Coil, Martha Jane 108
Coil, Nancy 109
Coil, Susan 108
Coil, William 114
Coin, Thomas 44
Coins, Chas. 571
Coit, George 755
Colair, Margaret 458
Colbert, Ann 588
Colby, Joseph 543
Colby, Wm. H. 543
Coldson, Margaret 382
Coldwell, Jane 25, 718
Coldwell, Samuel 641
Cole, A. A. 321
Cole, Alzina 504
Cole, Amos 504
Cole, Andrew 284
Cole, Anna 135
Cole, Catharine 548
Cole, David M. 137
Cole, Diana 499
Cole, Eber 496
Cole, Edmund 504
Cole, Elizabeth 660
Cole, Emily Jane 520
Cole, Fanny 504
Cole, Francis 93
Cole, Hannah 94
Cole, Ira 504
Cole, John B. 672
Cole, Joshua 382
Cole, Laura 504
Cole, Lewis P. 519
Cole, Louisa 504, 516
Cole, Lucas 504
Cole, Marcus 504
Cole, Mary 64, 382
Cole, Mesach 87
Cole, Minene 504
Cole, N. W. 94
Cole, Nancy 549
Cole, Nathan (Jr.) 519
Cole, Phebe 504
Cole, Philomela 504
Cole, Polley 661
Cole, Polly 382, 496,
  504
Cole, Sally 31
Cole, Samuel 548
Cole, Silas 500, 502,
  504
Coleburn, Mary 368
Colegrove, Peleg 512
Colegrove, Sarah 502
Colegrove, Wm. 502
Coleman, A . . . 118
Coleman, Achsah S. 36
Coleman, Daniel 258, 716
Coleman, Darwin 137
Coleman, Deborah 280

Coleman, Edward 192
Coleman, Elizabeth 78,
  514, 716
Coleman, Emoline 549
Coleman, Guilford D. 621
Coleman, Henry 621
Coleman, Jacob 159, 160
Coleman, Jane 501
Coleman, Jasen 137
Coleman, John 86, 621
Coleman, Jos. 496
Coleman, Joseph 188
Coleman, Katharine 160
Coleman, Lydia 137
Coleman, Margaret 76
Coleman, Maria 124
Coleman, Nathan V. 124
Coleman, Nicholas 164
Coleman, Peggy 715
Coleman, Philip 543
Coleman, Polly 159
Coleman, Thomas 77, 86,
  548, 716
Coleman, Valentine 621
Coleman, Westley 137
Coleman, William 650
Coleman, Willis P. 163
Coleman, Wm. 92, 672
Colen, Anna 468
Coler, John 731
Coles, Joseph 654
Coleston, Nancy 386
Colgan, Daniel 751
Colgan, Eleanor 751
Colgan, Elinar 513
Colgan, Hannah 751
Colgan, Mary 751
Colgan, Susannah 751
Colgan, William 751
Colganlog, Mary 745
Colgin, Susannah 511
Colgun, Daniel 754
Colhoun, Andrew 211
Colhoun, Mary 211
Colins, John J. 505
Colison, John 262, 268
Collens, Ira 43
Coller, Sarah 749
Collet, Alesebeth 566
Collet, John 472, 473,
  477
Collet, Margret 577
Collet, Mary 568
Collet, Rachel 566
Collet, William 565
Collett, Daniel 697
Collett, Joshua 658
Collett, Lemuel G. 548
Collett, M. 697
Collett, R. 697
Collett, Sarah R. 697
Collett, Thomas 687
Collett, William R. 684
Collette, Abraham 571
Collier, Catharine 756
Collier, Harriet 756
Collier, Thomas 756
Colliett, T. W. 672
Collince, Catherine 572

Collings, Wm. 500
Collins, Alfred 106
Collins, Amelia 515
Collins, Andrew 106
Collins, Anna Bell 709
Collins, Arthur 358
Collins, Carrie E. 534
Collins, Catharine 635
Collins, Catherine 76
Collins, Charles 316,
  319, 405
Collins, Charles Otto
  106
Collins, Edward 358
Collins, Elizabeth 495,
  635
Collins, Elner 109
Collins, F. Bekora 109
Collins, Findla 263
Collins, Findlay 303
Collins, Francys 554
Collins, Frankie 534
Collins, Franklin 534
Collins, Geo. W. 143
Collins, Harriet 81, 330
Collins, Henry 358
Collins, Holdon 555
Collins, Isaac 254
Collins, Isaac (Jr.) 24
Collins, James 201, 392
Collins, James N. 143
Collins, John 106, 201,
  330, 344, 358, 427,
  469, 554, 635, 744
Collins, John F. 109
Collins, John M. 255
Collins, John S. 143
Collins, John V. 647
Collins, Joseph 492
Collins, Leticia 635
Collins, Levi 635
Collins, Lewis 106, 254
Collins, Louisa 507
Collins, Lucinda 751
Collins, Major R. 109
Collins, Manda 635
Collins, Margaret 278
Collins, Margaret J. 255
Collins, Martha 106
Collins, Martin 512
Collins, Mary 405, 516,
  635
Collins, Mathias 589
Collins, Nancy 80, 109,
  254, 570
Collins, Orra Ann 30
Collins, Phelise Jane
  109
Collins, Rachael Anne
  106
Collins, Rosannah 344
Collins, S. M. (Dr.) 534
Collins, Saml. 255
Collins, Samuel 731
Collins, Sara Ann E. W.
  109
Collins, Sarah 555
Collins, Solomon 109
Collins, Solomon J. 109

Collins, Sophia 534
Collins, Tarlton 405
Collins, Thomas 502, 512
Collins, William 635
Collins, Wm. 455
Collison, John 262,
  268, 270, 273, 500
Colly, Isaac 644
Colly, Samuel 644
Colman, Jacob 224
Colmary, John 280
Colmer, Susan 82
Colney, Clarissa B. 764
Colney, James B. 764
Colp, Catherine 519
Colt, Richard E. 28
Colten, John 502
Colter, Philip 20
Columber, E. S. 43
Columbia, Dana 320, 322
Colver, Benjamin 529
Colver, Daniel 51
Colver, Handish 585
Colver, Joel 744
Colver, John 561
Colver, Nathaniel 561
Colver, Polly 561
Colver, Sarah 587
Colvin, Acklin 629
Colvin, Daniel 11
Colvin, Esther 514
Colvin, Jacob 629
Colvin, John 512
Colvin, Mahala 629
Colvin, Martha 629
Colvin, Martin 629
Colvin, Polly 629
Colvin, Saml. 713
Colvin, William 629, 632
Colvin, William P. 589
Colyer, Maream 13
Colyer, Mary 15
Comadoll, C. 329
Comadoll, Dennis 329
Comadoll, P. 329
Comans, Charity 77
Comaway, Simon 512
Comber, Mary 466
Comber, Temer 453
Combs, Charles 359
Combs, Christena
  Catherine 359
Combs, Eleanor 358
Combs, Elenora 359
Combs, George 359
Combs, James 358, 359
Combs, John 358, 359,
  488, 571
Combs, Levi 359
Combs, Lewis 359
Combs, Mary 358, 359
Combs, Rebecca 359, 466
Combs, Sarah 577
Combs, Thomas 359
Combs, William 358
Combs, Wm. 372
Combs, Wm. Henry 359
Comean, Smith 462
Comely, Lucinda 593

Comer, David 597
Comer, Eliza 597
Comer, Elizabeth 529,
  593
Comer, John 451, 462
Comer, Mary 453, 589,
  715
Comer, Polly 597
Comer, Rachel 586, 589,
  597
Comer, Rebeccah 452
Comer, Samuel Bear 597
Comer, William 249, 451
Comfort, Bridget 46
Comley, Charlotte 378
Comley, John 360
Comlin, Ann 160
Comlin, David 160
Comly, Catherine 357
Comly, John 357, 382
Comly, Joshua 357
Commer, Hetty 464
Common, Margaret M. 555
Commons, Lester 28
Comnton, Amos 698
Comnton, D. 698
Comnton, Wm. 698
Comparet, Joseph 744
Compton, Adelaide 701
Compton, Ally 698
Compton, Amos 651, 699,
  700
Compton, Amos S. 700
Compton, Ann 654, 699
Compton, Ann R. 697
Compton, Anna Elle 701
Compton, Catharine 699
Compton, Catherine M.
  700
Compton, Christopher 698
Compton, Clarissa 654
Compton, Dinah 700
Compton, E. 701
Compton, Edward 701
Compton, Eli 599, 701
Compton, Elijah 701
Compton, Elizabeth 651
Compton, Ella S. 699
Compton, Esther 698
Compton, Eunice 701
Compton, Hannah 699
Compton, Henry 654, 700
Compton, Hester 651
Compton, Isaac P. 681
Compton, J. Orville 699
Compton, J. T. 697
Compton, James 487, 697
Compton, Jesse 698
Compton, Joel T. 697
Compton, John 651, 699,
  700
Compton, Joseph 654, 697
Compton, Judith 699
Compton, Louisa J. 699
Compton, Maria 699
Compton, Martha 698
Compton, Mary 699, 701
Compton, Mary A. 701
Compton, Mary E. 701

Compton, Matilda 654
Compton, Matthew 651
Compton, Nancy 516,
  697, 698
Compton, Obediah 651
Compton, Patty 654
Compton, Phares 654, 697
Compton, Phebe 698, 701
Compton, Phebe E. 701
Compton, Polly 465
Compton, Rachael 651
Compton, Rebecca 651,
  698, 700
Compton, Rhesa A. 699
Compton, Runion 124
Compton, Ruth 698, 701
Compton, S. 701
Compton, Samuel 654,
  698, 701
Compton, Samuel B. 701
Compton, Sarah 664
Compton, Sarah Jane 701
Compton, Seth 701
Compton, Stephen 651,
  700
Compton, Susannah D. 697
Compton, Theresa 701
Compton, William 208,
  698
Compton, William Foster
  699
Compton, Wm. 698
Comwell, Harriet 498
Conally, Nancy 631
Conant, Calvin 269
Conant, Jane 85
Conant, Rufus 543
Conaut, Olive 90
Conaway, Amos 271
Conaway, Basil 357
Conaway, Jeremiah 263,
  264
Conaway, Moses 658
Concannon, Ann 136
Concannon, Catharine 136
Concannon, J. 136
Concannon, Polly 136
Concannon, Sally 136
Concannon, William 136
Conckright, Hollis 589
Concleton, Wm. 585
Condit, Philip 763
Condon, Richard 445
Cone, Amanda 585
Cone, Asa H. 279
Cone, Nelson 589
Conelly, Mary 383
Conger, David 156
Conger, Elias 154
Conger, Elias (Sr.) 158
Conger, Elizabeth 163
Conger, Gershom 156, 160
Conger, John 163
Conger, Mahala 160
Conger, Sarah 156
Conger, Stephen 178
Congleton, David 708
Congleton, Jane 708
Congleton, William 708

Congreve, William 90
Conine, Jeremiah 444
Conius, Abigail 713
Conius, Easter 715
Conkel, John 408
Conkilton, Gimmima 585
Conklin, Gideon 512
Conklin, Hannah 506
Conklin, Jacob 543
Conklin, Joseph 506
Conklin, Mary 512
Conklin, Smith 687
Conklin, William 506, 512
Conkling, John 46
Conkright, Sarah 710
Conley, Barton 462, 465
Conley, Beannah 667
Conn, Alexander 270
Conn, Anna 293
Conn, Geo. 571
Conn, James 273
Conn, John W. 601
Conndy, --- (Dr.) 220
Connel, Alexander 512
Connel, James 11
Connel, Martha 14
Connelly, Charles 231
Connelly, Deborah 231
Connelly, Elisabeth 231
Connelly, Elizabeth 231
Connelly, Fountain Scott 193
Connelly, Pamela 193
Connelly, Rebecca 231
Conner, Betsey 463
Conner, Boyne 40
Conner, David 487, 596
Conner, Deborah 596
Conner, Eleanor 80
Conner, Eliza J. 301
Conner, Elizabeth 12
Conner, Esther 487
Conner, Isaac 487
Conner, James 11, 86, 143, 585, 596
Conner, John S. 306
Conner, Josiah (Dr.) 220
Conner, Madelina 488
Conner, Matilda 143
Conner, Priscilla 152, 155
Conner, Rebecca 113
Conner, Richard 152, 155, 530
Conner, Robert 143
Conner, Samuel 488
Conner, William 451
Conners, Jacob 487
Connery, John 672
Connet, B. P. 539
Connit, Catharine 120
Conover, Alexander 211
Conover, Alexander G. 194, 205
Conover, Caty Ann 123
Conover, Elizabeth 650
Conover, Garret 194
Conover, Hannah 650

Conover, Joseph H. 194, 205, 211
Conover, Obadiah 192, 202
Conover, Obadiah B. 201
Conover, Peter 650
Conover, Sophia 650
Conover, Susan T. 211
Conover, Thomas 199
Conoway, Isaiah 378
Conoway, Jeremiah 339
Conrad, Adam A. 528
Conrad, Jacob 291, 571
Conrad, Rebecca 291
Conrad, Thomas 93
Conroy, Edward 543
Conroy, Elizabeth 551
Conroy, Isaac 543
Constable, Levin 649, 673
Conter, George 564
Contriman, Elizabeth 454
Contrman, Christian 454
Convers, Benjamin 720
Convers, Esther 720
Convers, Leicester G. 250, 251
Converse, Benjamin G. 250, 251
Converse, Daniel 285, 296, 297, 716
Converse, Danl. 298
Converse, James 713
Converse, Lester G. 266
Converse, Phebe 52
Converse, Polly Lucens 718
Converse, Sophah 250, 251
Conway, Samuel 284
Conwell, Mary 76
Conyser, Peter 390
Cooc, Catherine 458
Cooder, Solomon 399
Cook, Abel 439
Cook, Abiah 599
Cook, Abraham 534
Cook, Augustus 543
Cook, Charity 697
Cook, Christian 196
Cook, D. 698
Cook, Daniel 165, 442, 599, 601, 603
Cook, David 280, 390
Cook, Dinah 698
Cook, Erastus H. 526
Cook, Frederick 196
Cook, Hannah 699
Cook, Henry 383, 393
Cook, J. 698
Cook, John 455, 654, 698
Cook, John A. 668
Cook, John J. 46
Cook, Joseph 487, 571
Cook, K. 698
Cook, Leonard 519, 527
Cook, Levi 669
Cook, Maria 699
Cook, Martha 439

Cook, Mary A. 698
Cook, Mathew Bryant 439
Cook, Nancy 46, 512
Cook, Noah B. 439
Cook, Peggy 439
Cook, Peter 519
Cook, Polly 453
Cook, Russell G. 77
Cook, Ruth 390
Cook, S. 698
Cook, Sally 717
Cook, Samuel 698, 699
Cook, Sarah 609
Cook, Sarah M. 534
Cook, Solomon 439
Cook, Stephen 601, 603, 683
Cook, William 462, 698
Cook, Wm. 91
Cook, Zeba 439
Cooke, Charles 40
Cooke, Dinah 657
Cooke, Pheebe 714
Cooke, Richard 40
Cooke, Sally 717
Cookery, Josiah 298
Cooley, Easter 716
Cooley, Elizabeth 29
Cooley, Henry 487
Cooley, Malon 88
Cooley, Moses B. 28
Cooley, Nathaniel 396
Cooley, Rensellear 28
Cooley, Roger 28
Cooley, William 519
Coolidge, Augustus 596, 597
Coolidge, George W. 597
Coolidge, George Washington 597
Coolidge, James F. 597
Coolidge, John 596, 597
Coolidge, Lucy 597
Coolidge, Phebe 586
Coollidge, Maryann 585
Cooly, Alvin 519
Cooly, Matilda 290
Coombs, Joseph 432
Coon, Abraham 648
Coon, Adam 53, 487
Coon, Betsey Jane 752
Coon, Charles 492
Coon, David 543
Coon, George 383
Coon, Hannah 456
Coon, Henry 52
Coon, James 752
Coon, Joel 752
Coon, John 442, 442
Coon, Joseph 548
Coon, Luke (Jr.) 502
Coon, Peggy 384
Coon, Samuel 492
Coon, Stephen 648
Coon, Susannah 682
Coone, Adam 451
Coone, Louisa 497
Cooney, Lucinda 93
Coonrod, Adam 391

Coonrod, Barbary 391
Coonrod, Betsey 385
Coonrod, Catharine 391
Coonrod, Elizabeth 391
Coonrod, George 391
Coonrod, Henry 391
Coonrod, Jacob 391
Coonrod, John 391
Coonrod, Peter 391
Coonrod, Woolery 751
Coonrod, Woollery 391
Coonrod, Woollery (Sr.) 391
Coonrod, Woolsey 744
Coons, Elizabeth 461
Coony, Charles Frederick 344
Coony, Mary 344
Coony, Patrick 344
Cooper, --- 762
Cooper, Abigail J. 9
Cooper, Abijah 198, 204, 212
Cooper, Abner 728
Cooper, Alexander 427
Cooper, Alfred F. 10
Cooper, Allen 198, 204, 212
Cooper, Caroline 255
Cooper, Charles 728
Cooper, Daniel C. 182, 223
Cooper, David 255
Cooper, E. 692
Cooper, Elisha 731
Cooper, Elisha (Jr.) 731
Cooper, Elizabeth 422
Cooper, Em. 474
Cooper, Felix 429
Cooper, Francis 178
Cooper, Frederick 728
Cooper, George W. 89
Cooper, Hannah 429, 728
Cooper, Hulda 429
Cooper, Isaac 9, 198, 204, 212
Cooper, Isaac A. 10
Cooper, J. 692
Cooper, Jacob 284, 339, 340, 728
Cooper, Jacob H. 405
Cooper, Jakie 692
Cooper, James 255
Cooper, Jeremiah 728
Cooper, Joel 455
Cooper, John 255, 451, 496, 731
Cooper, Joseph 198, 204, 339
Cooper, Joseph C. 212
Cooper, Joseph L. 10
Cooper, Lat 202
Cooper, Lemuel 728
Cooper, Lucinda 405
Cooper, Margaret 178
Cooper, Mary 9, 198, 204
Cooper, Mary J. 10
Cooper, Nancy Ann 9
Cooper, Polly 718

Cooper, Rachel 429
Cooper, Reuben 28
Cooper, Rhoda 78, 117, 198, 204
Cooper, Robert 473, 475
Cooper, Royal B. 319
Cooper, Royal D. 335
Cooper, Ruel 361
Cooper, Samuel 77
Cooper, Sarah 429, 591
Cooper, Spencer 462
Cooper, Thomas 255
Cooper, Thomas B. 9
Cooper, William 429, 470, 471, 473
Cooper, Wm. 474, 477, 478
Cooperider, Elizabeth 375
Cooperider, Hannah 370
Cooperider, Manuel 375
Cooperider, Peter 370
Cooperider, Polly 377
Coopper, Eli B. 302
Coor, John 483
Coover, Laura 241
Coover, S. H. 241
Coover, Samuel 462
Cope, Ann E. 257
Cope, Caleb 5, 6
Cope, Daniel 492
Cope, Edith 5
Cope, Eli 6
Cope, Elias 257
Cope, Emalina 257
Cope, Emmy 6
Cope, Eve 492
Cope, Henry 6
Cope, Israel 5, 6
Cope, James 257
Cope, John 6
Cope, Lucretia 257
Cope, Margaret 6
Cope, Mary 5, 6
Cope, Ruth 5
Cope, Samuel 6
Cope, Simeon 5
Cope, Thomas 303
Cope, William 257
Copeland, Ann 158, 160
Copeland, David 158, 160
Copeland, Jeremiah 441
Copper, Roda 608
Coppoc, Mary Charles 419
Coppock, Allen 143
Coppock, Barbara 137
Coppock, Benjamin 131, 143
Coppock, Edney 119
Coppock, Elizabeth 119
Coppock, Henry 143
Coppock, Jane 125, 127
Coppock, John 116, 137, 182
Coppock, Lavina 121
Coppock, Margaret 123
Coppock, Mary 128
Coppock, Mary Elizabeth 137

Coppock, Nancy 137
Coppock, Samuel 128, 137
Coppock, Sarah J. 137
Coppock, Susannah 666
Coppock, Thomas 137, 182
Coppock, William 116
Coppock, Wm. 143
Copsy, Elizabeth 465
Corban, Marinda 31
Corbett, James 487
Corbett, Jane 488
Corbett, William 488
Corbett, Wm. 488
Corbin, Roxa 36
Corbit, Andrew 58
Corbit, Sarah 58
Corbley, Isaiah M. 689
Corbley, Mary Ann 689
Corder, Elizabeth 43
Corder, George 455
Cordery, Noble 565
Cordon, Lydia 344
Cordon, Wm. 344
Cordon, Wm. M. 344
Cordra, Sarah 566
Core, Catharine 740
Core, Gasper 471
Corey, Addison 55
Corey, Ambrose 763
Corey, David 487
Corey, Elizabeth 452
Corey, Elnathan 638
Corey, George D. 763
Corey, Henry 55
Corey, James 638
Corey, Jeremiah 638
Corey, Joanna 55
Corey, John 55
Corey, Joshua 55
Corey, Louisa C. 763
Corey, Mahala 55
Corey, Mary 638
Corey, Mary E. 763
Corey, Moses 638
Corey, Orrin I. 763
Corey, Polly 715
Corey, Rebecca 55
Corey, Sally 55
Corey, Samuel R. 763
Corey, Simeon 488
Corey, Sophronia 55
Corey, Thomas 713
Corey, Uriah 638
Corle, Wm. 266
Corn, Elizabeth 152
Corn, John 504
Corn, Levi 152
Corn, William 77
Cornel, Richard 168
Cornel, Sylvanus 645, 673
Cornelius, Benjamin 20
Cornell, James 374
Cornell, Joel 496
Cornell, Mary 374
Cornell, Sarah 583
Cornell, William 526
Corner, Edwin 254, 260, 266, 267, 268, 269, 273

Corner, Geo. L. 275
Corner, Rachael 591
Corner, William 249, 731
Corns, Anna 459
Corns, Chas. 571
Cornwell, Sally 117
Cornwell, Sylvester 40
Cornwell, Tabitha A. 46
Corran, William C. 46
Correll, Jacob 565
Correll, Mag. 46
Corsey, Cuiah 466
Corsey, Dinah 466
Corson, Henry 502
Corson, John 46
Cortright, John 589
Corus, Silas 548
Corwin, Benjamin 665
Corwin, David B. 679
Corwin, Ebe 505
Corwin, Emeline Amelia
  653
Corwin, Franklin 653
Corwin, Icabod 642, 649
Corwin, Ichabod 640, 653
Corwin, Ichabode 639
Corwin, James 505
Corwin, John 462
Corwin, Joseph 638,
  653, 679
Corwin, Joseph (Sr.) 653
Corwin, Matthias 639,
  641, 649, 650, 651,
  653, 670
Corwin, Matthias (Jr.)
  672
Corwin, Moses B. 665
Corwin, Oliver 383
Corwin, Pheanus 462
Corwin, Ruth 382, 453
Corwin, Sarah 658
Corwin, Thomas 654, 678
Corwin, Wm. M. 689
Corwine, Samuel 462
Cory, Abija 383
Cory, Alanson W. 526
Cory, Ambrose 764
Cory, Arbitty 526
Cory, Charles S. 711
Cory, Daniel 131
Cory, David J. 132
Cory, Edy 406
Cory, Elisha 406
Cory, Elizabeth 120
Cory, Elnathan 132
Cory, Ezra 149
Cory, Jane M. 137
Cory, Jemima 526
Cory, Jeremiah 658
Cory, John 119, 548
Cory, John B. 40
Cory, Julia 526
Cory, Mary 657
Cory, Moses 665
Cory, Nathan 391
Cory, Noah 642
Cory, Orin 526
Cory, Orin J. 526
Cory, Phebe 149, 526

Cory, Polly 117, 526
Cory, Samuel 526
Cory, Solomon 406
Cory, Uzel 526
Cosbey, Rebecca 413
Cosbindas, Magdalena 577
Coshner, Anna 399
Coshner, Peter 399
Cosot, Peter 642
Coss, Charrity 458
Cossairt, Peter 427
Cossett, John 29
Cossiart, Francis 427
Costigan, Cecilia 344
Costigan, Jacob 344, 377
Costigan, Mary A. 344
Costigan, Michael 344
Costlow, Joshua 635
Costonian, Alexander 351
Costonian, Marillas 351
Cote, Henry 134
Cote, James 134
Cote, Jesse 134
Cote, John 134
Cote, Marmaduk 134
Cote, Marmaduke 134
Cote, Mary 134
Cote, Moses 134
Cote, Samuel 134
Cote, Sarah 134
Cote, William 134
Cotem, Elizabeth 573
Cotes, Mary 123
Cothran, Jesse 116, 137
Cothran, John 137
Cothron, Hannah 136
Cotter, Margaret 519
Cotter, Mary 520
Cotter, Philip 519
Cotterman, Elias 222
Cotterman, Randolph 414
Cottingham, James 147,
  185
Cottingham, William 185
Cotton, Luther 633
Cottons, Thomas 185
Cottran, Alexander 137
Cottran, David Steaman
  137
Cottrell, A. W. 89
Cottrell, Andrew 82, 89
Cottrell, Elam 534
Cottrell, Emma C. 330
Cottrell, M. A. 330
Cottrell, N. . . . 330
Couden, Catharina 236
Couden, Markeret Em 236
Couden, Waschenton 236
Coughlin, Dennis 333
Coughlin, Michael 333
Coughlin, Sarah Jane 333
Coughren, Unas 116
Cougle, Alexander 451
Coulter, Alpheus W. 176
Coulter, David 439, 445
Coulter, Edward 166
Coulter, Eloner 574
Coulter, John 389
Coulter, John L. 450

Coulter, Jonathan 441
Coulter, Margaret 176
Coulter, Mary 716
Coulton, Ann 401
Coulton, Betsy Molly 401
Coulton, Ellen 401
Coulton, Hanis 401
Coulton, Hannis 401
Coulton, Hermon 401
Coulton, Jane Esther 401
Coulton, Keturah 401
Council, Isaac 262
Counee, Philip 512
Countant, John Lewis 722
Counter, John 82
Counterman, Derastus 114
Counterman, Jno. 618
Counterman, Lavina 606
Counterman, Mary Z. 606
Counts, Adam 543
Counts, Daniel (Sr.) 46
Counts, Joseph 451
Counts, Peter 56
Counts, Sarah 124
Countz, Daniel 462
Couples, Samuel 46
Courdate, Catherine 529
Courtaell, Lawrence 531
Courtney, John 361
Courtney, Neal 713
Courtney, Priscilla 401
Courtney, Robert 401,
  402
Courtode, John Peter 529
Courtright, Fanny 497
Courtwright, Isabella
  397
Courtwright, Jacob 397
Courtwright, John 397
Cousins, Suzan 30
Couzens, Elizabeth 284
Covault, Alex 143
Covault, Alexander 143
Covault, Eliz. 143
Covault, Israel 143
Covault, Lewis 143
Covault, Margaret E. 143
Covault, Robt. J. 143
Covault, Timothy N. 143
Covault, Watkins 143
Covault, Wm. S. 143
Covenhoven, Isaac 665
Covenhoven, Thomas 645,
  674
Cover, Catherine 357
Cover, Henry 357
Cover, Jacob 357
Cover, John 357
Cover, Lawrence 357
Cover, Mary 357
Cover, Michael 357
Cover, Samuel 357
Coverdill, John 291
Covert, Catharine 688
Covert, Joseph 688
Covert, Robert B. 665
Covert, Sarah 688
Covill, William 543
Covington, Anne 11

Cowan, Abigail 638, 671
Cowan, Elizabeth 16
Cowan, James 671
Cowan, Jane 671
Cowan, John 638, 671
Cowan, John (Jr.) 671
Cowan, Mary 658, 671
Cowan, Mary Ann 655
Cowan, Polly 662
Cowan, Thomas 357
Cowan, William 655
Cowber, Mary 466
Cowden, Eliza 354
Cowdery, Jacob 77
Cowdery, Joel 77
Cowdery, Nancy 77
Cowdery, Roswell 77
Cowdery, Samuel 283
Cowdery, Sarah 83
Cowdery, Sophia 80
Cowdery, Squire 77
Cowell, Andrew 166
Cowell, Mary 166
Cowen, Benjamin S. 171
Cowen, Charles 357
Cowen, Eliza Jane 377, 378
Cowen, Elizabeth 357
Cowen, Frances 357
Cowen, George 357
Cowen, Harriet 357, 378
Cowen, Horatio 357
Cowen, Jacob P. 606
Cowen, James 16
Cowen, Jane 357, 662
Cowen, John 357, 366
Cowen, Mariah 357
Cowen, Martha 357
Cowen, Mary 357
Cowen, Robert 357, 377
Cowen, Susanna 357
Cowen, Thomas 357, 364, 373, 379
Cowen, Walter 357
Cowenhooven, Elias 651
Cowens, John 475
Cowgall, George 640
Cowgel, Daniel 17
Cowgel, Elisha 24
Cowgel, Elizabeth 659
Cowgele, Polly 24
Cowgill, George J. 678
Cowgill, Henry 10
Cowgill, Joseph 485
Cowgill, Martha 588
Cowgill, Mary 21
Cowgill, Rebecca 12
Cowling, Edward 43
Cowling, Richard 46
Cowrser, Edward 40
Cox, Absalom 116
Cox, Alvina 420
Cox, Balding 171
Cox, Barbara 232
Cox, Benj. 134
Cox, Benjamin 392, 678
Cox, Benjamin S. 124
Cox, Bethsheba 116
Cox, Catherine 458

Cox, Charles 507
Cox, Charrety 458
Cox, Cyrus 740
Cox, Daniel 223
Cox, David 665
Cox, Deborah 12
Cox, Elijah 232
Cox, Elizabeth 160, 420, 630
Cox, Ellen 679
Cox, Ellen E. 740
Cox, Enogh 539
Cox, Griessal 120
Cox, Hannah 121, 138, 468, 630, 679
Cox, Henry 220
Cox, Hetty 120
Cox, Horatio J. 293
Cox, Jacob 192, 630
Cox, James 320, 720
Cox, Jane 679, 740
Cox, Jessee 539
Cox, John 132, 143, 160, 192, 224, 439, 483, 540, 679
Cox, Joseph 462, 679, 740
Cox, Joshua 543
Cox, Levi 740, 741
Cox, M. E. 540
Cox, Malon 630
Cox, Margaret 679
Cox, Maria E. 740
Cox, Martha Jane 678
Cox, Mary 118, 320, 414, 455, 539
Cox, Mary A. 539
Cox, Matilda 630
Cox, Michael 320, 321
Cox, N. 540
Cox, Nancy 114, 125, 138, 143, 451
Cox, Nathan 455
Cox, Nicholas 630
Cox, Phebe 664, 667
Cox, Polly 232, 467
Cox, Rachel 453
Cox, Richard 224
Cox, Rosannah 540
Cox, Rush 488
Cox, Sally 461
Cox, Samuel 420, 488
Cox, Sarah 143
Cox, Solomon 488
Cox, Terressa 740
Cox, Unice 138
Cox, William 143, 192, 232, 488, 658, 678, 679, 679, 740
Coy, Adam 751
Coy, Cristopher 87
Coy, Cyrus 40
Coy, Daniel 752
Coy, Henry 751
Coy, Jacob 751
Coy, Mary 744, 746, 751
Coy, Nancy Ann 751
Coyle, Gabriel 477
Cozad, Abba 464
Cozad, Abraham 630

Cozad, Catharine 630
Cozad, Charity 630
Cozad, Daniel 492
Cozad, Elizabeth 630
Cozad, Henry 630
Cozad, Job 630
Cozad, John 492, 630
Cozad, Levi 630
Cozad, Mary 630
Cozad, Susan 630
Cozart, Elisha 688
Cozart, Susan Rilla 87
Cozen, Horatio G. 40
Cozens, H. 733
Cozens, Hezekiah 731
Crabb, Edward 456
Crabb, Henderson 462
Crabb, Henry 456
Crabb, Jacob 456
Crabb, Jeremiah 456
Crabb, Mary 464
Crabb, Ozmond 456
Crabb, Reuben 451
Crabill, Christian 531
Crable, Polly 386
Crabtree, --- 408
Crabtree, Madison 410
Crabtree, Sarah 410
Crabtree, Thomas 512
Crack, Wm. 474
Cracraft, Charles 512
Craft, David A. 524
Craft, John 658
Craft, Sarah 700
Craft, Thomas 40
Craft, Timothy 658
Crafts, Samuel S. 621
Crage, Mary 456
Crager, Jacob 529
Crago, Deborah 463
Crago, Jonathan 456
Craig, Abraham 1
Craig, Alexander 187, 190, 230, 471, 472, 492
Craig, Andrew 585
Craig, Ann 180
Craig, Charles 484, 485
Craig, David 187, 190, 230
Craig, David H. 158
Craig, Delilah 4
Craig, Eli 682, 687
Craig, Eliza Jane 4
Craig, Elizabeth 4, 11, 113, 230
Craig, Emily 1
Craig, Fawcet 177
Craig, George 312
Craig, Harriet Jane 432
Craig, Isaac 731
Craig, James 4, 187, 230, 548, 682, 744
Craig, James W. 744
Craig, Jeremiah 230
Craig, Jeremiah S. 187
Craig, Jesse 687
Craig, John 187, 190, 230, 743

Craig, Joseph Seymore 432
Craig, Joshua 180
Craig, Margaret 12
Craig, Martha 230
Craig, Martin 687
Craig, Mary 230, 383
Craig, Merinda 113
Craig, Minerva 687
Craig, Nancy 127, 187, 230
Craig, Perry W. 1
Craig, Phebe 187, 230
Craig, Rachel Ann 4
Craig, Rosana 166
Craig, Samuel 113, 488, 687, 716
Craig, Sarah 113, 230, 746
Craig, Seymour 113, 187, 190, 230
Craig, Shoogart 220
Craig, William 166, 303, 484, 488, 512, 731
Craig, William H. 1
Craig, Wm. 220, 298, 474
Craige, John 565
Craigg, Joel 713
Craighed, John B. 449
Craighed, Mary 449
Craighton, Daniel 525
Craigsen, Wm. 480
Craigue, Alexander 471
Crain, Daniel 680
Crain, George 640
Crain, James 351
Crain, Polly 660
Cralinger, Sarah 593
Cram, Mary 569
Cram, Sarah A. 708
Cramblet, Sion 257
Crame, Mary 577
Cramer, Abigail 509
Cramer, Catharine 586
Cramer, Elizabeth 512
Cramer, Eve 512
Cramer, John 507, 543
Cramer, Mary 524
Cramer, Rachel 517
Cramer, Susanna 529
Cramer, William S. 278
Crampton, Jesse 432
Crampton, John 432
Crampton, Letta Charlotte 432
Crampton, Mallissa 432
Crampton, Margaret 432
Crampton, Margaret C. 432
Crampton, Margaret Cath. 432
Crampton, Rebecca C. 432
Crampton, Sarah 432
Crampton, Smith 432
Crandall, Aseneth D. 37
Crandall, Joshua 37
Crandall, Maria H. 37
Crandall, Mary L. 37
Crandall, N. 37
Crandall, P. 37

Crandall, Pardon 37
Crandall, S. M. 37
Crandall, S. S. 37
Crandall, Sarah C. 37
Crandel, Sophronia 29
Crandell, Sophronia 29
Crandle, Zedakiah 710
Crandle, Zedrick 712
Crane, Amos 496, 647
Crane, Caleb 644
Crane, Daniel 653, 680
Crane, Ezra 647
Crane, Francis 640
Crane, George 284
Crane, Hulda 647
Crane, Joseph H. 224
Crane, Miranda 766
Crane, Noah 649
Crane, Phebe 647
Crane, Sarah 680
Crane, William 649
Craner, Christian 278
Crassan, John 294
Crassen, Mary 665
Crasson, John 294
Crath, William 46
Cratty, Robert 585
Crauch, Harding 477
Craw, John 760
Craw, Richard 760
Crawford, Abijah 67
Crawford, Alexander 640
Crawford, Alexandria 649
Crawford, Andrew 132, 640
Crawford, Ann 565
Crawford, Betsy 467
Crawford, Charlotte 132
Crawford, David 169
Crawford, Edward 731
Crawford, Eli 571
Crawford, Eligah 749
Crawford, George 440
Crawford, Hannah 124
Crawford, Hannah C. 132
Crawford, Hannah H. 592
Crawford, Hugh 451
Crawford, Jacob 291
Crawford, James 480, 487
Crawford, James H. 589
Crawford, James Lee 132
Crawford, James M. 596
Crawford, Jane 586
Crawford, John 640
Crawford, John H. 131, 132
Crawford, Mary 169
Crawford, Mattie 410
Crawford, Noble 470
Crawford, Oliver 642, 665
Crawford, Rebecca 749
Crawford, Rhoda 506
Crawford, Robert 132, 637
Crawford, Robert C. 200
Crawford, Samuel 640
Crawford, Sarah 67, 590
Crawford, Temperance 29

Crawford, Thomas 640
Crawford, William 153, 170, 171, 180, 285, 286, 333
Crawford, William H. 47
Crawford, Wm. 154
Crawmer, John 524
Cray, Mathias 11
Craybill, Caty 386
Creager, Abraham 207
Creager, Catharine 207
Creager, Peter 203, 211
Creager, William 207
Creamer, Alexander 652
Creamer, Barbara 665
Creamer, David 665
Creamer, Eliza 652
Creamer, Jacob 665
Creamer, John 652
Creamer, Nancy 652
Creamor, Francis 487
Creanor, Aaron 487
Creary, Robert M. 333
Creasley, John 462
Creater, Andrew 571
Creath, Catharine A. 43
Creath, Elizabeth 46
Creath, William 51
Cree, Isabela 152
Cree, Isabella 175
Cree, James 152, 156, 175, 176
Cree, John 164
Creed, John 730
Creeger, Lawrence 519
Creek, Samuel 606
Creemer, Francis 485
Creemer, Henry 565
Creemor, Frances 485
Creerfield, Moses 456
Creetors, Ezekiel 672
Cregan, Cath. 138
Cregan, Danl. 138
Cregan, James 138
Cregan, Mary 138
Cregan, Nancy 138
Cregan, Sarah 138
Crege, Catherine 570
Creger, Ellen 497
Crego, Rachel 46
Creig, Rhoda 466
Creighton, Anna 555
Creighton, James 343, 555
Creighton, John 343
Creighton, John (Jr.) 555
Creighton, John (Sr.) 555
Creighton, Margaret 555
Creighton, Robert 555
Creighton, Will 470
Creighton, William 472
Creighton, William H. 46
Creighton, Wm. 470, 477
Creits, George 565
Creitz, Susannah 568
Crem, Margret 574
Cremean, Jas. 606

813

Cremean, Smith (Jr.) 606
Cremeen, Curtis 492
Cremor, Francis 484
Cress, Elizabeth 240
Creswell, William 582
Creter, Andrew 563
Cretzer, Susanna 743
Creu, Joseph 88
Crevaster, Jacob 283
Creviston, Barbary 457
Creviston, Jacob 11
Creviston, John 383
Creviston, Nicholas 488
Creviston, Peggy 387
Creviston, Polly 453
Crew, Casper 138
Crew, Jacob 708
Crew, James 19
Crew, Mannalius S. 138
Crew, Rachel 708
Crew, Wester 138
Crew, William 708
Cribbs, George 558
Cribs, George 556
Crichton, Andrew 508
Crickbaum, Daniel 213
Crider, Emanuel 462
Crider, Eve 462
Crider, Jacob 456
Crider, John 213
Crider, Michael 456
Crietz, Andrew 565
Criger, Amanda 419
Criger, John 419
Crillery, Josinnus 562
Cripe, Catharine 195
Cripe, Hannah 195
Cripe, Joseph 195
Cripleavor, John 571
Cripliver, Jacob 565
Crisley, Lawrence 339
Crisoin, Rebecca 465
Crispey, William 753
Crispin, John 456
Crispin, Phebe 464
Crissel, Wilson 364
Crist, Abraham 397
Crist, Betsey 356
Crist, Catherine 356
Crist, Christiana 356
Crist, Cyrus 612
Crist, Daniel 356, 613
Crist, E. 612, 613
Crist, Eliza 613
Crist, Frederick 356
Crist, Henry 224
Crist, Henry C. 432
Crist, J. 612, 613
Crist, Jacob 356
Crist, Jobes 613
Crist, John 356
Crist, Joseph 613
Crist, Laura Jane 613
Crist, Mary 567
Crist, Medora Ellen 613
Crist, Peter 640
Crist, Philip 356
Crist, Sarah 356
Crist, Urselah 577

Crist, William 356
Crister, Eli 642
Crister, George 642
Criswell, Larkin 280
Critchett, Ann 358
Critchett, Michael 358
Critchfield, John 658
Crits, Nicholas 565
Crits, Peggy 573
Critsswister, John 636
Critz, Andrew 562
Critz, Elizabeth 562
Critz, George 562
Critz, Harry 562
Critz, Jacob 562
Critz, John 562, 571
Critz, Katy 562
Critz, Margaret 562
Critz, Peter 562
Critz, Sarah 562
Critz, Susan 562
Critzer, Betsy 646, 674
Critzer, George 646, 674
Croan, Jacob 528
Croan, Mary Ann 520
Crocket, Andrew 665
Crocket, James R. 114
Crocket, John W. 114
Crocket, Mary Anne 114
Crocket, Patsy 16
Crocket, Payten 11
Crocket, Robert 16
Crockett, Chas. 138
Crockett, John 526
Crockett, Marmoduk 138
Crockett, Mordecai 138
Crockett, Oliver A. 519
Crockhaw, George L. 462
Croffert, An Mary 554
Croffert, Catharine 554
Croffert, Christina 554
Croffert, Jacob 554
Croffert, John 554
Croffert, Joseph 554
Croffert, Magdalena 554
Croffert, Margaret 554
Croft, George 347
Croft, John 347
Croghan, Nancy 95
Croghan, Nathaniel 95
Crom, John (Jr.) 764
Crom, John (Sr.) 760
Crom, Jonathan 756
Crom, Maria 756
Cromer, Isa Mayo 138
Cromer, John 138
Crone, John 675
Cronice, Henry 525
Croninger, A. E. 612
Croninger, Calvin 617
Croninger, Carl W. 612
Croninger, Joseph 553
Croninger, L. A. 617
Croninger, Lydia A. 617
Croninger, M. (Dr.) 612, 617
Cronkite, James 530
Cronkite, Martha Ellen 530

Cronkite, Mary E. 530
Cronkite, Nancy 530
Cronkite, Seth 530
Cronkite, Soloman 530
Cronkite, Tunis 530
Cronkite, Wilhelmus 530
Crook, Henry 297
Crook, John 368
Crook, Joseph 451
Crook, Thomas 209
Crookhaw, George L. 462
Crooks, Alexander 88, 90
Crooks, Oratio N. 82
Crosbie, Ed. 357
Crosbie, Nancy 357
Crosbie, Sarah 357
Crosby, Betsey 363
Crosby, Daniel 364
Crosby, Hannah 357
Crosby, James 357
Crosby, John 357
Crose, Barbary 463
Crose, Philip 383
Crosier, Ludy 31
Croskey, Cathrine 376
Crosky, Mary 65
Crosky, Robert 65
Crosley, Moses 688
Crosley, William 683
Crosly, Eunice S. 759
Crosly, Lucy M. 759
Crosly, Oris 759
Cross, A. 614
Cross, Alonzo 606, 614
Cross, B. 613, 614
Cross, Betsey 613
Cross, Bolivar 606
Cross, Cotilda 614
Cross, D. D. 613, 614
Cross, Daniel 571
Cross, Daniel D. 613, 614
Cross, Daniel P. 599
Cross, E. 613, 614
Cross, Edmond 606
Cross, George D. 614
Cross, Isaac 565
Cross, Iver 614
Cross, Jane 613
Cross, Joseph 512
Cross, M. 613
Cross, M. A. 614
Cross, M. Z. 613, 614
Cross, Marenda 614
Cross, Mary A. 614
Cross, Mary Ann 614
Cross, Mary M. 614
Cross, Mary Z. 614
Cross, Nancy 534
Cross, Oliver 534
Cross, R. D. 613
Cross, Solomon 11
Cross, William 483
Crossan, Geo. 357
Crossan, Wm. 682
Crossen, Ann 358
Crossen, Catherine 358
Crossen, Cornelius 358
Crossen, Emanuel 365

Crossen, Frances 358
Crossen, John 358
Crossen, Margaret 358
Crossen, Sally 368
Crossen, Sam. 358
Crossen, Wm. R. 368
Crosson, Barney 684
Crosson, John 321, 322
Crosson, William 684, 688, 689
Crosson, Wm. 690
Crosthwait, Bertha 438
Crosthwait, John 438
Crosthwait, Robert 438
Crosthwaite, Sarah 438
Crothers, Andrew 280
Crothers, David W. 764
Crothers, Elizabeth 764
Crothers, Ellen 764
Crothers, F. 764
Crothers, Francis 764
Crothers, James H. 764
Crothers, Jane 609
Crothers, John Wm. 731
Crothers, Lewis Cass 764
Crothers, Mary Margaret 764
Crothers, Nancy Jane 764
Crothers, Samuel 764
Crothers, Susanna 609
Crothers, Wm. R. 764
Crouch, Andrew 451
Crouch, George 43
Crouch, Harding 478
Crouch, John 462, 487
Crouch, Joseph 451
Crouch, Mary 453
Crouch, Patience 502
Crouch, Rebecca 453
Crouse, David 456
Crouse, Harding 482
Crouse, Lydia 588
Crouse, Ruth 459
Croush, Eleoner 451
Crow, Abraham 512
Crow, Catharine 631
Crow, David 383, 390
Crow, Elizabeth 390
Crow, G. F. 176
Crow, Geo. 264, 271
Crow, George 106, 154, 160
Crow, George Frederick 155
Crow, Isaac 155, 175
Crow, Jacob 155
Crow, Jacob W. 488
Crow, John 390
Crow, Joseph 390
Crow, Mary 390, 451, 514, 636
Crow, Mathias 636
Crow, Michael 173, 176
Crow, Nicholas 744
Crow, Peter 178
Crow, Rachel 155
Crow, Robert 390
Crow, Samuel 390
Crow, Susannah 390

Crow, Thomas 390
Crow, William 390
Crowder, Mary 384
Crowel, Alsina 29
Crowel, Charity 187
Crowel, Elizabeth 187, 238
Crowel, Henry 238, 565
Crowel, Mary 187
Crowel, Samuel 187
Crowel, Sophia 238
Crowell, Anna 79
Crowell, Benj. 89
Crowell, Lydia 84
Crowell, Mary 238
Crowell, Moses 653
Crowell, Phebe 187
Crowell, Seth 653
Crowsaur, John 82
Crowsaw, Elizabeth 78
Crowser, Nancy 93
Croy, Amy 143
Croy, Daniel 200
Croy, Jacob 543
Croy, James 200, 548
Croy, John 200
Crozier, John 548
Crozier, Richard J. 548
Crozier, Robert 543
Crozier, Sarah 548
Crque, Charles 473
Crucher, Jabez 18
Crucher, Nathan 11
Crue, Casper W. 138
Crue, Menalcus S. 138
Crull, Anna 507
Crull, Asseneth 507
Crull, Betsey 356
Crull, Caleb 507
Crull, Charles 501, 507, 509, 512
Crull, David 507
Crull, Elinor 507
Crull, Jane 501
Crull, Jemima 507, 517
Crull, John 356
Crull, Joshua 507
Crull, Martha 507
Crull, Mary 507
Crull, Maryann 507
Crull, Nancy 507
Crull, Rachel 507
Crull, Samuel 501, 507
Crull, Susannah 507, 516
Crull, Thomas 507
Crull, Thomas J. 509
Crull, William 507, 512
Crull, Wm. M. 507
Crum, Abraham 524
Crum, Agnes 302
Crum, David 302
Crum, George 524
Crum, John 524
Crume, Geo. F. M. 432
Crume, Martha Jane 432
Crume, Mary 425
Crume, McConnel 432
Crume, P. M. (Dr.) 425
Crume, Pliny 432

Crume, Thos. M. 432
Crume, Wm. Wallace 433
Crumer, Peggy 118
Cruse, John 537
Cruse, Martha A. 537
Cruse, Martha Ann 537
Cruse, Martha Ann M. 537
Cruse, Peter 537
Cruse, Ruth Ann 537
Crusen, Sarah 492
Crusin, Isaac 487
Crussel, Elizabeth 130
Crutcher, Jabez 18
Crybill, Catharine 736
Cryder, Diana 492
Cryder, Joseph 582
Cryder, Michael 492, 493
Cuarr, Ann 574
Cubbison, Andrew M. 376
Cuddington, Zecheriah 259
Cudley, Charles E. 86
Cuierson, Sarah 467
Culbertson, Acenith 187
Culbertson, Alex 300
Culbertson, Alexander 286, 298
Culbertson, Andrew 128
Culbertson, Henry W. 124, 148
Culbertson, James 300, 356, 366, 738
Culbertson, John 134, 187, 223, 233
Culbertson, Joseph 134
Culbertson, Joseph R. 134
Culbertson, Mary 128
Culbertson, Mary Jane 740
Culbertson, Nancy 125
Culbertson, Robert 187, 233
Culbertson, Robt. 233
Culbertson, S. W. 296
Culbertson, Sam. 300
Culbertson, Saml. W. 274
Culbertson, Samuel 138, 298
Culbertson, Samuel W. 259
Culeshine, Elizabeth 589
Cull, Bernard 357
Cull, Felix 354, 357
Cull, Mary 344
Cull, Michael 344
Cullanghand, Patrick 339
Cullenbaugh, Mary Ann 749
Culler, Gideon B. 589
Culling, Hannah 739
Cullman, George 519
Cullum, George 209
Cullum, James 209
Cullumber, Allen 62
Cullumber, John 62
Cullumber, Thomas 62
Cullums, Harriet 82
Culner, Levi 273

Culp, George 479
Culp, Jacob 512
Culter, D. C. 731
Culver, Amanda 29
Culver, Benjamin 529
Culver, Carpenter 524
Culver, Catharine 590
Culver, Chester 524
Culver, David 524
Culver, Diana 524
Culver, Ebenezer 730
Culver, Frances 524
Culver, Levi 273
Culver, Lewis 601, 621
Culver, Mary F. 589
Culver, Priscilla 730
Culver, Rachel 464, 593
Culver, Russell 589
Culver, Sarah 590
Culver, Sashel 589
Culver, Tabatha 523, 529
Cumberlin, Aley 754
Cume, John 695
Cumman, John 627
Cummings, Emanuel 621
Cummings, James 519
Cummings, Joseph 729
Cummins, Charlie G. 692
Cummins, Chloe 692
Cummins, David 529
Cummins, Eva 692
Cummins, Francis M. 692
Cummins, George 529
Cummins, Jacob 529
Cummins, James 173,
   529, 658
Cummins, Jeals 653
Cummins, John 492
Cummins, Julia 80
Cummins, Margaret 30
Cummins, Mary 173, 670
Cummins, Mathias 529
Cummins, Phebe 529
Cummins, Rebecca 589
Cummins, Robert 665
Cummins, Sarah Jane
   653, 655
Cummins, Thomas 170,
   653, 655
Cummins, William 529,
   665
Cunager, Joseph 40
Cuningham, Cushman 740
Cuningham, James 737
Cuningham, John 740
Cuningham, John T. 374
Cuningham, Maria E. 740
Cuningham, Rebecca B.
   740
Cunn, John 524
Cunning, Richard 571
Cunningham, Calvin 629
Cunningham, Catharine A.
   738
Cunningham, David 629
Cunningham, E. A. 413
Cunningham, Edward 629
Cunningham, Francis 647
Cunningham, Hugh 438

Cunningham, Isaac P. 507
Cunningham, Isabella 290
Cunningham, James 166
Cunningham, James Duncan
   438
Cunningham, John 438,
   629
Cunningham, John I. 371
Cunningham, Levi 752
Cunningham, Luke 629
Cunningham, Margaret 457
Cunningham, Moses
   Richard 638
Cunningham, Nicholas 629
Cunningham, Polly 657
Cunningham, Rahel 658
Cunningham, Richard 658
Cunningham, Robert 250,
   251
Cunningham, Simon 709
Cunningham, Thomas 629,
   647
Cunningham, William
   156, 225, 438
Cunningham, Wm. 116, 571
Cunnings, Thomas 571
Cupliver, Philip 40
Cupp, John 372
Cupp, Samuel 372
Cuppert, Catharina 236
Cuppert, Peter 236
Cuppert, Sara 236
Cuppy, Abraham 438
Curch, Joel 512
Curestone, Henry 119
Curk, Joseph 244
Curk, M. 244
Curk, Mary 244
Curk, Michael 244
Curk, P. 244
Curk, Sarah 244
Curl, Hannah 11
Curl, James R. 11
Curl, Jesse C. 606
Curl, Joseph 24
Curl, Joseph S. 11
Curl, Mary 16
Curl, Samuel 11, 16, 27
Curl, Thomas 658
Curn, David J. 487
Currain, Betsey 660
Curran, Alexander 441,
   446
Curran, Alexr. 500
Curran, Ann 357
Curran, Cartmell 446
Curran, Eliza 446
Curran, Hamilton 446
Curran, Hannah 446
Curran, James 358
Curran, John 446
Curran, Joseph 446
Curran, Mathew 500
Curran, Sam. 353, 357,
   358, 359
Curran, Samuel 361,
   366, 368, 370, 372,
   373, 377
Curran, Stephen B. 446

Curran, Thos. 359
Curran, William F. 446
Currants, Mary 459
Currard, Susannah 664
Currell, Mary 383
Currence, Lorenzo 312
Currey, William 383
Currier, Jacob L. 631
Currington, Benjamin 267
Currington, Lovisa 270
Curry, George H. 342
Curry, Henderson 512
Curry, James 462, 596
Curry, James A. 597
Curry, John 429, 433
Curry, John (Jr.) 428
Curry, Louisa 589
Curry, Mary Jane 429,
   433
Curry, Otway 589
Curry, Rachel 342
Curry, Stephenson 589
Curry, Susanah 568
Curry, Thomas 641
Curryer, Joseph C. 543
Curtin, Mary 46
Curtis, Abigail 291
Curtis, Atlanta 92
Curtis, Benjamin 496
Curtis, Catharine 495
Curtis, David L. 316
Curtis, Eleazer 729
Curtis, Eleazor 729
Curtis, Eli 178
Curtis, Eliza Jane 337
Curtis, Elizabeth 29,
   167, 178, 443, 518,
   664
Curtis, Emily S. 71
Curtis, Frederick 337
Curtis, Harvey A. 29
Curtis, Henry B. 443
Curtis, Herman J. 316
Curtis, Hiram 167
Curtis, Hiron 124
Curtis, Horatio N. 320,
   744
Curtis, Iram 167
Curtis, James 116
Curtis, Jared R. 29
Curtis, John 71, 658
Curtis, Jonathan 159
Curtis, Joseph 178, 665
Curtis, Joseph H. 496
Curtis, Lanson 18
Curtis, Laura 30
Curtis, Lewis 29
Curtis, Liberty 167
Curtis, Peter 91, 92
Curtis, Samuel J. 29
Curtis, Sarah 117
Curtis, Sibel 159
Curtis, William 429
Curtis, William Wiley
   124
Curtiss, Joshua 543
Curtner, Christopher
   183, 184, 223, 232,
   233

Curtner, Henry 232
Curtner, Jacob 232
Curtner, John 232
Curtner, Peter 543
Curts, Hector 383
Curts, Joseph 534, 535
Curts, Julia Ann 535
Curts, Lawrence 535
Curts, Mary 534
Curts, Pricella 534
Curts, Thomas 535
Curts, Thomas (Jr.) 534
Curts, William 534
Curts, William P. 534
Curtwright, Wm. E. 91
Cury, Ezra 512
Cusac, Andrew 284, 340
Cusac, Daniel 338
Cusack, Edmond C. 361, 372
Cusak, Catharine 343
Cusak, E. C. 343
Cush, Daniel D. 621
Cushing, Anne 648
Cushing, Clarisa 648
Cushing, Cortland 648
Cushing, Daniel 648
Cushing, Elizabeth 643
Cushing, Hannah 648
Cushing, Jonathan 648
Cushing, Mary Ward 643
Cushing, Milton B. 290
Cushing, Nathaniel 721
Cushing, Rebecca 643
Cushing, Rowland Owen 643
Cushing, Sally 717
Cushing, Samuel 713
Cushing, William 648
Cusing, M. B. 290
Custard, Daniel 60
Custer, Catherine 574
Custer, Eli 642
Custice, Thomas 512
Custice, William 512
Cutland, Joseph 25
Cutler, Chloe 30
Cutler, Emily 143
Cutler, Ephrain 727
Cutler, Jesse 29
Cutler, John 383
Cutler, Lavina 143
Cutler, Mary B. 143
Cutler, Sarah 383
Cutliff, Jane 465
Cutliss, George 487
Cutright, Andrew 456
Cutright, Catherine 452
Cutright, Nancy 459
Cutter, John 456
Cutter, William 86
Cuttey, William P. 507
Cutting, Linus 4
Cyphers, Catherine 465
Cypress, Andrew 64
Cypress, Hannah 64
Cypress, John 64
Cypress, Nancy 64
Cypress, Rebecca 64

--- D ---

D.Nacht, Joseph Winon 713
Dabney, Abigail Mason 86
Daely, Charles 441
Daggett, Caroline E. 38
Daggett, Henry S. 38
Daggett, Henry Smith 38
Daggett, Sarah 38
Daggett, Smith 40
Daggett, William F. 38
Daggett, William Fred. 38
Daggett, William K. 317
Dahr, Eleanor 298
Dailey, A. T. 615
Dailey, Andrew R. 29
Dailey, E. 615
Dailey, E. J. 615
Dailey, Eliza 82, 303
Dailey, Esaias 615
Dailey, Kane 155
Dailey, L. J. 615
Dailey, M. A. 615
Dailey, Mary Ann 615
Dailey, Mary Susan 615
Dailey, Nimrod 615
Dailey, Orainiewind 615
Dailey, Robert 82
Dailey, William 488
Daily, Anna Katharine 433
Daily, Francis 453
Daily, Hannah 28
Daily, James T. 606
Daily, John 160, 165
Daily, John Edmund 433
Daily, Joseph Wm. Henry 433
Daily, Mercy 30
Daily, Rebecca 281
Daily, Roswell 29
Daines, Jane 76
Daines, Wm. M. 261, 263, 273
Daives, Wm. 270
Daken, Thomas 164
Dalby, John 383
Dalby, Peter 492
Dale, John 584, 589
Dale, Molly 126
Daley, Ann 517
Daley, Peggy 516
Dalliez, Maria 727
Dalliez, Maria J. 727
Dalliez, Maria Josephine 727
Dally, Charles 441
Dally, Hannah 441
Dally, John 441
Dally, Vincent 441
Daly, Betsey 458
Daly, Sarah 713
Daly, William A. R. 565
Dame, Clarissa 739
Damen, Almira 71
Damen, Emily 71

Damen, Hannah 71
Damen, Harrison 71
Damen, Jane 71
Damen, Julius 71
Damen, Maria 71
Damen, Nathan 71
Damen, Roxy 71
Damico, Dortha M. 700
Damsheath, Sarah 335
Dana, Benjamin 713
Dana, Betsy H. 731
Dana, Betsy M. 731
Dana, George 731
Dana, Louisa C. 763
Dana, Luther 716
Dana, William 716, 731
Dana, Wm. W. 731
Danah, Joshua 406
Dandridge, Alexander 5
Dane, Phebe 659
Danelson, Katharine 550
Danford, Hiram 159
Danford, James 155, 301
Danford, Mary 155
Danford, Michael 159
Danford, Samuel 165
Danford, Sarah 313
Danford, William 313
Danhaur, Elias 284
Daniel, Hannah C. 571
Daniel, James 50
Daniel, Jasper 558
Daniel, Jenny 718
Daniel, John 370
Daniel, N. S. 508
Daniel, Pheba 508
Daniel, Samuel M. 11
Daniels, Cassey 363
Daniels, Catharine 336
Daniels, Ellah 38
Daniels, Fredrick 74
Daniels, Hannah 669
Daniels, James 462, 589, 669
Daniels, Kate 38
Daniels, Lucy 38
Daniels, Mary C. 38
Daniels, Munson H. 40
Daniels, Nathan 669
Daniels, Willard W. 38
Danley, Mary 128
Danner, Catharina 301
Danner, Clarisa V. 535
Danner, E. H. 535
Danner, Eliza 549
Danner, L. C. 535
Danniels, Jane 121
Dans, Priscilla 413
Dant, Calvin 589
Darby, Daniel 77
Darby, Mary 503
Darby, Rufus 280
Darby, Samuel 634
Darby, Sander 503
Darby, Saunders 502
Darby, Stephen 630
Darby, William 463
D'Arco, Mannes S. 358
Darist, Mary 79

Dark, William H. 38
Darley, Joanna 47
Darlington, Belinda 507
Darlington, Daniel 507
Darlington, Elisha 512
Darlington, Joseph 507
Darlington, Julia 507
Darlington, Robert 507
Darlington, Samuel 507
Darnon, Kethura 169
Darnon, Samuel 169
Darr, Ann 398
Darr, Catharine 398
Darr, David 398
Darr, Elizabeth 398
Darr, George 398
Darr, John 398
Darr, Margaret 398
Darr, Peter 398
Darr, Sarah 398
Darr, William 398
Darrah, B. 420
Darrah, Benjamin (Jr.) 420
Darrah, Rebecca 420
Darsham, Catherine 360
Darsham, Christian 360
Darsham, Christian (Jr.) 360
Darsham, Jacob 360
Darsham, Tobias 360
Darst, Abraham 191, 192, 207, 216
Darst, Daniel 492
Darst, Henry 406
Darst, Jacob 406
Darst, Mary 406
Darst, Wm. P. 354, 357, 361, 373
Dart, Titus 52
Dash, Adam 298
Dasring, Arnold 389
Datch, Elendor 47
Dathe, Charles Francis 713
Daugherty, Barnard 362
Daugherty, Charles 61
Daugherty, Isaac 606
Daugherty, John 61
Daugherty, Lavina 61
Daugherty, Mary 498
Daugherty, Mary E. 61
Daugherty, Mathew 178
Daugherty, Michael 463
Daugherty, Sarah 61, 292
Daugherty, Thomas 685
Daugherty, William 61
Daughter, Marmaduke 753
Daughter, Mary M. 753
Daughter, Stephen I. 753
Daughter, Stephen J. 753
Daughterty, Polly 60
Daulph, Benjamin 11
Dauterman, Jacob 758
Davenport, Abraham 463, 543
Davenport, Anthony S. 471, 474
Davenport, Edson 496

Davenport, Elizabeth 543
Davenport, Euice 495
Davenport, Jesse 223
Davenport, John 181, 548
Davenport, Peggy 715
David, Benj. 269
David, Charles 262
David, Elizabeth C. 20
David, James 492
David, Joseph 202
David, Stephen 202
Davidson, Ann 279
Davidson, Douglas N. 138
Davidson, Elizabeth 54
Davidson, Ephrain 543
Davidson, Jane 47
Davidson, John 53, 54, 543
Davidson, John B. 622
Davidson, Martha 47
Davidson, Patrick 44
Davidson, Rachel 54
Davidson, Samuel 456
Davidson, Sarah 44
Davidson, Thomas 472, 482, 485
Davidson, Thos. 477
Davidson, William 11, 135, 225, 710
Davis, Aaron 429
Davis, Abraham 119, 155, 269
Davis, Achsey 272
Davis, Alexander 169
Davis, Allie F. 37
Davis, Amasa 285
Davis, Amelia 387
Davis, Amsa 716
Davis, Ann 163
Davis, Anna 717
Davis, Asa 716, 730
Davis, Belle M. 37
Davis, Benjamin 383, 451
Davis, Benjamon 512
Davis, Betsey 76
Davis, Catharine 386, 445
Davis, Catherine 744
Davis, Charles 650
Davis, Chas. G. 138
Davis, Christena 574
Davis, Curella 413
Davis, Dalinda 543
Davis, Daniel 182, 215, 429, 549, 713, 716, 723, 730
Davis, Daniel (Jr.) 730
Davis, Dave 534
Davis, David 215, 483, 686
Davis, David W. 456
Davis, Diney 467
Davis, Doctor 429
Davis, Ebenezer 406, 445
Davis, Edward 445
Davis, Edwin Olney 730
Davis, Eleazor B. 40
Davis, Eliakim 82
Davis, Elijah 271

Davis, Eliza 248, 270
Davis, Elizabeth 14, 21, 44, 125, 406, 453
Davis, Ellen R. 419
Davis, Elnathan 512
Davis, Elvina 610
Davis, Emma 534
Davis, Enoch 669
Davis, Enos 383
Davis, Ephraim P. 232
Davis, Esther 182
Davis, Eunes 741
Davis, Evan 91, 231
Davis, Ezekiel 270
Davis, Frances 27
Davis, Francis 40, 642, 650, 672
Davis, Geo. 138
Davis, George 196, 215, 383, 445, 658
Davis, George C. 192, 232
Davis, George G. 138
Davis, George L. 696
Davis, Grove 138
Davis, H. B. 731
Davis, H. W. 357
Davis, Hannah 11, 124, 184, 223, 224
Davis, Harriet 422
Davis, Harriet D. 376
Davis, Harry 534
Davis, Henery 561
Davis, Hezekiel 716
Davis, I. Baron 40
Davis, Isaac 271, 451, 469, 472, 473, 476, 477
Davis, J. T. 37
Davis, Jacob 571
Davis, James 16, 124, 184, 247, 396, 549
Davis, James M. 376
Davis, James Oliver 606, 626
Davis, Jane 626
Davis, Jared 484
Davis, Jean 452
Davis, Jesse 168
Davis, Jesse (Sr.) 168
Davis, Jno. 285, 406
Davis, Joanna 730
Davis, John 12, 16, 135, 171, 184, 196, 249, 259, 279, 383, 416, 433, 463, 496, 606, 658, 670, 731
Davis, John (Jr.) 77
Davis, John (II) 171
Davis, John F. 3
Davis, John P. 101
Davis, John T. 37
Davis, John W. 376
Davis, Jonas 265, 723
Davis, Jonathan 658, 670
Davis, Joseph 148, 263
Davis, Joseph N. 422
Davis, Joshua 163, 172, 248, 255, 264, 272
Davis, Josiah 422

818

Davis, Katy 376
Davis, Kindall 646
Davis, Kindrey 483
Davis, Kiney 163
Davis, Laomi 29
Davis, Letticia 231
Davis, Levi 184, 259, 270, 529
Davis, Lewis 182, 184, 196, 215, 224, 647, 654, 655, 658, 670, 680
Davis, Lewis S. 419
Davis, Lon 534
Davis, Lucena 717
Davis, Luther 429
Davis, Lydia 670
Davis, M. 37
Davis, Margaret 445
Davis, Maria 80
Davis, Martha 406, 576
Davis, Martha Jane 523
Davis, Martin Van Buren 410
Davis, Mary 76, 77, 126, 182, 184, 223, 224, 445, 543, 593
Davis, Mary Eglin 37
Davis, Mehala 572
Davis, Michael 584
Davis, Moses 416, 429
Davis, Nancy 82, 383, 607
Davis, Nancy Ann 47
Davis, Nathaniel 163, 720, 721
Davis, Oliver P. 543
Davis, Patience 445
Davis, Patsey 15
Davis, Phebe 82
Davis, Polly 16, 89
Davis, Rachel 88, 400
Davis, Rebeca 588
Davis, Rebecca 457
Davis, Rebecchah 462
Davis, Rees 372
Davis, Rembrance W. 686
Davis, Remembrance W. 686
Davis, Robert 486
Davis, Ruth 445, 576
Davis, Sally 72
Davis, Samuel 482
Davis, Samuel D. 119
Davis, Saphrona 730
Davis, Sarah 88, 168, 196, 224, 417, 418, 517, 592
Davis, Sarah Ann 609
Davis, Silas 655, 678
Davis, Susan 509
Davis, Susanna 670
Davis, Thomas 16, 182, 184, 223, 224
Davis, Tobiatha 543
Davis, Tubal C. 549
Davis, Viney 467
Davis, William 16, 19, 27, 258, 263, 264, 290, 383, 445, 621, 626, 658, 727

Davis, William A. 12
Davis, William H. 12
Davis, Wm. 249, 259, 262, 270, 376, 406, 512, 589
Davis, Wm. B. 358
Davis, Wm. J. 88
Davison, Abisha 363
Davison, Abraham 585
Davison, Absolom 359
Davison, Artist 359
Davison, Daniel 594
Davison, Darkey 359
Davison, Edward 359, 380
Davison, Frederick 363
Davison, Isaac (Jr.) 50
Davison, Isaac (Sr.) 50
Davison, Isaac W. 359
Davison, Jacob 744
Davison, John 359
Davison, Lucy 359
Davison, Nancy 385
Davison, Polly 52
Davison, Sally 359
Davison, Thomas 472
Davison, Zeruah 359
Davisson, Edward S. 396
Davisson, Isaac 658
Davisson, Jane 657
Davisson, Josiah 427
Davisson, Margaret 429, 512
Davist, Mary 79
Davor, Francis 116
Davous, Francis 713, 727
Davrange, Constance 716
Davy, Charlotte 567
Davy, Wm. 571
Dawes, Henry 271
Dawes, William M. 258
Dawes, Wm. 266, 271, 274
Dawes, Wm. M. 268
Dawsen, Edward 503
Dawsen, Otho 506
Dawson, Abijah 512
Dawson, David 463, 488
Dawson, Edward 503
Dawson, Eliza 745
Dawson, Elizabeth 503
Dawson, I. B. 752
Dawson, Isaac 482
Dawson, James 405
Dawson, Jane 747
Dawson, John 503, 581, 649, 650
Dawson, Katharine 503
Dawson, Kesiah 582
Dawson, Mahlon 650
Dawson, Malon 649, 650
Dawson, Mary 405
Dawson, Matilda 466
Dawson, Millia 454
Dawson, Otho 509
Dawson, Parthenia 405
Dawson, Polly 52
Dawson, William 751, 752
Dawson, Wm. 405
Dawxon, James 512
Day, Clarissa 739

Day, David P. 739
Day, Diadema 739
Day, Elam 739
Day, Eli H. 319
Day, Elijah 260, 262
Day, Elizabeth 456, 551
Day, Ezekiel 512
Day, Hannah 739
Day, Henry 543
Day, Isaac 319
Day, James 77
Day, James H. 439, 445
Day, John 731
Day, John W. 549
Day, Lewis 543
Day, Lydia 551
Day, Margaret 739
Day, Martha J. 537
Day, Mary 537, 548
Day, Minerva 537
Day, Nancy 666
Day, Noah 537, 716
Day, Oliver 739
Day, Peter 456, 492
Day, Samuel 492
Day, Sarah 549
Day, Schugler 496
Day, Sylvester 755
Day, Thos. (Corpl.) 537
Dayhoff, Elizabeth 557
Dayler, Anne 359
Daylong, Margaret E. 520
Dazet, Joseph 716
Dcamp, Caroline 609
Dcamp, John 606
Deabler, George 488
Deacon, Elizabeth Jane 143
Deacon, Margaret 143
Deakens, John 585
Deal, Anna 352
Deal, Christian 352
Deal, David 352
Deal, Elizabeth 111
Deal, Henry 190
Deal, John 352
Deal, Philip 190
Deal, Sarah 352
Deal, Sophia 352
Deal, Susanna 352
Deal, Will 469
Deal, William 352
Deal, Wm. 479
Dealy, Henry 334
Deam, Adam 211
Dean, Abraham 470, 485, 488
Dean, Abrm. 486
Dean, Catherine 359
Dean, Elizabeth 488
Dean, George 582
Dean, George W. 59
Dean, H. D. 527
Dean, Hugh 376
Dean, James 344, 359, 470
Dean, John 59
Dean, Lucinda 583
Dean, Mary 523

Dean, Mary Ann 344, 359
Dean, Masson 359
Dean, Matthias 496
Dean, Seth C. 764
Dean, Teresa 376
Deaner, Joseph 621
Deaper, John 40
Deaper, Susan 38
Dearbin, Nicholas 271
Dearborn, Henry B. 250,
251
Dearborn, Julia 263
Dearborn, Luther 260,
263
Dearborn, Nathan 263,
264, 272
Deardoff, Elizabeth 665
Deardorf, Geo.
Washington 433
Deardorff, Adaline 684
Deardorff, Christian
560, 565
Dearduff, Abraham 476
Dearduff, Daniel 12, 463
Dearidoff, Elizabeth 574
Dearman, Ann 738
Dearman, Elizabeth 738
Dearman, James 738
Dearman, Margaret 738
Dearman, Mary 738
Dearman, Robert 738
Dearman, Samuel 738
Dearmont, Catharine 348
Dearmont, William 348
Dearth, Ann 662
Death, Ann 674
Death, Asahel 589
Death, Daniel 653
Death, Elizabeth 653
Death, Hannah 653
Death, Hugh 653
Death, Isaac 644, 673
Death, James 645, 653,
658, 674
Death, James (Jr.) 668,
671
Death, John C. 638,
658, 668, 671
Death, Mary Ann 653
Death, Priscilla 665
Death, Sarah 653, 658
Deaver, Elizabeth 517
Deaver, John 504
Deaver, John T. 298
Deaver, Joseph 621
Deaver, Levi 259
Deaver, Sarah E. 315
Debo, Ann 550
DeCamp, Melissa Janie
429
Decamp, Caroline 609
DeCamp, Gavin 429
DeCamp, Hannah 610
DeCamp, James 673
Decamp, John 606
Decan, James 669
Decan, John 669
Decan, Peggy 669
Decan, Thomas 669

Decan, William 669
Dechant, George
Frederick 225
Dechant, John Peter 225
Decker, Anna 385
Decker, Catherine 528
Decker, Hannah 519
Decker, Henry 165, 528
Decker, Isaac 383
Decker, Jacob 710
Decker, John 711
Decker, Joseph 383
Decker, Mary 165
Decker, Rudolphus 519
Decorsey, Anna 429
Decorsey, Samuel 429
Decorsey, Seth 429
Dedham, John 274
Dedick, Clarke 112
Deeds, Daniel 565
Deeds, John R. 549
Deem, Elizabeth 209
Deem, Hannah 116
Deem, J. C. (Rev.) 425
Deem, James Argus 209
Deem, John A. 209
Deem, John C. 419
Deem, Mary 425
Deem, Willson 209
Deemer, Jane 410
Deen, George W. 59
Deen, James 59, 213
Deen, Jeptha 441
Deen, John Graham 59
Deen, John Thomas 213
Deen, Mary Anderson 59
Deen, Mary Elizabeth 213
Deen, Nancy 213
Deen, Robert 59
Deen, Robert George 59
Deen, Walter 59
Deen, Walter Angus 59
Deen, Walter Myers 59
Deen, William 512
Deerduff, Abraham 485
Deerwerter, John S. 702
Deeter, Catharine 138
Deeter, Daniel 138
Deeter, Daniel (Sr.) 195
Deeter, David 133
Deeter, Emanuel 138
Deeter, Samuel 195
Deeter, Susan 138
Deeter, Susannah 120
Deetz, Mary 565
Deetz, Wm. 571
Defenbaugh, George 375
Defenbaugh, Isaiah 371
Defenbaugh, Rebecca 371
Deffendoffer, Elizabeth
740
Defner, Abraham 392
De Frague, Archie 541
Defrees, Archibald 119
Defrees, Joseph 543
Defrees, Polly 121
Defrees, Thomas J. 549
Defur, Daniel 710
Defur, Sarah 710

DeGarmo, Cashing 248
Dehaven, Abraham 463
Dehaven, Herman 492
Dehaven, Peter 383, 488
DeHaven, Peter 689
Dehays, C. D. 99
Dehays, Christena 98
Dehays, E. 99
Dehays, Fredrick 99
Dehays, John 98
Dehayse, William 658
Dehert, Cath. 404
Dehert, Elizabeth B. 404
Dehert, Jno. 404
Dehl, Jacob 188
Dehl, Justus 225
Deime, Philip 373
Deirdorff, Elizabeth 70
Deirdorff, Henry 70
Deirdorff, Jane 70
Deirdorff, John 70
Deirdorff, Jonas 70
Deirdorff, Joseph 70
Deirdorff, Martha Ann 70
Deirdorff, Mary 70
Deirdorff, Rebecca 70
Deirdorff, Susan 70
Deity, Elizabeth 571
Deitz, Henry 571
Delan, Elizabeth 219
Delaney, Sarah 44
Delaney, William 165
Delano, Cornelius 713
Delany, Isaac 105, 456
DeLarguillon, Francis
713
Delay, Elizabeth 454
Delay, James 481
Delay, Jonathan 451
Delcever, Michael 456
Deldine, John H. 519
Deldine, William M. 519
Delea, Jean 515
Deleshmot, Van B. 383
Delia, Elenor 515
Dell, Eva 331
Dell, Magdalen 464
Dellinger, Emma 612
Dellinger, Joseph Kemy
612
Dellinger, Lucinda J.
612
Dellinger, M. 612, 615
Dellinger, Margaret 95
Dellinger, N. 612, 615
Dellinger, Nancy 612
Dellinger, W. 612
Dellinger, Wm. 95, 612,
615
Delong, Augustine 359
DeLong, Catharine 750
Delong, Cecelia 359
DeLong, Columbus 750
Delong, David 359, 731
DeLong, David 750
DeLong, Eleanor 750
Delong, Elizabeth 359
DeLong, Elizabeth 344
DeLong, Eve 745, 750

Delong, George 360
Delong, Hannah 715
Delong, Isaac 359, 360, 373, 621
Delong, Jacob 138
DeLong, Jacob 750
Delong, Jane 574
DeLong, Jefferson 744, 750
Delong, John 301, 311, 360
Delong, Joseph 359, 373
DeLong, Joseph 344
Delong, Joseph Edward 359
Delong, Josiah 603
Delong, Lucinda 359
Delong, Lydia 359
Delong, Mary 359, 360, 370, 567
Delong, Nancy 360, 569
DeLong, Nicholas 750
Delong, Philip 360
Delong, Sarah 44, 359, 567
Delong, Solomon 335
Delong, William 359, 360
Delorar, Alse 665
Delran, Elizabeth 219
Deman, Abner 138
Deman, Benejah 138
Deman, Olive 138
Deman, Susannah 138
Dement, George 178
Dement, Vincent 160, 174
Dement, William 155, 160
Dement, Wm. 160
Demier, Jeannette 713
Deming, Lunin 70
Deming, Mathias 571
Deming, Simeon 730
Deming, Simon 70
Demint, Rhody 462
Demitt, William 658
Demming, Simion 727
Demmit, Moses 488
Demoss, Hannah 657
Demoss, Thomas 496
Demott, Aaron 429
Demott, John 429
DeMott, Samuel 40
Dempsey, Samuel 635
Dempsey, Wm. 355, 356, 372
Demun, Sarah 497
Demuth, Abigail 574
Demuth, Anna Maria 568
Demuth, Christopher 571
Demuth, Lydia 565, 572
Demuth, Margaret 566
Demuth, Sarah 568
Den, John 477
Denen, Michael 262
Denham, Josephus 672
Dening, Lunin 70
Dening, Simon 70
Denise, Elenor 196
Denise, George 196
Denise, John 196

Denise, John H. 690
Denise, Margaret 196
Denise, Obadiah 690
Denise, Rhoda Jane 690
Denise, Sarah Ann 196
Denise, Sidney 187, 188, 196, 199
Denison, Agnesd 30
Deniston, Alex. 486
Deniston, Seges 413
Denmon, John 606
Dennedy, David 444
Dennen, Polly 127
Denney, Azariah 97
Denney, C. F. 97
Denney, J. 97
Dennis, David 344
Dennis, John 347, 380
Dennis, N. 344
Dennis, R. 344
Dennis, Samuel 347
Dennis, Sarah 347
Dennis, Susannah 347
Dennison, George 526
Denny, David 488
Denny, George 658
Denny, George B. 691
Denny, Isaac 357
Denny, James 390
Denny, John 713
Denny, Lettitia 384
Denny, Rebecca Jane 414
Denny, Samuel S. 543
Denny, William H. P. 691
Densell, Sarah Ann 607
Denson, Nancy D. 15
Dent, John E. 298
Dent, Lewis 283
Dent, Rebecca 295
Dent, Samuel 33
Dention, Robert 51
Denton, Jonas 739
Deomoss, Sally 498
Deonnl, Samuel 507
Depen, Margaret 302
Depo, Charles W. 744
Deppe, Charles 543
Deppe, Julius 543
Deppen, Joseph 112
Depra, Betsy 138
Depra, Daniel 138
Depra, David 138
Depra, Henry 138
Depra, John 138
Depra, Jonathan 138
Depra, Molly 138
Depray, Jacob 138
Deprey, Daniel 198
Deprey, John 198
DePu, George 716
Depue, Benjamin 530
Derby, H. A. 735
Derby, Mary E. 735
Derby, W. R. 735
Dereau, Catharine 385
Derner, Jacob 286
Derner, Jacob (Sr.) 286
Derr, John 469
Derrah, Joseph 296

Dershom, Tobias 348
Derth, Mordeica 166
Derth, Susanna 166
Derumple, Mary Catharine 433
Derumple, Peter S. 433
Derush, John 483
Derwater, Anna 295
Derwater, Barbara 295
Derwater, Catharine 295
Derwater, Elizabeth 295
Derwater, Eve 295
Derwater, Fanny 295
Derwater, Jacob 295
Derwater, John 295
Derwater, Naomia 295
Desbord, Metilda 452
Desbrow, Henry 469
Deselin, Jacob 496
Deselmno, Elenor 496
Deselms, Alice 175
Deselms, Benjamin 175
Deselms, Jonathan 496
Desheter, Joseph 496
Deshetter, Malinda 497
Deshler, Amelia 72
Deshler, Catharine 72
Deshler, Caty Ann 72
Deshler, David 72
Deshler, Sally 72
Deshler, Thomas 72
Desman, Geo. 274
Dess, Joseph 112
Detambel, Elizabeth 709
Deter, Betsey 127
Deterick, . . . 179
Deterly, Mary 710
Deterow, Elizabeth 657
Detrick, Baker 284
Detrick, Jacob 65
Detrick, Jane 65
Detrick, Peter 20
Detterich, Catharine 525
Dettmer, E. J. 614
Dettmer, Ernest J. 614
Dettmer, Ernst Justice 225
Dettmer, Frankie 614
Dettmer, G. A. 614
Dettmer, Jacob E. 614
Dettmer, John W. 614
Dettmer, Justus 226
Dettmer, M. M. Wilhelmine 614
Dettmer, Mahala A. 614
Dettmer, Nancy E. 614
Dettmer, R. 614
Dettmer, Rachel 614
Detwiler, Susannah 742
DeVacht, Francis Joseph 726
Devacht, Francis Joseph Winnocus 724
Devacht, Francis Joseph Winocus 725
Devacht, J. W. 725
Devall, Mary 746
Devalld, Clark 301
Devalt, Nicholas 456

821

Devalt, Noah 3
Devan, Jacob 492
Devaughn, Hezekiah 178
Devaul, Conrad 165, 181
Devaul, Conrad (Jr.) 181
Devaul, John 165, 181
Devaul, Kesiah 181
Devaul, Mary 181
Devault, Levina 44
Develin, Elizabeth 433
Develin, Eunice Louisa 433
Develin, Jemima 433
Devellers, Jules Amane 713
Develly, Phidelia 498
Deven, John D. 356
Deven, Thomas 266
Devenport, Anthony S. 473
Devenport, John 55
Dever, Betsey Betsey 504
Dever, Evan 621
Dever, Hanna 507
Dever, Hannah 504
Dever, Henry 543
Dever, James 504
Dever, John 504, 507
Dever, Joseph 507
Dever, Levi 259
Dever, Louisa 507
Dever, Loyd 532
Dever, Malvina 507
Dever, Mary 501, 513
Dever, Mary Alvira 507
Dever, Mary Jane 519
Dever, Michael 260
Dever, Polly 504
Dever, Rachel 504
Dever, Sarah 504, 514
Dever, William 504, 507
Devereaux, Joseph 258, 260, 264
Deverny, William 760
Devin, John D. 356
Devin, Thomas 269, 270
Devol, Arphasad 274
Devol, Batheheba 713
Devol, Charlotte 707, 718
Devol, Elizabeth 716
Devol, Gilbert 713
Devol, Jonathan 713
Devol, Nancy 713
Devol, Polly 713
Devol, Presburry 716
Devol, Wing 716
Devoll, Presilla 715
Devoll, Wanton 729
Devolld, Clark 306
Devon, John 463
Devor, Hannah 513
Devor, John 224
Devore, Jesse 82
Devore, Josias 451
Devore, Luke 283
Devors, John 463
Devorse, Joseph 456
Devowe, Hiram 500

Dew, James H. 496
Dewalt, Magdalen 554
Dewalt, Magdalena 554
Dewalt, Philip 554
Dewalt, Valentine 554
Dewalt, W. 555
Dewas, Mary 164
Dewas, Owen 164
Dewees, Elizabeth 118
Dewees, Mary 172
Dewees, Owen 172
Deweese, Andrew 138
Deweese, Ann 138
DeWeese, Benjamin 539
Deweese, David 138, 532
Deweese, David M. 143
Deweese, Elizabeth 138
Deweese, Hannah 138
Deweese, J. B. 540
DeWeese, J. D. 539
Deweese, J. H. 540
Deweese, James 143, 532
Deweese, Jas. A. 143
Deweese, Jethro 543
Deweese, John 138
Deweese, John G. 138
Deweese, John M. 540, 543
Deweese, John Runyan 540
Deweese, Joshua 124
Deweese, Joshua (Elder) 532
Deweese, Katharine 138
DeWeese, L. 539
Deweese, Malinda I. 143
Deweese, Margaret 119
Deweese, Mary 138
Deweese, Mary J. 138
Deweese, Melissa 138
Deweese, Meme 532
Deweese, Olive 143
Deweese, Peggy 138
Deweese, Polly 138
Deweese, Sally 138
Deweese, Samuel 138
Deweese, Sarah E. 143
Deweese, Susannah 540
Deweese, Sylvester E. 143
Deweese, Thos. L. 138
Deweese, Tracy 138
Deweese, Wm. 138, 143
Dewese, Anna 125
Dewese, Samuel 558
Dewey, Erastus H. 509
Dewey, Joseph 509
Dewey, Reuben 74
Dewey, Rosanna 509
Dewgan, Andrew 265
Dewit, Debby 585
Dewit, Delilah 588
Dewit, Peggy 386
Dewitt, John 463
Dewitt, Martin 383
DeWitt, Paul 519
Dewitte, Joseph 519
DeWolf, Nancy 88
Dewpew, Isabell 618
Dewpew, John 618

Dhafer, Charles 85
D'Hebecourt, Francis 722
Dibble, Levi 112
Dibble, Lyman 109, 112
Dibble, Rebecca 112
Dice, Frances 638
Dick, A. 525
Dick, Samuel 639
Dick, Sarah 407
Dick, Thomas 469, 471, 473, 474, 475, 484
Dickason, Ruth 466
Dicken, Mary 523
Dickensheets, Frederick 239
Dickensheets, Samuel A. 239
Dickensheets, Sarah 239
Dickenson, Lydia 465
Dickerson, Asa 279
Dickerson, Caleb 658
Dickerson, David 274
Dickerson, Deborah 719
Dickerson, Gulana 274
Dickerson, Harriet 274
Dickerson, Mary 274
Dickerson, Rhoda 274
Dickerson, William R. 157
Dickerson, Zadoc 258
Dickerson, Zadock (Jr.) 274
Dickerson, Zodock (Sr.) 274
Dickey, John 74
Dickey, Michael 50
Dickey, Washington 492
Dickey, William 492
Dickin, Abeah 630
Dickin, Abner 630
Dickinson, Augustus M. 38
Dickinson, Barney P. 38
Dickinson, Ellen I. 38
Dickinson, Harriet 591
Dickinson, Henry 161
Dickinson, Rebecca 15
Dickinson, Richard 12
Dickinson, Thomas 488
Dickinson, Walter 639
Dickison, Christopher 716
Dickison, Isaac 451, 456
Dickison, William 383
Dickman, C. H. 104
Dickman, Carl H. 104, 107
Dickman, Charles H. 104
Dickman, Maria Angela 104
Dickon, Nicholas 119
Dickson, Alexander 383
Dickson, High 736
Dickson, J. H. 37
Dickson, Jenny 117
Dickson, John 393, 440, 446, 589
Dickson, Joseph 469
Dickson, Joseph H. 37

Dickson, Mary A. Laudon 37
Dickson, Mary L. Manley 37
Dickson, Nathan 630
Dickson, Robert 132
Dickson, Robert Spence 383
Dickson, Salathiel 40
Dickson, Sally 121
Dickson, Sarah 452
Dickson, Thomas 736
Dickson, Thompson 12
Didaway, Augustine 517
Die, Andrew 665
Die, Polly 467
Dieben, --- 34
Diebine, William 226
Diebold, John 111
Diehl, Jacob 420
Diel, Benjamin 636
Dieluwit, Zera 506
Dieluwit, Zeru 506
Diem, Ann Maria 522
Dietrick, Katharine 607
Dietz, Catherine C. 578
Diffendall, Elizabeth S. 433
Diffendall, Mary 433
Diffendall, Sarah 433
Diffendall, Susannah 433
Diggans, Betsy 714
Dike, Saml. M. 263
Dike, Sarah 663
Dilbone, John 138
Dilbone, Margaret 138
Dilbone, Priscilla 138
Dilbone, Wm. H. 138
Dilcard, Lizzie Fishburn 735
Dilcever, Michael 456
Dile, Aron 658
Dill, Amy 198
Dill, Augustus 199
Dill, Catharine 433
Dill, Ellinor 459
Dill, Francis 433, 640
Dill, Henry H. 658
Dill, Jane 664
Dill, John C. 198, 199
Dill, John Wesley 433
Dill, Josiah 82, 86
Dill, Julia Ann 433
Dill, Lewis 198
Dill, Lewis E. 419
Dill, Lucinda Jane 433
Dill, Mary 199
Dill, Sarah 660
Dill, Tiresa 433
Dill, Welthy 665
Dill, William 665
Dillaha, Polly 384
Dillan, Nancy 512
Dillan, Polly 462
Dille, Caleb 164
Dille, Elizabeth 170
Dille, John 273
Dille, Joseph 170
Dille, Luke 168

Dille, Rebecca 164
Dillen, Mary W. 635
Dilley, Oliver P. 315
Dilliha, Polly 461
Dillin, Becky 465
Dillin, Frederick 12
Dillin, Isaac B. 12
Dillman, David 433
Dillman, John 433
Dillman, Joseph 418, 433
Dillman, Mary 433
Dillon, Asa 748
Dillon, Daugherty 160
Dillon, James 368
Dillon, Jesse 665
Dillon, John J. 519
Dillon, John L. 634
Dillon, Jonathan 748
Dillon, Josiah 160
Dillon, Mary 748
Dillon, Moses 287
Dillon, Thomas 519, 658
Dillon, William 634
Dills, George 340
Dills, John 359
Dillseiver, John 589
Dilman, Elizabeth 385
Dilman, Jacob 749
Dilon, Josiah M. 178
Dils, George 295
Dilseiver, Sarah 591
Dilts, Wm. F. 369
Diltz, Catharine 218
Diltz, Cornelius 218
Diltz, Eliza 218
Diltz, John 218
Diltz, Susan 218
Dimick, Augustus R. 29
Dimick, E. B. 35
Dimmick, Matthew 272
Dimmock, Seneca 321
Dines, James 451
Dines, Jeremiah 488
Dines, Rebecca 492
Dingler, H. 541
Dingler, Henry 541
Dingler, Isaac 541
Dingler, S. 541
Dingler, Susanna 541
Dingman, Abraham 124
Dingman, James 116
Dininger, Catharine 202
Dininger, Elizabeth 202
Dininger, Jacob 202
Dininger, John 202, 226
Dinnan, Mary 126
Dins, George 284
Dinsmore, John 134
Dinsmore, Matthew 134
Dinsmore, Robert 134
Dinwiddle, Robert 585
Dippra, Daniel 138
Dirrdoff, Dorothy 70
Dirrdoff, Jonas 70
Dirrdorff, Dorothy 70
Dirst, Elizabeth 363
Dirst, Martin 363
Disbrow, Anna 753
Disbrow, Henry 182, 224

Disbrow, Jacob 753
Disbrow, Jonathan 29
Disbrow, Matilda 28
Disbrow, Polly 31
Disbrow, Rebecka 29
Diserd, Joseph 383
Disher, Daniel 420
Dismal, Teresa 30
Disney, Samuel 77
Dison, Matilda 6
Dison, Thomas 105
Ditmore, Daniel 244
Ditmore, Frederick 244
Dits, Francis 224
Ditterow, Jacob 672
Ditto, Sarah 549
Ditto, Solomon 519
Dittoe, Ann 344
Dittoe, Anne Catherine 359
Dittoe, Anthony 350, 359
Dittoe, Clara 344
Dittoe, Eleanor 368
Dittoe, Eleanora M. C. 359
Dittoe, Eve 373
Dittoe, Henry 359, 368, 373, 376
Dittoe, Jacob 339, 359, 361, 368
Dittoe, John 359, 373
Dittoe, John H. 368
Dittoe, Mary 368
Dittoe, Michael 350, 359, 368, 373
Dittoe, Peter 359, 375
Dittoe, Peter S. 344
Dittoe, Rachel 359
Dittoe, Sarah 359
Diver, Samuel 571
Dix, John 456
Dix, Mary 514
Dix, Peres Main 621
Dixon, Ann 455
Dixon, Cyrus 6
Dixon, Eli 512
Dixon, Elizabeth 5, 6
Dixon, Emmy 6
Dixon, Esther 80
Dixon, Hale 488
Dixon, Hannah 466
Dixon, Henry 6, 393
Dixon, Isaac 393
Dixon, Isaac (Jr.) 393
Dixon, Jacob 635
Dixon, Jane 15
Dixon, Jesse 488
Dixon, John 5, 6, 393, 580, 584, 589, 731
Dixon, Joseph 456, 470, 630
Dixon, Margaret 6
Dixon, Mary 6
Dixon, Mary Ann 591
Dixon, Nancy 588
Dixon, Peter 230
Dixon, Rachel 467
Dixon, Rebecca 5, 630
Dixon, Robert 60

Dixon, Ruth 6
Dixon, Samuel 473
Dixon, Sarah 6, 78, 458
Dixon, Simon 6
Dixon, Thomas 716
Dixon, William 77, 463
Dixson, Mary 367
Dixton, Joseph 473
D'Lashmutt, Anne 52
D'Lashmutt, Anne Maria 52
D'Lashmutt, Edmund Lyne 52
D'Lashmutt, Elias 52
D'Lashmutt, Elizabeth 52
D'Lashmutt, Francis Alexander 52
D'Lashmutt, Van B. 52
D'Lashmutt, Walter Collen 52
Doak, Mary 549
Doak, Patrick 543
Doan, A. 733
Doan, Argellous 731
Doan, David C. 761
Doan, Elizabeth 681
Doan, Hannah 681
Doan, Isaac 681
Doan, Jemima 681
Doan, John 658
Doan, Joseph C. 681
Doan, Lyman 22
Doan, Margaret 681
Doan, Ruth 659
Doan, Vinson 681
Dobbeling, Henrietta 104
Dobbins, Barbara 310
Dobbins, Charlotte C. 310
Dobbins, James 310
Dobbins, Joseph 543
Dobbins, Sarah M. 310
Dobson, Kesiah 334
Dobyns, Geroge Washington 408
Dock, Frederick 111
Dockum, Sarah 58
Doctor, Elizabeth V. 683
Doctor, James St. 683
Doctor, John 683
Doctor, John K. 683
Doctor, William L. 683
Docyor, Elizabeth V. 683
Dod, Isaac 512
Dodd, Isabella 186
Dodd, Joseph (Jr.) 186
Dodd, Samuel H. 589
Dodd, Thomas 589
Dodd, Wash. 353
Dodd, William 186, 187, 335
Dodderer, Andrew 82
Dodds, Andrew 585
Dodds, Hannah 586
Dodds, Jno. 270
Dodds, John 258, 633
Dodds, John F. 599
Dodds, William (Sr.) 189
Dodds, Wm. 378

Dodge, Hiram 585
Dodge, John 716
Dodge, Luther 627
Dodge, Lydia 575
Dodge, Mahitable 506
Dodge, Nathaniel 12
Dodge, Oliver 716
Dodge, P. O. 711
Dodge, Smantha 523
Dods, Benjamin 658
Dodson, J. C. 539
Dodson, John 2
Dodson, Mary 539
Dodson, Rachel 2
Dodson, William 196
Doe, John 469, 470
Doge, Elenor 586
Dogherty, James 82
Doherty, George 285
Doherty, Margret 336
Dolan, Charles 360
Dolan, Ellen O. 636
Dolan, Simon 636
Doland, John 258
Dolbier, Benjamin 589
Dolivar, Edy 758
Dolivar, Ira 758
Dolivar, Sarah Jane 758
Doll, Magdalen 464
Doll, Mary 452
Dollarhide, Kitty 513
Dollarson, Pricilla 665
Dollison, Daniel 496
Dollison, Hanna 119
Dollison, J. F. 366
Dollison, Mary A. 138
Dollison, William 138
Dolly, Elizabeth 461
Dome, Bridget D. 570
Domer, Susanna 571
Dominey, Alvin H. 47
Doming, Jeremiah 64
Donaghey, John 448
Donahoe, Polly 464
Donahue, Winifred 583
Donaldson, Andrew 755
Donaldson, Aras Berkley 757
Donaldson, David P. 359
Donaldson, Ebenezer R. 359
Donaldson, Elizabeth 359
Donaldson, Frances Amanda 757
Donaldson, George Thomas 757
Donaldson, Harriet Catharine 757
Donaldson, Harriett Catherine 757
Donaldson, Hiram 755
Donaldson, Hiram Alexander 757
Donaldson, James 359, 758
Donaldson, James H. 757
Donaldson, John 359, 473, 755
Donaldson, Martha 359

Donaldson, Mary 359
Donaldson, Mary Ann 755
Donaldson, Mathew 359
Donaldson, Nancy 757
Donaldson, Rebecca 359
Donaldson, Richard F. 757
Donaldson, Richard Franklin 757
Donaldson, Robert Safford 757
Donaldson, Sarah 359
Donaldson, Thomas 757, 760
Donaldson, William 760
Donaldson, William Thomas 760
Donalson, Wm. 755
Donallan, Nelson 208
Donally, Andrew 77
Donally, Henry 631
Donally, John 585
Donally, Nancy 631
Donally, Peggy 631
Donalson, James 40
Donalson, James E. 595
Donalston, John 51
Donaly, Henry 631
Donaly, Peggy 631
Donat, J. 330
Donat, John 330
Donat, Jonathan 330
Donat, Nancy 744
Donat, P. 330
Donat, Polly 330
Donely, Jane 119
Doner, Abraham 605
Doner, Mary 749
Doney, Barton 404
Doney, Jas. B. 404
Doney, Rachel 404
Doniface, James 758
Doniface, Susan 758
Donley, Hagre 313
Donley, Henry 744
Donley, James 344
Donley, Nancy 344
Donley, Rosanna 744
Donley, William 744
Donnel, Patrick 428
Donnell, John 703
Donnelly, James 40
Donnels, Mary 702
Donnels, Susan 21
Donner, Solomon 298
Donohoo, Susanna 182
Donough, Robert 488
Donough, Robt. 456
Donoughe, Robert 485
Donovan, Dennis 335
Donovan, Julia Ann 335
Donoven, Elizabeth 548
Donstn, Abraham 543
Doofman, John 665
Dooley, Agness 429
Dooley, Caleb W. 433
Dooley, Catharine Jane 433
Dooley, Elvina 433

Dooley, Henry 239
Dooley, John 303
Dooley, Kirtland 433
Dooley, Levi P. 433
Dooley, Martha 433
Dooley, Martin L. 429
Dooley, Orpha 433
Dooley, Rachel 429
Dooley, Richard 433
Dooley, Samuel 429, 433
Dooley, Selisa 433
Dooley, Silas 429
Doolittle, David 40
Doolittle, Harmon 754
Doolittle, Horace H. 754
Doolittle, John S. 754
Doolittle, Phebe Ann 754
Doolittle, Sophia C. 754
Door, Richard 260
Doore, Sarah 271
Doore, Wm. G. 271
Doorman, Solomon 433
Doorman, Susan 433
Dorhady, Elinor 457
Dorlan, George 40
Dorman, Christian 138
Dorman, David 138
Dorman, Elenor 138
Dorman, Elizabeth M. 135
Dorman, John B. 138
Dormer, Mary 567
Dorning, Abigal 52
Dorr, Edmon 716
Dorr, Edmund 728
Dorr, Matthew 728, 729
Dorrot, --- 745
Dorrough, Thomas 743
Dorsen, Zadock 456
Dorset, Jane 76
Dorsey, Hannah 293
Dorum, George 383
Dorwin, Philo 23
Doser, George 289
Dost, Titus 589
Doster, James 249, 293
Dotey, Ephraim 156
Dotson, Thomas 55
Doty, Ephraim 156, 157
Doty, Horatio 40
Doty, Mary 157, 588, 744
Doubleday, Mary 714
Doude, Andrew 713
Doudle, Peter 344
Doudna, Henry 255
Dougal, Johnm 692
Dougherty, Charles 524
Dougherty, David M. 82
Dougherty, Dennis 524
Dougherty, Elizabeth 663
Dougherty, Elizabeth A. 688
Dougherty, Hannah 25
Dougherty, James 449
Dougherty, James F. 688
Dougherty, John 524
Dougherty, John W. 688
Dougherty, Margery 718
Dougherty, Martha A. 688
Dougherty, Mary 524

Dougherty, Peter 524
Dougherty, Sarah E. 688
Dougherty, Thomas 124, 688
Dougherty, William 87
Dougherty, William K. 688
Dougherty, Wm. 89
Doughman, Daniel 688
Doughman, Eve 688
Doughty, Richard 298
Douglas, Andrew 383
Douglas, Clarissa 745
Douglas, David 658
Douglas, Elizabeth 658
Douglas, Gustavus 40
Douglas, James 492
Douglas, Jared E. 419
Douglas, Joshua 311
Douglas, Mary 79
Douglas, Mary E. L. 419
Douglas, Michael 439
Douglass, Elizabeth 763
Douglass, Ellen S. 763
Douglass, George 408
Douglass, John A. 763
Douglass, Margaret 568
Douglass, Martha C. 763
Douglass, Mary G. 763
Douglass, Robert 119
Douglass, Sally H. 763
Douglass, Sally W. 763
Douglass, Sarah 14
Douglass, William S. 17
Douk, William 549
Douner, Appleton 290
Dountz, Frederick 47
Dourson, Mary 710
Dourson, Thomas 710
Douthet, Sarah 663
Dover, Ann 672
Dow, Alvin 519
Dow, Ann 22
Dow, David 704
Dow, Mary Ann 753
Dowden, Lethe 15
Dowden, Sally 13
Dowden, Sophia 15
Dowell, John 731
Dowing, Mary 663
Dowman, Elizabeth 521
Downdride, Polly 467
Downey, Ephraim 303
Downey, Jeremiah 64
Downey, Polly 391
Downey, Summerset 391
Downey, William 450
Downhour, Betsey 359
Downhour, Catherine 359
Downhour, Elizabeth 354, 359
Downhour, George 359
Downhour, Jacob 359
Downhour, John 344, 359
Downhour, Magdalene 359
Downhour, Margaret 344
Downhour, Naomi 359
Downhour, Peter 359
Downhour, Stephen 359

Downing, Francis 451
Downing, Franklin 82
Downing, George 77
Downing, J. H. 736
Downing, Jemimah 462
Downing, John 383, 407
Downing, Meshair 451
Downing, Nancy 667
Downing, Rachel 58
Downing, Radner 77
Downing, Samuel 86
Downing, Sarah 451
Downing, William 543
Downs, Abigal 659
Downs, David 456
Downs, Henry 534
Downs, John 407, 456, 488
Downs, Martha M. 534
Downs, Mary F. 407
Downs, Rachel 98
Downs, Rebecca 456
Downs, Thos. 456
Downs, Wm. 98
Downy, Noah 519
Dowse, John 527
Dowse, Mary 527
Dowse, William 527
Doyal, Edward 427
Doyal, Isabella 420
Doyal, Mary 420
Doyl, Mary 718
Doyly, Hannah 456
Drake, Abraham 543
Drake, Amanda I. 692
Drake, Daniel 692
Drake, E. E. 692
Drake, Edward 639
Drake, Elizabeth 639
Drake, Elizabeth E. 692
Drake, Elmira 149
Drake, Elsy A. 149
Drake, Henry 658
Drake, Isabella 138
Drake, Isaih E. 692
Drake, Ithamer 668
Drake, J. C. 496
Drake, J. W. 692
Drake, Jane 639, 667
Drake, Jeremiah 138
Drake, Joel (Rev.) 692
Drake, John 658
Drake, John W. 692
Drake, Julia J. 692
Drake, Margaret 293
Drake, Martha 523
Drake, Martha J. 692
Drake, Mary 29, 149, 549, 667
Drake, Mary V. 692
Drake, Matilda 692
Drake, Patty 658
Drake, Peter 639, 684
Drake, Rebecca 684
Drake, Rebekah 666
Drake, Samuel 721
Drake, Sarah 692
Drake, William 543
Drake, William A. 149

Drake, William B. 692
Drake, Wm. A. 149
Drake, Wm. S. 149
Drakely, Thos. 404
Draper, John 263, 273
Draper, Rebecca 658
Draper, William 156, 658
Drees, John M. 104, 107
Drees, Michael 488
Drees, Tobias 543
Drennen, Thomas 472, 474
Dresbach, Catherine 390
Dresbach, Daniel 390
Dresbach, E. 524, 525
Dresbach, Henry 383
Dresbach, John 390
Dresser, Caroline 324
Dressman, Herman H. 543
Drew, Mary 655
Driggs, Dolly 156
Driggs, Joseph 156,
  159, 161, 167, 176
Driggs, Nelson 177
Driggs, Phebe 176
Drill, Amy Rebecca 215
Drill, George 215
Drill, George W. 215
Drill, Jacob A. 215
Drill, Jemima 215
Drill, John Wm. 215
Drim, Arthur 177
Driscol, John 223
Driscoll, Marguerite 34
Driver, Nancy 456
Driver, Rebecca 457
Driver, Sally 383
Droge, Ed. 361
Droulard, John 658
Drown, Benjamin 707
Drown, Delilah 707
Drown, Drusilla 707
Drown, John 707
Drown, John (Jr.) 707
Drown, Nancy 707
Drown, Notley 707
Droz, Peter 723, 724
Drum, Ann 292
Drum, Isaac 292
Drum, Levi 496
Drum, Mary 169
Drum, Samuel 288
Drum, Simon 152
Drum, William 403
Drumb, Mary 495
Drumm, Sarah 356
Drummond, Elizabeth 10
Drummond, John 10
Drummond, William 10
Drumn, Elizabeth 709
Drumo, William 496
Drurey, Edward 463
Drury, Abigal C. 502
Drury, James 112
Drury, Laura 112
Drury, Sybil 112
Dubois, Benjamin 215,
  650, 676
Dubois, Benjamin J. 650
DuBois, Francis 116

Duchallard, Prter 722
Duck, Philip 571
Duckworth, George 658
Duckworth, John 639
Duckworth, Robert 639
Dudley, Daniel 649
Dudley, David (Rev.) 594
Dudley, Emeline 649
Dudley, Gilman 264, 268
Dudley, Moses 648, 649
Dudley, Peter 649
Dudley, Ruby 649
Dudley, Washington 649
Duduit, Agalitha 513
Duduit, Caroline 516
Duduit, W. 507
Duduit, William 507
Duduit, Zaire 507
Dudwit, Augustine 517
Duey, Rebeckah 516
Dufer, Abel 711
Duff, Daniel 287
Duff, Harriet 8
Duff, Julia Ann 8
Duff, Silas C. 8
Duffe, Matthew 317
Duffee, Matthew 319
Duffee, Samuel 463
Duffield, John 628
Duffield, Lusina 628
Duffield, Susan
  Elizabeth 433
Duffin, Hugh 470, 486
Dufur, Abel 710
Dugan, Adison 500
Dugan, Andrew 265, 269,
  271, 290
Dugan, Benjamin 290
Dugan, Betsey 290
Dugan, Eliza 58
Dugan, James 500, 652
Dugan, James R. 652
Dugan, Jane 290
Dugan, John 290
Dugan, Lyddy 513
Dugan, Martha 290
Dugan, Mary 465
Dugan, Nancy 500
Dugan, Patrick 488
Dugan, Samuel 731
Dugan, Thomas 500
Dugan, Thos. 456
Dukes, Andrew 496
Duley, Charles 463
Duliel, Francis 501
Duliel, Peter 501
Duling, Zachariah 443
Dull, Catharine 606
Dull, Elizabeth 609
Dull, Hannah 606
Dull, Jacob 606
Dull, John 96
Dull, Lydia 606
Dull, Susan 96
Dulty, George 180
Dulty, John 286, 288
Dulty, Mary 180
Duly, Alexander 57
Duly, James 57

Duly, Sarah 57
Dum, Arthur 177
Duman, Geo. 270
Dumand, Joseph 124
Dumbauld, P. C. 377
Dumbauld, P. W. 377
Duming, James 302
Dummand, Joseph 124
Dumond, Isaac 524
Dunahoe, Precella 386
Dunaway, Elizabeth 657
Dunbar, Nancy 488
Dunbar, William 488
Duncan, Betsey 50
Duncan, Daniel 471
Duncan, David 472, 475,
  479
Duncan, Delilah 610
Duncan, Eliza 495
Duncan, James 558
Duncan, Joseph 607
Duncan, Lewis Langhorn
  50
Duncan, Mariah 385
Duncan, Mary 50
Duncan, Nancy 50, 607
Duncan, Patty 50, 85
Duncan, Polly 607
Duncan, Robert Peyton 50
Duncan, Sally 50
Duncan, Sarah Ann 117
Dunderman, Philip 334
Dune, Thomas 91
Dunfee, Elizabeth 172
Dunfee, John 169
Dunfee, Sarah 169
Dunfee, Thomas 172
Dungan, Ann Rebekah 467
Dungan, Cadwalder S. 152
Dungan, Eliza 58
Dungan, James 483
Dungan, Jane 51
Dungan, Jesse 51
Dungan, John 554
Dungan, Levi 637
Dungan, Nancy 514
Dungan, Sarah 47
Dunham, Abraham 652
Dunham, Amos 731
Dunham, Asa 124, 129
Dunham, Bathsheba 715,
  720
Dunham, Daniel 713,
  720, 722, 723
Dunham, Edward 658
Dunham, Eli 496
Dunham, Elizabeth 129
Dunham, James 652
Dunham, Jno. 723
Dunham, Joseph 638, 650
Dunham, Margaret 738
Dunham, Ruth 715
Dunham, Thomas 738, 743
Duniface, James 758
Dunkan, Amos 119
Dunkerly, Ann 226
Dunkerly, Enoch 226
Dunkerly, George 226
Dunkerly, James 226

Dunkerly, Joseph 226
Dunkerly, Luke 226
Dunkerly, Mary 226
Dunkerly, Susannah 226
Dunkin, Abigail 143
Dunkin, Amos 138
Dunkin, Amos E. 143
Dunkin, Amos W. 143
Dunkin, C. 330
Dunkin, Carolina 330
Dunkin, D. 330
Dunkin, David 143, 330
Dunkin, Eli 143
Dunkin, Elizabeth 143
Dunkin, George H. 330
Dunkin, Isaac 119, 143
Dunkin, Isaiah 138
Dunkin, John 138
Dunkin, Mary 118
Dunkin, Richard 138
Dunkin, Sally 138
Dunkin, Samuel 138
Dunkin, Saul 143
Dunkle, Rachel 634
Dunlap, Alexander 138
Dunlap, Ann 40
Dunlap, Catharine E. 419
Dunlap, Elizabeth 514, 551
Dunlap, James 473, 481, 482, 483, 571
Dunlap, Jane 575
Dunlap, Jas. 478
Dunlap, John 492
Dunlap, Joseph 12
Dunlap, Margaret 664
Dunlap, Mary 664
Dunlap, Robert 451
Dunlap, Sally 458
Dunlap, Wm. 571
Dunlavey, George 157
Dunlavy, Francis 646
Dunlavy, Geo. 174
Dunlevey, George 156
Dunlevy, Anthony H. 678, 679
Dunlevy, Francis 655
Dunlevy, George 265
Dunn, Abijah 124
Dunn, Alice 636
Dunn, Anne 11
Dunn, Arthur 177
Dunn, Casander 163
Dunn, Elijah 179
Dunn, George F. 12
Dunn, Isaac 690
Dunn, James 152
Dunn, John 18, 163, 164
Dunn, John R. 681
Dunn, Robert 549
Dunn, Stephen 138
Dunn, Washington 172, 175
Dunn, William 165
Dunnack, Joshua 383
Dunnen, Harriet 126
Dunnuch, Margaret 433
Dunscomb, Gilbert 744
Dunston, Eliza 14

Dunston, Temperance 14
Dunston, Thomas 12
Dunton, Samuel 34
Dunw . . . , Wm. 99
Dunwiddie, Almira 433
Dunwiddie, Debotah 433
Dunwiddie, Elizabeth 585
Dunwiddie, Hiram 213
Dunwiddie, John 213
Dunwiddie, Ruth 433
Dunwoody, Elizabeth 164
Dunwoody, James 164
Dunwoody, Wm. 99
Dupler, Elizabeth 353
Dupler, Fredk. 338
Dupler, Philip 338, 353
Dupler, Sarah 364
Duport, Marian 727
Duport, Marin 724
Durand, Samuel 321
Durbin, Anna 385
Durbin, Theresa R. 612
Durbin, Thomas 486
Durfey, E. L. 327
Durfey, Iloe M. 327
Durfey, M. A. 327
Durfey, Olive 328
Durfy, Delectus 519
Durgee, Silas 716
Durgens, Nancy 465
Durham, William 488
Duringer, Anthony 111
Durkee, Mary 168
Durlin, Hannah 252
Durlin, William 252
Durn, Mary 574
Durn, Stary 571
Durst, Abraham 77, 201
Durst, Henry 77
Durst, Mary 83
Durst, Michael 77
Durst, Samuel 82
Durst, Sophia 88
Durst, Susannah 84, 85
Durt, Elfinda 337
Dusaille, Jeanne Francois 713
Dusenberry, Benjamin 360
Dusenberry, Catherine 360
Dusenberry, Henry 360
Dusenberry, John 360
Dusenberry, William 282, 360
Dusenberry, Wm. 360
Duskey, Geo. 77
Dust, Mary 83
Dust, Nancy 576
Dust, Samuel 82
Dustan, Lydia 280
Dustan, Maria A. 152
Dustan, Seth B. 152
Dusten, Hannah M. 742
Dusten, Nathaniel (Dr.) 742
Dustimer, Catharena 567
Dustin, Miahill 731
Dutro, David 285
Dutrow, Andrew 266

Dutrow, John 266
Dutterer, Christian 323
Dutterer, Francis C. 334
Dutterow, Catharine 664
Dutton, Harison 731
Dutton, James 338, 731
Dutton, Joseph 731
Dutton, Pliny 66
Duval, Daniel 259
Duval, David 589
Duval, Elizabeth 589
Duval, Grafton 290, 291
Duval, Nancy 707
Duval, Rebecca 588
Duvall, Charles 753
Duvall, Jane 419
Duvall, Jas. A. 731
Duvall, John L. 419
Duvall, Marcam 406
Duvall, William 406
Duvege, F. 724
Duverge, Francis 725
Duverger, Anthony 724
Duverger, Francis 724
Duverger, Martha 724
Duverger, Stephen 724
Duvois, Elizabeth 452
Duvol, Arphaxad 258, 268
Dwellers, Jules Amane 713
Dwight, Seraph 730
Dyar, Jos. B. 731
Dyccas, Jacob 744
Dyce, Elizabeth 745
Dyce, George 284
Dyche, David R. 682
Dyche, George 682
Dyche, Mary 682
Dyche, Nancy 682
Dyche, Ruth 682
Dyche, William 682
Dye, A. 383
Dye, Abigail 714
Dye, Amos 731
Dye, Andrew 135
Dye, Andrew (Jr.) 119
Dye, Aniel 152
Dye, Belinda 138
Dye, Benj. L. 143
Dye, Benjamin 124, 135
Dye, Betsy 135
Dye, Dan. 731
Dye, Daniel 168
Dye, Daniel H. 731
Dye, David 152, 161, 164, 169
Dye, Dicy 152
Dye, Eliza 78
Dye, Elizabeth 124, 126, 135, 143, 170, 532
Dye, Ellen 143
Dye, Ezekiel 264, 731
Dye, Geo. 264
Dye, George 267
Dye, J. J. 532
Dye, James 124, 260
Dye, Jno. G. 731
Dye, Jno. W. 731
Dye, John 116, 135, 143, 731

Dye, John E.   138
Dye, John M.   135
Dye, John R.   170
Dye, Jonathan   731
Dye, Letitia   143
Dye, Margaret M.   138
Dye, Marshall A.   138
Dye, Martin   77
Dye, Mary   135, 138
Dye, Mary A.   138
Dye, Nelly   118
Dye, Philena   79
Dye, Precila   124
Dye, Priscilla   170
Dye, Rachel   118
Dye, Reuben   168
Dye, Robt.   731
Dye, Samuel   135, 138,
   711, 731
Dye, Sarah   118, 121, 143
Dye, Sarah A.   138
Dye, Sarah Ann   143
Dye, Stephen   124, 135
Dye, Thomas   262
Dye, Thos.   267
Dye, Vincent   124, 168,
   273
Dye, William   135
Dye, Wm.   143
Dye, Wm. H. H.   138
Dyer, James   481
Dyer, Jos. B.   731
Dyke, George   665
Dynis, William   658
Dys, Harriet   576
Dysart, Mary   591
Dysart, Rachel   515
Dysart, Stephen   512
Dysert, Ellen   96
Dysert, G. W.   96
Dysert, Geo. W.   96
Dysert, Ida Bell   96
Dysert, John   589
Dysert, John H.   96
Dysert, Julian   588
Dysert, Margaret   96
Dysert, Mary   96, 584,
   588
Dysert, S. E.   96
Dysert, Sarah E. Roebuck
   96
Dyson, John B.   303

--- E ---

Eachus, Mary   660
Eagle, David   194
Eagle, Jacob   194
Eagle, Peter   192, 194
Eagle, Sally   192
Eagler, Conrad   555
Eakan, James   665
Eaker, Margaret   387
Eakin, James L.   508
Eakin, Martha Ann   143
Eakins, Sarah   452
Eakins, Wm.   54

Eakman, Eliza   274
Ealladay, David   513
Eamins, John   456
Eamis, Elizabeth   576
Eanenfight, Christopher
   672
Earabaugh, Peter   320
Eare, George   503
Eare, Mary   503
Earhart, Barbara   680
Earhart, Catharine   414
Earhart, Daniel   433
Earhart, Elizabeth   433
Earhart, George   670, 673
Earhart, Martin   670,
   673, 680
Earhart, Martin (Sr.)
   639
Earhart, Mary   433, 670
Earhart, Michael   433
Earhart, Nancy   433
Earhart, Nicholas   673
Earhart, Peter   658
Earhart, Polly   662
Earl, Granthem   456
Earl, John   420
Earl, Mary   741
Earl, Mathew   383
Earl, Robert   741
Earlart, Margaret   295
Earley, Benoni   307
Earley, Demariaus   413
Earley, Elizabeth   307
Earley, John   281
Earley, Nancy   134
Earls, Rebecca   119
Early, Elisabeth   577
Early, James   167
Early, Nancy   167
Early, Patsy   93
Early, Peter   338, 463
Early, William   167
Earnest, Michael   383
Earnhart, Isebella   466
Earnhart, Lydia   653
Earnhart, Mary   399
Earnheart, William   383
Eartabough, Peter   335
Eastburn, Philip   513
Easten, Margaret   14
Eastep, Elizabeth   522
Easterd, C.   697
Easterd, Charissa   697
Easterd, M.   697
Easterd, N.   697
Easterd, Nomona A.   697
Easterday, Christ.   216
Easterday, Christian   398
Easterday, John W.   398
Easterday, Mary   398
Easterday, Noah   398
Easterday, Sarah Ellen
   398
Easterday, Thomas Nelson
   398
Easterland, Mary   663
Eastman, Apples   589
Eastman, Martha   55
Easton, Charlotte   23

Easton, William   58
Eaton, Abijah   178
Eaton, Ahijah   153
Eaton, Betsy   334
Eaton, David   153, 162,
   178, 180
Eaton, David (Jr.)   161
Eaton, Elizabeth   178
Eaton, Emily R.   336
Eaton, Hannah   153, 162
Eaton, Henen M.   143
Eaton, Isaac   472
Eaton, Ivers   143
Eaton, Jane   153, 178
Eaton, John   496
Eaton, Mary Ann   337
Eaton, Polly   499
Eaton, Rachel   178
Eaton, Roene   143
Eaton, William   12
Eators, Jacob   451
Ebbert, Peter   303
Eberman, Jacob M.   738
Eberman, Sarah   738
Ebersbach, Philip   91
Ebersole, Eliza   429
Ebersole, Harman   429
Ebersole, Henry   528
Ebersole, Jacob   429
Ebersole, Mary   429
Ebersole, Peter   529
Ebert, . . .   235
Ebert, Carloim   235
Ebert, Lydia   235
Ebert, Maria   235
Ebert, Mehely   235
Ebert, William   235
Ebie, Joseph   558
Eblen, Sally   79
Ebulin, Rachel   79
Eby, Abraham   360
Eby, Andrew   360
Eby, Barbara   360
Eby, Catherine   360
Eby, David   360
Eby, Eve   360
Eby, Jacob   360
Eby, John   360
Eby, Magdaline   360
Eby, Mary Ann   519
Eby, Noah   519
Eby, Peter   360
Eby, Simon   217
Eccles, Mary   67
Eccles, Samuel   67
Eccord, Samuel   160,
   180, 181
Eccord, Susanna   180
Eckard, Peter   571
Eckels, Daniel   44
Eckenrode, John   368
Eckert, Daniel   237
Eckert, Fidelia   334
Eckert, Gottlieb   237
Eckert, Jacob   237
Eckert, Maria   237
Eckler, Ambrose Rice
   757, 762
Eckles, Julia   360

Eckles, Margaret 360
Eckles, Richard 360
Eckles, Sally 360
Eckles, William 360
Eckley, John 40
Eckman, Ann 231
Eckman, Daniel 231
Eckman, George 519
Eckols, Charles H. 40
Eddings, Hannah 116
Eddington, Jonathan 256, 272
Eddington, Olive 256
Eddington, Susan 256
Eddington, Ursula 256
Eddison, Elizabeth 517
Eddleman, Caty 572
Eddy, Abigail 666
Eddy, Enneny 659
Eddy, Hannah 80
Eddy, Isaac 177
Eddy, Joseph 654
Eddy, Laodicea 76
Eddy, Mevilla 654
Eddy, Nancy 177
Eddy, Peter 161
Eddy, Phebe 654
Eddyburn, Anna 333
Edgar, Andrew 478
Edgar, Catharine 210
Edgar, Daniel 581
Edgar, George B. 210, 217
Edgar, Hannah 581
Edgar, John 486, 581
Edgar, John W. 589
Edgar, Robert A. 210, 217
Edgar, William 589
Edgecomb, Amy 606
Edger, John 510
Edger, Joseph 510
Edger, Mary 510
Edger, Robert 182, 184
Edgerly, Daniel W. 571
Edgerton, Abraham D. 764
Edgerton, D. 764
Edgerton, Elizabeth 13
Edgerton, Lydia 764
Edgerton, Nathaniel 764
Edgerton, Susan G. 764
Edgington, Aaron 553
Edgington, Isaac 553
Edgington, Jesse 555
Edgington, John 553
Edgington, Nancy 553
Edgington, Noah 553
Edgington, Peggy 553
Edgington, Rebecah 553
Edgington, Sally 553
Edginton, John 553
Edie, David 669
Edie, Margret 669
Edington, John 442, 669
Edison, James 500
Edison, Jas. 504
Edison, Margaret 513
Edmiston, Abraham 98
Edmiston, C. 98

Edmiston, Catharine 98
Edmiston, J. 98
Edmiston, Jacob 98
Edmiston, Thomas 488
Edmonds, David 565
Edmonds, Edward 565
Edmonds, Nathaniel 565
Edmonds, Peter 561
Edmonds, Peter (Jr.) 561
Edmonds, Sylvena Jain 29
Edmons, Peter (Jr.) 566
Edmonson, Enoch 418
Edsall, John 446
Edsall, Samuel 446
Edson, Charles P. 604
Edson, John 413
Edward, David 77
Edward, Peggy 456
Edwards, Amanda 683
Edwards, Archabald 669
Edwards, Benjamin 634
Edwards, Catharine 176
Edwards, Eden 683
Edwards, Elizabeth 645, 673
Edwards, Forster 260, 274
Edwards, Foster 260
Edwards, Henry 762
Edwards, Homer 734
Edwards, Isaac 731
Edwards, James 176, 658, 672
Edwards, John 182, 189, 470, 566, 645, 669, 673
Edwards, John S. 549
Edwards, Joseph 645, 673, 683
Edwards, Josias 645, 673
Edwards, Justice 12
Edwards, Lemuel James 189
Edwards, Maria 734
Edwards, Martin 519
Edwards, Nancy 645, 673
Edwards, Nathaniel 669
Edwards, Olive 138
Edwards, Rachel 521
Edwards, Rezin B. 689
Edwards, Ruth 669
Edwards, Sarah 144
Edwards, William 383, 669
Edwards, Wm. 124
Edwin, Hiram 433
Edy, Alexander 644
Edy, David 644
Edy, Jane 644
Eely, Peter 124
Egbert, David P. 688
Egbert, Delilah 433
Egbert, James 433
Egbert, John H. 543
Egbert, Nancy 433
Egbert, Nettie May 541
Egbert, Samuel 681
Egbert, Sarah 523
Egbert, Uriah 527

Egenbroad, Lewis 124
Eger, Ludwig 161
Eglin, Mary 37
Ehert, Jacob 268
Ehrhart, . . . 11y 234
Ehrhart, Abraham 234, 235
Ehrhart, Anna Elisabeth 235
Ehrhart, Anna Maria 234
Ehrhart, Daniel 234
Ehrhart, Elisabeth 234
Ehrhart, Maria 234
Ehrhart, Nancy 234
Ehrhart, Rebeka 235
Ehrhart, Rebeke 234
Ehrhart, Sara 234
Ehrhart, Susana 234
Ehrhart, Susanna 234
Ehrhart, William 234
Ehrhert, Jacob 238
Ehrhert, John 238
Ehrhert, Susannah 238
Ehrstine, John 194
Eich, Anna Maria 105
Eich, John 105
Eich, Jonnes 105
Eichar, Geo. W. 114
Eichar, Henry 114
Eichar, John Alexander 114
Eichen, Elener 497
Eichinger, John J. 92
Eichur, Elener 497
Eickey, John 565
Eidemuller, Peter 709
Eidmullet, Dorothea Margaretha 709
Eidson, Elizabeth 504
Eidson, James 504
Eidson, Jas. 502
Eidson, Margaret 504
Eidson, Sarah 504
Eikenbary, David 420
Eikenbary, Reuben 420
Eikenberry, Christiana 433
Eikenberry, Elizabeth 433
Eikenberry, John 433
Eikenberry, Joseph 433
Eikenberry, Lydia 433
Eikenberry, Mary 433
Eikenberry, Peter 433
Eikman, Ephraim 274
Eikman, John 415
Fikman, Sally 415
Ekins, Benj. F. 144
Ekins, Clementine 144
Elarton, John 527
Elbert, John D. (Sr.) 27
Elder, Abraham 4
Elder, Ann 308
Elder, Asbury 379
Elder, Benedict 207, 208
Elder, Charles 207, 208, 365
Elder, Eliza Ann 376
Elder, Elizabeth 207, 208

Elder, Eve 207, 208
Elder, James 731
Elder, John 363, 365, 761
Elder, Jos. 528
Elder, Mary Ann 608
Elder, Samuel 104, 469, 483
Elder, Steward 308
Elder, Stewart 301
Elder, William 104, 351, 433, 665
Eldor, Charles 119
Eldred, Aaron 29
Eldred, Mary P. 28
Eldred, Noah 29
Eldred, Samuel 513
Eldredg, James 554
Eldredg, William 554
Eldredge, Abigail 554
Eldredge, James 554
Eldredge, Nathan 554
Eldredge, Polly 554
Eldredge, Sarah 554
Eldredge, Stephen 554
Eldredge, Thomas 554
Eldredge, William 554
Eldridge, Elijah 549
Eldridge, Prudence 551
Eleman, John 131
Elenwood, Daniel 713
Eley, Andrew 530
Elfrits, Abraham 589
Elgee, Robert 398
Elifrits, George 585
Elifrits, Mary 588
Elifritz, Silicia 589
Elinton, Pleasant 513
Elkins, Nancy 336
Elkins, William 47
Ellars, Carty 47
Elleman, James 138
Elleman, Jane 138
Elleman, Joseph 138
Elleman, Margaret 138
Elleman, Wm. 138
Ellemon, David 124
Ellemon, John 116
Ellemon, Temperence 117
Ellemon, William 134
Ellender, Sally 12
Ellenwood, Daniel 728
Eller, Daniel 144, 433
Eller, Eliz. 144
Eller, Enoch 144
Eller, Frederick 602
Eller, Henry 119, 144
Eller, John 116, 144
Eller, Joseph 119
Eller, Leonard 185
Eller, Lucinda J. 602
Eller, Philip 144
Eller, Sally 119
Eller, Samuel 144
Eller, Susan 144
Ellers, Elizabeth 118
Elles, Richard 566
Ellinwood, Saml. 731
Elliot, Bernard 113

Elliot, Francis 559
Elliot, Fuller 82
Elliot, John (Dr.) 224
Elliot, Joseph F. 86
Elliot, Mary 81, 429, 559
Elliot, Melison 429
Elliot, Nancy G. 77
Elliot, Rachel 429
Elliot, Sophia 593
Elliot, Sophia A. 113
Elliott, Ambrose 267
Elliott, Ann 313
Elliott, Anne 739
Elliott, Bertha 535
Elliott, Charity 739
Elliott, Crenus (Jr.) 602
Elliott, Cyrenus 105
Elliott, David 456
Elliott, Ebenezer 416
Elliott, Eleanor 739
Elliott, Elizabeth 75, 313, 535, 663
Elliott, F. 535
Elliott, Francis 602
Elliott, Hannah 592
Elliott, Harrison P. 589
Elliott, Horance 433
Elliott, Isaac 313
Elliott, James 6, 215
Elliott, Jane 739
Elliott, Jesse 313
Elliott, John 6, 463, 589, 739
Elliott, John C. 541
Elliott, John W. 313
Elliott, Jos. W. 488
Elliott, Joseph 488, 535
Elliott, L. (?). 541
Elliott, Laura 602
Elliott, Lucinda 590
Elliott, Margaret 419, 488, 535, 739
Elliott, Margrette 75
Elliott, Maria 85
Elliott, Martha 22
Elliott, Martha Ann 433
Elliott, Mary 313
Elliott, Nathaniel 419
Elliott, R. C. 535
Elliott, Rebecca 535
Elliott, Richard 535
Elliott, Robert 182, 543
Elliott, Ruth 313
Elliott, S. 535
Elliott, Samuel 284, 535
Elliott, Sarah 535
Elliott, Simeon 739
Elliott, Susanna 658
Elliott, Termitha 541
Elliott, Thomas 176, 287, 739
Elliott, Thos. 75
Elliott, William 182, 429, 535, 739
Elliott, William A. 535
Elliott, Wm. 535
Elliott, Wm. Joseph 535

Ellis, Benj. 367
Ellis, Benjamin 360
Ellis, Betsey 360
Ellis, Catharine 26
Ellis, Chatrain 416
Ellis, Cynthian 549
Ellis, Daniel G. 372
Ellis, David C. 580
Ellis, Elias 293
Ellis, Eliza 293
Ellis, Ephraim 263
Ellis, Ephraim C. 266
Ellis, Ezer 165
Ellis, Francis 360
Ellis, George 360
Ellis, Hannah 106, 293
Ellis, Henry 360
Ellis, Indiana Lindley 699
Ellis, Ira 360
Ellis, James 177
Ellis, Jane 13
Ellis, Joannah 22
Ellis, John 12, 292, 440
Ellis, John F. 22
Ellis, Levi 259
Ellis, Martha 440, 444
Ellis, Mary 550
Ellis, Michael 360
Ellis, Patsey 360
Ellis, Phillip 114
Ellis, Reuben 360
Ellis, Robert 17
Ellis, Sarah 440
Ellis, Silas 731
Ellis, Stephen 360
Ellis, Susannah 360
Ellis, Thomas 293, 440, 444
Ellis, Wesley 360
Ellis, William 17, 106, 360
Ellison, Nancy 717
Ellison, Wm. 270
Ellmon, Elizabeth 118
Ellor, Henry 119
Ellsworth, John 543
Ellsworth, Martha 548
Ellsworth, Phebe 548
Elmore, Joseph 124
Elmore, Mary 462
Elmore, Rachel 144
Elmore, Ruth 658
Elmore, Sarah 464, 661
Elsen, Ann Maria 107
Elsen, Anna Maria 104
Elsey, Sally 384
Elson, Anna 742
Elson, Harriet 175
Elson, James 175
Elson, Wm. 558
Elsworth, Aquilla 543
Elsworth, William 124
Eltaroth, John 688
Eltzroth, Valentine 665
Elwell, Josiah 658
Elwell, Sarah 35
Ely, Francis M. 330
Ely, George 752

Ely, Isaiah 179
Ely, J. A. 330
Ely, Jane 647
Ely, John 390, 393, 647
Ely, Joseph 647, 674
Ely, Mary 647
Ely, Mary Ann 519
Ely, Michael 741
Ely, N. H. 330
Ely, Noah 519
Ely, Sally 647
Ely, William 647
Elyfrits, David 589
Elzy, Pheby 455
Emberson, James 384
Embra, Lydia 118
Embra, Rebecca 117
Embra, Sally 116
Embree, Isaac 124, 134
Embree, Ruth 134
Embres, James 116
Emerick, Aaron 217
Emerick, Caroline 217
Emerick, Catharine Ann 442
Emerick, Charles 217
Emerick, Christian 442
Emerick, Christopher C. 217
Emerick, Elizabeth 419, 442
Emerick, Jacob 229
Emerick, Joel 433
Emerick, John 217, 439, 442, 443
Emerick, John C. 217
Emerick, Lavina 229
Emerick, Leah 217
Emerick, Lucinda 442
Emerick, Philip 217
Emerick, Rachael 217
Emerick, Rebecca Ann 442
Emerson, Asa 258, 262, 267
Emerson, Asa (Jr.) 259, 264
Emerson, David 259, 263, 270
Emerson, Jesse 496
Emerson, John 335
Emerson, Loris 498
Emerson, Paulina 498
Emerson, Thomas 496, 755
Emerson, W. J. (Rev.) 221
Emery, Eliza 20
Emery, George 741
Emery, Henry 743
Emery, Lucy 466
Emery, Van 571
Emett, John 463
Emick, David 211
Emily, Lucy 666
Emlen, Susan 278
Emlin, Susan 279
Emmele, Sarah 464
Emmerson, Margaret 467
Emmery, Geo. 456
Emmery, Margaret 453

Emmick, Catherine 123
Emminger, Jacob 229
Emmitt, James 492
Emmons, Abraham 433
Emmons, Ann 414
Emmons, Eunice 28
Emmons, Ichabod 29
Emmons, Isaac 433, 727
Emmons, John 433
Emmons, Loisa 29
Emmons, Maria 28
Emmons, Marilla 28
Emmory, Marcia 454
Emrich, Elizabeth 232
Emrich, Henry 232
Emrich, William 224
Emrick, Abraham 232
Emrick, Andrew 189
Emrick, Catharine 229
Emrick, Catherine 189, 229
Emrick, Christopher 189, 223
Emrick, Christopher W. 229
Emrick, Elizabeth 189
Emrick, George 189
Emrick, Hannah 232
Emrick, John 189, 229, 419
Emrick, Magdaline 232
Emrick, Mary 229
Emrick, Peter 189
Emrick, Polly 189
Emrick, Samuel 189
Emrick, Susan 419
Emrick, William 183, 229, 232
Emrick, William R. 229
Emry, Mary 118
Enard, Benjamin 658
Eneland, Frederic 270
Eneland, Wm. 274
Enfant, Peter Charles L. 283
Enfield, Jonas 350, 375
Engal, Elizabeth 572
Engal, Mary 573
England, Barbara 461
England, Elizabeth 386, 457
England, Jacob 463
England, John 451
England, Nancy Ona 463
England, Sally 464
England, Titus 488
Englash, Thomas E. 124
Engle, Annie 636
Engle, Barbara 461
Engle, Henry 488
Engle, Job 161
Engle, Joseph H. 636
Engle, William 636
Engler, Casper 561
Engler, Lovina 575
Engleright, Samuel 603
Engles, Ann 518
Engles, Valentine 463
English, Andrew F. 433

English, E. 407
English, Isabel C. 433
English, J. 407
English, James 448
English, James W. 571
English, Joseph 40
English, Martha E. 433
English, Rebecca 433
English, Saml. B. 433
Englishman, John Charles Adam 607
Enick, Mary 518
Enkins, Cary J. 697
Enkmann, Z. Gerd. 102
Enlaw, David 294
Ennes, Thompson 223
Ennis, Absalom 195
Ennis, John 195
Ennis, Lemuel 210
Ennis, Rebecca 195
Ennis, Thompson 210
Ennis, William 195, 519
Enoch, Betsy 25
Enoch, Francis 543
Enoch, Jane 414
Enoch, John 12
Enochs, Abraham 173, 179
Enochs, Catharine 179
Enochs, Enoch 91
Enochs, Joseph 91, 179
Enochs, Lavisa 163
Enochs, Sarah 173, 179
Enochs, William 163, 179
Ensely, Nancy 577
Ensey, Dennis 210
Ensey, Elizabeth 210
Ensey, Mary 210
Ensign, Silas 440
Ensminger, Andrew 360
Ensminger, Ann Maria 360
Ensminger, Cornelius 360
Ensminger, Daniel 360
Ensminger, Elizabeth 360
Ensminger, Henry 360
Ensminger, Jane 741
Ensminger, John 360
Ensminger, Lawrence 360
Ensminger, Mary 360
Ensminger, Philip 360
Ensminger, Rachel 360
Ensminger, Rebecca 360
Ensminger, Samuel 360
Ensworth, Andw. 390
Enter, Betsy 495
Entley, Barney 379
Entsminger, John Lewis 82
Enyeart, Jane 144
Enyeart, John 144
Enyeart, Margaret 144
Enyeart, Sarah 144
Eoffe, Jacob 732
Eowds, Martin 565
Epley, Margaret 746
Eppas, Wm. 589
Epperson, Elijah 649
Eppes, Susannah 593
Eppley, James B. 425
Epps, Susanna 593

Erb, Jacob 738
Erbe, Elisabeth 235, 236
Erbe, Heinrich 235
Erbe, Henry 236
Erbe, Susanna 236
Erel, Bilberthorp 554
Erel, Gilberthorp 554
Erhart, Elizabeth 238
Erhart, Jacob 238
Erhart, Nicholas 488
Erisman, Elizabeth 151
Erisman, Jacob 151
Erl, Francys 554
Erlewine, David 176
Erlougher, Australia 429
Erlougher, Catherine 429
Erlougher, John 429
Ernest, Gottfried 626
Ernst, Catherine 88
Ervin, Etitille 593
Ervin, Jane 571
Erving, Peter 104
Ervins, James 556
Erwin, Amelia 51
Erwin, Benjamin 56
Erwin, Elizabeth 89
Erwin, James 56
Erwin, Jane 51, 76
Erwin, John 56, 82
Erwin, Joseph 51
Erwin, Lucy 84
Erwin, Mary 51
Erwin, Peggy 51
Erwin, Rhoda S. 56
Erwin, Richard 55
Erwin, Sally 51
Erwin, Samuel 56
Erwin, Smzeys 56
Erwin, William 51
Erwin, William B. 56
Erwin, Wm. 54
Esch, Bernard 602, 603,
   607
Eskew, Wm. W. 144
Eslinger, Kaziah 414
Espich, Chas. F. 572
Espich, Christian 561,
   562
Espich, Christian G. 201
Espich, Elizabeth 577
Espich, Jacob 566
Espick, John 566
Essex, Nathan 268, 270
Essex, Nathan (Sr.) 303
Essey, Abner 488
Essey, Jonathan 456
Essig, Simon 553
Estel, Levi 658
Etienne, Christopher 724
Etswiler, Frederick 743
Etswiler, Mary Elizabeth
   743
Etter, David 211
Etter, Eliz. 144
Etter, Eve 144
Etter, Fanny 144
Etter, Joseph 211
Etter, Lydia 144
Etter, Mary 144

Etter, William 211
Etzler, Abdel 429
Etzler, Mary C. 414
Etzler, Mary Magdelean
   429
Etzweler, Christena 743
Etzweler, Daniel 743
Etzweler, Frederick 743
Etzweler, George 743
Etzweler, Jacob 743
Etzweler, John 743
Etzweler, Joseph 743
Eullas, Jacob 658
Euningham, Maria E. 740
Eutelbush, John 732
Euter, Betsy 495
Eutsler, Henry 631
Eutsler, Henry (Jr.) 631
Eutzler, Andrew 632
Evan, Robert 472
Evans, --- 128
Evans, Abigail 634
Evans, Alexander 634
Evans, Alvin 40
Evans, Amanda 407
Evans, Amos 47, 59
Evans, Asher 91
Evans, Aurora L. 497
Evans, Carey 754
Evans, Catharine 166
Evans, Charles 634
Evans, Christenia 634
Evans, Daniel 155, 634
Evans, David 88, 91,
   589, 634, 683
Evans, Edward J. 119
Evans, Effie M. 613
Evans, Elizabeth 399,
   410, 456, 609, 634,
   681, 754
Evans, Ephraim 155
Evans, Euphemia 421
Evans, Ezra E. 256
Evans, George 383, 392
Evans, George W. 681
Evans, Gilbert 456
Evans, Horasio 488
Evans, I. K. 105
Evans, Isaac 294, 297,
   500, 634, 751
Evans, Isabel 636
Evans, Issabella 634
Evans, James (Jr.) 738
Evans, James W. 589
Evans, John 8, 179,
   261, 407, 471, 483,
   486, 750, 751, 754
Evans, Jona 383
Evans, Joseph 24, 47,
   189, 248, 681
Evans, Karn 421
Evans, Lewis 189
Evans, Margaret 80
Evans, Martha J. 407
Evans, Merica 754
Evans, Milly 386
Evans, Moses 24
Evans, Phebe 24, 77
Evans, Pierce 754

Evans, Rachel 135
Evans, Rebecca 24, 125
Evans, Richard 86, 634
Evans, Robert 463, 470,
   471, 472, 474
Evans, Roy A. 613
Evans, Rush 754
Evans, Ruth 386
Evans, Samuel 261, 399
Evans, Sary 744
Evans, Silas 24
Evans, Simeon 717
Evans, Solomon 634
Evans, Susanna 127
Evans, T. W. 380
Evans, Tabitha 81
Evans, Thomas 166, 171,
   463, 654
Evans, W. G. 754
Evans, Walter 549
Evans, William 24, 169,
   226
Evans, William M. 248,
   613
Evans, Wm. 665
Eveland, Frederick 713
Eveman, Philip 665
Even, James 290
Evens, Isaac 744
Everet, Charles 561
Everet, John 561
Everet, Phebe 105
Everett, Chas. 572
Everett, Henry 561, 566
Everett, Jacob 572
Everett, Jeremiah 496
Everett, Joel 496
Everett, John 444, 566
Everett, Joseph 561, 566
Everett, Joseph (Sr.)
   566
Everett, Moses 566
Everhart, George 658
Everheart, Calvin 748
Everheart, Catharine 644
Everheart, George 566
Everheart, Lydia 644
Everheart, Samuel 644
Everinger, Nathaniel 676
Everitt, A. 150
Everitt, A. A. 151
Everitt, Charles E. 151
Everitt, E. 150
Everitt, E. N. 149
Everitt, Elizabeth 149
Everitt, Epenetus 149
Everitt, Epenetus (Sr.)
   149
Everitt, Geo. J. 151
Everitt, J. S. 150
Everitt, Jeremiah A. 150
Everitt, Levi 149
Everitt, Rebecca 149
Everitt, Sarah 150
Everitt, Susannah 149
Everitt, Van Buren E.
   150
Everling, Adam 236
Everling, Frederick 236

Everling, Jacob 236
Everling, Margareta 236
Everling, Margaritta 236
Everling, Wilhelm 236
Everly, Daniel 433
Everly, Jacob 543
Everly, John 433
Everly, Peter 433
Everly, Rachael 543
Everly, Rebecca 378
Everly, Wm. Eli 433
Everman, Barbara 660
Everman, Betsey 658
Everman, Mary 661
Everran, Susanna 661
Evers, Celinda 758
Evers, Darias 607
Evers, Elias 600
Evers, John 758, 764
Evers, Perry 607
Eversole, Balultzer 375
Eversole, John 373, 375
Eversole, Peter 348
Eversolt, Valentine 427
Everson, Isaac C. 35
Evert, Thomas 561
Everton, Nancy 80
Everton, Polly 80
Everton, Sally 84
Everts, Gustavus 672
Every, George 282
Evey, Nathaniel 209
Evins, George 77
Evritt, Maria 717
Ewart, F. W. 732
Ewell, Barton 483
Ewell, James 483
Ewen, Emiline 418
Ewen, Polly 418
Ewens, Moris 27
Ewers, George 174
Ewett, John G. 144
Ewing, A. G. (Rev.) 307
Ewing, Cynthia Annes 595
Ewing, Eliza Mitchale 595
Ewing, Elizabeth 466
Ewing, George Jamison 595
Ewing, Harriet Newel 595
Ewing, Henry E. 634
Ewing, James 29, 595
Ewing, John 188
Ewing, Joshua 595
Ewing, Joshua Green 595
Ewing, Joshuah 595
Ewing, Margaret 595
Ewing, Martha Ramsey 595
Ewing, Peggy Jamison 595
Ewing, Polly J. 595
Ewing, Sophia 121
Ewing, Thomas 456
Ewing, Thomas M. 589
Ewing, Thos. 356
Ewing, William 383
Ewing, William G. 211
Ewing, William Gardner 188
Ewings, James 29

Ewins, Joseph 12
Eye, Ann 135
Eyestone, Abraham 527
Eyestone, Jene 462, 465
Eyler, Elias 519
Eyler, G. 617
Eyler, Geo. 617
Eyler, George 617
Eyler, George W. 617
Eyler, S. 617
Eyler, Sarah 617
Eyler, William H. 617
Eyre, John 488
Eystone, Casper 488

--- F ---

Faber, Godleib 631
Faber, John 710
Fackler, Amanda 326
Fackler, Barbara 563
Fackler, E. 326
Fackler, Godfove 566
Fackler, Godlieb 563
Fackler, Henry 563
Fackler, W. 326
Fadler, Catharina 133
Fadler, George 133
Fadler, Wentel 133
Fager, Catharine 138
Fagy, Christina 568
Fahee, John 319
Fahy, John 321
Fail, Samuel 492
Fair, Benjamin 504
Fair, James 297
Fairbanks, Lewis 583
Fairchild, Ann 723
Fairchild, Lewis 688
Fairchild, Major 723, 724
Fairchild, Sarah 58
Fairfield, Jacob 50
Fairfield, William 63
Fairley, Andrew 732
Fairman, Julia Ann 30
Faker, Havir 572
Fakes, Harriot 116
Falconer, Samuel 29
Falder, Rebecca A. 144
Falenstine, Amanda 420
Fales, Twipin 723
Falkerer, Thomas 637
Falkner, David 665
Falkner, Joseph 138
Falkner, Levi 144
Falkner, Thomas 665
Fall, Andrew 429
Fall, Anna 429
Fall, Benjamin N. 648
Fall, Daniel 426
Fall, Elizabeth 429
Fall, Jacob 429
Fall, John 429
Fall, Mary 426, 429
Fall, Sarah 429
Fallenash, Dorcas 661

Falsan, Alexander 162
Falsan, Eleanor 162
Falscroff, Elizabeth 166
Falscroff, Michael 166, 172
Falson, Alexander 162, 173
Falson, Eleanor 173
Faltz, John 640
Famil, William 696
Fancher, James 35
Fancher, Jane 21
Fangman, John 104
Fansler, Absolom 433
Fara, Samuel 269
Farden, Abigail 572
Farding, James 492
Fare, George 124
Fare, Sophia 127
Farel, Polly 658
Fargus, James 477
Farier, Eliza 357
Faris, Daniel 651
Faris, John 3
Farley, James 303
Farley, John 270
Farley, Thomas 164
Farlin, Daniel M. 470
Farlow, Benjamin 492
Farmer, Anna 716
Farmer, Elizabeth 123
Farmer, Mary 577
Farmer, Sarah 716
Farmon, Robert 654
Farner, George 645, 647, 673
Farner, Margaret 645, 647, 673
Farner, Michael 645, 647, 673
Farner, Peter 647
Farnow, Archa 716
Farnsworth, Charlotte 74
Farnsworth, Ralph 40
Farnum, Samuel 543
Farnum, Susan 591
Farquehar, Charles 677
Farquer, David 647
Farquer, Hugh 647
Farquer, John 647
Farquer, Theophilus S. 690
Farquer, Thomas 672
Farquhar, Iradel 699
Farquhar, Linden 699
Farquhar, P. 699
Farquhar, Philip 699
Farquhar, S. E. 699
Farquhar, Sarah E. 699
Farquhar, William Henry 699
Farquhar, Willie A. 699
Farquher, Charles 677
Farr, Catharine 130
Farr, Elizabeth 130, 748
Farr, George 130
Farr, John Clark 130
Farr, Michael 130
Farr, Philemon 29

Farr, Sophia 130
Farr, Susqnnah 130
Farra, James (Jr.) 256
Farra, William 250, 251
Farrar, Jonathan 47
Farras, Loring 765
Farrel, Cornelius 262
Farrell, James 40
Farrell, Martha 314
Farrell, Mary 711
Farrell, Thomas 314
Farrell, Wm. S. 314
Farris, Charity 660, 670
Farris, David 647, 670
Farris, Dolly 670
Farris, Elizabeth 670
Farris, James 647, 670
Farris, Jane 670
Farris, John 647, 670
Farris, Nancy 670
Farris, Polly 670
Farris, Priscilla 670
Farris, Rebecca 670
Farris, William 651, 670
Farrow, Susannah 550
Farver, Feorge 645
Farver, George 144
Farver, Margaret 645
Farver, Michael 645
Farver, William 144
Fashbaugh, John 572
Fashbough, Elizabeth 573
Fate, George 361
Fate, George A. 226
Fate, John 361
Fate, Leah 361
Fate, Martin 361
Fate, Shadrack 361
Fate, Thomas 361
Fatey, John 317
Fathus, Eve 529
Faucher, Samuel 621
Fauekler, Catharine 568
Faukhouser, Nicholas 153
Faulk, Mary Ann 555
Faulkner, Catharine 109
Faulkner, Margaret 453
Faulknor, David 671
Faulknor, Thomas 665
Faulks, Andrew 557
Faulks, Anna 607
Faulks, John 557
Faulks, Mary A. 557
Faulks, Mary Ann 557
Faulks, Nancy Ann 557
Faulks, Sophia 557
Fausnought, David 621
Faux, Charlotte 280
Favorite, Abram 144
Favorite, Geo. 144
Favorite, George 199
Favorite, Henry F. 144
Favorite, Margaret 144
Favorite, Polly 124
Favorite, Rebecca 144
Fawcett, Jesse 23
Fay, Benjamin A. 61
Fay, Hollis 765
Fay, Nathaniel T. 763

Fayles, Turpin 722
Fealdon, Nancy 117
Fealher, Elizabeth 451
Fealty, Ann 362
Fealty, Bernard 362
Fealty, David 362
Fealty, Morgan 362
Feams, Crumlin 180
Feams, Erunlin 180
Feams, Letitia 303, 304
Fearing, Christina 47
Fearing, Henry 636
Fearing, Paul 713, 727
Fease, Betsy 125
Feasel, Henry 527
Feasle, Catherine 519
Featherly, Henry 75
Fee, Belinda 744
Fee, Dennis 317
Fee, Hannah 745
Fee, John 744
Fee, Sarah 745
Fee, Sntha 744
Feefield, Daniel 519
Feeling, Wm. 320
Feerer, Hannah E. 543
Feerer, Peter 678
Feering, Noah 714
Fees, Henry 124
Feight, Charles 678
Feiter, Nicholas 114
Felch, Ebenezer 726, 730
Felch, Sarah 726
Feldhaus, Frederick 112
Feldheiser, Johan 111
Feldman, John Bernd. 102
Feldmann, J. Henry 102
Feldwisch, William 543
Felger, Jacob 740
Fell, Ann 580
Feller, Maria 433
Fellers, Abraham 566
Fellers, Sally 127
Fellows, Jacob 665
Fellshan, Samuel 723
Fellure, Nicholas 166
Felming, Margaret 745
Felony, Andrew 318
Felton, --- 87
Fen, Richard 477
Fender, Mary 607
Fenn, Ira I. 202
Fenn, Ira J. 206, 207
Fenn, Norman 204
Fenner, Benj. 589
Fenner, Phebe 590
Fenstemacher, Cath. 220
Fenstemaker, Mary 743
Fenstemaker, Sarah 743
Fenton, Robert 742
Fenton, Smith 742
Fentress, Ann 206
Fentress, Edward 148, 206
Fentress, Elizabeth 206
Fentress, George 148, 206
Fentress, Joseph 206
Fentress, Mary 206

Fentress, Rosannah 206
Feoter, Nicholas 114
Ferard, P. 724
Fergason, Hannah 528
Fergus, James 477
Fergus, John 543
Ferguson, Charles 492
Ferguson, Clements 429
Ferguson, James 473, 478, 484, 488
Ferguson, Jesse B. 63, 626
Ferguson, John 168
Ferguson, Julia 498
Ferguson, Lucinda V. 63
Ferguson, Magaret 429
Ferguson, Margery 511
Ferguson, Martha 168
Ferguson, Mary 678
Ferguson, Mary Timanda 429
Ferguson, Robert 168
Ferguson, Samuel 513, 743
Ferguson, William 646, 652, 654, 658, 674, 678
Ferin, Polly 456
Fernal, Noah 710
Fernean, John 492
Fernean, Philip 488
Ferneau, John 492
Ferneau, Philip 488
Fernhold, John Herman 105
Fernley, Hannah 709
Fernover, John 52
Fernsler, Mary 278
Ferr, Richard 469
Ferrard, Peter 717
Ferraro, John Baptist 724
Ferree, Peter 543
Ferrel, Alexander 161, 170
Ferrel, Esther 160
Ferrel, Jane 157, 159
Ferrel, Jno. T. 267
Ferrel, John 159, 161, 170
Ferrel, John P. 270
Ferrel, Joseph 157, 159
Ferrel, Joseph (Jr.) 157
Ferrel, Joseph (Sr.) 157
Ferrel, Josiah 160
Ferrel, Nancy 170
Ferrel, Rebecca 170
Ferrel, Samuel 268
Ferrell, Alexander 153
Ferrell, James 412
Ferrier, William 753
Ferril, Alexander 179
Ferril, Esther 158
Ferril, Hiram 179
Ferril, Joseph 158
Ferril, Matilda 179
Ferrill, Joseph 155
Ferris, Forest 29
Ferris, John L. 531

Ferris, Lucy 28
Ferris, Zina 637
Ferry, Julyann 414
Fesler, Barsheba 80
Fetch, Nancy 15
Fetheroff, Samuel 383
Fetter, Catharine 196
Fetter, Jacob 196
Fetter, John 196
Fetter, Peter 192, 196
Fetter, Polly 196
Fetterman, Alfred 60
Fetterman, Frances 60
Fetterman, George 60
Fetterman, Gertrude 60
Fetterman, Gilbert 60
Fetterman, Sarah 60
Fetterman, W. W. 60
Fetterman, Washington
    Welssed 60
Fetters, Caroline 144
Fetters, Catharine 144
Fetters, Catherine 144
Fetters, Daniel 224
Fetters, Elizabeth 123
Fetters, George 214
Fetters, Hannah 144
Fetters, Jacob 214
Fetters, John 144, 214
Fetters, Julia Ann 214
Fetters, Mary 144
Fetters, Nancy 144
Fetters, Sally 127
Fetters, Samuel 217
Fetters, William 108
Fetts, Jesse 553
Fetts, Shadrah 553
Feurl, Benjamin 504
Feurl, Polly 504
Feurquay, Nancy 512
Feurt, Benjamin 513
Feurt, Gabriel 513
Feurt, Gabriel (Jr.) 503
Feurt, Gabriel (Sr.) 503
Feurt, Isabella 503
Feurt, Rachell 511
Feurt, Susannah 515
Ficke, Sally 742
Fickle, Ann 378
Fickle, Benjamin 286,
    360
Fickle, Catherine 360
Fickle, Jonathan 375
Fickle, Joseph 283,
    340, 360
Fickle, Joseph G. 360
Field, Richard 709
Field, Rozetta 664
Fielder, Charles 390
Fielder, Matilda 23
Fielder, Sally 11
Fielding, Danual 144
Fielding, Harrietta 144
Fielding, Jeremiah 144
Fielding, Margaret 123
Fielding, Maria 144
Fields, Abia 662
Fields, Charles 278
Fields, David 284

Fields, James 421
Fields, Lyman 65
Fields, Robert 383
Fields, Sarah 662
Fields, Selina 65
Fierney, Henry 503
Fierney, Jane 503
Fiester, Magdalena 236
Fiester, Peter 236
Fiester, Pfilip 236
Figart, Susannah 456
Figley, Mary 583, 584
Fike, Sally 742
Filkins, Almon 72
Filkins, Amelia 80
Filkins, David 72
Filkins, Jane 72
Filkins, Lydia 72
Filkins, Martin Van
    Buren 72
Filkins, Mary 72
Fillerry, John 124
Filmer, Daniel W. 2
Filmer, John 2
Filmer, Robert 2
Finch, Cornelius P. 258
Finch, Elizabeth 153
Finch, Hannah 530
Finch, Humphrey 157
Finch, Humphry 153
Finch, Ira 60, 530
Finch, John 448, 530
Finch, Lewis 530
Finch, Margaret 530
Finch, Polly 460
Finch, Samuel 530
Finch, Sarah 521
Finch, Solomon 383, 530
Fincher, Jane 123
Fincher, Lemuel 119
Fincher, Rosanna 121
Fincher, William 116,
    191
Finck, --- 345
Finck, Adam 361, 367
Finck, Anthony 344,
    361, 367
Finck, Daniel 360
Finck, David 361
Finck, David P. 344
Finck, E. 344
Finck, Edmund Thadeus
    344
Finck, Elizabeth 361
Finck, Frances 361
Finck, George 344
Finck, Jacob 361
Finck, John 344, 361
Finck, John (Jr.) 344
Finck, John (Sr.) 344
Finck, Joseph 360, 361
Finck, Mary 344, 360,
    361
Finck, Mary Spurck 344
Finck, Philip 360
Finck, Sarah 360, 361
Finck, W. E. 363
Finck, William 360
Findlay, William 3

Findley, David 298
Findley, Eliz. P. 138
Findley, Elvira H. 138
Findley, James 285, 651
Findley, James W. 138
Findley, John P. 138
Findley, Margaret 88
Findley, Saml. 477
Findley, Saml. P. 138
Findley, Samuel 481
Findley, Wm. M. 138
Findly, Hannah 652
Findly, Hiram Merrick
    652
Findly, Levina 652
Findly, Mary Thompson
    652
Findly, Rebecca 652
Findly, Robert P. 652
Findly, Samuel C. 652
Findly, William P. 652
Finfrock, Jonathan 607
Fink, Adam 344, 361, 376
Fink, Alice 344
Fink, Anthony 344, 360,
    361, 365
Fink, David 361
Fink, Elizabeth 361, 379
Fink, Elizabeth Ann 379
Fink, Eve 360
Fink, Frances 361
Fink, Jacob 361
Fink, James 361
Fink, John 361, 379
Fink, Joseph 361, 368
Fink, Mary 361
Fink, Mary Ann 361
Fink, Mary E. 344
Fink, Sarah 361
Finke, William 105
Finkel, Peter 709
Finkle, Mary 571
Finley, Ebenezer 737
Finley, Elizabeth 737
Finley, Hanna 452
Finley, James 297, 303
Finley, John 301, 320
Finley, John P. 451
Finley, Martha 458
Finley, Michael 737
Finley, Robert 479
Finley, Robert W. 472
Finley, Robt. W. 476
Finley, Saml. 478
Finley, Samuel 469,
    471, 482, 483, 485
Finly, Samuel 472
Finnegan, John 686
Finney, James 442
Finney, Marget 509
Finney, Mary C. 695
Finney, Patrick 690
Finney, Robert 132, 442
Finney, William 287,
    318, 442
Finton, Elizabeth 577
Finton, James 572
Finton, Mary E. 3
Finton, Sarah Elizabeth 3

Finton, Vanranssalaer 496
Finton, William 3
Firebaugh, John 566
Fires, Almond A. 692
Firestone, Daniel 24
Firestone, George 24, 558
Firestone, Nancy 24
Firestone, Rebekah 24
Firestone, Sally 24
Firestone, Samuel 24, 26
Firestone, Sarah 14
Fisel, Catherina 234
Fisel, Johannes 234
Fisel, Lessa 234
Fisel, Rebeka 234
Fish, Benjamin 66
Fish, Christian 709
Fish, David 58
Fish, Eliza 58
Fish, Elizabeth 58, 709
Fish, James H. 583
Fish, Lydia 58
Fish, Margreth 709
Fish, Rachel 58
Fish, Sarah 58
Fish, Stephen 58
Fishburn, Abraham 734
Fishburn, Clementnie 735
Fishburn, Cora Ellen 735
Fishburn, Edward D. 735
Fishburn, F. 734
Fishburn, Henry 734
Fishburn, Leah 734
Fishburn, Levi 735
Fishburn, Lizzie 735
Fishburn, Mary 735
Fishburn, Nancy Jane 734
Fishburn, S. 734
Fishburn, William H. 734
Fishel, Daniel 239
Fisher, Abijah 183
Fisher, Abraham 732
Fisher, Adam 361, 364
Fisher, Andrew 361
Fisher, Ann 107
Fisher, Anthony 114, 361
Fisher, Anthony More 107
Fisher, Barak 173
Fisher, Barbara 361
Fisher, Barick 167
Fisher, Benjamin 603, 604, 607
Fisher, Catharine 361, 413
Fisher, Catherine 523
Fisher, Cephas 27
Fisher, Clark 99
Fisher, David 111
Fisher, Elias 681, 687
Fisher, Eliza 361
Fisher, Elizabeth 747
Fisher, Emanuel 372
Fisher, Eva Maria 361
Fisher, Genevieve 361
Fisher, George 361
Fisher, Gunan 361
Fisher, Hannah 162, 361

Fisher, Henry 519, 572
Fisher, J. 361
Fisher, Jacob 361, 367
Fisher, James 519
Fisher, Jane 173
Fisher, John 44, 107, 339, 361, 393, 519
Fisher, John H. 114
Fisher, Joseph 361
Fisher, Joshua 711
Fisher, Leonard 361
Fisher, Magdalene 361
Fisher, Marcia 99
Fisher, Margaret 361
Fisher, Maria 356, 361
Fisher, Martha A. 47
Fisher, Martha Maria 74
Fisher, Mary 361, 375, 522
Fisher, Mary Jane 107, 114
Fisher, Mary R. 334
Fisher, Matilda 107
Fisher, Michael 353, 361
Fisher, Nikolaus 88
Fisher, Peter 107, 519
Fisher, Philip 361
Fisher, Richard 162, 174
Fisher, Samuel 361
Fisher, Sarah Ellen 107, 114
Fisher, Schuyler 751
Fisher, Silas 114
Fisher, Sophia 361
Fisher, Stephen 519, 526
Fisher, Susannah 361
Fisher, Thomas 285, 448
Fisher, William 107, 361
Fisht, John 740
Fisinger, Peter 599
Fissel, Henry 238
Fissel, Magdelena 238
Fistler, Catharine 497
Fitch, Abi 759
Fitch, Amaza S. 759
Fitch, Charlotte E. 759
Fitch, Eliza J. 759
Fitch, James M. 759
Fitch, Lydia 759
Fitch, Mary S. 759
Fitch, Montgomery H. 524, 759
Fitch, William H. 759
Fitrow, Joseph 44
Fitscharles, Nelly 452
Fitscharles, Sarah 453
Fitsgarret, Fanny 661
Fitsgerael, Thomas 665
Fitsgerald, Thomas 641
Fitsimmons, Stephen 273
Fitsworth, Isaac 463
Fitzgarald, Nancy 388
Fitzgerald, Edward 58, 61
Fitzgerald, Elenor 383
Fitzgerald, Elizabeth 649
Fitzgerald, Polly 385
Fitzgerald, Reuben 303

Fitzgerald, Rose 373
Fitzpatrick, Benjamin 474
Fitzpatrick, Mary Rosa 330
Flack, Analiza 525
Flack, Barbara 527
Flack, Delila 525
Flack, George 525
Flack, George Dixon 525
Flack, Henry Jeremiah 525
Flack, Hiram 525
Flack, Jacob 449, 527
Flack, James 732
Flack, John Jackson 525
Flack, John L. 527
Flack, Josiah 525
Flack, Lewis L. 527
Flack, Lewis W. 525
Flack, Lydia 527
Flack, Magdelana 525
Flack, Sarah Carter 411
Flag, Abraham 673
Flag, Anna 642
Flag, Jacob 648, 673
Flag, Woodruff 642
Flagal, E. J. 405
Flagel, Mary L. 405
Flagg, Abraham 645
Flagg, Anne 645, 673
Flagg, Editha 715, 722
Flagg, Jacob 645
Flagg, James 722
Flagg, Junius 40
Flagg, Miriah 648
Flaherty, James 283, 288
Flanigan, John 355
Flannagen, Samuel 469
Flannakerr, Samuel C. 483
Flarnenan, Cintia 719
Flay, Anna 642
Flay, Jacob 648
Flay, Woodruff 642
Fleath, John 451
Fleck, Rebecca 743
Fleckenger, Stephen 581
Fleckinger, Jacob 556
Fleckinger, John 556
Fleckinger, Michael 556
Fleeharty, John 383
Fleek, Mary 574
Fleemin, Nancy 452
Fleet, William 519
Fleming, Abraham 29
Fleming, Aveline 433
Fleming, Barthalomew 82
Fleming, Betsey 452
Fleming, Desin 433
Fleming, Eliza 429
Fleming, Elizabeth 517
Fleming, Ferguson 383
Fleming, James 429
Fleming, Jane 433
Fleming, John 41, 463, 658
Fleming, John C. 429
Fleming, Juliett 433

Fleming, Madison 433
Fleming, Margaret 745
Fleming, Matthew 336
Fleming, Nancy 464, 658
Fleming, Nathan 299
Fleming, Rebecca 588
Fleming, Robert 383
Fleming, Robt. 456
Fleming, Sally 429
Fleming, William 706
Flemming, Abraham 29
Flemming, Elizabeth 583
Flemmor, Rebecca 588
Flemor, John 589
Flenagan, Samuel G. 52
Flenegen, Samuel 451
Flesher, Ann 292
Flesher, Balsar 292
Flesher, Balser 292
Flesher, Catharine 292
Flesher, Henry 292
Flesher, John 292
Flesher, Mary 292
Flesher, Matilda 292
Flesher, Peter 292
Flesher, Sarah 292
Fletcher, Catharine 290
Fletcher, Daniel M. 739
Fletcher, Edward 87
Fletcher, Elizabeth 498
Fletcher, Francis 572
Fletcher, Hannah 38
Fletcher, Henry 659
Fletcher, Jacob 47
Fletcher, Joseph 713
Fletcher, Mary 517
Fletcher, Sally 514
Fletcher, Tene 290
Fletcher, William 290
Fletcher, William (Sr.) 290
Flickenger, Catharine 568
Flickenger, Elizabeth 566
Flickenger, John 566
Flickinger, Becky 567
Flickinger, Christian 556
Flickinger, Peggy 556
Flickinger, Polly 556
Fling, James 361
Fling, John 555
Fling, Nacy 406
Fling, Nathan W. 406
Fling, Sally 368
Fling, Sarah 361
Fling, Wm. 406
Flinn, Bazel 488
Flinn, Daniel C. 552
Flinn, Elizabeth 116
Flinn, George N. 552
Flinn, Hugh 488
Flinn, James 543, 552
Flinn, James (Sr.) 552
Flinn, Jane 550
Flinn, John 116
Flinn, Lucinda 548
Flinn, Margaret 120, 551

Flinn, Mary 549, 552
Flinn, Nancy 125, 488
Flinn, Polly 117
Flinn, William 119, 124, 552
Flint, Ariel 543
Flint, Daniel 278
Flint, Joseph 456
Flisher, Eve 520
Flock, Isaac 144
Flock, Joshua 144
Flock, Lydia 144
Floid, Lydia 180
Floid, Thomas (Jr.) 180
Flood, Anna 303
Flood, Betsey 451
Flood, Geo. N. 290
Flood, Geo. W. 292
Flood, John 303
Flood, Thomas 290, 292
Flora, David 196
Flora, Elizabeth 198
Flora, Emanuel 194, 196, 197
Flora, Henry 196, 198, 203
Flora, Jesse 645, 654, 673
Flora, John 29, 196, 645
Flora, Jonathan 196
Flora, Joseph 194
Flora, Magdalene 553
Flora, Mary 194
Flora, Michael 194
Flora, Nancy 667
Flora, Nathaniel 196
Flora, Rachel 196, 203
Flord, William 714
Florence, Fanny 393
Florence, Robinson 58
Florence, Wm. 393
Flory, Elizabeth 383
Flory, Henry 211, 213
Flory, Jonas 211
Flory, Nathaniel 213
Flouson, Deborey 453
Flowers, Adam 12
Flowers, F. L. 372
Flowers, Henry 344
Flowers, Nickalas Dominic 344
Flowers, Susannah 344
Floyd, D . . . illa 164
Floyd, Elizabeth 161
Floyd, Michael 161
Floyd, Thomas 164
Fluckey, Geo. 363
Fluckey, George 340, 348
Flucky, George 284
Flumer, Mary 551
Flurry, Sarah 398
Focht, Ann 242
Focht, Jacob 360
Focht, Peter 242
Fogal, Jacob 260
Fogalsang, Fredrick H. 107
Fogalsang, Fredrick Henry 107

Fogalsang, Sophia Margarette 107
Fogelsong, Barbara 224
Fogelsong, Christian 186, 224
Fogelsong, George 186
Fogelsong, Jacob 186
Fogg, Laswell 401
Foggin, James 154
Foght, Jacob 355, 370
Foght, Michael 364
Fogle, Catharine 156, 158
Fogle, Elizabeth 157
Fogle, Frederick 158, 166
Fogle, Frederick (Jr.) 156
Fogle, Frederick (Sr.) 156, 158
Fogle, George 556, 558
Fogle, Henry 157, 158
Fogle, Jacob 264
Fogle, Melissa 306
Fogle, Melissa Ann 306
Fogler, Henry 383
Foglesong, George 644, 669, 680
Foglesong, John S. 680
Foglesong, Margaret C. 680
Foglesong, Prudence 680
Foglesong, Sarah 680
Foglesong, William G. 680
Foland, Daniel 124
Foland, Elizabeth 125
Foley, James 463
Foley, Roger 156
Folgate, --- 735
Folgate, John 734
Folger, Mary 558
Folger, Mayhew 558
Folglesong, George 644
Folk, John 371
Folkerth, Christopher 216
Folkerth, John 126, 133, 203, 223
Folkerth, Samuel 189
Folkner, Bailary 138
Folkner, Mary 138
Follett, Abel D. 496
Follett, Julia 497
Folmer, Catharine 737
Folmer, Jacob 737
Folsom, Catharine 6
Folsom, Charles 6
Folsom, Eliza Ann 79
Folsom, George 5, 6
Folsom, Henry 6
Folsom, Joshua 6
Folsom, Mary 6
Folsom, Samuel 717
Folson, Alexander 181
Folson, Eleanor 181
Folten, Anna 452
Foltz, Barbara 280
Foltz, David 740

Foltz, Eli Jackson 740
Foltz, Eliza 740
Foltz, Elizabeth 740
Foltz, Frederick 740
Foltz, Gideon 740
Foltz, John 383, 740
Foltz, Jonathan 740
Foltz, Joseph 740
Foltz, Julia A. 740
Foltz, Mary 740
Foltz, Rebecca 740
Foltz, Samuel 740
Foltz, William 740
Fomash, Ann 333
Fomash, William 333
Foncannon, Elizabeth 363
Foncannon, Mary 363
Foncannon, William 496
Foos, Clarissa 58
Foos, Gustavus 58
Foos, John 58
Foos, Joseph 58
Foos, Lewis 58
Foos, Sarah 63
Foos, William 58, 63, 626
Foose, Mary 87
Foot, Amos B. 685
Foot, Elijah C. 685
Foot, Joseph 672
Foot, M. D. 496
Foot, Mary 166
Foote, Anna 33
Foote, Henry B. 543
Foote, John B. 543
Foote, Wm. McLean 543
Footman, Margaret 344
Footman, Wm. 344
Forbes, Asahel 100
Forbes, Catharine 498
Forbes, Eli 100
Forbes, Erastus K. 41
Forbes, Joanna 100
Forbes, Jonathan 100
Forbush, Lyman 530
Ford, A. 614
Ford, Albert 29
Ford, Amon 732
Ford, Diana 719
Ford, Edward 185
Ford, Elijah 665
Ford, Francis X. A. 422
Ford, Giles 726
Ford, J. L. 614
Ford, James 443, 589
Ford, James K. 425
Ford, John 287
Ford, Leah 77
Ford, Mary Ann 422
Ford, Nicholas 443
Ford, Phenas 714
Ford, Rosian 57
Ford, Roxana B. 614
Ford, Sarah 714
Ford, Stephen 185
Ford, Susannah 751
Ford, Thomas 422
Fordice, Nelson 271
Fordice, William 271

Fordyce, David 659
Fordyce, William 659
Fore, Elizabeth 366
Foreacre, Wm. 262, 263
Foreaker, Mary 373
Foree, Bridgart 729
Foree, Bridget 729
Foreman, Alexander 743
Foreman, David 743
Foreman, India Pearce 617
Foreman, Martha 743
Foreman, Philip 572
Foreman, Sidna 743
Foreman, Susan 576
Forenark, Charles 717
Foreniger, Julia Ann 88
Foreshey, Joseph 171
Foresman, Hugh 400
Forgerson, Holsy 496
Forges, Jas. 478
Forgeson, Eleanor 448
Forgeson, Elizabeth 448
Forgeson, Henry 448
Forgeson, James 440, 448
Forgeson, Jane 448
Forgeson, Jane (Jr.) 448
Forgeson, John 448
Forgeson, Margaret 448
Forgeson, Nimrod 448
Forgeson, Ruth 448
Forgeson, William 448
Forgrave, Robert 380
Forguson, Edward 351
Forguson, Elizabeth 361
Forguson, Harriet 361
Forguson, Nancy 126
Forguson, Rebecca 361
Forguson, Thomas 496
Forkner, James 77
Formash, Ann 333
Formey, Magdalene 570
Formish, William 303
Fornash, William 333
Forney, . . . 579
Forney, Christian 572
Forney, Mary 570
Forney, Peter 572
Forquer, Cecily 362
Forquer, Charles 362
Forquer, Jane 380
Forquer, John (Sr.) 361
Forquer, Michael 361
Forquer, Michael D. 362
Forquer, Rosanna 361
Forquer, Sarah Elizabeth 362
Forquer, William 361, 362
Forquer, Wm. 361
Forquer, Wm. (Jr.) 361
Forrer, Christian 221
Forrest, Betsey 80
Forrest, Elizabeth 83
Forrest, Gabriel 708
Forrest, Gilbert 708
Forrest, John 708
Forrest, Joseph 717
Forrest, Rachel 708

Forseman, Henry 383
Forseman, Jane 383
Forshey, Abraham 177
Forshey, Asa 174
Forshey, Catharine 166, 177
Forshey, Catherine 155
Forshey, Hiram 166
Forshey, John 166
Forshey, Joseph 167
Forshey, Nancy L. 178
Forshey, Rachel 166
Forshey, Richard 178
Forshey, Sally 177
Forshey, Sarah 174
Forshey, Thomas 155, 177
Forsman, Agness 392
Forsman, Alexander 391, 392
Forsman, George 391, 392
Forsman, Hugh 391, 392
Forsman, Jane 391, 392
Forsman, Joseph 391, 392
Forsman, Margaret 385
Forsman, Philip 391, 392
Forsman, Robert 391, 392
Forsman, Samuel 391, 392
Forsman, William 391, 392
Forster, Polly 517
Forsyth, James 271
Forsyth, Samuel 358
Forsyth, Thos. L. 358
Forsythe, Hannah 362
Forsythe, James 543
Forsythe, John 362
Forsythe, Robert A. 12
Forsythe, Thos. L. (Rev.) 372
Forsythe, William 378
Fortney, Adam 607
Fose, Anna 429
Fose, Elizabeth 429
Fose, John 429
Foseth, John E. 26
Fosler, Margaret 661
Fosnaught, Elias 607
Fosnight, George 543
Fosnight, Henry 543
Fosnight, Martin 543
Fosnutt, Jacob 659
Fossett, Jadiah 44
Foster, Alexander 254
Foster, Anna 581
Foster, Archibald 29
Foster, Benjamin 572, 585
Foster, Betsey 462
Foster, Betsy Marietta 730
Foster, Catherine 462
Foster, Cathrine 574
Foster, Christiana 355
Foster, Dwight 730
Foster, Edwin 89
Foster, Elenor 659
Foster, Elizabeth 451, 626
Foster, Experience 581

Foster, Frederick
  Augustus 730
Foster, George 635
Foster, Hannah 498, 746
Foster, Henry 607, 626
Foster, Hugh 433
Foster, Jacob 451
Foster, James 413
Foster, James B. 433
Foster, James O. 690
Foster, Jesse 607, 626
Foster, Joel 626
Foster, John 47, 488,
  581, 752
Foster, Lawrence 463
Foster, M. 538
Foster, M. A. 59
Foster, Macinda 626
Foster, Marth 626
Foster, Martha 575
Foster, Mary 626, 730,
  752
Foster, Mary B. 538
Foster, Mary Jane 625
Foster, Moses 572
Foster, Nancy 752
Foster, Paegrine 730
Foster, Peregrine 730
Foster, Peregrine Pitt
  730
Foster, Polly 453, 514,
  716, 730
Foster, Rachel 626
Foster, Rainy 752
Foster, Rebecca 523
Foster, Rebeccah 454
Foster, Robert 324, 752
Foster, Saml. 599
Foster, Samuel 572, 626
Foster, Sarah 577, 626,
  717
Foster, Seraph 730
Foster, Susan 495
Foster, Theodore 730
Foster, Theodore
  Sedgwick 730
Foster, Thomas H. 433
Foster, W. S. 538
Foster, William 741
Foster, William H. 626
Foster, William S. 538
Foster, Zeptha 138
Fouckler, Adam 562
Fouckler, Catharine 562
Fouckler, Daniel 562
Fouckler, Eve 562
Fouckler, Godlieb 562
Fouckler, Henery 562
Fouckler, Jacob 562
Fouckler, Magdaline 562
Fouckler, Maria Barbara
  562
Fouckler, Phillip 562
Fouglar, Caty 387
Fourman, Eleazer 41
Fourman, Eleazun 41
Fourny, Mary 334
Fourt, Gabriel 503
Foust, Catharine 229

Foust, Charity 404
Foust, Daniel 229
Foust, John 68
Foust, Sally 68
Fout, Adam 412
Fout, Dova Beatrice 409
Fout, George 409, 410
Fout, John 410
Fout, Mary Anne 411
Fout, Ransom 29
Fouts, Andrew 274
Fouts, Barbara 134
Fouts, Caleb W. 247, 248
Fouts, Elizabeth 134
Fouts, Frederick 717
Fouts, Henry 134
Fouts, Jacob 223, 268
Fouts, Jenny 186
Fouts, Joel 188
Fouts, John 134
Fouts, Joseph 186
Fouts, Mary 127
Fouts, Matilda 134
Fouts, Peter 199
Fouts, Rebecca 134
Fouts, Samuel 274
Fouts, Susanna 134
Fouts, Wm. 265
Foutz, Henry 215
Fowler, Caroline 313
Fowler, Deborah 313
Fowler, Fanny 752
Fowler, Fidelia 313
Fowler, Filetus 313
Fowler, Jacob 255
Fowler, James 255
Fowler, Lemuel 313
Fowler, Lorinda 314
Fowler, Margaret 313
Fowler, Nathan 255
Fowler, Olla 313
Fowler, William 392
Fowler, Wm. 361
Fowler, Wm. S. 255
Fowler, Zachariah 288
Fox, Absalam 665
Fox, Absolom 654
Fox, Amasa 525
Fox, Anna 665
Fox, Anne 650, 695
Fox, Anson 761
Fox, Archabald 138
Fox, Betsey 659
Fox, Daniel L. 549
Fox, David 526, 671
Fox, Delight 525
Fox, Elijah 29
Fox, Eliza 660
Fox, Elizabeth 526, 662
Fox, Emily 401
Fox, George 676
Fox, Henrietta 433
Fox, Isaac 526
Fox, Jane 636
Fox, John 543, 670, 695
Fox, Joseph 508, 659
Fox, Levi F. 29
Fox, Lydia 630
Fox, Margaret 665

Fox, Mary Ann 433
Fox, Michael 526, 695
Fox, Rhodolphus 525
Fox, Sarah 526
Fox, Susannah 695
Fox, Thomas 543
Fox, Wm. 433
Foxter, Luke 513
Foy, Jacob 463
Frader, Catharine 118
Frail, John 157, 164
Frain, Daniel 463
Frakes, John 270
Fralling, Clennus 108
Frame, Elon 488
Frame, Levi 429
Frame, Rachel 429
Frame, Sarah B. 488
Frame, William 429
France, Christian 572
France, Jacob 153
France, John W. 407
France, M. 407
France, Magdalena 576
France, Ruth 153
France, W. 407
Frances, Jacob 153
Frances, Ruth 153
Francis, Adonjah 689
Francis, Alfred P. 279
Francis, Amelia 418
Francis, Ann 456
Francis, Anna 696
Francis, Betsey 453
Francis, Chrispen 47
Francis, Cornelius 488
Francis, Daniel F. 418
Francis, Daniel T. 761
Francis, Elinor 465
Francis, George W. 761
Francis, Jacob 54, 159
Francis, James Y. 419
Francis, Jemima 543
Francis, Jonathan 549
Francis, Lydia Ann 419,
  689
Francis, Reason 54
Francis, Richard 549
Francis, Ruth 159
Francis, Samuel 47
Francis, Tobias 689
Francis, William 488
Frank, Daniel 749
Frank, Henry 739
Frank, Hiram 109
Frank, Jacob 109
Frank, Luther M. 530
Frank, Mary Ann 616
Frankeberger, Eli 589
Frankeberger, Joel 543
Franklin, Alexander 301
Franklin, Calvin 269
Franklin, Henry 12
Franklin, Hezekiah 370
Franklin, James 463
Franklin, P. 367
Franklin, Ruth A. 549
Franklin, Saml. 451
Franklin, Sarah 549

839

Franks, Aaron 736, 743
Franks, Jacob 362
Franks, Jonathan 362
Franks, Peggy 363
Franks, Peter 362
Franks, Sally 363
Franks, Sarah 362
Frantce, Eve 574
Frantner, Caty 119
Frantner, Mary 120
Frants, Mary 573
Frantz, Abraham 12
Frantz, Abram 17
Frantz, Betsey 12
Frantz, David 566
Frantz, Mary 571
Frantz, Sarah 568
Frary, Milton 526
Fraser, James 704
Frasier, Sarah Crabtree 410
Frast, Lucy 83
Frasy, Laure 499
Frazee, Dulcina P. 144
Frazee, Jeresha 144
Frazee, John (Jr.) 634
Frazee, John W. 144
Frazee, Morris 144
Frazee, Moses 138, 144
Frazee, Nancy A. 692
Frazee, Priscilla 144
Frazee, R. A. 692
Frazee, Sarah 144
Frazee, W. T. (Dr.) 692
Frazell, Warren 594
Frazer, Alexander (Jr.) 383
Frazer, Benj. 283
Frazier, Daniel 287, 289
Frazier, David 138
Frazier, Israel 148
Frazier, Isreal 138
Frazier, Jacob 396
Frazier, James 650, 672
Frazier, James (Jr.) 383
Frazier, John 83, 138
Frazier, Matilda 138, 148
Frazier, Nathan 144
Frazier, Rebecca Jane 433
Freal, Mary 313
Freas, Ann 525
Freas, Catharine 525
Freas, Elizabeth 525
Freas, Jacob 525
Freas, John 525
Freas, Martin 525
Freas, Mary 525
Freas, Peter 525
Freas, Rachel 525
Freas, Susanna 525
Freas, William 525
Frease, Mary 403
Frebis, Anna 272
Frebis, Henry 272
Frederick, Abraham 572
Frederick, Adam 178
Frederick, Barbara 570

Frederick, Henry 456
Frederick, Joseph 572
Frederick, Martha 583
Frederick, Mary 567
Frederick, Peter 334, 492, 566
Frederick, Solomon 488
Fredericks, I. B. 105
Fredericks, John B. 110
Fredrick, Daniel 463
Free, Elizabeth 531
Free, Frederick 531
Free, John 445
Free, William 264
Free, Wm. 264
Freel, Levi J. 313
Freel, Sarah 657
Freeland, Luke 451
Freeman, Ann 451
Freeman, Anna 33
Freeman, B. N. 519
Freeman, Benjn. 384
Freeman, Caleb 138
Freeman, Clark C. 634
Freeman, Daniel 429, 634
Freeman, Eben Shaw 642
Freeman, Eliza 634
Freeman, Ervin 429
Freeman, George W. 634
Freeman, Henry 429
Freeman, Isaac 384
Freeman, James 155, 463, 644, 672
Freeman, Jesse 101
Freeman, John 376
Freeman, John A. 621
Freeman, John K. 634
Freeman, John W. 634
Freeman, Lauretta 429
Freeman, Lavina 120
Freeman, Magdalena 525
Freeman, Mahala 634
Freeman, Mary 138, 676
Freeman, Matilda 138
Freeman, Nancy 376
Freeman, Philip 634
Freeman, Priscilla 138
Freeman, Robert 138
Freeman, Ruth 382
Freeman, Samuel 130
Freeman, Samuel (Jr.) 116
Freeman, Sarah Ann 634
Freeman, Stephen 525
Freeman, Stephen S. 634
Freeman, Thomas 647, 672
Frees, Daniel H. 695
Frees, Hannah 495
Frees, Polly 382
Freestone, Danl. 670
Freitman, Geo. 113
French, Ambrose Rice 757, 762
French, Asa 124
French, Barbary 121
French, Catherine 575
French, Eliza 149
French, Harriet Amanda 333

French, Hiram 149
French, Isaac 711
French, James 116, 138, 144
French, Johannah 138
French, John 138
French, John P. 41
French, Jos. W. 144
French, Joseph 711
French, Michael 144
French, Moses F. 144
French, Otho 732
French, Philas 144
French, Polly 664
French, Rachel 138
French, Ralph 182
French, Russell 91
French, Salethy 570
French, Sarah 662
French, Susana 572
French, William 138
French, Wm. 144
Frese, Barbara 388
Fresh, Henry 153
Freshour, Abraham 52
Freshour, Elizabeth 52
Freshour, Henry 52
Freshour, John 52
Freshour, Margaret 52
Fressler, John 368
Frew, McKnight 492
Frewill, Jonathan 481
Frey, Abraham 347
Frey, Samuel 291
Freyer, Isaac H. 108
Friberger, George 231
Fribley, Jerome 105
Frick, Caroline 631
Frick, Christiana 631
Frick, Frederick 631
Frick, Jacob 409
Frick, Jacob F. 631
Frick, Mary 631
Frickle, Mary 387
Frieghton, Wm. 476
Friend, Andrew 138
Friend, Catharine 138
Friend, Elizabeth 138, 566
Friend, George 330
Friend, Hannah 727
Friend, Henry 138
Friend, Hester 138
Friend, James 116
Friend, Jesse 119, 138
Friend, John 138, 727
Friend, Joseph 643
Friend, Margaret 330
Friend, Rachel 118, 128
Friend, Rebecca 138
Friend, Sarah 138
Friend, Susannah 116
Friend, William 643
Friend, Wm. 138, 456
Frier, Julia 12
Frisbe, Theodore G. 763
Frisbey, Jonathan 261, 262
Frisbey, Sarah 262

Frisbie, Nathaniel K. 92
Frisbie, T. G. 765
Frisble, Theodonus H. C. 765
Frisble, Theodore G. 765
Frisby, James 258
Frisel, Nancy 515
Frishe, Gered Henry 226
Frishey, Jonathan 263
Frishey, Sarah 263
Frisinger, D. 613
Frisinger, David 613
Frisinger, Jacob 101
Frisinger, Noah 600
Frisinger, R. A. 613
Frisinger, Rachel E. 613
Frisinger, Rebecca Ann 613
Frisinger, William 101
Frisner, John 627
Fristoe, Mary V. 617
Fristoe, N. 617
Fristoe, Wm. H. 617
Fritch, Anthony 367
Fritsch, Hirommus 754
Fritsch, John 754
Fritsch, Lewis 754
Fritz, Catharine 609
Fritz, Christian 182
Fritz, Jacob 361
Frizell, Tabitha 515
Frizzell, Alice J. 138
Frizzell, Elizabeth 138
Frizzell, Harriet E. 138
Frizzell, Mary A. 138
Frizzle, Jacob 138
Frobes, Augustus 38
Frobes, Henry Ernst 38, 41
Frobes, William Ernst 38
Frock, Michael 564
From, Fredk. 367
From, Henry 572
Frone, Chas. Tobias 572
Fronie, Polly 663
Frontfield, William 607
Frost, Stephen 717, 727
Frothingham, Eben. 721
Frothingham, Ebenezer (Jr.) 721
Frothingham, Ebn. (Jr.) 721
Frothingham, Hannah 721, 726
Frothingham, John 721, 726
Frothingham, Lydia 721, 726
Frothingham, Peter 721, 726
Frothingham, Samuel 721, 726
Frow, Rhenmia 467
Fruch, Vaslita 75
Fruchey, Mary 383
Frungott, Susannah 88
Frush, Henry 153, 174
Frust, Henry 169
Frust, Mary 169

Fry, --- 518
Fry, Christian 543
Fry, Daniel 359, 513
Fry, Elizabeth 664
Fry, Enoch 527
Fry, Henry 492
Fry, Jonathan 659
Fry, M. 380
Fry, Margret 576
Fry, Mary 21
Fry, Philip 655
Fry, Samuel 566
Fry, Sarah 657
Fry, Susanna 658
Fry, Thomas 89
Fry, Thos. 572
Fry, Timothy 83
Fryback, Anna 384
Fryback, Catharine 384
Frybarger, Anna 238
Frybarger, Anna M. 238
Frybarger, Elizabeth 231
Frybarger, George 231
Frybarger, Jacob 238
Frybarger, Martin 231
Frybarger, Valentine 231
Fryberger, Hannah 684
Fryberger, Jacob 684
Fryer, Henry W. 692
Fryer, James M. 692
Fryer, Margaret 692
Fryer, S. 692
Fryer, Sarah 692
Fryer, Thomas 692
Fryer, W. 692
Fryman, Elizabeth 244
Fryman, Jacob 244
Fryman, John 244
Fryman, Joseph 244
Fryman, Joseph E. 244
Fryman, Stephen 71
Fuce, Margaret 519
Fudge, Adam 659
Fudge, Daniel 428
Fudge, Jacob 418, 427
Fudge, Mary Ann 433
Fudge, Rebecca Jane 433
Fudge, Sarah Elizabeth 433
Fuert, Anderson 513
Fugate, Edward 154
Fugate, Eliza 551
Fugate, James 683, 687
Fugate, Nancy 154
Fuge, David 659
Fulham, John 725, 728
Fulham, Thomas 725
Fulis, John 41
Fulkmore, Asa 500
Fulkreth, Abigail 308
Fullar, Alphonso 513
Fullen, Mary 550
Fuller, Dorcas 29
Fuller, Eliza 247
Fuller, Elizabeth 732
Fuller, George 597
Fuller, Harriet Ann 745
Fuller, James 273
Fuller, Jedediah B. 597

Fuller, John 496
Fuller, Joseph 714, 717
Fuller, Mary 138, 464
Fuller, Moses 732
Fuller, Russell 732
Fuller, Sally 497
Fuller, Samuel H. 732
Fuller, Solomon 732
Fullerton, Catherine 361
Fullerton, George 372
Fullerton, James 361
Fullerton, Jane 361
Fullerton, John 361
Fullerton, Mary 361, 510
Fullerton, Robert 361
Fullerton, Samuel 361
Fullerton, Wm. 368
Fullington, Eliza 58
Fullington, Moses 62
Fulmer, Mary 23
Fulton, Benjamin 543, 556
Fulton, David 267, 272, 355
Fulton, Elizabeth 556, 716
Fulton, George 556
Fulton, Isabella 556
Fulton, James 476, 477, 488
Fulton, Jane 294
Fulton, Jas. 477
Fulton, Jesse 297
Fulton, John 294, 556
Fulton, John S. 488
Fulton, Lawrence (Dr.) 105
Fulton, Lyle 360, 370
Fulton, Phebe Low 44
Fulton, Rachael 556
Fulton, Rachel 558
Fulton, Robert 284, 287, 298
Fulton, Robt. 272
Fulton, Saml. 294
Fulton, Samuel 294
Fulton, William 294, 556
Fultz, Catharine 216
Fultz, Elizabeth 216
Fultz, Isaac 216
Fultz, John 216
Fultz, Samuel 216
Fultz, William 216
Funderberg, Barbara 373
Funderburg, Barbara 361
Funderburg, Catherine 361
Funderburg, Eliza 361
Funderburg, Hetty 361
Funderburg, Jacob 361
Funderburg, Mary 361
Funderburg, Noah 361, 373
Funderburg, Rachel 361
Funderburg, Samuel 361
Funderburg, Sarah 361
Funk, Abraham 451
Funk, Barbara 509
Funk, Betsy 509

Funk, Catharine 509
Funk, Frederick 398
Funk, Hetty 568
Funk, Jacob 398, 509
Funk, John 509, 513
Funk, M. 740
Funk, Margaret 579
Funk, Martin 509
Funk, Polly 509
Funk, Ralph 737
Funk, Samuel 694
Funkhauser, Wentesty
　Piglar 162
Funston, Margaret 456
Funston, Wm. 384
Furgeson, William 23
Furguson, James 473, 478
Furguson, Mary 281
Furing, Noah 714
Furman, Abiah 602
Furman, Joel 543
Furman, Margaret 457
Furman, Sabria I. 608
Furman, Solomon 601, 603
Furnam, Sylvia Ann 610
Furnas, Hannah 699
Furnas, Isaac 681
Furnas, John 697
Furnas, Joseph 681
Furnas, M. W. 131
Furnas, Mary 117
Furnas, N. 697
Furnas, R. 697
Furnas, Rachel 138
Furnas, Rebecca 699
Furnas, Robert 679, 699
Furnas, Robert W. 138
Furnas, Ruth 697
Furnas, Solomon 697
Furnis, Rebecca 123
Furrow, Daniel 590
Furrow, James G. 543
Furrow, John 44, 116
Furrow, John P. 543
Fury, Elizabeth 628
Fury, Geo. B. 379
Fury, James 628
Fury, James M. 628
Fuson, Jane 543
Fuson, William 605
Fute, Eliza 466
Fute, Liza 466
Fwinchen, James 470
Fye, Charles 652
Fye, Elizabeth 355
Fye, Jacob 355, 358
Fye, Nicholas 665
Fyffe, Ann B. 13

--- G ---

Gab, William 683
Gabby, Robert 22
Gabby, Sarah Ann 22
Gabhart, Andrew 230
Gabhart, Catharine 230
Gabhart, Daniel 230

Gabhart, Elizabeth 230
Gabhart, John 230
Gabhart, Marier 230
Gabhart, Philip 230
Gabhart, Polly 230
Gabhart, Valentine 230
Gabriel, John F. 595
Gabriel, Mary 593
Gabriel, Nancy 585
Gabriel, Richard 582,
　596, 597
Gabriel, Thomas 736
Gadd, Elizabeth 154
Gadd, Giles 154
Gaddis, --- 639
Gaffield, Mary 23
Gage, Alden 51
Gage, Alden A. 51
Gage, Ambrose Rice 757,
　762
Gage, Horace M. 51
Gage, James L. 273,
　274, 762
Gage, Nancy M. 51
Gageby, David 607
Gagle, Matthias 114
Gagle, William 114
Gahagan, Maria 138
Gahm, Katheryne Meldick
　410
Gaitz, David 173
Galagher, Patrick 339
Galahan, Elizabeth 188
Galand, Katharine 716
Galaspie, George 303
Galaspy, Mary 665
Galbraith, John 717
Galbreath, Catharine 399
Galbreath, Elizabeth 392
Galbreath, Henry 399
Galbreath, Jane 399
Galbreath, John 399, 530
Galbreath, Margaret 399
Galbreath, Sarah 386
Galbreath, William 399
Galbreth, Betsey 458
Galbreth, John 116
Gale, Benjamin 496
Gale, Electa 41
Gale, Harrison 519
Gale, James 38, 279
Galeener, Peter 665
Galen, Andrew 717
Galer, Peter 717
Galey, David 607
Galigher, Ellen 371
Galiher, Peter 284
Galinger, A. B. 356
Galinger, Abraham B. 356
Gallagher, Adam 669
Gallagher, Anne 344
Gallagher, Charles 344
Gallagher, Edmund 303
Gallagher, Francis 344
Gallagher, John 317, 651
Gallagher, William 669
Gallahan, Edward 188,
　202, 210
Gallahan, Eliza 188

Gallahan, Eliza Ann 210
Gallahan, John 188,
　202, 210
Gallahan, Mary 202
Gallahan, Polly 188
Gallaher, John 319
Galland, Mary 593
Gallant, John 496, 513
Gallant, Sarah 496
Gallaspie, Jane 451
Gallatin, Francis A. 257
Gallatin, Jerusha 303
Gallatin, Susannah 257
Gallatin, Susannah G.
　257
Gallentine, John 12
Gallher, Manfield 513
Galligher, John 44
Galligher, M. 354
Galloher, Wm. 669
Galloway, Achsy 595
Galloway, James (Jr.) 50
Galloway, John 474, 590
Galloway, Samuel 595
Galpin, Jane 28
Galt, W. C. 26
Galt, William 529
Gamage, Hannah O. 510
Gamaye, Hannah O. 510
Gambal, John 590
Gambal, Matilda 593
Gambe, William 732
Gambert, Henry (Rev.)
　531
Gamble, Catharine 593
Gamble, Eliza 591
Gamble, Elizabeth 543
Gamble, George P. T. 336
Gamble, Henry 732
Gamble, Jane 425
Gamble, John G. 57
Gamble, Robt. 572
Gamble, Samuel 543
Gamble, William 563
Gammanthaller, Christian
　323
Gandee, Levi T. 77
Gandy, Acksah 590
Gandy, Elma 589
Gandy, Isaac 590
Gandy, Jacob 590
Gandy, Lucinda 584
Gannett, Parnell 271
Gannon, Elizabeth 108
Gannon, Emily 108
Gannon, Frederick 108
Gannon, Fredrick 108
Gannon, Mary 108
Gannon, Romanias 108
Gannon, Sarah Eliza 108
Ganon, Sabina 522
Gans, Daniel 226
Ganshaw, Abigail 321
Ganshaw, Frederick 321
Gant, Buy 666
Gant, Joel 303
Ganuge, Catharine 495
Garabant, Zachariah 572
Garard, Abner 116

Garard, Elizabeth 138
Garard, Esther 120
Garard, Esther A. 245
Garard, Henry 230
Garard, Isabella 548
Garard, J. 245
Garard, John 119
Garard, Johnathan 124
Garard, Joseph 119
Garard, Mary 120, 138
Garard, R. 245
Garard, Rhoda 119
Garber, Abraham 1
Garber, Catherine 540
Garber, Elizabeth 429
Garber, Henry 420, 429
Garber, John 217, 429
Garber, Joseph 540
Garber, Joseph (Rev.) 540
Garber, Martin 540
Garber, Mary 420, 429
Garber, Samuel 1
Garber, Solomon 2
Gard, Aaron 433
Gard, Levi 413
Gard, Lewis 433
Gard, Lydia 433
Gard, Mary 576
Gard, Mary Ann 433
Gard, Sarah 567
Gard, Simeon 433
Gard, Stephen 433, 672
Gardiner, Charles 77
Gardiner, Elizabeth 743
Gardiner, Fanny 743
Gardiner, George 743
Gardiner, George (Sr.) 743
Gardiner, James 743
Gardiner, John 714
Gardiner, Martha 743
Gardiner, Sally 714, 743
Gardiner, Sidna 743
Gardner, --- 279, 748
Gardner, Abner 44, 47
Gardner, Absolem 475
Gardner, Alfred 83
Gardner, Anna 79
Gardner, Archibald 29
Gardner, Charles 336
Gardner, Edward T. 298
Gardner, Edwin W. 433
Gardner, Elihua 632
Gardner, Elizabeth Ann 433
Gardner, Elizabeth P. 636
Gardner, Emeline Mary 433
Gardner, George 375
Gardner, George (Sr.) 742
Gardner, Gilbert Lafayette 433
Gardner, Isaac S. 18
Gardner, James 417, 422
Gardner, John 339, 357, 722, 724

Gardner, John Franklin 433
Gardner, Joshua 77, 566
Gardner, Margaret Little 722
Gardner, Nancy G. 84
Gardner, Patty 82
Gardner, Perry V. 433
Gardner, Sarah 553
Gardner, Silena 718
Gardner, Stephen D. 519
Gardner, William 60, 636
Garhagan, Maria 144
Garlach, Feith 112
Garlinger, Elizabeth 363
Garlinger, George 363
Garlinger, Jacob 363
Garlinger, John 363
Garlinger, Joseph 363
Garlinger, Magdalena 363
Garlinger, Mary 363
Garlinger, Sarah 363
Garlington, Conway 248
Garlock, Henry 213
Garlock, Jacob 213
Garmire, Christopher 563
Garmire, Elizabeth 563
Garmire, Francis 563
Garmire, John 563
Garmire, William 563
Garmore, Hariet 573
Garmore, John 572
Garn, John 519
Garner, Ben J. 692
Garner, James 58
Garner, Jeremiah 598
Garner, John 231
Garner, Peggy 121
Garnett, Ann 54
Garon, John 35
Garrard, Elizabeth 230
Garrard, Isaac 116
Garrard, Jonah 171
Garrard, Jonathan 230
Garrard, Mary 124, 171
Garrard, Milton 230
Garrard, Moses 659
Garrard, Nathaniel 119
Garrard, Thomas J. 135
Garrat, John 226
Garreard, John 119
Garret, Prescella 591
Garret, Russell 513
Garretson, Abiel 26
Garretson, Hannah 732
Garretson, Rebecca 658
Garrett, John C. 138
Garrett, Mary 125
Garrett, Mary Ann 633
Garrettson, J. 301
Garrison, Harriet 509
Garrison, John 179, 659
Garrison, Josiah 585
Garrison, Reuben 679
Garry, John M. 175
Garry, Patrick 704
Garst, Mary 498
Garthrop, Thomas 65
Gartley, George W. 535

Garver, Elizabeth 429
Garver, Henry 429
Garver, John 429
Garver, Mary 113
Garvey, John 119
Garvin, Mathew 732
Garvin, William 58
Garwick, Daniel 112
Garwick, E. 112
Garwick, M. 112
Garwood, Aaron 2, 7
Garwood, Alexander 2
Garwood, Carlisle H. 2, 7
Garwood, Charles 2
Garwood, Clarinda 7
Garwood, Clirinda 2
Garwood, Cynthanetta 15
Garwood, Daniel 12, 17
Garwood, Elizabeth 2
Garwood, Esther 2
Garwood, Hepsabeth 17
Garwood, Hester 591
Garwood, Hope 2
Garwood, Hosia 659
Garwood, James 2, 12
Garwood, Jane 7
Garwood, Jehu G. 12
Garwood, Jesse H. 17
Garwood, Job 2, 12
Garwood, John 2, 16, 17, 24, 25, 27
Garwood, John (Sr.) 17
Garwood, Joseph 6
Garwood, Levi 2, 7, 17
Garwood, Nathaniel 2
Garwood, Newton 5
Garwood, Rachel 2
Garwood, Rebecca 15
Garwood, Sally 11
Garwood, Sarah 2
Garwood, Sarah Jane 2
Garwood, Silas 2, 7
Garwood, Susan 2
Garwood, Susannah 13
Garwood, Synthia 2
Garwood, William 2, 12
Gasche, Gotlieb 741
Gase, Appellonia 521
Gaseugh, Thos. 572
Gashey, Charles 741
Gaskill, Cephas 649
Gaskill, Daniel 559
Gaskill, Nathan 559
Gaskill, Sarah 606
Gaskins, James 452
Gass, John 519
Gassard, Mehetable 659
Gassaway, Amelia 173
Gassaway, Henry 665, 677
Gassaway, Mary 677
Gassaway, Nich . . . 173
Gaston, Eunice 506
Gaston, Jared 77
Gaston, John 77
Gaston, Polly 80
Gaston, Salencia 82
Gaston, William 65
Gates, Abbott G. 138
Gates, Bittsa 716

Gates, David 474, 549
Gates, Fanny 601
Gates, George 153
Gates, Jared 601, 607
Gates, Lemuel B. 29
Gates, Mary 585
Gates, Prudence 589
Gates, Robens 590
Gates, Saml. T. 268
Gates, Samuel 260
Gates, Sarah T. 33
Gates, Stephen 267
Gates, Timoth M. 262
Gates, Timothy 717
Gates, Timothy G. 138
Gates, Timothy M. 258, 259, 260, 263, 267, 270
Gates, Wilson 508
Gates, Wm. A. 138
Gatewood, Phillip 384
Gatez, George 154
Gatis, Wilson 507
Gatliff, Jane 465
Gatz, Felty 152
Gault, John 449
Gault, William 527
Gause, D. 614
Gause, Enoch 616
Gause, Jesse 274
Gause, Mary Ann 606, 614
Gause, Missouri 616
Gause, Sarah A. 614
Gaven, Nancy 92
Gavit, Asa B. 496
Gawthrop, Richard 65
Gay, Eliza 467
Gay, Jacob 463
Gay, John 390
Gay, Molly 387
Gaylord, Harriet W. 275
Gaylord, James 270
Gaylord, James M. 275
Gaylord, Mary 714
Gaylord, Mary Jane 275
Gaylord, Timoth 262, 263, 264, 265
Gaylord, Timothy 258, 259, 263, 275
Gazaway, Saml. 260
Gaze, Mary 515
Geapam, Margaret 38
Gearhard, Lewis 133
Gearhart, John Y. 124
Gearhart, Polly 127
Gearheard, Lewis 132
Gearheard, William 132
Gearheart, James F. 543
Geary, Edward R. 741
Geary, Michael 335
Gebhardt, Henry 222
Gebhart, A. S. 356
Gebhart, Abraham 187
Gebhart, Barbara 187
Gebhart, Catharine 230
Gebhart, Catherine 187
Gebhart, David 420
Gebhart, George 230
Gebhart, Jacob 187

Gebhart, John 187
Gebhart, Margaret 187, 230, 420
Gebhart, Peter 242
Gebhart, Valentine 230
Gebhart, William 420
Gebheart, Maria 420
Geddis, Hamilton 253
Geddis, Horatio 253
Geddis, James 253
Geddis, John 253
Geddis, William 253
Geddis, Wm. 253
Gee, Clarcy 657
Gee, Henry 520
Geeheart, Samuel 463
Geer, Anna Viola 47
Geer, Earl P. 628
Geer, Mariah 586
Geer, Maxamilla 628
Geer, Smith 41
Geerhart, Catherine 126
Geers, Joseph 585
Geffery, E. 337
Geffery, Oliver T. 337
Gehbart, Elizabeth 242
Gehbart, Florence M. 242
Gehbart, Henry D. 242
Gehbart, John 242
Gehbart, John A. 242
Gehbart, Julia Ann 242
Gehbart, Mary 242
Gehbart, P. 242
Gehbart, Peter 242
Gehbart, S. 242
Gehbart, Wm. 242
Gehbart, Wm. F. 242
Gehbart, Wm. Henry 242
Geiger, Henry 388
Geigler, John 763
Geigler, John (Dr.) 763
Geilding, John 710
Geip, E. 735
Geip, J. 735
Geip, Rosana 735
Geise, Casper 604
Geiser, Casper 607
Geisler, Philip 543
Geisweit, Abigail 229
Geisweit, Jacob 229
Gendee, Uriah 77
Genethan, Philip 699
Genshaw, Frederick 318
Gentit, Susan 748
Gentle, Hannah 224
Gentle, John 224
Gentry, Abigail 184
Gentry, Ephraim 184
Gentry, Hannah 184
Gentry, John 184
Gentry, Margaret 184
Gentry, Samuel 184
Gentzer, Elizabeth 523
George, Alexander 285
George, Gohn 371
George, Isaac 339
George, Jacob 287
George, Jane 281
George, John 267, 272

George, Maria 371
George, Michael 268
George, Rebecca 385
George, Rhoda 497
George, Susannah 373
George, Weibly 749
George, William 286
Georges, Solomon 290
Georghegan, Anthony 672
Geotz, George 158
Geotz, George (Jr.) 158
Geotz, George (Sr.) 158
Geotz, Seville 158
Geotz, Solomon 158
Gephart, Abraham 198
Gephart, Barbara 198
Gephart, Betsy 186
Gephart, Catharine 192, 223, 231
Gephart, Daniel 187, 192, 205
Gephart, Elizabeth 182, 192, 200, 205, 231
Gephart, Emanuel 207
Gephart, George 187, 193, 194, 200
Gephart, Henry 187, 205
Gephart, Jacob 192, 193
Gephart, Jane 413
Gephart, John 182, 186, 187, 192, 198, 231
Gephart, Margaret 198
Gephart, Mary 200
Gephart, Peter 182, 186, 223, 231
Gephart, Rebecca 200
Gephart, Sarah 200
Gephart, Valentine 182
Gerard, Abner 138, 230
Gerard, Ann 230
Gerard, E. F. 607
Gerard, Ezra F. 599
Gerard, John 182, 223
Gerard, Jonah 171
Gerard, Mahitabel 549
Gerard, Margaret 123
Gerard, Mary 171
Gerard, Sarah 550
Gerard, Thomas I. 230
Gerard, Thomas J. 230
Gerber, Daniel 711
Gerberich, Johana 276
Gerberich, Levi 276
Gerhart, John 33
Gerk, William N. 520
Gerkin, Gerd 732
German, Amelia 574
German, Anthony 496
German, Catharine 608
German, Charles 601, 607
German, Charles P. 600, 602
German, George P. 602
German, Jacob 601, 602, 603
German, Peter 600, 602, 603
German, Sally 85
Germann, Anne E. 607

844

Germann, Henry 600
Germann, Jacob 600
Germann, Mary 607
Germann, Peter 607
Germann, Philip C. 607
Germy, Jacob 572
Gernert, Elizabeth 103
Gernon, Richard 282
Gerod, A. 326
Gerod, Emma 326
Gerod, S. 326
Gerrard, David W. 543
Gerrard, Jesse 130
Gerrard, John 124, 655
Gerron, John 35
Gervais, John Gabriel 722
Gess, Fanny 467
Gess, Joseph 116
Gester, Sarah 337
Gett, W. C. 505
Gettner, Peter E. 62
Getz, Daniel 163
Getz, Nancy 163
Getz, Valentine 152
Geyer, Andrew 66
Geyer, George 420
Geyer, Mary C. 420
Ghopes, Elizabeth 517
Gibb, James 463
Gibblin, Ann 47
Gibbons, Abraham 520
Gibbons, Wm. 456
Gibbs, Almon 760
Gibbs, Breadison 496
Gibbs, Charlotte 496
Gibbs, Cintha 496
Gibbs, Dennis 259, 264, 274
Gibbs, Elizabeth 516
Gibbs, James 456
Gibbs, Jane 566
Gibbs, John 138
Gibbs, Melinda 458
Gibbs, Miles H. 77
Gibbs, Milinda 458
Gibbs, Thomas 644, 656
Giblar, Susannah 451
Gibson, Catharine 181
Gibson, Cyrus 87
Gibson, Elizabeth 549
Gibson, Ester V. 734
Gibson, Israel T. 650
Gibson, Jane 200
Gibson, Jno. 177
Gibson, John 168, 171, 174, 178, 181, 271, 376, 485, 526
Gibson, John K. 530
Gibson, John M. 247
Gibson, John N. 260
Gibson, Jonathan 138
Gibson, Joseph 164, 530, 590
Gibson, Lydia 587
Gibson, Margaret 311
Gibson, Mary 113, 666
Gibson, Milo W. 734
Gibson, Rebecca 82

Gibson, Robert 384
Gibson, Ruth 79, 593
Gibson, Samuel D. 247
Gibson, Sarah 591
Gibson, Sarah Jane 311
Gibson, William 99, 456
Gibson, Wm. 271, 552
Giddings, Hannah 710
Giddings, John 710, 711
Giegler, Susan 569
Giel, John 189
Giel, Samuel 295
Giering, Mary 567
Giesaman, Anne Maria 133
Giesaman, Catharine 133
Giesaman, Maria 133
Giesler, John 603
Giesman, John 133
Gifford, Jesse 429
Gifford, Joseph 384, 472, 474
Gifford, Marvin 268
Gifford, Nathan 429
Gifford, Timothy 456
Gil, Andrew 596
Gilball, Aaron 144
Gilball, Louisa 144
Gilbert, Abel 257
Gilbert, Alice Roselle Jane 241
Gilbert, Alixes M. 73
Gilbert, Carcus G. 73
Gilbert, Charity 519
Gilbert, Chas. C. 292
Gilbert, Elizabeth 549
Gilbert, Elma A. 73
Gilbert, Emily J. 73
Gilbert, Esther 76
Gilbert, H. J. 151
Gilbert, Hannah 241
Gilbert, Hannah M. 73
Gilbert, J. T. 748
Gilbert, Jesse 241
Gilbert, John 119
Gilbert, Lester 760
Gilbert, Maria 73
Gilbert, Sarvis 760
Gilbert, William H. 73
Gilbert, Wm. R. 73
Gilbreath, Joseph 659
Gilchrist, James Parks 649
Gilchrist, Jane 649
Gilchrist, Margaret Anne 649
Gilchrist, Mary 649
Gilchrist, Miriah 649
Gilchrist, Robert 649
Gilchrist, Robert Willson 649
Gilchrist, Sarah 649
Giles, Charles 83
Giles, Joseph 86
Giles, Joseph (Jr.) 77
Giles, Maria E. 92
Giles, Polly 79
Giles, Sally 383
Gilespey, James A. 265
Gilespie, Evan 105

Gilfellin, Adam 477
Gilfillen, Adam 476
Gilfillin, Adam 476, 485
Gilhous, John H. 543
Gililan, Hana 513
Gilimore, Margaret 535
Gilimore, Mark 535
Gilimore, Samuel 535
Gilkison, Jane 511
Gilkison, Sarah 516
Gill, Andrew 595
Gill, David 585
Gill, Elizabeth 595
Gill, Gundy 77
Gill, James 83
Gill, Robert 641
Gillaland, Mariam 82
Gillan, Presley 513
Gilland, James Gordon 622
Gillas, Reubin 665
Gillaspie, Alexander 68
Gillaspie, Sarah 68
Gilleland, Abrham P. 83
Gilleland, Reuben 83
Gilleland, Robert 599
Gillen, William Bails 124
Gilles, Ruth 150
Gilles, Thomas 150
Gillespe, Jas. A. 270
Gillespie, Catharine 689
Gillespie, Ebenezer M. 433
Gillespie, Elizabeth 689
Gillespie, George 695
Gillespie, George (Jr.) 695
Gillespie, Isabel 640
Gillespie, James 659
Gillespie, James A. 269
Gillespie, James M. 751
Gillespie, Jane 695
Gillespie, Jas. A. 269
Gillespie, John 433, 543, 652, 689
Gillespie, M. 293
Gillespie, Mary 652
Gillespie, Sarah Ann 689
Gillespie, William 689
Gillespie, William H. 689
Gillespie, Wm. 433
Gillet, Emily 32
Gillet, Eunice 30
Gillet, Gersham 29
Gillet, Minerva 28
Gillett, Betsy 34
Gillfillan, John 492
Gillgillan, Thomas 492
Gillian, James 17
Gillian, Nathan 17
Gilliand, Nathan 17
Gillilan, Andrew 406
Gillilan, Elizabeth 406
Gillilan, Saml. 406
Gilliland, Abigal Allard 408
Gilliland, Adam 621

845

Gilliland, Charles 607
Gilliland, Elizabeth
  91, 609
Gilliland, Hugh 607
Gilliland, Jane 13
Gilliland, Jane E. 608
Gilliland, R. 626
Gilliland, Robert 603,
  607, 627
Gilliland, Robt. 627
Gilliland, Samuel 61
Gilliland, Sarah 607
Gilliland, Thomas 607
Gillim, Thomas 659
Gillimore, E. 535
Gillimore, Esabell 535
Gillimore, S. 535
Gillimore, U. M. 533
Gillispie, Ebenezer
  McGuffin 416
Gillispie, Joseph 349
Gillispie, Martha T. 416
Gillispie, Mary Jane 416
Gillmore, Martha 413
Gilloland, John 401
Gillruth, Hanorah 503
Gillruth, James 503
Gillruth, Mary 503
Gillruth, Thomas 503
Gillruth, William 503
Gillwell, Richard 263
Gilman, Benj. Ives 283
Gilman, Matilda 78
Gilman, Nicholas 283
Gilmore, Daniel 164
Gilmore, Isaac A. 535
Gilmore, John 160, 169
Gilmore, Lewis C. 535
Gilmore, Margaret 169
Gilmore, Mathew 154
Gilmore, Sally 78
Gilmore, Samuel 155
Gilmore, Thomas 164
Gilmore, Wm. 416
Gilpin, Caleb C. 732
Gilpin, Enos 433
Gilpin, Mary Agnes 433
Gilpin, Samuel 563
Gilpin, Sarah 563
Gimberman, Jacob 168
Gimer, Perry U. 98
Gimer, Wm. M. 98
Gimes, Cornelius 429
Gimling, Margaret 567
Gimlins, Barbara 563
Gimlins, Bernhart 563
Gimlins, Catharine 563
Gimlins, Elizabeth 563
Gimlins, George 563
Gimlins, Joab 563
Gimlins, John 563
Gimlins, Margaret 563
Gimlins, Sarah 563
Ginat, John Baptist 724
Ginatt, John B. 513
Ginlina, Jacob 572
Ginn, John 549
Ginnall, Jane 497
Ginter, Abraham 561

Ginter, Catherine 561
Ginter, Christian 561
Ginter, Elizabeth 561
Ginter, Frederick 362
Ginter, Henry 362
Ginter, Jacob 362
Ginter, John 561
Ginter, Justina 561
Ginter, Mary 561
Ginter, Mary Eve 362
Ginter, Peter 561
Ginter, Peter (Sr.) 561
Ginter, Susan 561
Ginther, Catharine 568
Ginther, Daniel 572
Ginther, Elizabeth 570
Ginther, Mary 568
Gipe, John 735
Gipe, LAH 735
Gipson, Charles W. 315
Gipson, Eliza 83
Giraga, Sarah 577
Girton, George 754
Girton, M. 702
Girton, S. A. 702
Gisons, George 478
Gist, Geo. W. 524, 525
Gitling, William 283
Givans, William 513
Given, Barbara 455
Given, William 463
Givens, Daniel 181
Givens, Elizabeth 166
Givens, William 166
Givens, Wm. 513
Givins, George 479
Givson, William 456
Gladman, Thomas 287
Gladwin, Mary 330
Glagrove, Henry B. 55
Glasford, William 665
Glasgow, James 686
Glasgow, James C. 755
Glasgow, John 755
Glasgow, Mary 755
Glasgow, William W. 755
Glasmore, Mary 744
Glass, Catharine 563,
  576
Glass, Elizabeth 563
Glass, Eve 563
Glass, Jacob 563
Glass, John 563
Glass, Joseph 384
Glass, Marton 563
Glass, Mary 563
Glass, Mathias 572
Glass, Matthias 563
Glass, Sarah 563, 573
Glass, Solomon 563
Glassmire, Abraham 321
Glassmire, Nancy 336
Glaze, Abraham 513
Glaze, Airhart 513
Glaze, Andrew (Jr.) 513
Glaze, Elizabeth 387,
  511
Glaze, John 384, 513
Glaze, Mary Eve 386

Glaze, Polly 387
Glaze, Rachael 383
Glaze, Rachel 400
Glaze, Rebecca 47
Glaze, Thomas 400
Glazier, Joseph 384
Gleason, Abigail 621
Gleason, Alford 36
Gleason, Alfred 36
Gleason, Cahen 744
Gleason, Clarissa 621
Gleason, Emily 607
Gleason, Joseph 599,
  600, 602, 603, 604,
  621, 625
Gleason, Mary 610, 621
Gleason, Sarah 752
Gleason, Sarah Jane 609
Gleason, Stephen 599,
  621, 626
Gleckler, Gotlieb 226
Glen, Aaron 659
Glenn, Charles 138
Glenn, Eliza 59
Glenn, Henry 219
Glenn, Jane 626
Glenn, John 561
Glenn, Margaret 59
Glenn, Solon J. 607
Glesser, David 761
Glesser, Sarah 761
Glick, Elizabeth 496
Glick, Esther 496
Glick, Jacob 535
Glick, Joad 541
Glick, John 405
Glick, L. F. 541
Glick, Margaret J. 541
Glick, Mary 541
Glick, Philip 405
Glick, R. 541
Glick, S. 541
Glick, Sarah Jane 541
Glick, Solomon 384
Glidden, Jefferson 274
Glidden, John 264
Glidden, Sidney 264
Glines, James 433
Glines, John 429
Glockner, Anna M. 92
Gloeckner, George 87
Glosser, Abraham 449
Glosser, Ann 449
Glosser, George 761
Glosser, Gillman 449
Glosser, Henry 449
Glosser, Margaret 449
Glove, Jane 457
Glove, June 457
Glover, Ann Massie 505
Glover, Anna 515
Glover, Catherine 505
Glover, Crawford 152,
  176
Glover, Eli 505
Glover, Elijah 505
Glover, Elizabeth 87
Glover, Elizabeth B. 505
Glover, Enos 313

Glover, Jemima 176
Glover, Jemina 152
Glover, John 505
Glover, Lydia 87
Glover, Margaret 513
Glover, Nathan 500, 513
Glover, Samuel 505
Glover, Sarah 516
Glover, Vincent 87
Glunt, John Samuel 433
Glunt, Susannah 433
Gnaggy, Anna 38
Gnaggy, Francis 38
Gobel, Sarah 342
Goben, Hugh 566
Goble, Charlota 116
Goble, Clarinda 543
Goble, Elizabeth 362
Goble, Enos 362
Goble, Eve 362
Goble, Evi 362
Goble, Hannah 362
Goble, Isaac 362
Goble, Joseph 116
Goble, Rhoda 657
Goble, Robert 362
Goble, Sally 125
Goble, Sarah 362
Goble, Simeon 362
Gocke, Herman 104
Gockemeyer, Henry M. 543
Godard, Abbott 672
Godard, Anson A. 29
Godard, E. A. 616
Godard, Hannah 616
Godard, J. A. 103
Godard, Rachel D. 616
Godard, Susan 616
Godard, Th . . . M. 616
Godard, William 616
Godare, James 513
Godare, Mary 513
Goddard, Chas. B. 291
Godden, Eleanor 127
Godfrey, Isaac 583
Godfrey, Joseph 492
Godfrey, Prince 264
Godman, Aulena 144
Godman, Cornelia 144
Godman, Eliz. B. 144
Godman, Julia H. 144
Godrey, Abagail 264
Goepper, Leopold 686
Goepper, Mary M. 686
Goepper, Maxamillian 686
Goepper, Michael 686
Goepper, Willhemina 686
Goerges, Philip 558
Goess, Mary 523
Goets, George 158
Goets, Seville 158
Goetschins, Maria 518
Goettel, John 41
Gofarth, Jemima 125
Goff, Betsey 580
Goff, David 739
Goff, James C. 86
Goff, Lorezo C. 508
Goff, Samuel 580

Gofset, John 474
Gofsett, John 476
Gohagan, Mary 123
Gohagan, William 119
Goings, George 543
Goings, Joseph 384
Goings, Samuel W. 543
Goke, Bernd. Herman 104
Goke, Gerd. Henery 104
Goke, Herman 104
Goke, Johann Dirk 104
Golden, Margaret 154
Golden, Nancy 663
Golder, Jane 594
Goldon, Thomas 665
Goldsberry, Benj. 492
Goldsberry, Benjamin 456
Goldsberry, James 60
Goldsbury, Humphrey 44
Goldsmith, James 710
Goldsmith, James J. 712
Goldwin, Elizabeth 666
Golleher, John 659
Golliver, William 607
Gonklin, --- 735
Good, Anna E. 326
Good, Barbara 362
Good, Benj. 364
Good, Benjamin 362
Good, Betsy 205
Good, Catharine 565
Good, Catherine 362
Good, Christian 362
Good, D. C. 326
Good, Eliza Anjelus 344
Good, Elizabeth 362,
    568, 571
Good, Eve 563
Good, Hannah 362
Good, Jacob 20, 205,
    563, 572
Good, John 205
Good, John (Jr.) 362
Good, John (Sr.) 362
Good, Joseph 357, 362
Good, Mary 563
Good, Nancy 125, 568
Good, Rachel 362
Good, Sarah J. 326
Good, Susannah 362
Goodah, Elizabeth 713
Goodal, Diadema 739
Goodale, Cynthia 713
Goodale, Nathan 723
Goodale, Sarah 713
Goodale, Susan 718
Goodale, Timothy 724
Goode, Burwell 659
Goodell, Martha 31
Gooden, Asa 362
Gooden, Daniel 513
Gooden, Davis 362
Gooden, Elizabeth 362
Gooden, Jane 362
Gooden, Martha 362
Gooden, Moses (Jr.) 362
Gooden, Moses (Sr.) 362
Gooden, Phebe 362
Gooden, Polly 362

Gooden, Samuel 362
Gooden, Smith 362
Goodfellow, Wm. 740
Goodforth, Jonas 526
Goodhue, John 173
Goodin, Elizabeth 359
Goodin, Isaac (Sr.) 739
Goodin, James 301, 484
Goodin, Jane 342
Goodin, Moses 342
Goodin, Moses (Sr.) 362
Goodin, Nancy 301, 375,
    551
Goodin, Samuel 342
Goodin, Sarah 342
Goodin, Susanah 342
Gooding, Clarrissa R.
    592
Gooding, Hannah 463
Gooding, James 65, 484,
    485
Gooding, Sarah D. 592
Goodleaf, Abraham 266
Goodleaf, Jacob 266
Goodlick, Samuel 210
Goodman, Catherine 458
Goodman, Christana 465
Goodman, John 384
Goodman, William 463
Goodno, Daniel 717
Goodpaster, Solomon 690
Goodpaster, Susannah 690
Goodpasture, Elizabeth
    660
Goodpasture, James 659
Goodpasture, Peggy 667
Goodrich, Geo. 572
Goodrich, James B. 501
Goodrich, John 630
Goodrich, Nelson 607
Goodwell, John 302
Goodwin, Abigail 433
Goodwin, Alexander 684
Goodwin, Amos 627
Goodwin, Angeline 627
Goodwin, Benjamin 627
Goodwin, Jacob 607, 627
Goodwin, Jehu 627
Goodwin, John 627
Goodwin, Joshua 627
Goodwin, Lavina 433
Goodwin, Marenday 31
Goodwin, Mary 29, 433
Goodwin, Noab 337
Goodwin, Noah 337
Goodwin, Sarah 627
Goodwin, Sarah Ann 627
Goodwin, William 684
Goodwin, William H. 684
Goodwin, William R. 668
Gorden, James 286
Gorden, Peggy 121
Gorden, William 659
Gordin, Abigail 66
Gordin, Charles 66
Gordin, Erastus 66
Gordin, Harriet 66
Gordin, John 659
Gordin, Laura 66

Gordin, Maria 66
Gordin, Stephen 66
Gordin, William 66
Gordineer, John A. 41
Gordon, . . . es 167
Gordon, A. G. 328
Gordon, Abraham 363
Gordon, Alice G. 328
Gordon, Anna 327, 498
Gordon, Bazel 362
Gordon, Bazzel 362
Gordon, Betsey 363
Gordon, Cassandra 363
Gordon, Charge 340
Gordon, Charles 285,
362, 363
Gordon, Coe 328
Gordon, D. A. 409
Gordon, Eleanor 363
Gordon, Elizabeth 363,
746
Gordon, Emma C. 363
Gordon, George 362, 363
Gordon, George F. R. 334
Gordon, George W. 363
Gordon, Hannah 363, 364
Gordon, Harriett 746
Gordon, Harry 328, 285,
340, 362
Gordon, Hester 362
Gordon, James 362, 524,
682
Gordon, Jane 363
Gordon, Jeremiah 362
Gordon, John 362, 363
Gordon, L. 328
Gordon, Lucy 363
Gordon, M. 328
Gordon, Malinda 328
Gordon, Margaret 363
Gordon, Martha C. 328
Gordon, Mary 344, 362,
363
Gordon, Moses 167
Gordon, Nancy 362, 363
Gordon, Peggy 363
Gordon, Pheby 571
Gordon, Rebecca 496
Gordon, Robert F. 363
Gordon, S. E. 328
Gordon, Sally 363
Gordon, Samuel 327, 328
Gordon, Samuel H. 362,
363
Gordon, Samuel H. (Dr.)
368
Gordon, Sarah 327, 362,
363
Gordon, Sarah E. 363
Gordon, Sarah M. C. 330
Gordon, Stewart 314
Gordon, Susanna 363
Gordon, William 328,
344, 362, 363, 744
Gordon, William B. 411
Gordon, Wm. 344
Gordy, Anne 387
Gordy, Polly 387
Gordy, Sally 388

Gore, John 422
Gore, Martha Ann 422
Gore, Peter 267
Gorey, Michael 47
Gorham, Amos T. 702
Gorham, Mary E. 702
Gorham, Richmond Holmes
702
Gormly, Jane 382
Gorrill, Thomas 765
Gorsuch, Elijah 211
Gorton, Benjamin 585
Gorton, Mary 588
Gosage, Mary 576
Goschert, Johannes
Frenkling 234
Goschert, Maria 234
Goschert, Samuel 234
Goslee, Samuel 463
Goslee, Thomas 44
Gosman, Agnes 264
Gosman, Andrew 264, 269
Goss, Elizabeth 714
Gossard, Catherine 457
Gossard, Philip 488
Gossard, Phillip 463
Gosset, John 476
Gossett, John 475, 481
Gossine, Edward 403
Gossom, Nancy 467
Gothard, Maria 492
Gotschald, Christina 236
Gotschald, Jacob 236
Gotschald, Sahra 236
Gott, David (Jr.) 29
Gott, Elizabeth 738
Gottschalk, Christina
236, 237
Gottschalk, George 236
Gottschalk, Jacob 234,
236, 237
Gottschalk, Johan 235,
236
Gottschalk, Johannes
234, 237
Gottschalk, Lusinda 235
Gottschalk, Michael 236
Gottschalk, Sara 234,
235, 236
Gottschall, John 237
Gottschall, Mary Ann 237
Gottschall, Sarah 237
Goudy, Catharine 739
Gouge, Robert 543
Gould, Aaron 308
Gould, Benjamin 732
Gould, Enos 29
Gould, Hannah 30
Gould, James 303
Gould, Joseph 29
Gould, M. C. 421
Gould, W. C. 421
Gouldsbury, John 590
Gouser, David 566
Gouter, George 566
Gouter, Nicholas 226
Gouty, Polly 382
Goveter, Jacob 566
Gowdy, John 680

Gowens, Catharine 452
Gower, Jacob R. 749
Gower, John S. 749
Graber, John 755
Gradhouse, George 169
Gradhouse, Jno. B. 169
Grady, Earl 628
Grady, John 463
Grady, Maxamilla 628
Graft, John 653
Graft, Marcus Z. 525
Gragg, Edward 590
Gragg, Isabella 593
Gragg, James 272
Gragg, John 268, 271,
272
Graham, Amy 711
Graham, Anna W. 28
Graham, Cathrine 636
Graham, Christiann 59
Graham, Eddy 460
Graham, Elizabeth 59,
512, 572
Graham, Esther 707
Graham, Felix 492
Graham, George 269, 311
Graham, Hannah 591
Graham, Helen 59
Graham, James 86
Graham, James B. 685
Graham, James R. 77
Graham, Jane 59
Graham, Jean 59
Graham, John 47, 51,
59, 159, 384, 448,
483, 492, 513, 543,
572, 707
Graham, Liddea 51
Graham, Lucy 359
Graham, Margaret 386,
716
Graham, Mary A. 407
Graham, Mary Ann 740
Graham, Patrick 416
Graham, Phebe 512
Graham, Rebecca 269
Graham, Robert 163, 463
Graham, Ruth 448
Graham, Samuel 77
Graham, Seth 513
Graham, Thomas 585, 648
Graham, William 138,
208, 585, 636
Grahan, James 513
Gralle, Phillip 384
Gram, Harriet 330
Gram, Henery 561, 572
Gram, Henry 561
Gram, Hester 561
Gram, John W. 330
Gram, S. 330
Grambel, Daniel 452
Gran, E. 151
Gran, J. 151
Gran, Joseph 151
Grandan, Enoch 163
Grandon, Enoch 170
Grandstaff, John 288,
291

Grandstaff, Joseph 636
Granger, Ebenezer 298
Granstaff, Adam 288
Grant, Alexander 101
Grant, Edwin 450
Grant, James 101
Grant, James A. 741
Grant, John 389
Grant, Jonathan 492
Grant, Landress 77
Grant, Lovina 522
Grant, Peter 384
Grant, Rachel 503
Grant, Zachariah 496
Grapes, Catharine 290
Grapes, David 290
Grapes, George 290
Grapes, Henry 290
Grapes, Jacob 290
Grapes, John 290
Grapes, Sarah 290
Graren, Daniel 47
Gratton, Mary 363
Gratton, Nancy 382
Graves, Amelia 499
Graves, Amy 509
Graves, Asa 496
Graves, Caroline 509
Graves, Eleanor 509
Graves, Elexander 452
Graves, Eli 635
Graves, Elize 496
Graves, George 509
Graves, Harriet 509
Graves, Inerean 496
Graves, Inerear 496
Graves, James D. 744
Graves, James Q. 599
Graves, John 509, 629, 635
Graves, Lovena 509
Graves, Mary 30, 509
Graves, Nancy 746
Graves, Nelly 453
Graves, Noah 503
Graves, Sarah 509
Graves, Susanna 509
Graves, Susannah 511, 746
Graves, Tyler 496
Graves, William 456, 509, 513
Graves, William B. 75
Graves, Zachariah 318, 319
Gray, --- 20, 400, 473
Gray, Abner 433
Gray, Achsah M. P. 363
Gray, Amos 665
Gray, Ann 109, 175
Gray, Anna 678
Gray, Caroline 109
Gray, Catharine 109, 180
Gray, Collins 109
Gray, Daniel 155, 161, 164, 166, 167, 172, 174
Gray, Danuel 535
Gray, David 109

Gray, Deborah 109, 155, 166, 167
Gray, Elijah 180
Gray, Eliza 350
Gray, Elizabeth 109, 175, 535
Gray, Ellen 350
Gray, Francis 175
Gray, Hannah 181, 678
Gray, Herbert W. 95
Gray, Ida J. 95
Gray, Ivy 692
Gray, James 23, 50, 83, 109, 175, 678
Gray, Jane 224
Gray, John 167, 180, 181, 590, 678
Gray, John M. 424
Gray, John W. 62
Gray, Jonas 350
Gray, Jonas H. 363
Gray, Jonathan 725
Gray, Joseph 109
Gray, Joseph M. 535
Gray, Lemuel 47
Gray, Maria 175
Gray, Mary 109
Gray, Nancy 350
Gray, Phebe 678
Gray, Philina 109
Gray, Rachel 184
Gray, Richard 175, 224
Gray, S. 95
Gray, Samuel 175, 535
Gray, Samuel T. 109
Gray, Sarah 109, 577
Gray, T. 95
Gray, Thomas 171, 180
Gray, Thomas B. 135
Gray, Truman 95
Gray, William 652, 653, 732
Gray, Wm. 643
Grayham, John 51
Grayham, Margaret 592
Grayham, Mary Ann 592
Grayham, Robert 590
Grayus, --- (Dr.) 12
Greague, Susan M. 748
Greaser, Christian 41
Greaser, Maria E. 91
Greathouse, James 272
Greaves, James Q. 599
Greben, Isaac 443
Greben, John 443
Greeg, --- 479
Greeg, Ann B. 684
Greelee, Jenny 455
Greeley, Edward 723
Greely, Daniel 684
Greely, Lavina E. 684
Greemen, Caleb 207
Green, . . . uel 170
Green, Abigail 125, 131, 159
Green, Achsah 211
Green, Alexander 41
Green, Allen 452
Green, Amos H. 582

Green, Amy 173
Green, Atsey 383
Green, Benjamin 685
Green, Betsey 461
Green, Catharine 589
Green, Charles 51, 501
Green, Charles (Jr.) 488
Green, Charlotte 263, 266
Green, Christopher 144
Green, Clarke 513
Green, Daniel 83, 144
Green, David 334
Green, Deborah 387
Green, Dianna D. 519
Green, Duff 61
Green, E. 94
Green, Elenor 144
Green, Elias 286
Green, Eliza A. 583
Green, Elizabeth 375, 415, 514, 685, 718
Green, Elmira 685
Green, Etthrine 50
Green, Experunie 50
Green, Francis M. 38
Green, Frederick 685
Green, Freelove 555
Green, George 12, 131
Green, George W. 116
Green, Hannah 685
Green, Harriet 420
Green, Harriet T. 38
Green, Henry 51, 433
Green, Henry H. 582
Green, Hillery 420
Green, Horace 41
Green, J. M. 94
Green, James 50, 503, 513
Green, James Monroe 417
Green, Jesse 91
Green, John 106, 124, 144, 350, 362, 415, 685, 760
Green, Joseph 50, 144, 286, 685
Green, Joshua 341
Green, Lewther F. 496
Green, Loran 514
Green, Lorenzo 50
Green, Lydia 685
Green, Margaret 12, 584
Green, Maria 420
Green, Mary 92, 163, 266
Green, Mary A. 171
Green, Mary Eddy 30
Green, Milton, A. 38
Green, Miner 526
Green, Moses 51, 585
Green, Myles 362, 367
Green, Nancy 350
Green, Nehmiah 12
Green, Olive S. 38
Green, Oliver W. 263, 266
Green, Ourns 90
Green, Randolph 665
Green, Rebecca 350

Green, Richard 350
Green, Robert 350
Green, Ruth 136
Green, Sampson 173
Green, Samuel 50, 51, 153, 163, 171, 350
Green, Sarah 127, 333
Green, Sarah A. 337
Green, Simeon F. 38
Green, Simion C. 41
Green, Susan 303
Green, Susan C. 550
Green, Thomas 47, 131, 290, 350
Green, Timothy 100, 526
Green, Wilkerson 139
Green, William 12, 44, 121, 159, 161, 176, 350, 420, 452
Green, William W. 420
Greene, Catharine 718
Greene, Charles Henry 212
Greene, Charles R. 212
Greene, Eleanor 356
Greene, Eliza J. 211
Greene, Elizabeth 394, 395
Greene, Griffin 730
Greene, Harriet 394, 395
Greene, Harriet C. 212
Greene, Isaac 732
Greene, Isaac N. 420
Greene, James 356, 394
Greene, John 356, 394, 395
Greene, John J. 367
Greene, Lucy Ann Teigler 211
Greene, Lucy M. 29
Greene, Martha 394, 395
Greene, Mary Sophia 212
Greene, P. S. 368
Greene, Phebe 714
Greene, Philip 730
Greene, Richard 730
Greene, William 395
Greene, William Henry 394
Greene, Zechariah 116
Greener, Philip 158
Greenfield, Elizabeth 556
Greenfield, Thomas 389
Greenham, N. 124
Greenlee, Alex. 268
Greenlee, David 153
Greenlee, Elizabeth 459
Greenlee, Mary 451
Greenlee, Rachel 716
Greenslit, Moses 29
Greenslit, Susan 29
Greenup, Charlotte V. C. 57
Greenup, Christ. 57
Greenup, Christopher 57
Greenup, Lucetta P. 57
Greenup, Nancy 57
Greenup, Susan 57

Greenup, Wilson 57
Greenup, William P. 57
Greenwood, Elizabeth 452
Greer, Jacob W. 543
Greer, James 681, 683, 688
Greer, Joseph 101, 105, 255
Greer, Joshua 203
Greer, Mary 384
Greer, Moses 204
Greer, Paul 717
Greg, Robert 474
Greg, Thomas 473
Gregary, James 44
Gregg, Abner 163
Gregg, Alexander J. 684
Gregg, Amor 492
Gregg, Druzela 414
Gregg, Harman 433
Gregg, Israel 684
Gregg, Jacob 315, 488
Gregg, James 590
Gregg, Lydia 12
Gregg, Nathan 484, 492
Gregg, Rhoda 414
Gregg, Robert 484, 488
Gregg, S. S. 486
Gregg, Sarah 560
Gregg, Thomas 472, 475, 482, 485, 488
Gregg, Thos. 479
Gregg, Uriah 303
Gregg, Wesley 492
Gregg, Zillah 11
Gregnon, John B. 496
Gregory, Benedict 655
Gregory, David 77
Gregory, Emma M. 655
Gregory, George 554
Gregory, Henry 428
Gregory, Joseph 47
Gregory, Lydia 58
Gregory, M. 509, 510
Gregory, Sally C. 655
Gregory, Selah 58
Gregory, William 44
Gregory, William S. 655
Greham, Susannah 383
Greife, --- 604
Greisinger, John 69
Greisinger, Susanna 69
Greisinger, Susannah 69
Greisse, --- 604
Grell, Hanrietta 523
Greosser, Peter 177
Greseman, John William 133
Gressel, Franz 92
Gretchell, David 12
Grewell, John 572
Grey, Amos 208
Grey, Caroline Lovisa 114
Grey, Catherine 666
Grey, David 109
Grey, Sarah 14
Grey, Sarah Philena 114
Grey, Thomas 154

Grey, W. H. 692
Grey, William 672
Grey, Wm. Collins 114
Greybill, John I. 210
Gribbin, John 492
Gribbs, Edward Young 653
Grice, John F. 336
Griddinger, --- 593
Griem, Cattiarina 33
Griener, Philip 158
Grier, James 384
Griesman, Catharine 133
Griesman, Curella 133
Griesman, George 133
Griesman, Magdalene 133
Griesman, Susanna 133
Grieve, David L. 492
Griffee, Hannah 293
Griffen, Winford 126
Griffeth, John 172, 392, 590
Griffeth, Mary Jane 741
Griffeth, Rebecca 741
Griffeth, Sarah Ann 741
Griffeth, William 562
Griffey, E. 405
Griffey, Geo. 405
Griffey, Jesse 348
Griffey, S. 405
Griffin, Adam 460
Griffin, Alexander 488
Griffin, Asael 717
Griffin, Charlotte 581
Griffin, David 643
Griffin, George W. 627
Griffin, Hezekiah 520
Griffin, Joseph 77
Griffin, Levin 590
Griffin, Mina 13
Griffin, William 41
Griffin, William C. 750
Griffith, Daniel 367
Griffith, Edwin 250, 251
Griffith, Eleazer 195
Griffith, Epienis 463
Griffith, George W. 164
Griffith, Hiram 744
Griffith, Isaac 195
Griffith, Joseph 195
Griffith, Nathan 572
Griffith, Sally 488
Griffith, William 179
Griffy, Laury 666
Griffy, Thomas 210
Griggs, Daniel 379, 381
Griggs, Deborah 363
Griggs, Ebenezer 653
Griggs, Elizabeth 363
Griggs, Elmira 653
Griggs, John 363
Griggs, Samuel 363
Grigsby, Elias 86
Grigsby, Lucy 363
Grigsby, Lucy C. 363
Grigsby, Moses 363
Grigsby, Moses B. (Jr.) 363
Grim, Barbara 44
Grim, Catharine 83

Grim, David 384
Grim, Jacob 83
Grimes, Ann 520
Grimes, Barbara 215
Grimes, Barby 220
Grimes, Bernard 353
Grimes, Cornelius 215
Grimes, Elizabeth 456, 520, 609
Grimes, Hannah 658
Grimes, Harrison 215
Grimes, Isabel 551
Grimes, James 447
Grimes, James M. 416
Grimes, Jeremiah 215
Grimes, John 183, 223, 444, 492
Grimes, Lemuel 711
Grimes, Lucinda 215
Grimes, Manerva 215
Grimes, Maria 496
Grimes, Matthew 264
Grimes, Samuel 224
Grimes, Thomas 452, 488
Grimes, William 215
Grin, E. 151
Grin, J. 151
Grin, Joseph 151
Griner, Christian L. 360, 365, 367
Griner, Mary 221
Grinning, Ebenezer 714
Grintner, Catharine 677
Grintner, Frederick 677
Grintner, Henry 677
Grintner, Mary Ann 677
Gripe, Catharine 202
Gripe, David 193
Gripe, Elizabeth 193
Gripe, Hannah 193
Gripe, Henry 202
Gripe, Jacob 202
Gripe, John 193
Gripe, Mary 202
Gripe, Samuel 202
Gripe, Stephen 193
Gripp, Rebecca 458
Grisbey, James 261
Grissell, Nathan P. 177
Grist, Magdalena 520
Grist, Susanna 253
Griswold, Jared 748
Griswold, Mary Ann 519
Grit, Mary 533
Grit, William 533
Grittery, Andrew 680
Grittery, Cephas 680
Grittery, Sarah 680
Grizzel, Edward 154
Grizzel, Hannah 154
Grizzle, Edward 154, 174
Grizzle, Hannah 154
Groce, Bentley 395
Groce, Betsey Ann 395
Groce, John 395
Groce, Lydia 395
Groce, Mahlon 395
Groce, Margaret 395
Groff, Benjamin 631

Groff, Catharine 631
Groff, Christian 631
Groff, David 631
Groff, Elizabeth 631
Groff, Ignatius 371
Groff, Jacob 631
Groff, Martin 631
Groff, Mary 631
Groff, Richard 631
Groff, Samuel 631
Groff, Susan 631
Groninger, Elizabeth 516
Groom, Job 384
Groom, Wm. 384
Gros . . . endyke, Samuel 380
Grose, Ida M. 330
Gross, John D. 312
Grossenbandur, Samuel 334
Grosvenor, Daniel 680
Grosvenor, Launson 543
Groth, Fred (Rev.) 221
Grottenthaler, George M. 543
Grove, Abijah 744
Grove, Catharine 2
Grove, Christopher 2
Grove, David 2
Grove, Elizabeth 2, 336
Grove, Fredrick 463
Grove, George 223, 224
Grove, Henry 210, 212
Grove, Jacob 212, 528
Grove, Jeptha 744
Grove, Lampson 745
Grove, Martin 2
Grove, Mary 2
Grove, Michael 520
Grove, Orpha 747
Grove, Philip 212
Grove, Phillip 210
Grove, Samuel 2
Grove, Stephen 210
Grove, Susannah 2
Grove, William 456
Grover, Ebenezer R. 101
Grover, Elijah 732
Grover, Ezra 86
Grover, Isaiah 504
Grover, Jonathan 21, 22
Grover, Leonard 504
Grover, Oliver 496
Grover, Sarah 504
Groves, Abraham 362
Groves, Catharine 383
Groves, George 362
Groves, Henry 53
Groves, James 362
Groves, John 362
Groves, John Selby 375
Groves, Luis 384
Groves, Mary 362
Groves, Nancy 362
Groves, Rebecca 362
Groves, Rhoda 274
Groves, William S. 336
Grow, Becca 83
Grow, Catharine 144

Grow, Herbert 409
Grow, Mary 144
Grow, Peter 86
Gruax, Mary 153
Gruax, Richard 153
Grubb, Andrew 24
Grubb, Anna 371
Grubb, Daniel 452
Grubb, Elizabeth 139
Grubb, George 365
Grubb, Henry 492
Grubb, Jacob 488
Grubb, James 264, 267, 470, 471, 472, 473, 474, 488, 492
Grubb, John 139
Grubb, William 720
Gruber, Jacob 229
Gruber, Mary Elizabeth 433
Gruber, Susannah 229
Grubs, Atlanlick 12
Grubs, Daniel 12
Grubs, Mary 14
Grueser, Mary E. 90
Gruey, Joseph 742
Grumble, Curtis 560
Grumble, Sally 127
Grumell, Timothy 553
Grumrine, John 572
Grun, E. 151
Grun, J. 151
Grun, Joseph 151
Grunden, J. F. 95
Grunden, Nellie 95
Grundner, Frederick 207
Grundner, Henry Frederick 207
Grundy, Mary 337
Gruner, Philip 158
Grussam, James 41
Guard, Elias 116
Guest, Pitney 555
Guier, Frederick 298
Guiler, Mary A. 313
Guiler, William 313
Guinall, Eleanor 498
Guinall, Sarah 495
Guires, Sherman S. 74
Guisinger, Emily J. 344
Guisinger, Jacob 344
Guisinger, John 340
Guisinger, Mary 344
Guisinger, Nancy 354
Guittean, Annie I. 712
Guiver, Joseph 317
Gulick, A. 618
Gulick, Amos 618
Gulick, Anna 617
Gulick, George W. 618
Gulick, Jeddiah 672
Gulick, S. M. 618
Gulick, Sarah M. 618
Gump, Daniel 124
Gump, George 144
Gump, John 543
Gump, Lavina 144
Gump, Levi 144
Gump, Lucy 144

Gump, Mary 127, 144
Gump, Wm. 144
Gunckel, Henry 217
Gunckel, Michael 204
Gunckel, Philip 184, 186, 224
Gunday, Catherine 457
Gunderman, George 580
Gundner, Catharine 202
Gundner, Charles Frederick 202
Gundner, Frederick 202
Gundner, Henry Theodore 202
Gundy, Jacob 486
Gundy, Mary V. 463
Gundy, Matty 466
Gundy, Polly 468
Gunkel, Barbary Anna 235
Gunkel, Christian 235
Gunkel, Maria 235
Gunkel, Maria Catherina 235
Gunn, Amanda 515
Gunn, Ann Eliza 750
Gunn, Ausman 745
Gunn, Carver 745, 750
Gunn, Carver S. 750
Gunn, Charles 750
Gunn, Enos 508
Gunn, Eve 750
Gunn, Fanny 12
Gunn, Havillah 509
Gunn, Mary Ann 744
Gunn, Zina 509
Gunsaulles, Levi 447
Gunset, Henry 607
Gunstead, James A. 59
Gunther, Elisabeth 571
Gunther, John 572
Gurner, Martha 22
Gushen, Catharine 574
Gustin, Bethana 677
Gustin, Cynthia 677
Gustin, Jane 663, 677
Gustin, John 677
Gustin, Mary 677
Gustin, Naomi 677
Gustin, Renee Jane 677
Gustin, Samuel 655
Gustin, Thomas 677
Guthery, Hannah 504
Guthery, John 484
Guthery, Rebecca 462
Guthey, Nathan 17
Guthree, John 475, 483
Guthrey, --- 451
Guthrey, Andrew 652
Guthrey, Charles 77
Guthrey, George 452
Guthrey, John 452
Guthrey, Mary 76
Guthrie, A. A. 290
Guthrie, Catharine Ann 746
Guthrie, Elias 77
Guthrie, George N. 607
Guthrie, Henman 77
Guthrie, Herman 77

Guthrie, James 232, 762
Guthrie, James G. 544
Guthrie, Jas. 762
Guthrie, John 477, 607
Guthrie, Joseph 513
Guthrie, Louisa 544
Guthrie, Percila 455
Guthrie, Rebecca 163, 175, 180
Guthrie, Rebecca G. 161, 177
Guthrie, Samuel 177
Guthrie, Samuel H. 161, 162, 163, 167, 168, 175, 176, 180
Guthrie, Stephen 77
Guthrie, Thomas 745
Guthrie, Trueman 714
Guthry, John 473
Gutridge, Hester 128
Gutridge, William 128
Guttery, Andrew 653
Guttery, Aseneth 653
Guttery, Belinda 652
Guttery, Cephus 651
Guttery, Demos 653
Guttery, Maria 655
Guttery, Samuel 653
Guttery, William 651, 653
Guttrey, William 651
Guy, Ann 398
Guy, Catharine 398
Guy, Charles 62
Guy, Cyrus 711
Guy, George 398, 607
Guy, Harrison 114
Guy, Hezekiah 398
Guy, James 58, 62
Guy, John 398
Guy, Margaret 398
Guy, Martha 114
Guy, Mary 44, 398
Guy, Nelson 398
Guy, Polly 44
Guy, Samuel 398
Guy, Wilkinson 47
Guy, William 62
Guy, Willis 398
Guygar, Elizabeth 568
Guymon, Noah 77
Guyton, Henry 556
Guyton, Jane 363
Guyton, John 556
Gwathney, Anna 508
Gwathney, George S. 508
Gwynne, Thomas 50
Gysinger, John 285

--- H ---

Habb, Sally 459
Hackenwelder, John 729
Hackly, James 124
Hackman, Teresa 607
Hackney, C. P. 366
Hadden, John 286

Hadden, Lemuel 685
Haddick, Wm. 456
Haddix, John 189
Haddix, Ninrod 189
Haddix, William 489
Haddix, Winny 493
Haddy, John 473
Haden, Elizabeth 77
Haden, John 83
Hadlee, Jacob 170
Hadley, Abraham 41
Hadley, Ann 6
Hadley, Elisabeth 393
Hadley, Elizabeth 5
Hadley, Emey 393
Hadley, Hannah 393
Hadley, John 6, 393
Hadley, Mary 393
Hadley, Phebe 6
Hadley, Phobe 393
Hadley, Samuel 6, 393
Hadley, Sarah 393
Hadley, Simeon 5, 6
Hadley, Simon 392, 393
Hadley, William 248
Haefner, Cathrine 521
Haft, Isabella 303
Haga, Godfrey 296
Haga, Jacob 303
Hagaman, Eli J. 252
Hagaman, Elizabeth 626
Hagaman, Jacob 626
Hagaman, John 626
Hagaman, Mary Ann 626
Hagaman, Sarah Jane 626
Hagaman, William 626
Hagan, Henry B. 144
Hagan, John 198
Hagar, Samuel 197
Hagar, Simeon 585
Hagelbarger, Peter 544
Hagelbarger, Philip J. 544
Hageman, Anna Martha 36
Hageman, Catharine 609
Hageman, Elizabeth 604
Hageman, Isaac 604
Hageman, Jacob 604
Hager, Aurelius 64
Hager, Polly 64
Hager, Samuel 209
Hager, Simeon 44
Hager, Simion 64
Hager, William B. 64
Hager, Wm. B. 64
Hagerman, Elizabeth 626
Hagerman, Jacob 626
Hagerman, John 626
Hagerman, John J. 753
Hagerman, Mary Ann 607, 626
Hagerman, Phebe Ann 744
Hagerman, Sarah Jane 626
Hagerman, Simon 678
Hagerman, William 626
Hagers, Polly 586
Haggin, John 482
Haggins, Charles 305
Hague, John 177

852

Hague, Margaret 741
Hague, William 741
Hahn, Mary 522
Haigg, James R. 560
Haight, Victory 520
Hail, Thomas 659
Hain, Hester 139
Hain, James 139
Hain, Rosannah 139
Hainer, Joel 266
Haines, Auston 20
Haines, Benj. 456
Haines, Bethuel 684
Haines, Catharine 347, 631
Haines, Catherine S. 214
Haines, Charles 631
Haines, Charles Beatty 214
Haines, Christiana 347
Haines, David R. 520
Haines, Deborah W. 684
Haines, E. 701
Haines, E. S. 701
Haines, Eli 697
Haines, Ella C. 697
Haines, Emily S. 697
Haines, Harriet S. 214
Haines, Jacob 347, 489
Haines, Jennie 697
Haines, Jesse 12
Haines, Job 214
Haines, Joel 265
Haines, John 347
Haines, Jonathan 24
Haines, Letitia 684
Haines, Mary 347, 489
Haines, Mary Ann 684
Haines, Mary E. 701
Haines, Peter 347
Haines, Philip 24
Haines, Rachel W. 684
Haines, Rebecca 15
Haines, Samuel 20
Haines, Samuel H. 684
Haines, Stephen A. 701
Haines, Susanna 347
Haines, Thos. 265
Haines, Wilkins 684
Haines, William 741
Haines, William H. 12
Haines, Wm. J. 374
Haines, Zimri F. 697
Hains, Christian 488
Hains, Elizabeth 126
Hains, George 478
Hains, Jonathan 651
Hains, Joseph 659
Hains, Joshua 659
Hains, Sarah Ann 15
Hake, Andrew 337
Hakes, Caroline 317, 324
Hakes, Robert 317, 320, 321, 324
Haldeman, Allen 429
Halderman, C. 403
Halderman, Eleaner 403
Halderman, Geo. 403
Halderman, Jacob 216

Halderman, John 74
Halderman, Nelson 403
Hale, Anna 239
Hale, Betsy 537
Hale, Catharine 117
Hale, Eliza 537
Hale, G. 537
Hale, Geo. 537
Hale, George 537
Hale, Henry 537
Hale, Jeneora G. 35
Hale, John 216, 238, 239
Hale, Leonard 590
Hale, M. 537
Hale, Maria 537
Hale, Martin 537
Hale, Owen 176
Hale, Polly 13, 513
Hale, Reubin 17
Hale, Samuel 537
Hale, Sarah 80
Hale, Stephen 732
Hale, Thomas 124
Hales, Ann 523
Hales, Joel 520
Haley, Carter 513
Haley, John 77
Haley, Sarah 85
Haley, Wm. L. 633
Halferty, Edward 448
Halferty, Elizabeth 448
Halferty, Isabella 448
Halferty, James 448
Halferty, Jane 448
Halferty, John 448
Halferty, Margaret 448
Halferty, Mary 448
Halferty, Robert 448
Halferty, William 448
Hall, A. 702
Hall, Aaron 504, 513
Hall, Able 554
Hall, Actious 382
Hall, Alexander 703
Hall, Alfred Gower 324
Hall, Alfred Gower 318
Hall, Andrew 205
Hall, Anthony 5, 456
Hall, Arad 520
Hall, Aron 504
Hall, Benjamin 398
Hall, Benjamin F. 20
Hall, Charlista Ann 449
Hall, Daniel 622
Hall, David 41
Hall, Elias 729
Hall, Elizabeth 449
Hall, Elle 83
Hall, Eskridge 502
Hall, George 714
Hall, Horace 745
Hall, Isaac 449, 554, 752
Hall, Isaac (Dr.) 763
Hall, Isreal 114
Hall, Jacob 751
Hall, James 77, 330, 438, 452
Hall, James Madison 205

Hall, Jenenerah 35
Hall, Joab H. 83
Hall, John 12, 86, 449, 529
Hall, John T. 679
Hall, Joseph 26, 205
Hall, Lititia 554
Hall, Lucy 676
Hall, Luther A. 520
Hall, Lydia 449
Hall, M. J. 702
Hall, Margaret 14, 489
Hall, Mary 449, 462
Hall, Melinda 449
Hall, Mills 263, 265
Hall, Molly 703
Hall, Nathan 340
Hall, Olivia M. 144
Hall, Parnel 554
Hall, Peggy 493
Hall, Peter L. 544
Hall, Phoebe 318, 324
Hall, Rebecca 5, 663
Hall, Richard 659
Hall, Sally 459
Hall, Sally Ann 523
Hall, Samuel 124, 566, 659
Hall, Sarah 449
Hall, Selden 29
Hall, Thomas 489, 665, 705
Hall, Vachel 259
Hall, W. 462
Hall, William 205, 335, 384, 449, 474, 544
Hall, William A. 702
Hall, John 678
Halland, James 124
Halleday, Sarah 667
Haller, Andrews 751
Haller, Henry 390
Haller, Henry Raper 751
Haller, John 751
Haller, John Milton 751
Haller, John Mitton 751
Haller, John S. 655
Haller, Julia 751
Haller, Lucinda 751
Haller, Luisa Gertrude 751
Haller, Mary 751
Haller, Mary Ann 751
Haller, Wesley 751
Haller, William 751
Hallerman, Henry 112
Halley, Harriet 752
Halley, John 752
Hallgen, Frederick 520
Halliday, Samuel 77
Hallock, Wesley 590
Hallom, Edward 41
Halloway, Daylon 124
Hally, Saml. 267
Halsey, John 422, 640
Halsey, Joseph 655
Halsey, Lucy 31
Halsey, Mark 78
Halsey, Sidney 90

Haltbey, Mary 527
Halteman, Scynthia E. 219
Halter, Hannah 90
Haltery, Edward 607
Halton, Eleanor 751
Haltrey, John 417
Haly, Maria 84
Hamand, Elijah 366
Hamand, Nancy 366
Hamand, Rebecca 366
Hamand, Thos. (Sr.) 366
Hamand, Wm. 366
Hambleton, Daniel 471
Hambleton, Martha 708
Hambleton, Samuel N. 708
Hambleton, Wm. 708
Hamell, Enoch 683
Hamelton, Daniel 479
Hamiel, Wm. 207
Hamilton, Allen 754
Hamilton, Benj. 152, 295
Hamilton, Benjamin 155, 295
Hamilton, Cassandrea 295
Hamilton, Daniel 470, 472, 473, 476, 477, 483
Hamilton, Edward 504
Hamilton, Elizabeth 295, 651
Hamilton, Frances 365
Hamilton, Hannah 751
Hamilton, Henry 260, 737
Hamilton, Isaac 651
Hamilton, Jacob 651
Hamilton, James 344, 365, 651, 677
Hamilton, James W. 7
Hamilton, Job 651
Hamilton, John 479, 590, 683, 684, 751
Hamilton, Jude 78
Hamilton, Justin 106, 109
Hamilton, Margaret 344
Hamilton, Mary N. 635
Hamilton, Mary W. 635
Hamilton, Rachel 295
Hamilton, Rebecca 295
Hamilton, Rebecca M. 737
Hamilton, Robert 681
Hamilton, Ruben 513
Hamilton, Samuel 295, 635
Hamilton, Sarah 651
Hamilton, Susanna 295
Hamilton, Wile 41
Hamilton, William 105, 106, 107, 295, 298
Hamilton, William H. 679
Hamilton, William L. 527
Hamilton, Wm. 107
Hamilton, Wm. L. 528
Hamisfar, Abraham 364, 377
Hamisfar, Charles 364
Hamisfar, Charles W. 365
Hamisfar, David L. 365

Hamisfar, Hannah 364
Hamisfar, Isaac 365
Hamisfar, Katherine 364
Hamisfar, Thomas 365
Hamker, Mathias 607
Hamler, Jacob 275
Hamler, Rachel 275
Hamlet, Benjamin 116
Hamlet, Mary 119
Hamlin, John 553
Hamlin, William 553
Hammel, Charles 109
Hammel, Enoch 687
Hammel, John 109, 433
Hammel, Mary 576
Hammel, Samuel 433
Hammel, Sophia 433
Hammell, Samuel 290
Hammen, Michael 114
Hammer, Ann 363
Hammer, Barbara 363
Hammer, Barnet 360, 363, 365
Hammer, Catherine 363
Hammer, Charlotte 365
Hammer, Esther 363
Hammer, George 363, 365
Hammer, Hulda 20
Hammer, Jacob 283, 363, 365
Hammer, Jacob W. 365
Hammer, John 360, 363, 365
Hammer, Martha 363
Hammer, Mary 363
Hammer, Sarah 365
Hammers, Barnet 362
Hammet, Kathrine 515
Hammet, Mary Ann 515
Hammett, Elizabeth 510
Hammett, George 510
Hammett, Lucinda 514
Hammett, Priscilla 514
Hammill, Margaret 290
Hammill, Samuel 290
Hammon, Allen 392
Hammon, Anna 715
Hammon, Betsey 392
Hammon, John 354
Hammon, Lucy 392
Hammon, Mark 392
Hammon, Nancy 392
Hammon, Rebecca 401
Hammon, William 392
Hammon, Zoeth 729
Hammond, Allen 392
Hammond, Betsey 392
Hammond, Charles 297, 555
Hammond, Eliza Ellen 247, 250, 251
Hammond, Elon O. 4
Hammond, George 287
Hammond, James 247, 257
Hammond, Jas. 247
Hammond, Jno. 269
Hammond, John 50, 290
Hammond, Juliana 378
Hammond, Lucy 392, 585

Hammond, Margaret 411
Hammond, Mark 392
Hammond, Meriban 717
Hammond, Michael 714
Hammond, Nancy 392
Hammond, Rebecca 364
Hammond, Sally Ann 250, 251
Hammond, Sarah 555
Hammond, Thos. (Jr.) 355
Hammond, William 392
Hammond, William C. 250, 251
Hammond, Wm. 247
Hammond, Zoath 730
Hammond, Zoeth 714
Hammons, Allen 392
Hammons, Betsey 392
Hammons, Hannah 717
Hammons, Lucy 392
Hammons, Mark 392
Hammons, Nancy 126, 392
Hammons, William 392
Hamond, Roxanna N. 376
Hamor, Amos Theobald 401
Hamor, Henrietta 401
Hamor, Jacob 401
Hamors, Jacob 401
Hampshire, Elizabeth 274
Hampshire, John 274
Hampson, John 470
Hampton, Betsy 111
Hampton, Jno. 273
Hampton, Thomas 273
Hamrick, Albert 618
Hamrick, Mary 618
Hamrick, Rachel 618
Hamsberger, George 646
Hamstead, Betsy 505
Han, Catherine 519
Hanahman, Polly 585
Hanbey, George 365
Hanby, Eliza Ann 365
Hanby, George 365
Hanby, John 365
Hanby, Martha 365
Hanby, Samuel 365
Hanby, Sarah 365
Hanby, William 365
Hance, Elias 481
Hance, Elisha 478, 480
Hance, Margaret 126
Hance, William 124
Hance, Willis 121
Hanch, John 732
Hancock, Almira 31
Hancock, David 38, 41
Hancock, Mary J. 38
Hancock, Rhoda 457
Hand, Elisha 264, 267, 270
Hand, Emily 590
Hand, George 463
Hand, Peter 270
Hand, Willis 121
Hander, Thomas 226
Handley, John 443
Handly, Isaac 443
Handly, James 443

Handraham, Joshua 23
Handricks, William 139
Handshaw, Margaret 77
Handycock, Rhoda 457
Hanell, C. 62
Hanenkrat, Anna E. 327
Hanes, Carlisle 17
Hanes, Darcus 17
Hanes, Isaac 273
Hanes, Jacob 172
Hanes, Joseph 752
Hanes, Mary 120, 717
Hanes, Phebe 12
Hanesworth, Aaron 260, 264, 268
Hanesworth, Robt. 268
Haney, Abraham 646, 653, 674
Haney, Elizabeth 610
Haney, Margaret 669
Haney, Peggy 666
Haney, William 201
Hanford, Henry 4
Hanford, James 520
Hank, Fred 483
Hank, Nancy 337
Hank, Susan 337
Hanker, Catherine M. 607
Hankins, Ann 337
Hankins, Ann P. 322
Hankins, Daniel 695
Hankins, David 463
Hankins, Jane 455
Hankins, Samuel 316
Hankins, Samuel S. 316, 317, 318, 320
Hankins, William E. 17
Hankinson, Hugh L. 366
Hankinson, Joshua 372
Hanks, Martha 135
Hanks, Noah 134
Hanks, Rachal 120
Hanks, Rachel 22
Hanks, Thomas 116
Hanlen, James 480
Hanlin, Felix 732
Hanlin, Jas. 732
Hanlon, James 354
Hann, Robert 121
Hann, William 256
Hanna, --- 174
Hanna, Amos Thompson 189
Hanna, Archd. 737
Hanna, Eveline 538
Hanna, Harriet N. 139
Hanna, Harriet Newel 189
Hanna, James 182, 189, 191, 224, 233, 323
Hanna, Jno. E. 273
Hanna, John E. 760
Hanna, Jonathan 538
Hanna, S. E. J. 316
Hanna, Sarah 323, 520
Hanna, William 78, 316, 323
Hanna, Wm. 323
Hannah, Betsy 638
Hannah, James 191, 196, 233

Hannah, Jane 147
Hannah, John 638
Hannahman, Robert L. 585
Hannam, Perry 520
Hannaman, Dorothea 68
Hannaman, Franklin 68
Hannaman, Nancy 512
Hannaman, Susannah 512
Hannan, Elizabeth 518
Hannard, John 124
Hannel, James 181
Hannold, Isaiah M. 732
Hansbarger, George 645
Hansberger, G. 672
Hansberger, George 675
Hanshaw, Rachel 387
Hanson, Bayille 124
Hanson, Catharine 106
Hanson, Daniel 47, 397
Hanson, Fletcher 106
Hanson, Harriet 106
Hanson, Maria 106
Hanson, Newton 106
Hanson, Peggy 718
Hanson, Raper 106
Hanson, Rufus 106
Hanson, Samuel 106
Hanson, Sanford 106
Hanson, Wesley 106
Hanver, Sally 25
Hanver, Samuel 25
Hany, Jacob 124
Hapner, Jacob 428
Hapner, John 414
Hapner, Nelson 433
Haraman, Caty 574
Harb, A. C. 618
Harb, Birdie 618
Harb, C. 618
Harb, Carolina 618
Harb, Frankie 618
Harb, Jimmy 618
Harb, M. L. 618
Harb, Wm. B. 618
Harbar, Sally 465
Harbaugh, Amalia 564
Harbaugh, Amos 564
Harbaugh, Benjamin (Jr.) 564
Harbaugh, David 564
Harbaugh, Elizabeth 564
Harbaugh, Frederick 572
Harbaugh, Frederick G. 334
Harbaugh, Harris B. 749
Harbaugh, Isaac 564
Harbaugh, John 564
Harbaugh, John (Jr.) 564
Harbaugh, John (Sr.) 564
Harbaugh, Peter 572
Harbaugh, Samuel 564
Harbaugh, Uriah 520
Harber, Mary 465
Harber, Wm. 456
Harbert, Abigail 391
Harbert, Eligah 593
Harbert, Richard 452
Harbert, Sarah 391
Harbert, William 506

Harbet, Henry 506
Harbet, John 506
Harbet, Samuel 506
Harbet, William 506
Harbin, John 179
Harbin, Rachel 179
Harbison, Amanda 429
Harbison, Henry 429
Harbison, John H. 109
Harbison, Mariah 429
Harbor, Auug 463
Harbough, Eliza Ann 570
Harbough, Margret 574
Harbut, Mary 465
Hard, Elisha 52
Hardar, John 238
Hardar, Sophia 238
Harden, Alven 83
Harden, Hiram 463
Harden, Isaac 384
Harden, James 717
Harden, Margaret 376, 746
Harden, Mary 718
Harden, Nancy 717
Harden, Thomas 29
Harden, Wm. 88
Hardenburg, Aaron 520
Hardesty, Anne 548
Hardesty, Benjamin 308, 544
Hardesty, Elizabeth 120
Hardesty, Phebe 551
Hardesty, Robert 544
Hardesty, William 556
Hardgrove, Richard 554
Hardin, --- 400
Hardin, Benj. 273
Hardin, Benjamin 364
Hardin, Daniel 501
Hardin, David 364
Hardin, Elender 501
Hardin, Elizabeth 364, 501
Hardin, Ellanor 501
Hardin, Even 364
Hardin, Ignatius 364
Hardin, James 364, 501
Hardin, John 364, 501
Hardin, Joseph 364
Hardin, Nancy 364
Hardin, Polly 364
Hardin, Rachel 364, 501
Hardin, Rebecca 364
Hardin, Sally 501
Hardin, Sarah 364
Hardin, Taylor 549
Hardin, Thomas 501
Harding, Benjamin 273, 275
Harding, Ransom 78
Harding, Selenda 79
Hardisty, Jesse 672
Hardisty, Margaret 126
Hardisty, Robert 283
Hardman, Abin 68
Hardman, Abner 68
Hardman, Anthony 761
Hardman, Daniel 68

Hardman, David 68
Hardman, Eleanor 68
Hardman, Elizabeth 68, 187
Hardman, Henry 68
Hardman, Jacob 557
Hardman, John 68
Hardman, Joseph 187
Hardman, Mary 187
Hardman, Nancy 68, 187
Hardman, Naomia 68
Hardman, Sarah 187
Hardman, Solomon 187
Hardman, Susaa 187
Hardman, William 187
Hardy, Elizabeth 433
Hardy, Farnum 86
Hardy, Henry 337
Hardy, Henry Sarah 433
Hardy, John 366, 433
Hardy, Joseph 433
Hardy, Mary 366
Hardy, Melinda 433
Hardy, Polly 498
Hardy, Sarah Ann 433
Hare, Catharine 488
Hare, Charles 38
Hare, Eliza 38
Hare, Henry 355
Hare, Henry I. 41
Harel, Ezra 503
Haresman, D. 483
Harfer, Wm. 572
Harfester, David 520
Harger, Mary 334
Hargrave, Richard 566
Hargus, John 474, 483
Harholtcer, Mary Ann 520
Harinard, Charles 273
Haring, Joseph C. (Dr.) 708
Haris, Garret 585
Haris, Martha 585
Harison, Moses 585
Harkenhoff, --- 114
Harker, Adelaid 144
Harker, Caroline 144
Harker, John F. 144
Harkey, Eliza 518
Harkless, Aaron 268
Harkless, James 637
Harkness, John 47
Harkness, Lamon G. (Dr.) 497
Harkness, Loiza 495
Harkrader, David 690
Harkrader, Elizabeth 690
Harkrader, Sarah Ann 690
Harkum, James 155
Harlan, Charles 312
Harlan, Hannah 661
Harlan, John G. 433
Harlan, Jonathan 659
Harlan, Nancy E. 433
Harlan, Nathan 689
Harlan, Sarah 689
Harless, Richard
  Wardrobe 133
Harley, Julian 336

Harley, Lucinda 513
Harlshom, Leonard 732
Harman, Adam 655
Harman, Barbara 576
Harman, Bowshier 406
Harman, Coonrod 266
Harman, F. 406
Harman, Geo. 572
Harman, George 384
Harman, Michael 572
Harman, Richard 651
Harman, Susann 570
Harman, Tena 655
Harman, Thomas 12
Harman, William 267
Harmer, Michael 106
Harmes, Henry 544
Harmeston, Fanny 272
Harmiston, Matthew 272
Harmon, Caroline 139
Harmon, Esebeth 515
Harmon, John 727
Harmon, Marcice 123
Harmon, Martha 513
Harmon, Mary 21
Harmon, Samuel 745
Harmon, Sarah 658
Harmon, William 271, 732
Harmon, Wm. 273
Harmond, Mary 550
Harmount, Alexander
  (Rev.) 605
Harms, Lena 544
Harmus, Israel 527
Harnahan, Patrick 47
Harner, Clement L. 700
Harner, Elizabeth 353
Harner, James 105
Harner, Lucina 693
Harner, M. 693
Harner, R. 693
Harness, Cenia 44
Harney, Peter 370
Harnsberger, George 649
Harp, Amos 108
Harp, Jacob R. 124
Harp, Jonas 607
Harp, Margaret 108
Harp, Reuben 607
Harper, Abigail 76
Harper, Alexr. 291
Harper, Amos 78
Harper, Andrew 78
Harper, Ann 394
Harper, Anna 77
Harper, Betsey 253
Harper, Catharine 649, 650
Harper, Daniel 86, 253
Harper, Daniel F. 268
Harper, Elizabeth 345, 650
Harper, Fenton 253
Harper, Henderson 637
Harper, Isabella 716
Harper, Jacob M. 599, 601, 604, 612
Harper, Jacob W. 599
Harper, James 29

Harper, Jane 459
Harper, John 12, 253, 650
Harper, Lavina 83
Harper, Margaret 253, 365
Harper, Mary 253, 458
Harper, Polly 466
Harper, Rachel 253, 274
Harper, Rebecca 274
Harper, Rhoda 253
Harper, Samuel 365
Harper, Samuel D. 253
Harper, Sophia 464
Harper, Thomas 365
Harper, William 345
Harple, Conrod 22
Harpold, Adam 89
Harpole, Barbary 391
Harpster, Daniel 29
Harpster, Solomon 520
Harr, David 456
Harr, Everard 493
Harr, Everrard 475
Harrah, James 303
Harramon, Elizabeth 667
Harrell, Lydia 335
Harret, Elizabeth 506
Harret, Maragarett 506
Harret, Susanna 506
Harret, William 506
Harrier, Samuel 549
Harriett, Robert 539
Harriman, David 22
Harrinaton, George M. 41
Harrington, Amelia 496
Harrington, Amina Ann 590
Harrington, D. W. 4
Harrington, David 585
Harrington, David W. 4
Harrington, Elizabeth 582
Harrington, George S. 4
Harrington, Loiza 591
Harrington, Mary 76
Harrington, Mary Sophia 4
Harrington, Merandy 590
Harrington, Mina Ann 590
Harrington, Nelson 590, 681
Harrington, O. W. 374
Harrington, Parmelia K. 4
Harrington, Samuel W. 681
Harrington, Wesley 497
Harriott, E. M. 583
Harris, Amos 644
Harris, Anna 429
Harris, Betsy 498
Harris, Celia N. 550
Harris, Christena 248
Harris, Colbert 161
Harris, Cyrus 273
Harris, Daniel 170, 585
Harris, David 273
Harris, Diantha 745
Harris, Edward (Sr.) 86
Harris, Elenor 555

Harris, Elisha 268
Harris, Elizabeth 457, 512
Harris, F. 331
Harris, Geo. 216
Harris, George 38, 229, 563
Harris, Hannah 44, 713
Harris, Harriet 216
Harris, Henry A. 762
Harris, Isaac 247, 248, 284
Harris, Isaac D. 248
Harris, Israel 164
Harris, J. 331
Harris, James 259, 279
Harris, Jane 280
Harris, Jno. 407
Harris, John 259, 260, 271, 273, 429, 572, 659, 717
Harris, John H. 737
Harris, Jonathan 174, 433
Harris, Josiah 34
Harris, Lydia Ann 248
Harris, Mahala 407
Harris, Margaret 268
Harris, Margaret Elizabeth 433
Harris, Mary 164, 407
Harris, Mary A. 337
Harris, Mary Ann 523
Harris, Minerva 495
Harris, Morgan 268
Harris, Mos 433
Harris, Nancy 247, 429
Harris, Peggy 714
Harris, Phoebe 429
Harris, Rachel 247
Harris, Rebecca 273
Harris, Richard 116
Harris, Robert 429, 433
Harris, Ruth B. 29
Harris, Samantha 337, 745
Harris, Samuel 252, 471, 472, 670
Harris, Sarah 174
Harris, Smith 248
Harris, Squire 337
Harris, Stephen 556
Harris, Susannah 91
Harris, Thomas 745
Harris, Uriah 264, 272
Harris, William 513, 563
Harris, Winnie B. 331
Harris, Wm. 572
Harrisbarger, George 640
Harrise, Aaron 83
Harrison, Aaron 590
Harrison, Alexander 590
Harrison, America 590
Harrison, Benjamin 6
Harrison, Caroline 207
Harrison, Cassandrea 295
Harrison, Catharine 626
Harrison, Charles 207
Harrison, Edmon 207

Harrison, Eli 463
Harrison, Elizabeth 593
Harrison, James G. 62
Harrison, Jesse 170
Harrison, Leonard B. 207
Harrison, Margaret 736
Harrison, Mary M. 707
Harrison, Mathew 736
Harrison, Nancy 544
Harrison, P. 383
Harrison, Rachel 119
Harrison, Sarah 462
Harrison, Talmon 41
Harrison, William 6, 590
Harrison, William H. 207
Harritt, C. 539
Harritt, S. 539
Harrod, Samuel 55
Harroun, John 41
Harrown, Sarah Jane 38
Harruf, --- 96
Harsh, Peter 428
Harshbarger, Abigail 144
Harshbarger, Benj. 144
Harshbarger, George 144
Harshbarger, Hester 144
Harshbarger, Mary 144
Harshbarger, Samuel 144
Harshberger, Jacob 202
Harshberger, Jonas 202
Harshberger, Samuel 202
Harshman, Anna 433, 667
Harshman, Barbara 429
Harshman, Christina 429
Harshman, Daniel 433
Harshman, Eliza 433
Harshman, Harvey 433
Harshman, Isaac 433
Harshman, James 433
Harshman, John 429, 433
Harshman, John W. 434
Harshman, Moses 429
Harshman, Peter 429, 659
Harsman, Rachel 571
Hart, Levi 180
Hart, Amon 555
Hart, Amos 555
Hart, Andrew 299
Hart, Benjamin 708
Hart, Betsey 716
Hart, Clara 716
Hart, David 195, 434
Hart, Elijah 297, 299
Hart, Elizabeth 365
Hart, Emma L. 36
Hart, Esther 30
Hart, George 434
Hart, Hartel 299
Hart, Henry 195
Hart, Hugh Peter 199
Hart, Jacob 195
Hart, James 669, 686
Hart, Jane 177, 299
Hart, John 195, 199, 299, 365, 600
Hart, Joseph 365
Hart, Josiah (Dr.) 714
Hart, Judah B. 29
Hart, Levi 177

Hart, Loiza 337
Hart, Lyman 337
Hart, Margaret 686
Hart, Martin 299
Hart, Mary 299, 659
Hart, Mary Ann 202
Hart, Mary Brill 330
Hart, Mary E. 518
Hart, Matilda 429
Hart, Neal 199
Hart, Peggy 299
Hart, Peter 199, 202, 607
Hart, Sally 367
Hart, Saml. 665
Hart, Sarah 199, 666
Hart, Susan 365
Hart, William 195, 365, 686
Hart, William E. 686
Hart, Wm. 377
Harter, Amanda 610
Harter, Benjamin 116
Harter, Elizabeth 602, 606
Harter, George 416
Harter, George Ann 602
Harter, George W. 601, 602
Harter, Henry 165
Harter, Jane 610
Harter, John 165, 745
Harter, Louisa 144
Harter, Margaret 746
Harter, Matthias 165
Harter, Peter 102
Harter, Polly 610
Harter, Rachel 609, 744
Harter, Sarah Jane 602, 608
Hartford, Ann 291
Hartford, Jane 291
Hartford, John 289, 291
Hartford, Mary 291
Hartford, William G. 291
Hartlan, James 219
Hartle, Jacob 384
Hartley, Aaron 155
Hartley, Elizabeth 117
Hartley, Phoeba 155
Hartline, Christian 165, 172, 174
Hartline, Mary 174
Hartline, Samuel 307
Hartman, Benjamin 229, 443
Hartman, Joshua 229
Hartman, Margaret 302
Hartman, Mary 229, 548
Hartman, Peter 544
Hartman, Soloman 229
Hartman, Solomon 229
Hartman, Susannah 544
Hartsel, George 200
Hartsel, John 343
Hartshorn, John W. 167
Hartsock, Jenima 520
Hartz, John 601
Hartz, Mary 609

Hartzell, Verina 333
Hartzog, Catharine 626
Hartzog, Eli 626
Hartzog, George 626
Hartzog, George W. 607
Hartzog, Israel 626
Hartzog, Mary 373, 609
Hartzog, Sarah 606
Harvey, Athelia 434
Harvey, Caleb 670
Harvey, Delila 52
Harvey, Delilah 386
Harvey, Eli 670
Harvey, Elijah 717
Harvey, Eliza 762
Harvey, Elizabeth 610
Harvey, Hannah 497
Harvey, Harden 595
Harvey, James 706, 732
Harvey, Jesse 685
Harvey, Jonathan 489
Harvey, Mary Jane 434
Harvey, Obadiah 607
Harvey, Peggy 666
Harvey, Philip 359, 361
Harvey, Richard 452
Harvey, Samuel 390
Harvey, Sylva 497
Harvey, William 35
Harvis, Squire 337
Harviy, Amos 714
Harvy, James 384
Harward, Eliza 255
Harward, Geo. 271
Harward, Henry 255
Harward, Madeson 255
Harwitt, Elisa 179
Harword, Chas. 274
Harword, Geo. 272
Harzog, Benjamin 604
Harzog, Eliza 604
Harzog, Jesse 604
Harzog, King 604
Harzog, Leo 604
Harzog, Mary 604
Harzog, Sarah 608
Harzog, Soloman 607
Harzog, Solomon 604
Harzog, Susannah 604
Harzogg, Elizabeth 606
Hasch, Betty Lou 329
Hasch, Caroline 329
Hasch, Cleo 329
Hasch, Clifford H. 329
Hasch, Floyd J. 329
Hasch, John 329
Hasch, Leo A. 329
Haselton, Jacob 384
Haselton, James 89
Hashan, Nancy 551
Hasher, George 469
Hashman, Elijah 665
Haskel, Jonathan (Maj.) 714
Hasket, Isaac 132, 210
Hasket, John 261
Hasket, Orren 47
Haskins, Benoni 646
Haskins, Collister 12

Haskins, Harris H. 78
Haskins, Joel 86
Hass, Isaac 637
Hastings, --- 44
Hastings, Alvi 70
Hastings, Elner 109
Hastings, Justus 70
Hastings, Lucius 70
Hastings, Nathan 70
Hastings, Pamelia 70
Hastings, Robert 70
Hastings, Sally L. 70
Hastings, Waitman 109
Hastings, Wartstill 70
Hastings, Wm. B. 535
Haston, William 120
Hasty, Ezra F. 434
Hasty, Ezra Franklin 434
Hasty, Hester Ann 434
Haswell, A. J. 405
Haswell, Henry 405
Haswell, Mary C. 405
Hatch, Sylvanus 759
Hatcher, Joshua 12
Hatcher, Rebecca 15
Hatcher, Samuel 2
Hatchur, Rachel 12
Hatery, Mary 572
Hatfield, Aaron 738
Hatfield, Adam 738
Hatfield, Alfred 212
Hatfield, Amey 224
Hatfield, Benjamin 190
Hatfield, Catharine A. 738
Hatfield, Cyrus 738
Hatfield, Elizabeth 212
Hatfield, George A. 218
Hatfield, George D. 738
Hatfield, Jeremiah 212
Hatfield, John 212
Hatfield, Jonas 419
Hatfield, Jonathan 190, 224
Hatfield, Joseph L. 683
Hatfield, Levin 184, 224
Hatfield, Margaret 738
Hatfield, Mary 190, 738
Hatfield, Mary E. 212
Hatfield, Morgan 212
Hatfield, Moses 419
Hatfield, Nancy 737, 738
Hatfield, Phebe 741
Hatfield, Robert 737, 738
Hatfield, Sah 120
Hatfield, Sarah 212, 224, 738
Hatfield, William 190, 738
Hath, Rebecca 388
Hathaway, Abraham 116, 659, 665
Hathaway, Albert K. 544
Hathaway, E. 692
Hathaway, Ebenezer 659
Hathaway, Eleazer 116
Hathaway, Ephraim 672
Hathaway, Ephrain 659

Hathaway, Florence E. 544
Hathaway, Francis M. 692
Hathaway, Henry 631
Hathaway, James 631
Hathaway, Jemima 658
Hathaway, Joanna C. 586
Hathaway, John 672
Hathaway, Mary 544
Hathaway, Nicholas 585, 595, 597
Hathaway, Phebe 666
Hathaway, Polly 650
Hathaway, Richard 117, 650
Hathaway, S. 692
Hathaway, Saml. 665
Hathaway, Sarah 119, 549, 662
Hathaway, Silas D. 549
Haton, Nathaniel 572
Hatt, Catharine 522
Hattan, John 513
Hatterman, --- 221
Hattery, Allen 578
Hattery, Emeline 578
Hattery, Ephraim 578
Hattery, Isaiah 578
Hattery, John 579
Hattery, Mary 578
Hattery, Noah 578
Hattery, Sarah 608
Hattery, Susan 579
Hatton, Ann 556
Hatton, Aquil 556
Hatton, Aquilla 556
Hatton, Caleb 556
Hatton, Elizabeth 556
Hatton, Francis Asbury 556
Hatton, John 556
Hatton, Joshua 556
Hatton, Mary 556
Hatton, Polly 455
Hatton, Wesley 556
Hatton, William 463
Hatton, Zachariah 556
Hauby, Julia 15
Hauck, Frederick 294
Hauck, George 294
Hauck, Jacob 294
Hauck, Margaret 294
Hauck, William 294
Haughman, David 482
Haughran, Eliz. 344
Haughran, John 344
Haughran, Patrick 344
Hauk, David 425
Hauk, Fred 483
Hause, John Gottleib 388
Hausel, Anthony 558
Hausher, Jacob 336
Hauvermale, Joseph 214
Hauzer, William 112
Haven, --- 74
Haven, Delia B. 34
Haven, John (Jr.) 669
Havens, Elijah 294
Havens, Mary 419

Haver, Charlot 595
Haver, Sarah 595
Haverback, Atono 105
Haverling, Christianna 347
Havner, H. Z. 761
Havner, Jacob 428
Haweiller, Jacob 165
Hawes, Sally 26
Hawes, Willia 732
Hawiller, Jacob 161
Hawiller, Mary 161
Hawk, David 421, 644, 650
Hawk, Elizabeth 293
Hawk, I. S. 636
Hawk, Isaac 83
Hawk, Jane 421
Hawk, John S. 637
Hawk, Peggy 650
Hawk, Sally 496
Hawkins, A. 699
Hawkins, Abraham 679
Hawkins, Amos 697, 699
Hawkins, Benjamin H. 699
Hawkins, Byrd 425
Hawkins, Charles 699
Hawkins, Elizabeth 679
Hawkins, Henry 325, 699
Hawkins, Huldah 325
Hawkins, Isaac 679
Hawkins, J. H. 698
Hawkins, James 697, 698
Hawkins, Jehu S. 697
Hawkins, Jesse 697
Hawkins, John 497
Hawkins, John J. 416, 417
Hawkins, Jos. Campbel 434
Hawkins, Joseph 749
Hawkins, Joseph S. 423
Hawkins, Margaret 679
Hawkins, Mary 325, 679
Hawkins, Mary M. 697, 698
Hawkins, Massie 697
Hawkins, Morris J. 698
Hawkins, Nancy 325
Hawkins, Nancy W. 697
Hawkins, Noah 699
Hawkins, R. 699
Hawkins, Rachel 325
Hawkins, Reuben 325
Hawkins, Robert 325
Hawkins, Ruth 679
Hawkins, Samuel 416
Hawkins, Sarah 679, 698
Hawkins, Seth 679
Hawkins, William 699
Hawkins, Willie S. 698
Hawkins, Wm. 263, 265, 266
Hawks, Frances 406
Hawks, Martha D. 406
Hawley, David W. 41
Hawley, Eri 414
Hawley, William 422
Hawn, Christian 648

Hawn, Daniel 644, 648, 659, 670
Hawn, David 670
Hawn, Eliza 648
Hawn, Elizabeth 670
Hawn, George 647
Hawn, Harriet 647
Hawn, Jacob 644, 647, 659, 670
Hawn, Mary 647
Hawn, Sally 644, 647, 670
Hawn, Sarah 648
Haworth, Betsey 124
Haworth, James 134, 135, 144
Haworth, Sarah 125, 662
Haworth, William 659
Hawthorn, B. C. 421
Hawvermake, Daniel 217
Hay, Ann 223
Hay, George 187, 188, 191
Hay, Gloria L. 94
Hay, Jacob 187, 188, 191
Hay, James 117, 223
Hay, Jane 127
Hay, Jean 139
Hay, John A. 124
Hay, Joseph 117, 139
Hay, Michael 187, 188, 191
Hay, Noah 144
Hay, Polly 118
Hay, William 223
Hayden, John 170, 171
Hayden, Joseph 622
Hayden, Margaret 79
Hayer, William Robinson 520
Hayes, Andrew 488
Hayes, David 488
Hayes, James 41, 469
Hayes, John 92
Hayes, Joseph 520
Hayes, Mary Ann 384
Hayes, Oden 4
Hayes, Samuel 616
Hayes, Theresa B. 616
Hayes, Timothy 322
Hayman, Jeptha 83
Hayman, John H. 83
Haynes, Barbara 413
Haynes, Betsey 466
Haynes, Charles 659
Haynes, Delezon E. 70
Haynes, Frederick 430
Haynes, Jacob 41
Haynes, John 430
Haynes, William 430, 452
Hays, Alfred 21
Hays, Andrew 60, 223, 761
Hays, Anne 60
Hays, Campbell 60
Hays, Catharine 113
Hays, David 109, 470, 472, 473, 476, 477, 478, 482, 485, 572, 659, 665, 761

Hays, Edmond 180
Hays, Elizabeth 160, 664
Hays, Francis 132
Hays, Frederick 160
Hays, George 376, 384
Hays, George Philip 144
Hays, Henry 761, 765
Hays, Isaac 398
Hays, James 130, 132, 470, 476, 633, 761, 765
Hays, James (Jr.) 761
Hays, Jane 761
Hays, Jemima 21
Hays, John 60, 434, 665, 761, 765
Hays, John A. 132
Hays, Loas A. 761
Hays, Marshal 761
Hays, Martha J. 144
Hays, Mary 577
Hays, Michael 60
Hays, Nancy 348, 590
Hays, Nolly 153
Hays, Notley 154, 156
Hays, Oden 7
Hays, Polly 434
Hays, Rebecca 434
Hays, Robert 398
Hays, Samuel 144
Hays, Sarah 154, 156
Hays, Thomas 434, 677, 761
Hays, Wm. D. 144
Hays, Wm. Robt. 434
Hayse, Jesse 83
Hayward, Charlotte 708
Hayward, E. J. 732
Hayward, Ed T. 708
Hayward, Solomon 83
Hayward, Wm. G. 708
Haywood, Alex H. 144
Haywood, Thos. P. 144
Haywood, Wm. H. 144
Hayworth, Joseph 139
Hayworth, Mary 139
Hayworth, Sampson 139
Hayworth, Wade 139
Hazal, Elizabeth 462
Hazelett, Cunningham 449
Hazelton, Barbara 364
Hazelton, Elizabeth 364
Hazelton, Henry 364
Hazelton, James 364
Hazelton, John 364
Hazelton, Joseph 364
Hazelton, Lot 364
Hazelton, Mary 364
Hazelton, Samuel 364
Hazelton, Sarah 364
Hazelton, William 364
Hazen, Elizabeth 554
Hazlet, Jane 90
Hazlett, Cunningham 449
Hazlett, Sarah 449
Hazlewood, Eliza 89
Heacock, Davis 29
Heacock, Erastus 29
Head, Asa 488

Head, Bigger 750
Headley, Cynthia 180
Headley, Jacob 180
Headley, Samuel 745
Headly, William H. 178
Heain, Samuel 186
Healey, Wm. 268
Health, Jonathan 463
Healy, Benjamin 36
Heann, Elizabeth 522
Hearholtzen, John B. 345
Hearholtzen, Joseph 345
Hearholzer, Elizabeth 365
Hearholzer, Helena 365
Hearholzer, John 365
Hearholzer, John B. 365
Hearholzer, Joseph 365
Hearholzer, Magdalena 365
Hearholzer, Mariana 365
Hearing, Jacob 356
Hearing, Samuel 374
Hearkless, James 637
Hearn, Daniel 732
Hearn, Elizabeth 522
Heart, --- (Capt.) 721
Heart, Andrew 248
Heart, Elizabeth 451
Heart, Jonathan (Capt.) 720
Heart, Peter 602
Heart, Selah 714
Heartless, Richard
  Wardrobe 133
Heartline, Peter 566
Heartly, Eliza J. 518
Heartly, John 566
Hearvey, Delany 716
Heasler, Barbary 514
Heastand, Mary 575
Heate, Helen 519
Heater, E. 404
Heater, Elizabeth 404
Heater, Helen 519
Heater, Jno. 404
Heater, Polly 382
Heater, Solomon 384
Heath, Alcina 649
Heath, Anna Jane 114
Heath, Barbary E. 609
Heath, Bridget 709
Heath, Elizabeth 609
Heath, George 472
Heath, Hanah 613
Heath, Hannah 22
Heath, James 645
Heath, James C. 613, 614
Heath, James T. 108, 109
Heath, Jesse 549
Heath, John 22, 107, 114
Heath, Joseph 649
Heath, Levi 649
Heath, Levina 114
Heath, Maria 649
Heath, Mary 609
Heath, Matilda 47
Heath, Nancey 613
Heath, Nancy 614

Heath, Nancy T. 114
Heath, Rebecca 388
Heath, Rebecca Elizabeth 613
Heath, Rody 11
Heath, Susanna 295
Heath, William 649
Heath, Wm. 456
Heaton, D. F. 672
Heaton, Elizabeth 666
Heaton, Isaac 489
Heaton, Jane M. 92
Heaton, Margaret 663
Heaton, Richard 685
Heaton, Samuel 659
Heaton, William 659, 672
Heavelo, Rachel 392
Heaveto, William 392
Heazlit, Caroline M. 328
Heazlit, D. W. 328
Heberling, Christiana 368
Heblock, Jane 573
Hecheweelder, John 282
Heck, Alexander 378
Heck, Catharine 519
Heck, George 520
Heck, Henry 378
Heck, John 153, 156, 158, 172, 180, 378
Heck, Margaret 375
Heck, Mary 156, 158, 172, 180
Heck, Peggy 374
Heckerthorn, Mary 388
Heckerthorn, Sarah 567
Heckewelder, Salome 568
Heckman, Abraham 210
Heckman, Catharine 210
Heckman, Mary 210
Heckman, Peter 210
Heckman, Phebe 210
Heckox, George 745
Heckwelder, John 561
Hecox, Adaline 87
Hecox, Jertha 87
Hecox, Marilla 87
Hecox, Truman 78
Hector, David 460
Hedden, Edward 268, 272
Hedden, Emmet 268, 272
Hedden, Enos 265, 268
Hedden, James 268, 272
Hedden, Mary 268, 272
Hedden, Phoebe 265, 268
Hedden, Susan 272
Hedge, Abby 178
Hedge, Cecelia 257
Hedge, Emily Jane 257
Hedge, Mary Ellen 257
Hedges, Alexander 530
Hedges, Charles 530
Hedges, Clarinda 520
Hedges, Cynthia Ann 520
Hedges, Dorcas 530
Hedges, Elizabeth 176
Hedges, Ellzey 441
Hedges, Emelia 530
Hedges, George 176

Hedges, Hannah 530
Hedges, Isaac 258, 263, 274, 530
Hedges, John 384, 393, 530
Hedges, Joseph 384
Hedges, Josiah 527
Hedges, Mary 383, 393
Hedges, Mary Jane 518
Hedges, Rhoda 387
Hedges, Susannah 393, 530
Hedges, William 139
Hedges, Wm. B. 103, 108
Hedly, Gabriel 572
Hedrich, Elizabeth 89
Hedrick, Peter 340
Hedtles, W. B. 105
Heekman, Joseph 124
Heely, Betsy 508
Heeter, Abraham 246
Heeter, Catherine 246
Heeter, Daniel 246
Heeter, David 246, 384
Heeter, Dick 246
Heeter, Elizabeth 246
Heeter, Frederick 246
Heeter, Henry 246
Heeter, Jacob 246
Heeter, Joseph 246
Heeter, Otto 246
Heeter, Polly 246
Heeter, Samuel 246
Heeter, Sebastian 246
Heffelbower, Barbara 38
Heffelbower, David 38
Heffelbower, Sarah 38
Hefflebower, John 41
Heffley, Lucy 363
Heffner, John 736
Heflin, William 44
Hegnerman, H. 626
Hehemann, Henry 102
Heincke, Henry (Rev.) 222
Heinrich, Catharine 114
Heinrich, Dorothy 114
Heinrich, Gertrude 114
Heinrich, John 114
Heinrich, Paul 114
Heird, Daniel D. F. 507
Heird, Ezra 507
Heiser, Elizabeth 739
Heiser, John 739
Heiser, William 739
Heiskell, David 61
Heistand, Daniel 188, 189
Heistand, John 188
Heistand, Peter 188, 196, 200
Heistand, Rosannah 200
Heistand, Samuel 196, 200
Heite, Levi 62
Heizer, John 739
Hekimer, Elizabeth 352
Helfield, Clark 659
Hell, Jacob 430

Hell, John 430
Hell, Polly 430
Hell, Samuel 666
Hellem, Adam 169
Heller, Elizth. 413
Heller, Francis 614
Heller, J. L. 614
Heller, Mary A. 614
Heller, P. 614
Heller, Sarah C. 609
Hellerman, Adam 242
Hellings, John 493
Hellyer, Elijah 249
Hellyer, Thos. 269
Helm, A. 510
Helm, Abraham 510
Helm, Catharine 510
Helm, J. H. (Dr.) 423,
424, 426
Helm, Jacob 384
Helm, John B. C. 426
Helm, Margaret 302, 426
Helm, Mary 423, 424
Helmeck, William 124
Helmer, Elizabeth 512
Helmes, James 732
Helmic, Thomas Jefferson
650
Helmick, Alexander 139
Helmick, David 271
Helmick, Eli 644, 672
Helmick, Elizabeth 139
Helmick, Isiah 144
Helmick, Jacob 139,
643, 644, 647, 672
Helmick, John Harrison
139
Helmick, John R. 336
Helmick, Mary Ann 139
Helmick, Nathan 647
Helmick, Prudence 647
Helms, Abraham 510
Helms, Catharine 510
Helphenstine, Elizabeth
52
Helscher, Barney W. 544
Helser, Ameline 365
Helser, Anna 365
Helser, Catherine 365
Helser, Daniel 357,
364, 365
Helser, Daniel (Jr.) 364
Helser, David 364, 369
Helser, Elijah 361
Helser, Elizabeth 364,
365, 374
Helser, George 364
Helser, Hannah 365
Helser, Jacob 364
Helser, John 364, 365
Helser, Liza 365
Helser, Margaret 364
Helser, Polly 365
Helser, Sally 364, 365
Helser, Samuel 364
Helser, Solomon 364, 369
Helser, Susanna 365
Helsey, Henry 488
Helten, Nancy 11

Helwig, Christieena 568
Helworth, Michael 108
Hemelgarn, Anna M. 112
Hemesaeth, Henry 104
Heming, Catharine 521
Heminger, Andrew 566
Heminger, Catharine 575
Heminger, Geo. 572
Hemmelgard, John Henry
110
Hemmelgard, John
Theodore 110
Hemmelrich, Elizabeth 80
Hemminger, Hannah 566
Hempfield, William 274
Hemphill, A. 737
Hemphill, Fanny 607
Hemphill, James 601, 602
Hemphill, Johnson 393
Hemphill, Johnston 384
Hemphill, Johnstone 478
Hemphill, Jos. 478
Hemphill, Matthew 493
Hempstead, G. S. B. 509
Hemstead, G. S. B. 509,
510
Henarix, William 132
Hendal, Rachel 503
Hendall, Amelia F. 521
Hendall, Rachel 502
Hendershot, David 157,
168, 170, 172, 176,
180
Hendershot, Eleaner 180
Hendershot, Eleanor
168, 172, 176
Hendershot, Elizabeth
167, 172
Hendershot, George 167,
172
Hendershot, John 154,
155, 156, 157, 158,
159, 164, 178
Hendershot, Mary 153
Hendershot, Susana 157,
159
Hendershot, Susanah
157, 159
Hendershot, Susanna
155, 158, 159, 178
Hendershot, Susannah
154, 156, 158, 164
Hendershot, Thomas 153
Hendershott, Addison 139
Hendershott, David 139,
549
Hendershott, Elizabeth
161
Hendershott, Jemima 124
Hendershott, John F. 139
Hendershott, Jonathan
161
Hendershott, Ruth 163
Hendershott, Samuel 163
Hendershott, Washington
139
Henderson, Abigail 463
Henderson, Alva W. 366
Henderson, Amelia 611

Henderson, Ann 557
Henderson, B. M. 611
Henderson, Bushrod H.
611
Henderson, Catherine
256, 457
Henderson, Charles 531,
584, 611
Henderson, Chas. 256,
611
Henderson, David 440,
463, 472
Henderson, Drusilla 256
Henderson, Ebenezer B.
366
Henderson, Edward 714,
728, 730
Henderson, Eliza Jane
366
Henderson, Elizabeth
213, 360, 366, 430,
440
Henderson, George (Sr.)
249
Henderson, Hannah 440
Henderson, Hugh 169
Henderson, J. 374
Henderson, James 194,
204, 213, 379, 384,
464, 474, 566
Henderson, James C. 366
Henderson, Jane 204
Henderson, Jane H. 213
Henderson, John 132,
256, 549
Henderson, John P. 366
Henderson, M. 611
Henderson, Martha W.
204, 213
Henderson, Mary 280
Henderson, Nancy 132
Henderson, Nancy T. 204
Henderson, Polly 453
Henderson, Rachel 384
Henderson, Sally 728
Henderson, Saml. 367
Henderson, Samuel 430,
486
Henderson, Samuel (Sr.)
486
Henderson, Samuel R. 366
Henderson, Sarah 440
Henderson, Thomas L. 366
Henderson, William 254,
257
Henderson, William C.
204, 213
Henderson, William F.
366
Henderson, Wm. 248
Henderspott, David 117
Hendey, Samuel 35
Hendley, William 144
Hendly, John 438
Hendrick, Edward 492
Hendricks, Catharine 139
Hendricks, David 415
Hendricks, David E. 415
Hendricks, Elizabeth 415

861

Hendricks, Elmira 425
Hendricks, Frederick H. 425
Hendricks, G. D. (Col.) 425
Hendricks, George 415
Hendricks, George Drummond 428
Hendricks, Isaac 144
Hendricks, Jacob 360
Hendricks, James 415
Hendricks, Jane 415
Hendricks, John 144, 294, 360
Hendricks, Julia 415
Hendricks, Mary 467
Hendricks, Nancy 415
Hendricks, Peter 339
Hendricks, Polly 139
Hendricks, Rachel 415
Hendricks, Rhoda 130
Hendricks, Rosannah 415
Hendricks, Samuel 144
Hendricks, Sara 144
Hendricks, Scynthia 415
Hendricks, William 415
Hendrickson, Maria 654
Hendrickson, Peter 654
Hendrisson, Hanah 430
Hendrix, Catherine 522
Hendrix, William H. 124
Hendrix, Wm. 659
Henely, Samuel 566
Heneman, George 709
Heney, Elizabeth 610
Henger, Barbara 523
Heninger, Jacob 497
Henish, Polly 742
Henkel, Andrew 357
Henkel, Andrew (Rev.) 369
Henkel, Charles 381
Henkel, Chas. 358, 378, 381
Henkle, Isaac 607
Henley, Catherine 231
Henley, Caty 232
Henley, Jacob 231, 232
Henley, John 446
Henman, Titus B. 264
Hennamon, Henry 709
Henney, Sarea 276
Henney, William 627
Henning, Jacob 193
Henning, John Henry 100
Henningshot, Elizabeth 149
Henningshot, J. T. 149
Henny, Jacob 276
Henny, Margaretha 276
Henphill, John 23
Henrich, Catharine 114
Henrich, Christian 520
Henrich, Dorothy 114
Henrich, Gertrude 114
Henrich, John 114
Henrich, Paul 114
Henricks, Daniel 364
Henricks, Elijah 364

Henricks, Elizabeth 364
Henricks, George 364
Henricks, Jacob 294, 364
Henricks, John 362, 364
Henricks, Margaret 364
Henricks, Peter 364
Henricks, Rathieme 497
Henricks, Samuel 362, 364
Henry, Aaron 696
Henry, Abraham 566
Henry, Alexander 5
Henry, Consard 319
Henry, Coonrod 603
Henry, David 544
Henry, Enoch 384
Henry, George 5, 12, 381
Henry, Harriet Elizabeth 5
Henry, J. D. 702
Henry, Jacob 292
Henry, James 5
Henry, James D. 702
Henry, Joel 5
Henry, John 268, 681, 732
Henry, John B. 710
Henry, Lucinda A. 702
Henry, Lucy 14
Henry, Margaret 292
Henry, Margaret L. 548
Henry, Mary Ann 5
Henry, Mellen 696
Henry, Nancy 5, 22
Henry, Peggy 12
Henry, Priscilla 5
Henry, Robt. 265
Henry, Saml. 264, 266, 270, 274
Henry, Samuel 258, 262, 263, 264, 452
Henry, Sanford 5
Henry, Sarah 5
Henry, Sarah Jane 702
Henry, William 7, 544, 681, 745
Henry, Wm. 555, 572
Hensley, Simon 124
Henthorn, Adam 153, 175
Henthorn, Eleanor 351
Henthorn, Elizabeth 177
Henthorn, Fanny 172
Henthorn, James 339, 341
Henthorn, Jas. L. 171
Henthorn, Jesse 351
Henthorn, John 154, 177
Henthorn, John C. 351
Henthorn, Mary 177
Henthorn, Nathan 339
Henthorn, Nimrod E. 166
Henthorn, Stephen 179
Henthorn, Susah. 165
Henthorn, Susan 157
Henthorn, Susannah 153, 156, 159
Henthorn, Susy 155, 156, 157
Henthorn, William 157, 172, 177

Henthorn, William D. 153, 155, 156, 157, 159
Henthron, James L. 177
Henthron, Rachel 177
Heousmen, Jemima 520
Heousmen, Jumma 520
Hepburn, Elizabeth 179
Hepburn, James 156, 179
Hepler, Barbary 514
Hepner, Henry 224
Heppes, Jacobpiennie 281
Herb, Carolina 618
Herb, W. B. 618
Herbach, Benjamin 566
Herbaugh, Amelia 568
Herbaugh, Catharine 565
Herbaugh, Daniel 566
Herbaugh, David 566
Herbaugh, Frederick 566
Herbaugh, Isaac 566
Herbaugh, Mary 565
Herbaugh, Samuel 566
Herbert, Joseph 622
Herbert, Thos. 393
Herbest, Elizabeth 424
Herbest, Frederick 424
Herbey, Mary Elizabeth 104
Herbison, Hugh 645
Herbison, James 645, 674
Herbison, Jane 645, 674
Herbison, John 645, 674
Herbison, Ruth 645, 674
Hercanchoff, John Henry 103
Herchel, Elizabeth 107
Herchfelt, Clerment 103
Herder, Simeon 384
Herder, Simon 50
Herdman, Catharine 557
Herdman, Christian 557
Herdman, Daniel 557
Herdman, George 557
Herdman, Jacob 557
Herdman, Magdaleen 557
Herdman, Susana 557
Herin, James 525
Hering, Judith 111
Herkedron, Rosannah 567
Herkenschoff, John Henry 103
Herkenscoff, John Henry 103
Herless, Geo. 572
Herly, Rebecca 665
Herman, Catty 573
Herman, Levi 566
Hermon, Jacob 374
Hermon, Margaret 553
Herod, Thomas 482
Heron, Barbara 47
Herrad, J. H. 47
Herrall, Eliza 745
Herrel, Daniel 464
Herricks, Samuel 144
Herriman, Adron 590
Herriman, Parthena 336
Herrin, Ellin J. 17

Herrin, William B. 17
Herring, Elenor I. 13
Herring, Geo. 265, 272
Herrington, Benjamin 29
Herriott, James 472
Herriott, Samuel 584
Herris, Isarel 573
Herris, Mary 89
Herrod, Jane 13
Herrod, Polly 11
Herrol, Jacob I. 108
Herrold, Mary 386
Herron, Elizabeth 574
Herron, Isaiah 573
Herron, Wm. H. 359
Herron, Wm. Henry 360
Hersey, Achsah 272
Hersey, Adriel 259
Hersey, Betsey 272
Hersey, Elmer Wilson 502
Hersey, Franklin 272
Hersey, George 305
Hersey, Isaac B. 272
Hersey, Marth E. 502
Hersey, Martin 728, 729
Hersey, Mary 728, 729
Hersey, Mercy 716
Hersey, Nathan 502
Hersey, Thomas (Dr.) 502
Hershberger, Jacob 187
Hershey, John 578
Hershey, John A. 578
Hershey, Magdalina 578
Herst, Israel 172
Heskett, Joseph 634
Hesler, Catherine 364
Hesler, Elizabeth 364
Hesler, Hannah 364
Hesler, Jacob 364
Hesler, Jenny 364
Hesler, John 364
Hesler, Nancy 364
Hesler, Rebecca 364
Hesler, Sarah 364
Hesler, Susanna 364
Hesmer, Henry 72
Hess, Angeline 208
Hess, Babzer 464
Hess, Frances 208
Hess, Jane 157, 160
Hess, John 208
Hess, Michael 157, 158,
  160
Hessong, E. S. 95
Hessong, Eliza J. 95
Hessong, L. 95
Hester, Abigail 667
Hester, Abraham 659
Hester, Elizabeth 657
Hester, Euphema 566
Hester, Masey 659
Hester, Peggy 659
Heth, George 470
Heth, William 397
Heth, Wm. 397
Hetrick, Peter 355
Hetzer, George 92
Hetzer, Philip 90
Hewell, Sally 90

Hewet, Moses 714
Hewet, Sally 714
Hewit, Frances 361
Hewit, Susanna 363
Hewitt, B. P. 635
Hewitt, Bethial 716
Hewitt, Catharine 555
Hewitt, Fanny 555
Hewitt, James 470, 555
Hewitt, John 555
Hewitt, Margaret 555
Hewitt, Mary Ann 555
Hewitt, Nancy 456, 555
Hewitt, Peter 601
Hewitt, William 555
Hewlings, John G. 25
Hews, Aaron 259
Hews, Abraham 258, 259
Hews, Charity 746
Hews, Hiram 23
Hews, Jonathan 263
Hews, Wm. 258
Hewston, Caty 430
Hewston, Rachel 430
Heymrod, Aaron R. 66
Heyser, Abraham 226
Heyward, Philip S. 508
Heywood, Elliott A. 144
Heywood, Esther 144
Heywood, Isa E. 144
Heywood, Wm. 144
Hezler, Abraham 573
Hiatt, Eby 120
Hiatt, William 409
Hiatt, Wm. 409
Hibard, Lucy 586
Hibbard, Alanson 83
Hibbard, Elisha 41
Hibbard, James R. 38
Hibbard, Jason 757
Hibbard, Jason R. 762
Hibbard, Lorenzo D. 590
Hibbard, Mortimer D. 762
Hibbard, Oscar 757
Hibbard, Oscar J. 38
Hibbard, Oscar S. 762
Hibbard, Robert A. 757
Hibberd, Eliza 589
Hibbs, Charlotte 648
Hibbs, Easton 648
Hibbs, John 384
Hibbs, Massy 388
Hice, Hulda 426
Hice, Philip 513
Hichley, Mary 23
Hickenbotton, Uriah 156
Hickethorn, Ann 525
Hickman, Benjamin 144
Hickman, Cyrus 311
Hickman, Daniel 160, 166
Hickman, Elizabeth 139,
  144
Hickman, Jeremiah 139
Hickman, John Frederick
  104
Hickman, Jonathan 139
Hickman, Martha 160
Hickman, Morgan 305
Hickman, Nancy 139

Hickman, Oliver 139
Hickman, Sarah 403
Hickman, Sarey 511
Hickox, Florinda 75
Hickox, Huldah 75
Hickox, Wm. 75
Hicks, --- 176
Hicks, David 41, 642
Hicks, Elizabeth 642
Hicks, Evra 642
Hicks, Frances 44
Hicks, Hannah 660, 686
Hicks, Henry 8
Hicks, Jeremiah 170
Hicks, Joseph 642
Hicks, Mary Ann 170
Hicks, Milcah 467
Hicks, Moses 544, 552
Hicks, Samuel 642, 686
Hicks, Sarah 593, 686
Hicks, Thomas 493, 686
Hicy, John 761
Hidegrass, Henry 563
Hidigh, Catharine 558
Hidlebaugh, Catharine 348
Hidlebaugh, George 376
Hiencke, Henry 226
Hier, Jacob 464
Hier, Leonard 199
Hier, Rudy 199
Hiet, Jesse 717
Hiett, Elizabeth 519
Higby, Brewster 729
Higby, John 29
Higgens, Robert 330
Higgins, Almira 373
Higgins, Anna 511
Higgins, Archibald 488,
  638
Higgins, Delilah 61
Higgins, Elizabeth 61,
  161, 718
Higgins, Francis 549
Higgins, Geo. 357
Higgins, Isaac N. 61
Higgins, John 161, 513
Higgins, John V. 544
Higgins, Johnathan 120
Higgins, Judiah 638
Higgins, Mary 548
Higgins, Nelly 544
Higgins, Robert 384
Higgins, Sarah 638, 658
Higgins, Thomas 544
Higgins, William 549
High, David 520
High, Edward 607
High, Jacob 607
Highday, Elizabeth 661
Highlands, John 478
Highlund, Sarah 495
Highway, Samuel 665
Higinbothom, Delila 172
Higinbothom, George 172
Higinbotton, Elizabeth
  153
Higinbotton, Uriah 153
Higley, Cyrus 83
Higley, Elam 78

Higley, Lucius 78
Higley, Maria 83
Higley, Ransom B. 88
Higley, Theressa 85
Hilbrant, E. J. 535
Hilbrant, Ferdinand 535
Hilbrant, Henry E. 535
Hilbrant, I. 535
Hilbrant, Joseph 535
Hilbrant, Mary 535
Hilbrenk, Francis 544
Hilbum, Jane 131
Hilbum, Levi 131
Hilburn, Jane 131
Hilburn, Levi 131
Hilburn, Ruth 131
Hildebrand, Ann M. 580
Hildebrand, E. J. 535
Hildebrand, Emely 21
Hildebrand, Irvan 535
Hilderbrand, John 732
Hildreth, Jonathan 195
Hildreth, Lewis A. 195
Hildreth, Rhoda C. 709
Hildreth, Saml. P. 732
Hile, Abraham 88
Hile, Nancy 11
Hileman, Daniel 434
Hileman, David 434
Hileman, Elizabeth 434
Hileman, Henry 434
Hileman, Mary Jane 434
Hileman, Peter 434
Hileman, Philip 434
Hill, Aaron 92
Hill, Alanso 672
Hill, Alexander 717
Hill, Amelia 702
Hill, Archibald 644
Hill, Benjamin 72, 105,
  702
Hill, Benjamin (Jr.) 72
Hill, Betsy 34
Hill, C. 611
Hill, Catherine 457
Hill, Chas. (Jr.) 573
Hill, Cyntha 430
Hill, Daniel 573
Hill, David 644
Hill, Deborah 689
Hill, Duke 105
Hill, Eleanor 393
Hill, Eliza 430, 702
Hill, Elizabeth 22,
  134, 702, 703, 754
Hill, Elizabeth Ann 434
Hill, Francis 393
Hill, George 369
Hill, George W. 745, 751
Hill, Hannah 176, 590
Hill, Harvey 430
Hill, Henry 452
Hill, Hilip 702
Hill, Isaac 268
Hill, Isarael 581
Hill, Jacob 635
Hill, James 12, 430,
  656, 672, 689, 702,
  751

Hill, James O. 464
Hill, James V. 464
Hill, James W. 527
Hill, Jane 649
Hill, Jesse 563
Hill, John 68, 120, 134,
  167, 464, 520, 625,
  649, 665, 703, 732
Hill, John (Rev.) 601
Hill, Joseph H. 698
Hill, Joshua 649
Hill, Julia Ann 702
Hill, Leonard 531
Hill, Margaret 393
Hill, Mary 571
Hill, Mary Ellen 744
Hill, Nancy 15
Hill, Nathan 117, 134
Hill, Omilla 72
Hill, P. 611
Hill, P. W. 702
Hill, Patrick 434
Hill, Patsy 116
Hill, Peggy 13
Hill, Philip 611, 702
Hill, Polly 44, 369
Hill, Rebecca 458
Hill, Robert 176
Hill, Robt. 573
Hill, Rosanna 625
Hill, Sally 72, 134,
  453, 461
Hill, Saml. 390
Hill, Samuel 390, 484,
  644
Hill, Sanford W. 590
Hill, Sarah 13, 134,
  565, 649
Hill, Selina 430
Hill, Simeon 83
Hill, Stephen 585
Hill, Susannah 14
Hill, Thomas 130, 134,
  401, 644
Hill, Thos. 434
Hill, W. 613
Hill, Welcome 72, 520
Hill, William 393, 544,
  603, 622, 673, 702,
  717
Hill, William (Jr.) 393
Hill, Wm. 573
Hillard, Lydia 587
Hillear, Benjamin
  Franklin 299
Hillengs, Margaret 21
Hiller, Jacob 399
Hiller, John 112, 392
Hiller, Kitty 386
Hillery, Ann 577
Hillery, Comfort 567
Hillery, Elizabeth 576
Hillery, John 384
Hillery, Peggy 467
Hilliar, Ann 299
Hilliard, Amanda 540
Hilliard, Daniel 117
Hilliard, E. 540
Hilliard, Fielding 139

Hilliard, H. 540
Hilliard, Joseph 117
Hilliard, Martha K. 540
Hilliard, Nancy 540
Hilliard, Patterson 139
Hilliard, Robert P. 259
Hillings, John 9
Hillis, Elizabeth 518
Hilman, Eleanor 79
Hilt, Nancy 695
Hilterbrack, Harriet 523
Hilton, Ann 499
Hilton, Brice 745
Hilton, Eliza 745
Hilton, Ezra 745
Hilton, Jesse 745
Hilton, Mary 746, 747
Hilzet, George 78
Himes, Francis 188
Himes, George 188
Himes, John 188
Himes, Martin 188
Himes, Matthias 446
Himes, Nancy 188
Himes, Peter 573
Himes, Rachel 188
Himes, Samuel 199
Himes, Thomas 188
Himmel, Jacob 728
Himmel, Thomas 728
Himrod, Ann 405
Himrod, Elijah 405
Hinchman, Benjamin 157
Hinckley, Nathl. 714
Hindman, Elizabeth 447
Hindman, Harriet 447
Hindman, John 447
Hindman, Susan 447
Hine, Elizabeth 527
Hinebaugh, Jacob 353
Hines, Abram 683
Hines, Amy 364
Hines, Anna 114
Hines, Daniel 743
Hines, Elizabeth 364
Hines, Elizabeth Ellen
  410
Hines, Hugh 683
Hines, John 457
Hines, Margaret 398, 461
Hines, Martin 364
Hines, Myer 371
Hines, Nancy 683
Hines, Peter 114
Hines, Philip 464
Hines, Philip J. (Dr.)
  607
Hines, Phillip 114
Hines, William 683
Hines, Wm. 573
Hinkelman, Elis. 709
Hinkins, David 692
Hinkins, George S. 692
Hinkins, J. 692
Hinkins, Jacob 692, 693
Hinkins, John W. 692
Hinkins, R. 692
Hinkins, Rachel 692, 693
Hinkins, Van Buren 692

864

Hinkle, David 424
Hinkle, Jacob 457
Hinkle, Lucy 116
Hinkley, John 648
Hinkley, Ophiah 648
Hinman, Titus B. 263
Hinsdale, Francis 761
Hinsdale, Jacob 35
Hinselman, Barbara 519
Hinshaw, John 464
Hinsky, Ada 536
Hinsky, Adam 535, 536
Hinsky, Ida May 535, 536
Hintelang, Casper 345
Hinton, David 464
Hinton, Elizabeth 574
Hinton, Levi 590
Hinton, Polly 388
Hinton, Rebeccah 453
Hinton, Thomas 457
Hipkins, James (Jr.) 677
Hipple, Adam M. 243
Hipple, Charles E. 243
Hipple, Daniel 243
Hipple, Elizabeth 243
Hipple, Eve 575
Hipple, Henry 195, 199,
    203, 206, 207
Hipple, J. 243
Hipple, John W. 243
Hipple, M. 243
Hipple, Mary 243
Hipple, Peter James 243
Hipple, William 198
Hipsheer, Sarah 607
Hipshire, John 607
Hipshire, Jonathan 607
Hipsley, Andrew 308
Hipsley, Elizabeth 308
Hipsley, Harriet 308
Hipsley, Josephus 308
Hipsley, Sarah 308
Hire, Elijah 607
Hire, Jeremiah 607
Hire, John 608
Hire, Mary 610
Hirt, Almira 139
Hiser, Charles 309
Hiser, Cyntha 211
Hiser, Mary 211, 309
Hiser, Peter 211
Hisey, Joseph 761
Hisle, Mary 83
Hisle, Robert 83
Hissebinger, Michael 161
Hissong, John 195
Hitchcock, Caleb 253
Hitchcock, Isaac 440
Hitchcock, Isabel 512
Hitchcock, Israel 356,
    377
Hitchcock, Jesse 503
Hitchcock, Joanna 515
Hitchcock, Lucretia 515
Hitchcock, Lydia 513
Hitchcock, Nicholas 374
Hitchcock, Pelatiah 730
Hitchcock, Samuel 34
Hitchcock, Washington 356

Hitchen, Wm. 139
Hitchens, George 464
Hite, Abraham 88
Hite, Isaac 520
Hitesman, Frederick 520
Hitler, Abraham 393, 399
Hitler, Caty 382
Hitler, Elizabeth 393
Hitler, George 393, 399
Hitler, Jacob 393, 399
Hitler, John 399
Hitler, Joseph 393, 399
Hitler, Polly 393
Hitler, Sarah 393
Hitler, Susannah 393,
    399
Hitsman, Jacob L. 35
Hittle, Sarah 119
Hitton, Ann 499
Hiveley, Elizabeth 750
Hiveley, John 750
Hiveley, Polly 750
Hively, Adam 750
Hively, Elizabeth 745,
    750
Hively, Isaac 745, 750
Hively, Jacob 520, 750
Hively, John 750
Hively, Joseph 750
Hively, Mary 744
Hively, Michael 750
Hively, Polly 750
Hively, Rebecca 750
Hively, Thomas 750
Hixon, David L. 758
Hixon, Elizabeth 758
Hixon, Henry 758
Hixon, John 464
Hixon, Mary 758
Hixon, Rachel 464
Hixon, Samuel 573
Hixson, Daniel 457
Hizer, John 186
Hizer, Susannah 572
Hoadley, Almancy 29
Hoadley, Calvin R. 29
Hoadley, Nelson 29
Hoadley, Sally 31
Hoagland, Vaste 576
Hoagland, Voste 576
Hoaglin, E. M. 626, 627
Hoaglin, Enoch M. 622
Hoaglin, Roszillah 607
Hobb, Jackson 34
Hobbs, Ephraim 488
Hobbs, Mary 385
Hobbs, Richard 384
Hobouch, Mary 11
Hobouch, Solomon 12
Hobson, Charles 430, 630
Hobson, Isaac 430
Hobson, Mary 430
Hobson, Rachel 430
Hobson, Sarah 430
Hobson, William 665
Hock, Cath. 220
Hockenberg, Christeena
    743
Hockenberg, Delila 743

Hockenberg, George 743
Hockenberg, Harmon 743
Hockenberg, John 743
Hockenberg, Lazarus 743
Hockenberg, Mary 743
Hockenberg, Michael 743
Hockenberg, Peter 743
Hockenberg, Sophia 743
Hocks, Samuel 434
Hockstetler, Jacob 573
Hoddy, John 474
Hoddy, Richard 472
Hoddy, William 452, 472
Hodge, Agness 180
Hodge, Hugh L. 54
Hodge, James 180
Hodge, Joseph 345
Hodge, Rachel 359
Hodge, Rachel C. 345
Hodges, Daniel 457
Hodges, Joseph 369
Hodges, Polly 457
Hodges, Thomas 457, 489
Hodgin, Jno. 269
Hoelzel, George 176
Hoeschel, P. 114
Hoeschel, William 114
Hoff, Phillip 737
Hoff, Thankful 498
Hoffkins, Abraham 633
Hoffkins, Sarah Mariah
    633
Hoffman, Adolph 242
Hoffman, C. 99
Hoffman, Charlotte Agnes
    242
Hoffman, D. 99
Hoffman, David 404
Hoffman, Eli 201
Hoffman, Enoch 99
Hoffman, George 520
Hoffman, Jacob 388
Hoffman, Jacob M. 709
Hoffman, John 401, 404
Hoffman, Julia Ann 404
Hoffman, Magdalene 420
Hoffmeister, Henry
    Rudolph 227
Hofkins, Henry 633
Hofkins, Polly 633
Hofkins, Voss 633
Hoftsinger, Christianna
    572
Hogan, Isabella 741
Hogan, Jacob 648
Hogan, Joseph 648
Hoge, Ann K. 400
Hoge, Ann Lacy 400
Hoge, Danuel 400
Hoge, Elizabeth Ann 400
Hoge, Elizabeth K. 400
Hoge, Elizabeth P. 400
Hoge, John B. 400
Hoge, John Blair 400
Hoge, Moses Duery 400
Hoge, Thomas D. 400
Hoge, William James 400
Hogen, Elisabeth 393
Hogen, Elizabeth 393

Hoggins, Charles 305
Hogland, Henry 573
Hogland, John 563, 573
Hogseed, Jacob 285
Hogseed, James 286
Hogseed, Walter 286
Hogue, Lucy Ann 171
Hogue, Nelson 171, 176
Hohtt, John Henry 104
Hohtt, Margaretta 104
Hohtt, Sally Alexandria 104
Hohtt, Sophia 104
Hohtt, Werner 104
Hoit, Betsy 333
Hoit, Evelina 77
Hoit, James 83
Hoit, Joseph 83
Hoit, Mary 11
Hoit, Syloy 15
Hokech, Rachel 13
Hokinson, Anna 517
Holand, George L. 58
Holand, William 513
Holawell, John 152
Holben, David D. 74
Holbrook, Jonathan 248
Holbrook, Malissa 248
Holbrook, Nancy 248
Holcomb, Buris 365
Holcomb, Charles H. 41
Holcomb, Elijah 365
Holcomb, Jacob 355
Holcomb, Jane Ann 29
Holcomb, John B. 365
Holcomb, Johnathan A. 622
Holcomb, Loami 29
Holcomb, Margaret 373
Holcomb, Mary Ann 409
Holcomb, Rachel 365
Holcomb, Thomas 365
Holcombe, Charles Ogden 520
Holden, Joseph 709, 732
Holden, Maria 709
Holden, Mary 718
Holder, Caroline 456
Holder, Emanuel 41
Holderman, Abraham 68, 399, 457
Holderman, Christopher 68, 399
Holderman, Christopher (Jr.) 68, 399
Holderman, Christopher (Sr.) 399
Holderman, David 68
Holderman, David (Jr.) 399
Holderman, Eleanor 399
Holderman, George 68, 399
Holderman, Isaac 68, 399
Holderman, Jacob 399
Holderman, Jacob S. 425
Holderman, John 68, 399, 434
Holderman, Julian 68

Holderman, Mary 68, 399
Holderman, Susannah 68
Holdermon, Jacob 218
Holdheid, Bernard 103
Holdheid, Elizabeth 103
Holdheid, Gerherd 103
Holdridge, Alanson 292
Holdridge, George W. 322, 324
Holdridge, Hulda 337
Holdridge, Huldah 324
Holdridge, James 324
Holdridge, Rosannah 292
Holdrige, Huldah 322
Holdrige, James C. 322
Holdron, Colman 732
Hole, Allen 492
Hole, John 184
Hole, John (Dr.) 184
Hole, Mary 670
Hole, Matilda 184
Hole, Nancy 661
Hole, Phebe 184, 658
Hole, Rebecca 94
Hole, War . . . 94
Hole, William 230
Hole, Zachariah 223
Holeman, Henry 688
Holenbeck, Casper 270
Holensworth, Carter 117
Holeton, Christeena 291
Holeton, Eliza 291
Holeton, Elizabeth 291
Holeton, Francis 291
Holeton, Gomailial 291
Holeton, John 291
Holeton, Mary Ann 291
Holeton, N. L. 291
Holeton, Nicholas C. 291
Holeton, Rebecca 291
Holeton, Samuel 291
Holeton, Silas 291
Holeton, Tabitha 291
Holeton, Washington 291
Holiday, Samuel 670
Holister, John 758
Holl, Matilda 85
Holland, Betsy 488
Holland, Elliot 153
Holland, Elliott 155, 160, 165, 168
Holland, Francis 513
Holland, Horace 732
Holland, James W. 273
Holland, John 493
Holland, Joshua 668
Holland, Mary 513, 515
Holland, Urania 155
Holland, William 489
Hollandship, George W. 60
Hollaway, Nancy 495
Holle, Mary 670
Hollenback, Daniel 365
Hollenback, Eliza 378
Hollenback, Hamsen 365
Hollenback, Jacob 365
Hollenback, Jacob (Sr.) 365

Hollenback, John 365
Hollenback, Martha 378
Hollenback, Nancy 365
Hollenback, Sarah 365
Hollenback, Susana 365
Hollenback, Susanna 365
Hollenback, Susannah 365
Hollenkuk, Chasper 717
Hollepeter, Elizabeth 139
Hollepeter, Mary 139
Hollepeter, Rudolph 139
Holler, Adam 480
Holler, Catharine 608
Holler, Julia 745
Holler, Philip 201
Holler, Susannah 213
Holliday, Anne 651
Holliday, Betsy 670
Holliday, Cynthia 651
Holliday, Lititia 651
Holliday, Samuel 651, 670
Hollinger, Barbara 710, 711
Hollingshead, John 745
Hollingshead, Susanah 155
Hollingshead, Thomas 155
Hollingsworth, David 697
Hollingsworth, Ely 125
Hollingsworth, James 684
Hollingsworth, Jane 121
Hollingsworth, John 117
Hollingsworth, Joshua 672, 683
Hollingsworth, Lydia 683
Hollingsworth, Mary 683, 684
Hollingsworth, Wm. 106
Hollinshead, Deborah 451
Hollinshead, Samuel 497
Hollis, Allen 144
Hollis, Edmund 144
Hollis, John B. 144
Hollis, Mary 144
Hollister, Abigail 158
Hollister, Jeremiah 159, 165
Hollister, John 154, 758
Hollister, Nathan 158, 732
Hollister, Rich. D. 732
Hollister, Sally 165
Hollopeter, Elizabeth 523
Holloway, Alpheus S. 41
Holloway, Amos 553
Holloway, Cyrus 41
Holloway, E. 151
Holloway, G. P. 151
Holloway, George 38
Holloway, Hephzibah 553
Holloway, Herbert 38
Holloway, Job 559
Holloway, Lucy J. 151
Holloway, Mary Jane 38
Hollway, William 464
Holly, Manning 549

866

Hollycross, David 590
Hollyday, Susannah 457
Holman, Wm. 493
Holmes, Abraham 392
Holmes, Anna E. 538
Holmes, Elijah 538
Holmes, Elizabeth 399
Holmes, Fanny 544
Holmes, Hannah 434
Holmes, Isaac 399
Holmes, James 399
Holmes, Jane 399
Holmes, Janett 434
Holmes, John 41
Holmes, John (Sr.) 520
Holmes, Jonathan 392,
  399
Holmes, Joshua 392
Holmes, Juliann 399
Holmes, Levi E. 538
Holmes, Manlove 8
Holmes, Margaret 434
Holmes, Martha 569
Holmes, Mary 399
Holmes, Mary E. 538
Holmes, Peter 290
Holmes, Rachel 399
Holmes, Robert 493
Holmes, Sally 518
Holmes, Samuel 573
Holmes, Sarah 574
Holmes, Thomas 544, 665
Holmes, Thos. 544
Holms, John 528
Holms, Saml. 310
Holms, William D. 424
Holopeter, Isaiah 520
Holsappel, Adam 244
Holsappel, Samuel 244
Holsapple, John 244
Holsapple, Mary 244
Holsapple, Sarah 244
Holsen, Gerhard 104
Holson, Hannah 661
Holsople, Frederick 190
Holsopple, Moses 434
Holt, Brittany 82
Holt, Christiana 387
Holt, Eliza 79
Holt, Hiram 83
Holt, Horace 78
Holt, Jerom 223, 224
Holt, Justice 745
Holt, Polly 76
Holtgraven, Francis 103
Holton, Benjamin 464
Holton, Mary Ann B. 744
Holtzenbuler, Henry 488
Holycross, Benj. 590
Holycross, Edmond 585
Holycross, James 590
Holycross, William 590
Holzgrave, Franz Jos.
  102
Homan, E. 245
Homan, Elizabeth 245
Homan, Fredrick 647
Homan, Hannah 647
Homan, John H. 245

Homan, Martha 245
Homan, Mary O. 245
Homan, Nelson 414
Homan, Peter 414
Homan, Polly 647
Homan, Samuel 647
Homan, W. L. 245
Homan, Wm. 245
Homan, Wm. H. 245
Homan, Wm. L. 245
Homeer, Alexander 520
Homerichouse, Polly 573
Homes, Susanah 574
Hon, Daniel 695
Honell, C. 62
Honnah, Versilla 749
Honnstett, Frederick W.
  604
Honstett, William 601
Hoobler, Michael 187
Hood, Andrew 745
Hood, Charles C. 347,
  355, 369
Hood, Chas. C. 375,
  378, 380
Hood, Chas. H. 378, 380
Hood, Chas. H. (Rev.) 371
Hood, Frances 364
Hood, Margaret 364
Hood, Temperance 364
Hood, Thos. 366, 378
Hook, . . . 330
Hook, Elisha (Rev.) 605
Hook, Elizabeth 240
Hook, J. 330
Hook, J. M. 330
Hook, James 240
Hook, John 330, 717
Hook, Levi 330
Hook, M. 330
Hook, Margaret 330
Hook, Mary 220, 221,
  240, 330, 331
Hook, Mary E. 311
Hook, Mary Elizabeth 311
Hook, Sarah 633
Hooker, Richard 286
Hoopengarden, Jacob 566
Hoopengarener, John 573
Hoopengarner, Daniel 573
Hooper, Ezekiel 348, 363
Hooper, George 721
Hooper, Jacob 348, 363,
  367, 380
Hooper, James 348, 363,
  379
Hooper, John 348, 363
Hooper, Lititia 348
Hooper, Philip 348, 363
Hooper, Polly 363
Hooper, Rebecca 363
Hooper, Samuel 348, 363
Hoopes, Eli 177
Hoopes, Eliza 177
Hoopes, Joel 6
Hoopes, Rebecca 6
Hoopingarner, Catharine
  570
Hoots, Marrilla 336

Hoover, Abraham 189, 191
Hoover, Alonzo 423
Hoover, Alonzo H. 144
Hoover, Andrew 185
Hoover, Anna Mariah 162
Hoover, Barbara 134
Hoover, Caroline 434
Hoover, Catherine 189
Hoover, Christian 558
Hoover, Daniel 144, 185
Hoover, Daniel (Jr.)
  130, 193, 224
Hoover, David 130, 144,
  208, 210, 558
Hoover, Elizabeth 122
Hoover, Esther 189, 191
Hoover, Frederic 185
Hoover, Geo. 144, 434
Hoover, George 423
Hoover, George H. 331
Hoover, Henry 117, 134,
  144, 162, 206, 630
Hoover, I. 752
Hoover, Isaac L. 307
Hoover, Jacob 144, 185,
  520
Hoover, Jesse 125
Hoover, John 20, 134,
  193, 558
Hoover, John L. 144
Hoover, Jonas 189
Hoover, Joseph 520
Hoover, Joshua 580
Hoover, Levi 144
Hoover, Louisa Jane 144
Hoover, Louise 434
Hoover, Martin 189, 191
Hoover, Mary 193, 630
Hoover, Mary E. 144
Hoover, Matilda 337
Hoover, Michael 630
Hoover, Noah 120
Hoover, Peggy 189
Hoover, Permelia Keys
  409
Hoover, Rachel 307
Hoover, Rebecca A. 423
Hoover, Rebeccah 134
Hoover, Sally 193
Hoover, Saml. 12
Hoover, Samuel 252
Hoover, Sarah 434
Hoover, Sarah F. 144
Hoover, Solomon 120, 125
Hoover, Susanna 119
Hoover, Susannah 193
Hoover, William 125
Hoover, William P. 139
Hoover, Wm. 434
Hope, Anna M. 612
Hope, John 612
Hopkin, Joseph 464
Hopkins, Alexander 669
Hopkins, Almon 5
Hopkins, Anvilley 497
Hopkins, Arch. 488
Hopkins, Arnal 36
Hopkins, Benjamin 581,
  598

Hopkins, Cloy 464
Hopkins, Cty. 464
Hopkins, Dan 5
Hopkins, David 653, 669
Hopkins, David O. 144
Hopkins, Eliza 5
Hopkins, Elizabeth 5, 498, 584
Hopkins, Eppenetus 524
Hopkins, Frank 5
Hopkins, Herty 5
Hopkins, Hester Jane 5
Hopkins, James 292, 647, 651, 653, 669
Hopkins, James (Sr.) 669
Hopkins, Jemima 5
Hopkins, Jno. 669
Hopkins, John 489, 647, 666, 669
Hopkins, John H. 12
Hopkins, John W. 581
Hopkins, John Y. 314
Hopkins, Jonathan 649
Hopkins, Lida 455
Hopkins, Martha 669
Hopkins, Martha Ann 5
Hopkins, Mary Ann 524
Hopkins, Mary J. 144
Hopkins, Mary Olivia 766
Hopkins, Owen Johnston 5
Hopkins, Polly 524
Hopkins, Rachel 669
Hopkins, Robt. R. 144
Hopkins, Samuel 520, 651, 669
Hopkins, Sarah 5, 292, 548, 653, 669
Hopkins, Steward 255
Hopkins, William 5, 464, 647, 650, 651, 653, 669, 677, 766
Hopkins, William A. 207
Hopkins, Wm. 677
Hopkins, Wm. H. 208
Hopkins, Wm. K. 144
Hopp, John 710
Hoppelberger, Elizabeth 36
Hopper, Laton 331
Hopper, Robert 158
Hoppers, Nancy 84
Hoppes, George 86
Hoppes, William 502
Hopton, William 177
Hormal, John 666
Hormell, Rebecca 660
Hormish, Christly 563
Hormish, Elizabeth 563
Horn, Daniel 464
Horn, George 420
Horn, George L. 414
Horn, George M. 420
Horn, Sally 382
Hornaday, Christopher 690
Hornaday, Ezra 434
Hornaday, Lucinda 690
Hornback, Claris 398
Hornback, Curtis 398

Hornback, Dolly 464
Hornback, Dorothy 398
Hornback, Elizabeth 464
Hornback, George 398
Hornback, James 398
Hornback, John 384
Hornback, Joseph B. 398
Hornback, Lydia 398
Hornback, Marinda 398
Hornback, Michael 398
Hornback, Robison 398
Hornback, Samuel 54
Hornbeck, James 44
Horne, Daniel 287
Horne, Lydia 760
Horner, Geo. 206
Horner, George 192, 528, 544
Horner, Hannah 665
Horner, James 471
Horner, John 192, 486
Horner, Nancy 517
Horner, Wm. 266, 267, 272
Horninger, George 562
Hornsberger, George 649
Horrise, Aaron 83
Horsbrook, Daniel 659
Horseman, John 417
Horton, Amos 86
Horton, Seth 75
Hoser, John 191
Hosford, Abigail 31
Hoshan, Margaret 551
Hoshour, Elizabeth 488
Hoshour, Henry 488
Hoskens, Erastus 267
Hoskin, Wait 303
Hoskins, Ann 499
Hoskins, Elnora 312
Hoskins, Erastus 265, 266, 267, 271
Hoskins, Henry 312
Hoskins, Lewis 312
Hoskins, Mary 33
Hoskins, Richard 583, 590
Hoskins, Wait 312
Hoskinson, Ezekiel 732
Hoskinson, Geo. W. 732
Hosmer, Hezekiah L. 762
Hosselton, Eve 384
Hosselton, Jacob 384
Hostenton, Jacob 464
Hoster, Barbara 232
Hostetter, Abraham 231, 232
Hostetter, Adam 231
Hostetter, Anna 231
Hostetter, Barbara 570
Hostetter, Catherine 231
Hostetter, Christian 231, 232
Hostetter, Christian H. 232
Hostetter, Daniel 232
Hostetter, David 231, 232
Hostetter, Elizabeth 231

Hostetter, Hannah 231, 232
Hostetter, James 232
Hostetter, Jeremiah 573
Hostetter, John 231
Hostetter, Ulila 232
Hotchkiss, Titus 281
Hotsonpillen, Jacob 395
Hotton, Rachel 459
Hottzgaver, August 114
Hottzgaver, Caroline 114
Hottzgaver, Charles 114
Hotzebuler, David 488
Houanstein, Anna 522
Houber, Christian 608
Houbert, Margaret 20
Houbougher, . . . 162
Houck, Catharine 564
Houck, Elizabeth 564
Houck, Henry 564
Houck, Isaac 520
Houck, Jacob 564
Houck, Margaret 564
Houflech, John 90
Hough, Benjamin 492
Hough, Ellen M. 493
Hough, John 290, 366
Hough, Joseph 376
Hough, Nancy 366
Houk, Charlotte W. 521
Houk, Fredk. 486
Houk, Henry 681
Houk, John 161
Houkimer, Eleanor 709
Houlton, John 745
Houlton, Samuel 745
Houp, John 434
Houpes, Martin 558
House, Conrad 41
House, Elizabeth 74
House, Harriet 38
House, James 38
House, Joseph 489
Householder, Adam 376
Householder, Christena 376
Houser, Abraham 139
Houser, Amelia 735
Houser, Anna 139
Houser, Austen 745
Houser, Barbara 230
Houser, Barbary 548
Houser, Charlotte 537
Houser, Christian 139
Houser, Daniel 544
Houser, Eliza 139
Houser, Elizabeth 220
Houser, Jacob 139, 537
Houser, Jasoe 735
Houser, Jonah 139
Houser, Martin 230
Houser, Mary E. 61
Houser, Michael 493
Houser, Susanna 139
Houser, Wm. T. 99
Houseworth, Ruth 30
Houstead, Frederick W. 608
Housted, Conrod 604

Houston, David 549
Houston, George L. 191
Houston, John 114
Houston, John S. 107
Houston, Margaret 552
Houston, Marietta 74
Houston, Mary 74, 551
Houston, Robert 74, 114
Houston, Robert (Sr.) 134
Houts, William 497
Houtz, Catharine 12
Houtz, Christian 756
Houtz, Henry 12, 17
Houtz, Leonard 17, 24
Hover, Charlot 595
Hover, Emeline 4
Hover, Jacob 1
Hover, Polly 464
Hover, Sarah 595
Hover, Susanah 23
Hoverstock, Conrad 566
Hoverstock, Elizabeth 569
Hoverstock, Tobias 566
Hovey, Anna M. 83
Hovey, Edmond 596, 597
Hovey, Eliza 585, 597
Hovey, Harden 585, 596
Hovey, Samuel 586
Hovey, Samuel T. 596
Hovey, Simon (Dr.) 473
Hovey, Sophiah 83
How, George 717
How, Henry 650
How, Jacob 562
Howalt, John 162
Howalt, Mary 162
Howard, Alexander 760
Howard, Angenette 756
Howard, Anjanett 761
Howard, Anjenette 756, 757
Howard, Ann 155, 404
Howard, Anson 595, 597
Howard, Basha 608
Howard, David 253, 257, 760
Howard, David R. 281
Howard, Dresden 757
Howard, Dresden W. H. 756, 761
Howard, Dresden Winfield Huston 760
Howard, E. 761
Howard, Edward 729, 756, 757, 760, 761, 762
Howard, Edward W. 729, 730
Howard, Edwin R. 756
Howard, Eliner 452
Howard, Elizabeth 756
Howard, Harton 155
Howard, Henry 155, 488, 729
Howard, Horton 156
Howard, Jno. 404
Howard, John 760
Howard, Lewis 78, 125, 452

Howard, Lida 452
Howard, Margaret 404
Howard, Mary 155
Howard, Megomi 461
Howard, Nancy 757, 761
Howard, Nathan 513
Howard, Negomi 461
Howard, Orange 765
Howard, Orange (Jr.) 765
Howard, Peter 12
Howard, Phebe 386
Howard, Philander 765
Howard, Pike M. 760
Howard, Pike Moroe 760
Howard, Polly 666
Howard, Ransom 765
Howard, Rebecca 253, 257
Howard, Richard M. W. 760
Howard, Robert 760
Howard, Robert A. 762
Howard, Saml. 477
Howard, Samuel 489
Howard, Sanford 765
Howard, Sarah 81, 452
Howard, Sarah Ann 591
Howard, Sidney 760
Howard, Simeon B. 497
Howard, Simon B. 497
Howard, Thomas 760
Howard, Thos. 760
Howard, Vetchel 384
Howard, William 489, 760
Howden, A. (Jr.) 291
Howden, Andrew (Jr.) 291
Howden, Ann B. 291
Howden, Emely 38
Howden, Jane 38
Howden, John 38
Howden, Martha 38
Howden, Matilda 38
Howden, Theophilus 291
Howden, Thomas 38, 291
Howden, William 291
Howdesheldt, Samuel 629
Howdyshelt, Catharine 84
Howe, Aaron 729
Howe, Charles E. 699
Howe, Chester 707
Howe, George 717
Howe, Hester 659
Howe, Jessie B. 699
Howe, John D. 139
Howe, Martin 125
Howe, Morris 544
Howe, Nancy 634
Howe, Pearley 714
Howe, Saml. M. 139
Howel, Charles 672
Howel, George W. 139
Howel, John 78
Howel, John Duncan 50
Howel, Joseph 78
Howell, A. J. 538
Howell, A. R. 538
Howell, A. R. W. 538
Howell, Amanda L. 538
Howell, Catherine 333
Howell, David 535
Howell, E. 538

Howell, E. Neal 358
Howell, Edgar O. 538
Howell, Elizabeth 538
Howell, J. 538
Howell, Jefferson 549
Howell, Jeremiah 161
Howell, Jonathan 538
Howell, Mandy 535
Howell, Mariam 538
Howell, Plazzie 538
Howell, Rebecca 538, 665
Howell, Samantha 538
Howell, Sarah E. 538
Howell, Silas 497
Howell, Simeon N. 538
Howell, T. R. E. 538
Howell, Thomas 156, 160
Howell, W. L. 538
Howell, William 83
Howell, Wm. 92
Hower, Christian 739
Howey, Aaron 36
Howey, Mary J. 328
Howey, Mary M. 328
Howey, Robert H. 328
Howey, William A. 328
Howk, Alanson 29
Howlet, Polly 85
Howman, Barbara 574
Howser, Catharine 139
Howser, Isaac 139
Howser, John 139
Howser, Polly 139
Howshour, John 464
Howsman, Frances 47
Hoy, Charles 558
Hoy, Daniel 558
Hoy, Margaret 363
Hoy, Matilda 23
Hoyde, John 92
Hoyer, John 573
Hoyerware, Elizabeth 522
Hoyt, Abagail 84
Hoyt, Andrew 56
Hoyt, Anne 56
Hoyt, Cyriel 87
Hoyt, Eunice 56
Hoyt, Josiah B. A. 56
Hoyt, Mary 757
Hoyt, Mercy 77
Hoyt, Robert 87
Hoyt, Susannah 87
Hoyt, William M. 757
Hren, George R. 497
Hster, Abigail 667
Hu . . . ell, Joseph 4
Hubard, Polly 386
Hubb, Mary 456
Hubbard, Alexander 561
Hubbard, Altie F. 498
Hubbard, Benjamin 426
Hubbard, Clara 426
Hubbard, Cyrus 497
Hubbard, Ebenezer 530
Hubbard, Ebern. 29
Hubbard, Emeline F. 30
Hubbard, Harriet B. 32
Hubbard, Jacob 452, 464, 489

Hubbard, John 457, 489
Hubbard, Minerva 426
Hubbard, Nancy 499
Hubbard, Owen 12
Hubbard, Phielden 457
Hubbard, Sarah 455
Hubbard, Titus 452
Hubbard, William 5
Hubbart, Catharine 67
Hubbart, Philip 67
Hubbel, Hezekiah 223
Hubbel, John R. 434
Hubbel, Samuel B. 497
Hubbel, Sarah 76
Hubbell, Abijah 86
Hubbell, Barailla 83
Hubbell, Calvin 38
Hubbell, Christiana 38
Hubbell, Hannah 38
Hubbell, Hezekiah 41
Hubbell, Jerusha 549
Hubbell, Mary Ann 38
Hubbell, Polly 79
Hubbell, Samuel 29
Hubbell, Thomas 38
Hubbell, William 416
Hubbert, Lucy 586
Hubble, Asa 120, 544
Hubble, Elizabeth 550
Hubble, Hezekiah 544,
  549
Hubble, Jane 416
Hubble, Minerva 549
Huber, John 562
Hubert, John 527
Hubler, Andrew J. 229
Hubler, Joseph 214
Hubler, Mary 229
Hucher, Catharine 95
Hucher, Jonathan 95
Hucheson, Jimpsey 741
Huckle, Benjamin 402
Huckle, John F. 402
Hudaon, Phoebe 694
Hudgel, Rachel 663
Hudgel, Thomas 659
Hudson, Abby 123
Hudson, Abigail 324
Hudson, Abraham 316
Hudson, Abram 323, 324
Hudson, David 86
Hudson, Elijah 153, 176
Hudson, Elizabeth 316,
  323, 324
Hudson, Elizabeth L. 336
Hudson, Ella 324
Hudson, Frances
  Elizabeth 324
Hudson, George 464
Hudson, James 316, 321,
  323, 324
Hudson, John 316, 323,
  324
Hudson, Mary 84
Hudson, Mary Anna 320
Hudson, Phebe 323, 324
Hudson, Phoebe 746
Hudson, Robert 464
Hudson, Rolla C. 320, 324

Hudson, Samuel 316,
  319, 323, 324
Hudson, Samuel W. 319,
  320, 324, 336
Hudson, Sarah 323, 324,
  746
Hudson, Shadrack 316,
  321, 323, 324
Hudson, Shadrack R.
  320, 321
Hudson, Thomas 341
Hudspeth, John 608
Hudspeth, Susan 608
Hudspeth, Thomas 608
Hues, Richard 573
Hues, Thomas 527
Huet, Isarael 717
Huet, John 654
Huet, Moses 714
Huet, Thomas 654
Huett, Solomon 520
Huey, Albert R. 223
Huey, Nancy 182
Huey, Robert 182
Huey, Robert (Jr.) 223
Huff, Ausila 575
Huff, Benjamin 349, 376
Huff, Bushrod 732
Huff, Catharine 444
Huff, Caty 575
Huff, Charity 444
Huff, Edwin 364
Huff, Eli 710
Huff, Gamaiel 440
Huff, Gameal 444
Huff, Gamiel 443
Huff, George 737
Huff, Henry 573, 737
Huff, Jacob 737
Huff, Jona 732
Huff, Joseph 452, 562
Huff, M. 701
Huff, Peter 443, 737
Huff, Philip 737
Huff, Robert 443, 444
Huff, Samuel 566
Huff, Thomas 78
Huff, William 440
Huffine, Mary J. 583
Huffman, Abraham 201
Huffman, Amos 44
Huffman, Daniel 742
Huffman, David T. 477
Huffman, Deliverance A.
  589
Huffman, Elizabeth 174,
  200
Huffman, Fanny 200
Huffman, George 200
Huffman, Jacob 152
Huffman, John 92, 174,
  200
Huffman, John M. 305
Huffman, Lydia 200
Huffman, Margaret E. 434
Huffman, Mary 200
Huffman, Nancy 152
Huffman, Rachael 385
Huffman, Roven 732

Huffman, Sarah 200
Huffman, Wm. 590
Huffner, Elizabeth 736
Huffner, Frederick 322
Huffner, John 736
Hufford, William 683
Huflines, Adam 457
Hufman, Stephen 666
Hugg, John 92
Huggins, Bryr 637
Huggins, Elizabeth 166,
  171
Huggins, John 165, 166,
  171
Hughbanks, Perry 590
Hughel, Cynthia 144
Hughes, A. L. 328
Hughes, Andre S. 337
Hughes, Anna 514
Hughes, Elisabeth 715
Hughes, Eliza Jane 335
Hughes, Elizabeth 328
Hughes, Jane 41
Hughes, John 489
Hughes, Margaret 93
Hughes, Nancy 337, 515
Hughes, Samuel 544
Hughes, Sarah 713
Hughes, William 513
Hughey, Alexander 188
Hughey, Elizabeth 123
Hughman, David 478
Hughs, Aaron 267
Hughs, Avon 294
Hughs, Ellen 47
Hughs, Hanery P. 168
Hughs, James 83
Hughs, John 457
Hughs, Jonathan 266, 267
Hughs, Lurania 80
Hughs, Margaret 128,
  129, 717
Hughs, Mary 718
Hughs, Montreville 745
Hughs, Richard 128, 129
Hughs, Sophia 268
Hughs, William 717
Hughs, Wm. 259
Hughy, Jane 126
Huhl, Louisa 712
Huhn, John 634
Huhn, Joseph 125
Huit, Deborah 109
Huit, Elisha 109
Huit, Elizabeth 109
Huit, Jefferson 109
Huit, John 109
Huit, Levi 109
Huit, Mary 109
Huit, Nathan 109
Huit, Nathaniel 109
Huit, Smith 109
Huit, William 635
Hulbert, Abigail 718
Hulbert, Hiram 635
Hulce, John 41
Huling, William 666
Hulings, Mary 38
Hulit, Sarah 519

Hull, Almira 12
Hull, Ann 508
Hull, Benjamin 342, 363
Hull, Catherine 363
Hull, Charles 279
Hull, Daniel 342, 362, 363
Hull, David 44
Hull, Ebenezer 105
Hull, Elizabeth 363, 737
Hull, Esther 449
Hull, Ezekiel 488
Hull, Hannah 342, 363
Hull, Harriet 84
Hull, Henry 89
Hull, Isaac 508, 513
Hull, Jacob 363, 481
Hull, Joel 342
Hull, John 258, 259, 260, 263, 292, 350, 363, 500
Hull, Leicester 78
Hull, Mary Ann 496
Hull, Nabby 78
Hull, Nancy 65
Hull, Nathan 283
Hull, Nathaniel 65
Hull, Polly 83
Hull, Rebecca 342, 508
Hull, Reuel S. 342
Hull, Robert M. 686, 687
Hull, Sally 12
Hull, Samuel 363
Hull, Sarah 281
Hull, Seth 449
Hull, W. 510
Hull, William 20, 86, 509, 510
Hull, Wm. 78, 510
Hulleraff, Gratry 715
Hullister, Jeremiah 154
Hulse, Henry 586
Hulse, James R. 384
Hulse, Joseph 590
Hulse, Mariah 280
Hulsly, Thomas 552
Humbarger, Adam 364
Humbarger, Benjamin 364
Humbarger, Catherine 364
Humbarger, Hannah 364
Humbarger, Henry 364
Humbarger, Jacob 364
Humbarger, John 357, 361, 364
Humbarger, Margaret 364
Humbarger, Mary 364
Humbarger, Peter 364
Humbarger, Rebecca 364
Humbarger, Susanna 364
Humberger, Peter 354
Humbert, Lewis 125, 148
Humble, Casear 52
Humble, Harriet 58
Hume, A. A. 58, 63
Hume, John 489
Hume, Mary E. 580
Hume, Robert 55
Humel, Susana 565
Humerichouse, Sarah 570

Humes, Isaac 689
Hummel, David 174
Hummel, Jacob 360, 729
Hummel, John 360
Humphrey, Benj. 353
Humphrey, Benjamin 364
Humphrey, Benjamin (Jr.) 364
Humphrey, Benjamin A. 363
Humphrey, Betty 364
Humphrey, David 364
Humphrey, Eliza 71
Humphrey, Elizabeth 458
Humphrey, Maria 31
Humphrey, Orson J. 33
Humphrey, Royal 47
Humphrey, Wm. 78
Humphreys, Elizabeth 12
Humphreys, Isaac 732
Humphreys, Jacob 12
Humphreys, Sarah 691
Humphreys, Thomas 691
Humphries, Andrew J. 2
Humphries, Augustus W. 2
Humphries, Eliza A. 2
Humphries, Elizabeth 2
Humphries, Lucilda 2
Humpnrey, Wm. 91
Humy, Joseph 608
Hundsucker, Samuel 366
Hunmell, Charles 283
Hunphrey, Gabriel 508
Hunphrey, Henry 508
Hunphrey, John 508
Hunphrey, Morris 508
Hunphrey, Thomas 508
Hunphrey, William 508
Hunphry, Elizabeth 508
Hunphry, Rachel 508
Hunphry, Sally 508
Hunt, Aaron 649
Hunt, Ann 295
Hunt, Byron 535
Hunt, Dora 535
Hunt, Doran T. 549
Hunt, Eleazer 16, 25
Hunt, Enoch 544
Hunt, Enoch S. 549
Hunt, George W. 544
Hunt, Harley E. 535
Hunt, Ira 544
Hunt, Isaac 659
Hunt, John 267, 273, 274, 649
Hunt, John (Rev.) 269
Hunt, Klune 335
Hunt, Margaret 280
Hunt, Martha 649
Hunt, Mary 535, 666
Hunt, P. 535
Hunt, Rachael 667
Hunt, Rebecca 369
Hunt, Reuben 13
Hunt, Samuel 434
Hunt, Wm. 477
Hunter, Annie 113
Hunter, Catherine 393, 434

Hunter, Cyrus 751
Hunter, Cyrus Robinson 751
Hunter, David 434
Hunter, Elizabeth 78, 659, 744
Hunter, George Henry 765
Hunter, Henry 260
Hunter, Ione 434
Hunter, James 271, 291
Hunter, John 13, 393, 434
Hunter, John J. 497
Hunter, John K. 600
Hunter, Joseph 469, 471, 480, 482, 483, 486, 745
Hunter, Julian 82
Hunter, Margaret 469, 696
Hunter, Maria 434
Hunter, Mary 408, 660, 744, 751
Hunter, Mary Jane 751
Hunter, Peggy 659
Hunter, Philander 765
Hunter, Robert 109, 434
Hunter, Samuel B. 696
Hunter, Stephen 765
Hunter, Thomas 120
Hunter, William 13, 520
Hunter, William Addison 751
Hunter, Wm. 57, 109
Huntington, E. 764
Huntington, Elijah 763
Huntington, William H. 544
Huntley, Sidney 34
Huntsman, Catharine 440, 442, 443, 544
Huntsman, James 442, 443
Huntsman, Jonathan 440, 442
Huntsman, Margaret 442
Huntsman, Mark E. 711
Huntsman, Mary 313
Huntsman, Samuel 443
Hupp, Daniel 312
Hupp, Daniel (Jr.) 312
Hupp, Eloner 312
Hupp, Emmanuel 173
Hupp, Eveline 312
Hupp, Henry 179
Hupp, Jackson 312
Hupp, John 86, 163, 173, 312
Hupp, Lucinda 312
Hupp, Margaret 312
Hupp, Mary 173
Hupp, Mary Ann 312
Hupp, Nancy 312
Hupp, Samuel 312
Hupp, Sarah 173, 312
Hupp, Silas 312
Hupp, Susan 163
Hurd, Cordelia Jane 336
Hurd, Emily 31
Hurd, Horace 29

Hurd, Jno. 169
Hurd, John 152
Hurd, Robert 227
Hurd, Samuel 172, 174
Hurd, Sarah 152
Hurdle, Mary Catharine 403
Hurdle, R. 403
Hurin, Ann 642
Hurin, Benjamin A. 642
Hurin, Berthia 642
Hurin, Bethiel 642
Hurin, Experience 642
Hurin, Hannah 642
Hurin, Otherie 642
Hurin, Phebe 642
Hurin, Rebecca 642
Hurin, Seth 642
Hurin, Silas 638
Hurin, Thallia 642
Hurlbut, Lydia 723
Hurley, Eleanor 126
Hurley, Leven 659
Hurley, Mary 552
Hurley, Thomas 544, 552
Hurley, Zadock 659
Hurlin, Elizabeth 100
Hurly, Cornelius 125
Hurly, Henry 125
Hurly, Jane 124
Hurly, Julian 336
Hurly, Rebecca 126
Hurly, Sally 127
Hurst, Abraham 473
Hurst, Cath. 405
Hurst, Drewey 544
Hurst, Geo. W. 405
Hurst, Joseph 396, 681, 684, 688
Hurst, Mary 335
Hurst, Sophia O. 405
Hurst, Thomas 489
Hurt, Sally 464
Hurtt, William 472
Huse, Avon 294
Huse, Polly 501
Hush, Peter 340
Hushan, Nancy 551
Husher, George 471
Hushor, Samuel 469, 470
Huss, Nancy 529
Hussa, Margery 84
Hussey, Lucy 83
Hussey, Mary 658
Hussey, William 106
Hust, Elizabeth 488
Husten, Levicy 693
Hustler, George 148
Hustler, Simon 148
Huston, Andrew 331, 394, 395
Huston, Archibald 364
Huston, Catharine 568
Huston, Christopher 374
Huston, David 193, 216, 229
Huston, Eli 644, 659
Huston, Elizabeth 468, 509

Huston, Ellener 364
Huston, Hannah 364
Huston, Henry 482, 613
Huston, James 464, 676
Huston, Jane 364
Huston, John 186, 187, 364, 384, 434
Huston, Joseph 125
Huston, Joseph C. 292
Huston, Joseph P. 290
Huston, Julia 511
Huston, Luther B. 216
Huston, Marjory 118
Huston, Mary 119, 364, 517, 567, 577
Huston, Middleton 509
Huston, Paul 470, 480, 482
Huston, Robert 364, 553
Huston, Robert E. 376
Huston, Sarah 456
Huston, Sarrah E. 613
Huston, Susan 369
Huston, William 120
Huston, Wm. 503
Huston, Wm. Riley 434
Hustone, Nancy 458
Hut, Elizabeth 382
Hut, Mary 522
Hutchen, David W. 58
Hutchen, Louisa 58
Hutchens, Bartlett 314
Hutchens, Bradbury 265
Hutchens, Daniel 195, 265
Hutchens, Jesse 195
Hutchens, Jonathan 125
Hutchens, Joseph 268, 314
Hutchens, Joseph (Sr.) 269
Hutchens, Stephen 260
Hutchenson, James 268
Hutcher, James 354
Hutcheson, James 741
Hutcheson, John Q. 738, 742
Hutcheson, Wm. 268
Hutchin, John 58
Hutchins, A. 328
Hutchins, Albert 328
Hutchins, Alexander 83
Hutchins, Alice 144
Hutchins, Benjamin 200
Hutchins, Cyrus 78
Hutchins, Dessie F. 328
Hutchins, George 337
Hutchins, Hollis 261, 265
Hutchins, James 366
Hutchins, Jefferson 314
Hutchins, Jemina 328
Hutchins, Joseph 314
Hutchins, Joshua 333
Hutchins, Lucena 314
Hutchins, M. 328
Hutchins, Mary 351
Hutchins, Polly 458
Hutchins, Roxalina 303

Hutchinson, David 371
Hutchinson, Elizabeth 371
Hutchinson, Hezekiah 178
Hutchinson, James R. 166, 174
Hutchinson, Jesse 647
Hutchinson, Joel 647
Hutchinson, John 371, 758
Hutchinson, Jonathan 659
Hutchinson, Joseph 659
Hutchinson, Patrick 59
Hutchinson, R. J. 668
Hutchinson, Samuel 177
Hutchinson, Sarah H. 758
Hutchinson, Thomas 714
Hutchison, Joseph 41
Hutchison, Laura 589
Hutchison, Robert M. 47
Hutingter, Christian 464
Hutson, Austin 54
Hutson, Frances 422
Hutson, Jane 54
Hutson, John 54
Hutson, John K. 47
Hutson, Skinner 54
Hutt, Adel Heit 104
Hutt, Ludwick 104
Hutt, William 471, 473, 482
Hutt, William S. 482
Hutt, Wm. 477, 478, 485
Hutton, Hannah 559
Hutton, Maranda 306
Hutton, Middleton 509
Hutton, Nancy 515
Hutton, William 559
Hutts, Sarah 560
Huttsell, John W. 139
Hyate, John 464
Hyate, Joseph 468
Hyatt, Ezekiel 259
Hyatt, Polley 386
Hyatt, Simon 65
Hyde, Christiana A. 64
Hyde, William 36
Hyer, Abraham 194
Hyer, Absalom 194
Hyer, Belinda 194
Hyer, David 194
Hyer, Isaac 194
Hyer, Moses 194
Hyer, Nancy 194
Hyer, Solomon 194
Hyette, Ezekiel 258
Hykes, W. D. (Rev.) 221
Hymes, George 566
Hymes, Sarah 568
Hymrod, Aaron 66
Hymrod, Aaron R. 66, 67
Hymrod, George 66
Hymrod, Hester 66
Hyre, Susannah 467
Hyrod, Aaron R. 66
Hysel, Boswell 78
Hysel, Owen 78
Hysell, Christiana 78
Hysell, Elizabeth 79

Hysell, James B. 86
Hysell, John C. 78
Hysell, Mary 83
Hysell, Robert 83
Hysell, Sally 93
Hyser, Charles 309
Hyser, Henry 680
Hysle, Smith 78
Hyter, Margaret 519

--- I ---

Iams, Isaac 303
Iams, Joseph Henry
    Harrison 366
Icasnogh, Abraham 428
Ice, Elizabeth 152
Ice, Frederick 152
Iddings, Benjamin 136,
    210, 217
Iddings, Elizabeth 144
Iddings, Hannah 136, 139
Iddings, James P. 144
Iddings, Joseph 134, 136
Iddings, Martha H. 144
Iddings, Mary 136
Iddings, Milley 136
Iddings, Phebe 136
Iddings, Pheby 118
Iddings, Ruth 136
Iddings, Sarah 139
Iddings, Susan M. 144
Iddings, Talbert 136
Iddings, Talbott 136
Idle, Elizabeth 11
Iiams, William 544
Ijams, Isaac H. 366
Ijams, John H. 375
Ike, Paul 549
Ike, Samuel 549
Ike, Sophia 550
Ike, William 544
Iles, David 352
Iliams, Caroline
    Elizabeth 366
Iliams, Comfort 366
Iliams, Elizabeth 366
Iliams, F. R. 366
Iliams, Isaac H. 366
Iliams, Sarah 366
Iliams, Wm. E. 366
Ilief, Fredrick 370
Ilief, Mary 370
Iliff, Isaac H. 366
Iliff, John 364
Iliff, Joseph 489
Iliff, Thos. 356
Illige, George Ph. 174
Ilree, Wm. M. 292
Iltere, Mairum 109
Imberson, James 384
Imbush, John Gerard 544
Imlay, Caleb 125
Imlay, Geo. T. 434
Imlay, Lydia Ann 434
Immel, John 489
Immill, Isaih 608

Impson, Ann 591
Impson, Elizabeth 590
Impson, Huldah 592
Impson, Malinay 590
Impson, Meranda 590
Indacut, Polly 118
Ingals, Fanny 713
Ingals, Olive 77
Ingersol, Elizabeth 434
Ingersol, Ezra 434
Ingersol, Hannah 434
Ingersol, Jane 434
Ingersol, Nancy Ann 434
Ingersoll, James 29
Ingle, Abraham 125, 139
Ingle, David 139, 356
Ingle, Edith 356
Ingle, Isaac 526
Ingle, John 117
Ingle, Lydia 139
Ingle, Michael 120
Ingle, Peter 573
Ingle, Philip 125
Ingle, Sally 139
Ingles, Anson 83
Ingles, Boon 232
Ingles, Elizabeth 232
Ingles, George 78
Ingles, James 78
Ingmand, E. 739
Ingmand, Edmund 739
Ingols, George 83
Ingraham, Mason 520
Ingraham, Wrathey 179
Ingram, H. 506
Ingram, Mary 153
Ingram, Rathey 153
Ingram, Thomas 739
Inman, Benjamin 430
Inman, Brazilla 430
Inman, David 337
Inman, Elizabeth 74
Inman, George 125
Inman, Jacob 430
Inman, Job 430
Inman, Joseph 430
Inman, Lorena 124
Inman, Noah 144
Inman, Samuel 430
Inman, Theodore 336
Inman, William 144
Inmon, Asa 135
Inmon, Eli 125
Innes, Francis 184
Innes, Nathaniel 184
Insco, James 198
Insco, Rebecca 198
Inskip, Annamaria 25
Inskip, Eliza 11
Inskip, Job 13, 25
Inskip, John 17, 24
Inskip, Levi 17
Inskip, Lot 17, 25
Inskip, Margaretann 25
Inskip, Mary 11
Inskip, Matilda 13
Inskip, Nancy Star 13
Inyard, Benjamin 672
Iredick, Andrew 457

Ireland, Robert 608
Ireland, Samuel 430
Ireland, Thomas 686
Irick, Andrew 419
Irick, David 419
Irick, Joseph 419
Irish, Nathan 33
Irvin, Nancy 593
Irvin, Sally 747
Irvin, Susan 608
Irvin, Thomas 505
Irvin, Wm. 273
Irvine, Nancy 583
Irwin, Abigail 434
Irwin, Andrew 202
Irwin, Andrew Barr 202
Irwin, Benjamin 83
Irwin, Betsy 434
Irwin, Catherine 155
Irwin, Catherine P. 202
Irwin, Cynthia 587
Irwin, David 125
Irwin, Eliza 216
Irwin, Eliza B. 582
Irwin, Elizabeth 216,
    501, 596
Irwin, Francis 544
Irwin, George 8
Irwin, Isaac 216
Irwin, James 202, 549
Irwin, James P. 590
Irwin, John 50, 78, 590
Irwin, John A. 216
Irwin, John B. 434
Irwin, Martha 216
Irwin, Mary 84, 591
Irwin, Mary Ellen 8
Irwin, Mary Jane 202,
    216
Irwin, Minerva 216
Irwin, Nathaniel 22
Irwin, Robert 686
Irwin, Samuel 216
Irwin, Thomas 13, 640,
    649, 650
Irwin, William 8, 155,
    216
Irwine, Elizabeth 84
Irwing, Jane 83
Isenagle, John 566
Isenhart, C. 97
Isenhart, Eliza 97
Isenhart, Elizabeth 97
Isenhart, Henry 97
Isenhart, Jac. 97
Isenhart, Jacob 97
Isenhart, Jane 97
Isenogle, David 566
Isham, George I. 642
Isham, Russell 714
Ishmael, Elizabeth 506
Iston, Jene 462, 465
Istone, Jasper 489
Itzen, Elizabeth 560
Itzen, Frances 560
Itzen, Philip 560
Itzken, Ann Mareah 560
Itzken, Christopher 560
Itzken, Elizabeth 567

Itzken, John 560
Itzken, Lewis 560
Itzken, Mary 565
Itzken, Philip 560
Itzken, Phillip 560
Itzken, William 560
Itzkin, Anna Mariah 571
Itzkin, Lewis 573
Iumister, Artimetia 520
Ivelt, Nicholas 389
Iwicolulc, I. 616
Iwicolulc, Isaac N. 616
Iwicolulc, R. 616
Izor, Daniel 209
Izor, Elizabeth 209
Izor, Joshua D. 209
Izor, Lewis 209
Izor, Margaret 209
Izor, Mariah 209

--- J ---

Jack, James 649, 670
Jack, John 649
Jack, John J. 651
Jack, John T. 651, 670
Jack, Mary 660
Jack, Robert L. 651
Jackson, Abner 630
Jackson, Albert M. 328
Jackson, Alexander 120
Jackson, Amanda 535
Jackson, Andrew 700
Jackson, Andrew J. 47
Jackson, Ann 700
Jackson, Annie Jos. 411
Jackson, B. 535
Jackson, Belinda A. 434
Jackson, Betsey 453
Jackson, Catherine 540
Jackson, Cathrin 80
Jackson, Chloe 28
Jackson, Clarinda Jane 114
Jackson, Clinton W. 700
Jackson, Cora M. 328
Jackson, Daniel 83
Jackson, Delila 548
Jackson, E. 535
Jackson, Edward 464
Jackson, Elizabeth 78, 345
Jackson, Elizabeth H. 434
Jackson, Ella Blanche 700
Jackson, Geo. 357
Jackson, George 366
Jackson, Giles 120, 182
Jackson, H. L. 540
Jackson, Hanah 453
Jackson, Hannah 498
Jackson, Henry 120, 540, 736
Jackson, Henry L. 540
Jackson, J. J. 345
Jackson, Jacob 294

Jackson, James 41, 125, 400, 434, 513
Jackson, Jane 164
Jackson, Jesse 163, 164
Jackson, John 47, 113, 384
Jackson, John C. 295
Jackson, John George 284
Jackson, John J. 363, 366
Jackson, Lucinda 520
Jackson, Mahala 535
Jackson, Martha 434, 455
Jackson, Mary 366, 391, 400, 548, 591, 714
Jackson, Mary Ann 544
Jackson, Morris W. 549
Jackson, Nancy 44, 434, 515
Jackson, Peter 391
Jackson, Pleasant 120
Jackson, Polly 120
Jackson, Rachel 120
Jackson, Richard 535
Jackson, Robt. 270, 274
Jackson, Ruth 540
Jackson, S. H. 345
Jackson, Sally 117
Jackson, Saml. D. 477
Jackson, Samuel 472, 483
Jackson, Sarah 366, 455
Jackson, Sarah I. 535
Jackson, Stephen O. 328
Jackson, Thomas 44, 303, 535
Jackson, Truman 30
Jackson, Uriah 700
Jackson, William 182, 366, 400
Jackson, William C. 139
Jackson, Wm. J. 411
Jackson, Zenobin 700
Jacky, Philip 754
Jacob, Nancy 180
Jacob, Zachariah 180
Jacobs, Annie M. 113
Jacobs, Cad. W. 133
Jacobs, Cadwalder 125
Jacobs, Elizabeth 23, 123, 575
Jacobs, Jacob 260, 513
Jacobs, Jasper 393
Jacobs, Jehu 690
Jacobs, John 13, 513
Jacobs, Margaret 133
Jacobs, Mark 133
Jacobs, Milly 467
Jacobs, Patty 514
Jacobs, Sally 117
Jacobs, Thomas K. 622
Jacobs, Wm. 264
Jajor, Jonathan 601
Jakeway, David 580
James, --- 470, 471, 472, 473
James, Aaron 648
James, Ann 671
James, Anne 713
James, Barton 352

James, Charlotte 279
James, Cordelia 30
James, Cynthia 408
James, Danl. 407
James, David 290, 671
James, Eliza 290
James, Elizabeth 643
James, Griffith 290
James, Hannah 290, 714
James, Harriet 337
James, Henry 489
James, Isaac 13, 175, 263, 265, 266, 267, 290
James, Isaac E. 65
James, Jane 671
James, Jno. 407
James, John 290, 355, 407, 671
James, Jonathan 659, 671
James, Joseph 359, 642
James, Lena 14
James, Levi 391
James, Luke 302
James, Mary 464
James, Mary Ann 290
James, Nancy 290, 657
James, Nicholas 476, 477, 478, 482
James, Rachel 671
James, Richard 671
James, Rufus 290
James, S. 407
James, Samuel 643, 648, 682
James, Sarah 407, 671
James, Saran 643
James, Susan 643
James, Thomas 13, 24, 27, 290, 303, 457, 475, 478, 479, 481, 485, 566
James, Thos. 477
James, Westly 643
James, William 642, 648, 671
Jameson, Joseph B. 33
Jameson, Nancy S. 737
Jameson, Stephen M. 737
Jameson, Susan 608
Jamieson, Charles 484
Jamieson, Wm. 484
Jamison, Betsy 509
Jamison, Charles 471, 472
Jamison, George 452
Jamison, Jacob 464
Jamison, John 292
Jamison, John G. 417
Jamison, Joseph 686
Jamison, Polly 123
Jamison, Rebecca Jane 737
Jamison, Rodney Carr 737
Jamison, Samuel 489
Jamison, Sarah 455
Jamison, Stephen M. 737
Jamison, Stephen Rush 737

Jamison, William 489
Janes, Abigail 163
Janes, Abraham 167
Janes, Cisne 167
Janes, Cornelius N. 169
Janes, Isaac 163, 168, 169
Janes, James 166, 167
Janes, Joseph 166, 167, 169
Janes, Margaret 166, 167, 169
Janes, Mary 167
Janes, R. B. 751
Janes, Samuel 167
Janes, Susanna 166
Janes, Wm. 260
Janie, George 613
Janie, Hanah 613
Janie, Rachel 613
Janney, Carter 493
Janney, Joseph 493
January, Catharine 3
January, Elizabeth 3
January, Houston 3
January, James 3
January, Martha 3
January, Mary 3
January, Nesbit 3
Janye, Lydia 514
Jaqua, Darius 418
Jaqua, Joshua 418
Jaque, Alford 608
Jaques, David 445
Jaques, Jeremiah 445
Jaques, Jesse 445
Jaques, John 445
Jaques, Margaret 445
Jaques, Nancy 445
Jaques, Samuel 445
Jaques, Sanford 445
Jaques, Warren 445
Jaquith, Abigail Rebecca 70
Jaquith, Charles Wesley 70
Jaquith, Josiah 70
Jaquith, Josiah (Jr.) 70
Jaquith, Lucy 70
Jaquith, Miranda 70
Jaquith, Sibil 70
Jaquith, Thomas 70
Jaquith, William Henry 70
Jarrard, Phebe C. 583
Jarvis, Andrew 307
Jarvis, Bazel 306
Jarvis, Elizabeth 174, 180, 352
Jarvis, Ezekiel 307
Jarvis, James 352
Jarvis, James W. 306
Jarvis, Jesse 352
Jarvis, John 306
Jarvis, John L. 306
Jarvis, Joseph A. 306
Jarvis, Maranda 306
Jarvis, Mary 306, 307, 352

Jarvis, Meed 306
Jarvis, Miriam 306, 307
Jarvis, Moses 352
Jarvis, Nancy 306
Jarvis, Philip 306, 307, 352
Jarvis, Rebecca 306, 352
Jarvis, Ruth A. 306, 307
Jarvis, Sarah 306, 352
Jarvis, Thomas 352
Jarvis, William 174, 180, 306, 307, 352
Jarvis, Wm. V. 307
Jasper, Phebe 82
Jay, Abigail 131
Jay, Anna 131
Jay, Charity 144
Jay, Charles 117, 147
Jay, Charlotte 127
Jay, David 131, 669
Jay, Denny 117, 204
Jay, Elijah 131
Jay, Elisha 144
Jay, Eliza Ann 147
Jay, Elizabeth 92, 127, 131
Jay, George 285
Jay, Insco 187
Jay, James 131
Jay, Jane 144
Jay, Joanna 187
Jay, John 131, 698, 700
Jay, Jonathan K. 363
Jay, L. 698
Jay, Layton 131, 671, 698
Jay, Lot B. 144
Jay, Lotty 131
Jay, Lydia 700
Jay, Martha 144
Jay, Martha C. 144
Jay, Mary 131, 144
Jay, Patience 131
Jay, Rebecca 144, 698, 699
Jay, Stephen 223
Jay, Tabitha 116
Jay, Tamer 121
Jay, Thomas 139, 187
Jay, Walter D. 134
Jay, William 125, 131, 659, 660
Jayne, Henry 732
Jayne, Nelson 732
Jayne, Robert F. 732
Jeans, Isaac 464
Jedkins, Joel 666
Jee, Caty 383
Jefferies, James 291
Jefferies, Joseph 481, 482
Jefferies, Sarah 291
Jefferies, W. 291
Jeffers, Barbara 22
Jeffers, George 666
Jeffers, Margaret 548
Jeffers, Mary 166
Jeffers, Moses 166
Jefferson, Henry 489

Jefferson, John 489
Jeffery, Eleanor 682
Jeffery, Francis 682, 693
Jeffery, Jacob 682
Jeffery, James 682
Jeffery, Mary 682
Jeffery, Oliver 318
Jeffery, Sarah 693
Jeffery, William 682
Jeffirs, Prudence 664
Jeffories, Henry 507
Jeffres, Hannah 658
Jeffreth, William 117
Jeffrey, Amy Ann 319, 321
Jeffrey, Charlotte 319, 321
Jeffrey, Gilbert 318, 319, 321
Jeffrey, Gilbert L. 321, 752
Jeffrey, Hannah 319
Jeffrey, Oliver 319
Jeffrey, Oliver (Sr.) 321
Jeffrey, Oliver T. 321, 336
Jeffrey, Robert F. 278
Jeffrey, Sylvester 319
Jeffrey, Sylvester Wilson 321
Jeffreys, Joseph 464
Jeffries, Alexander 139
Jeffries, Elias 156
Jeffries, Hannah 139, 401
Jeffries, James 288, 434
Jeffries, James J. C. 401
Jeffries, Jane 119
Jeffries, Jones 139
Jeffries, Joseph 472
Jeffries, Juliet 401
Jeffries, Polly 116
Jeffries, Sally 119
Jeffries, Sarah J. 139
Jellison, Samuel 413
Jellison, Sarah 414
Jemim, Jacob 556
Jeming, Lot 564
Jemison, Eliza 497
Jemison, George 41
Jencks, Mary 85
Jencks, Rebecca Carter 86
Jencks, Semilla 79
Jenes, Frederick 452
Jenes, Mary 403
Jenison, Charles V. 756
Jenison, Francis 756
Jenison, George 756
Jenison, Harriett 756
Jenison, Jonathan H. 756
Jenison, Martha 756
Jenison, Mary 756
Jenison, Nathaniel 756
Jenison, Olive 756
Jenison, Ralph 756

Jenison, Sally 756
Jenkens, Mary 131
Jenkens, William 131
Jenkins, Alex 478
Jenkins, Alexander 483
Jenkins, Amos 130, 132, 135, 147
Jenkins, Anderson 527
Jenkins, Benj. 527
Jenkins, Benjamin 527
Jenkins, Cary S. 701
Jenkins, David 130, 132, 133, 208
Jenkins, David (Jr.) 133, 135
Jenkins, Davis 147
Jenkins, Eda J. 281
Jenkins, Elizabeth 125, 130, 135
Jenkins, Ely 132, 135
Jenkins, Enoch 130, 132
Jenkins, Hannah 116, 135, 139
Jenkins, Harriott 123
Jenkins, Henry 430
Jenkins, Isaac 132
Jenkins, Isachac 132
Jenkins, Issacher 117
Jenkins, J. N. 327
Jenkins, James 753
Jenkins, Jas. H. 430
Jenkins, Jesse 130, 132, 135, 139
Jenkins, John 527, 580
Jenkins, Joseph 132
Jenkins, Margaret 527
Jenkins, Mary 130, 131
Jenkins, Mary Amanda 337
Jenkins, Mary Jane 90
Jenkins, Nancy 712
Jenkins, Patty 117
Jenkins, Phineas 132, 133
Jenkins, Phinehos 135
Jenkins, Phinias 147
Jenkins, R. 327
Jenkins, Richard 260
Jenkins, Robert 132
Jenkins, Rosanna 135
Jenkins, Samuel 132
Jenkins, Tena 196
Jenkins, Thomas 130, 132, 262, 263, 269
Jenkins, Tryphania Y. 279
Jenkins, William 130, 131, 132, 384
Jenkins, Wm. 469
Jenkinson, J. 135
Jenkinson, Martha 280
Jenks, John 476
Jennings, Amos 566
Jennings, Catherine 637
Jennings, Cornelius 25
Jennings, Cyrenius 655
Jennings, David 169, 645, 674
Jennings, Drusilla 569
Jennings, Elizabeth Jane 434

Jennings, Enos 637
Jennings, Enox 637
Jennings, Henry 271
Jennings, Isaac 25
Jennings, Jacob 555
Jennings, Joana 25
Jennings, John 677
Jennings, John P. 434
Jennings, Levi (Sr.) 209
Jennings, Lewis 573
Jennings, Mary 271, 565, 569
Jennings, Mary F. 434
Jennings, Minerva 625
Jennings, Nathan 266, 275
Jennings, Sarah 569, 682
Jennings, Sarah M. 434
Jennings, Zebulon 732
Jennison, James 751
Jens, Katharine M. 36
Jentry, Ephraim 125
Jerome, J. H. 756
Jerome, Jonathan H. 756, 762
Jerome, William 144
Jerrome, William 120
Jessop, Charles 676
Jessop, Daniel 676
Jessop, Jonathan 676
Jessop, Patience 676
Jessop, Thomas 676
Jessop, William 676
Jester, John 125
Jester, Rachael 123
Jett, Lucina 708
Jett, Owen 708
Jett, Thomas 708
Jett, Thos. (Jr.) 732
Jewel, G. 613
Jewel, George 613
Jewel, Ida M. 613
Jewel, M. 613
Jewell, John 583
Jewell, Walter 23
Jimmeson, Andrew 573
Jininger, John 193
Jinings, Belly 566
Jinkans, Phineas 117
Jinnings, Elenor 561
Jinnings, Hetebel 561
Jinnings, Mary 561
Jinnings, Simeon 561
Jinnings, Washington 561
Joachim, Barbara 91
Joachim, Henry 87
Joat, Jane 451
Jocky, Philip 754
John, Abraham 208
John, Anna 185
John, Benjamin 208
John, Bouch 185
John, Catharine 208
John, Daniel 185
John, David 185
John, Eleanor 185
John, Elizabeth 208
John, Isaac 689
John, Jesse 289

John, Joseph B. 208
John, Joseph R. 147, 148
John, Mary 185, 208
John, Powell 185
John, Sally 185
John, Samuel 185
John, Sarah 121
John, Thos. 233
John, William 208
Johns, Hannah 114
Johns, Jacob W. 602, 626
Johns, John 120
Johns, Nancy 664
Johns, William A. 106
Johnson, --- 750
Johnson, Aaron 367
Johnson, Aaron M. 634
Johnson, Abigail 119
Johnson, Abner 38
Johnson, Abraham 47, 248
Johnson, Adison 8
Johnson, Alexander 336, 434
Johnson, Almira 76
Johnson, Amos 566
Johnson, Amy Jane 212
Johnson, Andrew 256
Johnson, Anna 33
Johnson, Anne 681
Johnson, Aretemus 78
Johnson, Baley 47
Johnson, Benj. 357
Johnson, Benjamin 258, 622, 714
Johnson, Caroline 212
Johnson, Catharine 348, 591
Johnson, Charles 470, 681
Johnson, Cornelia 144
Johnson, David 13, 78, 187, 303, 613, 628, 636, 648
Johnson, Davis 626
Johnson, Dennis C. 212
Johnson, E. 611
Johnson, Edward 505
Johnson, Edwd. 26
Johnson, Eleanor 8, 628
Johnson, Eliza 434, 608
Johnson, Elizabeth 8, 139, 256, 345, 619, 634
Johnson, Enoch 41
Johnson, Ephraim 256
Johnson, Esther 629
Johnson, Fanny 416, 716
Johnson, Frances 392
Johnson, Geo. 273, 292
Johnson, Geo. Ferguson 434
Johnson, George 273, 726, 745
Johnson, George W. 248, 617
Johnson, Giles 120
Johnson, Grifn. 613
Johnson, Guy 38
Johnson, Henrietta 212

Johnson, Hester 357
Johnson, Hetty Ann 8
Johnson, Irene 31
Johnson, Isaac 8, 83, 502
Johnson, Isabelle 345
Johnson, Isadoria 611
Johnson, J. F. 611
Johnson, J. H. 634
Johnson, Jacob 502
Johnson, Jacob H. 634
Johnson, James 30, 139, 189, 345, 367, 416, 464, 573, 634, 638, 660, 726, 727
Johnson, James F. 611
Johnson, Jamima 613
Johnson, Jamina 613
Johnson, Jane 256, 502
Johnson, Jas. 248
Johnson, Jeremiah 41
Johnson, Jesse 47
Johnson, Joel M. 38
Johnson, John 13, 78, 187, 202, 248, 256, 273, 470, 628, 634, 638, 648, 660
Johnson, John (Rev.) 594
Johnson, John W. 1, 8, 271
Johnson, Joseph 195, 212, 372, 395, 406, 567, 599, 626, 684, 717
Johnson, Joseph C. 684
Johnson, Joshua 86, 91
Johnson, Jotham 586
Johnson, Julia 31
Johnson, Julius 622
Johnson, Leonard 30
Johnson, Letcher 242
Johnson, Levi 497, 717
Johnson, Levina 406
Johnson, Lucinda 172, 607
Johnson, Lydia 765
Johnson, Margaret 638, 698, 700
Johnson, Margaret Ann 407
Johnson, Margarete 452
Johnson, Martha 139, 572
Johnson, Mary 5, 8, 11, 406, 606, 659
Johnson, Mary Ann 345
Johnson, Mary E. 212
Johnson, Mary F. 606
Johnson, Matilda 637
Johnson, Maxwell 434
Johnson, Michael H. 669
Johnson, Nancy 634
Johnson, Nancy M. 617
Johnson, Nancy Taylor 717
Johnson, Obediah 55
Johnson, Orlistis R. 700
Johnson, Parley B. 271
Johnson, Perley B. 268, 269

Johnson, Permela 589
Johnson, Peter 556
Johnson, Phinehas M. 30
Johnson, Polly 187
Johnson, Rachel 342, 634
Johnson, Rebecca 79, 571, 634
Johnson, Richd. 406
Johnson, Robert 8, 367, 392, 700
Johnson, Robert T. 700
Johnson, Sally 121
Johnson, Samuel 30
Johnson, Sara 345
Johnson, Sara Jane 345
Johnson, Sarah 4, 361, 363, 372, 577
Johnson, Sarah Craft 700
Johnson, Simon 338
Johnson, Stephen 586
Johnson, Susan 82
Johnson, T. W. 48
Johnson, Thomas 83, 632
Johnson, Thomas B. 48
Johnson, Thomas F. 434
Johnson, Thos. 619
Johnson, Thos. Maxwell 434
Johnson, Valentine 727
Johnson, William 125, 172, 248, 470, 567
Johnson, William S. 544
Johnson, Willis H. 613
Johnson, Willson D. 634
Johnson, Wm. 362, 407
Johnson, Wm. C. 265, 266
Johnson, Wm. Henry Harrison 434
Johnson, Wm. T. 355
Johnston, A. W. 331
Johnston, Abner 131
Johnston, Agness 385
Johnston, Alvira A. 94
Johnston, Amasa 449
Johnston, Andrew 56, 120
Johnston, Ann 154
Johnston, Anna 154
Johnston, Anne 512
Johnston, Archibald 154
Johnston, Augustus T. 449
Johnston, Benjamin 660
Johnston, Britain 553
Johnston, Britan 553
Johnston, C. E. 331
Johnston, Caroline 139
Johnston, Caroline G. 167
Johnston, Catharine E. 551
Johnston, Charles 484, 485
Johnston, Charles C. 94
Johnston, Charles F. 666
Johnston, Charlotte 107
Johnston, Daniel 443, 449
Johnston, Daniel A. 139
Johnston, David 139, 363

Johnston, Deborah 544
Johnston, Drusilla 553
Johnston, Eleanor 8
Johnston, Elijah 154
Johnston, Eliza 139, 449
Johnston, Elizabeth 363, 586, 717, 740
Johnston, Ellen 15
Johnston, Ely 553
Johnston, Ephraim 256
Johnston, Esther 174
Johnston, F. W. 139
Johnston, G. M. 94
Johnston, George 672
Johnston, George W. 98
Johnston, Gratz M. 94
Johnston, Griffeth 13
Johnston, Guian 660
Johnston, Hannah 388
Johnston, Harriet 139
Johnston, Henry 56, 544, 704
Johnston, Hordah 553
Johnston, Hugh 405
Johnston, James 139, 156, 157, 161, 405, 439, 443, 452, 469, 474, 479, 493, 750
Johnston, James (Rev.) 438
Johnston, James A. 144
Johnston, James J. 144, 449
Johnston, Jane 123, 139
Johnston, Jane P. 139
Johnston, Jesse 27, 489
Johnston, John 120, 134, 139, 476, 489, 544, 549, 553
Johnston, John B. 549
Johnston, John E. 94
Johnston, Jonathan 131
Johnston, Joseph 315, 469, 478, 482
Johnston, M. I. 94
Johnston, M. J. 94
Johnston, M. S. 94
Johnston, Margaret 489, 739
Johnston, Margarett 144
Johnston, Margret 144
Johnston, Mary 12, 116, 125, 144, 455, 498, 575, 738
Johnston, Mary Ann 549
Johnston, Mary E. 94
Johnston, Mary F. 139
Johnston, Mary J. 94
Johnston, Matilda 449, 493
Johnston, Nancy 94, 117
Johnston, Patrick 489
Johnston, Peter 174
Johnston, Rachel 449, 457
Johnston, Randall 139
Johnston, Rebecca Ann 634
Johnston, Robert 439, 544, 553, 739

Johnston, Robt. E. 144
Johnston, Sally Ann 449
Johnston, Samuel 385, 449
Johnston, Samuel R. 544
Johnston, Samuel S. 449
Johnston, Sarah 118,
  125, 131
Johnston, Seth S. 139
Johnston, Simmion D. 331
Johnston, Stanton 20
Johnston, Stephen 139
Johnston, Sterling 159
Johnston, Sukey 464
Johnston, Thomas 544
Johnston, Thomas S. 449
Johnston, Valentine 296
Johnston, Vance 167
Johnston, Walter 485
Johnston, William 117,
  139, 174, 457, 470,
  480, 484, 485, 485,
  544, 549
Johnston, William A. 443
Johnston, William D. 449
Johnston, Wilson V. 331
Johnston, Wm. 139, 144,
  369, 480, 672
Johnston, Wm. E. 262
Johnston, Wm. F. W. 139
Johnston, Wm. Geo. 573
Johnstone, --- 479
Johnstone, Charles 486
Johnstone, David 472
Johnstone, James 485
Johnstone, John 471,
  472, 473
Johnstone, Jos. 477, 478
Johnstone, W. 472
Johnstone, William 484,
  486
Johnstone, Wm. 472, 477
Joliff, Peter 735
Joliff, Rebecca 735
Jolliff, Aaron 735
Jolliff, Christian 735
Jolliff, Mary 734
Jolliff, Moses 734
Jolliff, Peter 735
Jolliff, Reuban 735
Jolliff, Thomas 734
Jolly, Agnes 750
Jolly, David 489
Jolly, James 750
Jolly, Joel 590
Jolly, Mary 588, 718
Jolly, Sarah 744
Jolly, Wm. 457
Jonas, Samuel 341
Jones, Abigail 154,
  160, 170, 509
Jones, Abraham 176
Jones, Albert W. 608
Jones, Amos 63
Jones, Amos Buell 157
Jones, Ande 513
Jones, Andrew 631
Jones, Ann 413
Jones, Benjamin 117, 660
Jones, Betsey 716

Jones, Catharine 617
Jones, Catherine 334
Jones, Caty 457
Jones, Charles 83
Jones, Chloe 33
Jones, Cisner 176
Jones, Daniel 98
Jones, David 8, 128,
  147, 503, 505, 507,
  509, 732
Jones, Deborah Ann 434
Jones, E. W. 125
Jones, Ebenezer 30
Jones, Edward 321
Jones, Edwin 493
Jones, Elanor C. 139
Jones, Eleanor 521
Jones, Eleazer 41
Jones, Elenor C. 139
Jones, Elihu G. 139
Jones, Elijah 135
Jones, Elisha 132, 528
Jones, Eliza 88, 509
Jones, Elizabeth 311,
  572, 666
Jones, Elizabeth Ann 434
Jones, Ellen 401
Jones, Emma L. 617
Jones, Ephraim 160
Jones, Esther 82
Jones, Evan 608
Jones, Evan B. 600
Jones, Even 617
Jones, Even B. 600
Jones, Francis 120,
  131, 135
Jones, George 497
Jones, George O. 509
Jones, George W. 98, 430
Jones, Hanna 509
Jones, Hannah 13, 84, 280
Jones, Hardy 63
Jones, Harriet 77
Jones, Harrison 366
Jones, Heeth 505
Jones, Henry C. 672
Jones, Henry Newton 434
Jones, Huth 505
Jones, Isaac 47, 60,
  154, 154, 160, 165,
  170, 371, 594
Jones, Isaac N. 59
Jones, Isabella 139, 466
Jones, Israel 660
Jones, James 59, 311,
  385, 464, 759, 765
Jones, Jane 402
Jones, Jarred 311
Jones, Jasper 144
Jones, Jno. B. 274
Jones, John 44, 155,
  157, 163, 264, 299,
  311, 353, 366, 617,
  660, 682
Jones, John Hannah 147
Jones, John Lucas 509
Jones, Joseph 13, 63,
  117, 139, 148, 489,
  608

Jones, Keturah 401
Jones, Keziah 434
Jones, Lindley M. 139
Jones, Lucinda A. 622
Jones, M. 617
Jones, M. C. 47, 617
Jones, Macy B. 434
Jones, Martha 139, 155
Jones, Martha J. 144
Jones, Mary 14, 35, 63,
  91, 92, 120, 139,
  144, 311
Jones, Mary Ann 401, 430
Jones, Mary V. 148
Jones, Matilda 63
Jones, Matrimor Allen
  125
Jones, Miles C. 617
Jones, Morgan 155
Jones, Moses 187
Jones, Nancy 11, 63, 462
Jones, Nathan 125, 679
Jones, Oliver 125
Jones, Orphania 83
Jones, Owen 139
Jones, Patty 456
Jones, Phebe Ann 139
Jones, Philip 91
Jones, Phoebe Ann F. 148
Jones, Polly 120, 513
Jones, Prudence 139
Jones, Rachel 413, 509,
  662
Jones, Rebecca 139,
  459, 509, 714
Jones, Rebeckah 511
Jones, Robert 385
Jones, Robert F. 632
Jones, Rosanna 608
Jones, Ruth 664
Jones, Sabrah 311
Jones, Salem 139
Jones, Sally 452
Jones, Samuel 117, 135,
  176, 311, 464, 489,
  493
Jones, Samuel P. 154
Jones, Sarah 8, 29, 98,
  120, 127, 299, 458
Jones, Sarah Ann 366
Jones, Sarah B. 311
Jones, Sarah Jane 434
Jones, Seth 86
Jones, Sina 85
Jones, Stephen 187, 214
Jones, Susan 401, 430,
  631
Jones, Susanna 353, 434
Jones, Susannah 139
Jones, Thomas 63, 120,
  311, 366, 398, 464,
  717
Jones, Thomas C. 509
Jones, Wileber 413
Jones, William 41, 54,
  63, 88, 120, 660
Jones, William L. 311
Jones, William S. 98
Jones, Wm. Kendall 509

878

Jones, Wm. L. 311
Jones, Zacariah 549
Jones, Zelpha 139
Jonkey, John 212
Jonson, Mary Ann 527
Jonson, Rensellear 732
Jonson, William 8
Jonston, William 173
Jops, Sarah 521
Jordan, Abraham 266
Jordan, Elizabeth 89
Jordan, Garet 266
Jordan, Garret 262
Jordan, Henry 622
Jordan, Isaac 270
Jordan, Jacob 266, 267, 301
Jordan, John 274
Jordan, Joseph 287
Jordan, Louisa Ann 612
Jordan, S. 612
Jordan, Sarah 612
Jordan, Sarah Jane 612
Jordan, Sias 612
Jorden, Adam 303
Jorden, James 660
Joseph, Alonzo H. 150
Joseph, Annis 8
Joseph, Daniel 8
Joseph, David 8
Joseph, Eva Jane 8
Joseph, H. J. 150
Joseph, Harvey 8
Joseph, Isabella 8
Joseph, John 8
Joseph, Julianna 8
Joseph, M. 150
Joseph, Mary Eleanor 8
Joseph, Priscilla 8
Joseph, Ruth Amy 291
Joseph, Thomas Joseph 8
Joseph, William 8
Josephs, Catherine 523
Joslen, Lucreca 661
Josling, Sarah 354
Jourdon, Catharine 23
Joy, Benjamin 86
Joya, Job 281
Joynt, Micajh Macy 553
Juda, Catherine 467
Juday, Jacob 427
Juday, John (Jr.) 427
Judd, Alvin 497
Judkins, James 560
Judkins, William 560
Judy, Catherine 430
Judy, Elizabeth 565
Judy, John 430
Judy, John (Sr.) 427
Judy, Margaret 414
Julian, Isaac 120, 544
Julian, Jesse 544
Julian, Oliver N. P. 544
Julian, Pleasant 544
Julian, Rebecca 337
Julian, Ruth 120
Julian, Sarah A. 544
Julian, Sarah Ann 521
Julian, Stephen 117, 544

Julien, Elza 144
Julien, Harvey 148
Julin, Catharine 127
Julin, Jesse 125
Julyon, Hannah 660
Jumble, Michael 489
Jumps, Samuel 159
Junipher, George 299
Jushman, Mary 116
Justice, Ann 382
Justice, Ava 38
Justice, Daniel 385
Justice, Elizabeth An 765
Justice, Hannah Rosetta 38
Justice, James Armstrong 765
Justice, Jane 765
Justice, Jessee 385
Justice, John 38, 457, 765
Justice, Mary 765
Justice, Nancy 38
Justice, Rachael 383
Justice, Susan 765
Justice, Susannah 382
Justice, Thos. Jefferson 38
Justice, Westly 38
Justine, Michael 549
Justis, Phebe 404
Justus, Aquilla 404
Juvenal, David 489
Juvenal, Jacob 489

--- K ---

Kackley, George 308
Kackley, Mary 308
Kackley, Samuel (Sr.) 303
Kadell, James 248
Kaelhle, John 520
Kagy, Henry 520
Kahal, Elizabeth 513
Kahler, Jacob 255, 260, 263
Kahler, Philip 258
Kail, Mary 572
Kain, Dalia 462
Kain, Lookey 462
Kake, Andrew 337
Kalb, John S. 605
Kalb, Michael 88
Kalkhoff, Henry 111
Kallback, Henry 338
Kammon, Fredrick August 107
Kammon, John C. Wm. 107
Kammon, Mary Louise 107
Kampf, Anthony 738
Kampf, Elizabeth 738
Kampf, John 738
Kampf, Mariah 738
Kampf, Sarah 738
Kandal, Dewault 526

Kane, Alexander 418
Kane, Eliza 354
Kane, Isaiah 354
Kane, James 354
Kane, John 354
Kane, Louis 354
Kane, Margaret 417
Kane, Mary 354
Karar, Nelson 590
Karges, Lydia 199
Karn, Hannah 520
Karn, Moses D. 671
Karnes, Peter 303
Karns, Abigail 291
Karns, Cassia 291
Karns, Eleanor 291
Karns, Henry 291
Karns, Jacob 291, 527
Karns, John 291
Karns, Lewis 291
Karns, Lewis (Jr.) 291
Karns, Mary 291
Karns, Michael 291
Karns, Ruth Amy 291
Karns, Sanford 291
Karns, Stephen D. 291
Karns, Susannah 291
Karns, William 291
Karr, Elizabeth Jane 634
Karr, Hamilton 78
Karr, John 634, 636
Karr, Margaret 78
Karr, Mary Maria 634
Karr, Nathan 732
Karr, Rebecca 634
Karr, Robert 212
Karr, William 634
Karr, Wm. 364
Kart, George 2
Karter, Hannah 451
Kasebeer, Catharine 569
Kasebeer, John 560
Kasebeer, Samuel 567
Kaseberr, Agnes 560
Kaseberr, Catherine 560
Kaseberr, David 560
Kaseberr, Elizabeth 560
Kaseberr, Hannah 560
Kaseberr, Jacob 560
Kaseberr, John 560
Kaseberr, John (Jr.) 560
Kaseberr, Mary 560
Kashman, Elijah 665
Kassber, David 567
Kauderman, David 352
Kauderman, Eliza 352
Kauderman, Eve 352
Kauderman, George 352
Kauderman, Henry 352
Kauderman, Lewis 352
Kauderman, Mary 352
Kauderman, Susan 352
Kauffman, Christian 217
Kauffman, Conrad 192
Kauffman, David 738, 741, 743
Kauffman, Henry 743
Kaw, Charles C. 89
Kay, Charles 650

Kay, John S. 650
Kay, Mary Ann 650
Kay, Matthias 650
Kay, Rebecca 650
Kayler, Arthur 413
Kayler, Jacob 413
Kaylor, Christiana 368
Kaylor, Frederick 368
Kaylor, Jacob 368
Kaylor, Margaret 368
Kaylor, Sally 368
Kazan, Nathaniel 597
Kazar, Nelson 590
Kazer, Henry 600, 602
Kazy, William 717
Keairnes, John W. 409
Kean, Edward 283
Kean, Huffman 457
Kean, Jacob 296
Kean, Jane 296
Kean, John H. 672
Kean, Joseph 296
Kean, Margaret 296
Kean, Mary 296
Kear, Thomas 600
Kear, Thomas R. 599,
    600, 601
Keath, John 599
Keath, Johnzee 608
Keating, John 531
Keaton, Calvin 629
Keaton, John A. 629
Keaton, Josephine 629
Kebb, Hugh W. 481
Keck, Adam 262
Keck, David 739
Keckley, Samuel (Sr.)
    303
Keefer, Charles 520
Keefer, Henry 622
Keefer, Samuel 337
Keeler, Catharine 38
Keeler, Coleman I. (Jr.)
    41
Keeler, Coleman J. (Jr.)
    38
Keeler, Electa Amelia 758
Keeler, George 30
Keeler, Mahitabel 28
Keeler, Margaret 31
Keeler, Olmsted 758
Keeler, Orlandhia Jane
    758
Keeler, Orlanthia Jane
    758
Keeler, Ralph O. 758
Keeler, Sarah Grace 758
Keeler, William Olmsted
    758
Keeling, Elizabeth 121
Keeling, Polly 127
Keely, Albner 117
Keen, Benjamin 178
Keen, G. J. 529
Keen, Jesse 732
Keen, Mary 48
Keen, Rebecca 524
Keenan, Eleanor 368
Keenan, Elizabeth 368

Keenan, John 368
Keenan, Joseph 666, 672
Keenan, Mary 368
Keenan, Patrick 368
Keenan, Peter 348
Keenan, Susan 101
Keene, Daniel 44
Keene, Samuel Y. 286
Keener, Adam 464
Keener, Catharine 207
Keenin, Ed. 359
Keenin, Edward 370
Kees, James 660
Keeseman, George 117
Keeth, --- 606
Keeth, John 599
Keever, Adam 428, 640,
    660
Keever, George 647
Keever, Martin 660
Kefover, Jacob 367, 373
Kegan, John 41
Keifer, John 91
Keiffe, Edmund 520
Keihl, Charles 608
Keiker, Catarina 236
Keiker, Catharina 236
Keiker, David 236
Keiker, Maria 236
Keiker, Michel 236
Keiler, Daniel 211
Keiler, Daniel W. 211
Keinan, Peter 348
Keiser, Daniel 213
Keiser, George 213
Keiser, Jacob 215
Keiser, John 213, 215
Keiser, John Q. 213
Keiser, Joseph 215
Keiser, Mary 213, 215
Keiser, Mary Ann
    Elizabeth 213
Keiser, Rebecca 112
Keiser, William 213
Keith, Adam 262, 272
Keith, Andrew 311
Keith, Balser 311
Keith, Benjamin 268,
    303, 311
Keith, Edward 111
Keith, Elizabeth 311
Keith, Henry 438
Keith, John 599, 622
Keith, Joseph 272, 761
Keith, Levi 17
Keith, Michael 17, 438
Keith, Peter 257, 268
Keith, William 369
Kelgore, James 54
Kell, Samuel 666
Kellenberger, George
    216, 388
Keller, Betsey 718
Keller, Enos 200
Keller, Eva 560
Keller, George 452
Keller, Hannah 313
Keller, Henry 313, 560,
    567

Keller, Hezekiah 39
Keller, Jerome 238
Keller, John 113, 573
Keller, Levi 314, 529
Keller, Lewis 238
Keller, Martha 570
Keller, Martin 560
Keller, Martin (Jr.) 573
Keller, Martin (Sr.) 560
Keller, Mary 572
Keller, Mary J. 619
Keller, Rachel 718
Keller, S. R. 113
Keller, Samuel 544
Keller, Sarah 113
Keller, Ulrich 164
Keller, Verona 560
Keller, Verone 566
Kellerman, George 9
Kelley, Catharine 11
Kelley, Charles 109
Kelley, Ezra 660
Kelley, G. 532
Kelley, Henry 360, 369,
    380
Kelley, James 364, 372
Kelley, John A. 764
Kelley, Margaret 36
Kelley, Mary 519
Kelley, Nancy 532
Kelley, Nathan 646
Kelley, Owen 520
Kelley, Samuel 135, 354
Kelley, William 475, 489
Kelley, Wm. 464
Kelley, Wm. (Jr.) 732
Kelling, Jacob 88
Kellison, Dorcas 1
Kellison, Eli 5
Kellison, Zilpha 5
Kellog, Errilla 30
Kellog, James 324
Kellogg, Adeline 761
Kellogg, Chloe 761
Kellogg, Christopher S.
    761
Kellogg, D. M. 761
Kellogg, Daniel M. 761
Kellogg, Giles C. 761
Kellogg, John C. 761
Kellogg, Joseph E. 41
Kellogg, Justin 761
Kellogg, Martha A. 761
Kellough, --- 454
Kellough, Allen 493
Kellum, John P. (Rev.)
    605
Kelly, Abet 673
Kelly, Achsah 682
Kelly, Andrew 452
Kelly, Ann 665
Kelly, Anne 682
Kelly, Betsey 12, 350
Kelly, Betsy 25
Kelly, C. 150
Kelly, Catharine 201
Kelly, Caty 25
Kelly, Charles 78
Kelly, Charlotte 575

Kelly, Clinton 201
Kelly, Cornelius 434
Kelly, D. J. 220
Kelly, Dan 549
Kelly, David 636
Kelly, Elizabeth 758
Kelly, Emerline 201
Kelly, Ezekiel 470
Kelly, Galader A. 590
Kelly, George 717
Kelly, Hannah 386, 682
Kelly, Hannah Ann 201
Kelly, Isaac 682
Kelly, J. W. 150
Kelly, James 13, 567, 660, 758
Kelly, James H. 758
Kelly, Jane 657
Kelly, Jeremiah 434
Kelly, John 24, 25, 201, 350, 367, 388, 434, 513, 634
Kelly, John A. 759, 763
Kelly, John L. 78
Kelly, John R. 758
Kelly, Joseph 59, 340, 343, 385, 513
Kelly, Joseph B. 150
Kelly, Keziah 434
Kelly, Lucinda 548
Kelly, Margaret 35, 682, 713
Kelly, Mary 25, 201, 343, 350, 515, 516, 660
Kelly, Mary Ann 544
Kelly, Mathew 459
Kelly, Nancy 350
Kelly, Nathan 644, 645, 652, 673, 675
Kelly, Nathaniel 25
Kelly, Nehemiah 723
Kelly, Nicholas 489
Kelly, Patrick 636
Kelly, Patty 25
Kelly, Peter 13, 24, 25
Kelly, Peter (Sr.) 25
Kelly, Robert H. 758
Kelly, Ruth 565
Kelly, Sally 25
Kelly, Samuel 125, 150, 201, 682
Kelly, Sara 666
Kelly, Sissey 661
Kelly, Solomon 117
Kelly, Thomas 173, 286
Kelly, William 150
Kelly, Wm. 475
Keloy, Susannah 458
Kelser, Daniel 364
Kelsey, Abner 13
Kelsey, Betsey 665
Kelsey, Calvin 544
Kelsey, Cyrus 580
Kelsey, Daniel 193
Kelsey, David 684
Kelsey, Elizabeth 353
Kelsey, Jessey 666
Kelsey, John 269

Kelsey, M. D. 581
Kelsey, Mary 665
Kelsey, Phebe 658
Kelsey, Thomas 193, 684
Kelsy, Daniel 652
Kelsy, Elmira 652
Kelsy, Israel 652
Kelsy, Joel 652
Kelsy, John 652
Kelsy, Levina 652
Kelsy, Rebecca 652
Keltner, Catharine 434
Keltner, Emeline 434
Keltner, Henry Martin 434
Keltner, Sarah 434
Kelton, Elias 86
Kelton, Prudence 79
Kelzor, George 180
Kelzor, Jacob 180
Kemly, James 717
Kemmer, William J. 331
Kemmerer, Becca A. 331
Kemmerer, Lydia 331
Kemmerer, Manda 331
Kemp, Benjamin 681
Kemp, Daniel 223
Kemp, John 405
Kemp, Martin W. 599
Kemp, Mary 522
Kemp, Thomas 520
Kemp, Ulrick 41
Kemper, Amos R. 367
Kemper, Daniel 353, 378
Kemper, Elijah 353
Kemper, Henry 111
Kemper, Jacob 353
Kemper, Wesley 353
Kempt, Mariah 337
Kenady, Hezekiah 586
Kenady, John 586
Kenady, Michael 345
Kendal, Hannah 502
Kendal, J. 502
Kendal, William 500
Kendall, Benjamin 549
Kendall, Connie 689
Kendall, Ellen 689
Kendall, Lewis 689
Kendall, Mary 689
Kendall, Sarah Ann 689
Kendall, William (Gen.) 507
Kendall, Wm. 509
Kendel, Margaret 466
Kenedy, John 394
Kenedy, Rachel 457
Keness, Anna 548
Kenestirck, Margaret 571
Kenestrick, Polly 577
Kenis, Nancy 92
Kenison, Job 263
Kennady, Edward 393
Kennady, George Washington 193
Kennady, Irwin 303
Kennady, Robert 660
Kennard, A. C. 544
Kennard, A. D. 549

Kennard, Ezra 113
Kennard, George 544
Kennard, Isaac 544
Kennard, Susan 353
Kenne, Nathan 714
Kennear, Elizabeth Ann 606
Kenneday, Polly 415
Kennedy, Abigail 366
Kennedy, Bridget 345
Kennedy, Dennis 366
Kennedy, James 169, 170, 366, 670
Kennedy, Jane 660
Kennedy, John 366, 469, 489
Kennedy, Joseph 207
Kennedy, Nancy 457
Kennedy, Nathan 478
Kennedy, Polly 666
Kennedy, Prucy 366
Kennedy, Ruth 366
Kennedy, Sally 366
Kennedy, Samuel 51
Kennedy, Seath 366
Kennedy, Seth 366
Kenneir, Polly 121
Kenner, John 207, 457
Kennet, Pressly 476
Kennett, Pressly 473
Kenney, David 544
Kenney, John 633
Kenney, Nancy 544
Kenney, Richard 159
Kenny, Elizabeth 434
Kenny, George 434
Kenny, Jefferson 434
Kenny, Susan 434
Kenny, Wm. 434
Kenrich, Edward L. 688
Kenrich, Patience 688
Kenser, Jacob 117
Kent, Ann 567
Kent, Charity 569
Kent, Eliza 310
Kent, Frederick 573
Kent, George 745
Kent, Hiram 590
Kent, James 307, 310
Kent, Jesse 489
Kent, John 307, 310, 590
Kent, Josiah 307, 310
Kent, Mariah 310
Kent, Marinda 268
Kent, Mary Ann 307, 310
Kent, Rebecca 307, 310
Kent, Sarah 310
Kent, Susan 307, 310
Kent, William 158, 307, 310
Kent, William T. 310
Kentner, George 608
Kenton, Ann 61
Kenton, Claricy 61
Kenton, Elizabeth 61
Kenton, Lucy 61
Kenton, Martha 61
Kenton, Polly 14
Kenton, Sarah W. 61

Kenton, Simeon 13
Kenton, Simon 61
Kentworth, David 413
Kenzie, John 280
Kephart, Daniel 497
Kephart, Thomas 645, 674
Keplar, Frederick 41
Kepler, Barbara 360
Kepler, Catherine 199
Kepler, George 199
Kepler, Joseph 193
Keplinger, Jacob 544
Keppel, Ann 521
Keppel, George 520
Keppel, Hannah 522
Ker, James 476
Kerew, Elizabeth 592
Kerger, Jacob 230
Kerger, Margaret 230
Kerkendall, William 63
Kerkman, Hannah 585
Kern, Frederick 640
Kern, John Frederick 640
Kern, Margaret 22
Kern, Wm. 478
Kerner, Lewis 227
Kerns, Abraham 7
Kerns, Daniel (Rev.) 605
Kerns, Elizabeth 7
Kerns, George A. 7
Kerns, Hannah 7, 465
Kerns, Job 94
Kerns, Lucinda 7
Kerns, Mary 7
Kerns, Michael 7
Kerns, Peggy 123
Kerns, Phebe 94
Kerns, W. S. 94
Kerr, Charles 732
Kerr, David 3, 489
Kerr, Eliza Jane 3
Kerr, Elizabeth 385
Kerr, G. N. 61
Kerr, George 3, 257
Kerr, Gideon 385
Kerr, Hamilton 714
Kerr, Hamilton (Sr.) 86
Kerr, Harvey 139
Kerr, James 3, 139,
   278, 464, 489
Kerr, James W. 217
Kerr, Jane 82
Kerr, John 3, 184, 464
Kerr, Joseph 3
Kerr, Katherine 3
Kerr, Margaret Ann 3
Kerr, Martha 3, 139
Kerr, Mary 3, 139, 144,
   489
Kerr, Michael 596
Kerr, Morrison 3
Kerr, Patterson 3
Kerr, Peggy 382
Kerr, Rachel 451
Kerr, Reuben 596
Kerr, Robert S. 3
Kerr, Samuel 3
Kerr, Thomas L. 3
Kerr, William 3, 78

Kerr, William H. 144
Kerr, Wily M. 3
Kerr, Wm. 3, 362
Kerr, Wm. J. 139, 144
Kerrigan, Henry 303
Kerrigan, Terrence 389
Kers, Nancy 92
Kershaw, Jane 22
Kershner, David 544
Kersner, Daniel 229
Kersner, Mary 229
Kesinger, Cynthia Jane
   408
Kesler, Amanda Mariah
   434
Kesler, Elizabeth 665
Kesler, John 685
Kesling, Geo. 672
Kesling, George 645,
   647, 648, 673, 686
Kesling, Henry 660
Kesling, Peter 640
Kessler, Abraham 622
Kessler, An Eliza 144
Kessler, Catharine 120
Kessler, Charles 216
Kessler, Godfrey 216
Kessler, Joseph 200
Kessner, Benjamin 393
Kester, Andrew 430
Kester, Diana 430
Kester, Jacob 430
Kester, Samuel 430
Ketch, Benjamin 732
Ketcham, Alice 367
Ketcham, Andrew 367
Ketcham, Cynthia Mariah
   367
Ketcham, Esther 356
Ketcham, Esther Jane 367
Ketcham, Hiram 367
Ketcham, Holmes 367
Ketcham, John H. 367
Ketcham, Keturah Ann 367
Ketcham, Mary 367
Ketcham, Nancy 367
Ketcham, Obadiah 367
Ketchan, Valantine A. 69
Ketchem, Philip 622
Kethart, Catharine 661
Ketrick, George 497
Ketstadt, John M. 404
Ketstadt, M. 404
Ketstadt, Mary 404
Kettering, B. 735
Kettering, Barbara 735
Kettering, Moses 735
Kettering, P. 735
Kettering, Philip 735
Kettle, Samuel 497
Ketzer, John 227
Keuck, Matilda Jane 712
Keutch, Jacob 111
Kever, Amy 610
Kever, George 660
Kever, James 608
Keyes, Amery 274
Keyes, Andrew 590
Keyes, Thos. S. 371

Keyler, Conrad 720
Keys, Elsy 463
Keys, Horation R. 385
Keys, Phinias 253
Keys, William 439, 470,
   472, 480
Keys, Wm. H. 741
Keyser, Elizabeth 116
Keyser, Isaac 255
Keyser, Oliver 255, 257
Keyt, John 125
Keyte, James 145
Keyte, Margaret J. 145
Keyte, Mary 145
Keyte, Wm. J. 145
Khoar, Casper 486
Kibbe, Rufus (Dr.) 751
Kibble, John 83
Kibby, Elizabeth 663
Kibby, Ephraim 668
Kibby, Jarusha 665
Kibby, Julian 662
Kiblinger, Nancy 241
Kiby, Jonathan 573
Kichenbotton, James 514
Kidd, John 721
Kidd, Joseph 262
Kidder, Amos M. 520
Kidder, Gideon 732
Kieholtz, William 520
Kierchhoff, Greel
   Aeleheit Egeborn 105
Kierchhoff, John Arn 105
Kiertschhoff, John Arnt
   105
Kies, Edna R. 533
Kigar, Hannah 590
Kigar, Isaac 590
Kiger, George 709
Kiger, Jeremiah 764
Kiger, Rachael 589
Kiggins, Lydia B. 711
Kiggins, Mary 548
Kikendall, Minerva 510
Kilborn, Sally 465
Kilbourn, Lemuel 493
Kilbreth, Nancy 463
Kile, John 710
Kile, Nancy 48
Kiler, Sally 291
Kilgor, Matthew Lasley
   717
Kilgore, George 482
Kilgore, James 452, 476
Kilgore, Robert M. 573
Kilgore, Samuel 48
Kilgore, Sarah 48
Kilgore, Thomas 60
Kilgore, William 489
Killajor, Hector 745
Killem, Elizabeth 420
Killgore, George 470
Killian, B. 535
Killian, Mary 535
Killian, Mc. 535
Killian, Philip 535
Killison, Moses 464
Killough, John 454, 457
Kilmer, Philip 622

Kilpatrick, Benj. 473
Kilpatrick, James 484
Kilroy, Letitia 303
Kim, Adolphus 367
Kim, Augustin 367
Kim, Maria Ann 367
Kimball, Margaret 521
Kimball, Rosana 28
Kimberlin, Henry 763
Kimble, Edward 125
Kimble, Eliza Jane 749
Kimble, Hiram 643
Kimble, Hiram D. 590
Kimble, Isabel 125
Kimble, John 474
Kimble, Jonathan 385
Kimble, Mary S. 125
Kimble, Patsey 665
Kimble, Polly 119
Kimble, Susanah 126
Kime, Rebecca Ann 521
Kimes, Abraham 86
Kimes, John 83
Kimes, Samuel 83
Kimmel, Caroline 335
Kimmel, Daniel 205
Kimmel, Elizabeth 336
Kimmel, Hannah 205
Kimmel, John 196
Kimmel, Jonas 205
Kimmel, Martha 337
Kimmell, John 316
Kimmey, A. 407
Kimmey, M. 407
Kincaid, John 413
Kincaid, Robert 685
Kincaide, Nancy 172
Kincaide, Samuel 172
Kindal, Enoch 413
Kindall, John 549
Kindall, William 514
Kindel, Ammeta 95
Kindel, Charles 94
Kindel, Ima 94
Kindel, Joseph 94
Kindel, June 94
Kindel, Pricilla 94
Kindel, William A.
  (Rev.) 94
Kindel, Wm. (Rev.) 95
Kindel, Wm. J. 94
Kinder, Abraham 668, 695
Kinder, Abrm. 668
Kinder, George 651,
  668, 681, 695
Kinder, John 668
Kinder, Margaret 668
Kinder, Nancy 668
Kinder, Polly 668
Kindig, Francis 413
Kindle, Agnes 671
Kindle, Amelia 671
Kindle, Charity 671
Kindle, Elenor 671
Kindle, Hiram 145
Kindle, Mary 671
Kindle, Rholan 671
Kindle, Sarah 583
Kindle, Susannah 671

Kindle, William 671
Kindle, William V. 544
Kindrick, Hannah 15
Kineer, Parnel 554
Kineer, Thomas 554
Kinfall, Jeremiah 732
King, A. W. 693
King, Alice 72
King, Allis 548
King, Almira 114
King, Amos 114
King, Amy 177
King, Andrew 114
King, Ann 335
King, Anna 430
King, Anne 717
King, B. Harrison 544
King, Balsor 597
King, Belinda 85
King, Catharine 321
King, Catherine 693
King, Christian 338,
  341, 351, 356
King, David 17, 167,
  367, 544, 599, 622
King, David B. 597
King, David S. 368
King, Ealdon 463
King, Elizabeth 85,
  108, 167
King, Eve 592
King, Frances 78
King, Freeman 457
King, George 520, 597,
  681
King, George W. 63
King, Henry 44, 351,
  639, 686
King, Ignatius 521
King, Jacob 22, 430
King, Jacob G. 220
King, James 321, 430
King, Jane 367
King, Jefferson 681
King, Jephthat 434
King, Jesse 108
King, Joanna 523
King, John 160, 340,
  351, 430, 464, 514,
  590, 597, 681, 689
King, Joseph 763
King, Josias 108, 114
King, Leavitt H. 72
King, Lewis 745
King, Lydia 725
King, Marillas 351
King, Martha 114, 597
King, Martha J. 368
King, Mary 85, 127, 430
King, Mary Jane 145
King, Matilda 76
King, Michael 266, 269
King, Moses 367
King, Nancy 367, 607
King, Noah 114
King, Peter 351, 375
King, Priscilla 17
King, Pruella 15
King, Rachel 367

King, Rhoda 80
King, Robert 493
King, Ruth 590
King, Samuel 205, 430
King, Sarah 62, 76, 81,
  368, 374
King, Sarepta 52
King, Seymour 177
King, T. W. 608
King, Thomas 62, 78,
  192, 363, 367, 573
King, Thomas S. 368
King, Thos. 354, 357,
  364, 375, 376, 378
King, William 185, 341,
  374
King, William George 39
King, William L. 368
Kingam, Grace 457
Kingem, Grace 457
Kingery, Hester T. 337
Kingery, John 316, 319,
  323, 337, 750
Kingery, John E. 337
Kingery, Samuel 457
Kingrey, John 752
Kingry, John 316, 590
Kingsberry, Harley 83
Kingsbury, Honor M. 29
Kingseer, Endney 521
Kingsley, Manning 608
Kinkaid, Elizabeth 459
Kinkead, Tace 501
Kinkle, C. 329
Kinkle, Conrad 329
Kinkle, Konrad 333
Kinkle, Susanna 329
Kinman, Elizabeth 551 —
Kinnaman, John T. 200
Kinnaman, Samuel 199
Kinnaman, Samuel J. 199
Kinnaman, Walter 199
Kinnaman, Washington 199
Kinnard, William 549
Kinnear, David 390
Kinnear, Mary 383
Kinnear, Nancy 404
Kinnedy, Phillip 345
Kinney, Aaron 502, 505
Kinney, George W. 544
Kinney, John 438
Kinney, John C. 681, 685
Kinney, Lewis 438
Kinney, Patrick 529
Kinney, Richard 159
Kinney, Thomas 285
Kinney, Thomas E. 161
Kinney, Uri 497
Kinney, W. 508
Kinny, Elizabeth 156
Kinny, George 156
Kinple, Lena A. 584
Kinsel, D. B. 280
Kinser, George 385, 457
Kinser, John 117
Kinsey, Aaron 174
Kinsey, Abraham 203
Kinsey, Anna 203
Kinsey, David 192

Kinsey, E. 244
Kinsey, Enos 244
Kinsey, Jacob 192
Kinsey, John 192, 216
Kinsey, Jonas 192, 216
Kinsey, Joseph 192
Kinsey, Lewis 192, 203
Kinsey, Lydia 145
Kinsey, M. 244
Kinsey, Margaret 203
Kinsey, Noah 145, 192
Kinsey, Philip 203
Kinsey, Polly 192
Kinsey, Samuel 145
Kinsey, Susanna 192
Kinsey, Susannah 216
Kinsie, Abraham 203
Kinsie, Mary 203
Kinsman, Frederick 108
Kinsmin, Frederick 626
Kinson, Peter 338
Kinsy, Aaron 159
Kintz, Anthony 368
Kintz, Charles 368
Kintz, Frederick 368
Kintz, George 368
Kintz, Mary 368
Kintz, Mary Jane 368
Kintz, Nancy 368
Kintz, Polly 368
Kinzer, A. M. 329
Kinzer, Anna M. 329
Kinzer, Gottlop 329
Kinzer, J. C. 329
Kinzer, J. D. 329
Kinzer, Jacob 329
Kinzer, John D. 329
Kinzer, Mary 329
Kiplinger, Elizabeth 544
Kiplinger, Jas. H. 544
Kirbey, Mary 662
Kirby, Anna 670
Kirby, Anne 670
Kirby, Benjamin 660
Kirby, James 660
Kirby, John 249
Kirby, Joseph 660
Kirby, Joseph (Sr.) 641
Kirby, Mary 670
Kirby, Rebecah 670
Kirby, Richard 670
Kirby, Samuel 670
Kircher, Christiana 367
Kircher, Michael 367
Kirchner, Catherine 530
Kirchner, Eva Barbara
530
Kirchner, Henry 530
Kirchner, John Michael
530
Kirchner, Mary Margaret
530
Kirk, Geo. W. 732
Kirk, James J. 145
Kirk, Jane 301
Kirk, John 263, 301
Kirk, Margaret A. 145
Kirk, Mary 145, 454
Kirk, Samuel 489

Kirk, William 206, 301
Kirkbride, Catharine 156,
159, 170, 175, 178
Kirkbride, David 170,
172, 175
Kirkbride, David (Jr.)
170
Kirkbride, Henry 156,
157, 159, 168, 170,
174, 175, 178
Kirkbright, John 464
Kirkendall, Anna 515
Kirkendall, Archibald
737
Kirkendall, Christopher
737
Kirkendall, Daniel D.
521
Kirkendall, David 514
Kirkendall, Eliza 737
Kirkendall, Elizabeth
737
Kirkendall, Henry 489,
502
Kirkendall, James 737
Kirkendall, John 489,
493
Kirkendall, Joseph C.
631
Kirkendall, Mary 737
Kirkendall, Noah 493
Kirkendall, Phoebe 737
Kirkendall, Samuel 737
Kirkendall, Sarah 737
Kirkendol, John 476
Kirkendoll, Hannah 514
Kirker, James 284, 296
Kirker, Martha 296
Kirker, Mary 296
Kirker, Thomas 296
Kirker, William C. 296
Kirkham, H. L. 531
Kirkley, Ann 131
Kirkpatrick, Benj. 477,
478
Kirkpatrick, David 434
Kirkpatrick, Elizabeth
453, 596
Kirkpatrick, Esther Ann
434
Kirkpatrick, James 485,
717
Kirkpatrick, Jane 595,
596
Kirkpatrick, Jas. 477
Kirkpatrick, Jean 50
Kirkpatrick, John 434,
472
Kirkpatrick, Jos. 485
Kirkpatrick, Melissa 336
Kirkpatrick, Samuel
595, 596
Kirkwood, Anna 224
Kirkwood, David 182
Kirkwood, Joseph 27,
182, 639
Kirkwood, Nancy 20
Kirkwood, Polly 27
Kirkwood, Rhoda 27

Kirkwood, Robert 224
Kirmann, John Berned 103
Kirschner, Magdalena 234
Kirschner, Michael 234
Kirschner, Willhelm
Jacob 234
Kirstine, John 90
Kirtlan, William 549
Kirtley, Ezekiel 135
Kirtley, John 544
Kirtley, William H. 544
Kisaer, Rollo M. 616
Kisaer, S. S. 616
Kisaer, T. J. 616
Kiser, Charity 116
Kiser, Daniel 567
Kiser, Daniel H. 125
Kiser, Huldah 544
Kiser, Isaac 573
Kiser, Mary 575
Kiser, Thomas 117
Kishler, Geo. 371, 372
Kishler, George 368
Kisler, Geo. 371
Kisler, William 521
Kisling, Peter 666
Kisor, George 159
Kissabeth, Elizabeth 520
Kissabeth, Philip 521
Kissler, John 521
Kitch, David 573
Kitchel, . . . 657
Kitchel, Ashbel 643
Kitchel, Calvin 687
Kitchel, Harriet 663
Kitchell, Percy 642
Kitchen, Ann 21
Kitchen, Daniel 339
Kitchen, Edward 8
Kitchen, Henry 135
Kite, John 457
Kitson, Geo. 426
Kitson, Sarah 426
Kitt, Eli 41
Kittoe, Jacob 350
Kitts, Christian 732
Kitwiler, Mary 573
Kizer, Gerherd H. 103
Kizer, Granville 114
Kizer, Nicholas 544
Kizer, Peter 464, 493
Klamon, Philip 686
Klavalage, Henry 105
Klazz, Georg 235
Klazz, George 235
Klazz, Lydia 234, 235
Klazz, Maria Anna 235
Klee, Margretha 708
Kleforth, G. 107
Klein, Adam 236
Klein, Ann Elizabeth 608
Klein, Henrich 236
Klein, Jacob 710
Klein, James Vallentein
236
Klein, Luesa 236
Klein, Suse 236
Kleinfelter, Henry 521
Klender, Carl 328

Klender, D. 328
Klender, Dora 328
Klender, F. 328
Klender, Frederick 328
Klesthlic, Theressa 523
Klienfelter, Jacob 83
Klinck, Mary Malinda 222
Kline, Barbara 568
Kline, Catharine 239
Kline, Catharine B. 734
Kline, David 573
Kline, Elizabeth 336,
    499, 568
Kline, Eve 570
Kline, Henry 239, 567
Kline, Jacob 385, 734
Kline, John 567
Kline, Jonas 573
Kline, Louisa 239
Kline, Maria Ann 521
Kline, Mathias 239
Kline, Philip 567
Klingenpeel, Benj. 434
Klingenpeel, Margaret
    434
Klinger, Adam 338
Klinger, Daniel 434
Klinger, Elizabeth 434
Klinger, Jackson 434
Klinger, Joseph 434
Klinger, Peter 434
Klinger, Samuel 434
Klingler, Adam 367, 370
Klingler, David 367
Klingler, John 376
Klinglesmith, Peter 567
Klinker, Joseph 622
Klipner, Lewis 181
Klotz, Catharine 737
Klrick, P. H. 334
Klyne, Margaret 451
Knable, Catharine 565
Knace, Abraham 573
Knagg, John 41
Knaggs, Matilda 41
Knaht, James 573
Knap, Kiziah 52
Knap, Porter 590
Knapke, Bernard 110
Knapp, Abraham 78
Knapp, Alfred 30
Knapp, Ezra 41
Knapp, John 497
Knapp, Mary 78
Knapp, Phebe 44
Knapp, Sarah 90
Knapp, Sylvester 521
Knaus, Elizabeth 565
Knaus, Judith 566
Knaus, Mary Magdalene
    567
Knaus, Sarah Ane 568
Knaus, Susana 575
Knaus, Thomas 567
Knause, George 97
Knause, Isabel 97
Knause, Lucy 97
Knecht, Ruby 578
Kneeger, Peter 573

Knepsly, Lawrence 227
Knestrick, Catharine 560
Knestrick, Elizabeth 560
Knestrick, Frederick 560
Knestrick, Henry 560
Knestrick, Jeremiah 560
Knestrick, John 560
Knestrick, Margaret 560
Knestrick, Mary 560
Knestrick, Nancy 560
Knestrick, Sally 560
Knestrick, William 560
Kniesly, Benjamin 216
Kniesly, Zenuah 216
Kniester, Jacob 567
Knife, Amy 135
Knife, Aney 135
Knife, Catherine 198
Knife, Charles 198
Knife, Conrad 198
Knife, Elizabeth 135
Knife, Hannah 135
Knife, John 135, 198
Knife, Jonathan 135
Knife, Mary 198
Knife, Michael 135
Knife, Michal 135
Knife, Nancy 135
Knife, Samuel 139
Knife, Susannah 198
Kniff, George 514
Kniff, Mary 512
Knight, Benjamin 92
Knight, Betsey M. 83
Knight, Clarissa 139
Knight, Corbly 139
Knight, David 135
Knight, E. N. 762
Knight, Eliz. 139
Knight, Fielding 493
Knight, George 514
Knight, Hugh 139
Knight, James 130
Knight, Joanna 663
Knight, John 22, 125
Knight, Jonathan 139
Knight, Margaret 139
Knight, Mary 720
Knight, Mary A. 139
Knight, Michael 720
Knight, Nacy 116
Knight, Paul 139
Knight, Phebe M. 80
Knight, Polly 119
Knight, Precilla 121
Knight, Priscilla 139
Knight, Priscilla Corbly
    139
Knight, Rachel 123
Knight, Samuel 564
Knight, Silas W. 83
Knight, Stephen 139
Knight, Westbrook 586
Knight, Willard 497
Knight, Wm. 139
Knipple, Henry C. 695
Knipple, Louis 695
Knise, John 544
Knisely, Abraham 560

Knisely, Elizabeth 565
Knisely, Jacob 560, 567
Knisely, John 560
Knisely, Mary 569, 570
Knisely, Susanah 568
Knistrick, Catharine 575
Knitz, John 361
Kniza, Caroline 139
Kniza, Isaac 139
Kniza, Jane 139
Kniza, Sarah 139
Kniza, Susan 139
Knoop, Michael 125
Knop, J. F. 104
Knopp, George 239
Knott, Zachariah 48
Knotts, Lydia 223
Knotts, Nathaniel 223
Knouskop, Mercey 11
Knowles, Adam 464
Knowles, Levi 20
Knowls, Rebecca 661
Knowlton, Hiram 41
Knowlton, J. K. 306
Knowly, Adam 464
Knox, Bethnel 262, 268
Knox, Charles 262
Knox, Eliz. 139
Knox, George 262, 268,
    601
Knox, Hennetta 262
Knox, Hennitta 262
Knox, James A. 139
Knox, John 5, 22, 268
Knox, John G. 139
Knox, John W. 262, 268
Knox, John Whaley 262
Knox, Levi 601
Knox, Lydia 601
Knox, Margaret 139
Knox, Martha 601
Knox, Miles 139
Knox, Norman 601
Knox, Patty 25
Knox, Rettay B. 262
Knox, Sally 262
Knox, Sally M. 499
Knox, Samuel 112
Knox, Squire 112
Knox, Susan 601
Knox, Thomas 268
Knox, Tilman 262
Kober, Hannah 373
Koberlein, Nicholas 544
Koch, Betsy 186
Koch, Christian 186
Koch, Christiana 186
Koch, Frederick 186
Koch, Henry 171, 186
Koch, Margaret 186
Koch, Michael 186
Koch, Polly 186
Koch, Sally 186
Kock, E. (Dr.) 220
Koeberlein, N. 544
Koehne, Bernard 112
Koehner, Jacob 227
Kohendorf, John M. 749
Kohlman, Jacob 559

885

Kohne, Bernard 112
Kohrig, Elizabeth 368
Kokemiller, Caroline 114
Kokemiller, Eliza 114
Kokemiller, Frederick 114
Kokemiller, Wilhelmina 114
Kolbock, Henry 341
Kollar, Andrew 742
Kollar, Catharine 568
Kollar, George 749
Kollar, Peggy 566
Kone, Lucretia C. 407
Konhright, Lymon 590
Konklin, Joseph 591
Konrad, Adam A. 528
Konrad, Caroline 528
Konrad, Emilia 528
Konrad, Wilhilmina 528
Kontz, John 41
Koof, Ann 403
Koof, James 403
Koof, Polly W. 403
Kook, John 227
Koon, Nathan 102
Koonce, Rachael 384
Koons, Ephraim 366
Koons, Ephriam 366
Koop, Bernard 107
Koos, Christian 39
Koos, George 39
Koos, Margaret 39
Kopp, Jacob 328
Kopp, Liza 328
Kore, Elizabeth 573
Kore, Michaek 560
Kouhlman, Catherine 559
Kouhlman, George 559
Kouhlman, Jacob 559
Kouhlman, John 559
Kouhlman, Jonas 559
Kouhlman, Machderline 559
Kouhlman, Machtalena 559
Kouhlman, William 559
Kountz, John 82
Kourdate, Catherine 529
Kover, Adam 367
Kover, Elizabeth 367
Kover, Henry H. 367
Kover, John 367
Kover, Katherine 367
Kover, Mary 367
Kover, Sally 367
Kover, Samuel 367
Kraft, Conrad 93
Kramer, B. H. 102, 103
Kramer, Bernard Henry 103
Kramer, D. T. 622
Kramer, Engel 103
Kramer, Johann Heinrich 102
Kranemiller, Catherina 235
Kranemiller, Jacob 235
Kranemiller, Marcreda 235

Kranemiller, Marcreta 235
Krapps, Jacob 248
Kratch, Leonard 674
Kratzer, Catherina 235
Kratzer, Emanuel 235
Kratzer, Georg 235
Kratzer, Samuel 338
Krauss, John 528
Krebbs, Benedict 161
Krebbs, Elizabeth 161
Krebs, Benedict 161
Kreisher, Jacob 601
Kreisher, Peter 608
Kreisher, Philip Michael 601
Kridler, Frederick 497
Kring, Catharine 139
Kring, Philip 139
Krites, Jonas 521
Kritz, Elizabeth 572
Kritzer, Elizabeth 745
Kroft, Frederick 556
Kroft, Jno. 556
Kroft, Phillip 556
Kronmiller, Barbara 236
Kronmiller, Jacob 236
Kronmiller, Markereta 236
Kronmiller, Markertta 236
Kronmiller, Susanna 236
Krontz, Caroline 39
Krontz, Jacob 39
Krontz, Lucinda 39
Krontz, Manuel 39
Krontz, Simon 39
Krotzer, Isaac 756
Krotzer, Joseph 756
Krotzer, Peter 756
Krotzer, Rebecca 756
Krotzer, William 756
Krouskap, George (Jr.) 24
Krumryne, Catharine 366
Krumryne, Christian 366
Krumryne, Eliza 366
Krumryne, Elizabeth 366
Krumryne, Henry 366
Krumryne, Jacob 366
Krumryne, John 366
Krumryne, Malena 366
Krumryne, Margaret 366
Krumryne, Martin 366
Krumryne, Mary 366
Krumryne, Michael 366
Krumryne, Peter 366
Krumryne, Philip 366
Krumryne, Susanna 366
Kruse, Hellen Maria 107
Kruson, Geo. 457
Kruson, Isaac 489
Kruson, Sally 489
Kryder, John 555
Kuchenbecker, Mary 413
Kuder, Robert 385
Kuhn, Abraham 41
Kuhn, C. 242
Kuhn, Caroline Antonia 522

Kuhn, Charles 242
Kuhn, George 563
Kuhn, George William 567
Kuhn, H. 527
Kuhn, John Geo. 573
Kuhn, M. 242
Kuhn, Manorva 242
Kuhn, Mary 242
Kuhns, John 452
Kukman, Hannah 585
Kulentz, John 301
Kunce, Catherine 367
Kunce, George 367
Kunce, Sally 367
Kunce, Samuel 367
Kunce, Susanna 367
Kuncle, Conrod 41
Kunkle, Elizabeth 239
Kunkle, George Henry 749
Kunkle, Henry 239
Kunkler, Christian 345
Kuns, Catherine 367
Kuns, George 367
Kuns, Jacob 214
Kuns, Lydia 214
Kuns, Sally 367
Kuns, Samuel 367
Kuns, Susanna 367
Kuntz, Andrew 314
Kuntz, Magdaline 518
Kunz, Margreth 709
Kuostman, Henry 105
Kureth, Elizabeth 367
Kureth, Frantz 367
Kureth, Maria Ann 367
Kureth, Martin 367
Kurns, Supple 564
Kusman, Frederick 753
Kuykendall, Henry 493
Kuykendall, Rebecca 467
Kuykendoll, Jacob 441
Kuykendoll, William 441
Kuzsen, Lydia 606
Kyes, Samuel 30
Kyger, Anne 168, 170, 171, 175
Kyger, Daniel 168, 170, 171, 175, 176
Kyger, John 162
Kyger, Mary 162
Kyle, Ann 131
Kyle, Betsey 131
Kyle, Elizabeth 118
Kyle, George H. 521
Kyle, Isaac 739
Kyle, James 268, 274, 427
Kyle, John 385
Kyle, Joseph 356
Kyle, Lucy 121, 131
Kyle, Mary 131
Kyle, Sam. 356
Kyle, Samuel 131, 133, 135
Kyle, Samuel (Sr.) 131
Kyles, Rebecca 384
Kyser, Cactrena 568
Kyser, Catharine 569
Kyser, Rosannah 569

--- L ---

Laban, Elizabeth 288
Laban, Vincent 733
Labourne, John 41
Lacey, Anna 369
Lacey, Mahlon 369
Lacey, Mahlon Albert 369
Lacey, Sarah 569
Lacey, William 567
Lackey, Richard 689
Lacroix, Cecilla 506
Lacroix, Emily 506
Lacroix, Katherine 506
Lacroix, Michael 506
Lacroix, William 506
Lacroix, Zera 506
Lacroix, Zeru 506
Lacy, Benjamin 368
Lacy, James 368
Lacy, John Thomas 368
Lacy, Joseph 368
Lacy, Manuel 368
Lacy, Maria 368
Lacy, Mary 368
Lad, Hampton 497
Ladd, David 766
Ladd, Henry 521
Ladd, James Elison 745
Ladd, Jeremiah 13
Ladd, Mercy 613
Lafaber, Leonhard 711
Lafabre, Katharina 711
LaFerte, Creatus 714
Laffand, Patrick 265
Laffen, Patrick 265
Laffer, Bartholow 567
Laffer, Charlotte 565
Laffer, Henry 564
Laffer, Mary 571
Laffer, Philip 567
Laffer, Susanne 575
Lafferty, John 646, 675
Lafferty, Richard 646,
   660, 675
Laffin, Sally 577
Laffin, W. 480
Laflen, William 170
Lafleur, Archange 496
Lafleur, Mary 495
Laflin, Martha Ann 34
Lafontain, Alexander 497
Laforce, Agnes 653
Laforce, Archibald 653
Laforce, Archibald S.
   497
Laforce, Margaret 653
Laforce, Robinson 653
Laforce, William 653
LaForge, Maria Gaberiel
   715
Lafour, Bezry 497
Laid, Elizabeth 585
Laird, Davis 369
Laird, Elijah 369
Laird, Eliza 369
Laird, Elizabeth 672
Laird, James 369

Laird, John 369
Laird, Luther 642
Laird, Mary 369
Laird, Mary Ann 369
Laird, Moses 369
Laird, Rachel 369
Laird, Rebecca 369
Laird, Rees D. 369
Laird, Sarah Jane 369
Laird, Susan 369
Laird, William 369
Laird, William D. 369
Laird, Wm. D. 369
Lake, Andrew 714, 727
Lake, Archibald 727
Lake, Hannah 520
Lake, Henry 41
Lake, Joseph L. 497
Lake, Salley 462
Lake, William 622
Laky, Nelson 521
LaLance, Katherine 715
Lalance, Peter 717
LaLanu, Katherine 715
Lallance, Adam 78
Lallance, Jacob 83
Lalon, Deborah 461
Laman, John 117
Lamb, Ance 115
Lamb, Benj. 434
Lamb, Bird B. 426
Lamb, Charles 365
Lamb, D. G. 115
Lamb, Daniel 434
Lamb, Esther 290
Lamb, Helen M. 426
Lamb, Jacob T. 247
Lamb, James 385
Lamb, Jodrph 638
Lamb, Joseph 638, 648
Lamb, Margaret 292
Lamb, Martha J. 614
Lamb, Maxwell 457
Lamb, Pen the Mon 434
Lamb, Sarah 658
Lamb, Thomas F. 419
Lamb, Thompson 682
Lamb, William 469, 472,
   474
Lambat, Barnabas 475
Lambe, Christenah 567
Lamberson, Samuel 577
Lamberson, Timothy 567
Lambert, Abigail 513
Lambert, Amos 544
Lambert, James 508
Lambert, John 508, 523
Lambert, Joseph C. 333
Lambert, Rachel 662
Lambert, Richard 514
Lambert, Rochard 514
Lambert, Sarah 514
Lambson, Hannah 642
Lambson, Thomas 642
Lame, Clanend 92
Lame, Sally 14
Lamen, Joseph 586
Lamm, Aaron 434
Lamm, Henry 434

Lamma, William 260
Lamme, David 211
Lamme, James 120
Lamon, Joseph 489
Lamont, Mary 22
Lamoreaux, John L. 96
Lamoreaux, Rebecca 96
Lamp, Henry 172
Lamperson, Timothy 560
Lamphear, Abner 75
Lamping, Justina
   Wilhelmina 115
Lamson, Abigal 642
Lamson, Amos 642
Lamson, Eleaser 642, 666
Lanam, Caroline 312
Lanam, Eloner 312
Lanam, Henry 312
Lanam, Mary 169
Lanam, Mary Ann 312
Lanam, Maryann 312
Lanam, Thomas 169
Lance, Catherine 459
Lance, Miles V. 109
Lance, Wm. 739
Land, Lucy 457
Landerman, Peter 286
Landers, George 668
Landes, Elizabeth 207
Landes, Jacob 125
Landes, Jesse 207
Landes, Mary 207
Landes, Rebecca 573
Landis, Abraham 160,
   161, 164
Landis, Abram 164
Landis, Betsey 392
Landis, David 145, 341
Landis, Elizabeth 430
Landis, G. Frances 328
Landis, Henry 338, 430
Landis, J. 328
Landis, Jacob 393
Landis, John 333
Landis, Maria 335
Landis, Rebecca 430
Landis, S. 328
Landis, Sarah 161
Landis, Solomon 334
Landon, Levin 83
Landon, Nancy 127
Landon, Polly 397
Landon, Sally 79
Landon, Theron 745
Landre, Richard 139
Landre, Simon 147
Landree, Daniel 139
Landree, Richard 147
Landry, John 139
Landry, Susan 125
Lane, Abraham Vinton 637
Lane, Abrm. 295
Lane, Austin 637
Lane, B. D. 94
Lane, Benjamin D. V. 94
Lane, Betsey 348
Lane, Catharine 295, 300
Lane, Charity 295
Lane, Clarissa 637

Lane, Dannis 457
Lane, David P. 2
Lane, David Pitman 13
Lane, Dennis 55
Lane, Dotton 300
Lane, Dutton 295
Lane, Edward 169
Lane, Edward R. 174, 175
Lane, Electa 637
Lane, Eliz. M. 467
Lane, Eliza 12
Lane, Elizabeth 61, 295
Lane, Fanny 585
Lane, George 187, 227
Lane, Gilbert 209
Lane, Hannah 416
Lane, Henry 108, 626, 753
Lane, Hooper 55
Lane, Houlbur 83
Lane, Jamiana 295
Lane, John 55, 591
Lane, John C. 187
Lane, John G. 209
Lane, Jose 473
Lane, Joseph 472
Lane, Joseph K. 549
Lane, Junea 48
Lane, Lemuel 637, 721
Lane, Lilly 55
Lane, Lorenzo 637
Lane, Louanna 637
Lane, Luther 36
Lane, Mary 352, 661
Lane, Mitchell 55
Lane, Nancy 295
Lane, Noble 55
Lane, Orpha 637
Lane, Patrick 317
Lane, Permius 637
Lane, Polly 298
Lane, Reynolds 55
Lane, Richard 227, 295, 298
Lane, Royal Hastings 637
Lane, S. 94
Lane, Sally 399
Lane, Samuel 295
Lane, Sarah 466
Lane, Suckey 55
Lane, Susannah 637
Lane, Thomas 714
Lane, Thomas M. 41
Lane, Thos. 721
Lane, William 83
Lane, Wm. 219
Lanea, Elizabeth 336
Lanehart, Daniel 567
Lanfersneiler, Mary 111
Lanford, Peley P. 762
Lang, Catharine 712
Lang, Daniel 712
Lang, David 710, 712
Lang, Johan 237
Lang, Johan Friderick 237
Lang, Nicholas 710
Lang, Sarah 230
Lang, Susana 237

Lang, William 521
Langan, Thomas 48
Langerege, Robt. 573
Langewaine, Joseph 521
Langewaine, Peter 521
Langford, Dudley 717
Langham, --- 470, 471, 472
Langham, E. 64
Langham, E. T. 486
Langham, Elias 469, 473, 475, 477, 478, 479, 481, 485
Langham, Elias (Col.) 52
Langham, Eliza 478
Langhan, Elias 396
Langley, Bennet W. 133
Langstaff, James H. 582
Lanier, Helena 695
Lanier, Henry 413
Lanier, James W. 677
Lanius, Elizabeth F. 422
Lanius, Lavina 424
Lanius, R. Y. 424
Lanius, Richard Y. 422
Lanphin, Pierce 598
Lansdown, Hester H. 583
Lanston, John 147
Lanston, Joseph 147
Lantis, Asenith 434
Lantis, Samuel 434
Lantz, Abraham 743
Lantz, Emanuel 734
Lantz, Geo. 633
Lantz, George 633
Lantz, Sarah 734
Lanunn, Brooks 179
Lapan, David 259
Lape, George 396
Laperry, Precilla 384
Lapham, E. J. 532
Lapham, S. J. 532
Lapham, Thomas E. 532
Lapper, Wm. 476
Lappin, Samuel (Jr.) 567
Lappin, William 482
Larance, Sinthy 84
Lareau, Hannah 548
Large, Mary 119
Large, Nathaniel 125
Largey, Patrick 354
Larimer, Dolly 60
Larimer, Isaac 366
Larimer, Robert 763
Larison, Abel 265
Larison, James 259, 266
Larkin, Julia 82
Larkings, Christian 455
Larkins, Edward 385
Larrick, Abraham 308
Larrick, Asa 315
Larrick, Benjamin 308, 489
Larrick, Casper 308
Larrick, Catharine 308
Larrick, Elizabeth 489
Larrick, J. H. B. 315
Larrick, Jacob 308
Larrick, James V. 315

Larrick, John 308
Larrick, Levi E. 315
Larrick, Mary 315
Larrick, Mordecai B. 315
Larrick, Moses 315
Larrick, Rachel 308
Larrick, Rosanna 315
Larrick, William T. 315
Larrison, Abel 268
Larrison, Abel 270
Larrison, Amos 660
Larrow, Jacob 714
Lars, Catharine 337
Larsh, Margaret 422
Larsh, T. J. 422
Larue, Cyntha 65
Larue, Lydia 77
LaRue, Rachel 380
Larue, William 65, 78
Laser, Evy 523
Lash, Michael 361
Lash, Sophia 361
Lasher, Frederick 41
Lasher, Jeremiah 171
Lashley, Aaron 352
Lashley, Alexander 352
Lashley, Caleb 732
Lashley, Elizabeth 352
Lashley, Henry 688
Lashley, John 688
Lashley, Margery 352
Lashley, Mary 352
Lashley, Rebecca 352
Lashley, Richard 685
Lashley, Teresa 352
Lashley, William 352
Lashure, David 172
Lashure, John 171
Lashure, Mary 172
Lashward, Joseph 497
Lasley, --- 637
Lasley, David 339
Lasley, Easther 79
Lasley, Polley 83
Lasner, John H. 117
Lasse, George 396
Laterna, Chloe 194
Laterno, Chloe 192
Laterno, Francis 192
Latham, Chester 41
Latham, Nancy 48
Latham, Wm. A. (Capt.) 366
Lathrop, Daniel 497
Lathrop, Emily 654
Lathrop, George 497
Lathrop, Hazael 78
Lathrop, Henry 497
Lathrop, Isaac 497
Lathrop, Julia 592
Lathrop, Martin 654
Lathrop, Rebecca 654
Latimer, Alexander 369
Latimer, Dimmis 584
Laton, Asher 457
Laton, Elias 452
Latson, Sarah 584
Latta, Thomas 286, 559
Latterna, Francis 194

Latty, Abraham 320
Latty, John 317
Laturno, Chloe 198
Laturno, Francis 198
Laubaugh, John 573
Laudaman, David 745
Laudrick, Conrad 602
Laughbaugh, Catharine 565
Laughead, Wm. 270
Laughery, Charles 521
Laughlin, All. 296
Laughlin, Christiana 443
Laughlin, Daniel M. 167
Laughlin, Eleanor 591
Laughlin, James 573
Laughlin, John 439, 443
Laughlin, John C. 567
Laughlin, Robert 544
Laughman, Mary 369
Laughrey, John 266
Lauk, Samuel 580
Launes, Margret 386
Laur, Katharine 710
Lauren, Katharina 711
Laurence, Benjn. (Rev.) 594
Laurence, D. C. 711
Laurence, Henry 710
Laurent, James 717
Laurignour, Francis 120
Lavett, Lavina 166
Lavett, James 166
Lavy, William 514
Law, Ada 315
Law, Andrew 377
Law, Edey 170
Law, Elizabeth 77, 170
Law, Hannah 315
Law, Hetta 170
Law, John 375
Law, John H. 544
Law, Lovey 170
Law, Rebecca 170
Law, Sarah 170, 715
Law, William 660
Lawer, Francis 511
Lawes, Henry 573
Lawhead, Mary 302
Lawhead, Mary L. 532
Lawhead, Mattie 541
Lawhead, P. C. 541
Lawhead, S. 541
Lawler, Michael 544
Lawrence, Ami 266
Lawrence, Amy 509
Lawrence, Catharine 161
Lawrence, Daniel 260
Lawrence, John 521
Lawrence, John McDougal 86
Lawrence, John Shul 161
Lawrence, Joseph 6, 596
Lawrence, Lydia 660
Lawrence, Mary 155, 523
Lawrence, Mary Ann 84
Lawrence, Rice B. 125
Lawrence, Sarah 386, 548
Lawrence, William 155, 172, 286, 290

Lawrence, Wm. 385
Lawrence, Zecheriah 266
Lawson, Catharine 506
Lawson, Dolly 515
Lawson, Eleaser 666
Lawson, Elizabeth 506
Lawson, Hannah 506
Lawson, James 484, 506, 722
Lawson, Jeremiah 638
Lawson, John 506
Lawson, John (Sr.) 506
Lawson, John Taylor 506
Lawson, Manassa 509
Lawson, Mary An 506
Lawson, Rebecca Jane 506
Lawson, Thomas 506
Lay, James M. 605
Lay, John 497
Lay, Lorenzo D. 13
Laylin, Charles 30
Layman, Elizabeth S. 551
Layman, Jacob 162
Layman, John 544, 549
Layman, Mary Ann 162
Laymon, Abraham 660
Laymon, Eli 331
Layport, Catherine 2
Layport, Charles A. W. 2
Layport, Charles D. 2
Layport, James C. 2
Layport, Margaret 2
Layport, Robinson 2
Layport, Sarah 2
Layton, David 385
Layton, James 120
Lazarus, Fanny 271
Lazarus, Highman 263
Lazarus, Hyman 263, 271
Lazier, Jeremiah 164
Leach, John 16
Leach, Nancy 354
Leach, Nathaniel 544
Leadly, John 549
Leaf, Catharine 666
Leaf, Susannah 745
Leaky, Judith 553
Leanhart, Rosa 520
Leapley, Jacob 533
Leapley, Otho 544
Lear, Mary 688
Leard, Lucy P. 615
Leard, Mary C. 615
Leas, Catharine 414
Leas, Daniel G. 4
Leas, Joseph 639
Leas, Julius E. 434
Leas, Rebecca Jane 4
Leas, Samuel 4
Leas, Stephen 4
Lease, Stephen 20
Lease, William 8
Leasor, Phillip 220
Leasure, Caroline 751
Leasure, Jesse 751
Leasure, John 751
Leasure, Joseph 751
Leasure, William 751
Leath, John 717

Leatherman, Barbara 232
Leatherman, Christian 232
Leatherman, Daniel 573
Leatherman, Elizabeth 232
Leatherman, Eve 522
Leatherman, Jacob 232
Leatherman, Sarah 575
Leatherman, Susanna 572
Leavens, Matilda 719
Leaver, Adam 647
Leaver, Elizabeth 592
Lebart, John 298
Lebourn, David 489
Lebrell, Nicholas 485
Lecheiter, Joseph 112
Lechlider, Adam 191
Lechlider, Conrad 191
Lechlider, Mary Ann 191
Lechlider, Ruhamah 191
Leckey, Elizabeth 369
Leckey, Hannah 369
Leckey, Ruth 369
Leckey, Thomas 369
Leckey, William M. 544
Leckrone, John 369
LeClerc, John Lewis 722
LeClerc, L. 724
Leclerc, Lewis 723
LeClerc, Lewis 722
Leclereg, Francis 514
LeClerg, Francis 726
Lecroin, Andrew 714
Ledore, Minerva 80
Lee, Alfred 686
Lee, Ambrose Rice 757
Lee, Anna 582
Lee, Cyprean 598
Lee, Cyprian 591
Lee, David 638
Lee, David L. 145
Lee, Deany 511
Lee, Elizabeth 75, 639
Lee, Elizabeth E. 518
Lee, Eloner 663
Lee, Esther 517
Lee, F. A. 145
Lee, Francis H. 145
Lee, Geo. F. 145
Lee, Harrison 145
Lee, Henry 638
Lee, Howard M. 145
Lee, James 497
Lee, John 660, 684
Lee, John C. 278
Lee, John H. 145
Lee, Julia Ann 145
Lee, Keziah 639
Lee, Martha 631
Lee, Martin 165
Lee, Mary C. 145
Lee, Mayet 11
Lee, Myet 11
Lee, Nancy 713
Lee, Oliver 514
Lee, Pamelia 12
Lee, Patsey 517
Lee, Polly 633

Lee, Rachel 657
Lee, Rhoda 639, 664
Lee, Robert 649, 652, 653, 654, 660
Lee, Ruth 441
Lee, Samuel 732
Lee, Susannah 165
Lee, William 484, 638, 639
Lee, William C. 441
Lee, Wm. 78, 639
Lee, Zephemiah 638
Lee, Zepheniah 660
Leech, Gilbert 741
Leedham, John 705
Leedis, Jacob 206
Leedy, John 426
Leek, Barbara 310
Leek, Resin 310
Leek, Robert 310
Leeland, Baldwin M. 314
Leeland, Rebecca 314
Leeper, Alfred B. 312
Leeper, Betsey 13
Leeper, George 13
Leeper, James 16
Leeper, Jerusha 312
Leeper, Mary E. 312
Leeper, Samuel 596
Leeper, Sarah A. 312
Leeper, Thomas 385
Leeper, Virginia 312
Leeper, William 312
Leeper, William P. 312
Leer, David 688
Leeth, Elizabeth 512
Leezer, Clarissa 498
Leezer, Eliza 495
Lefaver, Daniel 120
Lefavors, David 549
Lefavour, Christian 660
Lefever, Isaac 361
Le Fevre, Henry J. 544
Le Fevre, John 544
Leffler, Frances 629
Leffler, John 629
Leforce, Robinson 660
Leforge, John 514
Leg, T. J. 626
Legg, George 493
Leggett, James 252
Leggit, Daniel 385
Leghty, John 573
Legit, Benjamin 573
Lehman, Adam 753
Lehman, Ann B. 369
Lehman, Christian 369
Lehman, Daniel 753
Lehman, David 753
Lehman, Jacob 753
Lehman, Jacob A. 369
Lehman, John 187, 753
Lehman, Magdalena 753
Lehman, Margaret 753
Lehman, Mary 753
Lehman, Peter 185, 224
Lehman, Samuel 753
Lehman, Sarah 753
Lehman, Wm. F. 368

Lehorn, Margaret V. 115
Lehorn, William 115
Leichty, William 328
Leidler, Jacob 227
Leighner, Elias 403
Leighner, James 403
Leikart, Battea 115
Leikart, Catharine 115
Leikart, Gabriel 115
Leikart, John 115
Leininger, Margaret 567
Leiper, . . . mas 153
Leiper, Elizabeth 153
Leiper, George Gray 153
Leiper, Hester 12
Leiper, Michael 161
Leist, Alice 411
Leist, Catharine 411
Leist, Clara 411
Leist, Coon 411
Leist, Edward 411
Leist, George 388
Leister, James 10
Leisure, John 357
Leisure, Margaret 357
Leitner, David 521
Leitrick, Jacob 603
Lelan, Baldwin 250, 251
Lelan, John A. C. 250, 251
Lellard, Thomas 48
Lelly, Armiger 62
Leman, Gabrill 336
Leman, William 751
Lemans, Wm. 752
Lemaster, Lemuel Q. 544
Lemasters, Jane 550
Lemasters, Lemuel 550
Lemasters, Luman W. 550
Lemasters, Sally 545
Lemert, Lewis 288
Lemert, Thaddeus 288
Leming, Hugh 545
Leming, Warren 134
Lemix, James (Sr.) 303
Lemmon, B. 525
Lemmon, Ellen 523
Lemmon, John C. 525
Lemmon, Joseph 470
Lemmon, Julia 523
Lemmon, William 497
Lemon, John A. 22
Lemon, Joseph 482
Lemon, Martha Ellen 519
Lemon, William 151
Lemouyon, Stephen 567
Lemum, Frederick 305
Lenan, Anne 117
Lender, Charles F. 30
Lender, James F. 30
Lene, Jane 565
Lenes, Fredrick 457
Lenhard, John 287
Lenhart, Ann 287
Lenhart, Aviey 287
Lenhart, David 369
Lenhart, David A. 369
Lenhart, George 287
Lenhart, Harriet 369

Lenhart, John R. 287
Lenhart, John W. 145
Lenhart, Mary Ann 287
Lenhart, Peter 573
Lenhart, Sally 287
Lenherst, David 573
Lennox, John 125
Lennox, Mary 123
Lenon, Charlotte 268
Lenon, John 268
Lenon, Mary 116
Lenon, Michael 268
Lenox, Amanda 550
Lenox, Ellener 120
Lenox, James 125
Lenox, John 532, 550
Lenox, John W. 608
Lenox, Richard M. 532
Lent, Nun M. 30
Lent, Polly 31
Lentz, Catherina 235
Lentz, Chatarina 234
Lentz, Elizabeth 278
Lentz, Johan 234
Lentz, Johannes 235
Lentz, John 365
Lentz, John Hennrich 234
Lentz, Maria Elisabeth 235
Lenville, Joseph 366
Leonal, Jacob 554
Leonard, Patrick 104
Leonard, Abigail 662
Leonard, Adam 509
Leonard, Anne 104
Leonard, Caleb 660
Leonard, Catherine 746
Leonard, Charles 385
Leonard, Elizabeth 509
Leonard, George 18
Leonard, Jacob 509
Leonard, James 666
Leonard, James F. 554
Leonard, John 650
Leonard, Lucas D. 680
Leonard, Mary 660
Leonard, Mason 655
Leonard, Nancy 509
Leonard, Peggy 663
Leonard, Polly 509
Leonard, Rueben 745
Leonard, Sarah 509, 662
Leonard, Sophia 30
Leonard, Susan 509
Leonard, Sylva 489
Leonard, William B. 717
Leonardson, John (Jr.) 41
Leopold, Catharine 677
Leopold, John 677
Leopold, Valentine 677
Lerce, Zelinda H. 595
Lermore, Jacob 295
Lermore, John 295
LeRoi, Marie Francois Charlotte 714
Lerue, Jacob 717
LeSeusior, Pierre 714
Lesh, Daniel 426

Lesher, Adam 227
Lesher, Barbary 203
Lesher, Elizabeth 520
Lesher, Jacob 203
Lesley, Christian 216
Lesley, David 216
Leslie, Absalom 218
Leslie, David 211, 218
Leslie, George 599
Leslie, John 211
Leslie, Jonson 167
Lesscena, John 120
Lesslie, Robert 163
Lester, Elizabeth 571
Lester, Sarah 44, 48
LeSure, Nicholas 722
LeTaileur, --- 727
LeTaileur, John Baptist
   724
LeTailleur, J. B. 722,
   724
LeTailleur, John B.
   723, 724, 726
LeTailleur, John Baptist
   724
LeTalliur, John
   Basstiste 714
Leth, Nancy 516
Letherman, Catharine 576
Lett, Eliza Jane 409
LeTumo, Francis 117
Leturno, Chloe 185, 192
Leturno, Francis 185
Leues, John 574
Leuser, Margaret 521
Level, Benjamin 117
Levengood, Barbara 116
Levey, J. 326
Levey, John 326
Levey, S. 326
Levey, Susan 326
Levick, Robert 284
Levill, Ezekiel 13
Levins, Easter 726
Levins, Francis 714
Levins, John 726
Levins, Joseph 726
Levisay, Nancy 408
Leviston, Prudence 658
Lewallen, Ascy 13
Lewallen, Jane 13
Lewallen, Rebecca 13
Lewelland, Charity 425
Lewelland, Lewis 425
Lewellen, James 732
Lewellen, John L. 423
Lewellen, Mary Ann 423
Lewin, John 385
Lewis, Abel 296, 299
Lewis, Abigail 54
Lewis, Abram 41
Lewis, Anna Maria 508
Lewis, Betsey 467
Lewis, Catharine 44
Lewis, Charles 689
Lewis, Comfort 517
Lewis, Daniel 732
Lewis, David 489, 514
Lewis, E. 762

Lewis, Emaline 406
Lewis, Esther 106
Lewis, Evaline 744
Lewis, Francis 716
Lewis, George 521
Lewis, George A. 508
Lewis, Griffin 514
Lewis, Hester 662
Lewis, J. M. 508
Lewis, Jacob M. 508
Lewis, James 48
Lewis, James O. 508
Lewis, Jno. 407
Lewis, John 419, 602,
   630, 689
Lewis, John F. 508
Lewis, Laura 520
Lewis, Lyman 41
Lewis, Mahala 15
Lewis, Margaret 387
Lewis, Mary 74, 407,
   516, 716
Lewis, Morgan 560
Lewis, Nancy 382
Lewis, Oliver H. 30
Lewis, P. 52
Lewis, Paul 641, 660,
   677
Lewis, Paul (Jr.) 689
Lewis, Peter 406
Lewis, Philip (Sr.) 514
Lewis, Ransum 65
Lewis, Sarah 385, 465
Lewis, Silas 13
Lewis, Solomon 44
Lewis, Stephen G. 419
Lewis, Thomas 477, 763
Lewis, Thomas B. 508
Lewis, Thos. B. 508
Lewis, Tiliman 474
Lewis, Tilman 469
Lewis, Tilmen 471
Lewis, William 608,
   689, 745
Lewis, William R. 407
Lewis, Wm. 258, 259, 630
Lewis, Wm. A. 508
Ley, Andrew 521
Lezer, Abraham 554
Libcap, C. 242
Libcap, Catharine 242
Libcap, Charles 242
Libcap, J. 242
Libcap, Jacob 242
Libcap, Louis B. 242
Libcap, Michael 242
Libcap, Sarah 242
Libcap, Sarah C. 242
Libcap, Thomas 242
Lich, John 734
Lichty, Ann 333
Lick, John 695
Liday, John 378
Liddle, James 680
Lidenbender, Mary 462
Lidey, Daniel 350, 369
Lidey, John 358, 361,
   364, 369, 370, 371,
   375, 377

Liebing, John 389
Lieper, Thomas 86
Ligen, Samuel 457
Ligget, Alexander 641
Ligget, Elizabeth 661
Ligget, Mary 662
Ligget, Rebecca 641
Liggett, Sarah 581
Liggitt, Darnis 660
Ligh, John 734
Lightcap, Levi 521
Lighter, Catharine 199
Lighter, Christianna 199
Lighter, Daniel 199
Lighter, Elizabeth 199
Lighter, Frederick 199
Lighter, George 199
Lighter, Henry 199
Lighter, John 199
Lighter, Mary 199
Lightfoot, Jepthah 651
Lightner, Catherine 518
Lighty, Conrad 190
Lighty, George 190
Lihehart, Casemer 608
Likens, Leonard 165
Likens, Ruth 165
Likins, Elizabeth 68
Likins, Frances 68
Likins, James 68
Likins, John E. 68
Likins, Nancy 68
Lilley, Richard J. 369
Lilly, Fanny S. 28
Lilly, James 48
Lilly, John 608
Limboth, Frederick 574
Limes, . . . 532
Liming, Elizabeth L. 134
Linch, Elizabeth 665
Linch, Isabella 48
Lincicum, Caleb 173
Lincoln, Alfred 448
Lincoln, Betsey 273
Lincoln, David 434
Lincoln, Elizabeth 434
Lincoln, Henry 434
Lincoln, Joseph 714
Lincoln, Lucy Ann 434
Lincoln, Mary Jane 434
Lincoln, Obediah 714
Lincoln, Peleg 273
Lind, Caroline 690
Lind, John M. 690
Lind, Nancy 748
Lindemood, Jacob 166
Lindenberger, Evaline
   752
Lindenmuth, Jonathan 232
Lindermuth, Jonathan 232
Lindermuth, Susannah 232
Lindley, Denias 120
Lindley, Elizabeth 119
Lindley, Hannah 87
Lindley, Levi 87
Lindley, Mary 657
Lindley, Ruth 87
Lindly, Nancy 127
Lindsay, Daniel 766

Lindsay, Lemuel 644
Lindsay, Oliver 644
Lindsey, Betsy Ann 506
Lindsey, James 685
Lindsey, Margaret 164, 515
Lindsey, Mary 715
Lindsey, Mary Ann 302
Lindsey, Robert 227
Lindsey, Samuel 164
Lindsey, William 514
Lindsley, Aaron K. 71
Lindsley, Benjamin 71
Lindsley, Betsey 71 71
Lindsley, Henry B. 71
Lindsley, Jonathan 648, 656
Lindsley, Letty 656
Lindsley, Lewis 656
Lindsley, Margaret 117
Lindsley, Zenas C. 71
Lindsly, Hannah 648
Lindsly, Lewis 648
Lindwood, Jacob 152
Line, A. 539
Line, Amanda 539
Line, Ann 539
Line, D. M. 539
Line, E. 540
Line, Elizabeth 539, 540
Line, George 539
Line, H. C. 539
Line, Henry C. 539
Line, J. 539
Line, John 539
Line, Johnathan 539
Line, Levi S. 545
Line, Martin 539
Line, O. Belle 539
Line, Oscar E. 539
Line, S. 540
Line, S. A. 539
Line, Solomon 540
Liners, Caroline 528
Liners, John A. 528
Lingeral, Jeremiah 13
Lingree, Jenna 463
Lininger, John 111
Link, Athanon 430
Link, Barbara 430
Link, Betsy 430
Link, Eve 430
Link, Mary 430
Link, Mary U. 430
Link, Susannah 430
Linkens, Robert 249
Linkins, Henry 249
Linkins, James Wesley 249
Linkswiler, George 13, 17
Linksyller, Kitty 454
Linn, Caleb 162
Linn, Hannah 719
Linn, John 154, 157, 162, 177, 404, 545
Linn, John E. 362
Linn, Joseph C. 270
Linn, Joshua 162, 165, 173

Linn, Levi 162
Linn, Robert 284
Linn, Sarah 157, 177
Linn, Susan 404
Linn, Susannah 154
Linn, Wm. 404
Linnell, J. P. 75
Linscott, Heman 755
Linscott, Heman W. 755
Linscott, Sarah 755
Linsey, Levi 509
Linson, Anna 55
Linson, Betsey 55
Linson, Catharine 63
Linson, Dolly 55, 63
Linson, Edward 55, 63
Linson, Edward T. 55
Linson, George 55, 63
Linson, Jacob 55, 63
Linson, John 55, 63
Linson, Nancy 55, 63
Linson, Polly 55, 63
Linson, Ruth 63
Linson, Sally 55
Linson, Washington 63
Linteman, Frederick 608
Lintermuth, Solomon 608
Lintner, David M. 434
Lintner, Wm. Henry 434
Linton, Zacheriah 464
Linville, Benjamin 380
Linville, Joseph 372
Linville, Margaret 375
Linville, Rachel 375
Linzee, Andrew Jackson 109
Linzee, Caroline 109
Linzee, Franklin 106
Linzee, Robert 105, 109
Linzee, Ruth 109
Lionbarger, Peter (Jr.) 500
Lionbarger, Peter (Sr.) 500
Lions, Isaac 430
Lions, Tabitha 430
Lippencott, Jane 14
Lippets, Fayette 586
Lippincomb, Elisha 157
Lippincomb, Mary 157
Lippincout, . . . 160
Lippitt, Alfred 306
Lippitt, Benjamin 306
Lippitt, Christopher 306
Lippitt, Elihu 306
Lippitt, Joseph 259
Lippitt, Joseph W. 306
Lippitt, Malinda 306
Lippitt, Mariah 306
Lippitt, Otis 306
Lippitt, Sarah 306
Lippold, Casper 604
Lipps, Henry 115
Lipscomb, Isaac 489
List, George 385
Lister, Elecy 398
Lister, Elsey 398
Lister, William 464
Liston, Ebenezer 633

Liston, John 501
Liston, Mary 516, 633
Liston, Perry 501
Litener, Paul 521
Little, Betsey 462
Little, Elias 638, 660
Little, Jacob 457
Little, John 464
Little, Joseph 7, 660
Little, Levi 260, 660, 666
Little, Margaret 722
Little, Nancy 466
Little, Peter 493
Little, Thomas 169
Little, William 660
Littlejohn, Henry 117
Littlejohn, Nancy 116
Littlejohn, Samuel 130
Littlejohn, Vallentine 514
Littler, John 27
Littler, Laban 54
Littler, Samuel 27
Littleton, James 78
Littleton, Leah 451
Littleton, M. 405
Littleton, Matthew 464
Littleton, Sarah 406
Littleton, Wm. 406
Litzinger, Elen 345
Litzinger, Jacob 345, 368
Litzinger, John 368
Lively, Clarinda 630
Lively, Cottrell 630
Lively, David 630
Lively, Elizabeth 630
Lively, Mary 630
Lively, Neoma 630
Lively, Rebecca 630
Lively, Sarah 630
Lively, William 630
Lively, Wilson 630
Livengood, --- 127
Livengood, Catherine 297
Livengood, Jacob 284, 297
Livengood, Mary 297
Livengood, Peter 284, 297
Livermore, Jonas 732
Livers, Caroline 528
Livers, John A. 528
Livezy, Jno. H. 273
Livingood, Jacob 284
Livingston, Alexander 632
Livingston, Christina 558
Livingston, Eli 632
Livingston, Jane 662
Livingston, William 660
Livseney, John 521
Lloyd, John 170, 687
Locaud, Jean 464
Lochard, Joseph 464
Lochard, Thomas 545
Locier, Jacob 403

Lock, Abram 434
Lock, Adam 419, 434
Lock, Andrew 182
Lock, Benjamin 591
Lock, Catharine 524
Lock, Christina 434
Lock, Elam 524
Lock, Elizabeth 434
Lock, Ira 524
Lock, Isaac 434
Lock, Jacob 434
Lock, John 385
Lock, John S. 591
Lock, Jonathan 591
Lock, Josiah 524
Lock, Levi 765
Lock, Louisa 580
Lock, Milo 524
Lock, Myron 524
Lock, Rosannah Margaret 434
Lock, Sally 434
Lock, Sidney Erie 524
Lock, Solomon 434
Lock, Sophia 419
Lock, William Roberts 524
Lockard, Elijah 452
Lockard, Elizabeth 11
Locke, Benjamin 503, 514
Locker, Susan 74
Lockhard, Phillip 125
Lockhard, William 452
Lockhart, Elizabeth J. 583
Lockhart, William 448
Lockwood, Elizth. 413
Lockwood, Geo. 434
Lockwood, Israel 586
Lockwood, Sarah 593
Lockwood, Wm. 434
Locy, Phebe 441
Lodge, Jacob 125
Lodsdan, Bennett 483
Loffelt, Margret Ann 336
Loffer, Christian 398
Loffer, Daniel 398
Loffer, Daniel P. 398
Loffer, Ellen 398
Loffer, Henry 398
Loffer, Sarah 398
Loffer, Simon P. 398
Loffer, Solomon T. 398
Logan, Eliza 513
Logan, Geo. H. Emerette 145
Logan, James 78, 471, 472, 477, 483, 484, 485
Logan, James A. 145
Logan, Jas. 478
Logan, John 545
Logan, John A. 145
Logan, Lot 24
Logan, Mary 571
Logan, Rebeccah 516
Logan, Robert 148
Logan, Saml. M. 148
Logan, Samuel M. 148

Logan, Sarah Catharine 686
Logan, William 686
Logsdan, Bennett 483
Logue, Benjamin 129
Logue, Elizabeth 129
Logue, John 145
Logue, Polly 465
Lohr, Sarah 48
Loller, Elisha 638
Loller, Elizabeth 638
Loller, Joseph 638
Loller, Moses 638
Loller, Nancy 638
Loller, Phebe 638
Loller, Polly 638
Loman, Eliz. 463
Lombar, Peter 41
Lombard, Jesse 48
Long, Aaron 109
Long, Able 72
Long, Abraham 102
Long, Adam 30, 37
Long, Alex. 407
Long, Benjamin 13
Long, Betsey 121, 384
Long, Catharine 368
Long, Catherine 368, 459
Long, Catrin 276
Long, Charles 533
Long, Christiana 368
Long, Christianna 347
Long, Clestia 37
Long, Daniel 72
Long, Daniel K. 419
Long, David 72, 109, 257, 355
Long, Ed. 533, 534
Long, Ed. C. 533
Long, Edna R. Kies 533
Long, Edward 464
Long, Elizabeth 102, 132, 205, 347, 368
Long, Ethel I. 533
Long, Geo. 358
Long, Geo. W. 145
Long, George 340, 347, 368
Long, Henry 167
Long, Henry F. 145
Long, Isabella 524
Long, Jaclb 347
Long, Jacob 102, 109, 223, 224, 347, 358, 368, 743
Long, James 13, 120, 132, 205, 668
Long, Jane 205, 549
Long, Johan 237
Long, Johan Friderick 237
Long, John 72, 109, 125, 132, 157, 419, 457, 464
Long, John Christian 276
Long, John F. 72
Long, Johnathan 109
Long, Joseph 276, 567
Long, Katharine 72

Long, Katharine (II) 72
Long, Louella C. 533
Long, Lucinda 145
Long, Margaret 347
Long, Margaretha 368
Long, Martha 205
Long, Mary 37, 72, 461
Long, Mary L. 533
Long, Mathias 208
Long, Matthias 133
Long, Noah 37
Long, Peter 218
Long, Polly 132
Long, Rachel 132
Long, Robert 132, 452, 514
Long, Robt. 132
Long, Samuel 274, 524, 690
Long, Sarah 205
Long, Sophia Wade 533
Long, Stephen 132
Long, Susan 109
Long, Susana 237
Long, Susanna 119
Long, Susannah 205, 347
Long, Thomas 484
Long, Thos. 476
Long, Tracey 37
Long, William 132, 190, 205, 314, 514, 528
Long, Wm. 205, 477
Longanecker, Henry 145
Longanecker, Jeremiah 145
Longanecker, Joe 145
Longanecker, Samuel 145
Longanecker, Sarah 145
Longbrake, Caroline 23
Longbrake, Jacob 591
Longbrake, Mary 589
Longfellow, Joseph 9
Longham, Elias 469
Longintiefer, Stephen E. 41
Longnecker, William 417
Longshore, Clarinda 67
Longshore, James 457
Longshore, John 67
Longstretch, E. 535
Longstretch, Estelle 535
Longstretch, John 535
Longstretch, John H. 535
Longstreth, B. 365
Longstreth, Bartholomew 262, 264, 268
Longstreth, Cynthia 635
Longstreth, George F. 690
Longstreth, James 261
Longstreth, Philip 268
Longsworth, Enoch G. 627
Longsworth, Enoch George 627
Longsworth, Solomon 627
Longsworth, Solomon Reece 627
Longsworth, Solomon Reexe 627

Longwith, Thomas 484
Longworth, Eliza 101
Longworth, J. 101
Longworth, Jackson 101
Longworth, Jonathan 101
Longworth, Margery 101
Longworth, Nicholas 270, 678
Longworth, Samuel 101
Longworth, Thomas 101
Loofborrow, Barbara 368
Loofborrow, Jonathan 368
Loofborrow, Mary 368
Loofbourrow, Abigail 391
Loofbourrow, Benjamin 391
Loofbourrow, Ebenezer 391
Loofbourrow, Jacob 391
Loofbourrow, John 391
Loofbourrow, John W. 391
Loofbourrow, John Wade 391
Loofbourrow, Mary 391
Loofbourrow, Nathan 391
Loofbourrow, Rebecca 391
Loofbourrow, Sarah 391
Loofbourrow, Thomas 391
Loofbourrow, Wade 391
Lookenbill, Margaret 590
Looker, E. J. 149
Looker, Edgar 149
Looker, G. R. 149
Lookinbil, Peter 591
Lookingbill, Dorothy 588
Lookingbill, George 586
Loper, Enoch 258, 260
Lord, A. H. 25
Lord, Abiel H. 13
Lord, Thomas 714
Lorentz, Peter 227
Loring, Charlotte 715
Loring, D. 728
Loring, Jesse 732
Lorton, Barbara 128
Lorton, Barbary 125
Lorton, John 125, 128
Lorton, William 545
Losier, Matthias 347, 348
Losier, Rosannah 347
Lothain, Bicy 545
Lothrop, Sybbil 585
Lotspeecer, James Quincy 48
Lott, Aaron B. 274
Lott, Abraham 368
Lott, Charles 368
Lott, Daniel A. 83
Lott, Peter 368, 525
Lott, Sally 368
Lott, William 368
Louck, Adam 428
Louck, Samuel 580
Loucks, Abraham 497
Loucks, Adam 428
Loudenslager, Daniel 530
Loudenslager, William 521

Louder, Anthony 1
Louder, Daniel L. 1
Louder, Emeline A. 1
Louder, Emily A. 1
Louder, George W. P. 1
Louder, Henry I. 1
Louder, Jacob M. 1
Louder, Jno. A. 1
Louder, Mortimer H. 1
Louder, Samuel S. 1
Louder, Susan R. 1
Louderback, Hannah 513
Louderback, Polly 513
Louderbough, John 660
Louer, Catherine 520
Lough, Levi 430
Louirh, Benjamin 441
Loury, Catherine 215
Loury, David 215
Loury, George Maley 215
Loury, James 215
Loury, Nancy 215
Loury, Rosanna 215
Loury, Sarah Ann 215
Loury, William (Jr.) 215
Lout, Aaron 593
Louthain, Absalom 131
Louthain, George 131, 135
Louthain, Grissey 131
Louthain, Grizzey 121
Louthain, John 131
Louthain, Juley 131
Louthain, Milly 131
Louthain, Nancy 131
Louthain, Polly 131
Louthain, Sally 131
Louthain, Samuel D. 131
Louthain, Tabitha 131
Louther, Wm. Re. 508
Louthin, Sarah 550
Louvet, Daniel 714
Love, Abigail 529
Love, Alexander 293
Love, Andrew 525, 529
Love, Anna Jane 368
Love, Eleanor 135
Love, Elizabeth 657
Love, Ellen 373
Love, Hugh 359
Love, James 293, 368
Love, James W. 529
Love, Jane 293
Love, John 514
Love, Joseph 135
Love, Lettuce 293
Love, Lewis 139
Love, Magdalena 529
Love, Margaret 293
Love, Mary 368
Love, Polly 79
Love, Prudence 529
Love, Robert 283, 340
Love, Sarah 529
Love, Thomas 293
Love, William 529
Love, Wm. 378
Lovekin, Sally 714
Lovel, Harriet 709

Lovel, Rachel 517
Loveland, Aaron 497
Loveland, Abner (Jr.) 30
Loveland, Joseph 452, 457
Loveland, Luther 322
Loveless, John 457, 489
Loveless, Wm. 464
Lovell, Harriet 709
Lovell, Isaiah 381
Lovell, John 514
Lovell, Mary 84
Lovelys, Wm. 464
Lovenz, Henry 710
Lover, Margaret 518
Lovess, Elias 489
Lovet, John 293
Lovet, William 84
Lovett, John J. 761
Lovett, Stephen C. 139
Lovett, William 93
Loving, Catharine 628
Loving, Martha 628
Loving, Patten 628
Loving, Thomas 628
Low, Ann Maria Elizabeth 105
Low, C. H. 102, 105
Low, Carl H. 103, 105
Low, Catharine 443
Low, George 139
Low, Herry 117
Low, John 591, 732
Low, Joseph 443
Low, Katharine Louisa 105
Low, Lucas 591
Low, Margaret 592
Lowder, Peggy 462
Lowderback, Catherine 515
Lowderback, Michael 514
Lowe, Abraham 457
Lowe, Abraham D. 660
Lowe, Elizabeth 11
Lowe, Jacob 574
Lowe, Jacob D. 646, 652
Lowe, Jesse 198
Lowe, John 125
Lowe, John Bishop 278
Lowe, John D. 675
Lowe, Peter P. 205, 207
Lowell, Joseph M. 465
Lower, Geo. 574
Lower, Margaret 430
Lower, Michael 418
Lower, Nancy 418, 511
Lower, Sarah Ann 430
Lower, William 418, 430
Lowers, Griffin 514
Lowery, Geo. 356
Lowery, Margaret 515
Lowes, Hendley 91
Lownes, Hygett 473
Lowrey, William 303
Lowry, Abraham 642
Lowry, Ann E. P. 207
Lowry, Archibald 183
Lowry, David 183

Lowry, Fielding 199, 207
Lowry, Fielding (Jr.) 199
Lowry, George 653
Lowry, Harriet S. 207
Lowry, Jane 515
Lowry, Mary B. 207
Lowry, William 642, 648, 660
Lowry, Wm. 670, 672
Lowther, Catharine 391
Lowther, George 452
Lowther, Polly 453
Loy, Adam 420
Loy, Alfred 420
Loy, Christena 377
Loy, Christopher 434
Loy, Errilla 129
Loy, George William Washington 368
Loy, Henry 129
Loy, Jacob O. (Dr.) 368
Loy, Jane 434
Loy, Margaret Susanna 368
Loy, Mary Ann 420
Loy, Matilda Jane 434
Loy, Susannah 434
Loyd, James 180
Loyd, John 125
Loyd, John W. 701
Loyd, M. 701
Loyd, Michael 701
Loyd, P. 701
Loyd, Phebe 701
Loyd, Polly 387
Loyd, Sarah 180
Luas, And. 104
Luas, Rebecca 274
Lucabill, Polly 585
Lucanbill, Susannah 585
Lucas, A. W. 505
Lucas, Abigail 500, 512
Lucas, Adrian 508
Lucas, Annie 508
Lucas, Barbary 179
Lucas, Betsey 502, 508
Lucas, Brice 306
Lucas, Caleb 660
Lucas, David 182
Lucas, Demaris 550
Lucas, Elizabeth 503, 717
Lucas, Elizabeth (Sr.) 508
Lucas, Hannah 502
Lucas, Harrison 179
Lucas, Israel 272
Lucas, Jane 121
Lucas, John 258, 259, 500, 501, 504, 508, 550
Lucas, Joseph 500
Lucas, Joshua 550
Lucas, Lavise 500
Lucas, Levi 508
Lucas, Levise 516
Lucas, Minerva E. B. 502, 503

Lucas, Nathaniel 334
Lucas, Peggy 550, 568
Lucas, Rebeccah 500
Lucas, Robbert 503
Lucas, Robert 500, 502, 512, 514
Lucas, Samuel 500, 714
Lucas, Simeon 100
Lucas, Susannah 500
Lucas, Willerby 385
Lucas, William 59, 500, 714
Lucas, William (Jr.) 508
Lucas, William (Sr.) 500
Lucas, Wilmoth 551
Luce, Ann Ohio 230
Luce, Benjamin 230
Luce, Samuel 742
Luce, William 745
Luck, William 267
Luckenbaugh, Abraham 567
Luckenbill, John 591
Luckey, Samuel 714
Lucky, Joseph 84
Lucrois, Alexander 506
Lucrois, Andrew 506
Lucus, James 163
Lucus, Margaret 163
Ludlow, Cooper 660
Ludlow, George 637
Ludlow, Joseph 637
Ludlow, Richard 637
Ludlum, Ephrain 660
Ludlum, Nancy 662
Ludlum, Rebecca 660
Ludwig, Catharine 385
Ludy, David 194
Luehman, Henry 104
Luellen, Philip 78
Lugenbul, Andrew 531
Luhmann, Henry 104
Luhmann, Henry L. 104
Luis, Thomas 501
Luke, George 567
Luke, John 574
Lukins, A. 407
Lukins, M. 407
Lukins, Margaret E. 407
Lukins, Thos. E. 407
Lulter, Robert 441
Lumbarger, Peter 514
Lumhart, H. 403
Lumpkin, Amy B. 701
Lumpkin, Elmer T. 701
Lumpkin, W. H. 701
Lumpkin, Wayne E. 701
Lunbeck, Henry 493
Lunbeck, Mary 493
Lundy, Henry 758
Lundy, James 732
Lundy, Margaret 758
Lundy, Susanna 14
Lundy, Tamer 593
Lung, Jacob 550
Lupton, John 117
Lurge, Mary 119
Lush, John 477
Lutere, Victore Charlotte 714

Luther, Eli 497
Luther, Sarah 744
Lutton, Matthew 269
Luttrell, Lewis 545
Lutz, Abraham 626
Lutz, Henry 626
Lutz, Jacob D. 385
Lutz, John 90
Lutz, John H. 385
Lutz, Mary C. 90
Lybarger, Jacob 741
Lybrand, Archibald 399
Lybrand, Samuel 396
Lyel, David 374
Lyel, Gresoll 374
Lyle, Butler 633
Lyle, Foster 633
Lyle, George 633
Lyle, Harrison 633
Lyle, Jackson 633
Lyle, James 633
Lyle, Jane 633
Lyle, John 633
Lyle, Mary 633
Lyle, Mary Ann 633
Lyle, Robert 365, 374, 633
Lyle, Sarah 633
Lyle, William 633
Lynch, Edwin 424
Lynch, Eleanor 352
Lynch, Elizabeth 424
Lynch, Ellen 44
Lynch, Isaac 424
Lynch, John 352
Lynch, Mary 352
Lynch, Patrick 442
Lynch, Samuel 352
Lynch, Susanna 352
Lynch, Timothy 352
Lynch, Walter 352
Lynch, William 90, 352
Lynch, Willimina 352
Lynder, Sarah 280
Lynn, Adam 567
Lynn, Hugh 489
Lynn, Joshua 165
Lynn, Samuel 48
Lyon, Charles M. 528
Lyon, Chester 528
Lyon, Elizabeth 528, 591
Lyon, Frederick 318, 319, 320
Lyon, James 267
Lyon, Mary 528
Lyon, Nathaniel 223, 754
Lyon, Reuben D. 528
Lyon, Reuben D. (Jr.) 528
Lyon, Ruth Ann 528
Lyon, Sarah 528
Lyons, Henry 125
Lyons, Ira E. 360
Lyons, Jacob 550
Lyons, James 268
Lyons, John 78, 732
Lyons, John W. 410
Lyons, Levi 305
Lyons, Thomas 493

Lyons, W. B.   355
Lyons, Winfield L.   34
Lyons, Winfield S.   34
Lyons, Wm. B.   360
Lyron, James R.   574
Lysher, Matilda   334
Lytle, Andrew   556, 669
Lytle, Catharine   649
Lytle, David   649
Lytle, Elizabeth   75
Lytle, Esther   665
Lytle, Henry   732
Lytle, Hugh   497
Lytle, Margareta   556
Lytle, Robert   556
Lytle, Sarah   673
Lytle, William   670, 672
Lytte, Andrew J.   431
Lytte, Hetty   431
Lytte, Joseph   431
Lytte, Margaret   431
Lytte, Susan   431
Lyur, Samuel E.   39

--- M ---

M . . . , Benson   167
M . . . , William   567
Ma . . . er, William   41
Macamon, Adam   562
Macamon, Henery   562
Macamon, Lewis   562
Macan, John G.   494
Macanally, Uriah P. R.
    745
Macater, Charles   745
Mace, Andrew   493
Mace, Elizabeth   58
Mace, Isaac   58
Mace, Jacob   465
Mace, Sarah   58
Maceuterfer, Catharine
    558
Maceuterfer, Christian
    558
Maceuterfer, Christina
    558
Maceuterfer, George   558
Maceuterfer, George
    (Jr.)   558
Maceuterfer, Jacob   558
Maceuterfer, John   558
Maceuterfer, Mary   558
Maceuterfer, Susana   558
Maceuterfer, William   558
Macey, John   413
Macham, John   563
Maches, Jennie   452
Machier, Elizabeth   406
Machier, Henry   406
Machier, James   406
Machling, Philip P.   580
Mack, Florinda   75
Mack, Frederick   117
Mack, Jacob   288
Mack, Susanah   566
Mack, Thomas   59

Mackall, John D.   732
Mackaman, Adam   564
Mackaman, Catharine   574
Mackeltree, Eve   517
Mackerel, Joel   754
Mackerell, Joel   754
Mackey, Abraham   154
Mackey, Elizabeth   116
Mackey, Margaret   517
Mackey, Robert   465
Mackey, Thomas   154
Mackool, Martha   116
Mackrill, Robert   521
Macnemu, Joseph (Rev.)
    529
Macomb, Mary   62
Macoon, Isaac   39
Macy, Alexander   213
Macy, Elizabeth   127
Macy, Enoch   145
Macy, George   213
Macy, Isaac   213
Macy, John   213
Macy, Lucinda   663
Macy, Mary   117, 213
Macy, Moses   145
Macy, Nancy   213
Macy, Phebe   145
Macy, Samuel   145
Macy, Seth   661
Macy, Thomas   134, 145,
    213
Macy, William   213
Madden, Charley   115
Madden, Dennis   385
Madden, Eli   661
Madden, Henry   139, 550
Madden, Joseph   567
Madden, Margaret   139
Madden, Nancy   117
Madden, Rebecca   278
Madden, Sarah   120, 387
Madden, William   115, 182
Madden, Wm.   139
Maddington, John   10
Maddock, Mary   33
Maddox, John   661
Maddox, Sarah Hall   387
Maddox, Stephen   693
Maddux, Charles   625
Maddux, David   625
Maddux, Elizabeth   608
Maddux, James   625
Maddux, John   625
Maddux, Mary   607
Maddux, Mary Jane   609,
    625
Maddux, Melinda H.   608
Maddux, Minerva   625
Maddux, Nancy F.   608
Maddux, Peter   625
Maddux, Rachel   625
Maddux, Rosanna   625
Maddux, Samuel   602, 625
Maddux, Sarah Jane   625
Maddux, Thomas H.   625
Madens, John   172
Madens, Mary Ann   172
Madigan, John   10

Madins, John   156, 167
Madison, Joab   648, 652
Madison, John P.   78
Maefild, Jane   573
Maefild, Mary   576
Maetin, Jacob   545
Magaw, William (Jr.)   418
Magee, William Fairchild
    723
Mager, George   320
Maginess, Edward   162
Maginess, Jane   162
Maginnis, David   290, 762
Maginnis, T. J.   374
Maginnis, Thos. J.   371
Magness, Ann   382
Magnier, Peter   722
Magny, Forgy   574
Magoffin, Jacob C.   525
Magone, Arthur   158
Magoverin, Owein   104
Magraugh, James   48
Magruder, E. R.   365, 374
Magruder, E. R. (Dr.)
    376
Maguire, James   427
Maguire, Lewis   514
Mahaffey, John   435
Mahan, James   438
Mahan, Robt. M.   470
Mahan, William   465
Mahana, John   267
Mahigan, William   441
Mahl, Reinhardt   41
Mahney, Bartholomew   41
Mahnin, Isaac   133
Mahon, James   457
Mahon, Jean   463
Mahon, John   493
Mahurin, Anna   140
Mahurin, Belinda   140
Mahurin, Catharine   140
Mahusin, Elizabeth   207
Mahusin, Isaac   207
Maidens, John   152, 159
Maidens, Mary   159
Main, John   156
Main, Sanford   321
Maines, Henry   493
Mains, George   368
Mains, Jacob   369
Mains, Phillip   442
Mair, Wm. H.   292
Maitland, William H.   84
Majar, George   323
Major, Caleb   101
Major, Calinda   608
Major, David   603, 604,
    605, 608, 617
Major, David (Sr.)   615
Major, Elizabeth   615
Major, Evalina   617
Major, Evelinah   617
Major, George   100, 333,
    615
Major, Hannah E.   617
Major, Hannan J.   615
Major, J. M.   615
Major, James   599, 615

Major, James (Jr.) 615
Major, James W. 614
Major, James Willis 100
Major, Jonathan 600, 602
Major, Jonathan W. 600, 615
Major, Laura E. 615
Major, Martha 617
Major, Mary 751
Major, Nancy 615
Major, Rachel 614
Major, Robert 603, 617
Major, Sarah 617
Major, Sopt, Wr. 614
Major, W. 615
Major, William 614, 615
Major, Wm. 614, 615
Majors, Jonathan 600
Majors, William 623
Maken, Joseph H. 208
Makinson, George 173
Makinson, Margaret 13
Malaham, Mary 536
Malcon, Thomas 748
Maldan, John Lewis 724
Maldon, Hannah Mion 718
Maldon, John Lewis 714
Maldrick, Elizabeth 514
Mallary, Jasper 162, 177
Mallen, Ferdinand 340
Mallen, James 317
Mallen, Jane 321
Mallery, Harriet 158
Mallery, Jasper 158
Mallett, Esther 520
Mallett, Henry 333
Mallison, Reuben 529
Mallon, Jane 320
Mallon, Peter 661
Mallory, Casper 157
Mallory, Elizabeth 89
Mallory, Harriet 169
Mallory, Jasper 166, 169, 172, 177
Mallory, John 748
Mallory, John B. 178
Mallow, Peter 661
Malo, C. 533
Malo, Edward 533
Malo, P. 533
Maloe, Susannah 516
Malone, Daniel 637
Malone, Haatley 452
Malone, Rebeccah 457
Malone, Sally 516
Malone, Susannah 516
Maloon, Josiah 78
Maloon, Mary 78
Malott, Daniel 319
Maloy, Emme 659
Maloy, Geals 660
Maloy, John L. 125
Maloy, Margaret 659
Maloy, Martha 667
Maloy, Patrick 649
Malster, John 732
Maltbie, Hiram 623
Man, Charlott 630
Man, Cyrus 630

Man, Jeremiah 630
Man, Lorenz D. 44
Man, Margarett 630
Man, Sarah 630
Man, Sena 630
Man, Temperance 630
Man, Thomas 630
Man, Wm. 416
Manbeck, David 231
Manche, Anna Catharine 612
Manche, B. 612
Manche, Barbara 612
Manche, Ceorc 612
Manche, J. 612
Manche, John 612
Manche, Loeorc 612
Manchester, Anna 716
Manear, John 126
Maner, Alexander P. 39
Maner, Isaac 120
Maner, Julia Jane 39
Maner, Lewis W. 39
Maner, Mary Clarisa 39
Mangan, John 545, 552
Mangan, Reuben 545
Mangen, David K. 145
Mangen, Mary A. 145
Mangen, Rebecca 549
Mangin, John 120
Manhein, Levinia 140
Manhein, Rachel 140
Manley, Elizabeth 298
Manley, Isaac 514
Manley, Mary 609
Manley, Mary L. 37
Manley, Orwin 41
Manley, Robert 295, 298
Manlove, William 189
Manly, Asher Bruse 745
Manly, John S. 363
Manly, Robert 608
Manmant, Jane 555
Mann, --- 219
Mann, Able 140
Mann, Augusteen 117
Mann, Barnabas 120
Mann, Barnabass 140
Mann, Eliza Ann 29
Mann, Elizabeth 155, 166
Mann, Emmanuel 169
Mann, George 120
Mann, Hirum 41
Mann, Hulday 550
Mann, J. E. 356
Mann, Jacob 120
Mann, James 717
Mann, Jane 62
Mann, John 140, 441, 545, 550
Mann, Molly 140
Mann, Nancy 459
Mann, Peter 155, 158, 159, 160, 166
Mann, Ruth 140
Mann, Sally 120
Mann, Sally M. 29
Mann, Samuel B. 419
Manner, Betsy 458

Manning, Azariah 140
Manning, Benjamin 126
Manning, Daniel 672
Manning, Eliza 377, 378
Manning, Elizabeth 140, 665
Manning, Enos 120
Manning, James 379, 545
Manning, Jeminah 121
Manning, John 117, 140
Manning, Martha 658
Manning, Mary 140
Manning, N. 540
Manning, Nancy 117, 140
Manning, Nathaniel 540
Manning, Polly 121
Manning, Sarah 540
Manning, Sarah A. 140
Manning, Thomas 540
Manning, William 33, 120, 145
Manning, Wm. 140
Manon, Peter 41
Mansan, James 120
Mansfield, Charles W. 145
Mansfield, Hannah 128
Mansfield, Hannah E. 64
Mansfield, John 317
Mansfield, Richard S. 64
Mansfield, Rosana 334
Mansfield, Thomas W. 128
Manson, David 117
Manson, Jane 122
Manson, John 661
Manson, Mary 121
Manson, Wm. 140
Mantel, Jacob 301
Manter, Pamela 30
Mantle, Eleanor 152, 162
Mantle, William 152, 162
Manville, John 279
Maoarty, Hannah 516
Mapes, Benjamin 550
Mapes, Delight 581
Mapes, Thomas 140
Maps, Elenor 140
Maquet, Alexandriens 727
Maquet, P. N. 727
Maquet, Peter Robert 724
Marah, Cornelius 489
Marcellas, Hugh J. 336
Marcellus, Henry 321
March, Elizabet 395
March, Sarah 657
Marcuss, Martha 589
Mare, Ave 453
Marek, Hetty 666
Maretin, Margaret 747
Margaret, Marqueritte 713
Marger, John 453
Margraw, John 666
Marguiss, Sarah 382
Margut, Daniel 75
Marian, Francois 714
Marick, John 78
Marietta, Betsy 730
Marim, Richard 453

897

Maris, Clark 256
Maris, George 256
Maris, Marshall J. 256
Maris, Mary Anna 256
Maris, Owen 256
Maris, Rebecca 256
Mark, Eliza 63, 626
Mark, Elizabeth 63, 626
Mark, James 63, 626
Mark, James W. 63, 626
Mark, John 521
Mark, Lucind 626
Mark, Lucinda V. 63
Mark, Matthias 63, 626
Mark, Nancy 63, 626
Mark, Sarah 63, 626
Mark, Stephen 755
Mark, Washington 44,
  63, 599, 623, 626
Markel, Elizabeth 458
Marker, Catherina 235
Marker, Eli 235
Markey, Catherine 217
Markey, David 217
Markey, Henry G. 217
Markey, John 217
Markey, Joseph 217
Markey, Thomas 165
Markius, Barbary 589
Markle, Benjamin 489
Markle, Catharine 53
Markle, Catherine 53
Markle, Daniel 489
Markle, Elinor 53
Markle, Ezra 52, 53
Markle, Gabriel 53
Markle, Gabriel (Sr.) 53
Markle, Hanna 53
Markle, Hesther 53
Markle, Jacob 493
Markle, James 489
Markle, John 489, 493
Markle, Jonathan 53
Markle, Joseph 489
Markle, Rachel 53
Markle, Samuel 53
Markle, Susan 53
Markley, Catharine 556
Markley, Christina 556
Markley, Christopher 556
Markley, Daniel 556
Markley, Elizabeth 556
Markley, Esther 556
Markley, John 556
Markley, Joseph 444
Markley, Mary 556
Markley, Moses 126
Markley, Susana 556
Markly, Christopher 556
Marks, Emeline 735
Marks, James 567
Marks, Mason 303
Marlatt, William 695
Marman, Martin 19
Marman, Stephen 13
Marmen, Martin 13
Marmin, David 25
Marmin, Dorothy 25
Marmin, Edmond 25

Marmin, Elizabeth 14
Marmin, Martin 25
Marmin, Mary 25
Marmin, Peter 25
Marmin, Robert 25
Marmon, Ann 10
Marmon, Charles M. 10
Marmon, Daniel W. 10
Marmon, Dorothy 25
Marmon, Hannah 25
Marmon, James W. 10
Marmon, Jane 11
Marmon, Joshua 25
Marmon, Lettice 14
Marmon, Martin 10, 18,
  25
Marmon, Mary 10
Marmon, Mary Ann Rebecca
  13
Marmon, Obedience 25
Marmon, Peter 13, 25
Marmon, Pricilla 13
Marmon, Richard 13
Marmon, Richmond 25
Marmon, Robert 25
Marmon, Robert M. 25
Marmon, Stephen 25
Marmon, Zylpha 21
Marmun, David 25
Marner, Michael 109
Maroba, Levin 161
Marple, David J. 287
Marquand, Charles 285
Marquant, Jonathan 672
Marquast, Henry 224
Marquess, Nancy 586
Marquess, Polly 586
Marquest, Henry 184
Marquis, Addison 1
Marquis, Amanda 1
Marquis, Ann 25
Marquis, Anna 23
Marquis, Calvin 10
Marquis, Ellhusa 1
Marquis, Francis A. 257
Marquis, Gallatin S. 257
Marquis, Hannah 451
Marquis, James 1, 25
Marquis, Jane 25
Marquis, Jean 25
Marquis, John 1, 10
Marquis, Joseph 3, 9
Marquis, Larissa 1
Marquis, Lovina 589
Marquis, Lucinda 10
Marquis, Margaret 10
Marquis, Mary 1, 25
Marquis, Mary E. 592
Marquis, Moses 9
Marquis, Saml. 270
Marquis, Sarah 25
Marquis, Susannah 25
Marquis, Thomas 25
Marquis, Thomas (Rev.)
  23, 25
Marquis, William 25, 257
Marquis, William Vance
  10
Marquis, Wm. 400

Marquis, Wm. V. 10
Marr, Amanda 145
Marr, Jane 145
Marr, John 145
Marr, Marion 145
Marret, Elizabeth 513
Marret, Ruth 513
Marrs, Samuel 540
Marrs, William 545, 599
Marry, George 567
Marsh, --- 421
Marsh, Clement 30
Marsh, Coleman 41
Marsh, David 385
Marsh, Elizabeth 644
Marsh, Ezekiel 555
Marsh, George 13
Marsh, Griffin 120
Marsh, Henrietta C. 607
Marsh, Henry 33
Marsh, Hetty 435
Marsh, James 503
Marsh, James Johnson 644
Marsh, John 44, 417,
  422, 424
Marsh, Jonathan 231
Marsh, Joseph 656
Marsh, Lucy Ann 424
Marsh, Margaret 644
Marsh, Margaret M. 422
Marsh, Mariah 644
Marsh, Mary 245, 581
Marsh, Mary Ann 422
Marsh, Nancy 644
Marsh, Peter 525, 525
Marsh, Polly 463
Marsh, Rachel 117
Marsh, Timothy 417
Marsh, William 644
Marshal, Abina 515
Marshal, Elizabeth 166
Marshal, John 166
Marshall, Anne 119
Marshall, Charity 582
Marshall, Elizabeth 515
Marshall, I. 245
Marshall, Jacob 550
Marshall, James 48,
  126, 130, 274
Marshall, James A. 545
Marshall, Jane 293, 430
Marshall, Jesse 514
Marshall, Joseph 430
Marshall, Josiah 64
Marshall, Lorinda 191
Marshall, Lucilla 140
Marshall, Lucinda 181
Marshall, Margaret 116,
  140, 666
Marshall, Mary 218, 667
Marshall, Matilda W. 594
Marshall, Nancy 592
Marshall, Penhord 294
Marshall, Polly 118
Marshall, Robert 181
Marshall, Samuel 545
Marshall, Shab 140
Marshall, Susan 593
Marshall, Thomas 140

Marshall, Walter 13
Marshall, Washington 191
Marshall, William 191
Marshall, Zephaniah 191
Mart, Andrew 140
Mart, Elizabeth 140
Mart, Jacob 140
Mart, Peter 140
Mart, Polly 140
Marth, Jonas 48
Martin, Abijah 140
Martin, Abner 153
Martin, Adam 385
Martin, Aidy 512
Martin, Alexander 264, 630
Martin, Alfred 269, 690
Martin, Almira 62
Martin, Almy 60
Martin, Amanda 630
Martin, Amos 630
Martin, Ann E. 6
Martin, Ann H. 590
Martin, Anna 383
Martin, Anne 651
Martin, Archibald 13
Martin, Barbara 210, 680
Martin, Betsy 742
Martin, Betty 89
Martin, Casey 384
Martin, Catharine 22
Martin, Catherine 210
Martin, Charles 629
Martin, Charles
  Honeywood 714
Martin, Christena 217
Martin, Christian 217
Martin, Daniel 210, 224
Martin, Daniel V. 13
Martin, David 52, 210, 217, 629
Martin, David V. 13
Martin, Deborah 6
Martin, Delila 140
Martin, Dolly 382
Martin, Dugal C. 163
Martin, Ebenezer 741
Martin, Edson B. 404
Martin, Edward 500
Martin, Eliz. 140
Martin, Elizabeth 76, 90, 119, 404, 515, 574, 629, 657
Martin, Elizabeth Ann 123
Martin, George 6, 209, 370, 680
Martin, George Pinkney 266, 270
Martin, Green 140
Martin, Hannah 6, 140, 357
Martin, Henry 371
Martin, Isaac 84
Martin, J. M. 745
Martin, Jacob 210, 370, 385, 404
Martin, James 79, 256, 391, 457, 483, 661

Martin, James (Sr.) 483, 484
Martin, Jane 386, 585
Martin, Jesse 514
Martin, John 140, 166, 217, 260, 303, 385, 493, 647, 651
Martin, Joseph 256, 489, 629
Martin, Julia Anna 197
Martin, Laura 629
Martin, Lear 385
Martin, Levi 140, 145
Martin, Louis 140
Martin, Lucretia 745
Martin, M. T. 630
Martin, Magdalena 210
Martin, Margaret 74, 163, 496
Martin, Margaret M. 610
Martin, Martin 145
Martin, Mary 35, 152, 161, 168, 209, 210, 256, 371
Martin, Merrick 120
Martin, Morris 256
Martin, Nancy 80, 125, 629
Martin, Olive 744
Martin, Owen 354, 358, 371
Martin, Owens 707
Martin, Peggy 451, 456, 457
Martin, Phoeba Ann 48
Martin, Prudence 517
Martin, Rachael 6
Martin, Rachel 388
Martin, Rebecca 630
Martin, Richard 497
Martin, Robert 256, 366, 426, 651
Martin, Robert M. 371
Martin, Rosa 210
Martin, Samuel 6, 140, 163, 179, 258, 266, 651
Martin, Samuel (Dr.) 269
Martin, Sarah 145, 153, 163, 371, 387, 658, 680
Martin, Silas 608
Martin, Simon 6
Martin, Thomas 6, 152, 153, 167, 178, 256, 258
Martin, Thomas (Jr.) 6
Martin, Thos. 256, 359
Martin, Timothy 550
Martin, Tulman 385
Martin, Urias 163
Martin, Whitney 256
Martin, William 41, 145, 256, 338, 340, 629, 630
Martin, William (Jr.) 490
Martin, Wm. 140, 357, 764

Martin, Wm. B. 360
Martin, Zenas 62
Martindale, David 79
Martindale, James 661
Martindale, John 207, 651
Martindale, Martin 661
Martindale, Patty 660
Martindale, Rachel 658
Martindale, Samuel 187, 196
Martindale, William 639
Martindell, Andrew L. 84
Martindill, William 634
Martz, Abraham 401
Martz, Catharine 401
Martz, George 545
Martz, John 401
Martz, Mary A. 545
Martz, Michael 545
Martz, Polly 401
Martz, Samuel 401
Martz, Susannah 401
Marvel, Barbara 575
Marven, Picket 714
Marvin, Elen 530
Marvin, Hannah 530
Marvin, Samuel B. 594
Marvin, Zacharia 530
Marvin, Zachariah 530
Mary, George 564
MarBown, Helen 64
Masar, Catharina 92
Masey, John 391
Maskill, Eliza 590
Masloh, John 104
Mason, Amelia 744
Mason, Charles 545
Mason, Christopher 224
Mason, Cynthia 680
Mason, David 176, 214
Mason, Deborah 335
Mason, Frances 214
Mason, Gideon 159, 167, 181
Mason, Hannah 167, 181
Mason, Haseey 176
Mason, Henry 181
Mason, James 650
Mason, John 164, 316, 320, 323, 324, 574
Mason, Luke 41
Mason, Margaret 169
Mason, Maria 680
Mason, Mariah 650
Mason, Peleg 283
Mason, Rebecca 657
Mason, Richard 184, 211, 214
Mason, Sally 680
Mason, Saml. 680
Mason, Samuel 680, 683
Mason, Sarah 79
Mason, Sidney 250, 251
Mason, Simon 224
Mason, Thomas 465
Mason, Thompson 153
Mason, William 153, 169, 680, 714

Mason, Wm. 638
Massey, Henry 202
Massey, Wm. 263, 265, 267, 270, 271
Massie, Alexander 170
Massie, Charlotte 457
Massie, Constance 26, 505
Massie, Courtland 26
Massie, Elizabeth 489
Massie, H. 26, 505
Massie, Helen 26
Massie, Hellen 505
Massie, Henry 26, 398, 505
Massie, Mary 170
Massie, Nathaniel 26, 490, 505
Massie, Thomas 26, 505
Massie, Wingate 465
Massy, Eleanor 634
Mast, Absolem 210
Mast, Adam 317
Mast, Austin 240
Mast, Earhart 161
Mast, Elizabeth 240
Mast, John 203
Mast, Nancy 185
Mast, Rebecca 185
Mast, Sarah 185
Mast, Susanna 185
Masteller, Thos. 591
Master, Joseph 732
Masters, Ann 306
Masters, Anna 576
Masters, Benjamin 507
Masters, Catharine 303
Masters, Elizabeth 411, 507
Masters, Ezekiel 507
Masters, George 507
Masters, Isaac 564
Masters, Jas. 732
Masters, John 507
Masters, Joseph 574, 710
Masters, Melissa 507
Masters, Nancy 507
Masters, Nancy M. 710
Masters, Sarah 710
Masterson, Frank 48
Masterson, H. 60
Masterson, Hester 128
Mastin, James 84
Matcack, Jno. 219
Mater, Stephen 748
Mathena, Andrew 268
Mathena, Cyrus 268
Mathena, Martha 268
Mathena, Nathan 268
Matheney, Joseph 264
Matheny, William 309
Matheny, Wm. 309
Mather, Ebenezer 666
Mather, Increase 591
Mather, Jane 337
Mathers, David 150
Mathers, Elizabeth 337
Mathers, James 150, 497
Mathers, John 371

Mathers, Margaret 150
Mathers, Mary Ann 371
Mathers, Sarah 150
Mathers, Southard 586
Mathers, Wm. 591
Mathes, Margaret 463
Mathew, John 140
Mathews, --- 398
Mathews, Catharine 718
Mathews, Chauncey 41
Mathews, Chester 527
Mathews, Geo. 397
Mathews, Increase 285, 296, 297, 298
Mathews, James 52
Mathews, John 288, 722
Mathews, Lot 485
Mathews, Mary 11
Mathews, Nathan H. 10
Mathews, Philip 17
Mathews, Philish 18
Mathews, Polly 52
Mathews, Rachel 18
Mathews, Sarah 120
Mathewson, William B. 521
Mathias, Daniel 555
Mathias, Henry 393
Mathious, Sarah C. 539
Matison, David C. 84
Matle, William 179
Mats, Joseph 679
Matson, John 661
Mattack, Thomas 160
Matten, Sarah 12
Matthews, --- 395
Matthews, Alexander 682
Matthews, Andrew 168
Matthews, Betsey 121
Matthews, Catharine 682
Matthews, David 682
Matthews, Edmund P. 678
Matthews, Elias 199
Matthews, Eliza Jane 682
Matthews, Increase 282, 296
Matthews, Isaac 682
Matthews, Jonathan 682
Matthias, Barbary 393
Matthias, Catherine 393
Matthias, Caty 393
Matthias, Doratia 393
Matthias, Henry 393
Matthias, Henry (Sr.) 393
Matthias, Mary 393
Mattison, Darias 521
Mattoon, Jacob 41
Mattox, James L. 623
Mattox, Sally 464
Mattox, Thomas 126
Matzler, David 395
Matzler, Derissa 395
Matzler, George 394, 395
Matzler, John 394, 395
Matzler, Keturah 395
Matzler, Margaret 394
Maugan, John 552
Maughran, John 345

Mauk, Anthony 292
Mauk, Jacob 292
Mauk, Mary 292
Maulsby, Maria 223
Maulsby, William 223
Maulston, James 182
Mault, Charles 550
Maun, John 441
Maupetit, Casar 722
Mauppin, Frances 385
Maus, Andreas 237
Maus, Andrias 236
Maus, David 236
Maus, Elias 238
Maus, Markaret Elisabet 237
Maus, Mary 238
Maus, Susana 236, 237
Mauser, Abraham 112
Mautz, Conrad 371
Mauzy, James L. 419
Mauzy, Joseph H. 419
Max, Jeremiah 145
Max, Solomon 145
Maxson, Simon 545
Maxwell, Amos 694
Maxwell, Basel 272
Maxwell, David 310
Maxwell, Eliza 272
Maxwell, George 199
Maxwell, Jane 405
Maxwell, John 272
Maxwell, Mary 272
Maxwell, Mary D. 712
Maxwell, Nancy 274, 275
Maxwell, Nathaniel 199
Maxwell, Phebe 199
Maxwell, Samuel 210
Maxwell, Thomas 199, 272
Maxwell, William 272
May, Agnes 648
May, Alonzo 41
May, Eliza 648
May, Hannah 648
May, Henry 385, 648, 673
May, Isaac 497
May, Jacob 113, 334, 748
May, James 480, 484, 648
May, Jane 648
May, Jeremiah 648
May, John 379, 648
May, Margaret 648
May, Martin 413
Mayberry, Ebenezer 164
Mayberry, Joshua 164
Mayburn, Creighton Mead 63
Mayer, Christian 223
Mayer, Daniel 182
Mayer, Elizabeth 182, 223
Mayer, Frances 766
Mayer, Francis 766
Mayer, Francis I. 766
Mayer, Henry 182, 223
Mayer, Jacob 111, 182
Mayer, John 182, 469
Mayer, Michael 182, 223
Mayer, Peter 182

Mayers, Alexander 156
Mayes, Catharine 555
Mayhen, Fielding 79
Mayhew, Frederick 303
Maynard, Joshua 524, 526
Maynard, Levy 79
Mayo, Asa 148
Mayo, Daniel 714
Mayo, Joseph (Jr.) 59
Mays, Lancelot 596
Mays, Robert 586
Mayse, James 574
Mayson, Rebecca 461
Maze, Lancelot 596
Maze, Mary 596
Maze, Robert 596
McAdam, Samuel 484
McAdams, John 301
McAden, Thos. F. 2
McAdoo, James 267
McAdow, Rebecca 582
McAdow, Samuel 390, 484
McAdow, Samuel 485
Mcadue, James 574
McAfee, Nancy M. 710
McAfee, Sophronia 740
McAlister, Elizabeth 290
McAlla, Catherine 331
McAlla, David 331
McAlla, Hester 331
McAlla, Isaac 331
McAlla, Martha 331
McAlla, Rebecca 331
McAlla, Thomas 331
McAllister, Elizabeth 290
McAllister, Wm. 732
McAnally, James D. 324, 745
McAnelly, Henry 371
McAnully, John 336
McArthur Wm. A. 34
McArthur, Duncan 2, 7, 500
McArthur, Nancy 11
McArthur, Peter 13
McArthur, Wm. A. 34
McAuley, James 514
McAuley, Rachel 512
McAvoy, Thomas 84
McBeath, Margaret 498
McBerney, Benjamin 181
McBerney, Isaac 181
McBerney, Martha 181
McBeth, Catharine Sophia 7
McBeth, Demarris 7
McBeth, Edward R. 7
McBeth, James Henry 7
McBeth, Joseph 18
McBeth, Letitia Ann 7
McBeth, Margaret Francis 7
McBeth, Martha Jane 7
McBeth, Peggy 27
McBeth, Samuel 7
McBeth, William 16, 18, 27
McBrice, Jacob 78

McBride, Alexander 738, 742
McBride, Alexander (III) 440
McBride, Andrew 283, 288
McBride, Catherine 88
McBride, Duncan 441
McBride, Elizabeth 514
McBride, Hannah 76
McBride, Jane 378
McBride, Jas. 434
McBride, John 63, 160, 369
McBride, Mary 160, 165
McBride, Richard 283, 288, 296, 717
McBride, Robert 63
McBride, Thomas 440, 441
McBride, William 378, 660
McBurney, Benjamin 167
McCabe, Arlinda 551
McCabe, Betsy 206
McCabe, Deborah 687
McCabe, Isaiah 457
McCabe, John 182
McCabe, Okey 687
McCachlun, John 510
McCafferty, Betsey 451
McCafferty, Ellen 56
McCafferty, James 452
McCafferty, John 494
McCafferty, Jonathan 56, 465
McCafferty, Mary 56
McCafferty, Matthias 56
McCafferty, Polly 458
McCafferty, Rebecca 56
McCafferty, Richard 465
McCafferty, Samuel 465
McCafferty, Susannah 56
McCafferty, Thomas 457
McCaig, James 296
McCain, Absalom 654
McCain, Jacob 303
McCain, John 654, 666
McCain, Soloman 654
McCall, David 506
McCall, Margaret 451
McCall, Peggy 716
McCall, Rebecca 457
McCall, Robert 291
McCallay, Sarah 222
McCallie, John C. 430
McCallie, Mariah 430
McCally, Grizzy 747
McCally, James 442
McCalmon, Eliza 444
McCalmon, Elizabeth 445
McCalmon, Jane 444, 445
McCalmon, Martha 444, 445
McCalmon, Mary 444, 445
McCalmon, Samuel 444, 445
McCammart, Samuel 293
McCammert, Rebeccah 293
McCammon, John 167, 280
McCampbell, Andrew J. 608

McCampbell, Elmyra 434
McCampbell, James 60
McCampbell, James R. 145
McCampbell, Phebe Ann 434
McCampbell, Sarah E. 145
McCampbell, Wm. B. 145
McCanburgh, John 472
McCandes, William 483
McCandles, Elizabeth 696
McCandless, Alexander 175
McCandless, Ann 175
McCandless, William (Rev.) 740
McCandlish, Rebecca 371
McCandlish, William 371
McCane, Susan 548
McCann, James 224
McCann, Nancy 224
McCann, Squire 313
McCann, Thomas 313
McCardburgh, John 472
McCardy, James 666
McCarel, John 370
McCarley, Alexander 521
McCarley, Betsey 717
McCarlney, J. D. 408
McCarney, Henry 527
McCart, Abraham Perry 449
McCart, Amy 449
McCart, Esther 449
McCart, Henry 449
McCart, Jesse 449
McCart, Martha 449
McCart, Mary 449
McCart, Rachel 449
McCart, Sarah 449
McCartney, Ann 530
McCartney, Arthur 374
McCartney, Charles 530
McCartney, Elizabeth 451
McCartney, Henry 530
McCartney, Jane 530
McCartney, Jean 465
McCartney, John 457, 530
McCartney, Reuben 530
McCartney, Robert 530
McCartney, Rufus 530
McCarty, --- 174
McCarty, Chas. 270
McCarty, David 689
McCarty, Henry 583
McCarty, Jeremiah 684
McCarty, John 689
McCarty, John (Sr.) 689
McCarty, Margaret 458
McCarty, Mary 665
McCarty, William 169, 175, 660
McCary, Benj. 145
McCary, John 145
McCash, Ann 427
McCashen, Abigail 641
McCashen, Absalom 545
McCashen, James 638, 641, 660
McCashen, John 641, 668

McCashen, Mary Ann 641
McCashen, Nancy 545
McCashen, Sally 641
McCashion, Nancy 666
McCaskey, Sally 80
McCaslin, Susanna 353
McCaslin, Wm. 376, 378
McCaules, John 452
McCawkey, John 591
McCawley, Margaret 590
McCene, James 471
McCene, Jeremiah 469
McCery, Benjamin 574
McChord, John 666
McChriste, Francis 115
McChriste, Lucinda 115
McChristy, John 434
McChristy, Mary 434
McCien, Jeremiah 480
McCinne, Mary 552
McClain, Alazan 250, 251
McClain, Alex. 368
McClain, Duncan 489
McClain, Eleanor B. 250, 251
McClain, Hanabal 250, 251
McClain, Isabel 250, 251
McClain, James 457
McClain, Jeremiah 469
McClain, Matilda 250, 251
McClain, Polly 490
McClain, Susanna 353
McClain, William 250, 251
McClain, Wm. 250, 251
McClalin, Catharine 337
McClane, Daniel 294
McClane, James 475
McClary, James S. 371
McClary, John 120
McClary, Joshua 395
McClary, Thomas 157
McClary, Wm. 371
McClash, Robert 567
McClaskey, Peggy 80
McClaskey, Thomas 78
McClaughlin, Cornelius 457
McClean, Elexander 385
McClean, Hannah Maria 207
McClean, Moses 490
McClean, Sally 465
McClean, William 493
McCleary, Catharine 290
McCleary, Dorcas 670
McCleary, Elizabeth 573, 670
McCleary, Ephraim 646
McCleary, James 290
McCleary, Jane 290
McCleary, John 290
McCleary, Mary 670
McCleary, Mary Ellen 290
McCleary, Nancy 670
McCleary, Susan 290
McCleary, Thomas 670

McCleery, Rachel 567
McCleland, William 45
McClellan, Catharine 421
McClellan, John L. 422
McClellan, Martha Ann 422
McClellan, Mary 279
McClellan, Samuel 421
McClellan, Theodore 421
McClelland, Ann 738
McClelland, Francis 317
McClelland, Harriet 317
McClelland, Henry 317
McClelland, James 317
McClelland, Melissa 317
McClelland, Nancy 365
McClelland, Robert 365
McClelland, William 497
McClelland, Wilson 364
McClemson, Rebecca 13
McClene, James 469, 480
McCleneham, Wm. 476
McClenehan, Anna D. 551
McClerc, Lewis 726
McClerg, Betsey 119
McClery, Rebecca 574
McClilman, Peggy 457
McClimans, David 48
McClimans, Jean 718
McClinans, Esbel 717
McClintick, Samuel 268
McClintock, Adam 120
McClintock, Alexander 489
McClintock, Betsy 456
McClintock, John 120
McClintock, Saml. 267, 271
McClintock, Samuel 262
McClintock, William 48
McClish, Hislette 461
McClish, John 745
McClish, Violette 461
McClory, John 134
McCloskey, Betsey 76
McCloskey, Charles 376
McCloskey, Michael 545
McCloskey, William N. 545
McCloud, Betsy 585, 586
McCloud, Charles 60
McCloud, Elizabeth 13
McCloud, Hannah 659
McCloud, James 591
McCloud, Letitia 13
McCloud, Sally 14
McCloud, Samuel J. 510
McClreg, Alexander 24
McClue, Nancy 462
McCluer, Andrew 714
McCluer, James 84
McClun, Sally 118
McClune, James 478
McClung, Elizabeth 523
McClung, J. L. 527
McClung, James 418
McClung, James (Dr.) 524
McClung, Margaret 434
McClung, Robert 375

McClung, Samuel 530
McClung, William 286
McClung, Wm. B. 434
McClure, Albert A. 203
McClure, Alexander 182, 750
McClure, Andrew 140
McClure, Ann 4
McClure, Benjamin 474, 475
McClure, Betsy 121
McClure, Catharine 217
McClure, Charles 742
McClure, Daniel 217
McClure, Danl. 553
McClure, Eliza 4
McClure, Elizabeth 135, 750
McClure, Enoch 545
McClure, Harriet 4
McClure, Hugh 493
McClure, James 445, 476
McClure, Jane 750
McClure, Jeremiah 217
McClure, John 117, 120, 469, 475, 478, 480, 482, 485, 486
McClure, John B. 145
McClure, Joseph M. 545
McClure, Margaret 135
McClure, Margary 117
McClure, Martha 4, 750
McClure, Mary 116, 135
McClure, Nancy 550, 750
McClure, Randall 217
McClure, Robert 4, 120, 135, 545
McClure, Robert A. 4
McClure, Rosana 750
McClure, Rosanna 126
McClure, Samuel 550, 622, 750
McClure, Sarah 461
McClure, Thomas 117
McClure, William 135, 182, 217, 224, 485, 530, 622
McClure, William Scott 4
McClure, Wm. 203, 357, 367
McClure, Wm. C. 145
McClurg, John 117
McCluskey, Rebecca 291
McCoid, James 287
McCollam, Robert 545
McCollester, Michael 660
McColley, Samuel 497
McColloch, Noah Z. 18
McColloch, Samuel 20
McColloch, Wm. 5
McColloch, Zellah 15
McCollom, Ethan 186
McCollom, Ethan L. 201
McCollom, Hugh 186, 201
McCollom, John 186
McCollom, Lucinda 186
McCollom, Maria 186
McCollom, Martha 125
McCollom, Parry 186

McCollom, Rachel 186
McCollough, Robert 550
McCollum, Archibald
258, 269
McCollum, Jacob M. 545
McCollum, Mary 452
McColly, Esther 295
McColough, Samuel 660
McColovey, Polly 459
McComas, Daniel 286
McComas, Elizabeth Anne
161
McComas, James 161, 179
McComas, William 152
McComb, R. C. 63
McComb, Thomas 62
McCombs, John 669
McCommack, William 207
McConahey, Isabella 448
McConahey, William 448
McConica, James 278
McConkey, Thomas 740
McConkey, William 39
McConn, William 45
McConnal, Catharine 386
McConnal, Rose 385
McConnamicher, Margaret
462
McConnaughey, Thomas H.
145
McConnel, Alex. 261,
266, 270
McConnel, Alexander
189, 258, 263
McConnel, James 485, 635
McConnel, John 374,
385, 750
McConnel, Joseph 259,
263
McConnel, Margaret 374
McConnel, Robert 299
McConnel, Robt. 275
McConnel, Samuel 761
McConnell, Caroline A.
250, 251
McConnell, Elizabeth
454, 457, 635
McConnell, James 635
McConnell, Jane 299
McConnell, John 279, 635
McConnell, Mitchell 681
McConnell, Polly 383
McConnell, Robert 117,
132, 135, 283, 284,
287, 297, 299
McConnell, Sarah Ann
250, 251
McConnell, William 287,
452, 635
McCool, Elisha 125,
134, 145
McCool, Gabriel 117
McCool, Mark Alexander
140
McCool, Mary 123
McCool, Nathaniel 145
McCool, Sarah 145
McCool, Wells 117
McCoole, Elisha 135

McCoole, Elizabeth M.
135
McCoole, Gabriel 135
McCoole, Hester 135, 140
McCoole, James 135
McCoole, John 120, 135
McCoole, Mack Alexander
135
McCoole, Martha 135
McCoole, Nancy 135
McCoole, Pickering 135
McCoole, Rachel 135
McCoole, Sally 135
McCoole, Thomas 135
McCoole, Thomas W. 140
McCoole, Wells 135
McCord, Carnahan 497
McCord, Jane 413
McCorkel, Wm. 465
McCorkle, Chas. 145
McCorkle, David 145
McCorkle, Eliz. J. 145
McCorkle, Eliza 116
McCorkle, Jas. A. 145
McCorkle, John 134
McCorkle, Jos. 140
McCorkle, Mary E. 145
McCorkle, Mary J. 140
McCorkle, Nancy 140
McCorkle, Patsy 117
McCorkle, Polly 121
McCorkle, Zelpha 145
McCormack, Edward 48
McCormack, John 349
McCormack, William 349
McCormick, Adah 371
McCormick, Anna 370
McCormick, Catharine 496
McCormick, Christena 756
McCormick, Elizabeth
207, 370, 756
McCormick, George 756
McCormick, Hannah 292
McCormick, Harriet 331
McCormick, Hugh 371
McCormick, J. 331
McCormick, James 84,
370, 371, 545, 756
McCormick, Jane 371
McCormick, John 370, 401
McCormick, Johnson 371
McCormick, Martha 756
McCormick, Mary 370
McCormick, Mary Ann 371
McCormick, P. 331
McCormick, Province 165
McCormick, Rebecca 371
McCormick, Rebecca Jane
371
McCormick, Robert 371,
756
McCormick, Sarah 756
McCormick, Sarah Ann 370
McCormick, Thomas 370
McCormick, Thomas F. 756
McCormick, William 212,
370
McCormick, William F.
331

McCortney, Arthur 372,
376
McCourtney, Alexander
475
McCowan, John 655
McCowan, Phebe 655
McCowen, James 680
McCown, Banner 414
McCoy, Alexander 283,
717
McCoy, Andrew 622
McCoy, Archibald 434
McCoy, C. 505
McCoy, Chas. S. 427
McCoy, Cynthia 489
McCoy, Daniel 17
McCoy, Gilbert 140, 157
McCoy, James 17, 732
McCoy, James P. 25
McCoy, Jas. Irvin 434
McCoy, John 430, 465,
473, 475, 485
McCoy, Jonathan 322
McCoy, Joseph 452, 482,
490
McCoy, Joseph G. 140
McCoy, Mary 109, 322,
554
McCoy, Moses 608
McCoy, Nathan 430
McCoy, Nelly 430
McCoy, Polly 458
McCoy, Ruth 501
McCoy, Sally 15, 430
McCoy, Samuel 227
McCoy, William 45, 117,
475
McCoy, William (Jr.) 493
McCracken, Agnes 738
McCracken, Ann 738
McCracken, Elizabeth 738
McCracken, Henry 61, 738
McCracken, James 738
McCracken, John 738
McCracken, Nathaniel 738
McCracken, Nessy 738
McCracken, Rachel 738
McCracken, Susan 738
McCracken, Thomas 457,
738
McCracken, William 738
McCraden, Jane 465
McCraken, Polly 392
McCrary, Margaret 461
McCrary, Tower 99
McCraw, Francis 635
McCray, Daniel 685
McCray, James 125
McCray, John 660
McCray, Laceretia 637
McCready, George 3
McCreary, Hiram 682
McCreary, John 567
McCreary, William 200
McCreery, Thomas 567
McCreery, Thos. 562
McCreey, Rebecca 672
McCreight, Joseph 202
McCreight, Thomas 202

McCrerry, Thomas 562
McCrery, James 574
McCrery, Nathan 514
McCriester, Joseph 115
McCristal, Mary 371
McCristal, Patrick 354
McCristy, Charles T. 103
McCristy, David J. 103
McCristy, Elisha D. 103
McCristy, George W. 103
McCristy, Jesse 103
McCristy, John M. 103
McCristy, Levina 413
McCristy, Martha Jane 103
McCristy, Moses L. 103
McCristy, Nancy 103
McCristy, Phebe Ann 103
McCristy, Polly L. 103
McCristy, William 639
McCrola, Jane Elizabeth 168
McCrola, Levin 168
McCrory, Lydian 764
McCullaugh, Samuel 583
McCulloch, George 16
McCulloch, Hugh 754
McCulloch, Samuel 490
McCulloch, Samuel H. 550
McCullock, George 717
McCullock, John 485
McCullough, Alexander 50
McCullough, Cynthia 532
McCullough, Eliza 140
McCullough, Emily 651
McCullough, John 452, 545, 622
McCullough, Mary 140, 545, 651
McCullough, Robert 319
McCullough, Saml. 140
McCullough, Samuel 50
McCullough, William 317, 319, 356, 532
McCullough, Wm. 319, 356
McCully, John 486
McCully, Nancy 745
McCully, Patrick 291
McCully, Robert 745
McCully, Sarah 291
McCulough, Mary 711
McCun, Daniel 514
McCun, John 457
McCunber, Charetta 591
McCune, Anna 455
McCune, Betsey 453
McCune, Charles 315
McCune, David 489
McCune, Elizabeth 455
McCune, Franklin 315
McCune, George 315
McCune, Hannah 565
McCune, Isaac E. 315
McCune, James 315
McCune, James (II) 315
McCune, Jean 457
McCune, John 315, 586
McCune, John K. 298
McCune, Joseph 309, 315, 486, 489

McCune, Keziah 460
McCune, Margaret 466
McCune, Mary 497
McCune, Michael 315
McCune, Peggy 714
McCune, Robt. 260
McCune, Saml. 269, 271, 273
McCune, Samuel 254
McCune, Sebrah 315
McCune, William 315
McCune, William (II) 315
McCurdy, George T. 72
McCurdy, John S. 72
McCurdy, Sally Ann 355
McCurdy, Sarah A. 72
McCurdy, William 72
McCurdy, William (Jr.) 72
McCutchen, Mary G. 763
McCutchen, Warren 521
McCutchin, Susan 385
McDanal, Thomas 391
McDaniel, David 717
McDaniel, Elizabeth 99, 550
McDaniel, James W. 530
McDaniel, Theresa M. 530
McDaniel, Thomas 596
McDaniel, William 20
McDaniel, Wm. 98, 550
McDaniels, John 435
McDaniels, Lucinda 435
McDaniels, Mary Abigail 435
McDaniels, Olinda 435
McDaniels, Samuel Wm. 435
McDargh, John 234
McDargh, Susana 234
McDermit, Parney 413
McDermot, Martin 545
McDerny, Bernie 234
McDerny, Christofel Collumbus 234
McDerny, Elizabeth 234
McDill, A. C. (Dr.) 425
McDill, Sarah L. 425
McDimick, Merilla 518
McDonal, Joshua 688
McDonal, William 428
McDonald, Aaron 145
McDonald, Adgines 55
McDonald, Archibald 125, 486
McDonald, Daniel 370, 743
McDonald, David 514
McDonald, Dollie 299
McDonald, Elenor 370
McDonald, Elizabeth 345, 361, 456, 595
McDonald, Ellen Maria 345
McDonald, Felix 345
McDonald, George G. 62
McDonald, J. 465
McDonald, James 54, 61, 545, 688, 726

McDonald, Jane B. 693
McDonald, John 61, 368, 370, 452, 471, 473, 474, 477, 545, 586, 684
McDonald, Joseph 117
McDonald, Lydia 606
McDonald, Mahala 145
McDonald, Martha 647
McDonald, Mary 370, 532
McDonald, Michael 370
McDonald, Mitchal 338
McDonald, Nancy 370
McDonald, Patrick 345, 365, 372
McDonald, Phebea 693
McDonald, Rachel 647
McDonald, Richard 693
McDonald, Robert 370
McDonald, Ronald 303
McDonald, Rosanna 370
McDonald, Samantha 693
McDonald, Samuel 591, 647, 687
McDonald, Sarah 45, 647
McDonald, Susan 345
McDonald, Thomas 55, 471, 485, 486
McDonald, Thos. 476, 477, 478
McDonald, William 465, 471, 474, 484, 486, 502, 514, 647
McDonald, William (Jr.) 473, 474
McDonald, William S. 532
McDonald, Wm. 480
McDongal, John 473
McDonnal, John 666
McDonnald, Ebenezer 443
McDonnold, James 660, 661
McDonnold, John 661
McDonold, Nancy 714
McDonough, Hugh 623
McDougal, Elizabeth 634
McDougal, George 507
McDougal, James 452
McDougal, John 452, 473, 481, 482
McDougal, Margurett 628
McDougal, Nancy 513
McDougal, Richard 628
McDougle, Lucy Ann 521
McDowel, Sarah 504
McDowel, Wm. 514
McDowell, Andrew 61
McDowell, Ann 250, 251
McDowell, Austin Fay 61
McDowell, Betsy 117, 118
McDowell, Eber. 61
McDowell, Elizabeth 98, 250, 251
McDowell, James 250, 251, 486, 598
McDowell, Jinny 515
McDowell, John 98, 250, 251
McDowell, John S. 98

McDowell, Lucinda I. 145
McDowell, Lucy J. 61
McDowell, Margaret 98
McDowell, Mary 98
McDowell, Polly 586
McDowell, Rachael 98
McDowell, Rachel 98
McDowell, Samuel 98, 250, 251
McDowell, William 250, 251
McElhana, Richard 271
McElhaney, Jane 205
McElhaney, Richard 265
McElhany, Thomas Rowan 205
McElheney, Andrew 214
McElheney, Jane 214
McElheney, Richard 271
McElheny, Robert 205
McElheny, Robert (Sr.) 212
McElheny, Samuel 212
McElheny, William K. 212
McElroy, Henry 265
McElroy, James 260, 556
McElroy, John 88, 168, 732
McElroy, Nancy 168
McElroy, William 490
McElroy, Wm. 270
McElvain, John 171
McElvine, Moses 652
McElvine, Rebecca 652
McElwain, Samuel 480
McElwee, A. 374
McElwy, Catherine 93
McEntire, M. 407
McEntire, Mary 565
McEntire, Sarah 407, 590
McEntire, T. 407
McEwen, James 670
McFadden, Andrew 736
McFadden, Charles 738
McFadden, Hamilton 448
McFadden, Mary 739
McFadden, Samuel 207
McFadden, Samuel (Jr.) 736
McFadden, Sarah Elizabeth 5
McFadden, Thomas 5
McFadden, Thomas Vance 5
McFaddin, James 554
McFaden, Nancy 5
McFadgen, John 457
McFadgin, William 514
McFall, John B. 13
McFall, Patrick 24
McFarlan, Daniel 652
McFarlan, Delila 652
McFarlan, Elizabeth 652
McFarland, . . . 164
McFarland, Calender 493
McFarland, Daniel 489
McFarland, Elizabeth Bradley 708
McFarland, Frances M. 550

McFarland, Jane 665
McFarland, John 230, 465, 737, 738
McFarland, John Q. 550
McFarland, Robert 490
McFarland, Susanna 570
McFarland, William (Jr.) 341
McFarlin, James 370
McFarsan, Robert 574
McFerrin, Ezekiel 764
McFerson, Geo. 574
McFerson, Robert 574
McFisher, James 686
Mcfolurene, Susanna 570
McGanard, Henry 473
McGargle, Wm. 362
McGarlin, Joseph 354
McGarry, Ann 260
McGarry, David 260, 262, 264, 274
McGarry, John 265
McGarry, John (Sr.) 303
McGarvy, Elizabeth 609
McGarvy, Patrick 717
McGaw, Susanna 571
McGeady, Margaret 400
McGee, Andrew 303
McGee, James 634, 636
McGeorge, Saml. P. 78
McGhee, Catherine 435
McGhee, Geo. H. 435
McGhee, James 435
McGhee, Mary Jane 435
McGhee, Thomas Allen 435
McGill, Hugh 452
McGill, James 474
McGilliard, Francis 695
McGilliard, Mary Annah 695
McGilliard, Robert 695
McGilliard, William V. 695
McGillienddy, Daniel 336
McGilliguthy, Daniel 336
McGimpsey, Anna 118
McGinely, Ellen 371
McGinley, Bridget 371
McGinley, John 371, 377
McGinley, John (Judge) 373
McGinnis, Mary 643
McGintry, E. B. 545
McGish, Jacob 557
McGive, Michael 104
McGoldrick, Hannah 159
McGoldrick, Peter 159
McGomery, Humphrey 489
McGonigle, Richard 341
McGovern, Charles 252
McGovern, Elizabeth 252
McGovern, James 252
McGovern, Matthew 252
McGovern, Patrick 252
McGowen, Jesse G. 345
McGowen, Mary 345, 361
McGown, Matilda Ann 586
McGrahan, Daniel 140
McGraw, Henry 193

McGraw, Joseph 48
McGrew, James 206, 430
McGrew, James Harvey 206
McGrew, John 427, 430
McGrew, John Steele 206
McGrew, Nathan 567, 577
McGrew, Samuel 430
McGrew, Sarah 206
McGrew, Washington 430
McGrew, Wm. H. 753
McGriff, A. 661
McGriff, Caty 660
McGriff, Elizabeth 424
McGriff, Margaret 662
McGroth, Thos. 271
McGrue, Nathan 562
McGruy, James 414
McGuire, Ann 312
McGuire, Ann Eliza 312
McGuire, Christianna 493
McGuire, Edison 445
McGuire, Elizabeth 665
McGuire, Hetty 430
McGuire, James 292, 312, 427, 445
McGuire, James (Sr.) 445
McGuire, James Francis 312
McGuire, John 312, 490
McGuire, Joseph 430
McGuire, Luke 445
McGuire, Mary E. 312
McGuire, Matilda 430
McGuire, Mehala 430
McGuire, Nancy 452
McGuire, Nathan 430
McGuire, Nicholas 445
McGuire, Polley 665
McGuire, Putura 576
McGuire, Robert 452
McGuire, Sarah 493
McGuire, Sinthy 666
McGuire, Thomas 452
McGuire, William 312
McGunnegal, Dan 268
McHendry, Samuel 84
McHenry, Bartholomew 78
McHenry, Margaret 83
McHenry, Samuel 84
McHill, Daniel 745
McIlroy, Daniel 489
McIlvain, Elizabeth 10
McIlvain, Florence 10
McIlvain, Isabella 12
McIlvain, James 13
McIlvain, Jane 10
McIlvain, John I. 13
McIlvain, Margaret 15
McIlvain, Mary Ellen 10
McIlvain, Moses 10
McIlvain, Polly 11
McIlvain, Rebecca 10
McIlvain, Robert 10, 13
McIlwain, Samuel 472
McIntire, Elijah 504
McIntire, Henry 504
McIntire, John 297, 471
McIntire, John A. 145
McIntire, Lydia 714

McIntire, Margaret 569
McIntire, Rebecca A. 145
McIntire, Robert 117
McIntire, William 84, 613
McIntish, William 314
McIntosh, Catherine 660
McIntosh, Elizabeth 663
McIntosh, Enoch 263, 266
McIntosh, Enoch S. 269, 272
McIntosh, Hannah 314
McIntosh, James 117
McIntosh, Nathan 714
McIntosh, William 493
McIntosh, Wm. W. 732
McInturf, Christiana 347
McInturf, Daniel 347
McInturf, Elizabeth 347
McInturf, Frederick 347
McInturf, John 347
McInturf, Polly 347
McInturf, Susannah 347
McIntyre, Edward 115
McIntyre, Elizabeth 314
McIntyre, Elizabeth B. 499
McIntyre, Ephraim 115
McIntyre, Hannah 83
McIntyre, John 117, 250, 251
McIntyre, Sarah E. 115
McIntyre, William 115
McIntyre, Wilson F. 314
McJempsey, Susannah 140
McJempsey, Wm. 140
McJilton, John F. 145
McJilton, Sarah F. 145
McJilton, Wm. F. 145
McJinsey, William 117
McKachen, Jane 179
McKachen, William 179
McKaig, Hannah 124
McKane, Daniel 670
McKane, Elizabeth 670
McKane, James 670
McKane, John 670
McKane, Mary 670
McKane, Richard 670
McKane, Robert 670
McKane, William 670
McKay, Hannah 506
McKay, Jesse 401
McKay, William 704
McKean, John 674
McKee, Agnes 202
McKee, Barbara 756
McKee, Elizabeth 524
McKee, Hannah 278
McKee, Henry 623
McKee, James 545
McKee, Jno. 202
McKee, John 260, 262, 452, 506, 545, 756
McKee, Jos. 298
McKee, Louiza 696
McKee, Maria 545
McKee, Mary Ann 571
McKee, Reddick 154

McKee, Robert 262
McKee, Robt. 264, 266, 267
McKee, Sally 717
McKee, Samuel 102
McKee, Sarah 524, 545
McKee, Thomas 102, 283, 298
McKee, Thomas M. 545
McKee, William 147
McKee, William (Sr.) 147
McKeen, Hugh 756
McKeen, Jane 466
McKees, John 268
McKeever, Susanna 365
McKelfish, Joseph 55
McKelvey, James 442
McKenne, Mary 124
McKennen, Uriah 13
McKenney, John 298, 385
McKenney, Mary 451, 514, 662
McKenny, H. 385
McKensey, Sarah 131
McKenzee, Sarah 388
McKenzie, Jas. 385
McKenzie, John 87
McKenzie, William 125
McKenzy, Nancy 124
McKeown, Thos. 354
McKernan, Daniel 370
McKernan, James 370
McKeul, Neoma 337
McKewn, Arthur 154
McKibben, David 732
M'Kim, C. 618
M'Kim, Celestina 618
M'Kim, Celinda 618
M'Kim, Jane 83
M'Kim, R. P. 618
M'Kim, T. S. 618
McKim, Thomas S. 608
M'Kim, Thomas S. 618
M'Kimer, Mary A. 518
McKinan, Mary A. 518
McKiney, Daniel (Jr.) 514
McKinley, Mary 149
McKinley, Nancy B. 149
McKinley, Rodger 669
McKinley, William 149
McKinley, Wm. 149
McKinney, Cynthia 500
McKinney, Daniel 500
McKinney, Elizabeth 123
McKinney, George (Jr.) 514
McKinney, James M. 140
McKinney, Jesse 550
McKinney, John 117
McKinney, Joseph 35
McKinney, Mary 500
McKinney, Polly 118
McKinney, Samuel S. 140
McKinney, Seleh 500
McKinney, Solomon 500, 514
McKinney, Theodore 500
McKinney, Tishe 500

McKinney, William 500
McKinney, William Thomas Berry 500
McKinney, Wm. 136
McKinnon, William H. 7
McKinny, Stephen 670
McKinsey, Alex. 732
McKinsey, Daniel (Jr.) 514
McKinsey, John 88
McKinsey, Polley 386
McKinsey, Polly 517
McKinsey, Samuel 666
McKinster, James 430
McKinster, Matilda 430
McKinzey, John 514
McKnight, --- 680
McKnight, Catharine 140, 654, 678
McKnight, Jane 654
McKnight, Rebecca 140, 654, 678
McKnight, Robert 652, 678
McKnight, Sarah J. 140
McKnight, Sarah Jane 678
McKnight, Thoa. R. 760
McKnight, Thomas R. 760
McKnight, William 140, 652, 654, 678, 696
McKracken, Jane 173
McKracken, William 173
McKune, Squiss C. 23
McKy, Eliza Jane 653
McKy, William 653
McLain, Charles 84, 376
McLain, James 64
McLain, John 392
McLain, Melinda 749
McLain, Nancy 376
McLain, William 694
McLaine, Mary 72
McLanburg, John 477
McLanburgh, John 478
McLandburg, John 476, 485
McLane, Allen 282
McLane, Jas. 478
McLane, John 352
McLaughlen, Robert J. 21
McLaughlin, Amy 364
McLaughlin, Dennis 319
McLaughlin, James 545
McLaughlin, Jane 84
McLaughlin, Peggy 463
McLaughlin, Samuel 410
McLean, Benjamin 214
McLean, James 550
McLean, Jeremiah 452
McLean, John 189, 214, 639, 646
McLean, John S. 317
McLean, Nathaniel 661, 672
McLean, Polly 713
MClean, Sally 465
McLean, Tergus 670
McLean, William 654
McLean, Wm. 284

McLeane, Polly 713
McLeem, William 672
McLees, Rachel 514
McLene, John 482
McLene, Patrick 52
McLinchey, John 450
McLinchey, Michael 450
McLinchey, Nancy 450
McLinchy, John 450
McLoud, Sally 590
McLoud, Wm. 591
MClue, Nancy 462
MClure, John 485
MClure, Sarah 461
McLung, George Heber 140
Mclwain, Samuel 472
McMachlam, Benjamin 452
McMacken, Andrew 545
McMahan, John 764
McMahan, Nancy 387
McMahan, Robert 470,
  473, 474
McMahan, Robt. 474,
  476, 477, 478
McMahan, William 483
McMahon, Abraham 732
McMahon, Elijah 165
McMahon, Elizabeth 84
McMahon, James 157, 732
McMahon, John 287
McMahon, R. W. 366
McMahon, Thomas 165
McMahon, Wm. 736, 737
McMaken, Andrew 545
McMaken, Caleb 140
McMaken, Charlotte 145
McMaken, Ezekiel 208
McMaken, George 140, 145
McMaken, James 140
McMaken, Joseph 145
McMaken, Joseph G. 208
McMaken, Joseph H. 208
McMaken, Maria C. 208
McMaken, Mary 208
McMaken, William 140
McManas, Henry 599
McManas, Jacob 599
McManas, John (Jr.) 599
McManas, Philip 599
McManas, Rachel 599
McManas, William 599
McManinea, Mary Ann 610
McManis, E. 616
McManis, R. 616
McManis, Robert 616
McMann, Elizabeth 84
McMann, Joseph 451
McMannancy, Geo. 536
McMannancy, James 535
McMannas, Henry 636
McMannas, Joseph 636
McMannas, Mary 636
McMannima, Danl. L. 608
McManis, E. 616
McManis, Elizabeth
  616, 637
McMannis, Henry 637
McMannis, Jacob 637
McMannis, Joseph 637

McMannis, Louisa 637
McMannis, Mary 616, 637
McMannis, R. 616
McMannis, Robert 616
McMannis, Samuel 637
McMannis, William 616,
  637
McManus, John C. 423
McManus, Rachel 599
McManus, Wm. 423
McMaster, William 672
McMasters, Andrew 732
McMasters, Margaret 402
McMasters, Samuel 402
McMean, James 679
McMeans, John 194
McMeen, Elizabeth 679
McMeen, Grisella 679
McMeen, James 679
McMeen, James N. 679
McMeen, John 679
McMeen, John B. 679
McMeen, Joseph A. 679
McMeen, Mariah 679
McMeen, Mary 679
McMeen, William 679
McMellen, Mathew 584
McMichael, Eliza 21
McMickel, James 481
McMillan, David 668
McMillan, Henry 668
McMillan, Jonathan 668
McMillan, Lydia 668
McMillan, Mary 668
McMillan, Nancy 497
McMillan, Thomas 668
McMillan, William 668
McMillen, Alex. 270, 272
McMillen, Angeline 145
McMillen, Eresbia 145
McMillen, James 170
McMillen, Jane S. 17
McMillen, John 608
McMillen, Lucinda 145
McMillen, Margaret 170
McMillen, Rebecca B. 740
McMillen, Robert 17
McMillen, Robert S. 13
McMillen, Wm. 41
McMiller, Alex. 764
McMillian, Lydia 659
McMordee, Adam 294
McMordee, Francis 294
McMordee, Jean 294
McMordee, John 294
McMordee, Nancy 294
McMordee, Robert 294
McMullan, John 61
McMullen, Alexander 489
McMullen, Alonzo 370
McMullen, Annanias 370
McMullen, Daniel 545
McMullen, James 370
McMullen, Jane 370
McMullen, John 686
McMullen, Patrick 371,
  373
McMullen, Peter 358
McMullin, Alexander 163

McMullin, Chas. H. 140
McMullin, Jane 455, 458
McMullin, John 465
McMullin, June 455
McMullin, Mar . . . 163
McMullin, Mary 163
McMullin, Rebecca 140
McMunah, Robert 227
McMunn, Ann 493
McMunn, Samuel 493
McMunn, William 493
McMurdie, Adam 477,
  478, 482
McMurdy, Adam 477
McMurray, Alexander 45
McMurray, Wm. (Jr.) 270
McMurtee, Hugh 59
McMurtee, John 59
McNabb, Margaret 145
McNairy, Betsey 451
McNairy, Jenny 452
McNamara, Hugh 559
McNamara, James 333
McNamara, James Mag. 559
McNamara, Jane 559
McNamara, John 559
McNamara, Robert 559
McNamara, Sarah 559
McNamer, Brian 385
McNamer, Nancy 551
McNamer, Philip 545
McNay, David 17, 19
McNay, Jane 13
McNay, John 13
McNay, Lucinda 11
McNay, Rhoda 17
McNay, Samuel 279
McNeal, Ann 391
McNeal, Ashel C. 402
McNeal, Benjamin 402,
  489
McNeal, John 390
McNeal, John R. 402
McNeal, Margaret 510
McNeal, Milton 525
McNeal, Reese 402
McNeal, Samuel 402
McNear, Huldah 588
McNeel, John 13
McNeel, Polly 14
McNeely, George 661
McNeil, Chloe 28
McNeil, Lovicea 29
McNemer, Elizabeth 463
McNemor, Elizabeth 399
McNemor, Harriet 399
McNemor, Nicholas 399
McNemor, Noah 399
McNemor, Philip 399
McNemor, Sarah 399
McNemor, William 399
McNichols, George 158
McNichols, John 153, 171
McNichols, Maria 171,
  179
McNichols, Mariah 171
McNichols, Nathaniel 153
McNickle, Alexander 469
McNight, Lewis 195

McNomar, Eliza 515
McNutt, Alexander 497
McNutt, Barbara 351
McNutt, Eliza 351
McNutt, Eliza Ann 351,
369
McNutt, Heulda 518
McNutt, James 50, 52
McNutt, John 351, 369,
497
McNutt, Joseph 351, 369
McNutt, Joseph G. 435
McNutt, Mary 518, 523
McNutt, Samuel 50
McNutte, Aszubia 523
McOnnel, Robert 256
McPharrin, Silas 13
McPherin, Samuel 493
McPherrin, Thos. 574
McPherson, George 584
McPherson, George W. 697
McPherson, Henry H. 13,
18
McPherson, James 145
McPherson, John 145
McPherson, John W. H.
311
McPherson, Lydia 145
McPherson, Martha Ann
145
McPherson, Sarah 311
McPherson, Susannah 464
McPherson, Wealthy 333
McPherson, William 311
McPherson, Wm. 311
McPheter, John 88
McPheters, Nancy Jane
308
McQuality, James 490
McQuality, Jane 490
McQuality, Kiturah 494
McQueen, Adam J. 608
McQueen, Anthony 608
McQueen, C. S. 356
McQueen, Margaret 606
McQueen, Mary 606
McQuillen, Robert 120
McQuiston, Archable 413
McQuiston, David 435
McQuiston, Eliza 413
McQuiston, Hugh 417
McQuiston, Martha Jane
435
McQuown, Allsworth 448
McQuown, Andrew 448
McQuown, David 448
McQuown, Harrison 448
McQuown, Margaret 448
McQuown, Mary Eliza 448
McQuown, Peggy Jane 448
McQuown, Thomas 448
McRacin, Saml. N. 413
MCraden, Jane 465
MCrary, Margaret 461
McRea, Charles 493
McRea, Joseph 748
McRean, Joseph 749
McRoberts, Alexander 489
McRoberts, Jane 467

McSherry, Haley 461
McTaigue, Stephen 178
McTeague, Stephen 178
McTehu, John 13
McVay, A. 533
McVay, Alice 533
McVay, Benjamin (Jr.)
177
McVay, Edward 533
McVay, Eliza A. 532
McVay, G. W. 533
McVay, Hemlie W. 532
McVay, Henry 533
McVay, I. T. 532
McVay, J. 532
McVay, J. A. 533
McVay, John 533
McVay, John M. 533
McVay, Lizzie 532
McVay, M. 533
McVay, M. L. 533
McVay, Mary 548
McVay, Mellie 533
McVay, Reuben 255
McVay, Tarry 532
McVay, Thomas 532, 550
McVeigh, America 257
McVeigh, Catherine 257
McVeigh, Orsemus 257
McVeigh, Silas 257
McVeigh, Stacey 257
McVeigh, Stacy 257
McVey, Elizabeth 548
McVey, James M. 545
McVey, Renson 302
McVicker, Eleanor 166
McVicker, Elizabeth
166, 305
McVicker, James 166
McVicker, Martha 165
McVicker, Thomas D. 166
McVickers, Alexander 305
McVickers, Elizabeth 305
McWade, Arthur 26
McWaid, Achshah 26
McWanson, William 133
McWhinney, Cynthia 435
McWhinney, Eli 435
McWhinney, James 193
McWhinney, John 193, 207
McWhinney, Mary 435
McWhinney, Newton 435
McWhinney, Rachel 435
McWhinney, Sally 193
McWhinney, Samuel 435
McWhinney, Sarah 435
McWhinney, Thomas 207
McWhinney, William 193
McWhinney, Wm. H. 435
McWhinny, James 425
McWhinny, Mary 425
McWhorter, Hugh 514
McWilliams, Alexander 171
McWilliams, Asenath 592
McWilliams, Jane 591
McWilliams, Jas. 732
McWilliams, Mary 589
McWilliams, Patience T.
555

McWilliams, Philip 303
McWilliams, Sarah 520
McWueston, Wm. 574
Meachouse, Margaret 455
Meacon, John 554
Mead, Elizabeth B. 404
Mead, Esther 506
Mead, Hezekiah 493
Mead, Jabez 322
Mead, Jonathan 504
Mead, Joseph 208
Mead, Samuel 280
Mead, Semanthe 30
Meaden, Alfred 465
Meads, Elma L. 328
Meads, M. A. 328
Meads, S. J. 328
Meaguians, Thram 140
Mealhouse, John 473
Mealhouse, Margaret 455
Meanor, Benjamin 87
Means, Elizabeth W. 634
Means, Hugh 634
Means, James 634
Means, James W. 634
Means, John 19
Means, John William 634
Measle, John 521
Meccum, Deberah 83
Mechen, John 158
Mechen, Sarah 158
Mechling, Catherine 370
Mechling, Eliza 370
Mechling, Elizabeth 370
Mechling, Esther 370
Mechling, Frederick 370
Mechling, George 370
Mechling, Hannah 370
Mechling, Jacob 370, 373
Mechling, Jacob M. 370
Mechling, John 370
Mechling, Joshua 370
Mechling, Lovey M. 370
Mechling, Magdalene 370
Mechling, Mary 370
Mechling, Peter 370
Mechling, Sally 370
Mechling, Samuel 370
Mechling, William 370
Mechling, Wm. 355, 377
Mechling, Wulliam 370
Mecoy, Mary 109
Mecuham, Eliza 585
Mecum, John 84
Medaris, Elizabell W.
539
Medaris, Elizabeth
Salters 539
Medaris, Jonathan H. 550
Medaris, Sarah 550
Medaris, Washington 539
Medbery, A. V. 101
Medbery, Allen V. 115
Medders, Aaron 167
Medders, Esther 167
Medkirk, Desdemona 510
Medsker, George 385
Meech, Reinhard 41
Meek, Betsy 741

Meek, Henry 167
Meek, James 514
Meek, Lucas 41
Meek, Mary 124
Meek, Mary Ann 741
Meek, Samuel 728
Meek, Sarah 626
Meeke, Anna 76
Meeker, --- 483
Meeker, Abagail 140
Meeker, Abner 470, 471, 489
Meeker, Anna 76
Meeker, Clarissa 83
Meeker, Evalena 489
Meeker, Harvey 489
Meeker, Jonathan 640
Meeker, Margaret 610
Meeker, Nancy 82, 640
Meeker, Tandy 490
Meeks, Nancy 566
Meeks, Sarah 293
Meeks, William 737
Mees, Rachael 607
Meetz, Barbara 459
Megely, Caroline 420
Megely, Catharine C. 420
Meigs, Ansel 126
Meigs, Jonathan 721, 722
Meigs, R. J. 727
Meigs, Return Jonathan (Jr.) 723
Meines, William 100
Mekoy, Ephram 102
Melana, Martha A. 85
Melching, F. C. 582
Meldick, Katheryne 410
Melia, William 322
Melick, Eleanor 343
Melick, John 343, 366, 373
Melick, Sarah 359
Meline, Polly 515
Melinger, William 126
Mellen, Aaron 696
Mellen, Alvira 29
Mellen, Henry 696
Mellen, Richard 720
Mellender, Martha 116
Mellenger, Leah 337
Meller, Clark 507
Melline, Baltzer 165
Melling, Peter 126
Mellinger, Alidza 548
Mellinger, B. F. 545
Mellinger, Catherine 549
Mellinger, David 320
Mellinger, Eliza 549
Mellinger, Freeborn 337
Mellinger, Harrison 320, 337
Mellinger, Jane 545
Mellinger, Jasper 545
Mellinger, John 545
Mellinger, Joseph 320, 545
Mellinger, Louisa 545
Mellinger, Margaret 545
Mellinger, Nancy 125

Mellinger, William 126, 320
Melliseek, Jacob 574
Melloer, Edward 261
Melloer, George 258
Mellor, Edward 266, 269
Mellor, Geo. 270
Mellor, George 262, 264
Mellor, John 264
Mellor, Samuel 264
Mellor, Samuel (III) 264
Melmon, Barney 317
Melone, Elizabeth 465
Melone, John 514
Melone, William 465
Melott, Easter 168
Melott, Jacob 168
Melott, Jane 154, 178, 179
Melott, John 153
Melott, Mary 153
Melott, Peter 168
Melott, Samuel 166
Melott, Sarah 162, 177
Melott, Stephen 152, 154, 159, 161, 178, 179
Melott, Stillwel 162
Melott, Stilwell 159, 171, 177
Meloy, Asa 424
Meloy, Hannah 661
Meloy, John 652
Meloy, Patrick 650
Meloy, Wm. 380
Melsheimer, C. A. 616
Melsheimer, Charles Edwin 616
Melsheimer, E. A. M. 616
Melter, August 545
Melter, Gerhard H. 545
Melvin, Abigail 54, 61
Melvin, Ann Robison 61
Melvin, Bartholomew S. 54
Melvin, Benjamin 51
Melvin, Charles 54, 61
Melvin, Chas. 255
Melvin, Eliza Catharine 61
Melvin, Elizabeth 61
Melvin, George 285
Melvin, Isaac 255
Melvin, Jane 54
Melvin, Jane H. 54
Melvin, Jehu J. 54
Melvin, John 54
Melvin, Josep V. 48
Melvin, Joseph 54, 61
Melvin, Joseph B. 54
Melvin, Martha 285
Melvin, Martin 61
Melvin, Phebe 54
Melvin, Samuel 54
Melvin, Sarah 54
Melvin, Thomas 54
Mendenhall, Allen 701
Mendenhall, Angeline 145
Mendenhall, Anna R. 701

Mendenhall, Bette 701
Mendenhall, Bettie 701
Mendenhall, Betty 701
Mendenhall, Caleb 147, 148
Mendenhall, Chas. 698
Mendenhall, Elijah 430
Mendenhall, Eliza Ann 430
Mendenhall, Eunice 701
Mendenhall, Grace 430
Mendenhall, H. 293
Mendenhall, Hannah 293, 430
Mendenhall, Hazel E. 698
Mendenhall, Ida 701
Mendenhall, Ida A. 701
Mendenhall, John 701
Mendenhall, Jos. E. 430
Mendenhall, Joseph 145
Mendenhall, Marmaduke 430
Mendenhall, Mary 119, 430
Mendenhall, Mary Catharine 701
Mendenhall, Mary E. 545
Mendenhall, Mordecai 545
Mendenhall, Morris D. 701
Mendenhall, Nettie 698
Mendenhall, Priscilla 145
Mendenhall, R. C. 293
Mendenhall, Rachel 11, 145
Mendenhall, Richard 126
Mendenhall, Ruth 701
Mendenhall, Samuel 293, 701
Mendenhall, Sarah A. 315
Mendenhall, Susan 123
Mendenhall, Thadius 126
Mendenhall, Walter E. 701
Mendenhall, William 545, 700
Mendenhall, Wm. 701
Mendenhall, Wm. A. 701
Mendenhall, Wm. Allen 701
Mendenhall, Wm. B. 701
Meneley, Theodocia 386
Meng, Anna 739
Meng, John S. 736, 739
Meng, Mary Margaretha 739
Meng, Philip 739
Meng, Philip (Sr.) 736
Menger, Claude 722
Menick, Rachel 459
Menjard, Susan 573
Mennell, Anne 31
Menshall, Jonathan 44
Menson, John 457
Mentel, Auguste Waldman 714
Meook, Susan 521
Meranda, Newland 545

909

Meranda, Samuel   545
Meranda, Thomas   661
Mercer, --- 400
Mercer, David   92
Mercer, Edward   164, 174
Mercer, Elizabeth   399
Mercer, George   489, 764
Mercer, Mary   164, 174,
  291
Mercer, Nottingham   514
Mercer, Saml.   148
Mercer, Samuel   148
Mercer, Vernon   313
Merceran, Ellen Ann   39
Merceran, Sarah E.   39
Mercerean, Henry   41
Merchant, John   521
Merck, Anthony   41
Meredith, Dorcas   180
Meredith, John L.   148
Meredith, New   180
Meredith, Norvel D.   148
Meres, John   374
Merevin, Simon   265
Mergan, George   403
Merithew, Benjamin   745
Meriven, Simeon   261
Merk, Lucas   41
Merker, Catherina   235
Merker, Ely   235
Merker, Martin   235
Merkle, Catharine   489
Merlin, Peter N.   335
Merphy, Nathaniel   666
Merril, Unity   718
Merrill, Cornelius   79
Merrill, Elizabeth   301
Merrill, Jacob   115
Merrill, Moses   30
Merrill, Sally   115
Merrim, John   574
Merrit, Abraham   647
Merrit, Isaac   150
Merrit, Joseph   265, 666
Merrit, Margaret   150
Merrit, William   120
Merritt, A.   150
Merritt, F.   150
Merritt, Rachel   150
Merrweathers, David   402
Merry, Ambrose H.   167
Merry, Caltan   169
Merry, Margaret   167
Merryman, Laura   519
Mers, George W.   753
Merser, Edward   170
Merser, Mary   170
Mershawn, John   591
Mervin, Simeon   259
Mervin, Simon   259
Merwin, Caroline A.   31
Meryman, Catherine   364
Mesberis, Sarah   124
Mese, B. H.   110
Mesler, Wilhomina   695
Mesner, Frederick   740
Messenger, Peter   126
Messer, Elizabeth   634
Messick, George   385

Messick, Noah   400
Messick, Polly   461
Metcalf, Edward   738
Metcalf, Hannah   738
Metcalf, John   738
Metcalf, John H.   738
Metcalf, Margaret   738
Metcalf, Nancy   738
Metcalf, Olive   518
Metcalf, Orlando   450
Metcalf, Vachel   738
Metcalf, Z.   608
Metger, Polly   386
Methard, Jacob   202
Methard, James   202
Metheney, Andrew   305
Metheney, Cyrus   305
Metheney, Nancy Ann   305
Metheney, Rachel   305
Metheney, Samantha   305
Metheney, Thomas   305
Mettert, Amanda   435
Mettert, Christena   435
Mettert, David G.   435
Mettert, Lydia A.   435
Mettert, Martin C.   435
Mettert, Rachel   435
Mettert, Wm. G.   435
Mettous, Francis   227
Metzgar, Simon   71
Metzger, George   396
Metzher, William   41
Metzter, Saloma   748
Mewhister, Frederick   608
Mewhister, James   608
Mewhister, William   608
Mewhorter, John   385
Meyer, Catharine   112
Meyer, Conrath   235
Meyer, Elisabeth   235
Meyer, Elizabeth   737
Meyer, Ely Henrich   234
Meyer, Jacob   737
Meyer, Johannes   234, 235
Meyer, John B.   545
Meyer, John George   227
Meyer, Lewis Henry   103,
  107
Meyer, Lucus Henry   102
Meyer, Marceta   235
Meyer, Rebeka   234
Meyer, William   602
Meyers, . . .   537
Meyers, ---   115
Meyers, C.   537
Meyers, Christena   537
Meyers, Ferdinand   521
Meyers, H. H.   537
Meyers, Henry   599, 600
Meyers, Joseph   537
Miars, C. W.   700
Miars, Hetty   700
Micael, Rebecca   382
Michael, Anna Mary   238
Michael, Catharine   385
Michael, Cornelias   385
Michael, Daniel   171, 181
Michael, Elizabeth   576
Michael, Henry   126

Michael, Jesse   214
Michael, Leah   214
Michael, Margaret   181
Michaels, Jacob   702
Michaels, Sallie A.   702
Michaels, Sallie L.   702
Michel, Jacob   236
Michel, Johan   235
Michel, Marcreta   235
Michel, Maria   235
Michels, Solomon   117
Mick, Ange   727
Micker, Wheeler   465
Mickeus, Peter   41
Mickey, Ann   511
Mickle, William S.   681
Micklewait, Barbara   509
Micklewait, Joseph   509
Middaugh, A.   331
Middaugh, Alfred   331
Middaugh, Benjamin   578
Middaugh, D.   578
Middaugh, Daniel   578
Middaugh, E.   331
Middaugh, Ester V.   578
Middaugh, Jesse M.   578
Middaugh, John   347
Middaugh, Lovey L.   331
Middaugh, Peter   358, 378
Middaugh, S.   578
Middaugh, Sarah   578
Middaugh, Susan   578
Middleswart, Jacob   732
Middleswart, Tunis   93
Middleton, Anna   583
Middleton, Anna S.   44
Middleton, Catharine   606
Middleton, Isaac   187
Middleton, Jacob   574
Middleton, John   591
Middleton, Timothy   580
Middlington, Lansing   591
Midkins, James   514
Miedon, Putnam
Miers, Bolsom   666
Miers, Catherine   744
Miers, John   465
Miiranda, George W.   690
Mikee, Farlander   216
Mikee, Leah   216
Mikesell, Aaron   193, 430
Mikesell, Abraham   193
Mikesell, Elizth.   413
Mikesell, Ephrain   417
Mikesell, Jacob   140
Mikesell, John   223, 224
Mikesell, John B.   193
Mikesell, Katherine   140
Mikesell, Valentine B.
  417
Mikesell, Wm.   140
Mikesill, Mary   421
Mikesill, Valentine B.
  421
Milbourn, David   764
Miles, Abigail   130
Miles, Ann O.   145
Miles, Anna   118, 135
Miles, Anne   130

Miles, Catharine 130
Miles, David 130, 135
Miles, Elizabeth 130, 145
Miles, Enoch P. 145
Miles, Enos 184, 185
Miles, Isreal 145
Miles, James 193
Miles, John 130, 545
Miles, Jonathan 130,
135, 586
Miles, Mary 93
Miles, Polly O. 77
Miles, Rachel 130
Miles, Rebeca 135
Miles, Rhoda 130
Miles, Sally 130
Miles, Sally O. 77
Miles, Samuel 130
Miles, Sarah 131
Miles, Thompson 30
Miles, William 130,
135, 661
Milford, Christianna 297
Milford, James 297
Milham, David 273
Milhollin, Edward J. 545
Milhollin, Jonathan 545
Milhorn, John 303
Miliness, Martha 365
Mill, T. O. 636
Mill, T. R. 637
Millar, Joseph 574
Millar, William 285
Millard, Elizabeth 29
Millard, Timothy 666
Millas, Catharine 515
Millegan, James 224, 472
Millehan, John 457
Miller, A. W. 614
Miller, Aaron 227, 229
Miller, Abigail 90
Miller, Abner 578
Miller, Abraham 48,
184, 203, 292, 482,
489, 550
Miller, Abraham R. 578
Miller, Adam 30, 385
Miller, Alexander 552
Miller, Alvin (Rev.) 578
Miller, Ana Maria 237
Miller, Anderson J. 604
Miller, Andrew 298
Miller, Anna 140, 203,
371
Miller, Anna D. 579
Miller, Annie R. 578
Miller, Anthony 240
Miller, Aron 186
Miller, Barbara 294,
566, 736, 736
Miller, Barbary 336
Miller, Benedict B. 578
Miller, Benj. 476, 483
Miller, Benjamin 62,
470, 489
Miller, Betsey 393, 661
Miller, Betsy 571, 585
Miller, Bithicah
Catharine 613

Miller, C. 540
Miller, Casper 689
Miller, Catharine 207,
230, 231, 240, 348,
393, 555, 568, 736,
738
Miller, Catherine 360,
369, 373, 456, 540,
579
Miller, Charles 579
Miller, Charles L. 614
Miller, Charlotte 145,
608
Miller, Chas. 253
Miller, Christena 348
Miller, Christian 203,
736
Miller, Christiana 203
Miller, Christopher 292
Miller, Creslly 126
Miller, Daniel 223, 224,
231, 539, 613, 736
Miller, Danl. 140
Miller, David 140, 184,
229, 231, 261, 274,
350, 555, 574, 604,
661
Miller, David M. 140
Miller, Delilah 604
Miller, Dinah 537
Miller, Dorcas 70
Miller, Drusilla 578
Miller, Edward 269
Miller, Edward (Jr.) 269
Miller, Eliz. 140
Miller, Elizabeth 203,
229, 348, 371, 390,
393, 489, 523, 545,
578, 604, 708, 717,
718
Miller, Emanuel 133
Miller, Emily 210
Miller, Ephraim 34, 210
Miller, Esther 462
Miller, Fanny 125
Miller, Frances J. 578
Miller, Francey 573
Miller, Francis 163, 310
Miller, Franklin 540
Miller, Frederic Wales
70
Miller, Frederick 303,
310, 738
Miller, Frederick W. 70
Miller, Geo. 627
Miller, Geo. M. 140
Miller, George 545,
567, 604, 661, 741
Miller, George G. 561
Miller, Gilbert 741
Miller, H. 540
Miller, Hannah 210, 345,
364, 371, 383, 457
Miller, Heath Jones 26
Miller, Henry 195, 210,
348, 489, 540, 567,
574, 641, 669, 673
Miller, Henry H. 579
Miller, Henry J. 579

Miller, Henry R. 540
Miller, Huldah 435
Miller, Isaac 13, 279,
292, 338, 457, 661
Miller, Isaac A. 579
Miller, Isabella 741
Miller, Israel 608
Miller, Jacob 120, 154,
170, 184, 203, 208,
291, 292, 348, 369,
371, 477, 478, 489,
555, 557, 574, 616,
685, 737, 739, 742
Miller, Jacob J. 574
Miller, James 13, 223,
253, 482, 521, 537,
608, 616, 741
Miller, James C. 736
Miller, Jane 120, 387,
458, 659, 741
Miller, Jane M. 608
Miller, Jas. 477, 537
Miller, Jemima 579
Miller, Jeremiah 521
Miller, Jesse 521
Miller, Joash 393
Miller, Johannes 236
Miller, John 41, 108,
140, 182, 184, 188,
208, 210, 224, 227,
230, 335, 341, 345,
348, 368, 369, 371,
453, 489, 521, 537,
545, 604, 661, 732,
736, 741, 745, 753
Miller, John A. 132, 435
Miller, John D. 503
Miller, John E. 579
Miller, John H. 48, 578
Miller, John J. 574
Miller, Jonathan 555
Miller, Jonathan D. 118
Miller, Jonnie W. 614
Miller, Joseph 134,
316, 348, 393, 493,
555, 714, 741
Miller, Joseph M. 537
Miller, Joshua 608, 626
Miller, Josias 598
Miller, Julia Ann 203
Miller, Katherine R. 435
Miller, Lavisa 616
Miller, Leah 578
Miller, Leanhart 168
Miller, Lemuel 741
Miller, Leonard 208, 213
Miller, Lewis 336
Miller, Lillie 578
Miller, Lydia 578, 579
Miller, Magdalena 236,
736
Miller, Magdalene 348
Miller, Malinda 578
Miller, Margaret 203,
348, 357, 461
Miller, Maria 140, 236
Miller, Maria Ann 369
Miller, Martha 62, 140,
210, 216

Miller, Martha Jane 435
Miller, Mary 163, 165, 180, 210, 393, 555, 565, 566, 741
Miller, Mary A. 493
Miller, Mary C. 435
Miller, Mary Co. 140
Miller, Mary Susan 435
Miller, Meria 736
Miller, Michael 145, 195, 237, 555
Miller, Michel 236
Miller, Mikiel 292
Miller, Moses 207, 209, 579, 686
Miller, Moses A. 578
Miller, Moses M. 579
Miller, Myers 737
Miller, Nancy 140, 154, 170, 393, 565
Miller, Nathl. M. 60
Miller, Nicholas 253, 390, 482
Miller, Noah 292
Miller, Norton 70
Miller, Olive Durfey 328
Miller, Oliver 497
Miller, Percy 579
Miller, Peter 30, 362, 376, 393
Miller, Phebe 207, 520
Miller, Phillip 292
Miller, Philomela 586
Miller, Polly 369, 376
Miller, Polly Ann 537
Miller, Rachel 573, 619, 711
Miller, Rebecca 62, 74, 85, 291, 335, 393, 606
Miller, Rebecca Jane 690
Miller, Richard 253
Miller, Robert 120, 132, 153, 162, 163, 165, 180, 453, 493, 545, 604, 608
Miller, Roy F. 578
Miller, Ruby Knecht 578
Miller, S. E. 614
Miller, Sally 203
Miller, Samuel 41, 72, 195, 208, 210, 363, 457, 604, 741, 745
Miller, Samuel H. 578
Miller, Samuel K. 737
Miller, Sarah 210, 229, 537, 579, 579
Miller, Sarah Ann 578
Miller, Sarah E. 609
Miller, Sarah Jane 537
Miller, Seth 578
Miller, Silvius 578
Miller, Susan 348, 493, 747
Miller, Susanah 575
Miller, Susanna 224, 310, 384
Miller, Susannah 126, 393
Miller, Theobald 708

Miller, Thomas 498
Miller, Thomas C. 599, 603
Miller, Thos. C. 619
Miller, Victor M. 578
Miller, Warmack 457
Miller, Wilhelm 277
Miller, William 6, 210, 277, 385, 490, 604
Miller, William J. 578
Miller, William S. 741
Miller, Wm. 269
Milleson, Isaac 295
Millhouse, Catharine 118
Millhouse, Elizabeth 125
Millhouse, John (Jr.) 120
Millhouse, Susannah 118
Milligan, Benjn. 591
Milligan, George S. 62
Milligan, Grizzel 430
Milligan, Hugh 171, 623
Milligan, John 274, 430
Milligan, John M. 417
Milligan, Margaret 588
Milligan, Ruth 171
Milligan, Samuel 314, 430
Millikan, John 457
Milliken, John 435
Millikin, James 44, 58
Millin, Stephen D. 591
Millinger, John 120
Millmon, Elizabeth 516
Mills, Adam 386
Mills, Allie R. 698
Mills, Amos 435
Mills, Ann P. 699
Mills, Anne 658
Mills, Benjamin 282
Mills, Betsey 537
Mills, Catherine 574
Mills, Charity 698
Mills, Charles 714
Mills, Charles F. 698
Mills, Charley A. 698
Mills, D. B. 617
Mills, D. C. 537
Mills, David 401, 676
Mills, Debora 660
Mills, Delila 102
Mills, Dinah 698
Mills, E. R. 537
Mills, Eber 498
Mills, Elizabeth 435
Mills, Esther 462
Mills, George 417, 435, 699
Mills, Gideon 269
Mills, H. 693
Mills, H. F. 701
Mills, Hannah P. 698
Mills, Harry A. 74
Mills, Henry 435
Mills, Henry F. 699
Mills, Isaac 102
Mills, J. 537, 698
Mills, James 102, 282
Mills, Jane 435

Mills, Jessie 102
Mills, Job 698
Mills, John 427, 435, 693
Mills, John L. 699
Mills, John Linley 701
Mills, Jonathan 698
Mills, Joseph 260, 435, 550
Mills, Joshua 198
Mills, Laura A. 693
Mills, Lizzie 698
Mills, Lydia 698
Mills, M. 693, 698
Mills, Margaret 457
Mills, Mary 401, 516
Mills, Mary 698
Mills, Mary Ann 435
Mills, Mary J. 693
Mills, Nannie D. C. 697
Mills, Peggy 140
Mills, Philemon 545
Mills, Rachel 350, 660
Mills, Rebecca 435, 567, 657
Mills, Reuben 41, 435
Mills, Rhoda 663
Mills, Richard 457
Mills, Robert 177
Mills, Rosewell 370
Mills, Rosswell 369
Mills, Roswell 350, 354, 369, 374
Mills, S. W. 701
Mills, Sally Amarintha 537
Mills, Samuel 567
Mills, Sarah 126, 570
Mills, Sarah W. 699
Mills, Siles 102
Mills, Sophia 549
Mills, Squire 102
Mills, Stephen 698
Mills, Thomas 661
Mills, Thos. 574
Mills, W. 537
Mills, W. Elmer 697
Mills, William 282, 537, 689
Mills, Wm. 435, 537, 574
Milner, John 107
Milroy, Catharine 22
Milt, John 389
Miltenberger, Adam 687
Miltenberger, Catherine 687
Miltenberger, George 687
Miltenberger, John 687
Milter, Betsy 585
Milton, Betsy 585
Milton, John 618
Milton, Lydia 717
Milton, Sarah 618
Mimain, Peter 717
Minard, Caroline 609
Minden, Anna 162
Minden, John 162
Minder, John 153, 154, 161
Minear, Adam 594

912

Miner, Abiah 648, 651
Miner, Charlott 69
Miner, Henry 643
Miner, Joseph 69
Miner, Marcus 69
Miner, Mathew 732
Miner, Philip 453
Miner, Priscilla 75
Miner, William 643, 651
Miner, William A. 69
Mingus, Charles 299
Minney, Eve 155
Minney, John 155
Minniar, Philip 392
Minniar, Solomon 392
Minnich, Barbara 140
Minnich, Catharine 571
Minnich, David 140
Minnich, Eliz. 140
Minnich, Geo. 359
Minnir, Benston 668
Minnir, Levin 668
Minnir, Mary 668
Minnir, Noah 668
Minnix, --- 408
Minor, John 165
Minor, Phinias 435
Minor, Rossalie 413
Minor, Theophilus 156, 165
Minott, Henry C. 30
Minshall, Amos 493
Minshall, Elenor 52
Minshall, Ellis 51, 413, 493
Minshall, Isaac 2
Minshall, Jonathan 51, 52, 61
Minshall, Rachel 464
Minshall, Walter W. 48
Minshell, Edward 356
Minsky, Ada 536
Minsky, Adam 536
Minsky, Ida May 536
Minter, Mary 44
Mintle, Aaron 681
Mintlo, Aaron 687
Minton, Nancy 41
Miranda, Angelina 648
Miranda, Fanny 673
Miranda, George 648, 673
Miranda, George W. 690
Miranda, James 669
Mires, John 608
Mirewrather, David 400
Miser, Frederick 567
Misfer, Ann 574
Mishler, Abraham 574
Mishler, Ann 574
Misky, Ida May 535
Misner, Margaret 93
Misner, Rebecca 497
Misner, William L. 498
Misor, Frederick 574
Mitchel, Betsey 586
Mitchel, D. M. 672
Mitchel, David 445
Mitchel, Edward 223, 224, 230

Mitchel, Elizabeth 401
Mitchel, Isaac 169
Mitchel, James 247, 401
Mitchel, Jesse 586
Mitchel, John 661
Mitchel, Margaret 230
Mitchel, Melissa 507
Mitchel, Polly 465
Mitchel, Sarah 223
Mitchel, Sarah D. 586
Mitchel, William 514
Mitchell, Catharine 140
Mitchell, David 50, 445, 581, 595
Mitchell, David (Sr.) 50
Mitchell, David Seign. 586
Mitchell, Dixon 581
Mitchell, Eleanor 595
Mitchell, Elizabeth 595
Mitchell, Ezekiel 483, 484
Mitchell, Francis 438
Mitchell, Franklin 435
Mitchell, Frederick 457
Mitchell, George 126, 371, 438
Mitchell, Harrison 435
Mitchell, James 401, 489, 595, 732
Mitchell, Jean 489, 595
Mitchell, John 389, 643
Mitchell, John F. 371
Mitchell, John H. 380
Mitchell, Joseph 48, 438
Mitchell, Josettee 495
Mitchell, Lavina 435
Mitchell, Leonard 583
Mitchell, Letetia 119
Mitchell, Linney 123
Mitchell, Louisa 435
Mitchell, Lydia 371
Mitchell, Magill 48
Mitchell, Margaret 306, 595
Mitchell, Martha 581, 589
Mitchell, Mary Ann 140
Mitchell, Mathew 371
Mitchell, Matilda 48
Mitchell, Milton 435
Mitchell, Moses 50
Mitchell, Moses G. 140
Mitchell, Moses Grant 120
Mitchell, Polly 463
Mitchell, Randolph 371
Mitchell, Robert 298, 338
Mitchell, Robt. 298, 457
Mitchell, Ruhama 508
Mitchell, Sally 120
Mitchell, Samuel 50, 435, 595, 597
Mitchell, Samuel (Sr.) 50
Mitchell, Sarah 435, 595
Mitchell, Shadrack 173
Mitchell, Sidney 30

Mitchell, Solomon C. 371
Mitchell, Susan 371
Mitchell, Thomas 177, 178, 283, 288
Mitchell, Velinda 435
Mitchell, Violet 371
Mitchell, William 131, 371, 591
Mitchell, William F. 371
Mitchell, Wm. 296, 353
Mith, Sarah 568
Mitsher, Samuel H. 126
Mittower, Andrew 526
Mittower, John 526
Mittower, Mary 526
Mix, Lydia 608
Mixton, Samuel 498
MKeen, Jane 466
Mobley, John B. 167
Mobley, Levi 167
Mock, Frederick 574
Mock, Hannah 118
Mock, Leander 145
Mock, Michael 574
Moderwell, Nessy 738
Moe, Betsey 29
Moe, Edwin 30
Moe, Hannah 28
Moe, Polly 30
Moeker, Herman F. 115
Moeller, Otto H. 368
Moellers, Franz Anton 111
Moetz, Catharine 557
Moffet, Catherine 415
Moffet, Jane 123
Moffett, Eliz. 145
Moffett, Jane 117
Moffett, Nathan 458
Moffett, Peggy 124
Moffett, Robert 145
Moffit, Mary 739
Moffitt, Joshua 493
Moffitt, Nathan 465
Mohar, Patsy 48
Mohler, Jacob 354
Mohler, Martin 354
Mohr, Barbara Anna 234
Mohr, Bernhard 236
Mohr, Daniel 236
Mohr, Frederick 20
Mohr, Jacob 234, 236
Mohr, Maria 234, 236
Molden, Sarah 77
Moler, Anne 91
Moler, Henry 267
Moler, Mary Jane 247
Molfe, Henry 113
Mollers, Franz Anton 111
Molter, Magdalena 711
Momina, Anthony 498
Monarty, Edward 388
Monbeck, Daniel 205
Monch, Eve Dorothy 145
Money, Anna 108
Money, Thomas 574
Money, William 108
Monfort, Aaron 421
Monfort, Elizabeth 421

Monfort, John 656
Monfort, Peter 686
Mongram, John 661
Monier, Catherine 456
Monnett, William 465
Monor, J. 59
Monro, Josiah (Capt.)
720
Monroe, Bridget 501
Monroe, Charles 514
Monroe, George 94
Monroe, George H. 79
Monroe, Henry 94
Monroe, John 20, 501
Monroe, Lida 501
Monroe, Mary J. 94
Monroe, Moses 501
Monroe, Phebe 501
Monroe, Simeon 13
Monrow, Aaron 501
Monrow, Barnabus 501
Monrow, Cizy 501
Monrow, Daniel 501
Monrow, Jesse 501
Monrow, Moses 501
Monrow, Solloman 501
Monson, John 457
Montfort, Henry 641
Montfort, Lenah 661
Montfort, Peggy 664
Montgomery, Betsey 386
Montgomery, Christiney
524
Montgomery, David 688
Montgomery, Eli 360, 365
Montgomery, Elizabeth
123, 297, 456
Montgomery, Hannah 506
Montgomery, Hugh 62, 465
Montgomery, Humphrey
465, 483
Montgomery, Isabella 524
Montgomery, James 62,
470
Montgomery, John 465,
472, 484, 485, 506,
717
Montgomery, John W. 145
Montgomery, Katharine 62
Montgomery, Kezia 522
Montgomery, Laura 90
Montgomery, Mary A. 145
Montgomery, Mary M. 583
Montgomery, Milton 506
Montgomery, Nancy 505
Montgomery, Nancy J. 145
Montgomery, Robert 62,
529
Montgomery, Samuel 737
Montgomery, Simeon 262
Montgomery, William 297,
453, 505, 506, 524
Montgomery, Wm. 258,
261, 263, 265, 266,
267, 268, 270, 458
Mt Gomery, Hugh 62
Montonney, Jane 120
Mony, Mary 498
Moodie, George 582

Moodie, Roger 582
Moody, Charles 34
Moody, Elias 591
Moody, Elizabeth 591
Moody, Ezemiah 279
Moody, George 591
Moody, Henry 591
Moody, John 661
Moody, Mariah 145
Moody, Nathan 247, 365
Moody, Saml. 264
Moody, Samuel 267, 270
Moody, Simon 458
Moon, Abraham 732
Moon, Abraham A. 30
Moon, Betsey 11
Moon, Catharine 640, 669
Moon, Elenor 669
Moon, Emma C. 700
Moon, Eunice E. 700
Moon, Heman 30
Moon, Horton 35
Moon, James 655
Moon, Jemima 700
Moon, John 51
Moon, Lonnie 700
Moon, M. A. 700
Moon, Mary 655
Moon, Mary A. 700
Moon, N. 700
Moon, Neri 700
Moon, Oliver 33
Moon, Phineas 640, 669
Moon, Phinehas 661
Moon, Phinias 661
Moon, Rebecca 435
Moon, Robert 13, 70
Moon, Thomas H. G. 435
Moon, William B. 700
Mooney, David B. 41
Mooney, Elizabeth G. 126
Mooney, Fanny 453
Mooney, John 118, 489,
567
Mooney, Peter 608
Mooney, Priscilia 117
Mooney, Prudence 117
Mooney, Ruth 117
Mooninger, Elizabeth 564
Mooninger, George 564
Moons, Polly L. 458
Moor, Elizabeth 178
Moor, Henry 126
Moor, Isaac 150
Moor, Martha 573
Moor, Mary 150
Moor, Thirza 28
Moor, Thomas 444, 574
Moor, William 161, 178
Moor, William A. 150
Moore, Agnes 370
Moore, Alexander 333
Moore, Allen 514
Moore, Ann 154
Moore, Anna 510
Moore, Anne 11, 385
Moore, Benjamin 366,
370, 376
Moore, Chloe 370

Moore, David 514
Moore, Delila 515
Moore, Edmund 388
Moore, Eleanor 517
Moore, Elihu (Rev.) 424
Moore, Elijah 370
Moore, Elizabeth 6, 463
Moore, Elizabeth E. 520
Moore, Elliner 514
Moore, Elsie 708
Moore, Ezekiel 259
Moore, Fergus 386, 470,
476, 489
Moore, Forman 509, 510,
514
Moore, Foster 515
Moore, Francis 115
Moore, Furgus 472, 480,
481, 482
Moore, George 44
Moore, Hannah Elizabeth 6
Moore, Harriet E. 6
Moore, Henry 120, 263,
269, 270
Moore, Hugh 471, 474,
489
Moore, Isaac 386
Moore, Isaac S. 435
Moore, Jacob 154, 159,
515
Moore, James 16, 287,
370, 386, 498
Moore, James G. 370
Moore, James King 6
Moore, Jane 370
Moore, Jeptha F. 643
Moore, John 27, 52, 54,
55, 58, 61, 260, 288,
358, 370, 371, 375,
515
Moore, John S. 371
Moore, Joseph 370, 515,
732
Moore, Joseph D. 608
Moore, Levi 510, 515
Moore, Levi A. 430
Moore, Lewis 666
Moore, Linus 265
Moore, Littleton (Jr.)
341
Moore, Lusinda 550
Moore, Macena 28
Moore, Martha 370
Moore, Mary 14, 260,
370, 371, 516, 570,
571, 592
Moore, Minerva 549
Moore, Nancy 370, 371,
384
Moore, Nathan 765
Moore, Nathaniel B. 498
Moore, Oliver 115
Moore, Ozias 115
Moore, Peter 609
Moore, Phebe 64
Moore, Philip 259, 260,
515
Moore, Polly 14, 259,
458

Moore, Ransom 30
Moore, Raphael 16, 18
Moore, Rebeccah 451
Moore, Richard H. 545
Moore, Robert 13, 67,
208, 296, 370, 371,
376
Moore, Rubal 386
Moore, Samuel 126, 435
Moore, Sarah 22
Moore, Sarah Jane 607
Moore, Shadrach N. 30
Moore, Thomas 4, 13,
353, 435
Moore, William 6, 13,
14, 370, 490, 515
Moore, Wm. C. 371
Moore, Wm. G. 14
Moorehead, Thomas 287,
290
Moorhead, Betsey 451
Moorhead, Thomas 469
Moorman, Agnes 604
Moorman, Elizabeth 604
Moorman, William 604
Moors, Furges 479
Moose, Jacob 166
Moose, John 178
Moose, John (Jr.) 181
Moose, Rachel 178
Moot, Charles 475
Moot, Conrad 475
Moothart, Andrew 545
Moothart, Mary A. 545
Moots, John 14, 489
Moots, Phillip 458
Moots, Susannah 15
Mor, David 235
Mor, Jacob 235
Mor, Maria 235
Morahuse, Susannah 12
More, Azuba 716
More, Cynthia 508
More, Daniel 591
More, Hannah 551
More, Mary 158
More, Nancy 463
More, Nelly 386
More, Ruth 28
More, Samuel 158
Morehart, George 530
Morehead, C. 616
Morehead, Calvin 616
Morehead, Carrie 616
Morehead, Charles E. 616
Morehead, Emanuel 609
Morehead, H. M. 616
Morehead, Hannah M. 616
Morehead, Rachael 608
Morehead, Thomas 295
Moreheart, Thos. 298
Moreland, Alex. 140
Moreland, Byers 140
Moreland, James 140
Mores, Anna 51
Mores, Polly 464
Moress, Mary 390
Morford, Cornelius 661
Morford, Wm. 508

Morgan, Aaron 545
Morgan, Abraham 643
Morgan, Andrew Jackson
140
Morgan, Anna 503
Morgan, Charles 193
Morgan, Cornelius 211
Morgan, Daniel 643
Morgan, David 643
Morgan, E. Wm. 30
Morgan, Elizabeth 84,
211
Morgan, Ester 643
Morgan, Eve B. 295
Morgan, Ezra 765
Morgan, Felix 643
Morgan, Gabriel 643
Morgan, George 208
Morgan, Jacob 643
Morgan, James 113, 126
Morgan, James S. 126
Morgan, John 643
Morgan, John E. 386
Morgan, John J. 208
Morgan, Joseph 643
Morgan, Margaret 380
Morgan, Matilda 699
Morgan, Patty 208
Morgan, Ruth J. 699
Morgan, S. 765
Morgan, Samuel 208
Morgan, Sarah 193
Morgan, Simon 635
Morgan, Thomas 510, 661
Morgan, William 458,
490, 699
Morganstern, Adam 732
Morganstin, Katharina
708
Morgareidge, Simeon
259, 260, 265
Morgen, Subrution 503
Morgenthaler, Christana
529
Morgenthaler, Christine
529
Morgenthaler, Doretha
529
Morgenthaler, Godgred
529
Morgenthaler, Gotlape
529
Morgenthaler, Jacob 529
Morgenthaler, John 529
Morgenthaler, Katherine
529
Morgenthaler, Margaretta
529
Morgin, Elizabeth 501
Morgin, Lewis 574
Morgin, Mary 570
Morgon, George B. 41
Morgon, William 458
Morgridge, Sally 48
Moriarty, John 67
Moriarty, Margery 67
Moris, Rose 345
Morison, Charlotte C. 36
Morley, Alexander 328

Morley, Amelia E. 328
Morley, Hannah 328
Morley, Harry C. 328
Morley, J. 328
Morley, James H. 328
Morley, Joel 328
Morley, W. Nelson 328
Morley, William 328
Morrel, Elizabeth 391
Morrel, Pierre 714
Morrell, Jesse 386
Morreson, Jane 664
Morrett, Polly 119
Morricks, Peter 419
Morris, Alexander 489
Morris, Andrew 177, 706
Morris, Anne 10
Morris, Benadict 390
Morris, Benjamin 10,
167, 396, 458, 465
Morris, Caroline 631
Morris, Charity 176
Morris, Charles 748
Morris, Dan 745
Morris, Daniel 672
Morris, David 639
Morris, Davied 465
Morris, Davis (Dr.) 670
Morris, Elihu 178
Morris, Elijah 164
Morris, Elinor 458
Morris, Elizabeth 161,
176, 631, 665
Morris, Emily P. 170
Morris, Geo. 354
Morris, George 269, 368
Morris, George (Sr.) 552
Morris, Hannah 390
Morris, Hannah J. 310
Morris, Harriet 178
Morris, Henry 310, 396
Morris, Henry (Sr.) 303
Morris, Ignatious 390
Morris, Isaac 418, 666
Morris, Isabella 164
Morris, Isah 666
Morris, Isaiah F. 171
Morris, Jacob 396, 686
Morris, James 10, 41,
303, 396, 704
Morris, James (Sr.) 396
Morris, Jane 10, 706
Morris, Jesse 170
Morris, Jessie 465
Morris, Jessy 390
Morris, Job S. 178
Morris, John 10, 430,
631, 706
Morris, Jonathan 173
Morris, Joseph 10, 169,
274, 279, 396
Morris, Joseph P. 145
Morris, Joshua 173, 176
Morris, Lewis 165, 176,
631
Morris, Louisa 396
Morris, Lucinda 631
Morris, Margaret 518,
706

Morris, Maria 631
Morris, Martha Jane 145
Morris, Mary 153, 170,
  178, 386, 390, 665
Morris, Mary J. 312
Morris, Matilda 281, 396
Morris, Molly 396
Morris, Moses 396
Morris, Nancy 119, 385
Morris, Phebe 171, 631
Morris, Polly 159
Morris, Rebecca 176, 631
Morris, Rebecca Ann 631
Morris, Robert 159, 164
Morris, Samuel 418, 430
Morris, Sarah 173, 664
Morris, Sarah Ann 254
Morris, Sarah E. 310
Morris, Sarah McKenney
  662
Morris, Susannah 180
Morris, Thadeus 10
Morris, Thomas 153,
  160, 170, 175, 176,
  254, 386, 706
Morris, Thomas William
  254
Morris, William 161,
  176, 180, 681
Morris, William A. 312
Morris, William H. 631
Morris, William Harvey
  396
Morrison, Alexander 348
Morrison, Arthur 666
Morrison, Belinda 633
Morrison, Betsey H. 118
Morrison, Calvin 633
Morrison, Charlotte 132
Morrison, David 282
Morrison, Elizabeth
  175, 178
Morrison, Esther 629
Morrison, Francis 441
Morrison, Hannah 633,
  659
Morrison, Harrison 506
Morrison, Isaac 633
Morrison, James 334,
  627, 638
Morrison, James D. 420
Morrison, John 68, 175,
  627, 629, 633
Morrison, John (Sr.) 175
Morrison, Joseph 178
Morrison, Margaret 178
Morrison, Michael 268
Morrison, Morris 732
Morrison, Nancy 593
Morrison, Peggy 302
Morrison, Persey 633
Morrison, Priscilla 127
Morrison, Robert 132, 133
Morrison, Robt. 458
Morrison, Samuel 270,
  717
Morrison, Sarah 633
Morrison, Sarah A. 405
Morrison, Theodore 633

Morrison, Thomas 291
Morrison, William 297,
  627
Morrison, William B. 627
Morrison, Wm. 405
Morrison, Wm. V. 21
Morriss, Benedick 386
Morriss, Henry 386
Morriss, Joseph 386
Morriss, Lydia 386
Morros, David 739
Morrow, Adams 140
Morrow, Andrew 378
Morrow, Daniel 498
Morrow, David 742
Morrow, Eleanor 383
Morrow, Elizabeth 123,
  140, 357, 378, 659
Morrow, James 118, 185,
  591, 661, 676
Morrow, Jane 140
Morrow, Jeremiah 668
Morrow, John 357, 586
Morrow, Richard 135
Morrow, Rosanna 76
Morrow, Sarah Jane 695
Morrow, Susannah 127
Morrow, Watson 140
Morrow, William 490
Morrow, Wm. 591
Morse, Betsey 586
Morse, Caleb 48
Morse, Edmond 297
Morse, John 386
Morse, John G. 602,
  623, 627
Morse, Joseph 297
Morse, Maria 627
Morse, Mercy A. 627
Morse, Permelia 591
Morse, Phobe 606
Morse, Relief 607
Morse, Rha 591
Morse, Rhoda 609
Morse, William W. 627
Morten, Cassandra 89
Morton, Elizabeth 585
Morton, Evan L. 527
Morton, Hannah 435
Morton, Harriet A. 75
Morton, John 527
Morton, Matilda 527
Morton, Meeker Squire
  643
Morton, Samuel 642
Morton, Thomas 435, 642
Morton, Wm. 480
Morts, George (Jr.) 14
Morty, Mary 512
Mortz, Mary 512
Mory, Stephen H. 440
Moseney, Dennis 166
Moseney, Rachel 166
Moser, Abraham 313
Moser, Hannah 313
Moser, John 313
Moser, Morris 313
Moser, Samson 313
Moser, Sarah J. 313

Moses, Aaron 240
Moses, Elizabeth 240,
  493
Moses, James 435
Moses, Martha 435
Moses, Michael 197
Moses, Rebecca 197
Moses, Robert 240, 435
Moses, Robert K. 240
Moses, Roger 439
Moses, Wm. 435
Mosier, Nancy 278
Mosley, Abner (Dr.) 296
Moss, Aaron 145
Moss, Augustus 759
Moss, Jacob 145
Moss, Margaret 319
Moss, Mary 494
Moss, Nancy 456
Moss, Nathaniel 661
Moss, Roger 439
Moss, Samuel 759
Moss, Susannah 456
Moss, William 319
Mossbarger, Matilda 410
Mosser, Abraham 560, 563
Mosser, Catharine 566,
  567
Mosser, Catrena 560
Mosser, Elizabeth 563,
  567
Mosser, Eve 563
Mosser, Mary 563
Mosser, Samuel 560
Mossey, John 202
Most, Jacob 185
Mosure, D. 618
Mosure, James O. 618
Mosure, R. A. 618
Mote, Allen 193
Mote, Carolina M. 140
Mote, David 131, 132,
  140, 193, 216
Mote, Dorcas 132
Mote, Eli 216
Mote, Elias 140
Mote, Elizabeth 117
Mote, Ely 193
Mote, Ginsey 193
Mote, Hannah 140
Mote, James 194
Mote, Jeremiah 147
Mote, Jerome 185
Mote, Jesse 194
Mote, John 130, 140, 194
Mote, Jonathan 126, 216
Mote, Mary 124
Mote, Mary M. 140
Mote, Rebecca 126
Mote, Rhoda 140
Mote, Sally C. 140
Mote, William 118, 126
Mott, Gideon 599, 600
Mott, H. H. 168
Mott, Henry H. 154,
  169, 181
Mott, Mary 181
Mott, Thomas 599
Mott, Thomas R. 600

916

Mott, William 169
Mottice, Peter 555
Motts, David 577
Motts, George 465
Motts, Jacob 172
Mouhart, Valentine 171
Mouk, Caty 502
Mouk, Frederick 502
Mouk, Joseph 502
Mouk, Peter 502
Mouk, Samuel 502
Moulton, Anna 714, 723
Moulton, Edmund 723
Moulton, Joseph 723
Moulton, Katharine 723
Moulton, Lydia 723
Moulton, Molley 723
Moulton, William 723
Mount, Charles 599
Mount, Elijah 651
Mount, Jesse 651
Mount, Lenford 44
Mount, Patience 665
Mount, Watson 675
Mount, William 675
Mountain, James 453
Mt Gomery, Hugh 62
Mounts, Abner 480
Mounts, Asa 458
Mounts, Catherine 675
Mounts, Elenor 452
Mounts, Elizabeth 662
Mounts, Jesse 489
Mounts, John G. 648
Mounts, Joseph 661
Mounts, Nancy 657
Mounts, Providence 675
Mounts, Sarah 490
Mounts, Thomas 490
Mounts, Watson 646
Mounts, William 550, 646
Mouser, Jacob P. 407
Mouser, John A. 407
Mouton, William 723
Mowan, Leonard 553
Mowbray, Ben. 390
Mowder, Elizabeth 153
Mowery, Eliza 495
Mowry, --- 469
Mowry, Peter 479
Mowy, --- 479
Moyer, Adams 521
Moyer, Ann Maria 370
Moyer, Barbara 370, 385
Moyer, Catherine 4, 370
Moyer, Daniel 182
Moyer, Dina 4
Moyer, Dorothy 386
Moyer, Elizabeth 4,
  182, 231, 370
Moyer, George 231, 545
Moyer, George W. 4
Moyer, Henry 182, 223
Moyer, Isaac 222
Moyer, Jacob 182, 489
Moyer, John 4, 182, 370
Moyer, John (Jr.) 370
Moyer, Leah 4
Moyer, Lydia 4

Moyer, Margaret 4
Moyer, Michael 182,
  201, 370
Moyer, P. 201
Moyer, Peter 182
Moyer, Sally 370
Moyer, Sarah 4
Moyer, Solomon 370, 377
Moyers, Abraham 386
Moyers, George 231, 552
Muck, Catherine 212
Muck, George 212
Muck, John 212
Muck, Margaret 212
Muckelhany, Elizabeth
  456
Mucklewain, Andres 435
Mucklewain, Moses 435
Mucklewain, Naomy 435
Mudgett, Gilman C. 316
Mueller, Otto H. 368
Mugg, Harriet 495
Mugridge, Simeon 258
Muhleman, Anders 161
Muhleman, Barbary 161
Muker, Herman F. 115
Mulbourn, Jemima 523
Mulford, Caleb 669
Mulford, Daniel 718
Mulford, Elizabeth 48
Mulford, Jehu 688
Mulford, John R. 688
Mulford, Joseph 655, 688
Mulford, Phebe 670
Mulford, Rebecca 660
Mull, Margaret 518
Mullen, Ann 303
Mullen, Joseph 591
Mullen, Mary 592
Mullen, Nancy 588
Mullen, Peggy N. 467
Mullendore, Aaron 435
Mullendore, Catharine
  241
Mullendore, Daniel 241
Mullendore, David 241
Mullendore, George 435
Mullendore, Hannah 241
Mullendore, Harriet 241
Mullendore, Jacob 192,
  241
Mullendore, John Wesley
  241
Mullendore, Jos. 435
Mullendore, Joseph 241
Mullendore, Josiah 241
Mullendore, Maria 241
Mullendore, Noah 435
Mullendore, Ozro 241
Muller, Isaac 640
Muller, Katharine 710
Mullet, Nancy 463
Mullian, Elizabeth 745
Mullican, Rachel 746
Mullican, Sarah Ann 745
Mullin, James 661
Mullin, Jane 661
Mullin, Sarah 660, 665
Mullon, John M. 368

Mulvey, Arthur 545
Muma, Barbara 568
Mumford, Benjamin 371
Mumford, Elizabeth 371
Mumford, James 371
Mumford, Levi 371
Mumford, Marget 326
Mumford, Mary 371
Mumford, Thomas 371
Mumo, Joseph F. 297
Muncey, Peggy 574
Munch, Eli 545
Munch, Mary Jane 545
Muncy, Eliza 566
Munday, George 521
Mundel, Abner 169
Mundel, Delila 169
Munford, Anna Rebecca 56
Munford, George Wythe 56
Munford, Sarah 56
Munford, William 56
Munford, Wm. 56
Munger, Edmond 331
Munger, F. 331
Munger, Gains 498
Munger, Harvy 666
Munger, John D. 331
Munger, Luther W. 331
Munger, Nancy 241
Munger, Sophia 331
Munger, Trifena R. 331
Munger, William 596
Munger, Z. N. 331
Munger, Zenith N. 331
Munn, David 515
Munn, James 121
Munn, Nancy 514
Munn, Peggy 511
Munn, William 515
Munro, Josiah 723, 728
Munro, Sally 716
Munro, Susanna 717
Munroe, Daniel 288
Munroe, James L. 628
Munroe, Margurett 628
Munroe, Rassilas 732
Munroe, Richard 628
Munrow, Daniel 515
Munrow, Lydia 85
Munsell, Caroline 145
Munsell, Deborah 109
Munsell, Howard 145
Munsell, Jane 145
Munsell, Leander 145
Munsell, Levi 714
Munsell, Sarah 145
Munsell, Thos. 145
Munsell, Ward 145
Munsey, Albert S. 545
Munsey, John 545
Munson, Demtt C. 69
Munson, Elizabeth 69
Munson, Flora 69
Munson, Francis 69
Munson, Joel 323
Munson, Lucius B. 69
Munson, Lucy M. 69
Munson, Maria 69
Munson, Mary 79

Munson, Perry 69
Munson, Polly 69
Munson, Samuel B. 69
Munson, Samuel R. 69
Munts, Joseph 641
Muntz, Josiah 417
Munyon, Ellie 514
Munyon, George 340
Munyon, John 340
Murdock, Covington 635
Murdock, Dan 440
Murdock, Fanny 21
Murdock, John 100
Murdock, Lydia J. 369
Murdock, Nancy 100
Murdock, Patrick 635
Murdock, Theopolis 154
Murdock, William M. 101
Murfrey, Fanny 334
Murlin, Daniel 109
Murpha, David 336
Murphey, Amy 123
Murphey, David 502
Murphey, John 666
Murphey, Lydia 127
Murphey, Mary 124
Murphey, Thomas 550
Murphey, William 550
Murphy, Ann 317
Murphy, Anna 746
Murphy, Daniel 337, 416
Murphy, David 14, 336,
    504
Murphy, David P. J. 746
Murphy, Delilah 140
Murphy, Edward 140,
    644, 653, 654
Murphy, Eliza Jane 448
Murphy, Elizabeth 664
Murphy, Elizabeth I. 435
Murphy, Frederick 689
Murphy, Hannah 435
Murphy, Harriet 744
Murphy, Hester 337
Murphy, Hugh 363
Murphy, Isaac 48, 84
Murphy, James 140, 435,
    448, 609, 636, 644,
    678
Murphy, John 79, 86,
    121, 140, 262, 264
Murphy, Joseph H. 746
Murphy, Joseph K. 321
Murphy, Julia Ann 448
Murphy, Juliann 448
Murphy, Labin 689
Murphy, Mariah 448
Murphy, Martin P. 435
Murphy, Mary 689
Murphy, Mary Ann 435,
    448
Murphy, Nancy 744
Murphy, Rebecca 435, 644
Murphy, Richard 653
Murphy, Robert 317,
    321, 746
Murphy, Samuel 644,
    646, 661, 673
Murphy, Sara 336

Murphy, Sarah 456, 644,
    673
Murphy, Sary 646
Murphy, Stephen 689
Murphy, Susannah 661
Murphy, William 258,
    268, 453
Murphy, William (Dr.)
    224
Murphy, Wm. 261
Murray, Abner 30
Murray, Alexander H. 84
Murray, Ann Maria 202
Murray, Anna 464
Murray, Archibald 79
Murray, Betsey 29
Murray, Catharine 201
Murray, Catherine
    Margaret 369
Murray, Daniel 14, 201
Murray, Elias 202
Murray, Elizabeth 201
Murray, Hugh 369
Murray, Jacob 201
Murray, James 256
Murray, Jane 78
Murray, John 63, 201
Murray, Julian
    Huntington 202
Murray, Julius Abbott
    202
Murray, Lucius Junius
    202
Murray, Lydia 31
Murray, Malinda 637
Murray, Mary 28
Murray, Matilda 83
Murray, Rebecca 266
Murray, Saml. 266
Murray, Scanda 92
Murray, Thomas 262, 266
Murray, Thos. 259
Murray, William 84, 86,
    677
Murray, Wm. 79
Murre, Christina 499
Murry, Ambrose Rice 762
Murry, Charles 118
Murry, Daniel 14
Murry, Edward 443
Murry, Julyann 575
Murry, Margaret 121
Murry, Rouse 161
Murry, Rufus 161
Murry, Sally 161
Murry, Samuel S. 629
Murry, Seth W. 498
Mury, Thos. 259
Mushell, Nelly 499
Muskings, John 386
Musselman, Daniel 458
Musselman, Elizabeth 345
Musselman, Jane 545
Musselman, Peter 545
Musselman, Samuel 545
Musselman, Sara 345
Musselman, Wm. 345
Musser, Christiana 355
Musser, Elizabeth 399

Musser, Henry 305
Musser, Theabold 355
Mussetter, Christian 526
Mussetter, Susannah 519
Musshel, Mary Ann 499
Mussleman, David 201
Mussleman, John 201, 550
Mussleman, Osins 201
Mussulman, John 318, 320
Mustard, Catharine 500
Mustard, Elizabeth 500
Mustard, George 515
Mustard, Joseph 515
Mustard, Lydia 500, 516
Mustard, Nancy 515
Mustard, Sally 516
Mustard, Samuel 500
Mustard, William 485,
    515
Mutchner, P. A. (Rev.)
    421
Muter, Sarah 113
Mutes, Charles 470, 475
Mutten, Thomas 592
Myars, George 465
Myer, Daniel 521
Myer, Gerherd 112
Myer, Herman 112
Myer, Mary 112
Myers, Abraham 465
Myers, Adam 152, 169,
    172, 179, 583
Myers, Agnes 528
Myers, Amanda M. 634
Myers, Ann Eliza 627
Myers, Anna D. 618
Myers, Benjamin 67
Myers, Catherine 452,
    459
Myers, Caty 369
Myers, Christopher 591
Myers, David 545
Myers, Eleazer 401
Myers, Elias 521
Myers, Elizabeth 67,
    369, 528, 607
Myers, Frederick 166
Myers, George 231, 528,
    623
Myers, George (Sr.)
    172, 528
Myers, Hannah 166, 181,
    581
Myers, Henry 126, 369,
    599
Myers, Huldah 29
Myers, Isaac 27, 67, 528
Myers, Jacob 216, 369,
    443, 465, 528
Myers, James 121, 574
Myers, Jesse 67
Myers, Joel 67, 279
Myers, John 30, 327,
    369, 528, 574, 583,
    600, 609, 627
Myers, Jonathan 618
Myers, Jos . . . 532
Myers, Leah 67
Myers, Magdeline 23

Myers, Margaret 67, 369
Myers, Martin 369, 482, 486
Myers, Mary 169, 179, 281, 369
Myers, Mary Ann 67
Myers, Melissa Jane 627
Myers, Michael 186, 591
Myers, Moses 67
Myers, Nancy 575
Myers, Nathaniel 287
Myers, Peggy 369
Myers, Peter 369
Myers, Phebe 528
Myers, Philip 528
Myers, Polly 493
Myers, Rachel 67
Myers, Roesey 716
Myers, Rosanna 465
Myers, Ruth 516
Myers, Samuel 369, 746
Myers, Sarah 401, 514, 608
Myers, Thomas 627
Myers, William 166, 172, 179, 181, 498
Myres, Abram 126
Myres, Elisa 571
Myres, Jacob F. 550
Myres, Ragina 523
Myrick, Sarah M. 632
Myson, Frederick 746

--- N ---

Nace, Jacob 217
Nace, Noah 217
Nadel, Anne Marie 572
Naeff, Abraham 413
Nafe, Mary 520
Nafus, Cornelius 524
Nafus, Wm. S. 524
Nagel, Mary 519
Nager, Michael 190
Nagle, Henry 340
Nagley, John 57
Nailer, Louisa 503
Nanpur, James 295
Napp, Thomas 458
Nash, Jonah 88
Nash, Matilda 499
Nash, Thomas 266
Nash, Zachariah 275
Nashee, George 465
Nason, Alexander 760
Nason, Julia Ann 760
Nason, Stephen 760
Nason, William 760
Nathan, Catherine 467
Nathan, Nicholas 490
Nathan, Sarah 459
Nauman, John 753
Naylor, Joseph P. 249
Naylor, Mary 177
Naylor, Mary B. 173
Naylor, Robert F. 173, 177, 180

Neal, Abigail 715
Neal, Benjamin 136
Neal, Catharine 581
Neal, Elizth. 140
Neal, Hester 140
Neal, John 140, 430, 550
Neal, Mahlond 140
Neal, Martin 444
Neal, Mary 430
Neal, Rachel 140
Neal, Rebeccah 568
Neal, Richard A. 550
Neal, Ruth 116
Neal, Sarah 140
Neal, Thomas 205
Neal, Thos. C. 140
Neal, William 136
Neale, Harriet 140
Neale, Lucinda 140
Nealson, Clef 706
Nealy, Benjamin 140
Nealy, Peggy 665
Nealy, Sarah 117
Nean, John 711
Near, David 493
Near, William 493
Nearing, Guy 764
Nearing, Neptune 764
Nearing, Rosetta 764
Nearing, Stella 764
Nearon, Mary 413
Neas, John 79
Neau, John 711
Nebaker, Lucas 483
Nebell, Augustus 580
Nebincall, Jacob 465
Nebuccar, Lucas 474
Nebuckas, Lucas 471
Nebuker, Lucas 486
Nedey, Gibson 538
Nedey, Irene 538
Nedey, Mary C. 538
Nedrow, Anna L. 329
Nedrow, John 329
Needham, Athelia Belle 314
Needham, David Leander 314
Needham, Elizabeth 314
Needham, Jasper 732
Needham, John 272, 314
Needham, Margaret 314
Needham, Mariam 314
Needham, Mary Ann 314
Needham, Michael 389
Needham, Samuel 314
Needham, William 314
Needles, Adam 149
Needles, C. 149
Needles, Catharine 149
Needles, Catherine 149
Needles, Clara G. 149
Needles, David 149
Needles, Eliza Jane 149
Needles, J. 149
Needles, Jac. 149
Needles, Joseph 149
Needles, Sarah 149
Needles, William 149

Neeham, Hannah G. 75
Neel, George 567
Neel, John 350
Neel, Rachael 125
Neeley, Wm. 369
Neely, Elizabeth 118
Neely, Jane 663
Neely, William 131
Neeper, Margaret 140
Neer, Adam 20
Neer, Martin 20
Neff, Abraham 224, 230
Neff, Adam 230
Neff, Barbary 571
Neff, Christian 224, 232
Neff, Corneluis 458
Neff, Daniel 184, 224, 230
Neff, Henry 184, 224, 230
Neff, John 61, 224, 230
Neff, John (Jr.) 418
Neff, John (Sr.) 418
Neff, Josephus 430
Neff, Lewis 184, 230
Neff, North 430
Neff, Polly 184
Neff, Sarah 430
Negley, John 14
Neher, Adam 9
Neher, George 9
Neher, Rachel Ann 9
Neice, William 515
Neighbor, Elizabeth 571
Neighbour, Anna 574
Neighbour, Anne 573
Neighbour, Catharine 566
Neighbour, John 567
Neighbour, Margaret 567
Neighbour, Nicholas 563, 574
Neikirk, George 526
Neikirk, Michael 524
Neil, Jacob 386
Neil, Margaret 457
Neil, Sarah 218
Neil, Susannah 746
Neiley, John 648
Neily, John 648
Neiswanger, David 623
Neiswanger, Fanny 218
Neiswanger, George 218
Neiswanger, John 218
Neiswanger, Mary 218
Neiswanger, Susannah 218
Neiswanger, William 254
Neiter, Charles Frederick 101
Neiter, Katharine Louisa 101
Neithercut, William 427
Neithercutt, William 427
Nell, James 574
Nelson, Benj. 89, 357
Nelson, Benjamin 498
Nelson, C. J. 411
Nelson, Catharine 145
Nelson, Henry 256
Nelson, Howard (Gov.) 760

Nelson, Isaac 256
Nelson, James 263, 269, 271, 567
Nelson, James J. 256
Nelson, Jesse 503
Nelson, Jessey 503
Nelson, John 90, 256, 545, 721
Nelson, Joseph 503
Nelson, Joshua 760
Nelson, Josiah 503
Nelson, Katherine 357
Nelson, Lucinda 420
Nelson, Moses 420
Nelson, Nancy 80
Nelson, Oliver 706
Nelson, Priscilla 271
Nelson, Richard 711
Nelson, Robert 50, 256, 598
Nelson, Ruth A. 145
Nelson, Seth 256
Nelson, Thomas 171, 465, 515
Nelson, Wm. 145
Neme, Louise 714
Nep . . . , John 179
Nephur, George 334
Neptune, Lydia 616
Neptune, William 167
Neptune, Wm. 616
Neron, John 661
Nesbet, John 705
Nesbet, Thomas 294, 295
Nesbit, Margaret 372
Nesbit, Thomas 295, 296, 354, 355, 372
Nesbit, Thos. 353
Nesmith, Henry 362
Nesmith, John 71
Nesslerode, Elias 79
Nessonger, Betsy 119
Netsker, Henry 193
Neucomb, Mathew 136
Neuman, John Henry 103
Neuman, Johnn Bernd. 101
Neuton, Stephen 636
Nevill, Mary 384
Nevills, John 397
Nevius, Olitta 665
New, Nicy Dunnis 15
Newcom, Charlotte 184
Newcom, George 182, 186, 223
Newcom, Mary 184
Newcom, Matthew 223
Newcom, Robert 184, 223
Newcom, William 184
Newcomb, Mary Jane 115
Newcomb, Matthew 550
Newcum, Samuel 666
Newell, David 441
Newell, John 16
Newell, Joseph 21
Newell, Julia 441
Newell, Maria 593
Newell, Mary 25
Newell, Matilda 11, 27
Newell, Rosannah 18

Newell, Sally 76
Newell, Samuel 18, 19, 27
Newell, Samuel (Rev.) 682
Newell, Thomas 18, 27
Newell, William 715
Newhoun, Wm. 586
Newhous, Wm. 586
Newhouse, Mary 387
Newkirk, Mary 190
Newlon, David 247, 253
Newlon, James 247, 253
Newlon, John 247, 253
Newlon, Mary 247
Newlon, William 247
Newman, Allen 248
Newman, Amanda 499
Newman, Andrew 445
Newman, Catharine 445
Newman, Eve 211
Newman, Geo. 264, 272
Newman, Henry 445
Newman, Henry W. 248
Newman, Jacob 441, 445
Newman, Jonathan 643, 669
Newman, Joseph 441, 445, 661
Newman, Joseph J. 690
Newman, Lemuel 640
Newman, Mark A. 211
Newman, Mary 211
Newman, Michael 465
Newman, Naomi 239
Newman, Peggy 461
Newman, Ruth 211
Newman, Samuel P. 498
Newman, Susannah 445
Newman, Thomas 211, 224
Newman, William 211, 224, 239, 240
Newport, Betsey 667
Newport, Hannah 664
Newport, Henry 567
Newport, Thomas 684
News, Peggy 585
News, Unity 15
Newsom, Benjamin 22
Newton, Ann 571
Newton, Anna 77
Newton, Caroline E. 334
Newton, Charles H. 430
Newton, Crissy 571
Newton, Hananiah 260
Newton, Isaac 405
Newton, James 227
Newton, James H. 430
Newton, Marinda 28
Newton, Nathan 262
Newton, Sarah 713
Newton, Sofa 762
Newton, Sylvanus 258, 259, 270
Newton, Sylvenus 263, 267
Newton, Thos. 435
Newton, Wm. H. 430
Ney, Ebenezer 730

Neyland, Michael 339
Nial, Elizabeth 498
Nibert, Anthony 724, 725
Niblach, William 453
Niblack, Robt. 574
Niblack, William 490
Niblock, Jane 571
Nibpack, William 483
Niccum, Thos. D. 435
Nicely, Abraham 483
Nicewarner, Jacob 525
Nichelson, David I. 14
Nichol, James 91
Nichol, Thomas 84
Nicholas, Balace 460
Nicholas, Francis 391
Nicholas, Hariet 35
Nicholas, Hetty 464
Nicholas, Jonathan 545
Nicholas, William 555
Nicholl, Harriet 321
Nicholl, William 321, 336
Nicholls, William 320
Nichols, Balace 458
Nichols, C. C. 612
Nichols, Catharine 611
Nichols, David 611, 655
Nichols, Edward 271
Nichols, F. 611
Nichols, Fredrick
   Nichols (Sr.) 611
Nichols, Henry 266
Nichols, James 84, 611
Nichols, John 506
Nichols, K. 611
Nichols, Minerva 612
Nichols, Moses 498
Nichols, Solomon 636
Nichols, Solomon C. 21
Nichols, Thomas 515
Nichols, Wm. 108
Nicholson, Abner 458
Nicholson, Abraham 651
Nicholson, Daniel 177, 178
Nicholson, Henry 465
Nicholson, Huldah 463
Nicholson, Martha 177
Nicholson, Robert 465
Nicholson, Samuel 126
Nicholson, William 469, 651
Nickerson, A. 98
Nickerson, Hugh 265, 272
Nickerson, J. 98
Nickerson, Nancy C. 98
Nickerson, Sidney B. 75
Nickins, Polly 451
Nickius, Eve 452
Nickle, John B. 746
Nickles, Sarah 663
Nickom, Abigal 430
Nickom, Curtland 430
Nickom, Jesse 430
Nickom, John 430
Nickom, Nancy 430
Nicol, Joanna 435
Nicol, John 435

920

Nicol, John L.   582, 583
Nicoles, David   515
Nicoles, Joseph   515
Nicoles, William   515
Nicoll, William   324
Nicols, William   515
Nicolson, Dinah   453
Nider, Jacob   380
Niegeman, John   574
Niehting, J. H.   103
Niggle, Jacob   681
Nigh, Christiana   657
Night, William   386
Nikens, Agga   465
Nikens, James   465
Nil, Elizabeth   126
Niles, Jonathan   30
Niley, Hannah   279
Niley, Hugh   271
Nimsik, Solomon   280
Nisbet, Caroline   430
Nisbet, Elizabeth   430
Nisbet, Jane   430
Nisbet, John   430
Nisbet, Margaret   430
Nisbet, Mary   430
Nisbet, Thomas   294, 295
Nisbet, Thomas James   430
Nisbet, Walter   430
Nisbet, William   430
Nischwitz, Elizabeth   234
Nischwitz, Jacob   234
Nischwitz, Susanna   234
Nisely, Jacob   74
Nishwitz, Catharine A.
   M.   239
Nishwitz, Catherine M.
   239
Nishwitz, David   237
Nishwitz, Geo.   239
Nishwitz, Margaret Jane
   239
Nishwitz, Rebecca Ann
   237
Nishwitz, Theodore
   Augustus   237
Niswonger, Frances   232
Niswonger, George   232
Niswonger, John   715
Niswonger, Thomas   545
Nitcher, John   498
Niven, Mary   10
Niven, Thomas   10
Nixon, Ann   270
Nixon, Catherine   372
Nixon, Edward   270
Nixon, Elijah   372
Nixon, Eliza Ann   252
Nixon, Elizabeth   372
Nixon, Hugh   252, 261,
   263
Nixon, Isaac   372
Nixon, Jacob   736
Nixon, Jeremiah   270
Nixon, John   372, 490
Nixon, Jonathan   372
Nixon, Katharine   635
Nixon, Levi   372
Nixon, Mary Ann   372

Nixon, Phebe   270
Nixon, Rachel   252
Nixon, Robert   372
Nixon, Saml.   509
Nixon, Samuel   510, 649,
   661, 672
Nixon, Sarah   372, 376
Nixon, Susannah   372
Nixon, William   261,
   263, 732, 742
Nixon, William (Sr.)   742
Noble, Alexander   334
Noble, Alonzo M.   41
Noble, Caleb   490
Noble, Charity   490
Noble, Edward   688
Noble, Elizabeth   740
Noble, Esther   82
Noble, James   740
Noble, John   259, 266,
   267, 740
Noble, John C.   115
Noble, Justin   115
Noble, Levin (Jr.)   490
Noble, Levin (Sr.)   490
Noble, Nancy   459
Noble, Nathan   490
Noble, Robert   740
Noble, Summers   490
Noble, Tamey   490
Noble, William   490, 740
Nobles, Charles F.   91
Nobles, Julia   81
Nobles, Osmin   92
Noe, Lysander F.   149
Noe, Michael   526
Noe, P.   149
Noe, W.   149
Noe, William   149
Noel, Abraham G.   515
Noel, Caty   517
Noel, David   507
Noel, Drusilla   515
Noel, Hanna   523
Noel, Jacob   515
Noel, John   510, 515
Noel, Margaret   574
Noel, Mary   515, 516
Noel, Nicholas   515, 521
Noel, Peter   515
Noel, Rebecah   517
Noel, Susannah   513, 523
Noffsinger, Catharine
   203
Noffsinger, Daniel   196,
   203
Noffsinger, Eli   217, 218
Noffsinger, Henry   203
Noffsinger, James   152
Noffsinger, Samuel   203,
   214
Noffsinger, Susan   203
Noftsinger, Magdalena
   572
Noggle, John H.   337
Noggle, Polly   134
Noggle, Thomas I.   550
Nogle, Isaac   718
Nolan, James   140, 190

Nolan, Julia Ann   190
Noland, Cyrus   181
Noland, John   485
Noland, Martha   166, 181
Noland, Mary   115
Noland, Philip   166, 181
Noland, Thomas   115
Noland, William   115
Nold, Catharine   741
Nold, John   741
Nold, William   741
Nolder, Elizabeth   509
Nolder, James   509
Nolder, Jane   509
Nolder, John   509
Nolder, Lemuel   509
Nolder, Marget   509
Nolder, Mary   509
Nolder, Matilda   509
Nolder, Samuel   509
Nolder, Sarah   509
Nolder, William   509
Nolder, Wm.   509
Nolen, Samuel   528
Noles, Almeda   372
Noles, Ann Maria   372
Noles, Asbury Fletcher
   372
Noles, Barbara   372
Noles, Clara   372
Noles, Emeline   372
Noles, Harriet   372
Noles, Henry   372
Noles, Jacob   366, 372
Noles, Leroy   372
Noles, Matilda   372
Noles, Susanna   570
Nolin, Matthew   490
Nolin, Richard   490
Noll, Catharina   565
Noll, Roderick   672
Nolton, Lydia   78
Noon, James   341
Noon, John   338
Nooulen, Rosey   453
Nopp, John   458
Norbeck, John   60
Norcutt, Margaritt   123
Nores, Charles   567
Noris, Geo.   574
Norman, George   288
Norman, Peggy   461
Norman, Rebeckah   516
Norris, Anna   76
Norris, E. M.   583
Norris, Eli   529
Norris, Elided   567
Norris, Gersham   558
Norris, J. S.   583
Norris, John   765
Norris, Lovey   565
Norris, Sarah Ann   522
Norris, Susannah   126
Norris, William   301
North, Alida   39
North, Allen   140
North, Caleb   347, 354,
   755
North, Delany   123

North, Geo. 39
North, Harriet 39
North, Isaac 41
North, James 39
North, Joel 375
North, John 39, 510
North, Lavina 140
North, Martha 121
North, Nancy 125, 749
North, Oron 61
North, Samuel 126
North, Sarah 125
North, Tho. 390
North, Thomas 118
North, William 396
North, Zelotus 30
Northcut, Sarah 120
Northrup, William 337
Northup, Henry 285, 286
Northup, Lensy 718
Norton, Abigal 52
Norton, Alweda 74
Norton, Carlos A. 283
Norton, Cloe 52
Norton, Cyrus G. 521
Norton, David 14, 18, 26
Norton, Deabory 52
Norton, Ebenezer M. 70
Norton, Hezekiah 7
Norton, Hiram 42
Norton, Hugh 736
Norton, Isaac 529
Norton, James 52
Norton, John 52
Norton, Jonathan 5, 22
Norton, Kiziah 52
Norton, Mahley 14
Norton, Moses 453
Norton, Phebe 52
Norton, Sarah C. 279
Norton, Sarepta 52
Norton, Solomon 52
Norton, Wm. 478
Norwood, Joshua 493
Nosmer, Hez. L. 763
Noteman, Andrew 453
Noteman, Ann 54
Noteman, Betsey 54
Noteman, Charles 54
Noteman, Jane 586
Noteman, Mary 589
Noteman, William 54
Noteman, William
    Willshire 54
Nott, Benjamin 263
Nott, Elisabeth 714
Nott, Mary 716
Nottingham, John 106
Novers, William 715
Nubuker, Lucas 472
Nuel, Drusilla 515
Nugent, Patrick 339
Null, Adam 661
Null, Anna 640
Null, Anna Catherine 372
Null, Catharine 640
Null, Catherine 372
Null, Conrad 372
Null, Elizabeth 660

Null, Lucinda 372
Null, Margaret 372
Null, Polly 640
Null, Sally 640
Null, Susannah 372
Numan, John Henry 101
Numpleby, Jackson H. 410
Nun, Margaretha 710
Nunemaker, Daniel 374
Nurse, Joshua 510
Nut, Ally 293
Nut, Harriet 293
Nutland, Adam 670
Nutt, Aaron 187
Nutt, Adam 669
Nutt, Elizabeth 663
Nutt, Henry K. 121
Nutt, Hester 661
Nutt, Sarah 658
Nutter, E. L. 405
Nutter, Sarah 405
Nutts, Frederic 187
Nutts, Frederick 196
Nuttz, Frederick 185
Nye, Absalom 503
Nye, Adam 403
Nye, Arius 296, 732
Nye, Ebenezer 718
Nye, Elizabeth 659
Nye, George 386
Nye, Henry 503
Nye, Icahabod 732
Nye, Ichabod 722
Nye, Melzer (Jr.) 635
Nye, Minerva 721
Nye, Robert 288
Nye, Sarah 715
Nyghswonger, Suckey 714
Nyswonger, Sally 714

--- O ---

Oadewalt, Margaret 140
Oadewalt, Mary E. 140
Oadewalt, Sarah 140
Oaks, Eliz. 145
Oaks, John 145
Oaks, Margaret 145
Oaks, Mary 145
Oaks, Priscilla 145
Oarel, Joseph 506
Oatley, Phebe 362
Oats, Rebecca 361
Oaverman, Sarah 455
Obenouer, Frederick 558
Ober, William (Sr.) 411
Oberdorf, Anna 763
Oberdorf, Barberry May
    763
Oberdorf, Daniel 763
Oberdorf, Eava 763
Oberdorf, Mary 763
Oberdorf, Mathias 763
Oberdorf, Matthias 763
Oberdorf, Maugred 763
Oberdorf, Samuel 763
Obermeyer, Johannes 368

Oblinger, Christian 218
Oblinger, Horatio 218
Oblinger, Jacob 199
Oblinger, John 196
Oblinger, Martha Jane
    218
Oblinger, William John
    218
Oboils, Cornelius 48
Obrian, John 453
Obriant, John 490
O'Brien, James 317
O'Brien, Mathew (Rev.)
    360
O'Brien, Patrick 42
O'Conner, Daniel 164
O'Conner, David 158
O'Conner, Joseph M. 317
O'Connor, John 362
Odell, Charlotte 658
Odell, Henry 249
Odell, Thomas 249
Odle, Elizabeth 455
Odle, Mary 455, 462
Odle, Mary Cornhammah
    140
Odle, Wm. 458
Odlin, P. 379
Odling, T. 376
O'Donald, Cornelius 574
Odonnald, James 567
ODonnald, Rachel 566
O'Donnell, Amelia 577
ODonnell, Elizabeth 566
ODonnell, Mary 566
O'Donnold, Cornelius 561
O'Donnold, Daniel 561
O'Donnold, Eleanore 561
O'Donnold, Elisabeth 561
O'Donnold, Emelie 561
O'Donnold, James 561
O'Donnold, Patty 561
O'Donnold, Rachel 561
O'Donnold, William 561
Officer, James 286
Offil, William 118
Offner, Jacob 504
Offnere, Jacob 505, 510
O'Flinn, John 274
Ogborn, Samuel 378
Ogburn, Robert J. 498
Ogden, Abner 52
Ogden, Albert 52
Ogden, Benjamin 52
Ogden, Caroline 522
Ogden, Deborah 52
Ogden, Eliza 519
Ogden, Elizabeth 736
Ogden, Gilbert J. 530
Ogden, Gilbert M. 521
Ogden, John 52
Ogden, Jonathan 52
Ogden, Margaret 52
Ogden, Oliver 736
Ogden, Polly 52
Ogden, Sally 682
Ogden, Samuel 52
Ogden, Sarah L. 522
Ogden, Stephen M. 521

Ogden, Susan 52
Ogden, William H. 748
Ogdon, Benjamin 444
Ogdon, Henry 444
Ogdon, John 444
Ogg, George 338
Ogg, Jane 362
Ogg, Rebecca 172
Ogg, Robert W. 169, 172
Ogg, Vachel 270
Ogle, Alfred 303
Ogle, Evaline E. 498
Ogle, George 271
Ogle, Jacob 165, 167, 172
Ogle, James 247
Ogle, Jane 84
Ogle, Jas. 270
Ogle, Lucinda 302
Ogle, Mary 271
Ogle, Rebecca 545
Ogle, Thomas 521
Ogle, Willis 545
Ogle, Wm. 263
Oglesbee, Margaret 48
O'Hara, Anna Maria 372
Ohara, Arthur 52
O'Hara, Daniel 370, 372
O'Hara, David 372
O'Hara, John 372
O'Hara, Margaret 372
O'Hara, Patrick 372
Oharo, Polly 665
O'Harra, Hugh 405
Oharro, Esther 387
Ohaver, Asahel 14
Ohaver, Margaret 11
O'Kane, Margaret Ellen 435
O'Kane, Peter 435
Okely, Aaron 741
Okely, Abraham 741
Okely, Betsy 741
Okely, Mary 741
Okely, Rachel 741
Okely, William 741
Okely, Wm. 741
Okey, --- 176
Okey, Arthur 155, 181
Okey, Catharine 172, 180
Okey, Catherine 152
Okey, Cornelius 171
Okey, Elizabeth 174
Okey, Esther 155, 158
Okey, George 174
Okey, Hannah 171, 181
Okey, Henry 152
Okey, James 171
Okey, Katharine 174
Okey, Leven 153, 154
Okey, Levin 155, 156, 158, 181
Okey, Mine . . . 152
Okey, Nancy 181
Okey, Woodman 152, 155, 167, 172, 174, 180
Olbert, Katharine 512
Olbinger, Charles W. 218
Oldaker, Jesse 458

Oldfather, John 205
Oldfield, Reuben 605
Olds, Amasa M. 400
Olds, Ezra 498
Olds, John 395
Olds, Joseph 396, 400
Olds, Rachel 34
Olds, Sarah 400
Olds, Sary 503
Olds, Thomas 752
Olery, Samuel 490
Oleshouse, David 574
Olewine, Abraham 151
Olewine, Elizabeth 151
Olewine, Michael T. 151
Olinger, Anna M. 88
Olinger, Barbara 294
Olinger, Catharine 575
Olinger, George 200, 205, 211, 294
Olinger, Isaac 294
Olinger, John 194, 198
Olinger, Mary 294
Olinger, Philip 681
Olinger, Samuel 294
Olinger, Susanna 294
Oliphant, Wm. 260, 266
Olive, Cessley 296
Olive, David 296
Olive, James 299
Oliver, Alexander 293
Oliver, Allen 372, 661
Oliver, Christian 713
Oliver, Daniel 303
Oliver, David L. 336
Oliver, Elanor 714
Oliver, Eliza 78
Oliver, Elizabeth 746
Oliver, Elsey 465
Oliver, Hetty 293
Oliver, Isabella 716
Oliver, Jane 293
Oliver, John 440, 515, 718
Oliver, Liza 715
Oliver, Lucinda 718
Oliver, Lucretia 714
Oliver, Peggy 715
Oliver, Precilla 293
Oliver, Robert 262, 721, 725, 728, 730
Oliver, Samuel 79
Oliver, Thomas 293
Oliver, William 265, 293, 715
Oliver, Wm. 274
Ollive, Joseph 299
Olliver, Elizabeth 116
Ollom, Jacob 173, 175
Ollom, John 169, 175
Ollom, Joseph 179
Ollom, Mary 175
Ollom, Susana 175
Ollom, Susanna 169
Ollom, William 169
Olmsted, Geo. G. 498
Olmsted, Jesse S. 498
Olney, Catharine 259
Olney, Coggeshall 730

Olney, Coggshall 730
Olney, Discovery 718, 730
Olney, Drusilla 713
Olney, Gilbert 258, 265, 266
Olney, Huldah 730
Olney, Ithamar 618
Olney, Jenny 730
Olney, Joanna 730
Olney, Lois 713
Olney, Lucy 618
Olney, Oman 259
Olney, Patience 713
Olney, Sally 716, 730
Olney, Sarah 730
Olney, Sylvanus 271
Olney, Televenus 718
Olney, Washington 730
Olny, Joanna 716
Olwine, Barnhart 357
Olwine, Jacob 223
Oman, Elizabeth 525
Omy, Aantony 567
O'Neal, Abijah 131
Oneal, Ann 456
O'Neal, Charles 631
Oneal, Charlotte 457
O'Neal, Henry 631
O'Neal, Hugh 131
O'Neal, James 631
O'Neal, John 631
O'Neal, Thomas 631
Oneall, James S. 682
O'Neil, Bridget 345
O'Neil, Cain 84
O'Neil, Charles 486
O'Neil, Francis 345
O'Neil, Margaret 407
Oniel, C. 407
Oniel, F. 407
O'Niel, Joseph 407
Onstot, Jacob 291
Onstott, Peter 288
Opdycke, John 753
Opp, Catheryne 409
Opp, Jacob 562
Oppert, Andrew 557
Oppert, Elizabeth 557
Oppert, Susannah 557
Opt, John 521
Orahood, Anna 582
Orahood, Caleb 586
Orahood, Jemima 589
Orahood, Noah 583
Orahood, Ozillye 588
Orahood, Samuel 584
Oranoodt, Jacob 591
Orbeson, John 126
Orbison, Henry 118
Orbison, John 545
Orcher, Joseph 718
Orcutt, B. 48
Ording, Gerherd 112
O. Rily, Ellen 636
Ormiston, James 732
Ormsby, C. 721
Orn, Mary 168
Orn, William 168

Orndorff, Eve 372
Orndorff, George 372
Orndorff, Henry 372
Orndorff, Margaret 372
Orndorff, William 372
Orr, Alexander P. 435
Orr, Betsey 131, 596
Orr, George 596
Orr, Hervey 398
Orr, Jackson 113
Orr, James 118, 130, 131
Orr, James M. 435
Orr, John 741
Orr, John C. 435
Orr, Martha 140
Orr, Mary Jane 435
Orr, Polly 496
Orr, Samuel 739
Orr, Sarah 585
Orr, Smith 739
Orr, Susannah 596
Orr, Thomas 739
Orr, Thomas K. 140
Orr, William 596
Orrahood, Elijah 586
Orrahood, Elizabeth 589
Orsborn, Absalom 661
Orsborn, Daniel 661
Orsborn, Morris 661
Ortendorf, Joseph 609
Orton, John B. 350,
   352, 353, 361, 372,
   374, 375, 380
Orton, Matilda 380
Orum, Hiram 417
Osban, John 121
Osbin, Zimery 179
Osborn, Ann 402
Osborn, Anna 682
Osborn, Caleb 274
Osborn, Catharine 402
Osborn, Daniel 58
Osborn, Eliza 274
Osborn, Elizabeth 170,
   551
Osborn, Ezra 259, 260,
   502, 503, 504, 505,
   509, 510
Osborn, Geo. 274
Osborn, Gideon 170, 172
Osborn, Harriet 274
Osborn, Henry 402
Osborn, Henry L. 79
Osborn, Isaac 312
Osborn, Jabez 170
Osborn, James D. 402
Osborn, Jane 402
Osborn, Jane A. 510
Osborn, John 79, 172,
   682, 689
Osborn, John R. 402
Osborn, Joseph 357
Osborn, Kitty 391
Osborn, Lucy 402
Osborn, Lucy E. 29
Osborn, Marietta 29
Osborn, Mary 402
Osborn, Phebe 76
Osborn, Rachel 312, 682

Osborn, Ralph 52, 386
Osborn, Sarah 682
Osborn, Silas 54
Osborn, Squier 682
Osborn, Thomas 586
Osborn, Usual 54
Osborn, William Renick
   402
Osborne, Ezra 500, 510
Osborne, Hannah O. 510
Osbourn, Hugh 261
Osbourn, James 666
Osburn, Elizabeth 32
Osburn, Isaac 438, 443
Osburn, Jacob 440
Osburn, Jemima 55
Osburn, Joseph H. 609
Osburn, Mary 457
Osburn, Richard 490
Osgood, Rowland 30
Osler, Mary 577
Osman, Wm. 764
Ostin, Joel 666
Ostrander, John 763
Ostrander, Sarah 763
Oswalt, C. 331
Oswalt, Daniel 202
Oswalt, E. A. 331
Oswalt, Emily 331
Oswalt, Eva Dell 331
Oswalt, Florus 331
Oswalt, Frank 331
Oswalt, G. 331
Oswalt, George 443
Oswalt, Henry 331
Oswalt, Hook 330
Oswalt, J. 331
Oswalt, John 331
Oswalt, John (Corpl.)
   331
Oswalt, Mary Hook 331
Oswalt, Minerva A. 331
Oswalt, O. W. 331
Oswalt, Roy H. 331
Oswalt, Rozetta 331
Oswalt, Sarah 331
Oswalts, Jacob 526
Oswalts, John 526
Oswalts, Joseph 526
Oswalts, Michael 526
Oswalts, Samuel 526
Otis, Anna 708
Otis, Edward 554
Otis, Jesse 567
Otis, Stephen 732
Ott, Joseph 493
Ott, Philip 493
Otto, Elizabeth 739
Ours, Charles 328
Ours, Emma 328
Ours, Mary 90
Oustat, Delila 467
Ouster, John 444
Ousterhout, Elizabeth
   444
Ousterhout, James 444
Ousterhout, John 444
Outan, Jesse 386
Overfield, Benjamin 118

Overfield, Moses 456
Overhalser, Abraham 210
Overhalt, Abraham 562
Overhole, Joseph 568
Overholser, Christian
   435
Overholser, Henry 435
Overholser, Jacob 190
Overholser, Joel 435
Overholser, Magdalene
   210
Overholser, Mary 435
Overholt, Abraham 563,
   568
Overholt, Elizabeth 74
Overholt, Joseph 72
Overholt, Sarah 569, 562
Overholtz, Daniel 435
Overholtz, Elizabeth 435
Overholtz, Isaac 435
Overholtz, Jacob 435
Overholtz, John 435
Overholtz, Jonathan 435
Overholtz, Jos. 435
Overholtz, Julia Ann 435
Overholtz, Lewis 435
Overholtz, Mary 435
Overholtz, Phebe Ann 435
Overholtz, Wm. 435
Overleese, Abram 211
Overly, Boston 465
Overly, Eve 490
Overly, James S. 278
Overly, Martin 490
Overman, Abraham 507
Overman, Amanda 507, 508
Overman, Enlice 507
Overman, George 507, 508
Overman, John 507, 508
Overman, Margaret 507,
   508
Overman, Maria 111
Overman, Mary 508
Overman, Mary Ann 507,
   508
Overman, Polly 507
Overmeyer, Catherine 368
Overmeyer, Jacob 362,
   370
Overmeyer, Martin 370
Overmeyer, Peter 370
Overmire, Jamimah 499
Overmyer, Mary M. 345
Overpeck, George 130
Overton, Oliver 14
Owen, David E. 525
Owen, Elizabeth 193
Owen, Geo. W. 762
Owen, Godfrey 581
Owen, Ira 749
Owen, James 718
Owen, John 193
Owen, Mary P. 521
Owen, Moses 743
Owen, Nathaniel 530
Owen, Sally 15, 749
Owen, William 193
Owens, Benjamin 198, 204
Owens, George W. 765

Owens, George Washington 372
Owens, Isaac 472, 476
Owens, Margaret 372
Owens, Moses 743
Owens, Nancy 372
Owens, Permelier 372
Owens, Rebecca 372
Owens, Rhoda Ann 743
Owens, Sarah Ann 372
Owens, Sary 513
Owens, Stephen 372
Owens, Stephen William 372
Owens, Susannah 372
Owens, William 227
Owens, William T. 45
Oxford, Abel 386
Oxford, Nancy 384
Oxley, Lewis 648
Oxley, Noah 648
Oxley, William 648
Oyer, Francis 664
Ozenbaugh, Minerva 115
Ozias, Amanda Emeline Weekly 435
Ozias, Caty 659
Ozias, David Franklin 435
Ozias, Nancy 413
Ozias, Peggy 665

--- P ---

Pace, Almira 373
Pace, Amy 372
Pace, Charles 373
Pace, Chester 372
Pace, David 372
Pace, Elizabeth 372
Pace, Hannah 372
Pace, Jacob 372
Pace, Jacob (Jr.) 372
Pace, Joanna 372
Pace, John 373
Pace, Joseph 372
Pace, Margaret 372
Pace, Mary 372
Pace, Michael 372
Pace, Miner 373
Pace, Noah 373
Pace, Priscilla 372
Pace, William 373
Packard, Alonzo 521
Packard, Hannah 753
Packard, Lucretia 93
Packard, William B. 746
Packer, John P. 546
Packwood, Alonzo 521
Padget, Aquilla 248
Padget, Elizabeth 248
Page, Abraham 182
Page, Ebenezer 440
Page, Geo. B. 353, 355
Page, James S. 42
Page, John 453
Page, John C. 416

Page, John E. 440
Page, Lydia 80
Page, Mary 30
Page, Polly 279
Paige, Henry Folsom 6
Paine, James 521
Paine, John 386
Paine, Mercy 83
Paine, Nancy 523
Painte, Ann 200
Painteer, James 661
Painter, Adam 759
Painter, Alfred 9
Painter, Barbara 200
Painter, Benjamin 672, 673
Painter, Carroline 566
Painter, David 200
Painter, Elizabeth 523, 759
Painter, Elva Hinshaw 698
Painter, Ezekiel 673
Painter, George 283, 493, 661, 669
Painter, George (Maj.) 298
Painter, Gladys Sprain 698
Painter, Hannah S. 698
Painter, Henry 759
Painter, Isaac 9
Painter, J. C. 698
Painter, Jacob 490, 558
Painter, Jemima 45
Painter, Joel 48
Painter, John 427, 666, 669, 759
Painter, Joseph C. 698
Painter, Joseph Henry 698
Painter, Katharine Sarah 759
Painter, Margaret 669
Painter, Maria 759
Painter, Mary 298, 669
Painter, Mathias 200
Painter, Matilda 9
Painter, Michael 759
Painter, Peter 759
Painter, Robert 9
Painter, Samuel 759
Painter, Sophia 9, 666, 669
Painter, Susannah 718
Painter, Walter 9
Painter, William R. 9
Painter, Zelotus 759
Palch, Caroline 593
Palmer, Christena 566
Palmer, Daniel 303
Palmer, David 162, 239, 708
Palmer, Dennis 30
Palmer, Eliakim 292
Palmer, Elizabeth 292
Palmer, George T. 18
Palmer, Howard 292
Palmer, James 574, 732

Palmer, Jane 18
Palmer, Jane S. 14
Palmer, Jesse 670
Palmer, Jewett 732
Palmer, John 126, 174, 182, 371, 609, 627
Palmer, John C. 734
Palmer, John G. 734
Palmer, John N. 292
Palmer, Joseph 732
Palmer, Lucy 594
Palmer, Martha 135
Palmer, Mary 292, 734
Palmer, Mary Ann 292
Palmer, Otho 292
Palmer, Phoebe 162
Palmer, Polly 732
Palmer, Rebecca 75
Palmer, Robert 135
Palmer, Rody 459
Palmer, Sarah 292
Palmer, Soloman W. 746
Palmer, William H. 292
Palmer, Wm. 265
Palmer, Zua James 409
Palmor, John 163, 175
Palmor, Sarah 163
Pamerly, Hannah 524
Panabaker, Chas. Stephen 145
Panabaker, John 145
Pancake, Cephas 48
Pancake, Hannah 455
Pancake, Isaac 386
Pancake, John 391
Pancake, Joseph 51, 54
Pancake, Leaven 458
Pancake, Mary 45
Pancake, Sarah 463
Pancake, Susannah 452
Pancake, Valentine 458
Pancason, Senon 458
Pane, John W. 521
Pane, Saly S. 83
Pankake, Isaac 391
Pape, Peircy 726
Pappenbrock, Henry 112
Papwater, Eliza 406
Papwater, Isaac 406
Parcels, Elizabeth 390
Parcels, John 390
Parcels, Peter 394, 465
Parcher, Sarah 608
Pardee, Aaron 70
Pardee, David 350
Pardee, George K. 761
Pardee, John 72
Pardee, Nathan 71
Pardee, Seymon 71
Parent, Catherine 538
Pargin, Elizabeth 372
Pargin, James 372
Pargin, Margaret 372
Pargin, Nancy 372
Pargin, Sarah 372
Parham, Benajah 430
Parham, Deliah 431
Parham, Elizabeth 431
Parham, Mary 134

Paris, Lewis D. 693
Parish, Betsey 463
Parish, Evae 495
Parish, John 465
Parish, Jolly 458
Parish, Joshua 515
Parish, Levi 498
Parish, Meredith 386
Parish, Polly 463
Parish, Reuben 465
Park, Andrew 185
Park, Elizabeth 443
Park, Elizabeth D. 185
Park, George 498
Park, Isabella 185
Park, James 9, 185
Park, Joseph 185, 440
Park, Joseph (Jr.) 185
Park, Matthew 443
Park, Robert 185, 490
Park, Sarah 23
Park, Thomas B. 185
Park, Wm. 614
Parke, Jane 550
Parke, Samuel 293
Parke, Uriah 293
Parker, Ackley 498
Parker, Allen 319
Parker, Andrew 152
Parker, Christina 435
Parker, Ebenezer 79
Parker, Edwin W. 84
Parker, Eliza 77
Parker, Haquis 27
Parker, Hiram 79
Parker, Isaac 560
Parker, Jabex 439
Parker, Jabez 445
Parker, Jacob 446, 447
Parker, James 87, 285, 443
Parker, John 3, 285, 365, 591
Parker, Joseph 365
Parker, Joseph H. 23
Parker, Mary 3
Parker, Ormel 35
Parker, Pay C. 750
Parker, Payne C. 750
Parker, Prentice 458
Parker, Richard 574, 704
Parker, Samuel M. 35
Parker, Seth C. 531
Parker, Silas 465
Parker, Simeon 42
Parker, Thomas 14
Parker, William 8, 453, 546
Parkerson, Nancy 407
Parkes, Jonathan 661
Parkhurst, Columbus 695
Parkhurst, Edward 30
Parkhurst, Jeremiah 521
Parkinson, Daniel 361
Parkinson, Jacob 609
Parkinson, Margaretha 368
Parkinson, Wm. 591
Parkison, Margaret 347

Parks, Alexander 401
Parks, Betsy 671
Parks, Cornelius 401
Parks, Ebenezer W. 498
Parks, Elizabeth Dovey 192
Parks, Grizella 682
Parks, Isaac 546, 552
Parks, Isabella 671
Parks, James 401, 650, 671, 679, 682, 687
Parks, Jane 671
Parks, John 281, 671
Parks, John H. 401
Parks, Joseph 668, 670, 671, 682, 687
Parks, Joseph (Jr.) 670
Parks, Martha Ann 682
Parks, Mary 401
Parks, Rebecca 682, 687
Parks, Robert 192, 671
Parks, William 401, 627
Parks, Wm. 627
Parles, Peter 648
Parmenter, Asahel 586
Parmenter, George 586
Parmenter, Sylvester 591
Parmentier, Jeanne Francoise 725
Parmentier, John 723, 724, 725
Parmer, Mary 302
Parminter, Clarinda 585
Parmontier, Jean 713
Parnel, Hester 661
Parr, E. 536
Parr, Robert E. 536
Parr, Samuel 350, 536, 546
Parr, Samuel H. 536
Parr, W. A. 536
Parrell, Jas. 500
Parret, Ezra F. 599
Parril, Stafford 409
Parrish, Edward 268
Parrish, George 63
Parrish, Isaac 273
Parrish, J. R. 52
Parrish, Jolly 490
Parrish, Stephen 643
Parrish, William 302, 643
Parrot, Ellen 372
Parrot, George 372
Parrot, Philip 372
Parrot, Samuel 372
Parrott, Thomas 108, 109
Parry, Elizabeth 516
Parry, Robert 332
Parsall, Richard 672
Parsel, Cyrus 435
Parshall, Nathaniel 650
Parson, Enoch 720
Parson, George 348
Parson, Joseph 348
Parson, Joshua 348
Parson, Mary 79
Parson, Samuel Holden 720

Parsons, --- (Capt.) 228
Parsons, Ann 518
Parsons, Chs. C. 739
Parsons, Elizabeth 314
Parsons, Frances 211
Parsons, George 188, 215
Parsons, George L. 211
Parsons, George M. 214
Parsons, Israel 252
Parsons, Jesse 214
Parsons, Joab 84
Parsons, John A. 214
Parsons, John S. 211, 215, 764
Parsons, Nancy Jane 314
Parsons, Rachel M. 314
Parsons, Rhoda 213
Parsons, Richard M. 211, 214, 215
Parsons, Samuel Holden 720, 722, 725
Parsons, Stella M. 764
Parsons, William Walter 722
Parsons, Zadock 314
Partee, James 515
Partee, Laurence 746
Parter, John 164
Parthemor, Catharine 582
Parthemor, Frederick 582
Parthemor, John 582
Parthimore, Polly 586
Partington, Eliezer 700
Partington, Flora H. 700
Partington, Joseph 546
Partington, Richard 546
Partlow, Morgan 84
Paschal, . . . 162
Paschal, Isaac 166
Paschal, Sarah 386
Pascoll, Isaac 305
Pask, Joseph 440
Passwater, E. 618
Passwater, Jesse C. 618
Passwater, R. 618
Passwaters, Michael C. 615
Passwaters, N. 615
Passwaters, T. B. 615
Paston, Samuel 690
Patch, Caroline 593
Patch, Charity 593
Patch, Charles 557
Patch, Hannah N. 586
Patch, John Patterson 30
Patch, Stephen 591
Patchel, Edward 475, 477
Patchel, Edwd. 478
Patchell, Edward 473, 483
Patees, Isaac 568
Patent, James 112
Paterson, Daniel 153
Paterton, Jacob 458
Pathemore, Jacob 586
Patle, Henry 103
Patrick, Bulah 12
Patrick, David 68, 399, 546

Patrick, Hiram 26
Patrick, Ira 591
Patrick, J. 618
Patrick, James 574
Patrick, James W. 618
Patrick, John 580
Patrick, L. S. 618
Patrick, Louisa J. 618
Patrick, Lyman Y. 618
Patrick, Magdalene 68, 399
Patrick, Moses 50
Patrick, Phebe 26
Patrick, Samuel 26
Patrick, Thomas J. 583
Pattars, Geo. 574
Patten, Christianna 641
Patten, John 270
Patten, John H. 504
Patten, Nancy 718
Patten, Richard 728
Patten, Ruth 13
Patten, Ruth 728
Patten, Shepherd 14
Patten, Thomas 550
Patten, William 666, 718, 728
Patten, Wm. 641
Pattengill, Lidia 510
Patter, Jemima 125
Patterson, Aaron 568
Patterson, Andrew 420
Patterson, Andw. 140
Patterson, Ann 157
Patterson, Catharine 140
Patterson, Daniel H. 521
Patterson, David 145
Patterson, Elam 157
Patterson, Elizabeth 299
Patterson, Francis 194
Patterson, Garret 688
Patterson, Hannah 566
Patterson, Harriet 498
Patterson, James 224, 370, 723, 729
Patterson, Jane 383, 546, 548
Patterson, Jefferson 215
Patterson, Jno. 266, 267
Patterson, John 14, 145, 152, 224, 266, 270, 645, 674
Patterson, Joseph 23
Patterson, Margt. 140
Patterson, Mary 272
Patterson, Mary Ellen 140
Patterson, Obedience 11
Patterson, Pegay 719
Patterson, Robert 3, 145, 186, 299
Patterson, Robert (Col.) 182
Patterson, Robert C. 420
Patterson, Saml. 145
Patterson, Thomas 546
Patterson, William 190, 568
Patterson, William C. 209

Patterson, William M. 522
Patterson, Wm. 274
Patterson, Wm. R. 419
Pattis, Prissili 558
Pattit, Pessella 558
Patton, Abner 501
Patton, Elizabeth 515
Patton, Esther 256, 490
Patton, James 179, 501
Patton, Jared 256
Patton, Jenny 501
Patton, Jeremiah 501
Patton, John 476, 490, 501
Patton, Lydia 256
Patton, Mahlon 256, 732
Patton, Margaret 490
Patton, Margaret Ann 181
Patton, Mary 501
Patton, Matthew 224
Patton, Merrick 256
Patton, Nancy 501
Patton, Rachel 501, 512
Patton, Rebecca 490, 501
Patton, Ruth 501, 511
Patton, Samuel 501, 515
Patton, Sarah 490
Patton, Thomas 194, 501, 732
Patton, Thos. 501, 515
Patton, Uriah 501
Patton, William 469, 471, 481, 482, 483, 490
Patton, William D. 181
Patton, Wm. 256, 472, 473
Patton, Wm. H. 414
Pattrick, Mary A. 3
Patty, Charles 211
Patty, David 145
Patty, Delphia 126
Patty, Eli Alexander 435
Patty, Elizabeth 140
Patty, Hugh 140
Patty, James 132
Patty, Joseph 145
Patty, Lot 140
Pauellus, Daniel 554
Pauellus, Hanney 554
Pauellus, Jacob 554
Paugh, Mary 62
Paul, Agnes 609
Paul, Eliza 160, 169
Paul, Geo. 169
Paul, George 160
Paul, Henry H. 609
Paul, James 418, 431
Paul, Zachariah 386
Paules, Daniel 554
Pauley, Jno. 220
Pauley, Mary M. 220
Pauley, Wm. 220
Paulk, Cyrus A. 84
Paull, George 165
Paulsgrove, Catharine 393
Paver, Sarah 589

Paver, William 503
Paverman, Sarah 455
Paxon, Charles 6
Paxon, Eli 6
Paxon, Mary 5
Paxon, Nelson 6
Paxon, Ruth Ann 5
Paxon, Samuel 6
Paxton, Abiel 26
Paxton, Achsha 26
Paxton, Jacob 26
Paxton, John 26
Paxton, John (Sr.) 26
Paxton, Jonathan 435
Paxton, Mary 26
Paxton, Nancy 26
Paxton, Reubin 26
Paxton, Ruben 26
Paxton, Susanna 26
Paxton, Susannah 15
Paxton, William 26
Payne, Coulson 649, 650
Payne, Henry 637
Payne, Isaac 515
Payne, John R. 581
Payne, Lemuel 633
Payne, Lydia 514
Payne, Olney 515
Payne, Sally A. 36
Payne, Sumner 581, 586
Payne, Vincent 732
Payton, Bridget L. 510
Payton, Harry 48
Payton, Samuel 163
Peace, Isaac 254
Peaceable, Timothy 260
Peach, Richard I. 14
Peach, Richard J. 14
Peach, Sarah E. 14
Peacock, Abigal 39
Peacock, Isaac 690
Peacock, Peter 39
Peak, Horatio 72
Peak, Lewis R. 72
Peak, Urial H. 72
Peaksley, Elijah 715
Pear, Any 120
Pearce, Affalander S. 616
Pearce, C. I. 616
Pearce, Catharine I. 616
Pearce, Emaline 617
Pearce, Fanny 86
Pearce, George W. 52
Pearce, Hannah 149
Pearce, I. J. 616
Pearce, Isaac 574
Pearce, J. W. 616, 617, 626
Pearce, J. W. (Dr.) 617
Pearce, John W. 104
Pearce, Kittie 617
Pearce, L. D. 616
Pearce, M. E. 616
Pearce, Mary 52
Pearce, Mary Ann Frank 616
Pearce, R. 617
Pearce, Rebecca 617

Pearce, Samuel 79, 465, 493
Pearce, Sarah 616
Pearce, Silas 446
Pearce, Theresa V. 616
Pearce, Thomas A. 616
Pearce, W. H. (Dr.) 149
Pearch, Hannah 570
Pearch, Joseph 575
Pearsen, Elizabeth 661
Pearsen, Ruth 124
Pearson, Abegail E. 140
Pearson, Abel 126
Pearson, Abigail 140
Pearson, Alpha 145
Pearson, Ann 118, 124
Pearson, Benjamin 133, 136, 140
Pearson, Charles M. 550
Pearson, Christopher 145
Pearson, Danl. 145
Pearson, David 153
Pearson, David Wesley 145
Pearson, Eli 145
Pearson, Elizabeth 135
Pearson, Enoch 126, 135, 140
Pearson, Enos 145
Pearson, Geo. W. 145
Pearson, Hannah 126
Pearson, Isaac 133, 140
Pearson, Jacob 126, 130
Pearson, James 121, 145, 152
Pearson, John 140
Pearson, John F. 135
Pearson, John J. 546
Pearson, John M. 145
Pearson, Jonathan 14
Pearson, Joseph 126, 136
Pearson, Margaret 120
Pearson, Mary 140, 664
Pearson, Mary J. 145
Pearson, Milton 140
Pearson, Moses 126
Pearson, Noah 133, 140
Pearson, Paul 145
Pearson, Rachel 145
Pearson, Robert 131, 135
Pearson, Robert V. 145
Pearson, Sally 127
Pearson, Samuel 130
Pearson, Sarah 126, 140, 145, 664
Pearson, Susanna 119
Pearson, Thomas (Jr.) 131
Pearson, William 121
Pearsons, Thomas 3
Pearsons, Thorrel 30
Peas, Hezekiah 721
Peas, Peter 640
Pease, Hezekiah 721
Pease, Peter 644, 646
Peaslee, Zaccheus 282
Pebbless, Rachel Rodgers 505
Pebless, John 505

Pebless, John Geddis 505
Pebless, Joseph Scott 505
Pebless, Margaret 505
Pebless, Richard Rodgers 505
Pechen, David 739
Peck, Amelia 28
Peck, Anne 140
Peck, Coonrad 395
Peck, E. D. 766
Peck, Elisha 30
Peck, Elizabeth 385
Peck, Jane M. 28
Peck, Jeremiah (Dr.) 763
Peck, John 121
Peck, Joshua 140
Peck, Lavina 713
Peck, Samuel 84
Peck, Sarah 395
Peck, Simeon (Rev.) 531
Peck, Wm. 503
Pecken, Alphas 448
Pecken, Elizabeth 448
Pecken, Jane 448
Pecken, Matilda 448
Pecken, Matthew 448
Pecken, Sarah 448
Pecken, Susannah 448
Peden, Sarah 78
Pedick, Joshua 453
Pedicord, Thomas 732
Pedycoart, Ann 565
Pedycoart, Sophia 565
Pedycourt, John S. 568
Pee, Elizabeth Rebecca 366
Peebles, Betsy 505
Peebles, Jane Finley 505
Peebles, R. R. 510
Peebles, William 505
Peebles, Wm. 505
Peer, Thomas 550
Peerce, Thomas 453
Peeus, William 337
Peffer, Christeena 565
Pegg, David 644
Pegg, Nancy 548
Pegg, Nathan 644
Peirce, Benjamin D. 134
Peirce, David Zeigler 192
Peirce, Ebenezer 729
Peirce, Ebnezer 730
Peirce, Gainer 134
Peirce, George 134
Peirce, Henrietta E. 192
Peirce, Isaac 723, 724
Peirce, James 134
Peirce, Jeremiah Hunt 192
Peirce, John 134
Peirce, Joseph 192
Peirce, Lewis 288
Peirce, Lois 718
Peirce, Mary 134, 192
Peirce, Ruth 134
Peirce, Samuel 134
Peirce, Squeir Little 435

Peirce, Susannah 742
Pelefisch, Christian 666
Pellorten, Geo. 274
Pelster, I. H. 102
Pelton, David M. 48
Pelton, Josiah S. 30
Pelton, Sallie 48
Pelty, Ebenezer 386
Pember, Carlisle 757
Pemberton, Anna 119
Pemberton, Elizabeth 349
Pemberton, Isaah 118
Pemberton, Joseph 141
Pemberton, Lucy Ann 349
Pemberton, Lydia 141
Pemberton, Mary 116, 141
Pemberton, Prudence 141
Pemberton, Rachael 124
Pemberton, Rebecca 349
Pemberton, Richard 141
Pemberton, Robert 131, 141
Pemberton, Sarah 349
Pemberton, Thomas 349
Pemberton, Thomas O. 349
Pemberton, William 126
Penabaker, Mary 608
Pence, A. I. 539
Pence, Allie A. 539
Pence, Catherine 431
Pence, Elizabeth 356
Pence, Isaac 377
Pence, John 568
Pence, Joseph 186
Pence, M. J. 539
Pence, Mahala 419
Pence, Mary 126
Pence, Polly 368
Pence, Susanah 126
Pence, Thomas 431
Pence, William 419
Pendergrass, John W. 3
Pendergrass, Mary 3
Pendergrass, Sophronia 3
Pendergrass, Thomas 3, 26
Pendery, Ann 684
Pendery, Deborah Jane 684
Pendery, Eliza 684
Pendery, Jeremiah 684
Pendery, John G. 684
Pendery, Mary 684
Pendery, Thomas 684
Penett, Felix 431
Penett, Henry 431
Penett, Samuel 431
Penfield, Maria 36
Penfield, Truman 34
Pengel, Henry 103
Pengel, Henryetta 103
Pengle, Henry 103
Penick, Sally 557
Penick, William 557
Penix, Caleb 557
Penix, Hannah 557
Penix, Jacob 557
Penix, James 557
Penix, John 557

Penix, Nancy 557
Penix, Nelly 557
Penix, Sally 557
Penix, William 557
Penn, Edmund 394
Penn, George S. 699
Penn, Mary Ann 394
Penner, Catharine 26
Penner, James 26
Penner, John 26
Penner, Nelly 26
Penner, Rachel 13, 26
Penner, Rheda 26
Penner, Sally 26
Pennington, Ashberry S. 270
Pennington, Robert 522
Pennock, Ann 6
Pennock, Elizabeth 6
Pennock, Ira 748
Pennock, Margaret 518
Pennock, Moses 6
Pennock, Phoebe 6
Pennock, Samuel 393
Pennock, Sarah 6
Pennock, Simon 6
Pennock, Thomas 21
Pennwell, Clara 407
Pennwell, James 407
Penny, Elijah 126
Pennywell, George 391
Penquite, William 689
Penrod, Israel 378
Penrod, John 575
Penrod, Michael 546
Penrod, Peter 575
Penrod, Samuel 546
Penrod, Solomon 575
Penrose, Albert 257
Penrose, Joseph 257
Penrose, Mary Elvira 257
Penrose, Richard 250, 251
Pense, David 522
Pepoit, John 546
Peppard, David 741
Peppard, Francis 741
Peppard, Isaac 741
Peppard, Jane 741
Peppard, John 741
Peppard, Jonathan 741
Peppard, Mary 741
Peppard, Phebe 741
Peppard, Rebecca 741
Peppard, William 741
Pepper, Betsy 540
Pepper, Chas. AX. 540
Pepper, E. 540
Pepper, M. 540
Pepper, William 540
Pepperman, Samuel 121
Peppers, Abel C. 386
Peppers, John 465
Peppers, Sophia 465
Peppers, John 568
Pepple, Abraham 490
Perdu, Eli G. 550
Perkins, --- 331
Perkins, Alva 522

Perkins, Andrew 448
Perkins, Daniel M. 35
Perkins, Darius 35
Perkins, Darius M. 36
Perkins, Eliphas (Dr.) 718
Perkins, Elizabeth 746
Perkins, Ezra 79
Perkins, Garret 746, 748
Perkins, Geo. 35
Perkins, Henry 108, 753
Perkins, Henry B. 626
Perkins, Isaac 671, 746
Perkins, Jacob 108, 626, 753
Perkins, Joseph 108, 626, 753
Perkins, Lucinda 35
Perkins, Malinda 746
Perkins, Mary 745
Perkins, Nancy 108, 626, 753
Perkins, Simon 108, 623, 626, 753
Perkins, William 564
Perkins, Zenophon 155
Perkins, Zopper 175
Perky, Martin 752
Perlee, Peter 641
Perr, William 465
Perrill, Augustus L. 395
Perrill, Catherine 465
Perrin, Abel 299
Perrine, James 218, 653
Perrine, Jno. 219
Perrine, Johnson V. 219
Perrine, Urias B. 546
Perrott, Samuel 686, 687
Perrung, Jacob 345
Perrung, Sarah 345
Perry, Abraham H. 522
Perry, Adam 746
Perry, Amos 145
Perry, Andrew 145
Perry, Betsy 502
Perry, C. A. 332
Perry, Charlotte A. 332
Perry, E. J. 332
Perry, Ebenezer 30
Perry, Eliza A. 146
Perry, Elizabeth 440
Perry, Esther O. 332
Perry, Ethelinda L. 332
Perry, G. S. 332
Perry, Hannah 440
Perry, Herbert S. 332
Perry, Horatio 145
Perry, Isaac 515
Perry, James 298
Perry, Jane 271, 440
Perry, John 267, 274, 515
Perry, John B. 259
Perry, L. 332
Perry, Margaret 440
Perry, Mary 440
Perry, N. J. 332
Perry, Newton J. (Capt.) 332

Perry, Phebe 123
Perry, Sally 714
Perry, Samuel 440, 515, 639
Perry, Sophia Ann 30
Perry, Thomas 274
Perry, W. S. 332
Perry, William 440
Perry, Wm. 271
Perrygoy, Mary 293
Persinger, Jacob 546
Persinger, Madison 546
Persinger, Sarah 546
Person, Esther 117
Person, William 118
Personett, Leona 141
Persons, Joseph 84
Perth, John Rowan 762
Peteet, William 254
Peter, David 560
Peter, Dorcas Elist. 576
Peter, Rufus S. 42
Peterman, H. 616
Peterman, John 276
Peterman, Lena 276
Peterman, R. 616
Peters, Abraham 490
Peters, Eshan 42
Peters, Gershom M. 397
Peters, John 45, 416, 486
Peters, Jonathan 401
Peters, Nathan 65
Peters, R. H. 380
Peters, Rachel 387
Peters, Statira 33
Peters, Susan 413
Peters, Tunis 386
Peterson, Drusilla 575
Peterson, Garret 661
Peterson, Geo. 575
Peterson, John G. 442
Peterson, Sandferd 146
Peterson, Susan 49
Peterson, William 49, 515, 666
Petet, Gilbert 722
Peticord, Nathan 560
Petigrue, James 126
Petit, --- (Dr.) 724
Petit, John G. 715
Petit, John Gilbert 722, 724
Petit, Nicholas 726
Petit, Pryscilla 556
Petrel, Peter M. 90
Petro, Asa J. 111
Petro, Michael 666
Petry, Catharine 435
Petry, Jacob 427
Petry, Magdalena 435
Petry, Michael 435
Petry, Nancy 435
Petry, Sarah 435
Petry, Susannah 435
Pettay, Daniel 265, 268
Pettay, Frances 270
Pettay, Rebecca 265
Petterson, John G. 443

Pettery, Francis 301
Pettet, Eli 254
Pettet, Ellis 254
Pettet, John 133
Pettet, Jonathan 254
Pettet, Plummer 254
Pettigrew, Anna 199
Pettigrew, Armstrong 199
Pettigrew, David 199
Pettigrew, James 199
Pettit, John 126
Pettit, John (Rev.) 531
Pettit, Joseph 266, 270
Pettit, Margaret 267
Pettit, Peggy 118
Pettit, Prudende 517
Pettit, Rodalphus 3
Pettit, Samuel 267
Pettit, Thomas 361
Pettit, Thos. 271
Petty, Aaron 358
Petty, Absalom 386
Petty, Elam 20
Petty, Jesse 84
Petty, Joseph 5, 341, 372, 453
Petty, Nancy 5
Pettyjohn, James 490
Peurt, Gabriel 513
Pewters, John 515
Peyton, Ellener 517
Peyton, Hannah 512
Peyton, John 50
Peyton, Stephen 486
Peyton, William 515
Peyton, William N. 50
Pfaff, Jacob 710
Pfeifer, Conrod 754
Pfeil, Frederick 602
Pfifer, Abraham 48
Pfisterer, Jacob 235
Pfisterer, Magdalena 235
Pfisterer, Philip 235
Pfleger, Chas. 412
Pfleger, Henry 411
Pfleger, Magdalena 408
Pfleger, Philip Lewis 410
Pfouts, George (Jr.) 737
Pfoutz, Michael 575
Pharis, Sarah 660
Pharrow, Elizabeth 124
Phebus, Chas. 407
Phebus, G. 407
Phebus, James 58
Phebus, L. A. 407
Phebus, Nancy 458
Phebus, Polly 384
Phebus, S. A. 407
Phebus, Samuel 58, 386
Phebus, Sarah 58
Phelps, Ames 37
Phelps, Ann 37
Phelps, Charles 37
Phelps, Edward 336
Phelps, Edward M. 623
Phelps, Electy 495
Phelps, Horrace 591
Phelps, John 470

Phelps, John M. 321
Phelps, Levi 591
Phelps, Marietta 29
Phelps, Melinda 80
Phelps, Phebe 321
Phelps, Richard 321
Phelps, Seth 498
Phelps, Sham 321
Phelps, Solomon 721
Pherson, George 372
Pherson, Jane 372
Pherson, John 372
Pherson, Jonathan 372
Pherson, Margaret 372
Pherson, Margaret Lucinda 372
Pherson, Martha 372
Pherson, Rebecca 372
Pherson, William 372
Phifer, Abraham 58
Phifer, Catharine 58
Phifer, Clarissa 58
Phifer, Davis 58
Phifer, Duletha 58
Phifer, Elizabeth 58
Phifer, George 58
Phifer, John 58
Phifer, Margarett 58
Phifer, Maria 58
Phifer, Nancy 58
Phifer, Sarah 58
Philbee, J. 618
Philbee, James 618
Philbee, Jane 618
Philbrick, Clark 746
Philip, Jas. 478
Philipps, Major 490
Philips, Barbara 566
Philips, Elizabeth 546
Philips, Henry 414
Philips, Horasho G. 183
Philips, James 14, 126, 476
Philips, Jerman 435
Philips, John 349, 435, 490, 575
Philips, Joseph 490
Philips, Maria 738
Philips, Samuel M. 515
Philips, Susan 572
Phillipeau, Anthony 715
Phillips, Adam 575
Phillips, Alexander 153
Phillips, Allston 393
Phillips, Andrew 45
Phillips, Betsy 467
Phillips, Celestia 39
Phillips, Cora 220
Phillips, Daniel 79
Phillips, Elijah 640
Phillips, Elizabeth 187, 652
Phillips, Ezra 715
Phillips, Francis 686
Phillips, George 187
Phillips, George H. 316, 317
Phillips, H. G. 201
Phillips, Henry 42

Phillips, Hezekiah 414
Phillips, Homer 217
Phillips, Horace G. 678
Phillips, Horatio G. 185, 207, 224
Phillips, Isaac 689
Phillips, Jabish 685, 689
Phillips, James 415, 458, 475, 480, 483, 485
Phillips, Jane 153
Phillips, Jas. 477
Phillips, Jesse 642
Phillips, John 79, 217, 285, 340, 661
Phillips, Joseph 682
Phillips, Justus B. 79
Phillips, Margaret 457
Phillips, Mary 682
Phillips, Nancy 181
Phillips, Parker 431
Phillips, Polly 667
Phillips, Rebecca 460
Phillips, Richard 217
Phillips, Sarah 657, 660, 682
Phillips, Thomas 117, 118, 652, 682
Phillips, Thomas J. 427
Phillips, Urania 415
Phillips, William 187, 200
Philpot, Ruth 166
Philpot, William 166
Phinegar, Benjamin 2
Phinegar, Benjamin F. 1
Phipps, Elizabeth 65
Phipps, Isabella 446
Phipps, Jacob 65
Phipps, Margaret 446
Phipps, Mary 446
Phipps, Polly 446
Phipps, Robert 446
Phipps, Samuel 446
Phipps, Samuel (Jr.) 446
Phipps, Sarah 446
Phocia, Sarah 91
Phoebus, Polly 382
Pholsegrave, Elizabeth 169
Pholsegrave, Michael 169
Phouts, Barbary 125
Piatt, Benjamin 168
Piatt, James 245
Piatt, Lucinda 168
Piatt, Stephen 293
Piatt, Thomas 168
Picheral, Achsha 26
Picheral, Catherine 26
Picheral, Henry 26
Picheral, John 26
Picheral, Nancy 26
Picheral, Nicholas 18
Picherall, John 26
Pichrel, Henry 18
Pichrel, Nicholas 18
Picken, Alexander 448
Picken, Elias 172

Picken, Elizabeth 448
Picken, Jane 448
Picken, Matilda 448
Picken, Matthew 448
Picken, Sarah 448
Picken, Susannah 448
Picken, William 448
Pickens, Elizabeth 83
Pickens, James 84
Pickens, Jane 76
Pickens, Jean 76
Pickens, John 79, 84,
   458, 493, 500
Pickens, Martha 76
Pickens, Thompson 84
Pickeral, Nicholas 17
Pickerell, John 6, 14
Pickering, Benjamin 134
Pickering, Daniel 2
Pickering, Elias 180
Pickering, Isaac 2
Pickering, John (Jr.) 86
Pickering, Phineas 86
Pickering, Susan 2
Picket, Elizabeth 717
Picket, Hannah 255
Picket, James 269
Picket, Mary 582, 719
Picket, Matilda 255
Picket, Moses 269
Picket, Rachel 255
Picket, Sarah 255
Picket, Thomas 255, 269
Pickett, Sarah 575
Pickingpaugh, John 274
Pickins, Sara 85
Pickins, William 171
Pickle, Elizabeth 431
Pickle, George 431
Pickle, Henry 431
Pickle, Jacob 431
Pickle, John 732
Pickle, Mary 431
Pickle, Sarah 431
Pickle, Simon 431
Pickrel, Andrew Jackson
   115
Pickrel, Caroline 115
Pickrel, John 100
Pickrell, Temperance 22
Pidcock, Geo. 270
Pidcock, John 270
Pidcock, Kiturah 275
Pidecock, George 275
Pidgeon, Isaac 693
Pidgeon, Rhoda 693
Pierce, Benoni 298
Pierce, Elizabeth 298
Pierce, Griffith 490
Pierce, Isaac 723, 727
Pierce, J. 618
Pierce, Jacob 115
Pierce, Johamiah 78
Pierce, John 425
Pierce, Joseph 485
Pierce, Joshua 337
Pierce, Louisa 83
Pierce, Mary 86, 425,
   657

Pierce, Milley 136
Pierce, Polly 493
Pierce, Samuel 136
Pierce, Sarah Jane 369
Pierce, Thomas (Sr.) 115
Pierce, Thomas F. 522
Piercy, John A. 618
Piercy, M. 618
Pierpoint, Elenor 563
Pierpoint, Sarah 563
Pierson, Abel S. 582
Pierson, Amianih 280
Pierson, Amos 196
Pierson, Joseph 196
Pierson, Sampson 550
Pierson, Wyllis 646,
   651, 656, 675
Pigman, Susanna 461
Pigmon, Elizabeth 468
Pignolet, Jeanne
   Francoise 725
Pignolet, Joachim 725
Pike, Alanson 752, 753
Pike, Orsella 762
Pilchard, John (Sr.) 90
Pilchard, Peter 84
Pilcher, Abraham 79
Pilcher, Arian 77
Pilcher, J. M. M. 693
Pilcher, Pemelia 76
Pilcher, Rosalie 693
Piler, Peggy 127
Piles, Absalom 515
Piles, Eliza Ann 508
Piles, Jeremiah 508
Piles, Joseph 508
Piles, Lucinda 508
Piles, Matilda 508
Piles, Rachel 508
Piles, William 508
Pillars, Sarah 459
Pilsen, Hugh 431
Pilson, Esther 546
Pinay, Elizabeth 497
Pindle, Adolphus 690
Pindle, Charles Angus
   690
Pindle, Elizabeth 690
Pindle, Emaline 690
Pindle, Joseph Thomas
   690
Pindle, Rebecca 690
Pine, Clement 269
Pingree, John 126
Pinkerton, Alexander R.
   263
Pinkerton, John 416
Pinkerton, Jos. L. 435
Pinney, Benj. 732
Piper, Aliscander 109
Piper, Amasa 263
Piper, Elenor 585
Piper, Philip 458
Piper, Sylvanius 271
Piper, Sylvanus 273
Piper, Sylvenus 266, 268
Piper, William 596
Pipler, David 458
Pirelan, Margaret 130

Pirelin, Genny 130
Pirson, David 181
Pirson, Elizabeth 181
Pirth, Henry 762
Pisel, Elyser 236
Pisel, Johan 236
Pisel, Rebeke 236
Pitcher, Elizabeth 382
Pitman, Elias 157
Pitman, Elias (Jr.) 154
Pitman, Elias (Sr.) 155
Pitman, Ide 174
Pitman, Jacob O. 174
Pitman, John H. 86
Pitman, Katharine 154
Pitman, Sarah 157
Pitman, Saunders 86
Pittenger, Abraham 448
Pittenger, Benj. 525
Pitthoue, Nancy 516
Pittman, Aaron 676
Pittman, Benjamin 163
Pittman, Bethany 160
Pittman, Catharine 163,
   173
Pittman, Catherine 155
Pittman, David 676
Pittman, Edith 676
Pittman, Elias 163,
   164, 173
Pittman, Elias (Jr.)
   155, 158, 176
Pittman, Elias (Sr.)
   154, 158, 176
Pittman, George 676
Pittman, Ide 163, 168,
   171
Pittman, Jacob 163, 171
Pittman, Jacob O. 168
Pittman, Jane 676
Pittman, Jemima 163
Pittman, John 676
Pittman, Joseph 162, 676
Pittman, Lucy Ann 676
Pittman, Lydia Margaret
   676
Pittman, Moore 676
Pittman, Rachel 676
Pittman, Samuel 676
Pittman, Sarah 158,
   163, 176
Pittman, William 160,
   163, 676
Pitzer, Cath. 748
Pitzer, Jacob 301
Pitzer, Johann 301
Pitzer, M. 748
Pitzer, Margaret 302,
   748
Place, Asher 682
Place, David 682
Place, Joseph 682
Place, Mary 682
Place, Sarah 711
Place, Sarah Ann 682
Plaff, Margaret 708
Plaff, Peter 708, 710
Plain, Henry 35
Plank, Adam 373

Plank, Christena 373
Plank, Elizabeth 373
Plank, Hannah 373
Plank, Hubbard 373
Plank, Jeptha (Sr.) 738
Plank, John 22
Plank, Joseph 373
Plank, Mary 373
Plants, Jacob 522
Plate, John F. 228
Plattar, James 121
Platter, Catherine 123, 745
Platter, Elizabeth 746
Platter, George 386
Platter, Hannah 746
Platter, Joanna 126
Platter, Joseph 746
Platter, Lewis 746
Platter, M. A. 337
Platter, Mary 336
Pletcher, Catharine 247, 253
Pletcher, Jacob 247, 253
Pletcher, Phoebe 247, 252
Pletcher, Solomon 252, 253
Pletcher, Washington 247, 252
Plimpton, Dwight 498
Plotner, Hannah 278
Plum, Adam 337
Plum, Henry 386
Plum, Isaac 7
Plum, Jonathan 7
Plum, Mary 679
Plum, Polly 348
Plumb, Celarista 522
Plumb, Elizabeth W. 334
Plumb, John A. 410
Plumb, Samuel 411
Plumb, William 515
Plumber, Philemon 224
Plumer, Asa 596
Plummer, Anna 247
Plummer, Benjamin 1
Plummer, Clarinda A. 588
Plummer, Dorcas 1
Plummer, Ezra 682
Plummer, Fannie 709
Plummer, Fidelia 588
Plummer, Hannah 585
Plummer, John 746
Plummer, John Westley 591
Plummer, Joseph 337, 550
Plummer, Lucy 465
Plummer, Margaret 127
Plummer, Mary 548, 551
Plummer, Mary Ann 335
Plummer, Reuben 56, 597
Plummer, Sophia 56, 224
Plummer, Treesy 463
Plyley, John P. 637
Poal, Banister 748
Pobl, Elizabeth Anne 607
Pocock, Daniel 738
Pocock, Eli 575

Poe, Benjamin D. 341
Poe, George I. 765
Poe, George J. 765
Poe, John 69
Poe, Polly 69
Pogue, Lucy 497
Pohlman, F. Ludewick 104
Pohlmeyer, Henry 104
Poiner, Thomas C. 334
Poland, Enoch 252
Poland, Samuel 252
Poling, Richard 312
Poling, Samuel 583
Polk, William 661
Pollard, Juliet 401
Pollard, Smith John 401
Pollin, Uriah 471, 474, 475
Polloch, Geba 14
Polloch, John 21
Polloch, William 609
Pollock, Abigale H. 180
Pollock, David 508
Pollock, Eleanor 438
Pollock, Ephraim 180
Pollock, George 591
Pollock, George Retty 9
Pollock, Hugh 438
Pollock, James 9
Pollock, John 469, 515
Pollock, Joseph 9, 14
Pollock, Layton 9
Pollock, Mary 9, 608
Pollock, Robert 9
Pollock, Sarah 9, 11
Pollock, Thomas 9, 180, 508, 623
Pollock, William 9
Polluch, Margaret 14
Polly, Elizabeth 409
Polly, Henry 409
Polly, Stephen 359
Polock, David 515
Polock, Joseph 18
Polock, Thomas 623
Pomeroy, Rolf 282
Pompey, Jno. 285
Pond, John P. 42
Pond, Norman 84
Pontious, Andrew 243
Pontious, Benjamin 391
Pontious, Caty 385
Pontious, Clement Vallaningham 243
Pontious, Conrad 546
Pontious, Conrod 552
Pontious, Daniel 386
Pontious, Emma 243
Pontious, J. 243
Pontious, M. 243
Pontious, Malinda 243
Pontious, Margaret 383
Pontious, Samuel 386
Pontious, Susana 552
Pontius, Abraham 188, 243, 599
Pontius, Benjamin 465
Pontius, Catharine 240
Pontius, Catherine 466

Pontius, D. 243
Pontius, Daniel 243
Pontius, Elizabeth 243
Pontius, Eve 461
Pontius, Eve Catharine 243
Pontius, Frederic 240
Pontius, Frederick 240
Pontius, George 386
Pontius, Henry 243
Pontius, John 243, 623
Pontius, Mary M. 243
Pontius, Peter 240
Pontius, S. 243
Pontius, Samuel 243
Pontius, Sarah 243, 606
Pontius, Sarah Ann 243
Pontius, William 609
Ponyard, Francis 498
Pool, . . . us 154
Pool, Amy 412
Pool, Asbery 50
Pool, Emily Jane 307
Pool, Frederick 746
Pool, George 50, 546
Pool, Guy W. 271
Pool, Hannah 271, 274
Pool, Henry 50
Pool, John 599
Pool, Nancy 50
Pool, Robert 50, 546
Pool, Robert W. 307
Pool, Simeon 258, 259, 274
Pool, Simeon (Jr.) 271
Pool, Simeon (Sr.) 270
Pool, Thomas A. 21
Poole, Jacob 501
Poorman, Barbara 431
Poorman, Barney 374
Poorman, Bernard 339
Poorman, Daniel 214, 381
Poorman, Hannah 374
Poorman, Jacob 214, 374
Poorman, John 373
Poorman, Mary 373
Poorman, Peter 381
Pope, Emsley 14
Pope, John 57
Pope, Martha 11
Pope, Mary 14
Pope, Samuel 642
Popejoy, Frankey 456
Poppleton, L. W. 522
Pore, Susannah 466
Porket, Eliza 336
Port, William 469, 473, 490
Portemon, Sarah 591
Porter, Abner 732
Porter, Alvin 581
Porter, Arthur 178
Porter, Cath. 406
Porter, Ebenezer 33
Porter, Elenor 585
Porter, Eloner 565
Porter, George 490
Porter, Henry 490
Porter, Isaac 556

Porter, James 30, 223, 255, 358, 407, 446
Porter, Jesse 591
Porter, Jesse E. 358
Porter, Jno. 406
Porter, John 164, 173, 586, 596
Porter, John (Jr.) 586
Porter, Johnathan 259
Porter, Jonathan 264, 265, 266
Porter, Jonathan C. 257
Porter, Joseph 255, 732
Porter, Lavina 572
Porter, Louisia 502
Porter, Margaret 521
Porter, Mary 556
Porter, Mary Ann 407
Porter, Moses 556
Porter, Nancy 466
Porter, Nathaniel 661
Porter, Otho 172
Porter, Polly 467, 590
Porter, Prissilla 715
Porter, Ralph 257
Porter, Rebecca 719
Porter, Reison 575
Porter, Reuben 263, 266
Porter, Robert 661, 670
Porter, Rosa Ann 407
Porter, Rosanna 596
Porter, Ruby B. 257
Porter, Sarah 662
Porter, Seth S. 257
Porter, Solomon 51
Porter, Susanah 586
Porter, Susannah 596
Porter, William 448, 586
Porter, Wm. 319, 581
Porterfield, William 113
Porthemore, Frederick 591
Porthemore, George 591
Portz, John 522
Poss, Rachel 512
Post, Bernard 103
Post, Isreal 546
Post, Mary Ann 79
Post, Mary Elizabeth 105
Post, William 473, 478
Postal, Solomon 49
Postgate, Thomas 490
Postogate, Rachel 456
Poter, Hannah 45
Poterf, Gasper 435
Poterf, Squire James 435
Potes, Anna 522
Pott, James 141
Pottenger, Cecilia 435
Pottenger, Granville 435
Pottenger, Hester 435
Pottenger, Hiram 435
Pottenger, Margaretta 435
Pottenger, Mary F. 435
Pottenger, Wm. K. 435
Potter, --- 479
Potter, Abigail 372
Potter, Carlton 435

Potter, Edward 591
Potter, Esther 109
Potter, George Foglesong 672
Potter, Hannah 109
Potter, Henry 109
Potter, Jos. 478
Potter, Joseph 469, 470, 471, 473, 478, 480, 481, 490, 651, 656
Potter, Kelita 372
Potter, Levi 435
Potter, Lydia C. 29
Potter, Martha 490
Potter, Thomas 109, 278
Potter, William 109, 372, 650, 656
Potterf, Jefferson 431
Potterf, Nancy Jane 435
Pottinger, Prudence 435
Pottor, Noah 696
Pottorf, Henry 126
Potts, Anthony 386
Potts, Elizabeth 109
Potts, John 141
Potts, Mary Ann 664
Potts, Richard 141
Potts, Robert 715
Potts, Stephen 154, 175
Potts, Sylvester 141
Poulson, Elisha 386
Pound, D. 238
Pound, David M. 238
Pound, P. 238
Powel, Charles 172
Powel, David 480
Powel, Elizabeth 172
Powel, Henry 602
Powel, James 79
Powel, John B. 503
Powel, Louisa 80
Powel, Rebecca 172
Powel, Veneen 515
Powel, Wm. 79
Powell, Benjamin 160
Powell, Burk 711
Powell, Buthbert 57
Powell, Cuthbert 57
Powell, Jacob F. 14
Powell, James 439, 442, 690
Powell, Mary 664
Powell, Mary Ann 523
Powell, Samuel 546
Powell, Sarah 380
Powell, T. W. 760
Powell, Thos. W. 760
Powell, William 14, 162
Power, Anna 36
Power, Rebecca 510
Power, Wm. 510
Powers, Alweda 74
Powers, Anna 36
Powers, Benjamin 634
Powers, Charlotte 707
Powers, Chas. 410
Powers, Edward 661
Powers, Esther 511
Powers, George 763

Powers, Isaac 498
Powers, John 386
Powers, John N. 157, 160, 179
Powers, Joseph 61, 174
Powers, Margaret 45
Powers, Michael 490
Powers, Polly 712
Powers, Rhody 496
Powers, Robert 2
Powers, Sally 28, 74
Powers, Sarah 160, 179
Powers, Theophelus Stanford 718
Powers, Theophilus H. 707
Powers, Thomas 316, 317, 320, 321
Powersock, Jane 127
Powlson, William 386
Poynton, Cynthia 514
Pradel, Julien 723
Prate, Electa 637
Prater, John 14
Pratt, Almira 496
Pratt, Azariah 715
Pratt, Barney T. 259
Pratt, Elisha 661
Pratt, Ezekiel 279
Pratt, Fletcher W. 57
Pratt, John 20
Pratt, Lucinda 387
Pratt, Margaret Ann 759
Pratt, Phebe 524
Pratt, Seth (Dr.) 84
Pratt, William 546
Pratt, Wm. 761
Pray, Ambrose Rice 39, 757, 762
Pray, Hannah 42
Pray, Parris 42
Preble, Barnet 435
Preble, Mary 522
Preble, Scynthia 435
Prekens, William 164
Preliamon, William 126
Prentice, Anna 74
Prentice, Dorcas 321
Prentice, John B. 74
Prentice, Solomon M. 321
Prentice, William W. 74
Prentis, Joseph 42
Prentiss, David 141
Prescott, James B. 502, 515
Presher, Asa 105
Presho, Asa 105
Pressel, David 218
Pressell, David 217
Pressler, William 531
Presten, John 121
Prestock, Martin 575
Preston, Eliza Jane 4
Preston, Hannah 445
Preston, John 445, 498
Preston, Norman C. 609
Preston, Pheb 89
Preston, Ruth 445
Preston, Samuel 42

Preston, Sarah 445
Preston, Theodocea 445
Preston, William 445
Preston, William S. 35
Preston, Wm. C. 748
Prettyman, Jane 745
Prettyman, Mary M. 746
Prezel, Sarah 717
Pribble, Amelia 435
Pribble, Debby 162
Pribble, Flora 180
Pribble, James 160, 180
Pribble, Oliver O. H.
   435
Pribble, Thomas 160, 162
Price, Aaron 732
Price, Barbary 661
Price, Barnet 84
Price, Benjamin 563
Price, Betsey 515
Price, Betsy 121
Price, Catharine 121
Price, Charles 84
Price, Christian 415
Price, Christopher 568
Price, David 79
Price, David M. 623
Price, Delilah 126
Price, E. T. 612
Price, Elijah 248
Price, Elizabeth 76,
   117, 586
Price, Ester 48
Price, George 435
Price, Hannah 224
Price, Henry 121
Price, Isaac 505
Price, Isaac M. 107, 108
Price, Israel 121
Price, J. M. 612
Price, Jacob 419
Price, Jacob R. 248,
   265, 266, 267, 274
Price, James 575, 655
Price, James M. 655
Price, Jane Eliza 248
Price, Jefferson Jackson
   248
Price, Jeffrey 283,
   284, 298
Price, John 223, 224,
   262, 586
Price, Josiah 483
Price, Levenia 589
Price, Lucinda 77
Price, Martin 274
Price, Mary 575, 576,
   659
Price, Meredith 79
Price, Michael 121
Price, Nancy 415, 657
Price, Peggy 659
Price, Peter 536
Price, Polly 657
Price, Rachel 662
Price, Rece 248
Price, Reuben 59
Price, Sarah 461, 576
Price, Sarah Ann 248

Price, Sophia 669
Price, Susan 83
Price, Susannah 666, 709
Price, William 14
Price, William (Jr.) 490
Price, Wm. 515, 575, 591
Price, Zoie 612
Prichard, Resin 575
Pricket, Catharine 12
Prickett, Isaac 493
Priddy, John N. 609
Priddy, Thomas D. 609
Priddy, William 625
Prider, James 575
Prieau, Nicholas 726
Prier, Andrew D. 121
Priest, Barsheba 117
Priest, Elijah 118
Priest, Haggy 116
Priest, John (Jr.) 286
Priest, Levi 286
Priest, Stephen 732
Prilaman, Sally 118
Prileman, Polly 118
Prill, John 662, 672
Prilleman, Christian 546
Prilleman, Prudence 118
Prillman, Sally 120
Primrose, Hester 358
Prince, Peter 558
Princehouse, Henry 126
Prindle, Rachel 572
Pring, Elanor 608
Pring, Elizabeth 606
Pring, Jeremiah 609
Pring, John 609
Pring, Richard 626
Prior, Barbara 299
Prior, Elijah 732
Prior, George 36
Prior, Isaac 299, 303
Prior, John 498
Prior, Joseph 299
Prior, Mary 299
Prior, Sally 717
Prior, Timothy 299
Prioux, Nicholas 724,
   725, 729
Prioux, Timothy 729
Prise, Eva Margaret 580
Pritchard, Anne 395
Pritchard, Edward 395
Pritchard, Elizabeth 395
Pritchard, Mitchel 395
Pritchard, Mitchell 395
Pritchard, Nancy 571
Pritchard, Thomas 395
Probst, George 91
Proby, John 341
Procter, Jacob 715
Prong, Juliann 572
Prosser, Daniel 439
Prosser, James 5
Prosser, Margaret 5
Prosser, Thomas 5
Proudfit, Patterson 292
Prouty, Esther 29
Proutz, David 264
Proutz, Russel 271, 303

Provabb, Elizabeth 460
Provatt, Elizabeth 460
Province, Thomas 473
Prowebb, Peter 458
Prudy, Fannie 281
Prugh, George 53
Prugh, Hester 435
Prugh, Jno. 209
Pruitt, Susanna 411
Prunly, Samuel 732
Prusman, Daniel 236
Prusman, Jacob Nathaniel
   236
Pryer, Timothy 729
Pryor, Ann 163
Pryor, Henry 163
Pryor, Mary 461
Pucket, Catharine 48
Pugh, Abel 662
Pugh, Azariah 666
Pugh, Hannah 665
Pugh, Job 662
Pugh, John 448
Pugh, Mary 256, 448
Pugh, Peter 86
Pugh, Samuel 256
Pugh, Thos. 14
Pugh, Valinda 663
Pugsley, Joseph 718
Pugsley, Olive 718
Pulford, Severett 498
Pumel, Elizabeth 513
Punchus, Conrod 552
Purce, Maria 384
Purcel, Elizabeth 380
Purcell, George 1
Purcell, Mary 1
Purcell, Rhoda 1
Purcell, Thomas 1
Purchase, Margaret 84
Purdy, Alexander W. 449
Purdy, Archibald 449
Purdy, Catharine 606
Purdy, Francis 14
Purdy, George 612
Purdy, J. 331
Purdy, James 449
Purdy, Jane 449
Purdy, Jane (Sr.) 449
Purdy, Joseph 331
Purdy, Joseph M. 331
Purdy, Joseph Miller 334
Purdy, Nancy 13
Purdy, Nathaniel 331
Purdy, Patrick 449
Purdy, Rachael 616
Purdy, Rachel 103
Purdy, S. 331, 616
Purdy, Sarah Jane 331
Purdy, T. H. 616
Purdy, William H. 599,
   600, 601
Purdy, William M. H. 616
Purina, Orilla 496
Purington, Charles 633
Purinton, Phoebe 84
Purkins, Ruth 657
Purl, Margaret Ann 384
Pursell, Hannah 436, 457

Pursell, John 493
Pursley, Abel 485
Purtee, Deborah 455
Purtee, James 746
Purtee, Lewis 746
Purviance, Jane 424
Purviance, Patterson 424
Purviance, Patterson
  James 436
Pusey, Mary 23
Puterbaugh, George 210
Puthoff, G. H. 546
Putman, Alexander 609
Putman, Bethiah 727
Putman, Betsy 636
Putman, Catherine 453
Putman, David 636
Putman, Mary 607
Putman, William 727
Putman, William Pitt
  727, 729
Putnam, Aaron W. 732
Putnam, Aaron Waldo 715
Putnam, Abigail 713
Putnam, Betsey 713
Putnam, Calvin 75
Putnam, Charles March
  636
Putnam, David 732
Putnam, David (Jr.) 636
Putnam, Doughlas 733
Putnam, Douglas 636
Putnam, Edwin 296
Putnam, George 636, 718
Putnam, Horace 45
Putnam, Ira H. 498
Putnam, L. 733
Putnam, Mary 496
Putnam, P. 733
Putnam, Paris 714
Putnam, Patty 718
Putnam, Persis 714
Putnam, Peter 623
Putnam, Polly 714, 730
Putnam, Rufus 282
Putnam, Sarah 715
Putnam, Urzel 498
Putnam, William 96
Putnam, William Rufus
  730
Putnam, Wm. P. 733
Putnam, Wm. Pitt 733
Putt, Lewis 576
Pye, Thomas 458
Pyle, Elizabeth 636
Pyle, Jonathan 271
Pyle, Oliver 462, 465
Pyle, William 636

--- Q ---

Quade, Christopher 42
Quarles, John 50
Queen, Michael 14
Queen, William 84
Questel, Nicholas 723
Queyere, Geo. 575

Qugley, Jonathan 490
Quick, Elizabeth 751
Quick, Leno 386
Quick, Thomas P. 746,
  751
Quiffe, Remmy Thierry
  725
Quiffe, Remy Thierry 725
Quiffe, Remy Thiery 724
Quigley, Ann Mgnerva 275
Quigley, Columbus 275
Quigley, George C. 275
Quigley, Isabel 275
Quigley, John 264, 265,
  730
Quigley, Lucretia 275
Quigley, Wm. M. 275
Quillin, Absalom 239
Quillin, Amos 733
Quillin, J. 239
Quillin, O. 239
Quimbey, Jonathan 79
Quimbey, Nancy 457
Quimby, Enos 79
Quimby, John 726
Quimby, Martha R. 78
Quimey, Daniel 726
Quinch, Elizabeth 359
Quinn, Cynthia 57
Quinn, Ellen 546
Quinn, John B. 436
Quinn, Michael 546
Quinn, Nancy 335
Quinn, Peter 93
Quinn, Richard 57
Quinn, Thomas P. 424
Quinnians, Mary 665
Quirs, Joseph 648
Quough, Benjamin 45
Qyney, Richard 42

--- R ---

Rabb, Jane 695
Rabb, John 695
Rabb, Samuel 695
Raburn, Wm. 54
Racey, Landen 303
Radabach, Adam 757
Radabach, Betsey 757
Radabach, Catharine 757
Radabach, Christiana 757
Radabach, Daniel 757
Radabach, Eliza 757
Radabach, Elizabeth 757
Radabach, John 757
Radabach, Joseph 757
Radabach, Lydia 757
Radabach, Peter 757
Radabach, Rebecca 757
Radabach, Samuel 757
Radabach, Thomas 757
Radcleff, Isaac 386
Radcliff, C. F. 702
Radcliff, Ezekiel 490
Radcliff, James 169
Radcliff, Jesse 490

Radcliff, John 490
Radefeld, Christiana 234
Radefeld, Emma 234
Radefeld, Jacob 234
Rader, Susanna 58
Raderick, Catherine 457
Radford, Billy 89
Radford, Wm. 56
Radliff, Ann 456
Radubach, Adam 761
Radubach, Daniel 761
Radubach, Elizabeth 761
Radubach, John 761
Radubach, Joseph 761
Radubach, Katharine 761
Radubach, Peter 761
Radubach, Rebecca 761
Radubach, Samuel 761
Radubach, Thomas 761
Rafferty, Isabell 45
Rafferty, Joseph 62
Rafferty, Rebecca 62
Ragan, Bethany 113
Ragan, John 466
Ragan, Wilks 666
Ragan, Zadock 118
Ragem, Elijah 666
Ragen, Wright 662
Rager, Elizabeth 570
Rager, Eva 384
Rager, Jacob (Jr.) 575
Ragin, Sarah 15
Ragoi, Thomas John 453
Ragon, Henrietta 523
Ragon, Jacob 718
Ragsdale, Berry 516
Rail, Catherine 369, 373
Rail, Elizabeth 373
Rail, Esther 373
Rail, Eve 373
Rail, Hannah 373
Rail, Mary 373
Rail, Mary Magdalena 373
Rail, Susannah 373
Rail, William 373
Rail, Wm. 369
Railback, Daniel 79
Railey, John 273
Rain, Lookey 462
Raines, Bennett 694
Rains, Catherine 465
Rains, Elicabeth 461
Rains, Isaac 458, 466
Rains, Lawren 466
Rainy, Edward 302
Raitt, Elizabeth 763
Raitt, James 763
Raitt, Nancy 763
Raitt, Sally F. 763
Raitt, Sarah Jane 763
Rake, Jacob 733
Rakes, William 493
Rakestraw, Joseph 42
Ralph, Abigal 81
Ralph, Obediah 79
Ralph, Wealthy 76
Ralson, Robert 379
Ralston, Benjamin 493
Ralston, David 690

935

Ralston, Joseph 763
Ralston, Nancy 493
Ralston, Robert 490
Ram, John 575
Rambo, Catharine 729
Rambo, Jackson 729
Rambo, Jacob 729
Rambo, John 356
Rambo, Rebeckah 729
Ramburgh, Daniel 337
Ramey, Caleb 466
Rammage, Susanna 571
Ramsay, Thomas 224
Ramsberger, John 564
Ramsey, David 254
Ramsey, Elizabeth 750
Ramsey, Frances V. 702
Ramsey, H. C. 702
Ramsey, Hannah 291
Ramsey, James 445, 476, 477, 478, 482
Ramsey, James H. 366
Ramsey, Leander 146
Ramsey, Lucinda 146
Ramsey, Martha Agnes 436
Ramsey, Mary 89, 354
Ramsey, Mary E. 702
Ramsey, Preston B. 431
Ramsey, Robt. 146
Ramsey, Sally 359
Ramsey, Saml. Rutherford 436
Ramsey, Susannah 117
Ramsey, Thomas 729
Ramsey, Thomas Lacy 436
Ramsey, William 118
Ramsey, Wm. Gilmore 436
Ramssing, Adel 111
Ramsy, Elizabeth 670
Randaburgh, George 108
Randal, Matilda 591
Randal, Tabor 591
Randall, Elizabeth 14, 513
Randall, Jis 436
Randall, Martha 436
Randall, Mary 13
Randall, Nancy 436
Randall, Nathan 75, 436
Randall, Phebe 436
Randall, Rachel 550
Randall, Rebecca 436
Randall, Thomas 591
Randell, Margarett 526
Randell, Thomas 526
Randolf, David 294
Randolf, James 294
Randolf, Jane 294
Randolf, John 294
Randolf, Mariah 294
Randolf, Mary 294
Randolf, Neomy 294
Randolph, Crawford 164
Randolph, David 639
Randolph, Israel F. 170
Randolph, Joel F. 170, 172
Randolph, John F. 172
Randolph, John R. 373

Randolph, Jonah F. 175
Randolph, Rachel 748
Randolph, Thomas 377
Randols, Elizabeth 717
Raney, Jno. 269, 272
Raney, John 270
Ranger, Erastus 764
Rank, Barbara 569
Rank, Philip 575
Ranka, John 240
Ranka, Minnie 240
Ranken, John 466
Rankin, Daniel 351
Rankin, Hugh 466
Rankin, Joseph Buekels 507
Rankin, Nancy 466
Rankin, Phebe 466
Rankin, William 486, 516
Rankins, Mary 509
Rankins, Thomas 486
Rankins, Wm. 509
Rannell, Sam J. 635
Rannells, William 303
Rannells, Wm. 263
Rannels, William 258
Ranney, Hiram 633
Ranney, Orange (Dr.) 575
Ranney, Susan 33
Ransco, Elizabeth 117
Ransey, Charity 117
Ransom, Charles 720
Ransom, George P. 284
Ransom, Samuel 284
Ransom, Sibble 503
Ransom, Thurman 263
Ranson, Charles 721
Raper, Robert 420
Raper, William 156
Raper, William H. 594
Rapger, Holly 421
Rapger, William (Rev.) 421
Rapp, Dicy Melinda 411
Rapp, Jacob (Sr.) 410
Rapp, Michael 408
Rappe, Andrew 553
Rardin, Rachel 501
Rardon, Daniel 516
Rardon, David 84
Rardon, Elliner 511
Rardon, James 516
Raredon, James 516
Rarick, Catharine 141
Rarick, Elizabeth 141, 246, 347
Rarick, Henry 246
Rarick, Lydia 141
Raridan, Saml. 550
Raridin, Jane 716
Rarool, Frederick 323
Rarredon, Thomas 718
Raser, Barbara 246
Raser, Daniel 232, 246
Raser, Elizabeth 232
Raser, John 232
Rasly, John 282
Rasor, Dinnes 718
Rasor, Dora 244

Rasor, Earl 244
Rasp, George 87
Rasselly, John 282
Rassor, Elizabeth 718
Ratcliff, James 170
Ratcliff, John 466
Ratcliff, Margaret 464
Ratcliff, Rachael 490
Ratcliff, Rachel 467
Ratcliff, Simon 490
Ratcliff, Stephen 170
Ratcliff, Susannah 459
Ratekin, James 560
Ratekin, Jane 560
Ratekin, Sarah 560
Rathaas, Mary Louisa 146
Rathbone, George 30
Rathbone, John 282
Rathborn, Charles 592
Rathborn, Clarissa 28
Rathburn, Alvan 79
Rathburn, Cynthia 82
Rathburn, Elisha 79, 88
Rathburn, Sereno 79
Rathburn, W. P. 633
Ratliff, Benjamin 168
Ratliff, Mary 168
Ratliff, Moses C. 609
Ratliff, Stephen 168
Rauby, Catherine 112
Raukins, Rachael 717
Rauser, Henry 305
Raver, Henry 575
Raver, W. A. (Rev.) 425
Rawley, Luther 575
Rawling, David 386
Rawlings, Sarah 384
Rawlling, Charles 516
Rawls, John 392
Rawsaw, Catherine 77
Rawser, Mary 116
Rawser, Sally 117
Rawson, Abel 525, 529, 530
Rawson, Semtary 71
Ray, Abner 71
Ray, Andrew 55
Ray, Ann 273
Ray, Anne 658
Ray, Benjamin 400
Ray, Betsey 55
Ray, Elias 400
Ray, George 400
Ray, Hannah 55, 400
Ray, Horace 207
Ray, James 55
Ray, Jane 31
Ray, Jeremiah 400
Ray, Jesse 55
Ray, John 306, 400
Ray, Margaret 13, 400, 661
Ray, Mary 23
Ray, Mary A. 313
Ray, Pamelia J. 83
Ray, Polly 718
Ray, Reuben 400
Ray, Richard 273
Ray, Robert 55, 313

Ray, Sarah 357, 400, 658
Ray, Selathiel 313
Ray, Thomas 55
Ray, William 25, 55
Rayboune, Andrw 486
Rayburn, Albert 63
Rayburn, Clinton 63
Rayburn, Creighton M.
  49, 63
Rayburn, Creighton Mead
  63
Rayburn, David 63
Rayburn, James 63
Rayburn, John 63
Rayburn, Joseph 63
Rayburn, Margaret 63
Rayburn, Martha 63
Rayburn, Rebecca Jane 63
Rayburn, William 63
Rayburn, William John 63
Rayer, Noble 154
Rayl, Noble 157, 160
Rayl, William 160
Rayman, Charles 116
Raymond, John 127
Raymond, William 209
Raymor, Geo. 575
Rayner, Lida 72
Rayner, Nancy S. 302
Raynlas, James 79
Raynolds, John 298, 299
Raynolds, Mary 27
Raynolds, W. 294
Raynolds, Wm. 556
Rea, Allen 14
Rea, Benjamin 18
Rea, David 14, 21
Rea, Mathew 49
Rea, Moses 393
Rea, Permelia 49
Rea, Pricilla 18
Rea, Rebecca 11
Rea, Robert 14, 93
Rea, Thomas 180
Read, Edward 9
Read, Elijah 527
Read, Elizabeth 63
Read, Margaret 9
Read, Martha A. 10
Read, Mary 9, 63
Read, Nathaniel C. 10
Read, Obediah 9
Read, Rachel 9
Read, Rebecca 63
Read, Sarah 9, 63
Read, Seth 522
Read, Solomon 466
Read, Thomas A. 356
Reader, John 30
Reading, Betsey 31
Readle, John 52
Reagan, Mary 701
Reagel, Catherine 369
Reagel, Wm. 369
Reager, Anne 293
Reager, Anthony 293
Reager, Henry 293
Reager, Jacob 293
Reager, John 293

Ream, Andrew 358
Ream, Christian 338,
  341, 354
Ream, David 354, 358
Ream, Harriet 606
Ream, Horace 343
Ream, Jacob 352, 362
Ream, James 343
Ream, Leonard 366, 374
Ream, Rachel 367
Ream, Sam. 354
Ream, Samuel 367, 375
Ream, William 339
Reames, Edward 592
Reams, Aron 14
Reams, Caleb 14
Reams, Joel 14
Reams, Martha 14
Reams, Moses 14
Reams, Talner 14
Reams, Vincent 22
Reanes, James 564
Reanes, Luisa Wilhelmena
  564
Reardon, Catharine 568
Rearen, Elener 572
Reason, Samuel 386
Reath, John 164
Reator, David 526
Reator, Eli Benjamin 526
Reator, Nancy 526
Reator, Otho 526
Reaves, James 564
Reaves, Joseph 303
Reaves, Luisa Wilhelmena
  564
Rebble, Nicholas 285
Rebstock, George 568
Rebstock, Salome 572
Reburn, William 718
Receses, Mary 666
Recher, John 210
Recher, Lewis 210
Recher, Peter 210
Rechman, E. 354
Reckeldaffer, Susanna
  383
Recker, Daniel 214
Recker, Elizabeth 112
Recter, John 127
Rector, Calvard 392
Rector, Edward 392,
  397, 466
Rector, Elizabeth 511
Rector, Enoch 733
Rector, Frederick 516
Rector, Henry 395
Rector, John 121, 392,
  490
Rector, Joseph 550
Rector, Mary 451
Rector, Nancy 551
Rector, Pency 382
Rector, Polly 392
Rector, Sally 26
Rector, Sanford 392
Rector, Starling 392
Rector, William 485, 486
Redden, Reuben 64

Reddick, --- 400
Reddick, Elizabeth 146
Reddick, Sarah J. 146
Reddin, Elizabeth 382
Reddin, Nancy 387
Redding, Elizabeth 451
Redding, Mary 83
Redebaugh, Mary E. 609
Redenbaugh, David 550
Redenbaugh, John 127
Redenbo, E. 540
Redenbo, Eliza Jane 539
Redenbo, Elizabeth 540
Redenbo, Lewis P. 540
Redenbo, S. 540
Redenbo, Samuel 540
Redenbo, Sarah 540
Redenbough, John 546
Reder, Esther 107
Redfearn, John 466, 634
Redford, Moses 586
Redinbaugh, Eliza 549
Reding, Patty 451
Redinger, Michael 563
Redington, Charlott 34
Redington, Ransom 30
Redman, . . . ancis 619
Redman, George 546
Redman, Israel 262, 267
Redman, John 176, 436
Redman, Mary 419
Redman, Sarah E. 604,
  609, 619
Redman, Thomas J. 604,
  609, 619
Redman, William 623
Redmond, Israel 275
Redmond, Robert 375
Reeb, --- 331
Reeb, Charles 323
Reeb, Joseph 320, 322
Reece, Elizabeth 589
Reece, Rebecca 611
Reech, Salome 709
Reed, --- 176
Reed, Abraham 190, 191
Reed, Aget M. 191
Reed, Alexander 595
Reed, Alexr. 596
Reed, Allen 20, 493, 662
Reed, Alvin 232
Reed, Amos 746
Reed, Betsy 296, 596
Reed, Catharine 190,
  609, 659
Reed, Cephas 598
Reed, Charlett 458
Reed, Cynthia 598
Reed, David 183, 224,
  289, 290, 483, 592,
  596, 598
Reed, Drusilla 609
Reed, E. M. 406
Reed, Edward 155, 167
Reed, Eleanor R. 591
Reed, Elijah 733
Reed, Eliza 761
Reed, Elizabeth 141, 191,
  458, 657, 666, 667

Reed, Ellis 285
Reed, Elnor 593
Reed, Emelia 384
Reed, Ethan Allen 373
Reed, Ezekiel 733
Reed, Flavilla 590
Reed, Frederick 141
Reed, George 373
Reed, Hannah 293
Reed, Hugh M. 546
Reed, Jacob 366, 498, 592
Reed, James 232, 259,
   260, 271, 272, 299,
   307, 310, 386, 556,
   586, 592, 601, 609
Reed, James I. 431
Reed, James P. 310
Reed, Jane 83, 583,
   591, 596, 598
Reed, Jeremiah 373
Reed, John 14, 141, 154,
   168, 232, 260, 267,
   303, 364, 373, 386,
   559, 586, 595, 598
Reed, John (Jr.) 262
Reed, John M. 373
Reed, John P. 592
Reed, Joseph 9, 153,
   191, 592, 645
Reed, Joshua 726, 727
Reed, Josiah 431
Reed, Laurilla 76
Reed, Lydia 596, 598
Reed, Margaret 13, 116,
   373, 383, 385, 596,
   598
Reed, Mary 13, 83, 168,
   373, 406, 431, 519,
   726, 727
Reed, Mary Elizabeth 406
Reed, Mary W. 591
Reed, Matilda 191
Reed, Melissa C. 9
Reed, Nancy 15, 77
Reed, Nathan 14, 394
Reed, Nicey 466
Reed, Orrin 9
Reed, Patric 636
Reed, Polly 451
Reed, Quinton 599
Reed, Rachel 601
Reed, Rebeccah 500
Reed, Richard 42, 490,
   550
Reed, Robert 738
Reed, Sally 117
Reed, Samuel 79, 287,
   480, 592, 596, 598
Reed, Samuel (IV) 586
Reed, Sarah 141, 191,
   307, 513, 588
Reed, Sarah Jane 431
Reed, Seppas 596
Reed, Solomon 466
Reed, Stephen 297
Reed, Susanah 497
Reed, Synthia 596
Reed, Thomas 458, 466,
   586, 596, 598

Reed, Thos. 592
Reed, Willard 84
Reed, William 232, 431,
   466, 645
Reed, Wm. 554, 592
Reeder, Benjamin 662
Reeder, Daniel F. 643,
   662
Reeder, Elizabeth 660
Reeder, James 188
Reeder, James M. 58
Reeder, John 5
Reeder, Jonathan 662
Reeder, Mary 657
Reeder, Mechailth 638
Reeder, Miciah 648
Reeder, Polly 384
Reeder, Robert B. 763
Reeder, Sarah 213
Reeder, William 198
Reekwith, John 336
Rees, Carolina 627
Rees, Catharine 133
Rees, Christopher 627
Rees, Cyrus 133
Rees, David 133
Rees, Elizabeth 133
Rees, Frederick 627
Rees, Hariet 133
Rees, Henry 627
Rees, Jeremiah 127, 133
Rees, John 133
Rees, Miria 133
Rees, Nancy 133
Rees, Polly 133
Rees, Robert 662
Rees, Sally 133
Rees, Samuel 133, 147
Rees, Sophia 133
Rees, Susanna 525
Rees, Wilmina 627
Reese, Angeline 373
Reese, David 278
Reese, Elizabeth 373,
   664
Reese, Emeline 373
Reese, Francis D. 373
Reese, George 373, 602,
   604
Reese, Hannah 171
Reese, Jacob 373
Reese, James 171
Reese, Maria 602
Reese, Nicholas J. Y.
   373
Reese, Philip 602, 604
Reese, Thomas 662
Reesy, Daniel J. 460
Reeve, Elijah Barton 503
Reeve, Fanny Ann 503
Reeve, Gabriel 503
Reeve, Hannah 503
Reeve, Joshua 733
Reeve, Polly 512
Reeve, Theresa 510
Reeve, Tracy 503
Reeve, Volney 503, 510
Reever, James 298
Reeves, Diploma L. 436

Reeves, Elijah 506
Reeves, Elizabeth 382
Reeves, Jessee 473
Reeves, John 645, 647,
   648, 652, 666, 672,
   673
Reeves, John D. 493
Reeves, Joseph 568
Reeves, Josephine 436
Reeves, Louisa 436
Reeves, Lydia 82
Reeves, Mary J. 534
Reeves, Morgan 455
Reeves, Pensela 461
Reeves, Rebecca 573
Reeves, Richard (Jr.) 79
Reeves, Solomon 84
Reeves, Thomas 49, 61,
   506
Regan, Bernard 222
Regan, John 192
Regans, Henry 203
Regans, John 185, 203
Regenatt, Ambrose 228
Regester, Robert 355
Reggs, Kezia 661
Reghert, Conrad 568
Rehapman, Alonzo 34
Rehard, Anthoney 417
Rehard, Joseph 417
Rehling, Bernard 546
Rehm, Jacob 362
Rehm, Susannah 362
Reichard, Calvin 619
Reichard, David 214
Reichard, Elizabeth 214
Reichard, Henry 599,
   601, 619, 626
Reichard, Henry R. 619
Reichard, John Peter 222
Reichard, Joseph 215
Reichard, Magdalena 214
Reichard, Margaret 214
Reichard, Samuel 214
Reichard, Sarah 619
Reichelderfer, Rebecca
   403
Reicherderfer, Vinus 403
Reicherl, Kelleau 112
Reichie, George Gilmon
   525
Reichman, Susan 567
Reid, Abraham 196
Reid, Adget 196
Reid, Adgit 196
Reid, Andrew 186
Reid, Catharine 394
Reid, David 223
Reid, Elizabeth 196,
   394, 745
Reid, Francis 394
Reid, John 394
Reid, Joseph 261
Reid, Margaret 414
Reid, Maria 394
Reid, Mary Ann 394
Reid, Matilda 196
Reid, Nathan 394
Reid, Pamelia 394

Reid, Patsey 394
Reid, Sarah 196
Reid, Sophia T. 394
Reid, Thomas 753
Reid, William 394
Reider, Catharina 236, 237
Reider, David 236, 237
Reider, Emeleia 237
Reiners, Frederick 174
Reis, Elizabeth Ann 302
Reisinger, Rhoda Ellen 409
Reiter, Amos 736
Reiter, I. H. (Rev.) 222
Reiter, William 736
Reitz, Joseph 522
Reley, John 386
Reley, Mary 382
Relfe, --- 298
Relland, George 292
Relstock, Elizabeth Barbara 572
Remel, Catharine 297
Remel, Michael 297, 718
Remey, Lewis 263
Remington, Belinda 60
Remley, Eleanor 168, 176
Remley, George 168, 176
Remly, Eleanor 154
Remly, George 154
Remson, Isaac (Jr.) 285
Remy, Alexander 632
Remy, David 632
Remy, Ealinor 632
Remy, Eleanor 632
Remy, Elias 632
Remy, Eliza Ann 632
Remy, Emily 632
Remy, Harriet 632
Remy, Hiram 632
Remy, Ibie 632
Remy, Isabel 632
Remy, James 632, 633
Remy, Jane 632
Remy, John 632
Remy, John W. 632
Remy, Julia Ann 632
Remy, Letitia 632
Remy, Lewis 632
Remy, Margaret 632
Remy, Marian 632
Remy, Sarah Ann 632
Rench, Barbary 126
Rench, Daniel 141
Rench, David 127
Rench, Jacob 127, 148
Rench, Joseph 118
Rench, Molly 119
Rench, Susannah 125
Rendall, Chauncey 527
Rendols, Polly 556
Renick, A. 402
Renick, Abel 391, 402
Renick, Adam 466
Renick, Alexander 402
Renick, Ann 391, 402
Renick, Asahel 391, 400, 402

Renick, Ashel 391
Renick, Catharine 386, 402
Renick, Eliza 6
Renick, Ellen 6
Renick, Felix W. 6
Renick, Harriet L. 402
Renick, Hiram 6
Renick, James 391, 402
Renick, Jane 402
Renick, John 391
Renick, Jonathan 386, 391, 402
Renick, Joseph O. B. 6
Renick, Josiah 402
Renick, Kitty 391
Renick, Margaret 402
Renick, Marget 391
Renick, Mary 391, 402
Renick, Polly 391
Renick, Rachael 391
Renick, Rachel 402, 459
Renick, Seymore G. 6
Renick, Susanna 117
Renick, Thomas 402
Renick, William 6
Renke, Frowe 34
Renner, Christian 336
Rennick, William S. 507
Rensberger, Magdalena 565
Renshaw, John 62
Rentfrew, Isaac 184
Rentfrew, Jacob 184
Rentfrew, James 185
Rentfrew, John 184
Rentfrew, Turpin 184
Reomeor, Sarah Ann 113
Replogle, Sarah 141
Repper, Samuel 118
Rerick, Barbary 141
Rerick, Christian 141
Rerick, David 141
Rese, Warren 586
Reshel, Magdeline 749
Resiger, Ann 173
Resiger, Benedict 173
Resoner, Henry 284
Resseiker, Christian 162
Resslar, Isaac 283
Ressler, Andrew 228
Resten, Henry 398
Resuker, Christian 162
Retter, Henry 386
Reubart, Rachel 568
Reugers, Mary A. 113
Revel, Francis H. 423
Revel, Francis Henry 428
Revel, Thos. C. 575
Revese, James 575
Rex, Jonathan 267
Rexford, Eugene 146
Rexford, Hortensia 146
Rey, Elizabeth 333
Rey, Horatio 201
Rey, James 201
Rey, John 333
Rey, Verina 333
Reybikds, Thomas 592

Reycup, Catharine 373
Reycup, John 373
Reycup, Joseph 373
Reymer, Rachel 20
Reynard, John 662
Reynolds, Almedia 436
Reynolds, Caleb 42, 733
Reynolds, Carolina 450
Reynolds, Delila 592
Reynolds, Elizabeth 591
Reynolds, George 450
Reynolds, Harris 450
Reynolds, Hope 2
Reynolds, Isiah 413
Reynolds, James 406, 592
Reynolds, Jane 592
Reynolds, Jefferson 450
Reynolds, John 450
Reynolds, Joseph 670
Reynolds, Margaret 416
Reynolds, Martha 406
Reynolds, Mary 461
Reynolds, Polly 590
Reynolds, Rebekah 450
Reynolds, Saloma 348
Reynolds, Sarah 549
Reynolds, Serepta 2
Reynolds, Sodica 746
Reynolds, Susanna 745
Reynolds, Thomas 594, 733
Reynolds, William 416, 450, 490
Reystone, Betty 462
Rhea, Elias B. 436
Rhea, Elizabeth 436
Rhea, John Wm. Harmonius 436
Rhea, Rebecca 714
Rhea, Wm. 477
Rheidler, Charles 111
Rhey, Wm. 476
Rhine, John 676
Rhine, Joshua 676
Rhine, Joshua Wilson 676
Rhinefrank, Jacb 410
Rhinehart, Jonathan 141
Rhinehart, Magdeline 570
Rhinehart, Motelene 490
Rhinehart, William R. 400
Rhoades, Catharine 577
Rhoads, Elizabeth 68
Rhoads, James 68
Rhoads, Jesse 68
Rhoads, Meria 736
Rhoads, Samuel 575
Rhoads, Susana 565
Rhoads, Susannah 68
Rhodes, Abraham 458
Rhodes, Eliza 34
Rhodes, Elizabeth 399
Rhodes, Elizabeth Jane 305
Rhodes, George 305
Rhodes, Henry 305
Rhodes, Jeremiah 305
Rhodes, Jesse 399
Rhodes, John 18, 305

939

Rhodes, Lydia Ann 305
Rhodes, Mariah 305
Rhodes, Mary 18, 305
Rhodes, Polly 13
Rhodes, Rebecca 758
Rhodes, Sanford 303
Rhodes, William 22
Rhodes, Wm. W. 305
Rhon, Samuel 746
Rhonamar, Jacob 662
Rhone, Jacob 522
Rhone, Mary 746
Ri . . . , Darcas 178
Ri . . . , Paul 178
Ribble, Nicholas 285
Ribinson, Sarah Jane 591
Ric . . . ee, Wm. 458
Ric . . . ets, Chane 458
Ric . . . ets, Chas. 458
Rice, A. 757
Rice, Abel 723
Rice, Abigail 441
Rice, Adam 86, 484
Rice, Alexander 441
Rice, Ambrose 757, 760, 762
Rice, Ambrose (II) 757, 762
Rice, Amy 64
Rice, Anabela 760
Rice, Anne 760
Rice, Caroline 589
Rice, Charles 86
Rice, Chloe 30
Rice, Clark H. 441
Rice, Daniel 498, 760
Rice, David 51, 273
Rice, Ebenezer 441
Rice, Elizabeth 582, 760
Rice, Ezekiel 498, 718
Rice, Fany 760
Rice, George 582
Rice, Hannah 582, 590
Rice, Harvey 592
Rice, Henry 184
Rice, Isaac 760
Rice, Jason 592
Rice, Jeremiah 516
Rice, John 279, 493, 760
Rice, Joseph 568
Rice, Josiah 89
Rice, Kassy 85
Rice, Levi A. 441
Rice, Lydia 760
Rice, Margaret 760
Rice, Martha Ann 607
Rice, Mary 760
Rice, Mary A. 493
Rice, Nancy 582, 592, 760, 765
Rice, Nathan 64
Rice, Obidiah 582
Rice, Orson W. 441
Rice, Phelemie 586
Rice, Philena 29
Rice, Polly 760
Rice, Rebecca 662
Rice, Rosanna 15
Rice, Russel 187, 498

Rice, Samuel B. 441
Rice, Sarah 582
Rice, Silas 184
Rice, Wm. 79
Rich, Abram 42
Rich, Ann 305
Rich, Jane 305
Rich, Jeremiah 305
Rich, Jesse 169, 172
Rich, Mary 169, 172
Rich, Polly 305
Rich, Rolly 305
Richaback, Catharine 513
Richard, Elizabeth 453
Richard, John 63, 677
Richards, Augustus 750
Richards, Aurilla 71
Richards, Benjamin 298
Richards, Catharine 677
Richards, Celia 74
Richards, Christian 478, 490
Richards, Doran 111
Richards, Elizaett 71
Richards, Elizatt 71
Richards, Henry 292
Richards, Jacob 359, 453
Richards, John 473, 553
Richards, John N. 21
Richards, Joseph 180
Richards, Leonard 738
Richards, Lois 71
Richards, Margarett 496
Richards, Marshall 71
Richards, Mills 71
Richards, Nancy 573
Richards, Peter 498
Richards, Sally Ann 71
Richards, Samuel 634
Richards, Susan E. 414
Richardson, Aaron 662
Richardson, Allen 564
Richardson, Archbard 104
Richardson, Charles W. 84
Richardson, Daniel 191
Richardson, David 285
Richardson, Drusilla 567
Richardson, Elijah 666
Richardson, Elizabeth 298, 452
Richardson, Erie 550
Richardson, George 118, 253, 564
Richardson, John 191, 298, 458
Richardson, Jonas 101
Richardson, Lydia 18
Richardson, Margaret 280
Richardson, Mary 109
Richardson, Nancy 551
Richardson, Nancy Ann 551
Richardson, Nathan 642, 648
Richardson, Oliver 42
Richardson, Parmela 101
Richardson, Phebe 661
Richardson, Polly 120

Richardson, Rebecca 426
Richardson, Robert 466
Richardson, Rufus 286
Richardson, Samuel 453
Richardson, Sarah 566
Richardson, Snow 552
Richardson, Thomas 18, 550, 564
Richardson, William 118, 191
Richardson, Zebediah 546
Richee, Rachel 458
Richey, Adam 584
Richey, Ann 586
Richey, Cath. 406
Richey, Catherine 293
Richey, George 285, 293
Richey, Jane 293
Richey, John 741
Richey, Margaret 585
Richey, Martha 84
Richey, Mary 12, 293
Richey, Philip 580
Richey, Prudence 293
Richey, Samuel 440
Richey, Thomas 293, 303, 466, 741
Richey, William 14, 586
Richey, William E. 293
Richie, Drusilla 749
Richie, Frances Maria 525
Richie, Maria B. 525
Richie, Rachel 458
Richioin, Henry 39
Richison, George 130
Richison, Henry 39
Richler, Christap Henry 106
Richman, E. 373
Richmond, Freeman 30
Richmond, Peter 504
Richmond, Wm. 316
Richy, David 609
Rickabaugh, Peter 472, 473, 480
Rickard, John 84
Ricker, Anna 146
Ricker, Geo. 146
Ricker, Julia 146
Ricketts, Benjamin 285
Ricketts, Cindrilla 518
Rickley, S. S. 356
Ricksecker, Abraham 562
Rickseker, Maria 564
Ricksucker, Henry 479
Riclenger, Elizabeth 573
Riddle, Abigal 208
Riddle, Abner 592
Riddle, Isabella 208
Riddle, James 208
Riddle, John 118, 490
Riddle, Manning R. 146
Riddle, Nancy J. 146
Riddon, John 453
Ridebaugh, George P. 603
Ridenbaugh, John Philip 323
Ridenhour, Lott 413

Ridenour, Amicy 609
Ridenour, Catherine
   353, 374
Ridenour, Christian 374
Ridenour, David 341, 373
Ridenour, Diannah 374
Ridenour, Eliza 322
Ridenour, Elizabeth 89,
   374
Ridenour, Evy 373
Ridenour, Hannah 374
Ridenour, Isaac 373
Ridenour, Jacob 322, 373
Ridenour, John 341, 373
Ridenour, Joseph 369
Ridenour, Juleyan 374
Ridenour, Levi N. 436
Ridenour, Ludwick 353,
   373, 374
Ridenour, Martin 355,
   373
Ridenour, Mathias 373
Ridenour, Michael 746
Ridenour, Mottelene 373
Ridenour, Nancy 374
Ridenour, Noah 374
Ridenour, Samuel 374
Ridenour, Sophia 374
Rider, Anna 237
Rider, Caroline 751
Rider, Catharina 237
Rider, Chrisdana 555
Rider, Chrisdena 555
Rider, David 237
Rider, Emeline 237
Rider, Hanah 574
Rider, Henry 237
Rider, Jacob 237, 555
Rider, James 751
Rider, Johanes 237
Rider, John 237
Rider, Joseph 100
Rider, Maria 237
Rider, Mary 555, 751
Rider, Michael 237
Rider, Reuben 751
Rider, Sarah Ann 372
Ridgely, William 516
Ridgley, Frederick 482
Ridgway, Eliza 406
Ridgway, Ellen 61
Ridgway, Ester 61
Ridgway, Thomas 705
Ridgway, Thorbley 406
Ridgway, Thos. 406
Ridinger, Catharine 570
Ridinger, Paul 242
Ridl . . . n, John 458
Ridley, Dean 246
Ried, Kathran 497
Rieder, Daniel F. 643
Riegal, Elizabeth 103
Riegal, J. Michael 103
Riegel, George 242, 243
Riegel, Margaret 242
Riegel, Mathias 242
Rieseger, Peter 173
Riestine, Barnett 453
Rieter, Mary Ann 518

Rifer, Christopher 9
Riffel, Jacob 668
Riffle, Catharine 665
Riffle, David 223
Riffle, John 127
Riffle, Nancy 116
Riffle, Sarah 657
Rigal, Matthias 182
Rigby, George 207
Rigby, Isaac 609
Rigby, Mary R. 207
Rigby, Phebe 207
Rigby, Richard 207
Rigel, John 575
Rigg, James 164
Rigg, John 749
Riggans, Robert 121
Riggin, J. W. 49
Riggs, Arthur 436
Riggs, Asahel 436
Riggs, Benj. 436
Riggs, Cyrus 436
Riggs, Eli 436
Riggs, Hezekiah 733
Riggs, James 79
Riggs, Jeremiah 86, 718
Riggs, Jesse 177
Riggs, John 718
Riggs, Lydia G. 519
Riggs, Margaret 436
Riggs, Pamela 436
Riggs, Rebecka 80
Riggs, Samuel 375
Riggs, Thomas 684
Right, David 453
Right, Reioth 496
Right, Simeon 715
Rike, Adam 209
Rike, Catharine 209
Rike, Daniel 209
Rike, Henry 209
Rike, John William 209
Rike, Philip 209
Riker, Eliza 619
Riker, L. 619
Riker, Lafayette 619
Riler, Nancey 385
Riley, Bridget 406
Riley, Bryan 406
Riley, Daniel 605
Riley, Edward 546
Riley, Eliza 575
Riley, Elizabeth 572
Riley, George 413
Riley, Hugh 263, 270,
   361
Riley, James 113
Riley, James Watson
   100, 113
Riley, John 380
Riley, John A. B. 575
Riley, Mary 574
Riley, Phebe 113
Riley, Sarah 387, 388
Riley, Smith 362
Riley, Susannah 124
Rily, Ellen O. 636
Rimel, Michael 718
Rinard, Isaac 733

Rinard, John 733
Rinard, Nancy 141
Rinard, Saml. K. 733
Rinearson, Ann 667
Rinebold, Barbara 379
Rinebold, Henry 379
Rinehart, Adam 575
Rinehart, Barbara 539,
   546
Rinehart, Christena 549
Rinehart, John 575
Rinehart, Mary 413
Rinehart, Peter 539
Rinehart, Philip 575
Rineholt, Catherine 521
Rineholt, Francis 522
Rinely, Mary 511
Riner, Elizabeth 436
Riner, Rebecca 436
Ringland, John 481, 484
Ringlin, Eliza 93
Rings, John 752, 753
Rings, Rachel C. 753
Rinner, Dolly 517
Ripley, Catharine 569
Ripley, David 586
Riply, Elizabeth 560
Rippel, Jacob 668
Rippith, Elizabeth 576
Rishel, Magdeline 749
Rison, Milly 550
Rison, Rola 348
Risoz, Francis 436
Risoz, Milton 436
Ritchey, Gideon 343
Ritchey, James 357
Ritchey, James B. 365
Ritchey, Jane A. 343
Ritchie, John 224
Ritchie, Polly 513
Riter, Jacobe 148
Riter, Lawrence 341
Ritrmon, Peter 662
Ritter, Frederick 516
Ritter, John 186
Ritter, Sally 570
Roach, Ann 688
Roach, Elizabeth 711
Roach, Frederick (Jr.)
   315
Roach, Price 498
Roach, Richard 688
Roade, Marah 382
Roads, Catharine 387
Roads, John 670
Roads, Jonathan 477
Roads, Manday 385
Roads, Samuel 646
Roads, Samuel 674
Roarer, Catharine 186
Roarer, Jacob 186
Roarer, Jacob (Jr.) 186
Roarer, John 186
Roarer, Mary 186
Roark, John 684
Rob, Jacob 558
Roba, Jemima 667
Robb, Andrew 7, 654, 662
Robb, Barbara 7

941

Robb, Benjamin F. 7
Robb, David 7
Robb, Dorcus 7
Robb, Dorcus Jane 7
Robb, Hannah 7
Robb, James 7
Robb, John 7, 223, 662
Robb, Johnson 645, 674
Robb, Joseph 678
Robb, Joshua 25
Robb, Margaret 667
Robb, Mary 7
Robb, Rachel 661
Robb, Samuel 7
Robb, William 7
Robbins, Aaron 203
Robbins, Amos 141
Robbins, Amos H. 203
Robbins, Bathshebe 203
Robbins, Benjamin 536
Robbins, Bersheba 141
Robbins, Catharine 66
Robbins, Cerelda L. 536
Robbins, Charles Alonzo 536
Robbins, David 536
Robbins, Deborah 203
Robbins, E. A. 536
Robbins, Edward 66
Robbins, Effie 695
Robbins, Elenor H. 203
Robbins, Elizabeth 66
Robbins, Eppaah 66
Robbins, Frederick 66
Robbins, I. E. 536
Robbins, Isaac 66
Robbins, John 66, 218
Robbins, Jonathan 695
Robbins, Joseph H. 109
Robbins, Joseph H. (Jr.) 109
Robbins, Lawrence 66
Robbins, Margaret 66
Robbins, Mary E. 536
Robbins, Nancy Ann 66
Robbins, Orin 30
Robbins, Sally 663
Robbins, Samuel 203
Robbins, Thomas 546
Robbins, W. E. 536
Robenson, James 14
Robenson, Jane 592
Roberson, William 121
Robert, Adaline 593
Robert, Phebe 576
Roberts, Abel 51
Roberts, Abraham 248, 250, 251
Roberts, Amos 630
Roberts, Anderson 546, 550
Roberts, Andrew 550
Roberts, Ann 447
Roberts, Betsey 519
Roberts, Charles 66, 299, 466
Roberts, Cynthia 66
Roberts, Daniel 453
Roberts, Edward 389

Roberts, Eliza 66
Roberts, Elizabeth 51
Roberts, Fergus 250, 251
Roberts, Frances 293
Roberts, George 374
Roberts, Grace 714
Roberts, Harlon 66
Roberts, Henry 274, 355
Roberts, Isaac 86, 121, 466, 662
Roberts, James 374
Roberts, James M. 550
Roberts, Jane 51
Roberts, John 4, 66, 127, 207, 292, 339, 374, 436
Roberts, John L. 546
Roberts, John W. 609
Roberts, John Wesley 207
Roberts, Joseph 253, 275, 374
Roberts, Leonard 742
Roberts, Lydia 250, 251
Roberts, Margaret 45, 374
Roberts, Mary 66, 551
Roberts, Mary Ann 207, 248
Roberts, Mary Chloe 436
Roberts, Mary Jane 250, 251
Roberts, Nathan 265, 268, 279
Roberts, Phebe 663
Roberts, Phinias 662
Roberts, Pryor 79
Roberts, Rachel 447
Roberts, Rebecca 467, 742
Roberts, Rebecca Ann 250, 251
Roberts, Richard 447
Roberts, Richard E. 18
Roberts, Russel 66
Roberts, Ruth 279
Roberts, Saml. G. 79
Roberts, Saml. S. 269
Roberts, Samuel S. 263, 266
Roberts, Samuel T. 259
Roberts, Sarah 291, 374, 447
Roberts, Solomon 279
Roberts, Thomas 20, 291
Roberts, Timothy P. 528
Roberts, William 18, 51, 66, 283, 374
Roberts, William C. 420
Roberts, William R. 293
Roberts, Wm. R. 293
Robertson, Alexander 453
Robertson, Caroline 693
Robertson, Catharine 436
Robertson, David 666
Robertson, Eleanor 436
Robertson, Elizabeth 15, 714
Robertson, Eva 328
Robertson, Ezra 436

Robertson, Ezra R. 693
Robertson, Hannah 292
Robertson, Harriet 436
Robertson, Henry 18
Robertson, Huldah 436
Robertson, John 18, 168, 172, 178, 292, 413, 471
Robertson, Joshua 14, 15
Robertson, Mary 168
Robertson, Mary Ann 436
Robertson, Rachel 436
Robertson, Rhoda 436
Robertson, S. G. 328
Robertson, Sally 18
Robertson, Samuel 14
Robertson, Samuel G. 328
Robertson, Sarah 521
Robertson, William 550
Robertson, Wm. 436
Robeson, Abigail M. 436
Robeson, John 643
Robeson, Mary Jane 436
Robeson, Rhoda Ann 436
Robeson, Samuel H. 413
Robeson, Sarah Elizabeth 436
Robeson, Sidna 743
Robeson, Wilson 743
Robinett, James 568
Robins, Benj. 223
Robins, Daniel 458, 460, 481
Robins, David 141
Robins, John 481
Robins, Joseph 298
Robins, Matthias 386
Robins, Roswell 141
Robins, Samuel 141
Robins, Sezelda Ann 141
Robinson, Abraham 210, 516
Robinson, Alex 597
Robinson, Alexander 595
Robinson, Andrew 373, 647
Robinson, Angeline M. 588
Robinson, Barbara 347
Robinson, Charles 273
Robinson, Edmund 676, 681
Robinson, Eleanor 592
Robinson, Eliza W. 586
Robinson, Elizabeth 50, 347, 647, 676, 679
Robinson, Ella Wical 533
Robinson, Ezra 642
Robinson, Hannah 540
Robinson, Henry 746
Robinson, Henson 662
Robinson, Isaac H. 522
Robinson, James 294, 373, 444, 486, 524, 596
Robinson, James H. 493, 647
Robinson, James T. 386
Robinson, Jane 596, 647, 676

942

Robinson, Jean 727
Robinson, John 50, 210, 283, 347, 392, 444
Robinson, John C. 758
Robinson, John H. 647
Robinson, John J. 493
Robinson, John S. 688
Robinson, John W. 586
Robinson, Joseph 30, 33, 592, 647, 676
Robinson, Kennedy 286
Robinson, Louisa 84
Robinson, Lucinda 676
Robinson, Lydia Ann 676
Robinson, Margaret Letete 714
Robinson, Margaret M. 758
Robinson, Mary 592, 747
Robinson, Milton G. 647
Robinson, Nancy 676
Robinson, Nancy G. 589
Robinson, Noah 79
Robinson, Patterson 592
Robinson, Polly 347
Robinson, Reaves 586
Robinson, Richard 373
Robinson, Robert 283, 338
Robinson, Robt. 466
Robinson, Rose 373
Robinson, Samuel 596, 676
Robinson, Sarah 550, 589, 593
Robinson, Sarah Jane 210
Robinson, Solomon 540
Robinson, Sophronia 79
Robinson, Thomas B. 647
Robinson, Thos. R. 546
Robinson, William 285, 341, 466, 546, 592, 680, 727
Robinson, William L. 609
Robinson, Wm. M. 592
Robison, Alexander 146
Robison, David 737
Robison, Eliza 690
Robison, Elizabeth 388
Robison, Gresoll 374
Robison, Hannah Maria 690
Robison, Harold 700
Robison, James H. 671
Robison, John L. 690
Robison, John R. 64
Robison, Joseph 86, 141
Robison, Mary 374, 700
Robison, Mary Ann 690
Robison, Nancy 374
Robison, Philip 374
Robison, Robert 374, 670
Robison, Sally 743
Robison, Thomas 168
Robison, Thomas S. 62
Robison, William 374
Robuck, Naomi 20
Roby, Abby Ameria 766
Roby, Amelia 766

Roby, Catherine 280
Roby, Charles C. 766
Roby, Chs. C. 766
Roby, Horatio 575
Roby, Jane H. 575
Roby, John 345
Roby, Margaret 345
Roby, Precious R. 575
Roby, Ruel 546, 552
Roby, Ruel A. 546
Roby, William 516
Rochard, Margaret 465
Rochell, John (Capt.) 286
Rock, Doranda 438
Rock, Frederick 438
Rock, Jeanette 334
Rock, Samuel 493
Rockey, Barbara 242
Rockey, C. 242
Rockey, Catharine 242
Rockey, Charles 242
Rockey, J. H. 242
Rockey, Jacob 242
Rockford, Margaret 465
Rockhold, Elisha John 374
Rockhold, Ellen 374
Rockhold, Ephraim 374
Rockhold, Jacob 374
Rockhold, John 466
Rockwell, Doranda 438
Rockwell, Dorinda 439
Rockwell, Frederick 439, 440
Rockwell, George 440
Rockwell, James 439, 440
Rockwell, John H. 439
Rockwell, Joseph 439
Rockwell, William H. 522
Rockwood, David 30
Rockwood, Emeline 29
Rode, Cath. 403
Rode, John 662
Rodebaugh, David 210
Rodecher, George 25
Rodeheffer, Samuel 216
Rodenbaugh, Philip 333
Roderick, John 135
Roderick, Susannah 459
Rodes, Delilah 200
Rodes, Eden 200
Rodes, Henry 200
Rodes, Jacob 200
Rodes, James 458
Rodes, Jefferson 200
Rodes, Maria 200
Rodes, Mary 200
Rodgees, Willian 321
Rodger, Linas 498
Rodger, Susannah 501
Rodger . . . , Thomas 458
Rodgers, Connel 290
Rodgers, Dolly 457
Rodgers, Emily 436
Rodgers, Hamilton 490
Rodgers, Isaac 436
Rodgers, James 486, 490
Rodgers, Jennie 463
Rodgers, John 269, 275, 546

Rodgers, Keziah 436
Rodgers, Lewis 490
Rodgers, Lydia Ann 436
Rodgers, Richard 551
Rodgers, William 319, 320, 321
Rodkey, John 146
Rodkey, Jos. 146
Rodkey, Josiah 146
Rodywas, Jean 454
Roe, Em. 472
Roe, Richard 469, 470
Roe, Stephen 264
Roebuc . . . , Rose 458
Roebuck, Albert 96
Roebuck, Benj. 466
Roebuck, Benjamin 106, 115
Roebuck, Branson 96
Roebuck, Catharine 96
Roebuck, Catharine A. 96
Roebuck, Elizabeth 106
Roebuck, Elizabeth C. 96
Roebuck, Elizabeth G. 96
Roebuck, Garrison 96
Roebuck, Geo. 96
Roebuck, George 96
Roebuck, Greenley 105
Roebuck, Henry N. 96
Roebuck, I. M. 96
Roebuck, Ishmael 96
Roebuck, James 106
Roebuck, John 96, 115
Roebuck, Joseph 115
Roebuck, Lorenzo 106
Roebuck, Mary 96
Roebuck, Parley Ann 105
Roebuck, Phebe A. 96
Roebuck, Rewel 96
Roebuck, Ruel 96
Roebuck, Sarah 96
Roebuck, Sarah E. 96
Roebuck, Warren 96
Roeder, John C. 42
Roehm, Andrew 603, 609
Roerbaugh, John 293
Roesner, Elizabeth 115
Roesner, Margaret 115
Roesz, Henry 388
Roetwick, Manley 42
Roff, Edward 662, 670
Rogan, Nelly 13
Rogan, Patrick 389
Rogard, Mahala 466
Rogers, Aaron 695
Rogers, Abigail 695
Rogers, Alexander 182
Rogers, Amos St. 686
Rogers, Ann 521
Rogers, Benjamin 453
Rogers, Bennett 728
Rogers, Bernard 484
Rogers, Eliphalet 498
Rogers, Elizabeth 753
Rogers, Jacob 269
Rogers, James 466, 469, 471, 475, 476, 481, 482, 486
Rogers, James L. 182

Rogers, Jane 178
Rogers, John 715, 753
Rogers, Joseph 177, 721
Rogers, Lucy Ann 588
Rogers, Mary Ann 695
Rogers, Mathew 178
Rogers, Nancy 290
Rogers, Nelson 369
Rogers, Rachael 123
Rogers, S. S. 280
Rogers, Susannah 464
Rogers, Thomas 127, 472, 474
Rogers, Thomas O. B. 141
Rogers, Thos. 477
Rogers, William 522, 746
Rohleous, Clemmens 604
Rohleous, Henry 604
Rohn, Magdalene 133
Rohr, Christian 666
Rohrer, Catherine 232
Rohrer, Christian 217
Rohrer, John 232
Rohrer, Joseph 184
Rohrer, Samuel 200
Rohris, Mary 690
Roht, Leonard 388
Rohtsen, David 581
Roin, George 555
Rokhill, William 672
Roland, Edward 257
Roland, Jane 385
Roland, John Richard 516
Roland, Perry 257
Roland, Wm. 269
Rolands, James 160
Roledsco, Collier 746
Roler, Susan 77
Rolf, Edward 669
Roll, Abigail 657
Roll, Isaac 148
Roll, Joseph 672
Roll, Rachel 663
Rolland, Joseph 718
Rollens, John 297
Rollings, Mahitable 127
Rollings, Mary 124
Rollins, A. 759
Rollins, Almon 759
Rollins, Angeline 519
Rollins, Celesta Ann 759
Rollins, Eliza 498
Rollins, Esther 141
Rollins, Harriett Amanda 759
Rollins, Jonathan 141
Rollins, Joseph 134
Rollins, Julia Ann 759
Rollins, Mary 141, 511
Rollins, Mary Ann 518
Rollins, Mary E. 759
Rollins, Mary Jane 141
Rollins, Myhew 134, 141
Rollins, Myhow 127
Rollins, Nancy 498
Rollins, Sarah 121
Rollins, Sophia 759
Rollins, William 759
Rollins, Wm. F. 141

Rolston, Andrew 646, 675
Rolston, David 647
Rolston, Edward 646, 675
Rolston, Eleanor 646
Rolston, Elenor 647, 675
Rolston, James 647
Rolston, John 647
Rolston, Margaret 646, 647, 675
Rolston, Martha 646, 675
Rolston, Mary 646, 675
Rolston, Robert 646, 675
Rolston, William 647, 662
Romar, Barnard 108
Romich, Abraham 297
Romich, Hannah 297
Romig, Abraham 718
Romig, Gabriel 564, 575
Romig, John 561
Romine, A. 698
Romine, Emily 698
Romine, Jesse 698
Romine, Olivia 336
Romine, Rebecca 82
Romine, Thomas 466
Roming, John 562
Rommie, Phebe 458
Rondefelt, Jacob 228
Rood, Avery 34
Rood, Catharine 178
Rood, Ezra 755
Rood, Hiram 644
Rood, John 178, 644
Roof, Catherine 519
Roof, John W. 104
Roof, Sarah J. 239
Rook, Frederick 672
Rook, John 466
Rook, William 475
Rooker, Phebe 136
Rooks, Polly G. 458
Roop, A. 613
Roop, Amos 602, 613
Roop, Clara O. 611
Roop, Eliza 450
Roop, Frederick 104
Roop, Herny 450
Roop, John 613
Roop, M. 611
Roop, R. 613
Roop, Rachel 613
Roop, Rebecca Ann 613
Roop, S. 611
Roop, Simon P. 613
Roop, William Elden 611
Roop, William M. 450
Roope, Henry 450
Root, Abner 440
Root, Charles C. 672
Root, Elizabeth 440
Root, Jane 28
Root, Lorain 32
Root, M. 403
Root, Rachel 69
Root, Sarah 146
Root, Sylvester 403
Root, Wm. 403
Rooyse, Susanna 506

Roph, Hannah 761
Ropp, Jacob 556
Roreback, David 42
Rorer, Catherine 232
Rorer, John 232
Rorick, Henry 450
Rorick, Jesse 450
Rorick, Jonas 450
Rorick, Margaret 450
Rorick, Rowland P9 450
Rorick, William 450
Rosabone, Nancy 112
Rosaborn, William 94
Rose, Erasmus 260
Rose, John 366
Rose, Lewis 646, 674
Rose, Lucy 581
Rose, Maria 403
Rose, Nancy 253
Rose, Obadiah 609
Rose, Peter 253
Rose, Robt. 253
Rose, Stephen 646, 674
Rose, William D. 154
Roseberry, . . . y 760
Roseberry, Ebenezer 760
Roseberry, John 760
Roseberry, Joseph 592
Roseberry, Mary 760
Roseberry, Michael 575
Rosebrook, Helkiah 18
Rosebrook, Henry 18
Rosebrook, Susannah 18
Rosenberger, David 522
Rosenberger, Mary E. 520
Rosenberger, Nicholas 522
Rosenmiller, D. P. 237
Roses, Mary 87
Roshong, Daniel 575
Rosman, Mary Ann 497
Ross, . . . ames 458
Ross, . . . nn 458
Ross, A. 618
Ross, A. L. 112
Ross, Absalom 431
Ross, Alexander 50
Ross, Almina 20
Ross, Angus 50
Ross, Ann 493
Ross, Asten 671
Ross, Benjamin 671
Ross, Betsy 118
Ross, C. 619
Ross, Catharine 619
Ross, Charles 415
Ross, Clarissa 146, 685
Ross, Clement 314
Ross, Daniel 50, 611
Ross, Daniel (Sr.) 733
Ross, David 50, 441, 662
Ross, Deborah 387
Ross, Eliza A. 611
Ross, Elizabeth 314, 638, 671
Ross, Georganna 146
Ross, George D. 150
Ross, Gray 708
Ross, Griffin 611
Ross, Hannah 291

944

Ross, Henry 390
Ross, Henry C. 431
Ross, Henry I. 687
Ross, Hugh 584
Ross, Ignatius 223
Ross, Isaac 84
Ross, Isabella 291
Ross, J. 619
Ross, J. B. 619
Ross, J. H. 611
Ross, J. K. (Dr.) 611
Ross, Jacob 102
Ross, James 291, 357, 371, 466, 498, 611, 619
Ross, James H. 141
Ross, Jane 128, 291, 302, 314, 611, 657
Ross, Jas. B. 431
Ross, Jean 671
Ross, Jennie 455
Ross, John 50, 105, 291, 490, 611, 651, 666, 671, 685
Ross, John B. 303, 314
Ross, John W. 141, 150
Ross, Joseph 141, 611, 651, 666
Ross, Joseph B. 619
Ross, Juda 141
Ross, Kelita 619
Ross, Letitia 455
Ross, Lewis 141
Ross, Lurany 574
Ross, Margaret 611
Ross, Mary 50, 107, 291, 314, 708
Ross, Mary C. 611
Ross, Mary E. 141
Ross, Mary L. 623
Ross, Matthias 672
Ross, Milton J. 623
Ross, N . . . haniel 458
Ross, Nancy 608
Ross, Nathaniel 392
Ross, O. 618
Ross, Oliver S. 618
Ross, Perris B. 431
Ross, Philip 490
Ross, Phineas 666
Ross, Polly 105
Ross, Rachael 384
Ross, Rachel 146, 150, 664
Ross, Randall 314
Ross, Rebecca 291, 453, 611
Ross, Robert 150, 490, 651, 671
Ross, Robert E. 431
Ross, Saml. A. 150
Ross, Samuel 150, 291
Ross, Samuel A. 150
Ross, Sarah 415, 671
Ross, Sarah Ann 611
Ross, Sarah Ann D. 611
Ross, Sarah J. 619
Ross, Thomas 291, 387, 666, 685

Ross, Thomas A. 666
Ross, Thomas S. 146
Ross, Virginia S. 146
Ross, W. 611
Ross, William 50, 118, 314, 611
Ross, William R. 611
Ross, Willis 619
Ross, Winney 118
Ross, Winnie 671
Ross, Wm. 141, 611
Rossel, Debby 586
Rossman, Elizabeth 694
Roswell, Zachariah 284
Rotch, Thos. 555
Rotcher, Christian 546
Roth, Conrad 560
Roth, Eleanor 498
Roth, Solomon 746
Rotrick, Dan 477
Rott, Joseph 546
Rott, Wilhelmina 237
Rotten, Ellenor 467
Rottinghaus, Elizabeth 546
Rottinghouse, John F. 546
Rotuck, Daniel 485
Rougrant, E. X. 522
Rouh, Ignathus 113
Rouk, Jonathan D. 200
Rouker, Joseph 530
Rouley, Joseph 84
Roult, James 453
Roulton, Chas. 575
Round, James M. (Sr.) 304
Rounsifer, Quick 297
Rour, George 749
Rousculp, Anna Mary 373
Rousculp, Daniel 373
Rousculp, George 373
Rousculp, Jacob 373
Rousculp, John 373
Rousculp, Peter 373
Rousculp, Philip 373
Rousculp, Sally 373
Rousculp, Samuel 373
Rouse, Catharine 717
Rouse, Cynthia 713
Rouse, Jacob 428
Rouse, John 505
Rouse, Martha 505
Rouse, Mary 302
Rouse, Reason 505
Rouse, Thomas 49, 505
Rousey, Mary Ann 401
Rousey, Wm. B. 401
Roush, Catharine 81
Roush, Christina 575
Roush, Cornelius 516
Roush, Eliza 79
Roush, Elizabeth 154
Roush, Francis 91
Roush, Frederick 575
Roush, George 154, 156, 160
Roush, George B. 89
Roush, Jacob 79
Roush, John 575

Roush, Jonas 84
Roush, Lydia 84
Roush, Magilina 575
Roush, Mariah 161
Roush, Sarah 77
Roush, Thomas 161
Roush, Wm. 84
Rouskins, Rachael 717
Route, Charles 106
Routh, John 546
Routzon, Albert M. 146
Routzon, Jemima 146
Routzon, Mary E. 146
Routzsong, Daniel 436
Routzsong, Lucinda 436
Rouzer, John 133
Roveland, Mary 458
Row, Anna 399
Row, Catharine 399, 555
Row, Elizabeth 399, 555
Row, George 555, 740
Row, Jacob 399, 555
Row, John 399, 555
Row, Lydia 555
Row, Magdalena 555
Row, Margaret 399
Row, Michael 399
Row, Milton 436
Row, Sally 555
Rowan, Alice 762
Rowan, Elizabeth 762
Rowan, John 762
Rowan, Josephine 762
Rowe, Adison 407
Rowe, Conny 490
Rowe, D. 407
Rowe, Dudley 407
Rowe, Elizabeth 493, 590
Rowe, George 67, 206
Rowe, Jno. 407
Rowe, Sandridge 490
Rowe, Sarah 572
Rowe, Susannah 67
Rowe, William 493
Rowel, Jerusha 33
Rowell, William 522
Rowen, Alexr. 392
Rowland, Elenor 607
Rowland, Levi 623
Rowland, Matthew 553
Rowland, Robt. 261
Rowland, Wm. 733
Rowlen, Rebecca 49
Rowley, Betsey 79
Rowley, Diodeme 35
Rowley, Mary 76
Rowley, Ransom 746
Rownd, James M. 174
Rowyer, Abraham 197
Rowyer, Elizabeth 197
Rowyer, George 197
Rowyer, Henry 197
Rowyer, John 197
Rowyer, Polly 197
Royal, Charles 127
Royal, Hannah 124
Royce, Lodemia 609
Royce, Lodusky 610
Royce, Lydia 610

Royel, Merrall 592
Royer, Ann 521
Royer, Hannah 519
Royer, John 528
Ruark, Arthur 450
Rubble, Jos. 146
Rubble, Margaret 146
Rubble, Michael 146
Rubble, Susannah 146
Rubert, Amelia 568
Rubert, Elizabeth 45
Rubert, Hannah 576
Ruble, Simon 738
Ruby, Jacob 187
Ruch, Aaron 127
Ruch, George 709
Ruch, Salome 709
Ruch, Susannah 690
Rucker, Ambrose 156
Rucker, Eliza 310
Rucker, Elizabeth 307
Rucker, Garland 159
Rucker, George 307
Rucker, George W. 310
Rucker, Lemuel 156, 159
Rucker, Lemuel (Jr.) 159
Rucker, Lemuel (Sr.) 159
Rucker, Pascal 159
Rucker, Robert 307, 310
Rucker, Sally 156
Rucker, Sarah A. 310
Rucker, Sarah Ann 307
Ruckman, Peter 440
Ruckman, Thomas W. 551
Rud, Stephen 297
Rudersill, Tobias 763
Rudesill, Tobias 761
Rudie, William 453
Rudolph, Julia Ann 581
Rudy, Andrew J. 141
Rudy, Cath. 141
Rudy, Elias 146
Rudy, Elizabeth 141
Rudy, Harman 146
Rudy, James 141
Rudy, John 141, 163, 165
Rudy, Martha 123
Rudy, Mary Ann 141
Rudy, Nancy 146
Rudy, Sally 120
Rudy, Susann 141
Rue, Benjamin 680
Rue, Catharine 658
Rue, Mary 680
Rueff, John 508
Ruegger, Jacob 228
Ruffner, Frederick 337
Ruffner, Peter 352
Ruffner, Peter J. 352
Ruffner, Savillah 352
Rugg, David 33
Ruggels, George 127
Ruggles, Benjamin 152,
   153, 156, 159, 160,
   164, 173
Ruggles, Clarissa 152,
   153, 164
Ruggles, Elizabeth 546,
   552

Ruggles, John 546
Rugh, Michael 354
Rugles, Benjamin 159
Ruharts, Sarah 717
Ruhl, Elisbat 276
Ruhl, George 276
Ruhl, Michael 584
Ruker, William 118
Rule, Jacob 278
Rule, Lawrence 14
Rule, Susan 521
Rulor, Wm. 401
Rumbaugh, Daniel 337
Rumbaugh, Nathaniel 337
Rummell, Susanna 761
Rummes, Sarah 709
Rumnalds, Benjamin 466
Rumple, John 522
Rumsey, Lewis 42
Rumsey, Milow 141
Rumsvners, Sarah 454
Run, Gabriel J. 527
Rundle, Betsey 291
Runes, Lucreid 576
Runion, Absalam 666
Runion, Elizabeth 307
Runkle, Polly 379
Runkle, Samuel 379
Runnel, Amelia 125
Runnels, Ann 373
Runnels, Benjamin 373
Runnels, Elizabeth 373
Runnels, James 373
Runnels, Jane 373
Runnels, Joseph 373
Runnels, Mary 308, 373
Runnels, Nancy 373
Runnels, Sarah 373
Runnels, Susanna 609
Runnil, John 761
Runnion, Absalom 672
Runyan, Benham 662
Runyan, Christian 746
Runyan, Hugh E. 746
Runyan, John 428, 662
Runyan, Mary 659, 746
Runyan, Nancy 746
Runyon, Beall 436
Runyon, Benjamin 662
Runyon, Elias L. 689
Runyon, Elizabeth 436
Runyon, Henry 689
Runyon, Jacob 436
Runyon, John 436
Runyon, Joseph 662
Runyon, Martin 436
Runyon, Martin S. 336
Runyon, Massa 436
Rupe, Joshua 88
Rupel, Arche 479
Rupel, Thomas 466
Rupell, Archabald 471
Rupell, Arche 479
Rupell, Elizabeth 508
Rupp, Margaret 302
Ruppell, Arche 479
Ruse, Daniel 189
Ruse, George 190
Ruse, Jacob 190

Ruse, Mary 190
Ruse, Nancy 190
Ruse, Nicholas 189, 190
Ruse, Phebe 190
Rusell, Thomas 466
Rush, Aaron 392
Rush, Abner 490
Rush, Andrew 390, 392,
   466
Rush, Bethuel 173, 179
Rush, Catharine 127, 490
Rush, Catherine 392, 461
Rush, Darcas 173
Rush, Elias 165
Rush, Elizabeth 118
Rush, G . . . 458
Rush, George 392
Rush, Henry 392
Rush, Isaac 174
Rush, Isaiah 338
Rush, Jacob 153, 179,
   387
Rush, James 121, 392,
   453
Rush, Jeremiah 155, 165
Rush, Jesse 118, 546
Rush, John 390, 392, 490
Rush, Jonas 609
Rush, Joshua 166
Rush, Julian 548
Rush, Lemuel 141
Rush, Lewis 493
Rush, Liddie 461
Rush, Margaret 463
Rush, Maria 141
Rush, Mary 155, 165,
   166, 390, 392, 458
Rush, Moses 387, 392
Rush, Paul 162, 173
Rush, Peter 387, 392
Rush, Prudence 153, 179
Rush, Runnel 390
Rush, Samuel 490, 493
Rush, Sarah 173, 463
Rush, Susannah 392
Rush, Thomas 141
Rush, Westley 392
Rush, William 141, 390,
   453
Rushau, John Theodore
   115
Rushau, Mary Theresa
   Caroline 115
Rusk, Ann Maria 374
Rusk, James 373, 662
Rusk, John 374, 391
Rusk, Margaret 373
Rusk, Margaret Ann 374
Rusk, Mary Ann 374
Rusk, Samuel 380
Rusley, James 516
Russel, Benj. 406
Russel, George 262, 268
Russel, James 84
Russel, John 127
Russel, Luther 670
Russel, Norman 764
Russel, Samuel 568
Russell, --- 479

Russell, Alethia 684
Russell, Andrew 546, 552
Russell, Catharine 632
Russell, Elizabeth 466,
    508, 592
Russell, George 70
Russell, Hannah 146
Russell, Hiram N. 70
Russell, Isaac 133,
    141, 575
Russell, James 203,
    213, 473, 592
Russell, James H. 70
Russell, John 458
Russell, Joseph 546
Russell, Lois 612
Russell, Luther 662
Russell, Lydia 410
Russell, Mahala 146
Russell, Nancy 292
Russell, Phebe 70
Russell, Phineas S. 612
Russell, Rhoda 92
Russell, Robert 84
Russell, Samuel 632
Russell, Sarah 290, 546
Russell, Susan J. 70
Russell, William 79,
    161, 684
Russell, William A. 70
Russell, William M. 70
Russell, Wm. 146
Rust, Elijah 36
Rutan, Arsula 115
Rutcil, John N. 36
Ruteager, Valentine 522
Ruth, James 337
Rutherford, Danl. 733
Rutherford, John 485,
    486
Rutherford, M. S. 89
Rutherford, Moses 89
Ruthledge, William 342
Rutledge, Benjamin 14
Rutledge, Jacob 252
Rutledge, Jno. D. 261,
    268
Rutledge, John D. 266
Rutledge, Margaret 342
Rutledge, Samuel 14
Rutledge, Susan 374
Rutledge, Wm. 478
Rutter, Benjamin 360
Rutter, George 672
Rutter, John 156
Rutter, Joseph 564
Rutter, Mary 181
Rutter, Michael 177, 181
Rutter, William 516
Ryan, Ausman 733
Ryan, Benj. 466
Ryan, Dennis 706
Ryan, James 345, 580
Ryan, John 334, 374
Ryan, John D. 345
Ryan, Lawrence 389
Ryan, Mary 345
Ryan, Mary Elizabeth 374
Ryan, Rody 345

Ryan, Rose 374
Ryan, William 374
Ryan, Wm. 358
Ryder, C. 237
Ryder, Catharine Anna
    237
Ryder, D. 237
Ryder, Michael 237
Ryder, Sarah 237
Rye, Maria 266
Rykendall, Rebecca 467
Ryley, Mary 290
Ryley, Wm. F. 290
Rynard, Catharine 659
Rynearson, Minney 666
Ryner, Lida 72
Ryniar, Susannah 382
Ryon, Abigail 196
Ryon, Joseph 196
Ryther, James 718
Ryther, Mary 85
Ryther, Sally 79

--- S ---

Saary, Solomon 466
Sabin, Charles 146
Sabin, David 355
Sabin, James C. 689
Sabin, Lorenzo 146
Sabin, Nancy 355
Sabin, Warren 678
Sabin, William H. 42
Sabins, Rebecca 590
Sackett, Noahdiah 30
Sackman, Agnes Elizabeth
    436
Sackman, Chas. Soloman
    436
Sackman, Cornelius S.
    420
Sackman, Helen Alice 420
Sackman, Henry Wm. 436
Sackman, John Michael
    436
Sackman, Mary Elizabeth
    436
Sackman, Oliver 436
Sackman, Samantha 436
Sackman, Samuel 420
Sadderis, Frederick 568
Sadler, Alexander 467
Sadler, Amelia 467
Sadler, Susannah 459
Sadler, William 466
Saerford, Thos. H. 90
Saffer, Jonas 760
Saffle, David 375
Saffle, Deborah 375
Saffle, Martha 375
Saffle, Orlando 375
Saffley, Mary 45
Safford, Adeline 551
Safford, Catherine 727
Safford, John 86
Safford, John H. 79
Safford, Lydia 727

Safford, Robert 718,
    727, 728
Sagar, Abraham 592, 597
Sagar, Bengamin 586
Sagar, Hannah 593
Sagar, Henry 592
Sagar, Levi 592
Sagar, Margaret 593
Sagar, Mary Ann 590
Sagar, Rosanah 585
Sage, Alvin R. 280
Sage, Caroline Rhoda 765
Sage, Eleanor Amanda 765
Sage, Emelia 588
Sage, Emily 765
Sage, Emily Harriet 765
Sage, H. H. 405
Sage, Harlehigh 387
Sage, Harleleigh 392, 393
Sage, Harriet 765
Sage, Harry 405
Sage, John Wesley 765
Sage, Roswell 765
Sage, Sarah Marietta 765
Sage, Seymore Norton 765
Sager, Abraham 596
Sager, Adam 592
Sager, Christian 592
Sager, Margaret 586, 591
Sager, Michael 61
Sager, William 62
Sagere, Racheal 555
Sahee, Elizabeth 238
Sahee, Michael 238
Sahm, Elizabeth 377
Sahm, Jacob 377
Sahm, Susannah 373
Said, Elizabeth 585
Said, Susan 584
Sailer, Ulrich 186
Sailor, Jacob 491
Sailor, Mary 518
Sailor, Samuel 268
Sailor, Samuel (Jr.) 255
Sailsbery, Wm. H. 619
Sailsbury, --- 75
Sain, Christian Kiser
    377
Sain, David Wilson 377
Sain, Jacob 369, 377
Sain, Jacob (Jr.) 377
Sain, Levi 377
Sain, Luertisha 377
Sain, Margaret Ann
    Whitmer 377
Sain, Mary 364
Sain, Matilda McFadden
    377
Sain, Peter 376
Sain, Philip 377
Sain, Samuel Manley 377
Sain, Sarah 377
Sain, Wm. Reynolds 377
Saint, Mary 741
St.Clair, --- (Gen.) 98
St.Clair, Arthur (Gov.)
    469
St.Clair, Columbus 765
St.Clair, Daniel 283

St.Clair, Elizabeth 765
St.Clair, Eunice 765
St.Clair, Francis 765
St.Clair, George 765
St.Clair, George (Jr.)
765
St.Clair, Hannah 765
St.Clair, James 765
St.Clair, John 286
St.Clair, Joseph 765
St.Clair, Leonard 259
St.Clair, Mariah 765
St.Clair, Perry 516
St.Clair, Peter 765
St.Clair, Robert 297
St.Clair, Samuel 765
St.Clair, Sarah 765
St.John, Elizabeth 663
St.John, Henry 445
St.John, James 663
St.John, Jno. 642
St.John, Job 646
St.John, John 642, 646,
663
St.John, Mary 663
St.John, Noah 646
St.John, S. W. 765
St.John, Seth 667
St.John, Stephen 765
St.John, Thomas 420
St.Rogers, Amos 686
Saladay, Nancy 511
Sale, Lydia 64
Salee, William 417
Sales, Elmaretta 335
Sales, Mary Ann 746
Sales, Nathan G. 318
Sales, Phebe Ann 744
Salesbury, Peter 42
Salisberry, Edward 160
Salisbury, Edward 175,
310
Salisbury, John 516
Salisbury, S. S. 179
Salisbury, Sally 179
Salladay, Alonzo 504
Salladay, Christena 500
Salladay, David 500, 504
Salladay, Eliza Ann 305
Salladay, Elizabeth 500
Salladay, Emeline 504
Salladay, George 305,
500, 516
Salladay, John 500
Salladay, Josfus 504
Salladay, Mary 500, 504
Salladay, Minerva 504
Salladay, Nancy 500
Salladay, Neely 500
Salladay, Octavius 504
Salladay, Philip 500
Salladay, Sally 500
Salladay, Samuel 500,
516
Salladay, Sarah 305, 504
Salladay, Thomas 305
Sallady, Mary 514
Sallee, Nimrod 417
Sallee, William 662

Sallow, Sarah 85
Salmons, Elizabeth 634
Salmons, James 634
Salmons, Levi 634
Salmons, Levi Reed 634
Salmons, Mary 634
Salmons, Sarah 634
Salmons, William 634
Salsbury, Noah 681
Salsbury, Runel 42
Salsbury, William 516
Saltenright, Anne 760
Salters, Elizabeth 539
Salts, Edward 630
Salts, John 634
Salts, Matilda 630
Saltzgafer, Mary 347
Saltzgaver, Henry 347
Salyers, Sarah 573
Samard, Sarah 456
Sambauch, George 228
Sammas, Elizabeth 454,
457
Sammons, Eliza Ann 250,
251
Sammons, Elizabeth 250,
251
Sammons, John 250, 251
Sammons, Roseanna 250,
251
Sammons, Sarah Ellen
250, 251
Sammons, Walter 250, 251
Sample, Caldwell 672
Sample, Isaac N. W. 436
Sample, James 491
Sample, Jane 458
Sample, Levi T. 436
Sampsel, Catherine 746
Sampson, Caty 514
Sampson, Hamilton 531
Sampson, Matilda 518
Sams, Ann 174
Sams, Charlotte 449
Sams, Jonas 174
Samson, Amos 679
Samson, David 160, 165,
170
Samson, Susanna 165
Samuel, Maria 555
Sanaft, Rhoda 115
Sanaft, Sarah Jane 115
Sanborn, Geo. W. 255
Sanborn, Jno. W. 92
Sanborn, John 255
Sanborn, Mary Ann 255
Sanborn, Robert 361
Sanborne, R. 361
Sance, Wm. 739
Sanders, Aaron 141
Sanders, Amsea 127
Sanders, Charlotte 375
Sanders, Dennis 575
Sanders, Eliphalet 71
Sanders, George 375, 377
Sanders, Hezekiah 662
Sanders, Horace 30
Sanders, John 377
Sanders, Mary 377

Sanders, Moses 141
Sanders, Tamma 71
Sanders, William 377
Sanderson, Alexander 374
Sanderson, Elizabeth 374
Sanderson, Foster M. 609
Sanderson, George 374
Sanderson, Henry 447
Sanderson, Mary 447
Sanderson, Peggy 374
Sanderson, Robert 374,
376
Sanderson, William 374
Sanderson, William
Monroe 447
Sandham, Mary 238
Sandham, Richard 228,
238
Sands, Catharine 307
Sands, Christian 609
Sands, David 609
Sands, Elizabeth 739
Sands, George 148
Sands, Hetty 606
Sands, James 739
Sands, James B. 307
Sands, Jane 739
Sands, John 739
Sands, John W. 256
Sands, Joshua 180
Sands, Margaret 739
Sands, Mary 739
Sands, Rebecca 169
Sands, Richard 169, 249
Sands, Sarah 180, 739
Sands, William 739
Sanford, Charity 745
Sanford, Enoch 516
Sanford, Horace 58, 62
Sanford, Huldah 715
Sanford, Mary 708
Sanford, Nathan P. 58,
62
Sanford, Robinson 160
Sanford, Salmon 209
Sanft, Eliza 96
Sanft, W. H. H. 96
Sanm, Leah 610
Sans, Erastus 79
Sansel, Elizabeth 695
Sansom, Isabella 742
Sansom, Jane 742
Sansom, Joseph 742
Sansom, Mary 742
Sansom, Sarah 742
Sansom, William 742
Sapington, Thomas 516
Sappin, William 482
Sappington, Marththree
555
Sappington, Mary 555
Sappington, Racheal 555
Sappington, Thomas 555
Sarchet, Thomas 285
Sares, Peter 662
Sargart, Eli 484
Sargeant, Elizabeth 490
Sargent, Daniel 484
Sargent, Eli 484, 485

Sargent, George 89
Sargent, Robt. 575
Sargent, Saml. 476
Sargent, Sampson 643
Sargent, Samuel 476,
484, 485
Sargent, Snowder 491
Sargent, William 491
Sarmon, Robert 388
Saro, Mary 512
Sarot, Marry Catterine
714
Sarrasin, Francis Abel
722, 723, 724
Sarver, Samuel 546
Sater, Susanna 356
Saterthwaite, Mary
Elizabeth 691
Satham, John 183
Satterthwait, Joseph W.
176
Satterthwait, Mary 160
Satterthwait, Wm. W. 160
Satterthwaite, John 678
Satterthwaite, Martha
Jane 691
Satterthwaite, Samuel
691
Satterthwate, John 650
Saum, Cora Ann 241
Saum, Evaline 241
Saum, John H. 241
Saum, Joseph 241
Saum, Martha 241
Saum, Mathias 338
Saunan, Hannah 404
Saunan, R. 404
Saunders, Anthony J. 522
Saunders, Caroline 592
Saunders, Elihy 223
Saunders, Martha 586
Saunders, Mary 223
Saunders, Oliver 766
Saunders, Thomas 586
Saurres, William H. 45
Saushing, Sarah 91
Savage, Adam 79
Savage, Catharine 66,
551
Savage, Daniel 332
Savage, Dorothy 88
Savage, George P. 546
Savage, Gibson 51
Savage, Henry 56
Savage, Jacob 66
Savage, John 79
Savage, Lovina 78
Savage, Sarah 337
Savage, Thomas 286
Savely, Edward 633
Savely, George 633
Savely, Henry 633
Savely, James 633
Savely, Jeptha 633, 634
Savely, John 633
Savers, Charles 447
Savey, Elizabeth 96
Savey, W. M. 96
Savidge, Jane 608

Savidge, Morgan 601,
602, 603
Savidge, Reuben 291
Saviers, Charles 447
Sawyer, Amassa 684
Sawyer, Betsey 11
Sawyer, Elica 78
Sawyer, Elizabeth 670
Sawyer, James Hughs 249
Sawyer, Jane 666
Sawyer, Joseph 249, 638
Sawyer, Levi 599
Sawyer, Lydia 719
Sawyer, Mary 660
Sawyer, Mary Eunice 249
Sawyer, Stephen 42
Sawyer, Thomas 249
Sawyers, Joseph C. 431
Saxter, Mary 186
Saxton, Hannah 83
Saxton, Joseph 530
Saxton, Michael 79, 530
Saxton, Nancy 78
Say, Rebecca 141
Sayers, Fanny 135
Sayers, Rachael 123
Sayle, Amy 64
Sayle, David 64
Sayle, Lydia 64
Sayle, Mary 64
Sayle, Phebe 64
Sayle, Seneca 64
Sayler, Catharine 420
Sayler, Elizabeth 420
Sayler, John 420
Sayler, Nathan 417
Sayler, Rebecca 420
Sayler, Solomon 420
Saylor, Abraham 436
Saylor, Jacob 337
Saylor, Mary 385
Saylor, Philip 436
Saylor, Polly 436, 747
Saylor, Rebecca 436
Sayman, Lydia 591
Sayre, Benjamin 672
Sayre, Daniel 79
Sayre, Hanah 81
Sayre, Hannah 77
Sayre, Hope 343, 376
Sayre, John 343
Sayre, John G. 80
Sayre, John H. 86
Sayre, Jonathan 80, 84
Sayre, Lydia 79
Sayre, Margaret 173
Sayre, Messer 173, 178
Sayre, Messor 160
Sayre, Nancy 76
Sayre, Phebey 376
Sayre, Rachel 376
Sayre, Rebecca 343
Sayre, Reuben 376
Sayre, Reuel 343
Sayre, Robert 86
Sayre, Robt. 84
Sayre, Ruel 376
Sayre, Ruel (Jr.) 363,
376

Sayre, Sarah 76
Sayre, Uriah 80
Sayres, Israel 158
Sayres, Mary 523
Sayres, Sarah 127
Sayrs, James 127
Sayton, Ulrick 746
Scallan, James 375
Scallan, Mary 375
Scallan, Mary Ann 375
Scanlin, Bridget 90
Scantlen, Thos. 636
Scantlin, Thomas 163
Scarborough, John 500
Scarborough, Mary 500
Scarborugh, Joseph 294
Schaal, August C. 629
Schaeffer, Barbara 207
Schaeffer, George 206,
207
Schaeffer, Jacob 206,
207
Schaeffer, Samuel 206
Schaeffer, William 206
Schaeffer, William N.
682
Schaeffer, Wm. N. 690
Schaeffer, Wm. W. 687
Schafer, Eva Christena
411
Schaffer, Jacob 493
Schaffer, Samuel 748
Schaffer, Valentine 91,
304
Schalk, Frederick 522
Schapper, Christian 546
Schapper, Henry 546
Schardelmann, John Henry
100
Schardelmann, William
100
Scharrer, John Rudolph
609
Scheafer, Jacob 239
Scheaffer, J. 238
Scheaffer, John 238
Scheaffer, S. 238
Scheaffer, Sarah 238
Scheaffer, Susannah 238
Scheblaine, Eli 84
Schefer, Elisabet 236
Schefer, Elisabeth 236
Schefer, Henrich 236
Schefer, Jacob 236
Schefer, Johannes 236
Scheffer, Elisabet 236
Scheffer, Elisabeth 236
Scheffer, Henrich 236
Scheffer, Marien 236
Schemmel, John H. 105
Schemmell, Antany 103
Schemmell, Christopher
103
Schemmell, Edward Henry
103
Schemmell, Elizabeth 103
Schemmell, John Henry
103
Schemmell, Joseph 103

949

Schemmell, Theadore
   Herman 103
Schenck, Allis 214
Schenck, Cryonce 209
Schenck, Daniel 185, 209
Schenck, David 214
Schenck, Garret 199, 685
Schenck, Garret A. 653
Schenck, Hannah 654
Schenck, Idia Ann 199
Schenck, John 185, 654
Schenck, John H. 188,
   196
Schenck, John N. C. 655,
   674, 676, 677, 679
Schenck, Jonathan 654
Schenck, Mariah 209
Schenck, Nelly 654
Schenck, Obadiah 685
Schenck, Obediah 214
Schenck, Peter 654, 685
Schenck, Phebe 214
Schenck, Phebe Ann 685
Schenck, Sarah 209, 654
Schenck, Tunis 209
Schenck, William 209, 654
Schenck, William C. 651
Schenck, William L. 689
Schenck, William W. 685
Schenck, Wm. 185
Schenck, Wm. C. 668
Schendk, James P. 651
Scher, Valentine 522
Scherp, David 236
Scherp, Jacob 236
Scherp, Sarah 236
Scheurick, Sebastian 228
Schevetz, Christina 229
Schiblaire, Catharine 77
Schiefelin, Jacob 86
Schilling, George 409,
   411
Schilling, Martha 411
Schink, Philip 228
Schiper, Henry 104
Schively, Christian 195
Schlamann, John 103
Schlenker, Cornelius 236
Schlenker, David 236
Schlenker, David
   Carmellias 239
Schlenker, David
   Rosenmiller 236
Schlenker, Elizabeth 239
Schlenker, George 239
Schlenker, George Henry
   239
Schlenker, Mary
   Elizabeth 239
Schlenker, Salomon 236
Schlenker, Solomon 239
Schlenker, Susan 239
Schlenker, Susana 236
Schlenker, Susane 236
Schlosser, Henry 557
Schlosser, Jacob 557
Schlosser, Mary 557
Schlotteludever,
   Catharina Sophia 237

Schlotteludever, F. 237
Schlotteludever, S. 237
Schmit, Charles 603
Schmitt, . . . Heinrich
   277
Schmitt, Elizabeth 607
Schmitt, George 367
Schmitt, J . . . 277
Schmitt, Joseph 367
Schneck, David 694
Schneck, Maud Ann 694
Schnecl, Obediah 694
Schnelle, Christopher
   546
Schnelle, J. D. Victor
   546
Schnelli, Conrad 152
Schnep, Catharine 195
Schnep, Daniel 195
Schnep, John 195
Schnep, Lewis 195
Schnep, Peter 195
Schnep, Rinehart 195
Schnep, William 195
Schnepf, Louisa 709
Schnepp, Daniel 196
Schnepp, Philip 196
Schnepp, William 196
Schnider, Adam 283
Schnippel, Herman 536
Schock, H. 404
Schock, Henry 404
Schoerer, George 192
Schofield, Benjamin 375
Schofield, Daniel 375
Schofield, Dorcas 375
Schofield, Elias 375
Schofield, Elijah 375
Schofield, Elizabeth 375
Schofield, Henry 733
Schofield, Jesse 375
Schofield, John 360, 375
Schofield, Joseph 304
Schofield, Polly 375
Schofield, Rhoda 375
Schofield, Susanna 375
Scholfield, Edith 166
Scholfield, Elizabeth
   376
Scholfield, Issachar 166
Scholfield, Jane Mariah
   376
Scholfield, John 376
Scholfield, Joseph 376
Scholfield, Lemuel 376
Scholfield, Mahala 376
Scholfield, Margaret 376
Scholfield, Mary Ann 376
Scholfield, Rebecca 376
Scholfield, Susannah 376
Scholler, Wm. 90
School, Hannah Rebecca
   521
Schooler, William 14
Schooley, Andrew E.
   317, 336
Schooley, George S. 317
Schooley, O. B. 332
Schooley, O. F. 332

Schooley, Olivia S. 334
Schooly, Elizabeth 568
Schooly, Richard 568
Schoonover, James 101
Schoster, Herman 111
Schott, Ambrose 267
Schrader, Henry
   Frederick 409
Schrader, Lean 409
Schrader, Philip P. 409
Schragg, Benedict 42
Schramm, Jacob 710, 711
Schramm, Michael 710,
   711
Schreder, Francis 105
Schreeher, Henry 90
Schricker, Catharine 93
Schriut, Bernard Brugen
   106
Schrock, John 738
Schroeder, Antone 105
Schroeder, B. F. 115
Schroeder, Catharine
   Maria 104
Schroeder, Clements 104
Schroeder, Francis 104,
   112
Schroeder, Francis Wm.
   105
Schroeder, Frederick 104
Schroeder, John
   Frederick 104
Schroeder, Maria 105
Schroeder, Maria Anna
   104
Schrube, Anna Maria 87
Schryack, Isaiah 49
Schucker, J. W. 743
Schuckers, I. W. 738
Schuckers, Samuel 738
Schulz, Dinah 546
Schuman, John W. 546
Schumm, Frederick 601
Schumm, George 601
Schumm, Henry 601
Schumm, Jacob 601
Schumm, John 601
Schumm, Lewis 601
Schumoeller, Bernadiner
   Elisabeth 106
Schumoeller, Henry 106
Schumoeller, Mary Alice
   106
Schumoller, Bernadiner
   Elisabeth 106
Schumoller, Henry 106
Schumoller, Mary Alice
   106
Schupel, John F. 546
Schuppert, Chreistopher
   200
Schuych, Lewis 228
Schwartz, Benjamin 546
Schwartz, Henry 280
Schwartz, James 411
Schwartz, Martin 409
Schwartz, Mary Anne 411
Schwartzel, Matthias 224
Schwartzel, Philip 224

Schwegman, Elizabeth 112
Schwiederman, Mary 112
Scofield, Alva 655
Scofield, Elijah 364
Scofield, Jacob 295
Scofield, Joseph 639
Scofield, William 299
Scofille, Laura N. 519
Scoggen, Wm. 263
Scoot, John 466
Scot, Thomas 662
Scothern, Ann 519
Scothern, M. 382
Scothorn, Benjamin 498
Scothorn, William 498
Scott, . . . oseph 458
Scott, Abner 431
Scott, Abraham 65
Scott, Alexander 97,
    101, 736
Scott, Alexander (Jr.)
    101
Scott, Andrew 271
Scott, Ann 20, 100, 404
Scott, Anne 392
Scott, B. 97
Scott, Barnaby 377
Scott, Benjamin 755
Scott, Betsy 588
Scott, C. 97
Scott, Calvin 141
Scott, Charles 710
Scott, Charlot 79
Scott, David 16, 270
Scott, Eleanor 100, 455
Scott, Elijhu 466
Scott, Eliza 65, 100
Scott, Eliza Jane 683
Scott, Elizabeth 124,
    164, 345, 388, 490,
    608
Scott, Elizabeth R. 56
Scott, Frances 580
Scott, Francis 260,
    271, 304
Scott, Geo. W. 412
Scott, George 546
Scott, George L. 546
Scott, George W. 683
Scott, H. 97
Scott, Hannah 97
Scott, Henry H. 377
Scott, Hugh 127, 134,
    135
Scott, J. 97
Scott, James 266, 300,
    469, 473, 480
Scott, Jane 117, 248
Scott, Jas. 478
Scott, Jesse 271
Scott, John 97, 392,
    466, 494, 705, 710,
    737
Scott, John T. 14
Scott, John Wesley 436
Scott, Jonathan 682, 683
Scott, Joseph 164, 293,
    296, 398, 683
Scott, Joseph M. 56

Scott, Julia 377
Scott, Justus 248
Scott, Levi E. 683
Scott, Levina 459
Scott, Lewis 592
Scott, Louisa 248
Scott, Lowly 248
Scott, M. J. 97
Scott, M. T. 59
Scott, Malinda 592
Scott, Mandy 97
Scott, Margaret 11
Scott, Marion 97
Scott, Martin F. 377
Scott, Mary 65, 78, 97,
    100, 710
Scott, Mathew 377, 575
Scott, Moses 466
Scott, Nancy 97, 101,
    511, 580, 683
Scott, Naome 11
Scott, Norris 466
Scott, Nune P. 85
Scott, Obediah 248
Scott, Orasmus 1
Scott, Patty 14
Scott, Peter B. 584
Scott, Polly 715
Scott, Richard 97, 101
Scott, Robert 108, 516,
    522
Scott, Roderig A. 97
Scott, Ruth Anna 755
Scott, Sabert 102
Scott, Samuel 19, 85,
    97, 100, 248, 494, 683
Scott, Sarah 608, 718
Scott, Selina 65
Scott, Seybert 100
Scott, Susan 377, 683
Scott, Theodore 733
Scott, Theopilus 551
Scott, Thomas 100, 568,
    670, 683, 686, 718
Scott, Thos. A. 733
Scott, W. 97
Scott, William 14, 417,
    516, 705
Scott, William H. 97
Scott, William L. 127
Scott, William
    Washington 417
Scott, Wm. 274, 396
Scraffenberger, Daniel
    42
Scranton, James A. 498
Scranton, Laura 111
Scribner, Abraham 750
Scribner, Alvira 65
Scribner, Ann Eliza 750
Scribner, Edwin 746, 750
Scribner, Elisa Ann 745
Scribner, Elisha 750
Scribner, Elisha Husted
    750
Scribner, Nancy 750
Scribner, Nancy Ann 745
Scribner, Samuel 65
Scribner, Uri 750

Scribner, Zacheus Lewis
    750
Scudder, Mary 121
Scuddor, Thomas 127
Seabourn, David 490
Seagchrist, Christian
    522
Seal, Charity 157
Seal, Joseph 157
Seal, Mary 404
Seal, Samuel 404
Sealey, Elizabeth 82
Sealey, Orcon 85
Sealey, Thomas 268
Seals, Joseph 163
Seaman, David 249
Seaman, Harman 249
Seaman, Henry 24
Seaman, Jas. 249
Seaman, Jesse 249
Seaman, John 249, 258,
    263, 265, 275
Seaman, Jonas 672
Seaman, Perley J. 249
Seaman, Wm. B. 662
Seamans, Gilbert 715
Seamans, Joseph 715
Seamans, Patty 715
Seamans, Samuel 715
Seamans, Tabra 715
Seamin, Jacob 592
Seamon, Henry 662
Seamons, Bennajah 727
Seamons, Gilbert 727
Seamons, Martha 727
Seamons, Polly 716, 727
Seamons, Preserved 727
Seamons, Sabra 727
Seamons, Samuel Benjamin
    727
Seamons, Sarah 660
Seamons, Susanna 727
Searfause, Philip 387
Searing, Catherine 198
Searing, Henry 198
Searing, Philip 198
Searl, Miranda 504
Sears, Allison 583
Sears, Ephraim 563
Sears, Jane 563
Sears, John 267, 272,
    273
Seas, Abraham 141
Seas, Jacob 141
Seasbourn, Theodoius 391
Seashotts, Betsey 384
Seaton, Ebenezer 546
Sebrel, Wm. 524
Sebrell, Nicholas 485
Sebring, Elizabeth 500
Sebring, Thompson 500,
    502
Secoy, Asenth 84
Secrist, Henry 20
Secrist, Madison 305
Sedam, Ann Eliza 654
Sedam, Lydia 654
Sedam, Simon 654
Sedwick, Richard 473

Seeley, --- (Judge) 323
Seeley, Alexander P. 746
Seeley, H. E. 75
Seeley, James 15
Seely, A. R. 332
Seely, Avaline 83
Seeman, Anna M. 710
Sees, Susannah 573
Seevers, Anna 711
Segar, Artemelia 401
Segar, John 401
Segler, Peter 136
Segles, Frederick 398
Segur, Hezekiah 559
Seiferman, Caroline 113
Seiks, Henry 85
Seiler, Ann Maria 709
Seiler, Maria Kath. 710
Seinbeck, Sally 508
Seiner, Susana 558
Seiper, . . . mas 153
Seitner, David 521
Seitz, Catharine 521
Seitz, Mary 112
Seitz, Matthias 112
Seitz, Max 112
Seitz, Rebecca 521
Seix, George 741
Selach, Henry 180
Selach, Margaret 180
Selby, Eli 375
Selby, John 375
Selby, Joshua 375
Selby, Ruby 375
Selby, Thomas 375
Seldenright, Catharine 564
Seldenright, Christiana 564
Seldenright, David 564
Seldenright, David (Sr.) 564
Seldenright, Elizabeth 564
Seldenright, Mary 564
Seldenright, Modena 564
Seldenright, Rebecca 564
Seldonwright, Magdalena 566
Self, Mariah 49
Self, William 285
Sell, Adam 276
Sell, Amos 276
Sell, Christian 198
Sell, Hannah 567
Sell, Jonathan 568
Sell, Lydia 565
Sell, Peter 568
Sell, Susannah 198
Sellars, Elizabeth 377
Sellars, Jacob 377
Sellars, James Alva 377
Sellars, James S. 372
Sellars, John 373, 674
Sellars, John Harvey 436
Sellars, Louisa 377
Sellars, Mahala 377
Sellars, Margaret 377
Sellars, Mary 377

Sellars, Naomi 377
Sellars, Reuben 377
Sellars, Susan E. E. 436
Sellen, Mahetable 519
Seller, Mahetable 519
Sellers, Adam 648
Sellers, Adams 639
Sellers, Benjamin 684, 686
Sellers, Catherine 415
Sellers, Christena 659
Sellers, Cynthia Ann 683
Sellers, David M. 375
Sellers, Eliza Jane 683
Sellers, Elizabeth 639, 663
Sellers, Frederick 522
Sellers, Henry 340
Sellers, Henry D. 54
Sellers, Isaac 284, 340
Sellers, John 669
Sellers, Joseph 639, 648
Sellers, Mary 424
Sellers, Nathan (Jr.) 415
Sellers, Nathan (Sr.) 415
Sellers, Parthena 683
Sellers, Peter 639, 648
Sellers, William 639, 648, 683, 686
Selliman, W. 294
Selliman, Wyllis 298
Selliman, Wyllys 297
Selliman, Wylys 297
Sellinger, John 751
Sells, Benj. 483
Sells, Mary 577
Sels, Israel 575
Selsor, Christian 58
Selsor, Mary 59
Selsor, William 59
Seman, William 751
Semans, William 746
Semard, Sarah 456
Semple, Elizabeth 436
Semple, James 436
Semple, Lattin 436
Semple, Mary Rebecca 436
Semple, Sarah Jane 436
Senclair, James 298
Seney, J. 528
Seney, Joshua 527
Senff, Michael 339
Senft, Adam 376
Senft, Barbara 376
Senft, Christena 376
Senft, Henry 376
Senft, John 376
Senft, Katy 376
Senft, Nancy 376
Senft, Philip 376
Senft, Polly 376
Senn, John 522
Sennet, Gideon 592
Senton, Samuel 80
Sepernich, Mary 527
Serel, Jacob 260
Sergeant, Charlotte 28

Sergeant, Sampson 642, 674
Sergeant, Samuel 642
Sergent, Elizabeth 455
Sergent, John 15
Sergent, Lawrence 575
Sergent, Nancy 15
Sergent, Sampson 646
Seritihfield, Catharine 717
Serring, Elizabeth 658
Serring, Ezekiel 662
Serring, Peggy 661
Serring, Samuel 649
Serring, Theodorin 658
Serroll, Peter F. 506
Serrot, Maria Katharine Aveline 724
Serrot, Peter 724, 725
Service, Hugh 736
Service, Phoebe 736
Service, Samuel 80
Sesler, Damarius 10
Sesler, Elizabeth Groves 10
Sesler, Harriet 10
Sesler, Jacob 10
Sesler, Mary 10
Sesler, Sophronia Ann 10
Sesler, Thomas Jefferson 10
Sesler, William Hamilton 10
Sessions, Horace 321
Seston, Samuel 60
Sevall, Jno. 269
Severance, Mary 177
Severance, Silas 177
Severence, Alfred 753
Severence, Benjamin 753
Severence, Caroline 753
Severence, Daniel 753
Severence, David 753
Severence, Elizabeth 753
Severence, Hannah 753
Severence, Lucinda 753
Severence, Mary Ann 753
Severence, Nancy 753
Sevesay, Peter 55
Seveth, Keziah 713
Sewall, Frederick 108
Sewall, Henry 108
Sewall, Mary 108
Seward, Anne 659
Seward, Charlotte 573
Seward, Elizabeth 640
Seward, Mary Maria 436
Seward, Mason 654
Seward, Richard 640
Sewart, Alexander 662
Sewel, Timothy 671
Sewell, Abner 575
Sewell, David 141
Sewell, Hester 662
Sewell, Peter 58
Sewell, Sally Ann 141
Sewell, Sarah 660
Sexton, Ann 699
Sexton, Elizabeth 699

Sexton, Hannah 699
Sexton, John 699
Sexton, Mary 699
Sexton, Rebecca 699
Sexton, Samuel (Dr.) 699
Sexton, Sarah 699
Seybold, Anna Magtalena 235
Seybold, Anna Maria 235
Seybold, Georg 235
Seybold, Jacobbina 235
Seybold, Johannes 235
Seybold, Johannes Georg 235
Seymore, Amos 720
Seymore, Wm. 391
Seymour, Adam 397
Seymour, Catharine 397
Seymour, Corilla L. 397
Seymour, Richard 397
Shackelford, Frances 127
Shackelford, James 127
Shackelford, William 127
Shackford, Josiah 505
Shacklee, Peter 272
Shacklee, Wm. H. 272
Shackleford, Wm. 494
Shackley, Richard 15
Shaefer, Adam 522
Shaefer, Frederick 239
Shafer, Alexander 378
Shafer, Alexander R. 378
Shafer, Barbara 230
Shafer, Charles 85
Shafer, Daniel 556, 592
Shafer, Elizabeth 314, 385
Shafer, Emely 65
Shafer, George 178, 230, 313
Shafer, James 314, 378
Shafer, John 238, 378
Shafer, John C. 313
Shafer, John M. 65
Shafer, Joseph 378
Shafer, Margaret 314, 378
Shafer, Mary 313, 378, 382
Shafer, Mary Ann 314
Shafer, Matilda 378
Shafer, Nelson 313
Shafer, Peter 378, 556
Shafer, Samuel 314
Shafer, Samuel H. 378
Shafer, Sarah 378
Shafer, William 313
Shaffer, Abraham 738
Shaffer, Anton 546
Shaffer, Benedict 546
Shaffer, Catherine 133
Shaffer, Christena 603
Shaffer, Elizabeth 193, 436, 738
Shaffer, Francis 546
Shaffer, Francis M. 5
Shaffer, George 5, 516, 738
Shaffer, Hannah 5, 738

Shaffer, Henry 193
Shaffer, Jacob 193, 564, 738
Shaffer, John 39, 228, 603, 738
Shaffer, John Henry 436
Shaffer, Joshua 609
Shaffer, Judia 738
Shaffer, Lidi 738
Shaffer, Mary 146, 415, 738
Shaffer, Mary Anna 738
Shaffer, Michael 415
Shaffer, Miram M. 584
Shaffer, Peter 564
Shaffer, Rachel 146
Shaffer, Samuel 5
Shaffer, Sarah 607, 738
Shaffer, William 582
Shaffer, William H. 5
Shaffer, Wm. 146
Shagely, Jacob 491
Shagely, Joseph 493
Shagly, Jacob 127
Shahoon, Nancy 459
Shakelford, James 130
Shakelford, Peggy 130
Shakelford, Rebecca 130
Shakelford, Reuben 130
Shakelford, William 130
Shakleford, James 130
Shakleford, Peggy 130
Shakleford, Rebecca 130
Shakleford, Reuben 130
Shakleford, William 130
Shalenberger, Jacob 568
Shalk, Regina 523
Shall, August 631
Shall, Michael 498
Shallenberger, Nancy 452
Shaller, Rebecca 571
Shalli, William 163, 165
Shamel, George 568
Shamhart, Henry 304
Shanck, John 442
Shane, Hannah 574
Shane, Henry 556
Shane, John 556
Shane, Rhoda 660
Shanefeldt, Mary 215
Shanefeldt, William 215
Shaner, George 490
Shaner, Henry 367, 376
Shank, --- 74
Shank, Adam 309
Shank, Daniel 436
Shank, Elizabeth 232
Shank, George 436
Shank, Henry 232
Shank, Jacob 232, 436, 533, 576
Shank, John 436
Shank, Joseph 195
Shank, Polly 436
Shank, Reasin Beall 740
Shank, Sally Ann 436
Shank, Sarah 232
Shank, Thomas 42
Shank, William 400

Shank, Wm. 436
Shankland, Harrie 169
Shankland, Harriet 176
Shankland, James W. 170
Shankland, William G. 166, 169, 172, 181
Shankland, Wm. G. 176
Shanks, Christopher 327
Shanks, Elizabeth 230, 567
Shanks, James 568
Shanks, John 230
Shanks, Joseph 576
Shanks, Mary A. 327
Shannon, Charlotte 562
Shannon, Eliza 562
Shannon, Elizabeth 497
Shannon, Enos 562
Shannon, George 498
Shannon, Jane 304
Shannon, Joseph 562
Shannon, Lanty 623
Shannon, Nancy 562
Shannon, Rebecca 562
Shannon, Temperance 562
Shannon, Thomas 562
Shanon, Amon 576
Shanten, Abraham 453
Shanton, Mary 462
Shantz, Magdalina 23
Shapley, Hannah 551
Sharader, Harman 653
Share, Barbara 678
Share, Catharine 678
Share, Ephraim 678
Share, Henry 678
Share, Henry G. 696
Share, Letitia Hortensia 678
Share, Mary 678
Share, Peter Levi 678
Share, Simon L. 696
Sharer, John 765
Sharits, Clara Augusta 243
Sharits, John 243
Sharits, Rodia 243
Sharitt, Hiram 626
Sharkey, Barbara 376
Sharkey, Elizabeth 376
Sharkey, Hugh 346, 358, 376
Sharkey, Teresa 376
Sharky, John 80
Sharon, William 562
Sharp, Achshah 26
Sharp, Betsey 79
Sharp, Catharine 495
Sharp, Elizabeth 2, 27, 575
Sharp, Esther 26
Sharp, George 322
Sharp, Hester 504
Sharp, Isaac 22
Sharp, James T. 683
Sharp, Jane Ann 745
Sharp, Jesse 15, 17
Sharp, Job 15, 26, 27
Sharp, Job H. 26

953

Sharp, John 27, 370, 480
Sharp, John S. 57
Sharp, Joshua 26
Sharp, Julia Ann 747
Sharp, Margaret 573
Sharp, Maria 27
Sharp, Mary 27
Sharp, Nancy 27
Sharp, Nathan 649
Sharp, Peter 752
Sharp, Phebe 26
Sharp, Polly 79
Sharp, Rachel 27
Sharp, Sally 13
Sharp, Samuel 27
Sharp, Sarah 26, 459
Sharp, Thomas 718
Sharp, William 16
Sharr, Sarah 551
Sharret, C. 243
Sharret, Charles W. 243
Sharret, E. 243
Sharret, H. 243
Sharret, Laura A. 243
Sharret, Wm. A. 243
Sharret, Z. 243
Sharrits, Mahala 222
Sharrock, Tenty 304
Shartel, Philip 458
Shasteen, Lunicia 745
Shattuck, Samuel 261
Shaul, Mathew 662
Shaunding, Henry 616
Shaver, Alexander 375
Shaver, Eleanor 509
Shaver, Elizabeth 375
Shaver, Geo. 272
Shaver, George 375
Shaver, James 375
Shaver, Joseph 374, 375
Shaver, Lidey 375
Shaver, Margaret 375
Shaver, Samuel 375
Shaw, --- 170
Shaw, --- (Capt.) 670
Shaw, Alexander 546
Shaw, Alice 762
Shaw, Andrew 191, 218
Shaw, Archibald 642
Shaw, Catharine 350
Shaw, Ebenezer 556, 558
Shaw, Elizabeth 350
Shaw, Freeman 185, 191
Shaw, George 15
Shaw, Hannah 82
Shaw, Henry 470
Shaw, Hesekiah 153
Shaw, James 195, 662
Shaw, Jane 747
Shaw, Jane L. 546
Shaw, John 74, 350,
  357, 546, 558, 639,
  662, 668, 669
Shaw, John (Jr.) 638
Shaw, Margaret 350
Shaw, Mary 195, 218,
  292, 336, 350, 551
Shaw, Nancy 350, 413
Shaw, Nathan 350

Shaw, Nelly 658
Shaw, Patrick 662
Shaw, Peter 439
Shaw, Rachel 558
Shaw, Rebecca 551
Shaw, Richard 218
Shaw, Robert 15
Shaw, Sally 660, 713
Shaw, Samuel 453, 482,
  484, 551
Shaw, Sarah 15, 195, 667
Shaw, Scott 185
Shaw, Silas W. 522
Shaw, Solomon 653
Shaw, Stephen 350
Shaw, Thomas 118, 195,
  546
Shaw, William 298
Shaw, Zachariah 153
Shawhan, Amos 689
Shawhan, John 652, 681,
  687
Shawhan, Rhoda 658
Shawhen, David 662
Shawl, Benjamin 498
Shawl, Rebecca 499
Shawver, Emma 327
Shawver, S. D. 327
Sheable, Bartholomew 546
Shealy, Elizabeth 141
Shealy, Peggy 141
Shearbaugh, Michael 546
Shearer, Catharine 588
Shearer, Christian 202,
  210
Shearer, Daniel 348
Shearer, Hannah Sophia
  436
Shearer, Jacob 112
Shearer, Jane 202
Shearer, Peggy 742
Shearer, Sally 452
Sheater, Nancy 609
Sheath, Mary 82
Sheathner, John 688
Sheby, Hannah 459
Sheckle, Wm. 270
Shedd, James A. 218
Shedenhelnn, Henry 522
Sheeler, James 458
Sheeler, Wm. 364
Sheeling, Nancy 127
Sheely, Henry 472, 486
Sheely, Lawrence 466
Sheet, Martha 461
Sheet, Susannah 116
Sheets, Adam 609
Sheets, Andrew 130
Sheets, Barbary 141
Sheets, Catharine 130
Sheets, Dora H. 328
Sheets, Elizabeth 118
Sheets, Frederick 754
Sheets, Henry 754
Sheets, Jacob 130
Sheets, James 61
Sheets, Jane 124
Sheets, John 609
Sheets, Martin 130

Sheets, Mary 116
Sheets, Nancy 125, 141
Sheets, Robert 146
Sheets, Susannah 146
Sheets, William 85
Sheets, Wm. 141, 146
Sheetz, Adam 733
Sheffer, Hannah 276
Sheffer, Henry 276
Sheffer, John 276
Shefferty, John 522
Sheffield, Hannah 715
Shefus, Nancy 453
Shegley, Nancy 456
Sheibly, Christopher 190
Sheibly, Daniel 190
Sheibly, Susannah 190
Sheidler, Elias 188
Sheidler, George 188
Sheidler, Henry 224
Sheidler, Jacob 188
Sheidler, John 188
Sheidler, Mary 188
Sheidler, Sarah 188
Sheilds, Eliza Margaret
  436
Sheilds, John A. Wilson
  436
Sheilds, Maria Elizabeth
  436
Sheilds, Mary Catharine
  436
Sheilds, Sarah Jane 436
Shel, Elenor 76
Shelburt, John 522
Shelby, . . . ohn 458
Shelby, Charity 386
Shelby, John 17, 25
Shelby, Joseph 387
Shelden, Abrah 718
Shelden, George W. 105
Sheldon, Benjamin F. 318
Sheldon, Giles J. 627
Shell, Christian 121
Shell, Elizabeth 120
Shell, George 158
Shell, Joseph H. 127
Shell, Nancy 123
Shell, William 127
Shell, Wm. 141
Shellebarger, Eliz. 146
Shellenbarger, John 538
Shellenbarger, Susanna
  538
Sheller, Nancy 523
Shellers, Cath. 414
Shellers, Christian 418
Shellet, Francis 322
Shelley, Daniel 375
Shelley, Elizabeth 375
Shelley, George 375
Shelley, Margaret 375
Shelley, Michael 375
Shelley, Sally 375
Shellman, John 240
Shellman, Margaret 240
Shellman, Sarah A. 240
Shelly, George 375
Shelly, Mary 414

Shelpherd, Jacob 472
Shelpman, Cela 514
Shelpman, Cornelius 592
Shelpman, Jacob 516
Shelpman, Latitia 591
Shelpman, Sarah 587
Shemklin, --- 36
Shenebarger, John 558
Shenefield, Christiana 209
Shenefield, Jacob 209
Shenefield, Katherine 367
Shenefield, Peter 209
Shenefield, William 209
Sheneman, Adam 741
Shenk, Cyrus 740
Shenk, Hannah 568
Shenk, Julian 740
Shenk, Nancy C. 740
Shenk, Syres 741
Shenman, Henry 568
Shepard, Arnold 252
Shepard, Betsy C. 34, 35
Shepard, Catharine 333
Shepard, Charles 80
Shepard, Isaiah 373
Shepard, Jane 79
Shepard, Lorena 713
Shepard, Morris Kelly 252
Shepard, Nancy 78
Shepard, Nathaniel 258
Shepard, Rhoda 714
Shepardson, James P. 498
Sheperd, Nathaniel 259
Shephard, Andrew 49
Shephard, Henry 195
Shepher, Jeremiah R. 576
Shepher . . . , Jonathan 458
Shepherd, --- 266
Shepherd, Abraham 54
Shepherd, Adam 398
Shepherd, Albert 699
Shepherd, Anna 18
Shepherd, Catharine 684
Shepherd, Charles R. 698
Shepherd, Christianna 665
Shepherd, Clementine 131
Shepherd, Cora L. 698
Shepherd, David 453, 476, 477, 478
Shepherd, Elizabeth 557
Shepherd, Emma A. 699
Shepherd, Ernest 698
Shepherd, Esther 293
Shepherd, George W. 106
Shepherd, Hath. 267
Shepherd, Jacob 466
Shepherd, James 131, 453
Shepherd, Jane 109
Shepherd, John 18, 155, 179, 333, 466
Shepherd, Jonathan 667
Shepherd, Joseph 147, 466, 557
Shepherd, Lydia E. 698

Shepherd, Mary 333, 463
Shepherd, Maud 700
Shepherd, Nancy 45
Shepherd, Nathanel 264
Shepherd, Nathionel 263
Shepherd, Phebe 590
Shepherd, Richard 179
Shepherd, Richard (Sr.) 171
Shepherd, Sarah 179
Shepler, Abraham 557
Shepler, Mathias 557
Shepler, Matthias 557
Shepley, Samuel 645, 673
Shepperd, Anna 199
Shepperd, John 199, 228
Sherb, James 315
Shereman, Lucy 715
Sherer, Daniel J. (Dr.) 419
Sherer, Doanah 436
Sherer, Geo. H. 436
Sherer, Mary Elizabeth 436
Sherer, Perminia 436
Sherg, Jacob 283, 340
Sheridan, James 409
Sherk, Elizabeth 586
Sherley, Lewis 272
Sherlock, Abraham 341, 376
Sherlock, Edward 453
Sherlock, George 376
Sherlock, Henry 370, 376, 380
Sherlock, James 368, 371, 376, 380
Sherlock, Jane 376
Sherlock, John O. P. 376
Sherlock, Margaret 376
Sherlock, Nancy 376
Sherlock, Patrick 270
Sherlock, Sarah 376
Sherlock, William 321
Sherman, Abigal 588
Sherman, Clarissa 713
Sherman, Ely 297
Sherman, John 596, 597, 598
Sherman, Josiah 715
Sherman, Julian 597
Sherman, Juliann 598
Sherman, July Ann 590
Sherman, Justin 31
Sherman, Sally 587
Sherman, Wm. 269
Shermin, Thomas 662
Shermon, Lucy 717
Shern, Catherine 457
Sherod, Adam 564
Sherowwd, Samuel 597
Sherrard, Anna Rebecca 56
Sherrard, David 292
Sherrets, Christene 577
Sherry, Montgomery 469
Sherward, Rebecah 511
Sherwood, Henry 682, 690
Sherwood, Raymond 274

Sherwood, Thamur 715
Sherwood, William D. 498
Sherwood, Zuriel 274
Shesler, Ann 592
Shetly, . . . atthew 459
Shevinin, Nicholas 718
Shevoe, Elizabeth 571
Shew, John 627
Sheward, David 501
Sheward, Ezekiel 501
Sheward, Isaiah 501, 516
Sheward, James 501
Sheward, John 501
Sheward, Nathan 501
Sheward, Phebe 501
Sheward, Rebeckah 501
Sheward, Ruth 501
Sheward, Sally 501
Sheward, Tace 501
Shewey, Henry 217
Shewey, William 217
Shewmaker, Jacob 576
Shewrnan, Nancy 572
Shick, Catherine 376
Shick, Frederick 376
Shick, John 376
Shick, John Andrew 376
Shick, Margaret 376
Shick, Mary Ann 376
Shick, Rosannah 376
Shidaker, John 118
Shideaker, Eve 133
Shideaker, John 133
Shideaker, Michael 133
Shideaker, Volentine 133
Shidelar, Catharine 558
Shideler, Gabriel 218
Shideler, Hannah 522
Shideler, Henry 209, 218
Shideler, Henry B. 413
Shideler, Jonathan 218
Shideler, Joseph 218
Shideler, Josiah 218
Shidler, Henry 203
Shidler, Jacob 413
Shidler, Susan 84
Shidly, Catharine 521
Shiedler, Henry 203
Shield, Elizabeth 577
Shield, Henry 741
Shield, William 632
Shields, Alexander 60
Shields, Andrew 50
Shields, Betsy 27
Shields, Catharine 18
Shields, David 18, 27
Shields, Elenor 76
Shields, Isaac 428
Shields, John 27, 50, 80, 466
Shields, Joseph 288
Shields, Margt. 413
Shields, Martin 18, 27
Shields, Mary 459
Shields, Peggy 27
Shields, Polly 27
Shields, Rhoda 27
Shields, Robt. 50
Shields, Samuel 27

Shields, Samuel (Jr.) 18
Shields, William 80, 510
Shilt, Barbara Ann 419
Shilt, John 419
Shim, Charles 85
Shin, Hannah 131
Shine, Conrad 436
Shink, Cyrus 737
Shink, Mary Ann 742
Shink, Shibnah 742
Shinn, Clement I. 539
Shinn, Elizabeth 539
Shinn, F. W. 529
Shinn, George 662, 686
Shiny, Margaret 747
Shipler, Jane 657
Shiplett, Rowland 370
Shipley, John 551
Shipley, Mary 742
Shipman, Maria B. 709
Shippy, Jonathan 522
Shirder, Jacob 353
Shirey, Valentine 288
Shirk, Levi 592
Shirk, Sarah 581
Shirke, Polly 588
Shirkee, Nancy 85
Shirkley, Mary 77
Shirky, James 85
Shirky, Jane 82
Shirley, Elias 316,
   323, 324, 746,
Shirley, Elizas 752
Shirley, Elizx 324
Shirley, George 272
Shirley, James 752
Shirley, John 752
Shirley, John J. 334
Shirley, Joseph 272
Shirley, Mary 747
Shirley, Nathan 337, 752
Shirley, Phebe 316, 323
Shirley, Rachael 752
Shirley, Rachel 335
Shirley, Robert 316,
   320, 323, 324, 746,
   752
Shirley, Robert (Sr.)
   752
Shirley, Ruth 744, 752
Shirley, Sarah 316, 323
Shirley, William H. 337
Shirt, Katherine 744
Shirtliff, Amassa 282
Shisler, Catharine 588
Shisler, Henry 576
Shisler, Samuel 334, 576
Shive, Conrad 436
Shively, A. 94
Shively, Adam 206
Shively, Anny 431
Shively, Christian 191,
   203
Shively, D. 94
Shively, Daniel 190,
   230, 554
Shively, David 190, 194
Shively, Elizabeth 520,
   553

Shively, Esther 94
Shively, Hariot 206
Shively, Henry 758,
   762, 764
Shively, Hettie O. 94
Shively, Isaac 194
Shively, J. C. 94
Shively, Jacob 190,
   194, 431, 553, 554
Shively, John 190
Shively, Leah 431
Shively, Mary 206, 553,
   662
Shively, Sally 194
Shively, Sarah 206
Shively, Susan 553
Shively, Susanna 190
Shively, Susannah 230
Shively, Uly 553
Shively, William 206
Shlater, John 603
Shlater, Peter 108
Shlater, Phebe 603
Shlater, William R. 108
Shoaff, Miles F. 146
Shoap, Thomas 387
Shobe, Jacob 493
Shock, Michael 453
Shockey, G. W. 629
Shockey, Jacob 733
Shockey, Minerva 733
Shoemaker, Anna 512
Shoemaker, Catharine 738
Shoemaker, Charles 401
Shoemaker, Christian
   31, 738
Shoemaker, Daniel 401
Shoemaker, Harvy 557
Shoemaker, Isabelle
   Flack 409
Shoemaker, Jacob 401,
   505
Shoemaker, Joseph 401,
   505
Shoemaker, Molly 401
Shoemaker, Sophia 401
Shoeman, Jacob 431
Shoeman, John Conrad 715
Shoewalter, Wm. 280
Sholes, Stanton 31
Sholley, John 190
Sholley, Joseph 190
Sholtz, Valentine 90
Shong, Elizabeth 760
Shong, John 760
Shook, Elizabeth 120
Shook, Margrat 499
Shoomaker, Lida 501
Shoot, Richard 516
Shope, Bernard 490
Shope, Elianor 580
Shorb, Adam 553
Shorb, Andrew 553
Shorb, Jacob 553
Shorb, John 553, 556
Shorb, Mary 553
Shorb, Peter 553
Shorb, Stephen 553
Shore, Barbara 376

Shore, John 376
Shores, Ledea 517
Short, David 42
Short, Elizabeth 392,
   512, 537
Short, Geo. 537
Short, Isaac 537
Short, Jacob 672
Short, James 392
Short, John A. 207
Short, Mary 392
Short, Phebe 392
Short, Phoebe 383
Short, Rachel 392
Short, Richard 50
Short, Sarah 392
Short, Sarah Jane 537
Short, Stephen 5, 392,
   393
Short, Susan Ann 608
Shortz, George 216
Shott, John 555
Shotto, Joshua 306
Shoub, Barbara 186
Shoub, Catherine 186
Shoub, Elizabeth 186
Shoub, Henry 186
Shoub, John 186
Shoub, Lydia 186
Shoub, Martin 186
Shouf, John 522
Shoulwiler, Elizabeth
   512
Shoup, Catharine 188
Shoup, Christopher 180
Shoup, David 216
Shoup, Elizabeth 191,
   230
Shoup, Elizabeth M. 216
Shoup, George 230
Shoup, George W. 216
Shoup, Henry 186, 191
Shoup, John Jacob 568
Shoup, Lydia 194
Shoup, Martin 186, 188,
   191, 194
Shoup, Mary Ann 216
Shoup, Sally 573
Show, George 417
Showalter, Elizabeth 577
Showalter, Henry 602,
   609
Showalter, John 576
Showalter, Magtilena 567
Showalter, Martin 600,
   602, 604, 609
Showalter, Peter 576
Shower, Abraham 200
Shower, David 200
Shower, Delia 200
Shower, Polly Ann 200
Showers, Abraham 209
Showers, David 209
Showers, Delilah 209
Showers, Polly Ann 209
Shrader, Harman 653
Shrader, Jabez 440
Shrader, Margaret 440
Shreeve, Caleb 354

956

Shreeve, James 340
Shreeve, John 359
Shreeve, Martha 359
Shreve, Elizabeth 740
Shrick, Harriet 632
Shrick, Philip 632
Shrider, John 365
Shrider, Peter 371
Shriver, Michael 264
Shriver, Rachel 442
Shriver, William 522
Shroyer, John 217
Shroyer, Philip (Jr.) 284
Shryock, Polly 127
Shttock, Joseph 576
Shubert, Andrew 337
Shubridge, Charles 391
Shuck, Mary 386
Shue, Gottlieb 369
Shuemaker, Margaret 521
Shuey, Adam 191, 211, 213
Shuey, Lewis 189, 194, 196
Shuey, Martin 186, 223
Shugert, --- 266
Shull, Frederick 562, 568, 737
Shull, Isaac 568
Shull, Mary 567
Shull, Sarah 565, 572
Shuller, Henry 561
Shultz, Elizabeth 602, 609
Shultz, Eve 602
Shultz, Sarah 602, 749
Shultz, William 749
Shumaker, Eliazer 436
Shumaker, George 436
Shumaker, Solomon 436
Shuman, Allen 414
Shuman, Eli 192
Shuman, Isaac 192
Shumbarger, Jacob 553
Shunburger, Aolina 522
Shunk, Elizabeth 374
Shunk, Henry 374
Shunk, Isaac 374
Shunk, Polly 374
Shunway, Pearly 85
Shupe, Betsey 28
Shupe, Polly 31
Shupert, Carl M. 243
Shupert, Christopher 194
Shupert, Edna F. 243
Shupert, Geo. 243
Shupert, H. 243
Shupert, John 243
Shupert, John Peter 243
Shupert, Mary 243
Shupert, Mary M. 243
Shupert, Nelson 243
Shupert, P. 243
Shupert, Peter R. 243
Shupert, Sarah 243
Shupert, Sarah M. 243
Shupert, Wanda L. 700
Shurley, Jonathan 427

Shurly, William 60
Shurts, Andrew 637
Shurts, Huston 683
Shurts, John 683
Shurts, Ruben 683
Shurty, William 60
Shurtz, Andres 634
Shuster, Abraham 314
Shuster, Christena 567
Shuster, Daniel 562
Shuster, Henry 632
Shuster, John 562, 576
Shuster, Margaret 562
Shuster, Martin 282
Shuster, Samuel 562
Shuster, Sarah 562
Shutt, Jno. 271
Shutt, John 259, 265, 266, 274
Shutt, Magelan 574
Shutts, Henry 172
Sibbels, James 491
Sibbet, James 476
Sibbit, Aaron 653
Sibbit, Benjamin 653
Sibbit, James 474
Sibert, John 247
Siblet, Aron 668
Sibley, Nancy 28
Sibley, Solomon 718
Sibley, William 42
Sichty, Sarah Ann 337
Sicicum, Caleb 173
Sickles, Elias 753
Sickles, Jacob 753
Sickles, Susannah 753
Sicks, William 85
Sideler, Eliza 205
Sideler, Matilda 205
Sidell, Gotlieb 388
Sidenbender, Joseph 101
Sidener, Catharine 761
Sides, Jacob 18
Sidesinger, Leonard 22
Sidey, John 340
Sidle, William 740
Sidner, David 60
Sidner, Eliza 60
Sidner, John T. 60
Sidner, Margaret 60
Sidner, Marquis 60
Sidner, Nancy 45, 60
Sidoras, Jane 496
Sidwell, Jno. 273
Sidwell, Levi 491
Sidwell, Rebecca 491
Siemon, Anna Catherina 411
Sifford, Lewis 402
Sifford, Sarah 402
Sifrit, James 62
Sigler, Eli 80
Sigler, Geo. 576
Sigler, John 466
Sigler, Sarah 336
Sikes, Eve 741
Sikes, George 741
Sikes, Jemima 504
Sikes, Levi 504

Sikes, Polly 513
Sikes, Rachel 504
Sikes, Rhuamy 516
Silas, Alkier 462
Silber, Catharine 740
Silber, Christian 740
Silber, Daniel 740
Silber, Elizabeth 740
Silber, Jacob 740
Silber, John 740
Silber, Margaret 740
Silber, Michael 740
Silber, Sophia 740
Silbery, Mary 124
Silbey, Solomon 282
Silby, Benjamin 587
Siler, Abner 141
Siler, Jacob 141
Siler, Sarah A. 141
Sill, Mary 155
Sill, Mary E. 35
Sill, Mary Eliz. 34
Sill, Mary Wright 181
Sill, Michael 155
Sill, Oswald 155, 166, 169, 180, 181
Sill, Oswalt 158
Sill, Polly 509
Sillas, Rebecca 659
Silley, Hannah 571
Sillibridge, Jerome B. 637
Silliman, W. 295
Silliman, Wyllis 295
Sills, Henry 297
Sills, Thos. 260
Silver, David 553
Silvers, Elizabeth 667
Silvers, Ephraim T. 55
Silvers, Mary 659
Silverthorn, Ellen G. 278
Silvey, James 265
Silvey, Robert 265
Silvey, William 265
Silvey, Wm. 259, 263, 266, 268
Simcox, William 69
Simens, Susan 101
Simers, Hanah 575
Simers, Henry 576
Simers, Isaac 576
Simeson, John 101
Siminton, Cyrus 688
Siminton, Nancy 688
Simmerman, Alexander G. 59
Simmerman, Johann Gerhard 105
Simmers, Adah 572
Simmers, Elizabeth 574
Simmers, Jesse 568
Simmers, Mary 577
Simmers, Sarah 566
Simmers, Wm. 576
Simmon, Arrenda P. 514
Simmons, Adam 529
Simmons, Barbara 117
Simmons, Catharine 116

Simmons, Catherine 529
Simmons, Charles 551
Simmons, David 185
Simmons, Elizabeth 529
Simmons, Eve 529
Simmons, Hannah 516
Simmons, Henry 146
Simmons, Jacob 127
Simmons, John 118, 529, 718
Simmons, Lucretia C. 407
Simmons, Magdalena 529
Simmons, Margaret 529
Simmons, Mary 29, 113, 115
Simmons, Mary Ann 529
Simmons, Milly 407
Simmons, Peter 529
Simmons, Philip 146
Simmons, Richard 178
Simmons, Samuel 715
Simmons, Sarah 501
Simmons, Stephen 407
Simmons, Susanna 120
Simmons, Susannah 119
Simms, Catharine 57, 117
Simms, Charles 57
Simms, Dorcas 180
Simms, John D. 57
Simms, Nancy 57
Simms, Richard 180
Simms, William Douglas 57
Simms, Wm. D. 57
Simms, Wm. R. 615
Simon, Aaron 304
Simon, Fortner 254
Simon, James F. 254
Simon, John 753
Simon, John Adam 753
Simons, Benjamin 760
Simons, Fany 760
Simons, John 253
Simons, Maria 760
Simons, Peter 529
Simons, Polly 760
Simons, Susan 760
Simonton, Alonzo L. 702
Simonton, Caroline 198
Simonton, Cyrus 690
Simonton, Eliza Ellen 690
Simonton, Elizabeth 690
Simonton, Ellen 702
Simonton, James 690
Simonton, Jane 657
Simonton, Jno. 702
Simonton, Peggy 702
Simonton, Rebecca 690
Simonton, Richard H. 690
Simonton, Sarah Jane 690
Simonton, Susan 690
Simonton, Theophilus 643
Simonton, Theophulus 654
Simpkins, Ganer P. 60
Simpson, Alexander 247, 248, 249, 252, 257, 271
Simpson, Andrew 751
Simpson, Ann Eliza 33

Simpson, Catherine 461
Simpson, David 131
Simpson, Edward 369
Simpson, Eliza 78, 746
Simpson, Eliza Jane 751
Simpson, Elizabeth 751
Simpson, Evans W. 751
Simpson, Hannah 131, 751
Simpson, James 131, 423
Simpson, Jno. 269, 271
Simpson, John 131, 516, 647, 651
Simpson, Jonathan Elmore 647
Simpson, Josiah (Jr.) 85
Simpson, Juletta 423
Simpson, Maria 82
Simpson, Mary 641
Simpson, Nancy 85
Simpson, Oliver 340
Simpson, Rachel 465
Simpson, Rebecca 751
Simpson, Robert 475, 494
Simpson, Ruth 131
Simpson, Samuel 592
Simpson, Sophia 90
Simpson, Terris 188
Simpson, Thomas I. 641
Simpson, Varsalion 751
Simpson, William 651, 720
Simpson, William D. 641
Simpson, Wm. 369
Sims, Barnett 86
Sims, Chesley K. 150
Sims, Christiann 80
Sims, Emanuel 80
Sims, Mary 82, 150
Sims, Nancy 76
Sims, Rees W. 80
Sinard, William 662
Sinclair, Alexander 163, 166, 167, 170
Sinclair, Andrew 635
Sinclair, Betsey 88
Sinclair, Elizabeth 635
Sin Clair, George 765
Sinclair, Jane 166, 635
Sinclair, John 163, 166
Sinclair, Katharine 635
Sinclair, Martha 635
Sinclair, Nancy Margaret 635
Sinclair, Sarah Ann 635
Sinclair, Thomas 635
Sinclair, Thos. 298
Sinclair, William 635
Sinclaire, Robert 297
Sindenbender, Mary 462
Sinerd, Benj. 667
Sines, Jacob 369
Sines, Jacob (Jr.) 369
Singer, Joseph 317
Sinift, Adam 376
Sinift, Barbara 376
Sinift, Christena 376
Sinift, Henry 376
Sinift, John 376
Sinift, Katy 376

Sinift, Nancy 376
Sinift, Philip 376
Sinift, Polly 376
Sinkey, Charlotte 220
Sinkey, Jno. 220
Sinks, Andrew 224
Sinks, George (Jr.) 224
Sinnard, John 651
Sinnard, William 650, 651
Sinnard, Wm. 672
Sinnet, Jacob 592
Sinter, Sossannah 575
Sinto, Anthony 522
Sippel, Elizabeth 712
Sipson, Joseph 583
Sirely, John 635
Sisco, John 400
Sisco, Mary Ann 400
Sisco, Mary Jane 400
Sissel, Sarah 84
Sissell, John 80
Sisson, Hope 637
Sisson, James 206
Sisson, Rebecca Ann 336
Sisson, William 206
Sisson, William P. 637
Sisson, Wm. 80
Sisson, Wm. P. 637
Sisty, Margaret 519
Sites, Hannah 374
Sites, William 522
Sivertson, Christian Frederick 706
Sivett, Mary 79
Six, Nancy 301
Skeels, Harvey 580
Skeen, Wm. 220
Skeets, Isaac 564
Skehan, Patrick 388
Skelings, John 127
Skggs, John L. 743
Skid, Thomas 494
Skidmore, George 481
Skidmore, Jennie 452
Skidmore, Joseph 15
Skidmore, Ruth 14
Skidmore, Shady 14
Skidmore, William 580
Skiemore, Jennie 452
Skiles, Susan 61
Skillen, Jane 550
Skillen, William 546
Skimer, David 89
Skinner, Adaline 709
Skinner, Anderson 133
Skinner, Archebald 141
Skinner, Azel 147
Skinner, C. 379
Skinner, Catherine 364
Skinner, Cornelius 375, 645, 674
Skinner, Daniel 80, 642, 672
Skinner, E. 396
Skinner, Eleanor 375
Skinner, Elizabeth 342, 364, 375
Skinner, Eve 376

958

Skinner, Fany 342
Skinner, George 375
Skinner, Hannah 349
Skinner, Hariet 645
Skinner, Harriet 674
Skinner, James 376
Skinner, James (Jr.) 376
Skinner, Jane 342
Skinner, Jesse 360, 376
Skinner, John (Jr.) 375
Skinner, John (Sr.) 375
Skinner, Joseph 80, 127
Skinner, Martha 367
Skinner, Mary 342
Skinner, Nancy 15, 133, 375
Skinner, Nathaniel 339, 349
Skinner, Rebecca 375
Skinner, Richard 340, 672
Skinner, Robert 342
Skinner, Sally 11
Skinner, Sam. 358
Skinner, Samuel 127, 360, 365, 376, 380
Skinner, Sarah 342
Skinner, Thomas 133
Skinner, W. Harrison 367
Skinner, William 127, 342, 375, 727
Skinner, Wm. Harrison 367
Skipton, William 712
Skyles, Rachel 658
Slack, Abel 285
Slack, Catharine 167
Slack, David 167
Slack, Osia 80
Slack, Robert 687
Slade, Sarah M. 337
Slagal, George 121
Slagel, Susannah 386
Slagle, Elizabeth 127
Slagle, John 127
Slagmaker, Francis 522
Slago, Martin Lawden 298
Slate, Caroline 335
Slater, Nancy 517
Slatory, John 34
Slattery, John 34
Slaugher, R. F. 470
Slaugher, Robert F. 480
Slaughter, Anna 49
Slaughter, Annie J. 411
Slaughter, Annie Jos. 411
Slaughter, Gabl. 57
Slaughter, John 350, 378
Slaughter, Mary 350
Slaughter, R. F. 469, 470
Slaughter, Robert F. 470
Slaughterback, Henry 765
Slavens, Reuben 466
Slay, Edward 178
Sleasman, Christopher 662
Sleasman, Hannah 660
Sleeper, E. 697

Sleeper, Parker 85
Sleeth, David 86
Sleeth, Elizabeth 82
Slegar, Elizabeth 384
Slemmer, Peter 609
Slemner, George 609
Slevin, Barbara 345
Slevin, James 345
Slevin, Jane 345
Slevin, John 345
Slicer, Walter 2
Slifer, Jacob 214
Slifer, Mahala 214
Slifer, Mary 214
Slifer, Rachel 214
Slinger, Joseph 525
Sloan, Agnis 298
Sloan, Ann 300
Sloan, Benj. 298
Sloan, Charles 401
Sloan, David 401
Sloan, Deborah 88
Sloan, Elias 168
Sloan, Hannah 401
Sloan, John 164, 754
Sloan, Jonathan 70
Sloan, Joseph 85
Sloan, Richard 182, 401
Sloan, Sarah 401
Sloan, Susannah 164
Sloane, Lafayette 436
Sloat, Achea 518
Slocum, Elias 31, 444
Slone, Barbery 572
Slone, Richard (Jr.) 418
Slosser, E. 113
Slosser, Elizabeth 113
Slosser, Jacob 113
Slough, Nancy Ann 333
Slow, Clarissa 493
Slusher, Samuel 171
Sluss, John 554, 557
Slusser, George 252
Slusser, Henry H. 146
Slusser, John 146
Slusser, Jones P. 746
Slusser, Mary 151
Slusser, Peter 151
Slusser, Sarah 146
Slute, Caroline 335
Slute, Peggy 567
Sluthower, George 568
Sluts, John 568
Slyter, Richard 609
Smaley, Benj. 135
Smalley, Azeriah 159
Smalley, Freeman 118
Smallwood, Branson 99
Smallwood, Marion 99
Smallwood, Peter 635
Smallwood, William 637
Smally, Abagail D. 141
Smally, Benjamin 662
Smally, Jasper M. 439
Smally, Nancy E. 141
Smally, Prudence 141
Smarr, Daniel B. 87
Smart, Francis 105
Smart, John S. 592

Smart, Judith 105
Smehey, Elizabeth 87
Smehey, Emily J. 87
Smehey, John 87
Smeltzer, Reuben 141
Smiley, Isaac 424
Smiley, Nancy 571
Smiley, Sarah 565
Smiley, Wm. 576
Smilie, John A. 742
Smily, Rhody 566
Sminth, Millenet 124
Smit, Catharine 741
Smit, Samuel 741
Smith, A . . . hy 459
Smith, A. B. 96
Smith, A. H. 98
Smith, Abigail 690, 741
Smith, Abner 133, 650
Smith, Abraham 436, 529
Smith, Adam 546
Smith, Addison 133, 762
Smith, Adella Virginia 436
Smith, Adison 742
Smith, Agnes 132
Smith, Agness 132
Smith, Alexander 398
Smith, Alfred G. 8
Smith, Amelius 206
Smith, Amos 673
Smith, Andrew 339, 340, 373, 375, 381
Smith, Ann 28, 34, 178, 264
Smith, Ann Eliza 436
Smith, Ann R. 456
Smith, Anna 45, 280, 581
Smith, Anne 13
Smith, Aron 132
Smith, Arthur 282
Smith, Asa 756
Smith, Aurilius 216
Smith, Azeriah 31
Smith, Ballard 680
Smith, Barbara 124, 513
Smith, Belinda 396
Smith, Benj. 2
Smith, Benj. F. 42
Smith, Benjamin 15, 493, 715
Smith, Benjamin C. 609
Smith, Bennet 31
Smith, Bennett 31
Smith, Betsey 132, 272, 455, 589, 629
Smith, Brainard 202
Smith, Breggton 112
Smith, C. S. 507
Smith, Caleb 758
Smith, Caroline 762, 765
Smith, Cassandra 295
Smith, Catharine 11, 84, 449, 575, 717, 765
Smith, Catherine 83, 212, 526
Smith, Cathrin 498
Smith, Caty 132
Smith, Celia 498

959

Smith, Charity 254, 592
Smith, Charles 609, 742
Smith, Charlie 96
Smith, Chloe 216
Smith, Christian 26
Smith, Christianna 493
Smith, Clarkson Z. 506
Smith, Cloe 386
Smith, Conrad 680
Smith, D. 238, 239
Smith, D. M. 615
Smith, Daniel 31, 133, 390, 522, 576
Smith, Darias 295
Smith, David 8, 31, 141, 239, 265, 285, 507, 525, 609, 662
Smith, David B. 670
Smith, David H. 254, 688
Smith, Douglas 31
Smith, E. 238, 239
Smith, E. J. 322
Smith, Easter 457
Smith, Edward 285, 291, 592
Smith, Effamay 170
Smith, Eleanor 519, 741
Smith, Eleanor J. 742
Smith, Eli B. 742
Smith, Elijah 270, 272
Smith, Elisha 499
Smith, Eliza Jane 436
Smith, Elizabeth 80, 124, 133, 141, 169, 170, 179, 212, 239, 355, 370, 376, 398, 456, 458, 490, 576, 592, 609, 635, 659, 688, 742, 743, 755, 758
Smith, Elnathan William 132
Smith, Elvira 206
Smith, Emily 29
Smith, Enoch 15
Smith, Eunice 28
Smith, Evaline 592
Smith, Ezra J. 321, 322
Smith, Fanny 132, 462, 742
Smith, Gabriel V. 146
Smith, Gasper 449
Smith, Geo. Jackson 436
Smith, George 262, 276, 361, 397, 405, 436, 499, 546, 623, 629, 672, 680, 758
Smith, George J. 686
Smith, George P. 741
Smith, George W. 195, 208
Smith, Hannah 123, 206, 216, 276, 449
Smith, Harriet 81
Smith, Harriett 132
Smith, Harvey 742
Smith, Henry 141, 170, 212, 250, 251, 592, 681
Smith, Henry A. 741

Smith, Henry Augustus 212
Smith, Henry M. 115
Smith, Henry W. 64, 576
Smith, Hester 449, 662
Smith, Hezekiah 718
Smith, Hiram C. 146
Smith, Hiram H. 629
Smith, Holland 206, 216
Smith, Hosea 650
Smith, Howell G. 7, 8
Smith, Huldah 165
Smith, Hylam 80
Smith, Irena 8
Smith, Isaac 21, 31, 212, 284, 516
Smith, Isaac J. 742
Smith, Isaiah 635
Smith, J. 536
Smith, J. F. 96
Smith, Jacob 133, 158, 160, 284, 370, 449, 466, 576, 751, 758
Smith, Jacob H. 392
Smith, Jacob M. 257
Smith, James 15, 25, 54, 133, 152, 154, 155, 172, 176, 178, 186, 284, 310, 392, 398, 438, 466, 516, 592, 645, 673, 715, 718, 728, 730, 755, 758, 764
Smith, James B. 162, 175
Smith, James F. 96
Smith, James J. 765
Smith, James O. 741
Smith, James R. 576
Smith, James S. 157
Smith, James Valentine 765
Smith, Jane 7, 12, 132
Smith, Jason W. 499
Smith, Jeremiah 279, 387, 491
Smith, Jesse 420, 623
Smith, Jno. 269, 404
Smith, Joanna 742
Smith, Job 179, 592
Smith, Joel 31
Smith, John 54, 61, 75, 80, 91, 132, 141, 146, 152, 159, 162, 207, 212, 264, 267, 295, 310, 376, 436, 502, 516, 522, 546, 557, 592, 623, 693, 709, 742, 758, 762
Smith, John (Jr.) 161, 175, 680
Smith, John A. 367
Smith, John Alfred 141
Smith, John Arra 453
Smith, John B. 537
Smith, John C. 312
Smith, John Canfield 204
Smith, John F. 509
Smith, John H. 680
Smith, John J. 51, 52, 252, 536

Smith, John L. 169, 181
Smith, John M. 63, 85, 90, 529
Smith, John Y. 629
Smith, Jonas 405
Smith, Jonathan 118, 662
Smith, Jones 397
Smith, Joseph 8, 259, 263, 522, 742
Smith, Joseph James 304
Smith, Josephine 742
Smith, Joshua D. 254
Smith, Josiah 132, 206, 216, 223
Smith, Julia 206
Smith, Laura 496
Smith, Lettitia 223
Smith, Lewis 141
Smith, Litty Ann 115
Smith, Livingston 80
Smith, Lodemia 607
Smith, Lorin 766
Smith, Louisa 254, 504, 766
Smith, Lovinan 238
Smith, Lucinda 276
Smith, Lucy 707
Smith, Lucy Ann 436
Smith, Lydia 85, 595
Smith, M. 536
Smith, M. C. 280
Smith, Magdalene 361
Smith, Mahala 172, 179
Smith, Malinda J. 615
Smith, Margaret 12, 23, 376, 398, 404
Smith, Margareta L. 693
Smith, Margarett 753
Smith, Margarette 276
Smith, Margart 565
Smith, Margrat 276
Smith, Margret 573
Smith, Maria 398, 743
Smith, Mariah 162, 680
Smith, Martha 29, 396, 454, 491, 576
Smith, Martha Ellen 436
Smith, Martha I. 693
Smith, Martin 206, 392
Smith, Mary 13, 72, 84, 123, 124, 376, 397, 405, 436, 449, 465, 499, 521, 565, 670
Smith, Mary A. 310
Smith, Mary Amanda 436
Smith, Mary E. 115
Smith, Mary R. 414
Smith, Mathew 169
Smith, Mathias 536
Smith, Matilda 81, 396
Smith, Maud 49
Smith, Mercy 502
Smith, Merril 407
Smith, Merzy 382
Smith, Michael 562
Smith, Minerva 77
Smith, Nancy 82, 153, 176, 178, 407, 455, 456, 465, 756

Smith, Nathan 254, 255,
262, 263, 266, 267,
272, 273, 727
Smith, Nicholas 466,
743, 743
Smith, Nicholas S. 741
Smith, Otilda 146
Smith, Pamila 12
Smith, Patrick 42
Smith, Pe. 106
Smith, Pencey 398
Smith, Permelia 396
Smith, Peter 7, 8, 146,
186, 491, 688
Smith, Phebe 64, 132
Smith, Phebe A. 96
Smith, Philip 118, 127
Smith, Phillip 387
Smith, Pierson 426
Smith, Polly 397, 449,
514, 658, 715
Smith, Priscilla 728, 730
Smith, Rachel 78, 107,
252, 295, 397, 523,
662, 663, 680
Smith, Rebecca 254,
306, 741, 742
Smith, Rebecca J. 98
Smith, Rhuville V. 332
Smith, Richard 49, 174,
177, 491, 586
Smith, Robert 7, 25,
27, 442, 453, 466,
484, 485, 680
Smith, Robert J. 292
Smith, Robert Mc. 629
Smith, Robny 592
Smith, Rody 461
Smith, Rosanna 273
Smith, Roswell 31
Smith, Rozetta 58
Smith, Ruth 19
Smith, S. M. 98
Smith, Salla 132
Smith, Sally 13, 56, 79
Smith, Samuel 170, 338,
436, 469, 472, 482,
484, 494, 592, 742
Smith, Samuel Arron 453
Smith, Samuel F. 741
Smith, Samuel H. 416
Smith, Samuel Littler 54
Smith, Sarah 161, 172,
186, 282, 387, 392,
449, 499, 549, 657
Smith, Sarah A. 279
Smith, Sarah C. 92
Smith, Sarah Elizabeth 8
Smith, Shubiah 263
Smith, Simeon 26
Smith, Sophia 591
Smith, Spencer 15
Smith, Stephen 146, 295
Smith, Susanna 295
Smith, Susannah 253,
257, 680
Smith, Thomas 80, 153,
165, 284, 491, 650,
655, 681, 742, 758

Smith, Thomas Cory 132
Smith, Thomas W. 536
Smith, Thompson 491
Smith, Thos. 154
Smith, Timothy 680
Smith, Tunis 449
Smith, Ulrich 276
Smith, V. R. 765
Smith, Valentine G. 743
Smith, Van Ranslear 765
Smith, Warren 31
Smith, Willard 42
Smith, William 7, 10,
20, 170, 172, 178,
179, 295, 317, 491,
504, 516, 536, 650,
662, 742, 755
Smith, William (Jr.) 629
Smith, William (Sr.) 304
Smith, William G. 623
Smith, William H. 629
Smith, William H. H. 254
Smith, William Harvey
436
Smith, William J. 407
Smith, William Lane 288
Smith, William M. 193
Smith, William S. 753
Smith, Wm. 59, 158,
436, 459, 629
Smith, Wm. D. 404
Smith, Wm. G. 576
Smith, Wm. M. 42, 202
Smith, Zilleman 396
Smith, Zra J. 318
Smithson, Rebecca 710
Smock, Polly 383
Smoke, Lavina 496
Smoot, John 304
Smoot, Moses A. 363
Smoot, Stephen 363
Smoot, Susannah 363
Smote, John B. 299
Smote, Mary 299
Smyers, Frederick 516
Smyth, William 318
Snack, Henry 522
Snailer, Conrad 152
Snap, John 459
Snapp, John 491
Snatterly, Elizabeth 367
Snead, Benjamin F. 42
Sneath, Mary Ann 520
Snedeker, John F. 584
Snedoker, Louisa 115
Sneed, Achillis 57
Sneff, John 267
Snel, Thomas 453
Snelbakker, John 568
Snell, Andrew J. 328
Snell, Christene 125
Snell, John 662
Snell, William M. 328
Snellabarger, George 337
Snep, John 198, 206
Snep, Leonard 206
Snep, Maria 206
Snep, Sarah 206
Snepp, John 192

Sneyder, Mary 276
Snider, Aaron 207
Snider, Adam 347, 568
Snider, Anna 231, 232
Snider, Arnold 645
Snider, Barbara 555
Snider, Catharine 189,
568
Snider, Christian 172
Snider, Coonrad 649
Snider, Coonrod 641
Snider, Daniel 189,
673, 763
Snider, David 645, 673
Snider, Elizabeth 555,
645, 673
Snider, Esther 645, 673
Snider, George 208, 555
Snider, Henry 189, 207,
208, 563, 649
Snider, Jacob 141, 189,
365, 378, 522, 555
Snider, John 133, 444,
530, 677
Snider, Jonas 232
Snider, Magdalena 555
Snider, Margaret 708
Snider, Maria 608
Snider, Mary 208, 645,
673
Snider, Michael 555
Snider, Nicholas 555
Snider, Peter 376, 555
Snider, Philip 576
Snider, Samuel 763
Snider, Sarah 763
Snider, Susan 378, 609
Snider, Susanna 189, 555
Snider, Thomas 127, 231
Snider, William 189,
645, 673
Sniff, John 260, 263,
267, 271
Snitker, Jacob 576
Snitker, Ruthnita 576
Snoddy, Abner 15
Snode, William 304
Snodgrass, Agnes 597, 598
Snodgrass, Agnes (Jr.)
598
Snodgrass, Alexd. 559
Snodgrass, Andrew H. 436
Snodgrass, Hannah 581,
586
Snodgrass, James 202,
420, 436, 586, 597,
598
Snodgrass, James R.
592, 598
Snodgrass, James T. 199
Snodgrass, Jane 581,
586, 598
Snodgrass, Jane Ann 586
Snodgrass, Jean 586
Snodgrass, Polly 598
Snodgrass, Robert 581,
592, 596
Snodgrass, Samuel 581,
593, 598

Snodgrass, Sarah Jane 436
Snodgrass, William 182, 593, 598
Snook, Ann R. 521
Snook, Annie 334
Snook, Charlotte 663
Snook, Delila 495
Snook, Eli 529
Snook, Elizabeth 515
Snook, George 631, 751
Snook, Henry 631
Snook, Jacob 746
Snook, Jeremiah 516
Snook, Joab 645, 674
Snook, John 631, 669, 672
Snook, John M. 662
Snook, Johnson 645, 674
Snook, Martha 635
Snook, Parmelia 745
Snook, Perlina 631
Snook, Peter 320
Snook, Sarah 631
Snook, W. N. 321
Snook, William 631, 646, 662, 674
Snook, William N. 316, 336
Snook, Wilson H. 746
Snow, Henry 499
Snow, Rebeckah 752
Snow, Sarah 667
Snowbarger, John 203
Snuff, Abram 662
Snuffin, Mary 14
Snuke, Jeremiah 516
Snyder, Abraham 563
Snyder, Anna 739
Snyder, Anthony W. 98
Snyder, Arnold 673
Snyder, Becky 452
Snyder, Christina 555
Snyder, Daniel 203, 338, 649
Snyder, Elizabeth 570
Snyder, Francis L. 422
Snyder, Frederick 641
Snyder, George 553
Snyder, Henry 276, 576
Snyder, Isaac 453
Snyder, Jacob 66, 217, 228
Snyder, John 181, 677, 739
Snyder, Lear 606
Snyder, M. J. 98
Snyder, Margaret 66, 98
Snyder, Martha 576
Snyder, Mary A. 94
Snyder, N. 94
Snyder, Nicholas 555
Snyder, Roy 245
Snyder, Susannah 422
Snyder, Valentine 422
Snyder, W. 98
Snyder, William 203
Sockrider, John 387
Sodders, Lawrence 491

Sohn, Margaret 521
Sollars, Ann 455
Sollars, John 466
Sollars, Nancy 451
Sollars, Slashey 461
Sollebarger, Abraham 213
Sollebarger, Samuel 213
Solleberger, Anna 213
Soller, John Fredrick 107
Soller, William 632
Sollers, Sally 453
Solliday, Jacob 738
Sollinger, Adam 751
Solomon, Elehow Wm. 49
Solomon, George 599
Solomon, John 436
Soloven, Maria 744
Solsgarven, Catherine 465
Somer, Jacob 593
Somersett, Susan 606
Sommers, Jacob 546
Sonder, Deliah 529
Sonder, John 524
Sonders, John 127
Songer, Adam 127
Songer, John 121
Songer, Sally 127
Sopt, Gufane 614
Sopt, Herman 614
Sorrels, Robert 443
Souder, Christina 522
Souder, John 42
Souder, John Wesley 522
Souders, Samuel 420
Soule, Olive 79
Sourbray, George 232
Sourbray, Mary 232
Sourbray, William 183
Sous, Benjamin (Rev.) 594
Sousley, Geo. 363
Souslin, Mary Magdalena 373
Sout, Aaron 593
Souter, Barbara 518
Southall, Wm. 353
Southard, Hudson 466
Southard, Sarah 580
Southard, William 398, 593
Southerland, David 155
Southerland, Hannah 15
Southerland, Margaret 155
Southerland, Thomas 27
Southward, Betsey 385
Southward, Betsy 586
Southward, Samuel 86
Southwards, Leamon 466
Southworth, Isaac (Jr.) 393
Soward, Sarah 523
Sowers, Amy Mulvina 276
Sowers, Henry 276
Sowers, John 276
Sowers, Mary 413
Sowers, Philip 92

Soyez, Louis 712
Space, Elizabeth 29
Space, Philip 74
Spacht, Anthony 729
Spacht, Fanny E. 431
Spacht, Jacob 729
Spade, Caty 384
Spafford, Alfred Jarvis 766
Spafford, Amos 760
Spafford, Aurora 760, 766
Spafford, Clvey 760
Spafford, James Aurora 766
Spafford, Louisa 766
Spafford, Mary 766
Spafford, Mary Olivia 766
Spafford, Miranda 766
Spafford, Olive 760
Spafford, Samuel 760
Spaicer, Eliza Ann 336
Spain, Aaron 581
Spain, Edward 593
Spain, Hezekiah 593
Spain, John 52
Spain, Milly 593
Spain, Paschael 593
Spain, Thomas 15
Spalding, George 155
Spallman, Mary 111
Spangle, Caty 501
Spangle, George 524
Spangle, Henry 501
Spangle, John H. 522
Spangle, Lydia 501
Spangle, Nancy 501
Spangler, Ann Mc. 419
Spangler, Cath. 403
Spangler, Catharine 384
Spangler, Christian 297, 298
Spangler, David 273, 290, 399
Spangler, Elizabeth 501, 517
Spangler, George 501
Spangler, Henry 501
Spangler, J. 403
Spangler, Jacob 403, 501
Spangler, Lydia Ann 419
Spangler, Mathias (Jr.) 291
Spangler, Polly 384, 501, 557
Spangler, Rachel 501
Spangler, Samuel 401
Spangler, Sarah 501
Spangler, Susannah 501
Spare, Thomas 340
Sparks, Isaac 15
Sparks, Nancy 414
Sparks, Ruth 577
Sparling, Elizabeth 540
Sparling, J. M. 540
Sparling, N. 540
Spaulding, Elizabeth 507
Speace, Henry 551

962

Spealer, Elizabeth 627
Spear, Jane 292
Spear, John 141
Spear, John Ulerick 293
Spear, Louiza 609
Spear, Mary 141
Spear, Mary Jane 606
Spear, Stewart 283
Spears, Eliza 607
Spears, Mary 91
Spears, Richard C. 609
Spears, Samuel I. 609
Speasmake, Casner 49
Speck, Elizabeth 565
Speedman, John 264
Speelman, John 265
Speer, Eliza 292
Speer, J. 701
Speer, Lydia M. 701
Speer, M. 701
Speer, Margaret 292
Speer, Martha 292
Speer, Nancy 294
Speer, Nancy Ann 292
Speer, Polly 292
Speer, Rebecca 292
Speer, Robert 286, 292, 297
Speer, Sarah 292
Speer, Stuart 292
Speer, Thomas 286, 292, 294
Speer, William 292
Speers, Daniel 306
Speilman, Philip 522
Spence, Andrew 208
Spence, Isaac 652
Spence, Mary Ann 208
Spence, Samuel 208
Spence, Thomas 208
Spence, William B. 652
Spencer, --- (Capt.) 426
Spencer, Amos L. 179
Spencer, Anna 666
Spencer, Barby 220
Spencer, Chas. 141
Spencer, Conrad 220
Spencer, Daniel S. 86
Spencer, E. S. 366
Spencer, Edward S. 363
Spencer, Elisha 265
Spencer, Elizabeth 179, 220
Spencer, Elizabeth R. 591
Spencer, George 285
Spencer, Gustavus 491
Spencer, James 141, 259, 265, 285, 343, 350, 375
Spencer, Jesse 390
Spencer, John 127, 141, 415, 663
Spencer, John R. 690
Spencer, Levi 593
Spencer, Margaret 343
Spencer, Mary 76, 358, 570, 740
Spencer, Moses 525

Spencer, Moses T. 167
Spencer, Robert 364, 375, 378
Spencer, Samuel 741
Spencer, Sarah 375
Spencer, Thomas 343
Spencer, William 285, 375, 378, 379
Spencer, Wm. 364, 378
Spengler, Catharine 388
Spenk, Amanda 740
Spenk, Cyrust 740
Spenk, Julie 740
Spenk, Martha 740
Spenk, Nancy Ann Beall 740
Spenk, Nancy C. 740
Spenk, Reasin Beall 740
Spenk, Rebecca B. 740
Spenk, Sophrona 740
Spenk, Syres 741
Spenning, Hannah 658
Spergin, Jesse 593
Spergin, Susanna 588
Sperker, Harred Engel 103
Speva, George 743
Spicer, Daniel 288
Spicer, Hiram 141
Spicer, Jabiah (Rev.) 531
Spicer, John 286
Spicer, Moses 80
Spicer, Stephen 609
Spicker, Christian 576
Spiece, John 551
Spier, Samuel 691
Spies, Abraham S. 375
Spies, Adam 375
Spies, David 375
Spies, Jacob 375
Spies, Peter 375
Spies, Philip 375
Spies, Susannah 375
Spiker, Mary 572
Spillers, Peter 127
Spindler, Peter 711
Spink, J. C. 761
Spinning, Corydon 684
Spinning, Elias W. 214
Spinning, John 684
Spinning, Stephen 644
Spitler, Nathan 355
Spitler, Simon 554
Spitsnoggle, Sarah 337
Spoer, Jesse 141
Spoer, Robert 141
Spohn, Barbara 353
Spohn, Catherine 355
Spohn, Catrina 375
Spohn, Daniel 378
Spohn, Jacob 353
Spohn, John 375, 376
Spohn, Margaret 409
Spohn, Philip 354, 355, 375
Spohr, Adam 351
Spong, Eve 457
Spoon, Kathran 498

Spooner, Charles 448
Spore, John Ulerick 293
Spradling, Eva 700
Spradling, Wm. 700
Spragg, Nancy 363
Sprague, Abigail 496
Sprague, Benjamin 162
Sprague, Betsy 752
Sprague, Eliza 255
Sprague, Evaline 752
Sprague, Fredk. 733
Sprague, Gartry 268
Sprague, Isaac 268, 272
Sprague, John 551
Sprague, Jonathan 715
Sprague, Margaret 255
Sprague, Martha 255
Sprague, Martin 189
Sprague, Mary 752
Sprague, Nathan 19, 255
Sprague, Nathaniel 255
Sprague, Nehemiah 727
Sprague, Phebe 752
Sprague, Phoe 268
Sprague, Samuel 255, 715
Sprague, Sarah 290, 752
Sprague, Sidney S. 320
Sprague, Solomon 752
Sprague, Susan 255
Sprague, Susannah 162
Sprague, Wilber 259, 268
Sprague, Wilber 715
Sprague, William 255
Sprague, William B. 752
Sprague, Wm. 268
Sprake, Francis 104
Sprake, Wm. Henry 105
Spraklin, Alfred (Rev.) 531
Sprankle, Henry 362
Spray, A. 697
Spray, Alva G. 697
Spray, Amos 697
Spray, Benjamin 546
Spray, Charles F. 697
Spray, Dinah 697
Spray, E. E. 697
Spray, Elizabeth 697
Spray, Eunice 697
Spray, J. 697
Spray, James 546, 663
Spray, Jane 659
Spray, Jesse 681, 697, 698
Spray, John 697, 698
Spray, M. 697
Spray, Martin 697
Spray, Mary 550, 664, 697, 698
Spray, Mary Ann 698
Spray, Rebeca 666
Spray, Rebecca 697
Spray, S. 697
Spray, Samuel 697
Spray, Sarah 698
Spray, Sarah A. 697
Sprecher, Sarah 521
Sprigg, Wm. 469
Springe, Deborah 54

Springer, Benjamin 54
Springer, Charles 375
Springer, Charles R. 522
Springer, Cons. 286
Springer, Daniel 368
Springer, Deborah 54
Springer, Elizabeth 54
Springer, J. P. 260
Springer, Jacob 721
Springer, Jacob P. 258, 259, 260, 262, 264, 265
Springer, Joseph 270
Springer, Mathias 568
Springer, Peleg 715
Springer, Peter 499
Springer, Robert 54
Springer, Silas 54
Springer, Thomas 54
Springum, John 262
Sproat, E. 730
Sproat, Earl 156, 157, 161, 179
Sproat, Ebenezer 721, 730
Sproat, James 179
Sproat, Katherine 730
Sproat, Sally 718
Sproat, Sarah 179, 730
Sprock, Ann Maria 107
Sprock, Anna Maria 104
Sprock, Bernard Henry 107
Sprock, Bernd. Henry 104
Sprock, Elizabeth 108
Sprock, Gesina Maria 104
Sprock, Hellen Maria 107
Sprock, Hellen Mary 104
Sprock, J. B. 104
Sprock, John Bernard 104
Sprock, Margaretta Maria 104, 107
Sprock, Maria Elizabeth 107
Sprock, Martha Maria 107
Sprock, Mary Elizabeth 104
Sprock, Mary Engle 104
Sprouse, Rachel 508
Sprowl, Andrew 156
Sprowl, Jane 606
Spry, J. W. 291
Spur, John 551
Spurce, Zellah 90
Spurch, George 375
Spurck, Mary 346
Spurck, Peter 346
Spurgen, Sarah 589
Spurgeon, Elias 68
Spurgeon, Jane 68
Spurgin, Jeremiah 294
Spurgin, Nathaniel 169
Spurgin, Sarah 169
Spurier, Elenor 744
Spurrier, Elizabeth 336
Spurrier, Frederick 746
Spurrier, Louis 336
Spve, Jonathan 576
Spyker, Henry 387

Squier, Daniel 31
Squier, David 182, 223
Squier, James J. 313
Squiers, Ezra 31
Squiers, Marietta 31
Squire, David 185
Squire, Eliza 185
Squire, James 491
Squire, Juliet 185
Squire, Phebe 185
Squire, Rebecca 185
Squire, Sally G. 185
Squire, Sarah 608
Squires, Amasa 31
Squires, Justice 721
Squires, Lavina 522
Squires, Mary 506, 507
Squires, Nathaniel 507
Squires, Phineas 507
Squires, Samuel 507
Squires, William H. 64
Srashel, Henry 749
Srimplin, Lydia 569
Srouf, Lucy L. 336
Sroufe, Albert 750
Sroufe, Alfred 750
Sroufe, Christopher 750
Sroufe, George 551, 750
Sroufe, Joseph 750
Sroufe, Lewis 750
Sroufe, Mary 750
Sroufe, Sebastian 750
Sroufe, Susan 750
Sroufe, Thomas D. 750
Srousse, George 551
Sruon, Valentine 522
Staats, Abraham 715
Staats, Anna 302
Staats, Elijah 80
Staats, Isaac 80
Staats, Joseph 718
Staats, Rebecca 717
Stabaugh, George 609
Stabaugh, John 610
Stacey, Gideon 729
Stacey, William 729
Stachard, Elizabeth 462
Stacher, Abey 452
Stack, Anna 718
Stackham, Joseph 516
Stackham, Rachel 513
Stackhous, Margaret 591
Stackhouse, Alice 764
Stackhouse, Elizabeth 452
Stackhouse, Isaac 733
Stackhouse, Jonathan 168
Stackhouse, Phebe A. 764
Stacy, Cathrine 126
Stacy, Emily 609
Stacy, George 764
Stacy, Sally 415
Stacy, Susanna 714
Stacy, William 715
Staden, John 718
Stafel, Joseph 439
Staffin, Catharine 607
Stafford, Christiopher 130

Stafford, Elizabeth 444, 490
Stafford, Hannah 522
Stafford, James 439, 444
Stafford, Jemima 444
Stafford, John W. 146
Stafford, Maria H. 519
Stafford, Martha 146
Stafford, Mary 146
Stafford, Ralph 130
Stafford, Thomas 131
Stage, Richard 387
Stager, Sarah E. 115
Stager, William 115
Staggs, William 453
Stagner, Godfrey 166, 172
Stagner, Julianne 172
Stahl, Peter 396
Stahl, William 523
Stahman, John B. 106
Staib, Lewis 523
Stair, John 39
Stair, William 42
Staley, Catharine 141
Staley, Christian 157
Staley, Christopher 371
Staley, David 127, 141
Staley, John 201
Staley, Joseph 141
Staley, Levi 546
Staley, Mary 549
Staley, Nancy 538
Staley, Reben 538
Staley, Reuben 551
Staley, Vitale 538
Stall, C. 327
Stall, Christopher 333
Stall, E. 327
Stall, Elizabeth 565
Stall, Hugh 387
Stall, Israel 761
Stall, Sarah E. 327
Stall, William 349, 351
Stallcup, John 491
Staly, John 558
Stam, Matty 607
Stamman, Wilhelm 112
Stams, Jesse 610
Stanback, Silas 416
Stanberry, Jacob W. 248
Stanberry, Jeremiah 15
Stanberry, Jonas 287, 341
Stanberry, Samuel 63, 274
Stanbery, Ezra 274
Stanbery, Harriet 274
Stanbery, Ira 274
Stanbery, Joel 274
Stanbery, John 274
Stanbery, Letitia H. 274
Stanbery, Martha 274
Stanbery, Samuel 270
Stanbery, Sarah 274
Stanbury, Daniel 15
Stancity, Mary 521
Standford, Sally 79
Standish, Ellen 92

Standley, Betsey 80
Stanfield, Charity A. 700
Stanfield, Eli 15
Stanfield, Elizabeth 27, 701
Stanfield, Evan J. 700
Stanfield, George 228
Stanfield, Hannah 27
Stanfield, Lydia 27
Stanfield, M. 701
Stanfield, Mary 27
Stanfield, Massey Kennedy 701
Stanfield, Nancy 27
Stanfield, Neva 700
Stanfield, Phebe 27
Stanfield, Rachel 27
Stanfield, Rebekah 27
Stanfield, Ruth 700
Stanfield, S. 701
Stanfield, Samuel 701
Stanfield, Sarah 27
Stanfield, Thomas 27
Stanfield, Thomas (Jr.) 27
Stanfield, Thomas (Sr.) 27
Stanfield, Wm. M. 700
Stanford, Elizabeth 85, 667
Stanford, Polly 660
Stanley, Amzi 733
Stanley, John 80
Stanley, Lydia N. 82
Stanley, Robert 387
Stanley, Sarah 559
Stanley, Thomas 723
Stanley, Thomas W. 499
Stanley, William H. 523
Stanly, Susanna 509
Stannard, Catherine 528
Stannard, John 528
Stansberry, Jonas 339, 733
Stansberry, Recompense 672
Stansbery, William C. 610
Stansbury, Eliza W. 92
Stansbury, Mary 556
Stansbury, Nathan 460
Stansel, Jeremiah 684
Stansel, John 210
Stanter, Mary 13
Stanton, Aaron 553
Stanton, Deborah 553
Stanton, Hephzibah 553
Stanton, James 553
Stanton, Laccheus 553
Stanton, Latham 553
Stanton, Sarah 553
Stanton, William 553
Stanton, Zaccheus 553
Starage, Jane 15
Starage, Mary 15
Starbuck, Samuel 15
Starcher, Abraham 80
Starens, Milly 497
Stark, Elizabeth 667

Stark, John 157
Starkey, . . . 163
Starkey, Catherine 522
Starkey, David 527
Starkey, Elizabeth 527
Starkey, Gabriel 164, 171
Starkey, Jesse 527
Starkey, Katherine 527
Starkey, Levi 527
Starkey, Lewis 167
Starkey, Maliny 527
Starkey, Mary 164, 171
Starkey, Rebecca J. 527
Starkey, Sally 527
Starkey, Simon Peter 527
Starkley, Russell 171
Starky, Perlia 92
Starlin, Simon 730
Starlin, Simon (Jr.) 730
Starner, Fanny 295
Starner, John 295
Starr, Elizabeth 307
Starr, Hannah 307
Starr, Jabez 171
Starr, John W. 272
Starr, Levi 633
Starr, Mary 307
Starr, Mervick 560
Starr, Peter 629
Starr, Samuel 307
Starr, Sarah 307
Starr, Susannah 334
Starr, William 307
Starrage, Thomas 15
Starrage, William 15
Starret, Charles 50
Starret, James 177
Starrett, Charles 546
Starrett, Elizabeth 546
Starrett, J. D. M. 546
Starrett, James 291, 546
Starwat, Mervin 593
State, John 672
Stater, Malind 744
Statfield, Francis M. 610
Statler, Abraham 121
Statler, Camillus W. 141
Statler, Christena 135
Statler, Christian 147
Statler, Christley 135
Statler, Christly 118
Statler, Christopher 135
Statler, Elizabeth 356
Statler, George 135
Statler, Henry 349, 362
Statler, Henry (Jr.) 349
Statler, Hiram 349
Statler, Isaac 148
Statler, Jacob 135
Statler, Jerome 349
Statler, John 118, 135, 371
Statler, Joseph 349
Statler, Jule Ann 349
Statler, Julian 349
Statler, Mary 49
Statler, Nancy 115

Statler, Nicholas 349
Statler, Polly 135
Statler, Rachel 349
Statler, Samuel 115, 147
Statler, William 349
Staub, Elizabeth 520
Staubus, Elizabeth 371
Staubus, William 371
Stauffer, Abraham 2
Stauffer, Catharine 2
Stauffer, David 1
Stauffer, Elisabth 237
Stauffer, Elizabeth 1
Stauffer, Henry 237
Stauffer, Joseph 2
Stauffer, Mary 2
Stauffer, Mary Ann 237
Stauffer, Nancy 2
Stauffer, Sarah 1
Stauffer, Susannah 2
Stauley, Nancy 467
Staunton, B. 3
Staunton, Benjamin (Jr.) 3
Staunton, Jane 424
Staunton, Robert 424
Stauton, Elizabeth 682
Staver, Casper (Jr.) 186
Staver, Frederick 186
Stawbecker, Magdalin 520
Steadman, Alex 80
Steddom, John 654
Steddom, Martha 688
Steddom, Mary 659
Stedman, Almerin 31
Stedman, Harriet 78
Stedman, Levi 86
Stedman, Lucy 77
Stedman, Lyman 86
Stedman, Polly 80
Stedman, Sally 84
Steed, George 175
Steedom, Edward 699
Steedom, Martha E. 699
Steefe, Jacob 568
Steel, Ann 520
Steel, Elizabeth 92
Steel, Havey 522
Steel, Henry K. (Dr.) 220
Steel, Hugh 668
Steel, J. A. 406
Steel, James 17, 183, 443
Steel, Jane 14
Steel, John 466, 471
Steel, Julia 406
Steel, Mary 662
Steel, Miria 133
Steel, Nancy 158, 180
Steel, Robt. 459
Steel, Samuel 158, 176, 180
Steel, Thomas 467, 494
Steel, William 181
Steel, Wm. 177
Steel, Wm. Franklin 406
Steele, Barbary J. 39
Steele, George 490

Steele, Hiram 42
Steele, J. R. 762
Steele, James 200
Steele, James E. 141
Steele, John 200
Steele, Lee 42
Steele, Margret 549
Steele, Peggy 491
Steele, William 174
Steeley, Gwana 399
Steeley, Gwinna 399
Steeley, James 546
Steeley, Lemuel 399
Steelsmith, John 568
Steely, Gionea 68
Steely, Guinnia 68
Steely, Guynea 68
Steely, John 467
Steely, Lemuel 68
Steely, Sarah 387
Steen, James 23
Steen, Jane 463
Steen, John 398
Steen, Robert 546
Steen, Sally 463
Steen, Thomas 546
Steenbarger, Lewis 121
Steennbergar, Charles
  516
Steenrod, Ephraim 176
Steenrod, Mary 176
Steenrod, Nathaniel 169
Steenson, James 296
Steenson, Jane 296
Steenson, John 296
Steenson, Mary 296
Steenson, Peggy Ann 296
Steenson, Sarah 296
Steenson, William 296
Steer, Alphus Green 52
Steer, Angella 52
Steer, Clinla 52
Steer, Simon 52
Steer, Simon Berdsall 52
Steiner, Abraham 467
Steiner, Barbary 743
Steiner, Daniel 743
Steiner, Jacob 741, 743
Steiner, Jno. J. 525
Steiner, Peter 743
Steiner, Rachel 741
Steiner, Uley 743
Steinlage, Mary 111
Steinman, J. H. 106
Steinman, Jacob 327
Steinmyer, Henry 102
Steith, David 80
Stemple, Daniel 576
Stencart, Alex. 733
Steneson, Joseph 25
Stenman, I. H. 108
Steortes, Margaret 760
Stepenson, Aaron 475
Stepenson, Marcus 475
Stephen, A. G. 419
Stephen, Elijah 168
Stephen, John 168, 467
Stephen, Margara 168
Stephen, Nancy 170

Stephen, Thomas 170
Stephens, Abednigo 230
Stephens, Abraham 553
Stephens, Alexander 232
Stephens, Amos 523
Stephens, Apolo 169
Stephens, Austin 141
Stephens, Benjamin 170
Stephens, Dewitt C. 436
Stephens, Eliz. 141
Stephens, Eliza 45,
  232, 436, 546
Stephens, Elizabeth 146
Stephens, Evan 671
Stephens, Fanny 436
Stephens, Harriet 141
Stephens, Harriet N. 420
Stephens, Harry 146
Stephens, Hetabel 230
Stephens, Hetty 550
Stephens, John 426
Stephens, John B. 436
Stephens, Joseph 279,
  624
Stephens, Laura 436
Stephens, Lewis 423
Stephens, Margaret 419
Stephens, Martin F. 436
Stephens, Mary 337, 426
Stephens, Nancy 464
Stephens, Nathaniel B.
  436
Stephens, Oliver G. 582
Stephens, Precilla 456
Stephens, Richard 230,
  436
Stephens, Wm. D. 436
Stephens, Zacheriah 568
Stephenson, Caroline 641
Stephenson, Catharine
  107
Stephenson, Charlotte
  107
Stephenson, David A. R.
  687
Stephenson, Debarough
  641
Stephenson, Delilah 687
Stephenson, Ebenezer 499
Stephenson, Hiram 107
Stephenson, James 15
Stephenson, James D. 523
Stephenson, Jas. 15
Stephenson, John 107
Stephenson, Joseph (Jr.)
  3
Stephenson, Levi 444
Stephenson, Margaret 3,
  14
Stephenson, Mary 551
Stephenson, Mary E. 92
Stephenson, May 641
Stephenson, Minerva 687
Stephenson, Philip 107
Stephenson, Robert 491,
  641, 687
Stephenson, Robert W.
  546
Stephenson, Samuel 107

Stephenson, Sarah 512
Stephenson, Silas 107
Stephenson, Susanna 641
Stephenson, Thomas 141,
  546
Stephenson, Thomas St.
  687
Stephenson, Wm. 141
Stephenson, Wm. W. 146
Stephenson, Zachariah
  387
Stepheson, Mary Ann 687
Steps, Abraham 472
Sterett, Maria 431
Sterling, Adam 15
Sterling, Micah 42
Stern, Aaron 334
Sterns, Sullivan F. 688
Sterret, Eleanor 436
Sterret, James 154
Sterret, Margaret 154
Stersenbach, Jacob 420
Stetler, Abraham 615
Stetler, Alfred 619
Stetler, Alonzo 613
Stetler, Angeline 613
Stetler, C. 619
Stetler, Catharine 615
Stetler, Celia Jane 437
Stetler, D. 614
Stetler, Daniel 186,
  196, 205, 599, 615
Stetler, Dewey F. 615
Stetler, Eliza Jane 610
Stetler, Elizabeth 606
Stetler, Elizabeth
  Melvina 437
Stetler, Emaline 615
Stetler, Emanuel 615
Stetler, G. 615
Stetler, Geo. 615
Stetler, Harrod 615
Stetler, Harvey 613
Stetler, Henry 196, 615
Stetler, I. 614
Stetler, Iona F. 619
Stetler, J. 613, 615,
  618
Stetler, Jacob 196,
  610, 619
Stetler, James Dewey 613
Stetler, Jeffry 614
Stetler, Jeffry 618
Stetler, John 431, 613
Stetler, John W. 615
Stetler, Julia Ann 610
Stetler, Julia H. 618
Stetler, Levi 612, 614
Stetler, Lewis 615
Stetler, Lucinda 614
Stetler, Lydia 615, 619
Stetler, M. A. 615
Stetler, Mahala 618
Stetler, Margaret 614,
  615
Stetler, Mathda V. 618
Stetler, Nancy 618
Stetler, Nelson 618
Stetler, O. 615

966

Stetler, P. 613
Stetler, Phebe 613
Stetler, R. 614, 615, 618
Stetler, Rhoda 614
Stetler, Samuel 614
Stetler, Sarah Ida 618
Stetler, Thomason 618
Stetler, Threse E. 615
Stetler, W. L. 619
Stetler, William 186, 196
Stettler, Catharine 242
Stettler, D. D. 242
Stettler, Daniel 242
Stettler, Elizabeth 242
Stettler, Eva Catharine 242
Stettler, George 242
Stettler, George V. 242
Stettler, Henry 222, 242
Stettler, Henry (Jr.) 242
Stettler, J. W. 242
Stettler, J. William 242
Stettler, John George 242
Stettler, Mahala 242
Stettler, Mary 242
Stettler, Philip 242
Stettler, Thomas 242
Stevens, Amos 80
Stevens, Anna Mariah 315
Stevens, Benjamin 86
Stevens, Catharine 93
Stevens, Daniel L. 315
Stevens, David 258, 263
Stevens, Elijah 250, 251
Stevens, Eliza 555
Stevens, Elizabeth Jane 403
Stevens, Emmy 315
Stevens, Frederick F. 746
Stevens, George W. 710
Stevens, Hannah 315
Stevens, J. A. 94
Stevens, James 313, 315
Stevens, James Bascom 315
Stevens, James F. 315
Stevens, Jane 315
Stevens, Jesse 80
Stevens, John 315
Stevens, John A. 115
Stevens, Jonathan 315
Stevens, Josphus 275
Stevens, Ketty 451
Stevens, Lorenzo D. 115
Stevens, Louis 77
Stevens, Lydia 92
Stevens, Lydia A. 547
Stevens, M. 403
Stevens, Mary 313, 315
Stevens, Peter 115
Stevens, Polly 524
Stevens, Rachel 315
Stevens, Rebecca 115
Stevens, Sally 555

Stevens, Saml. 403
Stevens, Samuel 733
Stevens, Sarah 315
Stevens, T. 94
Stevens, Thomas M. 315
Stevens, Vernon 301
Stevens, Virgil 115
Stevens, W. A. 115
Stevens, William 121, 315
Stevens, William S. 315
Stevens, Wm. 269
Stevens, Wm. C. 523
Stevens, Xula R. 94
Stevenson, Comfort 366
Stevenson, David 387
Stevenson, Eleanor 358
Stevenson, Hetty 660
Stevenson, Joseph 3
Stevenson, Joseph D. 80
Stevenson, Rebecca 453
Stevenson, Robert 683
Stevenson, Sarah 25
Stevenson, Thomas 286, 667, 683
Steward, Elizabeth 13
Steward, George 168, 173
Steward, Ishmael 127
Steward, James 26
Steward, Phebe 649
Steward, William 121
Stewart, . . . 173
Stewart, Abraham 467
Stewart, Adaline 591, 597, 598
Stewart, Ann 141
Stewart, Anna 511
Stewart, Archibald 422
Stewart, Arthur 486
Stewart, Betsey 660
Stewart, Catherine 512
Stewart, Charity 558
Stewart, Charles 558
Stewart, Chas. 141
Stewart, Daniel 551, 733
Stewart, David 646, 652, 675
Stewart, Edith Ellen 700
Stewart, Edward 558
Stewart, Eleanor 593, 595, 597
Stewart, Elenor 558
Stewart, Eliz. G. 141
Stewart, Eliza 141
Stewart, Eliza Ann 376
Stewart, Elizabeth 33, 126, 146, 661, 697
Stewart, Elizah 547
Stewart, Evie 547
Stewart, Ezra H. 437
Stewart, Falander B. 718
Stewart, Faney 15
Stewart, G. W. 697
Stewart, George 174
Stewart, Hugh 510
Stewart, Isabel 558
Stewart, Isabella 167
Stewart, James 19, 257, 444, 493, 597, 598, 648, 652

Stewart, James A. 530
Stewart, James Doliver 409
Stewart, James L. 141
Stewart, Jermiah 459
Stewart, Jesse 557, 558
Stewart, John 141, 302, 355, 438, 439, 441, 448, 459, 472, 480, 484, 485, 505, 593, 597, 648
Stewart, John N. 377
Stewart, Joseph 419, 595, 598, 610
Stewart, Joseph M. 19
Stewart, Joseph P. 87
Stewart, Joseph S. 646, 675
Stewart, Lemuel J. 718
Stewart, Luertisha 377
Stewart, Margaret 382, 465, 496
Stewart, Marjary 550
Stewart, Mary 547, 591, 657, 661
Stewart, Mary Ann 419
Stewart, Mary Jane 257
Stewart, Mary W. 437
Stewart, Mathew 175, 179
Stewart, Mathew M. 700
Stewart, Moses B. 547
Stewart, Nancy 141, 174
Stewart, Polly 505
Stewart, Rebecca 523
Stewart, Richard 551
Stewart, Robert 160, 167, 358, 360, 376
Stewart, Sally 501
Stewart, Samuel 646, 663, 675
Stewart, Sarah 376, 486
Stewart, Sarah Ann 547
Stewart, Stephen 516
Stewart, Susan 19
Stewart, Thomas 19, 173, 558, 697
Stewart, Warner 675
Stewart, Warren 646, 652
Stewart, William 160, 174, 305, 486, 510, 597, 598, 648, 653
Stewart, William S. 663
Stewart, Wm. 141, 478
Stewart, Wm. T. 697
Stewat, John 649
Stibbins, Elijah 650
Stibbins, Jeremiah 650
Stibbins, Levi 650
Stibbs, Henrietta 737, 740
Stibbs, J. 737
Stibbs, Joseph 737, 740
Stibbs, Margaret 737, 740
Stibbs, Mary 737
Stibbs, Reasen Beall 740
Stibbs, Reasin B. 737
Stibbs, Reasin Beall 740, 741

967

Stibbs, Reason Beall 740
Stibbs, Thomas 737, 740
Stickle, Catherine 566
Stickle, Patty 572
Stickle, Sarah 585
Sticklebrook, John 112
Stickney, Edson 528
Stickney, Nathaniel 85
Stidman, James 459
Stien, Polly W. 403
Stienburger, Lavise 500
Stiers, Ann 376
Stiers, Benjamin 376
Stiers, Benjamin (Jr.) 376
Stiers, Catherine 376
Stiers, Elizabeth 376
Stiers, George 376
Stiers, Henry 376
Stiers, Jacob 376
Stiers, Maglin 376
Stiers, Samuel 376
Stierwalt, --- (Dr.) 220
Sties, Margaret 577
Stiffler, Aggy 576
Stiffler, David 576
Stiffler, Elizabeth 577
Stiffler, Geo. 576
Stiffler, John 568
Stiffler, Mary 568
Stiles, Celestia 701
Stiles, E. D. 20
Stiles, I. 701
Stiles, John 172, 507
Stiles, John G. 672
Stiles, Margery B. 213
Stiles, N. 701
Stiles, Sarah 213
Stiles, Victory 701
Stilgenbauer, Andreas 302
Still, Adeline P. 56
Still, Charles 564
Still, Ebenezer 718
Still, James H. 93
Still, John 93
Still, William 743
Stilley, Rachel 278
Stillman, Emerson 247
Stillwell, Barnett 146
Stillwell, John 528
Stillwell, Lydia 127
Stillwell, Susanna 528
Stilson, George A. 739
Stilson, Harriet 739
Stilson, Louisa 739
Stilson, William 739
Stilwell, Anna 758
Stilwell, Daniel 299
Stilwell, Elisha 42
Stilwell, Elizabeth 19
Stilwell, Francis M. 146
Stilwell, Nicholas (Sr.) 19
Stilwell, Richard 266
Stilwell, Stilwell 758
Stimmel, Betsey 348
Stimmel, Catharine 348
Stimmel, Daniel 348

Stimmel, Jacob 348
Stimmel, Magdalena 348
Stimmel, Mary Ann 348
Stimmel, Michael 348
Stimmel, Peter 348
Stimmel, Polly 348
Stinchcomb, Ann 380
Stinchcomb, David 118
Stinchcomb, Geo. 359
Stine, Benjamin 166, 173, 174
Stine, George W. 687
Stine, Henry 171
Stine, Jesse 531
Stine, Michael 171, 173
Stine, Nancy 368
Stinebough, Catharine 525
Stinebough, Philip 525, 526
Stiner, Christian 593
Stines, Herman Henry 103
Stingle, Anthony 167
Stingle, Elizabeth 167
Stingley, Elizabeth 465
Stinon, Elizabeth 464
Stinson, Elizabeth 456
Stinson, Horace 746
Stinson, Robert 491
Stinson, Seth 499
Stip, Abraham 472, 483
Stipp, Abraham 467
Stipp, Abram 485
Stipp, John 467
Stites, Benjamin 669
Stites, Benjamine 667
Stites, Elijah 669
Stites, Rach 663
Stitt, James 453
Stitt, John 302
Stitt, William 668
Stiver, Absalom 192
Stiver, Absolem 213
Stiver, Anna Maria 192
Stiver, Catherine 192, 213
Stiver, Cristina 232
Stiver, John 192, 213
Stiver, John (Jr.) 232
Stiver, Margaret 192
Stiver, Mary 229
Stiver, Mary Ann 213
Stiver, Samuel 229
Stiver, Solomon 192, 213
Stivers, Joseph 297
Stivers, Lucinda 523
Stivers, Ralph 297
Stives, Herman Henry 103
Stkinson, Cornelius 172
Stkinson, Mary 172
Stmy, Hollis 593
Stock, Anna 718
Stockbarger, John 367
Stockberger, Catharine 348, 350
Stockberger, Christena 377
Stockberger, Christiana 348

Stockberger, Christiann 350
Stockberger, Elizabeth 348, 377
Stockberger, Frederick 348
Stockberger, George 348, 350, 377
Stockberger, Hannah 377
Stockberger, John 348, 350, 377
Stockberger, Katharine 377
Stockberger, Mathias 348, 350
Stockberger, Meina 377
Stockberger, Michael 348, 350
Stockberger, Nancy 377
Stockberger, Polly 377
Stockberger, Sarah 348
Stockberger, Solomon 377
Stockberger, Susana 377
Stockbridge, Susan 123
Stockdale, Thomas 710
Stockdon, Caleb 471, 472
Stockdon, Margaret 452
Stocken, Caleb 472, 481
Stocker, Adam 563
Stocker, Elizabeth 576
Stocker, Jacob 211
Stocker, John 576
Stocker, Massa 211
Stocker, Susannah 536
Stockey, Abraham 453
Stockey, Joseph (Sr.) 173
Stockey, Rebecca 173
Stockham, Daniel P. 507
Stockham, Daniel Paine 501
Stockham, David 501
Stockham, Ruth 512
Stockham, Susanah 501
Stockham, William 501
Stockhan, Aaron 516
Stockon, David 472
Stockslager, Philip 229
Stockten, David 480
Stockton, Caleb 472, 474, 481, 482
Stockton, David 467, 490
Stockton, John 491
Stockton, John Cox 283
Stockton, Samuel 491
Stockton, Thomas 491
Stockton, William 491
Stocton, William 467
Stodard, Dorcas 752
Stodard, Dwite 752
Stodard, Israel 752
Stodard, Lois 752
Stodard, Sarah 752
Stoddard, Asa P. 212
Stoddard, David 653
Stoddard, George 653
Stoddard, Henry 195, 198, 206, 212, 231
Stoddard, Laommi 31

Stoddart, John 624
Stodgdon, Jane 55
Stohrs, John 336
Stoke, Maria L. 528
Stokely, David 718
Stokely, Samuel 161
Stoker, Allen O. 376
Stoker, Barbara 348, 374
Stoker, Betsy Ann 215
Stoker, Catharine 348
Stoker, Catherine 374
Stoker, Charity 212
Stoker, Charlotte 348, 374, 376
Stoker, Cornelius 547
Stoker, Elijah 551
Stoker, Elizabeth 206, 212
Stoker, George W. 206, 376
Stoker, Isaac 215
Stoker, Jacob 206, 215, 348, 374, 376, 551
Stoker, Jno. W. 551
Stoker, John 206, 215, 348, 374
Stoker, John Milton 376
Stoker, Lucy Ann 206
Stoker, Magdalena 348
Stoker, Magdalene 374
Stoker, Margaret 348, 374
Stoker, Maria 348
Stoker, Mary 374, 376
Stoker, Michael 348, 374
Stoker, Philander H. A. 376
Stoker, Rosanna 549
Stoker, Saloma 348
Stoker, Salome 374
Stoker, Sarah 206
Stoker, Sarah Jane 211
Stoker, Susannah 211
Stoker, William 206, 215
Stokes, Delilah 583
Stokes, Herman 56
Stokes, James 17
Stokes, Jarvis 679, 691
Stokes, Joel A. 686, 687, 688
Stokes, Joseph 17, 24, 593
Stokes, Mathew 474
Stokes, Matthew 471, 474, 480
Stokes, Nithie 388
Stokes, Phebe 24, 583
Stokes, Rhoda 590
Stokman, John Bernard 106
Stoll, E. 411
Stoltz, George 377
Stoltz, John 369
Stoltz, Lewis 376, 377
Stoltz, Rebecca 376
Stone, Annis D. 85
Stone, B. 355, 357
Stone, Benjamin Franklin 728

Stone, Christopher 499
Stone, Daniel 551, 764
Stone, Elias 648
Stone, Elizabeth 714
Stone, Francis 648, 651
Stone, Grace 716
Stone, Henry 764
Stone, Israel 715
Stone, James 718
Stone, Jasper 718
Stone, Joel 529
Stone, John 733
Stone, John B. 253, 257, 270
Stone, Jonathan 728, 729, 730
Stone, Marshal 52
Stone, Marshall 52
Stone, Mary 590
Stone, Nancy 78
Stone, Noyes 718
Stone, Rosanna 764
Stone, Rufus P. 258, 261, 265, 267, 269, 733
Stone, Sardine 715
Stone, Susanna 728, 729
Stone, Theophilus 651
Stone, William 672
Stoneberger, John 190
Stonebreaker, Margaret 740
Stoneburner, John 259, 268
Stoneburner, Michael 268
Stonehawer, John 576
Stoneking, Avy 308
Stoneking, George 308
Stoneman, Benjamin 576
Stoneman, Catharine 563
Stoneman, John 563
Stoneman, John (Jr.) 576
Stoneman, Polly 575
Stoner, Aaron 203
Stoner, Abraham 203, 209, 210, 211
Stoner, Abram 207
Stoner, Anna 189
Stoner, Barbara 431
Stoner, Christopher 593
Stoner, Daniel 203
Stoner, Elizabeth 203, 431
Stoner, Fanny 189
Stoner, Frederick 431
Stoner, George 499, 524
Stoner, Henry 203, 209, 431
Stoner, Jacob 189, 203
Stoner, John 189, 663, 738
Stoner, Polly 189
Stoner, Samuel 49, 203, 209, 210
Stoner, Sarah 203
Stoner, Susan 203
Stoner, William 214, 547
Stonerock, E. 407
Stonerock, George 387

Stonerock, H. 407
Stonerock, Henry 406
Stonerock, Jacob 406
Stonerock, Julia 406
Stonerock, Pheby 464
Stonerock, Samuel 547
Stonerock, William 459
Stones, James 265, 268
Stones, Jos. 265
Stoody, John 576
Stookey, Eli 49
Stookey, Jacob 467
Stookey, Joseph 163
Stoolmiller, Elizabeth 740
Stoolmiller, Lewis 740
Stoolmiller, Louisa 740
Stoops, Samuel 469, 470, 472, 473, 475, 482, 483, 486
Stores, Hur 336
Storms, Abraham 685
Storms, Daniel 663
Storms, Rachel 685
Storms, Rebecca 582
Story, Daniel 730
Story, Daniel (Rev.) 730
Story, Harrison 733
Story, Sarah 744
Story, William 506
Stothard, Cetty 466
Stotler, Jacob 422
Stouder, Peter 33
Stoudt, Mary 447
Stoudt, William 447
Stough, Lyman 748
Stough, Samuel 568
Stoughton, Jane 361
Stoup, Elizabeth 608
Stout, Abner 80
Stout, Ann C. 84
Stout, Bartholomew 523
Stout, Eliza Jane 550
Stout, Elizabeth 249
Stout, George 523, 568, 646
Stout, George (Jr.) 397
Stout, George W. 674
Stout, Hannah 27, 643
Stout, Henry 643, 646, 674
Stout, Jesse 54
Stout, John 249
Stout, Jonathan 397
Stout, Mary 563
Stout, Mary Ann 551
Stout, Moses 249
Stout, Nancy 512
Stout, Philip 27, 274
Stout, Rachel 643
Stout, Rachel Ann 646, 674
Stout, Raliph P. 667
Stout, Rebecca 249
Stout, Sarah 249, 658
Stoutenborough, Adaline 684
Stoutenborough, Eleanor 684

Stove, Alfred 612
Stove, Edwin A. 612
Stove, Frederick W. 612
Stove, Ida I. 612
Stove, Kate A. 612
Stove, Monroe 612
Stoveburner, Peter 266
Stover, Benj. Clinton
437
Stover, David Pendleton
437
Stover, Geo. Washington
437
Stover, John 500
Stover, Julian 521
Stover, Samuel 292
Stover, Sarah Jane 437
Stow, James 80
Stow, Jane 92
Stow, Lucy W. 30
Stow, Norris O. 31
Stow, Polly 84
Stowell, Sarah 82
Stowner, George 285
Strack, Conrod 737
Strader, Catherine 461
Strader, Harman 689
Strader, Michael 459
Strahl, Ann 159, 181
Strahl, Hannah Ann 253
Strahl, Hannah J. 162
Strahl, Hannah Jane 175
Strahl, Hannah N. 250,
252
Strahl, Jas. 253
Strahl, Joel 167
Strahl, John 157, 159,
177
Strahl, John (Jr.) 155,
162, 175
Strahl, John (Sr.) 181
Strahl, Joseph 253
Strahl, William 169
Strain, Elizabeth 466
Strain, Samuel 459
Strain, Sarah 451
Strait, Aron 718
Strait, Barbara 377
Strait, Betsy 377
Strait, Catherine 377
Strait, Christopher 377
Strait, Henry 377
Strait, Jacob 338
Strait, Leonard 373
Strait, Lois 356
Strait, Margaret 377
Strait, Mary 377
Strait, Samuel 377
Strait, Sarah 377
Strait, Sophia 377
Strait, William 377
Strake, John (Jr.) 155
Straker, Albert 576
Stralham, Henry 547
Stranathan, Thomas 304
Stranel, Elmer 712
Stratten, Abigal 431
Stratten, F. J. (Dr.)
423

Stratten, Hester A. 423
Stratten, Seward H. 423
Stratton, Benjamin 27
Stratton, Calvin 8
Stratton, Charles 502
Stratton, Ephraim 5
Stratton, Hannah 27
Stratton, Jacob 27
Stratton, Job 651
Stratton, Joel 8, 27
Stratton, Joseph 27
Stratton, Letitia 651
Stratton, Mary 27, 516
Stratton, Naomi 27
Stratton, Raymond 710,
712
Stratton, Zimri 651
Strausbaugh, George 523
Strawn, Catherine 574
Strawn, Hannah 343
Strawn, Jemima 496
Strawn, Joel 353, 378
Strawn, Lydia 359
Strawn, Sarah 343, 378
Strawn, Thomas 340, 343
Strawser, Abraham 490
Strawser, Christian 490
Strawser, Christiana 463
Strawser, John 491
Strawser, Solomon 494
Strayer, Daniel 21
Streavy, Caty 566
Streeby, Daniel 467
Streekfoot, George 610
Streely, Daniel 467
Street, Benjamin 163
Street, Benjamin M. 611
Street, C. H. 612
Street, Caroline A. 612
Street, Elijah F. 612
Street, Elizabeth 612
Street, Ephriam B. 611
Street, James L. 426
Street, Jon A. 612
Street, M. J. 611, 612
Street, Martha 461
Street, Martha J. 611,
612
Street, Mary Ann 426
Street, T. 611, 612
Street, Thomas 611, 612
Street, Thomas M. 611
Street, Thos. 612
Streevey, Daniel 490
Streider, Philip 476
Stretton, Charles 730
Strevey, Peter 459
Strevy, Barbary 452
Stricker, Anthony 115
Stricker, Clements 115
Stricker, Mary 115
Strickland, Peter 31
Strickler, Effam 619
Strickler, George 418
Strickler, John 418
Strickler, Lydia 619
Strickler, Wm. 619
Strickling, George 523
Strickling, Mary M. 519

Strider, Phillip 476
Stripe, Jacob 610, 626
Stripe, Jacob (Jr.) 624
Stripe, Jacob (Sr.) 624
Stripe, Warner 624
Stripe, William 610, 624
Strockline, Catherine
377
Strockline, Elizabeth
377
Strockline, Frances 377
Strockline, John 377
Strockline, Joseph 377
Strockline, Martha 377
Strockline, Mary Ann 377
Stroeder, B. F. 101
Stroefer, William 105
Strohl, Jacob 370
Strohm, Isaac 624
Strong, Albert (Sr.) 304
Strong, Eliza 82
Strong, Emory 31
Strong, Eri 593
Strong, Lucy 87
Strong, Ozias 90
Strong, Samuel 31
Strong, Silas G. 598
Strong, Stephen 86
Strong, W. R. 89
Strong, Warren 31
Stronger, Precilla 126
Strons, Michl. 453
Stroop, Isabella 62
Stroop, John 62
Stropen, Ellen Polly 411
Strother, Alexander 610
Strother, Benjamin 624
Strother, Benjamin D.
603
Strother, Geo. 726
Strother, Mary Ann 603
Strothers, Benjamin D.
610
Stroud, Martha 515
Stroud, Phebe 501
Stroud, Polly 387
Stroud, Rebecca 715
Stroud, William 715
Stroup, David 55
Stroup, Eliza 229
Stroup, John 229
Stroup, Polly 463
Stroup, Samuel 229
Strous, Michl. 453
Strouse, Philip 387
Strouser, Christiana 382
Strout, Richard 319, 320
Strout, Sunford 336
Struble, Nancy 278
Strugle, Christian 228
Struser, Elizabeth 529
Stryder, Philip 478
Ststfield, Francis M.
610
Stuart, John 224
Stuart, Peggy 224
Stuart, Samuel 652
Stuart, Sarah 415
Stuart, William 160

Stubblefield, David 63
Stubblefield, Edward 63
Stubblefield, Robert 63
Stubblefield, Sarah 63
Stubbs, Jacob 733
Stubbs, Joseph 746
Stubbs, Phebe 748
Stubbs, Polly 744
Stubbs, Polly H. 746
Stubbs, Rachel 745
Stubbs, Sarah 661
Stubbs, Thomas 416
Stubing, Archibald C. 154
Stubing, Catharine 154
Stuborn, Daniel 523
Stuck, Sarah 718
Stucke, Francesca 111
Stucker, Henry 476
Stucker, Lydia 476
Stuckey, Aaron 61
Stuckey, Archibald 61
Stuckey, David 61
Stuckey, Eli 61
Stuckey, Elizabeth 61
Stuckey, Mary 61
Stuckey, Mary Ann 61
Stuckey, Susan 61
Stucty, Margaret 569
Stucybaker, John 554
Studabaker, Abraham 663
Studabaker, Betsy 119
Studebaker, Barbara 663
Studebaker, Eliz. 141
Studebaker, Jacob 141
Studebaker, Mariah 146
Studebaker, Paggy 124
Studebaker, Saml. 141
Studebaker, Sarah 146
Studer, Joseph 111
Studibacher, Sally 127
Study, Catharine 570
Study, Elizabeth 570
Study, George 562
Studybaker, John 553, 557
Studybaker, Joseph 229
Stufflebean, E. 407
Stufflebean, Sarah 407
Stufflebean, W. 407
Stukey, Anthony 115
Stukey, Catharine 115
Stukey, Eve 115
Stukey, Mary 115
Stuleff, Barna 263
Stull, Abraham 168
Stull, Barbary 168
Stull, Betsy 499
Stull, Edward 530
Stull, Hannah 296, 530
Stull, Lavina 530
Stull, Martin 296
Stull, Mary 743
Stull, Michael 499
Stull, Rebecca 499
Stull, Susannah 530
Stults, Abegel M. 497
Stults, Ann 497
Stults, Hannah 499

Stults, Noah 733
Stultz, Henry 387
Stultz, John 499
Stultz, Nancy 372
Stultz, Sally 495
Stultz, Samuel 372
Stuly, Elizabeth 383
Stump, Elizabeth 184, 386
Stump, George 183, 189, 198, 224
Stump, John 194, 197, 202, 214, 232
Stump, Julianna 224
Stump, Leonard 183, 224, 293
Stump, Mary 516
Stump, Nicholas 557
Sturdybaker, John 554, 555
Sturgeon, Eliza 377, 378
Sturgeon, Eliza Jane 549
Sturgeon, Elizabeth 377, 378
Sturgeon, George 141
Sturgeon, George R. 204
Sturgeon, Harriet 378
Sturgeon, Isabella 551
Sturgeon, John 338, 357, 377, 378
Sturgeon, John P. 378
Sturgeon, Levi 141
Sturgeon, Margaret 551
Sturgeon, Mary 378
Sturgeon, Mitchel 377
Sturgeon, Mitchell 378
Sturgeon, Moses 378, 547
Sturgeon, Reuben 155
Sturgeon, Simpson 377, 378
Sturgeon, Susannah 204
Sturgeon, William 179, 491
Sturges, Solomon 288, 339, 341
Sturgis, Russell 86
Sturgis, Sol. 733
Sturgis, Solomon 733
Sturm, George 551
Sturm, Henry 547
Sturm, Henry S. 551
Sturm, Peggy Ann 547
Sturn, Mathias 576
Sturr, H. J. (Dr.) 426
Sturr, Henry (Dr.) 426
Sturr, Jacob 337
Sturr, John (Dr.) 421, 424
Sturr, Susan 421
Sturrett, Christena 549
Stutes, William L. 419
Stuthard, Betsey 457
Stuthard, Sarah 466
Stuthart, John 491
Stutsman, Abraham 215
Stutsman, Nathaniel 189
Stutz, Anna 235
Stutz, David 235
Stutz, Johannes 235

Styer, Joseph T. 584
Styles, Jonathan 536
Subbil, Simon 724
Suddeth, Lucender 386
Sudeow, Joseph 637
Sudsow, Richard 637
Suel, Peter 121
Suell, Thomas 667
Suelley, Sophia 573
Suetland, Fuller M. 278
Sufferins, Mary 662
Sufficool, Jane 746
Sugar, Fayette 592
Sulivan, Charles 708
Sulivant, Lucas 471
Suliven, Hannah 337
Sull, Anne 462
Sull, Thos. 459
Sullenbarger, Saml. 547
Sullenwright, Mary 567
Sullevan, Newton M. 551
Sullinger, John 751
Sullivan, Aaron 392, 459
Sullivan, Andrew 374
Sullivan, Aron 391
Sullivan, Artemasa 745
Sullivan, Burton 547
Sullivan, Charles 290
Sullivan, Christena 374
Sullivan, Clarisa 290
Sullivan, Cornelius 374
Sullivan, David 374
Sullivan, Elizabeth 374
Sullivan, George 169, 547
Sullivan, Jeremiah 523
Sullivan, Lucy 290
Sullivan, Margaret 374
Sullivan, Mary 374
Sullivan, Nancy 290
Sullivan, Sarah 169, 374
Sullivan, Susanna 374
Sullivan, Wiley 547
Sullivant, Lucas 482
Suman, Catherine 198
Suman, Eli 198
Suman, Isaac 192
Suman, Jacob 192
Suman, James 198
Suman, Manes 198
Suman, Peter 224
Suman, Sarah 198
Summa, Genny 130
Summa, Kitran 130
Summa, Margaret 130
Summa, Mary 130
Summa, Mikel 130
Summa, Peter 130
Summe, Genny 130
Summe, Margaret 130
Summe, Mary 130
Summe, Mikel 130
Summe, Peter 130
Summerlin, Malvina 518
Summers, George 547
Summers, John 547, 667
Summersett, John 627
Summersett, Sarah 607
Summersett, William F. 610

Sumner, Mary 128
Sumner, Rhoda 511
Sumners, Pheby 116
Sumption, Charles (Jr.) 118
Sumption, George 118
Sumption, Mary 118
Sumption, Rebecca 118
Sumption, Sarah 117
Sunderland, Aaron 216
Sunderland, Betsy 124
Sunderland, Catharine 131
Sunderland, Christenhen 131
Sunderland, Daniel 118, 184
Sunderland, Edward 131, 627
Sunderland, Emaline 131
Sunderland, Joseph 547
Sunderland, Peter 131
Sunderland, Peter (Sr.) 131
Sunderland, Samuel 184
Sunderland, Samuel G. 141
Sunderland, William 131
Surdybaker, John 554
Sureley, Rezen 516
Surface, Adam 640
Surface, Andrew 130
Surface, Elizabeth 130
Surface, John 130
Surface, Mary 664
Surfus, Samuel 491
Surng, Joshua 668
Surrain, Betsey 666
Surts, Polly 12
Sutherland, David 155, 165
Sutherland, Elmer 90
Sutherland, John 387
Sutherland, Margaret 155
Sutherland, Vachel 568
Suttiff, Bains 271
Suttiff, Barna 261
Sutton, Amos 155
Sutton, Anna 747
Sutton, Catharine 162, 176
Sutton, Catherine 356
Sutton, Cornelius 663
Sutton, David 155, 643, 670
Sutton, David (Jr.) 663
Sutton, Elizabeth 499
Sutton, Hannah 52, 496
Sutton, Ivy 666
Sutton, Levi 356
Sutton, Miriam 517
Sutton, Robert 715
Sutton, Sarah 155
Sutton, Susann 498
Sutton, Thomas P. 42
Sutton, William 162, 176
Suvell, John R. 118
Suver, Elizabeth 49
Svarts, Betsy 456

Svenchen, Frederick 737
Swackhammer, Wm. 359
Swager, Elizabeth 146
Swager, John 146
Swager, Mary J. 146
Swager, Sarah A. 146
Swager, Susan 146
Swager, Wm. 146
Swagler, Nancy 571
Swails, Rebecca 124
Swaim, John 630
Swaim, John D. 630
Swaim, Lydia 630
Swaim, Moses 630
Swaim, Nancy 630
Swaim, William 630
Swain, Elizabeth 413
Swain, Elizabeth Jane 437
Swain, Jacob 437
Swain, John Lindsay 437
Swain, Jos. B. 437
Swain, Martin Van Buren 437
Swain, Mary 513
Swain, Schlinda 437
Swaley, Mary 570
Swallee, George 166
Swalley, Chas. 576
Swallow, Daniel 678
Swallow, John D. 676
Swally, Susanah 575
Swan, Amanda 511
Swan, Andrew 681
Swan, Ann 413
Swan, Lauson 551
Swan, Letty 463
Swanck, Philip 564
Swaney, James 163
Swaney, Rebecca 163
Swanger, Isaac 663
Swanger, Jacob 667
Swanger, Sarah 657
Swank, Aaron 240
Swank, Alvin 246
Swank, Augustus 246
Swank, Betsy 202
Swank, C. 244
Swank, Catharine 193, 240
Swank, Catherine 373
Swank, Clement 244
Swank, Daniel 193
Swank, E. 246
Swank, Elizabeth 373, 657
Swank, Emaline 615
Swank, George 201, 202
Swank, George D. 246
Swank, Isaac 387
Swank, J. 615, 618
Swank, Jacob 193, 201, 202, 246
Swank, Jno. 267
Swank, John 193, 265, 610, 618
Swank, Louisa 618
Swank, Lydia A. 246
Swank, Mahala 240
Swank, Mary 246

Swank, Mary Etta 246
Swank, Michael 193, 202
Swank, Pamelia 716
Swank, Pemelia 716
Swank, Peter 193, 387
Swank, Philip 267
Swank, Rachel 384
Swank, Richd. 387
Swank, S. 244, 246
Swank, Sarah 246
Swank, Susannah 193
Swank, Waitman 246
Swank, William 387
Swank, Wm. 273
Swaringen, George 438
Swaringen, Samuel 438
Swarm, John 523
Swarthout, Juliann 650
Swarts, Aug. 734
Swarts, Elizabeth 612
Swarts, George W. 734
Swarts, Henry S. 612
Swarts, William 612
Swartz, Ann Jenette 735
Swartz, Anthony 346
Swartz, Benwell 734
Swartz, C. 734
Swartz, Harvey 734
Swartz, J. 734
Swartz, John 568
Swartz, Lucetta 734
Swartzel, Frederick 182
Swartzel, John 182
Swartzel, Matthias 182
Swartzel, Philip 210
Swartzel, Susanna 210
Swartzel, Susannah 182
Swaynie, Joseph S. 219
Swearer, John 228
Sweeney, Pat. W. 360
Sweeney, William 547
Sweeny, Hugh 282
Sweet, Benjamin 80
Sweet, Edith 120
Sweetland, Ellen M. 734
Sweetland, Robert A. 734
Sweinfroot, Anton 104
Swenk, Philip 568
Sweth, Keziah 713
Swezeey, Richard G. 501
Swift, Charlotta 337
Swift, Daniel 42
Swift, Elizabeth 648
Swift, Malahi 663
Swift, Nancy 662
Swift, Thomas 663
Swigart, Eliza 393
Swigart, John 387
Swigart, Lydia 609
Swihart, Francis 437
Swihart, Isarel 576
Swihart, Jacob 437
Swihart, Marion 437
Swihart, Nancy Margaret 437
Swihart, Noah 420
Swihart, Sarah Cath. 437
Swihart, Wm. Adam 437
Swim, Gitty 496

Swinehart, Adam 182, 192, 223
Swinehart, Andrew 375
Swinehart, Anna 182
Swinehart, Catherine 375
Swinehart, Christina 375
Swinehart, Daniel 375, 576
Swinehart, Elizabeth 182, 375, 576, 577
Swinehart, Frederick 562
Swinehart, Gabriel 182, 223
Swinehart, George 375
Swinehart, Jacob 357, 375
Swinehart, John 341, 375
Swinehart, Jonas 375
Swinehart, Julid 375
Swinehart, Peter 375
Swinehart, S. 378
Swinehart, Sally 375
Swinehart, Salome 182, 223
Swinehart, Samuel 375
Swineheart, Elizabeth 241
Swineheart, Gabriel 576
Swineheart, John 576
Swineheart, P. 241
Swinhart, Catharine 576
Swisher, --- 400
Swisher, Eliza Caroline 437
Swisher, Hannah 383
Swisher, Nancy Maria 437
Swisher, Robt. 437
Swisher, Sarah Catharine 437
Switzer, Fredrick 448
Switzer, Jacob 321, 323
Switzer, John 568
Swob, Jacob 260
Swomley, Jacob 283
Swope, Meribeah 523
Swope, Samuel R. 530
Swope, Sinthe 79
Swope, William 516
Swoveland, Ann 567
Syder, Menervy Beloat 505
Sykes, George S. 610
Sylvester, Ellen G. 278
Sylvester, Joseph 80
Sylvester, Lucena 84
Sympson, Oliver 593
Sype, Eliza 141
Sype, Semantha 141
Syphers, William 615
Sytte, Andrew J. 431
Sytte, Hetty 431
Sytte, Joseph 431
Sytte, Margaret 431
Sytte, Susan 431

--- T ---

Tabb, John L. 467
Tabeling, Anna Katherine Elizabeth 102

Tabeling, Joseph 102
Taber, Bennet 18
Taber, Elisha 640
Tabler, Eliza Ann 365
Tabler, John W. 1
Tabor, Elisha 663
Tachudy, Elizabeth 570
Tadron, John 284
Tadrow, John 284
Taff, Aaron 188, 655
Taff, Abraham 188, 663
Taff, Abram 655
Taggart, Arthur 371
Taggart, Lucy 757
Taggart, Samuel 742
Taggart, William 446, 743
Taggart, William M. 757
Taggert, James (Jr.) 293
Tague, Edward 379
Tague, Ellenor 379
Tague, John 379
Tague, Patrick 379
Tague, Peter 379
Tague, Rose 379
Tailor, John 568
Talbert, Elijah 431
Talbert, Nathan 431
Talbert, William 297
Talbot, Amirah 745
Talbot, Ann 500
Talbot, B. W. 259, 266
Talbot, Benj. W. 261, 269, 271
Talbot, Benjamin W. 258, 259, 260
Talbot, William 500
Talbot, Chas. 733
Talbott, Jonathan 525
Talbott, William 500
Tallage, Jean Baptist Nicholus 715
Tallman, Woodmince 22
Talmage, James M. 278
Talman, James C. 356
Tambert, John 523
Tamman, Priscilla 437
Tancke, John Rud. 102
Tanner, Courtney 396
Tanner, Edward 396
Tanner, Elizabeth 569
Tanner, George Shelley 367
Tanner, James 427
Tanner, John U. 441
Tanner, Mary Ann 51
Tanner, Thomas 111
Tappan, Elizabeth 660
Tappen, Thomas 663
Tapscot, John 202
Tapscott, Joseph 674
Tarbert, Eligah 593
Tarcuson, George 453
Tarner, Pamelia 519
Tarnpret, Daniel 689
Tarnpret, Ross 689
Tarparing, Lawrence 593
Tarpring, Laura 591
Tarr, Catharine 566

Tarr, David 85
Tarr, Samuel 636
Tastlebee, August 322
Taswell, Newcum 296
Tate, David 491
Tate, Lyle 318
Tate, Robt. 459
Tate, Thomas 738
Tate, William 336
Tatman, Abigail 582
Tatman, Bartholomew 380
Tatman, Benjamin 380
Taubeling, Anna Katherine Elizabeth 102
Taubeling, Joseph 102
Taubut, Catharine 506
Taufer, David 236
Taufer, Elisabet 236
Taufer, Elisabeth 236
Taufer, Henrich 236
Taufer, Susene 236
Tavers, Asa 459
Tawn, Amand 75
Tawn, Thos. 75
Tawney, Henry 554
Tayler, Isabel 12
Tayler, Mary Ann 15
Taylor, Abraham 446, 447, 547
Taylor, Ann 177, 178, 547
Taylor, Ann Maria 685
Taylor, Anna 167
Taylor, Anselm 272
Taylor, Asa 593
Taylor, Benjamin 446, 447
Taylor, Bennet 447
Taylor, Charles 447
Taylor, Christian 229
Taylor, Christopher 189
Taylor, David 547
Taylor, David S. 374
Taylor, Drake 453
Taylor, Ed 141
Taylor, Edward Heuit 304
Taylor, Elener 447
Taylor, Eliza 63, 709
Taylor, Elizabeth 50, 446, 447, 456, 464, 710
Taylor, Evelina 447
Taylor, Francis 446, 447
Taylor, Franklin 31
Taylor, George 31, 352, 459
Taylor, H. 507
Taylor, Hannah 447
Taylor, Hanton H. 174
Taylor, Henry 266, 272, 273, 447, 610, 624
Taylor, Henry J. 491
Taylor, Hugh 365
Taylor, Isaac 93, 446, 447
Taylor, Jacob 6
Taylor, James 4, 54, 167, 177, 178, 316, 459, 499

Taylor, James B. 423
Taylor, James Lee 437
Taylor, Jane 414, 516
Taylor, Jno. (Sr.) 274
Taylor, John 4, 15, 63,
  266, 267, 270, 304,
  336, 446, 447, 467,
  479, 491, 516, 563,
  586, 626, 667, 707
Taylor, John B. 291, 447
Taylor, John W. 266,
  272, 273
Taylor, John Williams
  437
Taylor, Jonathan B. 746
Taylor, Joseph 485
Taylor, Juliann 573
Taylor, Levi 593
Taylor, Lewis 182
Taylor, Luther 80
Taylor, Lydia 437
Taylor, Mahlon K. 21
Taylor, Margaret 197,
  547, 548, 607
Taylor, Martha 336
Taylor, Mary 6, 82, 447,
  494, 547, 563, 590
Taylor, Mary Ann 608
Taylor, Mary M. 707
Taylor, Mathine 387
Taylor, Michael B. 437
Taylor, Mordecai 689
Taylor, Mordicai (Sr.)
  689
Taylor, Moses 593
Taylor, Nancy 446, 447,
  464
Taylor, Nathan 668
Taylor, Nathaniel 185
Taylor, Nelly 182
Taylor, Nicholas H.
  365, 374
Taylor, Oran 525
Taylor, Patsey 592
Taylor, Paul 31
Taylor, Peter 304
Taylor, Pierce 316, 323
Taylor, Rebecah 451
Taylor, Rebecca 464
Taylor, Rebeccah 566
Taylor, Rhoda 585
Taylor, Richard 185, 210
Taylor, Robert 297,
  728, 729
Taylor, Salam 431
Taylor, Saml. 478
Taylor, Samuel 287,
  446, 447, 479
Taylor, Sarah 54, 447,
  659, 663
Taylor, Squire T. 437
Taylor, Stacy 106, 672
Taylor, Stephen 416
Taylor, Susan 607
Taylor, Susan E. 437
Taylor, Susan S. 335
Taylor, Tanday 507
Taylor, Thomas 88, 273,
  355, 558

Taylor, Thornton 359
Taylor, Walter 447
Taylor, Washington 581
Taylor, William 185,
  223, 446, 447, 728
Taylor, William G. 685
Taylor, Wm. 593
Taylor, Zach. 482
Teabault, Hiram 757
Teaboo, H. 757
Teaboo, Sophia 757
Teabott, Polly 665
Teagarden, Abraham 209
Teagarden, Calvin 209
Teagarden, Henry 209
Teague, Moses 127
Teague, Samuel 134, 135
Teal, Ann 378
Teal, Catherine 431
Teal, Joseph 431
Teal, Lawson 338
Teal, Nathaniel 340
Tear, Caesar 530
Teare, Ester 530
Teare, Jane 530
Teare, Thomas 530
Teas, Mathew 126
Teats, Elizabeth 336
Tebo, Jane 496
Tebugdin, Zacheriah 127
Tedrow, Catherine 367
Tedrow, Michael 367
Tedrow, Rachel 367
Teegardin, Viola L. 332
Teel, Ann 378
Teel, Losson 378
Teel, Noah 378
Teeney, L. 735
Teeney, M. 735
Teeney, Wilson E. 735
Teeter, Mary 464
Teeters, Samuel 596
Teeters, Sarah 385
Teischer, Henry 710
Telbill, Betsey 452
Telford, Alexander 223
Telford, John G. 121
Telford, Polly 118
Tell, Osson 338
Tellis, Frances 12
Tellus, Bitsy 27
Tellus, Dorothy 27
Tellus, Frances 27
Tellus, Griffeth 27
Tellus, India 27
Tellus, James 27
Tellus, John 27
Tellus, Lewis 27
Tellus, Lydia 27
Tellus, Nancy 27
Tellus, Rebecca 27
Templane, James 481
Templane, Robert 482
Temple, Mary 609
Templeton, Bulah 141
Templeton, David 679
Templeton, Geo. 733
Templeton, Hannah 679
Templeton, James 679

Templeton, James G. 146
Templeton, John 475, 679
Templeton, Joseph 480
Templeton, Malinda 146
Templeton, Mariah 141
Templeton, Samuel 312
Templeton, William 679
Templin, Solmon 453
Tenant, Alexander 350
Tenant, Ann 350
Tenery, Maria 116
Tengel, Heinrich 104
Tenley, Jacob Rambo 729
Tenley, Rebeckah 729
Tenmant, Ansin 668
Tennery, Joseph L. 15
Tennery, Sally 119
Tentus, George 118
Terrel, Barbara 235
Terrel, Heinrich Marty
  235
Terrel, Jacobus 235
Terrel, Lucinda 28
Terrel, Mathew 19
Terrel, Randal 31
Terrel, William 19
Terrell, Arminda 379
Terrell, Asa 379
Terrell, Barbara 235
Terrell, Elizabeth M. 31
Terrell, Jacobus 235
Terrell, James 379
Terrell, Jesse 379
Terrell, Johan William
  235
Terrell, Lucinda 379
Terrell, Randel 31
Terrell, Rebecca 379
Terrell, Ressa 28
Terrence, A. A. 405
Terrence, Caleb 405
Terrence, Joshua M. 405
Terril, Albert G. 31
Terril, Harriet 31
Terrill, Amanda 31
Terrill, Betsey 74
Terrill, Olive I. 30
Terry, Betsy 121
Terry, Elizabeth 230
Terry, Enos 187, 230
Terry, John 528
Terry, Mary 45
Terry, Nancy 118
Terry, Nathan 121
Terry, Truman 322
Tersterge, Joseph 547
Terstiege, Bernard 547
Terstiege, Henry 547
Terwillegar, Cornelius
  547
Terwilliger, Nathan 547
Terwilliger, Percy 35
Test, Benjm. 667
Tetarick, Nicholas 288
Teters, Daniel 491
Teters, Henry 267
Teters, John 476
Teters, Rosanna 267
Teters, Saml. 476

Teters, W. Samuel   474
Tettsworth, J.   387
Tevault, Andrew   272
Tew, Paul   499
Tewksbury, Elizabeth   92
Thacker, Martial   746
Tharley, Thomas   576
Tharp, Alvah   367
Tharp, Andrew   223
Tharp, Boaz   223
Tharp, D.   15
Tharp, Elijah   379
Tharp, Elisha   379
Tharp, Elizabeth   657
Tharp, Emily   379
Tharp, Henry D.   15
Tharp, Huldah   379
Tharp, James   378, 379
Tharp, Job   378
Tharp, John   642
Tharp, Lavina   379
Tharp, Lucy   378
Tharp, Margaret   379
Tharp, Nancy   12
Tharp, Prudence   497
Tharp, Reuben   379
Tharp, Rhoda   379
Tharp, Sarah   379
Tharp, Thalia   661
Thatcher, Almedia   527
Thatcher, Amos   427
Thatcher, Calvin   527
Thatcher, Caroline   527
Thatcher, Clarinda   527
Thatcher, Daniel   746
Thatcher, Jacob   551
Thatcher, James   527
Thatcher, Jesse   427
Thatcher, John   527
Thatcher, Lydia   527
Thatcher, Mariah   527
Thatcher, Mary   664, 669
Thatcher, Orin   527
Thatcher, Romelia   527
Thayer, Davis W.   127
Thayer, Eliza   587
Thayer, Mary   75
Theis, Jacob (Sr.)   709
Themle, Samuel   524
Thenthorn, Jesse   351
Therby, Elizabeth   121
Thereck, Elizabeth   133
Thereck, Jacob   133
Thervenin, Nicholas   724
Thiemann, George F.   547
Thierry, Francis   724
Thiller, Elizabeth   453
Thimble, Cloe   116
Thistel, Geo.   248
Thistell, Benjamin F.   248
Thistell, Ezra   248
Thistil, Ezra   248
Thoke, John H.   547
Thom, Jacob   602
Thomas, Aaron   378, 467
Thomas, Abel   15
Thomas, Abraham   654
Thomas, Absalom   671

Thomas, Almena B.   37
Thomas, Anna   91
Thomas, Benjamin   161, 164, 167
Thomas, Betsey   467
Thomas, Bridget   93
Thomas, Casaline   308
Thomas, Chalkly   653
Thomas, Charles   618
Thomas, Cynthia   516
Thomas, Cynthia Ann   31
Thomas, David   27, 378, 401
Thomas, David F.   91
Thomas, Dolly   401
Thomas, Edmond   88
Thomas, Edmund   88
Thomas, Edward   652, 653, 663
Thomas, Elizabeth   67, 85, 378, 401, 572, 576, 610
Thomas, Equilles   176
Thomas, Evan   378
Thomas, Ezekiel   551
Thomas, Francis   718
Thomas, G. M.   37
Thomas, George   568
Thomas, Hiram   42
Thomas, Isaac   67, 562, 653
Thomas, Jacob   366, 378, 467, 576
Thomas, James   67
Thomas, Jane   396
Thomas, Jesse   378, 653
Thomas, John   57, 401, 441, 453, 558, 652
Thomas, Jonathan   750
Thomas, Joseph   92, 652, 667
Thomas, Levi   42
Thomas, Louisa   335
Thomas, Lucinda   618
Thomas, Lucretia M.   279
Thomas, Martha   167, 657, 523
Thomas, Mary   27, 63, 88, 336, 396, 459, 553, 653, 662
Thomas, Mary A.   403
Thomas, Michael   470, 476, 477
Thomas, Moses   752
Thomas, Nancy   107, 401, 573
Thomas, Nathaniel L.   751
Thomas, Peggy   67
Thomas, Peter   560
Thomas, Peter Thomas   724, 725
Thomas, Polly   133
Thomas, Rebecca   161, 164, 273, 572
Thomas, Robert   401
Thomas, Rosanna   378
Thomas, Ruth   12
Thomas, Sabra   57
Thomas, Saml.   476

Thomas, Samuel   67, 378, 476, 491, 558, 663
Thomas, Scott   49
Thomas, Sophia   740
Thomas, Sophia Almona   588
Thomas, Susan   553, 572, 592
Thomas, Thos.   614
Thomas, Tibitha   459
Thomas, William   396, 494, 654
Thomas, William J.   148
Thomas, William S.   503
Thompkins, Felix   201
Thompson, Abraham   459
Thompson, Alexander   328
Thompson, Alfred   318, 319
Thompson, Amy   498
Thompson, Amy Pool   412
Thompson, Andrew   378
Thompson, Ann   131, 254, 378
Thompson, Anna   465
Thompson, Caleb   646
Thompson, Catharine   669
Thompson, Charles   663
Thompson, Chaucy   761
Thompson, D.   58
Thompson, Daddy   516
Thompson, Dafeney   89
Thompson, Daniel   285, 401
Thompson, Daphney   91
Thompson, David   146, 401, 690
Thompson, David Moore   378
Thompson, David W.   378
Thompson, Dennis Whalen   431
Thompson, Elijah   308, 437
Thompson, Eliza   588
Thompson, Elizabeth   26, 378, 391, 437, 505, 551
Thompson, Enus   718
Thompson, Esther   378
Thompson, Eunice M.   761
Thompson, Ezekiel   467
Thompson, Franklin   254
Thompson, Frederick   564
Thompson, Freeborn   547
Thompson, George   161, 663
Thompson, George W.   633
Thompson, H. B.   564
Thompson, Hannah   393, 588
Thompson, Henry   255, 443
Thompson, Isaac   161, 378, 437
Thompson, Jacob   45, 564
Thompson, James   21, 146, 322, 473, 480, 516, 593, 646, 675
Thompson, Jane   131, 378

975

Thompson, Jas. 477
Thompson, Jeremiah 146
Thompson, Joel 141
Thompson, John 51, 66,
  160, 247, 343, 378,
  387, 516, 547, 554,
  564, 624
Thompson, John (Jr.) 378
Thompson, John Benj. 437
Thompson, Jonathan 152
Thompson, Joseph 131,
  491, 624, 684, 728
Thompson, Joseph (Jr.)
  131
Thompson, Joseph L. 637
Thompson, Joseph Rees
  637
Thompson, Joshua 6,
  254, 255
Thompson, Katie A. 328
Thompson, L. G. 754
Thompson, Laura A. 328
Thompson, Lydia 91, 637
Thompson, Mahala 378
Thompson, Margaret 378,
  540
Thompson, Mariah 378
Thompson, Martha 230,
  540, 585
Thompson, Mary 131,
  335, 378, 419, 443,
  564, 665
Thompson, Mathew 453,
  482
Thompson, Matthew 127,
  491
Thompson, Michael 564
Thompson, Mordecai 247
Thompson, Nancy 49,
  120, 343, 378, 386,
  437, 582, 666
Thompson, Nathan 494
Thompson, Oswald 491
Thompson, Phebe 6
Thompson, Phebe Maria
  497
Thompson, Polly 119
Thompson, Polly Ann 378
Thompson, Rebecca 146
Thompson, Rebeccah 554
Thompson, Rees 637
Thompson, Rhoda 29
Thompson, Richard 131
Thompson, Robert 414,
  516
Thompson, Robert M. 624
Thompson, Robert P. 547
Thompson, Roxy 498
Thompson, Ruth 451
Thompson, Sally 386
Thompson, Saml. 298
Thompson, Samuel 127,
  259, 286, 378
Thompson, Sarah 123,
  254, 624
Thompson, Sarah A. 146
Thompson, Sary 131
Thompson, Smallwood 540
Thompson, Sophia Ann 521

Thompson, Stephen 551
Thompson, Susanna 564
Thompson, Susannah 248
Thompson, Thomas 16,
  45, 378, 667
Thompson, William 75,
  98, 247, 378, 470,
  475, 486, 491, 516,
  596, 663, 669
Thompson, Wm. 437, 470,
  477, 587, 593
Thompson, Zinni 437
Thoms, Eliza 80
Thoms, Tibitha 459
Thomson, Rebecca 393
Thomson, Samuel 182
Thorla, Benj. 263
Thorla, Benjamin 271,
  304
Thorla, Daniel 271
Thorla, Silas 271
Thorlee, Richard 304
Thorley, Patience 445
Thorley, Thomas 445
Thorls, Richard 270
Thorn, Benjamin 610, 624
Thorn, Garret 499
Thorn, Jacob 602, 610
Thorn, Lemuel 80
Thorn, Lucy 82
Thorn, Saly 662
Thorn, Sarah 610
Thorn, Thomas 603, 610,
  624
Thornberry, Richard 127
Thornberry, Warren 173
Thornberry, William 178
Thornburgh, Nancy 291
Thornburgh, Thomas 291
Thornburgh, Uriah 45
Thorne, Rebecca 514
Thornly, Samuel 715
Thornton, Elijah 172
Thornton, John 85
Thornton, John H. 516
Thornton, Nancy 719
Thornton, Rebecca 658
Thornton, Sarah C. 586
Thornton, William 172
Thorp, Allen 459
Thorp, Asa 628
Thorpe, Ruth 632
Thorpe, Wm. 632
Thos, John 475
Thrall, Ann 378
Thrall, Anson R. 4
Thrall, Charlotte 378
Thrall, Eliza 378
Thrall, Ellenor 378
Thrall, James 378
Thrall, Jos. 184
Thrall, Juliana 378
Thrall, Martha 378
Thrall, Mary 378
Thrall, Patience 378
Thrall, Samuel 184, 378
Thrall, Sophia 378
Thralls, Margaret Ann
  437

Thrapp, Mary 373
Thrasher, Nancy 49
Throckmorton, J. S. 89
Throckmorton, James 89
Throne, Conrod 516
Throop, Zebulon 721
Throp, Samuel W. 690
Throup, Wm. 459
Throup, Zebulon 722
Thrush, Robert 366
Thucly, Simon 387
Thurlo, Silas 266
Thurlo, Susannah 266
Thurlow, Silas 709
Thurman, Frederick
  William 605
Thurman, Sofiat 459
Thurston, Bathshebe 212
Thurston, Betsy 639
Thurston, Charles 639
Thurston, Charlotte
  Temple 212
Thurston, Durinda 212
Thurston, Henry 31
Thurston, Isaac 212
Thurston, Joseph 639
Thurston, Mary Valentine
  212
Thurston, Otho 212
Thurston, Prudence 639
Thurston, Samuel H. 760
Thurthaver, Adam 161
Tibballs, Margarett 499
Tibbells, Fayette 586
Tibbets, Lanson 523
Tibbitts, Horace 710
Tibbury, Betsy 608
Tical, Amy 123
Tice, Elizabeth 14
Tice, James 733
Tice, Sarah 549
Tice, Solomon 733
Ticer, Austen 663
Tichanor, Aaron 663
Tichanor, Jonathan 663
Tichenor, Abagail 655
Tichenor, Abigail 679
Tichenor, Ann Eliza
  655, 679
Tichenor, David 655, 679
Tichenor, Hannah M. 679
Tichenor, Nathaniel
  655, 679
Tichenor, Thomas Miranda
  655
Tichmann, George F. 104
Tickel, Jacob 615
Tickel, Margaret 615
Tickle, Anna 618
Tickle, E. 615, 618
Tickle, Elizabeth 618
Tickle, Emaline 618
Tickle, I. 613
Tickle, Idna V. 613
Tickle, J. 613, 615, 618
Tickle, John 618
Tickle, Peter 618
Tickle, Pheby J. 615
Tickle, Rachel A. 618

Tickle, Thompson 618
Tickle, William 618
Tidd, John 158
Tierman, Michael 445
Tierman, Michael (Jr.) 445
Tiernel, Ann 576
Tifany, --- 170
Tiff, Patience 29
Tiffin, E. 477
Tiffin, Edward 467, 469
Tiffin, John 387
Tiffin, Joseph 454, 469, 474, 476
Tiffin, Phebe 383
Tifrin, Joseph 471
Tiger, Samuel 454
Tilberry, Abraham 551
Tilberry, Hannah 550
Tilbury, Thomas 551
Tilby, Benjamin 587
Tillbery, Thomas 547
Tilliman, Willis 718
Tillinghast, Freelove 555
Tillinghast, Samuel 555
Tillotson, Reuben 499
Tillotson, Ruth 31
Tillotson, Sally 75
Tillotson, Sarah 709
Tillson, Lydia 715
Tillton, Joseph 715
Tillus, John 27
Tilsen, Ruth 82
Tilton, Benjamin 302
Tilton, Catharine 107
Tilton, Davis 271
Tilton, Elizabeth 107, 115
Tilton, Hebron 311
Tilton, Helron 304
Tilton, John 107, 115
Tilton, Joseph (Jr.) 269
Tilton, Nancy 311
Tilton, Phebe 710
Tilton, Rufus 311
Tilton, Smith 311
Tilton, Sylvester 107, 115
Tilton, Wm. 274
Timmonds, Catharine 509
Timmons, Abraham 491
Timmons, Anmanias 467
Timmons, Ann 630
Timmons, Catharine 64
Timmons, Charlotte 64
Timmons, Christiana A. 64
Timmons, Cotman 64
Timmons, Dorthea 64
Timmons, Drucilla 64
Timmons, Eleanor 452
Timmons, Eli 494
Timmons, Elizabeth 494
Timmons, Henry Clay 64
Timmons, Isby 61
Timmons, Jane 49
Timmons, John 61, 459, 491

Timmons, John W. 64
Timmons, John W. (Jr.) 61
Timmons, John Wesley (Jr.) 61
Timmons, Martha 64
Timmons, Mary Adams 64
Timmons, Mary Ellen 61
Timmons, Polly 494
Timmons, Rebecca 61
Timmons, Samuel 630
Timmons, Thomas 61
Timmons, Thomas W. 64
Timmons, Thos. J. 494
Timmons, William A. 64
Timmons, William H. H. 61
Timmons, Wm. H. H. 61
Timney, Daniel 624
Tinan, Patrick 547
Tindall, Hendrixson 523
Tindall, John 499
Tindall, Zachariah 624
Tingle, Clarissa 421
Tingle, Mary 664
Tingle, Samuel L. 421
Tingler, John 524
Tingley, Ebenezer 155, 733
Tingley, Isabella 733
Tingley, John 181
Tinkham, Seth 85
Tinkle, Priscilla 141
Tinlow, William 454
Tinnis, Peggy 14
Tinnus, David 15
Tinsley, Joseph 667
Tipner, C. 244
Tipner, D. 244
Tipner, Lear 244
Tippie, Michael 102
Tippins, Charlotte 173
Tippins, Elijah 173
Tipton, Delilah 462
Tipton, Jos. H. 695
Tipton, Sarah 695
Tipton, Thomas 387
Tire, Mary 45
Tirgman, Geo. 404
Tirgman, Mary 404
Tirvy, George 517
Tisdale, Mary J. 608
Tisher, Catarin 276
Tisher, Charles 276
Tisher, Eve 276
Tisher, Jacob 276
Titarick, Balser 288
Titerack, Balser 288
Tittle, Elizabeth 746
Tittle, George 746
Tittle, Henry 165
Tittle, Mary 746
Tittle, Peter 746
Tittle, Rachel 744
Titus, Ann 677
Titus, Edith 677
Titus, Israel 42
Titus, Jacob 677
Titus, James J. 42

Titus, John Avery 42
Titus, Margaretta L. 635
Titus, Mary 677
Titus, Phillip 677
Titus, Stephen 635
Titus, Steven 92
Titus, Timothy 677
Titus, Zellah 677
Tizzard, Elizabeth 421
Toast, Emily 279
Tobe, Agnes 115
Tobe, Anna 113
Tobe, Joseph 115
Tobias, Henry Arnold 244
Tobias, Joseph Anson 244
Tobias, Laura Ellen 244
Tobias, P. 244
Tobias, Paul 244
Tobias, Sarah 244
Tobias, Sarina 244
Tobias, Talitha 244
Tobin, Bridget 358
Tod, David 72
Tod, Samuel 467
Todd, Andrew R. 610
Todd, Anne 660
Todd, Elizabeth 124, 387, 548, 661
Todd, Ely 399
Todd, Gavin 437
Todd, Geo. 403
Todd, James 437, 643, 663
Todd, James C. 142
Todd, Joel 403
Todd, John 130, 141, 437, 547
Todd, John S. 681
Todd, Jonah 387
Todd, Maria 403
Todd, Michael 624
Todd, Owen 643, 670
Todd, Robert 273
Todd, Robt. 269
Todd, Samuel 467
Todd, Sarah J. 142
Todd, William 610
Todd, Wm. 437
Todhunter, Jacob 683
Todhunter, John 27
Toland, A. 60
Toland, Aquela 52
Toland, Isabella 142
Toland, John M. 106
Toland, Morgan 3
Toland, Rachel C. 142
Tolbert, John 576
Tolbert, Ruth 547
Tolen, Morgan 3
Tolgenkearst, C. F. 104
Toliver, Sarah Ann 609
Tolman, Chester 733
Tolman, Ebenezer 727
Tolman, Seth 727
Tolmon, Mary 715
Tom, Sally 465
Tom, Seley 465
Toman, Louisa 195
Toman, Lydia 195

Toman, Valentine 195
Tomas, John D. 576
Tombold, Abraham 347
Tombold, Mary 378
Tombough, Susannah 558
Tomlin, Catherine 454
Tomlin, John 454
Tomlin, Mary 454
Tomlin, Nancy 451
Tomlin, Richard 454
Tomlinson, Daniel 168
Tomlinson, Elizabeth 387, 399
Tomlinson, Emily 331
Tomlinson, James 107
Tomlinson, Jesse 107
Tomlinson, John 107, 331
Tomlinson, John F. 107
Tomlinson, Joseph 200, 485, 610
Tomlinson, Joseph F. 107
Tomlinson, Joseph Foster 107
Tomlinson, Lewis F. 107
Tomlinson, Margaret 460
Tomlinson, Mary 107
Tomlinson, Nancy 107
Tomlinson, Rachel 107
Tomlinson, Rebecca 107
Tomlinson, Thomas 288
Tompkins, Asabel 265
Tompkins, Asahel 266, 271
Tompkins, George R. 59
Tompkins, John 55, 687
Tomset, Samuel 663
Tong, Jane 466
Tong, Wm. 477
Tonget, Larkin 593
Tool, Patrick 733
Toole, Timothy 317
Toolman, Dinah 383
Toops, Henry 459
Toops, John 467, 494
Tootle, John 387
Tope, James Jefferson 410
Tope, John Nelson 408
Topkin, Gerard 283
Topping, Flavel 499
Topping, Helen 499
Torbert, Elizabeth 256
Torbert, Eskridge 256
Torbert, Wm. 256
Torence, Lucy 93
Torland, Jane M. 659
Torrence, Alebert 80
Torrence, John 65
Torrence, John (Jr.) 65
Torrence, John C. 220
Torrence, Polly 84
Torrence, William 85
Torry, Sally 714
Torulinder, John F. 105
Tosin, John 276
Tosin, Laky 276
Tosin, Mary 276
Totten, James 683
Toujon, Andrew 454

Toujou, Andrew 454
Towers, Thomas 387
Town, Enor 385
Town, Mary 422
Town, Susan 413
Townsen, Allen 80
Townsen, Daniel 80
Townsend, Allen 80
Townsend, Caty Ann 80
Townsend, Charles 755
Townsend, Elizabeth 77
Townsend, John 663
Townsend, Joseph 663
Townsend, Lydia 80
Townsend, Mariah 83
Townsend, Mary 31, 663
Townsend, Rebecca 497
Townsend, Sally 76
Townsend, Solomon 80
Townsend, Thos. S. 80
Townsley, Junius 356
Trace, Adam 132
Trace, Andrew 132
Trace, Christiana 132
Tracey, Janard 356
Tracey, Joshua 356
Tracy, Abigal 762
Tracy, Anna 313
Tracy, Bazel 313
Tracy, Charles 507
Tracy, Ebenezer 762
Tracy, Eliza 571
Tracy, Elizabeth 313
Tracy, Eloner 565
Tracy, Harriet 762
Tracy, Isaac 762
Tracy, John 762
Tracy, John (Jr.) 762
Tracy, Joseph R. 762
Tracy, Lydia 762
Tracy, Lyman 762
Tracy, Mason 762
Tracy, Matilda 571
Tracy, Mercena R. 762
Tracy, Nancy 569
Tracy, Orsella 762
Tracy, Patience 175, 179
Tracy, Ruth A. 762
Tracy, Samuel M. 502
Tracy, Sofa 762
Tracy, Thomas R. 762
Tracy, Thos. R. 762
Tracy, William 175, 179, 313, 762
Trader, Matilda 124
Train, Christopher 547
Traner, Thos. 353
Trapp, Andrew 42
Trask, Olive 497
Trassal, George 562
Trassel, George 562
Trauger, George 740
Trauger, Jacob H. 740
Trauger, John 740
Trauger, Martha Catharine 740
Trauger, Mary 740
Trauger, Paul 740
Trausdale, Samuel 643

Travis, Cynthia 745
Travis, Ezra 747
Travis, Hanna 509
Travis, John 336
Travis, Joseph 517
Travis, Noah 517
Travis, Sarah 513
Traxler, Catherine T. 745
Tray, Nathaniel 45
Treadway, Mary 711
Treadwell, John Dexter 86
Treckle, Edward 448
Trees, Michael 491
Treesum, Catharine 452
Tregs, Polly 517
Tremain, Calvin 42
Treman, George Elmore 762
Treman, Jeremiah 762
Treman, John M. 762
Treman, Julius 762
Treman, Julius Derwin 762
Treman, Nancy I. 762
Treman, Nancy J. 762
Tremble, Abigail 659
Tremble, Jacob 669
Treon, Henry 217
Treon, Peter 193
Tressler, Jonathan 748
Trevor, Maria 709
Trewet, Elizabeth 517
Trexler, Emanuel 501
Trexler, Hannah 514
Trexler, Rachel 516
Trexler, Samuel 501
Trexler, Susannah 513
Tribly, Jonathan 681, 685, 688
Trigger, Rachel 458
Triggs, Polly 517
Triggs, Susannah 511
Trimble, Daniel 663
Trimble, Elizabeth 666
Trimble, John 491
Trimble, Sarah 655
Trimble, Susanna 659
Trimbley, David 176
Trimbly, David 161
Trimbly, Jemima 162
Trimbly, John 162
Trimer, William 503
Trimplin, Drusilla 565
Trine, Christian 224
Trip, Sophia 636
Tripp, Abigail 90
Tripp, Betsy 632
Tripp, David 632
Tripp, Holden 632
Tripp, Jesse 632
Tripp, John 632
Tripp, Joseph 632
Tripp, Leonidas 632
Tripp, Louisa 632
Tripp, Lovina 632
Tripp, Mary Ann 632
Tripp, Nancy N. 632

978

Tripp, Oliver 632
Tripp, Rebecca 632
Tripp, Stephen 632
Tripp, William H. 632
Tripp, Wm. H. 632
Tripp, Wm. H. A. 632
Triss, Morris A. 467
Trohee, Martin 270
Tront, Casper 265
Troop, Andrew I. 610
Troop, David C. 747
Trotter, William 718
Troublesome, Thomas 260
Troup, Adam 355
Trousdale, John Lowry
  643
Trout, Ann Margaret 379
Trout, Eleanor 375
Trout, Elizabeth 378,
  379
Trout, Ephraim 378
Trout, Geo. 353, 378
Trout, George 354, 375
Trout, George (Jr.) 378
Trout, George (Judge)
  354
Trout, George (Sr.)
  366, 378
Trout, Harriet 379
Trout, Henry 378, 379
Trout, Jacob 378
Trout, John 378
Trout, Juliana S. 378
Trout, Lucinda 536
Trout, Margaret 378
Trout, Margaret M. 364
Trout, Mary 7
Trout, Michael 7, 378
Trout, Philip 378
Trout, Polly 378
Trout, Sophia 378
Trout, W. 536
Trout, Wilson 379
Trout, Zeddig 379
Troutner, C. 618
Troutner, C. W. 618
Troutner, Elizabeth 613
Troutner, George 467
Troutner, Peter 613
Trove, John 733
Trowbridge, William 49
Troxel, Abraham 188
Troxell, Abraham 192,
  209, 216
Troxell, Lewis 216
Troxell, Mary 216
Troxell, Rosanna 216
Troxell, Samuel 216
Truax, Benj. P. 164
Trusx, Benjamin 162, 172
Truax, David 425
Truax, Isaac (Jr.) 431
Truax, Jacob 175
Truax, Jane 164
Truax, John 166, 176
Truax, Katharine 178
Truax, Margaret 166
Truax, Mary 156, 173
Truax, Phebe 172

Truax, Phoebe 162
Truax, Rebecca 164, 176
Truax, Richard 156,
  164, 173
Truax, Samuel 176
Truax, Stilwell 156
Truax, Susanna 176
Truax, William 164
Truby, Obediah 547
True, Amlin 733
True, Ephraim 726
True, Haynes 523
True, Jabez 728
True, Jabez (Dr.) 722,
  723
Truet, Mary Ann 509
Truet, Susan 510
Truett, James D. 49
Truex, Bethenia 170
Truex, John 170
Truex, Mary 154, 157,
  159
Truex, Rachel 159
Truex, Richard 154,
  157, 159, 166
Truex, Samuel 157
Truex, Stillwell 159
Truex, Stilwell 155, 158
Truex, William 153,
  159, 164
Truit, Peggy 12
Truit, William 15
Truitt, Eli 672
Trullinger, Abraham 387
Trullinger, Jacob 387
Trullinger, Margaret 387
Trullinger, Phillip 387
Trumbo, Andrew 379
Trumbow, Emley 571
Trumbs, Charlotte 566
Trumf, Elisabeth 234
Trumf, Fridrich 234
Trumf, Maria 234
Trump, Elliott 685
Trump, John 559
Truner, William 431
Trunnel, Silas 346
Trusam, Catharine 457
Trusel, Ann 577
Trussell, George 564
Trussum, Phebe 466
Tryon, Truman 31
Tshappat, Jacob 169
Tshappat, Susannah 169
Tshudy, Martin 576
Tubble, Elizabeth 639
Tubbs, Daniel 86
Tubbs, Deborah 77
Tubbs, Elizabeth 82
Tubbs, Ezra 85
Tubbs, Mary 76
Tubbs, Ransler 80
Tubbs, Reuben 80
Tubbs, Russell 80
Tubbs, William 80
Tucker, --- 677
Tucker, Abraham 142
Tucker, Alexd. D. 295
Tucker, Jacob 142

Tucker, John 577
Tucker, John Wesley 341
Tucker, Jonathan 142
Tucker, Joseph 142
Tucker, Lemuel 593
Tucker, Margaret 512
Tucker, Mary 494
Tucker, Matibaner 142
Tucker, Nathaniel 142
Tucker, Nicholas 142
Tucker, Samuel 577
Tucker, Susan 142
Tucker, Thomas V. 437
Tucker, William B. 547
Tuckett, Craven P. 57
Tuerwerk, Christian 113
Tuff, James 667
Tufford, Elizabeth 572
Tuft, Thomas 259
Tuger, Henry 322
Tuley, William 551
Tulle, Rachael 119
Tuller, Sally 497
Tulles, John 27
Tulles, Nancy 119
Tullis, David 655
Tullis, David H. 655
Tullis, David R. 121
Tullis, Elenor 669
Tullis, Ezra 663
Tullis, Joel 655
Tullis, John 655
Tullis, John T. 121
Tullis, John W. 58
Tullis, Jonathan 58, 655
Tullis, Michael 58, 669
Tullis, Nancy 58
Tullis, Polly 121
Tullis, Racheal 665
Tullis, Rebecca A. 607
Tullis, Stephen 663
Tullis, William 118
Tullis, Wm. 108
Tully, James 428
Tumbleson, John 601, 624
Tumbold, Barbara 347
Tumbold, Elizabeth 347
Tumbold, Nancy 348
Tumbold, Peter 347
Tumbold, Rosannah 347
Tumbold, Sarah 348
Tunis, Lindley 547
Tunks, Philip 547
Tunks, Rachael E. 593
Tunlin, James 577
Tunness, Dullene 385
Tupper, Anselm 721, 722
Tupper, Benj. 296
Tupper, Benjamin 296,
  718, 720, 721, 722,
  726
Tupper, Benjamin (Jr.)
  722
Tupper, Benjn. 721
Tupper, Edw. W. 722
Tupper, Edward W. 296
Tupper, Edward White
  721, 726
Tupper, Huldah 721

979

Tupper, Minerva 721
Tupper, Patty 296
Tupper, Polly 296
Turell, John 663
Turhune, James 324
Turk, John 654
Turmor, William 467
Turnbaugh, John 208
Turnbaugh, Phebe Ann 208
Turner, Adaline 269
Turner, Adam 474, 477
Turner, Alexander 69
Turner, Aquilla 583
Turner, Benjamin 286
Turner, Bridget 515
Turner, Cynthia 12
Turner, David 711
Turner, Eliza 269
Turner, Elizabeth 142, 516
Turner, Isaac 366
Turner, Isabella 266
Turner, J. R. 508, 510
Turner, Jamima 580
Turner, John 16, 26, 31, 208, 269, 469, 472, 527
Turner, John R. 500, 507
Turner, Malinda 582
Turner, Martha 13
Turner, Mary 510, 511
Turner, Peter 725
Turner, Richard 474
Turner, Robert 80, 581
Turner, Samuel 266, 269
Turner, Thomas 15, 580
Turner, William 517, 531, 593
Turney, Daniel 391
Turney, Elizabeth 491
Turney, Henry 459, 491
Turney, James 494
Turpin, James 459
Turton, Richard 389
Tuschler, John 505
Tuttle, Elizabeth 666
Tuttle, Esther 173
Tuttle, Isabell 618
Tuttle, Isaiah 491
Tuttle, James 459
Tuttle, James (Jr.) 173
Tuttle, Joel 715
Tuttle, John 480, 639
Tuttle, Linus 715, 733
Tuttle, Walbet 499
Tuttle, William W. 499
Twallo, Jacob 577
Tweed, Margaret 468
Tweedy, John 247
Tweford, Clement 467
Twichell, Ephraim 80
Twiford, Nancy M. 584
Twiford, Thomas 593
Twiss, Russell 523
Twitchell, William 80
Twoney, Michael 526
Tyler, Emily 83
Tyler, Lewis 762
Tyler, Mary 45

Tyler, Morris 499
Tyler, Walter 491
Tyrrell, Cyrus 42
Tyson, Zephanrah 271
Tyson, Zepheneah 262
Tyson, Zepheniah 261

--- U ---

Uendler, John Henry 107
Uger, Johann Jacob 74
Uhlhorn, John Dederick Herman 102
Uhrich, Catherine 562
Uhrich, Hannah 562, 574
Uhrich, Jacob 562, 568
Uhrich, John 562
Uhrich, Michael 562, 568
Ulery, Betsey 120
Ulery, Jacob 213, 281
Ulery, John 667
Ulery, Samuel 194
Ulex, A. W. 529
Ullem, Hannah 513
Ullery, Aaron 447
Ullery, Catharine 142
Ullery, Elizabeth 142
Ullery, Ephraim 447
Ullery, George 447
Ullery, Henry 447
Ullery, Jacob 142
Ullery, John 127, 447
Ullery, Polly 447
Ullery, Rebecca 447
Ullery, Samuel 447
Ullery, Stephen 193
Ullery, Wm. 142
Ullom, Dan 178
Ullom, Eleanor 172
Ullom, John 166
Ullom, Judah 177
Ullom, Margaret 166
Ullom, Stephen 172
Ullom, William 177
Ulm, Edward 459
Ulrey, Henry 491
Ulrey, Hiram 494
Ulrey, Jesse 494
Ulrich, Barbara 230
Ulrich, David (Sr.) 230
Ulrich, Susannah 230
Umbarger, George 196
Umbarger, Sarah 196
Umbenhour, Sophia 745
Umsted, Aaron 529
Umsted, Deliah 529
Umsted, Eli 529
Umsted, Elisha 529
Umsted, Eliza 529
Umsted, Enoch 529
Umsted, Nancy 529
Umsted, Rebecca 529
Umsted, Sarah 529
Umsted, Susannah 529
Umstone, Benj. 476
Underwood, John 121, 547
Underwood, Lucinda 549

Underwood, Mary 609
Underwood, Robert 286
Underwood, William 15, 118
Unger, Aaron Andrew 437
Ungerer, Hannah 222
Ungry, Betsey 659
Unpdike, S. G. 108
Unser, John 523
Upcott, Ann 495
Upcott, Elizabeth 499
Updegraff, Joseph S. 547
Upduyke, Green 108
Upduyke, Isaac 108
Upduyke, Jacob W. 108
Upduyke, Sarah 108
Upduyke, Smith 108
Upham, Curtis Z. 735
Upham, E. 735
Upham, Elizabeth 735
Upham, Hannah L. 735
Upham, L. H. 735
Upham, Myra E. 735
Uphouse, Henry 107
Uphouse, Mary 107
Upshur, A. P. 59
Upton, Matthew B. 647
Urbn, I. 537
Urbn, M. 537
Urbn, Phillip 537
Urich, Jacob 561
Urmston, Benj. 484, 485
Urmstone, Benj. 476, 477, 480
Urmstone, Benjamin 485
Urnston, Benjamin 472
Urschel, Catharine P. 222
Urschel, Lewis 222
Urschell, Lewis 222
Ury, David 297
Usher, Elias P. 31
Utley, Jos. 766
Utley, Samuel 499
Utt, Adam 517
Utt, Hannah 513
Utt, Jacob 517
Utt, Peggy 517
Utter, Jabes 577
Utter, Johez 271
Uttz, Mary Ann 431
Uttz, Nancy 431
Uttz, Susannah 431
Uttz, William 431
Uttz, Wirenda 431
Utz, Elizabeth 420
Utz, Louisa F. 420

--- V ---

Vail, --- 355
Vail, Aaron 683
Vail, Ephraim 440
Vail, James 443
Vail, Samuel 683
Valaday, Francis 517
Vale, Ann 89

980

Vale, Mary Ann 574
Valentine, Benj. 733
Valentine, Catherine 453
Valentine, Daniel 547
Valentine, George 146
Valentine, Mary 383
Valentine, Obadiah 101
Valentine, Sophia 383
Vallentine, Lidey 574
Valodin, Francis 715
Van Alsdall, Anna 28
Van Alstine, Abraham 42
Vanamon, Edmond 569
Vananda, William Collet 749
Vanasdal, John 250, 251
Vanasdall, John 250, 251
Vanator, Benjamin 577
Vanatta, Elias 356
Vanatta, Elizabeth 372
Vanatta, James 372
Vanatta, John 353, 356, 362, 363
Vanatta, Stephen 372
Vanausdale, John 223
Vanbeblow, John 517
Vanberon, John 517
Vanblicome, John 551
Van Bluricum, Elizabeth 550
Vanborne, Thomas B. 639
Vanbrike, Barnard 663
Vanbuskirk, Ann 462
Van Buskirk, Michael 387
Vancamp, Thomas 551
Vance, Elisha 142, 387
Vance, George 390
Vance, Isaac 92
Vance, Joseph 474, 476
Vance, Samuel 15
Vance, Samuel C. 282
Vance, William 454
Vancell, Joseph 747
Van Cleve, Benjamin 192
Van Cleve, Catharine 192
Van Cleve, Henrietta Maria 192
Vancleve, John W. 203
Van Cleve, John W. 202
Van Cleve, Mary Cornelia 192
Van Cleve, Sarah Sophia 192
Van Cleve, Wiley 192
Vancleve, William 182
Van Cleve, William 182, 192
Vanclief, Emeline 253
Vanclief, Luther 253
Vanclief, Patience 253
Vanclief, Peter 253
Vandan, Rachel 663
Vandason, Catren 452
Vandegrift, Jesse 551
Vandeman, Elizabeth 465
Vandemark, Catharine 548
Vandemark, Catherine 547
Van Demark, E. 404
Van Demark, Margaret 404

Van Demark, Mary E. 404
Vandenbenden, John 727
Vanderbark, David 293
Vanderbenden, Mertnias 727
Vanderford, Alexander 636
Vanderford, Austin 636
Vanderford, Eli 459, 636
Vanderford, Jesse 636
Vanderford, Joel 636
Vanderford, Mary 636
Vanderford, Nancy 636
Vanderford, Richard 636
Vanderford, William 636
Vanderhoof, Isaac 75
Van Derliss, Hugh 42
Vanderman, E. 60
Vandervart, Nathaniel 494
Vanderventer, Cornelius 159
Vandervert, Nicholas 645
Vandervest, Jonas 667
Vandervort, James 387
Vandervort, John 688
Vanderwit, James 292
Vandevart, John 671
Vandevart, Jonah 671
Vandeventer, John 157
Vandevere, Benjamin 215
Vandike, Henry 643
Vandike, Jane 643
Vandike, John 643
Vandine, Mathew 663
Vandoran, William 387
Vandoren, Abraham 437, 499
Vandoren, Cornelius 437
Vandoren, Frances 437
Vandoren, G. M. 497
Vandorman, Charlotte 449
Van Dreser, Eleazer 31
Vandrevander, Betsy 585
Van Dusen, Andrew 71
Van Dusen, Don C. 71
Van Dusen, Esther A. 71
Van Dusen, June 71
Van Dusen, Martin B. 71
Van Dusen, Orpha 71
Van Dusen, Ralph H. 71
Van Dusen, Ray L. 71
Van Dusen, Roe G. 71
Van Dusen, Rush L. 71
Vanduyn, William B. 80
Vanduyne, Adrianne B. 77
Vandyke, Mary 520
VanDyke, Peter 656
Vandyke, Samuel 523
Van Eaton, John 655
Vanemark, Daniel 547
Vanemon, Robert 624
Vanfossan, Samuel 408
Van Gundy, Branson 109
Vangundy, Chris. 491
Van Gundy, Elbe 109
Van Gundy, Elizabeth 109
Van Gundy, Elmore 109
Van Gundy, Huldah 109

Van Gundy, John 109
Van Gundy, John Jefferson 109
Van Gundy, Joshua 109
Van Gundy, Margaret 109
Van Gundy, Samuel 109
Van Gundy, Washington 109
Van Gunten, John 42
Vanhise, Oaky 672
Vanhook, Samuel 500
Vanhook, Thomas 387
Vanhorn, Ann 142
Vanhorn, Betsy 142
Van Horn, Catharine 146
Vanhorn, Christian 96
Vanhorn, Clarissa 639
Vanhorn, David 96
Vanhorn, Elizabeth 254
Van Horn, Elizabeth 146, 658
Van Horn, Harriet 666
Vanhorn, Isaac 379
Van Horn, Isaac 258, 297, 298
Van Horn, Isaac (Jr.) 284
Vanhorn, James 142, 254
Van Horn, James 655
Vanhorn, John 142
Vanhorn, John T. Burk 254
Vanhorn, Julia Ann 142
Vanhorn, Margaret 254
Van Horn, Martha J. 146
Vanhorn, Mary 65
Van Horn, Mary 146
Vanhorn, Mary Elvina 254
Van Horn, Robert 655
Vanhorn, Sarah 379
Vanhorn, Thomas 65, 254
Vanhorn, Walter 387
Vanhorn, Wilkinson 142
Van Horne, Isaac 286
Van Horne, Isaac (Sr.) 298
Vanhorne, Jane 604
VanHorne, Thomas B. 648
Van Houton, Jacob 447
Vankirk, Anna 195
Van Kirk, Barnac 392
Van Kirk, Grace 392
Vankirk, Hannah 195
Vankirk, James 195
Vankirk, Jane 195
Van Kirk, Mary 392
Vankirk, Sarah 195
Van Lehn, Benjamin 564
Van Lehn, Henry 564
Van Lehn, Mary 564
Van Lehr, Benjamin 564
Van Lehr, Henry 564
Van Lehr, Mary 564
Van Matre, Abraham 673
VanMatre, Abraham 644
Van Matre, John Johnson 673
VanMatre, John Johnson 645

Van Matre, Lewis D. 673
VanMatre, Lewis D. 644
Van Matre, Malissa 673
Van Matre, Margaret 673
VanMatre, Margaret 644
VanMatre, Melissa 644
Van Matre, Morgan 673
VanMatre, Morgan 644,
  645
VanMatre, Thomas I. 644
Van Matre, Thomas J. 673
Vanmeter, Betsey 466
Vanmeter, Cecelia B. 402
Vanmeter, Daniel T. 402
Vanmeter, Henry 402, 494
Vanmeter, James 467
Vanmeter, James W. 402
Vanmeter, John 65
Vanmeter, Joseph 402,
  459
Vanmeter, Lydia 494
Van Meter, Marget 391
Vanmeter, Mary 402
Vanmeter, Murry 402
Van Meter, Rachael 391
Vanmeter, Rachel 402
Vanmeter, Rebecca 402
Van Metre, Rebecca 384
Vanmeter, Sarah 402
Vanmeter, Sidney 402
Vanmeter, Sophy 65
Vanmeter, Susannah 385
Vanmeter, Thomas 402
Vanmetre, Maria E. 740
Vanmickle, Nancy 452
Vannasdoll, Anna 28
Vannatta, Aaron 347
Vannatta, Elijah 351
Vannatta, Eliza Ann 351
Vannatte, Peter 523
Vannawald, John 228
Vannelzer, Lewit H. 272
Vannest, David 505
Vannetten, Mercy 30
Vannill, John 663
Vannorman, Amanda 449
Vannorman, Clarissa 449
Vannorman, Elizabeth 449
Vannorman, Ira 449
Vannorman, Jasper 449
Vannorman, Jerusha 449
Vannorman, Nancy 449
Vannorman, Rachel 449
Vannorman, Sophia 449
Vannorne, George 604
Vannosetstren, Margaret
  736
Van Nostren, James 736
Van Nostren, Margaret
  736
Van Nuys, Jacobus J. 100
Van Nuys, James 100
Van Nuys, John 100, 101
Van Nuys, Margaret 100
Van Nuys, Peter 100
Van Nuys, Peter M. 100,
  101
Van Nuys, Rachel 100
Vanorman, Elizabeth 449

Vanorman, Miles J. 449
Vanost, Sally 511
Vanostran, James 215
Vanostran, Joseph 215
Vanote, Ezekiel 663
Vanote, Rhoda 547
Vanoy, John 663
Vanpelt, Daniel 568
Van Schork, David 696
Vanschoych, John 663
Vanscoik, Aaron 127
Vanscoyac, Abraham 142
Vanscoyac, David 142
Vanscoyac, Harvey 142
Vanscoyac, Henry 142
Vanscoyac, Jane 142
Vanscoyck, Tobias 206
Vanscoyk, N. 661
Vansell, Elizabeth 663
Vansickle, Elizabeth 280
Vansickle, Peter A. 363
Van Tassel, Isaac 762,
  765
Van Tassell, Isaac 757
Van Tassell, L. B. 765
Vantz, Jonas 437
Van Valkinburg, J. G.
  605
Van Valkinburgh, Roxana
  610
Vanvey, Mary 380
Van Vleet, Abram 672,
  674
VanVleet, Abram 645
Vanvoorhes, John 293
Vanvoorhis, Matilda 9
Vanwey, Elizabeth 360
Vanwickle, Danl. 387
Vanwickle, Nancy 452
Vanwinkle, Robert 437
Varande, Aaron 568
Vard, Nahum 733
Varen, Detter 517
Varian, Charles M. 208
Varner, Elizabeth 664
Varner, Joseph 169, 663
Varner, Louanna 637
Varner, Lucy 169
Varner, Martin 284
Varney, Julia 13
Vastine, Abraham 507
Vastine, Frederic 507
Vastine, Gabriel 507
Vastine, John 507, 508
Vastine, John (Jr.) 507
Vastine, Mary 507
Vastine, William 507
Vaughn, Alexander 42
Vaughn, Phebe 279
Vaughn, Samuel 33
Vaughters, Thomas G. 637
Veecher, Elizabeth 498
Veichers, Katharine 100
Velder, Charlotte 220
Vellnagle, Julius 528
Vellnagle, Nanetta 528
Venaman, James 118
Venaman, James H. 146
Venaman, Mary J. 146

Venaman, Wm. G. 146
Venard, Francis 663
Venard, J. 150
Venard, James 150
Venard, Jane K. 150
Venard, Jas. 150
Venard, Jerusha 150
Venard, Thomas 647
Vent, Sarah 407
Verdicate, Allsain 499
Verdicate, John 499
Verline, Henry 387
Vernon, Ann 123
Vernon, Joseph 285
Vernon, Margaret 117
Vernon, Thomas 121, 132
Vertner, Daniel 485
Vertner, John 15
Vest, Andrew 268
Vestal, Elizabeth 466,
  639, 671
Vestal, Jemima 639
Vestal, John 639, 671
Vestal, Mary 639
Vestal, Rachel 639
Vestal, Samuel 639
Vetcher, Elizabeth 498
Veze, Samuel 387
Vial, Polly 554
Vibert, Anthony 725
Vicars, Elizabeth 386
Vickers, William Smith
  49
Viers, Eliza 364
Vigo, Frances 481
Vilette, Eliza T. 555
Vincent, Anthony
  Claudius 719
Vincent, George A. 252
Vincent, Harriet 762
Vincent, John 34, 707
Vincent, Laban 733
Vincent, Rachel 707
Vinden, Isaac 467
Viniki, Christian 170
Vining, Elizabeth 579
Vining, Joseph 88
Vining, Sylvia 77
Vining, Timothy B. 85
Vinson, Clarissa 106
Vinson, Curthbert 106
Vinson, James S. 106
Vinson, Malachi 106
Vinson, William 51, 459
Vinson, William A. 106
Vinton, Almus E. 214
Vinton, David P. 214
Vinton, Malvina 214
Vinton, Rosewell M. 214
Violet, Margaret 717
Violet, Sampson 517
Violette, John Lewis 722
Violette, Lewis 723
Virgin, Abraham 504
Virgin, George O. 504
Virgin, Jemima 504
Virgin, Kinzey 504
Virgin, Rachel 504
Virgin, Resin 504

982

Virgin, William 118
Virtal, Elizabeth 466
Virtue, Eleanor 352
Visinier, Charles
    Nicholas 715
Vogelly, Christena 335
Voglesong, John J. 42
Voll, Conrod 161
Voorhees, Joseph 690
Voorheis, Abraham 214
Voorhis, Albert 641
Voorhis, Cornelius 638,
    640, 675
Voorhis, Daniel 640,
    655, 675
Voorhis, Elizabeth 657
Voorhis, James 667
Voorhis, John 640, 641
Voorhis, Luke 638
Voorhis, Magdalene 675
Voorhis, Margaret 675
Voorhise, Cornelius 646
Voorhise, Magdalene 646
Voorhise, Margaret 646
Vorannon, Mary 592
Vore, Elizabeth 204
Vore, Joseph 204
Vore, Mary 203
Vore, Peter 142, 203
Vore, Rebecca 142, 203
Vore, Sally 142
Vore, Thomas 203
Vorhees, Cornelius 651
Vorhees, Eliza 221
Vorhis, Aaron (Sr.) 304
Vorhise, Daniel 646
Voris, Ralph 427
Vosnight, Mary 665

--- W ---

Wa . . . , James 153
Wabby, Isaac 547
Waddal, Joseph 387
Waddell, Charles 369
Waddell, James 391
Waddill, Charles 517
Waddle, Francis 459
Waddle, James 391
Waddle, James L. 388
Waddle, John 459
Waddle, Joseph 391, 756
Waddle, Polly 391
Waddle, Sally 391
Waddle, Samuel 467
Waddle, Thomas 391
Waddle, William 391
Wade, Elias 577
Wade, J. 533
Wade, John 569
Wade, Loas A. 761
Wade, Sophia 533
Wadell, Thomas 396
Wademan, Sarah 630
Wadsworth, Benjamin 86
Wadsworth, Decius 755
Wadsworth, George 755

Wadsworth, Hosea 142
Waggaman, Catharine 208
Waggamon, Anna 208
Waggamon, Elizabeth 208
Waggamon, Joel 208
Waggamon, Rachel 208
Waggamon, Samuel 208
Wagganer, Benjamin 210
Waggner, Elizabeth 527
Waggner, Frederick 527
Waggner, George 527
Waggner, John 527
Waggner, Mary Ann 527
Waggner, Nicols 527
Waggoner, Benjamin 189
Waggoner, Betsy 523
Waggoner, Catharine 522
Waggoner, Christian 523
Waggoner, Daniel 523
Waggoner, David 198
Waggoner, Elizabeth 377
Waggoner, Fariba 190
Waggoner, Frederick
    199, 205
Waggoner, George 367,
    527
Waggoner, John 147,
    185, 339, 341
Waggoner, John (Jr.) 349
Waggoner, John (Sr.) 370
Waggoner, John H. 190
Waggoner, Mary 522
Waggoner, Mathias 569
Waggoner, Michael 663
Waggoner, Peter 15
Waggoner, Reuben 190
Waggoner, Ruth 313
Wagner, Ann 581
Wagner, Annie Catharine
    617
Wagner, August 108
Wagner, Azariah 610
Wagner, Eve 522
Wagner, John 80, 577
Wagner, M. 346
Wagner, Magdalena 346
Wagner, Margaret 708
Wagner, Maria 709
Wagner, Michael H. 617
Wagner, Peter (Jr.) 526
Wagner, Philip 184
Wagoner, A. L. 734
Wagoner, Alvin 146
Wagoner, Anna L. 734
Wagoner, B. E. 540
Wagoner, B. J. 313
Wagoner, Barney 312, 313
Wagoner, Benjamin 201
Wagoner, David 201
Wagoner, Elisa 146
Wagoner, Eliz. 146
Wagoner, Elizabeth 201,
    312, 313, 734
Wagoner, Ellen 146
Wagoner, Esther 201
Wagoner, Frederick 172
Wagoner, Hamala 146
Wagoner, Henry P. 610
Wagoner, Isaac 312, 313

Wagoner, Isaiah 313
Wagoner, John 201, 313
Wagoner, John W. 146,
    312, 313
Wagoner, Margaret Adelma
    540
Wagoner, Mary 313
Wagoner, Mary C. 313
Wagoner, Mary E. 313
Wagoner, N. W. 313
Wagoner, Nancy 313
Wagoner, Richard 312, 313
Wagoner, Sarah A. 312,
    313
Wagoner, Sarah Ann 312
Wagoner, Susannah 201
Wagoner, Thomas 540
Wagoner, Valentine 555
Wagoner, W. H. 734
Wagoner, William 312
Wagoner, William W. 313
Wagoner, Wm. 734
Wagonery, Sarah 413
Wahl, Conrod 161
Wainright, William 31
Wait, Almida 20
Wait, Benj. 353
Wait, Benjamin 347
Wait, Cecilla 506
Wait, E. 75
Wait, Elizabeth 28
Wait, Marietta 31
Wait, Mary 347
Wait, Sally Ann 30
Wait, Thomas 31
Waite, Horace 42
Waits, Allen 163
Wakefield, Keziah 708
Wakefield, Letitia 304
Wakefield, Peter 708
Wakely, Lyman 31
Walace, William 445
Walbridge, Betsey 270
Walbridge, Eliza 270
Walbridge, Elvira 270
Walbridge, Ira 270
Walbridge, Isaac 262
Walbridge, Roinena
Walbridge, Sylvanus 270
Walburn, William 85
Walcott, Emery B. 764
Walden, Andrew 215
Walden, David 42
Walden, Drew 655
Walden, Margaret 655
Walden, Martha 655
Waldin, David 42
Waldo, John A. 34
Waldron, Elizabeth 637
Waldron, John 683, 687
Waldron, Julia 687
Waldron, Philip 637
Waldrop, Isaac 663
Wale, Ann 628
Walick, Geo. 577
Walker, Aaron 733
Walker, Agnes 359
Walker, Andrew 3, 355,
    359, 372

983

Walker, C. C. 413
Walker, Daniel 85
Walker, Daniel C. 255
Walker, Daniel D. 593
Walker, Dinah 698
Walker, Druscilla 506
Walker, Edith A. 409
Walker, Eliza 4
Walker, Elizabeth 379,
462, 664
Walker, Francis E. 39
Walker, George 121
Walker, Hannah 425
Walker, Henry 355, 379
Walker, Horatio 459
Walker, James 629
Walker, Joanna 379
Walker, John 121, 161,
388, 494, 663, 707,
719
Walker, Joseph 379, 527
Walker, Laura Jane 519
Walker, Lewis 698
Walker, Mabel 734
Walker, Martha 734
Walker, Mary 263, 379,
453, 513, 707
Walker, Mary Ann 495
Walker, Nancy 414
Walker, Nathan 439
Walker, Patience 510
Walker, Polly 84
Walker, Sally 495
Walker, Samuel 263,
287, 485
Walker, Samuel B. 652
Walker, Sarah 661
Walker, Theodoreck 334
Walker, Thomas W. 42
Walker, Viola 734
Walker, Wiliam 556
Walker, William 31, 60,
379
Walkins, Wm. 577
Wall, Benjamin 15, 19
Wall, Elenor 13
Wall, James (Sr.) 17
Wall, John 19
Wall, Polly 19
Wall, Susan 22
Wallace, Alexander G. 4
Wallace, Asa A. 146
Wallace, Cadawallader
398
Wallace, Charity 304
Wallace, D. W. 147
Wallace, David 4, 445
Wallace, Edward 319, 321
Wallace, Elenor 58
Wallace, Eliza 58, 499
Wallace, Harriet 58
Wallace, James 4, 319,
321
Wallace, James (Rev.) 4
Wallace, John 118, 643
Wallace, John P. 4
Wallace, Joseph 4
Wallace, Margaret 4
Wallace, Mary 4

Wallace, Mary A. 4
Wallace, Moses 127
Wallace, Nancy 58
Wallace, Reuben 127
Wallace, Ross 118
Wallace, Sally 123
Wallace, Samuel 491, 584
Wallace, Sarah 319, 321
Wallace, Stephen 58
Wallace, Thomas 471
Wallace, William 445,
475, 485, 582
Wallace, Wm. 459
Wallack, Phillip 577
Wallaston, George 208
Wallaston, Levi 208
Wallaston, Susan 208
Wallen, James 484
Wallensiegle, George 523
Wallenslagh, John 526
Waller, David 270
Waller, Jesse 272
Waller, John 264, 270,
475, 481
Waller, Lewis 272, 304
Waller, Phoebe 272
Wallerr, James 485
Wallic, Nancy 565
Wallick, Jacob 569
Wallick, Mary 572
Wallick, Nancy 570
Wallick, Rebeccah 568
Walling, Ann 745
Walling, Anna 750
Walling, Betsey 52
Walling, Casear 52
Walling, D'Lashmutt 52
Walling, Daniel 750
Walling, Elias 750
Walling, Elizabeth 52
Walling, Isaac Tiffin
750
Walling, Jacob 52
Walling, James 52
Walling, John 52
Walling, Margaret Ann
750
Walling, Mary 52
Walling, Nelson D. 52
Walling, Polly 52
Walling, Robert 750
Walling, Suckey 52
Walling, Thomas 52
Walling, William 52
Wallingford, Absalom 99
Wallingford, Martha Ann
99
Wallingford, Nancy 99
Wallon, Barbara 134
Wallon, Mary 497
Wallon, Reuben 134
Walls, Arcade 512
Walls, Joshua 517
Walls, Sally 465
Walls, Thomas 261
Walmire, Joseph 365
Walpole, John 248
Walpole, Martin 252,
265, 270

Walpole, Mathew 264
Walpole, Matthew 269
Walpole, Matthew (Jr.)
265
Walpole, Patrick 265
Walsinger, John 517
Walston, Rose 382
Walter, Barbara 90, 179
Walter, Casper 179
Walter, Catharine 734
Walter, Charles F. 734
Walter, Edward 734
Walter, Eliza 606
Walter, Elizabeth 563,
573
Walter, George 563
Walter, Henry G. 734
Walter, Jacob 171, 734
Walter, John 577, 610
Walter, Martin 563
Walter, Mary 263, 266,
521, 602
Walter, Michael 467
Walter, Peter 563
Walter, Samuel 263
Walter, William G. 734
Walters, --- 33
Walters, Alexander 602,
610
Walters, Andrew 153,
175, 177
Walters, Betsey 273
Walters, Catharine 567
Walters, Catherine 602
Walters, Charles 547
Walters, Clem 156
Walters, David 602
Walters, Elizabeth 177,
608, 764
Walters, Ephraim 499
Walters, George 302, 610
Walters, Jacob 764
Walters, James 406,
602, 610
Walters, John 297, 302,
686, 764
Walters, John J. 685
Walters, Joseph 764
Walters, Levi 406
Walters, Marten 74
Walters, Mary 406
Walters, Samuel 273
Walters, Sarah Catherine
764
Walters, William 177
Waltman, Catharena 568
Waltman, Philip 109
Walton, A. 700
Walton, Alice 700
Walton, Anna E. 700
Walton, Boaz 561, 577
Walton, Boaz (Sr.) 561
Walton, Caroline 571
Walton, Catharine 700
Walton, Cynthia 577
Walton, D. 700
Walton, Deborah 701
Walton, E. R. 700
Walton, Edward 701

Walton, Edward R.   700
Walton, Edward T.   700
Walton, Eunice   701
Walton, Hannah   50, 566
Walton, James   156, 160
Walton, Jeremiah   174, 175
Walton, Jesse   563
Walton, John   50, 675, 700
Walton, Joseph   50
Walton, Lydia   574
Walton, M.   700, 701
Walton, Maria   50, 593
Walton, Mary   576, 700, 701
Walton, Peres   50
Walton, Polly   50
Walton, Rachel   700, 701
Walton, Rebecca   701
Walton, Rebecca Catharine   700
Walton, Ruth   160
Walton, Ruthetta   700
Walton, Sally   50
Walton, Samuel   700, 701
Walton, William   229, 282
Walton, William C.   164
Walts, David   25
Walts, Madison   25
Waltz, Daniel   577
Waltz, Sarah   536
Waltz, Wm.   536
Wampler, Mary   206
Wampler, Nancy   206
Wanamacher, Susan   384
Wanger, Magdalena   736
Wannell, Isaac   499
Ward, ---   539
Ward, Abigail   14
Ward, Abraham   270, 373
Ward, Alexander P.   133
Ward, Amos   379
Ward, Ann   379
Ward, Aron   668
Ward, Catharine   557
Ward, Charles   337
Ward, Diadema   499
Ward, Edward   379
Ward, Edward   380
Ward, Elizabeth   557
Ward, Frank M.   146
Ward, George   388
Ward, Hannah   557
Ward, Isaac   379, 643
Ward, Israel   719
Ward, James   34, 171, 360, 364, 379
Ward, Jeremiah   379
Ward, Jesse   153
Ward, John   379, 557
Ward, John M.   270
Ward, Joseph   55, 663
Ward, Joshua   677
Ward, Juley   379
Ward, Ketsey   659
Ward, Lafayette   605
Ward, Lilly   55
Ward, Lucy   379, 380

Ward, Mahala S.   708
Ward, Mary   456, 663
Ward, Moses   171
Ward, Nahum   733
Ward, Peggy   292
Ward, Peter   557
Ward, Polly   557
Ward, Robert   517
Ward, Sarah   658
Ward, Seth   171
Ward, Stephen   373
Ward, Sutton   304
Ward, Tobias   557
Ward, William   379
Warden, Barnet   517
Warden, John   31, 556, 558
Warden, Margaret   556
Warden, Martha   556
Warden, Mary   556
Warden, Mary Jean   556
Warden, Robert   556
Warden, Ruth   556
Wards, Hugh   472
Wardsworth, Dacias   762
Wardsworth, Dacius   762
Wardsworth, George   762
Wardsworth, Homeo   762
Wardsworth, Romeo   762
Wardsworth, Sidney   762
Wardsworth, William   762
Ware, Ave   453
Ware, Elizabeth   349
Ware, Jacob   63
Ware, James   294
Ware, Jesse   215, 421
Ware, Joseph A.   421
Ware, William   349, 595
Wareham, Daniel   200
Wareham, Philip   200
Wares, Jane   565
Warfield, Richard   163
Warigh, Lemon   459
Wark, John   523
Warman, Catharine   644
Warman, Joshua   644
Warman, Juliet   644
Warman, Nancy   644
Warman, Sally   644
Warman, Stephen   663
Warnackley, David   547
Warner, Abijah   26
Warner, Amassa   577
Warner, Amos   238
Warner, Andrew   201
Warner, Catharine   208
Warner, Christian   201
Warner, D.   239
Warner, Daniel   146, 577
Warner, David   146, 208, 239
Warner, E.   239
Warner, Elizabeth   201, 202, 238, 239
Warner, Frances   45
Warner, G.   238
Warner, George   208, 238
Warner, George (Sr.)   238
Warner, H.   52

Warner, Henry   63
Warner, Hester   362
Warner, Isaac   26, 473, 484, 485
Warner, James   73
Warner, Joellen   238
Warner, John   17, 81, 362
Warner, Jonathan   561
Warner, Joseph   146
Warner, Levi   277, 459
Warner, Luvina   420
Warner, Lydia   146
Warner, Margaret   238
Warner, Margaret Ann   420
Warner, Mary   563
Warner, Mary Ann   208
Warner, Nathan   561
Warner, Rosanah   142
Warner, Ruth   278
Warner, S.   238
Warner, Sarah   519, 561
Warner, Silas   388
Warner, Susanna   238
Warner, Susannah   201, 208
Warner, William   88
Warner, Wm.   475
Warnock, Robt.   75
Warnock, Rolt   75
Warnock, Wm.   517
Warren, Ann   34
Warren, Anna   467
Warren, Benjamin   35
Warren, Charles   81
Warren, Clement   517
Warren, David   469
Warren, Elijah   715
Warren, James S.   274
Warren, Jas.   478
Warren, Joshua   22
Warren, Lucrecia   333
Warren, Nancy   708
Warren, Rebecca   455
Warren, Wm.   264, 478
Warring, Humphrey   467
Warrington, John   523
Warth, Catherine   713, 715
Warth, John   722
Warth, Polly   714
Warth, Robert   715, 722
Warton, Andrew   273
Warts, Christian   388
Waruff, Oliver   733
Warwick, Aby   693
Warwick, Albert   693
Wash, Barbara   384
Wash, Mary   383
Washburn, Azel   34
Washburn, James   454, 459
Washburn, Matthew   431
Washburn, Norman   747
Washburn, Samuel   750
Washington, George (Gen.)   478
Washington, Jennie   49
Waterbury, Hiram   42
Waterman, Adin   268
Waterman, Nancy   386

Waters, George 162
Waters, Henry B. 81
Waters, James 437
Waters, Mary 467, 571
Waters, Sally 714
Watkins, Alfred 39
Watkins, Amy 115, 612
Watkins, Barbara 81
Watkins, Caler 612
Watkins, Catharine 78
Watkins, Catharine A. 39
Watkins, Charles 106
Watkins, Chris topher 39
Watkins, Clarissa 206
Watkins, Ebenezer 142
Watkins, Elizabeth 206, 464
Watkins, J. 612
Watkins, James 25
Watkins, Jane 106
Watkins, Jane Anna 106
Watkins, John 667
Watkins, John W. 581
Watkins, Jonathan 142, 203, 206
Watkins, Joseph 281
Watkins, Joshua 115, 601, 612
Watkins, M. 612
Watkins, Nancy 612
Watkins, Obedience 25
Watkins, Phebe 206
Watkins, Robert 663
Watkins, Thoas. 203
Watkins, Thos. J. 142
Watkins, William 206
Watkins, Wm. 193, 577
Watred, E. 618
Watred, J. R. 618
Watred, Marion W. 618
Watrous, Sally 714
Wats, Samuel 663
Watson, Abraham 52
Watson, Alex. 285
Watson, Betsy 658
Watson, Catharine 313
Watson, Culbut 682
Watson, Culbut A. 682
Watson, David 52, 181
Watson, David (Sr.) 61
Watson, Delila 52
Watson, Elenor 52
Watson, Elizabeth 181
Watson, Eve 52
Watson, Isaac 683
Watson, James 52, 85, 181
Watson, Jesse 61
Watson, Jessie 49
Watson, John 308, 582, 644, 682
Watson, John B. 176
Watson, John V. 313
Watson, Joseph 200
Watson, Kesiah 181
Watson, Lydia 657
Watson, Margaret 582
Watson, Mary 308
Watson, Patrick 15

Watson, Peggy 658
Watson, Polly 52
Watson, Samuel 52
Watson, Sarah 644
Watson, Seth 390
Watson, Sylvester 523
Watson, Walter 52
Watson, Walter (Sr.) 52
Watson, William 15, 52
Watson, Wm. M. 582
Watt, David P. 437
Watt, Elizabeth M. 437
Watt, George 494
Watt, James 517
Watt, James H. 437
Watt, Jas. A. 437
Watt, John 491
Watt, John B. 437
Watt, Joseph 359
Watt, L. P. 437
Watt, Levi 437
Watt, Louisa 437
Watt, Margaret 437
Watt, Martha E. 437
Watt, Mary P. 437
Watt, Milton 437
Watt, Nancy Jane 437
Watt, Sarah E. 437
Watters, Samuel 171
Wattle, Joseph 569
Wattman, Isaac 491
Watts, Arthur 56
Watts, Benjamin 551
Watts, Betsey 56
Watts, Charity 106
Watts, Edward 56
Watts, Elizabeth R. 56
Watts, Jacob W. 172
Watts, James 106
Watts, John 56
Watts, John S. 106
Watts, Nicholas P. 106, 115
Watts, Sarah 56
Watts, William 56
Watz, John K. 643
Waugh, John 517
Waun, Thomas 747
Wavre, Foreman 504
Wax, Anthony 747
Way, Andrew I. H. 39
Way, Benjamin 640
Way, George 640
Way, Mary 640
Way, Samuel 283
Waybright, Jacob 215
Waybright, Martin (Sr.) 201
Waymire, Andrew 201
Waymire, Elizabeth 201
Waymire, Enoch 201
Waymire, Frederick 201
Waymire, Henry 211
Waymire, Huldah 201
Waymire, John 201
Waymire, Lydia 201
Waymire, Rebecca 201, 211
Waymire, Rosanna 211

Waymire, Sally 211
Waymire, Solomon 239
Wayne, --- (Gen.) 98
Wayt, Benjamin 640
Wayt, George 640
Wayt, Mary 640
Wead, Jane 200
Wead, John 200
Wead, Mary Jane 200
Wead, Robert 200
Weakfield, Letitia 303
Weakley, Thomas 210
Weaks, Charles 121
Weaks, Elizabeth 117
Weaks, Fanny 116
Wearly, John H. 427
Weast, Andrew S. 431
Weast, Christopher 42
Weast, Hannah 431
Weast, Henry R. 431
Weast, Jacob 431
Weast, John H. 431
Weatherhead, Eunice 146
Weatherhead, Jacob 146
Weatherhead, James A. 146
Weatherhead, John 118, 128
Weatherhead, Jos. R. 146
Weatherhead, Rachel 128, 146
Weaver, Abraham 211
Weaver, Amos 156
Weaver, Ann 556
Weaver, Barbara 232, 523
Weaver, Catherine 358
Weaver, Daniel 81, 136, 142, 199
Weaver, David 57, 199, 205
Weaver, Elijah 509
Weaver, Elizabeth 57, 164, 238, 245, 579
Weaver, Elnora 579
Weaver, Emery 579
Weaver, Emma 579
Weaver, Esther 220
Weaver, Frederick 569
Weaver, George 57, 155, 161, 164, 166, 523
Weaver, Harriet 497
Weaver, Henry 199, 205, 240
Weaver, Jacob 57, 195, 205
Weaver, James 355, 577
Weaver, Jane 136
Weaver, Jno. 220
Weaver, Jno. C. 220
Weaver, John 57, 232
Weaver, John J. 579
Weaver, Joseph 57
Weaver, Kenneth 246
Weaver, Lydia 515
Weaver, Margaret 57, 79, 121
Weaver, Mary 57, 199, 388
Weaver, Michael 205

Weaver, Moses 579
Weaver, Peter 118, 136, 176, 199, 224
Weaver, Phillip 205
Weaver, Richard 240
Weaver, Robert 136, 142
Weaver, Sally 205
Weaver, Samuel 51
Weaver, Sarah 57, 199, 240
Weaver, Solomon 57
Weaver, Susan 136, 142
Weaver, Susannah 84, 142
Weaver, Ward 57
Webb, Amanda Ann 100
Webb, David 676
Webb, Diadama 30
Webb, Dianna 746
Webb, Elisha 100, 454
Webb, Elizabeth 100
Webb, Gilbert 63
Webb, J. (Capt.) 424
Webb, James 517, 547
Webb, John 100, 121, 757, 762, 766
Webb, John R. 108
Webb, Joseph D. 100
Webb, Margaret 100
Webb, Michael 379
Webb, Nelly 384
Webb, Rachel 561, 676
Webb, Rebecca 379, 746
Webb, Rezin 100
Webb, Robert 388
Webb, Sally Ann 100
Webb, Stephen 649
Webb, Thomas 100
Webb, Thomas D. 108, 626, 753
Webb, Tirzah 100
Webb, William 100
Webb, Wm. 388
Webber, James 265
Webber, Jesse 247
Webber, John 111
Webber, Jonas 247
Webber, Noah 42
Weber, Conrad 238
Weber, Elisabeth 236
Weber, Heinrich 236
Weber, James 266
Weber, John 112
Weber, Maria 236
Weber, Sarah 236
Webster, Amanda M. 28
Webster, Andrew 715
Webster, Benj. H. 146
Webster, Catharine 36
Webster, David 33
Webster, Dickinson 380
Webster, Even 380
Webster, Hannah 33
Webster, Jacob 348
Webster, James 473
Webster, James Brice 454
Webster, James S. 472, 484, 485
Webster, Jas. 472
Webster, Jas. S. 476

Webster, John 459
Webster, Joseph 380
Webster, Judith 380
Webster, Letty 494
Webster, Lewis H. 146
Webster, Milton B. 31
Webster, Peggy 459
Webster, Permelia 380
Webster, Rhoda A. 146
Webster, Taylor 491
Webster, William B. 494
Webster, Wm. C. 146
Wedding, Nancy 507
Weed, B. A. 637
Weed, E. B. 637
Weed, Jonathan P. 437
Weeden, Charles W. 31
Weeder, Catherine 456
Weedman, John 352
Weedman, Rachel 352, 379
Weekley, Peggy 291
Weeks, Catty 453
Weeks, Clarisce 127
Weeks, Eddy 693
Weeks, J. 693
Weeks, James 693
Weeks, James M. 142
Weeks, Mary 142
Weeks, Rachel 516
Weeks, V. E. 693
Weeks, Victory E. 693
Weeland, Hanah 575
Wees, Sally 501
Wegeman, George 499
Wegesin, Hennan H. 610
Wehlman, Maria Elizabeth 107
Wehr, Elizabeth 523
Wehr, Levi 523
Wehrley, Johathan 427
Weibel, John 563
Weible, Henry 610
Weichman, Elizabeth 108
Weichman, Joseph 108
Weider, Christina 458
Weider, D. 403
Weider, E. J. 403
Weider, Mary 458
Weider, Mary A. 403
Weidman, John 738
Weidner, Jacob 427
Weil, Reuben 504
Weilhelm, Saleza 146
Weimer, Jacob 381
Weimer, Peter 526
Weingard, Eva 709
Weinmann, George 329
Weinmann, Mary A. 329
Weippert, Dorothy M. 329
Weippert, Glades R. 329
Weippert, Hettie 329
Weippert, J. J. 329
Weippert, Mildred L. 329
Weippert, Nettie 329
Weir, Eliza 346
Weir, George K. 346
Weirick, David 734
Weirick, Henry 735
Weirick, Mary 734

Weirick, Sarah 735
Weisenbach, Henry 87
Weisenberger, Frederick 690
Weissenberger, Frederick 688
Weissenborn, C. 237
Weissenborn, Catharina Sophia 237
Weissenborn, Cathrine S. 237
Weissenborn, Christopher 237
Weisz, George 339
Weit, Daniel Theadore 236
Weit, James 236
Weit, Maria 236
Weitzel, Frederick 228
Welbaum, Abraham 192
Welbaum, Charles 196
Welbauum, Chas. 146
Welbauum, David 146
Welbauum, John 146
Welbauum, Sarah 146
Welber, Constant 723
Welberage, Henry 81
Welch, Abigail 716
Welch, Andrew 262
Welch, Dilla 508
Welch, Dilly 508
Welch, Eleanor 514
Welch, Elizabeth 508, 664
Welch, Fidelia 584
Welch, Henrietta 508
Welch, Henry 508
Welch, James 272, 523
Welch, Jane 272, 446
Welch, John 446, 502, 508, 547
Welch, Louise 508
Welch, Margaret 272, 446
Welch, Martin 523
Welch, Mary 508
Welch, Nancy 502
Welch, Polly 521
Welch, Rebecca 608
Welch, Robert 259, 272
Welch, Robt. (II) 271
Welch, Sally 714
Welch, Samuel 35, 491, 649
Welch, Sarah 607
Welch, William 81, 747
Weldenken, Catharine 709
Welder, Moranda 88
Weldon, John 81
Weldy, Christian 193, 194
Weldy, Daniel 193
Weldy, Elizabeth 194, 565
Weldy, George 569
Weldy, Henry 193
Weldy, Jacob 193, 569
Weldy, John 569
Weldy, Mary Ann 193
Weldy, Philip 569

987

Weldy, Rebecca 193
Weleler, Benjamin 672
Welker, William N. 523
Well, Sarah 459, 717
Wella, Magdalena 522
Wellbaum, C. 244
Wellbaum, Charles 192
Wellbaum, Christian 244
Wellbaum, Sarah 244
Weller, Elizabeth 553
Weller, Emily 520
Welles, David 715
Welles, Nancy 713
Welles, Sally 715
Welles, Susanna 715
Welles, Woolsey 31
Wellington, Geo. 733
Wellman, Delilah 29
Wellman, Herman Fredrick 104
Wellman, Isaac 31
Wellman, Joseph 31
Wellman, Mary Ann 29
Wellman, Sophia Margaret 104
Wellmann, Henrietta 104
Wells, Abraham 747
Wells, Absolem 252, 593
Wells, Agrippa 85
Wells, Alexander S. 252
Wells, Amelia 765
Wells, Amon 252, 255, 257
Wells, Arman 296
Wells, Benjamin 257
Wells, Benjamin F. 252
Wells, Betsey 155
Wells, Betsy 296
Wells, Caleb 260, 262
Wells, Charles 160, 180
Wells, Clark 720
Wells, Cornelius 306
Wells, Daniel 719
Wells, David 264, 593, 678, 720, 765
Wells, Deborah 505
Wells, Edward R. 610, 625
Wells, Elisabeth 715
Wells, Elisha 296, 624
Wells, Elizabeth 115, 744
Wells, Emily 505
Wells, Evangely 505
Wells, Flora 252
Wells, Hannah 158
Wells, Harriet 255
Wells, Henery R. 81
Wells, James 505, 593
Wells, Jesse 155
Wells, John 252, 257, 290, 474
Wells, John D. 584
Wells, Joseph 296, 583, 720
Wells, Joshua 147
Wells, Julia H. 28
Wells, Justus 96, 115
Wells, Laura 296, 609

Wells, Laura Jane 255
Wells, Lydia Ann 633
Wells, Lyman S. 624
Wells, Margaret 96
Wells, Marietta 74
Wells, Martha 505, 583
Wells, Mary 255, 505
Wells, Mary R. 142
Wells, Mary W. 746
Wells, Matraly 336
Wells, Minerva 91
Wells, Nancy 255, 765
Wells, Rebecca 124
Wells, Richard 505
Wells, Roswell 115
Wells, Ruth 588
Wells, Sally 465
Wells, Samuel 158
Wells, Sarah 290, 583, 717, 718
Wells, Sarah Jane 765
Wells, Solomon 765
Wells, Sophia 633
Wells, Thimothy 505
Wells, Thomas 719, 720
Wells, Timothy 505
Wells, Willey 127
Wells, William 115, 296, 298, 547
Wells, Wm. 269, 271
Wells, Zerubabel 678
Wells, Zimry 633
Welmouth, Lemuel 494
Wels, Elizabeth 146
Welsh, Brice B. 368
Welsh, Jacob 368
Welsh, James 368
Welsh, John 562
Welsh, Mary Ann 368
Welsh, Polly 368
Welsh, Robert (Sr.) 272
Welsh, Sarah 49
Welsh, William 279
Welsh, Wm. 368
Welter, Jacob 400
Welter, Margaret 400
Welter, Molly 400
Welter, Peter 400
Welter, Sophia 400
Welter, William 400
Welton, Isaac T. 71
Welton, John 646, 647, 681
Welty, Michael 563
Welty, Peter 375
Welty, Sally 375
Wena, Joseph 61
Wendell, Joseph 104
Wendln, Antone 104
Wenner, John 23
Wentworth, Chare E. 336
Wentworth, David 337
Wentworth, Rachael 332
Wentworth, T. 332
Wenty, Philip 528
Wentz, H. M. (Dr.) 626
Werly, Elizabetha 87
Wernecke, John C. 307
Werner, Chatarina 237

Werner, David 237
Werner, Wilhelm 237
Werts, Delilah 134
Werts, Jacob 418
Werts, Susanna 133
Wertz, Emeline 146
Wesbrook, Joseph 110
Wesbrook, Maria Anna 110
Wesco, Henry 428
Wesco, Theodore 437
Wese, Bertha 409
Weshler, Barbara 553
Weshler, Catharine 553
Weshler, Christian 553
Weshler, George 553
Weshler, Henry 553
Weshler, Jacob 553
Weshler, Margaret 553
Weshler, Nancy 553
Wesler, Jacob 142
Wessel, Diedrick 105
Wessel, Theadore 105
West, Alexander 3
West, Ann B. 398, 401
West, Avery 165
West, Barbara 384
West, Calvin Benjamin 336
West, Caty 387
West, Charles 640
West, David 168, 405
West, Delia 371
West, E. H. 319
West, Edmund 31
West, Edward 27
West, Elizabeth 165
West, George 394
West, Hannah 667
West, James 366, 547
West, Jeremiah 127
West, Jobe 260
West, John 395, 593
West, John A. 172
West, Julia 31
West, L. A. 540
West, Levi 577
West, Margaret 49
West, Mary 405, 667
West, Mary A. 540
West, Morris 569
West, Nancy 385
West, Phebe 714
West, Rebecca 168
West, Rosana 157
West, S. 540
West, Saml. M. 733
West, Samuel 388, 645, 673
West, Sarah 405, 495
West, Sidney 733
West, Thomas 27
West, William 289, 517
West, Wm. K. 71
West, Zadok 156, 157, 158
Westcott, Sylvester 272
Westen, Austin 72
Westen, Dennis G. 72
Westen, Thomas H. 72

Westen, Thomas Hawley 72
Westenhaver, Jacob 393
Westenhaver, Rebecca 393
Westerfield, Caroline
431
Westerfield, Hannah E.
413
Westerfield, Isaac 431
Westerfield, James 663
Westerfield, Johannah
431
Westerfield, John M. 667
Westerfield, Stephen 437
Western, Warren 31
Westfale, Catharine 574
Westfall, Cornelius
118, 131, 454
Westfall, Delilah 121
Westfall, Elizabeth 121
Westfall, Job 121
Westfall, Joel 118
Westfall, Julia 461
Westfall, Levi 118
Westfall, Mary 142
Westfall, Rachel 135
Westfall, Reuben 131
Westfall, Sarah 467
Westhaver, Conrad 561
Westheaver, Godfry 561
Westhoever, Christian
561
Westlake, Elizabeth 588
Westlake, George 593
Westlake, Rebecca 589
Westlake, Welling 593
Westlake, William 594
Westlake, Zephaniah 593
Weston, Dennis G. 72
Weston, Elizabeth 496
Weston, Jeremie 261
Weston, Jeremy 263
Weston, Thomas 162, 179
Westor, Elizabeth 496
Westrow, Tho. 219
Wetherhead, James 121
Wetstone, Abraham 473
Wetzel, Ann E. 35
Wever, John 121
Wever, Margaret 175
Wever, Peter 175
Wever, Peter (Sr.) 127
Weybright, Christeny 232
Weybright, Jacob 213
Weybright, Martin 196,
232
Weybrighter, Jacob 213
Weyer, Anthoney 556
Weymer, Godfrey 284
Weyre, John 667
Weyrick, Peter 443
Weysant, Jacob 166
Weysant, Margaret 166
Whalen, John 121
Whalen, Thomas 317
Whaley, James 86
Whaley, Job 410
Whaley, Susanna 748
Whaley, Susannah 748
Whaley, Thomas 748

Whallen, James 115
Whartin, John 148
Wharton, Andrew 260,
263, 293
Wharton, Elizabeth 293,
685
Wharton, John 142
Wharton, Rebecca 685
Wharton, Timothy 685
Whealdon, Nathan 304
Wheatcraft, Catherine
380
Wheatcraft, Daniel 380
Wheatcraft, David H. 380
Wheatcraft, Deborah 380
Wheatcraft, Edward 380
Wheatcraft, Harmon 380
Wheatcraft, James Finley
380
Wheatcraft, Joseph 366,
380
Wheatcraft, Malachi 380
Wheatcraft, Nancy 380
Wheatcraft, Rachel 380
Wheatcraft, Samuel 380
Wheatley, Henry 85
Wheatly, Charles 45
Wheaton, Elmar 291
Wheaton, Precilla 457
Wheaton, Uriah 517
Wheeland, Barbara 296
Wheeland, George 467
Wheeland, Peter 296
Wheeler, Almira H. 78
Wheeler, Betsey A. 39
Wheeler, Elizabeth 511
Wheeler, Hanson 288
Wheeler, Luther 504, 510
Wheeler, Nancy 12
Wheeler, Nathan 502
Wheeler, Nathan (III)
517
Wheeler, Richard 181
Wheeler, Robert 467
Wheeler, Thomothy 284
Wheelock, Lymon 127
Wheelook, Mary 134
Whelan, Thomas 334
Wheller, Rebecha 504
Whelsley, Persis 30
Wherley, Elizah. 413
Wherley, Polly 414
Whetlow, Francis 467
Wheton, David 186
Wheton, John 186
Whetsel, Margaret 335
Whetsone, Catherine 451
Whetstone, Abraham (Jr.)
473
Whetzell, Daniel 454
Whip, Daniel 216
Whipple, Abraham 723,
730
Whipple, Eliza 296
Whipple, Levi 282, 296,
298, 299
Whips, Ezekiel 339
Whisler, Daniel 241
Whisler, Daniel L. 241

Whisler, Edward 663
Whisman, Sophia 551
Whistler, Caty 388
Whiston, Jesse 731, 733
Whitacre, Andrew 677
Whitacre, Edward M. 764
Whitacre, Frances 649
Whitacre, Isaac 764
Whitacre, John 677
Whitacre, John M. 649
Whitacre, Jonas 649, 663
Whitacre, Lydian 764
Whitacre, Mahlon 764
Whitacre, Martha 764
Whitacre, Nancy 649
Whitacre, Oliver 663
Whitacre, Preston 764
Whitacre, Price 649
Whitacre, Price S. 684,
689
Whitacre, Reason 764
Whitacre, Robert 649,
673, 677
Whitacre, Sarah R. 649
Whitacre, Thornton 577
Whitaker, David H. 146
Whitaker, David N. 142
Whitaker, James 258,
259, 263, 272
Whitaker, Jas. 271
Whitaker, Jonathan 142
Whitaker, Lewis 284
Whitaker, Mary E. 146
Whitaker, Mary J. 146
Whitaker, Rachel 498
Whitaker, Robert S. 146
Whitaker, Sarah A. 146
Whitaker, Thomas 365,
375
Whitaker, Thos. 365
Whitaker, Wm. M. 146
Whitamore, Daniel 263
Whitcomb, James 6
Whitcomb, Martha 6
Whitcraft, Mary 571
White, . . . 160, 168
White, Alfred 629
White, Ann 406
White, Anna 406
White, Asa 272
White, Austin 257
White, Benj. 478
White, Benjamin 168
White, Calvin 437
White, Celinda 758
White, Charles 108,
388, 612, 626, 753
White, Daniel Theodore
236
White, David 42, 499, 719
White, E. M. 151
White, Elisha 587
White, Eliza 336, 387
White, Elizabeth 458
White, Elvina C. 42
White, Eunice 267
White, Francis Ann 39
White, George 257, 336,
593

White, George W. 523
White, Gilbert 523
White, Hartshorn 687
White, Henry 55, 393
White, Hope 387
White, Huldah 714
White, Ira 42
White, Isaac G. 747
White, J. C. 151
White, Jacob 664
White, Jacob R. 379
White, James 236
White, Jane 437
White, Jeremiah 55,
476, 504, 747
White, John 265, 437,
459, 517, 577, 612,
676, 715, 719
White, John S. 81
White, Joseph 27, 42,
750
White, Joshua 15
White, Kalista 257
White, Lewis 257
White, M. 507
White, Margaret 610
White, Maria 236, 629
White, Mary 146, 257,
291, 464
White, Mary A. 421
White, Mary Jane 151
White, Mary Rosetta 612
White, Mathew 517
White, Micajah L. 421
White, Naomah 707
White, Nathaniel 719
White, Orpha 279
White, Pelatiah 715
White, Peter 393
White, Polly 512
White, Rebecca 336
White, Robert 121, 400
White, Saml. 406
White, Samuel 258, 262,
267
White, Sarah 168, 177,
590
White, Sarah Ellen 612
White, Sarah Jane 421
White, Sukey 461
White, Tapley 517
White, Thomas 42, 259,
470, 471, 472, 474,
499
White, Thos. M. 257
White, Uriah 517
White, William 34, 55,
127, 177
White, Wm. 257
Whitecotten, Sally 456
Whitecotton, Polly 453
Whitehead, David H. 569
Whitehead, Julia 377
Whitehill, John 22
Whitehown, Mary 717
Whiteman, Absalam 523
Whiteman, Christian 397
Whiteman, Hannah 519
Whiteman, Jacob 523

Whitemyer, Adrian 734
Whitenger, Sarah 495
Whiteside, Baxter 407
Whiteside, J. 407
Whiteside, M. 407
Whiteside, Margaret 494
Whiteside, Sarah 406
Whitesides, Mary 382
Whitfield, Ann 710
Whitfield, James 185
Whitham, Mehitabel 715
Whiting, Elsie 708
Whiting, Geo. 708
Whiting, Lucy 708
Whiting, Nathan 31
Whiting, Phebe 127
Whitinger, Elizabeth 495
Whitinger, Jane 498
Whitinger, Mary 497
Whitions, Richard 121
Whitley, C. B. 115
Whitlock, Benjamin 86
Whitlock, Conrad 365
Whitlock, Ellen S. 29
Whitlock, Jane 31
Whitman, --- 721
Whitman, George 388
Whitman, Rebecca 101
Whitmer, Daniel 379
Whitmer, Elizabeth 151
Whitmer, George 379
Whitmer, Jacob 379
Whitmer, John 379
Whitmer, Lydia 379
Whitmer, Magdalene 379
Whitmer, Mary 379
Whitmer, Peter 379
Whitmer, Rozyann 151
Whitmer, S. 151
Whitmer, S. H. 151
Whitmer, Samuel B. 151
Whitmer, Sarah 379
Whitmer, Solomon 379
Whitmer, Susanna 379
Whitmon, David 121
Whitmore, Francis 715
Whitmore, Isaiah 115
Whitmore, Leonard 756
Whitney, Eli 762
Whitney, Lydia 82
Whitney, Michael T. 42
Whitney, Michel J. 81
Whitney, Milton D. 42
Whitney, Thankful 82
Whitney, Thomas 454
Whitridge, Almira 437
Whitridge, Ann Eliza 437
Whitridge, Chas. J. 437
Whitridge, Eveline 437
Whitridge, Henry C. 437
Whitridge, John H. 437
Whitridge, Lorenzo 437
Whitridge, Louisa 437
Whitridge, Lydia E. 437
Whitridge, Milcah E. 437
Whitridge, Ruth J. 437
Whitridge, Wm. E. 437
Whitridge, Wm. F. 437
Whitsel, Catherine 520

Whitsel, Jacob 206, 523
Whitsel, James 206
Whitsel, Samuel 459
Whitsit, Alexander 150
Whitsit, Ann 150
Whitsit, John Wm. 150
Whitsit, Wm. 150
Whitson, Jordan 699
Whitson, Jorden 664
Whitson, Mary 699
Whittecar, E. D. 45
Whitten, Jonathan 91
Whitten, Joseph 223
Whitten, William 297
Whittesiy, Wm. A. 733
Whittlesey, Frederick 32
Whittlesey, Wm. A. 733
Whitton, Rebecca 219
Whitton, William 294
Whitworth, Emma 228
Whitworth, George
Frederick 228
Whitworth, Mathew 228
Whitworth, Susannah 228
Whorton, Andrew 266
Whrley, Samuel J. 428
Wiant, Jacob 577
Wibbling, Hiram 547
Wible, Betsey 431
Wible, Nicholas 431
Wical, Al 534
Wical, Carrie H. 533
Wical, Catherine 533
Wical, Elizabeth 533
Wical, Ella 533
Wical, I. 533
Wical, John 533
Wical, Shepard 533
Wical, W. 533
Wicherham, John 638
Wick, Moses 491
Wick, Solomon 32
Wickam, Elizabeth 87
Wickam, Saml. 263
Wickersham, Enock 668
Wickham, Benjamin 304
Wickham, John 284
Wickhum, Bernard R. 305
Wickoff, Garret P. 667
Wicks, John 547
Wicks, Unis 457
Wickson, Barna 502
Wickum, Mary 305
Wicoff, Garret P. 664
Widdle, Dorothea 572
Widener, Michael 499
Widner, Jacob 476, 478
Widney, Caroline 551
Widney, John 547
Widney, John W. 146
Widney, Margaret 125
Wiedman, Henry 391
Wiees, Sarah 666
Wieland, Peter 569
Wieners, Mary 111
Wier, Obed 467
Wierbrink, John 547
Wierick, Henry 735
Wiford, Catherine 536

990

Wiford, Ed. L. 534
Wiford, Jacob 536
Wiford, L. F. 534
Wiford, William 533
Wiford, Wm. 534
Wiggins, Benjamin 668
Wiggins, Jacob 231
Wiggins, Joseph 307
Wiggins, Richard 39
Wight, Edward R. 268
Wight, Ephraim C. 268
Wight, Ephrain 264
Wight, Frances 268
Wight, Rhoda 268
Wight, Royal C. 268
Wikle, Andrew 431
Wikle, Phebe 431
Wikle, William J. 420
Wikoff, Garet P. 683
Wikoff, Isaac 547
Wikoff, Peter 505
Wikoff, Peter W. 683
Wilard, James 593
Wilauer, Andrew 276
Wilauer, Heinrich 276
Wilbarger, Elizabeth 83
Wilber, Christopher 582
Wilber, Henry 523
Wilbin, Judith 105
Wilbourn, Mary 456
Wilcoby, Marian 574
Wilcock, Catherine 569
Wilcoff, Sacale Ann 665
Wilcox, Calvin 32
Wilcox, Eliza 30
Wilcox, Hiram 65, 633
Wilcox, Hugh 705, 706
Wilcox, John 5
Wilcox, Jonathan 593
Wilcox, Mary 65
Wilcoxen, Loyd 517
Wilcoxon, Henry W. 438
Wilcoxon, Levin 517
Wilcoxon, Walter 517
Wilcoxton, Thomas 93
Wild, George 302
Wildbahn, Rebecca 385
Wilder, Jacob G. 747
Wilder, Lemuel 91
Wilder, Lemuel L. 81
Wilder, Levi 499
Wilder, Moranda 88
Wilder, Samuel 91
Wilds, Samuel 757
Wiler, Christian 277
Wiler, John 441
Wiles, Aaron 641
Wiles, Aikens 639
Wiles, Barbara 232
Wiles, Elenor 661, 669
Wiles, James 639, 669
Wiles, John 639, 646, 647, 669, 675
Wiles, Martha 639
Wiles, Mary 641
Wiles, Peter 232
Wiles, Polly 639
Wiles, Samuel 757
Wiles, Thompson 639, 647

Wiles, William 669
Wiles, William M. 639, 669
Wiles, William N. 643, 652
Wiles, William R. 664
Wiles, Wm. M. 640, 672
Wiley, David 555
Wiley, George 494
Wiley, Harriet N. 653
Wiley, Isaac 610
Wiley, Jared 491
Wiley, Jessie 467
Wiley, Jno. 272
Wiley, John 551, 653
Wiley, John O. 146
Wiley, John O'Ferrell 146
Wiley, Joseph 298
Wiley, Marcissa 494
Wiley, Robert 103, 355, 364, 494
Wiley, Robt. 105
Wiley, Tamer 81
Wiley, Thomas W. 419
Wiley, William H. 551
Wilfong, Christian 459
Wilfong, David 454
Wilfong, Hiram 551
Wilfong, John 470
Wilfrong, Sophia 460
Wilhalm, Catarin 276
Wilhalm, Peter 276
Wilhelm, Elizabeth 229
Wilhelm, John 229
Wilhelm, Peter 280
Wilhelm, Saleza 146
Wilivan, George 459
Wilkasen, William 15
Wilkee, Thos. 220
Wilken, Charles (Jr.) 472
Wilken, John 472
Wilker, Samuel 667
Wilkerson, Aaron H. 655
Wilkerson, Israel 274
Wilkerson, John 669
Wilkerson, William 677
Wilkes, Ann 405
Wilkes, Charles 86
Wilkeson, James 669
Wilkie, Martin 219
Wilkie, Shoogart 220
Wilkin, S. 741
Wilkin, Sarah J. 547
Wilkin, Stephen 547
Wilking, Daniel 710, 711
Wilkins, --- 733
Wilkins, Belitha 101
Wilkins, David 3
Wilkins, Huldah 19
Wilkins, Joseph 19, 413
Wilkins, Mary 3
Wilkins, Nat. 405
Wilkins, Rebecca 372
Wilkins, Thos. 459
Wilkinson, --- (Gen.) 98
Wilkinson, Alice 42
Wilkinson, Booth B. 547

Wilkinson, Catharine 9
Wilkinson, Charles 413
Wilkinson, Deborah 9
Wilkinson, Elenor 462
Wilkinson, Elizabeth 655
Wilkinson, Frances 657
Wilkinson, George 9
Wilkinson, Isabella 7, 9
Wilkinson, James 15
Wilkinson, John 9, 467, 476, 491
Wilkinson, Joseph 690
Wilkinson, Keziah 655
Wilkinson, Mahlon 655
Wilkinson, Nancy 9
Wilkinson, Rachel 551
Wilkinson, Rebecca 655
Wilkinson, Richard 36
Wilkinson, Samuel 547, 552
Wilkinson, Samuel Scott 502
Wilkinson, Thomas 7, 9, 454, 547
Wilkison, Jacob 761
Wilkison, James 42
Wilkison, James H. 39
Wilkison, Richard 467
Wilkison, Sally 761
Wilkison, William 42
Will, John S. 469, 470
Willard, Abner S. 49
Willard, Anthony L. 42
Willard, Catharine 567
Willard, Henry 569
Willard, Isaac 177
Willard, John G. 763
Willard, Lewy 569
Willard, Sarah 177
Willard, William 177
Willas, Catharine 515
Willber, James 597
Willcockson, Betsey Betsey 504
Willcox, Hezekiah 19
Willcoxen, George D. H. 517
Willcoxen, Sally 517
Willcoxen, Thomas 517
Willcoxon, Betsey Betsey 504
Willer, Christopher 593
Willer, Elijah 593
Willermy, Stephen 726
Willes, John 121
Willet, Abigail 453
Willets, Isaiah 388
Willets, Jane 280
Willets, Rachel 14, 15
Willets, Susan 383
Willey, Amos 388
Willey, Austin 308
Willey, E. 614
Willey, Elizabeth 614
Willey, George 308
Willey, George E. 308
Willey, Henry 308
Willey, John F. 614
Willey, M. 614

Willey, Margaret 313
Willey, Marshall 313
Willey, Nancy 308
Willey, Nargaret 313
Willey, Sarah 175, 308
Willey, Sylvester 308
Willey, William 175
Willey, William F. 614
Willey, William W. 308
Willey, Wm. 266
Willey, Wm. P. 267, 270
Willey, Wm. W. 308
Willhous, Andrew 278
William, Fegary 667
William, Maria 54
William, Matthew 547
Williama, Catharine 120
Williams, --- 477
Williams, Abby C. 606
Williams, Abigail 452
Williams, Abner 394
Williams, Abraham 441
Williams, Abrm. J. 394
Williams, Ahira 730
Williams, Alexander
  536, 633
Williams, Amanda 387
Williams, Amos 467
Williams, Amos A. 593
Williams, Amy 59
Williams, Andrew 667
Williams, Ann 452, 464,
  497
Williams, Benjamin 394,
  569
Williams, Betsey 52, 658
Williams, Betsy 45
Williams, C. B. 536
Williams, Catharine
  266, 662
Williams, Charles 167,
  294, 297
Williams, Daniel 155,
  178
Williams, Daniel P. 551
Williams, Darcas 85
Williams, David 388,
  394, 427
Williams, David B. 547
Williams, David L. 547
Williams, E. 536
Williams, Edward 388,
  397
Williams, Edward (Rev.)
  605
Williams, Edwen 27
Williams, Eleanor 716
Williams, Eli 49, 517
Williams, Elias 454
Williams, Eliza 520, 716
Williams, Eliza Ann 397
Williams, Elizabeth 84,
  127, 362, 397, 437,
  494, 581, 640, 659
Williams, Ellis 189
Williams, Enoch 388
Williams, Enos 648, 650,
  668, 669, 670, 683
Williams, Ezra 440, 499

Williams, Fanny 117,
  124, 748
Williams, Frank 517
Williams, Geo. W. 9
Williams, George 27,
  362, 454, 459
Williams, George O. 32
Williams, George W. 316
Williams, Godfrey 459
Williams, Hannah 666
Williams, Henry 26,
  127, 523, 577
Williams, Henry F. 747
Williams, Henry H. 146
Williams, Ibby 567
Williams, Isaac 27,
  394, 397, 467, 503
Williams, Israel 151
Williams, J. 151, 536
Williams, Jacob 173,
  247, 257, 499
Williams, James 397,
  504, 577
Williams, Jane 121, 633
Williams, Jemima 640
Williams, Jeremiah 161,
  165
Williams, Jerome B. 536
Williams, Jesse 15, 85,
  517
Williams, Jessy 517
Williams, John 27, 32,
  85, 86, 130, 189,
  263, 388, 397, 443,
  467, 491, 494, 523,
  561, 624, 640
Williams, Jonas 115
Williams, Jonathan 15,
  18, 155, 266
Williams, Joseph 178,
  296, 297, 397, 684
Williams, Joseph S. 247
Williams, Josephine 397
Williams, Justin 32
Williams, Lery 458
Williams, Levi 356,
  378, 682
Williams, Levy 569
Williams, Lewis 121
Williams, Lorenzo Dow
  523
Williams, Lory 458
Williams, Lucinda 124
Williams, Lucy 462
Williams, Lukema 27
Williams, Lydia 606
Williams, Lysander 333
Williams, Margaret 13,
  91, 126, 168, 394,
  644, 673
Williams, Martha 178,
  571, 730
Williams, Mary 180,
  394, 397, 419, 461,
  568, 640
Williams, Mary Jane 437
Williams, Mathew 577
Williams, Matilda 189,
  550

Williams, Michael (Jr.)
  130
Williams, Miles 149
Williams, Minervia 582
Williams, N. 20
Williams, Nancy 26, 717
Williams, Nathan 491
Williams, Nathaniel 189
Williams, Nicholas 15
Williams, Nimrod 265
Williams, Noah 640
Williams, Obadiah 26
Williams, Patience 151
Williams, Pattey 117
Williams, Peter 42,
  560, 569
Williams, Phoebe Ann 247
Williams, Polly 662
Williams, Prudence S.
  593
Williams, Rachail 15
Williams, Rachel 247,
  280, 640
Williams, Rebecca 394,
  397
Williams, Rebekah 27
Williams, Richard 363
Williams, Richd. 529
Williams, Robert 247,
  257, 517
Williams, Ruth 12
Williams, S. R. 536
Williams, Salina 499
Williams, Salinah 167
Williams, Sally 550
Williams, Samuel 142
Williams, Samuel K. 142
Williams, Samuel O. 625
Williams, Sarah 15, 27,
  394, 397, 744
Williams, Sarah Ann 593
Williams, Silas 577
Williams, Soloman 664
Williams, Susannah J.
  437
Williams, Thomas 266,
  494, 561, 569
Williams, Thos. 577
Williams, Vincent 397
Williams, Walter 294,
  298, 547
Williams, Washington 58
Williams, William 27,
  91, 168, 189, 394,
  427, 494, 547, 644,
  673, 730
Williams, Wm. 362, 459,
  730
Williams, Wm. (Jr.) 358
Williams, Wm. H. H. 437
Williams, Wm. S. 397
Williams, Zedikiah 467
Williamson, Ann 232
Williamson, Anne 10
Williamson, Bartholomew
  438
Williamson, Catharine 10
Williamson, David V. 672
Williamson, Drusille 382

Williamson, Elizabeth 10
Williamson, Flora 88
Williamson, Florence 89
Williamson, Frances 506
Williamson, Geo. P. 690
Williamson, George 664
Williamson, George W. 336
Williamson, Hugh 10
Williamson, Isabella 10
Williamson, James 86, 180, 506
Williamson, Jane 10, 294
Williamson, Jas. 733
Williamson, John 690
Williamson, Joseph 10, 232, 506
Williamson, Margaret 517
Williamson, Margaret Ann 506
Williamson, Martha 506
Williamson, Mary 180, 459
Williamson, Moses 719
Williamson, Peter 506
Williamson, Prescella 382
Williamson, Robert 294
Williamson, Sally 506
Williamson, Saml. M. 90
Williamson, Samuel 719
Williamson, Thomas 199, 494, 506
Williamson, William 10, 294, 677
Williamson, Wm. 199
Williamson, Wm. G. 10
Williard, John G. 755
Willias, William 667
Williba, Anilla 461
Willis, James Franklin 49
Willis, Joseph 664
Willis, Mary Ann 465
Willis, Sarah 466
Willison, Easter 380
Willison, Harrison 380
Willison, John 380
Willison, William 380
Willits, Jesse 486
Willitts, Ellis 279
Willmeth, Lemuel 587
Willoby, Farlington B. 577
Willocks, Sarah 91
Willouer, Jacob 276
Willouer, Michael 276
Willouer, Peter 276
Willoughby, Andrew 459
Willoughby, Diana 530
Willoughby, Margaret 45
Willoughby, Nancy 49
Willoughby, Sarah 459
Willoughby, T. B. 530
Wills, Absolom 467
Wills, Charles 664
Wills, George 541
Wills, Henry 541
Wills, John 460

Wills, John S. 470, 475, 484
Wills, Margaret 457
Wills, Mary 610
Wills, Nancy 466
Wills, Peter 625
Wills, Roswell 499
Wills, William 541
Willson, Amos 156, 174
Willson, Catherine 654
Willson, David 6, 209, 715
Willson, Elizabeth 174, 209
Willson, George 654, 725
Willson, Hannah 586
Willson, Isaac 152
Willson, Isabell 153
Willson, James 209, 216, 649, 650
Willson, Jesse 653
Willson, John 19, 653, 673
Willson, John L. 420
Willson, Joshua 653
Willson, Lucy 551
Willson, Lydia 6
Willson, Mary 714
Willson, Nancy 649
Willson, Nathaniel 209
Willson, Phebe 6
Willson, Polly 586
Willson, Robert 551
Willson, Sarah 589
Willson, Sophrona 495
Willson, Stephen 6
Willson, Susan 593
Willson, Urana 585
Willson, William 725
Willyard, George L. 736
Wilman, Michael 276
Wilman, Peter 276
Wilman, Rebecca 276
Wilmason, Rebecca 337
Wilmeth, Elizabeth 588
Wilsen, James L. 15
Wilson, Agnes 453
Wilson, Alexander 187, 431, 460, 664
Wilson, Amos 65, 379, 577, 699
Wilson, Andrew 49, 577
Wilson, Andrew J. 693
Wilson, Ann 548, 698
Wilson, Anna 406, 547
Wilson, Archibald 380
Wilson, Asa 352, 379
Wilson, Benjamin E. 85
Wilson, C. C. 499
Wilson, Charles 67, 491, 761
Wilson, Cylvester 664
Wilson, Cyrus 547
Wilson, Daniel 60, 154, 388
Wilson, David 142, 270, 437, 689, 693
Wilson, Dolly 73
Wilson, E. 698, 699

Wilson, Eber 760, 761
Wilson, Eber (Jr.) 761
Wilson, Edgar J. 697
Wilson, Edward 352, 379
Wilson, Elijah 472
Wilson, Eliza 91, 352, 689, 761
Wilson, Elizabeth 336, 384, 465, 503, 571
Wilson, Elizabeth Margaret 437
Wilson, Ella 699
Wilson, Ellanora 699
Wilson, Elsey 212
Wilson, Elzey 737
Wilson, Enos 699
Wilson, Enos B. 699
Wilson, Esiah 379
Wilson, Esther 379, 547
Wilson, Fredinand 499
Wilson, Hannah 128, 212, 677
Wilson, Hans 633
Wilson, Henry 90, 105, 370
Wilson, Hugh 2, 547, 650, 677, 733
Wilson, Isaac 600, 664
Wilson, Isabella 153
Wilson, Isaiah 352
Wilson, Isiah 379
Wilson, J. 698
Wilson, J. J. 363
Wilson, J. M. 697
Wilson, James 3, 85, 181, 208, 216, 319, 363, 367, 376, 379, 426, 491, 503, 551, 650, 736, 741
Wilson, James (Sr.) 503
Wilson, James C. 693
Wilson, James H. 431
Wilson, James M. 3
Wilson, Jane 2, 116, 185, 367, 379, 380, 550, 633
Wilson, Jane E. 547
Wilson, Jesse 273
Wilson, John 3, 23, 45, 184, 186, 273, 283, 340, 355, 359, 363, 365, 369, 375, 377, 379, 460, 480, 482, 494, 503, 547, 577, 643, 650, 664, 667, 677, 699, 707, 733, 750
Wilson, John L. 431
Wilson, Joseph 121, 185, 186, 187, 431, 460, 469, 485, 569, 593, 625
Wilson, Josiah 460
Wilson, Liza 379
Wilson, Lydia 387
Wilson, M. 698
Wilson, Magdalena 363
Wilson, Mahala 652
Wilson, Mahlon 272, 274

993

Wilson, Malinda 497
Wilson, Margaret 693
Wilson, Martha 290
Wilson, Martha Ann 437
Wilson, Mary 74, 154,
  158, 159, 366, 380,
  462, 566, 677, 699
Wilson, Mary Ann 465
Wilson, Mary Jane 437
Wilson, Mathew 262, 291
Wilson, Matilda 127, 496
Wilson, Matthew F. 763
Wilson, Michael 339
Wilson, Milton 380
Wilson, Morrison 380
Wilson, Nancy 45, 642
Wilson, Nancy L. 522
Wilson, Nathan 42
Wilson, Nathaniel 196
Wilson, Nelly 384
Wilson, Patsey 503
Wilson, Peterson 600
Wilson, Polly 380, 650
Wilson, R. 693
Wilson, R. B. 698
Wilson, Rachael 652
Wilson, Rachel 352,
  379, 568, 693
Wilson, Rebecca 689, 761
Wilson, Rebecca B. 699
Wilson, Rebeckah 388
Wilson, Rhoda 514
Wilson, Robert 59, 158,
  159, 291, 547, 593,
  677, 688
Wilson, Robert (Jr.) 159
Wilson, Robert (Sr.) 156
Wilson, Robert B. 380
Wilson, Robert F. 17
Wilson, Robert G. 81
Wilson, Robert R. 494
Wilson, Robert S. 547
Wilson, Robert W. 431
Wilson, St.John 747
Wilson, Sally 125, 185
Wilson, Samuel 73, 160,
  213, 256, 379, 472,
  479, 486, 517, 699
Wilson, Samuel F. 760,
  761
Wilson, Samuel P. 416,
  417
Wilson, Sara 379, 698
Wilson, Sarah 352, 379,
  380, 426, 460, 718
Wilson, Simeon 212
Wilson, Solomon 118
Wilson, Sophronia 760
Wilson, Spencer 698
Wilson, Suffrona J. 437
Wilson, Susana 503
Wilson, Sylvester 652
Wilson, Thomas 180, 339,
  352, 367, 379, 380
Wilson, Thos. 269, 364
Wilson, Uzziah 359
Wilson, W. Gilbert 699
Wilson, W. T. 697
Wilson, Walter T. 697

Wilson, Wanda 693
Wilson, West 642, 649
Wilson, William 2, 15,
  39, 42, 81, 166, 185,
  224, 284, 301, 304,
  340, 380, 393, 402,
  467, 484, 485, 551,
  593, 650, 677, 693
Wilson, William D. 49
Wilson, Wm. 166, 374
Wilson, Wm. Joseph 437
Wilt, Catharine 607
Wilt, Elizabeth 572
Wilt, Jacob 610
Wilt, John 420
Wily, Thomas 302
Wiman, Henry 337
Wimer, Benjamin 261
Wimer, Mary 577
Wimer, Susanah 565
Wimmer, Isaac 677
Wimmer, Lydia 293
Wimp, James 287
Winans, Anna M. 146
Winans, Anthony 146
Winans, Benjamin 118
Winans, Betsy 119
Winans, Cory 146
Winans, Elizabeth 124
Winans, Fanny 118
Winans, Frazee M. 147
Winans, Hannah E. 146
Winans, John C. 648
Winans, Louisa 547
Winans, Mary F. 146
Winans, Matthias S. 747
Winans, Samuel 142
Winans, Sarah 116, 119
Winans, Sarah Ann 548
Winans, Stephen 147
Winans, Susannah 118
Winbigler, John 742
Winbigler, Mary 742
Winbigler, Sarah Ann 742
Wince, Daniel 437
Wince, Elizabeth 437
Wince, Mary 437
Wince, Peter 437
Wince, Philip 437
Winch, Jacob 561
Winchester, Robert 173
Winckleplech, Philip 569
Winckleplck, Jacob 569
Winclepleck, Catharine
  567
Windbigler, Wm. 280
Winder, Elizabeth 459
Winder, James 494
Winder, John 494
Winder, John (Jr.) 494
Winder, Massie 459
Winders, William 61
Windland, Elizabeth 154
Windland, John 154
Windon, Massee 459
Windsor, Enos 437
Wine, George 279
Winebrenner, Christian
  202, 207

Winegate, Elizabeth 576
Winehart, Jacob 389
Wineland, Elizabeth 165
Wineland, John (Jr.) 165
Wines, Sarah 632
Wines, William 632
Wing, Enoch 727
Wing, Polly 33
Wingate, Cyrus 577
Wingate, Isaac 577
Wingate, Patty 577
Winget, Calvin 595
Winget, Colvin 587
Winget, Daniel 664
Winget, Ezra 596
Winget, Louisa 547
Winget, Stephen 594
Winget, William 547
Wink, John 172
Winkler, E. 612
Winkler, M. 612
Winkler, Martin 612, 626
Winkler, Pauline 612
Winkler, Peter 90
Winkler, Rosina 612
Winkler, Theresa 612
Winkley, Ann 58
Winkley, Edward 58
Winkley, Eliza 437
Winkley, Irena 437
Winkley, Joel 58
Winkley, John 81
Winkley, Louis 437
Winland, Catharine 156,
  163, 171
Winland, Jacob 159, 165
Winland, James 161,
  169, 179
Winland, John 163, 169,
  171, 172, 174
Winland, Magaret 165
Winland, Mahala 165
Winland, Sarah 159
Winn, Armstrong 81
Winn, George 279
Winn, John 405
Winn, Lydia 80
Winn, S. 405
Winn, Sarah 516
Winn, Timothy 86
Winnans, Mary E. 547
Winniger, Geo. 437
Winniger, John 437
Winons, Mary 123
Winship, Edwin 390
Winship, Elizabeth 390
Winship, Harriott 390
Winship, Hetty 390
Winship, Mary 390
Winship, Nancy 390
Winship, Thomas 494
Winship, Thomas
  Jefferson 390
Winship, William Henry
  390
Winship, Winn 390
Winslow, Martin 42
Winson, Jacob 719
Winstanley, Peter 304

994

Winter, David 220
Winter, Philanda 765
Winterow, Adam 664
Winters, Ann 497
Winters, Robert 260
Wintroad, Daniel 643
Wintroad, Peter 643
Winzired, Christian 167
Wipen, Mary 309
Wipling, Ann Margaret 547
Wipling, Herman 547
Wire, Maria 113
Wirick, Catherine 232
Wirick, Jacob 232
Wirick, John 232
Wirick, Margaret 232
Wirick, Rebecca 232
Wirick, Rebekah 232
Wirick, Sarah J. 281
Wirick, Valentine 381
Wirick, William 232, 381
Wirrick, Jacob 217
Wirrick, Martin 217
Wirrick, Mary 217
Wirrick, Samuel 217
Wirrick, William 217
Wirt, Elizabeth 665
Wirts, John 115
Wirts, Joseph 115
Wirts, Maria 115
Wirts, Peter 285
Wisard, David (Jr.) 739
Wise, Abraham 558
Wise, Adam 525, 558
Wise, Andrew 558, 733
Wise, Aney 558
Wise, Catharine 525, 558
Wise, Catherine 360
Wise, Daniel 558
Wise, Daniel (Sr.) 89
Wise, Elias 558
Wise, Elizabeth 459, 525, 558
Wise, George 525, 558
Wise, Hannah 558
Wise, Jacob 237, 525, 547, 558, 733
Wise, John 127, 525
Wise, Margaret 520, 525
Wise, Mary 237
Wise, Molly 558
Wise, Peter 558
Wise, Rebecca 558
Wise, Sarah 558
Wise, Solomon 525
Wise, Sophia 525
Wise, Stephen 368
Wise, Susannah 525, 558
Wisecarver, Abraham 285
Wisegerver, Elisabeth 573
Wiseman, Adam 380
Wiseman, Ann 380
Wiseman, Barbara 379
Wiseman, Betsy 379
Wiseman, Cath. 346
Wiseman, Catharine 346
Wiseman, Catherine 379

Wiseman, Eliza Crabtree 408
Wiseman, Elizabeth 363, 380
Wiseman, Ellen 346
Wiseman, George 380, 526
Wiseman, Gottleib 161
Wiseman, Henry 379
Wiseman, Isaac 380
Wiseman, Jacob 379, 380
Wiseman, Jacob G. 380
Wiseman, Joel 380
Wiseman, John 380, 708
Wiseman, John R. 380
Wiseman, Joseph G. 380
Wiseman, Lewis T. 346
Wiseman, Margaret 380
Wiseman, Mary 379
Wiseman, Michael 265, 270
Wiseman, Peter 380
Wiseman, Philip S. 380
Wiseman, Polly 379
Wiseman, Rebecca 346
Wiseman, Sam. 363
Wiseman, Sarah 380
Wiseman, Susannah 380
Wiseman, Wm. 346
Wiseman, Wm. (Sr.) 346
Wiseman, Wm. H. 346
Wisener, Isaac 152
Wishon, Phebe 113
Wisong, Margaret 420
Wissen, Mary 309
Wiswell, John 350
Wiswell, Sarah 350, 375
Witham, Benjamin 258
Witham, Elisha 258
Witherow, Elizabeth 196
Witherow, James 196
Witherow, Jane 196
Witherow, Mary P. 196
Witherow, Samuel 196
Witherow, Samuel T. W. 196
Witherow, Sarah T. 196
Withington, Patience G. 56
Withrow, James 51, 52
Withrow, Mary 62
Withrow, Samuel 62, 472
Withrow, Washington 62
Witman, Elizabeth 570
Witmer, ... B. 151
Witmer, Christian 523
Witmer, E. 151
Witmer, Elizabeth 151
Witmer, Joseph 151
Witmer, Mary 520
Witmer, Peter 363, 371, 375, 378
Witmer, S. B. 151
Witmer, Solomon 356
Witner, Bitsey 382
Witner, Geo. 354
Witte, George 604
Wittenbrook, Randolph 179
Witter, Christopher 415

Witter, Elijah 593
Witter, Mary 415
Witter, Mary Jane 521
Witter, Samuel 415
Witters, George W. 414
Witters, Mahala 466
Wittierstine, Abraham 75
Witzel, John 494
Wodeman, Elizabeth 203
Wodeman, Jacob 203
Wodeman, Jno. 203
Wodeman, John 203
Wogerman, Joel 220
Woggle, Polly 134
Wolburn, John 85
Wolcott, Horace 707
Wolcott, Lucy 707
Wolf, Abraham 374, 380
Wolf, Alfred 418
Wolf, Andrew 629, 634
Wolf, Anne 249
Wolf, Barbary 229
Wolf, Catharine 77
Wolf, Daniel 229
Wolf, David 494, 517
Wolf, Dolly 84
Wolf, E. J. 327
Wolf, Edward 569
Wolf, Eliva J. 327
Wolf, Eliza 380
Wolf, Elizabeth 229, 327, 565
Wolf, Fred. 229
Wolf, Frederick 229
Wolf, Geo. 372
Wolf, George 85, 193, 229, 380, 467
Wolf, H. 533
Wolf, J. W. 327
Wolf, Jacob 229
Wolf, Jesse 517
Wolf, John 249, 362, 380, 418, 569, 577, 664
Wolf, John W. 327
Wolf, Joseph 523
Wolf, Josie E. 533
Wolf, Lizzie M. 327
Wolf, M. E. 533
Wolf, Maggie A. 533
Wolf, Margaret 462
Wolf, Margareth 229
Wolf, Maria 380
Wolf, Mary 88, 229
Wolf, Pamela D. 30
Wolf, Peter 380
Wolf, Philip 380, 460, 483
Wolf, Polly 458
Wolf, Priscella 464
Wolf, Rachel 327
Wolf, Rebecca 93
Wolf, Simon 327
Wolf, William 380, 569
Wolfe, Catharine 78
Wolfe, George 86
Wolfe, Joseph 81
Wolfe, Phillip 473
Wolfe, Rebecca 84

Wolfe, Sarah 572
Wolff, John 334
Wolford, H. S. 741
Wolford, Polly 585
Wollard, Elizabeth 437
Wollard, Frances Jane 437
Wollard, Patrick Marcus 437
Wollard, Robert 437
Wollaton, George 190
Wollaver, John 352
Wollet, Elizabeth 611
Wollet, John 611
Wolley, Ashur 673
Wollington, Thomas 388
Wollison, George 122
Wolverton, Nancy 386
Womkldorf, George 547
Wonderly Jacob 219
Wonderly, Mary 522
Wonutern, John 713
Wood, A. J. 617
Wood, Abigail 554
Wood, An 152
Wood, Ann 152
Wood, Archibalc 156
Wood, Archibald 152
Wood, Beriah 689
Wood, Bertha E. 617
Wood, Betsey 473
Wood, C. E. 617
Wood, Catharine 652
Wood, Charles 247
Wood, Christopher 19
Wood, Daniel 279
Wood, Eliza 247
Wood, Eliza K. 247
Wood, Emma S. 35
Wood, Esther 176
Wood, Frederick Mary 247
Wood, Garrett V. 523
Wood, George J. 146
Wood, Georgena 247
Wood, Harriet 247
Wood, Henry 304
Wood, Ira 598
Wood, Israel 58
Wood, Jane Finley 505
Wood, Jeremiah 185
Wood, John 247
Wood, Jonas 185
Wood, Jonathan 284
Wood, Jonathan P. 142
Wood, Joseph 15, 652, 721
Wood, Joshua 166, 171
Wood, Laticia 154
Wood, Leticia 169
Wood, Levi 181
Wood, Louisa 589
Wood, Lucy 554
Wood, Maria 593
Wood, Martha Jane 652
Wood, Mary 163, 591
Wood, Matilda 12
Wood, Michael 598
Wood, Michael S. 587
Wood, Nancy 14, 454

Wood, Otis M. 625
Wood, Phebe 181, 691
Wood, Rebecca 12
Wood, Rhoda 223
Wood, Robert 163, 647, 652
Wood, Rueben 58
Wood, Ruth 718
Wood, Sally 166, 171
Wood, Samuel 185
Wood, Sarah 11, 19, 247
Wood, Sarah J. 146
Wood, Silas 652
Wood, Thomas 154, 169
Wood, Uriah 598
Wood, William 19
Wood, William G. 16
Wood, Wm. D. 395
Woodard, Caleb 290
Woodard, Isaac M. 685
Woodard, Jane 685
Woodard, Mary 314
Woodard, William 685
Woodard, Wm. 672
Woodbridge, --- 733
Woodbridge, Dudley 282, 726
Woodbridge, Ebenezer 99
Woodbridge, Eliza S. 99
Woodbridge, Joseph Egbert 99
Woodbridge, Lucy 715
Woodbridge, Maria M. 712
Woodbury, Benjamin 763, 764
Woodbury, J. W. 763, 764
Woodbury, Mehitable 763
Woodcock, B. B. (Dr.) 327
Woodcock, Bernard B. 324
Woodcock, Hannah J. 327
Woodcox, Cornelius 747
Woodcox, Isaac 316, 317, 318, 320, 322, 333, 747
Woodcox, Nancy 744
Woodcox, Rebecca 745
Woodcox, Solomon 747
Woodcox, Susannah 744
Woodell, Ira H. 536
Woodell, Joe 534
Woodell, Martha M. 536
Woodfield, John 15
Woodfield, Margaret 458
Woodford, Elihu 733
Woodford, Oliver (Jr.) 733
Woodford, William 719
Woodington, James 267, 273
Woodington, John 667
Woodmansee, Mary 446
Woodmansee, Thomas 447
Woodring, Christiana 505
Woodring, Christina 505
Woodring, Elizabeth 566
Woodring, Jacob 505
Woodring, John 505
Woodring, Joseph 505
Woodring, Lucy 575

Woodring, Mary 505
Woodring, Philip 564
Woodrow, David 192
Woodrow, James 192
Woodrow, Patty 577
Woodruff, David 81
Woodruff, Eliza 65
Woodruff, Hampton 122
Woodruff, Isaac 65
Woodruff, John 81
Woodruff, John F. 603, 604, 610
Woodruff, Silas 284
Woodruff, William 686
Woodrull, Israel 653
Woods, Achbold 168
Woods, Agness 567
Woods, Alexander 742
Woods, Ann 156, 159
Woods, Anne 100
Woods, Archabald 159
Woods, Archd. 165
Woods, Archibald 156
Woods, Archibold 175
Woods, Christian 625
Woods, E. A. 532
Woods, Eliza 589
Woods, Elizabeth 5, 15
Woods, Harvey 742
Woods, Hugh 477, 482, 485
Woods, James 473
Woods, John 485
Woods, Joshua 165
Woods, Lydia 5
Woods, Martha 742
Woods, Mary 742
Woods, Perthena 121
Woods, Rebecca 5
Woods, Rebeeke 718
Woods, Reuben N. 742
Woods, Rhoda 663
Woods, Robert 224, 672
Woods, Ruth 5
Woods, Sally 165
Woods, Samuel 5, 223
Woods, Sarah 86
Woods, Stephen 721
Woods, Thomas 122
Woods, Thomas F. 587, 594
Woods, William 16, 122, 262, 532
Woods, Willie 532
Woods, Zachariah 460, 467
Woodson, --- 677
Woodward, Drusilla 448
Woodward, Eunice 79
Woodward, Ezra S. 448
Woodward, George 598
Woodward, John 441, 448, 688
Woodward, John R. 146
Woodward, Lewis 468
Woodward, Lydia 448, 598
Woodward, Lydia S. 448
Woodward, Mahlon 431
Woodward, Malvina 448
Woodward, Mary 733
Woodward, Nathan 431

Woodward, Oliver 85
Woodward, Oliver (Jr.) 733
Woodward, Ruth 441
Woodward, Samuel 428
Woodward, William 688
Woodward, Wm. W. 146
Woogert, Hannah 87
Wook, Rebecca 63
Wool . . . , Lewis 177
Woolap, Abraham 266
Woolap, Jacob 266
Woolcoat, John 478
Woolcott, Minor 594
Woolcut, John H. 135
Woolcut, Rachel 463
Woolcutt, John 499
Woolery, Henry 547
Woolery, Sarah 382
Woolery, Sylvester 601
Woolet, Joseph 523
Wooley, Charles 146
Wooley, Deborah 146
Wooley, Jane 512
Woolf, Sarah 663
Woolford, Adam 602, 708
Woolford, Elijah 594
Woolford, John 708
Woolford, Margaret 708
Woolley, Eunice 496
Woolley, Mary N. 150
Woolley, T. C. 150
Woolley, Thomas C. 150
Woolman, John 668
Wooloet, Saml. 551
Woolverton, Lewis 391
Woolwine, Ephraim A. 146
Woolwine, Wm. F. 146
Wooly, Sarah 13
Wooten, --- 408
Wooten, Caleb W. 610
Worden, Ira 333
Wordle, Friszilla 572
Worford, John 564
Worford, William 564
Work, Alexander 290
Work, David 103, 108, 273
Work, Elizabeth 273
Work, John 273
Work, Nancy 273
Work, Robert 273
Work, Sam. 356
Work, Samuel 272, 304
Work, Sarah 273
Workman, Benj. 284
Workman, Betsey 12
Workman, John 16, 19
Workman, Samuel 526
Worley, Akey 556
Worley, Anna 510, 514
Worley, Anthony 502
Worley, Betsy 502
Worley, Catharine 556
Worley, Daniel 556
Worley, David W. 584
Worley, Eaky 556
Worley, Elijah 502
Worley, Elizabeth 509

Worley, Harry 477
Worley, Isaac 504, 509, 510, 517
Worley, Jacob 509, 510, 556
Worley, James E. 509
Worley, Jane 502
Worley, Jesse P. 509
Worley, John 502, 509, 510, 556
Worley, John M. 510
Worley, Joseph 509, 510, 556
Worley, Joshua 198
Worley, Mahom 664
Worley, Maleom 671
Worley, Margaret 502
Worley, Mary 556
Worley, Mary Ann 509
Worley, Matilda 509
Worley, Michael 556
Worley, Moses 502
Worley, Nancy 502, 510, 556
Worley, Patience 502, 510
Worley, Philip 473, 474, 477
Worley, Polly 502
Worley, Rebecca 556
Worley, Richard M. 509
Worley, Sally 510, 517
Worley, Samuel F. 509
Worley, Stephen G. 551
Worley, Susan 510
Worley, Thomas 556
Worley, William 594
Worley, William N. C. 212
Worley, Wm. S. 509
Worlley, Rebecka 75
Worly, Caleb 122
Worly, Isaac 504, 509
Worman, George 184
Worman, Henry 184
Worrel, William 23
Worrell, Amanda 142
Worrell, Samuel 23
Worrell, Susan 142
Worstal, John 292
Worstall, John 287
Worth, James 569
Worthen, Hannah 78
Worthen, Rebecca 81
Worthington, Albert 62
Worthington, Albert G. 62
Worthington, Eleanor 62
Worthington, Elizabeth 62, 466, 592, 669
Worthington, Ester 146
Worthington, Francis 62
Worthington, Israel 49
Worthington, James 62
Worthington, James G. 62
Worthington, Joseph 669
Worthington, Margaret 62
Worthington, Mary 62
Worthington, Sarah 62
Worthington, T. 62
Worthington, Thomas 5, 62, 469, 484

Worthington, William 62
Wortman, Benjamin 286
Wortman, James 627
Wortman, Lot 284
Wortman, Mary 608
Wortman, Sarah 607
Wotts, David 577
Wow, Cloe 52
Wray, James 517
Wray, Nancy 13
Wren, John 337
Wright, --- 473, 723
Wright, Aaron 103
Wright, Abigail 103
Wright, Acre 98
Wright, Ajolin 103
Wright, Alford S. 69
Wright, Allen 650, 651, 667
Wright, Amos 419
Wright, Ann 54, 103
Wright, Anna 530
Wright, Barbara 395
Wright, Catharine 78
Wright, Catherine 395
Wright, Charles 733
Wright, Charlott 69
Wright, Cyrenus 499
Wright, Cyrus 103
Wright, David 103, 129, 475
Wright, Delilah 530
Wright, Eber 111
Wright, Edward 491
Wright, Eli 81, 530
Wright, Elizabeth 103, 394, 395, 608
Wright, Ely 530
Wright, Ethan 103
Wright, Gabriel 135, 142, 491
Wright, Geo. P. 111
Wright, George Washington 194
Wright, Gersham 175
Wright, Hamilton Tr. 530
Wright, Hannah 126, 511
Wright, Harriet 146
Wright, Hugh 395
Wright, Huldah 714
Wright, Isaac 517
Wright, James 15, 22, 51
Wright, Jane 453
Wright, Jesse 85
Wright, John 63, 135, 142, 395, 468, 491, 517, 551
Wright, John (Sr.) 394
Wright, John Q. 146
Wright, Jonathan 491, 731, 733
Wright, Joseph 81, 291, 395
Wright, Joshua D. 109
Wright, Josiah 85, 194, 256, 260, 270, 271, 530
Wright, July Ann 395
Wright, Lucinda 395

997

Wright, Martha 79, 530
Wright, Mary 82, 103, 152, 161, 181, 395, 610, 661
Wright, Mary Ann 395
Wright, Moses 491
Wright, Nancy 135
Wright, Nathan 98
Wright, Owen 103
Wright, Pacience 664
Wright, Peggy Jane 103
Wright, Permelia 663
Wright, Peter 419
Wright, Phenius 491
Wright, Polly 394
Wright, Rachel 98, 103
Wright, Rebecca 660
Wright, Rhoda 175
Wright, Robert 734
Wright, Rosy 498
Wright, Rual 738
Wright, Ruth 659
Wright, Sally 103, 116
Wright, Samuel 152, 161, 177, 738
Wright, Samuel T. 529
Wright, Sarah 111, 395, 414, 494
Wright, Simeon 715
Wright, Susanna 663
Wright, Sylva 111
Wright, Thomas 395, 449, 625, 664, 667
Wright, Thomas Coke 194
Wright, Valentine 738
Wright, Warren 146
Wright, William 103, 395, 414, 517, 551
Wright, Wm. 146
Write, Elizabeth 567
Write, Martha 79
Writter, Jacob 148
Wrocklage, Anna Mariah 627
Wrocklage, Bernardina 627
Wrocklage, Christian M. 627
Wrocklage, Christian Matthias 627
Wrocklage, Elisabeth 627
Wrocklage, Gerhard Matthias 627
Wrocklage, Gertrude 627
Wrocklage, Maria Agnes 627
Wrocklage, Maria Catharine 627
Wrocklage, Maria Elisabeth 627
Wrocklage, Theodore 627
Wuebbling, Anna M. 547
Wuick, Thomas P. 751
Wukkuans, Rosama 690
Wunderle, Anna M. 112
Wunsck, John 42
Wyant, Benjamin 523
Wyant, Frederick 295
Wyant, Samuel 528

Wyate, John 464
Wyate, Joseph 468
Wyatt, J. T. 95
Wyatt, J. W. 95
Wyatt, James E. 95
Wyatt, James H. 95
Wyatt, Jane 125
Wyatt, John T. 94
Wyatt, Lavinah 65
Wyatt, Martha 547
Wyatt, Mary 457
Wyatt, Mary C. 95
Wyatt, Minnie A. 95
Wyatt, Nancy 94
Wyatt, Naomi 146
Wyatt, Nathan (Jr.) 65
Wyatt, Samuel D. 65
Wyatt, Sarah 65
Wyatt, Sarah Elizabeth 94
Wyatt, V. A. 95
Wyatt, William 65
Wyatte, Sarah 121
Wybeaut, John 174
Wybrant, Hugh 304
Wycoff, Charity 458
Wycoff, Hannah 528
Wycoff, Henry 528
Wycoff, Maria 528
Wycoff, Mariah 528
Wycoff, Mary 528
Wycoff, Nicholas 468
Wycoff, Susanna 528
Wycoff, Wm. 460
Wydener, Jacob 483
Wydner, Jacob 476, 478, 482
Wyett, Susannah 548
Wygate, Elizabeth 119
Wyle, William 469
Wylie, John 284
Wylie, William 469
Wylie, Wm. 479
Wyllys, Samuel 86
Wyman, Sylva 517
Wynent, Jas. 594
Wyning, Jacob 569
Wynn, --- 284
Wynn, Nany 80
Wynter, Lynn 699
Wyse, John 738
Wysent, Jacob 166
Wysong, Valentine 413

--- Y ---

Zahm, Lewis 523
Zane, Isaac 283, 297
Zane, John 283
Zane, Matilda 12
Zane, Thomas 287
Zane, William 19
Zangler, Joseph 523
Zaring, E. 735
Zaring, Ida L. 735
Zaring, M. 735
Zartman, Alex. 356

Zartman, Alexander 355, 380, 381
Zartman, Barbara 361, 381
Zartman, Catharine 361
Zartman, Henry 361, 381
Zartman, Isaac 356, 369, 380, 381
Zartman, Israel 381
Zartman, Joshua 381
Zartman, Levi 381
Zartman, Magdalene 381
Zartman, Margaret 381
Zartman, Peter 340
Zartman, Saloma 381
Zartman, Samuel 361
Zartman, Sarah 381
Zearing, Catharine 193
Zearing, David 193
Zearing, Elizabeth 193
Zearing, Fanny 193
Zearing, Hannah 193
Zearing, Henry 193
Zearing, Jacob 194
Zearing, Maria 193
Zearing, Samuel 193
Zearing, Solomon 194
Zearing, Susannah 193
Zegar, Philip 400
Zegler, Peter 667
Zehring, Catharine 399
Zehring, Daniel 207
Zehring, Henry 207
Zehring, John 399
Zehring, Joseph 399
Zehring, Peter 399
Zehring, Sephas 399
Zehring, William 399
Zeibler, Jacob 21
Zeigler, David 381
Zeigler, David (Capt.) 720
Zeigler, Geo. 364
Zeigler, George 376, 381
Zeigler, Jacob 364, 381
Zeigler, Jane 763
Zeigler, John 381
Zeigler, Magdalena 381
Zeigler, Mary 381
Zeigler, Nicholas 381
Zeigler, Nicholas S. 379
Zeigler, Peter 370, 381
Zeigler, Sarah 381
Zeigler, Susanna 381
Zeller, Adam 194, 204, 428
Zeller, Catharine 194
Zeller, Daniel 194
Zeller, G. 734
Zeller, Henry 194, 204
Zeller, J. 734
Zeller, John 217, 734, 747
Zellers, Lucinda 431
Zellers, Reuben 431
Zellers, Sarah 431, 437
Zelloff, Peter 333
Zeloff, Peter 333
Zemer, George 551
Zemer, Margaret 550

998

INSERT

GATEWAY TO THE WEST, VOL. II

(between pp. 998 & 999.)

After <u>Gateway to the West</u> was published, we learned that the Index to Volume II had inadvertently omitted all entries under the letter "Y". In order to rectify this error, we are herewith furnishing the missing entries, which should be inserted between pp. 998 and 999 of Volume II. Please accept our sincere apologies for any inconvenience this may cause.

Genealogical Publishing Company

--- Y ---

Yancey, Joel 56
Yaney, A. 94
Yaney, Barbara 94
Yaney, Barbatha 94
Yaney, Elizabeth 94
Yaney, G. 94
Yaney, George 94
Yaney, H. 94
Yaney, Hannah 94
Yaney, J. 94
Yaney, Jacob 94
Yaney, John C. 94
Yaney, M. 94
Yaney, M. I. 94
Yaney, Sarah E. 94
Yankee, Martha 34
Yant, Henry 569
Yant, John (Jr.) 577
Yant, Mary 570
Yant, Michael 577
Yant, Susanna 576
Yarger, Albright 639
Yarger, George 639
Yarnall, Benjamin 304
Yates, Artis S. 134
Yates, Benjamin 491
Yates, C. 407
Yates, David 407
Yates, Delilah 491
Yates, Edmund S. 134
Yates, Elizabeth 659
Yates, Elizabeth L. 134
Yates, Jonathan L. 134
Yates, Joseph 395
Yates, Mary 142
Yates, Mary Magdelene 395
Yates, Morris 468
Yates, Nezer S. 134
Yates, Phebe 134
Yates, Rebecca 142
Yates, Samuel 719
Yates, Sophrania 142
Yates, Thomas 134
Yauger, Wm. 286
Yeager, Cathrine 636
Yeager, Christian 632, 636
Yeager, Eliza Ann 632
Yeager, Elizabeth 636

Yeager, Emarillis 632
Yeager, George W. 419
Yeager, George 632, 636
Yeager, Harvey 632
Yeager, John 632, 636
Yeager, Ladora 632
Yeager, Lavinia F. 632
Yeager, Mahala 632
Yeager, Margaret A. 632
Yeager, Mary 632, 636
Yeager, Mary Eliza 636
Yeager, Rachel 636
Yeager, Rebecca 632
Yeager, Sally Ann 632
Yeaman, Jemima 664
Yearling, Kattie 329
Yearling, Tomy 329
Yearsley, Mary H. 584
Yeazel, Christian 214
Yeazel, John 214
Yeazel, Seymour 214
Yeazle, Barbara 171
Yeazle, Joseph 171
Yeger, Philip (Jr.) 399
Yeoman, Samuel 640
Yeowmans, Louis 49
Yinger, Daniel 547
Yinger, Debora 532
Yinger, Dennis 142
Yinger, Elizabeth 142
Yinger, H. 532
Yinger, Sarah Ann 142
Yingling, Catherine 511
Yingling, Christian 517
Yingling, John 414
Yoakum, John 49
Yocum, Elijah 739
Yoder, Catharine 738
Yoder, David 738
Yoder, Elizabeth 738
Yoder, Isaac 738
Yoder, Magdalena 23
Yoho, Charlotte J. 315
Yoho, Jacob 304
Yoho, Mary 154
Yoho, Molly 158
Yoho, Patterson F. 315
Yoho, Reuben 152, 162
Yong, Jane 466
Yonston, Elizabeth 454
Yontes, Catherine 123
York, Diadema 437
York, James 720

Yost, Anna C. 712
Yost, Eleanor 343
Yost, Elizabeth 379
Yost, Isaac 363
Yost, Jacob 223
Yost, Joel 163
Yost, John 176
Yost, Margaret 176
Yost, Martha 343
Yost, Wm. 343, 367
Youart, Andrew S. 146
Youart, James 130, 131, 132
Youart, Phebe 146
Youart, William T. 142
Youc, Abraham 142
Youc, Alexander 142
Youc, Eliz. 142
Youc, Larkin 142
Youc, Philip 142
Youc, Phillip 135
Youc, Samuel 142
Young, . . . 557
Young, Aaron 547, 551, 719
Young, Abraham 446, 447
Young, Alexander 269
Young, Andrew S. 146
Young, Betsey 465
Young, C. M. 380
Young, Casper 136, 223
Young, Catharine 409
Young, Catherine 380
Young, Charlotte 573
Young, Christina 437
Young, Daniel 203
Young, David 427, 664
Young, Dorcas 32, 174
Young, Dorcus 153
Young, Elinor 569
Young, Eliza Ann 437
Young, Elizabeth 122, 446, 447, 461, 513, 566, 661
Young, Emeline 269
Young, Enos 215
Young, Frederick 63
Young, George 136, 190
Young, George W. 142
Young, Hannah 446, 447, 497, 748, 749
Young, Henry 569, 729
Young, Hes . . . 172

Young, Holesworth 304
Young, Hugh 86
Young, Isaac 551
Young, Jacob 61, 157, 159, 560, 709
Young, James 172, 258, 259, 260, 263, 268, 272, 274, 419, 599, 668
Young, Jane 261, 265, 266, 269, 313, 466
Young, Jefferson A. 203
Young, Jesse 506
Young, John 156, 157, 446, 502, 569, 668, 684, 747
Young, John H. 419
Young, John Henry 419
Young, Joseph 269, 468
Young, Margaret 466, 468, 710
Young, Mary 334, 446, 447, 677
Young, Mary Ann 548
Young, Michael 547, 556
Young, Nancy 125, 413, 550, 670
Young, Nicholas D. 361
Young, Peter A. 63
Young, Pressocy 549

Young, Rebecca 446, 447
Young, Robert 301, 668, 670, 671, 677
Young, Ruth 157, 159
Young, Samuel 547
Young, Sarah 39, 447, 684
Young, Sarah Jane 437
Young, Silas 468
Young, Sophia 125
Young, Susanna 157
Young, Thomas 173, 174
Young, William 32, 153, 174, 443, 446, 447
Young, William (Jr.) 174
Young, William B. 258, 261, 265, 482
Young, William H. 610
Young, William J. 313
Young, Willis S. 380
Young, Wm. 39, 269
Young, Wm. B. 263, 266, 269, 477
Youngblood, Catharine 443
Youngblood, John C. 443
Younkey, Daniel 212
Younkey, John 212
Younkey, Joseph 212

Younmon, Adam 273
Yount, Andrew 198
Yount, Daniel 185
Yount, Delilah 121, 134
Yount, Enos 215
Yount, Frederick 134
Yount, George 191, 195, 224
Yount, George (Jr.) 224
Yount, Henry 122, 134, 148, 206
Yount, Henry (Jr.) 191
Yount, Jacob 185, 187
Yount, John 134, 191, 195
Yount, Lucy 191
Yount, Mahala 125
Yount, Michel 120
Yount, Peter 185
Yount, Rebecah 125
Yount, Rebeccah 134
Yount, Sarah 191
Yount, Solomon 134, 206
Yount, William 191
Yountz, Mary 302
Yourty, John 142
Yourty, Mary 142
Youse, Catharine 609
Youtes, Elizabeth 127

Zentman, Henry   602
Zentmeyers, Dal   693
Zentmeyers, David   693
Zentmeyers, Elizabeth 693
Zentmeyers, George   693
Zentmeyers, George (Sr.)
   693
Zeperick, David   523
Zepernich, Daniel   527
Zepernich, David   527
Zepernich, Elizabeth   527
Zepernich, Frederick   527
Zepernich, John   527
Zepernich, Joseph   527
Zepernich, Sarah   527
Zephart, Peter   523
Zerbe, John   557
Zering, John   388
Ziegler, George   352
Zimerman, Isaac   95
Zimerman, Jane   95
Zimermon, Isaac   95
Zimmer, Jacob   222
Zimmer, Joannes   711
Zimmer, Johannes 710, 711
Zimmer, Mary Malinda   222
Zimmerly, Peter   743
Zimmerman, A.   23
Zimmerman, Eli A. K.   431
Zimmerman, Eli C.   95
Zimmerman, Elizabeth
   431, 531
Zimmerman, Isaac   95
Zimmerman, Jacob 287, 610
Zimmerman, Jane   95
Zimmerman, John   531
Zimmerman, John B.   431
Zimmerman, Mary   23
Zimmerman, Rachel   606
Zimmerman, William J. 431
Zin, Elizabeth   631
Zin, George   631
Zin, John   631
Zin, Minerva   631
Zin, Susan   631
Zin, William   631
Zinn, Elizabeth   629
Zinn, George   629
Zinn, James   503
Zinn, John   629
Zinn, Minerva   629
Zinn, William   629
Zitzer, Catharine   413
Zoller, Hannah   558
Zook, Catharine   195
Zook, Esther   195
Zook, Eve   195
Zook, Gideon   736, 738
Zook, Jacob   195
Zook, John   195
Zook, Samuel   195, 203
Zook, Susannah   203
Zook, William   195
Zorns, Thomas   517
Zorus, Thomas   517
Zroirline, Margaret   522
Zuber, E.   332
Zuber, Elizabeth   332
Zuber, J.   332

Zuber, Joseph   332
Zuber, Rozeta   332
Zumbro, Frans   711
Zumer, Abraham   551
Zwirlein, John   523

--- Illegible ---

. . . , . . . wy   97
. . . , Abner   157
. . . , Amanda   536
. . . , Amos   618
. . . , Annie   536
. . . , Barb . . .   94
. . . , Barbara Elen 537
. . . , Benjamin   170
. . . , Bethena   163
. . . , Byron   617
. . . , Calvin   618
. . . , Catharine   615
. . . , Charles   536
. . . , D . . .   94
. . . , David   94, 156,
   536
. . . , E. A.   618
. . . , Emnit   535
. . . , G.   94
. . . , H.   536
. . . , Henry   617
. . . , Ida   734
. . . , J.   618
. . . , Jacob   695
. . . , James   538
. . . , Jane   149
. . . , Johann   133
. . . , Johannes   554
. . . , John H.   536
. . . , Joseph   156
. . . , Lavina   536
. . . , Little Faran 149
. . . , M.   538
. . . , Margaret B.   97
. . . , Marlle . . . der
   97
. . . , Mary E.   94
. . . , Matilda D.   99
. . . , Orlando   616
. . . , R.   538
. . . , S. S.   97
. . . , Samuel   94
. . . , Sarah   616
. . . , Stephen   164
. . . , Will   734
. . . cachel, . . .   661
. . . chutt, Elizabeth 98
. . . ehays, Fredrick 99
. . . fee, Sarah
Gre . . .   532
. . . hite, . . .   173
. . . ick, Thomas   157
. . . nene, P. M.   55

--- No Surname ---

---, A. M.   614

---, Adam   460
---, Adazilla   241
---, Aggy   59
---, Alex   460
---, Ann Elizabeth   364
---, Annis   460
---, Betsey   59
---, Caleb   109
---, Clem   506
---, Dan   506
---, Daniel   113
---, David   528
---, Dennis   460
---, Dianna   247
---, Dinah   460, 528
---, Felzey J.   460
---, Eliza Ann   247
---, Elizabeth   297
---, Fanny   59
---, Florence   247
---, George   503, 648
---, Gilbert   57
---, Hagar   506
---, Henrich Adam   237
---, Henry   528
---, Isaiah   364
---, Jacob   460
---, Jane   506
---, Jasper   59
---, Jenny   59
---, Joe   472
---, John   247
---, John A.   113
---, Joseph   506
---, Kitt   364
---, Lettice   393
---, Levina   57
---, Lewis   647
---, Lucy   59
---, Lydia   247, 364
---, M.   614
---, Mariana   365
---, Mariann   59
---, Mary   59, 297, 366
---, Michael   297
---, Moses   506
---, Nancy   100
---, Nancy Jane   752
---, Nat   59
---, Nathan   652
---, Patience   113
---, Phebe   56
---, Polly   506
---, Pracilla   247
---, Rachel   135
---, Rebecca   364
---, Reesy   460
---, Sally   57
---, Sam   506
---, Sarah   472
---, Sarah Anne   648
---, Sarah Jane   364
---, Solomon   528
---, Squire   645
---, Tawohesuch   599
---, Tebitha   57
---, Tzwohesugh   599
---, William   59, 247,
   727